The National Hockey League

Official Guide & Record Book

1996-97

Published by the National Hockey League.
Compiled by the NHL Public Relations Department
and the 26 NHL Club Public Relations Directors.
Copyright © 1996 by the National Hockey League

THE NATIONAL HOCKEY LEAGUE
Official Guide & Record Book/1996-97

Staff

For the NHL: Charlie Schmitt, Elle Farrell; Supervising Editor: Greg Inglis;
Statistician: Benny Ercolani; Editorial Staff: David Keon, Sherry McKeown, Rod Pasma

Managing Editors: Ralph Dinger, James Duplacey

Contributing Editor: Igor Kuperman

Contributors:
Blue Line Publishing (Minneapolis), Gene Dupras, Peter Fillman, Ernie Fitzsimmons, Herb Morell (OHL), NHL Broadcasters' Association, NHL Central Registry, NHL Players' Association, Mark Paddock, Jim Price (CHL), Valentina Riazanova, Kevin Smith (Hockey International newsletter), Jeff Weiss (CCHA), Eric Zweig.

Consulting Publisher: Dan Diamond

Photo Credits

Historical and special event photos: Bruce Bennett, David Bier, Michael Burns, Graphic Artists Collection, NHL Images/Silvia Pecota, New York Rangers, Rice Studio, Robert Shaver, Imperial Oil Turofsky Collection, Hockey Hall of Fame.

Current photos: Graig Abel, Toronto; Joe Angeles, St. Louis; Steve Babineau, Boston; Bruce Bennett Studios, NY Islanders and Philadelphia; Bob Binder, Anaheim; Denis Brodeur, Montreal; Mark Buckner, St. Louis; Denny Cavanaugh, Pittsburgh; Steve Crandall, New Jersey; Edmonton Northlands; Bob Fisher, Montreal; Ray Grabowski, Chicago; John Hartman, Detroit; Jonathan Hayt, Tampa Bay; J. Henson Photographics, Washington; Glenn James, Dallas; George Kalinsky, NY Rangers; Deborah King, Washington; David Klutho, St. Louis; Robert Laberge, Montreal; V.J. Lovero, Anaheim; Jim Mackey, Detroit; Doug MacLellan; McElligott-Teckles Sports Focus Imaging, Ottawa; Al Messerschmidt, Florida; Jack Murray, Vancouver; Tim Parker, St. Louis; Andre Pichette, Montreal; Richard Pilling, New Jersey; Harry Scull, Jr., Buffalo; Don Smith, San Jose; Diane Sobolewski, Hartford; John Soohoo; Gerry Thomas, Edmonton; Jim Turner, New Jersey; Brad Watson, Calgary; Rocky Widner, San Jose; Bill Wippert, Buffalo.

Distribution

Canadian representatives:
North 49 Books, 193 Bartley Drive, Toronto, Ontario M4A 1E6
416/750-7777; FAX 416/750-2049

NHL Publishing, 194 Dovercourt Road, Toronto, Ontario M6J 3C8
416/531-6535; FAX 416/531-3939

U.S. representatives: Triumph Books,
644 South Clark Street, Chicago, Illinois 60605   312/939-3330; FAX 312/663-3557

International representatives: Barkers Worldwide Publications,
155 Maybury Road, Woking, Surrey, England GU21 5JR
Tel. and FAX: 011/44/483/776-141

Data Management and Typesetting: Caledon Data Management, Hillsburgh, Ontario
Film Output and Scanning: Stafford Graphics, Toronto, Ontario
Printing: Moore Data Management Services, Scarborough, Ontario
Production Management: Dan Diamond and Associates, Inc., Toronto, Ontario

The National Hockey League
1251 Avenue of the Americas, 47th Floor, New York, New York 10020-1198
1800 McGill College Ave., Suite 2600, Montreal, Quebec H3A 3J6
75 International Boulevard, Suite 300, Toronto, Ontario M9W 6L9

Table of Contents

Table of Contents *continued*

Introduction

WELCOME TO *THE NHL OFFICIAL GUIDE & RECORD BOOK FOR 1996-97.* This 65th edition of the *Guide* incorporates three new features, each of which has been added in response to comments and suggestions from readers like you.

Most significant is a reorganization of the record book sections of this edition. The 1996-97 *Guide* contains three separate record books: regular season, beginning on page 138; All-Star Game, page 207 and playoffs, page 226. Each of these is still divided into team and individual sections, but each is now organized by achievement (goals, assists, points, etc.) rather than by duration (career, single-season, one-game). We believe that by arranging the records in this manner, information will be easier to retrieve. In the regular-season record book, looking up "Goals" in the individual record section will reveal NHL marks for most goals in a career (Wayne Gretzky, 837), in a single season (Gretzky, 92 in 1981-82), in one game ("Phantom" Joe Malone, 7 on January 31, 1920) and in one period (Harvey "Busher" Jackson and nine others, 4).

A full-page chart of Year-by-Year Individual Regular-Season Leaders has been added on page 172. This table lists the NHL leaders in goals, assists, points and penalty minutes for each season from 1917-18 to 1995-96.

The Player Register begins on page 247. This comprehensive listing of career data for NHL players and prospects has been supplemented with the addition of a symbol (♦) to indicate each season in which a player has been a member of a Stanley Cup-winning team. This symbol is also used in the Goaltender Register that begins on page 421. Late additions to the registers are found on page 246. A key to abbreviations and symbols used in the individual player and goaltender data panels that make up the Registers is found on page 245.

For 1996-97, the NHL welcomes the Phoenix Coyotes who will play in the Central Division of the Western Conference. Roster, coaching information and franchise records can be found beginning on page 85. The Coyotes will play their home games in America West Arena (18,000 capacity).

Other new arenas will open in the 1996-97 season. The Buffalo Sabres will begin play in the Marine Midland Arena (19,500 capacity) on October 12 vs. Detroit. The Philadelphia Flyers will play their first regular-season game in the new 19,500-seat CoreStates Center on October 5 vs. Florida. Tampa Bay Lightning will open the Ice Palace, a 20,500-seat facility, on October 20 vs. the New York Rangers.

THE **1996-97 NHL S**CHEDULE will see each of the League's 26 member clubs play 82 games, 41 at home and 41 on the road. Each club will play either five or six games against its divisional opponents, four games against teams in the other division of its own conference and two games against each of the 13 teams in the League's other conference.

As always, our thanks to readers, correspondents and members of the media who take the time to comment on the *Guide & Record Book*. Thanks as well to the people working in the communications departments of the NHL's member clubs and to their counterparts in the AHL, IHL, ECHL, Central, Colonial and junior leagues as well as in college athletic conferences and European hockey federations.

Best wishes for an enjoyable 1996-97 NHL season.

ACCURACY REMAINS THE *GUIDE & RECORD BOOK*'S TOP PRIORITY.
We appreciate comments and clarification from our readers. Please direct these to:
Greg Inglis   47th floor, 1251 Avenue of the Americas, New York, New York 10020-1198 . . . or . . .
David Keon   75 International Blvd., suite 300, Rexdale, Ontario M9W 6L9.
Your involvement makes a better book.

NATIONAL HOCKEY LEAGUE

New York — 1251 Avenue of the Americas, 47th Floor, New York, NY 10020-1198, (212)789-2000, Fax: (212)789-2020
Montreal — 1800 McGill College Avenue, Suite 2600, Montreal, Quebec H3A 3J6, (514)288-9220, Fax: (514)284-0300
Toronto — 75 International Blvd., Suite 300, Rexdale, Ontario M9W 6L9, (416)798-0809, Fax: (416)798-0819
NHL Enterprises, L.P. — 1251 Avenue of the Americas, 47th Floor, New York, NY 10020-1198, (212)789-2000, Fax: (212)789-2020
NHL Enterprises Canada. L.P. — 75 International Blvd., Suite 301, Rexdale, Ontario M9W 6L9, 416/798-9388, Fax: 416/798-9395
NHL Productions — 183 Oak Tree Road, Tappan, NY 10983-2809, (914)365-6701, Fax: (914)365-6010
NHL Europe — Signaustrasse 1, 8008 Zurich — Switzerland

Directory

Commissioner	Gary B. Bettman
Senior Vice President and Chief Operating Officer	Stephen J. Solomon
Senior Vice President and General Counsel	Jeffrey Pash
Senior Vice President and Director of Hockey Operations	Brian P. Burke
Executive Assistant to the Commissioner	Debbie Walsh

Administration

Director	Janet A. Meyers

Broadcasting / NHL Productions

Vice President	Glenn Adamo
Coordinating Producer, NHL Productions	Ken Rosen
Assistant Director	Steve HatzePetros
Manager, Broadcasting	Adam Acone
Manager, Broadcast Operations	Patti Fallick
Manager, Video Services, NHL Productions	Mott Linn

Corporate Communications

Vice President	Bernadette Mansur
Director, Corporate Communications	Mary Pat Clarke
Manager, Corporate Communications	Tracey Cohen
Director, Creative Services	David F. Haney

Finance

Vice President and Chief Financial Officer	Craig Harnett
Vice President, Finance and Office Manager (Montreal)	Joseph DeSousa
Controller, Broadcasting	Megan O'Donnell
Assistant Controller (Montreal)	Olivia Pietrantonio
Assistant Controller	Patricia Cooper
Accounting Supervisor (Montreal)	Donna Gillman

Hockey Operations

Vice President (Toronto)	Jim Gregory
Director, Central Registry (Montreal)	Garry Lovegrove
Assistant Director, Central Registry (Montreal)	Madeleine Supino
Director of Central Scouting (Toronto)	Frank Bonello
Officiating Coordinator (Toronto)	Robert Bouchard
Supervisor of Officials (Toronto)	Wally Harris
Hockey Operations Manager	David Nonis
Consultant (Montreal)	Brian F. O'Neill
Video Director, Hockey Operations	Rob Schoenbach

Information Systems

Director (Montreal)	Mario Carangi
Assistant Director (Montreal)	Luc Coulombe

International

Managing Director, Europe	Guido Tognoni

Legal

Vice President and Associate General Counsel	David Zimmerman
Associate Counsel	Katherine Jones

Pension

Director (Montreal)	Yvon Chamberland
Controller, Pension (Montreal)	Mary Skiadopoulos
Manager, Pension (Montreal)	Lise DeJocas

Public Relations

Vice President	Arthur Pincus
Director, Public Relations (Toronto)	Gary Meagher
Chief Statistician (Toronto)	Benny Ercolani
Manager, Media Relations	Susan Aglietti
Manager, News Services	Greg Inglis
Manager, Public Relations and News Services	Andrew McGowan
Public Relations Assistant	David Keon
New Services Assistant	Tamir Lipton
Public Relations Assistant	Adam Schwartz

Security

Vice President and Director	Dennis Cunningham
Assistant Director	Joseph Caporicci

Special Events / Event Marketing

Vice President Special Events	Frank Supovitz
Director, Event Marketing	Karen Ayoub
Director, Special Events	Lori Boesch
Manager, Event Marketing	Patricia L. Conrad

Special Events / Event Marketing (continued)

Manager, Special Events	Ann Devney Marciano
Manager, Special Events	Anne I. Grotefeld
Manager, Special Events	Michael Santos

Television and Business Affairs

VP Television and Business Affairs	Ellis T. "Skip" Prince III
Director, New Business Development	Bryant S. McBride
Manager, Broadcast Business Affairs	Samuel Esposito, Jr.
Manager, New Business Development	John Knebel
Manager, New Business Development	Susanna Mandel-Mantello

NHL Enterprises, L.P.

President	Rick Dudley

Consumer Products / Retail Sales Marketing

Vice President	Brian Jennings
Group Director, Consumer Products Marketing, US	Glenn Horine
Managing Director, Consumer Products Marketing, Canada	Bob McLaughlin
Group Director, Youth	Tina Ellis
Director, Consumer Products Marketing, Canada	Karen Hanson
Director, Apparel	Jim Haskins
Director, Consumer Products Marketing, Canada	Fiona Hastie
Director, Trading Card and Collectibles	Ilene Kent
Director, Special Projects	Brendan McQuillan
Director, Gifts and Novelties	Judith Salsberg
Sales Manager, Mid-Western Region	Christopher Agnew
Sales Manager, Eastern Region	Brian Way
Manager, Youth	Ann Kiely
Manager of Retail Sales and Marketing, Canada	Barry Monaghan

Marketing

CORPORATE MARKETING

Group Vice President, Marketing	Ed Horne
Director, Corporate Marketing	Dina Gilbertie
Director, Corporate Marketing	Todd Parker
Director, Corporate Marketing, Canada	Paul MacLaren
Manager, Corporate Marketing	Tim Conway
Manager, Corporate Marketing	Gord Lang

CLUB MARKETING

Director, Club Marketing	Scott Carmichael

PRINTED PRODUCTS MARKETING

Manager	Elle Farrell

Fan Development

Vice President	Ken Yaffe
Director, Off-Ice Programs	Brian Mullen
Manager, Street Hockey Division	Kamini Sharma
Manager, Fan Development Programs	Alysse Soll

Finance

Controller, Consumer Products Marketing	Mary C. McCarthy
Assistant Controller, Corporate	Pamela Wakoff
Manager, Accounts Payable	Evelyn Torres
Manager, Information Systems	John Ho

International Consumer Products Marketing

Managing Director, NHL Enterprises B.V.	Brad Kwong
Director, Pacific Rim Licensing	Frank Nakano

Legal

Senior VP and General Counsel	Richard Zahnd
Associate General Counsel — Intellectual Property	Mary Sotis
Associate Counsel	Leslie Gittess
Associate Counsel	Douglas Perlman
Director, Consumer Products Marketing and Trademark Compliance	Ruth Gruhin
Manager of Contract Administration	Heather Bell

NHL Interactive Cyber Enterprises (NHL "ICE")

General Manager and Executive Producer	Charlie Schmitt

BOARD OF GOVERNORS
Chairman of the Board: Harley N. Hotchkiss

MIGHTY DUCKS OF ANAHEIM
Disney Sports Enterprises, Inc,

Michael D. Eisner .... Governor
Tony Tavares .... Alternate Governor

BOSTON BRUINS
Boston Professional Hockey Association, Inc.

Jeremy M. Jacobs .... Governor
Louis Jacobs .... Alternate Governor
Harry J. Sinden .... Alternate Governor

BUFFALO SABRES
Niagara Frontier Hockey, L.P.

Robert O. Swados .... Governor
Seymour H. Knox, IV .... Alternate Governor
Douglas G. Moss .... Alternate Governor
John J. Rigas .... Alternate Governor

CALGARY FLAMES
Calgary Flames Limited Partnership

Harley N. Hotchkiss .... Governor
Al Coates .... Alternate Governor
Ron Joyce .... Alternate Governor
Byron J. Seaman .... Alternate Governor

CHICAGO BLACKHAWKS
Chicago Blackhawks Hockey Team, Inc.

William W. Wirtz .... Governor
Gene Gozdecki .... Alternate Governor
Thomas N. Ivan .... Alternate Governor
Robert J. Pulford .... Alternate Governor
Arthur M. Wirtz, Jr. .... Alternate Governor
W. Rockwell Wirtz .... Alternate Governor

COLORADO AVALANCHE
Colorado Avalanche, LLC

Charlie Lyons .... Governor
Pierre Lacroix .... Alternate Governor

DALLAS STARS
Dallas Stars, L.P.

Tom Hicks .... Governor
James R. Lites .... Alternate Governor

DETROIT RED WINGS
Detroit Red Wings, Inc.

Michael Ilitch .... Governor
Jay A. Bielfield .... Alternate Governor
Jim Devellano .... Alternate Governor
Bill Evo .... Alternate Governor
Atanas Ilitch .... Alternate Governor
Christopher Ilitch .... Alternate Governor

EDMONTON OILERS
Oilers Hockey Inc.

Peter Pocklington .... Governor
Glen Sather .... Alternate Governor

FLORIDA PANTHERS
Florida Panthers Hockey Club, Ltd.

William A. Torrey .... Governor
Dean Jordan .... Alternate Governor

HARTFORD WHALERS
KTR Hockey Limited Partnership

Peter Karmanos, Jr. .... Governor
Jim Rutherford .... Alternate Governor

LOS ANGELES KINGS
Los Angeles Kings Hockey Club, L.P.

Robert Sanderman .... Governor
Philip F. Anschutz .... Alternate Governor
Timothy J. Leiweke .... Alternate Governor
Edward Roski, Jr. .... Alternate Governor
Rogie Vachon .... Alternate Governor

MONTRÉAL CANADIENS
Le Club de Hockey Canadien, Inc.

Ronald L. Corey .... Governor
Rejean Houle .... Alternate Governor
Fred Steer .... Alternate Governor

NEW JERSEY DEVILS
Meadowlanders, Inc.

Dr. John J. McMullen .... Governor
Louis A. Lamoriello .... Alternate Governor
Peter McMullen .... Alternate Governor

NEW YORK ISLANDERS
New York Islanders Hockey Club, L.P.

Steve Walsh .... Governor
John H. Krumpe .... Alternate Governor
Arthur J. McCarthy .... Alternate Governor
Ralph F. Palleschi .... Alternate Governor
Robert Rosenthal .... Alternate Governor

NEW YORK RANGERS
Madison Square Garden, L.P.

Charles F. Dolan .... Governor
Rand V. Araskog .... Alternate Governor
David Checketts .... Alternate Governor
James L. Dolan .... Alternate Governor
Ken Munoz .... Alternate Governor
Neil Smith .... Alternate Governor

OTTAWA SENATORS
Ottawa Senators Hockey Club Limited Partnership

Roderick M. Bryden .... Governor
Bernard J. Ashe .... Alternate Governor
David Ferguson .... Alternate Governor
Cyril Leeder .... Alternate Governor

PHILADELPHIA FLYERS
Philadelphia Flyers Limited Partnership

Edward M. Snider .... Governor
Bob Clarke .... Alternate Governor
Richard Ruben .... Alternate Governor
Ronald K. Ryan .... Alternate Governor
Philip I. Weinberg .... Alternate Governor

PHOENIX COYOTES
BG Hockey Ventures

Richard Burke .... Governor
Steven Gluckstern .... Alternate Governor

PITTSBURGH PENGUINS
Pittsburgh Hockey Associates

Howard L. Baldwin .... Governor
Craig Patrick .... Alternate Governor
Thomas V. Ruta .... Alternate Governor
Stephen Ryan .... Alternate Governor

ST. LOUIS BLUES
St. Louis Blues Hockey Club, L.P.

Jack Quinn .... Governor
Ron Caron .... Alternate Governor
Mike Keenan .... Alternate Governor

SAN JOSE SHARKS
San Jose Sharks, L.P.

George Gund III .... Governor
Gordon Gund .... Alternate Governor
Greg Jamison .... Alternate Governor
Irvin A. Leonard .... Alternate Governor
Dean Lombardi .... Alternate Governor

TAMPA BAY LIGHTNING
Lightning Partners, Ltd.

David E. LeFevre .... Governor
Phil Esposito .... Alternate Governor
Steve Oto .... Alternate Governor
Chris Phillips .... Alternate Governor

TORONTO MAPLE LEAFS
Maple Leaf Gardens Limited

Steve A. Stavro .... Governor
Brian P. Bellmore .... Alternate Governor
Cliff Fletcher .... Alternate Governor

VANCOUVER CANUCKS
Vancouver Hockey Club Ltd.

Arthur R. Griffiths .... Governor
John H. Chappelle .... Alternate Governor
John E. McCaw, Jr. .... Alternate Governor
George McPhee .... Alternate Governor
J.B. Patrick Quinn .... Alternate Governor

WASHINGTON CAPITALS
Washington Capitals, L.P.

Richard M. Patrick .... Governor
Abe Pollin .... Alternate Governor
Peter O'Malley .... Alternate Governor
David Osnos .... Alternate Governor
David R. Poile .... Alternate Governor

Commissioner and League Presidents

Gary B. Bettman

Gary B. Bettman took office as the NHL's first Commissioner on February 1, 1993. Since the League was formed in 1917, there have been five League Presidents.

NHL President	Years in Office
Frank Calder	1917-1943
Mervyn "Red" Dutton	1943-1946
Clarence Campbell	1946-1977
John A. Ziegler, Jr.	1977-1992
Gil Stein	1992-1993

NHL Enterprises B.V.
Polakweg 14
2288 GG Rijswijk
Nederland
Phone: 31-(0)70-390-7797
Fax: 31-(0)70-390-7625

Stephen J. Solomon – Director
Richard Zahnd – Director
Cyril Speijer – Director

Hockey Hall of Fame
BCE Place
30 Yonge Street
Toronto, Ontario M5E 1X8
Phone: 416/360-7735
Fax: 416/360-1501

Ian "Scotty" Morrison – Chairman
Ian Morrison – Chairman
Bryan Black – Vice-President, Marketing and Communications
Jeff Denomme – Vice-President, Finance and Operations
Kelly Massé – Executive Assistant
Phil Pritchard – Manager, Resource Centre and Acquisitions
Ray Paquet – Manager, Exhibit Development and Technology
Barry Eversley – Manager, Building Services
Christine Simpson – Manager, Marketing
Scott North – Manager, Special Events and Facility Sales
Sandra Buffone – Manager, Accounting and Office Services
Christena Wilson – Associate Manager, Guest Services
Jeff Graham – Associate Manager, Guest Services
Craig Beckim – Associate Manager, Merchandising
Tim McWilliams – Associate Manager, Retail Operations

National Hockey League Players' Association
777 Bay Street, Suite 2400
Toronto, Ontario M5G 2C8
Phone: 416/408-4040
Fax: 416/408-3685
E-mail: smcall@nhlpa.com   Internet: http://www.nhlpa.com
Robert W. Goodenow – Executive Director and
               General Counsel
Ian Pulver – Associate Counsel
Jeffrey Citron – Associate Counsel
JP Barry – Associate Counsel
Ted Saskin – Senior Director, Business Affairs and Licensing
Michael Merhab – Collectibles and Media Projects
Mike Ouellet – Associate Counsel, Licensing
Ken Kim – "Be A Player" and Promotional Licensing
Barbara Larcina – Director of Business Administration
Jeff Holloway – Manager, Accounting
Steve McAllister – Manager, Media Relations
Dominic Dodds – Manager, Information Systems
Kim Murdoch – Manager, Pensions and Benefits

NHL On-Ice Officials
Total NHL Games and 95-96 Games columns count regular-season games only.

Referees

#	Name	Birthplace	Birthdate	First NHL Game	Total NHL Games	95-96 Games
9	Blaine Angus	Shawville, Que.	9/25/61	10/17/92	33	14
30	Bernard Degrace	Lameque, N.B.	5/1/67	10/15/91	*157	0
10	Paul Devorski	Guelph, Ont.	8/18/58	10/14/89	320	65
11	Mark Faucette	Springfield, MA	6/9/58	12/23/87	435	65
2	Kerry Fraser	Sarnia, Ont.	5/30/52	4/6/75	977	57
4	Terry Gregson	Erin, Ont.	11/7/53	12/19/81	864	68
8	Dave Jackson	Montreal, Que.	11/28/64	12/23/90	191	68
18	Greg Kimmerly	Toronto, Ont.	12/8/64		0	0
12	Don Koharski	Halifax, N.S.	12/2/55	10/14/77	**996	68
14	Dennis LaRue	Savannah, GA	7/14/59	3/26/91	56	17
28	Mike Leggo	North Bay, Ont.	10/7/64		0	0
27	Kevin Maguire	Toronto, Ont.	5/1/63		0	0
6	Dan Marouelli	Edmonton, Alta.	7/16/55	11/2/84	706	60
26	Rob Martell	Winnipeg, Man.	10/21/63	3/14/84	**2	1
7	Bill McCreary	Guelph, Ont.	11/17/55	11/3/84	730	64
19	Mick McGeough	Regina, Sask.	6/20/57	1/19/89	318	67
15	Dan O'Halloran	Leamington, Ont.	3/25/64	10/14/95	10	10
20	Lance Roberts	Edmonton, Alta.	5/28/57	11/3/89	207	60
31	Lyle Seitz	Brooks, Alta.	1/22/69	10/6/92	*102	0
16	Rob Shick	Port Alberni, B.C.	12/4/57	4/6/86	527	63
22	Paul Stewart	Boston, MA	3/21/55	3/27/87	560	64
17	Richard Trottier	Laval, Que.	2/28/57	12/13/89	222	62
21	Don Van Massenhoven	London, Ont.	7/17/60	11/11/93	115	64
24	Stephen Walkom	North Bay, Ont.	8/8/63	10/18/92	120	67
23	Brad Watson	Regina, Sask.	10/4/61	2/5/94	2	1
29	Scott Zelkin	Wilmette, IL	9/12/68		0	0

* All games worked as a linesman.   ** Includes some games worked as a linesman.

Linesmen

#	Name	Birthplace	Birthdate	First NHL Game	Total NHL Games	95-96 Games
38	Ron Asselstine	Toronto, Ont.	11/6/46	10/10/79	1292	72
94	Wayne Bonney	Ottawa, Ont.	5/27/53	10/10/79	1169	65
55	Gord Broseker	Baltimore, MD	7/8/50	1/14/75	1521	75
74	Lonnie Cameron	Victoria, B.C.	7/15/64		0	0
35	Pierre Champoux	Ville St-Pierre, Que.	4/18/63	10/8/88	491	65
50	Kevin Collins	Springfield, MA	12/15/50	10/13/77	1466	77
88	Mike Cvik	Calgary, Alta.	7/6/62	10/8/87	577	68
98	Pat Dapuzzo	Hoboken, NJ	12/29/58	12/5/84	930	75
44	Greg Devorski	Guelph, Ont.	8/3/69	10/9/93	167	73
68	Scott Driscoll	Seaforth, Ont.	5/2/68	10/10/92	222	66
36	Gerard Gauthier	Montreal, Que.	9/5/48	10/16/71	1867	79
95	Conrad Haché	Sudbury, Ont.	5/15/72	2/27/95	20	16
91	Don Henderson	Calgary, Alta.	9/23/68	3/10/95	19	18
64	Shane Heyer	Summerland, B.C.	2/7/64	10/5/88	456	81
37	Bob Hodges	Hespeler, Ont.	8/16/44	10/14/72	1632	66
48	Swede Knox	Edmonton, Alta.	3/2/48	10/14/72	1774	44
71	Brad Kovachik	Woodstock, Ont.	3/7/71		0	0
86	Brad Lazarowich	Vancouver, B.C.	8/4/62	10/9/86	681	68
46	Dan McCourt	Falconbridge, Ont.	8/14/54	12/27/80	1070	74
90	Andy McElman	Chicago Heights, IL	8/4/61	10/7/93	165	62
39	Randy Mitton	Fredericton, N.B.	9/22/50	2/2/74	1612	75
41	Jean Morin	Sorel, Que.	8/10/63	10/5/91	277	68
93	Brian Murphy	Dover, NH	12/13/64	10/7/88	503	71
40	Thor Nelson	Westminister, CA	1/6/68	2/16/95	19	15
43	Tim Nowak	Buffalo, NY	9/6/67	10/8/93	163	76
79	Mark Paré	Windsor, Ont.	7/26/57	10/11/79	1255	68
51	Baron Parker	Vancouver, B.C.	3/5/67	1/25/95	106	68
72	Stephane Provost	Montreal, Que.	5/5/67	1/25/95	114	69
34	Pierre Racicot	Verdun, Que.	2/15/67	10/12/93	163	68
32	Ray Scapinello	Guelph, Ont.	11/5/46	10/17/71	1947	76
47	Dan Schachte	Madison, WI	7/13/58	10/6/82	983	68
57	Jay Sharrers	Jamaica, WI	7/3/67	10/6/90	359	74
33	Leon Stickle	Toronto, Ont.	4/20/48	10/17/70	1898	73
56	Mark Wheler	North Battleford, Sask.	9/20/65	10/10/92	244	71

NHL History

1917 — National Hockey League organized November 22 in Montreal following suspension of operations by the National Hockey Association of Canada Limited (NHA). Montreal Canadiens, Montreal Wanderers, Ottawa Senators and Quebec Bulldogs attended founding meeting. Delegates decided to use NHA rules.

Toronto Arenas were later admitted as fifth team; Quebec decided not to operate during the first season. Quebec players allocated to remaining four teams.

Frank Calder elected president and secretary-treasurer.

First NHL games played December 19, with Toronto only arena with artificial ice. Clubs played 22-game split schedule.

1918 — Emergency meeting held January 3 due to destruction by fire of Montreal Arena which was home ice for both Canadiens and Wanderers.

Wanderers withdrew, reducing the NHL to three teams; Canadiens played remaining home games at 3,250-seat Jubilee rink.

Quebec franchise sold to P.J. Quinn of Toronto on October 18 on the condition that the team operate in Quebec City for 1918-19 season. Quinn did not attend the November League meeting and Quebec did not play in 1918-19.

1919-20 — NHL reactivated Quebec Bulldogs franchise. Former Quebec players returned to the club. New Mount Royal Arena became home of Canadiens. Toronto Arenas changed name to St. Patricks. Clubs played 24-game split schedule.

1920-21 — H.P. Thompson of Hamilton, Ontario made application for the purchase of an NHL franchise. Quebec franchise shifted to Hamilton with other NHL teams providing players to strengthen the club.

1921-22 — Split schedule abandoned. First and second place teams at the end of full schedule to play for championship.

1922-23 — Clubs agreed that players could not be sold or traded to clubs in any other league without first being offered to all other clubs in the NHL. In March, Foster Hewitt broadcasts radio's first hockey game.

1923-24 — Ottawa's new 10,000-seat arena opened. First U.S. franchise granted to Boston for following season.

Dr. Cecil Hart Trophy donated to NHL to be awarded to the player judged most useful to his team.

1924-25 — Canadian Arena Company of Montreal granted a franchise to operate Montreal Maroons. NHL now six team league with two clubs in Montreal. Inaugural game in new Montreal Forum played November 29, 1924 as Canadiens defeated Toronto 7-1. Forum was home rink for the Maroons, but no ice was available in the Canadiens arena November 29, resulting in shift to Forum.

Hamilton finished first in the standings, receiving a bye into the finals. But Hamilton players, demanding $200 each for additional games in the playoffs, went on strike. The NHL suspended all players, fining them $200 each. Stanley Cup finalist to be the winner of NHL semi-final between Toronto and Canadiens.

Prince of Wales and Lady Byng trophies donated to NHL.

Clubs played 30-game schedule.

1925-26 — Hamilton club dropped from NHL. Players signed by new New York Americans franchise. Franchise granted to Pittsburgh.

Clubs played 36-game schedule.

1926-27 — New York Rangers granted franchise May 15, 1926. Chicago Black Hawks and Detroit Cougars granted franchises September 25, 1926. NHL now ten-team league with an American and a Canadian Division.

Stanley Cup came under the control of NHL. In previous seasons, winners of the now-defunct Western or Pacific Coast leagues would play NHL champion in Cup finals.

Toronto franchise sold to a new company controlled by Hugh Aird and Conn Smythe. Name changed from St. Patricks to Maple Leafs.

Clubs played 44-game schedule.

The Montreal Canadiens donated the Vezina Trophy to be awarded to the team allowing the fewest goals-against in regular season play. The winning team would, in turn, present the trophy to the goaltender playing in the greatest number of games during the season.

1929-30 — Detroit franchise changed name from Cougars to Falcons.

1930-31 — Pittsburgh transferred to Philadelphia for one season. Pirates changed name to Philadelphia Quakers. Trading deadline for teams set at February 15 of each year. NHL approved operation of farm teams by Rangers, Americans, Falcons and Bruins. Four-sided electric arena clock first demonstrated.

1931-32 — Philadelphia dropped out. Ottawa withdrew for one season. New Maple Leaf Gardens completed.

Clubs played 48-game schedule

1932-33 — Detroit franchise changed name from Falcons to Red Wings. Franchise application received from St. Louis but refused because of additional travel costs. Ottawa team resumed play.

1933-34 — First All-Star Game played as a benefit for injured player Ace Bailey. Leafs defeated All-Stars 7-3 in Toronto.

1934-35 — Ottawa franchise transferred to St. Louis. Team called St. Louis Eagles and consisted largely of Ottawa's players.

1935-36 — Ottawa-St. Louis franchise terminated. Montreal Canadiens finished season with very poor record. To strengthen the club, NHL gave Canadiens first call on the services of all French-Canadian players for three seasons.

1937-38 — Second benefit all-star game staged November 2 in Montreal in aid of the family of the late Canadiens star Howie Morenz.

Montreal Maroons withdrew from the NHL on June 22, 1938, leaving seven clubs in the League.

1938-39 — Expenses for each club regulated at $5 per man per day for meals and $2.50 per man per day for accommodation.

1939-40 — Benefit All-Star Game played October 29, 1939 in Montreal for the children of the late Albert (Babe) Siebert.

1940-41 — Ross-Tyer puck adopted as the official puck of the NHL. Early in the season it was apparent that this puck was too soft. The Spalding puck was adopted in its place.

After the playoffs, Arthur Ross, NHL governor from Boston, donated a perpetual trophy to be awarded annually to the player voted outstanding in the league.

1941-42 — New York Americans changed name to Brooklyn Americans.

1942-43 — Brooklyn Americans withdrew from NHL, leaving six teams: Boston, Chicago, Detroit, Montreal, New York and Toronto. Playoff format saw first-place team play third-place team and second play fourth.

Clubs played 50-game schedule.

Frank Calder, president of the NHL since its inception, died in Montreal. Meryn "Red" Dutton, former manager of the New York Americans, became president. The NHL commissioned the Calder Memorial Trophy to be awarded to the League's outstanding rookie each year.

1945-46 — Philadelphia, Los Angeles and San Francisco applied for NHL franchises.

The Philadelphia Arena Company of the American Hockey League applied for an injunction to prevent the possible operation of an NHL franchise in that city.

1946-47 — Mervyn Dutton retired as president of the NHL prior to the start of the season. He was succeeded by Clarence S. Campbell.

Individual trophy winners and all-star team members to receive $1,000 awards.

Playoff guarantees for players introduced.

Clubs played 60-game schedule.

1947-48 — The first annual All-Star Game for the benefit of the players' pension fund was played when the All-Stars defeated the Stanley Cup Champion Toronto Maple Leafs 4-3 in Toronto on October 13, 1947.

Ross Trophy, awarded to the NHL's outstanding player since 1941, to be awarded annually to the League's scoring leader.

Philadelphia and Los Angeles franchise applications refused.

National Hockey League Pension Society formed.

1949-50 — Clubs played 70-game schedule.

First intra-league draft held April 30, 1950. Clubs allowed to protect 30 players. Remaining players available for $25,000 each.

1951-52 — Referees included in the League's pension plan.

1952-53 — In May of 1952, City of Cleveland applied for NHL franchise. Application denied. In March of 1953, the Cleveland Barons of the AHL challenged the NHL champions for the Stanley Cup. The NHL governors did not accept this challenge.

1953-54 — The James Norris Memorial Trophy presented to the NHL for annual presentation to the League's best defenseman.

Intra-league draft rules amended to allow teams to protect 18 skaters and two goaltenders, claiming price reduced to $15,000.

1954-55 — Each arena to operate an "out-of-town" scoreboard. Referees and linesmen to wear shirts of black and white vertical stripes. Teams agree to wear colored uniforms at home and white uniforms on the road.

1956-57 — Standardized signals for referees and linesmen introduced.

1960-61 — Canadian National Exhibition, City of Toronto and NHL reach agreement for the construction of a Hockey Hall of Fame on the CNE grounds. Hall opens on August 26, 1961.

1963-64 — Player development league established with clubs operated by NHL franchises located in Minneapolis, St. Paul, Indianapolis, Omaha and, beginning in 1964-65, Tulsa. First universal amateur draft took place. All players of qualifying age (17) unaffected by sponsorship of junior teams available to be drafted.

1964-65 — Conn Smythe Trophy presented to the NHL to be awarded annually to the outstanding player in the Stanley Cup playoffs.

Minimum age of players subject to amateur draft changed to 18.

1965-66 — NHL announced expansion plans for a second six-team division to begin play in 1967-68.

1966-67 — Fourteen applications for NHL franchises received.

Lester Patrick Trophy presented to the NHL to be awarded annually for outstanding service to hockey in the United States.

NHL sponsorship of junior teams ceased, making all players of qualifying age not already on NHL-sponsored lists eligible for the amateur draft.

1967-68 — Six new teams added: California Seals, Los Angeles Kings, Minnesota North Stars, Philadelphia Flyers, Pittsburgh Penguins, St. Louis Blues. New teams to play in West Division. Remaining six teams to play in East Division.

Minimum age of players subject to amateur draft changed to 20.

Clubs played 74-game schedule.

Clarence S. Campbell Trophy awarded to team finishing the regular season in first place in West Division.

California Seals changed name to Oakland Seals on December 8, 1967.

1968-69 — Clubs played 76-game schedule.

Amateur draft expanded to cover any amateur player of qualifying age throughout the world.

1970-71 — Two new teams added: Buffalo Sabres and Vancouver Canucks. These teams joined East Division: Chicago switched to West Division.

Clubs played 78-game schedule.

1971-72 — Playoff format amended. In each division, first to play fourth; second to play third.

1972-73 — Soviet Nationals and Canadian NHL stars play eight-game pre-season series. Canadians win 4-3-1.

Two new teams added. Atlanta Flames join West Division; New York Islanders join East Division.

1974-75 — Two new teams added: Kansas City Scouts and Washington Capitals. Teams realigned into two nine-team conferences, the Prince of Wales made up of the Norris and Adams Divisions, and the Clarence Campbell made up of the Smythe and Patrick Divisions.

Clubs played 80-game schedule.

NHL History — *continued*

1976-77 — California franchise transferred to Cleveland. Team named Cleveland Barons. Kansas City franchise transferred to Denver. Team named Colorado Rockies.

1977-78 — Clarence S. Campbell retires as NHL president. Succeeded by John A. Ziegler, Jr.

1978-79 — Cleveland and Minnesota franchises merge, leaving NHL with 17 teams. Merged team placed in Adams Division, playing home games in Minnesota.

Minimum age of players subject to amateur draft changed to 19.

1979-80 — Four new teams added: Edmonton Oilers, Hartford Whalers, Quebec Nordiques and Winnipeg Jets.

Minimum age of players subject to entry draft changed to 18.

1980-81 — Atlanta franchise shifted to Calgary, retaining "Flames" name.

1981-82 — Teams realigned within existing divisions. New groupings based on geographical areas. Unbalanced schedule adopted.

1982-83 — Colorado Rockies franchise shifted to East Rutherford, New Jersey. Team named New Jersey Devils. Franchise moved to Patrick Division from Smythe; Winnipeg moved to Smythe Division from Norris.

1991-92 — San Jose Sharks added, making the NHL a 22-team league. NHL celebrates 75th Anniversary Season. The 1991-92 regular season suspended due to a strike by members of the NHL Players' Association on April 1, 1992. Play resumed April 12, 1992.

1992-93 — Gil Stein named NHL president (October, 1992). Gary Bettman named first NHL Commissioner (February, 1993). Ottawa Senators and Tampa Bay Lightning added, making the NHL a 24-team league. NHL celebrates Stanley Cup Centennial. Clubs played 84-game schedule.

1993-94 — Mighty Ducks of Anaheim and Florida Panthers added, making the NHL a 26-team league. Minnesota franchise shifted to Dallas, team named Dallas Stars. Prince of Wales and Clarence Campbell Conferences renamed Eastern and Western. Adams, Patrick, Norris and Smythe Divisions renamed Northeast, Atlantic, Central and Pacific. Winnipeg moved to Central Division from Pacific; Tampa Bay moved to Atlantic Division from Central; Pittsburgh moved to Northeast Division from Atlantic.

1994-95 — A labor disruption forced the cancellation of 468 games from October 1, 1994 to January 19, 1995. Clubs played a 48-game schedule that began January 20, 1995 and ended May 3, 1995. No inter-conference games were played.

1995-96 — Quebec franchise transferred to Denver. Team named Colorado Avalanche and placed in Pacific Division of Western Conference. Clubs to play 82-game schedule.

1996-97 — Winnipeg franchise transferred to Phoenix. Team named Phoenix Coyotes and placed in Central Division of Western Conference.

NHL Attendance

Season	Regular Season		Playoffs		Total
	Games	Attendance	Games	Attendance	Attendance
1960-61	210	2,317,142	17	242,000	2,559,142
1961-62	210	2,435,424	18	277,000	2,712,424
1962-63	210	2,590,574	16	220,906	2,811,480
1963-64	210	2,732,642	21	309,149	3,041,791
1964-65	210	2,822,635	20	303,859	3,126,494
1965-66	210	2,941,164	16	249,000	3,190,184
1966-67	210	3,084,759	16	248,336	3,333,095
1967-68[1]	444	4,938,043	40	495,089	5,433,132
1968-69	456	5,550,613	33	431,739	5,982,352
1969-70	456	5,992,065	34	461,694	6,453,759
1970-71[2]	546	7,257,677	43	707,633	7,965,310
1971-72	546	7,609,368	36	582,666	8,192,034
1972-73[3]	624	8,575,651	38	624,637	9,200,288
1973-74	624	8,640,978	38	600,442	9,241,420
1974-75[4]	720	9,521,536	51	784,181	10,305,717
1975-76	720	9,103,761	48	726,279	9,830,040
1976-77	720	8,563,890	44	646,279	9,210,169
1977-78	720	8,526,564	45	686,634	9,213,198
1978-79	680	7,758,053	45	694,521	8,452,574
1979-80[5]	840	10,533,623	63	976,699	11,510,322
1980-81	840	10,726,198	68	966,390	11,692,588
1981-82	840	10,710,894	71	1,058,948	11,769,842
1982-83	840	11,020,610	66	1,088,222	12,028,832
1983-84	840	11,359,386	70	1,107,400	12,466,786
1984-85	840	11,633,730	70	1,107,500	12,741,230
1985-86	840	11,621,000	72	1,152,503	12,773,503
1986-87	840	11,855,880	87	1,383,967	13,239,847
1987-88	840	12,117,512	83	1,336,901	13,454,413
1988-89	840	12,417,969	83	1,327,214	13,745,183
1989-90	840	12,579,651	85	1,355,593	13,935,244
1990-91	840	12,343,897	92	1,442,203	13,786,100
1991-92[7]	880	12,769,676	86	1,327,920	14,097,596
1992-93[7]	1,008	14,158,177 [8]	83	1,346,034	15,504,211
1993-94[9]	1,092	16,105,604 [10]	90	1,440,095	17,545,699
1994-95	624	9,233,884	81	1,329,130	10,563,014
1995-96	1,066	17,041,614*	86	1,540,140*	18,581,754*

[1] First expansion: Los Angeles, Pittsburgh, California (Cleveland), Philadelphia, St. Louis and Minnesota (Dallas)
[2] Second expansion: Buffalo and Vancouver
[3] Third expansion: Atlanta (Calgary) and New York Islanders
[4] Fourth expansion: Kansas City (Colorado, New Jersey) and Washington
[5] Fifth expansion: Edmonton, Hartford, Quebec (Colorado) and Winnipeg
[6] Sixth expansion: San Jose
[7] Seventh expansion: Ottawa and Tampa Bay
[8] Includes 24 neutral site games
[9] Eighth expansion: Anaheim and Florida
[10] Includes 26 neutral site games

* Published attendance

Major Rule Changes

1910-11 — Game changed from two 30-minute periods to three 20-minute periods.

1911-12 — National Hockey Association (forerunner of the NHL) originated six-man hockey, replacing seven-man game.

1917-18 — Goalies permitted to fall to the ice to make saves. Previously a goaltender was penalized for dropping to the ice.

1918-19 — Penalty rules amended. For minor fouls, substitutes not allowed until penalized player had served three minutes. For major fouls, no substitutes for five minutes. For match fouls, no substitutes allowed for the remainder of the game.

With the addition of two lines painted on the ice twenty feet from center, three playing zones were created, producing a forty-foot neutral center ice area in which forward passing was permitted. Kicking the puck was permitted in this neutral zone. Tabulation of assists began.

1921-22 — Goaltenders allowed to pass the puck forward up to their own blue line.

Overtime limited to twenty minutes.

Minor penalties changed from three minutes to two minutes.

1923-24 — Match foul defined as actions deliberately injuring or disabling an opponent. For such actions, a player was fined not less than $50 and ruled off the ice for the balance of the game. A player assessed a match penalty may be replaced by a substitute at the end of 20 minutes. Match penalty recipients must meet with the League president who can assess additional punishment.

1925-26 — Delayed penalty rules introduced. Each team must have a minimum of four players on the ice at all times.

Two rules were amended to encourage offense: No more than two defensemen permitted to remain inside a team's own blue line when the puck has left the defensive zone. A faceoff to be called for ragging the puck unless short-handed.

Team captains only players allowed to talk to referees.

Goaltender's leg pads limited to 12-inch width.

Timekeeper's gong to mark end of periods rather than referee's whistle. Teams to dress a maximum of 12 players for each game from a roster of no more than 14 players.

1926-27 — Blue lines repositioned to sixty feet from each goal-line, thereby enlarging the neutral zone and standardizing distance from blueline to goal.

Uniform goal nets adopted throughout NHL with goal posts securely fastened to the ice.

1927-28 — To further encourage offense, forward passes allowed in defending and neutral zones and goaltender's pads reduced in width from 12 to 10 inches.

Game standardized at three twenty-minute periods of stop-time separated by ten-minute intermissions.

Teams to change ends after each period.

Ten minutes of sudden-death overtime to be played if the score is tied after regulation time.

Minor penalty to be assessed to any player other than a goaltender for deliberately picking up the puck while it is in play. Minor penalty to be assessed for deliberately shooting the puck out of play.

The Art Ross goal net adopted as the official net of the NHL.

Maximum length of hockey sticks limited to 53 inches measured from heel of blade to end of handle. No minimum length stipulated.

Home teams given choice of goals to defend at start of game.

1928-29 — Forward passing permitted in defensive and neutral zones and into attacking zone if pass receiver is in neutral zone when pass is made. No forward passing allowed inside attacking zone.

Minor penalty to be assessed to any player who delays the game by passing the puck back into his defensive zone.

Ten-minute overtime without sudden-death provision to be played in games tied after regulation time. Games tied after this overtime period declared a draw.

Exclusive of goaltenders, team to dress at least 8 and no more than 12 skaters.

Major Rule Changes — *continued*

1929-30 — Forward passing permitted inside all three zones but not permitted across either blue line.

Kicking the puck allowed, but a goal cannot be scored by kicking the puck in.

No more than three players including the goaltender may remain in their defensive zone when the puck has gone up ice. Minor penalties to be assessed for the first two violations of this rule in a game; major penalties thereafter.

Goaltenders forbidden to hold the puck. Pucks caught must be cleared immediately. For infringement of this rule, a faceoff to be taken ten feet in front of the goal with no player except the goaltender standing between the faceoff spot and the goal-line.

Highsticking penalties introduced.

Maximum number of players in uniform increased from 12 to 15.

December 21, 1929 — Forward passing rules instituted at the beginning of the 1929-30 season more than doubled number of goals scored. Partway through the season, these rules were further amended to read, "No attacking player allowed to precede the play when entering the opposing defensive zone." This is similar to modern offside rule.

1930-31 — A player without a complete stick ruled out of play and forbidden from taking part in further action until a new stick is obtained. A player who has broken his stick must obtain a replacement at his bench.

A further refinement of the offside rule stated that the puck must first be propelled into the attacking zone before any player of the attacking side can enter that zone; for infringement of this rule a faceoff to take place at the spot where the infraction took place.

1931-32 — Though there is no record of a team attempting to play with two goaltenders on the ice, a rule was instituted which stated that each team was allowed only one goaltender on the ice at one time.

Attacking players forbidden to impede the movement or obstruct the vision of opposing goaltenders.

Defending players with the exception of the goaltender forbidden from falling on the puck within 10 feet of the net.

1932-33 — Each team to have captain on the ice at all times.

If the goaltender is removed from the ice to serve a penalty, the manager of the club to appoint a substitute.

Match penalty with substitution after five minutes instituted for kicking another player.

1933-34 — Number of players permitted to stand in defensive zone restricted to three including goaltender.

Visible time clocks required in each rink.

Two referees replace one referee and one linesman.

1934-35 — Penalty shot awarded when a player is tripped and thus prevented from having a clear shot on goal, having no player to pass to other than the offending player. Shot taken from inside a 10-foot circle located 38 feet from the goal. The goaltender must not advance more than one foot from his goal-line when the shot is taken.

1937-38 — Rules introduced governing icing the puck.

Penalty shot awarded when a player other than a goaltender falls on the puck within 10 feet of the goal.

1938-39 — Penalty shot modified to allow puck carrier to skate in before shooting.

One referee and one linesman replace two referee system.

Blue line widened to 12 inches.

Maximum number of players in uniform increased from 14 to 15.

1939-40 — A substitute replacing a goaltender removed from ice to serve a penalty may use a goaltender's stick and gloves but no other goaltending equipment.

1940-41 — Flooding ice surface between periods made obligatory.

1941-42 — Penalty shots classified as minor and major. Minor shot to be taken from a line 28 feet from the goal. Major shot, awarded when a player is tripped with only the goaltender to beat, permits the player taking the penalty shot to skate right into the goalkeeper and shoot from point-blank range.

One referee and two linesmen employed to officiate games.

For playoffs, standby minor league goaltenders employed by NHL as emergency substitutes.

1942-43 — Because of wartime restrictions on train scheduling, regular-season overtime was discontinued on November 21, 1942.

Player limit reduced from 15 to 14. Minimum of 12 men in uniform abolished.

1943-44 — Red line at center ice introduced to speed up the game and reduce offside calls. This rule is considered to mark the beginning of the modern era in the NHL.

Delayed penalty rules introduced.

1945-46 — Goal indicator lights synchronized with official time clock required at all rinks.

1946-47 — System of signals by officials to indicate infractions introduced.

Linesmen from neutral cities employed for all games.

1947-48 — Goal awarded when a player with the puck has an open net to shoot at and a thrown stick prevents the shot on goal. Major penalty to any player who throws his stick in any zone other than defending zone. If a stick is thrown by a player in his defending zone but the thrown stick is not considered to have prevented a goal, a penalty shot is awarded.

All playoff games played until a winner determined, with 20-minute sudden-death overtime periods separated by 10-minute intermissions.

1949-50 — Ice surface painted white.

Clubs allowed to dress 17 players exclusive of goaltenders.

Major penalties incurred by goaltenders served by a member of the goaltender's team instead of resulting in a penalty shot.

1950-51 — Each team required to provide an emergency goaltender in attendance with full equipment at each game for use by either team in the event of illness or injury to a regular goaltender.

1951-52 — Home teams to wear basic white uniforms; visiting teams basic colored uniforms.

Goal crease enlarged from 3 × 7 feet to 4 × 8 feet.

Number of players in uniform reduced to 15 plus goaltenders.

Faceoff circles enlarged from 10-foot to 15-foot radius.

1952-53 — Teams permitted to dress 15 skaters on the road and 16 at home.

1953-54 — Number of players in uniform set at 16 plus goaltenders.

1954-55 — Number of players in uniform set at 18 plus goaltenders up to December 1 and 16 plus goaltenders thereafter.

1956-57 — Player serving a minor penalty allowed to return to ice when a goal is scored by opposing team.

1959-60 — Players prevented from leaving their benches to enter into an altercation. Substitutions permitted providing substitutes do not enter into altercation.

Stan Mikita (21) attempts to swipe a loose puck out of the air near Johnny Bower's crease during action in the 1967 semi-finals between the Leafs and Black Hawks. Like many other NHL players, Mikita used a "banana-blade" curve on his stick, but he was forced to "straighten out" when the NHL limited the curve on a player's stick to 1¹/₂ inches the following season.

1960-61 — Number of players in uniform set at 16 plus goaltenders.

1961-62 — Penalty shots to be taken by the player against whom the foul was committed. In the event of a penalty shot called in a situation where a particular player hasn't been fouled, the penalty shot to be taken by any player on the ice when the foul was committed.

1964-65 — No bodily contact on faceoffs.

In playoff games, each team to have its substitute goaltender dressed in his regular uniform except for leg pads and body protector. All previous rules governing standby goaltenders terminated.

1965-66 — Teams required to dress two goaltenders for each regular-season game. Maximum stick length increased to 55 inches.

1966-67 — Substitution allowed on coincidental major penalties.

Between-periods intermissions fixed at 15 minutes.

1967-68 — If a penalty incurred by a goaltender is a co-incident major, the penalty to be served by a player of the goaltender's team on the ice at the time the penalty was called. Limit of curvature of hockey stick blade set at 1-¹/₂ inches.

1969-70 — Limit of curvature of hockey stick blade set at 1 inch.

1970-71 — Home teams to wear basic white uniforms; visiting teams basic colored uniforms.

Limit of curvature of hockey stick blade set at ¹/₂ inch.

Minor penalty for deliberately shooting the puck out of the playing area.

1971-72 — Number of players in uniform set at 17 plus 2 goaltenders.

Third man to enter an altercation assessed an automatic game misconduct penalty.

1972-73 — Minimum width of stick blade reduced to 2 inches from 2-¹/₂ inches.

1974-75 — Bench minor penalty imposed if a penalized player does not proceed directly and immediately to the penalty box.

1976-77 — Rule dealing with fighting amended to provide a major and game misconduct penalty for any player who is clearly the instigator of a fight.

1977-78 — Teams requesting a stick measurement to be assessed a minor penalty in the event that the measured stick does not violate the rules.

1980-81 — Maximum stick length increased to 58 inches.

1981-82 — If both of a team's listed goaltenders are incapacitated, the team can dress and play any eligible goaltender who is available.

1982-83 — Number of players in uniform set at 18 plus 2 goaltenders.

1983-84 — Five-minute sudden-death overtime to be played in regular-season games that are tied at the end of regulation time.

1985-86 — Substitutions allowed in the event of co-incidental minor penalties. Maximum stick length increased to 60 inches.

1986-87 — Delayed off-side is no longer in effect once the players of the offending team have cleared the opponents' defensive zone.

1991-92 — Video replays employed to assist referees in goal/no goal situations. Size of goal crease increased. Crease changed to semi-circular configuration. Time clock to record tenths of a second in last minute of each period and overtime. Major and game misconduct penalty for checking from behind into boards. Penalties added for crease infringement and unnecessary contact with goaltender. Goal disallowed if puck enters net while a player of the attacking team is standing on the goal crease line, is in the goal crease or places his stick in the goal crease.

1992-93 — No substitutions allowed in the event of coincidental minor penalties called when both teams are at full strength. Wearing of helmets made optional for forwards and defensemen. Minor penalty for attempting to draw a penalty ("diving"). Major and game misconduct penalty for checking from behind into goal frame. Game misconduct penalty for instigating a fight. Highsticking redefined to include any use of the stick above waist-height. Previous rule stipulated shoulder-height.

1993-94 — High sticking redefined to allow goals scored with a high stick below the height of the crossbar of the goal frame.

1996-97 — Maximum stick length increased to 63 inches.

Notes

Steve Yzerman became only the second player in the history of the Detroit Red Wings to score 500 career goals when he reached the milestone mark on January 17, 1996 in a 3-2 win over the Colorado Avalanche.

Mighty Ducks of Anaheim

1995-96 Results: 35W-39L-8T 78PTS. Fourth, Pacific Division

Schedule

Oct.	Sat.	5	at Toronto	Fri.	10	Buffalo
	Mon.	7	at Montreal	Sun.	12	at Vancouver*
	Wed.	9	at Chicago	Wed.	15	at Calgary
	Thur.	10	at Colorado	Wed.	22	New Jersey
	Sat.	12	at Phoenix	Thur.	23	at Phoenix
	Wed.	16	Philadelphia	Sat.	25	at Los Angeles*
	Fri.	18	San Jose	Mon.	27	at St. Louis
	Sun.	20	Boston	Wed.	29	at Dallas
	Tues.	22	at Philadelphia	Fri.	31	Hartford
	Thur.	24	at Hartford	**Feb.** Sun.	2	Colorado
	Sun.	27	Calgary	Tues.	4	at NY Islanders
	Wed.	30	Vancouver	Wed.	5	at Toronto
Nov.	Fri.	1	San Jose	Sat.	8	at Edmonton
	Sun.	3	Colorado	Sun.	9	at Calgary
	Wed.	6	Montreal	Wed.	12	Toronto
	Fri.	8	Los Angeles	Sat.	15	at Vancouver
	Mon.	11	Dallas	Mon.	17	Edmonton
	Wed.	13	Toronto	Thur.	20	at Los Angeles
	Fri.	15	at Dallas	Sat.	22	Phoenix*
	Sun.	17	at St. Louis	Sun.	23	Vancouver
	Wed.	20	NY Islanders	Wed.	26	Edmonton
	Sat.	23	at San Jose	Fri.	28	at Washington
	Sun.	24	Detroit	**Mar.** Sun.	2	at Detroit
	Wed.	27	St. Louis	Wed.	5	Ottawa
	Fri.	29	Chicago*	Fri.	7	NY Rangers
Dec.	Sun.	1	Edmonton	Sun.	9	at Colorado
	Wed.	4	Tampa Bay	Wed.	12	Detroit
	Fri.	6	at Buffalo	Fri.	14	St. Louis
	Sat.	7	at Pittsburgh	Sun.	16	Calgary
	Mon.	9	at Boston	Wed.	19	Los Angeles
	Wed.	11	Pittsburgh	Fri.	21	at Colorado
	Fri.	13	Washington	Sun.	23	at Edmonton*
	Fri.	20	Calgary	Tues.	25	at Calgary
	Mon.	23	Phoenix	Wed.	26	at Vancouver
	Fri.	27	at NY Rangers	Fri.	28	at Chicago
	Sat.	28	at New Jersey	Sun.	30	at Detroit*
	Mon.	30	at Ottawa	**Apr.** Tues.	1	Chicago
Jan.	Wed.	1	at Florida*	Wed.	2	at San Jose
	Fri.	3	at Tampa Bay	Fri.	4	Dallas
	Mon.	6	Vancouver	Wed.	9	Los Angeles
	Wed.	8	Florida	Fri.	11	at San Jose

* Denotes afternoon game.

Year-by-Year Record

Season	GP	Home			Road			Overall					Pts.	Finished		Playoff Result
		W	L	T	W	L	T	W	L	T	GF	GA				
1995-96	82	22	15	4	13	24	4	35	39	8	234	247	78	4th,	Pacific Div.	Out of Playoffs
1994-95	48	11	9	4	5	18	1	16	27	5	125	164	37	6th,	Pacific Div.	Out of Playoffs
1993-94	84	14	26	2	19	20	3	33	46	5	229	251	71	4th,	Pacific Div.	Out of Playoffs

Acquired from the Winnipeg Jets on February 7, 1996, Teemu Selanne collected 16 goals and 20 assists in 28 games with the Mighty Ducks.

Franchise date: June 15, 1993

4th NHL Season

PACIFIC DIVISION

1996-97 Player Personnel

FORWARDS	HT	WT	S	Place of Birth	Date	1995-96 Club
BANHAM, Frank	6-0	187	R	Calahoo, Alta.	4/14/75	Saskatoon-Baltimore
BAUMGARTNER, Ken	6-1	205	L	Flin Flon, Man.	3/11/66	Toronto-Anaheim
BROWN, Kevin	6-1	212	R	Birmingham, England	5/11/74	L.A.-Phx-Corw'll-Peo-P.E.I.
DAY, Joe	5-11	180	L	Chicago, IL	5/11/68	Detroit (IHL)-Las Vegas
HERPERGER, Chris	6-0	190	L	Esterhazy, Sask.	2/24/74	Hershey-Baltimore
HICKS, Alex	6-1	195	L	Calgary, Alta.	9/4/69	Anaheim-Baltimore
JOMPHE, Jean-Francois	6-1	195	L	Harve' St. Pierre, Que.	12/28/72	Anaheim-Baltimore
KARIYA, Paul	5-11	175	L	Vancouver, B.C.	10/16/74	Anaheim
KARPOV, Valeri	5-10	176	L	Chelyabinsk, USSR	8/5/71	Anaheim
KURRI, Jari	6-1	195	R	Helsinki, Finland	5/18/60	Los Angeles-NY Rangers
LeBOUTILLIER, Peter	6-1	198	L	Minnedosa, Man.	1/11/75	Baltimore
LECLERC, Mike	6-1	205	L	Winnipeg, Man.	11/10/76	Brandon
NIKULIN, Igor	6-1	190	L	Cherepovets, USSR	8/26/72	Cherepovets-Baltimore
OKSIUTA, Roman	6-3	229	L	Murmansk, USSR	8/21/70	Vancouver-Anaheim
PRONGER, Sean	6-2	205	L	Dryden, Ont.	11/30/72	Anaheim-Baltimore
REICHERT, Craig	6-1	196	R	Winnipeg, Man.	5/11/74	Baltimore
RUCCHIN, Steve	6-3	210	L	London, Ont.	7/4/71	Anaheim
RYCHEL, Warren	6-0	202	L	Tecumseh, Ont.	5/12/67	Colorado
SACCO, Joe	6-1	195	R	Medford, MA	2/4/69	Anaheim
SELANNE, Teemu	6-0	200	L	Helsinki, Finland	7/3/70	Winnipeg-Anaheim
STEVENSON, Jeremy	6-2	215	L	San Bernadino, CA	7/28/74	Anaheim-Baltimore
VALK, Garry	6-1	205	L	Edmonton, Alta.	11/27/67	Anaheim
VAN ALLEN, Shaun	6-1	200	L	Shaunavon, Sask.	8/29/67	Anaheim

DEFENSEMEN						
BRISKE, Byron	6-2	194	R	Humboldt, Sask.	1/23/76	Tri-City
CORCORAN, Brian	6-2	247	L	Baldwinsville, NY	4/23/72	Raleigh-Baltimore
DEEKS, Alain	6-5	230	R	Hawkesbury, Ont.	4/15/69	Baltimore
DOLLAS, Bobby	6-2	212	L	Montreal, Que.	1/31/65	Anaheim
HOLAN, Milos	5-11	191	L	Bilovec, Czech.	4/22/71	Anaheim
KARPA, Dave	6-1	202	R	Regina, Sask.	5/7/71	Anaheim
MARSHALL, Bobby	6-1	190	L	North York, Ont.	4/11/72	Saint John-Baltimore
MARSHALL, Jason	6-2	195	R	Cranbrook, B.C.	2/22/71	Anaheim-Baltimore
MIKULCHIK, Oleg	6-2	200	R	Minsk, USSR	6/27/64	Anaheim-Baltimore
OLAUSSON, Fredrik	6-2	195	R	Dadesjo, Sweden	10/5/66	Edmonton-Anaheim
PLAVSIC, Adrien	6-1	200	L	Montreal, Que.	1/13/70	Tampa Bay-Atlanta
SALEI, Ruslan	6-1	200	L	Minsk, USSR	11/2/74	Las Vegas
TREBIL, Daniel	6-3	185	R	Edina, MN	4/10/74	U. Minnesota
TRNKA, Pavel	6-3	190	L	Plzen, Czech.	7/27/76	Baltimore
TSULYGIN, Nikolai	6-4	205	R	Ufa, USSR	5/29/75	Baltimore
VAN IMPE, Darren	6-0	195	L	Saskatoon, Sask.	5/18/73	Anaheim-Baltimore
YORK, Jason	6-2	195	R	Nepean, Ont.	5/20/70	Anaheim

GOALTENDERS	HT	WT	C	Place of Birth	Date	1995-96 Club
ASKEY, Tom	6-2	185	L	Kenmore, NY	10/4/74	Ohio State
HEBERT, Guy	5-11	185	L	Troy, NY	1/7/67	Anaheim
O'NEILL, Mike	5-7	160	L	LaSalle, Que.	11/3/67	Baltimore
SHTALENKOV, Mikhail	6-2	180	L	Moscow, USSR	10/20/65	Anaheim
TORCHIA, Mike	5-11	215	L	Toronto, Ont.	2/23/72	Port (AHL)-Hamp Rds-Mich-Orlando-Baltimore

1995-96 Scoring

* – rookie

Regular Season

Pos	#	Player	Team	GP	G	A	Pts	+/–	PIM	PP	SH	GW	GT	S	%
L	9	Paul Kariya	ANA	82	50	58	108	9	20	20	3	9	0	349	14.3
R	8	Teemu Selanne	WPG	51	24	48	72	3	18	6	1	4	0	163	14.7
			ANA	28	16	20	36	2	4	3	0	1	0	104	15.4
			TOTAL	79	40	68	108	5	22	9	1	5	0	267	15.0
R	28	Roman Oksiuta	VAN	56	16	23	39	2	42	5	0	1	0	92	17.4
			ANA	14	7	5	12	2	18	6	0	0	0	27	25.9
			TOTAL	70	23	28	51	4	60	11	0	1	0	119	19.3
C	20	Steve Rucchin	ANA	64	19	25	44	3	12	8	1	4	0	113	16.8
D	2	Bobby Dollas	ANA	82	8	22	30	9	64	0	1	1	0	117	6.8
R	14	Joe Sacco	ANA	76	13	14	27	1	40	1	2	2	1	132	9.8
C	93	Anatoli Semenov	PHI	44	3	13	16	3	14	0	0	0	0	55	5.5
			ANA	12	1	9	10	-4	10	0	0	0	0	24	4.2
			TOTAL	56	4	22	26	-1	24	0	0	0	0	79	5.1
C	22	Shaun Van Allen	ANA	49	8	17	25	13	41	0	0	2	0	78	10.3
L	18	Garry Valk	ANA	79	12	12	24	8	125	1	1	2	0	108	11.1
D	3	Jason York	ANA	79	3	21	24	-7	88	0	0	0	0	106	2.8
D	4	Fredrik Olausson	EDM	20	0	6	6	-14	14	0	0	0	0	20	0.0
			ANA	36	2	16	18	7	24	1	0	0	0	63	3.2
			TOTAL	56	2	22	24	-7	38	1	0	0	0	83	2.4
C	32	Alex Hicks	ANA	64	10	11	21	11	37	0	0	2	0	83	12.0
D	17	Dave Karpa	ANA	72	3	16	19	-3	270	0	1	1	0	62	4.8
R	21	Patrik Carnback	ANA	34	6	12	18	3	34	1	0	0	0	54	11.1
L	11	Valeri Karpov	ANA	37	9	8	17	-1	10	0	0	1	0	42	21.4
R	16	Peter Douris	ANA	31	8	7	15	-3	9	2	0	3	0	45	17.8
C	12	* David Sacco	ANA	23	4	10	14	1	18	2	0	0	0	26	15.4
R	46	* Jean-Francois Jomphe	ANA	31	2	12	14	7	39	2	0	0	0	46	4.3
L	42	* Denny Lambert	ANA	33	0	8	8	-2	55	0	0	0	0	28	0.0
R	36	Todd Ewen	ANA	53	4	3	7	-5	285	0	0	1	0	52	7.7
L	24	Ken Baumgartner	TOR	60	2	3	5	-5	152	0	0	1	0	27	7.4
			ANA	12	0	1	1	0	41	0	0	0	0	5	0.0
			TOTAL	72	2	4	6	-5	193	0	0	1	0	32	6.3
C	21	* Jim Campbell	ANA	16	2	3	5	0	36	1	0	0	0	25	8.0
D	7	* Milos Holan	ANA	16	2	2	4	-12	24	0	0	0	0	47	4.3
D	29	Randy Ladouceur	ANA	63	1	3	4	5	47	0	0	0	0	48	2.1
D	48	* Darren Van Impe	ANA	16	1	2	3	8	14	0	0	1	0	13	7.7
R	24	Steven King	ANA	7	2	0	2	-1	15	1	0	1	0	5	40.0
G	35	M. Shtalenkov	ANA	30	0	2	2	0	2	0	0	0	0	0	0.0
C	15	Viacheslav Butsayev	ANA	7	1	0	1	-4	0	0	0	0	0	9	11.1
R	28	* Dwayne Norris	ANA	3	0	1	1	0	2	0	0	0	0	3	0.0
L	40	* Jeremy Stevenson	ANA	3	0	1	1	1	12	0	0	0	0	1	0.0
C	54	* Sean Pronger	ANA	7	0	1	1	0	6	0	0	0	0	3	0.0
D	23	* Jason Marshall	ANA	24	0	1	1	3	42	0	0	0	0	9	0.0
C	27	John Lilley	ANA	1	0	0	0	-1	0	0	0	0	0	0	0.0
D	6	Don McSween	ANA	4	0	0	0	0	4	0	0	0	0	1	0.0
D	44	Oleg Mikulchik	ANA	8	0	0	0	-2	4	0	0	0	0	5	0.0
G	31	Guy Hebert	ANA	59	0	0	0	0	6	0	0	0	0	0	0.0

Goaltending

No.	Goaltender	GPI	Mins	Avg	W	L	T	EN	SO	GA	SA	S%
31	Guy Hebert	59	3326	2.83	28	23	5	3	4	157	1820	.914
35	M. Shtalenkov	30	1637	3.12	7	16	3	2	0	85	814	.896
	Totals	**82**	**4982**	**2.97**	**35**	**39**	**8**	**5**	**4**	**247**	**2639**	**.906**

General Managers' History

Jack Ferreira, 1993-94 to date.

Coaching History

Ron Wilson, 1993-94 to date.

Captains' History

Troy Loney, 1993-94; Randy Ladouceur, 1994-95 to 1995-96.

General Manager

FERREIRA, JACK
Vice-President/General Manager, The Mighty Ducks of Anaheim.
Born in Providence, RI, June 9, 1944.

Jack Ferreira was named as the first vice president/general manager of the Mighty Ducks on March 23, 1993. A veteran of over 22 years in professional hockey, Ferreira's expertise lies in evaluating talent. He is responsible for the overall hockey operations of the club.

Experienced in building an NHL team from the ground up, Ferreira assembled a nucleus in Anaheim that tied a record for most wins by an NHL first-year club (33), as the Mighty Ducks stayed in contention for a Western Conference playoff berth for most of the season in 1993-94. During the second half of the 1995-96 season, he made trades that added veteran talent and experienced players including Ken Baumgartner, Roman Oksiuta and Teemu Selanne. Those additions were a big reason the Mighty Ducks had the second-best record in the Western Conference during the last two months of the regular season and almost landed the team in the playoffs. Anaheim finished the 1995-96 season with a franchise-record 78 points, including 35 wins.

Ferreira came to the Mighty Ducks from the Montreal Canadiens, where he served as director of pro scouting during the 1992-93 season for the eventual Stanley Cup champions.

A Providence, RI, native, Ferreira's professional career began in 1972 with the New England Whalers of the World Hockey Association, where he served in many capacities, including head scout, assistant coach and assistant general manager through 1977.

From 1977-80, Ferreira served as a New England scout for the NHL's Central Scouting Bureau before moving to the Calgary Flames as a U.S. and college scout from 1980-86.

Ferreira took a post as director of player development for the New York Rangers in 1986, serving in that capacity until 1988. He then joined the Minnesota North Stars, where he served as vice president and general manager from 1988-90.

Ferreira helped start the San Jose Sharks franchise, serving as the team's executive vice president and general manager from 1990-92. Ferreira made acquisitions during the Sharks' first season that would be part of the foundation in San Jose's recent success over the past two campaigns.

A former All-American goaltender at Boston University, Ferreira was an assistant coach on the collegiate level at Princeton in 1969. He also served as an assistant coach with Brown University from 1970-72.

Ferreira earned a bachelor's degree in history from Boston University. Ferreira and his wife Kathy have two daughters, Jennifer and Julie, and two sons, Eric and Kent.

Club Records

Team

(Figures in brackets for season records are games played; records for fewest points, wins, ties, losses, goals, goals against are for 70 or more games)

Most Points	78	1995-96 (82)
Most Wins	35	1995-96 (82)
Most Ties	8	1995-96 (82)
Most Losses	46	1993-94 (84)
Most Goals	234	1995-96 (82)
Most Goals Against	251	1993-94 (84)
Fewest Points	71	1993-94 (84)
Fewest Wins	33	1993-94 (84)
Fewest Ties	5	1993-94 (84)
Fewest Losses	39	1995-96 (82)
Fewest Goals	229	1993-94 (84)
Fewest Goals Against	247	1995-96 (82)

Longest Winning Streak

Overall	6	Mar. 8-22/96
Home	5	Twice
Away	4	Nov. 19-24/93

Longest Undefeated Streak

Overall	7	Mar. 8-24/96 (6 wins, 1 tie)
Home	9	Mar. 8-Apr. 14/96 (8 wins, 1 tie)
Away	5	Jan. 2-19/94 (3 wins, 2 ties)

Longest Losing Streak

Overall	6	Oct. 20-31/93
Home	4	Twice
Away	6	Three times

Longest Winless Streak

Overall	9	Nov. 21-Dec. 10/95 (6 losses, 3 ties)
Home	4	Six times
Away	10	Mar. 26-Oct. 11/95 (9 losses, 1 tie)
Most Shutouts, Season	4	1995-96 (82)
Most PIM, Season	1,707	1993-94 (84)
Most Goals, Game	7	Four times

Individual

Most Seasons	3	Numerous
Most Games	201	Joe Sacco
Most Goals, Career	68	Paul Kariya
Most Assists, Career	79	Paul Kariya
Most Points, Career	147	Paul Kariya (68G, 79A)
Most PIM, Career	650	Todd Ewen
Most Shutouts, Career	8	Guy Hebert
Longest Consecutive Games Streak	84	Joe Sacco
Most Goals, Season	50	Paul Kariya (1995-96)
Most Assists, Season	58	Paul Kariya (1995-96)
Most Points, Season	108	Paul Kariya (1995-96; 50G, 58A)
Most PIM, Season	285	Todd Ewen (1995-96)

Most Points, Defenseman		
Season	39	Bill Houlder (1993-94; 14G, 25A)
Most Points, Center		
Season	51	Bob Corkum (1993-94; 23G, 28A)
Most Points, Right Wing		
Season	52	Terry Yake (1993-94; 21G, 31A)
Most Points, Left Wing		
Season	108	Paul Kariya (1995-96; 50G, 58A)
Most Points, Rookie		
Season	39	Paul Kariya (1994-95; 18G, 21A)
Most Shutouts, Season	4	Guy Hebert (1995-96)
Most Goals, Game	3	Four times
Most Assists, Game	4	Shaun Van Allen (Mar. 9/95)
Most Points, Game	4	Eight times

* NHL Record.

© Mighty Ducks

Joe Sacco continued his strong two-way play for Anaheim in 1995-96, clicking for 13 goals, including a pair of short-handed markers.

All-time Record vs. Other Clubs

Regular Season

		At Home							On Road								Total					
	GP	W	L	T	GF	GA	PTS	GP	W	L	T	GF	GA	PTS	GP	W	L	T	GF	GA	PTS
Boston	2	1	0	1	5	4	3	2	0	2	0	5	12	0	4	1	2	1	10	16	3
Buffalo	2	1	1	0	3	5	2	2	1	0	6	5	2	4	2	2	0	9	10	4
Calgary	8	3	4	1	21	23	7	8	4	4	0	22	21	8	16	7	8	1	43	44	15
Chicago	6	1	5	0	12	19	2	7	1	5	1	10	20	3	13	2	10	1	22	39	5
Colorado	4	3	1	0	13	5	6	4	3	0	12	16	2	8	4	4	0	25	21	8
Dallas	7	3	4	0	18	21	6	6	0	6	1	11	27	2	13	4	9	0	29	48	8
Detroit	6	0	4	2	15	30	2	6	0	5	1	18	31	1	12	0	9	3	33	61	3
Edmonton	7	5	2	0	21	17	10	8	3	5	0	17	18	6	15	8	7	0	38	35	16
Florida	2	0	2	0	5	7	0	2	1	1	5	7	1	4	0	3	1	10	14	1
Hartford	2	1	1	0	9	7	2	2	1	1	0	5	5	2	4	2	2	0	14	12	4
Los Angeles	8	3	3	2	25	22	8	9	3	5	1	21	29	7	17	6	8	3	46	51	15
Montreal	2	1	1	0	7	7	2	2	1	0	4	6	2	4	2	2	0	11	13	4
New Jersey	2	1	1	0	9	7	2	2	1	0	4	6	2	4	2	2	0	13	13	4
NY Islanders	2	1	1	0	5	5	2	2	1	1	0	6	4	2	4	2	2	0	11	9	4
NY Rangers	2	2	0	0	10	6	4	2	1	1	5	7	2	4	3	1	0	15	13	6
Ottawa	2	2	0	0	9	3	4	2	1	0	4	6	2	4	3	1	0	13	9	6
Philadelphia	2	1	1	0	8	7	2	2	1	0	1	5	4	3	4	2	1	1	13	11	5
Pittsburgh	2	1	1	0	10	8	2	2	0	1	1	4	7	1	4	1	2	1	14	15	3
St. Louis	6	3	3	0	17	14	6	6	2	4	0	19	25	4	12	5	7	0	36	39	10
San Jose	9	4	5	0	28	32	8	7	4	3	0	24	22	8	16	8	8	0	52	54	16
Tampa Bay	2	0	1	1	4	6	1	1	0	1	0	5	3	2	4	1	2	1	9	9	3
Toronto	6	2	3	1	18	14	5	6	1	3	2	14	19	4	12	3	6	3	32	33	9
Vancouver	8	2	5	1	15	22	5	8	3	5	0	20	29	6	16	5	10	1	35	51	11
Washington	2	0	1	1	4	7	1	2	0	2	4	4	2	4	1	2	1	6	11	3
Winnipeg	6	6	0	0	25	10	12	6	4	2	0	24	21	8	12	10	2	0	49	31	20
Totals	**107**	**47**	**50**	**10**	**316**	**308**	**104**	**107**	**37**	**62**	**8**	**272**	**354**	**82**	**214**	**84**	**112**	**18**	**588**	**662**	**186**

Colorado totals include Quebec, 1993-94 to 1994-95.

1995-96 Results

Oct.	9	at	Winnipeg	3-4		7	at	Edmonton	1-3
	11	at	Hartford	2-3		9	at	Philadelphia	2-2
	13	at	Buffalo	4-1		11	at	Boston	2-7
	14	at	Pittsburgh	2-5		12	at	Chicago	0-3
	18		Vancouver	1-5		14	at	Winnipeg	6-4
	20		Philadelphia	2-4		17		Calgary	1-4
	22		Winnipeg	6-2		24	at	Vancouver	2-1
	23	at	Colorado	1-3		27	at	Los Angeles	4-5
	26	at	Dallas	2-5		31		Colorado	2-1
	27	at	St. Louis	2-4	**Feb.**	2		Hartford	3-4
	29		Calgary	7-2		4		Chicago	1-4
Nov.	1		St. Louis	3-0		7		Toronto	1-2
	3		NY Rangers	7-4		10	at	NY Islanders	3-4
	5		New Jersey	6-1		11	at	New Jersey	4-2
	7	at	Toronto	3-6		14	at	Edmonton	2-3
	8	at	Montreal	3-2		15	at	Vancouver	3-5
	11	at	Ottawa	3-2		17	at	Los Angeles	2-1
	13		Los Angeles	2-4		21		Boston	2-3
	15		Colorado	7-3		23	at	Calgary	2-3
	17		NY Islanders	2-1		25		San Jose	4-3
	19		Florida	3-4		26	at	Colorado	2-3
	21	at	Calgary	3-2		28		Montreal	5-2
	22	at	Edmonton	0-2	**Mar.**	3		Tampa Bay	2-2
	24		Chicago	4-5		5		Dallas	1-3
	29		Washington	2-2		8		Buffalo	3-2
Dec.	1	at	Detroit	2-5		10		Los Angeles	3-2
	2	at	Toronto	4-4		13		Colorado	4-0
	4	at	NY Rangers	1-5		17		St. Louis	5-1
	6	at	Tampa Bay	1-2		19	at	Washington	2-1
	7	at	Florida	3-3		22	at	St. Louis	6-1
	10		Edmonton	1-3		24	at	Chicago	2-2
	13		Pittsburgh	6-3		25	at	Detroit	1-5
	15		Ottawa	4-2		28	at	Dallas	1-3
	17		Toronto	2-3		31	at	San Jose	3-3
	19		San Jose	4-7	**Apr.**	3		Edmonton	1-0
	20		Detroit	1-6		5		Detroit	2-2
	22		Vancouver	2-6		7	at	San Jose	5-3
	27	at	Los Angeles	1-7		9		Vancouver	2-0
	29		San Jose	4-2		10	at	Colorado	3-7
	31		Los Angeles	2-2		12		Dallas	5-3
Jan.	5	at	Calgary	3-1		14		Winnipeg	5-2

Entry Draft
Selections 1996-93

1996
Pick
9	Ruslan Salei
35	Matt Cullen
117	Brendan Buckley
149	Blaine Russell
172	Timo Ahmaoja
198	Kevin Kellett
224	Tobias Johansson

1995
Pick
4	Chad Kilger
29	Brian Wesenberg
55	Mike Leclerc
107	Igor Nikulin
133	Peter Leboutillier
159	Mike Laplante
185	Igor Karpenko

1994
Pick
2	Oleg Tverdovsky
28	Johan Davidsson
67	Craig Reichert
80	Byron Briske
106	Pavel Trnka
132	Jon Battaglia
158	Mark (Rocky) Welsing
184	John Brad Englehart
236	Tommi Miettinen
262	Jeremy Stevenson

1993
Pick
4	Paul Kariya
30	Nikolai Tsulygin
56	Valeri Karpov
82	Joel Gagnon
108	Mikhail Shtalenkov
134	Antti Aalto
160	Matt Peterson
186	Tom Askey
212	Vitaly Kozel
238	Anatoli Fedotov
264	David Penney

Coach

WILSON, RON
Head Coach, The Mighty Ducks of Anaheim.
Born in Windsor, Ont., May 28, 1955.

On June 30, 1993 Disney Sports Enterprises, Inc., introduced Ron Wilson as the first head coach in Mighty Ducks history. In his first year as a head coach in the NHL, Wilson led Anaheim to a 33-46-5 record and 71 points as the Mighty Ducks made a substantial run at a playoff berth in the Western Conference. Wilson received 12 points in the voting for the Jack Adams NHL coach of the year Award, including one first-place vote.

The Mighty Ducks finished the 1995-96 season strong under Wilson, earning the second-best record in the Western Conference over the last two months of the regular season and missing the playoffs by the slimmest of margins. The Ducks tied for the eighth-and-final playoff spot with Winnipeg but lost the first tiebreaker of total wins. Anaheim played particularly well at home during the latter part of the season, closing out the year with a franchise-record nine-game home unbeaten streak (8-0-1).

Wilson was named as head coach of the U.S. National Team that skated to a bronze medal at the 1996 World Championships in Vienna, Austria. The top-three finish marked the first time a U.S. team earned a medal at the "A" level since 1962's bronze medal-winning squad.

Wilson, 41, came to the Mighty Ducks after serving the previous three seasons as an assistant coach to Pat Quinn for the Vancouver Canucks. During Wilson's three seasons in Vancouver, the Canucks posted a 116-98-30 record (.537) and qualified for the Stanley Cup playoffs all three years.

Prior to becoming an assistant coach with Vancouver, Wilson was an assistant coach for the Milwaukee Admirals (IHL) under Ron LaPointe.

Wilson has significant playing experience in professional, amateur and international hockey. He played four years at Providence College where he was a two-time All-American and four-time All-Hockey East. Wilson was Hockey East player of the year in 1975 when he led the nation in scoring with 26-61-87 points in 26 games. He remains Providence's all-time leading scorer and ranks as the all-time NCAA leading scorer among defensemen with 250 points. Wilson received a Bachelor of Arts Degree in economics from Providence College.

Drafted by the Toronto Maple Leafs (132nd overall) in 1975, Wilson began his professional hockey career in 1976-77 with the Dallas Blackhawks in the old Central Hockey League. He joined the Toronto Maple Leafs in 1977-78, playing in 64 NHL contests over three seasons. Wilson then moved to Switzerland in 1980 and competed for the Swiss teams Klöten and Davos for six seasons. The former defenseman/winger signed with the Minnesota North Stars as a free agent in 1985 where he played through 1988, closing out his pro career.

Though he was born in Canada, Wilson was raised in the United States. He is a four-time player for U.S. National Teams (1975, 1981, 1983, 1987) and coached the 1994 squad at the World Championships in Italy, leading Team USA to a 4-4-0 record with a fourth-place finish – its highest ranking since 1991. Wilson led the U.S. team to its first victory over Russia in international competition since the 1980 "miracle on ice" game during the 1980 Winter Olympics at Lake Placid, NY. Wilson was assisted by Mighty Ducks Assistant Coach Tim Army on the 1994 U.S. squad that included six players from the Mighty Ducks' inaugural season.

The Windsor, Ontario native also has some family ties to the NHL. His father, Larry, played six NHL seasons with the Detroit Red Wings and Chicago Blackhawks and coached pro hockey for 11 seasons, including one with Detroit. Ron Wilson's uncle, Johnny, played 13 years in the NHL and also coached for Detroit, Los Angeles, Colorado and Pittsburgh. Johnny Wilson once played 580 consecutive games in the NHL, a record at that time. Ron Wilson's brothers, Brad and Randy, played at Providence.

Wilson is active in all Disney GOALS charity events and is part of the Mighty Ducks' Speakers Bureau. He is known for his keen sense of humor and is an avid golfer. Wilson and his wife Maureen reside in Orange, CA. They have two daughters, Kristen, 19, and Lauren, 16.

Coaching Record

Season	Team	Games	Regular Season W	L	T	%	Playoffs Games	W	L	%
1993-94	Anaheim (NHL)	84	33	46	5	.423	....	....	....	....
1994-95	Anaheim (NHL)	48	16	27	5	.385	....	....	....	....
1995-96	Anaheim (NHL)	82	35	39	8	.476	....	....	....	....
	NHL Totals	214	84	112	18	.435	....	....	....	....

Club Directory

Disney Hockey Enterprises, Inc.
Arrowhead Pond of Anaheim
2695 Katella Ave.
Anaheim, CA 92806
Phone **714/704-2700**
FAX 714/704-2753
Capacity: 17,174

Executive Management
Governor	Michael Eisner
President and Alternate Governor	Tony Tavares
Vice President/General Manager	Jack Ferreira
Vice President of Finance/Administration	Andy Roundtree
Assistant General Manager	David McNab
Vice President of Hockey Operations	Kevin Gilmore
Administrative Assistant to the President	Jennifer Mitchell
Administrative Assistant to the General Manager	Mary Leer
Administrative Assistant to Hockey Operations	Tia Wood

Coaching Staff
Head Coach	Ron Wilson
Assistant Coaches	Walt Kyle, Tim Army

Hockey Club Operations
Chief Amateur Scout	Alain Chainey
Chief Pro Scout	Paul Fenton
Assistant to the General Manager	Angela Gorgone
Amateur Scouts	Thommie Bergman, Al Godfrey, Richard Green, David McNamara
Scouting Staff	Mike McGraw, Mark Odnokon, Ed Wright
Head Athletic Trainer/Physical Therapist	Paddy Turner
Equipment Manager	Mark O'Neill
Assistant Equipment Manager	John Allaway
Supervisor of Off-Ice Officials	Tony Guanci
Team Physicians	Dr. Ronald Glousman, Dr. Craig Milhouse
Oral Surgeon	Dr. Jeff Pulver
Visiting Team Equipment Attendant	Chris Kincaid
Athletic Trainer Interns	Todd Hull, William Yanowsky

Communications Department
Director of Public Relations	Bill Robertson
Manager of Media Services	Rob Scichili
Publications Manager	Doug Ward
Media Relations Coordinator	Marc Simon
Public Relations Intern	Jason Franks
Publications Intern	Brian Israel
Team Photographer	V.J. Lovero (Lovero Group)

Finance and Administration Department
Director of Finance	Martin Greenspun
Controller	Jon Sullivan
Assistant Controller	Cris Fisher, Melody Martin
Accountants	Shelly Baker, Doug McKechnie, Jean Onyang, Roseanna Sitzman
Accounting Clerk	Brett Gilliland
Manager of Human Resources	Jenny Price
Manager of Information Services	Andy Roe
Manager of Community Relations/ Game Operations	Tory Whittingham
Office Manager	Barbara Potts
General Manager of Disney ICE	Art Trottier
Human Resources Administrative Assistant	Cindy Williams
Office Assistant	Paul Desaulniers

Marketing Department
Director of Marketing	Bill Holford
Director of Advertising & Broadcast Sales	Bob Wagner
Director of Sales	Chuck Bruns
Manager of Marketing	Lisa Manning
Manager of Promotions and Sponsorship Services	Kerry Fopma
Sponsorship Services Coordinator	Matthew Stys
Advertising Sales Managers	John Covarrubias, Richard McClemmy, Dave Severson
Account Executives	June Blair, Jennifer Flaa, Joe Furmanski, Keith Rowe, John Siragusa, Laury Wedin
Merchandise Manager	Tom McMillin
Merchandise Operations Manager	Linda Bessant
Synergy/Game Operations	Susan Jackson
Administrative Assistants	Madeline Falco, C.J. Jacobs, Michelle Lagestee, Pat Lissy, Debbie Nielander

Television and Radio Broadcasting Department
Associate Producers	Mark Vittorio, Tim Davis
Television, KCAL (Ch. 9) & Prime Sports (Cable)	Chris Madsen and Brian Hayward
Radio, KEZY (95.9 FM)	Brian Hamilton and Pat Conacher
Video Producer	Aaron Teats

Ticketing Department
Ticket Operations Manager	Don Boudreau
Manager of Premium Ticket Services	Anne McNiff
Ticketing Supervisors	Rick Capstraw, Kevin Gidden, Heather Holter
Mighty Ducks Receptionist	Anne Mason
Disney Sports Enterprises, Inc. Receptionist	Susan Felix
Public Address Announcer	Mike Carlucci
Interns	John Drum, Jennifer Gran, Paul Kidwell, Darren Kotsovos, Paul Nowosad, Cheryl Parker, John Pesetski, Brian Strohecker, David Tenzer

Miscellaneous
Team Colors	Purple (PMS 518C), Jade (PMS 329C), Silver (PMS 429C) and White
Practice Facilities	Disney ICE (300 W. Lincoln Ave.) and the Arrowhead Pond (2695 Katella Ave.)
Primary Developmental Affiliate	Baltimore Bandits (AHL)
Secondary Affiliates	Ft. Wayne Komets (IHL) Long Beach Ice Dogs (IHL)
Press Box Phone	714/704-2623
Press Room	714/704-2514 or 2517

Boston Bruins

1995-96 Results: 40W-31L-11T 91PTS. Second, Northeast Division

Schedule

Oct.	Sat.	5	NY Rangers		Thur.	9	Montreal
	Mon.	7	Phoenix		Sat.	11	at Montreal
	Sat.	12	at San Jose		Mon.	13	Ottawa
	Mon.	14	at Vancouver*		Tues.	14	at New Jersey
	Thur.	17	at Los Angeles		Mon.	20	Washington*
	Sun.	20	at Anaheim		Wed.	22	at Ottawa
	Thur.	24	Toronto		Thur.	23	Florida
	Sat.	26	Detroit		Sat.	25	Colorado*
	Tues.	29	New Jersey		Thur.	30	at Florida
	Thur.	31	Hartford	Feb.	Sat.	1	at Tampa Bay*
Nov.	Sat.	2	NY Rangers		Sun.	2	at NY Rangers
	Mon.	4	Los Angeles		Tues.	4	Ottawa
	Wed.	6	at Hartford		Thur.	6	Hartford
	Thur.	7	Edmonton		Sat.	8	St. Louis*
	Sat.	9	at Ottawa		Tues.	11	at Calgary
	Thur.	14	Pittsburgh		Wed.	12	at Edmonton
	Sat.	16	at Buffalo		Sat.	15	at Phoenix*
	Mon.	18	San Jose		Tues.	18	at Colorado
	Tues.	19	at Washington		Thur.	20	at Chicago
	Thur.	21	Montreal		Sun.	23	at Buffalo
	Sat.	23	Buffalo		Mon.	24	at Washington
	Tues.	26	Philadelphia		Thur.	27	Tampa Bay
	Fri.	29	Vancouver*	Mar.	Sat.	1	Philadelphia*
	Sat.	30	at Pittsburgh		Mon.	3	at Toronto
Dec.	Wed.	4	at Montreal		Thur.	6	at NY Islanders
	Thur.	5	Hartford		Sat.	8	at Tampa Bay*
	Sat.	7	Calgary		Sun.	9	at Florida
	Mon.	9	Anaheim		Wed.	12	at Hartford
	Thur.	12	New Jersey		Thur.	13	Montreal
	Sat.	14	Buffalo		Sat.	15	NY Islanders*
	Sun.	15	at Philadelphia		Wed.	19	at Detroit
	Tues.	17	at Pittsburgh		Sat.	22	Ottawa*
	Thur.	19	Tampa Bay		Mon.	24	at Montreal
	Sat.	21	Washington		Thur.	27	NY Islanders
	Mon.	23	Chicago		Sat.	29	at NY Islanders*
	Fri.	27	at Dallas	Apr.	Thur.	3	at NY Rangers
	Sun.	29	at St. Louis		Sat.	5	Florida*
Jan.	Wed.	1	at Ottawa*		Tues.	8	at Pittsburgh
	Thur.	2	at Hartford		Thur.	10	Buffalo
	Sat.	4	Dallas		Fri.	11	at New Jersey
	Tues.	7	at Philadelphia		Sun.	13	Pittsburgh*

* Denotes afternoon game.

Franchise date: November 1, 1924

73rd NHL Season

NORTHEAST DIVISION

For the fourth consecutive season, Adam Oates led the Boston Bruins in both assists (67) and points (92).

Year-by-Year Record

Season	GP	Home			Road			Overall			GF	GA	Pts.	Finished	Playoff Result
		W	L	T	W	L	T	W	L	T					
1995-96	82	22	14	5	18	17	6	40	31	11	282	269	91	2nd, Northeast Div.	Lost Conf. Quarter-Final
1994-95	48	15	7	2	12	11	1	27	18	3	150	127	57	3rd, Northeast Div.	Lost Conf. Quarter-Final
1993-94	84	20	14	8	22	15	5	42	29	13	289	252	97	2nd, Northeast Div.	Lost Conf. Semi-Final
1992-93	84	29	10	3	22	16	4	51	26	7	332	268	109	1st, Adams Div.	Lost Div. Semi-Final
1991-92	80	23	11	6	13	21	6	36	32	12	270	275	84	2nd, Adams Div.	Lost Conf. Championship
1990-91	80	26	9	5	18	15	7	44	24	12	299	264	100	1st, Adams Div.	Lost Conf. Championship
1989-90	80	23	13	4	23	12	5	46	25	9	289	232	101	1st, Adams Div.	Lost Final
1988-89	80	17	15	8	20	14	6	37	29	14	289	256	88	2nd, Adams Div.	Lost Div. Final
1987-88	80	24	13	3	20	17	3	44	30	6	300	251	94	2nd, Adams Div.	Lost Final
1986-87	80	25	11	4	14	23	3	39	34	7	301	276	85	3rd, Adams Div.	Lost Div. Semi-Final
1985-86	80	24	9	7	13	22	5	37	31	12	311	288	86	3rd, Adams Div.	Lost Div. Semi-Final
1984-85	80	21	15	4	15	19	6	36	34	10	303	287	82	4th, Adams Div.	Lost Div. Semi-Final
1983-84	80	25	12	3	24	13	3	49	25	6	336	261	104	1st, Adams Div.	Lost Div. Semi-Final
1982-83	80	28	6	6	22	14	4	50	20	10	327	228	110	1st, Adams Div.	Lost Conf. Championship
1981-82	80	24	12	4	19	15	6	43	27	10	323	285	96	2nd, Adams Div.	Lost Div. Final
1980-81	80	26	10	4	11	20	9	37	30	13	316	272	87	2nd, Adams Div.	Lost Prelim. Round
1979-80	80	27	9	4	19	12	9	46	21	13	310	234	105	2nd, Adams Div.	Lost Quarter-Final
1978-79	80	25	10	5	18	13	9	43	23	14	316	270	100	1st, Adams Div.	Lost Semi-Final
1977-78	80	29	6	5	22	12	6	51	18	11	333	218	113	1st, Adams Div.	Lost Final
1976-77	80	27	7	6	22	16	2	49	23	8	312	240	106	1st, Adams Div.	Lost Final
1975-76	80	27	5	8	21	10	9	48	15	17	313	237	113	1st, Adams Div.	Lost Semi-Final
1974-75	80	29	5	6	11	21	8	40	26	14	345	245	94	2nd, Adams Div.	Lost Prelim. Round
1973-74	78	33	4	2	19	13	7	52	17	9	349	221	113	1st, East Div.	Lost Final
1972-73	78	27	10	2	24	12	3	51	22	5	330	235	107	2nd, East Div.	Lost Quarter-Final
1971-72	**78**	**28**	**4**	**7**	**26**	**9**	**4**	**54**	**13**	**11**	**330**	**204**	**119**	**1st, East Div.**	**Won Stanley Cup**
1970-71	78	33	4	2	24	10	5	57	14	7	399	207	121	1st, East Div.	Lost Quarter-Final
1969-70	**76**	**27**	**3**	**8**	**13**	**14**	**11**	**40**	**17**	**19**	**277**	**216**	**99**	**2nd, East Div.**	**Won Stanley Cup**
1968-69	76	29	3	6	13	15	10	42	18	16	303	221	100	2nd, East Div.	Lost Semi-Final
1967-68	74	22	9	6	15	18	4	37	27	10	259	216	84	3rd, East Div.	Lost Quarter-Final
1966-67	70	10	21	4	7	22	6	17	43	10	182	253	44	6th,	Out of Playoffs
1965-66	70	15	17	3	6	26	3	21	43	6	174	275	48	5th,	Out of Playoffs
1964-65	70	12	17	6	9	26	0	21	43	6	166	253	48	6th,	Out of Playoffs
1963-64	70	13	15	7	5	25	5	18	40	12	170	212	48	6th,	Out of Playoffs
1962-63	70	7	18	10	7	21	7	14	39	17	198	281	45	6th,	Out of Playoffs
1961-62	70	9	22	4	6	25	4	15	47	8	177	306	38	6th,	Out of Playoffs
1960-61	70	13	17	5	2	25	8	15	42	13	176	254	43	6th,	Out of Playoffs
1959-60	70	21	11	3	7	23	5	28	34	8	220	241	64	5th,	Out of Playoffs
1958-59	70	21	11	3	11	18	6	32	29	9	205	215	73	2nd,	Lost Semi-Final
1957-58	70	15	14	6	12	14	9	27	28	15	199	194	69	4th,	Lost Final
1956-57	70	20	9	6	14	15	6	34	24	12	195	174	80	3rd,	Lost Final
1955-56	70	14	14	7	9	20	6	23	34	13	147	185	59	5th,	Out of Playoffs
1954-55	70	16	10	9	7	16	12	23	26	21	169	188	67	4th,	Lost Semi-Final
1953-54	70	22	8	5	10	20	5	32	28	10	177	181	74	4th,	Lost Semi-Final
1952-53	70	19	10	6	9	19	7	28	29	13	152	172	69	3rd,	Lost Final
1951-52	70	15	12	8	10	17	8	25	29	16	162	176	66	4th,	Lost Semi-Final
1950-51	70	13	12	10	9	18	8	22	30	18	178	197	62	4th,	Lost Semi-Final
1949-50	70	15	12	8	7	20	8	22	32	16	198	228	60	5th,	Out of Playoffs
1948-49	60	18	10	2	11	13	6	29	23	8	178	163	66	2nd,	Lost Semi-Final
1947-48	60	12	8	10	11	16	3	23	24	13	167	168	59	3rd,	Lost Semi-Final
1946-47	60	18	7	5	8	16	6	26	23	11	190	175	63	3rd,	Lost Semi-Final
1945-46	50	11	5	4	13	13	4	24	18	8	167	156	56	2nd,	Lost Final
1944-45	50	11	12	2	5	18	2	16	30	4	179	219	36	4th,	Lost Semi-Final
1943-44	50	15	8	2	4	18	3	19	26	5	223	268	43	5th,	Out of Playoffs
1942-43	50	17	3	5	7	14	4	24	17	9	195	176	57	2nd,	Lost Final
1941-42	48	17	4	3	8	13	3	25	17	6	160	118	56	3rd,	Lost Semi-Final
1940-41	**48**	**15**	**4**	**5**	**12**	**4**	**8**	**27**	**8**	**13**	**168**	**102**	**67**	**1st,**	**Won Stanley Cup**
1939-40	48	20	3	1	11	9	4	31	12	5	170	98	67	1st,	Lost Semi-Final
1938-39	**48**	**20**	**2**	**2**	**16**	**8**	**0**	**36**	**10**	**2**	**156**	**76**	**74**	**1st,**	**Won Stanley Cup**
1937-38	48	18	3	3	12	8	4	30	11	7	142	89	67	1st, Amn. Div.	Lost Semi-Final
1936-37	48	9	11	4	14	7	3	23	18	7	120	110	53	2nd, Amn. Div.	Lost Quarter-Final
1935-36	48	15	8	1	7	12	5	22	20	6	92	83	50	2nd, Amn. Div.	Lost Quarter-Final
1934-35	48	17	7	0	9	9	6	26	16	6	129	112	58	1st, Amn. Div.	Lost Semi-Final
1933-34	48	11	11	2	7	14	3	18	25	5	111	130	41	4th, Amn. Div.	Out of Playoffs
1932-33	48	20	2	3	5	13	5	25	15	8	124	88	58	1st, Amn. Div.	Lost Semi-Final
1931-32	48	11	10	3	4	11	9	15	21	12	122	117	42	4th, Amn. Div.	Out of Playoffs
1930-31	44	17	1	5	11	9	1	28	10	6	143	90	62	1st, Amn. Div.	Lost Semi-Final
1929-30	44	23	1	0	15	4	1	38	5	1	179	98	77	1st, Amn. Div.	Lost Final
1928-29	**44**	**16**	**6**	**1**	**10**	**7**	**4**	**26**	**13**	**5**	**89**	**52**	**57**	**1st, Amn. Div.**	**Won Stanley Cup**
1927-28	44	13	4	5	7	9	6	20	13	11	77	70	51	1st, Amn. Div.	Lost Semi-Final
1926-27	44	15	7	0	6	13	3	21	20	3	97	89	45	2nd, Amn. Div.	Lost Final
1925-26	36	10	7	1	7	8	3	17	15	4	92	85	38	4th,	Out of Playoffs
1924-25	30	3	12	0	3	12	0	6	24	0	49	119	12	6th,	Out of Playoffs

1996-97 Player Personnel

FORWARDS	HT	WT	S	Place of Birth	Date	1995-96 Club
BEDDOES, Clayton	5-11	190	L	Bentley, Alta.	11/10/70	Boston-Providence (AHL)
DONATO, Ted	5-10	181	L	Boston, MA	4/28/69	Boston
DOYLE, Jason	6-1	200	R	Toronto, Ont.	5/15/78	London-S.S. Marie
ELIK, Todd	6-2	195	L	Brampton, Ont.	4/15/66	Boston-Providence (AHL)
HEINZE, Stephen	5-11	193	R	Lawrence, MA	1/30/70	Boston
KENNEDY, Sheldon	5-10	180	R	Elkhorn, Man.	6/15/69	Calgary-Saint John
KIRTON, Scott	6-4	215	R	Penetanguishene, Ont.	10/4/71	Providence (AHL)-Charlotte
KUSTER, Henry	6-0	195	R	Edmonton, Alta.	11/11/77	Medicine Hat
MALLETTE, Troy	6-2	210	L	Sudbury, Ont.	2/25/70	Ottawa
MANN, Cameron	6-0	190	R	Thompson, Man.	4/20/77	Peterborough
McCAULEY, Bill	6-1	195	L	Detroit, MI	4/20/75	Providence (AHL)
MCCLEARY, Trent	6-0	180	R	Swift Current, Sask.	10/10/72	Ottawa
MOGER, Sandy	6-3	208	R	100 Mile House, B.C.	3/21/69	Boston
NAUD, Eric	6-1	187	L	Lasarre, Que.	10/2/77	Laval-St-Hyacinthe
NEELY, Cam	6-1	218	R	Comox, B.C.	6/6/65	Boston
NIELSEN, Kirk	6-1	190	R	Grand Rapids, MN	10/19/73	Harvard
OATES, Adam	5-11	185	R	Weston, Ont.	8/27/62	Boston
ODGERS, Jeff	6-0	195	R	Spy Hill, Sask.	5/31/69	San Jose
PAYNE, Davis	6-2	205	L	Port Alberni, B.C.	9/24/70	Boston-Providence (AHL)
ROY, Andre	6-3	178	L	Port Chester, NY	2/8/75	Boston-Providence (AHL)
ROY, Jean-Yves	5-10	180	L	Rosemere, Que.	2/17/69	Ottawa-P.E.I.
SAWYER, Kevin	6-2	205	L	Christina Lake, B.C.	2/21/74	StL-Wor-Bos-Prov (AHL)
STEWART, Cam	5-11	196	L	Kitchener, Ont.	9/18/71	Boston-Providence (AHL)
STUMPEL, Jozef	6-1	208	R	Nitra, Czech.	6/20/72	Boston
SWEENEY, Tim	5-11	185	L	Boston, MA	4/12/67	Boston-Providence (AHL)
TOCCHET, Rick	6-0	205	R	Scarborough, Ont.	4/9/64	Los Angeles-Boston
WHITFIELD, Trent	5-10	176	L	Estevan, Sask.	6/17/77	Spokane
DEFENSEMEN						
ABRAHAMSSON, Elias	6-3	216	L	Uppsala, Sweden	6/15/77	Halifax
AITKEN, Johnathan	6-3	188	L	Edmonton, Alta.	5/24/78	Medicine Hat
BEERS, Bob	6-2	200	R	Pittsburgh, PA	5/20/67	NY Islanders-Utah
BOURQUE, Ray	5-11	215	L	Montreal, Que.	12/28/60	Boston
CHYNOWETH, Dean	6-1	190	R	Calgary, Alta.	10/30/68	NY Islanders-Boston
CORNFORTH, Mark	6-1	193	L	Montreal, Que.	11/13/72	Boston-Providence (AHL)
GRUDEN, John	6-0	190	L	Virginia, MN	6/4/70	Boston-Providence (AHL)
MASTAD, Milt	6-3	205	L	Regina, Sask.	3/5/75	Providence (AHL)
McLAREN, Kyle	6-4	210	L	Humbolt, Sask.	6/18/77	Boston
MOSER, Jay	6-2	170	L	Cottage Grove, MN	12/26/72	U. Minnesota
PAQUETTE, Charles	6-1	193	L	Lachute, Que.	6/17/75	Providence (AHL)-Charlotte
RICHTER, Barry	6-2	195	L	Madison, WI	9/11/70	NY Rangers-Binghamton
ROHLOFF, Jon	5-11	220	R	Mankato, MN	10/3/69	Boston
STAIOS, Steve	6-0	185	R	Hamilton, Ont.	7/28/73	Peo-Wor-Bos-Prov (AHL)
SWEENEY, Don	5-10	188	L	St. Stephen, N.B.	8/17/66	Boston
TIMANDER, Mattias	6-1	194	L	Solleftea, Sweden	4/16/74	MoDo

GOALTENDERS	HT	WT	C	Place of Birth	Date	1995-96 Club
BAILEY, Scott	6-0	195	L	Calgary, Alta.	5/2/72	Boston-Providence (AHL)
CHEVELDAE, Tim	5-10	195	L	Melville, Sask.	2/15/68	Winnipeg-Hershey
RANFORD, Bill	5-11	185	L	Brandon, Man.	12/14/66	Edmonton-Boston
RYABCHIKOV, Evgeny	5-11	167	L	Yaroslavl, Soviet Union	1/16/74	Char-Huntington-Erie-Prov (AHL)
SCHAFER, Paxton	5-9	152	L	Medicine Hat, Alta.	2/26/76	Medicine Hat
TALLAS, Robbie	6-0	178	L	Edmonton, Alta.	3/20/73	Boston-Providence (AHL)

General Managers' History

Arthur Ross, 1924-25 to 1953-54; Lynn Patrick, 1954-55 to 1964-65; Leighton "Hap" Emms, 1965-66 to 1966-67; Milt Schmidt, 1967-68 to 1971-72; Harry Sinden, 1972-73 to date.

Captains' History

No Captain, 1924-25 to 1926-27; Lionel Hitchman, 1927-28 to 1930-31; George Owen, 1931-32; "Dit" Clapper, 1932-33 to 1937-38; "Cooney" Weiland, 1938-39; "Dit" Clapper, 1939-40 to 1945-46; "Dit" Clapper and John Crawford, 1946-47; John Crawford 1947-48 to 1949-50; Milt Schmidt, 1950-51 to 1953-54; Milt Schmidt, Ed Sanford, 1954-55; Fern Flaman, 1955-56 to 1960-61; Don McKenney, 1961-62, 1962-63; Leo Boivin, 1963-64 to 1965-66; John Bucyk, 1966-67; no captain, 1967-68 to 1972-73; John Bucyk, 1973-74 to 1976-77; Wayne Cashman, 1977-78 to 1982-83; Terry O'Reilly, 1983-84, 1984-85; Ray Bourque, Rick Middleton (co-captains) 1985-86 to 1987-88; Ray Bourque, 1988-89 to date.

Coaching History

Arthur Ross, 1924-25 to 1927-28; Cy Denneny, 1928-29; Arthur Ross, 1929-30 to 1933-34; Frank Patrick, 1934-35 to 1935-36; Arthur Ross, 1936-37 to 1938-39; "Cooney" Weiland, 1939-40 to 1940-41; Arthur Ross, 1941-42 to 1944-45; "Dit" Clapper, 1945-46 to 1948-49; George Boucher, 1949-50; Lynn Patrick, 1950-51 to 1953-54; Lynn Patrick and Milt Schmidt, 1954-55; Milt Schmidt, 1955-56 to 1960-61; Phil Watson, 1961-62; Phil Watson and Milt Schmidt, 1962-63; Milt Schmidt, 1963-64 to 1965-66; Harry Sinden, 1966-67 to 1969-70; Tom Johnson, 1970-71 to 1971-72; Tom Johnson and "Bep" Guidolin, 1972-73; "Bep" Guidolin, 1973-74; Don Cherry, 1974-75 to 1978-79; Fred Creighton and Harry Sinden, 1979-80; Gerry Cheevers, 1980-81 to 1983-84; Gerry Cheevers and Harry Sinden, 1984-85; "Butch" Goring, 1985-86; "Butch" Goring and Terry O'Reilly, 1986-87; Terry O'Reilly, 1987-88 to 1988-89; Mike Milbury, 1989-90 to 1990-91; Rick Bowness, 1991-92; Brian Sutter, 1992-93 to 1994-95; Steve Kasper, 1995-96 to date.

1995-96 Scoring

* – rookie

Regular Season

Pos	#	Player	Team	GP	G	A	Pts	+/–	PIM	PP	SH	GW	GT	S	%
C	12	Adam Oates	BOS	70	25	67	92	16	18	7	1	2	0	183	13.7
D	77	Ray Bourque	BOS	82	20	62	82	31	58	9	2	2	1	390	5.1
R	22	Rick Tocchet	L.A.	44	13	23	36	3	117	4	0	0	1	100	13.0
			BOS	27	16	8	24	7	64	6	0	3	0	85	18.8
			TOTAL	71	29	31	60	10	181	10	0	3	1	185	15.7
R	16	Jozef Stumpel	BOS	76	18	36	54	–8	14	5	0	2	0	158	11.4
C	14	Shawn McEachern	BOS	82	24	29	53	–5	34	3	2	3	0	238	10.1
C	21	Ted Donato	BOS	82	23	26	49	6	46	7	0	1	0	152	15.1
R	8	Cam Neely	BOS	49	26	20	46	3	31	7	0	3	0	191	13.6
C	20	Todd Elik	BOS	59	13	33	46	2	40	6	0	2	0	108	12.0
L	17	Dave Reid	BOS	63	23	21	44	14	4	1	6	3	1	160	14.4
R	45	Sandy Moger	BOS	80	15	14	29	–9	65	4	0	6	0	103	14.6
R	23	Steve Heinze	BOS	76	16	12	28	–3	43	0	1	3	0	129	12.4
D	32	Don Sweeney	BOS	77	4	24	28	–4	42	2	0	3	0	142	2.8
D	46	* Kyle McLaren	BOS	74	5	12	17	16	73	0	0	0	0	74	6.8
L	42	Tim Sweeney	BOS	41	8	8	16	4	14	1	0	2	1	47	17.0
R	11	Joe Mullen	BOS	37	8	7	15	–2	0	4	0	1	0	60	13.3
D	34	Rick Zombo	BOS	67	4	10	14	–7	53	0	0	1	1	68	5.9
D	38	Jon Rohloff	BOS	79	1	12	13	–8	59	1	0	0	0	106	0.9
C	10	Ron Sutter	BOS	18	5	7	12	10	24	0	1	0	0	34	14.7
D	28	Dean Chynoweth	NYI	14	0	1	1	–4	40	0	0	0	0	6	0.0
			BOS	35	2	5	7	–1	88	0	0	0	0	32	6.3
			TOTAL	49	2	6	8	–5	128	0	0	0	0	38	5.3
C	37	* Clayton Beddoes	BOS	39	1	6	7	–5	44	0	0	0	0	18	5.6
D	41	Phil Vonstefenelli	BOS	27	0	4	4	2	16	0	0	0	0	20	0.0
G	30	Bill Ranford	EDM	37	0	1	1	0	2	0	0	0	0	0	0.0
			BOS	40	0	2	2	0	0	0	0	0	0	0	0.0
			TOTAL	77	0	3	3	0	2	0	0	0	0	0	0.0
D	6	Alexei Kasatonov	BOS	19	1	0	1	1	12	0	0	0	0	15	6.7
G	35	* Robbie Tallas	BOS	1	0	0	0	0	0	0	0	0	0	0	0.0
C	47	* Ryan Hughes	BOS	3	0	0	0	0	0	0	0	0	0	2	0.0
L	49	* Andre Roy	BOS	3	0	0	0	0	0	0	0	0	0	0	0.0
C	26	Cameron Stewart	BOS	6	0	0	0	–2	0	0	0	0	0	2	0.0
D	40	* Mark Cornforth	BOS	6	0	0	0	4	4	0	0	0	0	1	0.0
L	44	* Davis Payne	BOS	7	0	0	0	0	7	0	0	0	0	2	0.0
L	19	* Kevin Sawyer	STL	6	0	0	0	–2	23	0	0	0	0	1	0.0
			BOS	2	0	0	0	1	5	0	0	0	0	0	0.0
			TOTAL	8	0	0	0	–1	28	0	0	0	0	1	0.0
G	39	* Scott Bailey	BOS	11	0	0	0	0	0	0	0	0	0	0	0.0
D	48	* Steve Staios	BOS	12	0	0	0	–5	4	0	0	0	0	4	0.0
G	31	Blaine Lacher	BOS	12	0	0	0	0	4	0	0	0	0	0	0.0
D	36	John Gruden	BOS	14	0	0	0	–3	4	0	0	0	0	12	0.0
G	1	Craig Billington	BOS	27	0	0	0	0	2	0	0	0	0	0	0.0
R	29	Marc Potvin	BOS	27	0	0	0	–2	12	0	0	0	0	14	0.0

Goaltending

No.	Goaltender	GPI	Mins	Avg	W	L	T	EN	SO	GA	SA	S%
30	Bill Ranford	40	2307	2.83	21	12	4	0	1	109	1030	.894
35	* Robbie Tallas	1	60	3.00	1	0	0	0	0	3	29	.897
39	* Scott Bailey	11	571	3.26	5	1	2	0	0	31	264	.883
1	Craig Billington	27	1380	3.43	10	13	3	2	1	79	594	.867
31	Blaine Lacher	12	671	3.93	3	5	2	1	0	44	284	.845
	Totals	**82**	**4992**	**3.23**	**40**	**31**	**11**	**3**	**2**	**269**	**2204**	**.878**

Playoffs

Pos	#	Player	Team	GP	G	A	Pts	+/–	PIM	PP	SH	GW	OT	S	%
C	12	Adam Oates	BOS	5	2	5	7	–3	2	0	1	0	0	13	15.4
D	77	Ray Bourque	BOS	5	1	6	7	–4	2	1	0	0	0	28	3.6
R	22	Rick Tocchet	BOS	5	4	0	4	–7	21	3	0	1	0	20	20.0
R	45	Sandy Moger	BOS	5	2	2	4	–1	12	1	0	0	0	12	16.7
C	14	Shawn McEachern	BOS	5	2	1	3	–2	8	0	0	0	0	7	28.6
C	21	Ted Donato	BOS	5	1	2	3	–3	2	1	0	0	0	7	14.3
D	38	Jon Rohloff	BOS	5	1	2	3	–3	2	1	0	0	0	14	7.1
R	16	Jozef Stumpel	BOS	5	1	2	3	–2	0	0	0	0	0	7	14.3
R	23	Steve Heinze	BOS	5	1	1	2	1	4	0	1	0	0	20	5.0
C	20	Todd Elik	BOS	4	0	2	2	–1	16	0	0	0	0	9	0.0
L	17	Dave Reid	BOS	5	0	2	2	–3	2	0	0	0	0	4	0.0
D	32	Don Sweeney	BOS	5	0	2	2	–3	6	0	0	0	0	12	0.0
C	26	Cameron Stewart	BOS	5	1	0	1	0	2	0	0	0	0	2	50.0
D	36	John Gruden	BOS	3	0	1	1	0	0	0	0	0	0	2	0.0
R	29	Marc Potvin	BOS	5	0	1	1	–2	18	0	0	0	0	5	0.0
G	1	Craig Billington	BOS	1	0	0	0	0	2	0	0	0	0	0	0.0
L	42	Tim Sweeney	BOS	1	0	0	0	0	2	0	0	0	0	1	0.0
D	48	* Steve Staios	BOS	3	0	0	0	–1	0	0	0	0	0	5	0.0
D	28	Dean Chynoweth	BOS	4	0	0	0	–2	24	0	0	0	0	3	0.0
G	30	Bill Ranford	BOS	4	0	0	0	0	0	0	0	0	0	0	0.0
C	10	Ron Sutter	BOS	5	0	0	0	–2	8	0	0	0	0	4	0.0
D	46	* Kyle McLaren	BOS	5	0	0	0	–3	14	0	0	0	0	13	0.0

Goaltending

No.	Goaltender	GPI	Mins	Avg	W	L	EN	SO	GA	SA	S%
30	Bill Ranford	4	239	4.02	1	3	0	0	16	112	.857
1	Craig Billington	1	60	6.00	0	1	0	0	6	28	.786
	Totals	**5**	**300**	**4.40**	**1**	**4**	**0**	**0**	**22**	**140**	**.843**

Club Records

Team

(Figures in brackets for season records are games played; records for fewest points, wins, ties, losses, goals, goals against are for 70 or more games)

Most Points	**121**	1970-71 (78)
Most Wins	**57**	1970-71 (78)
Most Ties	**21**	1954-55 (70)
Most Losses	**47**	1961-62 (70)
Most Goals	**399**	1970-71 (78)
Most Goals Against	**306**	1961-62 (70)
Fewest Points	**38**	1961-62 (70)
Fewest Wins	**14**	1962-63 (70)
Fewest Ties	**5**	1972-73 (78)
Fewest Losses	**13**	1971-72 (78)
Fewest Goals	**147**	1955-56 (70)
Fewest Goals Against	**172**	1952-53 (70)
Longest Winning Streak		
Overall	**14**	Dec. 3/29-Jan. 9/30
Home	***20**	Dec. 3/29-Mar. 18/30
Away	**8**	Feb. 17-Mar. 8/72, Mar. 15-Apr. 14/93
Longest Undefeated Streak		
Overall	**23**	Dec. 22/40-Feb. 23/41 (15 wins, 8 ties)
Home	**27**	Nov. 22/70-Mar. 20/71 (26 wins, 1 tie)
Away	**15**	Dec. 22/40-Mar. 16/41 (9 wins, 6 ties)
Longest Losing Streak		
Overall	**11**	Dec. 3/24-Jan. 5/25
Home	***11**	Dec. 8/24-Feb. 17/25
Away	**14**	Dec. 27/64-Feb. 21/65
Longest Winless Streak		
Overall	**20**	Jan. 28-Mar. 11/62 (16 losses, 4 ties)
Home	**11**	Dec. 8/24-Feb. 17/25 (11 losses)
Away	**14**	Three times
Most Shutouts, Season	**15**	1927-28 (44)
Most PIM, Season	**2,443**	1987-88 (80)
Most Goals, Game	**14**	Jan. 21/45 (NYR 3 at Bos. 14)

Individual

Most Seasons	**21**	John Bucyk
Most Games	**1,436**	John Bucyk
Most Goals, Career	**545**	John Bucyk
Most Assists, Career	**970**	Ray Bourque
Most Points, Career	**1,339**	John Bucyk (545G, 794A)
Most PIM, Career	**2,095**	Terry O'Reilly
Most Shutouts, Career	**74**	Tiny Thompson
Longest Consecutive Games Streak	**418**	John Bucyk (Jan. 23/69-Mar. 2/75)
Most Goals, Season	**76**	Phil Esposito (1970-71)
Most Assists, Season	**102**	Bobby Orr (1970-71)
Most Points, Season	**152**	Phil Esposito (1970-71; 76G, 76A)
Most PIM, Season	**304**	Jay Miller (1987-88)
Most Points, Defenseman Season	***139**	Bobby Orr (1970-71; 37G, 102A)
Most Points, Center Season	**152**	Phil Esposito (1970-71; 76G, 76A)
Most Points, Right Wing Season	**105**	Ken Hodge (1970-71; 43G, 62A), Ken Hodge (1973-74; 50G, 55A), Rick Middleton (1983-84; 47G, 58A)
Most Points, Left Wing Season	**116**	John Bucyk (1970-71; 51G, 65A)
Most Points, Rookie Season	**102**	Joe Juneau (1992-93; 32G, 70A)
Most Shutouts, Season	**15**	Hal Winkler (1927-28)
Most Goals, Game	**4**	Several players
Most Assists, Game	**6**	Ken Hodge (Feb. 9/71), Bobby Orr (Jan. 1/73)
Most Points, Game	**7**	Bobby Orr (Nov. 15/73; 3G, 4A), Phil Esposito (Dec. 19/74; 3G, 4A), Barry Pederson (Apr. 4/82; 3G, 4A), Cam Neely (Oct. 16/88; 3G, 4A)

* NHL Record.

Retired Numbers

2	Eddie Shore	1926-1940
3	Lionel Hitchman	1925-1934
4	Bobby Orr	1966-1976
5	Dit Clapper	1927-1947
7	Phil Esposito	1967-1975
9	John Bucyk	1957-1978
15	Milt Schmidt	1936-1955

All-time Record vs. Other Clubs

Regular Season

	At Home							On Road							Total						
	GP	W	L	T	GF	GA	PTS	GP	W	L	T	GF	GA	PTS	GP	W	L	T	GF	GA	PTS
Anaheim	2	2	0	0	12	5	4	2	0	1	1	4	5	1	4	2	1	1	16	10	5
Buffalo	86	51	24	11	356	262	113	87	31	42	14	273	325	76	173	82	66	25	629	587	189
Calgary	40	25	10	5	144	110	55	39	21	15	3	142	145	45	79	46	25	8	286	255	100
Chicago	277	159	86	32	1005	783	350	279	93	142	44	745	899	230	556	252	228	76	1750	1682	580
Colorado	56	29	19	8	223	177	66	58	33	19	6	253	211	72	114	62	38	14	476	388	138
Dallas	54	39	6	9	245	129	87	54	29	14	11	203	151	69	108	68	20	20	448	280	156
Detroit	280	151	86	43	991	745	345	279	76	151	52	701	934	204	559	227	237	95	1692	1679	549
Edmonton	24	17	5	2	110	67	36	23	12	8	3	83	80	27	47	29	13	5	193	147	63
Florida	6	2	2	2	14	14	6	5	3	2	0	12	12	6	11	5	4	2	26	26	12
Hartford	60	43	12	5	243	154	91	58	26	25	7	208	200	59	118	69	37	12	451	354	150
Los Angeles	55	42	10	3	263	150	87	54	30	18	6	206	188	66	109	72	28	9	469	338	153
Montreal	314	144	116	54	931	850	342	313	87	181	45	729	1066	219	627	231	297	99	1660	1916	561
New Jersey	40	26	10	4	175	124	56	37	22	7	8	136	99	52	77	48	17	12	311	223	108
NY Islanders	43	24	9	10	169	122	58	45	23	17	5	154	144	51	88	47	26	15	323	266	109
NY Rangers	282	151	91	40	1023	791	342	286	108	124	54	802	868	270	568	259	215	94	1825	1659	612
Ottawa	11	11	0	0	55	29	22	10	8	0	2	39	18	18	21	19	0	2	94	47	40
Philadelphia	60	39	14	7	247	175	85	57	26	25	6	172	191	58	117	65	39	13	419	366	143
Pittsburgh	61	43	12	6	283	183	92	62	26	25	11	237	220	63	123	69	37	17	520	403	155
St. Louis	52	34	11	7	230	140	75	53	23	21	9	188	167	55	105	57	32	16	418	307	130
San Jose	4	3	0	1	17	13	7	4	2	0	2	19	10	6	8	5	0	3	36	23	13
Tampa Bay	6	4	1	1	22	16	9	7	2	3	2	19	22	6	13	6	4	3	41	38	15
Toronto	281	151	83	47	925	752	349	281	86	147	48	732	957	220	562	237	230	95	1657	1709	569
Vancouver	44	35	5	4	194	102	74	45	23	14	8	191	150	54	89	58	19	12	385	252	128
Washington	40	23	12	5	160	113	51	39	21	10	8	150	117	50	79	44	22	13	310	230	101
Winnipeg	23	17	3	3	110	74	37	24	13	9	2	91	86	28	47	30	12	5	201	160	65
Defunct Clubs	164	112	39	13	525	306	237	164	79	67	18	496	440	176	328	191	106	31	1021	746	413
Totals	**2365**	**1377**	**666**	**322**	**8672**	**6386**	**3076**	**2365**	**903**	**1087**	**375**	**6985**	**7705**	**2181**	**4730**	**2280**	**1753**	**697**	**15657**	**14091**	**5257**

Playoffs

	Series	W	L	GP	W	L	T	GF	GA	Last Mtg.	Round	Result
Buffalo	6	5	1	33	19	14	0	132	113	1993	DSF	L 0-4
Chicago	6	5	1	22	16	5	1	97	63	1978	QF	W 4-0
Colorado	2	1	1	11	6	5	0	37	36	1983	DSF	W 3-1
Dallas	1	0	1	3	0	3	0	13	20	1981	PR	L 0-3
Detroit	7	4	3	33	19	14	0	96	98	1957	SF	W 4-1
Edmonton	2	0	2	9	1	8	0	20	41	1990	F	L 1-4
Florida	1	0	1	5	1	4	0	16	22	1996	CQF	L 1-4
Hartford	2	2	0	13	8	5	0	24	17	1991	DSF	W 4-2
Los Angeles	2	2	0	13	8	5	0	56	38	1977	QF	W 4-2
Montreal	28	7	21	139	52	87	0	339	430	1994	CQF	W 4-3
New Jersey	3	1	2	18	7	11	0	52	55	1995	CQF	L 1-4
NY Islanders	2	0	2	11	3	8	0	35	49	1983	CF	L 2-4
NY Rangers	9	6	3	42	22	18	2	114	104	1973	QF	L 1-4
Philadelphia	4	2	2	20	11	9	0	60	57	1978	SF	W 4-1
Pittsburgh	4	2	2	19	9	10	0	62	67	1992	CF	L 0-4
St. Louis	2	2	0	8	8	0	0	48	15	1972	SF	W 4-0
Toronto	13	5	8	62	30	31	1	153	150	1974	QF	W 4-0
Washington	1	1	0	4	4	0	0	15	6	1990	CF	W 4-0
Defunct Clubs	3	1	2	11	4	5	2	20	20			
Totals	**98**	**46**	**52**	**476**	**228**	**242**	**6**	**1405**	**1422**			

Calgary totals include Atlanta, 1972-73 to 1979-80. Colorado totals include Quebec, 1979-80 to 1994-95.
Dallas totals include Minnesota, 1967-68 to 1992-93.
New Jersey totals include Kansas City, 1974-75 to 1975-76, and Colorado Rockies, 1976-77 to 1981-82.

Playoff Results 1996-92

Year	Round	Opponent	Result	GF	GA
1996	CQF	Florida	L 1-4	16	22
1995	CQF	New Jersey	L 1-4	5	14
1994	CSF	New Jersey	L 2-4	17	22
	CQF	Montreal	W 4-3	22	20
1993	DSF	Buffalo	L 0-4	12	19
1992	CF	Pittsburgh	L 0-4	7	19
	DF	Montreal	W 4-0	14	8
	DSF	Buffalo	W 4-3	19	24

Abbreviations: Round: F – Final; **CF** – conference final; **CQF** – conference quarter-final; **CSF** – conference semi-final; **DF** – division final; **DSF** – division semi-final; **SF** – semi-final; **QF** – quarter-final; **PR** – preliminary round.

1995-96 Results

Oct.	7		NY Islanders	4-4		16	at	New Jersey	4-2
	9		Buffalo	5-3		22	at	Pittsburgh	6-7
	11	at	Colorado	1-3		25		Tampa Bay	4-3
	12	at	San Jose	6-6		27		NY Rangers	3-5
	14	at	Dallas	5-6		28	at	Montreal	4-5
	17	at	St. Louis	7-4		31	at	Ottawa	3-1
	21	at	Detroit	2-4	**Feb.**	1		Florida	2-2
	26		Washington	2-4		3		Buffalo	4-2
	28		Hartford	3-0		6	at	Pittsburgh	5-6
	31		Montreal	1-3		7	at	Buffalo	1-2
Nov.	2		Detroit	5-6		10		Philadelphia	2-6
	4	at	Montreal	1-4		14	at	Hartford	3-0
	7	at	Washington	4-3		15	at	Chicago	0-3
	9		Ottawa	4-3		17	at	Vancouver	4-1
	11		Toronto	1-3		19	at	Los Angeles	3-3
	14	at	Tampa Bay	3-5		21	at	Anaheim	3-4
	16		New Jersey	2-2		23	at	Edmonton	7-4
	18		St. Louis	5-2		24	at	Calgary	2-1
	21		Winnipeg	5-4		27		Edmonton	3-4
	24		Los Angeles	2-1		28	at	NY Rangers	3-1
	25	at	Ottawa	3-3	**Mar.**	2		Washington	0-2
	30		Pittsburgh	6-9		5	at	NY Islanders	3-5
Dec.	2		Buffalo	6-4		7		NY Islanders	4-3
	3	at	Philadelphia	1-6		9		Philadelphia	3-2
	5		Dallas	6-4		10	at	Florida	4-1
	8	at	Tampa Bay	1-3		14		Pittsburgh	4-2
	9	at	Florida	1-3		15	at	Washington	5-2
	13	at	NY Rangers	2-4		18		San Jose	3-3
	14		Florida	6-4		20	at	New Jersey	2-1
	16		Calgary	6-3		21		Ottawa	3-1
	22	at	Buffalo	3-2		23		NY Rangers	4-5
	23		Tampa Bay	7-5		27	at	Hartford	6-5
	26	at	NY Islanders	3-3		28		Montreal	3-4
	31	at	Winnipeg	5-3		31	at	Buffalo	6-5
Jan.	2		Chicago	2-5	**Apr.**	1	at	Ottawa	1-1
	3	at	Toronto	4-4		3	at	Montreal	4-1
	6		Hartford	5-2		4		Montreal	3-3
	9		Colorado	0-3		7	at	Philadelphia	4-2
	11		Anaheim	7-2		11		Hartford	3-2
	13		New Jersey	3-2		13	at	Hartford	0-2
	15		Vancouver	0-6		14		Pittsburgh	6-5

Entry Draft
Selections 1996-82

1996
Pick
8	Johnathan Aitken
45	Henry Kuster
53	Eric Naud
80	Jason Doyle
100	Trent Whitfield
132	Elias Abrahamsson
155	Chris Lane
182	Thomas Brown
208	Bob Prier
234	Anders Soderberg

1995
Pick
9	Kyle McLaren
21	Sean Brown
47	Paxton Schafer
73	Bill McCauley
99	Cameron Mann
151	Yevgeny Shaldybin
177	Per Johan Axelsson
203	Sergei Zhukov
229	Jonathan Murphy

1994
Pick
21	Evgeni Ryabchikov
47	Daniel Goneau
99	Eric Nickulas
125	Darren Wright
151	Andre Roy
177	Jeremy Schaefer
229	John Grahame
255	Neil Savary
281	Andrei Yakhanov

1993
Pick
25	Kevyn Adams
51	Matt Alvey
88	Charles Paquette
103	Shawn Bates
129	Andrei Sapozhnikov
155	Milt Mastad
181	Ryan Golden
207	Hal Gill
233	Joel Prpic
259	Joakim Persson

1992
Pick
16	Dmitri Kvartalnov
55	Sergei Zholtok
112	Scott Bailey
133	Jiri Dopita
136	Grigori Panteleev
184	Kurt Seher
208	Mattias Timander
232	Chris Crombie
256	Denis Chervyakov
257	Evgeny Pavlov

1991
Pick
18	Glen Murray
40	Jozef Stumpel
62	Marcel Cousineau
84	Brad Tiley
106	Mariusz Czerkawski
150	Gary Golczewski
172	John Moser
194	Daniel Hodge
216	Steve Norton
238	Stephen Lombardi
260	Torsten Kienass

1990
Pick
21	Bryan Smolinski
63	Cameron Stewart
84	Jerome Buckley
105	Mike Bales
126	Mark Woolf
147	Jim Mackey
168	John Gruden
189	Darren Wetherill
210	Dean Capuano
231	Andy Bezeau
252	Ted Miskolczi

1989
Pick
17	Shayne Stevenson
38	Mike Parson
57	Wes Walz
80	Jackson Penney
101	Mark Montanari
122	Stephen Foster
143	Otto Hascak
164	Rick Allain
185	James Lavish
206	Geoff Simpson
227	David Franzosa

1988
Pick
18	Robert Cimetta
60	Stephen Heinze
81	Joe Juneau
102	Daniel Murphy
123	Derek Geary
165	Mark Krys
186	Jon Rohloff
228	Eric Reisman
249	Doug Jones

1987
Pick
3	Glen Wesley
14	Stephane Quintal
56	Todd Lalonde
67	Darwin McPherson
77	Matt Delguidice
98	Ted Donato
119	Matt Glennon
140	Rob Cheevers
161	Chris Winnes
182	Paul Ohman
203	Casey Jones
224	Eric Lemarque
245	Sean Gorman

1986
Pick
13	Craig Janney
34	Pekka Tirkkonen
76	Dean Hall
97	Matt Pesklewis
118	Garth Premak
139	Paul Beraldo
160	Brian Ferreira
181	Jeff Flaherty
202	Greg Hawgood
223	Staffan Malmqvist
244	Joel Gardner

1985
Pick
31	Alain Cote
52	Bill Ranford
73	Jaime Kelly
94	Steve Moore
115	Gord Hynes
136	Per Martinelle
157	Randy Burridge
178	Gord Cruickshank
199	Dave Buda
210	Bob Beers
220	John Byce
241	Marc West

1984
Pick
19	Dave Pasin
40	Ray Podloski
61	Jeff Cornelius
82	Robert Joyce
103	Mike Bishop
124	Randy Oswald
145	Mark Thietke
166	Don Sweeney
186	Kevin Heffernan
207	J.D. Urbanic
227	Bill Kopecky
248	Jim Newhouse

1983
Pick
21	Nevin Markwart
42	Greg Johnston
62	Greg Puhalski
82	Alain Larochelle
102	Allen Pederson
122	Terry Taillefer
142	Ian Armstrong
162	Francois Olivier
182	Harri Laurilla
202	Paul Fitzsimmons
222	Norm Foster
242	Greg Murphy

1982
Pick
1	Gord Kluzak
22	Brian Curran
39	Lyndon Byers
60	Dave Reid
102	Bob Nicholson
123	Bob Sweeney
144	John Meulenbroeks
165	Tony Fiore
186	Doug Kostynski
207	Tony Gilliard
228	Tommy Lehmann
249	Bruno Campese

Club Directory

FleetCenter
Boston, Massachusetts 02114
Phone **617/624-1050**
FAX 617/523-7184
Capacity: 17,565

Executive
Owner and Governor	Jeremy M. Jacobs
Alternative Governor	Louis Jacobs
President, General Manager and Alternative Governor	Harry Sinden
Vice President	Tom Johnson
Assistant General Manager	Mike O'Connell
Sr. Assistant to the President	Nate Greenberg
General Counsel	Michael Wall
Director of Administration	Dale Hamilton
Assistant to the President	Joe Curnane
Administrative Assistant	Carol Gould
Receptionist	Karen Ondo

Coaching Staff
Coach	Steve Kasper
Assistant Coach	Cap Raeder
Coach, Providence Bruins	Bobby Francis
Coach, Charlotte Checkers	John Marks

Scouting Staff
Director of Scouting	Scott Bradley
Director of Player Evaluation	Bart Bradley
Director of Development	Bob Tindall
Director of Scouting Information	Jeff Gorton
Scouting Staff	Don Saatzer, Jean Ratelle, Scott McLellan, Daniel Dore, Svenake Svensson (Europe), Yuri Karmanov (CIS), Gerry Cheevers (Pro), Jim Morrison (Pro)

Communications Staff
Director of Media Relations	Heidi Holland
Media Relations Assistant	Rusty Ingram
Director of Community Relations, Marketing Services	Sue Byrne
Community Relations & Marketing Services Assistant	Brian Oates
Director of Alumni Community Relations	John Bucyk
Administrative Assistant, Alumni Office	Mal Viola

Medical and Training Staff
Athletic Trainer	Don Del Negro
Physical Therapist	Tim Trahant
Rehabilitation Consultant	Jim Kausek, AdvantageHEALTH Corp.
Equipment Manager	Ken Fleger
Assistant Equipment Manager	Keith Robinson
Team Physicians	Dr. Bertram Zarins, Dr. Ashby Moncure, Dr. John J. Boyle
Team Dentists	Dr. John Kelly and Dr. Bruce Donoff
Team Psychologist	Dr. Fred Neff

Ticketing and Finance Staff
Director of Ticket Operations	Matt Brennan
Assistant Director of Ticket Operations	Jim Foley
Ticket Office Assistants	Linda Bartlett, Justin Brennan
Accounting Manager	Richard McGlinchey
Accounts Payable	Barbara Johnson

Television and Radio
Broadcasters (UPN 38 WSBK-TV)	Fred Cusick and Derek Sanderson
Broadcasters (NESN)	Dale Arnold and Gord Kluzak
Broadcasters (Radio)	Bob Neumeier and TBA
TV Channels	New England Sports Network (NESN) and UPN38 WSBK-TV
Radio Station	WBZ (1030 AM) and Bruins Radio Network

General Manager

SINDEN, HARRY JAMES
President and General Manager, Boston Bruins.
Born in Toronto, Ont., September 14, 1932.

Harry Sinden never played a game in the NHL but stepped into the Bruins' organization with an impressive coaching background in minor professional hockey and his continued excellence has earned him a place in the Hockey Hall of Fame as one of the true builders in hockey history. After five years in OHA Senior hockey — including 1958 with the IIHF World Amateur Champion Whitby Dunlops — Sinden became a playing-coach in the old Eastern Professional League and its successor, the Central Professional League. In 1965-66 as playing-coach of Oklahoma City Blazers in the CPHL, Sinden led the club to second place in the regular standings and then to eight straight playoff victories for the Jack Adams Trophy.

Under his guidance, the Bruins of 1967-68 made the playoffs for the first time in nine seasons, finishing third in the East Division, and were nosed out of first place in 1968-69 by Montreal. In 1969-70, Sinden led the Bruins to their first Stanley Cup win since 1940-41.

The season he went into private business but returned to the hockey scene in the summer of 1972 when he was appointed coach of Team Canada. He molded that group of NHL stars into a powerful unit and led them into an exciting eight-game series against the Soviet national team in September of 1972. Team Canada emerged the winner by a narrow margin with a record of four wins, three losses and one tie.

Sinden then returned to the Bruins organization early in the 1972-73 season. Sinden last took over as the Bruins' coach in February 1985, after replacing Gerry Cheevers. Boston finished 11-10-3 with Sinden behind the bench before being defeated by Montreal in five games in the Adams Division semi-finals.

NHL Coaching Record

Season	Team	Regular Season					Playoffs			
		Games	W	L	T	%	Games	W	L	%
1966-67	Boston	70	17	43	10	.314				
1967-68	Boston	74	37	27	10	.568	4	0	4	.000
1968-69	Boston	76	42	18	16	.658	10	6	4	.600
1969-70	Boston	76	40	17	19	.651	14	12	2	.857*
1979-80	Boston	10	4	6	0	.400	9	4	5	.444
1984-85	Boston	24	11	10	3	.521	5	2	3	.400
	NHL Totals	330	151	121	58	.545	42	24	18	.571

* Stanley Cup win.

Coach

KASPER, STEVE
Coach, Boston Bruins. Born in Montreal, Que., September 28, 1961.

Steve Kasper was named as the Bruins 21st head coach on May 25, 1995.

Kasper, 35, began his coaching career as an assistant coach with the Bruins during the 1993-94 season. On July 22, 1994, he was named as head coach of Boston's American Hockey League affiliate in Providence and in 1994-95 he led the AHL Bruins to fifth place overall in the AHL standings, with a 39-30-11 record. His club set team records for fewest losses, fewest goals against and longest win streak during the regular season and also set a club record for most playoff victories.

A native of Montreal, Kasper joined the coaching ranks following a 13-year playing career during which he earned a reputation as one of the top defensive forwards in the league. He was drafted by the Bruins as their third pick, 81st overall, in the 1980 NHL Entry Draft following a junior career in the Quebec Major Junior Hockey League. He played eight-plus seasons in a Bruins uniform, winning the Selke Trophy as the league's top defensive forward in 1981-82, and enjoyed his best offensive NHL season with 26 goals and 70 points in 1987-88 as the Bruins advanced to the Stanley Cup finals. He went to Los Angeles in a January, 1989 trade for Bobby Carpenter and played his final four-plus NHL seasons with Los Angeles, Philadelphia and Tampa Bay before retiring as a player at the conclusion of the 1992-93 season. Kasper and his wife, Kathy, reside in North Andover with their two sons, Jordan and Michael.

Coaching Record

Season	Team	Regular Season					Playoffs			
		Games	W	L	T	%	Games	W	L	%
1994-95	Providence (AHL)	80	39	30	11	.550	13	6	7	.460
1995-96	Boston (NHL)	82	40	31	11	.555	5	1	4	.200
	NHL Totals	82	40	31	11	.555	5	1	4	.200

Buffalo Sabres

1995-96 Results: 33W-42L-7T 73PTS. Fifth, Northeast Division

Schedule

Oct.	Fri.	4	at Edmonton	Tues.	7	at San Jose	
	Sun.	6	at Calgary	Thur.	9	at Los Angeles	
	Wed.	9	at Vancouver	Fri.	10	at Anaheim	
	Sat.	12	Detroit	Sun.	12	at Phoenix	
	Tues.	15	Tampa Bay	Wed.	15	at NY Islanders	
	Thur.	17	Pittsburgh	Mon.	20	Chicago	
	Fri.	18	at Washington	Wed.	22	Montreal	
	Thur.	24	Montreal	Fri.	24	Edmonton	
	Sat.	26	Hartford	Sat.	25	Hartford	
	Sun.	27	at NY Rangers	Wed.	29	Pittsburgh	
	Wed.	30	at Dallas	Fri.	31	Dallas	
Nov.	Fri.	1	at St. Louis	**Feb.** Sun.	2	Washington	
	Sat.	2	at Colorado	Tues.	4	at Philadelphia	
	Thur.	7	Philadelphia	Thur.	6	Florida	
	Sat.	9	at Hartford	Sat.	8	at Tampa Bay	
	Mon.	11	Florida	Sun.	9	Ottawa	
	Tues.	12	at Pittsburgh	Wed.	12	Montreal	
	Thur.	14	Colorado	Sun.	16	San Jose	
	Sat.	16	Boston	Tues.	18	Calgary	
	Tues.	19	at Toronto	Fri.	21	NY Islanders	
	Thur.	21	Toronto	Sun.	23	Boston	
	Sat.	23	at Boston	Thur.	27	at New Jersey	
	Tues.	26	at Florida	**Mar.** Sat.	1	at Ottawa	
	Wed.	27	at Tampa Bay	Wed.	5	Pittsburgh	
	Fri.	29	Ottawa	Sat.	8	at Montreal	
	Sat.	30	at NY Islanders	Sun.	9	New Jersey	
Dec.	Wed.	4	Vancouver	Sat.	15	at Philadelphia*	
	Fri.	6	Anaheim	Sun.	16	Philadelphia*	
	Sat.	7	at Hartford	Tues.	18	at Pittsburgh	
	Wed.	11	at Montreal	Fri.	21	at Washington	
	Fri.	13	NY Rangers	Sat.	22	at Florida	
	Sat.	14	at Boston	Wed.	26	NY Islanders	
	Wed.	18	Tampa Bay	Fri.	28	at Detroit	
	Fri.	20	Los Angeles	Sun.	30	at Chicago*	
	Sat.	21	at Ottawa	**Apr.** Tues.	1	at NY Rangers	
	Mon.	23	at New Jersey	Wed.	2	Ottawa	
	Thur.	26	Hartford	Fri.	4	NY Rangers	
	Sat.	28	at Pittsburgh	Mon.	7	at Hartford	
	Tues.	31	New Jersey	Thur.	10	at Boston	
Jan.	Fri.	3	St. Louis	Sat.	12	at Ottawa	
	Sun.	5	Phoenix	Sun.	13	Washington	

* Denotes afternoon game.

Franchise date: May 22, 1970

EASTERN
NHL CONFERENCE

27th NHL Season

NORTHEAST DIVISION

A trio of Buffalo veterans (left to right: Pat LaFontaine, Richard Smehlik and Donald Audette) display the new colors and uniforms the Sabres will wear in their new home – the Marine Midland Arena – in 1996-97.

Year-by-Year Record

		Home			Road			Overall							
Season	GP	W	L	T	W	L	T	W	L	T	GF	GA	Pts.	Finished	Playoff Result
1995-96	82	19	17	5	14	25	2	33	42	7	247	262	73	5th, Northeast Div.	Out of Playoffs
1994-95	48	15	8	1	7	11	6	22	19	7	130	119	51	4th, Northeast Div.	Lost Conf. Quarter-Final
1993-94	84	22	17	3	21	15	6	43	32	9	282	218	95	4th, Northeast Div.	Lost Conf. Quarter-Final
1992-93	84	25	15	2	13	21	8	38	36	10	335	297	86	4th, Adams Div.	Lost Div. Final
1991-92	80	22	13	5	9	24	7	31	37	12	289	299	74	3rd, Adams Div.	Lost Div. Semi-Final
1990-91	80	15	13	12	16	17	7	31	30	19	292	278	81	3rd, Adams Div.	Lost Div. Semi-Final
1989-90	80	27	11	2	18	16	6	45	27	8	286	248	98	2nd, Adams Div.	Lost Div. Semi-Final
1988-89	80	25	12	3	13	23	4	38	35	7	291	299	83	3rd, Adams Div.	Lost Div. Semi-Final
1987-88	80	19	14	7	18	18	4	37	32	11	283	305	85	3rd, Adams Div.	Lost Div. Semi-Final
1986-87	80	18	18	4	10	26	4	28	44	8	280	308	64	5th, Adams Div.	Out of Playoffs
1985-86	80	23	16	1	14	21	5	37	37	6	296	291	80	5th, Adams Div.	Out of Playoffs
1984-85	80	23	10	7	15	18	7	38	28	14	290	237	90	3rd, Adams Div.	Lost Div. Semi-Final
1983-84	80	25	9	6	23	16	1	48	25	7	315	257	103	2nd, Adams Div.	Lost Div. Semi-Final
1982-83	80	25	7	8	13	22	5	38	29	13	318	285	89	3rd, Adams Div.	Lost Div. Final
1981-82	80	23	8	9	16	18	6	39	26	15	307	273	93	3rd, Adams Div.	Lost Div. Semi-Final
1980-81	80	21	7	12	18	13	9	39	20	21	327	250	99	1st, Adams Div.	Lost Quarter-Final
1979-80	80	27	5	8	20	12	8	47	17	16	318	201	110	1st, Adams Div.	Lost Semi-Final
1978-79	80	19	13	8	17	15	8	36	28	16	280	263	88	2nd, Adams Div.	Lost Prelim. Round
1977-78	80	25	7	8	19	12	9	44	19	17	288	215	105	2nd, Adams Div.	Lost Quarter-Final
1976-77	80	27	8	5	21	16	3	48	24	8	301	220	104	2nd, Adams Div.	Lost Quarter-Final
1975-76	80	28	7	5	18	14	8	46	21	13	339	240	105	2nd, Adams Div.	Lost Quarter-Final
1974-75	80	28	6	6	21	10	9	49	16	15	354	240	113	1st, Adams Div.	Lost Final
1973-74	78	23	10	6	9	24	6	32	34	12	242	250	76	5th, East Div.	Out of Playoffs
1972-73	78	30	6	3	7	21	11	37	27	14	257	219	88	4th, East Div.	Lost Quarter-Final
1971-72	78	11	19	9	5	24	10	16	43	19	203	289	51	6th, East Div.	Out of Playoffs
1970-71	78	16	13	10	8	26	5	24	39	15	217	291	63	5th, East Div.	Out of Playoffs

1996-97 Player Personnel

FORWARDS	HT	WT	S	Place of Birth	Date	1995-96 Club
AUDETTE, Donald	5-8	175	R	Laval, Que.	9/23/69	Buffalo
BARNABY, Matthew	6-0	170	L	Ottawa, Ont.	5/4/73	Buffalo
BIENVENUE, Daniel	6-0	195	L	Val d'Or, Que.	6/10/77	Val d'Or
BROWN, Curtis	6-0	182	L	Unity, Sask.	2/12/76	M.Jaw-P.A.-Buf-Roch
BURRIDGE, Randy	5-9	185	L	Fort Erie, Ont.	1/7/66	Buffalo
DAVIDSON, Matt	6-2	190	R	Flin Flon, Man.	8/9/77	Portland (WHL)
DAWE, Jason	5-10	195	L	North York, Ont.	5/29/73	Buffalo-Rochester
DUTIAUME, Mark	6-0	200	L	Winnipeg, Man.	1/31/77	Brandon
GROSEK, Michal	6-2	196	R	Vyskov, Czech.	6/1/75	Winnipeg-Buffalo-Springfield
HAMEL, Denis	6-2	200	L	Lachute, Que.	5/10/77	Chicoutimi
HOLZINGER, Brian	5-11	180	R	Parma, OH	10/10/72	Buffalo-Rochester
JACKSON, Dane	6-1	200	R	Castlegar, B.C.	5/17/70	Buffalo-Rochester
LaFONTAINE, Pat	5-10	180	R	St. Louis, MO	2/22/65	Buffalo
MAY, Brad	6-1	210	L	Toronto, Ont.	11/29/71	Buffalo
METHOT, Francois	6-0	171	R	Montreal, Que.	4/26/78	St-Hyacinthe
MOORE, Barrie	5-11	175	L	London, Ont.	5/22/75	Buffalo-Rochester
MORTIER, Darren	6-1	175	R	Sarnia, Ont.	5/4/77	Sarnia
NICHOL, Scott	5-8	160	R	Edmonton, Alta.	12/31/74	Buffalo-Rochester
PECA, Mike	5-11	180	R	Toronto, Ont.	3/26/74	Buffalo
PLANTE, Derek	5-11	180	L	Cloquet, MN	1/17/71	Buffalo
PRIMEAU, Wayne	6-3	193	L	Scarborough, Ont.	6/4/76	Buf-Owen Sound-Oshawa-Roch
RASMUSSEN, Erik	6-2	191	L	Minneapolis, MN	3/28/77	U. Minnesota
RAY, Rob	6-0	203	L	Belleville, Ont.	6/8/68	Buffalo
RUSHFORTH, Paul	6-0	189	R	Prince George, B.C.	4/22/74	South Carolina
SCOTT, Brian	6-0	187	L	Brampton, Ont.	5/22/77	Kitchener-Sudbury
SKRLAC, Rob	6-4	230	L	Campbell, B.C.	6/10/76	Kamloops
SPAHNEL, Martin	6-2	187	L	Gottwaldov, Czech.	7/1/77	Lethbridge-Moose Jaw
SUNDERLAND, Mathieu	6-4	192	R	Quebec City, Que.	11/30/76	Drummondville-Halifax
VAN OENE, Darren	6-3	207	L	Edmonton, Alta.	1/18/78	Brandon
VARADA, Vaclav	6-0	200	L	Vsetin, Czech.	4/26/76	Kelowna-Buffalo-Rochester
WALSH, Kurt	6-2	205	R	St. John's, Nfld.	9/26/77	Oshawa-Owen Sound
WARD, Dixon	6-0	200	R	Leduc, Alta.	9/23/68	Buffalo-Rochester
YAKE, Terry	5-11	190	R	New Westminster, B.C.	10/22/68	Milwaukee
ZANUTTO, Mike	6-0	190	L	Burlington, Ont.	1/1/77	Oshawa
DEFENSEMEN						
BOUGHNER, Bob	6-0	205	R	Windsor, Ont.	3/8/71	Carolina-Buffalo
GALLEY, Garry	6-0	204	L	Montreal, Que.	4/16/63	Buffalo
GRAND PIERRE, Jean-Luc	6-2	197	L	Montreal, Que.	2/2/77	Val d'Or
HOLLINGER, Terry	6-1	200	L	Regina, Sask.	2/24/71	Rochester
HOUDA, Doug	6-2	190	R	Blairmore, Alta.	6/3/66	Buffalo-Rochester
KLIMENTJEV, Sergei	5-11	200	L	Kiev, USSR	4/5/75	Rochester
MARTONE, Mike	6-1	200	R	Sault Ste. Marie, Ont.	9/26/77	Peterborough
McKEE, Jay	6-3	195	L	Kingston, Ont.	9/8/77	Buffalo-Niagara Falls-Rochester
MENHART, Marian	6-3	220	L	Most, Czech.	2/14/77	Prince Albert
MILLAR, Craig	6-2	200	L	Winnipeg, Man.	7/12/76	Swift Current
NDUR, Rumun	6-2	200	L	Zaria, Nigeria	7/7/75	Rochester
POPP, Kevin	6-1	198	L	Surrey, B.C.	2/26/76	Seattle-Portland (WHL)
SARICH, Cory	6-3	175	R	Saskatoon, Sask.	8/16/78	Saskatoon
SHANNON, Darryl	6-2	200	L	Barrie, Ont.	6/21/68	Winnipeg-Buffalo
SMEHLIK, Richard	6-3	208	L	Ostrava, Czech.	1/23/70	Did Not Play
TEZIKOV, Alexei	6-1	198	L	Togliatti, USSR	6/22/78	Lada Togliatti
WILSON, Mike	6-6	210	L	Brampton, Ont.	2/26/75	Buffalo-Rochester
WRIGHT, Shayne	6-0	189	L	Welland, Ont.	6/30/75	Rochester
ZHITNIK, Alexei	5-11	204	L	Kiev, USSR	10/10/72	Buffalo

GOALTENDERS	HT	WT	C	Place of Birth	Date	1995-96 Club
BIRON, Martin	6-1	154	L	Lac St. Charles, Que.	8/15/77	Buffalo-Beauport
HASEK, Dominik	5-11	168	L	Pardubice, Czech.	1/29/65	Buffalo
SHIELDS, Steve	6-3	210	L	Toronto, Ont.	7/19/72	Buffalo-Rochester
TREFILOV, Andrei	6-0	180	L	Kirovo-Chepetsk, USSR	8/31/69	Buffalo-Rochester

General Manager

MUCKLER, JOHN
General Manager, Buffalo Sabres. Born in Midland, Ont., April 3, 1934.

In 1996-97, Muckler enters his sixth season with the Sabres. He was hired as the director of hockey operations in the summer of 1991 and also took over as coach in December of that season. His first full season behind the Buffalo bench came in 1992-93 when he helped lead Buffalo to its first appearance in the second round of the playoffs since 1983. John added g.m. duties to his job in the summer of 1993.

In two seasons as head coach in Edmonton prior to joining the Sabres, Muckler led the Oilers to the Stanley Cup in 1989-90, and to the Conference Finals in 1990-91.

NHL Coaching Record

		Regular Season					Playoffs			
Season	Team	Games	W	L	T	%	Games	W	L	%
1968-69	Minnesota	35	6	23	6	.257	....	....	....	....
1989-90	Edmonton	80	38	28	14	.563	22	16	6	.727*
1990-91	Edmonton	80	37	37	6	.500	18	9	9	.500
1991-92	Buffalo	52	22	22	8	.500	7	3	4	.429
1992-93	Buffalo	84	38	36	10	.512	8	4	4	.500
1993-94	Buffalo	84	43	32	9	.565	7	3	4	.429
1994-95	Buffalo	48	22	19	7	.531	5	1	4	.200
	NHL Totals	**463**	**206**	**197**	**60**	**.510**	**67**	**36**	**31**	**.537**

* Won Stanley Cup.

General Managers' History

George "Punch" Imlach, 1970-71 to 1977-78; John Anderson (acting), 1978-79; Scotty Bowman, 1979-80 to 1985-86; Scotty Bowman and Gerry Meehan, 1986-87; Gerry Meehan, 1987-88 to 1992-93; John Muckler, 1993-94 to date.

1995-96 Scoring

* – rookie

Regular Season

Pos	#	Player	Team	GP	G	A	Pts	+/–	PIM	PP	SH	GW	GT	S	%
C	16	Pat LaFontaine	BUF	76	40	51	91	–8	36	15	3	7	1	224	17.9
L	12	Randy Burridge	BUF	74	25	33	58	0	30	6	0	3	0	154	16.2
C	26	Derek Plante	BUF	76	23	33	56	–4	28	4	0	5	0	203	11.3
D	3	Garry Galley	BUF	78	10	44	54	–2	81	7	1	2	0	175	5.7
L	43	Jason Dawe	BUF	67	25	25	50	–8	33	8	1	0	2	130	19.2
L	10	Brad May	BUF	79	15	29	44	6	295	3	0	4	0	168	8.9
D	44	Alexei Zhitnik	BUF	80	6	30	36	–25	58	5	0	0	0	193	3.1
L	36	Matthew Barnaby	BUF	73	15	16	31	–2	335	0	0	0	0	131	11.5
C	27	Mike Peca	BUF	68	11	20	31	–1	67	4	3	1	0	109	10.1
R	28	Donald Audette	BUF	23	12	13	25	0	18	8	0	1	0	92	13.0
C	19 *	Brian Holzinger	BUF	58	10	10	20	–21	37	5	0	1	0	71	14.1
D	21	Mark Astley	BUF	60	2	18	20	–12	80	0	0	0	0	80	2.5
D	8	Darryl Shannon	WPG	48	2	7	9	5	72	0	0	0	0	34	5.9
			BUF	26	2	6	8	10	20	0	0	0	0	25	8.0
			TOTAL	74	4	13	17	15	92	0	0	0	0	59	6.8
L	17	Brent Hughes	BUF	76	5	10	15	–9	148	0	0	0	0	56	8.9
D	34 *	Mike Wilson	BUF	58	4	8	12	13	41	1	0	1	0	52	7.7
L	18	Michal Grosek	WPG	1	0	0	0	–1	0	0	0	0	0	1	0.0
			BUF	22	6	4	10	0	31	2	0	1	1	33	18.2
			TOTAL	23	6	4	10	–1	31	2	0	1	1	34	17.6
R	24 *	Dane Jackson	BUF	22	5	4	9	3	41	0	0	1	0	20	25.0
L	32	Rob Ray	BUF	71	3	6	9	–8	287	0	0	0	1	21	14.3
R	25	Rob Conn	BUF	28	2	5	7	–9	18	0	0	0	0	36	5.6
L	33	Scott Pearson	BUF	27	4	0	4	–4	67	0	0	1	0	26	15.4
R	15	Dixon Ward	BUF	8	2	2	4	1	6	0	0	1	0	12	16.7
D	6	Doug Houda	BUF	38	1	3	4	3	52	0	0	0	0	21	4.8
D	38 *	Jay McKee	BUF	1	0	1	1	1	2	0	0	0	0	2	0.0
D	4 *	Bob Boughner	BUF	31	0	1	1	3	104	0	0	0	0	14	0.0
G	39	Dominik Hasek	BUF	59	0	1	1	0	6	0	0	0	0	0	0.0
L	9 *	Vaclav Varada	BUF	1	0	0	0	0	0	0	0	0	0	2	0.0
G	31 *	Steve Shields	BUF	2	0	0	0	0	2	0	0	0	0	0	0.0
C	45 *	Scott Nichol	BUF	2	0	0	0	0	10	0	0	0	0	4	0.0
C	76 *	Wayne Primeau	BUF	2	0	0	0	0	0	0	0	0	0	0	0.0
L	37 *	Barrie Moore	BUF	3	0	0	0	0	0	0	0	0	0	3	0.0
G	00 *	Martin Biron	BUF	3	0	0	0	0	0	0	0	0	0	0	0.0
C	37 *	Curtis Brown	BUF	4	0	0	0	0	0	0	0	0	0	1	0.0
G	1	John Blue	BUF	5	0	0	0	0	0	0	0	0	0	0	0.0
D	4	Grant Jennings	BUF	6	0	0	0	1	28	0	0	0	0	3	0.0
G	30	Andrei Trefilov	BUF	22	0	0	0	0	4	0	0	0	0	0	0.0

Goaltending

No.	Goaltender	GPI	Mins	Avg	W	L	T	EN	SO	GA	SA	S%
39	Dominik Hasek	59	3417	2.83	22	30	6	5	2	161	2011	.920
31	* Steve Shields	2	75	3.20	1	0	0	0	0	4	32	.875
30	Andrei Trefilov	22	1094	3.51	8	8	1	2	0	64	660	.903
1	John Blue	5	255	3.53	2	2	0	1	0	15	137	.891
00	* Martin Biron	3	119	5.04	0	2	0	0	0	10	64	.844
	Totals	**82**	**4976**	**3.16**	**33**	**42**	**7**	**8**	**2**	**262**	**2912**	**.910**

Coach

NOLAN, TED
Coach, Buffalo Sabres. Born in Sault Ste. Marie, Ont., April 7, 1958.

Nolan was named the 14th person in team history to coach the Sabres on July 18, 1995. The move for Nolan came just 13 months after having been named as an assistant coach with the Hartford Whalers.

It came as no surprise that just over a year after Nolan got his first position on an NHL coaching staff he secured his first head coaching job. The 38-year old built a successful resume in junior hockey, guiding the 1992-93 Sault Ste. Marie Greyhounds of the Ontario Hockey League to the Memorial Cup championship, after having taken that team to the OHL title the two years prior.

An Ojibway Indian, he is no stranger to the NHL however, or the Sabres' organization for that matter. Nolan played 78 NHL games over the course of five seasons with Detroit and Pittsburgh from 1981-82 to 1985-86 after the Red Wings had made him their seventh draft choice (78th overall) in 1978. In between these two cities, Theodore John (Ted) Nolan had ties to Buffalo when he was signed as a free agent on March 7, 1985 by the Sabres, who sold his rights to the Penguins just over six months later. He also spent the entire 1984-85 season as a player with Rochester, being named team captain at the halfway mark of the season. His AHL days also included a Calder Cup championship while playing for Adirondack. In the final year of his NHL playing career ('85-86), he played in Pittsburgh with former Sabres Doug Bodger and Dave Hannan, as well as Penguin star Mario Lemieux.

One of 12 children (he has six brothers and five sisters), Ted is married to Sandra. They have two children, sons Brandon and Jordan.

Coaching Record

		Regular Season					Playoffs			
Season	Team	Games	W	L	T	%	Games	W	L	%
1988-89	S.S. Marie (OHL)	38	12	25	1	.329	....	....	....	....
1989-90	S.S. Marie (OHL)	66	18	42	6	.318	....	....	....	....
1990-91	S.S. Marie (OHL)	66	42	21	3	.659	14	12	2	.857
1991-92	S.S. Marie (OHL)	66	41	19	6	.667	19	12	7	.632
1992-93	S.S. Marie (OHL)	66	38	23	5	.614	18	13	5	.722
1993-94	S.S. Marie (OHL)	66	35	24	7	.583	14	10	4	.714
1995-96	**Buffalo (NHL)**	**82**	**33**	**42**	**7**	**.445**	....	....	....	....
	NHL Totals	**82**	**33**	**42**	**7**	**.445**	....	....	....	....

Coaching History

"Punch" Imlach, 1970-71; "Punch" Imlach, Floyd Smith and Joe Crozier, 1971-72; Joe Crozier, 1972-73 to 1973-74; Floyd Smith, 1974-75 to 1976-77; Marcel Pronovost, 1977-78; Marcel Pronovost and Billy Inglis, 1978-79; Scotty Bowman, 1979-80; Roger Neilson, 1980-81; Jim Roberts and Scotty Bowman, 1981-82; Scotty Bowman 1982-83 to 1984-85; Jim Schoenfeld and Scotty Bowman, 1985-86; Scotty Bowman, Craig Ramsay and Ted Sator, 1986-87; Ted Sator, 1987-88 to 1988-89; Rick Dudley, 1989-90 to 1990-91; Rick Dudley and John Muckler, 1991-92; John Muckler, 1992-93 to 1994-95; Ted Nolan, 1995-96 to date.

Club Records

Team

(Figures in brackets for season records are games played; records for fewest points, wins, ties, losses, goals, goals against are for 70 or more games)

Most Points	113	1974-75 (80)
Most Wins	49	1974-75 (80)
Most Ties	21	1980-81 (80)
Most Losses	44	1986-87 (80)
Most Goals	354	1974-75 (80)
Most Goals Against	308	1986-87 (80)
Fewest Points	51	1971-72 (78)
Fewest Wins	16	1971-72 (78)
Fewest Ties	6	1985-86 (80)
Fewest Losses	16	1974-75 (80)
Fewest Goals	203	1971-72 (78)
Fewest Goals Against	201	1979-80 (80)
Longest Winning Streak		
Overall	10	Jan. 4-23/84
Home	12	Nov. 12/72-Jan. 7/73, Oct. 13-Dec. 10/89
Away	*10	Dec. 10/83-Jan. 23/84
Longest Undefeated Streak		
Overall	14	Mar. 6-Apr. 6/80 (8 wins, 6 ties)
Home	21	Oct. 8/72-Jan. 7/73 (18 wins, 3 ties)
Away	*10	Dec. 10/83-Jan. 23/84 (10 wins)
Longest Losing Streak		
Overall	7	Oct. 25-Nov. 8/70, Apr. 3-15/93, Oct. 9-22/93
Home	6	Oct. 10-Nov. 10/93
Away	7	Oct. 14-Nov. 7/70, Feb. 6-27/71
Longest Winless Streak		
Overall	12	Nov. 23-Dec. 20/91 (8 losses, 4 ties)
Home	12	Jan. 27-Mar. 10/91 (7 losses, 5 ties)
Away	23	Oct. 30/71-Feb. 19/72 (15 losses, 8 ties)
Most Shutouts, Season	9	1993-94 (84)
Most PIM, Season	2,712	1991-92 (80)
Most Goals, Game	14	Jan. 21/75 (Wsh. 2 at Buf. 14), Mar. 19/81 (Tor. 4 at Buf. 14)

Individual

Most Seasons	17	Gilbert Perreault
Most Games	1,191	Gilbert Perreault
Most Goals, Career	512	Gilbert Perreault
Most Assists, Career	814	Gilbert Perreault
Most Points, Career	1,326	Gilbert Perreault
Most PIM, Career	1,746	Rob Ray
Most Shutouts, Career	14	Don Edwards, Dominik Hasek
Longest Consecutive Games Streak	776	Craig Ramsay (Mar. 27/73-Feb. 10/83)
Most Goals, Season	76	Alexander Mogilny (1992-93)
Most Assists, Season	95	Pat LaFontaine (1992-93)
Most Points, Season	148	Pat LaFontaine (1992-93; 53G, 95A)
Most PIM, Season	354	Rob Ray (1991-92)
Most Points, Defenseman Season	81	Phil Housley (1989-90; 21G, 60A)
Most Points, Center Season	148	Pat LaFontaine (1992-93; 53G, 95A)
Most Points, Right Wing Season	127	Alexander Mogilny (1992-93; 76G, 51A)
Most Points, Left Wing Season	95	Richard Martin (1974-75; 52G, 43A)
Most Points, Rookie Season	74	Richard Martin (1971-72; 44G, 30A)
Most Shutouts, Season	7	Dominik Hasek (1993-94)
Most Goals, Game	5	Dave Andreychuk (Feb. 6/86)
Most Assists, Game	5	Gilbert Perreault (Feb. 1/76, Mar. 9/80, Jan. 4/84), Dale Hawerchuk (Jan. 15/92), Pat LaFontaine (Dec. 31/92, Feb. 10/93)
Most Points, Game	7	Gilbert Perreault (Feb. 1/76; 2G, 5A)

* NHL Record.

Retired Numbers

2	Tim Horton	1972-1974
7	Rick Martin	1971-1981
11	Gilbert Perreault	1970-1987
14	Rene Robert	1971-1979

Captains' History

Floyd Smith, 1970-71; Gerry Meehan, 1971-72 to 1973-74; Gerry Meehan and Jim Schoenfeld, 1974-75; Jim Schoenfeld, 1975-76 to 1976-77; Danny Gare, 1977-78 to 1980-81; Danny Gare and Gil Perreault, 1981-82; Gil Perreault, 1982-83 to 1985-86; Gil Perreault and Lindy Ruff, 1986-87; Lindy Ruff, 1987-88; Lindy Ruff and Mike Foligno, 1988-89; Mike Foligno, 1989-90. Mike Foligno and Mike Ramsey, 1990-91; Mike Ramsey, 1991-92; Mike Ramsey and Pat LaFontaine, 1992-93; Pat LaFontaine and Alexander Mogilny, 1993-94; Pat LaFontaine, 1994-95 to date.

All-time Record vs. Other Clubs

Regular Season

	At Home							On Road							Total						
	GP	W	L	T	GF	GA	PTS	GP	W	L	T	GF	GA	PTS	GP	W	L	T	GF	GA	PTS
Anaheim	2	1	1	0	5	6	2	2	1	1	0	5	3	2	4	2	2	0	10	9	4
Boston	87	42	31	14	325	273	98	86	24	51	11	262	356	59	173	66	82	25	587	629	157
Calgary	39	22	13	4	161	118	48	39	15	14	10	134	140	40	78	37	27	14	295	258	88
Chicago	46	28	12	6	176	121	62	44	15	23	6	123	144	36	90	43	35	12	299	265	98
Colorado	57	33	16	8	230	185	74	57	18	29	10	182	218	46	114	51	45	18	412	403	120
Dallas	46	24	12	10	170	125	58	47	20	21	6	144	147	46	93	44	33	16	314	272	104
Detroit	46	32	7	7	211	125	71	48	18	25	5	147	180	41	94	50	32	12	358	305	112
Edmonton	24	10	9	5	99	91	25	23	4	17	2	63	102	10	47	14	26	7	162	193	35
Florida	6	5	1	0	26	6	10	5	2	3	0	14	15	4	11	7	4	0	40	21	14
Hartford	59	33	19	7	246	186	73	60	29	22	9	186	177	67	119	62	41	16	432	363	140
Los Angeles	46	22	15	9	185	143	53	47	22	17	8	168	160	52	93	44	32	17	353	303	105
Montreal	81	39	24	18	253	227	96	82	23	49	10	249	341	56	163	62	73	28	502	568	152
New Jersey	38	26	7	5	171	116	57	38	22	9	7	147	118	51	76	48	16	12	318	234	108
NY Islanders	45	24	14	7	159	131	55	45	18	20	7	129	133	43	90	42	34	14	288	264	98
NY Rangers	52	31	15	6	232	173	68	50	15	23	12	138	176	42	102	46	38	18	370	349	110
Ottawa	10	9	1	0	53	16	18	12	8	2	2	46	26	18	22	17	3	2	99	42	36
Philadelphia	47	23	18	6	171	146	52	51	12	31	8	136	190	32	98	35	49	14	307	336	84
Pittsburgh	54	26	13	15	231	153	67	53	16	24	13	187	210	45	107	42	37	28	418	363	112
St. Louis	45	29	12	4	188	140	62	44	12	26	6	113	165	30	89	41	38	10	301	305	92
San Jose	5	5	0	0	28	18	10	4	1	2	1	20	18	3	9	6	2	1	48	36	13
Tampa Bay	7	2	4	1	16	28	5	7	6	1	0	24	15	12	14	8	5	1	40	43	17
Toronto	51	32	16	3	215	146	67	50	23	18	9	185	154	55	101	55	34	12	400	300	122
Vancouver	46	23	15	8	164	133	54	45	13	22	10	148	173	36	91	36	37	18	312	306	90
Washington	40	28	7	5	170	106	61	40	23	10	7	151	110	53	80	51	17	12	321	216	114
Winnipeg	23	19	2	2	107	57	40	23	11	10	2	83	75	24	46	30	12	4	190	132	64
Defunct Clubs	23	13	5	5	94	63	31	23	12	8	3	97	76	27	46	25	13	8	191	139	58
Totals	**1025**	**581**	**289**	**155**	**4086**	**3032**	**1317**	**1025**	**383**	**478**	**164**	**3281**	**3622**	**930**	**2050**	**964**	**767**	**319**	**7367**	**6654**	**2247**

Playoffs

	Series	W	L	GP	W	L	T	GF	GA	Last Mtg.	Round	Result
Boston	6	1	5	33	14	19	0	113	132	1993	DSF	W 4-0
Chicago	2	2	0	9	8	1	0	36	17	1980	QF	W 4-0
Colorado	2	0	2	8	2	6	0	27	35	1985	DSF	L 2-3
Dallas	2	1	1	7	3	4	0	28	26	1981	QF	L 1-4
Montreal	6	2	4	31	13	18	0	94	114	1993	DF	L 0-4
New Jersey	1	0	1	7	3	4	0	14	14	1994	CQF	L 3-4
NY Islanders	3	0	3	16	4	12	0	45	59	1980	SF	L 2-4
NY Rangers	1	1	0	3	2	1	0	11	6	1978	PR	W 2-1
Philadelphia	3	0	3	16	4	12	0	36	53	1995	CQF	L 1-4
Pittsburgh	1	0	1	3	1	2	0	9	9	1979	PR	L 1-2
St. Louis	1	1	0	3	2	1	0	7	8	1976	PR	W 2-1
Vancouver	2	2	0	7	6	1	0	28	14	1981	PR	W 3-0
Totals	**30**	**10**	**20**	**143**	**62**	**81**	**0**	**448**	**480**			

Playoff Results 1996-92

Year	Round	Opponent	Result	GF	GA
1995	CQF	Philadelphia	L 1-4	13	18
1994	CQF	New Jersey	L 3-4	14	14
1993	DF	Montreal	L 0-4	12	16
	DSF	Boston	W 4-0	19	12
1992	DSF	Boston	L 3-4	24	19

Abbreviations: Round: F – Final; **CF** – conference final; **CQF** – conference quarter-final; **CSF** – conference semi-final; **DF** – division final; **DSF** – division semi-final; **SF** – semi-final; **QF** – quarter-final; **PR** – preliminary round.

Calgary totals include Atlanta, 1972-73 to 1979-80. Colorado totals include Quebec, 1979-80 to 1994-95.
Dallas totals include Minnesota, 1970-71 to 1992-93.
New Jersey totals include Kansas City, 1974-75 to 1975-76, and Colorado Rockies, 1976-77 to 1981-82.

1995-96 Results

Oct.	7	at	Ottawa	3-1		12	at	Calgary	1-3
	9	at	Boston	3-5		13	at	Edmonton	4-5
	13		Anaheim	1-4		17		Pittsburgh	0-1
	15		New Jersey	3-4		24		Hartford	4-2
	18		Edmonton	4-1		26	at	Washington	0-1
	20		NY Rangers	1-3		27	at	Florida	3-6
	22		St. Louis	5-2		30	at	NY Islanders	4-5
	24	at	Dallas	0-3		31		Florida	6-1
	27	at	Colorado	4-5	**Feb.**	3	at	Boston	2-4
	29	at	Chicago	3-6		4		Tampa Bay	2-5
Nov.	1		Detroit	2-1		7		Boston	2-1
	3		Pittsburgh	3-3		8	at	Philadelphia	2-1
	5		Winnipeg	3-4		10	at	Toronto	2-2
	8		San Jose	7-2		14		Los Angeles	2-2
	11	at	Florida	1-4		16		New Jersey	2-2
	12	at	Tampa Bay	6-4		17	at	Hartford	1-2
	15		Dallas	2-1		21		Pittsburgh	6-3
	18	at	New Jersey	5-4		23		Philadelphia	7-2
	19		Ottawa	6-0		25		Florida	6-1
	24		NY Islanders	1-1		28	at	Ottawa	3-2
	25	at	Pittsburgh	3-5	**Mar.**	1	at	NY Rangers	3-3
	27	at	St. Louis	2-0		3		Vancouver	0-3
	29	at	NY Rangers	3-5		6	at	Vancouver	2-5
Dec.	1		Hartford	2-1		8	at	Anaheim	2-3
	2	at	Boston	4-6		10	at	San Jose	4-6
	7	at	Philadelphia	3-7		13	at	Los Angeles	6-2
	8		Washington	2-2		15		Calgary	1-3
	11		Tampa Bay	1-6		16	at	Hartford	1-2
	13		Colorado	4-3		18	at	Montreal	2-3
	15		NY Rangers	5-4		22		Montreal	1-4
	16	at	New Jersey	3-2		23	at	Pittsburgh	7-5
	20		Montreal	2-1		27	at	Detroit	2-4
	22		Boston	2-3		29		Philadelphia	5-6
	23	at	Ottawa	4-2		31		Boston	5-6
	26	at	Pittsburgh	3-6	**Apr.**	1	at	Montreal	6-4
	27		Ottawa	3-4		3		Washington	1-5
	29		Chicago	2-5		5	at	Tampa Bay	4-3
	31		NY Islanders	2-5		6	at	NY Islanders	0-3
Jan.	5		Toronto	3-1		10		Ottawa	5-2
	6	at	Montreal	7-6		13	at	Washington	3-2
	10	at	Winnipeg	1-4		14		Hartford	4-1

Entry Draft Selections 1996-82

1996
Pick	
7	Erik Rasmussen
27	Cory Sarich
33	Darren Van Oene
54	Francois Methot
87	Kurt Walsh
106	Mike Martone
115	Alexei Tezikov
142	Ryan Davis
161	Darren Mortier
222	Scott Buhler

1995
Pick	
14	Jay McKee
16	Martin Biron
42	Mark Dutiaume
68	Mathieu Sunderland
94	Matt Davidson
111	Marian Menhart
119	Kevin Popp
123	Daniel Bienvenue
172	Brian Scott
198	Mike Zanutto
224	Rob Skrlac

1994
Pick	
17	Wayne Primeau
43	Curtis Brown
69	Rumun Ndur
121	Sergei Klimentjev
147	Cal Benazic
168	Steve Plouffe
173	Shane Hnidy
176	Steve Webb
199	Bob Westerby
225	Craig Millar
251	Mark Polak
277	Shayne Wright

1993
Pick	
38	Denis Tsygurov
64	Ethan Philpott
116	Richard Safarik
142	Kevin Pozzo
168	Sergei Petrenko
194	Mike Barrie
220	Barrie Moore
246	Chris Davis
272	Scott Nichol

1992
Pick	
11	David Cooper
35	Jozef Cierny
59	Ondrej Steiner
80	Dean Melanson
83	Matthew Barnaby
107	Markus Ketterer
108	Yuri Khmylev
131	Paul Rushforth
179	Dean Tiltgen
203	Todd Simon
227	Rick Kowalsky
251	Chris Clancy

1991
Pick	
13	Philippe Boucher
35	Jason Dawe
57	Jason Young
72	Peter Ambroziak
101	Steve Shields
123	Sean O'Donnell
124	Brian Holzinger
145	Chris Snell
162	Jiri Kuntos
189	Tony Iob
211	Spencer Meany
233	Mikhail Volkov
255	Michael Smith

1990
Pick	
14	Brad May
82	Brian McCarthy
97	Richard Smehlik
100	Todd Bojcun
103	Brad Pascall
142	Viktor Gordiyuk
166	Milan Nedoma
187	Jason Winch
208	Sylvain Naud
229	Kenneth Martin
250	Brad Rubachuk

1989
Pick	
14	Kevin Haller
56	John (Scott) Thomas
77	Doug MacDonald
98	Ken Sutton
107	Bill Pye
119	Mike Barkley
161	Derek Plante
183	Donald Audette
194	Mark Astley
203	John Nelson
224	Todd Henderson
245	Michael Bavis

1988
Pick	
13	Joel Savage
55	Darcy Loewen
76	Keith E. Carney
89	Alexander Mogilny
97	Robert Ray
106	David Di Vita
118	Mike McLaughlin
139	Mike Griffith
160	Daniel Ruoho
181	Wade Flaherty
223	Thomas Nieman
244	Robert Wallwork

1987
Pick	
1	Pierre Turgeon
22	Brad Miller
53	Andrew MacVicar
84	John Bradley
85	David Pergola
106	Chris Marshall
127	Paul Flanagan
148	Sean Dooley
153	Tim Roberts
169	Grant Tkachuk
190	Ian Herbers
211	David Littman
232	Allan MacIsaac

1986
Pick	
5	Shawn Anderson
26	Greg Brown
47	Bob Corkum
56	Kevin Kerr
68	David Baseggio
89	Larry Rooney
110	Miguel Baldris
131	Mike Hartman
152	Francois Guay
173	Shawn Whitham
194	Kenton Rein
215	Troy Arndt

1985
Pick	
14	Calle Johansson
35	Benoit Hogue
56	Keith Gretzky
77	Dave Moylan
98	Ken Priestlay
119	Joe Reekie
140	Petri Matikainen
161	Trent Kaese
182	Jiri Sejba
203	Boyd Sutton
224	Guy Larose
245	Ken Baumgartner

1984
Pick	
18	Mikael Andersson
39	Doug Trapp
60	Ray Sheppard
81	Bob Halkidis
102	Joey Rampton
123	James Gasseau
144	Darcy Wakaluk
165	Orvar Stambert
206	Brian McKinnon
226	Grant Delcourt
247	Sean Baker

1983
Pick	
5	Tom Barrasso
10	Normand Lacombe
11	Adam Creighton
31	John Tucker
34	Richard Hajdu
74	Daren Puppa
94	Jayson Meyer
114	Jim Hofford
134	Christian Ruutlu
154	Don McSween
174	Tim Hoover
194	Mark Ferner
214	Uwe Krupp
234	Marc Hamelin
235	Kermit Salfi

1982
Pick	
6	Phil Housley
9	Paul Cyr
16	Dave Andreychuk
26	Mike Anderson
30	Jens Johansson
68	Timo Jutila
79	Jeff Hamilton
100	Bob Logan
111	Jeff Parker
121	Jacob Gustavsson
142	Allen Bishop
163	Claude Verret
184	Rob Norman
205	Mike Craig
226	Jim Plankers

Club Directory

Marine Midland Arena
One Seymour H. Knox III Plaza
Buffalo, NY 14203
Phone **716/855-4100**
Fax 716/855-4110
Ticket Office: 716/888-4000
Capacity: 18,500

Board of Directors

Vice-Chairman of the Board and Counsel	Robert O. Swados
Vice-Chairman of the Board	Robert E. Rich, Jr.
Treasurer	Joseph T.J. Stewart
Board of Directors. **Niagara Frontier Hockey, L.P.** (includes above listed officers)	Edwin C. Andrews, Peter C. Andrews, George L. Collins, Jr. M.D., William C. Cox, III, John B. Fisher, George T. Gregory, John E. Houghton, Seymour H. Knox, IV, John J. Rigas, Michael J. Rigas, Richard W. Rupp, Howard T. Saperston, Jr., Paul A. Schoellkopf, George Strawbridge, Jr., William H. Weeks
Consultant	Northrup R. Knox

Executive Department

President/CEO	Douglas G. Moss
Assistant to the President	Seymour H. Knox, IV
Administrative Assistant to the President	Elaine Burzynski

Hockey Department

General Manager	John Muckler
Administrative Assistant	Cindy Zorker
Team Travel Coordinator	Verna Wojcik
Assistant to the General Manager	Larry Carriere
Head Coach	Ted Nolan
Assistant Coaches	Don Lever, Paul Theriault
Goaltender Consultant	Mitch Korn
Strength & Conditioning Coach	Doug McKenney
Head Trainer	Jim Pizzutelli
Equipment Manager	Rip Simonick
Assistant Equipment Manager	George Babcock

Scouting

Director of Player Personnel	Don Luce
Director of Scouting	Jack Bowman
Professional Scouting Consultant	Rudy Migay
Scouting Staff	Don Barrie, Jim Benning, Ross Mahoney, Terry Martin, Paul Merritt, Mike Racicot, Gleb Tchistyakov, David Volek

Medical

Club Doctor	John L. Butsch, M.D.
Orthopedic Consultant	John Marzo, M.D.
Club Dentist	Daniel Yustin, D.D.S., M.S.
Oral Surgeon	Steve Jensen, D.D.S.
Team Psychologists	Max Offenberger, Ph.D. & Dan Smith, Ph.D.

Administration

Senior Vice-President/Administration	George Bergantz
Human Resources Coordinator	Vanessa Barrons
Distribution Manager	Gerry Magill
Receptionists	Olive Anticola, Evelyn Battleson

Broadcast Production

Broadcast Manager	Joe Guarnieri
Administrative Assistant	Lisa Tzetzo
Staff Cameraman	Martin McCreary
Producer/Director	Phil Mollica
Game Producer	Lowell MacDonald
TV Broadcast Team	Rick Jeanneret (play-by-play), Jim Lorentz (color commentary), Dennis Williams (host)
Radio Broadcast Team	Peter Weber (play-by-play), Danny Gare (color commentary), Dave Miller (host/producer)

Communications

Vice President/Communications	Terry Dunford
Director of Public & Media Relations	Jeff Holbrook
Director of Information	Bruce Wawrzyniak
Media Relations Director	Gil Chorbajian
Director of Community Relations	Ken Martin, Jr.
Community Relations Coordinator	Deidre Daniels
Director of Alumni Relations	Larry Playfair

Empire Sports Sales

Vice President/Sales	Kerry Atkinson
Executive Assistant	Stephanie LeMaitre
Senior Account Managers	Nick DiVico, Dan Rozanski, Steve Cuccia, Jim DiMino
Vendor Programs Manager	Jim Harrington
Account Managers	Kathleen Kane, Matt Schobert
Sales Support Account Executive	Len Synor
Traffic Coordinators	Corinne Farrell, Terese Schmidle

Finance

Executive Vice President/Chief Financial Officer	Dan DiPofi
Director of Finance	John Cudmore
Assistant Financial Coordinator	Elizabeth McPartland
Administrative Assistant to Finance	Toni Addeo
Corporate Controller	Karen Korthals
Administrative Assistant	Felicia Osby
Accounting Manager	Chris Ivansitz
Payroll Manager	Birgid Haensel
Purchases and Payables Assistant	Mary Jones
Cash Receipts and Billings Assistant	Sally Lippert
Management Information Systems Manager	Ken Bass

Legal

Senior Vice-President/Legal and Business Affairs	Kevin Billet
Administrative Assistants	Eleanore MacKenzie, Karen Young

Marketing & Broadcast

VP/Marketing & Broadcast	Jennifer Smith
Director of Promotions & Advertising	Tanya Isherwood
Graphics & Advertising Manager	Robert Kane
Special Projects Director	Karen Bolin
Director of Game Presentation & Special Events	Kimberly Hargreaves
Game Presentation and Event Manager	Matt Rabinowitz

Marketing & Ticket Sales

Director of Club & Season Seat Sales	D. Rovell Jones
Sales Representatives	Dave Forman, Jr., Joe Graves
Director of Group & Retail Promotions	Gary Rabinowitz
Assistant Director of Group & Retail Promotions	Nick Turano
Manager, Telemarketing Operations	Chris Barlow
Director of Account Services	Lisa Wandass
Account Services Manager	Kurt Silcott
Club Services Coordinator	Rose Thompson
Account Service Representative	Roxanne Frazier
Database Manager	Ed Boddecker

Merchandise

Director of Merchandise	Julie Scully
Merchandise Manager	Mike Kaminska

Ticket Operations

Director of Ticket Operations	John Sinclair
Assistant Box Office Manager	Mike Tout
Ticket Administrators	Paul Barker, Lisa Gajewski, Christopher Makowski, Marty Maloney, Cindi Reuther
Cash & Settlement Administrator	Jennifer Glowny

Crossroads Arena L.L.C.

President/Chief Operating Officer	Larry Quinn
Executive Assistant	Debbie Driscoll
Project Director	Carolyn Hoyt
Director of Suite Sales & Services	Erin Wright
Suite Services Manager	Sue Smith
Coordinator of Suite Services	Pat Chimera
Events & Promotion Director	Chris Schoepflin
Coordinator of Amateur Athletic Events & Basketball Operations	Reggie Witherspoon
Administrative Assistant	Donna Webb

Centre Management

Director of Building Operations	Stan Makowski
Communications Director	Al Wiessman
Communications Engineer	Ted Neddy
Engineers	John Blake, Brian Drabek
Maintenance Supervisor	Bill Graf
Accounting Coordinator	Scott Haima
Operations Manager	Sam Aceti
Administrative Assistant	Tracy Gilbert
Cleaning Supervisor	Bud Redding
Director of Arena Administration	Pamela Riehl

General Information

Training Camp/Practice Site	Sabreland – Wheatfield, NY
Team Colors	Black, White, Red, Grey and Silver
TV Stations	Empire Sports Network, WIVB-TV
Radio Flagship Stations	WGR AM-550 & CJRN AM-710
AHL Affiliate	Rochester Americans

Calgary Flames

1995-96 Results: 34w-37L-11T 79PTS. Second, Pacific Division

Schedule

Oct.	Sat.	5	at Vancouver	Tues.	7	Toronto
	Sun.	6	Buffalo	Thur.	9	Hartford
	Wed.	9	St. Louis	Sat.	11	Florida
	Fri.	11	at Detroit	Wed.	15	Anaheim
	Sun.	13	at Philadelphia	Tues.	21	at Pittsburgh
	Mon.	14	at NY Rangers	Wed.	22	at Toronto
	Wed.	16	at Montreal	Fri.	24	at Ottawa
	Sun.	20	Edmonton	Tues.	28	NY Islanders
	Tues.	22	Colorado	Thur.	30	San Jose
	Thur.	24	Pittsburgh	**Feb.** Sat.	1	Vancouver
	Sat.	26	at Los Angeles	Mon.	3	Los Angeles
	Sun.	27	at Anaheim	Wed.	5	at Edmonton
	Wed.	30	at San Jose	Fri.	7	Washington
Nov.	Fri.	1	Phoenix	Sun.	9	Anaheim
	Sat.	2	at Vancouver	Tues.	11	Boston
	Sat.	9	St. Louis	Thur.	13	Edmonton
	Wed.	13	at Dallas	Sat.	15	Toronto
	Thur.	14	at Chicago	Tues.	18	at Buffalo
	Sat.	16	at St. Louis	Wed.	19	at Detroit
	Mon.	18	NY Rangers	Fri.	21	at Dallas
	Wed.	20	Dallas	Sun.	23	at St. Louis
	Fri.	22	Chicago	Wed.	26	Phoenix
	Sat.	23	at Edmonton	Fri.	28	Montreal
	Tues.	26	Edmonton	**Mar.** Sat.	1	Dallas
	Thur.	28	Los Angeles	Tues.	4	at Washington
	Sat.	30	at Phoenix	Wed.	5	at Hartford
Dec.	Tues.	3	at NY Islanders	Fri.	7	at Florida
	Thur.	5	at New Jersey	Sun.	9	at Tampa Bay*
	Sat.	7	at Boston	Wed.	12	at Colorado
	Tues.	10	Ottawa	Sat.	15	at Los Angeles
	Thur.	12	at Los Angeles	Sun.	16	at Anaheim
	Sat.	14	Colorado	Wed.	19	San Jose
	Mon.	16	New Jersey	Fri.	21	Tampa Bay
	Wed.	18	Detroit	Tues.	25	Anaheim
	Fri.	20	at Anaheim	Sat.	29	Vancouver*
	Sun.	22	at Phoenix	**Apr.** Wed.	2	Colorado
	Mon.	23	at Colorado	Fri.	4	at Vancouver
	Sun.	29	Philadelphia*	Sun.	6	Chicago*
	Tues.	31	San Jose	Tues.	8	Detroit
Jan.	Thur.	2	at Colorado	Fri.	11	at Chicago
	Sat.	4	at San Jose	Sat.	12	at Toronto

* Denotes afternoon game.

Theoren Fleury had one of the greatest seasons in the history of the Calgary Flames in 1995-96, leading the team in seven offensive categories – goals (46), assists (50), points (96), plus/minus (plus 17), power-play goals (17), short-handed goals (5) and shots on goal (353).

Franchise date: June 24, 1980
Transferred from Atlanta to Calgary.

**25th
NHL
Season**

**PACIFIC
DIVISION**

Year-by-Year Record

		Home			Road			Overall							
Season	GP	W	L	T	W	L	T	W	L	T	GF	GA	Pts.	Finished	Playoff Result
1995-96	82	18	18	5	16	19	6	34	37	11	241	240	79	2nd, Pacific Div.	Lost Conf. Quarter-Final
1994-95	48	15	7	2	9	10	5	24	17	7	163	135	55	1st, Pacific Div.	Lost Conf. Quarter-Final
1993-94	84	25	12	5	17	17	8	42	29	13	302	256	97	1st, Pacific Div.	Lost Conf. Quarter-Final
1992-93	84	23	14	5	20	16	6	43	30	11	322	282	97	2nd, Smythe Div.	Lost Div. Semi-Final
1991-92	80	19	14	7	12	23	5	31	37	12	296	305	74	5th, Smythe Div.	Out of Playoffs
1990-91	80	29	8	3	17	18	5	46	26	8	344	263	100	2nd, Smythe Div.	Lost Div. Semi-Final
1989-90	80	28	7	5	14	16	10	42	23	15	348	265	99	1st, Smythe Div.	Lost Div. Semi-Final
1988-89	**80**	**32**	**4**	**4**	**22**	**13**	**5**	**54**	**17**	**9**	**354**	**226**	**117**	**1st, Smythe Div.**	**Won Stanley Cup**
1987-88	80	26	11	3	22	12	6	48	23	9	397	305	105	1st, Smythe Div.	Lost Div. Final
1986-87	80	25	13	2	21	18	1	46	31	3	318	289	95	2nd, Smythe Div.	Lost Div. Semi-Final
1985-86	80	23	11	6	17	20	3	40	31	9	354	315	89	2nd, Smythe Div.	Lost Final
1984-85	80	23	11	6	18	16	6	41	27	12	363	302	94	3rd, Smythe Div.	Lost Div. Semi-Final
1983-84	80	22	11	7	12	21	7	34	32	14	311	314	82	2nd, Smythe Div.	Lost Div. Final
1982-83	80	21	12	7	11	22	7	32	34	14	321	317	78	2nd, Smythe Div.	Lost Div. Final
1981-82	80	20	11	9	9	23	8	29	34	17	334	345	75	3rd, Smythe Div.	Lost Div. Semi-Final
1980-81	80	25	5	10	14	22	4	39	27	14	329	298	92	3rd, Patrick Div.	Lost Semi-Final
1979-80*	80	18	15	7	17	17	6	35	32	13	282	269	83	4th, Patrick Div.	Lost Prelim. Round
1978-79*	80	25	11	4	16	20	4	41	31	8	327	280	90	4th, Patrick Div.	Lost Prelim. Round
1977-78*	80	20	13	7	14	14	12	34	27	19	274	252	87	3rd, Patrick Div.	Lost Prelim. Round
1976-77*	80	22	11	7	12	23	5	34	34	12	264	265	80	3rd, Patrick Div.	Lost Prelim. Round
1975-76*	80	19	14	7	16	19	5	35	33	12	262	237	82	3rd, Patrick Div.	Lost Prelim. Round
1974-75*	80	24	9	7	10	22	8	34	31	15	243	233	83	4th, Patrick Div.	Out of Playoffs
1973-74*	78	17	15	7	13	19	7	30	34	14	214	238	74	4th, West Div.	Lost Quarter-Final
1972-73*	78	16	16	7	9	22	8	25	38	15	191	239	65	7th, West Div.	Out of Playoffs

* Atlanta Flames

1996-97 Player Personnel

FORWARDS	HT	WT	S	Place of Birth	Date	1995-96 Club
DINGMAN, Chris	6-4	225	L	Edmonton, Alta.	7/6/76	Brandon-Saint John
FLEURY, Theoren	5-6	160	R	Oxbow, Sask.	6/29/68	Calgary
GAGNER, Dave	5-10	180	L	Chatham, Ont.	12/11/64	Dallas-Toronto
HLUSHKO, Todd	5-11	185	L	Toronto, Ont.	2/7/70	Calgary-Saint John
IGINLA, Jarome	6-1	193	R	Edmonton, Alta.	7/1/77	Kamloops-Calgary
KOHN, Ladislav	5-10	180	L	Uherske Hradiste, Czech.	3/4/75	Calgary-Saint John
KRUSE, Paul	6-0	202	L	Merritt, B.C.	3/15/70	Calgary
LING, David	5-9	185	R	Halifax, N.S.	1/9/75	Saint John
MATTSSON, Jesper	6-0	185	R	Malmo, Sweden	5/13/75	Saint John
McCARTHY, Sandy	6-3	225	R	Toronto, Ont.	6/15/72	Calgary
MILLEN, Corey	5-7	170	R	Cloquet, MN	3/30/64	Dallas-Michigan-Calgary
MURPHY, Burke	6-0	180	L	Gloucester, Ont.	6/5/73	St. Lawrence
MURRAY, Marty	5-9	175	L	Deloraine, Man.	2/16/75	Calgary-Saint John
MURRAY, Mike	6-1	200	R	Cumberland, RI	4/18/71	Dayton-Saint John
NYLANDER, Michael	5-11	190	L	Stockholm, Sweden	10/3/72	Calgary
REICHEL, Robert	5-10	185	L	Litvinov, Czech.	6/25/71	Frankfurt
SCHULTE, Paxton	6-2	217	L	Onaway, Alta.	7/16/72	Cornwall-Saint John
STERN, Ron	6-0	195	R	Ste. Agathe, Que.	1/11/67	Calgary
STILLMAN, Cory	6-0	180	L	Peterborough, Ont.	12/20/73	Calgary
SULLIVAN, Mike	6-2	190	L	Marshfield, MA	2/27/68	Calgary
TITOV, German	6-1	190	L	Moscow, USSR	10/16/65	Calgary
WILM, Clarke	6-0	202	L	Central Butte, Sask.	10/24/76	Saskatoon
YAKUBOV, Ravil	6-1	190	L	Moscow, USSR	7/26/70	Moscow D'amo
DEFENSEMEN						
ALBELIN, Tommy	6-1	190	L	Stockholm, Sweden	5/21/64	New Jersey-Calgary
ALLISON, Jamie	6-1	190	L	Lindsay, Ont.	5/13/75	Saint John
BOUCHARD, Joel	6-0	190	L	Montreal, Que.	1/23/74	Calgary-Saint John
CHIASSON, Steve	6-1	205	L	Barrie, Ont.	4/14/67	Calgary
GAUTHIER, Denis	6-2	195	L	Montreal, Que.	10/1/76	Drummondville-Saint John
HELENIUS, Sami	6-5	225	L	Helsinki, Finland	1/22/74	Saint John
HULSE, Cale	6-3	210	R	Edmonton, Alta.	11/10/73	N.J.-Albany-Cgy-Saint John
HUSCROFT, Jamie	6-2	200	R	Creston, B.C.	1/9/67	Calgary
McCAMBRIDGE, Keith	6-2	205	L	Thompson, Man.	2/1/74	Saint John
O'SULLIVAN, Chris	6-2	185	L	Dorchester, MA	5/15/74	Boston U.
PATRICK, James	6-2	198	R	Winnipeg, Man.	6/14/63	Calgary
SIMPSON, Todd	6-3	215	L	Edmonton, Alta.	5/28/73	Calgary-Saint John
ZALAPSKI, Zarley	6-1	215	L	Edmonton, Alta.	4/22/68	Calgary
GOALTENDERS	**HT**	**WT**	**C**	**Place of Birth**	**Date**	**1995-96 Club**
HALTIA, Patrik	6-1	176	L	Karlstad, Sweden	3/29/73	Farjestad
KIDD, Trevor	6-2	190	L	Dugald, Man.	3/29/72	Calgary
ROLOSON, Dwayne	6-1	180	L	Simcoe, Ont.	10/12/69	Saint John
TABARACCI, Rick	6-1	180	L	Toronto, Ont.	1/2/69	Calgary

General Manager

COATES, AL
Executive Vice President/General Manager, Calgary Flames.
Born in Listowel, Ont., December 3, 1945.

Al Coates was named executive vice president of the Calgary Flames on June 22, 1995. On November 3, he was designated the interim general manager, replacing Doug Risebrough. Coates' appointment as general manager became official on May 31, 1996. In this role, he is responsible for all aspects of hockey operations for the club.

Coates had been a member of the Flames senior management team since the club's arrival in Calgary in 1980. He has over 25 years of professional hockey experience, including 16 years of service with the Calgary Flames.

Following a playing career in Europe, Coates joined the Detroit Red Wings organization in 1971. He spent nine seasons with the Red Wings, working in various capacities. In the summer of 1980, he joined the Flames as the team's director of public relations. In August, 1982, Coates was named as the assistant to the president, working directly with then president and general manager Cliff Fletcher in a number of hockey administrative capacities. Later, on August 1, 1989, he was promoted to director of hockey administration. He continued his progression through the organization when, on September 8, 1991, he was named the team's assistant general manager, a position he held until his promotion to executive vice president and general manager.

Coates' work has involved player contracts, coordinating professional scouting, and working with the Flames development team in Saint John (AHL). Coates also now serves as the chairman of the executive committee of the American Hockey League. His progressive management and leadership style has helped shape the Flames franchise into a successful, respected organization both on and off the ice.

General Managers' History

Cliff Fletcher, 1972-73 to 1990-91; Doug Risebrough, 1991-92 to 1994-95; Doug Risebrough and Al Coates, 1995-96; Al Coates, 1996-97.

Coaching History

Bernie Geoffrion, 1972-73 to 1973-74; Bernie Geoffrion and Fred Creighton, 1974-75; Fred Creighton, 1975-76 to 1978-79; Al MacNeil, 1979-80 (Atlanta); 1980-81 to 1981-82 (Calgary); Bob Johnson, 1982-83 to 1986-87; Terry Crisp, 1987-88 to 1989-90; Doug Risebrough, 1990-91; Doug Risebrough and Guy Charron, 1991-92; Dave King, 1992-93 to 1994-95; Pierre Page, 1995-96 to date.

1995-96 Scoring

* – rookie

Regular Season

Pos	#	Player	Team	GP	G	A	Pts	+/–	PIM	PP	SH	GW	GT	S	%
R	14	Theoren Fleury	CGY	80	46	50	96	17	112	17	5	4	0	353	13.0
C	13	German Titov	CGY	82	28	39	67	9	24	13	2	2	2	214	13.1
C	92	Michael Nylander	CGY	73	17	38	55	0	20	4	0	6	0	163	10.4
L	10	Gary Roberts	CGY	35	22	20	42	15	78	9	0	5	1	84	26.2
C	16 *	Cory Stillman	CGY	74	16	19	35	–5	41	4	1	3	0	132	12.1
D	3	James Patrick	CGY	80	3	32	35	3	30	1	0	0	0	116	2.6
D	21	Steve Chiasson	CGY	76	8	25	33	3	62	5	0	2	0	175	4.6
D	33	Zarley Zalapski	CGY	80	12	17	29	11	115	5	0	1	0	145	8.3
C	32	Mike Sullivan	CGY	81	9	12	21	–6	24	0	1	1	1	106	8.5
C	34	Corey Millen	DAL	13	3	4	7	0	8	1	0	0	1	25	12.0
			CGY	31	4	10	14	8	10	1	0	1	0	48	8.3
			TOTAL	44	7	14	21	8	18	2	0	1	1	73	9.6
R	15	Sandy McCarthy	CGY	75	9	7	16	–8	173	3	0	1	0	98	9.2
L	18	Pavel Torgajev	CGY	41	6	10	16	2	14	0	0	0	0	50	12.0
R	22	Ronnie Stern	CGY	52	10	5	15	2	111	0	0	1	1	64	15.6
L	12	Paul Kruse	CGY	75	3	12	15	–5	145	0	0	0	0	83	3.6
C	20	Dean Evason	CGY	67	7	7	14	–6	38	1	0	1	0	68	10.3
C	17	Bob Sweeney	NYI	66	6	6	12	–23	59	0	1	1	0	54	11.1
			CGY	6	1	1	2	3	6	0	0	0	0	8	12.5
			TOTAL	72	7	7	14	–20	65	0	1	1	0	62	11.3
D	5	Tommy Albelin	N.J.	53	1	12	13	0	14	0	0	0	0	90	1.1
			CGY	20	0	1	1	1	4	0	0	0	0	31	0.0
			TOTAL	73	1	13	14	1	18	0	0	0	0	121	0.8
R	45	Jocelyn Lemieux	HFD	29	1	2	3	–11	31	0	0	0	0	43	2.3
			N.J.	18	0	1	1	–7	4	0	0	0	0	20	0.0
			CGY	20	4	4	8	–1	10	0	0	0	0	27	14.8
			TOTAL	67	5	7	12	–19	45	0	0	0	0	90	5.6
D	7	Jamie Huscroft	CGY	70	3	9	12	14	162	0	0	1	0	57	5.3
R	23	Sheldon Kennedy	CGY	41	3	7	10	3	36	0	0	1	0	54	5.6
C	47	Claude Lapointe	COL	3	0	0	0	–1	0	0	0	0	0	0	0.0
			CGY	32	4	5	9	2	20	0	2	1	0	44	9.1
			TOTAL	35	4	5	9	1	20	0	2	1	0	44	9.1
R	42 *	Ed Ward	CGY	41	3	5	8	–2	44	0	0	0	0	33	9.1
C	28 *	Marty Murray	CGY	15	3	3	6	–4	0	2	0	0	0	22	13.6
L	36 *	Yves Sarault	MTL	14	0	0	0	–7	4	0	0	0	0	14	0.0
			CGY	11	2	1	3	–2	4	0	0	1	0	12	16.7
			TOTAL	25	2	1	3	–9	8	0	0	1	0	26	7.7
D	8	Trent Yawney	CGY	69	0	3	3	–1	88	0	0	0	0	51	0.0
D	4	Kevin Dahl	CGY	32	1	1	2	–2	26	0	0	1	0	17	5.9
G	31	Rick Tabaracci	CGY	43	0	2	2	0	8	0	0	0	0	0	0.0
G	37	Trevor Kidd	CGY	47	0	2	2	0	4	0	0	0	0	0	0.0
R	46 *	Ladislav Kohn	CGY	5	1	0	1	–1	2	0	0	0	0	8	12.5
C	38 *	Craig Ferguson	MTL	10	1	0	1	–5	2	0	0	0	0	9	11.1
			CGY	8	0	0	0	–4	4	0	0	0	0	11	0.0
			TOTAL	18	1	0	1	–9	6	0	0	0	0	20	5.0
C	38	Jarrod Skalde	CGY	1	0	0	0	0	0	0	0	0	0	0	0.0
R	35 *	Niklas Sundblad	CGY	2	0	0	0	0	0	0	0	0	0	3	0.0
C	17 *	Todd Hlushko	CGY	4	0	0	0	0	6	0	0	0	0	6	0.0
D	5 *	Joel Bouchard	CGY	4	0	0	0	0	4	0	0	0	0	0	0.0
L	19 *	Vesa Viitakoski	CGY	5	0	0	0	–1	2	0	0	0	0	7	0.0
D	27 *	Todd Simpson	CGY	6	0	0	0	0	32	0	0	0	0	3	0.0
D	29 *	Cale Hulse	N.J.	8	0	0	0	–2	15	0	0	0	0	5	0.0
			CGY	3	0	0	0	3	5	0	0	0	0	4	0.0
			TOTAL	11	0	0	0	1	20	0	0	0	0	9	0.0
D	39	Dan Keczmer	CGY	13	0	0	0	–6	14	0	0	0	0	13	0.0

Goaltending

No.	Goaltender	GPI	Mins	Avg	W	L	T	EN	SO	GA	SA	S%
37	Trevor Kidd	47	2570	2.78	15	21	8	2	3	119	1130	.895
31	Rick Tabaracci	43	2391	2.94	19	16	3	2	3	117	1087	.892
	Totals	**82**	**4984**	**2.89**	**34**	**37**	**11**	**4**	**6**	**240**	**2221**	**.892**

Playoffs

Pos	#	Player	Team	GP	G	A	Pts	+/–	PIM	PP	SH	GW	OT	S	%
D	21	Steve Chiasson	CGY	4	2	1	3	0	0	0	0	0	0	20	10.0
R	14	Theoren Fleury	CGY	4	2	1	3	1	14	0	0	0	0	28	7.1
C	16 *	Cory Stillman	CGY	2	1	1	2	–2	0	0	0	0	0	5	20.0
C	24 *	Jarome Iginla	CGY	2	1	1	2	2	0	0	0	0	0	6	16.7
R	22	Ronnie Stern	CGY	4	0	2	2	2	8	0	0	0	0	7	0.0
C	13	German Titov	CGY	4	0	2	2	0	0	0	0	0	0	13	0.0
R	23	Sheldon Kennedy	CGY	3	1	0	1	–2	2	0	0	0	0	4	25.0
C	20	Dean Evason	CGY	3	0	1	1	–1	0	0	0	0	0	3	0.0
D	7	Jamie Huscroft	CGY	4	0	1	1	–2	4	0	0	0	0	4	0.0
D	33	Zarley Zalapski	CGY	4	0	1	1	1	10	0	0	0	0	5	0.0
D	4	Kevin Dahl	CGY	1	0	0	0	0	0	0	0	0	0	0	0.0
D	29 *	Cale Hulse	CGY	1	0	0	0	–2	0	0	0	0	0	2	0.0
L	18	Pavel Torgajev	CGY	1	0	0	0	0	0	0	0	0	0	1	0.0
C	47	Claude Lapointe	CGY	2	0	0	0	–2	0	0	0	0	0	3	0.0
C	17	Bob Sweeney	CGY	2	0	0	0	–1	0	0	0	0	0	3	0.0
G	37	Trevor Kidd	CGY	2	0	0	0	0	0	0	0	0	0	0	0.0
G	31	Rick Tabaracci	CGY	3	0	0	0	0	0	0	0	0	0	0	0.0
L	12	Paul Kruse	CGY	3	0	0	0	–1	4	0	0	0	0	3	0.0
D	5	Tommy Albelin	CGY	4	0	0	0	–2	0	0	0	0	0	8	0.0
R	45	Jocelyn Lemieux	CGY	4	0	0	0	0	0	0	0	0	0	5	0.0
D	3	James Patrick	CGY	4	0	0	0	–3	2	0	0	0	0	3	0.0
D	8	Trent Yawney	CGY	4	0	0	0	–3	2	0	0	0	0	1	0.0
C	32	Mike Sullivan	CGY	4	0	0	0	–1	0	0	0	0	0	5	0.0
R	15	Sandy McCarthy	CGY	4	0	0	0	–3	10	0	0	0	0	4	0.0
C	92	Michael Nylander	CGY	4	0	0	0	–4	0	0	0	0	0	9	0.0

Goaltending

No.	Goaltender	GPI	Mins	Avg	W	L	EN	SO	GA	SA	S%
31	Rick Tabaracci	3	204	2.06	0	3	0	0	7	84	.917
37	Trevor Kidd	2	83	6.51	0	1	0	0	9	40	.775
	Totals	**4**	**290**	**3.31**	**0**	**4**	**0**	**0**	**16**	**124**	**.871**

Club Records

Team

(Figures in brackets for season records are games played; records for fewest points, wins, ties, losses, goals, goals against are for 70 or more games)

Most Points	117	1988-89 (80)
Most Wins	54	1988-89 (80)
Most Ties	19	1977-78 (80)
Most Losses	38	1972-73 (78)
Most Goals	397	1987-88 (80)
Most Goals Against	345	1981-82 (80)
Fewest Points	65	1972-73 (78)
Fewest Wins	25	1972-73 (78)
Fewest Ties	3	1986-87 (80)
Fewest Losses	17	1988-89 (80)
Fewest Goals	191	1972-73 (78)
Fewest Goals Against	226	1988-89 (80)

Longest Winning Streak

Overall	10	Oct. 14-Nov. 3/78
Home	9	Oct. 17-Nov. 15/78, Jan. 3-Feb. 5/89, Mar. 3-Apr. 1/90, Feb. 21-Mar. 14/91
Away	7	Nov. 10-Dec. 4/88

Longest Undefeated Streak

Overall	13	Nov. 10-Dec. 8/88 (12 wins, 1 tie)
Home	18	Dec. 29/90-Mar. 14/91 (17 wins, 1 tie)
Away	9	Feb. 20-Mar. 21/88 (6 wins, 3 ties), Nov. 11-Dec. 16/90 (6 wins, 3 ties)

Longest Losing Streak

Overall	11	Dec. 14/85-Jan. 7/86
Home	4	Seven times
Away	9	Dec. 1/85-Jan. 12/86

Longest Winless Streak

Overall	11	Dec. 14/85-Jan. 7/86 (11 losses), Jan. 5-26/93 (9 losses, 2 ties)
Home	6	Nov. 25-Dec. 18/82 (5 losses, 1 tie), Nov. 18-Dec. 9/95 (4 losses, 2 ties)
Away	13	Feb. 3-Mar. 29/73 (10 losses, 3 ties)

Most Shutouts, Season	8	1974-75 (80)
Most PIM, Season	2,655	1991-92 (80)
Most Goals, Game	13	Feb. 10/93 (S.J. 1 at Cgy. 13)

Individual

Most Seasons	13	Al MacInnis
Most Games, Career	803	Al MacInnis
Most Goals, Career	314	Joe Nieuwendyk
Most Assists, Career	609	Al MacInnis
Most Points, Career	822	Al MacInnis (213G, 609A)
Most PIM, Career	2,405	Tim Hunter
Most Shutouts, Career	20	Dan Bouchard

Longest Consecutive

Games Streak	257	Brad Marsh (Oct. 11/78-Nov. 10/81)
Most Goals, Season	66	Lanny McDonald (1982-83)
Most Assists, Season	82	Kent Nilsson (1980-81)
Most Points, Season	131	Kent Nilsson (1980-81) (49G, 82A)
Most PIM, Season	375	Tim Hunter (1988-89)

Most Points, Defenseman

Season	103	Al MacInnis (1990-91; 28G, 75A)

Most Points, Center

Season	131	Kent Nilsson (1980-81; 49G, 82A)

Most Points, Right Wing

Season	110	Joe Mullen (1988-89; 51G, 59A)

Most Points, Left Wing

Season	90	Gary Roberts (1991-92; 53G, 37A)

Most Points, Rookie

Season	92	Joe Nieuwendyk (1987-88; 51G, 41A)
Most Shutouts, Season	5	Dan Bouchard (1973-74), Phil Myre (1974-75)
Most Goals, Game	5	Joe Nieuwendyk (Jan. 11/89)
Most Assists, Game	6	Guy Chouinard (Feb. 25/81), Gary Suter (Apr. 4/86)
Most Points, Game	7	Sergei Makarov (Feb. 25/90; 2G, 5A)

Retired Numbers

9   Lanny McDonald   1981-1989

Captains' History

Keith McCreary, 1972-73 to 1974-75; Pat Quinn, 1975-76, 1976-77; Tom Lysiak, 1977-78, 1978-79; Jean Pronovost, 1979-80; Brad Marsh, 1980-81; Phil Russell, 1981-82, 1982-83; Lanny McDonald, Doug Risebrough (co-captains), 1983-84; Lanny McDonald, Doug Risebrough, Jim Peplinski (tri-captains), 1984-85 to 1986-87; Lanny McDonald, Jim Peplinski (co-captains), 1987-88; Lanny McDonald, Jim Peplinski, Tim Hunter (tri-captains), 1988-89; Brad McCrimmon, 1989-90; alternating captains, 1990-91; Joe Nieuwendyk, 1991-92 to 1994-95; Theoren Fleury, 1995-96 to date.

All-time Record vs. Other Clubs

Regular Season

			At Home							On Road							Total				
	GP	W	L	T	GF	GA	PTS	GP	W	L	T	GF	GA	PTS	GP	W	L	T	GF	GA	PTS
Anaheim	8	4	4	0	21	22	8	8	4	3	1	23	21	9	16	8	7	1	44	43	17
Boston	39	15	21	3	145	142	33	40	10	25	5	110	144	25	79	25	46	8	255	286	58
Buffalo	39	14	15	10	140	134	38	39	13	22	4	118	161	30	78	27	37	14	258	295	68
Chicago	47	22	17	8	151	141	52	45	14	20	11	136	157	39	92	36	37	19	287	298	91
Colorado	25	13	6	6	108	80	32	25	9	9	7	97	108	25	50	22	15	13	205	188	57
Dallas	46	27	8	11	182	124	65	46	18	22	6	158	173	42	92	45	30	17	340	297	107
Detroit	44	26	13	5	184	140	57	43	13	22	8	138	166	34	87	39	35	13	322	306	91
Edmonton	59	33	20	6	273	212	72	60	22	30	8	222	248	52	119	55	50	14	495	460	124
Florida	2	2	0	0	6	2	4	2	0	2	0	4	6	0	4	2	2	0	10	8	4
Hartford	23	18	4	1	121	77	37	23	13	7	3	93	77	29	46	31	11	4	214	154	66
Los Angeles	77	48	20	9	367	257	105	73	28	37	8	272	293	64	150	76	57	17	639	550	169
Montreal	38	11	22	5	120	139	27	39	11	22	6	95	140	28	77	22	44	11	215	279	55
New Jersey	37	27	4	6	173	94	60	38	24	11	3	146	110	51	75	51	15	9	319	204	111
NY Islanders	44	20	13	11	158	135	51	44	11	24	9	120	181	31	88	31	37	20	278	316	82
NY Rangers	44	25	10	9	199	135	59	45	20	20	5	162	160	45	89	45	30	14	361	295	104
Ottawa	3	3	0	0	21	5	6	3	1	1	1	9	6	3	6	4	1	1	30	11	9
Philadelphia	46	23	14	9	190	151	55	45	12	31	2	121	183	26	91	35	45	11	311	334	81
Pittsburgh	39	23	9	7	170	117	53	39	10	19	10	126	146	30	78	33	28	17	296	263	83
St. Louis	46	24	18	4	166	135	52	47	17	20	10	148	166	46	93	43	38	12	314	301	98
San Jose	14	10	4	0	72	35	20	17	14	2	1	67	38	29	31	24	6	1	139	73	49
Tampa Bay	3	2	1	0	13	6	4	4	2	1	1	19	16	5	7	4	2	1	32	22	9
Toronto	46	28	13	5	201	147	61	44	17	20	7	169	170	41	90	45	33	12	370	317	102
Vancouver	77	52	14	11	341	218	115	77	33	28	16	261	274	82	154	85	42	27	602	492	197
Washington	33	22	6	5	144	81	49	34	13	16	5	123	130	31	67	35	22	10	267	211	80
Winnipeg	55	35	13	7	262	178	77	54	20	25	9	195	222	49	109	55	38	16	457	400	126
Defunct Clubs	13	8	4	1	51	34	17	13	7	3	3	43	33	17	26	15	7	4	94	67	34
Totals	**947**	**535**	**273**	**139**	**3979**	**2941**	**1209**	**947**	**358**		**442**	**147**	**3175**	**3529**	**863**	**1894**	**893**	**715**	**286**	**7154**	**6470**	**2072**

Playoffs

	Series	W	L	GP	W	L	T	GF	GA	Last Mtg.	Round	Result
Chicago	3	1	2	12	7	5	0	37	33	1996	CQF	L 0-4
Dallas	1	0	1	6	2	4	0	18	25	1981	SF	L 2-4
Detroit	1	0	1	2	0	2	0	5	8	1978	PR	L 0-2
Edmonton	5	1	4	30	11	19	0	96	132	1991	DSF	L 3-4
Los Angeles	6	2	4	26	13	13	0	102	105	1993	DSF	L 2-4
Montreal	2	1	1	11	5	6	0	32	31	1989	F	W 4-2
NY Rangers	1	0	1	4	1	3	0	8	14	1980	PR	L 1-3
Philadelphia	2	1	1	11	4	7	0	28	43	1981	QF	W 4-3
St. Louis	1	1	0	7	4	3	0	28	22	1986	CF	W 4-3
San Jose	1	0	1	7	3	4	0	35	26	1995	CQF	L 3-4
Toronto	1	0	1	2	0	2	0	5	9	1979	PR	L 0-2
Vancouver	5	3	2	25	13	12	0	82	80	1994	CQF	L 3-4
Winnipeg	3	1	2	13	6	7	0	43	45	1987	DSF	L 2-4
Totals	**32**	**12**	**20**	**156**	**69**	**87**	**0**	**529**	**590**			

Calgary totals include Atlanta, 1972-73 to 1979-80. Colorado totals include Quebec, 1979-80 to 1994-95.
Dallas totals include Minnesota, 1972-73 to 1992-93.
New Jersey totals include Kansas City, 1974-75 to 1975-76, and Colorado Rockies, 1976-77 to 1981-82.

Playoff Results 1996-92

Year	Round	Opponent	Result	GF	GA
1996	CQF	Chicago	L 0-4	7	16
1995	CQF	San Jose	L 3-4	35	26
1994	CQF	Vancouver	L 3-4	20	23
1993	DSF	Los Angeles	L 2-4	28	33

Abbreviations: Round: F – Final;
CF – conference final; **CQF** – conference quarter-final;
CSF – conference semi-final; **DF** – division final;
DSF – division semi-final; **SF** – semi-final;
QF – quarter-final; **PR** – preliminary round.

1995-96 Results

Oct.	7	at	Tampa Bay	3-3	6	Florida	2-0
	8	at	Florida	3-4	10	Hartford	3-2
	10	at	Dallas	3-7	12	Buffalo	3-1
	15	at	Chicago	1-1	14 at	Colorado	4-4
	17	at	Detroit	3-3	16 at	Los Angeles	5-5
	19	at	Ottawa	2-4	17 at	Anaheim	4-1
	20	at	Toronto	3-4	24	NY Islanders	4-1
	25		Colorado	2-3	26	Dallas	2-3
	27		Detroit	0-3	30	Edmonton	3-2
	29	at	Anaheim	2-7	Feb. 1	New Jersey	1-1
	31	at	Los Angeles	2-1	3	Los Angeles	2-1
Nov.	1		Colorado	1-6	6	Ottawa	3-3
	4		Vancouver	4-4	8	Washington	4-4
	6	at	NY Rangers	2-4	10	Winnipeg	2-3
	8	at	New Jersey	2-1	11 at	Edmonton	2-3
	9	at	Philadelphia	1-3	13 at	Washington	2-3
	11		Montreal	0-4	15 at	NY Islanders	6-3
	14		Edmonton	4-2	17 at	Montreal	1-5
	17		Colorado	3-5	20	San Jose	3-3
	18	at	Colorado	2-5	23	Anaheim	3-2
	21		Anaheim	2-3	24	Boston	1-2
	24		Edmonton	2-5	29	Pittsburgh	7-3
	26		Chicago	2-2	Mar. 3 at	St. Louis	5-1
	29	at	San Jose	5-3	7 at	St. Louis	4-2
Dec.	1	at	Edmonton	8-2	9 at	Toronto	3-4
	3	at	Winnipeg	2-5	12	St. Louis	4-2
	5		St. Louis	1-1	15 at	Buffalo	2-3
	9		Vancouver	3-4	17 at	Detroit	2-4
	11		Los Angeles	6-2	20 at	Chicago	3-2
	13	at	Dallas	8-4	22	San Jose	1-2
	14	at	St. Louis	3-3	23 at	Vancouver	4-0
	16	at	Boston	3-6	25	Toronto	2-4
	19	at	Pittsburgh	1-7	27	Chicago	1-0
	20	at	Hartford	3-2	29	Los Angeles	3-4
	22		Detroit	1-5	31	Winnipeg	1-4
	26		Vancouver	4-2	Apr. 3	Vancouver	4-3
	27		Toronto	4-0	6 at	Winnipeg	3-4
	29		Philadelphia	2-3	8 at	Edmonton	3-2
	31		NY Rangers	3-1	9	Dallas	2-4
Jan.	2		Tampa Bay	10-0	12 at	San Jose	6-0
	5		Anaheim	1-3	13 at	Vancouver	0-5

Entry Draft Selections 1996-82

1996
Pick
13 Derek Morris
39 Travis Brigley
40 Steve Begin
73 Dmitri Vlasenkov
89 Toni Lydman
94 Christian Lefebvre
122 Josef Straka
202 Ryan Wade
228 Ronald Petrovicky

1995
Pick
20 Denis Gauthier Jr.
46 Pavel Smirnov
72 Rocky Thompson
98 Jan Labraaten
150 Clarke Wilm
176 Ryan Gillis
233 Steve Shirreffs

1994
Pick
19 Chris Dingman
45 Dmitri Ryabykin
77 Chris Clark
91 Ryan Duthie
97 Johan Finnstrom
107 Nils Ekman
123 Frank Appel
149 Patrick Haltia
175 Ladislav Kohn
201 Keith McCambridge
227 Jorgen Jonsson
253 Mike Peluso
279 Pavel Torgayev

1993
Pick
18 Jesper Mattsson
44 Jamie Allison
70 Dan Tompkins
95 Jason Smith
96 Marty Murray
121 Darryl Lafrance
122 John Emmons
148 Andreas Karlsson
200 Derek Sylvester
252 German Titov
278 Burke Murphy

1992
Pick
6 Cory Stillman
30 Chris O'Sullivan
54 Mathias Johansson
78 Robert Svehla
102 Sami Helenius
126 Ravil Yakubov
129 Joel Bouchard
150 Pavel Rajnoha
174 Ryan Mulhern
198 Brandon Carper
222 Jonas Hoglund
246 Andrei Potaichuk

1991
Pick
19 Niklas Sundblad
41 Francois Groleau
52 Sandy McCarthy
63 Brian Caruso
85 Steven Magnusson
107 Jerome Butler
129 Bobby Marshall
140 Matt Hoffman
151 Kelly Harper
173 David St. Pierre
195 David Struch
217 Sergei Zolotov
239 Marko Jantunen
261 Andrei Trefilov

1990
Pick
11 Trevor Kidd
26 Nicolas P. Perreault
32 Vesa Viitakoski
41 Etienne Belzile
62 Glen Mears
83 Paul Kruse
125 Chris Tschupp
146 Dmitri Frolov
167 Shawn Murray
188 Mike Murray
209 Rob Sumner
230 invalid claim
251 Leo Gudas

1989
Pick
24 Kent Manderville
42 Ted Drury
50 Veli-Pekka Kautonen
63 Corey Lyons
70 Robert Reichel
84 Ryan O'Leary
105 F. (Toby) Kearney
147 Alex Nikolic
168 Kevin Wortman
189 Sergei Gomolyako
210 Dan Sawyer
231 Alexander Yudin
252 Kenneth Kennholt

1988
Pick
21 Jason Muzzatti
42 Todd Harkins
84 Gary Socha
85 Thomas Forslund
90 Scott Matusovich
126 Jonas Bergqvist
147 Stefan Nilsson
168 Troy Kennedy
189 Brett Peterson
210 Guy Darveau
231 Dave Tretowicz
252 Sergei Priakhan

1987
Pick
19 Bryan Deasley
25 Stephane Matteau
40 Kevin Grant
61 Scott Mahoney
70 Tim Harris
103 Tim Corkery
124 Joe Aloi
145 Peter Ciavaglia
166 Theoren Fleury
187 Mark Osiecki
208 William Sedergren
229 Peter Hasselblad
250 Magnus Svensson

1986
Pick
16 George Pelawa
37 Brian Glynn
79 Tom Quinlan
100 Scott Bloom
121 John Parker
142 Rick Lessard
163 Mark Olsen
184 Warren Sharples
205 Doug Pickell
226 Anders Lindstrom
247 Antonin Stavjana

1985
Pick
17 Chris Biotti
27 Joe Nieuwendyk
38 Jeff Wenaas
59 Lane MacDonald
80 Roger Johansson
101 Esa Keskinen
122 Tim Sweeney
143 Stu Grimson
164 Nate Smith
185 Darryl Olsen
206 Peter Romberg
227 Alexander Kozhevnikov
248 Bill Gregoire

1984
Pick
12 Gary Roberts
33 Ken Sabourin
38 Paul Ranheim
75 Petr Rosol
96 Joel Paunio
117 Brett Hull
138 Kevan Melrose
159 Jiri Hrdina
180 Gary Suter
200 Petr Rucka
221 Stefan Jonsson
241 Rudolf Suchanek

1983
Pick
13 Dan Quinn
51 Brian Bradley
55 Perry Berezan
66 John Bekkers
71 Kevan Guy
77 Bill Claviter
91 Igor Liba
111 Grant Blair
131 Jeff Hogg
151 Chris MacDonald
171 Rob Kivell
191 Tom Pratt
211 Jaroslav Benak
231 Sergei Makarov

1982
Pick
29 Dave Reierson
37 Richard Kromm
51 Jim Laing
65 Dave Meszaros
72 Mark Lamb
93 Lou Kiriakou
114 Jeff Vaive
118 Mats Kihlstrom
135 Brad Ramsden
156 Roy Myllari
177 Ted Pearson
198 Jim Uens
219 Rick Erdall
240 Dale Thompson

Coach

PAGE, PIERRE
Coach, Calgary Flames.
Born in St. Hermas, Que., April 30, 1948.

Pierre Page was named the ninth head coach in Flames franchise history on July 17, 1995. For Page, his head coaching appointment returns him to the organization with whom he began his NHL coaching career.

Page joined the Calgary Flames in 1980-81 as an assistant coach to Al MacNeil. He served in that capacity through the 1981-82 season before accepting a position as head coach and general manager of the Flames top development club in Denver (two seasons), and later, Moncton (one season). In 1985-86, Page returned to Calgary as an assistant to head coach Bob Johnson and remained in that capacity through the 1987-88 season under Terry Crisp.

Page left the Flames following the 1987-88 season to become the head coach of the Minnesota North Stars. In his rookie season with Minnesota, the club posted a 27-37-16 record for 70 points, a 19-point improvement over the previous year, and earned its first playoff berth since 1985-86. In 1989-90, the North Stars continued improving, finishing the season with 76 points (36-40-4).

After two seasons as head coach in Minnesota, Page was named general manager of the Quebec Nordiques on May 4, 1990. He added the Nordiques head coaching duties to his resume during 1991-92, replacing Dave Chambers 18 games into the season. Under Page's guidance, the Nordiques compiled their best record during the 1992-93 season, garnering a 56-point improvement and qualifying for the playoffs for the first time in six seasons. The 56-point improvement between the two seasons ranks as one of the largest improvements in NHL history. Page left the Nordiques following the 1993-94 season, serving as a pro scout with Toronto in 1994-95.

Before joining the Flames in 1980, Page was head coach of the Dalhousie University Tigers of the CIAU where in 1978-79, he guided his club to a second place finish in the national final. He also served as a guest coach with the 1980 Canadian Olympic Team and an assistant coach with Team Canada in the 1981 Canada Cup.

Club Directory

Canadian Airlines Saddledome
P.O. Box 1540 Station M
Calgary, Alberta T2P 3B9
Phone **403/777-2177**
FAX 403/777-2195
Capacity: 20,000

Owners Harley N. Hotchkiss, Byron J. Seaman, Daryl K. Seaman, Grant A. Bartlett, N. Murray Edwards, Ronald V. Joyce, Alvin G. Libin, Allan P. Markin, J.R. (Bud) McCaig

Management
President/Cheif Executive Officer . . . . . Ron Bremner
Executive Vice-President/General Manager . . . . . Al Coates
Vice-President, Finance and Administration . . . . . Clare Rhyasen
Vice-President, General Manager Canadian Airlines Saddledome . . . . . Jay Green
Vice-President, Corporate Communications . . . . . Lanny McDonald

Hockey Club Personnel
Director of Hockey Operations . . . . . Al MacNeil
Director, Pro Scouting . . . . . Nick Polano
Head Coach . . . . . Pierre Page
Assistant Coaches . . . . . Bill Hughes, Guy Lapointe, Kevin Constantine
Hockey Information . . . . . Mike Burke
St. John Head Coach . . . . . Paul Baxter
St. John Assistant Coach . . . . . TBA
St. John Trainer . . . . . Brian Miller
Director of Amateur Scouting . . . . . Tom Thompson
Scouts . . . . . Jiri Hrdina, Ian McKenzie, Kelly Kisio
Scouting Staff . . . . . Glen Giovanucci, Larry Popein, Ernie Vargas, Anders Steen, Lindsay Hall, Jim Bezdel, Normand Poisson
Secretary to President/CEO & VP, Finance . . . . . Yvette Mutcheson
Secretary to GM and Hockey Operations . . . . . Brenda Koyich

Administration
Controller . . . . . Michael Holditch
Assistant Controller . . . . . Dorothy Stuart

Corporate Resources
Manager, Corporate Resources . . . . . Brian Beavis

Marketing
Manager, Marketing and Special Events . . . . . Roger Lemire
Director, Executive Suites/Club Sales . . . . . Bob White
Director, Advertising and Publishing . . . . . Pat Halls
Account Executive . . . . . John Vidalin
Manager, Tickets . . . . . Anne Marie Malarchuk
Manager, Sales and Customer Service . . . . . Wendy Kennelly
Retail Operations Manager . . . . . Mark Mason

Public Relations
Director, Public Relations . . . . . Rick Skaggs
Assistant Director, Public Relations . . . . . Kathy Gieck

Medical/Training Staff
Physiotherapist and Fitness Coordinator . . . . . Terry Kane
Equipment Manager . . . . . Bobby Stewart
Head Trainer . . . . . Brain Patafie
Dressing Room Attendants . . . . . Cliff Stewart, Les Jarvis
Head Physician — Sport Medicine . . . . . Dr. William Meeuwisse
Internal Medicine . . . . . Dr. Terry Groves
Orthopedic Surgeon . . . . . Dr. Nicholas Mohtadi
Team Dentist . . . . . Dr. Bill Blair

Canadian Airlines Saddledome
Assistant Manager . . . . . Libby Raines
Operations Manager . . . . . George Greenwood
Food Services Manager . . . . . Nancy Cleveland
Food Services Asst. Manager . . . . . Art Hernandez
Event Services Coordinator . . . . . Tracey Bodnarchuk
Maintenance Superintendant . . . . . Ron Leopold
Concessions Manager . . . . . Sheila Parisien
Entertainment . . . . . Karla Piper

Facility
Location of Press Boxes . . . . . Print – north side
TV & Radio – south side
Dimensions of Rink . . . . . 200 feet by 85 feet

Broadcast Stations
Radio . . . . . 66 CFR Radio (660 AM)
Television . . . . . Channels 2 & 7

Coaching Record

		Regular Season					Playoffs			
Season	**Team**	**Games**	**W**	**L**	**T**	**%**	**Games**	**W**	**L**	**%**
1978-79	Dalhousie (CIAU)	....	....	....	....	....	....	....	....	....
1982-83	Denver (CHL)	80	41	36	3	.531	6	2	4	.333
1983-84	Denver (CHL)	76	48	25	3	.651	6	2	4	.333
1984-85	Moncton (AHL)	80	32	40	8	.450	....	....	....	....
1988-89	**Minnesota (NHL)**	**80**	**27**	**37**	**16**	**.438**	**5**	**1**	**4**	**.200**
1989-90	**Minnesota (NHL)**	**80**	**36**	**40**	**4**	**.475**	**7**	**3**	**4**	**.429**
1991-92	**Quebec (NHL)**	**62**	**17**	**34**	**11**	**.362**	....	....	....	....
1992-93	**Quebec (NHL)**	**84**	**47**	**27**	**10**	**.619**	**6**	**2**	**4**	**.333**
1993-94	**Quebec (NHL)**	**84**	**34**	**42**	**8**	**.452**	....	....	....	....
1995-96	**Calgary (NHL)**	**82**	**34**	**37**	**11**	**.482**	**4**	**0**	**4**	**.000**
	NHL Totals	**472**	**195**	**217**	**60**	**.477**	**22**	**6**	**16**	**.273**

Chicago Blackhawks

1995-96 Results: 40W-28L-14T 94PTS. Second, Central Division

Schedule

Oct.	Sat.	5	at Washington
	Sun.	6	at St. Louis
	Wed.	9	Anaheim
	Fri.	11	Colorado
	Sun.	13	Dallas
	Tues.	15	at Toronto
	Thur.	17	Detroit
	Sun.	20	Los Angeles*
	Thur.	24	St. Louis
	Fri.	25	at Detroit
	Sun.	27	San Jose*
	Tues.	29	at Tampa Bay
	Wed.	30	at Florida
Nov.	Fri.	1	at Dallas
	Sun.	3	Edmonton*
	Thur.	7	New Jersey
	Sat.	9	at Philadelphia*
	Sun.	10	Ottawa
	Thur.	14	Calgary
	Fri.	15	at Ottawa
	Sun.	17	Los Angeles*
	Tues.	19	at Edmonton
	Thur.	21	at Vancouver
	Fri.	22	at Calgary
	Wed.	27	at San Jose
	Fri.	29	at Anaheim*
	Sat.	30	at Los Angeles
Dec.	Fri.	6	Montreal
	Sat.	7	at Montreal
	Mon.	9	Toronto
	Thur.	12	at Detroit
	Fri.	13	at St. Louis
	Sun.	15	Pittsburgh*
	Wed.	18	Dallas
	Fri.	20	Florida
	Sun.	22	Philadelphia
	Mon.	23	at Boston
	Thur.	26	St. Louis
	Sat.	28	at Toronto
	Sun.	29	Hartford
	Tues.	31	Colorado
Jan.	Thur.	2	Phoenix
	Sun.	5	Detroit
	Wed.	8	Edmonton
	Fri.	10	at New Jersey
	Sat.	11	at Detroit
	Mon.	13	Tampa Bay
	Mon.	20	at Buffalo
	Wed.	22	Vancouver
	Fri.	24	Toronto
	Sat.	25	at NY Islanders
	Mon.	27	at NY Rangers
Feb.	Sat.	1	at Los Angeles
	Mon.	3	at San Jose
	Thur.	6	at Phoenix
	Sat.	8	at Colorado*
	Thur.	13	San Jose
	Sat.	15	NY Rangers*
	Mon.	17	at St. Louis
	Thur.	20	Boston
	Sat.	22	at Pittsburgh*
	Tues.	25	Dallas
Mar.	Sat.	1	at Colorado*
	Sun.	2	at Phoenix
	Wed.	5	at Vancouver
	Sat.	8	Phoenix
	Mon.	10	Vancouver
	Wed.	12	at Toronto
	Fri.	14	at Dallas
	Sun.	16	NY Islanders*
	Thur.	20	Phoenix
	Sun.	23	Detroit*
	Wed.	26	Washington
	Fri.	28	Anaheim
	Sun.	30	Buffalo*
Apr.	Tues.	1	at Anaheim
	Thur.	3	at Edmonton
	Sun.	6	at Calgary*
	Wed.	9	St. Louis
	Fri.	11	Calgary
	Sun.	13	at Dallas*

* Denotes afternoon game.

Franchise date: September 25, 1926

CENTRAL DIVISION

71st NHL Season

Tony Amonte showed why he is one of Chicago's most versatile performers, finishing among the team leaders in goals (31), short-handed goals (4) and game-winning goals (5).

Year-by-Year Record

Season	GP	Home W	L	T	Road W	L	T	Overall W	L	T	GF	GA	Pts.	Finished		Playoff Result
1995-96	82	22	13	6	18	15	8	40	28	14	273	220	94	2nd,	Central Div.	Lost Conf. Semi-Final
1994-95	48	11	10	3	13	9	2	24	19	5	156	115	53	3rd,	Central Div.	Lost Conf. Championship
1993-94	84	21	16	5	18	20	4	39	36	9	254	240	87	5th,	Central Div.	Lost Conf. Quarter-Final
1992-93	84	25	11	6	22	14	6	47	25	12	279	230	106	1st,	Norris Div.	Lost Div. Semi-Final
1991-92	80	23	9	8	13	20	7	36	29	15	257	236	87	2nd,	Norris Div.	Lost Final
1990-91	80	28	8	4	21	15	4	49	23	8	284	211	106	1st,	Norris Div.	Lost Div. Semi-Final
1989-90	80	25	13	2	16	20	4	41	33	6	316	294	88	1st,	Norris Div.	Lost Conf. Championship
1988-89	80	16	14	10	11	27	2	27	41	12	297	335	66	4th,	Norris Div.	Lost Conf. Championship
1987-88	80	21	17	2	9	24	7	30	41	9	284	328	69	3rd,	Norris Div.	Lost Div. Semi-Final
1986-87	80	18	13	9	11	24	5	29	37	14	290	310	72	3rd,	Norris Div.	Lost Div. Semi-Final
1985-86	80	23	12	5	16	21	3	39	33	8	351	349	86	1st,	Norris Div.	Lost Div. Semi-Final
1984-85	80	22	16	2	16	19	5	38	35	7	309	299	83	2nd,	Norris Div.	Lost Conf. Championship
1983-84	80	25	13	2	5	29	6	30	42	8	277	311	68	4th,	Norris Div.	Lost Div. Semi-Final
1982-83	80	29	8	3	18	15	7	47	23	10	338	268	104	1st,	Norris Div.	Lost Conf. Championship
1981-82	80	20	13	7	10	25	5	30	38	12	332	363	72	4th,	Norris Div.	Lost Conf. Championship
1980-81	80	21	11	8	10	22	8	31	33	16	304	315	78	2nd,	Smythe Div.	Lost Prelim. Round
1979-80	80	21	12	7	13	15	12	34	27	19	241	250	87	1st,	Smythe Div.	Lost Quarter-Final
1978-79	80	18	12	10	11	24	5	29	36	15	244	277	73	1st,	Smythe Div.	Lost Quarter-Final
1977-78	80	20	9	11	12	20	8	32	29	19	230	220	83	1st,	Smythe Div.	Lost Quarter-Final
1976-77	80	19	16	5	7	27	6	26	43	11	240	298	63	3rd,	Smythe Div.	Lost Prelim. Round
1975-76	80	17	15	8	15	15	10	32	30	18	254	261	82	1st,	Smythe Div.	Lost Quarter-Final
1974-75	80	24	12	4	13	23	4	37	35	8	268	241	82	3rd,	Smythe Div.	Lost Quarter-Final
1973-74	78	20	6	13	21	8	10	41	14	23	272	164	105	2nd,	West Div.	Lost Semi-Final
1972-73	78	26	9	4	16	18	5	42	27	9	284	225	93	1st,	West Div.	Lost Final
1971-72	78	28	3	8	18	14	7	46	17	15	256	166	107	1st,	West Div.	Lost Semi-Final
1970-71	78	30	6	3	19	14	6	49	20	9	277	184	107	1st,	West Div.	Lost Final
1969-70	76	26	7	5	19	15	4	45	22	9	250	170	99	1st,	East Div.	Lost Semi-Final
1968-69	76	20	14	4	14	19	5	34	33	9	280	246	77	6th,	East Div.	Out of Playoffs
1967-68	74	20	13	4	12	13	12	32	26	16	212	222	80	4th,	East Div.	Lost Semi-Final
1966-67	70	24	5	6	17	12	6	41	17	12	264	170	94	1st,		Lost Semi-Final
1965-66	70	21	8	6	16	17	2	37	25	8	240	187	82	2nd,		Lost Semi-Final
1964-65	70	20	13	2	14	15	6	34	28	8	224	176	76	3rd,		Lost Final
1963-64	70	26	4	5	10	18	7	36	22	12	218	169	84	2nd,		Lost Semi-Final
1962-63	70	17	9	9	15	12	8	32	21	17	194	178	81	2nd,		Lost Semi-Final
1961-62	70	20	10	5	11	16	8	31	26	13	217	186	75	3rd,		Lost Final
1960-61	**70**	**20**	**6**	**9**	**9**	**18**	**8**	**29**	**24**	**17**	**198**	**180**	**75**	**3rd,**		**Won Stanley Cup**
1959-60	70	18	11	6	10	18	7	28	29	13	191	180	69	3rd,		Lost Semi-Final
1958-59	70	14	12	9	14	17	4	28	29	13	197	208	69	3rd,		Lost Semi-Final
1957-58	70	15	17	3	9	22	4	24	39	7	163	202	55	5th,		Out of Playoffs
1956-57	70	12	15	8	4	24	7	16	39	15	169	225	47	6th,		Out of Playoffs
1955-56	70	9	19	7	10	20	5	19	39	12	155	216	50	6th,		Out of Playoffs
1954-55	70	6	21	8	7	19	9	13	40	17	161	235	43	6th,		Out of Playoffs
1953-54	70	8	21	6	4	30	1	12	51	7	133	242	31	6th,		Out of Playoffs
1952-53	70	14	11	10	13	17	5	27	28	15	169	175	69	4th,		Lost Semi-Final
1951-52	70	9	19	7	8	25	2	17	44	9	158	241	43	6th,		Out of Playoffs
1950-51	70	8	22	5	5	25	5	13	47	10	171	280	36	6th,		Out of Playoffs
1949-50	70	13	18	4	9	20	6	22	38	10	203	244	54	6th,		Out of Playoffs
1948-49	60	13	12	5	8	19	3	21	31	8	173	211	50	5th,		Out of Playoffs
1947-48	60	10	17	3	10	17	3	20	34	6	195	225	46	6th,		Out of Playoffs
1946-47	60	10	17	3	9	20	1	19	37	4	193	274	42	6th,		Out of Playoffs
1945-46	50	15	5	5	8	15	2	23	20	7	200	178	53	3rd,		Lost Semi-Final
1944-45	50	9	14	2	4	16	5	13	30	7	141	194	33	5th,		Out of Playoffs
1943-44	50	15	6	4	7	17	1	22	23	5	178	187	49	4th,		Lost Final
1942-43	50	14	3	8	3	15	7	17	18	15	179	180	49	4th,		Out of Playoffs
1941-42	48	15	8	1	7	15	2	22	23	3	145	155	47	4th,		Lost Quarter-Final
1940-41	48	11	10	3	5	15	4	16	25	7	112	139	39	5th,		Lost Semi-Final
1939-40	48	15	7	2	8	12	4	23	19	6	112	120	52	4th,		Lost Quarter-Final
1938-39	48	5	13	6	7	15	2	12	28	8	91	132	32	7th,		Out of Playoffs
1937-38	**48**	**10**	**10**	**4**	**4**	**15**	**5**	**14**	**25**	**9**	**97**	**139**	**37**	**3rd,**	**Amn. Div.**	**Won Stanley Cup**
1936-37	48	8	13	3	6	14	4	14	27	7	99	131	35	4th,	Amn. Div.	Out of Playoffs
1935-36	48	15	7	2	6	12	6	21	19	8	93	92	50	3rd,	Amn. Div.	Lost Quarter-Final
1934-35	48	12	9	3	14	8	2	26	17	5	118	88	57	2nd,	Amn. Div.	Lost Quarter-Final
1933-34	**48**	**13**	**4**	**7**	**7**	**13**	**4**	**20**	**17**	**11**	**88**	**83**	**51**	**2nd,**	**Amn. Div.**	**Won Stanley Cup**
1932-33	48	12	5	7	4	13	7	16	20	12	88	101	44	4th,	Amn. Div.	Out of Playoffs
1931-32	48	13	5	6	5	14	5	18	19	11	86	101	47	2nd,	Amn. Div.	Lost Quarter-Final
1930-31	44	13	8	1	11	9	2	24	17	3	108	78	51	2nd,	Amn. Div.	Lost Final
1929-30	44	12	9	1	9	9	4	21	18	5	117	111	47	2nd,	Amn. Div.	Lost Quarter-Final
1928-29	44	3	13	6	4	16	2	7	29	8	33	85	22	5th,	Amn. Div.	Out of Playoffs
1927-28	44	2	18	2	5	16	1	7	34	3	68	134	17	5th,	Amn. Div.	Out of Playoffs
1926-27	44	12	8	2	7	14	1	19	22	3	115	116	41	3rd,	Amn. Div.	Lost Quarter-Final

1996-97 Player Personnel

FORWARDS	HT	WT	S	Place of Birth	Date	1995-96 Club
AMONTE, Tony	6-0	190	L	Hingham, MA	8/2/70	Chicago
BLACK, James	5-11	185	L	Regina, Sask.	8/15/69	Chicago-Indianapolis
CRAVEN, Murray	6-2	185	L	Medicine Hat, Alta.	7/20/64	Chicago
CUMMINS, Jim	6-2	203	R	Dearborn, MI	5/17/70	Chicago
DAZE, Eric	6-4	215	L	Montreal, Que.	7/2/75	Chicago
DUBINSKY, Steve	6-0	190	L	Montreal, Que.	7/9/70	Chicago-Indianapolis
GUSMANOV, Ravil	6-3	185	L	Naberezhnye Chelny, USSR	7/25/72	Wpg-Springfield-Indianapolis
HANKINSON, Casey	6-1	187	L	Edina, MN	5/8/76	U. Minnesota
HUSKA, Ryan	6-2	194	L	Cranbrook, B.C.	7/2/75	Indianapolis
HYMOVITZ, David	5-11	170	L	Boston, MA	5/30/74	Boston College
KLIMOVICH, Sergei	6-3	189	R	Novosibirsk, USSR	3/8/74	Indianapolis
KRIVOKRASOV, Sergei	5-11	185	L	Angarsk, USSR	4/15/74	Chicago-Indianapolis
LeCOMPTE, Eric	6-4	190	L	Montreal, Que.	4/4/75	Indianapolis
LEROUX, Jean-Yves	6-2	193	L	Montreal, Que.	6/24/76	Beauport
MacINTYRE, Andy	6-1	190	L	Thunder Bay, Ont.	4/16/74	Indianapolis-Columbus
MANLOW, Eric	6-0	190	L	Belleville, Ont.	4/7/75	Indianapolis
MARA, Rob	6-1	175	R	Boston, MA	9/25/75	Colgate
MILLER, Kevin	5-11	190	R	Lansing, MI	9/2/65	San Jose-Pittsburgh
MILLER, Kip	5-10	190	L	Lansing, MI	6/11/69	Chicago-Indianapolis
MILLS, Craig	5-11	174	R	Toronto, Ont.	8/27/76	Wpg-Belleville-Springfield
MOREAU, Ethan	6-2	205	L	Huntsville, Ont.	9/22/75	Chicago-Indianapolis
OATES, Matt	6-3	208	L	Evanston, IL	12/20/72	Columbus
PETROV, Sergei	5-11	185	L	Leningrad, USSR	1/22/75	Unavailable
PITTMAN, Mike	6-0	180	R	Placentia, Nfld.	3/29/76	Guelph
PROBERT, Bob	6-3	225	L	Windsor, Ont.	6/5/65	Chicago
PROKOPEC, Mike	6-2	190	R	Toronto, Ont.	5/17/74	Chicago-Indianapolis
PYSZ, Patrik	5-11	187	L	Nowy Targ, Poland	1/15/75	Mannheim
ROYER, Gaetan	6-3	193	R	Donnacona, Que.	3/13/76	Sherbrooke-Beauport
SAVARD, Denis	5-10	175	R	Pointe Gatineau, Que.	2/4/61	Chicago
SHANTZ, Jeff	6-0	185	R	Duchess, Alta.	10/10/73	Chicago
SUTTER, Brent	5-11	180	R	Viking, Alta.	6/10/62	Chicago
WHITE, Tom	6-1	185	L	Chicago, IL	8/25/75	Miami-Ohio
ZHAMNOV, Alexei	6-1	195	L	Moscow, USSR	10/1/70	Winnipeg
DEFENSEMEN						
CARNEY, Keith E.	6-2	205	L	Providence, RI	2/3/70	Chicago
CHELIOS, Chris	6-1	186	R	Chicago, IL	1/25/62	Chicago
CICCONE, Enrico	6-5	220	L	Montreal, Que.	4/10/70	Tampa Bay-Chicago
DROPPA, Ivan	6-2	209	L	Liptovsky Mikulas, Czech.	2/1/72	Chicago-Indianapolis
GRONMAN, Tuomas	6-3	198	R	Viitasaari, Fin.	3/22/74	TPS
KRIZ, Pavel	6-1	205	R	Nymburk, Czech.	1/2/77	Saskatoon
LAFLAMME, Christian	6-1	195	R	St. Charles, Que.	11/24/76	Beauport
MCLAREN, Steve	6-0	194	L	Owen Sound, Ont.	2/3/75	Indianapolis
RUSK, Mike	6-1	175	L	Milton, Ont.	4/26/75	Columbus
RUSSELL, Cam	6-4	206	L	Halifax, N.S.	1/12/69	Chicago
SMITH, Steve	6-4	215	L	Glasgow, Scotland	4/30/63	Chicago
SNELL, Chris	5-11	200	L	Regina, Sask.	5/12/71	Phoenix-Binghamton
SUTER, Gary	6-0	200	L	Madison, WI	6/24/64	Chicago
THIESSEN, Travis	6-3	203	L	North Battleford, Sask.	7/11/72	Indianapolis-Peoria
WEINRICH, Eric	6-1	210	L	Roanoke, VA	12/19/66	Chicago
WERENKA, Brad	6-2	210	L	Two Hills, Alta.	2/12/69	Chicago-Indianapolis

GOALTENDERS	HT	WT	C	Place of Birth	Date	1995-96 Club
BELFOUR, Ed	5-11	182	L	Carman, Man.	4/21/65	Chicago
HACKETT, Jeff	6-1	180	L	London, Ont.	6/1/68	Chicago
NOBLE, Tom	5-10	165	L	Quincy, MA	3/21/75	Boston U.
RACICOT, Andre	5-11	165	L	Rouyn-Noranda, Que.	6/9/69	Alb-Colum-Ind-Peo
WAITE, Jimmy	6-1	180	L	Sherbrooke, Que.	4/15/69	Chicago-Indianapolis
WEIBEL, Lars	6-0	178	L	Rapperswil, Switz.	5/20/74	Lugano

Coach

HARTSBURG, CRAIG
Coach, Chicago Blackhawks. Born in Stratford, Ont., June 29, 1959.

Craig Hartsburg enters his second season as coach of the Chicago Blackhawks after guiding the team to a 40-28-14 record behind the bench in his rookie campaign.

The Blackhawks finished the regular season second in the Central Division and earned a No. 3 seed in the Western Conference for the Stanley Cup playoffs. After a sweep of Calgary in the opening round of the playoffs, the Blackhawks fell to the eventual Stanley Cup champion Colorado Avalanche in the Western Conference semi-finals.

Hartsburg was introduced as the 30th head coach in the history of the Chicago Blackhawks at a press conference on June 29, 1995. Hartsburg comes to the Blackhawks from the Guelph Storm (OHL), where he was named OHL coach of the year after leading the Storm to a 47-14-5 record.

Hartsburg received his first head coaching position at Guelph in 1994-95 after spending four seasons as an assistant coach from 1990-94 with the Philadelphia Flyers and one season as an assistant coach with the Minnesota North Stars during the 1989-90 season.

Hartsburg played his entire 10-year NHL career with Minnesota. Known as an offensive-defenseman, Hartsburg was the North Stars' captain for six seasons, until injuries forced him to retire from active play on January 13, 1988.

Hartsburg lists winning the Canada Cup championship in 1987 as his most memorable hockey moment. He participated in three NHL All-Star Games (1980, 1982 and 1983) and also competed in three World Championship tournaments for Team Canada — and was chosen best defenseman of the 1987 World Championships. In February of 1992, Hartsburg was voted to the North Stars' 25th Anniversary Dream Team by Minnesota fans.

Hartsburg, who turned 36 on the day he was announced as head coach, and his wife Peggy have two children, Christopher and Katie.

1995-96 Scoring

* – rookie

Regular Season

Pos	#	Player	Team	GP	G	A	Pts	+/–	PIM	PP	SH	GW	GT	S	%
D	7	Chris Chelios	CHI	81	14	58	72	25	140	7	0	3	0	219	6.4
C	27	Jeremy Roenick	CHI	66	32	35	67	9	109	12	4	2	2	171	18.7
D	20	Gary Suter	CHI	82	20	47	67	3	80	12	2	4	0	242	8.3
R	10	Tony Amonte	CHI	81	31	32	63	10	62	5	4	5	0	216	14.4
C	92	Bernie Nicholls	CHI	59	19	41	60	11	60	6	0	2	2	100	19.0
L	55 *	Eric Daze	CHI	80	30	23	53	16	18	2	0	2	0	167	18.0
R	17	Joe Murphy	CHI	70	22	29	51	–3	86	8	0	3	0	212	10.4
C	18	Denis Savard	CHI	69	13	35	48	20	102	2	0	1	0	110	11.8
L	32	Murray Craven	CHI	66	18	29	47	20	36	5	1	7	0	86	20.9
R	24	Bob Probert	CHI	78	19	21	40	15	237	1	0	3	0	97	19.6
C	12	Brent Sutter	CHI	80	13	27	40	14	56	0	0	3	0	102	12.7
C	11	Jeff Shantz	CHI	78	6	14	20	12	24	1	2	0	0	72	8.3
D	4	Keith Carney	CHI	82	5	14	19	31	94	1	0	1	0	69	7.2
R	25	Sergei Krivokrasov	CHI	46	6	10	16	10	32	0	0	1	0	52	11.5
D	2	Eric Weinrich	CHI	77	5	10	15	14	65	0	0	0	0	76	6.6
D	5	Steve Smith	CHI	37	0	9	9	12	71	0	0	0	0	17	0.0
C	38	James Black	CHI	13	3	3	6	1	16	0	0	1	0	23	13.0
L	19	Brent Grieve	CHI	28	2	4	6	5	28	0	0	0	0	22	9.1
R	15	Jim Cummins	CHI	52	2	4	6	–1	180	0	0	2	0	34	5.9
D	39	Enrico Ciccone	T.B.	55	2	3	5	–4	258	0	0	0	0	48	4.2
			CHI	11	0	1	1	5	48	0	0	0	0	12	0.0
			TOTAL	66	2	4	6	1	306	0	0	0	0	60	3.3
C	22	Steve Dubinsky	CHI	43	2	3	5	3	14	0	0	0	0	33	6.1
C	14	Kip Miller	CHI	10	1	4	5	1	2	0	0	0	1	12	8.3
D	8	Cam Russell	CHI	61	2	2	4	8	129	0	0	0	0	22	9.1
G	30	Ed Belfour	CHI	50	0	2	2	0	36	0	0	0	0	0	0.0
R	19	Danton Cole	NYI	10	1	0	1	0	0	0	0	0	0	5	20.0
			CHI	2	0	0	0	0	0	0	0	0	0	1	0.0
			TOTAL	12	1	0	1	0	0	0	0	0	0	6	16.7
L	40 *	Ethan Moreau	CHI	8	0	1	1	1	4	0	0	0	0	1	0.0
G	31	Jeff Hackett	CHI	35	0	1	1	0	8	0	0	0	0	0	0.0
G	29	Jim Waite	CHI	1	0	0	0	0	0	0	0	0	0	0	0.0
D	6 *	Ivan Droppa	CHI	7	0	0	0	2	2	0	0	0	0	1	0.0
D	3	Brad Werenka	CHI	9	0	0	0	–2	8	0	0	0	0	2	0.0
R	23 *	Mike Prokopec	CHI	9	0	0	0	–4	5	0	0	0	0	5	0.0

Goaltending

No.	Goaltender	GPI	Mins	Avg	W	L	T	EN	SO	GA	SA	S%
29	Jim Waite	1	31	.00	0	0	0	0	0	0	8	1.000
31	Jeff Hackett	35	2000	2.40	18	11	4	2	4	80	948	.916
30	Ed Belfour	50	2956	2.74	22	17	10	3	1	135	1373	.902
	Totals	**82**	**4999**	**2.64**	**40**	**28**	**14**	**5**	**5**	**220**	**2334**	**.906**

Playoffs

Pos	#	Player	Team	GP	G	A	Pts	+/–	PIM	PP	SH	GW	OT	S	%
C	27	Jeremy Roenick	CHI	10	5	7	12	6	2	1	0	1	1	21	23.8
C	92	Bernie Nicholls	CHI	10	2	7	9	3	4	1	0	0	0	11	18.2
R	17	Joe Murphy	CHI	10	6	2	8	1	33	0	0	2	1	38	15.8
L	55 *	Eric Daze	CHI	10	3	5	8	4	0	0	0	1	0	32	9.4
D	20	Gary Suter	CHI	10	3	3	6	1	8	2	0	1	0	27	11.1
R	10	Tony Amonte	CHI	7	2	4	6	2	6	1	0	0	0	14	14.3
C	11	Jeff Shantz	CHI	10	2	3	5	–2	6	0	0	0	0	9	22.2
L	32	Murray Craven	CHI	9	1	4	5	–1	2	1	0	0	0	17	5.9
D	2	Eric Weinrich	CHI	10	1	4	5	2	10	1	0	0	0	13	7.7
C	18	Denis Savard	CHI	10	1	2	3	0	8	1	0	0	0	12	8.3
D	7	Chris Chelios	CHI	9	0	3	3	2	8	0	0	0	0	28	0.0
D	4	Keith Carney	CHI	10	0	3	3	–1	4	0	0	0	0	11	0.0
C	12	Brent Sutter	CHI	10	1	1	2	–3	6	0	0	0	0	18	5.6
R	24	Bob Probert	CHI	10	0	2	2	–1	23	0	0	0	0	20	0.0
R	25	Sergei Krivokrasov	CHI	5	1	0	1	–4	2	0	0	1	1	6	16.7
C	38	James Black	CHI	8	1	0	1	–1	2	0	0	0	0	6	16.7
D	39	Enrico Ciccone	CHI	9	1	0	1	–1	30	0	0	0	0	4	25.0
G	31	Jeff Hackett	CHI	1	0	0	0	0	0	0	0	0	0	0	0.0
D	8	Cam Russell	CHI	6	0	0	0	–1	2	0	0	0	0	4	0.0
D	5	Steve Smith	CHI	6	0	0	0	–2	16	0	0	0	0	3	0.0
G	30	Ed Belfour	CHI	9	0	0	0	0	4	0	0	0	0	0	0.0
R	15	Jim Cummins	CHI	10	0	0	0	–1	2	0	0	0	0	3	0.0

Goaltending

No.	Goaltender	GPI	Mins	Avg	W	L	EN	SO	GA	SA	S%
30	Ed Belfour	9	666	2.07	6	3	0	1	23	323	.929
31	Jeff Hackett	1	60	5.00	0	1	0	0	5	32	.844
	Totals	**10**	**727**	**2.31**	**6**	**4**	**0**	**1**	**28**	**355**	**.921**

Coaching Record

		Regular Season					Playoffs			
Season	Team	Games	W	L	T	%	Games	W	L	%
1994-95	Guelph (OHL)	66	47	14	5	.750	14	10	4	.714
1995-96	**Chicago (NHL)**	**82**	**40**	**28**	**14**	**.573**	**10**	**6**	**4**	**.600**
	NHL Totals	**82**	**40**	**28**	**14**	**.573**	**10**	**6**	**4**	**.600**

Club Records

Team

(Figures in brackets for season records are games played; records for fewest points, wins, ties, losses, goals, goals against are for 70 or more games)

Most Points	**107**	1970-71 (78), 1971-72 (78)
Most Wins	**49**	1970-71 (78), 1990-91 (80)
Most Ties	**23**	1973-74 (78)
Most Losses	**51**	1953-54 (70)
Most Goals	**351**	1985-86 (80)
Most Goals Against	**363**	1981-82 (80)
Fewest Points	**31**	1953-54 (70)
Fewest Wins	**12**	1953-54 (70)
Fewest Ties	**6**	1989-90 (80)
Fewest Losses	**14**	1973-74 (78)
Fewest Goals	***133**	1953-54 (70)
Fewest Goals Against	**164**	1973-74 (78)
Longest Winning Streak		
Overall	**8**	Dec. 9-26/71, Jan. 4-21/81
Home	**13**	Nov. 11-Dec. 20/70
Away	**7**	Dec. 9-29/64
Longest Undefeated Streak		
Overall	**15**	Jan. 14-Feb. 16/67 (12 wins, 3 ties)
Home	**18**	Oct. 11-Dec. 20/70 (16 wins, 2 ties)
Away	**12**	Nov. 2-Dec. 16/67 (6 wins, 6 ties)
Longest Losing Streak		
Overall	**13**	Feb. 25-Oct. 11/51
Home	**11**	Feb. 8-Nov. 22/28
Away	**17**	Jan. 2-Oct. 7/54
Longest Winless Streak		
Overall	**21**	Dec. 17/50-Jan. 28/51 (18 losses, 3 ties)
Home	**15**	Dec. 16/28-Feb. 28/29 (11 losses, 4 ties)
Away	**23**	Dec. 19/50-Oct. 11/51 (15 losses, 8 ties)
Most Shutouts, Season	**15**	1969-70 (76)
Most PIM, Season	**2,663**	1991-92 (80)
Most Goals, Game	**12**	Jan. 30/69 (Chi. 12 at Phi. 0)

Individual

Most Seasons	**22**	Stan Mikita
Most Games	**1,394**	Stan Mikita
Most Goals, Career	**604**	Bobby Hull
Most Assists, Career	**926**	Stan Mikita
Most Points, Career	**1,467**	Stan Mikita (541G, 926A)
Most PIM, Career	**1,442**	Keith Magnuson
Most Shutouts, Career	**74**	Tony Esposito
Longest Consecutive Games Streak	**884**	Steve Larmer (1982-83 to 1992-93)
Most Goals, Season	**58**	Bobby Hull (1968-69)
Most Assists, Season	**87**	Denis Savard (1981-82, 1987-88)
Most Points, Season	**131**	Denis Savard (1987-88; 44G, 87A)
Most PIM, Season	**408**	Mike Peluso (1991-92)
Most Points, Defenseman Season	**85**	Doug Wilson (1981-82; 39G, 46A)
Most Points, Center, Season	**131**	Denis Savard (1987-88; 44G, 87A)
Most Points, Right Wing, Season	**101**	Steve Larmer (1990-91; 44G, 57A)
Most Points, Left Wing, Season	**107**	Bobby Hull (1968-69; 58G, 49A)
Most Points, Rookie, Season	**90**	Steve Larmer (1982-83; 43G, 47A)
Most Shutouts, Season	**15**	Tony Esposito (1969-70)
Most Goals, Game	**5**	Grant Mulvey (Feb. 3/82)
Most Assists, Game	**6**	Pat Stapleton (Mar. 30/69)
Most Points, Game	**7**	Max Bentley (Jan. 28/43; 4G, 3A), Grant Mulvey (Feb. 3/82; 5G, 2A)

* NHL Record.

Retired Numbers

1	Glenn Hall	1957-1967
9	Bobby Hull	1957-1972
21	Stan Mikita	1958-1980
35	Tony Esposito	1969-1984

Captains' History

Dick Irvin, 1926-27 to 1928-29; "Duke" Dutkowski, 1929-30; Ty Arbour, 1930-31; Cy Wentworth, 1931-32; Helge Bostrom, 1932-33; Chuck Gardiner, 1933-34; no captain, 1934-35; Johnny Gottselig, 1935-36 to 1939-40; Earl Seibert, 1940-41, 1941-42; Doug Bentley, 1942-43, 1943-44; Clint Smith 1944-45; John Mariucci, 1945-46; "Red" Hamill, 1946-47; John Mariucci, 1947-48; Gaye Stewart, 1948-49; Doug Bentley, 1949-50; Jack Stewart, 1950-51, 1951-52; Bill Gadsby, 1952-53, 1953-54; Gus Mortson, 1954-55 to 1956-57; no captain, 1957-58; Eddie Litzenberger, 1958-59 to 1960-61; Pierre Pilote, 1961-62 to 1967-68, no captain, 1968-69; Pat Stapleton, 1969-70; no captain, 1970-71 to 1974-75; Stan Mikita and "Pit" Martin, 1975-76; Stan Mikita, "Pit" Martin and Keith Magnuson, 1976-77; Keith Magnuson, 1977-78, 1978-79; Keith Magnuson, Terry Ruskowski, 1979-80; Terry Ruskowski, 1980-81, 1981-82; Darryl Sutter, 1982-83 to 1984-85; Darryl Sutter and Bob Murray, 1985-86; Darryl Sutter, 1986-87; no captain, 1987-88; Denis Savard and Dirk Graham, 1988-89; Dirk Graham, 1989-90 to 1994-95; Chris Chelios, 1995-96 to date.

All-time Record vs. Other Clubs

Regular Season

	At Home							On Road							Total						
	GP	W	L	T	GF	GA	PTS	GP	W	L	T	GF	GA	PTS	GP	W	L	T	GF	GA	PTS
Anaheim	7	5	1	1	20	10	11	6	5	1	0	19	12	10	13	10	2	1	39	22	21
Boston	279	142	93	44	899	745	328	277	86	159	32	783	1005	204	556	228	252	76	1682	1750	532
Buffalo	44	23	15	6	144	123	52	46	12	28	6	121	176	30	90	35	43	12	265	299	82
Calgary	45	20	14	11	157	136	51	47	17	22	8	141	151	42	92	37	36	19	298	287	93
Colorado	25	15	8	2	101	84	32	24	9	11	4	94	105	22	49	24	19	6	195	189	54
Dallas	92	61	21	10	383	239	132	94	40	40	14	302	313	94	186	101	61	24	685	552	226
Detroit	315	144	122	49	948	879	337	314	92	194	28	770	1076	212	629	236	316	77	1718	1955	549
Edmonton	28	15	9	4	118	108	34	29	14	14	1	114	117	29	57	29	23	5	232	225	63
Florida	2	1	0	1	12	8	3	2	2	0	0	9	5	4	4	3	0	1	21	13	7
Hartford	23	14	6	3	103	65	31	24	11	11	2	82	83	24	47	25	17	5	185	148	55
Los Angeles	59	30	21	8	229	179	68	58	27	25	6	207	200	60	117	57	46	14	436	379	128
Montreal	268	91	122	55	723	751	237	268	51	169	48	632	1042	150	536	142	291	103	1355	1793	387
New Jersey	40	23	9	8	168	112	54	39	15	15	9	119	116	39	79	38	24	17	287	228	93
NY Islanders	42	21	16	5	140	144	47	40	11	16	13	121	145	35	82	32	32	18	261	289	82
NY Rangers	279	125	112	42	851	778	292	280	109	116	55	795	832	273	559	234	228	97	1646	1610	565
Ottawa	3	1	1	1	9	10	3	3	3	0	0	12	5	6	6	4	1	1	21	15	9
Philadelphia	54	25	11	18	196	154	68	55	15	29	11	147	181	41	109	40	40	29	343	335	109
Pittsburgh	53	36	8	9	226	145	81	52	22	25	5	173	187	49	105	58	33	14	399	332	130
St. Louis	96	55	28	13	379	294	123	92	31	44	17	288	311	79	188	86	72	30	667	605	202
San Jose	9	6	2	1	32	21	13	10	5	5	0	30	26	10	19	11	7	1	62	47	23
Tampa Bay	6	3	1	2	17	13	8	5	2	3	0	15	16	4	11	5	4	2	32	29	12
Toronto	305	154	110	41	944	793	349	304	91	160	53	784	1040	235	609	245	270	94	1728	1833	584
Vancouver	55	37	13	5	215	129	79	56	17	26	13	164	174	47	111	54	39	18	379	303	126
Washington	33	20	8	5	136	100	45	34	11	19	4	106	128	26	67	31	27	9	242	228	71
Winnipeg	31	23	5	3	149	88	49	33	11	18	4	112	127	26	64	34	23	7	261	215	75
Defunct Clubs	139	79	40	20	408	268	178	140	52	67	21	316	346	125	279	131	107	41	724	614	303
Totals	**2332**	**1169**	**796**	**367**	**7707**	**6376**	**2705**	**2332**	**761**	**1217**	**354**	**6456**	**7919**	**1876**	**4664**	**1930**	**2013**	**721**	**14163**	**14295**	**4581**

Playoffs

	Series	W	L	GP	W	L	T	GF	GA	Last Mtg.	Round	Result
Boston	6	1	5	22	5	16	1	63	97	1978	QF	L 0-4
Buffalo	2	0	2	9	1	8	0	17	36	1980	QF	L 0-4
Calgary	3	1	2	12	5	7	0	33	37	1996	CQF	W 4-0
Colorado	1	0	1	6	2	4	0	14	21	1996	CSF	L 2-4
Dallas	6	4	2	33	19	14	0	119	119	1991	DSF	L 2-4
Detroit	14	8	6	69	38	31	0	210	190	1995	CF	L 1-4
Edmonton	4	1	3	20	8	12	0	77	102	1992	CF	W 4-0
Los Angeles	1	1	0	5	4	1	0	10	7	1974	QF	W 4-1
Montreal	17	5	12	81	29	50	2	185	261	1976	QF	L 0-4
NY Islanders	2	0	2	6	0	6	0	6	21	1979	QF	L 0-4
NY Rangers	5	4	1	24	14	10	0	66	54	1973	SF	W 4-1
Philadelphia	1	1	0	4	4	0	0	20	8	1971	QF	W 4-0
Pittsburgh	2	1	1	8	4	4	0	24	23	1992	F	L 0-4
St. Louis	9	7	2	45	27	18	0	166	129	1993	DSF	L 0-4
Toronto	9	3	6	38	15	22	1	89	111	1995	CQF	W 4-3
Vancouver	2	1	1	9	5	4	0	24	24	1995	CSF	W 4-0
Defunct Clubs	4	2	2	9	5	3	1	16	15			
Totals	**88**	**40**	**48**	**400**	**185**	**210**	**5**	**1139**	**1255**			

Calgary totals include Atlanta, 1972-73 to 1979-80. Colorado totals include Quebec, 1979-80 to 1994-95.
Dallas totals include Minnesota, 1967-68 to 1992-93.
New Jersey totals include Kansas City, 1974-75 to 1975-76, and Colorado Rockies, 1976-77 to 1981-82.

Playoff Results 1996-92

Year	Round	Opponent	Result	GF	GA
1996	CSF	Colorado	L 2-4	14	21
	CQF	Calgary	W 4-0	16	7
1995	CF	Detroit	L 1-4	12	13
	CSF	Vancouver	W 4-0	11	6
	CQF	Toronto	W 4-3	22	20
1994	CQF	Toronto	L 2-4	10	15
1993	DSF	St. Louis	L 0-4	6	13
1992	F	Pittsburgh	L 0-4	10	15
	CF	Edmonton	W 4-0	21	8
	DF	Detroit	W 4-0	11	6
	DSF	St. Louis	W 4-2	23	19

Abbreviations: Round: F – Final; **CF** – conference final; **CQF** – conference quarter-final; **CSF** – conference semi-final; **DF** – division final; **DSF** – division semi-final; **SF** – semi-final; **QF** – quarter-final; **PR** – preliminary round.

1995-96 Results

Oct.	7	at	San Jose	4-3		6	at	Detroit	0-3
	10	at	Los Angeles	5-6		7		Dallas	5-2
	12		Pittsburgh	5-1		9	at	NY Islanders	3-3
	14	at	Hartford	2-3		12		Anaheim	3-0
	15		Calgary	1-1		14		Los Angeles	5-2
	17	at	Florida	6-3		17		Washington	2-3
	19		Tampa Bay	1-4		22	at	Ottawa	7-3
	21	at	St. Louis	4-1		24	at	Toronto	2-2
	22		Philadelphia	5-4		25		San Jose	2-1
	26		Toronto	1-2		27		Detroit	5-5
	28	at	Montreal	3-5		31	at	Edmonton	4-0
	29		Buffalo	6-3	**Feb.**	3	at	San Jose	4-1
Nov.	1	at	Dallas	1-1		4	at	Anaheim	4-1
	5		Colorado	3-7		6	at	Los Angeles	5-2
	9		Vancouver	5-2		8	at	St. Louis	6-1
	11	at	Washington	4-1		10	at	Pittsburgh	3-6
	12		Edmonton	4-4		15		Boston	3-0
	14	at	Winnipeg	5-6		18		Edmonton	4-1
	16		NY Rangers	3-1		22		St. Louis	3-4
	19		San Jose	2-3		23	at	Winnipeg	0-1
	22	at	Colorado	2-6		25	at	Philadelphia	2-3
	24	at	Anaheim	5-4		29		Colorado	4-3
	26	at	Calgary	2-2	**Mar.**	1	at	Colorado	3-5
	28	at	Edmonton	5-3		3		Detroit	2-6
	29	at	Vancouver	2-2		5	at	Tampa Bay	0-2
Dec.	2	at	Winnipeg	2-2		8		Los Angeles	2-4
	6	at	NY Rangers	5-5		11		Florida	8-4
	7		Ottawa	2-5		14		Vancouver	5-1
	10		Hartford	4-1		17		NY Islanders	5-1
	13	at	Detroit	1-3		20		Calgary	2-3
	15		Montreal	1-4		22	at	New Jersey	4-2
	17		Winnipeg	3-1		24		Anaheim	2-2
	20	at	Toronto	4-2		27	at	Calgary	0-1
	21		Toronto	3-3		29	at	Vancouver	2-4
	23	at	Dallas	2-0		31		Dallas	5-3
	26		Dallas	5-3	**Apr.**	3	at	Toronto	5-2
	28		Winnipeg	4-3		5	at	Dallas	3-3
	29	at	Buffalo	5-2		7		Detroit	1-4
	31		New Jersey	5-0		11		Toronto	5-2
Jan.	2	at	Boston	5-2		12	at	Detroit	3-5
	4		St. Louis	1-3		14		St. Louis	2-2

Entry Draft
Selections 1996-82

1996
Pick
31	Remi Royer
42	Jeff Paul
46	Geoff Peters
130	Andy Johnson
184	Mike Vellinga
210	Chris Twerdun
236	Alexei Kozyrev

1995
Pick
19	Dimitri Nabokov
45	Christian Laflamme
71	Kevin McKay
82	Chris Van Dyk
97	Pavel Kriz
146	Marc Magliarditi
149	Marty Wilford
175	Steve Tardif
201	Casey Hankinson
227	Mike Pittman

1994
Pick
14	Ethan Moreau
40	Jean-Yves Leroux
85	Steve McLaren
118	Marc Dupuis
144	Jim Enson
170	Tyler Prosofsky
196	Mike Josephson
222	Lubomir Jandera
248	Lars Weibel
263	Rob Mara

1993
Pick
24	Eric Lecompte
50	Eric Manlow
54	Bogdan Savenko
76	Ryan Huska
90	Eric Daze
102	Patrik Pysz
128	Jonni Vauhkonen
180	Tom White
206	Sergei Petrov
232	Mike Rusk
258	Mike McGhan
284	Tom Noble

1992
Pick
12	Sergei Krivokrasov
36	Jeff Shantz
41	Sergei Klimovich
89	Andy MacIntyre
113	Tim Hogan
137	Gerry Skrypec
161	Mike Prokopec
185	Layne Roland
209	David Hymovitz
233	Richard Raymond

1991
Pick
22	Dean McAmmond
39	Michael Pomichter
44	Jamie Matthews
66	Bobby House
71	Igor Kravchuk
88	Zac Boyer
110	Maco Balkovec
112	Kevin St. Jacques
132	Jacques Auger
154	Scott Kirton
176	Roch Belley
198	Scott MacDonald
220	A. Andriyevsky
242	Mike Larkin
264	Scott Dean

1990
Pick
16	Karl Dykhuis
37	Ivan Droppa
79	Chris Tucker
121	Brett Stickney
124	Derek Edgerly
163	Hugo Belanger
184	Owen Lessard
205	Erik Peterson
226	Steve Dubinsky
247	Dino Grossi

1989
Pick
6	Adam Bennett
27	Michael Speer
48	Bob Kellogg
111	Tommi Pullola
132	Tracy Egeland
153	Milan Tichy
174	Jason Greyerbiehl
195	Matt Saunders
216	Mike Kozak
237	Michael Doneghey

1988
Pick
8	Jeremy Roenick
50	Trevor Dam
71	Stefan Elvenas
92	Joe Cleary
113	Justin Lafayette
134	Craig Woodcroft
155	Jon Pojar
176	Mathew Hentges
197	Daniel Maurice
218	Dirk Tenzer
239	Andreas Lupzig

1987
Pick
8	Jimmy Waite
29	Ryan McGill
50	Cam Russell
60	Mike Dagenais
92	Ulf Sandstrom
113	Mike McCormick
134	Stephen Tepper
155	John Reilly
176	Lance Werness
197	Dale Marquette
218	Bill Lacouture
239	Mike Lappin

1986
Pick
14	Everett Sanipass
35	Mark Kurzawski
77	Frantisek Kucera
98	Lonnie Loach
119	Mario Doyon
140	Mike Hudson
161	Marty Nanne
182	Geoff Benic
203	Glen Lowes
224	Chris Thayer
245	Sean Williams

1985
Pick
11	Dave Manson
53	Andy Helmuth
74	Dan Vincellette
87	Rick Herbert
95	Brad Belland
116	Jonas Heed
137	Victor Posa
158	John Reid
179	Richard LaPlante
200	Brad Hamilton
221	Ian Pound
242	Rick Braccia

1984
Pick
3	Ed Olczyk
45	Trent Yawney
66	Tommy Eriksson
90	Timo Lehkonen
101	Darin Sceviour
111	Chris Clifford
132	Mike Stapleton
153	Glen Greenough
174	Ralph DiFiorie
194	Joakim Persson
215	Bill Brown
224	David Mackey
235	Dan Williams

1983
Pick
18	Bruce Cassidy
39	Wayne Presley
59	Marc Bergevin
79	Tarek Howard
99	Kevin Robinson
115	Jari Torkki
119	Mark Lavarre
139	Scot Birnie
159	Kevin Paynter
179	Brian Noonan
199	Dominik Hasek
219	Steve Pepin

1982
Pick
7	Ken Yaremchuk
28	Rene Badeau
49	Tom McMurchy
70	Bill Watson
91	Brad Beck
112	Mark Hatcher
133	Jay Ness
154	Jeff Smith
175	Phil Patterson
196	Jim Camazzola
217	Mike James
238	Bob Andrea

General Managers' History

Major Frederic McLaughlin, 1926-27 to 1941-42; Bill Tobin, 1942-43 to 1953-54; Tommy Ivan, 1954-55 to 1976-77; Bob Pulford, 1977-78 to 1989-90; Mike Keenan, 1990-91 to 1991-92; Mike Keenan and Bob Pulford, 1992-93; Bob Pulford, 1993-94 to date.

General Manager

PULFORD, ROBERT JESSE (BOB)
Senior Vice President/General Manager, Chicago Blackhawks.
Born in Newton Robinson, Ont., March 31, 1936.

Bob Pulford has excelled at every aspect of the game of hockey: player, coach, general manager. In his playing career, which began in 1956, Pulford collected 643 points (281 goals, 362 assists) in 1,079 games. With the Toronto Maple Leafs in their glory days of the Sixties, Pulford earned a Stanley Cup ring in the 1962, 1963, 1964 and 1967. Known as an outstanding penalty killer, he registered four 20-or-more goal seasons and played in the NHL All-Star Game six times. To this date, he ranks among the Maple Leafs' top ten in goals, assists, points, and games played.

Retiring from active play, Pulford accepted the position of head coach with the Los Angeles Kings in 1972. The team developed rapidly under his direction, and in the 1974-75 season, the Kings posted a 42-17-21 record for 105 points. For his efforts, Pulford was named NHL coach of the year.

Following five successful seasons in L.A., Pulford joined the Chicago Blackhawks on July 6, 1977, as head coach and general manager. He promptly led the Blackhawks to a first place finish in the Smythe Division and again earned the honor of being named coach of the year as voted by *The Hockey News*. The Chicago Blackhawks have won eight division titles with Pulford as general manager and coach, and the team has made the playoffs in each of his 19 seasons with the Hawks.

In June of 1990, William Wirtz, president of the Chicago Blackhawks, appointed Pulford the club's senior vice president.

In 1967, Pulford became first president of the NHL Players' Association. Today, he plays a key role acting as alternate governor for the team and sitting on the advisory committee to league ownership. On June 21, 1991, he was inducted into the Hockey Hall of Fame.

Pulford also served as head coach of Team USA during the 1976 Canada Cup. In the 1991 Canada Cup, he served as co-general manager for Team USA.

Club Directory

United Center
1901 W. Madison St.
Chicago, IL 60612
Phone **312/455-7000**
Capacity: 20,500

President	William W. Wirtz
Executive Vice President	Arthur M. Wirtz, Jr.
Vice President & Assistant to the President	Thomas N. Ivan
Senior Vice President/General Manager	Robert J. Pulford
Vice President	Jack Davison
Assistant GM/Director of Player Personnel	Bob Murray
Head Coach	Craig Hartsburg
Assistant Coach	Lorne Henning
Assistant Coach	Newell Brown
Goaltending Consultant	Vladislav Tretiak
Special Assignments	Darryl Sutter
Video Coach	Rob Pulford
Chief Amateur Scout	Michel Dumas
Amateur Scouting Staff	Tim Higgins, Steve Richmond, Bruce Franklin, Dave Lucas, Steve Lyons, Jim Walker
European Scouts	Jan Blomgren, Lars Norrman
Director of Team Services	Phil Thibodeau
Executive Assistant	Cindy Bodnarchuk
Receptionist/Secretary	Vicki Littleton

Medical Staff
Club Doctors	Louis Kolb, Howard Baim
Head Trainer	Michael Gapski
Equipment Manager	Troy Parchman
Assistant Equipment Manager	Lou Varga
Strength and Conditioning Trainer	Mark Kling
Massage Therapist	Pawel Prylinski

Finance
Controller	Robert Rinkus
Assistant to the Controller	Penny Swenson
Staff Accountant	Dave Jorns
Accounting Secretary	Pat Dema

Public Relations/Marketing
Vice President of Marketing	Peter R. Wirtz
Executive Director of Public Relations	Jim DeMaria
Executive Director of Marketing/Merchandising	Jim Sofranko
Director of Corporate Sponsorships	Elliot Bell
Manager of Client Services	Kelly Bodnarchuk
Director of Community Relations/PR Assistant	Barbara Davidson
Director of Publications/PR Assistant	Brad Freeman
Director of Game Night Operations/Special Events	Tom Finks

Ticketing
Ticket Manager	Jim Bare
Team Photographers	Ray Grabowski, Rob Grabowski
Organist	Frank Pellico
Location of Press Box	North Side of United Center
Dimensions of Rink	200 feet by 85 feet
Club Colors	Red,Black & White
Uniforms	Home – Base color white trimmed with black & red; Away – Base color red trimmed with black & white
Radio Station	WMVP (AM 1000)
Television Station	SportsChannel
Broadcasters	Pat Foley, Dale Tallon, Darren Pang, Brian Davis, Jim Blaney, Bill Gardner

Coaching History

Pete Muldoon, 1926-27; Barney Stanley and Hugh Lehman, 1927-28; Herb Gardiner, 1928-29; Tom Shaughnessy and Bill Tobin, 1929-30; Dick Irvin, 1930-31; Dick Irvin and Bill Tobin, 1931-32; Emil Iverson, Godfrey Matheson and Tommy Gorman, 1932-33; Tommy Gorman, 1933-34; Clem Loughlin, 1934-35 to 1936-37; Bill Stewart, 1937-38; Bill Stewart and Paul Thompson, 1938-39; Paul Thompson, 1939-40 to 1943-44; Paul Thompson and Johnny Gottselig, 1944-45; Johnny Gottselig, 1945-46 to 1946-47; Johnny Gottselig and Charlie Conacher, 1947-48; Charlie Conacher, 1948-49, 1949-50; Ebbie Goodfellow, 1950-51 to 1951-52; Sid Abel, 1952-53 to 1953-54; Frank Eddolls, 1954-55; Dick Irvin, 1955-56; Tommy Ivan, 1956-57; Tommy Ivan and Rudy Pilous, 1957-58; Rudy Pilous, 1958-59 to 1962-63; Billy Reay, 1963-64 to 1975-76; Billy Reay and Bill White, 1976-77; Bob Pulford, 1977-78, 1978-79; Eddie Johnston, 1979-80; Keith Magnuson, 1980-81; Keith Magnuson and Bob Pulford, 1981-82; Orval Tessier, 1982-83 to 1983-84; Orval Tessier and Bob Pulford, 1984-85; Bob Pulford, 1985-86 to 1986-87; Bob Murdoch, 1987-88; Mike Keenan, 1988-89 to 1991-92; Darryl Sutter, 1992-93 to 1994-95; Craig Hartsburg, 1995-96 to date.

NHL Coaching Record

			Regular Season					Playoffs			
Season	Team	Games	W	L	T	%	Games	W	L	%
1972-73	Los Angeles	78	31	36	11	.468	....	....	....	....
1973-74	Los Angeles	78	33	33	12	.500	5	1	4	.200
1974-75	Los Angeles	80	42	17	21	.656	3	1	2	.333
1975-76	Los Angeles	80	38	33	9	.531	9	5	4	.556
1976-77	Los Angeles	80	34	31	15	.519	9	4	5	.444
1977-78	Chicago	80	32	29	19	.519	4	0	4	.000
1978-79	Chicago	80	29	36	15	.456	4	0	4	.000
1981-82	Chicago	28	13	13	2	.500	15	8	7	.533
1984-85	Chicago	27	16	7	4	.667	15	9	6	.600
1985-86	Chicago	80	39	33	8	.538	3	0	3	.000
1986-87	Chicago	80	29	37	14	.450	4	0	4	.000
	NHL Totals	**771**	**336**	**305**	**130**	**.520**	**71**	**28**	**43**	**.394**

Colorado Avalanche

1995-96 Results: 47W-25L-10T 104PTS. First, Pacific Division

Schedule

Oct.	Fri.	4	at St. Louis	Wed.	8	at New Jersey
	Sat.	5	at Dallas	Thur.	9	at Ottawa
	Tues.	8	San Jose	Sat.	11	at Toronto
	Thur.	10	Anaheim	Wed.	15	Tampa Bay
	Fri.	11	at Chicago	Mon.	20	at Florida
	Tues.	15	Edmonton	Tues.	21	at Tampa Bay
	Thur.	17	Florida	Thur.	23	at Pittsburgh
	Sat.	19	Vancouver	Sat.	25	at Boston*
	Tues.	22	at Calgary	Mon.	27	at Toronto
	Wed.	23	at Vancouver	Thur.	29	Los Angeles
	Sat.	26	at Edmonton	**Feb.** Sat.	1	at San Jose*
	Mon.	28	Washington	Sun.	2	at Anaheim
	Wed.	30	St. Louis	Sat.	8	Chicago*
Nov.	Sat.	2	Buffalo	Tues.	11	Los Angeles
	Sun.	3	at Anaheim	Thur.	13	at Phoenix
	Wed.	6	at San Jose	Sat.	15	at St. Louis*
	Fri.	8	at Phoenix	Tues.	18	Boston
	Sat.	9	Montreal	Fri.	21	at Edmonton
	Mon.	11	at NY Islanders	Sun.	23	Ottawa
	Wed.	13	at Detroit	Tues.	25	at Los Angeles
	Thur.	14	at Buffalo	Thur.	27	Dallas
	Sat.	16	Hartford	**Mar.** Sat.	1	Chicago*
	Wed.	20	Phoenix	Mon.	3	Vancouver
	Fri.	22	NY Islanders	Wed.	5	at Montreal
	Wed.	27	NY Rangers	Thur.	6	at Washington
	Sat.	30	New Jersey	Sun.	9	Anaheim
Dec.	Wed.	4	Edmonton	Wed.	12	Calgary
	Fri.	6	St. Louis	Fri.	14	Pittsburgh
	Sat.	7	at Los Angeles	Sun.	16	Detroit
	Wed.	11	at Vancouver	Tues.	18	Vancouver
	Sat.	14	at Calgary	Fri.	21	Anaheim
	Tues.	17	Detroit	Sun.	23	at Philadelphia
	Wed.	18	at Edmonton	Tues.	25	at Hartford
	Sat.	21	Toronto	Wed.	26	at Detroit
	Mon.	23	Calgary	Sat.	29	Toronto
	Sat.	28	at Los Angeles	**Apr.** Wed.	2	at Calgary
	Sun.	29	Dallas	Fri.	4	at San Jose
	Tues.	31	at Chicago	Sun.	6	Phoenix
Jan.	Thur.	2	Calgary	Wed.	9	San Jose
	Sat.	4	Philadelphia	Fri.	11	at Dallas
	Mon.	6	at NY Rangers	Sun.	13	Los Angeles

* Denotes afternoon game.

Joe Sakic reached the 50-goal plateau for the first time in his career with a third period marker on April 7, 1996, helping the Avalanche down the Dallas Stars 4-1.

Franchise date: June 22, 1979
Transferred from Quebec to Denver, June 21, 1995

PACIFIC DIVISION

18th NHL Season

Year-by-Year Record

		Home			Road			Overall							
Season	GP	W	L	T	W	L	T	W	L	T	GF	GA	Pts.	Finished	Playoff Result
1995-96	82	24	10	7	23	15	3	47	25	10	326	240	104	1st, Pacific Div.	Won Stanley Cup
1994-95*	48	19	1	4	11	12	1	30	13	5	185	134	65	1st, Northeast Div.	Lost Conf. Quarter-Final
1993-94*	84	19	17	6	15	25	2	34	42	8	277	292	76	5th, Northeast Div.	Out of Playoffs
1992-93*	84	23	17	2	24	10	8	47	27	10	351	300	104	2nd, Adams Div.	Lost Div. Semi-Final
1991-92*	80	18	19	3	2	29	9	20	48	12	255	318	52	5th, Adams Div.	Out of Playoffs
1990-91*	80	9	23	8	7	27	6	16	50	14	236	354	46	5th, Adams Div.	Out of Playoffs
1989-90*	80	8	26	6	4	35	1	12	61	7	240	407	31	5th, Adams Div.	Out of Playoffs
1988-89*	80	16	20	4	11	26	3	27	46	7	269	342	61	5th, Adams Div.	Out of Playoffs
1987-88*	80	15	23	2	17	20	3	32	43	5	271	306	69	5th, Adams Div.	Out of Playoffs
1986-87*	80	20	13	7	11	26	3	31	39	10	267	276	72	4th, Adams Div.	Lost Div. Final
1985-86*	80	23	13	4	20	18	2	43	31	6	330	289	92	1st, Adams Div.	Lost Div. Semi-Final
1984-85*	80	24	12	4	17	18	5	41	30	9	323	275	91	2nd, Adams Div.	Lost Conf. Championship
1983-84*	80	24	11	5	18	17	5	42	28	10	360	278	94	3rd, Adams Div.	Lost Div. Final
1982-83*	80	23	10	7	11	24	5	34	34	12	343	336	80	4th, Adams Div.	Lost Div. Semi-Final
1981-82*	80	24	13	3	9	18	13	33	31	16	356	345	82	4th, Adams Div.	Lost Conf. Championship
1980-81*	80	18	11	11	12	21	7	30	32	18	314	318	78	4th, Adams Div.	Lost Prelim. Round
1979-80*	80	17	16	7	8	28	4	25	44	11	248	313	61	5th, Adams Div.	Out of Playoffs

* Quebec Nordiques

1996-97 Player Personnel

FORWARDS	HT	WT	S	Place of Birth	Date	1995-96 Club
BABENKO, Yuri	6-0	185	L	Penza, USSR	1/2/78	Soviet Wings
BEAUDOIN, Nic	6-3	205	L	Ottawa, Ont.	12/25/76	Detroit (OHL)
CORBET, Rene	6-0	187	L	Victoriaville, Que.	6/25/73	Colorado-Cornwall
DEADMARSH, Adam	6-0	195	R	Trail, B.C.	5/10/75	Colorado
FORSBERG, Peter	6-0	190	L	Ornskoldsvik, Sweden	7/20/73	Colorado
HIRVONEN, Tomi	5-11	180	L	Tampere, Finland	1/11/77	Ilves-Koo-Vee-Ilves
KAMENSKY, Valeri	6-2	198	R	Voskresensk, USSR	4/18/66	Colorado
KEANE, Mike	5-10	185	R	Winnipeg, Man.	5/29/67	Montreal-Colorado
LACROIX, Eric	6-1	205	L	Montreal, Que.	7/15/71	Los Angeles
LEMIEUX, Claude	6-1	215	R	Buckingham, Que.	7/16/65	Colorado
MARHA, Josef	6-0	176	L	Havlickuv Brod, Czech.	6/2/76	Colorado-Cornwall
MATTE, Christian	5-11	166	R	Hull, Que.	1/20/75	Cornwall
RICCI, Mike	6-0	190	L	Scarborough, Ont.	10/27/71	Colorado
SAKIC, Joe	5-11	185	L	Burnaby, B.C.	7/7/69	Colorado
SIMON, Chris	6-3	219	L	Wawa, Ont.	1/30/72	Colorado
VEILLEUX, Eric	5-7	148	L	Quebec, Que.	2/20/72	Cornwall
WILSON, Landon	6-2	202	R	St. Louis, MO	3/13/75	Colorado-Cornwall
YELLE, Stephane	6-1	162	L	Ottawa, Ont.	5/9/74	Colorado
YOUNG, Scott	6-0	190	R	Clinton, MA	10/1/67	Colorado
DEFENSEMEN						
BELAK, Wade	6-4	213	R	Saskatoon, Sask.	7/3/76	Saskatoon-Cornwall
BRENNAN, Rich	6-2	200	R	Schenectady, NY	11/26/72	Brantford-Cornwall
FOOTE, Adam	6-1	202	R	Toronto, Ont.	7/10/71	Colorado
GUSAROV, Alexei	6-3	185	L	Leningrad, USSR	7/8/64	Colorado
KLEMM, Jon	6-3	200	R	Cranbrook, B.C.	1/8/70	Colorado
KRUPP, Uwe	6-6	235	R	Cologne, West Germany	6/24/65	Colorado
LEFEBVRE, Sylvain	6-2	205	L	Richmond, Que.	10/14/67	Colorado
LESCHYSHYN, Curtis	6-1	205	L	Thompson, Man.	9/21/69	Colorado
MILLER, Aaron	6-3	197	R	Buffalo, NY	8/11/71	Colorado-Cornwall
MYRVOLD, Anders	6-1	178	L	Lorenskog, Norway	8/12/75	Colorado-Cornwall
OZOLINSH, Sandis	6-1	195	L	Riga, Latvia	8/3/72	San Francisco-San Jose-Colorado
SMITH, Dan	5-11	180	L	Vernon, B.C.	5/2/76	Unavailable
TREPANIER, Pascal	6-0	205	R	Gaspe, Que.	4/9/73	Cornwall

GOALTENDERS	HT	WT	C	Place of Birth	Date	1995-96 Club
DENIS, Marc	6-0	188	L	Montreal, Que.	8/1/77	Chicoutimi
FISCHER, Kai	5-11	176	L	Forst, Germany	3/25/77	Dusseldorf
PETRUK, Randy	5-9	178	R	Cranbrook, B.C.	4/23/78	Kamloops
ROY, Patrick	6-0	192	L	Quebec City, Que.	10/5/65	Montreal-Colorado

General Manager

LACROIX, PIERRE
President of Hockey Operations and General Manager, Colorado Avalanche. Born in Montreal, Que., August 3, 1948.

Pierre Lacroix was appointed to the general manager's post on May 24, 1994 after 21 years as a respected player agent. In his first season (1994-95) as general manager, his leadership was instrumental in moving the team from 11th to second place in the NHL. Lacroix's second season began with the club's move to Denver. He set out to improve the team and did so through acquisitions that brought Claude Lemieux, Sandis Ozolinsh, Patrick Roy and Mike Keane to Colorado. The revamped Avs finished atop the Pacific Division and went on to win the Stanley Cup. He was named NHL Executive of the Year by *The Hockey News* and became president of the club's hockey operations in August, 1995.

Lacroix and his wife Colombe have two children. Martin (26) is a player agent. Eric (25) plays left wing for the Avalanche.

Coach

CRAWFORD, MARC
Coach, Colorado Avalanche. Born in Belleville, Ont., February 13, 1961.

Marc Crawford became the tenth head coach in franchise history on July 6th, 1994. In 1994-95, he led the franchise (Quebec) to second place overall in the NHL and became the first rookie coach to win the Jack Adams Award.

In June 1996, he led the Avalanche to the Stanley Cup, becoming the first coach to lead a team to the championship in its first year in a new city.

Crawford played seven seasons with the Vancouver Canucks beginning in 1981. He became general manager and coach of the Cornwall Royals in the Ontario Hockey League in 1989 and joined the Maple Leafs organization as coach of Toronto's AHL farm club two years later. He reached the Calder Cup finals in his first AHL season and was named top coach in the league in 1992.

One of nine children, his father and two of his brothers also played pro hockey. Crawford and his wife Helene have two children, Dylan and Kaitlin.

Coaching Record

		Regular Season					Playoffs			
Season	Team	Games	W	L	T	%	Games	W	L	%
1989-90	Cornwall (OHL)	66	24	38	4	.394	6	2	4	.333
1990-91	Cornwall (OHL)	66	23	42	1	.356	....	....	....	....
1991-92	St. John's (AHL)	80	39	29	12	.562	16	11	5	.688
1992-93	St. John's (AHL)	80	41	26	13	.594	9	4	5	.444
1993-94	St. John's (AHL)	80	45	23	12	.638	11	6	5	.545
1994-95	**Quebec (NHL)**	**48**	**30**	**13**	**5**	**.677**	**6**	**2**	**4**	**.333**
1995-96	**Colorado (NHL)**	**82**	**47**	**25**	**10**	**.634**	**22**	**16**	**6**	**.727***
	NHL Totals	**130**	**77**	**38**	**15**	**.650**	**28**	**18**	**10**	**.643**

* Stanley Cup win.

1995-96 Scoring

* – rookie

Regular Season

Pos	#	Player	Team	GP	G	A	Pts	+/–	PIM	PP	SH	GW	GT	S	%
C	19	Joe Sakic	COL	82	51	69	120	14	44	17	6	7	1	339	15.0
C	21	Peter Forsberg	COL	82	30	86	116	26	47	7	3	3	0	217	13.8
L	13	Valeri Kamensky	COL	81	38	47	85	14	85	18	1	5	0	220	17.3
R	22	Claude Lemieux	COL	79	39	32	71	14	117	9	2	10	0	315	12.4
R	48	Scott Young	COL	81	21	39	60	2	50	7	0	5	0	229	9.2
D	8	Sandis Ozolinsh	S.J.	7	1	3	4	2	4	1	0	0	0	21	4.8
			COL	66	13	37	50	0	50	7	1	1	1	145	9.0
			TOTAL	73	14	40	54	2	54	8	1	1	1	166	8.4
C	18	Adam Deadmarsh	COL	78	21	27	48	20	142	3	0	2	0	151	13.9
L	12	Chris Simon	COL	64	16	18	34	10	250	4	0	1	0	105	15.2
C	26	* Stephane Yelle	COL	71	13	14	27	15	30	0	2	1	0	93	14.0
R	25	Mike Keane	MTL	18	0	7	7	–6	6	0	0	0	0	17	0.0
			COL	55	10	10	20	1	40	0	2	2	0	67	14.9
			TOTAL	73	10	17	27	–5	46	0	2	2	0	84	11.9
D	6	Craig Wolanin	COL	75	7	20	27	25	50	0	3	0	0	73	9.6
C	9	Mike Ricci	COL	62	6	21	27	1	52	3	0	1	0	73	8.2
C	10	Troy Murray	COL	63	7	14	21	15	22	0	0	1	0	36	19.4
D	5	Alexei Gusarov	COL	65	5	15	20	29	56	0	0	0	0	42	11.9
D	7	Curtis Leschyshyn	COL	77	4	15	19	32	73	0	0	1	0	76	5.3
C	14	Dave Hannan	BUF	57	6	10	16	2	30	1	1	2	0	40	15.0
			COL	4	1	0	1	1	2	0	0	0	0	1	100.0
			TOTAL	61	7	10	17	3	32	1	1	2	0	41	17.1
D	52	Adam Foote	COL	73	5	11	16	27	88	1	0	1	0	49	10.2
D	2	Sylvain Lefebvre	COL	75	5	11	16	26	49	2	0	0	0	115	4.3
D	24	* Jon Klemm	COL	56	3	12	15	12	20	0	1	1	0	61	4.9
L	20	Rene Corbet	COL	33	3	6	9	10	33	0	0	0	0	35	8.6
L	16	Warren Rychel	COL	52	6	2	8	6	147	0	0	1	0	45	13.3
D	4	Uwe Krupp	COL	6	0	3	3	4	4	0	0	0	0	9	0.0
R	38	* Paul Brousseau	COL	8	1	1	2	1	2	0	0	0	1	10	10.0
R	14	* Landon Wilson	COL	7	1	0	1	3	6	0	0	0	0	6	16.7
C	15	* Josef Marha	COL	2	0	1	1	1	0	0	0	0	0	2	0.0
D	55	* Anders Myrvold	COL	4	0	1	1	–2	6	0	0	0	0	4	0.0
G	35	Stephane Fiset	COL	37	0	1	1	0	2	0	0	0	0	0	0.0
D	31	* Aaron Miller	COL	5	0	0	0	0	0	0	0	0	0	2	0.0
G	33	Patrick Roy	MTL	22	0	0	0	0	6	0	0	0	0	0	0.0
			COL	39	0	0	0	0	4	0	0	0	0	0	0.0
			TOTAL	61	0	0	0	0	10	0	0	0	0	0	0.0

Goaltending

No.	Goaltender	GPI	Mins	Avg	W	L	T	EN	SO	GA	SA	S%
33	Patrick Roy	39	2305	2.68	22	15	1	3	1	103	1130	.909
35	Stephane Fiset	37	2107	2.93	22	6	7	3	1	103	1012	.898
41	Jocelyn Thibault	10	558	3.01	3	4	2	0	0	28	222	.874
	Totals	**82**	**4982**	**2.89**	**47**	**25**	**10**	**6**	**2**	**240**	**2370**	**.899**

Playoffs

Pos	#	Player	Team	GP	G	A	Pts	+/–	PIM	PP	SH	GW	OT	S	%
C	19	Joe Sakic	COL	22	18	16	34	10	14	6	0	6	2	98	18.4
L	13	Valeri Kamensky	COL	22	10	12	22	11	28	3	0	2	0	56	17.9
C	21	Peter Forsberg	COL	22	10	11	21	10	18	3	0	1	0	50	20.0
D	8	Sandis Ozolinsh	COL	22	5	14	19	5	16	2	0	1	1	52	9.6
C	9	Mike Ricci	COL	22	6	11	17	–1	18	3	0	1	0	31	19.4
C	18	Adam Deadmarsh	COL	22	5	12	17	8	25	1	0	0	0	40	12.5
D	4	Uwe Krupp	COL	22	4	12	16	5	33	1	0	2	1	38	10.5
R	48	Scott Young	COL	22	3	12	15	6	10	0	0	0	0	61	4.9
R	22	Claude Lemieux	COL	19	5	7	12	5	55	3	0	0	0	81	6.2
D	5	Alexei Gusarov	COL	21	0	9	9	13	12	0	0	0	0	15	0.0
L	20	Rene Corbet	COL	8	3	2	5	3	2	1	0	1	0	9	33.3
R	25	Mike Keane	COL	22	3	2	5	1	16	0	0	1	1	22	13.6
C	26	* Stephane Yelle	COL	22	1	4	5	2	8	0	1	0	0	24	4.2
D	2	Sylvain Lefebvre	COL	22	0	5	5	6	12	0	0	0	0	22	0.0
D	52	Adam Foote	COL	22	1	3	4	11	36	0	0	0	0	20	5.0
D	24	* Jon Klemm	COL	15	2	1	3	6	0	1	0	0	0	11	18.2
L	12	Chris Simon	COL	12	1	2	3	–2	11	0	0	0	0	9	11.1
D	7	Curtis Leschyshyn	COL	17	1	2	3	4	8	0	0	0	0	9	11.1
C	14	Dave Hannan	COL	13	0	2	2	3	2	0	0	0	0	2	0.0
D	6	Craig Wolanin	COL	7	1	0	1	2	8	0	0	1	0	5	20.0
L	16	Warren Rychel	COL	12	1	0	1	4	23	0	0	0	0	4	25.0
G	35	Stephane Fiset	COL	1	0	0	0	0	0	0	0	0	0	0	0.0
C	10	Troy Murray	COL	8	0	0	0	–4	19	0	0	0	0	6	0.0
G	33	Patrick Roy	COL	22	0	0	0	0	0	0	0	0	0	0	0.0

Goaltending

No.	Goaltender	GPI	Mins	Avg	W	L	EN	SO	GA	SA	S%
35	Stephane Fiset	1	1	.00	0	0	0	0	0	0	.000
33	Patrick Roy	22	1454	2.10	16	6	0	3	51	649	.921
	Totals	**22**	**1460**	**2.10**	**16**	**6**	**0**	**3**	**51**	**649**	**.921**

General Managers' History

Maurice Filion, 1979-80 to 1987-88; Martin Madden 1988-89; Martin Madden and Maurice Filion, 1989-90; Pierre Page, 1990-91 to 1993-94; Pierre Lacroix, 1994-95 to date.

Coaching History

Jacques Demers, 1979-80; Maurice Filion and Michel Bergeron, 1980-81; Michel Bergeron, 1981-82 to 1986-87; André Savard and Ron Lapointe, 1987-88; Ron Lapointe and Jean Perron, 1988-89; Michel Bergeron, 1989-90; Dave Chambers, 1990-91; Dave Chambers and Pierre Page, 1991-92; Pierre Page, 1992-93 to 1993-94; Marc Crawford, 1994-95 to date.

Club Records

Team

(Figures in brackets for season records are games played; records for fewest points, wins, ties, losses, goals, goals against are for 70 or more games)

Most Points	104	1992-93 (84), 1995-96 (82)
Most Wins	47	1992-93 (84), 1995-96 (82)
Most Ties	18	1980-81 (80)
Most Losses	61	1989-90 (80)
Most Goals	360	1983-84 (80)
Most Goals Against	407	1989-90 (80)
Fewest Points	31	1989-90 (80)
Fewest Wins	12	1989-90 (80)
Fewest Ties	5	1987-88 (80)
Fewest Losses	25	1995-96 (82)
Fewest Goals	236	1990-91 (80)
Fewest Goals Against	240	1995-96 (82)

Longest Winning Streak
Overall .... 7 Four times
Home .... 10 Nov. 26/83-Jan. 10/84, Mar. 6-Apr. 16/95
Away .... 5 Feb. 28-Mar. 24/86

Longest Undefeated Streak
Overall .... 11 Mar. 10-31/81 (7 wins, 4 ties)
Home .... 14 Nov. 19/83-Jan. 21/84 (11 wins, 3 ties)
Away .... 8 Feb. 17/81-Mar. 22/81 (6 wins, 2 ties)

Longest Losing Streak
Overall .... 14 Oct. 21-Nov. 19/90
Home .... 8 Oct. 21-Nov. 24/90
Away .... 18 Jan. 18-Apr. 1/90

Longest Winless Streak
Overall .... 17 Oct. 21-Nov. 25/90 (15 losses, 2 ties)
Home .... 11 Nov. 14-Dec. 26/89 (7 losses, 4 ties)
Away .... 33 Oct. 8/91-Feb. 27/92 (25 losses, 8 ties)

Most Shutouts, Season	6	1985-86 (80)
Most PIM, Season	2,104	1989-90 (80)
Most Goals, Game	12	Feb. 1/83 (Hfd. 3 at Que. 12), Oct. 20/84 (Que. 12 at Tor. 3)

Individual

Most Seasons	11	Michel Goulet
Most Games	813	Michel Goulet
Most Goals, Career	456	Michel Goulet
Most Assists, Career	668	Peter Stastny
Most Points, Career	1,048	Peter Stastny (380G, 668A)
Most PIM, Career	1,545	Dale Hunter
Most Shutouts, Career	6	Mario Gosselin, Stephane Fiset

Longest Consecutive
Games Streak .... 312 Dale Hunter (Oct. 9/80-Mar. 13/84)
Most Goals, Season .... 57 Michel Goulet (1982-83)
Most Assists, Season .... 93 Peter Stastny (1981-82)
Most Points, Season .... 139 Peter Stastny (1981-82; 46G, 93A)
Most PIM, Season .... 301 Gord Donnelly (1987-88)
Most Points, Defenseman, Season .... 82 Steve Duchesne (1992-93; 20G, 62A)
Most Points, Center, Season .... 139 Peter Stastny (1981-82; 46G, 93A)
Most Points, Right Wing, Season .... 103 Jacques Richard (1980-81; 52G, 51A)
Most Points, Left Wing, Season .... 121 Michel Goulet (1983-84; 56G, 65A)
Most Points, Rookie, Season .... 109 Peter Stastny (1980-81; 39G, 70A)

Most Shutouts, Season	4	Clint Malarchuk (1985-86)
Most Goals, Game	5	Mats Sundin (Mar. 5/92), Mike Ricci (Feb. 17/94)
Most Assists, Game	5	Anton Stastny (Feb. 22/81), Michel Goulet (Jan. 3/84), Owen Nolan (Mar. 5/92), Mike Ricci (Dec. 12/92)
Most Points, Game	8	Peter Stastny (Feb. 22/81; 4G, 4A), Anton Stastny (Feb. 22/81; 3G, 5A)

Records include Quebec Nordiques, 1979-80 through 1994-95.

Retired Numbers

3	J.C. Tremblay	1972-1979
8	Marc Tardif	1979-1983
16	Michel Goulet	1979-1990

Captains' History

Marc Tardif, 1979-80, 1980-81; Robbie Ftorek and Andre Dupont, 1981-82; Mario Marois, 1982-83 to 1984-85; Mario Marois and Peter Stastny, 1985-86; Peter Stastny, 1986-87 to 1989-90; Joe Sakic and Steven Finn, 1990-91; Mike Hough, 1991-92; Joe Sakic, 1992-93 to date.

All-time Record vs. Other Clubs

Regular Season

		At Home						On Road						Total				
	GP	W	L	T	GF	GA	PTS	GP	W	L	T	GF	GA	PTS	GP	W	L	T	GF	GA	PTS
Anaheim	4	3	1	0	16	12	6	4	1	3	0	5	13	2	8	4	4	0	21	25	8
Boston	58	19	33	6	211	253	44	56	19	29	8	177	223	46	114	38	62	14	388	476	90
Buffalo	57	29	18	10	218	182	68	57	16	33	8	185	230	40	114	45	51	18	403	412	108
Calgary	25	9	9	7	108	97	25	25	6	13	6	80	108	18	50	15	22	13	188	205	43
Chicago	24	11	9	4	105	94	26	25	8	15	2	84	101	18	49	19	24	6	189	195	44
Dallas	25	16	6	3	114	70	35	24	9	13	2	82	90	20	49	25	19	5	196	160	55
Detroit	25	13	9	3	101	91	29	24	9	14	1	79	98	19	49	22	23	4	180	189	48
Edmonton	25	9	14	2	106	118	20	24	6	17	1	73	129	13	49	15	31	3	179	247	33
Florida	4	1	1	2	13	14	4	5	4	1	0	21	13	8	9	5	2	2	34	27	12
Hartford	58	34	17	7	248	176	75	56	21	24	11	195	193	53	114	55	41	18	443	369	128
Los Angeles	24	11	10	3	104	98	25	25	9	14	2	86	110	20	49	20	24	5	190	208	45
Montreal	58	28	26	4	195	209	60	57	9	36	12	178	244	33	115	40	62	13	373	453	93
New Jersey	27	14	10	3	106	84	31	29	12	15	2	105	122	26	56	26	25	5	211	206	57
NY Islanders	27	15	10	2	104	87	32	26	10	15	1	90	111	21	53	25	25	3	194	198	53
NY Rangers	28	15	10	3	121	108	33	26	6	17	3	74	112	15	54	21	27	6	195	220	48
Ottawa	9	9	0	0	51	23	18	11	6	3	2	56	36	14	20	15	3	2	107	59	32
Philadelphia	27	9	9	9	101	99	27	28	6	20	2	76	109	14	55	15	29	11	177	208	41
Pittsburgh	26	13	12	1	120	107	27	29	10	15	4	119	127	24	55	23	27	5	239	234	51
St. Louis	24	11	10	3	87	81	25	24	5	17	2	78	111	12	48	16	27	5	165	192	37
San Jose	6	5	1	0	37	17	10	7	5	2	0	38	27	10	13	10	3	0	75	44	20
Tampa Bay	6	4	1	1	29	16	9	6	1	5	0	16	23	2	12	5	6	1	45	39	11
Toronto	25	15	5	5	101	75	35	25	11	12	2	106	90	24	50	26	17	7	207	165	59
Vancouver	25	9	11	5	71	74	23	25	10	11	4	107	105	24	50	19	22	9	178	179	47
Washington	27	11	12	4	90	103	26	27	9	15	3	87	110	21	54	20	27	7	177	213	47
Winnipeg	25	11	11	3	100	102	25	24	9	10	5	97	98	23	49	20	21	8	197	200	48
Totals	**669**	**324**	**255**	**90**	**2657**	**2390**	**738**	**669**	**220**	**369**	**80**	**2294**	**2733**	**520**	**1338**	**544**	**624**	**170**	**4951**	**5123**	**1258**

Playoffs

	Series	W	L	GP	W	L	T	GF	GA	Last Mtg.	Round	Result
Boston	2	1	1	11	5	6	0	36	37	1983	DSF	L 1-3
Buffalo	2	2	0	8	6	2	0	35	27	1985	DSF	W 3-2
Chicago	1	1	0	6	4	2	0	21	14	1996	CSF	W 4-2
Detroit	1	1	0	6	4	2	0	20	16	1996	CF	W 4-2
Florida	1	1	0	4	4	0	0	15	4	1996	F	W 4-0
Hartford	2	1	1	9	4	5	0	34	35	1987	DSF	L 2-4
Montreal	5	2	3	31	14	17	0	85	105	1993	DSF	L 2-4
NY Islanders	1	0	1	4	0	4	0	9	18	1982	CF	L 0-4
NY Rangers	1	0	1	6	2	4	0	19	25	1995	CQF	L 2-4
Philadelphia	2	0	2	11	4	7	0	29	39	1985	CF	L 2-4
Vancouver	1	1	0	6	4	2	0	24	17	1996	CQF	W 4-2
Totals	**19**	**10**	**9**	**102**	**51**	**51**	**0**	**327**	**337**			

Playoff Results 1996-92

Year	Round	Opponent	Result	GF	GA
1996	**F**	**Florida**	**W 4-0**	**15**	**4**
	CF	Detroit	W 4-2	20	16
	CSF	Chicago	W 4-2	21	14
	CQF	Vancouver	W 4-2	24	17
1995	CQF	NY Rangers	L 2-4	19	25
1993	DSF	Montreal	L 2-4	16	19

Abbreviations: Round: F – Final;
CF – conference final; **CQF** – conference quarter-final;
CSF – conference semi-final; **DF** – division final;
DSF – division semi-final; **SF** – semi-final;
QF – quarter-final; **PR** – preliminary round.

Calgary totals include Atlanta, 1979-80. Colorado totals include Quebec, 1979-80 to 1994-95.
Dallas totals include Minnesota, 1979-80 to 1992-93. New Jersey totals include Colorado Rockies, 1979-80 to 1981-82.

1995-96 Results

Oct.	6		Detroit	3-2	9	at Boston	3-0
	7	at	Los Angeles	2-4	10	Florida	4-4
	9		Pittsburgh	6-6	14	Calgary	4-4
	11		Boston	3-1	16	at Pittsburgh	5-2
	13	at	Washington	1-3	17	at Detroit	2-3
	14	at	St. Louis	1-4	22	NY Islanders	4-3
	18		Washington	4-2	25	Vancouver	2-2
	23		Anaheim	3-1	27	at San Jose	4-3
	25	at	Calgary	3-2	31	at Anaheim	1-2
	27		Buffalo	5-4	**Feb.** 1	Winnipeg	6-4
	30	at	Dallas	6-1	3	NY Rangers	7-1
Nov.	1		Calgary	6-1	5	Montreal	2-5
	3	at	Winnipeg	5-2	7	Tampa Bay	4-4
	5	at	Chicago	7-3	9	Hartford	2-3
	9		Dallas	1-1	11	at Philadelphia	5-3
	11	at	Vancouver	8-4	15	at Tampa Bay	2-4
	15	at	Anaheim	3-7	16	at Florida	5-4
	17	at	Calgary	5-3	19	Edmonton	7-5
	18		Calgary	5-2	23	Los Angeles	6-2
	20	at	Edmonton	3-3	25	Ottawa	4-2
	22		Chicago	6-2	26	Anaheim	3-2
	25	at	Montreal	2-2	29	at Chicago	3-4
	28	at	NY Islanders	7-3	**Mar.** 1	Chicago	5-3
	29	at	New Jersey	3-4	3	Toronto	4-0
Dec.	1	at	NY Rangers	3-5	5	San Jose	3-5
	3		Dallas	6-7	8	Detroit	2-4
	5		San Jose	12-2	9	at Vancouver	7-5
	7		Phoenix	3-5	13	at Anaheim	0-4
	9	at	Ottawa	7-3	17	Edmonton	8-1
	11	at	Toronto	5-1	19	at Vancouver	4-3
	13	at	Buffalo	3-4	20	at Los Angeles	5-2
	15	at	Hartford	2-4	22	at Detroit	0-7
	18		Vancouver	2-4	24	at Winnipeg	5-2
	20	at	Edmonton	4-1	27	Winnipeg	1-3
	22		St. Louis	2-1	28	at San Jose	8-3
	23	at	Los Angeles	2-2	**Apr.** 3	St. Louis	3-6
	26	at	San Jose	5-1	5	San Jose	5-1
	29		Toronto	3-2	7	at Dallas	4-1
Jan.	3		New Jersey	0-1	10	Anaheim	7-3
	5		Philadelphia	2-2	11	at St. Louis	3-2
	6	at	Toronto	2-5	14	Los Angeles	4-5

Entry Draft
Selections 1996-82

1996
Pick
25 Peter Ratchuk
51 Yuri Babenko
79 Mark Parrish
98 Ben Storey
107 Randy Petruk
134 Luke Curtin
146 Brian Willsie
160 Kai Fischer
167 Dan Hinote
176 Samuel Pahlsson
188 Roman Pylner
214 Matthew Scorsune
240 Justin Clark

1995
Pick
25 Marc Denis
51 Nic Beaudoin
77 John Tripp
81 Tomi Kallio
159 Brent Johnson
155 John Cirjak
181 Dan Smith
207 Tomi Hirvonen
228 Chris George

1994
Pick
12 Wade Belak
22 Jeffrey Kealty
35 Josef Marha
61 Sebastien Bety
72 Chris Drury
87 Milan Hejduk
113 Tony Tuzzolino
139 Nicholas Windsor
165 Calvin Elfring
191 Jay Bertsch
217 Tim Thomas
243 Chris Pittman
285 Steven Low

1993
Pick
10 Jocelyn Thibault
14 Adam Deadmarsh
49 Ashley Buckberger
75 Bill Pierce
101 Ryan Tocher
127 Anders Myrvold
137 Nicholas Checco
153 Christian Matte
179 David Ling
205 Petr Franek
231 Vincent Auger
257 Mark Pivetz
283 John Hillman

1992
Pick
4 Todd Warriner
28 Paul Brousseau
29 Tuomas Gronman
52 Emmanuel Fernandez
76 Ian McIntyre
100 Charlie Wasley
124 Paxton Schulte
148 Martin LePage
172 Mike Jickling
196 Steve Passmore
220 Anson Carter
244 Aaron Ellis

1991
Pick
1 Eric Lindros
24 Rene Corbet
46 Richard Brennan
68 Dave Karpa
90 Patrick Labrecque
103 Bill Lindsay
134 Mikael Johansson
156 Janne Laukkanen
157 Aaron Asp
178 Adam Bartell
188 Brent Brekke
200 Paul Koch
222 Doug Friedman
244 Eric Meloche

1990
Pick
1 Owen Nolan
22 Ryan Hughes
43 Bradley Zavisha
106 Jeff Parrott
127 Dwayne Norris
148 Andrei Kovalenko
158 Alexander Karpovtsev
169 Pat Mazzoli
190 Scott Davis
211 Mika Stromberg
232 Wade Klippenstein

1989
Pick
1 Mats Sundin
22 Adam Foote
43 Stephane Morin
54 John Tanner
68 Niklas Andersson
76 Eric Dubois
85 Kevin Kaiser
106 Dan Lambert
127 Sergei Mylnikov
148 Paul Krake
169 Viacheslav Bykov
190 Andrei Khomutov
211 Byron Witkowski
232 Noel Rahn

1988
Pick
3 Curtis Leschyshyn
5 Daniel Dore
24 Stephane Fiset
45 Petri Aaltonen
66 Darin Kimble
87 Stephane Venne
108 Ed Ward
129 Valeri Kamensky
150 Sakari Lindfors
171 Dan Wiebe
213 Alexei Gusarov
234 Claude Lapointe

1987
Pick
9 Bryan Fogarty
15 Joe Sakic
51 Jim Sprott
72 Kip Miller
93 Rob Mendel
114 Garth Snow
135 Tim Hanus
156 Jake Enebak
177 Jaroslav Sevcik
183 Ladislav Tresl
198 Darren Nauss
219 Mike Williams

1986
Pick
18 Ken McRae
39 Jean-Marc Routhier
41 Stephane Guerard
81 Ron Tugnutt
102 Gerald Bzdel
117 Scott White
123 Morgan Samuelsson
134 Mark Vermette
144 Jean-Francois Nault
165 Keith Miller
186 Pierre Millier
207 Chris Lappin
228 Martin Latreille
249 Sean Boudreault

1985
Pick
15 David Latta
36 Jason Lafreniere
57 Max Middendorf
65 Peter Massey
78 David Espe
99 Bruce Major
120 Andy Akervik
141 Mike Oliverio
162 Mario Brunetta
183 Brit Peer
204 Tom Sasso
225 Gary Murphy
246 Jean Bois

1984
Pick
15 Trevor Stienburg
36 Jeff Brown
57 Steve Finn
78 Terry Perkins
120 Darren Cota
141 Henrik Cedergren
162 Jyrki Maki
183 Guy Ouellette
203 Ken Quinney
244 Peter Loob

1983
Pick
32 Yves Heroux
52 Bruce Bell
54 Iiro Jarvi
92 Luc Guenette
112 Brad Walcott
132 Craig Mack
152 Tommy Albelin
172 Wayne Groulx
192 Scott Shaunessy
232 Bo Berglund
239 Jindrich Kokrment

1982
Pick
13 David Shaw
34 Paul Gillis
55 Mario Gosselin
76 Jiri Lala
97 Phil Stanger
131 Daniel Poudrier
181 Mike Hough
202 Vincent Lukac
223 Andre Martin
244 Jozef Lukac
248 Jan Jasko

Club Directory

McNichols Sports Arena
1635 Clay Street
Denver, Colorado 80204
Phone **303/893-6700**
FAX 303/893-0614
Capacity: 16,061

Owner . . . . Ascent Entertainment Group, Inc.
Governor and Chairman. . . . . Charlie Lyons
Alternate Governor/President . . . . Pierre Lacroix

Hockey Operations
President and General Manager/
  Hockey Operations . . . . Pierre Lacroix
Executive Assistant . . . . Charlotte Grahame
Assistant General Manager. . . . . Francois Giguere
Administrative Assistant . . . . Jill Darnell
Head Coach . . . . Marc Crawford
Assistant Coach . . . . Joel Quenneville
Assistant Coach . . . . Jacques Cloutier
Video Coach. . . . . Paul Fixter
Director of Media Relations and Team Services . . Jean Martineau
Assistant Director of Media Relations . . . . Sally Christgau
Media Relations Assistant . . . . Jennifer Hofmeister
Strength and Conditioning Coach . . . . Skip Allen
Director of Player Development . . . . Michel Goulet
Chief Scout. . . . . Dave Draper
Scouts. . . . . Yvon Gendron, Jan Janda, John Gill,
Brian MacDonald, Don McKenney, Orval
Tessier, Don Paarup
Pro Scouts. . . . . Brad Smith, Shawn Dineen
Athletic Trainer. . . . . Pat Karns
Kinesiologist . . . . Matthew Sokolowski
Massage Therapist . . . . Leo Vyssokov
Equipment Manager. . . . . Rob McLean
Assistant Equipment Managers. . . . . Mike Kramer, Wayne Fleming
Team Physician/Orthopedist . . . . Andrew Parker
Team Physician/Cardiologist . . . . Steve Freidrich
Team Dentist . . . . Steve Barker

Business Operations
President – Ascent Sports . . . . Ellen Robinson
Executive Assistant . . . . Mary Draper
Senior Vice President/Business Affairs. . . . . Steve Story
Executive Assistant . . . . Jo Ann Kratz
Vice President/Sales and Marketing . . . . Mimi Brown
Director of Community Relations . . . . Kathleen MacDonald
General Counsel . . . . Ron Sally
Special Assistant to General Counsel . . . . Sharon Chinn
Vice President/Broadcasting . . . . Lou Personett

Finance
Vice President/Chief Financial Officer . . . . Mark Waggoner
Director of Accounting . . . . Jerry Girkin
Assistant Controller . . . . Greg Sherman
Accounting Assistant . . . . Karen Becker

Accounting Assistant . . . . Loretta Harmon
Accounting Assistant . . . . Lori McLaren
Accounting Assistant . . . . Devin Brown

Ticket Sales
Director of Ticket Operations . . . . Kirk Dyer
Ticket Operations Manager . . . . Rob Winston
Customer Services Managers . . . . Lori Blanche, Glenn Hives
Manager Ticket Bus . . . . Carlos Jimenez
Ticket Operations Assistants . . . . Ann Harmon, Flo Kunze

Sales
Manager of Ticket Sales . . . . Paul Andrews
Senior Account Executives . . . . Amy Seltenreich, Dan Sweeney
Account Executives. Aimee Ahlers, Amy Cashel, Robert Kinnard,
Allison Levy, Nikki Lockton, Jack Breeden
Account Coordinators. . . . . Scott Billups, Jason Johanning, Jason Linscott,
Bouker Pool
Customer Service Coordinator . . . . Denika Garnet

Marketing and Corporate Partnership
Director of Marketing . . . . TBA
Marketing Assistant/Traffic Coordinator . . . . . . Brooke Spaulding
Director of Corporate Sales Hockey . . . . Susan Cohig
Manager New Business Development. . . . . Dave Smrek
Director of Corporate Services . . . . Chris Whitney
Senior Corporate Account Executives . . . . Brian Jones, Mike Kurowski, Molly Mueller,
Deanna Poyfair
Corporate Account Executive . . . . Christy Baird, John Moore, Jeff Plush
Director of Sales/Pepsi Center . . . . Todd Goldstein

Game Operations
Director of Game Operations . . . . Chris Wiger
Marketing. . . . . Kenn Solomon
Game Operations Coordinators . . . . Kim Erwin, TBA
Director of Special Events . . . . TBA
Special Events Manager . . . . Cydni Bickerstaff
Special Events Coordinators . . . . Becky Grupe, Rene Doubleday
Special Events Assistant . . . . Kirsten Nissler

Broadcasting
Executive Producer . . . . Robb Moody
Associate Producer . . . . Mike Schanno
TV Play-by-Play Announcer . . . . John Kelly
TV Color Commentator . . . . Peter McNab
Radio Play-by-Play Announcer . . . . Michael Haynes
Radio Color Commentator . . . . Norm Jones

Retail
Director of Merchandising . . . . Scott Franklin
Manager Sports Gallery/16th Street Mall . . . . . . Tino Romero
Manager Sports Gallery/Cherry Creek. . . . . Bryan Curtis
Assistant Manager Sports Gallery/Cherry Creek . . . Kevin Walsh
Manager Sports Gallery/Colorado Springs . . . . . . Ryan Eichman
Mail Order/Central Dist. Manager. . . . . Bill McAdoo
Warehouse/Arena Retail Manager . . . . Johnny Duke

Creative Services
Creative Director. . . . . Daniel Price
Senior Art Director . . . . Michael Beindorff
Art Director. . . . . Rick Fillmon
Graphic Artist . . . . Krysia Gallagher

Community Relations
Community Fund President. . . . . Chopper Travaglini
Community Programs Coordinator . . . . Taunya Cordova
Community Programs Coordinator . . . . Meredith Kaplan
Community Relations Assistant. . . . . Tamara Walker
Community Relations Coordinator . . . . Derek Williams

Administration
Director of Administration . . . . Cheryl Miller
Administrative Services Coordinator . . . . Lou Carroll
Administrative Assistant . . . . Jennifer Walters
Receptionists. . . . . Heather Ellsworth, Gina Silletto
Courier . . . . Paul Fernandez

Dallas Stars

1995-96 Results: 26W-42L-14T 66PTS. Sixth, Central Division

Mike Modano topped all Dallas scorers for the fourth time in the past five seasons with a 36-goal, 45-assist effort during the 1995-96 season.

Schedule

Oct.	Sat.	5	Colorado	Wed.	8	Detroit	
	Tues.	8	Washington	Fri.	10	Phoenix	
	Thur.	10	at NY Rangers	Mon.	13	at Montreal	
	Sat.	12	at New Jersey	Tues.	14	at Pittsburgh	
	Sun.	13	at Chicago	Tues.	21	at Philadelphia	
	Tues.	15	Detroit	Fri.	24	at Washington	
	Thur.	17	Vancouver	Sat.	25	at Toronto	
	Sat.	19	Toronto	Mon.	27	Los Angeles	
	Wed.	23	at Detroit	Wed.	29	Anaheim	
	Sat.	26	Ottawa	Fri.	31	at Buffalo	
	Wed.	30	Buffalo	**Feb.** Sun.	2	at Detroit	
Nov.	Fri.	1	Chicago	Wed.	5	Tampa Bay	
	Sun.	3	at St. Louis	Thur.	6	at St. Louis	
	Wed.	6	at Phoenix	Sat.	8	at Phoenix	
	Fri.	8	at San Jose	Sun.	9	Los Angeles	
	Mon.	11	at Anaheim	Wed.	12	Phoenix	
	Wed.	13	Calgary	Fri.	14	Detroit	
	Fri.	15	Anaheim	Mon.	17	at Los Angeles*	
	Sun.	17	at Edmonton	Tues.	18	at San Jose	
	Tues.	19	at Vancouver	Fri.	21	Calgary	
	Wed.	20	at Calgary	Sun.	23	Edmonton*	
	Fri.	22	Florida	Tues.	25	at Chicago	
	Wed.	27	New Jersey	Thur.	27	at Colorado	
	Fri.	29	at Tampa Bay	**Mar.** Sat.	1	at Calgary	
	Sat.	30	Toronto	Wed.	5	St. Louis	
Dec.	Wed.	4	San Jose	Fri.	7	Edmonton	
	Fri.	6	Philadelphia	Mon.	10	at Toronto	
	Sun.	8	at Florida	Fri.	14	Chicago	
	Wed.	11	St. Louis	Sun.	16	Pittsburgh	
	Fri.	13	Vancouver	Wed.	19	Phoenix	
	Sun.	15	at Ottawa*	Fri.	21	Hartford	
	Wed.	18	at Chicago	Sun.	23	at St. Louis	
	Fri.	20	at Hartford	Sun.	30	at Vancouver*	
	Sat.	21	at NY Islanders	Mon.	31	at Edmonton	
	Mon.	23	San Jose	**Apr.** Wed.	2	NY Islanders	
	Fri.	27	Boston	Fri.	4	at Anaheim	
	Sun.	29	at Colorado	Sat.	5	at Los Angeles	
	Mon.	30	NY Rangers	Mon.	7	at Phoenix	
Jan.	Wed.	1	Montreal*	Wed.	9	Toronto	
	Fri.	3	at Detroit	Fri.	11	Colorado	
	Sat.	4	at Boston	Sun.	13	Chicago*	

* Denotes afternoon game.

Franchise date: June 5, 1967
Transferred from Minnesota to Dallas beginning with 1993-94 season.

CENTRAL DIVISION

30th NHL Season

Year-by-Year Record

		Home			Road			Overall						
Season	GP	W	L	T	W	L	T	W	L	T	GF	GA	Pts.	Finished	Playoff Result
1995-96	82	14	18	9	12	24	5	26	42	14	227	280	66	6th, Central Div.	Out of Playoffs
1994-95	48	9	10	5	8	13	3	17	23	8	136	135	42	5th, Central Div.	Lost Conf. Quarter-Final
1993-94	84	23	12	7	19	17	6	42	29	13	286	265	97	3rd, Central Div.	Lost Conf. Semi-Final
1992-93*	84	18	17	7	18	21	3	36	38	10	272	293	82	5th, Norris Div.	Out of Playoffs
1991-92*	80	20	16	4	12	26	2	32	42	6	246	278	70	4th, Norris Div.	Lost Div. Semi-Final
1990-91*	80	19	15	6	8	24	8	27	39	14	256	266	68	4th, Norris Div.	Lost Final
1989-90*	80	26	12	2	10	28	2	36	40	4	284	291	76	4th, Norris Div.	Lost Div. Semi-Final
1988-89*	80	17	15	8	10	22	8	27	37	16	258	278	70	3rd, Norris Div.	Lost Div. Semi-Final
1987-88*	80	10	24	6	9	24	7	19	48	13	242	349	51	5th, Norris Div.	Out of Playoffs
1986-87*	80	17	20	3	13	20	7	30	40	10	296	314	70	5th, Norris Div.	Out of Playoffs
1985-86*	80	21	15	4	17	18	5	38	33	9	327	305	85	2nd, Norris Div.	Lost Div. Semi-Final
1984-85*	80	14	19	7	11	24	5	25	43	12	268	321	62	4th, Norris Div.	Lost Div. Final
1983-84*	80	22	14	4	17	17	6	39	31	10	345	344	88	1st, Norris Div.	Lost Conf. Championship
1982-83*	80	23	6	11	17	18	5	40	24	16	321	290	96	2nd, Norris Div.	Lost Div. Final
1981-82*	80	21	7	12	16	16	8	37	23	20	346	288	94	1st, Norris Div.	Lost Div. Semi-Final
1980-81*	80	23	10	7	12	18	10	35	28	17	291	263	87	3rd, Adams Div.	Lost Final
1979-80*	80	25	8	7	11	20	9	36	28	16	311	253	88	3rd, Adams Div.	Lost Semi-Final
1978-79*	80	19	15	6	9	25	6	28	40	12	257	289	68	4th, Adams Div.	Out Of Playoffs
1977-78*	80	12	24	4	6	29	5	18	53	9	218	325	45	5th, Smythe Div.	Out of Playoffs
1976-77*	80	17	14	9	6	25	9	23	39	18	240	310	64	2nd, Smythe Div.	Lost Prelim. Round
1975-76*	80	15	22	3	5	31	4	20	53	7	195	303	47	4th, Smythe Div.	Out of Playoffs
1974-75*	80	17	20	3	6	30	4	23	50	7	221	341	53	4th, Smythe Div.	Out of Playoffs
1973-74	78	18	15	6	5	23	11	23	38	17	235	275	63	7th, West Div.	Out of Playoffs
1972-73*	78	26	8	5	11	22	6	37	30	11	254	230	85	3rd, West Div.	Lost Quarter-Final
1971-72*	78	22	11	6	15	18	6	37	29	12	212	191	86	2nd, West Div.	Lost Quarter-Final
1970-71*	78	16	15	8	12	19	8	28	34	16	191	223	72	4th, West Div.	Lost Semi-Final
1969-70*	76	11	16	11	8	19	11	19	35	22	224	257	60	3rd, West Div.	Lost Quarter-Final
1968-69*	76	11	21	6	7	22	9	18	43	15	189	270	51	6th, West Div.	Out of Playoffs
1967-68*	74	17	12	8	10	20	7	27	32	15	191	226	69	4th, West Div.	Lost Semi-Final

* Minnesota North Stars

1996-97 Player Personnel

FORWARDS	HT	WT	S	Place of Birth	Date	1995-96 Club
ADAMS, Greg	6-3	195	L	Nelson, B.C.	8/1/63	Dallas
BASSEN, Bob	5-10	185	L	Calgary, Alta.	5/6/65	Dallas-Michigan
BRADY, Neil	6-2	200	L	Montreal, Que.	4/12/68	Michigan
CARBONNEAU, Guy	5-11	186	R	Sept-Iles, Que.	3/18/60	Dallas
COTE, Patrick	6-3	199	L	Lasalle, Que.	1/24/75	Dallas-Michigan
ELYNUIK, Pat	6-0	185	R	Foam Lake, Sask.	10/30/67	Ottawa-Fort Wayne
FEDYK, Brent	6-0	194	R	Yorkton, Sask.	3/8/67	Philadelphia-Dallas
GILCHRIST, Brent	5-11	180	L	Moose Jaw, Sask.	4/3/67	Dallas
HARVEY, Todd	6-0	195	R	Hamilton, Ont.	2/17/75	Dallas-Michigan
HOGUE, Benoit	5-10	194	L	Repentigny, Que.	10/28/66	Toronto-Dallas
HUARD, Bill	6-1	215	L	Welland, Ont.	6/24/67	Dallas-Michigan
JINMAN, Lee	5-10	160	R	Toronto, Ont.	1/10/76	North Bay-Detroit (OHL)
KENNEDY, Mike	6-1	195	R	Vancouver, B.C.	4/13/72	Dallas
LABELLE, Marc	6-1	215	L	Maniwak, Que.	12/20/69	Cincinnati-Milwaukee
LANGENBRUNNER, Jamie	5-11	185	R	Duluth, MN	7/24/75	Dallas-Michigan
LAWRENCE, Mark	6-4	215	R	Burlington, Ont.	1/27/72	Dallas-Michigan
LEHTINEN, Jere	6-0	192	R	Espoo, Finland	6/24/73	Dallas-Michigan
LIND, Juha	5-11	160	L	Helsinki, Finland	1/2/74	Jokerit
MARSHALL, Grant	6-1	193	R	Mississauga, Ont.	6/9/73	Dallas
MITCHELL, Jeff	6-1	190	R	Wayne, MI	5/16/75	Michigan
MODANO, Mike	6-3	200	L	Livonia, MI	6/7/70	Dallas
NIEUWENDYK, Joe	6-1	195	L	Oshawa, Ont.	9/10/66	Dallas
REID, David	6-1	217	L	Toronto, Ont.	5/15/64	Boston
STORM, Jim	6-2	200	L	Milford, MI	2/5/71	Dallas-Michigan
VERBEEK, Pat	5-9	192	R	Sarnia, Ont.	5/24/64	NY Rangers
DEFENSEMEN						
BUZEK, Petr	6-0	200	L	Jihlava, Czech.	2/2/63	
GUSEV, Sergey	6-1	195	L	Nizhny Tagil, USSR	7/31/75	Michigan
HATCHER, Derian	6-5	225	L	Sterling Heights, MI	6/4/72	Dallas
KECZMER, Dan	6-1	190	L	Mt. Clemens, MI	5/25/68	Calgary-Saint John-Albany
LALOR, Mike	6-0	200	L	Buffalo, NY	3/8/63	Dallas-San Francisco
LEDYARD, Grant	6-2	195	L	Winnipeg, Man.	11/19/61	Dallas
LUDWIG, Craig	6-3	220	L	Rhinelander, WI	3/15/61	Dallas
LUKOWICH, Brad	6-1	170	L	Cranbrook, B.C.	8/12/76	Kamloops
MATVICHUK, Richard	6-2	200	L	Edmonton, Alta.	2/5/73	Dallas
SYDOR, Darryl	6-0	195	L	Edmonton, Alta.	5/13/72	Los Angeles-Dallas
ZUBOV, Sergei	6-1	200	R	Moscow, USSR	7/22/70	Pittsburgh

GOALTENDERS	HT	WT	C	Place of Birth	Date	1995-96 Club
FERNANDEZ, Emmanuel	6-0	185	L	Etobicoke, Ont.	8/27/74	Dallas-Michigan
IRBE, Arturs	5-8	175	L	Riga, Latvia	2/2/67	San Jose-Kansas City
MOOG, Andy	5-8	175	L	Penticton, B.C.	2/18/60	Dallas
TUREK, Roman	6-3	190	R	Pisek, Czech.	5/21/70	Nurnberg

Coach

HITCHCOCK, KEN
Coach, Dallas Stars. Born in Edmonton, Alberta, December 17, 1951.

Ken Hitchcock, who was named the new head coach of the Stars on January 8, 1996, arrived in Dallas with a very impressive list of credentials. The 44-year old native of Edmonton has posted a winning record in every season as a head coach prior to joining the Stars, including record-breaking numbers in the Western Hockey League in the late 1980s.

Getting his start behind the bench as a head coach in the Canadian Triple A Midget ranks with Sherwood Park, a suburb of Edmonton, Hitchcock posted an incredible 575-69 mark during his ten-year reign there. Honored as the Alberta Minor Hockey Association Coach of the Year in 1983-84, he also was awarded minor hockey coach of the year honors in 1982-83.

Named head coach of the Kamloops Blazers of the WHL in 1984, he began a dominating run at the junior level which saw his team finish first in the Western Division in five of his six seasons at the helm. The WHL coach of the year in 1986-87 and 1989-90, Hitchcock was named the top coach in all of Canadian Major Jr. Hockey in 1989-90 after the Blazers won the WHL title and finished third at the Memorial Cup. His .693 winning percentage (291-125-15) at Kamloops is the highest in the history of the Western Hockey League while his .695 playoff winning percentage (66-29) with the Blazers is fourth best in league annals. Adding to his amateur success, he served as an assistant coach for the gold medal-winning 1987 Team Canada squad at the World Juniors in Russia.

After a three-year stint (1990-93) as an assistant coach for the Philadelphia Flyers, Hitchcock returned to head coaching duties for the 1993-94 season, manning the bench for the Kalamazoo Wings, the Stars minor league affiliate in the International Hockey League. In his two-plus seasons with the team, he earned a record of 110-62-32, the second-best winning percentage (.624) in K-Wings' history. Finishing first in the Atlantic Division in 1993-94 before losing in the post-season quarterfinals, he guided his team to a second place finish during the regular season and a spot in the Eastern Conference Finals in 1994-95. Hitchcock also coached in both the 1993-94 and 1994-95 IHL All-Star Games.

Coaching Record

		Regular Season					Playoffs			
Season	Team	Games	W	L	T	%	Games	W	L	%
1984-85	Kamloops (WHL)	71	52	17	2	.746	15	10	5	.667
1985-86	Kamloops (WHL)	72	49	19	4	.708	16	14	2	.875
1986-87	Kamloops (WHL)	72	55	14	3	.785	13	8	5	.615
1987-88	Kamloops (WHL)	72	45	26	1	.632	18	12	6	.667
1988-89	Kamloops (WHL)	72	34	33	5	.507	16	8	8	.500
1989-90	Kamloops (WHL)	72	56	16	0	.778	17	14	3	.824
1993-94	Kalamazoo (IHL)	81	48	26	7	.636	5	1	4	.200
1994-95	Kalamazoo (IHL)	81	43	24	14	.617	16	10	6	.625
1995-96	Michigan (IHL)	40	19	10	11	.613	....	....	....	....
	Dallas (NHL)	**43**	**15**	**23**	**5**	**.407**	....	....	....	....
	NHL Totals	**43**	**15**	**23**	**5**	**.407**	....	....	....	....

1995-96 Scoring

* – rookie

Regular Season

Pos	#	Player	Team	GP	G	A	Pts	+/–	PIM	PP	SH	GW	GT	S	%
C	9	Mike Modano	DAL	78	36	45	81	–12	63	8	4	4	1	320	11.3
C	33	Benoit Hogue	TOR	44	12	25	37	6	68	3	0	5	0	94	12.8
			DAL	34	7	20	27	4	36	2	0	0	0	61	11.5
			TOTAL	78	19	45	64	10	104	5	0	5	0	155	12.3
L	23	Greg Adams	DAL	66	22	21	43	–21	33	11	1	1	0	140	15.7
C	41	Brent Gilchrist	DAL	77	20	22	42	–11	36	6	1	2	0	164	12.2
D	4	Kevin Hatcher	DAL	74	15	26	41	–24	58	7	0	3	2	237	6.3
L	20	Brent Fedyk	PHI	24	10	5	15	1	24	4	0	0	0	42	23.8
			DAL	41	10	9	19	–17	30	4	0	0	0	71	14.1
			TOTAL	65	20	14	34	–16	54	8	0	0	0	113	17.7
C	25	Joe Nieuwendyk	DAL	52	14	18	32	–17	41	8	0	3	0	138	10.1
D	2	Derian Hatcher	DAL	79	8	23	31	–12	129	2	0	1	0	125	6.4
C	10	Todd Harvey	DAL	69	9	20	29	–13	136	3	0	1	0	101	8.9
R	29	* Grant Marshall	DAL	70	9	19	28	0	111	0	0	0	1	62	14.5
R	26	* Jere Lehtinen	DAL	57	6	22	28	5	16	0	0	1	0	109	5.5
L	39	Mike Kennedy	DAL	61	9	17	26	–7	48	4	0	1	0	111	8.1
D	12	Grant Ledyard	DAL	73	5	19	24	–15	20	2	0	1	0	123	4.1
C	21	Guy Carbonneau	DAL	71	8	15	23	–2	38	0	2	1	0	54	14.8
D	24	Richard Matvichuk	DAL	73	6	16	22	4	71	0	0	1	0	81	7.4
L	44	Randy Wood	TOR	46	7	9	16	–4	36	1	0	0	0	101	6.9
			DAL	30	1	4	5	–11	26	0	0	0	0	58	1.7
			TOTAL	76	8	13	21	–15	62	1	0	0	0	159	5.0
D	6	Darryl Sydor	L.A.	58	1	11	12	–11	34	1	0	0	0	84	1.2
			DAL	26	2	6	8	–1	41	1	0	0	0	33	6.1
			TOTAL	84	3	17	20	–12	75	2	0	0	0	117	2.6
L	17	Bill Huard	DAL	51	6	6	12	3	176	0	0	0	0	34	17.6
L	11	Mike Donnelly	DAL	24	2	5	7	–2	10	0	0	0	0	21	9.5
C	16	* Jamie Langenbrunner	DAL	12	2	2	4	–2	6	1	0	0	0	15	13.3
R	20	Nikolai Borschevsky	DAL	12	1	3	4	–7	6	0	0	1	0	22	4.5
L	43	Jim Storm	DAL	10	1	2	3	–1	17	0	0	1	0	11	9.1
D	18	Mike Lalor	DAL	63	1	2	3	–10	31	0	0	0	0	46	2.2
D	3	Craig Ludwig	DAL	65	1	2	3	–17	70	0	0	0	0	47	2.1
C	22	Robert Petrovicky	DAL	5	1	1	2	1	0	1	0	1	0	3	33.3
C	28	Bob Bassen	DAL	13	0	1	1	–6	15	0	0	0	0	9	0.0
R	38	* Mark Lawrence	DAL	13	0	1	1	0	17	0	0	0	0	13	0.0
D	32	* Travis Richards	DAL	1	0	0	0	–1	2	0	0	0	0	0	0.0
G	31	* Jordan Willis	DAL	1	0	0	0	0	0	0	0	0	0	0	0.0
D	40	Pat MacLeod	DAL	2	0	0	0	0	0	0	0	0	0	2	0.0
R	37	* Zac Boyer	DAL	2	0	0	0	0	0	0	0	0	0	3	0.0
L	40	* Patrick Cote	DAL	2	0	0	0	–2	5	0	0	0	0	0	0.0
R	14	Dan Marois	DAL	3	0	0	0	0	2	0	0	0	0	1	0.0
R	25	* Dan Kesa	DAL	3	0	0	0	–1	0	0	0	0	0	0	0.0
G	30	Emmanuel Fernandez	DAL	5	0	0	0	0	0	0	0	0	0	0	0.0
D	14	Paul Cavallini	DAL	8	0	0	0	–3	6	0	0	0	0	5	0.0
G	45	Allan Bester	DAL	10	0	0	0	0	2	0	0	0	0	0	0.0
G	34	Darcy Wakaluk	DAL	37	0	0	0	0	6	0	0	0	0	1	0.0
G	35	Andy Moog	DAL	41	0	0	0	0	28	0	0	0	0	0	0.0

Goaltending

No.	Goaltender	GPI	Mins	Avg	W	L	T	EN	SO	GA	SA	S%
35	Andy Moog	41	2228	2.99	13	19	7	6	1	111	1106	.900
45	Allan Bester	10	601	3.00	4	5	1	3	0	30	297	.899
31	* Jordan Willis	1	19	3.16	0	1	0	0	0	1	14	.929
34	Darcy Wakaluk	37	1875	3.39	9	16	5	4	1	106	975	.891
30	Emmanuel Fernandez	5	249	4.58	0	1	1	0	0	19	121	.843
	Totals	**82**	**4992**	**3.37**	**26**	**42**	**14**	**13**	**2**	**280**	**2526**	**.889**

General Managers' History

Wren A. Blair, 1967-68 to 1973-74; Jack Gordon, 1974-75 to 1976-77; Lou Nanne, 1977-78 to 1987-88; Jack Ferreira, 1988-89 to 1989-90; Bob Clarke 1990-91 to 1991-92; Bob Gainey, 1992-93 to date.

Coaching History

Wren Blair, 1967-68; Wren Blair and John Muckler, 1968-69; Wren Blair and Charlie Burns, 1969-70; Jackie Gordon, 1970-71 to 1972-73; Jackie Gordon and Parker MacDonald, 1973-74; Jackie Gordon and Charlie Burns, 1974-75; Ted Harris, 1975-76, 1976-77; Ted Harris, André Beaulieu and Lou Nanne, 1977-78; Harry Howell and Glen Sonmor, 1978-79; Glen Sonmor, 1979-80 to 1981-82; Glen Sonmor and Murray Oliver, 1982-83; Bill Mahoney, 1983-84 to 1984-85; Lorne Henning, 1985-86; Lorne Henning and Glen Sonmor, 1986-87; Herb Brooks, 1987-88; Pierre Page, 1988-89 to 1989-90; Bob Gainey, 1990-91 to 1994-95; Bob Gainey and Ken Hitchcock, 1995-96; Ken Hitchcock, 1996-97.

Captains' History

Bob Woytowich, 1967-68; "Moose" Vasko, 1968-69; Claude Larose, 1969-70; Ted Harris, 1970-71 to 1973-74; Bill Goldsworthy, 1974-75, 1975-76; Bill Hogaboam, 1976-77; Nick Beverley, 1977-78; J.P. Parise, 1978-79; Paul Shmyr, 1979-80, 1980-81; Tim Young, 1981-82; Craig Hartsburg, 1982-83; Craig Hartsburg, Brian Bellows, 1983-84; Craig Hartsburg, 1984-85 to 1987-88; Curt Fraser, Bob Rouse and Curt Giles, 1988-89; Curt Giles, 1989-90 to 1990-91; Mark Tinordi, 1991-92 to 1993-94; Neal Broten and Derian Hatcher, 1994-95; Derian Hatcher, 1995-96 to date.

Retired Numbers

8	Bill Goldsworthy	1967-1976
19	Bill Masterton	1967-1968

Club Records

Team

(Figures in brackets for season records are games played; records for fewest points, wins, ties, losses, goals, goals against are for 70 or more games)

Most Points	97	1993-94 (84)
Most Wins	42	1993-94 (84)
Most Ties	22	1969-70 (76)
Most Losses	53	1975-76, 1977-78 (80)
Most Goals	346	1981-82 (80)
Most Goals Against	349	1987-88 (80)
Fewest Points	45	1977-78 (80)
Fewest Wins	18	1968-69 (76), 1977-78 (80)
Fewest Ties	4	1989-90 (80)
Fewest Losses	23	1981-82 (80)
Fewest Goals	189	1968-69 (76)
Fewest Goals Against	191	1971-72 (78)

Longest Winning Streak

Overall	7	Mar. 16-28/80
Home	11	Nov. 4-Dec. 27/72
Away	7	Nov. 18-Dec. 5/92, Jan. 26-Feb. 21/94

Longest Undefeated Streak

Overall	12	Feb. 18-Mar. 15/82 (9 wins, 3 ties)
Home	13	Oct. 28-Dec. 27/72 (12 wins, 1 tie), Nov. 21-Jan. 9/80 (10 wins, 3 ties), Jan. 17-Mar. 17/91 (11 wins, 2 ties)
Away	8	Jan. 26-Feb. 21/94 (7 wins, 1 tie)

Longest Losing Streak

Overall	10	Feb. 1-20/76
Home	6	Jan. 17-Feb. 4/70
Away	8	Oct. 19-Nov. 13/75, Jan. 28-Mar. 3/88

Longest Winless Streak

Overall	20	Jan. 15-Feb. 28/70 (15 losses, 5 ties)
Home	12	Jan. 17-Feb. 25/70 (8 losses, 4 ties)
Away	23	Oct. 25/74-Jan. 28/75 (19 losses, 4 ties)

Most Shutouts, Season	7	1972-73 (78)
Most PIM, Season	2,313	1987-88 (80)
Most Goals, Game	15	Nov. 11/81 (Wpg. 2 at Min. 15)

Individual

Most Seasons	15	Neal Broten
Most Games	972	Neal Broten
Most Goals, Career	342	Brian Bellows
Most Assists, Career	586	Neal Broten
Most Points Career	852	Neal Broten (266G, 586A)
Most PIM, Career	1,883	Shane Churla
Most Shutouts, Career	26	Cesare Maniago
Longest Consecutive Games Streak	442	Danny Grant (Dec. 4/68-Apr. 7/74)
Most Goals, Season	55	Dino Ciccarelli (1981-82), Brian Bellows (1989-90)
Most Assists, Season	76	Neal Broten (1985-86)
Most Points, Season	114	Bobby Smith (1981-82; 43G, 71A)

Most PIM, Season	382	Basil McRae (1987-88)
Most Points, Defenseman Season	77	Craig Hartsburg (1981-82; 17G, 60A)
Most Points, Center, Season	114	Bobby Smith (1981-82; 43G, 71A)
Most Points, Right Wing, Season	107	Dino Ciccarelli (1981-82; 55G, 52A)
Most Point, Left Wing, Season	99	Brian Bellows (1989-90; 55G, 44A)
Most Points, Rookie, Season	98	Neal Broten (1981-82; 38G, 60A)
Most Shutouts, Season	6	Cesare Maniago (1967-68)
Most Goals, Game	5	Tim Young (Jan. 15/79)
Most Assists, Game	5	Murray Oliver (Oct. 24/71), Larry Murphy (Oct. 17/89)
Most Points, Game	7	Bobby Smith (Nov. 11/81; 4G, 3A)

Records include Minnesota North Stars 1967-68 through 1992-93.

All-time Record vs. Other Clubs

Regular Season

	At Home							On Road							Total						
	GP	W	L	T	GF	GA	PTS	GP	W	L	T	GF	GA	PTS	GP	W	L	T	GF	GA	PTS
Anaheim	6	5	1	0	27	11	10	7	4	3	0	21	18	8	13	9	4	0	48	29	18
Boston	54	14	29	11	151	203	39	54	6	39	9	129	245	21	108	20	68	20	280	448	60
Buffalo	47	21	20	6	147	144	48	46	12	24	10	125	170	34	93	33	44	16	272	314	82
Calgary	46	22	18	6	173	158	50	46	8	27	11	124	182	27	92	30	45	17	297	340	77
Chicago	94	40	40	14	313	302	94	92	21	61	10	239	383	52	186	61	101	24	552	685	146
Colorado	24	13	9	2	90	82	28	25	6	16	3	70	114	15	49	19	25	5	160	196	43
Detroit	89	45	30	14	325	270	104	88	30	45	13	295	359	73	177	75	75	27	620	629	177
Edmonton	29	10	13	6	106	101	26	28	6	16	6	94	132	18	57	16	29	12	200	233	44
Florida	2	0	0	2	10	10	2	2	1	1	0	9	10	2	4	1	1	2	19	20	4
Hartford	23	12	10	1	96	77	25	24	12	9	3	93	86	27	47	24	19	4	189	163	52
Los Angeles	63	36	16	11	259	180	83	62	18	27	17	186	222	53	125	54	43	28	445	402	136
Montreal	53	14	28	11	137	190	39	52	9	36	7	126	234	25	105	23	64	18	263	424	64
New Jersey	38	23	9	6	152	100	52	38	16	19	3	117	130	35	76	39	28	9	269	230	87
NY Islanders	40	14	19	7	117	151	35	40	9	23	8	114	159	26	80	23	42	15	231	310	61
NY Rangers	54	16	29	9	163	206	41	55	11	34	10	150	197	32	109	27	63	19	313	403	73
Ottawa	4	3	1	0	20	10	6	3	2	1	0	10	14	4	7	5	2	0	30	20	10
Philadelphia	60	24	22	14	201	200	62	60	9	41	10	137	241	28	120	33	63	24	338	441	90
Pittsburgh	58	32	21	5	219	197	69	57	17	35	5	160	220	39	115	49	56	10	379	417	108
St. Louis	98	44	36	18	335	292	106	100	27	54	19	283	366	73	198	71	90	37	618	658	179
San Jose	9	6	2	1	38	26	13	9	4	5	0	35	24	12	18	12	5	1	73	50	25
Tampa Bay	5	3	1	1	18	15	7	6	3	1	2	15	11	8	11	6	2	3	33	26	15
Toronto	88	44	33	11	339	288	99	92	30	47	15	288	333	75	180	74	80	26	627	621	174
Vancouver	55	33	14	10	220	161	72	55	20	25	10	174	213	50	110	53	39	20	394	374	122
Washington	33	14	11	8	125	98	36	34	13	14	7	106	108	33	67	27	25	15	231	206	69
Winnipeg	33	18	11	4	140	110	40	31	14	16	1	111	113	29	64	32	27	5	251	223	69
Defunct Clubs	33	19	8	6	123	86	44	32	10	16	6	84	105	26	65	29	24	12	207	191	70
Totals	**1138**	**523**	**431**	**184**	**4044**	**3668**	**1230**	**1138**	**320**	**633**	**185**	**3295**	**4385**	**825**	**2276**	**843**	**1064**	**369**	**7339**	**8053**	**2055**

Playoffs

	Series	W	L	GP	W	L	T	GF	GA	Mtg.	Last Round	Result
Boston	1	1	0	3	3	0	0	20	13	1981	PR	W 3-0
Buffalo	2	1	1	7	4	3	0	26	28	1981	QF	W 4-1
Calgary	1	1	0	6	4	2	0	25	18	1981	SF	W 4-2
Chicago	6	2	4	33	14	19	0	119	119	1991	DSF	W 4-2
Detroit	2	0	2	12	4	8	0	29	40	1995	CQF	L 1-4
Edmonton	2	1	1	9	4	5	0	30	36	1991	CF	W 4-1
Los Angeles	1	1	0	7	4	3	0	26	21	1968	QF	W 4-3
Montreal	2	1	1	13	6	7	0	37	48	1980	QF	W 4-3
NY Islanders	1	0	1	5	1	4	0	16	26	1981	F	L 1-4
Philadelphia	2	0	2	11	3	8	0	26	41	1980	SF	L 1-4
Pittsburgh	1	0	1	6	2	4	0	16	28	1991	F	L 2-4
St. Louis	10	5	5	56	30	26	0	174	162	1994	CQF	W 4-0
Toronto	2	2	0	7	6	1	0	35	26	1983	DSF	W 3-1
Vancouver	1	0	1	5	1	4	0	11	18	1994	CSF	L 1-4
Totals	**34**	**15**	**19**	**180**	**86**	**94**	**0**	**590**	**624**			

Calgary totals include Atlanta, 1972-73 to 1979-80. Colorado totals include Quebec, 1979-80 to 1994-95.
Dallas totals include Minnesota, 1967-68 to 1992-93.
New Jersey totals include Kansas City, 1974-75 to 1975-76, and Colorado Rockies, 1976-77 to 1981-82.

Playoff Results 1996-92

Year	Round	Opponent	Result	GF	GA
1995	CQF	Detroit	L 1-4	10	17
1994	CSF	Vancouver	L 1-4	11	18
	CQF	St. Louis	W 4-0	16	10
1992	DSF	Detroit	L 3-4	19	23

Abbreviations: Round: F – Final;
CF – conference final; **CQF** – conference quarter-final;
CSF – conference semi-final; **DF** – division final;
DSF – division semi-final; **SF** – semi-final;
QF – quarter-final; **PR** – preliminary round.

1995-96 Results

Oct.	7	at	Winnipeg	5-7	14	at	New Jersey	2-7
	10		Calgary	7-3	15	at	Philadelphia	1-6
	12		St. Louis	1-3	17		Edmonton	3-4
	14		Boston	6-5	22	at	Vancouver	6-4
	17		Washington	3-4	24	at	Edmonton	5-3
	19	at	St. Louis	1-1	26	at	Calgary	4-2
	21		Tampa Bay	3-3	29		Winnipeg	1-2
	24		Buffalo	3-0	31		NY Rangers	1-1
	26		Anaheim	5-2	Feb. 2		Vancouver	4-5
	28	at	San Jose	4-3	4	at	NY Islanders	3-5
	30		Colorado	1-6	6	at	St. Louis	5-2
Nov.	1		Chicago	1-1	7		Montreal	2-4
	4	at	Detroit	1-5	10		St. Louis	3-6
	8		Los Angeles	3-3	11		Hartford	3-5
	9	at	Colorado	1-1	16		Edmonton	6-1
	14	at	Pittsburgh	2-4	18	at	Florida	4-6
	15	at	Buffalo	1-2	19	at	Tampa Bay	2-4
	17		San Jose	2-1	22		Ottawa	3-2
	22		Vancouver	4-3	24	at	Toronto	3-2
	25		New Jersey	2-0	25	at	Hartford	6-2
Dec.	2	at	Los Angeles	2-2	28		Philadelphia	4-4
	3	at	Colorado	7-6	Mar. 2		Toronto	5-1
	5	at	Boston	4-6	5	at	Anaheim	3-1
	7	at	Detroit	1-3	6	at	San Jose	2-1
	9	at	Toronto	1-3	11	at	Montreal	1-4
	11	at	NY Rangers	2-3	13	at	Ottawa	1-4
	13		Calgary	4-8	15	at	Toronto	0-3
	15		Pittsburgh	1-5	17	at	Washington	1-2
	17		San Jose	4-2	20		St. Louis	2-1
	21		NY Islanders	3-3	22	at	Vancouver	2-5
	23		Chicago	0-2	23	at	Los Angeles	4-4
	26	at	Chicago	3-5	26		Winnipeg	2-8
	28	at	St. Louis	1-4	28		Anaheim	3-1
	29		Detroit	1-2	31	at	Chicago	3-5
Jan.	1		Toronto	0-1	Apr. 3	at	Winnipeg	1-3
	3	at	Detroit	3-3	5		Chicago	3-3
	5		Winnipeg	5-4	7		Colorado	1-4
	7	at	Chicago	2-5	9	at	Calgary	4-3
	8		Los Angeles	4-4	10	at	Edmonton	3-3
	10		Detroit	0-4	12	at	Anaheim	3-5
	12		Florida	6-6	14		Detroit	1-5

Entry Draft
Selections 1996-82

1996
Pick
5	Richard Jackman
70	Jonathan Sim
90	Mike Hurley
112	Ryan Christie
113	Evgeny Tysbuk
166	Eoin McInerney
194	Joel Kwiatkowski
220	Nick Bootland

1995
Pick
11	Jarome Iginla
37	Patrick Cote
63	Petr Buzek
69	Sergei Gusev
115	Wade Strand
141	Dominic Marleau
173	Jeff Dewar
193	Anatoli Kovesnikov
202	Sergei Luchinkin
219	Stephen Lowe

1994
Pick
20	Jason Botterill
46	Lee Jinman
98	Jamie Wright
124	Marty Turco
150	Yevgeny Petrochinin
228	Marty Flichel
254	Jimmy Roy
280	Chris Szysky

1993
Pick
9	Todd Harvey
35	Jamie Langenbrunner
87	Chad Lang
136	Rick Mrozik
139	Per Svartvadet
165	Jeremy Stasiuk
191	Rob Lurtsema
243	Jordan Willis
249	Bill Lang
269	Cory Peterson

1992
Pick
34	Jarkko Varvio
58	Jeff Bes
88	Jere Lehtinen
130	Michael Johnson
154	Kyle Peterson
178	Juha Lind
202	Lars Edstrom
226	Jeff Romfo
250	Jeffrey Moen

1991
Pick
8	Richard Matvichuk
74	Mike Torchia
97	Mike Kennedy
118	Mark Lawrence
137	Geoff Finch
174	MichaelBurkett
184	Derek Herlofsky
206	Tom Nemeth
228	Shayne Green
250	Jukka Suomalainen

1990
Pick
8	Derian Hatcher
50	Laurie Billeck
70	Cal McGowan
71	Frank Kovacs
92	Enrico Ciccone
113	Roman Turek
134	Jeff Levy
155	Doug Barrault
176	Joe Biondi
197	Troy Binnie
218	Ole-Eskild Dahlstrom
239	John McKersie

1989
Pick
7	Doug Zmolek
28	Mike Craig
60	Murray Garbutt
75	Jean-François Quintin
87	Pat MacLeod
91	Bryan Schoen
97	Rhys Hollyman
112	Scott Cashman
154	Jonathan Pratt
175	Kenneth Blum
196	Arturs Irbe
217	Tom Pederson
238	Helmut Balderis

1988
Pick
1	Mike Modano
40	Link Gaetz
43	Shaun Kane
64	Jeffrey Stop
148	Ken MacArthur
169	Travis Richards
190	Ari Matilainen
211	Grant Bischoff
232	Trent Andison

1987
Pick
6	David Archibald
35	Scott McCrady
48	Kevin Kaminski
73	John Weisbrod
88	Teppo Kivela
109	Darcy Norton
130	Timo Kulonen
151	Don Schmidt
172	Jarmo Myllys
193	Larry Olimb
214	Mark Felicio
235	Dave hields

1986
Pick
12	Warren Babe
30	Neil Wilkinson
33	Dean Kolstad
54	Eric Bennett
55	Rob Zettler
58	Brad Turner
75	Kirk Tomlinson
96	Jari Gronstrand
159	Scott Mathias
180	Lance Pitlick
201	Dan Keczmer
222	Garth Joy
243	Kurt Stahura

1985
Pick
51	Stephane Roy
69	Mike Berger
90	Dwight Mullins
111	MikeMullowney
132	Mike Kelfer
153	Ross Johnson
174	Tim Helmer
195	Gordon Ernst
216	Ladislav Lubina
237	Tommy Sjodin

1984
Pick
13	David Quinn
46	Ken Hodge
76	Miroslav Maly
89	Jiri Poner
97	Kari Takko
118	Gary McColgan
139	Vladimir Kyhos
160	Darin MacInnis
181	Duane Wahlin
201	Mike Orn
222	Tom Terwilliger
242	Mike Nightenale

1983
Pick
1	Brian Lawton
36	Malcolm Parks
38	Frantisek Musil
56	Mitch Messier
76	Brian Durand
96	Rich Geist
116	Tom McComb
136	Sean Toomey
156	Don Biggs
176	Paul Pulis
196	Milos Riha
212	Oldrich Valek
236	Paul Roff

1982
Pick
2	Brian Bellows
59	Wally Chapman
80	Rob Rouse
81	Dusan Pasek
101	Marty Wiitala
122	Todd Carlile
143	Victor Zhluktov
164	Paul Miller
185	Pat Micheletti
206	Arnold Kadlec
227	Scott Knutson

Club Directory

Reunion Arena

Dallas Stars Hockey Club, Inc.
Dr Pepper StarCenter
211 Cowboys Parkway
Irving, TX 75063
Phone **214/868-2890**
FAX 214/868-2860
P.R. Office 214/868-2807 or 2818
Capacity: 16,924

Executive
Chairman of the Board and Owner	Thomas O. Hicks
President and Alternate Governor	James R. Lites
Vice President of Hockey Operations	Bob Gainey
Vice President of Marketing and Broadcasting	Bill Strong
Vice President of Marketing and Promotion	Jeff Cogen
Vice President and Chief Financial Officer	Rick McLaughlin
Vice President of Business Operations/ General Counsel	Len Perna
Office Manager	Rene Marshall
Assistant to the President	Kim Smith

Hockey
General Manager	Bob Gainey
Assistant General Manager	Les Jackson
Head Coach	Ken Hitchcock
Assistant Coaches	Doug Jarvis, Rick Wilson
Assistant to the General Manager	Doug Armstrong
Director of Scouting	Craig Button
Chief Scout	Bob Gernander
Scout	Tim Bernhardt
Pro Scout	Doug Overton
Regional Scouts	Brad Robson, Jeff Twohey, Ray Robson, Serge Savard Jr., Kevin Pottle, Bob Richardson, Jim Pederson, Martin Pouiliot, Hans Edlund, Evgeny Larionov
Director of Team Services	Dan Stuchal
Head Athletic Trainer	Dave Surprenant
Equipment Manager	Dave Smith
Equipment Manager	Lance Vogt
Strength Coach	J.J. McQueen
Video Coordinator	Paul McGrath
Administrative Assistant	Lesa Moake

Public Relations
Director of Public Relations	Larry Kelly
Public Relations Manager	Kurt Daniels
Community Relations Manager	Susan Turner
Community Relations Assistant	Suzannah Jones

Ticket Sales
Director of Ticket Sales	Brian Byrnes
Senior Account Executives	Tom Fireoved, Frank Hubach, Jamie Norman
Account Executives	Brad Alberts, David Deering, Paige Jackson, Jason Sivils, Jeff Tummonds
Sales Coordinator	Leah Deniger
Sales/Marketing Assistant	Becky Thielen

Advertising and Promotion
Director of Advertising and Promotion	Christy Martinez
Manager of Events & Sponsor Services	Lee Smith

Merchandising
Director of Merchandising	Steve Shilts
Retail Manager	Tiffani McCallon
Merchandise Operations Manager	Jeff Casanova
Warehouse Manager	Oscar Garza

Corporate Sales
Assistant V.P. of Advertising Sales	David Peart
Director of Corporate Sales	Dana Summers

Broadcasting
Producer/Director	Kevin Spivey
Announcers, TV/Radio	Ralph Strangis, Daryl Reaugh
Announcer, Arena	Bill Oellerman
Manager, Broadcast and Sales Services	Hilary Roberts

Finance
Director of Finance	Therese Baird
Manager of Accounting	Sharon Arellano
Senior Accountant	Debbie Lalone
Staff Accountant	Mike Groom
Payroll Accountant	Dina Ferreira
Accounting Assistant	Cliff Johnson

Box Office Operations
Director of Box Office Operations	Augie Manfredo
Box Office Manager	Jenny Cauhorn
Assistant Box Office Manager	Stacey Marthaler
Phone Room Supervisor	Ben Marthaler

StarCenter Division
Director of Business Operations	Ed Reusch
Assistant Business Manager	Lance Lankford
Director of Marketing	Rebecca Miller
Director of Building Operations	Geoff Moore
Director of Corporate Hospitality	Jill Cogen
Hockey Programs Manager	Barbara Patten
Skating Programs Manager	Alexandra LaFave
Hockey Programs Manager	Jouni Lehtola
Coordinator of Hockey Programs/Building Manager	Louis Iglesias
Coordinator of Hockey Programs/Building Manager	Dan Ryan
Superintendent	Robert Santana

Operations
Receptionist	Mary Shartouny
Office Assistant	Kim Stewart
Practice Facility	Dr Pepper StarCenter
Radio flagship station	WBAP (820 AM)
TV Stations	KDFW (Ch. 4), KDFI (Ch. 27), Fox Sports (Cable)
Colors	Black, Green, Gold and White

General Manager

GAINEY, BOB
Vice President of Hockey Operations/General Manager, Dallas Stars.
Born in Peterborough, Ont., December 13, 1953.

Bob Gainey enters his first season as the full-time general manager for the Dallas Stars after relinquishing his head coaching duties on January 8, 1996. Named general manager of the team on June 8, 1992, he held the dual role of coach and g.m. for over four seasons. Having been appointed head coach for the Stars on June 19, 1990, his five-plus consecutive seasons behind the bench was the longest tenure of any head coach in franchise history. He is the Stars' sixth general manager and was the team's 16th head coach.

Under Gainey's tutelage, the Stars improved their regular-season record in each of Gainey's first four seasons as coach, going from 27 wins and 68 points in his first year to 42 wins and 97 points in 1993-94. In his first season, 1990-91, Gainey led the Stars through to the Stanley Cup finals, surprising Chicago and St. Louis and eliminating defending champion Edmonton before bowing in six games to Pittsburgh. He finished his reign behind the Stars bench with a 165-190-60 regular season record.

Elected to the Hockey Hall of Fame in 1992, Gainey was Montreal's first choice (eighth overall) in the 1973 Amateur Draft. During his 16-year career with the Canadiens, Gainey was a member of five Stanley Cup-winning teams and was named the Conn Smythe Trophy winner in 1979. He was a four-time recipient of the Frank Selke Trophy (1978-81), awarded the League's top defensive forward, and participated in four NHL All-Star Games (1977, 1978, 1980 and 1981). He served as team captain for eight seasons (1981-89). During his career, he played in 1,160 regular-season games, registering 239 goals and 262 assists for 501 points. In addition, he tallied 73 points (25-48-73) in 182 post-season games.

NHL Coaching Record

		Regular Season					Playoffs			
Season	Team	Games	W	L	T	%	Games	W	L	%
1990-91	Minnesota (NHL)	80	27	39	14	.425	23	14	9	.643
1991-92	Minnesota (NHL)	80	32	42	6	.438	7	3	4	.429
1992-93	Minnesota (NHL)	84	36	38	10	.488	....	....	....	....
1993-94	Dallas (NHL)	84	42	29	13	.577	9	5	4	.556
1994-95	Dallas (NHL)	48	17	23	8	.438	5	1	4	.200
1995-96	Dallas (NHL)	39	11	19	9	.397	....	....	....	....
	NHL Totals	**415**	**165**	**190**	**60**	**.470**	**44**	**23**	**21**	**.523**

Detroit Red Wings

1995-96 Results: 62W-13L-7T 131PTS. First, Central Division

Sergei Fedorov continued his impressive two-way play with the Detroit Red Wings during the 1995-96 schedule. The innovative center, who captured his second Selke Trophy as the league's top defensive forward, led the Wings in goals (39), assists (68), points (107) and game-winning goals (11).

Schedule

Oct.	Sat.	5	at New Jersey
	Wed.	9	Edmonton
	Fri.	11	Calgary
	Sat.	12	at Buffalo
	Tues.	15	at Dallas
	Thur.	17	at Chicago
	Sat.	19	NY Islanders
	Mon.	21	Los Angeles
	Wed.	23	Dallas
	Fri.	25	Chicago
	Sat.	26	at Boston
	Wed.	30	Montreal
Nov.	Fri.	1	at Ottawa
	Sat.	2	at Toronto
	Mon.	4	Hartford
	Wed.	6	New Jersey
	Fri.	8	at Hartford
	Sun.	10	Tampa Bay
	Wed.	13	Colorado
	Fri.	15	San Jose
	Mon.	18	at Phoenix
	Thur.	21	at San Jose
	Sat.	23	at Los Angeles
	Sun.	24	at Anaheim
	Wed.	27	Toronto
Dec.	Sun.	1	Florida*
	Tues.	3	Vancouver
	Wed.	4	at Washington
	Tues.	10	Edmonton
	Thur.	12	Chicago
	Sun.	15	Toronto
	Tues.	17	at Colorado
	Wed.	18	at Calgary
	Fri.	20	at Vancouver
	Sun.	22	at Edmonton
	Thur.	26	Washington
	Sat.	28	at NY Islanders
	Mon.	30	Phoenix
Jan.	Fri.	3	Dallas
	Sun.	5	at Chicago
	Wed.	8	at Dallas

	Thur.	9	at Phoenix
	Sat.	11	Chicago
	Tues.	14	Los Angeles
	Mon.	20	at Montreal
	Wed.	22	Philadelphia
	Sat.	25	at Philadelphia*
	Wed.	29	Phoenix
Feb.	Sat.	1	at St. Louis*
	Sun.	2	Dallas
	Tues.	4	St. Louis
	Thur.	6	Vancouver
	Sat.	8	at Pittsburgh*
	Wed.	12	San Jose
	Fri.	14	at Dallas
	Sun.	16	at Florida
	Mon.	17	at Tampa Bay
	Wed.	19	Calgary
	Sat.	22	at St. Louis*
	Mon.	24	at Phoenix
	Thur.	27	Pittsburgh
Mar.	Sat.	1	NY Rangers*
	Sun.	2	Anaheim
	Wed.	5	at Toronto
	Sat.	8	at Vancouver
	Mon.	10	at Los Angeles
	Wed.	12	at Anaheim
	Sat.	15	at San Jose
	Sun.	16	at Colorado
	Wed.	19	Boston
	Fri.	21	at NY Rangers
	Sun.	23	at Chicago*
	Wed.	26	Colorado
	Fri.	28	Buffalo
	Sun.	30	Anaheim*
Apr.	Tues.	1	St. Louis
	Thur.	3	Toronto
	Sat.	5	at Toronto
	Tues.	8	at Calgary
	Wed.	9	at Edmonton
	Fri.	11	Ottawa
	Sun.	13	St. Louis*

* Denotes afternoon game.

Franchise date: September 25, 1926

71st NHL Season

CENTRAL DIVISION

Year-by-Year Record

		Home			Road			Overall							
Season	GP	W	L	T	W	L	T	W	L	T	GF	GA	Pts.	Finished	Playoff Result
1995-96	82	36	3	2	26	10	5	62	13	7	325	181	131	1st, Central Div.	Lost Conf. Championship
1994-95	48	17	4	3	16	7	1	33	11	4	180	117	70	1st, Central Div.	Lost Final
1993-94	84	23	13	6	23	17	2	46	30	8	356	275	100	1st, Central Div.	Lost Conf. Quarter-Final
1992-93	84	25	14	3	22	14	6	47	28	9	369	280	103	2nd, Norris Div.	Lost Div. Semi-Final
1991-92	80	24	12	4	19	13	8	43	25	12	320	256	98	1st, Norris Div.	Lost Div. Final
1990-91	80	26	14	0	8	24	8	34	38	8	273	298	76	3rd, Norris Div.	Lost Div. Semi-Final
1989-90	80	20	14	6	8	24	8	28	38	14	288	323	70	5th, Norris Div.	Out of Playoffs
1988-89	80	20	14	6	14	20	6	34	34	12	313	316	80	1st, Norris Div.	Lost Div. Semi-Final
1987-88	80	24	10	6	17	18	5	41	28	11	322	269	93	1st, Norris Div.	Lost Conf. Championship
1986-87	80	20	14	6	14	22	4	34	36	10	260	274	78	2nd, Norris Div.	Lost Conf. Championship
1985-86	80	10	26	4	7	31	2	17	57	6	266	415	40	5th, Norris Div.	Out of Playoffs
1984-85	80	19	14	7	8	27	5	27	41	12	313	357	66	3rd, Norris Div.	Lost Div. Semi-Final
1983-84	80	18	20	2	13	22	5	31	42	7	298	323	69	3rd, Norris Div.	Lost Div. Semi-Final
1982-83	80	14	19	7	7	25	8	21	44	15	263	344	57	5th, Norris Div.	Out of Playoffs
1981-82	80	15	19	6	6	28	6	21	47	12	270	351	54	6th, Norris Div.	Out of Playoffs
1980-81	80	16	15	9	3	28	9	19	43	18	252	339	56	5th, Norris Div.	Out of Playoffs
1979-80	80	14	21	5	12	22	6	26	43	11	268	306	63	5th, Norris Div.	Out of Playoffs
1978-79	80	15	17	8	8	24	8	23	41	16	252	295	62	5th, Norris Div.	Out of Playoffs
1977-78	80	22	11	7	10	23	7	32	34	14	252	266	78	2nd, Norris Div.	Lost Quarter-Final
1976-77	80	12	22	6	4	33	3	16	55	9	183	309	41	5th, Norris Div.	Out of Playoffs
1975-76	80	17	15	8	9	29	2	26	44	10	226	300	62	4th, Norris Div.	Out of Playoffs
1974-75	80	17	17	6	6	28	6	23	45	12	259	335	58	4th, Norris Div.	Out of Playoffs
1973-74	78	21	12	6	8	27	4	29	39	10	255	319	68	6th, East Div.	Out of Playoffs
1972-73	78	22	12	5	15	17	7	37	29	12	265	243	86	5th, East Div.	Out of Playoffs
1971-72	78	25	11	3	8	24	7	33	35	10	261	262	76	5th, East Div.	Out of Playoffs
1970-71	78	17	15	7	5	30	4	22	45	11	209	308	55	7th, East Div.	Out of Playoffs
1969-70	76	20	11	7	20	10	8	40	21	15	246	199	95	3rd, East Div.	Lost Quarter-Final
1968-69	76	23	8	7	10	23	5	33	31	12	239	221	78	5th, East Div.	Out of Playoffs
1967-68	74	18	15	4	9	20	8	27	35	12	245	257	66	6th, East Div.	Out of Playoffs
1966-67	70	21	11	3	6	28	1	27	39	4	212	241	58	5th,	Out of Playoffs
1965-66	70	20	8	7	11	19	5	31	27	12	221	194	74	4th,	Lost Final
1964-65	70	25	7	3	15	16	4	40	23	7	224	175	87	1st,	Lost Semi-Final
1963-64	70	23	9	3	7	20	8	30	29	11	191	204	71	4th,	Lost Final
1962-63	70	19	10	6	13	15	7	32	25	13	200	194	77	4th,	Lost Final
1961-62	70	17	11	7	6	22	7	23	33	14	184	219	60	5th,	Out of Playoffs
1960-61	70	15	13	7	10	16	9	25	29	16	195	215	66	4th,	Lost Final
1959-60	70	18	14	3	8	15	12	26	29	15	186	197	67	4th,	Lost Semi-Final
1958-59	70	13	17	5	12	20	3	25	37	8	167	218	58	6th,	Out of Playoffs
1957-58	70	16	11	8	13	18	4	29	29	12	176	207	70	3rd,	Lost Semi-Final
1956-57	70	23	7	5	15	13	7	38	20	12	198	157	88	1st,	Lost Semi-Final
1955-56	70	21	6	8	9	18	8	30	24	16	183	148	76	2nd,	Lost Final
1954-55	70	25	5	5	17	12	6	42	17	11	204	134	95	1st,	**Won Stanley Cup**
1953-54	70	24	4	7	13	15	7	37	19	14	191	132	88	1st,	**Won Stanley Cup**
1952-53	70	20	5	10	16	11	8	36	16	18	222	133	90	1st,	Lost Semi-Final
1951-52	70	24	7	4	20	7	8	44	14	12	215	133	100	1st,	**Won Stanley Cup**
1950-51	70	25	3	7	19	10	6	44	13	13	236	139	101	1st,	Lost Semi-Final
1949-50	70	19	9	7	18	10	7	37	19	14	229	164	88	1st,	**Won Stanley Cup**
1948-49	60	21	6	3	13	13	4	34	19	7	195	145	75	1st,	Lost Final
1947-48	60	16	9	5	14	9	7	30	18	12	187	148	72	2nd,	Lost Final
1946-47	60	14	10	6	8	17	5	22	27	11	190	193	55	4th,	Lost Semi-Final
1945-46	50	16	5	4	4	15	6	20	20	10	146	159	50	4th,	Lost Semi-Final
1944-45	50	19	5	1	12	9	4	31	14	5	218	161	67	2nd,	Lost Final
1943-44	50	18	5	2	8	13	4	26	18	6	214	177	58	2nd,	Lost Semi-Final
1942-43	50	16	4	5	9	10	6	25	14	11	169	124	61	1st,	**Won Stanley Cup**
1941-42	48	14	7	3	5	18	1	19	25	4	140	147	42	5th,	Lost Final
1940-41	48	14	5	5	7	11	6	21	16	11	112	102	53	3rd,	Lost Final
1939-40	48	11	10	3	5	16	3	16	26	6	90	126	38	5th,	Lost Semi-Final
1938-39	48	14	8	2	4	16	4	18	24	6	107	128	42	5th,	Lost Semi-Final
1937-38	48	8	10	6	4	15	5	12	25	11	99	133	35	4th, Amn. Div.	Out of Playoffs
1936-37	48	14	5	5	11	9	4	25	14	9	128	102	59	1st, **Amn. Div.**	**Won Stanley Cup**
1935-36	48	14	5	5	10	11	3	24	16	8	124	103	56	1st, **Amn. Div.**	**Won Stanley Cup**
1934-35	48	11	8	5	8	14	2	19	22	7	127	114	45	4th, Amn. Div.	Out of Playoffs
1933-34	48	15	5	4	9	9	6	24	14	10	113	98	58	1st, Amn. Div.	Lost Final
1932-33*	48	17	3	4	8	12	4	25	15	8	111	93	58	2nd, Amn. Div.	Lost Semi-Final
1931-32	48	15	3	6	3	17	4	18	20	10	95	108	46	3rd, Amn. Div.	Lost Quarter-Final
1930-31**	44	11	5	6	5	14	3	16	21	7	102	105	39	4th, Amn. Div.	Out of Playoffs
1929-30	44	9	10	3	5	14	3	14	24	6	117	133	34	4th, Amn. Div.	Out of Playoffs
1928-29	44	11	6	5	8	10	4	19	16	9	72	63	47	3rd, Amn. Div.	Lost Quarter-Final
1927-28	44	9	10	3	10	9	3	19	19	6	88	79	44	4th, Amn. Div.	Out of Playoffs
1926-27***	44	5	16	0	7	12	4	12	28	4	76	105	28	5th, Amn. Div.	Out of Playoffs

* Team name changed to Red Wings. ** Team name changed to Falcons. *** Team named Cougars.

1996-97 Player Personnel

FORWARDS	HT	WT	S	Place of Birth	Date	1995-96 Club
BOWEN, Curtis	6-1	195	L	Kenora, Ont.	3/24/74	Cdn. National-Adirondack
BROWN, Doug	5-10	185	R	Southborough, MA	6/12/64	Detroit
CLOUTIER, Sylvain	6-0	195	L	Mont-Laurier, Que.	2/13/74	Adirondack-Toledo
DANDENAULT, Mathieu	6-0	174	R	Sherbrooke, Que.	2/3/76	Detroit-Adirondack
DRAPER, Kris	5-11	185	L	Toronto, Ont.	5/24/71	Detroit
ERREY, Bob	5-10	185	L	Montreal, Que.	9/21/64	Detroit
FEDOROV, Sergei	6-1	200	L	Pskov, USSR	12/13/69	Detroit
GRIMSON, Stu	6-5	227	L	Kamloops, B.C.	5/20/65	Detroit
HOLMSTROM, Tomas	6-0	200	L	Pitea, Sweden	1/23/73	Lulea
JOHNSON, Greg	5-10	185	L	Thunder Bay, Ont.	3/16/71	Detroit
KNUBLE, Michael	6-3	208	R	Toronto, Ont.	7/4/72	Adirondack
KOZLOV, Vyacheslav	5-10	180	L	Voskresensk, USSR	5/3/72	Detroit
LAPOINTE, Martin	5-11	200	R	Ville Ste. Pierre, Que.	9/12/73	Detroit
LARIONOV, Igor	5-9	170	L	Voskresensk, USSR	12/3/60	San Jose-Detroit
MacDONALD, Jason	6-0	195	R	Charlottetown, P.E.I.	4/1/74	Adirondack-Toledo
MAJOR, Mark	6-3	223	L	Toronto, Ont.	3/20/70	Adirondack
MALTBY, Kirk	6-0	180	R	Guelph, Ont.	12/22/72	Edmonton-Cape Breton-Detroit
McCARTY, Darren	6-1	210	R	Burnaby, B.C.	4/1/72	Detroit
PRIMEAU, Keith	6-4	210	L	Toronto, Ont.	11/24/71	Detroit
TAYLOR, Tim	6-1	185	L	Stratford, Ont.	2/6/69	Detroit
YZERMAN, Steve	5-11	185	R	Cranbrook, B.C.	5/9/65	Detroit
DEFENSEMEN						
BLOEMBERG, Jeff	6-2	205	R	Listowel, Ont.	1/31/68	Adirondack
COFFEY, Paul	6-0	190	L	Weston, Ont.	6/1/61	Detroit
ERIKSSON, Anders	6-3	218	L	Bollnas, Sweden	1/9/75	Detroit-Adirondack
FETISOV, Viacheslav	6-1	220	L	Moscow, USSR	4/20/58	Detroit
GILLAM, Sean	6-2	187	R	Lethbridge, Alta.	5/7/76	Spokane
GOLUBOVSKY, Yan	6-3	183	R	Novosibirsk, USSR	3/9/76	Adirondack
KONSTANTINOV, Vladimir	5-11	190	R	Murmansk, USSR	3/19/67	Detroit
LIDSTROM, Nicklas	6-2	185	L	Vasteras, Sweden	4/28/70	Detroit
PUSHOR, Jamie	6-3	192	R	Lethbridge, Alta.	2/11/73	Detroit-Adirondack
ROUSE, Bob	6-1	210	R	Surrey, B.C.	6/18/64	Detroit
WARD, Aaron	6-2	200	R	Windsor, Ont.	1/17/73	Adirondack

GOALTENDERS	HT	WT	C	Place of Birth	Date	1995-96 Club
ARSENAULT, David	6-2	165	L	Frankfurt, Germany	3/21/77	Drummondville-Chicoutimi
HODSON, Kevin	6-0	182	L	Winnipeg, Man.	3/27/72	Detroit-Adirondack
MARACLE, Norm	5-9	175	L	Belleville, Ont.	10/2/74	Adirondack
OSGOOD, Chris	5-10	160	L	Peace River, Alta.	11/26/72	Detroit
VERNON, Mike	5-9	165	L	Calgary, Alta.	2/24/63	Detroit

1995-96 Scoring

* – rookie

Regular Season

Pos	#	Player	Team	GP	G	A	Pts	+/–	PIM	PP	SH	GW	GT	S	%
C	91	Sergei Fedorov	DET	78	39	68	107	49	48	11	3	11	1	306	12.7
C	19	Steve Yzerman	DET	80	36	59	95	29	64	16	2	8	0	220	16.4
D	77	Paul Coffey	DET	76	14	60	74	19	90	3	1	3	0	234	6.0
C	13	Vyacheslav Kozlov	DET	82	36	37	73	33	70	9	0	7	0	237	15.2
C	8	Igor Larionov	S.J.	4	1	1	2	–6	0	1	0	0	0	5	20.0
			DET	69	21	50	71	37	34	9	1	5	0	108	19.4
			TOTAL	73	22	51	73	31	34	10	1	5	0	113	19.5
D	5	Nicklas Lidstrom	DET	81	17	50	67	29	20	8	1	1	1	211	8.1
L	55	Keith Primeau	DET	74	27	25	52	19	168	6	2	7	0	150	18.0
R	22	Dino Ciccarelli	DET	64	22	21	43	14	99	13	0	5	0	107	20.6
D	2	Viacheslav Fetisov	DET	69	7	35	42	37	96	1	1	1	0	127	5.5
C	23	Greg Johnson	DET	60	18	22	40	6	30	5	0	2	0	87	20.7
D	16	Vlad. Konstantinov	DET	81	14	20	34	60	139	3	1	3	0	168	8.3
L	21	Bob Errey	DET	71	11	21	32	30	66	2	2	2	1	85	12.9
R	25	Darren McCarty	DET	63	15	14	29	14	158	8	0	1	1	102	14.7
R	17	Doug Brown	DET	62	12	15	27	11	4	0	1	1	0	115	10.4
C	37	Tim Taylor	DET	72	11	14	25	11	39	1	1	4	0	81	13.6
C	33	Kris Draper	DET	52	7	9	16	2	32	0	1	0	0	51	13.7
R	11	* Mathieu Dandenault	DET	34	5	7	12	6	6	1	0	0	0	32	15.6
D	27	Marc Bergevin	DET	70	1	9	10	7	33	0	0	0	0	26	3.8
R	20	Martin Lapointe	DET	58	6	3	9	0	93	1	0	0	0	76	7.9
R	18	Kirk Maltby	EDM	49	2	6	8	–16	61	0	0	1	0	51	3.9
			DET	6	1	0	1	0	6	0	0	0	0	4	25.0
			TOTAL	55	3	6	9	–16	67	0	0	1	0	55	5.5
D	15	Mike Ramsey	DET	47	2	4	6	17	35	0	0	0	0	35	5.7
D	3	Bob Rouse	DET	58	0	6	6	5	48	0	0	0	0	49	0.0
G	30	Chris Osgood	DET	50	1	2	3	0	4	0	0	0	0	1	100.0
D	4	* Jamie Pushor	DET	5	0	1	1	2	17	0	0	0	0	6	0.0
L	32	Stu Grimson	DET	56	0	1	1	–10	128	0	0	0	0	19	0.0
D	34	* Anders Eriksson	DET	1	0	0	0	1	2	0	0	0	0	0	0.0
C	26	Wes Walz	DET	2	0	0	0	0	0	0	0	0	0	2	0.0
G	31	* Kevin Hodson	DET	4	0	0	0	0	0	0	0	0	0	0	0.0
G	29	Mike Vernon	DET	32	0	0	0	0	2	0	0	0	0	0	0.0

Goaltending

No.	Goaltender	GPI	Mins	Avg	W	L	T	EN	SO	GA	SA	S%
31	* Kevin Hodson	4	163	1.10	2	0	0	0	1	3	67	.955
30	Chris Osgood	50	2933	2.17	39	6	5	1	5	106	1190	.911
29	Mike Vernon	32	1855	2.26	21	7	2	1	3	70	723	.903
	Totals	**82**	**4961**	**2.19**	**62**	**13**	**7**	**2**	**9**	**181**	**1982**	**.909**

Director of Player Personnel/Coach

BOWMAN, WILLIAM SCOTT (SCOTTY)
Director of Player Personnel/Coach, Detroit Red Wings.
Born in Montreal, Que. September 18, 1933.

Scotty Bowman is in his fourth year behind the Red Wings' bench. 1996-97 will be his third season as Detroit's director of player personnel. This is the third time that Bowman has held a front-office position while working as an NHL head coach. Bowman holds the NHL regular-season record for coaching wins (975) and winning percentage (.664) and has also recorded more post-season victories than any other coach, compiling a 162-101 mark in playoff encounters.

He is the only coach to guide four different teams into the Stanley Cup Finals, Bowman's six Cup victories are second only to Montreal's Toe Blake. After guiding the St. Louis Blues into the championship round in three consecutive seasons from 1968-70, Bowman was appointed head coach of the Montreal Canadiens, who captured five Stanley Cup titles under Bowman's supervision.

Following an eight season term as the general manager of the Buffalo Sabres, and a brief stint as a commentator for CBC Television, Bowman joined the Pittsburgh Penguins as director of player development, but returned to coaching when head coach Bob Johnson became ill in September, 1991. Bowman was elected to the Hockey Hall of Fame as a builder in 1991.

NHL Coaching Record

		Regular Season					Playoffs			
Season	Team	Games	W	L	T	%	Games	W	L	%
1967-68	St. Louis	58	23	21	14	.517	18	8	10	.444
1968-69	St. Louis	76	37	25	14	.579	12	8	4	.667
1969-70	St. Louis	76	37	27	12	.566	16	8	8	.500
1970-71	St. Louis	28	13	10	5	.554	6	2	4	.333
1971-72	Montreal	78	46	16	16	.692	6	2	4	.333
1972-73	Montreal	78	52	10	16	.769	17	12	5	.706*
1973-74	Montreal	78	45	24	9	.635	6	2	4	.333
1974-75	Montreal	80	47	14	19	.706	11	6	5	.545
1975-76	Montreal	80	58	11	11	.794	13	12	1	.923*
1976-77	Montreal	80	60	8	12	.825	14	12	2	.857*
1977-78	Montreal	80	59	10	11	.806	15	12	3	.800*
1978-79	Montreal	80	52	17	11	.719	16	12	4	.750*
1979-80	Buffalo	80	47	17	16	.688	14	9	5	.643
1981-82	Buffalo	35	18	10	7	.614	4	1	3	.250
1982-83	Buffalo	80	38	29	13	.556	10	6	4	.600
1983-84	Buffalo	80	48	25	7	.644	3	0	3	.000
1984-85	Buffalo	80	38	28	14	.563	5	2	3	.400
1985-86	Buffalo	37	18	18	1	.500	....	....	....	....
1986-87	Buffalo	12	3	7	2	.333	....	....	....	....
1991-92	Pittsburgh	80	39	32	9	.544	21	16	5	.762*
1992-93	Pittsburgh	84	56	21	7	.708	12	7	5	.583
1993-94	Detroit	84	46	30	8	.595	7	3	4	.429
1994-95	Detroit	48	33	11	4	.729	18	12	6	.667
1995-96	Detroit	82	62	13	7	.799	19	10	9	.526
	NHL Totals	**1654**	**975**	**434**	**245**	**.664**	**263**	**162**	**101**	**.616**

* Stanley Cup win.

Playoffs

Pos	#	Player	Team	GP	G	A	Pts	+/–	PIM	PP	SH	GW	OT	S	%
C	19	Steve Yzerman	DET	18	8	12	20	–1	4	4	0	1	1	52	15.4
C	91	Sergei Fedorov	DET	19	2	18	20	8	10	0	0	2	0	59	3.4
D	77	Paul Coffey	DET	17	5	9	14	–3	30	3	2	1	0	49	10.2
D	5	Nicklas Lidstrom	DET	19	5	9	14	2	10	1	0	0	0	50	10.0
C	8	Igor Larionov	DET	19	6	7	13	5	6	3	0	2	0	46	13.0
C	13	Vyacheslav Kozlov	DET	19	5	7	12	3	10	2	0	1	0	38	13.2
D	16	Vlad. Konstantinov	DET	19	4	5	9	4	28	0	1	0	0	41	9.8
R	22	Dino Ciccarelli	DET	17	6	2	8	–6	26	6	0	1	0	36	16.7
C	33	Kris Draper	DET	18	4	2	6	2	18	0	1	0	0	25	16.0
R	17	Doug Brown	DET	13	3	3	6	0	4	0	1	0	0	18	16.7
R	25	Darren McCarty	DET	19	3	2	5	–2	20	0	0	1	0	30	10.0
L	55	Keith Primeau	DET	17	1	4	5	–1	28	0	0	0	0	40	2.5
D	2	Viacheslav Fetisov	DET	19	1	4	5	3	34	0	0	1	0	24	4.2
C	23	Greg Johnson	DET	13	3	1	4	–3	8	0	0	0	0	11	27.3
L	21	Bob Errey	DET	14	0	4	4	1	8	0	0	0	0	21	0.0
D	15	Mike Ramsey	DET	15	0	4	4	1	10	0	0	0	0	11	0.0
C	37	Tim Taylor	DET	18	0	4	4	0	4	0	0	0	0	10	0.0
R	20	Martin Lapointe	DET	11	1	2	3	2	12	0	0	0	0	15	6.7
D	27	Marc Bergevin	DET	17	1	0	1	–4	14	1	0	0	0	14	7.1
D	3	Bob Rouse	DET	7	0	1	1	4	4	0	0	0	0	11	0.0
R	18	Kirk Maltby	DET	8	0	1	1	0	4	0	0	0	0	5	0.0
L	32	Stu Grimson	DET	2	0	0	0	0	0	0	0	0	0	0	0.0
D	34	* Anders Eriksson	DET	3	0	0	0	2	0	0	0	0	0	1	0.0
G	29	Mike Vernon	DET	4	0	0	0	0	2	0	0	0	0	0	0.0
G	30	Chris Osgood	DET	15	0	0	0	0	4	0	0	0	0	0	0.0

Goaltending

No.	Goaltender	GPI	Mins	Avg	W	L	EN	SO	GA	SA	S%
30	Chris Osgood	15	936	2.12	8	7	2	2	33	322	.898
29	Mike Vernon	4	243	2.72	2	2	0	0	11	81	.864
	Totals	**19**	**1182**	**2.34**	**10**	**9**	**2**	**2**	**46**	**405**	**.886**

Club Records

Team

(Figures in brackets for season records are games played; records for fewest points, wins, ties, losses, goals, goals against are for 70 or more games)

Most Points	**131**	1995-96 (82)
Most Wins	***62**	1995-96 (82)
Most Ties	**18**	1952-53 (70), 1980-81 (80)
Most Losses	**57**	1985-86 (80)
Most Goals	**369**	1992-93 (84)
Most Goals Against	**415**	1985-86 (80)
Fewest Points	**40**	1985-86 (80)
Fewest Wins	**16**	1976-77 (80)
Fewest Ties	**4**	1966-67 (70)
Fewest Losses	**13**	1950-51 (70), 1995-96 (82)
Fewest Goals	**167**	1958-59 (70)
Fewest Goals Against	**132**	1953-54 (70)
Longest Winning Streak		
Overall	**9**	Mar. 3-21/51, Feb. 27-Mar. 20/55
Home	**14**	Jan. 21-Mar. 25/65
Away	**7**	Mar. 25-Apr. 14/95
Longest Undefeated Streak		
Overall	**15**	Nov. 27-Dec. 28/52 (8 wins, 7 ties)
Home	**18**	Dec. 26/54-Mar. 20/55 (13 wins, 5 ties)
Away	**15**	Oct. 18-Dec. 20/51 (10 wins, 5 ties)
Longest Losing Streak		
Overall	**14**	Feb. 24-Mar. 25/82
Home	**7**	Feb. 20-Mar. 25/82
Away	**14**	Oct. 19-Dec. 21/66
Longest Winless Streak		
Overall	**19**	Feb. 26-Apr. 3/77 (18 losses, 1 tie)
Home	**10**	Dec. 11/85-Jan. 18/86 (9 losses, 1 tie)
Away	**26**	Dec. 15/76-Apr. 3/77 (23 losses, 3 ties)
Most Shutouts, Season	**13**	1953-54 (70)
Most. PIM, Season	**2,393**	1985-86 (80)
Most Goals, Game	**15**	Jan. 23/44 (NYR 0 at Det. 15)

Individual

Most Seasons	**25**	Gordie Howe
Most Games	**1,687**	Gordie Howe
Most Goals, Career	**786**	Gordie Howe
Most Assists, Career	**1,023**	Gordie Howe
Most Points, Career	**1,809**	Gordie Howe (786G, 1,023A)
Most PIM, Career	**2,090**	Bob Probert
Most Shutouts, Career	**85**	Terry Sawchuk
Longest Consecutive Games Streak	**548**	Alex Delvecchio (Dec. 13/56-Nov. 11/64)
Most Goals, Season	**65**	Steve Yzerman (1988-89)
Most Assists, Season	**90**	Steve Yzerman (1988-89)
Most Points, Season	**155**	Steve Yzerman (1988-89; 65G, 90A)
Most PIM, Season	**398**	Bob Probert (1987-88)
Most Points, Defenseman Season	**77**	Paul Coffey (1993-94; 14G, 63A)
Most Points, Center, Season	**155**	Steve Yzerman (1988-89; 65G, 90A)
Most Points, Right Wing, Season	**103**	Gordie Howe (1968-69; 44G, 59A)
Most Points, Left Wing, Season	**105**	John Ogrodnick (1984-85; 55G, 50A)
Most Points, Rookie, Season	**87**	Steve Yzerman (1983-84; 39G, 48A)
Most Shutouts, Season	**12**	Terry Sawchuk (1951-52, 1953-54, 1954-55), Glenn Hall (1955-56)
Most Goals, Game	**6**	Syd Howe (Feb. 3/44)
Most Assists, Game	***7**	Billy Taylor (Mar. 16/47)
Most Points, Game	**7**	Carl Liscombe (Nov. 5/42; 3G, 4A), Don Grosso (Feb. 3/44; 1G, 6A), Billy Taylor (Mar. 16/47; 7A)

* NHL Record

Retired Numbers

1	Terry Sawchuk	1949-55, 57-64, 68-69
6	Larry Aurie	1927-1939
7	Ted Lindsay	1944-57, 64-65
9	Gordie Howe	1946-1971
10	Alex Delvecchio	1951-1973
12	Sid Abel	1938-43, 45-52

All-time Record vs. Other Clubs

Regular Season

	At Home							On Road							Total						
	GP	**W**	**L**	**T**	**GF**	**GA**	**PTS**	**GP**	**W**	**L**	**T**	**GF**	**GA**	**PTS**	**GP**	**W**	**L**	**T**	**GF**	**GA**	**PTS**
Anaheim	6	5	0	1	31	18	11	6	4	0	2	30	15	10	12	9	0	3	61	33	21
Boston	279	151	76	52	934	701	354	280	86	151	43	745	991	215	559	237	227	95	1679	1692	569
Buffalo	48	25	18	5	180	147	55	46	7	32	7	125	211	21	94	32	50	12	305	358	76
Calgary	43	22	13	8	166	138	52	44	13	26	5	140	184	31	87	35	39	13	306	322	83
Chicago	314	194	92	28	1076	770	416	315	122	144	49	879	948	293	629	316	236	77	1955	1718	709
Colorado	24	14	9	1	98	79	29	25	9	13	3	91	101	21	49	23	22	4	189	180	50
Dallas	88	45	30	13	359	295	103	89	30	45	14	270	325	74	177	75	75	27	629	620	177
Edmonton	28	13	13	2	114	113	28	28	10	14	4	112	131	24	56	23	27	6	226	244	52
Florida	2	2	0	0	11	5	4	2	1	1	0	5	6	2	4	3	1	0	16	11	6
Hartford	24	11	7	6	91	70	28	23	8	14	1	64	87	17	47	19	21	7	155	157	45
Los Angeles	63	27	27	9	259	237	63	64	17	35	12	199	276	46	127	44	62	21	458	513	109
Montreal	275	126	96	53	785	705	305	275	63	169	43	619	979	169	550	189	265	96	1404	1684	474
New Jersey	33	19	12	2	141	115	40	34	10	16	8	99	122	28	67	29	28	10	240	237	68
NY Islanders	38	20	16	2	136	124	42	39	15	22	2	115	150	32	77	35	38	4	251	274	74
NY Rangers	279	159	75	45	980	689	363	277	87	132	58	711	854	232	556	246	207	103	1691	1543	595
Ottawa	3	2	1	0	14	7	4	3	2	1	0	11	9	4	6	4	2	0	25	16	8
Philadelphia	52	25	18	9	189	171	59	53	12	30	11	157	214	35	105	37	48	20	346	385	94
Pittsburgh	59	37	11	11	235	164	85	58	14	40	4	171	259	32	117	51	51	15	406	423	117
St. Louis	87	37	37	13	320	283	87	89	26	49	14	251	325	66	176	63	86	27	571	608	153
San Jose	9	9	0	0	46	14	18	10	7	2	1	50	32	15	19	16	2	1	96	46	33
Tampa Bay	5	4	1	0	22	13	8	7	6	1	0	42	23	12	12	10	2	0	64	36	20
Toronto	307	161	101	45	920	751	367	305	100	161	44	811	1016	244	612	261	262	89	1731	1767	611
Vancouver	50	30	14	6	210	147	66	49	18	24	7	158	192	43	99	48	38	13	368	339	109
Washington	41	17	13	11	146	121	45	39	15	20	4	124	154	34	80	32	33	15	270	275	79
Winnipeg	34	19	11	4	149	120	42	31	9	13	9	98	105	27	65	28	24	13	247	225	69
Defunct Clubs	141	76	40	25	430	307	177	141	49	63	29	364	375	127	282	125	103	54	794	682	304
Totals	**2332**	**1250**	**731**	**351**	**8042**	**6304**	**2851**	**2332**	**740**	**1218**	**374**	**6441**	**8084**	**1854**	**4664**	**1990**	**1949**	**725**	**14483**	**14388**	**4705**

Playoffs

	Series	**W**	**L**	**GP**	**W**	**L**	**T**	**GF**	**GA**	**Last Mtg.**	**Round**	**Result**
Boston	7	3	4	33	14	19	0	98	96	1957	SF	L 1-4
Calgary	1	1	0	2	2	0	0	8	5	1978	PR	W 2-0
Chicago	14	6	8	69	31	38	0	190	210	1995	CF	W 4-1
Colorado	1	0	1	6	2	4	0	16	20	1996	CF	L 2-4
Dallas	2	2	0	12	8	4	0	40	29	1995	CQF	W 4-1
Edmonton	2	0	2	10	2	8	0	26	39	1988	CF	L 1-4
Montreal	12	7	5	62	29	33	0	149	161	1978	QF	L 1-4
New Jersey	1	0	1	4	0	4	0	7	16	1995	F	L 0-4
NY Rangers	5	4	1	23	13	10	0	57	49	1950	F	W 4-3
St. Louis	4	2	2	23	12	11	0	75	67	1996	CSF	W 4-3
San Jose	2	1	1	11	7	4	0	51	27	1995	CSF	W 4-0
Toronto	23	11	12	117	59	58	0	321	311	1993	DSF	L 3-4
Winnipeg	1	1	0	6	4	2	0	20	10	1996	CQF	W 4-2
Defunct Clubs	4	3	1	10	7	2	1	21	13			
Totals	**79**	**41**	**38**	**388**	**190**	**197**	**1**	**1079**	**1053**			

Playoff Results 1996-92

Year	**Round**	**Opponent**	**Result**	**GF**	**GA**
1996	CF	Colorado	L 2-4	16	20
	CSF	St. Louis	W 4-3	22	16
	CQF	Winnipeg	W 4-2	20	10
1995	F	New Jersey	L 0-4	7	16
	CF	Chicago	W 4-1	13	12
	CSF	San Jose	W 4-0	24	6
	CQF	Dallas	W 4-1	17	10
1994	CQF	San Jose	L 3-4	27	21
1993	DSF	Toronto	L 3-4	30	24
1992	DF	Chicago	L 0-4	6	11
	DSF	Minnesota	W 4-3	23	19

Abbreviations: Round: F – Final; **CF** – conference final; **CQF** – conference quarter-final; **CSF** – conference semi-final; **DF** – division final; **DSF** – division semi-final; **SF** – semi-final; **QF** – quarter-final; **PR** – preliminary round.

Calgary totals include Atlanta, 1972-73 to 1979-80. Colorado totals include Quebec, 1979-80 to 1994-95.
Dallas totals include Minnesota, 1967-68 to 1992-93.
New Jersey totals include Kansas City, 1974-75 to 1975-76, and Colorado Rockies, 1976-77 to 1981-82.

1995-96 Results

Oct.	6	at	Colorado	2-3		12		Los Angeles	3-2
	8	at	Edmonton	3-1		13	at	Washington	4-2
	9	at	Vancouver	5-3		17		Colorado	3-2
	13		Edmonton	9-0		24		San Jose	4-2
	15	at	Winnipeg	5-5		25	at	Ottawa	4-2
	17		Calgary	3-3		27	at	Chicago	5-5
	19	at	New Jersey	2-4		30		Toronto	4-2
	21		Boston	4-2	**Feb.**	3		Pittsburgh	3-0
	24		Ottawa	1-2		6		Florida	4-2
	27	at	Calgary	3-0		8	at	Florida	1-3
	30	at	Winnipeg	2-3		10	at	Tampa Bay	3-2
Nov.	1	at	Buffalo	1-2		13		Los Angeles	9-4
	2	at	Boston	6-5		15		Washington	4-3
	4		Dallas	5-1		16	at	St. Louis	3-4
	7		Edmonton	4-2		18	at	Toronto	3-2
	11	at	San Jose	5-2		19		Vancouver	4-3
	14	at	Los Angeles	6-5		22		Toronto	5-3
	17	at	Edmonton	5-4		24		Tampa Bay	2-0
	22		San Jose	5-2		27	at	NY Islanders	6-2
	24	at	Philadelphia	1-4		29		NY Islanders	5-1
	25		NY Rangers	2-0	**Mar.**	2		Vancouver	2-3
	28		Montreal	3-2		3	at	Chicago	6-2
Dec.	1		Anaheim	5-2		6	at	Hartford	4-2
	2	at	Montreal	11-1		8	at	Colorado	4-2
	5		Philadelphia	5-3		10	at	Winnipeg	5-2
	7		Dallas	3-1		12		Winnipeg	5-2
	8	at	NY Rangers	1-2		17		Calgary	4-2
	12	at	St. Louis	5-2		19		Toronto	6-5
	13		Chicago	3-1		20	at	Toronto	4-3
	15		New Jersey	3-1		22		Colorado	7-0
	20	at	Anaheim	6-1		24	at	St. Louis	2-2
	22	at	Calgary	5-1		25		Anaheim	5-1
	23	at	Vancouver	1-0		27		Buffalo	4-2
	26		St. Louis	3-2		31		St. Louis	8-1
	29	at	Dallas	2-1	**Apr.**	2	at	San Jose	3-6
	31		Hartford	3-2		3	at	Los Angeles	2-2
Jan.	3		Dallas	3-3		5	at	Anaheim	2-2
	5	at	Pittsburgh	2-5		7	at	Chicago	4-1
	6		Chicago	3-0		10		Winnipeg	5-2
	8		Winnipeg	4-6		12		Chicago	5-3
	10	at	Dallas	4-0		14	at	Dallas	5-1

Entry Draft
Selections 1996-82

1996 Pick	**1992** Pick	**1988** Pick	**1984** Pick
26 Jesse Wallin	22 Curtis Bowen	17 Kory Kocur	7 Shawn Burr
52 Aren Miller	46 Darren McCarty	38 Serge Anglehart	28 Doug Houda
108 Johan Forsander	70 Sylvain Cloutier	47 Guy Dupuis	49 Milan Chalupa
135 Michal Podolka	118 Mike Sullivan	59 Petr Hrbek	91 Mats Lundstrom
144 Magnus Nilsson	142 Jason MacDonald	80 Sheldon Kennedy	112 Randy Hansch
162 Alexandre Jacques	166 Greg Scott	143 Kelly Hurd	133 Stefan Larsson
189 Colin Beardsmore	183 Justin Krall	164 Brian McCormack	152 Lars Karlsson
215 Craig Stahl	189 C.J. Denomme	185 Jody Praznik	154 Urban Nordin
241 Evgeniy Afanasiev	214 Jeff Walker	206 Glen Goodall	175 Bill Shibicky
	238 Daniel McGillis	227 Darren Colbourne	195 Jay Rose
1995 Pick	262 Ryan Bach	248 Donald Stone	216 Tim Kaiser
26 Maxim Kuznetsov			236 Tom Nickolau
52 Philippe Audet	**1991** Pick	**1987** Pick	
58 Darryl Laplante	10 Martin Lapointe	11 Yves Racine	**1983** Pick
104 Anatoly Ustugov	32 Jamie Pushor	32 Gordon Kruppke	4 Steve Yzerman
125 David Arsenault	54 Chris Osgood	41 Bob Wilkie	25 Lane Lambert
126 David Arsenault	76 Michael Knuble	52 Dennis Holland	46 Bob Probert
156 Tyler Perry	98 Dmitri Motkov	74 Mark Reimer	68 David Korol
182 Per Eklund	142 Igor Malykhin	95 Radomir Brazda	86 Petr Klima
208 Andrei Samokvalov	186 Jim Bermingham	116 Sean Clifford	88 Joey Kocur
234 David Engblom	208 Jason Firth	137 Mike Gober	106 Chris Pusey
	230 Bart Turner	158 Kevin Scott	126 Bob Pierson
1994 Pick	252 Andrew Miller	179 Mikko Haapakoski	146 Craig Butz
23 Yan Golubovsky		200 Darin Bannister	166 Dave Sikorski
49 Mathieu Dandenault	**1990** Pick	221 Craig Quinlan	186 Stu Grimson
75 Sean Gillam	3 Keith Primeau	242 Tomas Jansson	206 Jeff Frank
114 Frederic Deschenes	45 Vyacheslav Kozlov		226 Charles Chiatto
127 Doug Battaglia	66 Stewart Malgunas	**1986** Pick	
153 Pavel Agarkov	87 Tony Burns	1 Joe Murphy	**1982** Pick
205 Jason Elliot	108 Claude Barthe	22 Adam Graves	17 Murray Craven
231 Jeff Mikesch	129 Jason York	43 Derek Mayer	23 Yves Courteau
257 Tomas Holmstrom	150 Wes McCauley	64 Tim Cheveldae	44 Carmine Vani
283 Toivo Suursoo	171 Anthony Gruba	85 Johan Garpenlov	66 Craig Coxe
	192 Travis Tucker	106 Jay Stark	86 Brad Shaw
1993 Pick	213 Brett Larson	127 Per Djoos	107 Claude Vilgrain
22 Anders Eriksson	234 John Hendry	148 Dean Morton	128 Greg Hudas
48 Jonathan Coleman		169 Marc Potvin	149 Pat Lahey
74 Kevin Hilton	**1989** Pick	190 Scott King	170 Gary Cullen
97 John Jakopin	11 Mike Sillinger	211 Tom Bissett	191 Brent Meckling
100 Benoit Larose	32 Bob Boughner	232 Peter Ekroth	212 Mike Stern
126 Norm Maracle	53 Nicklas Lidstrom		233 Shaun Reagan
152 Tim Spitzig	74 Sergei Fedorov	**1985** Pick	
178 Yuri Yeresko	95 Shawn McCosh	8 Brent Fedyk	
204 Vitezslav Skuta	116 Dallas Drake	29 Jeff Sharples	
230 Ryan Shanahan	137 Scott Zygulski	50 Steve Chiasson	
256 James Kosecki	158 Andy Suhy	71 Mark Gowans	
282 Gordon Hunt	179 Bob Jones	92 Chris Luongo	
	200 Greg Bignell	113 Randy McKay	
	204 Rick Judson	134 Thomas Bjur	
	221 Vladimir Konstantinov	155 Mike Luckraft	
	242 Joseph Frederick	176 Rob Schenna	
	246 Jason Glickman	197 Erik Hamalainen	
		218 Bo Svanberg	
		239 Mikael Lindman	

Club Directory

Joe Louis Arena
600 Civic Center Drive
Detroit, Michigan 48226
Phone **(313) 396-7544**
FAX PR: (313) 567-0296
Capacity: 19,275

Owner/President	Mike Ilitch
Owner/Secretary-Treasurer	Marian Ilitch
Vice-Presidents	Atanas Ilitch, Christopher Ilitch
Senior Vice-President/Hockey Operations	Jim Devellano
Director of Player Personnel/Head Coach	Scotty Bowman
Assistant General Manager/Goaltending Consultant	Ken Holland
Associate Coaches	Barry Smith, Dave Lewis
NHL Scout	Dan Belisle
Director of Player Development/AHL-IHL Scout	Jim Nill
Eastern Canada Scout	Joe McDonnell
Western Scout	Bruce Haralson
Eastern USA Scout	Mark Leach
Western USA Scout	Chris Coury
Director of European Scouting	Hakan Andersson
Czech Republic Scout	Vladimir HavLug
Controller	Paul MacDonald
Marketing Director	Ted Speers
Public Relations Director	TBA
Broadcast Coordinator	Jason O'Connell
Public Relations Assistants	Karen Davis, Tony Lasher
Box Office Manager	Bob Kerlin
Season Ticket Sales Director	Brad Ebben
Executive Assistant	Nancy Beard
Accounting Assistant	Cathy Witzke
Athletic Trainer	John Wharton
Equipment Manager/Trainer	Paul Boyer
Assistant Equipment Manager	Tim Abbott
Team Physicians	Dr. John Finley, D.O., Dr. David Collon, M.D.
Team Dentist	Dr. C.J. Regula, D.M.D.
Team Ophthalmologist	Dr. Charles Slater, M.D.
Home Ice/Training Camp Site	Joe Louis Arena
Press Box & Radio-TV Booths	Jefferson Avenue side of arena, top of seats
Media Lounge	First-floor hallway near Red Wings' dressing room
Rink Dimensions	200 feet by 85 feet
Uniforms	Home: Base color white, trimmed in red
	Road: Base color red, trimmed in white
Radio flagship station	WJR-AM (760)
TV stations	UPN-50; PASS Sports;
	Special Order Sports
Radio announcers	Ken Kal, Paul Woods
TV announcers	TBA, Mickey Redmond

Senior Vice-President

DEVELLANO, JAMES (JIM)
Senior Vice-President, Detroit Red Wings.
Born in Toronto, Ont., January 18, 1943.

Jim Devellano is in his 15th season with the Red Wings and has played a major role in the team's success. He served eight years as general manager before being appointed senior vice-president.

Devellano, respected throughout the league as an astute judge of talent, scouts players on all levels and also helps the scouting staff to prepare for the Entry Draft. In addition, he is involved with administrative matters and serves as the team's alternate on the NHL's Board of Governors.

Devellano, who is in his 29th season in the NHL in various capacities, came to Detroit as general manager July 12, 1982, and built a team through the draft, trades and free agency that finished first in its division in five of the past eight seasons and won the Presidents' Trophy as the NHL's best club in 1994-95 regular-season play. He also developed a top farm club in Adirondack that under his direction, won the AHL's Calder Cup championship in 1986 and 1989.

Devellano, 53, didn't play professional hockey but worked in various levels of the game in his hometown of Toronto. He joined the St. Louis Blues as a scout in 1967 when the NHL expanded from six to 12 teams. The Blues reached the Stanley Cup Finals in each of their first three seasons.

When the New York Islanders were founded in 1972, Devellano came aboard and helped to build a club that won four consecutive Stanley Cup titles (1980-89). In 1979-80, he became g.m. of the Islanders' Indianapolis (CHL) farm club and was named minor league executive of the year by *The Hockey News* in his first year. He returned to Long Island in 1981 as the Islanders' asssistant g.m.

Mike Ilitch bought the Red Wings in June of 1982 and brought in Devellano the following month. Jim became a team vice-president December 30, 1985, and assumed his present position July 13, 1990.

''Jimmy D '' is single and resides in Detroit.

General Managers' History

Art Duncan, 1926-27; Jack Adams, 1927-28 to 1961-62; Sid Abel, 1962-63 to 1969-70; Sid Abel and Ned Harkness, 1970-71; Ned Harkness, 1971-72 to 1973-74; Alex Delvecchio, 1974-75 to 1975-76; Alex Delvecchio and Ted Lindsay, 1976-77; Ted Lindsay, 1977-78 to 1979-80; Jimmy Skinner, 1980-81 to 1981-82; Jim Devellano, 1982-83 to 1989-90; Bryan Murray, 1990-91 to 1993-94; Jim Devellano (Senior Vice President), 1994-95 to date.

Coaching History

Art Duncan, 1926-27; Jack Adams, 1927-28 to 1946-47; Tommy Ivan, 1947-48 to 1953-54; Jimmy Skinner, 1954-55 to 1956-57; Jimmy Skinner and Sid Abel, 1957-58; Sid Abel, 1958-59 to 1967-68; Bill Gadsby, 1968-69; Bill Gadsby and Sid Abel, 1969-70; Ned Harkness and Doug Barkley, 1970-71; Doug Barkley and John Wilson, 1971-72; John Wilson, 1972-73; Ted Garvin and Alex Delvecchio, 1973-74; Alex Delvecchio, 1974-75; Doug Barkley and Alex Delvecchio, 1975-76; Alex Delvecchio and Larry Wilson, 1976-77; Bobby Kromm, 1977-78 to 1978-79; Bobby Kromm and Ted Lindsay, 1979-80; Ted Lindsay and Wayne Maxner, 1980-81; Wayne Maxner and Billy Dea, 1981-82; Nick Polano, 1982-83 to 1984-85; Harry Neale and Brad Park, 1985-86; Jacques Demers, 1986-87 to 1989-90; Bryan Murray, 1990-91 to 1992-93; Scotty Bowman, 1993-94 to date.

Captains' History

Art Duncan, 1926-27; Reg Noble, 1927-28 to 1929-30; George Hay, 1930-31; Carson Cooper, 1931-32; Larry Aurie, 1932-33; Herbie Lewis, 1933-34; Ebbie Goodfellow, 1934-35; Doug Young, 1935-36 to 1937-38; Ebbie Goodfellow, 1938-39 to 1940-41; Ebbie Goodfellow and Syd Howe, 1941-42; Sid Abel, 1942-43; ''Mud'' Bruneteau, Bill Hollett (co-captains), 1943-44; Bill Hollett, 1944-45; Bill Hollett and Sid Abel, 1945-46; Sid Abel, 1946-47 to 1951-52; Ted Lindsay, 1952-53 to 1955-56; Red Kelly, 1956-57; 1957-58; Gordie Howe, 1958-59 to 1961-62; Alex Delvecchio, 1962-63 to 1972-73; Alex Delvecchio, Nick Libett, Red Berenson, Gary Bergman, Ted Harris, Mickey Redmond, Larry Johnston, 1973-74; Marcel Dionne, 1974-75; Danny Grant, Terry Harper, 1975-76; Danny Grant, Dennis Polonich, 1976-77; Dan Maloney, Dennis Hextall, 1977-78; Dennis Hextall, Nick Libett, Paul Woods, 1978-79; Dale McCourt, 1979-80; Errol Thompson, Reed Larson, 1980-81; Reed Larson, 1981-82; Danny Gare, 1982-83 to 1985-86; Steve Yzerman, 1986-87 to date.

Edmonton Oilers

1995-96 Results: 30W-44L-8T 68PTS. Fifth, Pacific Division

Schedule

Oct.	Fri.	4	Buffalo
	Sun.	6	Vancouver
	Tues.	8	at Toronto
	Wed.	9	at Detroit
	Fri.	11	St. Louis
	Mon.	14	at Phoenix
	Tues.	15	at Colorado
	Sun.	20	at Calgary
	Tues.	22	Pittsburgh
	Thur.	24	at Los Angeles
	Sat.	26	Colorado
	Wed.	30	Phoenix
Nov.	Fri.	1	Vancouver
	Sun.	3	at Chicago*
	Wed.	6	at Pittsburgh
	Thur.	7	at Boston
	Sat.	9	at Toronto
	Mon.	11	at Montreal
	Wed.	13	at Ottawa
	Sun.	17	Dallas
	Tues.	19	Chicago
	Thur.	21	NY Rangers
	Sat.	23	Calgary
	Tues.	26	at Calgary
	Wed.	27	Los Angeles
	Fri.	29	at San Jose
Dec.	Sun.	1	at Anaheim
	Wed.	4	at Colorado
	Fri.	6	Ottawa
	Sun.	8	St. Louis
	Tues.	10	at Detroit
	Thur.	12	at Tampa Bay
	Sat.	14	at Florida
	Wed.	18	Colorado
	Fri.	20	New Jersey
	Sun.	22	Detroit
	Mon.	23	at Vancouver
	Fri.	27	Philadelphia
	Sat.	28	San Jose
	Mon.	30	Los Angeles
Jan.	Fri.	3	Toronto
	Tues.	7	at St. Louis
	Wed.	8	at Chicago
	Sat.	11	San Jose
	Sun.	12	Hartford
	Wed.	15	Florida
	Tues.	21	at NY Rangers
	Wed.	22	at NY Islanders
	Fri.	24	at Buffalo
	Sun.	26	at Washington*
	Wed.	29	San Jose
	Fri.	31	NY Islanders
Feb.	Wed.	5	Calgary
	Sat.	8	Anaheim
	Sun.	9	Washington
	Wed.	12	Boston
	Thur.	13	at Calgary
	Sat.	15	at Los Angeles
	Mon.	17	at Anaheim
	Wed.	19	Toronto
	Fri.	21	Colorado
	Sun.	23	at Dallas*
	Wed.	26	at Anaheim
	Thur.	27	at Los Angeles
Mar.	Sat.	1	Montreal
	Tues.	4	Los Angeles
	Fri.	7	at Dallas
	Sun.	9	at St. Louis
	Tues.	11	at New Jersey
	Thur.	13	at Philadelphia
	Sat.	15	at Hartford*
	Wed.	19	Tampa Bay
	Sun.	23	Anaheim*
	Mon.	24	at San Jose
	Fri.	28	at San Jose
	Sat.	29	at Phoenix
	Mon.	31	Dallas
Apr.	Thur.	3	Chicago
	Sat.	5	Vancouver
	Wed.	9	Detroit
	Fri.	11	Phoenix
	Sat.	12	at Vancouver

* Denotes afternoon game.

Year-by-Year Record

		Home			Road			Overall						
Season	GP	W	L	T	W	L	T	W	L	T	GF	GA	Pts.	Finished	Playoff Result
1995-96	82	15	21	5	15	23	3	30	44	8	240	304	68	5th, Pacific Div.	Out of Playoffs
1994-95	48	11	12	1	6	15	3	17	27	4	136	183	38	5th, Pacific Div.	Out of Playoffs
1993-94	84	17	22	3	8	23	11	25	45	14	261	305	64	6th, Pacific Div.	Out of Playoffs
1992-93	84	16	21	3	10	29	3	26	50	8	242	337	60	5th, Smythe Div.	Out of Playoffs
1991-92	80	22	13	5	14	21	5	36	34	10	295	297	82	3rd, Smythe Div.	Lost Conf. Championship
1990-91	80	22	15	3	15	22	3	37	37	6	272	272	80	3rd, Smythe Div.	Lost Conf. Championship
1989-90	80	23	11	6	15	17	8	38	28	14	315	283	90	2nd, Smythe Div.	**Won Stanley Cup**
1988-89	80	21	16	3	17	18	5	38	34	8	325	306	84	3rd, Smythe Div.	Lost Div. Semi-Final
1987-88	80	28	8	4	16	17	7	44	25	11	363	288	99	2nd, Smythe Div.	**Won Stanley Cup**
1986-87	80	29	6	5	21	18	1	50	24	6	372	284	106	1st, Smythe Div.	**Won Stanley Cup**
1985-86	80	32	6	2	24	11	5	56	17	7	426	310	119	1st, Smythe Div.	Lost Div. Final
1984-85	80	26	7	7	23	13	4	49	20	11	401	298	111	1st, Smythe Div.	**Won Stanley Cup**
1983-84	80	31	5	4	26	13	1	57	18	5	446	314	119	1st, Smythe Div.	**Won Stanley Cup**
1982-83	80	25	9	6	22	12	6	47	21	12	424	315	106	1st, Smythe Div.	Lost Final
1981-82	80	31	5	4	17	12	11	48	17	15	417	295	111	1st, Smythe Div.	Lost Div. Semi-Final
1980-81	80	17	13	10	12	22	6	29	35	16	328	327	74	4th, Smythe Div.	Lost Quarter-Final
1979-80	80	17	14	9	11	25	4	28	39	13	301	322	69	4th, Smythe Div.	Lost Prelim. Round

Although he missed 18 games during the 1995-96 season because of injury and knee surgery, Jason Arnott still finished third in goals (28) and first in game-winning goals (5) for the Edmonton Oilers.

Franchise date: June 22, 1979

PACIFIC DIVISION

18th NHL Season

1996-97 Player Personnel

FORWARDS	HT	WT	S	Place of Birth	Date	1995-96 Club
ARNOTT, Jason	6-3	220	R	Collingwood, Ont.	10/11/74	Edmonton
BELANGER, Jesse	6-1	190	R	St. Georges de Beauce, Que	6/15/69	Florida-Vancouver
BONSIGNORE, Jason	6-4	220	R	Rochester, NY	4/15/76	Edmonton-Sudbury-Cape Breton
BONVIE, Dennis	5-11	205	R	Antigonish, N.S.	7/23/73	Edmonton-Cape Breton
BREEN, George	6-2	200	R	Webster, MA	8/3/73	Cape Breton
BUCHBERGER, Kelly	6-2	200	L	Langenburg, Sask.	12/2/66	Edmonton
CERVEN, Martin	6-4	200	L	Trencin, Czech.	3/7/77	Spokane-Seattle
CIGER, Zdeno	6-1	190	L	Martin, Czech.	10/19/69	Edmonton
COPELAND, Adam	6-1	185	R	St. Catharines, Ont.	6/5/76	Miami-Ohio
CZERKAWSKI, Mariusz	6-0	195	R	Radomsko, Poland	4/13/72	Boston-Edmonton
DeBRUSK, Louie	6-2	215	L	Cambridge, Ont.	3/19/71	Edmonton
DEVEREAUX, Boyd	6-0	175	L	Seaforth, Ont.	4/16/78	Kitchener
GRIER, Michael	6-1	232	R	Detroit, Mich.	1/5/75	Boston U.
HAGGERTY, Ryan	6-1	195	L	Rye, NY	5/2/73	Cape Breton-Wheeling
INTRANUOVO, Ralph	5-8	185	L	East York, Ont.	12/11/73	Edmonton-Cape Breton
KELLY, Steve	6-1	190	L	Vancouver, B.C.	10/26/76	Prince Albert
LARAQUE, Georges	6-3	235	R	Montreal, Que.	12/7/76	Laval-St-Hyacinthe-Granby
LINDGREN, Mats	6-2	200	L	Skelleftea, Sweden	10/1/74	Cape Breton
MARCHANT, Todd	5-10	175	L	Buffalo, NY	8/12/73	Edmonton
McAMMOND, Dean	5-11	185	L	Grand Cache, Alta.	6/15/73	Edmonton-Cape Breton
OLIVER, David	6-0	190	R	Sechelt, B.C.	4/17/71	Edmonton
PADEN, Kevin	6-3	190	L	Woodhaven, MI	2/12/75	C.B.-Tallahassee-Huntington
SATAN, Miroslav	6-1	185	L	Topolcany, Czech.	10/22/74	Edmonton
SMYTH, Ryan	6-1	195	L	Banff, Alta.	2/21/76	Edmonton-Cape Breton
THORNTON, Scott	6-3	210	L	London, Ont.	1/9/71	Edmonton
TUOMAINEN, Marko	6-3	203	R	Kuopio, Finland	4/25/72	Cape Breton
WEIGHT, Doug	5-11	191	L	Warren, MI	1/21/71	Edmonton

DEFENSEMEN						
ANTONIN, Jiri	6-3	207	L	Pardubice, Czech.	11/15/75	Pardubice
BROWN, Sean	6-2	205	L	Oshawa, Ont.	11/5/76	Belleville-Sarnia
De VRIES, Greg	6-3	218	L	Sundridge, Ont.	1/4/73	Edmonton-Cape Breton
DESCOTEAUX, Matthieu	6-3	190	L	Pierreville, Que.	9/23/77	Shawinigan
FAFARD, Dominic	6-5	230	R	Longueuil, Que.	7/13/74	Wheeling-Raleigh-Oklahoma City
HAJT, Chris	6-3	206	L	Saskatoon, Sask.	7/5/78	Guelph
HAUER, Brett	6-2	200	R	Richfield, MN	7/11/71	Edmonton-Cape Breton
MARCHMENT, Bryan	6-1	205	L	Scarborough, Ont.	5/1/69	Edmonton
MIRONOV, Boris	6-3	220	R	Moscow, USSR	3/21/72	Edmonton
MUIR, Bryan	6-4	220	L	Winnipeg, Man.	6/8/73	Cdn. National-Edmonton
NORTON, Brad	6-4	225	L	Cambridge, MA	2/13/75	Massachusetts
NORTON, Jeff	6-2	200	L	Acton, MA	11/25/65	St. Louis-Edmonton
RICHARDSON, Luke	6-4	210	L	Ottawa, Ont.	3/26/69	Edmonton
SLEGR, Jiri	6-1	205	L	Jihlava, Czech.	5/30/71	Edmonton-Cape Breton
SNOPEK, Jan	6-3	212	R	Prague, Czech.	6/22/76	Oshawa
STAJDUHAR, Nick	6-3	200	L	Kitchener, Ont.	12/6/74	Edm-Cdn. National-Cape Breton
SYMES, Brad	6-2	210	L	Edmonton, Alta.	4/26/76	Portland (WHL)
ZHURIK, Alexander	6-3	195	L	Minsk, USSR	5/29/75	Cape Breton

GOALTENDERS	HT	WT	C	Place of Birth	Date	1995-96 Club
ESSENSA, Bob	6-0	185	L	Toronto, Ont.	1/14/65	Adirondack-Fort Wayne
GAGE, Joaquin	6-0	200	L	Vancouver, B.C.	10/19/73	Edmonton-Cape Breton
JOSEPH, Curtis	5-10	182	L	Keswick, Ont.	4/29/67	Las Vegas-Edmonton
MINARD, Mike	6-3	205	L	Owen Sound, Ont.	11/1/76	Barrie-Detroit (OHL)
PASSMORE, Steve	5-9	165	L	Thunder Bay, Ont.	1/29/73	Cape Breton
WICKENHEISER, Chris	6-1	185	L	Lethbridge, Alta.	1/20/76	Red Deer

General Managers' History

Larry Gordon, 1979-80; Glen Sather, 1980-81 to date.

Coaching History

Glen Sather, 1979-80; Bryan Watson and Glen Sather, 1980-81; Glen Sather, 1981-82 to 1988-89; John Muckler, 1989-90 to 1990-91; Ted Green, 1991-92 to 1992-93; Ted Green and Glen Sather, 1993-94; George Burnett and Ron Low, 1994-95; Ron Low, 1995-96 to date.

Captains' History

Ron Chipperfield, 1979-80; Blair MacDonald and Lee Fogolin, 1980-81; Lee Fogolin, 1981-82 to 1982-83; Wayne Gretzky, 1983-84 to 1987-88; Mark Messier, 1988-89 to 1990-91; Kevin Lowe, 1991-92; Craig MacTavish, 1992-93 to 1993-94; Shayne Corson, 1994-95; Kelly Buchberger, 1995-96.

Retired Numbers

3   Al Hamilton   1972-1980

1995-96 Scoring

* – rookie

Regular Season

Pos	#	Player	Team	GP	G	A	Pts	+/-	PIM	PP	SH	GW	GT	S	%
C	39	Doug Weight	EDM	82	25	79	104	-19	95	9	0	2	1	204	12.3
L	8	Zdeno Ciger	EDM	78	31	39	70	-15	41	12	0	3	0	184	16.8
C	7	Jason Arnott	EDM	64	28	31	59	-6	87	8	0	5	1	244	11.5
R	10	Mariusz Czerkawski	BOS	33	5	6	11	-11	10	1	0	0	0	63	7.9
			EDM	37	12	17	29	7	8	2	0	1	0	79	15.2
			TOTAL	70	17	23	40	-4	18	3	0	1	0	142	12.0
R	20	David Oliver	EDM	80	20	19	39	-22	34	14	0	0	0	131	15.3
C	26	Todd Marchant	EDM	81	19	19	38	-19	66	2	3	2	1	221	8.6
L	32	* Miroslav Satan	EDM	62	18	17	35	0	22	6	0	4	0	113	15.9
D	2	Boris Mironov	EDM	78	8	24	32	-23	101	7	0	1	0	158	5.1
D	6	Jeff Norton	STL	36	4	7	11	4	26	0	0	1	0	33	12.1
			EDM	30	4	16	20	5	16	1	0	1	0	52	7.7
			TOTAL	66	8	23	31	9	42	1	0	2	0	85	9.4
L	37	Dean McAmmond	EDM	53	15	15	30	6	23	4	0	0	0	79	19.0
L	16	Kelly Buchberger	EDM	82	11	14	25	-20	184	0	2	3	0	119	9.2
L	17	Scott Thornton	EDM	77	9	9	18	-25	149	0	2	3	0	95	9.5
D	24	Bryan Marchment	EDM	78	3	15	18	-7	202	0	0	0	0	96	3.1
D	28	Jiri Slegr	EDM	57	4	13	17	-1	74	0	1	1	0	91	4.4
L	15	* David Roberts	STL	28	1	6	7	-7	12	1	0	1	0	35	2.9
			EDM	6	2	4	6	0	6	0	0	0	0	12	16.7
			TOTAL	34	3	10	13	-7	18	1	0	1	0	47	6.4
L	94	* Ryan Smyth	EDM	48	2	9	11	-10	28	1	0	0	0	65	3.1
D	22	Luke Richardson	EDM	82	2	9	11	-27	108	0	0	0	0	61	3.3
L	19	Kent Manderville	EDM	37	3	5	8	-5	38	0	2	0	0	63	4.8
D	34	Donald Dufresne	STL	3	0	0	0	-2	4	0	0	0	0	1	0.0
			EDM	42	1	6	7	-2	16	0	0	0	0	20	5.0
			TOTAL	45	1	6	7	-4	20	0	0	0	0	21	4.8
D	5	* Brett Hauer	EDM	29	4	2	6	-11	30	2	1	0	0	53	7.5
L	29	Louie Debrusk	EDM	38	1	3	4	-7	96	0	0	1	0	17	5.9
C	27	* Ralph Intranuovo	EDM	13	1	2	3	-3	4	0	0	0	0	19	5.3
C	25	* Greg De Vries	EDM	13	1	1	2	-2	12	0	0	0	0	8	12.5
C	64	* Jason Bonsignore	EDM	20	0	2	2	-6	4	0	0	0	0	13	0.0
C	12	* Tyler Wright	EDM	23	1	0	1	-7	33	0	0	0	0	18	5.6
G	31	Curtis Joseph	EDM	34	0	1	1	0	4	0	0	0	0	1	0.0
D	23	* Nick Stajduhar	EDM	2	0	0	0	2	4	0	0	0	0	1	0.0
D	35	* Bryan Muir	EDM	5	0	0	0	-4	6	0	0	0	0	4	0.0
G	40	* Fred Brathwaite	EDM	7	0	0	0	0	2	0	0	0	0	0	0.0
R	36	* Dennis Bonvie	EDM	8	0	0	0	-3	47	0	0	0	0	0	0.0
G	1	* Joaquin Gage	EDM	16	0	0	0	0	4	0	0	0	0	0	0.0

Goaltending

No.	Goaltender	GPI	Mins	Avg	W	L	T	EN	SO	GA	SA	S%
40	Fred Brathwaite	7	293	2.46	0	2	0	1	0	12	140	.914
31	Curtis Joseph	34	1936	3.44	15	16	2	4	0	111	971	.886
1	* Joaquin Gage	16	717	3.77	2	8	1	1	0	45	350	.871
30	Bill Ranford	37	2015	3.81	13	18	5	2	1	128	1024	.875
	Totals	82	4978	3.66	30	44	8	8	1	304	2493	.878

Coach

LOW, RONALD ALBERT (RON)
Coach, Edmonton Oilers. Born in Birtle, Man., June 21, 1950.

The 1996-97 season sees Ron Low enter his third season as head coach of the Edmonton Oilers. After serving as an assistant coach with the Edmonton Oilers for six seasons, Ron Low became the team's sixth head coach when he was named to the position on April 6, 1995. Low relieved George Burnett after 35 games of the abbreviated 1994-95 season and guided the Oilers to a 5-7-1 (.423) record over the final 13 games of the campaign. In his first full season behind the Edmonton bench, Low had a record of 30-44-8 (.415) in 1995-96 and his career NHL record is 35-51-9 (.416).

On August 3, 1989, Low was appointed to the Edmonton Oilers' coaching staff as an assistant coach. During his tenure in that role, he was a member of the 1990 Stanley Cup championship team.

Low first became involved with the Oilers as a player during the 1979-80 season when Edmonton obtained his rights from the Quebec Nordiques in exchange for Ron Chipperfield. Playing parts of four seasons with Edmonton from 1979-80 to 1982-83, Low compiled a record of 30-23-5 and a 4.03 goals-against average in 67 regular season games.

The Oilers were one of six teams the Birtle, Manitoba native played for in an 11-year NHL career that saw him tend goal for Toronto, Washington, Detroit, Quebec, Edmonton and New Jersey. From 1972-73 to 1984-85, he played 382 NHL games and registered a 4.28 goals-against average with four shutouts and a 102-203-37 record.

In 1985-86 he was named assistant playing coach of the Nova Scotia Oilers, Edmonton's American Hockey League affiliate. Following two years as an assistant coach he was named Nova Scotia's head coach in 1987-88 and kept that position when the team became the Cape Breton Oilers in 1988-89. Low compiled a 62-83-15 record as an AHL head coach before joining the NHL coaching ranks.

Ron and his wife, Linda, have one daughter, Alexandra Juliana, born in June of 1992, and are expecting their second child in September.

Coaching Record

Season	Team	Regular Season					Playoffs			
		Games	W	L	T	%	Games	W	L	%
1987-88	Nova Scotia (AHL)	80	35	36	9	.506	5	1	4	.200
1988-89	Cape Breton (AHL)	80	27	47	6	.375	....	....	....	....
1994-95	**Edmonton (NHL)**	13	5	7	1	.423	....	....	....	....
1995-96	**Edmonton (NHL)**	82	30	44	8	.415	....	....	....	....
	NHL Totals	95	35	51	9	.416	....	....	....	....

Club Records

Team

(Figures in brackets for season records are games played; records for fewest points, wins, ties, losses, goals, goals against are for 70 or more games)

Most Points	119	1983-84 (80), 1985-86 (80)
Most Wins	57	1983-84 (80)
Most Ties	16	1980-81 (80)
Most Losses	50	1992-93 (84)
Most Goals	*446	1983-84 (80)
Most Goals Against	327	1980-81 (80)
Fewest Points	60	1992-93 (84)
Fewest Wins	25	1993-94 (84)
Fewest Ties	5	1983-84 (80)
Fewest Losses	17	1981-82 (80), 1985-86 (82)
Fewest Goals	240	1995-96 (82)
Fewest Goals Against	272	1990-91 (80)

Longest Winning Streak

Overall	8	Five times
Home	8	Jan. 19-Feb. 22/85, Feb. 24-Apr. 2/86
Away	8	Dec. 9/86-Jan. 17/87

Longest Undefeated Streak

Overall	15	Oct. 11-Nov. 9/84 (12 wins, 3 ties)
Home	14	Nov. 15/89-Jan. 6/90 (11 wins, 3 ties)
Away	9	Jan. 17-Mar. 2/82 (6 wins, 3 ties), Nov. 23/82-Jan. 18/83 (7 wins, 2 ties)

Longest Losing Streak

Overall	11	Oct. 16-Nov. 7/93
Home	9	Oct. 16-Nov. 24/93
Away	9	Nov. 25-Dec. 30/80

Longest Winless Streak

Overall	14	Oct. 11-Nov. 7/93 (13 losses, 1 tie)
Home	9	Oct. 16-Nov. 24/93 (9 losses)
Away	9	Three times
Most Shutouts, Season	4	1987-88 (80)
Most PIM, Season	2,173	1987-88 (80)
Most Goals, Game	13	Nov. 19/83 (N.J. 4 at Edm. 13), Nov 8/85 (Van. 0 at Edm. 13)

Individual

Most Seasons	13	Kevin Lowe
Most Games	966	Kevin Lowe
Most Goals, Career	583	Wayne Gretzky
Most Assists, Career	1,086	Wayne Gretzky
Most Points, Career	1,669	Wayne Gretzky (583G, 1,086A)
Most PIM, Career	1,386	Kelly Buchberger
Most Shutouts, Career	9	Grant Fuhr
Longest Consecutive Games Streak	521	Craig MacTavish (Oct. 11/86-Jan. 2/93)
Most Goals, Season	*92	Wayne Gretzky (1981-82)
Most Assists, Season	*163	Wayne Gretzky (1985-86)
Most Points, Season	*215	Wayne Gretzky (1985-86; 52G, 163A)
Most PIM, Season	286	Steve Smith (1987-88)
Most Points, Defenseman, Season	138	Paul Coffey (1985-86; 48G, 90A)
Most Points, Center, Season	*215	Wayne Gretzky (1985-86; 52G, 163A)
Most Points, Right Wing, Season	135	Jari Kurri (1984-85; 71G, 64A)
Most Points, Left Wing, Season	106	Mark Messier (1982-83; 48G, 58A)
Most Points, Rookie, Season	75	Jari Kurri (1980-81; 32G, 43A)
Most Shutouts, Season	4	Grant Fuhr (1987-88)
Most Goals, Game	5	Wayne Gretzky (Feb. 18/81, Dec. 30/81, Dec. 15/84, Dec. 6/87), Jari Kurri (Nov. 19/83), Pat Hughes (Feb. 3/84)
Most Assists, Game	*7	Wayne Gretzky (Feb. 15/80, Dec. 11/85, Feb. 14/86)
Most Points, Game	8	Wayne Gretzky (Nov. 19/83; 3G, 5A), Wayne Gretzky (Jan. 4/84; 4G, 4A), Paul Coffey (Mar. 14/86; 2G, 6A)

* NHL Record.

All-time Record vs. Other Clubs

Regular Season

	GP	W	L	T	GF	GA	PTS	GP	W	L	T	GF	GA	PTS	GP	W	L	T	GF	GA	PTS
				At Home							**On Road**							**Total**			
Anaheim	8	5	3	0	18	17	10	7	2	5	0	17	21	4	15	7	8	0	35	38	14
Boston	23	8	12	3	80	83	19	24	5	17	2	67	110	12	47	13	29	5	147	193	31
Buffalo	23	17	4	2	102	63	36	24	5	10	5	91	99	23	47	26	14	7	193	162	59
Calgary	60	30	22	8	248	222	68	59	20	33	6	212	273	46	119	50	55	14	460	495	114
Chicago	29	14	14	1	117	114	29	28	9	15	4	108	118	22	57	23	29	5	225	232	51
Colorado	24	17	6	1	129	73	35	25	14	9	2	118	106	30	49	31	15	3	247	179	65
Dallas	28	16	6	6	132	94	38	29	13	10	6	101	106	32	57	29	16	12	233	200	70
Detroit	28	14	10	4	131	112	32	28	13	13	2	113	114	28	56	27	23	6	244	226	60
Florida	2	0	2	0	5	8	0	1	1	0	0	5	6	1	4	0	3	1	10	14	1
Hartford	24	17	4	3	103	72	37	23	9	9	5	87	98	23	47	26	13	8	190	170	60
Los Angeles	60	31	15	14	302	233	76	59	24	23	12	258	252	60	119	55	38	26	560	485	136
Montreal	24	13	11	0	83	75	26	23	7	13	3	73	84	17	47	20	24	3	156	159	43
New Jersey	26	14	7	5	126	98	33	26	13	11	2	91	89	28	52	27	18	7	217	187	61
NY Islanders	24	15	5	4	97	71	34	24	5	11	8	92	101	18	48	20	16	12	189	172	52
NY Rangers	23	10	12	1	89	85	21	23	13	6	4	94	88	30	46	23	18	5	183	173	51
Ottawa	3	2	1	0	13	10	4	3	1	2	0	8	9	2	6	3	3	0	21	19	6
Philadelphia	23	14	5	4	86	65	32	24	6	17	1	68	109	13	47	20	22	5	154	174	45
Pittsburgh	24	18	5	1	129	85	37	24	12	11	1	114	95	25	48	30	16	2	243	180	62
St. Louis	28	15	10	3	120	111	33	28	11	13	4	113	114	26	56	26	23	7	233	225	59
San Jose	15	11	1	3	64	34	25	15	5	9	1	44	58	11	30	16	10	4	108	92	36
Tampa Bay	4	3	1	0	9	11	6	4	1	2	1	10	16	3	8	4	3	1	19	27	9
Toronto	28	15	7	6	139	97	36	28	13	13	2	129	116	28	56	28	20	8	268	213	64
Vancouver	59	40	14	5	292	187	85	61	30	23	8	257	236	68	120	70	37	13	549	423	153
Washington	23	9	10	4	89	80	22	23	8	13	2	84	102	18	46	17	23	6	173	182	40
Winnipeg	56	35	17	4	256	189	74	55	29	22	4	251	231	62	111	64	39	8	507	420	136
Totals	**669**	**383**	**204**	**82**	**2959**	**2289**	**848**	**669**	**272**	**311**	**86**	**2605**	**2751**	**630**	**1338**	**655**	**515**	**168**	**5564**	**5040**	**1478**

Playoffs

	Series	W	L	GP	W	L	T	GF	GA	Last Mtg.	Round	Result
Boston	2	2	0	9	8	1	0	41	20	1990	F	W 4-1
Calgary	5	4	1	30	19	11	0	132	96	1991	DSF	W 4-3
Chicago	4	3	1	20	12	8	0	102	77	1992	CF	L 0-4
Dallas	2	1	1	9	5	4	0	36	30	1991	CF	L 1-4
Detroit	2	2	0	10	8	2	0	39	26	1988	CF	W 4-1
Los Angeles	7	5	2	36	24	12	0	154	127	1992	DSF	W 4-2
Montreal	1	1	0	3	3	0	0	15	6	1981	PR	W 3-0
NY Islanders	3	1	2	15	6	9	0	47	58	1984	F	W 4-1
Philadelphia	3	2	1	15	8	7	0	49	44	1987	F	W 4-3
Vancouver	2	2	0	7	7	0	0	35	20	1992	DF	W 4-3
Winnipeg	6	6	0	26	22	4	0	120	75	1990	DSF	W 4-3
Totals	**37**	**29**	**8**	**182**	**122**	**60**	**0**	**770**	**579**			

Playoff Results 1996-92

Year	Round	Opponent	Result	GF	GA
1992	CF	Chicago	L 0-4	8	21
	DF	Vancouver	W 4-2	18	15
	DSF	Los Angeles	W 4-2	23	18

Abbreviations: Round: F – Final; CF – conference final; CQF – conference quarter-final; CSF – conference semi-final; DF – division final; DSF – division semi-final; SF – semi-final; QF – quarter-final; PR – preliminary round.

Calgary totals include Atlanta, 1979-80. Colorado totals include Quebec, 1979-80 to 1994-95.
Dallas totals include Minnesota, 1979-80 to 1992-93. New Jersey totals include Colorado Rockies, 1979-80 to 1981-82.

1995-96 Results

Oct.	8		Detroit	1-3		7		Anaheim	3-1
	10	at	St. Louis	3-5		9		Hartford	1-5
	13	at	Detroit	0-9		13		Buffalo	5-4
	15	at	Philadelphia	1-7		16	at	St. Louis	5-1
	17	at	New Jersey	3-1		17	at	Dallas	4-3
	18	at	Buffalo	1-4		24		Dallas	3-5
	21		Vancouver	6-4		26		NY Islanders	4-1
	22		San Jose	1-1		30	at	Calgary	2-3
	27		Winnipeg	7-5		31		Chicago	0-4
	31		New Jersey	2-1	**Feb.**	7		Washington	1-2
Nov.	1	at	Vancouver	3-3		9		Vancouver	2-3
	4		Toronto	3-3		11		Calgary	4-2
	7	at	Detroit	2-4		14		Anaheim	3-2
	9	at	Florida	1-2		16	at	Dallas	1-6
	10	at	Tampa Bay	4-3		18	at	Chicago	1-4
	12	at	Chicago	4-4		19	at	Colorado	5-7
	14	at	Calgary	2-4		21		Los Angeles	7-2
	15		Montreal	1-4		23		Boston	4-7
	17		Detroit	4-5		25	at	NY Islanders	0-2
	20		Colorado	3-3		27	at	Boston	4-3
	22		Anaheim	2-0		28	at	Hartford	4-3
	24	at	Calgary	5-2	**Mar.**	1		Pittsburgh	4-5
	26	at	Winnipeg	0-4		3		St. Louis	3-4
	28		Chicago	3-5		6	at	Los Angeles	2-3
Dec.	1		Calgary	2-8		8		San Jose	4-2
	2		St. Louis	3-7		13	at	San Jose	8-3
	5	at	Vancouver	2-6		16	at	Los Angeles	5-2
	7	at	Colorado	5-3		17	at	Colorado	1-8
	9	at	San Jose	3-1		19	at	NY Rangers	0-4
	10	at	Anaheim	3-1		21	at	Pittsburgh	4-5
	13		Vancouver	2-2		23	at	Montreal	6-5
	15	at	Winnipeg	4-9		24	at	Ottawa	3-2
	18		Ottawa	3-1		27		Los Angeles	3-3
	20		Colorado	1-4		29		Winnipeg	3-2
	22	at	Washington	3-6		30		Toronto	3-4
	23	at	Toronto	1-6	**Apr.**	1	at	Vancouver	6-2
	27		Philadelphia	3-3		3	at	Anaheim	0-1
	29		Los Angeles	5-4		4	at	San Jose	3-5
	30		NY Rangers	3-8		8		Calgary	2-3
Jan.	3		Tampa Bay	0-5		10		Dallas	2-4
	5		Florida	2-3		13	at	Toronto	3-6

Entry Draft
Selections 1996-82

1996
Pick
- 6 Boyd Devereaux
- 19 Matthieu Descoteaux
- 32 Chris Hajt
- 59 Tom Poti
- 114 Brian Urick
- 141 Bryan Randall
- 168 David Bernier
- 170 Brandon Lafrance
- 195 Fernando Pisani
- 221 John Hultberg

1995
Pick
- 6 Steve Kelly
- 31 Georges Laraque
- 57 Lukas Zib
- 83 Mike Minard
- 109 Jan Snopek
- 161 Martin Cerven
- 187 Stephen Douglas
- 213 Jiri Antonin

1994
Pick
- 4 Jason Bonsignore
- 6 Ryan Smyth
- 32 Mike Watt
- 53 Corey Neilson
- 60 Brad Symes
- 79 Adam Copeland
- 95 Jussi Tarvainen
- 110 Jon Gaskins
- 136 Terry Marchant
- 160 Curtis Sheptak
- 162 Dmitri Shulga
- 179 Chris Wickenheiser
- 185 Rob Guinn
- 188 Jason Reid
- 214 Jeremy Jablonski
- 266 Ladislav Benysek

1993
Pick
- 7 Jason Arnott
- 16 Nick Stajduhar
- 33 David Vyborny
- 59 Kevin Paden
- 60 Alexander Kerch
- 111 Miroslav Satan
- 163 Alexander Zhurik
- 189 Martin Bakula
- 215 Brad Norton
- 241 Oleg Maltsev
- 267 Ilja Byakin

1992
Pick
- 13 Joe Hulbig
- 37 Martin Reichel
- 61 Simon Roy
- 65 Kirk Maltby
- 96 Ralph Intranuovo
- 109 Joaquin Gage
- 157 Steve Gibson
- 181 Kyuin Shim
- 190 Colin Schmidt
- 205 Marko Tuomainen
- 253 Bryan Rasmussen

1991
Pick
- 12 Tyler Wright
- 20 Martin Rucinsky
- 34 Andrew Verner
- 56 George Breen
- 78 Mario Nobili
- 93 Ryan Haggerty
- 144 David Oliver
- 166 Gary Kitching
- 210 Vegar Barlie
- 232 Evgeny Belosheikin
- 254 Juha Riihijarvi

1990
Pick
- 17 Scott Allison
- 38 Alexandre Legault
- 59 Joe Crowley
- 67 Joel Blain
- 101 Greg Louder
- 122 Keijo Sailynoja
- 143 Mike Power
- 164 Roman Mejzlik
- 185 Richard Zemlicka
- 206 Petr Korinek
- 227 invalid claim
- 248 Sami Nuutinen

1989
Pick
- 15 Jason Soules
- 36 Richard Borgo
- 78 Josef Beranek
- 92 Peter White
- 120 Anatoli Semenov
- 140 Davis Payne
- 141 Sergei Yashin
- 162 Darcy Martini
- 225 Roman Bozek

1988
Pick
- 19 Francois Leroux
- 39 Petro Koivunen
- 53 Trevor Sim
- 61 Collin Bauer
- 82 Cam Brauer
- 103 Don Martin
- 124 Len Barrie
- 145 Mike Glover
- 166 Shjon Podein
- 187 Tom Cole
- 208 Vladimir Zubkov
- 229 Darin MacDonald
- 250 Tim Tisdale

1987
Pick
- 21 Peter Soberlak
- 42 Brad Werenka
- 63 Geoff Smith
- 64 Peter Eriksson
- 105 Shaun Van Allen
- 126 Radek Toupal
- 147 Tomas Srsen
- 168 Age Ellingsen
- 189 Gavin Armstrong
- 210 Mike Tinkham
- 231 Jeff Pauletti
- 241 Jesper Duus
- 252 Igor Vyazmikin

1986
Pick
- 21 Kim Issel
- 42 Jamie Nichols
- 63 Ron Shudra
- 84 Dan Currie
- 105 David Haas
- 126 Jim Ennis
- 147 Ivan Matulik
- 168 Nicolas Beaulieu
- 189 Mike Greenlay
- 210 Matt Lanza
- 231 Mojmir Bozik
- 252 Tony Hand

1985
Pick
- 20 Scott Metcalfe
- 41 Todd Carnelley
- 62 Mike Ware
- 104 Tomas Kapusta
- 125 Brian Tessier
- 146 Shawn Tyers
- 167 Tony Fairfield
- 188 Kelly Buchberger
- 209 Mario Barbe
- 230 Peter Headon
- 251 John Haley

1984
Pick
- 21 Selmar Odelein
- 42 Daryl Reaugh
- 63 Todd Norman
- 84 Rich Novak
- 105 Richard Lambert
- 106 Emanuel Viveiros
- 126 Ivan Dornic
- 147 Heikki Riihijarvi
- 168 Todd Ewen
- 209 Joel Curtis
- 229 Simon Wheeldon
- 250 Darren Gani

1983
Pick
- 19 Jeff Beukeboom
- 40 Mike Golden
- 60 Mike Flanagan
- 80 Esa Tikkanen
- 120 Don Barber
- 140 Dale Derkatch
- 160 Ralph Vos
- 180 Dave Roach
- 200 Warren Yadlowski
- 220 John Miner
- 240 Steve Woodburn

1982
Pick
- 20 Jim Playfair
- 41 Steve Graves
- 62 Brent Loney
- 83 Jaroslav Pouzar
- 104 Dwayne Boettger
- 125 Raimo Summanen
- 146 Brian Small
- 167 Dean Clark
- 188 Ian Wood
- 209 Grant Dion
- 230 Chris Smith
- 251 Jeff Crawford

General Manager

SATHER, GLEN CAMERON
President and General Manager, Edmonton Oilers.
Born in High River, Alta., Sept. 2, 1943.

The architect of the Edmonton Oilers' five Stanley Cup championships, Glen Sather is one of the most respected administrators in the NHL. The 1996-97 season is his 17th as general manager of the Oilers and his 21st with Edmonton since joining the organization in August of 1976.

Sather was the Oilers' coach and general manager for nine of the team's first ten seasons and returned to the coaching ranks in 1993-94, relieving Ted Green in late November. In 60 games, Sather guided the team to a 22-27-11 record. In 842 regular season games as coach, Sather has compiled a 464-268-110 record for a .616 winning percentage. He ranks seventh on the NHL's all-time coaching list while his .706 winning percentage in the playoffs is the best mark in NHL history.

Sather played for six different teams during his nine-year NHL career, registering 80 goals and 113 points in 660 games.

NHL Coaching Record

Season	Team	Games	W	L	T	%	Games	W	L	%
			Regular Season					Playoffs		
1979-80	Edmonton (NHL)	80	28	39	13	.431	3	0	3	.000
1980-81	Edmonton (NHL)	62	25	26	11	.492	9	5	4	.555
1981-82	Edmonton (NHL)	80	48	17	15	.694	5	2	3	.400
1982-83	Edmonton (NHL)	80	47	21	12	.663	16	11	5	.687
1983-84	Edmonton (NHL)	80	57	18	5	.744	19	15	4	.789*
1984-85	Edmonton (NHL)	80	49	20	11	.681	18	15	3	.833*
1985-86	Edmonton (NHL)	80	56	17	7	.744	10	6	4	.600
1986-87	Edmonton (NHL)	80	50	24	6	.663	21	16	5	.762*
1987-88	Edmonton (NHL)	80	44	25	11	.619	18	16	2	.889*
1988-89	Edmonton (NHL)	80	38	34	8	.538	7	3	4	.429
1993-94	Edmonton (NHL)	60	22	27	11	.458	....	....	....	....
	NHL Totals	842	464	268	110	.616	126	89	37	.706

* Stanley Cup win.

Club Directory

Edmonton Oilers
11230 – 110 Street
Edmonton, Alberta T5G 3G8
Phone **403/474-8561**
Ticketing 403/491-3291
FAX 403/477-9625
Capacity: 16,437

Owner/Governor	Peter Pocklington
Alternate Governor	Glen Sather
President/General Manager	Glen Sather
Exec. Vice-President/Assistant G.M.	Bruce MacGregor
Assistant to the President	Ted Green
Coach	Ron Low
Assistant Coaches	Kevin Primeau, Bob McCammon
Chief Scout	Barry Fraser
Director of Player Personnel/Hockey Operations	Kevin Prendergast
Director of Hockey Administration	Steve Pellegrini
Scouting Staff	Ed Chadwick, Lorne Davis, Harry Howell, Chris McCarthy, Kent Nilsson, Brad MacGregor, Peter Mahovlich, Michel Georges
Executive Secretary to the President	Betsy Freedman
Executive Secretary	Yvonne Ewaskow
Receptionist/Secretary	Melahna Matan

Medical and Training Staff

Athletic Trainer/Therapist	Ken Lowe
Athletic Trainer	Barrie Stafford
Assistant Trainer	Lyle Kulchisky
Massage Therapist	Roland Kelly
Team Medical Chief of Staff/Director of Glen Sather Sports Medicine Clinic	Dr. David C. Reid
Team Physicians	Dr. Don Groot, Dr. Boris Boyko
Team Dentists	Dr. Tony Sneazwell, Dr. Brian Nord
Fitness Consultant	Dr. Art Quinney
Physical Therapy Consultant	Dr. Dave Magee
Team Acupuncturist	Dr. Steven Aung
Fitness Consultant	Daryl Duke

Finance

Vice-President, Finance	Richard Hughes
Payroll	Donna Barnes
Accountants	Rhonda Holgersen, Fatima Mawani
Systems Administrator	Terry Rhoades

Public Relations

Director of Public Relations	Bill Tuele
Director of Community Relations/Special Events	Trish Kerr
Coordinator of Publications and Statistics	Steve Knowles
Public Relations Secretary	Fiona Liew
Service Representative	Ryan Gillis

Marketing

Executive VP of Business Operations	Doug Piper
Director of Marketing	Stew MacDonald
Manager, Corporate Sponsorships	Brad MacGregor
Manager, Corporate Sponsorships	Greg McDannold
Corporate Sponsorship Representative	Sean Price
Marketing Coordinator	Dave Myers
Executive Secretary	Jennifer Koehli

Properties

Director of Properties	Darrell Holowaychuk
Assistant Properties Manager	Ray MacDonald
Administrative Assistant Properties	Linda Malito
Merchandising Clerk	Kerri Hill
Properties Assistant	John Provis
Secretary	Heather Allen

Ticketing Operations

Director of Ticketing Operations	Sheila MacDonald
Ticket Client Services	Sheila McCaskill, Marcella Kinsman, Victor Liew, Dave Semenko, Sandy Langley, Sherry Smith

Ticketing Sales

Director of Ticket Sales	Kyle Draper
Sales and Marketing Assistant	Melanie Dudek
Client Services Representative	Lisa Johnson
Manager, Group Sales	Michael Lake
Group Sales Representatives	Brian Furman, Greg Hope
Corporate Sales Representatives	Stephanie Beaulieu, John Cutler, David Grout, Robbin Tylor, Mark Wollen

Miscellaneous

Team Administration Offices	Edmonton Coliseum, Edmonton, Alta., Canada T5B 4M9
Location of Press Box	East Side at top (Radio/TV) West Side at top (Media)
Dimensions of Rink	200 feet by 85 feet
Ends of Rink	Herculite extends above boards around rink

Team Information

Team Founded	1972 (WHA), 1979-80 (NHL)
Club Colours	Midnight Blue, Metallic Copper, Red & White
Team Uniforms	Home: Base colour White, trimmed with blue, copper and red Away: Base colour Blue, trimmed with white, copper and red
Training Camp Site	Edmonton Coliseum, Edmonton, Alberta
Television Outlets	CFRN (Channel 3, Cable 2) Dennis Beyak, Roger Millons CBXT TV (Channel 5, Cable 4)
Radio Flagship Station	630 CHED (AM) Rod Phillips, Morley Scott

Florida Panthers

1995-96 Results: 41w-31L-10T 92PTS. Third, Atlantic Division

Year-by-Year Record

		Home			Road			Overall						
Season	GP	W	L	T	W	L	T	W	L	T	GF	GA	Pts.	Finished	Playoff Result
1995-96	82	25	12	4	16	19	6	41	31	10	254	234	92	3rd, Atlantic Div.	Lost Final
1994-95	48	9	12	3	11	10	3	20	22	6	115	127	46	5th, Atlantic Div.	Out of Playoffs
1993-94	84	15	18	9	18	16	8	33	34	17	233	233	83	5th, Atlantic Div.	Out of Playoffs

Schedule

Oct.
Sat. 5 at Philadelphia
Sun. 6 at NY Rangers
Tues. 8 NY Rangers
Sat. 12 Hartford
Wed. 16 at San Jose
Thur. 17 at Colorado
Sun. 20 at Phoenix
Wed. 23 Ottawa
Fri. 25 NY Rangers
Sun. 27 at Philadelphia
Tues. 29 at NY Rangers
Wed. 30 Chicago

Nov.
Sat. 2 Philadelphia
Thur. 7 Washington
Sat. 9 Pittsburgh
Mon. 11 at Buffalo
Wed. 13 at Montreal
Fri. 15 NY Islanders
Mon. 18 Washington
Wed. 20 Los Angeles
Fri. 22 at Dallas
Sat. 23 at St. Louis
Tues. 26 Buffalo
Fri. 29 Hartford

Dec.
Sun. 1 at Detroit*
Tues. 3 at New Jersey
Thur. 5 NY Islanders
Sun. 8 Dallas
Tues. 10 at Philadelphia
Wed. 11 at Hartford
Sat. 14 Edmonton
Thur. 19 at Ottawa
Fri. 20 at Chicago
Sun. 22 at NY Rangers
Mon. 23 at NY Islanders
Thur. 26 at Tampa Bay
Sat. 28 at Washington
Sun. 29 Montreal

Jan.
Wed. 1 Anaheim*
Sat. 4 at Los Angeles
Wed. 8 at Anaheim

Sat. 11 at Calgary
Tues. 14 at Vancouver
Wed. 15 at Edmonton
Mon. 20 Colorado
Wed. 22 at Hartford
Thur. 23 at Boston
Sat. 25 Tampa Bay*
Tues. 28 Montreal
Thur. 30 Boston

Feb.
Sat. 1 Washington*
Mon. 3 at Montreal
Thur. 6 at Buffalo
Fri. 7 at New Jersey
Sun. 9 NY Rangers
Wed. 12 Tampa Bay
Sat. 15 at NY Islanders
Sun. 16 Detroit
Tues. 18 at Pittsburgh
Thur. 20 New Jersey
Sat. 22 Philadelphia*
Tues. 25 San Jose
Thur. 27 St. Louis

Mar.
Sat. 1 at Tampa Bay*
Wed. 5 Phoenix
Fri. 7 Calgary
Sun. 9 Boston
Tues. 11 NY Islanders
Thur. 13 Vancouver
Sat. 15 Toronto
Mon. 17 at New Jersey
Wed. 19 at NY Islanders
Thur. 20 at Ottawa
Sat. 22 Buffalo
Thur. 27 Ottawa
Sat. 29 Tampa Bay
Mon. 31 at Pittsburgh

Apr.
Wed. 2 at Toronto
Sat. 5 at Boston*
Sun. 6 at Washington*
Wed. 9 New Jersey
Fri. 11 Pittsburgh

* Denotes afternoon game.

Center Rob Niedermayer played a key role in helping the Florida Panthers reach the playoffs for the first time in franchise history in 1995-96, setting personal highs for goals (26), assists (35) and points (61).

Franchise date: June 14, 1993

EASTERN NHL CONFERENCE
ATLANTIC DIVISION

4th NHL Season

1996-97 Player Personnel

FORWARDS	HT	WT	S	Place of Birth	Date	1995-96 Club
BARNES, Stu	5-11	174	R	Edmonton, Alta.	12/25/70	Florida
BUCKBERGER, Ashley	6-2	206	R	Esterhazy, Sask.	2/19/75	Carolina
CABANA, Chad	6-1	200	L	Bonnyville, Alta.	10/1/74	Carolina
CASSELMAN, Mike	5-11	190	L	Morrisburg, Ont.	8/23/68	Florida-Carolina
DIONNE, Gilbert	6-0	194	L	Drummondville, Que.	9/19/70	Philadelphia-Florida-Carolina
DVORAK, Radek	6-2	187	R	Tabor, Czech.	3/9/77	Florida
FERGUSON, Craig	5-11	190	L	Castro Valley, CA	4/8/70	Mtl-Cgy-Saint John-Phoenix
FITZGERALD, Tom	6-1	191	R	Melrose, MA	8/28/68	Florida
GARPENLOV, Johan	5-11	184	L	Stockholm, Sweden	3/21/68	Florida
HOUGH, Mike	6-1	197	L	Montreal, Que.	2/6/63	Florida
HULL, Jody	6-2	195	R	Cambridge, Ont.	2/2/69	Florida
JOHNSON, Ryan	6-2	185	L	Thunder Bay, Ont.	6/14/76	North Dakota-Cdn. National
KVASHA, Oleg	6-5	205	R	Moscow, USSR	7/26/78	CSKA
LINDEN, Jamie	6-3	185	R	Medicine Hat, Alta.	7/19/72	Carolina
LINDSAY, Bill	5-11	190	L	Big Fork, MT	5/17/71	Florida
LOWRY, Dave	6-1	200	L	Sudbury, Ont.	2/14/65	Florida
MARTIN, Craig	6-2	215	R	Amherst, N.S.	1/21/71	Springfield
MELLANBY, Scott	6-1	199	R	Montreal, Que.	6/11/66	Florida
MONTREUIL, Eric	6-1	177	L	Verdun, Que.	5/18/75	Carolina
NEMIROVSKY, David	6-1	192	R	Toronto, Ont.	8/1/76	Florida-Sarnia-Carolina
NIEDERMAYER, Rob	6-2	201	L	Cassiar, B.C.	12/28/74	Florida
NILSON, Marcus	6-1	183	R	Stockholm, Sweden	3/1/78	Djurgarden-Djurgarden
PODOLLAN, Jason	6-1	192	R	Vernon, B.C.	2/18/76	Spokane
POIRIER, Gaetan	6-2	200	L	Moncton, N.B.	12/28/76	Merrimack
SHEPPARD, Ray	6-1	195	R	Pembroke, Ont.	5/27/66	Detroit-San Jose-Florida
SKRUDLAND, Brian	6-0	195	L	Peace River, Alta.	7/31/63	Florida
SMYTH, Brad	6-0	200	R	Ottawa, Ont.	3/13/73	Florida-Carolina
STRAKA, Martin	5-10	178	L	Plzen, Czech.	9/3/72	Ottawa-NY Islanders-Florida
WASHBURN, Steve	6-2	191	L	Ottawa, Ont.	4/10/75	Florida-Carolina
WORRELL, Peter	6-6	249	L	Pierre Fonds, Que.	8/18/77	Hull
DEFENSEMEN						
ARMSTRONG, Chris	6-0	198	L	Regina, Sask.	6/26/75	Carolina
CARKNER, Terry	6-3	210	L	Smiths Falls, Ont.	3/7/66	Florida
DOYLE, Trevor	6-3	212	R	Ottawa, Ont.	1/1/74	Carolina
GUSTAFSSON, Per	6-2	190	L	Osterham, Sweden	6/6/70	HV-71
HALKIDIS, Bob	5-11	205	L	Toronto, Ont.	3/5/66	T.B.-Atlanta-NYI-Utah
JOVANOVSKI, Ed	6-2	205	L	Windsor, Ont.	6/26/76	Florida
KUBA, Filip	6-3	202	L	Ostrava, Czech.	12/29/76	Vitkovice
LAUS, Paul	6-1	216	R	Beamsville, Ont.	9/26/70	Florida
MURPHY, Gord	6-2	191	R	Willowdale, Ont.	3/23/67	Florida
NASREDDINE, Alain	6-1	201	L	Montreal, Que.	7/10/75	Carolina
RATUSHNY, Dan	6-1	205	R	Nepean, Ont.	10/29/70	Peoria-Carolina
SMITH, Geoff	6-3	194	L	Edmonton, Alta.	3/7/69	Florida
SVEHLA, Robert	6-1	190	R	Martin, Czech.	1/2/69	Florida
WARRENER, Rhett	6-1	209	L	Shaunavon, Sask.	1/27/76	Florida-Carolina
WOOLLEY, Jason	6-0	188	L	Toronto, Ont.	7/27/69	Florida

GOALTENDERS	HT	WT	C	Place of Birth	Date	1995-96 Club
FITZPATRICK, Mark	6-2	198	L	Toronto, Ont.	11/13/68	Florida
LEMANOWICZ, David	6-2	190	L	Edmonton, Alta.	3/8/76	Spokane
MacDONALD, Todd	6-0	167	L	Charlottetown, P.E.I.	7/5/75	Carolina-Detroit (ColHL)
VANBIESBROUCK, John	5-8	176	L	Detroit, MI	9/4/63	Florida
WEEKES, Kevin	6-0	158	L	Toronto, Ont.	4/4/75	Carolina

General Manager

MURRAY, BRYAN CLARENCE
General Manager, Florida Panthers.
Born in Shawville, Que., December 5, 1942.

Bryan Murray is entering his third season as general manager of the Florida Panthers. Since being named to the position on August 1, 1994, he has helped construct a team that reached the Stanley Cup Final in its third year of existence. Under Murray's guidance, the Panthers have gone 61-53-16, good for a winning percentage of .531.

Murray acquired several players who helped the Panthers win the Prince of Wales Trophy in 1995-96 as champions of the NHL's Eastern Conference. Defensemen Robert Svehla and Terry Carkner excelled during the playoffs, while Ray Sheppard, Martin Straka and 1995 first-round draft pick Radek Dvorak added plenty of offense. Murray's shrewdest move, however, was made on July 24, 1995 when he hired Doug MacLean as coach. MacLean was named a finalist for the Jack Adams Trophy (NHL coach of the year) after guiding the Panthers to a fourth-place finish in the Eastern Conference.

This is Bryan's seventh season as a general manager. Before joining the Panthers, he served as coach and general manager of the Detroit Red Wings from 1990-93 and as general manager during the 1993-94 campaign. In 328 games under Murray's control, the Wings won a total of 170 games, while losing 121 and tying 37, an average of 43 wins 94 points a season. Murray, 53, left his mark in the NHL record book as a coach with a career record of 467-337-112 (.571 winning pct.) in 916 regular-season games, placing him sixth on the all-time victory list.

Murray broke into the NHL coaching ranks with the Washington Capitals on November 11, 1981. He spent the next 8 1/2 seasons with the Caps and earned the Jack Adams Award as the NHL's coach of the year in 1983-84. In 1988-89, he led the Capitals to the Patrick Division title, the only first-place finish in team history. On January 15, 1990, Bryan was replaced by his brother, Terry, who is currently the Flyers head coach.

1995-96 Scoring

* – rookie

Regular Season

Pos	#	Player	Team	GP	G	A	Pts	+/–	PIM	PP	SH	GW	GT	S	%
R	27	Scott Mellanby	FLA	79	32	38	70	4	160	19	0	3	1	225	14.2
C	44	Rob Niedermayer	FLA	82	26	35	61	1	107	11	0	6	0	155	16.8
R	26	Ray Sheppard	DET	5	2	2	4	0	2	0	0	1	0	9	22.2
			S.J.	51	27	19	46	–19	10	12	0	4	0	170	15.9
			FLA	14	8	2	10	0	4	2	0	2	0	52	15.4
			TOTAL	70	37	23	60	–19	16	14	0	7	0	231	16.0
D	24	Robert Svehla	FLA	81	8	49	57	–3	94	7	0	0	0	146	5.5
L	29	Johan Garpenlov	FLA	82	23	28	51	–10	36	8	0	7	1	130	17.7
C	14	Stu Barnes	FLA	72	19	25	44	–12	46	8	0	5	2	158	12.0
R	28	Martin Straka	OTT	43	9	16	25	–14	29	5	0	1	0	63	14.3
			NYI	22	2	10	12	–6	6	0	0	0	0	18	11.1
			FLA	12	2	4	6	1	6	1	0	0	0	17	11.8
			TOTAL	77	13	30	43	–19	41	6	0	1	0	98	13.3
R	12	Jody Hull	FLA	78	20	17	37	5	25	2	0	3	1	120	16.7
R	21	Tom Fitzgerald	FLA	82	13	21	34	–3	75	1	6	2	0	141	9.2
L	11	Bill Lindsay	FLA	73	12	22	34	13	57	0	3	2	0	118	10.2
D	6	Jason Woolley	FLA	52	6	28	34	–9	32	3	0	0	0	98	6.1
D	5	Gord Murphy	FLA	70	8	22	30	5	30	4	0	0	0	125	6.4
L	9	* Radek Dvorak	FLA	77	13	14	27	5	20	0	0	4	0	126	10.3
C	20	Brian Skrudland	FLA	79	7	20	27	6	129	0	1	1	0	90	7.8
L	10	Dave Lowry	FLA	63	10	14	24	–2	36	0	0	1	0	83	12.0
L	18	Mike Hough	FLA	64	7	16	23	4	37	0	1	1	0	66	10.6
D	55	* Ed Jovanovski	FLA	70	10	11	21	–3	137	2	0	2	0	116	8.6
D	2	Terry Carkner	FLA	73	3	10	13	10	80	1	0	0	0	42	7.1
D	8	Magnus Svensson	FLA	27	2	9	11	–1	21	2	0	1	0	58	3.4
D	25	Geoff Smith	FLA	31	3	7	10	–4	20	2	0	0	0	34	8.8
D	3	Paul Laus	FLA	78	3	6	9	–2	236	0	0	0	0	45	6.7
L	16	Gilbert Dionne	PHI	2	0	1	1	0	0	0	0	0	0	0	0.0
			FLA	5	1	2	3	0	0	0	0	0	0	12	8.3
			TOTAL	7	1	3	4	0	0	0	0	0	0	12	8.3
L	15	* Brett Harkins	FLA	8	0	3	3	–2	6	0	0	0	0	4	0.0
D	23	* Rhett Warrener	FLA	28	0	3	3	4	46	0	0	0	0	19	0.0
R	19	Brad Smyth	FLA	7	1	1	2	–3	4	1	0	0	0	12	8.3
R	51	* David Nemirovsky	FLA	9	0	2	2	–1	2	0	0	0	0	6	0.0
G	34	J. Vanbiesbrouck	FLA	57	0	2	2	0	10	0	0	0	0	0	0.0
C	40	* Steve Washburn	FLA	1	0	1	1	1	0	0	0	0	0	1	0.0
R	22	Bob Kudelski	FLA	13	0	1	1	1	0	0	0	0	0	23	0.0
C	7	Mike Casselman	FLA	3	0	0	0	–1	0	0	0	0	0	2	0.0
G	30	Mark Fitzpatrick	FLA	34	0	0	0	0	12	0	0	0	0	0	0.0

Goaltending

No.	Goaltender	GPI	Mins	Avg	W	L	T	EN	SO	GA	SA	S%
34	J. Vanbiesbrouck	57	3178	2.68	26	20	7	2	2	142	1473	.904
30	Mark Fitzpatrick	34	1786	2.96	15	11	3	2	0	88	810	.891
	Totals	**82**	**4979**	**2.82**	**41**	**31**	**10**	**4**	**2**	**234**	**2287**	**.898**

Playoffs

Pos	#	Player	Team	GP	G	A	Pts	+/–	PIM	PP	SH	GW	OT	S	%
L	10	Dave Lowry	FLA	22	10	7	17	8	39	4	0	2	1	45	22.2
R	26	Ray Sheppard	FLA	21	8	8	16	4	0	3	0	0	0	47	17.0
C	14	Stu Barnes	FLA	22	6	10	16	10	4	2	0	2	0	57	10.5
L	11	Bill Lindsay	FLA	22	5	5	10	6	18	0	1	1	0	33	15.2
R	27	Scott Mellanby	FLA	22	3	6	9	–10	44	2	0	0	0	57	5.3
D	55	* Ed Jovanovski	FLA	22	1	8	9	2	52	0	0	0	0	51	2.0
C	44	Rob Niedermayer	FLA	22	5	3	8	–8	12	2	0	2	0	48	10.4
R	21	Tom Fitzgerald	FLA	22	4	4	8	3	34	0	0	2	0	31	12.9
D	6	Jason Woolley	FLA	13	2	6	8	3	14	1	0	1	0	27	7.4
D	3	Paul Laus	FLA	21	2	6	8	3	62	0	0	0	0	18	11.1
L	29	Johan Garpenlov	FLA	20	4	2	6	–2	8	0	0	0	0	35	11.4
D	24	Robert Svehla	FLA	22	0	6	6	3	32	0	0	0	0	38	0.0
L	18	Mike Hough	FLA	22	4	1	5	5	8	0	0	2	1	38	10.5
R	12	Jody Hull	FLA	14	3	2	5	4	0	0	0	0	0	18	16.7
R	28	Martin Straka	FLA	13	2	2	4	–2	2	0	0	0	0	20	10.0
L	9	* Radek Dvorak	FLA	16	1	3	4	2	0	0	0	0	0	36	2.8
C	20	Brian Skrudland	FLA	21	1	3	4	6	18	0	0	0	0	27	3.7
D	5	Gord Murphy	FLA	14	0	4	4	1	6	0	0	0	0	53	0.0
D	2	Terry Carkner	FLA	22	0	4	4	8	10	0	0	0	0	15	0.0
D	23	* Rhett Warrener	FLA	21	0	3	3	3	10	0	0	0	0	14	0.0
C	40	* Steve Washburn	FLA	1	0	1	1	0	0	0	0	0	0	0	0.0
G	34	J. Vanbiesbrouck	FLA	22	0	1	1	0	20	0	0	0	0	0	0.0
D	25	Geoff Smith	FLA	1	0	0	0	–1	2	0	0	0	0	0	0.0
G	30	Mark Fitzpatrick	FLA	2	0	0	0	0	0	0	0	0	0	0	0.0

Goaltending

No.	Goaltender	GPI	Mins	Avg	W	L	EN	SO	GA	SA	S%
34	J. Vanbiesbrouck	22	1332	2.25	12	10	1	1	50	735	.932
30	Mark Fitzpatrick	2	60	6.00	0	0	0	0	6	30	.800
	Totals	**22**	**1397**	**2.45**	**12**	**10**	**1**	**1**	**57**	**766**	**.926**

NHL Coaching Record

		Regular Season					Playoffs			
Season	Team	Games	W	L	T	%	Games	W	L	%
1981-82	Washington	76	25	28	13	.477	....	....	....	....
1982-83	Washington	80	39	25	16	.588	4	1	3	.250
1983-84	Washington	80	48	27	5	.631	8	4	4	.500
1984-85	Washington	80	46	25	9	.631	5	2	3	.400
1985-86	Washington	80	50	23	7	.669	9	5	4	.556
1986-87	Washington	80	38	32	10	.538	7	3	4	.429
1987-88	Washington	80	38	33	9	.531	14	7	7	.500
1988-89	Washington	80	41	29	10	.575	6	2	4	.333
1989-90	Washington	46	18	24	4	.435	....	....	....	....
1990-91	Detroit	80	34	38	8	.475	7	3	4	.429
1991-92	Detroit	80	43	25	12	.613	11	4	7	.364
1992-93	Detroit	84	47	28	9	.613	7	3	4	.429
	NHL Totals	**916**	**467**	**337**	**112**	**.571**	**78**	**34**	**44**	**.436**

Club Records

Team

(Figures in brackets for season records are games played; records for fewest points, wins, ties, losses, goals, goals against are for 70 or more games)

Most Points	92	1995-96 (82)
Most Wins	41	1995-96 (82)
Most Ties	17	1993-94 (84)
Most Losses	34	1993-94 (84)
Most Goals	254	1995-96 (82)
Most Goals Against	234	1995-96 (82)
Fewest Points	83	1993-94 (84)
Fewest Wins	33	1993-94 (84)
Fewest Ties	10	1995-96 (82)
Fewest Losses	31	1995-96 (82)
Fewest Goals	233	1993-94 (84)
Fewest Goals Against	233	1993-94 (84)

Longest Winning Streak

Overall	7	Nov. 2-14/95
Home	5	Nov. 5-14/95
Away	4	Dec. 2-12/95

Longest Undefeated Streak

Overall	9	Jan. 8-Jan. 30/94 (5 wins, 4 ties)
Home	8	Nov. 5-26/95 (7 wins, 1 tie)
Away	7	Dec. 7-Dec. 29/93 (5 wins, 2 ties)

Longest Losing Streak

Overall	5	Twice
Home	5	Feb. 20-Mar. 4/94
Away	5	Feb. 25-Mar. 11/96

Longest Winless Streak

Overall	9	Feb. 24-Mar. 13/96 (7 losses, 2 ties)
Home	6	Mar. 21-Apr. 12/94 (3 losses, 3 ties)
Away	10	Feb. 25-Apr. 6/96 (9 losses, 1 tie)
Most Shutouts, Season	6	1994-95 (48)
Most PIM, Season	1,620	1993-94 (84)
Most Goals, Game	8	Jan. 24/94 (Mtl. 3 at Fla. 8)

Individual

Most Seasons	3	Several Players
Most Games	213	Tom Fitzgerald
Most Goals, Career	75	Scott Mellanby
Most Assists, Career	80	Scott Mellanby
Most Points, Career	155	Scott Mellanby (75G, 80A)
Most PIM, Career	483	Paul Laus
Most Shutouts, Career	7	John Vanbiesbrouck

Longest Consecutive

Games Streak	191	Bill Lindsay
Most Goals, Season	32	Scott Mellanby (1995-96)
Most Assists, Season	49	Robert Svehla (1995-96)
Most Points, Season	70	Scott Mellanby (1995-96; 32G, 38A)
Most PIM, Season	236	Paul Laus (1995-96)
Most Shutouts, Season	4	John Vanbiesbrouck (1994-95)

Most Points, Defenseman

Season	57	Robert Svehla (1995-96; 8G, 49A)

Most Points, Center

Season	61	Rob Niedermayer (1995-96; 26G, 35A)

Most Points, Right Wing

Season	70	Scott Mellanby (1995-96; 32G, 38A)

Most Points, Left Wing

Season	51	Johan Garpenlov (1995-96; 23G, 28A)

Most Points, Rookie

Season	50	Jesse Belanger (1993-94; 17G, 33A)
Most Goals, Game	3	Two players
Most Assists, Game	3	Seven players
Most Points, Game	4	Jesse Belanger (Jan. 19/94; 2G, 2A)

* NHL Record.

Robert Svehla emerged as one of Florida's top young defensemen in 1995-96, leading all Panther rearguards in scoring with eight goals and 49 points while playing a controlled, confident game in his own zone.

All-time Record vs. Other Clubs

Regular Season

	At Home							On Road							Total						
	GP	W	L	T	GF	GA	PTS	GP	W	L	T	GF	GA	PTS	GP	W	L	T	GF	GA	PTS
Anaheim	2	1	0	1	7	5	3	2	2	0	0	7	5	4	4	3	0	1	14	10	7
Boston	5	2	3	0	12	12	4	6	2	2	2	14	14	6	11	4	5	2	26	26	10
Buffalo	5	3	2	0	15	14	6	6	1	5	0	6	26	2	11	4	7	0	21	40	8
Calgary	2	2	0	0	6	4	4	2	0	2	0	2	6	0	4	2	2	0	8	10	4
Chicago	2	0	2	0	5	9	0	2	0	1	1	8	12	1	4	0	3	1	13	21	1
Colorado	5	1	4	0	13	21	2	4	1	1	2	14	13	4	9	2	5	2	27	34	6
Dallas	2	1	1	0	10	9	2	2	0	2	0	10	10	2	4	1	1	2	20	19	4
Detroit	2	1	1	0	6	5	2	2	0	2	0	5	11	0	4	1	3	0	11	16	2
Edmonton	2	1	0	1	6	5	3	2	2	0	0	8	5	4	4	3	0	1	14	10	7
Hartford	6	3	2	1	16	13	7	6	4	2	0	17	19	8	12	7	4	1	33	32	15
Los Angeles	2	1	0	1	7	3	3	3	2	1	0	8	8	4	5	3	1	1	15	11	5
Montreal	6	2	2	2	22	19	6	5	3	2	0	14	14	6	11	5	4	2	36	33	12
New Jersey	8	4	2	2	19	16	10	7	2	5	0	10	21	4	15	6	7	2	29	37	14
NY Islanders	7	4	3	0	23	21	8	7	4	1	2	16	11	10	14	8	4	2	39	32	18
NY Rangers	7	3	4	0	15	22	6	7	2	3	2	16	18	6	14	5	7	2	31	40	12
Ottawa	6	5	0	1	23	12	11	6	5	1	0	24	11	10	12	10	1	1	47	23	21
Philadelphia	7	2	5	0	19	22	4	7	2	3	2	17	15	7	14	4	8	2	36	37	11
Pittsburgh	6	2	4	0	15	16	4	6	1	4	1	16	22	3	12	3	8	1	31	38	7
St. Louis	2	0	1	1	3	5	1	2	0	2	0	3	7	0	4	0	3	1	6	12	1
San Jose	2	1	0	1	7	4	3	2	1	1	0	6	4	2	4	2	1	1	13	8	5
Tampa Bay	7	4	2	1	19	12	9	8	5	2	1	26	15	11	15	9	4	2	45	27	20
Toronto	3	1	1	1	9	7	3	2	1	1	0	9	7	2	5	2	2	1	18	14	5
Vancouver	2	1	0	1	4	3	3	2	1	1	0	4	8	2	4	2	1	1	8	11	5
Washington	7	3	2	2	23	16	8	7	3	3	1	19	22	7	14	6	5	3	42	38	15
Winnipeg	2	1	1	0	8	6	2	3	2	1	0	11	9	4	5	3	2	0	19	15	6
Totals	**107**	**49**	**42**	**16**	**312**	**281**	**114**	**107**	**45**	**45**	**17**	**290**	**313**	**107**	**214**	**94**	**87**	**33**	**602**	**594**	**221**

Playoffs

	Series	W	L	GP	W	L	T	GF	GA	Last Mtg.	Round	Result
Boston	1	1	0	5	4	1	0	22	16	1996	CQF	W 4-1
Colorado	1	0	1	4	0	4	0	4	15	1996	F	L 0-4
Philadelphia	1	1	0	6	4	2	0	15	11	1996	CSF	W 4-2
Pittsburgh	1	1	0	7	4	3	0	20	15	1996	CF	W 4-3
Totals	**4**	**3**	**1**	**22**	**12**	**10**	**0**	**61**	**57**			

Playoff Results 1996-94

Year	Round	Opponent	Result	GF	GA
1996	F	Colorado	L 0-4	4	15
	CF	Pittsburgh	W 4-3	20	15
	CSF	Philadelphia	W 4-2	15	11
	CQF	Boston	W 4-1	22	16

Abbreviations: Round: **F** – Final;
CF – conference final; **CQF** – conference quarter-final;
CSF – conference semi-final; **DF** – division final;
DSF – division semi-final; **SF** – semi-final;
QF – quarter-final; **PR** – preliminary round.

Colorado totals include Quebec, 1993-94 to 1994-95.

1995-96 Results

Oct.	7	at	New Jersey	0-4		10	at Colorado	4-4
	8		Calgary	4-3		12	at Dallas	6-6
	11		Montreal	6-1		16	San Jose	4-1
	13		Ottawa	6-2		22	at Philadelphia	1-1
	15		NY Islanders	5-3		23	at Washington	5-4
	17		Chicago	3-6		25	Montreal	2-6
	21		Hartford	3-0		27	Buffalo	6-3
	24	at	Toronto	6-1		29	Pittsburgh	2-1
	25	at	Montreal	2-7		31	at Buffalo	1-6
	28	at	Ottawa	4-1	Feb. 3	at Tampa Bay	5-3
	31		NY Islanders	4-5		5	at Detroit	2-4
Nov.	2	at	Philadelphia	2-1		6	at Detroit	2-4
	3	at	Washington	3-2		8	Detroit	3-1
	5		Tampa Bay	4-1		11	St. Louis	2-6
	7		Philadelphia	4-2		14	Philadelphia	2-4
	9		Edmonton	2-1		16	Colorado	4-5
	11		Buffalo	4-1		18	Dallas	6-4
	14		Toronto	5-2		21	at New Jersey	4-1
	16		Vancouver	2-2		24	NY Rangers	0-4
	18	at	Los Angeles	2-3		25	at Buffalo	1-6
	19	at	Anaheim	4-3		29	at Washington	2-2
	21		New Jersey	4-3	Mar. 2	at Hartford	1-7
	26		Los Angeles	5-1		2	at St. Louis	0-2
	29		Philadelphia	1-2		7	at Winnipeg	3-5
Dec.	1	at	Pittsburgh	1-2		10	Boston	1-4
	2	at	Hartford	5-3		11	at Chicago	4-8
	5	at	Washington	4-3		13	at NY Rangers	3-3
	7		Anaheim	3-3		17	New Jersey	3-0
	9		Boston	3-1		19	Ottawa	5-2
	11	at	New Jersey	2-1		21	NY Islanders	3-2
	12	at	NY Islanders	3-1		23	at Tampa Bay	2-4
	14	at	Boston	4-6		27	at NY Rangers	0-3
	16	at	Tampa Bay	7-2		28	Pittsburgh	2-5
	21		Winnipeg	6-1		30	Tampa Bay	1-2
	23		New Jersey	2-1	Apr. 1	Hartford	3-2
	28		Washington	4-5		3	at Ottawa	2-3
	30	at	Pittsburgh	5-6		6	at Montreal	2-3
Jan.	3	at	Vancouver	2-7		8	at NY Rangers	5-3
	5	at	Edmonton	3-2		10	Tampa Bay	1-2
	6	at	Calgary	0-2		12	at NY Islanders	1-1
	8	at	San Jose	5-2		14	NY Rangers	5-1

Entry Draft
Selections 1996-93

1996 Pick		**1995** Pick		**1994** Pick		**1993** Pick	
20	Marcus Nilson	10	Radek Dvorak	1	Ed Jovanovski	5	Rob Niedermayer
60	Chris Allen	36	Aaron MacDonald	27	Rhett Warrener	41	Kevin Weekes
65	Oleg Kvasha	62	Mike O'Grady	31	Jason Podollan	57	Chris Armstrong
82	Joey Tetarenko	80	Dave Duerden	36	Ryan Johnson	67	Mikael Tjallden
129	Andrew Long	88	Daniel Tjarnqvist	84	David Nemirovsky	78	Steve Washburn
156	Gaetan Poirier	114	Francois Cloutier	105	Dave Geris	83	Bill McCauley
183	Alexandre Couture	166	Peter Worrell	157	Matt O'Dette	109	Todd MacDonald
209	Denis Khloptonov	192	Filip Kuba	183	Jasson Boudrias	135	Alain Nasreddine
235	Russell Smith	218	David Lemanowicz	235	Tero Lehtera	161	Trevor Doyle
				261	Per Gustafsson	187	Briane Thompson
						213	Chad Cabana
						239	John Demarco
						265	Eric Montreuil

Coach

MacLEAN, DOUG
Coach, Florida Panthers. Born in Summerside, P.E.I., April 12, 1954.

MacLean, 42, made quite a name for himself in his first year as an NHL head coach. In 1995-96, he guided the Panthers to the Eastern Conference championship and a berth in the Stanley Cup final against the Colorado Avalanche. Known for his wit and the ability to get the most out of his players, MacLean was also named a finalist for the Jack Adams Award as the NHL's coach of the year.

MacLean's NHL career began in 1986-87 when he was hired by the St. Louis Blues as an assistant to head coach Jacques Martin. MacLean spent two seasons in St. Louis, helping guide the Blues to first- and second-place finishes in the Norris Division, before becoming Bryan Murray's assistant coach in Washington at the start of the 1988-89 campaign.

MacLean spent two seasons in the Capitals' organization. He spent all of 1988-89 as Murray's assistant and began the 1989-90 campaign in that capacity until he was named head coach of the Capitals' American Hockey League affiliate in Baltimore midway through the season. MacLean was Baltimore's head coach for the final 35 games of 1989-90 and he compiled a record of 17-13-5, finishing third in the AHL's South Division with an overall record of 43-30-7.

The following season, 1990-91, MacLean left the Capitals' organization to become Murray's assistant coach in Detroit. MacLean spent two seasons behind the Red Wings bench, the second season as associate coach, and helped guide Detroit to third- and first-place finishes, respectively. In 1992-93, he left the coaching ranks to concentrate on the Red Wings' player development. MacLean spent the entire 1992-93 and 1993-94 seasons as Detroit's assistant general manager, as well as general manager of the Adirondack Red Wings, Detroit's AHL affiliate. MacLean left the Wings' organization before the start of 1994-95 and once again was reunited with Bryan Murray. MacLean became the Panthers' director of player development and pro scout in October 1994 and was named the team's head coach on July 24, 1995.

A native of Summerside, Prince Edward Island, MacLean played collegiate hockey at the University of P.E.I., where he graduated with a bachelors degree in education. MacLean also played for the Montreal Junior Canadiens, and in 1974, was invited to attend the St. Louis Blues' training camp. After his playing career, he enrolled at the University of Western Ontario, where he received his masters degree in educational psychology. While attending Western, MacLean began his coaching career as an assistant with the London Knights of the Ontario Hockey League. After graduating from Western, he returned home where he taught high school and became head coach of Summerside's junior A hockey team. In 1985-86, MacLean became head coach at the University of New Brunswick, and after only one season there, was tabbed by Jacques Martin to join his coaching staff in St. Louis.

MacLean and his wife, Jill, have two children, a son, Clark (8) and a daughter, MacKenzie (5).

Coaching Record

Season	Team	Games	**Regular Season** W	L	T	%	Games	**Playoffs** W	L	%
1985-86	U. of New Brunswick (CIAU)	22	8	14	0	.364	....	....	....	....
1989-90	Baltimore (AHL)	35	17	13	5	.557	12	6	6	.500
1995-96	**Florida (NHL)**	**82**	**41**	**31**	**10**	**.561**	**22**	**12**	**10**	**.545**
	NHL Totals	**82**	**41**	**31**	**10**	**.561**	**22**	**12**	**10**	**.545**

Club Directory

Miami Arena
100 Northeast Third Avenue
2nd Floor
Fort Lauderdale, FL 33301
Phone **954/768-1900**
FAX 954/768-9870
Capacity: 14,703

Chairman and CEO	H. Wayne Huizenga
President & Governor	William A. Torrey
Executive Vice President & Alternate Governor	Dean J. Jordan
Special Consultant	Richard C. Rochon
Executive Assistants to Presidents	Deanna Cocozzelli, Cathy Stevenson
Executive Assistant to Executive Vice President	Janine Shea

Finance & Administration

Vice President of Finance and Administration	Steve Dauria
Director of Finance	Evelyn Lopez
Staff Accountants	Laura Barrera, Ana Carrasquilla
MIS Coordinator	Jay Royer
Executive Assistant to Vice President Finance & Administration	Jackie Ortega
Office Services	Anthony Vandaley

Hockey Operations

Vice President and General Manager	Bryan Murray
Assistant General Manager	Chuck Fletcher
Head Coach	Doug MacLean
Assistant Coaches	Lindy Ruff, Duane Sutter
Goaltending Coach	Bill Smith
Amateur Scouts	Paul Henry, Ron Harris, Matti Vaisanen, Tim Murray, Wayne Meier, Billy Dea
Pro Scouts	Micheal Abbamont, Jim Clark
Assistant to the General Manager	Kevin Dessart
Head Medical Trainer	David Smith
Equipment Manager	Mark Brennan
Training Staff	Tim Leroy, Scott Tinkler
Team Services	Marni Share
Training Staff Assistant	Andre Szucko
Internist	Charles Posternack, M.D.
Orthopedic Surgeons	David E. Attarian, M.D.
Assistant Physicians	Stephen R. Southworth, M.D., James Guerra, M.D.
Plastic Surgeon	Harry K. Moon
Minor League Affiliates	Carolina (AHL), Cincinnati (IHL), Tallahassee (ECHL) & Port Huron (ColHL)

Communications Department

Director, Public/Media Relations	Greg Bouris
Public/Media Relations Associate	Jon Kramer
Public/Media Relations Assistant	Tom Zlermann
Manager of Archives	Ed Krajewski
Administrative Assistant, Public/Media Relations	Aza Krotz

Marketing Department

Vice President of Marketing	Declan Bolger
Director of Corporate Sales & Sponsorship	Kimberly Terranova
Director of Merchandising	Ron Dennis
Senior Manager of Promotions	Lauren Menella
Manager, Corporate Sales & Sponsorship	Matthew Wintner
Corporate Account Coordinator	Brette Zalkin
Coordinator, Promotions & Youth Hockey	Elizabeth Ridley
Mascot Coordinator	George Russo
Senior Sales Manager	Chris Trinceri
Sales Manager	Greg Hanessian
Account Executive	Craig Petrus, Chris Gallagher, Leo Sarmiento
Executive Assistant to Vice President of Marketing	Andria Cunningham
Administrative Assistant to Director of Corporate Sales & Sponsorship	Susan Ferro
Coordinator of Merchandising	Mary Lou Poag

Ticket Operations

Vice President of Operations	Steve Dangerfield
Director of Ticket Operations	Scott Wampold
Manager of Ticket Operations	Matt Coyne
Ticket Operations Representative	Lauri Carr
Executive Assistant to Vice President of Operations	TBA

General Information

Arena Phone Number	(305) 530-4444
Location of Press Box	Mezzanine, Sec. 211
Dimensions of Rink	200 feet by 85 feet
Practice Arena	Gold Coast Ice Arena (954) 784-5500
Team Colors	Red, Navy Blue, Yellow-Gold
Television Station	SportsChannel
Television Announcers	Jeff Rimer, Denis Potvin
Panthers Radio Network	WQAM, 560 AM
Radio Announcers	Chris Moore
Panthers Spanish Radio	WCMQ, 1210 AM
Spanish Radio Announcer	Felix DeJesus

General Managers' History

Bob Clarke, 1993-94; Bryan Murray, 1994-95 to date.

Coaching History

Roger Neilson, 1993-94 to 1994-95; Doug MacLean, 1995-96 to date.

Captains' History

Brian Skrudland, 1993-94 to date.

Hartford Whalers

1995-96 Results: 34W-39L-9T 77PTS. Fourth, Northeast Division

Year-by-Year Record

		Home			Road			Overall							
Season	GP	W	L	T	W	L	T	W	L	T	GF	GA	Pts.	Finished	Playoff Result
1995-96	82	22	15	4	12	24	5	34	39	9	237	259	77	4th, Northeast Div.	Out of Playoffs
1994-95	48	12	10	2	7	14	3	19	24	5	127	141	43	5th, Northeast Div.	Out of Playoffs
1993-94	84	14	22	6	13	26	3	27	48	9	227	288	63	6th, Northeast Div.	Out of Playoffs
1992-93	84	12	25	5	14	27	1	26	52	6	284	369	58	5th, Adams Div.	Out of Playoffs
1991-92	80	13	17	10	13	24	3	26	41	13	247	283	65	4th, Adams Div.	Lost Div. Semi-Final
1990-91	80	18	16	6	13	22	5	31	38	11	238	276	73	4th, Adams Div.	Lost Div. Semi-Final
1989-90	80	17	18	5	21	15	4	38	33	9	275	268	85	4th, Adams Div.	Lost Div. Semi-Final
1988-89	80	21	17	2	16	21	3	37	38	5	299	290	79	4th, Adams Div.	Lost Div. Semi-Final
1987-88	80	21	14	5	14	24	2	35	38	7	249	267	77	4th, Adams Div.	Lost Div. Semi-Final
1986-87	80	26	9	5	17	21	2	43	30	7	287	270	93	1st, Adams Div.	Lost Div. Semi-Final
1985-86	80	21	17	2	19	19	2	40	36	4	332	302	84	4th, Adams Div.	Lost Div. Final
1984-85	80	17	18	5	13	23	4	30	41	9	268	318	69	5th, Adams Div.	Out of Playoffs
1983-84	80	19	16	5	9	26	5	28	42	10	288	320	66	5th, Adams Div.	Out of Playoffs
1982-83	80	13	22	5	6	32	2	19	54	7	261	403	45	5th, Adams Div.	Out of Playoffs
1981-82	80	13	17	10	8	24	8	21	41	18	264	351	60	5th, Adams Div.	Out of Playoffs
1980-81	80	14	17	9	7	24	9	21	41	18	292	372	60	4th, Norris Div.	Out of Playoffs
1979-80	80	22	12	6	5	22	13	27	34	19	303	312	73	4th, Norris Div.	Lost Prelim. Round

---

Schedule

Oct.	Sat.	5	Phoenix		Fri.	10	at Vancouver
	Tues.	8	Pittsburgh		Sun.	12	at Edmonton
	Sat.	12	at Florida		Wed.	15	Pittsburgh
	Thur.	17	at NY Islanders		Mon.	20	Toronto
	Sat.	19	New Jersey		Wed.	22	Florida
	Thur.	24	Anaheim		Fri.	24	NY Islanders
	Sat.	26	at Buffalo		Sat.	25	at Buffalo
	Wed.	30	NY Islanders		Thur.	30	at Los Angeles
	Thur.	31	at Boston		Fri.	31	at Anaheim
Nov.	Sat.	2	Los Angeles	Feb.	Wed.	5	at NY Rangers
	Mon.	4	at Detroit		Thur.	6	at Boston
	Wed.	6	Boston		Sat.	8	at Montreal
	Fri.	8	Detroit		Wed.	12	New Jersey
	Sat.	9	Buffalo		Thur.	13	at New Jersey
	Tues.	12	at San Jose		Sat.	15	Ottawa*
	Thur.	14	at Phoenix		Sun.	16	at Ottawa*
	Sat.	16	at Colorado		Wed.	19	at Philadelphia
	Wed.	20	Montreal		Fri.	21	NY Rangers
	Fri.	22	Pittsburgh		Sat.	22	Washington
	Sat.	23	at Ottawa		Wed.	26	Chicago
	Wed.	27	Vancouver		Fri.	28	San Jose
	Fri.	29	at Florida	Mar.	Sun.	2	Philadelphia*
	Sat.	30	at Tampa Bay		Wed.	5	Calgary
Dec.	Tues.	3	at Pittsburgh		Fri.	7	Montreal
	Thur.	5	at Boston		Sat.	8	at Toronto
	Sat.	7	Buffalo		Wed.	12	Boston
	Wed.	11	Florida		Thur.	13	at New Jersey
	Thur.	12	at Philadelphia		Sat.	15	Edmonton*
	Sat.	14	Philadelphia		Sun.	16	at Washington*
	Mon.	16	at NY Rangers		Thur.	20	at St. Louis
	Tues.	17	St. Louis		Fri.	21	at Dallas
	Fri.	20	Dallas		Tues.	25	Colorado
	Sat.	21	Tampa Bay		Thur.	27	at Tampa Bay
	Thur.	26	at Buffalo		Sat.	29	NY Rangers*
	Sat.	28	Ottawa	Apr.	Wed.	2	Montreal
	Sun.	29	at Chicago		Thur.	3	at Pittsburgh
Jan.	Wed.	1	at Washington*		Sat.	5	at Montreal
	Thur.	2	Boston		Mon.	7	Buffalo
	Sat.	4	Washington		Wed.	9	at Ottawa
	Mon.	6	at Montreal		Fri.	11	at NY Islanders
	Thur.	9	at Calgary		Sun.	13	Tampa Bay*

* Denotes afternoon game.

Franchise date: June 22, 1979

EASTERN CONFERENCE NHL

NORTHEAST DIVISION

18th NHL Season

Sean Burke had one of his finest seasons in 1995-96, establishing career-highs in games (66), wins (28), and shutouts (4) while registering an impressive 3.11 goals-against average for the Hartford Whalers.

1996-97 Player Personnel

FORWARDS

	HT	WT	S	Place of Birth	Date	1995-96 Club
BUCKLEY, Tom	6-1	204	L	Buffalo, NY	5/26/76	Detroit (OHL)
CASSELS, Andrew	5-11	177	L	Bramalea, Ont.	7/23/69	Hartford
CHASE, Kelly	5-11	193	R	Porcupine Plain, Sask.	10/25/67	Hartford
DANIELS, Jeff	6-1	200	L	Oshawa, Ont.	6/24/68	Springfield
DINEEN, Kevin	5-11	190	R	Quebec City, Que.	10/28/63	Philadelphia-Hartford
DOMENICHELLI, Hnat	6-0	175	L	Edmonton, Alta.	2/17/76	Kamloops
EMERSON, Nelson	5-11	175	R	Hamilton, Ont.	8/17/67	Hartford
HARDING, Mike	6-4	225	R	Edmonton, Alta.	2/24/71	Springfield-Richmond
JANSSENS, Mark	6-3	212	L	Surrey, B.C.	5/19/68	Hartford
KAPANEN, Sami	5-10	170	L	Vantaa, Finland	6/14/73	Hartford-Springfield
KESA, Dan	6-0	198	R	Vancouver, B.C.	11/23/71	Dal-Mich-Sprfld-Det (IHL)
KRON, Robert	5-11	185	L	Brno, Czech.	2/27/67	Hartford
MARTINS, Steve	5-9	175	L	Gatineau, Que.	4/13/72	Hartford-Springfield
NIKOLISHIN, Andrei	5-11	180	L	Vorkuta, USSR	3/25/73	Hartford
O'NEILL, Jeff	6-1	190	R	Richmond Hill, Ont.	2/23/76	Hartford
RANHEIM, Paul	6-1	210	R	St. Louis, MO	1/25/66	Hartford
RICE, Steven	6-0	217	R	Kitchener, Ont.	5/26/71	Hartford
RITCHIE, Byron	5-10	180	L	Burnaby, B.C.	4/24/77	Lethbridge
SANDERSON, Geoff	6-0	185	L	Hay River, N.W.T.	2/1/72	Hartford
SECORD, Brian	5-11	180	L	Ridgetown, Ont.	6/19/75	Belv'le-SSM-Sprfld
SHANAHAN, Brendan	6-3	218	L	Mimico, Ont.	1/23/69	Hartford
SMYTH, Kevin	6-2	217	L	Banff, Alta.	11/22/73	Hartford-Springfield

DEFENSEMEN

	HT	WT	S	Place of Birth	Date	1995-96 Club
BROWN, Jeff	6-1	204	R	Ottawa, Ont.	4/30/66	Vancouver-Hartford
BURT, Adam	6-2	207	L	Detroit, MI	1/15/69	Hartford
DIDUCK, Gerald	6-2	217	R	Edmonton, Alta.	4/6/65	Hartford
FEATHERSTONE, Glen	6-4	209	L	Toronto, Ont.	7/8/68	Hartford
FEDOTOV, Sergei	6-1	185	L	Moscow, USSR	1/24/77	Magnitogorsk-Moscow D'amo-Saratov
GLYNN, Brian	6-4	218	L	Iserlohn, West Germany	11/23/67	Hartford
GODYNYUK, Alexander	6-0	207	L	Kiev, Ukraine	1/27/70	Hfd-Sprfld-Det (IHL)-Minn
MALIK, Marek	6-5	190	L	Ostrava, Czech.	6/24/75	Hartford-Springfield
McBAIN, Jason	6-2	180	L	Ilion, NY	4/12/74	Hartford-Springfield
MUELLER, Brian	5-11	225	L	Liverpool, NY	6/2/72	Springfield-Richmond
PRATT, Nolan	6-2	195	L	Fort McMurray, Alta.	8/14/75	Springfield-Richmond
RISODORE, Ryan	6-4	195	L	Hamilton, Ont.	4/4/76	Guelph
RUCINSKI, Mike	5-11	179	L	Trenton, MI	3/30/75	Detroit (OHL)
WESLEY, Glen	6-1	197	L	Red Deer, Alta.	10/2/68	Hartford

GOALTENDERS

	HT	WT	C	Place of Birth	Date	1995-96 Club
BURKE, Sean	6-4	208	L	Windsor, Ont.	1/29/67	Hartford
GIGUERE, Jean-Sebastien	6-0	175	L	Montreal, Que.	5/16/77	Halifax
LEGACE, Manny	5-9	162	L	Toronto, Ont.	2/4/73	Springfield
MUZZATTI, Jason	6-1	190	L	Toronto, Ont.	2/3/70	Hartford-Springfield

Retired Numbers

2	Rick Ley	1972-1981
9	Gordie Howe	1977-1980
19	John McKenzie	1976-1979

General Managers' History

Jack Kelly, 1979-80 to 1980-81; Larry Pleau, 1981-82 to 1982-83; Emile Francis, 1983-84 to 1988-89; Ed Johnston, 1989-90 to 1991-92; Brian Burke, 1992-93; Paul Holmgren, 1993-94; Jim Rutherford, 1994-95 to date.

Coaching History

Don Blackburn, 1979-80; Don Blackburn and Larry Pleau, 1980-81; Larry Pleau, 1981-82; Larry Kish, Larry Pleau and John Cuniff, 1982- 83; Jack "Tex" Evans, 1983-84 to 1986-87; Jack "Tex" Evans and Larry Pleau, 1987-88; Larry Pleau, 1988-89; Rick Ley, 1989-90 to 1990-91; Jim Roberts, 1991-92; Paul Holmgren, 1992-93; Paul Holmgren and Pierre Maguire, 1993-94; Paul Holmgren, 1994-95; Paul Holmgren and Paul Maurice, 1995-96; Paul Maurice, 1996-97.

Captains' History

Rick Ley, 1979-80; Rick Ley and Mike Rogers, 1980-81. Dave Keon, 1981-82; Russ Anderson, 1982-83; Mark Johnson, 1983-84; Mark Johnson and Ron Francis, 1984-85; Ron Francis, 1985-86 to 1990-91; Randy Ladouceur, 1991-92; Pat Verbeek, 1992-93 to 1994-95; Brendan Shanahan, 1995-96.

1995-96 Scoring

*– rookie

Regular Season

Pos	#	Player	Team	GP	G	A	Pts	+/–	PIM	PP	SH	GW	GT	S	%
L	94	Brendan Shanahan	HFD	74	44	34	78	2	125	17	2	6	0	280	15.7
L	8	Geoff Sanderson	HFD	81	34	31	65	0	40	6	0	7	0	314	10.8
C	21	Andrew Cassels	HFD	81	20	43	63	8	39	6	0	1	2	135	14.8
R	16	Nelson Emerson	HFD	81	29	29	58	-7	78	12	2	5	0	247	11.7
D	27	Jeff Brown	VAN	28	1	16	17	6	18	0	0	0	0	62	1.6
			HFD	48	7	31	38	2	38	5	0	0	0	115	6.1
			TOTAL	76	8	47	55	8	56	5	0	0	0	177	4.5
C	13	Andrei Nikolishin	HFD	61	14	37	51	-2	34	4	1	3	0	83	16.9
R	18	Robert Kron	HFD	77	22	28	50	-1	6	8	1	3	0	203	10.8
L	28	Paul Ranheim	HFD	73	10	20	30	-2	14	0	1	1	0	126	7.9
C	92 *	Jeff O'Neill	HFD	65	8	19	27	-3	40	1	0	1	0	65	12.3
D	20	Glen Wesley	HFD	68	8	16	24	-9	88	6	0	1	0	129	6.2
R	12	Steven Rice	HFD	59	10	12	22	-4	47	1	0	2	0	108	9.3
D	6	Adam Burt	HFD	78	4	9	13	-4	121	0	0	1	0	90	4.4
D	36	Glen Featherstone	HFD	68	2	10	12	10	138	0	0	1	0	62	3.2
R	11	Kevin Dineen	PHI	26	0	2	2	-8	50	0	0	0	0	31	0.0
			HFD	20	2	7	9	7	67	0	0	0	0	35	5.7
			TOTAL	46	2	9	11	-1	117	0	0	0	0	66	3.0
D	4	Gerald Diduck	HFD	79	1	9	10	7	88	0	0	0	0	93	1.1
L	24 *	Sami Kapanen	HFD	35	5	4	9	0	6	0	0	0	0	46	10.9
D	10	Brad McCrimmon	HFD	58	3	6	9	15	62	0	1	0	0	39	7.7
C	22	Mark Janssens	HFD	81	2	7	9	-13	155	0	0	0	0	63	3.2
L	15 *	Scott Daniels	HFD	53	3	4	7	-4	254	0	0	0	0	43	7.0
R	39	Kelly Chase	HFD	55	2	4	6	-4	230	0	0	1	0	19	10.5
G	1	Sean Burke	HFD	66	0	6	6	0	16	0	0	0	0	1	0.0
C	32 *	Steve Martins	HFD	23	1	3	4	-3	8	0	0	0	0	27	3.7
D	7	Brian Glynn	HFD	54	0	4	4	-15	44	0	0	0	0	46	0.0
L	14	Kevin Smyth	HFD	21	2	1	3	-5	8	1	0	0	0	27	7.4
C	33	Jimmy Carson	HFD	11	1	0	1	1	0	0	0	0	0	9	11.1
D	5	Alexander Godynyuk	HFD	3	0	1	1	-1	2	0	0	0	0	1	0.0
D	25 *	Jason McBain	HFD	3	0	0	0	-1	0	0	0	0	0	0	0.0
D	23 *	Marek Malik	HFD	7	0	0	0	-3	4	0	0	0	0	2	0.0
G	29 *	Jason Muzzatti	HFD	22	0	0	0	0	33	0	0	0	0	0	0.0

Goaltending

No.	Goaltender	GPI	Mins	Avg	W	L	T	EN	SO	GA	SA	S%
29	* Jason Muzzatti	22	1013	2.90	4	8	3	3	1	49	551	.911
1	Jeff Reese	7	275	3.05	2	3	0	0	1	14	170	.918
1	Sean Burke	66	3669	3.11	28	28	6	3	4	190	2034	.907
	Totals	**82**	**4979**	**3.12**	**34**	**39**	**9**	**6**	**6**	**259**	**2761**	**.906**

Coach

MAURICE, PAUL
Coach, Hartford Whalers. Born January 30, 1967.

Paul Maurice became the Whalers' tenth coach in the 17-year history of the franchise on November 6, 1995 after Paul Holmgren was dismissed as the team's coach 12 games into the 1995-96 season. Maurice, who was born on January 30, 1967, stepped in as the youngest coach in the National Hockey League.

Under Maurice's direction, the Whalers were 29-33-8 (.471). Hartford finished fourth in the Northeast Division and tenth overall in the Eastern Conference. The Whalers missed the final playoff position by 11 points.

Maurice, who has been a member of the Compuware hockey organization for the past 11 years, joined the Whalers in June of 1995 as an assistant coach after serving as the head coach of the Detroit Junior Red Wings for two seasons. The Junior Wings won the OHL Western Division regular-season title and played for the 1995 Memorial Cup by winning the OHL playoffs. The Wings lost in the Cup finals to Kamloops. For his efforts, Maurice was the runner-up for OHL coach of the year Honors in 1995. In the 1993-94 season, Maurice's squad won the OHL Hap Emms Division title and advanced to the finals of the OHL playoffs before losing in seven games to North Bay.

Maurice began his coaching career in 1986 as an assistant coach for the Detroit Junior Red Wings after an eye injury ended his junior playing career. He served six seasons in that capacity before taking over the head coaching responsibilities in the 1993-94 season.

Maurice resides in West Hartford, Connecticut, with his wife, Michelle.

Coaching Record

		Regular Season					Playoffs			
Season	Team	Games	W	L	T	%	Games	W	L	%
1993-94	Detroit (OHL)	66	42	20	4	.697	17	11	6	.647
1994-95	Detroit (OHL)	66	44	18	4	.727	21	16	5	.762
1995-96	**Hartford (NHL)**	70	29	33	8	.471	....	....	....	....
	NHL Totals	70	29	33	8	.471	....	....	....	....

Club Records

Team

(Figures in brackets for season records are games played; records for fewest points, wins, ties, losses, goals, goals against are for 70 or more games)

Most Points	93	1986-87 (80)
Most Wins	43	1986-87 (80)
Most Ties	19	1979-80 (80)
Most Losses	54	1982-83 (80)
Most Goals	332	1985-86 (80)
Most Goals Against	403	1982-83 (80)
Fewest Points	45	1982-83 (80)
Fewest Wins	19	1982-83 (80)
Fewest Ties	4	1985-86 (80)
Fewest Losses	30	1986-87 (80)
Fewest Goals	227	1993-94 (84)
Fewest Goals Against	259	1995-96 (82)

Longest Winning Streak

Overall	7	Mar. 16-29/85
Home	5	Mar. 17-29/85
Away	6	Nov. 10-Dec. 7/90

Longest Undefeated Streak

Overall	10	Jan. 20-Feb. 10/82 (6 wins, 4 ties)
Home	7	Mar. 15-Apr. 5/86 (5 wins, 2 ties)
Away	6	Jan. 23-Feb. 10/82 (3 wins, 3 ties), Nov. 30-Dec. 26/89 (5 wins, 1 tie), Nov. 10-Dec. 7/90 (6 wins)

Longest Losing Streak

Overall	9	Feb. 19/83-Mar. 8/83
Home	6	Feb. 19/83-Mar. 12/83, Feb. 10-Mar. 3/85
Away	13	Dec. 18/82-Feb. 5/83

Longest Winless Streak

Overall	14	Jan. 4/92-Feb. 9/92 (8 losses, 6 ties)
Home	13	Jan. 15-Mar. 10/85 (11 losses, 2 ties)
Away	15	Nov. 11/79-Jan. 9/80 (11 losses, 4 ties)

Most Shutouts, Season	6	1995-96 (82)
Most PIM, Season	2,354	1992-93 (84)
Most Goals, Game	11	Feb. 12/84 (Edm. 0 at Hfd. 11), Oct. 19/85 (Mtl. 6 at Hfd. 11), Jan. 17/86 (Que. 6 at Hfd. 11), Mar. 15/86 (Chi. 4 at Hfd. 11)

Individual

Most Seasons	10	Ron Francis
Most Games	714	Ron Francis
Most Goals, Career	264	Ron Francis
Most Assists, Career	557	Ron Francis
Most Points, Career	821	Ron Francis (264G, 557A)
Most PIM, Career	1,368	Torrie Robertson
Most Shutouts, Career	13	Mike Liut
Longest Consecutive Games Streak	419	Dave Tippett (Mar. 3/84-Oct. 7/89)
Most Goals, Season	56	Blaine Stoughton (1979-80)
Most Assists, Season	69	Ron Francis (1989-90)
Most Points, Season	105	Mike Rogers (1979-80; 44G, 61A), (1980-81; 40G, 65A)
Most PIM, Season	358	Torrie Robertson (1985-86)

Most Points, Defenseman Season	69	Dave Babych (1985-86; 14G, 55A)
Most Points, Center, Season	105	Mike Rogers (1979-80; 44G, 61A), Mike Rogers (1980-81; 40G, 65A)
Most Points, Right Wing, Season	100	Blaine Stoughton (1979-80; 56G, 44A)
Most Points, Left Wing, Season	89	Geoff Sanderson (1992-93; 46G, 43A)
Most Points, Rookie, Season	72	Sylvain Turgeon (1983-84; 40G, 32A)
Most Shutouts, Season	4	Mike Liut (1986-87), Peter Sidorkiewicz (1988-89), Sean Burke (1995-96)
Most Goals, Game	4	Jordy Douglas (Feb. 3/80), Ron Francis (Feb. 12/84)
Most Assists, Game	6	Ron Francis (Mar. 5/87)
Most Points, Game	6	Paul Lawless (Jan. 4/87; 2G, 4A), Ron Francis (Mar. 5/87; 6A, Oct. 8/89; 3G, 3A)

All-time Record vs. Other Clubs

Regular Season

				At Home						On Road						Total				
	GP	W	L	T	GF	GA	PTS	GP	W	L	T	GF	GA	PTS	GP	W	L	T	GF	GA	PTS
Anaheim	2	1	1	0	5	5	2	2	1	1	0	7	9	2	4	2	2	0	12	14	4
Boston	58	25	26	7	200	208	57	60	12	43	5	154	243	29	118	37	69	12	354	451	86
Buffalo	60	22	29	9	177	186	53	59	19	33	7	186	246	45	119	41	62	16	363	432	98
Calgary	23	7	13	3	77	93	17	23	4	18	1	77	121	9	46	11	31	4	154	214	26
Chicago	24	11	11	2	83	82	24	23	6	14	3	65	103	15	47	17	25	5	148	185	39
Colorado	56	24	21	11	193	195	59	58	17	34	7	176	248	41	114	41	55	18	369	443	100
Dallas	24	9	12	3	86	93	21	23	10	12	1	77	96	21	47	19	24	4	163	189	42
Detroit	23	14	8	1	87	64	29	24	7	11	6	70	91	20	47	21	19	7	157	155	49
Edmonton	23	9	9	5	98	87	23	24	4	17	3	72	103	11	47	13	26	8	170	190	34
Florida	6	2	4	0	19	17	4	6	2	3	1	13	16	5	12	4	7	1	32	33	9
Los Angeles	24	13	8	3	98	96	29	23	7	13	3	93	104	17	47	20	21	6	191	200	46
Montreal	60	22	30	8	186	223	52	58	11	40	7	171	263	29	118	33	70	15	357	486	81
New Jersey	27	12	8	7	99	87	31	29	11	15	3	101	104	25	56	23	23	10	200	191	56
NY Islanders	29	14	11	4	111	107	32	27	8	15	4	73	102	20	56	22	26	8	184	209	52
NY Rangers	27	14	10	3	99	95	31	28	9	16	3	85	121	21	55	23	26	6	184	216	52
Ottawa	10	9	1	0	39	23	18	11	8	1	2	38	22	18	21	17	2	2	77	45	36
Philadelphia	28	10	13	5	110	117	25	27	7	19	1	74	113	15	55	17	32	6	184	230	40
Pittsburgh	30	16	12	2	129	115	34	29	10	16	3	118	142	23	59	26	28	5	247	257	57
St. Louis	25	9	14	2	76	80	20	24	8	14	2	80	97	18	49	17	28	4	156	177	38
San Jose	5	3	2	0	20	13	6	4	1	3	0	16	27	2	9	4	5	0	36	40	8
Tampa Bay	7	5	2	0	24	17	10	7	1	5	1	14	23	3	14	6	7	1	38	40	13
Toronto	23	13	6	4	109	78	30	23	13	8	2	94	82	28	46	26	14	6	203	160	58
Vancouver	23	10	9	4	76	79	24	24	9	9	6	71	85	24	47	19	18	10	147	164	48
Washington	29	10	15	4	85	106	24	28	10	16	2	82	98	22	57	20	31	6	167	204	46
Winnipeg	23	11	7	5	94	76	27	25	12	12	1	91	88	25	48	23	19	6	185	164	52
Totals	**669**	**295**	**282**	**92**	**2380**	**2342**	**682**	**669**	**207**	**388**	**74**	**2098**	**2747**	**488**	**1338**	**502**	**670**	**166**	**4478**	**5089**	**1170**

Playoffs

	Series	W	L	GP	W	L	T	GF	GA	Last Mtg.	Round	Result
Boston	2	0	2	13	5	8	0	38	47	1991	DSF	L 2-4
Colorado	2	1	1	9	5	4	0	35	34	1987	DSF	L 2-4
Montreal	5	0	5	27	8	19	0	70	96	1992	DSF	L 3-4
Totals	**9**	**1**	**8**	**49**	**18**	**31**	**0**	**143**	**177**			

Playoff Results 1996-92

Year	Round	Opponent	Result	GF	GA
1992	DSF	Montreal	L 3-4	18	21

Abbreviations: Round: F – Final; **CF** – conference final; **CQF** – conference quarter-final; **CSF** – conference semi-final; **DF** – division final; **DSF** – division semi-final; **SF** – semi-final; **QF** – quarter-final; **PR** – preliminary round.

Calgary totals include Atlanta, 1979-80. Colorado totals include Quebec, 1979-80 to 1994-95.
Dallas totals include Minnesota, 1979-80 to 1992-93. New Jersey totals include Colorado Rockies, 1979-80 to 1981-82.

1995-96 Results

Oct.	7		NY Rangers	2-0		10	at	Calgary	2-3
	11		Anaheim	3-2		12	at	Winnipeg	3-2
	14		Chicago	3-2		16		Vancouver	3-0
	16	at	NY Rangers	7-5		17	at	NY Islanders	6-3
	20		Pittsburgh	2-2		24	at	Buffalo	2-4
	21	at	Florida	0-3		25		Los Angeles	8-2
	25		St. Louis	2-4		27		New Jersey	4-4
	27		Montreal	1-4		30	at	San Jose	2-8
	28	at	Boston	0-3		31	at	Los Angeles	6-4
Nov.	2		Ottawa	0-5	Feb.	2	at	Anaheim	4-3
	4	at	Ottawa	5-4		7	at	Vancouver	3-2
	5	at	Philadelphia	1-6		9	at	Colorado	3-2
	7		San Jose	7-3		11	at	Dallas	5-3
	11		NY Rangers	1-4		14		Boston	0-3
	14	at	New Jersey	0-1		17		Buffalo	2-1
	15		Ottawa	3-2		21		Montreal	5-3
	18		Philadelphia	2-4		23	at	Pittsburgh	4-5
	20	at	Montreal	3-4		25		Dallas	2-6
	22		Montreal	4-2		28		Edmonton	4-4
	24	at	Toronto	4-0	Mar.	1		Winnipeg	2-5
	25		Washington	2-4		2		Florida	7-1
	29	at	Tampa Bay	2-2		6		Detroit	2-4
Dec.	1	at	Buffalo	1-2		8		Toronto	7-4
	2		Florida	3-5		9	at	St. Louis	3-6
	6		NY Islanders	7-4		13		Pittsburgh	3-2
	9	at	Pittsburgh	0-6		16		Buffalo	2-0
	10	at	Chicago	1-4		18		Tampa Bay	6-3
	13		Tampa Bay	2-3		20	at	Montreal	2-3
	15		Colorado	4-2		22	at	Ottawa	1-1
	16	at	NY Islanders	3-3		23	at	Washington	0-3
	18	at	Montreal	2-3		25	at	Philadelphia	0-3
	20		Calgary	2-3		27		Boston	5-6
	22	at	NY Rangers	3-3		30		NY Islanders	3-1
	23		Philadelphia	3-3	Apr.	1	at	Florida	2-3
	28	at	Pittsburgh	4-9		3	at	Tampa Bay	2-4
	30	at	Washington	2-3		4		New Jersey	1-0
	31	at	Detroit	2-3		6		New Jersey	3-6
Jan.	3		Washington	2-0		8		Pittsburgh	5-4
	5		Ottawa	4-2		11	at	Boston	2-3
	6	at	Boston	2-5		13		Boston	2-0
	9	at	Edmonton	5-1		14	at	Buffalo	1-4

Entry Draft
Selections 1996-82

1996 Pick		1992 Pick		1989 Pick		1985 Pick	
34	Trevor Wasyluk	9	Robert Petrovicky	10	Robert Holik	5	Dana Murzyn
61	Andrei Petrunin	47	Andrei Nikolishin	52	Blair Atcheynum	26	Kay Whitmore
88	Craig MacDonald	57	Jan Vopat	73	Jim McKenzie	68	Gary Callaghan
104	Steve Wasylko	79	Kevin Smyth	94	James Black	110	Shane Churla
116	Mark McMahon	81	Jason McBain	115	Jerome Bechard	131	Chris Brant
143	Aaron Baker	143	Jarret Reid	136	Scott Daniels	152	Brian Puhalsky
171	Greg Kuznik	153	Ken Belanger	157	Raymond Saumier	173	Greg Dornbach
197	Kevin Marsh	177	Konstantin Korotkov	178	Michel Picard	194	Paul Tory
223	Craig Adams	201	Greg Zwakman	199	Trevor Buchanan	215	Jerry Pawlowski
231	Askhat Rakhmatullin	225	Steven Halko	220	John Battice	236	Bruce Hill
		249	Joacim Esbjors	241	Peter Kasowski		

1995 Pick		1991 Pick		1988 Pick		1984 Pick	
13	J-Sebastien Giguere			11	Chris Govedaris	11	Sylvain Cote
35	Sergei Fedotov	9	Patrick Poulin	32	Barry Richter	110	Mike Millar
85	Ian MacNeil	31	Martin Hamrlik	74	Dean Dyer	131	Mike Vellucci
87	Sami Kapanen	53	Todd Hall	95	Scott Morrow	173	John Devereaux
113	Hugh Hamilton	59	Mikael Nylander	116	Corey Beaulieu	193	Brent Regan
165	Byron Ritchie	75	Jim Storm	137	Kerry Russell	214	Jim Culhane
191	Milan Kostolny	119	Mike Harding	158	Jim Burke	234	Pete Abric
217	Mike Rucinski	141	Brian Mueller	179	Mark Hirth		
		163	Steve Yule	200	Wayde Bucsis	1983 Pick	
1994 Pick		185	Chris Belanger	221	Rob White	2	Sylvain Turgeon
5	Jeff O'Neill	207	Jason Currie	242	Dan Slatalla	20	David Jensen
83	Hnat Domenichelli	229	Mike Santonelli			23	Ville Siren
109	Ryan Risidore	251	Rob Peters	1987 Pick		61	Leif Carlsson
187	Tom Buckley			18	Jody Hull	64	Dave MacLean
213	Ashlin Halfnight	1990 Pick		39	Adam Burt	72	Ron Chyzowski
230	Matt Ball	15	Mark Greig	81	Terry Yake	104	Brian Johnson
239	Brian Regan	36	Geoff Sanderson	102	Marc Rousseau	124	Joe Reekie
265	Steve Nimigon	57	Mike Lenarduzzi	123	Jeff St. Cyr	143	Chris Duperron
		78	Chris Bright	144	Greg Wolf	144	James Falle
1993 Pick		120	Cory Keenan	165	John Moore	164	Bill Fordy
2	Chris Pronger	141	Jergus Baca	186	Joe Day	193	Reine Karlsson
72	Marek Malik	162	Martin D'Orsonnens	228	Kevin Sullivan	204	Allan Acton
84	Trevor Roenick	183	Corey Osmak	249	Steve Laurin	224	Darcy Kaminski
115	Nolan Pratt	204	Espen Knutsen				
188	Emmanuel Legace	225	Tommie Eriksen	1986 Pick		1982 Pick	
214	Dmitri Gorenko	246	Denis Chalifoux	11	Scott Young	14	Paul Lawless
240	Wes Swinson			32	Marc Laforge	35	Mark Paterson
266	Igor Chibirev			74	Brian Chapman	56	Kevin Dineen
				95	Bill Horn	67	Ulf Samuelsson
				116	Joe Quinn	88	Ray Ferraro
				137	Steve Torrel	109	Randy Gilhen
				158	Ron Hoover	130	Jim Johannson
				179	Robert Glasgow	151	Mickey Krampotich
				200	Sean Evoy	172	Kevin Skilliter
				221	Cal Brown	214	Martin Linse
				242	Brian Verbeek	235	Randy Cameron

Club Directory

Hartford Whalers
242 Trumbull Street
Eighth Floor
Hartford, Connecticut 06103
Phone **860/728-3366**
GM FAX 860/493-2423
FAX 860/522-7707
Capacity: 15,635

Ownership
Chief Executive Officer/Governor . . . . Peter Karmanos Jr.
General Partner . . . . Thomas Thewes
Chief Operating Officer/President/General Manager. Jim Rutherford

Coaching Staff
Head Coach . . . . Paul Maurice
Assistant Coaches. . . . . Randy Ladouceur, Tom Webster, Steve Weeks

Hockey Operations
Vice President of Hockey Operations . . . . Terry McDonnell
Strength and Conditioning Consultant . . . . TBA
Director of Amateur Scouting/Player Personnel. . . . Sheldon Ferguson
Scouting Staff. . . . . Claude Larose, Willy Langer, Willy Lindstrom,
Ken Schinkel, Tony MacDonald, Bill Terry, Bert
Marshall, Lawrence Ferguson
Medical Trainer. . . . . Bud Gouveia
Equipment Managers . . . . Skip Cunningham, Wally Tatomir
Assistant Equipment Managers. . . . . Bob Gorman, Rick Szuber
Executive Secretary, Hockey Operations . . . . Cathy Merrick
Executive Secretary, Hockey Operations . . . . Anne Sullivan
Team Physicians . . . . Dr. David Grise, Dr. John Fulkerson
Consulting Physician . . . . Dr. John Rogers
Club Dentist . . . . Dr. Robert Hall
Motivational Consultant . . . . Doris Barksdale

Finance and Administration
Vice President of Finance and Administration . . . . . Mike Amendola
Consultant on Business Affairs . . . . Lou Beer
Accounting Staff. . . . . Lori Bengtson, Joyce Dextradeur,
Debbie Mierzejewski
Receptionist . . . . Dorothy Cronin

Merchandise
Team Store Manager . . . . Dave Freedman
Team Store Assistant Manager . . . . Rick Zablocki

Marketing
Vice President of Marketing and Sales . . . . Rick Francis
Director of Advertising Sales . . . . Kevin Bauer
Director of Sponsorship Sales . . . . Bill McMinn
Director of Corporate Sales. . . . . Jim Jacen
Marketing Services Representative . . . . Mickee Todd
Corporate Sales Services Representative . . . . Jill Pachla

Public Relations
Director of Public Relations. . . . . Chris Brown
Director of Publications/Statistics . . . . Frank Polnaszek
Director of Community Relations . . . . Mary Lynn Gorman
Director of Amateur Hockey Development . . . . Mike Veisor
Public Relations Assistant . . . . Wendy Mascetti
Public Relations Administrative Assistant . . . . Bruce Gold

Ticket Sales
Director of Ticket Operations . . . . Jim Baldwin
Ticket Sales Manager . . . . Bryan Dooley
Ticket Office Managers . . . . Mike Barnes, Chris O'Connor
Assistant Ticket Office Manager . . . . Adam Mehan
Account Executives. . . . . Mike Gilsenan, Joe Barbetta, Connie Cavallo

Television and Radio Broadcast
Radio Play-by-Play/Director of Broadcasting . . . . . . Chuck Kaiton
Radio Color. . . . . TBA
TV/Cable Play-by-Play . . . . John Forslund
TV/Cable Commentator . . . . TBA
Cable TV Outlet . . . . SportsChannel - New England
Radio Network Flagship Station . . . . WTIC-AM (1080)

General Information
Home Ice . . . . Hartford Civic Center
Veterans Memorial Coliseum
Dimensions of Rink . . . . 200 feet by 85 feet
Practice Facilities . . . . Hartford Civic Center and
Avon Old Farms
Developmental Club . . . . Springfield Falcons (AHL)
Team Colors . . . . Blue (PMS 281), Silver (PMS 877), Green (PMS 349)
Team Store Phone . . . . (800) T1WHALE
Ticket Information . . . . (800) WHALERS

General Manager

RUTHERFORD, JIM
General Manager, Hartford Whalers. Born in Beeton, Ont., February 17, 1949.

Jim Rutherford was named the president and general manager of the Hartford Whalers on June 28, 1994. He is the Whalers' seventh general manager in the history of the organization. Entering his third season, Rutherford has taken an aggressive approach towards turning the fortunes of the franchise through trades and the NHL draft. Few players remain on the roster from when he accepted the general manager's position.

The team's .470 winning percentage in the 1995-96 season marks the Whalers' best record since the 1989-90 season and a considerable improvement over the 1993-94 season (.375).

After his playing days with the Red Wings, Rutherford joined Compuware to serve as the director of hockey operations for Compuware Sports Corporation. Rutherford gained a wealth of experience in youth hockey and junior programs.

He started his management career by guiding Compuware Sports Corporation's purchase of the Windsor Spitfires of the Ontario Hockey League in April of 1984. During the next four years, Rutherford acted as general manager of the Spitfires. After the Spitfires advanced to the 1988 Memorial Cup finals, Rutherford led Compuware's efforts to bring the first American-based OHL franchise to Detroit on December 11, 1989. In the following five years, the Detroit Junior Whalers became one of the premier teams in the OHL. The 1993-94 Detroit team won the Emms Division championship and Rutherford was voted the 1993 executive of the year award again in 1994.

A veteran of 13 NHL seasons, Rutherford began his professional goaltending career in 1969 as a first-round selection of the Detroit Red Wings. While playing for Pittsburgh, Toronto, Los Angeles, and Detroit, Rutherford collected 14 career shutouts. For five seasons he also served as the Red Wings' player representative. Rutherford also played for Team Canada in the World Championships in Vienna in 1977 and Moscow in 1979.

Los Angeles Kings

1995-96 Results: 24W-40L-18T 66PTS. Sixth, Pacific Division

Schedule

Oct.	Fri.	4	NY Islanders		Thur.	9	Buffalo
	Sun.	6	San Jose		Sat.	11	St. Louis
	Wed.	9	at Montreal		Tues.	14	at Detroit
	Thur.	10	at Philadelphia		Wed.	15	at Toronto
	Sat.	12	at Washington		Tues.	21	New Jersey
	Tues.	15	Philadelphia		Wed.	22	at San Jose
	Thur.	17	Boston		Sat.	25	Anaheim*
	Sun.	20	at Chicago*		Mon.	27	at Dallas
	Mon.	21	at Detroit		Wed.	29	at Colorado
	Thur.	24	Edmonton		Thur.	30	Hartford
	Sat.	26	Calgary	**Feb.**	Sat.	1	Chicago
	Tues.	29	at Toronto		Mon.	3	at Calgary
	Wed.	30	at Ottawa		Wed.	5	at San Jose
Nov.	Sat.	2	at Hartford		Sun.	9	at Dallas
	Mon.	4	at Boston		Tues.	11	at Colorado
	Thur.	7	Montreal		Thur.	13	Toronto
	Fri.	8	at Anaheim		Sat.	15	Edmonton
	Thur.	14	Toronto		Mon.	17	Dallas*
	Sun.	17	at Chicago*		Tues.	18	at Phoenix
	Tues.	19	at Tampa Bay		Thur.	20	Anaheim
	Wed.	20	at Florida		Sat.	22	Vancouver
	Sat.	23	Detroit		Tues.	25	Colorado
	Wed.	27	at Edmonton		Thur.	27	Edmonton
	Thur.	28	at Calgary	**Mar.**	Sat.	1	at Vancouver
	Sat.	30	Chicago		Tues.	4	at Edmonton
Dec.	Tues.	3	at Phoenix		Thur.	6	NY Rangers
	Thur.	5	Tampa Bay		Sat.	8	Ottawa
	Sat.	7	Colorado		Mon.	10	Detroit
	Tues.	10	Pittsburgh		Thur.	13	St. Louis
	Thur.	12	Calgary		Sat.	15	Calgary
	Sat.	14	Washington		Wed.	19	at Anaheim
	Tues.	17	at NY Islanders		Sat.	22	San Jose
	Wed.	18	at NY Rangers		Mon.	24	at Vancouver
	Fri.	20	at Buffalo		Thur.	27	at St. Louis
	Sun.	22	at St. Louis		Sat.	29	at Pittsburgh*
	Thur.	26	Phoenix		Sun.	30	at New Jersey*
	Sat.	28	Colorado	**Apr.**	Thur.	3	Phoenix
	Mon.	30	at Edmonton		Sat.	5	Dallas
Jan.	Thur.	2	at Vancouver		Wed.	9	at Anaheim
	Sat.	4	Florida		Sat.	12	San Jose
	Tues.	7	Vancouver		Sun.	13	at Colorado

*Denotes afternoon game.

Acquired from the Washington Capitals in the off-season, Dimitri Khristich quickly became one of the Kings' offensive leaders in 1995-96, collecting 27 goals, 37 assists and a team-leading 12 power-play goals.

Franchise date: June 5, 1967

PACIFIC DIVISION

30th NHL Season

Year-by-Year Record

		Home			Road			Overall						
Season	**GP**	**W**	**L**	**T**	**W**	**L**	**T**	**W**	**L**	**T**	**GF**	**GA**	**Pts.**	**Finished**	**Playoff Result**
1995-96	82	16	16	9	8	24	9	24	40	18	256	302	66	6th, Pacific Div.	Out of Playoffs
1994-95	48	7	11	6	9	12	3	16	23	9	142	174	41	4th, Pacific Div.	Out of Playoffs
1993-94	84	18	19	5	9	26	7	27	45	12	294	322	66	5th, Pacific Div.	Out of Playoffs
1992-93	84	22	15	5	17	20	5	39	35	10	338	340	88	3rd, Smythe Div.	Lost Final
1991-92	80	20	11	9	15	20	5	35	31	14	287	296	84	2nd, Smythe Div.	Lost Div. Semi-Final
1990-91	80	26	9	5	20	15	5	46	24	10	340	254	102	1st, Smythe Div.	Lost Div. Final
1989-90	80	21	16	3	13	23	4	34	39	7	338	337	75	4th, Smythe Div.	Lost Div. Final
1988-89	80	25	12	3	17	19	4	42	31	7	376	335	91	2nd, Smythe Div.	Lost Div. Final
1987-88	80	19	18	3	11	24	5	30	42	8	318	359	68	4th, Smythe Div.	Lost Div. Semi-Final
1986-87	80	20	17	3	11	24	5	31	41	8	318	341	70	4th, Smythe Div.	Lost Div. Semi-Final
1985-86	80	9	27	4	14	22	4	23	49	8	284	389	54	5th, Smythe Div.	Out of Playoffs
1984-85	80	20	14	6	14	18	8	34	32	14	339	326	82	4th, Smythe Div.	Lost Div. Semi-Final
1983-84	80	13	19	8	10	25	5	23	44	13	309	376	59	5th, Smythe Div.	Out of Playoffs
1982-83	80	20	13	7	7	28	5	27	41	12	308	365	66	5th, Smythe Div.	Out of Playoffs
1981-82	80	19	15	6	5	26	9	24	41	15	314	369	63	4th, Smythe Div.	Lost Div. Final
1980-81	80	22	11	7	21	13	6	43	24	13	337	290	99	2nd, Norris Div.	Lost Prelim. Round
1979-80	80	18	13	9	12	23	5	30	36	14	290	313	74	2nd, Norris Div.	Lost Prelim. Round
1978-79	80	20	13	7	14	21	5	34	34	12	292	286	80	3rd, Norris Div.	Lost Prelim. Round
1977-78	80	18	16	6	13	18	9	31	34	15	243	245	77	3rd, Norris Div.	Lost Prelim. Round
1976-77	80	20	13	7	14	18	8	34	31	15	271	241	83	2nd, Norris Div.	Lost Quarter-Final
1975-76	80	22	13	5	16	20	4	38	33	9	263	265	85	2nd, Norris Div.	Lost Quarter-Final
1974-75	80	22	7	11	20	10	10	42	17	21	269	185	105	2nd, Norris Div.	Lost Prelim. Round
1973-74	78	22	13	4	11	20	8	33	33	12	233	231	78	3rd, West Div.	Lost Quarter-Final
1972-73	78	21	11	7	10	25	4	31	36	11	232	245	73	6th, West Div.	Out of Playoffs
1971-72	78	14	23	2	6	26	7	20	49	9	206	305	49	7th, West Div.	Out of Playoffs
1970-71	78	17	14	8	8	26	5	25	40	13	239	303	63	5th, West Div.	Out of Playoffs
1969-70	76	12	22	4	2	30	6	14	52	10	168	290	38	6th, West Div.	Out of Playoffs
1968-69	76	19	14	5	5	28	5	24	42	10	185	260	58	4th, West Div.	Lost Semi-Final
1967-68	74	20	13	4	11	20	6	31	33	10	200	224	72	2nd, West Div.	Lost Quarter-Final

1996-97 Player Personnel

FORWARDS	HT	WT	S	Place of Birth	Date	1995-96 Club
BYLSMA, Dan	6-2	215	L	Grand Rapids, MI	9/19/70	Los Angeles-Phoenix
DALE, Andrew	6-1	196	L	Sudbury, Ont.	2/16/76	Sudbury-Kitchener
DI PIETRO, Paul	5-9	181	R	Sault Ste. Marie, Ont.	9/8/70	Tor-St. John's-Houston-Las Vegas
FERRARO, Ray	5-10	185	L	Trail, B.C.	8/23/64	NY Rangers-Los Angeles
GRIEVE, Brent	6-1	202	L	Oshawa, Ont.	5/9/69	Chicago-Indianapolis-Phoenix
JOHNSON, Craig	6-2	197	L	St. Paul, MN	3/8/72	St. Louis-Worcester-Los Angeles
JOHNSON, Matt	6-5	230	L	Welland, Ont.	11/23/75	Los Angeles-Phoenix
KHRISTICH, Dimitri	6-2	195	R	Kiev, USSR	7/23/69	Los Angeles
KLIMA, Petr	6-0	190	R	Chomutov, Czech.	12/23/64	Tampa Bay
LaFAYETTE, Nathan	6-1	200	R	New Westminster, B.C.	2/17/73	NYR-Binghamton-L.A.
LANG, Robert	6-2	200	R	Teplice, Czech.	12/19/70	Los Angeles
LAPERRIERE, Ian	6-1	195	R	Montreal, Que.	1/19/74	StL-Worcester-NYR-L.A.
McRAE, Ken	6-1	195	R	Winchester, Ont.	4/23/68	Phoenix
MORGAN, Jason	6-1	185	L	St. John's, Nfld.	10/9/76	Kingston
NURMINEN, Kai	6-1	198	L	Turku, Finland	3/29/69	HV 71
OLCZYK, Ed	6-1	205	L	Chicago, IL	8/16/66	Winnipeg
PERREAULT, Yanic	5-11	182	L	Sherbrooke, Que.	4/4/71	Los Angeles
POTOMSKI, Barry	6-2	215	L	Windsor, Ont.	11/24/72	Los Angeles-Phoenix
ROSA, Pavel	5-11	178	R	Most, Czech.	6/7/77	Hull
SCHMIDT, Chris	6-3	200	L	Beaverlodge, Alta.	3/1/76	Seattle
SHEVALIER, Jeff	5-11	185	.L	Mississauga, Ont.	3/14/74	Phoenix
SOULLIERE, Stephane	5-11	180	L	Greenfield Park, Que.	5/30/75	Knoxville-Phoenix
STEVENS, Kevin	6-3	217	L	Brockton, MA	4/15/65	Boston-Los Angeles
TARDIF, Patrice	6-2	202	L	Thetford Mines, Que.	10/30/70	St. Louis-Worcester-Los Angeles
TSYPLAKOV, Vladimir	6-0	185	L	Moscow, USSR	4/18/69	Los Angeles-Las Vegas
VACHON, Nick	5-10	185	L	Montreal, Que.	7/20/72	Phoenix
VOPAT, Roman	6-3	216	L	Litvinov, Czech.	4/21/76	StL-Wor-M.Jaw-P.A.
YACHMENEV, Vitali	5-9	180	L	Chelyabinsk, USSR	1/8/75	Los Angeles

DEFENSEMEN						
BATYRSHIN, Ruslan	6-1	185	L	Moscow, USSR	2/19/75	Los Angeles-Phoenix
BERG, Aki-Petteri	6-3	198	L	Turku, Finland	2/28/77	Los Angeles-Phoenix
BLAKE, Rob	6-3	215	R	Simcoe, Ont.	12/10/69	Los Angeles
BOUCHER, Philippe	6-3	190	R	St. Apollinaire, Que.	3/24/73	Los Angeles-Phoenix
FINN, Steven	6-0	200	L	Laval, Que.	8/20/66	Tampa Bay-Los Angeles
McKENNA, Steve	6-8	247	L	Toronto, Ont.	8/21/73	Merrimack
MODRY, Jaroslav	6-2	195	L	Ceske-Budejovice, Czech.	2/27/71	Ottawa-Los Angeles
NORSTROM, Mattias	6-1	205	L	Stockholm, Sweden	1/2/72	NY Rangers-Los Angeles
O'DONNELL, Sean	6-2	225	L	Ottawa, Ont.	10/13/71	Los Angeles
SLANEY, John	6-0	185	L	St. John's, Nfld.	2/7/72	Colorado-Cornwall-Los Angeles
VOPAT, Jan	6-0	198	L	Most, Czech.	3/22/73	Los Angeles-Phoenix
ZMOLEK, Doug	6-2	220	L	Rochester, MN	11/3/70	Dallas-Los Angeles

GOALTENDERS	HT	WT	C	Place of Birth	Date	1995-96 Club
BEAUBIEN, Frederick	6-1	204	L	Lauzon, Que.	4/1/75	Phoenix
BERGERON, Jean-Claude	6-2	192	L	Hauterive, Que.	10/14/68	Tampa Bay-Atlanta
DAFOE, Byron	5-11	175	L	Sussex, England	2/25/71	Los Angeles
FISET, Stephane	6-1	195	L	Montreal, Que.	6/17/70	Colorado
GUZDA, Brad	6-3	180	L	Banff, Alta.	4/28/73	Knoxville-Muskegon
STORR, Jamie	6-0	170	L	Brampton, Ont.	12/28/75	Los Angeles-Phoenix

General Managers' History

Larry Regan, 1967-68 to 1972-73; Larry Regan and Jake Milford, 1973-74; Jake Milford, 1974-75 to 1976-77; George Maguire, 1977-78 to 1982-83; George Maguire and Rogatien Vachon, 1983-84; Rogatien Vachon, 1984-85 to 1991-92; Nick Beverley, 1992-93 to 1993-94; Sam McMaster, 1994-95 to date.

Coaching History

"Red" Kelly, 1967-68 to 1968-69; Hal Laycoe and John Wilson, 1969-70; Larry Regan, 1970-71; Larry Regan and Fred Glover, 1971-72; Bob Pulford, 1972-73 to 1976-77; Ron Stewart, 1977-78; Bob Berry, 1978-79 to 1980-81; Parker MacDonald and Don Perry, 1981-82; Don Perry, 1982-83; Don Perry, Rogie Vachon and Roger Neilson, 1983-84; Pat Quinn, 1984-85 to 1985-86; Pat Quinn and Mike Murphy 1986-87; Mike Murphy, Rogie Vachon and Robbie Ftorek, 1987-88; Robbie Ftorek, 1988-89; Tom Webster, 1989-90 to 1991-92; Barry Melrose, 1992-93 to 1993-94; Barry Melrose and Rogie Vachon, 1994-95; Larry Robinson, 1995-96 to date.

Captains' History

Bob Wall, 1967-68, 1968-69; Larry Cahan, 1969-70, 1970-71; Bob Pulford, 1971-72, 1972-73; Terry Harper, 1973-74, 1974-75; Mike Murphy, 1975-76 to 1980-81; Dave Lewis, 1981-82, 1982-83; Terry Ruskowski, 1983-84, 1984-85; Dave Taylor, 1985-86 to 1988-89; Wayne Gretzky, 1989-90 to 1991-92; Wayne Gretzky and Luc Robitaille, 1992-93; Wayne Gretzky, 1993-94 to 1995-96.

1995-96 Scoring

*– rookie

Regular Season

Pos	#	Player	Team	GP	G	A	Pts	+/−	PIM	PP	SH	GW	GT	S	%
L	8	Dimitri Khristich	L.A.	76	27	37	64	0	44	12	0	3	0	204	13.2
C	20	Ray Ferraro	NYR	65	25	29	54	13	82	8	0	4	0	160	15.6
			L.A.	11	4	2	6	−13	10	1	0	0	0	18	22.2
			TOTAL	76	29	31	60	0	92	9	0	4	0	178	16.3
R	43 *	Vitali Yachmenev	L.A.	80	19	34	53	−3	16	6	1	2	0	133	14.3
C	44	Yanic Perreault	L.A.	78	25	24	49	−11	16	8	3	7	0	175	14.3
C	12	Kevin Todd	L.A.	74	16	27	43	6	38	0	2	4	0	132	12.1
L	25	Kevin Stevens	BOS	41	10	13	23	1	49	3	0	1	0	101	9.9
			L.A.	20	3	10	13	−11	22	3	0	0	0	69	4.3
			TOTAL	61	13	23	36	−10	71	6	0	1	0	170	7.6
L	21	Tony Granato	L.A.	49	17	18	35	−5	46	5	0	1	0	156	10.9
L	28	Eric Lacroix	L.A.	72	16	16	32	−11	110	3	0	1	0	107	15.0
C	23 *	Craig Johnson	STL	49	8	7	15	−4	30	1	0	0	0	69	11.6
			L.A.	11	5	4	9	−4	6	3	0	0	0	28	17.9
			TOTAL	60	13	11	24	−8	36	4	0	0	0	97	13.4
D	26	Philippe Boucher	L.A.	53	7	16	23	−26	31	5	0	1	1	145	4.8
C	13	Robert Lang	L.A.	68	6	16	22	−15	10	0	2	0	1	71	8.5
D	15	Jaroslav Modry	OTT	64	4	14	18	−17	38	1	0	1	0	89	4.5
			L.A.	9	0	3	3	−4	6	0	0	0	0	17	0.0
			TOTAL	73	4	17	21	−21	44	1	0	1	0	106	3.8
D	27	John Slaney	COL	7	0	3	3	2	4	0	0	0	0	12	0.0
			L.A.	31	6	11	17	5	10	3	1	0	0	63	9.5
			TOTAL	38	6	14	20	7	14	3	1	0	0	75	8.0
C	22	Ian Laperriere	STL	33	3	5	8	−9	87	1	0	0	0	31	9.7
			NYR	28	1	2	3	−5	53	0	0	0	0	21	4.8
			L.A.	10	2	3	5	−2	15	0	0	1	0	18	11.1
			TOTAL	71	6	11	17	−11	155	1	0	1	1	70	8.6
C	14	Gary Shuchuk	L.A.	33	4	10	14	3	12	0	0	0	0	22	18.2
L	9	Vladimir Tsyplakov	L.A.	23	5	5	10	1	4	0	0	0	0	40	12.5
D	77	Rob Cowie	L.A.	46	5	5	10	−16	32	2	0	0	1	86	5.8
D	2	Doug Zmolek	DAL	42	1	5	6	1	65	0	0	0	0	26	3.8
			L.A.	16	1	0	1	−6	22	0	0	0	0	10	10.0
			TOTAL	58	2	5	7	−5	87	0	0	0	0	36	5.6
D	6 *	Sean O'Donnell	L.A.	71	2	5	7	3	127	0	0	0	0	65	3.1
D	5 *	Aki Berg	L.A.	51	0	7	7	−13	29	0	0	0	0	56	0.0
C	24	Nathan Lafayette	NYR	5	0	0	0	−1	2	0	0	0	0	5	0.0
			L.A.	12	2	4	6	−3	6	1	0	0	0	23	8.7
			TOTAL	17	2	4	6	−4	8	1	0	0	0	28	7.1
D	3	Denis Tsygurov	L.A.	18	1	5	6	0	22	1	0	0	0	21	4.8
C	37	Patrice Tardif	STL	23	3	0	3	−2	12	0	0	1	0	21	14.3
			L.A.	15	1	2	3	−9	37	1	0	0	0	29	3.4
			TOTAL	38	4	1	5	−11	49	1	0	1	0	50	8.0
L	40 *	Barry Potomski	L.A.	33	3	2	5	−7	104	0	0	0	0	23	13.0
D	29	Steven Finn	T.B.	16	0	0	0	−6	24	0	0	0	0	12	0.0
			L.A.	50	3	2	5	−6	102	0	0	0	0	42	7.1
			TOTAL	66	3	2	5	−12	126	0	0	0	0	54	5.6
D	3 *	Jan Vopat	L.A.	11	1	4	5	3	4	0	0	0	0	13	7.7
D	11	Mattias Norstrom	NYR	25	1	3	4	5	22	0	0	0	0	17	11.8
			L.A.	11	0	1	1	−8	18	0	0	0	0	17	0.0
			TOTAL	36	2	2	4	−3	40	0	0	0	0	34	5.9
D	4	Rob Blake	L.A.	6	1	2	3	0	8	0	0	0	0	13	7.7
C	20 *	Steve Larouche	NYR	1	0	0	0	0	0	0	0	0	0	1	0.0
			L.A.	7	1	2	3	0	4	1	0	0	0	13	7.7
			TOTAL	8	1	2	3	0	4	1	0	0	0	14	7.1
R	7 *	Kevin Brown	L.A.	7	1	0	1	−2	4	0	0	0	0	9	11.1
R	55	Troy Crowder	L.A.	15	1	0	1	−3	42	0	0	0	0	11	9.1
D	35	Arto Blomsten	L.A.	2	0	1	1	1	0	0	0	0	0	1	0.0
L	34 *	Matt Johnson	L.A.	1	0	0	0	0	5	0	0	0	0	1	0.0
D	45 *	Ruslan Batyrshin	L.A.	2	0	0	0	0	4	0	0	0	0	0	0.0
L	42 *	Dan Bylsma	L.A.	4	0	0	0	0	0	0	0	0	0	6	0.0
G	1 *	Jamie Storr	L.A.	5	0	0	0	0	0	0	0	0	0	0	0.0
G	32	Kelly Hrudey	L.A.	36	0	0	0	0	6	0	0	0	0	0	0.0
G	31 *	Byron Dafoe	L.A.	47	0	0	0	0	6	0	0	0	0	0	0.0

Goaltending

No.	Goaltender	GPI	Mins	Avg	W	L	T	EN	SO	GA	SA	S%
1	* Jamie Storr	5	262	2.75	3	1	0	0	0	12	147	.918
32	Kelly Hrudey	36	2077	3.26	7	15	10	2	0	113	1214	.907
31	* Byron Dafoe	47	2666	3.87	14	24	8	3	1	172	1539	.888
	Totals	82	5025	3.61	24	40	18	5	1	302	2905	.896

Club Records

Team

(Figures in brackets for season records are games played; records for fewest points, wins, ties, losses, goals, goals against are for 70 or more games)

Most Points	105	1974-75 (80)	
Most Wins	46	1990-91 (80)	
Most Ties	21	1974-75 (80)	
Most Losses	52	1969-70 (76)	
Most Goals	376	1988-89 (80)	
Most Goals Against	389	1985-86 (80)	
Fewest Points	38	1969-70 (76)	
Fewest Wins	14	1969-70 (76)	
Fewest Ties	7	1988-89 (80), 1989-90 (80)	
Fewest Losses	17	1974-75 (80)	
Fewest Goals	168	1969-70 (76)	
Fewest Goals Against	185	1974-75 (80)	

Longest Winning Streak
Overall 8   Oct. 21-Nov. 7/72
Home 12   Oct. 10-Dec. 5/92
Away 8   Dec. 18/74-Jan. 16/75

Longest Undefeated Streak
Overall 11   Feb. 28-Mar. 24/74
  (9 wins, 2 ties)
Home 13   Oct. 10-Dec. 8/92
  (12 wins, 1 tie)
Away 11   Oct. 10-Dec. 11/74
  (6 wins, 5 ties)

Longest Losing Streak
Overall 10   Feb. 22-Mar. 9/84
Home 9   Feb. 8-Mar. 12/86
Away 12   Jan. 11-Feb. 15/70

Longest Winless Streak
Overall 17   Jan. 29-Mar. 5/70
  (13 losses, 4 ties)
Home 9   Jan. 29-Mar. 5/70
  (8 losses, 1 tie),
  Feb. 8-Mar. 12/86
  (9 losses)
Away 21   Jan. 11-Apr. 3/70
  (17 losses, 4 ties)

Most Shutouts, Season 9   1974-75 (80)
Most PIM, Season 2,228   1990-91 (80)
Most Goals, Game 12   Nov. 28/84
  (Van. 1 at L.A. 12)

Individual

Most Seasons	17	Dave Taylor
Most Games	1,111	Dave Taylor
Most Goals, Career	550	Marcel Dionne
Most Assists, Career	757	Marcel Dionne
Most Points Career	1,307	Marcel Dionne
Most PIM, Career	1,846	Marty McSorley
Most Shutouts, Career	32	Rogie Vachon

Longest Consecutive
Games Streak 324   Marcel Dionne
  (Jan. 7/78-Jan. 9/82)
Most Goals, Season 70   Bernie Nicholls
  (1988-89)
Most Assists, Season 122   Wayne Gretzky
  (1990-91)
Most Points, Season 168   Wayne Gretzky
  (1988-89; 54G, 114A)
Most PIM, Season 399   Marty McSorley
  (1992-93)

Most Points, Defenseman
  Season 76   Larry Murphy
  (1980-81; 16G, 60A)
Most Points, Center,
  Season 168   Wayne Gretzky
  (1988-89; 54G, 114A)
Most Points, Right Wing,
  Season 112   Dave Taylor
  (1980-81; 47G, 65A)
Most Points, Left Wing,
  Season .... *125   Luc Robitaille
  (1992-93; 63G, 62A)
Most Points, Rookie,
  Season 84   Luc Robitaille
  (1986-87; 45G, 39A)
Most Shutouts, Season 8   Rogie Vachon
  (1976-77)
Most Goals, Game 4   Several players
Most Assists, Game 6   Bernie Nicholls
  (Dec. 1/88),
  Tomas Sandstrom
  (Oct. 9/93)
Most Points, Game 8   Bernie Nicholls
  (Dec. 1/88; 2G, 6A)

* NHL Record

Retired Numbers

16	Marcel Dionne	1975-1987
18	Dave Taylor	1977-1994
30	Rogatien Vachon	1971-1978

All-time Record vs. Other Clubs

Regular Season

		At Home							On Road							Total				
	GP	W	L	T	GF	GA	PTS	GP	W	L	T	GF	GA	PTS	GP	W	L	T	GF	GA	PTS
Anaheim	9	5	3	1	29	21	11	8	3	3	2	22	25	8	17	8	6	3	51	46	19
Boston	54	18	30	6	188	206	42	55	10	42	3	150	263	23	109	28	72	9	338	469	65
Buffalo	47	17	22	8	160	168	42	46	15	22	9	143	185	39	93	32	44	17	303	353	81
Calgary	73	37	28	8	293	272	82	77	20	48	9	257	367	49	150	57	76	17	550	639	131
Chicago	58	25	27	6	200	207	56	59	21	30	8	179	229	50	117	46	57	14	379	436	106
Colorado	25	14	9	2	110	86	30	24	10	11	3	98	104	23	49	24	20	5	208	,190	53
Dallas	62	27	18	17	222	186	71	63	16	36	11	180	259	43	125	43	54	28	402	445	114
Detroit	64	35	17	12	276	199	82	63	27	27	9	237	259	63	127	62	44	21	513	458	145
Edmonton	59	23	24	12	252	258	58	60	15	31	14	233	302	44	119	38	55	26	485	560	102
Florida	2	1	1	0	8	8	2	2	0	1	1	3	7	1	4	1	2	1	11	15	3
Hartford	23	13	7	3	104	93	29	24	8	13	3	96	98	19	47	21	20	6	200	191	48
Montreal	59	16	34	9	183	238	41	58	7	40	11	150	271	25	117	23	74	20	333	509	66
New Jersey	36	26	4	6	191	111	58	36	15	16	5	131	124	35	72	41	20	11	322	235	93
NY Islanders	38	17	14	7	141	127	41	38	13	21	4	110	145	30	76	30	35	11	251	272	71
NY Rangers	53	21	23	9	179	190	51	52	15	32	5	151	210	35	105	36	55	14	330	400	86
Ottawa	3	3	0	0	21	8	6	3	1	2	0	9	12	2	6	4	2	0	30	20	8
Philadelphia	59	17	34	8	172	205	42	57	15	35	7	147	222	37	116	32	69	15	319	427	79
Pittsburgh	63	41	14	8	248	163	90	65	20	37	8	206	245	48	128	61	51	16	454	408	138
St. Louis	62	32	21	9	227	177	73	62	15	39	8	162	235	38	124	47	60	17	389	412	111
San Jose	15	10	4	1	56	41	21	16	6	7	3	57	60	15	31	16	11	4	113	101	36
Tampa Bay	4	0	4	0	10	19	0	3	2	1	0	9	7	4	7	2	5	0	19	26	4
Toronto	60	32	20	8	216	178	72	59	17	31	11	199	241	45	119	49	51	19	415	419	117
Vancouver	82	41	29	12	338	277	94	79	25	41	13	262	318	63	161	66	70	25	600	595	157
Washington	40	24	12	4	162	125	52	39	16	17	6	147	170	38	79	40	29	10	309	295	90
Winnipeg	53	20	23	10	228	223	50	56	20	27	9	205	239	49	109	40	50	19	433	462	99
Defunct Clubs	35	27	6	2	141	76	56	34	11	14	9	91	109	31	69	38	20	11	232	185	87
Totals	**1138**	**542**	**428**	**168**	**4355**	**3862**	**1252**	**1138**	**343**	**624**	**171**	**3634**	**4706**	**857**	**2276**	**885**	**1052**	**339**	**7989**	**8568**	**2109**

Playoffs

	Series	W	L	GP	W	L	T	GF	GA	Last Mtg.	Round	Result
Boston	2	0	2	13	5	8	0	38	56	1977	QF	L 2-4
Calgary	6	4	2	26	13	13	0	105	112	1993	DSF	W 4-2
Chicago	1	0	1	5	1	4	0	7	10	1974	QF	L 1-4
Dallas	1	0	1	7	3	4	0	21	26	1968	QF	L 3-4
Edmonton	7	2	5	36	12	24	0	124	150	1992	DSF	L 2-4
Montreal	1	0	1	5	1	4	0	12	15	1993	F	L 1-4
NY Islanders	1	0	1	4	1	3	0	10	21	1980	PR	L 1-3
NY Rangers	2	0	2	6	1	5	0	14	32	1981	PR	L 1-3
St. Louis	1	0	1	4	0	4	0	5	16	1969	SF	L 0-4
Toronto	3	1	2	12	5	7	0	31	41	1993	CF	W 4-3
Vancouver	2	2	1	17	9	8	0	66	60	1993	DF	W 4-2
Defunct Clubs	1	1	0	7	4	3	0	23	25			
Totals	**29**	**10**	**19**	**142**	**55**	**87**	**0**	**459**	**568**			

Calgary totals include Atlanta, 1972-73 to 1979-80.   Colorado totals include Quebec, 1979-80 to 1994-95.
Dallas totals include Minnesota, 1967-68 to 1992-93.
New Jersey totals include Kansas City, 1974-75 to 1975-76, and Colorado Rockies, 1976-77 to 1981-82.

Playoff Results 1996-92

Year	Round	Opponent	Result	GF	GA
1993	F	Montreal	L 1-4	12	15
	CF	Toronto	W 4-3	22	23
	DF	Vancouver	W 4-2	26	25
	DSF	Calgary	W 4-2	33	28
1992	DSF	Edmonton	L 2-4	18	23

Abbreviations: Round: F – Final;
CF – conference final; **CQF** – conference quarter-final;
CSF – conference semi-final; **DF** – division final;
DSF – division semi-final; **SF** – semi-final;
QF – quarter-final; **PR** – preliminary round.

Oct.	7	Colorado	4-2	8	at Dallas	4-4
	10	Chicago	6-5	10	at Toronto	4-5
	12	Vancouver	7-7	12	at Detroit	2-3
	15	at Vancouver	3-3	14	at Chicago	2-5
	18	Philadelphia	1-1	16	Calgary	5-5
	20	at Washington	7-4	22	at NY Rangers	1-3
	21	at Pittsburgh	3-2	23	at New Jersey	1-3
	23	at Montreal	3-6	25	at Hartford	2-8
	26	at Ottawa	4-5	27	Anaheim	5-4
	28	at Toronto	2-2	31	Hartford	4-6
	31	Calgary	1-2	**Feb.** 1	at San Jose	6-6
Nov.	2	NY Rangers	5-3	3	at Calgary	1-2
	4	New Jersey	2-4	6	Chicago	2-5
	7	at St. Louis	1-0	8	Toronto	4-3
	8	at Dallas	3-3	10	San Jose	1-6
	11	Pittsburgh	3-2	13	at Detroit	4-9
	13	at Anaheim	4-2	14	at Buffalo	2-2
	14	Detroit	5-6	17	Anaheim	1-2
	16	NY Islanders	9-2	19	Boston	3-3
	18	Florida	3-2	21	at Edmonton	2-7
	21	at Philadelphia	2-5	23	at Colorado	2-6
	22	at NY Islanders	2-5	24	at St. Louis	2-2
	24	at Boston	1-2	26	at Winnipeg	3-4
	26	at Florida	1-5	28	Tampa Bay	1-5
	27	at Tampa Bay	0-2	**Mar.** 2	Montreal	5-4
	30	Washington	3-2	6	Edmonton	3-2
Dec.	2	Dallas	2-2	8	at Chicago	4-2
	6	Winnipeg	6-3	10	at Anaheim	2-3
	9	St. Louis	1-2	13	Buffalo	2-6
	11	at Calgary	2-6	16	Edmonton	2-5
	13	Ottawa	6-2	18	St. Louis	1-3
	16	Toronto	3-6	20	Colorado	3-3
	20	Vancouver	2-2	23	Dallas	4-4
	22	at San Jose	3-4	25	at Vancouver	1-4
	23	Colorado	2-2	27	at Edmonton	3-3
	27	Anaheim	7-1	29	at Calgary	4-3
	29	at Edmonton	4-5	**Apr.** 2	at Detroit	2-2
	31	at Anaheim	2-2	6	at Vancouver	2-4
Jan.	3	Winnipeg	4-5	10	at San Jose	6-2
	5	at San Jose	5-2	12	at Winnipeg	3-5
	6	San Jose	7-5	14	at Colorado	5-4

Entry Draft Selections 1996-82

1996
Pick
30 Josh Green
37 Marian Cisar
57 Greg Phillips
84 Mikael Simons
96 Eric Belanger
120 Jesse Black
123 Peter Hogan
190 Stephen Valiquette
193 Kai Nurminen
219 Sebastien Simard

1995
Pick
3 Aki-Petteri Berg
33 Donald MacLean
50 Pavel Rosa
59 Vladimir Tsyplakov
118 Jason Morgan
137 Igor Melyakov
157 Benoit Larose
163 Juha Vuorivirta
215 Brian Stewart

1994
Pick
7 Jamie Storr
33 Matt Johnson
59 Vitali Yachmenev
111 Chris Schmidt
163 Luc Gagne
189 Andrew Dale
215 Jan Nemecek
241 Sergei Shalomai

1993
Pick
42 Shayne Toporowski
68 Jeffrey Mitchell
94 Bob Wren
105 Frederick Beaubien
117 Jason Saal
120 Tomas Vlasak
146 Jere Karalahti
172 Justin Martin
198 John-Tra Dillabough
224 Martin Strbak
250 Kimmo Timonen
276 Patrick Howald

1992
Pick
39 Justin Hocking
63 Sandy Allan
87 Kevin Brown
111 Jeff Shevalier
135 Raymond Murray
207 Magnus Wernblom
231 Ryan Pisiak
255 Jukka Tiilikainen

1991
Pick
42 Guy Leveque
79 Keith Redmond
81 Alexei Zhitnik
108 Pauli Jaks
130 Brett Seguin
152 Kelly Fairchild
196 Craig Brown
218 Mattias Olsson
240 Andre Bouliane
262 Michael Gaul

1990
Pick
7 Darryl Sydor
28 Brandy Semchuk
49 Bob Berg
91 David Goverde
112 Erik Andersson
133 Robert Lang
154 Dean Hulett
175 Denis LeBlanc
196 Patrik Ross
217 K.J. (Kevin) White
238 Troy Mohns

1989
Pick
39 Brent Thompson
81 Jim Maher
102 Eric Ricard
103 Thomas Newman
123 Daniel Rydmark
144 Ted Kramer
165 Sean Whyte
182 Jim Giacin
186 Martin Maskarinec
207 Jim Hiller
228 Steve Jaques
249 Kevin Sneddon

1988
Pick
7 Martin Gelinas
28 Paul Holden
49 John Van Kessel
70 Rob Blake
91 Jeff Robison
109 Micah Aivazoff
112 Robert Larsson
133 Jeff Kruesel
154 Timo Peltomaa
175 Jim Larkin
196 Brad Hyatt
217 Doug Laprade
238 Joe Flanagan

1987
Pick
4 Wayne McBean
27 Mark Fitzpatrick
43 Ross Wilson
90 Mike Vukonich
111 Greg Batters
132 Kyosti Karjalainen
174 Jeff Gawlicki
195 John Preston
216 Rostislav Vlach
237 Mikael Lindholm

1986
Pick
2 Jimmy Carson
44 Denis Larocque
65 Sylvain Couturier
86 Dave Guden
107 Robb Stauber
128 Sean Krakiwsky
149 Rene Chapdelaine
170 Trevor Pochipinski
191 Paul Kelly
212 Russ Mann
233 Brian Hayton

1985
Pick
9 Craig Duncanson
10 Dan Gratton
30 Par Edlund
72 Perry Florio
93 Petr Prajsler
135 Tim Flannigan
156 John Hyduke
177 Steve Horner
219 Trent Ciprick
240 Marian Horwath

1984
Pick
6 Craig Redmond
24 Brian Wilks
48 John English
69 Tom Glavine
87 Dave Grannis
108 Greg Strome
129 Tim Hanley
150 Shannon Deegan
171 Luc Robitaille
191 Jeff Crossman
212 Paul Kenny
232 Brian Martin

1983
Pick
47 Bruce Shoebottom
67 Guy Benoit
87 Bob LaForest
100 Garry Galley
107 Dave Lundmark
108 Kevin Stevens
127 Tim Burgess
147 Ken Hammond
167 Bruce Fishback
187 Thomas Ahlen
207 Miroslav Blaha
227 Chad Johnson

1982
Pick
27 Mike Heidt
48 Steve Seguin
64 Dave Gans
82 Dave Ross
90 Darcy Roy
95 Ulf Isaksson
132 Victor Nechaev
153 Peter Helander
174 Dave Chartier
195 John Franzosa
216 Ray Shero
237 Mats Ulander

General Manager

McMASTER, SAM
General Manager, Los Angeles Kings. Born in Vancouver, B.C., March 3, 1944.

Sam McMaster is entering his third season as general manager of the Los Angeles Kings in 1996-97. He was named the sixth general manager in Los Angeles franchise history on May 24, 1994. He spent the six years prior to his appointment as general manager and director of hockey operations for the Sudbury Wolves of the Ontario Hockey League, earning league executive of the year honors in 1991. Prior to his tenure at Sudbury, McMaster served as assistant director of player personnel for the Washington Capitals from 1985 to 1988. He was also general manager of the OHL's Sault Ste. Marie Greyhounds from 1980 to 1985. These Soo teams won over 70 percent of their games and captured three OHL titles.

Coach

ROBINSON, LARRY
Coach, Los Angeles Kings. Born in Winchester, Ont., June 2, 1951.

Larry Robinson enters his second season as head coach in 1996-97. Robinson became the 18th head coach of the Los Angeles Kings on July 26, 1995, replacing Barry Melrose (Rogie Vachon served as interim coach for the final seven games of 1994-95 season). He served as an assistant coach with the New Jersey Devils the previous two seasons, helping them win the Stanley Cup in 1995. One of the great defensemen in NHL history, Robinson enjoyed a stellar 20-year playing career with the Montreal Canadiens and the Kings (1972-73–1991-92). In his 17 seasons with Montreal, the Habs won five Stanley Cups, including four straight (1975-76–1978-79). Robinson played in 1,384 career games (9th all-time), scoring 208 goals, 750 assists (3rd all-time defenseman) and 958 points (4th all-time defenseman). In playoff action, he holds NHL records for most career games played (227) and most consecutive years in playoffs (20). Robinson's individual honors include two Norris Trophies as the NHL's top defenseman, a Conn Smythe Trophy as playoff MVP, three seasons each as a First Team All-Star and Second Team All-Star, and 10 appearances in the NHL All-Star Game.

Coaching Record

		Regular Season					Playoffs			
Season	Team	Games	W	L	T	%	Games	W	L	%
1995-96	Los Angeles (NHL)	82	24	40	18	.402	....	....	....	....
	NHL Totals	82	24	40	18	.402	....	....	....	....

Club Directory

The Great Western Forum
3900 West Manchester Blvd.
Inglewood, California 90308
Phone **310/419-3160**
GM FAX 310/672-1490
PR FAX 310/673-8927
Capacity: 16,005

Executive

Owner	Philip F. Anschutz
Owner	Edward P. Roski
Governor	Robert Sanderman
President	Tim Leiweke
Vice President, Business Operations	Lorne Rubis
Vice President, Marketing & Communications	John Cimperman
Executive Assistant to the President	Celeste Grant
Executive Assistant to Vice President, Business Operations	Terry Carra
Executive Assistant to Vice President, Marketing	Jackie Howard

Hockey Operations

Chief Hockey Operations Officer	Rogatien Vachon
General Manager	Sam McMaster
Assistant General Manager/Director of Player Development	Dave Taylor
Assistant to General Manager	John Wolf
Executive Assistant to General Manager	Marcia Galloway
Head Coach	Larry Robinson
Assistant Coaches	Rick Green, Jay Leach
Goaltending Coach	Don Edwards
Director of Amateur Scouting	Al Murray
Director of Pro Scouting	Ace Bailey
Scouting Staff	Serge Aubry, Greg Dreschel, Rob Laird, Vaclav Nedomansky, John Stanton
Video Coordinator	Bill Gurney

Medical Staff

Trainer	Pete Demers
Equipment Manager	Peter Millar
Assistant Equipment Manager	Rick Garcia
Massage Therapist/Assistant Trainer	Pete Radulovic
Team Physicians	Kerlan/Jobe Orthopaedic Clinic directed by Dr. Ronald Kvitne
Internist	Dr. Michael Mellman
Dentist	Dr. Jeffrey Hoy
Opthamologist	Dr. Howard Lazerson

Communications

Director, Public Relations	Nick Salata
Director, Community Relations	Sheridan Issel
Manager, Media Relations	Mike Altieri
Media Relations Assistant	Justin Kischefsky
Community Relations Coordinator	Jill Berke
Reception and Guest Services	Lily Dunlop
Team Photographer	Art Foxall

Personnel/Accounting

Director, Human Resources	Barbara Mendez
Director, Finance	Peter Mazur
Manager, Accounting	Lisa Ashworth
Accounts Payable	Emma Harris
Accounts Receivable	Heather O'Conner
Assistant, Human Resources	Elizabeth Tutt

Marketing/Corporate Sales

Director, Corporate Sales	Sergio del Prado
Director, Promotions	Bob Zev
Manager, Corporate Sales	Susan Long
Corporate Account Executives	Bill Hirsch, Karen Marumoto
Client Service Coordinator	Tami Cole
Client Service Coordinator	Annie Goshert

Ticket Sales/Operations

Director, Sales	Steve DeLay
Director, Ticket Operations	Bill Chapin
Director, Group Sales	Andrew Silverman
Manager, Ticket Operations	Chris Cockrell
Senior Account Executive	Keith Jacobson
Senior Account Executive	Kerrie Gipe
Account Executives	Michael Carpenter, Matthew Cohen, Anthony Jones, Christopher McGowan, Fernando Valle, Lynn Wittenburg, Christopher Wyland

Entertainment and Events

Director, Entertainment and Events	Steve Dobo
Public Address Announcer	David Courtney
Music Coordinator	Dan Stein
Supervisor, Off-Ice Officials	Bill Meuris

Broadcasting

Play-by-Play Announcer, Television	Bob Miller
Color Commentator, Television	Jim Fox
Play-by-Play Announcer, Radio	Nick Nickson
Color Commentator, Radio	Mike Allison
Television Station	Prime Sports West
Radio Station	XTRA Sports (690 AM)
Spanish Radio Station	KWIZ (1480 AM)

General Information

Home Ice	Great Western Forum
Dimensions of Rink	200 feet by 85 feet
Colors	Black, White and Silver
Training Camp	Iceoplex, North Hills, CA
Location of Press Box	West Colonnade, Sec. 28, Rows 1-12
Web Site Address	www.lakings.com

Montreal Canadiens

1995-96 Results: 40W-32L-10T 90PTS. Third, Northeast Division

Pierre Turgeon fulfilled expectations in 1995-96, leading the Canadiens in assists (58), points (96) and power-play goals (17) while tying for top spot on the club in goals (38) and game-winning goals (6).

Schedule

Oct.	Sat.	5	Ottawa		Mon.	6	Hartford
	Mon.	7	Anaheim		Thur.	9	at Boston
	Wed.	9	Los Angeles		Sat.	11	Boston
	Sat.	12	NY Rangers		Mon.	13	Dallas
	Tues.	15	at New Jersey		Tues.	14	at Philadelphia
	Wed.	16	Calgary		Mon.	20	Detroit
	Sat.	19	at Ottawa		Wed.	22	at Buffalo
	Thur.	24	at Buffalo		Sat.	25	St. Louis*
	Sat.	26	Philadelphia		Sun.	26	Pittsburgh*
	Mon.	28	Phoenix		Tues.	28	at Florida
	Wed.	30	at Detroit		Thur.	30	at Tampa Bay
Nov.	Sat.	2	at San Jose	Feb.	Sat.	1	New Jersey
	Sun.	3	at Phoenix		Mon.	3	Florida
	Wed.	6	at Anaheim		Wed.	5	Pittsburgh
	Thur.	7	at Los Angeles		Thur.	6	at Philadelphia
	Sat.	9	at Colorado		Sat.	8	Hartford
	Mon.	11	Edmonton		Mon.	10	San Jose
	Wed.	13	Florida		Wed.	12	at Buffalo
	Fri.	15	at Washington		Sat.	15	New Jersey
	Sat.	16	Vancouver		Mon.	17	at NY Islanders*
	Wed.	20	at Hartford		Sat.	22	Toronto
	Thur.	21	at Boston		Tues.	25	at Vancouver
	Sat.	23	at Toronto		Fri.	28	at Calgary
	Mon.	25	Tampa Bay	Mar.	Sat.	1	at Edmonton
	Wed.	27	at Pittsburgh		Wed.	5	Colorado
	Sat.	30	Washington		Fri.	7	at Hartford
Dec.	Sun.	1	at NY Rangers		Sat.	8	Buffalo
	Wed.	4	Boston		Mon.	10	at Pittsburgh
	Fri.	6	at Chicago		Thur.	13	at Boston
	Sat.	7	Chicago		Sat.	15	Ottawa
	Wed.	11	Buffalo		Wed.	19	at NY Rangers
	Sat.	14	at New Jersey		Sat.	22	Washington
	Mon.	16	Tampa Bay		Mon.	24	Boston
	Sat.	21	NY Rangers		Wed.	26	Pittsburgh
	Mon.	23	Ottawa		Sat.	29	at Ottawa
	Thur.	26	at Pittsburgh	Apr.	Wed.	2	at Hartford
	Sat.	28	at Tampa Bay		Sat.	5	Hartford
	Sun.	29	at Florida		Mon.	7	NY Islanders
Jan.	Wed.	1	at Dallas*		Wed.	9	at NY Islanders
	Thur.	2	at St. Louis		Thur.	10	at Washington
	Sat.	4	NY Islanders		Sat.	12	Philadelphia

* Denotes afternoon game.

Franchise date: November 22, 1917

EASTERN CONFERENCE

NORTHEAST DIVISION

80th NHL Season

Year-by-Year Record

		Home			Road			Overall						
Season	GP	W	L	T	W	L	T	W	L	T	GF	GA	Pts.	Finished	Playoff Result
1995-96	82	23	12	6	17	20	4	40	32	10	265	248	90	3rd, Northeast Div.	Lost Conf. Quarter-Final
1994-95	48	15	5	4	3	18	3	18	23	7	125	148	43	6th, Northeast Div.	Out of Playoffs
1993-94	84	26	12	4	15	17	10	41	29	14	283	248	96	3rd, Northeast Div.	Lost Conf. Quarter-Final
1992-93	**84**	**27**	**13**	**2**	**21**	**17**	**4**	**48**	**30**	**6**	**326**	**280**	**102**	**3rd, Adams Div.**	**Won Stanley Cup**
1991-92	80	27	8	5	14	20	6	41	28	11	267	207	93	1st, Adams Div.	Lost Div. Final
1990-91	80	23	12	5	16	18	6	39	30	11	273	249	89	2nd, Adams Div.	Lost Div. Final
1989-90	80	26	8	6	15	20	5	41	28	11	288	234	93	3rd, Adams Div.	Lost Div. Final
1988-89	80	30	6	4	23	12	5	53	18	9	315	218	115	1st, Adams Div.	Lost Final
1987-88	80	26	8	6	19	14	7	45	22	13	298	238	103	1st, Adams Div.	Lost Div. Final
1986-87	80	27	9	4	14	20	6	41	29	10	277	241	92	2nd, Adams Div.	Lost Conf. Championship
1985-86	**80**	**25**	**11**	**4**	**15**	**22**	**3**	**40**	**33**	**7**	**330**	**280**	**87**	**2nd, Adams Div.**	**Won Stanley Cup**
1984-85	80	24	10	6	17	17	6	41	27	12	309	262	94	1st, Adams Div.	Lost Div. Final
1983-84	80	19	19	2	16	21	3	35	40	5	286	295	75	4th, Adams Div.	Lost Conf. Championship
1982-83	80	25	6	9	17	18	5	42	24	14	350	286	98	2nd, Adams Div.	Lost Div. Semi-Final
1981-82	80	25	6	9	21	11	8	46	17	17	360	223	109	1st, Adams Div.	Lost Div. Semi-Final
1980-81	80	31	7	2	14	15	11	45	22	13	332	232	103	1st, Norris Div.	Lost Prelim. Round
1979-80	80	30	7	3	17	13	10	47	20	13	328	240	107	1st, Norris Div.	Lost Quarter-Final
1978-79	**80**	**29**	**6**	**5**	**23**	**11**	**6**	**52**	**17**	**11**	**337**	**204**	**115**	**1st, Norris Div.**	**Won Stanley Cup**
1977-78	**80**	**32**	**4**	**4**	**27**	**6**	**7**	**59**	**10**	**11**	**359**	**183**	**129**	**1st, Norris Div.**	**Won Stanley Cup**
1976-77	**80**	**33**	**1**	**6**	**27**	**7**	**6**	**60**	**8**	**12**	**387**	**171**	**132**	**1st, Norris Div.**	**Won Stanley Cup**
1975-76	**80**	**32**	**3**	**5**	**26**	**8**	**6**	**58**	**11**	**11**	**337**	**174**	**127**	**1st, Norris Div.**	**Won Stanley Cup**
1974-75	80	27	8	5	20	6	14	47	14	19	374	225	113	1st, Norris Div.	Lost Semi-Final
1972-73	**78**	**29**	**6**	**4**	**23**	**6**	**10**	**52**	**10**	**16**	**329**	**184**	**120**	**1st, East Div.**	**Won Stanley Cup**
1973-74	78	24	12	3	21	12	6	45	24	9	293	240	99	2nd, East Div.	Lost Quarter-inal
1971-72	78	29	3	7	17	13	9	46	16	16	307	205	108	3rd, East Div.	Lost Quarter-Final
1970-71	**78**	**29**	**7**	**3**	**13**	**16**	**10**	**42**	**23**	**13**	**291**	**216**	**97**	**3rd, East Div.**	**Won Stanley Cup**
1969-70	76	21	9	8	17	13	8	38	22	16	244	201	92	5th, East Div.	Out of Playoffs
1968-69	**76**	**26**	**7**	**5**	**20**	**12**	**6**	**46**	**19**	**11**	**271**	**202**	**103**	**1st, East Div.**	**Won Stanley Cup**
1967-68	**74**	**26**	**5**	**6**	**16**	**17**	**4**	**42**	**22**	**10**	**236**	**167**	**94**	**1st, East Div.**	**Won Stanley Cup**
1966-67	70	19	9	7	13	16	6	32	25	13	202	188	77	2nd,	Lost Final
1965-66	**70**	**23**	**11**	**1**	**18**	**10**	**7**	**41**	**21**	**8**	**239**	**173**	**90**	**1st,**	**Won Stanley Cup**
1964-65	**70**	**20**	**8**	**7**	**16**	**15**	**4**	**36**	**23**	**11**	**211**	**185**	**83**	**2nd,**	**Won Stanley Cup**
1963-64	70	22	7	6	14	14	7	36	21	13	209	167	85	1st,	Lost Semi-Final
1962-63	70	15	10	10	13	9	13	28	19	23	225	183	79	3rd,	Lost Semi-Final
1961-62	70	26	2	7	16	12	7	42	14	14	259	166	98	1st,	Lost Semi-Final
1960-61	70	24	6	5	17	13	5	41	19	10	254	188	92	1st,	Lost Semi-Final
1959-60	**70**	**23**	**4**	**8**	**17**	**14**	**4**	**40**	**18**	**12**	**255**	**178**	**92**	**1st,**	**Won Stanley Cup**
1958-59	**70**	**23**	**8**	**6**	**18**	**10**	**7**	**39**	**18**	**13**	**258**	**158**	**91**	**1st,**	**Won Stanley Cup**
1957-58	**70**	**23**	**8**	**4**	**20**	**9**	**6**	**43**	**17**	**10**	**250**	**158**	**96**	**1st,**	**Won Stanley Cup**
1956-57	**70**	**23**	**6**	**6**	**12**	**17**	**6**	**35**	**23**	**12**	**210**	**155**	**82**	**2nd,**	**Won Stanley Cup**
1955-56	**70**	**29**	**5**	**1**	**16**	**10**	**9**	**45**	**15**	**10**	**222**	**131**	**100**	**1st,**	**Won Stanley Cup**
1954-55	70	26	5	4	15	13	7	41	18	11	228	157	93	2nd,	Lost Final
1953-54	70	27	5	3	8	19	8	35	24	11	195	141	81	2nd,	Lost Final
1952-53	**70**	**18**	**12**	**5**	**10**	**11**	**14**	**28**	**23**	**19**	**155**	**148**	**75**	**2nd,**	**Won Stanley Cup**
1951-52	70	22	8	5	12	18	5	34	26	10	195	164	78	2nd,	Lost Final
1950-51	70	17	10	8	8	20	7	25	30	15	173	184	65	3rd,	Lost Final
1949-50	70	17	8	10	12	14	9	29	22	19	172	150	77	2nd,	Lost Semi-Final
1948-49	60	19	8	3	9	15	6	28	23	9	152	126	65	3rd,	Lost Semi-Final
1947-48	60	13	13	4	7	16	7	20	29	11	147	169	51	5th,	Out of Playoffs
1946-47	60	19	6	5	15	10	5	34	16	10	189	138	78	1st,	Lost Final
1945-46	**50**	**16**	**6**	**3**	**12**	**11**	**2**	**28**	**17**	**5**	**172**	**134**	**61**	**1st,**	**Won Stanley Cup**
1944-45	50	21	2	2	17	6	2	38	8	4	228	121	80	1st,	Lost Semi-Final
1943-44	**50**	**22**	**0**	**3**	**16**	**5**	**4**	**38**	**5**	**7**	**234**	**109**	**83**	**1st,**	**Won Stanley Cup**
1942-43	50	14	4	7	5	15	5	19	19	12	181	191	50	4th,	Lost Semi-Final
1941-42	48	12	10	2	6	17	1	18	27	3	134	173	39	6th,	Lost Quarter-Final
1940-41	48	11	9	4	5	17	2	16	26	6	121	147	38	6th,	Lost Quarter-Final
1939-40	48	5	14	5	5	19	0	10	33	5	90	167	25	7th,	Out of Playoffs
1938-39	48	8	11	5	7	13	4	15	24	9	115	146	39	6th,	Lost Quarter-Final
1937-38	48	13	4	7	5	13	6	18	17	13	123	128	49	1st, Cdn. Div.	Lost Quarter-Final
1936-37	48	16	8	0	8	10	6	24	18	6	115	111	54	1st, Cdn. Div.	Lost Semi-Final
1935-36	48	5	11	8	6	15	3	11	26	11	82	123	33	4th, Cdn. Div.	Out of Playoffs
1934-35	48	11	11	2	8	12	4	19	23	6	110	145	44	3rd, Cdn. Div.	Lost Quarter-Final
1933-34	48	16	6	2	6	14	4	22	20	6	99	101	50	2nd, Cdn. Div.	Lost Quarter-Final
1932-33	48	15	5	4	3	20	1	18	25	5	92	115	41	3rd, Cdn. Div.	Lost Quarter-Final
1931-32	48	18	3	3	7	13	4	25	16	7	128	111	57	1st, Cdn. Div.	Lost Semi-Final
1930-31	**44**	**15**	**3**	**4**	**11**	**7**	**4**	**26**	**10**	**8**	**129**	**89**	**60**	**1st, Cdn. Div.**	**Won Stanley Cup**
1929-30	**44**	**13**	**5**	**4**	**8**	**9**	**5**	**21**	**14**	**9**	**142**	**114**	**51**	**2nd, Cdn. Div.**	**Won Stanley Cup**
1928-29	44	12	4	6	10	3	9	22	7	15	71	43	59	1st, Cdn. Div.	Lost Semi-Final
1927-28	44	12	7	3	14	4	4	26	11	7	116	48	59	1st, Cdn. Div.	Lost Semi-Final
1926-27	44	15	5	2	13	9	0	28	14	2	99	67	58	2nd, Cdn. Div.	Lost Semi-Final
1925-26	36	5	12	1	6	12	0	11	24	1	79	108	23	7th,	Out of Playoffs
1924-25	30	10	5	0	7	6	2	17	11	2	93	56	36	3rd,	Lost Final
1923-24	**24**	**10**	**2**	**0**	**3**	**9**	**0**	**13**	**11**	**0**	**59**	**48**	**26**	**2nd,**	**Won Stanley Cup**
1922-23	24	10	2	0	3	7	2	13	9	2	73	61	28	2nd,	Lost NHL Final
1921-22	24	8	3	1	4	8	0	12	11	1	88	94	25	3rd,	Out of Playoffs
1920-21	24	9	3	0	4	8	0	13	11	0	112	99	26	3rd and 2nd*	Out of Playoffs
1919-20	24	8	4	0	5	7	0	13	11	0	129	113	26	2nd and 3rd*	Out of Playoffs
1918-19	18	7	2	0	3	6	0	10	8	0	88	78	20	1st and 2nd*	Cup Final but no Decision
1917-18	22	8	3	0	5	6	0	13	9	0	115	84	26	1st and 3rd*	Lost NHL Final

** Season played in two halves with no combined standing at end.
From 1917-18 through 1925-26, NHL champions played against PCHA champions for Stanley Cup.*

1996-97 Player Personnel

FORWARDS	HT	WT	S	Place of Birth	Date	1995-96 Club
BORDELEAU, Sebastien	5-10	180	R	Vancouver, B.C.	2/15/75	Montreal-Fredericton
BRASHEAR, Donald	6-2	220	L	Bedford, IN	1/7/72	Montreal
BRUNET, Benoit	5-11	195	L	Pointe-Claire, Que.	8/24/68	Montreal-Fredericton
BURE, Valeri	5-10	168	R	Moscow, USSR	6/13/74	Montreal
BUREAU, Marc	6-1	198	R	Trois-Rivières, Que.	5/19/66	Montreal
CONROY, Craig	6-2	198	R	Potsdam, NY	9/4/71	Montreal-Fredericton
DAMPHOUSSE, Vincent	6-1	195	L	Montreal, Que.	12/17/67	Montreal
DELISLE, Jonathan	5-10	186	R	Ste-Anne-des-Plaines, Que.	6/30/77	Hull
FLEMING, Gerry	6-5	253	L	Montreal, Que.	10/16/67	Fredericton
FRASER, Scott	6-1	178	R	Moncton, N.B.	5/3/72	Montreal-Fredericton
HOUDE, Eric	5-11	190	L	Montreal, Que.	12/19/76	Halifax
KOIVU, Saku	5-9	175	L	Turku, Finland	11/23/74	Montreal
KOVALENKO, Andrei	5-10	215	L	Balakovo, USSR	6/7/70	Colorado-Montreal
MURRAY, Chris	6-2	209	R	Port Hardy, B.C.	10/25/74	Montreal-Fredericton
OLSON, Boyd	6-1	170	L	Edmonton, Alta.	4/4/76	Tri-City-Fredericton
RECCHI, Mark	5-10	180	L	Kamloops, B.C.	2/1/68	Montreal
RICHER, Stephane J. J.	6-2	215	R	Ripon, Que.	6/7/66	New Jersey
RUCINSKY, Martin	6-0	198	L	Most, Czech.	3/11/71	Vsetin-Colorado-Montreal
SAVAGE, Brian	6-1	190	L	Sudbury, Ont.	2/24/71	Montreal
SEVIGNY, Pierre	6-0	195	L	Trois-Rivières, Que.	9/8/71	Fredericton
STEVENSON, Turner	6-3	215	R	Prince George, B.C.	5/18/72	Montreal
TUCKER, Darcy	5-10	170	L	Castor, Alta.	3/15/75	Montreal-Fredericton
TURGEON, Pierre	6-1	195	L	Rouyn, Que.	8/28/69	Montreal
DEFENSEMEN						
BRISEBOIS, Patrice	6-1	188	R	Montreal, Que.	1/27/71	Montreal
BROWN, Brad	6-3	220	R	Baie Verte, Nfld.	12/27/75	Regina-Fredericton
DARLING, Dion	6-3	205	L	Edmonton, Alta.	10/22/74	Fredericton
DROLET, Jimmy	6-1	180	L	Vanier, Que.	2/19/76	St-Hyacinthe-Granby
FITZPATRICK, Rory	6-1	205	R	Rochester, NY	1/11/75	Montreal-Fredericton
GROLEAU, Francois	6-0	200	L	Longueuil, Que.	1/23/73	Mtl-S. Francisco-Fredericton
GUREN, Miloslav	6-2	205	L	Uherske. Hradiste, Czech.	9/24/76	ZPS Zlin
LETANG, Alan	6-0	185	L	Renfrew, Ont.	9/4/75	Fredericton
MAGUIRE, Derek	5-10	210	R	Rochester, NY	12/9/71	Fredericton
MALAKHOV, Vladimir	6-3	220	L	Sverdlovsk, USSR	8/30/68	Montreal
POPOVIC, Peter	6-6	235	R	Koping, Sweden	2/10/68	Montreal
QUINTAL, Stephane	6-3	225	R	Boucherville, Que.	10/22/68	Montreal
RIVET, Craig	6-1	190	R	North Bay, Ont.	9/13/74	Montreal-Fredericton
WIESEL, Adam	6-3	210	R	Holyoke, MA	1/25/75	Fredericton
WILKIE, David	6-2	210	R	Ellensburgh, WA	5/30/74	Montreal-Fredericton

GOALTENDERS	HT	WT	C	Place of Birth	Date	1995-96 Club
CAVICCHI, Trent	6-3	180	L	Halifax, N.S.	8/11/74	N. Hampshire
JABLONSKI, Pat	6-0	180	R	Toledo, OH	6/20/67	St. Louis-Montreal
LABRECQUE, Patrick	6-0	190	L	Laval, Que.	3/6/71	Montreal-Fredericton
THEODORE, Jose	5-11	180	R	Laval, Que.	9/13/76	Montreal-Hull
THIBAULT, Jocelyn	5-11	170	L	Montreal, Que.	1/12/75	Colorado-Montreal
VOKOUN, Tomas	5-11	180	R	Karlovy Vary, Czech.	7/2/76	Wheeling-Fredericton

Coach

TREMBLAY, MARIO

Coach, Montreal Canadiens. Born in Alma, Que., September 2, 1956.

Named as the 22nd head coach in the history of the Montreal Canadiens on October 21, 1995, Mario Tremblay guided the Canadiens to a 40-27-10 record during his first ever season as a coach. Under Tremblay, the Canadiens finished sixth in the Eastern Conference and secured a playoff spot after missing the post-season in 1994-95. Tremblay became the youngest player ever to play with the Canadiens when he joined the NHL team at age 18 in 1974. He helped the Canadiens win five Stanley Cups during his playing career, from 1974 to 1986. In 852 NHL games, Tremblay recorded a total of 584 points (258 goals, 326 assists) and 1,043 minutes in penalty.

Coaching Record

		Regular Season					Playoffs			
Season	Team	Games	W	L	T	%	Games	W	L	%
1995-96	Montreal (NHL)	77	40	27	10	.597	6	2	4	.333
	NHL Totals	77	40	27	10	.597	6	2	4	.333

Coaching History

"Jack" Laviolette, 1909-10; Adolphe Lecours, 1910-11; Napoleon Dorval, 1911-12 to 1912-13; Jimmy Gardner, 1913-14 to 1914-15; "Newsy" Lalonde, 1915-16 to 1920-21; "Newsy" Lalonde and Léo Dandurand, 1921-22; Léo Dandurand, 1922-23 to 1925-26; Cecil Hart, 1926-27 to 1931-32; "Newsy" Lalonde, 1932-33 to 1933-34; "Newsy" Lalonde and Léo Dandurand, 1934-35; Sylvio Mantha, 1935-36; Cecil Hart, 1936-37 to 1937-38; Cecil Hart and Jules Dugal, 1938-39; "Babe" Siebert, 1939*; "Pit" Lepine, 1939-40; Dick Irvin 1940-41 to 1954-55; "Toe" Blake, 1955-56 to 1967-68; Claude Ruel, 1968-69 to 1969-70; Claude Ruel and Al MacNeil, 1970-71; Scotty Bowman, 1971-72 to 1978-79; Bernie Geoffrion and Claude Ruel, 1979-80; Claude Ruel, 1980-81; Bob Berry, 1981-82 to 1982-83; Bob Berry and Jacques Lemaire, 1983-84; Jacques Lemaire, 1984-85; Jean Perron, 1985-86 to 1987-88; Pat Burns, 1988-89 to 1991-92; Jacques Demers, 1992-93 to 1994-95; Jacques Demers and Mario Tremblay, 1995-96; Mario Tremblay, 1996-97.

* Named coach in summer but died before 1939-40 season began.

1995-96 Scoring

* – rookie

Regular Season

Pos	#	Player	Team	GP	G	A	Pts	+/–	PIM	PP	SH	GW	GT	S	%
C	77	Pierre Turgeon	MTL	80	38	58	96	19	44	17	1	6	0	297	12.8
C	25	Vincent Damphousse	MTL	80	38	56	94	5	158	11	4	3	0	254	15.0
R	8	Mark Recchi	MTL	82	28	50	78	20	69	11	2	6	0	191	14.7
L	26	Martin Rucinsky	COL	22	4	11	15	10	14	0	0	1	0	39	10.3
			MTL	56	25	35	60	8	54	9	2	3	0	142	17.6
			TOTAL	78	29	46	75	18	68	9	2	4	0	181	16.0
R	51	Andrei Kovalenko	COL	26	11	11	22	11	16	3	0	3	0	46	23.9
			MTL	51	17	17	34	9	33	3	0	3	1	85	20.0
			TOTAL	77	28	28	56	20	49	6	0	6	1	131	21.4
L	11	* Saku Koivu	MTL	82	20	25	45	–7	40	8	3	2	1	136	14.7
R	18	* Valeri Bure	MTL	77	22	20	42	10	28	5	0	1	2	143	15.4
D	43	Patrice Brisebois	MTL	69	9	27	36	10	65	3	0	1	0	127	7.1
L	49	Brian Savage	MTL	75	25	8	33	–8	28	4	0	4	0	150	16.7
D	38	Vladimir Malakhov	MTL	61	5	23	28	7	79	2	0	0	0	122	4.1
R	30	Turner Stevenson	MTL	80	9	16	25	–2	167	0	0	2	0	101	8.9
D	24	Lyle Odelein	MTL	79	3	14	17	8	230	0	1	0	0	74	4.1
D	5	Stephane Quintal	MTL	68	2	14	16	–4	117	0	1	1	1	104	1.9
L	22	Benoit Brunet	MTL	26	7	8	15	–4	17	3	1	4	0	48	14.6
D	34	Peter Popovic	MTL	76	2	12	14	21	69	0	0	0	0	59	3.4
R	6	Oleg Petrov	MTL	36	4	7	11	–9	23	0	0	2	0	44	9.1
C	28	Marc Bureau	MTL	65	3	7	10	–3	46	0	0	1	0	43	7.0
R	57	* Chris Murray	MTL	48	3	4	7	5	163	0	0	1	0	32	9.4
D	27	* David Wilkie	MTL	24	1	5	6	–10	10	1	0	0	0	39	2.6
D	52	* Craig Rivet	MTL	19	1	4	5	4	54	0	0	0	0	9	11.1
D	23	* Marko Kiprusoff	MTL	24	0	4	4	–3	8	0	0	0	0	36	0.0
L	35	Donald Brashear	MTL	67	0	4	4	–10	223	0	0	0	0	25	0.0
D	3	Robert Dirk	ANA	44	1	2	3	8	42	0	0	0	0	20	5.0
			MTL	3	0	0	0	0	6	0	0	0	0	0	0.0
			TOTAL	47	1	2	3	8	48	0	0	0	0	20	5.0
C	56	* Scott Fraser	MTL	15	2	0	2	–1	4	0	0	0	0	9	22.2
D	53	* Rory Fitzpatrick	MTL	42	0	2	2	–7	18	0	0	0	0	31	0.0
D	48	* Francois Groleau	MTL	2	0	1	1	2	2	0	0	0	0	1	0.0
G	39	Pat Jablonski	STL	1	0	0	0	0	0	0	0	0	0	0	0.0
			MTL	23	0	1	1	0	2	0	0	0	0	0	0.0
			TOTAL	24	0	1	1	0	2	0	0	0	0	0	0.0
C	17	Mark Lamb	MTL	1	0	0	0	0	0	0	0	0	0	0	0.0
G	37	* Jose Theodore	MTL	1	0	0	0	0	0	0	0	0	0	0	0.0
G	31	* Patrick Labrecque	MTL	2	0	0	0	0	2	0	0	0	0	0	0.0
C	42	* Darcy Tucker	MTL	3	0	0	0	–1	0	0	0	0	0	1	0.0
C	71	* Sebastien Bordeleau	MTL	4	0	0	0	–1	0	0	0	0	0	0	0.0
C	20	* Craig Conroy	MTL	7	0	0	0	–4	2	0	0	0	0	1	0.0
G	41	Jocelyn Thibault	COL	10	0	0	0	0	0	0	0	0	0	0	0.0
			MTL	40	0	0	0	0	2	0	0	0	0	0	0.0
			TOTAL	50	0	0	0	0	2	0	0	0	0	0	0.0

Goaltending

No.	Goaltender	GPI	Mins	Avg	W	L	T	EN	SO	GA	SA	S%
41	Jocelyn Thibault	40	2334	2.83	23	13	3	2	3	110	1258	.913
39	Pat Jablonski	23	1264	2.94	5	9	6	4	0	62	676	.908
33	Patrick Roy	22	1260	2.95	12	9	1	0	1	62	667	.907
31	* Patrick Labrecque	2	98	4.29	0	1	0	0	0	7	47	.851
37	* Jose Theodore	1	9	6.67	0	0	0	0	0	1	2	.500
	Totals	**82**	**4987**	**2.98**	**40**	**32**	**10**	**6**	**4**	**248**	**2656**	**.907**

Playoffs

Pos	#	Player	Team	GP	G	A	Pts	+/–	PIM	PP	SH	GW	GT	S	%
C	25	Vincent Damphousse	MTL	6	4	4	8	2	0	0	1	2	1	26	15.4
R	8	Mark Recchi	MTL	6	3	3	6	1	0	3	0	0	0	13	23.1
C	77	Pierre Turgeon	MTL	6	2	4	6	1	2	0	0	0	0	18	11.1
L	11	* Saku Koivu	MTL	6	3	1	4	2	8	0	0	0	0	13	23.1
D	43	Patrice Brisebois	MTL	6	1	2	3	2	6	0	0	0	0	8	12.5
D	27	* David Wilkie	MTL	6	1	2	3	1	12	0	0	0	0	11	9.1
C	28	Marc Bureau	MTL	6	1	1	2	2	4	0	0	0	0	6	16.7
D	24	Lyle Odelein	MTL	6	1	1	2	1	6	0	1	0	0	5	20.0
D	53	* Rory Fitzpatrick	MTL	6	1	1	2	–1	0	0	0	0	0	5	20.0
L	22	Benoit Brunet	MTL	3	0	2	2	1	0	0	0	0	0	10	0.0
D	34	Peter Popovic	MTL	6	0	2	2	3	4	0	0	0	0	2	0.0
L	49	Brian Savage	MTL	6	0	2	2	2	2	0	0	0	0	9	0.0
R	6	Oleg Petrov	MTL	5	0	1	1	–1	0	0	0	0	0	1	0.0
D	5	Stephane Quintal	MTL	6	0	1	1	1	6	0	0	0	0	3	0.0
R	30	Turner Stevenson	MTL	6	0	1	1	–1	2	0	0	0	0	7	0.0
R	18	* Valeri Bure	MTL	6	0	1	1	–1	6	0	0	0	0	19	0.0
G	39	Pat Jablonski	MTL	1	0	0	0	0	0	0	0	0	0	0	0.0
R	57	* Chris Murray	MTL	4	0	0	0	0	4	0	0	0	0	1	0.0
R	51	Andrei Kovalenko	MTL	6	0	0	0	–2	6	0	0	0	0	9	0.0
L	35	Donald Brashear	MTL	6	0	0	0	–1	2	0	0	0	0	0	0.0
G	41	Jocelyn Thibault	MTL	6	0	0	0	0	0	0	0	0	0	0	0.0

Goaltending

No.	Goaltender	GPI	Mins	Avg	W	L	EN	SO	GA	SA	S%
39	Pat Jablonski	1	49	1.22	0	0	0	0	1	17	.941
41	Jocelyn Thibault	6	311	3.47	2	4	0	0	18	188	.904
	Totals	**6**	**365**	**3.12**	**2**	**4**	**0**	**0**	**19**	**205**	**.907**

Club Records

Team

(Figures in brackets for season records are games played; records for fewest points, wins, ties, losses, goals, goals against are for 70 or more games)

Most Points	***132**	1976-77 (80)
Most Wins	**60**	1976-77 (80)
Most Ties	**23**	1962-63 (70)
Most Losses	**40**	1983-84 (80)
Most Goals	**387**	1976-77 (80)
Most Goals Against	**295**	1983-84 (80)
Fewest Points	**65**	1950-51 (70)
Fewest Wins	**25**	1950-51 (70)
Fewest Ties	**5**	1983-84 (80)
Fewest Losses	***8**	1976-77 (80)
Fewest Goals	**155**	1952-53 (70)
Fewest Goals Against	***131**	1955-56 (70)
Longest WinningStreak		
Overall	**12**	Jan. 6-Feb. 3/68
Home	**13**	Nov. 2/43-Jan. 8/44, Jan. 30-Mar. 26/77
Away	**8**	Dec. 18/77-Jan. 18/78, Jan. 21-Feb. 21/82
Longest Undefeated Streak		
Overall	**28**	Dec. 18/77-Feb. 23/78 (23 wins, 5 ties)
Home	***34**	Nov. 1/76-Apr. 2/77 (28 wins, 6 ties)
Away	***23**	Nov. 27/74-Mar. 12/75 (14 wins, 9 ties)
Longest Losing Streak		
Overall	**12**	Feb. 13/26-Mar. 13/26
Home	**7**	Dec. 16/39-Jan. 18/40
Away	**10**	Jan. 16-Mar. 13/26
Longest Winless Streak		
Overall	**12**	Feb. 13-Mar. 13/26 (12 losses), Nov. 28-Dec. 29/35 (8 losses, 4 ties)
Home	**15**	Dec. 16/39-Mar. 7/40 (12 losses, 3 ties)
Away	**12**	Nov. 26/33-Jan. 28/34 (8 losses, 4 ties), Oct. 20/50-Dec. 13/51 (8 losses, 4 ties)
Most Shutouts, Season	***22**	1928-29 (44)
Most PIM, Season	**1,847**	1995-96 (82)
Most Goals, Game	***16**	Mar. 3/20 (Mtl. 16 at Que. 3)

Individual

Most Seasons	**20**	Henri Richard, Jean Beliveau
Most Games	**1,256**	Henri Richard
Most Goals Career	**544**	Maurice Richard
Most Assists, Career	**728**	Guy Lafleur
Most Points Career	**1,246**	Guy Lafleur (518G, 728A)
Most PIM, Career	**2,248**	Chris Nilan
Most Shutouts, Career	**75**	George Hainsworth
Longest Consecutive Games Streak	**560**	Doug Jarvis (Oct. 8/75-Apr. 4/82)
Most Goals, Season	**60**	Steve Shutt (1976-77), Guy Lafleur (1977-78)
Most Assists, Season	**82**	Peter Mahovlich (1974-75)
Most Points, Season	**136**	Guy Lafleur (1976-77; 56G, 80A)
Most PIM, Season	**358**	Chris Nilan (1984-85)
Most Points, Defenseman Season	**85**	Larry Robinson (1976-77; 19G, 66A)
Most Points, Center, Season	**117**	Peter Mahovlich (1974-75; 35G, 82A)
Most Points, Right Wing, Season	**136**	Guy Lafleur (1976-77; 56G, 80A)
Most Points, Left Wing, Season	**110**	Mats Naslund (1985-86; 43G, 67A)
Most Points, Rookie, Season	**71**	Mats Naslund (1982-83; 26G, 45A), Kjell Dahlin (1985-86; 32G, 39A)
Most Shutouts, Season	***22**	George Hainsworth (1928-29)
Most Goals, Game	**6**	Newsy Lalonde (Jan. 10/20)
Most Assists, Game	**6**	Elmer Lach (Feb. 6/43)
Most Points, Game	**8**	Maurice Richard (Dec. 28/44; 5G, 3A), Bert Olmstead (Jan. 9/54; 4G, 4A)

* NHL Record.

Retired Numbers

1	Jacques Plante	1952-1963
2	Doug Harvey	1947-1961
4	Jean Béliveau	1950-1971
7	Howie Morenz	1923-1937
9	Maurice Richard	1942-1960
10	Guy Lafleur	1971-1984
16	Henri Richard	1955-1975

All-time Record vs. Other Clubs

Regular Season

	At Home							On Road							Total						
	GP	W	L	T	GF	GA	PTS	GP	W	L	T	GF	GA	PTS	GP	W	L	T	GF	GA	PTS
Anaheim	2	1	1	0	6	4	2	2	1	1	0	7	7	2	4	2	2	0	13	11	4
Boston	313	181	87	45	1066	729	407	314	116	144	54	850	931	286	627	297	231	99	1916	1660	693
Buffalo	82	49	23	10	341	249	108	81	24	39	18	227	253	66	163	73	62	28	568	502	174
Calgary	39	22	11	6	140	95	50	38	22	11	5	139	120	49	77	44	22	11	279	215	99
Chicago	268	169	51	48	1042	632	386	268	122	91	55	751	723	299	536	291	142	103	1793	1355	685
Colorado	57	36	12	9	244	178	81	58	26	28	4	209	195	56	115	62	40	13	453	373	137
Dallas	52	36	9	7	234	126	79	53	28	14	11	190	137	67	105	64	23	18	424	263	146
Detroit	275	169	63	43	979	619	381	275	96	126	53	705	785	245	550	265	189	96	1684	1404	626
Edmonton	23	13	7	3	84	73	29	24	11	13	0	75	83	22	47	24	20	3	159	156	51
Florida	5	2	3	0	14	14	4	6	2	2	2	19	22	6	11	4	5	2	33	36	10
Hartford	58	40	11	7	263	171	87	60	30	22	8	223	186	68	118	70	33	15	486	357	155
Los Angeles	58	40	7	11	271	150	91	59	34	16	9	238	183	77	117	74	23	20	509	333	168
New Jersey	38	27	7	4	153	96	58	38	24	13	1	167	111	49	76	51	20	5	320	207	107
NY Islanders	44	25	11	8	171	136	58	44	19	20	5	130	145	43	88	44	31	13	301	281	101
NY Rangers	274	184	55	35	1080	630	403	274	109	111	54	799	798	272	548	293	166	89	1879	1428	675
Ottawa	12	9	3	0	43	32	18	10	9	1	0	39	22	18	22	18	4	0	82	54	36
Philadelphia	58	29	17	12	214	179	70	57	21	23	13	172	171	55	115	50	40	25	386	350	125
Pittsburgh	64	53	4	7	325	151	113	64	32	23	9	235	198	73	128	85	27	16	560	349	186
St. Louis	53	38	8	7	238	137	83	52	27	11	14	187	134	68	105	65	19	21	425	271	151
San Jose	5	5	0	0	24	7	10	5	2	1	2	12	13	6	10	7	1	2	36	20	16
Tampa Bay	6	3	2	1	13	14	7	7	0	6	1	10	21	1	13	3	8	2	23	35	8
Toronto	315	192	83	40	1123	776	424	316	112	160	44	828	955	268	631	304	243	84	1951	1731	692
Vancouver	46	35	8	3	228	122	73	44	29	7	8	176	109	66	90	64	15	11	404	231	139
Washington	44	30	8	6	193	89	66	43	18	18	7	139	118	43	87	48	26	13	332	207	109
Winnipeg	23	21	2	0	123	52	42	23	10	8	5	90	76	25	46	31	10	5	213	128	67
Defunct Clubs	231	148	58	25	779	469	321	230	98	97	35	586	606	231	461	246	155	60	1365	1075	552
Totals	**2445**	**1557**	**551**	**337**	**9391**	**5930**	**3451**	**2445**	**1022**	**1006**	**417**	**7203**	**7102**	**2461**	**4890**	**2579**	**1557**	**754**	**16594**	**13032**	**5912**

Playoffs

	Series	W	L	GP	W	L	T	GF	GA	Last Mtg.	Round	Result
Boston	28	21	7	139	87	52	0	430	339	1994	CQF	L 3-4
Buffalo	6	4	2	31	18	13	0	114	94	1993	DF	W 4-0
Calgary	2	1	1	11	6	5	0	31	32	1989	F	L 2-4
Chicago	17	12	5	81	50	29	2	261	185	1976	QF	W 4-0
Colorado	5	3	2	31	17	14	0	105	85	1993	DSF	W 4-2
Dallas	2	1	1	13	7	6	0	48	37	1980	QF	L 3-4
Detroit	12	5	7	62	33	29	0	161	149	1978	QF	W 4-1
Edmonton	1	0	1	3	0	3	0	6	15	1981	PR	L 0-3
Hartford	5	5	0	27	19	8	0	96	70	1992	DSF	W 4-3
Los Angeles	1	1	0	5	4	1	0	15	12	1993	F	W 4-1
NY Islanders	4	3	1	22	14	8	0	64	55	1993	CF	W 4-1
NY Rangers	14	7	7	61	34	25	2	188	158	1996	CQF	L 2-4
Philadelphia	4	3	1	21	14	7	0	72	52	1989	CF	W 4-2
St. Louis	3	3	0	12	12	0	0	42	14	1977	QF	W 4-0
Toronto	15	8	7	71	42	29	0	215	160	1979	QF	W 4-0
Vancouver	1	1	0	5	4	1	0	20	9	1975	QF	W 4-1
Defunct Clubs	11*	6	4	28	15	9	4	70	71			
Totals	**131***	**84**	**46**	**623**	**376**	**239**	**8**	**1938**	**1537**			

* 1919 Final incomplete due to influenza epidemic.

Calgary totals include Atlanta, 1972-73 to 1979-80. Colorado totals include Quebec, 1979-80 to 1994-95.
Dallas totals include Minnesota, 1967-68 to 1992-93.
New Jersey totals include Kansas City, 1974-75 to 1975-76, and Colorado Rockies, 1976-77 to 1981-82.

Playoff Results 1996-92

Year	Round	Opponent	Result	GF	GA
1996	CQF	NY Rangers	L 2-4	17	19
1994	CQF	Boston	L 3-4	20	22
1993	**F**	**Los Angeles**	**W 4-1**	**15**	**12**
	CF	NY Islanders	W 4-1	16	11
	DF	Buffalo	W 4-0	16	12
	DSF	Quebec	W 4-2	19	16
1992	DF	Boston	L 0-4	8	14
	DSF	Hartford	W 4-3	21	18

Abbreviations: Round: F – Final; **CF** – conference final; **CQF** – conference quarter-final; **CSF** – conference semi-final; **DF** – division final; **DSF** – division semi-final; **SF** – semi-final; **QF** – quarter-final; **PR** – preliminary round.

1995-96 Results

Oct.	7		Philadelphia	1-7		10		Vancouver	2-2
	11	at	Florida	1-6		12	at	Pittsburgh	6-5
	12	at	Tampa Bay	1-3		13		St. Louis	3-3
	14		New Jersey	1-4		17	at	Ottawa	3-0
	20	at	NY Islanders	0-2		22		Tampa Bay	1-4
	21		Toronto	4-3		25	at	Florida	6-2
	23		Los Angeles	6-3		27		Winnipeg	4-1
	25		Florida	7-2		28		Boston	5-4
	27	at	Hartford	4-1		31		Washington	5-3
	28		Chicago	5-3	**Feb.**	1	at	Philadelphia	2-3
	31	at	Boston	3-1		3	at	Toronto	4-1
Nov.	1	at	Washington	2-5		5	at	Colorado	2-4
	4		Boston	4-1		7	at	Dallas	4-2
	8		Anaheim	2-3		10		Ottawa	3-5
	11	at	Calgary	4-0		12		San Jose	3-0
	12	at	Vancouver	4-2		15	at	NY Rangers	2-2
	15	at	Edmonton	4-1		17		Calgary	5-1
	18		Ottawa	5-1		21	at	Hartford	3-5
	20		Hartford	4-3		23	at	New Jersey	5-6
	22	at	Hartford	2-4		24		Pittsburgh	7-3
	25		Colorado	2-2		26	at	San Jose	4-7
	28	at	Detroit	2-3		28	at	Anaheim	2-5
	29	at	St. Louis	4-5	**Mar.**	2	at	Los Angeles	4-5
Dec.	2		Detroit	1-11		9		Ottawa	3-2
	6		New Jersey	4-2		11		Dallas	4-1
	7	at	Pittsburgh	5-7		13	at	New Jersey	1-1
	9		NY Rangers	2-2		16		NY Rangers	4-2
	12	at	Winnipeg	6-5		18		Buffalo	3-2
	15	at	Chicago	4-1		20		Hartford	3-2
	16		Philadelphia	2-4		22	at	Buffalo	4-1
	18		Hartford	3-2		23		Edmonton	5-6
	20	at	Buffalo	1-2		25		NY Islanders	4-1
	22	at	Pittsburgh	4-2		27		Washington	0-1
	23		Pittsburgh	1-0		28	at	Boston	4-3
	26	at	Washington	0-4		30	at	Ottawa	3-1
	28	at	Tampa Bay	1-3	**Apr.**	1		Buffalo	4-6
	30	at	Ottawa	4-1		3		Boston	1-4
Jan.	3	at	NY Rangers	4-7		4	at	Boston	3-3
	4	at	NY Islanders	2-2		6		Florida	2-1
	6		Buffalo	6-7		11	at	Philadelphia	2-3
	8		Tampa Bay	3-3		13		NY Islanders	5-5

Entry Draft
Selections 1996-82

1996		1992		1988		1984	
Pick		**Pick**		**Pick**		**Pick**	
18	Matt Higgins	20	David Wilkie	20	Eric Charron	5	Petr Svoboda
44	Mathieu Garon	33	Valeri Bure	34	Martin St. Amour	8	Shayne Corson
71	Arron Asham	44	Keli Corpse	46	Neil Carnes	29	Stephane Richer
92	Kim Staal	68	Craig Rivet	83	Patrik Kjellberg	51	Patrick Roy
99	Etienne Drapeau	82	Louis Bernard	93	Peter Popovic	54	Graeme Bonar
127	Daniel Archambault	92	Marc Lamothe	104	Jean-Claude Bergeron	65	Lee Brodeur
154	Brett Clark	116	Don Chase	125	Patrik Carnback	95	Gerald Johannson
181	Timo Vertala	140	Martin Sychra	146	Tim Chase	116	Jim Nesich
207	Mattia Baldi	164	Christian Proulx	167	Sean Hill	137	Scott MacTavish
233	Michel Tremblay	188	Michael Burman	188	Harijs Vitolinsh	158	Brad McCughey
		212	Earl Cronan	209	Yuri Krivokhizha	179	Eric Demers
1995		236	Trent Cavicchi	230	Kevin Dahl	199	Ron Annear
Pick		260	Hiroyuki Miura	251	Dave Kunda	220	Dave Tanner
8	Terry Ryan					240	Troy Crosby
60	Miroslav Guren	**1991**		**1987**			
74	Martin Hohenberger	**Pick**		**Pick**		**1983**	
86	Jonathan Delisle	17	Brent Bilodeau	17	Andrew Cassels	**Pick**	
112	Niklas Anger	28	Jim Campbll	33	John LeClair	17	Alfie Turcotte
138	Boyd Olson	43	Craig Darby	38	Eric Desjardins	26	Claude Lemieux
164	Stephane Robidas	61	Yves Sarault	44	Mathieu Schneider	27	Sergio Momesso
190	Greg Hart	73	Vladimir Vujtek	58	Francois Gravel	35	Todd Francis
216	Eric Houde	83	Sylvain Lapointe	80	Kris Miller	45	Daniel Letendre
		100	Brad Layzell	101	Steve McCool	78	John Kordic
1994		105	Tony Prpic	122	Les Kuntar	98	Dan Wurst
Pick		127	Oleg Petrov	143	Rob Kelley	118	Arto Javanainen
18	Brad Brown	149	Brady Kramer	164	Will Geist	138	Vladislav Tretiak
44	Jose Theodore	171	Brian Savage	185	Eric Tremblay	158	Rob Bryden
54	Chris Murray	193	Scott Fraser	206	Barry McKinlay	178	Grant MacKay
70	Marko Kiprusoff	215	Greg MacEachern	227	Ed Ronan	198	Thomas Rundqvist
74	Martin Belanger	237	Paul Lepler	248	Bryan Herring	218	Jeff Perpich
96	Arto Kuki	259	Dale Hooper			238	Jean-Guy Bergeron
122	Jimmy Drolet			**1986**			
148	Joel Irving	**1990**		**Pick**		**1982**	
174	Jessie Rezansoff	**Pick**		15	Mark Pederson	**Pick**	
200	Peter Strom	12	Turner Stevenson	27	Benoit Brunet	19	Alain Heroux
226	Tomas Vokoun	39	Ryan Kuwabara	57	Jyrki Lumme	31	Jocelyn Gauvreau
252	Chris Aldous	58	Charles Poulin	78	Brent Bobyck	32	Kent Carlson
278	Ross Parsons	60	Robert Guillet	94	Eric Aubertin	33	David Maley
		81	Gilbert Dionne	99	Mario Milani	40	Scott Sandelin
1993		102	Paul DiPietro	120	Steve Bisson	61	Scott Harlow
Pick		123	Craig Conroy	141	Lyle Odelein	69	John Devoe
21	Saku Koivu	144	Stephen Rohr	162	Rick Hayward	103	Kevin Houle
47	Rory Fitzpatrick	165	Brent Fleetwood	183	Antonin Routa	117	Ernie Vargas
73	Sebastien Bordeleau	186	Derek Maguire	204	Eric Bohemier	124	Michael Dark
85	Adam Wiesel	207	Mark Kettelhut	225	Charlie Moore	145	Hannu Jarvenpaa
99	Jean-Francois Houle	228	John Uniac	246	Karel Svoboda	150	Steve Smith
113	Jeff Lank	249	Sergei Martynyuk			166	Tom Kolioupoulos
125	Dion Darling			**1985**		187	Brian Williams
151	Darcy Tucker	**1989**		**Pick**		208	Bob Emery
177	David Ruhly	**Pick**		12	Jose Charbonneau	229	Darren Acheson
203	Alan Letang	13	Lindsay Vallis	16	Tom Chorske	250	Bill Brauer
229	Alexandre Duchesne	30	Patrice Brisebois	33	Todd Richards		
255	Brian Larochelle	41	Steve Larouche	47	Rocky Dundas		
281	Russell Guzior	51	Pierre Sevigny	75	Martin Desjardins		
		83	Andre Racicot	79	Brent Gilchrist		
		104	Marc Deschamps	96	Tom Sagissor		
		146	Craig Ferguson	117	Donald Dufresne		
		167	Patrick Lebeu	142	Ed Cristofoli		
		188	Roy Mitchell	163	Mike Claringbull		
		209	Ed Henrich	184	Roger Beedon		
		230	Justin Duberman	198	Maurice Mansi		
		251	Steve Cadieux	205	Chad Authur		
				226	Mike Bishop		
				247	John Ferguson Jr.		

General Manager

HOULE, RÉJEAN
Vice President, Hockey and General Manager, Montreal Canadiens.
Born in Rouyn-Noranda, Que., October 25, 1949.

Réjean Houle was appointed general manager of the Montreal Canadiens on October 21, 1995. Along with new head coach Mario Tremblay, Houle guided the Canadiens to a playoff spot, after the team got off to a 0-5 start and missed the post-season in 1994-95. Houle played for the Canadiens from 1969 to 1983, with the exception of a three-year stint with the Quebec Nordiques (WHA), and was a recipient of five Stanley Cups with Montreal. Houle played in 635 NHL regular season games, posting totals of 161 goals and 247 assists. Prior to becoming general manager of the Canadiens, and following his playing career, Réjean Houle was an executive with Molson-O'Keefe Breweries.

General Managers' History

Joseph Cattarinich, 1909-1910; George Kennedy, 1910-11 to 1919-20; Leo Dandurand, 1920-21 to 1934-35; Ernest Savard, 1935-36; Cecil Hart, 1936-37 to 1938-39; Jules Dugal, 1939-40; Tom P. Gorman, 1940-41 to 1945-46; Frank J. Selke, 1946-47 to 1963-64; Sam Pollock, 1964-65 to 1977-78; Irving Grundman, 1978-79 to 1982-83; Serge Savard, 1983-84 to 1994-95; Serge Savard and Réjean Houle, 1995-96; Réjean Houle, 1996-97.

Club Directory

Centre Molson
1260 de La Gauchetière St. W.
Montréal, Québec H3B 5E8
Phone **514/932-2582**
FAX (Hockey) 514/932-8736
Team Services 514/989-2717
P.R. 514/932-9296
Media 514/932-8285
Capacity: 21,273

Owner: The Molson Companies Limited

Chairman of the Board, President and Governor	Ronald Corey
Vice-President, Hockey, General Manager and Alternate Governor	Réjean Houle
Vice-President, Finance and Administration and Alternate Governor	Fred Steer
Vice-President and General Manager, Centre Molson	Aldo Giampaolo
Vice-President, Communications and Marketing Services	Bernard Brisset
Administrative Assistant to the General Manager	Phil Scheuer
Head Coach	Mario Tremblay
Assistant Coaches	Jacques Laperrière, Steve Shutt, Yvan Cournoyer
Goaltending Instructor	Benoit Allaire
Director of Scouting	Pierre Mondou
Director of Player Development and Scout	Claude Ruel
Pro Scout	Jacques Demers
Director of Team Services	Michèle Lapointe
Chief Scout	Doug Robinson
Scouting Staff	Neil Armstrong, Scott Baker, Fred E. Bandel, Elmer Benning, Pierre Dorion, Mats Naslund, Gerry O'Flaherty, Sakari Pietila, Richard Scammell, Antonin Routa

AHL Affiliation	Fredericton Canadiens
Governor	Phil Scheuer
General Manager and Head Coach	Paulin Bordeleau
Assistant Coach	Luc Gauthier
Director of Operations	Wayne Gamble

Medical and Training Staff	
Club Physician	Dr. D.G. Kinnear
Athletic Trainer	Gaétan Lefebvre
Assistant to the Athletic Trainer	John Shipman
Equipment Manager	Eddy Palchak
Assistants to the Equipment Manager	Pierre Gervais, Robert Boulanger, Pierre Ouellette

Advertising and Sponsorship	
EFFIX Inc.	François-Xavier Seigneur

Communications	
Director of Communications	Donald Beauchamp
Assistant to the Director of Communications	Dominick Saillant
Assistant — Communications	Frédérique Cardinal
Assistant — Photos and Archives	Claude Rompré

Finance	
Director of Finance	François Trudel
Controller	Dennis McKinley
Administrative Supervisor	Dave Poulton
Manager of Financial Analysis and Control	Françoise Brault
Accounting Supervisors	Gilles Viens, Paule Jolicoeur
M.I.S. Director	Sylvain Roy

Centre Molson	
Director, Building and Operations	Alain Gauthier
Director, Concessions, Food & Beverage	Michel T. Tremblay
Director, Box Office and Customer Service	Richard Primeau
Director, Events	Louise Laliberté
Director, Boutiques Souvenirs	Yves Renaud
Assistant Director, Building and Operations	Jean-François Garneau
Supervisor, Box Office	Cathy D'Ascoli
Supervisor, Customer Services	Lucie Robert
Chief of Security	Fernand Fichaud

Executive Assistants
President, Lise Beaudry; General Manager, Donna Stuart; V.P. and General Manager (Centre Molson), Vicki Mercuri; V.P. Finance, Susan Cryans; Hockey, Claudine Crépin; Communications, Normande Herget

Location of Press Box	Suspended above ice — East side
Location of Radio and TV booths	Suspended above ice — West side
Dimensions of rink	200 feet by 85 feet
Club colors	Red, White and Blue
Club trains at	Centre Molson
Play-by-Play — Radio/TV	Dick Irvin, Dino Sisto (English) Claude Quenneville, André Côté, Pierre Houde, René Pothier (French)
TV Channels	CBFT (2), TQS (35) (French), CBMT (6) (English)
Cable TV	RDS (25)
Radio Stations	CBF (690) (French), CJAD (800) (English)

Captains' History

"Jack" Laviolette, 1909-10; "Newsy" Lalonde, 1910-11; "Jack" Laviolette, 1911-12; "Newsy" Lalonde, 1912-13; Jimmy Gardner, 1913-14 to 1914-15; Howard McNamara, 1915-16; "Newsy" Lalonde, 1916-17 to 1921-22; Sprague Cleghorn, 1922-23 to 1924-25; Bill Couture, 1925-26; Sylvio Mantha, 1926-27 to 1931-32; George Hainsworth, 1932-33; Sylvio Mantha, 1933-34 to 1935-36; "Babe" Seibert, 1936-37 to 1938-39; Walter Buswell, 1939-40; "Toe" Blake, 1940-41 to 1946-47; "Toe" Blake and Bill Durnan, 1947-48; Emile Bouchard, 1948-49 to 1955-56; Maurice Richard, 1956-57 to 1959-60; Doug Harvey, 1960-61; Jean Beliveau, 1961-62 to 1970-71; Henri Richard, 1971-72 to 1974-75; Yvan Cournoyer, 1975-76 to 1978-79; Serge Savard, 1979-80, 1980-81; Bob Gainey, 1981-82 to 1988-89; Guy Carbonneau and Chris Chelios (co-captains), 1989-90; Guy Carbonneau, 1990-91 to 1993-94; Kirk Muller and Mike Keane, 1994-95; Mike Keane and Pierre Turgeon, 1995-96.

New Jersey Devils

1995-96 Results: 37W-33L-12T 86PTS. Sixth, Atlantic Division

Schedule

Oct.	Sat.	5	Detroit	Sun.	12	at NY Rangers
	Mon.	7	at Philadelphia	Tues.	14	Boston
	Sat.	12	Dallas	Tues.	21	at Los Angeles
	Tues.	15	Montreal	Wed.	22	at Anaheim
	Fri.	18	Ottawa	Fri.	24	at San Jose
	Sat.	19	at Hartford	Wed.	29	Ottawa
	Thur.	24	San Jose	Fri.	31	Toronto
	Sat.	26	at Tampa Bay	Feb.	Sat.	1	at Montreal
	Tues.	29	at Boston	Wed.	5	NY Islanders
	Wed.	30	NY Rangers	Fri.	7	Florida
Nov.	Sat.	2	Tampa Bay*	Sat.	8	Philadelphia
	Wed.	6	at Detroit	Wed.	12	at Hartford
	Thur.	7	at Chicago	Thur.	13	Hartford
	Sat.	9	NY Islanders	Sat.	15	at Montreal
	Tues.	12	Washington	Mon.	17	at NY Rangers*
	Thur.	14	Vancouver	Wed.	19	NY Rangers
	Sat.	16	Tampa Bay*	Thur.	20	at Florida
	Tues.	19	at Ottawa	Sat.	22	at Tampa Bay*
	Fri.	22	Washington	Wed.	26	at NY Islanders
	Sat.	23	at Washington	Thur.	27	Buffalo
	Wed.	27	at Dallas	Mar.	Sat.	1	Pittsburgh*
	Thur.	28	at Phoenix	Tues.	4	at Pittsburgh
	Sat.	30	at Colorado	Wed.	5	at Philadelphia
Dec.	Tues.	3	Florida	Sat.	8	at NY Islanders
	Thur.	5	Calgary	Sun.	9	at Buffalo
	Sat.	7	Phoenix*	Tues.	11	Edmonton
	Tues.	10	at Toronto	Thur.	13	Hartford
	Thur.	12	at Boston	Sat.	15	Washington*
	Sat.	14	Montreal	Mon.	17	Florida
	Mon.	16	at Calgary	Wed.	19	at Washington
	Wed.	18	at Vancouver	Sat.	22	at Pittsburgh*
	Fri.	20	at Edmonton	Tues.	25	Philadelphia
	Mon.	23	Buffalo	Thur.	27	NY Rangers
	Thur.	26	at NY Islanders	Sun.	30	Los Angeles*
	Sat.	28	Anaheim	Apr.	Tues.	1	at Washington
	Tues.	31	at Buffalo	Fri.	4	Tampa Bay
Jan.	Thur.	2	Pittsburgh	Sun.	6	at St. Louis
	Fri.	3	at Ottawa	Tues.	8	at Tampa Bay
	Sun.	5	St. Louis	Wed.	9	at Florida
	Wed.	8	Colorado	Fri.	11	Boston
	Fri.	10	Chicago	Sun.	13	at Philadelphia

* Denotes afternoon game.

Year-by-Year Record

		Home			Road			Overall						
Season	GP	W	L	T	W	L	T	W	L	T	GF	GA	Pts.	Finished	Playoff Result
1995-96	82	22	17	2	15	16	10	37	33	12	215	202	86	6th, Atlantic Div.	Out of Playoffs
1994-95	**48**	**14**	**4**	**6**	**8**	**14**	**2**	**22**	**18**	**8**	**136**	**121**	**52**	**2nd, Atlantic Div.**	**Won Stanley Cup**
1993-94	84	29	11	2	18	14	10	47	25	12	306	220	106	2nd, Atlantic Div.	Lost Conf. Championship
1992-93	84	24	14	4	16	23	3	40	37	7	308	299	87	4th, Patrick Div.	Lost Div. Semi-Final
1991-92	80	24	12	4	14	19	3	38	31	11	289	259	87	4th, Patrick Div.	Lost Div. Semi-Final
1990-91	80	23	10	7	9	23	8	32	33	15	272	264	79	4th, Patrick Div.	Lost Div. Semi-Final
1989-90	80	22	15	3	15	19	6	37	34	9	295	288	83	2nd, Patrick Div.	Lost Div. Semi-Final
1988-89	80	17	18	5	10	23	7	27	41	12	281	325	66	5th, Patrick Div.	Out of Playoffs
1987-88	80	23	16	1	15	20	5	38	36	6	295	296	82	4th, Patrick Div.	Lost Conf. Championship
1986-87	80	20	17	3	9	28	3	29	45	6	293	368	64	6th, Patrick Div.	Out of Playoffs
1985-86	80	17	21	2	11	28	1	28	49	3	300	374	59	6th, Patrick Div.	Out of Playoffs
1984-85	80	13	21	6	9	27	4	22	48	10	264	346	54	5th, Patrick Div.	Out of Playoffs
1983-84	80	10	28	2	7	28	5	17	56	7	231	350	41	5th, Patrick Div.	Out of Playoffs
1982-83	80	11	20	9	6	29	5	17	49	14	230	338	48	5th, Patrick Div.	Out of Playoffs
1981-82**	80	14	21	5	4	28	8	18	49	13	241	362	49	5th, Smythe Div.	Out of Playoffs
1980-81**	80	15	16	9	7	29	4	22	45	13	258	344	57	5th, Smythe Div.	Out of Playoffs
1979-80**	80	12	20	8	7	28	5	19	48	13	234	308	51	6th, Smythe Div.	Out of Playoffs
1978-79**	80	8	24	8	7	29	4	15	53	12	210	331	42	4th, Smythe Div.	Out of Playoffs
1977-78**	80	17	14	9	2	26	12	19	40	21	257	305	59	2nd, Smythe Div.	Lost Prelim. Round
1976-77**	80	12	20	8	8	26	6	20	46	14	226	307	54	5th, Smythe Div.	Out of Playoffs
1975-76*	80	8	24	8	4	32	4	12	56	12	190	351	36	5th, Smythe Div.	Out of Playoffs
1974-75*	80	12	20	8	3	34	3	15	54	11	184	328	41	5th, Smythe Div.	Out of Playoffs

* Kansas City Scouts. ** Colorado Rockies.

Rookie sensation Petr Sykora was a pleasant surprise for New Jersey in 1995-96, leading all Devils' freshmen in goals (18), assists (24) and points (42).

Franchise date: June 30, 1982
Transferred from Denver to New Jersey, previously transferred from Kansas City to Denver, Colorado.

EASTERN
NHL
CONFERENCE

ATLANTIC DIVISION

23rd NHL Season

1996-97 Player Personnel

FORWARDS	HT	WT	S	Place of Birth	Date	1995-96 Club
ANDREYCHUK, Dave	6-3	220	R	Hamilton, Ont.	9/29/63	Toronto-New Jersey
BERTRAND, Eric	6-1	205	L	St. Ephrem, Que.	4/16/75	Albany
BERTSCH, Jay	6-4	205	R	Lethbridge, Alta.	7/14/76	Spokane
BROTEN, Neal	5-9	175	L	Roseau, MN	11/29/59	New Jersey
BRULE, Steve	5-11	185	R	Montreal, Que.	1/15/75	Albany
BRYLIN, Sergei	5-9	175	L	Moscow, USSR	1/13/74	New Jersey
CARPENTER, Bob	6-0	200	L	Beverly, MA	7/13/63	New Jersey
CRAWFORD, Glenn	5-11	175	L	Orillia, Ont.	2/27/78	Windsor
DAGENAIS, Pierre	6-3	185	L	Blainville, Que.	3/4/78	Moncton
ELIAS, Patrik	6-0	175	L	Trebic, Czech.	4/13/76	New Jersey-Albany
GOSSELIN, David	6-0	175	R	Levis, Que.	6/22/77	Sherbrooke
GUERIN, Bill	6-2	200	R	Wilbraham, MA	11/9/70	New Jersey
HOLIK, Bobby	6-3	220	R	Jihlava, Czech.	1/1/71	New Jersey
HOUSE, Bobby	6-1	200	R	Whitehorse, Yukon	1/7/73	Albany
MacLEAN, John	6-0	200	R	Oshawa, Ont.	11/20/64	New Jersey
MASON, Wes	6-2	180	L	Windsor, Ont.	12/12/77	Sarnia
McCAULEY, Alyn	5-11	185	L	Brockville, Ont.	5/29/77	Ottawa (OHL)
McKAY, Randy	6-1	205	R	Montreal, Que.	1/25/67	New Jersey
OLIWA, Krzysztof	6-5	235	L	Tychy, Poland	4/12/73	Albany-Raleigh
PANDOLFO, Jay	6-1	195	L	Winchester, MA	12/27/74	Boston U.-Albany
PARKER, Scott	6-4	220	R	Hanford, CA	1/29/78	Kelowna
PATTISON, Rob	6-0	195	L	Sherborn, MA	9/18/71	Raleigh-Albany
PEDERSON, Denis	6-2	190	R	Prince Albert, Sask.	9/10/75	New Jersey-Albany
PELUSO, Mike	6-4	220	L	Pengilly, MN	11/8/65	New Jersey
PERROTT, Nathan	6-0	215	R	Owen Sound, Ont.	12/8/76	Oshawa-Albany
RHEAUME, Pascal	6-1	200	L	Quebec, Que.	6/21/73	Albany
ROCHEFORT, Richard	5-9	180	R	North Bay, Ont.	1/7/77	Sudbury
ROLSTON, Brian	6-2	185	L	Flint, MI	2/21/73	New Jersey
SHARIFIJANOV, Vadim	5-11	210	L	Ufa, USSR	12/23/75	Albany
SIMPSON, Reid	6-1	210	L	Flin Flon, Man.	5/21/69	New Jersey-Albany
SKOREPA, Zdenek	6-0	185	L	Duchcov, Czech.	8/10/76	Kingston
SULLIVAN, Steve	5-9	155	R	Timmins, Ont.	7/6/74	New Jersey-Albany
SYKORA, Petr	5-11	185	L	Plzen, Czech.	11/19/76	New Jersey-Albany
THOMAS, Steve	5-11	185	L	Stockport, England	7/15/63	New Jersey
WILLIAMS, Jeff	6-0	175	L	Pointe-Claire, Que.	2/11/76	Guelph
ZELEPUKIN, Valeri	5-11	190	L	Voskresensk, USSR	9/17/68	New Jersey

DEFENSEMEN						
BOMBARDIR, Brad	6-2	190	L	Powell River, B.C.	5/5/72	Albany
CHAMBERS, Shawn	6-2	200	L	Sterling Hts., MI	10/11/66	New Jersey
DANEYKO, Ken	6-0	210	L	Windsor, Ont.	4/17/64	New Jersey
DEAN, Kevin	6-2	195	L	Madison, WI	4/1/69	New Jersey-Albany
HELMER, Bryan	6-1	200	R	Sault Ste. Marie, Ont.	7/15/72	Albany
KINNEAR, Geordie	6-1	200	L	Simcoe, Ont.	7/9/73	Albany
McALPINE, Chris	6-0	210	R	Roseville, MN	12/1/71	Albany
NIEDERMAYER, Scott	6-0	200	L	Edmonton, Alta.	8/31/73	New Jersey
ODELEIN, Lyle	5-11	210	R	Quill Lake, Sask.	7/21/68	Montreal
PERSSON, Ricard	6-2	205	L	Ostersund, Sweden	8/24/69	New Jersey-Albany
SMITH, Jason	6-3	205	R	Calgary, Alta.	11/2/73	New Jersey
SOURAY, Sheldon	6-2	210	L	Elk Point, Alta.	7/13/76	Prince George-Kelowna-Albany
STEVENS, Scott	6-2	210	L	Kitchener, Ont.	4/1/64	New Jersey
STROBEL, Mark	6-0	200	L	St. Paul, MN	8/15/73	Albany-Raleigh
VYSHEDKEVICH, Sergei	6-0	185	L	Dedovsk, USSR	1/3/75	Moscow D'amo
WARD, Lance	6-3	195	L	Lloydminster, Alta.	6/2/78	Red Deer
WHITE, Colin	6-3	190	L	New Glasgow, N.S.	12/12/77	Hull

GOALTENDERS	HT	WT	C	Place of Birth	Date	1995-96 Club
BRODEUR, Martin	6-1	205	L	Montreal, Que.	5/6/72	New Jersey
DUNHAM, Michael	6-3	185	L	Johnson City, NY	6/1/72	Albany
HENRY, Frederic	5-11	155	L	Cap-Rouge, Que.	8/9/77	Granby
MASON, Chris	5-11	180	L	Red Deer, Alta.	4/20/76	Prince George
REESE, Jeff	5-9	180	L	Brantford, Ont.	3/24/66	Hartford-Tampa Bay
SIDORKIEWICZ, Peter	5-9	180	L	Dabrowa Bialostocka, Pol.	6/29/63	Albany

General Manager

LAMORIELLO, LOU
President and General Manager, New Jersey Devils.
Born in Providence, Rhode Island, October 21, 1942.

Lou Lamoriello's life-long dedication to the game of hockey was rewarded in 1992 when he was named a recipient of the Lester Patrick Trophy for outstanding service to hockey in the United States. Lamoriello is entering his tenth season as president and general manager of the Devils following more than 20 years with Providence College as a player, coach and administrator. His trades, signings and draft choices helped lead the Devils to their first-ever Stanley Cup championship in 1995. A member of the varsity hockey Friars during his undergraduate days, he became an assistant coach with the college club after graduating in 1963. Lamoriello was later named head coach and in the ensuing 15 years, led his teams to a 248-179-13 record, a .578 winning percentage and appearances in 10 post-season tournaments, including the 1983 NCAA Final Four. Lamoriello also served a five-year term as athletic director at Providence and was a co-founder of Hockey East, one of the strongest collegiate hockey conferences in the U.S. He remained as athletic director until he was hired as president of the Devils on April 30, 1987. He assumed the dual responsibility of general manager on September 10, 1987. He was g.m. of Team USA for the first World Cup of Hockey this past summer.

1995-96 Scoring

* – rookie

Regular Season

Pos	#	Player	Team	GP	G	A	Pts	+/–	PIM	PP	SH	GW	GT	S	%
D	6	Phil Housley	CGY	59	16	36	52	–2	22	6	0	1	0	155	10.3
			N.J.	22	1	15	16	–4	8	0	0	0	0	50	2.0
			TOTAL	81	17	51	68	–6	30	6	0	1	0	205	8.3
L	32	Steve Thomas	N.J.	81	26	35	61	–2	98	6	0	6	1	192	13.5
L	23	Dave Andreychuk	TOR	61	20	24	44	–11	54	12	2	3	1	200	10.0
			N.J.	15	8	5	13	2	10	2	0	0	0	41	19.5
			TOTAL	76	28	29	57	–9	64	14	2	3	1	241	11.6
R	12	Bill Guerin	N.J.	80	23	30	53	7	116	8	0	6	1	216	10.6
R	15	John MacLean	N.J.	76	20	28	48	3	91	3	3	3	0	237	8.4
C	17	* Petr Sykora	N.J.	63	18	24	42	7	32	8	0	3	0	128	14.1
D	27	Scott Niedermayer	N.J.	79	8	25	33	5	46	6	0	1	0	179	4.5
R	44	Stephane Richer	N.J.	73	20	12	32	–8	30	3	4	3	0	192	10.4
L	16	Bobby Holik	N.J.	63	13	17	30	9	58	1	0	1	1	157	8.3
D	4	Scott Stevens	N.J.	82	5	23	28	7	100	2	1	1	0	174	2.9
L	14	Brian Rolston	N.J.	58	13	11	24	9	8	3	1	4	1	139	9.4
C	9	Neal Broten	N.J.	55	7	16	23	–3	14	1	1	1	0	73	9.6
D	29	Shawn Chambers	N.J.	64	2	21	23	1	18	2	0	1	0	112	1.8
R	21	Randy McKay	N.J.	76	11	10	21	7	145	3	0	3	1	97	11.3
L	25	Valeri Zelepukin	N.J.	61	6	9	15	–10	107	3	0	1	0	86	7.0
L	8	Mike Peluso	N.J.	57	3	8	11	4	146	0	0	0	0	41	7.3
L	19	Bob Carpenter	N.J.	52	5	5	10	–10	14	0	1	0	0	63	7.9
C	24	* Steve Sullivan	N.J.	16	5	4	9	3	8	2	0	1	0	23	21.7
C	18	Sergei Brylin	N.J.	50	4	5	9	–2	26	0	0	1	0	51	7.8
D	3	Ken Daneyko	N.J.	80	2	4	6	–10	115	0	0	0	0	67	3.0
L	33	Reid Simpson	N.J.	23	1	5	6	2	79	0	0	0	0	8	12.5
D	28	Kevin Dean	N.J.	41	0	6	6	4	28	0	0	0	0	29	0.0
C	10	* Denis Pederson	N.J.	10	3	1	4	–1	0	1	0	2	0	6	50.0
R	20	Scott Pellerin	N.J.	6	2	1	3	1	0	0	0	0	0	9	22.2
D	5	Ricard Persson	N.J.	12	2	1	3	5	8	1	0	0	0	41	4.9
D	26	Jason Smith	N.J.	64	2	1	3	5	86	0	0	0	0	52	3.8
G	30	Martin Brodeur	N.J.	77	0	1	1	0	0	0	0	0	0	1	0.0
R	24	* Patrik Elias	N.J.	1	0	0	0	–1	0	0	0	0	0	2	0.0
G	35	* Corey Schwab	N.J.	10	0	0	0	0	31	0	0	0	0	0	0.0

Goaltending

No.	Goaltender	GPI	Mins	Avg	W	L	T	EN	SO	GA	SA	S%
35	* Corey Schwab	10	331	2.18	0	3	0	0	0	12	119	.899
30	Martin Brodeur	77	4433	2.34	34	30	12	8	6	173	1954	.911
30	Chris Terreri	4	210	2.57	3	0	0	0	0	9	92	.902
	Totals	**82**	**4995**	**2.43**	**37**	**33**	**12**	**8**	**6**	**202**	**2173**	**.907**

Acquired from the Toronto Maple Leafs late in the 1995-96 season to add some extra zip to New Jersey's offense, Dave Andreychuk scored eight goals in his 15 games with the Devils.

General Managers' History

(Kansas City) Sid Abel, 1974-75 to 1975-76; (Colorado) Ray Miron, 1976-77 to 1980-81; Billy MacMillan, 1981-82 to 1982-83; Billy MacMillan and Max McNab, 1983-84; Max McNab 1984-85 to 1986-87; Lou Lamoriello, 1987-88 to date.

Coaching History

(Kansas City) "Bep" Guidolin, 1974-75; "Bep" Guidolin, Sid Abel, and Eddie Bush, 1975-76; (Colorado) John Wilson, 1976-77; Pat Kelly, 1977-78; Pat Kelly and Aldo Guidolin, 1978-79; Don Cherry, 1979-80; Bill MacMillan, 1980-81; Bert Marshall and Marshall Johnston, 1981-82; (New Jersey) Bill MacMillan, 1982-83; Bill MacMillan and Tom McVie, 1983-84; Doug Carpenter, 1984-85 to 1986-87; Doug Carpenter and Jim Schoenfeld, 1987-88; Jim Schoenfeld, 1988-89; Jim Schoenfeld and John Cunniff, 1989-90; John Cunniff and Tom McVie, 1990-91; Tom McVie, 1991-92; Herb Brooks, 1992-93; Jacques Lemaire, 1993-94 to date.

Captains' History

Simon Nolet, 1974-75 to 1976-77; Wilf Paiement, 1977-78; Gary Croteau, 1978-79; Mike Christie, Rene Robert, Lanny McDonald, 1979-80; Lanny McDonald, 1980-81; Lanny McDonald, Rob Ramage, 1981-82; Don Lever, 1982-83; Don Lever and Mel Bridgman, 1983-84; Mel Bridgman, 1984-85 to 1986-87; Kirk Muller, 1987-88 to 1990-91; Bruce Driver, 1991-92; Scott Stevens, 1992-93 to date.

Club Records

Team

(Figures in brackets for season records are games played; records for fewest points, wins, ties, losses, goals, goals against are for 70 or more games)

Most Points	106	1993-94 (84)
Most Wins	47	1993-94 (84)
Most Ties	21	1977-78 (80)
Most Losses	56	1983-84 (80),
		1975-76 (80)
Most Goals	308	1992-93 (84)
Most Goals Against	374	1985-86 (80)
Fewest Points	*36	1975-76 (80)
	41	1983-84 (80)
Fewest Wins	*12	1975-76 (80)
	17	1982-83 (80),
		1983-84 (80)
Fewest Ties	3	1985-86 (80)
Fewest Losses	25	1993-94 (84)
Fewest Goals	*184	1974-75 (80)
	230	1982-83 (80)
Fewest Goals Against	202	1995-96 (82)

Longest Winning Streak

Overall	7	Oct. 6-Oct. 23/93
Home	8	Oct. 9-Nov. 7/87
Away	4	Oct. 5-23/89,
		Dec. 31/91-Jan. 31/92,
		Nov. 5-Nov. 18/93

Longest Undefeated Streak

Overall	10	Feb. 23-Mar. 15/96
		(7 wins, 3 ties)
Home	10	Feb. 28-Mar. 29/94
		(9 wins, 1 tie)
Away	8	Nov. 5-Dec. 2/93
		(5 wins, 3 ties)

Longest Losing Streak

Overall	*14	Dec. 30/75-Jan. 29/76
	10	Oct. 14-Nov. 4/83
Home	9	Dec. 22/85-Feb. 6/86
Away	12	Oct. 19/83-Dec. 1/83

Longest Winless Streak

Overall	*27	Feb. 12-Apr. 4/76
		(21 losses, 6 ties)
	18	Oct. 20-Nov. 26/82
		(14 losses 4 ties)
Home	*14	Feb. 12-Mar. 30/76
		(10 losses, 4 ties),
		Feb. 4-Mar. 31/79
		(12 losses, 2 ties)
	9	Dec. 22/85-Feb. 6/86
		(9 losses)
Away	*32	Nov. 12/77-Mar. 15/78
		(22 losses, 10 ties)
	14	Dec. 26/82-Mar. 5/83
		(13 losses, 1 tie)

Most Shutouts, Season	6	1995-96 (82)
Most PIM, Season	2,494	1988-89 (80)
Most Goals, Game	9	Seven times

Individual

Most Seasons	13	Ken Daneyko
Most Games	828	John MacLean
Most Goals, Career	315	John MacLean
Most Assists, Career	335	Kirk Muller
Most Points, Career	636	John MacLean
		(315G, 321A)
Most PIM, Career	2,051	Ken Daneyko
Most Shutouts, Career	12	Martin Brodeur

Longest Consecutive

Games Streak	388	Ken Daneyko
		(Nov. 4/89-Mar. 29/94)
Most Goals, Season	46	Pat Verbeek
		(1987-88)
Most Assists, Season	60	Scott Stevens
		(1993-94)
Most Points, Season	94	Kirk Muller
		(1987-88; 37G, 57A)
Most PIM, Season	283	Ken Daneyko
		(1988-89)

Most Points, Defenseman

Season	78	Scott Stevens
		(1993-94; 18G, 60A)

Most Points, Center

Season	94	Kirk Muller
		(1987-88; 37G, 57A)

Most Points, Right Wing,

Season	*87	Wilf Paiement
		(1977-78; 31G, 56A)
	87	John MacLean
		(1988-89; 42G, 45A)

Most Points, Left Wing,

Season	86	Kirk Muller
		(1989-90; 30G, 56A)

Most Points, Rookie,

Season	63	Kevin Todd
		(1991-92; 21G, 42A)
Most Shutouts, Season	6	Martin Brodeur
		(1995-96)
Most Goals, Game	4	Bob MacMillan
		(Jan. 8/82),
		Pat Verbeek
		(Feb. 28/88)
Most Assists, Game	5	Kirk Muller
		(Mar. 25/87),
		Greg Adams
		(Oct. 10/86),
		Tom Kurvers
		(Feb. 13/89)
Most Points, Game	6	Kirk Muller
		(Nov. 29/86; 3G, 3A)

* Records include Kansas City Scouts and Colorado Rockies from 1974-75 through 1981-82.

All-time Record vs. Other Clubs

Regular Season

			At Home					On Road						Total					
	GP	W	L	T	GF	GA	PTS	GP	W	L	T	GF	GA	PTS	GP	W	L	T	GF	GA	PTS
Anaheim	2	1	1	0	6	4	2	2	1	1	0	7	9	2	4	2	2	0	13	13	4
Boston	37	7	22	8	99	136	22	40	10	26	4	124	175	24	77	17	48	12	223	311	46
Buffalo	38	9	22	7	118	147	25	38	7	26	5	116	171	19	76	16	48	12	234	318	44
Calgary	38	11	24	3	110	146	25	37	4	27	6	94	173	14	75	15	51	9	204	319	39
Chicago	39	15	15	9	116	119	39	40	9	23	8	112	168	26	79	24	38	17	228	287	65
Colorado	29	15	12	2	122	105	32	27	10	14	3	84	106	23	56	25	26	5	206	211	55
Dallas	38	19	16	3	130	117	41	38	9	23	6	100	152	24	76	28	39	9	230	269	65
Detroit	34	16	10	8	122	99	40	33	12	19	2	115	141	26	67	28	29	10	237	240	66
Edmonton	26	11	13	2	89	91	24	26	7	14	5	98	126	19	52	18	27	7	187	217	43
Florida	7	5	2	0	21	10	10	8	2	4	2	16	19	6	15	7	6	2	37	29	16
Hartford	29	15	11	3	104	101	33	27	8	12	7	87	99	23	56	23	23	10	191	200	56
Los Angeles	36	16	15	5	124	131	37	36	4	26	6	111	191	14	72	20	41	11	235	322	51
Montreal	38	13	24	1	111	167	27	38	7	27	4	96	153	18	76	20	51	5	207	320	45
NY Islanders	64	23	31	10	217	252	56	63	7	47	9	176	297	23	127	30	78	19	393	549	79
NY Rangers	64	29	31	4	219	236	62	64	16	38	10	198	277	42	128	45	69	14	417	513	104
Ottawa	7	6	1	0	30	17	12	8	6	1	1	29	14	13	15	12	2	1	59	31	25
Philadelphia	63	31	28	4	230	242	66	64	14	43	7	157	270	35	127	45	71	11	387	512	101
Pittsburgh	61	29	20	12	236	210	70	60	20	36	4	210	252	44	121	49	56	16	446	462	114
St. Louis	40	18	15	7	132	116	43	39	8	25	6	122	176	22	79	26	40	13	254	292	65
San Jose	5	3	2	0	21	9	6	4	2	1	1	13	8	5	9	5	3	1	34	17	11
Tampa Bay	8	6	1	1	30	13	13	8	4	2	2	24	21	10	16	10	3	3	54	34	23
Toronto	33	13	11	9	121	105	35	34	6	24	4	109	153	16	67	19	35	13	230	258	51
Vancouver	42	18	18	6	132	141	42	42	7	24	11	121	162	25	84	25	42	17	253	303	67
Washington	61	27	27	7	196	189	61	61	18	40	3	182	258	39	122	45	67	10	378	447	100
Winnipeg	22	7	9	6	70	71	20	24	4	17	3	64	97	11	46	11	26	9	134	168	31
Defunct Clubs	8	4	2	2	25	19	10	8	2	3	3	19	27	7	16	6	5	5	44	46	17
Totals	**869**	**367**	**383**	**119**	**2931**	**2993**	**853**	**869**	**204**	**543**	**122**	**2584**	**3695**	**530**	**1738**	**571**	**926**	**241**	**5515**	**6688**	**1383**

Playoffs

	Series	W	L	GP	W	L	T	GF	GA	Last Mtg.	Round	Result
Boston	3	2	1	18	11	7	0	55	52	1995	CQF	W 4-1
Buffalo	1	1	0	7	4	3	0	14	14	1994	CQF	W 4-3
Detroit	1	1	0	4	4	0	0	16	7	1995	F	W 4-0
NY Islanders	1	1	0	6	4	2	0	23	18	1988	DSF	W 4-2
NY Rangers	2	0	2	14	6	8	0	41	46	1994	CF	L 3-4
Philadelphia	2	1	1	8	4	4	0	23	20	1995	CF	W 4-2
Pittsburgh	3	1	2	17	8	9	0	47	56	1995	CSF	W 4-1
Washington	2	1	1	6	3	3	0	43	44	1990	DSF	L 2-4
Totals	**15**	**8**	**7**	**87**	**47**	**40**	**0**	**262**	**257**			

Playoff Results 1996-92

Year	Round	Opponent	Result	GF	GA
1995	F	**Detroit**	**W 4-0**	**16**	**7**
	CF	Philadelphia	W 4-2	20	14
	CSF	Pittsburgh	W 4-1	17	8
	CQF	Boston	W 4-1	14	5
1994	CF	NY Rangers	L 3-4	16	18
	CSF	Boston	W 4-2	22	17
	CQF	Buffalo	W 4-3	14	14
1993	DSF	Pittsburgh	L 1-4	13	23
1992	DSF	NY Rangers	L 3-4	25	28

Abbreviations: Round: F – Final;
CF – conference final; **CQF** – conference quarter-final;
CSF – conference semi-final; **DF** – division final;
DSF – division semi-final; **SF** – semi-final;
QF – quarter-final; **PR** – preliminary round.

Calgary totals include Atlanta, 1974-75 to 1979-80.   Colorado totals include Quebec, 1979-80 to 1994-95.
Dallas totals include Minnesota, 1974-75 to 1992-93.
New Jersey totals include Kansas City, 1974-75 to 1975-76, and Colorado Rockies, 1976-77 to 1981-82.

1995-96 Results

Oct.	7		Florida	4-0		11		San Jose	1-2
	12		Winnipeg	4-1		13	at	Boston	2-3
	14	at	Montreal	4-1		14		Dallas	7-2
	15	at	Buffalo	4-3		16		Boston	2-3
	17		Edmonton	1-3		23		Los Angeles	3-1
	19		Detroit	4-2		25		Washington	3-1
	21		Ottawa	4-1		27	at	Hartford	4-4
	25		Vancouver	2-4		30	at	Vancouver	3-2
	28		Pittsburgh	3-5	Feb.	1	at	Calgary	1-1
	31	at	Edmonton	1-2		3	at	Ottawa	3-2
Nov.	2	at	San Jose	3-3		7		Pittsburgh	1-1
	4	at	Los Angeles	4-2		10		NY Rangers	3-0
	5	at	Anaheim	1-6		11		Anaheim	2-4
	8		Calgary	1-2		16	at	Buffalo	2-2
	11		Philadelphia	4-2		18		Washington	3-0
	12	at	Philadelphia	3-2		19	at	Philadelphia	1-4
	14		Hartford	1-0		21		Florida	1-4
	16	at	Boston	2-2		23		Montreal	6-5
	18		Buffalo	4-5		24	at	Washington	2-1
	21	at	Florida	3-4	Mar.	1		NY Islanders	6-2
	22	at	Tampa Bay	1-3		2	at	Ottawa	4-1
	25	at	Dallas	0-2		4	at	NY Rangers	2-2
	27	at	NY Rangers	4-1		6	at	Toronto	2-2
	29		Colorado	4-3		9	at	Pittsburgh	4-3
Dec.	1		Tampa Bay	5-1		10	at	Philadelphia	3-2
	2	at	NY Islanders	1-4		13		Montreal	1-1
	6	at	Montreal	2-4		15		Tampa Bay	5-0
	7		Toronto	1-2		17	at	Florida	0-3
	9		NY Islanders	4-2		20		Boston	1-2
	11		Florida	1-2		22		Chicago	2-4
	15	at	Detroit	1-3		23	at	NY Islanders	3-3
	16		Buffalo	2-3		26	at	Tampa Bay	6-4
	19		Philadelphia	5-4		28	at	St. Louis	4-4
	21	at	Tampa Bay	2-2		30	at	Pittsburgh	1-2
	23	at	Florida	2-3	Apr.	2	at	NY Rangers	1-3
	27		NY Islanders	5-3		4		Hartford	0-1
	29	at	Winnipeg	3-5		6	at	Hartford	6-3
	31	at	Chicago	0-5		9		NY Rangers	4-2
Jan.	3	at	Colorado	1-0		10		Philadelphia	1-5
	6		Washington	3-1		11	at	Washington	3-1
	9		St. Louis	4-2		13		Ottawa	2-5

Entry Draft
Selections 1996-82

1996
Pick
10	Lance Ward
38	Wesley Mason
41	Joshua Dewolf
47	Pierre Dagenais
49	Colin White
63	Scott Parker
91	Josef Boumedienne
101	Josh MacNevin
118	Glenn Crawford
145	Sean Ritchlin
173	Daryl Andrews
199	Willie Mitchell
205	Jay Bertsch
225	Pasi Petrilainen

1995
Pick
18	Petr Sykora
44	Nathan Perrott
70	Sergei Vyshedkevich
78	David Gosselin
79	Alyn McCauley
96	Henrik Rehnberg
122	Chris Mason
148	Adam Young
174	Richard Rochefort
200	Frederic Henry
226	Colin O'Hara

1994
Pick
25	Vadim Sharifijanov
51	Patrik Elias
71	Sheldon Souray
103	Zdenek Skorepa
129	Christian Gosselin
134	Ryan Smart
155	Luciano Caravaggio
181	Jeff Williams
207	Eric Bertrand
233	Steve Sullivan
259	Scott Swanjord
269	Mike Hanson

1993
Pick
13	Denis Pederson
32	Jay Pandolfo
39	Brendan Morrison
65	Krzysztof Oliwa
110	John Guirestante
143	Steve Brule
169	Nikolai Zavarukhin
195	Thomas Cullen
221	Judd Lambert
247	Jimmy Provencher
273	Michael Legg

1992
Pick
18	Jason Smith
42	Sergei Brylin
66	Cale Hulse
90	Vitali Tomilin
94	Scott McCabe
114	Ryan Black
138	Daniel Trebil
162	Geordie Kinnear
186	Stephane Yelle
210	Jeff Toms
234	Heath Weenk
258	Vladislav Yakovenko

1991
Pick
3	Scott Niedermayer
11	Brian Rolston
33	Donevan Hextall
55	Fredrik Lindqvist
77	Bradley Willner
121	Curt Regnier
143	David Craievich
165	Paul Wolanski
187	Daniel Reimann
231	Kevin Riehl
253	Jason Hehr

1990
Pick
20	Martin Brodeur
24	David Harlock
29	Chris Gotziaman
53	Michael Dunham
56	Brad Bombardir
64	Mike Bodnarchuk
95	Dean Malkoc
104	Petr Kuchyna
116	Lubomir Kolnik
137	Chris McAlpine
179	Jaroslav Modry
200	Corey Schwab
221	Valeri Zelepukin
242	Todd Reirden

1989
Pick
5	Bill Guerin
18	Jason Miller
26	Jarrod Skalde
47	Scott Pellerin
89	Mike Heinke
110	David Emma
152	Sergei Starikov
173	Andre Faust
215	Jason Simon
236	Peter Larsson

1988
Pick
12	Corey Foster
23	Jeff Christian
54	Zdeno Ciger
65	Matt Ruchty
75	Scott Luik
96	Chris Nelson
117	Chad Johnson
138	Chad Erickson
159	Bryan Lafort
180	Sergei Svetlov
201	Bob Woods
207	Alexander Semak
222	Charles Hughes
243	Michael Pohl

1987
Pick
2	Brendan Shanahan
23	Rickard Persson
65	Brian Sullivan
86	Kevin Dean
107	Ben Hankinson
128	Tom Neziol
149	Jim Dowd
170	John Blessman
191	Peter Fry
212	Alain Charland

1986
Pick
3	Neil Brady
24	Todd Copeland
45	Janne Ojanen
62	Marc Laniel
66	Anders Carlsson
108	Troy Crowder
129	Kevin Todd
150	Ryan Pardoski
171	Scott McCormack
192	Frederic Chabot
213	John Andersen
236	Doug Kirton

1985
Pick
3	Craig Wolanin
24	Sean Burke
32	Eric Weinrich
45	Myles O'Connor
66	Gregg Polak
108	Bill McMillan
129	Kevin Schrader
150	Ed Krayer
171	Jamie Huscroft
192	Terry Shold
213	Jamie McKinley
234	David Williams

1984
Pick
2	Kirk Muller
23	Craig Billington
44	Neil Davey
74	Paul Ysebaert
86	Jon Morris
107	Kirk McLean
128	Ian Ferguson
149	Vladimir Kames
170	Mike Roth
190	Mike Peluso
211	Jarkko Piiparinen
231	Chris Kiene

1983
Pick
6	John MacLean
24	Shawn Evans
85	Chris Terreri
105	Gordon Mark
125	Greg Evtushevski
145	Viacheslav Fetisov
165	Jay Octeau
185	Alexander Chernykh
205	Allan Stewart
225	Alexei Kasatonov

1982
Pick
8	Rocky Trottier
18	Ken Daneyko
43	Pat Verbeek
54	Dave Kasper
5	Scott Brydges
106	Mike Moher
127	Paul Fulcher
148	John Hutchings
169	Alan Hepple
190	Brent Shaw
207	Tony Gilliard
211	Scott Fusco
232	Dan Dorion

Coach

LEMAIRE, JACQUES GERARD
Coach, New Jersey Devils. Born in LaSalle, Quebec, September 7, 1945.

Jacques Lemaire is entering his fourth season as head coach of the New Jersey Devils. In 1994-95 Lemaire led the Devils to a record of 22-18-8 and their first Stanley Cup championship that included a four-game sweep in the finals. In 1993-94, his first season behind the Devils' bench, he led the team to a franchise-record 106 points and guided the team to the Conference Finals for the first time since 1988. Lemaire was named the winner of the Jack Adams Award as the NHL's outstanding coach and was also honored by *The Sporting News* and *The Hockey News*. Lemaire, who served as the assistant to the managing director of the Montreal Canadiens for seven years, coached the Canadiens from February 24, 1984 to the end of the 1984-85 season. During his successful term as the Habs' coach, he led the team to the Conference Finals in 1984 and to a first place finish in the Adams Division in 1984-85.

A member of the Hockey Hall of Fame as a player, Lemaire coached Sierre of the Swiss League and Longueuil of the Quebec Major Junior Hockey League before joining the Canadiens' organization in 1983.

Coaching Record

Season	Team	Games	W	L	T	%	Games	W	L	%
1979-80	Sierre (Switzerland)					UNAVAILABLE				
1980-81	Sierre (Switzerland)					UNAVAILABLE				
1982-83	Longueuil (QMJHL)	70	37	29	4	.557	15	9	6	.600
1983-84	**Montreal (NHL)**	17	7	10	0	.412	15	9	6	.600
1984-85	**Montreal (NHL)**	80	41	27	12	.588	12	6	6	.500
1993-94	**New Jersey (NHL)**	84	47	25	12	.631	20	11	9	.550
1994-95	**New Jersey (NHL)**	48	22	18	8	.542	20	16	4	.800*
1995-96	**New Jersey (NHL)**	82	37	33	12	.524	....	....	....	....
	NHL Totals	311	154	113	44	.566	67	42	25	.627

*Stanley Cup win.

Club Directory

Continental Airlines Arena
50 Route 120 North
P.O. Box 504
East Rutherford, NJ 07073
Phone **201/935-6050**
FAX 201/935-2127
Capacity: 19,040

Chairman	John J. McMullen
President & General Manager	Louis A. Lamoriello
Senior Vice President, Finance	Chris Modrzynski
Vice President, General Counsel	Joseph C. Benedetti
Vice President, Ticket Operations	Terry Farmer
Vice President, Sales & Marketing	Michael G. McCall
Vice President, Operations & Human Resources	Peter McMullen
Executive Assistants to the President/GM	Marie Carnevale, Mary K. Morrison

Hockey Club Personnel
Head Coach	Jacques Lemaire
Assistant Coach	Robbie Ftorek
Goaltending Coach	Jacques Caron
Director of Scouting	David Conte
Scouting Staff	Claude Carrier, Glen Dirk, Milt Fisher, Ferny Flaman, Dan Labraaten, Chris Lamoriello, Joe Mahoney, Larry Perris, Marcel Pronovost, Lou Reycroft, Ed Thomlinson, Les Widdifield
Pro Scouting Staff	Bob Hoffmeyer, Jan Ludvig
Hockey Operations Video Coordinator	Taran Singleton
Scouting Staff Assistant	Callie A. Smith
Strength & Conditioning Coach	Michael Vasalani
Medical Trainer	Bill Murray
Equipment Manager	Dave Nichols
Assistant Equipment Manager	Alex Abasto, Joe Summers
Team Cardiologist	Dr. Joseph Niznik
Team Dentist	Dr. H. Hugh Gardy
Team Orthopedists	Dr. Barry Fisher, Dr. Len Jaffe
Exercise Physiologist	Dr. Garret Caffrey
Physical Therapist	David M. Feniger
Video Consultant	Mitch Kaufman

Finance Department
Senior Director, Finance	Scott Struble
Staff Accountants	Jerry Angelo, Dan Burgers, Gina Durante, Kevin Sevinsky
Secretary	Eileen Musikant
Systems Administrator	Mike Tukes
Merchandising Manager	David Perricone
Merchandising Assistant	Bethany Guldin

Ticket Department
Director, Ticket Operations	Tom Bates
Director, Customer Service/Gold Circle	Gail DeRisi
Customer Service Representative	Andrea Gebhardt
Director, Group Sales	Neil Desormeaux
Group Account Manager	Dan Sawyer

Marketing Department
Senior Director, Corporate Sponsorship	Ken Ferriter
Director, Radio Sales	Greg Stroud
Director, Season Ticket Sales	Kevin Morgan
Coordinator, Sponsor Services	Eileen Begg
Coordinator, Game Presentation	Joe Schilp
Community Development Assistant	Paul Viola
Secretary	Karen Pietz
Sales Receptionist	Margaret Scarinzi
Account Managers	David Beck, Blaise Bozzelli, Dan Carpenter, Michael DeMartino, John Donaldson, Megan Gardner, Rich Toland, Mike Yencik
Coordinator, Marketing Services	Jackie Dooley
Community Development Assistant	Paul Viola
Secretary	Karen Pietz
Sales Receptionist	Margaret Scarinzi

Communications Department
Director, Public Relations	Michael Gilbert
Director, Information & Publications	Mike Levine
Media Relations Assistant	Audra Ottimo
Public Relations Assistant	Mark Dalton
Staff Assistants	Karen Bouloucon, Phil Ratchford
Receptionists	Jelsa Belotta, Pat Maione
Team Photographer	Bruce Bennett Studios

Television/Radio
Television Outlet	SportsChannel
Broadcasters	Mike Emrick, Play-by-Play; Glenn "Chico" Resch, Color
Radio Outlet	WABC (770 AM)
Broadcasters	Mike Miller, Play-by-Play; Randy Velischek, Color
Dimensions of Rink	200 feet by 85 feet
Club Colors	Red, Black and White

New York Islanders

1995-96 Results: 22W-50L-10T 54PTS. Seventh, Atlantic Division

Schedule

Oct.	Fri.	4	at Los Angeles		Sat.	11	at Tampa Bay
	Sat.	5	at San Jose		Mon.	13	at NY Rangers
	Wed.	9	at Ottawa		Wed.	15	Buffalo
	Sat.	12	Philadelphia		Mon.	20	St. Louis*
	Thur.	17	Hartford		Wed.	22	Edmonton
	Sat.	19	at Detroit		Fri.	24	at Hartford
	Tues.	22	Tampa Bay		Sat.	25	Chicago
	Sat.	26	San Jose*		Tues.	28	at Calgary
	Wed.	30	at Hartford		Thur.	30	at Vancouver
	Thur.	31	Toronto		Fri.	31	at Edmonton
Nov.	Sat.	2	Washington	Feb.	Tues.	4	Anaheim
	Mon.	4	at Philadelphia		Wed.	5	at New Jersey
	Wed.	6	NY Rangers		Sat.	8	NY Rangers*
	Sat.	9	at New Jersey		Tues.	11	Ottawa
	Mon.	11	Colorado		Wed.	12	at Pittsburgh
	Wed.	13	Vancouver		Sat.	15	Florida
	Fri.	15	at Florida		Mon.	17	Montreal*
	Sat.	16	Ottawa		Fri.	21	at Buffalo
	Wed.	20	at Anaheim		Sun.	23	Pittsburgh*
	Fri.	22	at Colorado		Wed.	26	New Jersey
	Sat.	23	at Phoenix		Fri.	28	at Ottawa
	Wed.	27	Philadelphia	Mar.	Sun.	2	at Washington*
	Fri.	29	at Washington		Tues.	4	Tampa Bay
	Sat.	30	Buffalo		Thur.	6	Boston
Dec.	Tues.	3	Calgary		Sat.	8	New Jersey
	Thur.	5	at Florida		Tues.	11	at Florida
	Sat.	7	Washington		Thur.	13	at Tampa Bay
	Tues.	10	Phoenix		Sat.	15	at Boston*
	Wed.	11	at NY Rangers		Sun.	16	at Chicago*
	Sat.	14	at Tampa Bay		Wed.	19	Florida
	Tues.	17	Los Angeles		Sat.	22	Philadelphia
	Thur.	19	at Philadelphia		Wed.	26	at Buffalo
	Sat.	21	Dallas		Thur.	27	at Boston
	Mon.	23	Florida		Sat.	29	Boston*
	Thur.	26	New Jersey	Apr.	Wed.	2	at Dallas
	Sat.	28	Detroit		Thur.	3	at St. Louis
	Mon.	30	at Toronto		Sat.	5	Tampa Bay
Jan.	Thur.	2	at NY Rangers		Mon.	7	at Montreal
	Sat.	4	at Montreal		Wed.	9	Montreal
	Tues.	7	Pittsburgh		Fri.	11	Hartford
	Fri.	10	at Pittsburgh		Sat.	12	at Washington

* Denotes afternoon game.

Franchise date: June 6, 1972

ATLANTIC DIVISION

25th NHL Season

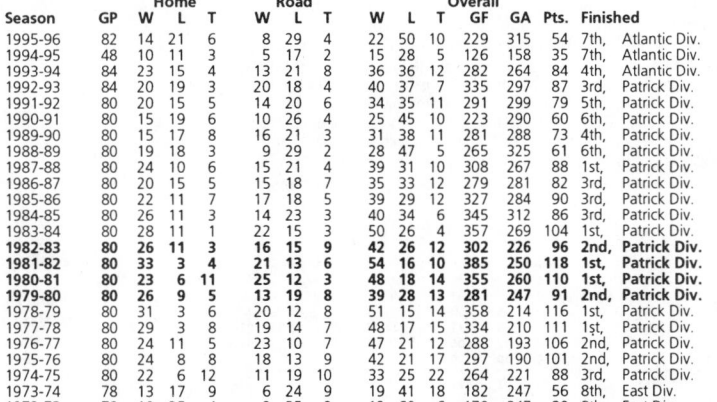

One of the top prospects in the Islanders' system, Travis Green had a career year in 1995-96, establishing personal highs in goals (25), assists (45) and points (70) while finishing second in team scoring.

Year-by-Year Record

		Home			Road			Overall							
Season	GP	W	L	T	W	L	T	W	L	T	GF	GA	Pts.	Finished	Playoff Result
1995-96	82	14	21	6	8	29	4	22	50	10	229	315	54	7th, Atlantic Div.	Out of Playoffs
1994-95	48	10	11	3	5	17	2	15	28	5	126	158	35	7th, Atlantic Div.	Out of Playoffs
1993-94	84	23	15	4	13	21	8	36	36	12	282	264	84	4th, Atlantic Div.	Lost Conf. Quarter-Final
1992-93	84	20	19	3	20	18	4	40	37	7	335	297	87	3rd, Patrick Div.	Lost Conf. Championship
1991-92	80	20	15	5	14	20	6	34	35	11	291	299	79	5th, Patrick Div.	Out of Playoffs
1990-91	80	15	19	6	10	26	4	25	45	10	223	290	60	6th, Patrick Div.	Out of Playoffs
1989-90	80	15	17	8	16	21	3	31	38	11	281	288	73	4th, Patrick Div.	Lost Div. Semi-Final
1988-89	80	19	18	3	9	29	2	28	47	5	265	325	61	6th, Patrick Div.	Out of Playoffs
1987-88	80	24	10	6	15	21	4	39	31	10	308	267	88	1st, Patrick Div.	Lost Div. Semi-Final
1986-87	80	20	15	5	15	18	7	35	33	12	279	281	82	3rd, Patrick Div.	Lost Div. Final
1985-86	80	22	11	7	17	18	5	39	29	12	327	284	90	3rd, Patrick Div.	Lost Div. Semi-Final
1984-85	80	26	11	3	14	23	3	40	34	6	345	312	86	3rd, Patrick Div.	Lost Div. Final
1983-84	80	28	11	1	22	15	3	50	26	4	357	269	104	1st, Patrick Div.	Lost Final
1982-83	**80**	**26**	**11**	**3**	**16**	**15**	**9**	**42**	**26**	**12**	**302**	**226**	**96**	**2nd, Patrick Div.**	**Won Stanley Cup**
1981-82	**80**	**33**	**3**	**4**	**21**	**13**	**6**	**54**	**16**	**10**	**385**	**250**	**118**	**1st, Patrick Div.**	**Won Stanley Cup**
1980-81	**80**	**23**	**6**	**11**	**25**	**12**	**3**	**48**	**18**	**14**	**355**	**260**	**110**	**1st, Patrick Div.**	**Won Stanley Cup**
1979-80	**80**	**26**	**9**	**5**	**13**	**19**	**8**	**39**	**28**	**13**	**281**	**247**	**91**	**2nd, Patrick Div.**	**Won Stanley Cup**
1978-79	80	31	3	6	20	12	8	51	15	14	358	214	116	1st, Patrick Div.	Lost Semi-Final
1977-78	80	29	3	8	19	14	7	48	17	15	334	210	111	1st, Patrick Div.	Lost Quarter-Final
1976-77	80	24	11	5	23	10	7	47	21	12	288	193	106	2nd, Patrick Div.	Lost Semi-Final
1975-76	80	24	8	8	18	13	9	42	21	17	297	190	101	2nd, Patrick Div.	Lost Semi-Final
1974-75	80	22	6	12	11	19	10	33	25	22	264	221	88	3rd, Patrick Div.	Lost Semi-Final
1973-74	78	13	17	9	6	24	9	19	41	18	182	247	56	8th, East Div.	Out of Playoffs
1972-73	78	10	25	4	2	35	2	12	60	6	170	347	30	8th, East Div.	Out of Playoffs

1996-97 Player Personnel

FORWARDS	HT	WT	S	Place of Birth	Date	1995-96 Club
ANDERSSON, Niklas	5-9	175	L	Kungalv, Sweden	5/20/71	NY Islanders-Utah
ARMSTRONG, Derek	5-11	188	R	Ottawa, Ont.	4/23/73	NY Islanders-Worcester
BELANGER, Ken	6-4	225	L	Sault Ste. Marie, Ont.	5/14/74	St. John's-NY Islanders
BERTUZZI, Todd	6-3	224	L	Sudbury, Ont.	2/2/75	NY Islanders
DEULING, Jarrett	6-0	202	L	Vernon, B.C.	3/4/74	NY Islanders-Worcester
DONNELLY, Mike	5-11	185	L	Detroit, MI	10/10/63	Dallas-Michigan
DUMONT, Jean-Pierre	6-1	187	L	Montreal, Que.	4/1/78	Val d'Or
FISHER, Craig	6-3	180	L	Oshawa, Ont.	6/30/70	Orlando
GREEN, Travis	6-1	193	R	Castlegar, B.C.	12/20/70	NY Islanders
HAGGERTY, Sean	6-1	186	L	Rye, NY	2/11/76	Toronto-Detroit (OHL)-Worcester
HENDRICKSON, Darby	6-0	185	L	Richfield, MN	8/28/72	Toronto-NY Islanders
HLAVAC, Jan	6-0	183	L	Prague, Czech.	9/20/76	HC Sparta
HUGHES, Brent	5-11	195	L	New Westminster, B.C.	4/5/66	Buffalo
JOHANSSON, Andreas	6-0	205	L	Hofors, Sweden	5/19/73	NY Islanders-Worcester-Utah
KING, Derek	6-0	212	L	Hamilton, Ont.	2/11/67	NY Islanders
LACOUTURE, Dan	6-2	201	L	Hyannis, MA	4/18/77	Jr. Whalers
LAPOINTE, Claude	5-9	181	L	Lachine, Que.	10/11/68	Colorado-Calgary-Saint John
MARINUCCI, Chris	6-0	188	L	Grand Rapids, MN	12/29/71	Utah
McINNIS, Marty	5-11	183	R	Hingham, MA.	6/2/70	NY Islanders
McLLWAIN, Dave	6-0	185	L	Seaforth, Ont.	1/9/67	Ottawa-Cleveland-Pittsburgh
MILLER, Todd	6-0	174	R	Elliot Lake, Ont.	5/24/78	Sarnia
ORSZAGH, Vladimir	5-11	173	L	Banska Bystrica, Czech.	5/24/77	B. Bystrica
PALFFY, Zigmund	5-10	183	L	Skalica, Czech.	5/5/72	NY Islanders
PLANTE, Dan	5-11	202	R	Hayward, WI	10/5/71	NY Islanders
SACHL, Peter	6-1	194	L	Jindrichuv Hradec, Czech.	12/2/77	Budejovice-Budejovice
SEMAK, Alexander	5-10	185	R	Ufa, USSR	2/11/66	NY Islanders
TAYLOR, Andrew	6-1	182	L	Stratford, Ont.	1/17/77	Detroit (OHL)
TAYLOR, Chris	6-0	189	L	Stratford, Ont.	3/6/72	NY Islanders-Utah
VUKOTA, Mick	6-1	225	R	Saskatoon, Sask.	9/14/66	NY Islanders
WALSH, Gord	6-1	186	L	St. John's, Nfld.	12/12/75	Kingston
DEFENSEMEN						
BERARD, Bryan	6-1	190	L	Woonsocket, RI	3/5/77	Detroit (OHL)
BERENZWEIG, Andy	6-2	195	L	Chicago, IL	8/8/77	U. of Michigan
CHARA, Zdeno	6-8	231	L	Trencin, Czech.	3/18/77	Trencin-Piestany-Sparta-Sparta
CHEBATURKIN, Vladimir	6-2	213	L	Tyumen, USSR	4/23/75	Elektrostal
HOLLAND, Jason	6-2	193	R	Morinville, Alta.	4/30/76	Kamloops
JONSSON, Kenny	6-3	195	L	Angelholm, Sweden	10/6/74	Toronto-NY Islanders
KASPARAITIS, Darius	5-10	205	L	Elektrenai, USSR	10/16/72	NY Islanders
LACHANCE, Scott	6-1	196	L	Charlottesville, VA	10/22/72	NY Islanders
LUONGO, Chris	5-10	206	R	Detroit, MI	3/17/67	NY Islanders
MCCABE, Bryan	6-1	204	L	St. Catharines, Ont.	6/8/75	NY Islanders
PILON, Richard	6-0	205	L	Saskatoon, Sask.	4/30/68	NY Islanders
SEVERYN, Brent	6-2	211	L	Vegreville, Alta.	2/22/66	NY Islanders
STRUDWICK, Jason	6-3	207	L	Edmonton, Alta.	7/17/75	NY Islanders-Worcester
VASKE, Dennis	6-2	210	L	Rockford, IL	10/11/67	NY Islanders

GOALTENDERS	HT	WT	C	Place of Birth	Date	1995-96 Club
FICHAUD, Eric	5-11	171	L	Anjou, Que.	11/4/75	NY Islanders-Worcester
GARNER, Tyrone	6-1	164	L	Stoney Creek, Ont.	7/27/78	Oshawa
MACDONALD, David	5-10	185	L	St. Thomas, Ont.	9/23/76	Sudbury
MCARTHUR, Mark	5-10	175	L	East York, Ont.	11/16/75	Utah
SALO, Tommy	5-11	173	L	Surahammar, Sweden	2/1/71	NY Islanders-Utah
SODERSTROM, Tommy	5-7	157	L	Stockholm, Sweden	7/17/69	NY Islanders

Coach and General Manager

MILBURY, MIKE
Coach and General Manager, New York Islanders.
Born in Walpole, MA, June 17, 1952.

Milbury, 44, came to the Islanders with 20 years of professional hockey experience with the Boston Bruins — as a player, assistant coach, assistant general manager, general manager and coach on both the NHL and AHL levels. Milbury took over as general manager from Don Maloney on December 12, 1995.

The Walpole, MA native joined the Boston organization after graduating from Colgate University with a degree in urban sociology and enjoyed a nine-year playing career with the team. He retired May 6, 1985 and took over as assistant coach. He returned to the ice late in the 1985-86 season when injuries decimated the Bruins' defense.

Milbury's playing career concluded on July 16, 1987 when he took over as coach of the Maine Mariners, Boston's top AHL affiliate. In his first year with the team he guided the Mariners to the AHL's Northern Division title and was named both AHL coach of the year and *The Hockey News* minor league coach of the year.

He was named the assistant general manager and coach of the Boston Bruins May 16, 1989. In two years behind the bench Milbury was the NHL's most successful coach: He guided the Bruins to consecutive 100-point seasons and Adams Division titles, the 1990 Presidents' Trophy and Wales Conference championship, and an appearance in the Stanley Cup finals in 1990. He earned coach of the year honors from both *The Hockey News* and *The Sporting News* for this effort.

Milbury and his wife, Debbie, have two sons, Owen and Luke, and two daughters, Alison and Caitlin.

Coaching Record

		Regular Season					Playoffs			
Season	Team	Games	W	L	T	%	Games	W	L	%
1987-88	Maine (AHL)	80	44	29	7	.594	10	5	5	.500
1988-89	Maine (AHL)	80	32	40	8	.450	....	....	....	....
1989-90	**Boston (NHL)**	**80**	**46**	**25**	**9**	**.631**	**21**	**13**	**8**	**.619**
1990-91	**Boston (NHL)**	**80**	**44**	**24**	**12**	**.606**	**19**	**10**	**9**	**.526**
1995-96	**NY Islanders (NHL)**	**82**	**22**	**50**	**10**	**.329**	....	....	....	....
	NHL Totals	**242**	**112**	**99**	**31**	**.527**	**40**	**23**	**17**	**.575**

1995-96 Scoring

* – rookie

Regular Season

Pos	#	Player	Team	GP	G	A	Pts	+/–	PIM	PP	SH	GW	GT	S	%
R	16	Zigmund Palffy	NYI	81	43	44	87	–17	56	17	1	6	0	257	16.7
C	39	Travis Green	NYI	69	25	45	70	–20	42	14	1	2	1	186	13.4
L	18	Marty McInnis	NYI	74	12	34	46	–11	39	2	0	1	0	167	7.2
R	44 *	Todd Bertuzzi	NYI	76	18	21	39	–14	83	4	0	2	0	127	14.2
C	28	Alexander Semak	NYI	69	20	14	34	–4	68	6	0	2	1	128	15.6
L	27	Derek King	NYI	61	12	20	32	–10	23	5	1	0	1	154	7.8
D	3	Kenny Jonsson	TOR	50	4	22	26	12	22	3	0	1	0	90	4.4
			NYI	16	0	4	4	–5	10	0	0	0	0	40	0.0
			TOTAL	66	4	26	30	7	32	3	0	1	0	130	3.1
L	32 *	Niklas Andersson	NYI	47	14	12	26	–3	12	3	2	1	0	89	15.7
D	4 *	Bryan McCabe	NYI	82	7	16	23	–24	156	3	0	1	0	130	5.4
R	26	Patrick Flatley	NYI	56	8	9	17	–24	21	0	0	0	0	89	9.0
C	17 *	Darby Hendrickson	TOR	46	6	6	12	–2	47	0	0	0	0	43	14.0
			NYI	16	1	4	5	–6	33	0	0	1	0	30	3.3
			TOTAL	62	7	10	17	–8	80	0	0	1	0	73	9.6
D	7	Scott Lachance	NYI	55	3	10	13	–19	54	1	0	0	0	81	3.7
D	6	Chris Luongo	NYI	74	3	7	10	–23	55	1	0	0	0	46	6.5
L	25	Pat Conacher	L.A.	35	5	2	7	–8	18	0	1	2	0	35	14.3
			CGY	7	0	0	0	–1	0	0	0	0	0	1	0.0
			NYI	13	1	1	2	–4	0	0	0	0	0	9	11.1
			TOTAL	55	6	3	9	–13	18	0	1	2	0	45	13.3
D	24	Brent Severyn	NYI	65	1	8	9	3	180	0	0	0	0	40	2.5
R	21 *	Dan Plante	NYI	73	5	3	8	–22	50	0	2	0	0	103	4.9
D	11	Darius Kasparaitis	NYI	46	1	7	8	–12	93	0	0	0	0	34	2.9
L	34 *	Andrey Vasilyev	NYI	10	2	5	7	4	2	0	0	1	0	12	16.7
D	37	Dennis Vaske	NYI	19	1	6	7	–13	21	1	0	1	0	19	5.3
D	2	Bob Beers	NYI	13	0	5	5	–2	10	0	0	0	0	9	0.0
C	14 *	Derek Armstrong	NYI	19	1	3	4	–6	14	0	0	0	0	23	4.3
D	33 *	Milan Tichy	NYI	8	0	4	4	3	8	0	0	0	0	6	0.0
R	15	Brad Dalgarno	NYI	18	1	2	3	–2	14	0	0	0	0	11	9.1
R	75	Brett Lindros	NYI	18	1	2	3	–6	47	0	0	0	0	10	10.0
D	47	Richard Pilon	NYI	27	0	3	3	–9	72	0	0	0	0	7	0.0
R	12	Mick Vukota	NYI	32	1	1	2	–3	106	0	0	0	0	11	9.1
C	10 *	Craig Darby	NYI	10	0	2	2	–1	0	0	0	0	0	1	0.0
D	34 *	Jason Herter	NYI	1	0	1	1	1	0	0	0	0	0	1	0.0
C	38 *	Andreas Johansson	NYI	3	0	1	1	1	0	0	0	0	0	6	0.0
C	43 *	Chris Taylor	NYI	11	0	1	1	1	2	0	0	0	0	4	0.0
C	36	Micah Aivazoff	NYI	12	0	1	1	–6	6	0	0	0	0	8	0.0
L	34 *	Jarrett Deuling	NYI	14	0	1	1	–1	11	0	0	0	0	11	0.0
G	1 *	Eric Fichaud	NYI	24	0	1	1	0	0	0	0	0	0	0	0.0
D	36 *	Jason Strudwick	NYI	1	0	0	0	0	7	0	0	0	0	0	0.0
L	32	Grigori Panteleev	NYI	4	0	0	0	–3	0	0	0	0	0	1	0.0
D	34 *	Jason Widmer	NYI	4	0	0	0	0	7	0	0	0	0	1	0.0
C	43	Michael MacWilliam	NYI	6	0	0	0	–1	14	0	0	0	0	4	0.0
L	33 *	Ken Belanger	NYI	7	0	0	0	–2	27	0	0	0	0	0	0.0
D	36	Bob Halkidis	T.B.	3	0	0	0	–1	7	0	0	0	0	0	0.0
			NYI	5	0	0	0	–3	30	0	0	0	0	2	0.0
			TOTAL	8	0	0	0	–4	37	0	0	0	0	2	0.0
G	35 *	Tommy Salo	NYI	10	0	0	0	0	0	0	0	0	0	0	0.0
G	29	Jamie McLennan	NYI	13	0	0	0	0	2	0	0	0	0	0	0.0
G	30	Tommy Soderstrom	NYI	51	0	0	0	0	7	0	0	0	0	0	0.0

Goaltending

No.	Goaltender	GPI	Mins	Avg	W	L	T	EN	SO	GA	SA	S%
1	* Eric Fichaud	24	1234	3.31	7	12	2	2	1	68	659	.897
29	Jamie McLennan	13	636	3.68	3	9	1	1	0	39	342	.886
30	Tommy Soderstrom	51	2590	3.87	11	22	6	0	2	167	1370	.878
35	* Tommy Salo	10	523	4.02	1	7	1	3	0	35	250	.860
	Totals	**82**	**4993**	**3.79**	**22**	**50**	**10**	**6**	**3**	**315**	**2627**	**.880**

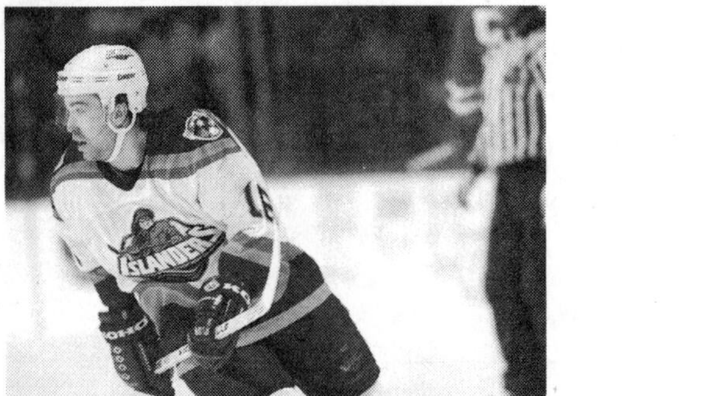

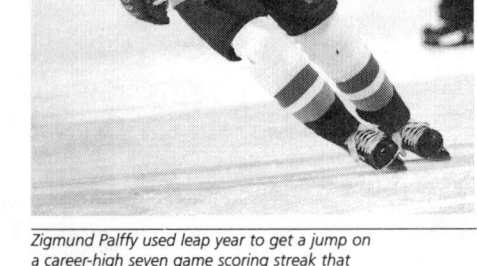

Zigmund Palffy used leap year to get a jump on a career-high seven game scoring streak that lasted from February 29 to March 16, 1996. He scored 11 goals in that seven game span.

Club Records

Team

(Figures in brackets for season records are games played; records for fewest points, wins, ties, losses, goals, goals against are for 70 or more games)

Most Points	118	1981-82 (80)
Most Wins	54	1981-82 (80)
Most Ties	22	1974-75 (80)
Most Losses	60	1972-73 (78)
Most Goals	385	1981-82 (80)
Most Goals Against	347	1972-73 (78)
Fewest Points	30	1972-73 (78)
Fewest Wins	12	1972-73 (78)
Fewest Ties	4	1983-84 (80)
Fewest Losses	15	1978-79 (80)
Fewest Goals	170	1972-73 (78)
Fewest Goals Against	190	1975-76 (80)

Longest Winning Streak

Overall	15	Jan. 21/82-Feb. 20/82
Home	14	Jan. 2/82-Feb. 27/82
Away	8	Feb. 27/81-Mar. 31/81

Longest Undefeated Streak

Overall	15	Jan. 21-Feb. 20/82 (15 wins), Nov. 4-Dec. 4/80 (13 wins, 2 ties)
Home	23	Oct. 17/78-Jan. 27/79 (19 wins, 4 ties), Jan. 2/82-Apr. 3/82 (21 wins, 2 ties)
Away	8	Four times

Longest Losing Streak

Overall	12	Dec. 27/72-Jan. 18/73, Nov. 22-Dec. 17/88
Home	5	Jan. 2-23/73, Feb. 28-Mar. 19/74, Nov. 22-Dec. 17/88
Away	15	Jan. 20-Apr. 1/73

Longest Winless Streak

Overall	15	Nov. 22-Dec. 23/72 (12 losses, 3 ties)
Home	7	Oct. 14-Nov. 21/72 (6 losses, 1 tie), Nov. 28-Dec. 23/72 (5 losses, 2 ties), Feb. 13-Mar. 13/90 (4 losses, 3 ties)
Away	20	Nov. 3/72-Jan. 13/73 (19 losses, 1 tie)

Most Shutouts, Season	10	1975-76 (80)
Most PIM, Season	1,857	1986-87 (80)
Most Goals, Game	11	Dec. 20/83 (Pit. 3 at NYI 11), Mar. 3/84 (NYI 11 at Tor. 6)

Individual

Most Seasons	17	Billy Smith
Most Games	1,123	Bryan Trottier
Most Goals, Career	573	Mike Bossy
Most Assists, Career	853	Bryan Trottier
Most Points, Career	1,353	Bryan Trottier (500G, 853A)
Most PIM, Career	1,808	Mick Vukota
Most Shutouts, Career	25	Glenn Resch

Longest Consecutive Games Streak .... 576 Bill Harris (Oct. 7/72-Nov. 30/79)

Most Goals, Season	69	Mike Bossy (1978-79)
Most Assists, Season	87	Bryan Trottier (1978-79)
Most Points, Season	147	Mike Bossy (1981-82; 64G, 83A)
Most PIM, Season	356	Brian Curran (1986-87)
Most Points, Defenseman, Season	101	Denis Potvin (1978-79; 31G, 70A)
Most Points, Center, Season	134	Bryan Trottier (1978-79; 47G, 87A)
Most Points, Right Wing, Season	*147	Mike Bossy (1981-82; 64G, 83A)
Most Points, Left Wing, Season	100	John Tonelli (1984-85; 42G, 58A)
Most Points, Rookie, Season	95	Bryan Trottier (1975-76; 32G, 63A)
Most Shutouts, Season	7	Glenn Resch (1975-76)
Most Goals, Game	5	Bryan Trottier (Dec. 23/78, Feb. 13/82), John Tonelli (Jan. 6/81)
Most Assists, Game	6	Mike Bossy (Jan. 6/81)
Most Points, Game	8	Bryan Trottier (Dec. 23/78; 5G, 3A)

* NHL Record.

Retired Numbers

5	Denis Potvin	1973-1988
22	Mike Bossy	1977-1987
23	Bob Nystrom	1972-1986
31	Billy Smith	1972-1989

All-time Record vs. Other Clubs

Regular Season

		At Home							On Road							Total					
	GP	W	L	T	GF	GA	PTS	GP	W	L	T	GF	GA	PTS	GP	W	L	T	GF	GA	PTS
Anaheim	2	1	1	0	4	6	2	2	1	1	0	5	5	2	4	2	2	0	9	11	4
Boston	45	17	23	5	144	154	39	43	9	24	10	122	169	28	88	26	47	15	266	323	67
Buffalo	45	20	18	7	133	129	47	45	14	24	7	131	159	35	90	34	42	14	264	288	82
Calgary	44	24	11	9	181	120	57	44	13	20	11	135	158	37	88	37	31	20	316	278	94
Chicago	40	16	11	13	145	121	45	42	16	21	5	144	140	37	82	32	32	18	289	261	82
Colorado	26	15	10	1	111	90	31	27	10	15	2	87	104	22	53	25	25	3	198	194	53
Dallas	40	23	9	8	159	114	54	40	19	14	7	151	117	45	80	42	23	15	310	231	99
Detroit	39	22	15	2	150	115	46	38	16	20	2	124	136	34	77	38	35	4	274	251	80
Edmonton	24	11	5	8	101	92	30	24	5	15	4	71	97	14	48	16	20	12	172	189	44
Florida	7	1	4	2	11	16	4	7	3	4	0	21	23	6	14	4	8	2	32	39	10
Hartford	27	15	8	4	102	73	34	29	11	14	4	107	111	26	56	26	22	8	209	184	60
Los Angeles	38	21	13	4	145	110	46	38	14	17	7	127	141	35	76	35	30	11	272	251	81
Montreal	44	20	19	5	145	130	45	44	11	25	8	136	171	30	88	31	44	13	281	301	75
New Jersey	63	47	7	9	297	176	103	64	31	23	10	252	217	72	127	78	30	19	549	393	175
NY Rangers	76	49	21	6	318	236	104	75	22	45	8	227	299	52	151	71	66	14	545	535	156
Ottawa	8	3	3	2	32	27	8	7	3	3	1	29	20	7	15	6	6	3	61	47	15
Philadelphia	77	41	24	12	301	230	94	75	22	45	8	229	286	52	152	63	69	20	530	516	146
Pittsburgh	67	35	24	8	278	224	78	68	25	32	11	239	263	61	135	60	56	19	517	487	139
St. Louis	42	23	9	10	162	102	56	41	17	17	7	135	150	41	83	40	26	17	297	252	97
San Jose	5	5	0	0	31	17	10	4	2	2	0	17	11	4	9	7	2	0	48	28	14
Tampa Bay	8	3	5	0	26	26	6	8	3	5	0	25	26	6	16	6	10	0	45	52	12
Toronto	39	23	13	3	170	120	49	41	20	18	3	152	142	43	80	43	31	6	322	262	92
Vancouver	40	22	10	8	152	107	52	42	20	19	3	141	141	43	82	42	29	11	293	248	95
Washington	64	38	25	1	258	204	77	63	27	27	9	214	205	63	127	65	52	10	472	409	140
Winnipeg	24	11	7	6	92	78	28	23	14	7	2	91	72	30	47	25	14	8	183	150	58
Defunct Clubs	13	11	0	2	75	33	24	13	4	5	4	35	41	12	26	15	5	6	110	74	36
Totals	947	517	295	135	3717	2850	1169	947	352	462	133	3147	3404	837	1894	869	757	268	6864	6254	2006

Playoffs

	Series	W	L	GP	W	L	T	GF	GA	Last Mtg.	Round	Result
Boston	2	2	0	11	8	3	0	49	35	1983	CF	W 4-2
Buffalo	3	3	0	16	12	4	0	59	45	1980	SF	W 4-2
Chicago	2	2	0	6	6	0	0	21	6	1979	QF	W 4-0
Colorado	1	1	0	4	4	0	0	18	9	1982	CF	W 4-0
Dallas	1	1	0	5	4	1	0	26	16	1981	F	W 4-1
Edmonton	3	2	1	15	9	6	0	58	47	1984	F	L 1-4
Los Angeles	1	1	0	4	3	1	0	21	10	1980	PR	W 3-1
Montreal	4	1	3	22	8	14	0	55	64	1993	CF	L 1-4
New Jersey	1	0	1	6	2	4	0	18	23	1988	DSF	L 2-4
NY Rangers	8	5	3	39	20	19	0	129	132	1994	CQF	L 0-4
Philadelphia	4	1	3	25	11	14	0	69	83	1987	DF	L 3-4
Pittsburgh	3	3	0	19	11	8	0	67	58	1993	DF	W 4-3
Toronto	2	1	1	10	6	4	0	33	20	1981	PR	W 3-0
Vancouver	2	2	0	6	6	0	0	26	14	1982	F	W 4-0
Washington	6	5	1	30	18	12	0	99	88	1993	DSF	W 4-2
Totals	43	30	13	218	128	90	0	748	650			

Calgary totals include Atlanta, 1972-73 to 1979-80.   Colorado totals include Quebec, 1979-80 to 1994-95.
Dallas totals include Minnesota, 1972-73 to 1992-93.
New Jersey totals include Kansas City, 1974-75 to 1975-76, and Colorado Rockies, 1976-77 to 1981-82.

Playoff Results 1996-92

Year	Round	Opponent	Result	GF	GA
1994	CQF	NY Rangers	L 0-4	3	22
1993	CF	Montreal	L 1-4	11	16
	DF	Pittsburgh	W 4-3	24	27
	DSF	Washington	W 4-2	23	22

Abbreviations: Round: F – Final;
CF – conference final; **CQF** – conference quarter-final;
CSF – conference semi-final; **DF** – division final;
DSF – division semi-final; **SF** – semi-final;
QF – quarter-final; **PR** – preliminary round.

1995-96 Results

Oct.	7	at	Boston	4-4	15	Tampa Bay	3-2
	10	at	Toronto	3-7	17	Hartford	3-6
	14		Philadelphia	0-3	22 at	Colorado	3-4
	15	at	Florida	3-5	24 at	Calgary	1-4
	17		NY Rangers	1-5	26 at	Edmonton	1-4
	20		Montreal	2-0	27 at	Vancouver	3-6
	25	at	Philadelphia	1-3	30	Buffalo	5-4
	26		Pittsburgh	5-7	**Feb.** 3 at	Washington	5-6
	28		Philadelphia	5-5	4	Dallas	5-3
	31	at	Florida	5-4	6	NY Rangers	2-4
Nov.	3	at	Tampa Bay	3-5	8 at	NY Rangers	2-6
	4		Washington	2-3	10	Anaheim	4-3
	7		Vancouver	2-5	12	Ottawa	1-4
	10	at	NY Rangers	1-4	15	Calgary	3-6
	11		St. Louis	1-4	17	San Jose	4-2
	14	at	San Jose	5-3	22 at	NY Rangers	5-3
	16	at	Los Angeles	2-9	23	Tampa Bay	3-5
	17	at	Anaheim	1-2	25	Edmonton	2-0
	22		Los Angeles	5-2	27	Detroit	2-6
	24	at	Buffalo	3-5	29 at	Detroit	1-5
	25		Tampa Bay	1-2	**Mar.** 1 at	New Jersey	2-5
	28		Colorado	3-7	3	Winnipeg	5-7
	30	at	Ottawa	5-3	5	Boston	5-3
Dec.	2		New Jersey	4-1	7 at	Boston	3-4
	5		Pittsburgh	3-6	9 at	Winnipeg	4-2
	6	at	Hartford	4-7	16 at	Pittsburgh	2-4
	9	at	New Jersey	2-4	17 at	Chicago	1-5
	10	at	Philadelphia	6-2	19 at	Philadelphia	1-4
	12		Florida	1-3	21 at	Florida	2-3
	14	at	Washington	3-4	23	New Jersey	2-3
	16		Hartford	3-3	25 at	Montreal	1-4
	19	at	St. Louis	3-3	26	Washington	1-7
	21	at	Dallas	3-3	30 at	Hartford	1-3
	23		Washington	3-1	31	NY Rangers	1-4
	26		Boston	3-3	**Apr.** 2	Philadelphia	2-6
	27	at	New Jersey	3-3	5 at	Ottawa	2-4
	31	at	Buffalo	5-2	6	Buffalo	3-0
Jan.	4		Montreal	2-2	8 at	Tampa Bay	3-4
	6		Ottawa	5-4	10 at	Pittsburgh	6-2
	9		Chicago	3-3	12	Florida	1-1
	11		Toronto	4-3	13 at	Montreal	5-5

Entry Draft
Selections 1996-82

1996
Pick
3 Jean-Pierre Dumont
29 Dan Lacouture
56 Zdeno Chara
83 Tyrone Garner
109 Andy Berenzweig
128 Petr Sachl
138 Todd Miller
165 Joe Prestifilippo
192 Evgeny Korolev
218 Mike Muzechka

1995
Pick
2 Wade Redden
28 Jan Hlavac
41 Denis Smith
106 Vladimir Orszagh
158 Andrew Taylor
210 David MacDonald
211 Mike Broda

1994
Pick
9 Brett Lindros
38 Jason Holland
63 Jason Strudwick
90 Brad Lukowich
112 Mark McArthur
116 Albert O'Connell
142 Jason Stewart
194 Mike Loach
203 Peter Hogardh
220 Gord Walsh
246 Kirk Dewaele
272 Dick Tarnstrom

1993
Pick
23 Todd Bertuzzi
40 Bryan McCabe
66 Vladim Chebaturkin
92 Warren Luhning
118 Tommy Salo
144 Peter Leboutillier
170 Darren Van Impe
196 Rod Hinks
222 Daniel Johansson
248 Stephane Larocque
274 Carl Charland

1992
Pick
5 Darius Kasparaitis
56 Jarrett Deuling
104 Tomas Klimt
105 Ryan Duthie
128 Derek Armstrong
152 Vladimir Grachev
159 Steve O'Rourke
176 Jason Widmer
200 Daniel Paradis
224 David Wainwright
248 Andrei Vasiljev

1991
Pick
4 Scott Lachance
26 Zigmund Palffy
48 Jamie McLennan
70 Milan Hnilicka
92 Steve Junker
114 Robert Valicevic
136 Andreas Johansson
158 Todd Sparks
180 John Johnson
202 Robert Canavan
224 Marcus Thuresson
246 Marty Schriner

1990
Pick
6 Scott Scissons
27 Chris Taylor
48 Dan Plante
90 Chris Marinucci
111 Joni Lehto
132 Michael Guilbert
153 Sylvain Fleury
174 John Joyce
195 Richard Enga
216 Martin Lacroix
237 Andy Shirr

1989
Pick
2 Dave Chyzowski
23 Travis Green
44 Jason Zent
65 Brent Grieve
86 Jace Reed
90 Steve Young
99 Kevin O'Sullivan
128 Jon Larson
133 Brett Harkins
149 Phil Huber
170 Matthew Robbins
191 Vladimir Malakhov
212 Kelly Ens
233 Iain Fraser

1988
Pick
16 Kevin Cheveldayoff
29 Wayne Doucet
37 Sean LeBrun
58 Danny Lorenz
79 Andre Brassard
100 Paul Rutherford
111 Pavel Gross
121 Jason Rathbone
142 Yves Gaucher
163 Marty McInnis
184 Jeff Blumer
205 Jeff Kampersal
226 Phillip Neururer
247 Joe Capprini

1987
Pick
13 Dean Chynoweth
34 Jeff Hackett
55 Dean Ewen
76 George Maneluk
97 Petr Vlk
118 Rob DiMaio
139 Knut Walbye
160 Jeff Saterdalen
181 Shawn Howard
202 John Herlihy
223 Michael Erickson
244 Will Averill

1986
Pick
17 Tom Fitzgerald
38 Dennis Vaske
59 Bill Berg
80 Shawn Byram
101 Dean Sexsmith
104 Todd McLellan
122 Tony Schmalzbauer
138 Will Anderson
143 Richard Pilon
164 Peter Harris
185 Jeff Jablonski
206 Kerry Clark
227 Dan Beaudette
248 Paul Thompson

1985
Pick
6 Brad Dalgarno
13 Derek King
34 Brad Lauer
55 Jeff Finley
76 Kevin Herom
89 Tommy Hedlund
97 Jeff Sveen
118 Rod Dallman
139 Kurt Lackten
160 Hank Lammens
181 Rich Wiest
202 Real Arsenault
223 Mike Volpe
244 Tony Grenier

1984
Pick
20 Duncan MacPherson
41 Bruce Melanson
62 Jeff Norton
70 Doug Wieck
83 Ari Haanpaa
104 Mike Murray
125 Jim Wilharm
146 Kelly Murphy
167 Franco Desantis
187 Tom Warden
208 David Volek
228 Russ Becker
249 Allister Brown

1983
Pick
3 Pat LaFontaine
16 Gerald Diduck
37 Garnet McKechney
57 Mike Neill
65 Mikko Maklla
84 Bob Caulfield
97 Ron Viglasi
117 Darin Illikainen
·137 Jim Sprenger
157 Dale Henry
177 Kevin Vescio
197 Dave Shellington
217 John Bjorkman
237 Peter McGeough

1982
Pick
21 Patrick Flatley
42 Vern Smith
63 Garry Lacey
84 Alan Kerr
105 Rene Breton
126 Roger Kortko
147 John Tiano
168 Todd Okerlund
189 Gord Paddock
210 Eric Faust
231 Pat Goff
252 Jim Koudys

Club Directory

**Nassau Veterans'
Memorial Coliseum**
Uniondale, NY 11553
Phone **516/794-4100**
GM FAX 516/542-9350
FAX 516/542-9348
Capacity: 16,297

Co-Chairmen	Robert Rosenthal, Stephen Walsh
Chief Operating Officer	Ralph Palleschi
Executive Vice-President	Paul Greenwood
Senior Vice-President & CFO	Arthur McCarthy
Consultant	John Krumpe
General Counsel	William Skehan

Hockey Staff

General Manager/Head Coach	Mike Milbury
Vice-President of Hockey Operations	Al Arbour
Assistant General Manager	Darcy Regier
Director of Player Personnel	Gordie Clark
Associate Coach	Rick Bowness
Assistant Coach	Guy Charron
Director of Pro Scouting	Ken Morrow
Video Coordinator	Bob Smith

Communications Staff

Vice-President/Communications	Patrick Calabria
Director of Amateur Hockey Development/ Alumni Relations	Bob Nystrom
25th Anniversary Ambassadors	Clark Gillies, John Tonelli, Ed Westfall
Director of Game Events	Tim Beach
Director of Media and Public Relations	Ginger Killian Serby
Director of Publications/Public Relations Associate	Chris Botta
Director of Special Events	Maureen Brady
Assistant Director of Media Relations	Eric Mirlis
Public Relations Assistant	Tom Bigliani

Sales and Administration

Vice-President/Media Sales	Arthur Adler
Controller	Ralph Sellitti
Assistant Controller	Ginna Cotton
Director of Administration	Joseph Dreyer
Director of Corporate Sales	Bill Kain
Director of Executive Suites	Tracy F. Matthews
Director of Marketing and Ticket Sales	Brian Edwards
Director of Merchandising	Mike Walsh
Director of Suite Operations	Sam Buonogura
Marketing Manager	Jennifer Garone
Ticket Manager	Vincent DiOrio
Account Representatives	Tom Engel, Richard Gaudet, Scott Lindquist, Brian Rabinowitz, Brian Reynolds, Eric Schiebe, Andy Smith
Accountants	Christine Bowler, Sue Meares
Assistant Ticket Manager	Joy Rusciano
Administrative Assistant	Margaret Barrett
Office Manager/Group Administrator	Kathleen Maloney
Receptionists	Colleen Touhey-Ramirez, Jennifer Guadagno

Medical and Training Staff

Athletic Trainer	Rich Campbell
Equipment Manager	Joe McMahon
Assistant Athletic Trainer	Sean Donellan
Assistant Equipment Manager	Eric Miklich
Team Orthopedists	Dr. Elliott Hershman, Dr. Stephen J. Nicholas
Team Internists	Dr. Elliot Pellman, Dr. Clifford Cooper
Team Dentists	Dr. Bruce Michnik, Dr. Jan Sherman

Team Information

Colors	Orange, blue, white, silver, Atlantic green
Television Coverage	SportsChannel
Announcers	Howie Rose, Ed Westfall, Stan Fischler
Radio	WLIR – 92.7 & 98.5
Announcers	Barry Landers, Bob Nystrom

General Managers' History

William A. Torrey, 1972-73 to 1991-92; Don Maloney, 1992-93 to 1994-95; Don Maloney and Mike Milbury, 1995-96; Mike Milbury, 1996-97.

Coaching History

Phil Goyette and Earl Ingarfield, 1972-73; Al Arbour, 1973-74 to 1985-86; Terry Simpson, 1986-87 to 1987-88; Terry Simpson and Al Arbour, 1988-89; Al Arbour, 1989-90 to 1993-94; Lorne Henning, 1994-95; Mike Milbury, 1995-96 to date.

Captains' History

Ed Westfall, 1972-73 to 1975-76; Ed Westfall, Clark Gillies, 1976-77; Clark Gillies, 1977-78, 1978-79; Denis Potvin, 1979-80 to 1986-87; Brent Sutter, 1987-88 to 1990-91; Brent Sutter and Patrick Flatley, 1991-92; Patrick Flatley, 1992-93 to 1995-96.

New York Rangers

1995-96 Results: 41W-27L-14T 96PTS. Second, Atlantic Division

A mainstay of the Rangers' offensive attack and the undisputed leader along the blueline, Brian Leetch had another tremendous season in 1995-96, leading the Rangers with 44 power-play points while earning his third Second All-Star Team berth.

Schedule

Oct.	Sat.	5	at Boston		Jan.	Thur.	2	NY Islanders
	Sun.	6	Florida			Sat.	4	Ottawa
	Tues.	8	at Florida			Mon.	6	Colorado
	Thur.	10	Dallas			Wed.	8	Tampa Bay
	Sat.	12	at Montreal			Thur.	9	at Washington
	Mon.	14	Calgary			Sun.	12	New Jersey
	Wed.	16	Pittsburgh			Mon.	13	NY Islanders
	Fri.	18	St. Louis			Tues.	21	Edmonton
	Sun.	20	at Tampa Bay			Wed.	22	at Washington
	Wed.	23	Washington			Sat.	25	at Pittsburgh*
	Fri.	25	at Florida			Mon.	27	Chicago
	Sun.	27	Buffalo		Feb.	Sat.	1	at Philadelphia*
	Tues.	29	Florida			Sun.	2	Boston
	Wed.	30	at New Jersey			Wed.	5	Hartford
Nov.	Sat.	2	at Boston			Sat.	8	at NY Islanders*
	Mon.	4	Tampa Bay			Sun.	9	at Florida
	Wed.	6	at NY Islanders			Thur.	13	at St. Louis
	Sat.	9	at Washington			Sat.	15	at Chicago*
	Mon.	11	Vancouver			Mon.	17	New Jersey*
	Wed.	13	Philadelphia			Wed.	19	at New Jersey
	Sat.	16	at Pittsburgh			Fri.	21	at Hartford
	Mon.	18	at Calgary			Sun.	23	at Philadelphia
	Thur.	21	at Edmonton		Mar.	Sat.	1	at Detroit*
	Sat.	23	at Vancouver			Mon.	3	San Jose
	Tues.	26	at Phoenix			Thur.	6	at Los Angeles
	Wed.	27	at Colorado			Fri.	7	at Anaheim
Dec.	Sun.	1	Montreal			Sun.	9	at San Jose*
	Wed.	4	Philadelphia			Wed.	12	Washington
	Fri.	6	Toronto			Fri.	14	at Ottawa
	Sat.	7	at Toronto			Mon.	17	Ottawa
	Mon.	9	Phoenix			Wed.	19	Montreal
	Wed.	11	NY Islanders			Fri.	21	Detroit
	Fri.	13	at Buffalo			Mon.	24	Pittsburgh
	Mon.	16	Hartford			Thur.	27	at New Jersey
	Wed.	18	Los Angeles			Sat.	29	at Hartford*
	Sat.	21	at Montreal		Apr.	Tues.	1	Buffalo
	Sun.	22	Florida			Thur.	3	Boston
	Thur.	26	at Ottawa			Fri.	4	at Buffalo
	Fri.	27	Anaheim			Mon.	7	Philadelphia
	Mon.	30	at Dallas			Thur.	10	at Philadelphia
	Tues.	31	at Tampa Bay			Fri.	11	Tampa Bay

* Denotes afternoon game.

Franchise date: May 15, 1926

ATLANTIC DIVISION

71st NHL Season

Year-by-Year Record

Season	GP	Home W	L	T	Road W	L	T	Overall W	L	T	GF	GA	Pts.	Finished		Playoff Result
1995-96	82	22	10	9	19	17	5	41	27	14	272	237	96	2nd,	Atlantic Div.	Lost Conf. Semi-Final
1994-95	48	11	10	3	11	13	0	22	23	3	139	134	47	4th,	Atlantic Div.	Lost Conf. Semi-Final
1993-94	**84**	**28**	**8**	**6**	**24**	**16**	**2**	**52**	**24**	**8**	**299**	**231**	**112**	**1st,**	**Atlantic Div.**	**Won Stanley Cup**
1992-93	84	20	17	5	14	22	6	34	39	11	304	308	79	6th,	Patrick Div.	Out of Playoffs
1991-92	80	28	8	4	22	17	1	50	25	5	321	246	105	1st,	Patrick Div.	Lost Div. Final
1990-91	80	22	11	7	14	20	6	36	31	13	297	265	85	2nd,	Patrick Div.	Lost Div. Semi-Final
1989-90	80	20	11	9	16	20	4	36	31	13	279	267	85	1st,	Patrick Div.	Lost Div. Final
1988-89	80	21	17	2	16	18	6	37	35	8	310	307	82	3rd,	Patrick Div.	Lost Div. Semi-Final
1987-88	80	22	13	5	14	21	5	36	34	10	300	283	82	5th,	Patrick Div.	Out of Playoffs
1986-87	80	18	18	4	16	20	4	34	38	8	307	323	76	4th,	Patrick Div.	Lost Div. Semi-Final
1985-86	80	20	18	2	16	20	4	36	38	6	280	276	78	4th,	Patick Div.	Lost Conf. Championship
1984-85	80	16	18	6	10	26	4	26	44	10	295	345	62	4th,	Patrick Div.	Lost Div. Semi-Final
1983-84	80	27	12	1	15	17	8	42	29	9	314	304	93	4th,	Patrick Div.	Lost Div. Semi-Final
1982-83	80	24	13	3	11	22	7	35	35	10	306	287	80	4th,	Patrick Div.	Lost Div. Final
1981-82	80	19	15	6	20	12	8	39	27	14	316	306	92	2nd,	Patrick Div.	Lost Div. Final
1980-81	80	17	13	10	13	23	4	30	36	14	312	317	74	4th,	Patrick Div.	Lost Semi-Final
1979-80	80	22	10	8	16	22	2	38	32	10	308	284	86	3rd,	Patrick Div.	Lost Quarter-Final
1978-79	80	19	13	8	21	16	3	40	29	11	316	292	91	3rd,	Patrick Div.	Lost Final
1977-78	80	18	15	7	12	22	6	30	37	13	279	280	73	4th,	Patrick Div.	Lost Prelim. Round
1976-77	80	17	18	5	12	19	9	29	37	14	272	310	72	4th,	Patrick Div.	Out of Playoffs
1975-76	80	16	16	8	13	26	1	29	42	9	262	333	67	4th,	Patrick Div.	Out of Playoffs
1974-75	80	21	11	8	16	18	6	37	29	14	319	276	88	2nd,	Patrick Div.	Lost Prelim. Round
1973-74	78	26	7	6	14	17	8	40	24	14	300	251	94	3rd,	East Div.	Lost Semi-Final
1972-73	78	26	8	5	21	15	3	47	23	8	297	208	102	3rd,	East Div.	Lost Semi-Final
1971-72	78	26	6	7	22	11	6	48	17	13	317	192	109	2nd,	East Div.	Lost Final
1970-71	78	30	2	7	19	16	4	49	18	11	259	177	109	2nd,	East Div.	Lost Semi-Final
1969-70	76	22	8	8	16	14	8	38	22	16	246	189	92	4th,	East Div.	Lost Quarter-Final
1968-69	76	27	7	4	14	19	5	41	26	9	231	196	91	3rd,	East Div.	Lost Quarter-Final
1967-68	74	22	8	7	17	15	5	39	23	12	226	183	90	2nd,	East Div.	Lost Quarter-Final
1966-67	70	18	12	5	12	16	7	30	28	12	188	189	72	4th,		Lost Semi-Final
1965-66	70	12	16	7	6	25	4	18	41	11	195	261	47	6th,		Out of Playoffs
1964-65	70	8	19	8	12	19	4	20	38	12	179	246	52	5th,		Out of Playoffs
1963-64	70	14	13	8	8	25	2	22	38	10	186	242	54	5th,		Out of Playoffs
1962-63	70	12	17	6	10	19	6	22	36	12	211	233	56	5th,		Out of Playoffs
1961-62	70	16	11	8	10	21	4	26	32	12	195	207	64	4th,		Lost Semi-Final
1960-61	70	15	15	5	7	23	5	22	38	10	204	248	54	5th,		Out of Playoffs
1959-60	70	10	15	10	7	23	5	17	38	15	187	247	49	6th,		Out of Playoffs
1958-59	70	14	16	5	12	16	7	26	32	12	201	217	64	5th,		Out of Playoffs
1957-58	70	14	15	6	18	10	7	32	25	13	195	188	77	2nd,		Lost Semi-Final
1956-57	70	15	12	8	11	18	6	26	30	14	184	227	66	4th,		Lost Semi-Final
1955-56	70	20	7	8	12	21	2	32	28	10	204	203	74	3rd,		Lost Semi-Final
1954-55	70	10	12	13	7	23	5	17	35	18	150	210	52	5th,		Out of Playoffs
1953-54	70	18	12	5	11	19	5	29	31	10	161	182	68	5th,		Out of Playoffs
1952-53	70	11	14	10	6	23	6	17	37	16	152	211	50	6th,		Out of Playoffs
1951-52	70	16	13	6	7	21	7	23	34	13	192	219	59	5th,		Out of Playoffs
1950-51	70	14	11	10	6	18	11	20	29	21	169	201	61	5th,		Out of Playoffs
1949-50	70	19	12	4	9	19	7	28	31	11	170	189	67	4th,		Lost Final
1948-49	60	13	12	5	5	19	6	18	31	11	133	172	47	6th,		Out of Playoffs
1947-48	60	11	12	7	10	14	6	21	26	13	176	201	55	4th,		Lost Semi-Final
1946-47	60	11	14	5	11	18	1	22	32	6	167	186	50	5th,		Out of Playoffs
1945-46	50	8	12	5	5	16	4	13	28	9	144	191	35	6th,		Out of Playoffs
1944-45	50	7	11	7	4	18	3	11	29	10	154	247	32	6th,		Out of Playoffs
1943-44	50	4	17	4	2	22	1	6	39	5	162	310	17	6th,		Out of Playoffs
1942-43	50	7	13	5	4	18	3	11	31	8	161	253	30	6th,		Out of Playoffs
1941-42	48	15	8	1	14	9	1	29	17	2	177	143	60	1st,		Lost Semi-Final
1940-41	48	13	7	4	8	12	4	21	19	8	143	125	50	4th,		Lost Quarter-Final
1939-40	**48**	**17**	**4**	**3**	**10**	**7**	**7**	**27**	**11**	**10**	**136**	**77**	**64**	**2nd,**		**Won Stanley Cup**
1938-39	48	13	8	3	13	8	3	26	16	6	149	105	58	2nd,		Lost Semi-Final
1937-38	48	15	5	4	12	10	2	27	15	6	149	96	60	2nd,	Amn. Div.	Lost Quarter-Final
1936-37	48	9	7	8	10	13	1	19	20	9	117	106	47	3rd,	Amn. Div.	Lost Final
1935-36	48	11	6	7	8	11	5	19	17	12	91	96	50	4th,	Amn. Div.	Out of Playoffs
1934-35	48	11	8	5	11	12	1	22	20	6	137	139	50	3rd,	Amn. Div.	Lost Semi-Final
1933-34	48	11	7	6	10	12	2	21	19	8	120	113	50	3rd,	Amn. Div.	Lost Quarter-Final
1932-33	**48**	**12**	**7**	**5**	**11**	**10**	**3**	**23**	**17**	**8**	**135**	**107**	**54**	**3rd,**	**Amn. Div.**	**Won Stanley Cup**
1931-32	48	13	7	4	10	10	4	23	17	8	134	112	54	1st,	Amn. Div.	Lost Final
1930-31	44	10	9	3	9	7	6	19	16	9	106	87	47	3rd,	Amn. Div.	Lost Semi-Final
1929-30	44	11	5	6	6	12	4	17	17	10	136	143	44	3rd,	Amn. Div.	Lost Semi-Final
1928-29	44	12	6	4	9	7	6	21	13	10	72	65	52	2nd,	Amn. Div.	Lost Final
1927-28	**44**	**10**	**8**	**4**	**9**	**8**	**5**	**19**	**16**	**9**	**94**	**79**	**47**	**2nd, Amn. Div.**		**Won Stanley Cup**
1926-27	44	13	5	4	12	8	2	25	13	6	95	72	56	1st,	Amn. Div.	Lost Quarter-Final

1996-97 Player Personnel

FORWARDS	HT	WT	S	Place of Birth	Date	1995-96 Club
BERG, Bill	6-1	205	L	St. Catharines, Ont.	10/21/67	Toronto-NY Rangers
BLOUIN, Sylvain	6-2	225	L	Montreal, Que.	5/21/74	Binghamton
BOULTON, Eric	6-0	201	L	Halifax, N.S.	8/17/76	Sarnia
BROSSEAU, David	6-2	189	R	Montreal, Que.	1/16/76	Granby
CHURLA, Shane	6-1	200	R	Fernie, B.C.	6/24/65	Dallas-Los Angeles-NY Rangers
DUBE, Christian	5-11	170	R	Sherbrooke, Que.	4/25/77	Sherbrooke
FERRARO, Chris	5-10	175	R	Port Jefferson, NY	1/24/73	NY Rangers-Binghamton
FERRARO, Peter	5-10	175	R	Port Jefferson, NY	1/24/73	NY Rangers-Binghamton
FLINTON, Eric	6-2	200	L	William Lake, B.C.	2/2/72	Charlotte
GERNANDER, Ken	5-10	180	L	Coleraine, MN	6/30/69	NY Rangers-Binghamton
GONEAU, Daniel	6-1	196	L	Montreal, Que.	1/16/76	Granby
GRAVES, Adam	6-0	205	L	Toronto, Ont.	4/12/68	NY Rangers
GRETZKY, Wayne	6-0	180	L	Brantford, Ont.	1/26/61	Los Angeles-St. Louis
KOVALEV, Alexei	6-0	205	L	Togliatti, USSR	2/24/73	NY Rangers
LANGDON, Darren	6-1	205	L	Deer Lake, Nfld.	1/8/71	NY Rangers-Binghamton
MAUDIE, Bob	5-11	180	L	Cranbrook, B.C.	9/17/76	Kamloops
MESSIER, Mark	6-1	205	L	Edmonton, Alta.	1/18/61	NY Rangers
MOMESSO, Sergio	6-3	215	L	Montreal, Que.	9/4/65	Toronto-NY Rangers
NEMCHINOV, Sergei	6-0	200	L	Moscow, USSR	1/14/64	NY Rangers
NIELSEN, Jeff	6-0	200	R	Grand Rapids, MN	9/20/71	Binghamton
PEPPERALL, Colin	5-10	155	L	Niagara Falls, Ont.	4/28/78	Niagara Falls
ROBITAILLE, Luc	6-1	195	L	Montreal, Que.	2/17/66	NY Rangers
SMELNITSKI, Maxim	6-3	207	L	Chelyabinsk, USSR	3/24/74	Chelyabinsk
STAROSTENKO, Dimitri	6-0	195	L	Minsk, USSR	3/18/73	Binghamton
SUNDSTROM, Niklas	6-0	185	L	Ornskoldsvik, Sweden	6/6/75	NY Rangers
VANDENBUSSCHE, Ryan	5-11	187	R	Simcoe, Ont.	2/28/73	Binghamton
VOROBIEV, Vladimir	5-11	185	R	Cherepovets, USSR	10/2/72	Moscow D'amo
WILLIS, Rick	6-0	190	L	Lynn, MA	1/12/72	Charlotte-Binghamton
DEFENSEMEN						
BEUKEBOOM, Jeff	6-5	230	R	Ajax, Ont.	3/28/65	NY Rangers
BROWN, Jeff	6-1	217	R	Mississauga, Ont.	4/24/78	Sarnia
CAIRNS, Eric	6-5	225	L	Oakville, Ont.	6/27/74	Binghamton-Charlotte
CAMPBELL, Ed	6-2	212	L	Worcester, MA	11/26/74	Lowell
DRIVER, Bruce	6-0	185	L	Toronto, Ont.	4/29/62	NY Rangers
FIORENTINO, Peter	6-1	205	R	Niagara Falls, Ont.	12/22/68	Las Vegas-Indianapolis
GALANOV, Maxim	6-1	175	L	Krasnoyarsk, USSR	3/13/74	Binghamton
KARPOVTSEV, Alexander	6-1	200	R	Moscow, USSR	4/7/70	NY Rangers
LEETCH, Brian	5-11	190	L	Corpus Christi, TX	3/3/68	NY Rangers
LIDSTER, Doug	6-1	190	R	Kamloops, B.C.	10/18/60	NY Rangers
LOWE, Kevin	6-2	190	L	Lachute, Que.	4/15/59	NY Rangers
MALONE, Scott	6-0	195	L	Boston, MA	1/16/71	Binghamton
MARTIN, Mike	6-2	204	R	Stratford, Ont.	10/27/76	Windsor
MORE, Jayson	6-2	210	R	Souris, Man.	1/12/69	San Jose
REID, Shawn	6-0	200	L	Toronto, Ont.	9/21/70	Binghamton-Charlotte
SAMUELSSON, Ulf	6-1	195	L	Fagersta, Sweden	3/26/64	NY Rangers
SILVERMAN, Andrew	6-3	205	L	Beverly, MA	8/23/72	Binghamton
SMITH, Adam	6-0	190	L	Digby, N.S.	5/24/76	Kelowna
SOROCHAN, Lee	6-1	210	L	Edmonton, Alta.	9/9/75	Binghamton

GOALTENDERS	HT	WT	C	Place of Birth	Date	1995-96 Club
CLOUTIER, Dan	6-1	182	L	Mont-Laurier, Que.	4/22/76	S.S. Marie-Guelph
HEALY, Glenn	5-10	185	L	Pickering, Ont.	8/23/62	NY Rangers
HILLEBRANDT, Jon	5-10	185	L	Cottage Grove, WI	12/18/71	Binghamton
RAM, Jamie	5-11	175	L	Scarborough, Ont.	1/18/71	NY Rangers-Binghamton
RICHTER, Mike	5-11	185	L	Abington, PA	9/22/66	NY Rangers
SHEPARD, Ken	5-10	192	L	Toronto, Ont.	1/20/74	Binghamton-Charlotte

General Manager

SMITH, NEIL

General Manager, New York Rangers. Born in Toronto, Ont., January 9, 1954.

Through his first seven years at the helm of the Rangers, Neil Smith has enjoyed great success. The club has posted an overall record of 271-200-67, ranking fifth among NHL teams since 1989-90. New York has captured three divisional titles, two Presidents' Trophies and one Stanley Cup championship.

In 1993-94, the Rangers captured the fourth Stanley Cup in franchise history, defeating Vancouver four games to three. The championship was the culmination of a season in which New York set a club record with 52 wins and 112 points. The Rangers captured their second Presidents' Trophy in three years and became the first team since the Presidents' Trophy was established to win it, along with the Conference Championship and Stanley Cup in the same year. Following the season, Neil was awarded with *The Hockey News* executive of the year award.

In his first three seasons as general manager after joining the Rangers on July 17, 1989, New York enjoyed the best three consecutive finishes in club history.

On June 19, 1992, he was promoted to the position of president and general manager, becoming the ninth president in Rangers' history and the first president to also hold the title of general manager.

A native of Toronto, Ontario, Smith played junior hockey at Brockville, Ontario, before entering Western Michigan University where he became an All-American defenseman as a freshman and team captain in his second year.

After being selected by the New York Islanders in the NHL Amateur Draft and playing two seasons in the International Hockey League, Neil joined the Islanders scouting department during the '80-81 season. Following two seasons in that capacity, he joined the Detroit Red Wings in 1982 as director of professional scouting and soon after became director of their farm system.

Smith was then named director of scouting, and general manager/governor of the Adirondack Red Wings of the AHL, where he won two Calder Cup championships.

1995-96 Scoring

* – rookie

Regular Season

Pos	#	Player	Team	GP	G	A	Pts	+/–	PIM	PP	SH	GW	GT	S	%
C	11	Mark Messier	NYR	74	47	52	99	29	122	14	1	5	1	241	19.5
D	2	Brian Leetch	NYR	82	15	70	85	12	30	7	0	3	0	276	5.4
R	16	Pat Verbeek	NYR	69	41	41	82	29	129	17	0	6	2	252	16.3
L	20	Luc Robitaille	NYR	77	23	46	69	13	80	11	0	4	2	223	10.3
R	27	Alexei Kovalev	NYR	81	24	34	58	5	98	8	1	7	0	206	11.7
L	9	Adam Graves	NYR	82	22	36	58	18	100	9	1	2	0	266	8.3
L	17	Jari Kurri	L.A.	57	17	23	40	–12	37	5	1	0	2	131	13.0
			NYR	14	1	4	5	–4	2	0	0	0	0	27	3.7
			TOTAL	71	18	27	45	–16	39	5	1	0	2	158	11.4
D	33	Bruce Driver	NYR	66	3	34	37	2	42	3	0	0	1	140	2.1
D	55	Marty McSorley	L.A.	59	10	21	31	–14	148	1	1	1	0	118	8.5
			NYR	9	0	2	2	–6	21	0	0	0	0	12	0.0
			TOTAL	68	10	23	33	–20	169	1	1	1	0	130	7.7
C	13	Sergei Nemchinov	NYR	78	17	15	32	9	38	0	0	2	0	118	14.4
L	32	Sergio Momesso	TOR	54	7	8	15	–11	112	4	0	1	2	91	7.7
			NYR	19	4	4	8	–2	30	2	0	0	0	35	11.4
			TOTAL	73	11	12	23	–13	142	6	0	1	2	126	8.7
L	24 *	Niklas Sundstrom	NYR	82	9	12	21	2	14	1	1	2	0	90	10.0
D	5	Ulf Samuelsson	NYR	74	1	18	19	9	122	0	0	0	0	66	1.5
D	25	A. Karpovtsev	NYR	40	2	16	18	12	26	1	0	1	0	71	2.8
D	6	Doug Lidster	NYR	59	5	9	14	11	50	0	0	0	0	73	6.8
D	23	Jeff Beukeboom	NYR	82	3	11	14	19	220	0	0	1	1	65	4.6
L	15 *	Darren Langdon	NYR	64	7	4	11	2	175	0	0	1	1	29	24.1
R	22	Shane Churla	DAL	34	3	4	7	4	168	0	0	0	0	18	16.7
			L.A.	11	1	2	3	–9	37	0	0	0	0	9	11.1
			NYR	10	0	0	0	–3	26	0	0	0	0	5	0.0
			TOTAL	55	4	6	10	–8	231	0	0	0	0	32	12.5
D	4	Kevin Lowe	NYR	53	1	5	6	20	76	0	0	0	0	30	3.3
L	18	Bill Berg	TOR	23	1	1	2	–6	33	0	0	0	0	33	3.0
			NYR	18	2	1	3	0	8	0	1	0	0	27	7.4
			TOTAL	41	3	2	5	–6	41	0	1	0	0	60	5.0
C	12	Ken Gernander	NYR	10	2	3	5	–3	4	2	0	0	0	10	20.0
L	37	Dan Lacroix	NYR	25	2	2	4	–1	30	0	0	0	0	14	14.3
R	14 *	Chris Ferraro	NYR	2	1	0	1	–3	0	1	0	0	0	4	25.0
D	29 *	Barry Richter	NYR	4	0	1	1	2	0	0	0	0	0	3	0.0
C	21 *	Peter Ferraro	NYR	5	0	1	1	–5	0	0	0	0	0	6	0.0
G	35	Mike Richter	NYR	41	0	1	1	0	4	0	0	0	0	0	0.0
G	30	Glenn Healy	NYR	44	0	1	1	0	8	0	0	0	0	0	0.0
G	34 *	Jamie Ram	NYR	1	0	0	0	0	0	0	0	0	0	0	0.0

Goaltending

No.	Goaltender	GPI	Mins	Avg	W	L	T	EN	SO	GA	SA	S%
34	* Jamie Ram	1	27	.00	0	0	0	0	0	0	9	1.000
35	Mike Richter	41	2396	2.68	24	13	3	3	3	107	1221	.912
30	Glenn Healy	44	2564	2.90	17	14	11	3	2	124	1237	.900
	Totals	**82**	**4995**	**2.85**	**41**	**27**	**14**	**6**	**5**	**237**	**2473**	**.904**

Playoffs

Pos	#	Player	Team	GP	G	A	Pts	+/–	PIM	PP	SH	GW	OT	S	%
C	11	Mark Messier	NYR	11	4	7	11	–10	16	2	0	1	0	41	9.8
R	16	Pat Verbeek	NYR	11	3	6	9	–8	12	1	0	0	0	38	7.9
L	9	Adam Graves	NYR	10	7	1	8	–9	4	6	0	2	0	43	16.3
L	17	Jari Kurri	NYR	11	3	5	8	–2	2	0	1	1	0	31	9.7
L	24 *	Niklas Sundstrom	NYR	11	4	3	7	1	4	1	0	0	0	27	14.8
R	27	Alexei Kovalev	NYR	11	3	4	7	0	14	0	0	1	0	31	9.7
D	2	Brian Leetch	NYR	11	1	6	7	–11	4	1	0	0	0	34	2.9
D	33	Bruce Driver	NYR	11	0	7	7	1	4	0	0	0	0	23	0.0
L	20	Luc Robitaille	NYR	11	1	5	6	1	8	0	0	0	0	36	2.8
D	5	Ulf Samuelsson	NYR	11	1	5	6	–1	16	0	0	0	0	6	16.7
L	32	Sergio Momesso	NYR	11	3	1	4	0	14	0	0	0	0	12	25.0
R	22	Shane Churla	NYR	11	2	2	4	–2	14	0	0	0	0	10	20.0
D	4	Kevin Lowe	NYR	10	0	4	4	5	4	0	0	0	0	7	0.0
D	23	Jeff Beukeboom	NYR	11	0	3	3	–1	6	0	0	0	0	12	0.0
D	6	Doug Lidster	NYR	7	1	0	1	–4	6	1	0	0	0	5	20.0
L	18	Bill Berg	NYR	10	1	0	1	–1	0	0	0	0	0	8	12.5
D	25	A. Karpovtsev	NYR	6	0	1	1	–2	4	0	0	0	0	5	0.0
C	13	Sergei Nemchinov	NYR	6	0	1	1	2	2	0	0	0	0	5	0.0
L	15 *	Darren Langdon	NYR	2	0	0	0	0	0	0	0	0	0	0	0.0
D	55	Marty McSorley	NYR	4	0	0	0	–1	0	0	0	0	0	3	0.0
C	12	Ken Gernander	NYR	6	0	0	0	0	0	0	0	0	0	1	0.0
G	35	Mike Richter	NYR	11	0	0	0	0	0	0	0	0	0	0	0.0

Goaltending

No.	Goaltender	GPI	Mins	Avg	W	L	EN	SO	GA	SA	S%
35	Mike Richter	11	661	3.27	5	6	2	0	36	308	.883
	Totals	**11**	**665**	**3.43**	**5**	**6**	**2**	**0**	**38**	**310**	**.877**

Captains' History

Bill Cook, 1926-27 to 1936-37; Art Coulter, 1937-38 to 1941-42; Ott Heller, 1942-43 to 1944-45; Neil Colville 1945-46 to 1948-49; Buddy O'Connor, 1949-50; Frank Eddolls, 1950-51; Frank Eddolls and Allan Stanley, 1951-52; Allan Stanley, 1952-53; Allan Stanley and Don Raleigh, 1953-54; Don Raleigh, 1954-55; Harry Howell, 1955-56, 1956-57; George Sullivan, 1957-58 to 1960-61; Andy Bathgate, 1961-62, 1962-63; Andy Bathgate and Camille Henry, 1963-64; Camille Henry and Bob Nevin, 1964-65; Bob Nevin 1965-66 to 1970-71; Vic Hadfield, 1971-72 to 1973-74; Brad Park, 1974-75; Brad Park and Phil Esposito, 1975-76; Phil Esposito, 1976-77, 1977-78; Dave Maloney, 1978-79, 1979-80; Dave Maloney, Walt Tkaczuk and Barry Beck, 1980-81; Barry Beck, 1981-82 to 1985-86; Ron Greschner, 1986-87; Ron Greschner and Kelly Kisio, 1987-88; Kelly Kisio, 1988-89 to 1990-91; Mark Messier, 1991-92 to date.

Club Records

Team

(Figures in brackets for season records are games played; records for fewest points, wins, ties, losses, goals, goals against are for 70 or more games)

Most Points	112	1993-94 (84)
Most Wins	52	1993-94 (84)
Most Ties	21	1950-51 (70)
Most Losses	44	1984-85 (80)
Most Goals	371	1991-92 (80)
Most Goals Against	345	1984-85 (80)
Fewest Points	47	1965-66 (70)
Fewest Wins	17	1952-53, 1954-55, 1959-60 (70)
Fewest Ties	5	1991-92 (80)
Fewest Losses	17	1971-72 (78)
Fewest Goals	150	1954-55 (70)
Fewest Goals Against	177	1970-71 (78)

Longest Winning Streak

Overall	10	Dec. 19/39-Jan. 13/40, Jan. 19-Feb. 10/73
Home	14	Dec. 19/39-Feb. 25/40
Away	7	Jan. 12-Feb. 12/35, Oct. 28-Nov. 29/78

Longest Undefeated Streak

Overall	19	Nov. 23/39-Jan. 13/40 (14 wins, 5 ties)
Home	26	Mar. 29/70-Feb. 2/71 (19 wins, 7 ties)
Away	11	Nov. 5/39-Jan. 13/40 (6 wins, 5 ties)

Longest Losing Streak

Overall	11	Oct. 30-Nov. 27/43
Home	7	Oct. 20-Nov. 14/76, Mar. 24-Apr. 14/93
Away	10	Oct. 30-Dec. 23/43

Longest Winless Streak

Overall	21	Jan. 23-Mar. 19/44 (17 losses, 4 ties)
Home	10	Jan. 30-Mar. 19/44 (7 losses, 3 ties)
Away	16	Oct. 9-Dec. 20/52 (12 losses, 4 ties)

Most Shutouts, Season	13	1928-29 (44)
Most PIM, Season	2,018	1989-90 (80)
Most Goals, Game	12	Nov. 21/71 (Cal. 1 at NYR 12)

Individual

Most Seasons	17	Harry Howell
Most Games	1,160	Harry Howell
Most Goals, Career	406	Rod Gilbert
Most Assists, Career	615	Rod Gilbert
Most Points, Career	1,021	Rod Gilbert (406G, 615A)
Most PIM, Career	1,226	Ron Greschner
Most Shutouts, Career	49	Ed Giacomin

Longest Consecutive

Games Streak	560	Andy Hebenton (Oct. 7/55-Mar. 24/63)
Most Goals, Season	52	Adam Graves (1993-94)
Most Assists, Season	80	Brian Leetch (1991-92)
Most Points, Season	109	Jean Ratelle (1971-72; 46G, 63A)
Most PIM, Season	305	Troy Mallette (1989-90)

Most Points, Defenseman

Season	102	Brian Leetch (1991-92; 22G, 80A)

Most Points, Center,

Season	109	Jean Ratelle (1971-72; 46G, 63A)

Most Points, Right Wing,

Season	97	Rod Gilbert (1971-72; 43G, 54A), Rod Gilbert (1974-75; 36G, 61A)

Most Points, Left Wing,

Season	106	Vic Hadfield (1971-72; 50G, 56A)

Most Points, Rookie,

Season	76	Mark Pavelich (1981-82; 33G, 43A)
Most Shutouts, Season	13	John Ross Roach (1928-29)
Most Goals, Game	5	Don Murdoch (Oct. 12/76), Mark Pavelich (Feb. 23/83)
Most Assists, Game	5	Walt Tkaczuk (Feb. 12/72), Rod Gilbert (Mar. 2/75, Mar. 30/75, Oct. 8/76), Don Maloney (Jan. 3/87)
Most Points, Game	7	Steve Vickers (Feb. 18/76; 3G, 4A)

Retired Numbers

1	Eddie Giacomin	1965-1976
7	Rod Gilbert	1960-1978

General Managers' History

Lester Patrick, 1927-28 to 1945-46; Frank Boucher, 1946-47 to 1954-55; "Muzz" Patrick, 1955-56 to 1963-64; Emile Francis, 1964-65 to 1974-75; Emile Francis and John Ferguson, 1975-76; John Ferguson, 1976-77 to 1977-78; John Ferguson and Fred Shero, 1978-79; Fred Shero, 1979-80; Fred Shero and Craig Patrick, 1980-81; Craig Patrick, 1981-82 to 1985-86; Phil Esposito, 1986-87 to 1988-89; Neil Smith, 1989-90 to date.

All-time Record vs. Other Clubs

Regular Season

	At Home						PTS	On Road						PTS	Total						PTS
	GP	W	L	T	GF	GA		GP	W	L	T	GF	GA		GP	W	L	T	GF	GA	
Anaheim	2	1	1	0	7	5	2	2	2	0	0	6	10	0	4	3	1	0	13	15	2
Boston	286	124	108	54	868	802	302	282	91	151	40	791	1023	222	568	215	259	94	1659	1825	524
Buffalo	50	23	15	12	176	138	58	52	15	31	6	173	232	36	102	38	46	18	349	370	94
Calgary	45	20	20	5	160	162	45	44	10	25	9	135	199	29	89	30	45	14	295	361	74
Chicago	280	116	109	55	832	795	287	279	112	125	42	778	851	266	559	228	234	97	1610	1646	553
Colorado	26	17	6	3	112	74	37	28	10	15	3	108	121	23	54	27	21	6	220	195	60
Dallas	55	34	11	10	197	150	78	54	29	16	9	206	163	67	109	63	27	19	403	313	145
Detroit	277	132	87	58	854	711	322	279	75	159	45	689	980	195	556	207	246	103	1543	1691	517
Edmonton	23	6	13	4	88	94	16	23	2	13	2	85	89	25	46	18	23	5	173	183	41
Florida	7	3	2	2	18	16	8	7	4	3	0	22	15	8	14	7	5	2	40	31	16
Hartford	28	16	9	3	121	85	35	27	10	14	3	95	99	23	55	26	23	6	216	184	58
Los Angeles	52	32	15	5	210	151	69	53	23	21	9	190	179	55	105	55	36	14	400	330	124
Montreal	274	111	109	54	790	799	276	274	55	184	35	630	1080	145	548	166	293	89	1428	1879	421
New Jersey	64	38	16	10	277	198	86	64	31	29	4	236	219	66	128	69	45	14	513	417	152
NY Islanders	75	45	22	8	299	227	98	76	21	49	6	236	318	48	151	66	71	14	535	545	146
Ottawa	7	6	1	0	33	18	12	7	7	0	0	27	14	14	14	13	1	0	60	32	26
Philadelphia	89	41	27	21	300	258	103	88	32	43	13	254	300	77	177	73	70	34	554	558	180
Pittsburgh	81	42	32	7	333	288	91	81	37	33	11	304	295	85	162	79	65	18	637	583	176
St. Louis	54	42	6	6	231	123	90	56	26	21	9	184	164	61	110	68	27	15	415	287	151
San Jose	4	3	0	1	22	11	7	5	5	0	0	27	12	10	9	8	0	1	49	23	17
Tampa Bay	9	5	3	1	36	36	11	8	5	2	1	29	25	11	17	10	5	2	65	61	22
Toronto	269	112	101	56	824	787	280	268	79	151	38	694	920	196	537	191	252	94	1518	1707	476
Vancouver	48	36	7	5	220	119	77	46	32	11	3	190	146	67	94	68	18	8	410	265	144
Washington	65	33	26	6	263	234	72	66	25	32	9	225	253	59	131	58	58	15	488	487	131
Winnipeg	23	13	8	2	110	93	28	24	12	10	2	90	90	26	47	25	18	4	200	183	54
Defunct Clubs	139	87	30	22	460	290	196	139	82	34	23	441	291	187	278	169	64	45	901	581	383
Totals	**2332**	**1138**	**784**	**410**	**7849**	**6664**	**2686**	**2332**	**840**	**1171**	**321**	**6845**	**8088**	**2001**	**4664**	**1978**	**1955**	**731**	**14694**	**14752**	**4687**

Playoffs

	Series	W	L	GP	W	L	T	GF	GA	Last Mtg.	Round	Result
Boston	9	3	6	42	18	22	2	104	114	1973	QF	W 4-1
Buffalo	1	0	1	3	1	2	0	6	11	1978	PR	L 1-2
Calgary	1	1	0	4	3	1	0	14	8	1980	PR	W 3-1
Chicago	5	1	4	24	10	14	0	54	66	1973	SF	L 1-4
Colorado	1	1	0	6	4	2	0	25	19	1995	CQF	W 4-2
Detroit	5	1	4	23	10	13	0	49	57	1950	F	L 3-4
Los Angeles	2	2	0	5	5	1	0	32	14	1981	PR	W 3-1
Montreal	14	7	7	61	25	34	2	158	188	1996	CQF	W 4-2
New Jersey	2	2	0	14	8	6	0	46	41	1994	CF	W 4-3
NY Islanders	8	3	5	39	19	20	0	132	129	1994	CQF	W 4-0
Philadelphia	9	4	5	42	19	23	0	140	137	1995	CSF	L 0-4
Pittsburgh	3	0	3	15	3	12	0	45	65	1996	CSF	L 1-4
St. Louis	1	1	0	6	4	2	0	29	22	1981	QF	W 4-2
Toronto	8	5	3	35	19	16	0	86	86	1971	QF	W 4-2
Vancouver	1	1	0	7	4	3	0	21	19	1994	F	W 4-3
Washington	4	2	2	22	11	11	0	71	75	1994	CSF	W 4-1
Defunct	9	6	3	22	11	7	4	43	29			
Totals	**83**	**40**	**43**	**371**	**174**	**189**	**8**	**1055**	**1079**			

Calgary totals include Atlanta, 1972-73 to 1979-80.   Colorado totals include Quebec, 1979-80 to 1994-95. Dallas totals include Minnesota, 1967-68 to 1992-93. New Jersey totals include Kansas City, 1974-75 to 1975-76, and Colorado Rockies, 1976-77 to 1981-82.

Playoff Results 1996-92

Year	Round	Opponent	Result	GF	GA
1996	CSF	Pittsburgh	L 1-4	15	21
	CQF	Montreal	W 4-2	19	17
1995	CSF	Philadelphia	L 0-4	10	18
	CQF	Quebec	W 4-2	25	19
1994	F	Vancouver	W 4-3	21	19
	CF	New Jersey	W 4-3	18	16
	CSF	Washington	W 4-1	20	12
	CQF	NY Islanders	W 4-0	22	3
1992	DF	Pittsburgh	L 2-4	19	24
	DSF	New Jersey	W 4-3	28	25

Abbreviations: Round: F – Final; **CF** – conference final; **CQF** – conference quarter-final; **CSF** – conference semi-final; **DF** – division final; **DSF** – division semi-final; **SF** – semi-final; **QF** – quarter-final; **PR** – preliminary round.

Entry Draft
Selections 1996-82

1996
Pick
22 Jeff Brown
48 Daniel Goneau
76 Dmitri Subbotin
131 Colin Pepperall
158 Ola Sandberg
185 Jeff Dessner
211 Ryan McKie
237 Ronnie Sundin

1995
Pick
39 Christian Dube
65 Mike Martin
91 Marc Savard
110 Alexei Vasiliev
117 Dale Purinton
143 Peter Slamiar
169 Jeff Heil
195 Ilja Gorohov
221 Bob Maudie

1994
Pick
26 Dan Cloutier
52 Rudolf Vercik
78 Adam Smith
100 Alexander Korobolin
104 Sylvain Blouin
130 Martin Ethier
135 Yuri Litvinov
156 David Brosseau
182 Alexei Lazarenko
208 Craig Anderson
209 Vitali Yeremeyev
234 Eric Boulton
260 Radoslav Kropac
267 Jamie Butt
286 Kim Johnsson

1993
Pick
8 Niklas Sundstrom
34 Lee Sorochan
61 Maxim Galanov
86 Sergei Olimpiyev
112 Gary Roach
138 Dave Trofimenkoff
162 Sergei Kondrashkin
164 Todd Marchant
190 Eddy Campbell
216 Ken Shepard
242 Andrei Kudinov
261 Pavel Komarov
268 Maxim Smelnitsky

1992
Pick
24 Peter Ferraro
48 Mattias Norstrom
72 Eric Cairns
85 Chris Ferraro
120 Dmitri Starostenko
144 David Dal Grande
168 Matt Oates
192 Mickey Elick
216 Dan Brierley
240 Vladimir Vorobjev

1991
Pick
15 Alexei Kovalev
37 Darcy Werenka
96 Corey Machanic
125 Fredrik Jax
128 Barry Young
147 John Rushin
169 Corey Hirsch
191 Viacheslav Uvayev
213 Jamie Ram
235 Vitali Chinakhov
257 Brian Wiseman

1990
Pick
13 Michael Stewart
34 Doug Weight
55 John Vary
69 Jeff Nielsen
76 Rick Willis
85 Sergei Zubov
99 Lubos Rob
118 Jason Weinrich
139 Bryan Lonsinger
160 Todd Hedlund
181 Andrew Silverman
202 Jon Hillebrandt
223 Brett Lievers
244 Sergei Nemchinov

1989
Pick
20 Steven Rice
40 Jason Prosofsky
45 Rob Zamuner
49 Louie DeBrusk
67 Jim Cummins
88 Aaron Miller
118 Joby Messier
139 Greg Leahy
160 Greg Spenrath
181 Mark Bavis
202 Roman Oksyuta
223 Steve Locke
244 Ken MacDermid

1988
Pick
22 Troy Mallette
26 Murray Duval
68 Tony Amonte
99 Martin Bergeron
110 Dennis Vial
131 Mike Rosati
152 Eric Couvrette
173 Shorty Forrest
194 Paul Cain
202 Eric Fenton
215 Peter Fiorentino
236 Keith Slifstien

1987
Pick
10 Jayson More
31 Daniel Lacroix
46 Simon Gagne
69 Michael Sullivan
94 Eric O'Borsky
115 Ludek Cajka
136 Clint Thomas
157 Charles Wiegand
178 Eric Burrill
199 David Porter
205 Brett Barnett
220 Lance Marciano

1986
Pick
9 Brian Leetch
51 Bret Walter
53 Shawn Clouston
72 Mark Janssens
93 Jeff Bloemberg
114 Darren Turcotte
135 Robb Graham
156 Barry Chyzowski
177 Pat Scanlon
198 Joe Ranger
219 Russell Parent
240 Soren True

1985
Pick
7 Ulf Dahlen
28 Mike Richter
49 Sam Lindstahl
70 Pat Janostin
91 Brad Stephan
112 Brian McReynolds
133 Neil Pilon
154 Larry Bernard
175 Stephane Brochu
196 Steve Nemeth
217 Robert Burakowsky
238 Rudy Poeschek

1984
Pick
14 Terry Carkner
35 Raimo Helminen
77 Paul Broten
98 Clark Donatelli
119 Kjell Samuelsson
140 Thomas Hussey
161 Brian Nelson
182 Ville Kentala
188 Heinz Ehlers
202 Kevin Miller
223 Tom Lorentz
243 Scott Brower

1983
Pick
12 Dave Gagner
33 Randy Heath
49 Vesa Salo
53 Gordie Walker
73 Peter Andersson
93 Jim Andonoff
113 Bob Alexander
133 Steve Orth
153 Peter Marcov
173 Paul Jerrard
213 Bryan Walker
233 Ulf Nilsson

1982
Pick
15 Chris Kontos
36 Tomas Sandstrom
57 Corey Millen
78 Chris Jensen
120 Tony Granato
141 Sergei Kapustin
160 Brian Glynn
162 Jan Karlsson
183 Kelly Miller
193 Simo Saarinen
204 Bob Lowes
225 Andy Otto
246 Dwayne Robinson

Coach

CAMPBELL, COLIN
Coach, New York Rangers. Born in London, Ontario, January 28, 1953.

Colin Campbell begins his third season as head coach of the Rangers after being named to the post on August 9, 1994. He was promoted to the position after serving in various capacities in the organization over the previous five years, including assistant coach, associate coach and half of the 1992-93 season as head coach of the Rangers American Hockey League affiliate at Binghamton. Colin made his head coaching debut on January 20 vs. Buffalo and earned his first NHL victory on January 21 vs. Montreal.

Campbell, 43, began his coaching career in 1985-86 with Detroit, following his retirement as a player after the 1984-85 season. He worked a total of five seasons as a Red Wings assistant coach, one season under coach Harry Neale and four seasons under coach Jacques Demers.

The native of London, Ontario, joined the Rangers organization in August of 1990 as an assistant coach to Roger Neilson. He served in that role until January 4, 1993, when he became head coach of the Binghamton Rangers, New York's American Hockey League affiliate. He guided Binghamton to a record of 29-8-5, helping the club set AHL records for wins (57) and points (124) in a single season.

On June 21, 1993, Campbell was promoted to associate coach of New York, under head coach Mike Keenan, helping the Rangers capture the Presidents' Trophy, given to the team with the best regular-season record, and the Stanley Cup.

Before joining the coaching ranks, Campbell played 12 seasons of professional hockey as a defensive defenseman. He played in a total of 636 NHL contests, collecting 25 goals and 103 assists for 128 points along with 1292 penalty minutes.

Coaching Record

Season	Team	Regular Season					Playoffs			
		Games	W	L	T	%	Games	W	L	%
1992-93	Binghamton (AHL)	42	29	8	5	.750	14	7	7	.500
1994-95	**NY Rangers (NHL)**	48	22	23	3	.490	10	4	6	.400
1995-96	**NY Rangers (NHL)**	82	41	27	14	.585	11	5	6	.455
	NHL Totals	130	63	50	17	.550	21	9	12	.429

Club Directory

Madison Square Garden
14th Floor
2 Pennsylvania Plaza
New York, New York 10121
Phone **212/465-6000**
PR FAX 212/465-6494
Capacity: 18,200

Executive Management
President and General Manager . . . . Neil Smith
Executive Vice-President and General Counsel . . . . . Kenneth W. Munoz
Vice-President and Business Manager . . . . Francis P. Murphy
Governor . . . . Charles Dolan
Alternate Governors . . . . Neil Smith, David W. Checketts, Kenneth W. Munoz, Rand Araskog, James Dolan

Hockey Club Personnel
Vice-President of Player Personnel . . . . Larry Pleau
Head Coach . . . . Colin Campbell
Assistant Coach . . . . Dick Todd
Assistant Coach . . . . TBA
Development Coach . . . . George Burnett
Assistant Development Coach . . . . Mike Busniuk
Goaltending Analyst . . . . Sam St. Laurent
Scouting Staff . . . . Darwin Bennett, Ray Clearwater, Herb Hammond, Martin Madden, Kevin McDonald, Christer Rockstrom
Director of Business Administration . . . . John Gentile
Director of Team Operations . . . . Matthew Loughran
Scouting Manager . . . . Bill Short
Executive Administrative Assistant . . . . Barbara Cahill

Medical/Training Staff
Team Physician and Orthopedic Surgeon . . . . Dr. Barton Nisonson
Assistant Team Physician . . . . Dr. Tony Maddalo
Medical Consultants . . . . Dr. Howard Chester, Dr. Frank Gardner, Dr. Ronald Weissman
Team Dentists . . . . Dr. Irwin Miller, Dr. Don Soloman
Sports Physiologist . . . . Howie Wenger
Medical Trainer . . . . Jim Ramsay
Equipment Manager . . . . Mike Folga
Massage Therapist . . . . Bruce Lifrieri
Video Assistant . . . . Jerry Dineen

Public Relations Department
Director of Public Relations . . . . John Rosasco
Assistant Director of Public Relations . . . . Rob Koch
Public Relations Assistant . . . . Frank Buonomo
Administrative Assistant . . . . Ann Marie Gilmartin

Marketing Department
Vice-President of Marketing . . . . Kevin Kennedy
Director of Community Relations . . . . Rod Gilbert
Director of Community and Marketing Operations . . Jim Pfeifer
Promotions Manager . . . . Caroline Calabrese
Manager of Event Presentation . . . . Jeanie Baumgartner

Home Ice . . . . Madison Square Garden
Press Facilities . . . . 33rd Street
Television Facilities . . . . 31st Street
Radio Facilities . . . . 33rd Street
Rink Dimensions . . . . 200 feet by 85 feet
Ends and Sides of Rink . . . . Plexiglass (8 feet)
Club Colors . . . . Blue, Red and White
Practice Facility . . . . Rye, New York
TV Announcers . . . . John Davidson, Sam Rosen, Al Trautwig
Radio Announcers . . . . Marv Albert, Sal Messina, Kenny Albert
Television Outlets . . . . Madison Square Garden Cable Network
Radio Outlet . . . . MSG Radio – WFAN (66 AM), WEVD (1050 AM), WXPS (107 1 FM)

The New York Rangers Hockey Club is part of Madison Square Garden

Coaching History

Lester Patrick, 1926-27 to 1938-39; Frank Boucher, 1939-40 to 1947-48; Frank Boucher and Lynn Patrick, 1948-49; Lynn Patrick, 1949-50; Neil Colville, 1950-51; Neil Colville and Bill Cook, 1951-52; Bill Cook, 1952-53; Frank Boucher and "Muzz" Patrick, 1953-54; "Muzz" Patrick, 1954-55; Phil Watson, 1955-56 to 1958-59; Phil Watson and Alf Pike, 1959-60; Alf Pike, 1960-61; Doug Harvey, 1961-62; "Muzz" Patrick and George Sullivan, 1962-63; George Sullivan, 1963-64 to 1964-65; George Sullivan and Emile Francis, 1965-66; Emile Francis, 1966-67 to 1967-68; Bernie Geoffrion and Emile Francis, 1968-69; Emile Francis, 1969-70 to 1972-73; Larry Popein and Emile Francis, 1973-74; Emile Francis, 1974-75; Ron Stewart and John Ferguson, 1975-76; John Ferguson, 1976-77; Jean-Guy Talbot, 1977-78; Fred Shero, 1978-79 to 1979-80; Fred Shero and Craig Patrick, 1980-81; Herb Brooks, 1981-82 to 1983-84; Herb Brooks and Craig Patrick, 1984-85; Ted Sator, 1985-86; Ted Sator, Tom Webster and Phil Esposito 1986-87; Michel Bergeron, 1987-88; Michel Bergeron and Phil Esposito, 1988-89; Roger Neilson, 1989-90 to 1991-92; Roger Neilson and Ron Smith, 1992-93; Mike Keenan, 1993-94; Colin Campbell, 1994-95 to date.

Ottawa Senators

1995-96 Results: 18W-59L-5T 41PTS. Sixth, Northeast Division

Schedule

Oct.	Sat.	5	at Montreal		
	Wed.	9	NY Islanders		
	Fri.	11	Pittsburgh		
	Sat.	12	at Pittsburgh		
	Fri.	18	at New Jersey		
	Sat.	19	Montreal		
	Wed.	23	at Florida		
	Thur.	24	at Tampa Bay		
	Sat.	26	at Dallas		
	Wed.	30	Los Angeles		
Nov.	Fri.	1	Detroit		
	Sat.	2	at Pittsburgh		
	Thur.	7	Toronto		
	Sat.	9	Boston		
	Sun.	10	at Chicago		
	Wed.	13	Edmonton		
	Fri.	15	Chicago		
	Sat.	16	at NY Islanders		
	Tues.	19	New Jersey		
	Sat.	23	Hartford		
	Wed.	27	at Washington		
	Fri.	29	at Buffalo		
	Sat.	30	Philadelphia		
Dec.	Wed.	4	Pittsburgh		
	Fri.	6	at Edmonton		
	Sat.	7	at Vancouver		
	Tues.	10	at Calgary		
	Fri.	13	Phoenix		
	Sun.	15	Dallas*		
	Thur.	19	Florida		
	Sat.	21	Buffalo		
	Mon.	23	at Montreal		
	Thur.	26	NY Rangers		
	Sat.	28	at Hartford		
	Mon.	30	Anaheim		
Jan.	Wed.	1	Boston*		
	Fri.	3	New Jersey		
	Sat.	4	at NY Rangers		
	Mon.	6	Tampa Bay		
	Thur.	9	Colorado		
	Sat.	11	Pittsburgh		

Mon.	13	at Boston	
Wed.	15	Washington	
Wed.	22	Boston	
Fri.	24	Calgary	
Mon.	27	Tampa Bay	
Wed.	29	at New Jersey	
Thur.	30	St. Louis	
Feb. Sat.	1	at Toronto	
Mon.	3	Vancouver	
Tues.	4	at Boston	
Sat.	8	San Jose	
Sun.	9	at Buffalo	
Tues.	11	at NY Islanders	
Thur.	13	at Philadelphia	
Sat.	15	at Hartford*	
Sun.	16	Hartford*	
Tues.	18	at Washington	
Thur.	20	at St. Louis	
Sun.	23	at Colorado	
Wed.	26	Philadelphia	
Fri.	28	NY Islanders	
Mar. Sat.	1	Buffalo	
Wed.	5	at Anaheim	
Thur.	6	at San Jose	
Sat.	8	at Los Angeles	
Mon.	10	at Phoenix	
Fri.	14	NY Rangers	
Sat.	15	at Montreal	
Mon.	17	at NY Rangers	
Thur.	20	Florida	
Sat.	22	at Boston*	
Tues.	25	at Tampa Bay	
Thur.	27	at Florida	
Sat.	29	Montreal	
Apr. Wed.	2	at Buffalo	
Thur.	3	Washington	
Sat.	5	at Pittsburgh*	
Sun.	6	at Philadelphia*	
Wed.	9	Hartford	
Fri.	11	at Detroit	
Sat.	12	Buffalo	

* Denotes afternoon game.

Franchise date: December 16, 1991

NORTHEAST DIVISION

5th NHL Season

Year-by-Year Record

		Home			Road			Overall						
Season	GP	W	L	T	W	L	T	W	L	T	GF	GA	Pts.	Finished	Playoff Result
1995-96	82	8	28	5	10	31	0	18	59	5	191	291	41	6th, Northeast Div.	Out of Playoffs
1994-95	48	5	16	3	4	18	2	9	34	5	117	174	23	7th, Northeast Div.	Out of Playoffs
1993-94	84	8	30	4	6	31	5	14	61	9	201	397	37	7th, Northeast Div.	Out of Playoffs
1992-93	84	9	29	4	1	41	0	10	70	4	202	395	24	6th, Adams Div.	Out of Playoffs

Despite missing 36 games during the 1995-96 season, Alexei Yashin still finished second in team scoring with 15 goals and 39 points.

1996-97 Player Personnel

FORWARDS	HT	WT	S	Place of Birth	Date	1995-96 Club
ALFREDSSON, Daniel	5-11	187	R	Grums, Sweden	12/11/72	Ottawa
BONK, Radek	6-3	215	L	Krnov, Czech.	1/9/76	Ottawa
CHORSKE, Tom	6-1	205	R	Minneapolis, MN	9/18/66	Ottawa
CROWE, Philip	6-2	220	L	Nanton, Alta.	4/14/70	Philadelphia-Hershey
CUNNEYWORTH, Randy	6-0	180	L	Etobicoke, Ont.	5/10/61	Ottawa
DACKELL, Andreas	5-10	191	R	Gavle, Sweden	12/29/72	Brynas
DAIGLE, Alexandre	6-0	185	L	Montreal, Que.	2/7/75	Ottawa
DEMITRA, Pavol	6-0	189	L	Dubnica, Czech.	11/29/74	Ottawa-P.E.I.
DRURY, Ted	6-0	185	L	Boston, MA	9/13/71	Ottawa
GARDINER, Bruce	6-1	185	R	Barrie, Ont.	2/11/71	P.E.I.
HANNAN, Dave	5-10	180	L	Sudbury, Ont.	11/26/61	Buffalo-Colorado
HOCKING, Justin	6-4	205	R	Stettler, Alta.	1/9/74	P.E.I.
LAMBERT, Denny	5-11	200	L	Wawa, Ont.	1/7/70	Anaheim-Baltimore
MANELUK, Mike	5-11	188	R	Winnipeg, Man.	10/1/73	Baltimore
McEACHERN, Shawn	5-11	195	L	Waltham, MA	2/28/69	Boston
TORMANEN, Antti	6-1	198	L	Espoo, Finland	9/19/70	Ottawa-P.E.I.
VIAL, Dennis	6-2	218	L	Sault Ste. Marie, Ont.	4/10/69	Ottawa
YASHIN, Alexei	6-3	215	R	Sverdlovsk, USSR	11/5/73	CSKA-Ottawa
ZENT, Jason	5-11	180	L	Buffalo, NY	4/15/71	P.E.I.
ZHOLTOK, Sergei	6-0	190	R	Riga, Latvia	12/2/72	Las Vegas

DEFENSEMEN						
BICANEK, Radim	6-1	195	L	Uherske Hradiste, Czech.	1/18/75	P.E.I.
DUCHESNE, Steve	5-11	195	L	Sept-Iles, Que.	6/30/65	Ottawa
HILL, Sean	6-0	195	R	Duluth, MN	2/14/70	Ottawa
LAUKKANEN, Janne	6-0	180	L	Lahti, Finland	3/19/70	Colorado-Cornwall-Ottawa
MUSIL, Frank	6-3	215	L	Pardubice, Czech.	12/17/64	Karlovy Vary-Ottawa
NECKAR, Stanislav	6-1	196	L	Ceske Budejovice, Czech.	12/22/75	Ottawa
PHILLIPS, Chris	6-2	200	L	Calgary, Alta.	3/9/78	Prince Albert
PITLICK, Lance	6-0	180	R	Minneapolis, MN	11/5/67	Ottawa-P.E.I.
REDDEN, Wade	6-2	193	L	Lloydminster, Sask.	6/12/77	Brandon
TRAVERSE, Patrick	6-3	200	L	Montreal, Que.	3/14/74	Ottawa-P.E.I.
VON STEFENELLI, Phil	6-1	200	L	Vancouver, B.C.	4/10/69	Boston-Providence (AHL)

GOALTENDERS	HT	WT	C	Place of Birth	Date	1995-96 Club
BALES, Michael	6-1	180	L	Prince Albert, Sask.	8/6/71	Ottawa-P.E.I.
CASSIVI, Frederic	6-3	193	L	Sorel, Que.	6/12/75	Thunder Bay-P.E.I.
CHARBONNEAU, Patrick	5-11	205	L	St-Jean sur Richelieu, Que.	7/22/75	Thunder Bay-P.E.I.
RHODES, Damian	6-0	190	L	St. Paul, MN	5/28/69	Toronto-Ottawa
TUGNUTT, Ron	5-11	155	L	Scarborough, Ont.	10/22/67	Portland (AHL)

1995-96 Scoring
*– rookie

Regular Season

Pos	#	Player	Team	GP	G	A	Pts	+/–	PIM	PP	SH	GW	GT	S	%
R	11	*Daniel Alfredsson	OTT	82	26	35	61	-18	28	8	2	3	1	212	12.3
C	19	Alexei Yashin	OTT	46	15	24	39	-15	28	8	0	1	0	143	10.5
L	7	Randy Cunneyworth	OTT	81	17	19	36	-31	130	4	0	2	0	142	12.0
D	28	Steve Duchesne	OTT	62	12	24	36	-23	42	7	0	2	0	163	7.4
C	76	Radek Bonk	OTT	76	16	19	35	-5	36	5	0	1	0	161	9.9
L	17	Tom Chorske	OTT	72	15	14	29	-9	21	0	2	1	0	118	12.7
D	4	Sean Hill	OTT	80	7	14	21	-26	94	2	0	2	0	157	4.5
R	78	Pavol Demitra	OTT	31	7	10	17	-3	6	2	0	1	0	66	10.6
C	91	Alexandre Daigle	OTT	50	5	12	17	-30	24	1	0	0	0	77	6.5
C	13	Ted Drury	OTT	42	9	7	16	-19	54	1	0	1	1	80	11.3
R	22	*Antti Tormanen	OTT	50	7	8	15	-15	28	0	0	0	0	68	10.3
R	20	*Trent McCleary	OTT	75	4	10	14	-15	68	0	1	0	0	58	6.9
C	10	Rob Gaudreau	OTT	52	8	5	13	-19	15	1	1	0	0	76	10.5
D	94	Stanislav Neckar	OTT	82	3	9	12	-16	54	1	0	0	0	57	5.3
C	12	David Archibald	OTT	44	6	4	10	-14	18	0	0	1	0	56	10.7
L	49	Michel Picard	OTT	17	2	6	8	-1	10	0	0	1	0	21	9.5
D	2	Lance Pitlick	OTT	28	1	6	7	-8	20	0	0	0	0	13	7.7
L	36	Troy Mallette	OTT	64	2	3	5	-7	171	0	0	0	0	51	3.9
D	21	Dennis Vial	OTT	64	1	4	5	-13	276	0	0	0	0	33	3.0
D	3	Frank Musil	OTT	65	1	3	4	-10	85	0	0	0	0	37	2.7
D	27	*Janne Laukkanen	COL	3	1	0	1	-1	0	1	0	0	0	4	25.0
			OTT	20	0	2	2	0	14	0	0	0	0	31	0.0
			TOTAL	23	1	2	3	-1	14	1	0	0	0	35	2.9
R	25	Pat Elynuik	OTT	29	1	2	3	2	16	0	0	0	0	27	3.7
R	14	Jean-Yves Roy	OTT	4	1	1	2	3	2	0	0	0	0	6	16.7
L	29	Phil Bourque	OTT	13	1	1	2	-3	14	0	0	0	0	12	8.3
D	6	Chris Dahlquist	OTT	24	1	1	2	-7	14	0	0	0	0	13	7.7
R	26	Scott Levins	OTT	27	0	2	2	-3	80	0	0	0	0	6	0.0
G	1	Damian Rhodes	TOR	11	0	0	0	0	0	0	0	0	0	0	0.0
			OTT	36	0	2	2	0	4	0	0	0	0	0	0.0
			TOTAL	47	0	2	2	0	4	0	0	0	0	0	0.0
D	18	*Patrick Traverse	OTT	5	0	0	0	-1	2	0	0	0	0	2	0.0
D	27	Joe Cirella	OTT	6	0	0	0	-3	4	0	0	0	0	3	0.0
D	24	Daniel Laperriere	OTT	6	0	0	0	2	4	0	0	0	0	12	0.0
G	35	*Mike Bales	OTT	20	0	0	0	0	2	0	0	0	0	0	0.0

Goaltending

No.	Goaltender	GPI	Mins	Avg	W	L	T	EN	SO	GA	SA	S%
1	Damian Rhodes	36	2123	2.77	10	22	4	1	2	98	1041	.906
33	Don Beaupre	33	1770	3.73	6	23	0	9	1	110	892	.877
35	*Mike Bales	20	1040	4.15	2	14	1	1	0	72	560	.871
	Totals	**82**	**4953**	**3.53**	**18**	**59**	**5**	**11**	**3**	**291**	**2504**	**.884**

Although he wasn't selected until the sixth round of the 1994 Entry Draft, Daniel Alfredsson led the Ottawa Senators in scoring with 61 points and won the Calder Trophy as the league's top rookie in 1995-96.

General Manager

GAUTHIER, PIERRE
General Manager, Ottawa Senators. Born in Montreal, Que., May 28, 1953.

Pierre Gauthier was appointed the second general manager in Senators history on December 11, 1995.

As the club's general manager, Gauthier quickly improved the team's goaltending by acquiring Damian Rhodes in a three-way deal on January 23, 1996. Rhodes was eventually named the club's 1995-96 Molson Cup winner, having played in 36 of the last 38 games. Defenseman prospect Wade Redden, a two-time gold medal champion with the Canadian National Junior Team was also acquired in that deal.

Prior to joining the Senators, Pierre Gauthier was acting as assistant general manager with the Mighty Ducks of Anaheim. He was a key part of management in starting up the NHL franchise in 1993.

Pierre Gauthier had previously spent 12 years in the scouting department of the Quebec Nordiques. He had joined the Nordiques in 1983 as a scout, working in that capacity for three years before being named assistant director of scouting in 1986. He was promoted to chief scout in 1988, serving at that post until he joined Anaheim.

Pierre Gauthier received a master's degree in sports administration from the University of Minnesota in 1983. He is also a graduate of Syracuse University, where he earned a bachelor's of science degree in physical education.

Pierre is married to Manon Roberge; they have a daughter, Catherine, born January 17, 1992.

Club Records

Team

(Figures in brackets for season records are games played; records for fewest points, wins, ties, losses, goals, goals against are for 70 or more games)

Most Points	41	1995-96 (82)
Most Wins	18	1995-96 (82)
Most Ties	9	1993-94 (84)
Most Losses	70	1992-93 (84)
Most Goals	202	1992-93 (84)
Most Goals Against	397	1993-94 (84)
Fewest Points	24	1992-93 (84)
Fewest Wins	10	1992-93 (84)
Fewest Ties	4	1992-93 (84)
Fewest Losses	59	1995-96 (82)
Fewest Goals	191	1995-96 (82)
Fewest Goals Against	291	1995-96 (82)

Longest Winning Streak

Overall	3	Four times
Home	3	Mar. 23-Apr. 6/94, Mar. 13-17/96
Away	3	Oct. 30-Nov. 5/93, Feb. 10-20/96

Longest Undefeated Streak

Overall	3	Eight times
Home	4	Jan. 28-Feb. 8/93 (3 wins, 1 tie), Mar. 13-22/96 (3 wins, 1 tie)
Away	3	Oct. 30-Nov. 5/93 (3 wins), Feb. 10-20/96 (3 wins)

** NHL records do not include neutral site games

Longest Losing Streak

Overall	14	Mar. 2-Apr. 7/93
Home	*11	Oct. 27-Dec. 8/93
Away	*38	Oct. 10/92-Apr. 3/93**

Longest Winless Streak

Overall	21	Oct. 10-Nov. 23/92 (20 losses, 1 tie)
Home	*17	Oct. 28/95-Jan. 27/96 (15 losses, 2 ties)
Away	*38	Oct. 10/92-Apr. 3/93 (38 losses)

Most Shutouts, Season	3	1995-96 (82)
Most PIM, Season	1,716	1992-93 (84)
Most Goals, Game	7	Four times

Individual

Most Seasons	4	Dave Archibald
Most Games, Career	181	Alexandre Daigle
Most Goals, Career	66	Alexei Yashin
Most Assists, Career	96	Alexei Yashin
Most Points, Career	162	Alexei Yashin (66G, 96A)
Most PIM, Career	575	Dennis Vial
Most Shutouts, Career	2	Don Beaupre, Damian Rhodes

Longest Consecutive

Games Streak	130	Stan Neckar (Jan. 22/95-Apr. 13/96)

Most Goals, Season	30	Alexei Yashin (1993-94)
Most Assists, Season	49	Alexei Yashin (1993-94)
Most Points, Season	79	Alexei Yashin (1993-94; 30G, 49A)
Most PIM, Season	318	Mike Peluso (1992-93)

Most Points, Defenseman

Season	63	Norm Maciver (1992-93; 17G, 46A)

Most Points, Center

Season	79	Alexei Yashin (1993-94; 30G, 49A)

Most Points, Right Wing

Season	61	Daniel Alfredsson (1995-96; 26G, 35A)

Most Points, Left Wing

Season	43	Sylvain Turgeon (1992-93; 25G, 18A)

Most Points, Rookie

Season	79	Alexei Yashin (1993-94; 30G, 49A)

Most Shutouts, Season	2	Damian Rhodes (1995-96)
Most Goals, Game	3	Eleven times
Most Assists, Game	4	Alexei Yashin (Nov. 5/95)
Most Points, Game	6	Dan Quinn (Oct. 15/95; 3G, 3A)

* NHL Record.

General Managers' History

Mel Bridgman, 1992-93; Randy Sexton, 1993-94 to 1994-95; Randy Sexton and Pierre Gauthier, 1995-96; Pierre Gauthier, 1996-97.

Coaching History

Rick Bowness, 1992-93 to 1994-95; Rick Bowness, Dave Allison and Jacques Martin, 1995-96; Jacques Martin, 1996-97.

Captains' History

Laurie Boschman, 1992-93; Brad Shaw, Mark Lamb and Gord Dineen, 1993-94; Randy Cunneyworth, 1994-95 to 1995-96.

Retired Numbers

8 Frank Finnigan 1924-1934

Steve Duchesne gives the Ottawa Senators an established leader along the blueline and a creative quarterback for the powerplay.

All-time Record vs. Other Clubs

Regular Season

	At Home							On Road							Total						
	GP	W	L	T	GF	GA	PTS	GP	W	L	T	GF	GA	PTS	GP	W	L	T	GF	GA	PTS
Anaheim	2	1	1	0	6	4	2	2	2	0	0	2	0	3	9	0	4	1	3	0	9	13	2
Boston	10	0	8	2	18	39	2	11	0	11	0	29	55	0	21	0	19	2	47	94	2
Buffalo	12	2	8	2	26	46	6	10	1	9	0	16	53	2	22	3	17	2	42	99	8
Calgary	3	1	1	1	6	9	3	3	0	3	0	5	21	0	6	1	4	1	11	30	3
Chicago	3	0	3	0	5	12	0	3	1	1	1	10	9	3	6	1	4	1	15	21	3
Colorado	11	3	6	2	36	56	8	9	0	9	0	23	51	0	20	3	15	2	59	107	8
Dallas	3	1	2	0	10	10	2	4	1	3	0	10	20	2	7	2	5	0	20	30	4
Detroit	3	1	2	0	9	11	2	3	1	2	0	7	14	2	6	2	4	0	16	25	4
Edmonton	3	2	1	0	9	8	4	3	1	2	0	10	13	2	6	3	3	0	19	21	6
Florida	6	1	5	0	11	24	2	6	0	5	1	12	23	1	12	1	10	1	23	47	3
Hartford	11	1	8	2	22	38	4	10	1	9	0	23	39	2	21	2	17	2	45	77	6
Los Angeles	3	2	1	0	12	9	4	3	0	3	0	8	21	0	6	2	4	0	20	30	4
Montreal	10	1	9	0	22	39	2	12	3	9	0	32	43	6	22	4	18	0	54	82	8
New Jersey	8	1	6	1	14	29	3	7	1	6	0	17	30	2	15	2	12	1	31	59	5
NY Islanders	7	3	3	1	20	29	7	8	3	3	2	27	32	8	15	6	6	3	47	61	15
NY Rangers	7	0	7	0	14	27	0	7	1	6	0	18	33	2	14	1	13	0	32	60	2
Philadelphia	7	2	4	1	16	20	5	7	1	6	0	16	39	2	14	3	10	1	32	59	7
Pittsburgh	9	1	8	0	18	40	2	10	0	9	1	20	49	1	19	1	17	1	38	89	3
St. Louis	3	1	2	0	6	17	2	3	1	2	0	13	13	2	6	2	4	0	19	30	4
San Jose	3	2	0	1	11	8	5	3	1	2	0	5	9	2	6	3	2	1	16	14	7
Tampa Bay	7	2	5	0	17	19	4	7	3	4	0	18	21	6	14	5	9	0	35	40	10
Toronto	3	0	2	1	4	9	1	4	0	4	0	8	20	0	7	0	6	1	12	29	1
Vancouver	3	1	2	0	4	6	2	3	0	3	0	5	14	0	6	1	5	0	9	20	2
Washington	7	1	5	1	25	34	3	8	0	7	1	14	44	1	15	1	12	2	39	78	4
Winnipeg	5	0	4	1	10	24	1	2	0	2	0	12	18	2	6	1	6	1	22	42	3
Totals	**149**	**30**	**103**	**16**	**351**	**571**	**76**	**149**	**21**	**121**	**7**	**360**	**686**	**49**	**298**	**51**	**224**	**23**	**711**	**1257**	**125**

Colorado totals include Quebec, 1992-93 to 1994-95.   Dallas totals include Minnesota, 1992-93.

1995-96 Results

Oct.	7		Buffalo	1-3	13	at	Tampa Bay	1-4
	13	at	Florida	2-6	17		Montreal	0-3
	15	at	Tampa Bay	7-4	22		Chicago	3-7
	19		Calgary	4-2	24		Pittsburgh	3-4
	21	at	New Jersey	1-4	25		Detroit	2-4
	22	at	NY Rangers	4-2	27		Toronto	2-2
	24	at	Detroit	2-1	29		St. Louis	4-2
	26		Los Angeles	5-4	31		Boston	2-3
	28		Florida	1-4	Feb.	1		Washington	1-4
	29	at	Philadelphia	2-5		3		New Jersey	2-3
Nov.	2		Hartford	5-0		6	at	Calgary	1-3
	4		Hartford	4-5		8	at	Winnipeg	2-6
	8		Pittsburgh	1-7		10	at	Montreal	5-3
	9	at	Boston	3-4		12	at	NY Islanders	4-1
	11		Anaheim	2-3		15		San Jose	2-2
	15	at	Hartford	2-3		17		NY Rangers	1-2
	16	at	Philadelphia	3-5		20	at	St. Louis	7-1
	18	at	Montreal	1-5		22	at	Dallas	2-3
	19	at	Buffalo	0-6		25	at	Colorado	2-4
	22		Winnipeg	1-3		28		Buffalo	2-5
	25		Boston	3-3	Mar.	1		Philadelphia	2-3
	28	at	Pittsburgh	2-7		2		New Jersey	1-4
	30		NY Islanders	3-5		7	at	Pittsburgh	1-5
Dec.	2		NY Rangers	2-4		9	at	Montreal	2-3
	5	at	Toronto	1-4		13		Dallas	4-1
	7	at	Chicago	5-2		15		Vancouver	2-0
	9		Colorado	3-7		17		Tampa Bay	5-0
	12	at	San Jose	1-2		19	at	Florida	2-5
	13	at	Los Angeles	2-6		21	at	Boston	1-3
	15	at	Anaheim	2-4		22		Hartford	1-1
	17	at	Vancouver	1-4		24		Edmonton	2-3
	18	at	Edmonton	1-3		27		Philadelphia	2-4
	23		Buffalo	2-4		29	at	Washington	0-5
	26	at	NY Rangers	4-6		30		Montreal	1-3
	27	at	Buffalo	4-3	Apr.	1		Boston	1-1
	30		Montreal	1-4		3		Florida	3-2
	31		Tampa Bay	0-3		5		NY Islanders	4-2
Jan.	3	at	Pittsburgh	1-4		6		Washington	3-4
	5	at	Hartford	2-4		10	at	Buffalo	2-5
	6	at	NY Islanders	4-5		11		Pittsburgh	3-5
	11	at	Washington	1-6		13	at	New Jersey	5-2

Entry Draft Selections 1996-92

1996

Pick	
1	Chris Phillips
81	Antti-Jussi Niemi
136	Andreas Dackell
163	Francois Hardy
212	Erich Goldmann
216	Ivan Ciernik
239	Sami Salo

1995

Pick	
1	Bryan Berard
27	Marc Moro
53	Brad Larsen
89	Kevin Bolibruck
103	Kevin Boyd
131	David Hruska
183	Kaj Linna
184	Ray Schultz
231	Erik Kaminski

1994

Pick	
3	Radek Bonk
29	Stanislav Neckar
81	Bryan Masotta
131	Mike Gaffney
133	Daniel Alfredsson
159	Doug Sproule
210	Frederic Cassivi
211	Danny Dupont
237	Stephen MacKinnon
274	Antti Tormanen

1993

Pick	
1	Alexandre Daigle
27	Radim Bicanek
53	Patrick Charbonneau
91	Cosmo Dupaul
131	Rick Bodkin
157	Sergei Poleschuk
183	Jason Disher
209	Toby Kvalevog
227	Pavol Demitra
235	Rick Schuwerk

1992

Pick	
2	Alexei Yashin
25	Chad Penney
50	Patrick Traverse
73	Radek Hamr
98	Daniel Guerard
121	Al Sinclair
146	Jaroslav Miklenda
169	Jay Kenney
194	Claude Savoie
217	Jake Grimes
242	Tomas Jelinek
264	Petter Ronnqvist

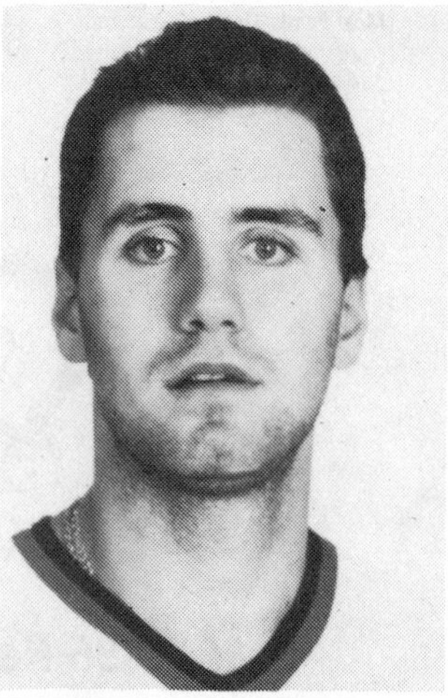

A skilled left-winger who doubles as the Senators' top face-off man, Radek Bonk adds both size and skill to the Ottawa attack.

Coach

MARTIN, JACQUES
Coach, Ottawa Senators. Born in Rockland, Ont., October 1, 1952.

When appointed the Senators' third head coach on January 24, 1996, Jacques Martin brought to the club ten years of NHL coaching experience, including five with the Quebec Nordiques, an organization he often compared with his new club, in that both teams were built around young, talented players who required patience and teaching.

Prior to Martin coming on board, the Senators held an 8-35-1 record (.193) and had allowed an average of 4.09 goals against per game. Under Martin, the Senators improved to a 10-24-4 record (.316), bringing the goals against down to a 2.92 average. In their last 29 games, the Senators played .362 hockey, and .412 hockey in their last 17.

Martin's coaching career began at the collegiate level in 1976. He was appointed head coach of the Guelph Platers (now Storm) in 1986, winning the OHL title, the Memorial Cup and CHL coach of the year award. That summer, Martin became head coach of the St. Louis Blues. In his NHL rookie year, he led that club to the Norris Division championship and, in two seasons with the Blues, posted a 66-71-23 record. He then spent two seasons as an assistant to Chicago's head coach Mike Keenan, before joining the Nordiques in 1990. With Quebec, he worked four years as an assistant coach and one year (1993-94) as both head coach and general manager of the AHL Cornwall Aces.

Jacques, his wife Patricia and their two daughters, Angela and Nathalee, have found a new home near Kanata.

Coaching Record

		Regular Season					Playoffs			
Season	Team	Games	W	L	T	%	Games	W	L	%
1983-84	Peterborough (OHL)	70	43	23	4	.643	....	....	....	....
1984-85	Peterborough (OHL)	66	42	20	4	.667	....	....	....	....
1985-86	Guelph (OHL)	66	41	23	2	.636	....	....	....	....
1986-87	**St. Louis (NHL)**	**80**	**32**	**33**	**15**	**.494**	**6**	**2**	**4**	**.333**
1987-88	**St. Louis (NHL)**	**80**	**34**	**38**	**8**	**.475**	**10**	**5**	**5**	**.500**
1995-96	**Ottawa (NHL)**	**38**	**10**	**24**	**4**	**.316**	....	....	....	....
	NHL Totals	**198**	**76**	**95**	**27**	**.452**	**16**	**7**	**9**	**.438**

Club Directory

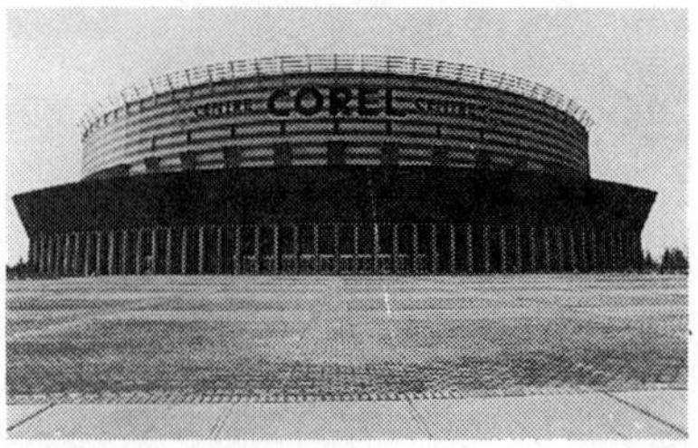

Ottawa Senators
301 Moodie Drive
Suite 200
Nepean, Ontario
K2H 9C4
Phone **613/721-0115**
FAX 613/726-1419
Capacity: 18,500

Executive
Chairman and Governor . . . . . Rod Bryden
President and CEO . . . . . Roy Mlakar
Chief Operating Officer and Alternate Governor . . . Bernie Ashe
General Manager and Alternate Governor . . . . . Pierre Gauthier

Assistants
Secretary to the Governor . . . . . Sharry Dozois
Executive Assistant to the Chief Operating Officer . . Cheryl Blake
Secretary to the General Manager . . . . . Allison Vaughan

Hockey Operations
Assistant General Manager . . . . . Ray Shero
Director of Player Personnel . . . . . Marshall Johnston
Head Coach . . . . . Jacques Martin
Assistant Coach . . . . . Perry Pearn
Assistant Coach . . . . . Craig Ramsay
Head Equipment Trainer . . . . . Ed Georgica
Athletic Therapist . . . . . Conrad Lackten
Assistant Trainer . . . . . John Gervais
Massage Therapist . . . . . Brad Joyal
Scouting Coordinator . . . . . Trevor Timmins
Chief Scout . . . . . Andre Savard
Scout . . . . . John Phelan
European Scout . . . . . Jarmo Kekalainen
Scout . . . . . Paul Castron
Pro Scout . . . . . Phil Myre
Scout . . . . . Don Boyd
Scout . . . . . Dale Engel
Team Doctor . . . . . Jamie Kissick M.D.
Strength and Conditioning Coach . . . . . Lorne Goldenberg
Video Coach . . . . . Randy Lee

Media Relations
Director . . . . . Phil Legault
Assistant . . . . . Lisa Hillary

Finance
Director . . . . . Mark Goudie
Manager, Computer and Internet Services . . . . . Sean Shrubsole
Payroll Supervisor . . . . . Sandi Horner
Senior Accountants . . . . . Lynda Rozon, Dave Spooner
Accounts Payable . . . . . Laurel Neill, Lisa Saumure
Accounts Receivable . . . . . Anne Hersey

Corporate Sales, Senators and Corel Centre
Vice President . . . . . Mark Bonneau
Secretaries . . . . . Christine Clancy, Jennifer Kearns
Manager, Sponsorship and Corporate Properties . . . Dan Quinn
Senior Account Managers . . . . . Brian Jokat, Darren McCartney
Corporate Account Managers . . . . . John Macbeth, Gina Hillcoat, Craig Purcell, James Cotie

Outaouais Office
Director, Business Development . . . . . Enrico Valente
Administrative Assistant . . . . . Marie-Danielle Davis

Ticketing and Game Day Operations
Vice-President . . . . . Jeff Kyle
Administrative Assistant . . . . . Jody Thorson
Director of Promotions . . . . . Patti Zebchuck
Coordinator, Promotions . . . . . Erik Vogel
Manager, Ticket Sales . . . . . Pat Whalen
Administrative Assistant . . . . . Paulette Surette
Sales Representatives . . . . . Shawn Williams, Jim Armstrong, Gus Ayoub, Mike Dagenais, Robert Campagna, Gianni Farinon, Robert Buchanan
Ticketing Coordinator . . . . . Tracey Drennan
Customer Service Coordinator . . . . . Cindy Kruger
Customer Service Representatives . . . . . Laurie Hamilton, Natalie Grandmaison-Farmer

Broadcast and Marketing Services
Vice President . . . . . Jim Steel
Administrative Assistant . . . . . Krista Pogue
Merchandise Manager . . . . . Bob Maxwell
Retail Supervisor . . . . . Tracey Ogilby
Managing Editor . . . . . Carl Lavigne
Graphic Designer . . . . . Kevin Caradonna

Community Development
Director . . . . . Brad Marsh
Coordinator . . . . . Marie Olney
Coordinator . . . . . Sherry Doiron
Coordinator . . . . . Sylvie Guenette-Craig

Administration
Administrative Assistant . . . . . Kelly MacCallum
Office Coordinator . . . . . Katrina Phelps

The Palladium Corporation
President and Alternate Governor . . . . . Cyril Leeder
Secretary to the President . . . . . Gail Martineau
Controller . . . . . Marc Beisham
Manager, Corporate Services . . . . . Greg Graham
Administrative Assistant . . . . . Linda MacKenzie

The Corel Centre
Executive Director . . . . . Roger Newton
Assistant Executive Director . . . . . Beth Lindquist
Executive Assistant . . . . . Linda Julian

Philadelphia Flyers

1995-96 Results: 45W-24L-13T 103PTS. First, Atlantic Division

Schedule

Oct.	Sat.	5	Florida		Tues.	7	Boston	
	Mon.	7	New Jersey		Thur.	9	Tampa Bay	
	Thur.	10	Los Angeles		Sat.	11	Washington	
	Sat.	12	at NY Islanders		Tues.	14	Montreal	
	Sun.	13	Calgary		Tues.	21	Dallas	
	Tues.	15	at Los Angeles		Wed.	22	at Detroit	
	Wed.	16	at Anaheim		Sat.	25	Detroit*	
	Fri.	18	at Phoenix		Tues.	28	Phoenix	
	Tues.	22	Anaheim		Wed.	29	at Washington	
	Sat.	26	at Montreal	**Feb.**	Sat.	1	NY Rangers*	
	Sun.	27	Florida		Tues.	4	Buffalo	
	Wed.	30	at Washington		Thur.	6	Montreal	
	Thur.	31	at Tampa Bay		Sat.	8	at New Jersey	
Nov.	Sat.	2	at Florida		Thur.	13	Ottawa	
	Mon.	4	NY Islanders		Sat.	15	Pittsburgh*	
	Thur.	7	at Buffalo		Sun.	16	at Pittsburgh	
	Sat.	9	Chicago*		Wed.	19	Hartford	
	Sun.	10	Toronto		Thur.	20	at Tampa Bay	
	Wed.	13	at NY Rangers		Sat.	22	at Florida*	
	Thur.	14	Washington		Sun.	23	NY Rangers	
	Sat.	16	San Jose		Wed.	26	at Ottawa	
	Thur.	21	Pittsburgh	**Mar.**	Sat.	1	at Boston*	
	Sat.	23	at Tampa Bay		Sun.	2	at Hartford*	
	Tues.	26	at Boston		Wed.	5	New Jersey	
	Wed.	27	at NY Islanders		Sat.	8	at Pittsburgh*	
	Sat.	30	at Ottawa		Sun.	9	Washington*	
Dec.	Sun.	1	Vancouver		Thur.	13	Edmonton	
	Wed.	4	at NY Rangers		Sat.	15	Buffalo*	
	Fri.	6	at Dallas		Sun.	16	at Buffalo*	
	Tues.	10	Florida		Wed.	19	at Toronto	
	Thur.	12	Hartford		Sat.	22	at NY Islanders	
	Sat.	14	at Hartford		Sun.	23	Colorado	
	Sun.	15	Boston		Tues.	25	at New Jersey	
	Thur.	19	NY Islanders		Sat.	29	at Washington	
	Sat.	21	St. Louis*		Sun.	30	at St. Louis	
	Sun.	22	at Chicago	**Apr.**	Tues.	1	Tampa Bay	
	Fri.	27	at Edmonton		Sun.	6	Ottawa*	
	Sun.	29	at Calgary*		Mon.	7	at NY Rangers	
	Tues.	31	at Vancouver		Thur.	10	NY Rangers	
Jan.	Thur.	2	at San Jose		Sat.	12	at Montreal	
	Sat.	4	at Colorado		Sun.	13	New Jersey	

* Denotes afternoon game.

Franchise date: June 5, 1967

30th
NHL
Season

The heart and soul of the Philadelphia Flyers offensive assault, Eric Lindros established personal highs in goals (47), assists (68), points (115) and plus/minus rating (+26).

Year-by-Year Record

		Home			Road			Overall							Playoff Result
Season	GP	W	L	T	W	L	T	W	L	T	GF	GA	Pts.	Finished	
1995-96	82	27	9	5	18	15	8	45	24	13	282	208	103	1st, Atlantic Div.	Lost Conf. Semi-Final
1994-95	48	16	7	1	12	9	3	28	16	4	150	132	60	1st, Atlantic Div.	Lost Conf. Championship
1993-94	84	19	20	3	16	19	7	35	39	10	294	314	80	6th, Atlantic Div.	Out of Playoffs
1992-93	84	23	14	5	13	23	6	36	37	11	319	319	83	5th, Patrick Div.	Out of Playoffs
1991-92	80	22	11	7	10	26	4	32	37	11	252	273	75	6th, Patrick Div.	Out of Playoffs
1990-91	80	18	16	6	15	21	4	33	37	10	252	267	76	5th, Patrick Div.	Out of Playoffs
1989-90	80	17	19	4	13	20	7	30	39	11	290	297	71	6th, Patrick Div.	Out of Playoffs
1988-89	80	22	15	3	14	21	5	36	36	8	307	285	80	4th, Patrick Div.	Lost Conf. Championship
1987-88	80	20	14	6	18	19	3	38	33	9	292	292	85	3rd, Patrick Div.	Lost Div. Semi-Final
1986-87	80	29	9	2	17	17	6	46	26	8	310	245	100	1st, Patrick Div.	Lost Final
1985-86	80	33	6	1	20	17	3	53	23	4	335	241	110	1st, Patrick Div.	Lost Div. Semi-Final
1984-85	80	32	4	4	21	16	3	53	20	7	348	241	113	1st, Patrick Div.	Lost Final
1983-84	80	25	10	5	19	16	5	44	26	10	350	290	98	3rd, Patrick Div.	Lost Div. Semi-Final
1982-83	80	29	8	3	20	15	5	49	23	8	326	240	106	1st, Patrick Div.	Lost Div. Semi-Final
1981-82	80	25	10	5	13	21	6	38	31	11	325	313	87	3rd, Patrick Div.	Lost Div. Semi-Final
1980-81	80	23	9	8	18	15	7	41	24	15	313	249	97	2nd, Patrick Div.	Lost Quarter-Final
1979-80	80	27	5	8	21	7	12	48	12	20	327	254	116	1st, Patrick Div.	Lost Final
1978-79	80	26	10	4	14	15	11	40	25	15	281	248	95	2nd, Patrick Div.	Lost Quarter-Final
1977-78	80	29	6	5	16	14	10	45	20	15	296	200	105	2nd, Patrick Div.	Lost Semi-Final
1976-77	80	33	6	1	15	10	15	48	16	16	323	213	112	1st, Patrick Div.	Lost Semi-Final
1975-76	80	36	2	2	15	11	14	51	13	16	348	209	118	1st, Patrick Div.	Lost Final
1974-75	80	32	6	2	19	12	9	51	18	11	293	181	113	1st, **Patrick Div.**	**Won Stanley Cup**
1973-74	78	28	6	5	22	10	7	50	16	12	273	164	112	1st, **West Div.**	**Won Stanley Cup**
1972-73	78	27	8	4	10	22	7	37	30	11	296	256	85	2nd, West Div.	Lost Semi-Final
1971-72	78	19	13	7	7	25	7	26	38	14	200	236	66	5th, West Div.	Out of Playoffs
1970-71	78	20	10	9	8	23	8	28	33	17	207	225	73	3rd, West Div.	Lost Quarter-Final
1969-70	76	11	14	13	6	21	11	17	35	24	197	225	58	5th, West Div.	Out of Playoffs
1968-69	76	14	16	8	6	19	13	20	35	21	174	225	61	3rd, West Div.	Lost Quarter-Final
1967-68	74	17	13	7	14	19	4	31	32	11	173	179	73	1st, West Div.	Lost Quarter-Final

1996-97 Player Personnel

FORWARDS	HT	WT	S	Place of Birth	Date	1995-96 Club
BIALOWAS, Frank	5-11	220	L	Winnipeg, Man.	9/25/70	Portland (AHL)
BOWEN, Jason	6-4	215	L	Port Alice, B.C.	11/9/73	Philadelphia-Hershey
BRIND'AMOUR, Rod	6-1	202	L	Ottawa, Ont.	8/9/70	Philadelphia
COLES, Bruce	5-9	183	L	Montreal, Que.	1/12/68	Hershey
CORKUM, Bob	6-2	210	R	Salisbury, MA	12/18/67	Anaheim-Philadelphia
DANIELS, Scott	6-3	200	L	Prince Albert, Sask.	9/19/69	Hartford-Springfield
DARBY, Craig	6-3	200	R	Oneida, NY	9/26/72	NY Islanders-Worcester
DiMAIO, Rob	5-10	190	R	Calgary, Alta.	2/19/68	Philadelphia
DRUCE, John	6-2	195	R	Peterborough, Ont.	2/23/66	Los Angeles-Philadelphia
FALLOON, Pat	5-11	190	R	Foxwarren, Man.	9/22/72	San Jose-Philadelphia
FORBES, Colin	6-3	205	L	New Westminster, B.C.	2/16/76	Portland (WHL)-Hershey
GALLANT, Chester	6-1	184	R	Thunder Bay, Ont.	12/22/77	Niagara Falls
HAWERCHUK, Dale	5-11	190	L	Toronto, Ont.	4/4/63	St. Louis-Philadelphia
HEALEY, Paul	6-2	196	R	Edmonton, Alta.	3/20/75	Hershey
HORACEK, Tony	6-4	210	L	Vancouver, B.C.	2/3/67	Hershey
JUHLIN, Patrik	6-0	194	L	Huddinge, Sweden	4/24/70	Philadelphia-Hershey
KING, Steven	6-0	195	R	Greenwich, RI	7/22/69	Anaheim-Baltimore
KLATT, Trent	6-1	205	R	Robbinsdale, MN	1/30/71	Dallas-Michigan-Philadelphia
KORDIC, Dan	6-5	234	L	Edmonton, Alta.	4/18/71	Philadelphia-Hershey
LACROIX, Daniel	6-2	205	L	Montreal, Que.	3/11/69	NY Rangers-Binghamton
LeCLAIR, John	6-3	226	L	St. Albans, VT	7/5/69	Philadelphia
LINDROS, Eric	6-4	236	R	London, Ont.	2/28/73	Philadelphia
McCOSH, Shawn	6-0	188	R	Oshawa, Ont.	6/5/69	Hershey
NORRIS, Clayton	6-2	205	R	Edmonton, Alta.	3/8/72	Hershey
OTTO, Joel	6-4	220	R	Elk River, MN	10/29/61	Philadelphia
PAYETTE, Andre	6-2	205	L	Cornwall, Ont.	7/29/76	S.S. Marie
PODEIN, Shjon	6-2	200	L	Rochester, MN	3/5/68	Philadelphia
PROSPAL, Vaclav	6-2	185	L	Ceske-Budejovice, Czech.	2/17/75	Hershey
RENBERG, Mikael	6-2	218	L	Pitea, Sweden	5/5/72	Philadelphia
WESENBERG, Brian	6-3	173	R	Peterborough, Ont.	5/9/77	Guelph
WHITE, Peter	5-11	200	L	Montreal, Que.	3/15/69	Edm-Tor-St. John's-Atlanta
ZUBRUS, Dainius	6-3	215	L	Elektrenai, USSR	6/16/78	Pembroke-Caledon
DEFENSEMEN						
BOULERICE, Jesse	6-1	200	R	Plattsburgh, NY	8/10/78	Detroit (OHL)
BOULIN, Vladislav	6-1	210	L	Penza, USSR	5/18/72	Hershey
BRIMANIS, Aris	6-3	210	R	Cleveland, OH	3/14/72	Philadelphia-Hershey
DESJARDINS, Eric	6-1	200	R	Rouyn, Que.	6/14/69	Philadelphia
DYKHUIS, Karl	6-3	205	L	Sept-Iles, Que.	7/8/72	Philadelphia
HALLER, Kevin	6-2	195	L	Trochu, Alta.	12/5/70	Philadelphia
KENNY, Shane	6-2	230	L	Oromocto, N.B.	3/1/77	Owen Sound
LANK, Jeff	6-3	205	L	Indian Head, Sask.	3/1/75	Hershey
MacISAAC, David	6-2	225	L	Arlington, MA	4/23/72	Milwaukee
NIINIMAA, Janne	6-1	196	L	Raahe, Finland	5/22/75	Jokerit
RUMBLE, Darren	6-1	200	L	Barrie, Ont.	1/23/69	Philadelphia-Hershey
SAMUELSSON, Kjell	6-6	235	R	Tyngsryd, Sweden	10/18/58	Philadelphia
STAPLES, Jeff	6-2	207	L	Kitimat, B.C.	3/4/75	Hershey
STEVENS, John	6-1	195	L	Completon, N.B.	5/4/66	Springfield
SVOBODA, Petr	6-1	190	L	Most, Czech.	2/14/66	Philadelphia
THERIEN, Chris	6-4	230	L	Ottawa, Ont.	12/14/71	Philadelphia

GOALTENDERS	HT	WT	C	Place of Birth	Date	1995-96 Club
BOUCHER, Brian	6-1	190	L	Woonsocket, RI	1/2/77	Tri-City
HEXTALL, Ron	6-3	192	L	Brandon, Man.	5/3/64	Philadelphia
KUNTAR, Les	6-2	195	L	Elma, NY	7/28/69	Hershey-Fort Wayne
LITTLE, Neil	6-1	193	L	Medicine Hat, Alta.	12/18/71	Hershey
ROUSSEL, Dominic	6-1	191	L	Hull, Que.	2/22/70	Philadelphia-Hershey-Winnipeg
SNOW, Garth	6-3	200	L	Wrentham, MA	7/28/69	Philadelphia

General Manager

CLARKE, ROBERT EARLE (BOB)
President/General Manager, Philadelphia Flyers.
Born in Flin Flon, Man., August 13, 1949.

Bob Clarke was named president and general manager of the Philadelphia Flyers on June 15, 1994. Prior to re-joining the Flyers' family, Clarke served as vice president and general manager of the Florida Panthers. In 1993-94, their first season in the NHL, the Panthers established NHL records for wins (33) and points (83) by an expansion franchise. Clarke also served as the vice president and general manager of the Minnesota North Stars from 1990-92, guiding the team to the Stanley Cup finals in 1990-91.

Clarke's appointment marks the second time he has served as the Flyers' general manager. The Flin Flon native was the Flyers' vice president and general manager from 1984-90, when the team posted a 256-177-47 record. During his six years as general manager, the Flyers won three divisional titles, two conference championships, reached the Stanley Cup semi-finals three times and the finals twice.

As a player, the former Philadelphia captain led his club to Stanley Cup championships in 1974 and 1975 and captured numerous individual awards, including the Hart Trophy as the League's most valuable player in 1973, 1975 and 1976. The four-time All-Star also received the Masterton Memorial Trophy (perseverance and dedication) in 1972 and the Frank J. Selke Trophy (top defensive forward) in 1983. He appeared in nine All-Star Games and was elected to the Hockey Hall of Fame in 1987. He was awarded the Lester Patrick Trophy in 1979-80 in recognition of his contribution to hockey in the United States. Clarke appeared in 1144 regular-season games, recording 358 goals and 852 assists for 1210 points. He also added 119 points in 136 playoff games.

1995-96 Scoring

* – rookie

Regular Season

Pos	#	Player	Team	GP	G	A	Pts	+/-	PIM	PP	SH	GW	GT	S	%
C	88	Eric Lindros	PHI	73	47	68	115	26	163	15	0	4	0	294	16.0
L	10	John LeClair	PHI	82	51	46	97	21	64	19	0	10	2	270	18.9
C	17	Rod Brind'Amour	PHI	82	26	61	87	20	110	4	4	5	4	213	12.2
C	18	Dale Hawerchuk	STL	66	13	28	41	5	22	5	0	1	0	136	9.6
			PHI	16	4	16	20	10	4	1	0	1	0	44	9.1
			TOTAL	82	17	44	61	15	26	6	0	2	0	180	9.4
R	15	Pat Falloon	S.J.	9	3	0	3	-1	4	0	0	0	1	18	16.7
			PHI	62	22	26	48	15	6	9	0	2	0	152	14.5
			TOTAL	71	25	26	51	14	10	9	0	2	1	170	14.7
D	37	Eric Desjardins	PHI	80	7	40	47	19	45	5	0	2	0	184	3.8
C	11	Dan Quinn	OTT	28	6	18	24	-8	24	4	0	0	0	62	9.7
			PHI	35	7	14	21	2	22	3	0	0	0	47	14.9
			TOTAL	63	13	32	45	-6	46	7	0	0	0	109	11.9
R	19	Mikael Renberg	PHI	51	23	20	43	8	45	9	0	4	0	198	11.6
C	29	Joel Otto	PHI	67	12	29	41	11	115	6	1	1	0	91	13.2
R	26	John Druce	L.A.	64	9	12	21	-26	14	0	0	0	0	103	8.7
			PHI	13	4	4	8	6	13	0	0	0	0	25	16.0
			TOTAL	77	13	16	29	-20	27	0	0	0	0	128	10.2
D	23	Petr Svoboda	PHI	73	1	28	29	28	105	0	0	0	0	91	1.1
L	25	Shjon Podein	PHI	79	15	10	25	25	89	0	4	4	0	115	13.0
D	6	Chris Therien	PHI	82	6	17	23	16	89	3	0	1	0	123	4.9
R	9	Rob Dimaio	PHI	59	6	15	21	0	58	1	1	0	0	49	12.2
D	24	Karl Dykhuis	PHI	82	5	15	20	12	101	1	0	0	0	104	4.8
C	22	Bob Corkum	ANA	48	5	7	12	0	26	0	0	1	0	88	5.7
			PHI	28	4	3	7	3	8	0	0	2	0	38	10.5
			TOTAL	76	9	10	19	3	34	0	0	3	0	126	7.1
R	20	Trent Klatt	DAL	22	4	4	8	0	23	0	0	1	0	37	10.8
			PHI	49	3	8	11	2	21	0	0	1	0	64	4.7
			TOTAL	71	7	12	19	2	44	0	0	2	0	101	6.9
D	2	Kerry Huffman	OTT	43	4	11	15	-18	63	3	0	0	0	88	4.5
			PHI	4	1	1	2	0	6	0	0	1	0	3	33.3
			TOTAL	47	5	12	17	-18	69	3	0	1	0	91	5.5
D	5	Kevin Haller	PHI	69	5	9	14	18	92	0	2	2	0	89	5.6
D	28	Kjell Samuelsson	PHI	75	3	11	14	20	81	0	0	1	1	62	4.8
R	12	Patrik Juhlin	PHI	14	3	3	6	4	17	1	0	0	0	14	21.4
L	8	Shawn Antoski	PHI	64	1	3	4	-4	204	0	0	0	0	34	2.9
L	42	Russ Romaniuk	PHI	17	3	0	3	-2	17	1	0	0	0	13	23.1
C	22	Jim Montgomery	PHI	5	1	2	3	1	9	0	0	0	0	4	25.0
L	18	* Yanick Dupre	PHI	12	2	0	2	0	8	0	0	1	0	10	20.0
L	26	Philip Crowe	PHI	16	1	1	2	0	28	0	0	0	0	6	16.7
D	40	* Aris Brimanis	PHI	17	0	2	2	-1	12	0	0	0	0	11	0.0
D	21	Dan Kordic	PHI	9	1	0	1	1	31	0	0	0	0	2	50.0
G	27	Ron Hextall	PHI	53	0	1	1	0	28	0	0	0	0	1	0.0
D	53	Jason Bowen	PHI	2	0	0	0	0	2	0	0	0	0	2	0.0
D	3	Darren Rumble	PHI	5	0	0	0	0	4	0	0	0	0	7	0.0
G	30	Garth Snow	PHI	26	0	0	0	0	18	0	0	0	0	0	0.0

Goaltending

No.	Goaltender	GPI	Mins	Avg	W	L	T	EN	SO	GA	SA	S%
27	Ron Hextall	53	3102	2.17	31	13	7	2	4	112	1292	.913
30	Garth Snow	26	1437	2.88	12	8	4	3	0	69	648	.894
37	Dominic Roussel	9	456	2.89	2	3	2	0	1	22	178	.876
	Totals	**82**	**5009**	**2.49**	**45**	**24**	**13**	**5**	**5**	**208**	**2123**	**.902**

Playoffs

Pos	#	Player	Team	GP	G	A	Pts	+/-	PIM	PP	SH	GW	OT	S	%
C	88	Eric Lindros	PHI	12	6	6	12	-1	43	3	0	2	0	46	13.0
L	10	John LeClair	PHI	11	6	5	11	3	6	4	0	1	0	25	24.0
R	19	Mikael Renberg	PHI	11	3	6	9	1	14	1	0	0	0	22	13.6
C	18	Dale Hawerchuk	PHI	12	3	6	9	0	12	1	0	0	0	48	6.3
C	29	Joel Otto	PHI	12	3	4	7	4	11	1	0	1	0	12	25.0
C	17	Rod Brind'Amour	PHI	12	2	5	7	-2	6	1	0	0	0	34	5.9
D	37	Eric Desjardins	PHI	12	0	6	6	-5	2	0	0	0	0	26	0.0
D	23	Petr Svoboda	PHI	12	0	6	6	6	22	0	0	0	0	17	0.0
R	20	Trent Klatt	PHI	12	4	1	5	1	0	0	0	0	0	16	25.0
R	15	Pat Falloon	PHI	12	3	2	5	-2	2	2	0	0	0	37	8.1
C	11	Dan Quinn	PHI	12	1	4	5	-3	6	1	0	0	0	19	5.3
D	24	Karl Dykhuis	PHI	12	2	2	4	6	22	1	0	0	0	18	11.1
C	22	Bob Corkum	PHI	12	1	2	3	-1	6	0	0	0	0	11	9.1
L	25	Shjon Podein	PHI	12	1	2	3	2	50	0	0	1	0	19	5.3
L	8	Shawn Antoski	PHI	7	1	1	2	3	28	0	0	1	0	3	33.3
R	26	John Druce	PHI	2	0	2	2	1	2	0	0	0	0	8	0.0
D	28	Kjell Samuelsson	PHI	12	1	0	1	0	24	0	0	0	0	7	14.3
D	5	Kevin Haller	PHI	6	0	1	1	0	8	0	0	0	0	6	0.0
L	42	Russ Romaniuk	PHI	1	0	0	0	-1	0	0	0	0	0	1	0.0
G	30	Garth Snow	PHI	1	0	0	0	0	0	0	0	0	0	0	0.0
C	32	Jim Montgomery	PHI	1	0	0	0	-1	0	0	0	0	0	0	0.0
R	9	Rob Dimaio	PHI	3	0	0	0	-1	0	0	0	0	0	1	0.0
D	2	Kerry Huffman	PHI	6	0	0	0	0	2	0	0	0	0	8	0.0
G	27	Ron Hextall	PHI	12	0	0	0	0	6	0	0	0	0	0	0.0
D	6	Chris Therien	PHI	12	0	0	0	-5	18	0	0	0	0	17	0.0

Goaltending

No.	Goaltender	GPI	Mins	Avg	W	L	EN	SO	GA	SA	S%
30	Garth Snow	1	1	.00	0	0	0	0	0	0	.000
27	Ron Hextall	12	760	2.13	6	6	1	0	27	319	.915
	Totals	**12**	**763**	**2.20**	**6**	**6**	**1**	**0**	**28**	**320**	**.913**

General Managers' History

"Bud" Poile, 1967-68 to 1968-69; "Bud" Poile and Keith Allen, 1969-70; Keith Allen, 1970-71 to 1982-83; Bob McCammon, 1983-84; Bob Clarke, 1984-85 to 1989-90; Russ Farwell, 1990-91 to 1993-94; Bob Clarke, 1994-95 to date.

Club Records

Team

(Figures in brackets for season records are games played; records for fewest points, wins, ties, losses, goals, goals against are for 70 or more games)

Most Points	**118**	1975-76 (80)
Most Wins	**53**	1984-85 (80), 1985-86 (80)
Most Ties	***24**	1969-70 (76)
Most Losses	**39**	1993-94 (84)
Most Goals	**350**	1983-84 (80)
Most Goals Against	**319**	1992-93 (84)
Fewest Points	**58**	1969-70 (76)
Fewest Wins	**17**	1969-70 (76)
Fewest Ties	**4**	1985-86 (80)
Fewest Losses	**12**	1979-80 (80)
Fewest Goals	**173**	1967-68 (74)
Fewest Goals Against	**164**	1973-74 (78)
Longest Winning Streak		
Overall	**13**	Oct. 19-Nov. 17/85
Home	***20**	Jan. 4-Apr. 3/76
Away	**8**	Dec. 22/82-Jan. 16/83
Longest Undefeated Streak		
Overall	***35**	Oct. 14/79-Jan. 6/80 (25 wins, 10 ties)
Home	**26**	Oct. 11/79-Feb. 3/80 (19 wins, 7 ties)
Away	**16**	Oct. 20/79-Jan. 6/80 (11 wins, 5 ties)
Longest Losing Streak		
Overall	**6**	Mar. 25-Apr. 4/70, Dec. 5-Dec. 17/92, Jan. 25-Feb. 5/94
Home	**5**	Jan. 30-Feb. 15/69
Away	**8**	Oct. 25-Nov. 26/72
Longest Winless Streak		
Overall	**11**	Nov. 21-Dec. 14/69 (9 losses, 2 ties), Dec. 10/70-Jan. 3/71 (9 losses, 2 ties)
Home	**8**	Dec. 19/68-Jan. 18/69 (4 losses, 4 ties)
Away	**19**	Oct. 23/71-Jan. 27/72 (15 losses, 4 ties)
Most Shutouts, Season	**13**	1974-75 (80)
Most PIM, Season	**2,621**	1980-81 (80)
Most Goals, Game	**13**	Mar. 22/84 (Pit. 4 at Phi. 13), Oct. 18/84 (Van. 2 at Phi. 13)

Individual

Most Seasons	**15**	Bobby Clarke
Most Games	**1,144**	Bobby Clarke
Most Goals, Career	**420**	Bill Barber
Most Assists, Career	**852**	Bobby Clarke
Most Points, Career	**1,210**	Bobby Clarke (358G, 852A)
Most PIM, Career	**1,683**	Rick Tocchet
Most Shutouts, Career	**50**	Bernie Parent
Longest Consecutive Game Streak	**287**	Rick MacLeish (Oct. 6/72-Feb. 5/76)
Most Goals, Season	**61**	Reggie Leach (1975-76)
Most Assists, Season	**89**	Bobby Clarke (1974-75, 1975-76)
Most Points, Season	**123**	Mark Recchi (1992-93; 53G, 70A)
Most PIM, Season	***472**	Dave Schultz (1974-75)
Most Points, Defenseman, Season	**82**	Mark Howe (1985-86; 24G, 58A)
Most Points, Center, Season	**119**	Bobby Clarke (1975-76; 30G, 89A)
Most Points, Right Wing, Season	**123**	Mark Recchi (1992-93; 53G, 70A)
Most Points, Left Wing, Season	**112**	Bill Barber (1975-76; 50G, 62A)
Most Points, Rookie, Season	**82**	Mikael Renberg (1993-94; 38G, 44A)
Most Shutouts, Season	**12**	Bernie Parent (1973-74, 1974-75)
Most Goals, Game	**4**	Rick MacLeish (Feb. 13/73, Mar. 4/73), Tom Bladon (Dec. 11/77), Tim Kerr (Oct. 25/84, Jan. 17/85, Feb. 9/85, Nov. 20/86), Brian Propp (Dec. 2/86), Rick Tocchet (Feb. 27/88, Jan. 25/90), Kevin Dineen (Oct. 31/93)
Most Assists, Game	**5**	Bobby Clarke (Apr. 1/76), Eric Lindros (Mar. 10/94)
Most Points, Game	**8**	Tom Bladon (Dec. 11/77; 4G, 4A)

* NHL Record

Retired Numbers

1	Bernie Parent	1967-1971 and 1973-1979
4	Barry Ashbee	1970-1974
7	Bill Barber	1972-1985
16	Bobby Clarke	1969-1984

All-time Record vs. Other Clubs

Regular Season

	At Home							On Road							Total						
	GP	**W**	**L**	**T**	**GF**	**GA**	**PTS**	**GP**	**W**	**L**	**T**	**GF**	**GA**	**PTS**	**GP**	**W**	**L**	**T**	**GF**	**GA**	**PTS**
Anaheim	2	0	1	1	4	5	1	2	1	1	0	7	8	2	4	1	2	1	11	13	3
Boston	57	25	26	6	191	172	56	60	14	39	7	175	247	35	117	39	65	13	366	419	91
Buffalo	51	31	12	8	190	136	70	47	18	23	6	146	171	42	98	49	35	14	336	307	112
Calgary	45	31	12	2	183	121	64	46	14	23	9	151	190	37	91	45	35	11	334	311	101
Chicago	55	29	15	11	181	147	69	54	11	25	18	154	196	40	109	40	40	29	335	343	109
Colorado	28	20	6	2	109	76	42	27	9	9	9	99	101	27	55	29	15	11	208	177	69
Dallas	60	41	9	10	241	137	92	60	22	24	14	200	201	58	120	63	33	24	441	338	150
Detroit	53	30	12	11	214	157	71	52	18	25	9	171	189	45	105	48	37	20	385	346	116
Edmonton	24	17	6	1	109	68	35	23	5	14	4	65	86	14	47	22	20	5	174	154	49
Florida	7	2	2	3	15	17	7	7	5	2	0	22	19	10	14	7	4	3	37	36	17
Hartford	27	19	7	1	113	74	39	28	13	10	5	117	110	31	55	32	17	6	230	184	70
Los Angeles	57	35	15	7	222	147	77	59	34	17	8	205	172	76	116	69	32	15	427	319	153
Montreal	57	23	21	13	171	172	59	58	17	29	12	179	214	46	115	40	50	25	350	386	105
New Jersey	64	43	14	7	270	157	93	63	28	31	4	242	230	60	127	71	45	11	512	387	153
NY Islanders	75	45	22	8	286	229	98	77	24	41	12	230	301	60	152	69	63	20	516	530	158
NY Rangers	88	43	32	13	300	254	99	89	27	41	21	258	300	75	177	70	73	34	558	554	174
Ottawa	7	6	1	0	39	16	12	7	4	2	1	20	16	9	14	10	3	1	59	32	21
Pittsburgh	87	65	15	7	380	225	137	86	31	38	17	278	303	79	173	96	53	24	658	528	216
St. Louis	60	40	10	10	241	139	90	60	30	23	7	190	176	67	120	70	33	17	431	315	157
San Jose	4	3	1	0	20	9	6	5	4	1	0	17	10	8	9	7	2	0	37	19	14
Tampa Bay	8	5	0	3	29	16	13	8	5	3	0	24	23	10	16	10	3	3	53	39	23
Toronto	53	34	11	8	214	125	76	53	21	19	13	181	180	55	106	55	30	21	395	305	131
Vancouver	46	31	14	1	205	137	63	46	24	10	12	179	136	60	92	55	24	13	384	273	123
Washington	65	39	22	4	249	186	82	63	27	24	12	219	219	66	128	66	46	16	468	405	148
Winnipeg	24	18	6	0	110	69	36	23	11	10	2	79	76	24	47	29	16	2	189	145	60
Defunct Clubs	34	24	4	6	137	67	54	35	13	14	8	102	89	34	69	37	18	14	239	156	88
Totals	**1138**	**699**	**296**	**143**	**4423**	**3058**	**1541**	**1138**	**430**	**498**	**210**	**3710**	**3963**	**1070**	**2276**	**1129**	**794**	**353**	**8133**	**7021**	**2611**

Playoffs

	Series	**W**	**L**	**GP**	**W**	**L**	**T**	**GF**	**GA**	**Last Mtg.**	**Round**	**Result**
Boston	4	2	2	20	9	11	0	57	60	1978	QF	L 1-4
Buffalo	3	3	0	16	12	4	0	53	36	1995	CQF	W 4-1
Calgary	2	1	1	11	7	4	0	43	28	1981	QF	L 3-4
Chicago	1	0	1	4	0	4	0	8	20	1971	QF	L 0-4
Colorado	2	2	0	11	7	4	0	39	29	1985	CF	W 4-2
Dallas	2	2	0	11	8	3	0	41	26	1980	SF	W 4-1
Edmonton	3	1	2	15	7	8	0	44	49	1987	F	L 3-4
Florida	1	0	1	6	2	4	0	11	15	1996	CSF	L 2-4
Montreal	4	1	3	21	6	15	0	52	72	1989	CF	L 2-4
New Jersey	2	1	1	8	4	4	0	20	23	1995	CF	L 2-4
NY Islanders	4	3	1	25	14	11	0	83	69	1987	DF	W 4-3
NY Rangers	9	5	4	42	23	19	0	137	140	1995	CSF	W 4-0
Pittsburgh	1	1	0	7	4	3	0	31	24	1989	DF	W 4-3
St. Louis	2	0	2	11	3	8	0	20	34	1969	QF	L 0-4
Tampa Bay	1	1	0	6	4	2	0	26	13	1996	CQF	W 4-2
Toronto	3	3	0	17	12	5	0	67	47	1977	QF	W 4-2
Vancouver	1	1	0	3	2	1	0	15	9	1979	PR	W 2-1
Washington	3	1	2	16	7	9	0	55	65	1989	DSF	W 4-2
Totals	**48**	**28**	**20**	**250**	**132**	**118**	**0**	**802**	**759**			

Calgary totals include Atlanta, 1972-73 to 1979-80. Colorado totals include Quebec, 1979-80 to 1994-95.
Dallas totals include Minnesota, 1967-68 to 1992-93.
New Jersey totals include Kansas City, 1974-75 to 1975-76, and Colorado Rockies, 1976-77 to 1981-82.

Playoff Results 1996-92

Year	**Round**	**Opponent**	**Result**	**GF**	**GA**
1996	CSF	Florida	L 2-4	11	15
	CQF	Tampa Bay	W 4-2	26	13
1995	CF	New Jersey	L 2-4	14	20
	CSF	NY Rangers	W 4-0	18	10
	CQF	Buffalo	W 4-1	18	13

Abbreviations: Round: F – Final; **CF** – conference final; **CQF** – conference quarter-final; **CSF** – conference semi-final; **DF** – division final; **DSF** – division semi-final; **SF** – semi-final; **QF** – quarter-final; **PR** – preliminary round.

1995-96 Results

Oct.	7	at	Montreal	7-1		9		Anaheim	2-2
	11		Washington	2-1		11		St. Louis	4-4
	14	at	NY Islanders	3-0		13		NY Rangers	0-4
	15		Edmonton	7-1		15		Dallas	6-1
	18	at	Los Angeles	1-1		22		Florida	1-1
	20	at	Anaheim	4-2		24	at	NY Rangers	4-4
	22	at	Chicago	4-5		27	at	Pittsburgh	4-7
	25		NY Islanders	3-1		28	at	Washington	2-3
	28	at	NY Islanders	5-5	**Feb.**	1		Montreal	3-2
	29		Ottawa	5-2		3	at	St. Louis	7-3
	31		Tampa Bay	2-2		8		Buffalo	1-2
Nov.	2		Florida	1-2		10	at	Boston	6-2
	4	at	Pittsburgh	4-7		11		Colorado	3-5
	5		Hartford	6-1		14	at	Florida	4-2
	7	at	Florida	2-4		17	at	Tampa Bay	2-5
	9		Calgary	3-1		19		New Jersey	4-1
	11	at	New Jersey	2-4		22		Washington	5-3
	12		New Jersey	2-3		23	at	Buffalo	2-7
	14	at	Washington	2-2		25		Chicago	3-2
	16		Ottawa	5-3		28	at	Dallas	4-4
	18	at	Hartford	4-2	**Mar.**	1	at	Ottawa	3-2
	19		Vancouver	3-2		3	at	Washington	0-3
	21		Los Angeles	5-2		9	at	Boston	2-3
	24		Detroit	4-1		10		New Jersey	2-3
	29	at	Florida	2-1		13		Tampa Bay	1-1
	30		Toronto	3-2		16		Winnipeg	3-0
Dec.	3		Boston	6-1		17		San Jose	8-2
	5	at	Detroit	3-5		19		NY Islanders	4-1
	7		Buffalo	7-3		22	at	Winnipeg	1-4
	10		NY Islanders	2-6		23	at	Toronto	4-0
	14		Tampa Bay	4-0		25		Hartford	3-0
	16	at	Montreal	4-2		27	at	Ottawa	4-2
	17		Pittsburgh	6-5		29	at	Buffalo	6-5
	19	at	New Jersey	4-5		31		Pittsburgh	4-1
	21		NY Rangers	1-2	**Apr.**	2	at	NY Islanders	6-2
	23	at	Hartford	3-3		4		NY Rangers	4-1
	27	at	Edmonton	2-3		5	at	NY Rangers	1-3
	29	at	Calgary	3-2		7		Boston	2-4
	31	at	Vancouver	5-5		10	at	New Jersey	5-1
Jan.	3	at	San Jose	3-1		11		Montreal	3-2
	4	at	Colorado	2-2		14	at	Tampa Bay	3-1

Entry Draft
Selections 1996-82

1996
Pick
15	Dainius Zubrus
64	Chester Gallant
124	Per-Ragna Bergqvist
133	Jesse Boulerice
187	Roman Malov
213	Jeff Milleker

1995
Pick
22	Brian Boucher
48	Shane Kenny
100	Radovan Somik
132	Dimitri Tertyshny
135	Jamie Sokolsky
152	Martin Spanhel
178	Martin Streit
204	Ruslan Shafikov
230	Jeff Lank

1994
Pick
62	Artem Anisimov
88	Adam Magarrell
101	Sebastien Vallee
140	Alexander Selivanov
166	Colin Forbes
192	Derek Diener
202	Raymond Giroux
218	Johan Hedberg
244	Andre Payette
270	Jan Lipiansky

1993
Pick
36	Janne Niinimaa
71	Vaclav Prospal
77	Milos Holan
114	Vladimir Krechin
140	Mike Crowley
166	Aaron Israel
192	Paul Healey
218	Tripp Tracy
226	E.J. Bradley
244	Jeffrey Staples
270	Kenneth Hemmenway

1992
Pick
7	Ryan Sittler
15	Jason Bowen
31	Denis Metlyuk
103	Vladislav Buljin
127	Roman Zolotov
151	Kirk Daubenspeck
175	Claude Jutras Jr.
199	Jonas Hakansson
223	Chris Herperger
247	Patrice Paquin

1991
Pick
6	Peter Forsberg
50	Yanick Dupre
86	Aris Brimanis
94	Yanick Degrace
116	Clayton Norris
122	Dmitri Yushkevich
138	Andrei Lomakin
182	James Bode
204	Josh Bartell
226	Neil Little
248	John Porco

1990
Pick
4	Mike Ricci
25	Chris Simon
40	Mikael Renberg
42	Terran Sandwith
44	Kimbi Daniels
46	Bill Armstrong
47	Chris Therien
52	Al Kinisky
88	Dan Kordic
109	Viacheslav Butsayev
151	Patrik Englund
172	Toni Porkka
193	Greg Hanson
214	Tommy Soderstrom
235	William Lund

1989
Pick
33	Greg Johnson
34	Patrik Juhlin
72	Reid Simpson
117	Niklas Eriksson
138	John Callahan Jr.
159	Sverre Sears
180	Glen Wisser
201	Al Kummu
222	Matt Brait
243	James Pollio

1988
Pick
14	Claude Boivin
35	Pat Murray
56	Craig Fisher
63	Dominic Roussel
77	Scott Lagrand
98	Edward O'Brien
119	Gordie Frantti
140	Jamie Cooke
161	Johan Salle
182	Brian Arthur
203	Jeff Dandreta
224	Scott Billey
245	Drahomir Kadlec

1987
Pick
20	Darren Rumble
30	Jeff Harding
62	Martin Hostak
83	Tomaz Eriksson
104	Bill Gall
125	Tony Link
146	Mark Strapon
167	Darryl Ingham
188	Bruce McDonald
209	Steve Morrow
230	Darius Rusnak
251	Dale Roehl

1986
Pick
20	Kerry Huffman
23	Jukka Seppo
28	Kent Hawley
83	Mark Bar
125	Steve Scheifele
146	Sami Wahlsten
167	Murray Baron
188	Blaine Rude
209	Shawn Sabol
230	Brett Lawrence
251	Daniel Stephano

1985
Pick
21	Glen Seabrooke
42	Bruce Rendall
48	Darryl Gilmour
63	Shane Whelan
84	Paul Marshall
105	Daril Holmes
126	Ken Alexander
147	Tony Horacek
168	Mike Cusack
189	Gordon Murphy
231	Rod Williams
252	Paul Maurice

1984
Pick
22	Greg Smyth
27	Scott Mellanby
37	Jeff Chychrun
43	Dave McLay
47	John Stevens
79	Dave Hanson
100	Brian Dobbin
121	John Dzikowski
142	Tom Allen
163	Luke Vitale
184	Bill Powers
204	Daryn Fersovitch
245	Juraj Bakos

1983
Pick
41	Peter Zezel
44	Derrick Smith
81	Alan Bourbeau
101	Jerome Carrier
121	Rick Tocchet
141	Bobby Mormina
161	Per-Erik Eklund
181	Rob Nichols
201	William McCormick
221	Brian Jopling
241	Harold Duvall

1982
Pick
4	Ron Sutter
46	Miroslav Dvorak
47	Bill Campbell
77	Mikael Hjalm
98	Todd Bergen
119	Ron Hextall
140	Dave Brown
161	Alain Lavigne
182	Magnus Roupe
203	Tom Allen
224	Rick Gal
245	Mark Vichorek

Coach

MURRAY, TERRY RODNEY
Coach, Philadelphia Flyers. Born in Shawville, Que., July 20, 1950.

Terry Murray was named as the tenth coach of the Philadelphia Flyers on June 23, 1994. He is the second former Flyers' player to return to the team as head coach, joining Paul Holmgren, who coached the team from 1988-91. Prior to joining the Flyers, Murray served as the head coach of the Washington Capitals for five seasons from January 20, 1990 to January 27, 1994. As coach of the Capitals, Murray's team posted an overall record of 163-134-28 for a .545 winning percentage. After leaving the Capitals, Murray served as head coach of the Cincinnati Cyclones, the Florida Panthers' IHL affiliate, leading the team to a 17-7-4 record in 28 games. The Shawville, Quebec native also spent two seasons as the head coach of the AHL's Baltimore Skipjacks.

Murray was selected 88th overall by California in the 1970 Amateur Draft. He enjoyed a successful playing career in both the NHL and American Hockey League. He led the Maine Mariners to two Calder Cup championships in 1977-78 and 1978-79, and was awarded the AHL's Eddie Shore Plaque as the league's outstanding defenseman in both seasons. He was an AHL First Team All-Star in three seasons, 1975-76, 1977-78 and 1978-79. Terry played in 302 NHL games over eight seasons, concluding his career with the Capitals in 1981-82. He was the first ex-Capital to coach the club.

Coaching Record

		Regular Season					Playoffs			
Season	Team	Games	W	L	T	%	Games	W	L	%
1988-89	Baltimore (AHL)	80	30	46	4	.400	....	....	....	....
1989-90	Baltimore (AHL)	44	26	17	1	.603	....	....	....	....
1989-90	**Washington (NHL)**	34	18	14	2	.559	15	8	7	.533
1990-91	**Washington (NHL)**	80	37	36	7	.506	11	5	6	.455
1991-92	**Washington (NHL)**	80	45	27	8	.613	7	3	4	.429
1992-93	**Washington (NHL)**	84	43	34	7	.554	6	2	4	.333
1993-94	**Washington (NHL)**	47	20	23	4	.468	....	....	....	....
	Cincinnati (IHL)	28	17	7	4	.679	11	6	5	.545
1994-95	**Philadelphia (NHL)**	48	28	16	4	.625	15	10	5	.667
1995-96	**Philadelphia (NHL)**	82	45	24	13	.628	12	6	6	.500
	NHL Totals	455	236	174	45	.568	66	34	32	.515

Club Directory

CoreStates Center
1 CoreStates Complex
Philadelphia, PA 19148
Phone **215/465-4500**
PR FAX 215/389-9403
Capacity: 19,500

Executive Management

Chairman	Ed Snider
Limited Partners	Sylvan and Fran Tobin
President and General Manager	Bob Clarke
Chairman of the Board, Emeritus	Joe Scott
Chief Operating Officer	Ron Ryan
Executive Vice-President	Keith Allen
Governor	Ed Snider
Alternate Governors	Bob Clarke, Rich Ruben, Ron Ryan, Phil Weinberg
Executive Assistant	Kathy Nasevich
Receptionist	Aggie Preston

Hockey Club Personnel
Head Coach	Terry Murray
Assistant General Manager	John Blackwell
Assistant Coaches	Keith Acton, Dave Brown
Director of Pro Scouting	Paul Holmgren
Goaltending Coach	Rejean Lemelin
Chief Scout	Dennis Patterson
Scouting Staff	John Chapman, Bill Dineen, Inge Hammarstrom, Jerry Melnyk, Simon Nolet, Blair Reid, Vaclav Slansky, Evgeny Zimin
Director of Team Services	Joe Kadlec
Computer Analyst	David Gelberg
Executive Assistant	Dianna Taylor

Medical/Training Staff
Team Physicians	Arthur Bartolozzi, M.D., Jeff Hartzell, M.D., Gary Dorshimer, M.D., Mike Weinik, M.D., Guy Lanzi, D.D.S.
Athletic Trainer	John Worley
Head Equipment Manager	Dave Settlemyre
Assistant Equipment Managers	Jim Evers, Rusty Pearl

Public Relations Department
Vice President, Public Relations	Mark Piazza
Director of Public Relations	Joe Klueg
Director of Community Relations	Linda Panasci
Director of Fan Development	Greg Scott
Assistant Director of Public Relations	Linda Held
Public Relations Assistant	Jody Clarke
Youth Hockey Assistant	Melissa Wilson

Sales/Marketing Department
Vice President, Marketing	Bob Schwartz
Vice President, Sales	Jack Betson
Director of Sales and Marketing	Frank Miceli
Ticket Manager	Ceil Baker
Assistant Director of Season Tickets	Bill Kearns
Sales/Marketing Assistant	Helen Hubbard
Ticket Office Assistants	Jason Zahor, Pat Piazza, Linda DiTommaso

Finance Department
Vice President, Finance	Dan Clemmens
Director of Finance	Jeff Niessen
Controller	Lisa Cataldo
Payroll Accountant	Susann Schaffer

Advertising/Sales Department
General Manager, Advertising/Sales	Dave Resnick
Sponsorship Manager	Carolyn Wollman
Sales Staff	Michael Buono, Steve Coates, Lisa Fusco, Jeff Kirk, Ivan Shlichtman, Joe Watson
Advertising/Sales Assistants	Suzanne Carlin, Mary Purcell Davis, Alyson Rochvary

Broadcast Department
TV Play-by-Play, Color Commentary	Jim Jackson, Gary Dornhoefer
Radio Play-by-Play, Color Commentary	John Wiedeman, Steve Coates
Broadcast Consultant	Mike Finocchiaro
Broadcast Advisor	Gene Hart
Public Address Announcer	Lou Nolan

Flyers Wives Charities
Executive Director	Fran Tobin
Director of Marketing	Rita Johanson
Marketing Coordinator	Laurie Podall

Coaching History

Keith Allen, 1967-68 to 1968-69; Vic Stasiuk, 1969-70 to 1970-71; Fred Shero, 1971-72 to 1977-78; Bob McCammon and Pat Quinn, 1978-79; Pat Quinn, 1979-80 to 1980-81; Pat Quinn and Bob McCammon, 1981-82; Bob McCammon, 1982-83 to 1983-84; Mike Keenan, 1984-85 to 1987-88; Paul Holmgren, 1988-89 to 1990-91; Paul Holmgren and Bill Dineen, 1991-92; Bill Dineen, 1992-93; Terry Simpson, 1993-94; Terry Murray, 1994-95 to date.

Captains' History

Lou Angotti, 1967-68; Ed Van Impe, 1968-69 to 1971-72; Ed Van Impe and Bobby Clarke, 1972-73; Bobby Clarke, 1973-74 to 1978-79; Mel Bridgman, 1979-80, 1980-81; Bill Barber, 1981-82; Bill Barber and Bobby Clarke, 1982-83; Bobby Clarke, 1983-84; Dave Poulin, 1984-85 to 1988-89; Dave Poulin and Ron Sutter, 1989-90; Ron Sutter, 1990-91; Rick Tocchet, 1991-92; no captain, 1992-93; Kevin Dineen, 1993-94; Eric Lindros, 1994-95 to date.

Phoenix Coyotes

1995-96 Results: 36W-40L-6T 78PTS. Fifth, Central Division

Schedule

Oct.	Sat.	5	at Hartford	Thur.	9	Detroit	
	Mon.	7	at Boston	Fri.	10	at Dallas	
	Thur.	10	San Jose	Sun.	12	Buffalo	
	Sat.	12	Anaheim	Mon.	13	at San Jose	
	Mon.	14	Edmonton	Wed.	15	St. Louis	
	Fri.	18	Philadelphia	Thur.	23	Anaheim	
	Sun.	20	Florida	Sat.	25	Vancouver	
	Tues.	22	St. Louis	Tues.	28	at Philadelphia	
	Sat.	26	at Toronto	Wed.	29	at Detroit	
	Mon.	28	at Montreal	Feb. Sat.	1	at Pittsburgh*	
	Wed.	30	at Edmonton	Tues.	4	Tampa Bay	
Nov.	Fri.	1	at Calgary	Thur.	6	Chicago	
	Sun.	3	Montreal	Sat.	8	Dallas	
	Wed.	6	Dallas	Mon.	10	at St. Louis	
	Fri.	8	Colorado	Wed.	12	at Dallas	
	Thur.	14	Hartford	Thur.	13	Colorado	
	Sat.	16	Toronto	Sat.	15	Boston*	
	Mon.	18	Detroit	Tues.	18	Los Angeles	
	Wed.	20	at Colorado	Sat.	22	at Anaheim*	
	Thur.	21	at St. Louis	Mon.	24	Detroit	
	Sat.	23	NY Islanders	Wed.	26	at Calgary	
	Tues.	26	NY Rangers	Thur.	27	at Vancouver	
	Thur.	28	New Jersey	Mar. Sun.	2	Chicago	
	Sat.	30	Calgary	Wed.	5	at Florida	
Dec.	Tues.	3	Los Angeles	Thur.	6	at Tampa Bay	
	Thur.	5	at St. Louis	Sat.	8	at Chicago	
	Sat.	7	at New Jersey*	Mon.	10	Ottawa	
	Mon.	9	at NY Rangers	Wed.	12	Pittsburgh	
	Tues.	10	at NY Islanders	Fri.	14	at San Jose	
	Fri.	13	at Ottawa	Mon.	17	St. Louis	
	Sat.	14	at Toronto	Wed.	19	at Dallas	
	Tues.	17	Washington	Thur.	20	at Chicago	
	Fri.	20	Toronto	Sat.	22	at Toronto	
	Sun.	22	Calgary	Thur.	27	Toronto	
	Mon.	23	at Anaheim	Sat.	29	Edmonton	
	Thur.	26	at Los Angeles	Apr. Tues.	1	San Jose	
	Fri.	27	Vancouver	Thur.	3	at Los Angeles	
	Mon.	30	at Detroit	Sun.	6	at Colorado	
Jan.	Thur.	2	at Chicago	Mon.	7	Dallas	
	Fri.	3	at Washington	Wed.	9	at Vancouver	
	Sun.	5	at Buffalo	Fri.	11	at Edmonton	

* Denotes afternoon game.

Kris King's dedication to his community off the ice coupled with his determined play were the main reasons why the Phoenix Coyote winger was honored as 1995's winner of the King Clancy Memorial Trophy.

Franchise date: June 22, 1979
Transferred from Winnipeg to Phoenix, July 1, 1996

CENTRAL DIVISION

18th NHL Season

Year-by-Year Record

		Home			Road			Overall							
Season	GP	W	L	T	W	L	T	W	L	T	GF	GA	Pts.	Finished		Playoff Result
1995-96*	82	22	16	3	14	24	3	36	40	6	275	291	78	5th,	Central Div.	Lost Conf. Quarter-Final
1994-95*	48	10	10	4	6	15	3	16	25	7	157	177	39	6th,	Central Div.	Out of Playoffs
1993-94*	84	15	23	4	9	28	5	24	51	9	245	344	57	6th,	Central Div.	Out of Playoffs
1992-93*	84	23	16	3	17	21	4	40	37	7	322	320	87	4th,	Smythe Div.	Lost Div. Semi-Final
1991-92*	80	20	14	6	13	18	9	33	32	15	251	244	81	4th,	Smythe Div.	Lost Div. Semi-Final
1990-91*	80	17	18	5	9	25	6	26	43	11	260	288	63	5th,	Smythe Div.	Out of Playoffs
1989-90*	80	22	13	5	15	19	6	37	32	11	298	290	85	3rd,	Smythe Div.	Lost Div. Semi-Final
1988-89*	80	17	18	5	9	24	7	26	42	12	300	355	64	5th,	Smythe Div.	Out of Playoffs
1987-88*	80	20	14	6	13	22	5	33	36	11	292	310	77	3rd,	Smythe Div.	Lost Div. Semi-Final
1986-87*	80	25	12	3	15	20	5	40	32	8	279	271	88	3rd,	Smythe Div.	Lost Div. Final
1985-86*	80	18	19	3	8	28	4	26	47	7	295	372	59	3rd,	Smythe Div.	Lost Div. Semi-Final
1984-85*	80	21	13	6	22	14	4	43	27	10	358	332	96	2nd,	Smythe Div.	Lost Div. Final
1983-84*	80	17	15	8	14	23	3	31	38	11	340	374	73	4th,	Smythe Div.	Lost Div. Semi-Final
1982-83*	80	22	16	2	11	23	6	33	39	8	311	333	74	4th,	Smythe Div.	Lost Div. Semi-Final
1981-82*	80	18	13	9	15	20	5	33	33	14	319	332	80	2nd,	Norris Div.	Lost Div. Semi-Final
1980-81*	80	7	25	8	2	32	6	9	57	14	246	400	32	6th,	Smythe Div.	Out of Playoffs
1979-80*	80	13	19	8	7	30	3	20	49	11	214	314	51	5th,	Smythe Div.	Out of Playoffs

* Winnipeg Jets

1996-97 Player Personnel

FORWARDS	HT	WT	S	Place of Birth	Date	1995-96 Club
DOAN, Shane	6-1	215	R	Halkirk, Alta.	10/10/76	Winnipeg
DRAKE, Dallas	6-0	180	L	Trail, B.C.	2/4/69	Winnipeg
EASTWOOD, Mike	6-3	205	R	Ottawa, Ont.	7/1/67	Winnipeg
GARTNER, Mike	6-0	187	R	Ottawa, Ont.	10/29/59	Toronto
GORDON, Rhett	5-11	175	R	Regina, Sask.	8/26/76	Regina-Springfield
HANSEN, Tavis	6-1	180	R	Prince Albert, Sask.	6/17/75	Springfield
JANNEY, Craig	6-1	190	L	Hartford, CT	9/26/67	San Jose-Winnipeg
KILGER, Chad	6-3	204	L	Cornwall, Ont.	11/27/76	Anaheim-Winnipeg
KING, Kris	5-11	208	L	Bracebridge, Ont.	2/18/66	Winnipeg
KOROLEV, Igor	6-1	187	L	Moscow, USSR	9/6/70	Winnipeg
McKENZIE, Jim	6-3	205	L	Gull Lake, Sask.	11/3/69	Winnipeg
MURRAY, Rob	6-1	180	R	Toronto, Ont.	4/4/67	Winnipeg-Springfield
ROENICK, Jeremy	6-0	170	R	Boston, MA	1/17/70	Chicago
RONNING, Cliff	5-8	170	L	Burnaby, B.C.	10/1/65	Vancouver
SAVAGE, Reggie	5-10	192	L	Montreal, Que.	5/1/70	Atlanta-Syracuse
SHANNON, Darrin	6-2	210	L	Barrie, Ont.	12/8/69	Winnipeg
SIMON, Jason	6-1	190	L	Sarnia, Ont.	3/21/69	Springfield
STAPLETON, Mike	5-10	183	R	Sarnia, Ont.	5/5/66	Winnipeg
TKACHUK, Keith	6-2	210	L	Melrose, MA	3/28/72	Winnipeg
YLONEN, Juha	6-0	180	L	Helsinki, Finland	2/13/72	Jokerit
DEFENSEMEN						
CHEREDARYK, Steve	6-2	197	L	Calgary, Alta.	11/20/75	Springfield-Knoxville
DOIG, Jason	6-3	216	R	Montreal, Que.	1/29/77	Wpg-Laval-Granby-Springfield
EAKINS, Dallas	6-2	195	L	Dade City, FL	2/27/67	St. Louis-Worcester-Winnipeg
FINLEY, Jeff	6-2	204	L	Edmonton, Alta.	4/14/67	Winnipeg-Springfield
JOHNSON, Jim	6-1	190	L	New Hope, MN	8/9/62	Washington
MACIVER, Norm	5-11	180	L	Thunder Bay, Ont.	9/8/64	Pittsburgh-Winnipeg
MANSON, Dave	6-2	202	L	Prince Albert, Sask.	1/27/67	Winnipeg
McCRIMMON, Brad	5-11	197	L	Dodsland, Sask.	3/29/59	Hartford
NUMMINEN, Teppo	6-1	190	R	Tampere, Finland	7/3/68	Winnipeg
QUINT, Deron	6-1	182	L	Durham, NH	3/12/76	Winnipeg-Springfield-Seattle
THOMPSON, Brent	6-2	200	L	Calgary, Alta.	1/9/71	Winnipeg-Springfield
TVERDOVSKY, Oleg	6-0	185	L	Donetsk, USSR	5/18/76	Anaheim-Winnipeg

GOALTENDERS	HT	WT	C	Place of Birth	Date	1995-96 Club
DUFFUS, Parris	6-2	192	L	Denver, CO	1/27/70	Minnesota
KHABIBULIN, Nikolai	6-1	176	L	Sverdlovsk, USSR	1/13/73	Winnipeg
LANGKOW, Scott	5-11	190	L	Sherwood Park, Alta.	4/21/75	Winnipeg-Springfield
WAKALUK, Darcy	5-11	180	L	Pincher Creek, Alta.	3/14/66	Dallas

Coach

HAY, DON

Coach, Phoenix Coyotes. Born in Kamloops, B.C., February 13, 1954.

Don Hay was named as the first head coach of the Phoenix Coyotes Hockey Club on July 1, 1996, after serving one season as an assistant coach with the Calgary Flames.

As head coach of the Canadian National Junior Team, Hay guided the Canadian squad to the gold medal and a World Championship. Hay joined the Calgary Flames organization on June 20, 1995 after serving as head coach of the Kamloops Blazers (WHL). In 216 career games as head coach of the Blazers, the team compiled an impressive 144-58-14 record (.699%), one of the top Major Junior hockey records in that period.

Along with many significant regular season achievements, Kamloops also enjoyed tremendous playoff success. Under Hay's direction, the Blazers won two consecutive Memorial Cup championships.

Kamloops captured the 1993-94 Western Hockey League championship with a 12-7 playoff record. The WHL champions followed their league title with a Memorial Cup championship two weeks later in Laval, Quebec.

The following season, the 1994-95 Kamloops team responded with a 52-14-6 record (.764%), the best regular-season record of Hay's tenure. The team compiled a 15-6 record through the 1995 playoffs, capturing their second consecutive Western Hockey League championship. In May, 1995, in front of a sold-out Kamloops crowd, the Blazers won their second consecutive Memorial Cup title.

After three seasons as head coach, Hay left the Blazers with two Western Hockey League championships, two Memorial Cup championships, and a remarkable 35-18 (.660%) playoff record.

In between the Blazers' two championship seasons, Hay coached Canada's entry at the 1995 World Junior Championships in Red Deer, Alberta. Hay led the Canadian Junior squad to a perfect 7-0 record — the first time a team had gone undefeated in the tournament — and captured the gold medal for Canada.

In addition to his three seasons as head coach of Kamloops, Hay also spent seven years with the Blazers as an assistant coach (1985-92). In his 10 seasons with Kamloops, he was a member of three Memorial Cup champions (also 1991-92) and four Western Hockey League champions.

Coaching Record

		Regular Season					Playoffs			
Season	Team	Games	W	L	T	%	Games	W	L	%
1992-93	Kamloops (WHL)	72	42	28	2	.597	13	8	5	.615
1993-94	Kamloops (WHL)	72	50	16	6	.736	19	12	7	.632
1994-95	Kamloops (WHL)	72	52	14	6	.764	21	15	6	.714

Coaching History

Tom McVie and Bill Sutherland, 1979-80; Tom McVie, Bill Sutherland and Mike Smith, 1980-81; Tom Watt, 1981-82 to 1982-83; Tom Watt and Barry Long, 1983-84; Barry Long, 1984-85; Barry Long and John Ferguson, 1985-86. Dan Maloney, 1986-87 to 1987-88, Dan Maloney and Rick Bowness 1988-89; Bob Murdoch, 1989-90, 1990-91; John Paddock, 1991-92 to 1993-94; John Paddock and Terry Simpson, 1994-95; Terry Simpson, 1995-96; Don Hay, 1996-97.

1995-96 Scoring

* – rookie

Regular Season

Pos	#	Player	Team	GP	G	A	Pts	+/–	PIM	PP	SH	GW	GT	S	%
L	7	Keith Tkachuk	WPG	76	50	48	98	11	156	20	2	6	0	249	20.1
C	29	Craig Janney	S.J.	71	13	49	62	–35	26	5	0	1	0	78	16.7
			WPG	13	7	13	20	2	0	2	0	1	0	13	53.8
			TOTAL	84	20	62	82	–33	26	7	0	2	0	91	22.0
C	10	Alexei Zhamnov	WPG	58	22	37	59	–4	65	5	0	2	0	199	11.1
D	27	Teppo Numminen	WPG	74	11	43	54	–4	22	6	0	3	0	165	6.7
D	44	Norm Maciver	PIT	32	2	21	23	12	32	1	0	0	0	30	6.7
			WPG	39	5	25	30	–6	26	2	0	0	0	49	10.2
			TOTAL	71	7	46	53	6	58	3	0	0	0	79	8.9
R	23	Igor Korolev	WPG	73	22	29	51	1	42	8	0	5	1	165	13.3
C	16	Ed Olczyk	WPG	51	27	22	49	0	65	16	0	1	0	147	18.4
C	11	Dallas Drake	WPG	69	19	20	39	–7	36	4	4	2	1	121	15.7
D	4	Dave Manson	WPG	82	7	23	30	8	205	3	0	0	0	189	3.7
D	20	Oleg Tverdovsky	ANA	51	7	15	22	0	35	2	0	0	0	84	8.3
			WPG	31	0	8	8	–7	6	0	0	0	0	35	0.0
			TOTAL	82	7	23	30	–7	41	2	0	0	0	119	5.9
C	32	Mike Eastwood	WPG	80	14	14	28	–14	20	2	0	3	1	94	14.9
C	14	Mike Stapleton	WPG	58	10	14	24	–4	37	3	1	0	0	91	11.0
L	34	Darrin Shannon	WPG	63	5	18	23	–5	28	0	0	1	0	74	6.8
L	17	Kris King	WPG	81	9	11	20	–7	151	0	1	2	0	89	10.1
D	5*	Deron Quint	WPG	51	5	13	18	–2	22	2	0	0	0	97	5.2
C	18*	Chad Kilger	ANA	45	5	7	12	–2	22	0	0	1	0	38	13.2
			WPG	29	2	3	5	–2	12	0	0	0	0	19	10.5
			TOTAL	74	7	10	17	–4	34	0	0	1	0	57	12.3
R	19*	Shane Doan	WPG	74	7	10	17	–9	101	1	0	3	0	106	6.6
D	28	Craig Muni	BUF	47	0	4	4	–12	69	0	0	0	0	25	0.0
			WPG	25	1	3	4	6	37	0	0	0	0	16	6.3
			TOTAL	72	1	7	8	–6	106	0	0	0	0	41	2.4
L	33	Jim McKenzie	WPG	73	4	2	6	–4	202	0	0	0	0	28	14.3
D	26	Jeff Finley	WPG	65	1	5	6	–2	81	0	0	0	0	27	3.7
C	15	Randy Gilhen	WPG	22	2	3	5	1	12	0	0	0	0	26	7.7
R	21	Denis Chasse	STL	42	3	0	3	–9	108	1	0	1	0	25	12.0
			WSH	3	0	0	0	–1	5	0	0	0	0	3	0.0
			WPG	15	0	0	0	–4	12	0	0	0	0	3	0.0
			TOTAL	60	3	0	3	–14	125	1	0	1	0	31	9.7
C	39	Iain Fraser	WPG	12	1	1	2	1	4	0	0	0	0	12	8.3
D	55*	Jason Doig	WPG	15	1	1	2	–2	28	0	0	0	0	7	14.3
R	22*	Craig Mills	WPG	4	0	2	2	0	0	0	0	0	0	0	0.0
D	3	Brent Thompson	WPG	10	0	1	1	–2	21	0	0	0	0	7	0.0
D	6	Dallas Eakins	STL	16	0	1	1	–2	34	0	0	0	0	6	0.0
			WPG	2	0	0	0	1	0	0	0	0	0	0	0.0
			TOTAL	18	0	1	1	–1	34	0	0	0	0	6	0.0
G	37	Tom Draper	WPG	1	0	0	0	0	0	0	0	0	0	0	0.0
C	12	Rob Murray	WPG	1	0	0	0	–1	2	0	0	0	0	1	0.0
G	31*	Scott Langkow	WPG	1	0	0	0	0	0	0	0	0	0	0	0.0
R	43*	Ravil Gusmanov	WPG	4	0	0	0	–3	0	0	0	0	0	6	0.0
G	37	Dominic Roussel	PHI	9	0	0	0	0	0	0	0	0	0	0	0.0
			WPG	7	0	0	0	0	2	0	0	0	0	0	0.0
			TOTAL	16	0	0	0	0	2	0	0	0	0	0	0.0
R	30	Ed Ronan	WPG	17	0	0	0	–3	16	0	0	0	0	13	0.0
G	29	Tim Cheveldae	WPG	30	0	0	0	0	0	0	0	0	0	0	0.0
G	35	N. Khabibulin	WPG	53	0	0	0	0	12	0	0	0	0	0	0.0

Goaltending

No.	Goaltender	GPI	Mins	Avg	W	L	T	EN	SO	GA	SA	S%
31	* Scott Langkow	1	6	.00	0	0	0	0	0	0	2	1.000
35	N. Khabibulin	53	2914	3.13	26	20	3	4	2	152	1656	.908
37	Dominic Roussel	7	285	3.37	2	2	0	0	0	16	134	.881
29	Tim Cheveldae	30	1695	3.93	8	18	3	5	0	111	948	.883
37	Tom Draper	1	34	5.29	0	0	0	0	0	3	14	.786
	Totals	**82**	**4951**	**3.53**	**36**	**40**	**6**	**9**	**2**	**291**	**2763**	**.895**

Playoffs

Pos	#	Player	Team	GP	G	A	Pts	+/–	PIM	PP	SH	GW	OT	S	%
D	4	Dave Manson	WPG	6	2	1	3	3	30	0	0	1	0	12	16.7
C	10	Alexei Zhamnov	WPG	6	2	1	3	0	8	0	0	0	0	11	18.2
C	29	Craig Janney	WPG	6	1	2	3	0	0	0	0	0	0	6	16.7
C	16	Ed Olczyk	WPG	6	1	2	3	0	6	0	0	0	0	15	6.7
L	7	Keith Tkachuk	WPG	6	1	2	3	0	22	0	0	0	0	16	6.3
R	23	Igor Korolev	WPG	6	0	3	3	–2	0	0	0	0	0	4	0.0
C	18*	Chad Kilger	WPG	4	1	0	1	0	0	0	0	1	0	2	50.0
D	44	Norm Maciver	WPG	6	1	0	1	3	2	0	0	0	0	10	10.0
L	34	Darrin Shannon	WPG	6	1	0	1	0	6	0	0	0	0	2	50.0
L	17	Kris King	WPG	5	0	1	1	1	4	0	0	0	0	3	0.0
D	28	Craig Muni	WPG	6	0	1	1	–2	2	0	0	0	0	1	0.0
C	32	Mike Eastwood	WPG	6	0	1	1	–1	2	0	0	0	0	2	0.0
D	20	Oleg Tverdovsky	WPG	6	0	1	1	–2	0	0	0	0	0	8	0.0
L	33	Jim McKenzie	WPG	1	0	0	0	0	2	0	0	0	0	0	0.0
R	22*	Craig Mills	WPG	1	0	0	0	0	0	0	0	0	0	0	0.0
C	11	Dallas Drake	WPG	3	0	0	0	–2	0	0	0	0	0	3	0.0
C	39	Iain Fraser	WPG	4	0	0	0	0	0	0	0	0	0	0	0.0
D	26	Jeff Finley	WPG	6	0	0	0	–4	4	0	0	0	0	3	0.0
D	27	Teppo Numminen	WPG	6	0	0	0	–3	2	0	0	0	0	6	0.0
C	14	Mike Stapleton	WPG	6	0	0	0	–1	21	0	0	0	0	1	0.0
G	35	N. Khabibulin	WPG	6	0	0	0	0	0	0	0	0	0	0	0.0
R	19*	Shane Doan	WPG	6	0	0	0	0	6	0	0	0	0	2	0.0

Goaltending

No.	Goaltender	GPI	Mins	Avg	W	L	EN	SO	GA	SA	S%
35	N. Khabibulin	6	359	3.18	2	4	1	0	19	214	.911
	Totals	**6**	**360**	**3.33**	**2**	**4**	**1**	**0**	**20**	**215**	**.907**

Club Records

Team

(Figures in brackets for season records are games played; records for fewest points, wins, ties, losses, goals, goals against are for 70 or more games)

Most Points	96	1984-85 (80)
Most Wins	43	1984-85 (80)
Most Ties	15	1991-92 (80)
Most Losses	57	1980-81 (80)
Most Goals	358	1984-85 (80)
Most Goals Against	400	1980-81 (80)
Fewest Points	32	1980-81 (80)
Fewest Wins	9	1980-81 (80)
Fewest Ties	7	1985-86 (80), 1992-93 (84)
Fewest Losses	27	1984-85 (80)
Fewest Goals	214	1979-80 (80)
Fewest Goals Against	244	1991-92 (80)
Longest Winning Streak		
Overall	9	Mar. 8-27/85
Home	9	Dec. 27/92-Jan. 23/93
Away	8	Feb. 25-Apr. 6/85
Longest Undefeated Streak		
Overall	13	Mar. 8-Apr. 7/85 (10 wins, 3 ties)
Home	11	Dec. 23/83-Feb. 5/84 (6 wins, 5 ties)
Away	9	Feb. 25-Apr. 7/85 (8 wins, 1 tie)
Longest Losing Streak		
Overall	10	Nov. 30-Dec. 20/80, Feb. 6-25/94
Home	5	Oct. 29-Nov. 13/93
Away	13	Jan. 26-Apr. 14/94
Longest Winless Streak		
Overall	*30	Oct. 19-Dec. 20/80 (23 losses, 7 ties)
Home	14	Oct. 19-Dec. 14/80 (9 losses, 5 ties)
Away	18	Oct. 10-Dec. 20/80 (16 losses, 2 ties)
Most Shutouts, Season	7	1991-92 (80)
Most PIM, Season	2,278	1987-88 (80)
Most Goals, Game	12	Feb. 25/85 (Wpg. 12 at NYR 5)

Individual

Most Seasons	14	Thomas Steen
Most Games	950	Thomas Steen
Most Goals, Career	379	Dale Hawerchuk
Most Assists, Career	553	Thomas Steen
Most Points, Career	929	Dale Hawerchuk (379G, 550A)
Most PIM, Career	1,338	Laurie Boschman
Most Shutouts, Career	14	Bob Essensa
Longest Consecutive Games Streak	475	Dale Hawerchuk (Dec. 19/82-Dec. 10/88)
Most Goals, Season	76	Teemu Selanne (1992-93)
Most Assists, Season	79	Phil Housley (1992-93)
Most Points, Season	132	Teemu Selanne (1992-93; 76G, 56A)
Most PIM, Season	347	Tie Domi (1993-94)
Most Points, Defenseman Season	97	Phil Housley (1992-93; 18G, 79A)
Most Points, Center, Season	130	Dale Hawerchuk (1984-85; 53G, 77A)
Most Points, Right Wing, Season	132	Teemu Selanne (1992-93; 76G, 56A)
Most Points, Left Wing, Season	98	Keith Tkachuk (1995-96; 50G, 48A)
Most Points, Rookie, Season	*132	Teemu Selanne (1992-93; 76G, 56A)
Most Shutouts, Season	5	Bob Essensa (1991-92)
Most Goals, Game	5	Willy Lindstrom (Mar. 2/82), Alexei Zhamnov (Apr. 1/95)
Most Assists, Game	5	Dale Hawerchuk (Mar. 6/84, Mar. 18/89, Mar. 4/90), Phil Housley (Jan. 18/93)
Most Points, Game	6	Willy Lindstrom (Mar. 2/82; 5G, 1A), Dale Hawerchuk (Dec. 14/83; 3G, 3A, Mar. 5/88; 2G, 4A, Mar. 18/89; 1G, 5A), Thomas Steen (Oct. 24/84; 2G, 4A), Eddie Olczyk (Dec. 21/91; 2G, 4A)

* NHL Record.
Records include Winnipeg Jets, 1979-80 through 1995-96.

Retired Numbers

9	Bobby Hull	1972-1980
25	Thomas Steen	1981-1995

Captains' History

Lars-Erik Sjoberg, 1979-80; Morris Lukowich, 1980-81; Dave Christian, 1981-82; Dave Christian and Lucien DeBlois, 1982-83; Lucien DeBlois, 1983-84; Dale Hawerchuk, 1984-85 to 1988-89; Randy Carlyle, Dale Hawerchuk and Thomas Steen (tri-captains), 1989-90; Randy Carlyle and Thomas Steen (co-captains), 1990-91; Troy Murray, 1991-92; Troy Murray and Dean Kennedy, 1992-93; Dean Kennedy and Keith Tkachuk, 1993-94; Keith Tkachuk, 1994-95; Kris King, 1995-96.

All-time Record vs. Other Clubs

Regular Season

	At Home							On Road							Total						
	GP	W	L	T	GF	GA	PTS	GP	W	L	T	GF	GA	PTS	GP	W	L	T	GF	GA	PTS
Anaheim	6	2	4	0	21	24	4	6	0	6	0	10	25	0	12	2	10	0	31	49	4
Boston	24	9	13	2	86	91	20	23	3	17	3	74	110	9	47	12	30	5	160	201	29
Buffalo	23	10	11	2	75	83	22	23	2	19	2	57	107	6	46	12	30	4	132	190	28
Calgary	54	25	20	9	222	195	59	55	13	35	7	178	262	33	109	38	55	16	400	457	92
Chicago	33	18	11	4	127	112	40	31	5	23	3	88	149	13	64	23	34	7	215	261	53
Colorado	24	10	9	5	98	97	25	25	11	11	3	102	100	25	49	21	20	8	200	197	50
Dallas	31	16	14	1	113	111	33	33	11	18	4	110	140	26	64	27	32	5	223	251	59
Detroit	31	13	9	9	105	98	35	34	11	19	4	120	149	26	65	24	28	13	225	247	61
Edmonton	55	22	29	4	231	251	48	56	17	35	4	189	256	38	111	39	64	8	420	507	86
Florida	3	1	2	0	9	11	2	2	1	1	0	6	8	2	5	2	3	0	15	19	4
Hartford	25	12	12	1	88	91	25	23	7	11	5	76	94	19	48	19	23	6	164	185	44
Los Angeles	56	27	20	9	239	205	63	53	23	20	10	223	228	56	109	50	40	19	462	433	119
Montreal	23	8	10	5	76	90	21	23	2	21	0	52	123	4	46	10	31	5	128	213	25
New Jersey	24	17	4	3	97	64	37	22	9	7	6	71	70	24	46	26	11	9	168	134	61
NY Islanders	23	7	14	2	72	91	16	24	7	11	6	78	92	20	47	14	25	8	150	183	36
NY Rangers	24	10	12	2	90	90	22	23	8	13	2	93	110	18	47	18	25	4	183	200	40
Ottawa	3	2	1	0	18	12	4	5	4	0	1	24	10	9	8	6	1	1	42	22	13
Philadelphia	23	10	11	2	76	79	22	24	6	18	0	69	110	12	47	16	29	2	145	189	34
Pittsburgh	23	9	13	1	83	84	19	24	7	17	0	73	105	14	47	16	30	1	156	189	33
St. Louis	34	17	11	6	117	105	40	32	7	16	9	95	126	23	66	24	27	15	212	231	63
San Jose	14	7	4	3	49	45	17	12	4	6	2	49	52	10	26	11	10	5	98	97	27
Tampa Bay	4	2	2	0	13	11	4	4	3	1	0	17	16	6	8	5	3	0	30	27	10
Toronto	32	16	11	5	140	127	37	33	17	14	2	130	123	36	65	33	25	7	270	250	73
Vancouver	53	25	20	8	207	204	58	56	16	32	8	164	217	40	109	41	52	16	371	421	98
Washington	24	12	7	5	91	89	29	23	5	15	3	71	105	13	47	17	22	8	162	194	42
Totals	**669**	**307**	**274**	**88**	**2543**	**2460**	**702**	**669**	**199**	**386**	**84**	**2219**	**2887**	**482**	**1338**	**506**	**660**	**172**	**4762**	**5347**	**1184**

Playoffs

	Series	W	L	GP	W	L	T	GF	GA	Last Mtg.	Round	Result
Calgary	3	2	1	13	7	6	0	45	43	1987	DSF	W 4-2
Detroit	1	0	1	6	2	4	0	10	20	1996	CQF	L 2-4
Edmonton	6	0	6	26	4	22	0	75	120	1990	DSF	L 3-4
St. Louis	1	0	1	4	1	3	0	13	20	1982	DSF	L 1-3
Vancouver	2	0	2	13	5	8	0	34	50	1993	DSF	L 2-4
Totals	**13**	**2**	**11**	**62**	**19**	**43**	**0**	**177**	**253**			

Playoff Results 1996-92

Year	Round	Opponent	Result	GF	GA
1996	CQF	Detroit	L 2-4	10	20
1993	DSF	Vancouver	L 2-4	17	21
1992	DSF	Vancouver	L 3-4	17	29

Abbreviations: Round: F – Final; **CF** – conference final; **CQF** – conference quarter-final; **CSF** – conference semi-final; **DF** – division final; **DSF** – division semi-final; **SF** – semi-final; **QF** – quarter-final; **PR** – preliminary round.

Calgary totals include Atlanta, 1979-80. Colorado totals include Quebec, 1979-80 to 1994-95.
Dallas totals include Minnesota, 1979-80 to 1992-93. New Jersey totals include Colorado Rockies, 1979-80 to 1981-82.

1995-96 Results

Oct.	7		Dallas	7-5		10		Buffalo	4-1
	9		Anaheim	4-3		12		Hartford	2-3
	11	at	NY Rangers	4-6		14		Anaheim	4-6
	12	at	New Jersey	1-4		16	at	Washington	1-1
	15		Detroit	5-5		17	at	Toronto	4-2
	17		Tampa Bay	5-2		24		St. Louis	5-6
	19		San Jose	3-3		27	at	Montreal	1-4
	22	at	Anaheim	2-6		29	at	Dallas	2-1
	25	at	San Jose	6-1	**Feb.**	1	at	Colorado	4-6
	27	at	Edmonton	5-7		4		Vancouver	2-4
	28	at	Vancouver	4-1		8		Ottawa	6-2
	30		Detroit	3-2		10	at	Calgary	3-2
Nov.	1		Toronto	2-4		13	at	Vancouver	4-5
	3		Colorado	2-5		16		Pittsburgh	0-1
	5	at	Buffalo	4-3		18	at	St. Louis	0-3
	10	at	St. Louis	2-3		21		Vancouver	3-5
	14		Chicago	6-5		23		Chicago	1-0
	17		NY Rangers	6-3		26		Los Angeles	4-3
	18	at	Toronto	1-2		28		Toronto	4-3
	21	at	Boston	4-5	**Mar.**	1	at	Hartford	5-2
	22	at	Ottawa	3-1		3	at	NY Islanders	7-5
	26		Edmonton	4-0		5	at	Pittsburgh	4-9
	28		Toronto	4-3		7		Florida	5-3
	30		St. Louis	1-4		9		NY Islanders	2-4
Dec.	2		Chicago	2-2		10		Detroit	2-5
	3		Calgary	5-2		12	at	Detroit	2-5
	6	at	Los Angeles	3-6		13	at	Toronto	3-3
	7	at	San Jose	3-5		16	at	Philadelphia	0-3
	10		Washington	1-6		20		San Jose	1-7
	12		Montreal	5-6		22		Philadelphia	4-1
	15		Edmonton	9-4		24		Colorado	2-5
	17	at	Chicago	1-3		26	at	Dallas	8-2
	19	at	Tampa Bay	3-6		27	at	Colorado	3-1
	21	at	Florida	1-6		29	at	Edmonton	2-3
	23		St. Louis	2-1		31	at	Calgary	4-1
	28	at	Chicago	3-4	**Apr.**	3		Dallas	3-1
	29		New Jersey	5-3		6		Calgary	4-3
	31		Boston	3-5		8	at	St. Louis	2-2
Jan.	3	at	Los Angeles	5-4		10	at	Detroit	2-5
	5	at	Dallas	4-5		12		Los Angeles	5-3
	8	at	Detroit	6-4		14	at	Anaheim	2-5

Entry Draft
Selections 1996-82

1996
Pick
11 Dan Focht
24 Daniel Briere
62 Per-Anton Lundstrom
119 Richard Lintner
139 Robert Esche
174 Trevor Letowski
200 Nicholas Lent
226 Marc-Etienne Hubert

1995
Pick
7 Shane Doan
32 Marc Chouinard
34 Jason Doig
67 Brad Isbister
84 Jason Kurtz
121 Brian Elder
136 Sylvain Daigle
162 Paul Traynor
188 Jaroslav Obsut
189 Frederik Loven
214 Rob Deciantis

1994
Pick
30 Deron Quint
56 Dorian Anneck
58 Tavis Hansen
82 Steve Cheredaryk
108 Craig Mills
143 Steve Vezina
146 Chris Kibermanis
186 Ramil Saifullin
212 Henrik Smangs
238 Mike Mader
264 Jason Issel

1993
Pick
15 Mats Lindgren
31 Scott Langkow
43 Alexei Budayev
79 Ruslan Batyrshin
93 Ravil Gusmanov
119 Larry Courville
145 Michal Grosek
171 Martin Woods
197 Adrian Murray
217 Vladimir Potapov
223 Ilja Stashenkov
228 Harijs Vitolinsh
285 Russell Hewson

1992
Pick
17 Sergei Bautin
27 Boris Mironov
60 Jeremy Stevenson
84 Mark Visheau
132 Alexander Alexeyev
155 Artur Oktyabrev
156 Andrei Raisky
204 Nikolai Khaibulin
228 Yevgeny Garanin
229 Teemu Numminen
252 Andrei Karpovtsev
254 Ivan Vologzhaninov

1991
Pick
5 Aaron Ward
49 Dmitri Filimonov
91 Juha Ylonen
99 Yan Kaminsky
115 Jeff Sebastian
159 Jeff Ricciardi
181 Sean Gauthier
203 Igor Ulanov
225 Jason Jennings
247 Sergei Sorokin

1990
Pick
19 Keith Tkachuk
35 Mike Muller
74 Roman Meluzin
75 Scott Levins
77 Alexei Zhamnov
98 Craig Martin
119 Daniel Jardemyr
140 John Lilley
161 Henrik Andersson
182 Rauli Raitanen
203 Mika Alatalo
224 Sergei Selyanin
245 Keith Morris

1989
Pick
4 Stu Barnes
25 Dan Ratushny
46 Jason Cirone
62 Kris Draper
64 Mark Brownschidle
69 Alain Roy
109 Dan Bylsma
130 Pekka Peltola
131 Doug Evans
151 Jim Solly
172 Stephane Gauvin
193 Joe Larson
214 Bradley Podiak
235 Evgeny Davydov
240 Sergei Kharin

1988
Pick
10 Teemu Selanne
31 Russell Romaniuk
52 Stephane Beauregard
73 Brian Hunt
94 Anthony Joseph
101 Benoit Lebeau
115 Ronald Jones
127 Markus Akerblom
136 Jukka Marttila
157 Mark Smith
178 Mike Helber
199 Pavel Kostichkin
220 Kevin Heise
241 Kyle Galloway

1987
Pick
16 Bryan Marchment
37 Patrik Erickson
79 Don McLennan
96 Ken Gernander
100 Darrin Amundson
121 Joe Harwell
142 Tod Hartje
163 Markku Kyllonen
184 Jim Fernholz
226 Roger Rougelot
247 Hans Goran Elo

1986
Pick
8 Pat Elynuik
29 Teppo Numminen
50 Esa Palosaari
71 Hannu Jarvenpaa
92 Craig Endean
113 Robertson Bateman
155 Frank Furlan
176 Mark Green
197 John Blue
218 Matt Cote
239 Arto Blomsten

1985
Pick
18 Ryan Stewart
39 Roger Ohman
60 Daniel Berthiaume
81 Fredrik Olausson
102 John Borrell
123 Danton Cole
144 Brent Mowery
165 Tom Draper
186 Nevin Kardum
207 Dave Quigley
228 Chris Norton
249 Anssi Melametsa

1984
Pick
30 Peter Douris
68 Chris Mills
72 Sean Clement
93 Scott Schneider
99 Brent Severyn
114 Gary Lorden
135 Luciano Borsato
156 Brad Jones
177 Gord Whitaker
197 Rick Forst
218 Mike Warus
238 Jim Edmonds

1983
Pick
8 Andrew McBain
14 Bobby Dollas
29 Brad Berry
43 Peter Taglianetti
69 Bob Essensa
89 Harry Armstrong
109 Joel Baillargeon
129 Iain Duncan
149 Ron Pessetti
169 Todd Flichel
189 Cory Wright
209 Eric Cormier
229 Jamie Husgen

1982
Pick
12 Jim Kyte
74 Tom Martin
75 Dave Ellett
96 Tim Mishler
138 Derek Ray
159 Guy Gosselin
180 Tom Ward
201 Mike Savage
222 Bob Shaw
243 Jan Urban Ericson

General Manager

PADDOCK, JOHN
General Manager, Phoenix Coyotes.
Born in Brandon, Man., June 9, 1954.

John Paddock was named the interim general manager of the Winnipeg Jets on January 19, 1994, replacing Mike Smith who was the g.m. from 1988-93. On June 3, 1994, Paddock was officially named the Jets' g.m. and head coach. He is the Jets' third general manager since joining the NHL in 1979 and the fifth g.m. in the club's history.

Paddock has excelled at every level of hockey. As a player and a coach, he has been a winner. In his professional career (1975-1983), Paddock played 87 games in the NHL with Washington, Philadelphia and Quebec. In the American Hockey League, he played 445 games, recording 132 goals and 141 assists for 273 points and 1291 penalty minutes. He was a fierce competitor who helped Maine win an American Hockey League championship in 1978-79 with his hard-nosed, physical style of play.

Paddock, a 42-year-old native of Oak River, Manitoba, was named head coach of the Jets on June 17, 1991 after coaching one season at Binghamton, NY, the New York Rangers' AHL affiliate. On April 5, 1995, Paddock handed the head coach's portfolio to veteran coach Terry Simpson, enabling him to devote full attention to his general manager's duties. In four seasons with the Jets, Paddock posted a coaching record of 106-138-37. He was the first Jets coach to lead the team to two consecutive winning seasons ('91-92 and '92-93). His coaching career began with Maine of the AHL in 1983 and continued with a move to Hershey to work for the Philadelphia Flyers organization between 1985 and 1989. Paddock won Calder Cups in both Maine and Hershey and was a two-time recipient of the Louis A.R. Pieri Memorial Award as coach of the year in the AHL. In 1989-90, Paddock moved to Philadelphia to become the Flyers' assistant general manager under Bobby Clarke.

This season, Paddock will continue his efforts to assemble a winning team comprised of players who exemplify his own characteristics: hard work, dedication, pride and commitment to excellence.

John and his wife, Jill reside in Charleswood, Manitoba, with their four daughters, Jenny, Sally, Anna and Alyssa.

Club Directory

Phoenix Coyotes Hockey Club
One Renaissance Square
2 North Central, Suite 1930
Phoenix, AZ 85004
Phone **602/379-2800**
FAX 602/379-2828
America West Arena
Capacity: TBA

CEO & Governor . . . . Richard Burke
President & Alternate Governor . . . . Steven Gluckstern
Chief Operating Officer . . . . Shawn Hunter
Executive Vice President of Hockey Operations . . . . Bobby Smith
Vice President of Finance and Administration . . . . . Don Binda

Hockey Operations
General Manager . . . . John Paddock
Vice President of Hockey Administration . . . . Mike O'Hearn
Assistant General Manager . . . . Taylor Burke
Head Coach . . . . Don Hay
Assistant Coach . . . . Paul MacLean
Assistant Coach . . . . Zinetula Bilyaletdinov
Goaltending Coach . . . . Pete Peeters
Director of Scouting . . . . Bill Lesuk
Director of Player Personnel . . . . Sean Coady
Assistant Director of Scouting . . . . Joe Yannetti
Scouts . . . . Vaughn Karpan, Terry Doran, Connie Broden,
                                                      Larry Hornung, Claes Wallin, Evzen Slansky,
                                                      Boris Yemeljanov, Blair Mackasey
Director of Player Development . . . . Gordie Roberts
Legal Counsel . . . . Laurence Gilman
Director of Hockey Information . . . . Igor Kuperman
Video Coordinator . . . . Aaron Neurer
Administrative Assistant — Hockey Operations . . . . Lesa Senker

Broadcasting
Director of Broadcasting . . . . Mark Hulsey
Broadcasting Coordinator . . . . Craig Amazeen
TV Play-by-Play . . . . Doug McLeod
TV Color Commentator . . . . Charlie Simmer
Radio Play-by-Play . . . . Curt Keilback
Radio Color Commentator . . . . Steve Konroyd

Corporate Sales and Service
Vice President of Marketing . . . . Mike Blake
Director of Corporate Sales . . . . Tim Weil
Senior Corporate Account Executive . . . . Rip Reynolds
Corporate Account Executives . . . . Rob Childs, Kelly Staley

Ticket Sales and Service
Vice President of Sales & Service . . . . Brenda Tinnen
Director of Ticket Operations . . . . Bruce Bielenberg
Director of Marketing . . . . Tim McBride
Game Operations Coordinator . . . . Staci Grevillius
Director of Premium Seats . . . . Renee Tauer
Receptionist . . . . Geraldine Coscas
Ticket Sales Coordinator . . . . Jeff Lane
Account Executives . . . . Michell Corr, Shawn Duguid, Mike McIlroy,
                                                      Nick Roe, Brian Tollefson
Administrative Assistant to the Chief
  Operating Officer . . . . Lisa Mardeusz

Communications
Director of Media & Player Relations . . . . Richard Nairn
Manager of Media Relations . . . . Jeffrey Hecht
Publications Coordinator . . . . Rick Braunstein
Director of Community Relations/Executive
  Director of Phoenix Coyotes Goals
  For Kids Foundation . . . . Lori Summers
Coordinator of Fan Development . . . . Justin Maloof

Finance & Administration
Controller . . . . Joe Leibfried
Payroll Administrator . . . . Cheri Sedor
Accounting Assistants . . . . Joanna Savage, June Reynolds

Dressing Room
Athletic Therapist . . . . Gord Hart
Strength & Conditioning Coach . . . . Phil Walker
Massage Therapist . . . . Jukka Nieminen
Equipment Managers . . . . Stan Wilson, Tony DaCosta
Team Physician . . . . Matthew Maddox, D.O., Dana Seltzer, M.D.
Team Dentist . . . . Dr. Rick Lawson

Team Information
Team Colours . . . . Red, Green, Sand, Sienna & Purple
Dimensions of Rink . . . . 200 feet by 85 feet
Training Camp . . . . Phoenix
Press Box Location . . . . East Side of Arena
Television Stations . . . . KTVK Channel 3 and WB-61, Fox Sports Arizona
Radio Stations . . . . KDKB FM (93.3), KUPD-2 AM (1060)

General Managers' History

John Ferguson, 1979-80 to 1987-88; John Ferguson and Mike Smith, 1988-89; Mike Smith, 1989-90 to 1992-93; Mike Smith and John Paddock, 1993-94; John Paddock, 1994-95 to date.

NHL Coaching Record

			Regular Season					Playoffs		
Season	Team	Games	W	L	T	%	Games	W	L	%
1991-92	Winnipeg	80	33	32	15	.506	7	3	4	.429
1992-93	Winnipeg	84	40	37	7	.518	6	2	4	.333
1993-94	Winnipeg	84	24	51	9	.339	....	....	....	....
1994-95	Winnipeg	33	9	18	6	.364	....	....	....	....
NHL Totals		**281**	**106**	**138**	**37**	**.443**	**13**	**5**	**8**	**.385**

Pittsburgh Penguins

1995-96 Results: 49W-29L-4T 102PTS. First, Northeast Division

Schedule

Oct.	Sat.	5	Tampa Bay		Fri.	10	NY Islanders
	Tues.	8	at Hartford		Sat.	11	at Ottawa
	Fri.	11	at Ottawa		Tues.	14	Dallas
	Sat.	12	Ottawa		Wed.	15	at Hartford
	Wed.	16	at NY Rangers		Tues.	21	Calgary
	Thur.	17	at Buffalo		Thur.	23	Colorado
	Sat.	19	Washington		Sat.	25	NY Rangers*
	Tues.	22	at Edmonton		Sun.	26	at Montreal*
	Thur.	24	at Calgary		Wed.	29	at Buffalo
	Sat.	26	at Vancouver	**Feb.**	Sat.	1	Phoenix*
Nov.	Fri.	1	at Washington		Tues.	4	Vancouver
	Sat.	2	Ottawa		Wed.	5	at Montreal
	Wed.	6	Edmonton		Sat.	8	Detroit*
	Fri.	8	at Tampa Bay		Wed.	12	NY Islanders
	Sat.	9	at Florida		Sat.	15	at Philadelphia*
	Tues.	12	Buffalo		Sun.	16	Philadelphia
	Thur.	14	at Boston		Tues.	18	Florida
	Sat.	16	NY Rangers		Sat.	22	Chicago*
	Tues.	19	St. Louis		Sun.	23	at NY Islanders*
	Thur.	21	at Philadelphia		Thur.	27	at Detroit
	Fri.	22	at Hartford	**Mar.**	Sat.	1	at New Jersey*
	Wed.	27	Montreal		Tues.	4	New Jersey
	Sat.	30	Boston		Wed.	5	at Buffalo
Dec.	Tues.	3	Hartford		Sat.	8	Philadelphia*
	Wed.	4	at Ottawa		Mon.	10	Montreal
	Fri.	6	at Washington		Wed.	12	at Phoenix
	Sat.	7	Anaheim		Fri.	14	at Colorado
	Tues.	10	at Los Angeles		Sun.	16	at Dallas
	Wed.	11	at Anaheim		Tues.	18	Buffalo
	Fri.	13	at San Jose		Thur.	20	Toronto
	Sun.	15	at Chicago*		Sat.	22	New Jersey*
	Tues.	17	Boston		Mon.	24	at NY Rangers
	Thur.	19	at St. Louis		Wed.	26	at Montreal
	Sat.	21	San Jose		Sat.	29	Los Angeles*
	Mon.	23	at Toronto		Mon.	31	Florida
	Thur.	26	Montreal	**Apr.**	Thur.	3	Hartford
	Sat.	28	Buffalo		Sat.	5	Ottawa*
	Mon.	30	Washington		Tues.	8	Boston
Jan.	Thur.	2	at New Jersey		Thur.	10	at Tampa Bay
	Sat.	4	Tampa Bay		Fri.	11	at Florida
	Tues.	7	at NY Islanders		Sun.	13	at Boston*

* Denotes afternoon game.

Franchise date: June 5, 1967

NORTHEAST DIVISION

30th NHL Season

Year-by-Year Record

		Home			Road			Overall							
Season	GP	W	L	T	W	L	T	W	L	T	GF	GA	Pts.	Finished	Playoff Result
1995-96	82	32	9	0	17	20	4	49	29	4	362	284	102	1st, Northeast Div.	Lost Conf. Championship
1994-95	48	18	5	1	11	11	2	29	16	3	181	158	61	2nd, Northeast Div.	Lost Conf. Semi-Final
1993-94	84	25	9	8	19	18	5	44	27	13	299	285	101	1st, Northeast Div.	Lost Conf. Quarter-Final
1992-93	84	32	6	4	24	15	3	56	21	7	367	268	119	1st, Patrick Div.	Lost Div. Final
1991-92	**80**	**21**	**13**	**6**	**18**	**19**	**3**	**39**	**32**	**9**	**343**	**308**	**87**	**3rd, Patrick Div.**	**Won Stanley Cup**
1990-91	**80**	**25**	**12**	**3**	**16**	**21**	**3**	**41**	**33**	**6**	**342**	**305**	**88**	**1st, Patrick Div.**	**Won Stanley Cup**
1989-90	80	22	15	3	10	25	5	32	40	8	318	359	72	5th, Patrick Div.	Out of Playoffs
1988-89	80	24	13	3	16	20	4	40	33	7	347	349	87	2nd, Patrick Div.	Lost Div. Final
1987-88	80	22	12	6	14	23	3	36	35	9	319	316	81	6th, Patrick Div.	Out of Playoffs
1986-87	80	19	15	6	11	23	6	30	38	12	297	290	72	5th, Patrick Div.	Out of Playoffs
1985-86	80	20	15	5	14	23	3	34	38	8	313	305	76	5th, Patrick Div.	Out of Playoffs
1984-85	80	17	20	3	7	31	2	24	51	5	276	385	53	6th, Patrick Div.	Out of Playoffs
1983-84	80	7	29	4	9	29	2	16	58	6	254	390	38	6th, Patrick Div.	Out of Playoffs
1982-83	80	14	22	4	4	31	5	18	53	9	257	394	45	6th, Patrick Div.	Out of Playoffs
1981-82	80	21	11	8	10	25	5	31	36	13	310	337	75	4th, Patrick Div.	Lost Div. Semi-Final
1980-81	80	21	16	3	9	21	10	30	37	13	302	345	73	3rd, Norris Div.	Lost Prelim. Round
1979-80	80	20	13	7	10	24	6	30	37	13	251	303	73	3rd, Norris Div.	Lost Prelim. Round
1978-79	80	23	12	5	13	19	8	36	31	13	281	279	85	2nd, Norris Div.	Lost Quarter-Final
1977-78	80	16	15	9	9	22	9	25	37	18	254	321	68	4th, Norris Div.	Out of Playoffs
1976-77	80	22	12	6	12	21	7	34	33	13	240	252	81	3rd, Norris Div.	Lost Prelim. Round
1975-76	80	23	11	6	12	22	6	35	33	12	339	303	82	3rd, Norris Div.	Lost Prelim. Round
1974-75	80	25	5	10	12	23	5	37	28	15	326	289	89	3rd, Norris Div.	Lost Quarter-Final
1973-74	78	15	18	6	13	23	3	28	41	9	242	273	65	5th, West Div.	Out of Playoffs
1972-73	78	24	11	4	8	26	5	32	37	9	257	265	73	5th, West Div.	Out of Playoffs
1971-72	78	18	15	6	8	23	8	26	38	14	220	258	66	4th, West Div.	Lost Quarter-Final
1970-71	78	18	12	9	3	25	11	21	37	20	221	240	62	6th, West Div.	Out of Playoffs
1969-70	76	17	13	8	9	25	4	26	38	12	182	238	64	2nd, West Div.	Lost Semi-Final
1968-69	76	12	20	6	8	25	5	20	45	11	189	252	51	5th, West Div.	Out of Playoffs
1967-68	74	15	12	10	12	22	3	27	34	13	195	216	67	5th, West Div.	Out of Playoffs

Jaromir Jagr became only the eighth right winger in NHL history to score more than 60 goals in a season when the talented Pittsburgh forward recorded a career-high 62 goals in 1995-96.

1996-97 Player Personnel

FORWARDS	HT	WT	S	Place of Birth	Date	1995-96 Club
ANTOSKI, Shawn	6-4	235	L	Brantford, Ont.	3/25/70	Philadelphia
AUBIN, Serge	6-1	194	L	Val d'Or, Que.	2/15/75	Hampton Rds.-Cleveland
BELOV, Oleg	6-0	185	L	Moscow, USSR	4/20/73	Cleveland
BERGMAN, Peter	6-1	195	L	Regina, Sask.	4/14/78	Kamloops
BONIN, Brian	5-10	185	L	White Bear Lake, MN	11/28/73	U. Minnesota
CHRISTIAN, Jeff	6-2	210	L	Burlington, Ont.	7/30/70	Pittsburgh-Cleveland
CLIFFORD, Brian	6-0	185	R	Buffalo, NY	6/18/73	Michigan State
DZIEDZIC, Joe	6-3	227	L	Minneapolis, MN	12/18/71	Pittsburgh
FITZGERALD, Rusty	6-0	210	L	Minneapolis, MN	10/4/72	Pittsburgh-Cleveland
FRANCIS, Ron	6-2	200	L	Sault Ste. Marie, Ont.	3/1/63	Pittsburgh
HRDINA, Jan	6-0	190	R	Hradec Kralove, Czech.	2/5/76	Seattle-Spokane
JAGR, Jaromir	6-2	216	L	Kladno, Czech.	2/15/72	Pittsburgh
KANE, Boyd	6-1	207	L	Swift Current, Sask.	4/18/78	Regina
LAUER, Brad	6-0	195	L	Humboldt, Sask.	10/27/66	Pittsburgh-Cleveland
LEMIEUX, Mario	6-4	225	R	Montreal, Que.	10/5/65	Pittsburgh
MURRAY, Glen	6-2	220	R	Halifax, N.S.	11/1/72	Pittsburgh
NEDVED, Petr	6-3	195	L	Liberec, Czech.	12/9/71	Pittsburgh
PARK, Richard	5-11	190	R	Seoul, S. Korea	5/27/76	Pittsburgh-Belleville
PATTERSON, Ed	6-2	213	R	Delta, B.C.	11/14/72	Pittsburgh
PITTIS, Domenic	5-11	185	L	Calgary, Alta.	10/1/74	Cleveland
PROTSENKO, Boris	6-0	185	R	Kiev, USSR	8/21/78	Calgary (WHL)
QUINN, Dan	5-11	182	L	Ottawa, Ont.	6/1/65	Ott-Detroit (IHL)-Phi
ROCHE, Dave	6-4	224	L	Lindsay, Ont.	6/13/75	Pittsburgh
SANDSTROM, Tomas	6-2	205	L	Jakobstad, Finland	9/4/64	Pittsburgh
SAVOIA, Ryan	6-0	195	R	Thorold, Ont.	5/6/73	Cleveland
SMOLINSKI, Bryan	6-1	200	R	Toledo, OH	12/27/71	Pittsburgh
STOJANOV, Alek	6-4	220	L	Windsor, Ont.	4/25/73	Vancouver-Pittsburgh
TODD, Kevin	5-10	180	L	Winnipeg, Man.	5/4/68	Los Angeles
WELLS, Chris	6-6	223	L	Calgary, Alta.	11/12/75	Pittsburgh
WRIGHT, Tyler	5-11	185	R	Canora, Sask.	4/6/73	Edmonton-Cape Breton
ZELENKO, Boris	6-1	172	R	Moscow, USSR	9/12/75	CSKA
DEFENSEMEN						
ALLEN, Peter	6-2	195	R	Calgary, Alta.	3/6/70	Pittsburgh-Cleveland
BERGKVIST, Stefan	6-2	224	L	Leksand, Sweden	3/10/75	Pittsburgh-Cleveland
BUTENSCHON, Sven	6-5	201	L	Itzehoe, West Germany	3/22/76	Brandon
DAIGNEAULT, Jean-Jacques	5-10	186	L	Montreal, Que.	10/12/65	Mtl-StL-Worcester-Pit
FOSTER, Corey	6-3	204	L	Ottawa, Ont.	10/27/69	Pittsburgh-Cleveland
HATCHER, Kevin	6-4	225	R	Detroit, MI	9/9/66	Dallas
JOSEPH, Chris	6-2	202	R	Burnaby, B.C.	9/10/69	Pittsburgh
KRIVCHENKOV, Alexei	6-0	190	L	Novosibirsk, USSR	6/11/74	Hampton Rds.-Cleveland
LEROUX, Francois	6-5	235	L	Ste.-Adele, Que.	4/18/70	Pittsburgh
MIRONOV, Dmitri	6-2	214	R	Moscow, USSR	12/25/65	Pittsburgh
MORAN, Ian	5-11	195	R	Cleveland, OH	8/24/72	Pittsburgh
ROZSIVAL, Michal	6-1	189	R	Vlasim, Czech.	9/3/78	Dukla Jihlava
TAMER, Chris	6-2	212	L	Dearborn, MI	11/17/70	Pittsburgh
VORONOV, Sergei	6-2	200	L	Moscow, USSR	2/5/71	Cleveland-Hampton Rds.
WILKINSON, Neil	6-3	190	R	Selkirk, Man.	8/15/67	Winnipeg-Pittsburgh
GOALTENDERS	**HT**	**WT**	**C**	**Place of Birth**	**Date**	**1995-96 Club**
AUBIN, Jean-Sebastien	5-11	179	R	Montreal, Que.	7/19/77	Sherbrooke
BARRASSO, Tom	6-3	211	R	Boston, MA	3/31/65	Pittsburgh
DeROUVILLE, Philippe	6-1	185	L	Victoriaville, Que.	8/7/74	Cleveland
HILLIER, Craig	6-1	174	L	Cole Harbour, N.S.	2/28/78	Ottawa (OHL)
LALIME, Patrick	6-2	170	L	St. Bonaventure, Que.	7/7/74	Cleveland
WREGGET, Ken	6-1	200	L	Brandon, Man.	3/25/64	Pittsburgh

Coach

JOHNSTON, ED
Coach, Pittsburgh Penguins. Born in Montreal, Que., November 24, 1935.

Ed Johnston enters his seventh season as Pittsburgh head coach in 1996-97. He is the Penguins all-time leader among coaches in wins (201) and games (454). He began his second stint as coach of the Penguins in 1993-94 having previously coached the team, from 1980-81 to 1982-83, compiling a record of 79-126-35. He was named general manager of the club on May 27, 1983, a position he held for five seasons. During the 1988-89 season, his last with the Penguins, Johnston served as assistant general manager. In 1989, Johnston was named vice president and general manager of the Hartford Whalers, serving three seasons in Connecticut. During Johnston's first season in Hartford (1989-90), the Whalers recorded the second-best record (38-33-9) in their NHL history.

Johnston played in the NHL for 16 seasons with Boston, Toronto, St. Louis and Chicago. He was a member of two Stanley Cup championship teams with the Boston Bruins, and was the last goaltender to play every minute of a season, when he played all 70 games in 1963-64 for the Bruins. Overall, Johnston played in 592 games, recording 236 wins, 32 shutouts and a 3.25 goals-against average.

Coaching Record

		Regular Season					Playoffs			
Season	Team	Games	W	L	T	%	Games	W	L	%
1979-80	Chicago (NHL)	80	34	27	19	.544	7	3	4	.429
1980-81	Pittsburgh (NHL)	80	30	37	13	.456	5	2	3	.400
1981-82	Pittsburgh (NHL)	80	31	36	13	.469	5	2	3	.400
1982-83	Pittsburgh (NHL)	80	18	53	9	.281	....	....	....	....
1993-94	Pittsburgh (NHL)	84	44	27	13	.601	6	2	4	.333
1994-95	Pittsburgh (NHL)	48	29	16	3	.635	12	5	7	.417
1995-96	Pittsburgh (NHL)	82	49	29	4	.622	18	11	7	.611
	NHL Totals	534	235	225	74	.509	53	25	28	.472

Coaching History

George Sullivan, 1967-68 to 1968-69; Red Kelly, 1969-70 to 1971-72; Red Kelly and Ken Schinkel, 1972-73; Ken Schinkel and Marc Boileau, 1973-74; Marc Boileau, 1974-75; Marc Boileau and Ken Schinkel, 1975-76; Ken Schinkel, 1976-77; John Wilson, 1977-78 to 1979-80; Eddie Johnston, 1980-81 to 1982-83; Lou Angotti, 1983-84; Bob Berry, 1984-85 to 1986-87; Pierre Creamer, 1987-88; Gene Ubriaco, 1988-89; Gene Ubriaco and Craig Patrick, 1989-90; Bob Johnson, 1990-91 to 1991-92; Scotty Bowman, 1991-92 to 1992-93; Eddie Johnston, 1993-94 to date.

1995-96 Scoring

* – rookie

Regular Season

Pos	#	Player	Team	GP	G	A	Pts	+/–	PIM	PP	SH	GW	GT	S	%
C	66	Mario Lemieux	PIT	70	69	92	161	10	54	31	8	8	0	338	20.4
R	68	Jaromir Jagr	PIT	82	62	87	149	31	96	20	1	12	1	403	15.4
C	10	Ron Francis	PIT	77	27	92	119	25	56	12	1	4	0	158	17.1
C	93	Petr Nedved	PIT	80	45	54	99	37	68	8	1	5	1	204	22.1
R	17	Tomas Sandstrom	PIT	58	35	35	70	4	69	17	1	2	0	187	18.7
D	56	Sergei Zubov	PIT	64	11	55	66	28	22	3	2	1	0	141	7.8
C	20	Bryan Smolinski	PIT	81	24	40	64	6	69	8	2	1	0	229	10.5
R	8	Kevin Miller	S.J.	68	22	20	42	–8	41	2	2	2	2	146	15.1
			PIT	13	6	5	11	4	4	1	0	0	0	33	18.2
			TOTAL	81	28	25	53	–4	45	3	2	2	2	179	15.6
D	15	Dmitri Mironov	PIT	72	3	31	34	19	88	1	0	1	1	86	3.5
R	27	Glen Murray	PIT	69	14	15	29	4	57	0	0	2	0	100	14.0
D	23	Chris Joseph	PIT	70	5	14	19	6	71	0	0	1	0	94	5.3
D	6	Neil Wilkinson	WPG	21	1	4	5	0	33	0	1	1	0	17	5.9
			PIT	41	2	10	12	12	87	0	0	0	0	42	4.8
			TOTAL	62	3	14	17	12	120	0	1	1	0	59	5.1
L	51	* Dave Roche	PIT	71	7	7	14	–5	130	0	0	1	0	65	10.8
D	2	Chris Tamer	PIT	70	4	10	14	20	153	0	0	1	0	75	5.3
D	36	J.J. Daigneault	MTL	7	0	1	1	0	6	0	0	0	0	3	0.0
			STL	37	1	3	4	–6	24	0	0	0	0	45	2.2
			PIT	13	3	3	6	0	23	2	0	0	0	13	23.1
			TOTAL	57	4	7	11	–6	53	2	0	0	0	61	6.6
D	18	Francois Leroux	PIT	66	2	9	11	2	161	0	0	0	0	43	4.7
L	16	* Joe Dziedzic	PIT	69	5	5	10	–5	68	0	0	3	0	44	11.4
C	76	* Richard Park	PIT	56	4	6	10	3	36	0	1	1	0	62	6.5
C	26	Dave McLlwain	OTT	1	0	1	1	0	2	0	0	0	0	1	0.0
			PIT	18	2	4	6	–5	4	0	0	1	0	19	10.5
			TOTAL	19	2	5	7	–5	6	0	0	1	0	20	10.0
R	14	Brad Lauer	PIT	21	4	1	5	–5	6	1	0	1	0	29	13.8
D	4	Corey Foster	PIT	11	2	2	4	–2	2	1	0	0	0	8	25.0
C	12	* Chris Wells	PIT	54	2	2	4	–6	59	0	1	0	0	25	8.0
C	52	* Rusty Fitzgerald	PIT	21	1	2	3	7	12	0	0	0	0	15	6.7
G	35	Tom Barrasso	PIT	49	0	3	3	0	18	0	0	0	0	0	0.0
D	24	* Ian Moran	PIT	51	1	1	2	–1	47	0	0	0	0	44	2.3
R	11	* Alek Stojanov	VAN	58	0	1	1	–12	123	0	0	0	0	16	0.0
			PIT	10	1	0	1	–1	7	0	0	0	0	4	25.0
			TOTAL	68	1	1	2	–13	130	0	0	0	0	20	5.0
R	44	Ed Patterson	PIT	35	0	2	2	–5	38	0	0	0	0	17	0.0
G	31	Ken Wregget	PIT	37	0	2	2	0	8	0	0	0	0	0	0.0
D	55	Drake Berehowsky	PIT	1	0	0	0	1	0	0	0	0	0	0	0.0
D	28	* Greg Andrusak	PIT	2	0	0	0	–1	0	0	0	0	0	1	0.0
D	33	* Stefan Bergkvist	PIT	2	0	0	0	0	2	0	0	0	0	4	0.0
L	28	* Jeff Christian	PIT	3	0	0	0	0	2	0	0	0	0	0	0.0
C	9	Len Barrie	PIT	5	0	0	0	–1	18	0	0	0	0	5	0.0
D	38	* Peter Allen	PIT	8	0	0	0	2	8	0	0	0	0	2	0.0

Goaltending

No.	Goaltender	GPI	Mins	Avg	W	L	T	EN	SO	GA	SA	S%
31	Ken Wregget	37	2132	3.24	20	13	2	4	3	115	1205	.905
35	Tom Barrasso	49	2799	3.43	29	16	2	5	2	160	1626	.902
	Totals	**82**	**4948**	**3.44**	**49**	**29**	**4**	**9**	**5**	**284**	**2840**	**.900**

Playoffs

Pos	#	Player	Team	GP	G	A	Pts	+/–	PIM	PP	SH	GW	OT	S	%
C	66	Mario Lemieux	PIT	18	11	16	27	3	33	3	1	2	0	78	14.1
R	68	Jaromir Jagr	PIT	18	11	12	23	7	18	5	1	1	0	74	14.9
C	93	Petr Nedved	PIT	18	10	10	20	3	16	4	0	2	1	54	18.5
D	56	Sergei Zubov	PIT	18	1	14	15	9	26	1	0	0	0	53	1.9
D	36	J.J. Daigneault	PIT	17	1	9	10	4	36	1	0	1	0	30	3.3
C	20	Bryan Smolinski	PIT	18	5	4	9	–4	10	0	0	1	0	46	10.9
C	10	Ron Francis	PIT	11	3	6	9	3	4	2	0	1	0	23	13.0
L	51	* Dave Roche	PIT	16	2	7	9	1	26	0	0	0	0	18	11.1
R	27	Glen Murray	PIT	18	2	6	8	2	10	0	0	1	0	21	9.5
D	2	Chris Tamer	PIT	18	0	7	7	0	24	0	0	0	0	23	0.0
R	17	Tomas Sandstrom	PIT	18	4	2	6	–6	30	0	0	1	0	44	9.1
R	8	Kevin Miller	PIT	18	3	2	5	–6	8	0	0	0	0	36	8.3
L	16	* Joe Dziedzic	PIT	16	1	2	3	1	19	0	0	0	0	6	16.7
R	14	Brad Lauer	PIT	12	1	1	2	0	4	0	0	0	0	8	12.5
D	18	Francois Leroux	PIT	18	1	1	2	2	20	0	0	1	0	8	12.5
D	23	Chris Joseph	PIT	15	1	0	1	1	8	0	0	0	0	15	6.7
G	31	Ken Wregget	PIT	9	0	1	1	0	0	0	0	0	0	0	0.0
D	6	Neil Wilkinson	PIT	15	0	1	1	–2	14	0	0	0	0	20	0.0
D	15	Dmitri Mironov	PIT	15	0	1	1	–6	10	0	0	0	0	10	0.0
C	76	* Richard Park	PIT	1	0	0	0	0	0	0	0	0	0	0	0.0
D	4	Corey Foster	PIT	3	0	0	0	–2	4	0	0	0	0	4	0.0
D	3	* Stefan Bergkvist	PIT	4	0	0	0	–1	2	0	0	0	0	0	0.0
C	26	Dave McLlwain	PIT	6	0	0	0	0	0	0	0	0	0	3	0.0
R	11	* Alek Stojanov	PIT	9	0	0	0	0	19	0	0	0	0	1	0.0
G	35	Tom Barrasso	PIT	10	0	0	0	0	8	0	0	0	0	0	0.0

Goaltending

No.	Goaltender	GPI	Mins	Avg	W	L	EN	SO	GA	SA	S%
31	Ken Wregget	9	599	2.30	7	2	1	0	23	328	.930
35	Tom Barrasso	10	558	2.80	4	5	2	1	26	337	.923
	Totals	**18**	**1159**	**2.69**	**11**	**7**	**3**	**1**	**52**	**668**	**.922**

Captains' History

Ab McDonald, 1967-68; no captain, 1968-69 to 1972-73; Ron Schock, 1973-74 to 1976-77; Jean Pronovost, 1977-78; Orest Kindrachuk, 1978-79 to 1980-81; Randy Carlyle, 1981-82 to 1983-84; Mike Bullard, 1984-85, 1985-86; Mike Bullard and Terry Ruskowski, 1986-87; Dan Frawley and Mario Lemieux, 1987-88; Mario Lemieux, 1988-89 to 1993-94; Ron Francis, 1994-95; Mario Lemieux, 1995-96 to date.

Club Records

Team

(Figures in brackets for season records are games played; records for fewest points, wins, ties, losses, goals, goals against are for 70 or more games)

Most Points	119	1992-93 (84)
Most Wins	56	1992-93 (84)
Most Ties	20	1970-71 (78)
Most Losses	58	1983-84 (80)
Most Goals	367	1992-93 (84)
Most Goals Against	394	1982-83 (80)
Fewest Points	38	1983-84 (80)
Fewest Wins	16	1983-84 (80)
Fewest Ties	4	1995-96 (82)
Fewest Losses	21	1992-93 (84)
Fewest Goals	182	1969-70 (76)
Fewest Goals Against	216	1967-68 (74)
Longest Winning Streak		
Overall	*17	Mar. 9-Apr. 10/93
Home	11	Jan. 5-Mar. 7/91
Away	6	Mar. 14-Apr. 9/93
Longest Undefeated Streak		
Overall	18	Mar. 9-Apr. 14/93 (17 wins, 1 tie)
Home	20	Nov. 30/74-Feb. 22/75 (12 wins, 8 ties)
Away	7	Twice
Longest Losing Streak		
Overall	11	Jan. 22/83-Feb. 10/83
Home	7	Oct. 8-29/83
Away	18	Dec. 23/82-Mar. 4/83
Longest Winless Streak		
Overall	18	Jan. 2-Feb. 10/83 (17 losses, 1 tie)
Home	11	Oct. 8-Nov. 19/83 (9 losses, 2 ties)
Away	18	Oct. 25/70-Jan. 14/71 (11 losses, 7 ties), Dec. 23/82-Mar. 4/83 (18 losses)
Most Shutouts, Season	6	1967-68 (74), 1976-77 (80)
Most PIM, Season	*2,670	1988-89 (80)
Most Goals, Game	12	Mar. 15/75 (Wsh. 1 at Pit. 12), Dec. 26/91 (Tor. 1 at Pit. 12)

Individual

Most Seasons	11	Rick Kehoe
Most Games	753	Jean Pronovost
Most Goals, Career	563	Mario Lemieux
Most Assists, Career	809	Mario Lemieux
Most Points, Career	1,372	Mario Lemieux (563G, 809A)
Most PIM, Career	980	Troy Loney
Most Shutouts, Career	11	Les Binkley
Longest Consecutive Games Streak	320	Ron Schock (Oct. 24/73-Apr. 3/77)
Most Goals, Season	85	Mario Lemieux (1988-89)
Most Assists, Season	114	Mario Lemieux (1988-89)
Most Points, Season	199	Mario Lemieux (1988-89; 85G, 114A)
Most PIM, Season	409	Paul Baxter (1981-82)
Most Points, Defenseman, Season	113	Paul Coffey (1988-89; 30G, 83A)
Most Points, Center, Season	199	Mario Lemieux (1988-89; 85G, 114A)
Most Points, Right Wing, Season	149	Jaromir Jagr (1995-96; 62G, 87A)
Most Points, Left Wing, Season	123	Kevin Stevens (1991-92; 54G, 69A)
Most Points, Rookie, Season	100	Mario Lemieux (1984-85; 43G, 57A)
Most Shutouts, Season	6	Les Binkley (1967-68)
Most Goals, Game	5	Mario Lemieux (Three times)
Most Assists, Game	6	Ron Stackhouse (Mar. 8/75), Greg Malone (Nov. 28/79), Mario Lemieux (Three times)
Most Points, Game	8	Mario Lemieux (Oct. 15/88; 3G, 5A, Dec. 31/88; 5G, 3A)

* NHL Record.

Retired Numbers

21	Michel Brière	1969-1970

All-time Record vs. Other Clubs

Regular Season

	At Home							On Road							Total						
	GP	W	L	T	GF	GA	PTS	GP	W	L	T	GF	GA	PTS	GP	W	L	T	GF	GA	PTS
Anaheim	2	1	0	1	7	4	3	2	1	1	0	8	10	2	4	2	1	1	15	14	5
Boston	62	25	26	11	220	237	61	61	12	43	6	183	283	30	123	37	69	17	403	520	91
Buffalo	53	24	16	13	210	187	61	54	13	26	15	153	231	41	107	37	42	28	363	418	102
Calgary	39	19	10	10	146	126	48	39	9	23	7	117	170	25	78	28	33	17	263	296	73
Chicago	52	25	22	5	187	173	55	53	8	36	9	145	226	25	105	33	58	14	332	399	80
Colorado	29	15	10	4	127	119	34	26	12	13	1	107	120	25	55	27	23	5	234	239	59
Dallas	57	35	17	5	220	160	75	58	21	32	5	197	219	47	115	56	49	10	417	379	122
Detroit	58	40	14	4	259	171	84	59	11	37	11	164	235	33	117	51	51	15	423	406	117
Edmonton	24	11	12	1	95	114	23	24	5	18	1	85	129	11	48	16	30	2	180	243	34
Florida	6	4	1	1	22	16	9	6	4	2	0	16	15	8	12	8	3	1	38	31	17
Hartford	29	16	10	3	142	118	35	30	12	16	2	115	129	26	59	28	26	5	257	247	61
Los Angeles	65	37	20	8	245	206	82	63	14	41	8	163	248	36	128	51	61	16	408	454	118
Montreal	64	23	32	9	198	235	55	64	4	53	7	151	325	15	128	27	85	16	349	560	70
New Jersey	60	36	20	4	252	210	76	61	20	29	12	210	236	52	121	56	49	16	462	446	128
NY Islanders	68	32	25	11	263	239	75	67	24	35	8	224	278	56	135	56	60	19	487	517	131
NY Rangers	81	33	37	11	295	304	77	81	32	42	7	288	333	71	162	65	79	18	583	637	148
Ottawa	10	9	0	1	49	20	19	9	8	1	0	40	18	16	19	17	1	1	89	38	35
Philadelphia	86	38	31	17	303	278	93	87	15	65	7	225	380	37	173	53	96	24	528	658	130
St. Louis	57	26	19	12	217	176	64	58	13	39	6	156	231	32	115	39	58	18	373	407	96
San Jose	4	2	1	1	27	16	5	5	4	0	1	36	11	9	9	6	1	2	63	27	14
Tampa Bay	7	5	1	1	33	15	11	6	4	2	0	24	21	8	13	9	3	1	57	36	19
Toronto	55	29	20	6	231	179	64	54	17	26	11	179	224	45	109	46	46	17	410	403	109
Vancouver	44	29	8	7	202	149	65	44	21	20	3	172	163	45	88	50	28	10	374	312	110
Washington	67	35	26	6	268	225	76	70	28	36	6	263	305	62	137	63	62	12	531	530	138
Winnipeg	24	17	7	0	105	73	34	23	13	9	1	84	83	27	47	30	16	1	189	156	61
Defunct Clubs	35	22	6	7	148	93	51	34	13	10	11	108	101	37	69	35	16	18	256	194	88
Totals	**1138**	**588**	**391**	**159**	**4471**	**3843**	**1335**	**1138**	**338**	**655**	**145**	**3613**	**4724**	**821**	**2276**	**926**	**1046**	**304**	**8084**	**8567**	**2156**

Playoffs

	Series	W	L	GP	W	L	T	GF	GA	Last Mtg.	Round	Result
Boston	4	2	2	19	10	9	0	67	62	1992	CF	W 4-0
Buffalo	1	1	0	3	2	1	0	9	9	1979	PR	W 2-1
Chicago	2	1	1	8	4	4	0	23	24	1992	F	W 4-0
Dallas	1	1	0	6	4	2	0	28	16	1991	F	W 4-2
Florida	1	0	1	7	3	4	0	15	20	1996	CF	L 3-4
New Jersey	3	2	1	17	9	8	0	56	47	1995	CSF	L 1-4
NY Islanders	3	0	3	19	8	11	0	58	67	1993	DF	L 3-4
NY Rangers	3	3	0	15	12	3	0	65	45	1996	CSF	W 4-1
Philadelphia	1	0	1	7	3	4	0	24	31	1989	DF	L 3-4
St. Louis	3	1	2	13	6	7	0	40	45	1981	PR	L 2-3
Toronto	2	0	2	6	2	4	0	13	21	1977	PR	L 1-2
Washington	5	4	1	31	18	13	0	106	103	1996	CQF	W 4-2
Defunct Clubs	1	1	0	4	4	0	0	13	6			
Totals	**30**	**16**	**14**	**155**	**85**	**70**	**0**	**516**	**496**			

Playoff Results 1996-92

Year	Round	Opponent	Result	GF	GA
1996	CF	Florida	L 3-4	15	20
	CSF	NY Rangers	W 4-1	21	15
	CQF	Washington	W 4-2	21	17
1995	CSF	New Jersey	L 1-4	8	17
	CQF	Washington	W 4-3	29	26
1994	CQF	Washington	L 2-4	12	20
1993	DF	NY Islanders	L 3-4	27	24
	DSF	New Jersey	W 4-1	23	13
1992	**F**	**Chicago**	**W 4-0**	**15**	**10**
	CF	Boston	W 4-0	19	7
	DF	NY Rangers	W 4-2	24	19
	DSF	Washington	W 4-3	25	27

Abbreviations: Round: F – Final; **CF** – conference final; **CQF** – conference quarter-final; **CSF** – conference semi-final; **DF** – division final; **DSF** – division semi-final; **SF** – semi-final; **QF** – quarter-final; **PR** – preliminary round.

Calgary totals include Atlanta, 1972-73 to 1979-80. Colorado totals include Quebec, 1979-80 to 1994-95.
Dallas totals include Minnesota, 1967-68 to 1992-93.
New Jersey totals include Kansas City, 1974-75 to 1975-76, and Colorado Rockies, 1976-77 to 1981-82.

1995-96 Results

Oct.	7		Toronto	8-3		12		Montreal	5-6
	9	at	Colorado	6-6		13		San Jose	8-10
	12	at	Chicago	1-5		16		Colorado	2-5
	14		Anaheim	5-2		17	at	Buffalo	1-0
	20	at	Hartford	2-2		22		Boston	7-6
	21		Los Angeles	2-3		24	at	Ottawa	4-3
	26	at	NY Islanders	7-5		27		Philadelphia	7-4
	28	at	New Jersey	5-3		29	at	Florida	1-2
Nov.	1		Tampa Bay	10-0		31	at	Tampa Bay	1-4
	3	at	Buffalo	3-3	**Feb.**	3	at	Detroit	0-3
	4		Philadelphia	7-4		6		Boston	6-5
	8	at	Ottawa	7-1		7	at	New Jersey	1-1
	10	at	San Jose	9-1		10		Chicago	6-3
	11	at	Los Angeles	2-3		12	at	Toronto	1-4
	14		Dallas	4-2		16	at	Winnipeg	1-0
	17	at	Washington	3-2		18		NY Rangers	4-3
	18		Washington	3-0		21	at	Buffalo	3-6
	21	at	NY Rangers	4-9		23		Hartford	5-4
	22		NY Rangers	3-4		24	at	Montreal	3-7
	25		Buffalo	5-3		27	at	Vancouver	7-4
	28		Ottawa	7-2		29	at	Calgary	3-7
	30	at	Boston	9-6	**Mar.**	1	at	Edmonton	5-4
Dec.	1		Florida	2-1		5		Winnipeg	9-4
	3	at	Tampa Bay	5-4		7		Ottawa	5-1
	5	at	NY Islanders	6-3		9		New Jersey	3-4
	7		Montreal	7-5		13	at	Hartford	2-3
	9		Hartford	6-0		14	at	Boston	2-4
	13	at	Anaheim	3-6		16		NY Islanders	4-2
	15	at	Dallas	5-1		21		Edmonton	5-4
	17	at	Philadelphia	5-6		23		Buffalo	5-7
	19		Calgary	7-1		24	at	NY Rangers	8-2
	22		Montreal	2-4		26		St. Louis	8-4
	23	at	Montreal	0-1		28	at	Florida	3-2
	26		Buffalo	6-3		30		New Jersey	2-1
	28		Hartford	9-4		31	at	Philadelphia	1-4
	30		Florida	6-5	**Apr.**	4		Washington	4-2
Jan.	1	at	Washington	2-4		6		Tampa Bay	2-1
	3		Ottawa	4-1		8	at	Hartford	4-5
	5		Detroit	5-2		10		NY Islanders	2-6
	6	at	St. Louis	2-3		11	at	Ottawa	5-3
	8		Vancouver	8-5		14	at	Boston	5-6

Entry Draft
Selections 1996-82

1996
Pick
23	Craig Hillier
28	Pavel Skrbek
72	Boyd Kane
77	Boris Protsenko
105	Michal Rozsival
150	Peter Bergman
186	Eric Meloche
238	Timo Seikkula

1995
Pick
24	Alexei Morozov
76	J-Sebastien Aubin
102	Oleg Belov
128	Jan Hrdina
154	Alexei Kolkunov
180	Derrick Pyke
206	Sergei Voronov
232	Frank Ivankovic

1994
Pick
24	Chris Wells
50	Richard Park
57	Sven Butenschon
73	Greg Crozier
76	Alexei Krivchenkov
102	Thomas O'Connor
128	Clint Johnson
154	Valentin Morozov
161	Serge Aubin
180	Drew Palmer
206	Boris Zelenko
232	Jason Godbout
258	Mikhail Kazakevich
284	Brian Leitza

1993
Pick
26	Stefan Bergkvist
52	Domenic Pittis
62	Dave Roche
104	Jonas Andersson-Junkka
130	Chris Kelleher
156	Patrick Lalime
182	Sean Selmser
208	Larry McMorran
234	Timothy Harberts
260	Leonid Toropchenko
286	Hans Jonsson

1992
Pick
19	Martin Straka
43	Marc Hussey
67	Travis Thiessen
91	Todd Klassen
115	Philipp De Rouville
139	Artem Kopot
163	Jan Alinc
187	Fran Bussey
211	Brian Bonin
235	Brian Callahan

1991
Pick
16	Markus Naslund
38	Rusty Fitzgerald
60	Shane Peacock
82	Joe Tamminen
104	Robert Melanson
126	Brian Clifford
148	Ed Patterson
170	Peter McLaughlin
192	Jeff Lembke
214	Chris Tok
236	Paul Dyck
258	Pasi Huura

1990
Pick
5	Jaromir Jagr
61	Joe Dziedzic
68	Chris Tamer
89	Brian Farrell
107	Ian Moran
110	Denis Casey
130	Mika Valila
131	Ken Plaquin
145	Pat Neaton
152	Petteri Koskimaki
173	Ladislav Karabin
194	Timothy Fingerhut
215	Michael Thompson
236	Brian Bruininks

1989
Pick
16	Jamie Heward
37	Paul Laus
58	John Brill
79	Todd Nelson
100	Tom Nevers
121	Mike Markovich
126	Mike Needham
142	Patrick Schafhauser
163	Dave Shute
184	Andrew Wolf
205	Greg Hagen
226	Scott Farrell
247	Jason Smart

1988
Pick
4	Darrin Shannon
25	Mark Major
62	Daniel Gauthier
67	Mark Recchi
88	Greg Andrusak
130	Troy Mick
151	Jeff Blaeser
172	Rob Gaudreau
193	Donald Pancoe
214	Cory Laylin
235	Darren Stolk

1987
Pick
5	Chris Joseph
26	Richard Tabaracci
47	Jamie Leach
68	Risto Kurkinen
89	Jeff Waver
110	Shawn McEachern
131	Jim Bodden
152	Jiri Kucera
173	Jack MacDougall
194	Daryn McBride
215	Mark Carlson
236	Ake Lilljebjorn

1986
Pick
4	Zarley Zalapski
25	Dave Capuano
46	Brad Aitken
67	Rob Brown
88	Sandy Smith
109	Jeff Daniels
130	Doug Hobson
151	Steve Rohlik
172	Dave McLwain
193	Kelly Cain
214	Stan Drulia
235	Rob Wilson

1985
Pick
2	Craig Simpson
23	Lee Giffin
58	Bruce Racine
86	Steve Gotaas
107	Kevin Clemens
114	Stuart Marston
128	Steve Titus
149	Paul Stanton
170	Jim Paek
191	Steve Shaunessy
212	Doug Greschuk
233	Gregory Choules

1984
Pick
1	Mario Lemieux
9	Doug Bodger
16	Roger Belanger
64	Mark Teevens
85	Arto Javanainen
127	Tom Ryan
169	John Del Col
189	Steve Hurt
210	Jim Steen
230	Mark Ziliotto

1983
Pick
15	Bob Errey
22	Todd Charlesworth
58	Mike Rowe
63	Frank Pietrangelo
103	Patrick Emond
123	Paul Ames
163	Marty Ketola
183	Alec Haidy
203	Garth Hildebrand
223	Dave Goertz

1982
Pick
10	Rich Sutter
38	Tim Hrynewich
52	Troy Loney
94	Grant Sasser
136	Grant Couture
157	Peter Derksen
178	Greg Gravel
199	Stu Wenaas
220	Chris McCauley
241	Stan Bautch

Club Directory

Civic Arena
Pittsburgh, PA 15219
Phone **412/642-1300**
FAX 412/642-1859
PR FAX 412/281-3005
Media Relations FAX
412/281-1322
Capacity: 17,181

Ownership	Howard Baldwin, Morris Belzberg, Thomas Ruta
Chairman of the Board & Governor	Howard Baldwin

Administration
President & Chief Operating Officer – PGH Sports Associates	Steve Ryan
President	Jack Kelley
Executive Vice President, Operations	Donn Patton
Vice President, General Counsel	Greg Cribbs
Assistant to the Chairman	Nick Ruta
Director of Planning and Design	Scott Baldwin
Marketing Consultant	Bill Barnes
Executive Assistants	Elaine Heufelder, Paula Nichols, Charlene Stone
Administrative Assistants	Christine Black, Amy Hirsh

Hockey Operations
Executive Vice President & General Manager	Craig Patrick
Head Coach	Ed Johnston
Assistant Coaches	Rick Kehoe, Bryan Trottier
Goaltending Coach and Scout	Gilles Meloche
Head Scout	Greg Malone
Scouting Staff	Les Binkley, Herb Brooks, Charlie Hodge, Mark Kelley, Ralph Cox
Professional Scouts	Glenn Patrick, Phil Russell
Strength and Conditioning Coach	John Welday
Equipment Manager	Steve Latin
Trainer	Charles "Skip" Thayer
Team Physician	Dr. Charles Burke
Team Dentist	Dr. David Donatelli
Executive Assistant	Tracey Botsford
Assistant Equipment Manager	Paul Flati
Assistant Trainer	Greg Thayer

Communications
Vice President, Communications	Tom McMillan
Director of Public Relations	Cindy Himes
Director of Media Relations	Steve Bovino
Director of Publishing	Phil Langan
Director of Entertainment	Kevin Smith
Manager, Community Relations	Renee Petrichevich

Finance
Vice President, Finance & Administration	Bob Vogel
Controller	Kevin Hart
Assistant Controller	Bill Snyder
Accounting Staff	Lisa Kreutzer, Tawni Love

Ticketing
Vice President, Ticket Sales	Jeff Barrett
Senior Manager, Corporate Ticket	Jeff Mercer
Director, Premium Seating	Rich Hixon
Manager, Premium Services	Erinn Dickson
Managers, Corporate Ticket Sales	Jim Carolan, Doug Sanborn, Brian Magness, Mark Anderson
Group Sales Director	Fred Traynor
Group Sales	Ward Russell
Box Office Manager	Carol Coulson
Assistant Box Office Manager	Debbie Campbell
Customer Service Manager	Allison Quigley
Telemarketing Manager	James Santilli

Marketing
Vice President, Marketing	Steve Violetta
Director of Advertising Sales	Taylor Baldwin
Advertising Sales Representatives	Jackie Mateosky, Arden Robbins
Director of Event Marketing	Bill Miller
Manager of Sales Services	Marie Mays
Sales Administrator	Barb Pilarski

Iceoplex at Southpointe
Vice President, General Manager	Howard Baldwin, Jr.
Director of Ice Hockey	Alain Lemieux
Director of Skating	Patricia Daurora
Director of Operations	Dan Kaschalk
Director of Off-Ice Events	Vikki Hultquist
Administrative Assistant	Nicole Kaschalk
Associate Director of Ice Hockey	Brian Coe
Director of Publicity and Youth Hockey	Harry Sanders

General Information
Home Ice	Civic Arena
Dimensions of Rink	200 feet by 85 feet
Location of Press Box	West Side of Building
Team Colors	Black, Gold and White
Flagship Radio Station	WTAE (1250 AM)
TV Stations	Prime Sports & KBL WPTT/UPN 22 and WPGH/Fox 53
Announcers	Mike Lange, Matt McConnell, Paul Steigerwald
Practice Facility	Iceoplex at Southpointe
Minor League Affiliation	Cleveland Lumberjacks (IHL) and Johnstown Chiefs (ECHL)

General Manager

PATRICK, CRAIG
General Manager, Pittsburgh Penguins. Born in Detroit, MI, May 20, 1946.

Appointed general manager of the Penguins on December 5, 1989, Patrick's teams have since won two Stanley Cup titles (1991 and 1992), the Presidents' Trophy (1993) and four division titles.

A 1969 graduate of the University of Denver, Patrick was captain of the Pioneers' NCAA championship hockey team that year. He returned to his alma mater in 1986 where he served as director of athletics and recreation for two years. Patrick served as administrative assistant to the president of the Amateur Hockey Association of the United States in 1980 and as an assistant coach/assistant general manager for the 1980 gold medal-winning U.S. Olympic hockey team. He joined the New York Rangers in 1980 as director of operations and became the youngest general manager in team history on June 14, 1981. Patrick served the Rangers in that capacity through the 1985-86 season. Before pursuing a coaching career, Patrick played professional hockey with Washington, Kansas City, St. Louis, Minnesota and California from 1971-79. In eight seasons, Patrick tallied 163 points (72-91-163) in 401 games.

NHL Coaching Record

		Regular Season					Playoffs			
Season	Team	Games	W	L	T	%	Games	W	L	%
1980-81	NY Rangers	59	26	23	10	.525	14	7	7	.500
1984-85	NY Rangers	35	11	22	2	.343	3	0	3	.000
1989-90	Pittsburgh	54	22	26	6	.463	....	....	....	....
	NHL Totals	**148**	**59**	**71**	**18**	**.459**	**17**	**7**	**10**	**.412**

General Managers' History

Jack Riley, 1967-68 to 1969-70; "Red" Kelly, 1970-71; "Red" Kelly and Jack Riley, 1971-72; Jack Riley, 1972-73; Jack Riley and Jack Button, 1973-74; Jack Button, 1974-75; Wren Blair, 1975-76; Wren A. Blair and Baz Bastien, 1976-77; Baz Bastien, 1977-78 to 1982-83; Ed Johnston, 1983-84 to 1987-88; Tony Esposito, 1988-89; Tony Esposito and Craig Patrick, 1989-90; Craig Patrick, 1990-91 to date.

St. Louis Blues

1995-96 Results: 32w-34l-16t 80pts. Fourth, Central Division

Year-by-Year Record

		Home			Road			Overall						
Season	GP	W	L	T	W	L	T	W	L	T	GF	GA	Pts.	Finished	Playoff Result
1995-96	82	15	17	9	17	17	7	32	34	16	219	248	80	4th, Central Div.	Lost Conf. Semi-Final
1994-95	48	16	6	2	12	9	3	28	15	5	178	135	61	2nd, Central Div.	Lost Conf. Quarter-Final
1993-94	84	23	11	8	17	22	3	40	33	11	270	283	91	4th, Central Div.	Lost Conf. Quarter-Final
1992-93	84	22	13	7	15	23	4	37	36	11	282	278	85	4th, Norris Div.	Lost Div. Final
1991-92	80	25	12	3	11	21	8	36	33	11	279	266	83	3rd, Norris Div.	Lost Div. Semi-Final
1990-91	80	24	9	7	23	13	4	47	22	11	310	250	105	2nd, Norris Div.	Lost Div. Final
1989-90	80	20	15	5	17	19	4	37	34	9	295	279	83	2nd, Norris Div.	Lost Div. Final
1988-89	80	22	11	7	11	24	5	33	35	12	275	285	78	2nd, Norris Div.	Lost Div. Final
1987-88	80	18	17	5	16	21	3	34	38	8	278	294	76	2nd, Norris Div.	Lost Div. Final
1986-87	80	21	12	7	11	21	8	32	33	15	281	293	79	1st, Norris Div.	Lost Div. Semi-Final
1985-86	80	23	11	6	14	23	3	37	34	9	302	291	83	3rd, Norris Div.	Lost Conf. Championship
1984-85	80	21	12	7	16	19	5	37	31	12	299	288	86	1st, Norris Div.	Lost Div. Semi-Final
1983-84	80	23	14	3	9	27	4	32	41	7	293	316	71	2nd, Norris Div.	Lost Div. Final
1982-83	80	16	16	8	9	24	7	25	40	15	285	316	65	4th, Norris Div.	Lost Div. Semi-Final
1981-82	80	22	14	4	10	26	4	32	40	8	315	349	72	3rd Norris Div.	Lost Div. Final
1980-81	80	29	7	4	16	11	13	45	18	17	352	281	107	1st, Smythe Div.	Lost Quarter-Final
1979-80	80	20	13	7	14	21	5	34	34	12	266	278	80	2nd, Smythe Div.	Lost Prelim. Round
1978-79	80	14	20	6	4	30	6	18	50	12	249	348	48	3rd, Smythe Div.	Out of Playoffs
1977-78	80	12	20	8	8	27	5	20	47	13	195	304	53	4th, Smythe Div.	Out of Playoffs
1976-77	80	22	13	5	10	26	4	32	39	9	239	276	73	1st, Smythe Div.	Lost Quarter-Final
1975-76	80	20	12	8	9	25	6	29	37	14	249	290	72	3rd, Smythe Div.	Lost Prelim. Round
1974-75	80	23	13	4	12	18	10	35	31	14	269	267	84	2nd, Smythe Div.	Lost Prelim. Round
1973-74	78	16	16	7	10	24	5	26	40	12	206	248	64	6th, West Div.	Out of Playoffs
1972-73	78	21	11	7	11	23	5	32	34	12	233	251	76	4th, West Div.	Lost Quarter-Final
1971-72	78	17	17	5	11	22	6	28	39	11	208	247	67	3rd, West Div.	Lost Semi-Final
1970-71	78	23	7	9	11	18	10	34	25	19	223	208	87	2nd, West Div.	Lost Quarter-Final
1969-70	76	24	9	5	13	18	7	37	27	12	224	179	86	1st, West Div.	Lost Final
1968-69	76	21	8	9	16	17	5	37	25	14	204	157	88	1st, West Div.	Lost Final
1967-68	74	18	12	7	9	19	9	27	31	16	177	191	70	3rd, West Div.	Lost Final

Schedule

Oct.	Fri.	4	Colorado		Sun.	5	at New Jersey
	Sun.	6	Chicago		Tues.	7	Edmonton
	Wed.	9	at Calgary		Thur.	9	at San Jose
	Fri.	11	at Edmonton		Sat.	11	at Los Angeles
	Sat.	12	at Vancouver		Wed.	15	at Phoenix
	Thur.	17	Toronto		Mon.	20	at NY Islanders*
	Fri.	18	at NY Rangers		Thur.	23	Vancouver
	Sun.	20	San Jose		Sat.	25	at Montreal*
	Tues.	22	at Phoenix		Mon.	27	Anaheim
	Thur.	24	at Chicago		Wed.	29	at Toronto
	Sat.	26	Washington		Thur.	30	at Ottawa
	Wed.	30	at Colorado	Feb.	Sat.	1	Detroit*
Nov.	Fri.	1	Buffalo		Tues.	4	at Detroit
	Sun.	3	Dallas		Thur.	6	Dallas
	Tues.	5	at Toronto		Sat.	8	at Boston*
	Fri.	8	at Vancouver		Mon.	10	Phoenix
	Sat.	9	at Calgary		Thur.	13	NY Rangers
	Thur.	14	Tampa Bay		Sat.	15	Colorado*
	Sat.	16	Calgary		Mon.	17	Chicago
	Sun.	17	Anaheim		Thur.	20	Ottawa
	Tues.	19	at Pittsburgh		Sat.	22	Detroit*
	Thur.	21	Phoenix		Sun.	23	Calgary
	Sat.	23	Florida		Tues.	25	at Tampa Bay
	Wed.	27	at Anaheim		Thur.	27	at Florida
Dec.	Sun.	1	San Jose	Mar.	Wed.	5	at Dallas
	Tues.	3	at Toronto		Sun.	9	Edmonton
	Thur.	5	Phoenix		Tues.	11	at San Jose
	Fri.	6	at Colorado		Thur.	13	at Los Angeles
	Sun.	8	at Edmonton		Fri.	14	at Anaheim
	Wed.	11	at Dallas		Mon.	17	at Phoenix
	Fri.	13	Chicago		Thur.	20	Hartford
	Sun.	15	Vancouver		Sun.	23	Dallas
	Tues.	17	at Hartford		Tues.	25	at Washington
	Thur.	19	Pittsburgh		Thur.	27	Los Angeles
	Sat.	21	at Philadelphia*		Sun.	30	Philadelphia
	Sun.	22	Los Angeles	Apr.	Tues.	1	at Detroit
	Thur.	26	at Chicago		Thur.	3	NY Islanders
	Fri.	27	Toronto		Sun.	6	New Jersey
	Sun.	29	Boston		Wed.	9	at Chicago
Jan.	Thur.	2	Montreal		Thur.	10	Toronto
	Fri.	3	at Buffalo		Sun.	13	at Detroit*

* Denotes afternoon game.

Franchise date: June 5, 1967

WESTERN CONFERENCE

CENTRAL DIVISION

30th NHL Season

St. Louis Blues' left winger Shayne Corson saved some of his best performances in 1995-96 for the post-season, finishing among the league-leaders in goals (8), points (14) and power-play goals (6).

1996-97 Player Personnel

FORWARDS	HT	WT	S	Place of Birth	Date	1995-96 Club
AMBROSIO, Jeff	6-1	188	L	Toronto, Ont.	4/26/77	Belleville-Kitchener
CAMPBELL, Jim	6-2	185	R	Worcester, MA	4/3/73	Fredericton-Anaheim-Baltimore
CORSON, Shayne	6-1	200	L	Midland, Ont.	8/13/66	St. Louis
COURTNALL, Geoff	6-1	195	L	Duncan, B.C.	8/18/62	St. Louis
CREIGHTON, Adam	6-5	220	L	Burlington, Ont.	6/2/65	St. Louis
DWYER, Gordie	6-2	190	L	Dalhousie, NB	1/25/78	Hull-Laval-Beauport
HANDZUS, Michal	6-3	191	L	Banska Bystrica, Czech.	3/11/77	B. Bystrica
HECHT, Jochen	6-1	180	L	Mannheim, Germany	6/21/77	Mannheim
HUDSON, Mike	6-1	205	L	Guelph, Ont.	2/6/67	Toronto-St. Louis
HULL, Brett	5-10	201	R	Belleville, Ont.	8/9/64	St. Louis
KENADY, Chris	6-2	195	R	Mound, MN	4/10/73	Worcester
KHMYLEV, Yuri	6-1	189	R	Moscow, USSR	8/9/64	Buffalo-St. Louis
LACHANCE, Bob	5-11	180	R	Northampton, MA	2/1/74	Boston U.-Worcester
LEACH, Stephen	5-11	197	R	Cambridge, MA	1/16/66	Boston-St. Louis
MacTAVISH, Craig	6-1	195	L	London, Ont.	8/15/58	Philadelphia-St. Louis
MATTEAU, Stephane	6-3	210	L	Rouyn-Noranda, Que.	9/2/69	NY Rangers-St. Louis
MAYERS, Jamal	6-0	190	R	Toronto, Ont.	10/24/74	W. Michigan
McRAE, Basil	6-2	210	L	Beaverton, Ont.	1/5/61	St. Louis
MURPHY, Joe	6-1	190	L	London, Ont.	10/16/67	Chicago
NOONAN, Brian	6-1	200	R	Boston, MA	5/29/65	St. Louis
PEARSON, Rob	6-3	198	R	Oshawa, Ont.	3/8/71	Portland (AHL)-St. Louis
PELLERIN, Scott	5-11	180	L	Shediac, N.B.	1/9/70	New Jersey-Albany
PETRAKOV, Andrei	6-0	198	L	Sverdlovsk, USSR	4/26/76	Yekaterinburg
PLAGER, Kevin	6-1	210	R	St. Louis, MO	4/27/71	U. Wisc.-St. Pt.
REASONER, Marty	6-1	185	L	Rochester, NY	2/26/77	Boston College
ROY, Stephane	5-10	173	L	Ste-Martine, Que.	1/26/76	Val d'Or
SHAFRANOV, Konstantin	5-11	176	L	Moscow, USSR	9/11/68	Ft. Wayne
TWIST, Tony	6-1	220	L	Sherwood Park, Alta.	5/9/68	St. Louis
VASILEVSKY, Alexander	5-11	190	L	Kiev, USSR	1/8/75	St. Louis-Worcester
YORK, Harry	6-2	215	L	Panoka, Alta.	4/16/74	Nashville-Worcester
ZEZEL, Peter	5-11	200	L	Toronto, Ont.	4/22/65	St. Louis
ZUKIWSKY, Jonathan	6-2	185	L	St. Paul, Alta.	10/7/77	Red Deer
DEFENSEMEN						
BARON, Murray	6-3	215	L	Prince George, B.C.	6/1/67	St. Louis
BERGEVIN, Marc	6-1	197	L	Montreal, Que.	8/11/65	Detroit
KRAVCHUK, Igor	6-1	200	L	Ufa, USSR	9/13/66	Edmonton-St. Louis
MacINNIS, Al	6-2	196	R	Inverness, N.S.	7/11/63	St. Louis
OLSSON, Christer	5-11	190	L	Arboga, Sweden	7/24/70	St. Louis-Worcester
PRONGER, Chris	6-5	220	L	Dryden, Ont.	10/10/74	St. Louis
RIVERS, Jamie	6-0	190	L	Ottawa, Ont.	3/16/75	St. Louis-Worcester
VIRTUE, Terry	6-0	200	R	Scarborough, Ont.	8/12/70	Worcester
WILLIAMS, David	6-2	195	R	Plainfield, NJ	8/25/67	Detroit (IHL)
YAWNEY, Trent	6-3	195	L	Hudson Bay, Sask.	9/29/65	Calgary
ZABRANSKY, Libor	6-3	196	L	Brno, Czech.	11/25/73	Budejovice
GOALTENDERS	**HT**	**WT**	**C**	**Place of Birth**	**Date**	**1995-96 Club**
BUZAK, Mike	6-3	183	L	Edson, Alta.	2/10/73	Worcester
CASEY, Jon	5-10	155	L	Grand Rapids, MN	3/29/62	St. Louis-Peoria
FUHR, Grant	5-9	190	R	Spruce Grove, Alta.	9/28/62	St. Louis
McLENNAN, Jamie	6-0	190	L	Edmonton, Alta.	6/30/71	NY Islanders-Utah-Worcester
ROCHE, Scott	6-4	220	L	Lindsay, Ont.	3/19/77	North Bay
VEISOR, Mike	6-2	195	R	Dallas, TX	12/7/72	Northeastern

General Managers' History

Lynn Patrick, 1967-68; Scotty Bowman, 1968-69 to 1970-71; Lynn Patrick, 1971-72; Sid Abel, 1972-73; Charles Catto, 1973-74; Gerry Ehman, 1974-75; Dennis Ball, 1975-76; Emile Francis, 1976-77 to 1982-83; Ron Caron, 1983-84 to 1993-94; Mike Keenan, 1994-95 to date.

Coaching History

Lynn Patrick and Scotty Bowman, 1967-68; Scotty Bowman, 1968-69 to 1969-70; Al Arbour and Scotty Bowman, 1970-71; Sid Abel, Bill McCreary and Al Arbour, 1971-72; Al Arbour and Jean-Guy Talbot, 1972-73; Jean-Guy Talbot and Lou Angotti, 1973-74; Lou Angotti, Lynn Patrck and Garry Young, 1974-75; Garry Young, Lynn Patrick and Leo Boivin, 1975-76; Emile Francis, 1976-77; Leo Boivin and Barclay Plager, 1977-78; Barclay Plager, 1978-79; Barclay Plager and Red Berenson, 1979-80; Red Berenson, 1980-81; Red Berenson and Emile Francis, 1981-82; Emile Francis and Barclay Plager, 1982-83; Jacques Demers, 1983-84 to 1985-86; Jacques Martin, 1986-87 to 1987-88. Brian Sutter, 1988-89 to 1991-92; Bob Plager and Bob Berry, 1992-93; Bob Berry, 1993-94; Mike Keenan, 1994-95 to date.

Captains' History

Al Arbour, 1967-68 to 1969-70; Red Berenson and Barclay Plager, 1970-71; Barclay Plager, 1971-72 to 1975-76; no captain, 1976-77; Red Berenson, 1977-78; Barry Gibbs, 1978-79; Brian Sutter, 1979-80 to 1987-88; Bernie Federko, 1988-89; Rick Meagher, 1989-90; Scott Stevens, 1990-91; Garth Butcher, 1991-92; Brett Hull, 1992-93 to 1994-95; Brett Hull, Shayne Corson and Wayne Gretzky, 1995-96.

1995-96 Scoring

* – rookie

Regular Season

Pos	#	Player	Team	GP	G	A	Pts	+/–	PIM	PP	SH	GW	GT	S	%
C	99	Wayne Gretzky	L.A.	62	15	66	81	–7	32	5	0	2	1	144	10.4
			STL	18	8	13	21	–6	2	1	1	1	0	51	15.7
			TOTAL	80	23	79	102	–13	34	6	1	3	1	195	11.8
R	16	Brett Hull	STL	70	43	40	83	4	30	16	5	6	0	327	13.1
D	2	Al MacInnis	STL	82	17	44	61	5	88	9	1	1	1	317	5.4
L	9	Shayne Corson	STL	77	18	28	46	3	192	13	0	0	2	150	12.0
L	14	Geoff Courtnall	STL	69	24	16	40	–9	101	7	1	1	2	228	10.5
R	28	Brian Noonan	STL	81	13	22	35	2	84	3	1	6	0	131	9.9
L	13	Yuri Khmylev	BUF	66	8	20	28	–12	40	5	1	1	1	123	6.5
			STL	7	0	1	1	–5	0	0	0	0	0	13	0.0
			TOTAL	73	8	21	29	–17	40	5	1	1	1	136	5.9
R	27	Stephen Leach	BOS	59	9	13	22	–4	86	1	0	2	0	124	7.3
			STL	14	2	4	6	–3	22	0	0	0	0	33	6.1
			TOTAL	73	11	17	28	–7	108	1	0	2	0	157	7.0
L	32	Stephane Matteau	NYR	32	4	2	6	–4	22	1	0	0	0	39	10.3
			STL	46	7	13	20	–4	65	3	0	2	1	70	10.0
			TOTAL	78	11	15	26	–8	87	4	0	2	1	109	10.1
D	44	Chris Pronger	STL	78	7	18	25	–18	110	3	1	1	0	138	5.1
D	5	Igor Kravchuk	EDM	26	4	4	8	–13	10	3	0	0	0	59	6.8
			STL	40	3	12	15	–6	24	0	0	1	0	114	2.6
			TOTAL	66	7	16	23	–19	34	3	0	1	0	173	4.0
C	20	Adam Creighton	STL	61	11	10	21	0	78	2	0	3	1	98	11.2
C	25	Peter Zezel	STL	57	8	13	21	–2	12	2	0	1	0	87	9.2
C	15	Mike Hudson	TOR	27	2	0	2	–5	29	0	0	0	0	27	7.4
			STL	32	3	12	15	7	26	0	0	0	0	32	9.4
			TOTAL	59	5	12	17	2	55	0	0	0	0	59	8.5
R	36	Glenn Anderson	EDM	17	4	6	10	0	27	0	0	1	0	36	11.1
			STL	15	2	2	4	–11	6	2	0	0	0	35	5.7
			TOTAL	32	6	8	14	–11	33	2	0	1	0	71	8.5
C	23	Craig MacTavish	PHI	55	5	8	13	–3	62	0	0	1	1	42	11.9
			STL	13	0	1	1	–6	8	0	0	0	0	16	0.0
			TOTAL	68	5	9	14	–9	70	0	0	1	1	58	8.6
D	34	Murray Baron	STL	82	2	9	11	3	190	0	0	0	0	86	2.3
R	12	Rob Pearson	STL	27	6	4	10	4	54	1	0	1	0	51	11.8
D	22	Charlie Huddy	BUF	52	5	5	10	–5	59	2	0	1	0	57	8.8
			STL	12	0	0	0	–7	6	0	0	0	0	13	0.0
			TOTAL	64	5	5	10	–12	65	2	0	1	0	70	7.1
D	35 *	Christer Olsson	STL	26	2	8	10	–6	14	2	0	0	0	32	6.3
D	33	Ken Sutton	EDM	32	0	8	8	–12	39	0	0	0	0	38	0.0
			STL	6	0	0	0	–1	4	0	0	0	0	3	0.0
			TOTAL	38	0	8	8	–13	43	0	0	0	0	41	0.0
L	18	Tony Twist	STL	51	3	2	5	–1	100	0	0	1	0	12	25.0
C	37 *	Roman Vopat	STL	25	2	3	5	–8	48	1	0	1	0	33	6.1
D	26	Jay Wells	STL	76	0	3	3	–8	67	0	0	0	0	24	0.0
L	17	Basil McRae	STL	18	1	1	2	–5	40	0	0	0	0	5	20.0
R	21	Paul Broten	STL	17	0	1	1	–1	4	0	0	0	0	11	0.0
L	7	Greg Gilbert	STL	17	0	1	1	–1	8	0	0	0	0	9	0.0
G	31	Grant Fuhr	STL	79	0	1	1	0	8	0	0	0	0	0	0.0
R	41 *	Alexander Vasilevskii	STL	1	0	0	0	–1	0	0	0	0	0	0	0.0
L	33	fred Knipscheer	STL	1	0	0	0	0	2	0	0	0	0	2	0.0
D	6 *	Jamie Rivers	STL	3	0	0	0	–1	2	0	0	0	0	5	0.0
G	30	Jon Casey	STL	9	0	0	0	0	0	0	0	0	0	0	0.0
G	29	Bruce Racine	STL	11	0	0	0	0	2	0	0	0	0	0	0.0

Goaltending

No.	Goaltender	GPI	Mins	Avg	W	L	T	EN	SO	GA	SA	S%
31	Grant Fuhr	79	4365	2.87	30	28	16	1	3	209	2157	.903
29	Bruce Racine	11	230	3.13	0	3	0	0	0	12	101	.881
30	Jon Casey	9	395	3.80	2	3	0	0	0	25	180	.861
39	Pat Jablonski	1	8	7.50	0	0	0	0	0	1	5	.800
	Totals	**82**	**5003**	**2.97**	**32**	**34**	**16**	**1**	**3**	**248**	**2444**	**.899**

Playoffs

Pos	#	Player	Team	GP	G	A	Pts	+/–	PIM	PP	SH	GW	OT	S	%
C	99	Wayne Gretzky	STL	13	2	14	16	2	0	1	0	1	0	25	8.0
L	9	Shayne Corson	STL	13	8	6	14	–1	22	6	1	1	0	37	21.6
R	16	Brett Hull	STL	13	6	5	11	2	10	2	1	1	0	52	11.5
D	2	Al MacInnis	STL	13	3	4	7	2	20	1	0	0	0	48	6.3
D	5	Igor Kravchuk	STL	10	1	5	6	0	4	0	0	1	1	14	7.1
D	44	Chris Pronger	STL	13	1	5	6	0	16	0	0	0	0	20	5.0
R	28	Brian Noonan	STL	13	4	1	5	–5	10	0	0	0	0	21	19.0
R	27	Stephen Leach	STL	11	3	2	5	4	10	1	0	1	0	11	27.3
R	36	Glenn Anderson	STL	11	1	4	5	5	6	0	0	1	1	20	5.0
C	25	Peter Zezel	STL	10	3	0	3	4	2	0	1	0	0	17	17.6
L	14	Geoff Courtnall	STL	13	0	3	3	2	14	0	0	0	0	26	0.0
L	13	Yuri Khmylev	STL	6	1	1	2	1	4	0	0	1	0	8	12.5
L	18	Tony Twist	STL	10	1	1	2	0	16	0	0	0	0	1	100.0
C	20	Adam Creighton	STL	13	1	1	2	–4	8	0	0	0	0	18	5.6
L	32	Stephane Matteau	STL	11	0	2	2	–2	8	0	0	0	0	13	0.0
G	30	Jon Casey	STL	12	0	2	2	0	8	0	0	0	0	0	0.0
C	23	Craig MacTavish	STL	13	0	2	2	0	6	0	0	0	0	11	0.0
D	34	Murray Baron	STL	13	1	0	1	4	20	0	1	0	0	10	10.0
D	22	Charlie Huddy	STL	13	1	0	1	1	8	0	0	0	0	14	7.1
C	15	Mike Hudson	STL	2	0	1	1	1	4	0	0	0	0	0	0.0
D	26	Jay Wells	STL	12	0	1	1	0	2	0	0	0	0	2	0.0
G	29	Bruce Racine	STL	1	0	0	0	0	0	0	0	0	0	0	0.0
D	33	Ken Sutton	STL	1	0	0	0	0	0	0	0	0	0	1	0.0
G	31	Grant Fuhr	STL	2	0	0	0	0	0	0	0	0	0	0	0.0
L	17	Basil Mcrae	STL	2	0	0	0	0	0	0	0	0	0	2	0.0
R	12	Rob Pearson	STL	2	0	0	0	1	14	0	0	0	0	2	0.0
D	35 *	Christer Olsson	STL	3	0	0	0	–1	0	0	0	0	0	0	0.0

Goaltending

No.	Goaltender	GPI	Mins	Avg	W	L	EN	SO	GA	SA	S%
29	Bruce Racine	1	1	.00	0	0	0	0	0	0	.000
31	Grant Fuhr	2	69	.87	1	0	0	0	1	45	.978
30	Jon Casey	12	747	2.89	6	6	0	1	36	378	.905
	Totals	**13**	**818**	**2.71**	**7**	**6**	**0**	**1**	**37**	**423**	**.913**

Club Records

Team

(Figures in brackets for season records are games played; records for fewest points, wins, ties, losses, goals, goals against are for 70 or more games)

Most Points	107	1980-81 (80)
Most Wins	47	1990-91 (80)
Most Ties	19	1970-71 (78)
Most Losses	50	1978-79 (80)
Most Goals	352	1980-81 (80)
Most Goals Against	349	1981-82 (80)
Fewest Points	48	1978-79 (80)
Fewest Wins	18	1978-79 (80)
Fewest Ties	7	1983-84 (80)
Fewest Losses	18	1980-81 (80)
Fewest Goals	177	1967-68 (74)
Fewest Goals Against	157	1968-69 (76)

Longest Winning Streak

Overall .... 7 Jan. 21-Feb. 3/88,
Mar. 19-31/91
Home .... 9 Jan. 26-Feb. 26/91
Away .... 4 Four times

Longest Undefeated Streak

Overall .... 12 Nov. 10-Dec. 8/68
(5 wins, 7 ties)
Home .... 11 Feb. 12-Mar. 19/69
(5 wins, 6 ties),
Feb. 7-Mar. 29/75
(9 wins, 2 ties),
Oct. 7-Nov. 26/93
(7 wins, 4 ties)
Away .... 7 Dec. 9-26/87
(4 wins, 3 ties)

Longest Losing Streak

Overall .... 7 Nov. 12-26/67,
Feb. 12-25/89
Home .... 5 Nov. 19-Dec. 6/77
Away .... 10 Jan. 20/82-Mar. 8/82

Longest Winless Streak

Overall .... 12 Jan. 17-Feb. 15/78
(10 losses, 2 ties)
Home .... 7 Dec. 28/82-Jan. 25/83
(5 losses, 2 ties)
Away .... 17 Jan. 23-Apr. 7/74
(14 losses, 3 ties)
Most Shutouts, Season 13 1968-69 (76)
Most PIM, Season 2,041 1990-91 (80)
Most Goals, Game .... 11 Feb. 26/94
(St.L. 11 at Ott. 1)

Individual

Most Seasons	13	Bernie Federko
Most Games	927	Bernie Federko
Most Goals, Career	458	Brett Hull
Most Assists, Career	721	Bernie Federko
Most Points, Career	1,073	Bernie Federko
Most PIM, Career	1,786	Brian Sutter
Most Shutouts, Career	16	Glenn Hall

Longest Consecutive
Games Streak .... 662 Garry Unger
(Feb. 7/71-Apr. 8/79)
Most Goals, Season .... 86 Brett Hull
(1990-91)
Most Assists, Season .... 90 Adam Oates
(1990-91)
Most Points, Season .... 131 Brett Hull
(1990-91)
(86G, 45A)
Most PIM, Season .... 306 Bob Gassoff
(1975-76)

Most Points, Defenseman
Season .... 78 Jeff Brown
(1992-93; 25G, 53A)

Most Points, Center,
Season .... 115 Adam Oates
(1990-91; 25G, 90A)

Most Points, Right Wing,
Season .... 131 Brett Hull
(1990-91; 86G, 45A)

Most Points, Left Wing,
Season .... 102 Brendan Shanahan
(1993-94; 52G, 50A)

Most Points, Rookie,
Season .... 73 Jorgen Pettersson
(1980-81; 37G, 36A)
Most Shutouts, Season .... 8 Glenn Hall
(1968-69)
Most Goals, Game .... 6 Red Berenson
(Nov. 7/68)
Most Assists, Game .... 5 Brian Sutter
(Nov. 22/88),
Bernie Federko
(Feb. 27/88),
Adam Oates
(Jan. 26/91)
Most Points, Game........... 7 Red Berenson
(Nov. 7/68; 6G, 1A),
Garry Unger
(Mar. 13/71; 3G, 4A)

Retired Numbers

3	Bob Gassoff	1973-1977
8	Barclay Plager	1967-1977
11	Brian Sutter	1976-1988
24	Bernie Federko	1976-1989

All-time Record vs. Other Clubs

Regular Season

		At Home							On Road							Total					
	GP	W	L	T	GF	GA	PTS	GP	W	L	T	GF	GA	PTS	GP	W	L	T	GF	GA	PTS
Anaheim	6	4	2	0	25	19	8	6	3	3	0	14	17	6	12	7	5	0	39	36	14
Boston	53	21	23	9	167	188	51	52	11	34	7	140	230	29	105	32	57	16	307	418	80
Buffalo	44	26	12	6	165	113	58	45	12	29	4	140	188	28	89	38	41	10	305	301	80
Calgary	47	20	19	8	166	148	48	46	18	24	4	135	166	40	93	38	43	12	301	314	88
Chicago	92	44	31	17	311	288	105	96	28	55	13	294	379	69	188	72	86	30	605	667	174
Colorado	24	17	5	2	111	78	36	24	10	11	3	81	87	23	48	27	16	5	192	165	59
Dallas	100	54	27	19	366	283	127	98	26	44	18	292	335	90	198	90	71	37	658	618	217
Detroit	89	49	26	14	325	251	112	87	37	37	13	283	320	87	176	86	63	27	608	571	199
Edmonton	28	13	11	4	114	113	30	28	10	15	3	111	120	23	56	23	26	7	225	233	53
Florida	2	2	0	0	7	3	4	2	1	1	0	5	3	3	4	3	1	0	12	6	7
Hartford	24	14	8	2	97	80	30	25	14	9	2	80	76	30	49	28	17	4	177	156	60
Los Angeles	62	39	15	8	235	162	86	62	21	32	9	177	227	51	124	60	47	17	412	389	137
Montreal	52	11	27	14	134	187	36	53	8	38	7	137	238	23	105	19	65	21	271	425	59
New Jersey	39	25	8	6	176	122	56	40	15	18	7	116	132	37	79	40	26	13	292	254	93
NY Islanders	41	17	17	7	150	135	41	42	9	23	10	102	162	28	83	26	40	17	252	297	69
NY Rangers	56	21	26	9	164	184	51	54	6	42	6	123	231	18	110	27	68	15	287	415	69
Ottawa	3	2	1	0	13	13	4	3	2	1	0	17	6	4	6	4	2	0	30	19	8
Philadelphia	60	23	30	7	176	190	53	60	10	40	10	139	241	30	120	33	70	17	315	431	83
Pittsburgh	58	39	13	6	231	156	84	57	19	26	12	176	217	50	115	58	39	18	407	373	134
San Jose	11	10	1	0	45	22	20	8	7	1	0	30	20	14	19	17	2	0	75	42	34
Tampa Bay	5	4	1	0	20	14	8	6	3	2	1	21	19	7	11	7	3	1	41	33	15
Toronto	89	51	25	13	310	254	115	88	23	55	10	255	339	56	177	74	80	23	565	593	171
Vancouver	55	30	17	8	207	164	68	56	25	24	7	176	173	57	111	55	41	15	383	337	125
Washington	34	14	12	8	140	114	36	33	12	18	3	99	122	27	67	26	30	11	239	236	63
Winnipeg	32	16	7	9	126	95	41	34	11	17	6	105	117	28	66	27	24	15	231	212	69
Defunct Clubs	32	25	4	3	131	55	53	33	11	10	12	95	100	34	65	36	14	15	226	155	87
Totals	**1138**	**591**	**368**	**179**	**4112**	**3431**	**1361**	**1138**	**362**	**608**	**168**	**3343**	**4265**	**892**	**2276**	**953**	**976**	**347**	**7455**	**7696**	**2253**

Playoffs

	Series	W	L	GP	W	L	T	GF	GA	Last Mtg.	Round	Result
Boston	2	0	2	8	0	8	0	15	48	1972	SF	L 0-4
Buffalo	1	0	1	3	1	2	0	8	7	1976	PR	L 1-2
Calgary	1	0	1	7	3	4	0	22	28	1986	CF	L 3-4
Chicago	9	2	7	45	18	27	0	129	166	1993	DSF	W 4-0
Dallas	10	5	5	56	26	30	0	162	174	1994	CQF	L 0-4
Detroit	4	2	2	23	11	12	0	67	75	1996	CSF	L 3-4
Los Angeles	1	1	0	4	4	0	0	16	5	1969	SF	W 4-0
Montreal	3	0	3	12	0	12	0	14	42	1977	QF	L 0-4
NY Rangers	1	0	1	6	2	4	0	22	29	1981	QF	L 2-4
Philadelphia	2	1	1	11	8	3	0	34	20	1969	QF	W 4-0
Pittsburgh	3	2	1	13	7	6	0	45	40	1981	PR	W 3-2
Toronto	5	3	2	31	17	14	0	88	90	1996	CQF	W 4-2
Vancouver	1	0	1	7	3	4	0	27	27	1995	CQF	L 3-4
Winnipeg	1	1	0	4	3	1	0	20	13	1982	DSF	W 3-1
Totals	**44**	**18**	**26**	**230**	**103**	**127**	**0**	**669**	**764**			

Calgary totals include Atlanta, 1972-73 to 1979-80.   Colorado totals include Quebec, 1979-80 to 1994-95.
Dallas totals include Minnesota, 1967-68 to 1992-93.
New Jersey totals include Kansas City, 1974-75 to 1975-76, and Colorado Rockies, 1976-77 to 1981-82.

Playoff Results 1996-92

Year	Round	Opponent	Result	GF	GA
1996	CSF	Detroit	L 3-4	16	22
	CQF	Toronto	W 4-2	21	15
1995	CQF	Vancouver	L 3-4	27	27
1994	CQF	Dallas	L 0-4	10	16
1993	DF	Toronto	L 3-4	11	22
	DSF	Chicago	W 4-0	13	6
1992	DSF	Chicago	L 2-4	19	23

Abbreviations: Round: F – Final;
CF – conference final; **CQF** – conference quarter-final;
CSF – conference semi-final; **DF** – division final;
DSF – division semi-final; **SF** – semi-final;
QF – quarter-final; **PR** – preliminary round.

1995-96 Results

Oct.	7	at Washington	1-4		11	at Philadelphia	4-4
	10	Edmonton	5-3		13	at Montreal	3-3
	12	at Dallas	3-1		14	at NY Rangers	3-3
	14	Colorado	4-1		16	Edmonton	1-5
	17	Boston	4-7		24	at Winnipeg	6-5
	19	Dallas	1-1		27	Tampa Bay	2-1
	21	Chicago	1-4		29	at Ottawa	2-4
	22	at Buffalo	2-5		31	at Toronto	4-0
	25	at Hartford	4-2	Feb.	1	Vancouver	2-3
	27	Anaheim	4-2		3	Philadelphia	3-7
	29	Washington	1-3		6	Dallas	2-5
Nov.	1	at Anaheim	0-3		8	Chicago	1-6
	4	at San Jose	3-7		10	at Dallas	6-3
	7	Los Angeles	0-1		11	at Florida	2-2
	10	Winnipeg	3-2		13	at Tampa Bay	3-2
	11	at NY Islanders	4-1		16	Detroit	4-3
	14	San Jose	3-1		18	Winnipeg	3-0
	16	at Boston	2-5		20	Ottawa	1-7
	18	at Toronto	2-5		22	at Chicago	4-3
	21	Vancouver	2-3		24	Los Angeles	2-2
	23	Toronto	2-2		29	at Vancouver	2-2
	25	Buffalo	0-2	Mar.	3	at Edmonton	4-3
	27	Montreal	5-4		5	Florida	2-0
	29	at Winnipeg	4-1		7	Calgary	2-4
	30	at Edmonton	7-3		9	Hartford	6-3
Dec.	2	at Calgary	1-1		12	at Calgary	2-4
	5	at Vancouver	6-3		15	at San Jose	4-2
	8	at Los Angeles	2-1		17	at Anaheim	1-5
	9	at Los Angeles	3-1		18	at Los Angeles	3-1
	12	Detroit	2-5		20	at Dallas	1-2
	14	Calgary	3-3		22	Anaheim	1-6
	16	San Jose	3-2		24	Detroit	2-2
	19	NY Islanders	4-1		26	at Pittsburgh	4-8
	22	at Colorado	1-2		28	New Jersey	4-4
	23	at Winnipeg	1-2		31	at Detroit	1-8
	26	at Detroit	2-3	Apr.	3	at Colorado	6-3
	28	Dallas	3-4		5	at Toronto	1-5
	30	Toronto	3-4		6	at Toronto	1-5
Jan.	4	at Chicago	3-1		8	Winnipeg	2-5
	6	Pittsburgh	3-2		11	Colorado	2-3
	9	at New Jersey	2-4		14	at Chicago	2-2

Entry Draft
Selections 1996-82

1996
Pick
14	Marty Reasoner
67	Gordie Dwyer
95	Jonathan Zukiwsky
97	Andrei Petrakov
159	Stephen Wagner
169	Daniel Corso
177	Reed Low
196	Andrei Podkonicky
203	Anthony Hutchins
229	Konstantin Shafranov

1995
Pick
49	Jochen Hecht
75	Scott Roche
101	Michal Handzus
127	Jeff Ambrosio
153	Denis Hamel
179	J-Luc Grand-Pierre
205	Derek Bekar
209	Libor Zabransky

1994
Pick
68	Stephane Roy
94	Tyler Harlton
120	Edvin Frylen
172	Roman Vopat
198	Steve Noble
224	Marc Stephan
250	Kevin Harper
276	Scott Fankhouser

1993
Pick
37	Maxim Bets
63	Jamie Rivers
89	Jamal Mayers
141	Todd Kelman
167	Mike Buzak
193	Eric Boguniecki
219	Michael Grier
245	Libor Prochazka
271	Alexander Vasilevsky
275	Christer Olsson

1992
Pick
38	Igor Korolev
62	Vitali Karamnov
64	Vitali Prokhorov
86	Lee J. Leslie
134	Bob Lachance
158	Ian LaPerriere
160	Lance Burns
180	Igor Boldin
182	Nicholas Naumenko
206	Todd Harris
230	Yuri Gunko
259	Wade Salzman

1991
Pick
27	Steve Staios
64	Kyle Reeves
65	Nathan Lafayette
87	Grayden Reid
109	Jeff Callinan
131	Bruce Gardiner
153	Terry Hollinger
175	Christopher Kenady
197	Jed Fiebelkorn
219	Chris MacKenzie
241	Kevin Rappana
263	Mike Veisor

1990
Pick
33	Craig Johnson
54	Patrice Tardif
96	Jason Ruff
117	Kurtis Miller
138	Wayne Conlan
180	Parris Duffus
201	Steve Widmeyer
222	Joe Hawley
243	Joe Fleming

1989
Pick
9	Jason Marshall
31	Rick Corriveau
55	Denny Felsner
93	Daniel Laperriere
114	David Roberts
124	Derek Frenette
135	Jeff Batters
156	Kevin Plager
177	John Roderick
198	John Valo
219	Brian Lukowski

1988
Pick
9	Rod Brind' Amour
30	Adrien Plavsic
51	Rob Fournier
72	Jaan Luik
105	Dave Lacouture
114	Dan Fowler
135	Matt Hayes
156	John McCoy
177	Tony Twist
198	Bret Hedican
219	Heath DeBoer
240	Michael Francis

1987
Pick
12	Keith Osborne
54	Kevin Miehm
59	Robert Nordmark
75	Darin Smith
82	Andy Rymsha
117	Rob Robinson
138	Todd Crabtree
159	Guy Hebert
180	Robert Dumas
201	David Marvin
207	Andy Cesarski
222	Dan Rolfe
243	Ray Savard

1986
Pick
10	Jocelyn Lemieux
31	Mike Posma
52	Tony Hejna
73	Glen Featherstone
87	Michael Wolak
115	Mike O'Toole
136	Andy May
157	Randy Skarda
178	Martyn Ball
199	Rod Thacker
220	Terry MacLean
234	Bill Butler
241	David O'Brien

1985
Pick
37	Herb Raglan
44	Nelson Emerson
54	Ned Desmond
100	Dan Brooks
121	Rich Burchill
138	Pat Jablonski
159	Scott Brickey
180	Jeff Urban
201	Vince Guidotti
222	Ron Saatzer
243	Dave Jecha

1984
Pick
26	Brian Benning
32	Tony Hrkac
50	Toby Ducolon
53	Robert Dirk
56	Alan Perry
71	Graham Herring
92	Scott Paluch
113	Steve Tuttle
134	Cliff Ronning
148	Don Porter
155	Jim Vesey
176	Daniel Jomphe
196	Tom Tilley
217	Mark Cupolo
237	Mark Lanigan

1983
DID NOT DRAFT

1982
Pick
50	Mike Posavad
92	Scott Machej
113	Perry Ganchar
134	Doug Gilmour
155	Chris Delaney
176	Matt Christensen
197	John Shumski
218	Brian Ahern
239	Peter Smith

Club Directory

Kiel Center
1401 Clark Avenue
St. Louis, MO 63103-2709
Phone **314/622-2500**
FAX 314/622-2582
Capacity: 19,260

Executive
Chairman of the Board . . . . Jerry Ritter
President and CEO . . . . Jack Quinn
General Manager and Head Coach . . . . Mike Keenan
Assistant General Manager. . . . . Bob Berry
Executive Vice-President . . . . Ronald Caron
Senior Vice-President, Marketing . . . . Tom Maurer
Vice-President, Sales . . . . Bruce Affleck
Vice-President, Finance and Administration . . . . . . Jerry Jasiek
Executive Assistant to President . . . . Lynn Diederichsen
Executive Assistant to General Manager . . . . Janiece Chambers

Hockey Operations
Director of Amateur Player Personnel and Scouting . Ted Hampson
Assistant Director of Scouting. . . . . Jack Evans
Scouting Staff. . . . . Pat Ginnell, Matt Keator, Peter Stastny,
Dick Cherry, Ken Williamson
Director of Professional Playing Personnel. . . . . . . Jim Pappin
Professional Scouts . . . . Bob Plager, Rick Meagher
Associate Coaches . . . . Roger Nielson, Jim Roberts
Director of Team Services . . . . Michael Caruso
Video Coordinator . . . . Arne Pappin
Head Coach, Worcester IceCats . . . . Greg Gilbert
Assistant Coach, Worcester IceCats . . . . Paul Pickard

Medical Staff
Medical Trainer . . . . Ray Barile
Massage Therapist . . . . Jeff Cope
Equipment Manager . . . . Terry Roof
Assistant Equipment Manager . . . . Mark Roof
Equipment Assistant . . . . Eric Bechtol
Orthopedic Surgeon . . . . Dr. Rick Lehman
Internist . . . . Dr. Aaron Birenbaum
Dentist . . . . Dr. Glenn Edwards
Optometrist . . . . Dr. N. Rex Ghormley
Strength & Conditioning Coach . . . . Bob Kersee

Public Relations/Marketing
Public Relations/Hockey Operations . . . . Christopher Taylor
Director of Promotions/Community Relations . . . . . Stacy Solomon
Marketing/Public Relations Assistant. . . . . Donna Quirk
Receptionist . . . . Pam Barrett

Finance/Sales
Director of Retail Operations. . . . . Andy Cotlar
Sales Representatives . . . . Paula Barnes, Wes Edwards, John Casson,
Tammy Iuli, Jill Mann
Accounting Staff. . . . . Jim Bergman, Craig Bryant, Marsha McBride

Miscellaneous
Television Stations . . . . Prime Sports and KMOV-TV, KTVI-TV
Radio Station . . . . KMOX (1120 AM)
Team Colors . . . . Blue, Gold & Red

General Manager and Coach

KEENAN, MICHAEL (MIKE)
General Manager and Coach, St. Louis Blues.
Born in Toronto, Ontario, October 21, 1949.

Mike Keenan became the 18th head coach and ninth general manager in St. Louis Blues' history on July 18, 1994. In his first two seasons in St. Louis, Keenan has guided the Blues to a cumulative 60-49-21 record. In Keenan's initial season in St. Louis (1994-95), he led the Blues to the third-best overall record in the National Hockey League (28-15-5), marking the third-highest winning percentage (.635) in club history.

In 854 career NHL games, Keenan owns a 455-301-98 career coaching record. In 160 playoff games, Keenan sports a 91-69 mark and has coached his team to the Stanley Cup Finals four times, leading the NY Rangers to their first Stanley Cup in 54 years in 1994. Keenan has guided his clubs to six division titles. He has finished with the best record in the National Hockey League three times with three different teams, averaging 43 wins and 95 points per season (minimum 80-game schedule).

He started in the NHL with Philadelphia in 1984-85, taking the Flyers from a third-place finish the previous season to the best record in the NHL with 113 points. He coached the Flyers for three more seasons and posted a mark of 190-102-28 in 320 games. He then moved to Chicago in 1988-89 and coached the Blackhawks for four seasons and 320 games. He left in 1991-92 with a record of 153-126-41 having coached the Hawks to the NHL's best record in 1990-91 with 106 points and a Stanley Cup final appearance in 1992. Keenan also served as the Blackhawks' general manager from 1989-90 to his departure in 1991-92.

Keenan joined the New York Rangers on April 17, 1993 and guided the club to its best record ever (52-24-8, 113 PTS) and his first Stanley Cup championship.

Mike has one daughter, Gayla, and resides in St. Louis.

Coaching Record

		Regular Season					Playoffs			
Season	Team	Games	W	L	T	%	Games	W	L	%
1979-80	Peterborough (OHL)	68	47	20	1	.699	18	15	3	.833
1980-81	Rochester (AHL)	80	30	42	8	.425	....	....	....	....
1981-82	Rochester (AHL)	80	40	31	9	.556	9	4	5	.444
1982-83	Rochester (AHL)	80	46	25	9	.631	16	12	4	.750
1983-84	U. of Toronto (CIAU)	49	41	5	3	.867	....	....	....	....
1984-85	Philadelphia (NHL)	80	53	20	7	.706	19	12	7	.632
1985-86	Philadelphia (NHL)	80	53	23	4	.688	5	2	3	.400
1986-87	Philadelphia (NHL)	80	46	26	8	.625	26	15	11	.577
1987-88	Philadelphia (NHL)	80	38	33	9	.531	7	3	4	.429
1988-89	Chicago (NHL)	80	27	41	12	.413	16	9	7	.563
1989-90	Chicago (NHL)	80	41	33	6	.550	20	10	10	.500
1990-91	Chicago (NHL)	80	49	23	8	.663	6	2	4	.333
1991-92	Chicago (NHL)	80	36	29	15	.544	18	12	6	.667
1993-94	NY Rangers (NHL)	84	52	24	8	.667	23	16	7	.696*
1994-95	St. Louis (NHL)	48	28	15	5	.635	7	3	4	.429
1995-96	St. Louis (NHL)	82	32	34	16	.488	13	7	6	.538
	NHL Totals	**854**	**455**	**301**	**98**	**.590**	**160**	**91**	**69**	**.569**

* Stanley Cup win.

San Jose Sharks

1995-96 Results: 20w-55L-7t 47pts. Seventh, Pacific Division

Year-by-Year Record

		Home			Road			Overall							
Season	GP	W	L	T	W	L	T	W	L	T	GF	GA	Pts.	Finished	Playoff Result
1995-96	82	12	26	3	8	29	4	20	55	7	252	357	47	7th, Pacific Div.	Out of Playoffs
1994-95	48	10	13	1	9	12	3	19	25	4	129	161	42	3rd, Pacific Div.	Lost Conf. Semi-Final
1993-94	84	19	13	10	14	22	6	33	35	16	252	265	82	3rd, Pacific Div.	Lost Conf. Semi-Final
1992-93	84	8	33	1	3	38	1	11	71	2	218	414	24	6th, Smythe Div.	Out of Playoffs
1991-92	80	14	23	3	3	35	2	17	58	5	219	359	39	6th, Smythe Div.	Out of Playoffs

Schedule

Oct.	Sat.	5	NY Islanders
	Sun.	6	at Los Angeles
	Tues.	8	at Colorado
	Thur.	10	at Phoenix
	Sat.	12	Boston
	Wed.	16	Florida
	Fri.	18	at Anaheim
	Sun.	20	at St. Louis
	Tues.	22	at Toronto
	Thur.	24	at New Jersey
	Sat.	26	at NY Islanders*
	Sun.	27	at Chicago*
	Wed.	30	Calgary
Nov.	Fri.	1	at Anaheim
	Sat.	2	Montreal
	Wed.	6	Colorado
	Fri.	8	Dallas
	Tues.	12	Hartford
	Fri.	15	at Detroit
	Sat.	16	at Philadelphia
	Mon.	18	at Boston
	Thur.	21	Detroit
	Sat.	23	Anaheim
	Wed.	27	Chicago
	Fri.	29	Edmonton
Dec.	Sun.	1	at St. Louis
	Wed.	4	at Dallas
	Sat.	7	Tampa Bay
	Wed.	11	Washington
	Fri.	13	Pittsburgh
	Tues.	17	Toronto
	Fri.	20	at Washington
	Sat.	21	at Pittsburgh
	Mon.	23	at Dallas
	Thur.	26	Vancouver
	Sat.	28	at Edmonton
	Sun.	29	at Vancouver
	Tues.	31	at Calgary
Jan.	Thur.	2	Philadelphia
	Sat.	4	Calgary
	Tues.	7	Buffalo
	Thur.	9	St. Louis
	Sat.	11	at Edmonton
	Mon.	13	Phoenix
	Wed.	22	Los Angeles
	Fri.	24	New Jersey
	Mon.	27	at Vancouver
	Wed.	29	at Edmonton
	Thur.	30	at Calgary
Feb.	Sat.	1	Colorado*
	Mon.	3	Chicago
	Wed.	5	Los Angeles
	Sat.	8	at Ottawa
	Mon.	10	at Montreal
	Wed.	12	at Detroit
	Thur.	13	at Chicago
	Sun.	16	at Buffalo
	Tues.	18	Dallas
	Thur.	20	Vancouver
	Sun.	23	at Tampa Bay*
	Tues.	25	at Florida
	Fri.	28	at Hartford
Mar.	Sat.	1	at Toronto
	Mon.	3	at NY Rangers
	Thur.	6	Ottawa
	Sun.	9	NY Rangers*
	Tues.	11	St. Louis
	Fri.	14	Phoenix
	Sat.	15	Detroit
	Wed.	19	at Calgary
	Thur.	20	at Vancouver
	Sat.	22	at Los Angeles
	Mon.	24	Edmonton
	Wed.	26	Toronto
	Fri.	28	Edmonton
Apr.	Tues.	1	at Phoenix
	Wed.	2	Anaheim
	Fri.	4	Colorado
	Mon.	7	Vancouver
	Wed.	9	at Colorado
	Fri.	11	Anaheim
	Sat.	12	at Los Angeles

* Denotes afternoon game.

Franchise date: May 9, 1990

WESTERN
CONFERENCE

PACIFIC DIVISION

6th NHL Season

Although he wasn't acquired by the Sharks until October 26, 1995, Owen Nolan still led the San Jose club in most offensive categories, including goals (29), assists (32), points (61) and power-play goals (12).

1996-97 Player Personnel

FORWARDS	HT	WT	S	Place of Birth	Date	1995-96 Club
CALOUN, Jan	5-10	175	R	Usti-Nad-Labem, Czech.	12/20/72	San Jose-Kansas City
DAHLEN, Ulf	6-2	195	L	Ostersund, Sweden	1/12/67	San Jose
DONOVAN, Shean	6-2	190	R	Timmins, Ont.	1/22/75	San Jose-Kansas City
EWEN, Todd	6-2	220	R	Saskatoon, Sask.	3/22/66	Anaheim
FRASER, Iain	5-10	175	L	Scarborough, Ont.	8/10/69	Winnipeg-Springfield
FRIESEN, Jeff	6-0	185	L	Meadow Lake, Sask.	8/5/76	San Jose
GRANATO, Tony	5-10	185	R	Downers Grove, IL	7/25/64	Los Angeles
GRILLO, Dean	6-2	210	R	Bemidji, MN	12/8/72	Kansas City
GUOLLA, Stephen	6-0	180	L	Scarborough, Ont.	3/15/73	P.E.I.
HUNTER, Tim	6-2	202	R	Calgary, Alta.	9/10/60	Vancouver
KOROLYUK, Alexander	5-9	170	L	Moscow, USSR	1/15/76	Soviet Wings
KOZLOV, Viktor	6-5	225	L	Togliatti, USSR	2/14/75	San Jose-Kansas City
KUDRNA, Jaroslav	6-0	180	L	Hradec Kralove, Czech.	12/5/75	Pardubice
MEHALKO, Brad	5-11	182	R	Lethbridge, Alta.	1/4/77	Lethbridge-Prince George
NAZAROV, Andrei	6-5	230	R	Chelyabinsk, USSR	5/22/74	San Jose-Kansas City
NICHOLLS, Bernie	6-1	185	R	Haliburton, Ont.	6/24/61	Chicago
NOLAN, Owen	6-1	201	R	Belfast, Ireland	9/22/71	Colorado-San Jose
PELTONEN, Ville	5-11	172	L	Vantaa, Finland	5/24/73	San Jose-Kansas City
ROED, Peter	5-10	210	L	St. Paul, MN	11/15/76	Prince George
TANCILL, Chris	5-10	185	L	Livonia, MI	2/7/68	San Jose-Kansas City
TURCOTTE, Darren	6-0	178	L	Boston, MA	3/2/68	Winnipeg-San Jose
WHITNEY, Ray	5-9	160	R	Fort Saskatchewan, Alta.	5/8/72	San Jose
WOOD, Dody	5-11	181	L	Chetwynd, B.C.	3/10/72	San Jose
YEGOROV, Alexei	5-11	185	L	St. Petersburg, USSR	5/21/75	San Jose-Kansas City

DEFENSEMEN	HT	WT	S	Place of Birth	Date	1995-96 Club
BODGER, Doug	6-2	213	L	Chemainus, B.C.	6/18/66	Buffalo-San Jose
BOIKOV, Alexander	6-0	180	L	Chelyabinsk, USSR	2/7/75	Tri-City
GILL, Todd	6-0	180	L	Cardinal, Ont.	11/9/65	Toronto
IAFRATE, Al	6-3	235	L	Dearborn, MI	3/21/66	Did Not Play
KROUPA, Vlastimil	6-3	210	L	Most, Czech.	4/27/75	San Jose-Kansas City
LIPUMA, Chris	6-0	183	L	Bridgeview, IL	3/23/71	Tampa Bay-Atlanta
McSORLEY, Marty	6-1	225	R	Hamilton, Ont.	5/18/63	Los Angeles-NY Rangers
ODUYA, Fredrik	6-2	185	L	Stockholm, Sweden	5/31/75	Kansas City
OSADCHY, Alexander	5-11	190	R	Kharkov, USSR	7/19/75	Wichita-Mobile-Kansas City
RACINE, Yves	6-0	205	L	Matane, Que.	2/7/69	Montreal-San Jose
RAGNARSSON, Marcus	6-1	200	L	Ostervala, Sweden	8/13/71	San Jose
RATHJE, Mike	6-6	220	L	Mannville, Alta.	5/11/74	San Jose-Kansas City
SYKORA, Michal	6-5	225	L	Pardubice, Czech.	7/5/73	San Jose
WIDMER, Jason	6-0	205	L	Calgary, Alta.	8/1/73	NY Islanders-Worcester

GOALTENDERS	HT	WT	C	Place of Birth	Date	1995-96 Club
FLAHERTY, Wade	6-0	170	L	Terrace, B.C.	1/11/68	San Jose
HRUDEY, Kelly	5-10	189	L	Edmonton, Alta.	1/13/61	Los Angeles-Phoenix
TERRERI, Chris	5-8	160	L	Providence, RI	11/15/64	New Jersey-San Jose

1995-96 Scoring
* – rookie

Regular Season

Pos	#	Player	Team	GP	G	A	Pts	+/-	PIM	PP	SH	GW	GT	S	%
R	11	Owen Nolan	COL	9	4	4	8	–3	9	4	0	0	0	23	17.4
			S.J.	72	29	32	61	–30	137	12	1	2	0	184	15.8
			TOTAL	81	33	36	69	–33	146	16	1	2	0	207	15.9
L	39	Jeff Friesen	S.J.	79	15	31	46	–19	42	2	0	0	0	123	12.2
C	9	Darren Turcotte	WPG	59	16	16	32	–3	26	2	0	2	0	134	11.9
			S.J.	9	6	5	11	8	4	0	1	2	0	33	18.2
			TOTAL	68	22	21	43	5	30	2	1	4	0	167	13.2
C	14	Ray Whitney	S.J.	60	17	24	41	–23	16	4	2	2	0	106	16.0
D	33 *	Marcus Ragnarsson	S.J.	71	8	31	39	–24	42	4	0	0	0	94	8.5
C	13	Jamie Baker	S.J.	77	16	17	33	–19	79	2	6	0	0	117	13.7
R	22	Ulf Dahlen	S.J.	59	16	12	28	–21	27	5	0	2	1	103	15.5
D	3	Doug Bodger	BUF	16	0	5	5	–6	18	0	0	0	0	27	0.0
			S.J.	57	4	19	23	–18	50	3	0	0	0	94	4.3
			TOTAL	73	4	24	28	–24	68	3	0	0	0	121	3.3
C	18	Chris Tancill	S.J.	45	7	16	23	–12	20	0	1	0	0	93	7.5
R	42 *	Shean Donovan	S.J.	74	13	8	21	–17	39	0	1	2	0	73	17.8
D	38	Michal Sykora	S.J.	79	4	16	20	–14	54	1	0	0	0	80	5.0
D	34	Yves Racine	MTL	25	0	3	3	–7	26	0	0	0	0	16	0.0
			S.J.	32	1	16	17	–3	28	0	0	0	0	35	2.9
			TOTAL	57	1	19	20	–10	54	0	0	0	0	51	2.0
R	25 *	Viktor Kozlov	S.J.	62	6	13	19	–15	6	1	0	0	0	107	5.6
L	36 *	Jeff Odgers	S.J.	78	12	4	16	–4	192	0	0	1	1	84	14.3
R	23	Andrei Nazarov	S.J.	42	7	7	14	–15	62	2	0	1	0	55	12.7
L	37 *	Ville Peltonen	S.J.	31	2	11	13	–7	14	0	0	0	0	58	3.4
R	43 *	Jan Caloun	S.J.	11	8	3	11	4	0	2	0	0	0	20	40.0
C	16 *	Dody Wood	S.J.	32	3	6	9	0	138	0	1	0	0	33	9.1
D	4	Jay More	S.J.	74	2	7	9	–32	147	0	0	0	0	67	3.0
D	44	Vlastimil Kroupa	S.J.	27	1	7	8	–17	18	0	0	0	0	11	9.1
D	2	Jim Kyte	S.J.	57	1	7	8	–12	146	0	0	0	0	32	3.1
D	40	Mike Rathje	S.J.	27	0	7	7	–16	14	0	0	0	0	26	0.0
R	48 *	Alexei Yegorov	S.J.	9	3	2	5	–5	2	2	0	0	0	10	30.0
D	41	Tom Pederson	S.J.	60	1	4	5	–9	40	1	0	1	0	59	1.7
G	30	Chris Terreri	N.J.	4	0	0	0	0	0	0	0	0	0	0	0.0
			S.J.	46	0	5	5	4	0	0	0	0	0	0	0.0
			TOTAL	50	0	5	5	4	0	0	0	0	0	0	0.0
R	21	Dave Brown	S.J.	37	3	1	4	4	46	0	0	0	0	8	37.5
D	28	Sergei Bautin	S.J.	1	0	0	0	–1	2	0	0	0	0	0	0.0
G	29 *	Geoff Sarjeant	S.J.	4	0	0	0	0	2	0	0	0	0	0	0.0
G	32	Arturs Irbe	S.J.	22	0	0	0	0	0	0	0	0	0	0	0.0
G	31	Wade Flaherty	S.J.	24	0	0	0	0	0	0	0	0	0	0	0.0

Goaltending

No.	Goaltender	GPI	Mins	Avg	W	L	T	EN	SO	GA	SA	S%
30	Chris Terreri	46	2516	3.70	13	29	1	10	0	155	1322	.883
32	Arturs Irbe	22	1112	4.59	4	12	4	0	0	85	607	.860
31	Wade Flaherty	24	1137	4.85	3	12	1	0	0	92	689	.866
29 *	Geoff Sarjeant	4	171	4.91	0	2	1	1	0	14	87	.839
	Totals	82	4959	4.32	20	55	7	11	0	357	2716	.869

Coach

SIMS, AL
Coach, San Jose Sharks. Born in Toronto, Ont., April 18, 1953.

As the fourth head coach in franchise history, Sims' knowledge of the National Hockey League, the NHL's Western Conference and the San Jose Sharks (as one of the Mighty Ducks division-rivals) are important assets in his new position.

The Toronto, Ontario native earned the Sharks head coach position by working his way up the ranks as a player and coach. With extensive experiences as both an NHL player and one who has competed in Europe, Sims brings an ability to relate to today's players on several levels. Sims was a virtual one-man show in Fort Wayne, where he learned the nuances of being a general manager, talent evaluator and head coach, operating that franchise as an independent club with no NHL affiliation. Sims' efforts with Fort Wayne resulted in marked improvement and success each season.

Sims is regarded around the league for his knowledge, expertise in coaching hockey at the pro level, accomplished bench-management skills and a solid track record for success. He has received much of the credit for Anaheim's successful defensive system and has garnered a strong reputation of relating well to his players.

Prior to his stint in Anaheim, Sims spent the previous four seasons (1989-93) with the Fort Wayne Komets of the International Hockey League where he served as head coach and director of hockey operations. He compiled an overall coaching record of 207-135-30 (including playoffs). In addition, he spent one season (1988-89) with the Komets as a player/assistant coach.

As Komets head coach, the former NHL defenseman led Fort Wayne to a playoff berth in all four seasons, including two trips to the finals and winning the Turner Cup in his last season as head coach in 1992-93. In capturing that league championship, the Komets won an IHL record 12 consecutive post-season games.

Sims was drafted by the Boston Bruins in 1973 (4th round, 47th overall) as a speedy six-foot, 185-pound defenseman and went on to play 10 NHL seasons. He recorded 165 points (49 goals, 116 assists) in 475 career games with Boston (1973-1979), Hartford (1979-1981) and Los Angeles (1982-83).

Coaching Record

Season	Team	Games	Regular Season				Games	Playoffs			
			W	L	T	%		W	L	%
1989-90	Fort Wayne (IHL)	82	37	34	11	.518	5	1	4	.200
1990-91	Fort Wayne (IHL)	83	43	35	5	.548	19	10	9	.526
1991-92	Fort Wayne (IHL)	82	52	22	8	.683	7	3	4	.429
1992-93	Fort Wayne (IHL)	82	49	27	6	.634	12	12	0	1.000

General Managers' History

Jack Ferreira, 1991-92; Office of the General Manager: Chuck Grillo (V.P. Director of Player Personnel) and Dean Lombardi (V.P. Director of Hockey Operations), 1992-93 to 1995-96; Dean Lombardi, 1996-97.

Coaching History

George Kingston, 1991-92 to 1992-93; Kevin Constantine, 1993-94 to 1994-95; Kevin Constantine and Jim Wiley, 1995-96; Al Sims, 1996-97.

Captains' History

Doug Wilson, 1991-92 to 1992-93; Bob Errey, 1993-94; Bob Errey and Jeff Odgers, 1994-95; Jeff Odgers, 1995-96.

A fan favorite in San Jose because of his aggressive play and relentless fore-checking, sophomore Jeff Friesen finished second in team scoring with 15 goals and 31 assists.

Club Records

Team

(Figures in brackets for season records are games played; records for fewest points, wins, ties, losses, goals, goals against are for 70 or more games)

Most Points	82	1993-94 (84)
Most Wins	33	1993-94 (84)
Most Ties	16	1993-94 (84)
Most Losses	*71	1992-93 (84)
Most Goals...............	252	1993-94 (84),
		1995-96 (82)
Most Goals Against........	414	1992-93 (84)
Fewest Points.............	24	1992-93 (84)
Fewest Wins...............	11	1992-93 (84)
Fewest Ties	*2	1992-93 (84)
Fewest Losses	35	1993-94 (84)
Fewest Goals	218	1992-93 (84)
Fewest Goals Against	265	1993-94 (84)

Longest Winning Streak

Overall	7	Mar. 24-Apr. 5/94
Home.....................	5	Jan. 21-Feb. 15/95
Away	4	Mar. 24-Apr. 5/94

Longest Undefeated Streak

Overall	9	Mar. 20-Apr. 5/94
		(7 wins, 2 ties)
Home.....................	6	Mar. 20-Apr. 13/94
		(4 wins, 2 ties)
Away	5	Two times

Longest Losing Streak

Overall	*17	Jan. 4/93-Feb. 12/93
Home.....................	9	Nov. 19/92-Dec. 19/92
Away	19	Nov. 27/92-Feb. 12/93

Longest Winless Streak

Overall	20	Dec. 29/92-Feb. 12/93
		(19 losses, 1 tie)
Home.....................	9	Nov. 19/92-Dec. 18/92
		(9 losses)
Away	19	Nov. 27/92-Feb. 12/93
		(19 losses)
Most Shutouts, Season	5	1994-95 (48)
Most PIM, Season..........	2134	1992-93 (84)
Most Goals, Game	10	Jan. 13/96
		(S.J. 10 at Pit. 8)

Individual

Most Seasons	5	Pat Falloon,
		Jayson More,
		Jeff Odgers
Most Games, Career........	334	Jeff Odgers
Most Goals, Career..........	76	Pat Falloon
Most Assists, Career.........	86	Johan Garpenlov,
		Pat Falloon
Most Points, Career	162	Pat Falloon
		(76G, 86A)
Most PIM, Career	1,001	Jeff Odgers
Most Shutouts, Career........	8	Arturs Irbe

Longest Consecutive

Games Streak	117	Doug Zmolek
		(Oct. 8/92-Dec. 15/93),
		Gaetan Dechesne
		(Oct. 6/93-Apr. 2/95)
Most Goals, Season	30	Sergei Makarov
		(1993-94)
Most Assists, Season	52	Kelly Kisio
		(1992-93)
Most Points, Season	78	Kelly Kisio
		(1992-93; 26G, 52A)
Most PIM, Season	326	Link Gaetz
		(1991-92)
Most Shutouts, Season	4	Arturs Irbe
		(1994-95)

Most Points,

Defenseman Season	64	Sandis Ozolnish
		(1993-94; 26G, 38A)

Most Points, Center,

Season	78	Kelly Kisio
		(1992-93; 26G, 52A)

Most Points, Right Wing,

Season	68	Sergei Makarov
		(1993-94; 30G, 38A)

Most Points, Left Wing,

Season	66	Johan Garpenlov
		(1992-93; 22G, 44A)

Most Points, Rookie,

Season	59	Pat Falloon
		(1991-92; 25G, 34A)
Most Goals, Game	4	Owen Nolan
		(Dec. 19/95)
Most Assists, Game	4	Three times
Most Points, Game...........	5	Owen Nolan
		(Dec. 19/95; 4G, 1A)

* NHL Record.

All-time Record vs. Other Clubs

Regular Season

		At Home							**On Road**							**Total**					
	GP	W	L	T	GF	GA	PTS	GP	W	L	T	GF	GA	PTS	GP	W	L	T	GF	GA	PTS
Anaheim	7	3	4	0	22	24	6	9	5	4	0	32	28	10	16	8	8	0	54	52	16
Boston	4	0	2	2	10	19	2	4	0	3	1	13	17	1	8	0	5	3	23	36	3
Buffalo	4	2	1	1	18	20	5	5	0	5	0	18	28	0	9	2	6	1	36	48	5
Calgary	17	2	14	1	38	67	5	14	4	10	0	35	72	8	31	6	24	1	73	139	13
Chicago	10	5	5	0	26	30	10	9	2	6	1	21	32	5	19	7	11	1	47	62	15
Colorado	7	2	5	0	27	38	4	6	1	5	0	17	37	2	13	3	10	0	44	75	6
Dallas	9	3	6	0	24	35	6	9	2	6	1	26	38	5	18	5	12	1	50	73	11
Detroit	10	2	7	1	32	50	5	9	0	9	0	14	46	0	19	2	16	1	46	96	5
Edmonton	15	9	5	1	58	44	19	15	1	11	3	34	64	5	30	10	16	4	92	108	24
Florida	2	1	1	0	4	6	2	2	0	1	1	4	7	1	4	1	2	1	8	13	3
Hartford	4	3	1	0	27	16	6	5	2	3	0	13	20	4	9	5	4	0	40	36	10
Los Angeles	16	7	6	3	60	57	17	15	4	10	1	41	56	9	31	11	16	4	101	113	26
Montreal	5	1	2	2	13	12	4	5	0	5	0	7	24	0	10	1	7	2	20	36	4
New Jersey	4	1	2	1	8	13	3	5	2	3	0	9	21	4	9	3	5	1	17	34	7
NY Islanders	4	2	2	0	11	17	4	5	0	5	0	17	31	0	9	2	7	0	28	48	4
NY Rangers	5	0	5	0	12	27	0	4	0	3	1	11	22	1	9	0	8	1	23	49	1
Ottawa	3	2	1	0	6	5	4	3	0	2	1	8	11	1	6	2	3	1	14	16	5
Philadelphia	5	1	4	0	10	17	2	4	2	1	0	9	20	2	9	3	5	0	19	37	4
Pittsburgh	5	0	4	1	11	36	1	4	1	2	1	16	27	3	9	1	6	2	27	63	4
St. Louis	8	1	7	0	20	30	2	11	1	10	0	22	45	2	19	2	17	0	42	75	4
Tampa Bay	4	0	4	0	12	20	0	4	2	2	0	9	13	4	8	2	6	0	21	33	4
Toronto	10	4	5	1	23	28	9	9	2	6	1	19	38	5	19	6	11	2	42	66	14
Vancouver	15	5	8	2	52	56	12	15	2	12	1	33	64	5	30	7	20	3	85	120	17
Washington	4	1	3	0	12	15	2	4	1	3	0	9	15	2	8	2	6	0	21	30	4
Winnipeg	12	6	4	2	52	49	14	14	4	7	3	45	49	11	26	10	11	5	97	98	25
Totals	**189**	**63**	**108**	**18**	**588**	**731**	**144**	**189**	**37**	**136**	**16**	**482**	**825**	**90**	**378**	**100**	**244**	**34**	**1070**	**1556**	**234**

Playoffs

	Series	W	L	GP	W	L	T	GF	GA	Last Mtg.	Round	Result
Calgary	1	1	0	7	4	3	0	26	35	1995	CQF	W 4-3
Detroit	2	1	1	11	4	7	0	27	51	1995	CSF	L 0-4
Toronto	1	0	1	7	3	4	0	21	26	1994	CSF	L 3-4
Totals	**4**	**2**	**2**	**25**	**11**	**14**	**0**	**74**	**112**			

Playoff Results 1996-92

Year	Round	Opponent	Result	GF	GA
1995	CSF	Detroit	L 0-4	6	24
	CQF	Calgary	W 4-3	26	35
1994	CSF	Toronto	L 3-4	21	26
	CQF	Detroit	W 4-3	21	27

Abbreviations: Round: F – Final;
CF – conference final; **CQF** – conference quarter-final;
CSF – conference semi-final; **DF** – division final;
DSF – division semi-final; **SF** – semi-final;
QF – quarter-final; **PR** – preliminary round.

Colorado totals include Quebec, 1991-92 to 1994-95.   Dallas totals include Minnesota, 1991-92 to 1992-93.

1995-96 Results

Oct.	7		Chicago	3-4		10	at NY Rangers	4-7
	12		Boston	6-6		11	at New Jersey	2-1
	14		Vancouver	6-7		13	at Pittsburgh	10-8
	17	at	Toronto	2-7		16	at Florida	1-4
	19	at	Winnipeg	3-3		17	at Tampa Bay	4-6
	22	at	Edmonton	1-1		24	at Detroit	2-4
	25		Winnipeg	1-6		25	at Chicago	1-2
	28		Dallas	3-4		27	Colorado	3-4
	30	at	Vancouver	3-4		30	Hartford	8-2
	31		NY Rangers	3-5	Feb. 1	Los Angeles	6-6
Nov.	2		New Jersey	3-3		3	Chicago	1-4
	4		St. Louis	7-3		5	Toronto	6-4
	7	at	Hartford	3-7		10	at Los Angeles	6-1
	8	at	Buffalo	2-7		12	at Montreal	0-3
	10		Pittsburgh	1-9		14	at Toronto	3-4
	11		Detroit	2-5		15	at Ottawa	2-2
	14		NY Islanders	3-5		17	at NY Islanders	2-4
	16	at	St. Louis	1-3		20	at Calgary	3-5
	17	at	Dallas	1-2		23	at Vancouver	1-3
	19	at	Chicago	3-2		25	at Anaheim	3-4
	21	at	Washington	2-3		26	Montreal	7-4
	22	at	Detroit	2-5	Mar. 1	Tampa Bay	3-7
	25		Vancouver	7-2		3	Calgary	1-5
	29		Calgary	3-5		5	at Colorado	5-3
Dec.	1	at	Vancouver	2-7		6	Dallas	1-2
	2		Washington	5-3		8	at Edmonton	2-4
	5	at	Colorado	2-12		10	Buffalo	6-4
	7		Winnipeg	5-3		13	Edmonton	3-8
	9		Edmonton	2-4		15	St. Louis	2-4
	12		Ottawa	2-1		17	at Philadelphia	2-8
	14		Toronto	1-4		18	at Boston	2-3
	16	at	St. Louis	2-3		20	at Winnipeg	7-1
	17	at	Dallas	2-4		22	at Calgary	2-1
	19	at	Anaheim	7-4		28	Colorado	3-8
	22		Los Angeles	4-3		31	Anaheim	3-4
	26		Colorado	1-5	Apr. 2	Detroit	6-3
	29	at	Anaheim	2-4		4	Edmonton	5-3
Jan.	3		Philadelphia	1-3		6	at Colorado	1-5
	5	at	Los Angeles	2-5		7	Anaheim	3-5
	6	at	Los Angeles	5-7		10	at Los Angeles	2-6
	8		Florida	2-5		12	Calgary	0-6

Entry Draft Selections 1996-91

1996

Pick	
2	Andrei Zyuzin
21	Marco Sturm
55	Terry Friesen
102	Matt Bradley
137	Michel Larocque
164	Jake Deadmarsh
191	Cory Cyrenne
217	David Thibeault

1995

Pick	
12	Teemu Riihijarvi
38	Peter Roed
64	Marko Makinen
90	Vesa Toskala
116	Miikka Kiprusoff
130	Michal Bros
140	Timo Hakanen
142	Jaroslav Kudrna
167	Brad Mehalko
168	Robert Jindrich
194	Ryan Kraft
220	Miiko Markkanen

1994

Pick	
11	Jeff Friesen
37	Angel Nikolov
66	Alexei Yegorov
89	Vaclav Varada
115	Brian Swanson
141	Alexander Korolyuk
167	Sergei Gorbachev
193	Eric Landry
219	Yevgeny Nabokov
240	Tomas Pisa
245	Aniket Dhadphale
271	David Beauregard

1993

Pick	
6	Viktor Kozlov
28	Shean Donovan
45	Vlastimil Kroupa
58	Ville Peltonen
80	Alexander Osadchy
106	Andrei Buschan
132	Petri Varis
154	Fredrik Oduya
158	Anatoli Filatov
184	Todd Holt
210	Jonas Forsberg
236	Jeff Salajko
262	Jamie Matthews

1992

Pick	
3	Mike Rathje
10	Andrei Nazarov
51	Alexander Cherbajev
75	Jan Caloun
99	Marcus Ragnarsson
123	Michal Sykora
147	Eric Bellerose
171	Ryan Smith
195	Chris Burns
219	A. Kholomeyev
243	Victor Ignatjev

1991

Pick	
2	Pat Falloon
23	Ray Whitney
30	Sandis Ozolinsh
45	Dody Wood
67	Kerry Toporowski
89	Dan Ryder
111	Fredrik Nilsson
133	Jaroslav Otevrel
155	Dean Grillo
177	Corwin Saurdiff
199	Dale Craigwell
221	Aaron Kriss
243	Mikhail Kravets

General Manager

LOMBARDI, DEAN
Executive Vice President and Director of Hockey Operations, San Jose Sharks. Born in Holyoke, Massachusetts, March 5, 1958.

Dean Lombardi enters his ninth year in the National Hockey League and his seventh with the Sharks. Well respected by his NHL colleagues, Lombardi was named to the position on Oct. 12, 1995 having previously served as executive vice president and director of hockey operations for several seasons.

As the team's top hockey executive, Lombardi has overall authority regarding all hockey-related operations for the sixth-year club. He oversees all player personnel decisions, negotiates player contracts, coordinates the evaluation efforts of the team's scouting department and administers the club's player evaluation process at all professional, minor and junior levels. Well versed in contract negotiations and the NHL's business and legal workings, Lombardi has developed a strong network throughout hockey circles to facilitate player trades and acquisitions.

After a disappointing 1995-96 season, Lombardi, 38, spent much energy in decisively implementing significant changes to strengthen the Sharks hockey department, both internally and on the ice. This offseason, with additions to the hockey department and personnel roster, Lombardi has added nearly 5,000 NHL games of playing experience to the franchise, including several members of various league championship teams at every level, and countless years of hockey executive experience. His efforts have fostered a renewed attitude of determination and success that runs deep throughout the organization.

With a proven track record in player acquisitions, Lombardi has assembled a host of veteran players to provide the proper on-ice leadership and character for one of the youngest teams in the league. The most notable off-ice decision was hiring 22-year player and coaching veteran Al Sims as head coach, ending Lombardi's comprehensive and detailed search. In addition, former Boston Bruins star Wayne Cashman was hired as an assistant coach, former assistant coach and NHL veteran Wayne Thomas was promoted to assistant general manager and Don Maloney and John Ferguson, two former NHL general managers and players, were hired to key positions on the professional scouting staff. Several support staff, including a new head athletic trainer and equipment manager, were also hired this offseason.

Lombardi is instrumental in constructing the key player acquisitions that have brought valuable NHL veterans into the Sharks stable, including forwards Owen Nolan, Darren Turcotte and Ulf Dahlen, goaltender Chris Terreri and defensemen Doug Bodger, Todd Gill, Al Iafrate, Marty McSorley and Yves Racine.

Club Directory

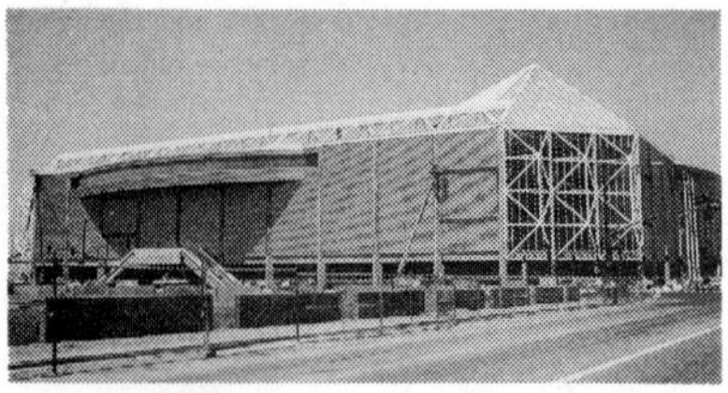

San Jose Arena
525 West Santa Clara Street
San Jose, California 95113
Phone **408/287-7070**
FAX 408/999-5797
Internet hhtp://www.sj-sharks.com
Capacity: 17,190

Executive Staff

Majority Owner & Chairman	George Gund III
Co-Owner	Gordon Gund
President & Chief Executive Officer	Greg Jamison
Vice Chairman	Tom McEnery
Senior Executive Vice President & Chief Operating Officer	Frank Jirik
Exec. Vice President, Development	Matt Levine
Exec. Vice President, General Manager	Dean Lombardi
Exec. Vice President, Chief Financial Officer	Gregg Olson
Vice President of Business Operations	Malcolm Bordelon
Vice President, General Manager (Arena)	Jim Goddard
Vice President of Marketing	Elaine Sullivan-Digre
Executive Assistant to President and CEO	Michelle Simmons

Hockey

Assistant General Manager	Wayne Thomas
Head Coach	Al Sims
Assistant Coaches	Wayne Cashman, Roy Sommer
Strength & Conditioning Specialist	Steve Millard
Eastern Professional Scout	Don Maloney
Western Professional Scout	John Ferguson
Director of Amateur Scouting	Tim Burke
Chief Scout	Ray Payne
Scouts	Rob Grillo, Pat Funk
Scouts	Karel Masopust, Jack Morganstern, Bruce Southern
Scouting Coordinator	Joe Will
Executive Assistant	Brenda Will
Video Scouting Coordinator	Bob Friedlander
Team Travel Coordinator	Steve Perry
Head Athletic Trainer	Ray Tufts, ATC
Athletic Trainer	Tom Woodcock
Massage Therapist	TBA
Hockey Equipment Manager	Mike Aldrich
Hockey Equipment Assistant	Kurt Harvey
Equipment Assistant/Equipment Transportation	Jason Rudee
Equipment Assistant	Tony Silva
Head Coach, Kentucky Thoroughblades	Jim Wiley
Assistant Coaches, Kentucky Thoroughblades	Mark Kaufman, Vasily Tikhonov
Head Trainer, Kentucky Thoroughblades	Jerry Iannarelli
Team Physician	Arthur J. Ting, M.D.
Team Dentist	Robert Bonahoom, D.D.S.
Team Vision Specialist	Vincent S. Zuccaro, O.D., F.A.A.O.
Medical Staff	Warren King, M.D., Mark Sontag, M.D., Will Straw, M.D.

Business Operations

Director of Media Relations	Ken Arnold
Director of Community Development	Lori Smith
Director of Sponsorship Sales	Greg Elliot
Director of Broadcasting	Mark Stulberger
Director of Event Services	Kimberley Hargreaves
Media Relations Manager	Roger Ross
Sponsorship Sales Managers	Kirk Berridge, Jim Josel, TBA
Youth & Amateur Hockey Program Manager	J.D. Kershaw
Mascot Operations Manager	Jason Minsky
Community Development Coordinator	Lou Siville
Sponsorship Services Coordinator	Valerie Bigelow
Broadcast Traffic & Promotions Coordinator	Patti Sircus
Educational Programs & Arena Tours Coordinator	Dianna Carthew
Media Relations Assistant	Chris Kelleher
Event Services Assistant	Jim Sparaco
Administrative Assistant	Dawn Beres

Marketing

Director of Ticket Sales	TBA
Director of Marketing	TBA
Account Service Managers	Elizabeth Smith, Pat Swan, Annie Chan-Zien
Group Accounts Manager	Gene Wiggins
Ticket Operations Manager	Mary Enriquez
Suite Hospitality Manager	Coleen Duncan
Marketing Manager	Beth Brigino
Ticket Operations Coordinator	John Castro
Suite Hospitality Coordinator	Mike Hollywood
Marketing Coordinator	Birgit Fink-Jensen
Administrative Assistants	Steward Diner, Kris Lyon

Development

Executive Assistant	Kim Brown

Finance

Director of Finance	Ken Caveney
Finance Manager	Steve Calamia
Management Information Systems Manager	TBA
Human Resources Manager	Carol Ross
Staff Accountant	Sarah McEnery
Payroll Accounting Associate	Sue Feachen
Accounts Payable Accounting Associate	Tina Park
Accounts Receivable Accounting Associate	Diane Rubino
Systems Analyst	TBA
Network & Telecommunications Coordinator	Lucas Handelsman
Executive Assistant	Tricia Nordquist

Building Operations

Director of Guest Services	Colleen Reilly
Director of Ticket Operations	Daniel DeBoer
Director of Building Operations	Rich Sotello
Director of Facilities	TBA
Ticket Operations Manager	Judy Jones
Building Services Manager	Bruce Tharaldson
Booking & Events Manager	Steve Kirsner, Bob Herrfeldt
Building Services Coordinators	George Gund IV, Greg Gund
Mailroom Coordinator	Rich Perez
Ticket Office Coordinator	Rossanna Lira
Executive Assistant	Chris Palmer
Administrative Assistant	Beth Ganeff

Aramark

General Manager	Dale Haynes
Concessions Manager	Steve Reuben
Financial Controller	Larry Tokarski
Executive Chef	Jurgen Pauer
Restaurant Manager	Tracy Ingram
Merchandise Manager	Dawn Haney
Suites & Catering Manager	Wendy Riggs
Human Resources Director	Gretchen La Due

Miscellaneous

Team Colors	Pacific Teal, Gray, Black, White
Dimensions of Rink	200 feet by 85 feet
Television Stations	KICU-TV 36, SportsChannel
Radio Network Flagship	KFRC (610-AM)
Play-By-Play (Radio)	Dan Rusanowsky
Play-By-Play (Television)	Randy Hahn
Color Commentator (TV/Radio)	Chris Collins
P.A. Announcer	Joe Ike
Organist	Dieter Ruehle

Tampa Bay Lightning

1995-96 Results: 38W-32L-12T 88PTS. Fifth, Atlantic Division

Year-by-Year Record

Season	GP	Home			Road			Overall			GF	GA	Pts.	Finished	Playoff Result
		W	L	T	W	L	T	W	L	T					
1995-96	82	22	14	5	16	18	7	38	32	12	238	248	88	5th, Atlantic Div.	Lost Conf. Quarter-Final
1994-95	48	10	14	0	7	14	3	17	28	3	120	144	37	6th, Atlantic Div.	Out of Playoffs
1993-94	84	14	22	6	16	21	5	30	43	11	224	251	71	7th, Atlantic Div.	Out of Playoffs
1992-93	84	12	27	3	11	27	4	23	54	7	245	332	53	6th, Norris Div.	Out of Playoffs

Schedule

Oct.	Sat.	5	at Pittsburgh
	Fri.	11	at Washington
	Sat.	12	at Toronto
	Tues.	15	at Buffalo
	Sun.	20	NY Rangers
	Tues.	22	at NY Islanders
	Thur.	24	Ottawa
	Sat.	26	New Jersey
	Tues.	29	Chicago
	Thur.	31	Philadelphia
Nov.	Sat.	2	at New Jersey*
	Mon.	4	at NY Rangers
	Wed.	6	Washington
	Fri.	8	Pittsburgh
	Sun.	10	at Detroit
	Thur.	14	at St. Louis
	Sat.	16	at New Jersey*
	Tues.	19	Los Angeles
	Sat.	23	Philadelphia
	Mon.	25	at Montreal
	Wed.	27	Buffalo
	Fri.	29	Dallas
	Sat.	30	Hartford
Dec.	Wed.	4	at Anaheim
	Thur.	5	at Los Angeles
	Sat.	7	at San Jose
	Thur.	12	Edmonton
	Sat.	14	NY Islanders
	Mon.	16	at Montreal
	Wed.	18	at Buffalo
	Thur.	19	at Boston
	Sat.	21	at Hartford
	Mon.	23	Washington
	Thur.	26	Florida
	Sat.	28	Montreal
	Tues.	31	NY Rangers
Jan.	Fri.	3	Anaheim
	Sat.	4	at Pittsburgh
	Mon.	6	at Ottawa
	Wed.	8	at NY Rangers
	Thur.	9	at Philadelphia

	Sat.	11	NY Islanders
	Mon.	13	at Chicago
	Wed.	15	at Colorado
	Tues.	21	Colorado
	Sat.	25	at Florida*
	Mon.	27	at Ottawa
	Thur.	30	Montreal
Feb.	Sat.	1	Boston*
	Tues.	4	at Phoenix
	Wed.	5	at Dallas
	Sat.	8	Buffalo
	Wed.	12	at Florida
	Fri.	14	at Washington
	Sat.	15	Washington
	Mon.	17	Detroit
	Thur.	20	Philadelphia
	Sat.	22	New Jersey*
	Sun.	23	San Jose
	Tues.	25	St. Louis
	Thur.	27	at Boston
Mar.	Sat.	1	Florida*
	Tues.	4	at NY Islanders
	Thur.	6	Phoenix
	Sat.	8	Boston*
	Sun.	9	Calgary*
	Thur.	13	NY Islanders
	Sat.	15	Vancouver*
	Sun.	16	Toronto
	Wed.	19	at Edmonton
	Fri.	21	at Calgary
	Sat.	22	at Vancouver
	Tues.	25	Ottawa
	Thur.	27	Hartford
	Sat.	29	at Florida
Apr.	Tues.	1	at Philadelphia
	Fri.	4	at New Jersey
	Sat.	5	at NY Islanders
	Tues.	8	New Jersey
	Thur.	10	Pittsburgh
	Fri.	11	at NY Rangers
	Sun.	13	at Hartford*

* Denotes afternoon game.

Franchise date: December 16, 1991

**ATLANTIC
DIVISION**

**5th
NHL
Season**

For the third consecutive season, Brian Bradley led all Tampa Bay players in total points, notching 23 goals and a personal-high 56 assists for 79 points, the second-highest total of his career.

1996-97 Player Personnel

FORWARDS	HT	WT	S	Place of Birth	Date	1995-96 Club
ANDERSSON, Mikael	5-11	185	L	Malmo, Sweden	5/10/66	Tampa Bay
BELLOWS, Brian	5-11	210	R	St. Catharines, Ont.	9/1/64	Tampa Bay
BRADLEY, Brian	5-10	177	R	Kitchener, Ont.	1/21/65	Tampa Bay
BURR, Shawn	6-1	202	L	Sarnia, Ont.	7/1/66	Tampa Bay
CARDARELLI, Joe	6-0	203	L	Vancouver, B.C.	6/13/77	Spokane
CICCARELLI, Dino	5-10	185	R	Sarnia, Ont.	2/8/60	Detroit
CLOUTIER, Colin	6-3	224	L	Winnipeg, Man.	1/27/76	Brandon-Lethbridge
CULLEN, John	5-10	180	R	Puslinch, Ont.	8/2/64	Tampa Bay
DELISLE, Xavier	5-11	182	R	Quebec City, Que.	5/24/77	Granby
EGELAND, Allan	6-0	184	L	Lethbridge, Alta.	1/31/73	Tampa Bay-Atlanta
GAVEY, Aaron	6-1	194	L	Sudbury, Ont.	2/22/74	Tampa Bay
GOLOKHVASTOV, Konstantin	6-1	185	R	Dneprodzerzinsk, USSR	2/6/77	Nizhnekamsk
GRATTON, Chris	6-4	218	L	Brantford, Ont.	7/5/75	Tampa Bay
KACIR, Marian	6-1	195	L	Hodonin, Czech.	9/29/74	Nashville-Atlanta
LANGKOW, Daymond	5-11	175	L	Edmonton, Alta	9/27/76	Tri-City-Tampa Bay
MATSOS, David	6-1	201	L	Burlington, Ont.	11/12/73	Cdn. National
MYHRES, Brantt	6-3	220	R	Edmonton, Alta.	3/18/74	Atlanta
PERSHIN, Eduard	6-0	191	L	Nizhnekamsk, USSR	9/1/77	Moscow D'amo
PETERSON, Brent	6-3	200	L	Calgary, Alta.	7/20/72	Atlanta
POESCHEK, Rudy	6-2	218	R	Kamloops, B.C.	9/29/66	Tampa Bay
POULIN, Patrick	6-1	210	L	Vanier, Que.	4/23/73	Chicago-Indianapolis-Tampa Bay
SELIVANOV, Alexander	6-1	206	L	Moscow, USSR	3/23/71	Tampa Bay
SMIRNOV, Yuri	5-11	172	L	Moscow, USSR	1/10/76	Spartak 2
SPRING, Corey	6-4	214	R	Cranbrook, B.C.	5/31/71	Atlanta
TIPLER, Curtis	6-5	205	R	Wainwright, Alta.	5/9/78	Regina
TOMS, Jeff	6-5	205	L	Swift Current, Sask.	6/4/74	Tampa Bay-Atlanta
WIEMER, Jason	6-1	215	L	Kimberley, B.C.	4/14/76	Tampa Bay
WILLIS, Shane	6-0	176	R	Edmonton, Alta.	6/13/77	Prince Albert
YSEBAERT, Paul	6-1	190	L	Sarnia, Ont.	5/15/66	Tampa Bay
ZAMUNER, Rob	6-2	202	L	Oakville, Ont.	9/17/69	Tampa Bay
DEFENSEMEN						
BANNISTER, Drew	6-2	205	R	Belleville, Ont.	9/4/74	Tampa Bay-Atlanta
BARANOV, Alexei	6-1	174	R	Lipetsk, USSR	6/3/76	Lipetsk
CROSS, Cory	6-5	212	L	Lloydminster, Alta.	1/3/71	Tampa Bay
HAMRLIK, Roman	6-2	202	L	Gottwaldov, Czech.	4/12/74	Tampa Bay
HOULDER, Bill	6-3	211	L	Thunder Bay, Ont.	3/11/67	Tampa Bay
IGNATOV, Nikolai	6-2	200	L	Moscow, USSR	4/22/78	CSKA 2
LAPORTE, Alexandre	6-3	210	R	Cowansville, Que.	5/1/75	Nashville-Atlanta
LAROCQUE, Mario	6-2	182	L	Montreal, Que.	4/24/78	Hull
McBAIN, Mike	6-1	191	L	Kimberley, B.C.	1/12/77	Red Deer
MURPHY, Cory	6-2	202	L	Perth, Ont.	10/22/76	S.S. Marie
RABY, Mathieu	6-2	204	R	Hull, Que.	1/19/75	Nashville-Atlanta
ROBINSON, Jason	6-2	190	L	Goderich, Ont.	8/22/78	Niagara Falls
SHAW, David	6-2	205	R	St. Thomas, Ont.	5/25/64	Tampa Bay
ULANOV, Igor	6-1	205	L	Krasnokamsk, USSR	10/1/69	Chicago-Indianapolis-Tampa Bay
WELLS, Jay	6-1	210	L	Paris, Ont.	5/18/59	St. Louis
WHITE, Brian	6-1	180	R	Winchester, MA	2/7/76	U. of Maine
WOLANIN, Craig	6-4	215	L	Grosse Pointe, MI	7/27/67	Colorado

GOALTENDERS	HT	WT	C	Place of Birth	Date	1995-96 Club
BIERK, Zac	6-4	186	L	Peterborough, Ont.	9/17/76	Peterborough
MOSS, Tyler	6-0	184	R	Ottawa, Ont.	6/29/75	Atlanta
PUPPA, Daren	6-3	205	R	Kirkland Lake, Ont.	3/23/65	Tampa Bay
SCHWAB, Corey	6-0	180	L	North Battleford, Sask.	11/4/70	New Jersey-Albany
WILKINSON, Derek	6-0	170	L	Lasalle, Que.	7/29/74	Tampa Bay-Atlanta

Coach

CRISP, TERRY
Coach, Tampa Bay Lightning. Born in Parry Sound, Ont., May 28, 1943.

Terry Crisp was a finalist for the Jack Adams Award as the NHL's coach of the year for 1995-96. He enters 1996-97 with the longest tenure among active NHL coaches, having directed the Lightning bench since the franchise's first game in 1992. In that time, he has built the Lightning into a hard-working team that reached the playoffs for the first time in 1996.

Crisp has won Stanley Cups as a player with Philadelphia in 1974 and 1975 and as a coach with Calgary in 1989. After 11 seasons in the NHL, he began his coaching career as an assistant with the Flyers in 1977. He later served as a head coach in the OHL and AHL. He was named Calgary's fifth head coach in 1987 and directed the Flames for three seasons, amassing a combined record of 144-63-33. He was named *The Hockey News* Coach of the Year in 1987-88.

Coaching Record

		Regular Season					Playoffs				
Season	**Team**	**Games**	**W**	**L**	**T**	**%**	**Games**	**W**	**L**	**T**	**%**
1979-80	S.S. Marie (OHL)	68	22	45	1	.331	....	....	....	....	....
1980-81	S.S. Marie (OHL)	68	47	19	2	.706	19	8	7	4	.526
1981-82	S.S. Marie (OHL)	68	40	25	3	.610	13	4	6	3	.423
1982-83	S.S. Marie (OHL)	70	48	21	1	.693	16	7	6	3	.531
1983-84	S.S. Marie (OHL)	70	38	28	4	.571	16	8	4	4	.625
1984-85	S.S. Marie (OHL)	66	54	11	1	.826	16	12	2	2	.813
1985-86	Moncton (AHL)	80	34	34	12	.500	10	5	5	0	.500
1986-87	Moncton (AHL)	80	43	31	6	.575	6	2	4	0	.333
1987-88	**Calgary (NHL)**	**80**	**48**	**23**	**9**	**.656**	**9**	**4**	**5**	**0**	**.444**
1988-89	**Calgary (NHL)**	**80**	**54**	**17**	**9**	**.731**	**22**	**16**	**6**	**0**	**.727***
1989-90	**Calgary (NHL)**	**80**	**42**	**23**	**15**	**.619**	**6**	**2**	**4**	**0**	**.333**
1992-93	**Tampa Bay (NHL)**	**84**	**23**	**54**	**7**	**.315**	....	....	....	....	....
1993-94	**Tampa Bay (NHL)**	**84**	**30**	**43**	**11**	**.423**	....	....	....	....	....
1994-95	**Tampa Bay (NHL)**	**48**	**17**	**28**	**3**	**.385**	....	....	....	....	....
1995-96	**Tampa Bay (NHL)**	**82**	**38**	**32**	**12**	**.537**	**6**	**2**	**4**	**0**	**.333**
	NHL Totals	**538**	**252**	**220**	**66**	**.530**	**43**	**24**	**19**	**0**	**.558**

* Stanley Cup win.

1995-96 Scoring

* – rookie

Regular Season

Pos	#	Player	Team	GP	G	A	Pts	+/–	PIM	PP	SH	GW	GT	S	%
C	19	Brian Bradley	T.B.	75	23	56	79	–11	77	9	0	5	0	189	12.2
D	44	Roman Hamrlik	T.B.	82	16	49	65	–24	103	12	0	2	3	281	5.7
R	29	Alexander Selivanov	T.B.	79	31	21	52	3	93	13	0	5	2	215	14.4
R	85	Petr Klima	T.B.	67	22	30	52	–25	68	8	0	3	2	164	13.4
C	12	John Cullen	T.B.	76	16	34	50	1	65	8	0	3	0	152	10.5
L	23	Brian Bellows	T.B.	79	23	26	49	–14	39	13	0	4	0	190	12.1
C	77	Chris Gratton	T.B.	82	17	21	38	–13	105	7	0	3	0	183	9.3
L	7	Rob Zamuner	T.B.	72	15	20	35	11	62	0	3	4	0	152	9.9
L	15	Paul Ysebaert	T.B.	55	16	15	31	–19	16	4	1	1	0	135	11.9
L	11	Shawn Burr	T.B.	81	13	15	28	4	119	1	0	2	0	122	10.7
D	2	Bill Houlder	T.B.	61	5	23	28	1	22	3	0	0	1	90	5.6
L	34	Mikael Andersson	T.B.	64	8	11	19	0	2	0	0	1	0	104	7.7
L	24	Jason Wiemer	T.B.	66	9	9	18	–9	81	4	0	1	0	89	10.1
L	28	Patrick Poulin	CHI	38	7	8	15	7	16	1	0	0	1	40	17.5
			T.B.	8	0	1	1	0	0	0	0	0	0	11	0.0
			TOTAL	46	7	9	16	7	16	1	0	0	1	51	13.7
D	4	Cory Cross	T.B.	75	2	14	16	4	66	0	0	0	0	57	3.5
C	22	* Aaron Gavey	T.B.	73	8	4	12	–6	56	1	1	2	0	65	12.3
D	95	Michel Petit	L.A.	9	0	1	1	–1	27	0	0	0	0	12	0.0
			T.B.	45	4	7	11	–10	108	0	0	1	0	56	7.1
			TOTAL	54	4	8	12	–11	135	0	0	1	0	68	5.9
D	5	Igor Ulanov	CHI	53	1	8	9	12	92	0	0	0	0	24	4.2
			T.B.	11	2	1	3	–1	24	0	0	1	0	13	15.4
			TOTAL	64	3	9	12	11	116	0	0	1	0	37	8.1
D	27	David Shaw	T.B.	66	1	11	12	5	64	0	0	0	0	90	1.1
R	14	John Tucker	T.B.	63	3	7	10	–8	18	0	1	0	0	53	5.7
R	20	Rudy Poeschek	T.B.	57	1	3	4	–2	88	0	0	0	0	36	2.8
D	6	Adrien Plavsic	T.B.	7	1	2	3	5	6	0	0	0	0	4	25.0
C	18	* Daymond Langkow	T.B.	4	0	1	1	–1	0	0	0	0	0	4	0.0
D	5	* Drew Bannister	T.B.	13	0	1	1	–1	4	0	0	0	0	10	0.0
G	93	Daren Puppa	T.B.	57	0	1	1	0	4	0	0	0	0	0	0.0
L	9	* Jeff Toms	T.B.	1	0	0	0	0	0	0	0	0	0	1	0.0
G	35	* Derek Wilkinson	T.B.	4	0	0	0	0	2	0	0	0	0	0	0.0
C	25	* Alan Egeland	T.B.	5	0	0	0	0	2	0	0	0	0	1	0.0
G	30	J.C. Bergeron	T.B.	12	0	0	0	0	0	0	0	0	0	0	0.0
D	26	Chris Lipuma	T.B.	21	0	0	0	–7	13	0	0	0	0	8	0.0
G	1	Jeff Reese	HFD	7	0	0	0	0	0	0	0	0	0	0	0.0
			T.B.	19	0	0	0	0	0	0	0	0	0	0	0.0
			TOTAL	26	0	0	0	0	0	0	0	0	0	0	0.0

Goaltending

No.	Goaltender	GPI	Mins	Avg	W	L	T	EN	SO	GA	SA	S%
93	Daren Puppa	57	3189	2.46	29	16	9	2	5	131	1605	.918
1	Jeff Reese	19	994	3.26	7	7	1	2	0	54	464	.884
30	J.C. Bergeron	12	595	4.24	2	6	2	2	0	42	250	.832
35	* Derek Wilkinson	4	200	4.50	0	3	0	0	0	15	105	.857
	Totals	**82**	**4993**	**2.98**	**38**	**32**	**12**	**6**	**5**	**248**	**2430**	**.898**

Playoffs

Pos	#	Player	Team	GP	G	A	Pts	+/–	PIM	PP	SH	GW	OT	S	%
C	12	John Cullen	T.B.	5	3	3	6	4	0	0	1	0	0	6	50.0
L	7	Rob Zamuner	T.B.	6	2	3	5	–1	10	0	1	0	0	10	20.0
R	29	Alexander Selivanov	T.B.	6	2	2	4	2	6	0	0	1	1	22	9.1
C	19	Brian Bradley	T.B.	5	0	3	3	–5	6	0	0	0	0	7	0.0
R	85	Petr Klima	T.B.	4	2	0	2	0	14	2	0	0	0	9	22.2
L	23	Brian Bellows	T.B.	6	2	0	2	–2	4	0	0	1	1	19	10.5
L	34	Mikael Andersson	T.B.	6	1	1	2	0	0	0	0	0	0	4	25.0
L	11	Shawn Burr	T.B.	6	0	2	2	0	8	0	0	0	0	5	0.0
C	77	Chris Gratton	T.B.	6	0	2	2	–3	27	0	0	0	0	4	0.0
L	24	Jason Wiemer	T.B.	6	1	0	1	–3	28	1	0	0	0	11	9.1
D	44	Roman Hamrlik	T.B.	5	0	1	1	–1	4	0	0	0	0	10	0.0
D	2	Bill Houlder	T.B.	6	0	1	1	0	4	0	0	0	0	8	0.0
D	27	David Shaw	T.B.	6	0	1	1	–4	4	0	0	0	0	9	0.0
R	14	John Tucker	T.B.	2	0	0	0	–1	2	0	0	0	0	0	0.0
L	28	Patrick Poulin	T.B.	2	0	0	0	0	0	0	0	0	0	0	0.0
R	20	Rudy Poeschek	T.B.	3	0	0	0	0	12	0	0	0	0	2	0.0
G	93	Daren Puppa	T.B.	4	0	0	0	0	0	0	0	0	0	0	0.0
G	1	Jeff Reese	T.B.	5	0	0	0	0	0	0	0	0	0	0	0.0
L	15	Paul Ysebaert	T.B.	5	0	0	0	–6	0	0	0	0	0	4	0.0
D	5	Igor Ulanov	T.B.	5	0	0	0	–1	15	0	0	0	0	2	0.0
D	95	Michel Petit	T.B.	6	0	0	0	–3	20	0	0	0	0	7	0.0
D	4	Cory Cross	T.B.	6	0	0	0	–4	22	0	0	0	0	6	0.0
C	22	* Aaron Gavey	T.B.	6	0	0	0	–3	4	0	0	0	0	5	0.0

Goaltending

No.	Goaltender	GPI	Mins	Avg	W	L	EN	SO	GA	SA	S%
1	Jeff Reese	5	198	3.64	1	1	0	0	12	100	.880
93	Daren Puppa	4	173	4.86	1	3	0	0	14	86	.837
	Totals	**6**	**371**	**4.20**	**2**	**4**	**0**	**0**	**26**	**186**	**.860**

General Managers' History

Phil Esposito, 1992-93 to date.

Captains' History

No captain, 1992-93 to 1994-95; Paul Ysebaert, 1995-96 to date.

Coaching History

Terry Crisp, 1992-93 to date.

Club Records

Team

(Figures in brackets for season records are games played; records for fewest points, wins, ties, losses, goals, goals against are for 70 or more games)

Most Points 88 1995-96 (82)
Most Wins 38 1995-96 (82)
Most Ties 12 1995-96 (82)
Most Losses 54 1992-93 (84)
Most Goals 245 1992-93 (84)
Most Goals Against........ 332 1992-93 (84)
Fewest Points............. 53 1992-93 (84)
Fewest Wins.............. 23 1992-93 (84)
Fewest Ties 7 1992-93 (84)
Fewest Losses 32 1995-96 (82)
Fewest Goals 224 1993-94 (84)
Fewest Goals Against 248 1995-96 (82)
Longest Winning Streak
  Overall.................. 5 Twice
  Home.................... 6 Feb. 15-Mar. 10/96
  Away.................... 3 Dec. 3-7/93,
                             Jan. 4-12/94
Longest Undefeated Streak
  Overall.................. 7 Feb. 28-Mar. 13/96
                             (5 wins, 2 ties)
  Home.................... 8 Feb. 15-Mar. 13/96
                             (6 wins, 2 ties)
  Away.................... 6 Dec. 28/93-Jan. 12/94
                             (5 wins, 1 tie)
Longest Losing Streak
  Overall.................. 8 Mar. 9-23/93
  Home.................... 6 Mar. 9-Apr. 11/93
  Away.................... 6 Apr. 14-29/95
Longest Winless Streak
  Overall.................. 8 Mar. 9-23/93
                             (8 losses)
  Home.................... 9 Mar. 9-Apr. 10/93
                             (8 losses, 1 tie)
  Away.................... 10 Oct. 23-Nov. 26/93
                             (8 losses, 2 ties)
Most Shutouts, Season....... 5 1993-94 (84),
                             1995-96 (82)
Most PIM, Season 1,628 1995-96 (82)
Most Goals, Game........... 7 Four times

Individual

Most Seasons .... 4 Several players
Most Games, Career........ 279 Brian Bradley
Most Goals, Career......... 102 Brian Bradley
Most Assists, Career....... 167 Brian Bradley
Most Points, Career .... 269 Brian Bradley
                             (102G, 167A)
Most PIM, Career .... 535 Enrico Ciccone
Most Shutouts, Career....... 10 Daren Puppa
Longest Consecutive
  Games Streak............ 144 Roman Hamrlik
Most Goals, Season .... 42 Brian Bradley
                             (1992-93)
Most Assists, Season .... 56 Brian Bradley
                             (1995-96)
Most Points, Season........ 86 Brian Bradley
                             (1992-93; 42G, 44A)
Most PIM, Season.......... 258 Enrico Ciccone
                             (1995-96)
Most Shutouts, Season .... 5 Daren Puppa
                             (1995-96)
Most Points,
  Defenseman Season........ 65 Roman Hamrlik
                             (1995-96; 16G, 49A)
Most Points, Center,
  Season................. 86 Brian Bradley
                             (1992-93; 42G, 44A)
Most Points, Right Wing,
  Season................. 56 John Tucker
                             (1992-93; 17G, 39A)
Most Points, Left Wing,
  Season................. 51 Chris Kontos
                             (1992-93; 27G, 24A)
Most Points, Rookie,
  Season................. 43 Rob Zamuner
                             (1992-93; 15G, 28A)
Most Goals, Game .... 4 Chris Kontos
                             (Oct. 7/92)
Most Assists, Game .... 4 Joe Reekie
                             (Oct. 7/92),
                             Marc Bureau
                             (Dec. 16/92)
Most Points, Game .... 6 Doug Crossman
                             (Nov. 11/92; 3G, 3A)

Chris Gratton continued his steady improvement in 1995-96, helping the Tampa Bay Lightning reach the post-season for the first time in franchise history with a career-high 17 goals.

All-time Record vs. Other Clubs

Regular Season

		At Home							On Road								Total					
	GP	W	L	T	GF	GA	PTS	GP	W	L	T	GF	GA	PTS	GP	W	L	T	GF	GA	PTS
Anaheim	2	1	1	0	3	5	2	2	1	0	1	6	4	3	4	2	1	1	9	9	5
Boston	7	3	2	2	22	19	8	4	1	4	1	16	22	3	13	4	6	3	38	41	11
Buffalo	7	1	6	0	15	24	2	7	4	2	1	28	16	9	14	5	8	1	43	40	11
Calgary	4	1	2	1	16	19	3	3	1	2	0	6	13	2	7	2	4	1	22	32	5
Chicago	5	3	2	0	16	15	6	6	1	3	2	13	17	4	11	4	5	2	29	32	10
Colorado	6	5	1	0	23	16	10	6	1	4	1	16	29	3	12	6	5	1	39	45	13
Dallas	6	1	3	2	11	15	4	5	1	3	1	15	18	3	11	2	6	3	26	33	7
Detroit	7	1	6	0	23	42	2	5	1	4	0	13	22	2	12	2	10	0	36	64	4
Edmonton	4	2	1	1	16	10	5	4	1	3	0	11	9	2	8	3	4	1	27	19	7
Florida	8	2	5	1	15	26	5	7	2	4	1	12	19	5	15	4	9	2	27	45	10
Hartford	7	5	1	1	23	14	11	7	2	5	0	17	24	4	14	7	6	1	40	38	15
Los Angeles	3	1	2	0	7	9	2	4	4	0	0	19	10	8	7	5	2	0	26	19	10
Montreal	7	6	0	1	21	10	13	6	2	3	1	14	13	5	13	8	3	2	35	23	18
New Jersey	8	2	4	2	21	24	6	8	1	6	1	13	30	3	16	3	10	3	34	54	9
NY Islanders	8	5	3	0	26	25	10	8	5	3	0	26	20	10	16	10	6	0	52	45	20
NY Rangers	8	2	5	1	25	29	5	9	3	5	1	36	36	7	17	5	10	2	61	65	12
Ottawa	7	4	3	0	21	18	8	7	5	2	0	19	17	10	14	9	5	0	40	35	18
Philadelphia	8	3	5	0	23	24	6	8	0	5	3	16	29	3	16	3	10	3	39	53	9
Pittsburgh	6	2	4	0	21	24	4	7	1	5	1	15	33	3	13	3	9	1	36	57	7
St. Louis	6	2	3	1	19	21	5	5	1	4	0	14	20	2	11	3	7	1	33	41	7
San Jose	4	2	2	0	13	9	4	4	4	0	0	20	12	8	8	6	2	0	33	21	12
Toronto	6	1	5	0	12	23	2	8	4	4	0	17	26	8	14	5	9	0	29	49	10
Vancouver	3	1	2	0	10	12	2	4	0	4	0	5	23	0	7	1	6	0	15	35	2
Washington	8	1	6	1	12	26	3	9	2	4	3	19	24	8	17	3	9	5	31	50	11
Winnipeg	4	1	3	0	16	17	2	4	2	2	0	11	13	4	8	3	5	0	27	30	6
Totals	149	58	77	14	430	476	130	149	50	80	19	397	499	119	298	108	157	33	827	975	249

Playoffs

	Series	W	L	GP	W	L	T	GF	GA	Last Mtg.	Round	Result
Philadelphia	1	0	1	6	2	4	0	13	26	1996	CQF	L 2-4
Totals	**1**	**0**	**1**	**6**	**2**	**4**	**0**	**13**	**26**			

Playoff Results 1996-93

Year	Round	Opponent	Result	GF	GA
1996	CQF	Philadelphia	L 2-4	13	26

Abbreviations: Round: F – Final;
CF – conference final; **CQF** – conference quarter-final;
CSF – conference semi-final; **DF** – division final;
DSF – division semi-final; **SF** – semi-final;
QF – quarter-final; **PR** – preliminary round.

Colorado totals include Quebec, 1992-93 to 1994-95.   Dallas totals include Minnesota, 1992-93.

1995-96 Results

Oct.	7		Calgary	3-3		13		Ottawa	4-1
	12		Montreal	3-1		15	at	NY Islanders	2-3
	14	at	Washington	0-2		17		San Jose	6-4
	15		Ottawa	4-7		22	at	Montreal	4-1
	17	at	Winnipeg	2-5		25	at	Boston	3-4
	19	at	Chicago	3-3		27	at	St. Louis	1-2
	21	at	Dallas	3-3		31		Pittsburgh	4-1
	26		NY Rangers	4-4	Feb.	3		Florida	3-5
	28		Washington	2-4		4	at	Buffalo	5-2
	31		Chicago	3-3		7	at	Colorado	4-4
Nov.	1	at	Pittsburgh	0-10		10		Detroit	2-3
	3		NY Islanders	5-3		11		NY Rangers	2-6
	5	at	Florida	1-4		13		St. Louis	2-3
	8	at	NY Rangers	4-5		15		Colorado	4-4
	10		Edmonton	3-4		17		Philadelphia	5-2
	12		Buffalo	4-6		19		Dallas	4-2
	14		Boston	5-3		21	at	Toronto	3-2
	16		Toronto	4-5		23	at	NY Islanders	3-2
	18		Vancouver	5-4		24	at	Detroit	0-2
	22		New Jersey	3-1		28	at	Los Angeles	5-1
	24	at	Washington	2-1	Mar.	1	at	San Jose	7-3
	25	at	NY Islanders	2-1		3	at	Anaheim	2-2
	27		Los Angeles	2-0		5		Chicago	2-0
	29		Hartford	2-2		7		NY Rangers	5-2
Dec.	1	at	New Jersey	1-5		10		Washington	1-0
	3		Pittsburgh	4-5		13	at	Philadelphia	1-1
	6		Anaheim	2-1		15	at	New Jersey	0-5
	8		Boston	3-1		17	at	Ottawa	0-5
	11	at	Buffalo	6-1		18	at	Hartford	3-6
	13	at	Hartford	3-2		21		Washington	3-3
	14	at	Philadelphia	0-4		23		Florida	4-2
	16		Florida	2-7		26		New Jersey	4-6
	19		Winnipeg	6-3		30	at	Florida	2-1
	21		New Jersey	2-3		31	at	Washington	1-1
	23	at	Boston	5-7	Apr.	3		Hartford	4-2
	28		Montreal	3-1		5		Buffalo	3-4
	31	at	Ottawa	3-0		6	at	Pittsburgh	1-2
Jan.	2	at	Calgary	0-10		8		NY Islanders	4-3
	3	at	Edmonton	5-0		10	at	Florida	2-1
	6	at	Vancouver	2-9		12	at	NY Rangers	3-2
	8	at	Montreal	3-3		14		Philadelphia	1-3

Entry Draft
Selections 1996-92

1996 Pick	1994 Pick	1993 Pick	1992 Pick
16 Mario Larocque	8 Jason Wiemer	3 Chris Gratton	1 Roman Hamrlik
69 Curtis Tipler	34 Colin Cloutier	29 Tyler Moss	26 Drew Bannister
125 Jason Robinson	55 Vadim Epanchintsev	55 Allan Egeland	49 Brent Gretzky
152 Nikolai Ignatov	86 Dmitri Klevakin	81 Marian Kacir	74 Aaron Gavey
157 Xavier Delisle	137 Daniel Juden	107 Ryan Brown	97 Brantt Myhres
179 Pavel Kubina	138 Bryce Salvador	133 Kiley Hill	122 Martin Tanguay
	164 Chris Maillet	159 Mathieu Raby	145 Derek Wilkinson
1995 Pick	190 Alexei Baranov	185 Ryan Nauss	170 Dennis Maxwell
5 Daymond Langkow	216 Yuri Smirnov	211 Alexandre Laporte	193 Andrew Kemper
30 Mike McBain	242 Shawn Gervais	237 Brett Duncan	218 Marc Tardif
56 Shane Willis	268 Brian White	263 Mark Szoke	241 Tom MacDonald
108 Konsta Golokhvastov			
134 Eduard Pershin			
160 Cory Murphy			
186 Joe Cardarelli			
212 Zac Bierk			

General Manager

ESPOSITO, PHIL
General Manager, Tampa Bay Lightning.
Born in Sault Ste. Marie, Ont., February 20, 1942.

It was Phil Esposito's determination that led to the awarding of an NHL franchise to Tampa Bay. Beginning play in 1992-93, the Lightning rapidly became a respected NHL opponent and reached the playoffs for the first time in 1996.

As a player, Esposito was one of the game's most gifted scorers. He played 18 seasons in the NHL with Chicago, Boston and the Rangers and is the League's fourth leading all-time scorer with 717 goals in regular-season play. He was the first to exceed 100 points and 70 goals in a single season and won the Stanley Cup with Boston in 1970 and 1972. He also played a vital leadership role for Team Canada in its dramatic eight-game series win over the Soviet National Team in 1972. He is a member of the Hockey Hall of Fame.

He served as general manager of the New York Rangers from 1986 to 1988.

With Tampa Bay, he has demonstrated great skill in player acquisition, utilizing free agent signings and the Expansion, Entry and Supplemental drafts to build the Lightning roster.

Now 54, he resides in Tampa. He has three daughters, Laurie, Carrie and Cerise, and two grandsons, Dylan and Dakoda.

NHL Coaching Record

		Regular Season					Playoffs			
Season	Team	Games	W	L	T	%	Games	W	L	%
1986-87	NY Rangers (NHL)	43	24	19	0	.558	6	2	4	.333
1988-89	NY Rangers (NHL)	2	0	2	0	.000	4	0	4	.000
	NHL Totals	**45**	**24**	**21**	**0**	**.533**	**10**	**2**	**8**	**.200**

Club Directory

Ice Palace

401 Channelside Drive
Tampa, FL 33602
Phone **813/229-2658**
FAX 813/229-3350
Capacity: 26,000

Lightning Partners, Ltd.
General Partner . . . . Lightning Partners, Inc.

Board of Directors
Takashi Okubo, Phil Esposito, Yasukiyo Higashiyama, David LeFevre, Fukusaboro Maeda, Tadashige Oku, Saburo (Steve) Oto, Chris Phillips, Reece Smith, Jr., Yoshiuki Sugioka

Executive Staff
Majority Owner and Chairman . . . . Takashi Okubo
President, CEO and Alternate Governor . . . . Saburo (Steve) Oto
Governor . . . . David LeFevre
General Manager & Alternate Governor . . . . Phil Esposito
Executive Vice President & Alternate Governor . . . . Chris Phillips
Vice President and CFO . . . . Frank Sato

Administration
Assistant to the President and CEO . . . . Masahiro Yamshita
Executive Assistant . . . . Connie Troy

Hockey Operations
General Manager . . . . Phil Esposito
Director of Hockey Development & Scouting . . . . . Tony Esposito
Counsel . . . . Henry Lee Paul – Lazzara & Paul, P.A.
Head Coach . . . . Terry Crisp
Assistant Coach . . . . Dave MacQueen
Assistant Coach/Strength and Conditioning Coach . Chris Reichart
Head Scout . . . . Don Murdoch
Scouting Staff . . . . Angelo Bumbacco, Jake Goertzen, Doug Macauley, Richard Rose, Luke Williams
Director of Team Services . . . . Barry Hanrahan
Head Trainer . . . . Dennis Brogna
Equipment Manager . . . . Jocko Cayer
Assistant Trainer . . . . Bill Cronin
Administrative Assistant . . . . Teresa P. Huffman
Administrative Assistant . . . . Kathy Skelton
Ice System Supervisor . . . . Tim Friedenberger
Operations Manager . . . . Michael Wall
Video Coordinator . . . . Duncan McMillian

Finance
Vice President and CFO . . . . Frank Sato
Accounting Manager . . . . Vincent Ascanio
Accounting Supervisor . . . . Kevin Steiger
Executive Administrative Assistant . . . . Evelyn Hicks
Accounts Payable Supervisor/Staff Accountant . . . . Kris Swofford
Accounts Payable Clerk . . . . Jill Lopez
Human Resource Administrator . . . . Katie Lang

Marketing and Sales
Director of Marketing . . . . Paul D'Aiuto
Director of Fan Services . . . . Steve Woznick
Production Coordinator . . . . Killeen Mullen
Promotions Coordinator . . . . Nichole Reckner
Senior Sales Representative . . . . Karl Nickel
Marketing Assistant . . . . Kim Pryor
Director of Merchandising . . . . Kevin L. Murphy
Inventory Control Coordinator . . . . Phil Kessel

Ticket Operations
Vice President/Ticket Operations and Sales . . . . Jeff Morander
Director of Ticket Operations . . . . Kevin Brooks
Director of Ticket Sales . . . . Bill Makris
Assistant Director of Ticket Sales . . . . Dan Froehlich
Director of Group Sales . . . . Cliff Gault
Ticket Office Manager . . . . Marilyn Brace
Ticket Office Representatives . . . . Cleff Smith, Dan Pekarek
Season Ticket Service Manager . . . . Keith Brennan
Ticket Sales Manager . . . . Brendan Cunningham
Corporate Ticket Sales . . . . Joe Domingos
Senior Sales Representative . . . . Jason Baumgarten
Sales Representatives . . . . Matt Lemay, Matt Poore

Communications
Vice President/Communications . . . . Gerry Helper
Director of Publications/Corporate PR . . . . Jay Preble
Communications & Community Relations Coord . . . . Carrie Schuldt
Media Information Manager . . . . John Sternal
Director of Amateur Hockey . . . . Nigel Kirwan
Receptionist . . . . Natalie Cacciatore, Holly Clarkson

Medical Staff
Team Physician . . . . Dr. David Leffers
Team Dentist . . . . Dr. Joseph Spoto

Game Night Staff
Team Photographer . . . . Jonathan Hayt
Off-ice Officials . . . . Jim Galluzzi, Ron Brace, Gerry Dollmont, Ralph Emery, Chuck Fontana, Mark Losier, Tony Mancuso, Jeff Maust, Mike Rees, Gary Reilly, John Supak, Rich Wasilewski
Game Summary . . . . Rick Pratt
NHL Commercial Coordinator . . . . David Rice
Public Address Announcer . . . . Paul Porter
Game Night Music . . . . Mike Oliviero
Scoreboard Operation . . . . Bill Heald
Media Services . . . . Jan Porter, Phil Czochanski

Television and Radio
Television Stations . . . . Sunshine Network, & Lightning Television Network
Broadcasters . . . . Rick Peckham and Bobby Taylor
Radio Stations . . . . WFNS-AM 910, WSUN-AM 620 & Lightning Radio Network
Broadcasters . . . . Larry Hirsch and Bobby Taylor

Tampa Bay Arena, L.P. (Ice Palace)
General Partner . . . . Lightning Arena, Inc.

Executive Staff
Majority Owner and Chairman . . . . Takashi Okubo
President, CEO . . . . Saburo (Steve) Oto
Special Advisor . . . . David LeFevre
Executive Vice President . . . . Chris Phillips
Vice President & CFO . . . . Frank Sato

Administration
Vice President, Arena Construction . . . . Tetsuo Makino
Assistant to the President and CEO . . . . Masahiro Yamashita
Executive Assistant . . . . Connie Troy

Arena Operations
General Manager . . . . Bob Rice
Director of Marketing . . . . Eric Bresler
Ice Palace Engineer . . . . Tim Higgins
Director of Operations . . . . Jay Cooper
Marketing Manager . . . . Bob Sanders
Event Coordinator . . . . Beth DeGaetano
Box Office Manager . . . . Lamar Vernon
Administrative Assistant . . . . Loan Nguyen
Account Manager . . . . Valerie Marshall
Director of Finance . . . . Tom Davenport

Executive Services and Sales
Director of Executive Services & Sales . . . . Lisa Byrd Mulfinger
Executive Services Assistant . . . . Rhonda Johnson
Manager Suite Services & Sales . . . . Charlotte Martin
Coordinator/Special Projects/Suite Services . . . . . . Nicole Leigh
Coordinator Suite Service . . . . Cheryll Pricher

Toronto Maple Leafs

1995-96 Results: 34W-36L-12T 80PTS. Third, Central Division

For the second season in a row, Mats Sundin was the offensive catalyst of the Toronto Maple Leafs, topping the club in assists (50), points (83), short-handed goals (6), game-winning goals (7) and shots on goal (301)

Schedule

Oct.	Sat.	5	Anaheim
	Tues.	8	Edmonton
	Sat.	12	Tampa Bay
	Tues.	15	Chicago
	Thur.	17	at St. Louis
	Sat.	19	at Dallas
	Tues.	22	San Jose
	Thur.	24	at Boston
	Sat.	26	Phoenix
	Tues.	29	Los Angeles
	Thur.	31	at NY Islanders
	Tues.	7	at Calgary
	Sat.	11	Colorado
	Mon.	13	at Washington
	Wed.	15	Los Angeles
	Mon.	20	at Hartford
	Wed.	22	Calgary
	Fri.	24	at Chicago
	Sat.	25	Dallas
	Mon.	27	Colorado
	Wed.	29	St. Louis
	Fri.	31	at New Jersey
Nov.	Sat.	2	Detroit
	Tues.	5	St. Louis
	Thur.	7	at Ottawa
	Sat.	9	Edmonton
	Sun.	10	at Philadelphia
	Wed.	13	at Anaheim
	Thur.	14	at Los Angeles
	Sat.	16	at Phoenix
	Tues.	19	Buffalo
	Thur.	21	at Buffalo
	Sat.	23	Montreal
	Tues.	26	Vancouver
	Wed.	27	at Detroit
	Sat.	30	at Dallas
Feb.	Sat.	1	Ottawa
	Wed.	5	Anaheim
	Sat.	8	Vancouver
	Wed.	12	at Anaheim
	Thur.	13	at Los Angeles
	Sat.	15	at Calgary
	Tues.	18	at Vancouver
	Wed.	19	at Edmonton
	Sat.	22	at Montreal
	Wed.	26	Washington
Mar.	Sat.	1	San Jose
	Mon.	3	Boston
	Wed.	5	Detroit
	Sat.	8	Hartford
Dec.	Tues.	3	St. Louis
	Fri.	6	at NY Rangers
	Sat.	7	NY Rangers
	Mon.	9	at Chicago
	Tues.	10	New Jersey
	Sat.	14	Phoenix
	Sun.	15	at Detroit
	Tues.	17	at San Jose
	Fri.	20	at Phoenix
	Sat.	21	at Colorado
	Mon.	23	Pittsburgh
	Fri.	27	at St. Louis
	Sat.	28	Chicago
	Mon.	30	NY Islanders
	Mon.	10	Dallas
	Wed.	12	Chicago
	Sat.	15	at Florida
	Sun.	17	at Tampa Bay
	Wed.	19	Philadelphia
	Thur.	20	at Pittsburgh
	Sat.	22	Phoenix
	Wed.	26	at San Jose
	Thur.	27	at Phoenix
	Sat.	29	at Colorado
	Apr. Wed.	2	Florida
	Thur.	3	at Detroit
	Sat.	5	Detroit
	Wed.	9	at Dallas
Jan.	Fri.	3	at Edmonton
	Thur.	10	at St. Louis
	Sat.	4	at Vancouver
	Sat.	12	Calgary

* Denotes afternoon game.

Franchise date: November 22, 1917

CENTRAL DIVISION

80th NHL Season

Year-by-Year Record

Season	GP	Home W	L	T	Road W	L	T	Overall W	L	T	GF	GA	Pts.	Finished		Playoff Result
1995-96	82	19	15	7	15	21	5	34	36	12	247	252	80	3rd,	Central Div.	Lost Conf. Quarter-Final
1994-95	48	15	7	2	6	12	6	21	19	8	135	146	50	4th,	Central Div.	Lost Conf. Quarter-Final
1993-94	84	23	15	4	20	14	8	43	29	12	280	243	98	2nd,	Central Div.	Lost Conf. Championship
1992-93	84	25	11	6	19	18	5	44	29	11	288	241	99	3rd,	Norris Div.	Lost Conf. Championship
1991-92	80	21	16	3	9	27	4	30	43	7	234	294	67	5th,	Norris Div.	Out of Playoffs
1990-91	80	15	21	4	8	25	7	23	46	11	241	318	57	5th,	Norris Div.	Out of Playoffs
1989-90	80	24	14	2	14	24	2	38	38	4	337	358	80	3rd,	Norris Div.	Lost Div. Semi-Final
1988-89	80	15	20	5	13	26	1	28	46	6	259	342	62	5th,	Norris Div.	Out of Playoffs
1987-88	80	14	20	6	7	29	4	21	49	10	273	345	52	4th,	Norris Div.	Lost Div. Semi-Final
1986-87	80	22	14	4	10	28	2	32	42	6	286	319	70	4th,	Norris Div.	Lost Div. Final
1985-86	80	16	21	3	9	27	4	25	48	7	311	386	57	4th,	Norris Div.	Lost Div. Final
1984-85	80	10	28	2	10	24	6	20	52	8	253	358	48	5th,	Norris Div.	Out of Playoffs
1983-84	80	17	16	7	9	29	2	26	45	9	303	387	61	5th,	Norris Div.	Out of Playoffs
1982-83	80	20	15	5	8	25	7	28	40	12	293	330	68	3rd,	Norris Div.	Lost Div. Semi-Final
1981-82	80	12	20	8	8	24	8	20	44	16	298	380	56	5th,	Norris Div.	Out of Playoffs
1980-81	80	14	21	5	14	16	10	28	37	15	322	367	71	5th,	Adams Div.	Lost Prelim. Round
1979-80	80	17	19	4	18	21	1	35	40	5	304	327	75	4th,	Adams Div.	Lost Prelim. Round
1978-79	80	20	12	8	14	21	5	34	33	13	267	252	81	3rd,	Adams Div.	Lost Quarter-Final
1977-78	80	21	13	6	20	16	4	41	29	10	271	237	92	3rd,	Adams Div.	Lost Semi-Final
1976-77	80	18	13	9	15	19	6	33	32	15	301	285	81	3rd,	Adams Div.	Lost Quarter-Final
1975-76	80	23	12	5	11	19	10	34	31	15	294	276	83	3rd,	Adams Div.	Lost Quarter-Final
1974-75	80	19	12	9	12	21	7	31	33	16	280	309	78	3rd,	Adams Div.	Lost Quarter-Final
1973-74	78	21	11	7	14	16	9	35	27	16	274	230	86	4th,	East Div.	Lost Quarter-Final
1972-73	78	20	12	7	7	29	3	27	41	10	247	279	64	6th,	East Div.	Out of Playoffs
1971-72	78	21	11	7	12	20	7	33	31	14	209	208	80	4th,	East Div.	Lost Quarter-Final
1970-71	78	24	9	6	13	24	2	37	33	8	248	211	82	4th,	East Div.	Lost Quarter-Final
1969-70	76	18	13	7	11	21	6	29	34	13	222	242	71	6th,	East Div.	Out of Playoffs
1968-69	76	20	8	10	15	18	5	35	26	15	234	217	85	4th,	East Div.	Lost Quarter-Final
1967-68	74	24	9	4	9	22	6	33	31	10	209	176	76	5th,	East Div.	Out of Playoffs
1966-67	70	21	8	6	11	19	5	32	27	11	204	211	75	3rd,		**Won Stanley Cup**
1965-66	70	22	9	4	12	16	7	34	25	11	208	187	79	4th,		Lost Semi-Final
1964-65	70	17	15	3	13	11	11	30	26	14	204	173	74	4th,		Lost Semi-Final
1963-64	70	22	7	6	11	18	6	33	25	12	192	172	78	3rd,		**Won Stanley Cup**
1962-63	70	21	8	6	14	15	6	35	23	12	221	180	82	1st,		**Won Stanley Cup**
1961-62	70	25	5	5	12	17	6	37	22	11	232	180	85	2nd,		**Won Stanley Cup**
1960-61	70	21	6	8	18	13	4	39	19	12	234	176	90	2nd,		Lost Semi-Final
1959-60	70	20	9	6	15	17	3	35	26	9	199	195	79	2nd,		Lost Final
1958-59	70	17	13	5	10	19	6	27	32	11	189	201	65	4th,		Lost Final
1957-58	70	12	16	7	9	22	4	21	38	11	192	226	53	6th,		Out of Playoffs
1956-57	70	12	16	7	9	18	8	21	34	15	174	192	57	5th,		Out of Playoffs
1955-56	70	19	10	6	5	23	7	24	33	13	153	181	61	4th,		Lost Semi-Final
1954-55	70	14	10	11	10	14	11	24	24	22	147	135	70	3rd,		Lost Semi-Final
1953-54	70	22	6	7	10	18	7	32	24	14	152	131	78	3rd,		Lost Semi-Final
1952-53	70	17	12	6	10	18	7	27	30	13	156	167	67	5th,		Out of Playoffs
1951-52	70	17	10	8	12	15	8	29	25	16	168	157	74	3rd,		Lost Semi-Final
1950-51	70	22	8	5	19	8	8	41	16	13	212	138	95	2nd,		**Won Stanley Cup**
1949-50	70	18	9	8	13	18	4	31	27	12	176	173	74	3rd,		Lost Semi-Final
1948-49	60	12	8	10	10	17	3	22	25	13	147	161	57	4th,		**Won Stanley Cup**
1947-48	60	22	3	5	10	12	8	32	15	13	182	143	77	1st,		**Won Stanley Cup**
1946-47	60	20	8	2	11	11	8	31	19	10	209	172	72	2nd,		**Won Stanley Cup**
1945-46	50	10	13	2	9	11	5	19	24	7	174	185	45	5th,		Out of Playoffs
1944-45	50	13	9	3	11	13	1	24	22	4	183	161	52	3rd,		**Won Stanley Cup**
1943-44	50	13	11	1	10	12	3	23	23	4	214	174	50	3rd,		Lost Semi-Final
1942-43	50	17	6	2	5	13	7	22	19	9	198	159	53	3rd,		Lost Semi-Final
1941-42	48	18	6	0	9	12	3	27	18	3	158	136	57	2nd,		**Won Stanley Cup**
1940-41	48	16	5	3	12	9	3	28	14	6	145	99	62	2nd,		Lost Semi-Final
1939-40	48	15	3	6	10	14	0	25	17	6	134	110	56	3rd,		Lost Final
1938-39	48	13	8	3	6	12	6	19	20	9	114	107	47	3rd,		Lost Final
1937-38	48	13	6	5	11	9	4	24	15	9	151	127	57	1st,	Cdn. Div.	Lost Final
1936-37	48	14	9	1	8	12	4	22	21	5	119	115	49	3rd,	Cdn. Div.	Lost Quarter-Final
1935-36	48	15	4	5	8	15	1	23	19	6	126	106	52	2nd,	Cdn. Div.	Lost Final
1934-35	48	16	6	2	14	8	2	30	14	4	157	111	64	1st,	Cdn. Div.	Lost Final
1933-34	48	19	2	3	7	11	6	26	13	9	174	119	61	1st,	Cdn. Div.	Lost Semi-Final
1932-33	48	16	4	4	8	14	2	24	18	6	119	111	54	1st,	Cdn. Div.	Lost Final
1931-32	48	17	4	3	6	14	4	23	18	7	155	127	53	2nd,	Cdn. Div.	**Won Stanley Cup**
1930-31	44	15	4	3	7	9	6	22	13	9	118	99	53	2nd,	Cdn. Div.	Lost Quarter-Final
1929-30	44	10	8	4	7	13	2	17	21	6	116	124	40	4th,	Cdn. Div.	Out of Playoffs
1928-29	44	15	5	2	6	13	3	21	18	5	85	69	47	3rd,	Cdn. Div.	Lost Semi-Final
1927-28	44	9	8	5	9	10	3	18	18	8	89	88	44	4th,	Cdn. Div.	Out of Playoffs
1926-27*	44	10	10	2	5	14	3	15	24	5	79	94	35	5th,	Cdn. Div.	Out of Playoffs
1925-26	36	11	5	2	1	16	1	12	21	3	92	114	27	6th,		Out of Playoffs
1924-25	30	10	5	0	9	6	0	19	11	0	90	84	38	2nd,		Lost NHL S-Final
1923-24	24	7	5	0	3	9	0	10	14	0	59	85	20	3rd,		Out of Playoffs
1922-23	24	10	1	1	3	9	0	13	10	1	82	88	27	2nd,		Out of Playoffs
1921-22	24	8	4	0	5	6	1	13	10	1	98	97	27	2nd,		**Won Stanley Cup**
1920-21	24	9	3	0	6	6	0	15	9	0	105	100	30	2nd and 1st***		Lost NHL Final
1919-20**	24	8	4	0	4	8	0	12	12	0	119	106	24	3rd and 2nd***		Out of Playoffs
1918-19	18	5	4	0	0	9	0	5	13	0	64	92	10	3rd and 3rd***		Out of Playoffs
1917-18	22	10	1	0	3	9	0	13	9	0	108	109	26	2nd and 1st***		**Won Stanley Cup**

* Name changed from St. Patricks to Maple Leafs. ** Name changed from Arenas to St. Patricks.
*** Season played in two halves with no combined standing at end.

1996-97 Player Personnel

FORWARDS	HT	WT	S	Place of Birth	Date	1995-96 Club
ANTIPOV, Vladimir	5-11	180	L	Appatity, USSR	1/17/78	Yaroslavl 2
BAKER, Jamie	6-0	195	L	Ottawa, Ont.	8/31/66	San Jose
BEREZIN, Sergei	5-10	187	R	Voskresensk, USSR	11/5/71	Koln
BUTZ, Rob	6-3	191	L	Dewberry, Alta.	2/24/75	St. John's
CAVA, Peter	5-11	175	L	Thunder Bay, Ont.	2/14/78	S.S. Marie
CLARK, Wendel	5-11	194	L	Kelvington, Sask.	10/25/66	NY Islanders-Toronto
CONVERY, Brandon	6-1	182	R	Kingston, Ont.	2/4/74	Toronto-St. John's
CRAIG, Mike	6-1	180	R	St. Mary's, Ont.	6/6/71	Toronto
CRAIGHEAD, John	6-0	195	R	Vancouver, B.C.	11/23/71	Detroit (IHL)
DEMARTINIS, Lucio	6-2	182	L	Montreal, Que.	7/31/78	Shawinigan
DEMPSEY, Nathan	6-0	170	L	Spruce Grove, Alta.	7/14/74	St. John's
DEYELL, Mark	6-0	180	R	Regina, Sask.	3/26/76	Saskatoon
DOMI, Tie	5-10	200	R	Windsor, Ont.	11/1/69	Toronto
FAIRCHILD, Kelly	5-11	180	L	Hibbing, MN	4/9/73	Toronto-St. John's
GILMOUR, Doug	5-11	172	L	Kingston, Ont.	6/25/63	Toronto
HAKANSSON, Mikael	6-1	196	L	Stockholm, Sweden	5/31/74	MoDo
KALMIKOV, Konstantin	6-4	205	R	Kharkov, USSR	6/14/78	Flint-Detroit (ColHL)
KOLESAR, Mark	6-1	188	R	Brampton, Ont.	1/23/73	Toronto-St. John's
KUCHARCIK, Tomas	6-2	200	L	Vlasim, Czech.	5/10/70	ZPS Plzen-Slavia Praha
KYPREOS, Nick	6-0	205	L	Toronto, Ont.	6/4/66	NY Rangers-Toronto
MAROIS, Daniel	6-0	190	R	Montreal, Que.	10/3/68	Dallas-Michigan-Minnesota
MELENOVSKY, Marek	5-9	176	L	Humpolec, Czech.	3/30/77	Dukla Jihlava
MODIN, Fredrik	6-3	202	L	Sundsvall, Sweden	10/8/74	Brynas
MULLER, Kirk	6-0	205	L	Kingston, Ont.	2/8/66	NY Islanders-Toronto
MURPHY, Mark	5-11	200	L	Stoughton, MA	8/6/76	Stratford
NEDVED, Zdenek	6-0	180	L	Lany, Czech.	3/3/75	Toronto-St. John's
NOLAN, Doug	6-1	185	L	Quincy, MA	1/5/76	Lowell
PEARSON, Scott	6-1	205	L	Cornwall, Ont.	12/19/69	Buffalo-Rochester
PEPPERALL, Ryan	6-1	185	R	Niagara Falls, Ont.	1/26/77	Kitchener
POMICHTER, Michael	6-1	222	L	New Haven, CT	9/10/73	Corw'll-Ind-St.J's
PRESLEY, Wayne	5-11	195	R	Dearborn, MI	3/23/65	NY Rangers-Toronto
PROCHAZKA, Martin	5-11	180	R	Slany, Czech.	3/3/72	Poldi Kladno
SESSA, Jason	6-1	173	R	Long Island, NY	7/17/77	Lake Superior
SUNDIN, Mats	6-4	215	R	Bromma, Sweden	2/13/71	Toronto
TOPOROWSKI, Shayne	6-2	210	R	Paddockwood, Sask.	8/6/75	St. John's
VINCENT, Paul	6-4	200	L	Utica, NY	1/4/75	St. John's-Raleigh
WARE, Mike	6-1	193	L	Toronto, Ont.	2/27/74	St. John's
WARRINER, Todd	6-1	188	L	Blenheim, Ont.	1/3/74	Toronto-St. John's
DEFENSEMEN						
BOGAS, Chris	6-0	192	R	Cleveland, OH	11/12/76	Michigan State
CULL, Trent	6-3	210	L	Brampton, Ont.	9/27/73	St. John's
ELLETT, Dave	6-2	205	L	Cleveland, OH	3/30/64	Toronto
HEWARD, Jamie	6-2	207	R	Regina, Sask.	3/30/71	Toronto-St. John's
LANKSHEAR, Mike	6-2	185	L	Calgary, Alta.	9/8/78	Guelph
MACOUN, Jamie	6-2	200	L	Newmarket, Ont.	8/17/61	Toronto
MARKOV, Daniil	5-11	176	L	Moscow, USSR	7/11/76	Spartak
MARTIN, Matt	6-3	205	L	Hamden, CT	4/30/71	Toronto
MULLIN, Kory	6-2	185	L	Lethbridge, Alta.	5/24/75	Brantford-St. John's
MURPHY, Larry	6-2	210	R	Scarborough, Ont.	3/8/61	Toronto
POSMYK, Marek	6-5	220	R	Jihlava, Czech.	9/15/78	Dukla Jihlava-Dukla Jihlava
RAJAMAKI, Tommi	6-2	180	L	Pori, Finland	2/29/76	Assat
SCHNEIDER, Mathieu	5-11	192	L	New York, NY	6/12/69	NY Islanders-Toronto
SIMONOV, Sergei	6-3	194	L	Saratov, USSR	5/20/74	Magnitogorsk-Saratov
SMITH, Denis	6-1	200	L	Windsor, Ont.	5/13/77	Windsor
SMYTH, Greg	6-3	212	R	Oakville, Ont.	4/23/66	Chicago-Los Angeles (IHL)
SUGDEN, Brandon	6-2	178	R	Toronto, Ont.	6/23/78	London
TREMBLAY, Yanick	6-2	185	R	Pointe-aux-Trembles, Que.	11/15/75	Beauport-St. John's
WARE, Jeff	6-4	220	L	Toronto, Ont.	5/19/77	Oshawa-St. John's
YAKUSHIN, Dmitri	6-0	198	L	Kharkov, USSR	1/21/78	Pembroke
YUSHKEVICH, Dimitri	5-11	208	R	Yaroslavl, USSR	11/19/71	Toronto
ZETTLER, Rob	6-3	200	L	Sept Iles, Que.	3/8/68	Toronto

GOALTENDERS	HT	WT	C	Place of Birth	Date	1995-96 Club
BEAUPRE, Don	5-10	172	L	Waterloo, Ont.	9/19/61	Ottawa-Toronto
BONNER, Doug	5-10	175	L	Tacoma, WA	10/15/76	Seattle
COUSINEAU, Marcel	5-9	180	L	Delson, Que.	4/30/73	St. John's
LARIVEE, Francis	6-2	198	L	Montreal, Que.	11/8/77	Val d'Or-Laval
POTVIN, Felix	6-0	190	L	Anjou, Que.	6/23/71	Toronto
SAAL, Jason	5-11	175	L	Sterling Heights, MI	2/1/75	South Carolina-St. John's

General Manager

FLETCHER, CLIFF
President, General Manager and Chief Operating Officer, Toronto Maple Leafs. Born in Montreal, Que., August 16, 1935.

Cliff Fletcher's hockey career began as a scout in the farm system of the Montreal Canadiens. He became St. Louis' eastern Canada scout in 1967 and later became the Blues' assistant general manager. He became g,m, of the Atlanta Flames when that franchise began operation in 1972 and organized its transfer to Calgary in 1980 where the flames reached the finals in 1986 and won the Stanley Cup in 1989.

He became chief operating officer, president and g.m. of the Maple Leafs on July 1, 1991. During his tenure, the Leafs have played in 52 playoff games and twice reached the Conference Championships. In his second season of leadership, the Leafs established new club records with 44 wins and 99 points and came within one goal of a berth in the Stanley Cup finals. Fletcher was named *The Hockey News* Man of the Year for 1992-93.

General Managers' History

Conn Smythe, 1927-28 to 1956-57; "Hap" Day, 1957-58; "Punch" Imlach, 1958-59 to 1968-69; Jim Gregory, 1969-70 to 1978-79; "Punch" Imlach, 1979-80 to 1980-81; "Punch" Imlach and Gerry McNamara, 1981-82; Gerry McNamara, 1982-83 to 1987-88; Gord Stellick, 1988-89; Floyd Smith, 1989-90 to 1990-91; Cliff Fletcher, 1991-92 to date.

1995-96 Scoring

* – rookie

Regular Season

Pos	#	Player	Team	GP	G	A	Pts	+/–	PIM	PP	SH	GW	GT	S	%
C	13	Mats Sundin	TOR	76	33	50	83	8	46	7	6	7	1	301	11.0
C	93	Doug Gilmour	TOR	81	32	40	72	–5	77	10	2	3	0	180	17.8
D	55	Larry Murphy	TOR	82	12	49	61	–2	34	8	0	1	2	182	6.6
L	17	Wendel Clark	NYI	58	24	19	43	–12	60	6	0	2	1	192	12.5
			TOR	13	8	7	15	7	16	2	0	1	0	45	17.8
			TOTAL	71	32	26	58	–5	76	8	0	3	1	237	13.5
R	11	Mike Gartner	TOR	82	35	19	54	5	52	15	0	4	1	275	12.7
D	72	Mathieu Schneider	NYI	65	11	36	47	–18	93	7	0	1	0	155	7.1
			TOR	13	2	5	7	–2	10	0	0	0	0	36	5.6
			TOTAL	78	13	41	54	–20	103	7	0	1	0	191	6.8
C	15	Dave Gagner	DAL	45	14	13	27	–17	44	6	0	2	0	145	9.7
			TOR	28	7	15	22	–2	59	1	0	1	0	70	10.0
			TOTAL	73	21	28	49	–19	103	7	0	3	0	215	9.8
C	21	Kirk Muller	NYI	15	4	3	7	–10	15	0	0	0	0	23	17.4
			TOR	36	9	16	25	–3	42	7	0	1	0	79	11.4
			TOTAL	51	13	19	32	–13	57	7	0	1	0	102	12.7
D	23	Todd Gill	TOR	74	7	18	25	–15	116	1	0	2	0	109	6.4
D	4	Dave Ellett	TOR	80	3	19	22	–10	59	1	1	0	0	153	2.0
R	9	Mike Craig	TOR	70	8	12	20	–8	42	1	0	1	0	108	7.4
L	8 *	Todd Warriner	TOR	57	7	8	15	–11	26	1	0	0	0	79	8.9
R	18	Wayne Presley	NYR	61	4	6	10	7	71	0	1	2	0	85	4.7
			TOR	19	2	2	4	–4	14	1	0	0	0	28	7.1
			TOTAL	80	6	8	14	3	85	1	1	2	0	113	5.3
R	28	Tie Domi	TOR	72	7	6	13	–3	297	0	0	1	0	61	11.5
D	26	Dimitri Yushkevich	TOR	69	1	10	11	–14	54	1	0	0	0	96	1.0
L	32	Nick Kypreos	NYR	42	3	4	7	1	77	0	0	1	0	35	8.6
			TOR	19	1	1	2	0	30	0	0	0	0	14	7.1
			TOTAL	61	4	5	9	1	107	0	0	1	0	49	8.2
C	18	Peter White	EDM	26	5	3	8	–14	0	1	0	0	0	34	14.7
			TOR	1	0	0	0	0	0	0	0	0	0	0	0.0
			TOTAL	27	5	3	8	–14	0	1	0	0	0	34	14.7
C	25	Paul Di Pietro	TOR	20	4	4	8	–3	4	1	0	0	0	23	17.4
D	34	Jamie Macoun	TOR	82	0	8	8	2	87	0	0	0	0	74	0.0
C	12 *	Brandon Convery	TOR	11	5	2	7	–7	4	3	0	1	0	16	31.3
R	37 *	Mark Kolesar	TOR	21	2	2	4	0	14	0	0	0	0	10	20.0
R	20 *	Zdenek Nedved	TOR	7	1	1	2	–1	6	0	0	0	0	7	14.3
G	33	Don Beaupre	OTT	33	0	2	2	0	17	0	0	0	0	0	0.0
			TOR	8	0	0	0	0	14	0	0	0	0	0	0.0
			TOTAL	41	0	2	2	0	31	0	0	0	0	0	0.0
D	40 *	Kelly Fairchild	TOR	1	0	1	1	1	2	0	0	0	0	1	0.0
D	2	Rob Zettler	TOR	29	0	1	1	–1	48	0	0	0	0	11	0.0
D	38 *	David Harlock	TOR	1	0	0	0	0	0	0	0	0	0	0	0.0
L	52 *	Sean Haggerty	TOR	1	0	0	0	0	0	0	0	0	0	0	0.0
R	36 *	Jamie Heward	TOR	5	0	0	0	–1	0	0	0	0	0	8	0.0
D	3	Matt Martin	TOR	13	0	0	0	–1	14	0	0	0	0	3	0.0
G	29	Felix Potvin	TOR	69	0	0	0	0	4	0	0	0	0	0	0.0

Goaltending

No.	Goaltender	GPI	Mins	Avg	W	L	T	EN	SO	GA	SA	S%
1	Damian Rhodes	11	624	2.79	4	5	1	0	0	29	301	.904
29	Felix Potvin	69	4009	2.87	30	26	11	4	2	192	2135	.910
33	Don Beaupre	8	336	4.64	0	5	0	1	0	26	170	.847
	Totals	**82**	**4989**	**3.03**	**34**	**36**	**12**	**5**	**2**	**252**	**2611**	**.903**

Playoffs

Pos	#	Player	Team	GP	G	A	Pts	+/–	PIM	PP	SH	GW	OT	S	%
C	93	Doug Gilmour	TOR	6	1	7	8	–4	12	1	0	0	0	15	6.7
R	11	Mike Gartner	TOR	6	4	1	5	–5	4	2	0	1	1	18	22.2
C	21	Kirk Muller	TOR	6	3	2	5	–1	0	2	0	0	0	12	25.0
C	13	Mats Sundin	TOR	6	3	1	4	–8	4	2	0	1	1	23	13.0
L	17	Wendel Clark	TOR	6	2	2	4	–6	2	1	0	0	0	17	11.8
D	72	Mathieu Schneider	TOR	6	0	4	4	–7	8	0	0	0	0	13	0.0
L	8 *	Todd Warriner	TOR	6	1	1	2	0	2	0	0	0	0	13	7.7
R	28	Tie Domi	TOR	6	0	2	2	0	4	0	0	0	0	4	0.0
C	15	Dave Gagner	TOR	6	0	2	2	–5	6	0	0	0	0	8	0.0
D	34	Jamie Macoun	TOR	6	0	2	2	3	8	0	0	0	0	10	0.0
D	55	Larry Murphy	TOR	6	0	2	2	–8	4	0	0	0	0	16	0.0
R	37 *	Mark Kolesar	TOR	3	1	0	1	1	2	0	1	0	0	2	50.0
G	33	Don Beaupre	TOR	2	0	0	0	0	0	0	0	0	0	0	0.0
D	2	Rob Zettler	TOR	2	0	0	0	0	0	0	0	0	0	1	0.0
D	26	Dimitri Yushkevich	TOR	4	0	0	0	1	0	0	0	0	0	3	0.0
L	32	Nick Kypreos	TOR	5	0	0	0	0	4	0	0	0	0	5	0.0
R	18	Wayne Presley	TOR	5	0	0	0	0	2	0	0	0	0	4	0.0
C	12 *	Brandon Convery	TOR	5	0	0	0	0	2	0	0	0	0	4	0.0
R	9	Mike Craig	TOR	6	0	0	0	0	18	0	0	0	0	7	0.0
D	4	Dave Ellett	TOR	6	0	0	0	–5	4	0	0	0	0	16	0.0
D	23	Todd Gill	TOR	6	0	0	0	–2	24	0	0	0	0	9	0.0
G	29	Felix Potvin	TOR	6	0	0	0	0	2	0	0	0	0	0	0.0

Goaltending

No.	Goaltender	GPI	Mins	Avg	W	L	EN	SO	GA	SA	S%
29	Felix Potvin	6	350	3.26	2	4	0	0	19	198	.904
33	Don Beaupre	2	20	6.00	0	0	0	0	2	13	.846
	Totals	**6**	**373**	**3.38**	**2**	**4**	**0**	**0**	**21**	**211**	**.900**

Captains' History

"Hap" Day, 1927-28 to 1936-37; Charlie Conacher, 1937-38; Red Horner, 1938-39, 1939-40; Syl Apps, 1940-41 to 1942-43; Bob Davidson, 1943-44, 1944-45; Syl Apps, 1945-46 to 1947-48; Ted Kennedy, 1948-49 to 1954-55; Sid Smith, 1955-56; Jim Thomson, Ted Kennedy, 1956-57; George Armstrong, 1957-58 to 1968-69; Dave Keon, 1969-70 to 1974-75; Darryl Sittler, 1975-76 to 1980-81; Rick Vaive, 1981-82 to 1985-86; no captain, 1986-87 to 1988-89; Rob Ramage, 1989-90 to 1990-91; Wendel Clark, 1991-92 to 1993-94; Doug Gilmour, 1994-95 to date.

Club Records

Team

(Figures in brackets for season records are games played; records for fewest points, wins, ties, losses, goals, goals against are for 70 or more games)

Most Points	99	1992-93 (84)
Most Wins	44	1992-93 (84)
Most Ties	22	1954-55 (70)
Most Losses	52	1984-85 (80)
Most Goals	337	1989-90 (80)
Most Goals Against	387	1983-84 (80)
Fewest Points	48	1984-85 (80)
Fewest Wins	20	1981-82, 1984-85 (80)
Fewest Ties	4	1989-90 (80)
Fewest Losses	16	1950-51 (70)
Fewest Goals	147	1954-55 (70)
Fewest Goals Against	*131	1953-54 (70)

Longest Winning Streak

Overall	10	Oct. 7-28/93
Home	9	Nov. 11-Dec. 26/53
Away	7	Nov. 14-Dec. 15/40, Dec. 4/60-Jan. 5/61

Longest Undefeated Streak

Overall	11	Oct. 15-Nov. 8/50 (8 wins, 3 ties), Jan. 6-Feb. 1/94 (7 wins, 4 ties)
Home	18	Nov. 28/33-Mar. 10/34 (15 wins, 3 ties), Oct. 31/53-Jan. 23/54 (16 wins, 2 ties)
Away	9	Nov. 30/47-Jan. 11/48 (4 wins, 5 ties)

Longest Losing Streak

Overall	10	Jan. 15-Feb. 8/67
Home	7	Nov. 10-Dec. 5/84, Jan. 26-Feb. 25/85
Away	11	Feb. 20-Apr. 1/88

Longest Winless Streak

Overall	15	Dec. 26/87-Jan. 25/88 (11 losses, 4 ties)
Home	11	Dec. 19/87-Jan. 25/88 (7 losses, 4 ties)
Away	18	Oct. 6/82-Jan. 5/83 (13 losses, 5 ties)

Most Shutouts, Season	13	1953-54 (70)
Most PIM, Season	2,419	1989-90 (80)
Most Goals, Game	14	Mar. 16/57 (NYR 1 at Tor. 14)

Individual

Most Seasons	21	George Armstrong
Most Games	1,187	George Armstrong
Most Goals, Career	389	Darryl Sittler
Most Assists, Career	620	Borje Salming
Most Points, Career	916	Darryl Sittler (389G, 527A)
Most PIM, Career	1,670	Dave Williams
Most Shutouts, Career	62	Turk Broda
Longest Consecutive Games Streak	486	Tim Horton (Feb. 11/61-Feb. 4/68)
Most Goals, Season	54	Rick Vaive (1981-82)
Most Assists, Season	95	Doug Gilmour (1992-93)
Most Points, Season	127	Doug Gilmour (1992-93; 32G, 95A)
Most PIM, Season	351	Dave Williams (1977-78)

Most Points, Defenseman Season	79	Ian Turnbull (1976-77; 22G, 57A)
Most Points, Center Season	127	Doug Gilmour (1992-93; 32G, 95A)
Most Points, Right Wing, Season	97	Wilf Paiement (1980-81; 40G, 57A)
Most Points, Left Wing, Season	99	Dave Andreychuk (1993-94; 53G, 46A)
Most Points, Rookie, Season	66	Peter Ihnacak (1982-83; 28G, 38A)
Most Shutouts, Season	13	Harry Lumley (1953-54)
Most Goals, Game	6	Corb Denneny (Jan. 26/21), Darryl Sittler (Feb. 7/76)
Most Assists, Game	6	Babe Pratt (Jan. 8/44), Doug Gilmour (Feb. 13/93)
Most Points, Game	*10	Darryl Sittler (Feb. 7/76; 6G, 4A)

* NHL Record.

Retired Numbers

5	Bill Barilko	1946-1951
6	Irvine "Ace" Bailey	1927-1934

Honored Numbers

1	Walter "Turk" Broda	1936-43, 45-52
	Johnny Bower	1958-70
7	Francis "King" Clancy	1930-37
	Tim Horton	1949-50, 51-70
9	Ted Kennedy	1942-1955, 56-57
10	Syl Apps	1936-1948

All-time Record vs. Other Clubs

Regular Season

			At Home						On Road						Total				
	GP	W	L	T	GF	GA	PTS	GP	W	L	T	GF	GA	PTS	GP	W	L	T	GF	GA	PTS
Anaheim	6	3	1	2	19	14	8	6	3	2	1	14	18	7	12	6	3	3	33	32	15
Boston	281	147	86	48	957	732	342	281	83	151	47	752	925	213	562	230	237	95	1709	1657	555
Buffalo	50	18	23	9	154	185	45	51	16	32	3	146	215	35	101	34	55	12	300	400	80
Calgary	44	20	17	7	170	169	47	46	13	28	5	147	201	31	90	33	45	12	317	370	78
Chicago	304	160	91	53	1040	784	373	305	110	154	41	793	944	261	609	270	245	94	1833	1728	634
Colorado	25	12	11	2	90	106	26	25	5	15	5	75	101	15	50	17	26	7	165	207	41
Dallas	92	47	30	15	333	288	109	88	33	44	11	288	339	77	180	80	74	26	621	627	186
Detroit	305	161	100	44	1016	811	366	307	101	161	45	751	920	247	612	262	261	89	1767	1731	613
Edmonton	28	13	13	2	116	129	28	28	7	15	6	97	139	20	56	20	28	8	213	268	48
Florida	2	1	1	0	7	9	2	3	1	1	1	7	9	3	5	2	2	1	14	18	5
Hartford	23	8	13	2	82	94	18	23	6	13	4	78	109	16	46	14	26	6	160	203	34
Los Angeles	59	31	17	11	241	199	73	60	20	32	8	178	216	48	119	51	49	19	419	415	121
Montreal	316	160	112	44	955	828	364	315	83	192	40	776	1123	206	631	243	304	84	1731	1951	570
New Jersey	34	24	6	4	153	109	52	33	11	13	9	105	121	31	67	35	19	13	258	230	83
NY Islanders	41	18	20	3	142	152	39	39	13	23	3	120	170	29	80	31	43	6	262	322	68
NY Rangers	268	151	79	38	920	694	340	269	101	112	56	787	824	258	537	252	191	94	1707	1518	598
Ottawa	4	4	0	0	20	8	8	3	2	1	0	9	4	5	7	6	1	0	29	12	13
Philadelphia	53	19	21	13	180	181	51	53	11	34	8	125	214	30	106	30	55	21	305	395	81
Pittsburgh	54	26	17	11	224	179	63	55	20	29	6	179	231	46	109	46	46	17	403	410	109
St. Louis	88	55	23	10	339	255	120	89	25	51	13	254	310	63	177	80	74	23	593	565	183
San Jose	9	6	2	1	38	19	13	10	5	4	1	28	23	11	19	11	6	2	66	42	24
Tampa Bay	8	4	4	0	26	17	8	6	5	1	0	23	12	10	14	9	5	0	49	29	18
Vancouver	51	23	19	9	194	176	55	49	15	25	9	162	167	39	100	38	44	18	356	343	94
Washington	35	20	11	4	170	123	44	36	12	22	2	99	136	26	71	32	33	6	269	259	70
Winnipeg	33	14	17	2	123	130	30	32	11	16	5	127	140	27	65	25	33	7	250	270	57
Defunct Clubs	232	158	53	21	860	515	337	233	84	120	29	607	745	197	465	242	173	50	1467	1260	534
Totals	**2445**	**1303**	**787**	**355**	**8569**	**6906**	**2961**	**2445**	**796**	**1290**	**359**	**6727**	**8356**	**1951**	**4890**	**2099**	**2077**	**714**	**15296**	**15262**	**4912**

Playoffs

	Series	W	L	GP	W	L	T	GF	GA	Last Mtg.	Round	Result
Boston	13	5	8	62	31	30	1	150	153	1974	QF	L 0-4
Calgary	1	1	0	2	2	0	0	9	5	1979	PR	W 2-0
Chicago	9	6	3	38	22	15	1	111	89	1995	CQF	L 3-4
Dallas	2	0	2	7	1	6	0	26	35	1983	DSF	L 1-3
Detroit	23	12	11	117	58	59	0	311	321	1993	DSF	W 4-3
Los Angeles	3	2	1	12	7	5	0	41	31	1993	CF	L 3-4
Montreal	15	7	8	71	29	42	0	160	215	1979	QF	L 0-4
NY Islanders	2	1	1	10	4	6	0	20	33	1981	PR	L 0-3
NY Rangers	8	3	5	35	16	19	0	86	86	1971	QF	L 2-4
Philadelphia	3	0	3	17	5	12	0	47	67	1977	QF	L 2-4
Pittsburgh	2	2	0	6	4	2	0	21	13	1977	PR	W 2-1
St. Louis	5	2	3	31	14	17	0	90	88	1996	CQF	L 2-4
San Jose	1	1	0	7	4	3	0	26	21	1994	CSF	W 4-3
Vancouver	1	0	1	5	1	4	0	9	16	1994	CF	L 1-4
Defunct	8	6	2	24	9	14	2	59	57			
Totals	**96**	**51**	**45**	**444**	**210**	**230**	**4**	**1166**	**1246**			

Calgary totals include Atlanta, 1972-73 to 1979-80. Colorado totals include Quebec, 1979-80 to 1994-95.
Dallas totals include Minnesota, 1967-68 to 1992-93.
New Jersey totals include Kansas City, 1974-75 to 1975-76, and Colorado Rockies, 1976-77 to 1981-82.

Playoff Results 1996-92

Year	Round	Opponent	Result	GF	GA
1996	CQF	St. Louis	L 2-4	15	21
1995	CQF	Chicago	L 3-4	20	22
1994	CF	Vancouver	L 1-4	9	16
	CSF	San Jose	W 4-3	26	21
	CQF	Chicago	W 4-2	15	10
1993	CF	Los Angeles	L 3-4	23	22
	DF	St. Louis	W 4-3	22	11
	DSF	Detroit	W 4-3	24	30

Abbreviations: Round: F – Final;
CF – conference final; **CQF** – conference quarter-final;
CSF – conference semi-final; **DF** – division final;
DSF – division semi-final; **SF** – semi-final;
QF – quarter-final; **PR** – preliminary round.

Entry Draft
Selections 1996-82

1996
Pick
- 36 Marek Posmyk
- 50 Francis Larivee
- 66 Mike Lankshear
- 68 Konstantin Kalmikov
- 86 Jason Sessa
- 103 Vladimir Antipov
- 110 Peter Cava
- 111 Brandon Sugden
- 140 Dmitriy Yakushin
- 148 Chris Bogas
- 151 Lucio Demartinis
- 178 Reggie Berg
- 204 Tomas Kaberle
- 230 Jared Hope

1995
Pick
- 15 Jeff Ware
- 54 Ryan Pepperall
- 139 Doug Bonner
- 145 Yannick Tremblay
- 171 Marek Melenovsky
- 197 Mark Murphy
- 223 Danlil Markov

1994
Pick
- 16 Eric Fichaud
- 48 Sean Haggerty
- 64 Fredrik Modin
- 126 Mark Deyell
- 152 Kam White
- 178 Tommi Rajamaki
- 204 Rob Butler
- 256 Sergei Berezin
- 282 Doug Nolan

1993
Pick
- 12 Kenny Jonsson
- 19 Landon Wilson
- 123 Zdenek Nedved
- 149 Paul Vincent
- 175 Jeff Andrews
- 201 David Brumby
- 253 Kyle Ferguson
- 279 Mikhail Lapin

1992
Pick
- 8 Brandon Convery
- 23 Grant Marshall
- 77 Nikolai Borschevsky
- 95 Mark Raiter
- 101 Janne Gronvall
- 106 Chris Deruiter
- 125 Mikael Hakansson
- 149 Patrik Augusta
- 173 Ryan Vandenbussche
- 197 Wayne Clarke
- 221 Sergei Simonov
- 245 Nathan Dempsey

1991
Pick
- 47 Yanic Perreault
- 69 Terry Chitaroni
- 102 Alexei Kudashov
- 113 Jeff Perry
- 120 Alexander Kuzminsky
- 135 Martin Prochazka
- 160 Dmitri Mironov
- 164 Robb McIntyre
- 167 Tomas Kucharcik
- 179 Guy Lehoux
- 201 Gary Miller
- 223 Jonathan Kelley
- 245 Chris O'Rourke

1990
Pick
- 10 Drake Berehowsky
- 31 Felix Potvin
- 73 Darby Hendrickson
- 80 Greg Walters
- 115 Alexander Godynyuk
- 136 Eric Lacroix
- 157 Dan Stiver
- 178 Robert Horyna
- 199 Rob Chebator
- 220 Scott Malone
- 241 Nick Vachon

1989
Pick
- 3 Scott Thornton
- 12 Rob Pearson
- 21 Steve Bancroft
- 66 Matt Martin
- 96 Keith Carney
- 108 David Burke
- 125 Michael Doers
- 129 Keith Merkler
- 150 Derek Langille
- 171 Jeffrey St. Laurent
- 192 Justin Tomberlin
- 213 Mike Jackson
- 234 Steve Chartrand

1988
Pick
- 6 Scott Pearson
- 27 Tie Domi
- 48 Peter Ing
- 69 Ted Crowley
- 88 Leonard Esau
- 132 Matt Mallgrave
- 153 Roger Elvenas
- 174 Mike Delay
- 195 David Sacco
- 216 Mike Gregorio
- 237 Peter DeBoer

1987
Pick
- 7 Luke Richardson
- 28 Daniel Marois
- 49 John McIntyre
- 71 Joe Sacco
- 91 Mike Eastwood
- 112 Damian Rhodes
- 133 Trevor Jobe
- 154 Chris Jensen
- 175 Brian Blad
- 196 Ron Bernacci
- 217 Ken Alexander
- 238 Alex Weinrich

1986
Pick
- 6 Vincent Damphousse
- 36 Darryl Shannon
- 48 Sean Boland
- 69 Kent Hulst
- 90 Scott Taylor
- 111 Stephane Giguere
- 132 Danny Hie
- 153 Stephen Brennan
- 174 Brian Bellefeuille
- 195 Sean Davidson
- 216 Mark Holick
- 237 Brian Hoard

1985
Pick
- 1 Wendel Clark
- 22 Ken Spangler
- 43 Dave Thomlinson
- 64 Greg Vey
- 85 Jeff Serowik
- 106 Jiri Latal
- 127 Tim Bean
- 148 Andy Donahue
- 169 Todd Whittemore
- 190 Bob Reynolds
- 211 Tim Armstrong
- 232 Mitch Murphy

1984
Pick
- 4 Al Iafrate
- 25 Todd Gill
- 67 Jeff Reese
- 88 Jack Capuano
- 109 Joseph Fabian
- 130 Joe McInnis
- 151 Derek Laxdal
- 172 Dan Turner
- 192 David Buckley
- 213 Mikael Wurst
- 233 Peter Slanina

1983
Pick
- 7 Russ Courtnall
- 28 Jeff Jackson
- 48 Allan Bester
- 83 Dan Hodgson
- 128 Cam Plante
- 148 Paul Bifano
- 168 Cliff Albrecht
- 184 Greg Rolston
- 188 Brian Ross
- 208 Mike Tomlak
- 228 Ron Choules

1982
Pick
- 3 Gary Nylund
- 24 Gary Leeman
- 25 Peter Ihnacak
- 45 Ken Wregget
- 73 Vladimir Ruzicka
- 87 Eduard Uvira
- 99 Sylvain Charland
- 108 Ron Dreger
- 115 Craig Kales
- 129 Dom Campedelli
- 139 Jeff Triano
- 171 Miroslav Ihnacak
- 192 Leigh Verstraete
- 213 Tim Loven
- 234 Jim Appleby

Coach

MURPHY, MIKE
Coach, Toronto Maple Leafs. Born in Toronto, Ont., September 12, 1950.

Named as the Maple Leafs' 24th coach on July 3, 1996, Mike Murphy is familiar with the expectations that accompany coaching in his hometown. Murphy, 46, was an assistant coach with the Leafs from 1991-92 to 1993-94 and served in a similar capacity with the New York Rangers in 1994-95 and 1995-96.

He played 12 NHL seasons at right wing, scoring 328 goals and 318 assists in 821 games. He played for the Rangers and Blues before joining the Los Angeles Kings in 1973. He played 10 seasons with the Kings and served as the club's captain before joining the club's coaching staff in 1984. He worked as an assistant before taking over the head coaching job in January of 1987. He coached 65 games for the Kings before moving to Vancouver as an assistant in 1988. In 1991, he coached Milwaukee, the Canucks' IHL affiliate, before joining the Leafs.

Coaching Record

Season	Team	Regular Season					Playoffs			
		Games	W	L	T	%	Games	W	L	%
1986-87	Los Angeles (NHL)	38	13	21	4	.395	5	1	4	.200
1987-88	Los Angeles (NHL)	27	7	16	4	.333	....	....	....	....
1990-91	Milwaukee (IHL)	82	36	43	3	.452	6	2	4	.333
	NHL Totals	**65**	**20**	**37**	**8**	**.370**	**5**	**1**	**4**	**.200**

Coaching History

Conn Smythe, 1927-28 to 1929-30; Conn Smythe and Art Duncan, 1930-31; Art Duncan and Dick Irvin, 1931-32; Dick Irvin, 1932-33 to 1939-40; "Hap" Day, 1940-41 to 1949-50; Joe Primeau, 1950-51 to 1952-53; "King" Clancy, 1953-54 to 1955-56; Howie Meeker, 1956-57; Billy Reay, 1957-58; Billy Reay and "Punch" Imlach, 1958-59; "Punch" Imlach, 1959-60 to 1968-69; John McLellan, 1969-70 to 1970-71; John McLellan and "King" Clancy, 1971-72; John McLellan, 1972-73; "Red" Kelly, 1973-74 to 1976-77; Roger Neilson, 1977-78 to 1978-79; Floyd Smith, Dick Duff and "Punch" Imlach, 1979-80; "Punch" Imlach, Joe Crozier and Mike Nykoluk, 1980-81; Mike Nykoluk, 1981-82 to 1983-84; Dan Maloney, 1984-85 to 1985-86; John Brophy, 1986-87 to 1987-88; John Brophy and George Armstrong, 1988-89; Doug Carpenter, 1989-90; Doug Carpenter and Tom Watt, 1990-91; Tom Watt, 1991-92; Pat Burns, 1992-93 to 1994-95; Pat Burns and Nick Beverley, 1995-96; Mike Murphy, 1996-97.

Club Directory

Maple Leaf Gardens
60 Carlton Street
Toronto, Ontario M5B 1L1
Phone **416/977-1641**
FAX 416/977-5364
Capacity: 15,746 (standing 100)

Board of Directors
Brian P. Bellmore, Robert G. Bertram, William T. Brock, J. Donald Crump, George J. Engman, Terence V. Kelly, Q.C., Ted Nikolaou, W. Ron Pringle, Steve A. Stavro, Larry Tanenbaum, George E. Whyte, Q.C.

Management
Chairman of the Board and CEO	Steve A. Stavro
President, Chief Operating Officer and General Manager	Cliff Fletcher
Secretary-Treasurer	J. Donald Crump
Alternate Governor	Cliff Fletcher
Alternate Governor	Brian P. Bellmore
Assistant General Manager	Bill Watters
Special Consultant to the President	Darryl Sittler
Director of Scouting and Player Personnel	Nick Beverley
Director of Professional Development	Floyd Smith
Head Coach	Mike Murphy
Assistant Coach	Mike Kitchen
Assistant Coach	Terry Simpson
Goaltending Consultant/Pro Scout	Rick Wamsley
Pro Scout	Mike Foligno
Pro Scout	Tom Watt
Scouting Coordinator	Dan Marr
Scouts	George Armstrong, John Choyce, Anders Hedberg, Mark Hillier, Peter Johnson, Garth Malarchuk, Dick Bouchard, Jack Gardiner, Bob Johnson, Ernie Gare, Doug Woods

St. John's Maple Leafs
Head Coach	Mark Hunter
Assistant Coach	Rich Brown
Equipment Manager	Jim Carey
Athletic Therapist	Nick Addey-Jibb

Hockey Administration
Director of Business Operations and Communications	Bob Stellick
Travel Coordinator	Mary Speck
Administrative Assistant	Brenda Powers
Manager, Media Relations	Pat Park
Communications Coordinator	Casey Vanden Heuvel
Community Relations Coordinator	Kristy Fletcher
Community Relations Coordinator	Angela McManus
Executive Secretary to the President and G.M.	Shelley Usher
Executive Assistant to the Directors	Paul Perantinos

Medical and Training Staff
Head Athletic Therapist	Chris Broadhurst
Athletic Therapist	Brent Smith
Trainer	Brian Papineau
Trainer	Dave Aleo
Team Doctors	Dr. Michael Clarfield, Dr. Darrell Ogilvie-Harris, Dr. Leith Douglas, Dr. Rob Devenyi, Dr. Simon McGrail
Team Dentist	Dr. Ernie Lewis
Team Psychologist	Robert Offenberger, Ph.D.

Marketing and Promotions
Director of Marketing	Bill Cluff
Marketing and Promotions Manager	Denis Cordick
Marketing Representative	Chris Reed
Luxury Suites Coordinator	Nancy Read
Promotions Assistant	Mike Ferriman
Promotions Assistant	Nancy Gilks
Marketing Assistant	Christine McKenna

Retail
Retail Operations Manager	Jeff Newman
Assistant to Retail Operations	Ugo Naccarato

Ticketing
Box Office Manager	Donna Henderson
Box Office Coordinator	Bonnie Fox
Box Office Coordinator	Stephen Nichol

Finance and Building Operations
Vice-President of Building Operations	Brian Conacher
Controller	Ian Clarke
Assistant Controller	Paul Franck
Building Manager	Wayne Gillespie
Assistant Building Manager	Bernie Fournier

Vancouver Canucks

1995-96 Results: 32w-35L-15T 79PTS. Third, Pacific Division

Schedule

Oct.	Sat.	5	Calgary		Fri.	10	Hartford
	Sun.	6	at Edmonton		Sun.	12	Anaheim*
	Wed.	9	Buffalo		Tues.	14	Florida
	Sat.	12	St. Louis		Wed.	22	at Chicago
	Mon.	14	Boston*		Thur.	23	at St. Louis
	Thur.	17	at Dallas		Sat.	25	at Phoenix
	Sat.	19	at Colorado		Mon.	27	San Jose
	Wed.	23	Colorado		Thur.	30	NY Islanders
	Sat.	26	Pittsburgh	Feb.	Sat.	1	at Calgary
	Wed.	30	at Anaheim		Mon.	3	at Ottawa
Nov.	Fri.	1	at Edmonton		Tues.	4	at Pittsburgh
	Sat.	2	Calgary		Thur.	6	at Detroit
	Fri.	8	St. Louis		Sat.	8	at Toronto
	Mon.	11	at NY Rangers		Tues.	11	Washington
	Wed.	13	at NY Islanders		Sat.	15	Anaheim
	Thur.	14	at New Jersey		Tues.	18	Toronto
	Sat.	16	at Montreal		Thur.	20	at San Jose
	Tues.	19	Dallas		Sat.	22	at Los Angeles
	Thur.	21	Chicago		Sun.	23	at Anaheim
	Sat.	23	NY Rangers		Tues.	25	Montreal
	Tues.	26	at Toronto		Thur.	27	Phoenix
	Wed.	27	at Hartford	Mar.	Sat.	1	Los Angeles
	Fri.	29	at Boston*		Mon.	3	at Colorado
Dec.	Sun.	1	at Philadelphia		Wed.	5	Chicago
	Tues.	3	at Detroit		Sat.	8	Detroit
	Wed.	4	at Buffalo		Mon.	10	at Chicago
	Sat.	7	Ottawa		Tues.	11	at Washington
	Wed.	11	Colorado		Thur.	13	at Florida
	Fri.	13	at Dallas		Sat.	15	at Tampa Bay*
	Sun.	15	at St. Louis		Tues.	18	at Colorado
	Wed.	18	New Jersey		Thur.	20	San Jose
	Fri.	20	Detroit		Sat.	22	Tampa Bay
	Mon.	23	Edmonton		Mon.	24	Los Angeles
	Thur.	26	at San Jose		Wed.	26	Anaheim
	Fri.	27	at Phoenix		Sat.	29	at Calgary*
	Sun.	29	San Jose		Sun.	30	Dallas*
	Tues.	31	Philadelphia	Apr.	Fri.	4	Calgary
Jan.	Thur.	2	Los Angeles		Sat.	5	at Edmonton
	Sat.	4	Toronto		Mon.	7	at San Jose
	Mon.	6	at Anaheim		Wed.	9	Phoenix
	Tues.	7	at Los Angeles		Sat.	12	Edmonton

* Denotes afternoon game.

Year-by-Year Record

		Home			Road			Overall							
Season	GP	W	L	T	W	L	T	W	L	T	GF	GA	Pts.	Finished	Playoff Result
1995-96	82	15	19	7	17	16	8	32	35	15	278	278	79	3rd, Pacific Div.	Lost Conf. Quarter-Final
1994-95	48	10	8	6	8	10	6	18	18	12	153	148	48	2nd, Pacific Div.	Lost Conf. Semi-Final
1993-94	84	20	19	3	21	21	0	41	40	3	279	276	85	2nd, Pacific Div.	Lost Final
1992-93	84	27	11	4	19	18	5	46	29	9	346	278	101	1st, Smythe Div.	Lost Div. Final
1991-92	80	23	10	7	19	16	5	42	26	12	285	250	96	1st, Smythe Div.	Lost Div. Final
1990-91	80	18	17	5	10	26	4	28	43	9	243	315	65	4th, Smythe Div.	Lost Div. Semi-Final
1989-90	80	13	16	11	12	25	3	25	41	14	245	306	64	5th, Smythe Div.	Out of Playoffs
1988-89	80	19	15	6	14	24	2	33	39	8	251	253	74	4th, Smythe Div.	Lost Div. Semi-Final
1987-88	80	15	20	5	10	26	4	25	46	9	272	320	59	5th, Smythe Div.	Out of Playoffs
1986-87	80	17	19	4	12	24	4	29	43	8	282	314	66	5th, Smythe Div.	Out of Playoffs
1985-86	80	17	18	5	6	26	8	23	44	13	282	333	59	4th, Smythe Div.	Lost Div. Semi-Final
1984-85	80	15	21	4	10	25	5	25	46	9	284	401	59	5th, Smythe Div.	Out of Playoffs
1983-84	80	20	16	4	12	23	5	32	39	9	306	328	73	3rd, Smythe Div.	Lost Div. Semi-Final
1982-83	80	20	12	8	10	23	7	30	35	15	303	309	75	3rd, Smythe Div.	Lost Div. Semi-Final
1981-82	80	20	8	12	10	25	5	30	33	17	290	286	77	2nd, Smythe Div.	Lost Final
1980-81	80	17	12	11	11	20	9	28	32	20	289	301	76	3rd, Smythe Div.	Lost Prelim. Round
1979-80	80	14	17	9	13	20	7	27	37	16	256	281	70	3rd, Smythe Div.	Lost Prelim. Round
1978-79	80	15	18	7	10	24	6	25	42	13	217	291	63	2nd, Smythe Div.	Lost Prelim. Round
1977-78	80	13	15	12	7	28	5	20	43	17	239	320	57	3rd, Smythe Div.	Out of Playoffs
1976-77	80	13	21	6	12	21	7	25	42	13	235	294	63	4th, Smythe Div.	Out of Playoffs
1975-76	80	22	11	7	11	21	8	33	32	15	271	272	81	2nd, Smythe Div.	Lost Prelim. Round
1974-75	80	23	12	5	15	20	5	38	32	10	271	254	86	1st, Smythe Div.	Lost Quarter-Final
1973-74	78	14	18	7	10	25	4	24	43	11	224	296	59	7th, East Div.	Out of Playoffs
1972-73	78	17	18	4	5	29	5	22	47	9	233	339	53	7th, East Div.	Out of Playoffs
1971-72	78	14	20	5	6	30	3	20	50	8	203	297	48	7th, East Div.	Out of Playoffs
1970-71	78	17	18	4	7	28	4	24	46	8	229	296	56	6th, East Div.	Out of Playoffs

Vancouver captain Trevor Linden continued to be a leader both on the ice and in the dressing room, finishing second in team scoring with 80 points while leading the club with 12 power-play goals.

Franchise date: May 22, 1970

PACIFIC DIVISION

27th NHL Season

1996-97 Player Personnel

FORWARDS	HT	WT	S	Place of Birth	Date	1995-96 Club
BADDUKE, John	6-2	195	R	Watson, Sask.	6/21/72	Syracuse-Wheeling
BOHONOS, Lonny	5-11	190	R	Winnipeg, Man.	5/20/73	Vancouver-Syracuse
BURE, Pavel	5-10	189	L	Moscow, USSR	3/31/71	Vancouver
COURTNALL, Russ	5-11	185	R	Duncan, B.C.	6/2/65	Vancouver
COURVILLE, Larry	6-1	180	L	Timmins, Ont.	4/2/75	Vancouver-Syracuse
DOWD, Jim	6-1	190	R	Brick, NJ	12/25/68	New Jersey-Vancouver
GELINAS, Martin	5-11	195	L	Shawinigan, Que.	6/5/70	Vancouver
GIRARD, Rick	5-11	175	L	Edmonton, Alta.	5/1/74	Syracuse
LINDEN, Trevor	6-4	210	R	Medicine Hat, Alta.	4/11/70	Vancouver
LONEY, Brian	6-2	200	R	Winnipeg, Man.	8/9/72	Vancouver-Syracuse
MOGILNY, Alexander	5-11	187	L	Khabarovsk, USSR	2/18/69	Vancouver
NASH, Tyson	6-0	180	L	Edmonton, Alta.	3/11/75	Syracuse-Raleigh
NASLUND, Markus	6-0	186	L	Ornskoldsvik, Sweden	7/30/73	Pittsburgh-Vancouver
ODJICK, Gino	6-3	210	L	Maniwaki, Que.	9/7/70	Vancouver
POLASEK, Libor	6-3	220	R	Vitkovice, Czech.	4/22/74	Syracuse-HC Vitkovice
PROSOFSKY, Tyler	5-11	175	L	Saskatoon, Sask.	2/19/76	Kelowna
RIDLEY, Mike	6-0	195	L	Winnipeg, Man.	7/8/63	Vancouver
ROBERTS, David	6-0	185	L	Alameda, CA	5/28/70	St. Louis-Worcester-Edmonton
RUCHTY, Matthew	6-1	225	L	Kitchener, Ont.	11/27/69	Syracuse-Atlanta
SAVENKO, Bogdan	6-1	192	R	Kiev, USSR	11/20/74	Syracuse
SILLINGER, Mike	5-10	190	R	Regina, Sask.	6/29/71	Anaheim-Vancouver
STEVENS, Rod	5-10	175	L	Fort St. John, B.C.	4/5/74	Syracuse
TIKKANEN, Esa	6-1	190	L	Helsinki, Finland	1/25/65	St. Louis-New Jersey-Vancouver
DEFENSEMEN						
AUCOIN, Adrian	6-1	194	R	Ottawa, Ont.	7/3/73	Vancouver-Syracuse
BABYCH, Dave	6-2	215	L	Edmonton, Alta.	5/23/61	Vancouver
CULLIMORE, Jassen	6-5	225	L	Simcoe, Ont.	12/4/72	Vancouver
HEDICAN, Bret	6-2	195	L	St. Paul, MN	8/10/70	Vancouver
KUCERA, Frantisek	6-2	205	R	Prague, Czech.	2/3/68	Hartford-Vancouver
LUMME, Jyrki	6-1	205	L	Tampere, Finland	7/16/66	Vancouver
MALKOC, Dean	6-3	200	L	Vancouver, B.C.	1/26/70	Vancouver
McALLISTER, Chris	6-7	238	L	Saskatoon, Sask.	6/16/75	Syracuse
MURZYN, Dana	6-2	200	L	Calgary, Alta.	12/9/66	Vancouver
NAMESTNIKOV, Yevgeny	5-11	190	R	Arzamis-lg, USSR	10/9/71	Syracuse-Vancouver
OKTYABREV, Artur	5-11	183	L	Irkutsk, USSR	11/26/73	Syracuse
ROBERTSSON, Bert	6-2	198	L	Sodertalje, Sweden	6/30/74	Syracuse
ROHLIN, Leif	6-1	198	L	Vasteras, Sweden	2/26/68	Vancouver
TULLY, Brent	6-3	195	R	Peterborough, Ont.	3/26/74	Syracuse
WALKER, Scott	5-9	180	R	Montreal, Que.	7/19/73	Vancouver-Syracuse
WOTTON, Mark	5-11	187	L	Foxwarren, Man.	11/16/73	Syracuse

GOALTENDERS	HT	WT	C	Place of Birth	Date	1995-96 Club
CUGNET, Jason	6-1	176	L	North Battleford, Sask.	7/31/76	Kelowna
FOUNTAIN, Mike	6-1	176	L	North York, Ont.	1/26/72	Syracuse
HIRSCH, Corey	5-10	160	L	Medicine Hat, Alta.	7/1/72	Vancouver
McLEAN, Kirk	6-0	195	L	Willowdale, Ont.	6/26/66	Vancouver
TKACHENKO, Sergei	6-2	198	L	Kiev, USSR	6/6/71	Oklahoma City-Syracuse-Raleigh

Coach

RENNEY, TOM
Coach, Vancouver Canucks. Born in Cranbrook, B.C.

Tom Renney was named head coach of the Vancouver Canucks on June 4, 1996. Renney, a native of Cranbrook, B.C., joined the National Team program at the beginning of the 1992-93 season and was appointed head coach in August of 1993. Renney coached Canada's National Team to a bronze medal at the 1995 World Championships and won the silver medal at the 1996 World Championships in Vienna, Austria.

Tom Renney coached Canada's Olympic Hockey Team to a silver medal-victory at the 1994 Olympic Winter Games in Lillehammer, Norway and coached the gold medal-winning team at the 1994 World Hockey Championships in Milan, Italy.

Renney, 41, coached the Kamloops Blazers to two WHL regular season pennants during the 1990-91 and the 1991-92 seasons, posting a record of 101 wins, 37 losses and six ties. Under the guidance of Renney, the Kamloops Blazers became the 1991-92 Canadian Hockey League's Memorial Cup champions.

Renney has been honored with the following awards: Sport British Columbia Coach of the Year in 1991-92, 3M Coaches Canada Award, and WHL coach of the year in 1990-91. He was an assistant coach for the Canadian team at the International Ice Hockey Federation's 1992 World Junior Championship in Fussen, Germany and in the summer of 1992, was the head coach of Canada's National Under-18 Team winning the Phoenix Cup in Japan.

Tom Renney graduated from the University of North Dakota with a degree in physical education. Tom and his wife Glenda have two daughters; Jessica and Jamie.

Coaching Record

		Regular Season					Playoffs, Olympics, or World Championships				
Year	Team	Games	W	L	T	%	Games	W	L	T	%
1990-91	Kamloops (WHL)	72	50	20	2	.708	12	5	7	0	.417
1991-92	Kamloops (WHL)	72	51	17	4	.736	16	11	5	0	.647
1993-94	Canadian National	63	33	26	4	.556	8	5	2	1	.688*
1994-95	Canadian National	57	37	17	3	.675	8	4	2	2	.625**
1995-96	Canadian National	53	33	12	8	.698	8	4	2	2	.625***

* Olympics (silver medal)
** World Championships (bronze)
*** World Championships (silver)

1995-96 Scoring

* – rookie

Regular Season

Pos	#	Player	Team	GP	G	A	Pts	+/-	PIM	PP	SH	GW	GT	S	%
R	89	Alexander Mogilny	VAN	79	55	52	107	14	16	10	5	6	3	292	18.8
R	16	Trevor Linden	VAN	82	33	47	80	6	42	12	1	2	0	202	16.3
C	7	Cliff Ronning	VAN	79	22	45	67	16	42	5	0	1	1	187	11.8
R	9	Russ Courtnall	VAN	81	26	39	65	25	40	6	4	4	2	205	12.7
L	23	Martin Gelinas	VAN	81	30	26	56	8	59	3	4	5	1	181	16.6
R	22	Markus Naslund	PIT	66	19	33	52	17	36	3	0	4	0	125	15.2
			VAN	10	3	0	3	3	6	1	0	1	0	19	15.8
			TOTAL	76	22	33	55	20	42	4	0	5	0	144	15.3
D	21	Jyrki Lumme	VAN	80	17	37	54	-9	50	8	0	2	2	192	8.9
L	10	Esa Tikkanen	STL	11	1	4	5	1	18	0	1	0	0	19	5.3
			N.J.	9	0	2	2	-6	4	0	0	0	0	15	0.0
			VAN	38	13	24	37	6	14	8	0	2	0	61	21.3
			TOTAL	58	14	30	44	1	36	8	1	2	0	95	14.7
C	14	Jesse Belanger	FLA	63	17	21	38	-5	10	7	0	1	0	140	12.1
			VAN	9	3	0	3	0	4	1	0	1	0	11	27.3
			TOTAL	72	20	21	41	-5	14	8	0	2	0	151	13.2
R	26	Mike Sillinger	ANA	62	13	21	34	-20	32	7	0	2	0	143	9.1
			VAN	12	1	3	4	2	6	0	1	0	0	16	6.3
			TOTAL	74	14	24	38	-18	38	7	1	2	0	159	8.8
D	3	Bret Hedican	VAN	77	6	23	29	8	83	1	0	0	0	113	5.3
D	44	Dave Babych	VAN	53	3	21	24	-5	38	3	0	0	0	69	4.3
D	27	Leif Rohlin	VAN	56	6	16	22	0	32	1	0	0	0	72	8.3
C	17	Mike Ridley	VAN	37	6	15	21	-3	29	2	0	1	0	32	18.8
C	42	Josef Beranek	VAN	61	6	14	20	-11	60	0	0	1	0	131	4.6
C	15	Jim Dowd	N.J.	28	4	9	13	-1	17	0	0	0	0	41	9.8
			VAN	38	1	6	7	-8	6	0	0	0	0	35	2.9
			TOTAL	66	5	15	20	-9	23	0	0	0	0	76	6.6
D	6	* Adrian Aucoin	VAN	49	4	14	18	8	34	2	0	0	0	85	4.7
L	96	Pavel Bure	VAN	15	6	7	13	-2	8	1	1	0	0	78	7.7
D	24	* Scott Walker	VAN	63	4	8	12	-7	137	0	1	1	0	45	8.9
D	5	Dana Murzyn	VAN	69	2	10	12	9	130	0	0	0	0	68	2.9
D	2	Frantisek Kucera	HFD	30	2	6	8	-3	10	0	0	1	0	43	4.7
			VAN	24	1	0	1	5	10	0	0	0	0	34	2.9
			TOTAL	54	3	6	9	2	20	0	0	1	0	77	3.9
L	29	Gino Odjick	VAN	55	3	4	7	-16	181	0	0	0	0	59	5.1
R	25	Jim Sandlak	VAN	33	4	2	6	-3	6	0	1	1	0	44	9.1
R	36	* Brian Loney	VAN	12	2	3	5	2	6	0	0	0	1	19	10.5
R	28	Joey Kocur	NYR	38	1	2	3	-4	49	0	0	0	0	19	5.3
			VAN	7	0	1	1	-3	19	0	0	0	0	1	0.0
			TOTAL	45	1	3	4	-7	68	0	0	0	0	20	5.0
R	19	Tim Hunter	VAN	60	2	0	2	-8	122	0	0	1	0	26	7.7
D	34	Jassen Cullimore	VAN	27	1	1	2	4	21	0	0	1	0	12	8.3
D	32	* Dean Malkoc	VAN	41	0	2	2	-10	136	0	0	0	0	8	0.0
G	31	* Corey Hirsch	VAN	41	0	2	2	0	2	0	0	0	0	0	0.0
G	1	Kirk McLean	VAN	45	0	2	2	0	6	0	0	0	0	0	0.0
L	14	* Larry Courville	VAN	3	1	0	1	1	0	0	0	1	0	2	50.0
R	14	* Lonny Bohonos	VAN	3	0	1	1	1	0	0	0	0	0	3	0.0

Goaltending

No.	Goaltender	GPI	Mins	Avg	W	L	T	EN	SO	GA	SA	S%
31	* Corey Hirsch	41	2338	2.93	17	14	6	4	1	114	1173	.903
1	Kirk McLean	45	2645	3.54	15	21	9	4	2	156	1292	.879
	Totals	**82**	**5003**	**3.33**	**32**	**35**	**15**	**8**	**3**	**278**	**2473**	**.888**

Playoffs

Pos	#	Player	Team	GP	G	A	Pts	+/-	PIM	PP	SH	GW	OT	S	%
R	89	Alexander Mogilny	VAN	6	1	8	9	-1	8	0	0	0	0	18	5.6
R	16	Trevor Linden	VAN	6	4	4	8	-1	6	2	0	0	0	14	28.6
L	10	Esa Tikkanen	VAN	6	3	2	5	-3	2	2	0	0	0	13	23.1
L	29	Gino Odjick	VAN	6	3	1	4	2	6	0	0	2	0	6	50.0
R	9	Russ Courtnall	VAN	6	1	3	4	-4	2	0	0	0	0	8	12.5
D	21	Jyrki Lumme	VAN	6	1	3	4	-1	2	1	0	0	0	13	7.7
C	42	Josef Beranek	VAN	3	2	1	3	0	0	0	0	0	0	7	28.6
R	22	Markus Naslund	VAN	6	1	2	3	-2	8	1	0	0	0	16	6.3
L	23	Martin Gelinas	VAN	6	1	1	2	-1	12	1	0	0	0	8	12.5
C	14	Jesse Belanger	VAN	3	0	2	2	0	2	0	0	0	0	3	0.0
C	7	Cliff Ronning	VAN	6	0	2	2	0	6	0	0	0	0	12	0.0
D	2	Frantisek Kucera	VAN	6	0	1	1	-3	0	0	0	0	0	6	0.0
D	3	Bret Hedican	VAN	6	0	1	1	-2	10	0	0	0	0	2	0.0
R	28	Joey Kocur	VAN	1	0	0	0	0	0	0	0	0	0	0	0.0
G	1	Kirk McLean	VAN	1	0	0	0	0	0	0	0	0	0	0	0.0
C	15	Jim Dowd	VAN	1	0	0	0	-1	0	0	0	0	0	0	0.0
D	20	Yevgeny Namestnikov	VAN	1	0	0	0	0	0	0	0	0	0	1	0.0
C	17	Mike Ridley	VAN	5	0	0	0	-3	2	0	0	0	0	3	0.0
R	25	Jim Sandlak	VAN	5	0	0	0	2	2	0	0	0	0	5	0.0
D	27	Leif Rohlin	VAN	5	0	0	0	-1	0	0	0	0	0	7	0.0
D	5	Dana Murzyn	VAN	6	0	0	0	0	25	0	0	0	0	2	0.0
R	26	Mike Sillinger	VAN	6	0	0	0	-5	2	0	0	0	0	5	0.0
G	31	* Corey Hirsch	VAN	6	0	0	0	0	2	0	0	0	0	0	0.0
D	6	* Adrian Aucoin	VAN	6	0	0	0	-5	2	0	0	0	0	7	0.0

Goaltending

No.	Goaltender	GPI	Mins	Avg	W	L	EN	SO	GA	SA	S%
31	* Corey Hirsch	6	338	3.73	2	3	0	0	21	166	.873
1	Kirk McLean	1	21	8.57	0	1	0	0	3	12	.750
	Totals	**6**	**361**	**3.99**	**2**	**4**	**0**	**0**	**24**	**178**	**.865**

General Managers' History

Normand Robert Poile, 1970-71 to 1972-73; Hal Laycoe, 1973-74; Phil Maloney, 1974-75 to 1976-77; Jake Milford, 1977-78 to 1981-82; Harry Neale, 1982-83 to 1984-85; Jack Gordon, 1985-86 to 1986-87; Pat Quinn, 1987-88 to date.

Club Records

Team

(Figures in brackets for season records are games played; records for fewest points, wins, ties, losses, goals, goals against are for 70 or more games)

Most Points	**101**	1992-93 (84)
Most Wins	**46**	1992-93 (84)
Most Ties	**20**	1980-81 (80)
Most Losses	**50**	1971-72 (78)
Most Goals	**346**	1992-93 (84)
Most Goals Against	**401**	1984-85 (80)
Fewest Points	**48**	1971-72 (78)
Fewest Wins	**20**	1971-72 (78), 1977-78 (80)
Fewest Ties	**3**	1993-94 (84)
Fewest Losses	**26**	1991-92 (80)
Fewest Goals	**203**	1971-72 (78)
Fewest Goals Against	**250**	1991-92 (80)
Longest Winning Streak		
Overall	**7**	Feb. 10-23/89
Home	**9**	Nov. 6-Dec. 9/92
Away	**5**	Jan. 14-25/92, Oct. 6-Nov. 2/93
Longest Undefeated Streak		
Overall	**10**	Mar. 5-25/77 (5 wins, 5 ties)
Home	**18**	Oct. 30/92-Jan. 18/93 (16 wins, 2 ties)
Away	**5**	Five times
Longest Losing Streak		
Overall	**9**	Four times
Home	**6**	Dec. 18/70-Jan. 20/71
Away	**12**	Nov. 28/81-Feb. 7/82
Longest Winless Streak		
Overall	**13**	Nov. 9-Dec. 7/73 (10 losses, 3 ties)
Home	**11**	Dec. 18/70-Feb. 6/71 (10 losses, 1 tie)
Away	**20**	Jan. 2-Apr. 2/86 (14 losses, 6 ties)
Most Shutouts, Season	**8**	1974-75 (80)
Most PIM, Season	**2,326**	1992-93 (84)
Most Goals, Game	**11**	Mar. 28/71 (Cal. 5 at Van. 11), Nov. 25/86 (L.A. 5 at Van. 11), Mar. 1/92 (Cgy. 0 at Van. 11)

Individual

Most Seasons	**13**	Stan Smyl
Most Games	**896**	Stan Smyl
Most Goals, Career	**262**	Stan Smyl
Most Assists, Career	**411**	Stan Smyl
Most Points, Career	**673**	Stan Smyl (262G, 411A)
Most PIM, Career	**1,668**	Garth Butcher
Most Shutouts, Career	**19**	Kirk McLean
Longest Consecutive Games Streak	**458**	Trevor Linden (Oct. 4/90-present)
Most Goals, Season	**60**	Pavel Bure (1992-93, 1993-94)
Most Assists, Season	**62**	André Boudrias (1974-75)
Most Points, Season	**110**	Pavel Bure (1992-93; 60G, 50A)
Most PIM, Season	**370**	Gino Odjick (1992-93)
Most Points, Defenseman, Season	**63**	Doug Lidster (1986-87; 12G, 51A)
Most Points, Center, Season	**91**	Patrik Sundstrom (1983-84; 38G, 53A)
Most Points, Right Wing, Season	**110**	Pavel Bure (1992-93; 60G, 50A)
Most Points, Left Wing, Season	**81**	Darcy Rota (1982-83; 42G, 39A)
Most Points, Rookie, Season	**60**	Ivan Hlinka (1981-82; 23G, 37A), Pavel Bure (1991-92; 34G, 26A)
Most Shutouts, Season	**6**	Gary Smith (1974-75)
Most Goals, Game	**4**	Several players
Most Assists, Game	**6**	Patrik Sundstrom (Feb. 29/84)
Most Points, Game	**7**	Patrik Sundstrom (Feb. 29/84; 1G, 6A)

Retired Numbers

12	Stan Smyl	1978-1991

Captains' History

Orland Kurtenbach, 1970-71 to 1973-74; no captain, 1974-75; Andre Boudrias, 1975-76; Chris Oddleifson, 1976-77; Don Lever, 1977-78; Don Lever and Kevin McCarthy, 1978-79; Kevin McCarthy, 1979-80 to 1981-82; Stan Smyl, 1982-83 to 1989-90; Dan Quinn, Doug Lidster and Trevor Linden, 1990-91; Trevor Linden, 1991-92 to date.

Coaching History

Hal Laycoe, 1970-71 to 1971-72; Vic Stasiuk, 1972-73; Bill McCreary and Phil Maloney, 1973-74; Phil Maloney, 1974-75 to 1975-76; Phil Maloney and Orland Kurtenbach, 1976-77; Orland Kurtenbach, 1977-78; Harry Neale, 1978-79 to 1980-81; Harry Neale and Roger Neilson, 1981-82; Roger Neilson 1982-83; Roger Neilson and Harry Neale, 1983-84; Harry Neale and Bill Laforge, 1984-85; Tom Watt, 1985-86, 1986-87; Bob McCammon, 1987-88 to 1989-90. Bob McCammon and Pat Quinn, 1990-91; Pat Quinn, 1991-92 to 1993-94; Rick Ley, 1994-95; Rick Ley and Pat Quinn, 1995-96; Tom Renney, 1996-97.

All-time Record vs. Other Clubs

Regular Season

	At Home							On Road							Total						
	GP	W	L	T	GF	GA	PTS	GP	W	L	T	GF	GA	PTS	GP	W	L	T	GF	GA	PTS
Anaheim	8	5	3	0	29	20	10	8	5	2	1	22	15	11	16	10	5	1	51	35	21
Boston	45	14	23	8	150	191	36	44	5	35	4	102	194	14	89	19	58	12	252	385	50
Buffalo	45	22	13	10	173	148	54	46	15	23	8	133	164	38	91	37	36	18	306	312	92
Calgary	77	28	33	16	274	261	72	77	14	52	11	218	341	39	154	42	85	27	492	602	111
Chicago	56	26	17	13	174	164	65	55	13	37	5	129	215	31	111	39	54	18	303	379	96
Colorado	25	11	10	4	105	107	26	25	11	9	5	74	71	27	50	22	19	9	179	178	53
Dallas	55	25	20	10	213	174	60	55	14	31	10	161	220	38	110	39	51	20	374	394	98
Detroit	49	24	18	7	192	158	55	50	14	30	6	147	210	34	99	38	48	13	339	368	89
Edmonton	61	23	30	8	236	257	54	59	14	40	5	187	292	33	120	37	70	13	423	549	87
Florida	2	1	1	0	8	4	2	2	0	1	1	3	4	1	4	1	2	1	11	8	3
Hartford	24	9	9	6	85	71	24	23	9	10	4	79	76	22	47	18	19	10	164	147	46
Los Angeles	79	41	25	13	318	262	95	82	29	41	12	277	338	70	161	70	66	25	595	600	165
Montreal	44	7	29	8	109	176	22	46	8	35	3	122	228	19	90	15	64	11	231	404	41
New Jersey	42	24	7	11	162	121	59	42	18	18	6	141	132	42	84	42	25	17	303	253	101
NY Islanders	42	19	20	3	141	141	41	40	10	22	8	107	152	28	82	29	42	11	248	293	69
NY Rangers	46	11	32	3	146	190	25	48	7	36	5	119	220	19	94	18	68	8	265	410	44
Ottawa	3	2	0	1	10	4	5	3	2	1	0	10	4	4	6	4	1	1	20	8	9
Philadelphia	46	10	24	12	136	179	32	46	14	31	1	137	205	29	92	24	55	13	273	384	61
Pittsburgh	44	20	21	3	163	172	43	44	8	29	7	149	202	23	88	28	50	10	312	374	66
St. Louis	56	24	25	7	173	176	55	55	17	30	8	164	207	42	111	41	55	15	337	383	97
San Jose	15	12	2	1	64	33	25	15	8	5	2	56	52	18	30	20	7	3	120	85	43
Tampa Bay	4	4	0	0	23	5	8	3	2	1	0	12	10	4	7	6	1	0	35	15	12
Toronto	49	25	15	9	167	162	59	51	19	23	9	176	194	47	100	44	38	18	343	356	106
Washington	33	15	13	5	113	107	35	34	11	19	4	103	120	26	67	26	32	9	216	227	61
Winnipeg	56	32	16	8	217	164	72	53	20	25	8	204	207	48	109	52	41	16	421	371	120
Defunct Clubs	19	14	3	2	82	48	30	19	10	8	1	71	68	21	38	24	11	3	153	116	51
Totals	**1025**	**448**	**409**	**168**	**3663**	**3495**	**1064**	**1025**	**297**	**594**	**134**	**3103**	**4141**	**728**	**2050**	**745**	**1003**	**302**	**6766**	**7636**	**1792**

Playoffs

	Series	W	L	GP	W	L	T	GF	GA	Last Mtg.	Round	Result
Buffalo	2	0	2	7	1	6	0	14	28	1981	PR	L 0-3
Calgary	5	2	3	25	12	13	0	80	82	1994	CQF	W 4-3
Chicago	2	1	1	9	4	5	0	24	24	1995	CSF	L 0-4
Colorado	1	0	1	6	2	4	0	17	24	1996	CQF	L 2-4
Dallas	1	1	0	5	4	1	0	18	11	1994	CSF	W 4-1
Edmonton	2	0	2	9	2	7	0	20	35	1992	DF	L 2-4
Los Angeles	3	1	2	17	8	9	0	60	66	1993	DF	L 2-4
Montreal	1	0	1	5	1	4	0	9	20	1975	QF	L 1-4
NY Islanders	2	0	2	6	0	6	0	14	26	1982	F	L 0-4
NY Rangers	1	0	1	7	3	4	0	19	21	1994	F	L 3-4
Philadelphia	1	0	1	3	1	2	0	9	15	1979	PR	L 1-2
St. Louis	1	1	0	7	4	3	0	27	27	1995	CQF	W 4-3
Toronto	1	1	0	5	4	1	0	16	9	1994	CF	W 4-1
Winnipeg	2	2	0	13	8	5	0	50	34	1993	DSF	W 4-2
Totals	**25**	**9**	**16**	**124**	**54**	**70**	**0**	**377**	**422**			

Playoff Results 1996-92

Year	Round	Opponent	Result	GF	GA
1996	CQF	Colorado	L 2-4	17	24
1995	CSF	Chicago	L 0-4	6	11
	CQF	St. Louis	W 4-3	27	27
1994	F	NY Rangers	L 3-4	19	21
	CF	Toronto	W 4-1	16	9
	CSF	Dallas	W 4-1	18	11
	CQF	Calgary	W 4-3	23	20
1993	DF	Los Angeles	L 2-4	25	26
	DSF	Winnipeg	W 4-2	21	17
1992	DF	Edmonton	L 2-4	15	18
	DSF	Winnipeg	W 4-3	29	17

Abbreviations: Round: F – Final; **CF** – conference final; **CQF** – conference quarter-final; **CSF** – conference semi-final; **DF** – division final; **DSF** – division semi-final; **SF** – semi-final; **QF** – quarter-final; **PR** – preliminary round.

Calgary totals include Atlanta, 1972-73 to 1979-80. Colorado totals include Quebec, 1979-80 to 1994-95.
Dallas totals include Minnesota, 1970-71 to 1992-93.
New Jersey totals include Kansas City, 1974-75 to 1975-76, and Colorado Rockies, 1976-77 to 1981-82.

1995-96 Results

Oct.	9		Detroit	3-5		13	at	Toronto	5-2
	12	at	Los Angeles	7-7		15	at	Boston	6-0
	14	at	San Jose	7-6		16	at	Hartford	0-3
	15		Los Angeles	3-3		22		Dallas	4-6
	18	at	Anaheim	5-1		24		Anaheim	1-2
	21	at	Edmonton	4-6		25	at	Colorado	2-2
	24	at	NY Rangers	2-5		27		NY Islanders	6-3
	25	at	New Jersey	4-2		30		New Jersey	2-3
	28		Winnipeg	1-4	**Feb.**	1	at	St. Louis	2-2
	30		San Jose	4-3		2	at	Dallas	5-4
Nov.	1		Edmonton	3-3		4	at	Winnipeg	4-2
	3		Toronto	4-4		7		Hartford	3-5
	4	at	Calgary	4-4		9	at	Edmonton	3-2
	7	at	NY Islanders	5-2		10		Washington	4-4
	9	at	Chicago	2-5		13		Winnipeg	5-4
	11		Colorado	4-8		15		Anaheim	5-3
	12		Montreal	2-4		17		Boston	1-4
	16	at	Florida	2-2		19	at	Detroit	3-4
	18	at	Tampa Bay	4-5		21	at	Winnipeg	5-3
	19	at	Philadelphia	2-3		23		San Jose	3-1
	22	at	Dallas	3-4		27		Pittsburgh	4-7
	23	at	St. Louis	3-2		29		St. Louis	2-2
	25	at	San Jose	2-7	**Mar.**	2	at	Detroit	3-2
	29		Chicago	2-2		3	at	Buffalo	3-0
Dec.	1		San Jose	7-2		6		Buffalo	5-2
	5		Edmonton	6-2		9		Colorado	5-7
	8		St. Louis	3-6		12	at	Washington	0-9
	9	at	Calgary	4-3		14	at	Chicago	1-5
	13	at	Edmonton	2-2		15	at	Ottawa	0-2
	17		Ottawa	4-1		17	at	Toronto	2-4
	18	at	Colorado	4-2		19		Colorado	3-4
	20	at	Los Angeles	2-2		22		Dallas	5-2
	22	at	Anaheim	6-2		23		Calgary	0-4
	23		Detroit	0-1		25		Los Angeles	4-1
	26		Calgary	2-4		27		Toronto	2-6
	28		NY Rangers	2-3		29		Chicago	4-2
	31		Philadelphia	5-5	**Apr.**	1		Edmonton	2-6
Jan.	3		Florida	7-2		3	at	Calgary	3-4
	6		Tampa Bay	9-2		6	at	Los Angeles	4-2
	8	at	Pittsburgh	5-8		8	at	Anaheim	0-2
	10	at	Montreal	2-2		13		Calgary	5-0

Entry Draft Selections 1996-82

1996
Pick
12 Josh Holden
75 Zenith Komarniski
93 Jonas Soling
121 Tyler Prosofsky
147 Nolan McDonald
175 Clint Cabana
201 Jeff Scissons
227 Lubomir Vaic

1995
Pick
40 Chris McAllister
61 Larry Courville
66 Peter Schaefer
92 Lloyd Shaw
120 Todd Norman
144 Brent Sopel
170 Stewart Bodtker
196 Tyler Willis
222 Jason Cugnet

1994
Pick
13 Mattias Ohlund
39 Robb Gordon
42 Dave Scatchard
65 Chad Allan
92 Mike Dubinsky
117 Yanick Dube
169 Yuri Kuznetsov
195 Rob Trumbley
221 Bill Muckalt
247 Tyson Nash
273 Robert Longpre

1993
Pick
20 Mike Wilson
46 Rick Girard
98 Dieter Kochan
124 Scott Walker
150 Troy Creurer
176 Yevgeny Babariko
202 Sean Tallaire
254 Bert Robertsson
280 Sergei Tkachenko

1992
Pick
21 Libor Polasek
40 Mike Peca
45 Michael Fountain
69 Jeff Connolly
93 Brent Tully
110 Brian Loney
117 Adrian Aucoin
141 Jason Clark
165 Scott Hollis
213 Sonny Mignacca
237 Mark Wotton
261 Aaron Boh

1991
Pick
7 Alex Stojanov
29 Jassen Cullimore
51 Sean Pronger
95 Danny Kesa
117 Evgeny Namestnikov
139 Brent Thurston
161 Eric Johnson
183 David Neilson
205 Brad Barton
227 Jason Fitzsimmons
249 Xavier Majic

1990
Pick
2 Petr Nedved
18 Shawn Antoski
23 Jiri Slegr
65 Darin Bader
86 Gino Odjick
128 Daryl Filipek
149 Paul O'Hagan
170 Mark Cipriano
191 Troy Neumier
212 Tyler Ertel
233 Karri Kivi

1989
Pick
8 Jason Herter
29 Robert Woodward
71 Brett Hauer
113 Pavel Bure
134 James Revenberg
155 Rob Sangster
176 Sandy Moger
197 Gus Morschauser
218 Hayden O'Rear
239 Darcy Cahill
248 Jan Bergman

1988
Pick
2 Trevor Linden
33 Leif Rohlin
44 Dane Jackson
107 Corrie D'Alessio
122 Phil Von Stefenelli
128 Dixon Ward
149 Greg Geldart
170 Roger Akerstrom
191 Paul Constantin
212 Chris Wolanin
233 Stefan Nilsson

1987
Pick
24 Rob Murphy
45 Steve Veilleux
66 Doug Torrel
87 Sean Fabian
108 Garry Valk
129 Todd Fanning
150 Viktor Tumenev
171 Craig Daly
192 John Fletcher
213 Roger Hansson
233 Neil Eisenhut
234 Matt Evo

1986
Pick
7 Dan Woodley
49 Don Gibson
70 Ronnie Stern
91 Eric Murano
112 Steve Herniman
133 Jon Helgeson
154 Jeff Noble
175 Matt Merton
196 Marc Lyons
217 Todd Hawkins
238 Vladimir Krutov

1985
Pick
4 Jim Sandlak
25 Troy Gamble
46 Shane Doyle
67 Randy Siska
88 Robert Kron
109 Martin Hrstka
130 Brian McFarlane
151 Hakan Ahlund
172 Curtis Hunt
193 Carl Valimont
214 Igor Larionov
235 Darren Taylor

1984
Pick
10 J.J. Daigneault
31 Jeff Rohlicek
52 Dave Saunders
55 Landis Chaulk
58 Mike Stevens
73 Brian Bertuzzi
94 Brett MacDonald
115 Jeff Korchinski
136 Blaine Chrest
157 Jim Agnew
178 Rex Grant
198 Ed Lowney
219 Doug Clarke
239 Ed Kister

1983
Pick
9 Cam Neely
30 Dave Bruce
50 Scott Tottle
70 Tim Lorentz
90 Doug Quinn
110 Dave Lowry
130 Terry Maki
150 John Labatt
170 Allan Measures
190 Roger Grillo
210 Steve Kayser
230 Jay Mazur

1982
Pick
11 Michel Petit
53 Yves Lapointe
71 Shawn Kilroy
116 Taylor Hall
137 Parie Proft
158 Newell Brown
179 Don McLaren
200 Al Raymond
221 Steve Driscoll
242 Shawn Green

General Manager

QUINN, PAT
President and General Manager, Vancouver Canucks.
Born in Hamilton, Ont., January 29, 1943.

After guiding the Vancouver Canucks to their third straight season with 40+ wins and a berth in the Stanley Cup finals in 1994, Pat Quinn stepped down as the most successful coach in club history. In 1995-96, he completed his ninth season with the organization, concentrating on his duties as president, general manager and alternate governor. He also stepped behind the bench late in the season after replacing coach Rick Ley.

When Quinn joined the Canucks in 1987, he inherited a team that had endured 11 consecutive losing seasons. In just five years, he turned the club around, posting the franchise's first 40-win campaign in 1991-92. He has also earned a reputation as an outstanding judge of talent and a shrewd negotiator, acquiring numerous players that have helped the club through deals at the NHL's annual trading deadline. He was named *The Hockey News* executive of the year in 1992 and was runner-up for the award in 1994. Last season, he received the Jake Milford Award recognizing his contributions to hockey in British Columbia.

In three-and-a-half seasons as head coach, Quinn posted a .554 winning percentage and a record of 132-108-28, four victories shy of the club's coaching record. Under Quinn, the Canucks set single-season records for wins (48) and points (101) in 1992-93.

Quinn accepted the position of Vancouver's president and g.m. on January 9, 1987 and officially became the club's seventh g.m. on May 1, 1987. He added the coaching portfolio on January 31, 1991. In 1992, he won the Jack Adams Award as the NHL's coach of the year for the second time in his career and is one of only two coaches to win the award with two different teams.

He previously coached in Los Angeles from 1984 to 1987 and in Philadelphia from 1978 to 1982. In 1979-80, his Flyers were the NHL's top team (48-12-20) and posted a 35-game undefeated streak, earning Quinn his first NHL coach of the year honors. After leaving the Flyers, Quinn earned his law degree from Delaware Law School. As a player, he was an NHL defenseman who played 606 games over nine years with Vancouver, Toronto and Atlanta. An original member of the 1970-71 Canucks, he finished his NHL career with 18 goals, 113 assists and 950 penalty minutes.

Club Directory

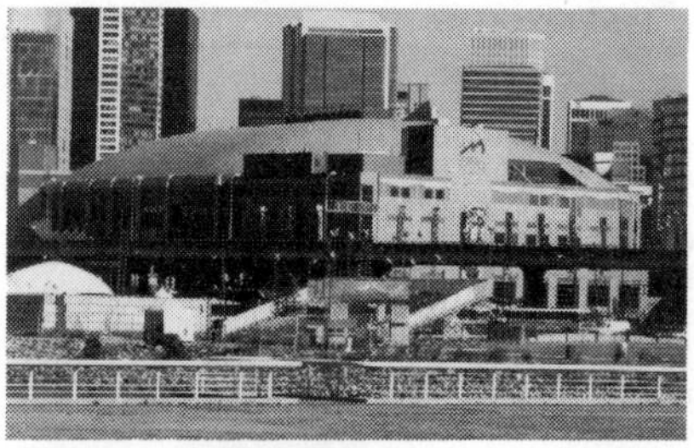

General Motors Place
800 Griffiths Way
Vancouver, B.C. V6B 6G1
Phone **604/899-4600**
FAX 604/899-4640
Capacity: 18,422

Orca Bay Sports & Entertainment
Chairman and Governor, NHL and NBA .... John E. McCaw, Jr.
Vice-Chairman, CEO and Alternate Governor, NHL and NBA .... Arthur R. Griffiths
Vice-Chairman, Orca Bay Sports & Entertainment .. Stanley B. McCammon
President and Chief Operating Officer Orca Bay Sports & Entertainment .... John H. Chapple
President, General Manager & Alternate Governor, Vancouver Canucks .... J.B. Patrick Quinn
President, General Manager, Vancouver Grizzlies... Tod Leiweke

Vancouver Canucks Staff
President, General Manager and Alternate Governor .... J.B. Patrick Quinn
Executive Assistant to President/GM .... Carolyn Marchese-Blanche
Vice President, Hockey Operations and Alternate Governor .... George McPhee
Executive Assistant to Hockey Operations .... Jeanne Mayne
Vice-President, Business Operations .... Steve Tambellini
Executive Assistant to Business Operations .... Kalli Quinn
Vice President, Finance, Hockey Operations .... Carlos Mascarenhas
Director, Scouting and Player Personnel .... Mike Penny
Assistant, Hockey Operations .... Frank Provenzano
Manager, Media Relations and Hockey Information . Devin Smith
Manager, Community Relations .... Veronica Varhaug
Community Relations Assistant .... Lisa Ryan
Office Assistant .... Brenda Eastcott
Head Coach .... Tom Renney
Assistant Coach .... Stan Smyl
Assistant Coach .... Glen Hanlon
Assistant Coach .... Terry Bangen
Strength and Conditioning Coach .... Peter Twist
Video Coordinator .... Doug Cole
Medical Trainer .... Mike Burnstein
Massage Therapist .... Dave Schima
Equipment Manager .... Pat O'Neill
Assistant Equipment Manager .... Darren Granger
Team Doctors .... Dr. Ross Davidson, Dr. Doug Clement
Team Dentist .... Dr. David Lawson
Team Chiropractor .... Dr. Sid Sheard
Head Coach/Syracuse Crunch .... Jack McIlhargey
Medical Trainer/Syracuse Crunch .... Ralph Krugler
Equipment Manager/Syracuse Crunch .... Rodney Blachford
Director of Pro Scouting .... Murray Oliver
Scouts .... Mike Backman, Jack Birch, Sergei Chibisov, Ron Delorme, Jim Eagle, Thomas Gradin, Rick Ley, Jack McCartan, Ed McColgan, Ray Miron, Ken Slater

Orca Bay Sports & Entertainment
Vice-President & Chief Financial Officer .... David Cobb
Vice-President, Corporate Communications and Community Investment .... Kevin Gass
Vice-President, People Development, Administration & Customer Care .... Linda McKenna
Vice-President, Business Development .... Leila Bell-Irving
Director of Business Development .... Ric Thomsen
Manager, Corporate Service .... Dave Cannon
Vice-President, Consumer Sales and Service .... John Rizzardini
Director, Customer Sales and Service .... John Rocha
Manager, Customer Communications .... Marla Taner
Account Manager .... Kelly Smith
Account Manager .... Reid Mitchell
Customer Sales and Service Assistant .... Michelle Carriere
Vice-President, Broadcast .... Chris Hebb
Director, Game Presentation and Special Events.... Greg von Schottenstein
Assistant Director, Game Presentation and Special Events .... Jane Bremmer
Game Presentation and Special Events Coordinator . Stephanie Willox
Game Presentation and Special Events Assistant.... Greg Bedard
Travel Coordinator .... Chantal Hassard
Accountant .... Mindy Chohan
Director of Publishing .... Norm Jewison
Production Coordinator .... Kathy McAdam
Editorial Coordinator .... Colin Stein

NHL Coaching Record

		Regular Season					Playoffs			
Season	**Team**	**Games**	**W**	**L**	**T**	**%**	**Games**	**W**	**L**	**%**
1978-79	Philadelphia	30	18	8	4	.667	8	3	5	.375
1979-80	Philadelphia	80	48	12	20	.725	19	13	6	.684
1980-81	Philadelphia	80	41	24	15	.606	12	6	6	.500
1981-82	Philadelphia	72	34	29	9	.535	....	....	....	....
1984-85	Los Angeles	80	34	32	14	.513	3	0	3	.000
1985-86	Los Angeles	80	23	49	8	.338	....	....	....	....
1986-87	Los Angeles	42	18	20	4	.476	....	....	....	....
1990-91	Vancouver	26	9	13	4	.423	6	2	4	.333
1991-92	Vancouver	80	42	26	12	.600	13	6	7	.462
1992-93	Vancouver	84	46	29	9	.601	12	6	6	.500
1993-94	Vancouver	84	41	40	3	.506	24	15	9	.625
1995-96	Vancouver	6	3	3	0	.500	6	2	4	.333
	NHL Totals	**744**	**357**	**285**	**102**	**.548**	**103**	**53**	**50**	**.515**

Washington Capitals

1995-96 Results: 39W-32L-11T 89PTS. Fourth, Atlantic Division

Schedule

Oct.	Sat.	5	Chicago		Thur.	9	NY Rangers
	Tues.	8	at Dallas		Sat.	11	at Philadelphia
	Fri.	11	Tampa Bay		Mon.	13	Toronto
	Sat.	12	Los Angeles		Wed.	15	at Ottawa
	Fri.	18	Buffalo		Mon.	20	at Boston*
	Sat.	19	at Pittsburgh		Wed.	22	NY Rangers
	Wed.	23	at NY Rangers		Fri.	24	Dallas
	Sat.	26	at St. Louis		Sun.	26	Edmonton*
	Mon.	28	at Colorado		Wed.	29	Philadelphia
	Wed.	30	Philadelphia	**Feb.**	Sat.	1	at Florida*
Nov.	Fri.	1	Pittsburgh		Sun.	2	at Buffalo
	Sat.	2	at NY Islanders		Fri.	7	at Calgary
	Wed.	6	at Tampa Bay		Sun.	9	at Edmonton
	Thur.	7	at Florida		Tues.	11	at Vancouver
	Sat.	9	NY Rangers		Fri.	14	Tampa Bay
	Tues.	12	at New Jersey		Sat.	15	at Tampa Bay
	Thur.	14	at Philadelphia		Tues.	18	Ottawa
	Fri.	15	Montreal		Sat.	22	at Hartford
	Mon.	18	at Florida		Mon.	24	Boston
	Tues.	19	Boston		Wed.	26	at Toronto
	Fri.	22	at New Jersey		Fri.	28	Anaheim
	Sat.	23	New Jersey	**Mar.**	Sun.	2	NY Islanders*
	Wed.	27	Ottawa		Tues.	4	Calgary
	Fri.	29	NY Islanders		Thur.	6	Colorado
	Sat.	30	at Montreal		Sun.	9	at Philadelphia*
Dec.	Wed.	4	Detroit		Tues.	11	Vancouver
	Fri.	6	Pittsburgh		Wed.	12	at NY Rangers
	Sat.	7	at NY Islanders		Sat.	15	at New Jersey*
	Wed.	11	at San Jose		Sun.	16	Hartford*
	Fri.	13	at Anaheim		Wed.	19	New Jersey
	Sat.	14	at Los Angeles		Fri.	21	Buffalo
	Tues.	17	at Phoenix		Sat.	22	at Montreal
	Fri.	20	San Jose		Tues.	25	St. Louis
	Sat.	21	at Boston		Wed.	26	at Chicago
	Mon.	23	at Tampa Bay		Sat.	29	Philadelphia
	Thur.	26	at Detroit	**Apr.**	Tues.	1	New Jersey
	Sat.	28	Florida		Thur.	3	at Ottawa
	Mon.	30	at Pittsburgh		Sun.	6	Florida*
Jan.	Wed.	1	Hartford*		Thur.	10	Montreal
	Fri.	3	Phoenix		Sat.	12	NY Islanders
	Sat.	4	at Hartford		Sun.	13	at Buffalo

* Denotes afternoon game.

A versatile centerman and crafty playmaker who is entering his 11th season in Washington, Michal Pivonka led the Capitals in scoring with 81 points (including a career-high 65 assists) during the 1995-96 season.

Franchise date: June 11, 1974

23rd NHL Season

ATLANTIC DIVISION

Year-by-Year Record

		Home			Road			Overall							Playoff Result
Season	GP	W	L	T	W	L	T	W	L	T	GF	GA	Pts.	Finished	
1995-96	82	21	15	5	18	17	6	39	32	11	234	204	89	4th, Atlantic Div.	Lost Conf. Quarter-Final
1994-95	48	15	6	3	7	12	5	22	18	8	136	120	52	3rd, Atlantic Div.	Lost Conf. Quarter-Final
1993-94	84	17	16	9	22	19	1	39	35	10	277	263	88	3rd, Atlantic Div.	Lost Conf. Semi-Final
1992-93	84	21	15	6	22	19	1	43	34	7	325	286	93	2nd, Patrick Div.	Lost Div. Semi-Final
1991-92	80	25	12	3	20	15	5	45	27	8	330	275	98	2nd, Patrick Div.	Lost Div. Semi-Final
1990-91	80	21	14	5	16	22	2	37	36	7	258	258	81	3rd, Patrick Div.	Lost Div. Final
1989-90	80	19	18	3	17	20	3	36	38	6	284	275	78	3rd, Patrick Div.	Lost Conf. Championship
1988-89	80	25	12	3	16	17	7	41	29	10	305	259	92	1st, Patrick Div.	Lost Div. Semi-Final
1987-88	80	22	14	4	16	19	5	38	33	9	281	249	85	2nd, Patrick Div.	Lost Div. Final
1986-87	80	22	15	3	16	17	7	38	32	10	285	278	86	2nd, Patrick Div.	Lost Div. Semi-Final
1985-86	80	30	8	2	20	15	5	50	23	7	315	272	107	2nd, Patrick Div.	Lost Div. Final
1984-85	80	27	11	2	19	14	7	46	25	9	322	240	101	2nd, Patrick Div.	Lost Div. Semi-Final
1983-84	80	26	11	3	22	16	2	48	27	5	308	226	101	2nd, Patrick Div.	Lost Div. Final
1982-83	80	22	12	6	17	13	10	39	25	16	306	283	94	3rd, Patrick Div.	Lost Div. Semi-Final
1981-82	80	16	16	8	10	25	5	26	41	13	319	338	65	5th, Patrick Div.	Out of Playoffs
1980-81	80	16	17	7	10	19	11	26	36	18	286	317	70	5th, Patrick Div.	Out of Playoffs
1979-80	80	20	14	6	7	26	7	27	40	13	261	293	67	5th, Patrick Div.	Out of Playoffs
1978-79	80	15	19	6	9	22	9	24	41	15	273	338	63	4th, Norris Div.	Out of Playoffs
1977-78	80	10	23	7	7	26	7	17	49	14	195	321	48	5th, Norris Div.	Out of Playoffs
1976-77	80	17	15	8	7	27	6	24	42	14	221	307	62	4th, Norris Div.	Out of Playoffs
1975-76	80	6	26	8	5	33	2	11	59	10	224	394	32	5th, Norris Div.	Out of Playoffs
1974-75	80	7	28	5	1	39	0	8	67	5	181	446	21	5th, Norris Div.	Out of Playoffs

1996-97 Player Personnel

FORWARDS	HT	WT	S	Place of Birth	Date	1995-96 Club
ALLISON, Jason	6-3	205	R	North York, Ont.	5/29/75	Washington-Portland (AHL)
BATHERSON, Norm	6-1	198	L	North Sydney, N.S.	3/27/69	Portland (AHL)
BERUBE, Craig	6-1	205	L	Calahoo, Alta.	12/17/65	Washington
BONDRA, Peter	6-1	200	L	Luck, USSR	2/7/68	Detroit (IHL)-Washington
BRUNETTE, Andrew	6-0	212	L	Sudbury, Ont.	8/24/73	Washington-Portland (AHL)
BULIS, Jan	6-0	194	L	Pardubice, Czech.	3/18/78	Barrie
CHURCH, Brad	6-1	210	L	Dauphin, Man.	11/14/76	Prince Albert
DAVIS, Justin	6-2	175	R	Burlington, Ont.	3/1/78	Kingston
EAGLES, Mike	5-10	190	L	Sussex, N.B.	3/7/63	Washington
ELOMO, Miika	6-0	180	L	Turku, Finland	4/21/77	TPS-Kiekko-67-TPS
GENDRON, Martin	5-9	190	R	Valleyfield, Que.	2/15/74	Washington-Portland (AHL)
GRATTON, Benoit	5-10	163	L	Montreal, Que.	12/28/76	Laval-Granby
HAY, Dwayne	6-1	183	L	London, Ont.	2/11/77	Guelph
HULST, Kent	6-0	180	L	St. Thomas, Ont.	4/8/68	Portland (AHL)
HUNTER, Dale	5-10	198	L	Petrolia, Ont.	7/31/60	Washington
JONES, Keith	6-2	200	L	Brantford, Ont.	11/8/68	Washington
JUNEAU, Joe	6-0	195	R	Pont-Rouge, Que.	1/5/68	Washington
KAMINSKI, Kevin	5-10	190	L	Churchbridge, Sask.	3/13/69	Washington
KHARLAMOV, Alexander	5-10	180	L	Moscow, USSR	9/23/75	Portland (AHL)
KLEE, Ken	6-1	205	R	Indianapolis, IN	4/24/71	Washington
KONOWALCHUK, Steve	6-1	195	L	Salt Lake City, UT	11/11/72	Washington
KRYGIER, Todd	6-0	185	L	Chicago Heights, MI	10/12/65	Anaheim-Washington
LAHEY, Matthew	6-1	216	L	Ottawa, Ont.	10/12/77	Peterborough
MCNEIL, Shawn	5-11	175	L	Pembroke, Ont.	3/17/78	Kamloops
MILLER, Kelly	5-11	197	L	Lansing, MI	3/3/63	Washington
NELSON, Jeff	6-0	190	L	Prince Albert, Sask.	12/18/72	Washington-Portland (AHL)
PEAKE, Pat	6-1	195	R	Rochester, MI	5/28/73	Washington
PIVONKA, Michal	6-2	195	L	Kladno, Czech.	1/28/66	Detroit (IHL)-Washington
POIRIER, Joel	6-1	190	L	Richmond Hill, Ont.	1/15/75	Portland (AHL)-Hampton Rds.
SVEJKOVSKY, Jaroslav	5-11	185	R	Plzen, Czech.	10/1/76	Tri-City
USTORF, Stefan	6-0	185	L	Kaufbeuren, Germany	1/3/74	Washington-Portland (AHL)
VOLCHKOV, Alexander	6-1	194	L	Moscow, USSR	9/25/77	Barrie
ZEDNIK, Richard	5-11	172	L	Bystrica, Czech.	1/6/76	Wsh-Port (WHL)-Port (AHL)
DEFENSEMEN						
BAUMGARTNER, Nolan	6-1	200	R	Calgary, Alta.	3/23/76	Kamloops-Washington
BOILEAU, Patrick	6-0	190	R	Montreal, Que.	2/22/75	Portland (AHL)
CHARRON, Eric	6-3	192	L	Verdun, Que.	1/14/70	T.B.-Wsh-Portland (AHL)
CORT, Joel	6-3	227	L	Hamilton, Ont.	4/30/77	Guelph
COTE, Sylvain	6-0	190	R	Quebec City, Que.	1/19/66	Washington
GONCHAR, Sergei	6-2	212	L	Chelyabinsk, USSR	4/13/74	Washington
HOUSLEY, Phil	5-10	185	L	St. Paul, MN	3/9/64	Calgary-New Jersey
JOBIN, Frederic	6-0	210	L	Montreal, Que.	1/28/77	Granby-Laval
JOHANSSON, Calle	5-11	200	L	Goteborg, Sweden	2/14/67	Washington
LAPERRIERE, Daniel	6-1	195	L	Laval, Que.	3/28/69	Ott-P.E.I.-Atlanta-Kansas City
MALGUNAS, Stewart	6-0	200	L	Prince George, B.C.	4/21/70	Wpg-Wsh-Portland (AHL)
POAPST, Steve	6-0	200	L	Cornwall, Ont.	1/3/69	Washington-Portland (AHL)
REEKIE, Joe	6-3	220	L	Victoria, B.C.	2/22/65	Washington
THERIAULT, Joel	6-3	201	R	Montreal, Que.	10/30/76	Halifax-Drummondville
TINORDI, Mark	6-4	213	L	Red Deer, Alta.	5/9/66	Washington
TURKOVSKY, Vasili	6-2	198	L	Saratov, USSR	9/3/74	CSKA
WITT, Brendan	6-1	205	L	Humbolt, Sask.	2/20/75	Washington

GOALTENDERS	HT	WT	C	Place of Birth	Date	1995-96 Club
CAREY, Jim	6-2	205	L	Dorchester, MA	5/31/74	Washington
CHARPENTIER, Sebastien	5-9	161	L	Drummondville, Que.	4/18/77	Laval-Val d'Or
KOLZIG, Olaf	6-3	225	L	Johannesburg, South Africa	4/9/70	Washington-Portland (AHL)
STAUBER, Robb	5-11	180	L	Duluth, MN	11/25/67	Rochester

Coach

SCHOENFELD, JAMES GRANT (JIM)
Coach, Washington Capitals. Born in Galt, Ont., September 4, 1952.

Youth and consistency have been trademarks for the Washington Capitals as Jim Schoenfeld begins his 4th season as head coach. Having made the playoffs in each of the last three seasons, Schoenfeld has proven he has what it takes to be a coach in the NHL.

Along with general manager David Poile, he has rebuilt his hockey club. This strategy is paying off as Peter Bondra, Michal Pivonka and goalie Jim Carey have rewritten the Capitals record books.

Schoenfeld's coaching career began in the Buffalo organization with Rochester of the AHL in 1984-85. He briefly returned to the NHL as a player before taking over as coach of the Sabres in 1985-86. He had coached 43 games when g.m. Scotty Bowman opted to return as head coach. Schoenfeld's next head coaching job was in 1988 with New Jersey when he led the Devils to within one game of the Stanley Cup finals.

Schoenfeld's success as a head coach in the NHL is shadowed only by his illustrious playing career, which spanned 13 years and three teams. Beginning in Buffalo, where he spent the majority of his career, Schoenfeld was voted top rookie defenseman for the 1972 season. His lifetime totals include 719 games played, 51 goals, 204 assists, and 1,132 penalty minutes. Last season, Schoenfeld became a member of the Sabres Hall of Fame.

Jim and Theresa, along with their four children, live in Annapolis, Maryland.

Coaching Record

		Regular Season					Playoffs			
Season	Team	Games	W	L	T	%	Games	W	L	%
1984-85	Rochester (AHL)	25	17	6	2	.720	....	....	....	....
1985-86	**Buffalo (NHL)**	**43**	**19**	**19**	**5**	**.500**	....	....	....	....
1987-88	**New Jersey (NHL)**	**30**	**17**	**12**	**1**	**.583**	**20**	**11**	**9**	**.550**
1988-89	**New Jersey (NHL)**	**80**	**27**	**41**	**12**	**.413**	....	....	....	....
1989-90	**New Jersey (NHL)**	**14**	**6**	**6**	**2**	**.500**	....	....	....	....
1993-94	**Washington (NHL)**	**37**	**19**	**12**	**6**	**.595**	**11**	**5**	**6**	**.455**
1994-95	**Washington (NHL)**	**48**	**22**	**18**	**8**	**.542**	**7**	**3**	**4**	**.429**
1995-96	**Washington (NHL)**	**82**	**39**	**32**	**11**	**.543**	**6**	**2**	**4**	**.333**
	NHL Totals	**334**	**149**	**140**	**45**	**.513**	**44**	**21**	**23**	**.477**

1995-96 Scoring

* – rookie

Regular Season

Pos	#	Player	Team	GP	G	A	Pts	+/–	PIM	PP	SH	GW	GT	S	%
C	20	Michal Pivonka	WSH	73	16	65	81	18	36	6	2	5	0	168	9.5
R	12	Peter Bondra	WSH	67	52	28	80	18	40	11	4	7	3	322	16.1
C	90	Joe Juneau	WSH	80	14	50	64	–3	30	7	2	2	0	176	8.0
L	21	Todd Krygier	ANA	60	9	28	37	–9	70	2	1	0	1	153	5.9
			WSH	16	6	5	11	8	12	1	0	0	0	28	21.4
			TOTAL	76	15	33	48	–1	82	3	1	0	1	181	8.3
C	22	Steve Konowalchuk	WSH	70	23	22	45	13	92	7	1	3	0	197	11.7
R	9	Keith Jones	WSH	68	18	23	41	8	103	5	0	2	0	155	11.6
D	55	Sergei Gonchar	WSH	78	15	26	41	25	60	4	0	4	0	139	10.8
D	3	Sylvain Cote	WSH	81	5	33	38	5	40	3	0	2	0	212	2.4
C	32	Dale Hunter	WSH	82	13	24	37	5	112	4	0	3	2	128	10.2
C	14	Pat Peake	WSH	62	17	19	36	7	46	8	0	3	0	129	13.2
D	6	Calle Johansson	WSH	78	10	25	35	13	50	4	0	0	0	182	5.5
L	10	Kelly Miller	WSH	74	7	13	20	7	30	0	2	1	0	93	7.5
R	16 *	Stefan Ustorf	WSH	48	7	10	17	8	14	0	0	1	0	39	17.9
D	24	Mark Tinordi	WSH	71	3	10	13	26	113	2	0	0	0	82	3.7
L	27	Craig Berube	WSH	50	2	10	12	1	151	1	0	1	0	28	7.1
D	2 *	Ken Klee	WSH	66	8	3	11	–1	60	0	1	2	0	76	10.5
C	36	Mike Eagles	WSH	70	4	7	11	–1	75	0	0	0	0	70	5.7
D	29	Joe Reekie	WSH	78	3	7	10	7	149	0	0	0	0	52	5.8
C	11 *	Jeff Nelson	WSH	33	0	7	7	3	16	0	0	0	0	21	0.0
L	18 *	Andrew Brunette	WSH	11	3	3	6	5	0	0	0	1	0	16	18.8
D	4	Jim Johnson	WSH	66	2	4	6	–3	34	0	0	0	0	49	4.1
D	19 *	Brendan Witt	WSH	48	2	3	5	–4	85	0	0	1	0	44	4.5
R	34 *	Martin Gendron	WSH	20	2	1	3	–5	8	0	0	0	0	22	9.1
C	23	Kevin Kaminski	WSH	54	1	2	3	–1	164	0	0	0	0	17	5.9
C	41 *	Jason Allison	WSH	19	0	3	3	–3	2	0	0	0	0	18	0.0
D	15	Steve Poapst	WSH	3	1	0	1	–1	0	0	0	1	0	2	50.0
D	28	Eric Charron	T.B.	14	0	0	0	–6	18	0	0	0	0	11	0.0
			WSH	4	0	1	1	3	4	0	0	0	0	2	0.0
			TOTAL	18	0	1	1	–3	22	0	0	0	0	13	0.0
D	26	Stewart Malgunas	WPG	29	0	1	1	–10	32	0	0	0	0	13	0.0
			WSH	1	0	0	0	0	0	0	0	0	0	0	0.0
			TOTAL	30	0	1	1	–10	32	0	0	0	0	13	0.0
G	30	Jim Carey	WSH	71	0	1	1	0	6	0	0	0	0	0	0.0
D	38 *	Nolan Baumgartner	WSH	1	0	0	0	–1	0	0	0	0	0	0	0.0
L	8 *	Richard Zednik	WSH	1	0	0	0	0	0	0	0	0	0	0	0.0
G	37	Olaf Kolzig	WSH	18	0	0	0	0	2	0	0	0	0	0	0.0

Goaltending

No.	Goaltender	GPI	Mins	Avg	W	L	T	EN	SO	GA	SA	S%
30	Jim Carey	71	4069	2.26	35	24	9	4	9	153	1631	.906
37	Olaf Kolzig	18	897	3.08	4	8	2	1	0	46	406	.887
	Totals	**82**	**4990**	**2.45**	**39**	**32**	**11**	**5**	**9**	**204**	**2042**	**.900**

Playoffs

Pos	#	Player	Team	GP	G	A	Pts	+/–	PIM	PP	SH	GW	OT	S	%
C	90	Joe Juneau	WSH	5	0	7	7	–4	6	0	0	0	0	20	0.0
D	55	Sergei Gonchar	WSH	6	2	4	6	–1	4	1	0	0	0	29	6.9
C	32	Dale Hunter	WSH	6	1	5	6	4	24	0	0	0	0	14	7.1
R	12	Peter Bondra	WSH	6	3	2	5	0	8	2	0	1	0	36	8.3
C	20	Michal Pivonka	WSH	6	3	2	5	1	18	1	0	0	0	17	17.6
L	18 *	Andrew Brunette	WSH	6	1	3	4	–5	0	0	0	0	0	7	14.3
C	14	Pat Peake	WSH	5	2	1	3	–4	12	2	0	0	0	9	22.2
D	3	Sylvain Cote	WSH	6	2	0	2	–3	12	1	0	0	0	25	8.0
L	21	Todd Krygier	WSH	6	2	0	2	–3	12	0	0	1	0	15	13.3
C	36	Mike Eagles	WSH	6	1	1	2	1	2	0	0	0	0	12	8.3
C	22	Steve Konowalchuk	WSH	2	0	2	2	1	0	0	0	0	0	1	0.0
L	10	Kelly Miller	WSH	6	0	1	1	–1	4	0	0	0	0	11	0.0
D	2 *	Ken Klee	WSH	1	0	0	0	0	0	0	0	0	0	2	0.0
D	38 *	Nolan Baumgartner	WSH	1	0	0	0	–1	10	0	0	0	0	0	0.0
L	27	Craig Berube	WSH	2	0	0	0	–1	19	0	0	0	0	3	0.0
R	9	Keith Jones	WSH	2	0	0	0	–1	7	0	0	0	0	3	0.0
C	23	Kevin Kaminski	WSH	3	0	0	0	0	16	0	0	0	0	1	0.0
C	11 *	Jeff Nelson	WSH	3	0	0	0	0	4	0	0	0	0	2	0.0
G	30	Jim Carey	WSH	3	0	0	0	0	0	0	0	0	0	0	0.0
G	37	Olaf Kolzig	WSH	5	0	0	0	0	4	0	0	0	0	0	0.0
R	16 *	Stefan Ustorf	WSH	5	0	0	0	–1	0	0	0	0	0	9	0.0
D	4	Jim Johnson	WSH	6	0	0	0	–2	6	0	0	0	0	15	0.0
D	24	Mark Tinordi	WSH	6	0	0	0	–2	16	0	0	0	0	9	0.0
D	28	Eric Charron	WSH	6	0	0	0	1	8	0	0	0	0	2	0.0
D	15	Steve Poapst	WSH	6	0	0	0	0	0	0	0	0	0	6	0.0

Goaltending

No.	Goaltender	GPI	Mins	Avg	W	L	EN	SO	GA	SA	S%
37	Olaf Kolzig	5	341	1.94	2	3	0	0	11	167	.934
30	Jim Carey	3	97	6.19	0	1	0	0	10	39	.744
	Totals	**6**	**439**	**2.87**	**2**	**4**	**0**	**0**	**21**	**206**	**.898**

General Managers' History

Milt Schmidt, 1974-75; Milt Schmidt and Max McNab, 1975-76; Max McNab, 1976-77 to 1980-81; Max McNab and Roger Crozier, 1981-82; David Poile, 1982-83 to date.

Coaching History

Jim Anderson, "Red" Sullivan and Milt Schmidt, 1974-75; Milt Schmidt and Tom McVie, 1975-76; Tom McVie, 1976-77 to 1977-78; Danny Belisle, 1978-79; Danny Belisle and Gary Green, 1979-80; Gary Green, 1980-81; Gary Green, Roger Crozier and Bryan Murray, 1981-82; Bryan Murray, 1982-83 to 1988-89; Bryan Murray and Terry Murray, 1989-90; Terry Murray, 1990-91 to 1992-93; Terry Murray and Jim Schoenfeld, 1993-94; Jim Schoenfeld, 1994-95 to date.

Club Records

Team

(Figures in brackets for season records are games played; records for fewest points, wins, ties, losses, goals, goals against are for 70 or more games)

Most Points	107	1985-86 (80)
Most Wins	50	1985-86 (80)
Most Ties	18	1980-81 (80)
Most Losses	67	1974-75 (80)
Most Goals	330	1991-92 (80)
Most Goals Against	*446	1974-75 (80)
Fewest Points	*21	1974-75 (80)
Fewest Wins	*8	1974-75 (80)
Fewest Ties	5	1974-75 (80), 1983-84 (80)
Fewest Losses	23	1985-86 (80)
Fewest Goals	181	1974-75 (80)
Fewest Goals Against	204	1995-96 (82)

Longest Winning Streak

Overall	10	Jan. 27-Feb. 18/84
Home	8	Feb. 1-Mar. 11/86, Mar. 3-Apr. 1/89
Away	6	Feb. 26-Apr. 1/84

Longest Undefeated Streak

Overall	14	Nov. 24-Dec. 23/82 (9 wins, 5 ties)
Home	13	Nov. 25/92-Feb. 2/93 (9 wins, 4 ties)
Away	10	Nov. 24/82-Jan. 8/83 (6 wins, 4 ties)

Longest Losing Streak

Overall	*17	Feb. 18-Mar. 26/75
Home	*11	Feb. 18-Mar. 30/75
Away	37	Oct. 9/74-Mar. 26/75

Longest Winless Streak

Overall	25	Nov. 29/75-Jan. 21/76 (22 losses, 3 ties)
Home	14	Dec. 3/75-Jan. 21/76 (11 losses, 3 ties)
Away	37	Oct. 9/74-Mar. 26/75 (37 losses)

Most Shutouts, Season	9	1995-96 (82)
Most PIM, Season	2,204	1989-90 (80)
Most Goals, Game	12	Feb. 6/90 (Que. 2 at Wsh. 12)

Individual

Most Seasons	11	Rod Langway
Most Games	758	Mike Gartner
Most Goals, Career	397	Mike Gartner
Most Assists, Career	392	Mike Gartner
Most Points, Career	789	Mike Gartner (397G, 392A)
Most PIM, Career	1,673	Dale Hunter
Most Shutouts, Career	13	Jim Carey
Longest Consecutive Games Streak	422	Bob Carpenter
Most Goals, Season	60	Dennis Maruk (1981-82)
Most Assists, Season	76	Dennis Maruk (1981-82)
Most Points, Season	136	Dennis Maruk (1981-82; 60G, 76A)
Most PIM, Season	339	Alan May (1989-90)

Most Points, Defenseman, Season	81	Larry Murphy (1986-87; 23G, 58A)
Most Points, Center, Season	136	Dennis Maruk (1981-82; 60G, 76A)
Most Points, Right Wing, Season	102	Mike Gartner (1984-85; 50G, 52A)
Most Points, Left Wing, Season	87	Ryan Walter (1981-82; 38G, 49A)
Most Points, Rookie, Season	67	Bobby Carpenter (1981-82; 32G, 35A), Chris Valentine (1981-82; 30G, 37A)
Most Shutouts, Season	9	Jim Carey (1995-96)
Most Goals, Game	5	Bengt Gustafsson (Jan. 8/84), Peter Bondra (Feb. 5/94)
Most Assists, Game	6	Mike Ridley (Jan. 7/89)
Most Points, Game	7	Dino Ciccarelli (Mar. 18/89; 4G, 3A)

* NHL Record.

Retired Numbers

7	Yvon Labre	1974-1981

Captains' History

Doug Mohns, 1974-75; Bill Clement and Yvon Labre, 1975-76; Yvon Labre, 1976-77, 1977-78; Guy Charron, 1978-79; Ryan Walter, 1979-80 to 1981-82; Rod Langway, 1982-83 to 1991-92; Rod Langway and Kevin Hatcher, 1992-93; Kevin Hatcher, 1993-94; Dale Hunter, 1994-95 to date.

All-time Record vs. Other Clubs

Regular Season

			At Home							On Road							Total			
	GP	W	L	T	GF	GA	PTS	GP	W	L	T	GF	GA	PTS	GP	W	L	T	GF	GA	PTS
Anaheim	2	1	1	0	4	2	2	2	1	0	1	7	4	3	4	2	1	1	11	6	5
Boston	39	10	21	8	117	150	28	40	12	23	5	113	160	29	79	22	44	13	230	310	57
Buffalo	40	10	23	7	110	151	27	40	7	28	5	106	170	19	80	17	51	12	216	321	46
Calgary	34	16	13	5	130	123	37	33	6	22	5	81	144	17	67	22	35	10	211	267	54
Chicago	34	19	11	4	128	106	42	33	8	20	5	100	136	21	67	27	31	9	228	242	63
Colorado	27	15	9	3	110	87	33	27	12	11	4	103	90	28	54	27	20	7	213	177	61
Dallas	34	14	13	7	108	106	35	33	11	14	8	98	125	30	67	25	27	15	206	231	65
Detroit	39	20	15	4	154	124	44	41	13	17	11	121	146	37	80	33	32	15	275	270	81
Edmonton	23	13	8	2	102	84	28	23	10	9	4	80	89	24	46	23	17	6	182	173	52
Florida	7	3	3	1	22	19	7	7	2	3	2	16	23	6	14	5	6	3	38	42	13
Hartford	28	16	10	2	98	82	34	29	15	10	4	106	85	34	57	31	20	6	204	167	68
Los Angeles	39	17	16	6	170	147	40	40	12	24	4	125	162	28	79	29	40	10	295	309	68
Montreal	43	18	18	7	118	139	43	44	8	30	6	89	193	22	87	26	48	13	207	332	65
New Jersey	61	40	18	3	258	182	83	61	27	27	7	189	196	61	122	67	45	10	447	378	144
NY Islanders	63	27	27	9	205	214	63	64	25	38	1	204	258	51	127	52	65	10	409	472	114
NY Rangers	66	32	25	9	253	225	73	65	26	33	6	234	263	58	131	58	58	15	487	488	131
Ottawa	8	7	0	1	44	14	15	7	5	1	1	34	25	11	15	12	1	2	78	39	26
Philadelphia	63	24	27	12	219	219	60	65	22	39	4	186	249	48	128	46	66	16	405	468	108
Pittsburgh	70	36	28	6	305	263	78	67	26	35	6	225	268	58	137	62	63	12	530	531	136
St. Louis	33	18	12	3	122	99	39	34	12	14	8	114	140	32	67	30	26	11	236	239	71
San Jose	4	3	1	0	15	9	6	4	3	1	0	15	12	6	8	6	2	0	30	21	12
Tampa Bay	9	3	2	4	24	19	10	8	6	1	1	26	12	13	17	9	3	5	50	31	23
Toronto	36	22	12	2	136	99	46	35	11	20	4	123	170	26	71	33	32	6	259	269	72
Vancouver	34	19	11	4	120	103	42	33	13	15	5	107	113	31	67	32	26	9	227	216	73
Winnipeg	23	15	5	3	105	71	33	24	7	12	5	89	91	19	47	22	17	8	194	162	52
Defunct Clubs	10	2	8	0	28	42	4	10	4	5	1	30	39	9	20	6	13	1	58	81	13
Totals	**869**	**420**	**337**	**112**	**3205**	**2879**	**952**	**869**	**304**	**452**	**113**	**2721**	**3363**	**721**	**1738**	**724**	**789**	**225**	**5926**	**6242**	**1673**

Playoffs

	Series	W	L	GP	W	L	T	GF	GA	Last Mtg.	Round	Result
Boston	1	0	1	4	0	4	0	6	15	1990	CF	L 0-4
New Jersey	2	1	1	13	7	6	0	44	43	1990	DSF	W 4-2
NY Islanders	6	1	5	30	12	18	0	88	89	1993	DSF	L 2-4
NY Rangers	4	2	2	22	11	11	0	75	71	1994	CSF	L 1-4
Philadelphia	3	2	1	16	9	7	0	65	55	1989	DSF	L 2-4
Pittsburgh	5	1	4	31	13	18	0	103	106	1996	CQF	L 2-4
Totals	**21**	**7**	**14**	**116**	**52**	**64**	**0**	**381**	**389**			

Playoff Results 1996-92

Year	Round	Opponent	Result	GF	GA
1996	CQF	Pittsburgh	L 3-4	17	21
1995	CQF	Pittsburgh	L 3-4	26	29
1994	CSF	NY Rangers	L 1-4	12	20
	CQF	Pittsburgh	W 4-2	20	12
1993	DSF	NY Islanders	L 2-4	22	23
1992	DSF	Pittsburgh	L 3-4	27	25

Abbreviations: Round: F – Final;
CF – conference final; CQF – conference quarter-final;
CSF – conference semi-final; DF – division final;
DSF – division semi-final; SF – semi-final;
QF – quarter-final; PR – preliminary round.

Calgary totals include Atlanta, 1974-75 to 1979-80.   Colorado totals include Quebec, 1979-80 to 1994-95.
Dallas totals include Minnesota, 1974-75 to 1992-93.
New Jersey totals include Kansas City, 1974-75 to 1975-76, and Colorado Rockies, 1976-77 to 1981-82.

1995-96 Results

Oct.	7		St. Louis	4-1		13	Detroit	2-4
	11	at	Philadelphia	1-2		16	Winnipeg	1-1
	13		Colorado	3-1		17	at Chicago	3-2
	14		Tampa Bay	2-0		23	Florida	4-5
	17	at	Dallas	4-3		25	at New Jersey	1-3
	18	at	Colorado	2-4		26	Buffalo	2-2
	20		Los Angeles	4-7		28	Philadelphia	3-2
	26	at	Boston	4-2		31	at Montreal	3-5
	28	at	Tampa Bay	4-2	Feb. 1	at Ottawa	4-2
	29	at	St. Louis	3-1		3	NY Islanders	6-5
Nov.	1		Montreal	5-2		7	at Edmonton	2-1
	3		Florida	2-3		8	at Calgary	4-4
	4	at	NY Islanders	3-2		10	at Vancouver	4-4
	7		Boston	3-4		13	Calgary	3-2
	10	at	Toronto	1-6		15	at Detroit	3-4
	11		Chicago	1-4		16	Toronto	4-3
	14		Philadelphia	2-2		18	at New Jersey	0-3
	17		Pittsburgh	2-3		22	at Philadelphia	1-5
	18	at	Pittsburgh	0-3		24	New Jersey	1-2
	21		San Jose	3-2		27	at NY Rangers	5-3
	24		Tampa Bay	1-2		29	at Florida	2-2
	25	at	Hartford	4-2	Mar. 2	at Boston	2-2
	29	at	Anaheim	2-2		3	Philadelphia	3-0
	30	at	Los Angeles	2-3		9	NY Rangers	1-6
Dec.	2	at	San Jose	3-5		10	at Tampa Bay	0-1
	5		Florida	3-4		12	Vancouver	9-0
	8	at	Buffalo	2-2		15	Boston	2-5
	10	at	Winnipeg	6-1		17	Dallas	2-1
	14		NY Islanders	4-3		19	Anaheim	1-2
	16		NY Rangers	3-2		21	at Tampa Bay	3-3
	18	at	NY Rangers	0-3		23	Hartford	2-2
	22		Edmonton	6-3		26	at NY Islanders	7-1
	23	at	NY Islanders	1-3		27	at Montreal	1-0
	26		Montreal	4-0		29	Ottawa	3-3
	28	at	Florida	5-4		31	Tampa Bay	1-1
	30		Hartford	3-0	Apr. 3	at Buffalo	5-1
Jan.	1		Pittsburgh	4-2		4	at Pittsburgh	2-4
	3	at	Hartford	0-2		6	at Ottawa	4-2
	5		NY Rangers	4-4		10	at NY Rangers	4-1
	6	at	New Jersey	1-3		11	New Jersey	2-3
	11		Ottawa	6-1		13	Buffalo	2-3

Entry Draft
Selections 1996-82

1996
Pick
4	Alexander Volchkov
17	Jaroslav Svejkovsky
43	Jan Bulis
58	Sergei Zimakov
74	Dave Weninger
78	Shawn McNeil
85	Justin Davis
126	Matthew Lahey
153	Andrew Van Bruggen
180	Michael Anderson
206	Oleg Orekhovsky
232	Chad Cavanagh

1995
Pick
17	Brad Church
23	Miikka Elomo
43	Dwayne Hay
93	Sebasti Charpentier
95	Joel Theriault
105	Benoit Gratton
124	Joel Cort
147	Frederick Jobin
199	Vasili Turkovsky
225	Scott Swanson

1994
Pick
10	Nolan Baumgartner
15	Alexander Kharlamov
41	Scott Cherrey
93	Matthew Herr
119	Yanick Jean
145	Dmitri Mekeshkin
171	Daniel Reja
197	Chris Patrick
223	John Tuohy
249	Richard Zednik
275	Sergei Tertyshny

1993
Pick
11	Brendan Witt
17	Jason Allison
69	Patrick Boileau
147	Frank Banham
173	Daniel Hendrickson
174	Andrew Brunette
199	Joel Poirier
225	Jason Gladney
251	Mark Seliger
277	Dany Bousquet

1992
Pick
14	Sergei Gonchar
32	Jim Carey
53	Stefan Ustorf
71	Martin Gendron
119	John Varga
167	Mark Matier
191	Mike Mathers
215	Brian Stagg
239	Gregory Callahan
263	Billy Jo MacPherson

1991
Pick
14	Pat Peake
21	Trevor Halverson
25	Eric Lavigne
36	Jeff Nelson
58	Steve Konowalchuk
80	Justin Morrison
146	Dave Morissette
168	Rick Corriveau
190	Trevor Duhaime
209	Rob Leask
212	Carl LeBlanc
234	Rob Puchniak
256	Bill Kovacs

1990
Pick
9	John Slaney
30	Rod Pasma
51	Chris Longo
72	Randy Pearce
93	Brian Sakic
94	Mark Ouimet
114	Andrei Kovalev
135	Roman Kontsek
156	Peter Bondra
159	Steve Martell
177	Ken Klee
198	Michael Boback
219	Alan Brown
240	Todd Hlushko

1989
Pick
19	Olaf Kolzig
35	Byron Dafoe
59	Jim Mathieson
61	Jason Woolley
82	Trent Klatt
145	Dave Lorentz
166	Dean Holoien
187	Victor Gervais
208	Jiri Vykoukal
229	Andrei Sidorov
250	Ken House

1988
Pick
15	Reginald Savage
36	Tim Taylor
41	Wade Bartley
57	Duane Derksen
78	Rob Krauss
120	Dmitri Khristich
141	Keith Jones
144	Brad Schlegel
162	Todd Hilditch
183	Petr Pavlas
192	Mark Sorensen
204	Claudio Scremin
225	Chris Venkus
246	Ron Pascucci

1987
Pick
36	Jeff Ballantyne
57	Steve Maltais
78	Tyler Larter
99	Pat Beauchesne
120	Rich Defreitas
141	Devon Oleniuk
162	Thomas Sjogren
204	Chris Clarke
225	Milos Vanik
240	Dan Brettschneider
246	Ryan Kummu

1986
Pick
19	Jeff Greenlaw
40	Steve Seftel
60	Shawn Simpson
61	Jimmy Hrivnak
82	Erin Ginnell
103	John Purves
124	Stefan Nilsson
145	Peter Choma
166	Lee Davidson
187	Tero Toivola
208	Bobby Bobcock
229	John Schratz
250	Scott McCrory

1985
Pick
19	Yvon Corriveau
40	John Druce
61	Rob Murray
82	Bill Houlder
83	Larry Shaw
103	Claude Dumas
124	Doug Stromback
145	Jamie Nadjiwan
166	Mark Haarmann
187	Steve Hollett
208	Dallas Eakins
229	Steve Hrynewich
250	Frank DiMuzio

1984
Pick
17	Kevin Hatcher
34	Steve Leach
59	Michal Pivonka
80	Kris King
122	Vito Cramarossa
143	Timo Iljina
164	Frank Joo
185	Jim Thomson
205	Paul Cavallini
225	Mikhail Tatarinov
246	Per Schedrin

1983
Pick
75	Tim Bergland
95	Martin Bouliane
135	Dwaine Hutton
155	Marty Abrams
175	David Cowan
195	Yves Beaudoin
215	Alain Raymond
216	Anders Huss

1982
Pick
5	Scott Stevens
58	Milan Novy
89	Dean Evason
110	Ed Kastelic
152	Wally Schreiber
173	Jamie Reeve
194	Juha Nurmi
215	Wayne Prestage
236	Jon Holden
247	Marco Kallas

General Manager

POILE, DAVID
Vice-President, General Manager and Alternate Governor,
Washington Capitals. Born in Toronto, Ont., February 14, 1949.

On August 30, 1982, David Poile was named g.m. of the Washington Capitals. His appointment would mark an era of change for the franchise, which, previously lacking a playoff appearance, would begin a string of 14 straight entries into the post season.

In 1989, the Capitals won their first division crown with a mark of 41-29-10. A year later, Washington advanced to the Conference finals under the leadership of David Poile. Entering this season, the Capitals have become one the NHL's most consistent clubs, compiling a record of 561-414-123 during Poile's 15-year tenure.

Poile has brought the Capitals to this level through both trades and the draft. Renowned Capitals players such as Dale Hunter, Joe Juneau, Kelly Miller, and Mark Tinordi have joined the team through trades, while the draft has provided depth, adding standout players Jim Carey, Michal Pivonka, and Peter Bondra.

Entering this season, Poile is the third-longest serving general manager in the league, behind only Boston's Harry Sinden and Edmonton's Glen Sather. His 561 victories rank fourth in the league, and he has twice been honored as *The Sporting News* NHL executive of the year. In 1992, Poile, also a member of the NHL general managers committee, was a major factor in the implementation of the NHL's instant replay rule. His leadership on the issue soon won him recognition throughout the league, and he was awarded *Inside Hockey's* man of the year.

Hockey has always been a part of David Poile's life, even early on. His father, Norman "Bud" Poile, played seven seasons in the NHL, before going on to be the general manager of the Philadelphia Flyers, and later the Vancouver Canucks. In 1989 Bud was a co-winner of the Lester Patrick Award, and would be inducted to the Hockey Hall of Fame a year later. David began his career with the Atlanta Flames, where he served as General Manager for a period of six years before joining the Capitals.

David Poile's influence and leadership on the Washington Capitals has proven to be invaluable. His commitment to winning, which has produced divisional finishes of third or higher in thirteen of the last fourteen years, is evident throughout the league and the Washington area.

Poile, 47, and his wife Elizabeth, make their home in Maryland along with their two children, Brian and Lauren.

Club Directory

USAir Arena
1 Harry S Truman Drive
Landover, Maryland 20785
Phone **301/386-7000**
PR FAX 301/386-7012
Capacity: 18,130

Executive Management
Chairman	Abe Pollin
Board of Directors	David P. Bindeman, Stuart L. Bindeman, James A. Cafritz, A. James Clark, Albert Cohen, J. Martin Irving, R. Robert Linowes, Arthur K. Mason, Dr. Jack Meshel, David M. Osnos, Richard M. Patrick

Management
President and Governor	Richard M. Patrick
Legal Counsel and Alternate Governor	David M. Osnos
Vice-President of Finance	Edmund Stelzer

Hockey Operations
Vice-President/General Manager	David Poile
Head Coach	Jim Schoenfeld
Assistant Coaches	Keith Allain, Tod Button
Head Trainer	Stan Wong
Assistant Trainer/Equipment Manager	Doug Shearer
Assistant Equipment Managers	Craig Leydig, Rick Harper
Strength and Conditioning Coach	Frank Costello
Massage Therapist	Curt Millar
Chief Pro Scout/Special Assignments	Shawn Simpson
Pro Scout/Special Assignments	Archie Henderson
Chief Amateur Scout	Craig Channell
Chief Eastern Scout	Bob Atrill
Chief Western Scout	Bob Schmidt
Scouting Staff	Fred Devereaux, Bud Quinn, Hugh Rogers, Niklas Wikegard, Darrell Young
Administrative Assistant to the General Manager	Pat Young
Director of Team Services	Todd Warren
Assistant to the Hockey Department	Larissa Cason
Piney Orchard Staff	Alex Walker

Medical Consultants
Team Physicians	Dr. Marc Connell, Dr. Richard Grossman, Dr. Stephen Haas, Dr. Peter Basch, Dr. Carl MacCartee
Team Ophthamologist	Dr. Michael Herr
Team Dentist	Dr. Howard Salob
Team Nutritionist	Dr. Pat Mann

Washington Sports and Entertainment
President	Susan O'Malley
Assistant to the President	Pam Medlock

Communications
Vice President of Communications	Matt Williams
Director of Public Relations	Nancy Yasharoff
Assistant Director of Broadcasting	Reed Laughlin
Communications Coordinator	Julie Hensley
Public Relations Assistant	Jerry Peters

Community Relations
Vice President of Community Relations	Judy Holland
Director of Special Programs	Yvon Labre
Assistant Director of Community Relations	Tara Greco
Community Relations Manager	Nicol Addison
Administrative Assistant	Kathy Moriarty

Customer Service
Executive Director of Customer Service	Rhonda Ballute
Director of Customer Service	Kerry Gregg
Assistant Directors of Customer Service	Glenn Morrill, Cathy Tessier
Special Events Coordinator	Aidan Duffy
Customer Service Coordinator	Jewel Smith
Ticket Operations Manager	Nancy Woodall
Box Office Supervisor	Greg Hall
Box Office Representatives	Wendy Kvancz, Greg Monares, Gregg Weiss
Mail Order Supervisor	Jason Sheer
Mail Order Representatives	Michelle Cook, Melanie Johnson

Advertising, Promotions and Game Operations
Director of Advertising, Promotions and Game Operations	Terri Maruca
Assistant Director of Game Operations	Chris Mulcahy
Advertising and Promotions Assistant	Katherine Quinn
Game Operations Assistant	Gina Spear

Finance
Vice President and Chief Financial Officer	Peter Biche
Controller	Aggie Ballard
Accounting Assistants	Crystal Coffren, Kathleen Brady, Deborah Kostakos, Melanie Loveless

Sales
Vice President of Sales	Rick Moreland
Director of Sales	Jerry Murphy
Regional Sales Managers	Darren Breuning, Bryan Maust, Ron Potter
Account Executives	Gail Bolden Adams, Bill Anderson, Ron Bates, Ken Bradford, Denise Doyle, Geoff Durham, Alvaro Gonzalez, Byron Hudtloff, Chrissie Kostyk, Laura Massard, Tim Munchmeyer, Eric Oppenheim, Mike Ragan, Kent Sites, Eric Shuster, Scott Tippins, Matt Trantham, Victoria Walker, Brian Walsh, Ed Wasielewski, Joe Zamoiski
Sales Coordinators	Bob Artman, Melissa Tindall, Chris Barr
Senior Administrative Assistant	TBA
Administrative Assistant	Vicki Miles, Connie Trott

1995-96 Final Statistics

Standings

Abbreviations: GA – goals against; **GF** – goals for; **GP** – games played; **L** – losses; **PTS** – points; **T** – ties; **W** – wins; **%** – percentage of games won.

EASTERN CONFERENCE

Northeast Division

	GP	W	L	T	GF	GA	PTS	%
Pittsburgh	82	49	29	4	362	284	102	.622
Boston	82	40	31	11	282	269	91	.555
Montreal	82	40	32	10	265	248	90	.549
Hartford	82	34	39	9	237	259	77	.470
Buffalo	82	33	42	7	247	262	73	.445
Ottawa	82	18	59	5	191	291	41	.250

Atlantic Division

Philadelphia	82	45	24	13	282	208	103	.628
NY Rangers	82	41	27	14	272	237	96	.585
Florida	82	41	31	10	254	234	92	.561
Washington	82	39	32	11	234	204	89	.543
Tampa Bay	82	38	32	12	238	248	88	.537
New Jersey	82	37	33	12	215	202	86	.524
NY Islanders	82	22	50	10	229	315	54	.329

WESTERN CONFERENCE

Central Division

Detroit	82	62	13	7	325	181	131	.799
Chicago	82	40	28	14	273	220	94	.573
Toronto	82	34	36	12	247	252	80	.488
St. Louis	82	32	34	16	219	248	80	.488
Winnipeg	82	36	40	6	275	291	78	.476
Dallas	82	26	42	14	227	280	66	.402

Pacific Division

Colorado	82	47	25	10	326	240	104	.634
Calgary	82	34	37	11	241	240	79	.482
Vancouver	82	32	35	15	278	278	79	.482
Anaheim	82	35	39	8	234	247	78	.476
Edmonton	82	30	44	8	240	304	68	.415
Los Angeles	82	24	40	18	256	302	66	.402
San Jose	82	20	55	7	252	357	47	.287

Rod Brind'Amour, who led the NHL with four game-tying goals, was also among the league leaders in points, assists and short-handed points.

INDIVIDUAL LEADERS

Goal Scoring

Player	Team	GP	G
Mario Lemieux	Pit.	70	69
Jaromir Jagr	Pit.	82	62
Alexander Mogilny	Van.	79	55
Peter Bondra	Wsh.	67	52
John LeClair	Phi.	82	51
Joe Sakic	Col.	82	51
Keith Tkachuk	Win.	76	50
Paul Kariya	Ana.	82	50
Eric Lindros	Phi.	73	47
Mark Messier	NYR	74	47

Assists

Player	Team	GP	A
Mario Lemieux	Pit.	70	92
Ron Francis	Pit.	77	92
Jaromir Jagr	Pit.	82	87
Peter Forsberg	Col.	82	86
Wayne Gretzky	L.A.-St.L.	80	79
Doug Weight	Edm.	82	79
Brian Leetch	NYR	82	70
Joe Sakic	Col.	82	69

Power-play Goals

Player	Team	GP	PP
Mario Lemieux	Pit.	70	31
Keith Tkachuk	Wpg.	76	20
Jaromir Jagr	Pit.	82	20
Paul Kariya	Ana.	82	20
Scott Mellanby	Fla.	79	19
John LeClair	Phi.	82	19
Valeri Kamensky	Col.	81	18
Tomas Sandstrom	Pit.	58	17
Pat Verbeek	NYR	69	17
Brendan Shanahan	Hfd.	74	17
Theoren Fleury	Cgy.	80	17
Pierre Turgeon	Mtl.	80	17
Zigmund Palffy	NYI	81	17
Joe Sakic	Col.	82	17

Short-handed Goals

Player	Team	GP	SH
Mario Lemieux	Pit.	70	8
Dave Reid	Bos.	63	6
Mats Sundin	Tor.	76	6
Jamie Baker	S.J.	77	6
Tom Fitzgerald	Fla.	82	6
Joe Sakic	Col.	82	6

Game-winning Goals

Player	Team	GP	GW
Jaromir Jagr	Pit.	82	12
Sergei Fedorov	Det.	78	11
Claude Lemieux	Col.	79	10
John LeClair	Phi.	82	10
Paul Kariya	Ana.	82	9

Game-tying Goals

Player	Team	GP	GT
Rod Brind'Amour	Phi.	82	4
Peter Bondra	Wsh.	67	3
Alexander Mogilny	Van.	79	3
Roman Hamrlik	T.B.	82	3

Shots

Player	Team	GP	S
Jaromir Jagr	Pit.	82	403
Ray Bourque	Bos.	82	390
Theoren Fleury	Cgy.	80	353
Paul Kariya	Ana.	82	349
Joe Sakic	Col.	82	339

Shooting Percentage

(minimum 48 shots)

Player	Team	GP	G	S	%
Gary Roberts	Cgy.	35	22	84	26.2
Petr Nedved	Pit.	80	45	204	22.1
Craig Janney	S.J.-Wpg.	84	20	91	22.0
Andrei Kovalenko	Col.-Mtl.	77	28	131	21.4
Murray Craven	Chi.	66	18	86	20.9

Penalty Minutes

Player	Team	GP	PIM
Matthew Barnaby	Buf.	73	335
Enrico Ciccone	T.B.-Chi.	66	306
Tie Domi	Tor.	72	297
Brad May	Buf.	79	295
Rob Ray	Buf.	71	287

Plus/Minus

Player	Team	GP	+/-
Vlad. Konstantinov	Det.	81	60
Sergei Fedorov	Det.	78	49
Viacheslav Fetisov	Det.	69	37
Petr Nedved	Pit.	80	37
Vyacheslav Kozlov	Det.	82	33

Individual Leaders

Abbreviations: * – rookie eligible for Calder Trophy; **A** – assists; **G** – goals; **GP** – games played; **GT** – game-tying goals; **GW** – game-winning goals; **PIM** – penalties in minutes; **PP** – power play goals; **Pts** – points; **S** – shots on goal; **SH** – short-handed goals; **%** – percentage of shots on goal resulting in goals; **+/–** – difference between Goals For (**GF**) scored when a player is on the ice with his team at even strength or short-handed and Goals Against (**GA**) scored when the same player is on the ice with his team at even strength or on a power play.

Individual Scoring Leaders for Art Ross Trophy

Player	Team	GP	G	A	Pts	+/–	PIM	PP	SH	GW	GT	S	%
Mario Lemieux	Pittsburgh	70	69	92	161	10	54	31	8	8	0	338	20.4
Jaromir Jagr	Pittsburgh	82	62	87	149	31	96	20	1	12	1	403	15.4
Joe Sakic	Colorado	82	51	69	120	14	44	17	6	7	1	339	15.0
Ron Francis	Pittsburgh	77	27	92	119	25	56	12	1	4	0	158	17.1
Peter Forsberg	Colorado	82	30	86	116	26	47	7	3	3	0	217	13.8
Eric Lindros	Philadelphia	73	47	68	115	26	163	15	0	4	0	294	16.0
Paul Kariya	Anaheim	82	50	58	108	9	20	20	3	9	0	349	14.3
Teemu Selanne	Wpg.-Ana.	79	40	68	108	5	22	9	1	5	0	267	15.0
Alexander Mogilny	Vancouver	79	55	52	107	14	16	10	5	6	3	292	18.8
Sergei Fedorov	Detroit	78	39	68	107	49	48	11	3	11	1	306	12.7
Doug Weight	Edmonton	82	25	79	104	–19	95	9	0	2	1	204	12.3
Wayne Gretzky	L.A.-St.L.	80	23	79	102	–13	34	6	1	3	1	195	11.8
Mark Messier	NY Rangers	74	47	52	99	29	122	14	1	5	1	241	19.5
Petr Nedved	Pittsburgh	80	45	54	99	37	68	8	1	5	1	204	22.1
Keith Tkachuk	Winnipeg	76	50	48	98	11	156	20	2	6	0	249	20.1
John LeClair	Philadelphia	82	51	46	97	21	64	19	0	10	2	270	18.9
Theoren Fleury	Calgary	80	46	50	96	17	112	17	5	4	0	353	13.0
Pierre Turgeon	Montreal	80	38	58	96	19	44	17	1	6	0	297	12.8
Steve Yzerman	Detroit	80	36	59	95	29	64	16	2	8	0	220	16.4
Vincent Damphousse	Montreal	80	38	56	94	5	158	11	4	3	0	254	15.0
Adam Oates	Boston	70	25	67	92	16	18	7	1	2	0	183	13.7
Pat LaFontaine	Buffalo	76	40	51	91	–8	36	15	3	7	1	224	17.9
Zigmund Palffy	NY Islanders	81	43	44	87	–17	56	17	1	6	0	257	16.7
Rod Brind'Amour	Philadelphia	82	26	61	87	20	110	4	4	5	4	213	12.2
Valeri Kamensky	Colorado	81	38	47	85	14	85	18	1	5	0	220	17.3
Brian Leetch	NY Rangers	82	15	70	85	12	30	7	0	3	0	276	5.4

Defensemen Scoring Leaders

Player	Team	GP	G	A	Pts	+/–	PIM	PP	SH	GW	GT	S	%
Brian Leetch	NY Rangers	82	15	70	85	12	30	7	0	3	0	276	5.4
Ray Bourque	Boston	82	20	62	82	31	58	9	2	2	1	390	5.1
Paul Coffey	Detroit	76	14	60	74	19	90	3	1	3	0	234	6.0
Chris Chelios	Chicago	81	14	58	72	25	140	7	0	3	0	219	6.4
Phil Housley	Cgy.-N.J.	81	17	51	68	–6	30	6	0	1	0	205	8.3
Gary Suter	Chicago	82	20	47	67	3	80	12	2	4	0	242	8.3
Nicklas Lidstrom	Detroit	81	17	50	67	29	20	8	1	1	1	211	8.1
Sergei Zubov	Pittsburgh	64	11	55	66	28	22	3	2	1	0	141	7.8
Roman Hamrlik	Tampa Bay	82	16	49	65	–24	103	12	0	2	3	281	5.7
Al MacInnis	St. Louis	82	17	44	61	5	88	9	1	1	1	317	5.4
Larry Murphy	Toronto	82	12	49	61	–2	34	8	0	1	2	182	6.6
Robert Svehla	Florida	81	8	49	57	–3	94	7	0	0	0	146	5.5
Jeff Brown	Van.-Hfd.	76	8	47	55	8	56	5	0	0	0	177	4.5
Jyrki Lumme	Vancouver	80	17	37	54	–9	50	8	0	2	2	192	8.9
Sandis Ozolinsh	S.J.-Col.	73	14	40	54	2	54	8	1	1	1	166	8.4
Mathieu Schneider	NYI-Tor.	78	13	41	54	–20	103	7	0	1	0	191	6.8
Teppo Numminen	Winnipeg	74	11	43	54	–4	22	6	0	3	0	165	6.7
Garry Galley	Buffalo	78	10	44	54	–2	81	7	1	2	0	175	5.7
Norm Maciver	Pit.-Wpg.	71	7	46	53	6	58	3	0	0	0	79	8.9
Eric Desjardins	Philadelphia	80	7	40	47	19	45	5	0	2	0	184	3.8
Viacheslav Fetisov	Detroit	69	7	35	42	37	96	1	1	1	0	127	5.5
Kevin Hatcher	Dallas	74	15	26	41	–24	58	7	0	3	2	237	6.3
Sergei Gonchar	Washington	78	15	26	41	25	60	4	0	4	0	139	10.8
*Marcus Ragnarsson	San Jose	71	8	31	39	–24	42	4	0	0	0	94	8.5
Sylvain Cote	Washington	81	5	33	38	5	40	3	0	2	0	212	2.4
Bruce Driver	NY Rangers	66	3	34	37	2	42	3	0	0	1	140	2.1

CONSECUTIVE SCORING STREAKS

Goals

Games	Player	Team	G
7	Zigmund Palffy	NY Islanders	11
7	Alexander Mogilny	Vancouver	7
6	Theoren Fleury	Calgary	9
6	John LeClair	Philadelphia	9
6	Petr Nedved	Pittsburgh	7
6	Mats Sundin	Toronto	6
5	Jaromir Jagr	Pittsburgh	8
5	Alexander Mogilny	Vancouver	8
5	Ed Olczyk	Winnipeg	8
5	Pat Verbeek	NY Rangers	8
5	Jaromir Jagr	Pittsburgh	7
5	Claude Lemieux	Colorado	7
5	Mark Messier	NY Rangers	7
5	Keith Tkachuk	Winnipeg	7
5	Benoit Brunet	Montreal	6
5	Russ Courtnall	Vancouver	6
5	Jaromir Jagr	Pittsburgh	6
5	Mario Lemieux	Pittsburgh	6
5	Greg Johnson	Detroit	6
5	Teemu Selanne	Winnipeg	6
5	Murray Craven	Chicago	5
5	Mike Sillinger	Anaheim	5
5	Andrei Kovalenko	Col.-Mtl.	5
5	Geoff Sanderson	Hartford	5
5	Eric Lindros	Philadelphia	5

Assists

Games	Player	Team	A
10	Ron Francis	Pittsburgh	19
10	Mario Lemieux	Pittsburgh	17
10	Benoit Hogue	Tor.-Dal.	12
10	Vincent Damphousse	Montreal	12
9	Teemu Selanne	Winnipeg	12
9	Chris Chelios	Chicago	11
9	Brian Leetch	NY Rangers	9
8	Eric Lindros	Philadelphia	18
8	Wayne Gretzky	Los Angeles	14
8	Wayne Gretzky	Los Angeles	14
8	Norm Maciver	Pittsburgh	13
8	Mark Recchi	Montreal	13
8	Brian Leetch	NY Rangers	9
8	Alexander Mogilny	Vancouver	11
7	Jozef Stumpel	Boston	10
7	Bruce Driver	NY Rangers	9
7	Craig Janney	San Jose	9
7	Igor Larionov	S.J.-Det.	9
7	Valeri Kamensky	Colorado	9
7	Doug Weight	Edmonton	9
7	Doug Gilmour	Toronto	8
7	Andrew Cassels	Hartford	7
7	Kevin Todd	Los Angeles	7

Points

Games	Player	Team	G	A	PTS
16	Mario Lemieux	Pittsburgh	13	23	36
16	Steve Yzerman	Detroit	10	16	26
15	Teemu Selanne	Winnipeg	5	18	23
15	Chris Chelios	Chicago	4	16	20
12	Jaromir Jagr	Pittsburgh	10	16	26
12	Ron Francis	Pittsburgh	2	20	22
12	Eric Lindros	Philadelphia	11	11	22
11	Jaromir Jagr	Pittsburgh	10	17	27
11	Jaromir Jagr	Pittsburgh	12	13	25
11	John LeClair	Philadelphia	15	8	23
11	Alexander Mogilny	Vancouver	9	8	17
11	Steve Thomas	New Jersey	8	9	17
11	Benoit Hogue	Tor.-Dal.	3	12	15
11	*Miroslav Satan	Edmonton	6	9	15

In his first season in Vancouver, Alexander Mogilny led the Canucks in goals (55), assists (52), points (107), short-handed goals (5), game-winning goals (6), game-tying goals (3), shots on goal (292) and hat-tricks (3).

In just his first full season in the NHL, Chicago rookie left-winger Eric Daze was already drawing favorable comparisons to Frank Mahovlich and Bobby Hull. Blessed with a graceful skating stride and an overpowering shot, Daze led all NHL freshmen with 30 goals in 1995-96.

Individual Rookie Scoring Leaders

Rookie	Team	GP	G	A	Pts	+/–	PIM	PP	SH	GW	GT	S	%
Daniel Alfredsson	Ottawa	82	26	35	61	–18	28	8	2	3	1	212	12.3
Eric Daze	Chicago	80	30	23	53	16	18	2	0	2	0	167	18.0
Vitali Yachmenev	Los Angeles	80	19	34	53	–3	16	6	1	2	0	133	14.3
Saku Koivu	Montreal	82	20	25	45	–7	40	8	3	2	1	136	14.7
Valeri Bure	Montreal	77	22	20	42	10	28	5	0	1	2	143	15.4
Petr Sykora	New Jersey	63	18	24	42	7	32	8	0	3	0	128	14.1
Todd Bertuzzi	NY Islanders	76	18	21	39	–14	83	4	0	2	0	127	14.2
Marcus Ragnarsson	San Jose	71	8	31	39	–24	42	4	0	0	0	94	8.5
Miroslav Satan	Edmonton	62	18	17	35	0	22	6	0	4	0	113	15.9
Cory Stillman	Calgary	74	16	19	35	–5	41	4	1	3	0	132	12.1
Grant Marshall	Dallas	70	9	19	28	0	111	0	0	0	1	62	14.5
Jere Lehtinen	Dallas	57	6	22	28	5	16	0	0	1	0	109	5.5
Stephane Yelle	Colorado	71	13	14	27	15	30	0	2	1	0	93	14.0
Radek Dvorak	Florida	77	13	14	27	5	20	0	0	4	0	126	10.3
Jeff O'Neill	Hartford	65	8	19	27	–3	40	1	0	1	0	65	12.3
Niklas Andersson	NY Islanders	47	14	12	26	–3	12	3	2	1	0	89	15.7
Craig Johnson	St.L.-L.A.	60	13	11	24	–8	36	4	0	0	0	97	13.4
Bryan McCabe	NY Islanders	82	7	16	23	–24	156	3	0	1	0	130	5.4
Shean Donovan	San Jose	74	13	8	21	–17	39	0	1	2	0	73	17.8
Ed Jovanovski	Florida	70	10	11	21	–3	137	2	0	2	0	116	8.6
Niklas Sundstrom	NY Rangers	82	9	12	21	2	14	1	1	2	0	90	10.0
Brian Holzinger	Buffalo	58	10	10	20	–21	37	5	0	1	0	71	14.1
Viktor Kozlov	San Jose	62	6	13	19	–15	6	1	0	0	0	107	5.6
Deron Quint	Winnipeg	51	5	13	18	–2	22	2	0	0	0	97	5.2
Adrian Aucoin	Vancouver	49	4	14	18	8	34	2	0	0	0	85	4.7
Stefan Ustorf	Washington	48	7	10	17	8	14	0	0	1	0	39	17.9

Goal Scoring

Name	Team	GP	G
Eric Daze	Chicago	80	30
Daniel Alfredsson	Ottawa	82	26
Valeri Bure	Montreal	77	22
Saku Koivu	Montreal	82	20
Vitali Yachmenev	Los Angeles	80	19
Miroslav Satan	Edmonton	62	18
Petr Sykora	New Jersey	63	18
Todd Bertuzzi	NY Islanders	76	18
Cory Stillman	Calgary	74	16
Niklas Andersson	NY Islanders	47	14

Assists

Name	Team	GP	A
Daniel Alfredsson	Ottawa	82	35
Vitali Yachmenev	Los Angeles	80	34
Marcus Ragnarsson	San Jose	71	31
Saku Koivu	Montreal	82	25
Petr Sykora	New Jersey	63	24
Eric Daze	Chicago	80	23
Jere Lehtinen	Dallas	57	22
Todd Bertuzzi	NY Islanders	76	21
Valeri Bure	Montreal	77	20
Jeff O'Neill	Hartford	65	19
Grant Marshall	Dallas	70	19
Cory Stillman	Calgary	74	19

Power-Play Goals

Name	Team	GP	PP
Petr Sykora	New Jersey	63	8
Saku Koivu	Montreal	82	8
Daniel Alfredsson	Ottawa	82	8
Miroslav Satan	Edmonton	62	6
Vitali Yachmenev	Los Angeles	80	6
Brian Holzinger	Buffalo	58	5
Valeri Bure	Montreal	77	5

Short-Handed Goals

Name	Team	GP	SH
Saku Koivu	Montreal	82	3
Niklas Andersson	NY Islanders	47	2
Stephane Yelle	Colorado	71	2
Dan Plante	NY Islanders	73	2
Daniel Alfredsson	Ottawa	82	2

Game-Winning Goals

Name	Team	GP	GW
Miroslav Satan	Edmonton	62	4
Radek Dvorak	Florida	77	4
Petr Sykora	New Jersey	63	3
Joe Dziedzic	Pittsburgh	69	3
Cory Stillman	Calgary	74	3
Shane Doan	Winnipeg	74	3
Daniel Alfredsson	Ottawa	82	3

Game-Tying Goals

Name	Team	GP	GT
Valeri Bure	Montreal	77	2
Paul Brousseau	Colorado	8	1
Brian Loney	Vancouver	12	1
Darren Langdon	NY Rangers	64	1
Grant Marshall	Dallas	70	1
Saku Koivu	Montreal	82	1
Daniel Alfredsson	Ottawa	82	1

Shots

Name	Team	GP	S
Daniel Alfredsson	Ottawa	82	212
Eric Daze	Chicago	80	167
Valeri Bure	Montreal	77	143
Saku Koivu	Montreal	82	136
Vitali Yachmenev	Los Angeles	80	133
Cory Stillman	Calgary	74	132
Bryan McCabe	NY Islanders	82	130
Petr Sykora	New Jersey	63	128
Todd Bertuzzi	NY Islanders	76	127
Radek Dvorak	Florida	77	126

Shooting Percentage
(minimum 82 shots)

Name	Team	GP	G	S	%
Eric Daze	Chicago	80	30	167	18.0
Miroslav Satan	Edmonton	62	18	113	15.9
Niklas Andersson	NY Islanders	47	14	89	15.7
Valeri Bure	Montreal	77	22	143	15.4
Saku Koivu	Montreal	82	20	136	14.7
Vitali Yachmenev	Los Angeles	80	19	133	14.3
Todd Bertuzzi	NY Islanders	76	18	127	14.2
Petr Sykora	New Jersey	63	18	128	14.1
Stephane Yelle	Colorado	71	13	93	14.0
Craig Johnson	St.L.-L.A.	60	13	97	13.4

Plus/Minus

Name	Team	GP	+/–
Kyle McLaren	Boston	74	16
Eric Daze	Chicago	80	16
Stephane Yelle	Colorado	71	15
Mike Wilson	Buffalo	58	13
Jon Klemm	Colorado	56	12
Valeri Bure	Montreal	77	10
Darren Van Impe	Anaheim	16	8
Stefan Ustorf	Washington	48	8
Adrian Aucoin	Vancouver	49	8

Three-or-More-Goal Games

Player	Team	Date	Final Score		G
*Daniel Alfredsson	Ottawa	Nov. 02	Ott. 5	Hfd. 0	3
Tony Amonte	Chicago	Feb. 22	St.L. 4	Chi. 3	3
*Niklas Andersson	NY Islanders	Feb. 04	Dal. 3	NYI 5	3
Jason Arnott	Edmonton	Mar. 23	Edm. 6	Mtl. 5	3
Donald Audette	Buffalo	Nov. 08	S.J. 2	Buf. 7	3
Brian Bellows	Tampa Bay	Mar. 01	T.B. 7	S.J. 3	3
Peter Bondra	Washington	Jan. 11	Ott. 1	Wsh.6	3
Peter Bondra	Washington	Feb. 03	NYI 5	Wsh.6	4
Peter Bondra	Washington	Mar. 26	Wsh.7	NYI 1	3
Peter Bondra	Washington	Apr. 03	Wsh. 5	Buf. 1	4
Geoff Courtnall	St. Louis	Nov. 11	St.L. 4	NYI 1	3
Russ Courtnall	Vancouver	Mar. 06	Buf. 2	Van. 5	3
Jason Dawe	Buffalo	Jan. 06	Buf. 7	Mtl. 6	3
Ray Ferraro	NY Rangers	Jan. 03	Mtl. 4	NYR 7	3
Theoren Fleury	Calgary	Dec. 11	L.A. 2	Cgy. 6	3
Theoren Fleury	Calgary	Jan. 02	T.B. 0	Cgy.10	3
Theoren Fleury	Calgary	Jan. 16	Cgy. 5	L.A. 5	3
Peter Forsberg	Colorado	Feb. 11	Col. 5	Phi. 3	3
Peter Forsberg	Colorado	Feb. 19	Edm.5	Col. 7	3
Ron Francis	Pittsburgh	Nov. 10	Pit. 9	S.J. 1	3
Jeff Friesen	San Jose	Mar. 20	S.J. 7	Wpg.1	3
Johan Garpenlov	Florida	Jan. 23	Fla. 5	Wsh.4	3
Kevin Hatcher	Dallas	Jan. 24	Dal. 5	Edm.3	3
Steve Heinze	Boston	Mar. 23	NYR 5	Bos. 4	3
Brett Hull	St. Louis	Oct. 10	Edm.3	St.L. 5	4
Brett Hull	St. Louis	Mar. 15	St.L. 4	S.J. 2	3
Valeri Kamensky	Colorado	Dec. 05	S.J. 2	Col.12	3
Valeri Kamensky	Colorado	Mar. 20	Col. 5	L.A. 2	3
Steve Konowalchuk	Washington	Dec. 10	Wsh. 6	Wpg.1	3
Steve Konowalchuk	Washington	Mar. 23	NYR 4	Wsh.4	3
Igor Korolev	Winnipeg	Oct. 07	Dal. 5	Wpg.7	3
Vyacheslav Kozlov	Detroit	Dec. 02	Det.11	Mtl. 1	4
Jari Kurri	Los Angeles	Oct. 20	L.A. 7	Wsh.4	3
Pat LaFontaine	Buffalo	Feb. 25	Fla. 1	Buf. 6	3
John LeClair	Philadelphia	Mar. 17	S.J. 2	Phi. 8	3
John LeClair	Philadelphia	Mar. 31	Pit. 1	Phi. 4	3
Claude Lemieux	Colorado	Nov. 28	Col. 7	NYI 3	3
Claude Lemieux	Colorado	Jan. 16	Col. 5	Pit. 2	3
Mario Lemieux	Pittsburgh	Oct. 26	Pit. 7	NYI 5	3
Mario Lemieux	Pittsburgh	Oct. 28	Pit. 5	N.J. 3	3
Mario Lemieux	Pittsburgh	Nov. 30	Pit. 9	Bos. 6	4
Mario Lemieux	Pittsburgh	Dec. 30	Fla. 5	Pit. 6	3
Mario Lemieux	Pittsburgh	Jan. 27	Phi. 4	Pit. 7	3
Mario Lemieux	Pittsburgh	Mar. 26	St.L. 4	Pit. 8	5
Trevor Linden	Vancouver	Mar. 09	Col. 7	Van. 5	3
Eric Lindros	Philadelphia	Feb. 03	Phi. 7	St.L. 3	3
Mark Messier	NY Rangers	Nov. 06	Cgy. 2	NYR 4	3
Kevin Miller	San Jose	Jan. 30	Hfd. 2	S.J. 8	3
Mike Modano	Dallas	Feb. 16	Edm.1	Dal. 6	4
Alexander Mogilny	Vancouver	Oct. 14	Van. 7	S.J. 6	3
Alexander Mogilny	Vancouver	Dec. 22	Van. 6	Ana. 2	3
Alexander Mogilny	Vancouver	Jan. 06	T.B. 2	Van. 9	3
Kirk Muller	Toronto	Mar. 09	Cgy. 3	Tor. 4	3
Markus Naslund	Pittsburgh	Nov. 28	Ott. 2	Pit. 7	3
Markus Naslund	Vancouver	Apr. 13	Cgy. 0	Van. 5	3
Petr Nedved	Pittsburgh	Mar. 05	Wpg.4	Pit. 9	4
Cam Neely	Boston	Oct. 07	NYI 4	Bos. 4	3
Owen Nolan	San Jose	Dec. 19	S.J. 7	Ana. 4	4
Adam Oates	Boston	Dec. 14	Fla. 4	Bos. 6	4
Ed Olczyk	Winnipeg	Dec. 12	Mtl. 6	Wpg.5	3
Zigmund Palffy	NY Islanders	Mar. 03	Wpg.7	NYI 5	3
Zigmund Palffy	NY Islanders	Mar. 05	Bos. 3	NYI 5	3
Dan Quinn	Ottawa	Oct. 15	Ott. 7	T.B. 4	3
Dave Reid	Boston	Dec. 16	Cgy. 3	Bos. 6	3
Stephane Richer	New Jersey	Mar. 26	N.J. 6	T.B. 4	3
Gary Roberts	Calgary	Jan. 12	Buf. 1	Cgy. 3	3
Gary Roberts	Calgary	Feb. 20	S.J. 3	Cgy. 5	3
Gary Roberts	Calgary	Feb. 29	Pit. 3	Cgy. 7	3
Cliff Ronning	Vancouver	Dec. 01	S.J. 2	Van. 7	3
Martin Rucinsky	Montreal	Jan. 25	Mtl. 6	Fla. 2	3
Geoff Sanderson	Hartford	Dec. 28	Hfd. 4	Pit. 9	3
Geoff Sanderson	Hartford	Mar. 02	Fla. 1	Hfd. 7	3
Brian Savage	Montreal	Oct. 28	Chi. 3	Mtl. 5	3
Teemu Selanne	Winnipeg	Dec. 15	Edm. 4	Wpg.9	4
Teemu Selanne	Anaheim	Feb. 25	S.J. 3	Ana. 4	3
Teemu Selanne	Anaheim	Mar. 17	St.L. 1	Ana. 5	3
Brendan Shanahan	Hartford	Feb. 23	Hfd. 4	Pit. 5	3
Ray Sheppard	San Jose	Jan. 13	S.J. 10	Pit. 8	3
Ray Sheppard	Florida	Mar. 21	NYI 2	Fla. 3	3
Jozef Stumpel	Boston	Nov. 21	Wpg.4	Bos. 5	3
Keith Tkachuk	Winnipeg	Mar. 26	Wpg.8	Dal. 2	4
Rick Tocchet	Boston	Mar. 14	Pit. 2	Bos. 4	3
Rick Tocchet	Boston	Mar. 21	Ott. 1	Bos. 3	3
Pierre Turgeon	Montreal	Jan. 06	Buf. 7	Mtl. 6	3
Garry Valk	Anaheim	Mar. 22	Ana. 6	St.L. 2	3
Pat Verbeek	NY Rangers	Nov. 21	Pit. 4	NYR 9	3
Pat Verbeek	NY Rangers	Dec. 02	NYR 4	Ott. 2	3
Doug Weight	Edmonton	Nov. 20	Col. 3	Edm.3	3
Jason Wiemer	Tampa Bay	Mar. 01	T.B. 7	S.J. 3	3
*Vitali Yachmenev	Los Angeles	Mar. 02	Mtl. 4	L.A. 5	3
Alexei Yashin	Ottawa	Feb. 20	Ott. 1	Bos. 3	3
*Alexei Yegorov	San Jose	Feb. 20	S.J. 3	Cgy. 5	3
Alexei Zhamnov	Winnipeg	Feb. 01	Wpg.4	Col. 6	3

NOTE: **93 Three-or-more-goal games recorded in 1995-96.**

In addition to being one of the NHL's finest playmakers, Ron Francis, left, is also one of the league's most productive scorers. On November 10, 1995, he recorded his tenth career hat-trick in Pittsburgh's 9-1 win over the San Jose Sharks. Ron Hextall, below, recorded the lowest goals-against average of his stellar 10-year career in 1995-96, compiling a miniscule 2.17 GAA in 53 games for the Philadelphia Flyers.

Goaltending Leaders

Minimum 25 games

Goals Against Average

Goaltender	Team	GPI	Mins	GA	Avg
Ron Hextall	Philadelphia	53	3102	112	2.17
Chris Osgood	Detroit	50	2933	106	2.17
Jim Carey	Washington	71	4069	153	2.26
Mike Vernon	Detroit	32	1855	70	2.26
Martin Brodeur	New Jersey	77	4434	173	2.34

Wins

Goaltender	Team	GPI	MINS	W	L	T
Chris Osgood	Detroit	50	2933	39	6	5
Jim Carey	Washington	71	4069	35	24	9
Patrick Roy	Mtl.-Col.	61	3565	34	24	2
Bill Ranford	Edm.-Bos.	77	4322	34	30	9
Martin Brodeur	New Jersey	77	4434	34	30	12
Ron Hextall	Philadelphia	53	3102	31	13	7
Felix Potvin	Toronto	69	4009	30	26	11
Grant Fuhr	St. Louis	79	4365	30	28	16

Save Percentage

Goaltender	Team	GPI	MINS	GA	SA	S%	W	L	T
Dominik Hasek	Buffalo	59	3417	161	2011	.920	22	30	6
Daren Puppa	Tampa Bay	57	3189	131	1605	.918	29	16	9
Jeff Hackett	Chicago	35	2000	80	948	.915	18	11	4
Guy Hebert	Anaheim	59	3326	157	1820	.914	28	23	5
Ron Hextall	Philadelphia	53	3102	112	1292	.913	31	13	7
Mike Richter	NY Rangers	41	2396	107	1221	.912	24	13	3
Martin Brodeur	New Jersey	77	4434	173	1954	.911	34	30	12
Chris Osgood	Detroit	50	2933	106	1190	.911	39	6	5

Shutouts

Goaltender	Team	GPI	MINS	SO	W	L	T
Jim Carey	Washington	71	4069	9	35	24	9
Martin Brodeur	New Jersey	77	4434	6	34	30	12
Chris Osgood	Detroit	50	2933	5	39	6	5
Daren Puppa	Tampa Bay	57	3189	5	29	16	9

Team-by-Team Point Totals

1991-92 to 1995-96

(Ranked by five-year winning %)

	95-96	94-95	93-94	92-93	91-92	W%
Detroit	131	70	100	103	98	.664
Pittsburgh	102	61	101	119	87	.621
NY Rangers	96	47	112	79	105	.581
Boston	91	57	97	109	84	.579
Chicago	94	53	87	106	87	.565
Montreal	90	43	96	102	93	.561
Washington	89	52	88	93	98	.556
New Jersey	86	52	106	87	87	.553
Vancouver	79	48	85	101	96	.541
Calgary	79	55	97	97	74	.532
Colorado	104	65	76	104	52	.530
Philadelphia	103	60	80	83	75	.530
St. Louis	80	61	91	85	83	.529
Toronto	80	50	98	99	67	.521
Florida	92	46	83	–	–	.516
Buffalo	73	51	95	86	74	.501
Dallas	66	42	97	82	70	.472
Los Angeles	66	41	66	88	84	.456
Winnipeg	78	39	57	87	81	.452
NY Islanders	54	35	84	87	79	.448
Anaheim	78	37	71	–	–	.435
Tampa Bay	88	37	71	53	–	.418
Edmonton	68	38	64	60	82	.413
Hartford	77	43	63	58	65	.405
San Jose	47	42	82	24	39	.310
Ottawa	41	23	37	24	–	.209

Team Record When Scoring First Goal of a Game

Team	GP	FG	W	L	T
Detroit	82	56	45	6	5
Pittsburgh	82	51	39	10	2
Philadelphia	82	52	34	12	6
Colorado	82	44	33	5	6
NY Rangers	82	43	32	4	7
Montreal	82	46	31	7	8
Florida	82	49	31	11	7
Chicago	82	41	29	7	5
Toronto	82	41	28	9	4
New Jersey	82	42	27	10	5
Washington	82	35	26	4	5
Boston	82	41	25	10	6
Calgary	82	43	24	12	7
Tampa Bay	82	33	23	5	5
Anaheim	82	36	23	10	3
Hartford	82	38	23	12	3
St. Louis	82	43	23	11	9
Edmonton	82	41	22	15	4
Buffalo	82	33	21	9	3
Vancouver	82	35	19	12	4
Dallas	82	45	19	16	10
NY Islanders	82	46	19	21	6
Winnipeg	82	33	16	12	5
Los Angeles	82	36	16	13	7
San Jose	82	27	14	11	2
Ottawa	82	36	13	20	3

Team Plus/Minus Differential

Team	GF	PPGF	Net GF	GA	PPGA	Net GA	Goal Differential
Detroit	325	97	228	181	44	137	+ 91
Colorado	326	86	240	240	71	169	+ 71
Chicago	273	63	210	220	65	155	+ 55
Philadelphia	282	82	200	208	62	146	+ 54
Pittsburgh	362	109	253	284	78	206	+ 47
NY Rangers	272	85	187	237	89	148	+ 39
Washington	234	63	171	204	67	137	+ 34
Boston	282	68	214	269	67	202	+ 12
Calgary	241	71	170	240	80	160	+ 10
Vancouver	278	69	209	278	78	200	+ 9
Montreal	265	77	188	248	68	180	+ 8
Anaheim	234	60	174	247	81	166	+ 8
New Jersey	215	55	160	202	49	153	+ 7
Florida	254	81	173	234	63	171	+ 2
Hartford	237	67	170	259	83	176	– 6
Winnipeg	275	82	193	291	88	203	– 10
Buffalo	247	76	171	262	74	188	– 17
Toronto	247	83	164	252	70	182	– 18
St. Louis	219	74	145	248	82	166	– 21
Tampa Bay	238	83	155	248	68	180	– 25
Dallas	227	67	160	280	82	198	– 38
Los Angeles	256	72	184	302	72	230	– 46
Edmonton	240	72	168	304	80	224	– 56
NY Islanders	229	70	159	315	90	225	– 66
Ottawa	191	53	138	291	83	208	– 70
San Jose	252	62	190	357	93	264	– 74

Team Record when Leading, Trailing, Tied

Team	Leading after 1 period W	L	T	Leading after 2 periods W	L	T	Trailing after 1 period W	L	T	Trailing after 2 periods W	L	T	Tied after 1 period W	L	T	Tied after 2 periods W	L	T
Anaheim	15	3	3	24	3	3	6	21	4	5	34	3	14	15	1	6	2	2
Boston	18	3	5	25	2	7	10	18	2	5	23	3	12	10	4	10	6	1
Buffalo	16	7	0	23	3	1	7	22	2	5	32	3	10	13	5	5	7	3
Calgary	18	4	8	25	5	3	5	17	1	3	27	2	11	16	2	6	5	6
Chicago	25	2	4	33	3	5	4	18	6	3	21	4	11	8	4	4	4	5
Colorado	32	2	4	41	1	3	6	17	2	2	14	3	9	6	4	4	10	4
Dallas	13	6	7	20	3	8	3	22	4	4	32	2	10	14	3	2	7	4
Detroit	36	4	3	51	2	1	6	4	3	0	8	3	20	5	1	11	3	3
Edmonton	20	9	3	20	5	5	4	25	2	2	31	3	6	10	3	8	8	0
Florida	24	3	4	34	4	3	5	19	3	4	22	4	12	9	3	5	3	3
Hartford	18	3	3	21	1	3	5	20	5	3	31	2	11	16	1	10	7	4
Los Angeles	10	6	5	17	3	3	2	24	6	2	32	6	12	10	7	5	5	9
Montreal	24	5	4	31	3	4	5	16	1	2	22	4	11	11	5	7	7	2
New Jersey	21	7	3	24	4	3	6	15	4	2	22	2	10	11	5	11	7	7
NY Islanders	12	13	6	18	5	5	1	21	3	0	34	3	9	16	1	4	11	2
NY Rangers	23	1	3	34	1	1	7	16	5	2	25	7	11	10	6	5	1	6
Ottawa	8	9	2	12	4	2	4	30	1	3	45	1	6	20	2	3	10	2
Philadelphia	25	6	2	33	3	2	2	12	4	3	14	4	18	6	7	9	7	7
Pittsburgh	34	4	2	40	5	0	5	14	1	3	18	1	10	11	1	6	6	3
San Jose	12	5	1	12	2	1	3	34	6	4	44	4	5	16	0	4	9	2
St. Louis	19	3	4	24	2	6	5	20	3	3	28	1	8	11	9	5	4	9
Tampa Bay	18	4	3	25	2	3	7	20	4	4	25	5	13	8	5	9	5	4
Toronto	20	6	2	31	5	4	3	23	4	2	27	5	11	7	6	1	4	3
Vancouver	18	6	2	23	4	4	8	19	7	3	24	7	6	10	6	6	7	4
Washington	16	3	3	25	2	4	8	22	3	6	26	4	15	7	6	8	4	3
Winnipeg	17	10	2	25	4	3	7	23	1	6	30	1	5	7	3	5	6	2

Team Statistics

TEAMS' HOME-AND-ROAD RECORD

Northeast Division

			Home								Road				
	GP	W	L	T	GF	GA	PTS	%	GP	W	L	T	GF	GA	PTS	%
PIT	41	32	9	0	215	136	64	.780	41	17	20	4	147	148	38	.463
BOS	41	22	14	5	147	138	49	.598	41	18	17	6	135	131	42	.512
MTL	41	23	12	6	139	122	52	.634	41	17	20	4	126	126	38	.463
HFD	41	22	15	4	134	120	48	.585	41	12	24	5	103	139	29	.354
BUF	41	19	17	5	125	111	43	.524	41	14	25	2	122	151	30	.366
OTT	41	8	28	5	91	133	21	.256	41	10	31	0	100	158	20	.244
Total	**246**	**126**	**95**	**25**	**851**	**760**	**277**	**.563**	**246**	**88**	**137**	**21**	**733**	**853**	**197**	**.400**

Atlantic Division

	GP	W	L	T	GF	GA	PTS	%	GP	W	L	T	GF	GA	PTS	%
PHI	41	27	9	5	143	83	59	.720	41	18	15	8	139	125	44	.537
NYR	41	22	10	9	150	122	53	.646	41	19	17	5	122	115	43	.524
FLA	41	25	12	4	137	97	54	.659	41	16	19	6	117	137	38	.463
WSH	41	21	15	5	124	97	47	.573	41	18	17	6	110	107	42	.512
T.B.	41	22	14	5	138	121	49	.598	41	16	18	7	100	127	39	.476
N.J.	41	22	17	2	120	94	46	.561	41	15	16	10	95	108	40	.488
NYI	41	14	21	6	114	146	34	.415	41	8	29	4	115	169	20	.244
Total	**287**	**153**	**98**	**36**	**926**	**760**	**342**	**.596**	**287**	**110**	**131**	**46**	**798**	**888**	**266**	**.463**

Central Division

	GP	W	L	T	GF	GA	PTS	%	GP	W	L	T	GF	GA	PTS	%
DET	41	36	3	2	172	80	74	.902	41	26	10	5	153	101	57	.695
CHI	41	22	13	6	139	108	50	.610	41	18	15	8	134	112	44	.537
TOR	41	19	15	7	129	116	45	.549	41	15	21	5	118	136	35	.427
ST.L.	41	15	17	9	101	120	39	.476	41	17	17	7	118	128	41	.500
WPG	41	22	16	3	147	139	47	.573	41	14	24	3	128	152	31	.378
DAL	41	14	18	9	116	132	37	.451	41	12	24	5	111	148	29	.354
Total	**246**	**128**	**82**	**36**	**804**	**695**	**292**	**.593**	**246**	**102**	**111**	**33**	**762**	**777**	**237**	**.482**

Pacific Division

	GP	W	L	T	GF	GA	PTS	%	GP	W	L	T	GF	GA	PTS	%
COL	41	24	10	7	171	115	55	.671	41	23	15	3	155	125	49	.598
CGY	41	18	18	5	114	103	41	.500	41	16	19	6	127	137	38	.463
VAN	41	15	19	7	146	142	37	.451	41	17	16	8	132	136	42	.512
ANA	41	22	15	4	132	111	48	.585	41	13	24	4	102	136	30	.366
EDM	41	15	21	5	118	143	35	.427	41	15	23	3	122	161	33	.402
L.A.	41	16	16	9	144	144	41	.500	41	8	24	9	112	158	25	.305
S.J.	41	12	26	3	139	183	27	.329	41	8	29	4	113	174	20	.244
Total	**287**	**122**	**125**	**40**	**964**	**941**	**284**	**.495**	**287**	**100**	**150**	**37**	**863**	**1027**	**237**	**.413**
	1066	**529**	**400**	**137**	**3545**	**3156**	**1195**	**.561**	**1066**	**400**	**529**	**137**	**3156**	**3545**	**937**	**.439**

TEAMS' DIVISIONAL RECORD

Northeast Division

			Against Own Division								Against Other Divisions				
	GP	W	L	T	GF	GA	PTS	%	GP	W	L	T	GF	GA	PTS	%
PIT	28	16	10	2	129	101	34	.607	54	33	19	2	233	183	68	.630
BOS	28	16	9	3	102	87	35	.625	54	24	22	8	180	182	56	.519
MTL	28	19	8	1	101	78	39	.696	54	21	24	9	164	170	51	.472
HFD	28	10	16	2	67	93	22	.393	54	24	23	7	170	166	55	.509
BUF	28	14	13	1	94	85	29	.518	54	19	29	6	153	177	44	.407
OTT	28	3	22	3	55	104	9	.161	54	15	37	2	136	187	32	.296
Total	**168**	**78**	**78**	**12**	**548**	**548**	**168**	**.500**	**324**	**136**	**154**	**34**	**1036**	**1065**	**306**	**.472**

Atlantic Division

	GP	W	L	T	GF	GA	PTS	%	GP	W	L	T	GF	GA	PTS	%
PHI	32	13	13	6	85	77	32	.500	50	32	11	7	197	131	71	.710
NYR	32	15	11	6	100	81	36	.563	50	26	16	8	172	156	60	.600
FLA	32	18	10	4	92	76	40	.625	50	23	21	6	162	158	52	.520
WSH	32	12	15	5	82	85	29	.453	50	27	17	6	152	119	60	.600
T.B.	32	13	13	6	76	93	32	.500	50	25	19	6	162	155	56	.560
N.J.	32	19	10	3	90	70	41	.641	50	18	23	9	125	132	45	.450
NYI	32	6	24	2	78	121	14	.219	50	16	26	8	151	194	40	.400
Total	**224**	**96**	**96**	**32**	**603**	**603**	**224**	**.500**	**350**	**167**	**133**	**50**	**1121**	**1045**	**384**	**.549**

Central Division

	GP	W	L	T	GF	GA	PTS	%	GP	W	L	T	GF	GA	PTS	%
DET	28	21	3	4	117	65	46	.821	54	41	10	3	208	116	85	.787
CHI	28	11	10	7	83	75	29	.518	54	29	18	7	190	145	65	.602
TOR	28	10	14	4	74	82	24	.429	54	24	22	8	173	170	56	.519
ST.L.	28	11	12	5	71	81	27	.482	54	21	22	11	148	167	53	.491
WPG	28	12	12	4	87	90	28	.500	54	24	28	2	188	201	50	.463
DAL	28	5	19	4	55	94	14	.250	54	21	23	10	172	186	52	.481
Total	**168**	**70**	**70**	**28**	**487**	**487**	**168**	**.500**	**324**	**160**	**123**	**41**	**1079**	**985**	**361**	**.557**

Pacific Division

	GP	W	L	T	GF	GA	PTS	%	GP	W	L	T	GF	GA	PTS	%
COL	32	20	8	4	144	94	44	.688	50	27	17	6	182	146	60	.600
CGY	32	16	13	3	105	96	35	.547	50	18	24	8	136	144	44	.440
VAN	32	14	11	7	116	107	35	.547	50	18	24	8	162	171	44	.440
ANA	32	15	16	1	85	95	31	.484	50	20	23	7	149	152	47	.470
EDM	32	15	12	5	106	99	35	.547	50	15	32	3	134	205	33	.330
L.A.	32	10	14	8	106	118	28	.438	50	14	26	10	150	184	38	.380
S.J.	32	7	23	2	98	151	16	.250	50	13	32	5	154	206	31	.310
Total	**224**	**97**	**97**	**30**	**760**	**760**	**224**	**.500**	**350**	**125**	**178**	**47**	**1067**	**1208**	**297**	**.424**

TEAM STREAKS

Consecutive Wins

Games	Team	From	To
9	Detroit	Dec. 12	Dec. 31
9	Detroit	Mar. 3	Mar. 22
8	Colorado	Oct. 18	Nov. 5
8	Philadelphia	Nov. 16	Dec. 3
8	Pittsburgh	Nov. 25	Dec. 9
7	Detroit	Nov. 2	Nov. 22
7	Florida	Nov. 2	Nov. 14
7	Philadelphia	Mar. 23	Apr. 4
6	Montreal	Oct. 21	Oct. 31
6	Detroit	Nov. 25	Dec. 7
6	Chicago	Dec. 23	Jan. 2
6	Detroit	Jan. 10	Jan. 25
6	Detroit	Feb. 18	Feb. 29
6	Anaheim	Mar. 8	Mar. 22

Consecutive Home Wins

Games	Team	From	To
12	Detroit	Nov. 4	Dec. 31
12	Detroit	Jan. 12	Feb. 29
9	Detroit	Mar. 12	Apr. 12
8	Pittsburgh	Jan. 22	Mar. 7
8	Montreal	Feb. 12	Mar. 20
7	Philadelphia	Nov. 16	Dec. 7
6	NY Rangers	Oct. 24	Nov. 21
6	Pittsburgh	Nov. 25	Dec. 19
6	Washington	Dec. 14	Jan. 1
6	Pittsburgh	Dec. 26	Jan. 8
6	Tampa Bay	Feb. 15	Mar. 10
6	Colorado	Feb. 19	Mar. 3
6	Philadelphia	Mar. 16	Apr. 4

Consecutive Road Wins

Games	Team	From	To
7	Detroit	Feb. 18	Mar. 20
5	Colorado	Oct. 25	Nov. 11
5	Detroit	Dec. 12	Dec. 29
5	Chicago	Jan. 31	Feb. 8
5	Hartford	Jan. 31	Feb. 11
5	Boston	Mar. 10	Mar. 31
4	Washington	Oct. 26	Nov. 4
4	Detroit	Nov. 2	Nov. 17
4	Florida	Dec. 2	Dec. 12
4	Toronto	Dec. 7	Dec. 17
4	Chicago	Dec. 20	Jan. 2
4	Dallas	Feb. 24	Mar. 6
4	Philadelphia	Mar. 23	Apr. 2
4	Colorado	Mar. 24	Apr. 11
4	Toronto	Mar. 25	Apr. 4

Consecutive Undefeated

Games	Team	W	T	From	To
13	Detroit	12	1	Mar. 3	Mar. 31
10	Colorado	9	1	Oct. 18	Nov. 11
10	NY Rangers	7	3	Nov. 27	Dec. 13
10	Detroit	9	1	Dec. 12	Jan. 3
10	Detroit	9	1	Jan. 10	Feb. 6
10	New Jersey	7	3	Feb. 23	Mar. 15
9	Philadelphia	8	1	Nov. 14	Dec. 3
9	Chicago	8	1	Dec. 17	Jan. 2
9	NY Rangers	5	4	Jan. 3	Jan. 31
9	Chicago	7	2	Jan. 22	Feb. 8
8	Florida	7	1	Nov. 2	Nov. 16
8	Pittsburgh	8	0	Nov. 25	Dec. 9
8	New Jersey	5	3	Jan. 23	Feb. 10
8	Boston	7	1	Mar. 7	Mar. 21

Consecutive Home Undefeated

Games	Team	W	T	From	To
24	NY Rangers	18	6	Oct. 24	Feb. 15
14	Detroit	13	1	Nov. 4	Jan. 6
12	Detroit	12	0	Jan. 12	Feb. 29
10	Colorado	8	2	Oct. 6	Nov. 22
9	Colorado	4	5	Jan. 4	Feb. 7
9	Anaheim	8	1	Mar. 8	Apr. 14
9	Detroit	9	0	Mar. 12	Apr. 12
8	Florida	7	1	Nov. 5	Nov. 26
8	Washington	7	1	Dec. 14	Jan. 11
8	NY Islanders	4	4	Dec. 16	Jan. 15
8	Pittsburgh	8	0	Jan. 22	Mar. 7
8	Montreal	8	0	Feb. 12	Mar. 20
8	Tampa Bay	7	1	Feb. 15	Mar. 23

Consecutive Road Undefeated

Games	Team	W	T	From	To
8	Chicago	6	2	Jan. 9	Feb. 8
8	Detroit	7	1	Feb. 18	Mar. 24
8	Boston	7	1	Mar. 10	Apr. 7
7	St. Louis	5	2	Jan. 31	Mar. 3
6	Pittsburgh	4	2	Oct. 20	Nov. 10
6	Chicago	2	4	Nov. 24	Dec. 6
6	New Jersey	4	2	Feb. 24	Mar. 10

TEAM PENALTIES

Abbreviations: GP – games played; **PEN** – total penalty minutes including bench minutes; **BMI** – total bench minor minutes; **AVG** – average penalty minutes/game calculated by dividing total penalty minutes by games played

Team	GP	PEN	BMI	AVG
BOS	82	1039	10	12.7
L.A.	82	1460	18	17.8
S.J.	82	1480	20	18.0
N.J.	82	1486	4	18.1
FLA	82	1494	16	18.2
CGY	82	1524	24	18.6
COL	82	1536	22	18.7
DET	82	1551	18	18.9
OTT	82	1553	16	18.9
VAN	82	1546	18	18.9
WSH	82	1553	14	18.9
PIT	82	1623	12	19.8
WPG	82	1622	18	19.8
T.B.	82	1628	14	19.9
DAL	82	1652	12	20.1
NYI	82	1669	14	20.4
ANA	82	1707	22	20.8
EDM	82	1709	12	20.8
TOR	82	1742	18	21.2
PHI	82	1785	20	21.8
ST.L.	82	1823	26	22.2
HFD	82	1844	18	22.5
MTL	82	1847	34	22.5
NYR	82	1849	16	22.5
CHI	82	1880	20	22.9
BUF	82	2195	14	26.8
Total	**1066**	**42797**	**450**	**40.1**

Roman Hamrlik's 12 power-play goals helped the Tampa Bay Lightning to place fourth in power-play efficiency in 1995-96 after finishing 22nd the previous season.

TEAMS' POWER-PLAY RECORD

Abbreviations: ADV – total advantages; **PPGF** – power-play goals for;
% – calculated by dividing number of power-play goals by total advantages.

		Home					Road					Overall		
	Team	GP	ADV	PPGF	%	Team	GP	ADV	PPGF	%	Team	GP	ADV	PPGF	%
1	PIT	41	206	57	27.7	PIT	41	214	52	24.3	PIT	82	420	109	26.0
2	PHI	41	212	51	24.1	COL	41	192	42	21.9	COL	82	404	86	21.3
3	DET	41	212	51	24.1	NYI	41	192	37	19.3	DET	82	455	97	21.3
4	NYR	41	208	50	24.0	CHI	41	181	35	19.3	T.B.	82	400	83	20.8
5	T.B.	41	213	50	23.5	DET	41	243	46	18.9	NYR	82	429	85	19.8
6	L.A.	41	227	50	22.0	VAN	41	207	39	18.8	PHI	82	417	82	19.7
7	MTL	41	195	42	21.5	WPG	41	207	38	18.4	WPG	82	417	82	19.7
8	BOS	41	220	47	21.4	CGY	41	188	34	18.1	MTL	82	405	77	19.0
9	WPG	41	210	44	21.0	T.B.	41	187	33	17.6	TOR	82	438	83	18.9
10	COL	41	212	44	20.8	S.J.	41	186	32	17.2	NYI	82	372	70	18.8
11	BOS	41	196	40	20.4	EDM	41	223	38	17.0	BOS	82	363	68	18.7
12	HFD	41	207	42	20.3	FLA	41	214	36	16.8	CGY	82	386	71	18.4
13	CGY	41	198	37	18.7	BOS	41	167	28	16.8	HFD	82	372	67	18.0
14	NYI	41	180	33	18.3	ST.L.	41	227	38	16.7	L.A.	82	401	72	18.0
15	FLA	41	254	45	17.7	MTL	41	210	35	16.7	CHI	82	356	63	17.7
16	DAL	41	226	38	16.8	TOR	41	218	36	16.5	FLA	82	468	81	17.3
17	ST.L.	41	221	36	16.3	NYR	41	221	35	15.8	VAN	82	411	69	16.8
18	BUF	41	253	41	16.2	BUF	41	224	35	15.6	ST.L.	82	448	74	16.5
19	CHI	41	175	28	16.0	WSH	41	207	32	15.5	S.J.	82	385	62	16.1
20	WSH	41	196	31	15.8	HFD	41	165	25	15.2	BUF	82	477	76	15.9
21	N.J.	41	192	30	15.6	PHI	41	205	31	15.1	EDM	82	452	72	15.9
22	S.J.	41	199	30	15.1	N.J.	41	176	25	14.2	WSH	82	403	63	15.6
23	ANA	41	221	33	14.9	DAL	41	217	29	13.4	DAL	82	443	67	15.1
24	EDM	41	229	34	14.8	ANA	41	205	27	13.2	N.J.	82	368	55	14.9
25	VAN	41	204	30	14.7	L.A.	41	174	22	12.6	ANA	82	426	60	14.1
26	OTT	41	216	29	13.4	OTT	41	214	24	11.2	OTT	82	430	53	12.3
Total		**1066**	**5482**	**1043**	**19.0**		**1066**	**5264**	**884**	**16.8**		**1066**	**10746**	**1927**	**17.9**

TEAMS' PENALTY KILLING RECORD

Abbreviations: TSH – total times short-handed; **PPGA** – power-play goals against;
% – calculated by dividing times short minus power-play goals against by times short.

		Home					Road					Overall		
	TEAM	GP	TSH	PPGA	%	TEAM	GP	TSH	PPGA	%	TEAM	GP	TSH	PPGA	%
1	DET	41	169	14	91.7	DET	41	206	30	85.4	DET	82	375	44	88.3
2	N.J.	41	152	17	88.8	T.B.	41	222	33	85.1	PHI	82	437	62	85.8
3	CHI	41	222	26	88.3	PHI	41	227	34	85.0	CHI	82	447	65	85.5
4	PHI	41	210	28	86.7	MTL	41	192	30	84.4	N.J.	82	319	44	84.6
5	COL	41	216	29	86.6	BUF	41	222	37	83.3	T.B.	82	439	68	84.5
6	FLA	41	185	27	85.4	WSH	41	197	33	83.2	BUF	82	461	74	83.9
7	PIT	41	240	36	85.0	CHI	41	225	39	82.7	COL	82	439	71	83.8
8	TOR	41	185	28	84.9	NYR	41	256	45	82.4	PIT	82	467	78	83.3
9	ST.L.	41	245	38	84.5	L.A.	41	187	34	81.8	FLA	82	370	63	83.0
10	BUF	41	239	37	84.5	VAN	41	223	41	81.6	ST.L.	82	482	82	83.0
11	ANA	41	201	32	84.1	PIT	41	227	42	81.5	TOR	82	403	70	82.6
12	T.B.	41	217	35	83.9	ST.L.	41	237	44	81.4	WSH	82	385	67	82.6
13	EDM	41	204	34	83.3	COL	41	223	42	81.2	MTL	82	382	68	82.2
14	WSH	41	188	34	81.9	DAL	41	201	38	81.1	NYR	82	495	89	82.0
15	HFD	41	188	34	81.9	BOS	41	162	31	80.9	VAN	82	418	78	81.3
16	HFD	41	213	39	81.7	N.J.	41	167	32	80.8	L.A.	82	381	72	81.1
17	NYR	41	239	44	81.6	TOR	41	218	42	80.7	ANA	82	423	80	80.9
18	VAN	41	195	37	81.0	FLA	41	185	36	80.5	EDM	82	417	80	80.8
19	OTT	41	199	38	80.9	HFD	41	216	44	79.6	HFD	82	429	83	80.7
20	WPG	41	199	38	80.9	CGY	41	214	46	78.5	BOS	82	341	67	80.4
21	L.A.	41	194	38	80.4	EDM	41	213	46	78.4	DAL	82	418	82	80.4
22	MTL	41	190	38	80.0	WPG	41	231	50	78.4	CGY	82	402	80	80.1
23	BOS	41	179	36	79.9	ANA	41	222	49	77.9	WPG	82	430	88	79.5
24	DAL	41	217	44	79.7	NYI	41	227	52	77.1	NYI	82	414	90	78.3
25	NYI	41	187	45	79.7	S.J.	41	206	48	76.7	OTT	82	375	83	77.9
26	S.J.	41	191	45	76.4	OTT	41	176	45	74.4	S.J.	82	397	93	76.6
Total		**1066**	**5264**	**884**	**83.2**		**1066**	**5482**	**1043**	**81.0**		**1066**	**10746**	**1927**	**82.1**

SHORT-HANDED GOALS FOR

		Home		Road			Overall	
	Team	GP	SHGF	Team	GP	SHGF	Team	GP	SHGF
1	PIT	41	13	BOS	41	10	COL	82	21
2	COL	41	12	COL	41	9	PIT	82	18
3	DET	41	11	MTL	41	9	VAN	82	18
4	S.J.	41	10	FLA	41	8	DET	82	17
5	VAN	41	10	VAN	41	8	MTL	82	15
6	CHI	41	10	NYI	41	7	S.J.	82	15
7	L.A.	41	9	ST.L.	41	7	BOS	82	13
8	N.J.	41	7	CGY	41	7	CHI	82	13
9	WSH	41	7	EDM	41	7	PHI	82	12
10	PHI	41	7	DET	41	6	WSH	82	12
11	ANA	41	7	TOR	41	6	L.A.	82	12
12	MTL	41	6	BUF	41	5	TOR	82	11
13	WPG	41	5	PHI	41	5	N.J.	82	11
14	TOR	41	5	PIT	41	5	FLA	82	11
15	BUF	41	5	WPG	41	5	ST.L.	82	11
16	ST.L.	41	4	WSH	41	5	CGY	82	11
17	DAL	41	4	HFD	41	5	BUF	82	10
18	NYR	41	4	S.J.	41	5	WPG	82	10
19	CGY	41	4	DAL	41	4	EDM	82	10
20	BOS	41	3	N.J.	41	4	ANA	82	10
21	HFD	41	3	CHI	41	3	NYI	82	8
22	OTT	41	3	ANA	41	3	HFD	82	8
23	T.B.	41	3	OTT	41	3	DAL	82	8
24	FLA	41	3	T.B.	41	3	NYR	82	6
25	EDM	41	3	L.A.	41	3	OTT	82	6
26	NYI	41	1	NYR	41	2	T.B.	82	6
Total		**1066**	**159**		**1066**	**144**		**1066**	**303**

SHORT-HANDED GOALS AGAINST

		Home		Road			Overall	
	Team	GP	SHGA	Team	GP	SHGA	Team	GP	SHGA
1	PHI	41	1	TOR	41	3	ANA	82	5
2	ANA	41	1	ST.L.	41	3	BOS	82	7
3	BOS	41	2	HFD	41	3	PHI	82	7
4	DET	41	2	NYR	41	4	WSH	82	7
5	MTL	41	3	CHI	41	4	CHI	82	7
6	WSH	41	3	ANA	41	4	ST.L.	82	8
7	FLA	41	3	PIT	41	4	DET	82	9
8	CHI	41	3	WSH	41	4	HFD	82	9
9	N.J.	41	4	CGY	41	5	TOR	82	9
10	WPG	41	4	BOS	41	5	N.J.	82	9
11	CGY	41	4	N.J.	41	5	CGY	82	9
12	EDM	41	5	PHI	41	6	NYR	82	11
13	ST.L.	41	5	VAN	41	6	MTL	82	11
14	BUF	41	5	DET	41	7	PIT	82	12
15	HFD	41	6	BUF	41	7	BUF	82	12
16	T.B.	41	6	EDM	41	7	FLA	82	12
17	TOR	41	6	OTT	41	7	WPG	82	12
18	OTT	41	7	T.B.	41	7	EDM	82	12
19	VAN	41	7	L.A.	41	7	T.B.	82	13
20	NYR	41	7	NYI	41	8	VAN	82	14
21	NYI	41	7	DAL	41	8	OTT	82	14
22	PIT	41	8	WPG	41	8	NYI	82	15
23	COL	41	11	MTL	41	8	L.A.	82	18
24	S.J.	41	11	FLA	41	9	DAL	82	20
25	L.A.	41	11	S.J.	41	9	S.J.	82	20
26	DAL	41	12	COL	41	11	COL	82	22
Total		**1066**	**144**		**1066**	**159**		**1066**	**303**

Overtime Results

1986-87 to 1995-96

Team	1995-96 GP	W	L	T	1994-95 GP	W	L	T	1993-94 GP	W	L	T	1992-93 GP	W	L	T	1991-92 GP	W	L	T	1990-91 GP	W	L	T	1989-90 GP	W	L	T	1988-89 GP	W	L	T	1987-88 GP	W	L	T	1986-87 GP	W	L	T
ANA	16	6	2	8	7	2	0	5	12	2	5	5																												
BOS	19	2	6	11	8	2	3	3	17	2	2	13	15	5	3	7	20	6	2	12	17	5	0	12	14	3	2	9	19	3	2	14	14	4	4	6	12	2	3	7
BUF	15	2	6	7	9	1	1	7	13	0	4	9	18	4	4	10	16	2	2	12	24	3	2	19	15	4	3	8	13	2	4	7	12	0	1	11	13	1	4	8
CGY	16	2	3	11	9	1	1	7	18	3	2	13	19	4	4	11	19	2	5	12	15	3	4	8	21	3	3	15	17	5	3	9	15	2	4	9	4	1	0	3
CHI	19	1	4	14	7	2	0	5	16	2	5	9	16	1	3	12	19	2	2	15	12	3	1	8	10	2	2	6	17	2	3	12	15	4	2	9	15	1	0	14
COL	15	2	3	10	6	1	0	5	8	0	0	8	15	4	1	10	17	0	5	12	18	1	3	14	8	0	1	7	10	2	1	7	9	2	2	5	14	0	4	10
DAL	15	1	0	14	9	0	1	8	22	6	3	13	10	0	0	10	8	0	2	6	17	0	3	14	11	3	4	4	17	0	1	16	16	1	2	13	14	2	2	10
DET	11	3	1	7	4	0	0	4	15	5	2	8	11	2	0	9	16	3	1	12	14	2	4	8	17	2	1	14	16	3	1	12	16	2	3	11	17	2	5	10
EDM	14	4	2	8	7	1	2	4	21	1	6	14	17	5	4	8	12	0	2	10	15	4	5	6	20	5	1	14	15	4	3	8	16	3	2	11	14	5	3	6
FLA	13	0	3	10	9	0	3	6	24	2	5	17																												
HFD	14	2	3	9	9	4	0	5	14	4	1	9	18	3	9	6	18	2	3	13	18	2	5	11	9	0	0	9	10	1	4	5	12	3	2	7	9	2	0	7
L.A.	23	3	2	18	9	0	0	9	18	3	3	12	13	2	1	10	16	1	1	14	16	4	2	10	12	3	2	7	14	6	1	7	12	1	3	8	12	2	2	8
MTL	15	2	3	10	10	1	2	7	19	3	2	14	14	5	3	6	20	6	3	11	17	3	3	11	17	4	2	11	11	2	0	9	16	1	2	13	16	2	4	10
N.J.	19	7	0	12	11	1	2	8	14	1	1	12	11	4	0	7	17	2	4	11	17	1	1	15	16	3	4	9	17	1	4	12	12	4	2	6	13	3	4	6
NYI	17	2	5	10	7	1	1	5	19	5	2	12	13	3	3	7	16	3	2	11	15	2	3	10	16	3	2	11	11	3	3	5	13	3	0	10	20	5	3	12
NYR	17	2	1	14	3	0	0	3	12	3	1	8	17	2	4	11	11	5	1	5	16	1	2	13	17	2	2	13	10	1	1	8	11	0	1	10	19	5	6	8
OTT	8	0	3	5	7	1	1	5	17	4	4	9	10	0	6	4																								
PHI	20	4	3	13	8	3	1	4	18	3	5	10	17	4	2	11	17	2	4	11	11	1	0	10	18	2	5	11	14	1	5	8	13	1	3	9	10	1	1	8
PIT	9	3	2	4	5	1	1	3	19	4	2	13	10	3	0	7	12	2	1	9	12	4	2	6	14	3	3	8	10	2	1	7	16	5	2	9	21	5	4	12
ST.L.	18	1	1	16	7	1	1	5	17	4	2	11	17	2	4	11	15	2	2	11	18	3	4	11	15	2	4	9	16	3	1	12	14	2	4	8	21	4	2	15
S.J.	9	1	1	7	5	1	0	4	19	2	1	16	10	3	5	2	9	1	3	5																				
T.B.	18	3	3	12	7	2	2	3	18	3	4	11	14	3	4	7																								
TOR	18	4	2	12	8	0	0	8	17	4	1	12	13	1	1	11	11	4	0	7	17	4	2	11	11	3	4	4	11	1	4	6	13	1	2	10	13	3	4	6
VAN	20	1	4	15	13	0	1	12	12	5	4	3	10	1	0	9	17	4	1	12	15	3	3	9	21	2	5	14	14	2	4	8	11	0	2	9	10	2	0	8
WSH	16	4	1	11	9	0	1	8	14	2	2	10	11	2	2	7	17	4	1	12	12	2	2	8	14	4	3	7	16	2	4	10	15	2	4	9	17	5	2	10
WPG	8	2	0	6	9	0	2	7	15	1	5	9	11	2	2	7	20	1	4	15	14	1	2	11	19	4	4	11	20	6	2	12	21	8	2	11	11	2	1	8
Totals	201	64	137		101	26	75		214	74	140		165	65	100		169	52	117		166	54	112		155	55	100		149	52	97		146	49	97		148	55	93	

1995-96
Home Team Wins: 26
Visiting Team Wins: 38

1995-96 Penalty Shots

Scored

Igor Larionov (Detroit) scored against Arturs Irbe (San Jose), November 22. Final score: San Jose 2 at Detroit 5.

Jeff Friesen (San Jose) scored against Jim Carey (Washington), December 2. Final score: Washington 3 at San Jose 5.

Kevin Miller (San Jose) scored against Stephane Fiset (Colorado), December 5. Final score: San Jose 2 at Colorado 12.

Steve Chiasson (Calgary) scored against Byron Dafoe (Los Angeles), December 11. Final score: Los Angeles 2 at Calgary 6.

Joe Sakic (Colorado) scored against Trevor Kidd (Calgary), January 14. Final score: Calgary 4 at Colorado 4.

Tampa Bay's Daren Puppa protected his 15th career shutout by stoning Edmonton's Doug Weight on a penalty shot during the Lightning's 5-0 victory over the Oilers on January 3, 1996.

Stopped

Grant Fuhr (St. Louis) stopped Dave Hannan (Buffalo), October 22. Final score: St. Louis 2 at Buffalo 5.

Patrick Labrecque (Montreal) stopped Keith Jones (Washington), November 1. Final score: Montreal 2 at Washington 5.

Blaine Lacher (Boston) stopped Steve Yzerman (Detroit), November 2. Final score: Detroit 6 at Boston 5.

Don Beaupre (Ottawa) stopped Marc Bureau (Montreal), November 18. Final score: Ottawa 1 at Montreal 5.

Darcy Wakaluk (Dallas) stopped Wendel Clark (NY Islanders), December 21. Final score: NY Islanders 3 at Dallas 3.

Daren Puppa (Tampa Bay) stopped Doug Weight (Edmonton), January 3. Final score: Tampa Bay 5 at Edmonton 0.

Jeff Hackett (Chicago) stopped Brett Hull (St. Louis), January 4. Final score: St. Louis 3 at Chicago 1.

Mark Fitzpatrick (Florida) stopped Dean McAmmond (Edmonton), January 5. Final score: Florida 3 at Edmonton 2.

Daren Puppa (Tampa Bay) stopped Radek Bonk (Ottawa), January 13. Final score: Ottawa 1 at Tampa Bay 4.

Tim Cheveldae (Winnipeg) stopped Peter Forsberg (Colorado), February 1. Final score: Winnipeg 4 at Colorado 6.

Bill Ranford (Boston) stopped Randy Burridge (Buffalo), February 3. Final score: Buffalo 2 at Boston 4.

Ken Wregget (Pittsburgh) stopped Scott Niedermayer (New Jersey), February 7. Final score: Pittsburgh 1 at New Jersey 1.

N. Khabibulin (Winnipeg) stopped Kevin Stevens (Los Angeles), February 26. Final score: Los Angeles 3 at Winnipeg 4.

Olaf Kolzig (Washington) stopped Mike Hough (Florida), February 29. Final score: Washington 2 at Florida 2.

Patrick Roy (Colorado) stopped Ville Peltonen (San Jose), March 5. Final score: San Jose 5 at Colorado 3.

Sean Burke (Hartford) stopped Wayne Presley (Toronto), March 8. Final score: Toronto 4 at Hartford 7.

Geoff Sarjeant (San Jose) stopped Rick Tocchet (Boston), March 18. Final score: San Jose 3 at Boston 3.

Dominik Hasek (Buffalo) stopped Mario Lemieux (Pittsburgh), March 23. Final score: Buffalo 7 at Pittsburgh 5.

Patrick Roy (Colorado) stopped Jamie Baker (San Jose), March 28. Final score: Colorado 8 at San Jose 3.

Damian Rhodes (Ottawa) stopped Martin Straka (Florida), April 3. Final score: Florida 2 at Ottawa 3.

Sean Burke (Hartford) stopped Brian Bradley (Tampa Bay), April 3. Final score: Hartford 2 at Tampa Bay 4.

Mike Vernon (Detroit) stopped Jim Cummins (Chicago), April 7. Final score: Detroit 4 at Chicago 1.

Summary

27 penalty shots resulted in 5 goals.

NHL Record Book

All-Time Standings of NHL Teams
(ranked by percentage)
Active Clubs

Team	Games	Wins	Losses	Ties	Goals For	Goals Against	Points	%	First Season
Montreal	4890	2579	1557	754	16594	13032	5912	.604	1917-18
Philadelphia	2276	1129	794	353	8133	7021	2611	.574	1967-68
Boston	4730	2280	1753	697	15657	14091	5257	.556	1924-25
Edmonton	1338	655	515	168	5564	5040	1478	.552	1979-80
Buffalo	2050	964	767	319	7367	6654	2247	.548	1970-71
Calgary	1894	893	715	286	7154	6470	2072	.547	1972-73
NY Islanders	1894	869	757	268	6864	6254	2006	.530	1972-73
Florida	214	94	87	33	602	594	221	.516	1993-94
Detroit	4664	1990	1949	725	14482	14388	4705	.504	1926-27
NY Rangers	4664	1978	1955	731	14694	14752	4687	.502	1926-27
Toronto	4890	2099	2077	714	15296	15262	4912	.502	1917-18
St. Louis	2276	953	976	347	7455	7696	2253	.495	1967-68
Chicago	4664	1930	2013	721	14163	14296	4581	.491	1926-27
Washington	1738	724	789	225	5926	6242	1673	.481	1974-75
Pittsburgh	2276	926	1046	304	8084	8567	2156	.474	1967-68
Colorado	1338	544	624	170	4951	5123	1258	.470	1979-80
Los Angeles	2276	885	1052	339	7989	8568	2109	.463	1967-68
Dallas	2276	843	1064	369	7339	8053	2055	.451	1967-68
Winnipeg	1338	506	660	172	4762	5347	1184	.442	1979-80
Hartford	1338	502	670	166	4478	5089	1170	.437	1979-80
Vancouver	2050	745	1003	302	6766	7636	1792	.437	1970-71
Anaheim	214	84	112	18	588	662	186	.435	1993-94
Tampa Bay	298	108	157	33	827	975	249	.418	1992-93
New Jersey	1738	571	926	241	5515	6686	1383	.398	1974-75
San Jose	378	100	244	34	1070	1556	234	.310	1991-92
Ottawa	298	51	224	23	711	1257	125	.210	1992-93

Defunct Clubs

Team	Games	Wins	Losses	Ties	Goals For	Goals Against	Points	%	First Season	Last Season
Ottawa Senators	542	258	221	63	1458	1333	579	.534	1917-18	1933-34
Montreal Maroons	622	271	260	91	1474	1405	633	.509	1924-25	1937-38
NY/Brooklyn Americans	784	255	402	127	1643	2182	637	.406	1925-26	1941-42
Hamilton Tigers	126	47	78	1	414	475	95	.377	1920-21	1924-25
Cleveland Barons	160	47	87	26	470	617	120	.375	1976-77	1977-78
Pittsburgh Pirates	212	67	122	23	376	519	157	.370	1925-26	1929-30
Calif./Oakland Seals	698	182	401	115	1826	2580	479	.343	1967-68	1975-76
St. Louis Eagles	48	11	31	6	86	144	28	.292	1934-35	1934-35
Quebec Bulldogs	24	4	20	0	91	177	8	.167	1919-20	1919-20
Montreal Wanderers	6	1	5	0	17	35	2	.167	1917-18	1917-18
Philadelphia Quakers	44	4	36	4	76	184	12	.136	1930-31	1930-31

Calgary totals include Atlanta, 1972-73 to 1979-80.
Colorado totals include Quebec, 1979-80 to 1994-95.
Dallas totals include Minnesota, 1967-68 to 1992-93.
Detroit totals include Cougars, 1926-27 to 1928-29, and Falcons, 1929-30 to 1931-32.
New Jersey totals include Kansas City, 1974-75 to 1975-76, and Colorado Rockies, 1976-77 to 1981-82.
Toronto totals include Arenas, 1917-18 to 1918-19, and St. Patricks, 1919-20 to 1925-56.

Year-By-Year Final Standings & Leading Scorers

*Stanley Cup winner

1917-18

Team	GP	W	L	T	GF	GA	PTS
Montreal	22	13	9	0	115	84	26
*Toronto	22	13	9	0	108	109	26
Ottawa	22	9	13	0	102	114	18
**Mtl. Wanderers	6	1	5	0	17	35	2

**Montreal Arena burned down and Wanderers forced to withdraw from League. Canadiens and Toronto each counted a win for defaulted games with Wanderers.

Leading Scorers

Player	Club	GP	G	A	PTS
Malone, Joe	Montreal	20	44	—	44
Denneny, Cy	Ottawa	22	36	—	36
Noble, Reg	Toronto	20	28	—	28
Lalonde, Newsy	Montreal	14	23	—	23
Denneny, Corbett	Toronto	21	20	—	20
Pitre, Didier	Montreal	19	17	—	17
Cameron, Harry	Toronto	20	17	—	17
Darragh, Jack	Ottawa	18	14	—	14
Hyland, Harry	Mtl.W., Ott.	16	14	—	14
Skinner, Alf	Toronto	19	13	—	13
Gerard, Eddie	Ottawa	21	13	—	13

1918-19

Team	GP	W	L	T	GF	GA	PTS
Ottawa	18	12	6	0	71	53	24
Montreal	18	10	8	0	88	78	20
Toronto	18	5	13	0	64	92	10

Leading Scorers

Player	Club	GP	G	A	PTS	PIM
Lalonde, Newsy	Montreal	17	21	9	30	40
Cleghorn, Odie	Montreal	17	23	6	29	33
Denneny, Cy	Ottawa	18	18	4	22	43
Nighbor, Frank	Ottawa	18	18	4	22	27
Pitre, Didier	Montreal	17	14	4	18	9
Skinner, Alf	Toronto	17	12	3	15	26
Cameron, Harry	Tor., Ott.	14	11	3	14	35
Noble, Reg	Toronto	17	11	3	14	35
Darragh, Jack	Ottawa	14	12	1	13	27
Randall, Ken	Toronto	14	7	6	13	27

1919-20

Team	GP	W	L	T	GF	GA	PTS
*Ottawa	24	19	5	0	121	64	38
Montreal	24	13	11	0	129	113	26
Toronto	24	12	12	0	119	106	24
Quebec	24	4	20	0	91	177	8

Leading Scorers

Player	Club	GP	G	A	PTS	PIM
Malone, Joe	Quebec	24	39	9	48	12
Lalonde, Newsy	Montreal	23	36	6	42	33
Denneny, Corbett	Toronto	23	23	12	35	18
Nighbor, Frank	Ottawa	23	26	7	33	18
Noble, Reg	Toronto	24	24	7	31	51
Darragh, Jack	Ottawa	22	22	5	27	22
Arbour, Amos	Montreal	20	22	4	26	10
Wilson, Cully	Toronto	23	21	5	26	79
Broadbent, Punch	Ottawa	20	19	4	23	39
Cleghorn, Odie	Montreal	21	19	3	22	30
Pitre, Didier	Montreal	22	15	7	22	6

1920-21

Team	GP	W	L	T	GF	GA	PTS
Toronto	24	15	9	0	105	100	30
*Ottawa	24	14	10	0	97	75	28
Montreal	24	13	11	0	112	99	26
Hamilton	24	6	18	0	92	132	12

Leading Scorers

Player	Club	GP	G	A	PTS	PIM
Lalonde, Newsy	Montreal	24	33	8	41	36
Denneny, Cy	Ottawa	24	34	5	39	0
Dye, Babe	Ham., Tor.	24	35	2	37	32
Malone, Joe	Hamilton	20	30	4	34	2
Cameron, Harry	Toronto	24	18	9	27	35
Noble, Reg	Toronto	24	20	6	26	54
Prodgers, Goldie	Hamilton	23	18	8	26	8
Denneny, Corbett	Toronto	20	17	6	23	27
Nighbor, Frank	Ottawa	24	18	3	21	10
Berlinquette, Louis	Montreal	24	12	9	21	24

1921-22

Team	GP	W	L	T	GF	GA	PTS
Ottawa	24	14	8	2	106	84	30
*Toronto	24	13	10	1	98	97	27
Montreal	24	12	11	1	88	94	25
Hamilton	24	7	17	0	88	105	14

Leading Scorers

Player	Club	GP	G	A	PTS	PIM
Broadbent, Punch	Ottawa	24	32	14	46	24
Denneny, Cy	Ottawa	22	27	12	39	18
Dye, Babe	Toronto	24	30	7	37	18
Malone, Joe	Hamilton	24	25	7	32	4
Cameron, Harry	Toronto	24	19	8	27	18
Denneny, Corbett	Toronto	24	19	7	26	28
Noble, Reg	Toronto	24	17	8	25	10
Cleghorn, Odie	Montreal	23	21	3	24	26
Cleghorn, Sprague	Montreal	24	17	7	24	63
Reise, Leo	Hamilton	24	9	14	23	8

1922-23

Team	GP	W	L	T	GF	GA	PTS
*Ottawa	24	14	9	1	77	54	29
Montreal	24	13	9	2	73	61	28
Toronto	24	13	10	1	82	88	27
Hamilton	24	6	18	0	81	110	12

Leading Scorers

Player	Club	GP	G	A	PTS	PIM
Dye, Babe	Toronto	22	26	11	37	19
Denneny, Cy	Ottawa	24	21	10	31	20
Adams, Jack	Toronto	23	19	9	28	42
Boucher, Billy	Montreal	24	23	4	27	52
Cleghorn, Odie	Montreal	24	19	7	26	14
Roach, Mickey	Hamilton	23	17	8	25	8
Boucher, George	Ottawa	23	15	9	24	44
Joliat, Aurel	Montreal	24	13	9	22	31
Noble, Reg	Toronto	24	12	10	22	41
Wilson, Cully	Hamilton	23	16	3	19	46

1923-24

Team	GP	W	L	T	GF	GA	PTS
Ottawa	24	16	8	0	74	54	32
*Montreal	24	13	11	0	59	48	26
Toronto	24	10	14	0	59	85	20
Hamilton	24	9	15	0	63	68	18

Leading Scorers

Player	Club	GP	G	A	PTS	PIM
Denneny, Cy	Ottawa	21	22	1	23	10
Boucher, Billy	Montreal	23	16	6	22	33
Joliat, Aurel	Montreal	24	15	5	20	19
Dye, Babe	Toronto	19	17	2	19	23
Boucher, George	Ottawa	21	14	5	19	28
Burch, Billy	Hamilton	24	16	2	18	4
Clancy, King	Ottawa	24	9	8	17	18
Adams, Jack	Toronto	22	13	3	16	49
Morenz, Howie	Montreal	24	13	3	16	20
Noble, Reg	Toronto	23	12	3	15	23

1924-25

Team	GP	W	L	T	GF	GA	PTS
Hamilton	30	19	10	1	90	60	39
Toronto	30	19	11	0	90	84	38
Montreal	30	17	11	2	93	56	36
Ottawa	30	17	12	1	83	66	35
Mtl. Maroons	30	9	19	2	45	65	20
Boston	30	6	24	0	49	119	12

Leading Scorers

Player	Club	GP	G	A	PTS	PIM
Dye, Babe	Toronto	29	38	6	44	41
Denneny, Cy	Ottawa	28	27	15	42	16
Joliat, Aurel	Montreal	24	29	11	40	85
Morenz, Howie	Montreal	30	27	7	34	31
Boucher, Billy	Montreal	30	18	13	31	92
Adams, Jack	Toronto	27	21	8	29	66
Burch, Billy	Hamilton	27	20	4	24	10
Green, Red	Hamilton	30	19	4	23	63
Herberts, Jimmy	Boston	30	17	5	22	50
Day, Hap	Toronto	26	10	12	22	27

1925-26

Team	GP	W	L	T	GF	GA	PTS
Ottawa	36	24	8	4	77	42	52
*Mtl. Maroons	36	20	11	5	91	73	45
Pittsburgh	36	19	16	1	82	70	39
Boston	36	17	15	4	92	85	38
NY Americans	36	12	20	4	68	89	28
Toronto	36	12	21	3	92	114	27
Montreal	36	11	24	1	79	108	23

Leading Scorers

Player	Club	GP	G	A	PTS	PIM
Stewart, Nels	Mtl. Maroons	36	34	8	42	119
Denneny, Cy	Ottawa	36	24	12	36	18
Cooper, Carson	Boston	36	28	3	31	10
Herberts, Jimmy	Boston	36	26	5	31	47
Morenz, Howie	Montreal	31	23	3	26	39
Adams, Jack	Toronto	36	21	5	26	52
Joliat, Aurel	Montreal	35	17	9	26	52
Burch, Billy	NY Americans	36	22	3	25	33
Smith, Hooley	Ottawa	28	16	9	25	53
Nighbor, Frank	Ottawa	35	12	13	25	40

1926-27
Canadian Division

Team	GP	W	L	T	GF	GA	PTS
*Ottawa	44	30	10	4	86	69	64
Montreal	44	28	14	2	99	67	58
Mtl. Maroons	44	20	20	4	71	68	44
NY Americans	44	17	25	2	82	91	36
Toronto	44	15	24	5	79	94	35

American Division

Team	GP	W	L	T	GF	GA	PTS
New York	44	25	13	6	95	72	56
Boston	44	21	20	3	97	89	45
Chicago	44	19	22	3	115	116	41
Pittsburgh	44	15	26	3	79	108	33
Detroit	44	12	28	4	76	105	28

Leading Scorers

Player	Club	GP	G	A	PTS	PIM
Cook, Bill	New York	44	33	4	37	58
Irvin, Dick	Chicago	43	18	18	36	34
Morenz, Howie	Montreal	44	25	7	32	49
Fredrickson, Frank	Det., Bos.	41	18	13	31	46
Dye, Babe	Chicago	41	25	5	30	14
Bailey, Ace	Toronto	42	15	13	28	82
Boucher, Frank	New York	44	13	15	28	17
Burch, Billy	NY Americans	43	19	8	27	40
Oliver, Harry	Boston	42	18	6	24	17
Keats, Gordon	Bos., Det.	42	16	8	24	52

1927-28
Canadian Division

Team	GP	W	L	T	GF	GA	PTS
Montreal	44	26	11	7	116	48	59
Mtl. Maroons	44	24	14	6	96	77	54
Ottawa	44	20	14	10	78	57	50
Toronto	44	18	18	8	89	88	44
NY Americans	44	11	27	6	63	128	28

American Division

Team	GP	W	L	T	GF	GA	PTS
Boston	44	20	13	11	77	70	51
*New York	44	19	16	9	94	79	47
Pittsburgh	44	19	17	8	67	76	46
Detroit	44	19	19	6	88	79	44
Chicago	44	7	34	3	68	134	17

Leading Scorers

Player	Club	GP	G	A	PTS	PIM
Morenz, Howie	Montreal	43	33	18	51	66
Joliat, Aurel	Montreal	44	28	11	39	105
Boucher, Frank	New York	44	23	12	35	15
Hay, George	Detroit	42	22	13	35	20
Stewart, Nels	Mtl. Maroons	41	27	7	34	104
Gagne, Art	Montreal	44	20	10	30	75
Cook, Fred	New York	44	14	14	28	45
Carson, Bill	Toronto	32	20	6	26	36
Finnigan, Frank	Ottawa	38	20	5	25	34
Cook, Bill	New York	43	18	6	24	42
Keats, Gordon	Det., Chi..	38	14	10	24	60

1928-29
Canadian Division

Team	GP	W	L	T	GF	GA	PTS
Montreal	44	22	7	15	71	43	59
NY Americans	44	19	13	12	53	53	50
Toronto	44	21	18	5	85	69	47
Ottawa	44	14	17	13	54	67	41
Mtl. Maroons	44	15	20	9	67	65	39

American Division

Team	GP	W	L	T	GF	GA	PTS
*Boston	44	26	13	5	89	52	57
New York	44	21	13	10	72	65	52
Detroit	44	19	16	9	72	63	47
Pittsburgh	44	9	27	8	46	80	26
Chicago	44	7	29	8	33	85	22

Leading Scorers

Player	Club	GP	G	A	PTS	PIM
Bailey, Ace	Toronto	44	22	10	32	78
Stewart, Nels	Mtl. Maroons	44	21	8	29	74
Cooper, Carson	Detroit	43	18	9	27	14
Morenz, Howie	Montreal	42	17	10	27	47
Blair, Andy	Toronto	44	12	15	27	41
Boucher, Frank	New York	44	10	16	26	8
Oliver, Harry	Boston	43	17	6	23	24
Cook, Bill	New York	43	15	8	23	41
Ward, Jimmy	Mtl. Maroons	43	14	8	22	46

Seven players tied with 19 points

1929-30
Canadian Division

Team	GP	W	L	T	GF	GA	PTS
Mtl. Maroons	44	23	16	5	141	114	51
*Montreal	44	21	14	9	142	114	51
Ottawa	44	21	15	8	138	118	50
Toronto	44	17	21	6	116	124	40
NY Americans	44	14	25	5	113	161	33

American Division

Team	GP	W	L	T	GF	GA	PTS
Boston	44	38	5	1	179	98	77
Chicago	44	21	18	5	117	111	47
New York	44	17	17	10	136	143	44
Detroit	44	14	24	6	117	133	34
Pittsburgh	44	5	36	3	102	185	13

Leading Scorers

Player	Club	GP	G	A	PTS	PIM
Weiland, Cooney	Boston	44	43	30	73	27
Boucher, Frank	New York	42	26	36	62	16
Clapper, Dit	Boston	44	41	20	61	48
Cook, Bill	New York	44	29	30	59	56
Kilrea, Hec	Ottawa	44	36	22	58	72
Stewart, Nels	Mtl. Maroons	44	39	16	55	81
Morenz, Howie	Montreal	44	40	10	50	72
Himes, Norm	NY Americans	44	28	22	50	15
Lamb, Joe	Ottawa	44	29	20	49	119
Gainor, Norm	Boston	42	18	31	49	39

1930-31
Canadian Division

Team	GP	W	L	T	GF	GA	PTS
*Montreal	44	26	10	8	129	89	60
Toronto	44	22	13	9	118	99	53
Mtl. Maroons	44	20	18	6	105	106	46
NY Americans	44	18	16	10	76	74	46
Ottawa	44	10	30	4	91	142	24

American Division

Team	GP	W	L	T	GF	GA	PTS
Boston	44	28	10	6	143	90	62
Chicago	44	24	17	3	108	78	51
New York	44	19	16	9	106	87	47
Detroit	44	16	21	7	102	105	39
Philadelphia	44	4	36	4	76	184	12

Leading Scorers

Player	Club	GP	G	A	PTS	PIM
Morenz, Howie	Montreal	39	28	23	51	49
Goodfellow, Ebbie	Detroit	44	25	23	48	32
Conacher, Charlie	Toronto	37	31	12	43	78
Cook, Bill	New York	43	30	12	42	39
Bailey, Ace	Toronto	40	23	19	42	46
Primeau, Joe	Toronto	38	9	32	41	18
Stewart, Nels	Mtl. Maroons	42	25	14	39	75
Boucher, Frank	New York	44	12	27	39	20
Weiland, Cooney	Boston	44	25	13	38	14
Cook, Fred	New York	44	18	17	35	72
Joliat, Aurel	Montreal	43	13	22	35	73

1931-32
Canadian Division

Team	GP	W	L	T	GF	GA	PTS
Montreal	48	25	16	7	128	111	57
*Toronto	48	23	18	7	155	127	53
Mtl. Maroons	48	19	22	7	142	139	45
NY Americans	48	16	24	8	95	142	40

American Division

Team	GP	W	L	T	GF	GA	PTS
New York	48	23	17	8	134	112	54
Chicago	48	18	19	11	86	101	47
Detroit	48	18	20	10	95	108	46
Boston	48	15	21	12	122	117	42

Leading Scorers

Player	Club	GP	G	A	PTS	PIM
Jackson, Harvey	Toronto	48	28	25	53	63
Primeau, Joe	Toronto	46	13	37	50	25
Morenz, Howie	Montreal	48	24	25	49	46
Conacher, Charlie	Toronto	44	34	14	48	66
Cook, Bill	New York	48	34	14	48	33
Trottier, Dave	Mtl. Maroons	48	26	18	44	94
Smith, Reg	Mtl. Maroons	43	11	33	44	49
Siebert, Albert	Mtl. Maroons	48	21	18	39	64
Clapper, Dit	Boston	48	17	22	39	21
Joliat, Aurel	Montreal	48	15	24	39	46

A native of Ottawa, Jack Darragh played six NHL seasons with the Senators and helped lead the club to three Stanley Cup titles in the early 1920s.

1932-33

Canadian Division

Team	GP	W	L	T	GF	GA	PTS
Toronto	48	24	18	6	119	111	54
Mtl. Maroons	48	22	20	6	135	119	50
Montreal	48	18	25	5	92	115	41
NY Americans	48	15	22	11	91	118	41
Ottawa	48	11	27	10	88	131	32

American Division

Team	GP	W	L	T	GF	GA	PTS
Boston	48	25	15	8	124	88	58
Detroit	48	25	15	8	111	93	58
*New York	48	23	17	8	135	107	54
Chicago	48	16	20	12	88	101	44

Leading Scorers

Player	Club	GP	G	A	PTS	PIM
Cook, Bill	New York	48	28	22	50	51
Jackson, Harvey	Toronto	48	27	17	44	43
Northcott, Lawrence	Mtl. Maroons	48	22	21	43	30
Smith, Reg	Mtl. Maroons	48	20	21	41	66
Haynes, Paul	Mtl. Maroons	48	16	25	41	18
Joliat, Aurel	Montreal	48	18	21	39	53
Barry, Marty	Boston	48	24	13	37	40
Cook, Fred	New York	48	22	15	37	35
Stewart, Nels	Boston	47	18	18	36	62
Morenz, Howie	Montreal	46	14	21	35	32
Gagnon, Johnny	Montreal	48	12	23	35	64
Shore, Eddie	Boston	48	8	27	35	102
Boucher, Frank	New York	47	7	28	35	4

1933-34

Canadian Division

Team	GP	W	L	T	GF	GA	PTS
Toronto	48	26	13	9	174	119	61
Montreal	48	22	20	6	99	101	50
Mtl. Maroons	48	19	18	11	117	122	49
NY Americans	48	15	23	10	104	132	40
Ottawa	48	13	29	6	115	143	32

American Division

Team	GP	W	L	T	GF	GA	PTS
Detroit	48	24	14	10	113	98	58
*Chicago	48	20	17	11	88	83	51
New York	48	21	19	8	120	113	50
Boston	48	18	25	5	111	130	41

Leading Scorers

Player	Club	GP	G	A	PTS	PIM
Conacher, Charlie	Toronto	42	32	20	52	38
Primeau, Joe	Toronto	45	14	32	46	8
Boucher, Frank	New York	48	14	30	44	4
Barry, Marty	Boston	48	27	12	39	12
Dillon, Cecil	New York	48	13	26	39	10
Stewart, Nels	Boston	48	21	17	38	68
Jackson, Harvey	Toronto	38	20	18	38	38
Joliat, Aurel	Montreal	48	22	15	37	27
Smith, Reg	Mtl. Maroons	47	18	19	37	58
Thompson, Paul	Chicago	48	20	16	36	17

1934-35

Canadian Division

Team	GP	W	L	T	GF	GA	PTS
Toronto	48	30	14	4	157	111	64
*Mtl. Maroons	48	24	19	5	123	92	53
Montreal	48	19	23	6	110	145	44
NY Americans	48	12	27	9	100	142	33
St. Louis	48	11	31	6	86	144	28

American Division

Team	GP	W	L	T	GF	GA	PTS
Boston	48	26	16	6	129	112	58
Chicago	48	26	17	5	118	88	57
New York	48	22	20	6	137	139	50
Detroit	48	19	22	7	127	114	45

Leading Scorers

Player	Club	GP	G	A	PTS	PIM
Conacher, Charlie	Toronto	47	36	21	57	24
Howe, Syd	St.L., Det.	50	22	25	47	34
Aurie, Larry	Detroit	48	17	29	46	24
Boucher, Frank	New York	48	13	32	45	2
Jackson, Harvey	Toronto	42	22	22	44	27
Lewis, Herb	Detroit	47	16	27	43	26
Chapman, Art	NY Americans	47	9	34	43	4
Barry, Marty	Boston	48	20	20	40	33
Schriner, Sweeney	NY Americans	48	18	22	40	6
Stewart, Nels	Boston	47	21	18	39	45
Thompson, Paul	Chicago	48	16	23	39	20

1935-36

Canadian Division

Team	GP	W	L	T	GF	GA	PTS
Mtl. Maroons	48	22	16	10	114	106	54
Toronto	48	23	19	6	126	106	52
NY Americans	48	16	25	7	109	122	39
Montreal	48	11	26	11	82	123	33

American Division

Team	GP	W	L	T	GF	GA	PTS
*Detroit	48	24	16	8	124	103	56
Boston	48	22	20	6	92	83	50
Chicago	48	21	19	8	93	92	50
New York	48	19	17	12	91	96	50

Leading Scorers

Player	Club	GP	G	A	PTS	PIM
Schriner, Sweeney	NY Americans	48	19	26	45	8
Barry, Marty	Detroit	48	21	19	40	16
Thompson, Paul	Chicago	45	17	23	40	19
Thoms, Bill	Toronto	48	23	15	38	29
Conacher, Charlie	Toronto	44	23	15	38	74
Smith, Reg	Mtl. Maroons	47	19	19	38	75
Romnes, Doc	Chicago	48	13	25	38	6
Chapman, Art	NY Americans	47	10	28	38	14
Lewis, Herb	Detroit	45	14	23	37	25
Northcott, Lawrence	Mtl. Maroons	48	15	21	36	41

1936-37

Canadian Division

Team	GP	W	L	T	GF	GA	PTS
Montreal	48	24	18	6	115	111	54
Mtl. Maroons	48	22	17	9	126	110	53
Toronto	48	22	21	5	119	115	49
NY Americans	48	15	29	4	122	161	34

American Division

Team	GP	W	L	T	GF	GA	PTS
*Detroit	48	25	14	9	128	102	59
Boston	48	23	18	7	120	110	53
New York	48	19	20	9	117	106	47
Chicago	48	14	27	7	99	131	35

Leading Scorers

Player	Club	GP	G	A	PTS	PIM
Schriner, Sweeney	NY Americans	48	21	25	46	17
Apps, Syl	Toronto	48	16	29	45	10
Barry, Marty	Detroit	48	17	27	44	6
Aurie, Larry	Detroit	45	23	20	43	20
Jackson, Harvey	Toronto	46	21	19	40	12
Gagnon, Johnny	Montreal	48	20	16	36	38
Gracie, Bob	Mtl. Maroons	47	11	25	36	18
Stewart, Nels	Bos., NYA	43	23	12	35	37
Thompson, Paul	Chicago	47	17	18	35	28
Cowley, Bill	Boston	46	13	22	35	4

1937-38

Canadian Division

Team	GP	W	L	T	GF	GA	PTS
Toronto	48	24	15	9	151	127	57
NY Americans	48	19	18	11	110	111	49
Montreal	48	18	17	13	123	128	49
Mtl. Maroons	48	12	30	6	101	149	30

American Division

Team	GP	W	L	T	GF	GA	PTS
Boston	48	30	11	7	142	89	67
New York	48	27	15	6	149	96	60
*Chicago	48	14	25	9	97	139	37
Detroit	48	12	25	11	99	133	35

Leading Scorers

Player	Club	GP	G	A	PTS	PIM
Drillon, Gord	Toronto	48	26	26	52	4
Apps, Syl	Toronto	47	21	29	50	9
Thompson, Paul	Chicago	48	22	22	44	14
Mantha, Georges	Montreal	47	23	19	42	12
Dillon, Cecil	New York	48	21	18	39	6
Cowley, Bill	Boston	48	17	22	39	8
Schriner, Sweeney	NY Americans	49	21	17	38	22
Thoms, Bill	Toronto	48	14	24	38	14
Smith, Clint	New York	48	14	23	37	0
Stewart, Nels	NY Americans	48	19	17	36	29
Colville, Neil	New York	45	17	19	36	11

1938-39

Team	GP	W	L	T	GF	GA	PTS
*Boston	48	36	10	2	156	76	74
New York	48	26	16	6	149	105	58
Toronto	48	19	20	9	114	107	47
NY Americans	48	17	21	10	119	157	44
Detroit	48	18	24	6	107	128	42
Montreal	48	15	24	9	115	146	39
Chicago	48	12	28	8	91	132	32

Leading Scorers

Player	Club	GP	G	A	PTS	PIM
Blake, Hector	Montreal	48	24	23	47	10
Schriner, Sweeney	NY Americans	48	13	31	44	20
Cowley, Bill	Boston	34	8	34	42	2
Smith, Clint	New York	48	21	20	41	2
Barry, Marty	Detroit	48	13	28	41	4
Apps, Syl	Toronto	44	15	25	40	4
Anderson, Tom	NY Americans	48	13	27	40	14
Gottselig, Johnny	Chicago	48	16	23	39	15
Haynes, Paul	Montreal	47	5	33	38	27
Conacher, Roy	Boston	47	26	11	37	12
Carr, Lorne	NY Americans	46	19	18	37	16
Colville, Neil	New York	48	18	19	37	12
Watson, Phil	New York	48	15	22	37	42

1939-40

Team	GP	W	L	T	GF	GA	PTS
Boston	48	31	12	5	170	98	67
*New York	48	27	11	10	136	77	64
Toronto	48	25	17	6	134	110	56
Chicago	48	23	19	6	112	120	52
Detroit	48	16	26	6	90	126	38
NY Americans	48	15	29	4	106	140	34
Montreal	48	10	33	5	90	167	25

Leading Scorers

Player	Club	GP	G	A	PTS	PIM
Schmidt, Milt	Boston	48	22	30	52	37
Dumart, Woody	Boston	48	22	21	43	16
Bauer, Bob	Boston	48	17	26	43	2
Drillon, Gord	Toronto	43	21	19	40	13
Cowley, Bill	Boston	48	13	27	40	24
Hextall, Bryan	New York	48	24	15	39	52
Colville, Neil	New York	48	19	19	38	22
Howe, Syd	Detroit	46	14	23	37	17
Blake, Hector	Montreal	48	17	19	36	48
Armstrong, Murray	NY Americans	48	16	20	36	12

1940-41

Team	GP	W	L	T	GF	GA	PTS
*Boston	48	27	8	13	168	102	67
Toronto	48	28	14	6	145	99	62
Detroit	48	21	16	11	112	102	53
New York	48	21	19	8	143	125	50
Chicago	48	16	25	7	112	139	39
Montreal	48	16	26	6	121	147	38
NY Americans	48	8	29	11	99	186	27

Leading Scorers

Player	Club	GP	G	A	PTS	PIM
Cowley, Bill	Boston	46	17	45	62	16
Hextall, Bryan	New York	48	26	18	44	16
Drillon, Gord	Toronto	42	23	21	44	2
Apps, Syl	Toronto	41	20	24	44	6
Patrick, Lynn	New York	48	20	24	44	12
Howe, Syd	Detroit	48	20	24	44	8
Colville, Neil	New York	48	14	28	42	28
Wiseman, Eddie	Boston	48	16	24	40	10
Bauer, Bobby	Boston	48	17	22	39	2
Schriner, Sweeney	Toronto	48	24	14	38	6
Conacher, Roy	Boston	40	24	14	38	7
Schmidt, Milt	Boston	44	13	25	38	23

1941-42

Team	GP	W	L	T	GF	GA	PTS
New York	48	29	17	2	177	143	60
*Toronto	48	27	18	3	158	136	57
Boston	48	25	17	6	160	118	56
Chicago	48	22	23	3	145	155	47
Detroit	48	19	25	4	140	147	42
Montreal	48	18	27	3	134	173	39
Brooklyn	48	16	29	3	133	175	35

Leading Scorers

Player	Club	GP	G	A	PTS	PIM
Hextall, Bryan	New York	48	24	32	56	30
Patrick, Lynn	New York	47	32	22	54	18
Grosso, Don	Detroit	48	23	30	53	13
Watson, Phil	New York	48	15	37	52	48
Abel, Sid	Detroit	48	18	31	49	45
Blake, Hector	Montreal	47	17	28	45	19
Thoms, Bill	Chicago	47	15	30	45	8
Drillon, Gord	Toronto	48	23	18	41	6
Apps, Syl	Toronto	38	18	23	41	0
Anderson, Tom	Brooklyn	48	12	29	41	54

1942-43

Team	GP	W	L	T	GF	GA	PTS
*Detroit	50	25	14	11	169	124	61
Boston	50	24	17	9	195	176	57
Toronto	50	22	19	9	198	159	53
Montreal	50	19	19	12	181	191	50
Chicago	50	17	18	15	179	180	49
New York	50	11	31	8	161	253	30

Leading Scorers

Player	Club	GP	G	A	PTS	PIM
Bentley, Doug	Chicago	50	33	40	73	18
Cowley, Bill	Boston	48	27	45	72	10
Bentley, Max	Chicago	47	26	44	70	2
Patrick, Lynn	New York	50	22	39	61	28
Carr, Lorne	Toronto	50	27	33	60	15
Taylor, Billy	Toronto	50	18	42	60	2
Hextall, Bryan	New York	50	27	32	59	28
Blake, Hector	Montreal	48	23	36	59	28
Lach, Elmer	Montreal	45	18	40	58	14
O'Connor, Herb	Montreal	50	15	43	58	2

1943-44

Team	GP	W	L	T	GF	GA	PTS
*Montreal	50	38	5	7	234	109	83
Detroit	50	26	18	6	214	177	58
Toronto	50	23	23	4	214	174	50
Chicago	50	22	23	5	178	187	49
Boston	50	19	26	5	223	268	43
New York	50	6	39	5	162	310	17

Leading Scorers

Player	Club	GP	G	A	PTS	PIM
Cain, Herb	Boston	48	36	46	82	4
Bentley, Doug	Chicago	50	38	39	77	22
Carr, Lorne	Toronto	50	36	38	74	9
Liscombe, Carl	Detroit	50	36	37	73	17
Lach, Elmer	Montreal	48	24	48	72	23
Smith, Clint	Chicago	50	23	49	72	4
Cowley, Bill	Boston	36	30	41	71	12
Mosienko, Bill	Chicago	50	32	38	70	10
Jackson, Art	Boston	49	28	41	69	8
Bodnar, Gus	Toronto	50	22	40	62	18

1944-45

Team	GP	W	L	T	GF	GA	PTS
Montreal	50	38	8	4	228	121	80
Detroit	50	31	14	5	218	161	67
*Toronto	50	24	22	4	183	161	52
Boston	50	16	30	4	179	219	36
Chicago	50	13	30	7	141	194	33
New York	50	11	29	10	154	247	32

Leading Scorers

Player	Club	GP	G	A	PTS	PIM
Lach, Elmer	Montreal	50	26	54	80	37
Richard, Maurice	Montreal	50	50	23	73	36
Blake, Hector	Montreal	49	29	38	67	15
Cowley, Bill	Boston	49	25	40	65	2
Kennedy, Ted	Toronto	49	29	25	54	14
Mosienko, Bill	Chicago	50	28	26	54	0
Carveth, Joe	Detroit	50	26	28	54	6
DeMarco, Albert	New York	50	24	30	54	10
Smith, Clint	Chicago	50	23	31	54	0
Howe, Syd	Detroit	46	17	36	53	6

1945-46

Team	GP	W	L	T	GF	GA	PTS
*Montreal	50	28	17	5	172	134	61
Boston	50	24	18	8	167	156	56
Chicago	50	23	20	7	200	178	53
Detroit	50	20	20	10	146	159	50
Toronto	50	19	24	7	174	185	45
New York	50	13	28	9	144	191	35

Leading Scorers

Player	Club	GP	G	A	PTS	PIM
Bentley, Max	Chicago	47	31	30	61	6
Stewart, Gaye	Toronto	50	37	15	52	8
Blake, Hector	Montreal	50	29	21	50	2
Smith, Clint	Chicago	50	26	24	50	2
Richard, Maurice	Montreal	50	27	21	48	50
Mosienko, Bill	Chicago	40	18	30	48	12
DeMarco, Albert	New York	50	20	27	47	20
Lach, Elmer	Montreal	50	13	34	47	34
Kaleta, Alex	Chicago	49	19	27	46	17
Taylor, Billy	Toronto	48	23	18	41	14
Horeck, Pete	Chicago	50	20	21	41	34

Bill Cowley (seen here with teammate Dit Clapper) led the NHL in assists three times, including the 1940-41 season when he also captured the Art Ross Trophy as the league's top scorer.

1946-47

Team	GP	W	L	T	GF	GA	PTS
Montreal	60	34	16	10	189	138	78
*Toronto	60	31	19	10	209	172	72
Boston	60	26	23	11	190	175	63
Detroit	60	22	27	11	190	193	55
New York	60	22	32	6	167	186	50
Chicago	60	19	37	4	193	274	42

Leading Scorers

Player	Club	GP	G	A	PTS	PIM
Bentley, Max	Chicago	60	29	43	72	12
Richard, Maurice	Montreal	60	45	26	71	69
Taylor, Billy	Detroit	60	17	46	63	35
Schmidt, Milt	Boston	59	27	35	62	40
Kennedy, Ted	Toronto	60	28	32	60	27
Bentley, Doug	Chicago	52	21	34	55	18
Bauer, Bob	Boston	58	30	24	54	4
Conacher, Roy	Detroit	60	30	24	54	6
Mosienko, Bill	Chicago	59	25	27	52	2
Dumart, Woody	Boston	60	24	28	52	12

1947-48

Team	GP	W	L	T	GF	GA	PTS
*Toronto	60	32	15	13	182	143	77
Detroit	60	30	18	12	187	148	72
Boston	60	23	24	13	167	168	59
New York	60	21	26	13	176	201	55
Montreal	60	20	29	11	147	169	51
Chicago	60	20	34	6	195	225	46

Leading Scorers

Player	Club	GP	G	A	PTS	PIM
Lach, Elmer	Montreal	60	30	31	61	72
O'Connor, Buddy	New York	60	24	36	60	8
Bentley, Doug	Chicago	60	20	37	57	16
Stewart, Gaye	Tor., Chi.	61	27	29	56	83
Bentley, Max	Chi., Tor.	59	26	28	54	14
Poile, Bud	Tor., Chi.	58	25	29	54	17
Richard, Maurice	Montreal	53	28	25	53	89
Apps, Syl	Toronto	55	26	27	53	12
Lindsay, Ted	Detroit	60	33	19	52	95
Conacher, Roy	Chicago	52	22	27	49	4

1948-49

Team	GP	W	L	T	GF	GA	PTS
Detroit	60	34	19	7	195	145	75
Boston	60	29	23	8	178	163	66
Montreal	60	28	23	9	152	126	65
*Toronto	60	22	25	13	147	161	57
Chicago	60	21	31	8	173	211	50
New York	60	18	31	11	133	172	47

Leading Scorers

Player	Club	GP	G	A	PTS	PIM
Conacher, Roy	Chicago	60	26	42	68	8
Bentley, Doug	Chicago	58	23	43	66	38
Abel, Sid	Detroit	60	28	26	54	49
Lindsay, Ted	Detroit	50	26	28	54	97
Conacher, Jim	Det., Chi.	59	26	23	49	43
Ronty, Paul	Boston	60	20	29	49	11
Watson, Harry	Toronto	60	26	19	45	0
Reay, Billy	Montreal	60	22	23	45	33
Bodnar, Gus	Chicago	59	19	26	45	14
Peirson, John	Boston	59	22	21	43	45

1949-50

Team	GP	W	L	T	GF	GA	PTS
*Detroit	70	37	19	14	229	164	88
Montreal	70	29	22	19	172	150	77
Toronto	70	31	27	12	176	173	74
New York	70	28	31	11	170	189	67
Boston	70	22	32	16	198	228	60
Chicago	70	22	38	10	203	244	54

Leading Scorers

Player	Club	GP	G	A	PTS	PIM
Lindsay, Ted	Detroit	69	23	55	78	141
Abel, Sid	Detroit	69	34	35	69	46
Howe, Gordie	Detroit	70	35	33	68	69
Richard, Maurice	Montreal	70	43	22	65	114
Ronty, Paul	Boston	70	23	36	59	8
Conacher, Roy	Chicago	70	25	31	56	16
Bentley, Doug	Chicago	64	20	33	53	28
Peirson, John	Boston	57	27	25	52	49
Prystai, Metro	Chicago	65	29	22	51	31
Guidolin, Bep	Chicago	70	17	34	51	42

Ted Kennedy, right, attempts to bury a rebound past Detroit goaltender Harry Lumley during action between the Red Wings and Toronto in the 1950-51 season. The Leafs and Red Wings staged a year-long battle for top spot in the league, but Detroit pulled away in the final weeks to become the first team to reach the 100-point plateau.

1950-51

Team	GP	W	L	T	GF	GA	PTS
Detroit	70	44	13	13	236	139	101
*Toronto	70	41	16	13	212	138	95
Montreal	70	25	30	15	173	184	65
Boston	70	22	30	18	178	197	62
New York	70	20	29	21	169	201	61
Chicago	70	13	47	10	171	280	36

Leading Scorers

Player	Club	GP	G	A	PTS	PIM
Howe, Gordie	Detroit	70	43	43	86	74
Richard, Maurice	Montreal	65	42	24	66	97
Bentley, Max	Toronto	67	21	41	62	34
Abel, Sid	Detroit	69	23	38	61	30
Schmidt, Milt	Boston	62	22	39	61	33
Kennedy, Ted	Toronto	63	18	43	61	32
Lindsay, Ted	Detroit	67	24	35	59	110
Sloan, Tod	Toronto	70	31	25	56	105
Kelly, Red	Detroit	70	17	37	54	24
Smith, Sid	Toronto	70	30	21	51	10
Gardner, Cal	Toronto	66	23	28	51	42

1951-52

Team	GP	W	L	T	GF	GA	PTS
*Detroit	70	44	14	12	215	133	100
Montreal	70	34	26	10	195	164	78
Toronto	70	29	25	16	168	157	74
Boston	70	25	29	16	162	176	66
New York	70	23	34	13	192	219	59
Chicago	70	17	44	9	158	241	43

Leading Scorers

Player	Club	GP	G	A	PTS	PIM
Howe, Gordie	Detroit	70	47	39	86	78
Lindsay, Ted	Detroit	70	30	39	69	123
Lach, Elmer	Montreal	70	15	50	65	36
Raleigh, Don	New York	70	19	42	61	14
Smith, Sid	Toronto	70	27	30	57	6
Geoffrion, Bernie	Montreal	67	30	24	54	66
Mosienko, Bill	Chicago	70	31	22	53	10
Abel, Sid	Detroit	62	17	36	53	32
Kennedy, Ted	Toronto	70	19	33	52	33
Schmidt, Milt	Boston	69	21	29	50	57
Peirson, John	Boston	68	20	30	50	30

1952-53

Team	GP	W	L	T	GF	GA	PTS
Detroit	70	36	16	18	222	133	90
*Montreal	70	28	23	19	155	148	75
Boston	70	28	29	13	152	172	69
Chicago	70	27	28	15	169	175	69
Toronto	70	27	30	13	156	167	67
New York	70	17	37	16	152	211	50

Leading Scorers

Player	Club	GP	G	A	PTS	PIM
Howe, Gordie	Detroit	70	49	46	95	57
Lindsay, Ted	Detroit	70	32	39	71	111
Richard, Maurice	Montreal	70	28	33	61	112
Hergesheimer, Wally	New York	70	30	29	59	10
Delvecchio, Alex	Detroit	70	16	43	59	28
Ronty, Paul	New York	70	16	38	54	20
Prystai, Metro	Detroit	70	16	34	50	12
Kelly, Red	Detroit	70	19	27	46	8
Olmstead, Bert	Montreal	69	17	28	45	83
Mackell, Fleming	Boston	65	27	17	44	63
McFadden, Jim	Chicago	70	23	21	44	29

1953-54

Team	GP	W	L	T	GF	GA	PTS
*Detroit	70	37	19	14	191	132	88
Montreal	70	35	24	11	195	141	81
Toronto	70	32	24	14	152	131	78
Boston	70	32	28	10	177	181	74
New York	70	29	31	10	161	182	68
Chicago	70	12	51	7	133	242	31

Leading Scorers

Player	Club	GP	G	A	PTS	PIM
Howe, Gordie	Detroit	70	33	48	81	109
Richard, Maurice	Montreal	70	37	30	67	112
Lindsay, Ted	Detroit	70	26	36	62	110
Geoffrion, Bernie	Montreal	54	29	25	54	87
Olmstead, Bert	Montreal	70	15	37	52	85
Kelly, Red	Detroit	62	16	33	49	18
Reibel, Earl	Detroit	69	15	33	48	18
Sandford, Ed	Boston	70	16	31	47	42
Mackell, Fleming	Boston	67	15	32	47	60
Mosdell, Ken	Montreal	67	22	24	46	64
Ronty, Paul	New York	70	13	33	46	18

1954-55

Team	GP	W	L	T	GF	GA	PTS
*Detroit	70	42	17	11	204	134	95
Montreal	70	41	18	11	228	157	93
Toronto	70	24	24	22	147	135	70
Boston	70	23	26	21	169	188	67
New York	70	17	35	18	150	210	52
Chicago	70	13	40	17	161	235	43

Leading Scorers

Player	Club	GP	G	A	PTS	PIM
Geoffrion, Bernie	Montreal	70	38	37	75	57
Richard, Maurice	Montreal	67	38	36	74	125
Beliveau, Jean	Montreal	70	37	36	73	58
Reibel, Earl	Detroit	70	25	41	66	15
Howe, Gordie	Detroit	64	29	33	62	68
Sullivan, George	Chicago	69	19	42	61	51
Olmstead, Bert	Montreal	70	10	48	58	103
Smith, Sid	Toronto	70	33	21	54	14
Mosdell, Ken	Montreal	70	22	32	54	82
Lewicki, Danny	New York	70	29	24	53	8

1955-56

Team	GP	W	L	T	GF	GA	PTS
*Montreal	70	45	15	10	222	131	100
Detroit	70	30	24	16	183	148	76
New York	70	32	28	10	204	203	74
Toronto	70	24	33	13	153	181	61
Boston	70	23	34	13	147	185	59
Chicago	70	19	39	12	155	216	50

Leading Scorers

Player	Club	GP	G	A	PTS	PIM
Beliveau, Jean	Montreal	70	47	41	88	143
Howe, Gordie	Detroit	70	38	41	79	100
Richard, Maurice	Montreal	70	38	33	71	89
Olmstead, Bert	Montreal	70	14	56	70	94
Sloan, Tod	Toronto	70	37	29	66	100
Bathgate, Andy	New York	70	19	47	66	59
Geoffrion, Bernie	Montreal	59	29	33	62	66
Reibel, Earl	Detroit	68	17	39	56	10
Delvecchio, Alex	Detroit	70	25	26	51	24
Creighton, Dave	New York	70	20	31	51	43
Gadsby, Bill	New York	70	9	42	51	84

1956-57

Team	GP	W	L	T	GF	GA	PTS
Detroit	70	38	20	12	198	157	88
*Montreal	70	35	23	12	210	155	82
Boston	70	34	24	12	195	174	80
New York	70	26	30	14	184	227	66
Toronto	70	21	34	15	174	192	57
Chicago	70	16	39	15	169	225	47

Leading Scorers

Player	Club	GP	G	A	PTS	PIM
Howe, Gordie	Detroit	70	44	45	89	72
Lindsay, Ted	Detroit	70	30	55	85	103
Beliveau, Jean	Montreal	69	33	51	84	105
Bathgate, Andy	New York	70	27	50	77	60
Litzenberger, Ed	Chicago	70	32	32	64	48
Richard, Maurice	Montreal	63	33	29	62	74
McKenney, Don	Boston	69	21	39	60	31
Moore, Dickie	Montreal	70	29	29	58	56
Richard, Henri	Montreal	63	18	36	54	71
Ullman, Norm	Detroit	64	16	36	52	47

1957-58

Team	GP	W	L	T	GF	GA	PTS
*Montreal	70	43	17	10	250	158	96
New York	70	32	25	13	195	188	77
Detroit	70	29	29	12	176	207	70
Boston	70	27	28	15	199	194	69
Chicago	70	24	39	7	163	202	55
Toronto	70	21	38	11	192	226	53

Leading Scorers

Player	Club	GP	G	A	PTS	PIM
Moore, Dickie	Montreal	70	36	48	84	65
Richard, Henri	Montreal	67	28	52	80	56
Bathgate, Andy	New York	65	30	48	78	42
Howe, Gordie	Detroit	64	33	44	77	40
Horvath, Bronco	Boston	67	30	36	66	71
Litzenberger, Ed	Chicago	70	32	30	62	63
Mackell, Fleming	Boston	70	20	40	60	72
Beliveau, Jean	Montreal	55	27	32	59	93
Delvecchio, Alex	Detroit	70	21	38	59	22
McKenney, Don	Boston	70	28	30	58	22

1958-59

Team	GP	W	L	T	GF	GA	PTS
*Montreal	70	39	18	13	258	158	91
Boston	70	32	29	9	205	215	73
Chicago	70	28	29	13	197	208	69
Toronto	70	27	32	11	189	201	65
New York	70	26	32	12	201	217	64
Detroit	70	25	37	8	167	218	58

Leading Scorers

Player	Club	GP	G	A	PTS	PIM
Moore, Dickie	Montreal	70	41	55	96	61
Beliveau, Jean	Montreal	64	45	46	91	67
Bathgate, Andy	New York	70	40	48	88	48
Howe, Gordie	Detroit	70	32	46	78	57
Litzenberger, Ed	Chicago	70	33	44	77	37
Geoffrion, Bernie	Montreal	59	22	44	66	30
Sullivan, George	New York	70	21	42	63	56
Hebenton, Andy	New York	70	33	29	62	8
McKenney, Don	Boston	70	32	30	62	20
Sloan, Tod	Chicago	59	27	35	62	79

1959-60

Team	GP	W	L	T	GF	GA	PTS
*Montreal	70	40	18	12	255	178	92
Toronto	70	35	26	9	199	195	79
Chicago	70	28	29	13	191	180	69
Detroit	70	26	29	15	186	197	67
Boston	70	28	34	8	220	241	64
New York	70	17	38	15	187	247	49

Leading Scorers

Player	Club	GP	G	A	PTS	PIM
Hull, Bobby	Chicago	70	39	42	81	68
Horvath, Bronco	Boston	68	39	41	80	60
Beliveau, Jean	Montreal	60	34	40	74	57
Bathgate, Andy	New York	70	26	48	74	28
Richard, Henri	Montreal	70	30	43	73	66
Howe, Gordie	Detroit	70	28	45	73	46
Geoffrion, Bernie	Montreal	59	30	41	71	36
McKenney, Don	Boston	70	20	49	69	28
Stasiuk, Vic	Boston	69	29	39	68	121
Prentice, Dean	New York	70	32	34	66	43

1960-61

Team	GP	W	L	T	GF	GA	PTS
Montreal	70	41	19	10	254	188	92
Toronto	70	39	19	12	234	176	90
*Chicago	70	29	24	17	198	180	75
Detroit	70	25	29	16	195	215	66
New York	70	22	38	10	204	248	54
Boston	70	15	42	13	176	254	43

Leading Scorers

Player	Club	GP	G	A	PTS	PIM
Geoffrion, Bernie	Montreal	64	50	45	95	29
Béliveau, Jean	Montreal	69	32	58	90	57
Mahovlich, Frank	Toronto	70	48	36	84	131
Bathgate, Andy	New York	70	29	48	77	22
Howe, Gordie	Detroit	64	23	49	72	30
Ullman, Norm	Detroit	70	28	42	70	34
Kelly, Red	Toronto	64	20	50	70	12
Moore, Dickie	Montreal	57	35	34	69	62
Richard, Henri	Montreal	70	24	44	68	91
Delvecchio, Alex	Detroit	70	27	35	62	26

1961-62

Team	GP	W	L	T	GF	GA	PTS
Montreal	70	42	14	14	259	166	98
*Toronto	70	37	22	11	232	180	85
Chicago	70	31	26	13	217	186	75
New York	70	26	32	12	195	207	64
Detroit	70	23	33	14	184	219	60
Boston	70	15	47	8	177	306	38

Leading Scorers

Player	Club	GP	G	A	PTS	PIM
Hull, Bobby	Chicago	70	50	34	84	35
Bathgate, Andy	New York	70	28	56	84	44
Howe, Gordie	Detroit	70	33	44	77	54
Mikita, Stan	Chicago	70	25	52	77	97
Mahovlich, Frank	Toronto	70	33	38	71	87
Delvecchio, Alex	Detroit	70	26	43	69	18
Backstrom, Ralph	Montreal	66	27	38	65	29
Ullman, Norm	Detroit	70	26	38	64	54
Hay, Bill	Chicago	60	11	52	63	34
Provost, Claude	Montreal	70	33	29	62	22

John Bucyk, seen here squeezing past Murray Oliver of the Maple Leafs, led the Bruins in scoring four times in six years during the early 1960s. He is still the club leader in seasons, games, goals and points.

1962-63

Team	GP	W	L	T	GF	GA	PTS
*Toronto	70	35	23	12	221	180	82
Chicago	70	32	21	17	194	178	81
Montreal	70	28	19	23	225	183	79
Detroit	70	32	25	13	200	194	77
New York	70	22	36	12	211	233	56
Boston	70	14	39	17	198	281	45

Leading Scorers

Player	Club	GP	G	A	PTS	PIM
Howe, Gordie	Detroit	70	38	48	86	100
Bathgate, Andy	New York	70	35	46	81	54
Mikita, Stan	Chicago	65	31	45	76	69
Mahovlich, Frank	Toronto	67	36	37	73	56
Richard, Henri	Montreal	67	23	50	73	57
Beliveau, Jean	Montreal	69	18	49	67	68
Bucyk, John	Boston	69	27	39	66	36
Delvecchio, Alex	Detroit	70	20	44	64	8
Hull, Bobby	Chicago	65	31	31	62	27
Oliver, Murray	Boston	65	22	40	62	38

1963-64

Team	GP	W	L	T	GF	GA	PTS
Montreal	70	36	21	13	209	167	85
Chicago	70	36	22	12	218	169	84
*Toronto	70	33	25	12	192	172	78
Detroit	70	30	29	11	191	204	71
New York	70	22	38	10	186	242	54
Boston	70	18	40	12	170	212	48

Leading Scorers

Player	Club	GP	G	A	PTS	PIM
Mikita, Stan	Chicago	70	39	50	89	146
Hull, Bobby	Chicago	70	43	44	87	50
Beliveau, Jean	Montreal	68	28	50	78	42
Bathgate, Andy	NYR, Tor.	71	19	58	77	34
Howe, Gordie	Detroit	69	26	47	73	70
Wharram, Ken	Chicago	70	39	32	71	18
Oliver, Murray	Boston	70	24	44	68	41
Goyette, Phil	New York	67	24	41	65	15
Gilbert, Rod	New York	70	24	40	64	62
Keon, Dave	Toronto	70	23	37	60	6

1964-65

Team	GP	W	L	T	GF	GA	PTS
Detroit	70	40	23	7	224	175	87
*Montreal	70	36	23	11	211	185	83
Chicago	70	34	28	8	224	176	76
Toronto	70	30	26	14	204	173	74
New York	70	20	38	12	179	246	52
Boston	70	21	43	6	166	253	48

Leading Scorers

Player	Club	GP	G	A	PTS	PIM
Mikita, Stan	Chicago	70	28	59	87	154
Ullman, Norm	Detroit	70	42	41	83	70
Howe, Gordie	Detroit	70	29	47	76	104
Hull, Bobby	Chicago	61	39	32	71	32
Delvecchio, Alex	Detroit	68	25	42	67	16
Provost, Claude	Montreal	70	27	37	64	28
Gilbert, Rod	New York	70	25	36	61	52
Pilote, Pierre	Chicago	68	14	45	59	162
Bucyk, John	Boston	68	26	29	55	24
Backstrom, Ralph	Montreal	70	25	30	55	41
Esposito, Phil	Chicago	70	23	32	55	44

1965-66

Team	GP	W	L	T	GF	GA	PTS
*Montreal	70	41	21	8	239	173	90
Chicago	70	37	25	8	240	187	82
Toronto	70	34	25	11	208	187	79
Detroit	70	31	27	12	221	194	74
Boston	70	21	43	6	174	275	48
New York	70	18	41	11	195	261	47

Leading Scorers

Player	Club	GP	G	A	PTS	PIM
Hull, Bobby	Chicago	65	54	43	97	70
Mikita, Stan	Chicago	68	30	48	78	58
Rousseau, Bobby	Montreal	70	30	48	78	20
Beliveau, Jean	Montreal	67	29	48	77	50
Howe, Gordie	Detroit	70	29	46	75	83
Ullman, Norm	Detroit	70	31	41	72	35
Delvecchio, Alex	Detroit	70	31	38	69	16
Nevin, Bob	New York	69	29	33	62	10
Richard, Henri	Montreal	62	22	39	61	47
Oliver, Murray	Boston	70	18	42	60	30

1966-67

Team	GP	W	L	T	GF	GA	PTS
Chicago	70	41	17	12	264	170	94
Montreal	70	32	25	13	202	188	77
*Toronto	70	32	27	11	204	211	75
New York	70	30	28	12	188	189	72
Detroit	70	27	39	4	212	241	58
Boston	70	17	43	10	182	253	44

Leading Scorers

Player	Club	GP	G	A	PTS	PIM
Mikita, Stan	Chicago	70	35	62	97	12
Hull, Bobby	Chicago	66	52	28	80	52
Ullman, Norm	Detroit	68	26	44	70	26
Wharram, Ken	Chicago	70	31	34	65	21
Howe, Gordie	Detroit	69	25	40	65	53
Rousseau, Bobby	Montreal	68	19	44	63	58
Esposito, Phil	Chicago	69	21	40	61	40
Goyette, Phil	New York	70	12	49	61	6
Mohns, Doug	Chicago	61	25	35	60	58
Richard, Henri	Montreal	65	21	34	55	28
Delvecchio, Alex	Detroit	70	17	38	55	10

Bobby Hull (9), hockey's only Golden Jet, electrified NHL fans during the 1960s with his blazing speed, cannonading slap-shot and prodigious goal-scoring.

1967-68

East Division

Team	GP	W	L	T	GF	GA	PTS
*Montreal	74	42	22	10	236	167	94
New York	74	39	23	12	226	183	90
Boston	74	37	27	10	259	216	84
Chicago	74	32	26	16	212	222	80
Toronto	74	33	31	10	209	176	76
Detroit	74	27	35	12	245	257	66

West Division

Team	GP	W	L	T	GF	GA	PTS
Philadelphia	74	31	32	11	173	179	73
Los Angeles	74	31	33	10	200	224	72
St. Louis	74	27	31	16	177	191	70
Minnesota	74	27	32	15	191	226	69
Pittsburgh	74	27	34	13	195	216	67
Oakland	74	15	42	17	153	219	47

Leading Scorers

Player	Club	GP	G	A	PTS	PIM
Mikita, Stan	Chicago	72	40	47	87	14
Esposito, Phil	Boston	74	35	49	84	21
Howe, Gordie	Detroit	74	39	43	82	53
Ratelle, Jean	New York	74	32	46	78	18
Gilbert, Rod	New York	73	29	48	77	12
Hull, Bobby	Chicago	71	44	31	75	39
Ullman, Norm	Det., Tor.	71	35	37	72	28
Delvecchio, Alex	Detroit	74	22	48	70	14
Bucyk, John	Boston	72	30	39	69	8
Wharram, Ken	Chicago	74	27	42	69	18

1968-69

East Division

Team	GP	W	L	T	GF	GA	PTS
*Montreal	76	46	19	11	271	202	103
Boston	76	42	18	16	303	221	100
New York	76	41	26	9	231	196	91
Toronto	76	35	26	15	234	217	85
Detroit	76	33	31	12	239	221	78
Chicago	76	34	33	9	280	246	77

West Division

Team	GP	W	L	T	GF	GA	PTS
St. Louis	76	37	25	14	204	157	88
Oakland	76	29	36	11	219	251	69
Philadelphia	76	20	35	21	174	225	61
Los Angeles	76	24	42	10	185	260	58
Pittsburgh	76	20	45	11	189	252	51
Minnesota	76	18	43	5	189	270	51

Leading Scorers

Player	Club	GP	G	A	PTS	PIM
Esposito, Phil	Boston	74	49	77	126	79
Hull, Bobby	Chicago	74	58	49	107	48
Howe, Gordie	Detroit	76	44	59	103	58
Mikita, Stan	Chicago	74	30	67	97	52
Hodge, Ken	Boston	75	45	45	90	75
Cournoyer, Yvan	Montreal	76	43	44	87	31
Delvecchio, Alex	Detroit	72	25	58	83	8
Berenson, Red	St. Louis	76	35	47	82	43
Beliveau, Jean	Montreal	69	33	49	82	55
Mahovlich, Frank	Detroit	76	49	29	78	38
Ratelle, Jean	New York	75	32	46	78	26

1969-70

East Division

Team	GP	W	L	T	GF	GA	PTS
Chicago	76	45	22	9	250	170	99
*Boston	76	40	17	19	277	216	99
Detroit	76	40	21	15	246	199	95
New York	76	38	22	16	246	189	92
Montreal	76	38	22	16	244	201	92
Toronto	76	29	34	13	222	242	71

West Division

Team	GP	W	L	T	GF	GA	PTS
St. Louis	76	37	27	12	224	179	86
Pittsburgh	76	26	38	12	182	238	64
Minnesota	76	19	35	22	224	257	60
Oakland	76	22	40	14	169	243	58
Philadelphia	76	17	35	24	197	225	58
Los Angeles	76	14	52	10	168	290	38

Leading Scorers

Player	Club	GP	G	A	PTS	PIM
Orr, Bobby	Boston	76	33	87	120	125
Esposito, Phil	Boston	76	43	56	99	50
Mikita, Stan	Chicago	76	39	47	86	50
Goyette, Phil	St. Louis	72	29	49	78	16
Tkaczuk, Walt	New York	76	27	50	77	38
Ratelle, Jean	New York	75	32	42	74	28
Berenson, Red	St. Louis	67	33	39	72	38
Parise, Jean-Paul	Minnesota	74	24	48	72	72
Howe, Gordie	Detroit	76	31	40	71	58
Mahovlich, Frank	Detroit	74	38	32	70	59
Balon, Dave	New York	76	33	37	70	100
McKenzie, John	Boston	72	29	41	70	114

1970-71

East Division

Team	GP	W	L	T	GF	GA	PTS
Boston	78	57	14	7	399	207	121
New York	78	49	18	11	259	177	109
*Montreal	78	42	23	13	291	216	97
Toronto	78	37	33	8	248	211	82
Buffalo	78	24	39	15	217	291	63
Vancouver	78	24	46	8	229	296	56
Detroit	78	22	45	11	209	308	55

West Division

Team	GP	W	L	T	GF	GA	PTS
Chicago	78	49	20	9	277	184	107
St. Louis	78	34	25	19	223	208	87
Philadelphia	78	28	33	17	207	225	73
Minnesota	78	28	34	16	191	223	72
Los Angeles	78	25	40	13	239	303	63
Pittsburgh	78	21	37	20	221	240	62
California	78	20	53	5	199	320	45

Leading Scorers

Player	Club	GP	G	A	PTS	PIM
Esposito, Phil	Boston	78	76	76	152	71
Orr, Bobby	Boston	78	37	102	139	91
Bucyk, John	Boston	78	51	65	116	8
Hodge, Ken	Boston	78	43	62	105	113
Hull, Bobby	Chicago	78	44	52	96	32
Ullman, Norm	Toronto	73	34	51	85	24
Cashman, Wayne	Boston	77	21	58	79	100
McKenzie, John	Boston	65	31	46	77	120
Keon, Dave	Toronto	76	38	38	76	4
Beliveau, Jean	Montreal	70	25	51	76	40
Stanfield, Fred	Boston	75	24	52	76	12

1971-72

East Division

Team	GP	W	L	T	GF	GA	PTS
*Boston	78	54	13	11	330	204	119
New York	78	48	17	13	317	192	109
Montreal	78	46	16	16	307	205	108
Toronto	78	33	31	14	209	208	80
Detroit	78	33	35	10	261	262	76
Buffalo	78	16	43	19	203	289	51
Vancouver	78	20	50	8	203	297	48

West Division

Team	GP	W	L	T	GF	GA	PTS
Chicago	78	46	17	15	256	166	107
Minnesota	78	37	29	12	212	191	86
St. Louis	78	28	39	11	208	247	67
Pittsburgh	78	26	38	14	220	258	66
Philadelphia	78	26	38	14	200	236	66
California	78	21	39	18	216	288	60
Los Angeles	78	20	49	9	206	305	49

Leading Scorers

Player	Club	GP	G	A	PTS	PIM
Esposito, Phil	Boston	76	66	67	133	76
Orr, Bobby	Boston	76	37	80	117	106
Ratelle, Jean	New York	63	46	63	109	4
Hadfield, Vic	New York	78	50	56	106	142
Gilbert, Rod	New York	73	43	54	97	64
Mahovlich, Frank	Montreal	76	43	53	96	36
Hull, Bobby	Chicago	78	50	43	93	24
Cournoyer, Yvan	Montreal	73	47	36	83	15
Bucyk, John	Boston	78	32	51	83	4
Clarke, Bobby	Philadelphia	78	35	46	81	87
Lemaire, Jacques	Montreal	77	32	49	81	26

1972-73

East Division

Team	GP	W	L	T	GF	GA	PTS
*Montreal	78	52	10	16	329	184	120
Boston	78	51	22	5	330	235	107
NY Rangers	78	47	23	8	297	208	102
Buffalo	78	37	27	14	257	219	88
Detroit	78	37	29	12	265	243	86
Toronto	78	27	41	10	247	279	64
Vancouver	78	22	47	9	233	339	53
NY Islanders	78	12	60	6	170	347	30

West Division

Team	GP	W	L	T	GF	GA	PTS
Chicago	78	42	27	9	284	225	93
Philadelphia	78	37	30	11	296	256	85
Minnesota	78	37	30	11	254	230	85
St. Louis	78	32	34	12	233	251	76
Pittsburgh	78	32	37	9	257	265	73
Los Angeles	78	31	36	11	232	245	73
Atlanta	78	25	38	15	191	239	65
California	78	16	46	16	213	323	48

Leading Scorers

Player	Club	GP	G	A	PTS	PIM
Esposito, Phil	Boston	78	55	75	130	87
Clarke, Bobby	Philadelphia	78	37	67	104	80
Orr, Bobby	Boston	63	29	72	101	99
MacLeish, Rick	Philadelphia	78	50	50	100	69
Lemaire, Jacques	Montreal	77	44	51	95	16
Ratelle, Jean	NY Rangers	78	41	53	94	12
Redmond, Mickey	Detroit	76	52	41	93	24
Bucyk, John	Boston	78	40	53	93	12
Mahovlich, Frank	Montreal	78	38	55	93	51
Pappin, Jim	Chicago	76	41	51	92	82

1973-74

East Division

Team	GP	W	L	T	GF	GA	PTS
Boston	78	52	17	9	349	221	113
Montreal	78	45	24	9	293	240	99
NY Rangers	78	40	24	14	300	251	94
Toronto	78	35	27	16	274	230	86
Buffalo	78	32	34	12	242	250	76
Detroit	78	29	39	10	255	319	68
Vancouver	78	24	43	11	224	296	59
NY Islanders	78	19	41	18	182	247	56

West Division

Team	GP	W	L	T	GF	GA	PTS
*Philadelphia	78	50	16	12	273	164	112
Chicago	78	41	14	23	272	164	105
Los Angeles	78	33	33	12	233	231	78
Atlanta	78	30	34	14	214	238	74
Pittsburgh	78	28	41	9	242	273	65
St. Louis	78	26	40	12	206	248	64
Minnesota	78	23	38	17	235	275	63
California	78	13	55	10	195	342	36

Leading Scorers

Player	Club	GP	G	A	PTS	PIM
Esposito, Phil	Boston	78	68	77	145	58
Orr, Bobby	Boston	74	32	90	122	82
Hodge, Ken	Boston	76	50	55	105	43
Cashman, Wayne	Boston	78	30	59	89	111
Clarke, Bobby	Philadelphia	77	35	52	87	113
Martin, Rick	Buffalo	78	52	34	86	38
Apps, Syl	Pittsburgh	75	24	61	85	37
Sittler, Darryl	Toronto	78	38	46	84	55
MacDonald, Lowell	Pittsburgh	78	43	39	82	14
Park, Brad	NY Rangers	78	25	57	82	148
Hextall, Dennis	Minnesota	78	20	62	82	138

1974-75
PRINCE OF WALES CONFERENCE
Norris Division

Team	GP	W	L	T	GF	GA	PTS
Montreal	80	47	14	19	374	225	113
Los Angeles	80	42	17	21	269	185	105
Pittsburgh	80	37	28	15	326	289	89
Detroit	80	23	45	12	259	335	58
Washington	80	8	67	5	181	446	21

Adams Division

Buffalo	80	49	16	15	354	240	113
Boston	80	40	26	14	345	245	94
Toronto	80	31	33	16	280	309	78
California	80	19	48	13	212	316	51

CLARENCE CAMPBELL CONFERENCE
Patrick Division

*Philadelphia	80	51	18	11	293	181	113
NY Rangers	80	37	29	14	319	276	88
NY Islanders	80	33	25	22	264	221	88
Atlanta	80	34	31	15	243	233	83

Smythe Division

Vancouver	80	38	32	10	271	254	86
St. Louis	80	35	31	14	269	267	84
Chicago	80	37	35	8	268	241	82
Minnesota	80	23	50	7	221	341	53
Kansas City	80	15	54	11	184	328	41

Leading Scorers

Player	Club	GP	G	A	PTS	PIM
Orr, Bobby	Boston	80	46	89	135	101
Esposito, Phil	Boston	79	61	66	127	62
Dionne, Marcel	Detroit	80	47	74	121	14
Lafleur, Guy	Montreal	70	53	66	119	37
Mahovlich, Pete	Montreal	80	35	82	117	64
Clarke, Bobby	Philadelphia	80	27	89	116	125
Robert, Rene	Buffalo	74	40	60	100	75
Gilbert, Rod	NY Rangers	76	36	61	97	22
Perreault, Gilbert	Buffalo	68	39	57	96	36
Martin, Rick	Buffalo	68	52	43	95	72

1975-76
PRINCE OF WALES CONFERENCE
Norris Division

Team	GP	W	L	T	GF	GA	PTS
*Montreal	80	58	11	11	337	174	127
Los Angeles	80	38	33	9	263	265	85
Pittsburgh	80	35	33	12	339	303	82
Detroit	80	26	44	10	226	300	62
Washington	80	11	59	10	224	394	32

Adams Division

Boston	80	48	15	17	313	237	113
Buffalo	80	46	21	13	339	240	105
Toronto	80	34	31	15	294	276	83
California	80	27	42	11	250	278	65

CLARENCE CAMPBELL CONFERENCE
Patrick Division

Philadelphia	80	51	13	16	348	209	118
NY Islanders	80	42	21	17	297	190	101
Atlanta	80	35	33	12	262	237	82
NY Rangers	80	29	42	9	262	333	67

Smythe Division

Chicago	80	32	30	18	254	261	82
Vancouver	80	33	32	15	271	272	81
St. Louis	80	29	37	14	249	290	72
Minnesota	80	20	53	7	195	303	47
Kansas City	80	12	56	12	190	351	36

Leading Scorers

Player	Club	GP	G	A	PTS	PIM
Lafleur, Guy	Montreal	80	56	69	125	36
Clarke, Bobby	Philadelphia	76	30	89	119	13
Perreault, Gilbert	Buffalo	80	44	69	113	36
Barber, Bill	Philadelphia	80	50	62	112	104
Larouche, Pierre	Pittsburgh	76	53	58	111	33
Ratelle, Jean	Bos., NYR	80	36	69	105	18
Mahovlich, Pete	Montreal	80	34	71	105	76
Pronovost, Jean	Pittsburgh	80	52	52	104	24
Sittler, Darryl	Toronto	79	41	59	100	90
Apps, Syl	Pittsburgh	80	32	67	99	24

1976-77
PRINCE OF WALES CONFERENCE
Norris Division

Team	GP	W	L	T	GF	GA	PTS
*Montreal	80	60	8	12	387	171	132
Los Angeles	80	34	31	15	271	241	83
Pittsburgh	80	34	33	13	240	252	81
Washington	80	24	42	14	221	307	62
Detroit	80	16	55	9	183	309	41

Adams Division

Boston	80	49	23	8	312	240	106
Buffalo	80	48	24	8	301	220	104
Toronto	80	33	32	15	301	285	81
Cleveland	80	25	42	13	240	292	63

CLARENCE CAMPBELL CONFERENCE
Patrick Division

Philadelphia	80	48	16	16	323	213	112
NY Islanders	80	47	21	12	288	193	106
Atlanta	80	34	34	12	264	265	80
NY Rangers	80	29	37	14	272	310	72

Smythe Division

St. Louis	80	32	39	9	239	276	73
Minnesota	80	23	39	18	240	310	64
Chicago	80	26	43	11	240	298	63
Vancouver	80	25	42	13	235	294	63
Colorado	80	20	46	14	226	307	54

Leading Scorers

Player	Club	GP	G	A	PTS	PIM
Lafleur, Guy	Montreal	80	56	80	136	20
Dionne, Marcel	Los Angeles	80	53	69	122	12
Shutt, Steve	Montreal	80	60	45	105	28
MacLeish, Rick	Philadelphia	79	49	48	97	42
Perreault, Gilbert	Buffalo	80	39	56	95	30
Young, Tim	Minnesota	80	29	66	95	58
Ratelle, Jean	Boston	78	33	61	94	22
McDonald, Lanny	Toronto	80	46	44	90	77
Sittler, Darryl	Toronto	73	38	52	90	89
Clarke, Bobby	Philadelphia	80	27	63	90	71

1977-78
PRINCE OF WALES CONFERENCE
Norris Division

Team	GP	W	L	T	GF	GA	PTS
*Montreal	80	59	10	11	359	183	129
Detroit	80	32	34	14	252	266	78
Los Angeles	80	31	34	15	243	45	77
Pittsburgh	80	25	37	18	254	321	68
Washington	80	17	49	14	195	321	48

Adams Division

Boston	80	51	18	11	333	218	113
Buffalo	80	44	19	17	288	215	105
Toronto	80	41	29	10	271	237	92
Cleveland	80	22	45	13	230	325	57

CLARENCE CAMPBELL CONFERENCE
Patrick Division

NY Islanders	80	48	17	15	334	210	111
Philadelphia	80	45	20	15	296	200	105
Atlanta	80	34	27	19	274	252	87
NY Rangers	80	30	37	13	279	280	73

Smythe Division

Chicago	80	32	29	19	230	220	83
Colorado	80	19	40	21	257	305	59
Vancouver	80	20	43	17	239	320	57
St. Louis	80	20	47	13	195	304	53
Minnesota	80	18	53	9	218	325	45

Leading Scorers

Player	Club	GP	G	A	PTS	PIM
Lafleur, Guy	Montreal	79	60	72	132	26
Trottier, Bryan	NY Islanders	77	46	77	123	46
Sittler, Darryl	Toronto	80	45	72	117	100
Lemaire, Jacques	Montreal	76	36	61	97	14
Potvin, Denis	NY Islanders	80	30	64	94	81
Bossy, Mike	NY Islanders	73	53	38	91	6
O'Reilly, Terry	Boston	77	29	61	90	211
Perreault, Gilbert	Buffalo	79	41	48	89	20
Clarke, Bobby	Philadelphia	71	21	68	89	83
McDonald, Lanny	Toronto	74	47	40	87	54
Paiement, Wilf	Colorado	80	31	56	87	114

1978-79
PRINCE OF WALES CONFERENCE
Norris Division

Team	GP	W	L	T	GF	GA	PTS
*Montreal	80	52	17	11	337	204	115
Pittsburgh	80	36	31	13	281	279	85
Los Angeles	80	34	34	12	292	286	80
Washington	80	24	41	15	273	338	63
Detroit	80	23	41	16	252	295	62

Adams Division

Boston	80	43	23	14	316	270	100
Buffalo	80	36	28	16	280	263	88
Toronto	80	34	33	13	267	252	81
Minnesota	80	28	40	12	257	289	68

CLARENCE CAMPBELL CONFERENCE
Patrick Division

NY Islanders	80	51	15	14	358	214	116
Philadelphia	80	40	25	15	281	248	95
NY Rangers	80	40	29	11	316	292	91
Atlanta	80	41	31	8	327	280	90

Smythe Division

Chicago	80	29	36	15	244	277	73
Vancouver	80	25	42	13	217	291	63
St. Louis	80	18	50	12	249	348	48
Colorado	80	15	53	12	210	331	42

Leading Scorers

Player	Club	GP	G	A	PTS	PIM
Trottier, Bryan	NY Islanders	76	47	87	134	50
Dionne, Marcel	Los Angeles	80	59	71	130	30
Lafleur, Guy	Montreal	80	52	77	129	28
Bossy, Mike	NY Islanders	80	69	57	126	25
MacMillan, Bob	Atlanta	79	37	71	108	14
Chouinard, Guy	Atlanta	80	50	57	107	14
Potvin, Denis	NY Islanders	73	31	70	101	58
Federko, Bernie	St. Louis	74	31	64	95	14
Taylor, Dave	Los Angeles	78	43	48	91	124
Gillies, Clark	NY Islanders	75	35	56	91	68

Cesare Maniago, who saw action with Toronto, Montreal and the NY Rangers before joining the Minnesota North Stars in 1967, still holds six individual career goaltending marks with the Stars, including games played, wins and shutouts.

1979-80

PRINCE OF WALES CONFERENCE

Norris Division

Team	GP	W	L	T	GF	GA	PTS
Montreal	80	47	20	13	328	240	107
Los Angeles	80	30	36	14	290	313	74
Pittsburgh	80	30	37	13	251	303	73
Hartford	80	27	34	19	303	312	73
Detroit	80	26	43	11	268	306	63
Adams Division							
Buffalo	80	47	17	16	318	201	110
Boston	80	46	21	13	310	234	105
Minnesota	80	36	28	16	311	253	88
Toronto	80	35	40	5	304	327	75
Quebec	80	25	44	11	248	313	61

CLARENCE CAMPBELL CONFERENCE

Patrick Division

Team	GP	W	L	T	GF	GA	PTS
Philadelphia	80	48	12	20	327	254	116
*NY Islanders	80	39	28	13	281	247	91
NY Rangers	80	38	32	10	308	284	86
Atlanta	80	35	32	13	282	269	83
Washington	80	27	40	13	261	293	67
Smythe Division							
Chicago	80	34	27	19	241	250	87
St. Louis	80	34	34	12	266	278	80
Vancouver	80	27	37	16	256	281	70
Edmonton	80	28	39	13	301	322	69
Winnipeg	80	20	49	11	214	314	51
Colorado	80	19	48	13	234	308	51

Leading Scorers

Player	Club	GP	G	A	PTS	PIM
Dionne, Marcel	Los Angeles	80	53	84	137	32
Gretzky, Wayne	Edmonton	79	51	86	137	21
Lafleur, Guy	Montreal	74	50	75	125	12
Perreault, Gilbert	Buffalo	80	40	66	106	57
Rogers, Mike	Hartford	80	44	61	105	10
Trottier, Bryan	NY Islanders	78	42	62	104	68
Simmer, Charlie	Los Angeles	64	56	45	101	65
Stoughton, Blaine	Hartford	80	56	44	100	16
Sittler, Darryl	Toronto	73	40	57	97	62
MacDonald, Blair	Edmonton	80	46	48	94	6
Federko, Bernie	St. Louis	79	38	56	94	24

1980-81

PRINCE OF WALES CONFERENCE

Norris Division

Team	GP	W	L	T	GF	GA	PTS
Montreal	80	45	22	13	332	232	103
Los Angeles	80	43	24	13	337	290	99
Pittsburgh	80	30	37	13	302	345	73
Hartford	80	21	41	18	292	372	60
Detroit	80	19	43	18	252	339	56
Adams Division							
Buffalo	80	39	20	21	327	250	99
Boston	80	37	30	13	316	272	87
Minnesota	80	35	28	17	291	263	87
Quebec	80	30	32	18	314	318	78
Toronto	80	28	37	15	322	367	71

CLARENCE CAMPBELL CONFERENCE

Patrick Division

Team	GP	W	L	T	GF	GA	PTS
*NY Islanders	80	48	18	14	355	260	110
Philadelphia	80	41	24	15	313	249	97
Calgary	80	39	27	14	329	298	92
NY Rangers	80	30	36	14	312	317	74
Washington	80	26	36	18	286	317	70
Smythe Division							
St. Louis	80	45	18	17	352	281	107
Chicago	80	31	33	16	304	315	78
Vancouver	80	28	32	20	289	301	76
Edmonton	80	29	35	16	328	327	74
Colorado	80	22	45	13	258	344	57
Winnipeg	80	9	57	14	246	400	32

Leading Scorers

Player	Club	GP	G	A	PTS	PIM
Gretzky, Wayne	Edmonton	80	55	109	164	28
Dionne, Marcel	Los Angeles	80	58	77	135	70
Nilsson, Kent	Calgary	80	49	82	131	26
Bossy, Mike	NY Islanders	79	68	51	119	32
Taylor, Dave	Los Angeles	72	47	65	112	130
Stastny, Peter	Quebec	77	39	70	109	37
Simmer, Charlie	Los Angeles	65	56	49	105	62
Rogers, Mike	Hartford	80	40	65	105	32
Federko, Bernie	St. Louis	78	31	73	104	47
Richard, Jacques	Quebec	78	52	51	103	39
Middleton, Rick	Boston	80	44	59	103	16
Trottier, Bryan	NY Islanders	73	31	72	103	74

1981-82

CLARENCE CAMPBELL CONFERENCE

Norris Division

Team	GP	W	L	T	GF	GA	PTS
Minnesota	80	37	23	20	346	288	94
Winnipeg	80	33	33	14	319	332	80
St. Louis	80	32	40	8	315	349	72
Chicago	80	30	38	12	332	363	72
Toronto	80	20	44	16	298	380	56
Detroit	80	21	47	12	270	351	54
Smythe Division							
Edmonton	80	48	17	15	417	295	111
Vancouver	80	30	33	17	290	286	77
Calgary	80	29	34	17	334	345	75
Los Angeles	80	24	41	15	314	369	63
Colorado	80	18	49	13	241	362	49

PRINCE OF WALES CONFERENCE

Adams Division

Team	GP	W	L	T	GF	GA	PTS
Montreal	80	46	17	17	360	223	109
Boston	80	43	27	10	323	285	96
Buffalo	80	39	26	15	307	273	93
Quebec	80	33	31	16	356	345	82
Hartford	80	21	41	18	264	351	60
Patrick Division							
*NY Islanders	80	54	16	10	385	250	118
NY Rangers	80	39	27	14	316	306	92
Philadelphia	80	38	31	11	325	313	87
Pittsburgh	80	31	36	13	310	337	75
Washington	80	26	41	13	319	338	65

Leading Scorers

Player	Club	GP	G	A	PTS	PIM
Gretzky, Wayne	Edmonton	80	92	120	212	26
Bossy, Mike	NY Islanders	80	64	83	147	22
Stastny, Peter	Quebec	80	46	93	139	91
Maruk, Dennis	Washington	80	60	76	136	128
Trottier, Bryan	NY Islanders	80	50	79	129	88
Savard, Denis	Chicago	80	32	87	119	82
Dionne, Marcel	Los Angeles	78	50	67	117	50
Smith, Bobby	Minnesota	80	43	71	114	82
Ciccarelli, Dino	Minnesota	76	55	51	106	138
Taylor, Dave	Los Angeles	78	39	67	106	130

1982-83

CLARENCE CAMPBELL CONFERENCE

Norris Division

Team	GP	W	L	T	GF	GA	PTS
Chicago	80	47	23	10	338	268	104
Minnesota	80	40	24	16	321	290	96
Toronto	80	28	40	12	293	330	68
St. Louis	80	25	40	15	285	316	65
Detroit	80	21	44	15	263	344	57
Smythe Division							
Edmonton	80	47	21	12	424	315	106
Calgary	80	32	34	14	321	317	78
Vancouver	80	30	35	15	303	309	75
Winnipeg	80	33	39	8	311	333	74
Los Angeles	80	27	41	12	308	365	66

PRINCE OF WALES CONFERENCE

Adams Division

Team	GP	W	L	T	GF	GA	PTS
Boston	80	50	20	10	327	228	110
Montreal	80	42	24	14	350	286	98
Buffalo	80	38	29	13	318	285	89
Quebec	80	34	34	12	343	336	80
Hartford	80	19	54	7	261	403	45
Patrick Division							
Philadelphia	80	49	23	8	326	240	106
*NY Islanders	80	42	26	12	302	226	96
Washington	80	39	25	16	306	283	94
NY Rangers	80	35	35	10	306	287	80
New Jersey	80	17	49	14	230	338	48
Pittsburgh	80	18	53	9	257	394	45

Leading Scorers

Player	Club	GP	G	A	PTS	PIM
Gretzky, Wayne	Edmonton	80	71	125	196	59
Stastny, Peter	Quebec	75	47	77	124	78
Savard, Denis	Chicago	78	35	86	121	99
Bossy, Mike	NY Islanders	79	60	58	118	20
Dionne, Marcel	Los Angeles	80	56	51	107	22
Pederson, Barry	Boston	77	46	61	107	47
Messier, Mark	Edmonton	77	48	58	106	72
Goulet, Michel	Quebec	80	57	48	105	51
Anderson, Glenn	Edmonton	72	48	56	104	70
Nilsson, Kent	Calgary	80	46	58	104	10
Kurri, Jari	Edmonton	80	45	59	104	22

1983-84

CLARENCE CAMPBELL CONFERENCE

Norris Division

Team	GP	W	L	T	GF	GA	PTS
Minnesota	80	39	31	10	345	344	88
St. Louis	80	32	41	7	293	316	71
Detroit	80	31	42	7	298	323	69
Chicago	80	30	42	8	277	311	68
Toronto	80	26	45	9	303	387	61
Smythe Division							
*Edmonton	80	57	18	5	446	314	119
Calgary	80	34	32	14	311	314	82
Vancouver	80	32	39	9	306	328	73
Winnipeg	80	31	38	11	340	374	73
Los Angeles	80	23	44	13	309	376	59

PRINCE OF WALES CONFERENCE

Adams Division

Team	GP	W	L	T	GF	GA	PTS
Boston	80	49	25	6	336	261	104
Buffalo	80	48	25	7	315	257	103
Quebec	80	42	28	10	360	278	94
Montreal	80	35	40	5	286	295	75
Hartford	80	28	42	10	288	320	66
Patrick Division							
NY Islanders	80	50	26	4	357	269	104
Washington	80	48	27	5	308	226	101
Philadelphia	80	44	26	10	350	290	98
NY Rangers	80	42	29	9	314	304	93
New Jersey	80	17	56	7	231	350	41
Pittsburgh	80	16	58	6	254	390	38

Leading Scorers

Player	Club	GP	G	A	PTS	PIM
Gretzky, Wayne	Edmonton	74	87	118	205	39
Coffey, Paul	Edmonton	80	40	86	126	104
Goulet, Michel	Quebec	75	56	65	121	76
Stastny, Peter	Quebec	80	46	73	119	73
Bossy, Mike	NY Islanders	67	51	67	118	8
Pederson, Barry	Boston	80	39	77	116	64
Kurri, Jari	Edmonton	64	52	61	113	14
Trottier, Bryan	NY Islanders	68	40	71	111	59
Federko, Bernie	St. Louis	79	41	66	107	43
Middleton, Rick	Boston	80	47	58	105	14

1984-85

CLARENCE CAMPBELL CONFERENCE

Norris Division

Team	GP	W	L	T	GF	GA	PTS
St. Louis	80	37	31	12	299	288	86
Chicago	80	38	35	7	309	299	83
Detroit	80	27	41	12	313	357	66
Minnesota	80	25	43	12	268	321	62
Toronto	80	20	52	8	253	358	48
Smythe Division							
*Edmonton	80	49	20	11	401	298	109
Winnipeg	80	43	27	10	358	332	96
Calgary	80	41	27	12	363	302	94
Los Angeles	80	34	32	14	339	326	82
Vancouver	80	25	46	9	284	401	59

PRINCE OF WALES CONFERENCE

Adams Division

Team	GP	W	L	T	GF	GA	PTS
Montreal	80	41	27	12	309	262	94
Quebec	80	41	30	9	323	275	91
Buffalo	80	38	28	14	290	237	90
Boston	80	36	34	10	303	287	82
Hartford	80	30	41	9	268	318	69
Patrick Division							
Philadelphia	80	53	20	7	348	241	113
Washington	80	46	25	9	322	240	101
NY Islanders	80	40	34	6	345	312	86
NY Rangers	80	26	44	10	295	345	62
New Jersey	80	22	48	10	264	346	54
Pittsburgh	80	24	51	5	276	385	53

Leading Scorers

Player	Club	GP	G	A	PTS	PIM
Gretzky, Wayne	Edmonton	80	73	135	208	52
Kurri, Jari	Edmonton	73	71	64	135	30
Hawerchuk, Dale	Winnipeg	80	53	77	130	74
Dionne, Marcel	Los Angeles	80	46	80	126	46
Coffey, Paul	Edmonton	80	37	84	121	97
Bossy, Mike	NY Islanders	76	58	59	117	38
Ogrodnick, John	Detroit	79	55	50	105	30
Savard, Denis	Chicago	79	38	67	105	56
Federko, Bernie	St. Louis	76	30	73	103	27
Gartner, Mike	Washington	80	50	52	102	71

Marcel Dionne finished among the NHL's top-ten scorers for the final time in his Hall-of-Fame career during the 1984-85 season. His 46 goals and 80 assists were the fourth best totals in the league that year.

Mike Bossy, arguably the NHL's top marksman during his ten-year career, scored all four game-winning goals for the NY Islanders in their six-game victory over Boston in the 1983 Campbell Conference Finals.

1985-86
CLARENCE CAMPBELL CONFERENCE
Norris Division

Team	GP	W	L	T	GF	GA	PTS
Chicago	80	39	33	8	351	349	86
Minnesota	80	38	33	9	327	305	85
St. Louis	80	37	34	9	302	291	83
Toronto	80	25	48	7	311	386	57
Detroit	80	17	57	6	266	415	40

Smythe Division

Team	GP	W	L	T	GF	GA	PTS
Edmonton	80	56	17	7	426	310	119
Calgary	80	40	31	9	354	315	89
Winnipeg	80	26	47	7	295	372	59
Vancouver	80	23	44	13	282	333	59
Los Angeles	80	23	49	8	284	389	54

PRINCE OF WALES CONFERENCE
Adams Division

Team	GP	W	L	T	GF	GA	PTS
Quebec	80	43	31	6	330	289	92
*Montreal	80	40	33	7	330	280	87
Boston	80	37	31	12	311	288	86
Hartford	80	40	36	4	332	302	84
Buffalo	80	37	37	6	296	291	80

Patrick Division

Team	GP	W	L	T	GF	GA	PTS
Philadelphia	80	53	23	4	335	241	110
Washington	80	50	23	7	315	272	107
NY Islanders	80	39	29	12	327	284	90
NY Rangers	80	36	38	6	280	276	78
Pittsburgh	80	34	38	8	313	305	76
New Jersey	80	28	49	3	300	374	59

Leading Scorers

Player	Club	GP	G	A	PTS	PIM
Gretzky, Wayne	Edmonton	80	52	163	215	52
Lemieux, Mario	Pittsburgh	79	48	93	141	43
Coffey, Paul	Edmonton	79	48	90	138	120
Kurri, Jari	Edmonton	78	68	63	131	22
Bossy, Mike	NY Islanders	80	61	62	123	14
Stastny, Peter	Quebec	76	41	81	122	60
Savard, Denis	Chicago	80	47	69	116	111
Naslund, Mats	Montreal	80	43	67	110	16
Hawerchuk, Dale	Winnipeg	80	46	59	105	44
Broten, Neal	Minnesota	80	29	76	105	47

1986-87
CLARENCE CAMPBELL CONFERENCE
Norris Division

Team	GP	W	L	T	GF	GA	PTS
St. Louis	80	32	33	15	281	293	79
Detroit	80	34	36	10	260	274	78
Chicago	80	29	37	14	290	310	72
Toronto	80	32	42	6	286	319	70
Minnesota	80	30	40	10	296	314	70

Smythe Division

Team	GP	W	L	T	GF	GA	PTS
*Edmonton	80	50	24	6	372	284	106
Calgary	80	46	31	3	318	289	95
Winnipeg	80	40	32	8	279	271	88
Los Angeles	80	31	41	8	318	341	70
Vancouver	80	29	43	8	282	314	66

PRINCE OF WALES CONFERENCE
Adams Division

Team	GP	W	L	T	GF	GA	PTS
Hartford	80	43	30	7	287	270	93
Montreal	80	41	29	10	277	241	92
Boston	80	39	34	7	301	276	85
Quebec	80	31	39	10	267	276	72
Buffalo	80	28	44	8	280	308	64

Patrick Division

Team	GP	W	L	T	GF	GA	PTS
Philadelphia	80	46	26	8	310	245	100
Washington	80	38	32	10	285	278	86
NY Islanders	80	35	33	12	279	281	82
NY Rangers	80	34	38	8	307	323	76
Pittsburgh	80	30	38	12	297	290	72
New Jersey	80	29	45	6	293	368	64

Leading Scorers

Player	Club	GP	G	A	PTS	PIM
Gretzky, Wayne	Edmonton	79	62	121	183	28
Kurri, Jari	Edmonton	79	54	54	108	41
Lemieux, Mario	Pittsburgh	63	54	53	107	57
Messier, Mark	Edmonton	77	37	70	107	73
Gilmour, Doug	St. Louis	80	42	63	105	58
Ciccarelli, Dino	Minnesota	80	52	51	103	92
Hawerchuk, Dale	Winnipeg	80	47	53	100	54
Goulet, Michel	Quebec	75	49	47	96	61
Kerr, Tim	Philadelphia	75	58	37	95	57
Bourque, Ray	Boston	78	23	72	95	36

1987-88
CLARENCE CAMPBELL CONFERENCE
Norris Division

Team	GP	W	L	T	GF	GA	PTS
Detroit	80	41	28	11	322	269	93
St. Louis	80	34	38	8	278	294	76
Chicago	80	30	41	9	284	328	69
Toronto	80	21	49	10	273	345	52
Minnesota	80	19	48	13	242	349	51

Smythe Division

Team	GP	W	L	T	GF	GA	PTS
Calgary	80	48	23	9	397	305	105
*Edmonton	80	44	25	11	363	288	99
Winnipeg	80	33	36	11	292	310	77
Los Angeles	80	30	42	8	318	359	68
Vancouver	80	25	46	9	272	320	59

PRINCE OF WALES CONFERENCE
Adams Division

Team	GP	W	L	T	GF	GA	PTS
Montreal	80	45	22	13	298	238	103
Boston	80	44	30	6	300	251	94
Buffalo	80	37	32	11	283	305	85
Hartford	80	35	38	7	249	267	77
Quebec	80	32	43	5	271	306	69

Patrick Division

Team	GP	W	L	T	GF	GA	PTS
NY Islanders	80	39	31	10	308	267	88
Washington	80	38	33	9	281	249	85
Philadelphia	80	38	33	9	292	292	85
New Jersey	80	38	36	6	295	296	82
NY Rangers	80	36	34	10	300	283	82
Pittsburgh	80	36	35	9	319	316	81

Leading Scorers

Player	Club	GP	G	A	PTS	PIM
Lemieux, Mario	Pittsburgh	76	70	98	168	92
Gretzky, Wayne	Edmonton	64	40	109	149	24
Savard, Denis	Chicago	80	44	87	131	95
Hawerchuk, Dale	Winnipeg	80	44	77	121	59
Robitaille, Luc	Los Angeles	80	53	58	111	82
Stastny, Peter	Quebec	76	46	65	111	69
Messier, Mark	Edmonton	77	37	74	111	103
Carson, Jimmy	Los Angeles	80	55	52	107	45
Loob, Hakan	Calgary	80	50	56	106	47
Goulet, Michel	Quebec	80	48	58	106	56

1988-89
CLARENCE CAMPBELL CONFERENCE
Norris Division

Team	GP	W	L	T	GF	GA	PTS
Detroit	80	34	34	12	313	316	80
St. Louis	80	33	35	12	275	285	78
Minnesota	80	27	37	16	258	278	70
Chicago	80	27	41	12	297	335	66
Toronto	80	28	46	6	259	342	62

Smythe Division

Team	GP	W	L	T	GF	GA	PTS
*Calgary	80	54	17	9	354	226	117
Los Angeles	80	42	31	7	376	335	91
Edmonton	80	38	34	8	325	306	84
Vancouver	80	33	39	8	251	253	74
Winnipeg	80	26	42	12	300	355	64

PRINCE OF WALES CONFERENCE
Adams Division

Team	GP	W	L	T	GF	GA	PTS
Montreal	80	53	18	9	315	218	115
Boston	80	37	29	14	289	256	88
Buffalo	80	38	35	7	291	299	83
Hartford	80	37	38	5	299	290	79
Quebec	80	27	46	7	269	342	61

Patrick Division

Team	GP	W	L	T	GF	GA	PTS
Washington	80	41	29	10	305	259	92
Pittsburgh	80	40	33	7	347	349	87
NY Rangers	80	37	35	8	310	307	82
Philadelphia	80	36	36	8	307	285	80
New Jersey	80	27	41	12	281	325	66
NY Islanders	80	28	47	5	265	325	61

Leading Scorers

Player	Club	GP	G	A	PTS	PIM
Lemieux, Mario	Pittsburgh	76	85	114	199	100
Gretzky, Wayne	Los Angeles	78	54	114	168	26
Yzerman, Steve	Detroit	80	65	90	155	61
Nicholls, Bernie	Los Angeles	79	70	80	150	96
Brown, Rob	Pittsburgh	68	49	66	115	118
Coffey, Paul	Pittsburgh	75	30	83	113	193
Mullen, Joe	Calgary	79	51	59	110	16
Kurri, Jari	Edmonton	76	44	58	102	69
Carson, Jimmy	Edmonton	80	49	51	100	36
Robitaille, Luc	Los Angeles	78	46	52	98	65

1989-90
CLARENCE CAMPBELL CONFERENCE
Norris Division

Team	GP	W	L	T	GF	GA	PTS
Chicago	80	41	33	6	316	294	88
St. Louis	80	37	34	9	295	279	83
Toronto	80	38	38	4	337	358	80
Minnesota	80	36	40	4	284	291	76
Detroit	80	28	38	14	288	323	70

Smythe Division

Team	GP	W	L	T	GF	GA	PTS
Calgary	80	42	23	15	348	265	99
*Edmonton	80	38	28	14	315	283	90
Winnipeg	80	37	32	11	298	290	85
Los Angeles	80	34	39	7	338	337	75
Vancouver	80	25	41	14	245	306	64

PRINCE OF WALES CONFERENCE
Adams Division

Team	GP	W	L	T	GF	GA	PTS
Boston	80	46	25	9	289	232	101
Buffalo	80	45	27	8	286	248	98
Montreal	80	41	28	11	288	234	93
Hartford	80	38	33	9	275	268	85
Quebec	80	12	61	7	240	407	31

Patrick Division

Team	GP	W	L	T	GF	GA	PTS
NY Rangers	80	36	31	13	279	267	85
New Jersey	80	37	34	9	295	288	83
Washington	80	36	38	6	284	275	78
NY Islanders	80	31	38	11	281	288	73
Pittsburgh	80	32	40	8	318	359	72
Philadelphia	80	30	39	11	290	297	71

Leading Scorers

Player	Club	GP	G	A	PTS	PIM
Gretzky, Wayne	Los Angeles	73	40	102	142	42
Messier, Mark	Edmonton	79	45	84	129	79
Yzerman, Steve	Detroit	79	62	65	127	79
Lemieux, Mario	Pittsburgh	59	45	78	123	78
Hull, Brett	St. Louis	80	72	41	113	24
Nicholls, Bernie	L.A., NYR	79	39	73	112	86
Turgeon, Pierre	Buffalo	80	40	66	106	29
LaFontaine, Pat	NY Islanders	74	54	51	105	38
Coffey, Paul	Pittsburgh	80	29	74	103	95
Sakic, Joe	Quebec	80	39	63	102	27
Oates, Adam	St. Louis	80	23	79	102	30

1990-91
CLARENCE CAMPBELL CONFERENCE
Norris Division

Team	GP	W	L	T	GF	GA	PTS
Chicago	80	49	23	8	284	211	106
St. Louis	80	47	22	11	310	250	105
Detroit	80	34	38	8	273	298	76
Minnesota	80	27	39	14	256	266	68
Toronto	80	23	46	11	241	318	57

Smythe Division

Team	GP	W	L	T	GF	GA	PTS
Los Angeles	80	46	24	10	340	254	102
Calgary	80	46	26	8	344	263	100
Edmonton	80	37	37	6	272	272	80
Vancouver	80	28	43	9	243	315	65
Winnipeg	80	26	43	11	260	288	63

PRINCE OF WALES CONFERENCE
Adams Division

Team	GP	W	L	T	GF	GA	PTS
Boston	80	44	24	12	299	264	100
Montreal	80	39	30	11	273	249	89
Buffalo	80	31	30	19	292	278	81
Hartford	80	31	38	11	238	276	73
Quebec	80	16	50	14	236	354	46

Patrick Division

Team	GP	W	L	T	GF	GA	PTS
*Pittsburgh	80	41	33	6	342	305	88
NY Rangers	80	36	31	13	297	265	85
Washington	80	37	36	7	258	258	81
New Jersey	80	32	33	15	272	264	79
Philadelphia	80	33	37	10	252	267	76
NY Islanders	80	25	45	10	223	290	60

Leading Scorers

Player	Club	GP	G	A	PTS	PIM
Gretzky, Wayne	Los Angeles	78	41	122	163	16
Hull, Brett	St. Louis	78	86	45	131	22
Oates, Adam	St. Louis	61	25	90	115	29
Recchi, Mark	Pittsburgh	78	40	73	113	48
Cullen, John	Pit., Hfd.	78	39	71	110	101
Sakic, Joe	Quebec	80	48	61	109	24
Yzerman, Steve	Detroit	80	51	57	108	34
Fleury, Theo	Calgary	79	51	53	104	136
MacInnis, Al	Calgary	78	28	75	103	90
Larmer, Steve	Chicago	80	44	57	101	79

1991-92
CLARENCE CAMPBELL CONFERENCE
Norris Division

Team	GP	W	L	T	GF	GA	PTS
Detroit	80	43	25	12	320	256	98
Chicago	80	36	29	15	257	236	87
St. Louis	80	36	33	11	279	266	83
Minnesota	80	32	42	6	246	278	70
Toronto	80	30	43	7	234	294	67

Smythe Division

Team	GP	W	L	T	GF	GA	PTS
Vancouver	80	42	26	12	285	250	96
Los Angeles	80	35	31	14	287	296	84
Edmonton	80	36	34	10	295	297	82
Winnipeg	80	33	32	15	251	244	81
Calgary	80	31	37	12	296	305	74
San Jose	80	17	58	5	219	359	39

PRINCE OF WALES CONFERENCE
Adams Division

Team	GP	W	L	T	GF	GA	PTS
Montreal	80	41	28	11	267	207	93
Boston	80	36	32	12	270	275	84
Buffalo	80	31	37	12	289	299	74
Hartford	80	26	41	13	247	283	65
Quebec	80	20	48	12	255	318	52

Patrick Division

Team	GP	W	L	T	GF	GA	PTS
NY Rangers	80	50	25	5	321	246	105
Washington	80	45	27	8	330	275	98
*Pittsburgh	80	39	32	9	343	308	87
New Jersey	80	38	31	11	289	259	87
NY Islanders	80	34	35	11	291	299	79
Philadelphia	80	32	37	11	252	273	75

Leading Scorers

Player	Club	GP	G	A	PTS	PIM
Lemieux, Mario	Pittsburgh	64	44	87	131	94
Stevens, Kevin	Pittsburgh	80	54	69	123	254
Gretzky, Wayne	Los Angeles	74	31	90	121	34
Hull, Brett	St. Louis	73	70	39	109	48
Robitaille, Luc	Los Angeles	80	44	63	107	95
Messier, Mark	NY Rangers	79	35	72	107	76
Roenick, Jeremy	Chicago	80	53	50	103	23
Yzerman, Steve	Detroit	79	45	58	103	64
Leetch, Brian	NY Rangers	80	22	80	102	26
Oates, Adam	St. L., Bos.	80	20	79	99	22

1992-93
CLARENCE CAMPBELL CONFERENCE
Norris Division

Team	GP	W	L	T	GF	GA	PTS
Chicago	84	47	25	12	279	230	106
Detroit	84	47	28	9	369	280	103
Toronto	84	44	29	11	288	241	99
St. Louis	84	37	36	11	282	278	85
Minnesota	84	36	38	10	272	293	82
Tampa Bay	84	23	54	7	245	332	53

Smythe Division

Team	GP	W	L	T	GF	GA	PTS
Vancouver	84	46	29	9	346	278	101
Calgary	84	43	30	11	322	282	97
Los Angeles	84	39	35	10	338	340	88
Winnipeg	84	40	37	7	322	320	87
Edmonton	84	26	50	8	242	337	60
San Jose	84	11	71	2	218	414	24

PRINCE OF WALES CONFERENCE
Adams Division

Team	GP	W	L	T	GF	GA	PTS
Boston	84	51	26	7	332	268	109
Quebec	84	47	27	10	351	300	104
*Montreal	84	48	30	6	326	280	102
Buffalo	84	38	36	10	335	297	86
Hartford	84	26	52	6	284	369	58
Ottawa	84	10	70	4	202	395	24

Patrick Division

Team	GP	W	L	T	GF	GA	PTS
Pittsburgh	84	56	21	7	367	268	119
Washington	84	43	34	7	325	286	93
NY Islanders	84	40	37	7	335	297	87
New Jersey	84	40	37	7	308	299	87
Philadelphia	84	36	37	11	319	319	83
NY Rangers	84	34	39	11	304	308	79

Leading Scorers

Player	Club	GP	G	A	PTS	PIM
Lemieux, Mario	Pittsburgh	60	69	91	160	38
LaFontaine, Pat	Buffalo	84	53	95	148	63
Oates, Adam	Boston	84	45	97	142	32
Yzerman, Steve	Detroit	84	58	79	137	44
Selanne, Teemu	Winnipeg	84	76	56	132	45
Turgeon, Pierre	NY Islanders	83	58	74	132	26
Mogilny, Alexander	Buffalo	77	76	51	127	40
Gilmour, Doug	Toronto	83	32	95	127	100
Robitaille, Luc	Los Angeles	84	63	62	125	100
Recchi, Mark	Philadelphia	84	53	70	123	95

1993-94
EASTERN CONFERENCE
Northeast Division

Team	GP	W	L	T	GF	GA	PTS
Pittsburgh	84	44	27	13	299	285	101
Boston	84	42	29	13	289	252	97
Montreal	84	41	29	14	283	248	96
Buffalo	84	43	32	9	282	218	95
Quebec	84	34	42	8	277	292	76
Hartford	84	27	48	9	227	288	63
Ottawa	84	14	61	9	201	397	37

Atlantic Division

Team	GP	W	L	T	GF	GA	PTS
*NY Rangers	84	52	24	8	299	231	112
New Jersey	84	47	25	12	306	220	106
Washington	84	39	35	10	277	263	88
NY Islanders	84	36	36	12	282	264	84
Florida	84	33	34	17	233	233	83
Philadelphia	84	35	39	10	294	314	80
Tampa Bay	84	30	43	11	224	251	71

WESTERN CONFERENCE
Central Division

Team	GP	W	L	T	GF	GA	PTS
Detroit	84	46	30	8	356	275	100
Toronto	84	43	29	12	280	243	98
Dallas	84	42	29	13	286	265	97
St. Louis	84	40	33	11	270	283	91
Chicago	84	39	36	9	254	240	87
Winnipeg	84	24	51	9	245	344	57

Pacific Division

Team	GP	W	L	T	GF	GA	PTS
Calgary	84	42	29	13	302	256	97
Vancouver	84	41	40	3	279	276	85
San Jose	84	33	35	16	252	265	82
Anaheim	84	33	46	5	229	251	71
Los Angeles	84	27	45	12	294	322	66
Edmonton	84	25	45	14	261	305	64

Leading Scorers

Player	Club	GP	G	A	PTS	PIM
Gretzky, Wayne	Los Angeles	81	38	92	130	20
Fedorov, Sergei	Detroit	82	56	64	120	34
Oates, Adam	Boston	77	32	80	112	45
Gilmour, Doug	Toronto	83	27	84	111	105
Bure, Pavel	Vancouver	76	60	47	107	86
Roenick, Jeremy	Chicago	84	46	61	107	125
Recchi, Mark	Philadelphia	84	40	67	107	46
Shanahan, Brendan	St. Louis	81	52	50	102	211
Andreychuk, Dave	Toronto	83	53	46	99	98
Jagr, Jaromir	Pittsburgh	80	32	67	99	61

1994-95
EASTERN CONFERENCE
Northeast Division

Team	GP	W	L	T	GF	GA	PTS
Quebec	48	30	13	5	185	134	65
Pittsburgh	48	29	16	3	181	158	61
Boston	48	27	18	3	150	127	57
Buffalo	48	22	19	7	130	119	51
Hartford	48	19	24	5	127	141	43
Montreal	48	18	23	7	125	148	43
Ottawa	48	9	34	5	117	174	23

Atlantic Division

Team	GP	W	L	T	GF	GA	PTS
Philadelphia	48	28	16	4	150	132	60
*New Jersey	48	22	18	8	136	121	52
Washington	48	22	18	8	136	120	52
NY Rangers	48	22	23	3	139	134	47
Florida	48	20	22	6	115	127	46
Tampa Bay	48	17	28	3	120	144	37
NY Islanders	48	15	28	5	126	158	35

WESTERN CONFERENCE
Central Division

Team	GP	W	L	T	GF	GA	PTS
Detroit	48	33	11	4	180	117	70
St. Louis	48	28	15	5	178	135	61
Chicago	48	24	19	5	156	115	53
Toronto	48	21	19	8	135	146	50
Dallas	48	17	23	8	136	135	42
Winnipeg	48	16	25	7	157	177	39

Pacific Division

Team	GP	W	L	T	GF	GA	PTS
Calgary	48	24	17	7	163	135	55
Vancouver	48	18	18	12	153	148	48
San Jose	48	19	25	4	129	161	42
Los Angeles	48	16	23	9	142	174	41
Edmonton	48	17	27	4	136	183	38
Anaheim	48	16	27	5	125	164	37

Leading Scorers

Player	Club	GP	G	A	PTS	PIM
Jagr, Jaromir	Pittsburgh	48	32	38	70	37
Lindros, Eric	Philadelphia	46	29	41	70	60
Zhamnov, Alexei	Winnipeg	48	30	35	65	20
Sakic, Joe	Quebec	47	19	43	62	30
Francis, Ron	Pittsburgh	44	11	48	59	18
Fleury, Theoren	Calgary	47	29	29	58	112
Coffey, Paul	Detroit	45	14	44	58	72
Renberg, Mikael	Philadelphia	47	26	31	57	20
LeClair, John	Mtl., Phi.	46	26	28	54	30
Messier, Mark	NY Rangers	46	14	39	53	40
Oates, Adam	Boston	48	12	41	53	8

1995-96
EASTERN CONFERENCE
Northeast Division

Team	GP	W	L	T	GF	GA	PTS
Pittsburgh	82	49	29	4	362	284	102
Boston	82	40	31	11	282	269	91
Montreal	82	40	32	10	265	248	90
Hartford	82	34	39	9	237	259	77
Buffalo	82	33	42	7	247	262	73
Ottawa	82	18	59	5	191	291	41

Atlantic Division

Team	GP	W	L	T	GF	GA	PTS
Philadelphia	82	45	24	13	282	208	103
NY Rangers	82	41	27	14	272	237	96
Florida	82	41	31	10	254	234	92
Washington	82	39	32	11	234	204	89
Tampa Bay	82	38	32	12	238	248	88
New Jersey	82	37	33	12	215	202	86
NY Islanders	82	22	50	10	229	315	54

WESTERN CONFERENCE
Central Division

Team	GP	W	L	T	GF	GA	PTS
Detroit	82	62	13	7	325	181	131
Chicago	82	40	28	14	273	220	94
Toronto	82	34	36	12	247	252	80
St. Louis	82	32	34	16	219	248	80
Winnipeg	82	36	40	6	275	291	78
Dallas	82	26	42	14	227	280	66

Pacific Division

Team	GP	W	L	T	GF	GA	PTS
Colorado	82	47	25	10	326	240	104
Calgary	82	34	37	11	241	240	79
Vancouver	82	32	35	15	278	278	79
Anaheim	82	35	39	8	234	247	78
Edmonton	82	30	44	8	240	304	68
Los Angeles	82	24	40	18	256	302	66
San Jose	82	20	55	7	252	357	47

Leading Scorers

Player	Club	GP	G	A	PTS	PIM
Lemieux, Mario	Pittsburgh	70	69	92	161	54
Jagr, Jaromir	Pittsburgh	82	62	87	149	96
Sakic, Joe	Colorado	82	51	69	120	44
Francis, Ron	Pittsburgh	77	27	92	119	56
Forsberg, Peter	Colorado	82	30	86	116	47
Lindros, Eric	Philadelphia	73	47	68	115	163
Kariya, Paul	Anaheim	82	50	58	108	20
Selanne, Teemu	Wpg., Ana.	79	40	68	108	22
Mogilny, Alexander	Vancouver	79	55	52	107	16
Fedorov, Sergei	Detroit	78	39	68	107	48

Note: Detailed statistics for 1995-96 are listed in the Final Statistics, 1995-96 section of the **NHL Guide & Record Book.** See page 117.

Pavel Bure, whose dynamic speed has earned him the nickname "the Russian Rocket", became the first Vancouver Canuck to reach the 50-goal plateau when he slammed home 60 goals during the 1993-94 season.

Team Records

FINAL STANDINGS

MOST POINTS, ONE SEASON:
132 —Montreal Canadiens, 1976-77. 60w-8L-12T. 80GP
131 —Detroit Red Wings, 1995-96. 62w-13L-7T. 82GP
129 —Montreal Canadiens, 1977-78. 59w-10L-11T. 80GP

BEST WINNING PERCENTAGE, ONE SEASON:
.875 —Boston Bruins, 1929-30. 38w-5L-1T. 77PTS in 44GP
.830 —Montreal Canadiens, 1943-44. 38w-5L-7T. 83PTS in 50GP
.825 —Montreal Canadiens, 1976-77. 60w-8L-12T. 132PTS in 80GP
.806 —Montreal Canadiens, 1977-78. 59w-10L-11T. 129PTS in 80GP
.800 —Montreal Canadiens, 1944-45. 38w-8L-4T. 80PTS in 50GP

FEWEST POINTS, ONE SEASON:
8 —Quebec Bulldogs, 1919-20. 4w-20L-0T. 24GP
10 —Toronto Arenas, 1918-19. 5w-13L-0T. 18GP
12 —Hamilton Tigers, 1920-21. 6w-18L-0T. 24GP
—Hamilton Tigers, 1922-23. 6w-18L-0T. 24GP
—Boston Bruins, 1924-25. 6w-24L-0T. 30GP
—Philadelphia Quakers, 1930-31. 4w-36L-4T. 44GP

FEWEST POINTS, ONE SEASON (MINIMUM 70-GAME SCHEDULE):
21 —Washington Capitals, 1974-75. 8w-67L-5T. 80GP
24 —Ottawa Senators, 1992-93. 10w-70L-4T. 84GP
—San Jose Sharks, 1992-93. 11w-71L-2T. 84GP
30 —NY Islanders, 1972-73. 12w-60L-6T. 78GP

WORST WINNING PERCENTAGE, ONE SEASON:
.131 —Washington Capitals, 1974-75. 8w-67L-5T. 21PTS in 80GP
.136 —Philadelphia Quakers, 1930-31. 4w-36L-4T. 12PTS in 44GP
.143 —Ottawa Senators, 1992-93. 10w-70L-4T. 24PTS in 84GP
.143 —San Jose Sharks, 1992-93. 11w-71L-2T. 24PTS in 84GP
.148 —Pittsburgh Pirates, 1929-30. 5w-36L-3T. 13PTS in 44GP

TEAM WINS

Most Wins

MOST WINS, ONE SEASON:
62 —Detroit Red Wings, 1995-96. 82GP
60 —Montreal Canadiens, 1976-77. 80GP
59 —Montreal Canadiens, 1977-78. 80GP

MOST HOME WINS, ONE SEASON:
36 —Philadelphia Flyers, 1975-76. 40GP
—Detroit Red Wings, 1995-96. 41GP
33 —Boston Bruins, 1970-71. 39GP
—Boston Bruins, 1973-74. 39GP
—Montreal Canadiens, 1976-77. 40GP
—Philadelphia Flyers, 1976-77. 40GP
—NY Islanders, 1981-82. 40GP
—Philadelphia Flyers,1985-86. 40GP

MOST ROAD WINS, ONE SEASON:
27 —Montreal Canadiens, 1976-77. 40GP
—Montreal Canadiens, 1977-78. 40GP
26 —Boston Bruins, 1971-72. 39GP
—Montreal Canadiens, 1975-76. 40GP
—Edmonton Oilers, 1983-84. 40GP
—Detroit Red Wings, 1995-96. 41GP

Fewest Wins

FEWEST WINS, ONE SEASON:
4 —Quebec Bulldogs, 1919-20. 24GP
—Philadelphia Quakers, 1930-31. 44GP
5 —Toronto Arenas, 1918-19. 18GP
—Pittsburgh Pirates, 1929-30. 44GP

FEWEST WINS, ONE SEASON (MINIMUM 70-GAME SCHEDULE):
8 —Washington Capitals, 1974-75. 80GP
9 —Winnipeg Jets, 1980-81. 80GP
10 —Ottawa Senators, 1992-93. 84GP

FEWEST HOME WINS, ONE SEASON:
2 —Chicago Blackhawks, 1927-28. 22GP
3 —Boston Bruins, 1924-25. 15GP
—Chicago Blackhawks, 1928-29. 22GP
—Philadelphia Quakers, 1930-31. 22GP

FEWEST HOME WINS, ONE SEASON (MINIMUM 70-GAME SCHEDULE):
6 —Chicago Blackhawks, 1954-55. 35GP
—Washington Capitals, 1975-76. 40GP
7 —Boston Bruins, 1962-63. 35GP
—Washington Capitals, 1974-75. 40GP
—Winnipeg Jets, 1980-81. 40GP
—Pittsburgh Penguins, 1983-84. 40GP

FEWEST ROAD WINS, ONE SEASON:
0 —Toronto Arenas, 1918-19. 9GP
—Quebec Bulldogs, 1919-20. 12GP
—Pittsburgh Pirates, 1929-30. 22GP
1 —Hamilton Tigers, 1921-22. 12GP
—Toronto St. Patricks, 1925-26. 18GP
—Philadelphia Quakers, 1930-31. 22GP
—NY Americans, 1940-41. 24GP
—Washington Capitals, 1974-75. 40GP
* —Ottawa Senators, 1992-93. 41GP

FEWEST ROAD WINS, ONE SEASON (MINIMUM 70-GAME SCHEDULE):
1 —Washington Capitals, 1974-75. 40GP
* **—Ottawa Senators,** 1992-93. 41GP
2 —Boston Bruins, 1960-61. 35GP
—Los Angeles Kings, 1969-70. 38GP
—NY Islanders, 1972-73. 39GP
—California Seals, 1973-74. 39GP
—Colorado Rockies, 1977-78. 40GP
—Winnipeg Jets, 1980-81. 40GP
—Quebec Nordiques, 1991-92. 40GP

TEAM LOSSES

Fewest Losses

FEWEST LOSSES, ONE SEASON:
5 —Ottawa Senators, 1919-20. 24GP
—Boston Bruins, 1929-30. 44GP
—Montreal Canadiens, 1943-44. 50GP

FEWEST HOME LOSSES, ONE SEASON:
0 —Ottawa Senators, 1922-23. 12GP
—Montreal Canadiens, 1943-44. 25GP
1 —Toronto Arenas, 1917-18. 11GP
—Ottawa Senators, 1918-19. 9GP
—Ottawa Senators, 1919-20. 12GP
—Toronto St. Patricks, 1922-23. 12GP
—Boston Bruins, 1929-30 and 1930-31. 22GP
—Montreal Canadiens, 1976-77. 40GP
—Quebec Nordiques, 1994-95. 24GP

FEWEST ROAD LOSSES, ONE SEASON:
3 —Montreal Canadiens, 1928-29. 22GP
4 —Ottawa Senators, 1919-20. 12GP
—Montreal Canadiens, 1927-28. 22GP
—Boston Bruins, 1929-30. 20GP
—Boston Bruins, 1940-41. 24GP

FEWEST LOSSES, ONE SEASON (MINIMUM 70-GAME SCHEDULE):
8 —Montreal Canadiens, 1976-77. 80GP
10 —Montreal Canadiens, 1972-73. 78GP
—Montreal Canadiens, 1977-78. 80GP
11 —Montreal Canadiens, 1975-76. 80GP

FEWEST HOME LOSSES, ONE SEASON (MINIMUM 70-GAME SCHEDULE):
1 —Montreal Canadiens, 1976-77. 40GP
2 —Montreal Canadiens, 1961-62. 35GP
—NY Rangers, 1970-71. 39GP
—Philadelphia Flyers, 1975-76. 40GP

FEWEST ROAD LOSSES, ONE SEASON (MINIMUM 70-GAME SCHEDULE):
6 —Montreal Canadiens, 1972-73. 39GP
—Montreal Canadiens, 1974-75. 40GP
—Montreal Canadiens, 1977-78. 40GP
7 —Detroit Red Wings, 1951-52. 35GP
—Montreal Canadiens, 1976-77. 40GP
—Philadelphia Flyers, 1979-80. 40GP

Most Losses

MOST LOSSES, ONE SEASON:
71 —San Jose Sharks, 1992-93. 84GP
70 —Ottawa Senators, 1992-93. 84GP
67 —Washington Capitals, 1974-75. 80GP
61 —Quebec Nordiques, 1989-90. 80GP
—Ottawa Senators, 1993-94. 84GP

MOST HOME LOSSES, ONE SEASON:
***32 —San Jose Sharks,** 1992-93. 41GP
29 —Pittsburgh Penguins, 1983-84. 40GP
* —Ottawa Senators, 1993-94. 41GP

MOST ROAD LOSSES, ONE SEASON:
***40 —Ottawa Senators,** 1992-93. 41GP
39 —Washington Capitals, 1974-75. 40GP
37 —California Seals, 1973-74. 39GP
* —San Jose Sharks, 1992-93. 41GP

* Does not include neutral site games

TEAM TIES

Most Ties

MOST TIES, ONE SEASON:
24 — Philadelphia Flyers, 1969-70. 76GP
23 — Montreal Canadiens, 1962-63. 70GP
— Chicago Blackhawks, 1973-74. 78GP

MOST HOME TIES, ONE SEASON:
13 — NY Rangers, 1954-55. 35GP
— Philadelphia Flyers, 1969-70. 38GP
— California Seals, 1971-72. 39GP
— California Seals, 1972-73. 39GP
— Chicago Blackhawks, 1973-74. 39GP

MOST ROAD TIES, ONE SEASON:
15 — Philadelphia Flyers, 1976-77. 40GP
14 — Montreal Canadiens, 1952-53. 35GP
— Montreal Canadiens, 1974-75. 40GP
— Philadelphia Flyers, 1975-76. 40GP

Fewest Ties

FEWEST TIES, ONE SEASON (Since 1926-27):
1 — Boston Bruins, 1929-30. 44GP
2 — NY Americans, 1926-27. 44GP
— Montreal Canadiens, 1926-27. 44GP
— Boston Bruins, 1938-39. 48GP
— NY Rangers, 1941-42. 48GP
— San Jose Sharks, 1992-93. 84GP

FEWEST TIES, ONE SEASON (MINIMUM 70-GAME SCHEDULE):
2 — San Jose Sharks, 1992-93. 84GP
3 — New Jersey Devils, 1985-86. 80GP
— Calgary Flames, 1986-87. 80GP
— Vancouver Canucks, 1993-94. 84GP

WINNING STREAKS

LONGEST WINNING STREAK:
17 Games — Pittsburgh Penguins, Mar. 9, 1993 - Apr. 10, 1993.
15 Games — NY Islanders, Jan. 21, 1982 - Feb. 20, 1982.
14 Games — Boston Bruins, Dec. 3, 1929 - Jan. 9, 1930.
13 Games — Boston Bruins, Feb. 23, 1971 - Mar. 20, 1971.
— Philadelphia Flyers, Oct. 19, 1985 - Nov. 17, 1985.

LONGEST HOME WINNING STREAK, ONE SEASON:
20 Games — Boston Bruins, Dec. 3, 1929 - Mar. 18, 1930.
— Philadelphia Flyers, Jan. 4, 1976 - Apr. 3, 1976.

LONGEST ROAD WINNING STREAK, ONE SEASON:
10 Games — Buffalo Sabres, Dec. 10, 1983 - Jan. 23, 1984.
8 Games — Boston Bruins, Feb. 17, 1972 - Mar. 8, 1972.
— Los Angeles Kings, Dec. 18, 1974 - Jan. 16, 1975.
— Montreal Canadiens, Dec. 18, 1977 - Jan. 18, 1978.
— NY Islanders, Feb. 27, 1981 - Mar. 29, 1981.
— Montreal Canadiens, Jan. 21, 1982 - Feb. 21, 1982.
— Philadelphia Flyers, Dec. 22, 1982 - Jan. 16, 1983.
— Winnipeg Jets, Feb. 25, 1985 - Apr. 6, 1985.
— Edmonton Oilers, Dec. 9, 1986 - Jan. 17, 1987.
— Boston Bruins, Mar. 15, 1993 - Apr. 14, 1993.

LONGEST WINNING STREAK FROM START OF SEASON:
10 Games — Toronto Maple Leafs, 1993-94.
8 Games — Toronto Maple Leafs, 1934-35.
— Buffalo Sabres, 1975-76.
7 Games — Edmonton Oilers, 1983-84.
— Quebec Nordiques, 1985-86.
— Pittsburgh Penguins, 1986-87.
— Pittsburgh Penguins, 1994-95.

LONGEST HOME WINNING STREAK FROM START OF SEASON:
11 Games — Chicago Blackhawks, 1963-64
10 Games — Ottawa Senators, 1925-26
9 Games — Montreal Canadiens, 1953-54
— Chicago Blackhawks, 1971-72
8 Games — Boston Bruins, 1983-84
— Philadelphia Flyers, 1986-87
— New Jersey Devils, 1987-88

LONGEST WINNING STREAK, INCLUDING PLAYOFFS:
15 Games — Detroit Red Wings, Feb. 27, 1955 - Apr. 5, 1955. Nine regular-season games, six playoff games.

LONGEST HOME WINNING STREAK, INCLUDING PLAYOFFS:
24 Games — Philadelphia Flyers, Jan. 4, 1976 - Apr. 25, 1976. 20 regular-season games, 4 playoff games.

UNDEFEATED STREAKS

LONGEST UNDEFEATED STREAK, ONE SEASON:
35 Games — Philadelphia Flyers, Oct. 14, 1979 - Jan. 6, 1980. 25w-10T.
28 Games — Montreal Canadiens, Dec. 18, 1977 - Feb. 23, 1978. 23w-5T.
23 Games — Boston Bruins, Dec. 22, 1940 - Feb. 23, 1941. 15w-8T.
— Philadelphia Flyers, Jan. 29, 1976 - Mar. 18, 1976. 17w-6T.

LONGEST HOME UNDEFEATED STREAK, ONE SEASON:
34 Games — Montreal Canadiens, Nov. 1, 1976 - Apr. 2, 1977. 28w-6T.
27 Games — Boston Bruins, Nov. 22, 1970 - Mar. 20, 1971. 26w-1T.

LONGEST ROAD UNDEFEATED STREAK, ONE SEASON:
23 Games — Montreal Canadiens, Nov. 27, 1974 - Mar. 12, 1975. 14w-9T.
17 Games — Montreal Canadiens, Dec. 18, 1977 - Mar. 1, 1978. 14w-3T.
16 Games — Philadelphia Flyers, Oct. 20, 1979 - Jan. 6, 1980. 11w-5T.

LONGEST UNDEFEATED STREAK FROM START OF SEASON:
15 Games — Edmonton Oilers, 1984-85. 12w-3T.
14 Games — Montreal Canadiens, 1943-44. 11w-3T.
13 Games — Montreal Canadiens, 1972-73. 9w-4T.
— Pittsburgh Penguins, 1994-95. 12w-1T.

LONGEST HOME UNDEFEATED STREAK, INCLUDING PLAYOFFS:
38 Games — Montreal Canadiens, Nov. 1, 1976 - Apr. 26, 1977. 28w-6T in regular season and 4w in playoffs).

LOSING STREAKS

LONGEST LOSING STREAK, ONE SEASON:
17 Games — Washington Capitals, Feb. 18, 1975 - Mar. 26, 1975.
— San Jose Sharks, Jan. 4, 1993 - Feb. 12, 1993.
15 Games — Philadelphia Quakers, Nov. 29, 1930 - Jan. 8, 1931.

LONGEST HOME LOSING STREAK, ONE SEASON:
11 Games — Boston Bruins, Dec. 8, 1924 - Feb. 17, 1925.
— Washington Capitals, Feb. 18, 1975 - Mar. 30, 1975.
— Ottawa Senators, Oct. 27, 1993 - Dec. 8, 1993.

LONGEST ROAD LOSING STREAK, ONE SEASON:
***38 Games — Ottawa Senators,** Oct. 10, 1992 - Apr. 3, 1993.
37 Games — Washington Capitals, Oct. 9, 1974 - Mar. 26, 1975.
* – Does not include neutral site games.

LONGEST LOSING STREAK FROM START OF SEASON:
11 Games — NY Rangers, 1943-44.
7 Games — Montreal Canadiens, 1938-39.
— Chicago Blackhawks, 1947-48.
— Washington Capitals, 1983-84.

WINLESS STREAKS

LONGEST WINLESS STREAK, ONE SEASON:
30 Games — Winnipeg Jets, Oct. 19, 1980 - Dec. 20, 1980. 23L-7T.
27 Games — Kansas City Scouts, Feb. 12, 1976 - Apr. 4, 1976. 21L-6T.
25 Games — Washington Capitals, Nov. 29, 1975 - Jan. 21, 1976. 22L-3T.

LONGEST HOME WINLESS STREAK, ONE SEASON:
17 Games — Ottawa Senators, Oct. 28, 1995 - Jan. 27, 1996. 15L-2T.
15 Games — Chicago Blackhawks, Dec. 16, 1928 - Feb. 28, 1929. 11L-4T.
— Montreal Canadiens, Dec. 16, 1939 - Mar. 7, 1940. 12L-3T.

LONGEST ROAD WINLESS STREAK, ONE SEASON:
***38 Games — Ottawa Senators,** Oct. 10, 1992 - Apr. 3, 1993. 38L-0T.
37 Games — Washington Capitals, Oct. 9, 1974 - Mar. 26, 1975. 37L-0T.
* – Does not include neutral site games.

LONGEST WINLESS STREAK FROM START OF SEASON:
15 Games — NY Rangers, 1943-44. 14L-1T.
12 Games — Pittsburgh Pirates, 1927-28. 9L-3T.
11 Games — Minnesota North Stars, 1973-74. 5L-6T.
— San Jose Sharks, 1995-96. 7L-4T.

NON-SHUTOUT STREAKS

LONGEST NON-SHUTOUT STREAK:
264 Games — Calgary Flames, Nov. 12, 1981 - Jan. 9, 1985.
262 Games — Los Angeles Kings, Mar. 15, 1986 - Oct. 25, 1989.
244 Games — Washington Capitals, Oct. 31, 1989 - Nov. 11, 1993.
230 Games — Quebec Nordiques, Feb. 10, 1980 - Jan. 13, 1983.
229 Games — Edmonton Oilers, Mar. 15, 1981 - Feb. 11, 1984.

LONGEST NON-SHUTOUT STREAK INCLUDING PLAYOFFS:
264 Games — Los Angeles Kings, Mar. 15 1986 - Apr. 6, 1989. (5 playoff games in 1987; 5 in 1988; 2 in 1989)
262 Games — Chicago Blackhawks, Mar. 14, 1970 - Feb. 21, 1973. (8 playoff games in 1970; 18 in 1971; 8 in 1972.)
251 Games — Quebec Nordiques, Feb. 10, 1980 - Jan. 13, 1983. (5 playoff games in 1981; 16 in 1982.)
245 Games — Pittsburgh Penguins, Jan. 7, 1989 - Oct. 26, 1991. (11 playoff games in 1989; 23 in 1991.)

TEAM GOALS

Most Goals

MOST GOALS, ONE SEASON:
446 — Edmonton Oilers, 1983-84. 80GP
426 — Edmonton Oilers, 1985-86. 80GP
424 — Edmonton Oilers, 1982-83. 80GP
417 — Edmonton Oilers, 1981-82. 80GP
401 — Edmonton Oilers, 1984-85. 80GP

MOST GOALS, ONE TEAM, ONE GAME:
16 — Montreal Canadiens, Mar. 3, 1920, at Quebec. Defeated Quebec Bulldogs 16-3.

MOST GOALS, BOTH TEAMS, ONE GAME:
21 —**Montreal Canadiens, Toronto St. Patricks,** at Montreal, Jan. 10, 1920. Montreal won 14-7.
  —**Edmonton Oilers, Chicago Blackhawks,** at Chicago, Dec. 11, 1985. Edmonton won 12-9.
20 —Edmonton Oilers, Minnesota North Stars, at Edmonton, Jan. 4, 1984. Edmonton won 12-8.
  —Toronto Maple Leafs, Edmonton Oilers, at Toronto, Jan. 8, 1986. Toronto won 11-9.
19 —Montreal Wanderers, Toronto Arenas, at Montreal, Dec. 19, 1917. Montreal won 10-9.
  —Montreal Canadiens, Quebec Bulldogs, at Quebec, Mar. 3, 1920, Montreal won 16-3.
  —Montreal Canadiens, Hamilton Tigers, at Montreal, Feb. 26, 1921. Montreal won 13-6.
  —Boston Bruins, NY Rangers, at Boston, Mar. 4, 1944, Boston won 10-9.
  —Boston Bruins, Detroit Red Wings, at Detroit, Mar. 16, 1944. Detroit won 10-9.
  —Vancouver Canucks, Minnesota North Stars, at Vancouver, Oct. 7, 1983. Vancouver won 10-9.

MOST GOALS, ONE TEAM, ONE PERIOD:
9 —**Buffalo Sabres,** March 19, 1981, at Buffalo, second period during 14-4 win over Toronto.
8 —Detroit Red Wings, Jan. 23, 1944, at Detroit, third period during 15-0 win over NY Rangers.
  —Boston Bruins, March 16, 1969, at Boston, second period during 11-3 win over Toronto.
  —NY Rangers, Nov. 21, 1971, at New York, third period during 12-1 win over California.
  —Philadelphia Flyers, March 31, 1973, at Philadelphia, second period during 10-2 win over NY Islanders.
  —Buffalo Sabres, Dec. 21, 1975, at Buffalo, third period during 14-2 win over Washington.
  —Minnesota North Stars, Nov. 11, 1981, at Minnesota, second period during 15-2 win over Winnipeg.
  —Pittsburgh Penguins, Dec. 17, 1991, at Pittsburgh, second period during 10-2 win over San Jose.

MOST GOALS, BOTH TEAMS, ONE PERIOD:
12 —**Buffalo Sabres, Toronto Maple Leafs,** at Buffalo, March 19, 1981, second period. Buffalo scored 9 goals, Toronto 3. Buffalo won 14-4.
  —**Edmonton Oilers, Chicago Blackhawks,** at Chicago, Dec. 11, 1985, second period. Edmonton scored 6 goals, Chicago 6. Edmonton won 12-9.
10 —NY Rangers, NY Americans, at NY Americans, March 16, 1939, third period. NY Rangers scored 7 goals, NY Americans 3. NY Rangers won 11-5.
  —Toronto Maple Leafs, Detroit Red Wings, at Detroit, March 17, 1946, third period. Toronto scored 6 goals, Detroit 4. Toronto won 11-7.
  —Vancouver Canucks, Buffalo Sabres, at Buffalo, Jan. 8, 1976, third period. Buffalo scored 6 goals, Vancouver 4. Buffalo won 8-5.
  —Buffalo Sabres, Montreal Canadiens, at Montreal, Oct. 26, 1982, first period. Montreal scored 5 goals, Buffalo 5. 7-7 tie.
  —Boston Bruins, Quebec Nordiques, at Quebec, Dec. 7, 1982, second period. Quebec scored 6 goals, Boston 4. Quebec won 10-5.
  —Calgary Flames, Vancouver Canucks, at Vancouver, Jan. 16, 1987, first period. Vancouver scored 6 goals, Calgary 4. Vancouver won 9-5.
  —Winnipeg Jets, Detroit Red Wings, at Detroit, Nov. 25, 1987, third period. Detroit scored 7 goals, Winnipeg 3. Detroit won 10-8.
  —Chicago Blackhawks, St. Louis Blues, at St. Louis, March 15, 1988, third period. Chicago scored 5 goals, St. Louis 5. 7-7 tie.

MOST CONSECUTIVE GOALS, ONE TEAM, ONE GAME:
15 —**Detroit Red Wings,** Jan. 23, 1944, at Detroit. Defeated NY Rangers 15-0.

Murray Balfour, who is pictured here slipping the puck past a masked Don Simmons during game five of the 1962-Stanley Cup finals, was one of the top scorers in the 1961 playoffs,. collecting five goals ands five assists for the Cup-winning Black Hawks.

Fewest Goals

FEWEST GOALS, ONE SEASON:
33 —Chicago Blackhawks, 1928-29. 44GP
45 —Montreal Maroons, 1924-25. 30GP
46 —Pittsburgh Pirates, 1928-29. 44GP

FEWEST GOALS, ONE SEASON (MINIMUM 70-GAME SCHEDULE):
133 —Chicago Blackhawks, 1953-54. 70GP
147 —Toronto Maple Leafs, 1954-55. 70GP
  —Boston Bruins, 1955-56. 70GP
150 —NY Rangers, 1954-55. 70GP

TEAM POWER-PLAY GOALS

MOST POWER-PLAY GOALS, ONE SEASON:
119 —Pittsburgh Penguins, 1988-89. 80GP
113 —Detroit Red Wings, 1992-93. 84GP
111 —NY Rangers, 1987-88. 80GP
110 —Pittsburgh Penguins, 1987-88. 80GP
  —Winnipeg Jets, 1987-88, 80GP

TEAM SHORTHAND GOALS

MOST SHORTHAND GOALS, ONE SEASON:
36 —Edmonton Oilers, 1983-84. 80GP
28 —Edmonton Oilers, 1986-87. 80GP
27 —Edmonton Oilers, 1985-86. 80GP
  —Edmonton Oilers, 1988-89. 80GP

TEAM GOALS-PER-GAME

HIGHEST GOALS-PER-GAME AVERAGE, ONE SEASON:
5.58 —Edmonton Oilers, 1983-84. 446G in 80GP.
5.38 —Montreal Canadiens, 1919-20. 129G in 24GP.
5.33 —Edmonton Oilers, 1985-86. 426G in 80GP.
5.30 —Edmonton Oilers, 1982-83. 424G in 80GP.
5.23 —Montreal Canadiens, 1917-18. 115G in 22GP.

LOWEST GOALS-PER-GAME AVERAGE, ONE SEASON:
.75 —Chicago Blackhawks, 1928-29, 33G in 44GP.
1.05 —Pittsburgh Pirates, 1928-29. 46G in 44GP.
1.20 —NY Americans, 1928-29. 53G in 44GP.

TEAM ASSISTS

MOST ASSISTS, ONE SEASON:
737 —Edmonton Oilers, 1985-86. 80GP
736 —Edmonton Oilers, 1983-84. 80GP
706 —Edmonton Oilers, 1981-82. 80GP

FEWEST ASSISTS, ONE SEASON:
45 —NY Rangers, 1926-27. 44GP

FEWEST ASSISTS, ONE SEASON (MINIMUM 70-GAME SCHEDULE):
206 —Chicago Blackhawks, 1953-54. 70GP

TEAM TOTAL POINTS

MOST SCORING POINTS, ONE SEASON:
1,182 —Edmonton Oilers, 1983-84. 80GP
1,163 —Edmonton Oilers, 1985-86. 80GP
1,123 —Edmonton Oilers, 1981-82. 80GP

MOST SCORING POINTS, ONE TEAM, ONE GAME:
40 —Buffalo Sabres, Dec. 21, 1975, at Buffalo. Buffalo defeated Washington 14-2, receiving 26A.
39 —Minnesota North Stars, Nov. 11, 1981, at Minnesota. Minnesota defeated Winnipeg 15-2, receiving 24A.
37 —Detroit Red Wings, Jan. 23, 1944, at Detroit. Detroit defeated NY Rangers 15-0, receiving 22A.
  —Toronto Maple Leafs, Mar. 16, 1957, at Toronto. Toronto defeated NY Rangers 14-1, receiving 23A.
  —Buffalo Sabres, Feb. 25, 1978, at Cleveland. Buffalo defeated Cleveland 13-3, receiving 24A.
  —Calgary Flames, Feb. 10, 1993, at Calgary. Calgary defeated San Jose 13-1, receiving 24A.

MOST SCORING POINTS, BOTH TEAMS, ONE GAME:
62 —Edmonton Oilers, Chicago Blackhawks, at Chicago, Dec. 11, 1985. Edmonton won 12-9. Edmonton had 24A, Chicago, 17.
53 —Quebec Nordiques, Washington Capitals, at Washington, Feb. 22, 1981. Quebec won 11-7. Quebec had 22A, Washington, 13.
  —Edmonton Oilers, Minnesota North Stars, at Edmonton, Jan. 4, 1984. Edmonton won 12-8. Edmonton had 20A, Minnesota 13.
  —Minnesota North Stars, St. Louis Blues, at St. Louis, Jan. 27, 1984. Minnesota won 10-8. Minnesota had 19A, St. Louis 16.
  —Toronto Maple Leafs, Edmonton Oilers, at Toronto, Jan. 8, 1986. Toronto won 11-9. Toronto had 17A, Edmonton 16.
52 —Mtl. Maroons, NY Americans, at New York, Feb. 18, 1936. 8-8 tie. New York had 20A, Montreal 16. (3A allowed for each goal.)
  —Vancouver Canucks, Minnesota North Stars, at Vancouver, Oct. 7, 1983. Vancouver won 10-9. Vancouver had 16A, Minnesota 17.

MOST SCORING POINTS, ONE TEAM, ONE PERIOD:
23 —**NY Rangers,** Nov. 21, 1971, at New York, third period during 12-1 win over California. NY Rangers scored 8G and 15A.
— **Buffalo Sabres,** Dec. 21, 1975, at Buffalo, third period during 14-2 win over Washington. Buffalo scored 8G and 15A.
— **Buffalo Sabres,** March 19, 1981, at Buffalo, second period, during 14-4 win over Toronto. Buffalo scored 9G and 14A.
22 —**Detroit Red Wings,** Jan. 23, 1944, at Detroit, third period during 15-0 win over NY Rangers. Detroit scored 8G and 14A.
— **Boston Bruins,** March 16, 1969, at Boston, second period during 11-3 win over Toronto Maple Leafs. Boston scored 8G and 14A.
— **Minnesota North Stars,** Nov. 11, 1981, at Minnesota, second period during 15-2 win over Winnipeg. Minnesota scored 8G and 14A.
— **Pittsburgh Penguins,** Dec. 17, 1991, at Pittsburgh, second period during 10-2 win over San Jose. Pittsburgh scored 8G and 14A.

MOST SCORING POINTS, BOTH TEAMS, ONE PERIOD:
35 —**Edmonton, Oilers, Chicago Blackhawks,** at Chicago, Dec. 11, 1985, second period. Edmonton had 6G, 12A; Chicago, 6G, 11A. Edmonton won 12-9.
31 —**Buffalo Sabres, Toronto Maple Leafs,** at Buffalo, March 19, 1981, second period. Buffalo had 9G, 14A; Toronto, 3G, 5A. Buffalo won 14-4.
29 —**Winnipeg Jets, Detroit Red Wings,** at Detroit, Nov. 25, 1987, third period. Detroit had 7G, 13A; Winnipeg had 3G, 6A. Detroit won 10-8.
— **Chicago Blackhawks, St. Louis Blues,** at St. Louis, March 15, 1988, third period. St. Louis had 5G, 10A; Chicago had 5G, 9A. 7-7 tie.

FASTEST GOALS

FASTEST SIX GOALS, BOTH TEAMS
3 Minutes, 15 Seconds — Montreal Canadiens, Toronto Maple Leafs, at Montreal, Jan. 4, 1944, first period. Montreal scored 4G, Toronto 2. Montreal won 6-3.

FASTEST FIVE GOALS, BOTH TEAMS:
1 Minute, 24 Seconds — Chicago Blackhawks, Toronto Maple Leafs, at Toronto, Oct. 15, 1983, second period. Scorers were: Gaston Gingras, Toronto, 16:49; Denis Savard, Chicago, 17:12; Steve Larmer, Chicago, 17:27; Savard, 17:42; and John Anderson, Toronto, 18:13. Toronto won 10-8.
1 Minute, 39 Seconds — Detroit Red Wings, Toronto Maple Leafs, at Toronto, Nov. 15, 1944, third period. Scorers were: Ted Kennedy, Toronto, 10:36 and 10:55; Hal Jackson, Detroit, 11:48; Steve Wochy, Detroit, 12:02; Don Grosso, Detroit, 12:15. Detroit won 8-4.

FASTEST FIVE GOALS, ONE TEAM:
2 Minutes, 7 Seconds — Pittsburgh Penguins, at Pittsburgh, Nov. 22, 1972, third period. Scorers: Bryan Hextall, 12:00; Jean Pronovost, 12:18; Al McDonough, 13:40; Ken Schinkel, 13:49; Ron Schock, 14:07. Pittsburgh defeated St. Louis 10-4.
2 Minutes, 37 seconds — NY Islanders, at New York, Jan. 26, 1982, first period. Scorers: Duane Sutter, 1:31; John Tonelli, 2:30; Bryan Trottier, 2:46; Bryan Trottier, 3:31; Duane Sutter, 4:08. NY Islanders defeated Pittsburgh 9-2.
2 Minutes, 55 Seconds — Boston Bruins, at Boston, Dec. 19, 1974. Scorers: Bobby Schmautz, 19:13 (first period); Ken Hodge, 0:18; Phil Esposito, 0:43; Don Marcotte, 0:58; John Bucyk, 2:08 (second period). Boston defeated NY Rangers 11-3.

FASTEST FOUR GOALS, BOTH TEAMS:
53 Seconds — Chicago Blackhawks, Toronto Maple Leafs, at Toronto, Oct. 15, 1983, second period. Scorers were: Gaston Gingras, Toronto, 16:49; Denis Savard, Chicago, 17:12; Steve Larmer, Chicago, 17:27; and Savard at 17:42. Toronto won 10-8.
57 Seconds — Quebec Nordiques, Detroit Red Wings, at Quebec, Jan. 27, 1990, first period. Scorers were: Paul Gillis, Quebec, 18:01; Claude Loiselle, Quebec, 18:12; Joe Sakic, Quebec, 18:27; and Jimmy Carson, Detroit, 18:58. Detroit won 8-6.
1 Minute, 1 Second — Colorado Rockies, NY Rangers, at New York, Jan. 15, 1980, first period. Scorers were: Doug Sulliman, NY Rangers, 7:52; Ed Johnstone, NY Rangers, 7:57; Warren Miller, NY Rangers, 8:20; Rob Ramage, Colorado, 8:53. 6-6 tie.
— Chicago Blackhawks, Toronto Maple Leafs, at Toronto, Oct. 15, 1983, second period. Scorers were: Denis Savard, Chicago, 17:12; Steve Larmer, Chicago, 17:27; Savard, 17:42; John Anderson, Toronto, 18:13. Toronto won 10-8.

FASTEST FOUR GOALS, ONE TEAM:
1 Minute, 20 Seconds — Boston Bruins, at Boston, Jan. 21, 1945, second period. Scorers were: Bill Thoms at 6:34; Frank Mario at 7:08 and 7:27; and Ken Smith at 7:54. Boston defeated NY Rangers 14-3.

FASTEST THREE GOALS, BOTH TEAMS:
15 Seconds — Minnesota North Stars, NY Rangers, at Minnesota, Feb. 10, 1983, second period. Scorers were: Mark Pavelich, NY Rangers, 19:18; Ron Greschner, NY Rangers, 19:27; Willi Plett, Minnesota, 19:33. Minnesota won 7-5.
18 Seconds — Montreal Canadiens, NY Rangers, at Montreal, Dec. 12, 1963, first period. Scorers were: Dave Balon, Montreal, 0:58; Gilles Tremblay, Montreal, 1:04; Camille Henry, NY Rangers, 1:16. Montreal won 6-4.
18 Seconds — California Golden Seals, Buffalo Sabres, at California, Feb. 1, 1976, third period. Scorers were: Jim Moxey, California, 19:38; Wayne Merrick, California, 19:45; Danny Gare, Buffalo, 19:56. Buffalo won 9-5.

FASTEST THREE GOALS, ONE TEAM:
20 Seconds — Boston Bruins, at Boston, Feb. 25, 1971, third period. John Bucyk scored at 4:50; Ed Westfall at 5:02 and Ted Green at 5:10. Boston defeated Vancouver 8-3.
21 Seconds — Chicago Blackhawks, at New York, March 23, 1952, third period. Bill Mosienko scored all three goals, at 6:09, 6:20 and 6:30. Chicago defeated NY Rangers 7-6.
21 Seconds — Washington Capitals, at Washington, Nov. 23, 1990, first period. Michal Pivonka scored at 16:18 and Stephen Leach scored at 16:29 and 16:39. Washington defeated Pittsburgh 7-3.

FASTEST THREE GOALS FROM START OF PERIOD, BOTH TEAMS:
1 Minute, 5 seconds — Hartford Whalers, Montreal Canadiens, at Montreal, March 11, 1989, second period. Scorers were: Kevin Dineen, Hartford, 0:11; Guy Carbonneau, Montreal, 0:36; Petr Svoboda, Montreal, 1:05. Montreal won 5-3.

FASTEST THREE GOALS FROM START OF PERIOD, ONE TEAM:
53 Seconds — Calgary Flames, at Calgary, Feb. 10, 1993, third period. Scorers were: Gary Suter at 0:17, Chris Lindbergh at 0:40, Ron Stern at 0:53. Calgary defeated San Jose 13-1.

FASTEST TWO GOALS, BOTH TEAMS:
2 Seconds — St. Louis Blues, Boston Bruins, at Boston, Dec. 19, 1987, third period. Scorers were: Ken Linseman, Boston, at 19:50; Doug Gilmour, St. Louis, at 19:52. St. Louis won 7-5.
3 Seconds — Chicago Blackhawks, Minnesota North Stars, at Minnesota, November 5, 1988, third period. Scorers were: Steve Thomas, Chicago, at 6:03; Dave Gagner, Minnesota, at 6:06. 5-5 tie.

FASTEST TWO GOALS, ONE TEAM:
4 Seconds — Montreal Maroons, at Montreal, Jan. 3, 1931, third period. Nels Stewart scored both goals, at 8:24 and 8:28. Mtl. Maroons defeated Boston 5-3.
— **Buffalo Sabres,** at Buffalo, Oct. 17, 1974, third period. Scorers were: Lee Fogolin at 14:55 and Don Luce at 14:59. Buffalo defeated California 6-1.
— **Toronto Maple Leafs,** at Quebec, December 29, 1988, third period. Scorers were: Ed Olczyk at 5:24 and Gary Leeman at 5:28. Toronto defeated Quebec 6-5.
— **Calgary Flames,** at Quebec, October 17, 1989, third period. Scorers were: Doug Gilmour at 19:45 and Paul Ranheim at 19:49. Calgary and Quebec tied 8-8.
— **Winnipeg Jets,** at Winnipeg, December 15, 1995, second period. Deron Quint scored both goals, at 7:51 and 7:55. Winnipeg defeated Edmonton 9-4.

FASTEST TWO GOALS FROM START OF GAME, ONE TEAM:
24 Seconds — Edmonton Oilers, March 28, 1982, at Los Angeles. Mark Messier, at 0:14 and Dave Lumley, at 0:24, scored in first period. Edmonton defeated Los Angeles 6-2.
29 Seconds — Pittsburgh Penguins, Dec. 6, 1981, at Pittsburgh. George Ferguson, at 0:17 and Greg Malone, at 0:29, scored in first period. Pittsburgh defeated Chicago 6-4.
32 Seconds — Calgary Flames, March 11, 1987, at Hartford. Doug Risebrough at 0:09, and Colin Patterson, at 0:32, in first period. Calgary defeated Hartford 6-1.

FASTEST TWO GOALS FROM START OF PERIOD, BOTH TEAMS:
14 Seconds — NY Rangers, Quebec Nordiques, at Quebec, Nov. 5, 1983, third period. Scorers: Andre Savard, Quebec, 0:08; Pierre Larouche, NY Rangers, 0:14. 4-4 tie.
26 Seconds — Buffalo Sabres, St. Louis Blues, at Buffalo, Jan. 3, 1993, third period. Scorers: Alexander Mogilny, Buffalo, 0:08; Phillippe Bozon, St. Louis, 0:26. Buffalo won 6-5.
28 Seconds — Boston Bruins, Montreal Canadiens, at Montreal, Oct. 11, 1989, third period. Scorers: Jim Wiemer, Boston 0:10; Tom Chorske, Montreal, 0:28. Montreal won 4-2.

FASTEST TWO GOALS FROM START OF PERIOD, ONE TEAM:
21 Seconds — Chicago Blackhawks, Nov. 5, 1983, at Minnesota, second period. Ken Yaremchuk scored at 0:12 and Darryl Sutter at 0:21. Minnesota defeated Chicago 10-5.
30 Seconds — Washington Capitals, Jan. 27, 1980, at Washington, second period. Mike Gartner scored at 0:08 and Bengt Gustafsson at 0:30. Washington defeated NY Islanders 7-1.
31 Seconds —Buffalo Sabres, Jan. 10, 1974, at Buffalo, third period. Rene Robert scored at 0:21 and Rick Martin at 0:31. Buffalo defeated NY Rangers 7-2.
— NY Islanders, Feb. 22, 1986, at New York, third period. Roger Kortko scored at 0:10 and Bob Bourne at 0:31. NY Islanders defeated Detroit 5-2.

When Pittsburgh's Ron Schock put a wrist shot past Wayne Stephenson at the 14:07 mark of the third period on November 22, 1972, he also put the finishing touch on the fastest five goals by one team in league history. Schock and four of his Penguin teammates combined to score five goals in two minutes and seven seconds in their 10-4 win over the St. Louis Blues.

50, 40, 30, 20-GOAL SCORERS

MOST 50-OR-MORE-GOAL SCORERS, ONE SEASON:

3 —Edmonton Oilers, 1983-84. Wayne Gretzky, 87; Glenn Anderson, 54; Jari Kurri, 52 80GP.

—**Edmonton Oilers,** 1985-86. Jari Kurri, 68; Glenn Anderson, 54; Wayne Gretzky, 52. 80GP.

2 —Boston Bruins, 1970-71. Phil Esposito, 76; John Bucyk, 51. 78GP
—Boston Bruins, 1973-74. Phil Esposito, 68; Ken Hodge, 50. 78GP
—Philadelphia Flyers, 1975-76. Reggie Leach, 61; Bill Barber, 50. 80GP
—Pittsburgh Penguins, 1975-76. Pierre Larouche, 53; Jean Pronovost, 52. 80GP
—Montreal Canadiens, 1976-77. Steve Shutt, 60; Guy Lafleur, 56. 80GP
—Los Angeles Kings, 1979-80. Charlie Simmer, 56; Marcel Dionne, 53. 80GP
—Montreal Canadiens, 1979-80. Pierre Larouche, 50; Guy Lafleur, 50. 80GP
—Los Angeles Kings, 1980-81. Marcel Dionne, 58; Charlie Simmer, 56. 80GP
—Edmonton Oilers, 1981-82. Wayne Gretzky, 92; Mark Messier, 50. 80GP
—NY Islanders, 1981-82. Mike Bossy, 64; Bryan Trottier, 50. 80GP
—Edmonton Oilers, 1984-85. Wayne Gretzky, 73; Jari Kurri, 71. 80GP
—Washington Capitals, 1984-85. Bob Carpenter, 53; Mike Gartner, 50. 80GP
—Edmonton Oilers, 1986-87. Wayne Gretzky, 62; Jari Kurri, 54. 80GP
—Calgary Flames, 1987-88. Joe Nieuwendyk, 51; Hakan Loob, 50. 80GP
—Los Angeles Kings, 1987-88. Jimmy Carson, 55; Luc Robitaille, 53. 80GP
—Los Angeles Kings, 1988-89. Bernie Nicholls, 70; Wayne Gretzky, 54. 80GP
—Calgary Flames, 1988-89. Joe Nieuwendyk, 51; Joe Mullen, 51. 80GP
—Buffalo Sabres, 1992-93. Alexander Mogilny, 76; Pat LaFontaine, 53. 84GP
—Pittsburgh Penguins, 1992-93. Mario Lemieux, 69; Kevin Stevens, 55. 84GP
—St. Louis Blues, 1992-93. Brett Hull, 54; Brendan Shanahan, 51. 84GP
—St. Louis Blues, 1993-94. Brett Hull, 57; Brendan Shanahan, 52. 84GP
—Detroit Red Wings, 1993-94. Sergei Fedorov, 56; Ray Sheppard, 52. 84GP
—Pittsburgh Penguins, 1995-96. Mario Lemieux, 69; Jaromir Jagr, 62. 82GP

MOST 40-OR-MORE-GOAL SCORERS, ONE SEASON:

4 —Edmonton Oilers, 1982-83. Wayne Gretzky, 71; Glenn Anderson, 48; Mark Messier, 48; Jari Kurri, 45. 80GP

—**Edmonton Oilers,** 1983-84. Wayne Gretzky, 87; Glenn Anderson, 54; Jari Kurri, 52; Paul Coffey, 40. 80GP

—**Edmonton Oilers,** 1984-85. Wayne Gretzky, 73; Jari Kurri, 71; Mike Krushelnyski, 43; Glenn Anderson, 42. 80GP

—**Edmonton Oilers,** 1985-86. Jari Kurri, 68; Glenn Anderson, 54; Wayne Gretzky, 52; Paul Coffey, 48. 80GP

—**Calgary Flames,** 1987-88. Joe Nieuwendyk, 51; Hakan Loob, 50; Mike Bullard, 48; Joe Mullen, 40. 80GP

3 —Boston Bruins, 1970-71. Phil Esposito, 76; John Bucyk, 51; Ken Hodge, 43. 78GP
—NY Rangers, 1971-72. Vic Hadfield, 50; Jean Ratelle, 46; Rod Gilbert, 43. 78GP
—Buffalo Sabres, 1975-76. Danny Gare, 50; Rick Martin, 49; Gilbert Perreault, 44. 80GP
—Montreal Canadiens, 1979-80. Guy Lafleur, 50; Pierre Larouche, 50; Steve Shutt, 47. 80GP
—Buffalo Sabres, 1979-80. Danny Gare, 56; Rick Martin, 45; Gilbert Perreault, 40. 80GP
—Los Angeles Kings, 1980-81. Marcel Dionne, 58; Charlie Simmer, 56; Dave Taylor, 47. 80GP
—Los Angeles Kings, 1984-85. Marcel Dionne, 46; Bernie Nicholls, 46; Dave Taylor, 41. 80GP
—NY Islanders, 1984-85. Mike Bossy, 58; Brent Sutter, 42; John Tonelli; 42. 80GP
—Chicago Blackhawks, 1985-86. Denis Savard, 47; Troy Murray, 45; Al Secord, 40. 80GP
—Chicago Blackhawks, 1987-88. Denis Savard, 44; Rick Vaive, 43; Steve Larmer, 41. 80GP
—Edmonton Oilers, 1987-88. Craig Simpson, 43; Jari Kurri, 43; Wayne Gretzky, 40. 80GP
—Los Angeles Kings, 1988-89. Bernie Nicholls, 70; Wayne Gretzky 54; Luc Robitaille, 46. 80GP
—Los Angeles Kings, 1990-91. Luc Robitaille, 45; Tomas Sandstrom, 45; Wayne Gretzky 41. 80GP
—Pittsburgh Penguins, 1991-92. Kevin Stevens, 54; Mario Lemieux, 44; Joe Mullen, 42. 80GP
—Pittsburgh Penguins, 1992-93. Mario Lemieux, 69; Kevin Stevens, 55; Rick Tocchet, 48. 84GP
—Calgary Flames, 1993-94. Gary Roberts, 41; Robert Reichel, 40; Theoren Fleury, 40. 84GP
—Pittsburgh Penguins, 1995-96. Mario Lemieux, 69; Jaromir Jagr, 62; Petr Nedved, 45. 82GP

MOST 30-OR-MORE GOAL SCORERS, ONE SEASON:

6 —Buffalo Sabres, 1974-75. Rick Martin, 52; Rene Robert, 40; Gilbert Perreault, 39; Don Luce, 33; Rick Dudley, Danny Gare, 31 each. 80GP

—**NY Islanders,** 1977-78. Mike Bossy, 53; Bryan Trottier, 46; Clark Gillies, 35; Denis Potvin, Bob Nystrom, Bob Bourne, 30 each. 80GP

—**Winnipeg Jets,** 1984-85. Dale Hawerchuk, 53; Paul MacLean, 41; Laurie Boschman, 32; Brian Mullen, 32; Doug Smail, 31; Thomas Steen, 30. 80GP

5 —Chicago Blackhawks, 1968-69. 76GP
—Boston Bruins, 1970-71. 78GP
—Montreal Canadiens, 1971-72. 78GP
—Philadelphia Flyers, 1972-73. 78GP
—Boston Bruins, 1973-74. 78GP
—Montreal Canadiens, 1974-75. 80GP
—Montreal Canadiens, 1975-76. 80GP
—Pittsburgh Penguins, 1975-76. 80GP
—NY Islanders, 1978-79. 80GP
—Detroit Red Wings, 1979-80. 80GP
—Philadelphia Flyers, 1979-80. 80GP
—NY Islanders, 1980-81. 80GP
—St. Louis Blues, 1980-81. 80GP
—Chicago Blackhawks, 1981-82. 80GP
—Edmonton Oilers, 1981-82. 80GP
—Montreal Canadiens, 1981-82. 80GP
—Quebec Nordiques, 1981-82. 80GP
—Washington Capitals, 1981-82. 80GP
—Edmonton Oilers, 1982-83. 80GP
—Edmonton Oilers, 1983-84. 80GP
—Edmonton Oilers, 1984-85. 80GP
—Los Angeles Kings, 1984-85. 80GP
—Edmonton Oilers, 1985-86. 80GP
—Edmonton Oilers, 1986-87. 80GP
—Edmonton Oilers, 1987-88. 80GP
—Edmonton Oilers, 1988-89. 80GP
—Detroit Red Wings, 1991-92. 80GP
—NY Rangers, 1991-92. 80GP
—Pittsburgh Penguins, 1991-92. 80GP
—Detroit Red Wings, 1992-93. 84GP
—Pittsburgh Penguins, 1992-93. 84GP

MOST 20-OR-MORE GOAL SCORERS, ONE SEASON:

11 —Boston Bruins, 1977-78; Peter McNab, 41; Terry O'Reilly, 29; Bobby Schmautz, Stan Jonathan, 27 each; Jean Ratelle, Rick Middleton, 25 each; Wayne Cashman, 24; Gregg Sheppard, 23; Brad Park, 22; Don Marcotte, Bob Miller, 20 each. 80GP

10 —Boston Bruins, 1970-71. 78GP
—Montreal Canadiens, 1974-75. 80GP
—St. Louis Blues, 1980-81. 80GP

Peter McNab's 41 goals led the way for the 1977-78 Boston Bruins, the only team in league history to have 11 different players score at least 20 goals in a single season.

100-POINT SCORERS

MOST 100 OR-MORE-POINT SCORERS, ONE SEASON:
  4 — **Boston Bruins,** 1970-71, Phil Esposito, 76G-76A-152PTS; Bobby Orr, 37G-102A-139PTS; John Bucyk, 51G-65A-116PTS; Ken Hodge, 43G-62A-105PTS. 78GP.
   — **Edmonton Oilers,** 1982-83, Wayne Gretzky, 71G-125A-196PTS; Mark Messier, 48G-58A-106PTS; Glenn Anderson, 48G-56A-104PTS; Jari Kurri, 45G-59A-104PTS. 80GP.
   — **Edmonton Oilers,** 1983-84, Wayne Gretzky, 87G-118A-205PTS; Paul Coffey, 40G-86A-126PTS; Jari Kurri, 52G-61A-113PTS; Mark Messier, 37G-64A-101PTS. 80GP.
   — **Edmonton Oilers,** 1985-86, Wayne Gretzky, 52G-163A-215PTS; Paul Coffey, 48G-90A-138PTS; Jari Kurri, 68G-63A-131PTS; Glenn Anderson, 54G-48A-102PTS. 80GP.
   — **Pittsburgh Penguins,** 1992-93, Mario Lemieux, 69G-91A-160PTS; Kevin Stevens, 55G-56A-111PTS; Rick Tocchet, 48G-61A-109PTS; Ron Francis, 24G-76A-100PTS. 84GP.
  3 — Boston Bruins, 1973-74, Phil Esposito, 68G-77A-145PTS; Bobby Orr, 32G-90A-122PTS; Ken Hodge, 50G-55A-105PTS. 78GP.
   — NY Islanders, 1978-79, Bryan Trottier, 47G-87A-134PTS; Mike Bossy, 69G-57A-126PTS; Denis Potvin, 31G-70A-101PTS. 80GP.
   — Los Angeles Kings, 1980-81, Marcel Dionne, 58G-77A-135PTS; Dave Taylor, 47 G-65A-112PTS; Charlie Simmer, 56G-49A-105PTS. 80GP.
   — Edmonton Oilers, 1984-85, Wayne Gretzky, 73G-135A-208PTS; Jari Kurri, 71G-64A-135PTS; Paul Coffey, 37G-84A-121PTS. 80GP.
   — NY Islanders, 1984-85. Mike Bossy, 58G-59A-117PTS; Brent Sutter, 42G-60A-102PTS; John Tonelli, 42G-58A-100PTS. 80GP.
   — Edmonton Oilers, 1986-87, Wayne Gretzky, 62G-121A-183PTS; Jari Kurri, 54G-54A-108PTS; Mark Messier, 37G-70A-107PTS. 80GP.
   — Pittsburgh Penguins, 1988-89, Mario Lemieux, 85G-114A-199PTS; Rob Brown, 49G-66A-115PTS; Paul Coffey, 30G-83A-113PTS. 80GP.
   — Pittsburgh Penguins, 1995-96, Mario Lemieux, 69G-92A-161PTS; Jaromir Jagr, 62G-87A-149PTS; Ron Francis, 27G-92A-119PTS. 82GP.

SHOTS ON GOAL

MOST SHOTS, BOTH TEAMS, ONE GAME:
  141 — **NY Americans, Pittsburgh Pirates,** Dec. 26, 1925, at New York. NY Americans, who won game 3-1, had 73 shots; Pit. Pirates, 68 shots.

MOST SHOTS, ONE TEAM, ONE GAME:
  83 — **Boston Bruins,** March 4, 1941, at Boston. Boston defeated Chicago 3-2.
  73 — NY Americans, Dec. 26, 1925, at New York. NY Americans defeated Pit. Pirates 3-1.
   — Boston Bruins, March 21, 1991, at Boston. Boston tied Quebec 3-3.
  72 — Boston Bruins, Dec. 10, 1970, at Boston. Boston defeated Buffalo 8-2.

MOST SHOTS, ONE TEAM, ONE PERIOD:
  33 — **Boston Bruins,** March 4, 1941, at Boston, second period. Boston defeated Chicago 3-2.

TEAM GOALS-AGAINST

Fewest Goals-Against

FEWEST GOALS AGAINST, ONE SEASON:
  42 — **Ottawa Senators,** 1925-26. 36GP
  43 — Montreal Canadiens, 1928-29. 44GP
  48 — Montreal Canadiens, 1923-24. 24GP
   — Montreal Canadiens, 1927-28. 44GP

FEWEST GOALS AGAINST, ONE SEASON (MINIMUM 70-GAME SCHEDULE):
  131 — **Toronto Maple Leafs,** 1953-54. 70GP
   — **Montreal Canadiens,** 1955-56. 70GP
  132 — Detroit Red Wings, 1953-54. 70GP
  133 — Detroit Red Wings, 1951-52. 70GP
   — Detroit Red Wings, 1952-53. 70GP

LOWEST GOALS-AGAINST-PER-GAME AVERAGE, ONE SEASON:
  .98 — **Montreal Canadiens,** 1928-29. 43GA vs. in 44GP.
  1.09 — Montreal Canadiens, 1927-28. 48GA vs. in 44GP.
  1.17 — Ottawa Senators, 1925-26. 42GA vs. in 36GP.

Most Goals-Against

MOST GOALS AGAINST, ONE SEASON:
  446 — **Washington Capitals,** 1974-75. 80GP
  415 — Detroit Red Wings, 1985-86. 80GP
  414 — San Jose Sharks, 1992-93. 84GP
  407 — Quebec Nordiques, 1989-90. 80GP
  403 — Hartford Whalers, 1982-83. 80GP

HIGHEST GOALS-AGAINST-PER-GAME AVERAGE, ONE SEASON:
  7.38 — **Quebec Bulldogs,** 1919-20, 177GA vs. in 24GP.
  6.20 — NY Rangers, 1943-44, 310GA vs. in 50GP.
  5.58 — Washington Capitals, 1974-75, 446GA vs. in 80GP.

MOST POWER-PLAY GOALS AGAINST, ONE SEASON:
  122 — **Chicago Blackhawks,** 1988-89. 80GP
  120 — Pittsburgh Penguins, 1987-88. 80GP
  115 — New Jersey Devils, 1988-89. 80GP
   — Ottawa Senators, 1992-93. 84GP
  114 — Los Angeles Kings, 1992-93. 84GP
  113 — San Jose Sharks, 1992-93. 84GP

MOST SHORTHAND GOALS AGAINST, ONE SEASON:
  22 — **Pittsburgh Penguins,** 1984-85. 80GP
   — **Minnesota North Stars,** 1991-92. 80GP
   — **Colorado Avalanche,** 1995-96. 82GP
  21 — Calgary Flames, 1984-85. 80GP
   — Pittsburgh Penguins, 1989-90. 80GP

SHUTOUTS

MOST SHUTOUTS, ONE SEASON:
  22 — **Montreal Canadiens,** 1928-29. All by George Hainsworth. 44GP
  16 — NY Americans, 1928-29. Roy Worters had 13; Flat Walsh 3. 44GP
  15 — Ottawa Senators, 1925-26. All by Alex Connell. 36GP
   — Ottawa Senators, 1927-28. All by Alex Connell. 44GP
   — Boston Bruins, 1927-28. All by Hal Winkler. 44GP
   — Chicago Blackhawks, 1969-70. All by Tony Esposito. 76GP

MOST CONSECUTIVE GAMES SHUT OUT:
  8 — **Chicago Blackhawks,** 1928-29.

TEAM PENALTIES

MOST PENALTY MINUTES, ONE SEASON:
  2,713 — **Buffalo Sabres,** 1991-92. 80GP
  2,670 — Pittsburgh Penguins, 1988-89. 80GP
  2,663 — Chicago Blackhawks, 1991-92. 80GP
  2,643 — Calgary Flames, 1991-92. 80GP
  2,621 — Philadelphia Flyers, 1980-81. 80GP

MOST PENALTIES, BOTH TEAMS, ONE GAME:
  85 Penalties — **Edmonton Oilers (44), Los Angeles Kings (41)** at Los Angeles, Feb. 28, 1990. Edmonton received 26 minors, 7 majors, 6 10-minute misconducts, 4 game misconducts and 1 match penalty; Los Angeles received 26 minors, 9 majors, 3 10-minute misconducts and 3 game misconducts.

MOST PENALTY MINUTES, BOTH TEAMS, ONE GAME:
  406 Minutes — **Minnesota North Stars, Boston Bruins** at Boston, Feb. 26, 1981. Minnesota received 18 minors, 13 majors, 4 10-minute misconducts and 7 game misconducts; a total of 211PIM. Boston received 20 minors, 13 majors, 3 10-minute misconducts and six game misconducts; a total of 195PIM.

MOST PENALTIES, ONE TEAM, ONE GAME:
  44 — **Edmonton Oilers,** Feb. 28, 1990, at Los Angeles. Edmonton received 26 minors, 7 majors, 6 10-minute misconducts, 4 game misconducts and 1 match penalty.
  42 — Minnesota North Stars, Feb. 26, 1981, at Boston. Minnesota received 18 minors, 13 majors, 4 10-minute misconducts and 7 game misconducts.
   — Boston Bruins, Feb. 26, 1981, at Boston vs. Minnesota. Boston received 20 minors, 13 majors, 3 10-minute misconducts and 7 game misconducts.

MOST PENALTY MINUTES, ONE TEAM, ONE GAME:
  211 — **Minnesota North Stars,** Feb. 26, 1981, at Boston. Minnesota received 18 minors, 13 majors, 4 10-minute misconducts and 7 game misconducts.

MOST PENALTIES, BOTH TEAMS, ONE PERIOD:
  67 — **Minnesota North Stars, Boston Bruins,** at Boston, Feb. 26, 1981, first period. Minnesota received 15 minors, 8 majors, 4 10-minute misconducts and 7 game misconducts, a total of 34 penalties. Boston had 16 minors, 8 majors, 3 10-minute misconducts and 6 game misconducts, a total of 33 penalties.

MOST PENALTY MINUTES, BOTH TEAMS, ONE PERIOD:
  372 — **Los Angeles Kings, Philadelphia Flyers** at Philadelphia, March 11, 1979, first period. Philadelphia received 4 minors, 8 majors, 6 10-minute misconducts and 8 game misconducts for 188 minutes. Los Angeles received 2 minors, 8 majors, 6 10-minute misconducts and 8 game misconducts for 184 minutes.

MOST PENALTIES, ONE TEAM, ONE PERIOD:
  34 — **Minnesota North Stars,** Feb. 26, 1981, at Boston, first period. 15 minors, 8 majors, 4 10-minute misconducts, 7 game misconducts.

MOST PENALTY MINUTES, ONE TEAM, ONE PERIOD:
  188 — **Philadelphia Flyers,** March 11, 1979, at Philadelphia vs. Los Angeles, first period. Flyers received 4 minors, 8 majors, 6 10-minute misconducts and 8 game misconducts.

NHL Individual Scoring Records – History

SIX INDIVIDUAL SCORING RECORDS stand as benchmarks in the history of the game: most goals, single-season and career; most assists, single-season and career; and most points, single-season and career. The evolution of these six records is traced here, beginning with 1917-18, the NHL's first season.

MOST GOALS, ONE SEASON

44 – Joe Malone, Montreal, 1917-18.
Scored goal #44 against Toronto's Harry Holmes on March 2, 1918 and finished season with 44 goals.

50 – Maurice Richard, Montreal, 1944-45.
Scored goal #45 against Toronto's Frank McCool on February 25, 1945 and finished the season with 50 goals.

50 – Bernie Geoffrion, Montreal, 1960-61.
Scored goal #50 against Toronto's Cesare Maniago on March 16, 1961 and finished the season with 50 goals.

50 – Bobby Hull, Chicago, 1961-62.
Scored goal #50 against NY Rangers' Gump Worsley on March 25, 1962 and finished the season with 50 goals.

54 – Bobby Hull, Chicago, 1965-66.
Scored goal #51 against NY Rangers' Cesare Maniago on March 12, 1966 and finished the season with 54 goals.

58 – Bobby Hull, Chicago, 1968-69.
Scored goal #55 against Boston's Gerry Cheevers on March 20, 1969 and finished the season with 58 goals.

76 – Phil Esposito, Boston, 1970-71.
Scored goal #59 against Los Angeles' Denis DeJordy on March 11, 1971 and finished the season with 76 goals.

92 – Wayne Gretzky, Edmonton, 1981-82.
Scored goal #77 against Buffalo's Don Edwards on February 24, 1982 and finished the season with 92 goals.

MOST ASSISTS, ONE SEASON

9 – Newsy Lalonde, Montreal, 1918-19.
14 – Leo Reise, Sr., Hamilton, 1921-22.
14 – Punch Broadbent, Ottawa, 1921-22.
15 – Cy Denneny, Ottawa, 1924-25.
18 – Dick Irvin, Chicago, 1926-27.
18 – Howie Morenz, Montreal, 1927-28.
36 – Frank Boucher, NY Rangers, 1929-30.
37 – Joe Primeau, Toronto, 1931-32.
45 – Bill Cowley, Boston, 1940-41.
45 – Bill Cowley, Boston, 1942-43.
49 – Clint Smith, Chicago, 1943-44.
54 – Elmer Lach, Montreal, 1944-45.
55 – Ted Lindsay, Detroit, 1949-50.
56 – Bert Olmstead, Montreal, 1955-56.
58 – Jean Beliveau, Montreal, 1960-61.
58 – Andy Bathgate, NY Rangers/Toronto, 1963-64.
59 – Stan Mikita, Chicago, 1964-65.
62 – Stan Mikita, Chicago, 1966-67.
77 – Phil Esposito, Boston, 1968-69.
87 – Bobby Orr, Boston, 1969-70.
102 – Bobby Orr, Boston, 1970-71.
109 – Wayne Gretzky, Edmonton, 1980-81.
120 – Wayne Gretzky, Edmonton, 1981-82.
125 – Wayne Gretzky, Edmonton, 1982-83.
135 – Wayne Gretzky, Edmonton, 1984-85.
163 – Wayne Gretzky, Edmonton, 1985-86.

MOST POINTS, ONE SEASON

44 – Joe Malone, Montreal, 1917-18.
48 – Joe Malone, Montreal, 1919-20.
51 – Howie Morenz, Montreal, 1927-28.
73 – Cooney Weiland, Boston, 1929-30.
73 – Doug Bentley, Chicago, 1942-43.
82 – Herb Cain, Boston, 1943-44.
86 – Gordie Howe, Detroit, 1950-51.
95 – Gordie Howe, Detroit, 1952-53.
96 – Dickie Moore, Montreal, 1958-59.
97 – Bobby Hull, Chicago, 1965-66.
97 – Stan Mikita, Chicago, 1966-67.
126 – Phil Esposito, Boston, 1968-69.
152 – Phil Esposito, Boston, 1970-71.
164 – Wayne Gretzky, Edmonton, 1980-81.
212 – Wayne Gretzky, Edmonton, 1981-82.
215 – Wayne Gretzky, Edmonton, 1985-86.

Ted Lindsay, right, established a new NHL single-season record for assists when he set up Red Kelly's goal at the 6:39 mark of the first period on March 26, 1950. In this photo "Terrible Ted" is reunited with former junior teammate Gus Mortson.

MOST GOALS, CAREER

44 – Joe Malone, 1917-18, Montreal.
Malone led the NHL in goals in the league's first season and finished with 44 goals in 22 games in 1917-18.

54 – Cy Denneny, 1918-19, Ottawa.
Denneny passed Malone during the 1918-19 season, finishing the year with a two-year total of 54 goals. He held the career goal-scoring mark until 1919-20.

146 – Joe Malone, Montreal, Quebec Bulldogs, Hamilton.
Malone passed Denneny in 1919-20 and remained the NHL's career goal-scoring leader until his retirement. He finished with a career total of 146 goals.

246 – Cy Denneny, Ottawa, Boston.
Denneny passed Malone with goal #147 in 1922-23 and remained the NHL's career goal-scoring leader until his retirement. He finished with a career total of 246 goals.

270 – Howie Morenz, Montreal, NY Rangers, Chicago.
Morenz passed Denneny with goal #247 in 1933-34 and finished his career with 270 goals.

324 – Nels Stewart, Montreal Maroons, Boston, NY Americans.
Stewart passed Morenz with goal #271 in 1936-37 and remained the NHL's career goal-scoring leader until his retirement. He finished his career with 324 goals.

544 – Maurice Richard, Montreal.
Richard passed Nels Stewart with goal #325 on Nov. 8, 1952 and remained the NHL's career goal-scoring leader until his retirement. He finished his career with 544 goals.

801 – Gordie Howe, Detroit, Hartford.
Howe passed Richard with goal #545 on Nov. 10, 1963 and remained the NHL's career goal-scoring leader until his retirement. He finished his career with 801 goals.

837 – Wayne Gretzky, Edmonton, Los Angeles, St. Louis.
Gretzky passed Gordie Howe with goal #802 on March 23, 1994. He is the current career goal-scoring leader with 837.

Gordie Howe, right, was the NHL's all-time leading scorer for 29 years, the longest reign in the history of the game. Bobby Hull became the only player in NHL history to break his own single-season goal-scoring record when he scored his 55th goal of the 1968-69 season against Boston's Gerry Cheevers on March 20.

MOST ASSISTS, CAREER (minimum 100 assists)

Note: Assists were not tabulated in 1917-18, the NHL's first season. Newsy Lalonde of the Canadiens was the NHL's first career (and single-season) assist leader, recording nine in 1918-19

100 – Frank Boucher, Ottawa, NY Rangers.
In 1930-31, Boucher became the first NHL player to reach the 100-assist milestone.

262 – Frank Boucher, Ottawa, NY Rangers.
Boucher retired as the NHL's career assist leader in 1938 with 252. He returned to the NHL in 1943-44 and remained the NHL's career assist leader until he was overtaken by Bill Cowley in 1943-44. He finished his career with 262 assists.

353 – Bill Cowley, St. Louis Eagles, Boston.
Cowley passed Boucher with assist #263 in 1943-44. He retired as the NHL's career assist leader in 1947 with 353.

408 – Elmer Lach, Montreal.
Lach passed Cowley with assist #354 in 1951-52. He retired as the NHL's career assist leader in 1953 with 408.

1,049 – Gordie Howe, Detroit, Hartford.
Howe passed Lach with assist #409 in 1957-58. He retired as the NHL's career assist leader in 1980 with 1,049.

1,771 – Wayne Gretzky, Edmonton, Los Angeles, St. Louis.
Gretzky passed Howe with assist #1,050 in 1988-89. He is the current career assist leader with 1,771.

MOST POINTS, CAREER (minimum 100 points)

100 – Joe Malone, Montreal, Quebec Bulldogs, Hamilton.
In 1920-21, Malone became the first player in NHL history to record 100 points.

200 – Cy Denneny, Ottawa.
In 1923-24, Denneny became the first player in NHL history to record 200 points.

300 – Cy Denneny, Ottawa.
In 1926-27, Denneny became the first player in NHL history to record 300 points.

315 – Cy Denneny, Ottawa, Boston.
Denneny retired as the NHL's career point-scoring leader in 1929 with 315 points.

467 – Howie Morenz, Montreal, Chicago, NY Rangers.
Morenz passed Cy Denneny with point #316 in 1931-32. At the time his career ended in 1937, he was the NHL's career point-scoring leader with 467 points.

515 – Nels Stewart, Montreal Maroons, Boston, NY Americans.
Stewart passed Morenz with point #468 in 1938-39. He retired as the NHL's career point-scoring leader in 1940 with 515 points.

528 – Syd Howe, Ottawa, Philadelphia Quakers, Toronto, St. Louis Eagles, Detroit.
Howe passed Nels Stewart with point #516 on March 8, 1945. He retired as the NHL's career point-scoring leader in 1946 with 528 points.

548 – Bill Cowley, St. Louis Eagles, Boston.
Cowley passed Syd Howe with point #529 on Feb. 12, 1947. He retired as the NHL's career point-scoring leader in 1947 with 548 points.

610 – Elmer Lach, Montreal.
Lach passed Bill Cowley with point #549 on Feb. 23, 1952. He remained the NHL's career point-scoring leader until he was overtaken by Maurice Richard in 1953-54. He finished his career with 623 points.

946 – Maurice Richard, Montreal.
Richard passed teammate Elmer Lach with point #611 on Dec. 12, 1953. He remained the NHL's career point-scoring leader until he was overtaken by Gordie Howe in 1959-60. He finished his career with 965 points.

1,850 – Gordie Howe, Detroit, Hartford.
Howe passed Richard with point #947 on Jan. 16, 1960. He retired as the NHL's career point-scoring leader in 1980 with 1,850 points.

2,608 – Wayne Gretzky, Edmonton, Los Angeles, St. Louis.
Gretzky passed Howe with point #1,851 on Oct. 15, 1989. He is the current career point-scoring leader with 2,608.

Individual Records

SEASONS

MOST SEASONS:
26 — Gordie Howe, Detroit, 1946-47 – 1970-71; Hartford, 1979-80.
24 — Alex Delvecchio, Detroit, 1950-51 – 1973-74.
— Tim Horton, Toronto, NY Rangers, Pittsburgh, Buffalo, 1949-50, 1951-52 – 1973-74.
23 — John Bucyk, Detroit, Boston, 1955-56 – 1977-78.
22 — Dean Prentice, NY Rangers, Boston, Detroit, Pittsburgh, Minnesota, 1952-53 – 1973-74.
— Doug Mohns, Boston, Chicago, Minnesota, Atlanta, Washington, 1953-54 – 1974-75.
— Stan Mikita, Chicago, 1958-59 – 1979-80.

GAMES

MOST GAMES:
1,767 — Gordie Howe, Detroit, 1946-47 – 1970-71; Hartford, 1979-80.
1,549 — Alex Delvecchio, Detroit, 1950-51 – 1973-74.
1,540 — John Bucyk, Detroit, Boston, 1955-56 – 1977-78.

MOST GAMES, INCLUDING PLAYOFFS:
1,924 — Gordie Howe, Detroit, Hartford, 1,767 regular-season and 157 playoff games.
1,670 — Alex Delvecchio, Detroit, 1,549 regular-season and 121 playoff games.
1,664 — John Bucyk, Detroit, Boston, 1,540 regular-season and 124 playoff games.

MOST CONSECUTIVE GAMES:
964 — Doug Jarvis, Montreal, Washington, Hartford, from Oct. 8, 1975 – Oct. 10, 1987.
914 — Garry Unger, Toronto, Detroit, St. Louis, Atlanta from Feb. 24, 1968, – Dec. 21, 1979.
884 — Steve Larmer, Chicago, from Oct. 6, 1982 to April 16, 1993.
776 — Craig Ramsay, Buffalo, from March 27, 1973, – Feb. 10, 1983.
630 — Andy Hebenton, NY Rangers, Boston, nine complete 70-game seasons from 1955-56 – 1963-64.

GOALS

MOST GOALS:
837 — Wayne Gretzky, Edmonton, Los Angeles, St. Louis, in 17 seasons, 1,253GP.
801 — Gordie Howe, Detroit, Hartford, in 26 seasons, 1,767GP.
731 — Marcel Dionne, Detroit, Los Angeles, NY Rangers, in 18 seasons, 1,348GP.
717 — Phil Esposito, Chicago, Boston, NY Rangers, in 18 seasons, 1,282GP.
664 — Mike Gartner, Washington, Minnesota, NY Rangers, Toronto, in 17 seasons, 1,290GP.

MOST GOALS, INCLUDING PLAYOFFS:
949 — Wayne Gretzky, Edmonton, Los Angeles, St. Louis, 837 regular-season and 112 playoff goals.
869 — Gordie Howe, Detroit, Hartford, 801 regular-season and 68 playoff goals.
778 — Phil Esposito, Chicago, Boston, NY Rangers, 717 regular-season and 61 playoff goals.
752 — Marcel Dionne, Detroit, Los Angeles, NY Rangers, 731 regular-season and 21 playoff goals.

MOST GOALS, ONE SEASON:
92 — Wayne Gretzky, Edmonton, 1981-82. 80 game schedule.
87 — Wayne Gretzky, Edmonton, 1983-84. 80 game schedule.
86 — Brett Hull, St. Louis, 1990-91. 80 game schedule.
85 — Mario Lemieux, Pittsburgh, 1988-89. 80 game schedule.
76 — Phil Esposito, Boston, 1970-71. 78 game schedule.
— Alexander Mogilny, Buffalo, 1992-93. 84 game schedule.
— Teemu Selanne, Winnipeg, 1992-93. 84 game schedule.
73 — Wayne Gretzky, Edmonton, 1984-85. 80 game schedule.
72 — Brett Hull, St. Louis, 1989-90. 80 game schedule.
71 — Jari Kurri, Edmonton, 1984-85 80 game schedule.
— Wayne Gretzky, Edmonton, 1982-83. 80 game schedule.
70 — Mario Lemieux, Pittsburgh, 1987-1988. 80 game schedule.
— Bernie Nicholls, Los Angeles, 1988-89. 80 game schedule.
— Brett Hull, St. Louis, 1991-92. 80 game schedule.

MOST GOALS, ONE SEASON, INCLUDING PLAYOFFS:
100 — Wayne Gretzky, Edmonton, 1983-84, 87G in 74 regular-season games and 13G in 19 playoff games.
97 — Wayne Gretzky, Edmonton, 1981-82, 92G in 80 regular-season games and 5G in 5 playoff games.
— Mario Lemieux, Pittsburgh, 1988-89, 85G in 76 regular-season games and 12G in 11 playoff games.
— Brett Hull, St. Louis, 1990-91, 86G in 78 regular-season games and 11G in 13 playoff games.
90 — Wayne Gretzky, Edmonton, 1984-85, 73G in 80 regular season games and 17G in 18 playoff games.
— Jari Kurri, Edmonton, 1984-85, 71G in 80 regular season games and 19G in 18 playoff games.
85 — Mike Bossy, NY Islanders, 1980-81, 68G in 79 regular-season games and 17G in 18 playoff games.
— Brett Hull, St. Louis, 1989-90, 72G in 80 regular-season games and 13G in 12 playoff games.
83 — Wayne Gretzky, Edmonton, 1982-83, 71G in 73 regular-season games and 12G in 16 playoff games.
— Alexander Mogilny, Buffalo, 1992-93, 76G in 77 regular-season games and 7G in 7 playoff games.

No athlete in any sport has dominated the record books like Wayne Gretzky, who still holds or shares over 60 NHL marks in the NHL Official Guide & Record Book.

MOST GOALS, 50 GAMES FROM START OF SEASON:
61 — Wayne Gretzky, Edmonton, 1981-82. Oct. 7, 1981 - Jan. 22, 1982. (80-game schedule)
— **Wayne Gretzky,** Edmonton, 1983-84. Oct. 5, 1983 - Jan. 25, 1984. (80-game schedule)
54 — Mario Lemieux, Pittsburgh, 1988-89. Oct. 7, 1988 - Jan. 31, 1989. (80-game schedule)
53 — Wayne Gretzky, Edmonton, 1984-85. Oct. 11, 1984 - Jan. 28, 1985. (80-game schedule)
52 — Brett Hull, St. Louis, 1990-91. Oct. 4, 1990 - Jan. 26, 1991. (80-game schedule).
50 — Maurice Richard, Montreal, 1944-45. Oct. 28, 1944 - March 18, 1945. (50-game schedule)
— Mike Bossy, NY Islanders, 1980-81. Oct. 11, 1980 - Jan. 24, 1981. (80-game schedule)
— Brett Hull, St. Louis, 1991-92. Oct. 5, 1991 – Jan 28, 1992. (80 game schedule)

MOST GOALS, ONE GAME:
7 — Joe Malone, Quebec Bulldogs, Jan. 31, 1920, at Quebec. Quebec 10, Toronto 6.
6 — Newsy Lalonde, Montreal, Jan. 10, 1920, at Montreal. Montreal 14, Toronto 7.
— Joe Malone, Quebec Bulldogs, March 10, 1920, at Quebec. Quebec 10, Ottawa 4.
— Corb Denneny, Toronto, Jan. 26, 1921, at Toronto. Toronto 10, Hamilton 3.
— Cy Denneny, Ottawa, March 7, 1921, at Ottawa. Ottawa 12, Hamilton 5.
— Syd Howe, Detroit, Feb. 3, 1944, at Detroit. Detroit 12, NY Rangers 2.
— Red Berenson, St. Louis, Nov. 7, 1968, at Philadelphia. St. Louis 8, Philadelphia 0.
— Darryl Sittler, Toronto, Feb. 7, 1976, at Toronto. Toronto 11, Boston 4.

On November 7, 1968, Gordon "Red" Berenson set an NHL record by scoring six goals
in the St. Louis Blues' 8-0 victory over the Flyers at the Philadelphia Spectrum.

MOST GOALS, ONE ROAD GAME:
6 —Red Berenson, St. Louis, Nov. 7, 1968, at Philadelphia. St. Louis 8,
   Philadelphia 0.
5 —Joe Malone, Montreal, Dec. 19, 1917, at Ottawa. Montreal 9, Ottawa 4.
   —Redvers Green, Hamilton, Dec. 5, 1924, at Toronto. Hamilton 10,
   Toronto 3.
   —Babe Dye, Toronto, Dec. 22, 1924, at Boston. Toronto 10, Boston 2.
   —Harry Broadbent, Mtl. Maroons, Jan. 7, 1925, at Hamilton. Mtl. Maroons 6,
   Hamilton 2.
   —Don Murdoch, NY Rangers, Oct. 12, 1976, at Minnesota. NY Rangers 10,
   Minnesota 4.
   —Tim Young, Minnesota, Jan. 15, 1979, at NY Rangers. Minnesota 8,
   NY Rangers 1.
   —Willy Lindstrom, Winnipeg, March 2, 1982, at Philadelphia. Winnipeg 7,
   Philadelphia 6.
   —Bengt Gustafsson, Washington, Jan. 8, 1984, at Philadelphia.
   Washington 7, Philadelphia 1.
   —Wayne Gretzky, Edmonton, Dec. 15, 1984, at St. Louis. Edmonton 8,
   St. Louis 2.
   —Dave Andreychuk, Buffalo, Feb. 6, 1986, at Boston. Buffalo 8, Boston 6.
   —Mats Sundin, Quebec, Mar. 5, 1992, at Hartford. Quebec 10, Hartford 4.
   —Mario Lemieux, Pittsburgh, Apr. 9, 1993, at New York. Pittsburgh 10,
   NY Rangers 4.
   —Mike Ricci, Quebec, Feb. 17, 1994, at San Jose. Quebec 8, San Jose 2.
   —Alexei Zhamnov, Winnipeg, Apr. 1, 1995, at Los Angeles. Winnipeg 7, Los
   Angeles 7.

MOST GOALS, ONE PERIOD:
4 —Harvey (Busher) Jackson, Toronto, Nov. 20, 1934, at St. Louis, third period.
   Toronto 5, St. Louis Eagles 2.
   —**Max Bentley,** Chicago, Jan. 28, 1943, at Chicago, third period.
   Chicago 10, NY Rangers 1.
   —**Clint Smith,** Chicago, March 4, 1945, at Chicago, third period. Chicago 6,
   Montreal 4.
   —**Red Berenson,** St. Louis, Nov. 7, 1968, at Philadelphia, second period.
   St. Louis 8, Philadelphia 0.
   —**Wayne Gretzky,** Edmonton, Feb. 18, 1981, at Edmonton, third period.
   Edmonton 9, St. Louis 2.
   —**Grant Mulvey,** Chicago, Feb. 3, 1982, at Chicago, first period. Chicago 9,
   St. Louis 5.
   —**Bryan Trottier,** NY Islanders, Feb. 13, 1982, at New York, second period.
   NY Islanders 8, Philadelphia 2.
   —**Al Secord,** Chicago, Jan. 7, 1987 at Chicago, second period. Chicago 6,
   Toronto 4.
   —**Joe Nieuwendyk,** Calgary, Jan. 11, 1989, at Calgary, second period.
   Calgary 8, Winnipeg 3.
   —**Peter Bondra,** Washington, Feb. 5, 1994, at Washington, first period.
   Washington 6, Tampa Bay 3.

ASSISTS

MOST ASSISTS:
1,771 —Wayne Gretzky, Edmonton, Los Angeles, St. Louis, in 17 seasons, 1,253GP.
1,049 —Gordie Howe, Detroit, Hartford in 26 seasons, 1,767GP.
1,040 —Marcel Dionne, Detroit, Los Angeles, NY Rangers in 18 seasons, 1,348GP.
1,038 —Paul Coffey, Edmonton, Pittsburgh, Los Angeles, Detroit, in 16 seasons,
   1,154GP.
   970 —Ray Bourque, Boston, in 17 seasons, 1,228GP.

MOST ASSISTS, INCLUDING PLAYOFFS:
2,021 —Wayne Gretzky, Edmonton, Los Angeles, St. Louis, 1,771 regular-season
   and 250 playoff assists.
1,166 —Paul Coffey, Edmonton, Pittsburgh, Los Angeles, Detroit, 1,038
   regular-season and 128 playoff assists.
1,141 —Gordie Howe, Detroit, Hartford, 1,049 regular-season and 92 playoff assists.
1,106 —Mark Messier, Edmonton, NY Rangers, 929 regular-season and 177 playoff
   assists.
1,064 —Marcel Dionne, Detroit, Los Angeles, NY Rangers, 1,040 regular-season and
   24 playoff assists.

MOST ASSISTS, ONE SEASON:
163 —Wayne Gretzky, Edmonton , 1985-86. 80 game schedule.
135 —Wayne Gretzky, Edmonton, 1984-85. 80 game schedule.
125 —Wayne Gretzky, Edmonton, 1982-83. 80 game schedule.
122 —Wayne Gretzky, Los Angeles, 1990-91. 80 game schedule.
121 —Wayne Gretzky, Edmonton, 1986-87. 80 game schedule.
120 —Wayne Gretzky, Edmonton, 1981-82. 80 game schedule.
118 —Wayne Gretzky, Edmonton, 1983-84. 80 game schedule.
114 —Wayne Gretzky, Los Angeles, 1988-89. 80 game schedule.
   —Mario Lemieux, Pittsburgh, 1988-89. 80 game schedule.
109 —Wayne Gretzky, Edmonton, 1980-81. 80 game schedule.
   —Wayne Gretzky, Edmonton, 1987-88. 80 game schedule.
102 —Bobby Orr, Boston, 1970-71. 78 game schedule.
   —Wayne Gretzky, Los Angeles, 1989-90. 80 game schedule.

MOST ASSISTS, ONE SEASON, INCLUDING PLAYOFFS:
174 —Wayne Gretzky, Edmonton, 1985-86, 163A in 80 regular-season games and 11A in 10 playoff games.
165 —Wayne Gretzky, Edmonton, 1984-85, 135A in 80 regular-season games and 30A in 18 playoff games.
151 —Wayne Gretzky, Edmonton, 1982-83, 125A in 80 regular-season games and 26A in 16 playoff games.
150 —Wayne Gretzky, Edmonton, 1986-87, 121A in 79 regular-season games and 29A in 21 playoff games.
140 —Wayne Gretzky, Edmonton, 1983-84, 118A in 74 regular-season games and 22A in 19 playoff games.
—Wayne Gretzky, Edmonton, 1987-88, 109A in 64 regular-season games and 31A in 19 playoff games.
133 —Wayne Gretzky, Los Angeles, 1990-91, 122A in 78 regular-season games and 11A in 12 playoff games.
131 —Wayne Gretzky, Los Angeles, 1988-89, 114A in 78 regular-season games and 17A in 11 playoff games.
127 —Wayne Gretzky, Edmonton, 1981-82, 120A in 80 regular-season games and 7A in 5 playoff games.
123 —Wayne Gretzky, Edmonton, 1980-81, 109A in 80 regular-season games and 14A in 9 playoff games.
121 —Mario Lemieux, Pittsburgh, 1988-89, 114A in 76 regular-season games and 7A in 11 playoff games.

MOST ASSISTS, ONE GAME:
7 —Billy Taylor, Detroit, March 16, 1947, at Chicago. Detroit 10, Chicago 6.
—**Wayne Gretzky,** Edmonton, Feb. 15, 1980, at Edmonton. Edmonton 8, Washington 2.
—**Wayne Gretzky,** Edmonton, Dec. 11, 1985, at Chicago. Edmonton 12, Chicago 9.
—**Wayne Gretzky,** Edmonton, Feb. 14, 1986, at Edmonton. Edmonton 8, Quebec 2.
6 —Elmer Lach, Montreal, Feb. 6, 1943.
—Walter (Babe) Pratt, Toronto, Jan. 8, 1944.
—Don Grosso, Detroit, Feb. 3, 1944.
—Pat Stapleton, Chicago, March 30, 1969.
—Ken Hodge, Boston, Feb. 9, 1971.
—Bobby Orr, Boston, Jan. 1, 1973.
—Ron Stackhouse, Pittsburgh, March 8, 1975.
—Greg Malone, Pittsburgh, Nov. 28, 1979.
—Mike Bossy, NY Islanders, Jan. 6, 1981.
—Guy Chouinard, Calgary, Feb. 25, 1981.
—Mark Messier, Edmonton, Jan. 4, 1984.
—Patrik Sundstrom, Vancouver, Feb 29, 1984.
—Wayne Gretzky, Edmonton, Dec. 20, 1985.
—Paul Coffey, Edmonton, March 14, 1986.
—Gary Suter, Calgary, Apr. 4, 1986.
—Ron Francis, Hartford, March 5, 1987.
—Mario Lemieux, Pittsburgh, Oct. 15, 1988.
—Bernie Nicholls, Los Angeles, Dec. 1, 1988.
—Mario Lemieux, Pittsburgh, Dec. 31, 1988.
—Mario Lemieux, Pittsburgh, Dec. 5, 1992.
—Doug Gilmour, Toronto, Feb. 13, 1993.
—Tomas Sandstrom, Los Angeles, Oct. 9, 1993.

MOST ASSISTS, ONE ROAD GAME:
7 —Billy Taylor, Detroit, March 16, 1947, at Chicago. Detroit 10, Chicago 6.
—**Wayne Gretzky,** Edmonton, Dec. 11, 1985, at Chicago. Edmonton 12, Chicago 9.
6 —Bobby Orr, Boston, Jan. 1, 1973, at Vancouver. Boston 8, Vancouver 2.
—Patrik Sundstrom, Vancouver, Feb. 29, 1984, at Pittsburgh. Vancouver 9, Pittsburgh 5.
—Mario Lemieux, Pittsburgh, Dec. 5, 1992, at San Jose. Pittsburgh 9, San Jose 4.

MOST ASSISTS, ONE PERIOD:
5 —Dale Hawerchuk, Winnipeg, Mar. 6, 1984, at Los Angeles, second period. Winnipeg 7, Los Angeles 3.
4 —Four assists have been recorded in one period on 46 occasions since Buddy O'Connor of Montreal first accomplished the feat vs. NY Rangers on Nov. 8, 1942. Most recent player, Wendel Clark of NY Islanders (Mar. 3, 1996 vs Winnipeg).

POINTS

MOST POINTS:
2,608 —Wayne Gretzky, Edmonton, Los Angeles, St. Louis, in 17 seasons, 1,253GP (837G-1,771A).
1,850 —Gordie Howe, Detroit, Hartford, in 26 seasons, 1,767GP (801G-1,049A).
1,771 —Marcel Dionne, Detroit, Los Angeles, NY Rangers, in 18 seasons, 1,348GP (731G-1,040A).
1,590 —Phil Esposito, Chicago, Boston, NY Rangers in 18 seasons, 1,282GP (717G-873A).
1,468 —Mark Messier, Edmonton, NY Rangers in 17 seasons, 1,201GP (539G-929A).

MOST POINTS, INCLUDING PLAYOFFS:
2,970 —Wayne Gretzky, Edmonton, Los Angeles, St. Louis, 2,608 regular-season and 362 playoff points.
2,010 —Gordie Howe, Detroit, Hartford, 1,850 regular-season and 160 playoff assists.
1,816 —Marcel Dionne, Detroit, Los Angeles, NY Rangers, 1,771 regular-season and 45 playoff points.
1,751 —Mark Messier, Edmonton, NY Rangers, 1,468 regular-season and 283 playoff points.
1,727 —Phil Esposito, Chicago, Boston, NY Rangers, 1,590 regular-season and 137 playoff points.

MOST POINTS, ONE SEASON:
215 —Wayne Gretzky, Edmonton, 1985-86. 80 game schedule.
212 —Wayne Gretzky, Edmonton, 1981-82. 80 game schedule.
208 —Wayne Gretzky, Edmonton, 1984-85. 80 game schedule.
205 —Wayne Gretzky, Edmonton, 1983-84. 80 game schedule.
199 —Mario Lemieux, Pittsburgh, 1988-89. 80 game schedule.
196 —Wayne Gretzky, Edmonton, 1982-83. 80 game schedule.
183 —Wayne Gretzky, Edmonton, 1986-87. 80 game schedule.
168 —Mario Lemieux, Pittsburgh, 1987-88, 80 game schedule.
—Wayne Gretzky, Los Angeles, 1988-89. 80 game schedule.
164 —Wayne Gretzky, Edmonton, 1980-81. 80 game schedule.
163 —Wayne Gretzky, Los Angeles, 1990-91. 80 game schedule.
161 —Mario Lemieux, Pittsburgh, 1995-96. 82 game schedule.
160 —Mario Lemieux, Pittsburgh, 1992-93. 84 game schedule.

MOST POINTS, ONE SEASON, INCLUDING PLAYOFFS:
255 —Wayne Gretzky, Edmonton, 1984-85, 208PTS in 80 regular-season games and 47PTS in 18 playoff games.
240 —Wayne Gretzky, Edmonton, 1983-84, 205PTS in 74 regular-season games and 35PTS in 19 playoff games.
234 —Wayne Gretzky, Edmonton, 1982-83, 196PTS in 80 regular-season games and 38PTS in 16 playoff games.
—Wayne Gretzky, Edmonton, 1985-86, 215PTS in 80 regular-season games and 19PTS in 10 playoff games.
224 —Wayne Gretzky, Edmonton, 1981-82, 212PTS in 80 regular-season games and 12PTS in 5 playoff games.
218 —Mario Lemieux, Pittsburgh, 1988-89, 199PTS in 76 regular-season games and 19PTS in 11 playoff games.
217 —Wayne Gretzky, Edmonton, 1986-87, 183PTS in 79 regular-season games and 34PTS in 21 playoff games.
192 —Wayne Gretzky, Edmonton, 1987-88, 149PTS in 64 regular-season games and 43PTS in 19 playoff games.
190 —Wayne Gretzky, Los Angeles, 1988-89, 168PTS in 78 regular-season games and 22PTS in 11 playoff games.
188 —Mario Lemieux, Pittsburgh, 1995-96, 161PTS in 70 regular-season games and 27PTS in 18 playoff games.
185 —Wayne Gretzky, Edmonton, 1980-81, 164PTS in 80 regular-season games and 21PTS in 9 playoff games.

Mario Lemieux has recorded seven points in a road game twice in his career, once in a 7-4 win over Edmonton on January 21, 1989 and again in a 9-6 romp over the San Jose Sharks on December 5, 1992. In the San Jose game, Lemieux collected six assists, the second-highest total in history.

MOST POINTS, ONE GAME:

10 —**Darryl Sittler**, Toronto, Feb. 7, 1976, at Toronto, 6G-4A. Toronto 11, Boston 4.
8 —Maurice Richard, Montreal, Dec. 28, 1944, at Montreal, 5G-3A. Montreal 9, Detroit 1.
—Bert Olmstead, Montreal, Jan. 9, 1954, at Montreal, 4G-4A. Montreal 12, Chicago 1.
—Tom Bladon, Philadelphia, Dec. 11, 1977, at Philadelphia, 4G-4A. Philadelphia 11, Cleveland 1.
—Bryan Trottier, NY Islanders, Dec. 23, 1978, at New York, 5G-3A. NY Islanders 9, NY Rangers 4.
—Peter Stastny, Quebec, Feb. 22, 1981, at Washington, 4G-4A. Quebec 11, Washington 7.
—Anton Stastny, Quebec, Feb. 22, 1981, at Washington, 3G-5A. Quebec 11, Washington 7.
—Wayne Gretzky, Edmonton, Nov. 19, 1983, at Edmonton, 3G-5A. Edmonton 13, New Jersey 4.
—Wayne Gretzky, Edmonton, Jan. 4, 1984, at Edmonton, 4G-4A. Edmonton 12 Minnesota 8.
—Paul Coffey, Edmonton, March 14, 1986, at Edmonton, 2G-6A. Edmonton 12, Detroit 3.
—Mario Lemieux, Pittsburgh, Oct. 15, 1988, at Pittsburgh, 2G-6A. Pittsburgh 9, St. Louis 2.
—Mario Lemieux, Pittsburgh, Dec. 31, 1988, at Pittsburgh, 5G-3A. Pittsburgh 8, New Jersey 6.
—Bernie Nicholls, Los Angeles, Dec. 1, 1988, at Los Angeles, 2G-6A. Los Angeles 9, Toronto 3.

MOST POINTS, ONE ROAD GAME:

8 —**Peter Stastny**, Quebec, Feb. 22, 1981, at Washington, 4G-4A. Quebec 11, Washington 7.
—**Anton Stastny**, Quebec, Feb. 22, 1981, at Washington, 3G-5A. Quebec 11, Washington 7.
7 —Billy Taylor, Detroit, March 16, 1947, at Chicago, 7A. Detroit 10, Chicago 6.
—Red Berenson, St. Louis, Nov. 7, 1968, at Philadelphia, 6G-1A. St. Louis 8, Philadelphia 0.
—Gilbert Perreault, Buffalo, Feb. 1, 1976, at California, 2G-5A. Buffalo 9, California 5.
—Peter Stastny, Quebec, April 1, 1982, at Boston, 3G-4A. Quebec 8, Boston 5.
—Wayne Gretzky, Edmonton, Nov. 6, 1983, at Winnipeg, 4G-3A. Edmonton 8, Winnipeg 5.
—Patrik Sundstrom, Vancouver, Feb. 29, 1984, at Pittsburgh, 1G-6A. Vancouver 9, Pittsburgh 5.
—Wayne Gretzky, Edmonton, Dec. 11, 1985, at Chicago. 7A, Edmonton 12, Chicago 9.
—Mario Lemieux, Pittsburgh, Jan. 21, 1989, at Edmonton, 2G, 5A. Pittsburgh 7, Edmonton 4.
—Cam Neely, Boston, Oct. 16, 1988, at Chicago, 3G, 4A. Boston 10, Chicago 3.
—Dino Ciccarelli, Washington, March 18, 1989, at Hartford, 4G, 3A. Washington 8, Hartford 2.
—Mats Sundin, Quebec, Mar. 5, 1992, at Hartford, 5G, 2A. Quebec 10, Hartford 4.
—Mario Lemieux, Pittsburgh, Dec. 5, 1992, at San Jose, 1G, 6A. Pittsburgh 9, San Jose 4.

MOST POINTS, ONE PERIOD:

6 —**Bryan Trottier,** NY Islanders, Dec. 23, 1978, at NY Islanders, second period. 3G, 3A. NY Islanders 9, NY Rangers 4.
5 —Les Cunningham, Chicago, Jan. 28, 1940, at Chicago, third period. 2G, 3A. Chicago 8, Montreal 1.
—Max Bentley, Chicago, Jan. 28, 1943, at Chicago, third period. 4G, 1A, Chicago 10, NY Rangers 1.
—Leo Labine, Boston, Nov. 28, 1954, at Boston, second period, 3G, 2A. Boston 6, Detroit 2.
—Darryl Sittler, Toronto, Feb. 7, 1976, at Toronto, second period. 3G, 2A. Toronto 11, Boston 4.
—Dale Hawerchuk, Winnipeg, Mar. 6, 1984, at Los Angeles, second period. 5A. Winnipeg 7, Los Angeles 3.
—Jari Kurri, Edmonton, October 26, 1984 at Edmonton, second period. 2G, 3A. Edmonton 8, Los Angeles 2.
—Pat Elynuik, Winnipeg, Jan. 20, 1989, at Winnipeg, second period. 2G, 3A. Winnipeg 7, Pittsburgh 3.
—Ray Ferraro, Hartford, Dec. 9, 1989, at Hartford, first period. 3G, 2A. Hartford 7, New Jersey 3.
—Stephane Richer, Montreal, Feb. 14, 1990, at Montreal, first period. 2G, 3A. Montreal 10, Vancouver 1.
—Cliff Ronning, Vancouver, Apr. 15, 1993, at Los Angeles, third period. 3G, 2A. Vancouver 8, Los Angeles 6.

POWER-PLAY and SHORTHAND GOALS

MOST POWER-PLAY GOALS, ONE SEASON:

34 —**Tim Kerr,** Philadelphia, 1985-86. 80 game schedule.
32 —Dave Andreychuk; Buffalo, Toronto, 1992-93. 84 game schedule.
31 —Joe Nieuwendyk, Calgary, 1987-88. 80 game schedule.
—Mario Lemieux, Pittsburgh, 1988-89. 80 game schedule.
—Mario Lemieux, Pittsburgh, 1995-96. 82 game schedule.
29 —Michel Goulet, Quebec, 1987-88. 80 game schedule.
—Brett Hull, St. Louis, 1990-91. 80 game schedule.
—Brett Hull, St. Louis, 1992-93. 84 game schedule.

MOST SHORTHAND GOALS, ONE SEASON:

13 —**Mario Lemieux,** Pittsburgh, 1988-89. 80 game schedule.
12 —Wayne Gretzky, Edmonton, 1983-84. 80 game schedule.
11 —Wayne Gretzky, Edmonton, 1984-85. 80 game schedule.
10 —Marcel Dionne, Detroit, 1974-75. 80 game schedule.
—Mario Lemieux, Pittsburgh, 1987-88. 80 game schedule.
—Dirk Graham, Chicago, 1988-89. 80 game schedule.

Doug Gilmour, seen here scoring the winning goal in Toronto's 2-1 victory over St. Louis in game one of the 1993 Norris Division finals, has assisted on eleven regular-season overtime goals in his 13-season career, the second-highest total in league history.

OVERTIME SCORING

MOST OVERTIME GOALS, CAREER:

9 —**Mario Lemieux,** Pittsburgh.
8 —Bob Sweeney, Boston, Buffalo, Calgary.
—Steve Thomas, Toronto, Chicago, NY Islanders, New Jersey.
7 —Jari Kurri, Edmonton, Los Angeles, NY Rangers.
—Tomas Sandstrom, NY Rangers, Los Angeles, Pittsburgh.
—Murray Craven, Philadelphia, Hartford, Vancouver, Chicago.
—Stephane Richer, Montreal, New Jersey.

MOST OVERTIME ASSISTS, CAREER:

12 —**Wayne Gretzky,** Edmonton, Los Angeles, St. Louis.
11 —Mark Messier, Edmonton, NY Rangers.
—Doug Gilmour, St. Louis, Calgary, Toronto.
10 —Mario Lemieux, Pittsburgh.
—Paul Coffey, Edmonton, Pittsburgh, Los Angeles, Detroit.
—Adam Oates, Detroit, St. Louis, Boston.

MOST OVERTIME POINTS, CAREER:

19 —**Mario Lemieux,** Pittsburgh, 9G-10A
17 —Mark Messier, Edmonton, NY Rangers. 6G-11A
14 —Wayne Gretzky, Edmonton, Los Angeles, St. Louis. 2G-12A
13 —Jari Kurri, Edmonton, Los Angeles, NY Rangers. 7G-6A
—Paul MacLean, Winnipeg, Detroit, St. Louis. 6G-7A
—Dale Hawerchuk, Winnipeg, Buffalo, St. Louis, Philadelphia. 4G-9A
—Steve Thomas, Toronto, Chicago, NY Islanders, New Jersey. 8G-5A

SCORING BY A CENTER

MOST GOALS BY A CENTER, CAREER

837 —**Wayne Gretzky,** Edmonton, Los Angeles, St. Louis, in 17 seasons.
731 —Marcel Dionne, Detroit, Los Angeles, NY Rangers, in 18 seasons
717 —Phil Esposito, Chicago, Boston, NY Rangers, in 18 seasons.
563 —Mario Lemieux, Pittsburgh, in 11 seasons.
541 —Stan Mikita, Chicago, in 22 seasons.

MOST GOALS BY A CENTER, ONE SEASON:

92 —**Wayne Gretzky,** Edmonton, 1981-82. 80 game schedule.
87 —Wayne Gretzky, Edmonton, 1983-84. 80 game schedule.
85 —Wayne Gretzky, Edmonton, 1988-89. 80 game schedule.
76 —Phil Esposito, Boston, 1970-71. 78 game schedule.
73 —Wayne Gretzky, Edmonton, 1984-85. 80 game schedule.
71 —Wayne Gretzky, Edmonton, 1982-83. 80 game schedule.
70 —Mario Lemieux, Pittsburgh, 1987-88. 80 game schedule.
—Bernie Nicholls, Los Angeles, 1988-89. 80 game schedule.

MOST ASSISTS BY A CENTER, CAREER:
1,771 — Wayne Gretzky, Edmonton, Los Angeles, St. Louis, in 17 seasons.
1,040 — Marcel Dionne, Detroit, Los Angeles, NY Rangers, in 18 seasons.
  929 — Mark Messier, Edmonton, NY Rangers, in 17 seasons.
  926 — Stan Mikita, Chicago, in 22 seasons.
  901 — Bryan Trottier, NY Islanders, Pittsburgh, in 18 seasons.

MOST ASSISTS BY A CENTER, ONE SEASON:
163 — Wayne Gretzky, Edmonton, 1985-86. 80 game schedule.
135 — Wayne Gretzky, Edmonton, 1984-85. 80 game schedule.
125 — Wayne Gretzky, Edmonton, 1982-83. 80 game schedule.
122 — Wayne Gretzky, Los Angeles, 1990-91. 80 game schedule.
121 — Wayne Gretzky, Edmonton, 1986-87. 80 game schedule.

MOST POINTS BY A CENTER, CAREER:
2,608 — Wayne Gretzky, Edmonton, Los Angeles, St. Louis, in 17 seasons.
1,771 — Marcel Dionne, Detroit, Los Angeles, NY Rangers, in 18 seasons.
1,590 — Phil Esposito, Chicago, Boston, NY Rangers, in 18 seasons.
1,468 — Mark Messier, Edmonton, NY Rangers, in 17 seasons.
1,467 — Stan Mikita, Chicago, in 22 seasons

MOST POINTS BY A CENTER, ONE SEASON:
215 — Wayne Gretzky, Edmonton, 1985-86. 80 game schedule.
212 — Wayne Gretzky, Edmonton, 1981-82. 80 game schedule.
208 — Wayne Gretzky, Edmonton, 1984-85. 80 game schedule.
205 — Wayne Gretzky, Edmonton, 1983-84. 80 game schedule.
199 — Mario Lemieux, Pittsburgh, 1988-89. 80 game schedule.

SCORING BY A LEFT WING

MOST GOALS BY A LEFT WING, CAREER:
610 — Bobby Hull, Chicago, Winnipeg, Hartford, in 16 seasons.
556 — John Bucyk, Detroit, Boston, in 23 seasons.
548 — Michel Goulet, Quebec, Chicago, in 15 seasons.
533 — Frank Mahovlich, Toronto, Detroit, Montreal, in 18 seasons.
476 — Dave Andreychuk, Buffalo, Toronto, New Jersey, in 14 seasons.

MOST GOALS BY A LEFT WING, ONE SEASON:
63 — Luc Robitaille, Los Angeles, 1992-93. 84 game schedule.
60 — Steve Shutt, Montreal, 1976-77. 80 game schedule.
58 — Bobby Hull, Chicago, 1968-69. 76 game schedule.
57 — Michel Goulet, Quebec, 1982-83. 80 game schedule.
56 — Charlie Simmer, Los Angeles, 1979-80. 80 game schedule.
   — Charlie Simmer, Los Angeles, 1980-81. 80 game schedule.
   — Michel Goulet, Quebec, 1983-84. 80 game schedule.

*Known affectionately as the "Big M" during
his Hall-of-Fame career, Frank Mahovlich
still ranks among the top five left wingers
in career goals, assists and points.*

MOST ASSISTS BY A LEFT WING, CAREER:
813 — John Bucyk, Detroit, Boston, in 23 seasons.
604 — Michel Goulet, Quebec, Chicago, in 15 seasons.
579 — Brian Propp, Philadelphia, Boston, Minnesota, Hartford, in 15 seasons.
570 — Frank Mahovlich, Toronto, Detroit, Montreal, in 18 seasons.
560 — Bobby Hull, Chicago, Winnipeg, Hartford, in 16 seasons.

MOST ASSISTS BY A LEFT WING, ONE SEASON:
70 — Joe Juneau, Boston, 1992-93. 84 game schedule.
69 — Kevin Stevens, Pittsburgh, 1991-92. 80 game schedule.
67 — Mats Naslund, Montreal, 1985-86. 80 game schedule.
65 — John Bucyk, Boston, 1970-71. 78 game schedule.
   — Michel Goulet, Quebec, 1983-84. 80 game schedule.
64 — Mark Messier, Edmonton, 1983-84. 80 game schedule.

MOST POINTS BY A LEFT WING, CAREER:
1,369 — John Bucyk, Detroit, Boston, in 23 seasons.
1,170 — Bobby Hull, Chicago, Winnipeg, Hartford, in 16 seasons.
1,152 — Michel Goulet, Quebec, Chicago, in 15 seasons.
1,103 — Frank Mahovlich, Toronto, Detroit, Montreal, in 18 seasons.
1,004 — Brian Propp, Philadelphia, Boston, Minnesota, Hartford, in 15 seasons.

MOST POINTS BY A LEFT WING, ONE SEASON:
125 — Luc Robitaille, Los Angeles, 1992-93. 84 game schedule.
123 — Kevin Stevens, Pittsburgh, 1991-92. 80 game schedule.
121 — Michel Goulet, Quebec, 1983-84. 80 game schedule.
116 — John Bucyk, Boston, 1970-71. 78 game schedule.
112 — Bill Barber, Philadelphia, 1975-76. 80 game schedule.

SCORING BY A RIGHT WING

MOST GOALS BY A RIGHT WING, CAREER:
801 — Gordie Howe, Detroit, Hartford, in 26 seasons.
664 — Mike Gartner, Washington, Minnesota, NY Rangers, Toronto, in 17 seasons.
583 — Jari Kurri, Edmonton, Los Angeles, NY Rangers, in 15 seasons.
573 — Mike Bossy, NY Islanders, in 10 seasons.
560 — Guy Lafleur, Montreal, NY Rangers, Quebec, in 17 seasons.

MOST GOALS BY A RIGHT WING, ONE SEASON:
86 — Brett Hull, St. Louis, 1990-91. 80 game schedule.
76 — Alexander Mogilny, Buffalo, 1992-93. 84 game schedule.
   — Teemu Selanne, Winnipeg, 1992-93. 84 game schedule.
72 — Brett Hull, St. Louis, 1989-90. 80 game schedule.
71 — Jari Kurri, Edmonton, 1984-85. 80 game schedule.
70 — Brett Hull, St. Louis, 1991-92. 80 game schedule.

MOST ASSISTS BY A RIGHT WING, CAREER:
1,049 — Gordie Howe, Detroit, Hartford, in 26 seasons.
793 — Guy Lafleur, Montreal, NY Rangers, Quebec, in 17 seasons.
758 — Jari Kurri, Edmonton, Los Angeles, NY Rangers, in 15 seasons.
638 — Dave Taylor, Los Angeles, in 17 seasons.
624 — Andy Bathgate, NY Rangers, Toronto, Detroit, Pittsburgh in 17 seasons.

MOST ASSISTS BY A RIGHT WING, ONE SEASON:
87 — Jaromir Jagr, Pittsburgh, 1995-96. 82 game schedule.
83 — Mike Bossy, NY Islanders, 1981-82. 80 game schedule.
80 — Guy Lafleur, Montreal, 1976-77. 80 game schedule.
77 — Guy Lafleur, Montreal, 1978-79. 80 game schedule.

MOST POINTS BY A RIGHT WING, CAREER:
1,850 —**Gordie Howe,** Detroit, Hartford, in 26 seasons.
1,353 —Guy Lafleur, Montreal, NY Rangers, Quebec, in 17 seasons.
1,341 —Jari Kurri, Edmonton, Los Angeles, NY Rangers, in 15 seasons.
1,245 —Mike Gartner, Washington, Minnesota, NY Rangers, Toronto, in 17 seasons.

MOST POINTS BY A RIGHT WING, ONE SEASON:
149 —**Jaromir Jagr,** Pittsburgh, 1995-96. 82 game schedule.
147 —Mike Bossy, NY Islanders, 1981-82. 80 game schedule.
136 —Guy Lafleur, Montreal, 1976-77. 80 game schedule.
135 —Jari Kurri, Edmonton, 1984-85. 80 game schedule.
132 —Guy Lafleur, Montreal, 1977-78. 80 game schedule.
— Teemu Selanne, Winnipeg, 1992-93. 84 game schedule.

SCORING BY A DEFENSEMAN

MOST GOALS BY A DEFENSEMAN, CAREER:
372 —**Paul Coffey,** Edmonton, Pittsburgh, Los Angeles, Detroit, in 16 seasons.
343 —Ray Bourque, Boston, in 17 seasons.
310 —Denis Potvin, NY Islanders, in 15 seasons.
274 —Phil Housley, Buffalo, Winnipeg, St. Louis, Calgary, New Jersey, in 14 seasons.
270 —Bobby Orr, Boston, Chicago, in 12 seasons.

MOST GOALS BY A DEFENSEMAN, ONE SEASON:
48 —**Paul Coffey,** Edmonton, 1985-86. 80 game schedule.
46 —Bobby Orr, Boston, 1974-75. 80 game schedule.
40 —Paul Coffey, Edmonton, 1983-84. 80 game schedule.
39 —Doug Wilson, Chicago, 1981-82. 80 game schedule.
37 —Bobby Orr, Boston, 1970-71. 78 game schedule.
— Bobby Orr, Boston, 1971-72. 78 game schedule.
— Paul Coffey, Edmonton, 1984-85 80 game schedule..

In the 1982-83 season, the Flames' third campaign in Calgary, Lanny McDonald enthralled the fans by scoring a team record 66 goals, which still stands as the eighth highest total by a right winger in league history .

MOST GOALS BY A DEFENSEMAN, ONE GAME:
5 —**Ian Turnbull,** Toronto, Feb. 2, 1977, at Toronto. Toronto 9, Detroit 1.
4 —Harry Cameron, Toronto, Dec. 26, 1917, at Toronto. Toronto 7, Montreal 5.
— Harry Cameron, Montreal, March 3, 1920, at Quebec City. Montreal 16, Que. Bulldogs 3.
— Sprague Cleghorn, Montreal, Jan. 14, 1922, at Montreal. Montreal 10, Hamilton 6.
— Johnny McKinnon, Pit. Pirates, Nov. 19, 1929, at Pittsburgh. Pit. Pirates 10, Toronto 5.
— Hap Day, Toronto, Nov. 19, 1929, at Pittsburgh. Pit. Pirates 10, Toronto 5.
— Tom Bladon, Philadelphia, Dec. 11, 1977, at Philadelphia. Philadelphia 11, Cleveland 1.
— Ian Turnbull, Los Angeles, Dec. 12, 1981, at Los Angeles. Los Angeles 7, Vancouver 5.
— Paul Coffey, Edmonton, Oct. 26, 1984, at Calgary. Edmonton 6, Calgary 5.

MOST ASSISTS BY A DEFENSEMAN, CAREER:
1,038 —**Paul Coffey,** Edmonton, Pittsburgh, Los Angeles, Detroit, in 16 seasons.
970 —Ray Bourque, Boston, in 17 seasons.
761 —Larry Murphy, Los Angeles, Washington, Minnesota, Pittsburgh, Toronto, in 16 seasons.
750 —Larry Robinson, Montreal, Los Angeles, in 20 seasons.
742 —Denis Potvin, NY Islanders, in 15 seasons.

MOST ASSISTS BY A DEFENSEMAN, ONE SEASON:
102 —**Bobby Orr,** Boston, 1970-71. 78 game schedule.
90 —Paul Coffey, Edmonton, 1985-86. 80 game schedule.
90 —Bobby Orr, Boston, 1973-74. 78 game schedule.
89 —Bobby Orr, Boston, 1974-75. 80 game schedule.

MOST ASSISTS BY A DEFENSEMAN, ONE GAME:
6 —**Babe Pratt,** Toronto, Jan. 8, 1944, at Toronto. Toronto 12, Boston 3.
— **Pat Stapleton,** Chicago, March 30, 1969, at Chicago. Chicago 9, Detroit 5.
— **Bobby Orr,** Boston, Jan. 1, 1973, at Vancouver, Boston 8, Vancouver 2.
— **Ron Stackhouse,** Pittsburgh, March 8, 1975, at Pittsburgh. Pittsburgh 8, Philadelphia 2.
— **Paul Coffey,** Edmonton, Mar. 14, 1986, at Edmonton. Edmonton 12, Detroit 3.
— **Gary Suter,** Calgary, Apr. 4, 1986, at Calgary. Calgary 9, Edmonton 3.

MOST POINTS BY A DEFENSEMAN, CAREER:
1,410 —**Paul Coffey,** Edmonton, Pittsburgh, Los Angeles, Detroit, in 16 seasons.
1,313 —Ray Bourque, Boston, in 17 seasons.
1,052 —Denis Potvin, NY Islanders, in 15 seasons.
1,006 —Larry Murphy, Los Angeles, Washington, Minnesota, Pittsburgh, Toronto, in 16 seasons.
958 —Larry Robinson, Montreal, Los Angeles, in 20 seasons.

MOST POINTS BY A DEFENSEMAN, ONE SEASON:
139 —**Bobby Orr,** Boston, 1970-71. 78 game schedule.
138 —Paul Coffey, Edmonton,1985-86. 80 game schedule.
135 —Bobby Orr, Boston, 1974-75. 80 game schedule.
126 —Paul Coffey, Edmonton, 1983-84. 80 game schedule.
122 —Bobby Orr, Boston, 1973-74. 78 game schedule.

MOST POINTS BY A DEFENSEMAN, ONE GAME:
8 —**Tom Bladon,** Philadelphia, Dec. 11, 1977, at Philadelphia. 4G-4A. Philadelphia 11, Cleveland 1.
— **Paul Coffey,** Edmonton, Mar. 14, 1986, at Edmonton. 2G-6A. Edmonton 12, Detroit 3.
7 —Bobby Orr, Boston, Nov. 15, 1973, at Boston, 3G-4A. Boston 10, NY Rangers 2.

SCORING BY A GOALTENDER

MOST POINTS BY A GOALTENDER, ONE SEASON:
14 —**Grant Fuhr,** Edmonton, 1983-84. (14A)
9 —Curtis Joseph, St. Louis, 1991-92. (9A)
8 —Mike Palmateer, Washington, 1980-81. (8A)
— Grant Fuhr, Edmonton, 1987-88. (8A)
— Ron Hextall, Philadelphia, 1988-89. (8A)
— Tom Barrasso, Pittsburgh, 1992-93. (8A)
7 —Ron Hextall, Philadelphia, 1987-88. (1G-6A)
— Mike Vernon, Calgary, 1987-88. (7A)

MOST POINTS, ONE GAME, BY A GOALTENDER:
3 —**Jeff Reese,** Calgary, Feb. 10, 1993, at Calgary. Calgary 13, San Jose 1. (3A)

SCORING BY A ROOKIE

MOST GOALS BY A ROOKIE, ONE SEASON:
76 —Teemu Selanne, Winnipeg, 1992-93. 84 game schedule.
53 —Mike Bossy, NY Islanders, 1977-78. 80 game schedule.
51 —Joe Nieuwendyk, Calgary, 1987-88. 80 game schedule.
45 —Dale Hawerchuk, Winnipeg, 1981-82. 80 game schedule.
— Luc Robitaille, Los Angeles, 1986-87. 80 game schedule.
44 —Richard Martin, Buffalo, 1971-72. 78 game schedule.
— Barry Pederson, Boston, 1981-82. 80 game schedule.
43 —Steve Larmer, Chicago, 1982-83. 80 game schedule.
— Mario Lemieux, Pittsburgh, 1984-85. 80 game schedule.

MOST GOALS BY A PLAYER IN HIS FIRST NHL SEASON, ONE GAME:
5 —Howie Meeker, Toronto, Jan. 8, 1947, at Toronto. Toronto 10, Chicago 4.
— Don Murdoch, NY Rangers, Oct. 12, 1976, at Minnesota. NY Rangers 10, Minnesota 4.

MOST GOALS BY A PLAYER IN HIS FIRST NHL GAME:
3 —Alex Smart, Montreal, Jan. 14, 1943, at Montreal. Montreal 5, Chicago 1.
— Real Cloutier, Quebec, Oct. 10, 1979, at Quebec. Atlanta 5, Quebec 3.

MOST ASSISTS BY A ROOKIE, ONE SEASON:
70 —Peter Stastny, Quebec, 1980-81. 80 game schedule.
— Joe Juneau, Boston, 1992-93. 84 game schedule.
63 —Bryan Trottier, NY Islanders, 1975-76. 80 game schedule.
62 —Sergei Makarov, Calgary, 1989-90. 80 game schedule.
60 —Larry Murphy, Los Angeles, 1980-81. 80 game schedule.

MOST ASSISTS BY A PLAYER IN HIS FIRST NHL SEASON, ONE GAME:
7 —Wayne Gretzky, Edmonton, Feb. 15, 1980, at Edmonton. Edmonton 8, Washington 2.
6 —Gary Suter, Calgary, Apr. 4, 1986, at Calgary. Calgary 9, Edmonton 3.

MOST ASSISTS BY A PLAYER IN HIS FIRST NHL GAME:
4 —Earl (Dutch) Reibel, Detroit, Oct. 8, 1953, at Detroit. Detroit 4, NY Rangers 1.
— Roland Eriksson, Minnesota, Oct. 6, 1976, at New York. NY Rangers 6, Minnesota 5.
3 —Al Hill, Philadelphia, Feb. 14, 1977, at Philadelphia. Philadelphia 6, St. Louis 4.

MOST POINTS BY A ROOKIE, ONE SEASON:
132 —Teemu Selanne, Winnipeg, 1992-93, 84 game schedule.
109 —Peter Stastny, Quebec, 1980-81. 80 game schedule.
103 —Dale Hawerchuk, Winnipeg, 1981-82. 80 game schedule.
102 —Joe Juneau, Boston, 1992-93. 84 game schedule.
100 —Mario Lemieux, Pittsburgh, 1984-85. 80 game schedule.

MOST POINTS BY A PLAYER IN HIS FIRST NHL SEASON, ONE GAME:
8 —Peter Stastny, Quebec, Feb. 22, 1981, at Washington. 4G-4A. Quebec 11, Washington 7.
— Anton Stastny, Quebec, Feb. 22, 1981, at Washington. 3G-5A. Quebec 11, Washington 7.
7 —Wayne Gretzky, Edmonton, Feb. 15, 1980, at Edmonton. 7A. Edmonton 8, Washington 2.
— Sergei Makarov, Calgary, Feb. 25, 1990, at Calgary, 2G-5A. Calgary 10, Edmonton 3.
6 —Wayne Gretzky, Edmonton, March 29, 1980, at Toronto. 2G-4A. Edmonton 8, Toronto 5.
— Gary Suter, Calgary, Apr. 4, 1986, at Calgary. 6A. Calgary 9, Edmonton 3.

MOST POINTS BY A PLAYER IN HIS FIRST NHL GAME:
5 —Al Hill, Philadelphia, Feb. 14, 1977, at Philadelphia. 2G-3A. Philadelphia 6, St. Louis 4.
4 —Alex Smart, Montreal, Jan. 14, 1943, at Montreal, 3G-1A. Montreal 5, Chicago 1.
— Earl (Dutch) Reibel, Detroit, Oct. 8, 1953, at Detroit. 4A. Detroit 4, NY Rangers 1.
— Roland Eriksson, Minnesota, Oct. 6, 1976 at New York. 4A. NY Rangers 6, Minnesota 5.

SCORING BY A ROOKIE DEFENSEMAN

MOST GOALS BY A ROOKIE DEFENSEMAN, ONE SEASON:
23 —Brian Leetch, NY Rangers, 1988-89. 80 game schedule.
22 —Barry Beck, Colorado, 1977-78. 80 game schedule.
19 —Reed Larson, Detroit, 1977-78. 80 game schedule.
— Phil Housley, Buffalo, 1982-83. 80 game schedule.

MOST ASSISTS BY A ROOKIE DEFENSEMAN, ONE SEASON:
60 —Larry Murphy, Los Angeles, 1980-81. 80 game schedule.
55 —Chris Chelios, Montreal, 1984-85. 80 game schedule.
50 —Stefan Persson, NY Islanders, 1977-78. 80 game schedule.
— Gary Suter, Calgary, 1985-86, 80 game schedule.
49 —Nicklas Lidstrom, Detroit, 1991-92. 80 game schedule.
48 —Raymond Bourque, Boston, 1979-80. 80 game schedule.
— Brian Leetch, NY Rangers, 1988-89. 80 game schedule.

MOST POINTS BY A ROOKIE DEFENSEMAN, ONE SEASON:
76 —Larry Murphy, Los Angeles, 1980-81. 80 game schedule.
71 —Brian Leetch, NY Rangers, 1988-89. 80 game schedule.
68 —Gary Suter, Calgary, 1985-86. 80 game schedule.
66 —Phil Housley, Buffalo, 1982-83. 80 game schedule.
65 —Raymond Bourque, Boston, 1979-80. 80 game schedule.
64 —Chris Chelios, Montreal, 1984-85. 80 game schedule.

Dale Hawerchuk almost single-handedly revived the fortunes of the Winnipeg Jets in his rookie season by collecting 103 points to help lift the club out of the NHL cellar and into the playoffs.

PER-GAME SCORING AVERAGES

HIGHEST GOALS-PER-GAME AVERAGE, CAREER
(AMONG PLAYERS WITH 200 OR MORE GOALS):
.842 —**Mario Lemieux,** Pittsburgh, 563G, 669GP, from 1984-85 – 1995-96.
.767 —Cy Denneny, Ottawa, Boston, 250G, 326GP, from 1917-18 – 1928-29.
.762 —Mike Bossy, NY Islanders, 573G, 752GP, from 1977-78 – 1986-87.
.737 —Brett Hull, Calgary, St. Louis, 485G, 658GP, from 1986-87 – 1995-96.
.668 —Wayne Gretzky, Edmonton, Los Angeles, St. Louis, 837G, 1,253GP, from 1979-80 – 1995-96.

HIGHEST GOALS-PER-GAME AVERAGE, ONE SEASON
(AMONG PLAYERS WITH 20-OR-MORE GOALS):
2.20 —**Joe Malone,** Montreal, 1917-18, with 44G in 20GP.
1.64 —Cy Denneny, Ottawa, 1917-18, with 36G in 22GP.
— Newsy Lalonde, Montreal, 1917-18, with 23G in 14GP.
1.63 —Joe Malone, Quebec, 1919-20, with 39G in 24GP.
1.57 —Newsy Lalonde, Montreal, 1919-20, with 36G in 23GP.
1.50 —Joe Malone, Hamilton, 1920-21, with 30G in 20GP.

HIGHEST GOALS-PER-GAME AVERAGE, ONE SEASON
(AMONG PLAYERS WITH 50-OR-MORE GOALS):
1.18 —**Wayne Gretzky,** Edmonton, 1983-84, with 87G in 74GP.
1.15 —Wayne Gretzky, Edmonton, 1981-82, with 92G in 80GP.
— Mario Lemieux, Pittsburgh, 1992-93, with 69G in 60GP.
1.12 —Mario Lemieux, Pittsburgh, 1988-89, with 85G in 76GP.
1.10 —Brett Hull, St. Louis, 1990-91, with 86G in 78GP.
1.02 —Cam Neely, Boston, 1993-94, with 50G in 49GP.
1.00 —Maurice Richard, Montreal, 1944-45, with 50G in 50GP.
.99 —Alexander Mogilny, Buffalo, 1992-93, with 76G in 77GP.
— Mario Lemieux, Pittsburgh, 1995-96, with 69G in 70GP.

HIGHEST ASSIST-PER-GAME AVERAGE, CAREER
(AMONG PLAYERS WITH 300 OR MORE ASSISTS):
1.413 —**Wayne Gretzky,** Edmonton, Los Angeles, St. Louis, 1,771A, 1,253GP from 1979-80 – 1995-96.
1.209 —Mario Lemieux, Pittsburgh, 809A, 669GP from 1984-85 – 1995-96.
.982 —Bobby Orr, Boston, Chicago, 645A, 657GP from 1966-67 – 1978-79.
.909 —Adam Oates, Detroit, St. Louis, Boston, 678A, 746GP from 1984-85 – 1995-96.
.899 —Paul Coffey, Edmonton, Pittsburgh, Los Angeles, Detroit, 1,038A, 1,154GP from 1980-81 – 1995-96.

HIGHEST ASSISTS-PER-GAME AVERAGE, ONE SEASON
(AMONG PLAYERS WITH 35-OR-MORE ASSISTS):
2.04 —**Wayne Gretzky,** Edmonton, 1985-86, with 163A in 80GP.
1.70 —Wayne Gretzky, Edmonton, 1987-88, with 109A in 64GP.
1.69 —Wayne Gretzky, Edmonton, 1984-85, with 135A in 80GP.
1.59 —Wayne Gretzky, Edmonton, 1983-84, with 118A in 74GP.
1.56 —Wayne Gretzky, Edmonton, 1982-83, with 125A in 80GP.
1.56 —Wayne Gretzky, Los Angeles, 1990-91, with 122A in 78GP.
1.53 —Wayne Gretzky, Edmonton, 1986-87, with 121A in 79GP.
1.52 —Mario Lemieux, Pittsburgh, 1992-93, with 91A in 60GP.
1.50 —Wayne Gretzky, Edmonton, 1981-82, with 120A in 80GP.
1.50 —Mario Lemieux, Pittsburgh, 1988-89, with 114A in 76GP.

HIGHEST POINTS-PER-GAME AVERAGE, CAREER:
(AMONG PLAYERS WITH 500 OR MORE POINTS):
2.081 —**Wayne Gretzky,** Edmonton, Los Angeles, St. Louis, 2,608PTS (837G-1,771A), 1,253GP from 1979-80 – 1995-96.
2.051 —Mario Lemieux, Pittsburgh, 1,372PTS (563G-809A), 669GP from 1984-85 – 1995-96.
1.497 —Mike Bossy, NY Islanders, 1,126PTS (573G-553A), 752GP from 1978-79 – 1986-87.
1.393 —Bobby Orr, Boston, Chicago, 915PTS (270G-645A), 657GP from 1966-67 – 1978-79.
1.332 —Steve Yzerman, Detroit, 1,255PTS (517G-738A), 942GP from 1983-84 – 1995-96.

HIGHEST POINTS-PER-GAME AVERAGE, ONE SEASON
(AMONG PLAYERS WITH 50-OR-MORE POINTS):
2.77 —**Wayne Gretzky,** Edmonton, 1983-84, with 205PTS in 74GP.
2.69 —Wayne Gretzky, Edmonton, 1985-86, with 215PTS in 80GP.
2.67 —Mario Lemieux, Pittsburgh, 1992-93, with 160PTS in 60GP.
2.65 —Wayne Gretzky, Edmonton, 1981-82, with 212PTS in 80GP.
2.62 —Mario Lemieux, Pittsburgh, 1988-89, with 199PTS in 78GP.
2.60 —Wayne Gretzky, Edmonton, 1984-85, with 208PTS in 80GP.
2.45 —Wayne Gretzky, Edmonton, 1982-83, with 196PTS in 80GP.
2.33 —Wayne Gretzky, Edmonton, 1987-88, with 149PTS in 64GP.
2.32 —Wayne Gretzky, Edmonton, 1986-87, with 183PTS in 79GP.
2.30 —Mario Lemieux, Pittsburgh, 1995-96 with 161PTS in 70GP.
2.18 —Mario Lemieux, Pittsburgh, 1987-88 with 168PTS in 77GP.
2.15 —Wayne Gretzky, Edmonton, 1988-89, with 168PTS in 78GP.
2.09 —Wayne Gretzky, Los Angeles, 1990-91, with 163 PTS in 78GP.
2.08 —Mario Lemieux, Pittsburgh, 1989-90, with 123 PTS in 59GP.
2.05 —Wayne Gretzky, Edmonton, 1980-81, with 164PTS in 80GP.

SCORING PLATEAUS

MOST 20-OR-MORE GOAL SEASONS:
22 —**Gordie Howe,** Detroit, Hartford in 26 seasons.
17 —Marcel Dionne, Detroit, Los Angeles, NY Rangers, in 18 seasons.
16 —Norm Ullman, Detroit, Toronto, in 19 seasons.
— John Bucyk, Detroit, Boston, in 22 seasons.
— Mike Gartner, Washington, NY Rangers, Toronto, in 17 seasons.
15 —Frank Mahovlich, Toronto, Detroit, Montreal in 17 seasons.
— Gilbert Perreault, Buffalo, in 17 seasons.
— Wayne Gretzky, Edmonton, Los Angeles, St. Louis, in 17 seasons.

MOST CONSECUTIVE 20-OR-MORE GOAL SEASONS:
22 —**Gordie Howe,** Detroit, 1949-50 – 1970-71.
17 —Marcel Dionne, Detroit, Los Angeles, NY Rangers, 1971-72 – 1987-88.
16 —Phil Esposito, Chicago, Boston, NY Rangers, 1964-65 – 1979-80.
15 —Mike Gartner, Washington, Minnesota, NY Rangers, Toronto, 1979-80 – 1993-94.
14 —Maurice Richard, Montreal, 1943-44 – 1956-57.
— Stan Mikita, Chicago, 1961-62 – 1974-75.
— Michel Goulet, Quebec, Chicago, 1979-80 – 1992-93.
13 —Bobby Hull, Chicago, 1959-60 – 1971-72.
— Guy Lafleur, Montreal, 1971-72 – 1983-84.
— Bryan Trottier, NY Islanders, 1975-76 – 1987-88.
— Wayne Gretzky, Edmonton, Los Angeles, 1979-80 – 1991-92.
— Ron Francis, Hartford, Pittsburgh, 1981-82 – 1993-94.

MOST 30-OR-MORE GOAL SEASONS:
16 —**Mike Gartner,** Washington, Minnesota, NY Rangers, Toronto, in 17 seasons.
14 —Gordie Howe, Detroit, Hartford, in 26 seasons.
— Marcel Dionne, Detroit, Los Angeles, NY Rangers, in 18 seasons.
— Wayne Gretzky, Edmonton, Los Angeles, St. Louis, in 17 seasons.
13 —Bobby Hull, Chicago, Winnipeg, Hartford, in 16 seasons.
— Phil Esposito, Chicago, Boston, NY Rangers, in 18 seasons.

Brett Hull enjoyed his finest offensive season in 1990-91, scoring a league-high 86 goals in only 78 games, for a goals-per-game average of 1.10.
That mark stands as the the fourth-highest average in NHL history.

MOST CONSECUTIVE 30-OR-MORE GOAL SEASONS:
15 — Mike Gartner, Washington, Minnesota, NY Rangers, Toronto, 1979-80 –
1993-94.
13 — Bobby Hull, Chicago, 1959-60 – 1971-72.
— Phil Esposito, Boston, NY Rangers, 1967-68 – 1979-80.
— Wayne Gretzky, Edmonton, Los Angeles, 1979-80 – 1991-92.
12 — Marcel Dionne, Detroit, Los Angeles,1974-75 – 1985-86.
10 — Darryl Sittler, Toronto, Philadelphia, 1973-74 – 1982-83.
— Mike Bossy, NY Islanders, 1977-78 – 1986-87.
— Jari Kurri, Edmonton, 1980-81 – 1989-90.

MOST 40-OR-MORE GOAL SEASONS:
12 — Wayne Gretzky, Edmonton, Los Angeles, St. Louis, in 17 seasons.
10 — Marcel Dionne, Detroit, Los Angeles, NY Rangers, in 18 seasons.
9 — Mike Bossy, NY Islanders, in 10 seasons.
— Mike Gartner, Washington, Minnesota, NY Rangers, Toronto, in 17 seasons.
— Mario Lemieux, Pittsburgh, in 11 seasons.
8 — Bobby Hull, Chicago, Winnipeg, Hartford, in 16 seasons.
— Phil Esposito, Chicago, Boston, NY Rangers, in 18 seasons.
— Jari Kurri, Edmonton, Los Angeles, NY Rangers, in 15 seasons.
— Luc Robitaille, Los Angeles, Pittsburgh, NY Rangers, in 10 seasons.

MOST CONSECUTIVE 40-OR-MORE GOAL SEASONS:
12 — Wayne Gretzky, Edmonton, Los Angeles, 1979-80 – 1990-91.
9 — Mike Bossy, NY Islanders, 1977-78 – 1985-86.
8 — Luc Robitaille, Los Angeles, 1986-87 – 1993-94.
7 — Phil Esposito, Boston, 1968-69 – 1974-75.
— Michel Goulet, Quebec, 1981-82 – 1987-88.
— Jari Kurri, Edmonton, 1982-83 – 1988-89.
6 — Guy Lafleur, Montreal, 1974-75 – 1979-80.
— Joe Mullen, St. Louis, Calgary, 1983-84 – 1988-89.
— Mario Lemieux, Pittsburgh, 1984-85 – 1989-90.
— Steve Yzerman, Detroit, 1987-88 – 1992-93.
— Brett Hull, St. Louis, 1988-89 – 1993-94.

MOST 50-OR-MORE GOAL SEASONS:
9 — Mike Bossy, NY Islanders, in 10 seasons.
— Wayne Gretzky, Edmonton, Los Angeles, in 17 seasons.
6 — Guy Lafleur, Montreal, NY Rangers, Quebec, in 17 seasons.
— Marcel Dionne, Detroit, Los Angeles, NY Rangers, in 18 seasons.
5 — Bobby Hull, Chicago, Winnipeg, Hartford, in 16 seasons.
— Phil Esposito, Chicago, Boston, NY Rangers, in 18 seasons.
— Brett Hull, Calgary, St. Louis, in 10 seasons.
— Steve Yzerman, Detroit, in 13 seasons.

MOST CONSECUTIVE 50-OR-MORE GOAL SEASONS:
9 — Mike Bossy, NY Islanders, 1977-78 – 1985-86.
8 — Wayne Gretzky, Edmonton, 1979-80 – 1986-87.
6 — Guy Lafleur, Montreal, 1974-75 – 1979-80.
5 — Phil Esposito, Boston, 1970-71 – 1974-75.
— Marcel Dionne, Los Angeles, 1978-79 – 1982-83.
— Brett Hull, St. Louis, 1989-90 – 1993-94.

MOST 60-OR-MORE GOAL SEASONS:
5 — Mike Bossy, NY Islanders, in 10 seasons.
— Wayne Gretzky, Edmonton, Los Angeles, St. Louis, in 17 seasons.
4 — Phil Esposito, Chicago, Boston, NY Rangers, in 18 seasons.
— Mario Lemieux, Pittsburgh, in 11 seasons.

MOST CONSECUTIVE 60-OR-MORE GOAL SEASONS:
4 — Wayne Gretzky, Edmonton, 1981-82 – 1984-85.
3 — Mike Bossy, NY Islanders, 1980-81 – 1982-83.
— Brett Hull, St. Louis, 1989-90 – 1991-92.
2 — Phil Esposito, Boston, 1970-71 – 1971-72, 1973-74 – 1974-75.
— Jari Kurri, Edmonton, 1984-85 – 1985-86.
— Mario Lemieux, Pittsburgh, 1987-88 – 1988-89.
— Steve Yzerman, Detroit, 1988-89 – 1989-90.
— Pavel Bure, Vancouver, 1992-93 – 1993-94.

MOST 100-OR-MORE POINT SEASONS:
15 — Wayne Gretzky, Edmonton, Los Angeles, St. Louis, 1979-80 – 1991-92;
1993-94; 1995-96.
9 — Mario Lemieux, Pittsburgh, 1984-85 – 1989-90; 1991-92; 1992-93; 1995-96.
8 — Marcel Dionne, Detroit, 1974-75; Los Angeles, 1976-77; 1978-79 –
1982-83; 1984-85.
7 — Mike Bossy, NY Islanders, 1978-79; 1980-81 – 1985-86.
— Peter Stastny, Quebec, 1980-81 – 1985-86; 1987-88.
6 — Phil Esposito, Boston, 1968-69; 1970-71 – 1974-75.
— Bobby Orr, Boston, 1969-70 – 1974-75.
— Guy Lafleur, Montreal, 1974-75 – 1979-80.
— Bryan Trottier, NY Islanders, 1977-78 – 1981-82; 1983-84.
— Dale Hawerchuk, Winnipeg, 1981-82; 1983-84 – 1987-88.
— Jari Kurri, Edmonton, 1982-83 – 1986-87; 1988-89.
— Mark Messier, Edmonton, 1982-83 – 1983-84; 1986-87 – 1987-88; 1989-90;
NY Rangers, 1991-92.
— Steve Yzerman, Detroit, 1987-88 – 1992-93.

MOST CONSECUTIVE 100-OR-MORE POINT SEASONS:
13 — Wayne Gretzky, Edmonton, Los Angeles, 1979-80 – 1991-92.
6 — Bobby Orr, Boston, 1969-70 – 1974-75.
— Guy Lafleur, Montreal, 1974-75 – 1979-80.
— Mike Bossy, NY Islanders,1980-81 – 1985-86.
— Peter Stastny, Quebec, 1980-81 – 1985-86.
— Mario Lemieux, Pittsburgh, 1984-85 – 1989-90.
— Steve Yzerman, Detroit, 1987-88 – 1992-93.

THREE-OR-MORE-GOAL GAMES

MOST THREE-OR-MORE GOAL GAMES, CAREER:
49 — Wayne Gretzky, Edmonton, Los Angeles, St. Louis, in 17 seasons, 36
three-goal games, 9 four-goal games, 4 five-goal games.
39 — Mike Bossy, NY Islanders, in 10 seasons, 30 three-goal games,
9 four-goal games.
37 — Mario Lemieux, Pittsburgh, in 11 seasons, 25 three-goal games, 9 four-goal
games and 3 five-goal games.
32 — Phil Esposito, Chicago, Boston, NY Rangers, in 18 seasons, 27 three-goal
games, 5 four-goal games.
28 — Bobby Hull, Chicago, Winnipeg, Hartford, in 16 seasons, 24 three-goal
games, 4 four-goal games.
— Marcel Dionne, Detroit, Los Angeles, NY Rangers, in 18 seasons,
25 three-goal games, 3 four-goal games.
26 — Cy Denneny, Ottawa in 12 seasons. 20 three-goal games,
5 four-goal games, 1 six-goal game.
— Maurice Richard, Montreal, in 18 seasons, 23 three-goal games,
2 four-goal games, 1 five-goal game.

MOST THREE-OR-MORE GOAL GAMES, ONE SEASON:
10 — Wayne Gretzky, Edmonton, 1981-82. 6 three-goal games, 3 four-goal
games, 1 five-goal game.
— Wayne Gretzky, Edmonton, 1983-84. 6 three-goal games, 4 four-goal
games.
9 — Mike Bossy, NY Islanders, 1980-81. 6 three-goal games, 3 four-goal games.
— Mario Lemieux, Pittsburgh, 1988-89. 7 three-goal games, 1 four-goal game,
1 five-goal game.
8 — Brett Hull, St. Louis, 1991-92. 8 three-goal games.
7 — Joe Malone, Montreal, 1917-18. 2 three-goal games, 2 four-goal games,
3 five-goal games.
— Phil Esposito, Boston, 1970-71. 7 three-goal games.
— Rick Martin, Buffalo, 1975-76. 6 three-goal games, 1 four-goal game.
— Alexander Mogilny, Buffalo, 1992-93. 5 three-goal games, 2 four-goal games.

*Luc Robitaille is the only left winger in NHL history to have
recorded eight consecutive seasons with at least 40 goals.*

SCORING STREAKS

LONGEST CONSECUTIVE GOAL-SCORING STREAK:
    16 Games —Harry (Punch) Broadbent, Ottawa, 1921-22.
        25 goals during streak.
    14 Games —Joe Malone, Montreal, 1917-18. 35 goals during streak.
    13 Games —Newsy Lalonde, Montreal, 1920-21. 24 goals during streak.
        —Charlie Simmer, Los Angeles, 1979-80. 17 goals during streak.
    12 Games —Cy Denneny, Ottawa, 1917-18. 23 goals during streak.
        —Dave Lumley, Edmonton, 1981-82. 15 goals during streak.
        —Mario Lemieux, Pittsburgh, 1992-93. 18 goals during streak.

LONGEST CONSECUTIVE ASSIST-SCORING STREAK:
    23 Games —Wayne Gretzky, Los Angeles, 1990-91. 48A during streak.
    18 Games —Adam Oates, Boston, 1992-93. 28A during streak.
    17 Games —Wayne Gretzky, Edmonton, 1983-84. 38A during streak.
        —Paul Coffey, Edmonton, 1985-86. 27A during streak.
        —Wayne Gretzky, Los Angeles, 1989-90. 35A during streak.
    15 Games —Jari Kurri, Edmonton, 1983-84. 21A during streak.
        —Brian Leetch, NY Rangers, 1991-92. 23A during streak.

LONGEST CONSECUTIVE POINT SCORING STREAK:
    51 Games —Wayne Gretzky, Edmonton, 1983-84. 61G-92A-153PTS during streak.
    46 Games —Mario Lemieux, Pittsburgh, 1989-90. 39G-64A-103PTS during streak.
    39 Games —Wayne Gretzky, Edmonton, 1985-86. 33G-75A-108PTS during streak.
    30 Games —Wayne Gretzky, Edmonton, 1982-83. 24G52A76PTS during streak.
        —Mats Sundin, Quebec, 1992-93. 21G-25A-46PTS during streak.
    28 Games —Guy Lafleur, Montreal, 1976-77. 19G-42A-61PTS during streak.
        —Wayne Gretzky, Edmonton, 1984-85. 20G-43A-63PTS during streak.
        —Mario Lemieux, Pittsburgh, 1985-86. 21G-38A-59PTS during streak.
        —Paul Coffey, Edmonton, 1985-86. 16G-39A-55PTS during streak.
        —Steve Yzerman, Detroit, 1988-89. 29G-36A-65PTS during streak.

**LONGEST CONSECUTIVE POINT-SCORING STREAK
FROM START OF SEASON:**
    51 Games —Wayne Gretzky, Edmonton, 1983-84. 61G-92A-153PTS during
        streak which was stopped by goaltender Markus Mattsson and
        Los Angeles on Jan. 28, 1984.

LONGEST CONSECUTIVE POINT-SCORING STREAK BY A DEFENSEMAN:
    28 Games —Paul Coffey, Edmonton, 1985-86. 16G-39A-55PTS during streak.
    19 Games —Ray Bourque, Boston, 1987-88. 6G-21A-27PTS during streak.
    17 Games —Ray Bourque, Boston, 1984-85. 4G-24A-28PTS during streak.
        —Brian Leetch, NY Rangers, 1991-92. 5G-24A-29PTS during streak.
    16 Games —Gary Suter, Calgary, 1987-88. 8G-17A-25PTS during streak.
    15 Games —Bobby Orr, Boston, 1970-71. 10G-23A-33PTS during streak.
        —Bobby Orr, Boston, 1973-74. 8G-15A-23PTS during streak.
        —Steve Duchesne, Quebec, 1992-93. 4G-17A-21PTS during streak.
        —Chris Chelios, Chicago, 1995-96. 4G-16A-20PTS during streak.

FASTEST GOALS AND ASSISTS

FASTEST GOAL FROM START OF A GAME:
    5 Seconds — Doug Smail, Winnipeg, Dec. 20, 1981, at Winnipeg.
        Winnipeg 5, St. Louis 4.
    — Bryan Trottier, NY Islanders, Mar. 22, 1984, at Boston.
        NY Islanders 3, Boston 3
    — Alexander Mogilny, Buffalo, Dec. 21, 1991, at Toronto.
        Buffalo 4, Toronto 1.
    6 Seconds — Henry Boucha, Detroit, Jan. 28, 1973, at Montreal.
        Detroit 4, Montreal 2
    — Jean Pronovost, Pittsburgh, March 25, 1976, at St. Louis.
        St. Louis 5, Pittsburgh 2
    7 Seconds — Charlie Conacher, Toronto, Feb. 6, 1932, at Toronto.
        Toronto 6, Boston 0.
    — Danny Gare, Buffalo, Dec. 17, 1978, at Buffalo.
        Buffalo 6, Vancouver 3
    — Dave Williams, Los Angeles, Feb. 14, 1987 at Los Angeles.
        Los Angeles 5, Harford 2.
    8 Seconds — Ron Martin, NY Americans, Dec. 4, 1932, at New York.
        NY Americans 4, Montreal 2
    — Chuck Arnason, Colorado, Jan. 28, 1977, at Atlanta.
        Colorado 3, Atlanta 3
    — Wayne Gretzky, Edmonton, Dec. 14, 1983, at New York.
        Edmonton 9, NY Rangers 4
    — Gaetan Duchesne, Washington, Mar. 14, 1987, at St. Louis.
        Washington 3, St. Louis 3.
    — Tim Kerr, Philadelphia, March 7, 1989, at Philadelphia.
        Philadelphia 4, Edmonton 3.
    — Grant Ledyard, Buffalo, Dec. 4, 1991, at Winnipeg. Buffalo 4, Winnipeg 4.
    — Brent Sutter, Chicago, Feb. 5, 1995, at Vancouver. Chicago 9, Vancouver 4.

FASTEST GOAL FROM START OF A PERIOD:
    4 Seconds — Claude Provost, Montreal, Nov. 9, 1957, at Montreal, second period.
        Montreal 4, Boston 2.
    — Denis Savard, Chicago, Jan. 12, 1986, at Chicago, third period.
        Chicago 4, Hartford 2.

FASTEST GOAL BY A PLAYER IN HIS FIRST NHL GAME:
    15 Seconds — Gus Bodnar, Toronto, Oct. 30, 1943.
        Toronto 5, NY Rangers 2.
    18 Seconds — Danny Gare, Buffalo, Oct. 10, 1974. Buffalo 9, Boston 5.
    20 Seconds — Alexander Mogilny, Buffalo, Oct. 5, 1989. Buffalo 4, Quebec 3.

FASTEST TWO GOALS:
    4 Seconds — Nels Stewart, Mtl. Maroons, Jan. 3, 1931, at Montreal at 8:24 and
        8:28, third period. Mtl. Maroons 5, Boston 3.
    — Deron Quint, Winnipeg, Dec. 15, 1995, at Winnipeg at 7:51 and 7:55, second
        period. Winnipeg 9, Edmonton 4.
    5 Seconds — Pete Mahovlich, Montreal, Feb. 20, 1971, at Montreal at 12:16 and
        12:21, third period. Montreal 7, Chicago 1.
    6 Seconds — Jim Pappin, Chicago, Feb. 16, 1972, at Chicago at
        2:57 and 3:03, third period. Chicago 3, Philadelphia 3.
    — Ralph Backstrom, Los Angeles, Nov. 2, 1972, at Los Angeles at 8:30 and 8:36, third
        period. Los Angeles 5, Boston 2.
    — Lanny McDonald, Calgary, Mar. 22, 1984, at Calgary at 16:23 and 16:29, first
        period. Detroit 6, Calgary 4.
    — Sylvain Turgeon, Hartford, Mar. 28, 1987, at Hartford at 13:59 and 14:05, second
        period. Hartford 5, Pittsburgh 4.

FASTEST THREE GOALS:
    21 Seconds — Bill Mosienko, Chicago, March 23, 1952, at
        New York, against goaltender Lorne Anderson. Mosienko scored at 6:09,
        6:20 and 6:30 of third period, all with both teams at full strength. Chicago 7,
        NY Rangers 6.
    44 Seconds — Jean Béliveau, Montreal, Nov. 5, 1955, at Montreal, against goaltender
        Terry Sawchuk. Béliveau scored at :42, 1:08 and 1:26 of second period, all with
        Montreal holding a 6-4 man advantage. Montreal 4, Boston 2.

FASTEST THREE ASSISTS:
    21 Seconds — Gus Bodnar, Chicago, March 23, 1952, at New York, Bodnar assisted
        on Bill Mosienko's three goals at 6:09, 6:20, 6:30 of third period. Chicago 7,
        NY Rangers 6.
    44 Seconds — Bert Olmstead, Montreal, Nov. 5, 1955, at Montreal against Boston.
        Olmstead assisted on Jean Béliveau's three goals at :42, 1:08 and 1:26 of
        second period. Montreal 4, Boston 2.

SHOTS ON GOAL

MOST SHOTS ON GOAL, ONE SEASON:
    550 —Phil Esposito, Boston, 1970-71. 78 game schedule.
    426 —Phil Esposito, Boston, 1971-72. 78 game schedule.
    414 —Bobby Hull, Chicago, 1968-69. 76 game schedule.

PENALTIES

MOST PENALTY MINUTES:
    3,966 —Dave Williams, Toronto, Vancouver, Detroit, Los Angeles, Hartford,
        in 14 seasons, 962GP.
    3,218 —Dale Hunter, Quebec, Washington, in 16 seasons, 1,181GP.
    3,043 —Chris Nilan, Monteal, NY Rangers, Boston, in 13 seasons, 688GP.
    3,011 —Tim Hunter, Calgary, Quebec, Vancouver, in 15 seasons, 769GP.
    2,892 —Marty McSorley, Pittsburgh, Edmonton, Los Angeles, NY Rangers, in 13
        seasons, 775GP.

MOST PENALTY MINUTES, INCLUDING PLAYOFFS:
    4,421 —Dave Williams, Toronto, Vancouver, Detroit, Los Angeles, Hartford, 3,966 in
        regular season; 455 in playoffs.
    3,879 —Dale Hunter, Quebec, Washington, 3,218 in regular-season;
        661 in playoffs.
    3,584 —Chris Nilan, Montreal, NY Rangers, Boston, 3,043 in regular-season;
        541 in playoffs.
    3,437 —Tim Hunter, Calgary, Quebec, Vancouver, 3,011 regular-season;
        426 in playoffs.
    3,264 —Marty McSorley, Pittsburgh, Edmonton, Los Angeles, NY Rangers, 2,892 in
        regular-season; 372 in playoffs.

MOST PENALTY MINUTES, ONE SEASON:
    472 —Dave Schultz, Philadelphia, 1974-75.
    409 —Paul Baxter, Pittsburgh, 1981-82.
    408 —Mike Peluso, Chicago, 1991-92.
    405 —Dave Schultz, Los Angeles, Pittsburgh, 1977-78.

MOST PENALTIES, ONE GAME:
    10 —Chris Nilan, Boston, March 31, 1991, at Boston against Hartford.
        6 minors, 2 majors, 1 10-minute misconduct, 1 game misconduct.
    9 —Jim Dorey, Toronto, Oct. 16, 1968, at Toronto against Pittsburgh. 4 minors,
        2 majors, 2 10-minute misconducts, 1 game misconduct.
    —Dave Schultz, Pittsburgh, Apr. 6, 1978, at Detroit. 5 minors,
        2 majors, 2 10-minute misconducts.
    —Randy Holt, Los Angeles, Mar. 11, 1979, at Philadelphia. 1 minor,
        3 majors, 2 10-minute misconducts, 3 game misconducts.
    —Russ Anderson, Pittsburgh, Jan. 19, 1980, at Pittsburgh.
        3 minors, 3 majors, 3 game misconducts.
    —Kim Clackson, Quebec, March 8, 1981, at Quebec. 4 minors, 3 majors,
        2 game misconducts.
    —Terry O'Reilly, Boston, Dec. 19, 1984, at Hartford. 5 minors,
        3 majors, 1 game misconduct.
    —Larry Playfair, Los Angeles, Dec. 9, 1986, at NY Islanders. 6 minors,
        2 majors, 1 10-minute misconduct.
    —Marty McSorley, Los Angeles, Apr. 14, 1992, at Vancouver. 5 minors,
        2 majors, 1 10-minute misconduct, 1 game misconduct.

MOST PENALTY MINUTES, ONE GAME:
    67 —Randy Holt, Los Angeles, Mar. 11, 1979, at Philadelphia. 1 minor,
        3 majors, 2 10-minute misconducts, 3 game misconducts.
    55 —Frank Bathe, Philadelphia, Mar. 11, 1979, at Philadelphia.
        3 majors, 2 10-minute misconducts, 2 game misconducts.
    51 —Russ Anderson, Pittsburgh, Jan. 19, 1980, at Pittsburgh.
        3 minors, 3 majors, 3 game misconducts.

MOST PENALTIES, ONE PERIOD:
9 — Randy Holt, Los Angeles, Mar. 11, 1979, at Philadelphia, first period.
1 minor, 3 majors, 2 10-minute misconducts, 3 game misconducts.

MOST PENALTY MINUTES, ONE PERIOD:
67 — Randy Holt, Los Angeles, Mar. 11, 1979, at Philadelphia, first period.
1 minor, 3 majors, 2 10-minute misconducts, 3 game misconducts.

GOALTENDING

MOST GAMES APPEARED IN BY A GOALTENDER, CAREER:
971 — Terry Sawchuk, Detroit, Boston, Toronto, Los Angeles, NY Rangers
from 1949-50 – 1969-70.
906 — Glenn Hall, Detroit, Chicago, St. Louis from 1952-53 – 1970-71.
886 — Tony Esposito, Montreal, Chicago from 1968-69 – 1983-84.
861 — Lorne "Gump" Worsley, NY Rangers, Montreal, Minnesota from
1952-53 – 1973-74.

MOST GAMES, ONE SEASON, BY A GOALTENDER:
79 — Grant Fuhr, St. Louis, 1995-96.
77 — Martin Brodeur, New Jersey, 1995-96.
75 — Grant Fuhr, Edmonton, 1987-88.
74 — Ed Belfour, Chicago, 1990-91.
— Arturs Irbe, San Jose, 1993-94.
73 — Bernie Parent, Philadelphia, 1973-74.

MOST MINUTES PLAYED BY A GOALTENDER, CAREER:
57,184 — Terry Sawchuk, Detroit, Boston, Toronto, Los Angeles, NY Rangers, from
1949-50 – 1969-70.

MOST MINUTES PLAYED, ONE SEASON, BY A GOALTENDER:
4,433 — Martin Brodeur, New Jersey, 1995-96.

MOST CONSECUTIVE COMPLETE GAMES BY A GOALTENDER:
502 — Glenn Hall, Detroit, Chicago. Played 502 games from beginning of 1955-56
season - first 12 games of 1962-63. In his 503rd straight game, Nov. 7, 1962,
at Chicago, Hall was removed from the game against Boston with a back
injury in the first period.

MOST SHUTOUTS BY A GOALTENDER, CAREER:
103 — Terry Sawchuk, Detroit, Boston, Toronto, Los Angeles, NY Rangers
in 21 seasons.
94 — George Hainsworth, Montreal Canadiens, Toronto in 10 seasons.
84 — Glenn Hall, Detroit, Chicago, St. Louis in 16 seasons.

MOST SHUTOUTS, ONE SEASON:
22 — George Hainsworth, Montreal, 1928-29. 44GP
15 — Alex Connell, Ottawa, 1925-26. 36GP
— Alex Connell, Ottawa, 1927-28. 44GP
— Hal Winkler, Boston, 1927-28. 44GP
— Tony Esposito, Chicago, 1969-70. 63GP
14 — George Hainsworth, Montreal, 1926-27. 44GP

LONGEST SHUTOUT SEQUENCE BY A GOALTENDER:
461 Minutes, 29 Seconds — Alex Connell, Ottawa, 1927-28, six consecutive
shutouts. (Forward passing not permitted in attacking zones in 1927-1928.)
343 Minutes, 5 Seconds — George Hainsworth, Montreal, 1928-29, four consecutive
shutouts.
324 Minutes, 40 Seconds — Roy Worters, NY Americans, 1930-31, four consecutive
shutouts.
309 Minutes, 21 Seconds — Bill Durnan, Montreal, 1948-49, four consecutive shutouts.

MOST WINS, ONE SEASON, BY A GOALTENDER:
47 — Bernie Parent, Philadelphia, 1973-74.
44 — Bernie Parent, Philadelphia, 1974-75.
— Terry Sawchuk, Detroit, 1950-51.
— Terry Sawchuk, Detroit, 1951-52.

LONGEST WINNING STREAK, ONE SEASON, BY A GOALTENDER:
17 — Gilles Gilbert, Boston, 1975-76.
14 — Don Beaupre, Minnesota, 1985-86.
— Ross Brooks, Boston, 1973-74.
— Tiny Thompson, Boston, 1929-30.
— Tom Barrasso, Pittsburgh, 1992-93.

LONGEST UNDEFEATED STREAK, ONE SEASON, BY A GOALTENDER:
32 Games — Gerry Cheevers, Boston, 1971-72. 24w-8т.
31 Games — Pete Peeters, Boston, 1982-83. 26w-5т.
27 Games — Pete Peeters, Philadelphia, 1979-80. 22w-5т.
23 Games — Frank Brimsek, Boston, 1940-41. 15w-8т.
— Glenn Resch, NY Islanders, 1978-79. 15w-8т.
— Grant Fuhr, Edmonton, 1981-82. 15w-8т.

MOST 40-OR-MORE WIN SEASONS BY A GOALTENDER:
3 — Jacques Plante, Montreal, NY Rangers, St. Louis, Toronto, Boston
in 18 seasons.
2 — Terry Sawchuk, Detroit, Boston, Toronto, Los Angeles, NY Rangers
in 21 seasons.
— Bernie Parent, Boston, Philadelphia, Toronto in 13 seasons.
— Ken Dryden, Montreal, in 8 seasons.
— Ed Belfour, Chicago, in 6 seasons.

MOST CONSECUTIVE 40-OR-MORE WIN SEASONS BY A GOALTENDER:
2 — Terry Sawchuk, Detroit, 1950-51 – 1951-52.
— Bernie Parent, Philadelphia, 1973-74 – 1974-75.
— Ken Dryden, Montreal, 1975-76 – 1976-77.

MOST 30-OR-MORE WIN SEASONS BY A GOALTENDER:
8 — Tony Esposito, Montreal, Chicago in 16 seasons.
7 — Jacques Plante, Montreal, NY Rangers, St. Louis, Toronto, Boston
in 18 seasons.
— Ken Dryden, Montreal, in 8 seasons.
6 — Glenn Hall, Detroit, Chicago, St. Louis in 18 seasons.

MOST CONSECUTIVE 30-OR-MORE WIN SEASONS BY A GOALTENDER:
7 — Tony Esposito, Chicago, 1969-70 – 1975-76.
6 — Jacques Plante, Montreal, 1954-55 – 1959-60.
5 — Ken Dryden, Montreal, 1974-75 – 1978-79.
4 — Terry Sawchuk, Detroit, 1950-51 – 1953-54.
— Ed Giacomin, NY Rangers, 1966-67 – 1969-70.

Terry Sawchuk, surrounded by his teammates,
heads to the Maple Leaf dressing room after
posting his 100th regular-season shutout,
a 3-0 blanking of the Chicago Black Hawks
on March 4, 1967.

Active NHL Players' Three-or-More-Goal Games

Regular Season

Teams named are the ones the players were with at the time of their multiple-scoring games. Players listed alphabetically.

A 14-year veteran who has suited up with Minnesota, Montreal and Tampa Bay, Brian Bellows has scored at least three goals in a game nine times in his career, including a four-goal effort in the Montreal Canadiens' 8-4 win over Buffalo on February 27, 1993.

Player	Team	3-Goals	4-Goals	5-Goals
Adams, Greg	Vancouver	1	1	—
Alfredsson, Daniel	Ottawa	1	—	—
Amonte, Tony	NYR, Chi	2	—	—
Anderson, Glenn	Edm., Tor.	18	3	—
Andersson, Mikael	Tampa Bay	1	—	—
Andersson, Niklas	NY Islanders	1	—	—
Andreychuk, Dave	Buf., Tor.	7	2	1
Arnott, Jason	Edmonton	2	—	—
Audette, Donald	Buffalo	2	—	—
Babych, Dave	Vancouver	1	—	—
Barnes, Stu	Winnipeg	1	—	—
Barr, Dave	St.L., Det.	2	—	—
Bellows, Brian	Min., Mtl., T.B.	6	3	—
Beranek, Josef	Philadelphia	1	—	—
Bondra, Peter	Washington	4	2	1
Bourque, Phil	Pittsburgh	1	—	—
Bourque, Ray	Boston	1	—	—
Bradley, Brian	Tampa Bay	1	—	—
Brickley, Andy	Pit., Bos.	2	—	—
Brind'Amour, Rod	Philadelphia	1	—	—
Broten, Neal	Minnesota	6	—	—
Broten, Paul	NY Rangers	1	—	—
Brown, Rob	Pittsburgh	7	—	—
Buchberger, Kelly	Edmonton	1	—	—
Bure, Pavel	Vancouver	5	1	—
Burr, Shawn	Detroit	3	—	—
Burridge, Randy	Bos., Wsh.	4	—	—
Butsayev, Viacheslav	Philadelphia	1	—	—
Carbonneau, Guy	Montreal	1	1	—
Carpenter, Bob	Wsh, Bos.	2	1	—
Carson, Jimmy	L.A., Edm., Det.	9	1	—
Cavallini, Gino	St. Louis	1	—	—
Christian, Dave	Wpg., Wsh.	2	—	—
Ciccarelli, Dino	Min., Wsh.	14	4	—
Clark, Wendel	Tor., Que.	7	1	—
Coffey, Paul	Edmonton	4	1	—
Corson, Shayne	Mtl., Edm.	3	—	—
Courtnall, Geoff	Bos., Wsh., St.L.	3	—	—
Courtnall, Russ	Tor., Mtl., / Min., Van.	5	—	—
Craven, Murray	Philadelphia	3	—	—
Creighton, Adam	Buf., Chi.	2	—	—
Crossman, Doug	Tampa Bay	1	—	—
Cullen, John	Pit., Hfd.	3	—	—
Cunneyworth, R.	Pittsburgh	1	1	—
Dahlen, Ulf	NYR, Min., S.J.	4	—	—
Daigle, Alexandre	Ottawa	1	—	—
Damphousse, V.	Tor., Edm., Mtl.	7	1	—
Davydov, Evgeny	Winnipeg	1	—	—
Dawe, Jason	Buffalo	1	—	—
Dineen, Kevin	Hfd., Phi.	9	1	—
Dionne, Gilbert	Montreal	1	—	—
Donnelly, Mike	Los Angeles	2	—	—
Druce, John	Wsh., L.A.	2	—	—
Duchesne, Steve	L.A., Phi., St.L.	3	—	—
Emerson, Nelson	Winnipeg	1	—	—
Errey, Bob	Pittsburgh	1	—	—
Evason, Dean	Hartford	1	—	—
Fedorov, Sergei	Detroit	1	1	—
Ferraro, Ray	Hfd., NYI, NYR	7	1	—
Flatley, Patrick	NY Islanders	2	1	—
Fleury, Theo	Calgary	10	—	—
Fogarty, Bryan	Quebec	1	—	—
Forsberg, Peter	Colorado	2	—	—
Francis, Ron	Hfd., Pit.	9	1	—
Friesen, Jeff	San Jose	1	—	—
Gagner, Dave	Min., Dal.	3	1	—
Gallant, Gerard	Detroit	4	—	—
Garpenlov, Johan	Det., S.J., Fla.	2	1	—
Gartner, Mike	Wsh., Min., NYR	14	2	—
Gaudreau, Rob	San Jose	3	—	—
Gelinas, Martin	Edmonton	1	—	—
Gilbert, Greg	NY Islanders	2	—	—
Gilchrist, Brent	Montreal	1	—	—
Gilmour, Doug	St.L., Tor.	3	—	—
Graham, Dirk	Minnesota	1	—	—
Granato, Tony	NYR, L.A.	4	1	—
Graves, Adam	Edm., NYR	5	—	—
Green, Travis	NY Islanders	1	—	—
Gretzky, Wayne	Edm., L.A.	36	9	4
Grieve, Brent	Edmonton	1	—	—
Hannan, Dave	Edmonton	1	—	—
Harvey, Todd	Dallas	1	—	—
Hatcher, Kevin	Wsh., Dal.	2	—	—
Hawerchuk, Dale	Wpg., Buf.	13	—	—
Heinze, Stephen	Boston	2	—	—
Hogue, Benoit	NY Islanders	1	—	—
Holik, Bobby	New Jersey	2	—	—

Player	Team	3-Goal	4-Goal	5-Goal
Horacek, Tony	Philadelphia	1	—	—
Housley, Phil	Buffalo	2	—	—
Hull, Brett	Cgy., St.L.	23	2	—
Hull, Jody	Hartford	1	—	—
Hunter, Dale	Que., Wsh.	4	—	—
Jagr, Jaromir	Pittsburgh	2	—	—
Janney, Craig	Bos., St.L.	3	—	—
Juneau, Joe	Boston	1	—	—
Kamensky, Valeri	Colorado	2	—	—
Khmylev, Yuri	Buffalo	1	—	—
Khristich, Dimitri	Washington	2	—	—
King, Derek	NY Islanders	4	1	—
Klima, Petr	Det., Edm.	6	—	—
Konowalchuk, Steve	Washington	2	—	—
Kontos, Chris	Tampa Bay	—	1	—
Korolev, Igor	Winnipeg	1	—	—
Kovalenko, Andrei	Quebec	1	—	—
Kovalev, Alexei	NY Rangers	1	—	—
Kozlov, Vyacheslav	Detroit	1	1	—
Krupp, Uwe	Quebec	1	—	—
Krygier, Todd	Washington	1	—	—
Kudelski, Robert	L.A., Ott.	4	—	—
Kurri, Jari	Edm., L.A.	21	1	1
LaFontaine, Pat	NYI, Buf.	13	—	—
Larionov, Igor	Van., S.J.	4	—	—
Larouche, Steve	Ottawa	1	—	—
Lebeau, Stephan	Montreal	1	—	—
LeClair, John	Philadelphia	4	—	—
Lemieux, Claude	Mtl., N.J., Col.	2	—	—
Lemieux, Jocelyn	Chicago	2	—	—
Lemieux, Mario	Pittsburgh	25	9	3
Linden, Trevor	Vancouver	4	—	—
Lindros, Eric	Philadelphia	8	—	—
MacInnis, Al	Calgary	1	—	—
MacLean, John	New Jersey	6	—	—
MacTavish, Craig	Edmonton	2	—	—
Marois, Daniel	Toronto	3	—	—
Messier, Mark	Edm., NYR	13	4	—
Miller, Kevin	Det., St.L., S.J.	4	—	—
Modano, Mike	Min., Dal.	2	1	—
Mogilny, Alexander	Buf., Van.	11	2	—
Momesso, Sergio	Montreal	1	—	—
Mullen, Joe	St.L., Cgy., Pit.	7	4	—
Muller, Kirk	N.J., Mtl., Tor.	7	—	—
Murray, Troy	Chicago	4	—	—
Murzyn, Dana	Calgary	1	—	—
Naslund, Markus	Pit., Van.	2	—	—
Nedved, Petr	Pittsburgh	—	1	—
Neely, Cam	Boston	14	—	—
Nemchinov, Sergei	NY Rangers	1	—	—
Nicholls, Bernie	L.A., N.J., Chi.	14	4	—
Nieuwendyk, Joe	Calgary	7	2	1
Nolan, Owen	Que., S.J.	7	1	—
Noonan, Brian	Chi., NYR	3	1	—
Nylander, Michael	Hartford	1	—	—
Oates, Adam	Boston	5	1	—
Odelein, Lyle	Montreal	1	—	—
Olczyk, Ed	Tor., NYR, Wpg.	4	—	—
Oliver, David	Edmonton	1	—	—
Osborne, Mark	Detroit	1	—	—
Otto, Joel	Calgary	2	—	—
Palffy, Zigmund	NY Islanders	2	—	—
Petrov, Oleg	Montreal	1	—	—
Pivonka, Michal	Washington	1	—	—
Plante, Derek	Buffalo	1	—	—
Poulin, Dave	Philadelphia	5	—	—
Presley, Wayne	Chicago	1	—	—
Probert, Bob	Detroit	1	—	—
Prokhorov, Vitali	St. Louis	1	—	—
Quinn, Dan	Pit., Van., Ott.	5	—	—
Ranheim, Paul	Calgary	1	—	—

Player	Team	3-Goal	4-Goal	5-Goal
Recchi, Mark	Pittsburgh	1	—	—
Reichel, Robert	Calgary	3	—	—
Reid, Dave	Boston	1	—	—
Renberg, Mikael	Philadelphia	1	—	—
Ricci, Mike	Quebec	—	—	1
Rice, Steven	Hartford	1	—	—
Richer, Stephane	Mtl., N.J.	8	1	—
Ridley, Mike	NYR, Wsh.	3	1	—
Roberts, Gary	Calgary	9	1	—
Robitaille, Luc	L.A., Pit.	9	3	—
Roenick, Jeremy	Chicago	4	3	—
Ronning, Cliff	St.L., Van.	3	—	—
Rucinsky, Martin	Montreal	1	—	—
Sakic, Joe	Quebec	4	1	—
Sanderson, Geoff	Hartford	5	—	—
Sandlak, Jim	Vancouver	1	—	—
Sandstrom, Tomas	NYR, L.A.	7	1	—
Savage, Brian	Montreal	1	—	—
Savard, Denis	Chi., Mtl.	12	—	—
Selanne, Teemu	Wpg., Ana.	8	2	—
Semak, Alexander	New Jersey	1	—	—
Shanahan, Brendan	N.J., St.L., Hfd.	7	—	—
Sheppard, Ray	Buf., Det., S.J., Fla.	8	—	—
Simpson, Craig	Pit., Edm.	3	—	—
Smith, Derrick	Philadelphia	1	—	—
Smolinski, Bryan	Boston	1	—	—
Stern, Ronnie	Calgary	3	—	—
Stevens, Kevin	Pittsburgh	8	2	—
Straka, Martin	Pittsburgh	1	—	—
Stumpel, Jozef	Boston	1	—	—
Sundin, Mats	Quebec	3	—	1
Sutter, Brent	NY Islanders	6	—	—
Sweeney, Bob	Boston	1	—	—
Thomas, Steve	Chi., NYI	4	2	—
Tikkanen, Esa	Edmonton	3	—	—
Titov, German	Calgary	1	—	—
Tkachuk, Keith	Winnipeg	1	1	—
Tocchet, Rick	Phi., Pit., L.A., Bos.	12	2	—
Tucker, John	Buffalo	1	—	—
Turcotte, Darren	NY Rangers	4	—	—
Turgeon, Pierre	Buf., NYI, Mtl.	12	—	—
Turgeon, Sylvain	Hfd., N.J., Ott.	5	—	—
Valk, Garry	Anaheim	1	—	—
Verbeek, Pat	N.J., Hfd., NYR	10	1	—
Vukota, Mick	NY Islanders	1	—	—
Weight, Doug	Edmonton	1	—	—
Wesley, Glen	Boston	1	—	—
Wiemer, Jason	Tampa Bay	1	—	—
Wood, Randy	NY Islanders	1	—	—
Yachmenev, Vitali	Los Angeles	1	—	—
Yake, Terry	Anaheim	1	—	—
Yashin, Alexei	Ottawa	3	—	—
Yegorov, Alexei	San Jose	1	—	—
Young, Scott	Quebec	1	—	—
Yzerman, Steve	Detroit	17	1	—
Ysebaert, Paul	Detroit	1	—	—
Zezel, Peter	Philadelphia	1	—	—
Zhamnov, Alexei	Winnipeg	4	—	1

Top 100 All-Time Goal-Scoring Leaders

* active player

Player	Seasons	Games	Goals	Goals per game
* 1. Wayne Gretzky, Edm., L.A., St.L.	17	1253	837	.668
2. Gordie Howe, Det., Hfd.	26	1767	801	.453
3. Marcel Dionne, Det., L.A., NYR	18	1348	731	.542
4. Phil Esposito, Chi., Bos., NYR	18	1282	717	.559
* 5. Mike Gartner, Wsh., Min., NYR, Tor.	17	1290	664	.515
6. Bobby Hull, Chi., Wpg., Hfd.	16	1063	610	.574
* 7. Jari Kurri, Edm., L.A., NYR	15	1099	583	.530
8. Mike Bossy, NYI	10	752	573	.762
* 9. Mario Lemieux, Pit.	11	669	563	.842
10. Guy Lafleur, Mtl., NYR, Que.	17	1126	560	.497
11. John Bucyk, Det., Bos.	23	1540	556	.361
* 12. Dino Ciccarelli, Min., Wsh., Det.	16	1079	551	.511
13. Michel Goulet, Que., Chi.	15	1089	548	.503
14. Maurice Richard, Mtl.	18	978	544	.556
15. Stan Mikita, Chi.	22	1394	541	.388
* 16. Mark Messier, Edm., NYR	17	1201	539	.449
17. Frank Mahovlich, Tor., Det., Mtl.	18	1181	533	.451
18. Bryan Trottier, NYI, Pit.	18	1279	524	.410
* 19. Steve Yzerman, Det.	13	942	517	.549
20. Gilbert Perreault, Buf.	17	1191	512	.430
21. Jean Beliveau, Mtl.	20	1125	507	.451
* 22. Dale Hawerchuk, Wpg., Buf., St.L., Phi.	15	1137	506	.445
23. Lanny McDonald, Tor., Col., Cgy.	16	1111	500	.450
* 24. Glenn Anderson, Edm., Tor., NYR, St.L.	16	1129	498	.441
* 25. Joe Mullen, St.L., Cgy., Pit., Bos.	15	1008	495	.491
26. Jean Ratelle, NYR, Bos.	21	1281	491	.383
* 27. Brett Hull, Cgy., St.L.	10	658	485	.737
28. Darryl Sittler, Tor., Phi., Det.	15	1096	484	.442
* 29. Dave Andreychuk, Buf., Tor., N.J.	14	1001	476	.476
30. Norm Ullman, Det., Tor.	20	1410	476	.338
* 31. Denis Savard, Chi., Mtl., T.B.	16	1132	464	.410
* 32. Bernie Nicholls, L.A., NYR, Edm., N.J., Chi.	15	992	457	.461
33. Alex Delvecchio, Det.	24	1549	456	.294
34. Peter Stastny,	15	977	450	.461
35. Rick Middleton, NYR, Bos.	14	1005	448	.446
* 36. Brian Bellows, Min., Mtl., T.B.	14	1032	446	.432
* 37. Pat LaFontaine, NYI, Buf.	13	785	443	.564
38. Rick Vaive, Van., Tor., Chi., Buf.	13	876	441	.503
39. Steve Larmer, Chi., NYR.	15	1006	441	.438
* 40. Luc Robitaille, L.A., Pit., NYR	10	763	438	.574
41. Dave Taylor, L.A.	17	1111	431	.388
42. Yvan Cournoyer, Mtl.	16	968	428	.442
43. Brian Propp, Phi., Bos., Min., Hfd.	15	1016	425	.418
44. Steve Shutt, Mtl., L.A.	13	930	424	.456
45. Bill Barber, Phi.	12	903	420	.465
* 46. Pat Verbeek, N.J., Hfd., NYR	14	984	413	.420
47. Garry Unger, Tor., Det., St.L., Atl., L.A., Edm.	16	1105	413	.374
48. Rod Gilbert, NYR	18	1065	406	.381
49. John Ogrodnick, Det., Que., NYR	14	928	402	.433
50. Dave Keon, Tor., Hfd.	18	1296	396	.306
* 51. Cam Neely, Van., Bos.	13	726	395	.544
52. Pierre Larouche, Pit., Mtl., Hfd., NYR.	14	812	395	.486
53. Bernie Geoffrion, Mtl., NYR	16	883	393	.445
54. Jean Pronovost, Wsh., Pit., Atl.	14	998	391	.392
55. Dean Prentice, Pit., Min., NYR, Bos.	22	1378	391	.284
56. Rick Martin, Buf., L.A.	11	685	384	.561
57. Reggie Leach, Bos., Cal., Phi., Det.	13	934	381	.408
58. Ted Lindsay, Det., Chi.	17	1068	379	.355
* 59. Ron Francis, Hfd., Pit.	15	1085	376	.347
60. Butch Goring, L.A., NYI, Bos.	16	1107	375	.339
* 61. Paul Coffey, Edm., Pit., L.A., Det.	16	1154	372	.322
62. Rick Kehoe, Tor., Pit.	14	906	371	.409
63. Tim Kerr, Phi., NYR, Hfd.	13	655	370	.565
64. Bernie Federko, St.L., Det.	14	1000	369	.369
65. Jacques Lemaire, Mtl.	12	853	366	.429
66. Peter McNab, Buf., Bos., Van., N.J.	14	954	363	.381
67. Ivan Boldirev, Bos., Cal., Chi., Atl., Van., Det.	15	1052	361	.343
68. Bobby Clarke, Phi.	15	1144	358	.313
69. Henri Richard, Mtl.	20	1256	358	.285
70. Bobby Smith, Min., Mtl.	15	1077	357	.331
71. Dennis Maruk, Cal., Clev., Min., Wsh.	14	888	356	.401
72. Wilf Paiement, K.C. Col., Tor., Que., NYR, Buf., Pit.	14	946	356	.376
73. Mike Foligno, Det., Buf., Tor., Fla.	15	1018	355	.349
74. Danny Gare, Buf., Det., Edm.	13	827	354	.428
* 75. Brent Sutter, NYI, Chi.	16	1020	354	.347
* 76. Tomas Sandstrom, NYR, L.A., Pit.	12	774	352	.455
77. Rick MacLeish, Phi., Hfd., Pit., Det.	14	846	349	.413
78. Andy Bathgate, NYR, Tor., Det., Pit.	17	1069	349	.326
* 79. Doug Gilmour, St.L., Cgy., Tor.	13	981	346	.353

Player	Seasons	Games	Goals	Goals per game
* 80. Stephane J. J. Richer, Mtl., N.J.	12	763	344	.451
* 81. Ray Bourque, Bos.	17	1228	343	.279
82. Charlie Simmer, Cal., Cle., L.A., Bos., Pit.	14	712	342	.480
* 83. Dave Christian, Wpg., Wsh., Bos., St.L., Chi.	15	1009	340	.337
* 84. Rick Tocchet, Phi., Pit., L.A., Bos.	12	788	338	.429
85. Ron Ellis, Tor.	16	1034	332	.321
86. Mike Bullard, Pit., Cgy., St.L., Phi., Tor.	11	727	329	.453
* 87. Joe Nieuwendyk, Cgy., Dal.	10	629	328	.521
88. Ken Hodge, Chi., Bos., NYR	13	881	328	.372
89. John Tonelli, NYI, Cgy., L.A., Chi., Que.	14	1028	325	.316
90. Nels Stewart, Mtl.M., Bos., NYA.	15	650	324	.498
91. Paul MacLean, St.L., Wpg., Det.	11	719	324	.451
92. Pit Martin, Det., Bos., Chi., Van.	17	1101	324	.294
93. Vic Hadfield, NYR, Pit.	16	1002	323	.322
94. Tony McKegney, Buf., Que., Min., NYR, St. L., Det., Chi.	13	912	320	.351
95. Clark Gillies, NYI, Buf.	14	958	319	.333
* 96. Pierre Turgeon, Buf., NYI, Mtl.	9	672	318	.473
* 97. John MacLean, N.J.	12	828	315	.380
98. Don Lever, Van., Atl., Cgy., Col., N.J., Buf.	15	1020	313	.307
* 99. Geoff Courtnall, Bos., Edm., Wsh., St.L., Van.	13	857	312	.364
* 100. Petr Klima, Det., Edm., T.B.	11	740	310	.419

Ron Ellis, who scored at least 20 goals in 10 consecutive seasons for the Toronto Maple Leafs, stands 85th on the NHL's top-100 all-time goal scoring ladder.

Top 100 Active Goal-Scoring Leaders

Player	Games	Goals	Goals per game
1. **Wayne Gretzky**, Edm., L.A., St.L.	1253	**837**	.668
2. **Mike Gartner**, Wsh., Min., NYR, Tor.	1290	**664**	.515
3. **Jari Kurri**, Edm., L.A., NYR	1099	**583**	.530
4. **Mario Lemieux**, Pit.	669	**563**	.842
5. **Dino Ciccarelli**, Min., Wsh., Det.	1079	**551**	.511
6. **Mark Messier**, Edm., NYR	1201	**539**	.449
7. **Steve Yzerman**, Det.	942	**517**	.549
8. **Dale Hawerchuk**, Wpg., Buf., St.L., Phi.	1137	**506**	.445
9. **Glenn Anderson**, Edm., Tor., NYR, St.L.	1129	**498**	.441
10. **Joe Mullen**, St.L., Cgy., Pit., Bos.	1008	**495**	.491
11. **Brett Hull**, Cgy., St.L.	658	**485**	.737
12. **Dave Andreychuk**, Buf., Tor., N.J.	1001	**476**	.476
13. **Denis Savard**, Chi., Mtl., T.B.	1132	**464**	.410
14. **Bernie Nicholls**, L.A., NYR, Edm., N.J., Chi.	992	**457**	.461
15. **Brian Bellows**, Min., Mtl., T.B.	1032	**446**	.432
16. **Pat LaFontaine**, NYI, Buf.	785	**443**	.564
17. **Luc Robitaille**, L.A., Pit., NYR	763	**438**	.574
18. **Pat Verbeek**, N.J., Hfd., NYR	984	**413**	.420
19. **Cam Neely**, Van., Bos.	726	**395**	.544
20. **Ron Francis**, Hfd., Pit.	1085	**376**	.347
21. **Paul Coffey**, Edm., Pit., L.A., Det.	1154	**372**	.322
22. **Brent Sutter**, NYI, Chi.	1020	**354**	.347
23. **Tomas Sandstrom**, NYR, L.A., Pit.	774	**352**	.455
24. **Doug Gilmour**, St.L., Cgy., Tor.	981	**346**	.353
25. **Stephane J. J. Richer**, Mtl., N.J.	763	**344**	.451
26. **Ray Bourque**, Bos.	1228	**343**	.279
27. **Dave Christian**, Wpg., Wsh., Bos., St.L., Chi.	1009	**340**	.337
28. **Rick Tocchet**, Phi., Pit., L.A., Bos.	788	**338**	.429
29. **Joe Nieuwendyk**, Cgy., Dal.	629	**328**	.521
30. **Pierre Turgeon**, Buf., NYI, Mtl.	672	**318**	.473
31. **John MacLean**, N.J.	828	**315**	.380
32. **Geoff Courtnall**, Bos., Edm., Wsh., St.L., Van.	857	**312**	.364
33. **Petr Klima**, Det., Edm., T.B.	740	**310**	.419
34. **Kirk Muller**, N.J., Mtl., NYI, Tor.	886	**305**	.344
35. **Bob Carpenter**, Wsh., NYR, L.A., Bos., N.J.	994	**305**	.307
36. **Kevin Dineen**, Hfd., Phi.	793	**304**	.383
37. **Ray Ferraro**, Hfd., NYI, NYR, L.A.	834	**302**	.362
38. **Dale Hunter**, Que., Wsh.	1181	**299**	.253
39. **Steve Thomas**, Tor., Chi., NYI, N.J.	748	**295**	.394
40. **Ed Olczyk**, Chi., Tor., Wpg., NYR	802	**294**	.367
41. **Brendan Shanahan**, N.J., St.L., Hfd.	632	**288**	.456
42. **Joe Sakic**, Que., Col.	590	**285**	.483
43. **Vincent Damphousse**, Tor., Edm., Mtl.	770	**283**	.368
44. **Neal Broten**, Min., Dal., N.J.	1057	**281**	.266
45. **Theoren Fleury**, Cgy.	568	**278**	.489
46. **Ray Sheppard**, Buf., NYR, Det., S.J., Fla.	557	**275**	.494
47. **Jimmy Carson**, L.A., Edm., Det., Van., Hfd.	626	**275**	.439
48. **Phil Housley**, Buf., Wpg., St.L., Cgy., N.J.	990	**274**	.277
49. **Mike Ridley**, NYR, Wsh., Tor., Van.	791	**272**	.344
50. **Greg Adams**, N.J., Van., Dal.	753	**271**	.360
51. **Sylvain Turgeon**, Hfd., N.J., Mtl., Ott.	669	**269**	.402
52. **Russ Courtnall**, Tor., Mtl., Min., Dal., Van.	853	**268**	.314
53. **Jeremy Roenick**, Chi.	524	**267**	.510
54. **Alexander Mogilny**, Buf., Van.	460	**266**	.578
55. **Dan Quinn**, Cgy., Pit., Van., St.L., Phi., Min., Ott., L.A.	789	**266**	.337
56. **Dave Gagner**, NYR, Min., Dal., Tor.	717	**265**	.370
57. **Kevin Stevens**, Pit., Bos., L.A.	519	**264**	.509
58. **Claude Lemieux**, Mtl., N.J., Col.	713	**261**	.366
59. **Gary Roberts**, Cgy.	585	**257**	.439
60. **Wendel Clark**, Tor., Que., NYI	571	**252**	.441
61. **Mark Recchi**, Pit., Phi., Mtl.	546	**251**	.460
62. **Larry Murphy**, L.A., Wsh., Min., Pit., Tor.	1234	**245**	.199
63. **Murray Craven**, Det., Phi., Hfd., Van., Chi.	867	**242**	.279
64. **Al MacInnis**, Cgy., St.L.	917	**238**	.260
65. **Adam Oates**, Det., St.L., Bos.	746	**236**	.316
66. **Guy Carbonneau**, Mtl., St.L., Dal.	1025	**234**	.228
67. **Trevor Linden**, Van.	611	**231**	.378
68. **Troy Murray**, Chi., Wpg., Ott., Pit., Colorado	915	**230**	.251
69. **Esa Tikkanen**, Edm., NYR, St.L., N.J., Van.	721	**228**	.316
70. **Mike Modano**, Min., Dal.	501	**221**	.441
71. **Jaromir Jagr**, Pit.	441	**219**	.497
72. **Ulf Dahlen**, NYR, Min., Dal., S.J.	613	**217**	.354
73. **Sergei Fedorov**, Det.	432	**212**	.491
74. **Mark Osborne**, Det., NYR, Tor., Wpg.	919	**212**	.231
75. **Craig MacTavish**, Bos., Edm., NYR, Phi., St.L.	1043	**211**	.202
76. **Peter Zezel**, Phi., St.L., Wsh., Tor., Dal.	749	**204**	.272
77. **Scott Mellanby**, Phi., Edm., Fla.	711	**196**	.276
78. **Shayne Corson**, Mtl., Edm., St.L.	689	**192**	.279
79. **Mats Sundin**, Que., Tor.	447	**191**	.427
80. **Tony Granato**, NYR, L.A.	495	**191**	.386
81. **Ron Sutter**, Phi., St.L., Que., NYI, Bos.	800	**189**	.236
82. **Derek King**, NYI	568	**188**	.331
83. **Peter Bondra**, Wsh.	391	**187**	.478

The only man to lead three different teams in scoring in three consecutive seasons, Vincent Damphousse moved up to 43rd on the NHL's top-100 active goal scoring list after connecting for 38 goals in the 1995-96 season.

Player	Games	Goals	Goals per game
84. **Rod Brind'Amour**, St.L., Phi.	532	**186**	.350
85. **Adam Creighton**, Buf., Chi., NYI, T.B., St.L.	689	**186**	.270
86. **Randy Burridge**, Bos., Wsh., L.A., Buf.	621	**185**	.298
87. **Pavel Bure**, Van.	283	**180**	.636
88. **Joel Otto**, Cgy., Phi.	797	**179**	.225
89. **John Tucker**, Buf., Wsh., NYI, T.B.	656	**177**	.270
90. **Adam Graves**, Det., Edm., NYR	594	**176**	.296
91. **Kevin Hatcher**, Wsh., Dal.	806	**174**	.216
92. **Brian Bradley**, Cgy., Van., Tor., T.B.	602	**173**	.287
93. **Randy Cunneyworth**, Buf., Pit., Wpg., Hfd., Chi., Ott.	705	**173**	.245
94. **Benoit Hogue**, Buf., NYI, Tor., Dal.	544	**172**	.316
95. **John Cullen**, Pit., Hfd., Tor., T.B.	547	**169**	.309
96. **Randy Wood**, NYI, Buf., Dal.	676	**169**	.250
97. **Steve Duchesne**, L.A., Phi., Que., St.L., Ott.	687	**169**	.246
98. **Joe Murphy**, Det., Edm., Chi.	522	**166**	.318
99. **Cliff Ronning**, St.L., Van.	546	**166**	.304
100. **Michal Pivonka**, Wsh.	702	**166**	.236

Top 100 All-Time Assist Leaders

* active player

Player	Seasons	Games	Assists	Assist per game
* 1. **Wayne Gretzky**, Edm., L.A., St.L.	17	1253	**1771**	1.41
2. **Gordie Howe**, Det., Hfd.	26	1767	**1049**	.594
3. **Marcel Dionne**, Det., L.A., NYR	18	1348	**1040**	.772
* 4. **Paul Coffey**, Edm., Pit., L.A., Det. . . .	16	1154	**1038**	.899
* 5. **Ray Bourque**, Bos.	17	1228	**970**	.790
* 6. **Mark Messier**, Edm., NYR	17	1201	**929**	.774
7. **Stan Mikita**, Chi.	22	1394	**926**	.664
8. **Bryan Trottier**, NYI, Pit.	18	1279	**901**	.704
* 9. **Ron Francis**, Hfd., Pit.	15	1085	**881**	.812
10. **Phil Esposito**, Chi., Bos., NYR	18	1282	**873**	.681
* 11. **Dale Hawerchuk**, Wpg., Buf., St.L., Phi.	15	1137	**869**	.764
12. **Bobby Clarke**, Phi.	15	1144	**852**	.745
* 13. **Denis Savard**, Chi., Mtl., T.B.	16	1132	**847**	.748
14. **Alex Delvecchio**, Det.	24	1549	**825**	.533
15. **Gilbert Perreault**, Buf.	17	1191	**814**	.683
16. **John Bucyk**, Det., Bos., ...	23	1540	**813**	.528
* 17. **Mario Lemieux**, Pit.	11	669	**809**	1.21
18. **Guy Lafleur**, Mtl., NYR, Que.	17	1126	**793**	.704
19. **Peter Stastny**, ...	15	977	**789**	.808
20. **Jean Ratelle**, NYR, Bos.	21	1281	**776**	.606
21. **Bernie Federko**, St.L., Det.	14	1000	**761**	.761
* 22. **Larry Murphy**, L.A., Wsh., Min., Pit., Tor.	16	1234	**761**	.617
* 23. **Jari Kurri**, Edm., L.A., NYR	15	1099	**758**	.690
24. **Larry Robinson**, Mtl., L.A.	20	1384	**750**	.542
25. **Denis Potvin**, NYI.	15	1066	**742**	.696
* 26. **Steve Yzerman**, Det.	13	942	**738**	.783
27. **Norm Ullman**, Det., Tor.	20	1410	**719**	.510
28. **Jean Beliveau**, Mtl.	20	1125	**712**	.633
* 29. **Doug Gilmour**, St.L., Cgy., Tor.	13	981	**695**	.708
30. **Henri Richard**, Mtl.	20	1256	**688**	.548
31. **Brad Park**, NYR, Bos., Det.	17	1113	**683**	.614
32. **Bobby Smith**, Min., Mtl.	15	1077	**679**	.630
* 33. **Adam Oates**, Det., St.L., Bos.	11	746	**678**	.909
* 34. **Bernie Nicholls**, L.A., NYR, Edm., N.J., Chi.	15	992	**677**	.682
* 35. **Phil Housley**, Buf., Wpg., St.L., Cgy., N.J.	14	990	**676**	.683
* 36. **Al MacInnis**, Cgy., St.L.	15	917	**673**	.734
37. **Bobby Orr**, Bos., Chi.	12	657	**645**	.982
38. **Dave Taylor**, L.A.	17	1111	**638**	.574
* 39. **Dale Hunter**, Que., Wsh.	16	1181	**638**	.540
40. **Darryl Sittler**, Tor., Phi., Det.	15	1096	**637**	.581
41. **Borje Salming**, Tor., Det.	17	1148	**637**	.555
42. **Andy Bathgate**, NYR, Tor., Det., Pit. .	17	1069	**624**	.584
* 43. **Neal Broten**, Min., Dal., N.J.	16	1057	**622**	.588
44. **Rod Gilbert**, NYR	18	1065	**615**	.577
45. **Michel Goulet**, Que., Chi.	15	1089	**604**	.555
* 46. **Glenn Anderson**, Edm., Tor., NYR, St.L.	16	1129	**601**	.532
47. **Doug Wilson**, Chi., S.J.	16	1024	**590**	.576
48. **Dave Keon**, Tor., Hfd.	18	1296	**590**	.455
* 49. **Mike Gartner**, Wsh., Min., NYR, Tor. . .	17	1290	**581**	.450
50. **Brian Propp**, Phi., Bos., Min., Hfd. . . .	15	1016	**579**	.570
51. **Steve Larmer**, Chi., NYR.	15	1006	**571**	.568
52. **Frank Mahovlich**, Tor., Det., Mtl.	18	1181	**570**	.483
* 53. **Scott Stevens**, Wsh., St.L., N.J.	14	1041	**565**	.543
54. **Bobby Hull**, Chi., Wpg., Hfd.	16	1063	**560**	.527
55. **Mike Bossy**, NYI	10	752	**553**	.735
56. **Thomas Steen**, Wpg.	14	950	**553**	.582
57. **Ken Linseman**, Phi., Edm., Bos., Tor. . .	14	860	**551**	.641
58. **Tom Lysiak**, Atl., Chi.	13	919	**551**	.600
* 59. **Dino Ciccarelli**, Min., Wsh., Det.	16	1079	**549**	.509
* 60. **Joe Mullen**, St.L., Cgy., Pit., Bos.	15	1008	**546**	.542
61. **Mark Howe**, Phi., Hfd., Det.	16	929	**545**	.587
* 62. **Dave Babych**, Wpg., Hfd., Van.	16	1023	**544**	.532
63. **Red Kelly**, Det., Tor.	20	1316	**542**	.412
64. **Rick Middleton**, NYR, Bos.	14	1005	**540**	.537
* 65. **Chris Chelios**, Mtl., Chi.	13	848	**529**	.624
* 66. **Dave Andreychuk**, Buf., Tor., N.J.	14	1001	**527**	.526
67. **Dennis Maruk**, Cal., Clev., Min., Wsh. .	14	888	**522**	.588
68. **Wayne Cashman**, Bos.	17	1027	**516**	.502
* 69. **Gary Suter**, Cgy., Col.	11	763	**514**	.674
70. **Butch Goring**, L.A., NYI, Bos.	16	1107	**513**	.463
71. **John Tonelli**, NYI, Cgy., L.A., Chi., Que.	14	1028	**511**	.497
72. **Lanny McDonald**, Tor., Col., Cgy.	16	1111	**506**	.455
73. **Ivan Boldirev**, Bos., Cal., Chi., Atl., Van., Det.	15	1052	**505**	.480
* 74. **Kirk Muller**, N.J., Mtl., NYI, Tor.	12	886	**502**	.567
* 75. **Pat LaFontaine**, NYI, Buf.	13	785	**500**	.637
* 76. **Brian Bellows**, Min., Mtl., T.B.	14	1032	**500**	.484
77. **Randy Carlyle**, Tor., Pit., Wpg.	17	1055	**499**	.473
78. **Pete Mahovlich**, Det., Mtl., Pit.	16	884	**485**	.549
79. **Pit Martin**, Det., Bos., Chi., Van.	17	1101	**485**	.441
* 80. **Luc Robitaille**, L.A., Pit., NYR	10	763	**476**	.624

Mark Howe, who retired prior to the 1995-96 season after 22 seasons in the WHA and NHL, recorded 545 assists in his NHL career, the 61st-highest total in league history.

Player	Seasons	Games	Assists	Assists per game
81. **Ken Hodge**, Chi., Bos., NYR	13	881	**472**	.536
82. **Ted Lindsay**, Det., Chi.	17	1068	**472**	.442
83. **Jacques Lemaire**, Mtl.	12	853	**469**	.550
84. **Dean Prentice**, Pit., Min., Det., NYR, Bos.	22	1378	**469**	.340
85. **Phil Goyette**, Mtl., NYR, St.L., Buf. . . .	16	941	**467**	.496
86. **Bill Barber**, Phi.	12	903	**463**	.513
87. **Reed Larson**, Det., Bos., Edm., NYI, Min., Buf.	14	904	**463**	.512
88. **Doug Mohns**, Bos., Chi., Min., Atl., Wsh.	22	1390	**462**	.332
* 89. **Joe Sakic**, Que., Col.	8	590	**461**	.781
* 90. **Pierre Turgeon**, Buf., NYI, Mtl.	9	672	**461**	.686
* 91. **Craig Janney**, Bos., St.L., S.J., Wpg. . . .	9	559	**460**	.823
92. **Bobby Rousseau**, Mtl., Min., NYR.	15	942	**458**	.486
93. **Wilf Paiement**, K.C. Col., Tor., Que., NYR, Buf., Pit.	14	946	**458**	.484
* 94. **Vincent Damphousse**, Tor., Edm., Mtl. .	10	770	**457**	.594
95. **Murray Oliver**, Det., Bos., Tor., Min. . . .	17	1127	**454**	.403
* 96. **Brent Sutter**, NYI, Chi.	16	1020	**453**	.444
97. **Doug Harvey**, Mtl., NYR, Det., St.L. . . .	20	1113	**452**	.406
98. **Guy Lapointe**, Mtl., St.L., Bos.	16	884	**451**	.510
99. **Walt Tkaczuk**, NYR.	14	945	**451**	.477
100. **Peter McNab**, Buf., Bos., Van., N.J.	14	954	**450**	.472

Top 100 Active Assist Leaders

	Player	Games	Assists	Assists per game
1.	**Wayne Gretzky**, Edm., L.A., St.L.	1253	**1771**	1.413
2.	**Paul Coffey**, Edm., Pit., L.A., Det.	1154	**1038**	.899
3.	**Ray Bourque**, Bos.	1228	**970**	.790
4.	**Mark Messier**, Edm., NYR	1201	**929**	.774
5.	**Ron Francis**, Hfd., Pit.	1085	**881**	.812
6.	**Dale Hawerchuk**, Wpg., Buf., St.L., Phi.	1137	**869**	.764
7.	**Denis Savard**, Chi., Mtl., T.B.	1132	**847**	.748
8.	**Mario Lemieux**, Pit.	669	**809**	1.209
9.	**Larry Murphy**, L.A., Wsh., Min., Pit., Tor.	1234	**761**	.617
10.	**Jari Kurri**, Edm., L.A., NYR	1099	**758**	.690
11.	**Steve Yzerman**, Det.	942	**738**	.783
12.	**Doug Gilmour**, St.L., Cgy., Tor.	981	**695**	.708
13.	**Adam Oates**, Det., St.L., Bos.	746	**678**	.909
14.	**Bernie Nicholls**, L.A., NYR, Edm., N.J., Chi. . . .	992	**677**	.682
15.	**Phil Housley**, Buf., Wpg., St.L., Cgy., N.J.	990	**676**	.683
16.	**Al MacInnis**, Cgy., St.L.	917	**673**	.734
17.	**Dale Hunter**, Que., Wsh.	1181	**638**	.540
18.	**Neal Broten**, Min., Dal., N.J.	1057	**622**	.588
19.	**Glenn Anderson**, Edm., Tor., NYR, St.L.	1129	**601**	.532
20.	**Mike Gartner**, Wsh., Min., NYR, Tor.	1290	**581**	.450
21.	**Scott Stevens**, Wsh., St.L., N.J.	1041	**565**	.543
22.	**Dino Ciccarelli**, Min., Wsh., Det.	1079	**549**	.509
23.	**Joe Mullen**, St.L., Cgy., Pit., Bos.	1008	**546**	.542
24.	**Dave Babych**, Wpg., Hfd., Van.	1023	**544**	.532
25.	**Chris Chelios**, Mtl., Chi.	848	**529**	.624
26.	**Dave Andreychuk**, Buf., Tor., N.J.	1001	**527**	.526
27.	**Gary Suter**, Cgy., Chi.	763	**514**	.674
28	**Kirk Muller**, N.J., Mtl., NYI, Tor.	886	**502**	.567
29.	**Pat LaFontaine**, NYI, Buf.	785	**500**	.637
30.	**Brian Bellows**, Min., Mtl., T.B.	1032	**500**	.484
31.	**Luc Robitaille**, L.A., Pit., NYR	763	**476**	.624
32.	**Joe Sakic**, Que., Colorado	590	**461**	.781
33.	**Pierre Turgeon**, Buf., NYI, Mtl.	672	**461**	.686
34.	**Craig Janney**, Bos., St.L., S.J., Wpg.	559	**460**	.823
35.	**Vincent Damphousse**, Tor., Edm., Mtl.	770	**457**	.594
36.	**Brent Sutter**, NYI, Chi.	1020	**453**	.444
37.	**Brian Leetch**, NYR	567	**445**	.785
38.	**Murray Craven**, Det., Phi., Hfd., Van., Chi.	867	**437**	.504
39.	**Mike Ridley**, NYR, Wsh., Tor., Van.	791	**434**	.549
40.	**Dave Christian**, Wpg., Wsh., Bos., St.L., Chi. . . .	1009	**433**	.429
41.	**James Patrick**, NYR, Hfd., Cgy.	856	**427**	.499
42.	**Dan Quinn**, Cgy., Pit., Van., St.L., Phi., Min., Ott., L.A.	789	**416**	.527
43	**Tomas Sandstrom**, NYR, L.A., Pit.	774	**413**	.534
44.	**Pat Verbeek**, N.J., Hfd., NYR	984	**408**	.415
45.	**Jeff Brown**, Que., St.L., Van., Hfd.	686	**406**	.592
46.	**Russ Courtnall**, Tor., Mtl., Min., Dal., Van.	853	**404**	.474
47.	**Rick Tocchet**, Phi., Pit., L.A., Bos.	788	**398**	.505
48.	**Ed Olczyk**, Chi., Tor., Wpg., NYR	802	**394**	.491
49.	**Michal Pivonka**, Wsh.	702	**390**	.556
50.	**Mark Recchi**, Pit., Phi., Mtl.	546	**384**	.703
51.	**Doug Bodger**, Pit., Buf., S.J.	835	**384**	.460
52.	**Bob Carpenter**, Wsh., NYR, L.A., Bos., N.J.	994	**376**	.378
53.	**Steve Duchesne**, L.A., Phi., Que., Ott.	687	**366**	.533
54.	**Dave Ellett**, Wpg., Tor.	865	**366**	.423
55.	**Garry Galley**, L.A., Wsh., Bos., Phi., Buf.	818	**365**	.446
56.	**Peter Zezel**, Phi., St.L., Wsh., Tor., Dal.	749	**354**	.473
57.	**Troy Murray**, Chi., Wpg., Ott., Pit., Colorado . .	915	**354**	.387
58.	**Charlie Huddy**, Edm., L.A., Buf., St.L.	1016	**354**	.348
59.	**Geoff Courtnall**, Bos., Edm., Wsh., St.L., Van. . .	857	**352**	.411
60.	**Guy Carbonneau**, Mtl., St.L., Dal.	1025	**352**	.343
61.	**Bruce Driver**, N.J., NYR	768	**350**	.456
62.	**Brett Hull**, Cgy., St.L.	658	**348**	.529
63.	**Esa Tikkanen**, Edm., NYR, St.L., N.J., Van.	721	**348**	.483
64.	**Ray Ferraro**, Hfd., NYI, NYR, L.A.	834	**347**	.416
65.	**Steve Thomas**, Tor., Chi., NYI, N.J.	748	**343**	.459
66.	**Theoren Fleury**, Cgy.	568	**338**	.595
67.	**Kevin Lowe**, Edm., NYR	1183	**334**	.282
68.	**Jeremy Roenick**, Chi.	524	**329**	.628
69.	**Pat Flatley**, NYI	712	**328**	.461
70.	**Kevin Dineen**, Hfd., Phi.	793	**327**	.412
71.	**John Cullen**, Pit., Hfd., Tor., T.B.	547	**326**	.596
72.	**Kevin Hatcher**, Wsh., Dal.	806	**322**	.400
73.	**John MacLean**, N.J.	828	**321**	.388
74.	**Joe Nieuwendyk**, Cgy., Dal.	629	**320**	.509
75.	**Jaromir Jagr**, Pit.	441	**319**	.723
76.	**Mark Osborne**, Det., NYR, Tor., Wpg.	919	**319**	.347
77.	**Dave Gagner**, NYR, Min., Dal., Tor.	717	**318**	.444
78.	**Sergei Fedorov**, Det.	432	**317**	.734
79.	**Brad McCrimmon**, Bos., Phi., Cgy., Det., Hfd. . .	1185	**317**	.268
80.	**Rod Brind'Amour**, St.L., Phi.	532	**310**	.583
81.	**Brendan Shanahan**, N.J., St.L., Hfd.	632	**310**	.491
82.	**Stephane J. J. Richer**, Mtl., N.J.	763	**302**	.396
83.	**Fredrik Olausson**, Wpg., Edm., Ana.	640	**300**	.469

Chris Chelios, the 1996 Norris Trophy winner as the league's top rearguard, stands 25th on the NHL's top-100 active assists leaders with 529 helpers.

	Player	Games	Assists	Assists per game
84.	**Ron Sutter**, Phi., St.L., Que., NYI, Bos.	800	**300**	.375
85.	**Kevin Stevens**, Pit., Bos., L.A.	519	**299**	.576
86.	**Brian Bradley**, Cgy., Van., Tor., T.B.	602	**299**	.497
87.	**Cam Neely**, Van., Bos.	726	**299**	.412
88.	**Christian Ruuttu**, Buf., Chi., Van.	621	**298**	.480
89.	**Al Iafrate**, Tor., Wsh., Bos.	740	**295**	.399
90.	**Calle Johansson**, Buf., Wsh.	645	**292**	.453
91.	**Greg Adams**, N.J., Van., Dal.	753	**292**	.388
92.	**Mike Modano**, Min., Dal.	501	**291**	.581
93.	**Joel Otto**, Cgy., Phi.	797	**290**	.364
94.	**Cliff Ronning**, St.L., Van.	546	**287**	.526
95.	**Jimmy Carson**, L.A., Edm., Det., Van., Hfd.	626	**286**	.457
96.	**Alexander Mogilny**, Buf., Van.	460	**285**	.620
97.	**Steve Smith**, Edm., Chi.	681	**283**	.416
98.	**Shayne Corson**, Mtl., Edm., St.L.	689	**278**	.403
99.	**Trevor Linden**, Van.	611	**277**	.453
100.	**Mats Sundin**, Que., Tor.	447	**273**	.611

Top 100 All-Time Point Leaders

* active player

Player	Seasons	Games	Goal	s		Goals per game
* 1. Wayne Gretzky, Edm., L.A., St.L.	17	1253	837	1771	**2608**	2.08
2. Gordie Howe, Det., Hfd.	26	1767	801	1049	**1846**	1.05
3. Marcel Dionne, Det., L.A., NYR	18	1348	731	1040	**1771**	1.31
4. Phil Esposito, Chi., Bos., NYR	18	1282	717	873	**1590**	1.24
* 5. Mark Messier, Edm., NYR	17	1201	539	929	**1468**	1.22
6. Stan Mikita, Chi.	22	1394	541	926	**1467**	1.05
7. Bryan Trottier, NYI, Pit.	18	1279	524	901	**1425**	1.11
* 8. Paul Coffey, Edm., Pit., L.A., Det.	16	1154	372	1038	**1410**	1.22
* 9. Dale Hawerchuk, Wpg., Buf., St.L., Phi.	15	1137	506	869	**1375**	1.21
* 10. Mario Lemieux, Pit.	11	669	563	809	**1372**	2.05
11. John Bucyk, Det., Bos.	23	1540	556	813	**1369**	.889
12. Guy Lafleur, Mtl., NYR, Que.	17	1126	560	793	**1353**	1.20
* 13. Jari Kurri, Edm., L.A., NYR	15	1099	583	758	**1341**	1.22
14. Gilbert Perreault, Buf.	17	1191	512	814	**1326**	1.11
* 15. Ray Bourque, Bos.	17	1228	343	970	**1313**	1.07
* 16. Denis Savard, Chi., Mtl., T.B.	16	1132	464	847	**1311**	1.16
17. Alex Delvecchio, Det.	24	1549	456	825	**1281**	.827
18. Jean Ratelle, NYR, Bos.	21	1281	491	776	**1267**	.989
* 19. Ron Francis, Hfd., Pit.	15	1085	376	881	**1257**	1.16
* 20. Steve Yzerman, Det.	13	942	517	738	**1255**	1.33
* 21. Mike Gartner, Wsh., Min., NYR, Tor.	17	1290	664	581	**1245**	.965
22. Peter Stastny	15	977	450	789	**1239**	1.27
23. Jean Beliveau, Mtl.	20	1125	507	712	**1219**	1.08
24. Bobby Clarke, Phi.	15	1144	358	852	**1210**	1.06
25. Norm Ullman, Det., Tor.	20	1410	476	719	**1195**	.848
26. Bobby Hull, Chi., Wpg., Hfd.	16	1063	610	560	**1170**	1.10
27. Michel Goulet, Que., Chi.	15	1089	548	604	**1152**	1.06
* 28. Bernie Nicholls, L.A., NYR, Edm., N.J., Chi.	15	992	457	677	**1134**	1.14
29. Bernie Federko, St.L., Det.	14	1000	369	761	**1130**	1.13
30. Mike Bossy, NYI	10	752	573	553	**1126**	1.50
31. Darryl Sittler, Tor., Phi., Det.	15	1096	484	637	**1121**	1.02
32. Frank Mahovlich, Tor., Det., Mtl.	18	1181	533	570	**1103**	.934
* 33. Dino Ciccarelli, Min., Wsh., Det.	16	1079	551	549	**1100**	1.02
* 34. Glenn Anderson, Edm., Tor., NYR, St.L.	16	1129	498	601	**1099**	.973
35. Dave Taylor, L.A.	17	1111	431	638	**1069**	.962
36. Denis Potvin, NYI	15	1066	310	742	**1052**	.987
37. Henri Richard, Mtl.	20	1256	358	688	**1046**	.833
* 38. Doug Gilmour, St.L., Cgy., Tor.	13	981	346	695	**1041**	1.06
* 39. Joe Mullen, St.L., Cgy., Pit., Bos.	16	1008	495	546	**1041**	1.03
40. Bobby Smith, Min., Mtl.	15	1077	357	679	**1036**	.962
41. Rod Gilbert, NYR	18	1065	406	615	**1021**	.959
42. Steve Larmer, Chi., NYR	15	1006	441	571	**1012**	1.01
43. Lanny McDonald, Tor., Col., Cgy.	16	1111	500	506	**1006**	.905
* 44. Larry Murphy, L.A., Wsh., Min., Pit., Tor.	16	1234	245	761	**1006**	.815
45. Brian Propp, Phi., Bos., Min., Hfd.	15	1016	425	579	**1004**	.988
* 46. Dave Andreychuk, Buf., Tor., N.J.	14	1001	476	527	**1003**	1.00
47. Rick Middleton, NYR, Bos.	14	1005	448	540	**988**	.983
48. Dave Keon, Tor., Hfd.	18	1296	396	590	**986**	.761
49. Andy Bathgate, NYR, Tor., Det., Pit.	17	1069	349	624	**973**	.910
50. Maurice Richard, Mtl.	18	978	544	421	**965**	.987
51. Larry Robinson, Mtl., L.A.	20	1384	208	750	**958**	.692
* 52. Phil Housley, Buf., Wpg., St.L., Cgy., N.J.	14	990	274	676	**950**	.960
* 53. Brian Bellows, Min., Mtl., T.B.	14	1032	446	500	**946**	.917
* 54. Pat LaFontaine, NYI, Buf.	13	785	443	500	**943**	1.20
* 55. Dale Hunter, Que., Wsh.	16	1181	299	638	**937**	.793
56. Bobby Orr, Bos., Chi.	12	657	270	645	**915**	1.39
* 57. Adam Oates, Det., St.L., Bos.	11	746	236	678	**914**	1.23
* 58. Luc Robitaille, L.A., Pit., NYR	10	763	438	476	**914**	1.20
* 59. Al MacInnis, Cgy., St.L.	15	917	238	673	**911**	.993
* 60. Neal Broten, Min., Dal., N.J.	16	1057	281	622	**903**	.854
61. Brad Park, NYR, Bos., Det.	17	1113	213	683	**896**	.805
62. Butch Goring, L.A., NYI, Bos.	16	1107	375	513	**888**	.802
63. Bill Barber, Phi.	12	903	420	463	**883**	.978
64. Dennis Maruk, Cal., Clev., Min., Wsh.	14	888	356	522	**878**	.989
65. Ivan Boldirev, Bos., Cal., Chi., Atl., Van., Det.	15	1052	361	505	**866**	.823

Norm Ullman, a 20-year NHL veteran who suited up with Toronto and Detroit, scored a league-high 42 goals in 1964-65. He still stands 25th on the NHL's all-time career goal-scoring chart.

Player	Seasons	Games	Goals	Assists	Points	Points per game
66. Yvan Cournoyer, Mtl.	16	968	428	435	**863**	.892
67. Dean Prentice, Pit., Min., Det., NYR, Bos.	22	1378	391	469	**860**	.624
68. Ted Lindsay, Det., Chi.	17	1068	379	472	**851**	.797
69. Tom Lysiak, Atl., Chi.	13	919	292	551	**843**	.917
70. John Tonelli, NYI, Cgy., L.A., Chi., Que.	14	1028	325	511	**836**	.813
71. Jacques Lemaire, Mtl.	12	853	366	469	**835**	.979
* 72. Brett Hull, Cgy., St.L.	10	658	485	348	**833**	1.27
73. John Ogrodnick, Det., Que., NYR	14	928	402	425	**827**	.891
74. Doug Wilson, Chi., S.J.	16	1024	237	590	**827**	.808
75. Red Kelly, Det., Tor.	20	1316	281	542	**823**	.625
76. Pierre Larouche, Pit., Mtl., Hfd., NYR	14	812	395	427	**822**	1.01
77. Bernie Geoffrion, Mtl., NYR	16	883	393	429	**822**	.931
* 78. Pat Verbeek, N.J., Hfd., NYR	14	984	413	408	**821**	.834
79. Steve Shutt, Mtl., L.A.	13	930	424	393	**817**	.878
80. Thomas Steen, Wpg.	14	950	264	553	**817**	.860
81. Wilf Paiement, K.C., Col., Tor., Que., NYR, Buf., Pit.	14	946	356	458	**814**	.860
82. Peter McNab, Buf., Bos., Van., N.J.	14	954	363	450	**813**	.852
83. Pit Martin, Det., Bos., Chi., Van.	17	1101	324	485	**809**	.735
84. Ken Linseman, Phi., Edm., Bos., Tor.	14	860	256	551	**807**	.938
* 85. Kirk Muller, N.J., Mtl., NYI, Tor.	12	886	305	502	**807**	.911
* 86. Brent Sutter, NYI, Chi.	16	1020	354	453	**807**	.791
87. Garry Unger, Tor., Det., St.L., Atl., L.A., Edm.	16	1105	413	391	**804**	.728
88. Ken Hodge, Chi., Bos., NYR	13	881	328	472	**800**	.908
89. Wayne Cashman, Bos.	17	1027	277	516	**793**	.772
90. Rick Vaive, Van., Tor., Chi., Buf.	13	876	441	347	**788**	.900
91. Borje Salming, Tor., Det.	17	1148	150	637	**787**	.686
* 92. Pierre Turgeon, Buf., NYI, Mtl.	9	672	318	461	**779**	1.16
93. Jean Pronovost, Wsh., Pit., Atl.	14	998	391	383	**774**	.776
94. Pete Mahovlich, Det., Mtl., Pit.	16	884	288	485	**773**	.874
* 95. Dave Christian, Wpg., Wsh., Bos., St.L., Chi.	15	1009	340	433	**773**	.766
96. Rick Kehoe, Tor., Pit.	14	906	371	396	**767**	.847
* 97. Tomas Sandstrom, NYR, L.A., Pit.	12	774	352	413	**765**	.988
98. Rick MacLeish, Phi., Hfd., Pit., Det.	14	846	349	410	**759**	.897
* 99. Joe Sakic, Que., Col.	8	590	285	461	**746**	1.26
100. Mark Howe, Hfd., Phi., Det.	16	929	197	545	**742**	.799

Top 100 Active Points Leaders

Player	Games	Goals	Assists	Points	Points per game
1. **Wayne Gretzky**, Edm., L.A., St.L.	1253	837	1771	**2608**	2.081
2. **Mark Messier**, Edm., NYR	1201	539	929	**1468**	1.222
3. **Paul Coffey**, Edm., Pit., L.A., Det.	1154	372	1038	**1410**	1.222
4. **Dale Hawerchuk**, Wpg., Buf., St.L., Phi.	1137	506	869	**1375**	1.209
5. **Mario Lemieux**, Pit.	669	563	809	**1372**	2.051
6. **Jari Kurri**, Edm., L.A., NYR	1099	583	758	**1341**	1.220
7. **Ray Bourque**, Bos.	1228	343	970	**1313**	1.069
8. **Denis Savard**, Chi., Mtl., T.B.	1132	464	847	**1311**	1.158
9. **Ron Francis**, Hfd., Pit.	1085	376	881	**1257**	1.159
10. **Steve Yzerman**, Det.	942	517	738	**1255**	1.332
11. **Mike Gartner**, Wsh., Min., NYR, Tor.	1290	664	581	**1245**	.965
12. **Bernie Nicholls**, L.A., NYR, Edm., N.J., Chi.	992	457	677	**1134**	1.143
13. **Dino Ciccarelli**, Min., Wsh., Det.	1079	551	549	**1100**	1.019
14. **Glenn Anderson**, Edm., Tor., NYR, St.L.	1129	498	601	**1099**	.973
15. **Doug Gilmour**, St.L., Cgy., Tor.	981	346	695	**1041**	1.061
16. **Joe Mullen**, St.L., Cgy., Pit., Bos.	1008	495	546	**1041**	1.033
17. **Larry Murphy**, L.A., Wsh., Min., Pit., Tor.	1234	245	761	**1006**	.815
18. **Dave Andreychuk**, Buf., Tor., N.J.	1001	476	527	**1003**	1.002
19. **Phil Housley**, Buf., Wpg., St.L., Cgy., N.J.	990	274	676	**950**	.960
20. **Brian Bellows**, Min., Mtl., T.B.	1032	446	500	**946**	.917
21. **Pat LaFontaine**, NYI, Buf.	785	443	500	**943**	1.201
22. **Dale Hunter**, Que., Wsh.	1181	299	638	**937**	.793
23. **Adam Oates**, Det., St.L., Bos.	746	236	678	**914**	1.225
24. **Luc Robitaille**, L.A., Pit., NYR	763	438	476	**914**	1.198
25. **Al MacInnis**, Cgy., St.L.	917	238	673	**911**	.993
26. **Neal Broten**, Min., Dal., N.J.	1057	281	622	**903**	.854
27. **Brett Hull**, Cgy., St.L.	658	485	348	**833**	1.266
28. **Pat Verbeek**, N.J., Hfd., NYR	984	413	408	**821**	.834
29. **Kirk Muller**, N.J., Mtl., NYI, Tor.	886	305	502	**807**	.911
30. **Brent Sutter**, NYI, Chi.	1020	354	453	**807**	.791
31. **Pierre Turgeon**, Buf., NYI, Mtl.	672	318	461	**779**	1.159
32. **Dave Christian**, Wpg., Wsh., Bos., St.L., Chi.	1009	340	433	**773**	.766
33. **Tomas Sandstrom**, NYR, L.A., Pit.	774	352	413	**765**	.988
34. **Joe Sakic**, Que., Colorado	590	285	461	**746**	1.264
35. **Vincent Damphousse**, Tor., Edm., Mtl.	770	283	457	**740**	.961
36. **Rick Tocchet**, Phi., Pit., L.A., Bos.	788	338	398	**736**	.934
37. **Scott Stevens**, Wsh., St.L., N.J.	1041	157	565	**722**	.694
38. **Mike Ridley**, NYR, Wsh., Tor., Van.	791	272	434	**706**	.893
39. **Cam Neely**, Van., Bos.	726	395	299	**694**	.956
40. **Ed Olczyk**, Chi., Tor., Wpg., NYR	802	294	394	**688**	.858
41. **Dan Quinn**, Cgy., Pit., Van., St.L., Phi., Min., Ott., L.A.	789	266	416	**682**	.864
42. **Bob Carpenter**, Wsh., NYR, L.A., Bos., N.J.	994	305	376	**681**	.685
43. **Murray Craven**, Det., Phi., Hfd., Van., Chi.	867	242	437	**679**	.783
44. **Dave Babych**, Wpg., Hfd., Van.	1023	135	544	**679**	.664
45. **Gary Suter**, Cgy., Chi.	763	160	514	**674**	.883
46. **Chris Chelios**, Mtl., Chi.	848	143	529	**672**	.792
47. **Russ Courtnall**, Tor., Mtl., Min., Dal., Van.	853	268	404	**672**	.788
48. **Geoff Courtnall**, Bos., Edm., Wsh., St.L., Van.	857	312	352	**664**	.775
49. **Ray Ferraro**, Hfd., NYI, NYR, L.A.	834	302	347	**649**	.778
50. **Joe Nieuwendyk**, Cgy., Dal.	629	328	320	**648**	1.030
51. **Stephane J. J. Richer**, Mtl., N.J.	763	344	302	**646**	.847
52. **Steve Thomas**, Tor., Chi., NYI, N.J.	748	295	343	**638**	.853
53. **John MacLean**, N.J.	828	315	321	**636**	.768
54. **Mark Recchi**, Pit., Phi., Mtl.	546	251	384	**635**	1.163
55. **Kevin Dineen**, Hfd., Phi.	793	304	327	**631**	.796
56. **Craig Janney**, Bos., St.L., S.J., Wpg.	559	158	460	**618**	1.106
57. **Theoren Fleury**, Cgy.	568	278	338	**616**	1.085
58. **Brendan Shanahan**, N.J., St.L., Hfd.	632	288	310	**598**	.946
59. **Jeremy Roenick**, Chi.	524	267	329	**596**	1.137
60. **Guy Carbonneau**, Mtl., St.L., Dal.	1025	234	352	**586**	.572
61. **Troy Murray**, Chi., Wpg., Ott., Pit., Col.	915	230	354	**584**	.638
62. **Dave Gagner**, NYR, Min., Dal., Tor.	717	265	318	**583**	.813
63. **Esa Tikkanen**, Edm., NYR, St.L., N.J., Van.	721	228	348	**576**	.799
64. **Brian Leetch**, NYR	567	127	445	**572**	1.009
65. **Kevin Stevens**, Pit., Bos., L.A.	519	264	299	**563**	1.085
66. **Greg Adams**, N.J., Van., Dal.	753	271	292	**563**	.748
67. **Jimmy Carson**, L.A., Edm., Det., Van., Hfd.	626	275	286	**561**	.896
68. **Petr Klima**, Det., Edm., T.B.	740	310	248	**558**	.754
69. **Peter Zezel**, Phi., St.L., Wsh., Tor., Dal.	749	204	354	**558**	.745
70. **Jeff Brown**, Que., St.L., Van., Hfd.	686	150	406	**556**	.810
71. **Michal Pivonka**, Wsh.	702	166	390	**556**	.792
72. **Alexander Mogilny**, Buf., Van.	460	266	285	**551**	1.198
73. **James Patrick**, NYR, Hfd., Cgy.	856	117	427	**544**	.636
74. **Jaromir Jagr**, Pit.	441	219	319	**538**	1.220
75. **Steve Duchesne**, L.A., Phi., Que., St.L., Van.	687	169	366	**535**	.779
76. **Mark Osborne**, Det., NYR, Tor., Wpg.	919	212	319	**531**	.578
77. **Sergei Fedorov**, Det.	432	212	317	**529**	1.225
78. **Claude Lemieux**, Mtl., N.J., Col.	713	261	258	**519**	.728
79. **Mike Modano**, Min., Dal.	501	221	291	**512**	1.022
80. **Trevor Linden**, Van.	611	231	277	**508**	.831
81. **Dave Ellett**, Wpg., Tor.	865	142	366	**508**	.587
82. **Gary Roberts**, Cgy.	585	257	248	**505**	.863
83. **Rod Brind'Amour**, St.L., Phi.	532	186	310	**496**	.932
84. **Kevin Hatcher**, Wsh., Dal.	806	174	322	**496**	.615
85. **John Cullen**, Pit., Hfd., Tor., T.B.	547	169	326	**495**	.905
86. **Sylvain Turgeon**, Hfd., N.J., Mtl., Ott.	669	269	226	**495**	.740
87. **Ron Sutter**, Phi., St.L., Que., NYI, Bos.	800	189	300	**489**	.611
88. **Pat Flatley**, NYI.	712	160	328	**488**	.685
89. **Ray Sheppard**, Buf., NYR, Det., S.J., Fla.	557	275	207	**482**	.865
90. **Doug Bodger**, Pit., Buf., S.J.	835	93	384	**477**	.571
91. **Craig MacTavish**, Bos., Edm., NYR, Phi., St.L.	1043	211	262	**473**	.453
92. **Brian Bradley**, Cgy., Van., Tor., T.B.	602	173	299	**472**	.784
93. **Shayne Corson**, Mtl., Edm., St.L.	689	192	278	**470**	.682
94. **Joel Otto**, Cgy., Phi.	797	179	290	**469**	.588
95. **Mats Sundin**, Que., Tor.	447	191	273	**464**	1.038
96. **Garry Galley**, L.A., Wsh., Bos., Phi., Buf.	818	93	365	**458**	.560
97. **Cliff Ronning**, St.L., Van.	546	166	287	**453**	.830
98. **Charlie Huddy**, Edm., L.A., Buf., St.L.	1016	99	354	**453**	.446
99. **Ulf Dahlen**, NYR, Min., Dal., S.J.	613	217	230	**447**	.729
100. **Derek King**, NYI	568	188	258	**446**	.785

Mark Messier, who is second among active scorers with 1468 points, climbed past Stan Mikita into fifth place on the NHL's all-time scoring ladder with a goal in the Rangers' 3-1 win over New Jersey on April 2, 1996.

All-Time Games Played Leaders

Regular Season

* active player

#	Player	Team	Seasons	GP
1.	Gordie Howe	Detroit	25	1,687
		Hartford	1	80
		Total	**26**	**1,767**
2.	Alex Delvecchio	Detroit	24	1,549
3.	John Bucyk	Detroit	2	104
		Boston	21	1,436
		Total	**23**	**1,540**
4.	Tim Horton	Toronto	19¾	1,185
		NY Rangers	1¼	93
		Pittsburgh	1	44
		Buffalo	2	124
		Total	**24**	**1,446**
5.	Harry Howell	NY Rangers	17	1,160
		California	1½	83
		Los Angeles	2½	168
		Total	**21**	**1,411**
6.	Norm Ullman	Detroit	12½	875
		Toronto	7½	535
		Total	**20**	**1,410**
7.	Stan Mikita	**Chicago**	**22**	**1,394**
8.	Doug Mohns	Boston	11	710
		Chicago	6½	415
		Minnesota	2½	162
		Atlanta	1	28
		Washington	1	75
		Total	**22**	**1,390**
9.	Larry Robinson	Montreal	17	1,202
		Los Angeles	3	182
		Total	**20**	**1,384**
10.	Dean Prentice	NY Rangers	10½	666
		Boston	3	170
		Detroit	3½	230
		Pittsburgh	2	144
		Minnesota	3	168
		Total	**22**	**1,378**
11.	Ron Stewart	Toronto	13	838
		Boston	2	126
		St. Louis	½	19
		NY Rangers	4	306
		Vancouver	1	42
		NY Islanders	½	22
		Total	**21**	**1,353**
12.	Marcel Dionne	Detroit	4	309
		Los Angeles	11¾	921
		NY Rangers	2¼	118
		Total	**18**	**1,348**
13.	Red Kelly	Detroit	12½	846
		Toronto	7½	470
		Total	**20**	**1,316**
14.	Dave Keon	Toronto	15	1,062
		Hartford	3	234
		Total	**18**	**1,296**
* 15.	Mike Gartner	Washington	9¾	758
		Minnesota	1	80
		NY Rangers	4	322
		Toronto	2¼	120
		Total	**17**	**1,290**
16.	Phil Esposito	Chicago	4	235
		Boston	8¼	625
		NY Rangers	5¾	422
		Total	**18**	**1,282**
17.	Jean Ratelle	NY Rangers	15¼	862
		Boston	5¾	419
		Total	**21**	**1,281**
18.	Bryan Trottier	NY Islanders	15	1,123
		Pittsburgh	3	156
		Total	**18**	**1,279**
19.	Henri Richard	**Montreal**	**20**	**1,256**
* 20.	Wayne Gretzky	Edmonton	9	696
		Los Angeles	7¾	539
		St. Louis	¼	18
		Total	**17**	**1,253**
21.	Bill Gadsby	Chicago	8½	468
		NY Rangers	6½	457
		Detroit	5	323
		Total	**20**	**1,248**
22.	Allan Stanley	NY Rangers	6¼	307
		Chicago	1¾	111
		Boston	2	129
		Toronto	9	633
		Philadelphia	1	64
		Total	**21**	**1,244**
* 23.	Larry Murphy	Los Angeles	3¼	242
		Washington	5½	453
		Minnesota	1¾	121
		Pittsburgh	4½	336
		Toronto	1	82
		Total	**16**	**1,234**
* 24.	Ray Bourque	**Boston**	**17**	**1,228**
25.	Eddie Westfall	Boston	11	734
		NY Islanders	7	493
		Total	**18**	**1,227**
26.	Eric Nesterenko	Toronto	5	206
		Chicago	16	1,013
		Total	**21**	**1,219**
27.	Marcel Pronovost	Detroit	16	983
		Toronto	5	223
		Total	**21**	**1,206**
* 28.	Mark Messier	Edmonton	12	851
		NY Rangers	5	350
		Total	**17**	**1,201**
29.	Gilbert Perreault	**Buffalo**	**17**	**1,191**
30.	George Armstrong	**Toronto**	**21**	**1,187**
* 31.	Brad McCrimmon	Boston	3	228
		Philadelphia	5	367
		Calgary	3	231
		Detroit	3	203
		Hartford	3	156
		Total	**17**	**1,185**
* 32.	Kevin Lowe	Edmonton	13	966
		NY Rangers	4	217
		Total	**17**	**1,183**
33.	Frank Mahovlich	Toronto	11¾	720
		Detroit	2¾	198
		Montreal	3½	263
		Total	**18**	**1,181**
* 34.	Dale Hunter	Quebec	7	523
		Washington	9	658
		Total	**16**	**1,181**
35.	Don Marshall	Montreal	10	585
		NY Rangers	7	479
		Buffalo	1	62
		Toronto	1	50
		Total	**19**	**1,176**
36.	Bob Gainey	**Montreal**	**16**	**1,160**
* 37.	Paul Coffey	Edmonton	7	532
		Pittsburgh	4¾	331
		Los Angeles	¾	60
		Detroit	3½	231
		Total	**16**	**1,154**
38.	Leo Boivin	Toronto	3¼	137
		Boston	11½	717
		Detroit	1¼	85
		Pittsburgh	1½	114
		Minnesota	1½	97
		Total	**19**	**1,150**
39.	Borje Salming	Toronto	16	1,099
		Detroit	1	49
		Total	**17**	**1,148**
40.	Bobby Clarke	**Philadelphia**	**15**	**1,144**
* 41.	Dale Hawerchuk	Winnipeg	9	713
		Buffalo	5	342
		St. Louis	¾	66
		Philadelphia	¼	16
		Total	**15**	**1,137**
* 42.	Denis Savard	Chicago	11¼	817
		Montreal	3	210
		Tampa Bay	1¾	105
		Total	**16**	**1,132**
* 43.	Glenn Anderson	Edmonton	11½	845
		Toronto	2¾	221
		NY Rangers	¼	12
		St. Louis	1½	51
		Total	**16**	**1,129**
44.	Bob Nevin	Toronto	5¾	250
		NY Rangers	7¼	505
		Minnesota	3	138
		Los Angeles	3	235
		Total	**18**	**1,128**
45.	Murray Oliver	Detroit	2½	101
		Boston	6½	429
		Toronto	3	226
		Minnesota	5	371
		Total	**17**	**1,127**
46.	Guy Lafleur	Montreal	14	961
		NY Rangers	1	67
		Quebec	2	98
		Total	**17**	**1,126**
47.	Jean Beliveau	**Montreal**	**20**	**1,125**
48.	Doug Harvey	Montreal	14	890
		NY Rangers	3	151
		Detroit	1	2
		St. Louis	1	70
		Total	**19**	**1,113**
49.	Brad Park	NY Rangers	7½	465
		Boston	7½	501
		Detroit	2	147
		Total	**17**	**1,113**

George Armstrong and Gordie Howe, who both played their first NHL games in the 1940s and continued to play into the 1970s, combined to play 47 seasons and 2954 games during their remarkable Hall-of-Fame careers.

	Player	Team	Seasons	GP
50.	Lanny McDonald	Toronto	6½	477
		Colorado	1¾	142
		Calgary	7¾	441
		Total	**16**	**1,111**
51.	**Dave Taylor**	**Los Angeles**	**17**	**1,111**
52.	Butch Goring	Los Angeles	10¾	736
		NY Islanders	4¾	332
		Boston	½	39
		Total	**16**	**1,107**
53.	Garry Unger	Toronto	½	15
		Detroit	3	216
		St. Louis	8½	662
		Atlanta	1	79
		Los Angeles	¾	58
		Edmonton	2¼	75
		Total	**16**	**1,105**
54.	Pit Martin	Detroit	3¼	119
		Boston	1¾	111
		Chicago	10¼	740
		Vancouver	1¾	131
		Total	**17**	**1,101**
* 55.	Jari Kurri	Edmonton	10	754
		Los Angeles	4¾	331
		NY Rangers	¼	14
		Total	**15**	**1,099**
56.	Gordie Roberts	Hartford	1½	107
		Minnesota	7	555
		Philadelphia	¼	11
		St. Louis	2½	166
		Pittsburgh	1¾	134
		Boston	2	124
		Total	**15**	**1,097**
57.	Darryl Sittler	Toronto	11½	844
		Philadelphia	2½	191
		Detroit	1	61
		Total	**15**	**1,096**
58.	Michel Goulet	Quebec	10¾	813
		Chicago	4¼	276
		Total	**15**	**1,089**
59.	Carol Vadnais	Montreal	2	42
		Oakland	2	152
		California	1¾	94
		Boston	3½	263
		NY Rangers	6¾	485
		New Jersey	1	51
		Total	**17**	**1,087**
60.	Brad Marsh	Atlanta	2	160
		Calgary	1¼	97
		Philadelphia	6¾	514
		Toronto	2¾	181
		Detroit	1¼	75
		Ottawa	1	59
		Total	**15**	**1,086**
* 61.	Ron Francis	Hartford	9¾	714
		Pittsburgh	5¼	371
		Total	**15**	**1,085**
62.	Bob Pulford	Toronto	14	947
		Los Angeles	2	132
		Total	**16**	**1,079**
* 63.	Dino Ciccarelli	Minnesota	8¾	602
		Washington	3¼	223
		Detroit	4	254
		Total	**16**	**1,079**
64.	Bobby Smith	Minnesota	8¼	572
		Montreal	6¾	505
		Total	**15**	**1,077**
* 65.	Jay Wells	Los Angeles	9	604
		Philadelphia	1¾	126
		Buffalo	2	85
		NY Rangers	3¼	186
		St. Louis	1	76
		Total	**17**	**1,077**
66.	**Craig Ramsay**	**Buffalo**	**14**	**1,070**
67.	Andy Bathgate	NY Rangers	11¾	719
		Toronto	1¼	70
		Detroit	2	130
		Pittsburgh	2	150
		Total	**17**	**1,069**
68.	Ted Lindsay	Detroit	14	862
		Chicago	3	206
		Total	**17**	**1,068**
69.	Mike Ramsey	Buffalo	13¾	911
		Pittsburgh	1¼	77
		Detroit	2	80
		Total	**17**	**1,068**
70.	Terry Harper	Montreal	10	554
		Los Angeles	3	234
		Detroit	4	252
		St. Louis	1	11
		Colorado	1	15
		Total	**19**	**1,066**
71.	**Rod Gilbert**	**NY Rangers**	**18**	**1,065**
72.	Bobby Hull	Chicago	15	1,036
		Winnipeg	⅔	18
		Hartford	⅓	9
		Total	**16**	**1,063**
73.	**Denis Potvin**	**NY Islanders**	**15**	**1,060**
* 74.	Neal Broten	Minnesota	13	876
		Dallas	1½	96
		New Jersey	1½	85
		Total	**16**	**1,057**
75.	Jean Guy Talbot	Montreal	13	791
		Minnesota	¼	4
		Detroit	½	32
		St. Louis	2½	172
		Buffalo	¾	57
		Total	**17**	**1,056**
76.	Randy Carlyle	Toronto	2	94
		Pittsburgh	5¾	397
		Winnipeg	9¼	564
		Total	**17**	**1,055**
77.	Ivan Boldirev	Boston	1¼	13
		California	2¾	191
		Chicago	4¾	384
		Atlanta	1	65
		Vancouver	2¾	216
		Detroit	2½	183
		Total	**15**	**1,052**
78.	Eddie Shack	NY Rangers	2¼	141
		Toronto	8¾	504
		Boston	2	120
		Los Angeles	1¼	84
		Buffalo	1½	111
		Pittsburgh	1¼	87
		Total	**17**	**1,047**
79.	Rob Ramage	Colorado	3	234
		St. Louis	5¾	441
		Calgary	1¼	80
		Toronto	2	160
		Minnesota	1	34
		Tampa Bay	¾	66
		Montreal	½	14
		Philadelphia	¾	15
		Total	**15**	**1,044**
* 80.	Craig MacTavish	Boston	5	217
		Edmonton	8¾	701
		NY Rangers	¼	12
		Philadelphia	1¾	100
		St. Louis	¼	13
		Total	**16**	**1,043**
* 81.	Scott Stevens	Washington	8	601
		St. Louis	1	78
		New Jersey	5	362
		Total	**14**	**1,041**
82.	Serge Savard	Montreal	15	917
		Winnipeg	2	123
		Total	**17**	**1,040**
83.	**Ron Ellis**	**Toronto**	**16**	**1,034**
84.	Harold Snepsts	Vancouver	11¾	781
		Minnesota	1	71
		Detroit	3	120
		St. Louis	1¼	61
		Total	**17**	**1,033**
85.	Ralph Backstrom	Montreal	14½	844
		Los Angeles	2¼	172
		Chicago	¼	16
		Total	**17**	**1,032**
* 86.	Brian Bellows	Minnesota	10	753
		Montreal	3	200
		Tampa Bay	1	79
		Total	**14**	**1,032**
87.	Dick Duff	Toronto	9¾	582
		NY Rangers	¾	43
		Montreal	5	305
		Los Angeles	¾	39
		Buffalo	1¾	61
		Total	**18**	**1,030**
88.	John Tonelli	NY Islanders	7¾	584
		Calgary	2¼	161
		Los Angeles	3	231
		Chicago	¾	33
		Quebec	¼	19
		Total	**14**	**1,028**
89.	Gaetan Duchesne	Washington	6	451
		Quebec	2	150
		Minnesota	4	297
		San Jose	1¾	117
		Florida	¼	13
		Total	**14**	**1,028**
90.	**Wayne Cashman**	**Boston**	**17**	**1,027**
* 91.	Guy Carbonneau	Montreal	13	912
		St. Louis	1	42
		Dallas	1	71
		Total	**15**	**1,025**
92.	Doug Wilson	Chicago	14	938
		San Jose	2	86
		Total	**16**	**1,024**
93.	Jim Neilson	NY Rangers	12	810
		California	2	98
		Cleveland	2	115
		Total	**16**	**1,023**
94.	Keith Acton	Montreal	4¼	228
		Minnesota	4¼	343
		Edmonton	1	72
		Philadelphia	4½	303
		Washington	¼	6
		NY Islanders	¾	71
		Total	**15**	**1,023**
* 95.	Dave Babych	Winnipeg	5¼	390
		Hartford	5¾	349
		Vancouver	5	284
		Total	**16**	**1,023**
96.	Don Lever	Vancouver	7⅔	593
		Atlanta	⅓	28
		Calgary	1¼	85
		Colorado	¾	59
		New Jersey	3	216
		Buffalo	2	39
		Total	**15**	**1,020**
* 97.	Brent Sutter	NY Islanders	11¼	694
		Chicago	4¾	326
		Total	**16**	**1,020**
* 98.	Craig Ludwig	Montreal	8	597
		NY Islanders	1	75
		Minnesota	2	151
		Dallas	3	196
		Total	**14**	**1,019**
99.	Mike Foligno	Detroit	2½	186
		Buffalo	9	664
		Toronto	2¾	129
		Florida	¾	39
		Total	**15**	**1,018**
100.	Phil Russell	Chicago	6¾	504
		Atlanta	1¼	93
		Calgary	3	229
		New Jersey	2¾	172
		Buffalo	1¼	18
		Total	**15**	**1,016**
101.	Brian Propp	Philadelphia	10¾	790
		Boston	¼	14
		Minnesota	3	147
		Hartford	1	65
		Total	**15**	**1,016**
*102.	Charlie Huddy	Edmonton	11	694
		Los Angeles	3¼	226
		Buffalo	1½	84
		St. Louis	¼	12
		Total	**16**	**1,016**
103.	Laurie Boschman	Toronto	2¾	187
		Edmonton	1	73
		Winnipeg	7¼	526
		New Jersey	2	153
		Ottawa	1	70
		Total	**14**	**1,009**
*104.	Dave Christian	Winnipeg	4	230
		Washington	6½	504
		Boston	1½	128
		St. Louis	1	78
		Chicago	2	69
		Total	**15**	**1,009**
105.	Dave Lewis	NY Islanders	6¾	514
		Los Angeles	3¼	221
		New Jersey	3	209
		Detroit	2	64
		Total	**15**	**1,008**
106.	**Bob Murray**	**Chicago**	**15**	**1,008**
107.	Jim Roberts	Montreal	9⅔	611
		St. Louis	5⅓	395
		Total	**15**	**1,006**
*108.	Joe Mullen	St. Louis	4½	301
		Calgary	4½	345
		Pittsburgh	5	325
		Boston	1	37
		Total	**15**	**1,008**
109.	Steve Larmer	Chicago	13	891
		NY Rangers	2	115
		Total	**15**	**1,006**
110.	**Claude Provost**	**Montreal**	**15**	**1,005**
111.	Rick Middleton	NY Rangers	2	124
		Boston	12	881
		Total	**14**	**1,005**
112.	Ryan Walter	Washington	4	307
		Montreal	9	604
		Vancouver	2	92
		Total	**15**	**1,003**
113.	Vic Hadfield	NY Rangers	13	839
		Pittsburgh	3	163
		Total	**16**	**1,002**
*114.	Dave Andreychuk	Buffalo	10½	763
		Toronto	3¼	223
		New Jersey	¼	15
		Total	**14**	**1,001**
115.	Bernie Federko	St. Louis	14	927
		Detroit	1	73
		Total	**15**	**1,000**

Goaltending Records

All-Time Shutout Leaders

Goaltender	Team	Seasons	Games	Shutouts
Terry Sawchuk	Detroit	14	734	85
(1949-1970)	Boston	2	102	11
	Toronto	3	91	4
	Los Angeles	1	36	2
	NY Rangers	1	8	1
	Total	21	971	**103**
George Hainsworth	Montreal	7½	318	75
(1926-1937)	Toronto	3½	147	19
	Total	11	465	**94**
Glenn Hall	Detroit	4	148	17
(1952-1971)	Chicago	10	618	51
	St. Louis	4	140	16
	Total	18	906	**84**
Jacques Plante	Montreal	11	556	58
(1952-1973)	NY Rangers	2	98	5
	St. Louis	2	69	10
	Toronto	2¾	106	7
	Boston	¼	8	2
	Total	18	837	**82**
Tiny Thompson	Boston	10¼	468	74
(1928-1940)	Detroit	1¾	85	7
	Total	12	553	**81**
Alex Connell	Ottawa	8	293	64
(1924-1937)	Detroit	1	48	6
	NY Americans	1	1	0
	Mtl. Maroons	2	75	11
	Total	12	417	**81**
Tony Esposito	Montreal	1	13	2
(1968-1984)	Chicago	15	873	74
	Total	16	886	**76**
Lorne Chabot	NY Rangers	2	80	21
(1926-1937)	Toronto	5	214	33
	Montreal	1	47	8
	Chicago	1	48	8
	Mtl. Maroons	1	16	2
	NY Americans	1	6	1
	Total	11	411	**73**
Harry Lumley	Detroit	6½	324	26
(1943-1960)	NY Rangers	½	1	0
	Chicago	2	134	5
	Toronto	4	267	34
	Boston	3	78	6
	Total	16	804	**71**
Roy Worters	Pittsburgh Pirates	3	123	22
(1925-1937)	NY Americans	9	360	44
	* Montreal		1	0
	Total	12	484	**66**
Turk Broda	Toronto	14	629	**62**
(1936-1952)				
John Roach	Toronto	7	222	13
(1921-1935)	NY Rangers	4	89	30
	Detroit	3	180	15
	Total	14	491	**58**
Clint Benedict	Ottawa	7	158	19
(1917-1930)	Mtl. Maroons	6	204	38
	Total	13	362	**57**

Goaltender	Team	Seasons	Games	Shutouts
Bernie Parent	Boston	2	57	1
(1965-1979)	Philadelphia	9½	486	50
	Toronto	1½	65	4
	Total	13	608	**55**
Ed Giacomin	NY Rangers	10¼	539	49
(1965-1978)	Detroit	2¾	71	5
	Total	13	610	**54**
David Kerr	Mtl. Maroons	3	101	11
(1930-1941)	NY Americans	1	1	0
	NY Rangers	7	324	40
	Total	11	426	**51**
Rogie Vachon	Montreal	5¼	206	13
(1966-1982)	Los Angeles	6¾	389	32
	Detroit	2	109	4
	Boston	2	91	2
	Total	16	795	**51**
Ken Dryden	Montreal	8	397	**46**
(1970-1979)				
Gump Worsley	NY Rangers	10	582	24
(1952-1974)	Montreal	6½	172	16
	Minnesota	4½	107	3
	Total	21	861	**43**
Charlie Gardiner	Chicago	7	316	**42**
(1927-1934)				
Frank Brimsek	Boston	9	444	35
(1938-1950)	Chicago	1	70	5
	Total	10	514	**40**
Johnny Bower	NY Rangers	3	77	5
(1953-1970)	Toronto	12	475	32
	Total	15	552	**37**
Bill Durnan	Montreal	7	383	**34**
(1943-1950)				
Eddie Johnston	Boston	11	444	27
(1962-1978)	Toronto	1	26	1
	St. Louis	3⅔	118	4
	Chicago	⅓	4	0
	Total	16	592	**32**
Roger Crozier	Detroit	7	313	20
(1963-1977)	Buffalo	6	202	10
	Washington	1	3	0
	Total	14	518	**30**
Cesare Maniago	Toronto	1	7	0
(1960-1978)	Montreal	1	14	0
	NY Rangers	2	34	2
	Minnesota	9	420	26
	Vancouver	2	93	2
	Total	15	568	**30**
Patrick Roy	Montreal	11½	551	29
(1984-1996)	Colorado	½	39	1
	Total	12	590	**30**

*Played 1 game for Canadiens in 1929-30.

Ten or More Shutouts, One Season

Number of Shutouts	Goaltender	Team	Season	Length of Schedule
22	George Hainsworth	Montreal	1928-29	44
15	Alex Connell	Ottawa	1925-26	36
	Alex Connell	Ottawa	1927-28	44
	Hal Winkler	Boston	1927-28	44
	Tony Esposito	Chicago	1969-70	76
14	George Hainsworth	Montreal	1926-27	44
13	Clint Benedict	Mtl. Maroons	1926-27	44
	Alex Connell	Ottawa	1926-27	44
	George Hainsworth	Montreal	1927-28	44
	John Roach	NY Rangers	1928-29	44
	Roy Worters	NY Americans	1928-29	44
	Harry Lumley	Toronto	1953-54	70
12	Tiny Thompson	Boston	1928-29	44
	Lorne Chabot	Toronto	1928-29	44
	Chuck Gardiner	Chicago	1930-31	44
	Terry Sawchuk	Detroit	1951-52	70
	Terry Sawchuk	Detroit	1953-54	70
	Terry Sawchuk	Detroit	1954-55	70
	Glenn Hall	Detroit	1955-56	70
	Bernie Parent	Philadelphia	1973-74	78
	Bernie Parent	Philadelphia	1974-75	80

Number of Shutouts	Goaltender	Team	Season	Length of Schedule
11	Lorne Chabot	NY Rangers	1927-28	44
	Harry Holmes	Detroit	1927-28	44
	Clint Benedict	Mtl. Maroons	1928-29	44
	Joe Miller	Pittsburgh Pirates	1928-29	44
	Tiny Thompson	Boston	1932-33	48
	Terry Sawchuk	Detroit	1950-51	70
10	Lorne Chabot	NY Rangers	1926-27	44
	Roy Worters	Pittsburgh Pirates	1927-28	44
	Clarence Dolson	Detroit	1928-29	44
	John Roach	Detroit	1932-33	48
	Chuck Gardiner	Chicago	1933-34	48
	Tiny Thompson	Boston	1935-36	48
	Frank Brimsek	Boston	1938-39	48
	Bill Durnan	Montreal	1948-49	60
	Gerry McNeil	Montreal	1952-53	70
	Harry Lumley	Toronto	1952-53	70
	Tony Esposito	Chicago	1973-74	78
	Ken Dryden	Montreal	1976-77	80

All-Time Win Leaders

(Minimum 200 Wins)

Wins	Goaltender	GP	Decisions	Losses	Ties	%
447	Terry Sawchuk	971	950	330	173	.562
434	Jacques Plante	837	827	246	147	.614
423	Tony Esposito	886	881	306	152	.566
407	Glenn Hall	906	897	327	163	.545
355	Rogie Vachon	795	773	291	127	.541
335	Gump Worsley	861	838	353	150	.489
333	Harry Lumley	804	802	326	143	.504
326	* Andy Moog	623	583	179	78	.626
320	* Grant Fuhr	675	630	223	87	.577
311	* Patrick Roy	590	568	190	67	.607
305	Billy Smith	680	643	233	105	.556
302	Turk Broda	629	627	224	101	.562
295	* Tom Barrasso	597	571	213	63	.572
294	Mike Liut	663	639	271	74	.518
289	Ed Giacomin	610	592	206	97	.570
288	* Mike Vernon	529	436	168	57	.726
286	Dan Bouchard	655	631	232	113	.543
284	Tiny Thompson	553	553	194	75	.581
270	Bernie Parent	608	588	197	121	.562
270	Gilles Meloche	788	752	351	131	.446
268	* Don Beaupre	664	617	274	75	.495
261	* John Vanbiesbrouck	600	567	237	69	.521
258	Ken Dryden	397	389	57	74	.758
252	Frank Brimsek	514	514	182	80	.568
251	Johnny Bower	552	537	196	90	.551
251	* Kelly Hrudey	601	557	225	81	.523
246	George Hainsworth	465	465	145	74	.609
246	Pete Peeters	489	452	155	51	.601
236	Reggie Lemelin	507	461	162	63	.580
236	Eddie Johnston	592	573	256	81	.483
234	* Ron Hextall	484	461	174	53	.565
231	Glenn Resch	571	537	224	82	.507
230	Gerry Cheevers	418	407	103	74	.656
219	John Roach	491	491	204	68	.515
215	Greg Millen	604	588	284	89	.441
208	Bill Durnan	383	382	112	62	.626
208	Don Edwards	459	440	155	77	.560
206	Lorne Chabot	411	411	140	65	.580
206	Roger Crozier	518	474	198	70	.508
204	Rick Wamsley	407	381	131	46	.596
203	David Kerr	426	426	148	75	.565
203	* Bill Ranford	518	480	220	57	.482

* active player

Active Shutout Leaders

(Minimum 12 Shutouts)

Goaltender	Teams	Seasons	Games	Shutouts
Patrick Roy	Montreal, Colorado	12	590	30
Ed Belfour	Chicago	8	382	29
Tom Barrasso	Buffalo, Pittsburgh	13	597	23
John Vanbiesbrouck	NY Rangers, Florida	14	600	23
Andy Moog	Edm., Bos., Dal.	16	623	22
Kirk McLean	New Jersey, Vancouver	11	449	19
Daren Puppa	Buf., Tor., T.B.	11	379	17
Don Beaupre	Min., Wsh., Ott., Tor.	16	664	17
Grant Fuhr	Edm., Tor., Buf., L.A., St.L.	15	675	17
Jon Casey	Min., Bos., St.L.	11	410	16
Kelly Hrudey	NY Islanders, Los Angeles	13	601	16
Dominik Hasek	Chicago, Buffalo	6	211	15
Bob Essensa	Winnipeg, Detroit	6	294	15
Mike Richter	NY Rangers	7	291	14
Ron Hextall	Phi., Que., NYI	10	484	14
Jim Carey	Washington	2	99	13
Mike Vernon	Calgary, Detroit	13	529	13
Martin Brodeur	New Jersey	4	168	12
Bill Ranford	Boston, Edmonton	11	518	12

Active Goaltending Leaders

(Ranked by winning percentage; minimum 250 games played)

Goaltender	Teams	Seasons	GP	Deci-sions	W	L	T	Winning %
Andy Moog	Edm., Bos., Dal.	16	623	583	326	179	78	.626
Mike Vernon	Calgary, Detroit	13	529	513	288	168	57	.617
Mike Richter	NY Rangers	7	291	268	149	91	28	.608
Patrick Roy	Montreal, Colorado	12	590	568	311	190	67	.607
Ed Belfour	Chicago	8	382	363	190	123	50	.592
Grant Fuhr	Edm., Tor., Buf., L.A., St.L.	15	675	630	320	223	87	.577
Tom Barrasso	Buffalo, Pittsburgh	13	597	571	295	213	63	.572
Curtis Joseph	St. Louis, Edmonton	7	314	300	152	112	36	.567
Ron Hextall	Phi., Que., NYI	10	484	461	234	174	53	.565
Daren Puppa	Buf., Tor., T.B.	11	379	350	167	138	45	.541
Jon Casey	Min., Bos., St.L.	11	410	371	167	149	55	.524
Kelly Hrudey	NY Islanders, Los Angeles	13	601	557	251	225	81	.523
Tim Cheveldae	Detroit, Winnipeg	8	338	321	149	135	37	.522
John Vanbiesbrouck	NY Rangers, Florida	14	600	567	261	237	69	.521
Bob Essensa	Winnipeg, Detroit	6	294	275	120	121	34	.498
Don Beaupre	Min., Wsh., Ott., Tor.	16	664	617	268	274	75	.495
Kirk McLean	New Jersey, Vancouver	11	449	436	186	195	55	.490
Glenn Healy	L.A., NYI, NYR	10	349	324	138	148	38	.485
Bill Ranford	Boston, Edmonton	11	518	480	203	220	57	.482
Chris Terreri	New Jersey, San Jose	9	314	282	119	130	33	.480
Ken Wregget	Tor., Phi., Pit.	13	458	423	181	203	39	.474
Sean Burke	New Jersey, Hartford	8	367	345	140	164	41	.465

Goals Against Average Leaders

(minimum 13 games played, 1994-95; minimum 27 games played, 1992-93 to 1993-94, 1995-96; 25 games played, 1926-27 to 1991-92; 15 games played, 1917-18 to 1925-26.)

Season	Goaltender and Club	GP	Mins.	GA	SO	AVG.
1995-96	Ron Hextall, Philadelphia	53	3,102	112	4	2.17
1994-95	Dominik Hasek, Buffalo	41	2,416	85	5	2.11
1993-94	Dominik Hasek, Buffalo	58	3,358	109	7	1.95
1992-93	Felix Potvin, Toronto	48	2,781	116	2	2.50
1991-92	Patrick Roy, Montreal	67	3,935	155	5	2.36
1990-91	Ed Belfour, Chicago	74	4,127	170	4	2.47
1989-90	Mike Liut, Hartford, Washington	37	2,161	91	4	2.53
1988-89	Patrick Roy, Montreal	48	2,744	113	4	2.47
1987-88	Pete Peeters, Washington	35	1,896	88	2	2.78
1986-87	Brian Hayward, Montreal	37	2,178	102	1	2.81
1985-86	Bob Froese, Philadelphia	51	2,728	116	5	2.55
1984-85	Tom Barrasso, Buffalo	54	3,248	144	5	2.66
1983-84	Pat Riggin, Washington	41	2,299	102	4	2.66
1982-83	Pete Peeters, Boston	62	3,611	142	8	2.36
1981-82	Denis Herron, Montreal	27	1,547	68	3	2.64
1980-81	Richard Sevigny, Montreal	33	1,777	71	2	2.40
1979-80	Bob Sauve, Buffalo	32	1,880	74	4	2.36
1978-79	Ken Dryden, Montreal	47	2,814	108	5	2.30
1977-78	Ken Dryden, Montreal	52	3,071	105	5	2.05
1976-77	Michel Larocque, Montreal	26	1,525	53	4	2.09
1975-76	Ken Dryden, Montreal	62	3,580	121	8	2.03
1974-75	Bernie Parent, Philadelphia	68	4,041	137	12	2.03
1973-74	Bernie Parent, Philadelphia	73	4,314	136	12	1.89
1972-73	Ken Dryden, Montreal	54	3,165	119	6	2.26
1971-72	Tony Esposito, Chicago	48	2,780	82	9	1.77
1970-71	Jacques Plante, Toronto	40	2,329	73	4	1.88
1969-70	Ernie Wakely, St. Louis	30	1,651	58	4	2.11
1968-69	Jacques Plante, St. Louis	37	2,139	70	5	1.96
1967-68	Gump Worsley, Montreal	40	2,213	73	6	1.98
1966-67	Glenn Hall, Chicago	32	1,664	66	2	2.38
1965-66	Johnny Bower, Toronto	35	1,998	75	3	2.25
1964-65	Johnny Bower, Toronto	34	2,040	81	3	2.38
1963-64	Johnny Bower, Toronto	51	3,009	106	5	2.11
1962-63	Jacques Plante, Montreal	56	3,320	138	5	2.49
1961-62	Jacques Plante, Montreal	70	4,200	166	4	2.37
1960-61	Johnny Bower, Toronto	58	3,480	145	2	2.50
1959-60	Jacques Plante, Montreal	69	4,140	175	3	2.54
1958-59	Jacques Plante, Montreal	67	4,000	144	9	2.16
1957-58	Jacques Plante, Montreal	57	3,386	119	9	2.11
1956-57	Jacques Plante, Montreal	61	3,660	123	9	2.02

Season	Goaltender and Club	GP	Mins.	GA	SO	AVG.
1955-56	Jacques Plante, Montreal	64	3,840	119	7	1.86
1954-55	Terry Sawchuk, Detroit	68	4,080	132	12	1.94
1953-54	Harry Lumley, Toronto	69	4,140	128	13	1.86
1952-53	Terry Sawchuk, Detroit	63	3,780	120	9	1.90
1951-52	Terry Sawchuk, Detroit	70	4,200	133	12	1.90
1950-51	Al Rollins, Toronto	40	2,367	70	5	1.77
1949-50	Bill Durnan, Montreal	64	3,840	141	8	2.20
1948-49	Bill Durnan, Montreal	60	3,600	126	10	2.10
1947-48	Turk Broda, Toronto	60	3,600	143	5	2.38
1946-47	Bill Durnan, Montreal	60	3,600	138	4	2.30
1945-46	Bill Durnan, Montreal	40	2,400	104	4	2.60
1944-45	Bill Durnan, Montreal	50	3,000	121	1	2.42
1943-44	Bill Durnan, Montreal	50	3,000	109	2	2.18
1942-43	Johnny Mowers, Detroit	50	3,010	124	6	2.47
1941-42	Frank Brimsek, Boston	47	2,930	115	3	2.35
1940-41	Turk Broda, Toronto	48	2,970	99	5	2.00
1939-40	Dave Kerr, NY Rangers	48	3,000	77	8	1.54
1938-39	Frank Brimsek, Boston	43	2,610	68	10	1.56
1937-38	Tiny Thompson, Boston	48	2,970	89	7	1.80
1936-37	Normie Smith, Detroit	48	2,980	102	6	2.05
1935-36	Tiny Thompson, Boston	48	2,930	82	10	1.68
1934-35	Lorne Chabot, Chicago	48	2,940	88	8	1.80
1933-34	Wilf Cude, Detroit, Montreal	30	1,920	47	5	1.47
1932-33	Tiny Thompson, Boston	48	3,000	88	11	1.76
1931-32	Chuck Gardiner, Chicago	48	2,989	92	4	1.85
1930-31	Roy Worters, NY Americans	44	2,760	74	8	1.61
1929-30	Tiny Thompson, Boston	44	2,680	98	3	2.19
1928-29	George Hainsworth, Montreal	44	2,800	43	22	0.92
1927-28	George Hainsworth, Montreal	44	2,730	48	13	1.05
1926-27	Clint Benedict, Mtl. Maroons	43	2,748	65	13	1.42
1925-26	Alex Connell, Ottawa	36	2,251	42	15	1.12
1924-25	Georges Vezina, Montreal	30	1,860	56	5	1.81
1923-24	Georges Vezina, Montreal	24	1,459	48	3	1.97
1922-23	Clint Benedict, Ottawa	24	1,478	54	4	2.19
1921-22	Clint Benedict, Ottawa	24	1,508	84	2	3.34
1920-21	Clint Benedict, Ottawa	24	1,457	75	2	3.09
1919-20	Clint Benedict, Ottawa	24	1,444	64	5	2.66
1918-19	Clint Benedict, Ottawa	18	1,113	53	2	2.86
1917-18	Georges Vezina, Montreal	21	1,282	84	1	3.93

All-Time NHL Coaching Register

Regular Season, 1917-96

(figures in parentheses indicate ranking of top 25 in order of games coached)

Coach	Team	Games	Wins	Losses	Ties	%	Cup Wins	Seasons
Abel, Sid (6)	Chicago	140	39	79	22	.357	0	1952-54
	Detroit	811	340	339	132	.501	0	1957-68, 1969-70
	St. Louis	10	3	6	1	.350	0	1971-72
	Kansas City	3	0	3	0	.000	0	1975-76
	Total	**963**	**382**	**426**	**155**	**.477**	**0**	**1952-76**
Adams, Jack (5)	Toronto St. Pats	18	10	7	1	.583	0	1922-23
	Detroit	964	413	390	161	.512	3	1927-44
	Total	**982**	**423**	**397**	**162**	**.513**	**3**	**1922-44**
Allen, Keith	Philadelphia	150	51	67	32	.447	0	1967-69
Allison, Dave	Ottawa	25	2	22	1	.100	0	1995-96
Anderson, Jim	Washington	54	4	45	5	.120	0	1974-75
Angotti, Lou	St. Louis	32	6	20	6	.281	0	1973-75
	Pittsburgh	80	16	58	6	.238	0	1983-84
	Total	**112**	**22**	**78**	**12**	**.250**	**0**	**1973-84**
Arbour, Al (1)	St. Louis	107	42	40	25	.509	0	1970-71, 1971-73
	NY Islanders	1499	739	537	223	.567	4	1973-86, 1988-94
	Total	**1606**	**781**	**577**	**248**	**.564**	**4**	**1970-94**
Armstrong, George	Toronto	47	17	26	4	.404	0	1988-89
Barkley, Doug	Detroit	77	20	46	11	.331	0	1970-72, 1975-76
Beaulieu, Andre	Minnesota	31	6	22	3	.242	0	1977-78
Belisle, Danny	Washington	96	28	51	17	.380	0	1978-80
Berenson, Red	St. Louis	204	100	72	32	.569	0	1979-82
Bergeron, Michel (14)	Quebec	634	265	283	86	.486	0	1980-87, 1989-90
	NY Rangers	158	73	67	18	.519	0	1987-89
	Total	**792**	**338**	**350**	**104**	**.492**	**0**	**1980-89**
Berry, Bob (10)	Los Angeles	240	107	94	39	.527	0	1978-81
	Montreal	223	116	71	36	.601	0	1981-84
	Pittsburgh	240	88	127	25	.419	0	1984-87
	St. Louis	157	73	63	21	.532	0	1992-94
	Total	**860**	**384**	**355**	**121**	**.517**	**0**	**1978-94**
Beverley, Nick	Toronto	17	9	6	2	.588	0	1995-96
Blackburn, Don	Hartford	140	42	63	35	.425	0	1979-81
Blair, Wren	Minnesota	147	48	65	34	.442	0	1967-70
Blake, Toe (9)	Montreal	914	500	255	159	.634	8	1955-68
Bolieau, Marc	Pittsburgh	151	66	61	24	.517	0	1973-76
Boivin, Leo	St. Louis	97	28	53	16	.371	0	1975-76, 1977-78
Boucher, Frank	NY Rangers	525	179	263	83	.420	1	1939-49, 1953-54
Boucher, George	Mtl. Maroons	12	6	5	1	.542	0	1930-31
	Ottawa	48	13	29	6	.333	0	1933-34
	St.L. Eagles	35	9	20	6	.343	0	1934-35
	Boston	70	22	32	16	.429	0	1949-50
	Total	**165**	**50**	**86**	**29**	**.391**	**0**	**1930-50**
Bowman, Scott (2)	St. Louis	238	110	83	45	.557	0	1967-70, 1970-71
	Montreal	634	419	110	105	.744	5	1971-79
	Buffalo	404	210	134	60	.594	0	1979-80, 1981-85, 1985-87
	Pittsburgh	164	95	53	16	.628	1	1991-93
	Detroit	214	141	54	19	.703	0	1993-96
	Total	**1654**	**975**	**434**	**245**	**.664**	**6**	**1967-96**
Bowness, Rick	Winnipeg	28	8	17	3	.339	0	1988-89
	Boston	80	36	32	12	.525	0	1991-92
	Ottawa	235	39	178	18	.204	0	1992-96
	Total	**343**	**83**	**227**	**33**	**.290**	**0**	**1991-96**
Brooks, Herb	NY Rangers	285	131	113	41	.532	0	1981-85
	Minnesota	80	19	48	13	.319	0	1987-88
	New Jersey	84	40	37	7	.518	0	1992-93
	Total	**449**	**190**	**198**	**61**	**.491**	**0**	**1981-93**
Brophy, John	Toronto	160	53	91	16	.381	0	1986-88
Burnett, George	Edmonton	35	12	20	3	.386	0	1994-95
Burns, Charlie	Minnesota	86	22	50	14	.337	0	1969-70, 1974-75
Burns, Pat	Montreal	320	174	104	42	.609	0	1988-92
	Toronto	281	133	107	41	.546	0	1992-96
	Total	**601**	**307**	**211**	**83**	**.580**	**0**	**1988-96**
Bush, Eddie	Kansas City	32	1	23	8	.156	0	1975-76
Colin Campbell	NY Rangers	130	63	50	17	.550	0	1994-96
Doug Carpenter	New Jersey	290	100	166	24	.386	0	1984-88
	Toronto	91	39	47	5	.456	0	1989-91
	Total	**381**	**139**	**213**	**29**	**.403**	**0**	**1984-91**
Carroll, Dick	Toronto Arenas	40	18	22	0	.450	1	1917-19
	Toronto St. Pats	24	15	9	0	.625	0	1920-21
	Total	**64**	**33**	**31**	**0**	**.516**	**1**	**1917-21**
Cashman, Wayne	NY Rangers	2	0	2	0	.000	0	1986-87
Chambers, Dave	Quebec	98	19	64	15	.270	0	1990-92
Charron, Guy	Calgary	16	6	7	3	.469	0	1991-92
Cheevers, Gerry	Boston	376	204	126	46	.604	0	1980-85
Cherry, Don	Boston	400	231	105	64	.658	0	1974-79
	Colorado	80	19	48	13	.319	0	1979-80
	Total	**480**	**250**	**153**	**77**	**.601**	**0**	**1974-80**

Coach	Team	Games	Wins	Losses	Ties	%	Cup Wins	Seasons
Clancy, King	Mtl. Maroons	18	6	11	1	.361	0	1937-38
	Toronto	235	96	94	45	.504	0	1953-56, 1966-67, 1971-72
	Total	**253**	**102**	**105**	**46**	**.494**	**0**	**1937-72**
Clapper, Dit	Boston	230	102	88	40	.530	0	1945-49
Cleghorn, Odie	Pit. Pirates	168	62	86	20	.429	0	1925-29
Colville, Neil	NY Rangers	93	26	41	26	.419	0	1950-52
Conacher, Charlie	Chicago	162	56	84	22	.414	0	1947-50
Conacher, Lionel	NY Americans	44	14	25	5	.375	0	1929-30
Constantine, Kevin	San Jose	157	55	78	24	.427	0	1993-96
Cook, Bill	NY Rangers	117	34	59	24	.393	0	1951-53
Crawford, Marc	Quebec	48	30	13	5	.677	0	1994-95
	Colorado	82	47	25	10	.634	1	1995-96
	Total	**130**	**77**	**38**	**15**	**.650**	**1**	**1994-96**
Creamer, Pierre	Pittsburgh	80	36	35	9	.506	0	1987-88
Creighton, Fred	Atlanta	348	156	136	56	.529	0	1974-79
	Boston	73	40	20	13	.637	0	1979-80
	Total	**421**	**196**	**156**	**69**	**.548**	**0**	**1974-80**
Crisp, Terry	Calgary	240	144	63	33	.669	1	1987-90
	Tampa Bay	298	108	157	33	.417	0	1992-96
	Total	**538**	**252**	**220**	**66**	**.530**	**1**	**1987-96**
Crozier, Joe	Buffalo	192	77	80	35	.492	0	1971-74
	Toronto	40	13	22	5	.388	0	1980-81
	Total	**232**	**90**	**102**	**40**	**.474**	**0**	**1971-81**
Crozier, Roger	Washington	1	0	1	0	.000	0	1981-82
Cunniff, John	Hartford	13	3	9	1	.269	0	1982-83
	New Jersey	133	59	56	18	.511	0	1989-91
	Total	**146**	**62**	**65**	**19**	**.490**	**0**	**1983-91**
Dandurand, Leo	Montreal	158	82	68	8	.544	1	1920-25, 1934-35
Day, Hap	Toronto	546	259	206	81	.549	5	1940-50
Dea, Bill	Detroit	100	32	57	11	.375	0	1975-77, 1981-82
Delvecchio, Alex	Detroit	156	53	82	21	.407	0	1973-77
Demers, Jacques (11)	Quebec	80	25	44	11	.381	0	1979-80
	St. Louis	240	106	106	28	.500	0	1983-86
	Detroit	320	137	136	47	.502	0	1986-90
	Montreal	220	107	86	27	.548	1	1992-96
	Total	**860**	**375**	**372**	**113**	**.502**	**1**	**1979-96**
Denneny, Cy	Boston	44	26	13	5	.648	1	1928-29
	Ottawa	48	11	27	10	.333	0	1932-33
	Total	**92**	**37**	**40**	**15**	**.484**	**1**	**1928-33**
Dineen, Bill	Philadelphia	140	60	60	20	.500	0	1991-93
Dudley, Rick	Buffalo	188	85	72	31	.535	0	1989-92
Duff, Dick	Toronto	2	0	2	0	.000	0	1979-80
Dugal, Jules	Montreal	18	9	6	3	.583	0	1938-39
Duncan, Art	Detroit	33	10	21	2	.333	0	1926-27
	Toronto	47	21	16	10	.553	0	1930-32
	Total	**80**	**31**	**37**	**12**	**.463**	**0**	**1926-32**
Dutton, Red	NY Americans	336	106	180	50	.390	0	1935-42
Eddolls, Frank	Chicago	70	13	40	17	.307	0	1954-55
Esposito, Phil	NY Rangers	45	24	21	0	.533	0	1986-87, 1988-89

Although he lost his top billing on the NHL's all-time coaching register to Scotty Bowman, Al Arbour's 1499 games behind the bench of the New York Islanders still ranks as a single-team record.

Coach	Team	Games	Wins	Losses	Ties	%	Cup Wins	Seasons
Evans, Jack (23)	California	80	27	42	11	.406	0	1975-76
	Cleveland	160	47	87	26	.375	0	1976-78
	Hartford	374	163	174	37	.485	0	1983-88
	Total	**614**	**237**	**303**	**74**	**.446**	**0**	**1975-88**
Fashoway, Gordie	Oakland	10	4	5	1	.450	0	1967-68
Ferguson, John	NY Rangers	121	43	59	19	.434	0	1975-77
	Winnipeg	14	7	6	1	.536	0	1985-86
	Total	**135**	**50**	**65**	**20**	**.444**	**0**	**1975-86**
Filion, Maurice	Quebec	6	1	3	2	.333	0	1980-81
Francis, Emile (15)	NY Rangers	654	347	209	98	.606	0	1965-68, 1968-73, 1973-75
	St. Louis	124	46	64	14	.427	0	1976-77, 1981-83
	Total	**778**	**393**	**273**	**112**	**.577**	**0**	**1965-83**
Fredrickson, Frank	Pit. Pirates	44	5	36	3	.148	0	1929-30
Ftorek, Robbie	Los Angeles	132	65	56	11	.534	0	1987-89
Gadsby, Bill	Detroit	78	35	31	12	.526	0	1968-69
Gainey, Bob	Minnesota	244	95	119	30	.451	0	1990-93
	Dallas	171	70	71	30	.497	0	1993-96
	Total	**415**	**165**	**190**	**60**	**.470**	**0**	**1990-96**
Gardiner, Herb	Chicago	44	7	29	8	.250	0	1928-29
Gardner, Jimmy	Hamilton	30	19	10	1	.650	0	1924-25
Garvin, Ted	Detroit	11	2	8	1	.227	0	1973-74
Geoffrion, Bernie	NY Rangers	43	22	18	3	.547	0	1968-69
	Atlanta	208	77	92	39	.464	0	1972-75
	Montreal	30	15	9	6	.600	0	1979-80
	Total	**281**	**114**	**119**	**48**	**.491**	**0**	**1968-80**
Gerard, Eddie	Ottawa	22	9	13	0	.409	0	1917-18
	Mtl. Maroons	284	129	112	43	.530	1	1924-29, 1932-34
	NY Americans	102	34	50	18	.422	0	1930-32
	St.L. Eagles	13	2	11	0	.154	0	1934-35
	Total	**421**	**174**	**186**	**61**	**.486**	**1**	**1917-35**
Gill, David	Ottawa	132	64	41	27	.587	1	1926-29
Glover, Fred	California	356	96	207	53	.344	0	1968-72, 1972-74
	Los Angeles	68	18	42	8	.324	0	1971-72
	Total	**424**	**114**	**249**	**61**	**.341**	**0**	**1968-74**
Goodfellow, Ebbie	Chicago	140	30	91	19	.282	0	1950-52
Gordon, Jackie	Minnesota	289	116	123	50	.488	0	1970-74, 1974-75
Goring, Butch	Boston	93	42	38	13	.522	0	1985-87
Gorman, Tommy	NY Americans	80	31	33	16	.488	0	1925-26, 1928-29
	Chicago	73	28	28	17	.500	1	1932-34
	Mtl. Maroons	174	74	71	29	.509	1	1934-38
	Total	**327**	**133**	**132**	**62**	**.502**	**2**	**1925-38**
Gottselig, Johnny	Chicago	187	62	104	21	.388	0	1944-48
Goyette, Phil	NY Islanders	48	6	38	4	.167	0	1972-73
Green, Gary	Washington	157	50	78	29	.411	0	1979-82
Green, Pete	Ottawa	186	117	61	8	.651	3	1919-26
Green, Wilf	NY Americans	44	11	27	6	.318	0	1927-28
Green, Ted	Edmonton	188	65	102	21	.402	0	1991-94
Guidolin, Aldo	Colorado	59	12	39	8	.271	0	1978-79
Guidolin, Bep	Boston	104	72	23	9	.736	0	1972-74
	Kansas City	125	26	84	15	.268	0	1974-76
	Total	**229**	**98**	**107**	**24**	**.480**	**0**	**1972-76**
Harkness, Ned	Detroit	38	12	22	4	.368	0	1970-71
Harris, Ted	Minnesota	179	48	104	27	.344	0	1975-78
Hart, Cecil	Montreal	430	207	149	74	.567	2	1925-32, 1936-39
Hartsburg, Craig	Chicago	82	40	28	14	.573	0	1995-96
Harvey, Doug	NY Rangers	70	26	32	12	.457	0	1961-62
Heffernan, Frank	Toronto St. Pats	12	5	7	0	.417	0	1919-20
Henning, Lorne	Minnesota	158	68	72	18	.487	0	1985-87
	NY Islanders	48	15	28	5	.365	0	1994-95
	Total	**206**	**83**	**100**	**23**	**.459**	**0**	**1985-95**
Hitchcock, Ken	Dallas	43	15	23	5	.407	0	1995-96
Holmgren, Paul	Philadelphia	264	107	126	31	.464	0	1988-92
	Hartford	161	54	93	14	.379	0	1992-96
	Total	**425**	**161**	**219**	**45**	**.432**	**0**	**1988-96**
Howell, Harry	Minnesota	11	3	6	2	.364	0	1978-79
Imlach, Punch (7)	Toronto	760	363	274	123	.559	4	1958-69, 1979-80
	Buffalo	119	32	62	25	.374	0	1970-72
	Total	**879**	**395**	**336**	**148**	**.534**	**4**	**1958-80**
Ingarfield, Earl	NY Islanders	30	6	22	2	.233	0	1972-73
Inglis, Bill	Buffalo	56	28	18	10	.589	0	1978-79
Irvin, Dick (3)	Chicago	114	43	56	15	.443	0	1930-31, 1955-56
	Toronto	427	216	152	59	.575	1	1931-40
	Montreal	896	431	313	152	.566	3	1940-55
	Total	**1437**	**690**	**521**	**226**	**.559**	**4**	**1930-55**
Ivan, Tommy (25)	Detroit	470	262	118	90	.653	3	1947-54
	Chicago	103	26	56	21	.354	0	1956-58
	Total	**573**	**288**	**174**	**111**	**.599**	**3**	**1947-58**
Iverson, Emil	Chicago	71	26	28	17	.486	0	1931-33
Johnson, Bob	Calgary	400	193	155	52	.548	0	1982-87
	Pittsburgh	80	41	33	6	.550	1	1990-91
	Total	**480**	**234**	**188**	**58**	**.548**	**1**	**1982-91**
Johnson, Tom	Boston	208	142	43	23	.738	1	1970-73
Johnston, Eddie	Chicago	80	34	27	19	.544	0	1979-80
	Pittsburgh	454	201	198	55	.503	0	1980-83, 1993-96
	Total	**534**	**235**	**225**	**74**	**.509**	**0**	**1979-96**

Coach	Team	Games	Wins	Losses	Ties	%	Cup Wins	Seasons
Johnston, Marshall	California	69	13	45	11	.268	0	1973-75
	Colorado	56	15	32	9	.348	0	1981-82
	Total	**125**	**28**	**77**	**20**	**.304**	**0**	**1973-82**
Kasper, Steve	Boston	82	40	31	11	.555	0	1995-96
Keats, Duke	Detroit	11	2	7	2	.273	0	1926-27
Keenan, Mike (16)	Philadelphia	320	190	102	28	.638	0	1984-88
	Chicago	320	153	126	41	.542	0	1988-92
	NY Rangers	84	52	24	8	.667	1	1993-94
	St. Louis	130	60	49	21	.542	0	1994-96
	Total	**854**	**455**	**301**	**98**	**.590**	**1**	**1984-96**
Kelly, Pat	Colorado	101	22	54	25	.342	0	1977-79
Kelly, Red (19)	Los Angeles	150	55	75	20	.433	0	1967-69
	Pittsburgh	274	90	132	52	.423	0	1969-73
	Toronto	318	133	123	62	.516	0	1973-77
	Totals	**742**	**278**	**330**	**134**	**.465**	**0**	**1967-77**
Kennedy, George	Montreal	64	36	28	0	.563	0	1917-20
King, Dave	Calgary	216	109	76	31	.576	0	1992-95
Kingston, George	San Jose	164	28	129	7	.192	0	1991-93
Kish, Larry	Hartford	49	12	32	5	.296	0	1982-83
Kromm, Bobby	Detroit	231	79	111	41	.431	0	1977-80
Kurtenbach, Orland	Vancouver	125	36	62	27	.396	0	1976-78
LaForge, Bill	Vancouver	20	4	14	2	.250	0	1984-85
Lalonde, Newsy	NY Americans	44	17	25	2	.409	0	1926-27
	Ottawa	88	31	45	12	.420	0	1929-31
	Montreal	112	45	53	14	.464	0	1932-35
	Totals	**244**	**93**	**123**	**28**	**.439**	**0**	**1926-35**
Laperriere, Jacques	Montreal	1	0	1	0	.000	0	1995-96
Lapointe, Ron	Quebec	89	33	50	6	.404	0	1987-89
Laycoe, Hal	Los Angeles	24	5	18	1	.229	0	1969-70
	Vancouver	156	44	96	16	.333	0	1970-72
	Totals	**180**	**49**	**114**	**17**	**.319**	**0**	**1969-72**
Lehman, Hugh	Chicago	21	3	17	1	.167	0	1927-28
Lemaire, Jacques	Montreal	97	48	37	12	.557	0	1983-85
	New Jersey	214	106	76	32	.570	1	1993-96
	Total	**311**	**154**	**113**	**44**	**.566**	**1**	**1983-96**
Lepine, Pit	Montreal	48	10	33	5	.260	0	1939-40
Lesueur, Percy	Hamilton	24	9	15	0	.375	0	1923-24
Ley, Rick	Hartford	160	69	71	20	.494	0	1989-91
	Vancouver	124	47	50	27	.488	0	1994-96
	Total	**284**	**116**	**121**	**47**	**.491**	**0**	**1989-96**
Lindsay, Ted	Detroit	20	3	14	3	.225	0	1980-81
Long, Barry	Winnipeg	205	87	93	25	.485	0	1983-86
Loughlin, Clem	Chicago	144	61	63	20	.493	0	1934-37
Low, Ron	Edmonton	95	35	51	9	.416	0	1994-96
MacDonald, Parker	Minnesota	61	20	30	11	.418	0	1973-74
	Los Angeles	42	13	24	5	.369	0	1981-82
	Total	**103**	**33**	**54**	**16**	**.398**	**0**	**1973-82**
MacLean, Doug	Florida	82	41	31	10	.561	0	1995-96
MacMillan, Billy	Colorado	80	22	45	13	.356	0	1980-81
	New Jersey	100	19	67	14	.260	0	1982-84
	Total	**180**	**41**	**112**	**27**	**.303**	**0**	**1980-83**
MacNeil, Al	Montreal	55	31	15	9	.645	1	1970-71
	Atlanta	80	35	32	13	.519	0	1979-80
	Calgary	160	68	61	31	.522	0	1980-82
	Total	**295**	**134**	**108**	**53**	**.544**	**1**	**1970-82**
Mahoney, Bill	Minnesota	93	42	39	12	.516	0	1983-85
Magnuson, Keith	Chicago	132	49	57	26	.470	0	1980-82
Maguire, Pierre	Hartford	67	23	37	7	.396	0	1993-94
Maloney, Dan	Toronto	160	45	100	15	.328	0	1984-86
	Winnipeg	212	91	93	28	.495	0	1986-89
	Total	**372**	**136**	**193**	**43**	**.423**	**0**	**1984-89**
Maloney, Phil	Vancouver	232	95	105	32	.478	0	1973-77
Mantha, Sylvio	Montreal	48	11	26	11	.344	0	1935-36
Marshall, Bert	Colorado	24	3	17	4	.208	0	1981-82
Martin, Jacques	St. Louis	160	66	71	23	.484	0	1986-88
	Ottawa	38	10	24	4	.316	0	1995-96
	Total	**198**	**76**	**95**	**27**	**.452**	**0**	**1986-96**
Maurice, Paul	Hartford	70	29	33	8	.471	0	1995-96
Maxner, Wayne	Detroit	129	34	68	27	.368	0	1980-82
McCammon, Bob	Philadelphia	218	119	68	31	.617	0	1978-79, 1981-84
	Vancouver	294	102	156	36	.408	0	1987-91
	Total	**511**	**221**	**223**	**67**	**.498**	**0**	**1978-91**
McCreary, Bill	St. Louis	24	6	14	4	.333	0	1971-72
	Vancouver	41	9	25	7	.305	0	1973-74
	California	32	8	20	4	.313	0	1974-75
	Total	**97**	**23**	**59**	**15**	**.314**	**0**	**1971-75**
McLellan, John	Toronto	295	117	136	42	.468	0	1969-73
McVie, Tom	Washington	204	49	122	33	.321	0	1975-78
	Winnipeg	105	20	67	18	.276	0	1979-80, 1980-81
	New Jersey	153	57	74	22	.444	0	1983-84, 1990-92
	Total	**462**	**126**	**263**	**73**	**.352**	**0**	**1975-92**
Meeker, Howie	Toronto	70	21	34	15	.407	0	1956-57
Melrose, Barry	Los Angeles	209	79	101	29	.447	0	1992-95
Milbury, Mike	Boston	160	90	49	21	.628	0	1989-91
	NY Islanders	82	22	50	10	.329	0	1995-96
	Total	**242**	**112**	**99**	**31**	**.527**	**0**	**1989-96**
Muckler, John	Minnesota	35	6	23	6	.257	0	1968-69
	Edmonton	160	75	65	20	.531	1	1989-91
	Buffalo	268	125	109	34	.530	0	1991-95
	Total	**463**	**206**	**197**	**60**	**.510**	**1**	**1968-95**
Muldoon, Pete	Chicago	44	19	22	3	.466	0	1926-27
Munro, Dunc	Mtl. Maroons	76	37	29	10	.553	0	1929-31
Murdoch, Bob	Chicago	80	30	41	9	.431	0	1987-88
	Winnipeg	160	63	75	22	.463	0	1989-91
	Total	**240**	**93**	**116**	**31**	**.452**	**0**	**1987-91**

Coach	Team	Games	Wins	Losses	Ties	%	Cup Wins	Seasons
Murphy, Mike	Los Angeles	65	20	37	8	.369	0	1986-88
Murray, Bryan (8)	Washington	672	343	246	83	.572	0	1981-90
	Detroit	244	124	91	29	.568	0	1990-93
	Total	**916**	**467**	**337**	**112**	**.571**	**0**	**1981-93**
Murray, Terry	Washington	325	163	134	28	.545	0	1989-94
	Philadelphia	130	73	40	17	.627	0	1994-96
	Total	**455**	**236**	**174**	**45**	**.568**	**0**	**1989-96**
Nanne, Lou	Minnesota	29	7	18	4	.310	0	1977-78
Neale, Harry	Vancouver	407	142	189	76	.442	0	1978-82
	Detroit	35	8	23	4	.286	0	1985-86
	Total	**442**	**150**	**212**	**80**	**.430**	**0**	**1978-82, 1983-84, 1984-85**
Neilson, Roger (13)	Toronto	160	75	62	23	.541	0	1977-79
	Buffalo	80	39	20	21	.619	0	1980-81
	Vancouver	133	51	61	21	.462	0	1982-84
	Los Angeles	28	8	17	3	.339	0	1983-84
	NY Rangers	280	141	104	35	.566	0	1989-93
	Florida	132	53	56	23	.489	0	1993-95
	Total	**813**	**367**	**320**	**126**	**.529**	**0**	**1977-95**
Nolan, Ted	Buffalo	82	33	42	7	.445	0	1995-96
Nykoluk, Mike	Toronto	280	89	144	47	.402	0	1980-84
Oliver, Murray	Minnesota	40	21	11	8	.625	0	1981-83
Olmstead, Bert	Oakland	64	11	37	16	.297	0	1967-68
O'Reilly, Terry	Boston	227	115	86	26	.564	0	1986-89
Paddock, John	Winnipeg	281	106	138	37	.443	0	1991-95
Page, Pierre	Minnesota	160	63	77	20	.456	0	1988-90
	Quebec	230	98	103	29	.489	0	1991-94
	Calgary	82	34	37	11	.482	0	1995-96
	Total	**472**	**195**	**217**	**60**	**.477**	**0**	**1988-96**
Park, Brad	Detroit	45	9	34	2	.222	0	1985-86
Patrick, Craig	NY Rangers	94	37	45	12	.457	0	1980-81, 1984-85
	Pittsburgh	54	22	26	6	.463	0	1989-90
	Total	**148**	**59**	**71**	**18**	**.459**	**0**	**1980-89**
Patrick, Frank	Boston	96	48	36	12	.563	0	1934-36
Patrick, Lester (24)	NY Rangers	604	281	216	107	.554	2	1926-39
Patrick, Lynn	NY Rangers	107	40	51	16	.449	0	1948-50
	Boston	310	117	130	63	.479	0	1950-55
	St. Louis	26	8	15	3	.365	0	1967-68, 1974-75 1975-76
	Total	**443**	**165**	**186**	**82**	**.465**	**0**	**1948-76**
Patrick, Muzz	NY Rangers	135	44	65	26	.422	0	1953-55, 1962-63
Perron, Jean	Montreal	240	126	84	30	.588	1	1985-88
	Quebec	47	16	26	5	.394	0	1988-89
	Total	**287**	**142**	**110**	**35**	**.556**	**1**	**1985-89**
Perry, Don	Los Angeles	168	52	85	31	.402	0	1981-84
Pike, Alf	NY Rangers	125	36	67	22	.376	0	1959-61
Pilous, Rudy	Chicago	387	162	151	74	.514	1	1958-63
Plager, Barclay	St. Louis	178	49	96	33	.368	0	1977-80, 1982-83
Plager, Bob	St. Louis	11	4	6	1	.409	0	1992-93
Pleau, Larry	Hartford	224	81	117	26	.420	0	1980-83, 1987-89
Polano, Nick	Detroit	240	79	127	34	.400	0	1982-85
Popein, Larry	NY Rangers	41	18	14	9	.549	0	1973-74
Powers, Eddie	Toronto St. Pats	114	54	56	4	.491	1	1921-22, 1923-26
Primeau, Joe	Toronto	210	97	71	42	.562	1	1950-53
Pronovost, Marcel	Buffalo	104	52	29	23	.611	0	1977-79
	Detroit	9	2	7	0	.222	0	1979-80
	Total	**113**	**54**	**36**	**23**	**.580**	**0**	**1977-80**
Pulford, Bob (17)	Los Angeles	396	178	150	68	.535	0	1972-77
	Chicago	375	158	155	62	.504	0	1977-79, 1981-82, 1984-87
	Total	**771**	**336**	**305**	**130**	**.520**	**0**	**1972-87**
Querrie, Charlie	Toronto St. Pats	6	3	3	0	.500	0	1922-23
Quinn, Mike	Quebec Bulldogs	24	4	20	0	.167	0	1919-20
Quinn, Pat (20)	Philadelphia	262	141	73	48	.630	0	1978-82
	Los Angeles	202	75	101	26	.436	0	1984-87
	Vancouver	280	141	111	28	.554	0	1990-96
	Total	**746**	**357**	**285**	**102**	**.547**	**0**	**1978-96**
Ramsay, Craig	Buffalo	21	4	15	2	.238	0	1986-87
Reay, Billy (4)	Toronto	90	26	50	14	.367	0	1957-59
	Chicago	1012	516	335	161	.589	0	1963-77
	Total	**1102**	**542**	**385**	**175**	**.571**	**0**	**1957-77**
Regan, Larry	Los Angeles	88	27	47	14	.386	0	1970-72
Risebrough, Doug	Calgary	144	71	56	17	.552	0	1990-92
Roberts, Jim	Buffalo	45	21	16	8	.556	0	1981-82
	Hartford	80	26	41	13	.406	0	1991-92
	Total	**125**	**47**	**56**	**22**	**.464**	**0**	**1981-92**
Robinson, Larry	Los Angeles	82	24	40	18	.402	0	1995-96
Ross, Art (22)	Mtl. Wanderers	6	1	5	0	.167	0	1917-18
	Hamilton	24	6	18	0	.250	0	1922-23
	Boston	698	354	254	90	.572	1	1924-28, 1929-34, 1936-39, 1941-45
	Total	**728**	**361**	**277**	**90**	**.558**	**1**	**1917-45**
Ruel, Claude	Montreal	305	172	82	51	.648	1	1968-71, 1979-81
Sather, Glen (12)	Edmonton	842	464	268	110	.616	4	1979-80, 1980-89, 1993-94

Coach	Team	Games	Wins	Losses	Ties	%	Cup Wins	Seasons
Sator, Ted	NY Rangers	99	41	48	10	.465	0	1985-87
	Buffalo	207	96	89	22	.517	0	1986-89
	Total	**306**	**137**	**137**	**32**	**.500**	**0**	**1985-88**
Savard, Andre	Quebec	24	10	13	1	.438	0	1987-88
Schinkel, Ken	Pittsburgh	203	83	92	28	.478	0	1972-74, 1975-77
Schmidt, Milt (18)	Boston	726	245	360	121	.421	0	1954-61, 1962-66
	Washington	43	5	33	5	.174	0	1974-76
	Total	**769**	**250**	**393**	**126**	**.407**	**0**	**1954-66**
Schonfield, Jim	Buffalo	43	19	19	5	.500	0	1985-86
	New Jersey	124	50	59	15	.464	0	1987-90
	Washington	167	80	62	25	.554	0	1993-96
	Total	**334**	**149**	**140**	**45**	**.513**	**0**	**1985-96**
Shaughnessy, Tom	Chicago	21	10	8	3	.548	0	1929-30
Shero, Fred (21)	Philadelphia	554	308	151	95	.642	2	1971-78
	NY Rangers	180	82	74	24	.522	0	1978-81
	Total	**734**	**390**	**225**	**119**	**.612**	**2**	**1971-81**
Simpson, Joe	NY Americans	144	42	72	30	.396	0	1932-35
Simpson, Terry	NY Islanders	187	81	82	24	.497	0	1986-89
	Winnipeg	1	0	1	0	.000	0	1992-93
	Philadelphia	84	35	39	10	.476	0	1993-94
	Winnipeg	97	43	47	7	.479	0	1994-96
	Total	**353**	**152**	**161**	**40**	**.487**	**0**	**1986-96**
Sinden, Harry	Boston	330	151	121	58	.545	1	1966-70, 1979-80, 1984-85
Skinner, Jimmy	Detroit	247	123	78	46	.591	1	1954-58
Smeaton, Cooper	Phi. Quakers	44	4	36	4	.136	0	1930-31
Smith, Alf	Ottawa	18	12	6	0	.667	0	1918-19
Smith, Floyd	Buffalo	241	143	62	36	.668	0	1974-77
	Toronto	68	30	33	5	.478	0	1979-80
	Total	**309**	**173**	**95**	**41**	**.626**	**0**	**1971-80**
Smith, Mike	Winnipeg	23	2	17	4	.174	0	1980-81
Smith, Ron	NY Rangers	44	15	22	7	.420	0	1992-93
Smythe, Conn	Toronto	178	72	81	25	.475	0	1926-30
Sonmor, Glen	Minnesota	416	174	161	81	.516	0	1978-83, 1984-85, 1986-87
Sproule, Harry	Toronto St. Pats	12	7	5	0	.583	0	1919-20
Stanley, Barney	Chicago	23	4	17	2	.217	0	1927-28
Stasiuk, Vic	Philadelphia	154	45	68	41	.425	0	1969-71
	California	75	21	38	16	.387	0	1971-72
	Vancouver	78	22	47	9	.340	0	1972-73
	Total	**307**	**88**	**153**	**66**	**.394**	**0**	**1969-73**
Stewart, Bill	Chicago	69	22	35	12	.406	1	1937-39
Stewart, Ron	NY Rangers	39	15	20	4	.436	0	1975-76
	Los Angeles	80	31	34	15	.481	0	1977-78
	Total	**119**	**46**	**54**	**19**	**.466**	**0**	**1975-78**
Sullivan, Red	NY Rangers	196	58	103	35	.385	0	1962-66
	Pittsburgh	150	47	79	24	.393	0	1967-69
	Washington	19	2	17	0	.105	0	1974-75
	Total	**365**	**107**	**199**	**59**	**.374**	**0**	**1962-75**
Sutherland, Bill	Winnipeg	32	7	22	3	.266	0	1979-80, 1980-81
Sutter, Brian	St. Louis	320	153	124	43	.545	0	1988-92
	Boston	216	120	73	23	.609	0	1992-95
	Total	**488**	**246**	**179**	**63**	**.569**	**0**	**1988-95**
Sutter, Darryl	Chicago	216	110	80	26	.569	0	1992-95
Talbot, Jean-Guy	St. Louis	120	52	53	15	.496	0	1972-74
	NY Rangers	80	30	37	13	.456	0	1977-78
	Total	**200**	**82**	**90**	**28**	**.480**	**0**	**1972-78**
Tessier, Orval	Chicago	213	99	93	21	.514	0	1982-85
Thompson, Paul	Chicago	272	104	127	41	.458	0	1938-45
Thompson, Percy	Hamilton	48	14	34	0	.292	0	1920-22
Tobin, Bill	Chicago	23	11	10	2	.522	0	1929-30
Tremblay, Mario	Montreal	77	40	27	10	.597	0	1995-96
Ubriaco, Gene	Pittsburgh	106	50	47	9	.514	0	1988-90
Vachon, Rogie	Los Angeles	8	4	2	2	.625	0	1983-84, 1987-88, 1994-95
Watson, Bryan	Edmonton	18	4	9	5	.361	0	1980-81
Watson, Phil	NY Rangers	294	118	124	52	.490	0	1955-60
	Boston	84	16	55	13	.268	0	1961-63
	Total	**378**	**134**	**179**	**65**	**.440**	**0**	**1955-64**
Watt, Tom	Winnipeg	181	72	85	24	.464	0	1981-84
	Vancouver	160	52	87	21	.391	0	1985-87
	Toronto	149	52	80	17	.406	0	1990-92
	Total	**490**	**176**	**252**	**62**	**.422**	**0**	**1981-92**
Webster, Tom	NY Rangers	16	5	7	4	.438	0	1986-87
	Los Angeles	240	115	94	31	.544	0	1989-92
	Total	**256**	**120**	**101**	**35**	**.537**	**0**	**1986-92**
Weiland, Cooney	Boston	96	58	20	18	.698	1	1939-41
White, Bill	Chicago	46	16	24	6	.413	0	1976-77
Wiley, Jim	San Jose	57	17	37	3	.325	0	1995-96
Wilson, Johnny	Los Angeles	52	9	34	9	.260	0	1969-70
	Detroit	145	67	56	22	.538	0	1971-73
	Colorado	80	20	46	14	.338	0	1976-77
	Pittsburgh	240	91	105	44	.471	0	1977-80
	Total	**517**	**187**	**241**	**89**	**.448**	**0**	**1969-80**
Wilson, Larry	Detroit	36	3	29	4	.139	0	1976-77
Wilson, Ron	Anaheim	214	84	112	18	.435	0	1993-96
Young, Garry	California	12	2	7	3	.292	0	1972-73
	St. Louis	98	41	41	16	.500	0	1974-76
	Total	**110**	**43**	**48**	**19**	**.477**	**0**	**1972-76**

Toe Blake, seen here sharing the spotlight with Claude Provost during the 1962-63 season, cut his coaching teeth with the Houston Huskies of the USHL , the Buffalo Bisons of the AHL and the Valleyfield Braves of the Quebec Hockey League before joining the Montreal Canadiens prior to the 1955-56 season.

Bob Probert's combination of raw toughness and scoring ability has made him one of the league's top cops on the NHL beat.

All-Time Penalty-Minute Leaders

* active player

(Regular season. Minimum 1,500 minutes)

Player	Teams	Seasons	Games	Penalty Minutes	Mins. per game
Dave Williams, Tor., Van., Det., L.A., Hfd.		14	962	3966	4.12
*Dale Hunter, Que., Wsh.		16	1181	3218	2.73
Chris Nilan, Mtl., NYR, Bos.		13	688	3043	4.42
*Tim Hunter, Cgy., Que., Van.		15	769	3011	3.92
*Marty McSorley, Pit., Edm., L.A., NYR		13	775	2892	3.73
Willi Plett, Atl., Cgy., Min., Bos.		13	834	2574	3.09
*Basil McRae, Que., Tor., Det., Min., T.B., St.L.		15	568	2445	4.31
*Rick Tocchet, Phi., Pit., L.A., Bos.		12	788	2371	3.01
Jay Wells, L.A., Phi., Buf., NYR, St.L.		17	1077	2346	2.18
*Bob Probert, Det., Chi.		10	552	2327	4.22
Garth Butcher, Van., St. L., Que., Tor.		14	897	2302	2.57
Dave Schultz, Phi., L.A., Pit., Buf.		9	535	2294	4.29
*Scott Stevens, Wsh., St.L., N.J.		14	1041	2290	2.20
*Joe Kocur, Det., NYR, Van.		12	684	2270	3.32
Laurie Boschman, Tor., Edm., Wpg., N.J., Ott.		14	1009	2265	2.25
*Pat Verbeek, N.J., Hfd., NYR		14	984	2234	2.27
Rob Ramage, Col., St.L., Cgy., Tor., Min., T.B., Mtl., Phi.		15	1044	2226	2.13
Bryan Watson, Mtl., Oak., Pit., Det., St.L., Wsh.		16	878	2212	2.52
*Shane Churla, Hfd., Cgy., Min., Dal., L.A., NYR		10	443	2195	4.96
*Dave Manson, Chi., Edm., Wpg.		10	688	2140	3.11
Terry O'Reilly, Bos.		14	891	2095	2.35
Al Secord, Bos., Chi., Tor., Phi.		12	766	2093	2.73
*Gord Donnelly, Que., Wpg., Buf., Dal.		12	554	2069	3.74
*Craig Berube, Phi., Tor., Cgy., Wsh.		10	565	2050	3.63
Mike Foligno, Det., Buf., Tor., Fla.		15	1018	2049	2.01
*Ken Daneyko, N.J.		13	796	2048	2.57
Phil Russell, Chi., Atl., Cgy., N.J., Buf.		15	1016	2038	2.01
*Ulf Samuelsson, Hfd., Pit., NYR		12	814	2036	2.50
Harold Snepsts, Van., Min., Det., St.L.		17	1033	2009	1.95
Andre Dupont, NYR, St.L., Phi., Que.		13	800	1986	2.48
*Steve Smith, Edm., Chi.		12	681	1971	2.89
*Chris Chelios, Mtl., Chi.		13	848	1926	2.27
Garry Howatt, NYI, Hfd., N.J.		12	720	1836	2.55
Carol Vadnais, Mtl., Oak., Cal., Bos., NYR, N.J.		17	1087	1813	1.67
Larry Playfair, Buf., L.A.		12	688	1812	2.63
*Mick Vukota, NYI		9	493	1808	3.67
Ted Lindsay, Det., Chi.		17	1068	1808	1.69
Jim Korn, Det., Tor., Buf., N.J., Cgy.		10	597	1801	3.02
David Brown, Phi., Edm., S.J.		14	729	1789	2.45
Brian Sutter, St.L.		12	779	1786	2.29
Bob McGill, Tor., Chi., S.J., Det., NYI, Hfd.		13	705	1766	2.51
*Joel Otto, Cgy., Phi.		12	797	1757	2.21
Wilf Paiement, K.C. Col., Tor., Que., NYR, Buf., Pit.		14	946	1757	1.86
Torrie Robertson, Wsh., Hfd., Det.		10	442	1751	3.96
*Todd Ewen, St.L., Mtl., Ana.		10	467	1749	3.75
*Rob Ray, Buf.		7	424	1748	4.12
Mario Marois, NYR, Van., Que., Wpg., St.L.		15	955	1746	1.83
*Ken Baumgartner, L.A., NYI, Tor., Ana.		9	478	1744	3.65
Gary Roberts, Cgy.		10	585	1736	2.97
Ken Linseman, Phi., Edm., Bos., Tor.		14	860	1727	2.01
Jay Miller, Bos., L.A.		7	446	1723	3.86
Randy Moller, Que., NYR, Buf., Fla.		14	815	1692	2.08
*Michel Petit, Van., NYR, Que., Tor., Cgy., L.A., T.B.		14	757	1691	2.23
Paul Holmgren, Phi., Min.		10	527	1684	3.20
Gordie Howe, Det., Hfd.		26	1767	1675	.948
Gerard Gallant, Det., T.B.		11	615	1674	2.72
Kevin McClelland, Pit., Edm., Det., Tor., Wpg.		12	588	1672	2.84
*Steven Finn, Que., T.B., L.A.		11	671	1640	2.44
*Paul Coffey, Edm., Pit., L.A., Det.		16	1154	1636	1.42
*Kevin Dineen, Hfd., Phi.		12	793	1629	2.05
Jerry Korab, Chi., Van., Buf., L.A.		15	975	1629	1.67
Mel Bridgman, Phi., Cgy., N.J., Det., Van.		14	977	1625	1.66
*Tie Domi, Tor., NYR, Wpg.		7	326	1620	4.97
*Mike Peluso, Chi., Ott., N.J.		7	371	1612	4.35
*Ron Stern, Van., Cgy.		9	414	1611	3.89
Tim Horton, Tor., NYR, Buf., Pit.		24	1446	1611	1.11
Dave Taylor, L.A.		17	1111	1589	1.43
Gordie Roberts, Hfd., Min., Phi., St. L., Pit., Bos.		15	1097	1582	1.44
*Gino Odjick, Van.		6	339	1575	4.65
Paul Baxter, Que., Pit., Cgy.		8	472	1564	3.31
Glen Cochrane, Phi., Van., Chi., Edm.		10	411	1556	3.79
Stan Smyl, Van.		13	896	1556	1.74
Mike Milbury, Bos.		12	754	1552	2.06
Dave Hutchison, L.A., Tor., Chi., N.J.		10	584	1550	2.65
Doug Risebrough, Mtl., Cgy.		13	740	1542	2.08
Bill Gadsby, Chi., NYR, Det.		20	1248	1539	1.23
*Sergio Momesso, Mtl., St.L., Van., Tor., NYR		12	670	1509	2.25
*Mark Messier, Edm., NYR		17	1201	1508	1.26

Year-by-Year Individual Regular-Season Leaders

Season	Goals	G	Assists	A	Points	Pts.	Penalty Minutes	PIM
1917-18	Joe Malone	44	no assists recorded	...	Joe Malone	44	Joe Hall	60
1918-19	Newsy Lalonde	23	Newsy Lalonde	9	Newsy Lalonde	32	Joe Hall	85
1919-20	Joe Malone	39	Cy Denneny	12	Joe Malone	48	Cully Wilson	79
1920-21	Babe Dye	35	Harry Cameron	9	Newsy Lalonde	41	Bert Corbeau	86
			Louis Berlinquette	9				
			Joe Matte	9				
1921-22	Punch Broadbent	32	Punch Broadbent	14	Punch Broadbent	46	Sprague Cleghorn	63
			Leo Reise	14				
1922-23	Babe Dye	26	Edmond Bouchard	12	Babe Dye	37	Billy Boucher	52
1923-24	Cy Denneny	22	King Clancy	8	Cy Denneny	23	Bert Corbeau	55
1924-25	Babe Dye	38	Cy Denneny	15	Babe Dye	44	Billy Boucher	92
1925-26	Nels Stewart	34	Frank Nighbor	13	Nels Stewart	42	Bert Corbeau	121
1926-27	Bill Cook	33	Dick Irvin	18	Bill Cook	37	Nels Stewart	133
1927-28	Howie Morenz	33	Howie Morenz	18	Howie Morenz	51	Eddie Shore	165
1928-29	Ace Bailey	22	Frank Boucher	16	Ace Bailey	32	Red Dutton	139
1929-30	Cooney Weiland	43	Frank Boucher	36	Cooney Weiland	73	Joe Lamb	119
1930-31	Charlie Conacher	31	Joe Primeau	32	Howie Morenz	51	Harvey Rockburn	118
1931-32	Charlie Conacher	34	Joe Primeau	37	Busher Jackson	53	Red Dutton	107
	Bill Cook	34						
1932-33	Bill Cook	28	Frank Boucher	28	Bill Cook	50	Red Horner	144
1933-34	Charlie Conacher	32	Joe Primeau	32	Charlie Conacher	52	Red Horner	126*
1934-35	Charlie Conacher	36	Art Chapman	34	Charlie Conacher	57	Red Horner	125
1935-36	Charlie Conacher	23	Art Chapman	28	Sweeney Schriner	45	Red Horner	167
	Bill Thoms	23						
1936-37	Larry Aurie	23	Syl Apps	29	Sweeney Schriner	46	Red Horner	124
	Nels Stewart	23						
1937-38	Gordie Drillon	26	Syl Apps	29	Gordie Drillon	52	Red Horner	82*
1938-39	Roy Conacher	26	Bill Cowley	34	Toe Blake	47	Red Horner	85
1939-40	Bryan Hextall	24	Milt Schmidt	30	Milt Schmidt	52	Red Horner	87
1940-41	Bryan Hextall	26	Bill Cowley	45	Bill Cowley	62	Jimmy Orlando	99
1941-42	Lynn Patrick	32	Phil Watson	37	Bryan Hextall	56	Jimmy Orlando	81**
1942-43	Doug Bentley	33	Bill Cowley	45	Doug Bentley	73	Jimmy Orlando	89*
1943-44	Doug Bentley	38	Clint Smith	49	Herb Cain	82	Mike McMahon	98
1944-45	Maurice Richard	50	Elmer Lach	54	Elmer Lach	80	Pat Egan	86
1945-46	Gaye Stewart	37	Elmer Lach	34	Max Bentley	61	Jack Stewart	73
1946-47	Maurice Richard	45	Billy Taylor	46	Max Bentley	72	Gus Mortson	133
1947-48	Ted Lindsay	33	Doug Bentley	37	Elmer Lach	61	Bill Barilko	147
1948-49	Sid Abel	28	Doug Bentley	43	Roy Conacher	68	Bill Ezinicki	145
1949-50	Maurice Richard	43	Ted Lindsay	55	Ted Lindsay	78	Bill Ezinicki	144
1950-51	Gordie Howe	43	Gordie Howe	43	Gordie Howe	86	Gus Mortson	142
1951-52	Gordie Howe	47	Elmer Lach	50	Gordie Howe	86	Gus Kyle	127
1952-53	Gordie Howe	49	Gordie Howe	46	Gordie Howe	95	Maurice Richard	112
1953-54	Maurice Richard	37	Gordie Howe	48	Gordie Howe	81	Gus Mortson	132
1954-55	Maurice Richard	38	Bert Olmstead	48	Bernie Geoffrion	75	Fernie Flaman	150
	Bernie Geoffrion	38						
1955-56	Jean Beliveau	47	Bert Olmstead	56	Jean Beliveau	88	Lou Fontinato	202
1956-57	Gordie Howe	44	Ted Lindsay	55	Gordie Howe	89	Gus Mortson	147
1957-58	Dickie Moore	36	Henri Richard	52	Dickie Moore	84	Lou Fontinato	152
1958-59	Jean Beliveau	45	Dickie Moore	55	Dickie Moore	96	Ted Lindsay	184
1959-60	Bobby Hull	39	Don McKenney	49	Bobby Hull	81	Carl Brewer	150
1960-61	Bernie Geoffrion	50	Jean Beliveau	58	Bernie Geoffrion	95	Pierre Pilote	165
1961-62	Bobby Hull	50	Andy Bathgate	56	Bobby Hull	84	Lou Fontinato	167
					Andy Bathgate	84		
1962-63	Gordie Howe	38	Henri Richard	50	Gordie Howe	86	Howie Young	273
1963-64	Bobby Hull	43	Andy Bathgate	58	Stan Mikita	89	Vic Hadfield	151
1964-65	Norm Ullman	42	Stan Mikita	59	Stan Mikita	87	Carl Brewer	177
1965-66	Bobby Hull	54	Stan Mikita	48	Bobby Hull	97	Reg Fleming	166
			Bobby Rousseau	48				
			Jean Beliveau	48				
1966-67	Bobby Hull	52	Stan Mikita	62	Stan Mikita	97	John Ferguson	177
1967-68	Bobby Hull	44	Phil Esposito	49	Stan Mikita	87	Barclay Plager	153
1968-69	Bobby Hull	58	Phil Esposito	77	Phil Esposito	126	Forbes Kennedy	219
1969-70	Phil Esposito	43	Bobby Orr	87	Bobby Orr	120	Keith Magnuson	213
1970-71	Phil Esposito	76	Bobby Orr	102	Phil Esposito	152	Keith Magnuson	291
1971-72	Phil Esposito	66	Bobby Orr	80	Phil Esposito	133	Bryan Watson	212
1972-73	Phil Esposito	55	Phil Esposito	75	Phil Esposito	130	Dave Schultz	259
1973-74	Phil Esposito	68	Bobby Orr	90	Phil Esposito	145	Dave Schultz	348
1974-75	Phil Esposito	61	Bobby Orr	89	Bobby Orr	135	Dave Schultz	472
			Bobby Clarke	89				
1975-76	Reggie Leach	61	Bobby Clarke	89	Guy Lafleur	125	Steve Durbano	370
1976-77	Steve Shutt	60	Guy Lafleur	80	Guy Lafleur	136	Tiger Williams	338
1977-78	Guy Lafleur	60	Bryan Trottier	77	Guy Lafleur	132	Dave Schultz	405
1978-79	Mike Bossy	69	Bryan Trottier	87	Bryan Trottier	134	Tiger Williams	298
1979-80	Charlie Simmer	56	Wayne Gretzky	86	Marcel Dionne	137	Jimmy Mann	287
	Danny Gare	56			Wayne Gretzky	137		
	Blaine Stoughton	56						
1980-81	Mike Bossy	68	Wayne Gretzky	109	Wayne Gretzky	164	Tiger Williams	343
1981-82	Wayne Gretzky	92	Wayne Gretzky	120	Wayne Gretzky	212	Paul Baxter	409
1982-83	Wayne Gretzky	71	Wayne Gretzky	125	Wayne Gretzky	196	Randy Holt	275
1983-84	Wayne Gretzky	87	Wayne Gretzky	118	Wayne Gretzky	205	Chris Nilan	338
1984-85	Wayne Gretzky	73	Wayne Gretzky	135	Wayne Gretzky	208	Chris Nilan	358
1985-86	Jari Kurri	68	Wayne Gretzky	163	Wayne Gretzky	215	Joey Kocur	377
1986-87	Wayne Gretzky	62	Wayne Gretzky	121	Wayne Gretzky	183	Tim Hunter	375
1987-88	Mario Lemieux	70	Wayne Gretzky	109	Mario Lemieux	168	Bob Probert	398
1988-89	Mario Lemieux	85	Mario Lemieux	114	Mario Lemieux	199	Tim Hunter	375
			Wayne Gretzky	114				
1989-90	Brett Hull	72	Wayne Gretzky	102	Wayne Gretzky	142	Basil McRae	351
1990-91	Brett Hull	86	Wayne Gretzky	122	Wayne Gretzky	163	Rob Ray	350
1991-92	Brett Hull	70	Wayne Gretzky	90	Mario Lemieux	131	Mike Peluso	408
1992-93	Teemu Selanne	76	Adam Oates	97	Mario Lemeiux	160	Marty McSorley	399
	Alex Mogilny	76						
1993-94	Pavel Bure	60	Wayne Gretzky	92	Wayne Gretzky	130	Tie Domi	347
1994-95	Peter Bondra	34	Ron Francis	48	Jaromir Jagr	70	Enrico Ciccone	225
					Eric Lindros	70		
1995-96	Mario Lemieux	69	Mario Lemieux	92	Mario Lemieux	161	Matthew Barnaby	335
			Ron Francis	92				

* Match Misconduct penalty not included in total penalty minutes. ** Three Match Misconduct penalties not included in total penalty minutes. 1946-47 was the first season that a Match penalty was automatically written into the player's total penalty minutes as 20 minutes. Now all penalties, Match, Game Misconduct, and Misconduct, are written as 10 minutes.

One Season Scoring Records

Goals-Per-Game Leaders, One Season

(Among players with 20 goals or more in one season)

Player	Team	Season	Games	Goals	Average
Joe Malone	Montreal	1917-18	20	44	2.20
Cy Denneny	Ottawa	1917-18	22	36	1.64
Newsy Lalonde	Montreal	1917-18	14	23	1.64
Joe Malone	Quebec	1919-20	24	39	1.63
Newsy Lalonde	Montreal	1919-20	23	36	1.57
Joe Malone	Hamilton	1920-21	20	30	1.50
Babe Dye	Ham., Tor.	1920-21	24	35	1.46
Cy Denneny	Ottawa	1920-21	24	34	1.42
Reg Noble	Toronto	1917-18	20	28	1.40
Newsy Lalonde	Montreal	1920-21	24	33	1.38
Odie Cleghorn	Montreal	1918-19	17	23	1.35
Harry Broadbent	Ottawa	1921-22	24	32	1.33
Babe Dye	Toronto	1924-25	29	38	1.31
Babe Dye	Toronto	1921-22	24	30	1.25
Newsy Lalonde	Montreal	1918-19	17	21	1.24
Cy Denneny	Ottawa	1921-22	22	27	1.23
Aurel Joliat	Montreal	1924-25	24	29	1.21
Wayne Gretzky	Edmonton	1983-84	74	87	1.18
Babe Dye	Toronto	1922-23	22	26	1.18
Wayne Gretzky	Edmonton	1981-82	80	92	1.15
Mario Lemieux	Pittsburgh	1992-93	60	69	1.15
Frank Nighbor	Ottawa	1919-20	23	26	1.13
Mario Lemieux	Pittsburgh	1988-89	76	85	1.12
Brett Hull	St. Louis	1990-91	78	86	1.10
Amos Arbour	Montreal	1919-20	20	22	1.10
Cy Denneny	Ottawa	1923-24	21	22	1.05
Joe Malone	Hamilton	1921-22	24	25	1.04
Billy Boucher	Montreal	1922-23	24	25	1.04
Cam Neely	Boston	1993-94	49	50	1.02
Maurice Richard	Montreal	1944-45	50	50	1.00
Howie Morenz	Montreal	1924-25	30	30	1.00
Reg Noble	Toronto	1919-20	24	24	1.00
Corbett Denneny	Toronto	1919-20	23	23	1.00
Jack Darragh	Ottawa	1919-20	22	22	1.00
Alexander Mogilny	Buffalo	1992-93	77	76	.99
Mario Lemieux	Pittsburgh	**1995-96**	70	69	.99
Cooney Weiland	Boston	1929-30	44	43	.98
Phil Esposito	Boston	1970-71	78	76	.97
Jari Kurri	Edmonton	1984-85	73	71	.97

Reg Noble led the Toronto Arenas in scoring during the NHL's first season of 1917-18, finding the back of the net 28 times in 20 games for a goals-per-game average of 1.40.

Assists-Per-Game Leaders, One Season

(Among players with 35 assists or more in one season)

Player	Team	Season	Games	Assists	Average
Wayne Gretzky	Edmonton	1985-86	80	163	2.04
Wayne Gretzky	Edmonton	1987-88	64	109	1.70
Wayne Gretzky	Edmonton	1984-85	80	135	1.69
Wayne Gretzky	Edmonton	1983-84	74	118	1.59
Wayne Gretzky	Edmonton	1982-83	80	125	1.56
Wayne Gretzky	Los Angeles	1990-91	78	122	1.56
Wayne Gretzky	Edmonton	1986-87	79	121	1.53
Mario Lemieux	Pittsburgh	1992-93	60	91	1.52
Wayne Gretzky	Edmonton	1981-82	80	120	1.50
Mario Lemieux	Pittsburgh	1988-89	76	114	1.50
Adam Oates	St. Louis	1990-91	61	90	1.48
Wayne Gretzky	Los Angeles	1988-89	78	114	1.46
Wayne Gretzky	Los Angeles	1989-90	73	102	1.40
Wayne Gretzky	Edmonton	1980-81	80	109	1.36
Mario Lemieux	Pittsburgh	1991-92	64	87	1.36
Mario Lemieux	Pittsburgh	1989-90	59	78	1.32
Bobby Orr	Boston	1970-71	78	102	1.31
Mario Lemieux	Pittsburgh	**1995-96**	70	92	1.31
Mario Lemieux	Pittsburgh	1987-88	77	98	1.27
Bobby Orr	Boston	1973-74	74	90	1.22
Wayne Gretzky	Los Angeles	1991-92	74	90	1.22
Ron Francis	Pittsburgh	**1995-96**	77	92	1.19
Mario Lemieux	Pittsburgh	1985-86	79	93	1.18
Bobby Clarke	Philadelphia	1975-76	76	89	1.17
Peter Stastny	Quebec	1981-82	80	93	1.16
Adam Oates	Boston	1992-93	84	97	1.15
Doug Gilmour	Toronto	1992-93	83	95	1.14
Wayne Gretzky	Los Angeles	1993-94	81	92	1.14
Paul Coffey	Edmonton	1985-86	79	90	1.14
Bobby Orr	Boston	1969-70	76	87	1.14
Bryan Trottier	NY Islanders	1978-79	76	87	1.14
Bobby Orr	Boston	1972-73	63	72	1.14
Bill Cowley	Boston	1943-44	36	41	1.14
Pat LaFontaine	Buffalo	1992-93	84	95	1.13
Steve Yzerman	Detroit	1988-89	80	90	1.13
Paul Coffey	Pittsburgh	1987-88	46	52	1.13
Bobby Orr	Boston	1974-75	80	89	1.11

Player	Team	Season	Games	Assists	Average
Bobby Clarke	Philadelphia	1974-75	80	89	1.11
Paul Coffey	Pittsburgh	1988-89	75	83	1.11
Wayne Gretzky	Los Angeles	1992-93	45	49	1.11
Denis Savard	Chicago	1982-83	78	86	1.10
Ron Francis	Pittsburgh	1994-95	44	48	1.09
Denis Savard	Chicago	1981-82	80	87	1.09
Denis Savard	Chicago	1987-88	80	87	1.09
Wayne Gretzky	Edmonton	1979-80	79	86	1.09
Paul Coffey	Edmonton	1983-84	80	86	1.08
Elmer Lach	Montreal	1944-45	50	54	1.08
Peter Stastny	Quebec	1985-86	76	81	1.07
Jaromir Jagr	Pittsburgh	**1995-96**	82	87	1.06
Mark Messier	Edmonton	1989-90	79	84	1.06
Peter Forsberg	Colorado	**1995-96**	82	86	1.05
Paul Coffey	Edmonton	1984-85	80	84	1.05
Marcel Dionne	Los Angeles	1979-80	80	84	1.05
Bobby Orr	Boston	1971-72	76	80	1.05
Mike Bossy	NY Islanders	1981-82	80	83	1.04
Adam Oates	Boston	1993-94	77	80	1.04
Phil Esposito	Boston	1968-69	74	77	1.04
Bryan Trottier	NY Islanders	1983-84	68	71	1.04
Pete Mahovlich	Montreal	1974-75	80	82	1.03
Kent Nilsson	Calgary	1980-81	80	82	1.03
Peter Stastny	Quebec	1982-83	75	77	1.03
Doug Gilmour	Toronto	1993-94	83	84	1.01
Bernie Nicholls	Los Angeles	1988-89	79	80	1.01
Guy Lafleur	Montreal	1979-80	74	75	1.01
Guy Lafleur	Montreal	1976-77	80	80	1.00
Marcel Dionne	Los Angeles	1984-85	80	80	1.00
Brian Leetch	NY Rangers	1991-92	80	80	1.00
Bryan Trottier	NY Islanders	1977-78	77	77	1.00
Mike Bossy	NY Islanders	1983-84	67	67	1.00
Jean Ratelle	NY Rangers	1971-72	63	63	1.00
Steve Yzerman	Detroit	1993-94	58	58	1.00
Ron Francis	Hartford	1985-86	53	53	1.00
Guy Chouinard	Calgary	1980-81	52	52	1.00
Elmer Lach	Montreal	1943-44	48	48	1.00

Points-Per-Game Leaders, One Season

(Among players with 50 points or more in one season)

Player	Team	Season	Games	Points	Average	Player	Team	Season	Games	Points	Average
Wayne Gretzky	Edmonton	1983-84	74	205	2.77	Cooney Weiland	Boston	1929-30	44	73	1.66
Wayne Gretzky	Edmonton	1985-86	80	215	2.69	Alexander Mogilny	Buffalo	1992-93	77	127	1.65
Mario Lemieux	Pittsburgh	1992-93	60	160	2.67	Peter Stastny	Quebec	1982-83	75	124	1.65
Wayne Gretzky	Edmonton	1981-82	80	212	2.65	Bobby Orr	Boston	1973-74	74	122	1.65
Mario Lemieux	Pittsburgh	1988-89	76	199	2.62	Kent Nilsson	Calgary	1980-81	80	131	1.64
Wayne Gretzky	Edmonton	1984-85	80	208	2.60	Wayne Gretzky	Los Angeles	1991-92	74	121	1.64
Wayne Gretzky	Edmonton	1982-83	80	196	2.45	Denis Savard	Chicago	1987-88	80	131	1.64
Wayne Gretzky	Edmonton	1987-88	64	149	2.33	Steve Yzerman	Detroit	1992-93	84	137	1.63
Wayne Gretzky	Edmonton	1986-87	79	183	2.32	Marcel Dionne	Los Angeles	1978-79	80	130	1.63
Mario Lemieux	Pittsburgh	**1995-96**	70	161	2.30	Dale Hawerchuk	Winnipeg	1984-85	80	130	1.63
Mario Lemieux	Pittsburgh	1987-88	77	168	2.18	Mark Messier	Edmonton	1989-90	79	129	1.63
Wayne Gretzky	Los Angeles	1988-89	78	168	2.15	Bryan Trottier	NY Islanders	1983-84	68	111	1.63
Wayne Gretzky	Los Angeles	1990-91	78	163	2.09	Pat LaFontaine	Buffalo	1991-92	57	93	1.63
Mario Lemieux	Pittsburgh	1989-90	59	123	2.08	Charlie Simmer	Los Angeles	1980-81	65	105	1.62
Wayne Gretzky	Edmonton	1980-81	80	164	2.05	Guy Lafleur	Montreal	1978-79	80	129	1.61
Mario Lemieux	Pittsburgh	1991-92	64	131	2.05	Bryan Trottier	NY Islanders	1981-82	80	129	1.61
Bill Cowley	Boston	1943-44	36	71	1.97	Phil Esposito	Boston	1974-75	79	127	1.61
Phil Esposito	Boston	1970-71	78	152	1.95	Steve Yzerman	Detroit	1989-90	79	127	1.61
Wayne Gretzky	Los Angeles	1989-90	73	142	1.95	Peter Stastny	Quebec	1985-86	76	122	1.61
Steve Yzerman	Detroit	1988-89	80	155	1.94	Michel Goulet	Quebec	1983-84	75	121	1.61
Bernie Nicholls	Los Angeles	1988-89	79	150	1.90	Wayne Gretzky	Los Angeles	1993-94	81	130	1.60
Adam Oates	St. Louis	1990-91	61	115	1.89	Bryan Trottier	NY Islanders	1977-78	77	123	1.60
Phil Esposito	Boston	1973-74	78	145	1.86	Bobby Orr	Boston	1972-73	63	101	1.60
Jari Kurri	Edmonton	1984-85	73	135	1.85	Guy Chouinard	Calgary	1980-81	52	83	1.60
Mike Bossy	NY Islanders	1981-82	80	147	1.84	Elmer Lach	Montreal	1944-45	50	80	1.60
Jaromir Jagr	Pittsburgh	**1995-96**	82	149	1.82	Pierre Turgeon	NY Islanders	1992-93	83	132	1.59
Mario Lemieux	Pittsburgh	1985-86	79	141	1.78	Steve Yzerman	Detroit	1987-88	64	102	1.59
Bobby Orr	Boston	1970-71	78	139	1.78	Mike Bossy	NY Islanders	1978-79	80	126	1.58
Jari Kurri	Edmonton	1983-84	64	113	1.77	Paul Coffey	Edmonton	1983-84	80	126	1.58
Pat LaFontaine	Buffalo	1992-93	84	148	1.76	Marcel Dionne	Los Angeles	1984-85	80	126	1.58
Bryan Trottier	NY Islanders	1978-79	76	134	1.76	Bobby Orr	Boston	1969-70	76	120	1.58
Mike Bossy	NY Islanders	1983-84	67	118	1.76	Eric Lindros	Philadelphia	**1995-96**	73	115	1.58
Paul Coffey	Edmonton	1985-86	79	138	1.75	Charlie Simmer	Los Angeles	1979-80	64	101	1.58
Phil Esposito	Boston	1971-72	76	133	1.75	Teemu Selanne	Winnipeg	1992-93	84	132	1.57
Peter Stastny	Quebec	1981-82	80	139	1.74	Bobby Clarke	Philadelphia	1975-76	76	119	1.57
Wayne Gretzky	Edmonton	1979-80	79	137	1.73	Guy Lafleur	Montreal	1975-76	80	125	1.56
Jean Ratelle	NY Rangers	1971-72	63	109	1.73	Dave Taylor	Los Angeles	1980-81	72	112	1.56
Marcel Dionne	Los Angeles	1979-80	80	137	1.71	Denis Savard	Chicago	1982-83	78	121	1.55
Herb Cain	Boston	1943-44	48	82	1.71	Ron Francis	Pittsburgh	**1995-96**	77	119	1.55
Guy Lafleur	Montreal	1976-77	80	136	1.70	Mike Bossy	NY Islanders	1985-86	80	123	1.54
Dennis Maruk	Washington	1981-82	80	136	1.70	Bobby Orr	Boston	1971-72	76	117	1.54
Phil Esposito	Boston	1968-69	74	126	1.70	Kevin Stevens	Pittsburgh	1991-92	80	123	1.54
Guy Lafleur	Montreal	1974-75	70	119	1.70	Mike Bossy	NY Islanders	1984-85	76	117	1.54
Mario Lemieux	Pittsburgh	1986-87	63	107	1.70	Kevin Stevens	Pittsburgh	1992-93	72	111	1.54
Adam Oates	Boston	1992-93	84	142	1.69	Doug Bentley	Chicago	1943-44	50	77	1.54
Bobby Orr	Boston	1974-75	80	135	1.69	Doug Gilmour	Toronto	1992-93	83	127	1.53
Marcel Dionne	Los Angeles	1980-81	80	135	1.69	Marcel Dionne	Los Angeles	1976-77	80	122	1.53
Guy Lafleur	Montreal	1977-78	78	132	1.69	Eric Lindros	Philadelphia	1994-95	46	70	1.52
Guy Lafleur	Montreal	1979-80	74	125	1.69	Marcel Dionne	Detroit	1974-75	80	121	1.51
Rob Brown	Pittsburgh	1988-89	68	115	1.69	Dale Hawerchuk	Winnipeg	1987-88	80	121	1.51
Jari Kurri	Edmonton	1985-86	78	131	1.68	Paul Coffey	Pittsburgh	1988-89	75	113	1.51
Brett Hull	St. Louis	1990-91	78	131	1.68	Cam Neely	Boston	1993-94	49	74	1.51
Phil Esposito	Boston	1972-73	78	130	1.67						

Bobby Clarke, seen here celebrating his first NHL goal, was the emotional heart and offensive soul of the Philadelphia Flyers dynasty in the mid-1970s. He collected a career-high 119 points during the 1975-76 season for an average of 1.57 points-per-game.

When Bryan Trottier collected 95 points as a freshman with the New York Islanders during the 1975-76 season, he set a new rookie record that many experts felt might never be eclipsed. As it turns out, "never" came five seasons later when Peter Stastny broke Trottier's mark by becoming the first rookie to reach the 100-point plateau.

Rookie Scoring Records

All-Time Top 50 Goal-Scoring Rookies

	Rookie	Team	Position	Season	GP	G	A	PTS
1.	* Teemu Selanne	Winnipeg	Right wing	1992-93	84	**76**	56	132
2.	* Mike Bossy	NY Islanders	Right wing	1977-78	73	**53**	38	91
3.	* Joe Nieuwendyk	Calgary	Center	1987-88	75	**51**	41	92
4.	* Dale Hawerchuk	Winnipeg	Center	1981-82	80	**45**	58	103
5.	Luc Robitaille	Los Angeles	Left wing	1986-87	79	**45**	39	84
6.	Rick Martin	Buffalo	Left wing	1971-72	73	**44**	30	74
	Barry Pederson	Boston	Center	1981-82	80	**44**	48	92
8.	Steve Larmer	Chicago	Right wing	1982-83	80	**43**	47	90
	* Mario Lemieux	Pittsburgh	Center	1984-85	73	**43**	57	100
10.	Eric Lindros	Philadelphia	Center	1992-93	61	**41**	34	75
11.	Darryl Sutter	Chicago	Left wing	1980-81	76	**40**	22	62
	Sylvain Turgeon	Hartford	Left wing	1983-84	76	**40**	32	72
	Warren Young	Pittsburgh	Left wing	1984-85	80	**40**	32	72
14.	* Eric Vail	Atlanta	Left wing	1974-75	72	**39**	21	60
	Anton Stastny	Quebec	Left wing	1980-81	80	**39**	46	85
	* Peter Stastny	Quebec	Center	1980-81	77	**39**	70	109
	Steve Yzerman	Detroit	Center	1983-84	80	**39**	48	87
18.	* Gilbert Perreault	Buffalo	Center	1970-71	78	**38**	34	72
	Neal Broten	Minnesota	Center	1981-82	73	**38**	60	98
	Ray Sheppard	Buffalo	Right wing	1987-88	74	**38**	27	65
	Mikael Renberg	Philadelphia	Left wing	1993-94	83	**38**	44	82
22.	Jorgen Pettersson	St. Louis	Left wing	1980-81	62	**37**	36	73
	Jimmy Carson	Los Angeles	Centre	1986-87	80	**37**	42	79
24.	Mike Foligno	Detroit	Right wing	1979-80	80	**36**	35	71
	Mike Bullard	Pittsburgh	Center	1981-82	75	**36**	27	63
	Paul MacLean	Winnipeg	Right wing	1981-82	74	**36**	25	61
	Tony Granato	NY Rangers	Right wing	1988-89	78	**36**	27	63
28.	Marian Stastny	Quebec	Right wing	1981-82	74	**35**	54	89
	Brian Bellows	Minnesota	Right wing	1982-83	78	**35**	30	65
	Tony Amonte	NY Rangers	Right wing	1991-92	79	**35**	34	69
31.	Nels Stewart	Mtl. Maroons	Center	1925-26	36	**34**	8	42
	* Danny Grant	Minnesota	Left wing	1968-69	75	**34**	31	65
	Norm Ferguson	Oakland	Right wing	1968-69	76	**34**	20	54
	Brian Propp	Philadelphia	Left wing	1979-80	80	**34**	41	75
	Wendel Clark	Toronto	Left wing	1985-86	66	**34**	11	45
	* Pavel Bure	Vancouver	Right wing	1991-92	65	**34**	26	60
37.	* Willi Plett	Atlanta	Right wing	1976-77	64	**33**	23	56
	Dale McCourt	Detroit	Center	1977-78	76	**33**	39	72
	Mark Pavelich	NY Rangers	Center	1981-82	79	**33**	43	76
	Ron Flockhart	Philadelphia	Center	1981-82	72	**33**	39	72
	Steve Bozek	Los Angeles	Center	1981-82	71	**33**	23	56
	Jason Arnott	Edmonton	Center	1993-94	78	**33**	35	68
43.	Bill Mosienko	Chicago	Right wing	1943-44	50	**32**	38	70
	Michel Bergeron	Detroit	Right wing	1975-76	72	**32**	27	59
	* Bryan Trottier	NY Islanders	Center	1975-76	80	**32**	63	95
	Don Murdoch	NY Rangers	Right wing	1976-77	59	**32**	24	56
	Jari Kurri	Edmonton	Left wing	1980-81	75	**32**	43	75
	Bobby Carpenter	Washington	Center	1981-82	80	**32**	35	67
	Kjell Dahlin	Montreal	Right wing	1985-86	77	**32**	39	71
	Petr Klima	Detroit	Left wing	1985-86	74	**32**	24	56
	Darren Turcotte	NY Rangers	Right wing	1989-90	76	**32**	34	66
	Joe Juneau	Boston	Center	1992-93	84	**32**	70	102

All-Time Top 50 Point-Scoring Rookies

	Rookie	Team	Position	Season	GP	G	A	PTS
1.	* Teemu Selanne	Winnipeg	Right wing	1992-93	84	76	56	**132**
2.	* Peter Stastny	Quebec	Center	1980-81	77	39	70	**109**
3.	* Dale Hawerchuk	Winnipeg	Center	1981-82	80	45	58	**103**
4.	Joe Juneau	Boston	Center	1992-93	84	32	70	**102**
5.	* Mario Lemieux	Pittsburgh	Center	1984-85	73	43	57	**100**
6.	Neal Broten	Minnesota	Center	1981-82	73	38	60	**98**
7.	* Bryan Trottier	NY Islanders	Center	1975-76	80	32	63	**95**
8.	Barry Pederson	Boston	Center	1981-82	80	44	48	**92**
	* Joe Nieuwendyk	Calgary	Center	1987-88	75	51	41	**92**
10.	* Mike Bossy	NY Islanders	Right wing	1977-78	73	53	38	**91**
11.	* Steve Larmer	Chicago	Right wing	1982-83	80	43	47	**90**
12.	Marian Stastny	Quebec	Right wing	1981-82	74	35	54	**89**
13.	Steve Yzerman	Detroit	Center	1983-84	80	39	48	**87**
14.	* Sergei Makarov	Calgary	Right wing	1989-90	80	24	62	**86**
	Anton Stastny	Quebec	Left wing	1980-81	80	39	46	**85**
16.	Luc Robitaille	Los Angeles	Left wing	1986-87	79	45	39	**84**
17.	Mikael Renberg	Philadelphia	Left wing	1993-94	83	38	44	**82**
18.	Jimmy Carson	Los Angeles	Center	1986-87	80	37	42	**79**
	Sergei Fedorov	Detroit	Center	1990-91	77	31	48	**79**
	Alexei Yashin	Ottawa	Center	1993-94	83	30	49	**79**
21.	Marcel Dionne	Detroit	Center	1971-72	78	28	49	**77**
22.	Larry Murphy	Los Angeles	Defense	1980-81	80	16	60	**76**
	Mark Pavelich	NY Rangers	Center	1981-82	79	33	43	**76**
	Dave Poulin	Philadelphia	Center	1983-84	73	31	45	**76**
25.	Brian Propp	Philadelphia	Left wing	1979-80	80	34	41	**75**
	Jari Kurri	Edmonton	Left wing	1980-81	75	32	43	**75**
	Denis Savard	Chicago	Center	1980-81	76	28	47	**75**
	Mike Modano	Minnesota	Center	1989-90	80	29	46	**75**
	Eric Lindros	Philadelphia	Center	1992-93	61	41	34	**75**
30.	Rick Martin	Buffalo	Left wing	1971-72	73	44	30	**74**
	* Bobby Smith	Minnesota	Center	1978-79	80	30	44	**74**
32.	Jorgen Pettersson	St. Louis	Left wing	1980-81	62	37	36	**73**
33.	* Gilbert Perreault	Buffalo	Center	1970-71	78	38	34	**72**
	Dale McCourt	Detroit	Center	1977-78	76	33	39	**72**
	Ron Flockhart	Philadelphia	Center	1981-82	72	33	39	**72**
	Sylvain Turgeon	Hartford	Left wing	1983-84	76	40	32	**72**
	Warren Young	Pittsburgh	Left wing	1984-85	80	40	32	**72**
	Carey Wilson	Calgary	Center	1984-85	74	24	48	**72**
	Alexei Zhamnov	Winnipeg	Center	1992-93	68	25	47	**72**
40.	Mike Foligno	Detroit	Right wing	1979-80	80	36	35	**71**
	Dave Christian	Winnipeg	Center	1980-81	80	28	43	**71**
	Mats Naslund	Montreal	Left wing	1982-83	74	26	45	**71**
	Kjell Dahlin	Montreal	Right wing	1985-86	77	32	39	**71**
	* Brian Leetch	NY Rangers	Defense	1988-89	68	23	48	**71**
45.	Bill Mosienko	Chicago	Right wing	1943-44	50	32	38	**70**
46.	Roland Eriksson	Minnesota	Center	1976-77	80	25	44	**69**
	Tony Amonte	NY Rangers	Right wing	1991-92	79	35	34	**69**
48.	Jude Drouin	Minnesota	Center	1970-71	75	16	52	**68**
	Pierre Larouche	Pittsburgh	Center	1974-75	79	31	37	**68**
	Ron Francis	Hartford	Center	1981-82	59	25	43	**68**
	* Gary Suter	Calgary	Defense	1985-86	80	18	50	**68**
	Jason Arnott	Edmonton	Center	1993-94	84	33	35	**68**

* Calder Trophy Winner

50-Goal Seasons

Dennis Maruk

Bob Carpenter

Dave Andreychuk

Player	Team	Date of 50th Goal	Score			Goaltender	Player's Game No.	Team Game No.	Total Goals	Total Games	Age When First 50th Scored (Yrs. & Mos.)
Maurice Richard	Mtl.	18-3-45	Mtl. 4	at	Bos. 2	Harvey Bennett	50	50	50	50	23.7
Bernie Geoffrion	Mtl.	16-3-61	Tor. 2	at	Mtl. 5	Cesare Maniago	62	68	50	64	30.1
Bobby Hull	Chi.	25-3-62	Chi. 1	at	NYR 4	Gump Worsley	70	70	50	70	23.2
Bobby Hull	Chi.	2-3-66	Det. 4	at	Chi. 5	Hank Bassen	52	57	54	65	
Bobby Hull	Chi.	18-3-67	Chi. 5	at	Tor. 9	Bruce Gamble	63	66	52	66	
Bobby Hull	Chi.	5-3-69	NYR 4	at	Chi. 4	Ed Giacomin	64	66	58	74	
Phil Esposito	Bos.	20-2-71	Bos. 4	at	L.A. 5	Denis DeJordy	58	58	76	78	29.0
John Bucyk	Bos.	16-3-71	Bos. 11	at	Det. 4	Roy Edwards	69	69	51	78	35.10
Phil Esposito	Bos.	20-2-72	Bos. 3	at	Chi. 1	Tony Esposito	60	60	66	76	
Bobby Hull	Chi.	2-4-72	Det. 1	at	Chi. 6	Andy Brown	78	78	50	78	
Vic Hadfield	NYR	2-4-72	Mtl. 6	at	NYR 5	Denis DeJordy	78	78	50	78	31.6
Phil Esposito	Bos.	25-3-73	Buf. 1	at	Bos. 6	Roger Crozier	75	75	55	78	
Mickey Redmond	Det.	27-3-73	Det. 8	at	Tor. 1	Ron Low	73	75	52	76	25.3
Rick MacLeish	Phi.	1-4-73	Phi. 4	at	Pit. 5	Cam Newton	78	78	50	78	23.2
Phil Esposito	Bos.	20-2-74	Bos. 5	at	Min. 5	Cesare Maniago	56	56	68	78	
Mickey Redmond	Det.	23-3-74	NYR 3	at	Det 5	Ed Giacomin	69	71	51	76	
Ken Hodge	Bos.	6-4-74	Bos. 2	at	Mtl. 6	Michel Larocque	75	77	50	76	29.10
Rick Martin	Buf.	7-4-74	St. L. 2	at	Buf. 5	Wayne Stephenson	78	78	52	78	22.9
Phil Esposito	Bos.	8-2-75	Bos. 8	at	Det. 5	Jim Rutherford	54	54	61	79	
Guy Lafleur	Mtl.	29-3-75	K.C. 1	at	Mtl. 4	Denis Herron	66	76	53	70	23.6
Danny Grant	Det.	2-4-75	Wsh. 3	at	Det. 8	John Adams	78	78	50	80	29.2
Rick Martin	Buf.	3-4-75	Bos. 2	at	Buf. 4	Ken Broderick	67	79	52	68	
Reggie Leach	Phi.	14-3-76	Atl. 1	at	Phi. 6	Daniel Bouchard	69	69	61	80	25.11
Jean Pronovost	Pit.	24-3-76	Bos. 5	at	Pit. 5	Gilles Gilbert	74	74	52	80	30.3
Guy Lafleur	Mtl.	27-3-76	K.C. 2	at	Mtl. 8	Denis Herron	76	76	56	80	
Bill Barber	Phi.	3-4-76	Buf. 2	at	Phi. 5	Al Smith	79	79	50	80	23.9
Pierre Larouche	Pit.	3-4-76	Wsh. 5	at	Pit. 4	Ron Low	75	79	53	76	20.5
Danny Gare	Buf.	4-4-76	Tor. 2	at	Buf. 5	Gord McRae	79	80	50	79	21.11
Steve Shutt	Mtl.	1-3-77	Mtl. 5	at	NYI 4	Glenn Resch	65	65	60	80	24.8
Guy Lafleur	Mtl.	6-3-77	Mtl. 1	at	Buf. 4	Don Edwards	68	68	56	80	
Marcel Dionne	L.A.	2-4-77	Min. 2	at	L.A. 7	Pete LoPresti	79	79	53	80	25.8
Guy Lafleur	Mtl.	8-3-78	Wsh. 3	at	Mtl. 4	Jim Bedard	63	65	60	78	
Mike Bossy	NYI	1-4-78	Wsh. 2	at	NYI 3	Bernie Wolfe	69	76	53	73	21.2
Mike Bossy	NYI	24-2-79	Det. 1	at	NYI 3	Rogie Vachon	58	58	69	80	
Marcel Dionne	L.A.	11-3-79	L.A. 3	at	Phi. 6	Wayne Stephenson	68	68	59	80	
Guy Lafleur	Mtl.	31-3-79	Pit. 3	at	Mtl. 5	Denis Herron	76	76	52	80	
Guy Chouinard	Atl.	6-4-79	NYR 2	at	Atl. 9	John Davidson	79	79	50	80	22.5
Marcel Dionne	L.A.	12-3-80	L.A. 2	at	Pit. 4	Nick Ricci	70	70	53	80	
Mike Bossy	NYI	16-3-80	NYI 6	at	Chi. 1	Tony Esposito	68	71	51	75	
Charlie Simmer	L.A.	19-3-80	Det. 3	at	L.A. 4	Jim Rutherford	57	73	56	64	26.0
Pierre Larouche	Mtl.	25-3-80	Chi. 4	at	Mtl. 8	Tony Esposito	72	75	50	73	
Danny Gare	Buf.	27-3-80	Det. 1	at	Buf. 10	Jim Rutherford	71	75	56	76	
Blaine Stoughton	Hfd.	28-3-80	Hfd. 4	at	Van. 4	Glen Hanlon	75	75	56	80	27.0
Guy Lafleur	Mtl.	2-4-80	Mtl. 7	at	Det. 2	Rogie Vachon	72	78	50	74	
Wayne Gretzky	Edm.	2-4-80	Min. 1	at	Edm. 1	Gary Edwards	78	79	51	79	19.2
Reggie Leach	Phi.	3-4-80	Wsh. 2	at	Phi. 4	(empty net)	75	79	50	76	
Mike Bossy	NYI	24-1-81	Que. 3	at	NYI 7	Ron Grahame	50	50	68	79	
Charlie Simmer	L.A.	26-1-81	L.A. 7	at	Que. 5	Michel Dion	51	51	56	65	
Marcel Dionne	L.A.	8-3-81	L.A. 4	at	Wpg. 1	Markus Mattsson	68	68	58	80	
Wayne Babych	St. L.	12-3-81	St. L. 3	at	Mtl. 4	Richard Sevigny	70	68	54	78	22.9
Wayne Gretzky	Edm.	15-3-81	Edm. 3	at	Cgy. 3	Pat Riggin	69	69	55	80	
Rick Kehoe	Pit.	16-3-81	Pit. 7	at	Edm. 6	Eddie Mio	70	70	55	80	29.7
Jacques Richard	Que.	29-3-81	Mtl. 0	at	Que. 4	Richard Sevigny	76	75	52	78	28.6
Dennis Maruk	Wsh.	5-4-81	Det. 2	at	Wsh. 7	Larry Lozinski	80	80	50	80	25.3
Wayne Gretzky	Edm.	30-12-81	Phi. 5	at	Edm. 7	(empty net)	39	39	92	80	
Dennis Maruk	Wsh.	21-2-82	Wpg. 3	at	Wsh. 6	Doug Soetaert	61	61	60	80	
Mike Bossy	NYI	4-3-82	Tor. 1	at	NYI 10	Michel Larocque	66	66	64	80	
Dino Ciccarelli	Min.	8-3-82	St. L. 1	at	Min. 8	Mike Liut	67	68	55	76	21.7
Rick Vaive	Tor.	24-3-82	St. L. 3	at	Tor. 4	Mike Liut	72	75	54	77	22.10
Blaine Stoughton	Hfd.	28-3-82	Min. 5	at	Hfd. 2	Gilles Meloche	76	76	52	80	
Rick Middleton	Bos.	28-3-82	Bos. 5	at	Buf. 9	Paul Harrison	72	77	51	75	28.11
Marcel Dionne	L.A.	30-3-82	Cgy. 7	at	L.A. 5	Pat Riggin	75	77	50	78	
Mark Messier	Edm.	31-3-82	L.A. 3	at	Edm. 7	Mario Lessard	78	79	50	78	21.3
Bryan Trottier	NYI	3-4-82	Phi. 3	at	NYI 6	Pete Peeters	79	79	50	80	25.9
Lanny McDonald	Cgy.	18-2-83	Cgy. 1	at	Buf. 5	Bob Sauve	60	60	66	80	30.0
Wayne Gretzky	Edm.	19-2-83	Edm. 10	at	Pit. 7	Nick Ricci	60	60	71	80	
Michel Goulet	Que.	5-3-83	Hfd. 3	at	Que. 10	Mike Veisor	67	67	57	80	22.11
Mike Bossy	NYI	12-3-83	Wsh. 2	at	NYI 6	Al Jensen	70	71	60	79	
Marcel Dionne	L.A.	17-3-83	Que. 3	at	L.A. 4	Daniel Bouchard	71	71	56	80	
Al Secord	Chi.	20-3-83	Tor. 3	at	Chi. 7	Mike Palmateer	73	73	54	80	25.0
Rick Vaive	Tor.	30-3-83	Tor. 4	at	Det. 2	Gilles Gilbert	76	78	51	78	
Wayne Gretzky	Edm.	7-1-84	Hfd. 3	at	Edm. 5	Greg Millen	42	42	87	74	
Michel Goulet	Que.	8-3-84	Que. 8	at	Pit. 6	Denis Herron	63	69	56	75	
Rick Vaive	Tor.	14-3-84	Min. 3	at	Tor. 3	Gilles Meloche	69	72	52	76	
Mike Bullard	Pit.	14-3-84	Pit. 6	at	L.A. 7	Markus Mattsson	71	72	51	76	23.0

Player	Team	Date of 50th Goal	Score			Goaltender	Player's Game No.	Team Game No.	Total Goals	Total Games	Age When First 50th Scored (Yrs. & Mos.)
Jari Kurri	Edm.	15-3-84	Edm. 2	at	Mtl. 3	Rick Wamsley	57	73	52	64	23.10
Glenn Anderson	Edm.	21-3-84	Hfd. 3	at	Edm. 5	Greg Millen	76	76	54	80	23.6
Tim Kerr	Phi.	22-3-84	Pit. 4	at	Phi. 13	Denis Herron	74	75	54	79	24.3
Mike Bossy	NYI	31-3-84	NYI 3	at	Wsh. 1	Pat Riggin	67	79	51	67	
Wayne Gretzky	Edm.	26-1-85	Pit. 3	at	Edm. 6	Denis Herron	49	49	73	80	
Jari Kurri	Edm.	3-2-85	Hfd. 3	at	Edm. 6	Greg Millen	50	53	71	73	
Mike Bossy	NYI	5-3-85	Phi. 5	at	NYI 4	Bob Froese	61	65	58	76	
Michel Goulet	Que.	6-3-85	Buf. 3	at	Que. 4	Tom Barrasso	62	73	55	69	
Tim Kerr	Phi.	7-3-85	Wsh. 6	at	Phi. 9	Pat Riggin	63	65	54	74	
John Ogrodnick	Det.	13-3-85	Det. 6	at	Edm. 7	Grant Fuhr	69	69	55	79	25.9
Bob Carpenter	Wsh.	21-3-85	Wsh. 2	at	Mtl. 3	Steve Penney	72	72	53	80	21.9
Dale Hawerchuk	Wpg.	29-3-85	Chi. 5	at	Wpg. 5	W. Skorodenski	77	77	53	80	21.11
Mike Gartner	Wsh.	7-4-85	Pit. 3	at	Wsh. 7	Brian Ford	80	80	50	80	25.5
Jari Kurri	Edm.	4-3-86	Edm. 6	at	Van. 2	Richard Brodeur	63	65	68	78	
Mike Bossy	NYI	11-3-86	Cgy. 4	at	NYI 8	Rejean Lemelin	67	67	61	80	
Glenn Anderson	Edm.	14-3-86	Det. 3	at	Edm. 12	Greg Stefan	63	71	54	72	
Michel Goulet	Que.	17-3-86	Que. 8	at	Mtl. 6	Patrick Roy	67	72	53	75	
Wayne Gretzky	Edm.	18-3-86	Wpg. 2	at	Edm. 6	Brian Hayward	72	72	52	80	
Tim Kerr	Phi.	20-3-86	Pit. 1	at	Phi. 5	Roberto Romano	68	72	58	76	
Wayne Gretzky	Edm.	4-2-87	Edm. 6	at	Min. 5	Don Beaupre	55	55	62	79	
Dino Ciccarelli	Min.	7-3-87	Pit. 7	at	Min. 3	Gilles Meloche	66	66	52	80	
Mario Lemieux	Pit.	12-3-87	Que. 3	at	Pit. 6	Mario Gosselin	53	70	54	63	21.5
Tim Kerr	Phi.	17-3-87	NYR 1	at	Phi. 4	J. Vanbiesbrouck	67	71	58	75	
Jari Kurri	Edm.	17-3-87	N.J. 4	at	Edm. 7	Craig Billington	69	70	54	79	
Mario Lemieux	Pit.	2-2-88	Wsh. 2	at	Pit. 3	Pete Peeters	51	54	70	77	
Steve Yzerman	Det.	1-3-88	Buf. 0	at	Det. 4	Tom Barrasso	64	64	50	64	22.10
Joe Nieuwendyk	Cgy.	12-3-88	Buf. 4	at	Cgy. 10	Tom Barrasso	66	70	51	75	21.5
Craig Simpson	Edm.	15-3-88	Buf. 4	at	Edm. 6	Jacques Cloutier	71	71	56	80	21.1
Jimmy Carson	L.A.	26-3-88	Chi. 5	at	L.A. 9	Darren Pang	77	77	55	88	19.8
Luc Robitaille	L.A.	1-4-88	L.A. 6	at	Cgy. 3	Mike Vernon	79	79	53	80	21.10
Hakan Loob	Cgy.	3-4-88	Min. 1	at	Cgy. 4	Don Beaupre	80	80	50	80	27.9
Stephane Richer	Mtl.	3-4-88	Mtl. 4	at	Buf. 4	Tom Barrasso	72	80	50	72	21.10
Mario Lemieux	Pit.	20-1-89	Pit. 3	at	Wpg. 7	Eldon Reddick	44	46	85	76	
Bernie Nicholls	L.A.	28-1-89	Edm. 7	at	L.A. 6	Grant Fuhr	51	51	70	79	27.7
Steve Yzerman	Det.	5-2-89	Det. 6	at	Wpg. 2	Eldon Reddick	55	55	65	80	
Wayne Gretzky	L.A.	4-3-89	Phi. 2	at	L.A. 6	Ron Hextall	66	67	54	78	
Joe Nieuwendyk	Cgy.	21-3-89	NYI 1	at	Cgy. 4	Mark Fitzpatrick	72	74	51	77	
Joe Mullen	Cgy.	31-3-89	Wpg. 1	at	Cgy. 4	Bob Essensa	78	79	51	79	32.1
Brett Hull	St. L.	6-2-90	Tor. 4	at	St. L. 6	Jeff Reese	54	54	72	80	25.6
Steve Yzerman	Det.	24-2-90	Det. 3	at	NYI 3	Glenn Healy	63	63	62	79	
Cam Neely	Bos.	10-3-90	Bos. 3	at	NYI 3	Mark Fitzpatrick	69	71	55	76	24.9
Luc Robitaille	L.A.	21-3-90	L.A. 3	at	Van. 6	Kirk McLean	79	79	52	80	
Brian Bellows	Min.	22-3-90	Min. 5	at	Det. 1	Tim Cheveldae	75	75	55	80	25.6
Pat LaFontaine	NYI	24-3-90	NYI 5	at	Edm. 5	Bill Ranford	71	77	54	74	25.1
Stephane Richer	Mtl.	24-3-90	Mtl. 4	at	Hfd. 7	Peter Sidorkiewicz	75	77	51	75	
Gary Leeman	Tor.	28-3-90	NYI 6	at	Tor. 3	Mark Fitzpatrick	78	78	51	80	26.1
Brett Hull	St. L.	25-1-91	St. L. 9	at	Det. 4	Dave Gagnon	49	49	86	78	
Cam Neely	Bos.	26-3-91	Bos. 7	at	Que. 4	empty net	67	78	51	69	
Theoren Fleury	Cgy.	26-3-91	Van. 2	at	Cgy. 7	Bob Mason	77	77	51	79	22.9
Steve Yzerman	Det.	30-3-91	NYR 5	at	Det. 6	Mike Richter	79	79	51	80	
Brett Hull	St. L.	28-1-92	St. L. 3	at	L.A. 3	Kelly Hrudey	50	50	70	73	
Jeremy Roenick	Chi.	7-3-92	Chi. 2	at	Bos. 1	Daniel Berthiaume	67	67	53	80	22.2
Kevin Stevens	Pit.	24-3-92	Pit. 3	at	Det. 4	Tim Cheveldae	74	74	54	80	26.11
Gary Roberts	Cgy.	31-3-92	Edm. 2	at	Cgy. 5	Bill Ranford	73	77	53	76	25.10
Alexander Mogilny	Buf.	3-2-93	Hfd. 2	at	Buf. 3	Sean Burke	46	53	76	77	23.11
Teemu Selanne	Wpg.	28-2-93	Min. 6	at	Wpg. 7	Darcy Wakaluk	63	63	76	84	22.6
Pavel Bure	Van.	1-3-93	Van. 5	at	Buf. 2*	Grant Fuhr	63	63	60	83	21.11
Steve Yzerman	Det.	10-3-93	Det. 6	at	Edm. 3	Bill Ranford	70	70	58	84	
Luc Robitaille	L.A.	15-3-93	L.A. 4	at	Buf. 2	Grant Fuhr	69	69	63	84	
Brett Hull	St. L.	20-3-93	St. L. 2	at	L.A. 3	Robb Stauber	73	73	54	80	
Mario Lemieux	Pit.	21-3-93	Pit. 6	at	Edm. 4**	Ron Tugnutt	48	72	69	60	
Kevin Stevens	Pit.	21-3-93	Pit. 6	at	Edm. 4**	Ron Tugnutt	62	72	55	72	
Dave Andreychuk	Tor.	23-3-93	Tor. 5	at	Wpg. 4	Bob Essensa	72	73	54	83	29.6
Pat LaFontaine	Buf.	28-3-93	Ott. 1	at	Buf. 3	Peter Sidorkiewicz	75	75	53	84	
Pierre Turgeon	NYI	2-4-93	NYI 3	at	NYR 2	Mike Richter	75	76	58	83	23.8
Mark Recchi	Phi.	3-4-93	T.B. 2	at	Phi. 6	J-C Bergeron	77	77	53	84	25.2
Jeremy Roenick	Chi.	15-4-93	Tor. 2	at	Chi. 3	Felix Potvin	84	84	50	84	
Brendan Shanahan	St. L.	15-4-93	T.B. 5	at	St. L. 6	Pat Jablonski	71	84	51	71	24.3
Cam Neely	Bos.	7-3-94	Wsh. 3	at	Bos. 6	Don Beaupre	44	66	50	49	
Sergei Fedorov	Det.	15-3-94	Van. 2	at	Det. 5	Kirk McLean	67	69	56	82	24.3
Pavel Bure	Van.	23-3-94	Van. 6	at	L.A. 3	empty net	65	73	60	76	
Adam Graves	NYR	23-3-94	NYR 5	at	Edm. 3	Bill Ranford	74	74	51	84	25.11
Dave Andreychuk	Tor	24-3-94	S.J. 4	at	Tor. 1	Arturs Irbe	73	74	53	83	
Brett Hull	St.L.	25-3-94	Dal. 3	at	St. L. 5	Andy Moog	71	74	52	81	
Ray Sheppard	Det.	29-3-94	Hfd. 2	at	Det. 6	Sean Burke	74	76	52	82	27.10
Brendan Shanahan	St.L.	12-4-94	St.L. 5	at	Dal. 5	Andy Moog	80	83	52	81	
Mike Modano	Dal.	12-4-94	St.L. 5	at	Dal. 9	Curtis Joseph	75	83	50	76	23.11
Mario Lemieux	Pit.	23-2-96	Hfd. 4	at	Pit. 5	Sean Burke	50	59	69	70	
Jaromir Jagr	Pit.	23-2-96	Hfd. 4	at	Pit. 5	Sean Burke	59	59	62	82	24.0
Alexander Mogilny	Van.	29-2-96	St.L. 2	at	Van. 2	Grant Fuhr	60	63	55	79	
Peter Bondra	Wsh.	3-4-96	Wsh. 5	at	Buf. 1	Andrei Trefilov	62	77	52	67	28.1
Joe Sakic	Col.	7-4-96	Col. 4	at	Dal. 1	empty net	79	79	51	82	26.7
John LeClair	Phi.	10-4-96	Phi. 5	at	N.J. 1	Corey Schwab	80	80	51	82	26.7
Keith Tkachuk	Wpg.	12-4-96	L.A. 3	at	Wpg. 5	Empty Net	75	81	50	76	24.0
Paul Kariya	Ana.	14-4-96	Wpg. 2	at	Ana. 5	N. Khabibulin	82	82	50	82	21.5

* neutral site game played at Hamilton; ** neutral site game played at Cleveland

Peter Bondra

Paul Kariya

John LeClair

100-Point Seasons

Rene Robert

Guy Chouinard

Dino Ciccarelli

Player	Team	Date of 100th Point	G or A	Score		Player's Game No.	Team Game No.	Points G - A PTS	Total Games	Age when first 100th point scored (Yrs. & Mos.)
Phil Esposito	Bos.	2-3-69	(G)	Pit. 0	at Bos. 4	60	62	49-77 — 126	74	27.1
Bobby Hull	Chi.	20-3-69	(G)	Chi. 5	at Bos. 5	71	71	58-49 — 107	76	30.2
Gordie Howe	Det.	30-3-69	(G)	Det. 5	at Chi. 9	76	76	44-59 — 103	76	41.0
Bobby Orr	Bos.	15-3-70	(G)	Det. 5	at Bos. 5	67	67	33-87 — 120	76	22.11
Phil Esposito	Bos.	6-2-71	(A)	Buf. 3	at Bos. 4	51	51	76-76 — 152	78	
Bobby Orr	Bos.	22-2-71	(A)	Bos. 4	at L.A. 5	58	58	37-102 — 139	78	
John Bucyk	Bos.	13-3-71	(G)	Bos. 6	at Van. 3	68	68	51-65 — 116	78	35.10
Ken Hodge	Bos.	21-3-71	(A)	Buf. 7	at Bos. 5	72	72	43-62 — 105	78	26.9
Jean Ratelle	NYR	18-2-72	(A)	NYR 2	at Cal. 2	58	58	46-63 — 109	63	31.4
Phil Esposito	Bos.	19-2-72	(A)	Bos. 6	at Min. 4	59	59	66-67 — 133	76	
Bobby Orr	Bos.	2-3-72	(A)	Van. 3	at Bos. 6	64	64	37-80 — 117	76	
Vic Hadfield	NYR	25-3-72	(A)	NYR 3	at Mtl. 3	74	74	50-56 — 106	78	31.5
Phil Esposito	Bos.	3-3-73	(A)	Bos. 1	at Mtl. 5	64	64	55-75 — 130	78	
Bobby Clarke	Phi.	29-3-73	(G)	Atl. 2	at Phi. 4	76	76	37-67 — 104	78	23.7
Bobby Orr	Bos.	31-3-73	(G)	Bos. 3	at Tor. 7	62	77	29-72 — 101	63	
Rick MacLeish	Phi.	1-4-73	(G)	Phi. 4	at Pit. 5	78	78	50-50 — 100	78	23.3
Phil Esposito	Bos.	13-2-74	(A)	Bos. 9	at Cal. 6	53	53	68-77 — 145	78	
Bobby Orr	Bos.	12-3-74	(A)	Buf. 0	at Bos. 6	62	66	32-90 — 122	74	
Ken Hodge	Bos.	24-3-74	(A)	Mtl. 3	at Bos. 6	72	72	50-55 — 105	76	
Phil Esposito	Bos.	8-2-75	(A)	Bos. 8	at Det. 5	54	54	61-66 — 127	79	
Bobby Orr	Bos.	13-2-75	(A)	Bos. 1	at Buf. 3	57	57	46-89 — 135	80	
Guy Lafleur	Mtl.	7-3-75	(G)	Wsh. 4	at Mtl. 8	56	66	53-66 — 119	70	24.6
Pete Mahovlich	Mtl.	9-3-75	(A)	Mtl. 5	at NYR 3	67	67	35-82 — 117	80	29.5
Marcel Dionne	Det.	9-3-75	(A)	Det. 5	at Phi. 8	67	67	47-74 — 121	80	23.7
Bobby Clarke	Phi.	22-3-75	(A)	Min. 0	at Phi. 4	72	72	27-89 — 116	80	
Rene Robert	Buf.	5-4-75	(A)	Buf. 4	at Tor. 2	74	80	40-60 — 100	74	26.4
Guy Lafleur	Mtl.	10-3-76	(G)	Mtl. 5	at Chi. 1	69	69	56-69 — 125	80	
Bobby Clarke	Phi.	11-3-76	(A)	Buf. 1	at Phi. 6	64	68	30-89 — 119	76	
Bill Barber	Phi.	18-3-76	(A)	Van. 2	at Phi. 3	71	71	50-62 — 112	80	23.8
Gilbert Perreault	Buf.	21-3-76	(G)	K.C. 1	at Buf. 3	73	73	44-69 — 113	80	25.4
Pierre Larouche	Pit.	24-3-76	(G)	Bos. 5	at Pit. 5	70	74	53-58 — 111	76	20.4
Pete Mahovlich	Mtl.	28-3-76	(A)	Mtl. 2	at Bos. 2	77	77	34-71 — 105	80	
Jean Ratelle	Bos.	30-3-76	(A)	Buf. 4	at Bos. 4	77	77	36-69 — 105	80	
Jean Pronovost	Pit.	3-4-76	(A)	Wsh. 5	at Pit. 4	79	79	52-52 — 104	80	30.4
Darryl Sittler	Tor.	3-4-76	(A)	Bos. 4	at Tor. 2	78	79	41-59 — 100	79	26.7
Guy Lafleur	Mtl.	26-2-77	(A)	Clev. 3	at Mtl. 5	63	63	56-80 — 136	80	
Marcel Dionne	L.A.	5-3-77	(A)	Pit. 3	at L.A. 3	67	67	53-69 — 122	80	
Steve Shutt	Mtl.	27-3-77	(A)	Mtl. 6	at Det. 0	77	77	60-45 — 105	80	24.9
Bryan Trottier	NYI	25-2-78	(A)	Chi. 1	at NYI 7	59	60	46-77 — 123	77	21.7
Guy Lafleur	Mtl.	28-2-78	(G)	Det. 3	at Mtl. 9	69	61	60-72 — 132	78	
Darryl Sittler	Tor.	12-3-7?	(A)	Tor. 7	at Pit. 1	67	67	45-72 — 117	80	
Guy Lafleur	Mtl.	27-2-79	(A)	Mtl. 3	at NYI 7	61	61	52-77 — 129	80	
Bryan Trottier	NYI	6-3-79	(A)	Buf. 3	at NYI 2	59	63	47-87 — 134	76	
Marcel Dionne	L.A.	8-3-79	(A)	L.A. 4	at Buf. 6	66	66	59-71 — 130	80	
Mike Bossy	NYI	11-3-79	(G)	NYI 4	at Bos. 4	66	66	69-57 — 126	80	22.2
Bob MacMillan	Atl.	15-3-79	(A)	Atl. 4	at Phi. 5	68	69	37-71 — 108	79	26.6
Guy Chouinard	Atl.	30-3-79	(G)	L.A. 3	at Atl. 5	75	75	50-57 — 107	80	22.5
Denis Potvin	NYI	8-4-79	(A)	NYI 5	at NYR 2	73	80	31-70 — 101	73	25.5
Marcel Dionne	L.A.	6-2-80	(A)	L.A. 3	at Hfd. 7	53	53	53-84 — 137	80	
Guy Lafleur	Mtl.	10-2-80	(A)	Mtl. 3	at Bos. 2	55	55	50-75 — 125	74	
Wayne Gretzky	Edm.	24-2-80	(A)	Bos. 4	at Edm. 2	61	62	51-86 — 137	79	19.2
Bryan Trottier	NYI	30-3-80	(A)	NYI 9	at Que. 6	75	77	42-62 — 104	78	
Gilbert Perreault	Buf.	1-4-80	(A)	Buf. 5	at Atl. 2	77	77	40-66 — 106	80	
Mike Rogers	Hfd.	4-4-80	(A)	Que. 2	at Hfd. 9	79	79	44-61 — 105	80	25.5
Charlie Simmer	L.A.	5-4-80	(G)	Van. 5	at L.A. 3	64	80	56-45 — 101	64	26.0
Blaine Stoughton	Hfd.	6-4-80	(A)	Det. 3	at Hfd. 5	80	80	56-44 — 100	80	27.0
Wayne Gretzky	Edm.	6-2-81	(G)	Wpg. 4	at Edm. 10	53	53	55-109 — 164	80	
Marcel Dionne	L.A.	12-2-81	(A)	L.A. 5	at Chi. 5	58	58	58-77 — 135	80	
Charlie Simmer	L.A.	14-2-81	(A)	Bos. 5	at L.A. 4	59	59	56-49 — 105	65	
Kent Nilsson	Cgy.	27-2-81	(G)	Hfd. 1	at Cgy. 5	64	64	49-82 — 131	80	24.6
Mike Bossy	NYI	3-3-81	(G)	Edm. 8	at NYI 8	65	66	68-51 — 119	79	
Dave Taylor	L.A.	14-3-81	(G)	Min. 4	at L.A. 10	63	70	47-65 — 112	72	25.3
Mike Rogers	Hfd.	22-3-81	(G)	Tor. 3	at Hfd. 3	74	74	40-65 — 105	80	
Bernie Federko	St. L.	28-3-81	(A)	Buf. 4	at St. L. 7	74	76	31-73 — 104	78	24.10
Rick Middleton	Bos.	28-3-81	(A)	Chi. 2	at Bos. 5	76	76	44-59 — 103	80	27.4
Jacques Richard	Que.	29-3-81	(A)	Mtl. 0	at Que. 4	75	76	52-51 — 103	78	28.6
Bryan Trottier	NYI	29-3-81	(G)	NYI 5	at Wsh. 4	69	76	31-72 — 103	73	
Peter Stastny	Que.	29-3-81	(A)	Mtl. 0	at Que. 4	73	76	39-70 — 109	77	24.6
Wayne Gretzky	Edm.	27-12-81	(G)	L.A. 3	at Edm. 10	38	38	92-120 — 212	80	
Mike Bossy	NYI	13-2-82	(A)	Phi. 2	at NYI 8	55	55	64-83 — 147	80	
Peter Stastny	Que.	16-2-82	(A)	Wpg. 3	at Que. 7	60	60	46-93 — 139	80	
Dennis Maruk	Wsh.	20-2-82	(G)	Wsh. 3	at Min. 7	60	60	60-76 — 136	80	26.3
Bryan Trottier	NYI	23-2-82	(G)	Chi. 1	at NYI 5	61	61	50-79 — 129	80	
Denis Savard	Chi.	27-2-82	(A)	Chi. 5	at L.A. 3	64	64	32-87 — 119	80	21.1
Bobby Smith	Min.	3-3-82	(A)	Det. 4	at Min. 6	66	66	43-71 — 114	80	24.1
Marcel Dionne	L.A.	6-3-82	(G)	L.A. 6	at Hfd. 7	64	66	50-67 — 117	78	
Dave Taylor	L.A.	20-3-82	(G)	Pit. 5	at L.A. 7	71	72	39-67 — 106	78	
Dale Hawerchuk	Wpg.	24-3-82	(G)	L.A. 3	at Wpg.	74	74	45-58 — 103	80	18.11
Dino Ciccarelli	Min.	27-3-82	(G)	Min. 6	at Bos. 5	72	76	55-52 — 107	76	21.8
Glenn Anderson	Edm.	28-3-82	(G)	Edm. 6	at L.A. 2	78	78	38-67 — 105	80	21.7
Mike Rogers	NYR	2-4-82	(G)	Pit. 7	at NYR 5	79	79	38-65 — 103	80	

Player	Team	Date of 100th Point	G or A	Score		Player's Game No.	Team Game No.	Points G - A PTS	Total Games	Age when first 100th point scored (Yrs. & Mos.)
Wayne Gretzky	Edm.	5-1-83	(A)	Edm. 8	at Wpg. 3	42	42	71-125 — 196	80	
Mike Bossy	NYI	3-3-83	(A)	Tor. 1	at NYI. 5	66	67	60-58 — 118	79	
Peter Stastny	Que.	5-3-83	(A)	Hfd. 3	at Que. 10	62	67	47-77 — 124	75	
Denis Savard	Chi.	6-3-83	(G)	Mtl. 4	at Chi. 5	65	67	35-86 — 121	78	
Mark Messier	Edm.	23-3-83	(G)	Edm. 4	at Wpg. 7	73	76	48-58 — 106	77	22.2
Barry Pederson	Bos.	26-3-83	(A)	Hfd. 4	at Bos. 7	73	76	46-61 — 107	77	22.0
Marcel Dionne	L.A.	26-3-83	(A)	Edm. 9	at L.A. 3	75	75	56-51 — 107	80	
Michel Goulet	Que.	27-3-83	(A)	Que. 6	at Buf. 6	77	77	57-48 — 105	80	22.11
Glenn Anderson	Edm.	29-3-83	(A)	Edm. 7	at Van. 4	70	78	48-56 -- 104	72	
Jari Kurri	Edm.	29-3-83	(A)	Edm. 7	at Van. 4	78	78	45-59 — 104	80	22.10
Kent Nilsson	Cgy.	29-3-83	(G)	L.A. 3	at Cgy. 5	78	78	46-58 — 104	80	
Wayne Gretzky	Edm.	18-12-83	(G)	Edm. 7	at Wpg. 5	34	34	87-118 — 205	74	22.9
Paul Coffey	Edm.	4-3-84	(A)	Mtl. 1	at Edm. 6"	68	68	40-86 — 126	80	
Michel Goulet	Que.	4-3-84	(A)	Que. 1	at Buf. 1	62	67	56-65 — 121	75	
Jari Kurri	Edm.	7-3-84	(G)	Chi. 4	at Edm. 7	53	69	52-61 — 113	64	
Peter Stastny	Que.	8-3-84	(A)	Que. 8	at Pit. 6	69	69	46-73 — 119	80	
Mike Bossy	NYI	8-3-84	(A)	Tor. 5	at NYI 9	56	68	51-67 — 118	67	
Barry Pederson	Bos.	14-3-84	(A)	Bos. 4	at Det. 2	71	71	39-77 — 116	80	
Bryan Trottier	NYI	18-3-84	(G)	NYI 4	at Hfd. 5	62	73	40-71 — 111	68	
Bernie Federko	St. L.	20-3-84	(A)	Wpg. 3	at St. L. 9	75	76	41-66 — 107	79	
Rick Middleton	Bos.	27-3-84	(G)	Bos. 6	at Que. 4	77	77	47-58 — 105	80	
Dale Hawerchuk	Wpg.	27-3-84	(G)	Wpg. 3	at L.A. 3	77	77	37-65 — 102	80	
Mark Messier	Edm.	27-3-84	(A)	Edm. 9	at Cgy. 2	72	79	37-64 — 101	73	
Wayne Gretzky	Edm.	29-12-84	(A)	Det. 3	at Edm. 6	35	35	73-135 — 208	80	
Jari Kurri	Edm.	29-1-85	(G)	Edm. 4	at Cgy. 2	48	51	71-64 — 135	73	
Mike Bossy	NYI	23-2-85	(A)	Bos. 1	at NYI 7	56	60	58-59 — 117	76	
Dale Hawerchuk	Wpg.	25-2-85	(A)	Wpg. 12	at NYR 5	64	64	53-77 — 130	80	
Marcel Dionne	L.A.	5-3-85	(A)	Pit. 0	at L.A. 6	66	66	46-80 — 126	80	
Brent Sutter	NYI	12-3-85	(A)	NYI 6	at St. L. 5	68	68	42-60 — 102	72	22.10
John Ogrodnick	Det.	22-3-85	(A)	NYR 3	at Det. 5	73	73	55-50 — 105	79	25.9
Paul Coffey	Edm.	26-3-85	(G)	Edm. 7	at NYI 5	74	74	37-84 — 121	80	
Denis Savard	Chi.	29-3-85	(A)	Chi. 5	at Wpg. 5	75	76	38-67 — 105	79	
Peter Stastny	Que.	2-4-85	(A)	Bos. 4	at Que. 6	74	77	32-68 — 100	75	
Bernie Federko	St. L.	4-4-85	(A)	NYR 5	at St. L. 4	74	78	30-73 — 103	76	
John Tonelli	NYI	6-4-85	(G)	NJ 5	at NYI 5	80	80	42-58 — 100	80	28.1
Paul MacLean	Wpg.	6-4-85	(A)	Wpg. 6	at Edm. 5	78	79	41-60 — 101	79	27.1
Bernie Nicholls	L.A.	6-4-85	(A)	Van. 4	at L.A. 4	80	80	46-54 — 100	80	22.9
Mike Gartner	Wsh.	7-4-85	(G)	Pit. 3	at Wsh. 7	80	80	50-52 — 102	80	25.6
Mario Lemieux	Pit.	7-4-85	(A)	Pit. 3	at Wsh. 7	73	80	43-57 — 100	73	19.6
Wayne Gretzky	Edm.	4-1-86	(A)	Hfd. 3	at Edm. 4	39	39	52-163 — 215	80	
Mario Lemieux	Pit.	15-2-86	(G)	Van. 4	at Pit. 9	55	56	48-93 — 141	79	
Paul Coffey	Edm.	19-2-86	(A)	Tor. 5	at Edm. 9	59	60	48-90 — 138	79	
Peter Stastny	Que.	1-3-86	(A)	Buf. 8	at Que. 4	66	68	41-81 — 122	76	
Jari Kurri	Edm.	2-3-86	(G)	Phi. 1	at Edm. 2	62	64	68-63 — 131	78	
Mike Bossy	NYI	8-3-86	(G)	Wsh. 6	at NYI 7	65	65	61-62 — 123	80	
Denis Savard	Chi.	12-3-86	(A)	Buf. 7	at Chi. 6	69	69	47-69 — 116	80	
Mats Naslund	Mtl.	13-3-86	(A)	Mtl. 2	at Bos. 3	70	70	43-67 — 110	80	26.4
Michel Goulet	Que.	24-3-86	(A)	Que. 1	at Min. 0	70	75	53-50 — 103	75	
Glenn Anderson	Edm.	25-3-86	(G)	Edm. 7	at Det. 2	66	74	54-48 — 102	72	
Neal Broten	Min.	26-3-86	(A)	Min. 6	at Tor. 1	76	76	29-76 — 105	80	26.4
Dale Hawerchuk	Wpg.	31-3-86	(A)	Wpg. 5	at L.A. 2	78	78	46-59 — 105	80	
Bernie Federko	St. L.	5-4-86	(A)	Chi. 5	at St. L. 7	79	79	34-68 — 102	80	
Wayne Gretzky	Edm.	11-1-87	(A)	Cgy. 3	at Edm. 5	42	42	62-121 — 183	79	
Jari Kurri	Edm.	14-3-87	(A)	Buf. 3	at Edm. 5	67	68	54-54 — 108	79	
Mario Lemieux	Pit.	18-3-87	(A)	St. L. 4	at Pit. 5	55	72	54-53 — 107	63	
Mark Messier	Edm.	19-3-87	(A)	Edm. 4	at Cgy. 5	71	71	37-70 — 107	77	
Dino Ciccarelli	Min.	30-3-87	(A)	NYR 6	at Min. 5	78	78	52-51 — 103	80	
Doug Gilmour	St. L.	2-4-87	(A)	Buf. 3	at St. L. 5	78	78	42-63 — 105	80	23.10
Dale Hawerchuk	Wpg.	5-4-87	(A)	Wpg. 3	at Cgy. 1	80	80	47-53 — 100	80	
Mario Lemieux	Pit.	20-1-88	(G)	Plt. 8	at Chi. 3	45	48	70-98 — 168	77	
Wayne Gretzky	Edm.	11-2-88	(A)	Edm. 7	at Van. 2	43	56	40-109 — 149	64	
Denis Savard	Chi.	12-2-88	(A)	St. L. 3	at Chi. 4	57	57	44-87 — 131	80	
Dale Hawerchuk	Wpg.	23-2-88	(A)	Wpg. 4	at Pit. 3	61	61	44-77 — 121	80	
Steve Yzerman	Det.	27-2-88	(A)	Det. 4	at Que. 5	63	63	50-52 — 102	64	22.10
Peter Stastny	Que.	8-3-88	(A)	Hfd. 4	at Que. 6	63	67	46-65 — 111	76	
Mark Messier	Edm.	15-3-88	(A)	Buf. 4	at Edm. 6	68	71	37-74 — 111	77	
Jimmy Carson	L.A.	26-3-88	(A)	Chi. 5	at L.A. 9	77	77	55-52 — 107	80	19.8
Hakan Loob	Cgy.	26-3-88	(A)	Van. 1	at Cgy. 6	76	76	50-56 — 106	80	27.9
Mike Bullard	Cgy.	26-3-88	(A)	Van. 1	at Cgy. 6	76	76	48-55 — 103	79	27.1
Michel Goulet	Que.	27-3-88	(A)	Pit. 6	at Que. 3	76	76	48-58 — 106	80	
Luc Robitaille	L.A.	30-3-88	(G)	Cgy. 7	at L.A. 9	78	78	53-58 — 111	80	22.1
Mario Lemieux	Pit.	31-12-88	(A)	N.J. 6	at Pit. 8	36	38	85-114 — 199	76	
Wayne Gretzky	L.A.	21-1-89	(A)	L.A. 4	at Hfd. 5	47	48	54-114 — 168	78	
Bernie Nicholls	L.A.	21-1-89	(A)	L.A. 4	at Hfd. 5	48	48	70-80 — 150	79	
Steve Yzerman	Det.	27-1-89	(G)	Tor. 1	at Det. 8	50	50	65-90 — 155	80	
Rob Brown	Pit.	16-3-89	(A)	Pit. 2	at N.J. 1	60	72	49-66 — 115	68	20.11
Paul Coffey	Pit.	20-3-89	(A)	Pit. 2	at Min. 7	69	74	30-83 — 113	75	
Joe Mullen	Cgy.	23-3-89	(A)	L.A. 2	at Cgy. 4	74	75	51-59 — 110	79	32.1
Jari Kurri	Edm.	29-3-89	(A)	Edm. 5	at Van. 2	75	79	44-58 — 102	76	
Jimmy Carson	Edm.	2-4-89	(A)	Edm. 2	at Cgy. 4	80	80	49-51 — 100	80	
Mario Lemieux	Pit.	28-1-90	(G)	Pit. 2	at Buf. 7	50	50	45-78 — 123	59	
Wayne Gretzky	L.A.	30-1-90	(A)	N.J. 2	at L.A. 5	51	51	40-102 — 142	73	
Steve Yzerman	Det.	19-2-90	(A)	Mtl. 5	at Det. 5	61	61	62-65 — 127	79	
Mark Messier	Edm.	20-2-90	(A)	Edm. 4	at Cgy. 2	62	62	45-84 — 129	79	
Brett Hull	St. L.	3-3-90	(A)	NYI 4	at St. L. 5	67	67	72-41 — 113	80	25.7
Bernie Nicholls	NYR	12-3-90	(A)	L.A. 6	at NYR 2	70	71	39-73 — 112	79	
Pierre Turgeon	Buf.	25-3-90	(A)	N.J. 4	at Buf. 3	76	76	40-66 — 106	80	20.7
Paul Coffey	Pit.	25-3-90	(A)	Pit. 2	at Hfd. 4	77	77	29-74 — 103	80	
Pat LaFontaine	NYI	27-3-90	(G)	Cgy. 4	at NYI 2	72	78	54-51 — 105	74	25.1

Mike Rogers

Teemu Selanne

Joe Sakic

100-Point Seasons — *continued*

Player	Team	Date of 100th Point	G or A	Score		Player's Game No.	Team Game No.	Points G - A PTS	Total Games	Age when first 100th point scored (Yrs. & Mos.)
Adam Oates	St. L.	29-3-90	(G)	Pit 4	at St. L. 5	79	79	23-79 — 102	80	27.7
Joe Sakic	Que.	31-3-90	(G)	Hfd. 3	at Que. 2	79	79	39-63 — 102	80	20.8
Ron Francis	Hfd.	31-3-90	(G)	Hfd. 3	at Que. 2	79	79	32-69 — 101	80	27.0
Luc Robitaille	L.A.	1-4-90	(A)	L.A. 4	at Cgy. 8	80	80	52-49 — 101	80	
Wayne Gretzky	L.A.	30-1-91	(A)	N.J. 4	at L.A. 2	50	51	41-122 — 163	78	
Brett Hull	St. L.	23-2-91	(G)	Bos. 2	at St. L. 9	60	62	86-45 — 131	78	
Mark Recchi	Pit.	5-3-91	(G)	Van. 1	at Pit. 4	66	67	40-73 — 113	78	23.1
Steve Yzerman	Det.	10-3-91	(G)	Det. 4	at St. L. 1	72	72	51-57 — 108	80	
John Cullen	Hfd.	16-3-91	(G)	N.J. 2	at Hfd. 6	71	71	39-71 — 110	78	26.7
Adam Oates	St. L.	17-3-91	(A)	St. L. 4	at Chi. 6	54	73	25-90 — 115	61	
Joe Sakic	Que.	19-3-91	(A)	Edm. 7	at Que. 6	74	74	48-61 — 109	80	
Steve Larmer	Chi.	24-3-91	(A)	Min. 4	at Chi. 5	76	76	44-57 — 101	80	29.9
Theoren Fleury	Cgy.	26-3-91	(G)	Van. 2	at Cgy. 7	77	77	51-53 — 104	79	22.9
Al MacInnis	Cgy.	28-3-91	(A)	Edm. 4	at Cgy. 4	78	78	28-75 — 103	78	27.8
Brett Hull	St. L.	2-3-92	(G)	St. L. 5	at Van. 3	66	66	70-39 — 109	73	
Wayne Gretzky	L.A.	3-3-92	(A)	Phi. 1	at L.A. 4	60	66	31-90 — 121	74	
Kevin Stevens	Pit.	7-3-92	(A)	Pit. 3	at L.A. 5	66	66	54-69 — 123	80	26.11
Mario Lemieux	Pit.	10-03-92	(A)	Cgy. 2	at Pit. 5	53	67	44-87 — 131	64	
Luc Robitaille	L.A.	17-3-92	(A)	Wpg. 4	at L.A. 5	73	73	44-63 — 107	80	
Mark Messier	NYR	22-3-92	(A)	N.J. 3	at NYR 6	74	75	35-72 — 107	79	
Jeremy Roenick	Chi.	29-3-92	(G)	Tor. 1	at Chi. 5	77	77	53-50 — 103	80	22.2
Steve Yzerman	Det.	14-4-92	(G)	Det. 7	at Min. 4	79	80	45-58 — 103	79	
Brian Leetch	NYR	16-4-92	(G)	Pit. 1	at NYR 7	80	80	22-80 — 102	80	24.1
Mario Lemieux	Pit.	31-12-92	(G)	Tor. 3	at Pit. 3	38	39	69-91 — 160	60	
Pat LaFontaine	Buf.	10-2-93	(A)	Buf. 6	at Wpg. 2	55	55	53-95 — 148	84	
Adam Oates	Bos.	14-2-93	(A)	Bos. 3	at T.B. 3	58	58	45-97 — 142	84	
Steve Yzerman	Det.	24-2-93	(A)	Det. 7	at Buf. 10	64	64	58-79 — 137	84	
Pierre Turgeon	NYI	28-2-93	(G)	NYI 7	at Hfd. 6	62	63	58-74 — 132	83	
Doug Gilmour	Tor.	3-3-93	(A)	Min. 1	at Tor. 3	64	64	32-95 — 127	83	
Alexander Mogilny	Buf.	5-3-93	(A)	Hfd. 4	at Buf. 2	58	65	76-51 — 127	77	24.1
Mark Recchi	Phi.	7-3-93	(G)	Phi. 3	at N.J. 7	66	66	53-70 — 123	84	
Teemu Selanne	Wpg.	9-3-93	(G)	Wpg. 4	at T.B. 2	68	68	76-56 — 132	84	22.7
Luc Robitaille	L.A.	15-3-93	(A)	L.A. 4	at Buf. 2	69	69	63-62 — 125	84	
Kevin Stevens	Pit.	23-3-93	(A)	S.J. 2	at Pit. 7	63	73	55-56 — 111	72	
Mats Sundin	Que.	27-3-93	(G)	Phi. 3	at Que. 8	71	75	47-67 — 114	80	22.1
Pavel Bure	Van.	1-4-93	(G)	Van. 5	at T.B. 3	77	77	60-50 — 110	83	22.0
Jeremy Roenick	Chi.	4-4-93	(A)	St. L. 4	at Chi. 5	79	79	50-57 — 107	84	
Craig Janney	St. L.	4-4-93	(A)	St. L. 4	at Chi. 5	79	79	24-82 — 106	84	25.7
Rick Tocchet	Pit.	7-4-93	(G)	Mtl. 3	at Pit. 4	77	81	48-61 — 109	80	28.11
Joe Sakic	Que.	8-4-93	(A)	Que. 2	at Bos. 6	75	81	48-57 — 105	78	
Ron Francis	Pit.	9-4-93	(A)	Pit. 10	at NYR 4	82	82	24-76 — 100	84	
Brett Hull	St. L.	11-4-93	(G)	Min. 1	at St. L. 5	78	82	54-47 — 101	80	
Theoren Fleury	Cgy.	11-4-93	(G)	Cgy. 3	at Van. 6	82	82	34-66 — 100	83	
Joe Juneau	Bos.	14-4-93	(A)	Bos. 4	at Ott. 2	84	84	32-70 — 102	84	25.3
Wayne Gretzky	L.A.	14-2-94	(A)	Bos. 3	at L.A. 2	56	56	38-92 — 130	81	
Sergei Fedorov	Det.	1-3-94	(A)	Cgy. 2	at Det. 5	63	63	56-64 — 120	82	24.2
Doug Gilmour	Tor.	23-3-94	(G)	Tor. 1	at Fla. 1	74	74	27-84 — 111	83	
Adma Oates	Bos.	26-3-94	(A)	Mtl. 3	at Bos. 6	68	75	32-80 — 112	77	
Mark Recchi	Phi.	27-3-94	(A)	Ana. 3	at Phi. 2	76	76	40-67 — 107	84	
Pavel Bure	Van.	28-3-94	(A)	Tor. 2	at Van. 3	68	76	60-47 — 107	76	
Brendan Shanahan	St.L.	12-4-94	(G)	St.L. 5	at Dal. 9	80	83	52-50 — 102	81	25.2
Mario Lemieux	Pit.	16-1-96	(G)	Col. 5	at Pit. 2	38	44	69-92 — 161	70	
Jaromir Jagr	Pit.	6-2-96	(G)	Bos. 5	at Pit. 6	52	52	62-87 — 149	82	23.12
Ron Francis	Pit.	9-3-96	(A)	N.J. 4	at Pit. 3	61	66	27-92 — 119	77	
Peter Forsberg	Col.	9-3-96	(A)	Col. 7	at Van. 5	68	68	30-86 — 116	82	22.7
Joe Sakic	Col.	17-3-96	(A)	Edm. 1	at Col. 8	70	70	51-69 — 120	82	
Teemu Selanne	Ana.	25-3-96	(A)	Ana. 1	at Det. 5	70	73	40-68 — 108	79	
Alexander Mogilny	Van.	25-3-96	(A)	L.A. 1	at Van. 4	72	75	55-52 — 107	79	
Eric Lindros	Phi.	25-3-96	(A)	Hfd. 0	at Phi. 3	65	73	47-68 — 115	73	23.0
Wayne Gretzky	St.L.	28-3-96	(A)	N.J.4	at St.L. 4	76	75	23-79 — 102	80	
Doug Weight	Edm.	30-3-96	(G)	Tor. 4	at Edm. 3	76	76	25-79 — 104	82	25.3
Sergei Fedorov	Det.	2-4-96	(A)	Det. 3	at S.J. 6	72	76	39-68 — 107	78	
Paul Kariya	Ana.	7-4-96	(G)	Ana. 5	at S.J. 3	78	78	68-58 — 108	82	21.5

Eric Lindros

Doug Weight

New York Islanders' sparkplug John Tonelli shrugged off his traditional checking role to score five goals against the Maple Leafs on January 6, 1981.

Five-or-more-Goal Games

Player	Team	Date	Score		Opposing Goaltender
SEVEN GOALS					
Joe Malone	Quebec Bulldogs	Jan. 31/20	Tor. 6	at Que. 10	Ivan Mitchell
SIX GOALS					
Newsy Lalonde	Montreal	Jan. 10/20	Tor. 7	at Mtl. 14	Ivan Mitchell
Joe Malone	Quebec Bulldogs	Mar. 10/20	Ott. 4	at Que. 10	Clint Benedict
Corb Denneny	Toronto St. Pats	Jan. 26/21	Ham. 3	at Tor. 10	Howard Lockhart
Cy Denneny	Ottawa Senators	Mar. 7/21	Ham. 5	at Ott. 12	Howard Lockhart
Syd Howe	Detroit	Feb. 3/44	NYR 2	at Det. 12	Ken McAuley
Red Berenson	St. Louis	Nov. 7/68	St. L. 8	at Phil 0	Doug Favell
Darryl Sittler	Toronto	Feb. 7/76	Bos. 4	at Tor. 11	Dave Reece
FIVE GOALS					
Joe Malone	Montreal	Dec. 19/17	Mtl. 7	at Ott. 4	Clint Benedict
Harry Hyland	Mtl. Wanderers	Dec. 19/17	Tor. 9	at Mtl. W. 10	Arthur Brooks
Joe Malone	Montreal	Jan. 12/18	Ott. 4	at Mtl. 9	Clint Benedict
Joe Malone	Montreal	Feb. 2/18	Tor. 2	at Mtl. 11	Harry Holmes
Mickey Roach	Toronto St. Pats	Mar. 6/20	Que. 2	at Tor. 11	Frank Brophy
Newsy Lalonde	Montreal	Feb. 16/21	Ham. 5	at Mtl. 10	Howard Lockhart
Babe Dye	Toronto St. Pats	Dec. 16/22	Mtl. 2	at Tor. 7	Georges Vezina
Redvers Green	Hamilton Tigers	Dec. 5/24	Ham. 10	at Tor. 3	John Roach
Babe Dye	Toronto St. Pats	Dec. 22/24	Tor. 10	at Bos. 1	Charlie Stewart
Harry Broadbent	Mtl. Maroons	Jan. 7/25	Mtl. 6	at Ham. 2	Vernon Forbes
Pit Lepine	Montreal	Dec. 14/29	Ott. 4	at Mtl. 6	Alex Connell
Howie Morenz	Montreal	Mar. 18/30	NYA 3	at Mtl. 8	Roy Worters
Charlie Conacher	Toronto	Jan. 19/32	NYA 3	at Tor. 11	Roy Worters
Ray Getliffe	Montreal	Feb. 6/43	Bos. 3	at Mtl. 8	Frank Brimsek
Maurice Richard	Montreal	Dec. 28/44	Det. 1	at Mtl. 9	Harry Lumley
Howie Meeker	Toronto	Jan. 8/47	Chi. 4	at Tor. 10	Paul Bibeault
Bernie Geoffrion	Montreal	Feb. 19/55	NYR 2	at Mtl. 10	Gump Worsley
Bobby Rousseau	Montreal	Feb. 1/64	Det. 3	at Mtl. 9	Roger Crozier
Yvan Cournoyer	Montreal	Feb. 15/75	Chi. 3	at Mtl. 12	Mike Veisor
Don Murdoch	NY Rangers	Oct. 12/76	NYR 10	at Min. 4	Gary Smith
Ian Turnbull	Toronto	Feb. 2/77	Det. 1	at Tor. 9	Ed Giacomin (2) Jim Rutherford (3)
Bryan Trottier	NY Islanders	Dec. 23/78	NYR 4	at NYI 9	Wayne Thomas (4) John Davidson (1)
Tim Young	Minnesota	Jan. 15/79	Min. 8	at NYR 1	Doug Soetaert (3) Wayne Thomas (2)

Player	Team	Date	Score		Opposing Goaltender
John Tonelli	NY Islanders	Jan. 6/81	Tor. 3	at NYI 6	Jiri Crha (4) empty net (1)
Wayne Gretzky	Edmonton	Feb. 18/81	St. L. 2	at Edm. 9	Mike Liut (3) Ed Staniowski (2) empty net (1)
Wayne Gretzky	Edmonton	Dec. 30/81	Phi. 5	at Edm. 7	Pete Peeters (4) empty net (1)
Grant Mulvey	Chicago	Feb. 3/82	St. L. 5	at Chi. 9	Mike Liut (4) Gary Edwards (1)
Bryan Trottier	NY Islanders	Feb. 13/82	Phi. 2	at NYI 8	Pete Peeters
Willy Lindstrom	Winnipeg	Mar. 2/82	Wpg. 7	at Phi. 6	Pete Peeters
Mark Pavelich	NY Rangers	Feb. 23/83	Hfd. 3	at NYR 11	Greg Millen
Jari Kurri	Edmonton	Nov. 19/83	NJ. 4	at Edm. 13	Glenn Resch (3) Ron Low (2)
Bengt Gustafsson	Washington	Jan. 8/84	Wsh. 7	at Phi. 1	Pelle Lindbergh
Pat Hughes	Edmonton	Feb. 3/84	Cgy. 5	at Edm. 10	Don Edwards (3) Rejean Lemelin (2)
Wayne Gretzky	Edmonton	Dec. 15/84	Edm. 8	at St. L. 2	Rick Wamsley (4) Mike Liut(1)
Dave Andreychuk	Buffalo	Feb. 6/86	Buf. 8	at Bos. 6	Pat Riggin (1) Doug Keans (4)
Wayne Gretzky	Edmonton	Dec. 6/87	Min. 4	at Edm. 10	Don Beaupre (4) Kari Takko (1)
Mario Lemieux	Pittsburgh	Dec. 31/88	N.J. 6	at Pit. 8	Bob Sauve (3) Chris Terreri (2)
Joe Nieuwendyk	Calgary	Jan. 11/89	Wpg. 3	at Cgy. 8	Daniel Berthiaume
Mats Sundin	Quebec	Mar. 5/92	Que. 10	at Hfd. 4	Peter Sidorkiewicz (3) Kay Whitmore (2)
Mario Lemieux	Pittsburgh	Apr. 9/93	Pit. 10	at NYR 4	Corey Hirsch (3) Mike Richter (2)
Peter Bondra	Washington	Feb. 5/94	T.B. 3	at Wsh. 6	Darren Puppa (4) Pat Jablonski (1)
Mike Ricci	Quebec	Feb. 17/94	Que. 8	at S.J. 2	Arturs Irbe (3) Jimmy Waite (2)
Alexei Zhamnov	Winnipeg	Apr. 1/95	Wpg. 7	at L.A. 7	Grant Fuhr (2)
Mario Lemieux	Pittsburgh	Mar. 26/96	St. L. 4	at Pit. 8	Grant Fuhr (1) Jon Casey (4)

Players' 500th Goals

Player	Team	Date	Game No.	Score		Opposing Goaltender	Total Goals	Total Games
Maurice Richard	Montreal	Oct. 19/57	863	Chi. 1	at Mtl. 3	Glenn Hall	544	978
Gordie Howe	Detroit	Mar. 14/62	1,045	Det. 2	at NYR 3	Gump Worsley	801	1,767
Bobby Hull	Chicago	Feb. 21/70	861	NYR. 2	at Chi. 4	Ed Giacomin	610	1,063
Jean Béliveau	Montreal	Feb. 11/71	1,101	Min. 2	at Mtl. 6	Gilles Gilbert	507	1,125
Frank Mahovlich	Montreal	Mar. 21/73	1,105	Van. 2	at Mtl. 3	Dunc Wilson	533	1,181
Phil Esposito	Boston	Dec. 22/74	803	Det. 4	at Bos. 5	Jim Rutherford	717	1,282
John Bucyk	Boston	Oct. 30/75	1,370	St. L. 2	at Bos. 3	Yves Bélanger	556	1,540
Stan Mikita	Chicago	Feb. 27/77	1,221	Van. 4	at Chi. 3	Cesare Maniago	541	1,394
Marcel Dionne	Los Angeles	Dec. 14/82	887	L.A. 2	at Wsh. 7	Al Jensen	731	1,348
Guy Lafleur	Montreal	Dec. 20/83	918	Mtl. 6	at N.J. 0	Glenn Resch	560	1,126
Mike Bossy	NY Islanders	Jan. 2/86	647	Bos. 5	at NYI 7	empty net	573	752
Gilbert Perreault	Buffalo	Mar. 9/86	1,159	NJ 3	at Buf. 4	Alain Chevrier	512	1,191
*Wayne Gretzky	Edmonton	Nov. 22/86	575	Van. 2	at Edm. 5	empty net	837	1,253
Lanny McDonald	Calgary	Mar. 21/89	1,107	NYI 1	at Cgy. 4	Mark Fitzpatrick	500	1,111
Bryan Trottier	NY Islanders	Feb. 13/90	1,104	Cgy. 4	at NYI 2	Rick Wamsley	524	1,279
*Mike Gartner	NY Rangers	Oct. 14/91	936	Wsh. 5	at NYR 3	Mike Liut	664	1,290
Michel Goulet	Chicago	Feb. 16/92	951	Cgy. 5	at Chi. 5	Jeff Reese	548	1,089
*Jari Kurri	Los Angeles	Oct. 17/92	833	Bos. 6	at L.A. 8	empty net	583	1,099
*Dino Ciccarelli	Detroit	Jan. 8/94	946	Det. 6	at L.A. 3	Kelly Hrudey	551	1,079
*Mario Lemieux	Pittsburgh	Oct. 26/95	605	Pit. 7	at NYI 5	Tommy Soderstrom	563	669
*Mark Messier	NY Rangers	Nov. 6/95	1,141	NYR 4	at Cgy. 2	Rick Tabaracci	539	1,201
*Steve Yzerman	Detroit	Jan. 17/96	906	Col. 2	at Det. 3	Patrick Roy	517	942
*Dale Hawerchuk	St. Louis	Jan. 31/96	1,103	St. L. 4	at Tor. 0	Felix Potvin	506	1,137

*Active

Players' 1,000th Points

Player	Team	Date	Game No.	G or A		Score	Total Points G A PTS	Total Games
Gordie Howe	Detroit	Nov. 27/60	938	(A)	Tor. 0	at Det. 2	801-1,049–1,850	1,767
Jean Béliveau	Montreal	Mar. 3/68	911	(G)	Mtl. 2	at Det. 5	507-712–1,219	1,125
Alex Delvecchio	Detroit	Feb. 16/69	1,143	(A)	LA 3	at Det. 6	456-825–1,281	1,549
Bobby Hull	Chicago	Dec. 12/70	909	(A)	Minn. 3	at Chi. 5	610-560–1,170	1,063
Norm Ullman	Toronto	Oct. 16/71	1,113	(A)	NYR 5	at Tor. 3	490-739–1,229	1,410
Stan Mikita	Chicago	Oct. 15/72	924	(A)	St.L. 3	at Chi. 1	541-926–1,467	1,394
John Bucyk	Boston	Nov. 9/72	1,144	(G)	Det. 3	at Bos. 8	556-813–1,369	1,540
Frank Mahovlich	Montreal	Feb. 17/73	1,090	(A)	Phi. 7	at Mtl. 6	533-570–1,103	1,181
Henri Richard	Montreal	Dec. 20/73	1,194	(A)	Mtl. 2	at Buf. 2	358-688–1,046	1,256
Phil Esposito	Boston	Feb. 15/74	745	(A)	Bos. 4	at Van. 2	717-873–1,590	1,282
Rod Gilbert	NY Rangers	Feb. 19/77	1,027	(G)	NYR 2	at NYI 5	406-615–1,021	1,065
Jean Ratelle	Boston	Apr. 3/77	1,007	(A)	Tor. 4	at Bos. 7	491-776–1,267	1,281
Marcel Dionne	Los Angeles	Jan. 7/81	740	(G)	L.A. 5	at Hfd. 3	731-1,040–1,771	1,348
Guy Lafleur	Montreal	Mar. 4/81	720	(A)	Mtl. 9	at Wpg. 3	560-793–1,353	1,126
Bobby Clarke	Philadelphia	Mar. 19/81	922	(G)	Bos. 3	at Phi. 5	358-852–1,210	1,144
Gilbert Perreault	Buffalo	Apr. 3/82	871	(A)	Buf. 5	at Mtl.4	512-814–1,326	1,191
Darryl Sittler	Philadelphia	Jan. 20/83	927	(G)	Cgy 2	at Phi. 5	484-637–1,121	1,096
*Wayne Gretzky	Edmonton	Dec. 19/84	424	(A)	L.A. 3	at Edm. 7	837-1,771–2,608	1,253
Bryan Trottier	NY Islanders	Jan. 29/85	726	(A)	Min. 4	at NYI 4	524-901–1,425	1,279
Mike Bossy	NY Islanders	Jan. 24/86	656	(A)	NYI 7	at Wsh. 5	573-553–1,126	752
Denis Potvin	NY Islanders	Apr. 4/87	987	(G)	Buf. 6	at NYI 6	310-742–1,052	1,060
Bernie Federko	St. Louis	Mar 19/88	855	(A)	Hfd. 5	at St.L. 3	369-761–1,130	1,000
Lanny McDonald	Calgary	Mar. 7/89	1,101	(G)	Wpg. 5	at Cgy. 9	500-506–1,006	1,111
Peter Stastny	Quebec	Oct. 19/89	682	(G)	Que. 5	at Chi. 3	450-789–1,239	977
*Jari Kurri	Edmonton	Jan. 2/90	716	(A)	Edm. 6	at St.L. 4	583-758–1,341	1,099
*Denis Savard	Chicago	Mar. 11/90	727	(A)	St.L. 6	at Chi. 4	464-847–1,311	1,132
*Paul Coffey	Pittsburgh	Dec. 22/90	770	(A)	Pit. 4	at NYI 3	372-1,038–1,410	1,154
*Mark Messier	Edmonton	Jan. 13/91	822	(A)	Edm. 5	at Phi. 3	539-929–1,468	1,201
Dave Taylor	Los Angeles	Feb. 5/91	930	(A)	L.A. 3	at Phi. 2	431-638–1,069	1,111
Michel Goulet	Chicago	Feb. 23/91	878	(G)	Chi. 3	at Min. 4	548-604–1,152	1,089
*Dale Hawerchuk	Buffalo	Mar. 8/91	781	(G)	Chi. 5	at Buf. 3	506-869–1,375	1,137
Bobby Smith	Minnesota	Nov. 30/91	986	(A)	Min. 4	at Tor. 3	357-679–1,036	1,077
*Mike Gartner	NY Rangers	Jan. 4/92	971	(G)	NYR 4	at N.J. 6	664-581–1,245	1,290
*Ray Bourque	Boston	Feb. 29/92	933	(A)	Wsh. 5	at Bos. 5	343-970–1,313	1,228
*Mario Lemieux	Pittsburgh	Mar. 24/92	513	(A)	Pit. 3	at Det. 4	563-809–1,372	669
*Glenn Anderson	Toronto	Feb. 22/93	954	(A)	Tor. 8	at Van. 1	498-601–1,099	1,129
*Steve Yzerman	Detroit	Feb. 24/93	737	(A)	Det. 7	at Buf. 10	517-738–1,255	942
*Ron Francis	Pittsburgh	Oct. 28/93	893	(G)	Que. 7	at Pit. 3	376-881–1,257	1,085
*Bernie Nicholls	New Jersey	Feb. 13/94	858	(A)	N.J. 3	at T.B. 3	457-677–1,134	992
*Dino Ciccarelli	Detroit	Mar. 9/94	957	(G)	Det. 5	at Cgy. 1	551-549–1,100	1,079
Brian Propp	Hartford	Mar. 19/94	1,008	(G)	Hfd. 5	at Phi. 3	425-578–1,003	1,016
*Joe Mullen	Pittsburgh	Feb. 7/95	935	(A)	Fla. 3	at Pit. 7	495-546–1,041	1,008
Steve Larmer	NY Rangers	Mar. 8/95	983	(G)	N.J. 4	at NYR 6	441-571–1,012	1,006
*Doug Gilmour	Toronto	Dec. 23/95	935	(A)	Edm. 1	at Tor. 6	346-695–1,041	981
*Larry Murphy	Toronto	Mar. 27/96	1,228	(G)	Tor. 6	at Van. 2	245-761–1,006	1,234
*Dave Andreychuk	New Jersey	Apr. 7/96	998	(G)	NYR 2	at N.J. 4	476-527–1,003	1,001

*Active

Mario Lemieux, above, overcame both injury and illness to become the fourth active player to reach the 500-goal mark when he fired home a hat-trick in Pittsburgh's 7-5 victory over the NY Islanders on October 26, 1995. Two weeks after Lemieux's milestone marker, Mark Messier, below, snapped one of his patented off-wing wrist shots past Calgary's Rick Tabaracci for his 500th career goal as the New York Rangers edged the the Flames 4-2 on November 6, 1995.

Individual Awards

Hart Memorial Trophy

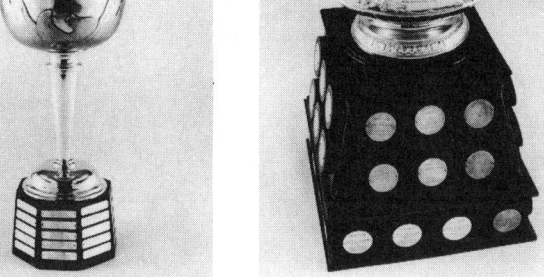

Art Ross Trophy

Calder Memorial Trophy

James Norris Memorial Trophy

HART MEMORIAL TROPHY

An annual award "to the player adjudged to be the most valuable to his team". Winner selected in poll by Professional Hockey Writers' Association in the 26 NHL cities at the end of the regular schedule. The winner receives $10,000 and the runners-up $6,000 and $4,000.

History: The Hart Memorial Trophy was presented by the National Hockey League in 1960 after the original Hart Trophy was retired to the Hockey Hall of Fame. The original Hart Trophy was donated to the NHL in 1923 by Dr. David A. Hart, father of Cecil Hart, former manager-coach of the Montreal Canadiens.

1995-96 Winner: **Mario Lemieux, Pittsburgh Penguins**
Runners-up: **Mark Messier, New York Rangers**
Eric Lindros, Philadelphia Flyers

Center Mario Lemieux of the Pittsburgh Penguins captured the Hart Memorial Trophy, awarded annually "to the player adjudged to be the most valuable to his team." Lemieux was a top five selection on 51 of 54 ballots, attracting 34 first place votes and 439 total points. New York Rangers center Mark Messier placed second, named on 43 of 54 ballots for 275 points.

In 1995-96 Lemieux captured the Art Ross Trophy as the NHL's scoring leader with 161 points (69-92-161) in 70 games, making a remarkable comeback to League play after missing the 1994-95 season recovering from Hodgkin's disease and an ailing back. Lemieux recorded his 500th career goal on Oct. 26, 1995 versus the New York Islanders.

This represents Lemieux's third career Hart Trophy and his first since the 1992-93 season.

ART ROSS TROPHY

An annual award "to the player who leads the league in scoring points at the end of the regular season." The winner receives $10,000 and the runners-up $6,000 and $4,000.

History: Arthur Howie Ross, former manager-coach of Boston Bruins, presented the trophy to the National Hockey League in 1947. If two players finish the schedule with the same number of points, the trophy is awarded in the following manner: 1. Player with most goals. 2. Player with fewer games played. 3. Player scoring first goal of the season.

1995-96 Winner: **Mario Lemieux, Pittsburgh Penguins**
Runners-up: **Jaromir Jagr, Pittsburgh Penguins**
Joe Sakic, Colorado Avalanche

Center Mario Lemieux of the Pittsburgh Penguins received his fifth career Art Ross Trophy in 1996.

Lemieux made a spectacular return to the NHL after missing the 1994-95 season recovering from Hodgkin's disease and an ailing back to record 161 points (69-92-161). Lemieux appeared in 70 games this season, averaging 2.3 points per game. Mario's 69 goals led the NHL and his 92 assists tied him with teammate Ron Francis for the League lead. This is the first Art Ross Trophy for Lemieux since the 1992-93 season, when he recorded 160 points (69-91-160) in 60 games. Lemieux, who has earned his five Art Ross Trophies in the last eight years, becomes just the fourth player in NHL history to

CALDER MEMORIAL TROPHY

An annual award "to the player selected as the most proficient in his first year of competition in the National Hockey League." Winner selected in poll by Professional Hockey Writers' Association at the end of the regular schedule. The winner receives $10,000 and the runners-up $6,000 and $4,000.

History: From 1936-37 until his death in 1943, Frank Calder, NHL President, bought a trophy each year to be given permanently to the outstanding rookie. After Calder's death, the NHL presented the Calder Memorial Trophy in his memory and the trophy is to be kept in perpetuity. To be eligible for the award, a player cannot have played more than 25 games in any single preceding season nor in six or more games in each of any two preceding seasons in any major professional league. Beginning in 1990-91, to be eligible for this award a player must not have attained his twenty-sixth birthday by September 15th of the season in which he is eligible.

1995-96 Winner: **Daniel Alfredsson, Ottawa Senators**
Runners-up: **Eric Daze, Chicago Blackhawks**
Ed Jovanovski, Florida Panthers

Right wing Daniel Alfredsson of the Ottawa Senators has been selected as the winner of the Calder Memorial Trophy, awarded "to the player selected as the most proficient in his first year of competition in the National Hockey League." Alfredsson was a top-five selection on all 54 ballots and polled 437 points, ahead of Chicago Blackhawks left wing Eric Daze (416 points) in the closest Calder balloting since 1986-87, when the Kings' Luc Robitaille edged Philadelphia's Ron Hextall by 18 points.

Alfredsson led all NHL rookies in scoring with 61 points (26-35-61) in 82 games, the only rookie to lead his club in scoring. He also led all rookies in assists (35), power play points (26) and shots (212). He was named the NHL Rookie of the Month twice, the only two-time winner this season, and he was the only rookie selected to play in this year's NHL All-Star Game in Boston. He is the second Swedish player to win the Calder Trophy, following Peter Forsberg in 1995.

JAMES NORRIS MEMORIAL TROPHY

An annual award "to the defense player who demonstrates throughout the season the greatest all-round ability in the position." Winner selected in poll by Professional Hockey Writers' Association at the end of the regular schedule. The winner receives $10,000 and the runners-up $6,000 and $4,000.

History: The James Norris Memorial Trophy was presented in 1953 by the four children of the late James Norris in memory of the former owner-president of the Detroit Red Wings.

1995-96 Winner: **Chris Chelios, Chicago Blackhawks**
Runners-up: **Ray Bourque, Boston Bruins**
Brian Leetch, New York Rangers

Chris Chelios of the Chicago Blackhawks won his third career Norris Trophy in the second-closest voting in the 42-year history of the trophy.

Chelios was named on all 54 ballots, including 22 first-place votes, and earned 408 points, just five more than Boston's Ray Bourque, who collected 403 points, including 23 first-place votes. Bourque was also named on all 54 ballots. Bourque was the victor in the closest race in Norris Trophy history when he edged New Jersey's Scott Stevens by four points in 1993-94.

Chelios led the Chicago Blackhawks in scoring with 72 points (14-58-72), playing in 81 of 82 games. He finished second on the club with a plus-minus rating of +25 and was one of two defensemen to lead his club in scoring (with New Jersey's Phil Housley). Chelios previously won the Norris Trophy with Montreal in 1989 and with the Blackhawks in 1993.

Vezina Trophy

Lady Byng Memorial Trophy

Frank J. Selke Trophy

Conn Smythe Trophy

VEZINA TROPHY

An annual award "to the goalkeeper adjudged to be the best at his position" as voted by the general managers of each of the 26 clubs. Over-all winner receives $10,000, runners-up $6,000 and $4,000.

History: Leo Dandurand, Louis Letourneau and Joe Cattarinich, former owners of the Montreal Canadiens, presented the trophy to the National Hockey League in 1926-27 in memory of Georges Vezina, outstanding goalkeeper of the Canadiens who collapsed during an NHL game November 28, 1925, and died of tuberculosis a few months later. Until the 1981-82 season, the goalkeeper(s) of the team allowing the fewest number of goals during the regular-season were awarded the Vezina Trophy.

1995-96 Winner: **Jim Carey, Washington Capitals**
    Runners-up: **Chris Osgood, Detroit Red Wings**
                    Daren Puppa, Tampa Bay Lightning

Carey was named on 18 of 26 ballots and earned 52 points overall to narrowly edge first-time nominee Chris Osgood of the Detroit Red Wings. Osgood received 46 points and was named on 14 of 26 ballots.

Carey, the first goaltender ever to be nominated for the Vezina Trophy in his first two seasons in the NHL, posted a 35-24-9 record, 2.26 goals-against average and .906 save percentage in 1995-96, appearing in 71 games. His nine shutouts led the NHL and he finished second in wins and third in goals-against average. In two seasons Carey has now posted 13 shutouts in 99 games played.

A 23-year-old native of Dorchester, MA, Carey becomes the third U.S.-born goaltender since 1982 to win the award, following Tom Barrasso (1984) and John Vanbiesbrouck (1986). He is also the first Washington Capitals goaltender to win the award.

LADY BYNG MEMORIAL TROPHY

An annual award "to the player adjudged to have exhibited the best type of sportsmanship and gentlemanly conduct combined with a high standard of playing ability." Winner selected in poll by Professional Hockey Writers' Association at the end of the regular schedule. The winner receives $10,000 and the runners-up $6,000 and $4,000.

History: Lady Byng, wife of Canada's Governor-General at the time, presented the Lady Byng Trophy in 1925. After Frank Boucher of New York Rangers won the award seven times in eight seasons, he was given the trophy to keep and Lady Byng donated another trophy in 1936. After Lady Byng's death in 1949, the National Hockey League presented a new trophy, changing the name to Lady Byng Memorial Trophy.

1995-96 Winner: **Paul Kariya, Mighty Ducks of Anaheim**
    Runners-up: **Adam Oates, Boston Bruins**
                    Teemu Selanne, Winnipeg, Anaheim

Kariya was named on 37 of the 54 ballots and received 255 points, winning a close race with Adam Oates of Boston, who finished as the Lady Byng runner-up for the fourth consecutive year. Kariya shared the scoring lead on the Mighty Ducks with fellow Lady Byng nominee Teemu Selanne, recording 108 points (50-58-108), the Ducks' first 50-goal man. He received just 20 penalty minutes all season.

FRANK J. SELKE TROPHY

An annual award "to the forward who best excels in the defensive aspects of the game." Winner selected in poll by Professional Hockey Writers' Association at the end of the regular schedule. The winner receives $10,000 and the runners-up $6,000 and $4,000.

History: Presented to the National Hockey League in 1977 by the Board of Governors of the NHL in honour of Frank J. Selke, one of the great architects of NHL championship teams.

1995-96 Winner: **Sergei Fedorov, Detroit Red Wings**
    Runners-up: **Ron Francis, Pittsburgh Penguins**
                    Steve Yzerman, Detroit Red Wings

Fedorov received 356 points and was named on 44 of 52 ballots to comfortably outdistance last year's winner Ron Francis of Pittsburgh (255 points) and Detroit teammate Steve Yzerman (57 pts).

A Selke finalist for the third time in his six-year NHL career, Fedorov earned his second career win after posting a plus-minus rating of +49, second in the NHL to teammate Vladimir Konstantinov (+60). Fedorov led the Red Wings in scoring with 107 points (39-68-107) in 78 games and also led the club with three shorthanded goals and 11 game-winning goals. The Red Wings allowed just 181 goals during the season, the fewest of any NHL club.

CONN SMYTHE TROPHY

An annual award "to the most valuable player for his team in the playoffs." Winner selected by the Professional Hockey Writers' Association at the conclusion of the final game in the Stanley Cup Finals. The winner receives $10,000.

History: Presented by Maple Leaf Gardens Limited in 1964 to honor Conn Smythe, the former coach, manager, president and owner-governor of the Toronto Maple Leafs.

1995-96 Winner: **Joe Sakic, Colorado Avalanche**

Colorado center Joe Sakic topped all playoff scorers with 18 goals in 22 playoff games. He was a key factor in all four series en route to the Avalanche's first Cup win. He scored six powerplay goals and six game-winning goals including two overtime goals.

WILLIAM M. JENNINGS TROPHY

An annual award "to the goalkeeper(s) having played a minimum of 25 games for the team with the fewest goals scored against it." Winners selected on regular-season play. Overall winner receives $10,000, runners-up $6,000 and $4,000.

History: The Jennings Trophy was presented in 1981-82 by the National Hockey League's Board of Governors to honor the late William M. Jennings, longtime governor and president of the New York Rangers and one of the great builders of hockey in the United States.

1995-96 Winner: **Mike Vernon, Chris Osgood, Detroit Red Wings**
    Runners-up: **Martin Brodeur, New Jersey Devils**
                    Jim Carey, Washington Capitals

The Detroit Red Wings allowed a League-low 181 goals-against in the regular season, the only NHL club to give up fewer than 200, and Osgood and Vernon combined to post 60 of Detroit's record-breaking 62 wins. They become the first Detroit goaltending combination to capture the Jennings Trophy since its inception in 1981-82. Osgood's 39 wins on the season (39-6-5) led the NHL and he finished second among goaltenders in goals-against average (2.19). Vernon finished the regular season with a 21-7-2 record; his 2.26 goals-against average was fourth-best among goaltenders.

LESTER B. PEARSON AWARD

An annual award presented to the NHL's outstanding player as selected by the members of the National Hockey League Players' Association. The winner receives $10,000.

History: The award was presented in 1970-71 by the NHLPA in honor of the late Lester B. Pearson, former Prime Minister of Canada.

1995-96 Winner: **Mario Lemieux, Pittsburgh Penguins**

Mario Lemieux returned from a year off in 1994-95 to again lead the League in scoring with 161 points in just 70 games. His 69 goals also led the NHL.

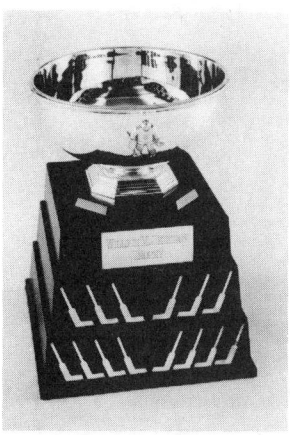

William M. Jennings Trophy

Jack Adams Award

Bill Masterton Trophy

Lester Patrick Trophy

Lester B. Pearson Award

JACK ADAMS AWARD

An annual award presented by the National Hockey League Broadcasters' Association to "the NHL coach adjudged to have contributed the most to his team's success." Winner selected by poll among members of the NHL Broadcasters' Association at the end of the regular season. The winner receives $1,000 from the NHLBA.

History: The award was presented by the NHL Broadcasters' Association in 1974 to commemorate the late Jack Adams, coach and general manager of the Detroit Red Wings, whose lifetime dedication to hockey serves as an inspiration to all who aspire to further the game.

1995-96 Winner: **Scotty Bowman, Detroit Red Wings**
Runners-up: **Doug MacLean, Florida Panthers**
                       Terry Crisp, Tampa Bay Lightning

Bowman polled 39 of a possible 72 first place votes in posting a total of 243 points, ahead of second place Doug MacLean of the Florida Panthers, who finished with 150 points. MacLean was named on 44 of 72 ballots, including 17 first place votes, for 150 points.

Bowman guided the Red Wings to the NHL's best record for the second consecutive year with a 62-13-7 record in 82 games. The 62 wins set an NHL record for most wins in one season. On Dec. 29, 1995, Bowman became the NHL's all-time leader in games coached (1,607), passing Al Arbour.

This represents Bowman's second career Adams win, having captured the award in 1977 with Montreal. He was a runner-up as coach of the Buffalo Sabres in 1984 and finished second to Quebec's Marc Crawford last season.

BILL MASTERTON MEMORIAL TROPHY

An annual award under the trusteeship of the Professional Hockey Writers' Association to "the National Hockey League player who best exemplifies the qualities of perseverance, sportsmanship and dedication to hockey." Winner selected by poll among the 26 chapters of the PHWA at the end of the regular season. A $2,500 grant from the PHWA is awarded annually to the Bill Masterton Scholarship Fund, based in Bloomington, MN, in the name of the Masterton Trophy winner.

History: The trophy was presented by the NHL Writers' Association in 1968 to commemorate the late William Masterton, a player of the Minnesota North Stars, who exhibited to a high degree the qualities of perseverance, sportsmanship and dedication to hockey, and who died January 15, 1968.

1995-96 Winner: **Gary Roberts, Calgary Flames**
Runners-up;   **Grant Fuhr, St. Louis**
                       Steve Smith, Chicago

Roberts made a successful return to the NHL last season after missing 11 months with a neck injury (cervical foraminal stenosis). Roberts, who had last appeared in a League game on Feb. 4, 1995, made his return in January after undergoing two major surgeries and extensive rehabilitation to correct degeneration and bone spurs that narrowed space available for nerves to exit his spine.

After learning he would miss the remainder of the 1994-95 regular season in February, 1995, it was a long and difficult road back. Under the supervision of specialist Dr. Robert Watkins of Los Angeles, Roberts underwent two cervical operations later that year, one in March and one in October, each requiring grueling rehabilitation work. He was cleared to resume ply by Dr. Watkins on January 9, 1996 and suited up for the Flames in a 3-2 win over Hartford on January 10, tallying a goal on his second shift of the game.

His return inspired the Flames, who overcame a slow start to the season and qualified for the Stanley Cup Playoffs by finishing sixth overall in the Western Conference. Limited to just 35 games played for Calgary in 1995-96, Roberts still finished fourth on the club in scoring with 42 points (22-20-42), despite being reinjured late in the season.

On June 17, 1996 Roberts announced his retirement, following careful consideration with his family on the long-term implications of extending his playing career.

LESTER PATRICK TROPHY

An annual award "for outstanding service to hockey in the United States." Eligible recipients are players, officials, coaches, executives and referees. Winner selected by an award committee consisting of the President of the NHL, an NHL Governor, a representative of the New York Rangers, a member of the Hockey Hall of Fame Builder's section, a member of the Hockey Hall of Fame Player's section, a member of the U.S. Hockey Hall of Fame, a member of the NHL Broadcasters' Association and a member of the Professional Hockey Writers' Association. Each except the League President is rotated annually. The winner receives a miniature of the trophy.

History: Presented by the New York Rangers in 1966 to honor the late Lester Patrick, longtime general manager and coach of the New York Rangers, whose teams finished out of the playoffs only once in his first 16 years with the club.

1995-96 Winners: **George Gund**
                       Ken Morrow
                       Milt Schmidt

George Gund, majority owner and chairman of the NHL's San Jose Sharks, has maintained a love affair with hockey that dates back to his days as a youth in his hometown of Cleveland, Ohio. He grew up playing hockey on outdoor ponds and later, as a student at Case Western Reserve University, organized the school's first hockey team.

A longtime supporter of amateur hockey, Gund was instrumental in building an indoor rink in Sun Valley, Idaho and starting senior, junior and women's ice hockey programs. He served on the 1991-92 Team USA Management Committee, is a member of the International Council of USA Hockey, a trustee of the USA Hockey Foundation and past chairman and current trustee of the United States Hockey Hall of Fame.

For the past 21 years, Gund has been involved in NHL team ownership, as a partner with the California Seals, president of the Cleveland Barons, chairman of the Minnesota North Stars and majority owner and president of the San Jose Sharks. Consistent with his devotion to the game, he is the only NHL owner who actively scouts for his team.

Ken Morrow left his mark during a long and successful playing career as one of the best United States-born defensemen in hockey history. Born in Flint, Mich., Morrow attended Bowling Green State University, winning CCHA Player of the Year honors in 1978-79 before joining the United States Olympic Team in 1979-80. He played a key role on the blueline of the "Miracle on Ice" club that captured the gold medal at the Olympic Winter Games in Lake Placid, N.Y., in February 1980.

A fourth round selection of the New York Islanders in the 1976 Amateur Draft, Morrow made his NHL debut with the Islanders immediately following the Lake Placid Olympics and helped the club win its first-ever Stanley Cup Championship. Morrow became the first player in hockey history to ever win an Olympic gold medal and Stanley Cup in the same season. The Islanders, and Morrow, went on to capture four straight Stanley Cups, from 1980 through 1983.

Morrow appeared in 550 career NHL regular season games with the Islanders over 10 seasons before retiring in 1989. He was subsequently named to an assistant coaching position with Flint of the International Hockey League in 1989-90 and later co-coach of the Kansas City Blades in 1990-91. In 1991-92 he joined the Islanders' coaching staff as an assistant to head coach Al Arbour and currently serves as the club's Director of Pro Scouting.

Milt Schmidt's contributions to the Boston Bruins in a career that spanned parts of seven decades as a player, coach, manager and administrator have made him one of the most revered figures in club history. Born in Kitchener, Ontario, he forged a Hockey Hall of Fame playing career with the Bruins from 1936-37 through 1954-55, with the exception of three years serving in the Royal Canadian Air Force during World War II. A center, Schmidt made up one third of the famous "Kraut Line" with wingers Bobby Bauer and Woody Dumart. He was a member of two Stanley Cup Championship clubs, in 1939 and 1941, and captured the Hart Trophy as the NHL's Most Valuable Player in 1951. He was inducted into the Hockey Hall of Fame in 1961.

After retiring as a player, Schmidt coached the Bruins from 1954-55 through 1960-61, and from 1962-63 through 1965-66. He later acted as the club's general manager from 1967-68 through 1971-72, with the Bruins capturing two Stanley Cups during that period, in 1970 and 1972. In 1974-75 Schmidt was hired as the first-ever general manager of the expansion Washington Capitals, where he remained until the 1975-76 season.

King Clancy Memorial Trophy

Alka-Seltzer Plus Award

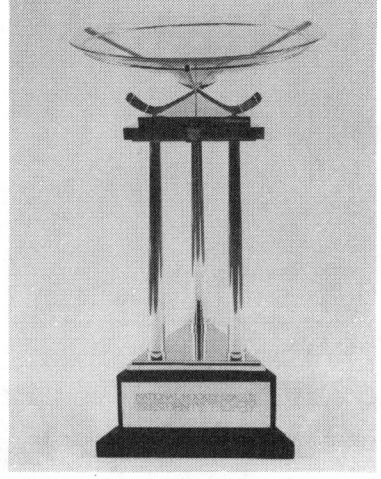

Presidents' Trophy

KING CLANCY MEMORIAL TROPHY

An annual award "to the player who best exemplifies leadership qualities on and off the ice and has made a noteworthy humanitarian contribution in his community."

History: The King Clancy Memorial Trophy was presented to the National Hockey League by the Board of Governors in 1988 to honor the late Frank "King" Clancy.

1995-96 Winner: Kris King, Winnipeg Jets

Kris King has been an inspirational leader, both in the dressing room and in the Winnipeg community, since his arrival in December, 1992 following a trade with the New York Rangers. Named the Jets' captain at the beginning of the 1995-96 season, his leadership was a crucial element in the club's return to the Stanley Cup playoffs for the first time in three years, helping a young club remain unified and focused throughout its last season in Winnipeg.

King has also been the club's most active player in the community, donating countless hours to the Ronald McDonald House of Manitoba, the Manitoba Muscular Dystrophy Association and the Goals For Kids Foundation, among others. He has acted as Honorary Chairman of the Ronald McDonald House of Manitoba for the last three and a half years, enthusiastically participating in fundraising efforts, hospital visits and other charity events, and has supplied Jets tickets to parents of children staying at the House. He has been his club's most active member in the Goals For Kids Foundation, the official charity of the Winnipeg Jets, donating his time to numerous charities the Foundation is involved with, and served as Guest Speaker this year at the Winnipeg Jets Goals For Kids/Manitoba Special Olympics Dinner.

He has served as Chairman of the Manitoba Muscular Dystrophy Association for the last three years, has worked with the Royal Canadian Mounted Police as part of their "On Side" program to help provide guidance and leadership to underprivileged juveniles, and frequently helps a "Make a Wish" request come true by taking sick children on a dressing room tour or skate. Fans of the new Phoenix Coyotes will soon discover their community enriched by the efforts of Kris King.

ALKA-SELTZER PLUS AWARD

An annual award "to the player, having played a minimum of 60 games (34 games in 1994-95), who leads the League in plus/minus statistics" at the end of the regular season. Miles, Inc. will contribute $5,000 on behalf of the winner to the charity of his choice and $1000 on behalf of each individual team winner.

History: The award was presented to the NHL in 1989-90 by Miles, Inc., to recognize the League leader in plus-minus statistics. Plus-minus statistics are calculated by giving a player a "plus" when on-ice for an even-strength or shorthand goal scored by his team. He receives a "minus" when on-ice for an even-strength or shorthand goal scored by the opposing team. A plus-minus award has been presented since the 1982-83 season.

1995-96 Winner: Vladimir Konstantinov, Detroit Red Wings

Detroit defenseman Vladimir Konstantinov was the NHL's leader in +/– in 1995-96 with a total of +60 in 81 games played. The second highest +/– figure belonged to Detroit's Sergei Fedorov who finished with a rating of +49. Tied for third were Petr Nedved of Pittsburgh and Viacheslav Fetisov of Detroit who each had a rating of +37. Team +/– leaders for 1995-96 were: Anaheim, Alex Hicks; Boston, Ray Bourque; Buffalo, Brad May; Calgary, Theoren Fleury; Chicago, Keith Carney; Colorado, Curtis Leschyshyn; Dallas, Richard Matvichuk; Detroit, Vladimir Konstantinov; Edmonton, Miroslav Satan; Florida, Bill Lindsay; Hartford, Glen Featherstone; Los Angeles, Kevin Todd; Montreal, Peter Popovic; New Jersey, Bobby Holik; NY Islanders, Brent Severyn; NY Rangers, Mark Messier and Pat Verbeek; Ottawa, Radek Bonk; Philadelphia, Petr Svoboda; Pittsburgh, Petr Nedved; St. Louis, Al MacInnis; San Jose, Jeff Odgers; Tampa Bay, Rob Zamuner; Toronto, Mats Sundin; Vancouver, Russ Courtnall; Washington, Mark Tinordi; Winnipeg, Keith Tkachuk.

PRESIDENTS' TROPHY

An annual award to the club finishing the regular-season with the best overall record. The winner receives $200,000, to be split evenly between the team and its players.

History: Presented to the National Hockey League in 1985-86 by the NHL Board of Governors to recognize the team compiling the top regular-season record.

1995-96 Winner: Detroit Red Wings
Runners-up: Colorado Avalanche
Philadelphia Flyers

The Detroit Red Wings set a single-season record for wins in capturing their second straight President's Trophy in 1995-96. The Red Wings finished comfortably atop the league standings with 131 points after going 62-13-7. Only the 1976-77 Montreal Canadiens, whose record for wins Detroit broke, have ever had more points in a season (60-8-12, 132).

The Colorado Avalanche finished second with a 47-25-10 record for 104 points while the Philadelphia Flyers had the third-best regular season mark with a record of 45-24-13 for 103 points.

PRESIDENTS' TROPHY

	Winner	Runner-up
1996	Detroit Red Wings	Colorado Avalanche
1995	Detroit Red Wings	Quebec Nordiques
1994	New York Rangers	New Jersey Devils
1993	Pittsburgh Penguins	Boston Bruins
1992	New York Rangers	Washington Capitals
1991	Chicago Blackhawks	St. Louis Blues
1990	Boston Bruins	Calgary Flames
1989	Calgary Flames	Montreal Canadiens
1988	Calgary Flames	Montreal Canadiens
1987	Edmonton Oilers	Philadelphia Flyers
1986	Edmonton Oilers	Philadelphia Flyers

NHL AWARD MONEY BREAKDOWN

(Players on each club determine how team award money is divided. All award monies are in U.S. funds.)

TEAM AWARDS

Stanley Cup Playoffs	Number of Clubs	Share Per Club	Total
Conference Quarter-Final Losers	8	$ 175,000	$1,400,000
Conference Semi-Final Losers	4	350,000	1,400,000
Conference Championship Losers	2	675,000	1,350,000
Stanley Cup Loser	1	1,075,000	1,075,000
Stanley Cup Winners	1	1,750,000	1,750,000
TOTAL PLAYOFF AWARD MONEY			$6,975,000

Final Standings, Regular Season	Number of Clubs	Share Per Club	Total
Presidents' Trophy			
Club's Share	1	$ 100,000	$ 100,000
Players' Share	1	250,000	250,000
Division Winners	4	425,000	1,700,000
Division Second Place	4	200,000	800,000
TOTAL REGULAR-SEASON AWARD MONEY			$2,850,000

INDIVIDUAL AWARDS	Winner	First Runner-up	Second Runner-up
Hart, Calder, Norris, Ross, Vezina, Byng, Selke, Jennings, Masterton Trophies	$10,000	$6,000	$4,000
Conn Smythe Trophy	$10,000		
TOTAL INDIVIDUAL AWARD MONEY			$190,000

ALL-STARS	Number of winners	Per Player	Total
First Team All-Stars	6	$10,000	$ 60,000
Second Team All-Stars	6	5,000	$ 30,000
TOTAL ALL-STAR AWARD MONEY			$ 90,000
TOTAL ALL AWARDS			**$10,105,000**

NATIONAL HOCKEY LEAGUE INDIVIDUAL AWARD WINNERS

ART ROSS TROPHY

	Winner	Runner-up
1996	Mario Lemieux, Pit.	Jaromir Jagr, Pit.
1995	Jaromir Jagr, Pit.	Eric Lindros, Phi.
1994	Wayne Gretzky, L.A.	Sergei Fedorov, Det.
1993	Mario Lemieux, Pit.	Pat LaFontaine, Buf.
1992	Mario Lemieux, Pit.	Kevin Stevens, Pit.
1991	Wayne Gretzky, L.A.	Brett Hull, St.L.
1990	Wayne Gretzky, L.A.	Mark Messier, Edm.
1989	Mario Lemieux, Pit.	Wayne Gretzky, L.A.
1988	Mario Lemieux, Pit.	Wayne Gretzky, Edm.
1987	Wayne Gretzky, Edm.	Jari Kurri, Edm.
1986	Wayne Gretzky, Edm.	Mario Lemieux, Pit.
1985	Wayne Gretzky, Edm.	Jari Kurri, Edm.
1984	Wayne Gretzky, Edm.	Paul Coffey, Edm.
1983	Wayne Gretzky, Edm.	Peter Stastny, Que.
1982	Wayne Gretzky, Edm.	Mike Bossy, NYI
1981	Wayne Gretzky, Edm.	Marcel Dionne, L.A.
1980	Marcel Dionne, L.A.	Wayne Gretzky, Edm.
1979	Bryan Trottier, NYI	Marcel Dionne, L.A.
1978	Guy Lafleur, Mtl.	Bryan Trottier, NYI
1977	Guy Lafleur, Mtl.	Marcel Dionne, L.A.
1976	Guy Lafleur, Mtl.	Bobby Clarke, Phi.
1975	Bobby Orr, Bos.	Phil Esposito, Bos.
1974	Phil Esposito, Bos.	Bobby Orr, Bos.
1973	Phil Esposito, Bos.	Bobby Clarke, Phi.
1972	Phil Esposito, Bos.	Bobby Orr, Bos.
1971	Phil Esposito, Bos.	Bobby Orr, Bos.
1970	Bobby Orr, Bos.	Phil Esposito, Bos.
1969	Phil Esposito, Bos.	Bobby Hull, Chi.
1968	Stan Mikita, Chi.	Phil Esposito, Bos.
1967	Stan Mikita, Chi.	Bobby Hull, Chi.
1966	Bobby Hull, Chi.	Stan Mikita, Chi.
1965	Stan Mikita, Chi.	Norm Ullman, Det.
1964	Stan Mikita, Chi.	Bobby Hull, Chi.
1963	Gordie Howe, Det.	Andy Bathgate, NYR
1962	Bobby Hull, Chi.	Andy Bathgate, NYR
1961	Bernie Geoffrion, Mtl.	Jean Beliveau, Mtl.
1960	Bobby Hull, Chi.	Bronco Horvath, Bos.
1959	Dickie Moore, Mtl.	Jean Beliveau, Mtl.
1958	Dickie Moore, Mtl.	Henri Richard, Mtl.
1957	Gordie Howe, Det.	Ted Lindsay, Det.
1956	Jean Beliveau, Mtl.	Gordie Howe, Det.
1955	Bernie Geoffrion, Mtl.	Maurice Richard, Mtl.
1954	Gordie Howe, Det.	Maurice Richard, Mtl.
1953	Gordie Howe, Det.	Ted Lindsay, Det.
1952	Gordie Howe, Det.	Ted Lindsay, Det.
1951	Gordie Howe, Det.	Maurice Richard, Mtl.
1950	Ted Lindsay, Det.	Sid Abel, Det.
1949	Roy Conacher, Chi.	Doug Bentley, Chi.
1948	Elmer Lach, Mtl.	Buddy O'Connor, NYR
1947*	Max Bentley, Chi.	Maurice Richard, Mtl.
1946	Max Bentley, Chi.	Gaye Stewart, Tor.
1945	Elmer Lach, Mtl.	Maurice Richard, Mtl.
1944	Herbie Cain, Bos.	Doug Bentley, Chi.
1943	Doug Bentley, Chi.	Bill Cowley, Bos.
1942	Bryan Hextall, NYR	Lynn Patrick, NYR
1941	Bill Cowley, Bos.	Bryan Hextall, NYR
1940	Milt Schmidt, Bos.	Woody Dumart, Bos.
1939	Toe Blake, Mtl.	Dave Schriner, NYA
1938	Gordie Drillon, Tor.	Syl Apps, Tor.
1937	Dave Schriner, NYA	Syl Apps, Tor.
1936	Dave Schriner, NYA	Marty Barry, Det.
1935	Charlie Conacher, Tor.	Syd Howe, St.L-Det.
1934	Charlie Conacher, Tor.	Joe Primeau, Tor
1933	Bill Cook, NYR	Harvey Jackson, Tor.
1932	Harvey Jackson, Tor.	Joe Primeau, Tor.
1931	Howie Morenz, Mtl.	Ebbie Goodfellow, Det.
1930	Cooney Weiland, Bos.	Frank Boucher, NYR
1929	Ace Bailey, Tor.	Nels Stewart, Mtl.M
1928	Howie Morenz, Mtl.	Aurel Joliat, Mtl.
1927	Bill Cook, NYR	Dick Irvin, Chi.
1926	Nels Stewart, Mtl.M.	Cy Denneny, Ott.
1925	Babe Dye, Tor.	Cy Denneny, Ott.
1924	Cy Denneny, Ott.	Billy Boucher, Mtl.
1923	Babe Dye, Tor.	Cy Denneny, Ott.
1922	Punch Broadbent, Ott.	Cy Denneny, Ott.
1921	Newsy Lalonde, Mtl.	Cy Denneny, Ott.
1920	Joe Malone, Que.	Newsy Lalonde, Mtl.
1919	Newsy Lalonde, Mtl.	Odie Cleghorn, Mtl.
1918	Joe Malone, Mtl.	Cy Denneny, Ott.

* Trophy first awarded in 1948.
  Scoring leaders listed from 1918 to 1947.

KING CLANCY MEMORIAL TROPHY WINNERS

1996	Kris King	Winnipeg
1995	Joe Nieuwendyk	Calgary
1994	Adam Graves	NY Rangers
1993	Dave Poulin	Boston
1992	Ray Bourque	Boston
1991	Dave Taylor	Los Angeles
1990	Kevin Lowe	Edmonton
1989	Bryan Trottier	NY Islanders
1988	Lanny McDonald	Calgary

HART TROPHY

	Winner	Runner-up
1996	Mario Lemieux, Pit.	Mark Messier, NYR
1995	Eric Lindros, Phi.	Jaromir Jagr, Pit.
1994	Sergei Fedorov, Det.	Dominik Hasek, Buf.
1993	Mario Lemieux, Pit.	Doug Gilmour, Tor.
1992	Mark Messier, NYR	Patrick Roy, Mtl.
1991	Brett Hull, St.L.	Wayne Gretzky, L.A.
1990	Mark Messier, Edm.	Ray Bourque, Bos.
1989	Wayne Gretzky, L.A.	Mario Lemieux, Pit.
1988	Mario Lemieux, Pit.	Grant Fuhr, Edm.
1987	Wayne Gretzky, Edm.	Ray Bourque, Bos.
1986	Wayne Gretzky, Edm.	Mario Lemieux, Pit.
1985	Wayne Gretzky, Edm.	Dale Hawerchuk, Wpg.
1984	Wayne Gretzky, Edm.	Rod Langway, Wsh.
1983	Wayne Gretzky, Edm.	Pete Peeters, Bos.
1982	Wayne Gretzky, Edm.	Bryan Trottier, NYI
1981	Wayne Gretzky, Edm.	Mike Liut, St.L.
1980	Wayne Gretzky, Edm.	Marcel Dionne, L.A.
1979	Bryan Trottier, NYI	Guy Lafleur, Mtl
1978	Guy Lafleur, Mtl.	Bryan Trottier, NYI
1977	Guy Lafleur, Mtl.	Bobby Clarke, Phi.
1976	Bobby Clarke, Phi.	Denis Potvin, NYI
1975	Bobby Clarke, Phi.	Rogatien Vachon, L.A.
1974	Phil Esposito, Bos.	Bernie Parent, Phi.
1973	Bobby Clarke, Phi.	Phil Esposito, Bos.
1972	Bobby Orr, Bos.	Ken Dryden, Mtl.
1971	Bobby Orr, Bos.	Phil Esposito, Bos.
1970	Bobby Orr, Bos.	Tony Esposito, Chi.
1969	Phil Esposito, Bos.	Jean Beliveau, Mtl.
1968	Stan Mikita, Chi.	Jean Beliveau, Mtl.
1967	Stan Mikita, Chi.	Ed Giacomin, NYR
1966	Bobby Hull, Chi.	Jean Beliveau, Mtl.
1965	Bobby Hull, Chi.	Norm Ullman, Det.
1964	Jean Beliveau, Mtl.	Bobby Hull, Chi.
1963	Gordie Howe, Det.	Stan Mikita, Chi.
1962	Jacques Plante, Mtl.	Doug Harvey, NYR
1961	Bernie Geoffrion, Mtl.	Johnny Bower, Tor.
1960	Gordie Howe, Det.	Bobby Hull, Chi.
1959	Andy Bathgate, NYR	Gordie Howe, Det.
1958	Gordie Howe, Det.	Andy Bathgate, NYR
1957	Gordie Howe, Det.	Jean Beliveau, Mtl.
1956	Jean Beliveau, Mtl.	Tod Sloan, Tor.
1955	Ted Kennedy, Tor.	Harry Lumley, Tor.
1954	Al Rollins, Chi.	Red Kelly, Det.
1953	Gordie Howe, Det.	Al Rollins, Chi.
1952	Gordie Howe, Det.	Elmer Lach, Mtl.
1951	Milt Schmidt, Bos.	Maurice Richard, Mtl.
1950	Charlie Rayner, NYR	Ted Kennedy, Tor.
1949	Sid Abel, Det.	Bill Durnan, Mtl.
1948	Buddy O'Connor, NYR	Frank Brimsek, Bos.
1947	Maurice Richard, Mtl.	Milt Schmidt, Bos.
1946	Max Bentley, Chi.	Gaye Stewart, Tor.
1945	Elmer Lach, Mtl.	Maurice Richard, Mtl.
1944	Babe Pratt, Tor.	Bill Cowley, Bos.
1943	Bill Cowley, Bos.	Doug Bentley, Chi.
1942	Tom Anderson, Bro.	Syl Apps, Tor.
1941	Bill Cowley, Bos.	Dit Clapper, Bos.
1940	Ebbie Goodfellow, Det.	Syl Apps, Tor.
1939	Toe Blake, Mtl.	Syl Apps, Tor.
1938	Eddie Shore, Bos.	Paul Thompson, Chi.
1937	Babe Siebert, Mtl.	Lionel Conacher, Mtl.M
1936	Eddie Shore, Bos.	Hooley Smith, Mtl.M
1935	Eddie Shore, Bos.	Charlie Conacher, Tor.
1934	Aurel Joliat, Mtl.	Lionel Conacher, Chi.
1933	Eddie Shore, Bos.	Bill Cook, NYR
1932	Howie Morenz, Mtl.	Ching Johnson, NYR
1931	Howie Morenz, Mtl.	Eddie Shore, Bos.
1930	Nels Stewart, Mtl.M.	Lionel Hitchman, Bos.
1929	Roy Worters, NYA	Ace Bailey, Tor.
1928	Howie Morenz, Mtl.	Roy Worters, Pit.
1927	Herb Gardiner, Mtl.	Bill Cook, NYR
1926	Nels Stewart, Mtl.M.	Sprague Cleghorn, Bos.
1925	Billy Burch, Ham.	Howie Morenz, Mtl.
1924	Frank Nighbor, Ott.	Sprague Cleghorn, Mtl.

FRANK J. SELKE TROPHY WINNERS

	Winner	Runner-up
1996	Sergei Fedorov, Det.	Ron Francis, Pit.
1995	Ron Francis, Pit.	Esa Tikkanen, St.L.
1994	Sergei Fedorov, Det.	Doug Gilmour, Tor.
1993	Doug Gilmour, Tor.	Dave Poulin, Bos.
1992	Guy Carbonneau, Mtl.	Sergei Fedorov, Det.
1991	Dirk Graham, Chi.	Esa Tikkanen, Edm.
1990	Rick Meagher, St.L.	Guy Carbonneau, Mtl.
1989	Guy Carbonneau, Mtl.	Esa Tikkanen, Edm.
1988	Guy Carbonneau, Mtl.	Steve Kasper, Bos.
1987	Dave Poulin, Phi.	Guy Carbonneau, Mtl.
1986	Troy Murray, Chi.	Ron Sutter, Phi.
1985	Craig Ramsay, Buf.	Doug Jarvis, Wsh.
1984	Doug Jarvis, Wsh.	Bryan Trottier, NYI
1983	Bobby Clarke, Phi.	Jari Kurri, Edm.
1982	Steve Kasper, Bos.	Bob Gainey, Mtl.
1981	Bob Gainey, Mtl.	Craig Ramsay, Buf.
1980	Bob Gainey, Mtl.	Craig Ramsay, Buf.
1979	Bob Gainey, Mtl.	Don Marcotte, Bos.
1978	Bob Gainey, Mtl.	Craig Ramsay, Buf.

1995-96 NHL Player of the Week Award Winners

Player of the Week

Week Ending	Player	Team
Oct. 16	**Mario Lemieux**	Pittsburgh
Oct. 23	**Bill Ranford**	Edmonton
Oct. 30	**Brian Savage**	Montreal
Nov. 6	**Mario Lemieux**	Pittsburgh
Nov. 13	**Mark Messier**	NY Rangers
Nov. 20	**Wayne Gretzky**	Los Angeles
Nov. 27	**Daren Puppa**	Tampa Bay
Dec. 4	**Mario Lemieux**	Pittsburgh
Dec. 11	**Peter Forsberg**	Colorado
Dec. 18	**Theoren Fleury**	Calgary
Dec. 25	**Jocelyn Thibault**	Montreal
Jan. 1	**Jim Carey**	Washington
Jan. 8	**Wayne Gretzky**	Los Angeles
Jan. 15	**Gary Roberts**	Calgary
Jan. 22	**Ray Bourque**	Boston
Jan. 29	**Mario Lemieux**	Pittsburgh
Feb. 5	**Martin Rucinsky**	Montreal
Feb. 12	**Jason Muzzatti**	Hartford
Feb. 19	**Mike Modano**	Dallas
	Grant Fuhr	St. Louis
Feb. 26	**Pat LaFontaine**	Buffalo
Mar. 4	**Jim Carey**	Washington
Mar. 11	**Daren Puppa**	Tampa Bay
Mar. 18	**Damien Rhodes**	Ottawa
Mar. 25	**Guy Hebert**	Anaheim
Apr. 1	**Keith Tkachuk**	Winnipeg
Apr. 8	**Paul Kariya**	Anaheim
Apr. 15	**Daren Puppa**	Tampa Bay

1995-96 Player of the Month

Month	Player	Team
Oct.	**Eric Lindros**	Philadelphia
Nov.	**Mario Lemieux**	Pittsburgh
Dec.	**Mark Messier**	NY Rangers
Jan.	**Theoren Fleury**	Calgary
Feb.	**Peter Forsberg**	Colorado
Mar.	**Jim Carey**	Washington
Apr.	**Paul Kariya**	Anaheim

1995-96 Rookie of the Month

Month	Player	Team
Oct.	**V. Yachmenev**	Los Angeles
Nov.	**D. Alfredsson**	Ottawa
Dec.	**Petr Sykora**	New Jersey
Jan.	**Eric Daze**	Chicago
Feb.	**Jere Lehtinen**	Dallas
Mar.	**Miroslav Satan**	Edmonton
Apr.	**D. Alfredsson**	Ottawa

LADY BYNG TROPHY

	Winner	Runner-up
1996	Paul Kariya, Ana.	Adam Oates, Bos.
1995	Ron Francis, Pit.	Adam Oates, Bos.
1994	Wayne Gretzky, L.A.	Adam Oates, Bos.
1993	Pierre Turgeon, NYI	Adam Oates, Bos.
1992	Wayne Gretzky, L.A.	Joe Sakic, Que.
1991	Wayne Gretzky, L.A.	Brett Hull, St.L.
1990	Brett Hull, St.L.	Wayne Gretzky, L.A.
1989	Joe Mullen, Cgy.	Wayne Gretzky, L.A.
1988	Mats Naslund, Mtl.	Wayne Gretzky, Edm.
1987	Joe Mullen, Cgy.	Wayne Gretzky, Edm.
1986	Mike Bossy, NYI	Jari Kurri, Edm.
1985	Jari Kurri, Edm.	Joe Mullen, St.L.
1984	Mike Bossy, NYI	Rick Middleton, Bos.
1983	Mike Bossy, NYI	Rick Middleton, Bos.
1982	Rick Middleton, Bos.	Mike Bossy, NYI
1981	Rick Kehoe, Pit.	Wayne Gretzky, Edm.
1980	Wayne Gretzky, Edm.	Marcel Dionne, L.A.
1979	Bob MacMillan, Atl.	Marcel Dionne, L.A.
1978	Butch Goring, L.A.	Peter McNab, Bos.
1977	Marcel Dionne, L.A.	Jean Ratelle, Bos.
1976	Jean Ratelle, NYR-Bos.	Jean Pronovost, Pit.
1975	Marcel Dionne, Det.	John Bucyk, Bos.
1974	John Bucyk, Bos.	Lowell MacDonald, Pit.
1973	Gilbert Perreault, Buf.	Jean Ratelle, NYR
1972	Jean Ratelle, NYR	John Bucyk, Bos.
1971	John Bucyk, Bos.	Dave Keon, Tor.
1970	Phil Goyette, St.L.	John Bucyk, Bos.
1969	Alex Delvecchio, Det.	Ted Hampson, Oak.
1968	Stan Mikita, Chi.	John Bucyk, Bos.
1967	Stan Mikita, Chi.	Dave Keon, Tor.
1966	Alex Delvecchio, Det.	Bobby Rousseau, Mtl.
1965	Bobby Hull, Chi.	Alex Delvecchio, Det.
1964	Ken Wharram, Chi.	Dave Keon, Tor.
1963	Dave Keon, Tor.	Camille Henry, NYR
1962	Dave Keon, Tor.	Claude Provost, Mtl.
1961	Red Kelly, Tor.	Norm Ullman, Det.
1960	Don McKenney, Bos.	Andy Hebenton, NYR
1959	Alex Delvecchio, Det.	Andy Hebenton, NYR
1958	Camille Henry, NYR	Don Marshall, Mtl.
1957	Andy Hebenton, NYR	Earl Reibel, Det.
1956	Earl Reibel, Det.	Floyd Curry, Mtl.
1955	Sid Smith, Tor.	Danny Lewicki, NYR
1954	Red Kelly, Det.	Don Raleigh, NYR
1953	Red Kelly, Det.	Wally Hergesheimer, NYR
1952	Sid Smith, Tor.	Red Kelly, Det.
1951	Red Kelly, Det.	Woody Dumart, Bos.
1950	Edgar Laprade, NYR	Red Kelly, Det.
1949	Bill Quackenbush, Det.	Harry Watson, Tor.
1948	Buddy O'Connor, NYR	Syl Apps, Tor.
1947	Bobby Bauer, Bos.	Syl Apps, Tor.
1946	Toe Blake, Mtl.	Clint Smith, Chi.
1945	Bill Mosienko, Chi.	Syd Howe, Det.
1944	Clint Smith, Chi.	Herb Cain, Bos.
1943	Max Bentley, Chi.	Buddy O'Connor, Mtl.
1942	Syl Apps, Tor.	Gordie Drillon, Tor.
1941	Bobby Bauer, Bos.	Gordie Drillon, Tor.
1940	Bobby Bauer, Bos.	Clint Smith, NYR
1939	Clint Smith, NYR	Marty Barry, Det.
1938	Gordie Drillon, Tor.	Clint Smith, NYR
1937	Marty Barry, Det.	Gordie Drillon, Tor.
1936	Doc Romnes, Chi.	Dave Schriner, NYA
1935	Frank Boucher, NYR	Russ Blinco, Mtl.M
1934	Frank Boucher, NYR	Joe Primeau, Tor.
1933	Frank Boucher, NYR	Joe Primeau, Tor.
1932	Joe Primeau, Tor.	Frank Boucher, NYR
1931	Frank Boucher, NYR	Normie Himes, NYA
1930	Frank Boucher, NYR	Normie Himes, NYA
1929	Frank Boucher, NYR	Harry Darragh, Pit.
1928	Frank Boucher, NYR	George Hay, Det.
1927	Billy Burch, NYA	Dick Irvin, Chi.
1926	Frank Nighbor, Ott.	Billy Burch, NYA
1925	Frank Nighbor, Ott.	none

VEZINA TROPHY

	Winner	Runner-up
1996	Jim Carey, Wsh.	Chris Osgood, Det.
1995	Dominik Hasek, Buf.	Ed Belfour, Chi.
1994	Dominik Hasek, Buf.	John Vanbiesbrouck, Fla.
1993	Ed Belfour, Chi.	Tom Barrasso, Pit.
1992	Patrick Roy, Mtl.	Kirk McLean, Van.
1991	Ed Belfour, Chi.	Patrick Roy, Mtl.
1990	Patrick Roy, Mtl.	Daren Puppa, Buf.
1989	Patrick Roy, Mtl.	Mike Vernon, Cgy.
1988	Grant Fuhr, Edm.	Tom Barrasso, Buf.
1987	Ron Hextall, Phi.	Mike Liut, Hfd.
1986	John Vanbiesbrouck, NYR	Bob Froese, Phi.
1985	Pelle Lindbergh, Phi.	Tom Barrasso, Buf.
1984	Tom Barrasso, Buf.	Rejean Lemelin, Cgy.
1983	Pete Peeters, Bos.	Roland Melanson, NYI
1982	Bill Smith, NYI	Grant Fuhr, Edm.
1981	Richard Sevigny, Mtl.	Pete Peeters, Phi.
	Denis Herron, Mtl.	Rick St. Croix, Phi.
	Michel Larocque, Mtl.	
1980	Bob Sauve, Buf.	Gerry Cheevers, Bos.
	Don Edwards, Buf.	Gilles Gilbert, Bos.
1979	Ken Dryden, Mtl.	Glenn Resch, NYI
	Michel Larocque, Mtl.	Bill Smith, NYI
1978	Ken Dryden, Mtl.	Bernie Parent, Phi.
	Michel Larocque	Wayne Stephenson, Phi.
1977	Ken Dryden, Mtl.	Glenn Resch, NYI
	Michel Larocque, Mtl.	Bill Smith, NYI
1976	Ken Dryden, Mtl.	Glenn Resch, NYI
		Bill Smith, NYI
1975	Bernie Parent, Phi.	Rogie Vachon, L.A.
		Gary Edwards, L.A.
1974	Bernie Parent, Phi. (tie)	Gilles Gilbert, Bos.
	Tony Esposito, Chi. (tie)	
1973	Ken Dryden, Mtl.	Ed Giacomin, NYR
		Gilles Villemure, NYR
1972	Tony Esposito, Chi.	Cesare Maniago, Min.
	Gary Smith, Chi.	Lorne Worsley, Min.
1971	Ed Giacomin, NYR	Tony Esposito, Chi.
	Gilles Villemure, NYR	
1970	Tony Esposito, Chi.	Jacques Plante, St.L.
		Ernie Wakely, St.L.
1969	Jacques Plante, St.L.	Ed Giacomin, NYR
	Glenn Hall, St.L.	
1968	Lorne Worsley, Mtl.	Johnny Bower, Tor.
	Rogatien Vachon, Mtl.	Bruce Gamble, Tor.
1967	Glenn Hall, Chi.	Charlie Hodge, Mtl.
	Denis Dejordy, Chi.	
1966	Lorne Worsley, Mtl.	Glenn Hall, Chi.
	Charlie Hodge, Mtl.	
1965	Terry Sawchuk, Tor.	Roger Crozier, Det.
	Johnny Bower, Tor.	
1964	Charlie Hodge, Mtl.	Glenn Hall, Chi.
1963	Glenn Hall, Chi.	Johnny Bower, Tor.
		Don Simmons, Tor.
1962	Jacques Plante, Mtl.	Johnny Bower, Tor.
1961	Johnny Bower, Tor.	Glenn Hall, Chi.
1960	Jacques Plante, Mtl.	Glenn Hall, Chi.
1959	Jacques Plante, Mtl.	Johnny Bower, Tor.
		Ed Chadwick, Tor.
1958	Jacques Plante, Mtl.	Lorne Worsley, NYR
		Marcel Paille, NYR
1957	Jacques Plante, Mtl.	Glenn Hall, Det.
1956	Jacques Plante, Mtl.	Glenn Hall, Det.
1955	Terry Sawchuk, Det.	Harry Lumley, Tor.
1954	Harry Lumley, Tor.	Terry Sawchuk, Det.
1953	Terry Sawchuk, Det.	Gerry McNeil, Mtl.
1952	Terry Sawchuk, Det.	Al Rollins, Tor.
1951	Al Rollins, Tor.	Terry Sawchuk, Det.
1950	Bill Durnan, Mtl.	Harry Lumley, Det.
1949	Bill Durnan, Mtl.	Harry Lumley, Det.
1948	Turk Broda, Tor.	Harry Lumley, Det.
1947	Bill Durnan, Mtl.	Turk Broda, Tor.
1946	Bill Durnan, Mtl.	Frank Brimsek, Bos.
1945	Bill Durnan, Mtl.	Frank McCool, Tor. (tie)
		Harry Lumley, Det. (tie)
1944	Bill Durnan, Mtl.	Paul Bibeault, Tor.
1943	Johnny Mowers, Det.	Turk Broda, Tor.
1942	Frank Brimsek, Bos.	Turk Broda, Tor.
1941	Turk Broda, Tor.	Frank Brimsek, Bos. (tie)
		Johnny Mowers, Det. (tie)
1940	Dave Kerr, NYR	Frank Brimsek, Bos.
1939	Frank Brimsek, Bos.	Dave Kerr, NYR
1938	Tiny Thompson, Bos.	Dave Kerr, NYR
1937	Normie Smith, Det.	Dave Kerr, NYR
1936	Tiny Thompson, Bos.	Mike Karakas, Chi.
1935	Lorne Chabot, Chi.	Alex Connell, Mtl.M
1934	Charlie Gardiner, Chi.	Wilf Cude, Det.
1933	Tiny Thompson, Bos.	John Roach, Det.
1932	Charlie Gardiner, Chi.	Alex Connell, Det.
1931	Roy Worters, NYA	Charlie Gardiner, Chi.
1930	Tiny Thompson, Bos.	Charlie Gardiner, Chi.
1929	George Hainsworth, Mtl.	Tiny Thompson, Bos.
1928	George Hainsworth, Mtl.	Alex Connell, Ott.
1927	George Hainsworth, Mtl.	Clint Benedict, Mtl.M

BILL MASTERTON TROPHY WINNERS

1996	Gary Roberts	Calgary
1995	Pat LaFontaine	Buffalo
1994	Cam Neely	Boston
1993	Mario Lemieux	Pittsburgh
1992	Mark Fitzpatrick	NY Islanders
1991	Dave Taylor	Los Angeles
1990	Gord Kluzak	Boston
1989	Tim Kerr	Philadelphia
1988	Bob Bourne	Los Angeles
1987	Doug Jarvis	Hartford
1986	Charlie Simmer	Boston
1985	Anders Hedberg	NY Rangers
1984	Brad Park	Detroit
1983	Lanny McDonald	Calgary
1982	Glenn Resch	Colorado
1981	Blake Dunlop	St. Louis
1980	Al MacAdam	Minnesota
1979	Serge Savard	Montreal
1978	Butch Goring	Los Angeles
1977	Ed Westfall	NY Islanders
1976	Rod Gilbert	NY Rangers
1975	Don Luce	Buffalo
1974	Henri Richard	Montreal
1973	Lowell MacDonald	Pittsburgh
1972	Bobby Clarke	Philadelphia
1971	Jean Ratelle	NY Rangers
1970	Pit Martin	Chicago
1969	Ted Hampson	Oakland
1968	Claude Provost	Montreal

CALDER MEMORIAL TROPHY WINNERS

	Winner	Runner-up
1996	Daniel Alfredsson, Ott.	Eric Daze, Chi.
1995	Peter Forsberg, Que.	Jim Carey, Wsh.
1994	Martin Brodeur, N.J.	Jason Arnott, Edm.
1993	Teemu Selanne, Wpg.	Joe Juneau, Bos.
1992	Pavel Bure, Van.	Nicklas Lidstrom, Det
1991	Ed Belfour, Chi.	Sergei Fedorov, Det.
1990	Sergei Makarov, Cgy.	Mike Modano, Min.
1989	Brian Leetch, NYR	Trevor Linden, Van.
1988	Joe Nieuwendyk, Cgy.	Ray Sheppard, Buf.
1987	Luc Robitaille, L.A.	Ron Hextall, Phi.
1986	Gary Suter, Cgy.	Wendel Clark, Tor.
1985	Mario Lemieux, Pit.	Chris Chelios, Mtl.
1984	Tom Barrasso, Buf.	Steve Yzerman, Det.
1983	Steve Larmer, Chi.	Phil Housley, Buf.
1982	Dale Hawerchuk, Wpg.	Barry Pederson, Bos.
1981	Peter Stastny, Que.	Larry Murphy, L.A.
1980	Ray Bourque, Bos.	Mike Foligno, Det.
1979	Bobby Smith, Min	Ryan Walter, Wsh.
1978	Mike Bossy, NYI	Barry Beck, Col.
1977	Willi Plett, Atl.	Don Murdoch, NYR
1976	Bryan Trottier, NYI	Glenn Resch, NYI
1975	Eric Vail, Atl.	Pierre Larouche, Pit.
1974	Denis Potvin, NYI	Tom Lysiak, Atl.
1973	Steve Vickers, NYR	Bill Barber, Phi.
1972	Ken Dryden, Mtl.	Rick Martin, Buf.
1971	Gilbert Perreault, Buf.	Jude Drouin, Min.
1970	Tony Esposito, Chi.	Bill Fairbairn, NYR
1969	Danny Grant, Min.	Norm Ferguson, Oak.
1968	Derek Sanderson, Bos.	Jacques Lemaire, Mtl.
1967	Bobby Orr, Bos.	Ed Van Impe, Chi.
1966	Brit Selby, Tor.	Bert Marshall, Det.
1965	Roger Crozier, Det.	Ron Ellis, Tor.
1964	Jacques Laperriere, Mtl.	John Ferguson, Mtl.
1963	Kent Douglas, Tor.	Doug Barkley, Det.
1962	Bobby Rousseu, Mtl.	Cliff Pennington, Bos.
1961	Dave Keon, Tor.	Bob Nevin, Tor.
1960	Bill Hay, Chi.	Murray Oliver, Det.
1959	Ralph Backstrom, Mtl.	Carl Brewer, Tor.
1958	Frank Mahovlich, Tor.	Bobby Hull, Chi.
1957	Larry Regan, Bos.	Ed Chadwick, Tor.
1956	Glenn Hall, Det.	Andy Hebenton, NYR
1955	Ed Litzenberger, Chi.	Don McKenney, Bos.
1954	Camille Henry, NYR	Earl Reibel, Det.
1953	Lorne Worsley, NYR	Gordie Hannigan, Tor.
1952	Bernie Geoffrion, Mtl.	Hy Buller, NYR
1951	Terry Sawchuk, Det.	Al Rollins, Tor.
1950	Jack Gelineau, Bos.	Phil Maloney, Bos.
1949	Pentti Lund, NYR	Allan Stanley, NYR
1948	Jim McFadden, Det.	Pete Babando, Bos.
1947	Howie Meeker, Tor.	Jimmy Conacher, Det.
1946	Edgar Laprade, NYR	George Gee, Chi.
1945	Frank McCool, Tor.	Ken Smith, Bos.
1944	Gus Bodnar, Tor.	Bill Durnan, Mtl.
1943	Gaye Stewart, Tor.	Glen Harmon, Mtl.
1942	Grant Warwick, NYR	Buddy O'Connor, Mtl.
1941	Johnny Quilty, Mtl.	Johnny Mowers, Det.
1940	Kilby MacDonald, NYR	Wally Stanowski, Tor.
1939	Frank Brimsek, Bos.	Roy Conacher, Bos.
1938	Cully Dahlstrom, Chi.	Murph Chamberlain, Tor.
1937	Syl Apps, Tor.	Gordie Drillon, Tor.
1936	Mike Karakas, Chi.	Bucko McDonald, Det.
1935	Dave Schriner, NYA	Bert Connolly, NYR
1934	Russ Blinko, Mtl.M.	
1933	Carl Voss, Det.	

CONN SMYTHE TROPHY WINNERS

1996	Joe Sakic	Colorado
1995	Claude Lemieux	New Jersey
1994	Brian Leetch	NY Rangers
1993	Patrick Roy	Montreal
1992	Mario Lemieux	Pittsburgh
1991	Mario Lemieux	Pittsburgh
1990	Bill Ranford	Edmonton
1989	Al MacInnis	Calgary
1988	Wayne Gretzky	Edmonton
1987	Ron Hextall	Philadelphia
1986	Patrick Roy	Montreal
1985	Wayne Gretzky	Edmonton
1984	Mark Messier	Edmonton
1983	Bill Smith	NY Islanders
1982	Mike Bossy	NY Islanders
1981	Butch Goring	NY Islanders
1980	Bryan Trottier	NY Islanders
1979	Bob Gainey	Montreal
1978	Larry Robinson	Montreal
1977	Guy Lafleur	Montreal
1976	Reggie Leach	Philadelphia
1975	Bernie Parent	Philadelphia
1974	Bernie Parent	Philadelphia
1973	Yvan Cournoyer	Montreal
1972	Bobby Orr	Boston
1971	Ken Dryden	Montreal
1970	Bobby Orr	Boston
1969	Serge Savard	Montreal
1968	Glenn Hall	St. Louis
1967	Dave Keon	Toronto
1966	Roger Crozier	Detroit
1965	Jean Béliveau	Montreal

JAMES NORRIS TROPHY WINNERS

	Winner	Runner-up
1996	Chris Chelios, Chi.	Ray Bourque, Bos.
1995	Paul Coffey, Det.	Chris Chelios, Chi.
1994	Ray Bourque, Bos.	Scott Stevens, N.J.
1993	Chris Chelios, Chi.	Ray Bourque, Bos.
1992	Brian Leetch, NYR	Ray Bourque, Bos.
1991	Ray Bourque, Bos.	Al MacInnis, Cgy.
1990	Ray Bourque, Bos.	Al MacInnis, Cgy.
1989	Chris Chelios, Mtl	Paul Coffey, Pit.
1988	Ray Bourque, Bos.	Scott Stevens, Wsh.
1987	Ray Bourque, Bos.	Mark Howe, Phi.
1986	Paul Coffey, Edm.	Mark Howe, Phi.
1985	Paul Coffey, Edm.	Ray Bourque, Bos.
1984	Rod Langway, Wsh.	Paul Coffey, Edm.
1983	Rod Langway, Wsh.	Mark Howe, Phi.
1982	Doug Wilson, Chi.	Ray Bourque, Bos.
1981	Randy Carlyle, Pit.	Denis Potvin, NYI
1980	Larry Robinson, Mtl.	Borje Salming, Tor.
1979	Denis Potvin, NYI	Larry Robinson, Mtl.
1978	Denis Potvin, NYI	Brad Park, Bos.
1977	Larry Robinson, Mtl.	Borje Salming, Tor.
1976	Denis Potvin, NYI	Brad Park, NYR-Bos.
1975	Bobby Orr, Bos.	Denis Potvin, NYI
1974	Bobby Orr, Bos.	Brad Park, NYR
1973	Bobby Orr, Bos.	Guy Lapointe, Mtl.
1972	Bobby Orr, Bos.	Brad Park, NYR
1971	Bobby Orr, Bos.	Brad Park, NYR
1970	Bobby Orr, Bos.	Brad Park, NYR
1969	Bobby Orr, Bos.	Tim Horton, Tor.
1968	Bobby Orr, Bos.	J.C. Tremblay, Mtl
1967	Harry Howell, NYR	Pierre Pilote, Chi.
1966	Jacques Laperriere, Mtl.	Pierre Pilote, Chi.
1965	Pierre Pilote, Chi.	Jacques Laperriere, Mtl.
1964	Pierre Pilote, Chi.	Tim Horton, Tor.
1963	Pierre Pilote, Chi.	Carl Brewer, Tor.
1962	Doug Harvey, NYR	Pierre Pilote, Chi.
1961	Doug Harvey, Mtl.	Marcel Pronovost, Det.
1960	Doug Harvey, Mtl.	Allan Stanley, Tor.
1959	Tom Johnson, Mtl.	Bill Gadsby, NYR
1958	Doug Harvey, Mtl.	Bill Gadsby, NYR
1957	Doug Harvey, Mtl.	Red Kelly, Det.
1956	Doug Harvey, Mtl.	Bill Gadsby, NYR
1955	Doug Harvey, Mtl.	Red Kelly, Det.
1954	Red Kelly, Det.	Doug Harvey, Mtl.

LESTER PATRICK TROPHY WINNERS

1996	George Gund
	Ken Morrow
	Milt Schmidt
1995	Joe Mullen
	Brian Mullen
	Bob Fleming
1994	Wayne Gretzky
	Robert Ridder
1993	*Frank Boucher
	*Mervyn (Red) Dutton
	Bruce McNall
	Gil Stein
1992	Al Arbour
	Art Berglund
	Lou Lamoriello
1991	Rod Gilbert
	Mike Ilitch
1990	Len Ceglarski
1989	Dan Kelly
	Lou Nanne
	*Lynn Patrick
	Bud Poile
1988	Keith Allen
	Fred Cusick
	Bob Johnson
1987	*Hobey Baker
	Frank Mathers
1986	John MacInnes
	Jack Riley
1985	Jack Butterfield
	Arthur M. Wirtz
1984	John A. Ziegler Jr.
	*Arthur Howie Ross
1983	Bill Torrey
1982	Emile P. Francis
1981	Charles M. Schulz
1980	Bobby Clarke
	Edward M. Snider
	Frederick A. Shero
	1980 U.S. Olympic Hockey Team
1979	Bobby Orr
1978	Phil Esposito
	Tom Fitzgerald
	William T. Tutt
	William W. Wirtz
1977	John P. Bucyk
	Murray A. Armstrong
	John Mariucci
1976	Stanley Mikita
	George A. Leader
	Bruce A. Norris
1975	Donald M. Clark
	William L. Chadwick
	Thomas N. Ivan
1974	Alex Delvecchio
	Murray Murdoch
	*Weston W. Adams, Sr.
	*Charles L. Crovat
1973	Walter L. Bush, Jr.
1972	Clarence S. Campbell
	John A. "Snooks" Kelly
	Ralph "Cooney" Weiland
	*James D. Norris
1971	William M. Jennings
	*John B. Sollenberger
	*Terrance G. Sawchuk
1970	Edward W. Shore
	*James C. V. Hendy
1969	Robert M. Hull
	*Edward J. Jeremiah
1968	Thomas F. Lockhart
	*Walter A. Brown
	*Gen. John R. Kilpatrick
1967	Gordon Howe
	*Charles F. Adams
	*James Norris, Sr.
1966	J.J. "Jack" Adams
	* awarded posthumously

ALKA-SELTZER PLUS AWARD WINNERS

1996	Vladimir Konstantinov	Detroit
1995	Ron Francis	Pittsburgh
1994	Scott Stevens	New Jersey
1993	Mario Lemieux	Pittsburgh
1992	Paul Ysebaert	Detroit
1991	Marty McSorley	Los Angeles
	Theoren Fleury	Calgary
1990	Paul Cavallini	St. Louis

WILLIAM M. JENNINGS TROPHY WINNERS

	Winner	Runner-up
1996	Chris Osgood, Det. Mike Vernon	Martin Brodeur, N.J.
1995	Ed Belfour, Chi.	Mike Vernon, Det. Chris Osgood
1994	Dominik Hasek, Buf. Grant Fuhr	Martin Brodeur, N.J. Chris Terreri
1993	Ed Belfour, Chi.	Felix Potvin, Tor. Grant Fuhr
1992	Patrick Roy, Mtl.	Ed Belfour, Chi.
1991	Ed Belfour, Chi.	Patrick Roy, Mtl.
1990	Andy Moog, Bos. Rejean Lemelin	Patrick Roy, Mtl. Brian Hayward
1989	Patrick Roy, Mtl. Brian Hayward	Mike Vernon, Cgy. Rick Wamsley
1988	Patrick Roy, Mtl. Brian Hayward	Clint Malarchuk, Wsh. Pete Peeters
1987	Patrick Roy, Mtl. Brian Hayward	Ron Hextall, Phi.
1986	Bob Froese, Phi. Darren Jensen	Al Jensen, Wsh. Pete Peeters
1985	Tom Barrasso, Buf. Bob Sauve	Pat Riggin, Wsh.
1984	Al Jensen, Wsh. Pat Riggin	Tom Barrasso, Buf. Bob Sauve
1983	Roland Melanson, NYI Bill Smith	Pete Peeters, Bos.
1982	Rick Wamsley, Mtl. Denis Herron	Billy Smith, NYI Roland Melanson

LESTER B. PEARSON AWARD WINNERS

1996	Mario Lemieux	Pittsburgh
1995	Eric Lindros	Philadelphia
1994	Sergei Fedorov	Detroit
1993	Mario Lemieux	Pittsburgh
1992	Mark Messier	NY Rangers
1991	Brett Hull	St. Louis
1990	Mark Messier	Edmonton
1989	Steve Yzerman	Detroit
1988	Mario Lemieux	Pittsburgh
1987	Wayne Gretzky	Edmonton
1986	Mario Lemieux	Pittsburgh
1985	Wayne Gretzky	Edmonton
1984	Wayne Gretzky	Edmonton
1983	Wayne Gretzky	Edmonton
1982	Wayne Gretzky	Edmonton
1981	Mike Liut	St. Louis
1980	Marcel Dionne	Los Angeles
1979	Marcel Dionne	Los Angeles
1978	Guy Lafleur	Montreal
1977	Guy Lafleur	Montreal
1976	Guy Lafleur	Montreal
1975	Bobby Orr	Boston
1974	Phil Esposito	Boston
1973	Bobby Clarke	Philadelphia
1972	Jean Ratelle	NY Rangers
1971	Phil Esposito	Boston

JACK ADAMS AWARD WINNERS

	Winner	Runner-up
1996	Scotty Bowman, Det.	Doug MacLean, Fla.
1995	Marc Crawford, Que.	Scotty Bowman, Det.
1994	Jacques Lemaire, N.J.	Kevin Constantine, S.J.
1993	Pat Burns, Tor.	Brian Sutter, Bos.
1992	Pat Quinn, Van.	Roger Neilson, NYR
1991	Brian Sutter, St.L.	Tom Webster, L.A.
1990	Bob Murdoch, Wpg.	Mike Milbury, Bos.
1989	Pat Burns, Mtl.	Bob McCammon, Van.
1988	Jacques Demers, Det.	Terry Crisp, Cgy.
1987	Jacques Demers, Det.	Jack Evans, Hfd.
1986	Glen Sather, Edm.	Jacques Demers, St.L.
1985	Mike Keenan, Phi.	Barry Long, Wpg.
1984	Bryan Murray, Wsh.	Scotty Bowman, Buf.
1983	Orval Tessier, Chi.	
1982	Tom Watt, Wpg.	
1981	Red Berenson, St.L.	Bob Berry, L.A.
1980	Pat Quinn, Phi.	
1979	Al Arbour, NYI	Fred Shero, NYR
1978	Bobby Kromm, Det.	Don Cherry, Bos.
1977	Scotty Bowman, Mtl.	Tom McVie, Wsh.
1976	Don Cherry, Bos.	
1975	Bob Pulford, L.A.	
1974	Fred Shero, Phi.	

NHL Amateur and Entry Draft

History

Year	Site	Date	Total Players Drafted
1963	Queen Elizabeth Hotel	June 5	21
1964	Queen Elizabeth Hotel	June 11	24
1965	Queen Elizabeth Hotel	April 27	11
1966	Mount Royal Hotel	April 25	24
1967	Queen Elizabeth Hotel	June 7	18
1968	Queen Elizabeth Hotel	June 13	24
1969	Queen Elizabeth Hotel	June 12	84
1970	Queen Elizabeth Hotel	June 11	115
1971	Queen Elizabeth Hotel	June 10	117
1972	Queen Elizabeth Hotel	June 8	152
1973	Mount Royal Hotel	May 15	168
1974	NHL Montreal Office	May 28	247
1975	NHL Montreal Office	June 3	217
1976	NHL Montreal Office	June 1	135
1977	NHL Montreal Office	June 14	185
1978	Queen Elizabeth Hotel	June 15	234
1979	Queen Elizabeth Hotel	August 9	126
1980	Montreal Forum	June 11	210
1981	Montreal Forum	June 10	211
1982	Montreal Forum	June 9	252
1983	Montreal Forum	June 8	242
1984	Montreal Forum	June 9	250
1985	Toronto Convention Centre	June 15	252
1986	Montreal Forum	June 21	252
1987	Joe Louis Sports Arena	June 13	252
1988	Montreal Forum	June 11	252
1989	Metropolitan Sports Center	June 17	252
1990	B. C. Place	June 16	250
1991	Memorial Auditorium	June 9	264
1992	Montreal Forum	June 20	264
1993	Colisée de Québec	June 26	286
1994	Hartford Civic Center	June 28-29	286
1995	Edmonton Coliseum	July 8	234
1996	Kiel Center	June 22	241

* The NHL Amateur Draft became the NHL Entry Draft in 1979

Defenseman Chris Phillips was chosen first overall by the Ottawa Senators in the 1996 Entry Draft. A rough 'n' ready rearguard who is at his best when the game is on the line, Phillips spent the 1995-96 season with the WHL's Prince Albert Raiders.

First Selections

Year	Player	Pos	Drafted By	Drafted From	Age
1969	Rejean Houle	LW	Montreal	Jr. Canadiens	19.8
1970	Gilbert Perreault	C	Buffalo	Jr. Canadiens	19.7
1971	Guy Lafleur	RW	Montreal	Quebec Remparts	19.9
1972	Billy Harris	RW	NY Islanders	Toronto Marlboros	20.4
1973	Denis Potvin	D	NY Islanders	Ottawa 67's	19.7
1974	Greg Joly	D	Washington	Regina Pats	20.0
1975	Mel Bridgman	C	Philadelphia	Victoria Cougars	20.1
1976	Rick Green	D	Washington	London Knights	20.3
1977	Dale McCourt	C	Detroit	St. Catharines Fincups	20.4
1978	Bobby Smith	C	Minnesota	Ottawa 67's	20.4
1979	Rob Ramage	D	Colorado	London Knights	20.5
1980	Doug Wickenheiser	C	Montreal	Regina Pats	19.2
1981	Dale Hawerchuk	C	Winnipeg	Cornwall Royals	18.2
1982	Gord Kluzak	D	Boston	Nanaimo Islanders	18.3
1983	Brian Lawton	C	Minnesota	Mount St. Charles HS	18.11
1984	Mario Lemieux	C	Pittsburgh	Laval Voisins	18.8
1985	Wendel Clark	LW/D	Toronto	Saskatoon Blades	18.7
1986	Joe Murphy	C	Detroit	Michigan State	18.8
1987	Pierre Turgeon	C	Buffalo	Granby Bisons	17.10
1988	Mike Modano	C	Minnesota	Prince Albert Raiders	18.0
1989	Mats Sundin	RW	Quebec	Nacka (Sweden)	18.4
1990	Owen Nolan	RW	Quebec	Cornwall Royals	18.4
1991	Eric Lindros	C	Quebec	Oshawa Generals	18.3
1992	Roman Hamrlik	D	Tampa Bay	ZPS Zlin (Czech.)	18.2
1993	Alexandre Daigle	C	Ottawa	Victoriaville Tigres	18.5
1994	Ed Jovanovski	D	Florida	Windsor Spitfires	18.0
1995	Bryan Berard	D	Ottawa	Detroit Jr. Red Wings	18.4
1996	Chris Phillips	D	Ottawa	Prince Albert Raiders	18.3

Draft Summary

Following is a summary of the number of players drafted from the Ontario Hockey League (OHL), Western Hockey League (WHL), Quebec Major Junior Hockey League (QMJHL), United States Colleges, United States High Schools, European Leagues and other Leagues throughout North America since 1969:

	OHL	WHL	QMJHL	US Colleges	US HS	International	Other
1969	36	20	11	7	0	1	9
1970	51	22	13	16	0	0	13
1971	41	28	13	22	0	0	13
1972	46	44	30	21	0	0	11
1973	56	49	24	25	0	0	14
1974	69	66	40	41	0	6	25
1975	55	57	28	59	0	6	12
1976	47	33	18	26	0	8	3
1977	42	44	40	49	0	5	5
1978	59	48	22	73	0	16	16
1979	48	37	19	15	0	6	1
1980	73	41	24	42	7	13	10
1981	59	37	28	21	17	32	17
1982	60	55	17	20	47	35	18
1983	57	41	24	14	35	34	37
1984	55	38	16	22	44	40	36
1985	59	47	15	20	48	31	31
1986	66	32	22	22	40	28	42
1987	32	36	17	40	69	38	20
1988	32	30	22	48	56	39	25
1989	39	44	16	48	47	38	20
1990	39	33	14	38	57	53	16
1991	43	40	25	43	37	55	21
1992	57	45	22	9	25	84	22
1993	60	44	23	17	33	78	31
1994	45	66	28	6	28	80	33
1995	54	55	35	5	2	69	14
1996	51	54	31	25	6	58	16
Total	1431	1186	637	794	598	853	531

Total Drafted, 1969-1996: 6,030

Ontario Hockey League

Club	'69	'70	'71	'72	'73	'74	'75	'76	'77	'78	'79	'80	'81	'82	'83	'84	'85	'86	'87	'88	'89	'90	'91	'92	'93	'94	'95	'96	Total
Peterborough	5	5	4	5	9	4	8	1	4	6	9	10	3	5	7	3	9	2	5	2	2	4	3	4	4	2	5	4	134
Oshawa	5	4	3	5	5	7	6	6	1	3	3	2	9	5	5	6	6	6	3	2	4	2	4	4	4	1	10	1	122
Kitchener	1	6	2	8	4	13	3	1	3	4	4	4	5	5	8	4	6	3	2	1	7	5	3	1	4	2	4	2	115
Ottawa	2	4	3	4	6	5	6	5	5	5	3	8	4	9	2	2	3	3	2	1	–	5	5	6	4	1	1	2	106
London	4	9	1	5	6	6	3	5	4	3	6	2	5	5	3	7	1	3	2	6	3	3	1	3	4	1	1	4	106
S.S. Marie	–	–	–	–	4	5	2	5	1	5	3	3	8	1	6	4	5	7	1	2	3	1	2	7	3	4	3	4	89
Sudbury	–	–	–	–	6	6	4	5	4	4	3	7	2	4	–	2	5	3	1	–	1	2	8	2	10	2	2	1	84
Kingston	–	–	–	–	–	4	4	6	4	9	2	8	5	2	1	3	3	4	1	1	–	2	2	3	5	2	3	4	78
Niagara Falls	4	2	1	4	–	–	–	–	2	3	5	8	6	6	–	–	–	–	–	–	4	4	4	4	4	3	2	6	72
Windsor	–	–	–	–	–	–	–	2	1	4	2	3	5	3	2	2	3	7	–	5	2	1	–	3	–	3	4	1	53
Guelph	–	–	–	–	–	–	–	–	–	–	–	–	–	–	1	5	3	8	2	–	4	–	–	2	2	7	5	6	45
North Bay	–	–	–	–	–	–	–	–	–	–	–	–	–	–	4	4	3	3	3	3	1	4	2	5	2	7	2	1	44
Belleville	–	–	–	–	–	–	–	–	–	–	–	–	–	–	3	4	4	5	2	–	4	2	1	4	–	3	3	–	35
Detroit	–	–	–	–	–	–	–	–	–	–	–	–	–	–	–	–	–	–	–	–	–	–	2	2	7	2	6	3	22
Owen Sound	–	–	–	–	–	–	–	–	–	–	–	–	–	–	–	–	–	–	–	–	–	1	1	2	4	3	2	3	16
Sarnia	–	–	–	–	–	–	–	–	–	–	–	–	–	–	–	–	–	–	–	–	–	–	–	–	–	–	1	7	8
Barrie	–	–	–	–	–	–	–	–	–	–	–	–	–	–	–	–	–	–	–	–	–	–	–	–	–	–	–	2	2
Teams no longer operating																													
Toronto	3	7	6	5	6	8	4	4	7	5	4	10	2	6	4	4	3	4	1	2	2	–	–	–	–	–	–	–	97
Hamilton	2	3	5	4	6	4	7	3	–	8	1	–	–	–	–	–	3	6	4	4	–	–	2	–	–	–	–	–	62
St. Catharines	5	5	8	5	4	7	8	4	6	–	–	–	–	–	–	–	–	–	–	–	–	–	–	–	–	–	–	–	52
Cornwall	–	–	–	–	–	–	–	–	–	–	–	–	–	7	4	3	2	2	3	3	2	3	3	5	–	–	–	–	37
Brantford	–	–	–	–	–	–	–	–	–	–	3	8	5	2	7	2	–	–	–	–	–	–	–	–	–	–	–	–	27
Montreal	5	6	8	1	–	–	–	–	–	–	–	–	–	–	–	–	–	–	–	–	–	–	–	–	–	–	–	–	20
Newmarket	–	–	–	–	–	–	–	–	–	–	–	–	–	–	–	–	–	–	–	–	–	–	–	–	3	2	–	–	5

Year	Total Ontario Drafted	Total Players Drafted	Ontario %
1969	36	84	42.9
1970	51	115	44.3
1971	41	117	35.0
1972	46	152	30.3
1973	56	168	33.3
1974	69	247	27.9
1975	55	217	25.3
1976	47	135	34.8
1977	42	185	22.7
1978	59	234	25.2
1979	48	126	38.1
1980	73	210	34.8
1981	59	211	28.0
1982	60	252	23.8
1983	57	242	23.6
1984	55	250	22.0
1985	59	252	23.4
1986	66	252	26.2
1987	32	252	12.7
1988	32	252	12.7
1989	39	252	15.5
1990	39	250	15.6
1991	43	264	16.3
1992	57	264	21.6
1993	60	286	21.0
1994	45	286	15.7
1995	54	234	23.1
1996	51	241	21.1
Total	**1431**	**6030**	**23.7**

Western Hockey League

Club	'69	'70	'71	'72	'73	'74	'75	'76	'77	'78	'79	'80	'81	'82	'83	'84	'85	'86	'87	'88	'89	'90	'91	'92	'93	'94	'95	'96	Total
Regina	–	–	5	5	1	8	5	3	1	4	1	3	5	6	8	4	4	3	2	–	5	1	–	4	–	3	2	4	87
Saskatoon	1	–	1	3	8	4	5	3	4	1	2	2	3	5	5	3	1	5	4	4	3	2	2	3	2	4	2	2	84
Portland	–	–	–	–	–	–	–	–	4	8	7	8	6	7	7	5	2	4	3	1	4	1	1	4	4	3	2	1	82
Medicine Hat	–	–	–	4	6	4	5	3	5	4	–	4	2	1	2	1	6	2	5	1	4	1	3	3	1	6	2	7	82
Brandon	–	3	1	5	2	7	4	–	3	1	10	5	2	2	1	3	2	1	3	3	–	1	1	1	2	5	6	2	76
Kamloops	–	–	–	–	–	4	4	4	4	–	–	–	–	2	4	4	4	4	3	1	5	4	6	3	2	9	5	4	76
Lethbridge	–	–	–	–	–	–	3	2	3	5	4	1	4	7	2	1	5	1	–	3	3	4	7	3	4	3	3	1	69
Seattle	–	–	–	–	–	–	–	–	–	4	2	3	–	6	–	1	3	1	2	4	2	6	3	2	4	5	5	1	54
Prince Albert	–	–	–	–	–	–	–	–	–	–	–	–	–	4	2	2	6	6	1	3	3	4	6	2	5	3	4	3	54
Swift Current	1	–	1	–	3	6	–	–	–	–	–	–	–	–	–	–	–	–	5	2	2	2	1	1	5	4	4	1	38
Spokane	–	–	–	–	–	–	–	–	–	–	–	–	1	–	–	–	–	–	1	3	2	1	5	7	4	4	4	5	37
Tri-City	–	–	–	–	–	–	–	–	–	–	–	–	–	–	–	–	–	–	–	–	4	3	3	5	2	2	6	6	31
Moose Jaw	–	–	–	–	–	–	–	–	–	–	–	–	–	–	–	–	4	1	3	–	3	1	2	3	2	3	4	4	30
Red Deer	–	–	–	–	–	–	–	–	–	–	–	–	–	–	–	–	–	–	–	–	–	–	–	–	3	5	2	4	14
Prince George	–	–	–	–	–	–	–	–	–	–	–	–	–	–	–	–	–	–	–	–	–	–	–	–	–	–	2	2	4
Kelowna	–	–	–	–	–	–	–	–	–	–	–	–	–	–	–	–	–	–	–	–	–	–	–	–	–	–	–	4	4
Calgary	–	–	–	–	–	–	–	–	–	–	–	–	–	–	–	–	–	–	–	–	–	–	–	–	–	–	–	3	3
Teams no longer operating																													
Victoria	–	–	–	2	2	5	7	4	3	3	1	8	6	2	3	4	2	1	2	4	4	2	–	1	2	2	–	–	70
Calgary	3	5	2	7	4	8	4	4	4	3	–	2	5	4	3	3	3	2	–	–	–	–	–	–	–	–	–	–	66
New Westm'r	–	–	–	6	8	7	9	5	8	6	5	1	–	–	–	2	1	1	2	1	–	–	–	–	–	–	–	–	62
Flin Flon	4	4	5	2	4	7	4	3	1	5	–	–	–	–	–	–	–	–	–	–	–	–	–	–	–	–	–	–	39
Winnipeg	3	2	4	2	5	4	4	–	4	–	–	–	1	4	1	–	–	–	–	–	–	–	–	–	–	–	–	–	34
Edmonton	4	4	5	6	6	2	3	2	–	–	2	–	–	–	–	–	–	–	–	–	–	–	–	–	–	–	–	–	34
Billings	–	–	–	–	–	–	–	–	–	4	3	4	2	–	–	–	–	–	–	–	–	–	–	–	–	–	–	–	13
Estevan	4	4	4	–	–	–	–	–	–	–	–	–	–	–	–	–	–	–	–	–	–	–	–	–	–	–	–	–	12
Tacoma	–	–	–	–	–	–	–	–	–	–	–	–	–	–	–	–	–	–	–	–	–	–	–	3	2	5	2	–	12
Kelowna	–	–	–	–	–	–	–	–	–	–	–	–	–	–	2	4	5	–	–	–	–	–	–	–	–	–	–	–	11
Nanaimo	–	–	–	–	–	–	–	–	–	–	–	–	–	5	1	–	–	–	–	–	–	–	–	–	–	–	–	–	6
Vancouver	–	–	–	2	–	–	–	–	–	–	–	–	–	–	–	–	–	–	–	–	–	–	–	–	–	–	–	–	2

Year	Total Western Drafted	Total Players Drafted	Western %
1969	20	84	23.8
1970	22	115	19.1
1971	28	117	23.9
1972	44	152	28.9
1973	49	168	29.2
1974	66	247	26.7
1975	57	217	26.3
1976	33	135	24.4
1977	44	185	23.8
1978	48	234	20.5
1979	37	126	29.4
1980	41	210	19.5
1981	37	211	17.5
1982	55	252	21.8
1983	41	242	16.9
1984	37	250	14.8
1985	48	252	19.0
1986	32	252	12.7
1987	36	252	14.3
1988	30	252	11.9
1989	44	252	17.5
1990	33	250	13.2
1991	40	264	15.2
1992	45	264	17.0
1993	44	286	15.4
1994	66	286	23.0
1995	55	234	23.5
1996	54	241	22.4
Total	**1186**	**6030**	**19.6**

Quebec Major Junior Hockey League

Club	'69	'70	'71	'72	'73	'74	'75	'76	'77	'78	'79	'80	'81	'82	'83	'84	'85	'86	'87	'88	'89	'90	'91	'92	'93	'94	'95	'96	Total
Shawinigan	3	2	1	6	1	5	3	–	3	–	–	2	2	5	5	2	–	2	1	–	2	–	2	3	1	1	2	4	58
Sherbrooke	–	–	2	2	4	3	7	5	6	3	4	1	5	2	–	–	–	–	–	–	–	–	–	–	3	2	4	–	53
Laval	–	–	–	1	–	2	1	1	4	2	1	–	–	2	1	2	–	5	3	1	3	3	4	1	2	5	4	2	50
Hull	–	–	–	–	–	–	3	2	2	3	–	3	1	–	3	1	–	4	3	2	2	3	3	3	3	1	3	3	48
Drummondville	2	4	1	4	2	1	–	–	–	–	–	–	–	–	–	1	2	2	2	4	1	–	4	2	2	1	4	3	42
Chicoutimi	–	–	–	–	–	1	–	–	5	1	1	3	6	1	3	–	3	1	2	2	1	1	–	1	1	3	2	–	38
Granby	–	–	–	–	–	–	–	–	–	–	–	–	–	2	1	3	2	2	4	–	2	–	2	–	1	5	2	3	29
Victoriaville	–	–	–	–	–	–	–	–	–	–	–	–	–	–	–	–	–	–	–	4	–	1	–	2	6	1	1	3	18
Beauport	–	–	–	–	–	–	–	–	–	–	–	–	–	–	–	–	–	–	–	–	–	–	1	3	1	3	7	3	18
St. Hyacinthe	–	–	–	–	–	–	–	–	–	–	–	–	–	–	–	–	–	–	–	–	–	3	1	2	1	4	–	4	15
Val D'Or	–	–	–	–	–	–	–	–	–	–	–	–	–	–	–	–	–	–	–	–	–	–	–	–	–	1	2	4	7
Halifax	–	–	–	–	–	–	–	–	–	–	–	–	–	–	–	–	–	–	–	–	–	–	–	–	–	–	3	1	4
Moncton	–	–	–	–	–	–	–	–	–	–	–	–	–	–	–	–	–	–	–	–	–	–	–	–	–	–	–	1	1
Teams no longer operating																													
Quebec	1	1	2	4	6	6	1	3	7	1	3	2	2	1	2	2	3	–	–	–	–	–	–	–	–	–	–	–	47
Trois Rivieres	–	1	2	2	2	2	3	2	6	3	2	2	2	1	3	–	3	–	1	3	3	1	2	1	–	–	–	–	47
Cornwall	2	1	2	6	4	8	1	3	1	6	1	5	5	–	–	–	–	–	–	–	–	–	–	–	–	–	–	–	45
Montreal	–	–	–	–	4	4	8	1	3	2	4	3	–	3	–	–	–	–	–	–	–	–	–	–	–	–	–	–	32
Sorel	2	3	1	3	1	8	1	1	3	–	–	–	5	–	–	–	–	–	–	–	–	–	–	–	–	–	–	–	28
Verdun	–	1	1	2	–	–	–	–	–	1	3	3	–	–	3	3	–	3	0	3	1	–	–	3	–	–	–	–	27
St. Jean	–	–	–	–	–	–	–	–	–	–	–	–	–	–	2	–	1	1	0	3	1	–	3	1	2	1	1	–	16
Longueuil	–	–	–	–	–	–	–	–	–	–	–	–	–	–	1	2	1	2	1	–	–	2	3	–	–	–	–	–	12
St. Jerome	1	–	1	–	–	–	–	–	–	–	–	–	–	–	–	–	–	–	–	–	–	–	–	–	–	–	–	–	2

Year	Total Quebec Drafted	Total Players Drafted	Quebec %
1969	11	84	13.1
1970	13	115	11.3
1971	13	117	11.1
1972	30	152	19.7
1973	24	168	14.3
1974	40	247	16.2
1975	28	217	12.9
1976	18	135	13.3
1977	40	185	21.6
1978	22	234	9.4
1979	19	126	15.1
1980	24	210	11.4
1981	28	211	13.3
1982	17	252	6.7
1983	24	242	9.9
1984	16	250	6.4
1985	15	252	5.9
1986	22	252	8.7
1987	17	252	6.7
1988	22	252	8.7
1989	16	252	6.3
1990	14	250	5.6
1991	25	264	9.5
1992	22	264	8.3
1993	23	286	8.0
1994	28	286	9.7
1995	35	234	14.9
1996	31	241	12.8
Total	**637**	**6030**	**10.5**

United States Colleges

Club	'69	'70	'71	'72	'73	'74	'75	'76	'77	'78	'79	'80	'81	'82	'83	'84	'85	'86	'87	'88	'89	'90	'91	'92	'93	'94	'95	'96	Total
Minnesota	1	3	2	–	–	9	4	4	5	5	2	3	1	1	1	–	–	2	1	1	1	–	–	–	–	–	2	3	51
Michigan	1	–	–	2	2	3	3	1	6	–	4	–	–	–	1	1	–	1	2	3	5	4	2	1	1	–	–	3	46
Michigan Tech	–	–	3	1	2	5	4	4	1	2	1	4	–	1	–	2	2	2	1	1	2	1	2	–	1	2	–	1	45
Boston U.	–	4	–	1	1	1	1	4	5	1	–	1	–	–	1	1	2	2	3	1	2	2	1	1	–	1	1	–	37
Wisconsin	–	1	2	4	5	4	4	2	3	–	1	–	3	2	–	1	1	–	1	–	–	1	–	–	–	–	–	–	36
Denver	1	3	2	4	2	3	1	2	2	2	2	1	–	1	–	–	1	2	4	1	1	–	–	–	–	–	–	–	35
Michigan State	–	–	1	–	1	1	1	1	–	–	2	–	2	–	2	–	1	1	4	4	5	4	1	1	1	–	1		34
North Dakota	2	3	3	1	4	2	1	–	1	2	3	3	1	–	–	1	–	–	–	2	1	1	–	–	–	–	–	–	31
Providence	–	–	–	–	–	3	2	3	4	–	5	4	1	2	–	1	1	–	–	–	1	–	–	–	–	–	–	–	27
Clarkson	–	–	2	2	1	–	2	–	2	2	1	1	1	1	1	–	–	1	1	1	3	2	1	1	–	–	–	–	27
New Hampshire	–	–	–	1	1	3	6	–	4	1	1	2	1	1	1	2	–	–	–	–	–	–	–	–	–	–	–	–	25
Cornell	–	–	–	2	1	1	–	1	1	1	–	1	1	1	–	1	2	–	1	2	5	2	–	–	–	–	–	–	23
Harvard	–	–	2	–	–	–	2	–	2	2	–	–	–	1	1	–	2	–	1	1	2	–	–	2	1	–	3		22
Bowling Green	–	–	–	–	1	3	2	1	1	1	1	–	–	1	–	–	–	3	2	1	3	1	–	–	–	–	–	–	21
Colorado	2	1	–	–	–	1	3	1	2	2	–	1	–	–	3	–	1	–	1	–	2	–	–	–	–	–	1	–	21
Lake Superior	–	–	–	1	1	1	–	–	3	–	–	–	–	1	–	3	–	3	2	3	1	–	1	–	–	1			21
W. Michigan	–	–	–	–	–	–	–	2	–	–	–	2	–	2	2	–	2	1	1	1	1	4	–	2	–	–	–	–	20
Notre Dame	–	–	2	3	–	7	2	–	3	1	1	–	–	–	–	–	–	1	–	–	–	–	–	–	–	–	–	1	20
St. Lawrence	–	–	–	–	–	1	–	1	4	–	–	–	3	–	1	1	1	1	1	1	2	–	1	–	–	–	–	1	20
RPI	–	–	–	1	–	–	1	3	–	1	2	1	1	–	1	–	2	2	–	–	3	1	–	–	–	–	–	2	19
Boston College	–	1	–	–	–	1	1	–	5	–	2	1	1	–	–	1	2	–	2	–	–	1	–	–	–	–	–	2	19
Northern Mich.	–	–	–	–	–	–	–	–	4	–	1	2	1	–	–	–	–	4	1	2	–	1	–	–	–	1	–	–	17
Vermont	–	–	–	1	–	4	1	1	–	1	1	–	1	1	2	–	1	1	2	–	–	1	–	–	–	1	–	1	17
Miami of Ohio	–	–	–	–	–	–	–	–	–	–	–	–	1	–	2	4	2	–	2	1	1	–	–	–	–	–	–	–	13
Ohio State	–	–	–	–	–	–	–	2	1	–	–	–	1	–	–	–	2	2	–	1	1	1	1	1	–	–	–	–	13
Minn.-Duluth	–	–	2	1	–	–	–	1	1	–	1	–	–	–	–	1	–	–	–	2	1	2	1	–	–	–	–	–	12
Brown	–	–	–	–	1	2	1	–	3	2	–	–	–	1	–	–	–	–	–	–	–	1	–	–	–	–	–	–	11
Maine	–	–	–	–	–	–	–	–	–	–	1	1	–	–	1	1	–	3	2	1	–	1	–	–	–	–	–	–	11
Colgate	–	–	–	–	–	1	–	–	–	2	1	–	–	–	–	–	–	–	1	1	2	2	–	–	–	–	–	–	10
Yale	–	–	–	1	–	1	–	–	2	–	1	–	–	–	–	–	1	2	–	1	–	–	1	–	–	–	–	–	10
Northeastern	–	–	–	–	1	–	–	–	1	–	1	–	1	–	1	1	–	1	1	–	–	1	–	–	–	–	–	–	8
Princeton	–	–	–	–	1	–	1	–	1	1	1	–	1	–	–	–	1	–	1	–	–	1	–	–	–	–	–	–	8
Ferris State	–	–	–	–	–	–	–	–	–	–	–	–	–	–	–	2	1	1	1	2	–	–	–	–	–	–	–	–	7
St. Louis	–	–	–	1	2	–	1	2	–	–	–	–	–	–	–	–	–	–	–	–	–	–	–	–	–	–	–	–	6
U. of Ill.-Chi.	–	–	–	–	–	–	–	–	–	1	–	2	1	2	–	–	–	–	–	–	–	–	–	–	–	–	–	–	6
Pennsylvania	–	–	–	1	2	1	–	–	–	1	–	–	–	–	–	–	–	–	–	–	–	–	–	–	–	–	–	–	5
Dartmouth	–	–	–	1	–	–	–	–	1	1	–	–	–	–	1	–	1	–	–	1	–	–	–	–	–	–	–		5
Merrimack	–	–	–	–	–	–	1	–	–	–	–	–	–	–	1	–	1	–	–	1	–	–	–	–	–	1			5
Union College	–	–	–	–	–	–	–	4	–	–	–	–	–	–	–	–	–	–	–	–	–	–	–	–	–	–	–	–	4
Lowell	–	–	–	–	–	1	1	–	1	–	1	–	–	–	–	–	–	–	–	–	–	–	–	–	–	–	–	–	4
Alaska-Anchorage	–	–	–	–	–	–	–	–	–	–	–	–	–	–	–	2	1	–	1	–	–	–	–	–	–	–	–		4
Babson College	–	–	–	–	–	–	–	–	–	–	–	–	1	–	1	1	–	–	–	–	–	–	–	–	–	–	–		3
St. Cloud State	–	–	–	–	–	–	–	–	–	–	–	–	–	–	–	1	–	–	–	–	–	–	–	–	2				3
Alaska-Fairbanks	–	–	–	–	–	–	–	–	–	–	–	–	–	–	–	–	1	1	–	–	–	–	–	–	–	–			2
Salem State	–	–	–	–	1	–	–	–	–	–	–	–	–	–	–	–	–	–	–	–	–	–	–	–	–	–	–	–	1
Bemidji State	–	1	–	–	–	–	–	–	–	–	–	–	–	–	–	–	–	–	–	–	–	–	–	–	–	–	–	–	1
San Diego U.	–	–	–	–	–	–	–	–	–	–	–	1	–	–	–	–	–	–	–	–	–	–	–	–	–	–	–	–	1
Greenway	–	–	–	–	–	–	–	–	–	–	–	–	1	–	–	–	–	–	–	–	–	–	–	–	–	–	–	–	1
St. Anselen College	–	–	–	–	–	–	–	–	–	–	–	–	1	–	–	–	–	–	–	–	–	–	–	–	–	–	–	–	1
Hamilton College	–	–	–	–	–	–	–	–	–	–	–	–	1	–	–	–	–	–	–	–	–	–	–	–	–	–	–	–	1
St. Thomas	–	–	–	–	–	–	–	–	–	–	–	–	–	1	–	–	–	–	–	–	–	–	–	–	–	–	–	–	1
Amer. Int'l College	–	–	–	–	–	–	–	–	–	–	–	–	–	–	1	–	–	–	–	–	–	–	–	–	–	–	–	–	1
Wisc.-River Falls	–	–	–	–	–	–	–	–	–	–	–	–	–	–	–	–	–	–	–	–	–	–	–	–	–	–	1	–	1
Army	–	–	–	–	–	–	–	–	–	–	–	–	–	–	–	–	–	–	–	–	–	–	–	–	–	–	–	1	1

Year	Total College Drafted	Total Players Drafted	College %
1969	7	84	8.3
1970	16	115	13.9
1971	22	117	18.8
1972	21	152	13.8
1973	25	168	14.9
1974	41	247	16.6
1975	59	217	26.7
1976	26	135	19.3
1977	49	185	26.5
1978	73	234	31.2
1979	15	126	11.9
1980	42	210	20.0
1981	21	211	10.0
1982	20	252	7.9
1983	14	242	5.8
1984	22	250	8.8
1985	20	252	7.9
1986	22	252	8.7
1987	40	252	15.9
1988	48	252	19.0
1989	48	252	19.0
1990	38	250	15.2
1991	43	264	16.3
1992	9	264	3.4
1993	17	286	5.9
1994	6	286	2.1
1995	5	234	2.1
1996	25	241	10.4
Total	**794**	**6030**	**13.1**

United States High Schools (selected)

Club	'80	'81	'82	'83	'84	'85	'86	'87	'88	'89	'90	'91	'92	'93	'94	'95	'96	Total
Northwood Prep (NY)	–	–	2	1	–	2	2	4	1	1	3	1	–	1	1	–	–	19
Belmont Hill (MA)	–	–	–	1	–	2	1	2	1	3	2	1	2	–	1	–	–	16
Edina (MN)	–	1	4	2	2	–	1	2	2	1	–	1	–	–	–	–	–	16
Hill-Murray (MN)	–	–	–	–	3	–	3	3	–	2	3	–	–	–	1	–	–	15
Cushing Acad. (MA)	–	–	–	–	1	–	–	–	3	2	3	1	–	2	2	–	1	15
Mount St. Charles (RI)	–	1	–	3	1	–	2	1	2	1	1	–	–	–	–	–	–	12
Culver Mil. Acad. (IN)	–	–	–	–	–	–	2	1	2	2	1	2	2	–	–	–	–	12
Catholic Memorial (MA)	–	–	–	–	–	2	–	1	1	2	–	–	2	1	2	–	–	11
Canterbury (CT)	–	–	–	–	–	–	2	–	3	–	2	2	1	–	–	–	–	10
Matignon (MA)	1	1	1	–	3	–	–	3	–	–	1	–	–	–	–	–	–	10
Roseau (MN)	1	–	1	1	1	–	1	–	–	1	3	1	–	–	–	–	–	10
Hotchkiss (CT)	–	–	–	–	–	–	–	–	–	–	–	–	–	–	–	1	2	3
White Bear Lake (MN)	–	–	–	–	–	–	–	–	–	–	–	–	–	–	–	1	–	1
Shattuck (NY)	–	–	–	–	–	–	–	–	–	–	–	–	–	–	–	1	–	1
Taft (IL)	–	–	–	–	–	–	–	–	–	–	–	–	–	–	–	1	–	1
Lawrence Acad. (NH)	–	–	–	–	–	–	–	–	–	–	–	–	–	–	–	1		1

Year	Total USHS Drafted	Total Players Drafted	USHS %
1980	7	210	3.3
1981	17	211	8.1
1982	47	252	18.6
1983	35	242	14.5
1984	44	250	17.6
1985	48	252	19.1
1986	40	252	15.9
1987	69	252	27.4
1988	56	252	22.2
1989	47	252	18.7
1990	57	250	22.8
1991	37	264	14.0
1992	25	264	9.5
1993	33	286	11.5
1994	28	286	9.7
1995	2	234	0.9
1996	6	241	2.4
Total	**598**	**6030**	**9.9**

International

Country	'69	'70	'71	'72	'73	'74	'75	'76	'77	'78	'79	'80	'81	'82	'83	'84	'85	'86	'87	'88	'89	'90	'91	'92	'93	'94	'95	'96	Total
USSR/CIS	–	–	–	–	–	1	–	–	2	–	–	3	5	1	2	1	2	11	18	14	25	45	31	35	27	17	–	–	240
Sweden	–	–	–	–	–	5	2	5	2	8	5	9	14	14	10	14	16	9	15	14	9	7	11	11	18	17	8	16	239
Czech Republic and Slovakia	–	–	–	–	–	–	–	–	–	2	1	–	4	13	8	6	11	5	8	21	9	17	15	18	21	14			195
Finland	1	–	–	1	3	2	3	2	–	4	12	5	9	10	4	10	6	7	3	9	6	8	9	8	12	7	–	–	141
Germany	–	–	–	–	–	–	2	–	–	2	–	1	2	1	–	1	2	–	1	1	3	1	1	3					22
Switzerland	–	–	–	–	–	1	–	–	–	–	–	–	–	–	–	–	–	–	–	–	–	2	1	–	1				6
Norway	–	–	–	–	–	–	–	–	–	–	–	–	–	–	–	–	–	–	2	–	2	1	–	–					5
Denmark	–	–	–	–	–	–	–	–	–	–	–	–	–	–	–	–	1	1	–	–	–	–	–	–					2
Scotland	–	–	–	–	–	–	–	–	–	–	–	–	–	–	–	1													1
Poland	–	–	–	–	–	–	–	–	–	–	–	–	–	–	–	–	–	–	–	–	–	1	–						1
Japan	–	–	–	–	–	–	–	–	–	–	–	–	–	–	–	–	–	–	–	–	1	–	–						1

Sweden

Club	'74	'75	'76	'77	'78	'79	'80	'81	'82	'83	'84	'85	'86	'87	'88	'89	'90	'91	'92	'93	'94	'95	'96	Total
Djurgarden Stockholm	1	1	1	–	–	1	2	–	1	2	1	–	1	2	–	1	1	2	1	1	–	3	2	24
Leksand	1	–	–	–	1	–	1	–	2	2	1	1	2	1	–	2	–	2	2	2	–	1		19
Farjestad Karlstad	–	–	2	2	1	2	1	1	2	–	–	1	–	1	2	1	–	1	2	1	1			19
MoDo Hockey Ornskoldsvik	–	1	–	1	–	1	2	–	1	–	–	1	–	–	–	2	2	5	–	–	3			18
AIK Solna	–	1	1	1	1	–	2	3	1	–	4	–	–	1	1	1	–	1	–	–				17
Brynas Gavle	1	–	1	1	1	1	1	2	–	4	–	–	–	–										14
Sodertalje	–	1	–	1	1	1	1	2	2	2	–	2	–	1	–									13
Vastra Frolunda Goteborg	–	–	2	1	–	1	1	1	–	1	3	1	1											12
Skelleftea	1	1	–	1	1	1	–	1	–															9
Vasteras									2	2	1	1	1											8
Rogle Angelholm								1	2	–	–	2	2	1										8
HV 71 Jonkoping						1	1	1	1	–	2	–	2											8
Lulea				1	1	1	1	1	1															6
Sundsvall Timra[1]					1	2	1	1																6
Malmo							1	1	1	1	2													6
Bjorkloven Umea				2	1	1	1																	5
Orebro	–	1	1	1	1	1																		5
Nacka								1	1	2														4
Hammarby Stockholm				1	1	1	1																	4
Falun					1	1	1																	3
Team Kiruna				1	1	1																		3
Boden	1	1	1																					3
Pitea					1	1	1																	3
Mora					1	1	1																1	3
Huddinge								1	1												2			3
Troja							1	1																2
Ostersund						1	1																	2
Almtuna					1																			1
Danderyd Hockey															1									1
Fagersta					1																			1
Karskoga	–	1																						1
Stocksund					1																			1
S/G Hockey 83 Gavle								1																1
Talje	–	1																						1
Tunabro	1																							1
Uppsala													1											1
Grums																1								1
Vallentuna																					1	–		1
Vita Hasten																						1		1

Former club names: [1]–Timra

Russia/C.I.S.

Club	'74	'75	'76	'77	'78	'79	'80	'81	'82	'83	'84	'85	'86	'87	'88	'89	'90	'91	'92	'93	'94	'95	'96	Total
CSKA Moscow	–	–	–	–	1	–	–	1	4	–	1	1	1	5	8	3	4	7	3	5	2	3		49
Dynamo Moscow	–	–	–	–	–	–	–	–	–	2	3	4	7	10	2	1	7	1	1					37
Krylja Sovetov Moscow	–	–	–	–	–	–	–	–	–	–	1	1	2	4	3	1	5	3	2					22
Spartak Moscow	–	–	–	–	1	–	1	–	1	–	–	1	4	–	6	1	–							15
Traktor Chelyabinsk	–	–	–	–	–	–	–	–	2	–	2	–	2	7	1	1	–							13
Sokol Kiev	–	–	–	–	–	–	–	1	–	1	2	3	1	–	2	–								11
Pardaugava Riga[1]	–	1	–	–	–	–	–	1	2	–	1	4	1	–	–									10
Torpedo Yaroslavl	–	–	–	–	–	–	–	–	–	–	–	2	–	1	5	1								10
Khimik Voskresensk	–	–	–	–	–	–	–	–	–	–	1	3	1	2	–									9
SKA St. Peterburg[2]	–	–	–	–	–	1	–	–	–	–	–	2	1	–	1									6
Salavat Yulayev Ufa	–	–	–	–	–	–	–	–	–	–	–	2	2	1	1									6
Dynamo-2 Moscow	–	–	–	–	–	–	–	–	–	–	2	1	2	–										5
Torpedo Ust Kamenogorsk	–	–	–	–	–	–	–	–	–	–	1	1	2	1										5
Tivali Minsk[3]	–	–	–	–	–	–	–	–	1	–	–	2	1	–										4
Lada Togliatti	–	–	–	–	–	–	–	–	–	–	1	2	–	–	1									4
Kristall Elektrostal	–	–	–	–	–	–	–	–	–	–	3	–	–											3
Avangard Omsk	–	–	–	–	–	–	–	–	–	–	–	3	–	1										4
Severstal Cherepovets[5]	–	–	–	–	–	–	–	–	–	–	1	1	–	1	1									4
Torpedo Nizhny Novgorod[4]	–	–	–	–	–	–	–	–	–	–	–	1	2	–										3
CSKA-2 Moscow	–	–	–	–	–	–	–	–	–	–	–	1	–	2										3
Torpedo-2 Yaroslavl	–	–	–	–	–	–	–	–	–	–	–	1	–	2										3
Molot Perm	–	–	–	–	–	–	–	–	–	–	1	1	–											2
Argus Moscow	–	–	–	–	–	–	–	–	–	–	1	–												1
Dizelist Penza	–	–	–	–	–	–	–	–	–	–	1	–												1
Dynamo Kharkov	–	–	–	–	–	–	–	1	–															1
Izhorets St. Peterburg	–	–	–	–	–	–	–	–	–	–	1	–												1
Khimik Novopolotsk	–	–	–	–	–	–	–	–	–	–	–	1	–											1
Kristall Saratov	–	–	–	–	–	–	–	–	–	–	–	1	–											1
Krylja Sovetov-2 Moscow	–	–	–	–	–	–	–	–	1	–														1
Itil Kazan	–	–	–	–	–	–	–	–	–	–	–	1	–											1
Mechel Chelyabinsk	–	–	–	–	–	–	–	–	–	–	–	1	–											1
CSK VVS Samara	–	–	–	–	–	–	–	–	–	–	–	1	–											1
Avtomobilist Yekaterinburg	–	–	–	–	–	–	–	–	–	–	–	–	1											1
Salavat Novoil Ufa	–	–	–	–	–	–	–	–	–	–	–	–	1											1

Former club names: [1]–Dynamo Riga, HC Riga, [2]–SKA Leningrad, [3]–Dynamo Minsk, [4]–Torpedo Gorky, [5]–Metallurg Cherepovets

Year	Total International Drafted	Total Players Drafted	International %
1969	1	84	1.2
1970	0	115	0
1971	0	117	0
1972	0	152	0
1973	0	168	0
1974	6	247	2.4
1975	6	217	2.8
1976	8	135	5.9
1977	5	185	2.7
1978	16	234	6.8
1979	6	126	4.8
1980	13	210	6.2
1981	32	211	15.2
1982	35	252	13.9
1983	34	242	14.0
1984	40	250	17.6
1985	31	252	12.3
1986	28	252	11.1
1987	38	252	15.1
1988	39	252	15.5
1989	38	252	15.1
1990	53	250	21.2
1991	55	264	20.8
1992	84	264	31.4
1993	78	286	27.3
1994	80	286	27.9
1995	69	234	29.5
1996	58	241	24.0
Total	**853**	**6030**	**14.1**

Note: Players drafted in the International category played outside North America in their draft year. European-born players drafted from the OHL, QMJHL, WHL or U.S. Colleges are not counted as International players. See Country of Origin, below.

1996 Entry Draft Analysis

Country of Origin

Country	Players Drafted
Canada	140
Russia	20
Czech Republic	11
USA	29
Finland	8
Sweden	15
Slovakia	7
Ukraine	3
Germany	3
Kazahkstan	1
Denmark	1
Belarus	1
Lithuania	1
Switzerland	1

Position

Position	Players Drafted
Defense	85
Center	54
Left Wing	35
Right Wing	44
Goaltender	23

Birth Year

Year	Players Drafted
1978	128
1977	84
1976	21
1975	1
1974	2
1973	1
1972	1
1970	1
1969	1
1968	1

Czech Republic and Slovakia

Club	'69	'70	'71	'72	'73	'74	'75	'76	'77	'78	'79	'80	'81	'82	'83	'84	'85	'86	'87	'88	'89	'90	'91	'92	'93	'94	'95	'96	Total
Dukla Jihlava	–	–	–	–	–	–	–	–	–	–	–	–	2	4	3	1	–	3	1	1	3	2	1	1	1	2	2	–	27
Chemopetrol Litvinov[1]	–	–	–	–	–	–	–	–	–	–	–	–	3	1	2	–	–	–	–	2	2	1	3	2	4	2	2	–	24
HC Ceske Budejovice[6]	–	–	–	–	–	–	–	–	–	–	–	–	–	–	2	1	1	–	–	1	–	1	2	–	1	2	3	1	15
Sparta Praha	–	–	–	–	–	–	–	–	–	–	–	–	–	1	–	2	1	1	1	2	1	2	–	1	1	–	1	–	14
HC Kladno[7]	–	–	–	–	–	–	–	2	1	–	1	–	1	–	–	1	2	–	1	2	–	2	–	–	–	–	–	–	13
Slovan Bratislava	–	–	–	–	–	–	1	1	–	2	–	–	1	1	1	–	1	–	–	3	–	1	–	–	–	–	–	–	12
Dukla Trencin	–	–	–	–	–	–	–	–	–	–	–	–	–	–	–	1	–	–	–	1	1	2	–	2	2	–	1	2	12
ZPS Zlin[2]	–	–	–	–	–	–	–	–	–	–	–	–	–	–	1	–	1	1	1	–	–	–	2	2	1	–	2	–	11
HC Vitkovice[8]	–	–	–	–	–	–	1	–	–	1	–	1	–	–	–	–	–	–	–	–	1	–	1	3	1	1	1	–	10
HC Kosice[3]	–	–	–	–	–	–	–	–	–	1	2	–	2	–	1	–	–	2	–	–	–	–	–	–	–	–	1	–	9
Interconex Plzen[9]	–	–	–	–	–	–	–	–	–	–	–	–	–	–	–	–	1	–	1	1	–	3	–	–	1	1	–	–	8
HC Pardubice[4]	–	–	–	–	–	–	–	–	–	–	–	–	–	–	2	–	2	–	1	–	–	2	1	–	–	–	–	–	8
Zetor Brno	–	–	–	–	–	–	–	–	–	–	–	–	–	–	–	–	1	–	3	–	–	2	–	1	–	–	–	–	7
HC Olomouc[5]	–	–	–	–	–	–	–	–	–	–	–	–	–	–	–	–	–	–	–	1	–	2	–	–	1	2	–	–	6
AC Nitra	–	–	–	–	–	–	–	–	–	–	–	–	–	–	–	–	–	–	–	–	2	–	1	–	–	–	1	–	4
ZTS Martin	–	–	–	–	–	–	–	–	–	–	–	–	–	–	–	–	1	–	–	–	–	–	–	–	–	2	–	–	3
ZTK Zvolen	–	–	–	–	–	–	–	–	–	–	–	–	–	–	–	–	–	–	–	–	1	–	–	–	–	–	1	1	3
Slavia Praha	–	–	–	–	–	–	–	–	–	–	–	–	–	–	–	1	–	–	–	–	–	–	1	–	–	–	–	–	2
IS Banska Bystrica	–	–	–	–	–	–	–	–	–	–	–	–	–	–	–	–	–	–	–	–	–	–	–	–	–	1	1	–	2
Ingstav Brno	–	–	–	–	–	–	–	–	–	–	–	–	–	–	–	1	–	–	–	–	–	–	–	–	–	–	–	–	1
Partizan Liptovsky Mikulas	–	–	–	–	–	–	–	–	–	–	–	–	–	–	–	–	–	–	–	–	1	–	–	–	–	–	–	–	1
VTJ Pisek	–	–	–	–	–	–	–	–	–	–	–	–	–	–	–	–	–	–	–	–	1	–	–	–	–	–	–	–	1
ZPA Presov	–	–	–	–	–	–	–	–	–	–	–	–	–	–	–	–	–	–	–	–	–	–	–	–	–	1	–	–	1
Banik Sokolov	–	–	–	–	–	–	–	–	–	–	–	–	–	–	–	–	–	–	–	–	–	–	–	–	–	–	1	–	1

Former club names: [1]–CHZ Litvinov, [2]–TJ Gottwaldov, TJ Zlin, [3]–VSZ Kosice, [4]–Tesla Pardubice, [5]–DS Olomouc, [6]–Motor Ceske Budejovice, [7]–Poldi Kladno, [8]–TJ Vitkovice, [9]–Skoda Plzen

Finland

Club	'69	'70	'71	'72	'73	'74	'75	'76	'77	'78	'79	'80	'81	'82	'83	'84	'85	'86	'87	'88	'89	'90	'91	'92	'93	'94	'95	'96	Total
TPS Turku	–	–	–	–	–	–	–	–	–	–	–	1	6	–	–	1	–	1	–	–	–	–	–	–	3	2	3	1	18
HIFK Helsinki	1	–	–	–	–	–	1	–	1	–	–	1	1	2	2	1	–	–	2	1	–	–	–	–	2	–	1	–	16
Ilves Tampere	–	–	–	–	–	1	–	2	–	–	–	2	–	2	–	2	1	–	–	1	–	1	1	–	–	–	2	–	15
Jokerit Helsinki	–	–	–	–	–	–	–	–	2	1	–	–	1	–	–	–	1	1	–	–	2	–	3	–	–	1	–	1	13
Assat Pori	–	–	–	–	2	–	–	–	–	–	–	–	1	–	2	2	–	–	1	–	1	–	–	1	1	1	–	–	12
Tappara Tampere	–	–	–	–	–	–	1	–	–	–	–	–	2	–	–	–	4	1	–	–	1	–	–	–	–	–	1	1	11
Karpat Oulu	–	–	–	–	–	–	–	–	–	–	1	–	1	–	1	–	–	2	2	–	–	1	–	1	–	–	–	–	9
Lukko Rauma	–	–	–	–	–	–	2	1	–	–	–	–	2	–	1	–	1	–	–	–	1	–	1	–	–	–	–	–	9
Kiekko-Espoo	–	–	–	–	–	–	–	–	–	–	–	–	–	–	–	–	–	–	–	1	1	1	2	–	2	1	–	–	8
Reipas Lahti	–	–	–	–	–	–	–	–	–	–	–	1	1	1	–	–	–	–	–	–	2	–	1	–	–	–	1	–	7
KalPa Kuopio	–	–	–	–	–	–	–	–	–	–	–	–	–	–	–	–	–	–	1	–	–	–	1	2	–	–	–	–	4
HPK Hameenlinna	–	–	–	–	–	–	–	–	–	–	–	–	–	–	–	–	–	–	–	1	–	–	2	–	–	–	–	–	3
Kiekoo-67 Turku	–	–	–	–	–	–	–	–	–	–	–	–	–	–	–	–	–	–	–	–	–	–	–	–	–	3	–	–	3
JyP HT Jyvaskyla	–	–	–	–	–	–	–	–	–	–	–	–	–	–	–	–	–	–	1	–	–	–	–	–	–	–	2	–	3
SaiPa Lappeenranta	–	–	–	–	–	–	–	–	–	–	1	–	–	–	–	–	–	–	–	–	–	1	–	–	–	–	–	–	2
Sapko Savonlinna	–	–	–	–	–	–	–	–	–	–	–	–	–	–	–	–	1	1	–	–	–	–	–	–	–	–	–	–	2
Sport Vaasa	–	–	–	–	–	–	–	–	–	–	–	–	–	–	–	–	–	1	–	1	–	–	–	–	–	–	–	–	2
GrIFK Kauniainen	–	–	–	–	–	–	–	–	–	–	–	–	–	–	–	–	–	–	–	–	–	–	1	–	–	–	–	–	1
Koo Koo Kouvola	–	–	–	–	–	–	–	–	–	–	–	–	–	–	–	–	–	–	–	–	–	–	1	–	–	–	–	–	1
S-Kiekko Seinajoki	–	–	–	–	–	–	–	–	–	–	–	–	–	–	–	–	–	–	–	–	–	1	–	–	–	–	–	–	1
Junkkarit Kalajoki	–	–	–	–	–	–	–	–	–	–	–	–	–	–	–	–	–	–	–	–	–	–	–	–	–	–	–	1	1

James Patrick, below, was the ninth player chosen overall in the 1981 Entry Draft by the New York Rangers. A two-time NCAA All-Star with the University of North Dakota, Patrick scored at least 10 goals in seven straight seasons with the Rangers. Defenseman Shawn Anderson, right, selected fifth overall by the Buffalo Sabres in the 1986 Entry Draft, had his finest season as a professional in 1995-96, recording 22 goals and 61 points with the IHL's Milwaukee Admirals.

First Round Draft Selections, 1996

1. OTTAWA • **CHRIS PHILLIPS** • D • Projected by many as a future NHL captain, Phillips was the WHL Rookie of the Year with the Prince Albert Raiders in 1995-96 and was named to the WHL Central/East All-Star Team. He was also the youngest member of the 1996 gold medal Canadian team at the World Junior Championships. A physical presence on the ice, Phillips tries to emulate the style of New Jersey's Scott Stevens. He has a quick stride, with good speed and acceleration.

2. SAN JOSE • **ANDREI ZYUZIN** • D • An excellent skater with speed, acceleration, and balance, Zyuzin also boasts tremendous puck skills and a very hard shot. He was a key performer for the Russian team at the World Junior Championships and was named the best player in the tournament at the European Junior tournament. Rated better offensively than on defense, Zyuzin can throw a bodycheck and be aggressive if needed. He's spent two seasons with Salavat Yulayev in his home town of Ufa, Russia.

3. NY ISLANDERS • **JEAN-PIERRE DUMONT** • RW • The first forward selected in the Draft, Dumont came into his own in 1995-96 with 48 goals and 57 assists for Val d'Or of the QMJHL. He tries to copy the style of Colorado's Joe Sakic, who is his favorite player. Dumont's improved skating dramatically enhanced his other skills, which include a quick wrist shot and tremendous passing ability. He uses his body effectively in front of the net. Dumont played for Team Quebec at the 1995 Canada Winter Games.

4. WASHINGTON • **ALEXANDER VOLCHKOV** • C • One of the premier offensive talents in the 1996 Entry Draft, Volchkov has the size, strength and speed to succeed in the NHL. Limited by injuries to just 47 games with the Barrie Colts of the OHL, he had 37 goals and 27 assists in 1995-96 after being drafted from the Central Red Army junior squad. A gifted scorer who can also set up the play, Volchkov boasts an impressive combination of speed, agility and quickness and doesn't back down in a physical game.

5. DALLAS • **RICHARD JACKMAN** • D • Jackman surprised some scouts when he turned down an opportunity to play in the CHL Prospects Game, but impressed others with the fact he did not want to miss any key contests with his Sault Ste. Marie club in the OHL. He had quickly become an important player with the Greyhounds after joining the team right out of midget hockey, seeing power play and penalty killing time in addition to his regular shift. Jackman is an excellent skater with good puck skills and a hard, accurate shot.

6. EDMONTON • **BOYD DEVEREAUX** • C • An all-around performer who may have been the best defensive forward available in the Draft, Devereaux has excellent speed and a hard shot. He spent the 1995-96 season with the OHL's Kitchener Rangers after winning the Ontario Jr. B championship the season before with the Stratford Cullitons. Devereaux combines a good hockey sense with a high skill level and finished third in the CHL's obstacle course skills test. He's a tireless worker who plays with enthusiasm.

7. BUFFALO • **ERIK RASMUSSEN** • C • The first American-born player to be selected in the Draft, Rasmussen would likely have been picked in 1995 had he not chosen to play college hockey. In 1995-96, he was named WCHA Rookie of the Year with the University of Minnesota after totalling 13 goals and 28 assists for 41 points in 31 games. He was a member of the U.S. National Junior Team at both the 1995 and 1996 World Junior Championships, and patterns his game after Chicago's Jeremy Roenick. Rasmussen plays a tough physical style.

8. BOSTON • **JONATHAN AITKEN** • D • Aitken was named Best Defenseman and Rookie of the Year for the Medicine Hat Tigers of the WHL in 1994-95, and improved all of his numbers in 1995-96. At 6'3" and 188 pounds, Aitken is a physical presence on the ice and is not afraid to throw big bodychecks. He'll likely fill out to over 200 pounds. Aitken is a good skater with quick acceleration and has a hard, accurate shot. He admires the play of Al Iafrate and Scott Niedermayer.

9. ANAHEIM • **RUSLAN SALEI** • D • A native of Minsk in Belarus, 21-year-old Salei was the elder statesman in this year's Draft. Being from Belarus, Salei never competed at the Four Nations, European Junior, or World Junior Championships, but attracted attention during the 1995-96 season with his strong play as a member of the Las Vegas Thunder in the IHL. A solid, defensive defenseman, Salei is a hard hitter who can pass well and has a good shot.

10. NEW JERSEY • **LANCE WARD** • D • A physical, stay-at-home defenseman, Lance Ward had just four goals all season with Red Deer of the WHL, but tallied twice in the CHL Prospects Game in Toronto. He enjoys being involved physically in the game and is a punishing checker. Ward has a hard shot but needs to improve his accuracy. He tries to pattern his game after New Jersey's Scott Stevens. Red Deer teammate Jesse Wallin was selected by Detroit later in the first round.

11. PHOENIX • **DAN FOCHT** • D • Dan Focht was a last-minute roster addition at the CHL Prospects Game and promptly went on to wow the scouts when he recorded the second-hardest shot in skills competition and won the c150-foot puck agility drill. At 6'5" and 226 pounds, Focht has an excellent physical presence on the ice as well being a very mobile defenseman. He tries to copy the on-ice style of Eric Lindros, who is his favorite player.

12. VANCOUVER • **JOSH HOLDEN** • C • A smallish center who makes up for his lack of size with a fierce competitive spirit, Josh Holden was the 1994-95 Regina Pats Rookie of the Year and was a CHL Central/East All-Star in 1995-96. He recorded 57 goals and 55 assists with the Pats last season, notching 28 of his goals over the club's final 24 games of the regular season. In the playoffs, he scored the winning goal in quadruple overtime in a 3-2 victory over Lethbridge in the longest game in WHL history. Holden is an excellent passer and playmaker.

13. CALGARY • **DEREK MORRIS** • D • A very competitive player who gives a solid offensive effort in all games, Derek Morris was voted the Best Defenseman at the 1995 Air Canada Cup midget tournament and was a First-Team All-Star in 1995-96. A good puckhandler who likes to rush the puck, Morris had 8 goals and 44 assists for Regina in the WHL last season. A good all-around skater with speed and acceleration, Morris tries to emulate the style of Paul Coffey.

14. ST. LOUIS • **MARTY REASONER** • C • Marty Reasoner was named to the New England Prep All-Star Team in 1993-94 and 1994-95. Moving on the Boston College for the 1995-96 season, Reasoner earned comparisons with BC alumnus Craig Janney. An exceptional stickhandler and agile skater, Reasoner is an offensive force who has yet to demonstrate a physical side to his game. He passes and shoots the puck well, recording 16 goals and 27 assists in 32 games last season.

15. PHILADELPHIA • **DAINIUS ZUBRUS** • RW • A skilled offensive player, Lithuania's Dainius Zubrus is a strong skater who handles the puck well and has an excellent shot with a quick release. Property of Laval in the QMJHL, Zubrus chose to play instead at the Tier II level in 1995-96 and had 19 goals and 13 assists for 32 points in 28 games with Pembroke. He can be a hard-hitting player at times, but prefers to play a finesse game. Sergei Fedorov is his on-ice role model.

16. TAMPA BAY • **MARIO LAROCQUE** • D • Mario Larocque was named to the QMJHL Rookie All-Star Team in 1995-96 after being selected first overall by Hull in the Quebec Midget Draft in 1995. The defenseman, who tries to pattern his play after Boston's Ray Bourque, participated in the 1996 CHL Prospects Game. An agile skater who moves well in all directions, he excels at playing in his own end and also possesses a good slap and wrist shot. Larocque is a hard worker who is not afraid to play a physical game.

17. WASHINGTON • **JAROSLAV SVEJKOVSKY** • RW • The top Czech player selected in the Draft, Jaroslav Svejkovsky is a goal-scorer who wants the puck when the game is on the line. After playing in the Czech Republic, Svejkovsky was a rookie with the Tri-City Americans of the WHL in 1995-96 and scored 58 goals along with 43 assists. A streak scorer, he had 21 games in which he scored at least two goals. Svejkovsky netted 24 power play goals and 13 game-winners. He has good speed, but is not overly aggressive.

18. MONTREAL • **MATT HIGGINS** • C • Scouts say Matt Higgins isn't a great skater and isn't very strong, but that he possess great hockey sense and a strong work ethic. Named the Most Gentlemanly Player for Moose Jaw of the WHL in his rookie campaign of 1993-94, Higgins enjoyed his best season the following year when he had 36 goals and 34 assists for 70 points in 72 games. He maintained similar numbers last season when he had 30 goals and 33 assists. Steve Yzerman is his favorite player.

19. EDMONTON • **MATTHIEU DESCOTEAUX** • D • Matthieu Descoteaux played alongside Chris Phillips in the 1996 CHL Prospects Game and impressed scouts both during the contest and in the skills competition. A strong skater who concentrates on defensive play, Descoteaux was converted from left wing to defense in 1994-95 by former NHLer Jean Pronovost, who coaches him at Shawinigan of the QMJHL. He is a solid, effective body checker who can also lug the puck out of his zone and make effective passes to his forwards.

20. FLORIDA • **MARCUS NILSON** • C • The only Swedish player selected in the first round of the draft, Marcus Nilson is an offensive talent with a strong hockey sense. He has played at both the European and World Junior tournaments and had the best plus-minus rating at the 1996 World Junior Championships. Nilson is a good passer and playmaker with good hands and outstanding puck skills. He has also represented his country on national youth teams in soccer.

21. SAN JOSE • **MARCO STURM** • C • The first German player ever selected in the first round of the NHL Draft, Marco Sturm was a key player on the German team that won a silver medal in the European Junior tournament in 1995. He has also played in two World Junior Championships. Smallish for a center at 5'11" and 178 pounds, Sturm compensates with blazing speed. He's also a good stickhandler with good hands around the net. Sturm is an excellent competitor, who is a heady and talented performer.

22. NY RANGERS • **JEFF BROWN** • D • Skating is the strongest part of Jeff Brown's game. He has good speed and balance and is very quick to get to the puck. He is an effective penalty killer who uses his quickness to force his opponents into mistakes. Brown is also a good passer. He was the first player chosen in the 1994 OHL midget draft when the Sarnia Sting selected him after a Rookie-of-the-Year season with the Thornhill Islanders. He improved all of his numbers in his second season with Sarnia in 1995-96.

23. PITTSBURGH • **CRAIG HILLIER** • G • The only goaltender chosen in the first round of the NHL Draft, Craig Hillier has excellent tools as well as an understanding of his position. He is a stand-up goalie with good quickness who is excellent at playing the puck. Hillier played for Team Nova Scotia at the 1995 Canada Winter Games and was invited to training camp with the 1996 Canadian National Junior Team. He also played in the 1996 CHL Prospects Game. He sported a 2.88 goals-against average in 44 games with Ottawa of the OHL last season.

24. PHOENIX • **DANIEL BRIERE** • C • At 5'9" and 160 pounds, Daniel Briere lacks only size, but has been overcoming that problem at every level. An impressive offensive talent, Briere has upped his point production in each of the last four seasons, scoring 67 goals and adding 96 assists last season with Drummondville of the QMJHL. The season before, he had been Rookie of the Year. Briere is an excellent skater and a tremendous passer on both his forehand and his backhand. He also possesses a good shot.

25. COLORADO • **PETER RATCHUK** • D • The last of three Americans to be selected in the first round, Peter Ratchuk was drafted right out of high school but will be attending Bowling Green State University before turning pro, hoping to follow in the footsteps of BGSU alumnae Rob Blake, Garry Galley and Dave Ellett, all of whom have excelled as NHL defenseman. Ratchuk is not overly physical, but is aggressive getting to the puck and will play the body one-on-one. He is a fluid skater who plays with a high level of intensity.

26. DETROIT • **JESSE WALLIN** • D • An offensive-minded defenseman with an accurate shot and the ability to move the puck from his own end, Jesse Wallin is a durable performer with a strong work ethic. He played on both the power play and penalty killing units with Red Deer of the WHL last season, and was named an alternate captain in just his second season in the league. Wallin has a smooth, long skating stride and his lateral movement and turns are especially good.

1996 Entry Draft

Transferred draft choice notation:

Example: Col.-Ana. represents a draft choice transferred
from Colorado **to** Anaheim.

Pick	Player	Claimed By	Amateur Club	Position
ROUND # 1				
1	PHILLIPS, Chris	Ott.	Prince Albert	D
2	ZYUZIN, Andrei	S.J.	Salavat Yulayev Ufa	D
3	DUMONT, Jean-Pierre	NYI	Val d'Or	RW
4	VOLCHKOV, Alexander	L.A.-Wsh.	Barrie	C
5	JACKMAN, Richard	Dal.	Sault Ste. Marie	D
6	DEVEREAUX, Boyd	Edm.	Kitchener	C
7	RASMUSSEN, Erik	Buf.	U. of Minnesota	C
8	AITKEN, Johnathan	Hfd.-Bos.	Medicine Hat	D
9	SALEI, Ruslan	Ana.	Las Vegas	D
10	WARD, Lance	N.J.	Red Deer	D
11	FOCHT, Dan	Pho.	Tri-City	D
12	HOLDEN, Josh	Van.	Regina	C
13	MORRIS, Derek	Cgy.	Regina	D
14	REASONER, Marty	St.L.-Edm.-St.L.	Boston College	C
15	ZUBRUS, Dainius	Tor.-Phi.	Pembroke	RW
16	LAROCQUE, Mario	T.B.	Hull	D
17	SVEJKOVSKY, Jaroslav	Wsh.	Tri-City	RW
18	HIGGINS, Matt	Mtl.	Moose Jaw	C
19	DESCOTEAUX, Matthieu	Bos.-Edm.	Shawinigan	D
20	NILSON, Marcus	Fla.	Djurgarden Stockholm	C
21	STURM, Marco	Chi.-S.J.	Landshut	C
22	BROWN, Jeff	NYR	Sarnia	D
23	HILLIER, Craig	Pit.	Ottawa	G
24	BRIERE, Daniel	Phi.-Pho.	Drummondville	C
25	RATCHUK, Peter	Col.	Shattuck St. Mary's	D
26	WALLIN, Jesse	Det.	Red Deer	D
ROUND # 2				
27	SARICH, Cory	Ott.-St.L.-Buf.	Saskatoon	D
28	SKRBEK, Pavel	S.J.-N.J.-Pit.	HC Kladno	D
29	LACOUTURE, Dan	NYI	Jr. Whalers	LW
30	GREEN, Josh	L.A.	Medicine Hat	LW
31	ROYER, Remi	Dal.-Pho.- S.J.-Chi.	St-Hyacinthe	D
32	HAJT, Chris	Edm.	Guelph	D
33	VAN OENE, Darren	Buf.	Brandon	LW
34	WASYLUK, Trevor	Hfd.	Medicine Hat	LW
35	CULLEN, Matt	Ana.	St. Cloud State	C
36	POSMYK, Marek	N.J.-Tor.	Dukla Jihlava	D
37	CISAR, Marian	Pho.-L.A.	Slovan Bratislava	W
38	MASON, Wesley	Van.-N.J.	Sarnia	LW
39	BRIGLEY, Travis	Cgy.	Lethbridge	LW
40	BEGIN, Steve	St.L.-Cgy.	Val d'Or	C
41	DEWOLF, Joshua	Tor.-Pit.-N.J.	Twin Cities	D
42	PAUL, Jeff	T.B.-Chi.	Niagara Falls	D
43	BULIS, Jan	Wsh.	Barrie	C
44	GARON, Mathieu	Mtl.	Victoriaville	G
45	KUSTER, Henry	Bos.	Medicine Hat	RW
46	PETERS, Geoff	Fla.-S.J.-Chi.	Niagara Falls	C
47	DAGENAIS, Pierre	Chi.-T.B.-N.J.	Moncton	LW
48	GONEAU, Daniel	NYR	Granby	LW
49	WHITE, Colin	Pit.-N.J.	Hull	D
50	LARIVEE, Francis	Phi.-Tor.	Laval	G
51	BABENKO, Yuri	Col.	Krylja Sovetov	C
52	MILLER, Aren	Det.	Spokane	G
ROUND # 3				
53	NAUD, Eric	Ott.-Bos.	St-Hyacinthe	LW
54	METHOT, Francois	Buf.	St-Hyacinthe	C
55	FRIESEN, Terry	S.J.	Swift Current	G
56	CHARA, Zdeno	NYI	Dukla Trencin	D
57	PHILLIPS, Greg	L.A.	Saskatoon	C
58	ZIMAKOV, Sergei	Dal.-Wsh.	Krylja Sovetov	D
59	POTI, Tom	Edm.	Cushing Academy	D
60	ALLEN, Chris	Buf.-Fla.	Kingston	D
61	PETRUNIN, Andrei	Hfd.	CSKA Moskow	W
62	LUNDSTROM, Per-Anton	Ana.-Pho	MoDo Ornskoldsvik	D
63	PARKER, Scott	N.J.	Kelowna	D
64	GALLANT, Chester	Pho.-Phi.	Niagara Falls	RW
65	KVASHA, Oleg	Van.-Fla.	CSKA Moskow	W
66	LANKSHEAR, Mike	Cgy.-Tor.	Guelph	D
67	DWYER, Gordie	St.L.	Beauport	LW
68	KALMIKOV, Konstantin	Tor.	Detroit	LW
69	TIPLER, Curtis	T.B.	Regina	RW
70	SIM, Jonathan	Wsh.-Dal.	Sarnia	C
71	ASHAM, Arron	Mtl.	Red Deer	C
72	KANE, Boyd	Bos.-Pit.	Regina	LW
73	VLASENKOV, Dmitri	Fla.-Cgy.	Yaroslavl	W
74	WENINGER, Dave	Chi.-Wsh.	Michigan Tech U.	G
75	KOMARNISKI, Zenith	Van.	Tri-City	D
76	SUBBOTIN, Dmitri	NYR	CSKA Moskow	LW
77	PROTSENKO, Boris	Pit.	Calgary	RW
78	McNEIL, Shawn	Phi.-Col.-Wsh	Kamloops	C
79	PARRISH, Mark	Col.	St. Cloud State	LW
80	DOYLE, Jason	Det.-T.B.-Bos.	Sault Ste. Marie	RW

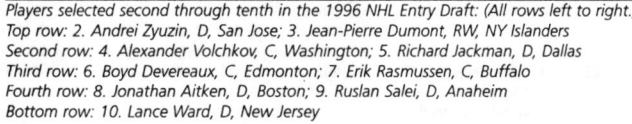

Players selected second through tenth in the 1996 NHL Entry Draft: (All rows left to right.)
Top row: 2. Andrei Zyuzin, D, San Jose; 3. Jean-Pierre Dumont, RW, NY Islanders
Second row: 4. Alexander Volchkov, C, Washington; 5. Richard Jackman, D, Dallas
Third row: 6. Boyd Devereaux, C, Edmonton; 7. Erik Rasmussen, C, Buffalo
Fourth row: 8. Jonathan Aitken, D, Boston; 9. Ruslan Salei, D, Anaheim
Bottom row: 10. Lance Ward, D, New Jersey

ROUND # 4

81	NIEMI, Antti-Jussi	Ott.	Jokerit Helsinki	D
82	TETARENKO, Joey	S.J.-Fla.	Portland	D
83	GARNER, Tyrone	NYI	Oshawa	G
84	SIMONS, Mikael	L.A.-Tor.-Phi.-L.A.	Mora	C
85	DAVIS, Justin	Dal.-L.A.-Wsh.	Kingston	RW
86	SESSA, Jason	Edm.-Tor.	Lake Superior	RW
87	WALSH, Kurt	Buf.	Owen Sound	RW
88	MacDONALD, Craig	Hfd.	Harvard University	C
89	LYDMAN, Toni	Cgy.	Reipas Lahti	D
90	HURLEY, Mike	Ana.-Wsh.-Dal.	Tri-City	RW
91	BOUMEDIENNE, Josef	N.J.	Huddinge	D
92	STAAL, Kim	Pho.-Ana.-Tor.-Mtl.	Malmo	C
93	SOLING, Jonas	Van.	Huddinge	W
94	LEFEBVRE, Christian	Cgy.	Granby	D
95	ZUKIWSKY, Jonathan	St.L.	Red Deer	C
96	BELANGER, Eric	Tor.-L.A.	Beauport	C
97	PETRAKOV, Andrei	T.B.-St.L.	Yekaterinburg	LW
98	STOREY, Ben	Wsh.-Col.	Harvard University	D
99	DRAPEAU, Etienne	Mtl.	Beauport	C
100	WHITFIELD, Trent	Bos.	Spokane	C
101	MacNEVIN, Josh	N.J.	Vernon	D
102	BRADLEY, Matt	Fla.-S.J.	Kingston	RW
103	ANTIPOV, Vladimir	Chi.-Pho.-Tor.	Yaroslavl	W
104	WASYLKO, Steve	NYR-Hfd.	Detroit	C
105	ROZSIVAL, Michal	Pit.	Dukla Jihlava	D
106	MARTONE, Mike	Phi.-S.J.-Buf.	Peterborough	D
107	PETRUK, Randy	Col.	Kamloops	G
108	FORSANDER, Johan	Det.	HV 71	W

ROUND # 5

109	BERENZWEIG, Andy	Ott.-NYI	U. of Michigan	D
110	CAVA, Peter	S.J.-Tor.	Sault Ste. Marie	C
111	SUGDEN, Brandon	NYI-Tor.	London	D
112	CHRISTIE, Ryan	L.A.-Dal.	Owen Sound	LW
113	TYSBUK, Evgeny	Dal.	Yaroslavl	D
114	URICK, Brian	Edm.	U. of Notre Dame	RW
115	TEZIKOV, Alexei	Buf.	Lada Togliatti	D
116	McMAHON, Mark	Hfd.	Kitchener	D
117	BUCKLEY, Brendan	Ana.	Boston College	D
118	CRAWFORD, Glenn	N.J.	Windsor	C
119	LINTNER, Richard	Pho.	Trencin Jr.	D
120	BLACK, Jesse	L.A.	Niagara Falls	D
121	PROSOFSKY, Tyler	Van.	Kelowna	C
122	STRAKA, Josef	Cgy.	Chemopetrol Litvinov	C
123	HOGAN, Peter	St.L.-L.A.	Oshawa	D
124	BERGQVIST, Per-Ragna	Tor.-Phi.	Leksand	G
125	ROBINSON, Jason	T.B.	Niagara Falls	D
126	LAHEY, Matthew	Wsh.	Peterborough	LW
127	ARCHAMBAULT, Daniel	Mtl.	Val d'Or	D
128	SACHL, Petr	Bos.-NYI	Budejovice Jr.	C
129	LONG, Andrew	Fla.	Guelph	RW
130	JOHNSON, Andy	Chi.	Peterborough	D
131	PEPPERALL, Colin	NYR	Niagara Falls	LW
132	ABRAHAMSSON, Elias	Pit.-S.J.-Bos.	Halifax	D
133	BOULERICE, Jesse	Phi.	Detroit	D
134	CURTIN, Luke	Col.	Kelowna	LW
135	PODOLKA, Michal	Det.	Sault Ste. Marie	G

ROUND # 6

136	DACKELL, Andreas	Ott.	Brynas Gavle	W
137	LAROCQUE, Michel	S.J.	Boston University	G
138	MILLER, Todd	NYI	Sarnia	C
139	ESCHE, Robert	L.A.-Pho.	Detroit	G
140	YAKUSHIN, Dmitriy	Dal.-Tor.	Pembroke	D
141	RANDALL, Bryan	Edm.	Medicine Hat	C
142	DAVIS, Ryan	Buf.	Owen Sound	RW
143	BAKER, Aaron	Hfd.	Tri-City	G
144	NILSSON, Magnus	Ana.-Det.	Vita Hasten	W
145	RITCHLIN, Sean	N.J.	U. of Michigan	RW
146	WILLSIE, Brian	Pho.-L.A.-Col.	Guelph	RW
147	McDONALD, Nolan	Van.	U. of Vermont	G
148	BOGAS, Chris	Cgy.-Tor.	Michigan State	D
149	RUSSELL, Blaine	St.L.-Ana.	Prince Albert	G
150	BERGMAN, Peter	Pit.	Kamloops	C
151	DEMARTINIS, Lucio	Tor.	Shawinigan	LW
152	IGNATOV, Nikolai	T.B.	CSKA Moskow	D
153	VAN BRUGGEN, Andrew	Wsh.	Northern Michigan U.	RW
154	CLARK, Brett	Mtl.	University of Maine	D
155	LANE, Chris	Bos.	Spokane	D
156	POIRIER, Gaetan	Fla.	Merrimack College	LW
157	DELISLE, Xavier	Chi.-T.B.	Granby	C
158	SANDBERG, Ola	NYR	Djurgarden Stockholm	D
159	WAGNER, Stephen	Pit.-St.L.	Olds	G
160	FISCHER, Kai	Phi.-Col.	Dusseldorf	G
161	MORTIER, Darren	Col.-Buf.	Sarnia	C
162	JACQUES, Alexandre	Det.	Shawinigan	C

ROUND # 7

163	HARDY, Francois	Ott.	Val d'Or	D
164	DEADMARSH, Jake	S.J.	Kamloops	D
165	PRESTIFILIPPO, Joe	NYI	Hotchkiss	G
166	McINERNEY, Eoin	L.A.-Dal.	London	G
167	HINOTE, Dan	Dal.-Col.	Army	RW
168	BERNIER, David	Edm.	St-Hyacinthe	C
169	CORSO, Daniel	Buf.-St.L.	Victoriaville	C
170	LAFRANCE, Brandon	Pit.-Edm.	Ohio State	RW
171	KUZNIK, Greg	Hfd.	Seattle	D
172	AHMAOJA, Timo	Ana.	JyP HT Jyvaskyla	D
173	ANDREWS, Daryl	N.J.	Melfort	D
174	LETOWSKI, Trevor	Pho.	Sarnia	C
175	CABANA, Clint	Van.	Medicine Hat	D
176	PAHLSSON, Samuel	Cgy.-Col.	MoDo Ornskoldsvik	C
177	LOW, Reed	St.L.	Moose Jaw	RW
178	BERG, Reggie	Tor.	U. of Minnesota	C
179	KUBINA, Pavel	T.B.	HC Vitkovice	D
180	ANDERSON, Michael	Wsh.	U. of Minnesota	RW
181	VERTALA, Timo	Mtl.	JyP HT Jyvaskyla	W
182	BROWN, Thomas	Bos.	Sarnia	D
183	COUTURE, Alexandre	Fla.	Victoriaville	D
184	VELLINGA, Mike	Chi.	Guelph	D
185	DESSNER, Jeff	NYR	Taft	RW
186	MELOCHE, Eric	Pit.	Cornwall	RW
187	MALOV, Roman	Phi.	Avangard Omsk	LW
188	PYLNER, Roman	Col.	Chemopetrol Litvinov	C
189	BEARDSMORE, Colin	Det.	North Bay	C

ROUND # 8

190	VALIQUETTE, Stephen	Ott.-L.A.	Sudbury	G
191	CYRENNE, Cory	S.J.	Brandon	C
192	KOROLEV, Evgeny	NYI	Peterborough	D
193	NURMINEN, Kai	L.A.	HV 71	W
194	KWIATKOWSKI, Joel	Dal.	Prince George	D
195	PISANI, Fernando	Edm.	St. Albert	C
196	PODKONICKY, Andrei	Buf.-St.L.	ZTK Zvolen	C
197	MARSH, Kevin	Hfd.	Calgary	LW
198	KELLETT, Kevin	Ana.	Prince Albert	D
199	MITCHELL, Willie	N.J.	Melfort	D
200	LENT, Nicholas	Pho.	Omaha Jr.A	RW
201	SCISSONS, Jeff	Van.	Vernon	F
202	WADE, Ryan	Cgy.	Kelowna	RW
203	HUTCHINS, Anthony	St.L.	Lawrence Academy	C
204	KABERLE, Tomas	Tor.	HC Kladno	D
205	BERTSCH, Jason	T.B.-N.J.	Spokane	RW
206	OREKHOVSKY, Oleg	Wsh.	Ambri	D
207	BALDI, Mattia	Mtl.	St. Lawrence U.	F
208	PRIER, Bob	Bos.	CSKA Moskow	RW
209	KHLOPTONOV, Denis	Fla.	Moose Jaw	G
210	TWERDUN, Chris	Chi.	London	D
211	McKIE, Ryan	NYR	Mannheim	D
212	GOLDMANN, Erich	Pit.-Ott.	Moose Jaw	D
213	MILLEKER, Jeff	Phi.	Hotchkiss	C
214	SCORSUNE, Matthew	Col.	Tri-City	C
215	STAHL, Craig	Det.		RW

ROUND # 9

216	CIERNIK, Ivan	Ott.	HC Nitra	RW
217	THIBEAULT, David	S.J.	Drummondville	LW
218	MUZECHKA, Mike	NYI	Calgary	D
219	SIMARD, Sebastien	L.A.	Drummondville	LW
220	BOOTLAND, Nick	Dal.	Guelph	LW
221	HULTBERG, John	Edm.	Kingston	G
222	BUHLER, Scott	Buf.	Medicine Hat	G
223	ADAMS, Craig	Hfd.	Harvard University	RW
224	JOHANSSON, Tobias	Ana.	Malmo Jr	W
225	PETRILAINEN, Pasi	N.J.	Tappara Tampere	D
226	HUBERT, Marc-Etienne	Pho.	Laval	C
227	VAIC, Lubomir	Van.	HC Kosice	C
228	PETROVICKY, Ronald	Cgy.	Prince George	RW
229	SHAFRANOV, Konstanti	St.L.	Fort Wayne	LW
230	HOPE, Jared	Tor.		C
231	RAKHMATULLIN, Askhat	T.B.-Hfd.		LW
232	CAVANAGH, Chad	Wsh.	London	LW
233	TREMBLAY, Michel	Mtl.	Shawinigan	LW
234	SODERBERG, Anders	Bos.	MoDo Ornskoldsvik	W
235	SMITH, Russell	Fla.	Hull	D
236	KOZYREV, Alexei	Chi.	Cherepovets	D
237	SUNDIN, Ronnie	NYR	Vastra F. Goteborg	D
238	SEIKKULA, Timo	Pit.	Junkkarit	C
239	SALO, Sami	Phi.-Ott.	TPS Turko	D
240	CLARK, Justin	Col.	U. of Michigan	RW
241	AFANASIEV, Evgeniy	Det.	Detroit L.C. Midgets	LW

Draft Choices, 1995-69

1995

FIRST ROUND

Selection	Claimed By	Amateur Club	
1. BERARD, Bryan	Ott.	Detroit	D
2. REDDEN, Wade	NYI	Brandon	D
3. BERG, Aki-Petteri	L.A.	Kiekko-67 Turku	D
4. KILGER, Chad	Ana.	Kingston	C
5. LANGKOW, Daymond	T.B.	Tri-City	C
6. KELLY, Steve	Edm.	Prince Albert	C
7. DOAN, Shane	Wpg.	Kamloops	RW
8. RYAN, Terry	Mtl.	Tri-City	LW
9. McLAREN, Kyle	Hfd.-Bos.	Tacoma	D
10. DVORAK, Radek	Fla.	HC Ceske Budejovice	W
11. IGINLA, Jarome	Dal.	Kamloops	C
12. RIIHIJARVI, Teemu	S.J.	Kiekko-Espoo Jr.	LW
13. GIGUERE, J-Sebastien	NYR-Hfd.	Halifax	G
14. McKEE, Jay	Van.-Buf.	Niagara Falls	D
15. WARE, Jeff	Tor.	Oshawa	D
16. BIRON, Martin	Buf.	Beauport	G
17. CHURCH, Brad	Wsh.	Prince Albert	LW
18. SYKORA, Petr	N.J.	Detroit	C
19. NABOKOV, Dmitri	Chi.	Krylja Sovetov	C
20. GAUTHIER, Denis Jr.	Cgy.	Drummondville	D
21. BROWN, Sean	Bos.	Belleville	D
22. BOUCHER, Brian	Phi.	Tri-City	G
23. ELOMO, Miika	St.L.-Wsh.	Kiekko-67 Turku	LW
24. MOROZOV, Alexei	Pit.	Krylja Sovetov	RW
25. DENIS, Marc	Col.	Chicoutimi	G
26. KUZNETSOV, Maxim	Det.	Dynamo Moscow	D

SECOND ROUND

Selection	Claimed By	Amateur Club	
27. MORO, Marc	Ott.	Kingston	D
28. HLAVAC, Jan	NYI	Sparta Praha	LW
29. WESENBERG, Brian	Ana.	Guelph	RW
30. McBAIN, Mike	T.B.	Red Deer	D
31. LARAQUE, Georges	Edm.	St-Jean	RW
32. CHOUINARD, Marc	Wpg.	Beauport	C
33. MacLEAN, Donald	L.A.	Beauport	C
34. DOIG, Jason	Mtl.-Wpg.	Laval	D
35. FEDOTOV, Sergei	Hfd.	Dynamo Moscow	D
36. MacDONALD, Aaron	Fla.	Swift Current	G
37. COTE, Patrick	Dal.	Beauport	LW
38. ROED, Peter	S.J.	White Bear Lake	C
39. DUBE, Christian	NYR	Sherbrooke	C
40. McALLISTER, Chris	Van.	Saskatoon	D
41. SMITH, Denis (D.J.)	Tor.-NYI	Windsor	D
42. DUTIAUME, Mark	Buf.	Brandon	LW
43. HAY, Dwayne	Wsh.	Guelph	LW
44. PERROTT, Nathan	N.J.	Oshawa	RW
45. LAFLAMME, Christian	Chi.	Beauport	D
46. SMIRNOV, Pavel	Cgy.	Molot Perm	RW/C
47. SCHAFER, Paxton	Bos.	Medicine Hat	G
48. KENNY, Shane	Phi.	Owen Sound	D
49. HECHT, Jochen	St.L.	Mannheim	C
50. ROSA, Pavel	Pit.-L.A.	Chemopetrol Litvinov	RW
51. BEAUDOIN, Nic	Col.	Detroit	LW
52. AUDET, Philippe	Det.	Granby	LW

1994

FIRST ROUND

Selection	Claimed By	Amateur Club	
1. JOVANOVSKI, Ed	Fla.	Windsor	D
2. TVERDOVSKY, Oleg	Ana.	Soviet Wings	D
3. BONK, Radek	Ott.	Las Vegas	C
4. BONSIGNORE, Jason	Wpg.-Edm.	Niagara Falls	C
5. O'NEILL, Jeff	Hfd.	Guelph	C
6. SMYTH, Ryan	Edm.	Moose Jaw	LW
7. STORR, Jamie	L.A.	Owen Sound	G
8. WIEMER, Jason	T.B.	Portland	LW
9. LINDROS, Brett	Que.-NYI	Kingston	RW
10. BAUMGARTNER, Nolan	Phi.-Que.-Tor.-Wsh.	Kamloops	D
11. FRIESEN, Jeff	S.J.	Regina	LW
12. BELAK, Wade	NYI-Que.	Saskatoon	D
13. OHLUND, Mattias	Van.	Pitea	D
14. MOREAU, Ethan	Chi.	Niagara Falls	LW
15. KHARLAMOV, Alexander	Wsh.	CSKA Moscow	C
16. FICHAUD, Eric	St.L.-Wsh.-Tor.	Chicoutimi	G
17. PRIMEAU, Wayne	Buf.	Owen Sound	C
18. BROWN, Brad	Mtl.	North Bay	D
19. DINGMAN, Chris	Cgy.	Brandon	LW
20. BOTTERILL, Jason	Dal.	U. of Michigan	LW
21. RYABCHIKOV, Evgeni	Bos.	Molot Perm	G
22. KEALTY, Jeffrey	Tor.-Que.	Catholic Memorial	D
23. GOLUBOVSKY, Yan	Det.	CSKA Jr. Moscow	D
24. WELLS, Chris	Pit.	Seattle	G
25. SHARIFIJANOV, Vadim	N.J.	Salavat Yulayev ufa	RW
26. CLOUTIER, Dan	NYR	Sault Ste. Marie	G

SECOND ROUND

Selection	Claimed By	Amateur Club	
27. WARRENER, Rhett	Fla.	Saskatoon	D
28. DAVIDSSON, Johan	Ana.	HV 71	C
29. NECKAR, Stanislav	Ott.	Ceske Budejovice	D
30. QUINT, Deron	Wpg.	Seattle	D
31. PODOLLAN, Jason	Hfd.-Fla.	Spokane	C
32. WATT, Mike	Edm.	Stratford Jr. B	LW
33. JOHNSON, Matt	L.A.	Peterborough	LW
34. CLOUTIER, Colin	T.B.	Brandon	C
35. MARHA, Josef	Que.	Dukla Jihlava	C
36. JOHNSON, Ryan	Phi.-Fla.	Thunder Bay Jr. A	C
37. NIKOLOV, Angel	S.J.	Litvinov	D
38. HOLLAND, Jason	NYI	Kamloops	D
39. GORDON, Robb	Van.	Powell River Jr. A	C
40. LEROUX, Jean-Yves	Chi.	Beauport	LW
41. CHERREY, Scott	Wsh.	North Bay	LW
42. SCATCHARD, Dave	St.L.-Van.	Portland	C
43. BROWN, Curtis	Buf.	Moose Jaw	C
44. THEODORE, Jose	Mtl.	St-Jean	G
45. RYABYKIN, Dmitri	Cgy.	Dynamo-2	D
46. JINMAN, Lee	Dal.	North Bay	C
47. GONEAU, Daniel	Bos.	Laval	LW
48. HAGGERTY, Sean	Tor.	Detroit	LW
49. DANDENAULT, Mathieu	Det.	Sherbrooke	RW
50. PARK, Richard	Pit.	Belleville	C
51. ELIAS, Patrik	N.J.	Kladno	LW
52. VERCIK, Rudolf	NYR	Slovan Bratislava	LW

1993

FIRST ROUND

Selection	Claimed By	Amateur Club	
1. DAIGLE, Alexandre	Ott.	Victoriaville	C
2. PRONGER, Chris	S.J.-Hfd.	Peterborough	D
3. GRATTON, Chris	T.B.	Kingston	C
4. KARIYA, Paul	Ana.	University of Maine	LW
5. NIEDERMAYER, Rob	Fla.	Medicine Hat	C
6. KOZLOV, Viktor	Hfd.-S.J.	Dynamo Moscow	LW
7. ARNOTT, Jason	Edm.	Oshawa	C
8. SUNDSTROM, Niklas	NYR	MoDo	LW
9. HARVEY, Todd	Dal.	Detroit	C
10. THIBAULT, Jocelyn	Phi.-Que.	Sherbrooke	G
11. WITT, Brendan	St. L.-Wsh.	Seattle	D
12. JONSSON, Kenny	Buf.-Tor.	Rogle Angelholm	D
13. PEDERSON, Denis	N.J.	Prince Albert	C
14. DEADMARSH, Adam	NYI-Que.	Portland	C
15. LINDGREN, Mats	Wpg.	Skelleftea	C
16. STAJDUHAR, Nick	L.A.-Edm.	London	D
17. ALLISON, Jason	Wsh.	London	C
18. MATTSSON, Jesper	Cgy.	Malmo	C
19. WILSON, Landon	Tor.	Dubuque Jr. A	RW
20. WILSON, Mike	Van.	Sudbury	D
21. KOIVU, Saku	Mtl.	TPS Turku	C
22. ERIKSSON, Anders	Det.	MoDo	D
23. BERTUZZI, Todd	Que.-NYI	Guelph	C
24. LECOMPTE, Eric	Chi.	Hull	LW
25. ADAMS, Kevyn	Bos.	Miami-Ohio	C
26. BERGQVIST, Stefan	Pit.	Leksand	D

SECOND ROUND

Selection	Claimed By	Amateur Club	
27. BICANEK, Radim	Ott.	Dukla Jihlava	D
28. DONOVAN, Shean	S.J.	Ottawa	RW
29. MOSS, Tyler	T.B.	Kingston	G
30. TSULYGIN, Nikolai	Ana.	Salavat Yulalev Ufa	D
31. LANGKOW, Scott	Fla.-Wpg.	Portland	G
32. PANDOLFO, Jay	Hfd.-N.J.	Boston University	LW
33. VYBORNY, David	Edm.	Sparta Praha	C
34. SOROCHAN, Lee	NYR	Lethbridge	D
35. LANGENBRUNNER, Jamie	Dal.	Cloquet	C
36. NIINIMAA, Janne	Phi.	Karpat Oulu	D
37. BETS, Maxim	St. L.	Spokane	LW
38. TSYGUROV, Denis	Buf.	Lada Togliatti	D
39. MORRISON, Brendan	N.J.	Penticton T-II Jr. A	C
40. McCABE, Bryan	NYI	Spokane	D
41. WEEKES, Kevin	Wpg.-Fla.	Owen Sound	G
42. TOPOROWSKI, Shayne	L.A.	Prince Albert	RW
43. BUDAYEV, Alexei	Wsh.-Wpg.	Kristall Elektrostal	C
44. ALLISON, Jamie	Cgy.	Detroit	D
45. KROUPA, Vlastimil	Tor.-Hfd.-S.J.	Chemopetrol Litvinov	D
46. GIRARD, Rick	Van.	Swift Current	C
47. FITZPATRICK, Rory	Mtl.	Sudbury	D
48. COLEMAN, Jonathan	Det.	Andover Academy	D
49. BUCKBERGER, Ashley	Que.	Swift Current	RW
50. MANLOW, Eric	Chi.	Kitchener	C
51. ALVEY, Matt	Bos.	Springfield Jr. B	RW
52. PITTIS, Domenic	Pit.	Lethbridge	C

1992

FIRST ROUND

Selection	Claimed By	Amateur Club	
1. HAMRLIK, Roman	T.B.	ZPS Zlin (Czech.)	D
2. YASHIN, Alexei	Ott.	Dynamo Moscow (CIS)	C
3. RATHJE, Mike	S.J.	Medicine Hat	D
4. WARRINER, Todd	Que.	Windsor	LW
5. KASPARAITIS, Darius	Tor.-NYI	Dynamo Moscow (CIS)	D
6. STILLMAN, Cory	Cgy.	Windsor	C
7. SITTLER, Ryan	Phi.	Nichols	LW
8. CONVERY, Brandon	NYI-Tor.	Sudbury	C
9. PETROVICKY, Robert	Hfd.	Dukla Trencin (Czech.)	C
10. NAZAROV, Andrei	Min.-S.J.	Dynamo Moscow	LW
11. COOPER, David	Buf.	Medicine Hat	D
12. KRIVOKRASOV, Sergei	Wpg.-Chi.	CSKA Moscow (CIS)	RW
13. HULBIG, Joe	Edm.	St. Sebastian's	LW
14. GONCHAR, Sergei	St.L.-Wsh.	Chelybinsk (CIS)	D
15. BOWEN, Jason	L.A.-Pit.-Phi.	Tri-City	LW
16. KVARTALNOV, Dmitri	Bos.	San Diego	LW
17. BAUTIN, Sergei	Chi.-Wpg.	Dynamo Moscow (CIS)	D
18. SMITH, Jason	N.J.	Regina	D
19. STRAKA, Martin	Pit.	Skoda Plzen (Czech.)	C
20. WILKIE, David	Mtl.	Kamloops	D
21. POLASEK, Libor	Van.	TJ Vitkovice (Czech.)	C
22. BOWEN, Curtis	Det.	Ottawa	LW
23. MARSHALL, Grant	Wsh.-Tor.	Ottawa	RW
24. FERRARO, Peter	NYR	Waterloo Jr. A	C

SECOND ROUND

Selection	Claimed By	Amateur Club	
25. PENNEY, Chad	Ott.	North Bay	LW
26. BANNISTER, Drew	T.B.	Sault-Ste-Marie	D
27. MIRANOV, Boris	S.J.-Chi.-Wpg.	CSKA Moscow (CIS)	D
28. BROUSSEAU, Paul	Que.	Hull	RW
29. GRONMAN, Toumas	Tor.-Que.	Tacoma	D
30. O'SULLIVAN, Chris	Cgy.	Catholic Memorial	D
31. METLYUK, Denis	Phi.	Lada Togliatti (CIS)	C
32. CAREY, Jim	NYI-Tor.-Wsh.	Catholic Memorial	G
33. BURE, Valeri	Hfd.-Mtl.	Spokane	LW
34. VARVIO, Jarkko	Min.	HPK (Finland)	RW
35. CIERNY, Jozef	Buf.	ZTK Zvolen (Czech.)	LW
36. SHANTZ, Jeff	Wpg.-Chi.	Regina	C
37. REICHEL, Martin	Edm.	Freiburg (Germany)	RW
38. KOROLEV, Igor	St.L.	Dynamo Moscow	RW
39. HOCKING, Justin	L.A.	Spokane	D
40. PECA, Mike	Bos.-Van.	Ottawa	C
41. KLIMOVICH, Sergei	Chi.	Dynamo Moscow	C
42. BRYLIN, Sergei	N.J.	CSKA Moscow (CIS)	C
43. HUSSEY, Marc	Pit.	Moose Jaw	D
44. CORPSE, Keli	Mtl.	Kingston	C
45. FOUNTAIN, Michael	Van.	Oshawa	G
46. McCARTY, Darren	Det.	Belleville	RW
47. NIKOLISHIN, Andrei	Wsh.-Hfd.	Dynamo Moscow	LW
48. NORSTROM, Mattias	NYR	AIK (Sweden)	D

1991

FIRST ROUND

Selection	Claimed By	Amateur Club	
1. LINDROS, Eric	Que.	Oshawa	C
2. FALLOON, Pat	S.J.	Spokane	RW
3. NIEDERMAYER, Scott	Tor.-N.J.	Kamloops	D
4. LACHANCE, Scott	NYI	Boston University	D
5. WARD, Aaron	Wpg.	U. of Michigan	D
6. FORSBERG, Peter	Phi.	MoDo (Sweden)	C
7. STOJANOV, Alex	Van.	Hamilton	RW
8. MATVICHUK, Richard	Min.	Saskatoon	D
9. POULIN, Patrick	Hfd.	St.-Hyacinthe	LW
10. LAPOINTE, Martin	Det.	Laval	RW
11. ROLSTON, Brian	N.J.	Detroit Comp. Jr. A	C
12. WRIGHT, Tyler	Edm.	Swift Current	C
13. BOUCHER, Phillipe	Buf.	Granby	D
14. PEAKE, Pat	Wsh.	Detroit	C
15. KOVALEV, Alexei	NYR	D'amo Moscow	RW
16. NASLUND, Markus	Pit.	MoDo	RW
17. BILODEAU, Brent	Mtl.	Seattle	D
18. MURRAY, Glen	Bos.	Sudbury	RW
19. SUNDBLAD, Niklas	Cgy.	AIK (Sweden)	RW
20. RUCINSKY, Martin	L.A.-Edm.	CHZ Litvinov (Czech.)	LW
21. HALVERSON, Trevor	St.L.-Wsh.	North Bay	LW
22. McAMMOND, Dean	Chi.	Prince Albert	C

SECOND ROUND

Selection	Claimed By	Amateur Club	
23. WHITNEY, Ray	S.J.	Spokane	C
24. CORBET, Rene	Que.	Drummondville	LW
25. LAVIGNE, Eric	Tor.-Que.-Wsh.	Hull	D
26. PALFFY, Zigmund	NYI	AC Nitra (Czech.)	LW
27. STAIOS, Steve	Wpg.-St.L.	Niagara Falls	D
28. CAMPBELL, Jim	Phi.-Mtl.	Northwood Prep	C
29. CULLIMORE, Jassen	Van.	Peterborough	D
30. OZOLINSH, Sandis	Min.-S.J.	Dynamo Riga (USSR)	D
31. HAMRLIK, Martin	Hfd.	TJ Zin (Czech.)	D
32. PUSHOR, Jamie	Det.	Lethbridge	D
33. HEXTALL, Donevan	N.J.	Prince Albert	LW
34. VERNER, Andrew	Edm.	Peterborough	G
35. DAWE, Jason	Buf.	Peterborough	LW
36. NELSON, Jeff	Wsh.	Prince Albert	C
37. WERENKA, Darcy	NYR	Lethbridge	D
38. FITZGERALD, Rusty	Pit.	Duluth East HS	C
39. POMICHTER, Michael	Mtl.-Chi.	Springfield Jr. B	C
40. STUMPEL, Jozef	Bos.	AC Nitra (Czech.)	RW
41. GROLEAU, Francois	Cgy.	Shawinigan	D
42. LEVEQUE, Guy	L.A.	Cornwall	C
43. DARBY, Craig	St.L.-Mtl.	Albany Academy	C
44. MATTHEWS, Jamie	Chi.	Sudbury	C

1990

FIRST ROUND

Selection	Claimed By	Amateur Club	
1. NOLAN, Owen	Que.	Cornwall	RW
2. NEDVED, Petr	Van.	Seattle	C
3. PRIMEAU, Keith	Det.	Niagara Falls	C
4. RICCI, Mike	Phi.	Peterborough	C
5. JAGR, Jaromir	Pit.	Poldi Kladno (Czech.)	LW
6. SCISSONS, Scott	NYI	Saskatoon	C
7. SYDOR, Darryl	L.A.	Kamloops	D
8. HATCHER, Derian	Min.	North Bay	D
9. SLANEY, John	Wsh.	Cornwall	D
10. BEREHOWSKY, Drake	Tor.	Kingston	D
11. KIDD, Trevor	N.J.-Cgy.	Brandon	G
12. STEVENSON, Turner	St.L.-Mtl.	Seattle	RW
13. STEWART, Michael	NYR	Michigan State	D
14. MAY, Brad	Wpg.-Buf.	Niagara Falls	LW
15. GREIG, Mark	Hfd.	Lethbridge	RW
16. DYKHUIS, Karl	Chi.	Hull	D
17. ALLISON, Scott	Edm.	Prince Albert	C
18. ANTOSKI, Shawn	Mtl.-St.L.-Van.	North Bay	LW
19. TKACHUK, Keith	Buf.-Wpg.	Malden Catholic	LW
20. BRODEUR, Martin	Cgy.-N.J.	St. Hyacinthe	G
21. SMOLINSKI, Bryan	Bos.	Michigan State	C

SECOND ROUND

Selection	Claimed By	Amateur Club	
22. HUGHES, Ryan	Que.	Cornell	C
23. SLEGR, Jiri	Van.	CHZ Litvinov (Czech.)	D
24. HARLOCK, David	Det.-Cgy.-N.J.	U. of Michigan	D
25. SIMON, Chris	Phi.	Ottawa	LW
26. PERREAULT, Nicolas P.	Pit.-Cgy.	Hawkesbury Jr. A	D
27. TAYLOR, Chris	NYI	London	C
28. SEMCHUK, Brandy	L.A.	Canadian National	RW
29. GOTZIAMAN, Chris	Min.-Cgy.-N.J.	Roseau	RW
30. PASMA, Rod	Wsh.	Cornwall	D
31. POTVIN, Felix	Tor.	Chicoutimi	G
32. VIITAKOSKI, Vesa	N.J.-Cgy.	SaiPa (Finland)	LW
33. JOHNSON, Craig	St.L.	Hill-Murray HS	C
34. WEIGHT, Doug	NYR	Lake Superior	C
35. MULLER, Mike	Wpg.	Wayzata	D
36. SANDERSON, Geoff	Hfd.	Swift Current	C
37. DROPPA, Ivan	Chi.	Partizan (Czech.)	D
38. LEGAULT, Alexandre	Edm.	Boston University	RW
39. KUWABARA, Ryan	Mtl.	Ottawa	RW
40. RENBERG, Mikael	Buf.-Phi.	Pitea (Sweden)	LW
41. BELZILE, Etienne	Cgy.	Cornell	D
42. SANDWITH, Terran	Bos.-Phi.	Tri-Cities	D

1989

FIRST ROUND

Selection	Claimed By	Amateur Club	
1. SUNDIN, Mats	Que.	Nacka (Sweden)	RW
2. CHYZOWSKI, Dave	NYI	Kamloops	LW
3. THORNTON, Scott	Tor.	Belleville	C
4. BARNES, Stu	Wpg.	Tri-Cities	C
5. GUERIN, Bill	N.J.	Springfield Jr. B	RW
6. BENNETT, Adam	Chi.	Sudbury	D
7. ZMOLEK, Doug	Min.	John Marshall	D
8. HERTER, Jason	Van.	U. of North Dakota	D
9. MARSHALL, Jason	St.L.	Vernon Jr. A	D
10. HOLIK, Robert	Hfd.	Dukla Jihlava (Czech.)	C
11. SILLINGER, Mike	Det.	Regina	C
12. PEARSON, Rob	Phi.-Tor.	Belleville	RW
13. VALLIS, Lindsay	NYR-Mtl.	Seattle	RW
14. HALLER, Kevin	Buf.	Regina	D
15. SOULES, Jason	Edm.	Niagara Falls	D
16. HEWARD, Jamie	Pit.	Regina	RW
17. STEVENSON, Shayne	Bos.	Kitchener	RW
18. MILLER, Jason	L.A.-Edm.-N.J.	Medicine Hat	C
19. KOLZIG, Olaf	Wsh.	Tri-Cities	G
20. RICE, Steven	Mtl.-NYR	Kitchener	RW
21. BANCROFT, Steve	Cgy.-Tor.	Belleville	D

SECOND ROUND

Selection	Claimed By	Amateur Club	
22. FOOTE, Adam	Que.	Sault Ste. Marie	D
23. GREEN, Travis	NYI	Spokane	C
24. MANDERVILLE, Kent	Tor.-Cgy.	Notre Dame Jr. A	LW
25. RATUSHNY, Dan	Wpg.	Cornell	D
26. SKALDE, Jarrod	N.J.	Oshawa	C
27. SPEER, Michael	Chi.	Guelph	D
28. CRAIG, Mike	Min.	Oshawa	RW
29. WOODWARD, Robert	Van.	Deerfield	LW
30. BRISEBOIS, Patrice	St.L.-Mtl.	Laval	D
31. CORRIVEAU, Rick	Hfd.-St.L.	London	D
32. BOUGHNER, Bob	Det.	Sault-Ste. Marie	D
33. JOHNSON, Greg	Phi.	Thunder Bay Jr. A	C
34. JUHLIN, Patrik	NYR-Phi.	Vasteras (Sweden)	LW
35. DAFOE, Byron	Buf.-Wsh.	Portland	G
36. BORGO, Richard	Edm.	Kitchener	G
37. LAUS, Paul	Pit.	Niagara Falls	D
38. PARSON, Mike	Bos.	Guelph	G
39. THOMPSON, Brent	L.A.	Medicine Hat	D
40. PROSOFSKY, Jason	Wsh.-NYR	Medicine Hat	RW
41. LAROUCHE, Steve	Mtl.	Trois-Rivieres	C
42. DRURY, Ted	Cgy.	Fairfield Prep	C

1988

FIRST ROUND

Selection	Claimed By	Amateur Club	
1. MODANO, Mike	Min.	Prince Albert	C
2. LINDEN, Trevor	Van.	Medicine Hat	RW
3. LESCHYSHYN, Curtis	Que.	Saskatoon	D
4. SHANNON, Darrin	Pit.	Windsor	LW
5. DORE, Daniel	NYR-Que.	Drummondville	RW
6. PEARSON, Scott	Tor.	Kingston	LW
7. GELINAS, Martin	L.A.	Hull	LW
8. ROENICK, Jeremy	Chi.	Thayer Academy	C
9. BRIND'AMOUR, Rod	St.L.	Notre Dame Jr. A	C
10. SELANNE, Teemu	Wpg.	Jokerit (Finland)	RW
11. GOVEDARIS, Chris	Hfd.	Toronto	LW
12. FOSTER, Corey	N.J.	Peterborough	D
13. SAVAGE, Joel	Buf.	Victoria	RW
14. BOIVIN, Claude	Phi.	Drummondville	LW
15. SAVAGE, Reginald	Wsh.	Victoriaville	C
16. CHEVELDAYOFF, Kevin	NYI	Brandon	D
17. KOCUR, Kory	Det.	Saskatoon	RW
18. CIMETTA, Robert	Bos.	Toronto	LW
19. LEROUX, Francois	Edm.	St. Jean	D
20. CHARRON, Eric	Mtl.	Trois-Rivieres	D
21. MUZZATTI, Jason	Cgy.	Michigan State	G

SECOND ROUND

Selection	Claimed By	Amateur Club	
22. MALLETTE, Troy	Min.-NYR	Sault Ste. Marie	C
23. CHRISTIAN, Jeff	Van.-N.J.	London	LW
24. FISET, Stephane	Que.	Victoriaville	G
25. MAJOR, Mark	Pit.	North Bay	D
26. DUVAL, Murray	NYR	Spokane	RW
27. DOMI, Tie	Tor.	Peterborough	RW
28. HOLDEN, Paul	L.A.	London	D
29. DOUCET, Wayne	Chi.-NYI	Hamilton	LW
30. PLAVSIC, Adrien	St.L.	U. of New Hampshire	D
31. ROMANIUK, Russell	Wpg.	St. Boniface Jr. A	LW
32. RICHTER, Barry	Hfd.	Culver Academy	D
33. ROHLIN, Leif	N.J.-Van.	Vasteras (Sweden)	D
34. ST. AMOUR, Martin	Buf.-Mtl.	Verdun	LW
35. MURRAY, Pat	Phi.	Michigan State	LW
36. TAYLOR, Tim	Wsh.	London	C
37. LEBRUN, Sean	NYI	New Westminster	LW
38. ANGLEHART, Serge	Det.	Drummondville	D
39. KOIVUNEN, Petro	Bos.-Edm.	Espoo (Finland)	C
40. GAETZ, Link	Edm.-Min.	Spokane	D
41. BARTLEY, Wade	Mtl.-St.L.-Wsh.	Dauphin Jr. A	D
42. HARKINS, Todd	Cgy.	Miami-Ohio	RW

1987

FIRST ROUND

Selection	Claimed By	Amateur Club	
1. TURGEON, Pierre	Buf.	Granby	C
2. SHANAHAN, Brendan	N.J.	London	C
3. WESLEY, Glen	Van.-Bos.	Portland	D
4. McBEAN, Wayne	Min.-L.A.	Medicine Hat	D
5. JOSEPH, Chris	Pit.	Seattle	D
6. ARCHIBALD, David	L.A.-Min.	Portland	C/LW
7. RICHARDSON, Luke	Tor.	Peterborough	D
8. WAITE, Jimmy	Chi.	Chicoutimi	G
9. FOGARTY, Bryan	Que.	Kingston	D
10. MORE, Jayson	NYR	New Westminster	D
11. RACINE, Yves	Det.	Longueuil	D
12. OSBORNE, Keith	St.L.	North Bay	RW
13. CHYNOWETH, Dean	NYI	Medicine Hat	D
14. QUINTAL, Stephane	Bos.	Granby	D
15. SAKIC, Joe	Wsh.-Que.	Swift Current	C
16. MARCHMENT, Bryan	Wpg.	Belleville	D
17. CASSELS, Andrew	Mtl.	Ottawa	C
18. HULL, Jody	Hfd.	Peterborough	RW
19. DEASLEY, Bryan	Cgy.	U. of Michigan	LW
20. RUMBLE, Darren	Phi.	Kitchener	D
21. SOBERLAK, Peter	Edm.	Swift Current	LW

SECOND ROUND

Selection	Claimed By	Amateur Club	
22. MILLER, Brad	Buf.	Regina	D
23. PERSSON, Rickard	N.J.	Ostersund (Sweden)	D
24. MURPHY, Rob	Van.	Laval	C
25. MATTEAU, Stephane	Min.-Cgy.	Hull	LW
26. TABARACCI, Richard	Pit.	Cornwall	G
27. FITZPATRICK, Mark	L.A.	Medicine Hat	G
28. MAROIS, Daniel	Tor.	Chicoutimi	RW
29. McGILL, Ryan	Chi.	Swift Current	D
30. HARDING, Jeff	Que.-Phi.	St. Michael's Jr. B	LW
31. LACROIX, Daniel	NYR	Granby	LW
32. KRUPPKE, Gordon	Det.	Prince Albert	D
33. LECLAIR, John	St.L.-Mtl.	Bellows Academy	D
34. HACKETT, Jeff	NYI	Oshawa	G
35. McCRADY, Scott	Bos.-Min.	Medicine Hat	D
36. BALLANTYNE, Jeff	Wsh.	Ottawa	D
37. ERICKSSON, Patrik	Wpg.	Brynas (Sweden)	C
38. DESJARDINS, Eric	Mtl.	Granby	D
39. BURT, Adam	Hfd.	North Bay	D
40. GRANT, Kevin	Cgy.	Kitchener	D
41. WILKIE, Bob	Phi.-Det.	Swift Current	D
42. WERENKA, Brad	Edm.	N. Michigan	D

1986

FIRST ROUND

Selection	Claimed By	Amateur Club	
1. MURPHY, Joe	Det.	Michigan State	C
2. CARSON, Jimmy	L.A.	Verdun	C
3. BRADY, Neil	N.J.	Medicine Hat	C
4. ZALAPSKI, Zarley	Pit.	Canadian National	D
5. ANDERSON, Shawn	Buf.	Canadian National	D
6. DAMPHOUSSE, Vincent	Tor.	Laval	LW
7. WOODLEY, Dan	Van.	Portland	C
8. ELYNUIK, Pat	Wpg.	Prince Albert	RW
9. LEETCH, Brian	NYR	Avon Old Farms HS	D
10. LEMIEUX, Jocelyn	St.L.	Laval	RW
11. YOUNG, Scott	Hfd.	Boston University	RW
12. BABE, Warren	Min.	Lethbridge	LW
13. JANNEY, Craig	Bos.	Boston College	C
14. SANIPASS, Everett	Chi.	Verdun	LW
15. PEDERSON, Mark	Mtl.	Medicine Hat	LW
16. PELAWA, George	Cgy.	Bemidji HS	RW
17. FITZGERALD, Tom	NYI	Austin Prep	C
18. McRAE, Ken	Que.	Sudbury	C
19. GREENLAW, Jeff	Wsh.	Canadian National	LW
20. HUFFMAN, Kerry	Phi.	Guelph	D
21. ISSEL, Kim	Edm.	Prince Albert	RW

SECOND ROUND

Selection	Claimed By	Amateur Club	
22. GRAVES, Adam	Det.	Windsor	C
23. SEPPO, Jukka	L.A.-Phi.	Sport (Finland)	LW
24. COPELAND, Todd	N.J.	Belmont Hill HS	D
25. CAPUANO, Dave	Pit.	Mt. St. Charles HS	C
26. BROWN, Greg	Buf.	St. Mark's	D
27. BRUNET, Benoit	Tor.-Mtl.	Hull	LW
28. HAWLEY, Kent	Van.-Phi.	Ottawa	C
29. NUMMINEN, Teppo	Wpg.	Tappara (Finland)	D
30. WILKINSON, Neil	NYR-Min.	Selkirk	D
31. POSMA, Mike	St.L.	Buffalo Jr. A	D
32. LaFORGE, Marc	Hfd.	Kingston	D
33. KOLSTAD, Dean	Min.	Prince Albert	D
34. TIRKKONEN, Pekka	Bos.	SaPKo (Finland)	C
35. KURZAWSKI, Mark	Chi.	Windsor	D
36. SHANNON, Darryl	Mtl.-Tor.	Windsor	D
37. GLYNN, Brian	Cgy.	Saskatoon	D
38. VASKE, Dennis	NYI	Armstrong HS	D
39. ROUTHIER, Jean-Marc	Que.	Hull	RW
40. SEFTEL, Steve	Wsh.	Kingston	LW
41. GUERARD, Stephane	Phi.-Que.	Shawinigan	D
42. NICHOLS, Jamie	Edm.	Portland	LW

1985

FIRST ROUND

Selection	Claimed By	Amateur Club	
1. CLARK, Wendel	Tor.	Saskatoon	D
2. SIMPSON, Craig	Pit.	Michigan State	C
3. WOLANIN, Craig	N.J.	Kitchener	D
4. SANDLAK, Jim	Van.	London	RW
5. MURZYN, Dana	Hfd.	Calgary	D
6. DALGARNO, Brad	Min.-NYI	Hamilton	RW
7. DAHLEN, Ulf	NYR	Ostersund (Sweden)	C
8. FEDYK, Brent	Det.	Regina	RW
9. DUNCANSON, Craig	L.A.	Sudbury	LW
10. GRATTON, Dan	Bos.-L.A.	Oshawa	C
11. MANSON, David	Chi.	Prince Albert	D
12. CHARBONNEAU, Jose	St.L.-Mtl.	Drummondville	RW
13. KING, Derek	NYI	Sault Ste. Marie	LW
14. JOHANSSON, Calle	Buf.	V. Frolunda (Sweden)	D
15. LATTA, Dave	Que.	Kitchener	LW
16. CHORSKE, Tom	Mtl.	Minneapolis SW HS	LW
17. BIOTTI, Chris	Cgy.	Belmont Hill HS	D
18. STEWART, Ryan	Wpg.	Kamloops	C
19. CORRIVEAU, Yvon	Wsh.	Toronto	LW
20. METCALFE, Scott	Edm.	Kingston	LW
21. SEABROOKE, Glen	Phi.	Peterborough	C

SECOND ROUND

Selection	Claimed By	Amateur Club	
22. SPANGLER, Ken	Tor.	Calgary	D
23. GIFFIN, Lee	Pit.	Oshawa	RW
24. BURKE, Sean	N.J.	Toronto	G
25. GAMBLE, Troy	Van.	Medicine Hat	G
26. WHITMORE, Kay	Hfd.	Peterborough	G
27. NIEUWENDYK, Joe	Min.-Cgy.	Cornell	C
28. RICHTER, Mike	NYR	Northwood Prep.	G
29. SHARPLES, Jeff	Det.	Kelowna	D
30. EDLUND, Par	L.A.	Bjorkloven (Sweden)	RW
31. COTE, Alain	Bos.	Quebec	D
32. WEINRICH, Eric	Chi.-N.J.	North Yarmouth	D
33. RICHARD, Todd	Mtl.	Armstrong HS	D
34. LAUER, Brad	NYI	Regina	RW
35. HOGUE, Benoit	Buf.	St-Jean	C
36. LAFRENIERE, Jason	Que.	Hamilton	C
37. RAGLAN, Herb	Mtl.-St.L.	Kingston	RW
38. WENAAS, Jeff	Cgy.	Medicine Hat	C
39. OHMAN, Roger	Wpg.	Leksand (Sweden)	D
40. DRUCE, John	Wsh.	Peterborough	RW
41. CARNELLEY, Todd	Edm.	Kamloops	D
42. RENDALL, Bruce	Phi.	Chatham	LW

1984

FIRST ROUND

Selection	Claimed By	Amateur Club	
1. LEMIEUX, Mario	Pit.	Laval	C
2. MULLER, Kirk	N.J.	Cdn-Nat.-Guelph	C
3. OLCZYK, Ed	L.A.-Chi.	U.S. National	RW
4. IAFRATE, Al	Tor.	U.S. National-Belleville	D
5. SVOBODA, Petr	Hfd.-Mtl.	CHZ (Czech.)	D
6. REDMOND, Craig	Chi.-L.A.	Canadian National	D
7. BURR, Shawn	Det.	Kitchener	C
8. CORSON, Shayne	St.L.-Mtl.	Brantford	C
9. BODGER, Doug	Wpg.-Pit.	Kamloops Jr. A	D
10. DAIGNEAULT, J.J.	Van.	Cdn. Nat.-Longueuil	D
11. COTE, Sylvain	Mtl.-Hfd.	Quebec	D
12. ROBERTS, Gary	Cgy.	Ottawa	LW
13. QUINN, David	Min.	Kent HS	D
14. CARKNER, Terry	NYR	Peterborough	D
15. STIENBURG, Trevor	Que.	Guelph	C
16. BELANGER, Roger	Phi.-Pit.	Kingston	D
17. HATCHER, Kevin	Wsh.	North Bay	D
18. ANDERSSON, Mikael	Buf.	V. Frolunda (Sweden)	C
19. PASIN, Dave	Bos.	Prince Albert	RW
20. MacPHERSON, Duncan	NYI	Saskatoon	D
21. ODELEIN, Selmar	Edm.	Regina	D

SECOND ROUND

Selection	Claimed By	Amateur Club	
22. SMYTH, Greg	Phi.	London	D
23. BILLINGTON, Craig	N.J.	Belleville	G
24. WILKS, Brian	L.A.	Kitchener	C
25. GILL, Todd	Tor.	Windsor	D
26. BENNING, Brian	Hfd.-St.L.	Portland	D
27. MELLANBY, Scott	Chi.-Phi.	Henry Carr Jr. B	RW
28. HOUDA, Doug	Det.	Calgary	D
29. RICHER, Stephane	St.L.-Mtl.	Granby	C
30. DOURIS, Peter	Wpg.	U. of New Hampshire	C
31. ROHLICEK, Jeff	Van.	Portland	LW
32. HRKAC, Anthony	Mtl.-St.L.	Orillia Jr. A	C
33. SABOURIN, Ken	Cgy.	Sault Ste. Marie	D
34. LEACH, Stephen	Min.-Wsh.	Matignon HS	RW
35. HELMINEN, Raimo	NYR	Ilves (Finland)	C
36. BROWN, Jeff	Que.	Sudbury	D
37. CHYCHRUN, Jeff	Phi.	Kingston	D
38. RANHEIM, Paul	Wsh.-Cgy.	Edina Hornets HS	C
39. TRAPP, Doug	Buf.	Regina	LW
40. PODLOSKI, Ray	Bos.	Portland	C
41. MELANSON, Bruce	NYI	Oshawa	RW
42. REAUGH, Daryl	Edm.	Kamloops Jr. A	G

1983

FIRST ROUND

Selection	Claimed By	Amateur Club	
1. LAWTON, Brian	Pit.-Min.	Mount St. Charles HS	C
2. TURGEON, Sylvain	Hfd.	Hull	C
3. LaFONTAINE, Pat	N.J.-NYI	Verdun	C
4. YZERMAN, Steve	Det.	Peterborough	C
5. BARRASSO, Tom	St.L.-Buf.	Acton-Boxboro HS	G
6. MacLEAN, John	L.A.-N.J.	Oshawa	RW
7. COURTNALL, Russ	Tor.	Victoria	C
8. McBAIN, Andrew	Wpg.	North Bay	RW
9. NEELY, Cam	Van.	Portland	RW
10. LACOMBE, Normand	Cgy.-Buf.	U. of New Hampshire	RW
11. CREIGHTON, Adam	Que.-Buf.	Ottawa	C
12. GAGNER, Dave	NYR	Brantford	C
13. QUINN, Dan	Buf.-Cgy.	Belleville	C
14. DOLLAS, Bobby	Wsh.-Wpg.	Laval	D
15. ERREY, Bob	Min.-Pit.	Peterborough	LW
16. DIDUCK, Gerald	NYI	Lethbridge	D
17. TURCOTTE, Alfie	Mtl.	Portland	C
18. CASSIDY, Bruce	Chi.	Ottawa	D
19. BEUKEBOOM, Jeff	Edm.	Sault Ste. Marie	D
20. JENSEN, David	Phi.-Hfd.	Lawrence	C
21. MARKWART, Nevin	Bos.	Regina	LW

SECOND ROUND

22. CHARLESWORTH, Todd	Pit.	Oshawa	D
23. SIREN, Ville	Hfd.	Ilves (Finland)	D
24. EVANS, Shawn	N.J.	Peterborough	D
25. LAMBERT, Lane	Det.	Saskatoon	RW
26. LEMIEUX, Claude	St.L.-Mtl.	Trois-Rivières	RW
27. MOMESSO, Sergio	L.A.-Mtl.	Shawinigan	C
28. JACKSON, Jeff	Tor.	Brantford	LW
29. BERRY, Brad	Wpg.	St. Albert	D
30. BRUCE, Dave	Van.	Kitchener	RW
31. TUCKER, John	Cgy.-Buf.	Kitchener	C
32. HEROUX, Yves	Que.	Chicoutimi	RW
33. HEATH, Randy	NYR	Portland	LW
34. HAJDU, Richard	Wsh.-Buf.	Kamloops Jr. A	LW
35. FRANCIS, Todd	Mtl.	Brantford	RW
36. PARKS, Malcolm	Min.	St. Albert	C
37. McKECHNEY, Garnet	NYI	Kitchener	RW
38. MUSIL, Frantisek	Mtl.-Min.	Tesla (Czech.)	D
39. PRESLEY, Wayne	Chi.	Kitchener	RW
40. GOLDEN, Mike	Edm.	Reading HS	C
41. ZEZEL, Peter	Phi.	Toronto	C
42. JOHNSTON, Greg	Bos.	Toronto	RW

1982

FIRST ROUND

Selection	Claimed By	Amateur Club	
1. KLUZAK, Gord	Col.-Bos.	Nanaimo	D
2. BELLOWS, Brian	Det.-Min.	Kitchener	RW
3. NYLUND, Gary	Tor.	Portland	D
4. SUTTER, Ron	Hfd.-Phi.	Lethbridge	C
5. STEVENS, Scott	L.A.-Wsh.	Kitchener	D
6. HOUSLEY, Phil	Wsh.-Buf.	S. St. Paul HS	D
7. YAREMCHUK, Ken	Chi.	Portland	C
8. TROTTIER, Rocky	St.L.-N.J.	Nanaimo	RW
9. CYR, Paul	Cgy.-Buf.	Victoria	LW
10. SUTTER, Rich	Pit.	Lethbridge	RW
11. PETIT, Michel	Van.	Sherbrooke	D
12. KYTE, Jim	Wpg.	Cornwall	D
13. SHAW, David	Que.	Kitchener	D
14. LAWLESS, Paul	Phi.-Hfd.	Windsor	LW
15. KONTOS, Chris	NYR	Toronto	C
16. ANDREYCHUK, Dave	Buf.	Oshawa	LW
17. CRAVEN, Murray	Min.-Det.	Medicine Hat	C
18. DANEYKO, Ken	Bos.-N.J.	Seattle	D
19. HEROUX, Alain	Mtl.	Chicoutimi	LW
20. PLAYFAIR, Jim	Edm.	Portland	D
21. FLATLEY, Pat	NYI	U. of Wisconsin	RW

SECOND ROUND

22. CURRAN, Brian	Col.-Bos.	Portland	D
23. COURTEAU, Yves	Det.	Laval	RW
24. LEEMAN, Gary	Tor.	Regina	D
25. IHNACAK, Peter	Hfd.-Tor.	Sparta (Czech.)	C
26. ANDERSON, Mike	L.A.-Buf.	N. St. Paul HS	C
27. HEIDT, Mike	Wsh.-L.A.	Calgary	D
28. BADEAU, Rene	St.L.-Chi.	Quebec	D
29. REIERSON, Dave	Cgy.	Prince Albert	D
30. JOHANSSON, Jens	Buf.	Pitea (Sweden)	D
31. GAUVREAU, Jocelyn	Pit.-Mtl.	Granby	D
32. CARLSON, Kent	Van.-Mtl.	St. Lawrence University	D
33. MALEY, David	Wpg.-Mtl.	Edina HS	C
34. GILLIS, Paul	Que.	Niagara Falls	C
35. PATERSON, Mark	Phi.-Hfd.	Ottawa	D
36. SANDSTROM, Tomas	NYR	Farjestads (Sweden)	RW
37. KROMM, Richard	Buf.-Cgy.	Portland	LW
38. HRYNEWICH, Tim	Min.-Pit.	Sudbury	LW
39. BYERS, Lyndon	Bos.	Regina	RW
40. SANDELIN, Scott	Mtl.	Hibbing HS	D
41. GRAVES, Steve	Edm.	Sault Ste. Marie	C
42. SMITH, Vern	NYI	Lethbridge	D

1981

FIRST ROUND

Selection	Claimed By	Amateur Club	
1. HAWERCHUK, Dale	Wpg.	Cornwall	C
2. SMITH, Doug	Det.-L.A.	Ottawa	C
3. CARPENTER, Bobby	Col.-Wsh.	St. John's HS	C
4. FRANCIS, Ron	Hfd.	Sault Ste. Marie	C
5. CIRELLA, Joe	Wsh.-Col.	Oshawa	D
6. BENNING, Jim	Tor.	Portland	D
7. HUNTER, Mark	Pit.-Mtl.	Brantford	RW
8. FUHR, Grant	Edm.	Victoria	G
9. PATRICK, James	NYR	Prince Albert	D
10. BUTCHER, Garth	Van.	Regina	D
11. MOLLER, Randy	Que.	Lethbridge	D
12. TANTI, Tony	Chi.	Oshawa	RW
13. MEIGHAN, Ron	Min.	Niagara Falls	D
14. LEVEILLE, Normand	Bos.	Chicoutimi	LW
15. MacINNIS, Allan	Cgy.	Kitchener	D
16. SMITH, Steve	Phi.	Sault Ste. Marie	D
17. DUDACEK, Jiri	Buf.	Poldi Kladno (Czech.)	RW
18. DELORME, Gilbert	L.A.-Mtl.	Chicoutimi	D
19. INGMAN, Jan	Mtl.	Farjestad (Sweden)	LW
20. RUFF, Marty	St.L.	Lethbridge	D
21. BOUTILIER, Paul	NYI	Sherbrooke	D

SECOND ROUND

22. ARNIEL, Scott	Wpg.	Cornwall	LW
23. LOISELLE, Claude	Det.	Windsor	C
24. YAREMCHUK, Gary	Col.-Tor.	Portland	C
25. GRIFFIN, Kevin	Hfd.-Chi.	Portland	LW
26. CHERNOMAZ, Rich	Wsh.-Col.	Victoria	C
27. DONNELLY, Dave	Tor.-Min.	St. Albert	C
28. GATZOS, Steve	Pit.	Sault Ste. Marie	RW
29. STRUEBY, Todd	Edm.	Regina	LW
30. ERIXON, Jan	NYR	Skelleftea (Sweden)	RW
31. SANDS, Mike	Van.-Min.	Sudbury	G
32. ERIKSSON, Lars	Que.-Mtl.	Brynas (Sweden)	G
33. HIRSCH, Tom	Chi.-Min.	Patrick Henry HS	D
34. PREUSS, Dave	Min.	St. Thomas Academy	C
35. DUFOUR, Luc	Bos.	Chicoutimi	RW
36. NORDIN, Hakan	Cgy.-St.L.	Farjestad (Sweden)	D
37. COSTELLO, Rich	Phi.	Natick HS	C
38. VIRTA, Hannu	Buf.	TPS (Finland)	D
39. KENNEDY, Dean	L.A.	Brandon	D
40. CHELIOS, Chris	Mtl.	Moose Jaw	D
41. WAHLSTEN, Jali	St.L.-Min.	TPS (Finland)	C
42. DINEEN, Gord	NYI	Sault Ste. Marie	D

1980

FIRST ROUND

Selection	Claimed By	Amateur Club	
1. WICKENHEISER, Doug	Col.-Mtl.	Regina	C
2. BABYCH, Dave	Wpg.	Portland	D
3. SAVARD, Denis	Que.-Chi.	Montreal	C
4. MURPHY, Larry	Det.-L.A.	Peterborough	D
5. VEITCH, Darren	Wsh.	Regina	D
6. COFFEY, Paul	Edm.	Kitchener	D
7. LANZ, Rick	Van.	Oshawa	D
8. ARTHUR, Fred	Hfd.	Cornwall	D
9. BULLARD, Mike	Pit.	Brantford	C
10. FOX, Jimmy	L.A.	Ottawa	RW
11. BLAISDELL, Mike	Tor.-Det.	Regina	RW
12. WILSON, Rik	St.L.	Kingston	D
13. CYR, Denis	Cgy.	Montreal	RW
14. MALONE, Jim	NYR	Toronto	C
15. DUPONT, Jerome	Chi.	Toronto	D
16. PALMER, Brad	Min.	Victoria	LW
17. SUTTER, Brent	NYI	Red Deer	C
18. PEDERSON, Barry	Bos.	Victoria	C
19. GAGNE, Paul	Mtl.-Col.	Windsor	LW
20. PATRICK, Steve	Buf.	Brandon	RW
21. STOTHERS, Mike	Phi.	Kingston	D

SECOND ROUND

22. WARD, Joe	Col.	Seattle	C
23. MANTHA, Moe	Wpg.	Toronto	D
24. ROCHEFORT, Normand	Que.	Quebec	D
25. MUNI, Craig	Det.-Tor.	Kingston	D
26. McGILL, Bob	Wsh.-Tor.	Victoria	D
27. NATTRESS, Ric	Edm.-Mtl.	Brantford	D
28. LUDZIK, Steve	Van.-Chi.	Niagara Falls	C
29. GALARNEAU, Michel	Hfd.	Hull	C
30. SOLHEIM, Ken	Pit.-Chi.	Medicine Hat	LW
31. CURTALE, Tony	L.A.-Cgy.	Brantford	D
32. LaVALLEE, Kevin	Tor.-Cgy.	Brantford	LW
33. TERRION, Greg	St.L.-L.A.	Brantford	LW
34. MORRISON, Dave	Cgy.-L.A.	Peterborough	RW
35. ALLISON, Mike	NYR	Sudbury	LW
36. DAWES, Len	Chi.	Victoria	D
37. BEAUPRE, Don	Min.	Sudbury	G
38. HRUDEY, Kelly	NYI	Medicine Hat	G
39. KONROYD, Steve	Cgy.	Oshawa	D
40. CHABOT, John	Mtl.	Hull	C
41. MOLLER, Mike	Buf.	Lethbridge	RW
42. FRASER, Jay	Phi.	Ottawa	LW

1979

FIRST ROUND

Selection	Claimed By	Amateur Club	
1. RAMAGE, Rob	Col.	London	D
2. TURNBULL, Perry	St.L.	Portland	C
3. FOLIGNO, Mike	Det.	Sudbury	RW
4. GARTNER, Mike	Wsh.	Niagara Falls	RW
5. VAIVE, Rick	Van.	Sherbrooke	RW
6. HARTSBURG, Craig	Min.	Sault St. Marie	D
7. BROWN, Keith	Chi.	Portland	D
8. BOURQUE, Raymond	L.A.-Bos.	Verdun	D
9. BOSCHMAN, Laurie	Tor.	Brandon	C
10. McCARTHY, Tom	Wsh.-Min.	Oshawa	LW
11. RAMSEY, Mike	Buf.	U. of Minnesota	D
12. REINHART, Paul	Atl.	Kitchener	D
13. SULLIMAN, Doug	NYR	Kitchener	RW
14. PROPP, Brian	Phi.	Brandon	LW
15. McCRIMMON, Brad	Bos.	Brandon	D
16. WELLS, Jay	Mtl.-L.A.	Kingston	D
17. SUTTER, Duane	NYI	Lethbridge	RW
18. ALLISON, Ray	Hfd.	Brandon	RW
19. MANN, Jimmy	Wpg.	Sherbrooke	RW
20. GOULET, Michel	Que.	Quebec	LW
21. LOWE, Kevin	Edm.	Quebec	D

SECOND ROUND

22. WESLEY, Blake	Col.-Phi.	Portland	D
23. PEROVICH, Mike	St.L.-Atl.	Brandon	D
24. RAUSSE, Errol	Det.-Wsh.	Seattle	LW
25. JONSSON, Tomas	Wsh.-NYI	MoDo AIK (Sweden)	D
26. ASHTON, Brent	Van.	Saskatoon	LW
27. GINGRAS, Gaston	Min.-Mtl.	Hamilton	D
28. TRIMPER, Tim	Chi.	Peterborough	LW
29. HOPKINS, Dean	L.A.	London	RW
30. HARDY, Mark	Tor.-L.A.	Montreal	D
31. MARSHALL, Paul	Wsh.-Pit.	Brantford	LW
32. RUFF, Lindy	Buf.	Lethbridge	D
33. RIGGIN, Pat	Atl.	London	G
34. HOSPODAR, Ed	NYR	Ottawa	D
35. LINDBERGH, Pelle	Phi.	AIK Solna (Sweden)	G
36. MORRISON, Doug	Bos.	Lethbridge	RW
37. NASLUND, Mats	Mtl.	Brynas IFK (Sweden)	LW
38. CARROLL, Billy	NYI	London	C
39. SMITH, Stuart	Hfd.	Peterborough	D
40. CHRISTIAN, Dave	Wpg.	U. of North Dakota	C
41. HUNTER, Dale	Que.	Sudbury	C
42. BROTEN, Neal	Min.	U. of Minnesota	C

1978

FIRST ROUND

Selection	Claimed By	Amateur Club	
1. SMITH, Bobby	Min.	Ottawa	C
2. WALTER, Ryan	Wsh.	Seattle	LW
3. BABYCH, Wayne	St.L.	Portland	RW
4. DERLAGO, Bill	Van.	Brandon	C
5. GILLIS, Mike	Col.	Kingston	LW
6. WILSON, Behn	Pit.-Phi.	Kingston	D
7. LINSEMAN, Ken	NYR-Phi.	Kingston	C
8. GEOFFRION, Danny	L.A.-Mtl.	Cornwall	RW
9. HUBER, Willie	Det.	Hamilton	D
10. HIGGINS, Tim	Chi.	Ottawa	RW
11. MARSH, Brad	Atl.	London	D
12. PETERSON, Brent	Tor.-Det.	Portland	C
13. PLAYFAIR, Larry	Buf.	Portland	D
14. LUCAS, Danny	Phi.	Sault Ste. Marie	RW
15. TAMBELLINI, Steve	NYI	Lethbridge	C
16. SECORD, Al	Bos.	Hamilton	LW
17. HUNTER, Dave	Mtl.	Sudbury	LW
18. COULIS, Tim	Wsh.	Hamilton	LW

SECOND ROUND

19. PAYNE, Steve	Min.	Ottawa	LW
20. MULVEY, Paul	Wsh.	Portland	RW
21. QUENNEVILLE, Joel	Tor.	Windsor	D
22. FRASER, Curt	Van.	Victoria	LW
23. MacKINNON, Paul	Wsh.	Peterborough	D
24. CHRISTOFF, Steve	Min.	U. of Minnesota	C
25. MEEKER, Mike	Pit.	Peterborough	RW
26. MALONEY, Don	NYR	Kitchener	LW
27. MALINOWSKI, Merlin	Col.	Medicine Hat	C
28. HICKS, Glenn	Det.	Flin Flon	LW
29. LECUYER, Doug	Chi.	Portland	LW
30. YAKIWCHUK, Dale	Mtl.	Portland	C
31. JENSEN, Al	Det.	Hamilton	G
32. McKEGNEY, Tony	Buf.	Kingston	LW
33. SIMURDA, Mike	Phi.	Kingston	RW
34. JOHNSTON, Randy	NYI	Peterborough	D
35. NICOLSON, Graeme	Bos.	Cornwall	D
36. CARTER, Ron	Mtl.	Sherbrooke	RW

1977

FIRST ROUND

Selection	Claimed By	Amateur Club	
1. McCOURT, Dale	Det.	St. Catharines	C
2. BECK, Barry	Col.	New Westminster	D
3. PICARD, Robert	Wsh.	Montreal	D
4. GILLIS, Jere	Van.	Sherbrooke	LW
5. CROMBEEN, Mike	Cle.	Kingston	RW
6. WILSON, Doug	Chi.	Ottawa	D
7. MAXWELL, Brad	Min.	New Westminster	D
8. DEBLOIS, Lucien	NYR	Sorel	C
9. CAMPBELL, Scott	St.L.	London	D
10. NAPIER, Mark	Atl.-Mtl.	Toronto	RW
11. ANDERSON, John	Tor.	Toronto	RW
12. JOHANSEN, Trevor	Pit.-Tor.	Toronto	D
13. DUGUAY, Ron	L.A.-NYR	Sudbury	C
14. SEILING, Ric	Buf.	St. Catharines	RW
15. BOSSY, Mike	NYI	Laval	RW
16. FOSTER, Dwight	Bos.	Kitchener	C/RW
17. McCARTHY, Kevin	Phi.	Winnipeg	D
18. DUPONT, Norm	Mtl.	Montreal	C

SECOND ROUND

Selection	Claimed By	Amateur Club	
19. SAVARD, Jean	Det.-Chi.	Quebec	C
20. ZAHARKO, Miles	Col.-Atl.	New Westminister	D
21. LOFTHOUSE, Mark	Wsh.	New Westminster	RW
22. BANDURA, Jeff	Van.	Portland	D
23. CHICOINE, Daniel	Cle.	Sherbrooke	RW
24. GLADNEY, Bob	Chi.-Tor.	Oshawa	D
25. SEMENKO, Dave	Min.	Brandon	LW
26. KEATING, Mike	NYR	St. Catherines	LW
27. LABATTE, Neil	St.L.	Toronto	D
28. LAURENCE, Don	Atl.	Kitchener	C
29. SAGANIUK, Rocky	Tor.	Lethbridge	RW
30. HAMILTON, Jim	Pit.	London	RW
31. HILL, Brian	L.A.-Atl.	Medicine Hat	RW
32. ARESHENKOFF, Ron	Buf.	Medicine Hat	C
33. TONELLI, John	NYI	Toronto	LW
34. PARRO, Dave	Bos.	Saskatoon	G
35. GORENCE, Tom	Phi.	U. of Minnesota	RW
36. LANGWAY, Rod	Mtl.	U. of New Hampshire	D

1976

FIRST ROUND

Selection	Claimed By	Amateur Club	
1. GREEN, Rick	K.C.-Wsh.	London	D
2. CHAPMAN, Blair	Pit.	Saskatoon	RW
3. SHARPLEY, Glen	Min.	Hull	C
4. WILLIAMS, Fred	Det.	Saskatoon	C
5. JOHANSSON, Bjorn	Cal.	Sweden	D
6. MURDOCH, Don	NYR	Medicine Hat	RW
7. FEDERKO, Bernie	St.L.	Saskatoon	C
8. SHAND, Dave	Van.-Atl.	Peterborough	D
9. CLOUTIER, Real	Chi.	Quebec	RW
10. PHILLIPOFF, Harold	Atl.	New Westminster	LW
11. GARDNER, Paul	Pit.-K.C.	Oshawa	C
12. LEE, Peter	Tor.-Mtl.	Ottawa	RW
13. SCHUTT, Rod	L.A.-Mtl.	Sudbury	LW
14. McKENDRY, Alex	NYI	Sudbury	LW
15. CARROLL, Greg	Buf.-Wsh.	Medicine Hat	C
16. PACHAL, Clayton	Bos.	New Westminster	C
17. SUZOR, Mark	Phi.	Kingston	D
18. BAKER, Bruce	Mtl.	Ottawa	RW

SECOND ROUND

Selection	Claimed By	Amateur Club	
19. MALONE, Greg	Wsh.-Pit.	Oshawa	C
20. SUTTER, Brian	K.C.-St.L.	Lethbridge	LW
21. CLIPPINGDALE, Steve	Min.-L.A.	New Westminster	LW
22. LARSON, Reed	Det.	U. of Minnesota	D
23. STENLUND, Vern	Cal.	London	C
24. FARRISH, Dave	NYR	Sudbury	D
25. SMRKE, John	St.L.	Toronto	LW
26. MANNO, Bob	Van.	St. Catharines	D
27. McDILL, Jeff	Chi.	Victoria	RW
28. SIMPSON, Bobby	Atl.	Sherbrooke	LW
29. MARSH, Peter	Pit.	Sherbrooke	RW
30. CARLYLE, Randy	Tor.	Sudbury	D
31. ROBERTS, Jim	L.A.-Min.	Ottawa	LW
32. KASZYCKI, Mike	NYI	Sault Ste. Marie	C
33. KOWAL, Joe	Buf.	Hamilton	LW
34. GLOECKNER, Larry	Bos.	Victoria	D
35. CALLANDER, Drew	Phi.	Regina	C
36. MELROSE, Barry	Mtl.	Kamloops	D

1975

FIRST ROUND

Selection	Claimed By	Amateur Club	
1. BRIDGMAN, Mel	Wsh.-Phi.	Victoria	C
2. DEAN, Barry	K.C.	Medicine Hat	LW
3. KLASSEN, Ralph	Cal.	Saskatoon	C
4. MAXWELL, Brian	Min.	Medicine Hat	D
5. LAPOINTE, Rick	Det.	Victoria	D
6. ASHBY, Don	Tor.	Calgary	C
7. VAYDIK, Greg	Chi.	Medicine Hat	C
8. MULHERN, Richard	Atl.	Sherbrooke	D
9. SADLER, Robin	St.L.-Mtl.	Edmonton	D
10. BLIGHT, Rick	Van.	Brandon	RW
11. PRICE, Pat	NYI	Saskatoon	D
12. DILLON, Wayne	NYR	Toronto	C
13. LAXTON, Gord	Pit.	New Westminster	G
14. HALWARD, Doug	Bos.	Peterborough	D
15. MONDOU, Pierre	L.A.-Mtl.	Montreal	C
16. YOUNG, Tim	Mtl.-L.A.	Ottawa	C
17. SAUVE, Bob	Buf.	Laval	G
18. FORSYTH, Alex	Phi.-Wsh.	Kingston	C

SECOND ROUND

Selection	Claimed By	Amateur Club	
19. SCAMURRA, Peter	Wsh.	Peterborough	D
20. CAIRNS, Don	K.C.	Victoria	LW
21. MARUK, Dennis	Cal.	London	C
22. ENGBLOM, Brian	Min.-Mtl.	U. of Wisconsin	D
23. ROLLINS, Jerry	Det.	Winnipeg	D
24. JARVIS, Doug	Tor.	Peterborough	C
25. ARNDT, Daniel	Chi.	Saskatoon	LW
26. BOWNESS, Rick	Atl.	Montreal	RW
27. STANIOWSKI, Ed	St.L.	Regina	G
28. GASSOFF, Brad	Van.	Kamloops	D
29. SALVIAN, David	NYI	St. Catharines	RW
30. SOETAERT, Doug	NYR	Edmonton	G
31. ANDERSON, Russ	Pit.	U. of Minnesota	D
32. SMITH, Barry	Bos.	New Westminster	C
33. BUCYK, Terry	L.A.	Lethbridge	RW
34. GREENBANK, Kelvin	Mtl.	Winnipeg	RW
35. BREITENBACH, Ken	Buf.	St. Catharines	D
36. MASTERS, Jamie	Phi.-St.L.	Ottawa	D

1974

FIRST ROUND

Selection	Claimed By	Amateur Club	
1. JOLY, Greg	Wsh.	Regina	D
2. PAIEMENT, Wilfred	K.C.	St. Catharines	RW
3. HAMPTON, Rick	Cal.	St. Catharines	D
4. GILLIES, Clark	NYI	Regina	LW
5. CONNOR, Cam	Van.-Mtl.	Flin Flon	RW
6. HICKS, Doug	Min.	Flin Flon	D
7. RISEBROUGH, Doug	St.L.-Mtl.	Kitchener	C
8. LAROUCHE, Pierre	Pit.	Sorel	C
9. LOCHEAD, Bill	Det.	Oshawa	LW
10. CHARTRAW, Rick	Atl.-Mtl.	Kitchener	D
11. FOGOLIN, Lee	Buf.	Oshawa	D
12. TREMBLAY, Mario	L.A.-Mtl.	Montreal	RW
13. VALIQUETTE, Jack	Tor.	Sault Ste. Marie	C
14. MALONEY, Dave	NYR	Kitchener	D
15. McTAVISH, Gord	Mtl.	Sudbury	C
16. MULVEY, Grant	Chi.	Calgary	RW
17. CHIPPERFIELD, Ron	Phi.-Cal.	Brandon	C
18. LARWAY, Don	Bos.	Swift Current	RW

SECOND ROUND

Selection	Claimed By	Amateur Club	
19. MARSON, Mike	Wsh.	Sudbury	LW
20. BURDON, Glen	K.C.	Regina	C
21. AFFLECK, Bruce	Cal.	U. of Denver	D
22. TROTTIER, Bryan	NYI	Swift Current	C
23. SEDLBAUER, Ron	Van.	Kitchener	LW
24. NANTAIS, Rick	Min.	Quebec	LW
25. HOWE, Mark	St.L.-Bos.	Toronto	D
26. HESS, Bob	Pit.-St.L.	New Westminster	D
27. COSSETTE, Jacques	Det.-Pit.	Sorel	RW
28. CHOUINARD, Guy	Atl.	Quebec	C
29. GARE, Danny	Buf.	Calgary	RW
30. MacGREGOR, Gary	L.A.-Mtl.	Cornwall	C
31. WILLIAMS, Dave	Tor.	Swift Current	LW
32. GRESCHNER, Ron	NYR	New Westminster	D
33. LUPIEN, Gilles	Mtl.	Montreal	D
34. DAIGLE, Alain	Chi.	Trois-Rivières	RW
35. McLEAN, Don	Phi.	Sudbury	D
36. STURGEON, Peter	Bos.	Kitchener	LW

1973

FIRST ROUND

Selection	Claimed By	Amateur Club	
1. POTVIN, Denis	NYI	Ottawa	D
2. LYSIAK, Tom	Cal.-Mtl.-Atl.	Medicine Hat	C
3. VERVERGAERT, Dennis	Van.	London	RW
4. McDONALD, Lanny	Tor.	Medicine Hat	RW
5. DAVIDSON, John	Atl.-Mtl.-St.L.	Calgary	G
6. SAVARD, Andre	L.A.-Bos.	Quebec	C
7. STOUGHTON, Blaine	Pit.	Flin Flon	RW
8. GAINEY, Bob	St.L.-Mtl.	Peterborough	LW
9. DAILEY, Bob	Min.-Mtl.-Van.	Toronto	D
10. NEELY, Bob	Phi.-Tor.	Peterborough	LW
11. RICHARDSON, Terry	Det.	New Westminster	G
12. TITANIC, Morris	Buf.	Sudbury	LW
13. ROTA, Darcy	Chi.	Edmonton	LW
14. MIDDLETON, Rick	NYR	Oshawa	RW
15. TURNBULL, Ian	Bos.-Tor.	Ottawa	D
16. MERCREDI, Vic	Mtl.-Atl.	New Westminster	C

SECOND ROUND

Selection	Claimed By	Amateur Club	
17. GOLDUP, Glen	NYI-Mtl.	Toronto	RW
18. DUNLOP, Blake	Cal.-Min.	Ottawa	C
19. BORDELEAU, Paulin	Van.	Toronto	RW
20. GOODENOUGH, Larry	Tor.-Phi.	London	D
21. VAIL, Eric	Atl.	Sudbury	LW
22. MARRIN, Peter	L.A.-Mtl.	Toronto	C
23. BIANCHIN, Wayne	Pit.	Flin Flon	LW
24. PESUT, George	St.L.	Saskatoon	D
25. ROGERS, John	Min.	Edmonton	RW
26. LEVINS, Brent	Phi.	Swift Current	
27. CAMPBELL, Colin	Det.-Pit.	Peterborough	D
28. LANDRY, Jean	Buf.	Quebec	D
29. THOMAS, Reg	Chi.	London	LW
30. HICKEY, Pat	NYR	Hamilton	LW
31. JONES, Jim	Bos.	Peterborough	RW
32. ANDRUFF, Ron	Mtl.	Flin Flon	C

1972

FIRST ROUND

Selection	Claimed By	Amateur Club	
1. HARRIS, Billy	NYI	Toronto	RW
2. RICHARD, Jacques	Atl.	Quebec	LW
3. LEVER, Don	Van.	Niagara Falls	C
4. SHUTT, Steve	L.A.-Mtl.	Toronto	LW
5. SCHOENFELD, Jim	Buf.	Niagara Falls	D
6. LAROCQUE, Michel	Cal.-Mtl.	Ottawa	G
7. BARBER, Bill	Phi.	Kitchener	LW
8. GARDNER, Dave	Pit.-Min.-Mtl.	Toronto	C
9. MERRICK, Wayne	St.L.	Ottawa	C
10. BLANCHARD, Albert	Det.-NYR	Kitchener	LW
11. FERGUSON, George	Tor.	Toronto	C
12. BYERS, Jerry	Min.	Kitchener	LW
13. RUSSELL, Phil	Chi.	Edmonton	D
14. VAN BOXMEER, John	Mtl.	Guelph	D
15. MacMILLAN, Bobby	NYR	St. Catharines	RW
16. BLOOM, Mike	Bos.	St. Catharines	LW

SECOND ROUND

Selection	Claimed By	Amateur Club	
17. HENNING Lorne	NYI	New Westminster	C
18. BIALOWAS, Dwight	Atl.	Regina	D
19. McSHEFFREY, Brian	Van.	Ottawa	RW
20. KOZAK, Don	L.A.	Edmonton	RW
21. SACHARUK, Larry	Buf.-NYR	Saskatoon	D
22. CASSIDY, Tom	Cal.	Kitchener	C
23. BLADON, Tom	Phi.	Edmonton	D
24. LYNCH, Jack	Pit.	Oshawa	D
25. CARRIERE, Larry	St.L.-Buf.	Loyola College	D
26. GUITE, Pierre	Det.	St. Catharines	LW
27. OSBURN, Randy	Tor.	London	LW
28. WEIR, Stan	Min.-Cal.	Medicine Hat	C
29. OGILVIE, Brian	Chi.	Edmonton	C
30. LUKOWICH, Bernie	Mtl.-Pit.	New Westminster	RW
31. VILLEMURE, Rene	NYR	Shawinigan	LW
32. ELDER, Wayne	Bos.	London	D

1971

FIRST ROUND

Selection	Claimed By	Amateur Club	
1. LAFLEUR, Guy	Cal.-Mtl.	Quebec	RW
2. DIONNE, Marcel	Det.	St. Catharines	C
3. GUEVREMONT, Jocelyn	Van.	Montreal	D
4. CARR, Gene	Pit.-St.L.	Flin Flon	C
5. MARTIN, Rick	Buf.	Montreal	LW
6. JONES, Ron	L.A.-Bos.	Edmonton	D
7. ARNASON, Chuck	Min.-Mtl.	Flin Flon	RW
8. WRIGHT, Larry	Phi.	Regina	C
9. PLANTE, Pierre	Tor.-Phi.	Drummondville	RW
10. VICKERS, Steve	St.L.-NYR	Toronto	LW
11. WILSON, Murray	Mtl.	Ottawa	LW
12. SPRING, Dan	Chi.	Edmonton	C
13. DURBANO, Steve	NYR	Toronto	D
14. O'REILLY, Terry	Bos.	Oshawa	RW

SECOND ROUND

Selection	Claimed By	Amateur Club	
15. BAIRD, Ken	Cal.	Flin Flon	D
16. BOUCHA, Henry	Det.	U.S. Nationals	C
17. LALONDE, Bobby	Van.	Montreal	C
18. McKENZIE, Brian	Pit.	St. Catharines	LW
19. RAMSAY, Craig	Buf.	Peterborough	LW
20. ROBINSON, Larry	L.A.-Mtl.	Kitchener	D
21. NORRISH, Rod	Min.	Regina	LW
22. KEHOE, Rick	Phi.-Tor.	Hamilton	RW
23. FORTIER, Dave	Tor.	St. Catharines	D
24. DEGUISE, Michel	St.L.-Mtl.	Sorel	G
25. FRENCH, Terry	Mtl.	Ottawa	C
26. KRYSKOW, Dave	Chi.	Edmonton	LW
27. WILLIAMS, Tom	NYR	Hamilton	LW
28. RIDLEY, Curt	Bos.	Portage	G

1970

FIRST ROUND

Selection	Claimed By	Amateur Club	
1. PERREAULT, Gilbert	Buf.	Montreal	C
2. TALLON, Dale	Van.	Toronto	D
3. LEACH, Reg	L.A.-Bos.	Flin Flon	LW
4. MacLEISH, Rick	Phi.-Bos.	Peterborough	C
5. MARTINIUK, Ray	Oak.-Mtl.	Flin Flon	G
6. LEFLEY, Chuck	Min.-Mtl.	Canadian Nationals	C
7. POLIS, Greg	Pit.	Estevan	LW
8. SITTLER, Darryl	Tor.	London	C
9. PLUMB, Ron	Bos.	Peterborough	D
10. ODDLEIFSON, Chris	St.L.-Oak.	Winnipeg	C
11. GRATTON, Norm	Mtl.-NYR	Montreal	LW
12. LAJEUNESSE, Serge	Det.	Montreal	RW
13. STEWART, Bob	Bos.	Oshawa	D
14. MALONEY, Dan	Chi.	London	LW

SECOND ROUND

Selection	Claimed By	Amateur Club	
15. DEADMARSH, Butch	Buf.	Brandon	LW
16. HARGREAVES, Jim	Van.	Winnipeg	D
17. HARVEY, Fred	L.A.-Min.	Hamilton	RW
18. CLEMENT, Bill	Phi.	Ottawa	C
19. LAFRAMBOISE, Pete	Oak.	Ottawa	C
20. BARRETT, Fred	Min.	Toronto	D
21. STEWART, John	Pit.	Flin Flon	LW
22. THOMPSON, Errol	Tor.	Charlottetown	LW
23. KEOGAN, Murray	St.L.	U. of Minnesota	C
24. McDONOUGH, Al	Mtl.-L.A.	St. Catharines	RW
25. MURPHY, Mike	NYR	Toronto	RW
26. GUINDON, Bobby	Det.	Montreal	LW
27. BOUCHARD, Dan	Bos.	London	G
28. ARCHAMBAULT, Mike	Chi.	Drummondville	LW

1969

FIRST ROUND

Selection	Claimed By	Amateur Club	
1. HOULE, Rejean	Mtl.	Montreal	LW
2. TARDIF, Marc	Mtl.	Montreal	LW
3. TANNAHILL, Don	Min.-Bos.	Niagara Falls	LW
4. SPRING, Frank	Pit.-Bos.	Edmonton	RW
5. REDMOND, Dick	L.A.-Mtl.-Min.	St. Catharines	D
6. CURRIER, Bob	Phi.	Cornwall	C
7. FEATHERSTONE, Tony	Oak.	Peterborough	RW
8. DUPONT, André	St.L.-NYR	Montreal	D
9. MOSER, Ernie	Det.-Tor.	Estevan	RW
10. RUTHERFORD, Jim	Det.	Hamilton	G
11. BOLDIREV, Ivan	Bos.	Oshawa	C
12. JARRY, Pierre	NYR	Ottawa	LW
13. BORDELEAU, J.-P.	Chi.	Montreal	RW
14. O'BRIEN, Dennis	Min.	St. Catharines	D

SECOND ROUND

Selection	Claimed By	Amateur Club	
15. KESSELL, Rick	Pit.	Oshawa	C
16. HOGANSON, Dale	L.A.	Estevan	D
17. CLARKE, Bobby	Phi.	Flin Flon	C
18. STACKHOUSE, Ron	Oak.	Peterborough	D
19. LOWE, Mike	St.L.	Loyola College	
20. BRINDLEY, Doug	Tor.	Niagara Falls	C
21. GARWASIUK, Ron	Det.	Regina	LW
22. QUOQUOCHI, Art	Bos.	Montreal	
23. WILSON, Bert	NYR	London	LW
24. ROMANCHYCH, Larry	Chi.	Flin Flon	RW
25. GILBERT, Gilles	Min.	London	G
26. BRIERE, Michel	Pit.	Shawinigan Falls	C
27. BODDY, Greg	L.A.	Edmonton	D
28. BROSSART, Bill	Phi.	Estevan	D

NHL All-Stars

Active Players' All-Star Selection Records

GOALTENDERS

Player	First Team Selections	Second Team Selections	Total
Patrick Roy	(3) 1988-89; 1989-90; 1991-92.	(2) 1987-88; 1990-91.	5
Ed Belfour	(2) 1990-91; 1992-93.	(1) 1994-95	3
Tom Barrasso	(1) 1983-84.	(2) 1984-85; 1992-93.	3
Dominik Hasek	(2) 1993-94; 1994-95.	(0)	2
Grant Fuhr	(1) 1987-88.	(1) 1981-82.	2
J. Vanbiesbrouck	(1) 1985-86.	(1) 1993-94.	2
Ron Hextall	(1) 1986-87.	(0)	1
Jim Carey	(1) 1995-96.	(0)	1
Mike Vernon	(0)	(1) 1988-89.	1
Daren Puppa	(0)	(1) 1989-90.	1
Kirk McLean	(0)	(1) 1991-92.	1
Chris Osgood	(0)	(1) 1995-96.	1

DEFENSEMEN

Player	First Team Selections	Second Team Selections	Total
Ray Bourque	(12) 1979-80; 1981-82; 1983-84; 1984-85; 1986-87; 1987-88; 1989-90; 1990-91; 1991-92; 1992-93; 1993-94; 1995-96.	(5) 1980-81; 1982-83; 1985-86; 1988-89; 1994-95.	17
Paul Coffey	(4) 1984-85; 1985-86; 1988-89; 1994-95.	(4) 1981-82; 1982-83; 1983-84; 1989-90.	8
Chris Chelios	(4) 1988-89; 1992-93; 1994-95; 1995-96.	(1) 1990-91.	5
Al MacInnis	(2) 1989-90; 1990-91.	(3) 1986-87; 1988-89; 1993-94.	5
Brian Leetch	(1) 1991-92.	(3) 1990-91; 1993-94; 1995-96.	4
Scott Stevens	(2) 1987-88; 1993-94.	(2) 1991-92.	3
Larry Murphy	(0)	(3) 1986-87; 1992-93; 1994-95.	3
Gary Suter	(0)	(1) 1987-88.	1
Brad McCrimmon	(0)	(1) 1987-88.	1
Phil Housley	(0)	(1) 1991-92.	1
Al Iafrate	(0)	(1) 1992-93.	1
V. Konstantinov	(0)	(1) 1995-96.	1

CENTERS

Player	First Team Selections	Second Team Selections	Total
Wayne Gretzky	(8) 1980-81; 1981-82; 1982-83; 1983-84; 1984-85; 1985-86; 1986-87; 1990-91.	(5) 1979-80; 1987-88; 1988-89; 1989-90; 1993-94.	13
Mario Lemieux	(4) 1987-88; 1988-89; 1992-93; 1995-96.	(3) 1985-86; 1986-87; 1991-92.	7
Mark Messier	(2) 1989-90; 1991-92.	(0)	2
Eric Lindros	(1) 1994-95.	(1) 1995-96.	2
Sergei Fedorov	(1) 1993-94.	(0)	1
Denis Savard	(0)	(1) 1982-83.	1
Dale Hawerchuk	(0)	(1) 1984-85.	1
Adam Oates	(0)	(1) 1990-91.	1
Pat LaFontaine	(0)	(1) 1992-93.	1
Alexei Zhamnov	(0)	(1) 1994-95.	1

RIGHT WINGERS

Player	First Team Selections	Second Team Selections	Total
Jari Kurri	(2) 1984-85; 1986-87.	(3) 1983-84; 1985-86; 1988-89.	5
Cam Neely	(0)	(4) 1987-88; 1989-90; 1990-91; 1993-94.	4
Brett Hull	(3) 1989-90; 1990-91; 1991-92.	(0)	3
Jaromir Jagr	(2) 1994-95; 1995-96.	(0)	2
Alexander Mogilny	(0)	(2) 1992-93; 1995-96.	2
Joe Mullen	(1) 1988-89.	(0)	1
Teemu Selanne	(1) 1992-93.	(0)	1
Pavel Bure	(1) 1993-94.	(0)	1
Mark Recchi	(0)	(1) 1991-92.	1
Theoren Fleury	(0)	(1) 1994-95.	1

LEFT WINGERS

Player	First Team Selections	Second Team Selections	Total
Luc Robitaille	(5) 1987-88; 1988-89; 1989-90; 1990-91; 1992-93.	(2) 1986-87; 1991-92.	7
Mark Messier	(2) 1981-82; 1982-83.	(1) 1983-84.	3
Kevin Stevens	(1) 1991-92.	(2) 1990-91; 1992-93.	3
John LeClair	(1) 1994-95.	(1) 1995-96.	2
Brendan Shanahan	(1) 1993-94.	(0)	1
Brian Bellows	(0)	(1) 1989-90.	1
Adam Graves	(0)	(1) 1993-94.	1
Keith Tkachuk	(0)	(1) 1994-95.	1
Paul Kariya	(1) 1995-96.	(0)	1

Leading NHL All-Stars   1930-96

Player	Pos	Team	NHL Seasons	First Team Selections	Second Team Selections	Total Selections
Howe, Gordie	RW	Detroit	26	12	9	21
* Bourque, Ray	D	Boston	17	12	5	17
Richard, Maurice	RW	Montreal	18	8	6	14
* Gretzky, Wayne	C	Edm., L.A.	16	8	5	13
Hull, Bobby	LW	Chicago	16	10	2	12
Harvey, Doug	D	Mtl., NYR	19	10	1	11
Hall, Glenn	G	Det., Chi., St.L.	18	7	4	11
Beliveau, Jean	C	Montreal	20	6	4	10
Seibert, Earl	D	NYR., Chi	15	4	6	10
Orr, Bobby	D	Boston	12	8	1	9
Lindsay, Ted	LW	Detroit	17	8	1	9
Mahovlich, Frank	LW	Tor., Det., Mtl.	18	3	6	9
Shore, Eddie	D	Boston	14	7	1	8
Mikita, Stan	C	Chicago	22	6	2	8
Kelly, Red	D	Detroit	20	6	2	8
Esposito, Phil	C	Boston	18	6	2	8
Pilote, Pierre	D	Chicago	14	5	3	8
* Coffey, Paul	D	Edm., Pit., Det.	15	4	4	8
Brimsek, Frank	G	Boston	10	2	6	8
Bossy, Mike	RW	NY Islanders	10	5	3	8
* Robitaille, Luc	LW	Los Angeles	9	5	2	7
Potvin, Denis	D	NY Islanders	15	5	2	7
Park, Brad	D	NYR, Bos.	17	5	2	7
* Lemieux, Mario	C	Pittsburgh	11	4	3	7
Plante, Jacques	G	Mtl., Tor.	18	3	4	7
Gadsby, Bill	D	Chi., NYR, Det.	20	3	4	7
Sawchuk, Terry	G	Detroit	21	3	4	7
Durnan, Bill	G	Montreal	7	6	0	6
Lafleur, Guy	RW	Montreal	16	6	0	6
Dryden, Ken	G	Montreal	8	5	1	6
Robinson, Larry	D	Montreal	20	3	3	6
Horton, Tim	D	Toronto	24	3	3	6
Salming, Borje	D	Toronto	17	1	5	6
Cowley, Bill	C	Boston	13	4	1	5
* Messier, Mark	LW/C	Edm., NYR	16	4	1	5
Jackson, Harvey	LW	Toronto	15	4	1	5
* Chelios, Chris	D	Mtl., Chi.	13	4	1	5
Goulet, Michel	LW	Quebec	15	3	2	5
Clapper, "Dit"	RW/D	Boston	20	3	2	5
Conacher, Charlie	RW	Toronto	12	3	2	5
Stewart, Jack	D	Detroit	12	3	2	5
Lach, Elmer	C	Montreal	14	3	2	5
Quackenbush, Bill	D	Det., Bos.	14	3	2	5
Blake, Toe	LW	Montreal	15	3	2	5
Esposito, Tony	G	Chicago	16	3	2	5
* Roy, Patrick	G	Montreal	11	2	3	5
Reardon, Ken	D	Montreal	7	2	3	5
* Kurri, Jari	RW	Edmonton	14	2	3	5
Apps, Syl	C	Toronto	10	2	3	5
Giacomin, Ed	G	NY Rangers	13	2	3	5
* MacInnis, Al	D	Calgary	15	2	3	5

* Active

Position Leaders in All-Star Selections

Position	Player	First Team	Second Team	Total
GOAL	Glenn Hall	7	4	11
	Frank Brimsek	2	6	8
	Jacques Plante	3	4	7
	Terry Sawchuk	3	4	7
	Bill Durnan	6	0	6
	Ken Dryden	5	1	6
DEFENSE	* Ray Bourque	12	5	17
	Doug Harvey	10	1	11
	Earl Seibert	4	6	10
	Bobby Orr	8	1	9
	Eddie Shore	7	1	8
	Red Kelly	6	2	8
	Pierre Pilote	5	3	8
	* Paul Coffey	4	4	8
LEFT WING	Bobby Hull	10	2	12
	Ted Lindsay	8	1	9
	Frank Mahovlich	3	6	9
	* Luc Robitaille	5	2	7
	Harvey Jackson	4	1	5
	Michel Goulet	3	2	5
	Toe Blake	3	2	5
RIGHT WING	Gordie Howe	12	9	21
	Maurice Richard	8	6	14
	Mike Bossy	5	3	8
	Guy Lafleur	6	0	6
	Charlie Conacher	3	2	5
	* Jari Kurri	2	3	5
CENTER	* Wayne Gretzky	8	5	13
	Jean Beliveau	6	4	10
	Stan Mikita	6	2	8
	Phil Esposito	6	2	8
	* Mario Lemieux	4	3	7

* active player

All-Star Teams

1930-96

Voting for the NHL All-Star Team is conducted among the representatives of the Professional Hockey Writers' Association at the end of the season.

Following is a list of the First and Second All-Star Teams since their inception in 1930-31.

First Team		Second Team
1995-96		
Carey, Jim, Wsh.	G	Osgood, Chris, Det.
Chelios, Chris, Chi.	D	Konstantinov, V., Det.
Bourque, Ray, Bos.	D	Leetch, Brian, NYR.
Lemieux, Mario, Pit.	C	Lindros, Eric, Phi.
Jagr, Jaromir, Pit.	RW	Mogilny, Alexander, Van.
Kariya, Paul, Ana.	LW	LeClair, John, Phi.
1994-95		
Hasek, Dominik, Buf.	G	Belfour, Ed, Chi.
Coffey, Paul, Det.	D	Bourque, Ray, Bos.
Chelios, Chris, Chi.	D	Murphy, Larry, Pit.
Lindros, Eric, Phi.	C	Zhamnov, Alexei, Wpg.
Jagr, Jaromir, Pit.	RW	Fleury, Theoren, Cgy.
LeClair, John, Mtl., Phi.	LW	Tkachuk, Keith, Wpg.
1993-94		
Hasek, Dominik, Buf.	G	Vanbiesbrouck, John, Fla.
Bourque, Ray, Bos.	D	MacInnis, Al, Cgy.
Stevens, Scott, N.J.	D	Leetch, Brian, NYR
Fedorov, Sergei, Det.	C	Gretzky, Wayne, L.A.
Bure, Pavel, Van.	RW	Neely, Cam, Bos.
Shanahan, Brendan, St. L.	LW	Graves, Adam, NYR
1992-93		
Belfour, Ed, Chi.	G	Barrasso, Tom, Pit.
Chelios, Chris, Chi.	D	Murphy, Larry, Pit.
Bourque, Ray, Bos.	D	Iafrate, Al, Wsh.
Lemieux, Mario, Pit.	C	LaFontaine, Pat, Buf.
Selanne, Teemu, Wpg.	RW	Mogilny, Alexander, Buf.
Robitaille, Luc, L.A.	LW	Stevens, Kevin, Pit.
1991-92		
Roy, Patrick, Mtl.	G	McLean, Kirk, Van.
Leetch, Brian, NYR	D	Housley, Phil, Wpg.
Bourque, Ray, Bos.	D	Stevens, Scott, N.J.
Messier, Mark, NYR	C	Lemieux, Mario, Pit.
Hull, Brett, St. L.	RW	Recchi, Mark, Pit., Phi.
Stevens, Kevin, Pit.	LW	Robitaille, Luc, L.A.
1990-91		
Belfour, Ed, Chi.	G	Roy, Patrick, Mtl.
Bourque, Ray, Bos.	D	Chelios, Chris, Chi.
MacInnis, Al, Cgy.	D	Leetch, Brian, NYR
Gretzky, Wayne, L.A.	C	Oates, Adam, St. L.
Hull, Brett, St. L.	RW	Neely, Cam, Bos.
Robitaille, Luc, L.A.	LW	Stevens, Kevin, Pit.
1989-90		
Roy, Patrick, Mtl.	G	Puppa, Daren, Buf.
Bourque, Ray, Bos.	D	Coffey, Paul, Pit.
MacInnis, Al, Cgy.	D	Wilson, Doug, Chi.
Messier, Mark, Edm.	C	Gretzky, Wayne, L.A.
Hull, Brett, St. L.	RW	Neely, Cam, Bos.
Robitaille, Luc, L.A.	LW	Bellows, Brian, Min.
1988-89		
Roy, Patrick, Mtl.	G	Vernon, Mike, Cgy.
Chelios, Chris, Mtl.	D	MacInnis, Al, Cgy.
Coffey, Paul, Pit.	D	Bourque, Ray, Bos.
Lemieux, Mario, Pit.	C	Gretzky, Wayne, L.A.
Mullen, Joe, Cgy.	RW	Kurri, Jari, Edm.
Robitaille, Luc, L.A.	LW	Gallant, Gerard, Det.

First Team		Second Team
1987-88		
Fuhr, Grant, Edm.	G	Roy, Patrick, Mtl.
Bourque, Ray, Bos.	D	Suter, Gary, Cgy.
Stevens, Scott, Wsh.	D	McCrimmon, Brad, Cgy.
Lemieux, Mario, Pit.	C	Gretzky, Wayne, Edm.
Loob, Hakan, Cgy.	RW	Neely, Cam, Bos.
Robitaille, Luc, L.A.	LW	Goulet, Michel, Que.
1986-87		
Hextall, Ron, Phi.	G	Liut, Mike, Hfd.
Bourque, Ray, Bos.	D	Murphy, Larry, Wsh.
Howe, Mark, Phi.	D	MacInnis, Al, Cgy.
Gretzky, Wayne, Edm.	C	Lemieux, Mario, Pit.
Kurri, Jari, Edm.	RW	Kerr, Tim, Phi.
Goulet, Michel, Que.	LW	Robitaille, Luc, L.A.

First Team		Second Team
1985-86		
Vanbiesbrouck, J., NYR	G	Froese, Bob, Phi.
Coffey, Paul, Edm.	D	Robinson, Larry, Mtl.
Howe, Mark, Phi.	D	Bourque, Ray, Bos.
Gretzky, Wayne, Edm.	C	Lemieux, Mario, Pit.
Bossy, Mike, NYI	RW	Kurri, Jari, Edm.
Goulet, Michel, Que.	LW	Naslund, Mats, Mtl.
1984-85		
Lindbergh, Pelle, Phi.	G	Barrasso, Tom, Buf.
Coffey, Paul, Edm.	D	Langway, Rod, Wsh.
Bourque, Ray, Bos.	D	Wilson, Doug, Chi.
Gretzky, Wayne, Edm.	C	Hawerchuk, Dale, Wpg.
Kurri, Jari, Edm.	RW	Bossy, Mike, NYI
Ogrodnick, John, Det.	LW	Tonelli, John, NYI

Detroit defenseman Vladimir Konstantinov, who led the league in plus/minus with a mark of +60, earned a berth on the NHL's Second All-Star Team in 1995-96.

First Team		Second Team

1983-84

First Team		Second Team
Barrasso, Tom, Buf.	G	Riggin, Pat, Wsh.
Langway, Rod, Wsh.	D	Coffey, Paul, Edm.
Bourque, Ray, Bos.	D	Potvin, Denis, NYI
Gretzky, Wayne, Edm.	C	Trottier, Bryan, NYI
Bossy, Mike, NYI	RW	Kurri, Jari, Edm.
Goulet, Michel, Que.	LW	Messier, Mark, Edm.

1982-83

Peeters, Pete, Bos.	G	Melanson, Roland, NYI
Howe, Mark, Phi.	D	Bourque, Ray, Bos.
Langway, Rod, Wsh.	D	Coffey, Paul, Edm.
Gretzky, Wayne, Edm.	C	Savard, Denis, Chi.
Bossy, Mike, NYI	RW	McDonald, Lanny, Cgy.
Messier, Mark, Edm.	LW	Goulet, Michel, Que.

1981-82

Smith, Bill, NYI	G	Fuhr, Grant, Edm.
Wilson, Doug, Chi.	D	Coffey, Paul, Edm.
Bourque, Ray, Bos.	D	Engblom, Brian, Mtl.
Gretzky, Wayne, Edm.	C	Trottier, Bryan, NYI
Bossy, Mike, NYI	RW	Middleton, Rick, Bos.
Messier, Mark, Edm.	LW	Tonelli, John, NYI

1980-81

Liut, Mike, St.L.	G	Lessard, Mario, L.A.
Potvin, Denis, NYI	D	Robinson, Larry, Mtl.
Carlyle, Randy, Pit.	D	Bourque, Ray, Bos.
Gretzky, Wayne, Edm.	C	Dionne, Marcel, L.A.
Bossy, Mike, NYI	RW	Taylor, Dave, L.A.
Simmer, Charlie, L.A.	LW	Barber, Bill, Phi.

1979-80

Esposito, Tony, Chi.	G	Edwards, Don, Buf.
Robinson, Larry, Mtl.	D	Salming, Borje, Tor.
Bourque, Ray, Bos.	D	Schoenfeld, Jim, Buf.
Dionne, Marcel, L.A.	C	Gretzky, Wayne, Edm.
Lafleur, Guy, Mtl.	RW	Gare, Danny, Buf.
Simmer, Charlie, L.A.	LW	Shutt, Steve, Mtl.

1978-79

Dryden, Ken, Mtl.	G	Resch, Glenn, NYI
Potvin, Denis, NYI	D	Salming, Borje, Tor.
Robinson, Larry, Mtl.	D	Savard, Serge, Mtl.
Trottier, Bryan, NYI	C	Dionne, Marcel, L.A.
Lafleur, Guy, Mtl.	RW	Bossy, Mike, NYI
Gillies, Clark, NYI	LW	Barber, Bill, Phi.

1977-78

Dryden, Ken, Mtl.	G	Edwards, Don, Buf.
Potvin, Denis, NYI	D	Robinson, Larry, Mtl.
Park, Brad, Bos.	D	Salming, Borje, Tor.
Trottier, Bryan, NYI	C	Sittler, Darryl, Tor.
Lafleur, Guy, Mtl.	RW	Bossy, Mike, NYI
Gillies, Clark, NYI	LW	Shutt, Steve, Mtl.

1976-77

Dryden, Ken, Mtl.	G	Vachon, Rogatien, L.A.
Robinson, Larry, Mtl.	D	Potvin, Denis, NYI
Salming, Borje, Tor.	D	Lapointe, Guy, Mtl.
Dionne, Marcel, L.A.	C	Perreault, Gilbert, Buf.
Lafleur, Guy, Mtl.	RW	McDonald, Lanny, Tor.
Shutt, Steve, Mtl.	LW	Martin, Richard, Buf.

1975-76

Dryden, Ken, Mtl.	G	Resch, Glenn, NYI
Potvin, Denis, NYI	D	Salming, Borje, Tor.
Park, Brad, Bos.	D	Lapointe, Guy, Mtl.
Clarke, Bobby, Phi.	C	Perreault, Gilbert, Buf.
Lafleur, Guy, Mtl.	RW	Leach, Reggie, Phi.
Barber, Bill, Phi.	LW	Martin, Richard, Buf.

1974-75

Parent, Bernie, Phi.	G	Vachon, Rogie, L.A.
Orr, Bobby, Bos.	D	Salming, Borje, Tor.
Potvin, Denis, NYI	D	Salming, Borje, Tor.
Clarke, Bobby, Phi.	C	Esposito, Phil, Bos.
Lafleur, Guy, Mtl.	RW	Robert, René, Buf.
Martin, Richard, Buf.	LW	Vickers, Steve, NYR

1973-74

Parent, Bernie, Phi.	G	Esposito, Tony, Chi.
Orr, Bobby, Bos.	D	White, Bill, Chi.
Park, Brad, NYR	D	Ashbee, Barry, Phi.
Esposito, Phil, Bos.	C	Clarke, Bobby, Phi.
Hodge, Ken, Bos.	RW	Redmond, Mickey, Det.
Martin, Richard, Buf.	LW	Cashman, Wayne, Bos.

1972-73

Dryden, Ken, Mtl.	G	Esposito, Tony, Chi.
Orr, Bobby, Bos.	D	Park, Brad, NYR
Lapointe, Guy, Mtl.	D	White, Bill, Chi.
Esposito, Phil, Bos.	C	Clarke, Bobby, Phi.
Redmond, Mickey, Det.	RW	Cournoyer, Yvan, Mtl.
Mahovlich, Frank, Mtl.	LW	Hull, Dennis, Chi.

1971-72

Esposito, Tony, Chi.	G	Dryden, Ken, Mtl.
Orr, Bobby, Bos.	D	White, Bill, Chi.
Park, Brad, NYR	D	Stapleton, Pat, Chi.
Esposito, Phil, Bos.	C	Ratelle, Jean, NYR
Gilbert, Rod, NYR	RW	Cournoyer, Yvan, Mtl.
Hull, Bobby, Chi.	LW	Hadfield, Vic, NYR

1970-71

Giacomin, Ed, NYR	G	Plante, Jacques, Tor.
Orr, Bobby, Bos.	D	Park, Brad, NYR
Tremblay, J.C., Mtl.	D	Stapleton, Pat, Chi.
Esposito, Phil, Bos.	C	Keon, Dave, Tor.
Hodge, Ken, Bos.	RW	Cournoyer, Yvan, Mtl.
Bucyk, John, Bos.	LW	Hull, Bobby, Chi.

1969-70

Esposito, Tony, Chi.	G	Giacomin, Ed, NYR
Orr, Bobby, Bos.	D	Brewer, Carl, Det.
Park, Brad, NYR	D	Laperriere, Jacques, Mtl.
Esposito, Phil, Bos.	C	Mikita, Stan, Chi.
Howe, Gordie, Det.	RW	McKenzie, John, Bos.
Hull, Bobby, Chi.	LW	Mahovlich, Frank, Det.

1968-69

Hall, Glenn, St.L.	G	Giacomin, Ed, NYR
Orr, Bobby, Bos.	D	Green, Ted, Bos.
Horton, Tim, Tor.	D	Harris, Ted, Mtl.
Esposito, Phil, Bos.	C	Béliveau, Jean, Mtl.
Howe, Gordie, Det.	RW	Cournoyer, Yvan, Mtl.
Hull, Bobby, Chi.	LW	Mahovlich, Frank, Det.

1967-68

Worsley, Lorne, Mtl.	G	Giacomin, Ed, NYR
Orr, Bobby, Bos.	D	Tremblay, J.C., Mtl.
Horton, Tim, Tor.	D	Neilson, Jim, NYR
Mikita, Stan, Chi.	C	Esposito, Phil, Bos.
Howe, Gordie, Det.	RW	Gilbert, Rod, NYR
Hull, Bobby, Chi.	LW	Bucyk, John, Bos.

1966-67

Giacomin, Ed, NYR	G	Hall, Glenn, Chi.
Pilote, Pierre, Chi.	D	Horton, Tim, Tor.
Howell, Harry, NYR	D	Orr, Bobby, Bos.
Mikita, Stan, Chi.	C	Ullman, Norm, Det.
Wharram, Ken, Chi.	RW	Howe, Gordie, Det.
Hull, Bobby, Chi.	LW	Marshall, Don, NYR

1965-66

Hall, Glenn, Chi.	G	Worsley, Lorne, Mtl.
Laperriere, Jacques, Mtl.	D	Stanley, Allan, Tor.
Pilote, Pierre, Chi.	D	Stapleton, Pat, Chi.
Mikita, Stan, Chi.	C	Béliveau, Jean, Mtl.
Howe, Gordie, Det.	RW	Rousseau, Bobby, Mtl.
Hull, Bobby, Chi.	LW	Mahovlich, Frank, Tor.

1964-65

Crozier, Roger, Det.	G	Hodge, Charlie, Mtl.
Pilote, Pierre, Chi.	D	Gadsby, Bill, Det.
Laperriere, Jacques, Mtl.	D	Brewer, Carl, Tor.
Ullman, Norm, Det.	C	Mikita, Stan, Chi.
Provost, Claude, Mtl.	RW	Howe, Gordie, Det.
Hull, Bobby, Chi.	LW	Mahovlich, Frank, Tor.

1963-64

Hall, Glenn, Chi.	G	Hodge, Charlie, Mtl.
Pilote, Pierre, Chi.	D	Vasko, Elmer, Chi.
Horton, Tim, Tor.	D	Laperriere, Jacques, Mtl.
Mikita, Stan, Chi.	C	Béliveau, Jean, Mtl.
Wharram, Ken, Chi.	RW	Howe, Gordie, Det.
Hull, Bobby, Chi.	LW	Mahovlich, Frank, Tor.

1962-63

Hall, Glenn, Chi.	G	Sawchuk, Terry, Det.
Pilote, Pierre, Chi.	D	Horton, Tim, Tor.
Brewer, Carl, Tor.	D	Vasko, Elmer, Chi.
Mikita, Stan, Chi.	C	Richard, Henri, Mtl.
Howe, Gordie, Det.	RW	Bathgate, Andy, NYR
Mahovlich, Frank, Tor.	LW	Hull, Bobby, Chi.

1961-62

Plante, Jacques, Mtl.	G	Hall, Glenn, Chi.
Harvey, Doug, NYR	D	Brewer, Carl, Tor.
Talbot, Jean-Guy, Mtl.	D	Pilote, Pierre, Chi.
Mikita, Stan, Chi.	C	Keon, Dave, Tor.
Bathgate, Andy, NYR	RW	Howe, Gordie, Det.
Hull, Bobby, Chi.	LW	Mahovlich, Frank, Tor.

1960-61

Bower, Johnny, Tor.	G	Hall, Glenn, Chi.
Harvey, Doug, Mtl.	D	Stanley, Allan, Tor.
Pronovost, Marcel, Det.	D	Pilote, Pierre, Chi.
Béliveau, Jean, Mtl.	C	Richard, Henri, Mtl.
Geoffrion, Bernie, Mtl.	RW	Howe, Gordie, Det.
Mahovlich, Frank, Tor.	LW	Moore, Dickie, Mtl.

1959-60

Hall, Glenn, Chi.	G	Plante, Jacques, Mtl.
Harvey, Doug, Mtl.	D	Stanley, Allan, Tor.
Pronovost, Marcel, Det.	D	Pilote, Pierre, Chi.
Béliveau, Jean, Mtl.	C	Horvath, Bronco, Bos.
Howe, Gordie, Det.	RW	Geoffrion, Bernie, Mtl.
Hull, Bobby, Chi.	LW	Prentice, Dean, NYR

1958-59

Plante, Jacques, Mtl.	G	Sawchuk, Terry, Det.
Johnson, Tom, Mtl.	D	Pronovost, Marcel, Det.
Gadsby, Bill, NYR	D	Harvey, Doug, Mtl.
Béliveau, Jean, Mtl.	C	Richard, Henri, Mtl.
Bathgate, Andy, NYR	RW	Howe, Gordie, Det.
Moore, Dickie, Mtl.	LW	Delvecchio, Alex, Det.

1957-58

Hall, Glenn, Chi.	G	Plante, Jacques, Mtl.
Harvey, Doug, Mtl.	D	Flaman, Fern, Bos.
Gadsby, Bill, NYR	D	Pronovost, Marcel, Det.
Richard, Henri, Mtl.	C	Béliveau, Jean, Mtl.
Howe, Gordie, Det.	RW	Bathgate, Andy, NYR
Moore, Dickie, Mtl.	LW	Henry, Camille, NYR

First Team		Second Team

1956-57

First Team		Second Team
Hall, Glenn, Det.	G	Plante, Jacques, Mtl.
Harvey, Doug, Mtl.	D	Flaman, Fern, Bos.
Kelly, Red, Det.	D	Gadsby, Bill, NYR
Béliveau, Jean, Mtl.	C	Litzenberger, Eddie, Chi.
Howe, Gordie, Det.	RW	Richard, Maurice, Mtl.
Lindsay, Ted, Det.	LW	Chevrefils, Real, Bos.

1955-56

Plante, Jacques, Mtl.	G	Hall, Glenn, Det.
Harvey, Doug, Mtl.	D	Kelly, Red, Det.
Gadsby, Bill, NYR	D	Johnson, Tom, Mtl.
Béliveau, Jean, Mtl.	C	Sloan, Tod, Tor.
Richard, Maurice, Mtl.	RW	Howe, Gordie, Det.
Lindsay, Ted, Det.	LW	Olmstead, Bert, Mtl.

1954-55

Lumley, Harry, Tor.	G	Sawchuk, Terry, Det.
Harvey, Doug, Mtl.	D	Goldham, Bob, Det.
Kelly, Red, Det.	D	Flaman, Fern, Bos.
Béliveau, Jean, Mtl.	C	Mosdell, Ken, Mtl.
Richard, Maurice, Mtl.	RW	Geoffrion, Bernie, Mtl.
Smith, Sid, Tor.	LW	Lewicki, Danny, NYR

1953-54

Lumley, Harry, Tor.	G	Sawchuk, Terry, Det.
Kelly, Red, Det.	D	Gadsby, Bill, Chi.
Harvey, Doug, Mtl.	D	Horton, Tim, Tor.
Mosdell, Ken, Mtl.	C	Kennedy, Ted, Tor.
Howe, Gordie, Det.	RW	Richard, Maurice, Mtl.
Lindsay, Ted, Det.	LW	Sandford, Ed, Bos.

1952-53

Sawchuk, Terry, Det.	G	McNeil, Gerry, Mtl.
Kelly, Red, Det.	D	Quackenbush, Bill, Bos.
Harvey, Doug, Mtl.	D	Gadsby, Bill, Chi.
Mackell, Fleming, Bos.	C	Delvecchio, Alex, Det.
Howe, Gordie, Det.	RW	Richard, Maurice, Mtl.
Lindsay, Ted, Det.	LW	Olmstead, Bert, Mtl.

1951-52

Sawchuk, Terry, Det.	G	Henry, Jim, Bos.
Kelly, Red, Det.	D	Buller, Hy, NYR
Harvey, Doug, Mtl.	D	Thomson, Jim, Tor.
Lach, Elmer, Mtl.	C	Schmidt, Milt, Bos.
Howe, Gordie, Det.	RW	Richard, Maurice, Mtl.
Lindsay, Ted, Det.	LW	Smith, Sid, Tor.

1950-51

Sawchuk, Terry, Det.	G	Rayner, Chuck, NYR
Kelly, Red, Det.	D	Thomson, Jim, Tor.
Quackenbush, Bill, Bos.	D	Reise, Leo, Det.
Schmidt, Milt, Bos.	C	Abel, Sid, Det.
	(tied)	Kennedy, Ted, Tor.
Howe, Gordie, Det.	RW	Richard, Maurice, Mtl.
Lindsay, Ted, Det.	LW	Smith, Sid, Tor.

1949-50

Durnan, Bill, Mtl.	G	Rayner, Chuck, NYR
Mortson, Gus, Tor.	D	Reise, Leo, Det.
Reardon, Kenny, Mtl.	D	Kelly, Red, Det.
Abel, Sid, Det.	C	Kennedy, Ted, Tor.
Richard, Maurice, Mtl.	RW	Howe, Gordie, Det.
Lindsay, Ted, Det.	LW	Leswick, Tony, NYR

1948-49

Durnan, Bill, Mtl.	G	Rayner, Chuck, NYR
Quackenbush, Bill, Det.	D	Harmon, Glen, Mtl.
Stewart, Jack, Det.	D	Reardon, Kenny, Mtl.
Abel, Sid, Det.	C	Bentley, Doug, Chi.
Richard, Maurice, Mtl.	RW	Howe, Gordie, Det.
Conacher, Roy, Chi.	LW	Lindsay, Ted, Det.

1947-48

Broda, W. "Turk", Tor.	G	Brimsek, Frank, Bos.
Quackenbush, Bill, Det.	D	Reardon, Kenny, Mtl.
Stewart, Jack, Det.	D	Colville, Neil, NYR
Lach, Elmer, Mtl.	C	O'Connor, "Buddy", NYR
Richard, Maurice, Mtl.	RW	Poile, "Bud", Chi.
Lindsay, Ted, Det.	LW	Stewart, Gaye, Chi.

1946-47

Durnan, Bill, Mtl.	G	Brimsek, Frank, Bos.
Reardon, Kenny, Mtl.	D	Stewart, Jack, Det.
Bouchard, Emile, Mtl.	D	Quackenbush, Bill, Det.
Schmidt, Milt, Bos.	C	Bentley, Max, Chi.
Richard, Maurice, Mtl.	RW	Bauer, Bobby, Bos.
Bentley, Doug, Chi.	LW	Dumart, Woody, Bos.

1945-46

Durnan, Bill, Mtl.	G	Brimsek, Frank, Bos.
Crawford, Jack, Bos.	D	Reardon, Kenny, Mtl.
Bouchard, Emile, Mtl.	D	Stewart, Jack, Det.
Bentley, Max, Chi.	C	Lach, Elmer, Mtl.
Richard, Maurice, Mtl.	RW	Mosienko, Bill, Chi.
Stewart, Gaye, Tor.	LW	Blake, "Toe", Mtl.
Irvin, Dick, Mtl.	Coach	Gottselig, John, Chi.

1944-45

Durnan, Bill, Mtl.	G	Karakas, Mike, Chi.
Bouchard, Emile, Mtl.	D	Harmon, Glen, Mtl.
Hollett, Bill, Det.	D	Pratt, "Babe", Tor.
Lach, Elmer, Mtl.	C	Cowley, Bill, Bos.
Richard, Maurice, Mtl.	RW	Mosienko, Bill, Chi.
Blake, "Toe", Mtl.	LW	Howe, Syd, Det.
Irvin, Dick, Mtl.	Coach	Adams, Jack, Det.

1943-44

Durnan, Bill, Mtl.	G	Bibeault, Paul, Tor.
Seibert, Earl, Chi.	D	Bouchard, Emile, Mtl.
Pratt, "Babe", Tor.	D	Clapper, "Dit", Bos.
Cowley, Bill, Bos.	C	Lach, Elmer, Mtl.
Carr, Lorne, Tor.	RW	Richard, Maurice, Mtl.
Bentley, Doug, Chi.	LW	Cain, Herb, Bos.
Irvin, Dick, Mtl.	Coach	Day, "Hap", Tor.

1942-43

Mowers, Johnny, Det.	G	Brimsek, Frank, Bos.
Seibert, Earl, Chi.	D	Crawford, Jack, Bos.
Stewart, Jack, Det.	D	Hollett, Bill, Bos.
Cowley, Bill, Bos.	C	Apps, Syl, Tor.
Carr, Lorne, Tor.	RW	Hextall, Bryan, NYR
Bentley, Doug, Chi.	LW	Patrick, Lynn, NYR
Adams, Jack, Det.	Coach	Ross, Art, Bos.

1941-42

Brimsek, Frank, Bos.	G	Broda, W. "Turk", Tor.
Seibert, Earl, Chi.	D	Egan, Pat, Bro.
Anderson, Tommy, Bro.	D	McDonald, Bucko, Tor.
Apps, Syl, Tor.	C	Watson, Phil, NYR
Hextall, Bryan, NYR	RW	Drillon, Gord, Tor.
Patrick, Lynn, NYR	LW	Abel, Sid, Det.
Boucher, Frank, NYR	Coach	Thompson, Paul, Chi.

1940-41

Broda, W. "Turk", Tor.	G	Brimsek, Frank, Bos.
Clapper, "Dit", Bos.	D	Seibert, Earl, Chi.
Stanowski, Wally, Tor.	D	Heller, Ott, NYR
Cowley, Bill, Bos.	C	Apps, Syl, Tor.
Hextall, Bryan, NYR	RW	Bauer, Bobby, Bos.
Schriner, Dave, Tor.	LW	Dumart, Woody, Bos.
Weiland, "Cooney", Bos.	Coach	Irvin, Dick, Mtl.

1939-40

Kerr, Dave, NYR	G	Brimsek, Frank, Bos.
Clapper, "Dit", Bos.	D	Coulter, Art, NYR
Goodfellow, Ebbie, Det.	D	Seibert, Earl, Chi.
Schmidt, Milt, Bos.	C	Colville, Neil, NYR
Hextall, Bryan, NYR	RW	Bauer, Bobby, Bos.
Blake, "Toe", Mtl.	LW	Dumart, Woody, Bos.
Thompson, Paul, Chi.	Coach	Boucher, Frank, NYR

1938-39

Brimsek, Frank, Bos.	G	Robertson, Earl, NYA
Shore, Eddie, Bos.	D	Seibert, Earl, Chi.
Clapper, "Dit", Bos.	D	Coulter, Art, NYR
Apps, Syl, Tor.	C	Colville, Neil, NYR
Drillon, Gord, Tor.	RW	Bauer, Bobby, Bos.
Blake, "Toe", Mtl.	LW	Gottselig, Johnny, Chi.
Ross, Art, Bos.	Coach	Dutton, "Red", NYA

1937-38

First Team		Second Team
Thompson, "Tiny", Bos.	G	Kerr, Dave, NYR
Shore, Eddie, Bos.	D	Coulter, Art, NYR
Siebert, "Babe", Mtl.	D	Seibert, Earl, Chi.
Cowley, Bill, Bos.	C	Apps, Syl, Tor.
Dillon, Cecil, NYR	RW	Dillon, Cecil, NYR
Drillon, Gord, Tor.	(tied)	Drillon, Gord, Tor.
Thompson, Paul, Chi.	LW	Blake, Toe, Mtl.
Patrick, Lester, NYR	Coach	Ross, Art, Bos.

1936-37

Smith, Norm, Det.	G	Cude, Wilf, Mtl.
Siebert, "Babe", Mtl.	D	Seibert, Earl, Chi.
Goodfellow, Ebbie, Det.	D	Conacher, Lionel, Mtl. M.
Barry, Marty, Det.	C	Chapman, Art, NYA
Aurie, Larry, Det.	RW	Dillon, Cecil, NYR
Jackson, Harvey, Tor.	LW	Schriner, Dave, NYA
Adams, Jack, Det.	Coach	Hart, Cecil, Mtl.

1935-36

Thompson, "Tiny", Bos.	G	Cude, Wilf, Mtl.
Shore, Eddie, Bos.	D	Seibert, Earl, Chi.
Siebert, "Babe", Bos.	D	Goodfellow, Ebbie, Det.
Smith, "Hooley", Mtl. M.	C	Thoms, Bill, Tor.
Conacher, Charlie, Tor.	RW	Dillon, Cecil, NYR
Schriner, Dave, NYA	LW	Thompson, Paul, Chi.
Patrick, Lester, NYR	Coach	Gorman, T.P., Mtl. M.

1934-35

Chabot, Lorne, Chi.	G	Thompson, "Tiny", Bos.
Shore, Eddie, Bos.	D	Wentworth, Cy, Mtl. M.
Seibert, Earl, NYR	D	Coulter, Art, Chi.
Boucher, Frank, NYR	C	Weiland, "Cooney", Det.
Conacher, Charlie, Tor.	RW	Clapper, "Dit", Bos.
Jackson, Harvey, Tor.	LW	Joliat, Aurel, Mtl.
Patrick, Lester, NYR	Coach	Irvin, Dick, Tor.

1933-34

Gardiner, Charlie, Chi.	G	Worters, Roy, NYA
Clancy, "King", Tor.	D	Shore, Eddie, Bos.
Conacher, Lionel, Chi.	D	Johnson, "Ching", NYR
Boucher, Frank, NYR	C	Primeau, Joe, Tor.
Conacher, Charlie, Tor.	RW	Cook, Bill, NYR
Jackson, Harvey, Tor.	LW	Joliat, Aurel, Mtl.
Patrick, Lester, NYR	Coach	Irvin, Dick, Tor.

1932-33

Roach, John Ross, Det.	G	Gardiner, Charlie, Chi.
Shore, Eddie, Bos.	D	Clancy, "King", Tor.
Johnson, "Ching", NYR	D	Conacher, Lionel, Mtl. M.
Boucher, Frank, NYR	C	Morenz, Howie, Mtl.
Cook, Bill, NYR	RW	Conacher, Charlie, Tor.
Northcott, "Baldy", Mtl M.	LW	Jackson, Harvey, Tor.
Patrick, Lester, NYR	Coach	Irvin, Dick, Tor.

1931-32

Gardiner, Charlie, Chi.	G	Worters, Roy, NYA
Shore, Eddie, Bos.	D	Mantha, Sylvio, Mtl.
Johnson, "Ching", NYR	D	Clancy, "King", Tor.
Morenz, Howie, Mtl.	C	Smith, "Hooley", Mtl. M.
Cook, Bill, NYR	RW	Conacher, Charlie, Tor.
Jackson, Harvey, Tor.	LW	Joliat, Aurel, Mtl.
Patrick, Lester, NYR	Coach	Irvin, Dick, Tor.

1930-31

Gardiner, Charlie, Chi.	G	Thompson, "Tiny", Bos.
Shore, Eddie, Bos.	D	Mantha, Sylvio, Mtl.
Clancy, "King", Tor.	D	Johnson, "Ching", NYR
Morenz, Howie, Mtl.	C	Boucher, Frank, NYR
Cook, Bill, NYR	RW	Clapper, "Dit", Bos.
Joliet, Aurel, Mtl.	LW	Cook, "Bun", NYR
Patrick, Lester, NYR	Coach	Irvin, Dick, Chi.

All-Star Game Results

Year	Venue	Score	Coaches	Attendance
1996	Boston	Eastern 5, Western 4	Doug MacLean, Scotty Bowman	17,565
1994	NY Rangers	Eastern 9, Western 8	Jacques Demers, Barry Melrose	18,200
1993	Montreal	Wales 16, Campbell 6	Scotty Bowman, Mike Keenan	17,137
1992	Philadelphia	Campbell 10, Wales 6	Bob Gainey, Scotty Bowman	17,380
1991	Chicago	Campbell 11, Wales 5	John Muckler, Mike Milbury	18,472
1990	Pittsburgh	Wales 12, Campbell 7	Pat Burns, Terry Crisp	16,236
1989	Edmonton	Campbell 9, Wales 5	Glen Sather, Terry O'Reilly	17,503
1988	St. Louis	Wales 6, Campbell 5 OT	Mike Keenan, Glen Sather	17,878
1986	Hartford	Wales 4, Campbell 3 OT	Mike Keenan, Glen Sather	15,100
1985	Calgary	Wales 6, Campbell 4	Al Arbour, Glen Sather	16,825
1984	New Jersey	Wales 7, Campbell 6	Al Arbour, Glen Sather	18,939
1983	NY Islanders	Campbell 9, Wales 3	Roger Neilson, Al Arbour	15,230
1982	Washington	Wales 4, Campbell 2	Al Arbour, Glen Sonmor	18,130
1981	Los Angeles	Campbell 4, Wales 1	Pat Quinn, Scotty Bowman	15,761
1980	Detroit	Wales 6, Campbell 3	Scotty Bowman, Al Arbour	21,002
1978	Buffalo	Wales 3, Campbell 2 OT	Scotty Bowman, Fred Shero	16,433
1977	Vancouver	Wales 4, Campbell 3	Scotty Bowman, Fred Shero	15,607
1976	Philadelphia	Wales 7, Campbell 5	Floyd Smith, Fred Shero	16,436
1975	Montreal	Wales 7, Campbell 1	Bep Guidolin, Fred Shero	16,080
1974	Chicago	West 6, East 4	Billy Reay, Scotty Bowman	16,426
1973	New York	East 5, West 4	Tom Johnson, Billy Reay	16,986
1972	Minnesota	East 3, West 2	Al MacNeil, Billy Reay	15,423
1971	Boston	West 2, East 1	Scotty Bowman, Harry Sinden	14,790
1970	St. Louis	East 4, West 1	Claude Ruel, Scotty Bowman	16,587
1969	Montreal	East 3, West 3	Toe Blake, Scotty Bowman	16,260
1968	Toronto	Toronto 4, All-Stars 3	Punch Imlach, Toe Blake	15,753
1967	Montreal	Montreal 3, All-Stars 0	Toe Blake, Sid Abel	14,284
1965	Montreal	All-Stars 5, Montreal 2	Billy Reay, Toe Blake	13,529
1964	Toronto	All-Stars 3, Toronto 2	Sid Abel, Punch Imlach	14,232
1963	Toronto	All-Stars 3, Toronto 3	Sid Abel, Punch Imlach	14,034
1962	Toronto	Toronto 4, All-Stars 1	Punch Imlach, Rudy Pilous	14,236
1961	Chicago	All-Stars 3, Chicago 1	Sid Abel, Rudy Pilous	14,534
1960	Montreal	All-Stars 2, Montreal 1	Punch Imlach, Toe Blake	13,949
1959	Montreal	Montreal 6, All-Stars 1	Toe Blake, Punch Imlach	13,818
1958	Montreal	Montreal 6, All-Stars 3	Toe Blake, Milt Schmidt	13,989
1957	Montreal	All-Stars 5, Montreal 3	Milt Schmidt, Toe Blake	13,003
1956	Montreal	All-Stars 1, Montreal 1	Jim Skinner, Toe Blake	13,095
1955	Detroit	Detroit 3, All-Stars 1	Jim Skinner, Dick Irvin	10,111
1954	Detroit	All-Stars 2, Detroit 2	King Clancy, Jim Skinner	10,689
1953	Montreal	All-Stars 3, Montreal 1	Lynn Patrick, Dick Irvin	14,153
1952	Detroit	1st team 1, 2nd team 1	Tommy Ivan, Dick Irvin	10,680
1951	Toronto	1st team 2, 2nd team 2	Joe Primeau, Hap Day	11,469
1950	Detroit	Detroit 7, All-Stars 1	Tommy Ivan, Lynn Patrick	9,166
1949	Toronto	All-Stars 3, Toronto 1	Tommy Ivan, Hap Day	13,541
1948	Chicago	All-Stars 3, Toronto 1	Tommy Ivan, Hap Day	12,794
1947	Toronto	All-Stars 4, Toronto 3	Dick Irvin, Hap Day	14,169

There was no All-Star contest during the calendar year of 1966 because the game was moved from the start of season to mid-season. In 1979, the Challenge Cup series between the Soviet Union and Team NHL replaced the All-Star Game. In 1987, Rendez-Vous '87, two games between the Soviet Union and Team NHL replaced the All-Star Game. Rendez-Vous '87 scores: game one, NHL All-Stars 4, Soviet Union 3; game two, Soviet Union 5, NHL All-Stars 3. There was no All-Star Game in 1995 due to a labor disruption.

1995-96 All-Star Game Summary

January 20, 1996 at Boston   Eastern 5, Western 4

PLAYERS ON ICE: **Western Conference** — Belfour, Osgood, Potvin, MacInnis, K. Hatcher, Lidstrom, Chelios, L. Murphy, Coffey, Selanne, Kariya, Nolan, Sundin, Fleury, Hull, Savard, Sakic, Forsberg, Gartner, Weight, Mogilny, Fedorov, Gretzky

Eastern Conference — Brodeur, Vanbiesbrouck, Hasek, Leetch, S. Stevens, Desjardins, Hamrlik, Schneider, Bourque, Turgeon, Neely, Francis, Messier, Bondra, MacTavish, Alfredsson, Verbeek, LeClair, Mellanby, Lemieux, Jagr, Lindros, Shanahan

GOALTENDERS				
	Western:	Belfour	20 minutes	2 goals against
		Osgood	20 minutes	2 goals against
		Potvin	20 minutes	1 goal against
	Eastern:	Brodeur	20 minutes	0 goals against
		Vanbiesbrouck	20 minutes	3 goals against
		Hasek	20 minutes	1 goal against

SUMMARY
First Period

1. Eastern	Lindros	(Leetch, LeClair)	11:05
2. Eastern	Verbeek	(Lemieux, Schneider)	13:49

PENALTIES: Western (too many men) 4:35

Second Period

3. Eastern	Jagr	(Lemieux, Francis)	2:07
4. Western	Hull	(Kariya, Coffey)	5:33
5. Eastern	Shanahan	(Turgeon, Neely)	8:57
6. Western	Coffey	(Fedorov, Mogilny)	11:42
7. Western	Kariya	(Sundin)	17:47

PENALTIES: Eastern (too many men) 15:14

Third Period

8. Western	Selanne		16:31
9. Eastern	Bourque	(Messier, Verbeek)	19:22

PENALTIES: None.

SHOTS ON GOAL BY:

Western Conference	12	7	13	**32**
Eastern Conference	18	15	8	**41**

Attendance: 17,565

Referee: Mark Faucette   Linesmen: Ron Asselstine, Brad Lazarowich

NHL ALL-ROOKIE TEAM

Voting for the NHL All-Rookie Team is conducted among the representatives of the Professional Hockey Writers' Association at the end of the season. The rookie all-star team was first selected for the 1982-83 season.

1995-96

Corey Hirsch, Vancouver	Goal
Ed Jovanovski, Florida	Defense
Kyle McLaren, Boston	Defense
Daniel Alfredsson, Ottawa	Forward
Eric Daze, Chicago	Forward
Petr Sykora, New Jersey	Forward

1993-94

Martin Brodeur, New Jersey	Goal
Chris Pronger, Hartford	Defense
Boris Mironov, Wpg., Edm.	Defense
Jason Arnott, Edmonton	Center
Mikael Renberg, Philadelphia	Wing
Oleg Petrov, Montreal	Wing

1991-92

Dominik Hasek, Chicago	Goal
Nicklas Lidstrom, Detroit	Defense
Vladimir Konstantinov, Detroit	Defense
Kevin Todd, New Jersey	Center
Tony Amonte, NY Rangers	Right Wing
Gilbert Dionne, Montreal	Left Wing

1989-90

Bob Essensa, Winnipeg	Goal
Brad Shaw, Hartford	Defense
Geoff Smith, Edmonton	Defense
Mike Modano, Minnesota	Center
Sergei Makarov, Calgary	Right Wing
Rod Brind'Amour, St. Louis	Left Wing

1994-95

Jim Carey, Washington	Goal
Chris Therien, Philadelphia	Defense
Kenny Jonsson, Toronto	Defense
Peter Forsberg, Quebec	Forward
Jeff Friesen, San Jose	Forward
Paul Kariya, Anaheim	Forward

1992-93

Felix Potvin, Toronto	Goal
Vladimir Malakhov, NY Islanders	Defense
Scott Niedermayer, New Jersey	Defense
Eric Lindros, Philadelphia	Center
Teemu Selanne, Winnipeg	Wing
Joe Juneau, Boston	Wing

1990-91

Ed Belfour, Chicago	Goal
Eric Weinrich, New Jersey	Defense
Rob Blake, Los Angeles	Defense
Sergei Fedorov, Detroit	Center
Ken Hodge, Boston	Wing
Jaromir Jagr, Pittsburgh	Wing

1988-89

Peter Sidorkiewicz, Hartford	Goal
Brian Leetch, NY Rangers	Defense
Zarley Zalapski, Pittsburgh	Defense
Trevor Linden, Vancouver	Center
Tony Granato, NY Rangers	Wing
David Volek, NY Islanders	Wing

1987-88

Darren Pang, Chicago	Goal
Glen Wesley, Boston	Defense
Calle Johansson, Buffalo	Defense
Joe Nieuwendyk, Calgary	Center
Ray Sheppard, Buffalo	Right Wing
Iain Duncan, Winnipeg	Left Wing

1985-86

Patrick Roy, Montreal	Goal
Gary Suter, Calgary	Defense
Dana Murzyn, Hartford	Defense
Mike Ridley, NY Rangers	Center
Kjell Dahlin, Montreal	Right Wing
Wendel Clark, Toronto	Left Wing

1983-84

Tom Barrasso, Buffalo	Goal
Thomas Eriksson, Philadelphia	Defense
Jamie Macoun, Calgary	Defense
Steve Yzerman, Detroit	Center
Hakan Loob, Calgary	Right Wing
Sylvain Turgeon, Hartford	Left Wing

1986-87

Ron Hextall, Philadelphia	Goal
Steve Duchesne, Los Angeles	Defense
Brian Benning, St. Louis	Defense
Jimmy Carson, Los Angeles	Center
Jim Sandlak, Vancouver	Right Wing
Luc Robitaille, Los Angeles	Left Wing

1984-85

Steve Penney, Montreal	Goal
Chris Chelios, Montreal	Defense
Bruce Bell, Quebec	Defense
Mario Lemieux, Pittsburgh	Center
Tomas Sandstrom, NY Rangers	Right Wing
Warren Young, Pittsburgh	Left Wing

1982-83

Pelle Lindbergh, Philadelphia	Goal
Scott Stevens, Washington	Defense
Phil Housley, Buffalo	Defense
Dan Daoust, Montreal/Toronto	Center
Steve Larmer, Chicago	Right Wing
Mats Naslund, Montreal	Left Wing

All-Star Game Records 1947 through 1996

TEAM RECORDS

MOST GOALS, BOTH TEAMS, ONE GAME:
22 — Wales 16, Campbell 6, 1993 at Montreal
19 — Wales 12, Campbell 7, 1990 at Pittsburgh
17 — East 9, West 8, 1994 at NY Rangers
16 — Campbell 11, Wales 5, 1991 at Chicago
— Campbell 10, Wales 6, 1992 at Philadelphia
14 — Campbell 9, Wales 5, 1989 at Edmonton
13 — Wales 7, Campbell 6, 1984 at New Jersey
12 — Campbell 9, Wales 3, 1983 at NY Islanders
— Wales 7, Campbell 5, 1976 at Philadelphia

FEWEST GOALS, BOTH TEAMS, ONE GAME:
  2 — NHL All-Stars 1, Montreal Canadiens 1, 1956 at Montreal
— First Team All-Stars 1, Second Team All-Stars 1, 1952 at Detroit
  3 — West 2, East 1, 1971 at Boston
— Montreal Canadiens 3, NHL All-Stars 0, 1967 at Montreal
— NHL All-Stars 2, Montreal Canadiens 1, 1960 at Montreal

MOST GOALS, ONE TEAM, ONE GAME:
16 — Wales 16, Campbell 6, 1993 at Montreal
12 — Wales 12, Campbell 7, 1990 at Pittsburgh
11 — Campbell 11, Wales 5, 1991 at Chicago
10 — Campbell 10, Wales 6, 1992 at Philadelphia
  9 — Campbell 9, Wales 3, 1983 at NY Islanders
— Campbell 9, Wales 5, 1989 at Edmonton
— East 9, West 8, 1994 at NY Rangers

FEWEST GOALS, ONE TEAM, ONE GAME:
0 — NHL All-Stars 0, Montreal Canadiens 3, 1967 at Montreal
  1 — 17 times (1981, 1975, 1971, 1970, 1962, 1961, 1960, 1959, both teams 1956, 1955, 1953, both teams 1952, 1950, 1949, 1948)

MOST SHOTS, BOTH TEAMS, ONE GAME (SINCE 1955):
102 — 1994 at NY Rangers — East 9 (56 shots)
              West 8 (46 shots)
90 — 1993 at Montreal — Wales 16 (49 shots),
              Campbell 6 (41 shots)
87 — 1990 at Pittsburgh — Wales 12 (45 shots),
              Campbell 7 (42 shots)
83 — 1992 at Philadelphia — Campbell 10 (42 shots),
              Wales 6 (41 shots)
82 — 1991 at Chicago — Campbell 11 (41 shots),
              Wales 5 (41 shots)

FEWEST SHOTS, BOTH TEAMS, ONE GAME (SINCE 1955):
52 — 1978 at Buffalo — Campbell 2 (12 shots)
              Wales 3 (40 shots)
53 — 1960 at Montreal — NHL All-Stars 2 (27 shots)
              Montreal Canadiens 1 (26 shots)
55 — 1956 at Montreal — NHL All-Stars 1 (28 shots)
              Montreal Canadiens 1 (27 shots)
— 1971 at Boston — West 2 (28 shots)
              East 1 (27 shots)

MOST SHOTS, ONE TEAM, ONE GAME (SINCE 1955):
56 — 1994 at NY Rangers — East (9-8 vs. West)
49 — 1993 at Montreal — Wales (16-6 vs. Campbell)
46 — 1994 at NY Rangers — West (8-9 vs. East)
45 — 1990 at Pittsburgh — Wales (12-7 vs. Campbell)
44 — 1955 at Detroit — Detroit Red Wings (3-1 vs. NHL All-Stars)
— 1970 at St. Louis — East (4-1 vs. West)
43 — 1981 at Los Angeles — Campbell (4-1 vs. Wales)

FEWEST SHOTS, ONE TEAM, ONE GAME (SINCE 1955):
12 — 1978 at Buffalo — Campbell (2-3 vs. Wales)
17 — 1970 at St. Louis — West (1-4 vs. East)
23 — 1961 at Chicago — Chicago Black Hawks (1-3 vs. NHL All-Stars)
24 — 1976 at Philadelphia — Campbell (5-7 vs. Wales)

MOST POWER-PLAY GOALS, BOTH TEAMS, ONE GAME (SINCE 1950):
3 — 1953 at Montreal — NHL All-Stars 3 (2 power-play goals),
              Montreal Canadiens 1 (1 power-play goal)
— 1954 at Detroit — NHL All-Stars 2 (1 power-play goal)
              Detroit Red Wings 2 (2 power-play goals)
— 1958 at Montreal — NHL All-Stars 3 (1 power-play goal)
              Montreal Canadiens 6 (2 power-play goals)

FEWEST POWER-PLAY GOALS, BOTH TEAMS, ONE GAME (SINCE 1950):
0 — 15 times (1952, 1959, 1960, 1967, 1968, 1969, 1972, 1973, 1976, 1980, 1981, 1984, 1985, 1992, 1994, 1996)

FASTEST TWO GOALS, BOTH TEAMS, FROM START OF GAME:
37 seconds — 1970 at St. Louis — Jacques Laperriere of East scored at 20 seconds and Dean Prentice of West scored at 37 seconds. Final score: East 4, West 1.
3:37 — 1993 at Montreal — Mike Gartner scored at 3:15 and at 3:37 for Wales. Final score: Wales 16, Campbell 6.
4:08 — 1963 at Toronto — Frank Mahovlich scored for Toronto Maple Leafs at 2:22 of first period and Henri Richard scored at 4:08 for NHL All-Stars. Final score: NHL All-Stars 3, Toronto Maple Leafs 3.

FASTEST TWO GOALS, BOTH TEAMS:
10 seconds — 1976 at Philadelphia — Dennis Ververgaert scored at 4:33 and at 4:43 of third period for Campbell. Final score: Wales 7, Campbell 5.
14 seconds — 1989 at Edmonton. Steve Yzerman and Gary Leeman scored at 17:21 and 17:35 of second period for Campbell. Final score: Campbell 9, Wales 5.
16 seconds — 1990 at Pittsburgh. Kirk Muller of Wales scored at 8:47 of second period and Al MacInnis of Campbell scored at 9:03. Final score: Wales 12, Campbell 7.

FASTEST THREE GOALS, BOTH TEAMS:
1:08 — 1993 at Montreal — all by Wales — Mike Gartner scored at 3:15 and at 3:37 of first period; Peter Bondra scored at 4:23. Final score: Wales 16, Campbell 6.
1:14 — 1994 at NY Rangers — Bob Kudelski scored at 9:46 of first period for East; Sergei Fedorov scored at 10:20 for West; Eric Lindros scored at 11:00 for East. Final score: East 9, West 8.
1:25 — 1992 at Philadelphia — Bryan Trottier scored at 4:03 of third period for Wales; Brian Bellows scored at 4:50 for Campbell; Alexander Mogilny scored at 5:28 for Wales. Final score: Campbell 10, Wales 6.

FASTEST FOUR GOALS, BOTH TEAMS:
3:29 — 1994 at NY Rangers — Jeremy Roenick scored at 7:31 of first period for West; Bob Kudelski scored at 9:46 of first period for East; Sergei Fedorov scored at 10:20 for West; Eric Lindros scored at 11:00 for East. Final score: East 9, West 8.
3:35 — 1994 at NY Rangers — Bob Kudelski scored at 9:46 of first period for East; Sergei Fedorov scored at 10:20 for West; Eric Lindros scored at 11:00 for East; Brendan Shanahan scored at 13:21 for West. Final score: East 9, West 8.
3:40 — 1993 at Montreal — Pierre Turgeon scored at 15:51 of third period for Wales; Teemu Selanne scored at 17:03 for Campbell; Pavel Bure scored at 18:44 and 19:31 for Campbell. Final score: Wales 16, Campbell 6.

FASTEST TWO GOALS, ONE TEAM, FROM START OF GAME:
3:37 — 1993 at Montreal — Wales — Mike Gartner scored at 3:15 and at 3:37. Final socre: Wales 16, Campbell 6.
4:19 — 1980 at Detroit — Wales — Larry Robinson scored at 3:58 and Steve Payne scored at 4:19. Final score: Wales 6, Campbell 3.
4:38 — 1971 at Boston — West — Chico Maki scored at 36 seconds and Bobby Hull scored at 4:38. Final score: West 2, East 1.

FASTEST TWO GOALS, ONE TEAM:
10 seconds — 1976 at Philadelphia — Campbell — Dennis Ververgaert scored at 4:33 and at 4:43 of third period. Final score: Wales 7, Campbell 5.
14 seconds — 1989 at Edmonton — Campbell — Steve Yzerman and Gary Leeman scored at 17:21 and 17:35 of second period. Final score: Campbell 9, Wales 5.
17 seconds — 1993 at Montreal — Wales — Pierre Turgeon scored at 13:05 of first period and Mike Gartner scored at 13:22. Final score: Wales 16, Campbell 6.

FASTEST THREE GOALS, ONE TEAM:
1:08 — 1993 at Montreal — Wales — Mike Gartner scored at 3:15 and 3:37 of first period; Peter Bondra scored at 4:23. Final score: Wales 16, Campbell 6.
1:32 — 1980 at Detroit — Wales — Ron Stackhouse scored at 11:40 of third period; Craig Hartsburg scored at 12:40; Reed Larson scored at 13:12. Final score: Wales 6, Campbell 3.
1:42 — 1993 at Montreal — Wales — Alexander Mogilny scored at 11:40 of first period; Pierre Turgeon scored at 13:05; Mike Gartner scored at 13:22. Final score: Wales 16, Campbell 6.

FASTEST FOUR GOALS, ONE TEAM:
4:19 — 1992 at Philadelphia — Campbell — Brian Bellows scored at 7:40 of second period, Jeremy Roenick scored at 8:13, Theoren Fleury scored at 11:06, Brett Hull scored at 11:59. Final score: Campbell 10, Wales 6.
4:26 — 1980 at Detroit — Wales — Ron Stackhouse scored at 11:40 of third period; Craig Hartsburg scored at 12:40; Reed Larson scored at 13:12; Real Cloutier scored at 16:06. Final score: Wales 6, Campbell 3.
5:34 — 1993 at Montreal — Campbell — Doug Gilmour scored at 13:57 of third period; Teemu Selanne scored at 17:03; Pavel Bure scored at 18:44 and 19:31. Final score: Wales 16, Campbell 6.

MOST GOALS, BOTH TEAMS, ONE PERIOD:
9 — 1990 at Pittsburgh — First Period — Wales (7), Campbell (2). Final score: Wales 12, Campbell 7.
8 — 1992 at Philadelphia — Second period — Campbell (6), Wales (2). Final Score: Campbell 10, Wales 6.
— 1993 at Montreal — Second period — Wales (6), Campbell (2). Final score: Wales 16, Campbell 6.
— 1993 at Montreal — Third period — Wales (4), Campbell (4). Final score: Wales 16, Campbell 6.

MOST GOALS, ONE TEAM, ONE PERIOD:
7 — 1990 at Pittsburgh — First period — Wales. Final score: Wales 12, Campbell 7.
6 — 1983 at NY Islanders — Third period — Campbell.
Final score: Campbell 9, Wales 3.
— 1992 at Philadelphia — Second Period — Campbell.
Final score: Campbell 10, Wales 6.
— 1993 at Montreal — First period — Wales.
Final score: Wales 16, Campbell 6.
— 1993 at Montreal — Second period — Wales.
Final score: Wales 16, Campbell 6.

MOST SHOTS, BOTH TEAMS, ONE PERIOD:
39 — 1994 at NY Rangers — Second period — West (21) East (18).
Final score: East 9, West 8.
36 — 1990 at Pittsburgh — Third period — Campbell (22), Wales (14).
Final score: Wales 12, Campbell 7.
— 1994 at NY Rangers — First period — East (19), West (17).
Final score: East 9, West 8.

MOST SHOTS, ONE TEAM, ONE PERIOD:
22 — 1990 at Pittsburgh — Third period — Campbell.
Final score: Wales 12, Campbell 7.
— 1991 at Chicago — Third Period — Wales.
Final score: Campbell 11, Wales 5.
— 1993 at Montreal — First period — Wales.
Final score: Wales 16, Campbell 6.
20 — 1970 at St. Louis — Third period — East. Final score: East 4, West 1.

FEWEST SHOTS, BOTH TEAMS, ONE PERIOD:
9 — 1971 at Boston — Third period — East (2), West (7).
Final score: West 2, East 1.
— 1980 at Detroit — Second period — Campbell (4), Wales (5).
Final score: Wales 6, Campbell 3.
13 — 1982 at Washington — Third period — Campbell (6), Wales (7).
Final score: Wales 4, Campbell 2.
14 — 1978 at Buffalo — First period — Campbell (7), Wales (7).
Final score: Wales 3, Campbell 2.
— 1986 at Hartford — First period — Campbell (6), Wales (8).
Final score: Wales 4, Campbell 3.

FEWEST SHOTS, ONE TEAM, ONE PERIOD:
2 — 1971 at Boston   Third period   East
Final score: West 2, East 1
— 1978 at Buffalo   Second period   Campbell
Final score: Wales 3, Campbell 2
3 — 1978 at Buffalo   Third period   Campbell
Final score: Wales 3, Campbell 2
4 — 1955 at Detroit   First period   NHL All-Stars
Final score: Detroit Red Wings 3, NHL All-Stars 1
4 — 1980 at Detroit   Second period   Campbell
Final score: Wales 6, Campbell 3

A weary group of NHL All-Stars pose for the camera in the dressing room following their 4-1 loss to the Toronto Maple Leafs in the 16th annual All-Star tilt on October 6, 1962. Note that both Jacques Plante, left, and Glenn Hall, right, who tended goal in the first and second periods respectively, are already out of uniform and ready for the post-game festivities.

INDIVIDUAL RECORDS

Games

MOST GAMES PLAYED:
23 — **Gordie Howe** from 1948 through 1980
15 — Frank Mahovlich from 1959 through 1974
— Wayne Gretzky from 1980 through 1996
14 — Ray Bourque from 1981 through 1996
13 — Jean Beliveau from 1953 through 1969
— Alex Delvecchio from 1953 through 1967
— Doug Harvey from 1951 through 1969
— Maurice Richard from 1947 through 1959
— Paul Coffey from 1982 through 1996

Goals

MOST GOALS (CAREER):
12 — **Wayne Gretzky** in 15GP
10 — Gordie Howe in 23GP
9 — Mario Lemieux in 7GP
8 — Frank Mahovlich in 15GP
7 — Maurice Richard in 13GP
6 — Mike Gartner in 7GP

MOST GOALS, ONE GAME:
4 — **Wayne Gretzky,** Campbell, 1983
— **Mario Lemieux,** Wales, 1990
— **Vince Damphousse,** Campbell, 1991
— **Mike Gartner,** Wales, 1993
3 — Ted Lindsay, Detroit Red Wings, 1950
— Mario Lemieux, Wales, 1988
— Pierre Turgeon, Wales, 1993
2 — Wally Hergesheimer, NHL All-Stars, 1953
— Earl Reibel, Detroit Red Wings, 1955
— Andy Bathgate, NHL All-Stars, 1958
— Maurice Richard, Montreal Canadiens, 1958
— Frank Mahovlich, Toronto Maple Leafs, 1963
— Gordie Howe, NHL All-Stars, 1965
— John Ferguson, Montreal Canadiens, 1967
— Frank Mahovlich, East All-Stars, 1969
— Greg Polis, West All-Stars, 1973
— Syl Apps, Wales, 1975
— Dennis Ververgaert, Campbell, 1976
— Richard Martin, Wales, 1977
— Lanny McDonald, Wales, 1977
— Mike Bossy, Wales, 1982
— Pierre Larouche, Wales, 1984
— Mario Lemieux, Wales, 1985
— Brian Propp, Wales, 1986
— Luc Robitaille, Campbell, 1988
— Joe Mullen, Campbell, 1989
— Pierre Turgeon, Wales, 1990
— Kirk Muller, Wales, 1990
— Luc Robitaille, Campbell, 1990
— Pat LaFontaine, Wales, 1991
— Brett Hull, Campbell, 1992
— Theoren Fleury, Campbell, 1992
— Rick Tocchet, Wales, 1993
— Pavel Bure, Campbell, 1993
— Sandis Ozolinsh, West All-Stars, 1994
— Brendan Shanahan, West All-Stars, 1994
— Bob Kudelski, East All-Stars, 1994
— Alexei Yashin, East All-Stars, 1994

MOST GOALS, ONE PERIOD:
4 — **Wayne Gretzky,** Campbell, Third period, 1983
3 — Mario Lemieux, Wales, First period, 1990
— Vince Damphousse, Campbell, Third period, 1991
— Mike Gartner, Wales, First period, 1993
2 — Ted Lindsay, Detroit Red Wings, First period, 1950
— Wally Hergesheimer, NHL All-Stars, First period, 1953
— Andy Bathgate, NHL All-Stars, Third period, 1958
— Frank Mahovlich, Toronto Maple Leafs, First period, 1963
— Dennis Ververgaert, Campbell, Third period, 1976
— Richard Martin, Wales, Third period, 1977
— Pierre Turgeon, Wales, First period, 1990
— Luc Robitaille, Campbell, Third period, 1990
— Theoren Fleury, Campbell, Second period, 1992
— Brett Hull, Campbell, Second period, 1992
— Rick Tocchet, Wales, Second period, 1993
— Pavel Bure, Campbell, Third period, 1993

Assists

MOST ASSISTS (CAREER):
11 — **Ray Bourque** in 14GP
10 — Adam Oates in 4GP
— Joe Sakic in 6GP
9 — Gordie Howe in 23GP
— Larry Robinson in 10GP
— Mark Messier in 11GP
8 — Mario Lemieux in 7GP
— Paul Coffey in 13GP

MOST ASSISTS, ONE GAME:
5 — Mats Naslund, Wales, 1988
4 — Ray Bourque, Wales, 1985
— Adam Oates, Campbell, 1991
— Adam Oates, Wales, 1993
— Mark Recchi, Wales, 1993
— Pierre Turgeon, East All-Stars, 1994
3 — Dickie Moore, Montreal Canadiens, 1958
— Doug Harvey, Montreal Canadiens, 1959
— Guy Lafleur, Wales, 1975
— Pete Mahovlich, Wales, 1976
— Mark Messier, Campbell, 1983
— Rick Vaive, Campbell, 1984
— Mark Johnson, Wales, 1984
— Don Maloney, Wales, 1984
— Mike Krushelnyski, Campbell, 1985
— Mario Lemieux, Wales, 1988
— Brett Hull, Campbell, 1990
— Luc Robitaille, Campbell, 1992
— Joe Sakic, Wales, 1993

MOST ASSISTS, ONE PERIOD:
4 — Adam Oates, Wales, First period, 1993
3 — Mark Messier, Campbell, Third period, 1983

Points

MOST POINTS (CAREER):
19 — Gordie Howe (10G-9A in 23GP)
— Wayne Gretzky (12G-7A in 15GP)
17 — Mario Lemieux (9G-8A in 7GP)
14 — Ray Bourque (3G-11A in 14GP)
13 — Frank Mahovlich (8G-5A in 15GP)
12 — Mark Messier (3G-9A in 11GP)
— Pierre Turgeon (5G-7A in 4GP)
11 — Adam Oates (1G-10A in 4GP)
— Joe Sakic (1G-10A in 6GP)

MOST POINTS, ONE GAME:
6 — Mario Lemieux, Wales, 1988 (3G-3A)
5 — Mats Naslund, Wales, 1988 (5A)
— Adam Oates, Campbell, 1991 (1G-4A)
— Mike Gartner, Wales, 1993 (4G-1A)
— Mark Recchi, Wales, 1993 (1G-4A)
— Pierre Turgeon, Wales, 1993 (3G-2A)

MOST POINTS, ONE PERIOD:
4 — Wayne Gretzky, Campbell, Third period, 1983 (4G)
— Mike Gartner, Wales, First period, 1993 (3G-1A)
— Adam Oates, Wales, First period, 1993 (4A)
3 — Gordie Howe, NHL All-Stars, Second period, 1965 (1G-2A)
— Pete Mahovlich, Wales, First period, 1976 (1G-2A)
— Mark Messier, Campbell, Third period, 1983 (3A)
— Mario Lemieux, Wales, Second period, 1988 (1G-2A)
— Mario Lemieux, Wales, First period, 1990 (3G)
— Vince Damphousse, Campbell, Third period, 1991 (3G)
— Mark Recchi, Wales, Second period, 1993 (1G-2A)

Power-Play Goals

MOST POWER-PLAY GOALS:
6 — Gordie Howe in 23GP
3 — Bobby Hull in 12GP
2 — Maurice Richard in 13GP

Fastest Goals

FASTEST GOAL FROM START OF GAME:
19 seconds — Ted Lindsay, Detroit Red Wings, 1950
20 seconds — Jacques Laperriere, East All-Stars, 1970
21 seconds — Mario Lemieux, Wales, 1990
36 seconds — Chico Maki, West All-Stars, 1971
37 seconds — Dean Prentice, West All-Stars, 1970

FASTEST GOAL FROM START OF A PERIOD:
19 seconds — Ted Lindsay, Detroit Red Wings, 1950 (first period)
— Rick Tocchet, Wales, 1993 (second period)
20 seconds — Jacques Laperriere, East, 1970 (first period)
21 seconds — Mario Lemieux, Wales, 1990 (first period)
26 seconds — Wayne Gretzky, Campbell, 1982 (second period)
28 seconds — Maurice Richard, NHL All-Stars, 1947 (third period)

FASTEST TWO GOALS (ONE PLAYER) FROM START OF GAME:
3:37 — Mike Gartner, Wales, 1993, at 3:15 and 3:37.
5:25 — Wally Hergesheimer, NHL All-Stars, 1953, at 4:06 and 5:25.
12:11 — Frank Mahovlich, Toronto, 1963, at 2:22 and 12:11.

FASTEST TWO GOALS (ONE PLAYER) FROM START OF A PERIOD:
3:37 — Mike Gartner, Wales, 1993, at 3:15 and 3:37 of first period.
4:43 — Dennis Ververgaert, Campbell, 1976, at 4:33 and 4:43 of third period.
4:57 — Rick Tocchet, Wales, 1993, at :19 and 4:57 of second period.

FASTEST TWO GOALS (ONE PLAYER):
10 seconds — Dennis Ververgaert, Campbell, 1976. Scored at 4:33 and 4:43 of third period.
22 seconds — Mike Gartner, Wales, 1993. Scored at 3:15 and 3:37 of first period.
47 seconds — Pavel Bure, Campbell, 1993. Scored at 18:44 and 19:31 of third period.

Penalties

MOST PENALTY MINUTES:
27 — Gordie Howe in 23GP
21 — Gus Mortson in 9GP
16 — Harry Howell in 7GP

Goaltenders

MOST GAMES PLAYED:
13 — Glenn Hall from 1955-1969
11 — Terry Sawchuk from 1950-1968
8 — Jacques Plante from 1956-1970
6 — Tony Esposito from 1970-1980
— Ed Giacomin from 1967-1973
— Grant Fuhr from 1982-1989

MOST MINUTES PLAYED:
467 — Terry Sawchuk in 11GP
421 — Glenn Hall in 13GP
370 — Jacques Plante in 8GP
209 — Turk Broda in 4GP
182 — Ed Giacomin in 6GP
177 — Grant Fuhr in 6GP
165 — Tony Esposito in 6GP

MOST GOALS AGAINST:
22 — Glenn Hall in 13GP
21 — Mike Vernon in 5GP
19 — Terry Sawchuk in 11GP
18 — Jacques Plante in 8GP

BEST GOALS-AGAINST-AVERAGE AMONG THOSE WITH AT LEAST TWO GAMES PLAYED:
0.68 — Gilles Villemure in 3GP
1.02 — Frank Brimsek in 2GP
1.59 — Johnny Bower in 4GP
1.64 — Lorne ''Gump'' Worsley in 4GP
1.98 — Gerry McNeil in 3GP
2.03 — Don Edwards in 2GP
2.44 — Terry Sawchuk in 11GP

Leaf defender Allan Stanley battles Gordie Howe for a loose puck during the 1962 All-Star Game in Toronto.

Hockey Hall of Fame

(Year of induction is listed after each Honored Members name)

Location: BCE Place, at the corner of Front and Yonge Streets in the heart of downtown Toronto. Easy access from all major highways running into Toronto. Close to TTC and Union Station.

Telephone: administration (416) 360-7735; information (416) 360-7765.

Summer and Christmas/March break hours: Monday to Saturday 9:30 a.m. to 6 p.m.; Sunday 10:00 a.m. to 6 p.m.

Fall/Winter/Spring hours (except Christmas/March break): Monday to Friday 10 a.m. to 5 p.m.; Saturday 9:30 a.m. to 6 p.m.; Sunday 10:30 a.m. to 5 p.m. The Hockey Hall of Fame can be booked for private functions after hours.

History: The Hockey Hall of Fame was established in 1943. Members were first honored in 1945. On August 26, 1961, the Hockey Hall of Fame opened its doors to the public in a building located on the grounds of the Canadian National Exhibition in Toronto. The Hockey Hall of Fame relocated to its new site at BCE Place and welcomed the hockey world on June 18, 1993.

Honor Roll: There are 304 Honored Members in the Hockey Hall of Fame. 207 have been inducted as players, 84 as builders and 13 as Referees/Linesmen. In addition, there are 53 media honorees.

Founding Sponsors: Special thanks to Blockbuster Video, Bell Canada, Coca-Cola Canada, Household Finance, Ford of Canada, Imperial Oil, Molson Breweries, London Life, TSN/RDS and The Toronto Sun.

PLAYERS

Abel, Sidney Gerald 1969
* Adams, John James "Jack" 1959
Apps, Charles Joseph Sylvanus "Syl" 1961
Armstrong, George Edward 1975
* Bailey, Irvine Wallace "Ace" 1975
* Bain, Donald H. "Dan" 1945
* Baker, Hobart "Hobey" 1945
Barber, William Charles "Bill" 1990
* Barry, Martin J. "Marty" 1965
Bathgate, Andrew James "Andy" 1978
Béliveau, Jean Arthur 1972
* Benedict, Clinton S. 1965
* Bentley, Douglas Wagner 1964
* Bentley, Maxwell H. L. 1966
* Blake, Hector "Toe" 1966
Boivin, Leo Joseph 1986
* Boon, Richard R. "Dickie" 1952
Bossy, Michael 1991
Bouchard, Emile Joseph "Butch" 1966
* Boucher, Frank 1958
* Boucher, George "Buck" 1960
Bower, John William 1976
* Bowie, Russell 1945
Brimsek, Francis Charles 1966
* Broadbent, Harry L. "Punch" 1962
* Broda, Walter Edward "Turk" 1967
Bucyk, John Paul 1981
* Burch, Billy 1974
* Cameron, Harold Hugh "Harry" 1962
Cheevers, Gerald Michael "Gerry" 1985
* Clancy, Francis Michael "King" 1958
* Clapper, Aubrey "Dit" 1947
Clarke, Robert "Bobby" 1987
* Cleghorn, Sprague 1958
* Colville, Neil MacNeil 1967
* Conacher, Charles W. 1961
* Conacher, Lionel Pretoria 1994
* Connell, Alex 1958
* Cook, Fred "Bun" 1995
* Cook, William Osser 1952
* Coulter, Arthur Edmund 1974
Cournoyer, Yvan Serge 1982
* Cowley, William Mailes 1968
* Crawford, Samuel Russell "Rusty" 1962
* Darragh, John Proctor "Jack" 1962
* Davidson, Allan M. "Scotty" 1950
* Day, Clarence Henry "Hap" 1961
Delvecchio, Alex 1977
* Denneny, Cyril "Cy" 1959
Dionne, Marcel 1992
* Drillon, Gordon Arthur 1975
* Drinkwater, Charles Graham 1950

Dryden, Kenneth Wayne 1983
Dumart, Woodrow "Woody" 1992
* Dunderdale, Thomas 1974
* Durnan, William Ronald 1964
* Dutton, Mervyn A. "Red" 1958
* Dye, Cecil Henry "Babe" 1970
Esposito, Anthony James "Tony" 1988
Esposito, Philip Anthony 1984
* Farrell, Arthur F. 1965
Flaman, Ferdinand Charles "Fern" 1990
* Foyston, Frank 1958
* Frederickson, Frank 1958
Gadsby, William Alexander 1970
Gainey, Bob 1992
* Gardiner, Charles Robert "Chuck" 1945
* Gardiner, Herbert Martin "Herb" 1958
* Gardner, James Henry "Jimmy" 1962
Geoffrion, Jos. A. Bernard "Boom Boom" 1972
* Gerard, Eddie 1945
Giacomin, Edward "Eddie" 1987
Gilbert, Rodrigue Gabriel "Rod" 1982
* Gilmour, Hamilton Livingstone "Billy" 1962
* Goheen, Frank Xavier "Moose" 1952
Goodfellow, Ebenezer R. "Ebbie" 1963
* Grant, Michael "Mike" 1950
* Green, Wilfred "Shorty" 1962
* Griffis, Silas Seth "Si" 1950
* Hainsworth, George 1961
Hall, Glenn Henry 1975
* Hall, Joseph Henry 1961
* Harvey, Douglas Norman 1973
* Hay, George 1958
* Hern, William Milton "Riley" 1962
* Hextall, Bryan Aldwyn 1969
* Holmes, Harry "Hap" 1972
* Hooper, Charles Thomas "Tom" 1962
Horner, George Reginald "Red" 1965
* Horton, Miles Gilbert "Tim" 1977
Howe, Gordon 1972
* Howe, Sydney Harris 1965
Howell, Henry Vernon "Harry" 1979
Hull, Robert Marvin 1983
* Hutton, John Bower "Bouse" 1962
* Hyland, Harry M. 1962
* Irvin, James Dickenson "Dick" 1958
* Jackson, Harvey "Busher" 1971
* Johnson, Ernest "Moose" 1952
* Johnson, Ivan "Ching" 1958
Johnson, Thomas Christian 1970
* Joliat, Aurel 1947
* Keats, Gordon "Duke" 1958
Kelly, Leonard Patrick "Red" 1969

Kennedy, Theodore Samuel "Teeder" 1966
Keon, David Michael 1986
Lach, Elmer James 1966
Lafleur, Guy Damien 1988
* Lalonde, Edouard Charles "Newsy" 1950
Laperriere, Jacques 1987
Lapointe, Guy 1993
Laprade, Edgar 1993
* Laviolette, Jean Baptiste "Jack" 1962
* Lehman, Hugh 1958
Lemaire, Jacques Gerard 1984
* LeSueur, Percy 1961
* Lewis, Herbert A. 1989
Lindsay, Robert Blake Theodore "Ted" 1966
Lumley, Harry 1980
* MacKay, Duncan "Mickey" 1952
Mahovlich, Frank William 1981
* Malone, Joseph "Joe" 1950
* Mantha, Sylvio 1960
* Marshall, John "Jack" 1965
* Maxwell, Fred G. "Steamer" 1962
McDonald, Lanny 1992
* McGee, Frank 1945
* McGimsie, William George "Billy" 1962
* McNamara, George 1958
Mikita, Stanley 1983
Moore, Richard Winston 1974
* Moran, Patrick Joseph "Paddy" 1958
* Morenz, Howie 1945
* Mosienko, William "Billy" 1965
* Nighbor, Frank 1947
* Noble, Edward Reginald "Reg" 1962
* O'Connor, Herbert William "Buddy" 1988
* Oliver, Harry 1967
Olmstead, Murray Bert "Bert" 1985
Orr, Robert Gordon 1979
Parent, Bernard Marcel 1984
Park, Douglas Bradford "Brad" 1988
* Patrick, Joseph Lynn 1980
* Patrick, Lester 1947
Perreault, Gilbert 1990
* Phillips, Tommy 1945
Pilote, Joseph Albert Pierre Paul 1975
* Pitre, Didier "Pit" 1962
* Plante, Joseph Jacques Omer 1978
Potvin, Denis 1991
* Pratt, Walter "Babe" 1966
* Primeau, A. Joseph 1963
Pronovost, Joseph René Marcel 1978
Pulford, Bob 1991
* Pulford, Harvey 1945
Quackenbush, Hubert George "Bill" 1976

BUILDERS

* Adams, Charles 1960
* Adams, Weston W. 1972
* Ahearn, Thomas Franklin "Frank" 1962
* Ahearne, John Francis "Bunny" 1977
* Allan, Sir Montagu (C.V.O.) 1945
  Allen, Keith 1992
* Ballard, Harold Edwin 1977
* Bauer, Father David 1989
* Bickell, John Paris 1978
  Bowman, Scott 1991
* Brown, George V. 1961
* Brown, Walter A. 1962
* Buckland, Frank 1975
  Butterfield, Jack Arlington 1980
* Calder, Frank 1947
* Campbell, Angus D. 1964
* Campbell, Clarence Sutherland 1966
* Cattarinich, Joseph 1977
* Dandurand, Joseph Viateur "Leo" 1963
  Dilio, Francis Paul 1964
* Dudley, George S. 1958
* Dunn, James A. 1968
  Eagleson, Robert Alan 1989
  Francis, Emile 1982
* Gibson, Dr. John L. "Jack" 1976
* Gorman, Thomas Patrick "Tommy" 1963
* Griffiths, Frank A. 1993
* Hanley, William 1986
* Hay, Charles 1974
* Hendy, James C. 1968
* Hewitt, Foster 1965
* Hewitt, William Abraham 1947
* Hume, Fred J. 1962
* Imlach, George "Punch" 1984
  Ivan, Thomas N. 1974
* Jennings, William M. 1975
* Johnson, Bob 1992
* Juckes, Gordon W. 1979
* Kilpatrick, Gen. John Reed 1960
* Knox, Seymour H. III 1993
* Leader, George Alfred 1969
  LeBel, Robert 1970
* Lockhart, Thomas F. 1965
* Loicq, Paul 1961
* Mariucci, John 1985
  Mathers, Frank 1992
* McLaughlin, Major Frederic 1963
* Milford, John "Jake" 1984
  Molson, Hon. Hartland de Montarville 1973
* Nelson, Francis 1947
* Norris, Bruce A. 1969
* Norris, Sr., James 1958
* Norris, James Dougan 1962
* Northey, William M. 1947
* O'Brien, John Ambrose 1962
  O'Neill, Brian 1994
  Page, Fred 1993
* Patrick, Frank 1958
* Pickard, Allan W. 1958
* Pilous, Rudy 1985
  Poile, Norman "Bud" 1990
  Pollock, Samuel Patterson Smyth 1978
* Raymond, Sen. Donat 1958
* Robertson, John Ross 1947
* Robinson, Claude C. 1947
* Ross, Philip D. 1976
  Sabetzki, Dr. Gunther 1995
* Selke, Frank J. 1960
  Sinden, Harry James 1983
* Smith, Frank D. 1962
* Smythe, Conn 1958
  Snider, Edward M. 1988
* Stanley of Preston, Lord (G.C.B.) 1945
* Sutherland, Cap. James T. 1947
* Tarasov, Anatoli V. 1974
  Torrey, Bill 1995
* Turner, Lloyd 1958
* Tutt, William Thayer 1978
* Voss, Carl Potter 1974
* Waghorn, Fred C. 1961
* Wirtz, Arthur Michael 1971
  Wirtz, William W. "Bill" 1976
  Ziegler, John A. Jr. 1987

REFEREES/LINESMEN

  Armstrong, Neil 1991
  Ashley, John George 1981
  Chadwick, William L. 1964
  D'Amico, John 1993
* Elliott, Chaucer 1961
* Hayes, George William 1988
* Hewitson, Robert W. 1963
* Ion, Fred J. "Mickey" 1961
  Pavelich, Matt 1987
* Rodden, Michael J. "Mike" 1962
* Smeaton, J. Cooper 1961
  Storey, Roy Alvin "Red" 1967
  Udvari, Frank Joseph 1973

* Rankin, Frank 1961
  Ratelle, Joseph Gilbert Yvan Jean "Jean" 1985
  Rayner, Claude Earl "Chuck" 1973
  Reardon, Kenneth Joseph 1966
  Richard, Joseph Henri 1979
  Richard, Joseph Henri Maurice "Rocket" 1961
* Richardson, George Taylor 1950
* Roberts, Gordon 1971
  Robinson, Larry 1995
* Ross, Arthur Howie 1945
* Russel, Blair 1965
* Russell, Ernest 1965
* Ruttan, J.D. "Jack" 1962
  Savard, Serge A. 1986
* Sawchuk, Terrance Gordon "Terry" 1971
* Scanlan, Fred 1965
  Schmidt, Milton Conrad "Milt" 1961
* Schriner, David "Sweeney" 1962
* Seibert, Earl Walter 1963
* Seibert, Oliver Levi 1961
* Shore, Edward W. "Eddie" 1947
  Shutt, Stephen 1993
* Siebert, Albert C. "Babe" 1964
* Simpson, Harold Edward "Bullet Joe" 1962
  Sittler, Darryl Glen 1989
* Smith, Alfred E. 1962
  Smith, Clint 1991
* Smith, Reginald "Hooley" 1972
* Smith, Thomas James 1973
  Smith, William John "Billy" 1993
  Stanley, Allan Herbert 1981
* Stanley, Russell "Barney" 1962
* Stewart, John Sherratt "Black Jack" 1964
* Stewart, Nelson "Nels" 1962
* Stuart, Bruce 1961
* Stuart, Hod 1945
* Taylor, Frederic "Cyclone" (O.B.E.) 1947
* Thompson, Cecil R. "Tiny" 1959
  Tretiak, Vladislav 1989
* Trihey, Col. Harry J. 1950
  Ullman, Norman V. Alexander "Norm" 1982
* Vezina, Georges 1945
* Walker, John Phillip "Jack" 1960
* Walsh, Martin "Marty" 1962
* Watson, Harry E. 1962
* Watson, Harry 1994
* Weiland, Ralph "Cooney" 1971
* Westwick, Harry 1962
* Whitcroft, Fred 1962
* Wilson, Gordon Allan "Phat" 1962
  Worsley, Lorne John "Gump" 1980
* Worters, Roy 1969

Elmer Ferguson Memorial Award Winners

In recognition of distinguished members of the newspaper profession whose words have brought honor to journalism and to hockey. Selected by the Professional Hockey Writers' Association.

* Barton, Charlie, Buffalo-Courier Express 1985
* Beauchamp, Jacques, Montreal Matin/Journal de Montréal 1984
* Brennan, Bill, Detroit News 1987
* Burchard, Jim, New York World Telegram 1984
* Burnett, Red, Toronto Star 1984
* Carroll, Dink, Montreal Gazette 1984
  Coleman, Jim, Southam Newspapers 1984
* Damata, Ted, Chicago Tribune 1984
  Delano, Hugh, New York Post 1991
  Desjardins, Marcel, Montréal La Presse 1984
  Dulmage, Jack, Windsor Star 1984
  Dunnell, Milt, Toronto Star 1984
* Ferguson, Elmer, Montreal Herald/Star 1984
  Fisher, Red, Montreal Star/Gazette 1985
* Fitzgerald, Tom, Boston Globe 1984
  Frayne, Trent, Toronto Telegram/Globe and Mail/ Sun 1984
  Gatecliff, Jack, St. Catherines Standard 1995
  Gross, George, Toronto Telegram/Sun 1985
  Johnston, Dick, Buffalo News 1986
* Laney, Al, New York Herald-Tribune 1984
  Larochelle, Claude, Le Soleil 1989
  L'Esperance, Zotique, Journal de Montréal/ le Petit Journal 1985
* Mayer, Charles, le Journal de Montréal/la Patrie 1985
  MacLeod, Rex, Toronto Globe and Mail/Star 1987
  Monahan, Leo, Boston Daily Record/ Record-American/Herald American 1986
  Moriarty, Tim, UPI/Newsday 1986
* Nichols, Joe, New York Times 1984
* O'Brien, Andy, Weekend Magazine 1985
  Orr, Frank, Toronto Star 1989
  Olan, Ben, New York Associated Press 1987
* O'Meara, Basil, Montreal Star 1984
  Proudfoot, Jim, Toronto Star 1988
  Raymond, Bertrand, le Journal de Montréal 1990
  Rosa, Fran, Boston Globe 1987
  Strachan, Al, Globe and Mail/Toronto Sun 1993
* Vipond, Jim, Toronto Globe and Mail 1984
  Walter, Lewis, Detroit Times 1984
  Young, Scott, Toronto Globe and Mail/Telegram 1988

Foster Hewitt Memorial Award Winners

In recognition of members of the radio and television industry who made outstanding contributions to their profession and the game during their career in hockey broadcasting. Selected by the NHL Broadcasters' Association.

  Cusick, Fred, Boston 1984
  Darling, Ted, Buffalo 1994
* Gallivan, Danny, Montreal 1984
* Hewitt, Foster, Toronto 1984
  Irvin, Dick, Montreal 1988
* Kelly, Dan, St. Louis 1989
  Lecavelier, René, Montreal 1984
  Lynch, Budd, Detroit 1985
  Martyn, Bruce, Detroit 1991
  McDonald, Jiggs, Los Angeles, Atlanta, NY Islanders 1990
  McFarlane, Brian, Hockey Night in Canada
* McKnight, Wes, Toronto 1986
  Pettit, Lloyd, Chicago 1986
  Robson, Jim, Vancouver 1992
  Shaver, Al, Minnesota 1993
* Smith, Doug, Montreal 1985
  Wilson, Bob, Boston 1987

* Deceased

United States Hockey Hall of Fame

The United States Hockey Hall of Fame is located in Eveleth, Minnesota, 60 miles north of Duluth, on Highway 53. The facility is open Monday to Saturday 9 a.m. to 5 p.m. and Sundays 11 a.m to 5 p.m.; Adult $3.00; Seniors $2.00; Juniors 13-17 $2.00; and Children 6-12 $1.75; Children under 6 free. Group rates available.

The Hall was dedicated and opened on June 21, 1973, largely as the result of the work of D. Kelly Campbell, Chairman of the Eveleth Civic Association's Project H Committee. There are now 89 enshrinees consisting of 54 players, 19 coaches, 16 administrators, and one referee. New members are inducted annually in October and must have made a significant contribution toward hockey in the United States through the vehicle of their careers. Support for the Hall comes from sponsorship and membership programs, grants from the hockey community, and government agencies.

PLAYERS

* Abel, Clarence "Taffy"
* Baker, Hobart "Hobey"
Bartholome, Earl
Bessone, Peter
Blake, Robert
Boucha, Henry
Brimsek, Frank
Cavanough, Joe
* Chaisson, Ray
Chase, John P.
Christian, Roger
Christian, William "Bill"
Cleary, Robert
Cleary, William
* Conroy, Anthony
Dahlstrom, Carl "Cully"
DesJardins, Victor
Desmond, Richard
* Dill, Robert
Everett, Doug
Ftorek, Robbie
* Garrison, John B.
Garrity, Jack
* Goheen, Frank "Moose"
Grant, Wally
Harding, Austin "Austie"
* Iglehart, Stewart
Johnson, Virgil
* Karakas, Mike
Kirrane, Jack
* Lane, Myles J.
Langevin, David R.
* Linder, Joseph
* LoPresti, Sam L.
* Mariucci, John
Matchefts, John
Mayasich, John
McCartan, Jack
Moe, William
Morrow, Ken
* Moseley, Fred
* Murray, Hugh "Muzz" Sr.
* Nelson, Hubert "Hub"
Olson , Eddie
* Owen, Jr., George
* Palmer, Winthrop
Paradise, Robert
Purpur, Clifford "Fido"
Riley, William
* Romnes, Elwin "Doc"
Rondeau, Richard
* Williams, Thomas
* Winters, Frank "Coddy"
* Yackel, Ken

COACHES

* Almquist, Oscar
Bessone, Amo
Brooks, Herbert
Ceglarski, Len
* Fullerton, James
* Gordon, Malcolm K.
Harkness, Nevin D. "Ned"
Heyliger, Victor
Ikola, Willard
* Jeremiah, Edward J.
* Johnson, Bob
* Kelley, John "Snooks"
Kelley, John H. "Jack"
Pleban, John "Connie"
Riley, Jack
* Ross, Larry
* Thompson, Clifford, R.
* Stewart, William
* Winsor, Alfred "Ralph"

ADMINISTRATORS

* Brown, George V.
* Brown, Walter A.
Bush, Walter
Clark, Donald
Claypool, James
* Gibson, J.C. "Doc"
* Jennings, William M.
* Kahler, Nick
* Lockhart, Thomas F.
Marvin, Cal
Ridder, Robert
Schulz, Charles M.
Trumble, Harold
* Tutt, William Thayer
Wirtz, William W. "Bill"
* Wright, Lyle Z.

REFEREE

Chadwick, William

*Deceased

Although he never played professionally, Francis Xavier "Moose" Goheen was one of the best players of his era. A member of both the Hockey Hall of Fame and the U.S. Hockey Hall of Fame, he was one of the first players to wear a helmet.

Results

1996 Stanley Cup Playoffs

CONFERENCE QUARTER-FINALS
(Best-of-seven series)

Eastern Conference

Series 'A'

Tue. Apr. 16	Tampa Bay 3	at	Philadelphia 7
Thu. Apr. 18	Tampa Bay 2	at	Philadelphia 1 OT
Sun. Apr. 21	Philadelphia 4	at	Tampa Bay 5 OT
Tue. Apr. 23	Philadelphia 4	at	Tampa Bay 1
Thu. Apr. 25	Tampa Bay 1	at	Philadelphia 4
Sat. Apr. 27	Philadelphia 6	at	Tampa Bay 1

Philadelphia won series 4-2

Series 'B'

Wed. Apr. 17	Washington 6	at	Pittsburgh 4
Fri. Apr. 19	Washington 5	at	Pittsburgh 3
Mon. Apr. 22	Pittsburgh 4	at	Washington 1
Wed. Apr. 24	Pittsburgh 3	at	Washington 2 OT
Fri. Apr. 26	Washington 1	at	Pittsburgh 4
Sun. Apr. 28	Pittsburgh 3	at	Washington 2

Pittsburgh won series 4-2

Series 'C'

Tue. Apr. 16	Montreal 3	at	NY Rangers 2 OT
Thu. Apr. 18	Montreal 5	at	NY Rangers 3
Sun. Apr. 21	NY Rangers 2	at	Montreal 1
Tue. Apr. 23	NY Rangers 4	at	Montreal 3
Fri. Apr. 26	Montreal 2	at	NY Rangers 3
Sun. Apr. 28	NY Rangers 5	at	Montreal 3

NY Rangers won series 4-2

Series 'D'

Wed. Apr. 17	Boston 3	at	Florida 6
Mon. Apr. 22	Boston 2	at	Florida 6
Wed. Apr. 24	Florida 4	at	Boston 2
Thu. Apr. 25	Florida 2	at	Boston 6
Sat. Apr. 27	Boston 3	at	Florida 4

Florida won series 4-1

Western Conference

Series 'E'

Wed. Apr. 17	Winnipeg 1	at	Detroit 4
Fri. Apr. 19	Winnipeg 0	at	Detroit 4
Sun. Apr. 21	Detroit 1	at	Winnipeg 4
Tue. Apr. 23	Detroit 6	at	Winnipeg 1
Fri. Apr. 26	Winnipeg 3	at	Detroit 1
Sun. Apr. 28	Detroit 4	at	Winnipeg 1

Detroit won series 4-2

Series 'F'

Tue. Apr. 16	Vancouver 2	at	Colorado 5
Thu. Apr. 18	Vancouver 5	at	Colorado 4
Sat. Apr. 20	Colorado 4	at	Vancouver 0
Mon. Apr. 22	Colorado 3	at	Vancouver 4
Thu. Apr. 25	Vancouver 4	at	Colorado 5 OT
Sat. Apr. 27	Colorado 3	at	Vancouver 2

Colorado won series 4-2

Series 'G'

Wed. Apr. 17	Calgary 1	at	Chicago 4
Fri. Apr. 19	Calgary 0	at	Chicago 3
Sun. Apr. 21	Chicago 7	at	Calgary 5
Tue. Apr. 23	Chicago 2	at	Calgary 1 OT

Chicago won series 4-0

Series 'H'

Tue. Apr. 16	St. Louis 3	at	Toronto 1
Thu. Apr. 18	St. Louis 4	at	Toronto 5 OT
Sun. Apr. 21	Toronto 2	at	St. Louis 3 OT
Tue. Apr. 23	Toronto 1	at	St. Louis 5
Thu. Apr. 25	St. Louis 4	at	Toronto 5 OT
Sat. Apr. 27	Toronto 1	at	St. Louis 2

St. Louis won series 4-2

CONFERENCE SEMI-FINALS
(Best-of-seven series)

Eastern Conference

Series 'I'

Thu. May 2	Florida 2	at	Philadelphia 0
Sat. May 4	Florida 2	at	Philadelphia 3
Tue. May 7	Philadelphia 3	at	Florida 1
Thu. May 9	Philadelphia 3	at	Florida 4 OT
Sun. May 12	Florida 2	at	Philadelphia 1 OT
Tue. May 14	Philadelphia 1	at	Florida 4

Florida won series 4-2

Series 'J'

Fri. May 3	NY Rangers 3	at	Pittsburgh 4
Sun. May 5	NY Rangers 6	at	Pittsburgh 3
Tue. May 7	Pittsburgh 3	at	NY Rangers 2
Thu. May 9	Pittsburgh 4	at	NY Rangers 1
Sat. May 11	NY Rangers 3	at	Pittsburgh 7

Pittsburgh won series 4-1

Western Conference

Series 'K'

Fri. May 3	St. Louis 2	at	Detroit 3
Sun. May 5	St. Louis 3	at	Detroit 8
Wed. May 8	Detroit 4	at	St. Louis 5 OT
Fri. May 10	Detroit 0	at	St. Louis 1
Sun. May 12	St. Louis 3	at	Detroit 2
Tue. May 14	Detroit 4	at	St. Louis 2
Thu. May 16	St. Louis 0	at	Detroit 1 OT

Detroit won series 4-3

Series 'L'

Thu. May 2	Chicago 3	at	Colorado 2 OT
Sat. May 4	Chicago 1	at	Colorado 5
Mon. May 6	Colorado 3	at	Chicago 4 OT
Wed. May 8	Colorado 3	at	Chicago 2 OT
Sat. May 11	Chicago 1	at	Colorado 4
Mon. May 13	Colorado 4	at	Chicago 3 OT

Colorado won series 4-2

CONFERENCE FINALS
(Best-of-seven series)

Eastern Conference

Series 'M'

Sat. May 18	Florida 5	at	Pittsburgh 1
Mon. May 20	Florida 2	at	Pittsburgh 3
Fri. May 24	Pittsburgh 2	at	Florida 5
Sun. May 26	Pittsburgh 2	at	Florida 1
Tue. May 28	Florida 0	at	Pittsburgh 3
Thu. May 30	Pittsburgh 3	at	Florida 4
Sat. Jun. 1	Florida 3	at	Pittsburgh 1

Florida won series 4-3

Western Conference

Series 'N'

Sun. May 19	Colorado 3	at	Detroit 2 OT
Tue. May 21	Colorado 3	at	Detroit 0
Thu. May 23	Detroit 6	at	Colorado 4
Sat. May 25	Detroit 2	at	Colorado 4
Mon. May 27	Colorado 2	at	Detroit 5
Wed. May 29	Detroit 1	at	Colorado 4

Colorado won series 4-2

STANLEY CUP CHAMPIONSHIP
(Best-of-seven series)

Series 'O'

Tue. Jun. 4	Florida 1	at	Colorado 3
Thu. Jun. 6	Florida 1	at	Colorado 8
Sat. Jun. 8	Colorado 3	at	Florida 2
Mon. Jun. 10	Colorado 1	at	Florida 0 OT

Colorado won series 4-0

Team Playoff Records

	GP	W	L	GF	GA	%
Colorado	22	16	6	80	51	.727
Florida	22	12	10	61	57	.545
Pittsburgh	18	11	7	57	52	.611
Detroit	19	10	9	58	46	.526
St. Louis	13	7	6	37	37	.538
Chicago	10	6	4	30	28	.600
Philadelphia	12	6	6	37	28	.500
NY Rangers	11	5	6	34	38	.455
Montreal	6	2	4	17	19	.333
Washington	6	2	4	17	21	.333
Toronto	6	2	4	15	21	.333
Vancouver	6	2	4	17	24	.333
Winnipeg	6	2	4	10	20	.333
Tampa bay	6	2	4	13	26	.333
Boston	5	1	4	16	22	.200
Calgary	4	0	4	7	16	.000

Individual Leaders

Abbreviations: * – rookie eligible for Calder Trophy; **A** – assists; **G** – goals; **GP** – Games Played; **OT** – overtime goals; **GW** – game-winning goals; **PIM** – penalties in minutes; **PP** – power play goals; **Pts** – points; **S** – shots on goal; **SH** – short-handed goals; **%** – percentage shots resulting in goals; **+/–** – difference between Goals For (**GF**) scored when a player is on the ice with his team at even strength or short-handed and Goals Against (**GA**) scored when the same player is on the ice with his team at even strength or on a power play.

Playoff Scoring Leaders

Player	Team	GP	G	A	Pts	+/–	PIM	PP	SH	GW	OT	S	%
Joe Sakic	Colorado	22	18	16	34	10	14	6	0	6	2	98	18.4
Mario Lemieux	Pittsburgh	18	11	16	27	3	33	3	1	2	0	78	14.1
Jaromir Jagr	Pittsburgh	18	11	12	23	7	18	5	1	1	0	74	14.9
Valeri Kamensky	Colorado	22	10	12	22	11	28	3	0	2	0	56	17.9
Peter Forsberg	Colorado	22	10	11	21	10	18	3	0	1	0	50	20.0
Petr Nedved	Pittsburgh	18	10	10	20	3	16	4	0	2	1	54	18.5
Steve Yzerman	Detroit	18	8	12	20	–1	4	4	0	1	1	52	15.4
Sergei Fedorov	Detroit	19	2	18	20	8	10	0	0	2	0	59	3.4
Sandis Ozolinsh	Colorado	22	5	14	19	5	16	2	0	1	1	52	9.6
Dave Lowry	Florida	22	10	7	17	8	39	4	0	2	1	45	22.2
Mike Ricci	Colorado	22	6	11	17	–1	18	3	0	1	0	31	19.4
Adam Deadmarsh	Colorado	22	5	12	17	8	25	1	0	0	0	40	12.5
Ray Sheppard	Florida	21	8	8	16	4	0	3	0	0	0	47	17.0
Stu Barnes	Florida	22	6	10	16	10	4	2	0	2	0	57	10.5
Uwe Krupp	Colorado	22	4	12	16	5	33	1	0	2	1	38	10.5
Wayne Gretzky	St. Louis	13	2	14	16	2	0	1	0	1	0	25	8.0
Scott Young	Colorado	22	3	12	15	6	10	0	0	0	0	61	4.9
Sergei Zubov	Pittsburgh	18	1	14	15	9	26	1	0	0	0	53	1.9
Shayne Corson	St. Louis	13	8	6	14	–1	22	6	1	1	0	37	21.6
Paul Coffey	Detroit	17	5	9	14	–3	30	3	2	1	0	49	10.2
Nicklas Lidstrom	Detroit	19	5	9	14	2	10	1	0	0	0	50	10.0
Igor Larionov	Detroit	19	6	7	13	5	6	3	0	2	0	46	13.0
Eric Lindros	Philadelphia	12	6	6	12	–1	43	3	0	2	0	46	13.0
Jeremy Roenick	Chicago	10	5	7	12	6	2	1	0	1	1	21	23.8
Claude Lemieux	Colorado	19	5	7	12	5	55	3	0	0	0	81	6.2
V. Kozlov	Detroit	19	5	7	12	3	10	2	0	1	0	38	13.2

Playoff Defensemen Scoring Leaders

Player	Team	GP	G	A	Pts	+/–	PIM	PP	SH	GW	OT	S	%
Sandis Ozolinsh	Colorado	22	5	14	19	5	16	2	0	1	1	52	9.6
Uwe Krupp	Colorado	22	4	12	16	5	33	1	0	2	1	38	10.5
Sergei Zubov	Pittsburgh	18	1	14	15	9	26	1	0	0	0	53	1.9
Paul Coffey	Detroit	17	5	9	14	–3	30	3	2	1	0	49	10.2
Nicklas Lidstrom	Detroit	19	5	9	14	2	10	1	0	0	0	50	10.0
J.J. Daigneault	Pittsburgh	17	1	9	10	4	36	1	0	1	0	30	3.3
V. Konstantinov	Detroit	19	4	5	9	4	28	0	1	0	0	41	9.8
*Ed Jovanovski	Florida	22	1	8	9	2	52	0	0	0	0	51	2.0
Alexei Gusarov	Colorado	21	0	9	9	13	12	0	0	0	0	15	.0
Jason Woolley	Florida	13	2	6	8	3	14	1	0	1	0	27	7.4
Paul Laus	Florida	21	2	6	8	3	62	0	0	0	0	18	11.1

GOALTENDING LEADERS

Goals Against Average

Goaltender	Team	GPI	Mins.	GA	Avg.
Ed Belfour	Chicago	9	666	23	2.07
Patrick Roy	Colorado	22	1454	51	2.10
Chris Osgood	Detroit	15	936	33	2.12
Ron Hextall	Philadelphia	12	760	27	2.13
J. Vanbiesbrouck	Florida	22	1332	50	2.25

Wins

Goaltender	Team	GPI	Mins.	W	L
Patrick Roy	Colorado	22	1454	16	6
J. Vanbiesbrouck	Florida	22	1332	12	10
Chris Osgood	Detroit	15	936	8	7
Ken Wregget	Pittsburgh	9	599	7	2
Ed Belfour	Chicago	9	666	6	3
Jon Casey	St. Louis	12	747	6	6
Ron Hextall	Philadelphia	12	760	6	6

Save Percentage

Goaltender	Team	GPI	Mins.	GA	SA	S%	W	L
J. Vanbiesbrouck	Florida	22	1332	50	735	.932	12	10
Ken Wregget	Pittsburgh	9	599	23	328	.930	7	2
Ed Belfour	Chicago	9	666	23	323	.929	6	3
Tom Barrasso	Pittsburgh	10	558	26	337	.922	4	5
Patrick Roy	Colorado	22	1454	51	649	.921	16	6

Shutouts

Goaltender	Team	GPI	Mins.	SO
Patrick Roy	Colorado	22	1454	3
Chris Osgood	Detroit	15	936	2
Tom Barrasso	Pittsburgh	10	558	1
Ed Belfour	Chicago	9	666	1
Jon Casey	St. Louis	12	747	1
J. Vanbiesbrouck	Florida	22	1332	1

Goal Scoring

Name	Team	GP	G
Joe Sakic	Colorado	22	18
Jaromir Jagr	Pittsburgh	18	11
Mario Lemieux	Pittsburgh	18	11
Petr Nedved	Pittsburgh	18	10
Dave Lowry	Florida	22	10
Valeri Kamensky	Colorado	22	10
Peter Forsberg	Colorado	22	10
Shayne Corson	St. Louis	13	8
Steve Yzerman	Detroit	18	8
Ray Sheppard	Florida	21	8
Adam Graves	NY Rangers	10	7

Assists

Name	Team	GP	A
Sergei Fedorov	Detroit	19	18
Mario Lemieux	Pittsburgh	18	16
Joe Sakic	Colorado	22	16
Wayne Gretzky	St. Louis	13	14
Sergei Zubov	Pittsburgh	18	14
Sandis Ozolinsh	Colorado	22	14
Jaromir Jagr	Pittsburgh	18	12
Steve Yzerman	Detroit	18	12
Uwe Krupp	Colorado	22	12
Scott Young	Colorado	22	12
Valeri Kamensky	Colorado	22	12
Adam Deadmarsh	Colorado	22	12

Power-play Goals

Name	Team	GP	PP
Adam Graves	NY Rangers	10	6
Shayne Corson	St. Louis	13	6
Dino Ciccarelli	Detroit	17	6
Joe Sakic	Colorado	22	6
Jaromir Jagr	Pittsburgh	18	5

Game-winning Goals

Name	Team	GP	GW
Joe Sakic	Colorado	22	6
Vincent Damphousse	Montreal	6	2
Gino Odjick	Vancouver	6	2
Adam Graves	NY Rangers	10	2
Joe Murphy	Chicago	10	2
Eric Lindros	Philadelphia	12	2
Mario Lemieux	Pittsburgh	18	2
Petr Nedved	Pittsburgh	18	2
Sergei Fedorov	Detroit	19	2
Igor Larionov	Detroit	19	2
Tom Fitzgerald	Florida	22	2
Mike Hough	Florida	22	2
Uwe Krupp	Colorado	22	2
Dave Lowry	Florida	22	2
Stu Barnes	Florida	22	2
Valeri Kamensky	Colorado	22	2
Rob Niedermayer	Florida	22	2

Short-handed Goals

Name	Team	GP	SH
Paul Coffey	Detroit	17	2
Mark Kolesar	Toronto	3	1
John Cullen	Tampa Bay	5	1
Adam Oates	Boston	5	1
Steve Heinze	Boston	5	1
Vincent Damphousse	Montreal	6	1

Overtime Goals

Name	Team	GP	OT
Joe Sakic	Colorado	22	2
Sergei Krivokrasov	Chicago	5	1
Brian Bellows	Tampa Bay	6	1
Vincent Damphousse	Montreal	6	1
Mike Gartner	Toronto	6	1

Shots

Name	Team	GP	S
Joe Sakic	Colorado	22	98
Claude Lemieux	Colorado	19	81
Mario Lemieux	Pittsburgh	18	78
Jaromir Jagr	Pittsburgh	18	74
Scott Young	Colorado	22	61

Plus/Minus

Name	Team	GP	+/–
Alexei Gusarov	Colorado	21	13
Adam Foote	Colorado	22	11
Valeri Kamensky	Colorado	22	11

Team Statistics

TEAMS' HOME-AND-ROAD RECORD

	Home						Road					
	GP	W	L	GF	GA	%	GP	W	L	GF	GA	%
COL	11	8	3	48	27	.727	11	8	3	32	24	.727
FLA	11	7	4	37	26	.636	11	5	6	24	31	.455
PIT	10	5	5	33	34	.500	8	6	2	24	18	.750
DET	10	6	4	30	20	.600	9	4	5	28	26	.444
ST.L.	6	5	1	18	12	.833	7	2	5	19	25	.286
CHI	5	3	2	16	11	.600	5	3	2	14	17	.600
PHI	6	3	3	16	12	.500	6	3	3	21	16	.500
NYR	5	1	4	11	17	.200	6	4	2	23	21	.667
MTL	3	0	3	7	11	.000	3	2	1	10	8	.667
WSH	3	0	3	5	10	.000	3	2	1	12	11	.667
TOR	3	2	1	11	11	.667	3	0	3	4	10	.000
VAN	3	1	2	6	10	.333	3	1	2	11	14	.333
WPG	3	1	2	6	11	.333	3	1	2	4	9	.333
T.B.	3	1	2	7	14	.333	3	1	2	6	12	.333
BOS	2	1	1	8	6	.500	3	0	3	8	16	.000
CGY	2	0	2	6	9	.000	2	0	2	1	7	.000
Total	**86**	**44**	**42**	**265**	**241**	**.512**	**86**	**42**	**44**	**241**	**265**	**.488**

TEAMS' POWER-PLAY RECORD

Abbreviations: Adv-total advantages; **PPGF**-power play goals for; **%** arrived by dividing number of power-play goals by total advantages.

		Home						Road						Overall		
	Team	GP	ADV	PPGF	%		Team	GP	ADV	PPGF	%		Team	GP	ADV	PPGF	%
1	TOR	3	19	6	31.6		NYR	6	31	9	29.0		BOS	5	27	7	25.9
2	BOS	2	8	2	25.0		BOS	3	19	5	26.3		TOR	6	32	8	25.0
3	COL	11	66	14	21.2		WSH	3	16	4	25.0		NYR	11	55	12	21.8
4	VAN	3	19	4	21.1		DET	9	48	12	25.0		COL	22	110	24	21.8
5	PHI	6	40	8	20.0		COL	11	44	10	22.7		PHI	12	71	15	21.1
6	PIT	10	59	11	18.6		PHI	6	31	7	22.6		WSH	6	38	7	18.4
7	FLA	11	57	8	14.0		ST.L.	7	38	8	21.1		VAN	6	39	7	17.9
8	WSH	3	22	3	13.6		CHI	5	23	4	17.4		DET	19	112	20	17.9
9	T.B.	3	15	2	13.3		TOR	3	13	2	15.4		PIT	18	100	16	16.0
10	CHI	5	23	3	13.0		VAN	3	20	3	15.0		ST.L.	13	69	11	15.9
11	NYR	5	24	3	12.5		PIT	8	41	5	12.2		CHI	10	46	7	15.2
12	DET	10	64	8	12.5		FLA	11	52	6	11.5		FLA	22	109	14	12.8
13	ST.L.	6	31	3	9.7		MTL	3	10	1	10.0		MTL	6	31	3	9.7
14	MTL	3	21	2	9.5		T.B.	3	20	1	5.0		T.B.	6	35	3	8.6
15	CGY	2	11	0	.0		CGY	2	10	0	.0		CGY	4	21	0	.0
16	WPG	3	13	0	.0		WPG	3	15	0	.0		WPG	6	28	0	.0
	Total	**86**	**492**	**77**	**15.7**			**86**	**431**	**77**	**17.9**			**86**	**923**	**154**	**16.7**

TEAMS' PENALTY KILLING RECORD

Abbreviations: TSH – Total times short-handed; **PPGA** – power-play goals against; **%** arrived by dividing times short minus power-play goals against by times short.

		Home						Road						Overall		
	Team	GP	TSH	PPGA	%		Team	GP	TSH	PPGA	%		Team	GP	TSH	PPGA	%
1	NYR	5	18	1	94.4		TOR	3	15	0	100.0		CHI	10	53	5	90.6
2	BOS	2	11	1	90.9		CHI	5	31	2	93.5		PHI	12	63	7	88.9
3	PHI	6	33	3	90.9		WSH	3	22	2	90.9		NYR	11	57	8	86.0
4	DET	10	47	6	87.2		PIT	8	49	5	89.8		PIT	18	96	14	85.4
5	CHI	5	22	3	86.4		MTL	3	15	2	86.7		DET	19	89	13	85.4
6	FLA	11	51	8	84.3		PHI	6	30	4	86.7		TOR	6	34	5	85.3
7	COL	11	63	10	84.1		WPG	3	22	3	86.4		COL	22	113	17	85.0
8	ST.L.	6	29	5	82.8		COL	11	50	7	86.0		BOS	5	30	5	83.3
9	PIT	10	47	9	80.9		CGY	2	12	2	83.3		WSH	6	42	7	83.3
10	CGY	2	9	2	77.8		DET	9	42	7	83.3		CGY	4	21	4	81.0
11	WSH	3	20	5	75.0		NYR	6	39	7	82.1		FLA	22	103	20	80.6
12	VAN	3	16	4	75.0		VAN	3	20	4	80.0		ST.L.	13	75	15	80.0
13	TOR	3	19	5	73.7		BOS	3	19	4	78.9		WPG	6	37	8	78.4
14	T.B.	3	15	4	73.3		T.B.	3	28	6	78.6		VAN	6	36	8	77.8
15	WPG	3	15	5	66.7		ST.L.	7	46	10	78.3		T.B.	6	43	10	76.7
16	MTL	3	16	6	62.5		FLA	11	52	12	76.9		MTL	6	31	8	74.2
	Total	**86**	**431**	**77**	**82.1**			**86**	**492**	**77**	**84.3**			**86**	**923**	**154**	**83.3**

SHORT-HANDED GOALS

	For			Against		
Team	Games	Goals	Team	Games	Goals	
DET	19	5	PIT	18	0	
ST.L.	13	4	CHI	10	0	
BOS	5	2	T.B.	6	0	
T.B.	6	2	VAN	6	0	
MTL	6	2	BOS	5	0	
PIT	18	2	CGY	4	0	
TOR	6	1	DET	19	1	
NYR	11	1	WSH	6	1	
FLA	22	1	MTL	6	1	
COL	22	1	FLA	22	2	
CGY	4	0	COL	22	2	
WSH	6	0	ST.L.	13	2	
WPG	6	0	WPG	6	2	
VAN	6	0	PHI	12	3	
CHI	10	0	NYR	11	3	
PHI	12	0	TOR	6	4	
Total	**86**	**21**	**Total**	**86**	**21**	

TEAM PENALTIES

Abbreviations: GP – games played; **PEN** – total penalty minutes, including bench penalties; **BMI** – total bench penalty minutes; **AVG** – average penalty minutes per game.

Team	GP	PEN	BMI	AVG
MTL	6	72	2	12.0
NYR	11	136	2	12.4
CGY	4	56	0	14.0
DET	19	302	4	15.9
ST.L.	13	214	2	16.5
VAN	6	99	0	16.5
COL	22	374	2	17.0
CHI	10	180	2	18.0
FLA	22	401	6	18.2
TOR	6	112	2	18.7
PIT	18	351	2	19.5
WPG	6	119	2	19.8
PHI	12	290	0	24.2
BOS	5	147	0	29.4
T.B.	6	190	0	31.7
WSH	6	194	2	32.3
Total	**86**	**3237**	**24**	**37.6**

Patrick Roy and Mike Keane, who last hugged the Mug as members of the Montreal Canadiens, pay homage to the Stanley Cup moments after the Avalanche completed its four-game sweep of the Florida Panthers on June 10, 1996.

Stanley Cup Record Book

History: The Stanley Cup, the oldest trophy competed for by professional athletes in North America, was donated by Frederick Arthur, Lord Stanley of Preston and son of the Earl of Derby, in 1893. Lord Stanley purchased the trophy for 10 guineas ($50 at that time) for presentation to the amateur hockey champions of Canada. Since 1910, when the National Hockey Association took possession of the Stanley Cup, the trophy has been the symbol of professional hockey supremacy. It has been competed for only by NHL teams since 1926 and has been under the exclusive control of the NHL since 1946.

Stanley Cup Standings

1918-96

(ranked by Cup wins)

Teams	Cup Wins	Yrs.	Series	Wins	Losses	Games	Wins	Losses	Ties	Goals For	Goals Against	Winning %
Montreal	23[1]	70	131[2]	84	46	623	376	239	8	1938	1537	.610
Toronto	13	58	96	51	45	444	210	230	4	1166	1230	.477
Detroit	7	45	79	41	38	388	190	197	1	1079	1053	.491
Boston	5	57	98	46	52	476	228	242	6	1405	1422	.485
Edmonton	5	13	37	29	8	180	120	60	0	770	579	.667
NY Rangers	4	47	83	40	43	371	174	189	8	1055	1079	.480
NY Islanders	4	17	43	30	13	218	128	90	0	748	650	.587
Chicago	3	51	88	40	48	400	185	210	5	1157	1270	.469
Philadelphia	2	22	48	28	20	250	132	118	0	802	759	.528
Pittsburgh	2	16	30	16	14	155	85	70	0	512	500	.548
Calgary[3]	1	21	32	12	20	156	69	87	0	529	573	.442
Colorado[4]	1	10	19	10	9	102	51	51	0	327	337	.500
New Jersey[5]	1	8	15	8	7	87	47	40	0	266	253	.540
St. Louis	0	26	44	18	26	230	103	127	0	669	764	.448
Buffalo	0	20	30	10	20	143	62	81	0	448	480	.434
Dallas[6]	0	19	34	15	19	180	86	94	0	591	624	.478
Los Angeles	0	19	29	10	19	142	55	87	0	459	568	.387
Vancouver	0	16	25	9	16	124	54	70	0	377	422	.435
Washington	0	14	21	7	14	116	52	64	0	381	389	.448
Phoenix[7]	0	11	13	2	11	62	19	43	0	177	253	.306
Hartford	0	8	9	1	8	49	18	31	0	143	177	.367
San Jose	0	2	4	2	2	25	11	14	0	74	112	.440
Florida	0	1	4	3	1	22	12	10	0	61	57	.545
Tampa Bay	0	1	1	2	4	6	2	4	0	13	26	.333

1. Montreal also won the Stanley Cup in 1916.
2. 1919 final incomplete due to influenza epidemic.
3. Includes totals of Atlanta 1972-80.
4. Includes totals of Quebec 1979-95.
5. Includes totals of Colorado Rockies 1976-82.
6. Includes totals of Minnesota 1967-93.
7. Includes totals of Winnipeg 1979-96.

Stanley Cup Winners Prior to Formation of NHL in 1917

Season	Champions	Manager	Coach
1916-17	Seattle Metropolitans	Pete Muldoon	Pete Muldoon
1915-16	Montreal Canadiens	George Kennedy	George Kennedy
1914-15	Vancouver Millionaires	Frank Patrick	Frank Patrick
1913-14	Toronto Blueshirts	Jack Marshall	Scotty Davidson*
1912-13**	Quebec Bulldogs	M.J. Quinn	Joe Malone*
1911-12	Quebec Bulldogs	M.J. Quinn	C. Nolan
1910-11	Ottawa Senators		Bruce Stuart*
1909-10	Montreal Wanderers	R. R. Boon	Pud Glass*
1908-09	Ottawa Senators		Bruce Stuart*
1907-08	Montreal Wanderers	R. R. Boon	Cecil Blachford
1906-07	Montreal Wanderers (March)	R. R. Boon	Cecil Blachford
1906-07	Kenora Thistles (January)	F.A. Hudson	Tommy Phillips*
1905-06	Montreal Wanderers		Cecil Blachford*
1904-05	Ottawa Silver Seven		A. T. Smith
1903-04	Ottawa Silver Seven		A. T. Smith
1902-03	Ottawa Silver Seven		A. T. Smith
1901-02	Montreal A.A.A.		C. McKerrow
1900-01	Winnipeg Victorias		D. H. Bain
1899-1900	Montreal Shamrocks		H.J. Trihey*
1898-99	Montreal Shamrocks		H.J. Trihey*
1897-98	Montreal Victorias		F. Richardson
1896-97	Montreal Victorias		Mike Grant*
1895-96 (December, 1896)	Montreal Victorias		Mike Grant*
1895-96 (February)	Winnipeg Victorias		J.C. G. Armytage
1894-95	Montreal Victorias		Mike Grant*
1893-94	Montreal A.A.A.		
1892-93	Montreal A.A.A.		

** Victoria defeated Quebec in challenge series. No official recognition.
* In the early years the teams were frequently run by the Captain. *Indicates Captain

Stanley Cup Winners

Year	W&L in Finals	Winner	Coach	Finalist	Coach
1996	4-0	Colorado	Marc Crawford	Florida	Doug MacLean
1995	4-0	New Jersey	Jacques Lemaire	Detroit	Scotty Bowman
1994	4-3	NY Rangers	Mike Keenan	Vancouver	Pat Quinn
1993	4-1	Montreal	Jacques Demers	Los Angeles	Barry Melrose
1992	4-0	Pittsburgh	Scotty Bowman	Chicago	Mike Keenan
1991	4-2	Pittsburgh	Bob Johnson	Minnesota	Bob Gainey
1990	4-1	Edmonton	John Muckler	Boston	Mike Milbury
1989	4-2	Calgary	Terry Crisp	Montreal	Pat Burns
1988	4-0	Edmonton	Glen Sather	Boston	Terry O'Reilly
1987	4-3	Edmonton	Glen Sather	Philadelphia	Mike Keenan
1986	4-1	Montreal	Jean Perron	Calgary Flames	Bob Johnson
1985	4-1	Edmonton	Glen Sather	Philadelphia	Mike Keenan
1984	4-1	Edmonton	Glen Sather	NY Islanders	Al Arbour
1983	4-0	NY Islanders	Al Arbour	Edmonton	Glen Sather
1982	4-0	NY Islanders	Al Arbour	Vancouver	Roger Neilson
1981	4-1	NY Islanders	Al Arbour	Minnesota	Glen Sonmor
1980	4-2	NY Islanders	Al Arbour	Philadelphia	Pat Quinn
1979	4-1	Montreal	Scotty Bowman	NY Rangers	Fred Shero
1978	4-2	Montreal	Scotty Bowman	Boston	Don Cherry
1977	4-0	Montreal	Scotty Bowman	Boston	Don Cherry
1976	4-0	Montreal	Scotty Bowman	Philadelphia	Fred Shero
1975	4-2	Philadelphia	Fred Shero	Buffalo Sabres	Floyd Smith
1974	4-2	Philadelphia	Fred Shero	Boston	Bep Guidolin
1973	4-2	Montreal	Scotty Bowman	Chicago	Billy Reay
1972	4-2	Boston	Tom Johnson	NY Rangers	Emile Francis
1971	4-3	Montreal	Al MacNeil	Chicago	Billy Reay
1970	4-0	Boston	Harry Sinden	St. Louis	Scotty Bowman
1969	4-0	Montreal	Claude Ruel	St. Louis	Scotty Bowman
1968	4-0	Montreal	Toe Blake	St. Louis	Scotty Bowman
1967	4-2	Toronto	Punch Imlach	Montreal	Toe Blake
1966	4-2	Montreal	Toe Blake	Detroit	Sid Abel
1965	4-3	Montreal	Toe Blake	Chicago	Billy Reay
1964	4-3	Toronto	Punch Imlach	Detroit	Sid Abel
1963	4-1	Toronto	Punch Imlach	Detroit	Sid Abel
1962	4-2	Toronto	Punch Imlach	Chicago	Rudy Pilous
1961	4-2	Chicago	Rudy Pilous	Detroit	Sid Abel
1960	4-3	Montreal	Toe Blake	Toronto	Punch Imlach
1959	4-1	Montreal	Toe Blake	Toronto	Punch Imlach
1958	4-2	Montreal	Toe Blake	Boston	Milt Schmidt
1957	4-1	Montreal	Toe Blake	Boston	Milt Schmidt
1956	4-1	Montreal	Toe Blake	Detroit	Jimmy Skinner
1955	4-3	Detroit	Jimmy Skinner	Montreal	Dick Irvin
1954	4-3	Detroit	Tommy Ivan	Montreal	Dick Irvin
1953	4-1	Montreal	Dick Irvin	Boston	Lynn Patrick
1952	4-0	Detroit	Tommy Ivan	Montreal	Dick Irvin
1951	4-1	Toronto	Joe Primeau	Montreal	Dick Irvin
1950	4-3	Detroit	Tommy Ivan	NY Rangers	Lynn Patrick
1949	4-0	Toronto	Hap Day	Detroit	Tommy Ivan
1948	4-0	Toronto	Hap Day	Detroit	Tommy Ivan
1947	4-2	Toronto	Hap Day	Montreal	Dick Irvin
1946	4-1	Montreal	Dick Irvin	Boston	Dit Clapper
1945	4-3	Toronto	Hap Day	Detroit	Jack Adams
1944	4-0	Montreal	Dick Irvin	Chicago	Paul Thompson
1943	4-0	Detroit	Jack Adams	Boston	Art Ross
1942	4-3	Toronto	Hap Day	Detroit	Jack Adams
1941	4-0	Boston	Cooney Weiland	Detroit	Ebbie Goodfellow
1940	4-2	NY Rangers	Frank Boucher	Toronto	Dick Irvin
1939	4-1	Boston	Art Ross	Toronto	Dick Irvin
1938	3-1	Chicago	Bill Stewart	Toronto	Dick Irvin
1937	3-2	Detroit	Jack Adams	NY Rangers	Lester Patrick
1936	3-1	Detroit	Jack Adams	Toronto	Dick Irvin
1935	3-0	Mtl. Maroons	Tommy Gorman	Toronto	Dick Irvin
1934	3-1	Chicago	Tommy Gorman	Detroit	Herbie Lewis
1933	3-1	NY Rangers	Lester Patrick	Toronto	Dick Irvin
1932	3-0	Toronto	Dick Irvin	NY Rangers	Lester Patrick
1931	3-2	Montreal	Cecil Hart	Chicago	Dick Irvin
1930	2-0	Montreal	Cecil Hart	Boston	Art Ross
1929	2-0	Boston	Cy Denneny	NY Rangers	Lester Patrick
1928	3-2	NY Rangers	Lester Patrick	Mtl. Maroons	Eddie Gerard
1927	2-0-2	Ottawa	Dave Gill	Boston	Art Ross

The National Hockey League assumed control of Stanley Cup competition after 1926

Year	W&L in Finals	Winner	Coach	Finalist	Coach
1926	3-1	Mtl. Maroons	Eddie Gerard	Victoria	Lester Patrick
1925	3-1	Victoria	Lester Patrick	Montreal	Leo Dandurand
1924	2-0 / 2-0	Montreal	Leo Dandurand	Cgy. Tigers / Van. Maroons	— / —
1923	2-0 / 3-1	Ottawa	Pete Green	Edm. Eskimos / Van. Maroons	— / —
1922	3-2	Tor. St. Pats	Eddie Powers	Van. Millionaires	Frank Patrick
1921	3-2	Ottawa	Pete Green	Van. Millionaires	Frank Patrick
1920	3-2	Ottawa	Pete Green	Seattle	—
1919	2-2-1	No decision - series between Montreal and Seattle cancelled due to influenza epidemic			
1918	3-2	Tor. Arenas	Dick Carroll	Van. Millionaires	Frank Patrick

Championship Trophies

PRINCE OF WALES TROPHY

Beginning with the 1993-94 season, the club which advances to the Stanley Cup Finals as the winner of the Eastern Conference Championship is presented with the Prince of Wales Trophy.

History: His Royal Highness, the Prince of Wales, donated the trophy to the National Hockey League in 1924. From 1927-28 through 1937-38, the award was presented to the team finishing first in the American Division of the NHL. From 1938-39, when the NHL reverted to one section, to 1966-67, it was presented to the team winning the NHL regular season championship. With expansion in 1967-68, it again became a divisional trophy, awarded to the regular season champions of the East Division through to the end of the 1973-74 season. Beginning in 1974-75, it was awarded to the regular-season winner of the conference bearing the name of the trophy. From 1981-82 to 1992-93 the trophy was presented to the playoff champion in the Wales Conference. Since 1993-94, the trophy has been presented to the playoff champion in the Eastern Conference.

1995-96 Winner: Florida Panthers

In just their third season, and first playoff appearance, the Florida Panthers won the Prince of Wales Trophy on June 1, 1996 with a 3-1 win over the Pittsburgh Penguins in game seven of the Eastern Conference Championship series. Previous series wins had come over the Boston Bruins and Philadelphia Flyers.

PRINCE OF WALES TROPHY WINNERS

1995-96	**Florida Panthers**	1958-59	Montreal Canadiens
1994-95	New Jersey Devils	1957-58	Montreal Canadiens
1993-94	New York Rangers	1956-57	Detroit Red Wings
1992-93	Montreal Canadiens	1955-56	Montreal Canadiens
1991-92	Pittsburgh Penguins	1954-55	Detroit Red Wings
1990-91	Pittsburgh Penguins	1953-54	Detroit Red Wings
1989-90	Boston Bruins	1952-53	Detroit Red Wings
1988-89	Montreal Canadiens	1951-52	Detroit Red Wings
1987-88	Boston Bruins	1950-51	Detroit Red Wings
1986-87	Philadelphia Flyers	1949-50	Detroit Red Wings
1985-86	Montreal Canadiens	1948-49	Detroit Red Wings
1984-85	Philadelphia Flyers	1947-48	Toronto Maple Leafs
1983-84	New York Islanders	1946-47	Montreal Canadiens
1982-83	New York Islanders	1945-46	Montreal Canadiens
1981-82	New York Islanders	1944-45	Montreal Canadiens
1980-81	Montreal Canadiens	1943-44	Montreal Canadiens
1979-80	Buffalo Sabres	1942-43	Detroit Red Wings
1978-79	Montreal Canadiens	1941-42	New York Rangers
1977-78	Montreal Canadiens	1940-41	Boston Bruins
1976-77	Montreal Canadiens	1939-40	Boston Bruins
1975-76	Montreal Canadiens	1938-39	Boston Bruins
1974-75	Buffalo Sabres	1937-38	Boston Bruins
1973-74	Boston Bruins	1936-37	Detroit Red Wings
1972-73	Montreal Canadiens	1935-36	Detroit Red Wings
1971-72	Boston Bruins	1934-35	Boston Bruins
1970-71	Boston Bruins	1933-34	Detroit Red Wings
1969-70	Chicago Blackhawks	1932-33	Boston Bruins
1968-69	Montreal Canadiens	1931-32	New York Rangers
1967-68	Montreal Canadiens	1930-31	Boston Bruins
1966-67	Chicago Blackhawks	1929-30	Boston Bruins
1965-66	Montreal Canadiens	1928-29	Boston Bruins
1964-65	Detroit Red Wings	1927-28	Boston Bruins
1963-64	Montreal Canadiens	1926-27	Ottawa Senators
1962-63	Toronto Maple Leafs	1925-26	Montreal Maroons
1961-62	Montreal Canadiens	1924-25	Montreal Canadiens
1960-61	Montreal Canadiens	1923-24	Montreal Canadiens
1959-60	Montreal Canadiens		

CLARENCE S. CAMPBELL BOWL

Beginning with the 1993-94 season, the club which advances to the Stanley Cup Finals as the winner of the Western Conference Championship is presented with the Clarence S. Campbell Bowl.

History: Presented by the member clubs in 1968 for perpetual competition by the National Hockey League in recognition of the services of Clarence S. Campbell, President of the NHL from 1946 to 1977. From 1967-68 through 1973-74, the trophy was awarded to the regular season champions of the West Division. Beginning in 1974-75, it was awarded to the regular-season winner of the conference bearing the name of the trophy. From 1981-82 to 1992-93 the trophy was presented to the playoff champion in the Campbell Conference. Since 1993-94, the trophy has been presented to the playoff champion in the Western Conference. The trophy itself is a hallmark piece made of sterling silver and was crafted by a British silversmith in 1878.

1995-96 Winner: Colorado Avalanche

In their first season after leaving Quebec, the Colorado Avalanche won the Clarence S. Campbell Bowl by defeating the Detroit Red Wings 4-1 in game six of the Western Conference Championship series. Before eliminating the Red Wings, Colorado had series wins over the Chicago Blackhawks and Vancouver Canucks.

CLARENCE S. CAMPBELL BOWL WINNERS

1995-96	**Colorado Avalanche**	1980-81	New York Islanders
1994-95	Detroit Red Wings	1979-80	Philadelphia Flyers
1993-94	Vancouver Canucks	1978-79	New York Islanders
1992-93	Los Angeles Kings	1977-78	New York Islanders
1991-92	Chicago Blackhawks	1976-77	Philadelphia Flyers
1990-91	Minnesota North Stars	1975-76	Philadelphia Flyers
1989-90	Edmonton Oilers	1974-75	Philadelphia Flyers
1988-89	Calgary Flames	1973-74	Philadelphia Flyers
1987-88	Edmonton Oilers	1972-73	Chicago Blackhawks
1986-87	Edmonton Oilers	1971-72	Chicago Blackhawks
1985-86	Calgary Flames	1970-71	Chicago Blackhawks
1984-85	Edmonton Oilers	1969-70	St. Louis Blues
1983-84	Edmonton Oilers	1968-69	St. Louis Blues
1982-83	Edmonton Oilers	1967-68	Philadelphia Flyers
1981-82	Vancouver Canucks		

Prince of Wales Trophy

Clarence S. Campbell Bowl

Stanley Cup

Stanley Cup Winners:

Rosters and Final Series Scores

1995-96 — Colorado Avalanche — Joe Sakic (Captain), Rene Corbet, Adam Deadmarsh, Stephane Fiset, Adam Foote, Peter Forsberg, Alexei Gusarov, Dave Hannan, Valeri Kamensky, Mike Keane, Jon Klemm, Uwe Krupp, Sylvain Lefebvre, Claude Lemieux, Curtis Leschyshyn, Troy Murray, Sandis Ozolinsh, Mike Ricci, Patrick Roy, Warren Rychel, Chris Simon, Craig Wolanin, Stephane Yelle, Scott Young, Charlie Lyons (Chairman, CEO), Pierre Lacroix (Exec. V.P., G.M.), Marc Crawford (Head Coach), Joel Quenneville (Assistant Coach), Jacques Cloutier (Assistant Coach), Francois Giguere (Assistant General Manager), Michel Goulet (Director of Player Personnel), Dave Draper (Chief Scout), Jean Martineau (Director of Public Relations), Pat Karns (Trainer), Matthew Sokolowski (Assistant Trainer), Rob McLean (Equipment Manager), Mike Kramer (Assistant Equipment Manager), Brock Gibbins (Assistant Equipment Manager), Skip Allen (Strength and Conditioning Coach), Paul Fixter (Video Coordinator), Leo Vyssokov (Massage Therapist).

Scores: June 4 at Colorado - Colorado 3, Florida 1; June 6 at Colorado - Colorado 8, Florida 1; June 8 at Florida - Colorado 3, Florida 2; June 10 at Florida - Colorado 1, Florida 0.

1994-95 — New Jersey Devils — R. Scott Stevens (Captain), Tommy Albelin, Martin Brodeur, Neil Broten, Sergei Brylin, Robert E. Carpenter, Jr., Shawn Chambers, Tom Chorske, Danton Cole, Ken Daneyko, Kevin Dean, Jim Dowd, Bruce Driver (Alternate Captain), Bill Guerin, Bobby Holik, Claude Lemieux, John MacLean (Alternate Captain), Chris McAlpine, Randy McKay, Scott Niedermayer, Mike Peluso, Stephane J.J. Richer, Brian Rolston, Chris Terreri, Valeri Zelepukin, Dr. John J. McMullen (Owner/Chairman), Peter S. McMullen (Owner), Lou Lamoriello (President/General Manager), Jacques Lemaire (Head Coach), Jacques Caron (Goaltender Coach), Dennis Gendron (Assistant Coach), Larry Robinson (Assistant Coach), Robbie Ftorek (AHL Coach), Alex Abasto (Assistant Equipment Manager), Bob Huddleston (Massage Therapist), David Nichols (Equipment Manager), Ted Schuch (Medical Trainer), Mike Vasalani (Strength Coach), David Conte (Director of Scouting) Claude Carrier (Scout), Milt Fisher (Scout), Dan Labraaten (Scout), Marcel Pronovost (Scout).

Scores: June 17 at Detroit — New Jersey 2, Detroit 1; June 20 at Detroit — New Jersey 4, Detroit 2; June 22 at New Jersey — New Jersey 5, Detroit 2; June 24 at New Jersey — New Jersey 5, Detroit 2.

1993-94 — New York Rangers — Mark Messier (Captain), Brian Leetch, Kevin Lowe, Adam Graves, Steve Larmer, Glenn Anderson, Jeff Beukeboom, Greg Gilbert, Mike Hartman, Glenn Healy, Mike Hudson, Alexander Karpovtsev, Joe Kocur, Alexei Kovalev, Nick Kypreos, Doug Lidster, Stephane Matteau, Craig MacTavish, Sergei Nemchinov, Brian Noonan, Ed Olczyk, Mike Richter, Esa Tikkanen, Jay Wells, Sergei Zubov, Neil Smith (President, General Manager and Governor), Robert Gutkowski, Stanley Jaffe, Kenneth Munoz (Governors), Larry Pleau (Assistant General Manager), Mike Keenan (Head Coach), Colin Campbell (Associate Coach), Dick Todd (Assistant Coach), Matthew Loughren (Manager, Team Operations), Barry Watkins (Director, Communications), Christer Rockstrom, Tony Feltrin, Martin Madden, Herb Hammond, Darwin Bennett (Scouts), Dave Smith, Joe Murphy, Mike Folga, Bruce Lifrieri (Trainers).
Scores: May 31 at New York — Vancouver 3, NY Rangers 2; June 2 at New York — NY Rangers 3, Vancouver 1; June 4 at Vancouver — NY Rangers 5, Vancouver 1; June 7 at Vancouver — NY Rangers 4, Vancouver 2; June 9 at New York — Vancouver 6 at NY Rangers 3; June 11 at Vancouver — Vancouver 4, NY Rangers 1; June 14 at New York — NY Rangers 3, Vancouver 2.

1992-93 — Montreal Canadiens — Guy Carbonneau (Captain), Patrick Roy, Mike Keane, Eric Desjardins, Stephan Lebeau, Mathieu Schneider, Jean-Jacques Daigneault, Denis Savard, Lyle Odelein, Todd Ewen, Kirk Muller, John LeClair, Gilbert Dionne, Benoit Brunet, Patrice Brisebois, Paul Di Pietro, Andre Racicot, Donald Dufresne, Mario Roberge, Sean Hill, Ed Ronan, Kevin Haller, Vincent Damphousse, Brian Bellows, Gary Leeman, Rob Ramage, Ronald Corey (President), Serge Savard (Managing Director & Vice-President Hockey), Jacques Demers (Head Coach), Jacques Laperriere (Assistant Coach), Charles Thiffault (Assistant Coach), Francois Allaire (Goaltending Instructor), Jean Béliveau (Senior Vice-President, Corporate Affairs), Fred Steer (Vice-President, Finance & Adminstration), Aldo Giampaolo (Vice-President, Operations), Bernard Brisset (Vice-President, Marketing & Communications), André Boudrias (Assistant to the Managing Director & Director of Scouting), Jacques Lemaire (Assistant to the Managing Director), Gaeten Lefebvre (Athletic Trainer), John Shipman (Assistant to the Athletic Trainer), Eddy Palchak (Equipment Manager), Pierre Gervais (Assistant to the Equipment Manager), Robert Boulanger (Assistant to the Equipment Manager), Pierre Ouellete (Assistant to the Equipment Manager).
Scores: June 1 at Montreal — Los Angeles 4, Montreal 1; June 2 at Montreal — Montreal 3, Los Angeles 2; June 5 at Los Angeles — Montreal 4, Los Angeles 3; June 7 at Los Angeles — Montreal 3, Los Angeles 2; June 9 at Montreal — Montreal 4, Los Angeles 1.

1991-92 — Pittsburgh Penguins — Mario Lemieux (Captain), Ron Francis, Bryan Trottier, Kevin Stevens, Bob Errey, Phil Bourque, Troy Loney, Rick Tocchet, Joe Mullen, Jaromir Jagr, Jiri Hrdina, Shawn McEachern, Ulf Samuelsson, Kjell Samuelsson, Larry Murphy, Gord Roberts, Jim Paek, Paul Stanton, Tom Barrasso, Ken Wregget, Jay Caufield, Jamie Leach, Wendell Young, Grant Jennings, Peter Taglianetti, Jock Callander, Dave Michayluk, Mike Needham, Jeff Chychrun, Ken Priestlay, Jeff Daniels, Howard Baldwin (Owner and President), Morris Belzberg (Owner), Thomas Ruta (Owner), Donn Patton (Executive Vice President and Chief Financial Officer), Paul Martha (Executive Vice President and General Counsel), Craig Patrick (Executive Vice President and General Manager), Bob Johnson (Coach), Scotty Bowman (Director of Player Development and Coach), Barry Smith, Rick Kehoe, Pierre McGuire, Gilles Meloche, Rick Paterson (Assistant Coaches), Steve Latin (Equipment Manager), Skip Thayer (Trainer), John Welday (Strength and Conditioning Coach), Greg Malone, Les Binkley, Charlie Hodge, John Gill, Ralph Cox (Scouts).
Scores: May 26 at Pittsburgh — Pittsburgh 5, Chicago 4; May 28 at Pittsburgh — Pittsburgh 3, Chicago 1; May 30 at Chicago — Pittsburgh 1, Chicago 0; June 1 at Chicago — Pittsburgh 6, Chicago 5.

1990-91 — Pittsburgh Penguins — Mario Lemieux (Captain), Paul Coffey, Randy Hillier, Bob Errey, Tom Barrasso, Phil Bourque, Jay Caufield, Ron Francis, Randy Gilhen, Jiri Hrdina, Jaromir Jagr, Grant Jennings, Troy Loney, Joe Mullen, Larry Murphy, Jim Paek, Frank Pietrangelo, Barry Pederson, Mark Recchi, Gordie Roberts, Ulf Samuelsson, Paul Stanton, Kevin Stevens, Peter Taglianetti, Bryan Trottier, Scott Young, Wendell Young, Edward J. DeBartolo, Sr. (Owner), Marie D. DeBartolo York (President), Paul Martha (Vice-President & General Counsel), Craig Patrick (General Manager), Scotty Bowman (Director of Player Development & Recruitment), Bob Johnson (Coach), Rick Kehoe (Assistant Coach), Gilles Meloche (Goaltending Coach & Scout), Rick Paterson (Assistant Coach), Barry Smith (Assistant Coach), Steve Latin (Equipment Manager), Skip Thayer (Trainer), John Welday (Strength & Conditioning Coach), Greg Malone (Scout).
Scores: May 15 at Pittsburgh — Minnesota 5, Pittsburgh 4; May 17 at Pittsburgh — Pittsburgh 4, Minnesota 1; May 19 at Minnesota — Minnesota 3, Pittsburgh 1; May 21 at Minnesota — Pittsburgh 5, Minnesota 3; May 23 at Pittsburgh — Pittsburgh 6, Minnesota 4; May 25 at Minnesota — Pittsburgh 8, Minnesota 0.

1989-90 — Edmonton Oilers — Kevin Lowe, Steve Smith, Jeff Beukeboom, Mark Lamb, Joe Murphy, Glenn Anderson, Mark Messier, Adam Graves, Craig MacTavish, Kelly Buchberger, Jari Kurri, Craig Simpson, Martin Gelinas, Randy Gregg, Charlie Huddy, Geoff Smith, Reijo Ruotsalainen, Craig Muni, Bill Ranford, Dave Brown, Eldon Reddick, Petr Klima, Esa Tikkanen, Grant Fuhr, Peter Pocklington (Owner), Glen Sather (President/General Manager), John Muckler (Coach), Ted Green (Co-Coach), Ron Low (Ass't Coach), Bruce MacGregor (Ass't General Manager), Barry Fraser (Director of Player Personnel), John Blackwell (Director of Operations, AHL), Ace Bailey, Ed Chadwick, Lorne Davis, Harry Howell, Matti Vaisanen and Albert Reeves (Scouts), Bill Tuele (Director of Public Relations), Werner Baum (Controller), Dr. Gordon Cameron (Medical Chief of Staff), Dr. David Reid (Team Physician), Barrie Stafford (Athletic Trainer), Ken Lowe (Athletic Therapist), Stuart Poirier (Massage Therapist), Lyle Kulchisky (Ass't Trainer).
Scores: May 15 at Boston — Edmonton 3, Boston 2; May 18 at Boston — Edmonton 7, Boston 2; May 20 at Edmonton — Boston 2, Edmonton 1; May 22 at Edmonton — Edmonton 5, Boston 1; May 24 at Boston — Edmonton 4, Boston 1.

1988-89 — Calgary Flames — Mike Vernon, Rick Wamsley, Al MacInnis, Brad McCrimmon, Dana Murzyn, Ric Nattress, Joe Mullen, Lanny McDonald (Co-captain), Gary Roberts, Colin Patterson, Hakan Loob, Theoren Fleury, Jiri Hrdina, Tim Hunter (Ass't. captain), Gary Suter, Mark Hunter, Jim Peplinski (Co-captain), Joe Nieuwendyk, Brian MacLellan, Joel Otto, Jamie Macoun, Doug Gilmour, Rob Ramage. Norman Green, Harley Hotchkiss, Norman Kwong, Sonia Scurfield, B.J. Seaman, D.K. Seaman (Owners), Cliff Fletcher (President and General Manager), Al MacNeil (Ass't General Manager), Al Coates (Ass't to the President), Terry Crisp (Head Coach), Doug Risebrough, Tom Watt (Ass't Coaches), Glenn Hall (Goaltending Consultant), Jim Murray (Trainer), Bob Stewart (Equipment Manager), Al Murray (Ass't Trainer).
Scores: May 14 at Calgary — Calgary 3, Montreal 2; May 17 at Calgary— Montreal 4, Calgary 2; May 19 at Montreal — Montreal 4, Calgary 3; May 21 at Montreal — Calgary 4, Montreal 2; May 23 at Calgary — Calgary 3, Montreal 2; May 25 at Montreal — Calgary 4, Montreal 2.

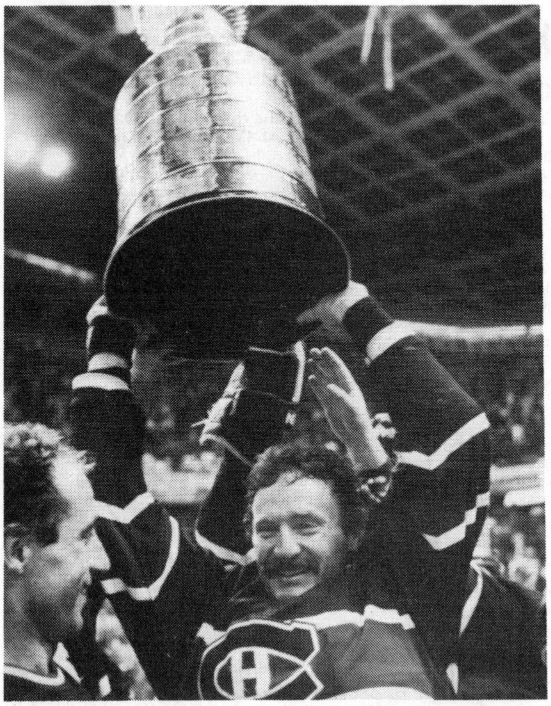

Larry Robinson hoists the Stanley Cup above his head for the final time as a player shortly after the Montreal Canadiens defeated the Calgary Flames in the 1986 Stanley Cup finals. Ten seasons later, in 1995, he would have his name engraved on the Cup once again, this time as an assistant coach with the New Jersey Devils.

1987-88 — Edmonton Oilers — Keith Acton, Glenn Anderson, Jeff Beukeboom, Geoff Courtnall, Grant Fuhr, Randy Gregg, Wayne Gretzky, Dave Hannan, Charlie Huddy, Mike Krushelnyski, Jari Kurri, Normand Lacombe, Kevin Lowe, Craig MacTavish, Kevin McClelland, Marty McSorley, Mark Messier, Craig Muni, Bill Ranford, Craig Simpson, Steve Smith, Esa Tikkanen, Peter Pocklington (Owner), Glen Sather (General Manager/Coach), John Muckler (Co-Coach), Ted Green (Ass't Coach), Bruce MacGregor (Ass't General Manager), Barry Fraser (Director of Player Personnel), Bill Tuele (Director of Public Relations), Dr. Gordon Cameron (Team Physician), Peter Millar (Athletic Therapist), Barrie Stafford (Trainer), Juergen Mers (Massage Therapist), Lyle Kulchisky (Ass't Trainer).
Scores: May 18 at Edmonton — Edmonton 2, Boston 1; May 20 at Edmonton — Edmonton 4, Boston 2; May 22 at Boston — Edmonton 6, Boston 3; May 24 at Boston — Boston 3, Edmonton 3 (suspended due to power failure); May 26 at Edmonton — Edmonton 6, Boston 3.

1986-87 — Edmonton Oilers — Glenn Anderson, Jeff Beukeboom, Kelly Buchberger, Paul Coffey, Grant Fuhr, Randy Gregg, Wayne Gretzky, Charlie Huddy, Dave Hunter, Mike Krushelnyski, Jari Kurri, Moe Lemay, Kevin Lowe, Craig MacTavish, Kevin McClelland, Marty McSorley, Mark Messier, Andy Moog, Craig Muni, Kent Nilsson, Jaroslav Pouzar, Reijo Ruotsalainen, Steve Smith, Esa Tikkanen, Peter Pocklington (Owner), Glen Sather (General Manager/Coach), John Muckler (Co-Coach), Ted Green (Ass't. Coach), Ron Low (Ass't. Coach), Bruce MacGregor (Ass't. General Manager), Barry Fraser (Director of Player Personnel), Peter Millar (Athletic Therapist), Barrie Stafford (Trainer), Lyle Kulchisky (Ass't Trainer).
Scores: May 17 at Edmonton — Edmonton 4, Philadelphia 2; May 20 at Edmonton — Edmonton 3, Philadelphia 2; May 22 at Philadelphia — Philadelphia 5, Edmonton 3; May 24 at Philadelphia — Edmonton 4, Philadelphia 1; May 26 at Edmonton — Philadelphia 4, Edmonton 3; May 28 at Philadelphia — Philadelphia 3, Edmonton 2; May 31 at Edmonton — Edmonton 3, Philadelphia 1.

1985-86 — Montreal Canadiens — Bob Gainey, Doug Soetaert, Patrick Roy, Rick Green, David Maley, Ryan Walter, Serge Boisvert, Mario Tremblay, Bobby Smith, Craig Ludwig, Tom Kurvers, Kjell Dahlin, Larry Robinson, Guy Carbonneau, Chris Chelios, Petr Svoboda, Mats Naslund, Lucien DeBlois, Steve Rooney, Gaston Gingras, Mike Lalor, Chris Nilan, John Kordic, Claude Lemieux, Mike McPhee, Brian Skrudland, Stephane Richer, Ronald Corey (President), Serge Savard (General Manager), Jean Perron (Coach), Jacques Laperrière (Ass't. Coach), Jean Béliveau (Vice President), Francois-Xavier Seigneur (Vice President), Fred Steer (Vice President), Jacques Lemaire (Ass't. General Manager), André Boudrias (Ass't. General Manager), Claude Ruel, Yves Belanger (Athletic Therapist), Gaetan Lefebvre (Ass't. Athletic Therapist), Eddy Palchek (Trainer), Sylvain Toupin (Ass't. Trainer).
Scores: May 16 at Calgary — Calgary 5, Montreal 2; May 18 at Calgary — Montreal 3, Calgary 2; May 20 at Montreal — Montreal 5, Calgary 3; May 22 at Montreal — Montreal 1, Calgary 0; May 24 at Calgary — Montreal 4, Calgary 3.

1984-85 — Edmonton Oilers — Glenn Anderson, Bill Carroll, Paul Coffey, Lee Fogolin, Grant Fuhr, Randy Gregg, Wayne Gretzky, Charlie Huddy, Pat Hughes, Dave Hunter, Don Jackson, Mike Krushelnyski, Jari Kurri, Willy Lindstrom, Kevin Lowe, Dave Lumley, Kevin McClelland, Larry Melnyk, Mark Messier, Andy Moog, Mark Napier, Jaroslav Pouzar, Dave Semenko, Esa Tikkanen, Peter Pocklington (Owner), Glen Sather (General Manager/Coach), John Muckler (Ass't. Coach), Ted Green (Ass't. Coach), Bruce MacGregor (Ass't. General Manager), Barry Fraser (Director of Player Personnel/Chief Scout), Peter Millar (Athletic Therapist), Barrie Stafford, Lyle Kulchisky (Trainers)
Scores: May 21 at Philadelphia — Philadelphia 4, Edmonton 1; May 23 at Philadelphia — Edmonton 3, Philadelphia 1; May 25 at Edmonton — Edmonton 4, Philadelphia 3; May 28 at Edmonton — Edmonton 5, Philadelphia 3; May 30 at Edmonton — Edmonton 8, Philadelphia 3.

1983-84 — Edmonton Oilers — Glenn Anderson, Paul Coffey, Pat Conacher, Lee Fogolin, Grant Fuhr, Randy Gregg, Wayne Gretzky, Charlie Huddy, Pat Hughes, Dave Hunter, Don Jackson, Jari Kurri, Willy Lindstrom, Ken Linseman, Kevin Lowe, Dave Lumley, Kevin McClelland, Mark Messier, Andy Moog, Jaroslav Pouzar, Dave Semenko, Peter Pocklington (Owner), Glen Sather (General Manager/Coach), John Muckler (Ass't. Coach), Ted Green (Ass't. Coach), Bruce MacGregor (Ass't. General Manager), Barry Fraser (Director of Player Personnel/Chief Scout), Peter Millar (Athletic Therapist), Barrie Stafford (Trainer)
Scores: May 10 at New York — Edmonton 1, NY Islanders 0; May 12 at New York — NY Islanders 6, Edmonton 1; May 15 at Edmonton — Edmonton 7, NY Islanders 2; May 17 at Edmonton — Edmonton 7, NY Islanders 2; May 19 at Edmonton — Edmonton 5, NY Islanders 2.

1982-83 — New York Islanders — Mike Bossy, Bob Bourne, Paul Boutilier, Bill Carroll, Greg Gilbert, Clark Gillies, Butch Goring, Mats Hallin, Tomas Jonsson, Anders Kallur, Gord Lane, Dave Langevin, Mike McEwen, Roland Melanson, Wayne Merrick, Ken Morrow, Bob Nystrom, Stefan Persson, Denis Potvin, Bill Smith, Brent Sutter, Duane Sutter, John Tonelli, Bryan Trottier, Al Arbour (coach), Lorne Henning (ass't coach), Bill Torrey (general manager), Ron Waske, Jim Pickard (trainers)
Scores: May 10 at Edmonton — NY Islanders 2, Edmonton 0; May 12 at Edmonton — NY Islanders 6, Edmonton 3; May 14 at New York — NY Islanders 5, Edmonton 1; May 17 at New York — NY Islanders 4, Edmonton 2

1981-82 — New York Islanders — Mike Bossy, Bob Bourne, Bill Carroll, Butch Goring, Greg Gilbert, Clark Gillies, Tomas Jonsson, Anders Kallur, Gord Lane, Dave Langevin, Hector Marini, Mike McEwen, Roland Melanson, Wayne Merrick, Ken Morrow, Bob Nystrom, Stefan Persson, Denis Potvin, Bill Smith, Brent Sutter, Duane Sutter, John Tonelli, Bryan Trottier, Al Arbour (coach), Lorne Henning (ass't coach), Bill Torrey (general manager), Ron Waske, Jim Pickard (trainers)
Scores: May 8 at New York — NY Islanders 6, Vancouver 5; May 11 at New York — NY Islanders 6, Vancouver 4; May 13 at Vancouver — NY Islanders 3, Vancouver 0; May 16 at Vancouver — NY Islanders 3, Vancouver 1

1980-81 — New York Islanders — Denis Potvin, Mike McEwen, Ken Morrow, Gord Lane, Bob Lorimer, Stefan Persson, Dave Langevin, Mike Bossy, Bryan Trottier, Butch Goring, Wayne Merrick, Clark Gillies, John Tonelli, Bob Nystrom, Bill Carroll, Bob Bourne, Hector Marini, Anders Kallur, Duane Sutter, Garry Howatt, Lorne Henning, Bill Smith, Roland Melanson, Al Arbour (coach), Bill Torrey (general manager), Ron Waske, Jim Pickard (trainers).
Scores: May 12 at New York — NY Islanders 6, Minnesota 3; May 14 at New York — NY Islanders 6, Minnesota 3; May 17 at Minnesota — NY Islanders 7, Minnesota 5; May 19 at Minnesota— Minnesota 4, NY Islanders 2; May 21 at New York — NY Islanders 5, Minnesota 1.

1979-80 — New York Islanders — Gord Lane, Jean Potvin, Bob Lorimer, Denis Potvin, Stefan Persson, Ken Morrow, Dave Langevin, Duane Sutter, Garry Howatt, Clark Gillies, Lorne Henning, Wayne Merrick, Bob Bourne, Steve Tambellini, Bryan Trottier, Mike Bossy, Bob Nystrom, John Tonelli, Anders Kallur, Butch Goring, Alex McKendry, Glenn Resch, Billy Smith, Al Arbour (coach), Bill Torrey (general manager), Ron Waske, Jim Pickard (trainers).
Scores: May 13 at Philadelphia — NY Islanders 4, Philadelphia 3; May 15 at Philadelphia — Philadelphia 8, NY Islanders 3; May 17 at New York — NY Islanders 6, Philadelphia 2; May 19 at New York — NY Islanders 5, Philadelphia 2; May 22 at Philadelphia — Philadelphia 6, NY Islanders 3; May 24 at New York — NY Islanders 5, Philadelphia 4.

1978-79 — Montreal Canadiens — Ken Dryden, Larry Robinson, Serge Savard, Guy Lapointe, Brian Engblom, Gilles Lupien, Rick Chartraw, Guy Lafleur, Steve Shutt, Jacques Lemaire, Yvan Cournoyer, Réjean Houle, Pierre Mondou, Bob Gainey, Doug Jarvis, Yvon Lambert, Doug Risebrough, Pierre Larouche, Mario Tremblay, Cam Connor, Pat Hughes, Rod Langway, Mark Napier, Michel Larocque, Richard Sévigny, Scotty Bowman (coach), Irving Grundman (managing director), Eddy Palchak, Pierre Meilleur (trainers).
Scores: May 13 at Montreal — NY Rangers 4, Montreal 1; May 15 at Montreal — Montreal 6, NY Rangers 2; May 17 at New York — Montreal 4, NY Rangers 1; May 19 at New York — Montreal 4, NY Rangers 3; May 21 at Montreal — Montreal 4, NY Rangers 1.

1977-78 — Montreal Canadiens — Ken Dryden, Larry Robinson, Serge Savard, Guy Lapointe, Bill Nyrop, Pierre Bouchard, Brian Engblom, Gilles Lupien, Rick Chartraw, Guy Lafleur, Steve Shutt, Jacques Lemaire, Yvan Cournoyer, Réjean Houle, Pierre Mondou, Bob Gainey, Doug Jarvis, Yvon Lambert, Doug Risebrough, Pierre Larouche, Mario Tremblay, Michel Larocque, Murray Wilson, Scotty Bowman (coach), Sam Pollock (general manager), Eddy Palchak, Pierre Meilleur (trainers).
Scores: May 13 at Montreal — Montreal 4, Boston 1; May 16 at Montreal — Montreal 3, Boston 2; May 18 at Boston — Boston 4, Montreal 0; May 21 at Boston — Boston 4, Montreal 3; May 23 at Montreal — Montreal 4, Boston 1; May 25 at Boston — Montreal 4, Boston 1.

1976-77 — Montreal Canadiens — Ken Dryden, Guy Lapointe, Larry Robinson, Serge Savard, Jimmy Roberts, Rick Chartraw, Bill Nyrop, Pierre Bouchard, Brian Engblom, Yvan Cournoyer, Guy Lafleur, Jacques Lemaire, Steve Shutt, Pete Mahovlich, Murray Wilson, Doug Jarvis, Yvon Lambert, Bob Gainey, Doug Risebrough, Mario Tremblay, Rejean Houle, Pierre Mondou, Mike Polich, Michel Larocque, Scotty Bowman (coach), Sam Pollock (general manager), Eddy Palchak, Pierre Meilleur (trainers).
Scores: May 7 at Montreal — Montreal 7, Boston 3; May 10 at Montreal — Montreal 3, Boston 0; May 12 at Boston — Montreal 4, Boston 2; May 14 at Boston — Montreal 2, Boston 1.

1975-76 — Montreal Canadiens — Ken Dryden, Serge Savard, Guy Lapointe, Larry Robinson, Bill Nyrop, Pierre Bouchard, Jim Roberts, Guy Lafleur, Steve Shutt, Pete Mahovlich, Yvan Cournoyer, Jacques Lemaire, Yvon Lambert, Bob Gainey, Doug Jarvis, Doug Risebrough, Murray Wilson, Mario Tremblay, Rick Chartraw, Michel Larocque, Scotty Bowman (coach), Sam Pollock (general manager), Eddy Palchak, Pierre Meilleur (trainers).
Scores: May 9 at Montreal — Montreal 4, Philadelphia 3; May 11 at Montreal — Montreal 2, Philadelphia 1; May 13 at Philadelphia — Montreal 3, Philadelphia 2; May 16 at Philadelphia — Montreal 5, Philadelphia 3.

1974-75 — Philadelphia Flyers — Bernie Parent, Wayne Stephenson, Ed Van Impe, Tom Bladon, André Dupont, Joe Watson, Jim Watson, Ted Harris, Larry Goodenough, Rick MacLeish, Bobby Clarke, Bill Barber, Reggie Leach, Gary Dornhoefer, Ross Lonsberry, Bob Kelly, Terry Crisp, Don Saleski, Dave Schultz, Orest Kindrachuk, Bill Clement, Fred Shero (coach), Keith Allen (general manager), Frank Lewis, Jim McKenzie (trainers).
Scores: May 15 at Philadelphia — Philadelphia 4, Buffalo 1; May 18 at Philadelphia — Philadelphia 2, Buffalo 1; May 20 at Buffalo — Buffalo 5, Philadelphia 4; May 22 at Buffalo — Buffalo 4, Philadelphia 2; May 25 at Philadelphia — Philadelphia 5, Buffalo 1; May 27 at Buffalo — Philadelphia 2, Buffalo 0.

1973-74 — Philadelphia Flyers — Bernie Parent, Ed Van Impe, Tom Bladon, André Dupont, Joe Watson, Jim Watson, Barry Ashbee, Bill Barber, Dave Schultz, Don Saleski, Gary Dornhoefer, Terry Crisp, Bobby Clarke, Simon Nolet, Ross Lonsberry, Rick MacLeish, Bill Flett, Orest Kindrachuk, Bill Clement, Bob Kelly, Bruce Cowick, Al MacAdam, Bobby Taylor, Fred Shero (coach), Keith Allen (general manager), Frank Lewis, Jim McKenzie (trainers).
Scores: May 7 at Boston — Boston 3, Philadelphia 2; May 9 at Boston — Philadelphia 3, Boston 2; May 12 at Philadelphia — Philadelphia 4, Boston 1; May 14 at Philadelphia — Philadelphia 4, Boston 2; May 16 at Boston — Boston 5, Philadelphia 1; May 19 at Philadelphia — Philadelphia 1, Boston 0.

1972-73 — Montreal Canadiens — Ken Dryden, Guy Lapointe, Serge Savard, Larry Robinson, Jacques Laperrière, Bob Murdoch, Pierre Bouchard, Jim Roberts, Yvan Cournoyer, Frank Mahovlich, Jacques Lemaire, Pete Mahovlich, Marc Tardif, Henri Richard, Réjean Houle, Guy Lafleur, Chuck Lefley, Claude Larose, Murray Wilson, Steve Shutt, Michel Plasse, Scotty Bowman (coach), Sam Pollock (general manager), Ed Palchak, Bob Williams (trainers).
Scores: April 29 at Montreal — Montreal 8, Chicago 3; May 1 at Montreal — Montreal 4, Chicago 1; May 3 at Chicago — Chicago 7, Montreal 4; May 6 at Chicago — Montreal 4, Chicago 0; May 8 at Montreal — Chicago 8, Montreal 7; May 10 at Chicago — Montreal 6, Chicago 4.

1971-72 — Boston Bruins — Gerry Cheevers, Ed Johnston, Bobby Orr, Ted Green, Carol Vadnais, Dallas Smith, Don Awrey, Phil Esposito, Ken Hodge, John Bucyk, Mike Walton, Wayne Cashman, Garnet Bailey, Derek Sanderson, Fred Stanfield, Ed Westfall, John McKenzie, Don Marcotte, Garry Peters, Chris Hayes, Tom Johnson (coach), Milt Schmidt (general manager), Dan Canney, John Forristall (trainers).
Scores: April 30 at Boston — Boston 6, NY Rangers 5; May 2 at Boston — Boston 2, NY Rangers 1; May 4 at New York — NY Rangers 5, Boston 2; May 7 at New York — Boston 3, NY Rangers 2; May 9 at Boston — NY Rangers 3, Boston 2; May 11 at New York — Boston 3, NY Rangers 0.

1970-71 — Montreal Canadiens — Ken Dryden, Rogatien Vachon, Jacques Laperrière, Jean-Claude Tremblay, Guy Lapointe, Terry Harper, Pierre Bouchard, Jean Béliveau, Marc Tardif, Yvan Cournoyer, Réjean Houle, Claude Larose, Henri Richard, Phil Roberto, Pete Mahovlich, Leon Rochefort, John Ferguson, Bobby Sheehan, Jacques Lemaire, Frank Mahovlich, Bob Murdoch, Chuck Lefley, Al MacNeil (coach), Sam Pollock (general manager), Yvon Belanger, Ed Palchak (trainers).
Scores: May 4 at Chicago — Chicago 2, Montreal 1; May 6 at Chicago — Chicago 5, Montreal 3; May 9 at Montreal — Montreal 4, Chicago 2; May 11 at Montreal — Montreal 5, Chicago 2; May 13 at Chicago — Chicago 2, Montreal 0; May 16 at Montreal — Montreal 4, Chicago 3; May 18 at Chicago — Montreal 3, Chicago 2.

1969-70 — Boston Bruins — Gerry Cheevers, Ed Johnston, Bobby Orr, Rick Smith, Dallas Smith, Bill Speer, Gary Doak, Don Awrey, Phil Esposito, Ken Hodge, John Bucyk, Wayne Carleton, Wayne Cashman, Derek Sanderson, Fred Stanfield, Ed Westfall, John McKenzie, Jim Lorentz, Don Marcotte, Bill Lesuk, Dan Schock, Harry Sinden (coach), Milt Schmidt (general manager), Dan Canney, John Forristall (trainers).
Scores: May 3 at St. Louis — Boston 6, St. Louis 1; May 5 at St. Louis — Boston 6, St. Louis 2; May 7 at Boston — Boston 4, St. Louis 1; May 10 at Boston — Boston 4, St. Louis 3.

1968-69 — Montreal Canadiens — Lorne Worsley, Rogatien Vachon, Jacques Laperrière, Jean-Claude Tremblay, Ted Harris, Serge Savard, Terry Harper, Larry Hillman, Jean Béliveau, Ralph Backstrom, Dick Duff, Yvan Cournoyer, Claude Provost, Bobby Rousseau, Henri Richard, John Ferguson, Christian Bordeleau, Mickey Redmond, Jacques Lemaire, Lucien Grenier, Tony Esposito, Claude Ruel (coach), Sam Pollock (general manager), Larry Aubut, Eddy Palchak (trainers).
Scores: April 27 at Montreal — Montreal 3, St. Louis 1; April 29 at Montreal — Montreal 3, St. Louis 1; May 1 at St. Louis — Montreal 4, St. Louis 0; May 4 at St. Louis — Montreal 2, St. Louis 1.

1967-68 — Montreal Canadiens — Lorne Worsley, Rogatien Vachon, Jacques Laperrière, Jean-Claude Tremblay, Ted Harris, Serge Savard, Terry Harper, Carol Vadnais, Jean Béliveau, Gilles Tremblay, Ralph Backstrom, Dick Duff, Claude Larose, Yvan Cournoyer, Claude Provost, Bobby Rousseau, Henri Richard, John Ferguson, Danny Grant, Jacques Lemaire, Mickey Redmond, Toe Blake (coach), Sam Pollock (general manager), Larry Aubut, Eddy Palchak (trainers).
Scores: May 5 at St. Louis — Montreal 3, St. Louis 2; May 7 at St. Louis — Montreal 1, St. Louis 0; May 9 at Montreal — Montreal 4, St. Louis 3; May 11 at Montreal — Montreal 3, St. Louis 2.

1966-67 — Toronto Maple Leafs — Johnny Bower, Terry Sawchuk, Larry Hillman, Marcel Pronovost, Tim Horton, Bob Baun, Aut Erickson, Allan Stanley, Red Kelly, Ron Ellis, George Armstrong, Pete Stemkowski, Dave Keon, Mike Walton, Jim Pappin, Bob Pulford, Brian Conacher, Eddie Shack, Frank Mahovlich, Milan Marcetta, Larry Jeffrey, Bruce Gamble, Punch Imlach (manager-coach), Bob Haggart (trainer).
Scores: April 20 at Montreal — Toronto 2, Montreal 6; April 22 at Montreal — Toronto 3, Montreal 0; April 25 at Toronto — Toronto 3, Montreal 2; April 27 at Toronto — Toronto 2, Montreal 6; April 29 at Montreal — Toronto 4, Montreal 1; May 2 at Toronto — Toronto 3, Montreal 1.

1965-66 — Montreal Canadiens — Lorne Worsley, Charlie Hodge, Jean-Claude Tremblay, Ted Harris, Jean-Guy Talbot, Terry Harper, Jacques Laperrière, Noel Price, Jean Béliveau, Ralph Backstrom, Dick Duff, Gilles Tremblay, Claude Larose, Yvan Cournoyer, Claude Provost, Bobby Rousseau, Henri Richard, Dave Balon, John Ferguson, Leon Rochefort, Jim Roberts, Toe Blake (coch), Sam Pollock (general manager), Larry Aubut, Andy Galley (trainers).
Scores: April 24 at Montreal — Detroit 3, Montreal 2; April 26 at Montreal — Detroit 5, Montreal 2; April 28 at Detroit — Montreal 4, Detroit 2; May 1 at Detroit — Montreal 2, Detroit 1; May 3 at Montreal — Montreal 5, Detroit 1; May 5 at Detroit — Montreal 3, Detroit 2.

1964-65 — Montreal Canadiens — Lorne Worsley, Charlie Hodge, Jean-Claude Tremblay, Ted Harris, Jean-Guy Talbot, Terry Harper, Jacques Laperrière, Jean Gauthier, Noel Picard, Jean Béliveau, Ralph Backstrom, Dick Duff, Claude Larose, Yvan Cournoyer, Claude Provost, Bobby Rousseau, Henri Richard, Dave Balon, John Ferguson, Jim Roberts, Toe Blake (coach), Sam Pollock (general manager), Larry Aubut, Andy Galley (trainers).
Scores: April 17 at Montreal — Montreal 3, Chicago 2; April 20 at Montreal — Montreal 2, Chicago 0; April 22 at Chicago — Montreal 1, Chicago 3; April 25 at Chicago — Montreal 1, Chicago 5; April 7 at Montreal — Montreal 6, Chicago 0; April 29 at Chicago — Montreal 1, Chicago 2; May 1 at Montreal — Montreal 4, Chicago 0.

1963-64 — Toronto Maple Leafs — Johnny Bower, Carl Brewer, Tim Horton, Bob Baun, Allan Stanley, Larry Hillman, Al Arbour, Red Kelly, Gerry Ehman, Andy Bathgate, George Armstrong, Ron Stewart, Dave Keon, Billy Harris, Bob Pulford, Eddie Shack, Frank Mahovlich, Eddie Litzenberger, Punch Imlach (manager-coach), Bob Haggert (trainer).
Scores April 11 at Toronto — Toronto 3, Detroit 2; April 14 at Toronto — Toronto 3, Detroit 4; April 16 at Detroit — Toronto 3, Detroit 4; April 18 at Detroit — Toronto 4, Detroit 2; April 21 at Toronto — Toronto 1, Detroit 2; April 23 at Detroit — Toronto 4, Detroit 3; April 25 at Toronto — Toronto 4, Detroit 0.

1962-63 — Toronto Maple Leafs — Johnny Bower, Don Simmons, Carl Brewer, Tim Horton, Kent Douglas, Allan Stanley, Bob Baun, Larry Hillman, Red Kelly, Dick Duff, George Armstrong, Bob Nevin, Ron Stewart, Dave Keon, Billy Harris, Bob Pulford, Eddie Shack, Ed Litzenberger, Frank Mahovlich, John MacMillan, Punch Imlach (manager-coach), Bob Haggert (trainer).
Scores: April 9 at Toronto — Toronto 4, Detroit 2; April 11 at Toronto — Toronto 4, Detroit 2; April 14 at Detroit — Toronto 2, Detroit 3; April 16 at Detroit — Toronto 4, Detroit 2; April 18 at Toronto — Toronto 3, Detroit 1.

1961-62 — Toronto Maple Leafs — Johnny Bower, Don Simmons, Carl Brewer, Tim Horton, Bob Baun, Allan Stanley, Al Arbour, Larry Hillman, Red Kelly, Dick Duff, George Armstrong, Frank Mahovlich, Bob Nevin, Ron Stewart, Bill Harris, Bert Olmstead, Bob Pulford, Eddie Shack, Dave Keon, Ed Litzenberger, John MacMillan, Punch Imlach (manager-coach), Bob Haggert (trainer).
Scores: April 10 at Toronto — Toronto 4, Chicago 1; April 12 at Toronto — Toronto 3, Chicago 2; April 15 at Chicago — Toronto 0, Chicago 3; April 17 at Chicago — Toronto 1, Chicago 4; April 19 at Toronto —Toronto 8, Chicago 4; April 22 at Chicago — Toronto 2, Chicago 1.

1960-61 — Chicago Black Hawks — Glenn Hall, Al Arbour, Pierre Pilote, Elmer Vasko, Jack Evans, Dollard St. Laurent, Reg Fleming, Tod Sloan, Ron Murphy, Eddie Litzenberger, Bill Hay, Bobby Hull, Ab McDonald, Eric Nesterenko, Ken Wharram, Earl Balfour, Stan Mikita, Murray Balfour, Chico Maki, Wayne Hicks, Tommy Ivan (manager), Rudy Pilous (coach), Nick Garen (trainer).
Scores: April 6 at Chicago — Chicago 3, Detroit 2; April 8 at Detroit — Detroit 3, Chicago 1; April 10 at Chicago — Chicago 3, Detroit 1; April 12 at Detroit — Detroit 2, Chicago 1; April 14 at Chicago — Chicago 6, Detroit 3; April 16 at Detroit — Chicago 5, Detroit 1.

1959-60 — Montreal Canadiens — Jacques Plante, Charlie Hodge, Doug Harvey, Tom Johnson, Bob Turner, Jean-Guy Talbot, Albert Langlois, Ralph Backstrom, Jean Béliveau, Marcel Bonin, Bernie Geoffrion, Bill Hicke, Don Marshall, Ab McDonald, Dickie Moore, André Pronovost, Claude Provost, Henri Richard, Maurice Richard, Frank Selke (manager), Toe Blake (coach), Hector Dubois, Larry Aubut (trainers).
Scores: April 7 at Montreal — Montreal 4, Toronto 2; April 9 at Montreal — Montreal 2, Toronto 1; April 12 at Toronto — Montreal 5, Toronto 2; April 14 at Toronto — Montreal 4, Toronto 0.

1958-59 — Montreal Canadiens — Jacques Plante, Charlie Hodge, Doug Harvey, Tom Johnson, Bob Turner, Jean-Guy Talbot, Albert Langlois, Bernie Geoffrion, Ralph Backstrom, Bill Hicke, Maurice Richard, Dickie Moore, Claude Provost, Ab McDonald, Henri Richard, Marcel Bonin, Phil Goyette, Don Marshall, Jean Béliveau, Frank Selke (manager), Toe Blake (coach), Hector Dubois, Larry Aubut (trainers).
Scores: April 9 at Montreal — Montreal 5, Toronto 3; April 11 at Montreal — Montreal 3, Toronto 1; April 14 at Toronto — Toronto 3, Montreal 2; April 16 at Toronto — Montreal 3, Toronto 2; April 18 at Montreal — Montreal 5, Toronto 3.

1957-58 — Montreal Canadiens — Jacques Plante, Gerry McNeil, Doug Harvey, Tom Johnson, Bob Turner, Dollard St-Laurent, Jean-Guy Talbot, Albert Langlois, Jean Béliveau, Bernie Geoffrion, Maurice Richard, Dickie Moore, Claude Provost, Floyd Curry, Bert Olmstead, Henri Richard, Marcel Bonin, Phil Goyette, Don Marshall, André Pronovost, Connie Broden, Frank Selke (manager), Toe Blake (coach), Hector Dubois, Larry Aubut (trainers).
Scores: April 8 at Montreal —Montreal 2, Boston 1; April 10 at Montreal — Boston 5, Montreal 2; April 13 at Boston — Montreal 3, Boston 0; April 15 at Boston — Boston 3, Montreal 1; April 17 at Montreal — Montreal 3, Boston 2; April 20 at Boston — Montreal 5, Boston 3.

The Montreal Canadiens downed the Boston Bruins twice on the way to their record five consecutive Stanley Cup titles in the 1950s. Here, Bernie Geoffrion begins the traditional post-goal celebration after firing the puck past Boston's Don Simmons in game five of the 1957 final.

1956-57 — Montreal Canadiens — Jacques Plante, Gerry McNeil, Doug Harvey, Tom Johnson, Bob Turner, Dollard St. Laurent, Jean-Guy Talbot, Jean Béliveau, Bernie Geoffrion, Floyd Curry, Dickie Moore, Maurice Richard, Claude Provost, Bert Olmstead, Henri Richard, Phil Goyette, Don Marshall, André Pronovost, Connie Broden, Frank Selke (manager), Toe Blake (coach), Hector Dubois, Larry Aubut (trainers).
Scores: April 6, at Montreal — Montreal 5, Boston 1; April 9, at Montreal — Montreal 1, Boston 0; April 11, at Boston — Montreal 4, Boston 2; April 14, at Boston — Boston 2, Montreal 0; April 16, at Montreal — Montreal 5, Boston 1.

1955-56 — Montreal Canadiens — Jacques Plante, Doug Harvey, Emile Bouchard, Bob Turner, Tom Johnson, Jean-Guy Talbot, Dollard St. Laurent, Jean Béliveau, Bernie Geoffrion, Bert Olmstead, Floyd Curry, Jackie Leclair, Maurice Richard, Dickie Moore, Henri Richard, Ken Mosdell, Don Marshall, Claude Provost, Frank Selke (manager), Toe Blake (coach), Hector Dubois (trainer).
Scores: March 31, at Montreal — Montreal 6, Detroit 4; April 3, at Montreal — Montreal 5, Detroit 1; April 5, at Detroit — Detroit 3, Montreal 1; April 8, at Detroit — Montreal 3, Detroit 0; April 10, at Montreal — Montreal 3, Detroit 1.

1954-55 — Detroit Red Wings — Terry Sawchuk, Red Kelly, Bob Goldham, Marcel Pronovost, Ben Woit, Jim Hay, Larry Hillman, Ted Lindsay, Tony Leswick, Gordie Howe, Alex Delvecchio, Marty Pavelich, Glen Skov, Earl Reibel, John Wilson, Bill Dineen, Vic Stasiuk, Marcel Bonin, Jack Adams (manager), Jimmy Skinner (coach), Carl Mattson (trainer).
Scores: April 3, at Detroit — Detroit 4, Montreal 2; April 5, at Detroit — Detroit 7, Montreal 1, April 7 at Montreal — Montreal 4, Detroit 2; April 9, at Montreal — Montreal 5, Detroit 3; April 10, at Detroit — Detroit 5, Montreal 1; April 12, at Montreal — Montreal 6, Detroit 3; April 14, at Detroit — Detroit 3, Montreal 1

1953-54 — Detroit Red Wings — Terry Sawchuk, Red Kelly, Bob Goldham, Ben Woit, Marcel Pronovost, Al Arbour, Keith Allen, Ted Lindsay, Tony Leswick, Gordie Howe, Marty Pavelich, Alex Delvecchio, Metro Prystai, Glen Skov, John Wilson, Bill Dineen, Jim Peters, Earl Reibel, Vic Stasiuk, Jack Adams (manager), Tommy Ivan (coach), Carl Mattson (trainer).
Scores: April 4, at Detroit — Detroit 3, Montreal 1; April 6, at Detroit — Montreal 3, Detroit 1; April 8, at Montreal — Detroit 5, Montreal 2; April 10, at Montreal — Detroit 2, Montreal 0; April 11, at Detroit — Montreal 1, Detroit 0; April 13, at Montreal — Montreal 4, Detroit 1; April 16, at Detroit — Detroit 2, Montreal 1.

1952-53 — Montreal Canadiens — Gerry McNeil, Jacques Plante, Doug Harvey, Emile Bouchard, Tom Johnson, Dollard St. Laurent, Bud MacPherson, Maurice Richard, Elmer Lach, Bert Olmstead, Bernie Geoffrion, Floyd Curry, Paul Masnick, Billy Reay, Dickie Moore, Ken Mosdell, Dick Gamble, Johnny McCormack, Lorne Davis, Calum McKay, Eddie Mazur, Frank Selke (manager), Dick Irvin (coach), Hector Dubois (trainer).
Scores: April 9, at Montreal — Montreal 4, Boston 2; April 11, at Montreal — Boston 4, Montreal 1; April 12, at Boston — Montreal 3, Boston 0; April 14, at Boston — Montreal 7, Boston 3; April 16, at Montreal — Montreal 1, Boston 0.

1951-52 — Detroit Red Wings — Terry Sawchuk, Bob Goldham, Ben Woit, Red Kelly, Leo Reise, Marcel Pronovost, Ted Lindsay, Tony Leswick, Gordie Howe, Metro Prystai, Marty Pavelich, Sid Abel, Glen Skov, Alex Delvecchio, John Wilson, Vic Stasiuk, Larry Zeidel, Jack Adams (manager) Tommy Ivan (coach), Carl Mattson (trainer).
Scores: April 10, at Montreal — Detroit 3, Montreal 1; April 12 at Montreal — Detroit 2, Montreal 1; April 13 — at Detroit — Detroit 3, Montreal 0; April 15 at Detroit — Detroit 3, Montreal 0.

1950-51 — Toronto Maple Leafs — Turk Broda, Al Rollins, Jim Thomson, Gus Mortson, Bill Barilko, Bill Juzda, Fern Flaman, Hugh Bolton, Ted Kennedy, Sid Smith, Tod Sloan, Cal Gardner, Howie Meeker, Harry Watson, Max Bentley, Joe Klukay, Danny Lewicki, Ray Timgren, Fleming Mackell, Johnny McCormack, Bob Hassard, Conn Smythe (manager), Joe Primeau (coach), Tim Daly (trainer).
Scores: April 11, at Toronto — Toronto 3, Montreal 2; April 14, at Toronto — Montreal 3, Toronto 2; April 17, at Montreal — Toronto 2, Montreal 1; April 19, at Montreal — Toronto 3, Montreal 2; April 21, at Toronto — Toronto 3, Montreal 2.

1949-50 — Detroit Red Wings — Harry Lumley, Jack Stewart, Leo Reise, Clare Martin, Al Dewsbury, Lee Fogolin, Marcel Pronovost, Red Kelly, Ted Lindsay, Sid Abel, Gordie Howe, George Gee, Jimmy Peters, Marty Pavelich, Pete Babando, Max McNab, Gerry Couture, Joe Carveth, Steve Black, John Wilson, Larry Wilson, Jack Adams (manager), Tommy Ivan (coach), Carl Mattson (trainer).
Scores: April 11, at Detroit — Detroit 4, NY Rangers 1; April 13, at Toronto* — NY Rangers 3, Detroit 1; April 15, at Toronto — Detroit 4, NY Rangers 0; April 18, at Detroit — NY Rangers 4, Detroit 3; April 20, at Detroit — NY Rangers 2, Detroit 1; April 22, at Detroit — Detroit 5, NY Rangers 4; April 23, at Detroit — Detroit 4, NY Rangers 3.
* Ice was unavailable in Madison Square Garden and Rangers elected to play second and third games on Toronto ice.

1948-49 — Toronto Maple Leafs — Turk Broda, Jim Thomson, Gus Mortson, Bill Barilko, Garth Boesch, Bill Juzda, Ted Kennedy, Howie Meeker, Vic Lynn, Harry Watson, Bill Ezinicki, Cal Gardner, Max Bentley, Joe Klukay, Sid Smith, Don Metz, Fleming Mackell, Harry Taylor, Bob Dawes, Tod Sloan, Conn Smythe (manager), Hap Day (coach), Tim Daly (trainer).
Scores: April 8, at Detroit — Toronto 3, Detroit 2; April 10, at Detroit — Toronto 3, Detroit 1; April 13, at Toronto — Toronto 3, Detroit 1; April 16, at Toronto — Toronto 3, Detroit 1.

1947-48 — Toronto Maple Leafs — Turk Broda, Jim Thomson, Wally Stanowski, Garth Boesch, Bill Barilko, Gus Mortson, Phil Samis, Syl Apps, Bill Ezinicki, Harry Watson, Ted Kennedy, Howie Meeker, Vic Lynn, Nick Metz, Max Bentley, Joe Klukay, Les Costello, Don Metz, Sid Smith, Conn Smythe (manager), Hap Day (coach), Tim Daly (trainer).
Scores: April 7, at Toronto — Toronto 5, Detroit 3; April 10, at Toronto — Toronto 4, Detroit 2; April 11, at Detroit — Toronto 2, Detroit 0; April 14, at Detroit — Toronto 7, Detroit 2.

The Toronto Maple Leafs and the Detroit Red Wings met 14 times in the Stanley Cup playoffs during the six-team era, with each club winning seven series apiece. In this action from the 1952 semi-finals, Terry Sawchuk makes a nifty pad save on Leaf forward Sid Smith (8), helping the Wings eliminate the Leafs in four straight games.

1946-47 — Toronto Maple Leafs — Turk Broda, Garth Boesch, Gus Mortson, Jim Thomson, Wally Stanowski, Bill Barilko, Harry Watson, Bud Poile, Ted Kennedy, Syl Apps, Don Metz, Nick Metz, Bill Ezinicki, Vic Lynn, Howie Meeker, Gaye Stewart, Joe Klukay, Gus Bodnar, Bob Goldham, Conn Smythe (manager), Hap Day (coach), Tim Daly (trainer).
Scores: April 8, at Montreal — Montreal 6, Toronto 0; April 10, at Montreal — Toronto 4, Montreal 0; April 12, at Toronto — Toronto 4, Montreal 2; April 15, at Toronto — Toronto 2, Montreal 1; April 17, at Montreal — Montreal 3, Toronto 1; April 19, at Toronto — Toronto 2, Montreal 1.

1945-46 — Montreal Canadiens — Elmer Lach, Toe Blake, Maurice Richard, Bob Fillion, Dutch Hiller, Murph Chamberlain, Ken Mosdell, Buddy O'Connor, Glen Harmon, Jim Peters, Emile Bouchard, Bill Reay, Ken Reardon, Leo Lamoureux, Frank Eddolls, Gerry Plamondon, Bill Durnan, Tommy Gorman (manager), Dick Irvin (coach), Ernie Cook (trainer).
Scores: March 30, at Montreal — Montreal 4, Boston 3; April 2, at Montreal — Montreal 3, Boston 2; April 4, at Boston — Montreal 4, Boston 2; April 7, at Boston — Boston 3, Montreal 2; April 9, at Montreal — Montreal 6, Boston 3.

1944-45 — Toronto Maple Leafs — Don Metz, Frank McCool, Wally Stanowski, Reg Hamilton, Elwyn Morris, Johnny McCreedy, Tommy O'Neill, Ted Kennedy, Babe Pratt, Gus Bodnar, Art Jackson, Jack McLean, Mel Hill, Nick Metz, Bob Davidson, Dave Schriner, Lorne Carr, Conn Smythe (manager), Frank Selke (business manager), Hap Day (coach), Tim Daly (trainer).
Scores: April 6, at Detroit — Toronto 1, Detroit 0; April 8, at Detroit — Toronto 2, Detroit 0; April 12, at Toronto — Toronto 1, Detroit 0; April 14, at Toronto — Detroit 5, Toronto 3; April 19, at Detroit — Detroit 2, Toronto 0; April 21, at Toronto — Detroit 1, Toronto 0; April 22, at Detroit — Toronto 2, Detroit 1.

1943-44 — Montreal Canadiens — Toe Blake, Maurice Richard, Elmer Lach, Ray Getliffe, Murph Chamberlain, Phil Watson, Emile Bouchard, Glen Harmon, Buddy O'Connor, Jerry Heffernan, Mike McMahon, Leo Lamoureux, Fernand Majeau, Bob Fillion, Bill Durnan, Tommy Gorman (manager), Dick Irvin (coach), Ernie Cook (trainer).
Scores: April 4, at Montreal — Montreal 5, Chicago 1; April 6, at Chicago — Montreal 3, Chicago 1; April 9, at Chicago — Montreal 3, Chicago 2; April 13, at Montreal — Montreal 5, Chicago 4.

1942-43 — Detroit Red Wings — Jack Stewart, Jimmy Orlando, Sid Abel, Alex Motter, Harry Watson, Joe Carveth, Mud Bruneteau, Eddie Wares, Johnny Mowers, Cully Simon, Don Grosso, Carl Liscombe, Connie Brown, Syd Howe, Les Douglas, Hal Jackson, Joe Fisher, Jack Adams (manager), Ebbie Goodfellow (playing-coach), Honey Walker (trainer).
Scores: April 1, at Detroit — Detroit 6, Boston 2; April 4, at Detroit — Detroit 4, Boston 3; April 7, at Boston — Detroit 4, Boston 0; April 8, at Boston — Detroit 2, Boston 0.

1941-42 — Toronto Maple Leafs — Wally Stanowski, Syl Apps, Bob Goldham, Gord Drillon, Hank Goldup, Ernie Dickens, Dave Schriner, Bucko McDonald, Bob Davidson, Nick Metz, Bingo Kampman, Don Metz, Gaye Stewart, Turk Broda, Johnny McCreedy, Lorne Carr, Pete Langelle, Billy Taylor, Conn Smythe (manager), Hap Day (coach), Frank Selke (business manager), Tim Daly (trainer).
Scores: April 4, at Toronto — Detroit 3, Toronto 2; April 7, at Toronto — Detroit 4, Toronto 2; April 9, at Detroit — Detroit 5, Toronto 2; April 12, at Detroit — Toronto 4, Detroit 3; April 14, at Toronto — Toronto 9, Detroit 3; April 16, at Detroit — Toronto 3, Detroit 0; April 18, at Toronto — Toronto 3, Detroit 1.

1940-41 — Boston Bruins — Bill Cowley, Des Smith, Dit Clapper, Frank Brimsek, Flash Hollett, John Crawford, Bobby Bauer, Pat McReavy, Herb Cain, Mel Hill, Milt Schmidt, Woody Dumart, Roy Conacher, Terry Reardon, Art Jackson, Eddie Wiseman, Art Ross (manager), Cooney Weiland (coach), Win Green (trainer).
Scores: April 6, at Boston — Detroit 2, Boston 3; April 8, at Boston — Detroit 1, Boston 2; April 10, at Detroit — Boston 4, Detroit 2; April 12, at Detroit — Boston 3, Detroit 1.

1939-40 — New York Rangers — Dave Kerr, Art Coulter, Ott Heller, Alex Shibicky, Mac Colville, Neil Colville, Phil Watson, Lynn Patrick, Clint Smith, Muzz Patrick, Babe Pratt, Bryan Hextall, Kilby Macdonald, Dutch Hiller, Alf Pike, Sanford Smith, Lester Patrick (manager), Frank Boucher (coach), Harry Westerby (trainer).
Scores: April 2, at New York — NY Rangers 2, Toronto 1; April 3, at New York — NY Rangers 6, Toronto 2; April 6, at Toronto — NY Rangers 1, Toronto 2; April 9, at Toronto — NY Rangers 0, Toronto 3; April 11, at Toronto — NY Rangers 2, Toronto 1; April 13, at Toronto — NY Rangers 3, Toronto 2.

1938-39 — Boston Bruins — Bobby Bauer, Mel Hill, Flash Hollett, Roy Conacher, Gord Pettinger, Milt Schmidt, Woody Dumart, Jack Crawford, Ray Getliffe, Frank Brimsek, Eddie Shore, Dit Clapper, Bill Cowley, Jack Portland, Red Hamill, Cooney Weiland, Art Ross (manager-coach), Win Green (trainer).
Scores: April 6, at Boston — Toronto 1, Boston 2; April 9, at Boston — Toronto 3, Boston 2; April 11, at Toronto — Toronto 1, Boston 3; April 13 at Toronto — Toronto 0, Boston 2; April 16, at Boston — Toronto 1, Boston 3.

1937-38 — Chicago Black Hawks — Art Wiebe, Carl Voss, Hal Jackson, Mike Karakas, Mush March, Jack Shill, Earl Seibert, Cully Dahlstrom, Alex Levinsky, Johnny Gottselig, Lou Trudel, Pete Palangio, Bill MacKenzie, Doc Romnes, Paul Thompson, Roger Jenkins, Alf Moore, Bert Connolly, Virgil Johnson, Paul Goodman, Bill Stewart (manager-coach), Eddie Froelich (trainer).
Scores: April 5, at Toronto — Chicago 3, Toronto 1; April 7, at Toronto — Chicago 1, Toronto 5; April 10 at Chicago — Chicago 2, Toronto 1; April 12, at Chicago — Chicago 4, Toronto 1.

1936-37 — Detroit Red Wings — Normie Smith, Pete Kelly, Larry Aurie, Herbie Lewis, Hec Kilrea, Mud Bruneteau, Syd Howe, Wally Kilrea, Jimmy Franks, Bucko McDonald, Gordon Pettinger, Ebbie Goodfellow, Johnny Gallagher, Scotty Bowman, Johnny Sorrell, Marty Barry, Earl Robertson, Johnny Sherf, Howard Mackie, Jack Adams (manager-coach), Honey Walker (trainer).
Scores: April 6, at New York — Detroit 1, NY Rangers 5; April 8, at Detroit — Detroit 4, NY Rangers 2; April 11, at Detroit — Detroit 0, NY Rangers 1; April 13, at Detroit — Detroit 1, NY Rangers 0; April 15, at Detroit — Detroit 3, NY Rangers 0.

1935-36 — Detroit Red Wings — Johnny Sorrell, Syd Howe, Marty Barry, Herbie Lewis, Mud Bruneteau, Wally Kilrea, Hec Kilrea, Gordon Pettinger, Bucko McDonald, Scotty Bowman, Pete Kelly, Doug Young, Ebbie Goodfellow, Normie Smith, Jack Adams (manager-coach), Honey Walker (trainer).
Scores: April 5, at Detroit — Detroit 3, Toronto 1; April 7, at Detroit — Detroit 9, Toronto 4; April 9, at Toronto — Detroit 3, Toronto 4; April 11, at Toronto — Detroit 3, Toronto 2.

1934-35 — Montreal Maroons — Marvin (Cy) Wentworth, Alex Connell, Toe Blake, Stew Evans, Earl Robinson, Bill Miller, Dave Trottier, Jimmy Ward, Larry Northcott, Hooley Smith, Russ Blinco, Allan Shields, Sammy McManus, Gus Marker, Bob Gracie, Herb Cain, Tommy Gorman (manager), Lionel Conacher (coach), Bill O'Brien (trainer).
Scores: April 4, at Toronto — Mtl. Maroons 3, Toronto 2; April 6, at Toronto — Mtl. Maroons 3, Toronto 1; April 9, at Montreal — Mtl. Maroons 4, Toronto 1.

1933-34 — Chicago Black Hawks — Taffy Abel, Lolo Couture, Lou Trudel, Lionel Conacher, Paul Thompson, Leroy Goldsworthy, Art Coulter, Roger Jenkins, Don McFayden, Tommy Cook, Doc Romnes, Johnny Gottselig, Mush March, Johnny Sheppard, Chuck Gardiner (captain), Bill Kendall, Tommy Gorman (manager-coach), Eddie Froelich (trainer).
Scores: April 3, at Detroit — Chicago 2, Detroit 1; April 5, at Detroit — Chicago 4, Detroit 1; April 8, at Chicago — Detroit 5, Chicago 2; April 10, at Chicago — Chicago 1, Detroit 0.

1932-33 — New York Rangers — Ching Johnson, Butch Keeling, Frank Boucher, Art Somers, Babe Siebert, Bun Cook, Andy Aitkenhead, Ott Heller, Ozzie Asmundson, Gord Pettinger, Doug Brennan, Cecil Dillon, Bill Cook (captain), Murray Murdoch, Earl Seibert, Lester Patrick (manager-coach), Harry Westerby (trainer).
Scores: April 4, at New York — NY Rangers 5, Toronto 1; April 8, at Toronto — NY Rangers 3, Toronto 1; April 11, at Toronto — Toronto 3, NY Rangers 2; April 13, at Toronto — NY Rangers 1, Toronto 0.

1931-32 — Toronto Maple Leafs — Charlie Conacher, Harvey Jackson, King Clancy, Andy Blair, Red Horner, Lorne Chabot, Alex Levinsky, Joe Primeau, Hal Darragh, Hal Cotton, Frank Finnigan, Hap Day, Ace Bailey, Bob Gracie, Fred Robertson, Earl Miller, Conn Smythe (manager), Dick Irvin (coach), Tim Daly (trainer).
Scores: April 5 at New York — Toronto 6, NY Rangers 4; April 7, at Boston* — Toronto 6, NY Rangers 2; April 9, at Toronto — Toronto 6, NY Rangers 4.
* Ice was unavailable in Madison Square Garden and Rangers elected to play the second game on neutral ice.

1930-31 — Montreal Canadiens — George Hainsworth, Wildor Larochelle, Marty Burke, Sylvio Mantha, Howie Morenz, Johnny Gagnon, Aurel Joliat, Armand Mondou, Pit Lepine, Albert Leduc, Georges Mantha, Art Lesieur, Nick Wasnie, Bert McCaffrey, Gus Rivers, Jean Pusie, Léo Dandurand (manager), Cecil Hart (coach), Ed Dufour (trainer).
Scores: April 3, at Chicago — Montreal 2, Chicago 1; April 5, at Chicago — Chicago 2, Montreal 1; April 9, at Montreal — Chicago 3, Montreal 2; April 11, at Montreal — Montreal 4, Chicago 2; April 14, at Montreal — Montreal 2, Chicago 0.

1929-30 — Montreal Canadiens — George Hainsworth, Marty Burke, Sylvio Mantha, Howie Morenz, Bert McCaffrey, Aurel Joliat, Albert Leduc, Pit Lepine, Wildor Larochelle, Nick Wasnie, Gerald Carson, Armand Mondou, Georges Mantha, Gus Rivers, Léo Dandurand (manager), Cecil Hart (coach), Ed Dufour (trainer).
Scores: April 1 at Boston — Montreal 3, Boston 0; April 3 at Montreal — Montreal 4, Boston 3.

1928-29 — Boston Bruins — Cecil (Tiny) Thompson, Eddie Shore, Lionel Hitchman, Perk Galbraith, Eric Pettinger, Frank Fredrickson, Mickey Mackay, Red Green, Dutch Gainor, Harry Oliver, Eddie Rodden, Dit Clapper, Cooney Weiland, Lloyd Klein, Cy Denneny, Bill Carson, George Owen, Myles Lane, Art Ross (manager-coach), Win Green (trainer).
Scores: March 28 at Boston — Boston 2, NY Rangers 0; March 29 at New York — Boston 2, NY Rangers 1.

1927-28 — New York Rangers — Lorne Chabot, Taffy Abel, Leon Bourgault, Ching Johnson, Bill Cook, Bun Cook, Frank Boucher, Billy Boyd, Murray Murdoch, Paul Thompson, Alex Gray, Joe Miller, Patsy Callighen, Lester Patrick (manager-coach), Harry Westerby (trainer).
Scores: April 5 at Montreal — Mtl. Maroons 2, NY Rangers 0; April 7 at Montreal — NY Rangers 2, Mtl. Maroons 1; April 10 at Montreal — Mtl. Maroons 2, NY Rangers 0; April 12 at Montreal — NY Rangers 1, Mtl. Maroons 0; April 14 at Montreal — NY Rangers 2, Mtl. Maroons 1.

1926-27 — Ottawa Senators — Alex Connell, King Clancy, George (Buck) Boucher, Ed Gorman, Frank Finnigan, Alex Smith, Hec Kilrea, Hooley Smith, Cy Denneny, Frank Nighbor, Jack Adams, Milt Halliday, Dave Gill (manager-coach).
Scores: April 7 at Boston — Ottawa 0, Boston 0; April 9 at Boston — Ottawa 3, Boston 1; April 11 at Ottawa — Boston 1, Ottawa 1; April 13 at Ottawa — Ottawa 3, Boston 1.

1925-26 — Montreal Maroons — Clint Benedict, Reg Noble, Frank Carson, Dunc Munro, Nels Stewart, Harry Broadbent, Babe Siebert, Dinny Dinsmore, Bill Phillips, Hobart (Hobie) Kitchen, Sammy Rothschield, Albert (Toots) Holway, Shorty Horne, Bern Brophy, Eddie Gerard (manager-coach), Bill O'Brien (trainer).
Scores: March 30 at Montreal — Mtl. Maroons 3, Victoria 0; April 1 at Montreal — Mtl. Maroons 3, Victoria 0; April 3 at Montreal — Victoria 3, Mtl. Maroons 2; April 6 at Montreal — Mtl. Maroons 2, Victoria 0.

The series in the spring of 1926 ended the annual playoffs between the champions of the East and the champions of the West. Since 1926-27 the annual playoffs in the National Hockey League have decided the Stanley Cup champions.

1924-25 — Victoria Cougars — Harry (Happy) Holmes, Clem Loughlin, Gordie Fraser, Frank Fredrickson, Jack Walker, Harold (Gizzy) Hart, Harold (Slim) Halderson, Frank Foyston, Wally Elmer, Harry Meeking, Jocko Anderson, Lester Patrick (manager-coach).
Scores: March 21 at Victoria — Victoria 5, Montreal 2; March 23 at Vancouver — Victoria 3, Montreal 1; March 27 at Victoria — Montreal 4, Victoria 2; March 30 at Victoria — Victoria 6, Montreal 1.

1923-24 — Montreal Canadiens — Georges Vezina, Sprague Cleghorn, Billy Couture, Howie Morenz, Aurel Joliat, Billy Boucher, Odie Cleghorn, Sylvio Mantha, Bobby Boucher, Billy Bell, Billy Cameron, Joe Malone, Charles Fortier, Leo Dandurand (manager-coach).
Scores: March 18 at Montreal — Montreal 3, Van. Maroons 2; March 20 at Montreal — Montreal 2, Van. Maroons 1. March 22 at Montreal — Montreal 6, Cgy. Tigers 1; March 25 at Ottawa* — Montreal 3, Cgy. Tigers 0.
* Game transferred to Ottawa to benefit from artificial ice surface.

1922-23 — Ottawa Senators — George (Buck) Boucher, Lionel Hitchman, Frank Nighbor, King Clancy, Harry Helman, Clint Benedict, Jack Darragh, Eddie Gerard, Cy Denneny, Harry Broadbent, Tommy Gorman (manager), Pete Green (coach), F. Dolan (trainer).
Scores: March 16 at Vancouver — Ottawa 1, Van. Maroons 0; March 19 at Vancouver — Van. Maroons 4, Ottawa 1; March 23 at Vancouver — Ottawa 3, Van. Maroons 2; March 26 at Vancouver — Ottawa 5, Van. Maroons 1; March 29 at Vancouver — Ottawa 2, Edm. Eskimos 1; March 31 at Vancouver — Ottawa 1, Edm. Eskimos 0.

The Ottawa Hockey Club, known as the Silver Seven during its glory days, successfully defended its Stanley Cup title ten times from March, 1903 to March 1906 against challenges from the Montreal Victorias, Montreal Wanderers, Rat Portage (twice), Brandon, Toronto, Winnipeg, Dawson City, Smiths Falls and Queen's University.

1921-22 — Toronto St. Pats — Ted Stackhouse, Corb Denneny, Rod Smylie, Lloyd Andrews, John Ross Roach, Harry Cameron, Bill (Red) Stuart, Cecil (Babe) Dye, Ken Randall, Reg Noble, Eddie Gerard (borrowed for one game from Ottawa), Stan Jackson, Nolan Mitchell, Charlie Querrie (manager), Eddie Powers (coach).
Scores: March 17 at Toronto — Van. Millionaires 4, Toronto 3; March 20 at Toronto — Toronto 2, Van. Millionaires 1; March 23 at Toronto — Van. Millionaires 3, Toronto 0; March 25 at Toronto — Toronto 6, Van. Millionaires 0; March 28 at Toronto — Toronto 5, Van. Millionaires 1.

1920-21 — Ottawa Senators — Jack McKell, Jack Darragh, Morley Bruce, George (Buck) Boucher, Eddie Gerard, Clint Benedict, Sprague Cleghorn, Frank Nighbor, Harry Broadbent, Cy Denneny, Leth Graham, Tommy Gorman (manager),Pete Green (coach), F. Dolan (trainer).
Scores: March 21 at Vancouver — Van. Millionaires 2, Ottawa 1; March 24 at Vancouver — Ottawa 4, Van. Millionaires 3; March 28 at Vancouver — Ottawa 3, Van. Millionaires 2; March 31 at Vancouver — Van. Millionaires 3, Ottawa 2; April 4 at Vancouver — Ottawa 2, Van. Millionaires 1

1919-20 — Ottawa Senators — Jack McKell, Jack Darragh, Morley Bruce, Horrace Merrill, George (Buck) Boucher, Eddie Gerard, Clint Benedict, Sprague Cleghorn, Frank Nighbor, Harry Broadbent, Cy Denneny, Price, Tommy Gorman (manager), Pete Green (coach).
Scores: March 22 at Ottawa — Ottawa 3, Seattle 2; March 24 at Ottawa — Ottawa 3, Seattle 0; March 27 at Ottawa — Seattle 3, Ottawa 1; March 30 at Toronto* — Seattle 5, Ottawa 2; April 1 at Toronto* — Ottawa 6, Seattle 1.
* Games transferred to Toronto to benefit from artificial ice surface.

1918-19 — No decision, Series halted by Spanish influenza epidemic, illness of several players and death of Joe Hall of Montreal Canadiens from flu. Five games had been played when the series was halted, each team having won two and tied one. The results are shown:
Scores: March 19 at Seattle — Seattle 7, Montreal 0; March 22 at Seattle — Montreal 4, Seattle 2; March 24 at Seattle — Seattle 7, Montreal 2; March 26 at Seattle — Montreal 0, Seattle 0; March 30 at Seattle — Montreal 4, Seattle 3.

1917-18 — Toronto Arenas — Rusty Crawford, Harry Meeking, Ken Randall, Corb Denneny, Harry Cameron, Jack Adams, Alf Skinner, Harry Mummery, Harry (Happy) Holmes, Reg Noble, Sammy Hebert, Jack Marks, Jack Coughlin, Neville, Charlie Querrie (manager), Dick Carroll (coach), Frank Carroll (trainer).
Scores: March 20 at Toronto — Toronto 5, Van. Millionaires 3; March 23 at Toronto — Van. Millionaires 6, Toronto 4; March 26 at Toronto — Toronto 6, Van. Millionaires 3; March 28 at Toronto — Van. Millionaires 8, Toronto 1; March 30 at Toronto — Toronto 2, Van. Millionaires 1.

1916-17 — Seattle Metropolitans — Harry (Happy) Holmes, Ed Carpenter, Cully Wilson, Jack Walker, Bernie Morris, Frank Foyston, Roy Rickey, Jim Riley, Bobby Rowe (captain), Peter Muldoon (manager).
Scores: March 17 at Seattle — Montreal 8, Seattle 4; March 20 at Seattle — Seattle 6, Montreal 1; March 23 at Seattle — Seattle 4, Montreal 1; March 25 at Seattle — Seattle 9, Montreal 1.

1915-16 — Montreal Canadiens — Georges Vezina, Bert Corbeau, Jack Laviolette, Newsy Lalonde, Louis Berlinguette, Goldie Prodgers, Howard McNamara, Didier Pitre, Skene Ronan, Amos Arbour, Georges Poulin, Jacques Fournier, George Kennedy (manager).
Scores: March 20 at Montreal — Portland 2, Montreal 0; March 22 at Montreal — Montreal 2, Portland 1; March 25 at Montreal — Montreal 6, Portland 3; March 28 at Montreal — Portland 6, Montreal 5; March 30 at Montreal — Montreal 2, Portland 1.

1914-15 — Vancouver Millionaires — Kenny Mallen, Frank Nighbor, Fred (Cyclone) Taylor, Hughie Lehman, Lloyd Cook, Mickey MacKay, Barney Stanley, Jim Seaborn, Si Griffis (captain), Jean Matz, Frank Patrick (playing manager).
Scores: March 22 at Vancouver — Van. Millionaires 6, Ottawa 2; March 24 at Vancouver — Van. Millionaires 8, Ottawa 3; March 26 at Vancouver — Van. Millionaires 12, Ottawa 3.

1913-14 — Toronto Blueshirts — Con Corbeau, F. Roy McGiffen, Jack Walker, George McNamara, Cully Wilson, Frank Foyston, Harry Cameron, Harry (Happy) Holmes, Alan M. Davidson (captain), Harriston, Jack Marshall (playing-manager), Frank and Dick Carroll (trainers).
Scores: March 14 at Toronto — Toronto 5, Victoria 2; March 17 at Toronto — Toronto 6, Victoria 5; March 19 at Toronto — Toronto 2, Victoria 1.

1912-13 — **Quebec Bulldogs** — Joe Malone, Joe Hall, Paddy Moran, Harry Mummery, Tommy Smith, Jack Marks, Russell Crawford, Billy Creighton, Jeff Malone, Rocket Power, M.J. Quinn (manager), D. Beland (trainer).
Scores: March 8 at Quebec — Que. Bulldogs 14, Sydney 3; March 10 at Quebec — Que. Bulldogs 6, Sydney 2.
Victoria challenged Quebec but the Bulldogs refused to put the Stanley Cup in competition so the two teams played an exhibition series with Victoria winning two games to one by scores of 7-5, 3-6, 6-1. It was the first meeting between the Eastern champions and the Western champions. The following year, and until the Western Hockey League disbanded after the 1926 playoffs, the Cup went to the winner of the series between East and West.

1911-12 — **Quebec Bulldogs** — Goldie Prodgers, Joe Hall, Walter Rooney, Paddy Moran, Jack Marks, Jack McDonald, Eddie Oatman, George Leonard, Joe Malone (captain), C. Nolan (coach), M.J. Quinn (manager), D. Beland (trainer).
Scores: March 11 at Quebec — Que. Bulldogs 9, Moncton 3; March 13 at Quebec — Que. Bulldogs 8, Moncton 0.
Prior to 1912, teams could challenge the Stanley Cup champions for the title, thus there was more than one Championship Series played in most of the seasons between 1894 and 1911.

1910-11 — **Ottawa Senators** — Hamby Shore, Percy LeSueur, Jack Darragh, Bruce Stuart, Marty Walsh, Bruce Ridpath, Fred Lake, Albert (Dubby) Kerr, Alex Currie, Horace Gaul.
Scores: March 13 at Ottawa — Ottawa 7, Galt 4; March 16 at Ottawa — Ottawa 13, Port Arthur 4.

1909-10 — **Montreal Wanderers** — Cecil W. Blachford, Ernie (Moose) Johnson, Ernie Russell, Riley Hern, Harry Hyland, Jack Marshall, Frank (Pud) Glass (captain), Jimmy Gardner, R. R. Boon (manager).
Scores: March 12 at Montreal — Mtl. Wanderers 7, Berlin (Kitchener) 3.

1908-09 — **Ottawa Senators** — Fred Lake, Percy LeSueur, Fred (Cyclone) Taylor, H.L. (Billy) Gilmour, Albert Kerr, Edgar Dey, Marty Walsh, Bruce Stuart (captain).
Scores: Ottawa, as champions of the Eastern Canada Hockey Association took over the Stanley Cup in 1909 and, although a challenge was accepted by the Cup trustees from Winnipeg Shamrocks, games could not be arranged because of the lateness of the season. No other challenges were made in 1909. The following season — 1909-10 — however, the Senators accepted two challenges as defending Cup Champions. The first was against Galt in a two-game, total-goals series, and the second against Edmonton, also a two-game, total-goals series. Results: January 5 at Ottawa —Ottawa 12, Galt 3; January 7 at Ottawa — Ottawa 3, Galt 1. January 18 at Ottawa — Ottawa 8, Edm. Eskimos 4; January 20 at Ottawa — Ottawa 13, Edm. Eskimos 7.

1907-08 — **Montreal Wanderers** — Riley Hern, Art Ross, Walter Smaill, Frank (Pud) Glass, Bruce Stuart, Ernie Russell, Ernie (Moose) Johnson, Cecil Blachford (captain), Tom Hooper, Larry Gilmour, Ernie Liffiton, R.R. Boon (manager).
Scores: Wanderers accepted four challenges for the Cup: January 9 at Montreal — Mtl. Wanderers 9, Ott. Victorias 3; January 13 at Montreal — Mtl. Wanderers 13, Ott. Victorias 1; March 10 at Montreal — Mtl. Wanderers 11, Wpg. Maple Leafs 5; March 12 at Montreal — Mtl. Wanderers 9, Wpg. Maple Leafs 3; March 14 at Montreal — Mtl. Wanderers 6, Toronto (OPHL) 4. At start of following season, 1908-09, Wanderers were challenged by Edmonton. Results: December 28 at Montreal — Mtl. Wanderers 7, Edm. Eskimos 3; December 30 at Montreal — Edm. Eskimos 7, Mtl. Wanderers 6. Total goals: Mtl. Wanderers 13, Edm. Eskimos 10.

1906-07 — (March) — **Montreal Wanderers** — W. S. (Billy) Strachan, Riley Hern, Lester Patrick, Hod Stuart, Frank (Pud) Glass, Ernie Russell, Cecil Blachford (captain), Ernie (Moose) Johnson, Rod Kennedy, Jack Marshall, R.R. Boon (manager).
Scores: March 23 at Winnipeg — Mtl. Wanderers 7, Kenora 2; March 25 at Winnipeg — Kenora 6, Mtl. Wanderers 5. Total goals: Mtl. Wanderers 12, Kenora 8.

1906-07 — (January) — **Kenora Thistles** — Eddie Geroux, Art Ross, Si Griffis, Tom Hooper, Billy McGimsie, Roxy Beaudro, Tom Phillips.
Scores: January 17 at Montreal — Kenora 4, Mtl. Wanderers 2; Jan. 21 at Montreal — Kenora 8, Mtl. Wanderers 6.

1905-06 — (March) — **Montreal Wanderers** — Henri Menard, Billy Strachan, Rod Kennedy, Lester Patrick, Frank (Pud) Glass, Ernie Russell, Ernie (Moose) Johnson, Cecil Blachford (captain), Josh Arnold, R.R. Boon (manager).
Scores: March 14 at Montreal — Mtl. Wanderers 9, Ottawa 1; March 17 at Ottawa — Ottawa 9, Mtl. Wanderers 3. Total goals: Mtl. Wanderers 12, Ottawa 10. Wanderers accepted a challenge from New Glasgow, N.S., prior to the start of the 1906-07 season. Results: December 27 at Montreal — Mtl. Wanderers 10, New Glasgow 3; December 29 at Montreal — Mtl. Wanderers 7, New Glasgow 2.

1905-06 — (February) — **Ottawa Silver Seven** — Harvey Pulford (captain), Arthur Moore, Harry Westwick, Frank McGee, Alf Smith (playing coach), Billy Gilmour, Billy Hague, Percy LeSueur, Harry Smith, Tommy Smith, Dion, Ebbs.
Scores: February 27 at Ottawa — Ottawa 16, Queen's University 7; February 28 at Ottawa — Ottawa 12, Queen's University 7; March 6 at Ottawa — Ottawa 6, Smiths Falls 5; March 8 at Ottawa — Ottawa 8, Smiths Falls 2.

1904-05 — **Ottawa Silver Seven** — Dave Finnie, Harvey Pulford (captain), Arthur Moore, Harry Westwick, Frank McGee, Alf Smith (playing coach), Billy Gilmour, Frank White, Horace Gaul, Hamby Shore, Bones Allen.
Scores: January 13 at Ottawa — Ottawa 9, Dawson City 2; January 16 at Ottawa — Ottawa 23, Dawson City 2; March 7 at Ottawa — Rat Portage 9, Ottawa 3; March 9 at Ottawa — Ottawa 4, Rat Portage 2; March 11 at Ottawa — Ottawa 5, Rat Portage 4.

1903-04 — **Ottawa Silver Seven** — S.C. (Suddy) Gilmour, Arthur Moore, Frank McGee, J.B. (Bouse) Hutton, H.L. (Billy) Gilmour, Jim McGee, Harry Westwick, E. H. (Harvey) Pulford (captain), Scott, Alf Smith (playing coach).
Scores: December 30 at Ottawa — Ottawa 9, Wpg. Rowing Club 1; January 1 at Ottawa — Wpg. Rowing Club 6, Ottawa 2; January 4 at Ottawa — Ottawa 2, Wpg. Rowing Club 0. February 23 at Ottawa — Ottawa 6, Tor. Marlboros 3; February 25 at Ottawa — Ottawa 11, Tor. Marlboros 2; March 2 at Montreal — Ottawa 5, Mtl. Wanderers 5. Following the tie game, a new two-game series was ordered to be played in Ottawa but the Wanderers refused unless the tie game was replayed in Montreal. When no settlement could be reached, the series was abandoned and Ottawa retained the Cup and accepted a two-game challenge from Brandon. Results: (both games at Ottawa), March 9, Ottawa 6, Brandon 3; March 11, Ottawa 9, Brandon 3.

1902-03 — (March) — **Ottawa Silver Seven** — S.C. (Suddy) Gilmour, P.T. (Percy) Sims, J.B. (Bouse) Hutton, D.J. (Dave) Gilmour, H.L. (Billy) Gilmour, Harry Westwick, Frank McGee, F.H. Wood, A.A. Fraser, Charles D. Spittal, E.H. (Harvey) Pulford (captain), Arthur Moore, Alf Smith (coach.)
Scores: March 7 at Montreal — Ottawa 1, Mtl. Victorias 1; March 10 at Ottawa — Ottawa 8, Mtl. Victorias 0. Total goals: Ottawa 9, Mtl. Victorias 1; March 12 at Ottawa — Ottawa 6, Rat Portage 2; March 14 at Ottawa — Ottawa 4, Rat Portage 2.

1902-03 — (February) — **Montreal AAA** — Tom Hodge, R.R. (Dickie) Boon, W.C. (Billy) Nicholson, Tom Phillips, Art Hooper, W.J. (Billy) Bellingham, Charles A. Liffiton, Jack Marshall, Jim Gardner, Cecil Blachford, George Smith.
Scores: January 29 at Montreal — Mtl. AAA 8, Wpg. Victorias 1; January 31 at Montreal — Wpg. Victorias 2, Mtl. AAA 2; February 2 at Montreal — Wpg. Victorias 4, Mtl. AAA 2; February 4 at Montreal — Mtl. AAA 5, Wpg. Victorias 1.

1901-02 — (March) — **Montreal AAA** — Tom Hodge, R.R. (Dickie) Boon, William C. (Billy) Nicholson, Archie Hooper, W.J. (Billy) Bellingham, Charles A. Liffiton, Jack Marshall, Roland Elliott, Jim Gardner.
Scores: March 13 at Winnipeg — Wpg. Victorias 1, Mtl. AAA 0; March 15 at Winnipeg — Mtl. AAA 5, Wpg. Victorias 0; March 17 at Winnipeg — Mtl. AAA 2, Wpg. Victorias 1.

1901-02 — (January) — **Winnipeg Victorias** — Burke Wood, A.B. (Tony) Gingras, Charles W. Johnstone, R.M. (Rod) Flett, Magnus L. Flett, Dan Bain (captain), Fred Scanlon, F. Cadham, G. Brown.
Scores: January 21 at Winnipeg — Wpg. Victorias 5, Tor Wellingtons 3; January 23 at Winnipeg — Wpg. Victorias 5, Tor. Wellingtons 3.

1900-01 — **Winnipeg Victorias** — Burke Wood, Jack Marshall, A.B. (Tony) Gingras, Charles W. Johnstone, R.M. (Rod) Flett, Magnus L. Flett, Dan Bain (captain), G. Brown.
Scores: January 29 at Montreal — Wpg. Victorias 4, Mtl. Shamrocks 3; January 31 at Montreal — Wpg. Victorias 2, Mtl. Shamrocks 1.

1899-1900 — **Montreal Shamrocks** — Joe McKenna, Frank Tansey, Frank Wall, Art Farrell, Fred Scanlon, Harry Trihey (captain), Jack Brannen.
Scores: February 12 at Montreal — Mtl. Shamrocks 4, Wpg. Victorias 3; February 14 at Montreal — Wpg. Victorias 3, Mtl. Shamrocks 2; February 16 at Montreal — Mtl. Shamrocks 5, Wpg. Victorias 4; March 5 at Montreal — Mtl. Shamrocks 10, Halifax 2; March 7 at Montreal — Mtl. Shamrocks 11, Halifax 0.

1898-99 — (March) — **Montreal Shamrocks** — Jim McKenna, Frank Tansey, Frank Wall, Harry Trihey (captain), Art Farrell, Fred Scanlon, Jack Brannen, John Dobby, Charles Hoerner.
Scores: March 14 at Montreal — Mtl. Shamrocks 6, Queen's University 2.

1898-99 — (February) — **Montreal Victorias** — Gordon Lewis, Mike Grant, Graham Drinkwater, Cam Davidson, Bob McDougall, Ernie McLea, Frank Richardson, Jack Ewing, Russell Bowie, Douglas Acer, Fred McRobie.
Scores: February 15 at Montreal — Mtl. Victorias 2, Wpg. Victorias 1; February 18 at Montreal — Mtl. Victorias 3, Wpg. Victorias 2.

1897-98 — **Montreal Victorias** — Gordon Lewis, Hartland McDougall, Mike Grant, Graham Drinkwater, Cam Davidson, Bob McDougall, Ernie McLea, Frank Richardson (captain), Jack Ewing. The Victorias as champions of the Amateur Hockey Association, retained the Cup and were not called upon to defend it.

1896-97 — **Montreal Victorias** — Gordon Lewis, Harold Henderson, Mike Grant (captain), Cam Davidson, Graham Drinkwater, Robert McDougall, Ernie McLea, Shirley Davidson, Hartland McDougall, Jack Ewing, Percy Molson, David Gillilan, McLellan.
Scores: December 27 at Montreal — Mtl. Victorias 15, Ott. Capitals 2.

1895-96 — (December) — **Montreal Victorias** — Harold Henderson, Mike Grant (captain), Robert McDougall, Graham Drinkwater, Shirley Davidson, Ernie McLea, Robert Jones, Cam Davidson, David Gillilan, Stanley Willett.
Scores: December 30 at Winnipeg — Mtl. Victorias 6, Wpg. Victorias 5.

1895-96 — (February) — **Winnipeg Victorias** — G.H. Merritt, Rod Flett, Fred Higginbotham, Jack Armitage (captain), C.J. (Tote) Campbell, Dan Bain, Charles Johnstone, H. Howard.
Scores: February 14 at Montreal — Wpg. Victorias 2, Mtl. Victorias 0.

1894-95 — **Montreal Victorias** — Robert Jones, Harold Henderson, Mike Grant (captain), Shirley Davidson, Bob McDougall, Norman Rankin, Graham Drinkwater, Roland Elliot, William Pullan, Hartland McDougall, Jim Fenwick, A. McDougall. Montreal Victorias, as champions of the Amateur Hockey Association, were prepared to defend the Stanley Cup. However, the Stanley Cup trustees had already accepted a challenge match between the 1894 champion Montreal AAA and Queen's University. It was declared that if Montreal AAA defeated Queen's University, Montreal Victorias would be declared Stanley Cup champions. If Queen's University won, the Cup would go to the university club. In a game played March 9, 1895, Montreal AAA defeated Queen's University 5-1. As a result, Montreal Victorias were awarded the Stanley Cup.

1893-94 — **Montreal AAA** — Herbert Collins, Allan Cameron, George James, Billy Barlow, Clare Mussen, Archie Hodgson, Haviland Routh, Alex Irving, James Stewart, A.C. (Toad) Wand, A. Kingan.
Scores: March 17 at Mtl. Victorias — Mtl. AAA 3, Mtl. Victorias 2; March 22 at Montreal — Mtl. AAA 3, Ott. Capitals 1.

1892-93 — **Montreal AAA** — Tom Paton, James Stewart, Allan Cameron, Haviland Routh, Archie Hodgson, Billy Barlow, A.B. Kingan, G.S. Lowe.
In accordance with the terms governing the presentation of the Stanley Cup, it was awarded for the first time to the Montreal AAA as champions of the Amateur Hockey Association in 1893. Once Montreal AAA had been declared holders of the Stanley Cup, any Canadian hockey team could challenge for the trophy.

All-Time NHL Playoff Formats

1917-18 — The regular-season was split into two halves. The winners of both halves faced each other in a two-game, total-goals series for the NHL championship and the right to meet the PCHA champion in the best-of-five Stanley Cup Finals.

1918-19 — Same as 1917-18, except that the Stanley Cup Finals was extended to a best-of-seven series.

1919-20 — Same as 1917-1918, except that Ottawa won both halves of the split regular-season schedule to earn an automatic berth into the best-of-five Stanley Cup Finals against the PCHA champions.

1921-22 — The top two teams at the conclusion of the regular-season faced each other in a two-game, total-goals series for the NHL championship. The NHL champion then moved on to play the winner of the PCHA-WCHL playoff series in the best-of-five Stanley Cup Finals.

1922-23 — The top two teams at the conclusion of the regular-season faced each other in a two-game, total-goals series for the NHL championship. The NHL champion then moved on to play the PCHA champion in the best-of-three Stanley Cup Semi-Finals, and the winner of the Semi-Finals played the WCHL champion, which had been given a bye, in the best-of-three Stanley Cup Finals.

1923-24 — The top two teams at the conclusion of the regular-season faced each other in a two-game, total-goals series for the NHL championship. The NHL champion then moved to play the loser of the PCHA-WCHL playoff (the winner of the PCHA-WCHL playoff earned a bye into the Stanley Cup Finals) in the best-of-three Stanley Cup Semi-Finals. The winner of this series met the PCHA-WCHL playoff winner in the best-of-three Stanley Cup Finals.

1924-25 — The first place team (Hamilton) at the conclusion of the regular-season was supposed to play the winner of a two-game, total goals series between the second (Toronto) and third (Montreal) place clubs. However, Hamilton refused to abide by this new format, demanding greater compensation than offered by the League. Thus, Toronto and Montreal played their two-game, total-goals series, and the winner (Montreal) earned the NHL title and then played the WCHL champion (Victoria) in the best-of-five Stanley Cup Finals.

1925-26 — The format which was intended for 1924-25 went into effect. The winner of the two-game, total-goals series between the second and third place teams squared off against the first place team in the two-game, total-goals NHL championship series. The NHL champion then moved on to play the WHL champion in the best-of-five Stanley Cup Finals.

After the 1925-26 season, the NHL was the only major professional hockey league still in existence and consequently took over sole control of the Stanley Cup competition.

1926-27 — The 10-team league was divided into two divisions — Canadian and American — of five teams apiece. In each division, the winner of the two-game, total-goals series between the second and third place teams faced the first place team in a two-game, total-goals series for the division title. The two division title winners then met in the best-of-five Stanley Cup Finals.

1928-29 — Both first place teams in the two divisions played each other in a best-of-five series. Both second place teams in the two divisions played each other in a two-game, total-goals series as did the two third place teams. The winners of these latter two series then played each other in a best-of-three series for the right to meet the winner of the series between the two first place clubs. This Stanley Cup Final was a best-of-three.

> Series A: First in Canadian Division versus first in American (best-of-five)
> Series B: Second in Canadian Division versus second in American (two-game, total-goals)
> Series C: Third in Canadian Division versus third in American (two-game, total-goals)
> Series D: Winner of Series B versus winner of Series C (best-of-three)
> Series E: Winner of Series A versus winner of Series D (best of three) for Stanley Cup

1931-32 — Same as 1928-29, except that Series D was changed to a two-game, total-goals format and Series E was changed to best of five.

1936-37 — Same as 1931-32, except that Series B, C, and D were each best-of-three.

1938-39 — With the NHL reduced to seven teams, the two-division system was replaced by one seven-team league. Based on final regular-season standings, the following playoff format was adopted:

> Series A: First versus Second (best-of-seven)
> Series B: Third versus Fourth (best-of-three)
> Series C: Fifth versus Sixth (best-of-three)
> Series D: Winner of Series B versus winner of Series C (best-of-three)
> Series E: Winner of Series A versus winner of Series D (best-of-seven)

1942-43 — With the NHL reduced to six teams (the ''original six''), only the top four finishers qualified for playoff action. The best-of-seven Semi-Finals pitted Team #1 vs Team #3 and Team #2 vs Team #4. The winners of each Semi-Final series met in the best-of-seven Stanley Cup Finals.

1967-68 — When it doubled in size from 6 to 12 teams, the NHL once again was divided into two divisions — East and West — of six teams apiece. The top four clubs in each division qualified for the playoffs (all series were best-of-seven):

> Series A; Team #1 (East) vs Team #3 (East)
> Series B: Team #2 (East) vs Team #4 (East)
> Series C: Team #1 (West) vs Team #3 (West)
> Series D: Team #2 (West) vs Team #4 (West)
> Series E: Winner of Series A vs winner of Series B
> Series F: Winner of Series C vs winner of Series D
> Series G: Winner of Series E vs Winner of Series F

1970-71 — Same as 1967-68 except that Series E matched the winners of Series A and D, and Series F matched the winners of Series B and C.

1971-72 — Same as 1970-71, except that Series A and C matched Team #1 vs Team #4, and Series B and D matched Team #2 vs Team #3.

1974-75 — With the League now expanded to 18 teams in four divisions, a completely new playoff format was introduced. First, the #2 and #3 teams in each of the four divisions were pooled together in the Preliminary round. These eight (#2 and #3) clubs were ranked #1 to #8 based on regular-season record:

> Series A: Team #1 vs Team #8 (best-of-three)
> Series B: Team #2 vs Team #7 (best-of-three)
> Series C: Team #3 vs Team #6 (best-of-three)
> Series D: Team #4 vs Team #5 (best-of-three)
> The winners of this Preliminary round then pooled together with the four division winners, which had received byes into this Quarter-Final round. These eight teams were again ranked #1 to #8 based on regular-season record:
> Series E: Team #1 vs Team #8 (best-of-seven)
> Series F: Team #2 vs Team #7 (best-of-seven)
> Series G: Team #3 vs Team #6 (best-of-seven)
> Series H: Team #4 vs Team #5 (best-of-seven)
> The four Quarter-Finals winners, which moved on to the Semi-Finals, were then ranked #1 to #4 based on regular season record:
> Series I: Team #1 vs Team #4 (best-of-seven)
> Series J: Team #2 vs Team #3 (best-of-seven)
> Series K: Winner of Series I vs winner of Series J (best-of-seven)

1977-78 — Same as 1974-75, except that the Preliminary round consisted of the #2 teams in the four divisions and the next four teams based on regular-season record (not their standings within their divisions).

1979-80 — With the addition of four WHA franchises, the League expanded its playoff structure to include 16 of its 21 teams. The four first place teams in the four divisions automatically earned playoff berths. Among the 17 other clubs, the top 12, according to regular-season record, also earned berths. All 16 teams were then pooled together and ranked #1 to #16 based on regular-season record:

> Series A: Team #1 vs Team #16 (best-of-five)
> Series B: Team #2 vs Team #15 (best-of-five)
> Series C: Team #3 vs Team #14 (best-of-five)
> Series D: Team #4 vs Team #13 (best-of-five)
> Series E: Team #5 vs Team #12 (best-of-five)
> Series F: Team #6 vs Team #11 (best-of-five)
> Series G: Team #7 vs Team #10 (best-of-five)
> Series H: Team #8 vs Team # 9 (best-of-five)
> The eight Preliminary round winners, ranked #1 to #8 based on regular-season record, moved on to the Quarter-Finals:
> Series I: Team #1 vs Team #8 (best-of-seven)
> Series J: Team #2 vs Team #7 (best-of-seven)
> Series K: Team #3 vs Team #6 (best-of-seven)
> Series L: Team #4 vs Team #5 (best-of-seven)
> The eight Quarter-Finals winners, ranked #1 to #4 based on regular-season record, moved on to the semi-finals:
> Series M: Team #1 vs Team #4 (best-of-seven)
> Series N: Team #2 vs Team #3 (best-of-seven)
> Series O: Winner of Series M vs winner of Series N (best-of-seven)

1981-82 — The first four teams in each division earned playoff berths. In each division, the first-place team opposed the fourth-place team and the second-place team opposed the third-place team in a best-of-five Division Semi-Final series (DSF). In each division, the two winners of the DSF met in a best-of-seven Division Final series (DF). The two winners in each conference met in a best-of-seven Conference Final series (CF). In the Prince of Wales Conference, the Adams Division winner opposed the Patrick Division winner; in the Clarence Campbell Conference, the Smythe Division winner opposed the Norris Division winner. The two CF winners met in a best-of-seven Stanley Cup Final (F) series.

1986-87 — Division Semi-Final series changed from best-of-five to best-of-seven.

1993-94 — The NHL's playoff draw conference-based rather than division-based. At the conclusion of the regular season, the top eight teams in each of the Eastern and Western Conferences qualify for the playoffs. The teams that finish in first place in each of the League's divisions are seeded first and second in each conference's playoff draw and are assured of home ice advantage in the first two playoff rounds. The remaining teams are seeded based on their regular-season point totals. In each conference, the team seeded #1 plays #8; #2 vs. #7; #3 vs. #6; and #4 vs. #5. All series are best-of-seven with home ice rotating on a 2-2-1-1-1 basis, with the exception of matchups between Central and Pacific Division teams. These matchups will be played on a 2-3-2 basis to reduce travel. In a 2-3-2 series, the team with the most points will have its choice to start the series at home or on the road. The Eastern Conference champion will face the Western Conference champion in the Stanley Cup Final.

1994-95 — Same as 1993-94, except that in first, second or third-round playoff series involving Central and Pacific Division teams, the team with the better record has the choice of using either a 2-3-2 or a 2-2-1-1-1 format. When a 2-3-2 format is selected, the higher-ranked team also has the choice of playing games 1, 2, 6 and 7 at home or playing games 3, 4 and 5 at home. The format for the Stanley Cup Final remains 2-2-1-1-1.

NHL Commissioner Gary Bettman presents Colorado's Joe Sakic with the Conn Smythe Trophy after the Avalanche captain was named the most valuable player of the 1996 playoffs.

Team Records

1918-1996

GAMES PLAYED

MOST GAMES PLAYED BY ALL TEAMS, ONE PLAYOFF YEAR:
92 — 1991. There were 51 DSF, 24 DF, 11 CF and 6 F games.
90 — 1994. There were 48 CQF, 23 CSF, 12 CF and 7 F games.
87 — 1987. There were 44 DSF, 25 DF, 11 CF and 7 F games.

MOST GAMES PLAYED, ONE TEAM, ONE PLAYOFF YEAR:
26 — Philadelphia Flyers, 1987. Won DSF 4-2 against NY Rangers, DF 4-3 against NY Islanders, CF 4-2 against Montreal, and lost F 4-3 against Edmonton.
24 — Pittsburgh Penguins,1991. Won DSF 4-3 against New Jersey, DF 4-1 against Washington, CF 4-2 against Boston, and F 4-2 against Minnesota.
— Los Angeles Kings, 1993. Won DSF 4-2 against Calgary, DF 4-2 against Vancouver, CF 4-3 against Toronto, and lost F 4-1 against Montreal.
— Vancouver Canucks, 1994. Won CQF 4-3 against Calgary, CSF 4-1 against Dallas, CF 4-1 against Toronto, and lost F 4-3 against NY Rangers.

PLAYOFF APPEARANCESS

MOST STANLEY CUP CHAMPIONSHIPS:
23 — Montreal Canadiens 1924-30-31-44-46-53-56-57-58-59-60-65-66-68-69-71-73-76-77-78-79-86-93
13 — Toronto Maple Leafs 1918-22-32-42-45-47-48-49-51-62-63-64-67
7 — Detroit Red Wings 1936-37-43-50-52-54-55

MOST CONSECUTIVE STANLEY CUP CHAMPIONSHIPS:
5 — Montreal Canadiens (1956-57-58-59-60)
4 — Montreal Canadiens (1976-77-78-79)
— NY Islanders (1980-81-82-83)

MOST FINAL SERIES APPEARANCES:
32 — Montreal Canadiens in 78-year history.
21 — Toronto Maple Leafs in 78-year history.
19 — Detroit Red Wings in 69-year history.

MOST CONSECUTIVE FINAL SERIES APPEARANCES:
10 — Montreal Canadiens (1951-60, inclusive)
5 — Montreal Canadiens, (1965-69, inclusive)
— NY Islanders, (1980-84, inclusive)

MOST YEARS IN PLAYOFFS:
70 — Montreal Canadiens in 79-year history.
58 — Toronto Maple Leafs in 79-year history.
57 — Boston Bruins in 72-year history.

MOST CONSECUTIVE PLAYOFF APPEARANCES:
29 — Boston Bruins (1968-96, inclusive)
27 — Chicago Blackhawks (1970-96, inclusive)
24 — Montreal Canadiens (1971-94, inclusive)
21 — Montreal Canadiens (1949-69, inclusive)
20 — Detroit Red Wings (1939-58, inclusive)

TEAM WINS

MOST HOME WINS, ONE TEAM, ONE PLAYOFF YEAR:
11 — Edmonton Oilers, 1988
10 — Edmonton Oilers, 1985 in 10 home-ice games.
— Montreal Canadiens, 1986
— Montreal Canadiens, 1993
9 — Philadelphia Flyers, 1974
— Philadelphia Flyers, 1980
— NY Islanders, 1981
— NY Islanders, 1983
— Edmonton Oilers, 1984
— Edmonton Oilers, 1987
— Calgary Flames, 1989
— Pittsburgh Penguins, 1991
— NY Rangers, 1994.

MOST ROAD WINS, ONE TEAM, ONE PLAYOFF YEAR:
10 — New Jersey Devils, 1995. Won three at Boston in CQF; two at Pittsburgh in CSF; three at Philadelphia in CF; and two at Detroit in F series.
8 — NY Islanders, 1980. Won two at Los Angeles in PR; three at Boston in QF; two at Buffalo in SF; and one at Philadelphia in F series.
— Philadelphia Flyers, 1987. Won two at NY Rangers in DSF; two at NY Islanders in DF; three at Montreal in CF; and one at Edmonton in F series.
— Edmonton Oilers, 1990. Won one at Winnipeg in DSF; two at Los Angeles in DF; two at Chicago in CF and three at Boston in F series.
— Pittsburgh Penguins, 1992. Won two at Washington in DSF; two at NY Rangers in DF; two at Boston in CF; and two at Chicago in F series.
— Vancouver Canucks, 1994. Won three at Calgary in CQF; two at Dallas in CSF; one at Toronto in CF; and two at NY Rangers in F series.
— Colorado Avalanche, 1996. Won two at Vancouver in CQF; two at Chicago in CSF; two at Detroit in CF; and two at Florida in F series.

MOST ROAD WINS, ALL TEAMS, ONE PLAYOFF YEAR:
46 — 1987. Of 87 games played, road teams won 46 (22 DSF, 14 DF, 8 CF and 2 Stanley Cup final).

PLAYOFF WINNING STREAKS

MOST CONSECUTIVE WINS, ONE TEAM, ONE PLAYOFF YEAR:
  11 — Chicago Blackhawks in 1992. Chicago won last three games of best-of-seven DSF against St. Louis to win series 4-2 and then defeated Detroit 4-0 in best-of-seven DF and Edmonton 4-0 in best-of-seven CF.
  — Pittsburgh Penguins in 1992. Pittsburgh won last three games of best-of-seven DF against NY Rangers to win series 4-2 and then defeated Boston 4-0 in best-of-seven CF and Chicago 4-0 in best-of-seven F.
  — Montreal Canadiens in 1993. Montreal won last four games of best-of-seven DSF against Quebec to win series 4-2, defeated Buffalo 4-0 in best-of-seven DF and won first three games of CF against NY Islanders.

MOST CONSECUTIVE PLAYOFF GAME WINS:
  14 — Pittsburgh Penguins. Streak started May 9, 1992, at Pittsburgh with a 5-4 win in fourth game of a DF series against NY Rangers, won by Pittsburgh 4-2. Continued with a four-game sweep over Boston in the 1992 CF and a four-game win over Chicago in the 1992 F. Pittsburgh then won the first three games of the 1993 DSF versus New Jersey. New Jersey ended the streak April 25, 1993, at New Jersey with a 4-1 win.
  12 — Edmonton Oilers. Streak began May 15, 1984 at Edmonton with a 7-2 win over NY Islanders in third game of F series, and ended May 9, 1985 when Chicago defeated Edmonton 5-2 at Chicago. Included in the streak were three wins over the NY Islanders, in 1984, three over Los Angeles, four over Winnipeg and two over Chicago, all in 1985.
  11 — Montreal Canadiens. Streak began April 16, 1959, at Toronto with 3-2 win in fourth game of F series, won by Montreal 4-1, and ended March 23, 1961, when Chicago defeated Montreal 4-3 in second game of SF series. Included in streak were eight straight victories in 1960.
  — Montreal Canadiens. Streak began April 28, 1968, at Montreal with 4-3 win in fifth game of SF series, won by Montreal 4-1, and ended April 17, 1969, at Boston when Boston defeated them 5-0 in third game of SF series. Included in the streak were four straight wins over St. Louis in the 1968 F and four straight wins over NY Rangers in a 1969 QF series.
  — Boston Bruins. Streak began April 14, 1970, at Boston with 3-2 victory over NY Rangers in fifth game of a QF series, won by Boston 4-2. It continued with a four-game victory over Chicago in the 1970 SF and four over St. Louis in the 1970 F. Boston then won the first game of a 1971 QF series against Montreal. Montreal ended the streak April 8, 1971, at Boston with a 7-5 victory.
  — Montreal Canadiens. Streak started May 6, 1976, at Montreal with 5-2 win in fifth game of a SF series against NY Islanders, won by Montreal 4-1. Continued with a four-game sweep over Philadelphia in the 1976 F and a four-game win against St. Louis in the 1977 QF. Montreal won the first two games of a 1977 SF series against the NY Islanders before NY Islanders ended the streak, April 2, 1977 at New York with a 5-3 victory.
  — Chicago Blackhawks. Streak started April 24, 1992, at St. Louis with a 5-3 win in fourth game of a DSF series against St. Louis, won by Chicago 4-2. Continued with a four-game sweep over Detroit in the 1992 DF and a four-game win over Edmonton in the 1992 CF. Pittsburgh ended the streak May 26, 1992, at Pittsburgh with a 5-4 victory.

MOST OVERTIME WINS, ONE TEAM, ONE PLAYOFF YEAR:
  10 — Montreal Canadiens, 1993. Two against Quebec in the DSF; three against Buffalo in the DF; two against NY Islanders in the CF; and three against Los Angeles in the F. Montreal played 20 games.
  6 — NY Islanders, 1980. One against Los Angeles in the PR; two against Boston in the QF; one against Buffalo in the SF; and two against Philadelphia in the F. Islanders played 21 games.
  — Vancouver Canucks, 1994. Three against Calgary in the CQF; one against Dallas in the CSF; one against Toronto in the CF; and one against NY Rangers in the F. Vancouver played 24 games.

PLAYOFF LOSING STREAKS

LONGEST PLAYOFF LOSING STREAK:
  16 Games — Chicago Blackhawks. Streak started in 1975 QF against Buffalo when Chicago lost last two games. Then Chicago lost four games to Montreal in 1976 QF; two games to NY Islanders in 1977 PR; four games to Boston in 1978 QF and four games to NY Islanders in 1979 QF. Streak ended on April 8, 1980 when Chicago defeated St. Louis 3-2 in the opening game of their 1980 PR series.
  12 Games — Toronto Maple Leafs. Streak started on April 16, 1979 as Toronto lost four straight games in a QF series against Montreal. Continued with three-game PR defeats versus Philadelphia and NY Islanders in 1980 and 1981 respectively. Toronto failed to qualify for the 1982 playoffs and lost the first two games of a 1983 DSF against Minnesota. Toronto ended the streak with a 6-3 win against the North Stars on April 9, 1983.
  10 Games — NY Rangers. Streak started in 1968 QF against Chicago when NY Rangers lost last four games and continued through 1969 (four straight losses to Montreal in QF) and 1970 (two straight losses to Boston in QF) before ending with a 4-3 win against Boston, at New York, April 11, 1970.
  — Philadelphia Flyers. Streak started on April 18, 1968, the last game in the 1968 QF series against St. Louis, and continued through 1969 (four straight losses to St. Louis in QF), 1971 (four straight losses to Chicago in QF) and 1973 (opening game loss to Minnesota in QF) before ending with a 4-1 win against Minnesota, at Philadelphia, April 5, 1973.
  — Chicago Blackhawks. Streak started on May 26, 1992 as Chicago lost four straight games in the F to Pittsburgh. Continued with four straight losses to St. Louis in 1993 DSF. Chicago lost the first two games of 1994 CQF to Toronto before ending the streak with a 5-4 win against Toronto on April 23, 1994.

MOST GOALS IN A SERIES, ONE TEAM

MOST GOALS, ONE TEAM, ONE PLAYOFF SERIES:
  44 — Edmonton Oilers in 1985 CF. Edmonton won best-of-seven series 4-2, outscoring Chicago 44-25.
  35 — Edmonton Oilers in 1983 DF. Edmonton won best-of-seven series 4-1, outscoring Calgary 35-13.
  — Calgary Flames in 1995 CQF. Calgary lost best-of-seven series 3-4, outscoring San Jose 35-26.

MOST GOALS, ONE TEAM, TWO-GAME SERIES:
  11 — Buffalo Sabres in 1977 PR. Buffalo won best-of-three series 2-0, outscoring Minnesota 11-3.
  — Toronto Maple Leafs in 1978 PR. Toronto won best-of-three series 2-0, outscoring Los Angeles 11-3.
  10 — Boston Bruins in 1927 QF. Boston won two-game total goal series 10-5.

MOST GOALS, ONE TEAM, THREE-GAME SERIES:
  23 — Chicago Blackhawks in 1985 DSF. Chicago won best-of-five series 3-0, outscoring Detroit 23-8.
  20 — Minnesota North Stars in 1981 PR. Minnesota won best-of-five series 3-0, outscoring Boston 20-13.
  — NY Islanders in 1981 PR. New York won best-of-five series 3-0, outscoring Toronto 20-4.

MOST GOALS, ONE TEAM, FOUR-GAME SERIES:
  28 — Boston Bruins in 1972 SF. Boston won best-of-seven series 4-0, outscoring St. Louis 28-8.

MOST GOALS, ONE TEAM, FIVE-GAME SERIES:
  35 — Edmonton Oilers in 1983 DF. Edmonton won best-of-seven series 4-1, outscoring Calgary 35-13.
  32 — Edmonton Oilers in 1987 DSF. Edmonton won best-of-seven series 4-1, outscoring Los Angeles 32-20.
  28 — NY Rangers in 1979 QF. NY Rangers won best-of-seven series 4-1, outscoring Philadelphia 28-8.
  27 — Philadelphia Flyers in 1980 SF. Philadelphia won best-of-seven series 4-1, outscoring Minnesota 27-14.
  — Los Angeles Kings, in 1982 DSF. Los Angeles won best-of-five series 3-2, outscoring Edmonton 27-23.

MOST GOALS, ONE TEAM, SIX-GAME SERIES:
  44 — Edmonton Oilers in 1985 CF. Edmonton won best-of-seven series 4-2, outscoring Chicago 44-25.
  33 — Chicago Blackhawks in 1985 DF. Chicago won best-of-seven series 4-2, outscoring Minnesota 33-29.
  — Montreal Canadiens in 1973 F. Montreal won best-of-seven series 4-2, outscoring Chicago 33-23.
  — Los Angeles Kings in 1993 DSF. Los Angeles won best-of-seven series 4-2, outscoring Calgary 33-28.

MOST GOALS, ONE TEAM, SEVEN-GAME SERIES:
  35 — Calgary Flames in 1995 CQF. Calgary lost best-of-seven series 3-4, outscoring San Jose 35-26.
  33 — Philadelphia Flyers in 1976 QF. Philadelphia won best-of-seven series 4-3, outscoring Toronto 33-23.
  — Boston Bruins in 1983 DF. Boston won best-of-seven series 4-3, outscoring Buffalo 33-23.
  — Edmonton Oilers in 1984 DF. Edmonton won best-of-seven series 4-3, outscoring Calgary 33-27.

FEWEST GOALS IN A SERIES, ONE TEAM

FEWEST GOALS, ONE TEAM, TWO-GAME SERIES:
  0 — NY Americans in 1929 SF. Lost two-game total-goal series 1-0 against NY Rangers.
  — Chicago Blackhawks in 1935 SF. Lost two-game total-goal series 1-0 against Mtl. Maroons.
  — Mtl. Maroons in 1937 SF. Lost best-of-three series 2-0 to NY Rangers while being outscored 5-0.
  — NY Americans in 1939 QF. Lost best-of-three series 2-0 to Toronto while being outscored 6-0.

FEWEST GOALS, ONE TEAM, THREE-GAME SERIES:
  1 — Mtl. Maroons in 1936 SF. Lost best-of-five series 3-0 to Detroit and were outscored 6-1.

FEWEST GOALS, ONE TEAM, FOUR-GAME SERIES:
  2 — Boston Bruins in 1935 SF. Toronto won best-of-five series 3-1, outscoring Boston 7-2.
  — Montreal Canadiens in 1952 F. Detroit won best-of-seven series 4-0, outscoring Montreal 11-2.

FEWEST GOALS, ONE TEAM, FIVE-GAME SERIES:
  5 — NY Rangers in 1928 F. NY Rangers won best-of-five series 3-2, while being outscored by Mtl. Maroons 6-5.
  — Boston Bruins in 1995 CQF. New Jersey won best-of-seven series 4-1, while outscoring Boston 14-5.

FEWEST GOALS, ONE TEAM, SIX-GAME SERIES:
  5 — Boston Bruins in 1951 SF. Toronto won best-of-seven series 4-1 with 1 tie, outscoring Boston 17-5.

FEWEST GOALS, ONE TEAM, SEVEN-GAME SERIES:
  9 — Toronto Maple Leafs, in 1945 F. Toronto won best-of-seven series 4-3; teams tied in scoring 9-9.
  — Detroit Red Wings, in 1945 F. Toronto won best-of-seven series 4-3; teams tied in scoring 9-9.

MOST GOALS IN A SERIES, BOTH TEAMS

MOST GOALS, BOTH TEAMS, ONE PLAYOFF SERIES:
69 — Edmonton Oilers, Chicago Blackhawks in 1985 CF. Edmonton won best-of-seven series 4-2, outscoring Chicago 44-25.
62 — Chicago Blackhawks, Minnesota North Stars in 1985 DF. Chicago won best-of-seven series 4-2, outscoring Minnesota 33-29.
61 — Los Angeles Kings, Calgary Flames in 1993 DSF. Los Angeles won best-of-seven series 4-2, outscoring Calgary 33-28.
— San Jose Sharks, Calgary Flames in 1995 CQF. San Jose won best-of-seven series 4-3, while being outscored 35-26.

MOST GOALS, BOTH TEAMS, TWO-GAME SERIES:
17 — Toronto St. Patricks, Montreal Canadiens in 1918 NHL F. Toronto won two-game total goal series 10-7.
15 — Boston Bruins, Chicago Blackhawks in 1927 QF. Boston won two-game total goal series 10-5.
— Pittsburgh Penguins, St. Louis Blues in 1975 PR. Pittsburgh won best-of-three series 2-0, outscoring St. Louis 9-6.

MOST GOALS, BOTH TEAMS, THREE-GAME SERIES:
33 — Minnesota North Stars, Boston Bruins in 1981 PR. Minnesota won best-of-five series 3-0, outscoring Boston 20-13.
31 — Chicago Blackhawks, Detroit Red Wings in 1985 DSF. Chicago won best-of-five series 3-0, outscoring Detroit 23-8.
28 — Toronto Maple Leafs, NY Rangers in 1932 F. Toronto won best-of-five series 3-0, outscoring New York 18-10.

MOST GOALS, BOTH TEAMS, FOUR-GAME SERIES:
36 — Boston Bruins, St. Louis Blues in 1972 SF. Boston won best-of-seven series 4-0, outscoring St. Louis 28-8.
— **Edmonton Oilers, Chicago Blackhawks** in 1983 CF. Edmonton won best-of-seven series 4-0, outscoring Chicago 25-11.
— **Minnesota North Stars, Toronto Maple Leafs** in 1983 DSF. Minnesota won best-of-five series 3-1; teams tied in scoring 18-18.
35 — NY Rangers, Los Angeles Kings in 1981 PR. NY Rangers won best-of-five series 3-1, outscoring Los Angeles 23-12.

MOST GOALS, BOTH TEAMS, FIVE-GAME SERIES:
52 — Edmonton Oilers, Los Angeles Kings in 1987 DSF. Edmonton won best-of-seven series 4-1, outscoring Los Angeles 32-20.
50 — Los Angeles Kings, Edmonton Oilers in 1982 DSF. Los Angeles won best-of-five series 3-2, outscoring Edmonton 27-23.
48 — Edmonton Oilers, Calgary Flames in 1983 DF. Edmonton won best-of-seven series 4-1, outscoring Calgary 35-13.
— Calgary Flames, Los Angeles Kings in 1988 DSF. Calgary won best-of-seven series 4-1, outscoring Los Angeles 30-18.

MOST GOALS, BOTH TEAMS, SIX-GAME SERIES:
69 — Edmonton Oilers, Chicago Blackhawks in 1985 CF. Edmonton won best-of-seven series 4-2, outscoring Chicago 44-25.
62 — Chicago Blackhawks, Minnesota North Stars in 1985 DF. Chicago won best-of-seven series 4-2, outscoring Minnesota 33-29.
61 — Los Angeles Kings, Calgary Flames in 1993 DSF. Los Angeles won best-of-seven series 4-2, outscoring Calgary 33-28.

MOST GOALS, BOTH TEAMS, SEVEN-GAME SERIES:
61 — San Jose Sharks, Calgary Flames in 1995 CQF. San Jose won best-of-seven series 4-3, while being outscored 35-26.
60 — Edmonton Oilers, Calgary Flames in 1984 DF. Edmonton won best-of-seven series 4-3, outscoring Calgary 33-27.

FEWEST GOALS IN A SERIES, BOTH TEAMS

FEWEST GOALS, BOTH TEAMS, TWO-GAME SERIES:
1 — NY Rangers, NY Americans, in 1929 SF. NY Rangers defeated NY Americans 1-0 in two-game, total-goal series.
— **Mtl. Maroons, Chicago Blackhawks** in 1935 SF. Mtl. Maroons defeated Chicago 1-0 in two-game, total-goal series.

FEWEST GOALS, BOTH TEAMS, THREE-GAME SERIES:
7 — Boston Bruins, Montreal Canadiens in 1929 SF. Boston won best-of-five series 3-0, outscoring Montreal 5-2.
— **Detroit Red Wings, Mtl. Maroons** in 1936 SF. Detroit won best-of-five series 3-0, outscoring Mtl. Maroons 6-1.

FEWEST GOALS, BOTH TEAMS, FOUR-GAME SERIES:
9 — Toronto Maple Leafs, Boston Bruins in 1935 SF. Toronto won best-of-five series 3-1, outscoring Boston 7-2.

FEWEST GOALS, BOTH TEAMS, FIVE-GAME SERIES:
11 — NY Rangers, Mtl. Maroons in 1928 F. NY Rangers won best-of-five series 3-2, while outscored by Mtl. Maroons 6-5.

FEWEST GOALS, BOTH TEAMS, SIX-GAME SERIES:
22 — Toronto Maple Leafs, Boston Bruins in 1951 SF. Toronto won best-of-seven series 4-1 with 1 tie, outscoring Boston 17-5.

FEWEST GOALS, BOTH TEAMS, SEVEN-GAME SERIES:
18 — Toronto Maple Leafs, Detroit Red Wings in 1945 F. Toronto won best-of-seven series 4-3; teams tied in scoring 9-9.

Willy Lindstrom basks in the Stanley Cup spotlight after helping the Edmonton Oilers derail the New York Islanders dynasty with a five-game final series win in 1984.

MOST GOALS IN A GAME OR PERIOD

MOST GOALS, ONE TEAM, ONE GAME:
13 — Edmonton Oilers at Edmonton, April 9, 1987. Edmonton 13, Los Angeles 3. Edmonton won best-of-seven DSF 4-1.
12 — Los Angeles Kings at Los Angeles, April 10, 1990. Los Angeles 12, Calgary 4. Los Angeles won best-of-seven DSF 4-2.
11 — Montreal Canadiens at Montreal, March 30, 1944. Montreal 11, Toronto 0. Canadiens won best-of-seven SF 4-1.
— Edmonton Oilers at Edmonton May 4, 1985. Edmonton 11, Chicago 2. Edmonton won best-of-seven CF 4-2.

MOST GOALS, ONE TEAM, ONE PERIOD:
7 — Montreal Canadiens, March 30, 1944, at Montreal in third period, during 11-0 win against Toronto.

MOST GOALS, BOTH TEAMS, ONE GAME:
18 — Los Angeles Kings, Edmonton Oilers at Edmonton, April 7, 1982. Los Angeles 10, Edmonton 8. Los Angeles won best-of-five DSF 3-2.
17 — Pittsburgh Penguins, Philadelphia Flyers at Pittsburgh, April 25, 1989. Pittsburgh 10, Philadelphia 7. Philadelphia won best-of-seven DF 4-3.
16 — Edmonton Oilers, Los Angeles Kings at Edmonton, April 9, 1987. Edmonton 13, Los Angeles 3. Edmonton won best-of-seven DSF 4-1.
— Los Angeles Kings, Calgary Flames at Los Angeles, April 10, 1990. Los Angeles 12, Calgary 4. Los Angeles won best-of-seven DF 4-2.

MOST GOALS, BOTH TEAMS, ONE PERIOD:
9 — NY Rangers, Philadelphia Flyers, April 24, 1979, at Philadelphia, third period. NY Rangers won 8-3 scoring six of nine third-period goals.
— **Los Angeles Kings, Calgary Flames** at Los Angeles, April 10, 1990, second period. Los Angeles won game 12-4, scoring five of nine second-period goals.
8 — Chicago Blackhawks, Montreal Canadiens at Montreal, May 8, 1973, in the second period. Chicago won 8-7 scoring five of eight second-period goals.
— Chicago Blackhawks, Edmonton Oilers at Chicago, May 12, 1985 in the first period. Chicago won 8-6, scoring five of eight first-period goals.
— Edmonton Oilers, Winnipeg Jets at Edmonton, April 6, 1988 in the third period. Edmonton won 7-4, scoring six of eight third-period goals.
— Hartford Whalers, Montreal Canadiens at Hartford, April 10, 1988 in the third period. Hartford won 7-5, scoring five of eight third-period goals.
— Vancouver Canucks, NY Rangers at New York, June 9, 1994 in the third period. Vancouver won 6-3, scoring five of eight third period goals.

TEAM POWER-PLAY GOALS

MOST POWER-PLAY GOALS BY ALL TEAMS, ONE PLAYOFF YEAR:
199 — 1988 in 83 games.

MOST POWER-PLAY GOALS, ONE TEAM, ONE PLAYOFF YEAR:
35 — Minnesota North Stars, 1991 in 23 games.
32 — Edmonton Oilers, 1988 in 18 games.
31 — NY Islanders, 1981, in 18 games.

MOST POWER-PLAY GOALS, ONE TEAM, ONE SERIES:
15 — NY Islanders in 1980 F against Philadelphia. NY Islanders won series 4-2.
— **Minnesota North Stars** in 1991 DSF against Chicago. Minnesota won series 4-2.
13 — NY Islanders in 1981 QF against Edmonton. NY Islanders won series 4-2.
— Calgary Flames in 1986 CF against St. Louis. Calgary won series 4-3.
12 — Toronto Maple Leafs in 1976 QF series won by Philadelphia 4-3.

MOST POWER-PLAY GOALS, BOTH TEAMS, ONE SERIES:
21 — NY Islanders, Philadelphia Flyers in 1980 F, won by NY Islanders 4-2. NY Islanders had 15 and Flyers 6.
— **NY Islanders, Edmonton Oilers** in 1981 QF, won by NY Islanders 4-2. NY Islanders had 13 and Edmonton 8.
— **Philadelphia Flyers, Pittsburgh Penguins** in 1989 DF, won by Philadelphia 4-3. Philadelphia had 11 and Pittsburgh 10.
— **Minnesota North Stars, Chicago Blackhawks** in 1991 DSF, won by Minnesota 4-2. Minnesota had 15 and Chicago 6.
20 — Toronto Maple Leafs, Philadelphia Flyers in 1976 QF series won by Philadelphia 4-3. Toronto had 12 power-play goals; Philadelphia 8.

MOST POWER-PLAY GOALS, ONE TEAM, ONE GAME:
6 — Boston Bruins, April 2, 1969, at Boston against Toronto. Boston won 10-0.

MOST POWER-PLAY GOALS, BOTH TEAMS, ONE GAME:
8 — Minnesota North Stars, St. Louis Blues, April 24, 1991 at Minnesota. Minnesota had 4, St. Louis 4. Minnesota won 8-4.
7 — Minnesota North Stars, Edmonton Oilers, April 28, 1984 at Minnesota. Minnesota had 4, Edmonton 3. Edmonton won 8-5.
— Philadelphia Flyers, NY Rangers, April 13, 1985 at New York. Philadelphia had 4, NY Rangers 3. Philadelphia won 6-5.
— Edmonton Oilers, Chicago Blackhawks, May 14, 1985 at Edmonton. Chicago had 5, Edmonton 2. Edmonton won 10-5.
— Edmonton Oilers, Los Angeles Kings, April 9, 1987 at Edmonton. Edmonton had 5, Los Angeles 2. Edmonton won 13-3.
— Vancouver Canucks, Calgary Flames, April 9, 1989 at Vancouver. Vancouver had 4, Calgary 3. Vancouver won 5-3.

MOST POWER-PLAY GOALS, ONE TEAM, ONE PERIOD:
4 — Toronto Maple Leafs, March 26, 1936, second period against Boston at Toronto. Toronto won 8-3.
— **Minnesota North Stars,** April 28, 1984, second period against Edmonton at Minnesota. Edmonton won 8-5.
— **Boston Bruins,** April 11, 1991, third period against Hartford at Boston. Boston won 6-1.
— **Minnesota North Stars,** April 24, 1991, second period against St. Louis at Minnesota. Minnesota won 8-4.

MOST POWER-PLAY GOALS, BOTH TEAMS, ONE PERIOD:
5 — Minnesota North Stars, Edmonton Oilers, April 28, 1984, second period, at Minnesota. Minnesota had 4 and Edmonton 1. Edmonton won 8-5.
— **Vancouver Canucks, Calgary Flames,** April 9, 1989, third period at Vancouver. Vancouver had 3 and Calgary 2. Vancouver won 5-3.
— **Minnesota North Stars, St. Louis Blues,** April 24, 1991, second period, at Minnesota. Minnesota had 4 and St. Louis 1. Minnesota won 8-4.

TEAM SHORTHAND GOALS

MOST SHORTHAND GOALS BY ALL TEAMS, ONE PLAYOFF YEAR:
33 — 1988, in 83 games.

MOST SHORTHAND GOALS, ONE TEAM, ONE PLAYOFF YEAR:
10 — Edmonton Oilers 1983, in 16 games.
9 — NY Islanders, 1981, in 19 games.
8 — Philadelphia Flyers, 1989, in 19 games.
7 — NY Islanders, 1980, in 21 games.
— Chicago Blackhawks, 1989, in 16 games.
— Vancouver Canucks, 1995, in 11 games.

MOST SHORTHAND GOALS, ONE TEAM, ONE SERIES:
6 — Calgary Flames in 1995 against San Jose in best-of-seven CQF won by San Jose 4-3.
— **Vancouver Canucks** in 1995 against St. Louis in best-of-seven CQF won by Vancouver 4-3.
5 — Edmonton Oilers in 1983 against Calgary in best-of-seven DF won by Edmonton 4-1.
— NY Rangers in 1979 against Philadelphia in best-of-seven QF, won by NY Rangers 4-1.

MOST SHORTHAND GOALS, BOTH TEAMS, ONE SERIES:
7 — Boston Bruins (4), NY Rangers (3), in 1958 SF, won by Boston 4-2.
— **Edmonton Oilers (5), Calgary Flames (2),** in 1983 DF won by Edmonton 4-1.
— **Vancouver Canucks (6), St. Louis Blues (1),** in 1995 CQF won by Vancouver 4-3.

MOST SHORTHAND GOALS, ONE TEAM, ONE GAME:
3 — Boston Bruins, April 11, 1981, at Minnesota. Minnesota won 6-3.
— **NY Islanders,** April 17, 1983, at NY Rangers. NY Rangers won 7-6.
— **Toronto Maple Leafs,** May 8, 1994, at San Jose. Toronto won 8-3.

MOST SHORTHAND GOALS, BOTH TEAMS, ONE GAME:
4 — NY Islanders, NY Rangers, April 17, 1983 at NY Rangers. NY Islanders had 3 shorthand goals, NY Rangers 1. NY Rangers won 7-6.
— **Boston Bruins, Minnesota North Stars,** April 11, 1981, at Minnesota. Boston had 3 shorthand goals, Minnesota 1. Minnesota won 6-3.
— **San Jose Sharks, Toronto Maple Leafs,** May 8, 1994 at San Jose. Toronto had 3 shorthanded goals, San Jose 1. Toronto won 8-3.
3 — Toronto Maple Leafs, Detroit Red Wings, April 5, 1947, at Toronto. Toronto had 2 shorthand goals, Detroit 1. Toronto won 6-1.
— NY Rangers, Boston Bruins, April 1, 1958, at Boston. NY Rangers had 2 shorthand goals, Boston 1. NY Rangers won 5-2.
— Minnesota North Stars, Philadelphia Flyers, May 4, 1980, at Minnesota. Minnesota had 2 shorthand goals, Philadelphia 1. Philadelphia won 5-3.
— Edmonton Oilers, Winnipeg Jets, April 9, 1988 at Winnipeg. Winnipeg had 2 shorthand goals, Edmonton 1. Winnipeg won 6-4.
— New Jersey Devils, NY Islanders, April 14, 1988 at New Jersey. NY Islanders had 2 shorthand goals, New Jersey 1. New Jersey won 6-5.

MOST SHORTHAND GOALS, ONE TEAM, ONE PERIOD:
2 — Toronto Maple Leafs, April 5, 1947, at Toronto against Detroit, first period. Toronto won 6-1.
— **Toronto Maple Leafs,** April 13, 1965, at Toronto against Montreal, first period. Montreal won 4-3.
— **Boston Bruins,** April 20, 1969, at Boston against Montreal, first period. Boston won 3-2.
— **Boston Bruins,** April 8, 1970, at Boston against NY Rangers, second period. Boston won 8-2.
— **Boston Bruins,** April 30, 1972, at Boston against NY Rangers, first period. Boston won 6-5.
— **Chicago Blackhawks,** May 3, 1973, at Chicago against Montreal, first period. Chicago won 7-4.
— **Montreal Canadiens,** April 23, 1978, at Detroit, first period. Montreal won 8-0.
— **NY Islanders,** April 8, 1980, at New York against Los Angeles, second period. NY Islanders won 8-1.
— **Los Angeles Kings,** April 9, 1980, at NY Islanders, first period. Los Angeles won 6-3.
— **Boston Bruins,** April 13, 1980, at Pittsburgh, second period. Boston won 8-3.
— **Minnesota North Stars,** May 4, 1980, at Minnesota against Philadelphia, second period. Philadelphia won 5-3.
— **Boston Bruins,** April 11, 1981, at Minnesota, third period. Minnesota won 6-3.
— **NY Islanders,** May 12, 1981, at New York against Minnesota, first period. NY Islanders won 6-3.
— **Montreal Canadiens,** April 7, 1982, at Montreal against Quebec, third period. Montreal won 5-1.
— **Edmonton Oilers,** April 24, 1983, at Edmonton against Chicago, third period. Edmonton won 8-4.
— **Winnipeg Jets,** April 14, 1985, at Calgary, second period. Winnipeg won 5-3.
— **Boston Bruins,** April 6, 1988 at Boston against Buffalo, first period. Boston won 7-3.
— **NY Islanders,** April 14, 1988 at New Jersey, third period. New Jersey won 6-5.
— **Detroit Red Wings,** April 29, 1993 at Toronto, second period. Detroit won 7-3.
— **Toronto Maple Leafs,** May 8, 1994 at San Jose, third period. Toronto won 8-3.
— **Calgary Flames,** May 11, 1995 at San Jose, first period. Calgary won 9-2.
— **Vancouver Canucks,** May 15, 1995 at St. Louis, second period. Vancouver won 6-5.

The Edmonton Oilers set a franchise record by scoring 32 power-play goals during the 1988 playoffs. Eight different Oilers, including Glenn Anderson, shown here, hit the scoresheet with Edmonton enjoying the odd-man advantage.

MOST SHORTHAND GOALS, BOTH TEAMS, ONE PERIOD:
3 — **Toronto Maple Leafs, Detroit Red Wings,** April 5, 1947, at Toronto, first period. Toronto had 2 shorthand goals, Detroit 1. Toronto won 6-1.
— **Toronto Maple Leafs, San Jose Sharks,** May 8, 1994, at San Jose, third period. Toronto had 2 shorthanded goals, San Jose 1. Toronto won 8-3.

Fastest Goals

FASTEST FIVE GOALS, BOTH TEAMS:
3 Minutes, 6 Seconds — **Chicago Blackhawks, Minnesota North Stars,** at Chicago April 21, 1985. Keith Brown scored for Chicago at 1:12, second period; Ken Yaremchuk, Chicago, 1:27; Dino Ciccarelli, Minnesota, 2:48; Tony McKegney, Minnesota, 4:07; and Curt Fraser, Chicago, 4:18. Chicago won 6-2 and best-of-seven DF 4-2.
3 Minutes, 20 Seconds — **Minnesota North Stars, Philadelphia Flyers,** at Philadelphia, April 21, 1980. Paul Shmyr scored for Minnesota at 13:20, first period; Steve Christoff, Minnesota, 13:59; Ken Linseman, Philadelphia, 14:54; Tom Gorence, Philadelphia, 15:36; and Linseman, 16:40. Minnesota won 6-5. Philadelphia won best-of-seven SF 4-1.
4 Minutes, 19 Seconds — **Toronto Maple Leafs, NY Rangers** at Toronto, April 9, 1932. Ace Bailey scored for Toronto at 15:07, third period; Fred Cook, NY Rangers, 16:32; Bob Gracie, Toronto, 17:36; Frank Boucher, NY Rangers, 18:26 and again at 19:26. Toronto won 6-4 and best-of-five F 3-0.

FASTEST FIVE GOALS, ONE TEAM:
3 Minutes, 36 Seconds — **Montreal Canadiens** at Montreal, March 30, 1944, against Toronto. Toe Blake scored at 7:58 of third period and again at 8:37; Maurice Richard, 9:17; Ray Getliffe, 10:33; and Buddy O'Connor, 11:34. Canadiens won 11-0 and best-of-seven SF 4-1.

FASTEST FOUR GOALS, BOTH TEAMS:
1 Minute, 33 Seconds — **Philadelphia Flyers, Toronto Maple Leafs** at Philadelphia, April 20, 1976. Don Saleski of Philadelphia scored at 10:04 of second period; Bob Neely, Toronto, 10:42; Gary Dornhoefer, Philadelphia, 11:24; and Don Saleski, 11:37. Philadelphia won 7-1 and best-of-seven QF series 4-3.
1 minute, 34 seconds — **Montreal Canadiens, Calgary Flames** at Montreal, May 20, 1986. Joel Otto of Calgary scored at 17:59 of first period; Bobby Smith, Montreal, 18:25; Mats Naslund, Montreal, 19:17; and Bob Gainey, Montreal, 19:33. Montreal won 5-3 and best-of-seven F series 4-1.
1 Minute, 38 Seconds — **Boston Bruins, Philadelphia Flyers** at Philadelphia, April 26, 1977. Gregg Sheppard of Boston scored at 14:01 of second period; Mike Milbury, Boston, 15:01; Gary Dornhoefer, Philadelphia, 15:16; and Jean Ratelle, Boston, 15:39. Boston won 5-4 and best-of-seven SF series 4-0.

FASTEST FOUR GOALS, ONE TEAM:
2 Minutes, 35 Seconds — **Montreal Canadiens** at Montreal, March 30, 1944, against Toronto. Toe Blake scored at 7:58 of third period and again at 8:37; Maurice Richard, 9:17; Ray Getliffe, 10:33. Montreal won 11-0 and best-of-seven SF 4-1.

FASTEST THREE GOALS, BOTH TEAMS:
21 Seconds — **Edmonton Oilers, Chicago Blackhawks** at Edmonton, May 7, 1985. Behn Wilson scored for Chicago at 19:22 of third period, Jari Kurri at 19:36 and Glenn Anderson at 19:43 for Edmonton. Edmonton won 7-3 and best-of-seven CF 4-2.
30 Seconds — Chicago Blackhawks, Pittsburgh Penguins at Chicago, June 1, 1992. Dirk Graham scored for Chicago at 6:21 of first period, Kevin Stevens for Pittsburgh at 6:33 and Graham for Chicago at 6:51. Pittsburgh won 6-5 and best-of-seven F 4-0.
31 Seconds — Edmonton Oilers, Philadelphia Flyers at Edmonton, May 25, 1985. Wayne Gretzky scored for Edmonton at 1:10 and 1:25 of first period, Derrick Smith scored for Philadelphia at 1:41. Edmonton won 4-3 and best-of-seven F 4-1.

FASTEST THREE GOALS, ONE TEAM:
23 Seconds — **Toronto Maple Leafs** at Toronto, April 12, 1979, against Atlanta. Darryl Sittler scored at 4:04 of first period and again at 4:16 and Ron Ellis at 4:27. Leafs won 7-4 and best-of-three PR 2-0.
38 Seconds — NY Rangers at New York, April 12, 1986. Jim Wiemer scored at 12:29 of third period, Bob Brooke at 12:43 and Ron Grescher at 13:07 against Philadelphia. NY Rangers won 5-2 and best-of-five DSF 3-2.
56 Seconds — Montreal Canadiens at Detroit, April 6, 1954. Dickie Moore scored at 15:03 of first period, Maurice Richard at 15:28 and again at 15:59. Montreal won 3-1. Detroit won best-of-seven F 4-3.

FASTEST TWO GOALS, BOTH TEAMS:
5 Seconds — **Pittsburgh Penguins, Buffalo Sabres** at Buffalo, April 14, 1979. Gilbert Perreault scored for Buffalo at 12:59 and Jim Hamilton for Pittsburgh at 13:04 of first period. Pittsburgh won 4-3 and best-of-three PR 2-1.
8 Seconds — Minnesota North Stars, St. Louis Blues at Minnesota, April 9, 1989. Bernie Federko scored for St. Louis at 2:28 of third period and Perry Berezan at 2:36 for Minnesota. Minnesota won 5-4. St. Louis won best-of-seven DSF 4-1.
9 Seconds — NY Islanders, Washington Capitals at Washington, April 10, 1986. Bryan Trottier scored for New York at 18:26 of second period and Scott Stevens at 18:35 for Washington. Washington won 5-2, and best-of-five DSF 3-0.
10 Seconds — Washington Capitals, New Jersey Devils at New Jersey, April 5, 1990. Pat Conacher scored for New Jersey at 8:02 of second period and Dale Hunter at 8:12 for Washington. Washington won 5-4, and best-of-seven DSF 4-2.
— Calgary Flames, Edmonton Oilers at Edmonton, April 8, 1991. Joe Nieuwendyk scored for Calgary at 2:03 of first period and Esa Tikkanen at 2:13 for Edmonton. Edmonton won 4-3, and best-of-seven DSF 4-3.

FASTEST TWO GOALS, ONE TEAM:
5 Seconds — **Detroit Red Wings** at Detroit, April 11, 1965, against Chicago. Norm Ullman scored at 17:35 and 17:40, second period. Detroit won 4-2. Chicago won best-of-seven SF 4-3.

Jari Kurri, seen here scoring a goal against Montreal, helped the Edmonton Oilers establish a playoff record for short-handed goals when the Oilers downed Chicago 8-4 in game one of the 1983 Campbell Conference Finals. With Dave Semenko serving a five-minute major in the third period, Kurri scored a pair of goals in a two-minute span to give the Oilers ten shorthanded markers in the 1983 playoffs, an NHL record that still stands.

Syl Apps raises his stick in triumph after scoring the overtime winner for Toronto in game one of the 1940 quarter-finals between the Leafs and Black Hawks. The Leafs went on to defeat Chicago and Detroit before dropping a six-game decision to the Rangers in the Stanley Cup championship round.

OVERTIME

SHORTEST OVERTIME:
9 Seconds — Montreal Canadiens, Calgary Flames, at Calgary, May 18, 1986. Montreal won 3-2 on Brian Skrudland's goal and captured the best-of-seven F 4-1.
11 Seconds — NY Islanders, NY Rangers, at NY Rangers, April 11, 1975. NY Islanders won 4-3 on Jean-Paul Parise's goal and captured the best-of-three PR 2-1.

LONGEST OVERTIME:
116 Minutes, 30 Seconds — Detroit Red Wings, Mtl. Maroons at Montreal, March 24, 25, 1936. Detroit 1, Mtl. Maroons 0. Mud Bruneteau scored, assisted by Hec Kilrea, at 16:30 of sixth overtime period, or after 176 minutes, 30 seconds from start of game, which ended at 2:25 a.m. Detroit won best-of-five SF 3-0.

MOST OVERTIME GAMES, ONE PLAYOFF YEAR:
28 — 1993. Of 85 games played, 28 went into overtime.
19 — 1996. Of 86 games played, 19 went into overtime.
18 — 1994. Of 90 games played, 18 went into overtime.
— 1995. Of 81 games played, 18 went into overtime.

FEWEST OVERTIME GAMES, ONE PLAYOFF YEAR:
0 — 1963. None of the 16 games went into overtime, the only year since 1926 that no overtime was required in any playoff series.

MOST OVERTIME GAMES, ONE SERIES:
5 — Toronto Maple Leafs, Montreal Canadiens in 1951. Toronto defeated Montreal 4-1 in best-of-seven F.
4 — Toronto Maple Leafs, Boston Bruins in 1933. Toronto won best-of-five SF 3-2.
— Boston Bruins, NY Rangers in 1939. Boston won best-of-seven SF 4-3.
— St. Louis Blues, Minnesota North Stars in 1968. St. Louis won best-of-seven SF 4-3.

THREE-OR-MORE GOAL GAMES

MOST THREE-OR-MORE GOAL GAMES BY ALL TEAMS, ONE PLAYOFF YEAR:
12 — **1983** in 66 games.
— **1988** in 83 games.
11 — 1985 in 70 games.
— 1992 in 86 games.

MOST THREE-OR-MORE GOAL GAMES, ONE TEAM, ONE PLAYOFF YEAR:
6 — Edmonton Oilers in 16 games, 1983.
— **Edmonton Oilers** in 18 games, 1985.

SHUTOUTS

MOST SHUTOUTS, ONE PLAYOFF YEAR, ALL TEAMS:
16 — 1994. Of 90 games played, NY Rangers and Vancouver had 4 each, Toronto had 3, Buffalo had 2, while Washington, Detroit and New Jersey had 1 each.
12 — 1992. Of 86 games played, Detroit, Edmonton and Vancouver had 2 each, while Boston, Buffalo, Chicago, Montreal, NY Rangers and Pittsburgh had 1 each.

FEWEST SHUTOUTS, ONE PLAYOFF YEAR, ALL TEAMS:
0 — 1959. 18 games played.

MOST SHUTOUTS, BOTH TEAMS, ONE SERIES:
5 — 1945 F, Toronto Maple Leafs, Detroit Red Wings. Toronto had 3 shutouts, Detroit 2. Toronto won best-of-seven series 4-3.
— **1950 SF, Toronto Maple Leafs, Detroit Red Wings.** Toronto had 3 shutouts, Detroit 2. Detroit won best-of-seven series 4-3.

TEAM PENALTIES

FEWEST PENALTIES, BOTH TEAMS, BEST-OF-SEVEN SERIES:
19 — Detroit Red Wings, Toronto Maple Leafs in 1945 F, won by Toronto 4-3. Detroit received 10 minors. Toronto 9 minors.

FEWEST PENALTIES, ONE TEAM, BEST-OF-SEVEN SERIES:
9 — Toronto Maple Leafs in 1945 F, won by Toronto 4-3 against Detroit.

MOST PENALTIES, BOTH TEAMS, ONE SERIES:
219 — New Jersey Devils, Washington Capitals in 1988 DF won by New Jersey 4-3. New Jersey received 98 minors, 11 majors, 9 misconducts and 1 match penalty. Washington received 80 minors, 11 majors, 8 misconducts and 1 match penalty.

MOST PENALTY MINUTES, BOTH TEAMS, ONE SERIES:
656 — New Jersey Devils, Washington Capitals in 1988 DF won by New Jersey 4-3. New Jersey had 351 minutes; Washington 305.

MOST PENALTIES, ONE TEAM, ONE SERIES:
119 — New Jersey Devils in 1988 DF versus Washington. New Jersey received 98 minors, 11 majors, 9 misconducts and 1 match penalty.

MOST PENALTY MINUTES, ONE TEAM, ONE SERIES:
351 — New Jersey Devils in 1988 DF versus Washington. Series won by New Jersey 4-3.

MOST PENALTIES, BOTH TEAMS, ONE GAME:
66 — Detroit Red Wings, St. Louis Blues, at St. Louis, April 12, 1991. Detroit received 33 penalties; St. Louis 33. St. Louis won 6-1.
62 — New Jersey Devils, Washington Capitals, at New Jersey, April 22, 1988. New Jersey received 32 penalties; Washington 30. New Jersey won 10-4.

MOST PENALTY MINUTES, BOTH TEAMS, ONE GAME:
298 Minutes — Detroit Red Wings, St. Louis Blues, at St. Louis, April 12, 1991. Detroit received 33 penalties for 152 minutes; St. Louis 33 penalties for 146 minutes. St. Louis won 6-1.
267 Minutes — NY Rangers, Los Angeles Kings, at Los Angeles, April 9, 1981. NY Rangers received 31 penalties for 142 minutes; Los Angeles 28 penalties for 125 minutes. Los Angeles won 5-4.

MOST PENALTIES, ONE TEAM, ONE GAME:
33 — Detroit Red Wings, at St. Louis, April 12,1991. St. Louis won 6-1.
— **St. Louis Blues,** at St. Louis, April 12, 1991. St. Louis won 6-1.
32 — New Jersey Devils, at Washington, April 22,1988. New Jersey won 10-4.
31 — NY Rangers, at Los Angeles, April 9, 1981. Los Angeles won 5-4.
30 — Philadelphia Flyers, at Toronto, April 15, 1976. Toronto won 5-4.

MOST PENALTY MINUTES, ONE TEAM, ONE GAME:
152 — Detroit Red Wings, at St. Louis, April 12, 1991. St. Louis won 6-1.
146 — St. Louis Blues, at St. Louis, April 12, 1991. St. Louis won 6-1.
142 — NY Rangers, at Los Angeles, April 9, 1981. Los Angeles won 5-4.

MOST PENALTIES, BOTH TEAMS, ONE PERIOD:
43 — NY Rangers, Los Angeles Kings, April 9, 1981, at Los Angeles, first period. NY Rangers had 24 penalties; Los Angeles 19. Los Angeles won 5-4.

MOST PENALTY MINUTES, BOTH TEAMS, ONE PERIOD:
248 — NY Islanders, Boston Bruins, April 17, 1980, first period, at Boston. Each team received 124 minutes. Islanders won 5-4.

MOST PENALTIES, ONE TEAM, ONE PERIOD: (AND) MOST PENALTY MINUTES, ONE TEAM, ONE PERIOD:
24 Penalties; 125 Minutes — NY Rangers, April 9, 1981, at Los Angeles, first period. Los Angeles won 5-4.

Individual Records

Career

GAMES PLAYED

MOST YEARS IN PLAYOFFS:
20 — Gordie Howe, Detroit, Hartford (1947-58 incl.; 60-61; 63-66 incl.; 70 & 80)
— Larry Robinson, Montreal, Los Angeles (1973-92 incl.)
19 — Red Kelly, Detroit, Toronto
18 — Stan Mikita, Chicago
— Henri Richard, Montreal

MOST CONSECUTIVE YEARS IN PLAYOFFS:
20 — Larry Robinson, Montreal, Los Angeles (1973-1992, inclusive).
17 — Brad Park, NY Rangers, Boston, Detroit (1969-1985, inclusive).
— Ray Bourque, Boston (1980-96, inclusive).
16 — Jean Beliveau, Montreal (1954-69, inclusive).
— Bob Gainey, Montreal (1974-89, inclusive).

MOST PLAYOFF GAMES:
227 — Larry Robinson, Montreal, Los Angeles
225 — Glenn Anderson, Edmonton, Toronto, NY Rangers, St. Louis
221 — Bryan Trottier, NY Islanders, Pittsburgh
— Mark Messier, Edmonton, NY Rangers
212 — Kevin Lowe, Edmonton, NY Rangers

GOALS

MOST GOALS IN PLAYOFFS (CAREER):
112 — Wayne Gretzky, Edmonton, Los Angeles, St. Louis
106 — Mark Messier, Edmonton, NY Rangers
105 — Jari Kurri, Edmonton, Los Angeles, NY Rangers
93 — Glenn Anderson, Edmonton, Toronto, NY Rangers, St. Louis
85 — Mike Bossy, NY Islanders

MOST GOALS, ONE PLAYOFF YEAR:
19 — Reggie Leach, Philadelphia, 1976. 16 games.
— Jari Kurri, Edmonton, 1985. 18 games.
18 — Joe Sakic, Colorado, 1996. 22 games.
17 — Newsy Lalonde, Montreal, 1919. 10 games.
— Mike Bossy, NY Islanders, 1981. 19 games.
— Steve Payne, Minnesota, 1981. 19 games.
— Mike Bossy, NY Islanders, 1982. 19 games.
— Mike Bossy, NY Islanders, 1983. 19 games.
— Wayne Gretzky, Edmonton, 1985. 18 games.
— Kevin Stevens, Pittsburgh, 1991. 24 games.

MOST GOALS IN ONE SERIES (OTHER THAN FINAL):
12 — Jari Kurri, Edmonton, in 1985 CF, 6 games vs. Chicago.
11 — Newsy Lalonde, Montreal, in 1919 NHL F, 5 games vs. Ottawa.
10 — Tim Kerr, Philadelphia, in 1989 DF, 7 games vs. Pittsburgh.
9 — Reggie Leach, Philadelphia, in 1976 SF, 5 games vs. Boston.
— Bill Barber, Philadelphia, in 1980 SF, 5 games vs. Minnesota.
— Mike Bossy, NY Islanders, in 1983 CF, 6 games vs. Boston.
— Mario Lemieux, Pittsburgh, in 1989 DF, 7 games vs. Philadelphia.

MOST GOALS IN FINAL SERIES:
9 — Babe Dye, Toronto, in 1922, 5 games vs. Van. Millionaires.
8 — Alf Skinner, Toronto, in 1918, 5 games vs. Van. Millionaires.
7 — Jean Beliveau, Montreal, in 1956, during 5 games vs. Detroit.
— Mike Bossy, NY Islanders, in 1982, during 4 games vs. Vancouver.
— Wayne Gretzky, Edmonton, in 1985, during 5 games vs. Philadelphia.

MOST GOALS, ONE GAME:
5 — Newsy Lalonde, Montreal, March 1, 1919, at Montreal. Final score: Montreal 6, Ottawa 3.
— Maurice Richard, Montreal, March 23, 1944, at Montreal. Final score: Montreal 5, Toronto 1.
— Darryl Sittler, Toronto, April 22, 1976, at Toronto. Final score: Toronto 8, Philadelphia 5.
— Reggie Leach, Philadelphia, May 6, 1976, at Philadelphia. Final score: Philadelphia 6, Boston 3.
— Mario Lemieux, Pittsburgh, April 25, 1989 at Pittsburgh. Final score: Pittsburgh 10, Philadelphia 7.

MOST GOALS, ONE PERIOD:
4 — Tim Kerr, Philadelphia, April 13, 1985, at New York vs. NY Rangers, second period. Final score: Philadelphia 6, NY Rangers 5.
— Mario Lemieux, Pittsburgh, April 25, 1989, at Pittsburgh vs. Philadelphia, first period. Final score: Pittsburgh 10, Philadelphia 7.

ASSISTS

MOST ASSISTS IN PLAYOFFS (CAREER):
250 — Wayne Gretzky, Edmonton, Los Angeles, St. Louis
177 — Mark Messier, Edmonton, NY Rangers
128 — Paul Coffey, Edmonton, Pittsburgh, Los Angeles, Detroit
125 — Jari Kurri, Edmonton, Los Angeles, NY Rangers
121 — Glenn Anderson, Edmonton, Toronto, NY Rangers, St. Louis

MOST ASSISTS, ONE PLAYOFF YEAR:
31 — Wayne Gretzky, Edmonton, 1988. 19 games.
30 — Wayne Gretzky, Edmonton, 1985. 18 games.
29 — Wayne Gretzky, Edmonton, 1987. 21 games.
28 — Mario Lemieux, Pittsburgh, 1991. 23 games.
26 — Wayne Gretzky, Edmonton, 1983. 16 games.

MOST ASSISTS IN ONE SERIES (OTHER THAN FINAL):
14 — Rick Middleton, Boston, in 1983 DF, 7 games vs. Buffalo.
— Wayne Gretzky, Edmonton, in 1985 CF, 6 games vs. Chicago.
13 — Wayne Gretzky, Edmonton, in 1987 DSF, 5 games vs. Los Angeles.
— Doug Gilmour, Toronto, in 1994 CSF, 7 games vs. San Jose.
11 — Mark Messier, Edmonton, in 1989 DSF, 7 games vs. Los Angeles.
— Al MacInnis, Calgary, in 1984 DF, 7 games vs. Edmonton.
— Mike Ridley, Washington, in 1992 DSF, 7 games vs. Pittsburgh.
— Ron Francis, Pittsburgh, in 1995 CQF, 7 games vs. Washington.
10 — Fleming Mackell, Boston, in 1958 SF, 6 games vs. NY Rangers.
— Stan Mikita, Chicago, in 1962 SF, 6 games vs. Montreal.
— Bob Bourne, NY Islanders, in 1983 DF, 6 games vs. NY Rangers.
— Wayne Gretzky, Edmonton, in 1988 DSF, 5 games vs. Winnipeg.
— Mario Lemieux, Pittsburgh, in 1992 DSF, 6 games vs. Washington.

MOST ASSISTS IN FINAL SERIES:
10 — Wayne Gretzky, Edmonton, in 1988, 4 games plus suspended game vs. Boston.
9 — Jacques Lemaire, Montreal, in 1973, 6 games vs. Chicago.
— Wayne Gretzky, Edmonton, in 1987, 7 games vs. Philadelphia.
— Larry Murphy, Pittsburgh, in 1991, 6 games vs. Minnesota.

MOST ASSISTS, ONE GAME:
6 — Mikko Leinonen, NY Rangers, April 8, 1982, at New York. Final score: NY Rangers 7, Philadelphia 3.
— Wayne Gretzky, Edmonton, April 9, 1987, at Edmonton. Final score: Edmonton 13, Los Angeles 3.
5 — Toe Blake, Montreal, March 23, 1944, at Montreal. Final score: Montreal 5, Toronto 1.
— Maurice Richard, Montreal, March 27, 1956, at Montreal. Final score: Montreal 7, NY Rangers 0.
— Bert Olmstead, Montreal, March 30, 1957, at Montreal. Final score: Montreal 8, NY Rangers 3.
— Don McKenney, Boston, April 5, 1958, at Boston. Final score: Boston 8, NY Rangers 2.
— Stan Mikita, Chicago, April 4, 1973, at Chicago. Final score: Chicago 7, St. Louis 1.
— Wayne Gretzky, Edmonton, April 8, 1981, at Montreal. Final score: Edmonton 6, Montreal 3.
— Paul Coffey, Edmonton, May 14, 1985, at Edmonton. Final score: Edmonton 10, Chicago 5.
— Doug Gilmour, St. Louis, April 15, 1986, at Minnesota. Final score: St. Louis 6, Minnesota 3.
— Risto Siltanen, Quebec, April 14, 1987 at Hartford. Final score: Quebec 7, Hartford 5.
— Patrik Sundstrom, New Jersey, April 22, 1988, at New Jersey. Final score: New Jersey 10, Washington 4.

MOST ASSISTS, ONE PERIOD:
3 — Three assists by one player in one period of a playoff game has been recorded on 64 occasions. Joe Sakic of the Colorado Avalanche is the most recent to equal this mark with 3 assists in the first period at Colorado, June 6, 1996. Final score: Colorado 8, Florida 1.
Wayne Gretzky has had 3 assists in one period 5 times; Ray Bourque, 3 times; Toe Blake, Jean Beliveau, Doug Harvey and Bobby Orr, twice. Nick Metz of Toronto was the first player to be credited with 3 assists in one period of a playoff game Mar. 21, 1941 at Toronto vs. Boston.

POINTS

MOST POINTS IN PLAYOFFS (CAREER):
362 — Wayne Gretzky, Edmonton, Los Angeles, St. Louis, 112G, 250A
283 — Mark Messier, Edmonton, NY Rangers, 106G, 177A
230 — Jari Kurri, Edmonton, Los Angeles, NY Rangers, 105G, 125A
214 — Glenn Anderson, Edmonton, Toronto, NY Rangers, St. Louis, 93G, 121A
184 — Bryan Trottier, NY Islanders, Pittsburgh 71G, 113A

MOST POINTS, ONE PLAYOFF YEAR:
47 — Wayne Gretzky, Edmonton, in 1985. 17 goals, 30 assists in 18 games.
44 — Mario Lemieux, Pittsburgh, in 1991. 16 goals, 28 assists in 23 games.
43 — Wayne Gretzky, Edmonton, in 1988. 12 goals, 31 assists in 19 games.
40 — Wayne Gretzky, Los Angeles, in 1993. 15 goals, 25 assists in 24 games.
38 — Wayne Gretzky, Edmonton, in 1983. 12 goals, 26 assists in 16 games.

MOST POINTS IN ONE SERIES (OTHER THAN FINAL):
19 — Rick Middleton, Boston, in 1983 DF, 7 games vs. Buffalo. 5 goals, 14 assists.
18 — Wayne Gretzky, Edmonton, in 1985 CF, 6 games vs. Chicago. 4 goals, 14 assists.
17 — Mario Lemieux, Pittsburgh, in 1992 DSF, 6 games vs. Washington. 7 goals, 10 assists.
16 — Barry Pederson, Boston, in 1983 DF, 7 games vs. Buffalo. 7 goals, 9 assists.
— Doug Gilmour, Toronto, in 1994 CSF, 7 games vs. San Jose. 3 goals, 13 assists.
15 — Jari Kurri, Edmonton, in 1985 CF, 6 games vs. Chicago. 12 goals, 3 assists.
— Wayne Gretzky, Edmonton, in 1987 DSF, 5 games vs. Los Angeles. 2 goals, 13 assists.
— Tim Kerr, Philadelphia, in 1989 DF, 7 games vs. Pittsburgh. 10 goals, 5 assists.
— Mario Lemieux, Pittsburgh, in 1991 CF, 6 games vs. Boston. 6 goals, 9 assists.

MOST POINTS IN FINAL SERIES:
- 13 — **Wayne Gretzky, Edmonton,** in 1988, 4 games plus suspended game vs. Boston. 3 goals, 10 assists.
- 12 — Gordie Howe, Detroit, in 1955, 7 games vs. Montreal. 5 goals, 7 assists.
  - — Yvan Cournoyer, Montreal, in 1973, 6 games vs. Chicago. 6 goals, 6 assists.
  - — Jacques Lemaire, Montreal, in 1973, 6 games vs. Chicago. 3 goals, 9 assists.
  - — Mario Lemieux, Pittsburgh, in 1991, 5 games vs. Minnesota. 5 goals, 7 assists.

MOST POINTS, ONE GAME:
- 8 — **Patrik Sundstrom, New Jersey,** April 22, 1988 at New Jersey during 10-4 win over Washington. Sundstrom had 3 goals, 5 assists.
  - — **Mario Lemieux, Pittsburgh,** April 25, 1989 at Pittsburgh during 10-7 win over Philadelphia. Lemieux had 5 goals, 3 assists.
- 7 — Wayne Gretzky, Edmonton, April 17, 1983 at Calgary during 10-2 win. Gretzky had 4 goals, 3 assists.
  - — Wayne Gretzky, Edmonton, April 25,1985 at Winnipeg during 8-3 win. Gretzky had 3 goals, 4 assists.
  - — Wayne Gretzky, Edmonton, April 9, 1987, at Edmonton during 13-3 win over Los Angeles. Gretzky had 1 goal, 6 assists.
- 6 — Dickie Moore, Montreal, March 25, 1954, at Montreal during 8-1 win over Boston. Moore had 2 goals, 4 assists.
  - — Phil Esposito, Boston, April 2, 1969, at Boston during 10-0 win over Toronto. Esposito had 4 goals, 2 assists.
  - — Darryl Sittler, Toronto, April 22, 1976, at Toronto during 8-5 win over Philadelphia. Sittler had 5 goals, 1 assist.
  - — Guy Lafleur, Montreal, April 11, 1977, at Montreal during 7-2 victory vs. St. Louis. Lafleur had 3 goals, 3 assists.
  - — Mikko Leinonen, NY Rangers, April 8, 1982, at New York during 7-3 win over Philadelphia. Leinonen had 6 assists.
  - — Paul Coffey, Edmonton, May 14, 1985 at Edmonton during 10-5 win over Chicago. Coffey had 1 goal, 5 assists.
  - — John Anderson, Hartford, April 12, 1986 at Hartford during 9-4 win over Quebec. Anderson had 2 goals, 4 assists.
  - — Mario Lemieux, Pittsburgh, April 23, 1992 at Pittsburgh during 6-4 win over Washington. Lemieux had 3 goals, 3 assists.

MOST POINTS, ONE PERIOD:
- 4 — **Maurice Richard, Montreal,** March 29, 1945, at Montreal vs. Toronto. Third period, 3 goals, 1 assist. Final score: Montreal 10, Toronto 3.
  - — **Dickie Moore, Montreal,** March 25, 1954, at Montreal vs. Boston. First period, 2 goals, 2 assists. Final score: Montreal 8, Boston 1.
  - — **Barry Pederson, Boston,** April 8, 1982, at Boston vs. Buffalo. Second period, 3 goals, 1 assist. Final score: Boston 7, Buffalo 3.
  - — **Peter McNab, Boston,** April 12, 1982, at Buffalo. Second period, 1 goal, 3 assists. Final score: Boston 5, Buffalo 2.
  - — **Tim Kerr, Philadelphia,** April 13, 1985 at New York. Second period, 4 goals. Final score: Philadelphia 6, Rangers 5.
  - — **Ken Linseman, Boston,** April 14, 1985 at Boston vs. Montreal. Second period, 2 goals, 2 assists. Final score: Boston 7, Montreal 6.
  - — **Wayne Gretzky, Edmonton,** April 12, 1987, at Los Angeles. Third period, 1 goal, 3 assists. Final score: Edmonton 6, Los Angeles 3.
  - — **Glenn Anderson, Edmonton,** April 6, 1988, at Edmonton vs. Winnipeg. Third period, 3 goals, 1 assist. Final score: Edmonton 7, Winnipeg 4.
  - — **Mario Lemieux, Pittsburgh,** April 25, 1989, at Pittsburgh vs. Philadelphia. First period, 4 goals. Final score: Pittsburgh 10, Philadelphia 7.
  - — **Dave Gagner, Minnesota,** April 8, 1991, at Minnesota vs. Chicago. First period, 2 goals, 2 assists. Final score: Chicago 6, Minnesota 5.
  - — **Mario Lemieux, Pittsburgh,** April 23, 1992, at Pittsburgh vs. Washington. Second period, 2 goals, 2 assists. Final score: Pittsburgh 6, Washington 4.

POWER-PLAY GOALS

MOST POWER-PLAY GOALS IN PLAYOFFS (CAREER):
- 35 — **Mike Bossy, NY Islanders**
- 34 — Dino Ciccarelli, Minnesota, Washington, Detroit
- 31 — Wayne Gretzky, Edmonton, Los Angeles, St. Louis
- 28 — Mario Lemieux, Pittsburgh
- 27 — Denis Potvin, NY Islanders
- 26 — Jean Beliveau, Montreal
- 25 — Jari Kurri, Edmonton, Los Angeles

MOST POWER-PLAY GOALS, ONE PLAYOFF YEAR:
- 9 — **Mike Bossy, NY Islanders,** 1981. 18 games against Toronto, Edmonton, NY Rangers and Minnesota.
  - — **Cam Neely, Boston,** 1991. 19 games against Hartford, Montreal, Pittsburgh.
- 8 — Tim Kerr, Philadelphia, 1989. 19 games.
  - — John Druce, Washington, 1990. 15 games.
  - — Brian Propp, Minnesota, 1991. 23 games.
  - — Mario Lemieux, Pittsburgh, 1992. 15 games.
- 7 — Michel Goulet, Quebec, 1985. 17 games.
  - — Mark Messier, Edmonton, 1988. 19 games.
  - — Mario Lemieux, Pittsburgh, 1989. 11 games.
  - — Brett Hull, St. Louis, 1990. 12 games.
  - — Kevin Stevens, Pittsburgh, 1991. 24 games.

MOST POWER-PLAY GOALS, ONE PLAYOFF SERIES:
- 6 — **Chris Kontos, Los Angeles,** 1989, DSF vs. Edmonton, won by Los Angeles 4-3.
- 5 — Andy Bathgate, Detroit, 1966, SF vs. Chicago, won by Detroit 4-2.
  - — Denis Potvin, NY Islanders, 1981, QF vs. Edmonton, won by NY Islanders 4-2.
  - — Ken Houston, Calgary, 1981, QF vs. Philadelphia, won by Calgary 4-3.
  - — Rick Vaive, Chicago, 1988, DSF vs. St. Louis, won by St. Louis 4-1.
  - — Tim Kerr, Philadelphia, 1989, DF vs. Pittsburgh, won by Philadelphia 4-3.
  - — Mario Lemieux, Pittsburgh, 1989, DF vs. Philadelphia won by Philadelphia 4-3.
  - — John Druce, Washington, 1990, DF vs. NY Rangers won by Washington 4-1.
  - — Pat LaFontaine, Buffalo, 1992, DSF vs. Boston won by Boston 4-3.
  - — Adam Graves, NY Rangers, 1996, CQF vs. Montreal, won by NY Rangers 4-2.

MOST POWER-PLAY GOALS, ONE GAME:
- 3 — **Syd Howe, Detroit,** March 23, 1939, at Detroit vs. Montreal, Detroit won 7-3.
  - — **Sid Smith, Toronto,** April 10, 1949, at Detroit. Toronto won 3-1.
  - — **Phil Esposito, Boston,** April 2, 1969, at Boston vs. Toronto. Boston won 10-0.
  - — **John Bucyk, Boston,** April 21, 1974, at Boston vs. Chicago. Boston won 8-6.
  - — **Denis Potvin, NY Islanders,** April 17, 1981, at New York vs. Edmonton. NY Islanders won 6-3.
  - — **Tim Kerr, Philadelphia,** April 13, 1985, at NY Rangers. Philadelphia won 6-5.
  - — **Jari Kurri, Edmonton,** April 9, 1987, at Edmonton vs. Los Angeles. Edmonton won 13-3.
  - — **Mark Johnson, New Jersey,** April 22, 1988, at New Jersey vs. Washington. New Jersey won 10-4.
  - — **Dino Ciccarelli, Detroit,** April 29, 1993, at Toronto, in 7-3 win by Detroit.
  - — **Dino Ciccarelli, Detroit,** May 11, 1995, at Dallas, in 5-1 win by Detroit.

MOST POWER-PLAY GOALS, ONE PERIOD:
- 3 — **Tim Kerr, Philadelphia,** April 13, 1985 at New York, second period in 6-5 win vs. NY Rangers.
- 2 — Two power-play goals have been scored by one player in one period on 48 occasions. Charlie Conacher of Toronto was the first to score two power-play goals in one period, setting the mark on Mar. 26, 1936. Peter Forsberg of Colorado is the most recent to equal this mark with two power-play goals in the first period at Colorado, June 6, 1996. Final score: Colorado 8, Florida 1.

SHORTHAND GOALS

MOST SHORTHAND GOALS IN PLAYOFFS (CAREER):
- 14 — **Mark Messier, Edmonton, NY Rangers**
- 11 — Wayne Gretzky, Edmonton, Los Angeles, St. Louis
- 10 — Jari Kurri, Edmonton, Los Angeles, NY Rangers
- 8 — Ed Westfall, Boston, NY Islanders
  - — Hakan Loob, Calgary

MOST SHORTHAND GOALS, ONE PLAYOFF YEAR:
- 3 — **Derek Sanderson, Boston,** 1969. 1 against Toronto in QF, won by Boston 4-0; 2 against Montreal in SF, won by Montreal 4-2.
  - — **Bill Barber, Philadelphia,** 1980. All against Minnesota in SF, won by Philadelphia 4-1.
  - — **Lorne Henning, NY Islanders,** 1980. 1 against Boston in QF won by NY Islanders 4-1; 1 against Buffalo in SF, won by NY Islanders 4-2, 1 against Philadelphia in F, won by NY Islanders 4-2.
  - — **Wayne Gretzky, Edmonton,** 1983. 2 against Winnipeg in DSF won by Edmonton 3-0; 1 against Calgary in DF, won by Edmonton 4-1.
  - — **Wayne Presley, Chicago,** 1989. All against Detroit in DSF won by Chicago 4-2.

MOST SHORTHAND GOALS, ONE PLAYOFF SERIES:
- 3 — **Bill Barber, Philadelphia,** 1980, SF vs. Minnesota, won by Philadelphia 4-1.
  - — **Wayne Presley, Chicago,** 1989, DSF vs. Detroit, won by Chicago 4-2.
- 2 — Mac Colville, NY Rangers, 1940, SF vs. Boston, won by NY Rangers 4-2.
  - — Jerry Toppazzini, Boston, 1958, SF vs. NY Rangers, won by Boston 4-2.
  - — Dave Keon, Toronto, 1963, F vs. Detroit, won by Toronto 4-1.
  - — Bob Pulford, Toronto, 1964, F vs. Detroit, won by Toronto 4-3.
  - — Serge Savard, Montreal, 1968, F vs. St. Louis, won by Montreal 4-0.
  - — Derek Sanderson, Boston, 1969, SF vs. Montreal, won by Montreal 4-2.
  - — Bryan Trottier, NY Islanders, 1980, PR vs. Los Angeles, won by NY Islanders 3-1.
  - — Bobby Lalonde, Boston, 1981, PR vs. Minnesota, won by Minnesota 3-0.
  - — Butch Goring, NY Islanders, 1981, SF vs. NY Rangers, won by NY Islanders 4-0.
  - — Wayne Gretzky, Edmonton, 1983, DSF vs. Winnipeg, won by Edmonton 3-0.
  - — Mark Messier, Edmonton, 1983, DF vs. Calgary, won by Edmonton 4-1.
  - — Jari Kurri, Edmonton, 1983, CF vs. Chicago, won by Edmonton 4-0.
  - — Wayne Gretzky, Edmonton, 1985, DF vs. Winnipeg, won by Edmonton 4-0.
  - — Kevin Lowe, Edmonton, 1987, F vs. Philadelphia, won by Edmonton 4-3.
  - — Bob Gould, Washington, 1988, DSF vs. Philadelphia, won by Washington 4-3.
  - — Dave Poulin, Philadelphia, 1989, DF vs. Pittsburgh, won by Philadelphia 4-3.
  - — Russ Courtnall, Montreal, 1991, DF vs. Boston, won by Boston 4-3.
  - — Sergei Fedorov, Detroit, 1992 DSF vs. Minnesota, won by Detroit 4-3.
  - — Mark Messier, NY Rangers, 1992, DSF vs. New Jersey, won by NY Rangers 4-3.
  - — Tom Fitzgerald, NY Islanders, 1993, DF vs. Pittsburgh, won by NY Islanders 4-3.
  - — Mark Osborne, Toronto, 1994, CSF vs. San Jose, won by Toronto 4-3.

MOST SHORTHAND GOALS, ONE GAME:
- 2 — **Dave Keon, Toronto,** April 18, 1963, at Toronto, in 3-1 win vs. Detroit.
  - — **Bryan Trottier, NY Islanders,** April 8, 1980 at New York, in 8-1 win vs. Los Angeles.
  - — **Bobby Lalonde, Boston,** April 11, 1981 at Minnesota, in 6-3 win by Minnesota.
  - — **Wayne Gretzky, Edmonton.** April 6, 1983 at Edmonton, in 6-3 win vs. Winnipeg.
  - — **Jari Kurri, Edmonton,** April 24, 1983, at Edmonton, in 8-3 win vs. Chicago.
  - — **Mark Messier, NY Rangers,** April 21, 1992, at New York, in 7-3 loss vs. New Jersey.
  - — **Tom Fitzgerald, NY Islanders,** May 8, 1993, at Long Island, in 6-5 win vs. Pittsburgh.

MOST SHORTHAND GOALS, ONE PERIOD:
- 2 — **Bryan Trottier, NY Islanders,** April 8, 1980, second period at New York in 8-1 win vs. Los Angeles.
  - — **Bobby Lalonde, Boston,** April 11, 1981, third period at Minnesota in 6-3 win by Minnesota.
  - — **Jari Kurri, Edmonton,** April 24, 1983, third period at Edmonton in 8-4 win vs. Chicago.

This goal by Pete Stemkowski at the 1:29 mark of the third overtime period gave the New York Rangers a 3-2 win over Chicago and tied their 1971 semi-final series at three games apiece. Three nights later, Chicago downed the Rangers 4-2 to advance to the Stanley Cup finals for the first time since 1965.

GAME-WINNING GOALS

MOST GAME-WINNING GOALS IN PLAYOFFS (CAREER):
22 — Wayne Gretzky, Edmonton, Los Angeles, St. Louis
18 — Maurice Richard, Montreal
17 — Mike Bossy, NY Islanders
— Glenn Anderson, Edmonton, Toronto, NY Rangers, St. Louis
15 — Jean Beliveau, Montreal
— Yvan Cournoyer, Montreal

MOST GAME-WINNING GOALS, ONE PLAYOFF YEAR:
6 — Joe Sakic, Colorado, 1996. 22 games.
5 — Mike Bossy, NY Islanders, 1983. 19 games.
— Jari Kurri, Edmonton, 1987. 21 games.
— Bobby Smith, Minnesota, 1991. 23 games.
— Mario Lemieux, Pittsburgh, 1992. 15 games.

MOST GAME-WINNING GOALS, ONE PLAYOFF SERIES:
4 — Mike Bossy, NY Islanders, 1983, CF vs. Boston, won by NY Islanders 4-2.

OVERTIME GOALS

MOST OVERTIME GOALS IN PLAYOFFS (CAREER):
6 — Maurice Richard, Montreal (1 in 1946; 3 in 1951; 1 in 1957; 1 in 1958.)
5 — Glenn Anderson, Edmonton, Toronto, NY Rangers, St. Louis
4 — Bob Nystrom, NY Islanders
— Dale Hunter, Quebec, Washington
— Wayne Gretzky, Edmonton, Los Angeles
— Stephane Richer, Montreal, New Jersey
— Joe Murphy, Edmonton, Chicago
3 — Mel Hill, Boston
— Rene Robert, Buffalo
— Danny Gare, Buffalo
— Jacques Lemaire, Montreal
— Bobby Clarke, Philadelphia
— Terry O'Reilly, Boston
— Mike Bossy, NY Islanders
— Steve Payne, Minnesota
— Ken Morrow, NY Islanders
— Lanny McDonald, Toronto, Calgary
— Peter Stastny, Quebec
— Dino Ciccarelli, Minnesota, Washington
— Russ Courtnall, Montreal
— Kirk Muller, Montreal
— Doug Gilmour, St. Louis, Calgary, Toronto
— Greg Adams, Vancouver

MOST OVERTIME GOALS, ONE PLAYOFF YEAR:
3 — Mel Hill, Boston, 1939. All against NY Rangers in best-of-seven SF, won by Boston 4-3.
— Maurice Richard, Montreal, 1951. 2 against Detroit in best-of-seven SF, won by Montreal 4-2; 1 against Toronto best-of-seven F, won by Toronto 4-1.

MOST OVERTIME GOALS, ONE PLAYOFF SERIES:
3 — Mel Hill, Boston, 1939, SF vs. NY Rangers, won by Boston 4-3. Hill scored at 59:25 overtime March 21 for a 2-1 win; at 8:24, March 23 for a 3-2 win; and at 48:00, April 2 for a 2-1 win.

SCORING BY A DEFENSEMAN

MOST GOALS BY A DEFENSEMAN, ONE PLAYOFF YEAR:
12 — Paul Coffey, Edmonton, 1985. 18 games.
11 — Brian Leetch, NY Rangers, 1994. 23 games.
9 — Bobby Orr, Boston, 1970. 14 games.
— Brad Park, Boston, 1978. 15 games.
8 — Denis Potvin, NY Islanders, 1981. 18 games.
— Raymond Bourque, Boston, 1983. 17 games.
— Denis Potvin, NY Islanders, 1983. 20 games.
— Paul Coffey, Edmonton, 1984. 19 games

MOST GOALS BY A DEFENSEMAN, ONE GAME:
3 — Bobby Orr, Boston, April 11, 1971 at Montreal. Final score: Boston 5, Montreal 2.
— **Dick Redmond, Chicago,** April 4, 1973 at Chicago. Final score: Chicago 7, St. Louis 1.
— **Denis Potvin, NY Islanders,** April 17, 1981 at New York. Final score: NY Islanders 6, Edmonton 3.
— **Paul Reinhart, Calgary,** April 14, 1983 at Edmonton. Final score: Edmonton 6, Calgary 3.
— **Paul Reinhart, Calgary,** April 8, 1984 at Vancouver. Final score: Calgary 5, Vancouver 1.
— **Doug Halward, Vancouver,** April 7, 1984 at Vancouver. Final score: Vancouver 7, Calgary 0.
— **Al Iafrate, Washington,** April 26, 1993 at Washington. Final score: Washington 6, NY Islanders 4.
— **Eric Desjardins, Montreal,** June 3, 1993 at Montreal. Final score: Montreal 3, Los Angeles 2.
— **Gary Suter, Chicago,** April 24, 1994, at Chicago. Final score: Chicago 4, Toronto 3.
— **Brian Leetch, NY Rangers,** May 22, 1995 at Philadelphia. Final score: Philadelphia 4, NY Rangers 3.

MOST ASSISTS BY A DEFENSEMAN, ONE PLAYOFF YEAR:
25 — Paul Coffey, Edmonton, 1985. 18 games.
24 — Al MacInnis, Calgary, 1989. 22 games.
23 — Brian Leetch, NY Rangers, 1994. 23 games.
19 — Bobby Orr, Boston, 1972. 15 games.
18 — Ray Bourque, Boston, 1988. 23 games.
— Ray Bourque, Boston, 1991. 19 games.
— Larry Murphy, Pittsburgh, 1991. 23 games.

MOST ASSISTS BY A DEFENSEMAN, ONE GAME:
5 — Paul Coffey, Edmonton, May 14, 1985 at Edmonton vs. Chicago. Edmonton won 10-5.
— Risto Siltanen, Quebec, April 14, 1987 at Hartford. Quebec won 7-5.

MOST POINTS BY A DEFENSEMAN, ONE PLAYOFF YEAR:
37 — Paul Coffey, Edmonton, in 1985. 12 goals, 25 assists in 18 games.
34 — Brian Leetch, NY Rangers, in 1994. 11 goals, 23 assists in 23 games.
31 — Al MacInnis, Calgary, in 1989. 7 goals, 24 assists in 18 games.
25 — Denis Potvin, NY Islanders, in 1981. 8 goals, 17 assists in 18 games.
— Ray Bourque, Boston, in 1991. 7 goals, 18 assists in 19 games.

MOST POINTS BY A DEFENSEMAN, ONE GAME:
6 — Paul Coffey, Edmonton, May 14, 1985 at Edmonton vs. Chicago. 1 goal, 5 assists. Edmonton won 10-5.
5 — Eddie Bush, Detroit, April 9, 1942, at Detroit vs. Toronto. 1 goal, 4 assists. Detroit won 5-2.
— Bob Dailey, Philadelphia, May 1, 1980, at Philadelphia vs. Minnesota. 1 goal, 4 assists. Philadelphia won 7-0.
— Denis Potvin, NY Islanders, April 17, 1981, at New York vs. Edmonton. 3 goals, 2 assists. NY Islanders won 6-3.
— Risto Siltanen, Quebec, April 14, 1987 at Hartford. 5 assists. Quebec won 7-5.

SCORING BY A ROOKIE

MOST GOALS BY A ROOKIE, ONE PLAYOFF YEAR:
14 — Dino Ciccarelli, Minnesota, 1981. 19 games.
11 — Jeremy Roenick, Chicago, 1990. 20 games.
10 — Claude Lemieux, Montreal, 1986. 20 games.
9 — Pat Flatley, NY Islanders, 1984. 21 games
8 — Steve Christoff, Minnesota, 1980. 14 games.
— Brad Palmer, Minnesota, 1981. 19 games.
— Mike Krushelnyski, Boston, 1983. 17 games.
— Bob Joyce, Boston, 1988. 23 games.

MOST POINTS BY A ROOKIE, ONE PLAYOFF YEAR:
21 — Dino Ciccarelli, Minnesota, in 1981. 14 goals, 7 assists in 19 games.
20 — Don Maloney, NY Rangers, in 1979. 7 goals, 13 assists in 18 games.

THREE-OR-MORE-GOAL GAMES

MOST THREE-OR-MORE-GOAL GAMES IN PLAYOFFS (CAREER):
8 — Wayne Gretzky, Edmonton, Los Angeles. Six three-goal games; two four-goal games.
7 — Maurice Richard, Montreal. Four three-goal games; two four-goal games; one five-goal game.
— Jari Kurri, Edmonton. Six three-goal games; one four-goal game.
6 — Dino Ciccarelli, Minnesota, Washington, Detroit. Five three-goal games; one four-goal game.
5 — Mike Bossy, NY Islanders. Four three-goal games; one four-goal game.

MOST THREE-OR-MORE-GOAL GAMES, ONE PLAYOFF YEAR:
4 — Jari Kurri, Edmonton, 1985. 1 four-goal game, 3 three-goal games.
3 — Mark Messier, Edmonton, 1983. 3 three-goal games.
— Mike Bossy, NY Islanders, 1983. 1 four-goal game, 2 three-goal games
2 — Newsy Lalonde, Montreal, 1919. 1 five-goal game, 1 four-goal game.
— Maurice Richard, Montreal, 1944. 1 five-goal game; 1 three-goal game.
— Doug Bentley, Chicago, 1944. 2 three-goal games.
— Norm Ullman, Detroit, 1964. 2 three-goal games.
— Phil Esposito, Boston, 1970. 2 three-goal games.
— Pit Martin, Chicago, 1973. 2 three-goal games.
— Rick MacLeish, Philadelphia, 1975. 2 three-goal games.
— Lanny McDonald, Toronto, 1977. 1 four-goal game; 1 three-goal game.
— Wayne Gretzky, Edmonton, 1981. 2 three-goal games.
— Wayne Gretzky, Edmonton, 1983. 2 four-goal games.
— Wayne Gretzky, Edmonton, 1985. 2 three-goal games.
— Petr Klima, Detroit, 1988. 2 three-goal games.
— Cam Neely, Boston, 1991. 2 three-goal games.

MOST THREE-OR-MORE-GOAL GAMES, ONE PLAYOFF SERIES:
3 — Jari Kurri, Edmonton 1985, CF vs. Chicago won by Edmonton 4-2. Kurri scored 3 G May 7 at Edmonton in 7-3 win, 3 G May 14 in 10-5 win and 4 G May 16 at Chicago in 8-2 win.
2 — Doug Bentley, Chicago, 1944, SF vs. Detroit, won by Chicago 4-1. Bentley scored 3 G Mar. 28 at Chicago in 7-1 win and 3 G Mar. 30 at Detroit in 5-2 win.
— Norm Ullman, Detroit, 1964, SF vs. Chicago, won by Detroit 4-3. Ullman scored 3 G Mar. 29 at Chicago in 7-1 win and 3 G April 7 at Detroit in 7-2 win.
— Mark Messier, Edmonton, 1983, DF vs. Calgary won by Edmonton 4-1. Messier scored 4 G April 14 at Edmonton in 6-3 win and 3 G April 17 at Calgary in 10-2 win.
— Mike Bossy, NY Islanders, 1983, CF vs. Boston won by NY Islanders 4-2. Bossy scored 3 G May 3 at New York in 8-3 win and 4 G on May 7 at New York in 8-4 win.

SCORING STREAKS

LONGEST CONSECUTIVE GOAL-SCORING STREAK, ONE PLAYOFF YEAR:
9 Games — Reggie Leach, Philadelphia, 1976. Streak started April 17 at Toronto and ended May 9 at Montreal. He scored one goal in each of seven games; two in one game; and five in another; a total of 14 goals.

LONGEST CONSECUTIVE POINT-SCORING STREAK, ONE PLAYOFF YEAR:
18 games — Bryan Trottier, NY Islanders, 1981. 11 goals, 18 assists, 29 points.
17 games — Wayne Gretzky, Edmonton, 1988. 12 goals, 29 assists, 41 points.
— Al MacInnis, Calgary, 1989. 7 goals, 19 assists, 24 points.

LONGEST CONSECUTIVE POINT-SCORING STREAK, MORE THAN ONE PLAYOFF YEAR:
27 games — Bryan Trottier, NY Islanders, 1980, 1981 and 1982. 7 games in 1980 (3 G, 5 A, 8 PTS), 18 games in 1981 (11 G, 18 A, 29 PTS), and two games in 1982 (2 G, 3 A, 5 PTS). Total points, 42.
19 games — Wayne Gretzky, Edmonton, Los Angeles 1988 and 1989. 17 games in 1988 (12 G, 29 A, 41 PTS with Edmonton), 2 games in 1989 (1 G, 2 A, 3 PTS with Los Angeles). Total points, 44.
18 games — Phil Esposito, Boston, 1970 and 1971. 13 G, 20 A, 33 PTS.

FASTEST GOALS

FASTEST GOAL FROM START OF GAME:
6 Seconds — Don Kozak, Los Angeles, April 17, 1977, at Los Angeles vs. Boston and goaltender Gerry Cheevers. Los Angeles won 7-4.
7 Seconds — Bob Gainey, Montreal, May 5, 1977, at New York vs. NY Islanders and goaltender Glenn Resch. Montreal won 2-1.
— Terry Murray, Philadelphia, April 12, 1981, at Quebec vs. goaltender Dan Bouchard. Quebec won 4-3 in overtime.
8 Seconds — Stan Smyl, Vancouver, April 7, 1982, at Vancouver vs. Calgary and goaltender Pat Riggin. Vancouver won 5-3.

FASTEST GOAL FROM START OF PERIOD (OTHER THAN FIRST):
6 Seconds — Pelle Eklund, Phiadelphia, April 25, 1989, at Pittsburgh vs. goaltender Tom Barrasso, second period. Pittsburgh won 10-7.
9 Seconds — Bill Collins, Minnesota, April 9, 1968, at Minnesota vs. Los Angeles and goaltender Wayne Rutledge, third period. Minnesota won 7-5.
— Dave Balon, Minnesota, April 25, 1968, at St. Louis vs. goaltender Glenn Hall, third period. Minnesota won 5-1.
— Murray Oliver, Minnesota, April 8, 1971, at St. Louis vs. goaltender Ernie Wakely, third period. St. Louis won 4-2.
— Clark Gillies, NY Islanders, April 15, 1977, at Buffalo vs. goaltender Don Edwards, third period. NY Islanders won 4-3.
— Eric Vail, Atlanta, April 11, 1978, at Atlanta vs. Detroit and goaltender Ron Low, third period. Detroit won 5-3.
— Stan Smyl, Vancouver, April 10, 1979, at Philadelphia vs. goaltender Wayne Stephenson, third period. Vancouver won 3-2.
— Wayne Gretzky, Edmonton, April 6, 1983, at Edmonton vs. Winnipeg and goaltender Brian Hayward, second period. Edmonton won 6-3.
— Mark Messier, Edmonton, April 16, 1984, at Calgary vs. goaltender Don Edwards, third period. Edmonton won 5-3.
— Brian Skrudland, Montreal, May 18, 1986 at Calgary and goaltender Mike Vernon, overtime. Montreal won 3-2.

FASTEST TWO GOALS:
5 Seconds — Norm Ullman, Detroit, at Detroit, April 11, 1965, vs. Chicago and goaltender Glenn Hall. Ullman scored at 17:35 and 17:40 of second period. Detroit won 4-2.

FASTEST TWO GOALS FROM START OF A GAME:
1 Minute, 8 Seconds — Dick Duff, Toronto, April 9, 1963 at Toronto vs. Detroit and goaltender Terry Sawchuk. Duff scored at 49 seconds and 1:08. Final score: Toronto 4, Detroit 2.

FASTEST TWO GOALS FROM START OF A PERIOD:
35 Seconds — Pat LaFontaine, NY Islanders, May 19, 1984 at Edmonton vs. goaltender Andy Moog. LaFontaine scored at 13 and 35 seconds of third period. Final score: Edmonton 5, NY Islanders 2.

PENALTIES

MOST PENALTY MINUTES IN PLAYOFFS (CAREER):
661 — Dale Hunter, Quebec, Washington
541 — Chris Nilan, Montreal, NY Rangers, Boston
466 — Willi Plett, Atlanta, Calgary, Minnesota, Boston
455 — Dave Williams, Toronto, Vancouver, Los Angeles
442 — Glenn Anderson, Edmonton, Toronto, NY Rangers, St. Louis

MOST PENALTIES, ONE GAME:
8 — Forbes Kennedy, Toronto, April 2, 1969, at Boston. Four minors, 2 majors, 1 10-minute misconduct, 1 game misconduct. Final score: Boston 10, Toronto 0.
— **Kim Clackson, Pittsburgh,** April 14, 1980, at Boston. Five minors, 2 majors, 1 10-minute misconduct. Final score: Boston 6, Pittsburgh 2
— Jaromir Jagr, Pittsburgh, May 11, 1996, at Pittsburgh vs NY Rangers, second period. Final score: Pittsburgh 7, NY Rangers 3.
— Peter Forsberg, Colorado, June 6, 1996, at Colorado vs Florida, first period. Final score: Colorado 8, Florida 1.

MOST PENALTY MINUTES, ONE GAME:
42 — Dave Schultz, Philadelphia, April 22, 1976, at Toronto. One minor, 2 majors, 1 10-minute misconduct and 2 game-misconducts. Final score: Toronto 8, Philadelphia 5.

MOST PENALTIES, ONE PERIOD AND MOST PENALTY MINUTES, ONE PERIOD:
6 Penalties; 39 Minutes — Ed Hospodar, NY Rangers, April 9, 1981, at Los Angeles, first period. Two minors, 1 major, 1 10-minute misconduct, 2 game misconducts. Final score: Los Angeles 5, NY Rangers 4.

GOALTENDING

MOST PLAYOFF GAMES APPEARED IN BY A GOALTENDER (CAREER):
136 — Patrick Roy, Montreal, Colorado
132 — Bill Smith, Los Angeles, NY Islanders
121 — Grant Fuhr, Edmonton, Toronto, Buffalo, St. Louis
116 — Andy Moog, Edmonton, Boston, Dallas
115 — Glenn Hall, Detroit, Chicago, St. Louis
112 — Jacques Plante, Montreal, St. Louis, Toronto, Boston
— Ken Dryden, Montreal

MOST MINUTES PLAYED BY A GOALTENDER (CAREER):
8,418 — Patrick Roy, Montreal, Colorado
7,645 — Bill Smith, Los Angeles, NY Islanders
7,071 — Grant Fuhr, Edmonton, Toronto, Buffalo, St. Louis
6,899 — Glenn Hall, Detroit, Chicago, St. Louis
6,846 — Ken Dryden, Montreal

MOST MINUTES PLAYED BY A GOALTENDER, ONE PLAYOFF YEAR:
1,544 — Kirk McLean, Vancouver, 1994. 24 games.
1,540 — Ron Hextall, Philadelphia, 1987. 26 games.
1,477 — Mike Richter, NY Rangers, 1994. 23 games.
1,454 — Patrick Roy, Colorado, 1996. 22 games.
1,401 — Bill Ranford, Edmonton, 1990. 22 games.

MOST SHUTOUTS IN PLAYOFFS (CAREER):
15 — Clint Benedict, Ottawa, Mtl. Maroons
14 — Jacques Plante, Montreal, St. Louis
13 — Turk Broda, Toronto
12 — Terry Sawchuk, Detroit, Toronto, Los Angeles

MOST SHUTOUTS, ONE PLAYOFF YEAR:
4 — Clint Benedict, Mtl. Maroons, 1926. 8 games.
— **Clint Benedict, Mtl. Maroons,** 1928. 9 games.
— **Dave Kerr, NY Rangers,** 1937. 9 games.
— **Frank McCool, Toronto,** 1945. 13 games.
— **Terry Sawchuk, Detroit,** 1952. 8 games.
— **Bernie Parent, Philadelphia,** 1975. 17 games.
— **Ken Dryden, Montreal,** 1977. 14 games.
— **Mike Richter, NY Rangers,** 1994. 23 games.
— **Kirk McLean, Vancouver,** 1994. 24 games.

MOST WINS BY A GOALTENDER, (CAREER):
88 — Bill Smith, Los Angeles, NY Islanders
86 — Patrick Roy, Montreal, Colorado
80 — Ken Dryden, Montreal
78 — Grant Fuhr, Edm., Buf., St.L.

MOST WINS BY A GOALTENDER, ONE PLAYOFF YEAR:
16 — Grant Fuhr, Edmonton, 1988. 19 games.
— **Mike Vernon, Calgary,** 1989. 22 games.
— **Bill Ranford, Edmonton,** 1990. 22 games.
— **Tom Barrasso, Pittsburgh,** 1992. 21 games.
— **Patrick Roy, Montreal,** 1993. 20 games.
— **Mike Richter, NY Rangers,** 1994. 23 games.
— **Martin Brodeur, New Jersey,** 1995. 20 games.
— **Patrick Roy, Colorado,** 1996. 22 games.
15 — Bill Smith, NY Islanders, 1980. 20 games.
— Bill Smith, NY Islanders, 1982. 18 games.
— Grant Fuhr, Edmonton, 1985. 18 games.
— Patrick Roy, Montreal, 1986. 20 games.
— Ron Hextall, Philadelphia, 1987. 26 games.
— Kirk McLean, Vancouver, 1994. 24 games.

MOST CONSECUTIVE WINS BY A GOALTENDER, ONE PLAYOFF YEAR:
11 — Ed Belfour, Chicago, 1992. 3 wins against St. Louis in DSF, won by Chicago 4-2; 4 wins against Detroit in DF, won by Chicago 4-0; and 4 wins against Edmonton in CF, won by Chicago 4-0.
— **Tom Barrasso, Pittsburgh,** 1992. 3 wins against NY Rangers in DF, won by Pittsburgh 4-2; 4 wins against Boston in CF, won by Pittsburgh 4-0; and 4 wins against Chicago in F, won by Pittsburgh 4-0.
— **Patrick Roy, Montreal,** 1993. 4 wins against Quebec in DSF, won by Montreal 4-2; 4 wins against Buffalo in DF, won by Montreal 4-0; and 3 wins against NY Islanders in CF, won by Montreal 4-1.

LONGEST SHUTOUT SEQUENCE:
248 Minutes, 32 Seconds — Norm Smith, Detroit, 1936. In best-of-five SF, Smith shut out Mtl. Maroons 1-0, March 24, in 116:30 overtime; shut out Maroons 3-0 in second game, March 26; and was scored against at 12:02 of first period, March 29, by Gus Marker. Detroit won SF 3-0.

MOST CONSECUTIVE SHUTOUTS:
3 — Clint Benedict, Mtl. Maroons, 1926. Benedict shut out Ottawa 1-0, Mar. 27; he then shut out Victoria twice, 3-0, Mar. 30; 3-0, Apr. 1. Mtl. Maroons won NHL F vs. Ottawa 2 goals to 1 and won the best-of-five F vs. Victoria 3-1.
— **John Roach, NY Rangers,** 1929. Roach shutout NY Americans twice, 0-0, Mar. 19; 1-0, Mar. 21; he then shutout Toronto 1-0, Mar. 24. NY Rangers won QF vs. NY Americans 1 goal to 0 and won the best-of-three SF vs. Toronto 2-0.
— **Frank McCool, Toronto,** 1945. McCool shut out Detroit 1-0, April 6; 2-0, April 8; 1-0, April 12. Toronto won the best-of-seven F 4-3.

Early Playoff Records

1893-1918
Team Records

MOST GOALS, BOTH TEAMS, ONE GAME:
25 — Ottawa Silver Seven, Dawson City at Ottawa, Jan. 16, 1905. Ottawa 23, Dawson City 2. Ottawa won best-of-three series 2-0.

MOST GOALS, ONE TEAM, ONE GAME:
23 — Ottawa Silver Seven at Ottawa, Jan. 16, 1905. Ottawa defeated Dawson City 23-2.

MOST GOALS, BOTH TEAMS, BEST-OF-THREE SERIES:
42 — Ottawa Silver Seven, Queen's University at Ottawa, 1906. Ottawa defeated Queen's 16-7, Feb. 27, and 12-7, Feb. 28.

MOST GOALS, ONE TEAM, BEST-OF-THREE SERIES:
32 — Ottawa Silver Seven in 1905 at Ottawa. Defeated Dawson City 9-2, Jan. 13, and 23-2, Jan. 16.

MOST GOALS, BOTH TEAMS, BEST-OF-FIVE SERIES:
39 — Toronto Arenas, Vancouver Millionaires at Toronto, 1918. Toronto won 5-3, Mar. 20; 6-3, Mar. 26; 2-1, Mar. 30. Vancouver won 6-4, Mar. 23, and 8-1, Mar. 28. Toronto scored 18 goals; Vancouver 21.

MOST GOALS, ONE TEAM, BEST-OF-FIVE SERIES:
26 — Vancouver Millionaires in 1915 at Vancouver. Defeated Ottawa Senators 6-2, Mar. 22; 8-3, Mar. 24; and 12-3 Mar. 26.

Individual Records

MOST GOALS IN PLAYOFFS:
63 — Frank McGee, Ottawa Silver Seven, in 22 playoff games. Seven goals in four games, 1903; 21 goals in eight games, 1904; 18 goals in four games, 1905; 17 goals in six games, 1906.

MOST GOALS, ONE PLAYOFF SERIES:
15 — Frank McGee, Ottawa Silver Seven, in two games in 1905 at Ottawa. Scored one goal, Jan. 13, in 9-2 victory over Dawson City and 14 goals, Jan. 16, in 23-2 victory.

MOST GOALS, ONE PLAYOFF GAME:
14 — Frank McGee, Ottawa Silver Seven, Jan. 16, 1905 at Ottawa in 23-2 victory over Dawson City.

FASTEST THREE GOALS:
40 Seconds — Marty Walsh, Ottawa Senators, at Ottawa, March 16, 1911, at 3:00, 3:10, and 3:40 of third period. Ottawa defeated Port Arthur 13-4.

Reggie "The Riverton Rifle" Leach is the only forward from a losing team in the Stanley Cup finals to be awarded the Conn Smythe Trophy. Leach connected for 47 goals in 94 playoff games during his career.

All-Time Playoff Goal Leaders since 1918

(40 or more goals)

Player	Teams	Yrs.	GP	G
* Wayne Gretzky	Edm., L.A., St.L.	15	193	112
* Mark Messier	Edm., NYR	16	221	106
* Jari Kurri	Edm., L.A., NYR	13	185	105
* Glenn Anderson	Edm., Tor., NYR, St.L.	15	225	93
Mike Bossy	NY Islanders	10	129	85
Maurice Richard	Montreal	15	133	82
Jean Beliveau	Montreal	17	162	79
* Dino Ciccarelli	Min., Wsh., Det.	14	141	73
Bryan Trottier	NYI, Pit.	17	221	71
Gordie Howe	Det., Hfd.	20	157	68
* Mario Lemieux	Pittsburgh	6	84	67
* Denis Savard	Chi., Mtl.	15	163	66
* Brett Hull	Cgy., St.L.	11	92	64
Yvan Cournoyer	Montreal	12	147	64
Brian Propp	Phi., Bos., Min.	13	160	64
Bobby Smith	Min., Mtl.	13	184	64
Bobby Hull	Chi., Hfd.	14	119	62
Phil Esposito	Chi., Bos., NYR	15	130	61
Jacques Lemaire	Montreal	11	145	61
* Joe Mullen	St.L., Cgy., Pit.	14	142	60
* Esa Tikkanen	Edm., NYR, St.L., Van.	11	150	60
Stan Mikita	Chicago	18	155	59
Guy Lafleur	Mtl., NYR	14	128	58
Bernie Geoffrion	Mtl., NYR	16	132	58
* Paul Coffey	Edm., Pit., L.A., Det.	14	172	58
* Cam Neely	Van., Bos.	9	93	57
* Claude Lemieux	Mtl., N.J., Col.	11	155	57
Steve Larmer	Chi., NYR	13	140	56
Denis Potvin	NY Islanders	14	185	56
Rick MacLeish	Phi., Pit., Det.	11	114	54
Bill Barber	Philadelphia	11	129	53
* Stephane Richer	Mtl., N.J.	10	123	52
Frank Mahovlich	Tor., Det., Mtl.	14	137	51
Steve Shutt	Mtl., L.A.	12	99	50
* Doug Gilmour	St.L., Cgy., Tor.	12	136	49
Henri Richard	Montreal	18	180	49
Reggie Leach	Bos., Phi.	8	94	47
Ted Lindsay	Det., Chi.	16	133	47
Clark Gillies	NYI, Buf.	13	164	47
Dickie Moore	Mtl., Tor., St.L.	14	135	46
Rick Middleton	NYR, Bos.	12	114	45
Lanny McDonald	Tor., Cgy.	13	117	44
* Kevin Stevens	Pit.	6	36	43
* Brian Bellows	Min., Mtl., T.B.	11	111	43
Ken Linseman	Phi., Edm., Bos.	11	113	43
* Luc Robitaille	L.A., Pit., NYR	9	96	42
* Bernie Nicholls	L.A., NYR, Edm., N.J., Chi.	12	112	42
Bobby Clarke	Philadelphia	13	136	42
* Jaromir Jagr	Pit.	6	93	42
* Rick Tocchet	Phi., Pit., L.A., Bos.	9	108	41
* Mike Gartner	Wsh., Min., NYR, Tor	13	110	41
John Bucyk	Det., Bos.	14	124	41
* Dale Hunter	Que., Wsh.	16	146	41
Tim Kerr	Phi., NYR	10	81	40
Peter McNab	Bos., Van.	10	107	40
Bob Bourne	NYI, L.A.	13	139	40
John Tonelli	NYI, Cgy., L.A.	13	172	40

* — Active player.

All-Time Playoff Assist Leaders since 1918

(60 or more assists)

Player	Teams	Yrs.	GP	A
* Wayne Gretzky	Edm., L.A., St.L.	15	193	250
* Mark Messier	Edm., NYR	16	221	177
* Paul Coffey	Edm., Pit., L.A., Det.	14	172	128
* Jari Kurri	Edm., L.A., NYR	13	185	125
* Glenn Anderson	Edm., Tor., NYR, St.L.	15	225	121
Larry Robinson	Mtl., L.A.	20	227	116
Bryan Trottier	NYI, Pit.	17	221	113
* Ray Bourque	Boston	17	162	112
* Doug Gilmour	St.L., Cgy., Tor.	12	136	111
Denis Potvin	NY Islanders	14	185	108
* Denis Savard	Chi., Mtl.	15	163	107
Jean Beliveau	Montreal	17	162	97
Bobby Smith	Min., Mtl.	13	184	96
Gordie Howe	Det., Hfd.	20	157	92
Stan Mikita	Chicago	18	155	91
Brad Park	NYR, Bos., Det.	17	161	90
* Adam Oates	Det., St.L., Bos.	10	105	89
* Larry Murphy	L.A., Wsh., Min., Pit., Tor.	15	148	88
* Chris Chelios	Mtl., Chi.	13	157	87
* Al MacInnis	Cgy., St.L.	12	115	86
Brian Propp	Phi., Bos., Min.	13	160	84
* Mario Lemieux	Pittsburgh	6	84	82
* Craig Janney	Bos., St. L., S.J., Wpg.	9	107	80
Henri Richard	Montreal	18	180	80
Jacques Lemaire	Montreal	11	145	78
Ken Linseman	Phi., Edm., Bos.	11	113	77
Bobby Clarke	Philadelphia	13	136	77
Guy Lafleur	Mtl., NYR	14	128	76
Phil Esposito	Chi., Bos., NYR	15	130	76
* Ron Francis	Hfd., Pit.	11	119	75
Mike Bossy	NY Islanders	10	129	75
Steve Larmer	Chi., NYR	13	140	75
John Tonelli	NYI, Cgy., L.A.	13	172	75
Peter Stastny	Que., N.J., St.L.	12	93	72
Gilbert Perreault	Buffalo	11	90	70
Alex Delvecchio	Detroit	14	121	69
* Dale Hunter	Que., Wsh.	16	146	69
* Bernie Nicholls	L.A., NYR, Edm., N.J., Chi.	12	112	67
Bobby Hull	Chi., Hfd.	14	119	67
Frank Mahovlich	Tor., Det., Mtl.	14	137	67
Bobby Orr	Boston	8	74	66
Bernie Federko	St. Louis	11	91	66
Jean Ratelle	NYR, Bos.	15	123	66
* Scott Stevens	Wsh., St. L., N.J.	13	132	66
* Charlie Huddy	Edm., L.A., Buf., St.L.	14	183	66
* Dale Hawerchuk	Wpg., Buf., Phi.	14	80	64
Dickie Moore	Mtl., Tor., St.L.	14	135	64
Doug Harvey	Mtl., NYR, St.L.	15	137	64
Yvan Cournoyer	Montreal	12	147	63
John Bucyk	Det., Bos.	14	124	62
* Neal Broten	Min., Dal., N.J.	12	133	62
Doug Wilson	Chicago	12	95	61
* Brian Bellows	Min., Mtl., T.B.	11	111	60
Bernie Geoffrion	Mtl., NYR	16	132	60

All-Time Playoff Point Leaders since 1918

(100 or more points)

Player	Teams	Yrs.	GP	G	A	Pts.
* Wayne Gretzky	Edm., L.A., St.L.	15	193	112	250	362
* Mark Messier	Edm., NYR	16	221	106	177	283
* Jari Kurri	Edm., L.A., NYR	13	185	105	125	230
* Glenn Anderson	Edm., Tor., NYR, St.L.	15	225	93	121	214
* Paul Coffey	Edm., Pit., L.A., Det.	14	172	58	128	186
Bryan Trottier	NYI, Pit.	17	221	71	113	184
Jean Beliveau	Montreal	17	162	79	97	176
* Denis Savard	Chi., Mtl.	15	163	66	107	173
Denis Potvin	NY Islanders	14	185	56	108	164
Mike Bossy	NY Islanders	10	129	85	75	160
* Doug Gilmour	St.L., Cgy., Tor.	12	136	49	111	160
Gordie Howe	Det., Hfd.	20	157	68	92	160
Bobby Smith	Min., Mtl.	13	184	64	96	160
Stan Mikita	Chicago	18	155	59	91	150
* Mario Lemieux	Pittsburgh	6	84	67	82	149
Brian Propp	Phi., Bos., Min.	13	160	64	84	148
* Ray Bourque	Boston	17	162	34	112	146
Larry Robinson	Mtl., L.A.	20	227	28	116	144
Jacques Lemaire	Montreal	11	145	61	78	139
Phil Esposito	Chi., Bos., NYR	15	130	61	76	137
Guy Lafleur	Mtl., NYR	14	128	58	76	134
Steve Larmer	Chi., NYR	13	140	56	75	131
Bobby Hull	Chi., Hfd.	14	119	62	67	129
Henri Richard	Montreal	18	180	49	80	129
Yvan Cournoyer	Montreal	12	147	64	63	127
Maurice Richard	Montreal	15	133	82	44	126
Brad Park	NYR, Bos., Det.	17	161	35	90	125
* Adam Oates	Det., St.L., Bos.	10	105	32	89	121
Ken Linseman	Phi., Edm., Bos.	11	113	43	77	120
Bobby Clarke	Philadelphia	13	136	42	77	119
Bernie Geoffrion	Mtl., NYR	16	132	58	60	118
Frank Mahovlich	Tor., Det., Mtl.	14	137	51	67	118
* Dino Ciccarelli	Min., Wsh., Det.	14	141	73	45	118
* Larry Murphy	L.A., Wsh., Min., Pit., Tor.	15	148	30	88	118
* Al MacInnis	Cgy., St.L.	12	115	29	86	115
* Chris Chelios	Mtl., Chi.	13	157	28	87	115
John Tonelli	NYI, Cgy., L.A.	13	172	40	75	115
* Esa Tikkanen	Edm., NYR, St.L., Van.	11	150	60	54	114
* Ron Francis	Hfd., Pit.	11	119	38	73	111
Dickie Moore	Mtl., Tor., St.L.	14	135	46	64	110
* Dale Hunter	Que., Wsh.	16	146	41	69	110
* Bernie Nicholls	L.A., NYR, Edm., N.J., Chi.	12	112	42	67	109
Bill Barber	Philadelphia	11	129	53	55	108
Rick MacLeish	Phi., Pit., Det.	11	114	54	53	107
* Joe Mullen	St.L., Cgy., Pit.	14	142	60	46	106
* Brett Hull	Cgy., St.L.	11	92	64	41	105
Peter Stastny	Que., N.J., St.L.	12	93	33	72	105
* Craig Janney	Bos., St. L., S.J., Wpg.	9	107	24	80	104
Alex Delvecchio	Detroit	14	121	35	69	104
* Claude Lemieux	Mtl., N.J., Col.	11	155	57	47	104
Gilbert Perreault	Buffalo	11	90	33	70	103
* Brian Bellows	Min., Mtl., T.B.	11	111	43	60	103
John Bucyk	Det., Bos.	14	124	41	62	103
Bernie Federko	St. Louis	11	91	35	66	101
* Kevin Stevens	Pit.	6	86	43	57	100
Rick Middleton	NYR, Bos.	12	114	45	55	100

Three-or-more-Goal Games, Playoffs 1918–1996

Player	Team	Date	City	Total Goals	Opposing Goaltender	Score	
Wayne Gretzky (8)	Edm.	Apr. 11/81	Edm.	3	Richard Sevigny	Edm. 6	Mtl. 2
		Apr. 19/81	Edm.	3	Billy Smith	Edm. 5	NYI 2
		Apr. 6/83	Edm.	4	Brian Hayward	Edm. 6	Wpg. 3
		Apr. 17/83	Cgy.	4	Rejean Lemelin	Edm. 10	Cgy. 2
		Apr. 25/85	Wpg.	3	Bryan Hayward (2) Marc Behrend (1)	Edm. 8	Wpg. 3
		May 25/85	Edm.	3	Pelle Lindbergh	Edm. 4	Phi. 3
		Apr. 24/86	Cgy.	3	Mike Vernon	Edm. 7	Cgy. 4
	L.A.	May 29/93	Tor.	3	Felix Potvin	L.A. 5	Tor. 4
Maurice Richard (7)	Mtl.	Mar. 23/44	Mtl.	5	Paul Bibeault	Mtl. 5	Tor. 1
		Apr. 7/44	Chi.	3	Mike Karakas	Mtl. 3	Chi. 1
		Mar. 29/45	Mtl.	4	Frank McCool	Mtl. 10	Tor. 3
		Apr. 14/53	Bos.	3	Gord Henry	Mtl. 7	Bos. 3
		Mar. 20/56	Mtl.	3	Lorne Worsley	Mtl. 7	NYR 1
		Apr. 6/57	Mtl.	4	Don Simmons	Mtl. 5	Bos. 1
		Apr. 1/58	Det.	3	Terry Sawchuk	Mtl. 4	Det. 3
Jari Kurri (7)	Edm.	Apr. 4/84	Edm.	3	Doug Soetaert (1) Mike Veisor (2)	Edm. 9	Wpg. 2
		Apr. 25/85	Wpg.	3	Bryan Hayward (2) Marc Behrend (1)	Edm. 8	Wpg. 3
		May 7/85	Edm.	3	Murray Bannerman	Edm. 7	Chi. 3
		May 14/85	Edm.	3	Murray Bannerman	Edm. 10	Chi. 5
		May 16/85	Chi.	4	Murray Bannerman	Edm. 8	Chi. 2
		Apr. 9/87	Edm.	4	Roland Melanson (2) Daren Eliot (2)	Edm. 13	L.A. 3
		May 18/90	Bos.	3	Andy Moog (2) Rejean Lemelin (1)	Edm. 7	Bos. 2
Dino Ciccarelli (6)	Min.	May 5/81	Min.	3	Pat Riggin	Min. 7	Cgy. 4
		Apr. 10/82	Min.	3	Murray Bannerman	Min. 7	Chi. 1
	Wsh.	Apr. 5/90	N.J.	3	Sean Burke	Wsh. 5	N.J. 4
		Apr. 25/92	Pit.	4	Tom Barrasso (1) Ken Wregget (3)	Wsh. 7	Pit. 2
	Det.	Apr. 29/93	Tor.	3	Felix Potvin (2) Daren Puppa (1)	Det. 7	Tor. 3
		May 11/95	Dal.	3	Andy Moog (2) Darcy Wakaluk (1)	Det. 5	Dal. 1
Mike Bossy (5)	NYI	Apr. 16/79	NYI	3	Tony Esposito	NYI 6	Chi. 2
		May 8/82	NYI	3	Richard Brodeur	NYI 6	Van. 5
		Apr. 10/83	Wsh.	3	Al Jensen	NYI 6	Wsh. 3
		May 3/83	NYI	3	Pete Peeters	NYI 8	Bos. 3
		May 7/83	NYI	4	Pete Peeters	NYI 8	Bos. 4
Phil Esposito (4)	Bos.	Apr. 2/69	Bos.	4	Bruce Gamble	Bos. 10	Tor. 0
		Apr. 8/70	Bos.	3	Ed Giacomin	Bos. 8	NYR 2
		Apr. 19/70	Chi.	3	Tony Esposito	Bos. 6	Chi. 3
		Apr. 8/75	Bos.	3	Tony Esposito (2) Michel Dumas (1)	Bos. 8	Chi. 2
Mark Messier (4)	Edm.	Apr. 14/83	Edm.	4	Rejean Lemelin	Edm. 6	Cgy. 3
		Apr. 17/83	Cgy.	3	Rejean Lemelin (1) Don Edwards (2)	Edm. 10	Cgy. 2
		Apr. 26/83	Edm.	3	Murray Bannerman	Edm. 8	Chi. 2
	NYR	May 25/94	N.J.	3	Martin Brodeur (2) ENG (1)	NYR 4	N.J. 2
Bernie Geoffrion (3)	Mtl.	Mar. 27/52	Mtl.	3	Jim Henry	Mtl. 4	Bos. 0
		Apr. 7/55	Mtl.	3	Terry Sawchuk	Mtl. 4	Det. 2
		Mar. 30/57	Mtl.	3	Lorne Worsley	Mtl. 8	NYR 3
Norm Ullman (3)	Det.	Mar. 29/64	Chi.	3	Glenn Hall	Det. 5	Chi. 4
		Apr. 7/64	Det.	3	Glenn Hall (2) Denis DeJordy (1)	Det. 7	Chi. 2
		Apr. 11/65	Det.	3	Glenn Hall	Det. 4	Chi. 2
John Bucyk (3)	Bos.	May 3/70	St. L.	3	Jacques Plante (1) Ernie Wakely (2)	Bos. 6	St. L. 1
		Apr. 20/72	Bos.	3	Jacques Caron (1) Ernie Wakely (2)	Bos. 10	St. L. 2
		Apr. 21/74	Bos.	3	Tony Esposito	Bos. 8	Chi. 6
Rick MacLeish (3)	Phi.	Apr. 11/74	Phi.	3	Phil Myre	Phi. 5	Atl. 1
		Apr. 13/75	Phi.	3	Gord McRae	Phi. 6	Tor. 3
		May 13/75	Phi.	3	Glenn Resch	Phi. 4	NYI 1
Denis Savard (3)	Chi.	Apr. 19/82	Chi.	3	Mike Liut	Chi. 7	StL. 4
		Apr. 10/86	Chi.	4	Ken Wregget	Tor. 6	Chi. 4
		Apr. 9/88	St. L.	3	Greg Millen	Chi. 6	St. L. 3
Tim Kerr (3)	Phi.	Apr. 13/85	NYR	4	Glen Hanlon	Phi. 6	NYR 5
		Apr. 20/87	Phi.	3	Kelly Hrudey	Phi. 4	NYI 2
		Apr. 19/89	Pit.	3	Tom Barrasso	Phi. 4	Pit. 2
Cam Neely (3)	Bos.	Apr. 9/87	Mtl.	3	Patrick Roy	Mtl. 4	Bos. 3
		Apr. 5/91	Bos.	3	Peter Sidorkiewicz	Bos. 4	Hfd. 3
		Apr. 25/91	Bos.	3	Patrick Roy	Bos. 4	Mtl. 1
Petr Klima (3)	Det.	Apr. 7/88	Tor.	3	Alan Bester (2) Ken Wregett (1)	Det. 6	Tor. 2
		Apr. 21/88	St. L.	3	Greg Millen	Det. 6	St. L. 0
	Edm.	May 4/91	Edm.	3	Jon Casey	Edm. 7	Min. 2
Esa Tikkanen (3)	Edm.	May 22/88	Edm.	3	Rejean Lemelin	Edm. 6	Bos. 3
		Apr. 16/91	Cgy.	3	Mike Vernon	Edm. 5	Cgy. 4
		Apr. 26/92	L.A.	3	Kelly Hrudey	Edm. 5	L.A. 2
Steve Yzerman (3)	Det.	Apr. 6/89	Det.	3	Alain Chevrier	Chi. 5	Det. 4
		Apr. 4/91	St. L.	3	Vincent Riendeau (2) Pat Jablonski (1)	Det. 6	St. L. 3
		May 8/96	St.L.	3	Jon Casey	St.L. 5	Det. 4
Mario Lemieux (3)	Pit.	Apr. 25/89	Pit.	5	Ron Hextall	Pit. 10	Phi. 7
		Apr. 23/92	Pit.	3	Don Beaupre	Pit. 6	Wsh. 4
		May 11/96	Pit.	3	Mike Richter	Pit. 7	NYR 3
Mike Gartner (3)	NYR	Apr. 13/90	NYR	3	Mark Fitzpatrick (2) Glenn Healy (1)	NYR 6	NYI 5
		Apr. 27/92	NYR	3	Chris Terreri	NYR 8	N.J. 5
	Tor.	Apr. 25/96	Tor.	3	Jon Casey	Tor. 5	St.L. 4
Newsy Lalonde (2)	Mtl.	Mar. 1/19	Mtl.	5	Clint Benedict	Mtl. 6	Ott. 3
		Mar. 22/19	Sea.	4	Harry Holmes	Mtl. 4	Sea. 2
Howie Morenz (2)	Mtl.	Mar. 22/24	Mtl.	3	Charles Reid	Mtl. 6	Cgy.T. 1
		Mar. 27/25	Mtl.	3	Harry Holmes	Mtl. 4	Vic. 2
Toe Blake (2)	Mtl.	Mar. 22/38	Mtl.	3	Mike Karakas	Mtl. 6	Chi. 4
		Mar. 26/46	Chi.	3	Mike Karakas	Mtl. 7	Chi. 2
Doug Bentley (2)	Chi.	Mar. 28/44	Chi.	3	Connie Dion	Chi. 7	Det. 1
		Mar. 30/44	Det.	3	Connie Dion	Chi. 5	Det. 2
Ted Kennedy (2)	Tor.	Apr. 14/45	Tor.	3	Harry Lumley	Det. 5	Tor. 3
		Mar. 27/48	Tor.	4	Frank Brimsek	Tor. 5	Bos. 3
Bobby Hull (2)	Chi.	Apr. 7/63	Det.	3	Terry Sawchuk	Det. 7	Chi. 4
		Apr. 9/72	Pit.	3	Jim Rutherford	Chi. 6	Pit. 5
F. St. Marseille (2)	St. L.	Apr. 28/70	St. L.	3	Al Smith	St. L. 5	Pit. 0
		Apr. 6/72	Min.	3	Cesare Maniago	Min. 6	St. L. 5
Pit Martin (2)	Chi.	Apr. 4/73	Chi.	3	W. Stephenson	Chi. 7	St. L. 1
		May 10/73	Chi.	3	Ken Dryden	Mtl. 6	Chi. 4
Yvan Cournoyer (2)	Mtl.	Apr. 5/73	Mtl.	3	Dave Dryden	Mtl. 7	Buf. 3
		Apr. 11/74	Mtl.	3	Ed Giacomin	Mtl. 4	NYR 1
Guy Lafleur (2)	Mtl.	May 1/75	Mtl.	3	Roger Crozier (1) Gerry Desjardins (2)	Mtl. 7	Buf. 0
		Apr. 11/77	Mtl.	3	Ed Staniowski	Mtl. 7	St. L. 2
Lanny McDonald (2)	Tor.	Apr. 9/77	Pit.	3	Denis Herron	Tor. 5	Pit. 2
		Apr. 17/77	Tor.	4	W. Stephenson	Phi. 6	Tor. 5
Butch Goring (2)	L.A.	Apr. 9/77	L.A.	3	Phil Myre	L.A. 4	Atl. 2
	NYI	May 17/81	Min.	3	Gilles Meloche	NYI 7	Min. 5
Bryan Trottier (2)	NYI	Apr. 8/80	NYI	3	Doug Keans	NYI 8	L.A. 1
		Apr. 9/81	NYI	3	Michel Larocque	NYI 5	Tor. 1
Bill Barber (2)	Phi.	May 4/80	Min.	4	Gilles Meloche	Phi. 5	Min. 3
		Apr. 9/81	Phi.	3	Dan Bouchard	Phi. 8	Que. 5
Brian Propp (2)	Phi.	Apr. 22/81	Phi.	3	Pat Riggin	Phi. 9	Cgy. 4
		Apr. 21/85	Phi.	3	Billy Smith	Phi. 5	NYI 2
Paul Reinhart (2)	Cgy	Apr. 14/83	Edm.	3	Andy Moog	Edm. 6	Cgy. 3
		Apr. 8/84	Van	3	Richard Brodeur	Cgy. 5	Van. 1
Peter Stastny (2)	Que.	Apr. 5/83	Bos.	3	Pete Peeters	Bos. 4	Que. 3
		Apr. 11/87	Que.	3	Mike Liut (2) Steve Weeks (1)	Que. 5	Hfd. 1
Glenn Anderson (2)	Edm.	Apr. 26/83	Edm.	4	Murray Bannerman	Edm. 8	Chi. 2
		Apr. 6/88	Wpg.	3	Daniel Berthiaume	Edm. 7	Wpg. 4
Michel Goulet (2)	Que.	Apr. 23/85	Que.	3	Steve Penney	Que. 7	Mtl. 6
		Apr. 12/87	Que.	3	Mike Liut	Que. 4	Hfd. 1
Peter Zezel (2)	Phi.	Apr. 13/86	NYR	3	J. Vanbiesbrouck	Phi. 7	NYR 1
	St. L.	Apr. 11/89	St. L.	3	Jon Casey (2) Kari Takko (1)	St. L. 6	Min. 1
Geoff Courtnall (2)	Van.	Apr. 4/91	L.A.	3	Kelly Hrudey	Van. 6	L.A. 5
		Apr. 30/92	Van.	3	Rick Tabaracci	Van. 5	Win. 0
Joe Sakic (2)	Que.	May 6/95	Que.	3	Mike Richter	Que. 5	NYR 4
	Col.	Apr. 25/96	Col.	3	Corey Hirsch	Col. 5	Van. 4
Harry Meeking	Tor.	Mar. 11/18	Tor.	3	Georges Vezina	Tor. 7	Mtl. 3
Alf Skinner	Tor.	Mar. 23/18	Tor.	3	Hugh Lehman	Van.M. 6	Tor. 4
Joe Malone	Mtl.	Feb. 23/19	Mtl.	3	Clint Benedict	Mtl. 8	Ott. 4
Odie Cleghorn	Mtl.	Feb. 27/19	Ott.	3	Clint Benedict	Mtl. 5	Ott. 3
Jack Darragh	Ott.	Apr. 1/20	Tor.	3	Harry Holmes	Ott. 6	Sea. 1
George Boucher	Ott.	Mar. 10/21	Ott.	3	Jake Forbes	Ott. 5	Tor. 0
Babe Dye	Tor.	Mar. 28/22	Tor.	4	Hugh Lehman	Tor. 5	Van.M. 1
Perk Galbraith	Bos.	Mar. 31/27	Bos.	3	Hugh Lehman	Bos. 4	Chi. 4
Busher Jackson	Tor.	Apr. 5/32	NYR	3	John Ross Roach	Tor. 6	NYR 4
Frank Boucher	NYR	Apr. 9/32	Tor.	3	Lorne Chabot	Tor. 6	NYR 4
Charlie Conacher	Tor.	Mar. 26/36	Tor.	3	Tiny Thompson	Tor. 8	Bos. 3
Syd Howe	Det.	Mar. 23/39	Det.	3	Claude Bourque	Det. 7	Mtl. 3
Bryan Hextall	NYR	Apr. 3/40	NYR	3	Turk Broda	NYR 6	Tor. 2
Joe Benoit	Mtl.	Mar. 22/41	Mtl.	3	Sam LoPresti	Mtl. 4	Chi. 3
Syl Apps	Tor.	Mar. 25/41	Tor.	3	Frank Brimsek	Tor. 7	Bos. 2
Jack McGill	Bos.	Mar. 29/42	Bos.	3	Johnny Mowers	Det. 6	Bos. 4
Don Metz	Tor.	Apr. 14/42	Tor.	3	Johnny Mowers	Tor. 9	Det. 3
Mud Bruneteau	Det.	Apr. 1/43	Det.	3	Frank Brimsek	Det. 6	Bos. 2
Don Grosso	Det.	Apr. 7/43	Bos.	3	Frank Brimsek	Det. 4	Bos. 0
Carl Liscombe	Det.	Apr. 3/45	Bos.	4	Paul Bibeault	Det. 5	Bos. 3
Billy Reay	Mtl.	Apr. 1/47	Bos.	4	Frank Brimsek	Mtl. 5	Bos. 1
Gerry Plamondon	Mtl.	Mar. 24/49	Det.	3	Harry Lumley	Mtl. 4	Det. 3
Sid Smith	Tor.	Apr. 10/49	Det.	3	Harry Lumley	Tor. 3	Det. 1
Pentti Lund	NYR	Apr. 2/50	NYR	3	Bill Durnan	NYR 4	Mtl. 1
Ted Lindsay	Det.	Apr. 5/55	Det.	4	Charlie Hodge (1) Jacques Plante (3)	Det. 7	Mtl. 1
Gordie Howe	Det.	Apr. 10/55	Det.	3	Jacques Plante	Det. 5	Mtl. 1
Phil Goyette	Mtl.	Mar. 25/58	Mtl.	3	Terry Sawchuk	Mtl. 8	Det. 1
Jerry Toppazzini	Bos.	Apr. 5/58	Bos.	3	Lorne Worsley	Bos. 8	NYR 2
Bob Pulford	Tor.	Apr. 19/62	Tor.	3	Glenn Hall	Tor. 8	Chi. 4
Dave Keon	Tor.	Apr. 9/64	Mtl.	3	Charlie Hodge	Tor. 3	Mtl. 1
Henri Richard	Mtl.	Apr. 20/67	Mtl.	3	Terry Sawchuk (2) Johnny Bower (1)	Mtl. 6	Tor. 2
Rosaire Paiement	Phi.	Apr. 13/68	Phi.	3	Glenn Hall (1) Seth Martin (2)	Phi. 6	St. L. 1
Jean Beliveau	Mtl.	Apr. 20/68	Mtl.	3	Denis DeJordy	Mtl. 4	Chi. 1
Red Berenson	St. L.	Apr. 15/69	St. L	3	Gerry Desjardins	St. L. 4	L.A. 0
Ken Schinkel	Pit.	Apr. 11/70	Oak.	3	Gary Smith	Pit. 5	Oak. 2
Jim Pappin	Chi.	Apr. 11/71	Phi.	3	Bruce Gamble	Chi. 6	Phi. 2
Bobby Orr	Bos.	Apr. 11/71	Mtl.	3	Ken Dryden	Bos. 5	Mtl. 2
Jacques Lemaire	Mtl.	Apr. 20/71	Mtl.	3	Lorne Worsley	Mtl. 7	Min. 2
Vic Hadfield	NYR	Apr. 22/71	NYR	3	Tony Esposito	NYR 4	Chi. 1

Player	Team	Date	City	Total Goals	Opposing Goaltender	Score	
Fred Stanfield	Bos.	Apr. 18/72	Bos.	3	Jacques Caron	Bos. 6	St. L. 1
Ken Hodge	Bos.	Apr. 30/72	Bos.	3	Ed Giacomin	Bos. 6	NYR 5
Steve Vickers	NYR	Apr. 10/73	Bos.	3	Ross Brooks (2) Ed Johnston (1)	NYR 6	Bos. 3
Dick Redmond	Chi.	Apr. 4/73	Chi.	3	Wayne Stephenson	Chi. 7	St. L. 1
Tom Williams	L.A.	Apr. 14/74	L.A.	3	Mike Veisor	L.A. 5	Chi. 1
Marcel Dionne	L.A.	Apr. 15/76	L.A.	3	Gilles Gilbert	L.A. 6	Bos. 4
Don Saleski	Phi.	Apr. 20/76	Phi.	3	Wayne Thomas	Phi. 7	Tor. 1
Darryl Sittler	Tor.	Apr. 22/76	Tor.	5	Bernie Parent	Tor. 8	Phi. 5
Reggie Leach	Phi.	May 6/76	Phi.	5	Gilles Gilbert	Phi. 6	Bos. 3
Jim Lorentz	Buf.	Apr. 7/77	Min.	3	Pete LoPresti (2) Gary Smith (1)	Buf. 7	Min. 1
Bobby Schmautz	Bos.	Apr. 11/77	Bos.	3	Rogatien Vachon	Bos. 8	L.A. 3
Billy Harris	NYI	Apr. 23/77	Mtl.	3	Ken Dryden	Mtl. 4	NYI 3
George Ferguson	Tor.	Apr. 11/78	Tor.	3	Rogatien Vachon	Tor. 7	L.A. 3
Jean Ratelle	Bos.	May 3/79	Bos.	3	Ken Dryden	Bos. 4	Mtl. 3
Stan Jonathan	Bos.	May 8/79	Bos.	3	Ken Dryden	Bos. 5	Mtl. 2
Ron Duguay	NYR	Apr. 20/80	NYR	3	Pete Peeters	NYR 4	Phi. 2
Steve Shutt	Mtl.	Apr. 22/80	Mtl.	3	Gilles Meloche	Mtl. 6	Min. 2
Gilbert Perreault	Buf.	May 6/80	NYI	3	Billy Smith (2) ENG (1)	Buf. 7	NYI 4
Paul Holmgren	Phi.	May 15/80	Phil	3	Billy Smith	Phi. 8	NYI 3
Steve Payne	Min.	Apr. 8/81	Bos.	3	Rogatien Vachon	Min. 5	Bos. 4
Denis Potvin	NYI	Apr. 17/81	NYI	3	Andy Moog	NYI 6	Edm. 3
Barry Pederson	Bos.	Apr. 8/82	Bos.	3	Don Edwards	Bos. 7	Buf. 3
Duane Sutter	NYI	Apr. 15/83	NYI	3	Glen Hanlon	NYI 5	NYR 0
Doug Halward	Van.	Apr. 7/84	Van.	3	Rejean Lemelin (2) Don Edwards (1)	Van. 7	Cgy. 0
Jorgen Pettersson	St. L.	Apr. 8/84	Det.	3	Ed Mio	St. L. 3	Det. 2
Clark Gillies	NYI	May 12/84	NYI	3	Grant Fuhr	NYI 6	Edm. 1
Ken Linseman	Bos.	Apr. 14/85	Bos.	3	Steve Penney	Bos. 7	Mtl. 6
Dave Andreychuk	Buf.	Apr. 14/85	Buf.	3	Dan Bouchard	Que. 4	Buf. 7
Greg Paslawski	StL.	Apr. 15/86	Min.	3	Don Beaupre	St. L. 6	Min. 3
Doug Risebrough	Cgy.	May 4/86	Cgy.	3	Rick Wamsley	Cgy. 8	St. L. 2
Mike McPhee	Mtl.	Apr. 11/87	Bos.	3	Doug Keans	Mtl. 5	Bos. 4
John Ogrodnick	Que.	Apr. 14/87	Hfd.	3	Mike Liut	Que. 7	Hfd. 5
Pelle Eklund	Phi.	May 10/87	Mtl.	3	Patrick Roy (1) Bryan Hayward (2)	Phi. 6	Mtl. 3
John Tucker	Buf.	Apr. 9/88	Bos.	4	Andy Moog	Buf. 6	Bos. 2
Tony Hrkac	St. L.	Apr. 10/88	St. L.	4	Darren Pang	St. L. 6	Chi. 5
Hakan Loob	Cgy.	Apr. 10/88	Cgy.	3	Glenn Healy	Cgy. 7	L.A. 3
Ed Olczyk	Tor.	Apr. 12/88	Tor.	3	Greg Stefan (2) Glen Hanlon (1)	Tor. 6	Det. 5
Aaron Broten	N.J.	Apr. 20/88	N.J.	3	Pete Peeters	N.J. 5	Wsh. 2
Mark Johnson	N.J.	Apr. 22/88	Wsh.	4	Pete Peeters	N.J. 10	Wsh. 4
Patrik Sundstrom	N.J.	Apr. 22/88	Wsh.	3	Pete Peeters (2) Clint Malarchuk (1)	N.J. 10	Wsh. 4
Bob Brooke	Min.	Apr. 5/89	St. L.	3	Greg Millen	St. L. 4	Min. 3
Chris Kontos	L.A.	Apr. 6/89	L.A.	3	Grant Fuhr	L.A. 5	Edm. 2
Wayne Presley	Chi.	Apr. 13/89	Chi.	3	Greg Stefan (1) Glen Hanlon (2)	Chi. 7	Det. 1
Tony Granato	L.A.	Apr. 10/90	L.A.	3	Mike Vernon (1) Rick Wamsley (2)	L.A. 12	Cgy. 4
Tomas Sandstrom	L.A.	Apr. 10/90	L.A.	3	Mike Vernon (1) Rick Wamsley (2)	L.A. 12	Cgy. 4
Dave Taylor	L.A.	Apr. 10/90	L.A.	3	Mike Vernon (1) Rick Wamsley (2)	L.A. 12	Cgy. 4
Bernie Nicholls	NYR	Apr. 19/90	NYR	3	Mike Liut	NYR 7	Wsh. 3
John Druce	Wsh.	Apr. 21/90	NYR	3	John Vanbiesbrouck	Wsh. 6	NYR 3
Adam Oates	St. L.	Apr. 12/91	St. L.	3	Tim Chevaldae	St. L. 6	Det. 1
Luc Robitaille	L.A.	Apr. 26/91	L.A.	3	Grant Fuhr	L.A. 5	Edm. 2
Ron Francis	Pit.	May 9/92	Pit.	3	Mike Richter (2) John V'brouck (1)	Pit. 5	NYR. 4
Dirk Graham	Chi.	June 1/92	Chi.	3	Tom Barrasso	Pit. 5	Chi. 2
Joe Murphy	Edm.	May 6/92	Edm.	3	Kirk McLean	Edm. 5	Van. 2
Ray Sheppard	Det.	Apr. 24/92	Min.	3	Jon Casey	Min. 5	Det. 2
Kevin Stevens	Pit.	May 21/92	Bos.	4	Andy Moog	Pit. 5	Bos. 2
Pavel Bure	Van.	Apr. 28/92	Wpg.	3	Rick Tabaracci	Van. 8	Wpg. 3
Brian Noonan	Chi.	Apr. 18/93	Chi.	3	Curtis Joseph	St. L. 4	Chi. 3
Dale Hunter	Wsh.	Apr. 20/93	Wsh.	3	Glenn Healy	NYI 5	Wsh. 4
Teemu Selanne	Wpg.	Apr. 23/93	Wpg.	3	Kirk McLean	Wpg. 5	Van. 4
Ray Ferraro	NYI	Apr. 26/93	Wsh.	4	Don Beaupre	Wsh. 6	NYI 4
Al Iafrate	Wsh.	Apr. 26/93	Wsh.	3	Glenn Healy (2) Mark Fitzpatrick (1)	Wsh. 6	NYI 4
Paul Di Pietro	Mtl.	Apr. 28/93	Mtl.	3	Ron Hextall	Mtl. 6	Que. 2
Wendel Clark	Tor.	May 27/93	L.A.	3	Kelly Hrudey	L.A. 5	Tor. 4
Eric Desjardins	Mtl.	Jun. 3/93	Mtl.	3	Kelly Hrudey	Mtl. 3	L.A. 2
Tony Amonte	Chi.	Apr. 23/94	Chi.	4	Felix Potvin	Chi. 5	Tor. 4
Gary Suter	Chi.	Apr. 24/94	Chi.	3	Felix Potvin	Chi. 4	Tor. 3
Ulf Dahlen	S.J.	May 6/94	S.J.	3	Felix Potvin	S.J. 5	Tor. 2
Mike Sullivan	Cgy.	May 11/95	S.J.	3	Arturs Irbe (2) Wade Flaherty (1)	Cgy. 9	S.J. 2
Theoren Fleury	Cgy.	May 13/95	S.J.	4	Arturs Irbe (3) ENG (1)	Cgy. 6	S.J. 4
Brendan Shanahan	St. L.	May 13/95	Van.	3	Kirk McLean	St. L. 5	Van. 2
John LeClair	Phi.	May 21/95	Phi.	3	Mike Richter	Phi. 5	NYR 4
Brian Leetch	NYR	May 22/95	Phi.	3	Ron Hextall	Phi. 4	NYR 3
Trevor Linden	Van.	Apr. 25/96	Col.	3	Patrick Roy	Col. 5	Van. 4
Jaromir Jagr	Pit.	May 11/96	Pit.	3	Mike Richter	Pit. 7	NYR 3
Peter Forsberg	Col.	Jun. 6/96	Col.	3	John Vanbiesbrouck	Col. 8	Fla. 1

Leading Playoff Scorers, 1918–1996

Season	Player and Club	Games Played	Goals	Assists	Points
1995-96	Joe Sakic, Colorado	22	18	16	34
1994-95	Sergei Fedorov, Detroit	17	7	17	24
1993-94	Brian Leetch, NY Rangers	23	11	23	34
1992-93	Wayne Gretzky, Los Angeles	24	15	25	40
1991-92	Mario Lemieux, Pittsburgh	15	16	18	34
1990-91	Mario Lemieux, Pittsburgh	23	16	28	44
1989-90	Craig Simpson, Edmonton	22	16	15	31
	Mark Messier, Edmonton	22	9	22	31
1988-89	Al MacInnis, Calgary	22	7	24	31
1987-88	Wayne Gretzky, Edmonton	19	12	31	43
1986-87	Wayne Gretzky, Edmonton	21	5	29	34
1985-86	Doug Gilmour, St. Louis	19	9	12	21
	Bernie Federko, St. Louis	19	7	14	21
1984-85	Wayne Gretzky, Edmonton	18	17	30	47
1983-84	Wayne Gretzky, Edmonton	19	13	22	35
1982-83	Wayne Gretzky, Edmonton	16	12	26	38
1981-82	Bryan Trottier, NY Islanders	19	6	23	29
1980-81	Mike Bossy, NY Islanders	18	17	18	35
1979-80	Bryan Trottier, NY Islanders	21	12	17	29
1978-79	Jacques Lemaire, Montreal	16	11	12	23
	Guy Lafleur, Montreal	16	10	13	23
1977-78	Guy Lafleur, Montreal	15	10	11	21
	Larry Robinson, Montreal	15	4	17	21
1976-77	Guy Lafleur, Montreal	14	9	17	26
1975-76	Reggie Leach, Philadelphia	16	19	5	24
1974-75	Rick MacLeish, Philadelphia	17	11	9	20
1973-74	Rick MacLeish, Philadelphia	17	13	9	22
1972-73	Yvan Cournoyer, Montreal	17	15	10	25
1971-72	Phil Esposito, Boston	15	9	15	24
	Bobby Orr, Boston	15	5	19	24
1970-71	Frank Mahovlich, Montreal	20	14	13	27
1969-70	Phil Esposito, Boston	14	13	14	27
1968-69	Phil Esposito, Boston	10	8	10	18
1967-68	Bill Goldsworthy, Minnesota	14	8	7	15
1966-67	Jim Pappin, Toronto	12	7	8	15
1965-66	Norm Ullman, Detroit	12	6	9	15
1964-65	Bobby Hull, Chicago	14	10	7	17
1963-64	Gordie Howe, Detroit	14	9	10	19
1962-63	Gordie Howe, Detroit	11	7	9	16
	Norm Ullman, Detroit	11	4	12	16
1961-62	Stan Mikita, Chicago	12	6	15	21
1960-61	Gordie Howe, Detroit	11	4	11	15
	Pierre Pilote, Chicago	12	3	12	15
1959-60	Henri Richard, Montreal	8	3	9	12
	Bernie Geoffrion, Montreal	8	2	10	12
1958-59	Dickie Moore, Montreal	11	5	12	17
1957-58	Fleming Mackell, Boston	12	5	14	19
1956-57	Bernie Geoffrion, Montreal	11	11	7	18
1955-56	Jean Béliveau, Montreal	10	12	7	19
1954-55	Gordie Howe, Detroit	11	9	11	20
1953-54	Dickie Moore, Montreal	11	5	8	13
1952-53	Ed Sanford, Boston	11	8	3	11
1951-52	Ted Lindsay, Detroit	8	5	2	7
	Floyd Curry, Montreal	11	4	3	7
	Metro Prystai, Detroit	8	2	5	7
	Gordie Howe, Detroit	8	2	5	7
1950-51	Maurice Richard, Montreal	11	9	4	13
	Max Bentley, Toronto	11	2	11	13
1949-50	Pentti Lund, NY Rangers	12	6	5	11
1948-49	Gordie Howe, Detroit	11	8	3	11
1947-48	Ted Kennedy, Toronto	9	8	6	14
1946-47	Maurice Richard, Montreal	10	6	5	11
1945-46	Elmer Lach, Montreal	9	5	12	17
1944-45	Joe Carveth, Detroit	14	5	6	11
1943-44	Toe Blake, Montreal	9	7	11	18
1942-43	Carl Liscombe, Detroit	10	6	8	14
1941-42	Don Grosso, Detroit	12	8	6	14
1940-41	Milt Schmidt, Boston	11	5	6	11
1939-40	Phil Watson, NY Rangers	12	3	6	9
	Neil Colville, NY Rangers	12	2	7	9
1938-39	Bill Cowley, Boston	12	3	11	14
1937-38	Johnny Gottselig, Chicago	10	5	3	8
1936-37	Marty Barry, Detroit	10	4	7	11
1935-36	Buzz Boll, Toronto	9	7	3	10
1934-35	Baldy Northcott, Mtl. Maroons	7	4	1	5
	Harvey Jackson, Toronto	7	3	2	5
	Marvin Wentworth, Mtl. Maroons	7	3	2	5
1933-34	Larry Aurie, Detroit	9	3	7	10
1932-33	Cecil Dillon, NY Rangers	8	8	2	10
1931-32	Frank Boucher, NY Rangers	7	3	6	9
1930-31	Cooney Weiland, Boston	5	6	3	9
1929-30	Marty Barry, Boston	6	3	3	6
	Cooney Weiland, Boston	6	1	5	6
1928-29	Andy Blair, Toronto	4	3	0	3
	Butch Keeling, NY Rangers	6	3	0	3
	Ace Bailey, Toronto	4	1	2	3
1927-28	Frank Boucher, NY Rangers	9	7	3	10
1926-27	Harry Oliver, Boston	8	4	2	6
	Perk Galbraith, Boston	8	3	3	6
	Frank Fredrickson, Boston	8	2	4	6
1925-26	Nels Stewart, Mtl. Maroons	8	6	3	9
1924-25	Howie Morenz, Montreal	6	7	1	8
1923-24	Howie Morenz, Montreal	6	7	2	9
1922-23	Punch Broadbent, Ottawa	8	6	1	7
1921-22	Babe Dye, Toronto	7	11	2	13
1920-21	Cy Denneny, Ottawa	7	4	2	6
1919-20	Frank Nighbor, Ottawa	5	6	1	7
	Jack Darragh, Ottawa	5	5	2	7
1918-19	Newsy Lalonde, Montreal	10	17	1	18
1917-18	Alf Skinner, Toronto	7	8	1	9

Overtime Games since 1918

Abbreviations: Teams/Cities: — **Atl.** - Atlanta; **Bos.** - Boston; **Buf.** - Buffalo; **Cgy.** - Calgary; **Cgy. T.** - Calgary Tigers (Western Canada Hockey League); **Chi.** - Chicago; **Col.** - Colorado; **Dal.** - Dallas; **Det.** - Detroit; **Edm.** - Edmonton; **Edm. E.** - Edmonton Eskimos (WCHL); **Fla.** - Florida; **Hfd.** - Hartford; **K.C.** - Kansas City; **L.A.** - Los Angeles; **Min.** - Minnesota; **Mtl.** - Montreal; **Mtl.M.** - Montreal Maroons; **N.J.** - New Jersey; **NYA** - NY Americans; **NYI** - New York Islanders; **NYR** - New York Rangers; **Oak.** - Oakland; **Ott.** - Ottawa; **Phi.** - Philadelphia; **Pit.** - Pittsburgh; **Que.** - Quebec; **St. L.** - St. Louis; **Sea.** - Seattle Metropolitans (Pacific Coast Hockey Association); **S.J.** - San Jose; **T.B.** - Tampa Bay; **Tor.** - Toronto; **Van.** - Vancouver; **Van. M** - Vancouver Millionaires (PCHA); **Vic.** - Victoria Cougars (WCHL); **Wpg.** - Winnipeg; **Wsh.** - Washington.

SERIES — **CF** - conference final; **CSF** - conference semi-final; **CQF** - conference quarter-final; **DF** - division final; **DSF** - division semi-final; **F** - final; **PR** - preliminary round; **QF** - quarter final; **SF** - semi-final.

Date	City	Series	Score		Scorer	Overtime	Series Winner
Mar. 26/19	Sea.	F	Mtl. 0	Sea. 0	no scorer	20:00	
Mar. 29/19	Sea.	F	Mtl. 4	Sea. 3	Odie Cleghorn	15:57	
Mar. 21/22	Tor.	F	Tor 2	Van.M. 1	Babe Dye	4:50	Tor.
Mar. 29/23	Van.	F	Ott. 2	Edm.E. 1	Cy Denneny	2:08	Ott.
Mar. 31/27	Mtl.	QF	Mtl. 1	Mtl. M. 0	Howie Morenz	12:05	Mtl.
Apr. 7/27	Bos.	F	Ott. 0	Bos. 0	no scorer	20:00	Ott.
Apr. 11/27	Ott.	F	Bos. 1	Ott. 1	no scorer	20:00	Ott.
Apr. 3/28	Mtl.	QF	Mtl. M. 1	Mtl. 0	Russ Oatman	8:20	Mtl. M.
Apr. 7/28	Mtl.	F	NYR 2	Mtl. M. 1	Frank Boucher	7:05	NYR
Mar. 21/29	NY	QF	NYR 1	NYA 0	Butch Keeling	29:50	NYR
Mar. 26/29	Tor.	SF	NYR 2	Tor. 1	Frank Boucher	2:03	NYR
Mar. 20/30	Mtl.	SF	Bos. 2	Mtl. M. 1	Harry Oliver	45:35	Bos.
Mar. 25/30	Bos.	SF	Mtl. M. 1	Bos. 0	Archie Wilcox	26:27	Bos.
Mar. 26/30	Mtl.	QF	Chi. 2	Mtl. 2	Howie Morenz (Mtl.)	51:43	Mtl.
Mar. 28/30	Mtl.	SF	Mtl. 2	NYR 1	Gus Rivers	68:52	Mtl.
Mar. 24/31	Bos.	SF	Bos. 5	Mtl. 4	Cooney Weiland	18:56	Mtl.
Mar. 26/31	Chi.	QF	Chi. 2	Tor. 1	Steward Adams	19:20	Chi.
Mar. 28/31	Mtl.	SF	Mtl. 4	Bos. 3	Georges Mantha	5:10	Mtl.
Apr. 1/31	Mtl.	SF	Mtl. 3	Bos. 2	Wildor Larochelle	19:00	Mtl.
Apr. 5/31	Chi.	F	Chi. 2	Mtl. 1	Johnny Gottselig	24:50	Mtl.
Apr. 9/31	Mtl.	F	Chi. 3	Mtl. 2	Cy Wentworth	53:50	Mtl.
Mar. 26/32	Mtl.	SF	NYR 4	Mtl. 3	Fred Cook	59:32	NYR
Apr. 2/32	Tor.	SF	Tor. 3	Mtl. M. 2	Bob Gracie	17:59	Tor.
Mar. 25/33	Bos.	SF	Bos. 2	Tor. 1	Marty Barry	14:14	Tor.
Mar. 28/33	Bos.	SF	Tor. 1	Bos. 0	Busher Jackson	15:03	Tor.
Mar. 30/33	Tor.	SF	Bos. 2	Tor. 1	Eddie Shore	4:23	Tor.
Apr. 3/33	Tor.	SF	Tor. 1	Bos. 0	Ken Doraty	104:46	Tor.
Apr. 13/33	Tor.	F	NYR 1	Tor. 0	Bill Cook	7:33	NYR
Mar. 22/34	Tor.	SF	Det. 2	Tor. 1	Herbie Lewis	1:33	Det.
Mar. 25/34	Chi.	QF	Chi. 1	Mtl. 1	Mush March (Chi)	11:05	Chi.
Apr. 3/34	Det.	F	Chi. 2	Det. 1	Paul Thompson	21:10	Chi.
Apr. 10/34	Chi.	F	Chi. 1	Det. 0	Mush March	30:05	Chi.
Mar. 23/35	Bos.	SF	Bos. 1	Tor. 0	Dit Clapper	33:26	Tor.
Mar. 26/35	Chi.	QF	Mtl. M. 1	Chi. 0	Baldy Northcott	4:02	Mtl. M.
Mar. 30/35	Tor.	SF	Tor. 2	Bos. 1	Pep Kelly	1:36	Tor.
Apr. 4/35	Tor.	F	Mtl. M. 3	Tor. 2	Dave Trottier	5:28	Mtl. M.
Mar. 24/36	Mtl.	SF	Det. 1	Mtl. M. 0	Mud Bruneteau	116:30	Det.
Apr. 9/36	Tor.	F	Tor. 4	Det. 3	Buzz Boll	0:31	Det.
Mar. 25/37	NY	QF	NYR 2	Tor. 1	Babe Pratt	13:05	NYR
Apr. 1/37	Mtl.	SF	Det. 2	Mtl. 1	Hec Kilrea	51:49	Det.
Mar. 22/38	NY	QF	NYA 2	NYR 1	Johnny Sorrell	21:25	NYA
Mar. 24/38	Tor.	SF	Tor. 1	Bos. 0	George Parsons	21:31	Tor.
Mar. 26/38	Mtl.	QF	Chi. 3	Mtl. 2	Paul Thompson	11:49	Chi.
Mar. 27/38	NY	QF	NYA 3	NYR 2	Lorne Carr	60:40	NYA
Mar. 29/38	Bos.	SF	Tor. 3	Bos. 2	Gord Drillon	10:04	Tor.
Mar. 31/38	Chi.	SF	Chi. 1	NYA 0	Cully Dahlstrom	33:01	Chi.
Mar. 21/39	NY	SF	Bos. 2	NYR 1	Mel Hill	59:25	Bos.
Mar. 23/39	Bos.	SF	Bos. 3	NYR 2	Mel Hill	8:24	Bos.
Mar. 26/39	Det.	QF	Det. 1	Mtl. 0	Marty Barry	7:47	Det.
Mar. 30/39	Bos.	SF	NYR 2	Bos. 1	Clint Smith	17:19	Bos.
Apr. 1/39	Tor.	SF	Tor. 5	Det. 4	Gord Drillon	5:42	Tor.
Apr. 2/39	Bos.	SF	Bos. 2	NYR 1	Mel Hill	48:00	Bos.
Apr. 9/39	Bos.	F	Tor. 3	Bos. 2	Doc Romnes	10:38	Bos.
Mar. 19/40	Det.	QF	Det. 2	NYA 1	Syd Howe	0:25	Det.
Mar. 19/40	Tor.	QF	Tor. 3	Chi. 2	Syl Apps	6:35	Tor.
Apr. 2/40	NY	F	NYR 2	Tor. 1	Alf Pike	15:30	NYR
Apr. 11/40	Tor.	F	NYR 2	Tor. 1	Muzz Patrick	31:43	NYR
Apr. 13/40	Tor.	F	NYR 3	Tor. 2	Bryan Hextall	2:07	NYR
Mar. 20/41	Det.	QF	Det. 2	NYR 1	Gus Giesebrecht	12:01	Det.
Mar. 22/41	Mtl.	QF	Mtl. 4	Chi. 3	Charlie Sands	34:04	Chi.
Mar. 29/41	Bos.	SF	Tor. 2	Bos. 1	Pete Langelle	17:31	Bos.
Mar. 30/41	Chi.	SF	Det. 2	Chi. 1	Gus Giesebrecht	9:15	Det.
Mar. 22/42	Chi.	QF	Bos. 2	Chi. 1	Des Smith	6:51	Bos.
Mar. 21/43	Bos.	SF	Bos. 5	Mtl. 4	Don Gallinger	12:30	Bos.
Mar. 23/43	Det.	SF	Tor. 3	Det. 2	Jack McLean	70:18	Det.
Mar. 25/43	Mtl.	SF	Bos. 3	Mtl. 2	Harvey Jackson	3:20	Bos.
Mar. 30/43	Tor.	SF	Det. 3	Tor. 2	Adam Brown	9:21	Det.
Mar. 30/43	Bos.	SF	Bos. 5	Mtl. 4	Ab DeMarco	3:41	Bos.
Apr. 13/44	Mtl.	F	Mtl. 5	Chi. 4	Toe Blake	9:12	Mtl.
Mar. 27/45	Tor.	SF	Tor. 4	Mtl. 3	Gus Bodnar	12:36	Tor.
Mar. 29/45	Det.	SF	Det. 3	Bos. 2	Mud Bruneteau	17:12	Det.
Apr. 21/45	Tor.	F	Det. 1	Tor. 0	Ed Bruneteau	14:16	Tor.
Mar. 28/46	Bos.	SF	Bos. 4	Det. 3	Don Gallinger	9:51	Bos.
Mar. 30/46	Mtl.	F	Mtl. 4	Bos. 3	Maurice Richard	9:08	Mtl.
Apr. 2/46	Mtl.	F	Mtl. 3	Bos. 2	Jim Peters	16:55	Mtl.
Apr. 7/46	Bos.	F	Bos. 3	Mtl. 2	Terry Reardon	15:13	Mtl.
Mar. 26/47	Tor.	SF	Tor. 3	Det. 2	Howie Meeker	3:05	Tor.
Mar. 27/47	Mtl.	SF	Mtl. 2	Bos. 1	Ken Mosdell	5:38	Mtl.
Apr. 3/47	Mtl.	SF	Mtl. 4	Bos. 3	John Quilty	36:40	Mtl.
Apr. 15/47	Tor.	F	Tor. 2	Mtl. 1	Syl Apps	16:36	Tor.
Mar. 24/48	Tor.	SF	Tor. 5	Bos. 4	Nick Metz	17:03	Tor.
Mar. 22/49	Det.	SF	Det. 2	Mtl. 1	Max McNab	44:52	Det.
Mar. 24/49	Det.	SF	Mtl. 4	Det. 3	Gerry Plamondon	2:59	Det.
Mar. 26/49	Tor.	SF	Bos. 5	Tor. 4	Woody Dumart	16:14	Tor.
Apr. 8/49	Det.	F	Tor. 3	Det. 2	Joe Klukay	17:31	Tor.

Date	City	Series	Score		Scorer	Overtime	Series Winner
Apr. 4/50	Tor.	SF	Det. 2	Tor. 1	Leo Reise	20:38	Det.
Apr. 4/50	Mtl.	SF	Mtl. 3	NYR 2	Elmer Lach	15:19	Mtl.
Apr. 9/50	Det.	SF	Det. 1	Tor. 0	Leo Reise	8:39	Det.
Apr. 18/50	Det.	F	NYR 4	Det. 3	Don Raleigh	8:34	Det.
Apr. 20/50	Det.	F	NYR 2	Det. 1	Don Raleigh	1:38	Det.
Apr. 23/50	Det.	F	Det. 4	NYR 3	Pete Babando	28:31	Det.
Mar. 27/51	Det.	SF	Mtl. 3	Det. 2	Maurice Richard	61:09	Mtl.
Mar. 29/51	Det.	SF	Mtl. 1	Det. 0	Maurice Richard	42:20	Mtl.
Mar. 31/51	Tor.	SF	Bos. 1	Tor. 1	no scorer	20:00	Tor.
Apr. 11/51	Tor.	F	Tor. 3	Mtl. 2	Sid Smith	5:51	Tor.
Apr. 14/51	Tor.	F	Mtl. 3	Tor. 2	Maurice Richard	2:55	Tor.
Apr. 17/51	Mtl.	F	Tor. 2	Mtl. 1	Ted Kennedy	4:47	Tor.
Apr. 19/51	Mtl.	F	Tor. 3	Mtl. 2	Harry Watson	5:15	Tor.
Apr. 21/51	Tor.	F	Tor. 3	Mtl. 2	Bill Barilko	2:53	Tor.
Apr. 6/52	Bos.	SF	Mtl. 3	Bos. 2	Paul Masnick	27:49	Mtl.
Mar. 29/53	Bos.	SF	Bos. 2	Det. 1	Jack McIntyre	12:29	Bos.
Mar. 29/53	Chi.	SF	Chi. 2	Mtl. 1	Al Dewsbury	5:18	Mtl.
Apr. 16/53	Mtl.	F	Mtl. 1	Bos. 0	Elmer Lach	1:22	Mtl.
Apr. 1/54	Det.	SF	Det. 4	Tor. 3	Ted Lindsay	21:01	Det.
Apr. 11/54	Det.	F	Mtl. 1	Det. 0	Ken Mosdell	5:45	Det.
Apr. 16/54	Det.	F	Det. 2	Mtl. 1	Tony Leswick	4:29	Det.
Mar. 29/55	Bos.	SF	Mtl. 4	Bos. 3	Don Marshall	3:05	Mtl.
Mar. 24/56	Tor.	SF	Det. 5	Tor. 4	Ted Lindsay	4:22	Det.
Mar. 28/57	NY	SF	NYR 4	Mtl. 3	Andy Hebenton	13:38	Mtl.
Apr. 4/57	Mtl.	SF	Mtl. 4	NYR 3	Maurice Richard	1:11	Mtl.
Mar. 27/58	NY	SF	Bos. 4	NYR 3	Jerry Toppazzini	4:46	Bos.
Mar. 30/58	Det.	SF	Mtl. 2	Det. 1	André Pronovost	11:52	Mtl.
Apr. 17/58	Mtl.	F	Mtl. 3	Bos. 2	Maurice Richard	5:45	Mtl.
Mar. 28/59	Tor.	SF	Tor. 3	Bos. 2	Gerry Ehman	5:02	Tor.
Mar. 31/59	Tor.	SF	Tor. 3	Bos. 2	Frank Mahovlich	11:21	Tor.
Apr. 14/59	Tor.	F	Tor. 3	Mtl. 2	Dick Duff	10:06	Mtl.
Mar. 26/60	Mtl.	SF	Mtl. 4	Chi. 3	Doug Harvey	8:38	Mtl.
Mar. 27/60	Det.	SF	Tor. 5	Det. 4	Frank Mahovlich	43:00	Tor.
Mar. 29/60	Det.	SF	Det. 2	Tor. 1	Gerry Melnyk	1:54	Tor.
Mar. 22/61	Tor.	SF	Tor. 3	Det. 2	George Armstrong	24:51	Det.
Mar. 26/61	Chi.	SF	Chi. 2	Mtl. 1	Murray Balfour	52:12	Chi.
Apr. 5/62	Tor.	SF	Tor. 3	NYR 2	Red Kelly	24:23	Tor.
Apr. 2/64	Det.	SF	Chi. 3	Det. 2	Murray Balfour	8:21	Det.
Apr. 14/64	Tor.	F	Det. 4	Tor. 3	Larry Jeffrey	7:52	Tor.
Apr. 23/64	Det.	F	Tor. 4	Det. 3	Bobby Baun	1:43	Tor.
Apr. 6/65	Tor.	SF	Tor. 3	Mtl. 2	Dave Keon	4:17	Mtl.
Apr. 13/65	Tor.	SF	Mtl. 4	Tor. 3	Claude Provost	16:33	Mtl.
May 5/66	Det.	F	Mtl. 3	Det. 2	Henri Richard	2:20	Mtl.
Apr. 13/67	NY	SF	Mtl. 2	NYR 1	John Ferguson	6:28	Mtl.
Apr. 25/67	Tor.	F	Tor. 3	Mtl. 2	Bob Pulford	28:26	Tor.
Apr. 10/68	St. L.	QF	St. L. 3	Phi. 2	Larry Keenan	24:10	St. L.
Apr. 16/68	St. L.	QF	Phi. 2	St. L. 1	Don Blackburn	31:18	St. L.
Apr. 16/68	Min.	QF	Min. 4	L.A. 3	Milan Marcetta	9:11	Min.
Apr. 22/68	Min.	SF	Min. 3	St. L. 2	Parker MacDonald	3:41	St. L.
Apr. 27/68	St. L.	SF	St. L. 4	Min. 3	Gary Sabourin	1:32	St. L.
Apr. 28/68	Mtl.	SF	Mtl. 4	Chi. 3	Jacques Lemaire	2:14	Mtl.
Apr. 29/68	St. L.	SF	St. L. 3	Min. 2	Bill McCreary	17:27	St. L.
May 3/68	St. L.	SF	St. L. 2	Min. 1	Ron Schock	22:50	St. L.
May 5/68	St. L.	F	Mtl. 3	St. L. 2	Jacques Lemaire	1:41	Mtl.
May 9/68	Mtl.	F	Mtl. 4	St. L. 3	Bobby Rousseau	1:13	Mtl.
Apr. 2/69	Oak.	QF	L.A. 5	Oak. 4	Ted Irvine	0:19	L.A.
Apr. 10/69	Mtl.	SF	Mtl. 3	Bos. 2	Ralph Backstrom	0:42	Mtl.
Apr. 13/69	Mtl.	SF	Mtl. 4	Bos. 3	Mickey Redmond	4:55	Mtl.
Apr. 24/69	Bos.	SF	Mtl. 2	Bos. 1	Jean Béliveau	31:28	Mtl.
Apr. 12/70	Oak.	QF	Pit. 3	Oak. 2	Michel Briere	8:28	Pit.
May 10/70	Bos.	F	Bos. 4	St. L. 3	Bobby Orr	0:40	Bos.
Apr. 15/71	Tor.	QF	NYR 2	Tor. 1	Bob Nevin	9:07	NYR
Apr. 18/71	Chi.	SF	NYR 2	Chi. 1	Pete Stemkowski	1:37	Chi.
Apr. 27/71	Chi.	SF	Chi. 3	NYR 2	Bobby Hull	6:35	Chi.
Apr. 29/71	NY	SF	NYR 3	Chi. 2	Pete Stemkowski	41:29	Chi.
May 4/71	Chi.	F	Chi. 2	Mtl. 1	Jim Pappin	21:11	Mtl.
Apr. 6/72	Bos.	QF	Tor. 4	Bos. 3	Jim Harrison	2:58	Bos.
Apr. 6/72	Min.	QF	Min. 6	St. L. 5	Bill Goldsworthy	1:36	St. L.
Apr. 9/72	Pit.	QF	Chi. 6	Pit. 5	Pit Martin	0:12	Chi.
Apr. 16/72	Min.	QF	St. L. 2	Min. 1	Kevin O'Shea	10:07	St. L.
Apr. 1/73	Mtl.	QF	Buf. 3	Mtl. 2	René Robert	9:18	Mtl.
Apr. 10/73	Phi.	QF	Phi. 3	Min. 2	Gary Dornhoefer	8:35	Phi.
Apr. 14/73	Mtl.	SF	Phi. 5	Mtl. 4	Rick MacLeish	2:56	Mtl.
Apr. 17/73	Mtl.	SF	Mtl. 4	Phi. 3	Larry Robinson	6:45	Mtl.
Apr. 14/74	Tor.	QF	Bos. 4	Tor. 3	Ken Hodge	1:27	Bos.
Apr. 14/74	Atl.	QF	Phi. 4	Atl. 3	Dave Schultz	5:40	Phi.
Apr. 16/74	Mtl.	QF	NYR 3	Mtl. 2	Ron Harris	4:07	NYR
Apr. 23/74	Chi.	SF	Chi. 4	Bos. 3	Jim Pappin	3:48	Bos.
Apr. 28/74	NY	SF	NYR 2	Phi. 1	Rod Gilbert	4:20	Phi.
May 9/74	Bos.	F	Phi. 3	Bos. 2	Bobby Clarke	12:01	Phi.
Apr. 8/75	L.A.	PR	L.A. 3	Tor. 2	Mike Murphy	8:53	Tor.
Apr. 10/75	Tor.	PR	Tor. 3	L.A. 2	Blaine Stoughton	10:19	Tor.
Apr. 10/75	Chi.	PR	Chi. 4	Bos. 3	Ivan Boldirev	7:33	Chi.
Apr. 11/75	NY	PR	NYI 4	NYR 3	Jean-Paul Parise	0:11	NYI
Apr. 19/75	Tor.	QF	Phi. 4	Tor. 3	André Dupont	1:45	Phi.
Apr. 17/75	Chi.	QF	Chi. 5	Buf. 4	Stan Mikita	2:31	Buf.
Apr. 22/75	Mtl.	QF	Mtl. 5	Van. 4	Guy Lafleur	17:06	Mtl.
May 1/75	Phi.	SF	Phi. 5	NYI 4	Bobby Clarke	2:56	Phi.
May 7/75	NYI	SF	NYI 4	Phi. 3	Jude Drouin	1:53	Phi.
Apr. 27/75	Buf.	SF	Buf. 6	Mtl. 5	Danny Gare	4:42	Buf.
May 6/75	Buf.	SF	Buf. 5	Mtl. 4	René Robert	5:56	Buf.
May 20/75	Buf.	F	Buf. 5	Phi. 4	René Robert	18:29	Phi.
Apr. 8/76	Buf.	PR	Buf. 3	St. L. 2	Danny Gare	11:43	Buf.
Apr. 9/76	Buf.	PR	Buf. 2	St. L. 1	Don Luce	14:27	Buf.
Apr. 13/76	Bos.	QF	L.A. 3	Bos. 2	Butch Goring	0:27	Bos.
Apr. 13/76	Buf.	QF	Buf. 3	NYI 2	Danny Gare	14:04	NYI
Apr. 22/76	L.A.	QF	L.A. 4	Bos. 3	Butch Goring	18:28	Bos.
Apr. 29/76	Phi.	SF	Phi. 2	Bos. 1	Reggie Leach	13:38	Phi.
Apr. 15/77	Tor.	QF	Phi. 4	Tor. 3	Rick MacLeish	2:55	Phi.
Apr. 17/77	Tor.	QF	Phi. 6	Tor. 5	Reggie Leach	19:10	Phi.
Apr. 24/77	Phi.	SF	Bos. 4	Phi. 3	Rick Middleton	2:57	Bos.
Apr. 26/77	Phi.	SF	Bos. 5	Phi. 4	Terry O'Reilly	30:07	Bos.
May 3/77	Mtl.	SF	NYI 4	Mtl. 3	Billy Harris	3:58	Mtl.

Date	City	Series	Score		Scorer	Overtime	Series Winner
May 14/77	Bos.	F	Mtl. 2	Bos. 1	Jacques Lemaire	4:32	Mtl.
Apr. 11/78	Phi.	PR	Phi. 3	Col. 2	Mel Bridgman	0:23	Phi.
Apr. 13/78	NY	PR	NYR 4	Buf. 3	Don Murdoch	1:37	Buf.
Apr. 19/78	Bos.	QF	Bos. 4	Chi. 3	Terry O'Reilly	1:50	Bos.
Apr. 19/78	NYI	QF	NYI 3	Tor. 2	Mike Bossy	2:50	Tor.
Apr. 21/78	Chi.	QF	Bos. 4	Chi. 3	Peter McNab	10:17	Bos.
Apr. 25/78	NYI	QF	NYI 2	Tor. 1	Bob Nystrom	8:02	Tor.
Apr. 29/78	NYI	QF	Tor. 2	NYI 1	Lanny McDonald	4:13	Tor.
May 2/78	Bos.	SF	Bos. 3	Phi. 2	Rick Middleton	1:43	Bos.
May 16/78	Mtl.	F	Mtl. 3	Bos. 2	Guy Lafleur	13:09	Mtl.
May 21/78	Bos.	F	Bos. 4	Mtl. 3	Bobby Schmautz	6:22	Mtl.
Apr. 12/79	L.A.	PR	NYR 2	L.A. 1	Phil Esposito	6:11	NYR
Apr. 14/79	Buf.	PR	Pit. 4	Buf. 3	George Ferguson	0:47	Pit.
Apr. 16/79	Phi.	PR	NYR 3	Phi. 2	Ken Linseman	0:44	NYR
Apr. 18/79	NYI	QF	NYI 1	Chi. 0	Mike Bossy	2:31	NYI
Apr. 21/79	Tor.	QF	Mtl. 4	Tor. 3	Cam Connor	25:25	Mtl.
Apr. 22/79	Tor.	QF	Mtl. 5	Tor. 4	Larry Robinson	4:14	Mtl.
Apr. 28/79	NYI	SF	NYI 4	NYR 3	Denis Potvin	8:02	NYR
May 3/79	NY	SF	NYI 3	NYR 2	Bob Nystrom	3:40	NYR
May 3/79	Bos.	SF	Bos. 4	Mtl. 3	Jean Ratelle	3:46	Mtl.
May 10/79	Mtl.	SF	Mtl. 5	Bos. 4	Yvon Lambert	9:33	Mtl.
May 19/79	NY	F	Mtl. 4	NYR 3	Serge Savard	7:25	Mtl.
Apr. 8/80	NY	PR	NYR 2	Atl. 1	Steve Vickers	0:33	NYR
Apr. 8/80	Phi.	PR	Phi. 4	Edm. 3	Bobby Clarke	8:06	Phi.
Apr. 8/80	Chi.	PR	Chi. 3	St. L. 2	Doug Lecuyer	12:34	Chi.
Apr. 11/80	Hfd.	PR	Mtl. 4	Hfd. 3	Yvon Lambert	0:29	Mtl.
Apr. 11/80	Tor.	PR	Min. 4	Tor. 3	Al MacAdam	0:32	Min.
Apr. 11/80	L.A.	PR	NYI 4	L.A. 3	Ken Morrow	6:55	NYI
Apr. 11/80	Edm.	PR	Phi. 3	Edm. 2	Ken Linseman	23:56	Phi.
Apr. 16/80	Bos.	QF	NYI 2	Bos. 1	Clark Gillies	1:02	NYI
Apr. 17/80	Bos.	QF	NYI 5	Bos. 4	Bob Bourne	1:24	NYI
Apr. 21/80	NYI	QF	Bos. 4	NYI 3	Terry O'Reilly	17:13	NYI
May 1/80	Buf.	SF	NYI 2	Buf. 1	Bob Nystrom	21:20	NYI
May 13/80	Phi.	F	NYI 4	Phi. 3	Denis Potvin	4:07	NYI
May 24/80	NYI	F	NYI 5	Phi. 4	Bob Nystrom	7:11	NYI
Apr. 8/81	Buf.	PR	Buf. 3	Van. 2	Alan Haworth	5:00	Buf.
Apr. 8/81	Bos.	PR	Min. 5	Bos. 4	Steve Payne	3:34	Min.
Apr. 11/81	Chi.	PR	Cgy. 5	Chi. 4	Willi Plett	35:17	Cgy.
Apr. 12/81	Que.	PR	Que. 4	Phi. 3	Dale Hunter	0:37	Phi.
Apr. 14/81	St. L.	PR	St. L. 4	Pit. 3	Mike Crombeen	25:16	St. L.
Apr. 16/81	Buf.	QF	Min. 4	Buf. 3	Steve Payne	0:22	Min.
Apr. 20/81	Min.	QF	Buf. 5	Min. 4	Craig Ramsay	16:32	Min.
Apr. 20/81	Edm.	QF	NYI 5	Edm. 4	Ken Morrow	5:41	NYI
Apr. 7/82	Min.	DSF	Chi. 3	Min. 2	Greg Fox	3:34	Chi.
Apr. 8/82	Edm.	DSF	Edm. 3	L.A. 2	Wayne Gretzky	6:20	L.A.
Apr. 8/82	Van.	DSF	Van. 2	Cgy. 1	Dave Williams	14:20	Van.
Apr. 10/82	Pit.	DSF	Pit. 2	NYI 1	Rick Kehoe	4:14	NYI
Apr. 10/82	L.A.	DSF	L.A. 6	Edm. 5	Daryl Evans	2:35	L.A.
Apr. 13/82	Mtl.	DSF	Que. 3	Mtl. 2	Dale Hunter	0:22	Que.
Apr. 13/82	NY	DSF	NYI 4	Pit. 3	John Tonelli	6:19	NYI
Apr. 16/82	Van.	DF	L.A. 3	Van. 2	Steve Bozek	4:33	Van.
Apr. 18/82	Que.	DF	Que. 3	Bos. 2	Wilf Paiement	11:44	Que.
Apr. 18/82	NY	DF	NYI 4	NYR 3	Bryan Trottier	3:00	NYI
Apr. 18/82	L.A.	DF	Van. 4	L.A. 3	Colin Campbell	1:23	Van.
Apr. 21/82	St. L.	DF	St. L. 3	Chi. 2	Bernie Federko	3:28	Chi.
Apr. 23/82	Que.	DF	Bos. 6	Que. 5	Peter McNab	10:54	Que.
Apr. 27/82	Chi.	CF	Van. 2	Chi. 1	Jim Nill	28:58	NYI
May 1/82	Que.	CF	NYI 5	Que. 4	Wayne Merrick	16:52	NYI
May 8/82	NYI	F	NYI 6	Van. 5	Mike Bossy	19:58	NYI
Apr. 5/83	Bos.	DSF	Bos. 4	Que. 3	Barry Pederson	1:46	Bos.
Apr. 6/83	Cgy.	DSF	Cgy. 4	Van. 3	Eddy Beers	12:27	Cgy.
Apr. 7/83	Min.	DSF	Min. 5	Tor. 4	Bobby Smith	5:03	Min.
Apr. 10/83	Tor.	DSF	Min. 5	Tor. 4	Dino Ciccarelli	8:05	Min.
Apr. 10/83	Van.	DSF	Cgy. 4	Van. 3	Greg Meredith	1:06	Cgy.
Apr. 18/83	Min.	DF	Chi. 4	Min. 3	Rich Preston	10:34	Chi.
Apr. 24/83	Bos.	DF	Bos. 3	Buf. 2	Brad Park	1:52	Bos.
Apr. 5/84	Edm.	DSF	Edm. 5	Wpg. 4	Randy Gregg	0:21	Edm.
Apr. 7/84	Det.	DSF	St. L. 4	Det. 3	Mark Reeds	37:07	St. L.
Apr. 8/84	Det.	DSF	St. L. 3	Det. 2	Jorgen Pettersson	2:42	St. L.
Apr. 10/84	NYI	DSF	NYI 3	NYR 2	Ken Morrow	8:56	NYI
Apr. 13/84	Min.	DF	St. L. 4	Min. 3	Doug Gilmour	16:16	Min.
Apr. 13/84	Edm.	DF	Cgy. 6	Edm. 5	Carey Wilson	3:42	Edm.
Apr. 13/84	NYI	DF	NYI 5	NYI 4	Anders Kallur	7:35	NYI
Apr. 16/84	Mtl.	DF	Que. 4	Mtl. 3	Bo Berglund	3:00	Mtl.
Apr. 20/84	Cgy.	DF	Cgy. 5	Edm. 4	Lanny McDonald	1:04	Edm.
Apr. 22/84	Min.	DF	Min. 4	St. L. 3	Steve Payne	6:00	Min.

Jean Beliveau, seen here battling Detroit defenseman Bob Goldham in the 1954 Stanley Cup finals, scored the only overtime goal of his career in the Canadiens' 2-1 win over Boston on April 24, 1969.

Date	City	Series	Score		Scorer	Overtime	Series Winner
Apr. 10/85	Phi.	DSF	Phi. 5	NYR 4	Mark Howe	8:01	Phi.
Apr. 10/85	Wsh.	DSF	Wsh. 4	NYI 3	Alan Haworth	2:28	NYI
Apr. 10/85	Edm.	DSF	Edm. 3	L.A. 2	Lee Fogolin	3:01	Edm.
Apr. 10/85	Wpg.	DSF	Wpg. 5	Cgy. 4	Brian Mullen	7:56	Wpg.
Apr. 11/85	Wsh.	DSF	Wsh. 2	NYI 1	Mike Gartner	21:23	NYI
Apr. 13/85	L.A.	DSF	Edm. 4	L.A. 3	Glenn Anderson	0:46	Edm.
Apr. 18/85	Mtl.	DF	Que. 2	Mtl. 1	Mark Kumpel	12:23	Que.
Apr. 23/85	Que.	DF	Que. 7	Mtl. 6	Dale Hunter	18:36	Que.
May 2/85	Mtl.	DF	Que. 3	Mtl. 2	Peter Stastny	2:22	Que.
Apr. 25/85	Min.	DF	Chi. 7	Min. 6	Darryl Sutter	21:57	Chi.
Apr. 28/85	Chi.	DF	Min. 5	Chi. 4	Dennis Maruk	1:14	Chi.
Apr. 30/85	Min.	DF	Chi. 6	Min. 5	Darryl Sutter	15:41	Chi.
May 5/85	Que.	CF	Que. 2	Phi. 1	Peter Stastny	6:20	Phi.
Apr. 9/86	Que.	DSF	Hfd. 3	Que. 2	Sylvain Turgeon	2:36	Hfd.
Apr. 12/86	Wpg.	DSF	Cgy. 4	Wpg. 3	Lanny McDonald	8:25	Cgy.
Apr. 17/86	Wsh.	DF	NYR 4	Wsh. 3	Brian MacLellan	1:16	NYR
Apr. 20/86	Edm.	DF	Edm. 6	Cgy. 5	Glenn Anderson	1:04	Cgy.
Apr. 23/86	Hfd.	DF	Hfd. 2	Mtl. 1	Kevin Dineen	1:07	Mtl.
Apr. 23/86	NYR	DF	NYR 6	Wsh. 5	Bob Brooke	2:40	NYR
Apr. 26/86	St L.	DF	St L. 4	Tor. 3	Mark Reeds	7:11	St L.
Apr. 29/86	Mtl.	DF	Mtl. 2	Hfd. 1	Claude Lemieux	5:55	Mtl.
May 5/86	NYR	CF	Mtl. 4	NYR 3	Claude Lemieux	9:41	Mtl.
May 12/86	St L.	CF	St L. 6	Cgy. 5	Doug Wickenheiser	7:30	Cgy.
May 18/86	Cgy.	F	Mtl. 3	Cgy. 2	Brian Skrudland	0:09	Mtl.
Apr. 8/87	Hfd.	DSF	Hfd. 3	Que. 2	Paul MacDermid	2:20	Que.
Apr. 9/87	Mtl.	DSF	Mtl. 4	Bos. 3	Mats Naslund	2:38	Mtl.
Apr. 9/87	St. L.	DSF	Tor. 3	St. L. 2	Rick Lanz	10:17	Tor.
Apr. 11/87	Wpg.	DSF	Cgy. 3	Wpg. 2	Mike Bullard	3:53	Wpg.
Apr. 11/87	Chi.	DSF	Det. 4	Chi. 3	Shawn Burr	4:51	Det.
Apr. 16/87	Que.	DSF	Que. 5	Hfd. 4	Peter Stastny	6:05	Que.
Apr. 18/87	Wsh.	DSF	NYI 3	Wsh. 2	Pat LaFontaine	68:47	NYI
Apr. 21/87	Edm.	DF	Edm. 3	Wpg. 2	Glenn Anderson	0:36	Edm.
Apr. 26/87	Que.	DF	Mtl. 3	Que. 2	Mats Naslund	5:30	Mtl.
Apr. 27/87	Tor.	DF	Tor. 3	Det. 2	Mike Allison	9:31	Det.
May 4/87	Phi.	CF	Phi. 4	Mtl. 3	Ilkka Sinislao	9:11	Phi.
May 20/87	Edm.	F	Edm. 3	Phi. 2	Jari Kurri	6:50	Edm.
Apr. 6/88	NYI	DSF	NYI 4	N.J. 3	Pat LaFontaine	6:11	N.J.
Apr. 10/88	Phi.	DSF	Phi. 5	Wsh. 4	Murray Craven	1:18	Wsh.
Apr. 10/88	N.J.	DSF	NYI 5	N.J. 4	Brent Sutter	15:07	N.J.
Apr. 10/88	Buf.	DSF	Buf. 6	Bos. 5	John Tucker	5:32	Bos.
Apr. 12/88	Det.	DSF	Tor. 6	Det. 5	Ed Olczyk	0:34	Det.
Apr. 16/88	Wsh.	DSF	Wsh. 5	Phi. 4	Dale Hunter	5:57	Wsh.
Apr. 21/88	Cgy.	DF	Edm. 5	Cgy. 4	Wayne Gretzky	7:54	Edm.
May 4/88	Bos.	CF	N.J. 3	Bos. 2	Doug Brown	17:46	Bos.
May 9/88	Det.	CF	Edm. 4	Det. 3	Jari Kurri	11:02	Edm.
Apr. 5/89	St. L.	DSF	St. L. 4	Min. 3	Brett Hull	11:55	St. L.
Apr. 5/89	Cgy.	DSF	Van. 4	Cgy. 3	Paul Reinhart	2:47	Cgy.
Apr. 6/89	St. L.	DSF	St. L. 4	Min. 3	Rick Meagher	5:30	St. L.
Apr. 6/89	Det.	DSF	Chi. 5	Det. 4	Duane Sutter	14:36	Chi.
Apr. 8/89	Hfd.	DSF	Mtl. 5	Hfd. 4	Stephane Richer	5:01	Mtl.
Apr. 8/89	Phi.	DSF	Wsh. 4	Phi. 3	Kelly Miller	0:51	Phi.
Apr. 9/89	Hfd.	DSF	Mtl. 4	Hfd. 3	Russ Courtnall	15:12	Mtl.
Apr. 15/89	Cgy.	DSF	Cgy. 4	Van. 3	Joel Otto	19:21	Cgy.
Apr. 18/89	Cgy.	DF	Cgy. 4	L.A. 3	Doug Gilmour	7:47	Cgy.
Apr. 19/89	Mtl.	DF	Mtl. 3	Bos. 2	Bobby Smith	12:24	Mtl.
Apr. 20/89	St. L.	DF	St. L. 5	Chi. 4	Tony Hrkac	33:49	Chi.
Apr. 21/89	Phi.	DF	Pit. 4	Phi. 3	Phil Bourque	12:08	Phi.
May 8/89	Chi.	CF	Cgy. 2	Chi. 1	Al MacInnis	15:05	Cgy.
May 9/89	Mtl.	CF	Phi. 2	Mtl. 1	Dave Poulin	5:02	Mtl.
May 19/89	Mtl.	F	Mtl. 4	Cgy. 3	Ryan Walter	38:08	Cgy.
Apr. 5/90	N.J.	DSF	Wsh. 5	N.J. 4	Dino Ciccarelli	5:34	Wsh.
Apr. 6/90	Edm.	DSF	Edm. 3	Wpg. 2	Mark Lamb	4:21	Edm.
Apr. 8/90	Tor.	DSF	St. L. 6	Tor. 5	Sergio Momesso	6:04	St. L.
Apr. 8/90	L.A.	DSF	L.A. 2	Cgy. 1	Tony Granato	8:37	L.A.
Apr. 9/90	Mtl.	DSF	Mtl. 2	Buf. 1	Brian Skrudland	12:35	Mtl.
Apr. 9/90	NYI	DSF	NYI 4	NYR 3	Brent Sutter	20:59	NYR
Apr. 10/90	Wpg.	DSF	Wpg. 4	Edm. 3	Dave Ellett	21:08	Edm.
Apr. 14/90	L.A.	DSF	L.A. 4	Cgy. 3	Mike Krushelnyski	23:14	L.A.
Apr. 15/90	Hfd.	DSF	Hfd. 3	Bos. 2	Kevin Dineen	12:30	Bos.
Apr. 21/90	Bos.	DF	Bos. 5	Mtl. 4	Garry Galley	3:42	Bos.
Apr. 24/90	L.A.	DF	Edm. 6	L.A. 5	Joe Murphy	4:42	Edm.
Apr. 25/90	Wsh.	DF	Wsh. 4	NYR 3	Rod Langway	0:34	Wsh.
Apr. 27/90	NYR	DF	Wsh. 2	NYR 1	John Druce	6:48	Wsh.
May 15/90	Bos.	F	Edm. 3	Bos. 2	Petr Klima	55:13	Edm.
Apr. 4/91	Chi.	DSF	Min. 4	Chi. 3	Brian Propp	4:14	Min.
Apr. 5/91	Pit.	DSF	Pit. 5	N.J. 4	Jaromir Jagr	8:52	Pit.
Apr. 6/91	L.A.	DSF	L.A. 3	Van. 2	Wayne Gretzky	11:08	L.A.
Apr. 8/91	Van.	DSF	Van. 2	L.A. 1	Cliff Ronning	3:12	L.A.
Apr. 11/91	NYR	DSF	Wsh. 5	NYR 4	Dino Ciccarelli	6:44	Wsh.
Apr. 11/91	Mtl.	DSF	Mtl. 4	Buf. 3	Russ Courtnall	5:56	Mtl.
Apr. 14/91	Edm.	DSF	Cgy. 2	Edm. 1	Theo Fleury	4:40	Edm.
Apr. 16/91	Cgy.	DSF	Edm. 5	Cgy. 4	Esa Tikkanen	6:58	Edm.
Apr. 18/91	L.A.	DF	L.A. 4	Edm. 3	Luc Robitaille	2:13	Edm.
Apr. 19/91	Bos.	DF	Mtl. 4	Bos. 3	Stephane Richer	0:27	Bos.
Apr. 19/91	Pit.	DF	Pit. 7	Wsh. 6	Kevin Stevens	8:10	Pit.
Apr. 20/91	L.A.	DF	Edm. 4	L.A. 3	Petr Klima	24:48	Edm.
Apr. 22/91	Edm.	DF	Edm. 4	L.A. 3	Esa Tikkanen	20:48	Edm.
Apr. 27/91	Mtl.	DF	Mtl. 3	Bos. 2	Shayne Corson	17:47	Bos.
Apr. 28/91	Edm.	DF	Edm. 4	L.A. 3	Craig MacTavish	16:57	Edm.
May 3/91	Bos.	CF	Bos. 5	Pit. 4	Vladimir Ruzicka	8:14	Pit.
Apr. 21/92	Bos.	DSF	Bos. 3	Buf. 2	Adam Oates	11:14	Bos.
Apr. 22/92	Min.	DSF	Det. 5	Min. 4	Yves Racine	1:15	Det.
Apr. 22/92	St. L.	DSF	St. L. 5	Chi. 4	Brett Hull	23:33	Chi.
Apr. 25/92	Buf.	DSF	Bos. 5	Buf. 4	Ted Donato	2:08	Bos.
Apr. 28/92	Min.	DSF	Det. 1	Min. 0	Sergei Fedorov	16:13	Det.
Apr. 29/92	Hfd.	DSF	Hfd. 2	Mon. 1	Yvon Corriveau	0:24	Mtl.
May 1/92	Mtl.	DSF	Mtl. 3	Hfd. 2	Russ Courtnall	25:26	Mtl.
May 3/92	Van.	DF	Edm. 4	Van. 3	Joe Murphy	8:36	Edm.
May 5/92	Mtl.	DF	Bos. 3	Mtl. 2	Peter Douris	3:12	Bos.
May 7/92	Pit.	DF	NYR 6	Pit. 5	Kris King	1:29	Pit.
May 9/92	Pit.	DF	Pit. 5	NYR 4	Ron Francis	2:47	Pit.
May 17/92	Pit.	CF	Pit. 4	Bos. 3	Jaromir Jagr	9:44	Pit.
May 20/92	Edm.	CF	Chi. 4	Edm. 3	Jeremy Roenick	2:45	Chi.
Apr. 18/93	Bos.	DSF	Buf. 5	Bos. 4	Bob Sweeney	11:03	Buf.
Apr. 18/93	Que.	DSF	Que. 3	Mtl. 2	Scott Young	16:49	Mtl.
Apr. 20/93	Wsh.	DSF	NYI 5	Wsh. 4	Brian Mullen	34:50	NYI
Apr. 22/93	Mtl.	DSF	Mtl. 2	Que. 1	Vincent Damphousse	10:30	Mtl.
Apr. 22/93	Buf.	DSF	Buf. 4	Bos. 3	Yuri Khmylev	1:05	Buf.
Apr. 22/93	NYI	DSF	NYI 4	Wsh. 3	Ray Ferraro	4:46	NYI
Apr. 24/93	Buf.	DSF	Buf. 6	Bos. 5	Brad May	4:48	Buf.
Apr. 24/93	NYI	DSF	NYI 4	Wsh. 3	Ray Ferraro	25:40	NYI
Apr. 25/93	St. L.	DSF	St. L. 4	Chi. 3	Craig Janney	10:43	St. L.
Apr. 26/93	Que.	DSF	Mtl. 5	Que. 4	Kirk Muller	8:17	Mtl.
Apr. 27/93	Det.	DSF	Tor. 5	Det. 4	Mike Foligno	2:05	Tor.
Apr. 27/93	Van.	DSF	Wpg. 4	Van. 3	Teemu Selanne	6:18	Van.
Apr. 29/93	Wpg.	DSF	Van. 4	Wpg. 3	Greg Adams	4:30	Van.
May 1/93	Det.	DSF	Tor. 4	Det. 3	Nikolai Borschevsky	2:35	Tor.
May 3/93	Tor.	DF	Tor. 2	St. L. 1	Doug Gilmour	23:16	Tor.
May 4/93	Mtl.	DF	Mtl. 4	Buf. 3	Guy Carbonneau	2:50	Mtl.
May 5/93	Tor.	DF	St. L. 2	Tor. 1	Jeff Brown	23:03	Tor.
May 6/93	Buf.	DF	Mtl. 4	Buf. 3	Gilbert Dionne	8:28	Mtl.
May 8/93	Buf.	DF	Mtl. 4	Buf. 3	Kirk Muller	11:37	Mtl.
May 11/93	Van.	DF	L.A. 4	Van. 3	Gary Shuchuk	26:31	L.A.
May 14/93	Pit.	DF	NYI 4	Pit. 3	Dave Volek	5:16	NYI
May 18/93	Mtl.	CF	Mtl. 4	NYI 3	Stephan Lebeau	26:21	Mtl.
May 20/93	NYI	CF	Mtl. 2	NYI 1	Guy Carbonneau	12:34	Mtl.
May 25/93	Tor.	CF	Tor. 3	L.A. 2	Glenn Anderson	19:20	L.A.
May 27/93	L.A.	CF	L.A. 5	Tor. 4	Wayne Gretzky	1:41	L.A.
Jun. 3/93	Mtl.	F	Mtl. 3	L.A. 2	Eric Desjardins	0:51	Mtl.
Jun. 5/93	L.A.	F	Mtl. 4	L.A. 3	John LeClair	0:34	Mtl.
Jun. 7/93	L.A.	F	Mtl. 3	L.A. 2	John LeClair	14:37	Mtl.
Apr. 20/94	Tor.	CQF	Tor. 1	Chi. 0	Todd Gill	2:15	Tor.
Apr. 22/94	St. L.	CQF	Dal. 5	St. L. 4	Paul Cavallini	8:34	Dal.
Apr. 24/94	Chi.	CQF	Chi. 4	Tor. 3	Jeremy Roenick	1:23	Tor.
Apr. 25/94	Bos.	CQF	Mtl. 2	Bos. 1	Kirk Muller	17:18	Bos.
Apr. 26/94	Cgy.	CQF	Van. 2	Cgy. 1	Geoff Courtnall	7:15	Van.
Apr. 27/94	Buf.	CQF	Buf. 1	N.J. 0	Dave Hannan	65:43	N.J.
Apr. 28/94	Van.	CQF	Van. 3	Cgy. 2	Trevor Linden	16:43	Van.
Apr. 30/94	Cgy.	CQF	Van. 4	Cgy. 3	Pavel Bure	22:20	Van.
May 3/94	N.J.	CSF	Bos. 6	N.J. 5	Don Sweeney	9:08	N.J.
May 7/94	Bos.	CSF	N.J. 5	Bos. 4	Stephane Richer	14:19	N.J.
May 8/94	Van.	CSF	Van. 2	Dal. 1	Sergio Momesso	11:01	Van.
May 12/94	Tor.	CSF	Tor. 3	S.J. 2	Mike Gartner	8:53	Tor.
May 15/94	NYR	CF	N.J. 4	NYR 3	Stephane Richer	35:23	NYR
May 16/94	Tor.	CF	Tor. 3	Van. 2	Peter Zezel	16:55	Van.
May 19/94	N.J.	CF	NYR 3	N.J. 2	Stephane Matteau	26:13	NYR
May 24/94	Van.	CF	Van. 4	Tor. 3	Greg Adams	20:14	Van.
May 27/94	NYR	CF	NYR 2	N.J. 1	Stephane Matteau	24:24	NYR
May 31/94	NYR	F	Van. 3	NYR 2	Greg Adams	19:26	NYR
May 7/95	Phi.	CQF	Phi. 4	Buf. 3	Karl Dykhuis	10:06	Phi.
May 9/95	Cgy.	CQF	S.J. 5	Cgy. 4	Ulf Dahlen	12:21	S.J.
May 12/95	NYR	CQF	NYR 3	Que. 2	Steve Larmer	8:09	NYR
May 12/95	N.J.	CQF	N.J. 1	Bos. 0	Randy McKay	8:51	N.J.
May 14/95	Pit.	CQF	Pit. 6	Wsh. 5	Luc Robitaille	4:30	Pit.
May 15/95	St. L.	CQF	Van. 6	St. L. 5	Cliff Ronning	1:48	Van.
May 17/95	Tor.	CQF	Tor. 5	Chi. 4	Randy Wood	10:00	Chi.
May 19/95	Cgy.	CQF	S.J. 5	Cgy. 4	Ray Whitney	21:54	S.J.
May 21/95	Phi.	CSF	Phi. 5	NYR 4	Eric Desjardins	7:03	Phi.
May 21/95	Chi.	CSF	Chi. 2	Van. 1	Joe Murphy	9:04	Chi.
May 22/95	Phi.	CSF	Phi. 4	NYR 3	Kevin Haller	0:25	Phi.
May 25/95	Van.	CSF	Chi. 3	Van. 2	Chris Chelios	6:22	Chi.
May 26/95	N.J.	CSF	N.J. 2	Pit. 1	Neal Broten	18:36	N.J.
May 27/95	Van.	CSF	Chi. 4	Van. 3	Chris Chelios	5:35	Chi.
Jun. 1/95	Det.	CF	Det. 2	Chi. 1	Nicklas Lidstrom	1:01	Det.
Jun. 6/95	Chi.	CF	Det. 4	Chi. 3	Vladimir Konstantinov	29:25	Det.
Jun. 7/95	N.J.	CF	Phi. 3	N.J. 2	Eric Lindros	4:19	N.J.
Jun. 11/95	Det.	CF	Det. 2	Chi. 1	Vyacheslav Kozlov	22:25	Det.
Apr. 16/96	NYR	CQF	Mtl. 3	NYR 2	Vincent Damphousse	5:04	NYR
Apr. 18/96	Tor.	CQF	Tor. 5	St. L. 4	Mats Sundin	4:02	St. L.
Apr. 18/96	Phi.	CQF	T.B. 2	Phi. 1	Brian Bellows	9:05	Phi.
Apr. 21/96	St. L.	CQF	St. L. 3	Tor. 2	Glenn Anderson	1:24	St. L.
Apr. 21/96	T.B.	CQF	T.B. 5	Phi. 4	Alexander Selivanov	2:04	Phi.
Apr. 23/96	Cgy.	CQF	Chi. 2	Cgy. 1	Joe Murphy	50:02	Chi.
Apr. 24/96	Wsh.	CQF	Pit. 3	Wsh. 2	Petr Nedved	79:15	Pit.
Apr. 25/96	Col.	CQF	Col. 5	Van. 4	Joe Sakic	0:51	Col.
Apr. 25/96	Tor.	CQF	Tor. 5	St. L. 4	Mike Gartner	7:31	St. L.
May 2/96	Col.	CSF	Chi. 3	Col. 2	Jeremy Roenick	6:29	Col.
May 6/96	Chi.	CSF	Chi. 4	Col. 3	Sergei Krivokrasov	0:46	Col.
May 8/96	St. L.	CSF	St. L. 5	Det. 4	Igor Kravchuk	3:23	Det.
May 8/96	Chi.	CSF	Col. 3	Chi. 2	Joe Sakic	44:33	Col.
May 9/96	Fla.	CSF	Fla. 4	Phi. 3	Dave Lowry	4:06	Fla.
May 12/96	Phi.	CSF	Fla. 2	Phi. 1	Mike Hough	28:05	Fla.
May 13/96	Chi.	CSF	Col. 4	Chi. 3	Sandis Ozolinsh	25:18	Col.
May 16/96	Det.	CSF	Det. 1	St. L. 0	Steve Yzerman	21:15	Det.
May 19/96	Det.	CF	Col. 3	Det. 2	Mike Keane	17:31	Col.
Jun. 10/96	Fla.	F	Col. 1	Fla. 0	Uwe Krupp	44:31	Col.

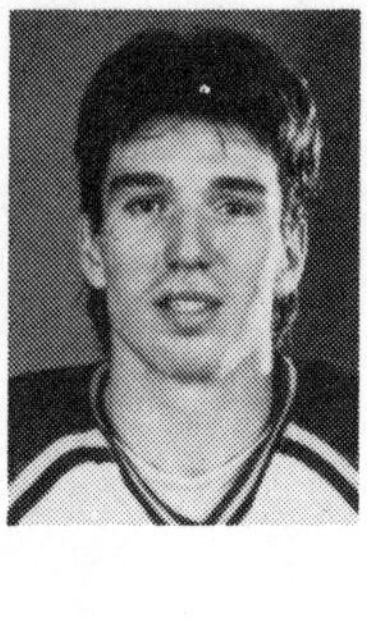

Colorado's Uwe Krupp, left, became the 12th player to score the Stanley Cup-winning goal in overtime. Dave Lowry, right, led the Florida Panthers in scoring in the 1996 playoffs with 17 points and tallied the first overtime winner of his career in the Panthers' 4-3 win over Philadelphia on May 9, 1996.

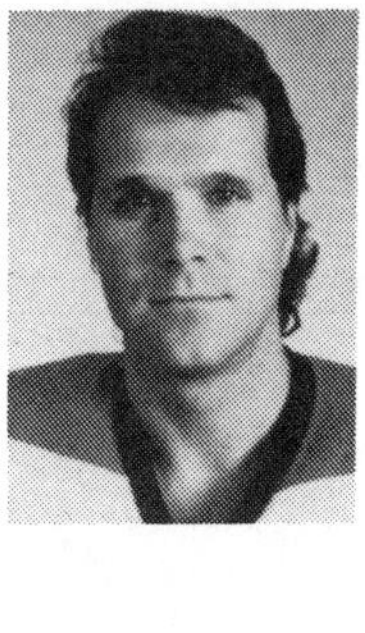

Punch Imlach, left, Scotty Bowman, center, and Sid Abel, right, each lost in their first two trips to the Stanley Cup finals as a coach. While Imlach and Bowman later went on to enjoy Stanley Cup success, Abel lost all four times he took the Red Wings to the finals.

Stanley Cup Coaching Records

Coaches listed in order of total games coached in playoffs. Minimum: 65 games.

Coach	Team	Years	Series	Series W	L	G	Games W	L	T	Cups	%
Bowman, Scott	St. Louis	4	10	6	4	52	26	26	0	0	.500
	Montreal	8	19	16	3	98	70	28	0	5	.714
	Buffalo	5	8	3	5	36	18	18	0	0	.500
	Pittsburgh	2	6	5	1	33	23	10	0	1	.696
	Detroit	3	8	5	3	44	25	19	0	0	.568
	Total	**22**	**51**	**35**	**16**	**263**	**162**	**101**	**0**	**6**	**.616**
Arbour, Al	St. Louis	1	2	1	1	11	4	7	0	0	.364
	NY Islanders	15	40	29	11	198	119	79	0	4	.601
	Total	**16**	**42**	**30**	**12**	**209**	**123**	**86**	**0**	**4**	**.589**
Irvin, Dick	Chicago	1	3	2	1	9	5	3	1	0	.611
	Toronto	9	20	12	8	66	33	32	1	1	.508
	Montreal	14	22	11	11	115	62	53	0	3	.539
	Total	**24**	**45**	**25**	**20**	**190**	**100**	**88**	**2**	**4**	**.532**
Keenan, Mike	Philadelphia	4	10	6	4	57	32	25	0	0	.561
	Chicago	4	11	7	4	60	33	27	0	0	.550
	NY Rangers	1	4	4	0	23	16	7	0	1	.695
	St. Louis	2	3	1	2	20	10	10	0	0	.500
	Total	**11**	**28**	**18**	**10**	**160**	**91**	**69**	**0**	**1**	**.569**
Sather, Glen	Edmonton	10	27	21	6	*126	89	37	0	4	.706
Blake, Toe	Montreal	13	23	18	5	119	82	37	0	8	.689
Reay, Billy	Chicago	12	22	10	12	117	57	60	0	0	.487
Shero, Fred	Philadelphia	6	16	12	4	83	48	35	0	2	.578
	NY Rangers	2	5	3	2	25	13	12	0	0	.520
	Total	**8**	**21**	**15**	**6**	**108**	**61**	**47**	**0**	**2**	**.565**
Adams, Jack	Detroit	15	27	15	12	105	52	52	1	3	.500
Demers, Jacques	St. Louis	3	6	3	3	33	16	17	0	0	.485
	Detroit	3	7	4	3	38	20	18	0	0	.526
	Montreal	2	5	4	1	27	19	8	0	1	.704
	Total	**8**	**18**	**11**	**7**	**98**	**55**	**43**	**0**	**1**	**.561**
Quinn, Pat	Philadelphia	3	8	5	3	39	22	17	0	0	.564
	Los Angeles	1	1	0	1	3	0	3	0	0	.000
	Vancouver	5	10	5	5	61	31	30	0	0	.508
	Total	**9**	**19**	**10**	**9**	**103**	**53**	**50**	**0**	**0**	**.515**
Burns, Pat	Montreal	4	10	6	4	56	30	26	0	0	.535
	Toronto	3	7	4	3	46	23	23	0	0	.500
	Total	**7**	**17**	**10**	**7**	**102**	**53**	**49**	**0**	**0**	**.519**
Francis, Emile	NY Rangers	9	14	5	9	75	34	41	0	0	.453
	St. Louis	3	4	1	3	18	6	12	0	0	.333
	Total	**12**	**18**	**6**	**12**	**93**	**40**	**53**	**0**	**0**	**.430**

Coach	Team	Years	Series	Series W	L	G	Games W	L	T	Cups	%
Imlach, Punch	Toronto	11	17	10	7	92	44	48	0	4	.478
Day, Hap	Toronto	9	14	10	4	80	49	31	0	5	.613
Murray, Bryan	Washington	7	10	3	7	53	24	29	0	0	.452
	Detroit	3	4	1	3	25	10	15	0	0	.400
	Total	**10**	**14**	**4**	**10**	**78**	**34**	**44**	**0**	**0**	**.435**
Johnson, Bob	Calgary	5	10	5	5	52	25	27	0	0	.481
	Pittsburgh	1	4	4	0	24	16	8	0	1	.666
	Total	**6**	**14**	**9**	**5**	**76**	**41**	**35**	**0**	**1**	**.539**
Abel, Sid	Chicago	1	1	0	1	7	3	4	0	0	.429
	Detroit	8	12	4	8	69	29	40	0	0	.420
	Total	**9**	**13**	**4**	**9**	**76**	**32**	**44**	**0**	**0**	**.421**
Ross, Art	Boston	12	19	9	10	70	32	33	5	1	.493
Bergeron, Michel	Quebec	7	13	6	7	68	31	37	0	0	.456
Lemaire, Jacques	Montreal	2	5	3	2	27	15	12	0	0	.555
	New Jersey	2	7	6	1	40	27	13	0	1	.675
	Total	**4**	**12**	**9**	**3**	**67**	**42**	**25**	**0**	**1**	**.626**
Muckler, John	Edmonton	2	7	6	1	40	25	15	0	1	.625
	Buffalo	4	5	1	4	27	11	16	0	0	.407
	Total	**6**	**12**	**7**	**5**	**67**	**36**	**31**	**0**	**1**	**.537**
Ivan, Tommy	Detroit	7	12	8	4	67	36	31	0	3	.537
Neilson, Roger	Toronto	2	5	3	2	19	8	11	0	0	.421
	Buffalo	1	2	1	1	8	4	4	0	0	.500
	Vancouver	2	5	3	2	21	12	9	0	0	.571
	NY Rangers	2	3	1	2	19	8	11	0	0	.421
	Total	**7**	**15**	**8**	**7**	**67**	**32**	**35**	**0**	**0**	**.473**
Pulford, Bob	Los Angeles	4	6	2	4	26	11	15	0	0	.423
	Chicago	5	9	4	5	41	17	24	0	0	.415
	Total	**9**	**15**	**6**	**9**	**67**	**28**	**39**	**0**	**0**	**.418**
Murray, Terry	Washington	4	7	3	4	39	18	21	0	0	.462
	Philadelphia	2	5	3	2	27	16	11	0	0	.593
	Total	**6**	**12**	**6**	**6**	**66**	**34**	**32**	**0**	**0**	**.515**
Patrick, Lester	NY Rangers	12	24	14	10	65	31	26	8	2	.538

* Does not include suspended game, May 24, 1988.

Penalty Shots in Stanley Cup Playoff Games

Date	Player	Goaltender	Scored	Final Score				Series
Mar. 25/37	Lionel Conacher, Mtl. Maroons	Tiny Thompson, Boston	No	Mtl. M. 0	at	Bos.	4	QF
Apr. 15/37	Alex Shibicky, NY Rangers	Earl Robertson, Detroit	No	NYR 0	at	Det.	3	F
Apr. 13/44	Virgil Johnson, Chicago	Bill Durnan, Montreal	No	Chi. 4	at	Mtl.	5*	F
Apr. 9/68	Wayne Connelly, Minnesota	Terry Sawchuk, Los Angeles	Yes	L.A. 4	at	Min.	7	QF
Apr. 27/68	Jim Roberts, St. Louis	Cesare Maniago, Minnesota	No	St. L. 4	at	Min.	3	SF
May 16/71	Frank Mahovlich, Montreal	Tony Esposito, Chicago	No	Chi. 3	at	Mtl.	4	F
May 7/75	Bill Barber, Philadelphia	Glenn Resch, NY Islanders	No	Phi. 3	at	NYI	4*	SF
Apr. 20/79	Mike Walton, Chicago	Glenn Resch, NY Islanders	No	NYI 4	at	Chi.	0	QF
Apr. 9/81	Peter McNab, Boston	Don Beaupre, Minnesota	No	Min. 5	at	Bos.	4*	PR
Apr. 17/81	Anders Hedberg, NY Rangers	Mike Liut, St. Louis	Yes	NYR 4	at	St. L.	4	QF
Apr. 9/83	Denis Potvin, NY Islanders	Pat Riggin, Washington	No	NYI 6	at	Wsh.	2	DSF
Apr. 28/84	Wayne Gretzky, Edmonton	Don Beaupre, Minnesota	Yes	Edm. 8	at	Min.	5	CF
May 1/84	Mats Naslund, Montreal	Bill Smith, NY Islanders	No	Mtl. 1	at	NYI	3	F
Apr. 14/85	Bob Carpenter, Washington	Bill Smith, NY Islanders	No	Wsh. 4	at	NYI.	6	DF
May 28/85	Ron Sutter, Philadelphia	Grant Fuhr, Edmonton	No	Phi. 3	at	Edm.	5	F
May 30/85	Dave Poulin, Philadelphia	Grant Fuhr, Edmonton	No	Phi. 3	at	Edm.	8	F
Apr. 9/88	John Tucker, Buffalo	Andy Moog, Boston	Yes	Bos. 2	at	Buf.	6	DSF
Apr. 9/88	Petr Klima, Detroit	Allan Bester, Toronto	Yes	Det. 6	at	Tor.	3	DSF
Apr. 8/89	Neal Broten, Minnesota	Greg Millen, St. Louis	Yes	St. L. 5	at	Min.	3	DSF
Apr. 4/90	Al MacInnis, Calgary	Kelly Hrudey, Los Angeles	Yes	L.A. 5	at	Cgy.	3	DSF
Apr. 5/90	Randy Wood, NY Islanders	Mike Richter, NY Rangers	No	NYI 1	at	NYR	2	DSF
May 3/90	Kelly Miller, Washington	Andy Moog, Boston	No	Wsh. 3	at	Bos.	5	CF
May 18/90	Petr Klima, Edmonton	Rejean Lemelin, Boston	No	Edm. 7	at	Bos.	2	F
Apr. 6/91	Basil McRae, Minnesota	Ed Belfour, Chicago	Yes	Min. 2	at	Chi.	5	DSF
Apr. 10/91	Steve Duchesne, Los Angeles	Kirk McLean, Vancouver	Yes	L.A. 6	at	Van.	1	DSF
May 11/92	Jaromir Jagr, Pittsburgh	John Vanbiesbrouck, NYR	Yes	Pit. 3	at	NYR	2	DF
May 13/92	Shawn McEachern, Pittsburgh	John Vanbiesbrouck, NYR	No	NYR 1	at	Pit.	5	DF
June 7/94	Pavel Bure, Vancouver	Mike Richter, NYR	No	NYR 4	at	Van.	2	F
May 9/95	Patrick Poulin, Chicago	Felix Potvin, Toronto	No	Tor. 3	at	Chi.	0	CQF
May 10/95	Michal Pivonka, Washington	Tom Barrasso, Pittsburgh	No	Pit. 2	at	Wsh.	6	CQF
Apr. 24/96	Joe Juneau, Washington	Ken Wregget, Pittsburgh	No	Pit. 3	at	Wsh.	2	CQF

* Game was decided in overtime, but shot taken during regulation time.

Ten Longest Overtime Games

Date	City	Series	Score				Scorer	Overtime	Series Winner
Mar. 24/36	Mtl.	SF	Det. 1		Mtl. M. 0		Mud Bruneteau	116:30	Det.
Apr. 3/33	Tor.	SF	Tor. 1		Bos. 0		Ken Doraty	104:46	Tor.
Apr. 24/96	**Wsh.**	**CQF**	**Pit. 3**		**Wsh. 2**		**Petr Nedved**	**79:15**	**Pit.**
Mar. 23/43	Det.	SF	Tor. 3		Det. 2		Jack McLean	70:18	Det.
Mar. 28/30	Mtl.	SF	Mtl. 2		NYR 1		Gus Rivers	68:52	Mtl.
Apr. 18/87	Wsh.	DSF	NYI 3		Wsh. 2		Pat LaFontaine	68:47	NYI
Apr. 27/94	Buf.	CQF	Buf. 1		N.J. 0		Dave Hannan	65:43	N.J.
Mar. 27/51	Det.	SF	Mtl. 3		Det. 2		Maurice Richard	61:09	Mtl.
Mar. 27/38	NY	QF	NYA 3		NYR 2		Lorne Carr	60:40	NYA
Mar. 26/32	Mtl.	SF	NYR 4		Mtl. 3		Fred Cook	59:32	NYR

Game four of the Washington-Pittsburgh quarter-final featured the first overtime penalty shot in Stanley Cup history. Penguins defenseman Chris Tamer knocked his own net off its moorings during a wild goal mouth scramble in the second overtime frame which meant an automatic penalty shot had to be called. Joe Juneau, below, was selected to take the shot, but Penguin goaltender Ken Wregget stoned the Capitals' center, allowing teammate Petr Nedved to eventually score the game-winner in the fourth extra period.

Overtime Record of Current Teams

(Listed by number of OT games played)

	Overall				Home					Road				
Team	GP	W	L	T	GP	W	L	T	Last OT Game	GP	W	L	T	Last OT Game
Montreal	116	67	47	2	53	35	17	1	Jun. 3/93	63	32	30	1	Apr. 16/96
Boston	93	36	54	3	43	20	22	1	May 9/94	50	16	32	2	May 12/94
Toronto	90	46	43	1	57	30	26	1	Apr. 25/96	33	16	17	0	Apr. 21/96
Chicago	61	29	30	2	29	15	13	1	May 13/96	32	14	17	1	May 2/96
NY Rangers	60	27	33	0	26	11	15	0	Apr. 16/96	34	16	18	0	May 22/95
Detroit	57	26	31	0	35	13	22	0	May 19/96	22	13	9	0	May 8/96
Philadelphia	42	22	20	0	18	11	7	0	May 12/96	24	11	13	0	May 9/96
NY Islanders	38	29	9	0	17	14	3	0	May 20/93	21	15	6	0	May 18/93
St. Louis	38	21	17	0	19	15	4	0	May 8/96	19	6	13	0	May 16/96
Los Angeles	30	12	18	0	16	8	8	0	Jun. 7/93	14	4	10	0	Jun. 3/93
* Calgary	30	11	19	0	14	4	10	0	Apr. 23/96	16	7	9	0	Apr. 28/94
Vancouver	29	13	16	0	12	5	7	0	May 27/95	17	8	9	0	Apr. 25/96
Buffalo	28	14	14	0	17	11	6	0	Apr. 27/94	11	3	8	0	May 7/95
** Dallas	28	12	16	0	14	5	9	0	Apr. 28/92	14	7	7	0	May 8/94
Edmonton	27	17	10	0	14	9	5	0	May 20/92	13	8	5	0	May 3/92
*** Colorado	26	15	11	0	13	7	6	0	May 2/96	13	8	5	0	Jun. 10/96
Washington	19	8	11	0	8	4	4	0	Apr. 24/96	11	4	7	0	May 14/95
Pittsburgh	17	10	7	0	9	6	3	0	May 14/95	8	4	4	0	Apr. 24/96
**** New Jersey	15	5	10	0	7	2	5	0	Jun. 7/95	8	3	5	0	May 27/94
Hartford	11	5	6	0	7	4	3	0	Apr. 29/92	4	1	3	0	May 1/92
Winnipeg	9	4	5	0	5	2	3	0	Apr. 29/93	4	2	2	0	Apr. 27/93
San Jose	3	2	1	0	0	0	0	0		3	2	1	0	May 19/95
Florida	3	2	1	0	2	1	1	0	Jun. 10/96	1	1	0	0	May 12/96
Tampa Bay	2	2	0	0	1	1	0	0	Apr. 21/96	1	1	0	0	Apr. 18/96

*Totals include those of Atlanta 1972-80.
**Totals include those of Minnesota 1967-93.
***Totals include those of Quebec 1979-95.
****Totals include those of Kansas City and Colorado 1974-82.

Key to Player and Goaltender Registers

Demographics: Position, shooting side (catching hand for goaltenders), height, weight, place and date of birth are found on first line. Draft information, if any, is located on second line.

Major Junior, NCAA, minor pro, senior European and NHL clubs form a permanent part of each player's data panel. If a player sees action with more than one club in any of the above categories, a separate line is included for each one.

High school, prep school, Tier II junior, European junior and U.S. junior listings are deleted if a player accumulates two or more years of Major Junior, NCAA or senior European experience.

Canadian and U.S. National and Olympic Team statistics are also listed. For Europeans, Olympic Team participation is included as a separate line if a player joins an NHL club at the conclusion of the Games.

Some data is unavailable at press time. Readers are encouraged to contribute. See page 5 for contact names and addresses

Player's NHL organization as of August 28, 1996. This includes players under contract, unsigned draft choices and other players on reserve lists. Free agents as of August 28, 1996 show a blank here.

The complete career data panels of players with NHL experience who announced their retirement before the start of the 1996-97 season are included in the 1996-97 Player Register. These newly-retired players also show a blank here.

Each NHL club's minor-pro affiliates are listed at the bottom of this page.

Footnotes are listed below player's year-by-year data and indicate league awards and all-star selections. Letter corresponding to footnote is placed beside the season in which awards or all-star selections were received.

PLAYER, JOHN SAMPLE   (PLAY-uhr)   **PHO.**

Center. Shoots left. 6'1", 200 lbs. Born, Moncton, N.B., April 14, 1974.
(Pittsburgh's 3rd choice, 62nd overall in the 1992 Entry Draft).

			Regular Season					Playoffs				
Season	Club	League	GP	G	A	TP	PIM	GP	G	A	TP	PIM
1990-91	Brandon	WHL	66	15	13	28	17	4	3	1	4	6
1991-92	Brandon	WHL	72	36	30	66	72	12	4	5	9	12
1992-93ab	Brandon	WHL	70	47	59	106	83	16	*16	8	*24	14
1993-94	**Pittsburgh**	**NHL**	10	1	2	3	6	....	....	....	....	....
	Cleveland	IHL	64	31	22	53	71	5	3	2	5	8
1994-95	**Montreal**	**NHL**	24	7	6	13	42	1	0	0	0	0
	Fredericton	AHL	47	41	31	72	106	....	....	....	....	....
1995-96	**Colorado**	**NHL**	68	27	35	62	88	14	4	6	10	12 ♦
	NHL Totals		102	35	43	78	136	15	4	6	10	12

a WHL East Second All-Star Team (1993)
b Won Stafford Smythe Memorial Trophy (Memorial Cup MVP) (1993)

Traded to **Montreal** by **Pittsburgh** for Montreal's third round choice in 1996 Entry Draft, June 14, 1994. Traded to **Colorado** by **Montreal** for Bill Winger, June 17, 1995. Signed as a free agent by **Phoenix**, August 23, 1996.

All trades, free agent signings and other transactions involving NHL clubs are listed in chronological order. Players selected by NHL clubs after re-entering the NHL Entry Draft are noted here. NHL All-Star Game appearances are listed above trade notes.

Asterisk (*) indicates league leader in this statistical category.

NEW FOR 1996-97: Member of Stanley Cup-winning team.

NHL Clubs and Minor League Affiliates 1996-97

NHL CLUB	MINOR LEAGUE AFFILIATE
Anaheim	Baltimore Bandits (IHL)
	Fort Wayne Komets (IHL)
	Long Beach Ice Dogs (IHL)
Boston	Providence Bruins (AHL)
	Charlotte Checkers (ECHL)
Buffalo	Rochester Americans (AHL)
	South Carolina Stingrays (ECHL)
Calgary	Saint John Flames (AHL)
	Roanoke Express (ECHL)
Chicago	Indianapolis Ice (IHL)
	Columbus Chill (ECHL)
Colorado	Hershey Bears (AHL)
Dallas	Michigan K-Wings (IHL)
	Dayton Bombers (ECHL)
Detroit	Adirondack Red Wings (AHL)
	Toledo Storm (ECHL)
Edmonton	Hamilton Bulldogs (AHL)
	Wheeling Thunderbirds (AHL)
Florida	Carolina Monarchs (AHL)
	Cincinnati Cyclones (IHL)
	Tallahassie Tiger-Sharks (ECHL)
	Port Huron Border Cats (ColHL)
Hartford	Springfield Falcons (AHL)
	Richmond Renegades (ECHL)
Los Angeles	Phoenix Roadrunners (IHL)
	Mississippi Seawolves (ECHL)
	Knoxville Cherokees (ECHL)

NHL CLUB	MINOR LEAGUE AFFILIATE
Montreal	Fredericton Canadiens (AHL)
	Rafales de Quebec (IHL)
	Wheeling Thunderbirds (ECHL)
New Jersey	Albany River Rats (AHL)
	Raleigh IceCaps (ECHL)
NY Islanders	Kentucky Thoroughblades (AHL)
	Utah Grizzlies (IHL)
NY Rangers	Binghamton Rangers (AHL)
Ottawa	Worcester IceCats (AHL)
	Raleigh IceCaps (ECHL)
Philadelphia	Philadelphia Phantoms (AHL)
Phoenix	Springfield Falcons (AHL)
	Las Vegas Thunder (IHL)
Pittsburgh	Cleveland Lumberjacks (IHL)
	Johnstown Chiefs (ECHL)
St. Louis	Worcester IceCats (AHL)
San Jose	Kentucky Thoroughblades (IHL)
	Louisville River Frogs (ECHL)
Tampa Bay	Adirondack Red Wings (AHL)
Toronto	St. John's Maple Leafs (AHL)
Vancouver	Syracuse Crunch (AHL)
Washington	Portland Pirates (AHL)
	Hampton Roads Admirals (ECHL)

Pronunciation of Player Names

United Press International phonetic style.

AY	long A as in mate
A	short A as in cat
AI	nasal A as on air
AH	short A as in father
AW	broad A as in talk
EE	long E as in meat
EH	short E as in get
UH	hollow E as in "the"
AY	French long E with acute accent as in Pathe
IH	middle E as in pretty
EW	EW dipthong as in few
IGH	long I as in time
EE	French long I as in machine
IH	short I as in pity
OH	long O as in note
AH	short O as in hot
AW	broad O as in fought
OO	long double OO as in fool
UH	short double O as in ouch
OW	OW dipthong as in how
EW	long U as in mule
OO	long U as in rule
U	middle U as in put
UH	short U as in shut or hurt
K	hard C as in cat
S	soft C as in cease
SH	soft CH as in machine
CH	hard CH or TCH as in catch
Z	hard S as in decrease
S	soft S as in sun
G	hard G as in gang
J	soft G as in general
ZH	soft J as in French version of Joliet

Late Additions to Player Register

BOIKOV, ALEXANDER · S.J.

Defense. Shoots left. 6', 180 lbs.   Born, Chelyabinsk, USSR, February 7, 1975.

Season	Club	Lea	Regular Season GP	G	A	TP	PIM	Playoffs GP	G	A	TP	PIM
1995-96	Tri-City	WHL	71	3	49	52	230	11	2	4	6	28

Signed as a free agent by **San Jose**, April 22, 1996.

MACISAAC, DAVID · PHI.

Defense. Shoots left. 6'2", 225 lbs.   Born, Arlington, MA, April 23, 1972.

Season	Club	Lea	Regular Season GP	G	A	TP	PIM	Playoffs GP	G	A	TP	PIM
1995-96	Milwaukee	IHL	71	7	16	23	165	....	....	....	....	....

Signed as a free agent by **Philadelphia**, July 30, 1996.

RATUSHNY, DAN   (rah-TOOSH-nee) · FLA.

Defense. Shoots right. 6'1", 205 lbs.   Born, Nepean, Ont., October 29, 1970.
(Winnipeg's 2nd choice, 25th overall, in 1989 Entry Draft).

Season	Club	Lea	Regular Season GP	G	A	TP	PIM	Playoffs GP	G	A	TP	PIM
1988-89	Cornell	ECAC	28	2	13	15	50	....	....	....	....	....
	Cdn. National	....	2	0	0	0	2	....	....	....	....	....
1989-90ab	Cornell	ECAC	26	5	14	19	54	....	....	....	....	....
1990-91ac	Cornell	ECAC	26	7	24	31	52	....	....	....	....	....
	Cdn. National	....	12	0	1	1	6	....	....	....	....	....
1991-92	Cdn. National	....	58	5	13	18	50	....	....	....	....	....
	Cdn. Olympic	....	8	0	0	0	4	....	....	....	....	....
1992-93	Fort Wayne	IHL	63	6	19	25	48	....	....	....	....	....
	Vancouver	**NHL**	1	0	1	1	2	....	....	....	....	....
1993-94	Hamilton	AHL	62	8	31	39	22	4	0	0	0	4
1994-95	Fort Wayne	IHL	72	3	25	28	46	4	0	1	1	8
1994-95	Ft. Wayne	IHL	72	3	25	28	46	4	0	1	1	8
1995-96	Peoria	IHL	45	7	15	22	45	12	3	4	7	10
	Carolina	AHL	23	5	10	15	28	....	....	....	....	....
	NHL Totals		**1**	**0**	**1**	**1**	**2**	....	....	....	....	....

a ECAC First All-Star Team (1990, 1991)
b NCAA East Second All-American Team (1990)
c NCAA East First All-American Team (1991)
Traded to **Vancouver** by **Winnipeg** for Vancouver's ninth round choice (Harijs Vitolinsh) in 1993 Entry Draft, March 22, 1993. Signed as a free agent by **Florida**, February 21, 1996.

SMELNITSKI, MAXIM · NYR

Right wing. Shoots left. 6'3", 207 lbs.   Born, Chelyabinsk, USSR, March 24, 1974.
(NY Rangers' 13th choice, 268th overall, in 1993 Entry Draft).

Season	Club	Lea	Regular Season GP	G	A	TP	PIM	Playoffs GP	G	A	TP	PIM
1992-93	Chelyabinsk	CIS	35	0	1	1	7	2	0	0	0	0
1993-94	Chelyabinsk	USSR	23	4	0	4	4	3	0	0	0	0
1994-95	Chelyabinsk	CIS	49	9	5	14	22	....	....	....	....	....
1995-96	Chelyabinsk	CIS	41	4	5	9	39	....	....	....	....	....

STROBEL, MARK · N.J.

Defense. Shoots left. 6', 200 lbs.   Born, St. Paul, MN, August 15, 1973.

Season	Club	Lea	Regular Season GP	G	A	TP	PIM	Playoffs GP	G	A	TP	PIM
1995-96	Albany	AHL	28	1	1	2	36	....	....	....	....	....
	Raleigh	ECHL	26	1	5	6	18	....	....	....	....	....

Signed as a free agent by **New Jersey**, August, 1996.

Trade Notes and Free Agent Signings

FLATLEY, PAT Signed as a free agent by NY Rangers, September 6, 1996.

HAWGOOD, GREG Signed as a free agent by San Jose, September 8, 1996.

KOVALENKO, ANDREI Traded to Edmonton by Montreal for Scott Thornton, September 6, 1996.

RONAN, ED Signed as a free agent by Buffalo, September 5, 1996.

SEMENOV, ANATOLI Signed as a free agent by Buffalo, September 5, 1996.

THORNTON, SCOTT Traded to Montreal by Edmonton for Andrei Kovalenko, September 6, 1996.

WARD, DIXON Signed as a free agent by Buffalo, September 5, 1996.

1996-97 Player Register

Note: The 1996-97 Player Register lists forwards and defensemen only. Goaltenders are listed separately. The Player Register lists every skater who appeared in an NHL game in the 1995-96 season, every skater drafted in the first six rounds of the 1996 Entry Draft, players on NHL Reserve Lists and other players. Trades and roster changes are current as of August 28, 1996.

Abbreviations: A – assists; **G** – goals; **GP** – games played; **Lea** – league; **PIM** – penalties in minutes; **TP** – total points; * – league-leading total; ♦ – member of Stanley Cup-winning team.

Pronunciations courtesy of the NHL Broadcasters' Association and Igor Kuperman, Phoenix Coyotes

Goaltender Register begins on page 421.

LEAGUES:

ACHL	Atlantic Coast Hockey League
AHL	American Hockey League
AJHL	Alberta Junior Hockey League
Alp.	Alpenliga
AUAA	Atlantic Universities Athletic Association
BCJHL	British Columbia Junior Hockey League
CCHA	Central Collegiate Hockey Association
CHL	Central Hockey League
CIAU	Canadian Interuniversity Athletic Union
COJHL	Central Ontario Junior Hockey League
ColHL	Colonial Hockey League
CWUAA	Canada West Universities Athletic Association
ECAC	Eastern Collegiate Athletic Association
ECHL	East Coast Hockey League
EJHL	Eastern Junior Hockey League
G.N.	Great Northern
GPAC	Great Plains Athletic Conference
H.E.	Hockey East
HS	High School
IHL	International Hockey League
Jr.	Junior
MJHA	(New York) Metropolitan Junior Hockey Association
MJHL	Manitoba Junior Hockey League
NAJHL	North American Junior Hockey League
NCAA	National Collegiate Athletic Association
NHL	**National Hockey League**
OHA	Ontario Hockey Association
OHL	Ontario Hockey League
OMJHL	Ontario Major Junior Hockey League
OPJHL	Ontario Provincial Junior Hockey League
OUAA	Ontario Universities Athletic Association
QJHL	Quebec Junior Hockey League
QMJHL	Quebec Major Junior Hockey League
SJHL	Saskatchewan Junior Hockey League
SOHL	Southern Ontario Hockey League
USHL	United States Hockey League (Junior)
WCHA	Western Collegiate Hockey Association
WHA	World Hockey Association
WHL	Western Hockey League

AALTO, ANTTI (AL-toh, AN-tee) ANA.

Center. Shoots left. 6'2", 185 lbs.   Born, Lappeenranta, Finland, March 4, 1975.
(Anaheim's 6th choice, 134th overall, in 1993 Entry Draft).

			Regular Season					Playoffs				
Season	Club	Lea	GP	G	A	TP	PIM	GP	G	A	TP	PIM
1991-92	SaiPa	Fin. 2	20	6	6	12	20	....	....	....	....	....
1992-93	SaiPa	Fin. 2	23	6	8	14	14	....	....	....	....	....
	TPS	Fin.	1	0	0	0	0	....	....	....	....	....
1993-94	TPS	Fin.	33	5	9	14	16	10	1	1	2	4
1994-95	TPS	Fin.	44	11	7	18	18	5	0	1	1	2
1995-96	TPS	Fin.	40	15	16	31	22	11	3	5	8	14
	Kiekko-67	Fin. 2	2	0	2	2	2	....	....	....	....	....

AALTONEN, PETRI (AL-tuh-nehn) COL.

Center. Shoots left. 5'10", 185 lbs.   Born, Tampere, Finland, May 31, 1970.
(Quebec's 4th choice, 45th overall, in 1988 Entry Draft).

			Regular Season					Playoffs				
Season	Club	Lea	GP	G	A	TP	PIM	GP	G	A	TP	PIM
1988-89	HIFK	Fin.	2	0	0	0	0	....	....	....	....	....
1989-90	HIFK	Fin.	3	0	0	0	0	....	....	....	....	....
1990-91	HIFK	Fin.	43	6	9	15	12	3	1	1	2	0
1991-92	Tappara	Fin.	36	3	4	7	18	....	....	....	....	....
1992-93	Vantaa	Fin. 2	33	15	11	26	50	....	....	....	....	....
1993-94	Tappara	Fin.	25	2	4	6	12	....	....	....	....	....
	Karhu-Kissat	Fin. 2	9	3	7	10	50	....	....	....	....	....
1994-95	Haukat	Fin. 2	39	19	24	43	115	3	0	1	1	4
1995-96	Haukat	Fin. 2	37	5	17	22	49	3	0	0	0	2

ABRAHAMSSON, ELIAS BOS.

Defense. Shoots left. 6'3", 216 lbs.   Born, Uppsala, Sweden, June 15, 1977.
(Boston's 6th choice, 132nd overall, in 1996 Entry Draft).

			Regular Season					Playoffs				
Season	Club	Lea	GP	G	A	TP	PIM	GP	G	A	TP	PIM
1994-95	Halifax	QMJHL	25	0	3	3	41	....	....	....	....	....
1995-96	Halifax	QMJHL	64	3	11	14	268	6	2	2	4	8

ADAMS, GREG DAL.

Left wing. Shoots left. 6'3", 195 lbs.   Born, Nelson, B.C., August 1, 1963.

			Regular Season					Playoffs				
Season	Club	Lea	GP	G	A	TP	PIM	GP	G	A	TP	PIM
1982-83	N. Arizona	NCAA	29	14	21	35	19	....	....	....	....	....
1983-84	N. Arizona	NCAA	26	44	29	73	24	....	....	....	....	....
1984-85	**New Jersey**	**NHL**	**36**	**12**	**9**	**21**	**14**	....	....	....	....	....
	Maine	AHL	41	15	20	35	12	11	3	4	7	0
1985-86	**New Jersey**	**NHL**	**78**	**35**	**42**	**77**	**30**	....	....	....	....	....
1986-87	**New Jersey**	**NHL**	**72**	**20**	**27**	**47**	**19**	....	....	....	....	....
1987-88	**Vancouver**	**NHL**	**80**	**36**	**40**	**76**	**30**	....	....	....	....	....
1988-89	**Vancouver**	**NHL**	**61**	**19**	**14**	**33**	**24**	**7**	**2**	**3**	**5**	**2**
1989-90	**Vancouver**	**NHL**	**65**	**30**	**20**	**50**	**18**	....	....	....	....	....
1990-91	**Vancouver**	**NHL**	**55**	**21**	**24**	**45**	**10**	**5**	**0**	**0**	**0**	**2**
1991-92	**Vancouver**	**NHL**	**76**	**30**	**27**	**57**	**26**	**6**	**0**	**2**	**2**	**4**
1992-93	**Vancouver**	**NHL**	**53**	**25**	**31**	**56**	**14**	**12**	**7**	**6**	**13**	**6**
1993-94	**Vancouver**	**NHL**	**68**	**13**	**24**	**37**	**20**	**23**	**6**	**8**	**14**	**2**
1994-95	**Vancouver**	**NHL**	**31**	**5**	**10**	**15**	**12**	....	....	....	....	....
	Dallas	**NHL**	**12**	**3**	**3**	**6**	**4**	**5**	**2**	**0**	**2**	**0**
1995-96	**Dallas**	**NHL**	**66**	**22**	**21**	**43**	**33**	....	....	....	....	....
	NHL Totals		**753**	**271**	**292**	**563**	**254**	**58**	**17**	**19**	**36**	**16**

Played in NHL All-Star Game (1988)

Signed as a free agent by **New Jersey**, June 25, 1984. Traded to **Vancouver** by **New Jersey** with Kirk McLean for Patrik Sundstrom and Vancouver's fourth round choice (Matt Ruchty) in 1988 Entry Draft, September 10, 1987. Traded to **Dallas** by **Vancouver** with Dan Kesa and Vancouver's fifth round choice (later traded to Los Angeles — Los Angeles selected Jason Morgan) in 1995 Entry Draft for Russ Courtnall, April 7, 1995.

ADAMS, KEVYN BOS.

Center. Shoots right. 6'1", 182 lbs.   Born, Washington, D.C., October 8, 1974.
(Boston's 1st choice, 25th overall, in 1993 Entry Draft).

			Regular Season					Playoffs				
Season	Club	Lea	GP	G	A	TP	PIM	GP	G	A	TP	PIM
1992-93	Miami-Ohio	CCHA	40	17	15	32	18	....	....	....	....	....
1993-94	Miami-Ohio	CCHA	36	15	28	43	24	....	....	....	....	....
1994-95a	Miami-Ohio	CCHA	38	20	29	49	30	....	....	....	....	....
1995-96	Miami-Ohio	CCHA	36	17	30	47	30	....	....	....	....	....

a   CCHA Second All-Star Team (1995)

AHLUND, HAKAN VAN.

Right wing. Shoots left. 6', 194 lbs.   Born, Orebro, Sweden, August 16, 1967.
(Vancouver's 8th choice, 151st overall, in 1985 Entry Draft).

			Regular Season					Playoffs				
Season	Club	Lea	GP	G	A	TP	PIM	GP	G	A	TP	PIM
1983-84	Orebro	Swe. 2	1	0	1	1	0	....	....	....	....	....
1984-85	Orebro	Swe. 2	25	2	6	8	10	....	....	....	....	....
1985-86	Orebro	Swe. 2	20	5	4	9	10	2	0	0	0	0
1986-87	Orebro	Swe. 2	27	16	9	25	6	6	0	3	3	6
1987-88	Orebro	Swe. 2	36	24	23	47	29	6	3	4	7	7
1988-89	Malmo	Swe. 2	35	20	27	47	44	....	....	....	....	....
1989-90	Malmo	Swe. 2	35	12	38	50	30	....	....	....	....	....
1990-91	Malmo	Swe.	39	9	18	27	46	2	0	0	0	0
1991-92	Malmo	Swe.	38	5	12	17	48	10	2	2	4	8
1992-93	Malmo	Swe.	33	5	10	15	30	6	2	1	3	6
1993-94	Malmo	Swe.	37	7	7	14	26	10	4	3	7	13
1994-95	Malmo	Swe.	37	4	10	14	26	9	4	5	9	10
1995-96	Malmo	Swe.	33	7	13	20	62	5	0	3	3	6

AITKEN, JOHNATHAN BOS.

Defense. Shoots left. 6'3", 188 lbs.   Born, Edmonton, Alta., May 24, 1978.
(Boston's 1st choice, 8th overall, in 1996 Entry Draft).

			Regular Season					Playoffs				
Season	Club	Lea	GP	G	A	TP	PIM	GP	G	A	TP	PIM
1994-95	Medicine Hat	WHL	53	0	5	5	71	5	0	0	0	0
1995-96	Medicine Hat	WHL	71	6	14	20	131	5	1	0	1	6

AIVAZOFF, MICAH (A-vuh-zahf, MIGH-kuh)

Center. Shoots left. 6', 195 lbs.   Born, Powell River, B.C., May 4, 1969.
(Los Angeles' 6th choice, 109th overall, in 1988 Entry Draft).

			Regular Season					Playoffs				
Season	Club	Lea	GP	G	A	TP	PIM	GP	G	A	TP	PIM
1986-87	Victoria	WHL	72	18	39	57	112	5	1	0	1	2
1987-88	Victoria	WHL	69	26	57	83	79	8	3	4	7	14
1988-89	Victoria	WHL	70	35	65	100	136	8	5	7	12	2
1989-90	New Haven	AHL	77	20	39	59	71	....	....	....	....	....
1990-91	New Haven	AHL	79	11	29	40	84	....	....	....	....	....
1991-92	Adirondack	AHL	61	9	20	29	50	19	2	8	10	25
1992-93	Adirondack	AHL	79	32	53	85	100	11	8	6	14	10
1993-94	**Detroit**	**NHL**	**59**	**4**	**4**	**8**	**38**	....	....	....	....	....
1994-95	**Edmonton**	**NHL**	**21**	**0**	**1**	**1**	**2**	....	....	....	....	....
1995-96	**NY Islanders**	**NHL**	**12**	**0**	**1**	**1**	**6**	....	....	....	....	....
	Utah	IHL	59	14	21	35	58	22	3	5	8	33
	NHL Totals		**92**	**4**	**6**	**10**	**46**	....	....	....	....	....

Signed as a free agent by **Detroit**, March 18, 1993. Claimed by **Pittsburgh** from **Detroit** in NHL Waiver Draft, January 18, 1995. Claimed by **Edmonton** from **Pittsburgh** in NHL Waiver Draft, January 18, 1995. Signed as a free agent by **NY Islanders**, August 23, 1995.

AKERSTROM, ROGER (OHK-uhr-struhm) VAN.

Defense. Shoots left. 5'11", 189 lbs. Born, Lulea, Sweden, April 5, 1967.
(Vancouver's 8th choice, 170th overall, in 1988 Entry Draft).

			Regular Season					Playoffs				
Season	Club	Lea	GP	G	A	TP	PIM	GP	G	A	TP	PIM
1987-88	Lulea	Swe.	34	4	3	7	28	....	....	....	....	....
1988-89	Lulea	Swe.	38	6	12	18	32	....	....	....	....	....
1989-90	Lulea	Swe.	36	5	10	15	44	5	3	2	5	2
1990-91	Lulea	Swe.	37	2	10	12	38	5	0	1	1	6
1991-92	Vasteras	Swe.	39	3	9	12	20	....	....	....	....	....
1992-93	Vasteras	Swe.	37	13	13	26	36	3	0	0	0	6
1993-94	Vasteras	Swe.	36	5	4	9	37	4	2	1	3	4
1994-95	Lulea	Swe.	39	5	16	21	38	8	1	1	2	12
1995-96	Lulea	Swe.	38	5	4	9	26	13	3	4	7	12

ALATALO, MIKA PHO.

Left wing. Shoots left. 5'11", 185 lbs. Born, Oulu, Finland, June 11, 1971.
(Winnipeg's 11th choice, 203rd overall, in 1990 Entry Draft).

			Regular Season					Playoffs				
Season	Club	Lea	GP	G	A	TP	PIM	GP	G	A	TP	PIM
1988-89	KooKoo	Fin.	34	8	6	14	10	....	....	....	....	....
1989-90	KooKoo	Fin.	41	3	5	8	22	....	....	....	....	....
1990-91	Lukko	Fin.	39	10	1	11	10	....	....	....	....	....
1991-92	Lukko	Fin.	43	20	17	37	32	2	0	0	0	0
1992-93	Lukko	Fin.	48	16	19	35	38	3	0	0	0	0
1993-94	Lukko	Fin.	45	19	15	34	77	9	2	2	4	4
1994-95	TPS	Fin.	44	23	13	36	79	13	2	5	7	8
1995-96	TPS	Fin.	49	19	18	37	44	11	3	4	7	8

ALBELIN, TOMMY (AL-buh-LEEN) CGY.

Defense. Shoots left. 6'1", 190 lbs. Born, Stockholm, Sweden, May 21, 1964.
(Quebec's 7th choice, 152nd overall, in 1983 Entry Draft).

			Regular Season					Playoffs				
Season	Club	Lea	GP	G	A	TP	PIM	GP	G	A	TP	PIM
1982-83	Djurgarden	Swe.	19	2	5	7	4	6	1	0	1	2
1983-84	Djurgarden	Swe.	30	9	5	14	26	4	0	1	1	2
1984-85	Djurgarden	Swe.	32	9	8	17	22	8	2	1	3	4
1985-86	Djurgarden	Swe.	35	4	8	12	26	....	....	....	....	....
1986-87	Djurgarden	Swe.	33	7	5	12	49	2	0	0	0	0
1987-88	**Quebec**	**NHL**	**60**	**3**	**23**	**26**	**47**	....	....	....	....	....
1988-89	**Quebec**	**NHL**	**14**	**2**	**4**	**6**	**27**	....	....	....	....	....
	Halifax	AHL	8	2	5	7	4	....	....	....	....	....
	New Jersey	**NHL**	**46**	**7**	**24**	**31**	**40**	....	....	....	....	....
1989-90	**New Jersey**	**NHL**	**68**	**6**	**23**	**29**	**63**	....	....	....	....	....
1990-91	**New Jersey**	**NHL**	**47**	**2**	**12**	**14**	**44**	**3**	**0**	**1**	**1**	**2**
	Utica	AHL	14	4	2	6	10	....	....	....	....	....
1991-92	**New Jersey**	**NHL**	**19**	**0**	**4**	**4**	**4**	**1**	**1**	**1**	**2**	**0**
	Utica	AHL	11	4	6	10	4	....	....	....	....	....
1992-93	**New Jersey**	**NHL**	**36**	**1**	**5**	**6**	**14**	**5**	**2**	**0**	**2**	**0**
1993-94	**New Jersey**	**NHL**	**62**	**2**	**17**	**19**	**36**	**20**	**2**	**5**	**7**	**14**
	Albany	AHL	4	0	2	2	17	....	....	....	....	....
1994-95	**New Jersey**	**NHL**	**48**	**5**	**10**	**15**	**20**	**20**	**1**	**7**	**8**	**2** ♦
1995-96	**New Jersey**	**NHL**	**53**	**1**	**12**	**13**	**14**	....	....	....	....	....
	Calgary	**NHL**	**20**	**0**	**1**	**1**	**4**	**4**	**0**	**0**	**0**	**0**
	NHL Totals		**473**	**29**	**135**	**164**	**313**	**53**	**6**	**14**	**20**	**18**

Traded to **New Jersey** by **Quebec** for New Jersey's fourth round choice (Niclas Andersson) in 1989 Entry Draft, December 12, 1988. Traded to **Calgary** by **New Jersey** with Cale Hulse and Jocelyn Lemieux for Phil Housley and Dan Keczmer, February 26, 1996.

ALDOUS, CHRIS MTL.

Defense. Shoots left. 6'3", 181 lbs. Born, Massena, NY, November 19, 1975.
(Montreal's 12th choice, 252nd overall, in 1994 Entry Draft).

			Regular Season					Playoffs				
Season	Club	Lea	GP	G	A	TP	PIM	GP	G	A	TP	PIM
1994-95	RPI	ECAC	31	0	1	1	4	....	....	....	....	....
1995-96	RPI	ECAC	35	1	3	4	26	....	....	....	....	....

ALFREDSSON, DANIEL (AHL-frehd-suhn) OTT.

Right wing. Shoots right. 5'11", 187 lbs. Born, Grums, Sweden, December 11, 1972.
(Ottawa's 5th choice, 133rd overall, in 1994 Entry Draft).

			Regular Season					Playoffs				
Season	Club	Lea	GP	G	A	TP	PIM	GP	G	A	TP	PIM
1991-92	Molndal	Swe. 2	32	12	8	20	43	....	....	....	....	....
1992-93	V. Frolunda	Swe.	20	1	5	6	8	....	....	....	....	....
1993-94	V. Frolunda	Swe.	39	20	10	30	18	4	1	1	2	....
1994-95	V. Frolunda	Swe.	22	7	11	18	22	....	....	....	....	....
1995-96ab	**Ottawa**	**NHL**	**82**	**26**	**35**	**61**	**28**	....	....	....	....	....
	NHL Totals		**82**	**26**	**35**	**61**	**28**	....	....	....	....	....

a NHL All-Rookie Team (1996)
b Won Calder Memorial Trophy (1996)

Played in NHL All-Star Game (1996)

ALINC, JAN (AH-lihnch, YAHN) PIT.

Center. Shoots left. 6'2", 190 lbs. Born, Most, Czech., May 27, 1972.
(Pittsburgh's 7th choice, 163rd overall, in 1992 Entry Draft).

			Regular Season					Playoffs				
Season	Club	Lea	GP	G	A	TP	PIM	GP	G	A	TP	PIM
1990-91	Litvinov	Czech.	7	1	1	2	....	....	....	....	....	....
1991-92	Litvinov	Czech.	45	21	16	37	24	....	....	....	....	....
1992-93	Litvinov	Czech.	36	16	13	29	....	....	....	....	....	....
1993-94	Litvinov	Czech.	36	16	25	41	....	4	1	4	5	....
1994-95	Litvinov	Czech.	42	16	32	48	50	4	3	2	5	2
1995-96	Litvinov	Czech.	38	15	29	44	....	16	2	5	7	....

ALLAN, CHAD VAN.

Defense. Shoots left. 6'1", 192 lbs. Born, Saskatoon, Sask., July 12, 1976.
(Vancouver's 4th choice, 65th overall, in 1994 Entry Draft).

			Regular Season					Playoffs				
Season	Club	Lea	GP	G	A	TP	PIM	GP	G	A	TP	PIM
1991-92	Saskatoon	WHL	1	0	0	0	2	....	....	....	....	....
1992-93	Saskatoon	WHL	69	2	10	12	67	9	0	0	0	25
1993-94	Saskatoon	WHL	70	6	16	22	123	16	1	1	2	21
1994-95a	Saskatoon	WHL	63	14	29	43	95	9	0	3	3	2
1995-96b	Saskatoon	WHL	57	8	30	38	106	4	0	0	0	5

a WHL East First All-Star Team (1995)
b WHL East Second All-Star Team (1996)

ALLEN, CHRIS FLA.

Defense. Shoots right. 6'2", 193 lbs. Born, Chatham, Ont., May 8, 1978.
(Florida's 2nd choice, 60th overall, in 1996 Entry Draft).

			Regular Season					Playoffs				
Season	Club	Lea	GP	G	A	TP	PIM	GP	G	A	TP	PIM
1994-95	Kingston	OHL	43	3	5	8	15	2	0	0	0	0
1995-96	Kingston	OHL	55	21	18	39	58	6	0	2	2	8

ALLEN, PETER PIT.

Defense. Shoots right. 6'2", 195 lbs. Born, Calgary, Alta., March 6, 1970.
(Boston's 1st choice, 24th overall, in 1991 Supplemental Draft).

			Regular Season					Playoffs				
Season	Club	Lea	GP	G	A	TP	PIM	GP	G	A	TP	PIM
1989-90	Yale	ECAC	26	2	4	6	16	....	....	....	....	....
1990-91	Yale	ECAC	17	0	6	6	14	....	....	....	....	....
1991-92	Yale	ECAC	26	5	13	18	26	....	....	....	....	....
1992-93	Yale	ECAC	30	3	15	18	32	....	....	....	....	....
1993-94	Richmond	ECHL	52	2	16	18	62	....	....	....	....	....
	P.E.I.	AHL	6	0	1	1	6	....	....	....	....	....
1994-95	Cdn. National	....	52	5	15	20	36	....	....	....	....	....
1995-96	**Pittsburgh**	**NHL**	**8**	**0**	**0**	**0**	**8**	....	....	....	....	....
	Cleveland	IHL	65	3	45	48	55	3	0	0	0	2
	NHL Totals		**8**	**0**	**0**	**0**	**8**	....	....	....	....	....

Signed as a free agent by **Pittsburgh**, August 10, 1995.

ALLISON, JAMIE CGY.

Defense. Shoots left. 6'1", 190 lbs. Born, Lindsay, Ont., May 13, 1975.
(Calgary's 2nd choice, 44th overall, in 1993 Entry Draft).

			Regular Season					Playoffs				
Season	Club	Lea	GP	G	A	TP	PIM	GP	G	A	TP	PIM
1991-92	Windsor	OHL	59	4	8	12	70	4	1	1	2	2
1992-93	Detroit	OHL	61	0	13	13	64	15	2	5	7	23
1993-94	Detroit	OHL	40	2	22	24	69	17	2	9	11	35
1994-95	Detroit	OHL	50	1	14	15	119	18	2	7	9	35
	Calgary	**NHL**	**1**	**0**	**0**	**0**	**0**	....	....	....	....	....
1995-96	Saint John	AHL	71	3	16	19	223	14	0	2	2	16
	NHL Totals		**1**	**0**	**0**	**0**	**0**	....	....	....	....	....

ALLISON, JASON WSH.

Center. Shoots right. 6'3", 205 lbs. Born, North York, Ont., May 29, 1975.
(Washington's 2nd choice, 17th overall, in 1993 Entry Draft).

			Regular Season					Playoffs				
Season	Club	Lea	GP	G	A	TP	PIM	GP	G	A	TP	PIM
1991-92	London	OHL	65	11	19	30	15	7	0	0	0	0
1992-93	London	OHL	66	42	76	118	50	12	7	13	20	8
1993-94	**Washington**	**NHL**	**2**	**0**	**1**	**1**	**0**	....	....	....	....	....
abc	London	OHL	56	55	87	*142	68	5	2	13	15	13
	Portland	AHL	....	....	....	....	....	6	2	1	3	0
1994-95	London	OHL	15	15	21	36	43	....	....	....	....	....
	Washington	**NHL**	**12**	**2**	**1**	**3**	**6**	....	....	....	....	....
	Portland	AHL	8	5	4	9	2	7	3	8	11	2
1995-96	**Washington**	**NHL**	**19**	**0**	**3**	**3**	**2**	....	....	....	....	....
	Portland	AHL	57	28	41	69	42	6	1	6	7	9
	NHL Totals		**33**	**2**	**5**	**7**	**8**	....	....	....	....	....

a OHL First All-Star Team (1994)
b Canadian Major Junior First All-Star Team (1994)
c Canadian Major Junior Player of the Year (1994)

ALVEY, MATT BOS.

Right wing. Shoots right. 6'5", 195 lbs. Born, Troy, NY, May 15, 1975.
(Boston's 2nd choice, 51st overall, in 1993 Entry Draft).

			Regular Season					Playoffs				
Season	Club	Lea	GP	G	A	TP	PIM	GP	G	A	TP	PIM
1993-94	Lake Superior	CCHA	41	6	8	14	16	....	....	....	....	....
1994-95	Lake Superior	CCHA	25	4	7	11	32	....	....	....	....	....
1995-96	Lake Superior	CCHA	39	14	8	22	40	....	....	....	....	....

AMBROSIO, JEFF ST.L.

Left wing. Shoots left. 6'1", 188 lbs. Born, Toronto, Ont., April 26, 1977.
(St. Louis' 4th choice, 127th overall, in 1995 Entry Draft).

			Regular Season					Playoffs				
Season	Club	Lea	GP	G	A	TP	PIM	GP	G	A	TP	PIM
1993-94	Belleville	OHL	59	13	17	30	18	11	1	0	1	6
1994-95	Belleville	OHL	47	10	10	20	10	16	1	7	8	8
1995-96	Belleville	OHL	14	8	8	16	6	....	....	....	....	....
	Kitchener	OHL	50	13	23	36	40	12	2	1	3	13

AMBROZIAK, PETER

Left wing. Shoots left. 6', 206 lbs. Born, Toronto, Ont., September 15, 1971.
(Buffalo's 4th choice, 72nd overall, in 1991 Entry Draft).

			Regular Season					Playoffs				
Season	Club	Lea	GP	G	A	TP	PIM	GP	G	A	TP	PIM
1990-91	Ottawa	OHL	62	30	32	62	56	17	15	9	24	24
1991-92	Ottawa	OHL	49	32	49	81	50	11	3	7	10	33
	Rochester	AHL	2	0	1	1	0	....	....	....	....	....
1992-93	Rochester	AHL	50	8	10	18	37	12	4	3	7	16
1993-94	Rochester	AHL	22	3	4	7	53	....	....	....	....	....
1994-95	Rochester	AHL	46	14	11	25	35	4	0	0	0	6
	Buffalo	**NHL**	**12**	**0**	**1**	**1**	**0**	....	....	....	....	....
1995-96	Albany	AHL	8	2	1	3	25	....	....	....	....	....
	Cornwall	AHL	50	9	15	24	42	8	1	1	2	4
	NHL Totals		**12**	**0**	**1**	**1**	**0**	....	....	....	....	....

AMONTE, TONY (eh-MAHN-tee) CHI.

Right wing. Shoots left. 6', 190 lbs. Born, Hingham, MA, August 2, 1970.
(NY Rangers' 3rd choice, 68th overall, in 1988 Entry Draft).

			Regular Season					Playoffs				
Season	Club	Lea	GP	G	A	TP	PIM	GP	G	A	TP	PIM
1989-90	Boston U.	H.E.	41	25	33	58	52	....	....	....	....	....
1990-91ab	Boston U.	H.E.	38	31	37	68	82	....	....	....	....	....
	NY Rangers	**NHL**	....	....	....	....	....	**2**	**0**	**2**	**2**	**2**
1991-92c	**NY Rangers**	**NHL**	**79**	**35**	**34**	**69**	**55**	**13**	**3**	**6**	**9**	**2**
1992-93	**NY Rangers**	**NHL**	**83**	**33**	**43**	**76**	**49**	....	....	....	....	....
1993-94	**NY Rangers**	**NHL**	**72**	**16**	**22**	**38**	**31**	....	....	....	....	....
	Chicago	**NHL**	**7**	**1**	**3**	**4**	**6**	**6**	**4**	**2**	**6**	**4**
1994-95	Fassa	Italy	14	22	16	38	10	....	....	....	....	....
	Chicago	**NHL**	**48**	**15**	**20**	**35**	**41**	**16**	**3**	**3**	**6**	**10**
1995-96	**Chicago**	**NHL**	**81**	**31**	**32**	**63**	**62**	**7**	**2**	**4**	**6**	**6**
	NHL Totals		**370**	**131**	**154**	**285**	**244**	**44**	**12**	**17**	**29**	**24**

a Hockey East Second All-Star Team (1991)
b NCAA Final Four All-Tournament Team (1991)
c NHL/Upper Deck All-Rookie Team (1992)

Traded to **Chicago** by **NY Rangers** with the rights to Matt Oates for Stephane Matteau and Brian Noonan, March 21, 1994.

ANDERSON, CRAIG NYR

Defense. Shoots left. 6'1", 171 lbs. Born, Minneapolis, MN, January 6, 1976.
(NY Rangers' 10th choice, 208th overall, in 1994 Entry Draft).

			Regular Season					Playoffs				
Season	Club	Lea	GP	G	A	TP	PIM	GP	G	A	TP	PIM
1994-95	U. Wisconsin	WCHA				DID NOT PLAY						
1995-96	U. Wisconsin	WCHA	16	1	3	4	2	....	....	....	....	....

ANDERSON, GLENN

Right wing. Shoots left. 6'1", 190 lbs. Born, Vancouver, B.C., October 2, 1960.
(Edmonton's 3rd choice, 69th overall, in 1979 Entry Draft).

			Regular Season					Playoffs				
Season	Club	Lea	GP	G	A	TP	PIM	GP	G	A	TP	PIM
1978-79	U. of Denver	WCHA	40	26	29	55	58	....	....	....	....	....
1979-80	Seattle	WHL	7	5	5	10	4	....	....	....	....	....
	Cdn. Olympic	....	49	21	21	42	46	....	....	....	....	....
1980-81	**Edmonton**	**NHL**	**58**	**30**	**23**	**53**	**24**	**9**	**5**	**7**	**12**	**12**
1981-82	**Edmonton**	**NHL**	**80**	**38**	**67**	**105**	**71**	**5**	**2**	**5**	**7**	**8**
1982-83	**Edmonton**	**NHL**	**72**	**48**	**56**	**104**	**70**	**16**	**10**	**10**	**20**	**32**
1983-84	**Edmonton**	**NHL**	**80**	**54**	**45**	**99**	**65**	**19**	**6**	**11**	**17**	**33** ♦
1984-85	**Edmonton**	**NHL**	**80**	**42**	**39**	**81**	**69**	**18**	**10**	**16**	**26**	**38** ♦
1985-86	**Edmonton**	**NHL**	**72**	**54**	**48**	**102**	**90**	**10**	**8**	**3**	**11**	**14**
1986-87	**Edmonton**	**NHL**	**80**	**35**	**38**	**73**	**65**	**21**	**14**	**13**	**27**	**59** ♦
1987-88	**Edmonton**	**NHL**	**80**	**38**	**50**	**88**	**58**	**19**	**9**	**16**	**25**	**49** ♦
1988-89	**Edmonton**	**NHL**	**79**	**16**	**48**	**64**	**93**	**7**	**1**	**2**	**3**	**8**
1989-90	**Edmonton**	**NHL**	**73**	**34**	**38**	**72**	**107**	**22**	**10**	**12**	**22**	**20** ♦
1990-91	**Edmonton**	**NHL**	**74**	**24**	**31**	**55**	**59**	**18**	**6**	**7**	**13**	**41**
1991-92	**Toronto**	**NHL**	**72**	**24**	**33**	**57**	**100**	....	....	....	....	....
1992-93	**Toronto**	**NHL**	**76**	**22**	**43**	**65**	**117**	**21**	**7**	**11**	**18**	**31**
1993-94	**Toronto**	**NHL**	**73**	**17**	**18**	**35**	**50**	....	....	....	....	....
	NY Rangers	**NHL**	**12**	**4**	**2**	**6**	**12**	**23**	**3**	**3**	**6**	**42** ♦
1994-95	Augsburg	Ger.	5	6	2	8	10	....	....	....	....	....
	Lukko	Fin.	4	1	1	2	0	....	....	....	....	....
	Cdn. National	....	26	11	8	19	40	....	....	....	....	....
	St. Louis	**NHL**	**36**	**12**	**14**	**26**	**37**	**6**	**1**	**1**	**2**	***49**
1995-96	Cdn. National	....	11	4	4	8	39	....	....	....	....	....
	Augsburg	Ger.	9	5	3	8	48	....	....	....	....	....
	Edmonton	**NHL**	**17**	**4**	**6**	**10**	**27**	....	....	....	....	....
	St. Louis	**NHL**	**15**	**2**	**2**	**4**	**6**	**11**	**1**	**4**	**5**	**6**
	NHL Totals		**1129**	**498**	**601**	**1099**	**1120**	**225**	**93**	**121**	**214**	**442**

Played in NHL All-Star Game (1984-86, 1988)

Traded to **Toronto** by **Edmonton** with Grant Fuhr and Craig Berube for Vincent Damphousse, Peter Ing, Scott Thornton, Luke Richardson, future considerations and cash, September 19, 1991. Traded to **NY Rangers** by **Toronto** with the rights to Scott Malone and Toronto's fourth round choice (Alexander Korobolin) in 1994 Entry Draft for Mike Gartner, March 21, 1994. Signed as a free agent by **St. Louis**, February 13, 1995. Signed as a free agent by **Vancouver**, January 22, 1996. Claimed on waivers by **Edmonton** from **Vancouver**, January 25, 1996. Claimed on waivers by **St. Louis** from **Edmonton**, March 12, 1996.

ANDERSON, SHAWN

Defense. Shoots left. 6'1", 200 lbs. Born, Montreal, Que., February 7, 1968.
(Buffalo's 1st choice, 5th overall, in 1986 Entry Draft).

			Regular Season					Playoffs				
Season	Club	Lea	GP	G	A	TP	PIM	GP	G	A	TP	PIM
1985-86	Maine	H.E.	16	5	8	13	22	....	....	....	....	....
	Cdn. National	....	33	2	6	8	16	....	....	....	....	....
1986-87	**Buffalo**	**NHL**	**41**	**2**	**11**	**13**	**23**	....	....	....	....	....
	Rochester	AHL	15	2	5	7	11	....	....	....	....	....
1987-88	**Buffalo**	**NHL**	**23**	**1**	**2**	**3**	**17**	....	....	....	....	....
	Rochester	AHL	22	5	16	21	19	6	0	0	0	0
1988-89	**Buffalo**	**NHL**	**33**	**2**	**10**	**12**	**18**	**5**	**0**	**1**	**1**	**4**
	Rochester	AHL	31	5	14	19	24	....	....	....	....	....
1989-90	**Buffalo**	**NHL**	**16**	**1**	**3**	**4**	**8**	....	....	....	....	....
	Rochester	AHL	39	2	16	18	41	9	1	0	1	4
1990-91	**Quebec**	**NHL**	**31**	**3**	**10**	**13**	**21**	....	....	....	....	....
	Halifax	AHL	4	0	1	1	2	....	....	....	....	....
1991-92	Weiswasser	Ger.	38	7	15	22	83	....	....	....	....	....
1992-93	**Washington**	**NHL**	**60**	**2**	**6**	**8**	**18**	**6**	**0**	**0**	**0**	**0**
	Baltimore	AHL	10	1	5	6	8	....	....	....	....	....
1993-94	**Washington**	**NHL**	**50**	**0**	**9**	**9**	**12**	**8**	**1**	**0**	**1**	**12**
1994-95	**Philadelphia**	**NHL**	**1**	**0**	**0**	**0**	**0**	....	....	....	....	....
	Hershey	AHL	31	9	21	30	18	6	2	3	5	19
1995-96	Milwaukee	IHL	79	22	39	61	68	5	0	7	7	0
	NHL Totals		**255**	**11**	**51**	**62**	**117**	**19**	**1**	**1**	**2**	**16**

Traded to **Washington** by **Buffalo** for Bill Houlder, September 30, 1990. Claimed by **Quebec** from **Washington** in NHL Waiver Draft, October 1, 1990. Traded to **Winnipeg** by **Quebec** for Sergei Kharin, October 22, 1991. Traded to **Washington** by **Winnipeg** for future considerations, October 23, 1991. Signed as a free agent by **Philadelphia**, August 16, 1994.

ANDERSSON, MIKAEL (AN-duhr-suhn) T.B.

Left wing. Shoots left. 5'11", 185 lbs. Born, Malmo, Sweden, May 10, 1966.
(Buffalo's 1st choice, 18th overall, in 1984 Entry Draft).

			Regular Season					Playoffs				
Season	Club	Lea	GP	G	A	TP	PIM	GP	G	A	TP	PIM
1982-83	V. Frolunda	Swe.	1	1	0	1	0	....	....	....	....	....
1983-84	V. Frolunda	Swe.	18	0	3	3	6	....	....	....	....	....
1984-85	V. Frolunda	Swe. 2	30	16	11	27	18	6	3	2	5	2
1985-86	**Buffalo**	**NHL**	**32**	**1**	**9**	**10**	**4**	....	....	....	....	....
	Rochester	AHL	20	10	4	14	6	....	....	....	....	....
1986-87	**Buffalo**	**NHL**	**16**	**0**	**3**	**3**	**0**	....	....	....	....	....
	Rochester	AHL	42	6	20	26	14	9	1	2	3	2
1987-88	**Buffalo**	**NHL**	**37**	**3**	**20**	**23**	**10**	**1**	**1**	**0**	**1**	**0**
	Rochester	AHL	35	12	24	36	16	....	....	....	....	....
1988-89	**Buffalo**	**NHL**	**14**	**0**	**1**	**1**	**4**	....	....	....	....	....
	Rochester	AHL	56	18	33	51	12	....	....	....	....	....
1989-90	**Hartford**	**NHL**	**50**	**13**	**24**	**37**	**6**	**5**	**0**	**3**	**3**	**2**
1990-91	**Hartford**	**NHL**	**41**	**4**	**7**	**11**	**8**	....	....	....	....	....
	Springfield	AHL	26	7	22	29	10	18	*10	8	18	12
1991-92	**Hartford**	**NHL**	**74**	**18**	**29**	**47**	**14**	**7**	**0**	**2**	**2**	**6**
1992-93	**Tampa Bay**	**NHL**	**77**	**16**	**11**	**27**	**14**	....	....	....	....	....
1993-94	**Tampa Bay**	**NHL**	**76**	**13**	**12**	**25**	**23**	....	....	....	....	....
1994-95	V. Frolunda	Swe.	7	1	0	1	31	....	....	....	....	....
	Tampa Bay	**NHL**	**36**	**4**	**7**	**11**	**4**	....	....	....	....	....
1995-96	**Tampa Bay**	**NHL**	**64**	**8**	**11**	**19**	**2**	**6**	**1**	**1**	**2**	**0**
	NHL Totals		**517**	**80**	**134**	**214**	**89**	**19**	**2**	**6**	**8**	**8**

Claimed by **Hartford** from **Buffalo** in NHL Waiver Draft, October 2, 1989. Signed as a free agent by **Tampa Bay**, June 29, 1992.

ANDERSSON, NIKLAS (AN-duhr-suhn) NYI

Left wing. Shoots left. 5'9", 175 lbs. Born, Kungalv, Sweden, May 20, 1971.
(Quebec's 5th choice, 68th overall, in 1989 Entry Draft).

			Regular Season					Playoffs				
Season	Club	Lea	GP	G	A	TP	PIM	GP	G	A	TP	PIM
1987-88	V. Frolunda	Swe. 2	15	5	5	10	6	8	6	4	10	4
1988-89	V. Frolunda	Swe. 2	30	13	24	37	24	....	....	....	....	....
1989-90	V. Frolunda	Swe.	38	10	21	31	14	....	....	....	....	....
1990-91	V. Frolunda	Swe.	22	6	10	16	16	....	....	....	....	....
1991-92	Halifax	AHL	57	8	26	34	41	....	....	....	....	....
1992-93	**Quebec**	**NHL**	**3**	**0**	**1**	**1**	**2**	....	....	....	....	....
	Halifax	AHL	76	32	50	82	42	....	....	....	....	....
1993-94	Cornwall	AHL	42	18	34	52	8	....	....	....	....	....
1994-95	Denver	IHL	66	22	39	61	28	15	8	13	21	10
1995-96	**NY Islanders**	**NHL**	**47**	**14**	**12**	**26**	**12**	....	....	....	....	....
	Utah	IHL	30	13	22	35	25	....	....	....	....	....
	NHL Totals		**50**	**14**	**13**	**27**	**14**	....	....	....	....	....

Signed as a free agent by **NY Islanders**, July 15, 1994.

ANDERSSON-JUNKKA, JONAS PIT.

Defense. Shoots right. 6'2", 170 lbs. Born, Kiruna, Sweden, May 4, 1975.
(Pittsburgh's 4th choice, 104th overall, in 1993 Entry Draft).

			Regular Season					Playoffs				
Season	Club	Lea	GP	G	A	TP	PIM	GP	G	A	TP	PIM
1991-92	Kiruna	Swe. 2	1	0	0	0	0	....	....	....	....	....
1992-93	Kiruna	Swe. 2	30	3	7	10	32	....	....	....	....	....
1993-94	Kiruna	Swe. 2	32	6	10	16	84	....	....	....	....	....
1994-95	V. Frolunda	Swe.	19	0	2	2	2	....	....	....	....	....
1995-96	V. Frolunda	Swe.	31	3	1	4	20	13	1	0	1	6

ANDREYCHUK, DAVE (AN-druh-chuhk) N.J.

Left wing. Shoots right. 6'3", 220 lbs. Born, Hamilton, Ont., September 29, 1963.
(Buffalo's 3rd choice, 16th overall, in 1982 Entry Draft).

			Regular Season					Playoffs				
Season	Club	Lea	GP	G	A	TP	PIM	GP	G	A	TP	PIM
1980-81	Oshawa	OHA	67	22	22	44	80	10	3	2	5	20
1981-82	Oshawa	OHL	67	57	43	100	71	3	1	4	5	16
1982-83	**Buffalo**	**NHL**	**43**	**14**	**23**	**37**	**16**	**4**	**1**	**0**	**1**	**4**
	Oshawa	OHL	14	8	24	32	6	....	....	....	....	....
1983-84	**Buffalo**	**NHL**	**78**	**38**	**42**	**80**	**42**	**2**	**0**	**1**	**1**	**2**
1984-85	**Buffalo**	**NHL**	**64**	**31**	**30**	**61**	**54**	**5**	**4**	**2**	**6**	**4**
1985-86	**Buffalo**	**NHL**	**80**	**36**	**51**	**87**	**61**	....	....	....	....	....
1986-87	**Buffalo**	**NHL**	**77**	**25**	**48**	**73**	**46**	....	....	....	....	....
1987-88	**Buffalo**	**NHL**	**80**	**30**	**48**	**78**	**112**	**6**	**2**	**4**	**6**	**0**
1988-89	**Buffalo**	**NHL**	**56**	**28**	**24**	**52**	**40**	**5**	**0**	**3**	**3**	**0**
1989-90	**Buffalo**	**NHL**	**73**	**40**	**42**	**82**	**42**	**6**	**2**	**5**	**7**	**2**
1990-91	**Buffalo**	**NHL**	**80**	**36**	**33**	**69**	**32**	**6**	**2**	**2**	**4**	**8**
1991-92	**Buffalo**	**NHL**	**80**	**41**	**50**	**91**	**71**	**7**	**1**	**3**	**4**	**12**
1992-93	**Buffalo**	**NHL**	**52**	**29**	**32**	**61**	**48**	....	....	....	....	....
	Toronto	**NHL**	**31**	**25**	**13**	**38**	**8**	**21**	**12**	**7**	**19**	**35**
1993-94	**Toronto**	**NHL**	**83**	**53**	**46**	**99**	**98**	**18**	**5**	**5**	**10**	**16**
1994-95	**Toronto**	**NHL**	**48**	**22**	**16**	**38**	**34**	**7**	**3**	**2**	**5**	**25**
1995-96	**Toronto**	**NHL**	**61**	**20**	**24**	**44**	**54**	....	....	....	....	....
	New Jersey	**NHL**	**15**	**8**	**5**	**13**	**10**	....	....	....	....	....
	NHL Totals		**1001**	**476**	**527**	**1003**	**768**	**87**	**32**	**34**	**66**	**108**

Played in NHL All-Star Game (1990, 1994)

Traded to **Toronto** by **Buffalo** with Daren Puppa and Buffalo's first round choice (Kenny Jonsson) in 1993 Entry Draft for Grant Fuhr and Toronto's fifth round choice (Kevin Popp) in 1995 Entry Draft, February 2, 1993. Traded to **New Jersey** by **Toronto** for New Jersey's second round choice (Marek Posmyk) in 1996 Entry Draft and a conditional choice in 1998 or 1999 Entry Draft, March 13, 1996.

ANDRUSAK, GREG (AN-druh-sak)

Defense. Shoots right. 6'1", 190 lbs. Born, Cranbrook, B.C., November 14, 1969.
(Pittsburgh's 5th choice, 88th overall, in 1988 Entry Draft).

			Regular Season					Playoffs				
Season	Club	Lea	GP	G	A	TP	PIM	GP	G	A	TP	PIM
1987-88	Minn.-Duluth	WCHA	37	4	5	9	42	....	....	....	....	....
1988-89	Minn.-Duluth	WCHA	35	4	8	12	74	....	....	....	....	....
	Cdn. National	....	2	0	0	0	0	....	....	....	....	....
1989-90	Minn.-Duluth	WCHA	35	5	29	34	74	....	....	....	....	....
1990-91	Cdn. National	....	53	4	11	15	34	....	....	....	....	....
1991-92a	Minn.-Duluth	WCHA	36	7	27	34	125	....	....	....	....	....
1992-93	Cleveland	IHL	55	3	22	25	78	2	0	0	0	2
	Muskegon	ColHL	2	0	3	3	7	....	....	....	....	....
1993-94	**Pittsburgh**	**NHL**	**3**	**0**	**0**	**0**	**2**	....	....	....	....	....
	Cleveland	IHL	69	13	26	39	109	....	....	....	....	....
1994-95	Detroit	IHL	37	5	26	31	50	....	....	....	....	....
	Pittsburgh	**NHL**	**7**	**0**	**4**	**4**	**6**	....	....	....	....	....
	Cleveland	IHL	8	0	8	8	14	....	....	....	....	....
1995-96	**Pittsburgh**	**NHL**	**2**	**0**	**0**	**0**	**0**	....	....	....	....	....
	Detroit	IHL	58	6	30	36	128	....	....	....	....	....
	Minnesota	IHL	5	0	4	4	8	....	....	....	....	....
	NHL Totals		**12**	**0**	**4**	**4**	**8**	....	....	....	....	....

a WCHA First All-Star Team (1992)

ANGER, NIKLAS MTL.

Right wing. Shoots left. 6'1", 185 lbs. Born, Gavle, Sweden, July 31, 1977.
(Montreal's 5th choice, 112th overall, in 1995 Entry Draft).

			Regular Season					Playoffs				
Season	Club	Lea	GP	G	A	TP	PIM	GP	G	A	TP	PIM
1994-95	Djurgarden	Swe. Jr.	30	14	12	26	26	....	....	....	....	....
	Djurgarden	Swe.	1	0	0	0	0	....	....	....	....	....
1995-96	Djurgarden	Swe.	10	0	0	0	2	....	....	....	....	....

ANISIMOV, ARTEM (ah-NIH-sih-mohv) PHI.

Defense. Shoots left. 6'1", 187 lbs. Born, Kazan, USSR, July 27, 1976.
(Philadelphia's 1st choice, 62nd overall, in 1994 Entry Draft).

			Regular Season					Playoffs				
Season	Club	Lea	GP	G	A	TP	PIM	GP	G	A	TP	PIM
1993-94	Kazan	CIS	38	0	1	1	12	5	0	0	0	0
1994-95	Kazan	CIS	46	3	2	5	55	1	0	0	0	0
1995-96	Kazan	CIS	30	0	2	2	8	....	....	....	....	....

ANTIPOV, VLADIMIR (an-TIH-pahv) TOR.

Right wing. Shoots left. 5'11", 180 lbs. Born, Appatity, USSR, January 17, 1978.
(Toronto's 6th choice, 103rd overall, in 1996 Entry Draft).

			Regular Season					Playoffs				
Season	Club	Lea	GP	G	A	TP	PIM	GP	G	A	TP	PIM
1995-96	Yaroslavl 2	CIS 2	39	14	11	25	....	....	....	....	....	....

ANTONIN, JIRI EDM.

Defense. Shoots left. 6'3", 207 lbs. Born, Pardubice, Czech., November 15, 1975.
(Edmonton's 8th choice, 213th overall, in 1995 Entry Draft).

			Regular Season					Playoffs				
Season	Club	Lea	GP	G	A	TP	PIM	GP	G	A	TP	PIM
1995-96	Pardubice	Czech.	20	1	1	2	....	....	....	....	....	....

ANTOSKI, SHAWN (an-TAW-skee) PIT.

Left wing. Shoots left. 6'4", 235 lbs. Born, Brantford, Ont., March 25, 1970.
(Vancouver's 2nd choice, 18th overall, in 1990 Entry Draft).

			Regular Season					Playoffs				
Season	Club	Lea	GP	G	A	TP	PIM	GP	G	A	TP	PIM
1987-88	North Bay	OHL	52	3	4	7	163	....	....	....	....	....
1988-89	North Bay	OHL	57	6	21	27	201	9	5	3	8	24
1989-90	North Bay	OHL	59	25	31	56	201	5	1	2	3	17
1990-91	**Vancouver**	**NHL**	**2**	**0**	**0**	**0**	**0**	....	....	....	....	....
	Milwaukee	IHL	62	17	7	24	330	5	1	2	3	10
1991-92	**Vancouver**	**NHL**	**4**	**0**	**0**	**0**	**29**	....	....	....	....	....
	Milwaukee	IHL	52	17	16	33	346	5	2	0	2	20
1992-93	**Vancouver**	**NHL**	**2**	**0**	**0**	**0**	**0**	....	....	....	....	....
	Hamilton	AHL	41	3	4	7	172	....	....	....	....	....
1993-94	**Vancouver**	**NHL**	**55**	**1**	**2**	**3**	**190**	**16**	**0**	**1**	**1**	**36**
1994-95	**Vancouver**	**NHL**	**7**	**0**	**0**	**0**	**46**	....	....	....	....	....
	Philadelphia	**NHL**	**25**	**0**	**0**	**0**	**61**	**13**	**0**	**1**	**1**	**10**
1995-96	**Philadelphia**	**NHL**	**64**	**1**	**3**	**4**	**204**	**7**	**1**	**1**	**2**	**28**
	NHL Totals		**159**	**2**	**5**	**7**	**530**	**36**	**1**	**3**	**4**	**74**

Traded to **Philadelphia** by **Vancouver** for Josef Beranek, February 15, 1995. Signed as a free agent by **Pittsburgh**, July 31, 1996.

APPEL, FRANK (AHP-pehl) CGY.

Defense. Shoots left. 6'4", 210 lbs. Born, Dusseldorf, West Germany, May 12, 1976.
(Calgary's 7th choice, 123rd overall, in 1994 Entry Draft).

			Regular Season					Playoffs				
Season	Club	Lea	GP	G	A	TP	PIM	GP	G	A	TP	PIM
1993-94	Dusseldorf	Ger.	4	0	0	0	4	....	....	....	....	....
1994-95	Eisbaren Berlin	Ger.	12	0	0	0	4	....	....	....	....	....
1995-96	Moncton	QMJHL	38	3	10	13	77	....	....	....	....	....

ARCHAMBAULT, DANIEL MTL.

Defense. Shoots left. 6', 202 lbs. Born, Ste-Agathe, Que., March 28, 1978.
(Montreal's 6th choice, 127th overall, in 1996 Entry Draft).

			Regular Season					Playoffs				
Season	Club	Lea	GP	G	A	TP	PIM	GP	G	A	TP	PIM
1994-95	Val d'Or	QMJHL	54	3	1	4	165	....	....	....	....	....
1995-96	Val d'Or	QMJHL	43	1	12	13	254	13	1	1	2	74

ARCHIBALD, DAVE

Center/Left wing. Shoots left. 6'1", 210 lbs. Born, Chilliwack, B.C., April 14, 1969.
(Minnesota's 1st choice, 6th overall, in 1987 Entry Draft).

			Regular Season					Playoffs				
Season	Club	Lea	GP	G	A	TP	PIM	GP	G	A	TP	PIM
1984-85	Portland	WHL	47	7	11	18	10	3	0	2	2	0
1985-86	Portland	WHL	70	29	35	64	56	15	6	7	13	11
1986-87	Portland	WHL	65	50	57	107	40	20	10	18	28	11
1987-88	**Minnesota**	**NHL**	**78**	**13**	**20**	**33**	**26**	....	....	....	....	....
1988-89	**Minnesota**	**NHL**	**72**	**14**	**19**	**33**	**14**	**5**	**0**	**1**	**1**	**0**
1989-90	**Minnesota**	**NHL**	**12**	**1**	**5**	**6**	**6**	....	....	....	....	....
	NY Rangers	**NHL**	**19**	**2**	**3**	**5**	**6**	....	....	....	....	....
	Flint	IHL	41	14	38	52	16	4	3	2	5	0
1990-91	Cdn. National	....	29	19	12	31	20	....	....	....	....	....
1991-92	Cdn. National	....	58	20	43	63	64	....	....	....	....	....
	Cdn. Olympic	....	8	7	1	8	18	....	....	....	....	....
	Bolzano	....	5	4	3	7	16	7	8	5	13	7
1992-93	Binghamton	AHL	8	6	3	9	10	....	....	....	....	....
	Ottawa	**NHL**	**44**	**9**	**6**	**15**	**32**	....	....	....	....	....
1993-94	**Ottawa**	**NHL**	**33**	**10**	**8**	**18**	**14**	....	....	....	....	....
1994-95	**Ottawa**	**NHL**	**14**	**2**	**2**	**4**	**19**	....	....	....	....	....
1995-96	**Ottawa**	**NHL**	**44**	**6**	**4**	**10**	**18**	....	....	....	....	....
	Utah	IHL	19	1	4	5	10	....	....	....	....	....
	NHL Totals		**316**	**57**	**67**	**124**	**135**	**5**	**0**	**1**	**1**	**0**

Traded to **NY Rangers** by **Minnesota** for Jayson More, November 1, 1989. Traded to **Ottawa** by **NY Rangers** for Ottawa's fifth round choice (later traded to Los Angeles — Los Angeles selected Frederick Beaubien) in 1993 Entry Draft, November 5, 1992.

ARMSTRONG, BILL H.

Center. Shoots left. 6'2", 195 lbs. Born, London, Ont., June 25, 1966.

			Regular Season					Playoffs				
Season	Club	Lea	GP	G	A	TP	PIM	GP	G	A	TP	PIM
1986-87	W. Michigan	CCHA	43	13	20	33	86	....	....	....	....	....
1987-88	W. Michigan	CCHA	41	22	17	39	88	....	....	....	....	....
1988-89	W. Michigan	CCHA	40	23	19	42	97	....	....	....	....	....
1989-90	Hershey	AHL	58	10	6	16	99	....	....	....	....	....
1990-91	**Philadelphia**	**NHL**	**1**	**0**	**1**	**1**	**0**	....	....	....	....	....
	Hershey	AHL	70	36	27	63	150	6	2	8	10	19
1991-92	Hershey	AHL	64	26	22	48	186	6	2	2	4	6
1992-93	Cincinnati	IHL	42	14	11	25	99	....	....	....	....	....
	Utica	AHL	32	18	21	39	60	....	....	....	....	....
1993-94	Albany	AHL	74	32	50	82	188	....	....	....	....	....
1994-95	Albany	AHL	76	32	47	79	115	13	6	5	11	20
1995-96	Albany	AHL	10	3	4	7	22	....	....	....	....	....
	Indianapolis	IHL	12	4	5	9	13	....	....	....	....	....
	Detroit	IHL	54	34	25	59	66	12	6	2	8	15
	NHL Totals		**1**	**0**	**1**	**1**	**0**	....	....	....	....	....

Signed as a free agent by **Philadelphia**, May 16, 1989. Signed as a free agent by **New Jersey**, March 21, 1993. Traded to **Chicago** by **New Jersey** with Michael Vukonich for Darin Kimble, November 1, 1995.

ARMSTRONG, CHRIS FLA.

Defense. Shoots left. 6', 198 lbs. Born, Regina, Sask., June 26, 1975.
(Florida's 3rd choice, 57th overall, in 1993 Entry Draft).

			Regular Season					Playoffs				
Season	Club	Lea	GP	G	A	TP	PIM	GP	G	A	TP	PIM
1991-92	Moose Jaw	WHL	43	2	7	9	19	4	0	0	0	0
1992-93	Moose Jaw	WHL	67	9	35	44	104	....	....	....	....	....
1993-94ab	Moose Jaw	WHL	64	13	55	68	54	....	....	....	....	....
	Cincinnati	IHL	1	0	0	0	0	10	1	3	4	2
1994-95c	Moose Jaw	WHL	66	17	54	71	61	10	2	12	14	22
	Cincinnati	IHL	....	....	....	....	....	9	1	3	4	10
1995-96	Carolina	AHL	78	9	33	42	65	....	....	....	....	....

a WHL East First All-Star Team (1994)
b Canadian Major Junior Second All-Star Team (1994)
c WHL East Second All-Star Team (1995)

ARMSTRONG, DEREK NYI

Center. Shoots right. 5'11", 188 lbs. Born, Ottawa, Ont., April 23, 1973.
(NY Islanders' 5th choice, 128th overall, in 1992 Entry Draft).

			Regular Season					Playoffs				
Season	Club	Lea	GP	G	A	TP	PIM	GP	G	A	TP	PIM
1991-92	Sudbury	OHL	66	31	54	85	22	9	2	2	4	2
1992-93	Sudbury	OHL	66	44	62	106	56	14	9	10	19	26
1993-94	**NY Islanders**	**NHL**	**1**	**0**	**0**	**0**	**0**	....	....	....	....	....
	Salt Lake	IHL	76	23	35	58	61	....	....	....	....	....
1994-95	Denver	IHL	59	13	18	31	65	6	0	2	2	0
1995-96	**NY Islanders**	**NHL**	**19**	**1**	**3**	**4**	**14**	....	....	....	....	....
	Worcester	AHL	51	11	15	26	33	4	2	1	3	0
	NHL Totals		**20**	**1**	**3**	**4**	**14**	....	....	....	....	....

ARNOTT, JASON (AHR-nawt) EDM.

Center. Shoots right. 6'3", 220 lbs. Born, Collingwood, Ont., October 11, 1974.
(Edmonton's 1st choice, 7th overall, in 1993 Entry Draft).

			Regular Season					Playoffs				
Season	Club	Lea	GP	G	A	TP	PIM	GP	G	A	TP	PIM
1991-92	Oshawa	OHL	57	9	15	24	12	....	....	....	....	....
1992-93	Oshawa	OHL	56	41	57	98	74	13	9	9	18	20
1993-94a	**Edmonton**	**NHL**	**78**	**33**	**35**	**68**	**104**	....	....	....	....	....
1994-95	**Edmonton**	**NHL**	**42**	**15**	**22**	**37**	**128**	....	....	....	....	....
1995-96	**Edmonton**	**NHL**	**64**	**28**	**31**	**59**	**87**	....	....	....	....	....
	NHL Totals		**184**	**76**	**88**	**164**	**319**	....	....	....	....	....

a NHL/Upper Deck All-Rookie Team (1994)

ASHAM, ARRON MTL.

Right wing. Shoots right. 5'10", 170 lbs. Born, Portage La Prairie, Man., April 13, 1978.
(Montreal's 3rd choice, 71st overall, in 1996 Entry Draft).

			Regular Season					Playoffs				
Season	Club	Lea	GP	G	A	TP	PIM	GP	G	A	TP	PIM
1994-95	Red Deer	WHL	62	11	16	27	126	....	....	....	....	....
1995-96	Red Deer	WHL	70	32	45	77	174	10	6	3	9	20

ASTLEY, MARK

Defense. Shoots left. 5'11", 185 lbs. Born, Calgary, Alta., March 30, 1969.
(Buffalo's 9th choice, 194th overall, in 1989 Entry Draft).

			Regular Season					Playoffs				
Season	Club	Lea	GP	G	A	TP	PIM	GP	G	A	TP	PIM
1988-89	Lake Superior	CCHA	42	3	12	15	26	....	....	....	....	....
1989-90	Lake Superior	CCHA	43	7	25	32	29	....	....	....	....	....
1990-91a	Lake Superior	CCHA	45	19	27	46	50	....	....	....	....	....
1991-92bcd	Lake Superior	CCHA	39	11	36	47	65	....	....	....	....	....
	Cdn. National	....	11	2	2	4	6	....	....	....	....	....
1992-93	Lugano	Switz.	30	10	12	22	57	....	....	....	....	....
	Cdn. National	....	22	4	14	18	14	....	....	....	....	....
1993-94	Ambri	Switz.	23	5	9	14	17	....	....	....	....	....
	Cdn. National	....	13	4	8	12	6	....	....	....	....	....
	Cdn. Olympic	....	8	0	1	1	4	....	....	....	....	....
	Buffalo	**NHL**	**1**	**0**	**0**	**0**	**0**	....	....	....	....	....
1994-95	Rochester	AHL	46	5	24	29	49	3	0	2	2	2
	Buffalo	**NHL**	**14**	**2**	**1**	**3**	**12**	**2**	**0**	**0**	**0**	**0**
1995-96	**Buffalo**	**NHL**	**60**	**2**	**18**	**20**	**80**	....	....	....	....	....
	NHL Totals		**75**	**4**	**19**	**23**	**92**	**2**	**0**	**0**	**0**	**0**

a CCHA Second All-Star Team (1991)
b CCHA First All-Star Team (1992)
c NCAA West First All-American Team (1992)
d NCAA All-Tournament Team (1992)

AUBIN, SERGE — PIT.

Center. Shoots left. 6'1", 194 lbs. Born, Val d'Or, Que., February 15, 1975.
(Pittsburgh's 9th choice, 161st overall, in 1994 Entry Draft).

			Regular Season					Playoffs				
Season	Club	Lea	GP	G	A	TP	PIM	GP	G	A	TP	PIM
1992-93	Drummondville	QMJHL	65	16	34	50	30	8	0	1	1	16
1993-94	Granby	QMJHL	63	42	32	74	80	7	2	3	5	8
1994-95	Granby	QMJHL	60	37	73	110	55	11	8	15	23	4
1995-96	Hampton Rds.	ECHL	62	24	62	86	74	3	1	4	5	10
	Cleveland	IHL	2	0	0	0	0	2	0	0	0	0

AUCOIN, ADRIAN (oh-KWEHN) — VAN.

Defense. Shoots right. 6'1", 194 lbs. Born, Ottawa, Ont., July 3, 1973.
(Vancouver's 7th choice, 117th overall, in 1992 Entry Draft).

			Regular Season					Playoffs				
Season	Club	Lea	GP	G	A	TP	PIM	GP	G	A	TP	PIM
1991-92	Boston U.	H.E.	32	2	10	12	60	....	....	....	....	....
1992-93	Cdn. National	....	42	8	10	18	71	....	....	....	....	....
1993-94	Cdn. National	....	59	5	12	17	80	....	....	....	....	....
	Cdn. Olympic	....	4	0	0	0	2	....	....	....	....	....
	Hamilton	AHL	13	1	2	3	19	4	0	2	2	6
1994-95	Syracuse	AHL	71	13	18	31	52	....	....	....	....	....
	Vancouver	**NHL**	**1**	**1**	**0**	**1**	**0**	**4**	**1**	**0**	**1**	**0**
1995-96	**Vancouver**	**NHL**	**49**	**4**	**14**	**18**	**34**	**6**	**0**	**0**	**0**	**2**
	Syracuse	AHL	29	5	13	18	47	....	....	....	....	....
	NHL Totals		**50**	**5**	**14**	**19**	**34**	**10**	**1**	**0**	**1**	**2**

AUDET, PHILIPPE — DET.

Left wing. Shoots left. 6'2", 175 lbs. Born, Ottawa, Ont., June 4, 1977.
(Detroit's 2nd choice, 52nd overall, in 1995 Entry Draft).

			Regular Season					Playoffs				
Season	Club	Lea	GP	G	A	TP	PIM	GP	G	A	TP	PIM
1994-95	Granby	QMJHL	62	19	17	36	93	13	2	5	7	10
1995-96a	Granby	QMJHL	67	40	43	83	162	21	12	18	30	32

a Memorial Cup All-Star Team (1996)

AUDETTE, DONALD (aw-DEHT) — BUF.

Right wing. Shoots right. 5'8", 175 lbs. Born, Laval, Que., September 23, 1969.
(Buffalo's 8th choice, 183rd overall, in 1989 Entry Draft).

			Regular Season					Playoffs				
Season	Club	Lea	GP	G	A	TP	PIM	GP	G	A	TP	PIM
1986-87	Laval	QMJHL	66	17	22	39	36	14	2	6	8	10
1987-88	Laval	QMJHL	63	48	61	109	56	14	7	12	19	20
1988-89a	Laval	QMJHL	70	76	85	161	123	17	17	12	29	43
1989-90bc	Rochester	AHL	70	42	46	88	78	15	9	8	17	29
	Buffalo	**NHL**	....	....	....	....	....	**2**	**0**	**0**	**0**	**0**
1990-91	**Buffalo**	**NHL**	**8**	**4**	**3**	**7**	**4**	....	....	....	....	....
	Rochester	AHL	5	4	0	4	2	....	....	....	....	....
1991-92	**Buffalo**	**NHL**	**63**	**31**	**17**	**48**	**75**	....	....	....	....	....
1992-93	**Buffalo**	**NHL**	**44**	**12**	**7**	**19**	**51**	**8**	**2**	**2**	**4**	**6**
	Rochester	AHL	6	8	4	12	10	....	....	....	....	....
1993-94	**Buffalo**	**NHL**	**77**	**29**	**30**	**59**	**41**	**7**	**0**	**1**	**1**	**6**
1994-95	**Buffalo**	**NHL**	**46**	**24**	**13**	**37**	**27**	**5**	**1**	**1**	**2**	**4**
1995-96	**Buffalo**	**NHL**	**23**	**12**	**13**	**25**	**18**	....	....	....	....	....
	NHL Totals		**261**	**112**	**83**	**195**	**216**	**22**	**3**	**4**	**7**	**16**

a QMJHL First All-Star Team (1989)
b AHL First All-Star Team (1990)
c Won Dudley "Red" Garret Memorial Trophy (Top Rookie - AHL) (1990)

AUGER, VINCENT (OH-zhay, VIHN-cehnt) — COL.

Center. Shoots left. 5'10", 175 lbs. Born, Quebec, Que., March 7, 1975.
(Quebec's 11th choice, 231st overall, in 1993 Entry Draft).

			Regular Season					Playoffs				
Season	Club	Lea	GP	G	A	TP	PIM	GP	G	A	TP	PIM
1993-94	Cornell	ECAC	29	11	13	24	33	....	....	....	....	....
1994-95					DID NOT PLAY							
1995-96	Cornell	ECAC	23	5	15	20	22	....	....	....	....	....

AUGUSTA, PATRIK (ah-GOOS-tuh, pa-TREEK)

Right wing. Shoots left. 5'10", 170 lbs. Born, Jihlava, Czech., November 13, 1969.
(Toronto's 8th choice, 149th overall, in 1992 Entry Draft).

			Regular Season					Playoffs				
Season	Club	Lea	GP	G	A	TP	PIM	GP	G	A	TP	PIM
1988-89	Dukla Jihlava	Czech.	15	3	1	4	4	....	....	....	....	....
1989-90	Dukla Jihlava	Czech.	46	12	12	24	....	....	....	....	....	....
1990-91	Dukla Jihlava	Czech.	51	20	23	43	....	....	....	....	....	....
1991-92	Dukla Jihlava	Czech.	42	16	16	32	26	....	....	....	....	....
1992-93	St. John's	AHL	75	32	45	77	74	8	3	3	6	23
1993-94	**Toronto**	**NHL**	**2**	**0**	**0**	**0**	**0**	....	....	....	....	....
a	St. John's	AHL	77	*53	43	96	105	11	4	8	12	4
1994-95	St. John's	AHL	71	37	32	69	98	4	2	0	2	7
1995-96	Los Angeles	IHL	79	34	51	85	83	....	....	....	....	....
	NHL Totals		**2**	**0**	**0**	**0**	**0**	....	....	....	....	....

a AHL Second All-Star Team (1994)

AXELSSON, PER-JOHAN — BOS.

Left wing. Shoots left. 6'1", 174 lbs. Born, Kungalv, Sweden, February 26, 1975.
(Boston's 7th choice, 177th overall, in 1995 Entry Draft).

			Regular Season					Playoffs				
Season	Club	Lea	GP	G	A	TP	PIM	GP	G	A	TP	PIM
1993-94	V. Frolunda	Swe.	11	0	0	0	4	4	0	0	0	0
1994-95	V. Frolunda	Swe.	8	2	1	3	6	....	....	....	....	....
1995-96	V. Frolunda	Swe.	36	15	5	20	10	13	3	0	3	10

BABARIKO, JEVGENI (boh-bah-RIH-koh) — VAN.

Center. Shoots left. 6'1", 183 lbs. Born, Gorky, USSR, March 3, 1974.
(Vancouver's 6th choice, 176th overall, in 1993 Entry Draft).

			Regular Season					Playoffs				
Season	Club	Lea	GP	G	A	TP	PIM	GP	G	A	TP	PIM
1991-92	Torpedo Niz.	CIS	17	5	0	5	4	....	....	....	....	....
1992-93	Torpedo Niz.	CIS	13	1	0	1	4	....	....	....	....	....
1993-94	Torpedo Niz.	CIS	44	3	5	8	12	....	....	....	....	....
1994-95	Torpedo Niz.	CIS	41	10	4	14	12	5	0	2	2	0
1995-96	Torpedo Niz.	CIS	49	16	18	34	20	3	2	1	3	2

BABENKO, YURI (bah-BEHN-koh) — COL.

Center. Shoots left. 6', 185 lbs. Born, Penza, USSR, January 2, 1978.
(Colorado's 2nd choice, 51st overall, in 1996 Entry Draft).

			Regular Season					Playoffs				
Season	Club	Lea	GP	G	A	TP	PIM	GP	G	A	TP	PIM
1995-96	Soviet Wings	CIS	21	0	0	0	16	....	....	....	....	....

BABYCH, DAVE (BAB-itch) — VAN.

Defense. Shoots left. 6'2", 215 lbs. Born, Edmonton, Alta., May 23, 1961.
(Winnipeg's 1st choice, 2nd overall, in 1980 Entry Draft).

			Regular Season					Playoffs				
Season	Club	Lea	GP	G	A	TP	PIM	GP	G	A	TP	PIM
1978-79	Portland	WHL	67	20	59	79	63	25	7	22	29	22
1979-80a	Portland	WHL	50	22	60	82	71	8	1	10	11	2
1980-81	**Winnipeg**	**NHL**	**69**	**6**	**38**	**44**	**90**	....	....	....	....	....
1981-82	**Winnipeg**	**NHL**	**79**	**19**	**49**	**68**	**92**	**4**	**1**	**2**	**3**	**29**
1982-83	**Winnipeg**	**NHL**	**79**	**13**	**61**	**74**	**56**	**3**	**0**	**0**	**0**	**0**
1983-84	**Winnipeg**	**NHL**	**66**	**18**	**39**	**57**	**62**	**3**	**1**	**1**	**2**	**0**
1984-85	**Winnipeg**	**NHL**	**78**	**13**	**49**	**62**	**78**	**8**	**2**	**7**	**9**	**6**
1985-86	**Winnipeg**	**NHL**	**19**	**4**	**12**	**16**	**14**	....	....	....	....	....
	Hartford	**NHL**	**62**	**10**	**43**	**53**	**36**	**8**	**1**	**3**	**4**	**14**
1986-87	**Hartford**	**NHL**	**66**	**8**	**33**	**41**	**44**	**6**	**1**	**1**	**2**	**14**
1987-88	**Hartford**	**NHL**	**71**	**14**	**36**	**50**	**54**	**6**	**3**	**2**	**5**	**2**
1988-89	**Hartford**	**NHL**	**70**	**6**	**41**	**47**	**54**	**4**	**1**	**5**	**6**	**2**
1989-90	**Hartford**	**NHL**	**72**	**6**	**37**	**43**	**62**	**7**	**1**	**2**	**3**	**0**
1990-91	**Hartford**	**NHL**	**8**	**0**	**6**	**6**	**4**	....	....	....	....	....
1991-92	**Vancouver**	**NHL**	**75**	**5**	**24**	**29**	**63**	**13**	**2**	**6**	**8**	**10**
1992-93	**Vancouver**	**NHL**	**43**	**3**	**16**	**19**	**44**	**12**	**2**	**5**	**7**	**6**
1993-94	**Vancouver**	**NHL**	**73**	**4**	**28**	**32**	**52**	**24**	**3**	**5**	**8**	**12**
1994-95	**Vancouver**	**NHL**	**40**	**3**	**11**	**14**	**18**	**11**	**2**	**2**	**4**	**14**
1995-96	**Vancouver**	**NHL**	**53**	**3**	**21**	**24**	**38**	....	....	....	....	....
	NHL Totals		**1023**	**135**	**544**	**679**	**861**	**109**	**20**	**41**	**61**	**109**

a WHL First All-Star Team (1980)

Played in NHL All-Star Game (1983, 1984)

Traded to **Hartford** by **Winnipeg** for Ray Neufeld, November 21, 1985. Claimed by **Minnesota** from **Hartford** in Expansion Draft, May 30, 1991. Traded to **Vancouver** by **Minnesota** for Tom Kurvers, June 22, 1991.

BADDUKE, JOHN — VAN.

Right wing. Shoots right. 6'2", 195 lbs. Born, Watson, Sask., June 21, 1972.

			Regular Season					Playoffs				
Season	Club	Lea	GP	G	A	TP	PIM	GP	G	A	TP	PIM
1988-89	Regina	WHL	8	0	0	0	4	....	....	....	....	....
1989-90	Victoria	WHL	49	1	2	3	138	....	....	....	....	....
1990-91	Victoria	WHL	66	8	9	17	305	....	....	....	....	....
1991-92	Portland	WHL	67	6	13	19	*335	6	1	1	2	42
1992-93	Portland	WHL	71	12	14	26	*367	16	3	4	7	57
1993-94	Hamilton	AHL	55	6	8	14	*356	4	0	1	1	18
	Columbus	ECHL	7	0	3	3	60	....	....	....	....	....
	Brantford	ColHL	1	1	0	1	2	....	....	....	....	....
1994-95	Syracuse	AHL	44	6	0	6	334	....	....	....	....	....
1995-96	Syracuse	AHL	46	2	2	4	245	2	0	0	0	19
	Wheeling	ECHL	4	1	2	3	15	....	....	....	....	....

Signed as a free agent by **Vancouver**, February 2, 1994.

BAKER, JAMIE — TOR.

Center. Shoots left. 6', 195 lbs. Born, Ottawa, Ont., August 31, 1966.
(Quebec's 2nd choice, 8th overall, in 1988 Supplemental Draft).

			Regular Season					Playoffs				
Season	Club	Lea	GP	G	A	TP	PIM	GP	G	A	TP	PIM
1985-86	St. Lawrence	ECAC	31	9	16	25	52	....	....	....	....	....
1986-87	St. Lawrence	ECAC	32	8	24	32	59	....	....	....	....	....
1987-88	St. Lawrence	ECAC	34	26	24	50	38	....	....	....	....	....
1988-89	St. Lawrence	ECAC	13	11	16	27	16	....	....	....	....	....
1989-90	**Quebec**	**NHL**	**1**	**0**	**0**	**0**	**0**	....	....	....	....	....
	Halifax	AHL	74	17	43	60	47	6	0	0	0	7
1990-91	**Quebec**	**NHL**	**18**	**2**	**0**	**2**	**8**	....	....	....	....	....
	Halifax	AHL	50	14	22	36	85	....	....	....	....	....
1991-92	**Quebec**	**NHL**	**52**	**7**	**10**	**17**	**32**	....	....	....	....	....
	Halifax	AHL	9	5	0	5	12	....	....	....	....	....
1992-93	**Ottawa**	**NHL**	**76**	**19**	**29**	**48**	**54**	....	....	....	....	....
1993-94	**San Jose**	**NHL**	**65**	**12**	**5**	**17**	**38**	**14**	**3**	**2**	**5**	**30**
1994-95	**San Jose**	**NHL**	**43**	**7**	**4**	**11**	**22**	**11**	**2**	**2**	**4**	**12**
1995-96	**San Jose**	**NHL**	**77**	**16**	**17**	**33**	**79**	....	....	....	....	....
	NHL Totals		**332**	**63**	**65**	**128**	**233**	**25**	**5**	**4**	**9**	**42**

Signed as a free agent by **Ottawa**, September 2, 1992. Signed as a free agent by **San Jose**, September 11, 1993. Traded to **Toronto** by **San Jose** with San Jose's fifth round choice (Peter Cava) in 1996 Entry Draft for Todd Gill, June 14, 1996.

BANCROFT, STEVE

Defense. Shoots left. 6'1", 214 lbs. Born, Toronto, Ont., October 6, 1970.
(Toronto's 3rd choice, 21st overall, in 1989 Entry Draft).

			Regular Season					Playoffs				
Season	Club	Lea	GP	G	A	TP	PIM	GP	G	A	TP	PIM
1987-88	Belleville	OHL	56	1	8	9	42	....	....	....	....	....
1988-89	Belleville	OHL	66	7	30	37	99	5	0	2	2	10
1989-90	Belleville	OHL	53	10	33	43	135	11	3	9	12	38
1990-91	Newmarket	AHL	9	0	3	3	22	....	....	....	....	....
	Maine	AHL	53	2	12	14	46	2	0	0	0	2
1991-92	Maine	AHL	26	1	3	4	45	....	....	....	....	....
	Indianapolis	IHL	36	8	23	31	49	....	....	....	....	....
1992-93	**Chicago**	**NHL**	**1**	**0**	**0**	**0**	**0**	....	....	....	....	....
	Indianapolis	IHL	53	10	35	45	138	....	....	....	....	....
	Moncton	AHL	21	3	13	16	16	5	0	0	0	16
1993-94	Cleveland	IHL	33	2	12	14	58	....	....	....	....	....
1994-95	Detroit	IHL	6	1	3	4	0	....	....	....	....	....
	Fort Wayne	IHL	50	7	17	24	100	....	....	....	....	....
	St. John's	AHL	4	2	0	2	2	5	0	3	3	8
1995-96	Los Angeles	IHL	15	3	10	13	22	....	....	....	....	....
	Chicago	IHL	64	9	41	50	91	9	1	7	8	22
	NHL Totals		**1**	**0**	**0**	**0**	**0**	....	....	....	....	....

Traded to **Boston** by **Toronto** for Rob Cimetta, November 9, 1990. Traded to **Chicago** by **Boston** with Boston's eleventh round choice (later traded to Winnipeg — Winnipeg selected Russel Hewson) in 1993 Entry Draft for Chicago's eleventh round choice (Eugene Pavlov) in 1992 Entry Draft, January 9, 1992. Traded to **Winnipeg** by **Chicago** with future considerations for Troy Murray, February 21, 1993. Claimed by **Florida** from **Winnipeg** in Expansion Draft, June 24, 1993. Signed as a free agent by **Pittsburgh**, August 2, 1993.

BANHAM, FRANK — ANA.

Right wing. Shoots right. 6', 187 lbs. Born, Calahoo, Alta., April 14, 1975.
(Washington's 4th choice, 147th overall, in 1993 Entry Draft).

			Regular Season					Playoffs				
Season	Club	Lea	GP	G	A	TP	PIM	GP	G	A	TP	PIM
1992-93	Saskatoon	WHL	71	29	33	62	55	9	2	7	9	8
1993-94	Saskatoon	WHL	65	28	39	67	99	16	8	11	19	36
1994-95	Saskatoon	WHL	70	50	39	89	63	8	2	6	8	12
1995-96a	Saskatoon	WHL	72	*83	69	152	116	4	6	0	6	2
	Baltimore	AHL	9	1	4	5	0	7	1	1	2	2

a WHL East First All-Star Team (1996)

Signed as a free agent by **Anaheim**, January 27, 1996.

BANNISTER, DREW — T.B.

Defense. Shoots right. 6'2", 205 lbs. Born, Belleville, Ont., September 4, 1974.
(Tampa Bay's 2nd choice, 26th overall, in 1992 Entry Draft).

			Regular Season					Playoffs				
Season	Club	Lea	GP	G	A	TP	PIM	GP	G	A	TP	PIM
1990-91	S.S. Marie	OHL	41	2	8	10	51	4	0	0	0	0
1991-92	S.S. Marie	OHL	64	4	21	25	122	16	3	10	13	36
1992-93a	S.S. Marie	OHL	59	5	28	33	114	18	2	7	9	12
1993-94b	S.S. Marie	OHL	58	7	43	50	108	14	6	9	15	20
1994-95	Atlanta	IHL	72	5	7	12	74	5	0	2	2	22
1995-96	**Tampa Bay**	**NHL**	**13**	**0**	**1**	**1**	**4**	....	....	....	....	....
	Atlanta	IHL	61	3	13	16	105	3	0	0	0	4
	NHL Totals		**13**	**0**	**1**	**1**	**4**	....	....	....	....	....

a Memorial Cup All-Star Team (1993)
b OHL Second All-Star Team (1994)

BARANOV, ALEXEI — T.B.

Defense. Shoots right. 6'1", 174 lbs. Born, Lipetsk, USSR, June 3, 1976.
(Tampa Bay's 8th choice, 190th overall, in 1994 Entry Draft).

			Regular Season					Playoffs				
Season	Club	Lea	GP	G	A	TP	PIM	GP	G	A	TP	PIM
1994-95	Moscow D'amo	CIS	1	0	0	0	0	....	....	....	....	....
1995-96	Lipetsk	CIS 2				UNAVAILABLE						

BARNABY, MATTHEW — BUF.

Right wing. Shoots left. 6', 170 lbs. Born, Ottawa, Ont., May 4, 1973.
(Buffalo's 5th choice, 83rd overall, in 1992 Entry Draft).

			Regular Season					Playoffs				
Season	Club	Lea	GP	G	A	TP	PIM	GP	G	A	TP	PIM
1990-91	Beauport	QMJHL	52	9	5	14	262	....	....	....	....	....
1991-92	Beauport	QMJHL	63	29	37	66	*476	....	....	....	....	....
1992-93	**Buffalo**	**NHL**	**2**	**1**	**0**	**1**	**10**	**1**	**0**	**1**	**1**	**4**
	Victoriaville	QMJHL	65	44	67	111	*448	6	2	4	6	44
1993-94	**Buffalo**	**NHL**	**35**	**2**	**4**	**6**	**106**	**3**	**0**	**0**	**0**	**17**
	Rochester	AHL	42	10	32	42	153	....	....	....	....	....
1994-95	Rochester	AHL	56	21	29	50	274	....	....	....	....	....
	Buffalo	**NHL**	**23**	**1**	**1**	**2**	**116**	....	....	....	....	....
1995-96	**Buffalo**	**NHL**	**73**	**15**	**16**	**31**	***335**	....	....	....	....	....
	NHL Totals		**133**	**19**	**21**	**40**	**567**	**4**	**0**	**1**	**1**	**21**

BARNES, STU — FLA.

Center. Shoots right. 5'11", 174 lbs. Born, Edmonton, Alta., December 25, 1970.
(Winnipeg's 1st choice, 4th overall, in 1989 Entry Draft).

			Regular Season					Playoffs				
Season	Club	Lea	GP	G	A	TP	PIM	GP	G	A	TP	PIM
1987-88	N. Westminster	WHL	71	37	64	101	88	5	2	3	5	6
1988-89a	Tri-City	WHL	70	59	82	141	117	7	6	5	11	10
1989-90	Tri-City	WHL	63	52	92	144	165	7	1	5	6	26
1990-91	Cdn. National	....	53	22	27	49	68	....	....	....	....	....
1991-92	**Winnipeg**	**NHL**	**46**	**8**	**9**	**17**	**26**	....	....	....	....	....
	Moncton	AHL	30	13	19	32	10	11	3	9	12	6
1992-93	**Winnipeg**	**NHL**	**38**	**12**	**10**	**22**	**10**	**6**	**1**	**3**	**4**	**2**
	Moncton	AHL	42	23	31	54	58	....	....	....	....	....
1993-94	**Winnipeg**	**NHL**	**18**	**5**	**4**	**9**	**8**	....	....	....	....	....
	Florida	**NHL**	**59**	**18**	**20**	**38**	**30**	....	....	....	....	....
1994-95	**Florida**	**NHL**	**41**	**10**	**19**	**29**	**8**	....	....	....	....	....
1995-96	**Florida**	**NHL**	**72**	**19**	**25**	**44**	**46**	**22**	**6**	**10**	**16**	**4**
	NHL Totals		**274**	**72**	**87**	**159**	**128**	**28**	**7**	**13**	**20**	**6**

a WHL West Second All-Star Team (1989)

Traded to **Florida** by **Winnipeg** with St. Louis' sixth round choice (previously acquired by Winnipeg — later traded to Edmonton — later traded to Winnipeg — Winnipeg selected Chris Kibermanis) for Randy Gilhen, November 25, 1993.

BARON, MURRAY — ST.L.

Defense. Shoots left. 6'3", 215 lbs. Born, Prince George, B.C., June 1, 1967.
(Philadelphia's 7th choice, 167th overall, in 1986 Entry Draft).

			Regular Season					Playoffs				
Season	Club	Lea	GP	G	A	TP	PIM	GP	G	A	TP	PIM
1986-87	North Dakota	WCHA	41	4	10	14	62	....	....	....	....	....
1987-88	North Dakota	WCHA	41	1	10	11	95	....	....	....	....	....
1988-89	North Dakota	WCHA	40	2	6	8	92	....	....	....	....	....
	Hershey	AHL	9	0	3	3	8	....	....	....	....	....
1989-90	**Philadelphia**	**NHL**	**16**	**2**	**2**	**4**	**12**	....	....	....	....	....
	Hershey	AHL	50	0	10	10	101	....	....	....	....	....
1990-91	**Philadelphia**	**NHL**	**67**	**8**	**8**	**16**	**74**	....	....	....	....	....
	Hershey	AHL	6	2	3	5	0	....	....	....	....	....
1991-92	**St. Louis**	**NHL**	**67**	**3**	**8**	**11**	**94**	**2**	**0**	**0**	**0**	**2**
1992-93	**St. Louis**	**NHL**	**53**	**2**	**2**	**4**	**59**	**11**	**0**	**0**	**0**	**12**
1993-94	**St. Louis**	**NHL**	**77**	**5**	**9**	**14**	**123**	**4**	**0**	**0**	**0**	**10**
1994-95	**St. Louis**	**NHL**	**39**	**0**	**5**	**5**	**93**	**7**	**1**	**1**	**2**	**2**
1995-96	**St. Louis**	**NHL**	**82**	**2**	**9**	**11**	**190**	**13**	**1**	**0**	**1**	**20**
	NHL Totals		**401**	**22**	**43**	**65**	**645**	**37**	**2**	**1**	**3**	**46**

Traded to **St. Louis** by **Philadelphia** with Ron Sutter for Dan Quinn and Rod Brind'Amour, September 22, 1991.

BARR, DAVE

Right wing. Shoots right. 6'1", 195 lbs. Born, Toronto, Ont., November 30, 1960.

			Regular Season					Playoffs				
Season	Club	Lea	GP	G	A	TP	PIM	GP	G	A	TP	PIM
1979-80	Lethbridge	WHL	60	16	38	54	47	....	....	....	....	....
1980-81	Lethbridge	WHL	72	26	62	88	106	10	4	10	14	4
1981-82	**Boston**	**NHL**	**2**	**0**	**0**	**0**	**0**	**5**	**1**	**0**	**1**	**0**
	Erie	AHL	76	18	48	66	29	....	....	....	....	....
1982-83	**Boston**	**NHL**	**10**	**1**	**1**	**2**	**7**	**10**	**0**	**0**	**0**	**2**
	Baltimore	AHL	72	27	51	78	67	....	....	....	....	....
1983-84	**NY Rangers**	**NHL**	**6**	**0**	**0**	**0**	**2**	....	....	....	....	....
	Tulsa	CHL	50	28	37	65	24	....	....	....	....	....
	St. Louis	**NHL**	**1**	**0**	**0**	**0**	**0**	....	....	....	....	....
1984-85	**St. Louis**	**NHL**	**75**	**16**	**18**	**34**	**32**	**2**	**0**	**0**	**0**	**2**
1985-86	**St. Louis**	**NHL**	**72**	**13**	**38**	**51**	**70**	**11**	**1**	**1**	**2**	**14**
1986-87	**St. Louis**	**NHL**	**2**	**0**	**0**	**0**	**0**	....	....	....	....	....
	Hartford	**NHL**	**30**	**2**	**4**	**6**	**19**	....	....	....	....	....
	Detroit	**NHL**	**37**	**13**	**13**	**26**	**49**	**13**	**1**	**0**	**1**	**14**
1987-88	**Detroit**	**NHL**	**51**	**14**	**26**	**40**	**58**	**16**	**5**	**7**	**12**	**22**
1988-89	**Detroit**	**NHL**	**73**	**27**	**32**	**59**	**69**	**6**	**3**	**1**	**4**	**6**
1989-90	**Detroit**	**NHL**	**62**	**10**	**25**	**35**	**45**	....	....	....	....	....
	Adirondack	AHL	9	1	14	15	17	....	....	....	....	....
1990-91	**Detroit**	**NHL**	**70**	**18**	**22**	**40**	**55**	....	....	....	....	....
1991-92	**New Jersey**	**NHL**	**41**	**6**	**12**	**18**	**32**	....	....	....	....	....
	Utica	AHL	1	0	0	0	7	....	....	....	....	....
1992-93	**New Jersey**	**NHL**	**62**	**6**	**8**	**14**	**61**	**5**	**1**	**0**	**1**	**6**
1993-94	**Dallas**	**NHL**	**20**	**2**	**5**	**7**	**21**	**3**	**0**	**1**	**1**	**4**
	Kalamazoo	IHL	4	3	2	5	5	....	....	....	....	....
1994-95	Kalamazoo	IHL	66	18	41	59	77	16	1	4	5	8
1995-96	Orlando	IHL	82	38	62	100	87	23	8	13	21	14
	NHL Totals		**614**	**128**	**204**	**332**	**520**	**71**	**12**	**10**	**22**	**70**

Signed as a free agent by **Boston**, September 28, 1981. Traded to **NY Rangers** by **Boston** for Dave Silk, October 5, 1983. Traded to **St. Louis** by **NY Rangers** with NY Rangers' third round choice (Alan Perry) in the 1984 Entry Draft for Larry Patey and Bob Brooke, March 5, 1984. Traded to **Hartford** by **St. Louis** for Tim Bothwell, October 21, 1986. Traded to **Detroit** by **Hartford** for Randy Ladouceur, January 12, 1987. Acquired by **New Jersey** from **Detroit** with Randy McKay as compensation for Detroit's signing of free agent Troy Crowder, September 9, 1991. Signed as a free agent by **Dallas**, August 28, 1993.

BARRAULT, DOUG (buh-ROH)

Right wing. Shoots right. 6'2", 205 lbs. Born, Golden, B.C., April 21, 1970.
(Minnesota's 8th choice, 155th overall, in 1990 Entry Draft).

			Regular Season					Playoffs				
Season	Club	Lea	GP	G	A	TP	PIM	GP	G	A	TP	PIM
1988-89	Lethbridge	WHL	57	14	13	27	34	....	....	....	....	....
1989-90	Lethbridge	WHL	54	14	16	30	36	19	7	3	10	0
1990-91a	Lethbridge	WHL	4	2	2	4	16	....	....	....	....	....
	Seattle	WHL	61	42	42	84	69	6	5	3	8	4
1991-92	Kalamazoo	IHL	60	5	14	19	26	....	....	....	....	....
1992-93	**Minnesota**	**NHL**	**2**	**0**	**0**	**0**	**2**	....	....	....	....	....
	Kalamazoo	IHL	78	32	34	66	74	....	....	....	....	....
1993-94	**Florida**	**NHL**	**2**	**0**	**0**	**0**	**0**	....	....	....	....	....
	Cincinnati	IHL	75	36	28	64	59	9	8	2	10	0
1994-95	Cincinnati	IHL	74	20	40	60	57	10	2	6	8	20
1995-96	Atlanta	IHL	19	5	9	14	16	....	....	....	....	....
	Chicago	IHL	54	12	18	30	39	9	2	3	5	6
	NHL Totals		**4**	**0**	**0**	**0**	**2**	....	....	....	....	....

a WHL West Second All-Star Team (1991)

Claimed by **Florida** from **Dallas** in Expansion Draft, June 24, 1993.

BARRIE, LEN

Center. Shoots left. 6', 200 lbs. Born, Kimberley, B.C., June 4, 1969.
(Edmonton's 7th choice, 124th overall, in 1988 Entry Draft).

			Regular Season					Playoffs				
Season	Club	Lea	GP	G	A	TP	PIM	GP	G	A	TP	PIM
1985-86	Calgary	WHL	32	3	0	3	18	....	....	....	....	....
1986-87	Calgary	WHL	34	13	13	26	81	....	....	....	....	....
	Victoria	WHL	34	7	6	13	92	5	0	1	1	15
1987-88	Victoria	WHL	70	37	49	86	192	8	2	0	2	29
1988-89	Victoria	WHL	67	39	48	87	157	7	5	2	7	23
1989-90	**Philadelphia**	**NHL**	**1**	**0**	**0**	**0**	**0**	....	....	....	....	....
a	Kamloops	WHL	70	*85	*100	*185	108	17	*14	23	*37	24
1990-91	Hershey	AHL	63	26	32	58	60	7	4	0	4	12
1991-92	Hershey	AHL	75	42	43	85	78	3	0	2	2	32
1992-93	**Philadelphia**	**NHL**	**8**	**2**	**2**	**4**	**9**	....	....	....	....	....
	Hershey	AHL	61	31	45	76	162	....	....	....	....	....
1993-94	**Florida**	**NHL**	**2**	**0**	**0**	**0**	**0**	....	....	....	....	....
b	Cincinnati	IHL	77	45	71	116	246	11	8	13	21	60
1994-95	Cleveland	IHL	28	13	30	43	137	....	....	....	....	....
	Pittsburgh	**NHL**	**48**	**3**	**11**	**14**	**66**	**4**	**1**	**0**	**1**	**8**
1995-96	**Pittsburgh**	**NHL**	**5**	**0**	**0**	**0**	**18**	....	....	....	....	....
	Cleveland	IHL	55	29	43	72	178	3	2	3	5	6
	NHL Totals		**64**	**5**	**13**	**18**	**93**	**4**	**1**	**0**	**1**	**8**

a WHL West First All-Star Team (1990)
b IHL Second All-Star Team (1994)

Signed as a free agent by **Philadelphia**, February 28, 1990. Signed as a free agent by **Florida**, July 20, 1993. Signed as a free agent by **Pittsburgh**, August 15, 1994.

BARTELL, JOSH — PHI.

Defense. Shoots left. 6'3", 205 lbs. Born, Syracuse, NY, April 14, 1973.
(Philadelphia's 9th choice, 204th overall, in 1991 Entry Draft).

			Regular Season					Playoffs				
Season	Club	Lea	GP	G	A	TP	PIM	GP	G	A	TP	PIM
1992-93	Clarkson	ECAC	22	1	0	1	24	....	....	....	....	....
1993-94	Clarkson	ECAC	29	1	2	3	42	....	....	....	....	....
1994-95	Clarkson	ECAC	29	0	3	3	77	....	....	....	....	....
1995-96	Clarkson	ECAC	34	1	7	8	66	....	....	....	....	....

BASSEN, BOB — DAL.

Center. Shoots left. 5'10", 185 lbs. Born, Calgary, Alta., May 6, 1965.

			Regular Season					Playoffs				
Season	Club	Lea	GP	G	A	TP	PIM	GP	G	A	TP	PIM
1982-83	Medicine Hat	WHL	4	3	2	5	0	3	0	0	0	4
1983-84	Medicine Hat	WHL	72	29	29	58	93	14	5	11	16	12
1984-85a	Medicine Hat	WHL	65	32	50	82	143	10	2	8	10	39
1985-86	**NY Islanders**	**NHL**	**11**	**2**	**1**	**3**	**6**	**3**	**0**	**1**	**1**	**0**
	Springfield	AHL	54	13	21	34	111	....	....	....	....	....
1986-87	**NY Islanders**	**NHL**	**77**	**7**	**10**	**17**	**89**	**14**	**1**	**2**	**3**	**21**
1987-88	**NY Islanders**	**NHL**	**77**	**6**	**16**	**22**	**99**	**6**	**0**	**1**	**1**	**23**
1988-89	**NY Islanders**	**NHL**	**19**	**1**	**4**	**5**	**21**	....	....	....	....	....
	Chicago	**NHL**	**49**	**4**	**12**	**16**	**62**	**10**	**1**	**1**	**2**	**34**
1989-90	**Chicago**	**NHL**	**6**	**1**	**1**	**2**	**8**	**1**	**0**	**0**	**0**	**2**
b	Indianapolis	IHL	73	22	32	54	179	12	3	8	11	33
1990-91	**St. Louis**	**NHL**	**79**	**16**	**18**	**34**	**183**	**13**	**1**	**3**	**4**	**24**
1991-92	**St. Louis**	**NHL**	**79**	**7**	**25**	**32**	**167**	**6**	**0**	**2**	**2**	**4**
1992-93	**St. Louis**	**NHL**	**53**	**9**	**10**	**19**	**63**	**11**	**0**	**0**	**0**	**10**
1993-94	**St. Louis**	**NHL**	**46**	**2**	**7**	**9**	**44**	....	....	....	....	....
	Quebec	**NHL**	**37**	**11**	**8**	**19**	**55**	....	....	....	....	....
1994-95	**Quebec**	**NHL**	**47**	**12**	**15**	**27**	**33**	**5**	**2**	**4**	**6**	**0**
1995-96	**Dallas**	**NHL**	**13**	**0**	**1**	**1**	**15**	....	....	....	....	....
	Michigan	IHL	1	0	0	0	4	....	....	....	....	....
	NHL Totals		**593**	**78**	**128**	**206**	**845**	**69**	**5**	**14**	**19**	**118**

a WHL First All-Star Team (1985)
b IHL First All-Star Team (1990)

Signed as a free agent by **NY Islanders**, October 19, 1984. Traded to **Chicago** by **NY Islanders** with Steve Konroyd for Marc Bergevin and Gary Nylund, November 25, 1988. Claimed by **St. Louis** from **Chicago** in NHL Waiver Draft, October 1, 1990. Traded to **Quebec** by **St. Louis** with Garth Butcher and Ron Sutter for Steve Duchesne and Denis Chasse, January 23, 1994. Signed as a free agent by **Dallas**, August 10, 1995.

BATES, SHAWN — BOS.

Center. Shoots right. 5'11", 160 lbs. Born, Melrose, MA, April 3, 1975.
(Boston's 4th choice, 103rd overall, in 1993 Entry Draft).

			Regular Season					Playoffs				
Season	Club	Lea	GP	G	A	TP	PIM	GP	G	A	TP	PIM
1993-94	Boston U.	H.E.	41	10	19	29	24	....	....	....	....	....
1994-95a	Boston U.	H.E.	38	18	12	30	48	....	....	....	....	....
1995-96	Boston U.	H.E.	40	28	22	50	54	....	....	....	....	....

a NCAA Final Four All-Tournament Team (1995)

BATHERSON, NORM — WSH.

Left wing. Shoots left. 6'1", 198 lbs. Born, North Sydney, N.S., March 27, 1969.

			Regular Season					Playoffs				
Season	Club	Lea	GP	G	A	TP	PIM	GP	G	A	TP	PIM
1992-93	Acadia	AUAA	20	16	21	37	44	....	....	....	....	....
1993-94	P.E.I.	AHL	67	14	23	37	85	....	....	....	....	....
1994-95	Portland	AHL	77	27	34	61	64	7	3	4	7	4
1995-96	Portland	AHL	45	6	21	27	72	24	11	8	19	16

Signed as a free agent by **Washington**, August 21, 1995.

BATTAGLIA, BATES — ANA.

Left wing. Shoots left. 6'2", 185 lbs. Born, Chicago, IL, December 13, 1975.
(Anaheim's 6th choice, 132nd overall, in 1994 Entry Draft).

			Regular Season					Playoffs				
Season	Club	Lea	GP	G	A	TP	PIM	GP	G	A	TP	PIM
1994-95	Lake Superior	CCHA	38	6	14	20	34	....	....	....	....	....
1995-96	Lake Superior	CCHA	40	13	22	35	48	....	....	....	....	....

BATTAGLIA, DOUG — DET.

Left wing. Shoots left. 6'1", 185 lbs. Born, Newmarket, Ont., October 26, 1975.
(Detroit's 5th choice, 127th overall, in 1994 Entry Draft).

			Regular Season					Playoffs				
Season	Club	Lea	GP	G	A	TP	PIM	GP	G	A	TP	PIM
1994-95	RPI	ECAC	34	1	4	5	57	....	....	....	....	....
1995-96	RPI	ECAC	33	5	5	10	37	....	....	....	....	....

BATYRSHIN, RUSLAN — (ba-TEER-shihn) — L.A.

Defense. Shoots left. 6'1", 185 lbs. Born, Moscow, USSR, February 19, 1975.
(Winnipeg's 4th choice, 79th overall, in 1993 Entry Draft).

			Regular Season					Playoffs				
Season	Club	Lea	GP	G	A	TP	PIM	GP	G	A	TP	PIM
1991-92	Mosc.D'amo-2	CIS 3	40	0	2	2	52	....	....	....	....	....
1992-93	Mosc.D'amo-2	CIS 2				UNAVAILABLE						
1993-94	Moscow D'amo	CIS	10	0	0	0	10	3	0	0	0	22
1994-95	Moscow D'amo	CIS	36	2	2	4	65	12	1	1	2	6
1995-96	**Los Angeles**	**NHL**	**2**	**0**	**0**	**0**	**6**	....	....	....	....	....
	Phoenix	IHL	71	1	9	10	144	2	0	0	0	2
	NHL Totals		**2**	**0**	**0**	**0**	**6**	....	....	....	....	....

Rights traded to **Los Angeles** by **Winnipeg** with Winnipeg's second round choice (Marian Cisar) in 1996 Entry Draft for Brent Thompson and future considerations, August 8, 1994.

BAUMGARTNER, KEN — ANA.

Left wing. Shoots left. 6'1", 205 lbs. Born, Flin Flon, Man., March 11, 1966.
(Buffalo's 12th choice, 245th overall, in 1985 Entry Draft).

			Regular Season					Playoffs				
Season	Club	Lea	GP	G	A	TP	PIM	GP	G	A	TP	PIM
1984-85	Prince Albert	WHL	60	3	9	12	252	13	1	3	4	89
1985-86	Prince Albert	WHL	70	4	23	27	277	20	3	9	12	112
1986-87	New Haven	AHL	13	0	3	3	99	6	0	0	0	60
1987-88	**Los Angeles**	**NHL**	**30**	**2**	**3**	**5**	**189**	**5**	**0**	**1**	**1**	**28**
	New Haven	AHL	48	1	5	6	181	....	....	....	....	....
1988-89	**Los Angeles**	**NHL**	**49**	**1**	**3**	**4**	**288**	**5**	**0**	**0**	**0**	**8**
	New Haven	AHL	10	1	3	4	26	....	....	....	....	....
1989-90	**Los Angeles**	**NHL**	**12**	**1**	**0**	**1**	**28**	....	....	....	....	....
	NY Islanders	**NHL**	**53**	**0**	**5**	**5**	**194**	**4**	**0**	**0**	**0**	**27**
1990-91	**NY Islanders**	**NHL**	**78**	**1**	**6**	**7**	**282**	....	....	....	....	....
1991-92	**NY Islanders**	**NHL**	**44**	**0**	**1**	**1**	**202**	....	....	....	....	....
	Toronto	**NHL**	**11**	**0**	**0**	**0**	**23**	....	....	....	....	....
1992-93	**Toronto**	**NHL**	**63**	**1**	**0**	**1**	**155**	**7**	**1**	**0**	**1**	**0**
1993-94	**Toronto**	**NHL**	**64**	**4**	**4**	**8**	**185**	**10**	**0**	**0**	**0**	**18**
1994-95	**Toronto**	**NHL**	**2**	**0**	**0**	**0**	**5**	....	....	....	....	....
1995-96	**Toronto**	**NHL**	**60**	**2**	**3**	**5**	**152**	....	....	....	....	....
	Anaheim	**NHL**	**12**	**0**	**1**	**1**	**41**	....	....	....	....	....
	NHL Totals		**478**	**12**	**26**	**38**	**1744**	**31**	**1**	**1**	**2**	**81**

Traded to **Los Angeles** by **Buffalo** with Sean McKenna and Larry Playfair for Brian Engblom and Doug Smith, January 29, 1986. Traded to **NY Islanders** by **Los Angeles** with Hubie McDonough for Mikko Makela, November 29, 1989. Traded to **Toronto** by **NY Islanders** with Dave McLlwain for Daniel Marois and Claude Loiselle, March 10, 1992. Traded to **Anaheim** by **Toronto** for Winnipeg's fourth round choice (previously acquired by Anaheim — later traded to Montreal — Montreal selected Kim Staal) in 1996 Entry Draft, March 20, 1996.

BAUMGARTNER, NOLAN — WSH.

Defense. Shoots right. 6'1", 200 lbs. Born, Calgary, Alta., March 23, 1976.
(Washington's 1st choice, 10th overall, in 1994 Entry Draft).

			Regular Season					Playoffs				
Season	Club	Lea	GP	G	A	TP	PIM	GP	G	A	TP	PIM
1992-93	Kamloops	WHL	43	0	5	5	30	11	1	1	2	0
1993-94a	Kamloops	WHL	69	13	42	55	109	19	3	14	17	33
1994-95abcd	Kamloops	WHL	62	8	36	44	71	21	4	13	17	16
1995-96b	Kamloops	WHL	28	13	15	28	45	16	1	9	10	26
	Washington	**NHL**	**1**	**0**	**0**	**0**	**0**	**1**	**0**	**0**	**0**	**10**
	NHL Totals		**1**	**0**	**0**	**0**	**0**	**1**	**0**	**0**	**0**	**10**

a Memorial Cup All-Star Team (1994, 1995)
b WHL West First All-Star Team (1995, 1996)
c Canadian Major Junior First All-Star Team (1995)
d Canadian Major Junior Defenseman of the Year (1995)

BAUTIN, SERGEI — (BOW-tin)

Defense. Shoots left. 6'3", 200 lbs. Born, Rogachev, USSR, March 11, 1967.
(Winnipeg's 1st choice, 17th overall, in 1992 Entry Draft).

			Regular Season					Playoffs				
Season	Club	Lea	GP	G	A	TP	PIM	GP	G	A	TP	PIM
1990-91	Moscow D'amo	USSR	33	2	0	2	28	....	....	....	....	....
1991-92	Moscow D'amo	CIS	37	1	3	4	88	....	....	....	....	....
1992-93	**Winnipeg**	**NHL**	**71**	**5**	**18**	**23**	**96**	**6**	**0**	**0**	**0**	**2**
1993-94	**Winnipeg**	**NHL**	**59**	**0**	**7**	**7**	**78**	....	....	....	....	....
	Detroit	**NHL**	**1**	**0**	**0**	**0**	**0**	....	....	....	....	....
	Adirondack	AHL	9	1	5	6	6	....	....	....	....	....
1994-95	Adirondack	AHL	32	0	10	10	57	1	0	0	0	4
1995-96	**San Jose**	**NHL**	**1**	**0**	**0**	**0**	**2**	....	....	....	....	....
	Kansas City	IHL	60	0	14	14	113	3	0	0	0	6
	NHL Totals		**132**	**5**	**25**	**30**	**176**	**6**	**0**	**0**	**0**	**2**

Traded to **Detroit** by **Winnipeg** with Bob Essensa for Tim Cheveldae and Dallas Drake, March 8, 1994. Signed as a free agent by **San Jose**, October 12, 1995.

BAWA, ROBIN — (BAH-wah)

Right wing. Shoots right. 6'2", 214 lbs. Born, Chemainus, B.C., March 26, 1966.

			Regular Season					Playoffs				
Season	Club	Lea	GP	G	A	TP	PIM	GP	G	A	TP	PIM
1982-83	Kamloops	WHL	66	10	24	34	17	7	1	2	3	0
1983-84	Kamloops	WHL	64	16	28	44	40	13	4	2	6	4
1984-85	Kamloops	WHL	52	6	19	25	45	15	4	9	13	14
1985-86	Kamloops	WHL	63	29	43	72	78	16	5	13	18	4
1986-87a	Kamloops	WHL	62	57	56	113	91	13	6	7	13	22
1987-88	Fort Wayne	IHL	55	12	27	39	239	6	1	3	4	24
1988-89	Baltimore	AHL	75	23	24	47	205	....	....	....	....	....
1989-90	**Washington**	**NHL**	**5**	**1**	**0**	**1**	**6**	....	....	....	....	....
	Baltimore	AHL	61	7	18	25	189	11	1	2	3	49
1990-91	Fort Wayne	IHL	72	21	26	47	381	18	4	4	8	87
1991-92	**Vancouver**	**NHL**	**2**	**0**	**0**	**0**	**0**	**1**	**0**	**0**	**0**	**0**
	Milwaukee	IHL	70	27	14	41	238	5	2	2	4	8
1992-93	Hamilton	AHL	23	3	4	7	58	....	....	....	....	....
	San Jose	**NHL**	**42**	**5**	**0**	**5**	**47**	....	....	....	....	....
	Kansas City	IHL	5	2	0	2	20	....	....	....	....	....
1993-94	**Anaheim**	**NHL**	**12**	**0**	**1**	**1**	**7**	....	....	....	....	....
	San Diego	IHL	25	6	15	21	54	6	0	0	0	52
1994-95	Kalamazoo	IHL	71	22	12	34	184	....	....	....	....	....
	Milwaukee	IHL	4	1	1	2	19	15	1	5	6	48
1995-96	San Francisco	IHL	77	23	25	48	234	4	0	2	2	4
	NHL Totals		**61**	**6**	**1**	**7**	**60**	**1**	**0**	**0**	**0**	**0**

a WHL West All-Star Team (1987)

Signed as a free agent by **Washington**, May 22, 1987. Traded to **Vancouver** by **Washington** for cash, July 31, 1991. Traded to **San Jose** by **Vancouver** for Rick Lessard, December 15, 1992. Claimed by **Anaheim** from **San Jose** in Expansion Draft, June 24, 1993. Signed as a free agent by **Dallas**, July 22, 1994.

BEAUDOIN, NIC — (BOH-dwehn) — COL.

Left wing. Shoots left. 6'3", 205 lbs. Born, Ottawa, Ont., December 25, 1976.
(Colorado's 2nd choice, 51st overall, in 1995 Entry Draft).

			Regular Season					Playoffs				
Season	Club	Lea	GP	G	A	TP	PIM	GP	G	A	TP	PIM
1993-94	Detroit	OHL	63	9	18	27	32	17	1	2	3	13
1994-95	Detroit	OHL	11	1	3	4	16	21	5	7	12	16
1995-96	Detroit	OHL	60	26	33	59	78	16	8	10	18	35

BEAUFAIT, MARK

Center. Shoots right. 5'9", 170 lbs. Born, Livonia, MI, May 13, 1970.
(San Jose's 2nd choice, 7th overall, in 1991 Supplemental Draft).

			Regular Season					Playoffs				
Season	Club	Lea	GP	G	A	TP	PIM	GP	G	A	TP	PIM
1988-89	N. Michigan	WCHA	11	2	1	3	2	....	....	....	....	....
1989-90	N. Michigan	WCHA	34	10	14	24	12	....	....	....	....	....
1990-91	N. Michigan	WCHA	47	19	30	49	18	....	....	....	....	....
1991-92	N. Michigan	WCHA	39	31	44	75	43	....	....	....	....	....
1992-93	**San Jose**	**NHL**	**5**	**1**	**0**	**1**	**0**	....	....	....	....	....
	Kansas City	IHL	66	19	40	59	22	9	1	1	2	8
1993-94	U.S. National	....	51	22	29	51	36	....	....	....	....	....
	U.S. Olympic	....	8	1	4	5	2	....	....	....	....	....
	Kansas City	IHL	21	12	9	21	18	....	....	....	....	....
1994-95	San Diego	IHL	68	24	39	63	22	5	2	2	4	2
1995-96	Orlando	IHL	77	30	79	109	87	22	9	*19	*28	22
	NHL Totals		**5**	**1**	**0**	**1**	**0**	....	....	....	....	....

BEDDOES, CLAYTON — BOS.

Center. Shoots left. 5'11", 190 lbs. Born, Bentley, Alta., November 10, 1970.

			Regular Season					Playoffs				
Season	Club	Lea	GP	G	A	TP	PIM	GP	G	A	TP	PIM
1990-91	Lake Superior	CCHA	45	14	28	42	26	....	....	....	....	....
1991-92	Lake Superior	CCHA	38	14	26	40	24	....	....	....	....	....
1992-93	Lake Superior	CCHA	43	18	40	58	30	....	....	....	....	....
1993-94ab	Lake Superior	CCHA	44	23	31	54	56	....	....	....	....	....
1994-95	Providence	AHL	65	16	20	36	39	13	3	1	4	18
1995-96	**Boston**	**NHL**	**39**	**1**	**6**	**7**	**44**	....	....	....	....	....
	Providence	AHL	32	10	15	25	24	4	2	3	5	0
	NHL Totals		**39**	**1**	**6**	**7**	**44**	....	....	....	....	....

a CCHA Second All-Star Team (1994)
b NCAA West Second All-American Team (1994)

Signed as a free agent by **Boston**, June 2, 1994.

BEERS, BOB — BOS.

Defense. Shoots right. 6'2", 200 lbs. Born, Pittsburgh, PA, May 20, 1967.
(Boston's 10th choice, 210th overall, in 1985 Entry Draft).

			Regular Season					Playoffs				
Season	Club	Lea	GP	G	A	TP	PIM	GP	G	A	TP	PIM
1985-86	N. Arizona	NCAA	28	11	39	50	96	....	....	....	....	....
1986-87	U. of Maine	H.E.	38	0	13	13	45	....	....	....	....	....
1987-88	U. of Maine	H.E.	41	3	11	14	72	....	....	....	....	....
1988-89ab	U. of Maine	H.E.	44	10	27	37	53	....	....	....	....	....
1989-90	**Boston**	**NHL**	**3**	**0**	**1**	**1**	**6**	**14**	**1**	**1**	**2**	**18**
	Maine	AHL	74	7	36	43	63	....	....	....	....	....
1990-91	**Boston**	**NHL**	**16**	**0**	**1**	**1**	**10**	**6**	**0**	**0**	**0**	**4**
	Maine	AHL	36	2	16	18	21	....	....	....	....	....
1991-92	**Boston**	**NHL**	**31**	**0**	**5**	**5**	**29**	**1**	**0**	**0**	**0**	**0**
	Maine	AHL	33	6	23	29	24	....	....	....	....	....
1992-93	Providence	AHL	6	1	2	3	10	....	....	....	....	....
	Tampa Bay	**NHL**	**64**	**12**	**24**	**36**	**70**	....	....	....	....	....
	Atlanta	IHL	1	0	0	0	0	....	....	....	....	....
1993-94	**Tampa Bay**	**NHL**	**16**	**1**	**5**	**6**	**12**	....	....	....	....	....
	Edmonton	**NHL**	**66**	**10**	**27**	**37**	**74**	....	....	....	....	....
1994-95	**NY Islanders**	**NHL**	**22**	**2**	**7**	**9**	**6**	....	....	....	....	....
1995-96	**NY Islanders**	**NHL**	**13**	**0**	**5**	**5**	**10**	....	....	....	....	....
	Utah	IHL	65	6	36	42	54	22	1	12	13	16
	NHL Totals		**231**	**25**	**75**	**100**	**217**	**21**	**1**	**1**	**2**	**22**

a Hockey East Second All-Star Team (1989)
b NCAA East Second All-American Team (1989)

Traded to **Tampa Bay** by **Boston** for Stephane Richer, October 28, 1992. Traded to **Edmonton** by **Tampa Bay** for Chris Joseph, November 11, 1993. Signed as a free agent by **NY Islanders**, August 29, 1994. Signed as a free agent by **Boston**, August 5, 1996.

BEGIN, STEVE (bay-ZHIN) — CGY.

Center. Shoots left. 5'11", 180 lbs. Born, Trois-Rivieres, Que., June 14, 1978.
(Calgary's 3rd choice, 40th overall, in 1996 Entry Draft).

			Regular Season					Playoffs				
Season	Club	Lea	GP	G	A	TP	PIM	GP	G	A	TP	PIM
1994-95	Cap de la Mad.	Midget	35	9	15	24	48	....	....	....	....	....
1995-96	Val d'Or	QMJHL	64	13	23	36	218	13	1	3	4	33

BEKAR, DEREK — ST.L.

Center. Shoots left. 6'3", 185 lbs. Born, Burnaby, B.C., September 15, 1975.
(St. Louis' 6th choice, 205th overall, in 1995 Entry Draft).

			Regular Season					Playoffs				
Season	Club	Lea	GP	G	A	TP	PIM	GP	G	A	TP	PIM
1994-95	Powell River	Jr. A	46	33	29	62	35	....	....	....	....	....
1995-96	N. Hampshire	H.E.	34	15	18	33	4	....	....	....	....	....

BELAK, WADE — COL.

Defense. Shoots right. 6'4", 213 lbs. Born, Saskatoon, Sask., July 3, 1976.
(Quebec's 1st choice, 12th overall, in 1994 Entry Draft).

			Regular Season					Playoffs				
Season	Club	Lea	GP	G	A	TP	PIM	GP	G	A	TP	PIM
1992-93	N. Battleford	Midget	50	5	15	20	146	....	....	....	....	....
	Saskatoon	WHL	7	0	0	0	23	7	0	0	0	0
1993-94	Saskatoon	WHL	69	4	13	17	226	16	2	2	4	43
1994-95	Saskatoon	WHL	72	4	14	18	290	9	0	0	0	36
	Cornwall	AHL	....	....	....	....	....	11	1	2	3	40
1995-96	Saskatoon	WHL	63	3	15	18	207	4	0	0	0	9
	Cornwall	AHL	5	0	0	0	18	2	0	0	0	2

BELANGER, ERIC — L.A.

Center. Shoots left. 5'11", 159 lbs. Born, Sherbrooke, Que., December 16, 1977.
(Los Angeles' 5th choice, 96th overall, in 1996 Entry Draft).

			Regular Season					Playoffs				
Season	Club	Lea	GP	G	A	TP	PIM	GP	G	A	TP	PIM
1994-95	Beauport	QMJHL	71	12	28	40	24	18	5	9	14	25
1995-96	Beauport	QMJHL	59	35	38	83	18	20	13	14	27	6

BELANGER, JESSE (buh-LAWN-zhay) — EDM.

Center. Shoots right. 6'1", 190 lbs. Born, St. Georges de Beauce, Que., June 15, 1969.

			Regular Season					Playoffs				
Season	Club	Lea	GP	G	A	TP	PIM	GP	G	A	TP	PIM
1987-88	Granby	QMJHL	69	33	43	76	10	5	3	3	6	0
1988-89	Granby	QMJHL	67	40	63	103	26	4	0	5	5	0
1989-90	Granby	QMJHL	67	53	54	107	53	....	....	....	....	....
1990-91	Fredericton	AHL	75	40	58	98	30	6	2	4	6	0
1991-92	**Montreal**	**NHL**	**4**	**0**	**0**	**0**	**0**	....	....	....	....	....
	Fredericton	AHL	65	30	41	71	26	7	3	3	6	2
1992-93	**Montreal**	**NHL**	**19**	**4**	**2**	**6**	**4**	**9**	**0**	**1**	**1**	**0**
	Fredericton	AHL	39	19	32	51	24	....	....	....	....	....
1993-94	**Florida**	**NHL**	**70**	**17**	**33**	**50**	**16**	....	....	....	....	....
1994-95	**Florida**	**NHL**	**47**	**15**	**14**	**29**	**18**	....	....	....	....	....
1995-96	**Florida**	**NHL**	**63**	**17**	**21**	**38**	**10**	....	....	....	....	....
	Vancouver	**NHL**	**9**	**3**	**0**	**3**	**4**	**3**	**0**	**2**	**2**	**2**
	NHL Totals		**212**	**56**	**70**	**126**	**52**	**12**	**0**	**3**	**3**	**2**

Signed as a free agent by **Montreal**, October 3, 1990. Claimed by **Florida** from **Montreal** in Expansion Draft, June 24, 1993. Traded to **Vancouver** by **Florida** for Vancouver's third round choice (Oleg Kvasha) in 1996 Entry Draft and future considerations, March 20, 1996. Signed as a free agent by **Edmonton**, August 28, 1996.

BELANGER, KEN (buh-LAWN-zhay) — NYI

Left wing. Shoots left. 6'4", 225 lbs. Born, Sault Ste. Marie, Ont., May 14, 1974.
(Hartford's 7th choice, 153rd overall, in 1992 Entry Draft).

			Regular Season					Playoffs				
Season	Club	Lea	GP	G	A	TP	PIM	GP	G	A	TP	PIM
1991-92	Ottawa	OHL	51	4	4	8	174	11	0	0	0	24
1992-93	Ottawa	OHL	34	6	12	18	139	....	....	....	....	....
	Guelph	OHL	29	10	14	24	86	5	2	1	3	14
1993-94	Guelph	OHL	55	11	22	33	185	9	2	3	5	30
1994-95	St. John's	AHL	47	5	5	10	246	4	0	0	0	30
	Toronto	**NHL**	**3**	**0**	**0**	**0**	**9**	....	....	....	....	....
1995-96	St. John's	AHL	40	16	14	30	222	....	....	....	....	....
	NY Islanders	**NHL**	**7**	**0**	**0**	**0**	**27**	....	....	....	....	....
	NHL Totals		**10**	**0**	**0**	**0**	**36**	....	....	....	....	....

Traded to **Toronto** by **Hartford** for Toronto's ninth round choice (Matt Ball) in 1994 Entry Draft, March 18, 1994. Traded to **NY Islanders** by **Toronto** with Damian Rhodes for future considerations, January 23, 1996.

BELANGER, MARTIN (buh-LAWN-zhay)

Defense. Shoots right. 6', 205 lbs. Born, Lasalle, Que., February 3, 1976.
(Montreal's 5th choice, 74th overall, in 1994 Entry Draft).

			Regular Season					Playoffs				
Season	Club	Lea	GP	G	A	TP	PIM	GP	G	A	TP	PIM
1992-93	Granby	QMJHL	49	2	19	21	24	....	....	....	....	....
1993-94	Granby	QMJHL	63	8	32	40	49	7	0	1	1	28
1994-95	Granby	QMJHL	43	0	11	11	32	12	0	1	1	6
1995-96	St-Hyacinthe	QMJHL	66	7	23	30	39	12	0	1	1	4

BELLOWS, BRIAN — T.B.

Left wing. Shoots right. 5'11", 210 lbs. Born, St. Catharines, Ont., September 1, 1964.
(Minnesota's 1st choice, 2nd overall, in 1982 Entry Draft).

			Regular Season					Playoffs				
Season	Club	Lea	GP	G	A	TP	PIM	GP	G	A	TP	PIM
1980-81	Kitchener	OHA	66	49	67	116	23	16	14	13	27	13
1981-82ab	Kitchener	OHL	47	45	52	97	23	15	16	13	29	11
1982-83	**Minnesota**	**NHL**	**78**	**35**	**30**	**65**	**27**	**9**	**5**	**4**	**9**	**18**
1983-84	**Minnesota**	**NHL**	**78**	**41**	**42**	**83**	**66**	**16**	**2**	**12**	**14**	**6**
1984-85	**Minnesota**	**NHL**	**78**	**26**	**36**	**62**	**72**	**9**	**2**	**4**	**6**	**9**
1985-86	**Minnesota**	**NHL**	**77**	**31**	**48**	**79**	**46**	**5**	**5**	**0**	**5**	**16**
1986-87	**Minnesota**	**NHL**	**65**	**26**	**27**	**53**	**34**	....	....	....	....	....
1987-88	**Minnesota**	**NHL**	**77**	**40**	**41**	**81**	**81**	....	....	....	....	....
1988-89	**Minnesota**	**NHL**	**60**	**23**	**27**	**50**	**55**	**5**	**2**	**3**	**5**	**8**
1989-90c	**Minnesota**	**NHL**	**80**	**55**	**44**	**99**	**72**	**7**	**4**	**3**	**7**	**10**
1990-91	**Minnesota**	**NHL**	**80**	**35**	**40**	**75**	**43**	**23**	**10**	**19**	**29**	**30**
1991-92	**Minnesota**	**NHL**	**80**	**30**	**45**	**75**	**41**	**7**	**4**	**4**	**8**	**14**
1992-93	**Montreal**	**NHL**	**82**	**40**	**48**	**88**	**44**	**18**	**6**	**9**	**15**	**18** ♦
1993-94	**Montreal**	**NHL**	**77**	**33**	**38**	**71**	**36**	**6**	**1**	**2**	**3**	**2**
1994-95	**Montreal**	**NHL**	**41**	**8**	**8**	**16**	**8**	....	....	....	....	....
1995-96	**Tampa Bay**	**NHL**	**79**	**23**	**26**	**49**	**39**	**6**	**2**	**0**	**2**	**4**
	NHL Totals		**1032**	**446**	**500**	**946**	**664**	**111**	**43**	**60**	**103**	**135**

a OHL First All-Star Team (1982)
b Won George Parsons Trophy (Memorial Cup Tournament Most Sportsmanlike Player) (1982)
c NHL Second All-Star Team (1990)

Played in NHL All-Star Game (1984, 1988, 1992)

Traded to **Montreal** by **Minnesota** for Russ Courtnall, August 31, 1992. Traded to **Tampa Bay** by **Montreal** for Marc Bureau, June 30, 1995.

BELOV, OLEG — PIT.

Center. Shoots left. 6', 185 lbs. Born, Moscow, USSR, April 20, 1973.
(Pittsburgh's 3rd choice, 102nd overall, in 1995 Entry Draft).

			Regular Season					Playoffs				
Season	Club	Lea	GP	G	A	TP	PIM	GP	G	A	TP	PIM
1991-92	CSKA	CIS	1	0	0	0	2	....	....	....	....	....
1992-93	CSKA	CIS	42	7	4	11	18	....	....	....	....	....
1993-94	CSKA	CIS	46	14	8	22	18	3	1	0	1	2
1994-95	CSKA	CIS	46	21	18	39	51	....	....	....	....	....
1995-96	Cleveland	IHL	68	14	15	29	34	3	0	0	0	0

BERANEK, JOSEF (buh-RAH-nehk, JOH-sehf)

Left wing. Shoots left. 6'2", 185 lbs. Born, Litvinov, Czechoslovakia, October 25, 1969.
(Edmonton's 3rd choice, 78th overall, in 1989 Entry Draft).

			Regular Season					Playoffs				
Season	Club	Lea	GP	G	A	TP	PIM	GP	G	A	TP	PIM
1987-88	Litvinov	Czech.	14	7	4	11	12	....	....	....	....	....
1988-89	Litvinov	Czech.	32	18	10	28	47	....	....	....	....	....
1989-90	Dukla Trencin	Czech.	49	19	23	42	....	....	....	....	....	....
1990-91	Litvinov	Czech.	58	29	31	60	98	....	....	....	....	....
1991-92	**Edmonton**	**NHL**	**58**	**12**	**16**	**28**	**18**	**12**	**2**	**1**	**3**	**0**
1992-93	**Edmonton**	**NHL**	**26**	**2**	**6**	**8**	**28**	....	....	....	....	....
	Cape Breton	AHL	6	1	2	3	8	....	....	....	....	....
	Philadelphia	**NHL**	**40**	**13**	**12**	**25**	**50**	....	....	....	....	....
1993-94	**Philadelphia**	**NHL**	**80**	**28**	**21**	**49**	**85**	....	....	....	....	....
1994-95	Vsetin	Czech.	16	7	7	14	26	....	....	....	....	....
	Philadelphia	**NHL**	**14**	**5**	**5**	**10**	**2**	....	....	....	....	....
	Vancouver	**NHL**	**37**	**8**	**13**	**21**	**28**	**11**	**1**	**1**	**2**	**12**
1995-96	**Vancouver**	**NHL**	**61**	**6**	**14**	**20**	**60**	**3**	**2**	**1**	**3**	**0**
	NHL Totals		**316**	**74**	**87**	**161**	**271**	**26**	**5**	**3**	**8**	**12**

Traded to **Philadelphia** by **Edmonton** with Greg Hawgood for Brian Benning, January 16, 1993. Traded to **Vancouver** by **Philadelphia** for Shawn Antoski, February 15, 1995.

BERARD, BRYAN — NYI

Defense. Shoots left. 6'1", 190 lbs. Born, Woonsocket, RI, March 5, 1977.
(Ottawa's 1st choice, 1st overall, in 1995 Entry Draft).

			Regular Season					Playoffs				
Season	Club	Lea	GP	G	A	TP	PIM	GP	G	A	TP	PIM
1994-95abc	Detroit	OHL	58	20	55	75	97	21	4	20	24	38
1995-96abd	Detroit	OHL	56	31	58	89	116	17	7	18	25	41

a OHL First All-Star Team (1995, 1996)
b Canadian Major Junior First All-Star Team (1995, 1996)
c Canadian Major Junior Rookie of the Year (1995)
d Canadian Major Junior Defenseman of the Year (1996)

Traded to **NY Islanders** by **Ottawa** with Don Beaupre and Martin Straka for Damian Rhodes and Wade Redden, January 23, 1996.

BEREHOWSKY, DRAKE (beh-reh-HOW-skee)

Defense. Shoots right. 6'1", 211 lbs. Born, Toronto, Ont., January 3, 1972.
(Toronto's 1st choice, 10th overall, in 1990 Entry Draft).

			Regular Season					Playoffs				
Season	Club	Lea	GP	G	A	TP	PIM	GP	G	A	TP	PIM
1988-89	Kingston	OHL	63	7	39	46	85	....	....	....	....	....
	Cdn. National	....	1	0	0	0	0	....	....	....	....	....
1989-90	Kingston	OHL	9	3	11	14	28	....	....	....	....	....
1990-91	**Toronto**	**NHL**	**8**	**0**	**1**	**1**	**25**	....	....	....	....	....
	Kingston	OHL	13	5	13	18	38	....	....	....	....	....
	North Bay	OHL	26	7	23	30	51	10	2	7	9	21
1991-92	**Toronto**	**NHL**	**1**	**0**	**0**	**0**	**0**	....	....	....	....	....
ab	North Bay	OHL	62	19	63	82	147	21	7	24	31	22
	St. John's	AHL	....	....	....	....	....	6	0	5	5	21
1992-93	**Toronto**	**NHL**	**41**	**4**	**15**	**19**	**61**	....	....	....	....	....
	St. John's	AHL	28	10	17	27	38	....	....	....	....	....
1993-94	**Toronto**	**NHL**	**49**	**2**	**8**	**10**	**63**	....	....	....	....	....
	St. John's	AHL	18	3	12	15	40	....	....	....	....	....
1994-95	**Toronto**	**NHL**	**25**	**0**	**2**	**2**	**15**	....	....	....	....	....
	Pittsburgh	**NHL**	**4**	**0**	**0**	**0**	**13**	**1**	**0**	**0**	**0**	**0**
1995-96	**Pittsburgh**	**NHL**	**1**	**0**	**0**	**0**	**0**	....	....	....	....	....
	Cleveland	IHL	74	6	28	34	141	3	0	3	3	6
	NHL Totals		**129**	**6**	**26**	**32**	**177**	**1**	**0**	**0**	**0**	**0**

a Canadian Major Junior Defenseman of the Year (1992)
b OHL First All-Star Team (1992)

Traded to **Pittsburgh** by **Toronto** for Grant Jennings, April 7, 1995.

BERENZWEIG, ANDY — NYI

Defense. Shoots left. 6'2", 195 lbs. Born, Chicago, IL, August 8, 1977.
(NY Islanders' 5th choice, 109th overall, in 1996 Entry Draft).

			Regular Season					Playoffs				
Season	Club	Lea	GP	G	A	TP	PIM	GP	G	A	TP	PIM
1994-95	Loomis-Chaffee	HS	23	19	23	42	10	....	....	....	....	....
1995-96	U. of Michigan	CCHA	42	4	8	12	4	....	....	....	....	....

BEREZIN, SERGEI — TOR.

Right wing. Shoots right. 5'10", 187 lbs. Born, Voskresensk, USSR, November 5, 1971.
(Toronto's 8th choice, 256th overall, in 1994 Entry Draft).

			Regular Season					Playoffs				
Season	Club	Lea	GP	G	A	TP	PIM	GP	G	A	TP	PIM
1990-91	Khimik	USSR	30	6	2	8	4	....	....	....	....	....
1991-92	Khimik	CIS	36	7	5	12	10	....	....	....	....	....
1992-93	Khimik	CIS	38	9	3	12	12	2	1	0	1	0
1993-94	Khimik	CIS	40	31	10	41	16	3	2	0	2	2
1994-95	Koln	Ger.	43	38	19	57	8	18	17	8	25	14
1995-96	Koln	Ger.	45	49	31	80	8	14	13	9	22	10

BERG, AKI-PETTERI — L.A.

Defense. Shoots left. 6'3", 198 lbs. Born, Turku, Finland, February 28, 1977.
(Los Angeles' 1st choice, 3rd overall, in 1995 Entry Draft).

			Regular Season					Playoffs				
Season	Club	Lea	GP	G	A	TP	PIM	GP	G	A	TP	PIM
1993-94	TPS	Fin.	6	0	6	6	4	....	....	....	....	....
1994-95	TPS	Fin.	5	0	0	0	4	....	....	....	....	....
	Kiekko-67	Fin. 2	28	3	9	12	34	....	....	....	....	....
1995-96	**Los Angeles**	**NHL**	**51**	**0**	**7**	**7**	**29**	....	....	....	....	....
	Phoenix	IHL	20	0	3	3	18	2	0	0	0	4
	NHL Totals		**51**	**0**	**7**	**7**	**29**	....	....	....	....	....

BERG, BILL — NYR

Left wing. Shoots left. 6'1", 205 lbs. Born, St. Catharines, Ont., October 21, 1967.
(NY Islanders' 3rd choice, 59th overall, in 1986 Entry Draft).

			Regular Season					Playoffs				
Season	Club	Lea	GP	G	A	TP	PIM	GP	G	A	TP	PIM
1985-86	Toronto	OHL	64	3	35	38	143	4	0	0	0	19
	Springfield	AHL	4	1	1	2	4	....	....	....	....	....
1986-87	Toronto	OHL	57	3	15	18	138	....	....	....	....	....
1987-88	Springfield	AHL	76	6	26	32	148	....	....	....	....	....
	Peoria	IHL	5	0	1	1	8	7	0	3	3	31
1988-89	**NY Islanders**	**NHL**	**7**	**1**	**2**	**3**	**10**	....	....	....	....	....
	Springfield	AHL	69	17	32	49	122	....	....	....	....	....
1989-90	Springfield	AHL	74	12	42	54	74	15	5	12	17	35
1990-91	**NY Islanders**	**NHL**	**78**	**9**	**14**	**23**	**67**	....	....	....	....	....
1991-92	**NY Islanders**	**NHL**	**47**	**5**	**9**	**14**	**28**	....	....	....	....	....
	Capital Dist.	AHL	3	0	2	2	16	....	....	....	....	....
1992-93	**NY Islanders**	**NHL**	**22**	**6**	**3**	**9**	**49**	....	....	....	....	....
	Toronto	**NHL**	**58**	**7**	**8**	**15**	**54**	**21**	**1**	**1**	**2**	**18**
1993-94	**Toronto**	**NHL**	**83**	**8**	**11**	**19**	**93**	**18**	**1**	**2**	**3**	**10**
1994-95	**Toronto**	**NHL**	**32**	**5**	**1**	**6**	**26**	**7**	**0**	**1**	**1**	**4**
1995-96	**Toronto**	**NHL**	**23**	**1**	**1**	**2**	**33**	....	....	....	....	....
	NY Rangers	**NHL**	**18**	**2**	**1**	**3**	**8**	**10**	**1**	**0**	**1**	**0**
	NHL Totals		**368**	**44**	**50**	**94**	**368**	**56**	**3**	**4**	**7**	**32**

Claimed on waivers by **Toronto** from **NY Islanders**, December 3, 1992. Traded to **NY Rangers** by **Toronto** for Nick Kypreos, February 29, 1996.

BERGEVIN, MARC — ST.L.

Defense. Shoots left. 6'1", 197 lbs. Born, Montreal, Que., August 11, 1965.
(Chicago's 3rd choice, 59th overall, in 1983 Entry Draft).

			Regular Season					Playoffs				
Season	Club	Lea	GP	G	A	TP	PIM	GP	G	A	TP	PIM
1982-83	Chicoutimi	QMJHL	64	3	27	30	113	....	....	....	....	....
1983-84	Chicoutimi	QMJHL	70	10	35	45	125	....	....	....	....	....
	Springfield	AHL	7	0	1	1	2	....	....	....	....	....
1984-85	**Chicago**	**NHL**	**60**	**0**	**6**	**6**	**54**	**6**	**0**	**3**	**3**	**2**
	Springfield	AHL	....	....	....	....	....	4	0	0	0	0
1985-86	**Chicago**	**NHL**	**71**	**7**	**7**	**14**	**60**	**3**	**0**	**0**	**0**	**0**
1986-87	**Chicago**	**NHL**	**66**	**4**	**10**	**14**	**66**	**3**	**1**	**0**	**1**	**2**
1987-88	**Chicago**	**NHL**	**58**	**1**	**6**	**7**	**85**	....	....	....	....	....
	Saginaw	IHL	10	2	7	9	20	....	....	....	....	....
1988-89	**Chicago**	**NHL**	**11**	**0**	**0**	**0**	**18**	....	....	....	....	....
	NY Islanders	**NHL**	**58**	**2**	**13**	**15**	**62**	....	....	....	....	....
1989-90	**NY Islanders**	**NHL**	**18**	**0**	**4**	**4**	**30**	....	....	....	....	....
	Springfield	AHL	47	7	16	23	66	17	2	11	13	16
1990-91	Capital Dist.	AHL	7	0	5	5	6	....	....	....	....	....
	Hartford	**NHL**	**4**	**0**	**0**	**0**	**4**	....	....	....	....	....
	Springfield	AHL	58	4	23	27	85	18	0	7	7	26
1991-92	**Hartford**	**NHL**	**75**	**7**	**17**	**24**	**64**	**5**	**0**	**0**	**0**	**2**
1992-93	**Tampa Bay**	**NHL**	**78**	**2**	**12**	**14**	**66**	....	....	....	....	....
1993-94	**Tampa Bay**	**NHL**	**83**	**1**	**15**	**16**	**87**	....	....	....	....	....
1994-95	**Tampa Bay**	**NHL**	**44**	**2**	**4**	**6**	**51**	....	....	....	....	....
1995-96	**Detroit**	**NHL**	**70**	**1**	**9**	**10**	**33**	**17**	**1**	**0**	**1**	**14**
	NHL Totals		**696**	**27**	**103**	**130**	**680**	**34**	**2**	**3**	**5**	**20**

Traded to **NY Islanders** by **Chicago** with Gary Nylund for Steve Konroyd and Bob Bassen, November 25, 1988. Traded to **Hartford** by **NY Islanders** for Hartford's fifth round choice (Ryan Duthie) in 1992 Entry Draft, October 30, 1990. Signed as a free agent by **Tampa Bay**, July 9, 1992. Traded to **Detroit** by **Tampa Bay** with Ben Hankinson for Shawn Burr and Detroit's third round choice (later traded to Boston — Boston selected Jason Doyle) in 1996 Entry Draft, August 17, 1995. Signed as a free agent by **St. Louis**, July 31, 1996.

BERGKVIST, STEFAN — PIT.

Defense. Shoots left. 6'2", 224 lbs. Born, Leksand, Sweden, March 10, 1975.
(Pittsburgh's 1st choice, 26th overall, in 1993 Entry Draft).

			Regular Season					Playoffs				
Season	Club	Lea	GP	G	A	TP	PIM	GP	G	A	TP	PIM
1992-93	Leksand	Swe.	15	0	0	0	6	....	....	....	....	....
1993-94	Leksand	Swe.	6	0	0	0	0	....	....	....	....	....
1994-95	London	OHL	64	3	17	20	93	4	0	0	0	5
1995-96	**Pittsburgh**	**NHL**	**2**	**0**	**0**	**0**	**2**	**4**	**0**	**0**	**0**	**2**
	Cleveland	IHL	61	2	8	10	58	3	0	0	0	14
	NHL Totals		**2**	**0**	**0**	**0**	**2**	**4**	**0**	**0**	**0**	**2**

BERGMAN, PETER — PIT.

Center. Shoots left. 6'1", 195 lbs. Born, Regina, Sask., April 14, 1978.
(Pittsburgh's 6th choice, 150th overall, in 1996 Entry Draft).

			Regular Season					Playoffs				
Season	Club	Lea	GP	G	A	TP	PIM	GP	G	A	TP	PIM
1995-96	Kamloops	WHL	53	8	7	15	23	10	1	2	3	10

BERRY, BRAD

Defense. Shoots left. 6'2", 190 lbs. Born, Bashaw, Alta., April 1, 1965.
(Winnipeg's 3rd choice, 29th overall, in 1983 Entry Draft).

			Regular Season					Playoffs				
Season	Club	Lea	GP	G	A	TP	PIM	GP	G	A	TP	PIM
1983-84	North Dakota	WCHA	32	2	7	9	8	....	....	....	....	....
1984-85	North Dakota	WCHA	40	4	26	30	26	....	....	....	....	....
1985-86	North Dakota	WCHA	40	6	29	35	26	....	....	....	....	....
	Winnipeg	**NHL**	**13**	**1**	**0**	**1**	**10**	**3**	**0**	**0**	**0**	**0**
1986-87	**Winnipeg**	**NHL**	**52**	**2**	**8**	**10**	**60**	**7**	**0**	**1**	**1**	**14**
1987-88	**Winnipeg**	**NHL**	**48**	**0**	**6**	**6**	**75**	....	....	....	....	....
	Moncton	AHL	10	1	3	4	14	....	....	....	....	....
1988-89	**Winnipeg**	**NHL**	**38**	**0**	**9**	**9**	**45**	....	....	....	....	....
	Moncton	AHL	38	3	16	19	39	....	....	....	....	....
1989-90	**Winnipeg**	**NHL**	**12**	**1**	**2**	**3**	**6**	**1**	**0**	**0**	**0**	**0**
	Moncton	AHL	38	1	9	10	58	....	....	....	....	....
1990-91	Brynas	Swe.	38	3	1	4	38	....	....	....	....	....
	Cdn. National	....	4	0	1	1	0	....	....	....	....	....
1991-92	**Minnesota**	**NHL**	**7**	**0**	**0**	**0**	**6**	**2**	**0**	**0**	**0**	**2**
	Kalamazoo	IHL	65	5	18	23	90	5	2	0	2	6
1992-93	**Minnesota**	**NHL**	**63**	**0**	**3**	**3**	**109**	....	....	....	....	....
1993-94	**Dallas**	**NHL**	**8**	**0**	**0**	**0**	**12**	....	....	....	....	....
	Kalamazoo	IHL	45	3	19	22	91	1	0	0	0	0
1994-95	Kalamazoo	IHL	65	4	11	15	146	1	0	0	0	0
1995-96	Michigan	IHL	80	4	13	17	73	10	0	5	5	12
	NHL Totals		**241**	**4**	**28**	**32**	**323**	**13**	**0**	**1**	**1**	**16**

Signed as a free agent by **Minnesota**, October 4, 1991.

BERTRAND, ERIC — N.J.

Left wing. Shoots left. 6'1", 205 lbs. Born, St. Ephrem, Que., April 16, 1975.
(New Jersey's 9th choice, 207th overall, in 1994 Entry Draft).

			Regular Season					Playoffs				
Season	Club	Lea	GP	G	A	TP	PIM	GP	G	A	TP	PIM
1992-93	Granby	QMJHL	64	10	15	25	82	....	....	....	....	....
1993-94	Granby	QMJHL	60	11	15	26	151	6	1	0	1	18
1994-95	Granby	QMJHL	56	14	26	40	268	13	3	8	11	50
1995-96	Albany	AHL	70	16	13	29	199	4	0	0	0	6

BERTSCH, JAY — N.J.

Right wing. Shoots right. 6'2", 208 lbs. Born, Lethbridge, Alta., July 14, 1976.
(Quebec's 10th choice, 191st overall, in 1994 Entry Draft).

			Regular Season					Playoffs				
Season	Club	Lea	GP	G	A	TP	PIM	GP	G	A	TP	PIM
1992-93	Lethbridge	WHL	49	3	2	5	80	1	0	0	0	0
1993-94	Lethbridge	WHL	36	1	6	7	61	....	....	....	....	....
	Spokane	WHL	29	5	4	9	87	3	0	0	0	16
1994-95	Spokane	WHL	47	5	7	12	147	9	3	0	3	34
1995-96	Spokane	WHL	69	15	24	39	293	18	1	3	4	35

Re-entered NHL Entry Draft, New Jersey's 13th choice, 250th overall, in 1996 Entry Draft.

BERTUZZI, TODD (buhr-TOO-zee) NYI

Center. Shoots left. 6'3", 224 lbs. Born, Sudbury, Ont., February 2, 1975.
(NY Islanders' 1st choice, 23rd overall, in 1993 Entry Draft).

			Regular Season					Playoffs				
Season	Club	Lea	GP	G	A	TP	PIM	GP	G	A	TP	PIM
1991-92	Guelph	OHL	47	7	14	21	145	....	....	....	....	....
1992-93	Guelph	OHL	59	27	32	59	164	5	2	2	4	6
1993-94	Guelph	OHL	61	28	54	82	165	9	2	6	8	30
1994-95a	Guelph	OHL	62	54	65	119	58	14	*15	18	33	41
1995-96	**NY Islanders**	**NHL**	**76**	**18**	**21**	**39**	**83**	....	....	....	....	....
	NHL Totals		**76**	**18**	**21**	**39**	**83**	....	....	....	....	....

a OHL Second All-Star team (1995)

BERUBE, CRAIG (buh-ROO-bee) WSH.

Left wing. Shoots left. 6'1", 205 lbs. Born, Calahoo, Alta., December 17, 1965.

			Regular Season					Playoffs				
Season	Club	Lea	GP	G	A	TP	PIM	GP	G	A	TP	PIM
1982-83	Kamloops	WHL	4	0	0	0	0	....	....	....	....	....
1983-84	N. Westminster	WHL	70	11	20	31	104	8	1	2	3	5
1984-85	N. Westminster	WHL	70	25	44	69	191	10	3	2	5	4
1985-86	Kamloops	WHL	32	17	14	31	119	....	....	....	....	....
	Medicine Hat	WHL	34	14	16	30	95	25	7	8	15	102
1986-87	**Philadelphia**	**NHL**	**7**	**0**	**0**	**0**	**57**	**5**	**0**	**0**	**0**	**17**
	Hershey	AHL	63	7	17	24	325	....	....	....	....	....
1987-88	**Philadelphia**	**NHL**	**27**	**3**	**2**	**5**	**108**	....	....	....	....	....
	Hershey	AHL	31	5	9	14	119	....	....	....	....	....
1988-89	**Philadelphia**	**NHL**	**53**	**1**	**1**	**2**	**199**	**16**	**0**	**0**	**0**	**56**
	Hershey	AHL	7	0	2	2	19	....	....	....	....	....
1989-90	**Philadelphia**	**NHL**	**74**	**4**	**14**	**18**	**291**	....	....	....	....	....
1990-91	**Philadelphia**	**NHL**	**74**	**8**	**9**	**17**	**293**	....	....	....	....	....
1991-92	**Toronto**	**NHL**	**40**	**5**	**7**	**12**	**109**	....	....	....	....	....
	Calgary	**NHL**	**36**	**1**	**4**	**5**	**155**	....	....	....	....	....
1992-93	**Calgary**	**NHL**	**77**	**4**	**8**	**12**	**209**	**6**	**0**	**1**	**1**	**21**
1993-94	**Washington**	**NHL**	**84**	**7**	**7**	**14**	**305**	**8**	**0**	**0**	**0**	**21**
1994-95	**Washington**	**NHL**	**43**	**2**	**4**	**6**	**173**	**7**	**0**	**0**	**0**	**29**
1995-96	**Washington**	**NHL**	**50**	**2**	**10**	**12**	**151**	**2**	**0**	**0**	**0**	**19**
	NHL Totals		**565**	**37**	**66**	**103**	**2050**	**44**	**0**	**1**	**1**	**163**

Signed as a free agent by **Philadelphia**, March 19, 1986. Traded to **Edmonton** by **Philadelphia** with Craig Fisher and Scott Mellanby for Dave Brown, Corey Foster and Jari Kurri, May 30, 1991. Traded to **Toronto** by **Edmonton** with Grant Fuhr and Glenn Anderson for Vincent Damphousse, Peter Ing, Scott Thornton, Luke Richardson, future considerations and cash, September 19, 1991. Traded to **Calgary** by **Toronto** with Alexander Godynyuk, Gary Leeman, Michel Petit and Jeff Reese for Doug Gilmour, Jamie Macoun, Ric Nattress, Rick Wamsley and Kent Manderville, January 2, 1992. Traded to **Washington** by **Calgary** for Washington's fifth round choice (Darryl Lafrance) in 1993 Entry Draft, June 26, 1993.

BES, JEFF

Center. Shoots left. 6', 190 lbs. Born, Tillsonburg, Ont., July 31, 1973.
(Minnesota's 2nd choice, 58th overall, in 1992 Entry Draft).

			Regular Season					Playoffs				
Season	Club	Lea	GP	G	A	TP	PIM	GP	G	A	TP	PIM
1990-91	Hamilton	OHL	66	23	47	70	53	4	1	4	5	4
1991-92	Guelph	OHL	62	40	62	102	123	....	....	....	....	....
1992-93	Guelph	OHL	59	48	67	115	128	5	3	5	8	4
	Kalamazoo	IHL	3	1	3	4	6	....	....	....	....	....
1993-94	Dayton	ECHL	2	2	0	2	12	....	....	....	....	....
	Kalamazoo	IHL	30	2	12	14	30	....	....	....	....	....
1994-95	Kalamazoo	IHL	52	8	17	25	47	....	....	....	....	....
1995-96	Springfield	AHL	57	20	23	43	77	9	3	4	7	13

Claimed on waivers by **Hartford** from **Dallas**, July 29, 1995.

BETS, MAXIM (BEHTS, MAKS-eem)

Left wing. Shoots left. 6'1", 185 lbs. Born, Chelyabinsk, USSR, January 31, 1974.
(St. Louis' 1st choice, 37th overall, in 1993 Entry Draft).

			Regular Season					Playoffs				
Season	Club	Lea	GP	G	A	TP	PIM	GP	G	A	TP	PIM
1991-92	Chelyabinsk	CIS	25	1	1	2	8	....	....	....	....	....
1992-93	Spokane	WHL	54	49	57	106	130	9	5	6	11	20
1993-94	Spokane	WHL	63	46	70	116	111	3	1	1	2	12
	Anaheim	**NHL**	**3**	**0**	**0**	**0**	**0**	....	....	....	....	....
	San Diego	IHL	....	....	....	....	....	9	0	2	2	0
1994-95	San Diego	IHL	36	2	6	8	31	....	....	....	....	....
	Worcester	AHL	9	1	1	2	6	....	....	....	....	....
1995-96	Baltimore	AHL	34	5	5	10	18	....	....	....	....	....
	Raleigh	ECHL	9	0	4	4	6	4	0	0	0	0
	NHL Totals		**3**	**0**	**0**	**0**	**0**	....	....	....	....	....

Traded to **Anaheim** by **St. Louis** with St. Louis' sixth round choice (later traded back to St. Louis — St. Louis selected Denis Hamel) in 1995 Entry Draft for Alexei Kasatonov, March 21, 1994.

BEUKEBOOM, JEFF (BOO-kuh-BOOM) NYR

Defense. Shoots right. 6'5", 230 lbs. Born, Ajax, Ont., March 28, 1965.
(Edmonton's 1st choice, 19th overall, in 1983 Entry Draft).

			Regular Season					Playoffs				
Season	Club	Lea	GP	G	A	TP	PIM	GP	G	A	TP	PIM
1982-83	S.S. Marie	OHL	70	0	25	25	143	16	1	4	5	46
1983-84	S.S. Marie	OHL	61	6	30	36	178	16	1	7	8	43
1984-85a	S.S. Marie	OHL	37	4	20	24	85	16	4	6	10	47
1985-86	Nova Scotia	AHL	77	9	20	29	175	....	....	....	....	....
	Edmonton	**NHL**	....	....	....	....	....	**1**	**0**	**0**	**0**	**4**
1986-87	**Edmonton**	**NHL**	**44**	**3**	**8**	**11**	**124**	....	....	....	....	.... ♦
	Nova Scotia	AHL	14	1	7	8	35	....	....	....	....	....
1987-88	**Edmonton**	**NHL**	**73**	**5**	**20**	**25**	**201**	**7**	**0**	**0**	**0**	**16** ♦
1988-89	**Edmonton**	**NHL**	**36**	**0**	**5**	**5**	**94**	**1**	**0**	**0**	**0**	**2**
	Cape Breton	AHL	8	0	4	4	36	....	....	....	....	....
1989-90	**Edmonton**	**NHL**	**46**	**1**	**12**	**13**	**86**	**2**	**0**	**0**	**0**	**0** ♦
1990-91	**Edmonton**	**NHL**	**67**	**3**	**7**	**10**	**150**	**18**	**1**	**3**	**4**	**28**
1991-92	**Edmonton**	**NHL**	**18**	**0**	**5**	**5**	**78**	....	....	....	....	....
	NY Rangers	**NHL**	**56**	**1**	**10**	**11**	**122**	**13**	**2**	**3**	**5**	**47**
1992-93	**NY Rangers**	**NHL**	**82**	**2**	**17**	**19**	**153**	....	....	....	....	....
1993-94	**NY Rangers**	**NHL**	**68**	**8**	**8**	**16**	**170**	**22**	**0**	**6**	**6**	**50** ♦
1994-95	**NY Rangers**	**NHL**	**44**	**1**	**3**	**4**	**70**	**9**	**0**	**0**	**0**	**10**
1995-96	**NY Rangers**	**NHL**	**82**	**3**	**11**	**14**	**220**	**11**	**0**	**3**	**3**	**6**
	NHL Totals		**616**	**27**	**106**	**133**	**1468**	**84**	**3**	**15**	**18**	**163**

a OHL First All-Star Team (1985)

Traded to **NY Rangers** by **Edmonton** for David Shaw, November 12, 1991.

BIALOWAS, FRANK (bigh-uh-LOH-uhs) PHI.

Left wing. Shoots left. 5'11", 220 lbs. Born, Winnipeg, Man., September 25, 1970.

			Regular Season					Playoffs				
Season	Club	Lea	GP	G	A	TP	PIM	GP	G	A	TP	PIM
1991-92	Roanoke	ECHL	23	4	2	6	150	3	0	0	0	4
1992-93	Richmond	ECHL	60	3	18	21	261	1	0	0	0	2
	St. John's	AHL	7	1	0	1	28	1	0	0	0	0
1993-94	St. John's	AHL	69	2	8	10	352	7	0	3	3	25
	Toronto	**NHL**	**3**	**0**	**0**	**0**	**12**	....	....	....	....	....
1994-95	St. John's	AHL	51	2	3	5	277	4	0	0	0	12
1995-96	Portland	AHL	65	4	3	7	211	7	0	0	0	42
	NHL Totals		**3**	**0**	**0**	**0**	**12**	....	....	....	....	....

Signed as a free agent by **Toronto**, March 20, 1994. Signed as a free agent by **Washington**, September 8, 1995. Traded to **Philadelphia** by **Washington** for future considerations, July 18, 1996.

BICANEK, RADIM (BEE-chah-nehk) OTT.

Defense. Shoots left. 6'1", 195 lbs. Born, Uherske Hradiste, Czech., January 18, 1975.
(Ottawa's 2nd choice, 27th overall, in 1993 Entry Draft).

			Regular Season					Playoffs				
Season	Club	Lea	GP	G	A	TP	PIM	GP	G	A	TP	PIM
1992-93	Dukla Jihlava	Czech.	43	2	3	5	....	....	....	....	....	....
1993-94	Belleville	OHL	63	16	27	43	49	12	2	8	10	21
1994-95	Belleville	OHL	49	13	26	39	61	16	6	5	11	30
	Ottawa	**NHL**	**6**	**0**	**0**	**0**	**0**	....	....	....	....	....
	P.E.I.	AHL	....	....	....	....	....	3	0	1	1	0
1995-96	P.E.I.	AHL	74	7	19	26	87	5	0	2	2	6
	NHL Totals		**6**	**0**	**0**	**0**	**0**	....	....	....	....	....

BIENVENUE, DANIEL BUF.

Left wing. Shoots left. 6', 195 lbs. Born, Val d'Or, Que., June 10, 1977.
(Buffalo's 8th choice, 123rd overall, in 1995 Entry Draft).

			Regular Season					Playoffs				
Season	Club	Lea	GP	G	A	TP	PIM	GP	G	A	TP	PIM
1993-94	Chicoutimi	QMJHL	42	2	7	9	4	....	....	....	....	....
1994-95	Val d'Or	QMJHL	67	27	14	41	40	....	....	....	....	....
1995-96	Val d'Or	QMJHL	67	30	42	72	65	13	6	1	7	0

BIGGS, DON

Center. Shoots right. 5'8", 185 lbs. Born, Mississauga, Ont., April 7, 1965.
(Minnesota's 9th choice, 156th overall, in 1983 Entry Draft).

			Regular Season					Playoffs				
Season	Club	Lea	GP	G	A	TP	PIM	GP	G	A	TP	PIM
1982-83	Oshawa	OHL	70	22	53	75	145	16	3	6	9	17
1983-84	Oshawa	OHL	58	31	60	91	149	7	4	4	8	18
1984-85	**Minnesota**	**NHL**	**1**	**0**	**0**	**0**	**0**	....	....	....	....	....
	Springfield	AHL	6	0	3	3	0	2	1	0	1	0
	Oshawa	OHL	60	48	69	117	105	5	3	4	7	6
1985-86	Springfield	AHL	28	15	16	31	46	....	....	....	....	....
	Nova Scotia	AHL	47	6	23	29	36	....	....	....	....	....
1986-87	Nova Scotia	AHL	80	22	25	47	165	5	1	2	3	4
1987-88	Hershey	AHL	77	38	41	79	151	12	5	*11	*16	22
1988-89	Hershey	AHL	76	36	67	103	158	11	5	9	14	30
1989-90	**Philadelphia**	**NHL**	**11**	**2**	**0**	**2**	**8**	....	....	....	....	....
	Hershey	AHL	66	39	53	92	125	....	....	....	....	....
1990-91	Rochester	AHL	65	31	57	88	115	15	9	*14	*23	14
1991-92	Binghamton	AHL	74	32	50	82	122	11	3	7	10	8
1992-93abc	Binghamton	AHL	78	54	*84	*138	112	14	3	9	12	32
1993-94	Cincinnati	IHL	80	30	59	89	128	11	8	9	17	29
1994-95	Cincinnati	IHL	77	27	49	76	152	10	1	9	10	29
1995-96	Cincinnati	IHL	82	27	57	84	160	17	9	10	19	24
	NHL Totals		**12**	**2**	**0**	**2**	**8**	....	....	....	....	....

a Won Les Cunningham Plaque (MVP - AHL) (1993)
b Won John B. Sollenberger Trophy (Top Scorer - AHL) (1993)
c AHL First All-Star Team (1993)

Traded to **Edmonton** by **Minnesota** with Gord Sherven for Marc Habscheid, Don Barber and Emanuel Viveiros, December 20, 1985. Signed as a free agent by **Philadelphia**, July 17, 1987. Traded to **NY Rangers** by **Philadelphia** for future considerations, August 8, 1991.

BILODEAU, BRENT (BIHL-uh-DOH)

Defense. Shoots left. 6'3", 217 lbs. Born, Dallas, TX, March 27, 1973.
(Montreal's 1st choice, 17th overall, in 1991 Entry Draft).

			Regular Season					Playoffs				
Season	Club	Lea	GP	G	A	TP	PIM	GP	G	A	TP	PIM
1989-90	Seattle	WHL	68	14	29	43	170	13	3	5	8	31
1990-91	Seattle	WHL	55	7	18	25	145	6	1	0	1	12
1991-92a	Seattle	WHL	7	1	2	3	43	....	....	....	....	....
	Swift Current	WHL	56	10	47	57	118	8	2	3	5	11
1992-93a	Swift Current	WHL	59	11	57	68	77	17	5	14	19	18
1993-94	Fredericton	AHL	72	2	5	7	89	....	....	....	....	....
1994-95	Fredericton	AHL	50	4	8	12	146	12	3	3	6	28
1995-96	San Francisco	IHL	65	3	14	17	123	4	1	0	1	2

a WHL East Second All-Star Team (1992, 1993)

BLACK, JAMES CHI.

Center. Shoots left. 5'11", 185 lbs. Born, Regina, Sask., August 15, 1969.
(Hartford's 4th choice, 94th overall, in 1989 Entry Draft).

			Regular Season					Playoffs				
Season	Club	Lea	GP	G	A	TP	PIM	GP	G	A	TP	PIM
1987-88	Portland	WHL	72	30	50	80	50	....	....	....	....	....
1988-89	Portland	WHL	71	45	51	96	57	19	13	6	19	28
1989-90	**Hartford**	**NHL**	**1**	**0**	**0**	**0**	**0**	....	....	....	....	....
	Binghamton	AHL	80	37	35	72	34	....	....	....	....	....
1990-91	**Hartford**	**NHL**	**1**	**0**	**0**	**0**	**0**	....	....	....	....	....
	Springfield	AHL	79	35	61	96	34	18	9	9	18	6
1991-92	**Hartford**	**NHL**	**30**	**4**	**6**	**10**	**10**	....	....	....	....	....
	Springfield	AHL	47	15	25	40	33	10	3	2	5	18
1992-93	**Minnesota**	**NHL**	**10**	**2**	**1**	**3**	**4**	....	....	....	....	....
	Kalamazoo	IHL	63	25	45	70	40	....	....	....	....	....
1993-94	**Dallas**	**NHL**	**13**	**2**	**3**	**5**	**2**	....	....	....	....	....
	Buffalo	**NHL**	**2**	**0**	**0**	**0**	**0**	....	....	....	....	....
	Rochester	AHL	45	19	32	51	28	4	2	3	5	0
1994-95	Las Vegas	IHL	78	29	44	73	54	10	1	6	7	4
1995-96	**Chicago**	**NHL**	**13**	**3**	**3**	**6**	**16**	**8**	**1**	**0**	**1**	**2**
	Indianapolis	IHL	67	32	50	82	56	....	....	....	....	....
	NHL Totals		**70**	**11**	**13**	**24**	**32**	**8**	**1**	**0**	**1**	**2**

Traded to **Minnesota** by **Hartford** for Mark Janssens, September 3, 1992. Traded to **Buffalo** by **Dallas** with Dallas' seventh round choice (Steve Webb) in 1994 Entry Draft for Gord Donnelly, December 15, 1993. Signed as a free agent by **Chicago**, September 18, 1995.

BLACK, JESSE — L.A.

Defense. Shoots right. 6'4", 197 lbs. Born, Thunder Bay, Ont., June 23, 1978.
(Los Angeles' 6th choice, 120th overall, in 1996 Entry Draft).

			Regular Season					Playoffs				
Season	**Club**	**Lea**	**GP**	**G**	**A**	**TP**	**PIM**	**GP**	**G**	**A**	**TP**	**PIM**
1994-95	Thunder Bay	Midget	70	3	20	23	86	....	....	....	....	....
1995-96	Niagara Falls	OHL	59	1	3	4	27	10	0	2	2	0

BLAKE, ROB — L.A.

Defense. Shoots right. 6'3", 215 lbs. Born, Simcoe, Ont., December 10, 1969.
(Los Angeles' 4th choice, 70th overall, in 1988 Entry Draft).

			Regular Season					Playoffs				
Season	**Club**	**Lea**	**GP**	**G**	**A**	**TP**	**PIM**	**GP**	**G**	**A**	**TP**	**PIM**
1987-88	Bowling Green	CCHA	43	5	8	13	88	....	....	....	....	....
1988-89a	Bowling Green	CCHA	46	11	21	32	140	....	....	....	....	....
1989-90bc	Bowling Green	CCHA	42	23	36	59	140	....	....	....	....	....
	Los Angeles	**NHL**	**4**	**0**	**0**	**0**	**4**	**8**	**1**	**3**	**4**	**4**
1990-91d	**Los Angeles**	**NHL**	**75**	**12**	**34**	**46**	**125**	**12**	**1**	**4**	**5**	**26**
1991-92	**Los Angeles**	**NHL**	**57**	**7**	**13**	**20**	**102**	**6**	**2**	**1**	**3**	**12**
1992-93	**Los Angeles**	**NHL**	**76**	**16**	**43**	**59**	**152**	**23**	**4**	**6**	**10**	**46**
1993-94	**Los Angeles**	**NHL**	**84**	**20**	**48**	**68**	**137**	....	....	....	....	....
1994-95	**Los Angeles**	**NHL**	**24**	**4**	**7**	**11**	**38**	....	....	....	....	....
1995-96	**Los Angeles**	**NHL**	**6**	**1**	**2**	**3**	**8**	....	....	....	....	....
	NHL Totals		**326**	**60**	**147**	**207**	**566**	**49**	**8**	**14**	**22**	**88**

a CCHA Second All-Star Team (1989)
b CCHA First All-Star Team (1990)
c NCAA West First All-American Team (1990)
d NHL/Upper Deck All-Rookie Team (1991)

Played in NHL All-Star Game (1994)

BLOEMBERG, JEFF (BLOOM-buhrg) — DET.

Defense. Shoots right. 6'2", 205 lbs. Born, Listowel, Ont., January 31, 1968.
(NY Rangers' 5th choice, 93rd overall, in 1986 Entry Draft).

			Regular Season					Playoffs				
Season	**Club**	**Lea**	**GP**	**G**	**A**	**TP**	**PIM**	**GP**	**G**	**A**	**TP**	**PIM**
1985-86	North Bay	OHL	60	2	11	13	76	8	1	2	3	9
1986-87	North Bay	OHL	60	5	13	18	91	21	1	6	7	13
1987-88	Colorado	IHL	5	0	0	0	0	11	1	0	1	8
	North Bay	OHL	46	9	26	35	60	4	1	4	5	2
1988-89	**NY Rangers**	**NHL**	**9**	**0**	**0**	**0**	**0**	....	....	....	....	....
	Denver	IHL	64	7	22	29	55	1	0	0	0	0
1989-90	**NY Rangers**	**NHL**	**28**	**3**	**3**	**6**	**25**	**7**	**0**	**3**	**3**	**5**
	Flint	IHL	41	7	14	21	24	....	....	....	....	....
1990-91	**NY Rangers**	**NHL**	**3**	**0**	**2**	**2**	**0**	....	....	....	....	....
a	Binghamton	AHL	77	16	46	62	28	10	0	6	6	10
1991-92	**NY Rangers**	**NHL**	**3**	**0**	**1**	**1**	**0**	....	....	....	....	....
	Binghamton	AHL	66	6	41	47	22	11	1	10	11	10
1992-93	Cape Breton	AHL	76	6	45	51	34	16	5	10	15	10
1993-94	Springfield	AHL	78	8	28	36	36	6	0	3	3	8
1994-95	Adirondack	AHL	44	5	19	24	10	4	0	0	0	0
1995-96	Adirondack	AHL	72	10	28	38	32	3	0	1	1	4
	NHL Totals		**43**	**3**	**6**	**9**	**25**	**7**	**0**	**3**	**3**	**5**

a AHL Second All-Star Team (1991)

Claimed by **Tampa Bay** from **NY Rangers** in Expansion Draft, June 18, 1992. Traded to **Edmonton** by **Tampa Bay** for future considerations, September 25, 1992. Signed as a free agent by **Hartford**, August 9, 1993. Signed as a free agent by **Detroit**, May 9, 1995.

BLOMSTEN, ARTO (BLOOM-stehn)

Defense. Shoots left. 6'3", 210 lbs. Born, Vaasa, Finland, March 16, 1965.
(Winnipeg's 11th choice, 239th overall, in 1986 Entry Draft).

			Regular Season					Playoffs				
Season	**Club**	**Lea**	**GP**	**G**	**A**	**TP**	**PIM**	**GP**	**G**	**A**	**TP**	**PIM**
1983-84	Djurgarden	Swe.	3	0	0	0	4	....	....	....	....	....
1984-85	Djurgarden	Swe.	19	3	1	4	22	8	0	0	0	8
1985-86	Djurgarden	Swe.	8	0	3	3	6	....	....	....	....	....
1986-87	Djurgarden	Swe.	29	2	4	6	28	....	....	....	....	....
1987-88	Djurgarden	Swe.	39	12	6	18	36	2	1	0	1	0
1988-89	Djurgarden	Swe.	40	10	9	19	38	....	....	....	....	....
1989-90	Djurgarden	Swe.	36	5	21	26	28	8	0	1	1	6
1990-91	Djurgarden	Swe.	38	2	9	11	38	7	2	1	3	12
1991-92	Djurgarden	Swe.	39	6	8	14	34	10	2	0	2	8
1992-93	Djurgarden	Swe.	40	4	16	20	52	....	....	....	....	....
1993-94	**Winnipeg**	**NHL**	**18**	**0**	**2**	**2**	**6**	....	....	....	....	....
	Moncton	AHL	44	6	27	33	25	20	4	10	14	8
1994-95	Springfield	AHL	27	3	16	19	20	....	....	....	....	....
	Winnipeg	**NHL**	**1**	**0**	**0**	**0**	**2**	....	....	....	....	....
	Los Angeles	**NHL**	**4**	**0**	**1**	**1**	**0**	....	....	....	....	....
	Phoenix	IHL	2	1	2	3	0	8	3	6	9	6
1995-96	**Los Angeles**	**NHL**	**2**	**0**	**1**	**1**	**0**	....	....	....	....	....
	Phoenix	IHL	47	4	15	19	10	4	0	4	4	2
	NHL Totals		**25**	**0**	**4**	**4**	**8**	....	....	....	....	....

Traded to **Los Angeles** by **Winnipeg** for Los Angeles' eighth round choice (Frederik Loven) in 1995 Entry Draft, March 27, 1995.

BLOUIN, SYLVAIN (bluh-WEHN) — NYR

Left wing. Shoots left. 6'2", 225 lbs. Born, Montreal, Que., May 21, 1974.
(NY Rangers' 5th choice, 104th overall, in 1994 Entry Draft).

			Regular Season					Playoffs				
Season	**Club**	**Lea**	**GP**	**G**	**A**	**TP**	**PIM**	**GP**	**G**	**A**	**TP**	**PIM**
1991-92	Laval	QMJHL	28	0	0	0	23	9	0	0	0	35
1992-93	Laval	QMJHL	68	0	10	10	373	13	1	0	1	*66
1993-94	Laval	QMJHL	62	18	22	40	*492	21	4	13	17	*177
1994-95	Chicago	IHL	1	0	0	0	2	....	....	....	....	....
	Charlotte	ECHL	50	5	7	12	280	3	0	0	0	6
	Binghamton	AHL	10	1	0	1	46	2	0	0	0	24
1995-96	Binghamton	AHL	71	5	8	13	*352	4	0	3	3	4

BODGER, DOUG — S.J.

Defense. Shoots left. 6'2", 213 lbs. Born, Chemainus, B.C., June 18, 1966.
(Pittsburgh's 2nd choice, 9th overall, in 1984 Entry Draft).

			Regular Season					Playoffs				
Season	**Club**	**Lea**	**GP**	**G**	**A**	**TP**	**PIM**	**GP**	**G**	**A**	**TP**	**PIM**
1982-83a	Kamloops	WHL	72	26	66	92	98	7	0	5	5	2
1983-84	Kamloops	WHL	70	21	77	98	90	17	2	15	17	12
1984-85	**Pittsburgh**	**NHL**	**65**	**5**	**26**	**31**	**67**	....	....	....	....	....
1985-86	**Pittsburgh**	**NHL**	**79**	**4**	**33**	**37**	**63**	....	....	....	....	....
1986-87	**Pittsburgh**	**NHL**	**76**	**11**	**38**	**49**	**52**	....	....	....	....	....
1987-88	**Pittsburgh**	**NHL**	**69**	**14**	**31**	**45**	**103**	....	....	....	....	....
1988-89	**Pittsburgh**	**NHL**	**10**	**1**	**4**	**5**	**7**	....	....	....	....	....
	Buffalo	**NHL**	**61**	**7**	**40**	**47**	**52**	**5**	**1**	**1**	**2**	**11**
1989-90	**Buffalo**	**NHL**	**71**	**12**	**36**	**48**	**64**	**6**	**1**	**5**	**6**	**6**
1990-91	**Buffalo**	**NHL**	**58**	**5**	**23**	**28**	**54**	**4**	**0**	**1**	**1**	**0**
1991-92	**Buffalo**	**NHL**	**73**	**11**	**35**	**46**	**108**	**7**	**2**	**1**	**3**	**2**
1992-93	**Buffalo**	**NHL**	**81**	**9**	**45**	**54**	**87**	**8**	**2**	**3**	**5**	**0**
1993-94	**Buffalo**	**NHL**	**75**	**7**	**32**	**39**	**76**	**7**	**0**	**3**	**3**	**6**
1994-95	**Buffalo**	**NHL**	**44**	**3**	**17**	**20**	**47**	**5**	**0**	**4**	**4**	**0**
1995-96	**Buffalo**	**NHL**	**16**	**0**	**5**	**5**	**18**	....	....	....	....	....
	San Jose	**NHL**	**57**	**4**	**19**	**23**	**50**	....	....	....	....	....
	NHL Totals		**835**	**93**	**384**	**477**	**848**	**42**	**6**	**18**	**24**	**25**

a WHL Second All-Star Team (1983)

Traded to **Buffalo** by **Pittsburgh** wih Darrin Shannon for Tom Barrasso and Buffalo's third round choice (Joe Dziedzic) in 1990 Entry Draft, November 12, 1988. Traded to **San Jose** by **Buffalo** for an optional first round choice in 1996 Entry Draft, Philadelphia's fourth round choice (previously acquired by San Jose — Buffalo selected Mike Martone) in 1996 Entry Draft, Vaclav Varada and Martin Spanhel, November 16, 1995.

BODTKER, STEWART — VAN.

Center. Shoots right. 6'1", 175 lbs. Born, Vancouver, B.C., September 15, 1976.
(Vancouver's 7th choice, 174th overall, in 1995 Entry Draft).

			Regular Season					Playoffs				
Season	**Club**	**Lea**	**GP**	**G**	**A**	**TP**	**PIM**	**GP**	**G**	**A**	**TP**	**PIM**
1994-95	Colorado	WCHA	27	6	4	10	22	....	....	....	....	....
1995-96	Colorado	WCHA	42	6	7	13	40	....	....	....	....	....

BOGAS, CHRIS — TOR.

Defense. Shoots right. 6', 192 lbs. Born, Cleveland, OH, November 12, 1976.
(Toronto's 10th choice, 148th overall, in 1996 Entry Draft).

			Regular Season					Playoffs				
Season	**Club**	**Lea**	**GP**	**G**	**A**	**TP**	**PIM**	**GP**	**G**	**A**	**TP**	**PIM**
1995-96	Michigan State	CCHA	39	1	19	20	55	....	....	....	....	....

BOGUNIECKI, ERIC — ST.L.

Center. Shoots right. 5'8", 192 lbs. Born, New Haven, CT, May 6, 1975.
(St. Louis' 6th choice, 193rd overall, in 1993 Entry Draft).

			Regular Season					Playoffs				
Season	**Club**	**Lea**	**GP**	**G**	**A**	**TP**	**PIM**	**GP**	**G**	**A**	**TP**	**PIM**
1993-94	N. Hampshire	H.E.	40	17	16	33	66	....	....	....	....	....
1994-95	N. Hampshire	H.E.	34	12	16	28	62	....	....	....	....	....
1995-96	N. Hampshire	H.E.	32	23	28	51	46	....	....	....	....	....

BOHONOS, LONNY (boh-HOH-nohz) — VAN.

Right wing. Shoots right. 5'11", 190 lbs. Born, Winnipeg, Man., May 20, 1973.

			Regular Season					Playoffs				
Season	**Club**	**Lea**	**GP**	**G**	**A**	**TP**	**PIM**	**GP**	**G**	**A**	**TP**	**PIM**
1991-92	Moose Jaw	WHL	8	1	1	2	0	....	....	....	....	....
1992-93	Seattle	WHL	46	13	13	26	27	....	....	....	....	....
	Portland	WHL	27	20	17	37	16	15	8	13	21	19
1993-94ab	Portland	WHL	70	*62	*90	*152	80	10	8	11	19	13
1994-95	Syracuse	AHL	67	30	45	75	71	....	....	....	....	....
1995-96	**Vancouver**	**NHL**	**3**	**0**	**1**	**1**	**0**	....	....	....	....	....
	Syracuse	AHL	74	40	39	79	82	16	14	8	22	16
	NHL Totals		**3**	**0**	**1**	**1**	**0**	....	....	....	....	....

a WHL West First All-Star Team (1994)
b Canadian Major Junior First All-Star Team (1994)

Signed as a free agent by **Vancouver**, May 31, 1994.

BOILEAU, PATRICK — WSH.

Defense. Shoots right. 6', 190 lbs. Born, Montreal, Que., February 22, 1975.
(Washington's 3rd choice, 69th overall, in 1993 Entry Draft).

			Regular Season					Playoffs				
Season	**Club**	**Lea**	**GP**	**G**	**A**	**TP**	**PIM**	**GP**	**G**	**A**	**TP**	**PIM**
1992-93	Laval	QMJHL	69	4	19	23	73	13	1	2	3	10
1993-94	Laval	QMJHL	64	13	57	70	56	21	1	7	8	24
1994-95	Laval	QMJHL	38	8	25	33	46	20	4	16	20	24
1995-96	Portland	AHL	78	10	28	38	41	19	1	3	4	12

BOLIBRUCK, KEVIN — OTT.

Defense. Shoots left. 6'1", 197 lbs. Born, Peterborough, Ont., February 8, 1977.
(Ottawa's 4th choice, 89th overall, in 1995 Entry Draft).

			Regular Season					Playoffs				
Season	**Club**	**Lea**	**GP**	**G**	**A**	**TP**	**PIM**	**GP**	**G**	**A**	**TP**	**PIM**
1994-95	Peterborough	OHL	66	2	16	18	88	11	1	1	2	14
1995-96a	Peterborough	OHL	57	6	21	27	105	24	3	6	9	46

a OHL First All-Star Team (1996)

BOMBARDIR, BRAD — N.J.

Defense. Shoots left. 6'2", 190 lbs. Born, Powell River, B.C., May 5, 1972.
(New Jersey's 5th choice, 56th overall, in 1990 Entry Draft).

			Regular Season					Playoffs				
Season	**Club**	**Lea**	**GP**	**G**	**A**	**TP**	**PIM**	**GP**	**G**	**A**	**TP**	**PIM**
1990-91	North Dakota	WCHA	33	3	6	9	18	....	....	....	....	....
1991-92	North Dakota	WCHA	35	3	14	17	54	....	....	....	....	....
1992-93	North Dakota	WCHA	38	8	15	23	34	....	....	....	....	....
1993-94	North Dakota	WCHA	38	5	17	22	38	....	....	....	....	....
1994-95	Albany	AHL	77	5	22	27	22	14	0	3	3	6
1995-96a	Albany	AHL	80	6	25	31	63	3	0	1	1	4

a AHL Second All-Star Team (1996)

BONDRA, PETER — WSH.

Right wing. Shoots left. 6'1", 200 lbs. Born, Luck, USSR, February 7, 1968.
(Washington's 9th choice, 156th overall, in 1990 Entry Draft).

			Regular Season					Playoffs				
Season	Club	Lea	GP	G	A	TP	PIM	GP	G	A	TP	PIM
1986-87	VSZ Kosice	Czech.	32	4	5	9	24	....	....	....	....	....
1987-88	VSZ Kosice	Czech.	45	27	11	38	20	....	....	....	....	....
1988-89	VSZ Kosice	Czech.	40	30	10	40	20	....	....	....	....	....
1989-90	VSZ Kosice	Czech.	49	36	19	55	....	....	....	....	....	....
1990-91	**Washington**	**NHL**	**54**	**12**	**16**	**28**	**47**	**4**	**0**	**1**	**1**	**2**
1991-92	**Washington**	**NHL**	**71**	**28**	**28**	**56**	**42**	**7**	**6**	**2**	**8**	**4**
1992-93	**Washington**	**NHL**	**83**	**37**	**48**	**85**	**70**	**6**	**0**	**6**	**6**	**0**
1993-94	**Washington**	**NHL**	**69**	**24**	**19**	**43**	**40**	**9**	**2**	**4**	**6**	**4**
1994-95	Kosice	Slov.	2	1	0	1	0	....	....	....	....	....
	Washington	**NHL**	**47**	***34**	**9**	**43**	**24**	**7**	**5**	**3**	**8**	**10**
1995-96	Detroit	IHL	7	8	1	9	0	....	....	....	....	....
	Washington	**NHL**	**67**	**52**	**28**	**80**	**40**	**6**	**3**	**2**	**5**	**8**
	NHL Totals		**391**	**187**	**148**	**335**	**263**	**39**	**16**	**18**	**34**	**28**

Played in NHL All-Star Game (1993, 1996)

BONIN, BRIAN — PIT.

Center. Shoots left. 5'10", 185 lbs. Born, White Bear Lake, MN, November 28, 1973.
(Pittsburgh's 9th choice, 211th overall, in 1992 Entry Draft).

			Regular Season					Playoffs				
Season	Club	Lea	GP	G	A	TP	PIM	GP	G	A	TP	PIM
1992-93	U. Minnesota	WCHA	38	10	18	28	10	....	....	....	....	....
1993-94	U. Minnesota	WCHA	42	24	20	44	14	....	....	....	....	....
1994-95ab	U. Minnesota	WCHA	44	32	31	*63	28	....	....	....	....	....
1995-96abc	U. Minnesota	WCHA	42	34	*47	*81	30	....	....	....	....	....

a WCHA First All-Star Team (1995, 1996)
b NCAA West First All-American Team (1995, 1996)
c Won Hobey Baker Memorial Award (Top U.S. Collegiate Player) (1996)

BONK, RADEK — (BOHNK) OTT.

Center. Shoots left. 6'3", 215 lbs. Born, Krnov, Czech., January 9, 1976.
(Ottawa's 1st choice, 3rd overall, in 1994 Entry Draft).

			Regular Season					Playoffs				
Season	Club	Lea	GP	G	A	TP	PIM	GP	G	A	TP	PIM
1992-93	ZPS Zlin	Czech.	30	5	5	10	10	....	....	....	....	....
1993-94a	Las Vegas	IHL	76	42	45	87	208	5	1	2	3	10
1994-95	Las Vegas	IHL	33	7	13	20	62	....	....	....	....	....
	Ottawa	**NHL**	**42**	**3**	**8**	**11**	**28**	....	....	....	....	....
	P.E.I.	AHL	....	....	....	....	....	1	0	0	0	0
1995-96	**Ottawa**	**NHL**	**76**	**16**	**19**	**35**	**36**	....	....	....	....	....
	NHL Totals		**118**	**19**	**27**	**46**	**64**	....	....	....	....	....

a Won Garry F. Longman Memorial Trophy (Top Rookie - IHL) (1994)

BONSIGNORE, JASON — (bohn-SEE-nohr) EDM.

Center. Shoots right. 6'4", 220 lbs. Born, Rochester, NY, April 15, 1976.
(Edmonton's 1st choice, 4th overall, in 1994 Entry Draft).

			Regular Season					Playoffs				
Season	Club	Lea	GP	G	A	TP	PIM	GP	G	A	TP	PIM
1992-93	Newmarket	OHL	66	22	20	42	6	7	0	3	3	0
1993-94	Newmarket	OHL	17	7	17	24	22	....	....	....	....	....
	U.S. National	....	5	0	2	2	0	....	....	....	....	....
	Niagara Falls	OHL	41	15	47	62	41	....	....	....	....	....
1994-95	Niagara Falls	OHL	26	12	21	33	51	....	....	....	....	....
	Sudbury	OHL	23	15	14	29	45	17	13	10	23	12
	Edmonton	**NHL**	**1**	**1**	**0**	**1**	**0**	....	....	....	....	....
1995-96	**Edmonton**	**NHL**	**20**	**0**	**2**	**2**	**4**	....	....	....	....	....
	Sudbury	OHL	18	10	16	26	37	....	....	....	....	....
	Cape Breton	AHL	12	1	4	5	12	....	....	....	....	....
	NHL Totals		**21**	**1**	**2**	**3**	**4**	....	....	....	....	....

BONVIE, DENNIS — EDM.

Right wing/Defense. Shoots right. 5'11", 205 lbs. Born, Antigonish, N.S., July 23, 1973.

			Regular Season					Playoffs				
Season	Club	Lea	GP	G	A	TP	PIM	GP	G	A	TP	PIM
1991-92	Kitchener	OHL	7	1	1	2	23	....	....	....	....	....
	North Bay	OHL	49	0	12	12	261	21	0	1	1	91
1992-93	North Bay	OHL	64	3	21	24	*316	5	0	0	0	34
1993-94	Cape Breton	AHL	63	1	10	11	278	4	0	0	0	11
1994-95	Cape Breton	AHL	74	5	15	20	422	....	....	....	....	....
	Edmonton	**NHL**	**2**	**0**	**0**	**0**	**0**	....	....	....	....	....
1995-96	**Edmonton**	**NHL**	**8**	**0**	**0**	**0**	**47**	....	....	....	....	....
	Cape Breton	AHL	38	13	14	27	269	....	....	....	....	....
	NHL Totals		**10**	**0**	**0**	**0**	**47**	....	....	....	....	....

Signed as a free agent by **Edmonton**, August 25, 1994.

BORDELEAU, SEBASTIEN — (BOHR-duh-loh) MTL.

Center. Shoots right. 5'10", 180 lbs. Born, Vancouver, B.C., February 15, 1975.
(Montreal's 3rd choice, 73rd overall, in 1993 Entry Draft).

			Regular Season					Playoffs				
Season	Club	Lea	GP	G	A	TP	PIM	GP	G	A	TP	PIM
1991-92	Hull	QMJHL	62	26	32	58	91	5	0	3	3	23
1992-93	Hull	QMJHL	60	18	39	57	95	10	3	8	11	20
1993-94	Hull	QMJHL	60	26	57	83	147	17	6	14	20	26
1994-95a	Hull	QMJHL	68	52	76	128	142	18	*13	19	*32	25
1995-96	**Montreal**	**NHL**	**4**	**0**	**0**	**0**	**0**	....	....	....	....	....
	Fredericton	AHL	43	17	29	46	68	7	0	2	2	8
	NHL Totals		**4**	**0**	**0**	**0**	**0**	....	....	....	....	....

a QMJHL First All-Star Team (1995)

BORSATO, LUCIANO — (bohr-SAH-toh, LOO-chee-AH-noh)

Center. Shoots right. 5'11", 190 lbs. Born, Richmond Hill, Ont., January 7, 1966.
(Winnipeg's 7th choice, 135th overall, in 1984 Entry Draft).

			Regular Season					Playoffs				
Season	Club	Lea	GP	G	A	TP	PIM	GP	G	A	TP	PIM
1984-85	Clarkson	ECAC	33	15	17	32	37	....	....	....	....	....
1985-86	Clarkson	ECAC	28	14	17	31	44	....	....	....	....	....
1986-87	Clarkson	ECAC	31	16	41	57	55	....	....	....	....	....
1987-88ab	Clarkson	ECAC	33	15	29	44	38	....	....	....	....	....
	Moncton	AHL	3	1	1	2	0	....	....	....	....	....
1988-89	Moncton	AHL	6	2	5	7	4	....	....	....	....	....
	Tappara	Fin.	44	31	36	67	69	7	0	3	3	4
1989-90	Moncton	AHL	1	1	0	1	0	....	....	....	....	....
1990-91	**Winnipeg**	**NHL**	**1**	**0**	**1**	**1**	**2**	....	....	....	....	....
	Moncton	AHL	41	14	24	38	40	9	3	7	10	22
1991-92	**Winnipeg**	**NHL**	**56**	**15**	**21**	**36**	**45**	**1**	**0**	**0**	**0**	**0**
	Moncton	AHL	14	2	7	9	39	....	....	....	....	....
1992-93	**Winnipeg**	**NHL**	**67**	**15**	**20**	**35**	**38**	**6**	**1**	**0**	**1**	**4**
1993-94	**Winnipeg**	**NHL**	**75**	**5**	**13**	**18**	**28**	....	....	....	....	....
1994-95	**Winnipeg**	**NHL**	**4**	**0**	**0**	**0**	**0**	....	....	....	....	....
	Springfield	AHL	22	9	11	20	14	....	....	....	....	....
1995-96	Koln	Ger.	49	25	36	61	52	12	6	8	14	28
	NHL Totals		**203**	**35**	**55**	**90**	**113**	**7**	**1**	**0**	**1**	**4**

a ECAC Second All-Star Team (1988)
b NCAA East Second All-American Team (1988)

BORSCHEVSKY, NIKOLAI — (bohr-SHEHV-skee)

Right wing. Shoots left. 5'9", 180 lbs. Born, Tomsk, USSR, January 12, 1965.
(Toronto's 3rd choice, 77th overall, in 1992 Entry Draft).

			Regular Season					Playoffs				
Season	Club	Lea	GP	G	A	TP	PIM	GP	G	A	TP	PIM
1983-84	Moscow D'amo	USSR	34	4	5	9	4	....	....	....	....	....
1984-85	Moscow D'amo	USSR	34	5	9	14	6	....	....	....	....	....
1985-86	Moscow D'amo	USSR	31	6	4	10	4	....	....	....	....	....
1986-87	Moscow D'amo	USSR	28	1	4	5	8	....	....	....	....	....
1987-88	Moscow D'amo	USSR	37	11	7	18	6	....	....	....	....	....
1988-89	Moscow D'amo	USSR	43	7	8	15	18	....	....	....	....	....
1989-90	Spartak	USSR	48	17	25	42	8	....	....	....	....	....
1990-91	Spartak	USSR	45	19	16	35	16	....	....	....	....	....
1991-92	Spartak	CIS	40	25	14	39	16	....	....	....	....	....
1992-93	**Toronto**	**NHL**	**78**	**34**	**40**	**74**	**28**	**16**	**2**	**7**	**9**	**0**
1993-94	**Toronto**	**NHL**	**45**	**14**	**20**	**34**	**10**	**15**	**2**	**2**	**4**	**4**
1994-95	Spartak	CIS	9	5	1	6	14	....	....	....	....	....
	Toronto	**NHL**	**19**	**0**	**5**	**5**	**0**	....	....	....	....	....
	Calgary	**NHL**	**8**	**0**	**5**	**5**	**0**	....	....	....	....	....
1995-96	**Dallas**	**NHL**	**12**	**1**	**3**	**4**	**6**	....	....	....	....	....
	Koln	Ger.	8	0	4	4	27	8	2	2	4	4
	NHL Totals		**162**	**49**	**73**	**122**	**44**	**31**	**4**	**9**	**13**	**4**

Traded to **Calgary** by **Toronto** for Calgary's sixth round choice (Chris Bogas) in 1996 Entry Draft, April 6, 1995. Signed as a free agent by **Dallas**, September 13, 1995.

BOTTERILL, JASON — (BOH-tuhr-ihl) DAL.

Left wing. Shoots left. 6'3", 205 lbs. Born, Edmonton, Alta., May 19, 1976.
(Dallas' 1st choice, 20th overall, in 1994 Entry Draft).

			Regular Season					Playoffs				
Season	Club	Lea	GP	G	A	TP	PIM	GP	G	A	TP	PIM
1993-94	U. of Michigan	CCHA	36	20	19	39	94	....	....	....	....	....
1994-95	U. of Michigan	CCHA	34	14	14	28	117	....	....	....	....	....
1995-96a	U. of Michigan	CCHA	37	*32	25	57	*143	....	....	....	....	....

a CCHA Second All-Star Team (1996)

BOUCHARD, JOEL — CGY.

Defense. Shoots left. 6', 190 lbs. Born, Montreal, Que., January 23, 1974.
(Calgary's 7th choice, 129th overall, in 1992 Entry Draft).

			Regular Season					Playoffs				
Season	Club	Lea	GP	G	A	TP	PIM	GP	G	A	TP	PIM
1990-91	Longueuil	QMJHL	53	3	19	22	34	8	1	0	1	11
1991-92	Verdun	QMJHL	70	9	20	29	55	19	1	7	8	20
1992-93	Verdun	QMJHL	60	10	49	59	126	4	0	2	2	4
1993-94a	Verdun	QMJHL	60	15	55	70	62	4	1	0	1	6
	Saint John	AHL	1	0	0	0	0	2	0	0	0	0
1994-95	Saint John	AHL	77	6	25	31	63	5	1	0	1	4
	Calgary	**NHL**	**2**	**0**	**0**	**0**	**0**	....	....	....	....	....
1995-96	**Calgary**	**NHL**	**4**	**0**	**0**	**0**	**4**	....	....	....	....	....
	Saint John	AHL	74	8	25	33	104	16	1	4	5	10
	NHL Totals		**6**	**0**	**0**	**0**	**4**	....	....	....	....	....

a QMJHL First All-Star Team (1994)

BOUCHER, PHILIPPE — L.A.

Defense. Shoots right. 6'3", 190 lbs. Born, St. Apollinaire, Que., March 24, 1973.
(Buffalo's 1st choice, 13th overall, in 1991 Entry Draft).

			Regular Season					Playoffs				
Season	Club	Lea	GP	G	A	TP	PIM	GP	G	A	TP	PIM
1990-91ab	Granby	QMJHL	69	21	46	67	92	....	....	....	....	....
1991-92	Granby	QMJHL	49	22	37	59	47	....	....	....	....	....
b	Laval	QMJHL	16	7	11	18	36	10	5	6	11	8
1992-93	**Buffalo**	**NHL**	**18**	**0**	**4**	**4**	**14**	....	....	....	....	....
	Laval	QMJHL	16	12	15	27	37	13	6	15	21	12
	Rochester	AHL	5	4	3	7	8	3	0	1	1	2
1993-94	**Buffalo**	**NHL**	**38**	**6**	**8**	**14**	**29**	**7**	**1**	**1**	**2**	**2**
	Rochester	AHL	31	10	22	32	51	....	....	....	....	....
1994-95	Rochester	AHL	43	14	27	41	26	....	....	....	....	....
	Buffalo	**NHL**	**9**	**1**	**4**	**5**	**0**	....	....	....	....	....
	Los Angeles	**NHL**	**6**	**1**	**0**	**1**	**4**	....	....	....	....	....
1995-96	**Los Angeles**	**NHL**	**53**	**7**	**16**	**23**	**31**	....	....	....	....	....
	Phoenix	IHL	10	4	3	7	4	....	....	....	....	....
	NHL Totals		**124**	**15**	**32**	**47**	**78**	**7**	**1**	**1**	**2**	**2**

a Canadian Major Junior Rookie of the Year (1991)
b QMJHL Second All-Star Team (1991, 1992)

Traded to **Los Angeles** by **Buffalo** with Denis Tsygurov and Grant Fuhr for Alexei Zhitnik, Robb Stauber, Charlie Huddy and Los Angeles' fifth round choice (Marian Menhart) in 1995 Entry Draft, February 14, 1995.

BOUGHNER, BOB (BOOG-nuhr) BUF.

Defense. Shoots right. 6', 205 lbs. Born, Windsor, Ont., March 8, 1971.
(Detroit's 2nd choice, 32nd overall, in 1989 Entry Draft).

			Regular Season					Playoffs				
Season	Club	Lea	GP	G	A	TP	PIM	GP	G	A	TP	PIM
1988-89	S.S. Marie	OHL	64	6	15	21	182	....	....	....	....	....
1989-90	S.S. Marie	OHL	49	7	23	30	122	....	....	....	....	....
1990-91	S.S. Marie	OHL	64	13	33	46	156	14	2	9	11	35
1991-92	Toledo	ECHL	28	3	10	13	79	5	2	0	2	15
	Adirondack	AHL	1	0	0	0	7	....	....	....	....	....
1992-93	Adirondack	AHL	69	1	16	17	190	....	....	....	....	....
1993-94	Adirondack	AHL	72	8	14	22	292	10	1	1	2	18
1994-95	Cincinnati	IHL	81	2	14	16	192	10	0	0	0	18
1995-96	Carolina	AHL	46	2	15	17	127	....	....	....	....	....
	Buffalo	**NHL**	**31**	**0**	**1**	**1**	**104**	....	....	....	....	....
	NHL Totals		**31**	**0**	**1**	**1**	**104**	....	....	....	....	....

Signed as a free agent by **Florida**, July 25, 1994. Traded to **Buffalo** by **Florida** for Buffalo's third round choice (Chris Allen) in 1996 Entry Draft, February 1, 1996.

BOULERICE, JESSE PHI.

Defense. Shoots right. 6'1", 200 lbs. Born, Plattsburgh, NY, August 10, 1978.
(Philadelphia's 4th choice, 133rd overall, in 1996 Entry Draft).

			Regular Season					Playoffs				
Season	Club	Lea	GP	G	A	TP	PIM	GP	G	A	TP	PIM
1995-96	Detroit	OHL	64	2	5	7	150	16	0	0	0	12

BOULIN, VLADISLAV PHI.

Defense. Shoots left. 6'1", 210 lbs. Born, Penza, USSR, May 18, 1972.
(Philadelphia's 4th choice, 103rd overall, in 1992 Entry Draft).

			Regular Season					Playoffs				
Season	Club	Lea	GP	G	A	TP	PIM	GP	G	A	TP	PIM
1992-93	Moscow D'amo	CIS	32	2	1	3	55	4	0	0	0	2
1993-94	Moscow D'amo	CIS	43	4	2	6	36	7	0	1	1	16
1994-95	Hershey	AHL	52	1	7	8	30	....	....	....	....	....
1995-96	Hershey	AHL	32	1	2	3	30	2	0	0	0	0

BOULTON, ERIC NYR

Left wing. Shoots left. 6', 201 lbs. Born, Halifax, N.S., August 17, 1976.
(NY Rangers' 12th choice, 234th overall, in 1994 Entry Draft).

			Regular Season					Playoffs				
Season	Club	Lea	GP	G	A	TP	PIM	GP	G	A	TP	PIM
1993-94	Oshawa	OHL	45	4	3	7	149	5	0	0	0	16
1994-95	Oshawa	OHL	27	7	5	12	125	....	....	....	....	....
	Sarnia	OHL	24	3	7	10	134	4	0	1	1	10
1995-96	Sarnia	OHL	66	14	29	43	243	9	0	3	3	29

BOUMEDIENNE, JOSEF N.J.

Defense. Shoots left. 6'1", 190 lbs. Born, Stockholm, Sweden, January 12, 1978.
(New Jersey's 7th choice, 91st overall, in 1996 Entry Draft).

			Regular Season					Playoffs				
Season	Club	Lea	GP	G	A	TP	PIM	GP	G	A	TP	PIM
1994-95	Huddinge	Swe. Jr.	10	0	2	2	57	....	....	....	....	....
1995-96	Huddinge	Swe. Jr.	25	2	4	6	66	....	....	....	....	....
	Huddinge	Swe. 2	7	0	0	0	14	....	....	....	....	....

BOURQUE, PHIL (BOHRK)

Left wing. Shoots left. 6'1", 196 lbs. Born, Chelmsford, MA, June 8, 1962.

			Regular Season					Playoffs				
Season	Club	Lea	GP	G	A	TP	PIM	GP	G	A	TP	PIM
1980-81	Kingston	OHL	47	4	4	8	46	6	0	0	0	10
1981-82	Kingston	OHL	67	11	40	51	111	4	0	0	0	0
1982-83	Baltimore	AHL	65	1	15	16	93	....	....	....	....	....
1983-84	**Pittsburgh**	**NHL**	**5**	**0**	**1**	**1**	**12**	....	....	....	....	....
	Baltimore	AHL	58	5	17	22	96	....	....	....	....	....
1984-85	Baltimore	AHL	79	6	15	21	164	13	2	5	7	23
1985-86	**Pittsburgh**	**NHL**	**4**	**0**	**0**	**0**	**2**	....	....	....	....	....
	Baltimore	AHL	74	8	18	26	226	....	....	....	....	....
1986-87	**Pittsburgh**	**NHL**	**22**	**2**	**3**	**5**	**32**	....	....	....	....	....
	Baltimore	AHL	49	15	16	31	183	....	....	....	....	....
1987-88	**Pittsburgh**	**NHL**	**21**	**4**	**12**	**16**	**20**	....	....	....	....	....
ab	Muskegon	IHL	52	16	36	52	66	6	1	2	3	16
1988-89	**Pittsburgh**	**NHL**	**80**	**17**	**26**	**43**	**97**	**11**	**4**	**1**	**5**	**66**
1989-90	**Pittsburgh**	**NHL**	**76**	**22**	**17**	**39**	**108**	....	....	....	....	....
1990-91	**Pittsburgh**	**NHL**	**78**	**20**	**14**	**34**	**106**	**24**	**6**	**7**	**13**	**16 ♦**
1991-92	**Pittsburgh**	**NHL**	**58**	**10**	**16**	**26**	**58**	**21**	**3**	**4**	**7**	**25 ♦**
1992-93	**NY Rangers**	**NHL**	**55**	**6**	**14**	**20**	**39**	....	....	....	....	....
1993-94	**NY Rangers**	**NHL**	**16**	**0**	**1**	**1**	**8**	....	....	....	....	....
	Ottawa	**NHL**	**11**	**2**	**3**	**5**	**0**	....	....	....	....	....
1994-95	**Ottawa**	**NHL**	**38**	**4**	**3**	**7**	**20**	....	....	....	....	....
1995-96	**Ottawa**	**NHL**	**13**	**1**	**1**	**2**	**14**	....	....	....	....	....
	Detroit	IHL	36	4	13	17	70	10	1	3	4	10
	NHL Totals		**477**	**88**	**111**	**199**	**516**	**56**	**13**	**12**	**25**	**107**

a IHL First All-Star Team (1988)
b Won Governor's Trophy (Outstanding Defenseman - IHL) (1988)

Signed as a free agent by **Pittsburgh**, October 4, 1982. Signed as a free agent by **NY Rangers**, August 31, 1992. Traded to **Ottawa** by **NY Rangers** for future considerations, March 21, 1994.

BOURQUE, RAY (BOHRK) BOS.

Defense. Shoots left. 5'11", 215 lbs. Born, Montreal, Que., December 28, 1960.
(Boston's 1st choice, 8th overall, in 1979 Entry Draft).

			Regular Season					Playoffs				
Season	Club	Lea	GP	G	A	TP	PIM	GP	G	A	TP	PIM
1976-77	Sorel	QJHL	69	12	36	48	61	....	....	....	....	....
1977-78	Verdun	QJHL	72	22	57	79	90	4	2	1	3	0
1978-79	Verdun	QJHL	63	22	71	93	44	11	3	16	19	18
1979-80ab	**Boston**	**NHL**	**80**	**17**	**48**	**65**	**73**	**10**	**2**	**9**	**11**	**27**
1980-81c	**Boston**	**NHL**	**67**	**27**	**29**	**56**	**96**	**3**	**0**	**1**	**1**	**2**
1981-82b	**Boston**	**NHL**	**65**	**17**	**49**	**66**	**51**	**9**	**1**	**5**	**6**	**16**
1982-83c	**Boston**	**NHL**	**65**	**22**	**51**	**73**	**20**	**17**	**8**	**15**	**23**	**10**
1983-84b	**Boston**	**NHL**	**78**	**31**	**65**	**96**	**57**	**3**	**0**	**2**	**2**	**0**
1984-85b	**Boston**	**NHL**	**73**	**20**	**66**	**86**	**53**	**5**	**0**	**3**	**3**	**4**
1985-86c	**Boston**	**NHL**	**74**	**19**	**58**	**77**	**68**	**3**	**0**	**0**	**0**	**0**
1986-87bd	**Boston**	**NHL**	**78**	**23**	**72**	**95**	**36**	**4**	**1**	**2**	**3**	**0**
1987-88bd	**Boston**	**NHL**	**78**	**17**	**64**	**81**	**72**	**23**	**3**	**18**	**21**	**26**
1988-89c	**Boston**	**NHL**	**60**	**18**	**43**	**61**	**52**	**10**	**0**	**4**	**4**	**6**
1989-90bd	**Boston**	**NHL**	**76**	**19**	**65**	**84**	**50**	**17**	**5**	**12**	**17**	**16**
1990-91bd	**Boston**	**NHL**	**76**	**21**	**73**	**94**	**75**	**19**	**7**	**18**	**25**	**12**
1991-92be	**Boston**	**NHL**	**80**	**21**	**60**	**81**	**56**	**12**	**3**	**6**	**9**	**12**
1992-93b	**Boston**	**NHL**	**78**	**19**	**63**	**82**	**40**	**4**	**1**	**0**	**1**	**2**
1993-94bd	**Boston**	**NHL**	**72**	**20**	**71**	**91**	**58**	**13**	**2**	**8**	**10**	**0**
1994-95c	**Boston**	**NHL**	**46**	**12**	**31**	**43**	**20**	**5**	**0**	**3**	**3**	**0**
1995-96b	**Boston**	**NHL**	**82**	**20**	**62**	**82**	**58**	**5**	**1**	**6**	**7**	**2**
	NHL Totals		**1228**	**343**	**970**	**1313**	**935**	**162**	**34**	**112**	**146**	**135**

a Won Calder Memorial Trophy (1980)
b NHL First All-Star Team (1980, 1982, 1984, 1985, 1987, 1988, 1990, 1991, 1992, 1993, 1994, 1996)
c NHL Second All-Star Team (1981, 1983, 1986, 1989, 1995)
d Won James Norris Memorial Trophy (1987, 1988, 1990, 1991, 1994)
e Won King Clancy Memorial Trophy (1992)

Played in NHL All-Star Game (1981-86, 1988-94, 1996)

BOWEN, CURTIS (BOW-ehn) DET.

Left wing. Shoots left. 6'1", 195 lbs. Born, Kenora, Ont., March 24, 1974.
(Detroit's 1st choice, 22nd overall, in 1992 Entry Draft).

			Regular Season					Playoffs				
Season	Club	Lea	GP	G	A	TP	PIM	GP	G	A	TP	PIM
1990-91	Ottawa	OHL	42	12	14	26	31	....	....	....	....	....
1991-92	Ottawa	OHL	65	31	45	76	94	11	3	7	10	11
1992-93	Ottawa	OHL	21	9	19	28	51	....	....	....	....	....
1993-94	Ottawa	OHL	52	25	37	62	98	17	8	13	21	14
1994-95	Adirondack	AHL	64	6	11	17	71	4	0	2	2	4
1995-96	Cdn. National	....	31	8	8	16	48	....	....	....	....	....
	Adirondack	AHL	3	0	0	0	0	....	....	....	....	....

BOWEN, JASON (BOW-ehn) PHI.

Left wing. Shoots left. 6'4", 215 lbs. Born, Port Alice, B.C., November 9, 1973.
(Philadelphia's 2nd choice, 15th overall, in 1992 Entry Draft).

			Regular Season					Playoffs				
Season	Club	Lea	GP	G	A	TP	PIM	GP	G	A	TP	PIM
1989-90	Tri-City	WHL	61	8	5	13	129	7	0	3	3	4
1990-91	Tri-City	WHL	60	7	13	20	252	6	2	2	4	18
1991-92	Tri-City	WHL	19	5	3	8	135	5	0	1	1	42
1992-93	**Philadelphia**	**NHL**	**7**	**1**	**0**	**1**	**2**	....	....	....	....	....
	Tri-City	WHL	62	10	12	22	219	3	1	1	2	18
1993-94	**Philadelphia**	**NHL**	**56**	**1**	**5**	**6**	**87**	....	....	....	....	....
1994-95	Hershey	AHL	55	5	5	10	116	6	0	0	0	46
	Philadelphia	**NHL**	**4**	**0**	**0**	**0**	**0**	....	....	....	....	....
1995-96	**Philadelphia**	**NHL**	**2**	**0**	**0**	**0**	**2**	....	....	....	....	....
	Hershey	AHL	72	6	7	13	128	4	2	0	2	13
	NHL Totals		**69**	**2**	**5**	**7**	**91**	....	....	....	....	....

BOYD, KEVIN OTT.

Left wing. Shoots left. 6'3", 195 lbs. Born, Newmarket, Ont., May 19, 1977.
(Ottawa's 5th choice, 103rd overall, in 1995 Entry Draft).

			Regular Season					Playoffs				
Season	Club	Lea	GP	G	A	TP	PIM	GP	G	A	TP	PIM
1994-95	London	OHL	65	5	5	10	125	4	0	0	0	0
1995-96	London	OHL	62	8	14	22	108	....	....	....	....	....

BOYER, ZAC

Right wing. Shoots right. 6'1", 199 lbs. Born, Inuvik, N.W.T., October 25, 1971.
(Chicago's 4th choice, 88th overall, in 1991 Entry Draft).

			Regular Season					Playoffs				
Season	Club	Lea	GP	G	A	TP	PIM	GP	G	A	TP	PIM
1988-89	Kamloops	WHL	42	10	17	27	22	16	9	8	17	10
1989-90	Kamloops	WHL	71	24	47	71	163	17	4	4	8	8
1990-91	Kamloops	WHL	64	45	60	105	58	12	6	10	16	8
1991-92	Kamloops	WHL	70	40	69	109	90	17	9	*20	*29	16
1992-93	Indianapolis	IHL	59	7	14	21	26	....	....	....	....	....
1993-94	Indianapolis	IHL	54	13	12	25	67	....	....	....	....	....
1994-95	Kalamazoo	IHL	22	9	7	16	22	15	3	9	12	8
	Dallas	**NHL**	**1**	**0**	**0**	**0**	**0**	**2**	**0**	**0**	**0**	**0**
1995-96	**Dallas**	**NHL**	**2**	**0**	**0**	**0**	**0**	....	....	....	....	....
	Michigan	IHL	67	24	27	51	58	10	11	6	17	0
	NHL Totals		**3**	**0**	**0**	**0**	**0**	**2**	**0**	**0**	**0**	**0**

Signed as a free agent by **Dallas**, July 25, 1994.

BRADLEY, BRIAN — T.B.

Center. Shoots right. 5'10", 177 lbs. Born, Kitchener, Ont., January 21, 1965.
(Calgary's 2nd choice, 51st overall, in 1983 Entry Draft).

			Regular Season					Playoffs				
Season	Club	Lea	GP	G	A	TP	PIM	GP	G	A	TP	PIM
1982-83	London	OHL	67	37	82	119	37	3	1	0	1	0
1983-84	London	OHL	49	40	60	100	24	4	2	4	6	0
1984-85	London	OHL	32	27	49	76	22	8	5	10	15	4
1985-86	**Calgary**	**NHL**	**5**	**0**	**1**	**1**	**0**	**1**	**0**	**0**	**0**	**0**
	Moncton	AHL	59	23	42	65	40	10	6	9	15	4
1986-87	**Calgary**	**NHL**	**40**	**10**	**18**	**28**	**16**	....	....	....	....	....
	Moncton	AHL	20	12	16	28	8	....	....	....	....	....
1987-88	Cdn. National	....	47	18	19	37	42	....	....	....	....	....
	Cdn. Olympic	....	7	0	4	4	0	....	....	....	....	....
	Vancouver	**NHL**	**11**	**3**	**5**	**8**	**6**	....	....	....	....	....
1988-89	**Vancouver**	**NHL**	**71**	**18**	**27**	**45**	**42**	**7**	**3**	**4**	**7**	**10**
1989-90	**Vancouver**	**NHL**	**67**	**19**	**29**	**48**	**65**	....	....	....	....	....
1990-91	**Vancouver**	**NHL**	**44**	**11**	**20**	**31**	**42**	....	....	....	....	....
	Toronto	**NHL**	**26**	**0**	**11**	**11**	**20**	....	....	....	....	....
1991-92	**Toronto**	**NHL**	**59**	**10**	**21**	**31**	**48**	....	....	....	....	....
1992-93	**Tampa Bay**	**NHL**	**80**	**42**	**44**	**86**	**92**	....	....	....	....	....
1993-94	**Tampa Bay**	**NHL**	**78**	**24**	**40**	**64**	**56**	....	....	....	....	....
1994-95	**Tampa Bay**	**NHL**	**46**	**13**	**27**	**40**	**42**	....	....	....	....	....
1995-96	**Tampa Bay**	**NHL**	**75**	**23**	**56**	**79**	**77**	**5**	**0**	**3**	**3**	**6**
	NHL Totals		**602**	**173**	**299**	**472**	**506**	**13**	**3**	**7**	**10**	**16**

Played in NHL All-Star Game (1993, 1994)

Traded to **Vancouver** by **Calgary** with Peter Bakovic and Kevin Guy for Craig Coxe, March 6, 1988. Traded to **Toronto** by **Vancouver** for Tom Kurvers, January 12, 1991. Claimed by **Tampa Bay** from **Toronto** in Expansion Draft, June 18, 1992.

BRADLEY, E.J. — PHI.

Center. Shoots left. 5'10", 182 lbs. Born, New Hyde Park, NY, January 2, 1975.
(Philadelphia's 9th choice, 226th overall, in 1993 Entry Draft).

			Regular Season					Playoffs				
Season	Club	Lea	GP	G	A	TP	PIM	GP	G	A	TP	PIM
1994-95	U. Wisconsin	WCHA	40	3	4	7	22	....	....	....	....	....
1995-96	U. Wisconsin	WCHA	26	1	6	7	39	....	....	....	....	....

BRADLEY, MATT — S.J.

Right wing. Shoots right. 6'1", 168 lbs. Born, Stittsville, Ont., June 13, 1978.
(San Jose's 4th choice, 102nd overall, in 1996 Entry Draft).

			Regular Season					Playoffs				
Season	Club	Lea	GP	G	A	TP	PIM	GP	G	A	TP	PIM
1994-95	Cumberland	CJHL	49	13	20	33	18	....	....	....	....	....
1995-96	Kingston	OHL	55	10	14	24	17	6	0	1	1	6

BRADY, NEIL — DAL.

Center. Shoots left. 6'2", 200 lbs. Born, Montreal, Que., April 12, 1968.
(New Jersey's 1st choice, 3rd overall, in 1986 Entry Draft).

			Regular Season					Playoffs				
Season	Club	Lea	GP	G	A	TP	PIM	GP	G	A	TP	PIM
1984-85	Calgary	Midget	37	25	50	75	75	....	....	....	....	....
	Medicine Hat	WHL	....	....	....	....	....	3	0	0	0	2
1985-86	Medicine Hat	WHL	72	21	60	81	104	21	9	11	20	23
1986-87	Medicine Hat	WHL	57	19	64	83	126	18	1	4	5	25
1987-88	Medicine Hat	WHL	61	16	35	51	110	15	0	3	3	19
1988-89	Utica	AHL	75	16	21	37	56	4	0	3	3	0
1989-90	**New Jersey**	**NHL**	**19**	**1**	**4**	**5**	**13**	....	....	....	....	....
	Utica	AHL	38	10	13	23	21	5	0	1	1	10
1990-91	**New Jersey**	**NHL**	**3**	**0**	**0**	**0**	**0**	....	....	....	....	....
	Utica	AHL	77	33	63	96	91	....	....	....	....	....
1991-92	**New Jersey**	**NHL**	**7**	**1**	**0**	**1**	**4**	....	....	....	....	....
	Utica	AHL	33	12	30	42	28	....	....	....	....	....
1992-93	**Ottawa**	**NHL**	**55**	**7**	**17**	**24**	**57**	....	....	....	....	....
	New Haven	AHL	8	6	3	9	2	....	....	....	....	....
1993-94	Kalamazoo	IHL	43	10	16	26	188	5	1	1	2	10
	Dallas	**NHL**	**5**	**0**	**1**	**1**	**21**	....	....	....	....	....
1994-95	Kalamazoo	IHL	70	13	45	58	140	15	5	14	19	22
1995-96	Michigan	IHL	61	14	20	34	127	10	1	4	5	8
	NHL Totals		**89**	**9**	**22**	**31**	**95**	....	....	....	....	....

Traded to **Ottawa** by **New Jersey** for future considerations, September 3, 1992. Signed as a free agent by **Dallas**, December 3, 1993.

BRASHEAR, DONALD — (bra-SHEER) — MTL.

Left wing. Shoots left. 6'2", 220 lbs. Born, Bedford, IN, January 7, 1972.

			Regular Season					Playoffs				
Season	Club	Lea	GP	G	A	TP	PIM	GP	G	A	TP	PIM
1989-90	Longueuil	QMJHL	64	12	14	26	169	7	0	0	0	11
1990-91	Longueuil	QMJHL	68	12	26	38	195	8	0	3	3	33
1991-92	Verdun	QMJHL	65	18	24	42	283	18	4	2	6	98
1992-93	Fredericton	AHL	76	11	3	14	261	5	0	0	0	8
1993-94	**Montreal**	**NHL**	**14**	**2**	**2**	**4**	**34**	**2**	**0**	**0**	**0**	**0**
	Fredericton	AHL	62	38	28	66	250	....	....	....	....	....
1994-95	Fredericton	AHL	29	10	9	19	182	17	7	5	12	77
	Montreal	**NHL**	**20**	**1**	**1**	**2**	**63**	....	....	....	....	....
1995-96	**Montreal**	**NHL**	**67**	**0**	**4**	**4**	**223**	**6**	**0**	**0**	**0**	**2**
	NHL Totals		**101**	**3**	**7**	**10**	**320**	**8**	**0**	**0**	**0**	**2**

Signed as a free agent by **Montreal**, July 28, 1992.

BREEN, GEORGE — EDM.

Right wing. Shoots right. 6'2", 200 lbs. Born, Webster, MA, August 3, 1973.
(Edmonton's 4th choice, 56th overall, in 1991 Entry Draft).

			Regular Season					Playoffs				
Season	Club	Lea	GP	G	A	TP	PIM	GP	G	A	TP	PIM
1991-92	Providence	H.E.	36	8	4	12	24	....	....	....	....	....
1992-93	Providence	H.E.	31	11	7	18	45	....	....	....	....	....
1993-94	Providence	H.E.	32	8	14	22	22	....	....	....	....	....
1994-95	Providence	H.E.	36	17	18	35	51	....	....	....	....	....
1995-96	Cape Breton	AHL	50	11	12	23	20	....	....	....	....	....

BRENNAN, RICH — COL.

Defense. Shoots right. 6'2", 200 lbs. Born, Schenectady, NY, November 26, 1972.
(Quebec's 3rd choice, 46th overall, in 1991 Entry Draft).

			Regular Season					Playoffs				
Season	Club	Lea	GP	G	A	TP	PIM	GP	G	A	TP	PIM
1991-92	Boston U.	H.E.	30	4	13	17	50	....	....	....	....	....
1992-93	Boston U.	H.E.	40	9	11	20	68	....	....	....	....	....
1993-94ab	Boston U.	H.E.	41	8	27	35	82	....	....	....	....	....
1994-95	Boston U.	H.E.	31	5	22	27	56	....	....	....	....	....
1995-96	Brantford	ColHL	5	1	2	3	2	....	....	....	....	....
	Cornwall	AHL	36	4	8	12	61	7	0	0	0	6

a Hockey East First All-Star Team (1994)
b NCAA East Second All-American Team (1994)

BRICKLEY, ANDY

Left wing/Center. Shoots left. 5'11", 200 lbs. Born, Melrose, MA, August 9, 1961.
(Philadelphia's 10th choice, 210th overall, in 1980 Entry Draft).

			Regular Season					Playoffs				
Season	Club	Lea	GP	G	A	TP	PIM	GP	G	A	TP	PIM
1979-80	N. Hampshire	ECAC	27	15	17	32	8	....	....	....	....	....
1980-81	N. Hampshire	ECAC	31	27	25	52	16	....	....	....	....	....
1981-82ab	N. Hampshire	ECAC	35	26	27	53	6	....	....	....	....	....
1982-83	**Philadelphia**	**NHL**	**3**	**1**	**1**	**2**	**0**	....	....	....	....	....
c	Maine	AHL	76	29	54	83	10	17	9	5	14	0
1983-84	Springfield	AHL	7	1	5	6	2	....	....	....	....	....
	Pittsburgh	**NHL**	**50**	**18**	**20**	**38**	**9**	....	....	....	....	....
	Baltimore	AHL	4	0	5	5	2	....	....	....	....	....
1984-85	**Pittsburgh**	**NHL**	**45**	**7**	**15**	**22**	**10**	....	....	....	....	....
	Baltimore	AHL	31	13	14	27	8	15	*10	8	18	0
1985-86	Maine	AHL	60	26	34	60	20	5	0	4	4	0
1986-87	**New Jersey**	**NHL**	**51**	**11**	**12**	**23**	**8**	....	....	....	....	....
1987-88	**New Jersey**	**NHL**	**45**	**8**	**14**	**22**	**14**	**4**	**0**	**1**	**1**	**4**
	Utica	AHL	9	5	8	13	4	....	....	....	....	....
1988-89	**Boston**	**NHL**	**71**	**13**	**22**	**35**	**20**	**10**	**0**	**2**	**2**	**0**
1989-90	**Boston**	**NHL**	**43**	**12**	**28**	**40**	**8**	**2**	**0**	**0**	**0**	**0**
1990-91	**Boston**	**NHL**	**40**	**2**	**9**	**11**	**8**	....	....	....	....	....
	Maine	AHL	17	8	17	25	2	1	0	0	0	0
1991-92	**Boston**	**NHL**	**23**	**10**	**17**	**27**	**2**	....	....	....	....	....
	Maine	AHL	14	5	15	20	2	....	....	....	....	....
1992-93	**Winnipeg**	**NHL**	**12**	**0**	**2**	**2**	**2**	**1**	**1**	**1**	**2**	**0**
	Moncton	AHL	38	15	36	51	10	5	4	2	6	0
1993-94	**Winnipeg**	**NHL**	**2**	**0**	**0**	**0**	**0**	....	....	....	....	....
	Moncton	AHL	53	20	39	59	20	19	8	*19	*27	4
1994-95	Denver	IHL	58	15	35	50	16	16	5	*25	*30	2
1995-96	Utah	IHL	36	12	34	46	24	16	6	13	19	8
	NHL Totals		**385**	**82**	**140**	**222**	**81**	**17**	**1**	**4**	**5**	**4**

a ECAC First All-Star Team (1982)
b NCAA All-American Team (1982)
c AHL Second All-Star Team (1983)

Traded to **Pittsburgh** by **Philadelphia** with Mark Taylor, Ron Flockhart, Philadelphia's first round (Roger Belanger) and third round (later traded to Vancouver — Vancouver selected Mike Stevens) choices in 1984 Entry Draft for Rich Sutter and Pittsburgh's second round (Greg Smyth) and third round (David McLay) choices in 1984 Entry Draft, October 23, 1983. Signed as a free agent by **New Jersey**, July 8, 1986. Claimed by **Boston** from **New Jersey** in NHL Waiver Draft, October 3, 1988. Signed as a free agent by **Winnipeg**, November 11, 1992. Signed as a free agent by **NY Islanders**, July 27, 1994.

BRIERE, DANIEL — (bree-AIR) — PHO.

Center. Shoots left. 5'9", 160 lbs. Born, Gatineau, Que., October 6, 1977.
(Phoenix's 2nd choice, 24th overall, in 1996 Entry Draft).

			Regular Season					Playoffs				
Season	Club	Lea	GP	G	A	TP	PIM	GP	G	A	TP	PIM
1994-95	Drummondville	QMJHL	72	51	72	123	54	4	2	3	5	2
1995-96a	Drummondville	QMJHL	67	*67	*96	*163	84	6	6	12	18	8

a QMJHL Second All-Star Team (1996)

BRIGLEY, TRAVIS — CGY.

Left wing. Shoots left. 6'1", 190 lbs. Born, Coronation, Alta., June 16, 1977.
(Calgary's 2nd choice, 39th overall, in 1996 Entry Draft).

			Regular Season					Playoffs				
Season	Club	Lea	GP	G	A	TP	PIM	GP	G	A	TP	PIM
1994-95	Lethbridge	WHL	64	14	18	32	14	....	....	....	....	....
1995-96	Lethbridge	WHL	69	34	43	77	94	4	2	3	5	8

BRIMANIS, ARIS — PHI.

Defense. Shoots right. 6'3", 210 lbs. Born, Cleveland, OH, March 14, 1972.
(Philadelphia's 3rd choice, 86th overall, in 1991 Entry Draft).

			Regular Season					Playoffs				
Season	Club	Lea	GP	G	A	TP	PIM	GP	G	A	TP	PIM
1990-91	Bowling Green	CCHA	38	3	6	9	42	....	....	....	....	....
1991-92	Bowling Green	CCHA	32	2	9	11	38	....	....	....	....	....
1992-93	Brandon	WHL	71	8	50	58	110	4	2	1	3	7
1993-94	**Philadelphia**	**NHL**	**1**	**0**	**0**	**0**	**0**	....	....	....	....	....
	Hershey	AHL	75	8	15	23	65	11	2	3	5	12
1994-95	Hershey	AHL	76	8	17	25	68	6	1	1	2	14
1995-96	**Philadelphia**	**NHL**	**17**	**0**	**2**	**2**	**12**	....	....	....	....	....
	Hershey	AHL	54	9	22	31	64	5	1	2	3	4
	NHL Totals		**18**	**0**	**2**	**2**	**12**	....	....	....	....	....

BRIND'AMOUR, ROD — (BRIHND-uh-MOHR) — PHI.

Center. Shoots left. 6'1", 202 lbs. Born, Ottawa, Ont., August 9, 1970.
(St. Louis' 1st choice, 9th overall, in 1988 Entry Draft).

			Regular Season					Playoffs				
Season	Club	Lea	GP	G	A	TP	PIM	GP	G	A	TP	PIM
1988-89	Michigan State	CCHA	42	27	32	59	63	....	....	....	....	....
	St. Louis	**NHL**	....	....	....	....	....	**5**	**2**	**0**	**2**	**4**
1989-90a	**St. Louis**	**NHL**	**79**	**26**	**35**	**61**	**46**	**12**	**5**	**8**	**13**	**6**
1990-91	**St. Louis**	**NHL**	**78**	**17**	**32**	**49**	**93**	**13**	**2**	**5**	**7**	**10**
1991-92	**Philadelphia**	**NHL**	**80**	**33**	**44**	**77**	**100**	....	....	....	....	....
1992-93	**Philadelphia**	**NHL**	**81**	**37**	**49**	**86**	**89**	....	....	....	....	....
1993-94	**Philadelphia**	**NHL**	**84**	**35**	**62**	**97**	**85**	....	....	....	....	....
1994-95	**Philadelphia**	**NHL**	**48**	**12**	**27**	**39**	**33**	**15**	**6**	**9**	**15**	**8**
1995-96	**Philadelphia**	**NHL**	**82**	**26**	**61**	**87**	**110**	**12**	**2**	**5**	**7**	**6**
	NHL Totals		**532**	**186**	**310**	**496**	**556**	**57**	**17**	**27**	**44**	**34**

a NHL All-Rookie Team (1990)

Played in NHL All-Star Game (1992)

Traded to **Philadelphia** by **St. Louis** with Dan Quinn for Ron Sutter and Murray Baron, September 22, 1991.

BRISEBOIS, PATRICE   (BREES-bwah, pa-TREEZ)   **MTL.**

Defense. Shoots right. 6'1", 188 lbs.   Born, Montreal, Que., January 27, 1971.
(Montreal's 2nd choice, 30th overall, in 1989 Entry Draft).

					Regular Season					Playoffs			
Season	Club	Lea	GP	G	A	TP	PIM	GP	G	A	TP	PIM
1987-88	Laval	QMJHL	48	10	34	44	95	6	0	2	2	2
1988-89	Laval	QMJHL	50	20	45	65	95	17	8	14	22	45
1989-90a	Laval	QMJHL	56	18	70	88	108	13	7	9	16	26
1990-91	**Montreal**	**NHL**	**10**	**0**	**2**	**2**	**4**	....	....	....	....	....
bcd	Drummondville	QMJHL	54	17	44	61	72	14	6	18	24	49
1991-92	**Montreal**	**NHL**	**26**	**2**	**8**	**10**	**20**	**11**	**2**	**4**	**6**	**6**
	Fredericton	AHL	53	12	27	39	51	....	....	....	....	....
1992-93	**Montreal**	**NHL**	**70**	**10**	**21**	**31**	**79**	**20**	**0**	**4**	**4**	**18 ♦**
1993-94	**Montreal**	**NHL**	**53**	**2**	**21**	**23**	**63**	**7**	**0**	**4**	**4**	**6**
1994-95	**Montreal**	**NHL**	**35**	**4**	**8**	**12**	**26**	....	....	....	....	....
1995-96	**Montreal**	**NHL**	**69**	**9**	**27**	**36**	**65**	**6**	**1**	**2**	**3**	**6**
	NHL Totals		**263**	**27**	**87**	**114**	**257**	**44**	**3**	**14**	**17**	**36**

a QMJHL Second All-Star Team (1990)
b Canadian Major Junior Defenseman of the Year (1991)
c QMJHL First All-Star Team (1991)
d Memorial Cup All-Star Team (1991)

BRISKE, BYRON   **ANA.**

Defense. Shoots right. 6'2", 194 lbs.   Born, Humboldt, Sask., January 23, 1976.
(Anaheim's 4th choice, 80th overall, in 1994 Entry Draft).

					Regular Season					Playoffs			
Season	Club	Lea	GP	G	A	TP	PIM	GP	G	A	TP	PIM
1992-93	Victoria	WHL	66	1	10	11	110	....	....	....	....	....
1993-94	Red Deer	WHL	61	6	21	27	174	....	....	....	....	....
1994-95	Red Deer	WHL	48	4	17	21	116	....	....	....	....	....
	Tri-City	WHL	15	0	1	1	22	13	0	0	0	18
1995-96	Tri-City	WHL	72	15	38	53	189	11	0	5	5	36

BROS, MICHAL   **S.J.**

Center. Shoots right. 6'1", 195 lbs.   Born, Olomouc, Czech., January 25, 1976.
(San Jose's 6th choice, 130th overall, in 1995 Entry Draft).

					Regular Season					Playoffs			
Season	Club	Lea	GP	G	A	TP	PIM	GP	G	A	TP	PIM
1994-95	Olomouc	Czech. Jr.	34	29	32	61	....	....	....	....	....	....
1995-96	Olomouc	Czech.	35	8	11	19	....	4	2	0	2	....

BROSSEAU, DAVID   **NYR**

Center. Shoots right. 6'2", 189 lbs.   Born, Montreal, Que., January 16, 1976.
(NY Rangers' 8th choice, 156th overall, in 1994 Entry Draft).

					Regular Season					Playoffs			
Season	Club	Lea	GP	G	A	TP	PIM	GP	G	A	TP	PIM
1992-93	Shawinigan	QMJHL	56	5	4	9	28	....	....	....	....	....
1993-94	Shawinigan	QMJHL	65	27	26	53	62	5	3	0	3	2
1994-95	Shawinigan	QMJHL	39	28	20	48	65	....	....	....	....	....
	Granby	QMJHL	26	9	6	15	37	13	2	2	4	4
1995-96	Granby	QMJHL	63	32	33	65	115	21	*22	12	34	30

BROTEN, NEAL   (BRAH-tuhn)   **N.J.**

Center. Shoots left. 5'9", 175 lbs.   Born, Roseau, MN, November 29, 1959.
(Minnesota's 3rd choice, 42nd overall, in 1979 Entry Draft).

					Regular Season					Playoffs			
Season	Club	Lea	GP	G	A	TP	PIM	GP	G	A	TP	PIM
1978-79	U. Minnesota	WCHA	40	21	50	71	18	....	....	....	....	....
1979-80	U.S. National	....	55	25	30	55	20	....	....	....	....	....
	U.S. Olympic	....	7	2	1	3	2	....	....	....	....	....
1980-81ab	U. Minnesota	WCHA	36	17	54	71	56	....	....	....	....	....
	Minnesota	**NHL**	**3**	**2**	**0**	**2**	**12**	**19**	**1**	**7**	**8**	**9**
1981-82	**Minnesota**	**NHL**	**73**	**38**	**60**	**98**	**42**	**4**	**0**	**2**	**2**	**0**
1982-83	**Minnesota**	**NHL**	**79**	**32**	**45**	**77**	**43**	**9**	**1**	**6**	**7**	**10**
1983-84	**Minnesota**	**NHL**	**76**	**28**	**61**	**89**	**43**	**16**	**5**	**5**	**10**	**4**
1984-85	**Minnesota**	**NHL**	**80**	**19**	**37**	**56**	**39**	**9**	**2**	**5**	**7**	**10**
1985-86	**Minnesota**	**NHL**	**80**	**29**	**76**	**105**	**47**	**5**	**3**	**2**	**5**	**2**
1986-87	**Minnesota**	**NHL**	**46**	**18**	**35**	**53**	**33**	....	....	....	....	....
1987-88	**Minnesota**	**NHL**	**54**	**9**	**30**	**39**	**32**	....	....	....	....	....
1988-89	**Minnesota**	**NHL**	**68**	**18**	**38**	**56**	**57**	**5**	**2**	**2**	**4**	**4**
1989-90	**Minnesota**	**NHL**	**80**	**23**	**62**	**85**	**45**	**7**	**2**	**2**	**4**	**18**
1990-91	**Minnesota**	**NHL**	**79**	**13**	**56**	**69**	**26**	**23**	**9**	**13**	**22**	**6**
1991-92	Preussen	Ger.	8	3	5	8	2	....	....	....	....	....
	Minnesota	**NHL**	**76**	**8**	**26**	**34**	**16**	**7**	**1**	**5**	**6**	**2**
1992-93	**Minnesota**	**NHL**	**82**	**12**	**21**	**33**	**22**	....	....	....	....	....
1993-94	**Dallas**	**NHL**	**79**	**17**	**35**	**52**	**62**	**9**	**2**	**1**	**3**	**6**
1994-95	**Dallas**	**NHL**	**17**	**0**	**4**	**4**	**4**	....	....	....	....	....
	New Jersey	**NHL**	**30**	**8**	**20**	**28**	**20**	**20**	**7**	**12**	**19**	**6 ♦**
1995-96	**New Jersey**	**NHL**	**55**	**7**	**16**	**23**	**14**	....	....	....	....	....
	NHL Totals		**1057**	**281**	**622**	**903**	**557**	**133**	**35**	**62**	**97**	**77**

a WCHA First All-Star Team (1981)
b Won Hobey Baker Memorial Award (Top U.S. Collegiate Player) (1981)

Played in NHL All-Star Game (1983, 1986)

Traded to **New Jersey** by **Dallas** for Corey Millen, February 27, 1995.

BROTEN, PAUL   (BRAH-tuhn)

Right wing. Shoots right. 5'11", 188 lbs.   Born, Roseau, MN, October 27, 1965.
(NY Rangers' 3rd choice, 77th overall, in 1984 Entry Draft).

					Regular Season					Playoffs			
Season	Club	Lea	GP	G	A	TP	PIM	GP	G	A	TP	PIM
1984-85	U. Minnesota	WCHA	44	8	8	16	26	....	....	....	....	....
1985-86	U. Minnesota	WCHA	38	6	16	22	24	....	....	....	....	....
1986-87	U. Minnesota	WCHA	48	17	22	39	52	....	....	....	....	....
1987-88	U. Minnesota	WCHA	38	18	21	39	42	....	....	....	....	....
1988-89	Denver	IHL	77	28	31	59	133	4	0	2	2	6
1989-90	**NY Rangers**	**NHL**	**32**	**5**	**3**	**8**	**26**	**6**	**1**	**1**	**2**	**2**
	Flint	IHL	28	17	9	26	55	....	....	....	....	....
1990-91	**NY Rangers**	**NHL**	**28**	**4**	**6**	**10**	**18**	**5**	**0**	**0**	**0**	**2**
	Binghamton	AHL	8	2	2	4	4	....	....	....	....	....
1991-92	**NY Rangers**	**NHL**	**74**	**13**	**15**	**28**	**102**	**13**	**1**	**2**	**3**	**10**
1992-93	**NY Rangers**	**NHL**	**60**	**5**	**9**	**14**	**48**	....	....	....	....	....
1993-94	**Dallas**	**NHL**	**64**	**12**	**12**	**24**	**30**	**9**	**1**	**1**	**2**	**2**
1994-95	**Dallas**	**NHL**	**47**	**7**	**9**	**16**	**36**	**5**	**1**	**2**	**3**	**2**
1995-96	**St. Louis**	**NHL**	**17**	**0**	**1**	**1**	**4**	....	....	....	....	....
	Worcester	AHL	50	22	21	43	42	3	0	0	0	0
	NHL Totals		**322**	**46**	**55**	**101**	**264**	**38**	**4**	**6**	**10**	**18**

Claimed by **Dallas** from **NY Rangers** in NHL Waiver Draft, October 3, 1993. Traded to **St. Louis** by **Dallas** for Guy Carbonneau, October 2, 1995.

BROUSSEAU, PAUL

Right wing. Shoots right. 6'2", 203 lbs.   Born, Pierrefonds, Que., September 18, 1973.
(Quebec's 2nd choice, 28th overall, in 1992 Entry Draft).

					Regular Season					Playoffs			
Season	Club	Lea	GP	G	A	TP	PIM	GP	G	A	TP	PIM
1989-90	Chicoutimi	QMJHL	57	17	24	41	32	7	0	3	3	0
1990-91	Trois-Rivières	QMJHL	67	30	66	96	48	6	3	2	5	2
1991-92	Hull	QMJHL	57	35	61	96	54	6	3	5	8	10
1992-93	Hull	QMJHL	59	27	48	75	49	10	7	8	15	6
1993-94	Cornwall	AHL	69	18	26	44	35	1	0	0	0	0
1994-95	Cornwall	AHL	57	19	17	36	29	7	2	1	3	10
1995-96	**Colorado**	**NHL**	**8**	**1**	**1**	**2**	**2**	....	....	....	....	....
	Cornwall	AHL	63	21	22	43	60	8	4	0	4	2
	NHL Totals		**8**	**1**	**1**	**2**	**2**	....	....	....	....	....

BROWN, BRAD   **MTL.**

Defense. Shoots right. 6'3", 220 lbs.   Born, Baie Verte, Nfld., December 27, 1975.
(Montreal's 1st choice, 18th overall, in 1994 Entry Draft).

					Regular Season					Playoffs			
Season	Club	Lea	GP	G	A	TP	PIM	GP	G	A	TP	PIM
1991-92	North Bay	OHL	49	2	9	11	170	18	0	6	6	43
1992-93	North Bay	OHL	61	4	9	13	228	2	0	2	2	13
1993-94	North Bay	OHL	66	8	24	32	196	18	3	12	15	33
1994-95	North Bay	OHL	64	8	38	46	172	6	1	4	5	8
1995-96	Regina	WHL	21	2	3	5	7	....	....	....	....	....
	Fredericton	AHL	38	0	3	3	148	10	2	1	3	6

BROWN, CURTIS   **BUF.**

Center. Shoots left. 6', 182 lbs.   Born, Unity, Sask., February 12, 1976.
(Buffalo's 2nd choice, 43rd overall, in 1994 Entry Draft).

					Regular Season					Playoffs			
Season	Club	Lea	GP	G	A	TP	PIM	GP	G	A	TP	PIM
1992-93	Moose Jaw	WHL	71	13	16	29	30	....	....	....	....	....
1993-94	Moose Jaw	WHL	72	27	38	65	82	....	....	....	....	....
1994-95a	Moose Jaw	WHL	70	51	53	104	63	10	8	7	15	20
	Buffalo	**NHL**	**1**	**1**	**1**	**2**	**2**	....	....	....	....	....
1995-96	Moose Jaw	WHL	25	20	18	38	30	....	....	....	....	....
b	Prince Albert	WHL	19	12	21	33	8	18	10	15	25	18
	Buffalo	**NHL**	**4**	**0**	**0**	**0**	**0**	....	....	....	....	....
	Rochester	AHL	....	....	....	....	....	12	0	1	1	2
	NHL Totals		**5**	**1**	**1**	**2**	**2**	....	....	....	....	....

a WHL East First All-Star Team (1995)
b WHL East Second All-Star Team (1996)

BROWN, DAVID

Right wing. Shoots right. 6'5", 222 lbs.   Born, Saskatoon, Sask., October 12, 1962.
(Philadelphia's 7th choice, 140th overall, in 1982 Entry Draft).

					Regular Season					Playoffs			
Season	Club	Lea	GP	G	A	TP	PIM	GP	G	A	TP	PIM
1980-81	Spokane	WHL	9	2	2	4	21	....	....	....	....	....
1981-82	Saskatoon	WHL	62	11	33	44	344	5	1	0	1	4
1982-83	**Philadelphia**	**NHL**	**2**	**0**	**0**	**0**	**5**	....	....	....	....	....
	Maine	AHL	71	8	6	14	*418	16	0	0	0	*107
1983-84	**Philadelphia**	**NHL**	**19**	**1**	**5**	**6**	**98**	**2**	**0**	**0**	**0**	**12**
	Springfield	AHL	59	17	14	31	150	....	....	....	....	....
1984-85	**Philadelphia**	**NHL**	**57**	**3**	**6**	**9**	**165**	**11**	**0**	**0**	**0**	**59**
1985-86	**Philadelphia**	**NHL**	**76**	**10**	**7**	**17**	**277**	**5**	**0**	**0**	**0**	**16**
1986-87	**Philadelphia**	**NHL**	**62**	**7**	**3**	**10**	**274**	**26**	**1**	**2**	**3**	**59**
1987-88	**Philadelphia**	**NHL**	**47**	**12**	**5**	**17**	**114**	**7**	**1**	**0**	**1**	**27**
1988-89	**Philadelphia**	**NHL**	**50**	**0**	**3**	**3**	**100**	....	....	....	....	....
	Edmonton	**NHL**	**22**	**0**	**2**	**2**	**56**	**7**	**0**	**0**	**0**	**6**
1989-90	**Edmonton**	**NHL**	**60**	**0**	**6**	**6**	**145**	**3**	**0**	**0**	**0**	**0 ♦**
1990-91	**Edmonton**	**NHL**	**58**	**3**	**4**	**7**	**160**	**16**	**0**	**1**	**1**	**30**
1991-92	**Philadelphia**	**NHL**	**70**	**4**	**2**	**6**	**81**	....	....	....	....	....
1992-93	**Philadelphia**	**NHL**	**70**	**0**	**2**	**2**	**78**	....	....	....	....	....
1993-94	**Philadelphia**	**NHL**	**71**	**1**	**4**	**5**	**137**	....	....	....	....	....
1994-95	**Philadelphia**	**NHL**	**28**	**1**	**2**	**3**	**53**	**3**	**0**	**0**	**0**	**0**
1995-96	**San Jose**	**NHL**	**37**	**3**	**1**	**4**	**46**	....	....	....	....	....
	NHL Totals		**729**	**45**	**52**	**97**	**1789**	**80**	**2**	**3**	**5**	**209**

Traded to **Edmonton** by **Philadelphia** for Keith Acton and Edmonton's fifth round choice (Dimitri Yushkevich) in 1991 Entry Draft, February 7, 1989. Traded to **Philadelphia** by **Edmonton** with Corey Foster and Jari Kurri for Craig Fisher, Scott Mellanby and Craig Berube, May 30, 1991. Signed as a free agent by **San Jose**, September 14, 1995.

BROWN, DOUG   **DET.**

Right wing. Shoots right. 5'10", 185 lbs.   Born, Southborough, MA, June 12, 1964.

					Regular Season					Playoffs			
Season	Club	Lea	GP	G	A	TP	PIM	GP	G	A	TP	PIM
1982-83	Boston College	ECAC	22	9	8	17	0	....	....	....	....	....
1983-84	Boston College	ECAC	38	11	10	21	6	....	....	....	....	....
1984-85a	Boston College	H.E.	45	37	31	68	10	....	....	....	....	....
1985-86a	Boston College	H.E.	38	16	40	56	16	....	....	....	....	....
1986-87	**New Jersey**	**NHL**	**4**	**0**	**1**	**1**	**0**	....	....	....	....	....
	Maine	AHL	73	24	34	58	15	....	....	....	....	....
1987-88	**New Jersey**	**NHL**	**70**	**14**	**11**	**25**	**20**	**19**	**5**	**1**	**6**	**6**
	Utica	AHL	2	0	2	2	2	....	....	....	....	....
1988-89	**New Jersey**	**NHL**	**63**	**15**	**10**	**25**	**15**	....	....	....	....	....
	Utica	AHL	4	1	4	5	0	....	....	....	....	....
1989-90	**New Jersey**	**NHL**	**69**	**14**	**20**	**34**	**16**	**6**	**0**	**1**	**1**	**2**
1990-91	**New Jersey**	**NHL**	**58**	**14**	**16**	**30**	**4**	**7**	**2**	**2**	**4**	**2**
1991-92	**New Jersey**	**NHL**	**71**	**11**	**17**	**28**	**27**	....	....	....	....	....
1992-93	**New Jersey**	**NHL**	**15**	**0**	**5**	**5**	**2**	....	....	....	....	....
	Utica	AHL	25	11	17	28	8	....	....	....	....	....
1993-94	**Pittsburgh**	**NHL**	**77**	**18**	**37**	**55**	**18**	**6**	**0**	**0**	**0**	**2**
1994-95	**Detroit**	**NHL**	**45**	**9**	**12**	**21**	**16**	**18**	**4**	**8**	**12**	**2**
1995-96	**Detroit**	**NHL**	**62**	**12**	**15**	**27**	**4**	**13**	**3**	**3**	**6**	**4**
	NHL Totals		**534**	**107**	**144**	**251**	**122**	**69**	**14**	**15**	**29**	**18**

a Hockey East First All-Star Team (1985, 1986)

Signed as a free agent by **New Jersey**, August 6, 1986. Signed as a free agent by **Pittsburgh**, September 28, 1993. Claimed by **Detroit** from **Pittsburgh** in NHL Waiver Draft, January 18, 1995.

BROWN, GREG

Defense. Shoots right. 6', 185 lbs. Born, Hartford, CT, March 7, 1968.
(Buffalo's 2nd choice, 26th overall, in 1986 Entry Draft).

			Regular Season					Playoffs				
Season	Club	Lea	GP	G	A	TP	PIM	GP	G	A	TP	PIM
1986-87	Boston College	H.E.	37	10	27	37	22	....	....	....	....	....
1987-88	U.S. National	....	55	6	29	35	22	....	....	....	....	....
	U.S. Olympic	....	6	0	4	4	2	....	....	....	....	....
1988-89abc	Boston College	H.E.	40	9	34	43	24	....	....	....	....	....
1989-90abc	Boston College	H.E.	42	5	35	40	42	....	....	....	....	....
1990-91	**Buffalo**	**NHL**	**39**	**1**	**2**	**3**	**35**	....	....	....	....	....
	Rochester	AHL	31	6	17	23	16	14	1	4	5	8
1991-92	Rochester	AHL	56	8	30	38	25	16	1	5	6	4
	U.S. National	....	8	0	0	0	5	....	....	....	....	....
	U.S. Olympic	....	7	0	0	0	2	....	....	....	....	....
1992-93	**Buffalo**	**NHL**	**10**	**0**	**1**	**1**	**6**	....	....	....	....	....
	Rochester	AHL	61	11	38	49	46	16	3	8	11	14
1993-94	**Pittsburgh**	**NHL**	**36**	**3**	**8**	**11**	**28**	**6**	**0**	**1**	**1**	**4**
	San Diego	IHL	42	8	25	33	26	....	....	....	....	....
1994-95	Cleveland	IHL	28	5	14	19	22	....	....	....	....	....
	Winnipeg	**NHL**	**9**	**0**	**3**	**3**	**17**	....	....	....	....	....
1995-96	Rogle	Swe.	22	4	7	11	32	....	....	....	....	....
	NHL Totals		**94**	**4**	**14**	**18**	**86**	**6**	**0**	**1**	**1**	**4**

a Hockey East First All-Star Team (1989, 1990)
b Hockey East Player of the Year (1989, 1990)
c NCAA East First All-American Team (1989, 1990)

Signed as a free agent by **Pittsburgh**, September 29, 1993. Traded to **Winnipeg** by **Pittsburgh** for a conditional eighth round choice in 1996 Entry Draft, April 7, 1995.

BROWN, JEFF — HFD.

Defense. Shoots right. 6'1", 204 lbs. Born, Ottawa, Ont., April 30, 1966.
(Quebec's 2nd choice, 36th overall, in 1984 Entry Draft).

			Regular Season					Playoffs				
Season	Club	Lea	GP	G	A	TP	PIM	GP	G	A	TP	PIM
1982-83	Sudbury	OHL	65	9	37	46	39	....	....	....	....	....
1983-84	Sudbury	OHL	68	17	60	77	39	....	....	....	....	....
1984-85	Sudbury	OHL	56	16	48	64	26	....	....	....	....	....
1985-86	**Quebec**	**NHL**	**8**	**3**	**2**	**5**	**6**	**1**	**0**	**0**	**0**	**0**
a	Sudbury	OHL	45	22	28	50	24	4	0	2	2	11
	Fredericton	AHL	....	....	....	....	....	1	0	1	1	0
1986-87	**Quebec**	**NHL**	**44**	**7**	**22**	**29**	**16**	**13**	**3**	**3**	**6**	**2**
	Fredericton	AHL	26	2	14	16	16	....	....	....	....	....
1987-88	**Quebec**	**NHL**	**78**	**16**	**36**	**52**	**64**	....	....	....	....	....
1988-89	**Quebec**	**NHL**	**78**	**21**	**47**	**68**	**62**	....	....	....	....	....
1989-90	**Quebec**	**NHL**	**29**	**6**	**10**	**16**	**18**	....	....	....	....	....
	St. Louis	**NHL**	**48**	**10**	**28**	**38**	**37**	**12**	**2**	**10**	**12**	**4**
1990-91	**St. Louis**	**NHL**	**67**	**12**	**47**	**59**	**39**	**13**	**3**	**9**	**12**	**6**
1991-92	**St. Louis**	**NHL**	**80**	**20**	**39**	**59**	**38**	**6**	**2**	**1**	**3**	**2**
1992-93	**St. Louis**	**NHL**	**71**	**25**	**53**	**78**	**58**	**11**	**3**	**8**	**11**	**6**
1993-94	**St. Louis**	**NHL**	**63**	**13**	**47**	**60**	**46**	....	....	....	....	....
	Vancouver	**NHL**	**11**	**1**	**5**	**6**	**10**	**24**	**6**	**9**	**15**	**37**
1994-95	**Vancouver**	**NHL**	**33**	**8**	**23**	**31**	**16**	**5**	**1**	**3**	**4**	**2**
1995-96	**Vancouver**	**NHL**	**28**	**1**	**16**	**17**	**18**	....	....	....	....	....
	Hartford	**NHL**	**48**	**7**	**31**	**38**	**38**	....	....	....	....	....
	NHL Totals		**686**	**150**	**406**	**556**	**466**	**85**	**20**	**43**	**63**	**59**

a OHL First All-Star Team (1986)

Traded to **St Louis** by **Quebec** for Tony Hrkac and Greg Millen, December 13, 1989. Traded to **Vancouver** by **St. Louis** with Bret Hedican and Nathan Lafayette for Craig Janney, March 21, 1994. Traded to **Hartford** by **Vancouver** with Vancouver's third round choice in 1998 Entry Draft for Jim Dowd, Frantisek Kucera and Hartford's second round choice in 1997 Entry Draft, December 19, 1995.

BROWN, JEFF — NYR

Defense. Shoots right. 6'1", 217 lbs. Born, Mississauga, Ont., April 24, 1978.
(NY Rangers' 1st choice, 22nd overall, in 1996 Entry Draft).

			Regular Season					Playoffs				
Season	Club	Lea	GP	G	A	TP	PIM	GP	G	A	TP	PIM
1994-95	Sarnia	OHL	58	2	14	16	52	4	0	2	2	2
1995-96	Sarnia	OHL	65	8	20	28	111	10	1	2	3	12

BROWN, KEVIN — ANA.

Right wing. Shoots right. 6'1", 212 lbs. Born, Birmingham, England, May 11, 1974.
(Los Angeles' 3rd choice, 87th overall, in 1992 Entry Draft).

			Regular Season					Playoffs				
Season	Club	Lea	GP	G	A	TP	PIM	GP	G	A	TP	PIM
1991-92	Belleville	OHL	66	24	24	48	52	5	1	4	5	8
1992-93a	Belleville	OHL	6	2	5	7	4	....	....	....	....	....
	Detroit	OHL	56	48	86	134	76	15	10	18	28	18
1993-94bc	Detroit	OHL	57	54	81	135	85	17	14	*26	*40	28
1994-95	Phoenix	IHL	48	19	31	50	64	....	....	....	....	....
	Los Angeles	**NHL**	**23**	**2**	**3**	**5**	**18**	....	....	....	....	....
1995-96	**Los Angeles**	**NHL**	**7**	**1**	**0**	**1**	**4**	....	....	....	....	....
	Phoenix	IHL	45	10	16	26	39	....	....	....	....	....
	Cornwall	AHL	2	0	0	0	0	....	....	....	....	....
	Peoria	IHL	3	2	1	3	0	....	....	....	....	....
	P.E.I.	AHL	8	3	6	9	2	3	1	3	4	0
	NHL Totals		**30**	**3**	**3**	**6**	**22**	....	....	....	....	....

a OHL Second All-Star Team (1993)
b OHL First All-Star Team (1994)
c Canadian Major Junior Second All-Star Team (1994)

Traded to **Ottawa** by **Los Angeles** for Jaroslav Modry and Ottawa's eighth round choice (Stephen Valiquette) in 1996 Entry Draft, March 20, 1996. Traded to **Anaheim** by **Ottawa** for Mike Maneluk, July 1, 1996.

BROWN, ROB

Right wing. Shoots left. 5'11", 185 lbs. Born, Kingston, Ont., April 10, 1968.
(Pittsburgh's 4th choice, 67th overall, in 1986 Entry Draft).

			Regular Season					Playoffs				
Season	Club	Lea	GP	G	A	TP	PIM	GP	G	A	TP	PIM
1984-85	Kamloops	WHL	60	29	50	79	95	15	8	8	26	28
1985-86a	Kamloops	WHL	69	58	*115	*173	171	16	*18	*28	*46	14
1986-87ab	Kamloops	WHL	63	*76	*136	*212	101	5	6	5	11	6
1987-88	**Pittsburgh**	**NHL**	**51**	**24**	**20**	**44**	**56**	....	....	....	....	....
1988-89	**Pittsburgh**	**NHL**	**68**	**49**	**66**	**115**	**118**	**11**	**5**	**3**	**8**	**22**
1989-90	**Pittsburgh**	**NHL**	**80**	**33**	**47**	**80**	**102**	....	....	....	....	....
1990-91	**Pittsburgh**	**NHL**	**25**	**6**	**10**	**16**	**31**	....	....	....	....	....
	Hartford	**NHL**	**44**	**18**	**24**	**42**	**101**	**5**	**1**	**0**	**1**	**7**
1991-92	**Hartford**	**NHL**	**42**	**16**	**15**	**31**	**39**	....	....	....	....	....
	Chicago	**NHL**	**25**	**5**	**11**	**16**	**34**	**8**	**2**	**4**	**6**	**4**
1992-93	**Chicago**	**NHL**	**15**	**1**	**6**	**7**	**33**	....	....	....	....	....
	Indianapolis	IHL	19	14	19	33	32	2	0	1	1	2
1993-94	**Dallas**	**NHL**	**1**	**0**	**0**	**0**	**0**	....	....	....	....	....
cde	Kalamazoo	IHL	79	42	*113	*155	188	5	1	3	4	6
1994-95f	Phoenix	IHL	69	34	73	107	135	9	4	12	16	0
	Los Angeles	**NHL**	**2**	**0**	**0**	**0**	**0**	....	....	....	....	....
1995-96cd	Chicago	IHL	79	52	*91	*143	100	9	4	11	15	6
	NHL Totals		**353**	**152**	**199**	**351**	**514**	**24**	**8**	**7**	**15**	**33**

a WHL First All-Star Team (1986, 1987)
b Canadian Major Junior Player of the Year (1987)
c IHL First All-Star Team (1994, 1996)
d Won Leo P. Lamoureux Memorial Trophy (Top Scorer - IHL) (1994, 1996)
e Won James Gatschene Memorial Trophy (MVP - IHL) (1994)
f IHL Second All-Star Team (1995)

Played in NHL All-Star Game (1989)

Traded to **Hartford** by **Pittsburgh** for Scott Young, December 21, 1990. Traded to **Chicago** by **Hartford** for Steve Konroyd, January 24, 1992. Signed as a free agent by **Dallas**, August 12, 1993. Signed as a free agent by **Los Angeles**, June 14, 1994.

BROWN, SEAN — EDM.

Defense. Shoots left. 6'2", 205 lbs. Born, Oshawa, Ont., November 5, 1976.
(Boston's 2nd choice, 21st overall, in 1995 Entry Draft).

			Regular Season					Playoffs				
Season	Club	Lea	GP	G	A	TP	PIM	GP	G	A	TP	PIM
1993-94	Belleville	OHL	28	1	2	3	53	8	0	0	0	17
1994-95	Belleville	OHL	58	2	16	18	200	16	4	2	6	*67
	Phoenix	IHL	3	0	1	1	0	....	....	....	....	....
1995-96	Belleville	OHL	37	10	23	33	150	....	....	....	....	....
a	Sarnia	OHL	26	8	17	25	112	10	1	0	1	38

a OHL Second All-Star Team (1996)

Traded to **Edmonton** by **Boston** with Mariusz Czerkawski and Boston's first round choice (Matthieu Descoteaux) in 1996 Entry Draft for Bill Ranford, January 11, 1996.

BRUCE, DAVID

Left wing. Shoots right. 5'11", 190 lbs. Born, Thunder Bay, Ont., October 7, 1964.
(Vancouver's 2nd choice, 30th overall, in 1983 Entry Draft).

			Regular Season					Playoffs				
Season	Club	Lea	GP	G	A	TP	PIM	GP	G	A	TP	PIM
1982-83	Kitchener	OHL	67	36	35	71	199	12	7	9	16	27
1983-84	Kitchener	OHL	62	52	40	92	203	10	5	8	13	20
1984-85	Fredericton	AHL	56	14	11	25	104	5	0	0	0	37
1985-86	**Vancouver**	**NHL**	**12**	**0**	**1**	**1**	**14**	**1**	**0**	**0**	**0**	**0**
	Fredericton	AHL	66	25	16	41	151	2	0	1	1	12
1986-87	**Vancouver**	**NHL**	**50**	**9**	**7**	**16**	**109**	....	....	....	....	....
	Fredericton	AHL	17	7	6	13	73	....	....	....	....	....
1987-88	**Vancouver**	**NHL**	**28**	**7**	**3**	**10**	**57**	....	....	....	....	....
	Fredericton	AHL	30	27	18	45	115	....	....	....	....	....
1988-89	**Vancouver**	**NHL**	**53**	**7**	**7**	**14**	**65**	....	....	....	....	....
1989-90a	Milwaukee	IHL	68	40	35	75	148	6	5	3	8	0
1990-91	**St. Louis**	**NHL**	**12**	**1**	**2**	**3**	**14**	**2**	**0**	**0**	**0**	**2**
ab	Peoria	IHL	60	*64	52	116	78	18	*18	11	*29	40
1991-92	**San Jose**	**NHL**	**60**	**22**	**16**	**38**	**46**	....	....	....	....	....
	Kansas City	IHL	7	5	5	10	6	....	....	....	....	....
1992-93	**San Jose**	**NHL**	**17**	**2**	**3**	**5**	**33**	....	....	....	....	....
1993-94	**San Jose**	**NHL**	**2**	**0**	**0**	**0**	**0**	....	....	....	....	....
	Kansas City	IHL	72	40	24	64	115	....	....	....	....	....
1994-95	Kansas City	IHL	63	33	25	58	80	....	....	....	....	....
1995-96	Kansas City	IHL	62	27	26	53	84	1	0	0	0	8
	NHL Totals		**234**	**48**	**39**	**87**	**338**	**3**	**0**	**0**	**0**	**2**

a IHL First All-Star Team (1990, 1991)
b Won James Gatschene Memorial Trophy (MVP - IHL) (1991)

Signed as a free agent by **St. Louis**, July 6, 1990. Claimed by **San Jose** from **St. Louis** in Expansion Draft, May 30, 1991.

BRULE, STEVE (broo-LAY) — N.J.

Center. Shoots right. 5'11", 185 lbs. Born, Montreal, Que., January 15, 1975.
(New Jersey's 6th choice, 143rd overall, in 1993 Entry Draft).

			Regular Season					Playoffs				
Season	Club	Lea	GP	G	A	TP	PIM	GP	G	A	TP	PIM
1992-93	St-Jean	QMJHL	70	33	47	80	46	4	0	0	0	9
1993-94	St-Jean	QMJHL	66	41	64	105	46	5	2	1	3	0
1994-95a	St-Jean	QMJHL	69	44	64	108	42	7	3	4	7	8
	Albany	AHL	3	1	4	5	0	14	9	5	14	4
1995-96	Albany	AHL	80	30	21	51	37	4	0	0	0	17

a QMJHL Second All-Star Team (1995)

BRUNET, BENOIT (broo-NAY, BEHN-wah) MTL.

Left wing. Shoots left. 5'11", 195 lbs. Born, Pointe-Claire, Que., August 24, 1968.
(Montreal's 2nd choice, 27th overall, in 1986 Entry Draft).

			Regular Season					Playoffs				
Season	Club	Lea	GP	G	A	TP	PIM	GP	G	A	TP	PIM
1985-86	Hull	QMJHL	71	33	37	70	81	....	....	....	....	....
1986-87a	Hull	QMJHL	60	43	67	110	105	6	7	5	12	8
1987-88	Hull	QMJHL	62	54	89	143	131	10	3	10	13	11
1988-89	**Montreal**	**NHL**	**2**	**0**	**1**	**1**	**0**	....	....	....	....	....
b	Sherbrooke	AHL	73	41	76	117	95	6	2	0	2	4
1989-90	Sherbrooke	AHL	72	32	35	67	82	12	8	7	15	20
1990-91	**Montreal**	**NHL**	**17**	**1**	**3**	**4**	**0**	....	....	....	....	....
	Fredericton	AHL	24	13	18	31	16	6	5	6	11	2
1991-92	**Montreal**	**NHL**	**18**	**4**	**6**	**10**	**14**	....	....	....	....	....
	Fredericton	AHL	6	7	9	16	27	....	....	....	....	....
1992-93	**Montreal**	**NHL**	**47**	**10**	**15**	**25**	**19**	**20**	**2**	**8**	**10**	**8 ♦**
1993-94	**Montreal**	**NHL**	**71**	**10**	**20**	**30**	**20**	**7**	**1**	**4**	**5**	**16**
1994-95	**Montreal**	**NHL**	**45**	**7**	**18**	**25**	**16**	....	....	....	....	....
1995-96	**Montreal**	**NHL**	**26**	**7**	**8**	**15**	**17**	**3**	**0**	**2**	**2**	**0**
	Fredericton	AHL	3	2	1	3	6	....	....	....	....	....
	NHL Totals		**226**	**39**	**71**	**110**	**86**	**30**	**3**	**14**	**17**	**24**

a QMJHL Second All-Star Team (1987)
b AHL First All-Star Team (1989)

BRUNETTE, ANDREW WSH.

Left wing. Shoots left. 6', 212 lbs. Born, Sudbury, Ont., August 24, 1973.
(Washington's 6th choice, 174th overall, in 1993 Entry Draft).

			Regular Season					Playoffs				
Season	Club	Lea	GP	G	A	TP	PIM	GP	G	A	TP	PIM
1990-91	Owen Sound	OHL	63	15	20	35	15	....	....	....	....	....
1991-92	Owen Sound	OHL	66	51	47	98	42	5	5	0	5	8
1992-93ab	Owen Sound	OHL	66	*62	*100	*162	91	8	8	6	14	16
1993-94	Portland	AHL	23	9	11	20	10	2	0	1	1	0
	Providence	AHL	3	0	0	0	0	....	....	....	....	....
	Hampton	ECHL	20	12	18	30	32	7	7	6	13	18
1994-95c	Portland	AHL	79	30	50	80	53	7	3	3	6	10
1995-96	**Washington**	**NHL**	**11**	**3**	**3**	**6**	**0**	**6**	**1**	**3**	**4**	**0**
	Portland	AHL	69	28	66	94	125	20	11	18	29	15
	NHL Totals		**11**	**3**	**3**	**6**	**0**	**6**	**1**	**3**	**4**	**0**

a OHL First All-Star Team (1993)
b Canadian Major Junior Second All-Star Team (1993)
c AHL Second All-Star Team (1995)

BRYLIN, SERGEI (BRIH-lin) N.J.

Center. Shoots left. 5'9", 175 lbs. Born, Moscow, USSR, January 13, 1974.
(New Jersey's 2nd choice, 42nd overall, in 1992 Entry Draft).

			Regular Season					Playoffs				
Season	Club	Lea	GP	G	A	TP	PIM	GP	G	A	TP	PIM
1991-92	CSKA	CIS	44	1	6	7	4	....	....	....	....	....
1992-93	CSKA	CIS	42	5	4	9	36	....	....	....	....	....
1993-94	CSKA	CIS	39	4	6	10	36	3	1	0	1	2
	Russian Pen's	IHL	13	4	5	9	18	....	....	....	....	....
1994-95	Albany	AHL	63	19	35	54	78	....	....	....	....	....
	New Jersey	**NHL**	**26**	**6**	**8**	**14**	**8**	**12**	**1**	**2**	**3**	**4 ♦**
1995-96	**New Jersey**	**NHL**	**50**	**4**	**5**	**9**	**26**	....	....	....	....	....
	NHL Totals		**76**	**10**	**13**	**23**	**34**	**12**	**1**	**2**	**3**	**4**

BUCHANAN, JEFF

Defense. Shoots right. 5'10", 165 lbs. Born, Swift Current, Sask., May 23, 1971.

			Regular Season					Playoffs				
Season	Club	Lea	GP	G	A	TP	PIM	GP	G	A	TP	PIM
1989-90	Saskatoon	WHL	66	7	12	19	96	9	0	2	2	2
1990-91	Saskatoon	WHL	69	10	26	36	123	....	....	....	....	....
1991-92	Saskatoon	WHL	72	17	37	54	145	22	10	14	24	39
1992-93	Atlanta	IHL	68	4	18	22	282	9	0	0	0	26
1993-94	Atlanta	IHL	76	5	24	29	253	14	0	1	1	20
1994-95	Atlanta	IHL	4	0	1	1	9	....	....	....	....	....
	Indianapolis	IHL	25	3	9	12	63	....	....	....	....	....
1995-96	Indianapolis	IHL	77	4	14	18	277	5	0	1	1	9

Signed as a free agent by **Tampa Bay**, July 13, 1992. Traded to **Chicago** by **Tampa Bay** with Jim Cummins and Tom Tilley for Paul Ysebaert and Rich Sutter, February 22, 1995.

BUCHBERGER, KELLY (BUK-buhr-guhr) EDM.

Left wing. Shoots left. 6'2", 200 lbs. Born, Langenburg, Sask., December 2, 1966.
(Edmonton's 8th choice, 188th overall, in 1985 Entry Draft).

			Regular Season					Playoffs				
Season	Club	Lea	GP	G	A	TP	PIM	GP	G	A	TP	PIM
1984-85	Moose Jaw	WHL	51	12	17	29	114	....	....	....	....	....
1985-86	Moose Jaw	WHL	72	14	22	36	206	13	11	4	15	37
1986-87	Nova Scotia	AHL	70	12	20	32	257	5	0	1	1	23
	Edmonton	**NHL**	....	....	....	....	....	**3**	**0**	**1**	**1**	**5 ♦**
1987-88	**Edmonton**	**NHL**	**19**	**1**	**0**	**1**	**81**	....	....	....	....	....
	Nova Scotia	AHL	49	21	23	44	206	2	0	0	0	11
1988-89	**Edmonton**	**NHL**	**66**	**5**	**9**	**14**	**234**	....	....	....	....	....
1989-90	**Edmonton**	**NHL**	**55**	**2**	**6**	**8**	**168**	**19**	**0**	**5**	**5**	**13 ♦**
1990-91	**Edmonton**	**NHL**	**64**	**3**	**1**	**4**	**160**	**12**	**2**	**1**	**3**	**25**
1991-92	**Edmonton**	**NHL**	**79**	**20**	**24**	**44**	**157**	**16**	**1**	**4**	**5**	**32**
1992-93	**Edmonton**	**NHL**	**83**	**12**	**18**	**30**	**133**	....	....	....	....	....
1993-94	**Edmonton**	**NHL**	**84**	**3**	**18**	**21**	**199**	....	....	....	....	....
1994-95	**Edmonton**	**NHL**	**48**	**7**	**17**	**24**	**82**	....	....	....	....	....
1995-96	**Edmonton**	**NHL**	**82**	**11**	**14**	**25**	**184**	....	....	....	....	....
	NHL Totals		**580**	**64**	**107**	**171**	**1398**	**50**	**3**	**11**	**14**	**75**

BUCKBERGER, ASHLEY FLA.

Right wing. Shoots right. 6'2", 206 lbs. Born, Esterhazy, Sask., February 19, 1975.
(Quebec's 3rd choice, 49th overall, in 1993 Entry Draft).

			Regular Season					Playoffs				
Season	Club	Lea	GP	G	A	TP	PIM	GP	G	A	TP	PIM
1991-92	Swift Current	WHL	67	23	22	45	38	8	2	1	3	2
1992-93	Swift Current	WHL	72	23	44	67	41	17	6	7	13	6
1993-94	Swift Current	WHL	67	42	45	87	42	7	0	1	1	6
1994-95	Swift Current	WHL	53	23	37	60	51	....	....	....	....	....
	Kamloops	WHL	21	9	13	22	13	19	7	11	18	22
1995-96	Carolina	AHL	67	8	9	17	25	....	....	....	....	....

Signed as a free agent by **Florida**, July 27, 1995.

BUCKLEY, BRENDAN ANA.

Defense. Shoots right. 6'2", 190 lbs. Born, Boston, MA, February 26, 1977.
(Anaheim's 3rd choice, 117th overall, in 1996 Entry Draft).

			Regular Season					Playoffs				
Season	Club	Lea	GP	G	A	TP	PIM	GP	G	A	TP	PIM
1994-95	Jr. Bruins	Jr. A	48	22	43	65	164	....	....	....	....	....
1995-96	Boston College	H.E.	34	0	4	4	72	....	....	....	....	....

BUCKLEY, TOM HFD.

Center. Shoots left. 6'1", 204 lbs. Born, Buffalo, NY, May 26, 1976.
(Hartford's 4th choice, 187th overall, in 1994 Entry Draft).

			Regular Season					Playoffs				
Season	Club	Lea	GP	G	A	TP	PIM	GP	G	A	TP	PIM
1994-95	Detroit	OHL	64	30	36	66	49	21	10	9	19	8
1995-96	Detroit	OHL	66	29	43	72	31	17	6	20	26	20

BUDAYEV, ALEXEI PHO.

Center. Shoots right. 6'2", 183 lbs. Born, Pavlov Posad, USSR, April 24, 1975.
(Winnipeg's 3rd choice, 43rd overall, in 1993 Entry Draft).

			Regular Season					Playoffs				
Season	Club	Lea	GP	G	A	TP	PIM	GP	G	A	TP	PIM
1993-94	Elektrostal	CIS 2	46	6	5	11	26	....	....	....	....	....
1994-95	Elektrostal	CIS	25	2	1	3	12	....	....	....	....	....
	Red Deer	WHL	30	15	12	27	6	....	....	....	....	....
1995-96	Red Deer	WHL	48	13	12	25	48	9	0	1	1	6

BULIS, JAN WSH.

Center. Shoots left. 6', 194 lbs. Born, Pardubice, Czech., March 18, 1978.
(Washington's 3rd choice, 43rd overall, in 1996 Entry Draft).

			Regular Season					Playoffs				
Season	Club	Lea	GP	G	A	TP	PIM	GP	G	A	TP	PIM
1994-95	Kelowna	Jr. A	51	23	25	48	36	....	....	....	....	....
1995-96	Barrie	OHL	59	29	30	59	22	7	2	3	5	2

BURE, PAVEL (boo-RAY) VAN.

Right wing. Shoots left. 5'10", 189 lbs. Born, Moscow, USSR, March 31, 1971.
(Vancouver's 4th choice, 113th overall, in 1989 Entry Draft).

			Regular Season					Playoffs				
Season	Club	Lea	GP	G	A	TP	PIM	GP	G	A	TP	PIM
1987-88	CSKA	USSR	5	1	1	2	0	....	....	....	....	....
1988-89a	CSKA	USSR	32	17	9	26	8	....	....	....	....	....
1989-90	CSKA	USSR	46	14	10	24	20	....	....	....	....	....
1990-91	CSKA	USSR	44	35	11	46	24	....	....	....	....	....
1991-92b	**Vancouver**	**NHL**	**65**	**34**	**26**	**60**	**30**	**13**	**6**	**4**	**10**	**14**
1992-93	**Vancouver**	**NHL**	**83**	**60**	**50**	**110**	**69**	**12**	**5**	**7**	**12**	**8**
1993-94c	**Vancouver**	**NHL**	**76**	***60**	**47**	**107**	**86**	**24**	***16**	**15**	**31**	**40**
1994-95	Landshut	Ger.	1	3	0	3	2	....	....	....	....	....
	Spartak	CIS	1	2	0	2	2	....	....	....	....	....
	Vancouver	**NHL**	**44**	**20**	**23**	**43**	**47**	**11**	**7**	**6**	**13**	**10**
1995-96	**Vancouver**	**NHL**	**15**	**6**	**7**	**13**	**8**	....	....	....	....	....
	NHL Totals		**283**	**180**	**153**	**333**	**240**	**60**	**34**	**32**	**66**	**72**

a Named Soviet National League Rookie-of-the-Year (1989)
b Won Calder Memorial Trophy (1992)
c NHL First All-Star Team (1994)

Played in NHL All-Star Game (1993, 1994)

BURE, VALERI (boo-RAY) MTL.

Right wing. Shoots right. 5'10", 168 lbs. Born, Moscow, USSR, June 13, 1974.
(Montreal's 2nd choice, 33rd overall, in 1992 Entry Draft).

			Regular Season					Playoffs				
Season	Club	Lea	GP	G	A	TP	PIM	GP	G	A	TP	PIM
1990-91	CSKA	USSR	3	0	0	0	0	....	....	....	....	....
1991-92	Spokane	WHL	53	27	22	49	78	10	11	6	17	10
1992-93a	Spokane	WHL	66	68	79	147	49	9	6	11	17	14
1993-94b	Spokane	WHL	59	40	62	102	48	3	5	3	8	2
1994-95	Fredericton	AHL	45	23	25	48	32	....	....	....	....	....
	Montreal	**NHL**	**24**	**3**	**1**	**4**	**6**	....	....	....	....	....
1995-96	**Montreal**	**NHL**	**77**	**22**	**20**	**42**	**28**	**6**	**0**	**1**	**1**	**6**
	NHL Totals		**101**	**25**	**21**	**46**	**34**	**6**	**0**	**1**	**1**	**6**

a WHL West First All-Star Team (1993)
b WHL West Second All-Star Team (1994)

BUREAU, MARC (BEWR-oh) MTL.

Center. Shoots right. 6'1", 198 lbs. Born, Trois-Rivières, Que., May 19, 1966.

			Regular Season					Playoffs				
Season	Club	Lea	GP	G	A	TP	PIM	GP	G	A	TP	PIM
1983-84	Chicoutimi	QMJHL	56	6	16	22	14	....	....	....	....	....
1984-85	Chicoutimi	QMJHL	41	30	25	55	15	....	....	....	....	....
	Granby	QMJHL	27	20	45	65	14	....	....	....	....	....
1985-86	Granby	QMJHL	19	6	17	23	36	....	....	....	....	....
	Chicoutimi	QMJHL	44	30	45	75	33	9	3	7	10	10
1986-87	Longueuil	QMJHL	66	54	58	112	68	20	17	20	37	12
1987-88	Salt Lake	IHL	69	7	20	27	86	7	0	3	3	8
1988-89	Salt Lake	IHL	76	28	36	64	119	14	7	5	12	31
1989-90	**Calgary**	**NHL**	**5**	**0**	**0**	**0**	**4**	....	....	....	....	....
a	Salt Lake	IHL	67	43	48	91	173	11	4	8	12	0
1990-91	**Calgary**	**NHL**	**5**	**0**	**0**	**0**	**2**	....	....	....	....	....
a	Salt Lake	IHL	54	40	48	88	101	....	....	....	....	....
	Minnesota	**NHL**	**9**	**0**	**6**	**6**	**4**	**23**	**3**	**2**	**5**	**20**
1991-92	**Minnesota**	**NHL**	**46**	**6**	**4**	**10**	**50**	**5**	**0**	**0**	**0**	**14**
	Kalamazoo	IHL	7	2	8	10	2	....	....	....	....	....
1992-93	**Tampa Bay**	**NHL**	**63**	**10**	**21**	**31**	**111**	....	....	....	....	....
1993-94	**Tampa Bay**	**NHL**	**75**	**8**	**7**	**15**	**30**	....	....	....	....	....
1994-95	**Tampa Bay**	**NHL**	**48**	**2**	**12**	**14**	**30**	....	....	....	....	....
1995-96	**Montreal**	**NHL**	**65**	**3**	**7**	**10**	**46**	**6**	**1**	**1**	**2**	**4**
	NHL Totals		**316**	**29**	**57**	**86**	**277**	**34**	**4**	**3**	**7**	**38**

a IHL Second All-Star Team (1990, 1991)

Signed as a free agent by **Calgary**, May 19, 1987. Traded to **Minnesota** by **Calgary** for Minnesota's third round choice (Sandy McCarthy) in 1991 Entry Draft, March 5, 1991. Claimed on waivers by **Tampa Bay** from **Minnesota**, October 16, 1992. Traded to **Montreal** by **Tampa Bay** for Brian Bellows, June 30, 1995.

BURR, SHAWN — T.B.

Left wing/Center. Shoots left. 6'1", 202 lbs. Born, Sarnia, Ont., July 1, 1966.
(Detroit's 1st choice, 7th overall, in 1984 Entry Draft).

Season	Club	Lea	Regular Season GP	G	A	TP	PIM	Playoffs GP	G	A	TP	PIM
1983-84	Kitchener	OHL	68	41	44	85	50	16	5	12	17	22
1984-85	**Detroit**	**NHL**	**9**	**0**	**0**	**0**	**2**	....	....	....	....	....
	Adirondack	AHL	4	0	0	0	2	....	....	....	....	....
	Kitchener	OHL	48	24	42	66	50	4	3	3	6	2
1985-86	**Detroit**	**NHL**	**5**	**1**	**0**	**1**	**4**	....	....	....	....	....
	Adirondack	AHL	3	2	2	4	2	17	5	7	12	32
a	Kitchener	OHL	59	60	67	127	104	5	2	3	5	8
1986-87	**Detroit**	**NHL**	**80**	**22**	**25**	**47**	**107**	**16**	**7**	**2**	**9**	**20**
1987-88	**Detroit**	**NHL**	**78**	**17**	**23**	**40**	**97**	**9**	**3**	**1**	**4**	**14**
1988-89	**Detroit**	**NHL**	**79**	**19**	**27**	**46**	**78**	**6**	**1**	**2**	**3**	**6**
1989-90	**Detroit**	**NHL**	**76**	**24**	**32**	**56**	**82**	....	....	....	....	....
	Adirondack	AHL	3	4	2	6	2	....	....	....	....	....
1990-91	**Detroit**	**NHL**	**80**	**20**	**30**	**50**	**112**	**7**	**0**	**4**	**4**	**15**
1991-92	**Detroit**	**NHL**	**79**	**19**	**32**	**51**	**118**	**11**	**1**	**5**	**6**	**10**
1992-93	**Detroit**	**NHL**	**80**	**10**	**25**	**35**	**74**	**7**	**2**	**1**	**3**	**2**
1993-94	**Detroit**	**NHL**	**51**	**10**	**12**	**22**	**31**	**7**	**2**	**0**	**2**	**6**
1994-95	**Detroit**	**NHL**	**42**	**6**	**8**	**14**	**60**	**16**	**0**	**2**	**2**	**6**
1995-96	**Tampa Bay**	**NHL**	**81**	**13**	**15**	**28**	**119**	**6**	**0**	**2**	**2**	**8**
	NHL Totals		**740**	**161**	**229**	**390**	**884**	**85**	**16**	**19**	**35**	**87**

a OHL Second All-Star Team (1986)

Traded to **Tampa Bay** by **Detroit** with Detroit's third round choice (later traded to Boston — Boston selected Jason Doyle) in 1996 Entry Draft for Marc Bergevin and Ben Hankinson, August 17, 1995.

BURRIDGE, RANDY — BUF.

Left wing. Shoots left. 5'9", 185 lbs. Born, Fort Erie, Ont., January 7, 1966.
(Boston's 7th choice, 157th overall, in 1985 Entry Draft).

Season	Club	Lea	Regular Season GP	G	A	TP	PIM	Playoffs GP	G	A	TP	PIM
1983-84	Peterborough	OHL	55	6	7	13	44	8	3	2	5	7
1984-85	Peterborough	OHL	66	49	57	106	88	17	9	16	25	18
1985-86	**Boston**	**NHL**	**52**	**17**	**25**	**42**	**28**	**3**	**0**	**4**	**4**	**12**
	Peterborough	OHL	17	15	11	26	23	3	1	3	4	2
	Moncton	AHL	....	....	....	....	....	3	0	2	2	2
1986-87	**Boston**	**NHL**	**23**	**1**	**4**	**5**	**16**	**2**	**1**	**0**	**1**	**2**
	Moncton	AHL	47	26	41	67	139	3	1	2	3	30
1987-88	**Boston**	**NHL**	**79**	**27**	**28**	**55**	**105**	**23**	**2**	**10**	**12**	**16**
1988-89	**Boston**	**NHL**	**80**	**31**	**30**	**61**	**39**	**10**	**5**	**2**	**7**	**6**
1989-90	**Boston**	**NHL**	**63**	**17**	**15**	**32**	**47**	**21**	**4**	**11**	**15**	**14**
1990-91	**Boston**	**NHL**	**62**	**15**	**13**	**28**	**40**	**19**	**0**	**3**	**3**	**39**
1991-92	**Washington**	**NHL**	**66**	**23**	**44**	**67**	**50**	**2**	**0**	**1**	**1**	**0**
1992-93	**Washington**	**NHL**	**4**	**0**	**0**	**0**	**0**	**4**	**1**	**0**	**1**	**0**
	Baltimore	AHL	2	0	1	1	2	....	....	....	....	....
1993-94	**Washington**	**NHL**	**78**	**25**	**17**	**42**	**73**	**11**	**0**	**2**	**2**	**12**
1994-95	**Washington**	**NHL**	**2**	**0**	**0**	**0**	**2**	....	....	....	....	....
	Los Angeles	**NHL**	**38**	**4**	**15**	**19**	**8**	....	....	....	....	....
1995-96	**Buffalo**	**NHL**	**74**	**25**	**33**	**58**	**30**	....	....	....	....	....
	NHL Totals		**621**	**185**	**224**	**409**	**438**	**95**	**13**	**33**	**46**	**101**

Played in NHL All-Star Game (1992)

Traded to **Washington** by **Boston** for Stephen Leach, June 21, 1991. Traded to **Los Angeles** by **Washington** for Warren Rychel, February 10, 1995. Signed as a free agent by **Buffalo**, October 5, 1995.

BURT, ADAM — HFD.

Defense. Shoots left. 6'2", 207 lbs. Born, Detroit, MI, January 15, 1969.
(Hartford's 2nd choice, 39th overall, in 1987 Entry Draft).

Season	Club	Lea	Regular Season GP	G	A	TP	PIM	Playoffs GP	G	A	TP	PIM
1985-86	North Bay	OHL	49	0	11	11	81	10	0	0	0	24
1986-87	North Bay	OHL	57	4	27	31	138	24	1	6	7	68
1987-88	Binghamton	AHL	....	....	....	....	....	2	1	1	2	0
a	North Bay	OHL	66	17	53	70	176	2	0	3	3	6
1988-89	**Hartford**	**NHL**	**5**	**0**	**0**	**0**	**6**	....	....	....	....	....
	Binghamton	AHL	5	0	2	2	13	....	....	....	....	....
	North Bay	OHL	23	4	11	15	45	12	2	12	14	12
1989-90	**Hartford**	**NHL**	**63**	**4**	**8**	**12**	**105**	**2**	**0**	**0**	**0**	**0**
1990-91	**Hartford**	**NHL**	**42**	**2**	**7**	**9**	**63**	....	....	....	....	....
	Springfield	AHL	9	1	3	4	22	....	....	....	....	....
1991-92	**Hartford**	**NHL**	**66**	**9**	**15**	**24**	**93**	**2**	**0**	**0**	**0**	**0**
1992-93	**Hartford**	**NHL**	**65**	**6**	**14**	**20**	**116**	....	....	....	....	....
1993-94	**Hartford**	**NHL**	**63**	**1**	**17**	**18**	**75**	....	....	....	....	....
1994-95	**Hartford**	**NHL**	**46**	**7**	**11**	**18**	**65**	....	....	....	....	....
1995-96	**Hartford**	**NHL**	**78**	**4**	**9**	**13**	**121**	....	....	....	....	....
	NHL Totals		**428**	**33**	**81**	**114**	**644**	**4**	**0**	**0**	**0**	**0**

a OHL Second All-Star Team (1988)

BUTENSCHON, SVEN — (BUH-tehn-shohn) — PIT.

Defense. Shoots left. 6'5", 201 lbs. Born, Itzehoe, West Germany, March 22, 1976.
(Pittsburgh's 3rd choice, 57th overall, in 1994 Entry Draft).

Season	Club	Lea	Regular Season GP	G	A	TP	PIM	Playoffs GP	G	A	TP	PIM
1993-94	Brandon	WHL	70	3	19	22	51	4	0	0	0	6
1994-95	Brandon	WHL	21	1	5	6	44	18	1	2	3	11
1995-96	Brandon	WHL	70	4	37	41	99	19	1	12	13	18

BUTSAYEV, VIACHESLAV — (boot-SIGH-yehf)

Center. Shoots left. 6'2", 200 lbs. Born, Togliatti, USSR, June 13, 1970.
(Philadelphia's 10th choice, 109th overall, in 1990 Entry Draft).

Season	Club	Lea	Regular Season GP	G	A	TP	PIM	Playoffs GP	G	A	TP	PIM
1989-90	CSKA	USSR	48	14	4	18	30	....	....	....	....	....
1990-91	CSKA	USSR	46	14	9	23	32	....	....	....	....	....
1991-92	CSKA	CIS	36	12	13	25	26	....	....	....	....	....
1992-93	CSKA	CIS	5	3	4	7	6	....	....	....	....	....
	Philadelphia	**NHL**	**52**	**2**	**14**	**16**	**61**	....	....	....	....	....
	Hershey	AHL	24	8	10	18	51	....	....	....	....	....
1993-94	**Philadelphia**	**NHL**	**47**	**12**	**9**	**21**	**58**	....	....	....	....	....
	San Jose	**NHL**	**12**	**0**	**2**	**2**	**10**	....	....	....	....	....
1994-95	Togliatti	CIS	9	2	6	8	6	....	....	....	....	....
	San Jose	**NHL**	**6**	**2**	**0**	**2**	**0**	....	....	....	....	....
	Kansas City	IHL	13	3	4	7	12	3	0	0	0	2
1995-96	**Anaheim**	**NHL**	**7**	**1**	**0**	**1**	**0**	....	....	....	....	....
	Baltimore	AHL	62	23	42	65	70	12	4	8	12	28
	NHL Totals		**124**	**17**	**25**	**42**	**129**	....	....	....	....	....

Traded to **San Jose** by **Philadelphia** for Rob Zettler, February 1, 1994. Signed as a free agent by **Anaheim**, October 19, 1995.

BUTZ, ROB — TOR.

Left wing. Shoots left. 6'3", 191 lbs. Born, Dewberry, Alta., February 24, 1975.

Season	Club	Lea	Regular Season GP	G	A	TP	PIM	Playoffs GP	G	A	TP	PIM
1992-93	Victoria	WHL	67	7	11	18	64	....	....	....	....	....
1993-94	Victoria	WHL	72	24	24	48	161	....	....	....	....	....
	St. John's	AHL	5	0	0	0	26	....	....	....	....	....
1994-95	Prince George	WHL	32	12	18	30	83	....	....	....	....	....
	Tri-City	WHL	17	4	8	12	38	17	4	5	9	22
1995-96	St. John's	AHL	74	10	20	30	127	4	1	0	1	4

Signed as a free agent by **Toronto**, April 1, 1993.

BUZEK, PETR — DAL.

Defense. Shoots left. 6', 205 lbs. Born, Jihlava, Czech., April 26, 1977.
(Dallas' 3rd choice, 63rd overall, in 1995 Entry Draft).

Season	Club	Lea	Regular Season GP	G	A	TP	PIM	Playoffs GP	G	A	TP	PIM
1993-94	Dukla Jihlava	Czech.	3	0	0	0	....	....	....	....	....	....
1994-95	Dukla Jihlava	Czech.	43	2	5	7	47	2	0	0	0	2
1995-96			DID NOT PLAY – INJURED									

BYAKIN, ILYA

Defense. Shoots left. 5'9", 185 lbs. Born, Sverdlovsk, USSR, February 2, 1963.
(Edmonton's 11th choice, 267th overall, in 1993 Entry Draft).

Season	Club	Lea	Regular Season GP	G	A	TP	PIM	Playoffs GP	G	A	TP	PIM
1983-84	Spartak	USSR	44	9	12	21	26	....	....	....	....	....
1984-85	Spartak	USSR	46	7	11	18	56	....	....	....	....	....
1985-86	Spartak	USSR	34	8	7	15	41	....	....	....	....	....
1986-87			DID NOT PLAY									
1987-88	Sverdlovsk	USSR	30	10	10	20	37	....	....	....	....	....
1988-89	Sverdlovsk	USSR	40	11	9	20	53	....	....	....	....	....
1989-90	Sverdlovsk	USSR	27	14	7	21	20	....	....	....	....	....
1990-91	CSKA	USSR	29	4	7	11	20	....	....	....	....	....
1991-92	Rapperswil	Switz.2	36	27	40	67	36	....	....	....	....	....
1992-93	Landshut	Ger.	44	12	19	31	43	6	5	6	11	6
1993-94	**Edmonton**	**NHL**	**44**	**8**	**20**	**28**	**30**	....	....	....	....	....
	Cape Breton	AHL	12	2	9	11	8	....	....	....	....	....
1994-95	Yekaterinburg	CIS	4	3	2	5	14	....	....	....	....	....
	San Jose	**NHL**	**13**	**0**	**5**	**5**	**14**	....	....	....	....	....
	Kansas City	IHL	1	0	2	2	0	16	4	10	14	43
1995-96	Malmo	Swe.	36	10	15	25	52	3	1	0	1	19
	NHL Totals		**57**	**8**	**25**	**33**	**44**	....	....	....	....	....

Signed as a free agent by **San Jose**, September 18, 1994.

BYLSMA, DAN — L.A.

Left wing. Shoots left. 6'2", 215 lbs. Born, Grand Rapids, MI, September 19, 1970.
(Winnipeg's 7th choice, 109th overall, in 1989 Entry Draft).

Season	Club	Lea	Regular Season GP	G	A	TP	PIM	Playoffs GP	G	A	TP	PIM
1988-89	Bowling Green	CCHA	32	3	7	10	10	....	....	....	....	....
1989-90	Bowling Green	CCHA	44	13	17	30	30	....	....	....	....	....
1990-91	Bowling Green	CCHA	40	9	12	21	48	....	....	....	....	....
1991-92	Bowling Green	CCHA	34	11	14	25	24	....	....	....	....	....
1992-93	Greensboro	ECHL	60	25	35	60	66	1	0	1	1	10
	Rochester	AHL	2	0	1	1	0	....	....	....	....	....
1993-94	Greensboro	ECHL	25	14	16	30	52	....	....	....	....	....
	Albany	AHL	3	0	1	1	2	....	....	....	....	....
	Moncton	AHL	50	12	16	28	25	21	3	4	7	31
1994-95	Phoenix	IHL	81	19	23	42	41	9	4	4	8	4
1995-96	**Los Angeles**	**NHL**	**4**	**0**	**0**	**0**	**0**	....	....	....	....	....
	Phoenix	IHL	78	22	20	42	48	4	1	0	1	2
	NHL Totals		**4**	**0**	**0**	**0**	**0**	....	....	....	....	....

Signed as a free agent by **Los Angeles**, July 7, 1994.

CABANA, CHAD — FLA.

Left wing. Shoots left. 6'1", 200 lbs. Born, Bonnyville, Alta., October 1, 1974.
(Florida's 11th choice, 213th overall, in 1993 Entry Draft).

Season	Club	Lea	Regular Season GP	G	A	TP	PIM	Playoffs GP	G	A	TP	PIM
1991-92	Tri-City	WHL	57	5	8	13	145	4	0	1	1	21
1992-93	Tri-City	WHL	68	19	23	42	104	4	1	0	1	10
1993-94	Tri-City	WHL	67	27	33	60	201	4	2	0	2	24
1994-95	Tri-City	WHL	68	25	34	59	252	17	10	11	21	47
1995-96	Carolina	AHL	59	4	9	13	159	....	....	....	....	....

CAIRNS, ERIC — NYR

Defense. Shoots left. 6'5", 225 lbs. Born, Oakville, Ont., June 27, 1974.
(NY Rangers' 3rd choice, 72nd overall, in 1992 Entry Draft).

Season	Club	Lea	Regular Season GP	G	A	TP	PIM	Playoffs GP	G	A	TP	PIM
1991-92	Detroit	OHL	64	1	11	12	232	7	0	0	0	31
1992-93	Detroit	OHL	64	3	13	16	194	15	0	3	3	24
1993-94	Detroit	OHL	59	7	35	42	204	17	0	4	4	46
1994-95	Birmingham	ECHL	11	1	3	4	49	....	....	....	....	....
	Binghamton	AHL	27	0	3	3	134	9	1	1	2	28
1995-96	Binghamton	AHL	46	1	13	14	192	4	0	0	0	37
	Charlotte	ECHL	6	0	1	1	34	....	....	....	....	....

CALLAHAN, BRIAN — PIT.

Center. Shoots left. 6'1", 190 lbs. Born, Melrose, MA, July 13, 1974.
(Pittsburgh's 10th choice, 235th overall, in 1992 Entry Draft).

Season	Club	Lea	Regular Season GP	G	A	TP	PIM	Playoffs GP	G	A	TP	PIM
1993-94	Boston College	H.E.	36	11	11	22	58	....	....	....	....	....
1994-95	Boston College	H.E.	34	10	1	11	58	....	....	....	....	....
1995-96	Boston College	H.E.	36	14	8	22	38	....	....	....	....	....

CALOUN, JAN (CHAH-loon) S.J.

Right wing. Shoots right. 5'10", 175 lbs. Born, Usti-Nad-Labem, Czech., December 20, 1972.
(San Jose's 4th choice, 75th overall, in 1992 Entry Draft).

			Regular Season					Playoffs				
Season	Club	Lea	GP	G	A	TP	PIM	GP	G	A	TP	PIM
1990-91	Litvinov	Czech.	50	28	19	47	12	....	....	....	....	....
1991-92	Litvinov	Czech.	46	39	13	52	24	....	....	....	....	....
1992-93	Litvinov	Czech.	47	45	22	67	....	....	....	....	....	....
1993-94	Litvinov	Czech.	38	25	17	42	....	4	2	2	4	....
1994-95	Kansas City	IHL	76	34	39	73	50	21	13	10	23	18
1995-96	**San Jose**	**NHL**	**11**	**8**	**3**	**11**	**0**	....	....	....	....	....
	Kansas City	IHL	61	38	30	68	58	5	0	1	1	6
	NHL Totals		**11**	**8**	**3**	**11**	**0**	....	....	....	....	....

CAMPBELL, ED NYR

Defense. Shoots left. 6'2", 212 lbs. Born, Worcester, MA, November 26, 1974.
(NY Rangers' 9th choice, 190th overall, in 1993 Entry Draft).

			Regular Season					Playoffs				
Season	Club	Lea	GP	G	A	TP	PIM	GP	G	A	TP	PIM
1993-94	Lowell	H.E.	40	8	16	24	114	....	....	....	....	....
1994-95	Lowell	H.E.	34	6	24	30	105	....	....	....	....	....
1995-96	Lowell	H.E.	39	6	33	39	*107	....	....	....	....	....

CAMPBELL, JIM ST.L.

Center. Shoots right. 6'2", 185 lbs. Born, Worcester, MA, April 3, 1973.
(Montreal's 2nd choice, 28th overall, in 1991 Entry Draft).

			Regular Season					Playoffs				
Season	Club	Lea	GP	G	A	TP	PIM	GP	G	A	TP	PIM
1991-92	Hull	QMJHL	64	41	44	85	51	6	7	3	10	8
1992-93	Hull	QMJHL	50	42	29	71	66	8	11	4	15	43
1993-94	U.S. National	....	56	24	33	57	59	....	....	....	....	....
	U.S. Olympic	....	8	0	0	0	6	....	....	....	....	....
	Fredericton	AHL	19	6	17	23	6	....	....	....	....	....
1994-95	Fredericton	AHL	77	27	24	51	103	12	0	7	7	8
1995-96	Fredericton	AHL	44	28	23	51	24	....	....	....	....	....
	Anaheim	**NHL**	**16**	**2**	**3**	**5**	**36**	....	....	....	....	....
	Baltimore	AHL	16	13	7	20	8	12	7	5	12	10
	NHL Totals		**16**	**2**	**3**	**5**	**36**	....	....	....	....	....

Traded to **Anaheim** by **Montreal** for Robert Dirk, January 21, 1996. Signed as a free agent by **St. Louis**, July 11, 1996.

CARBONNEAU, GUY (KAR-buhn-oh, GEE) DAL.

Center. Shoots right. 5'11", 186 lbs. Born, Sept-Iles, Que., March 18, 1960.
(Montreal's 4th choice, 44th overall, in 1979 Entry Draft).

			Regular Season					Playoffs				
Season	Club	Lea	GP	G	A	TP	PIM	GP	G	A	TP	PIM
1976-77	Chicoutimi	QJHL	59	9	20	29	8	4	1	0	1	0
1977-78	Chicoutimi	QJHL	70	28	55	83	60	....	....	....	....	....
1978-79	Chicoutimi	QJHL	72	62	79	141	47	4	2	1	3	4
1979-80	Chicoutimi	QJHL	72	72	110	182	66	12	9	15	24	28
	Nova Scotia	AHL	....	....	....	....	....	2	1	1	2	2
1980-81	**Montreal**	**NHL**	**2**	**0**	**1**	**1**	**0**	....	....	....	....	....
	Nova Scotia	AHL	78	35	53	88	87	6	1	3	4	9
1981-82	Nova Scotia	AHL	77	27	67	94	124	9	2	7	9	8
1982-83	**Montreal**	**NHL**	**77**	**18**	**29**	**47**	**68**	**3**	**0**	**0**	**0**	**2**
1983-84	**Montreal**	**NHL**	**78**	**24**	**30**	**54**	**75**	**15**	**4**	**3**	**7**	**12**
1984-85	**Montreal**	**NHL**	**79**	**23**	**34**	**57**	**43**	**12**	**4**	**3**	**7**	**8**
1985-86	**Montreal**	**NHL**	**80**	**20**	**36**	**56**	**57**	**20**	**7**	**5**	**12**	**35** ♦
1986-87	**Montreal**	**NHL**	**79**	**18**	**27**	**45**	**68**	**17**	**3**	**8**	**11**	**20**
1987-88a	**Montreal**	**NHL**	**80**	**17**	**21**	**38**	**61**	**11**	**0**	**4**	**4**	**2**
1988-89a	**Montreal**	**NHL**	**79**	**26**	**30**	**56**	**44**	**21**	**4**	**5**	**9**	**10**
1989-90	**Montreal**	**NHL**	**68**	**19**	**36**	**55**	**37**	**11**	**2**	**3**	**5**	**6**
1990-91	**Montreal**	**NHL**	**78**	**20**	**24**	**44**	**63**	**13**	**1**	**5**	**6**	**10**
1991-92a	**Montreal**	**NHL**	**72**	**18**	**21**	**39**	**39**	**11**	**1**	**1**	**2**	**6**
1992-93	**Montreal**	**NHL**	**61**	**4**	**13**	**17**	**20**	**20**	**3**	**3**	**6**	**10** ♦
1993-94	**Montreal**	**NHL**	**79**	**14**	**24**	**38**	**48**	**7**	**1**	**3**	**4**	**4**
1994-95	**St. Louis**	**NHL**	**42**	**5**	**11**	**16**	**16**	**7**	**1**	**2**	**3**	**6**
1995-96	**Dallas**	**NHL**	**71**	**8**	**15**	**23**	**38**	....	....	....	....	....
	NHL Totals		**1025**	**234**	**352**	**586**	**677**	**168**	**31**	**45**	**76**	**131**

a Won Frank J. Selke Trophy (1988, 1989, 1992)

Traded to **St. Louis** by **Montreal** for Jim Montgomery, August 19, 1994. Traded to **Dallas** by **St. Louis** for Paul Broten, October 2, 1995.

CARDARELLI, JOE T.B.

Left winger. Shoots left. 6', 203 lbs. Born, Vancouver, B.C., June 13, 1977.
(Tampa Bay's 7th choice, 186th overall, in 1995 Entry Draft).

			Regular Season					Playoffs				
Season	Club	Lea	GP	G	A	TP	PIM	GP	G	A	TP	PIM
1993-94	Spokane	WHL	51	7	11	18	9	2	0	0	0	0
1994-95	Spokane	WHL	71	27	22	49	20	11	4	9	13	0
1995-96	Spokane	WHL	44	25	19	44	21	18	4	0	4	4

CARKNER, TERRY FLA.

Defense. Shoots left. 6'3", 210 lbs. Born, Smiths Falls, Ont., March 7, 1966.
(NY Rangers' 1st choice, 14th overall, in 1984 Entry Draft).

			Regular Season					Playoffs				
Season	Club	Lea	GP	G	A	TP	PIM	GP	G	A	TP	PIM
1983-84	Peterborough	OHL	58	4	19	23	77	8	0	6	6	13
1984-85a	Peterborough	OHL	64	14	47	61	125	17	2	10	12	11
1985-86b	Peterborough	OHL	54	12	32	44	106	16	1	7	8	17
1986-87	**NY Rangers**	**NHL**	**52**	**2**	**13**	**15**	**118**	**1**	**0**	**0**	**0**	**0**
	New Haven	AHL	12	2	6	8	56	3	1	0	1	0
1987-88	**Quebec**	**NHL**	**63**	**3**	**24**	**27**	**159**	....	....	....	....	....
1988-89	**Philadelphia**	**NHL**	**78**	**11**	**32**	**43**	**149**	**19**	**1**	**5**	**6**	**28**
1989-90	**Philadelphia**	**NHL**	**63**	**4**	**18**	**22**	**169**	....	....	....	....	....
1990-91	**Philadelphia**	**NHL**	**79**	**7**	**25**	**32**	**204**	....	....	....	....	....
1991-92	**Philadelphia**	**NHL**	**73**	**4**	**12**	**16**	**195**	....	....	....	....	....
1992-93	**Philadelphia**	**NHL**	**83**	**3**	**16**	**19**	**150**	....	....	....	....	....
1993-94	**Detroit**	**NHL**	**68**	**1**	**6**	**7**	**130**	**7**	**0**	**0**	**0**	**4**
1994-95	**Detroit**	**NHL**	**20**	**1**	**2**	**3**	**21**	....	....	....	....	....
1995-96	**Florida**	**NHL**	**73**	**3**	**10**	**13**	**80**	**22**	**0**	**4**	**4**	**10**
	NHL Totals		**652**	**39**	**158**	**197**	**1375**	**49**	**1**	**9**	**10**	**42**

a OHL Second All-Star Team (1985)
b OHL First All-Star Team (1986)

Traded to **Quebec** by **NY Rangers** with Jeff Jackson for John Ogrodnick and David Shaw, September 30, 1987. Traded to **Philadelphia** by **Quebec** for Greg Smyth and Philadelphia's third round choice (John Tanner) in the 1989 Entry Draft, July 25, 1988. Traded to **Detroit** by **Philadelphia** for Yves Racine and Detroit's fourth round choice (Sebastien Vallee) in 1994 Entry Draft, October 5, 1993. Signed as a free agent by **Florida**, August 8, 1995.

CARNBACK, PATRIK (KAHRN-buhk)

Center. Shoots left. 6', 187 lbs. Born, Goteborg, Sweden, February 1, 1968.
(Montreal's 7th choice, 125th overall, in 1988 Entry Draft).

			Regular Season					Playoffs				
Season	Club	Lea	GP	G	A	TP	PIM	GP	G	A	TP	PIM
1986-87	V. Frolunda	Swe. 2	28	3	1	4	4	....	....	....	....	....
1987-88	V. Frolunda	Swe. 2	33	16	19	35	24	11	4	5	9	8
1988-89	V. Frolunda	Swe. 2	53	39	36	75	52	....	....	....	....	....
1989-90	V. Frolunda	Swe.	40	26	27	53	34	....	....	....	....	....
1990-91	V. Frolunda	Swe.	22	10	9	19	46	28	15	24	39	24
1991-92	V. Frolunda	Swe.	33	17	22	39	32	3	1	5	6	20
1992-93	**Montreal**	**NHL**	**6**	**0**	**0**	**0**	**2**	....	....	....	....	....
	Fredericton	AHL	45	20	37	57	45	5	0	3	3	14
1993-94	**Anaheim**	**NHL**	**73**	**12**	**11**	**23**	**54**	....	....	....	....	....
1994-95	V. Frolunda	Swe.	14	2	6	8	20	....	....	....	....	....
	Anaheim	**NHL**	**41**	**6**	**15**	**21**	**32**	....	....	....	....	....
1995-96	**Anaheim**	**NHL**	**34**	**6**	**12**	**18**	**34**	....	....	....	....	....
	Koln	Ger.	5	1	6	7	2	14	8	8	16	33
	NHL Totals		**154**	**24**	**38**	**62**	**122**	....	....	....	....	....

Traded to **Anaheim** by **Montreal** with Todd Ewen for Anaheim's third round choice (Chris Murray) in 1994 Entry Draft, August 10, 1993.

CARNEY, KEITH E. CHI.

Defense. Shoots left. 6'2", 205 lbs. Born, Providence, RI, February 3, 1970.
(Buffalo's 3rd choice, 76th overall, in 1988 Entry Draft).

			Regular Season					Playoffs				
Season	Club	Lea	GP	G	A	TP	PIM	GP	G	A	TP	PIM
1988-89	U. of Maine	H.E.	40	4	22	26	24	....	....	....	....	....
1989-90ab	U. of Maine	H.E.	41	3	41	44	43	....	....	....	....	....
1990-91cd	U. of Maine	H.E.	40	7	49	56	38	....	....	....	....	....
1991-92	U.S. National	....	49	2	17	19	16	....	....	....	....	....
	Buffalo	**NHL**	**14**	**1**	**2**	**3**	**18**	**7**	**0**	**3**	**3**	**0**
	Rochester	AHL	24	1	10	11	2	2	0	2	2	0
1992-93	**Buffalo**	**NHL**	**30**	**2**	**4**	**6**	**55**	**8**	**0**	**3**	**3**	**6**
	Rochester	AHL	41	5	21	26	32	....	....	....	....	....
1993-94	**Buffalo**	**NHL**	**7**	**1**	**3**	**4**	**4**	....	....	....	....	....
	Chicago	**NHL**	**30**	**3**	**5**	**8**	**35**	**6**	**0**	**1**	**1**	**4**
	Indianapolis	IHL	28	0	14	14	20	....	....	....	....	....
1994-95	**Chicago**	**NHL**	**18**	**1**	**0**	**1**	**11**	**4**	**0**	**1**	**1**	**0**
1995-96	**Chicago**	**NHL**	**82**	**5**	**14**	**19**	**94**	**10**	**0**	**3**	**3**	**4**
	NHL Totals		**181**	**13**	**28**	**41**	**217**	**35**	**0**	**11**	**11**	**14**

a Hockey East Second All-Star Team (1990)
b NCAA East Second All-American Team (1990)
c Hockey East First All-Star Team (1991)
d NCAA East First All-American Team (1991)

Traded to **Chicago** by **Buffalo** with Buffalo's sixth round choice (Marc Magliarditi) in 1995 Entry Draft for Craig Muni and Chicago's fifth round choice (Daniel Bienvenue) in 1995 Entry Draft, October 27, 1993.

CARPENTER, BOB N.J.

Center. Shoots left. 6', 200 lbs. Born, Beverly, MA, July 13, 1963.
(Washington's 1st choice, 3rd overall, in 1981 Entry Draft).

			Regular Season					Playoffs				
Season	Club	Lea	GP	G	A	TP	PIM	GP	G	A	TP	PIM
1980-81	St. John's	HS	18	14	24	38	....	....	....	....	....	....
1981-82	**Washington**	**NHL**	**80**	**32**	**35**	**67**	**69**	....	....	....	....	....
1982-83	**Washington**	**NHL**	**80**	**32**	**37**	**69**	**64**	**4**	**1**	**0**	**1**	**2**
1983-84	**Washington**	**NHL**	**80**	**28**	**40**	**68**	**51**	**8**	**2**	**1**	**3**	**25**
1984-85	**Washington**	**NHL**	**80**	**53**	**42**	**95**	**87**	**5**	**1**	**4**	**5**	**8**
1985-86	**Washington**	**NHL**	**80**	**27**	**29**	**56**	**105**	**9**	**5**	**4**	**9**	**12**
1986-87	**Washington**	**NHL**	**22**	**5**	**7**	**12**	**21**	....	....	....	....	....
	NY Rangers	**NHL**	**28**	**2**	**8**	**10**	**20**	....	....	....	....	....
	Los Angeles	**NHL**	**10**	**2**	**3**	**5**	**6**	**5**	**1**	**2**	**3**	**2**
1987-88	**Los Angeles**	**NHL**	**71**	**19**	**33**	**52**	**84**	**5**	**1**	**1**	**2**	**0**
1988-89	**Los Angeles**	**NHL**	**39**	**11**	**15**	**26**	**16**	....	....	....	....	....
	Boston	**NHL**	**18**	**5**	**9**	**14**	**10**	**8**	**1**	**1**	**2**	**4**
1989-90	**Boston**	**NHL**	**80**	**25**	**31**	**56**	**97**	**21**	**4**	**6**	**10**	**39**
1990-91	**Boston**	**NHL**	**29**	**8**	**8**	**16**	**22**	**1**	**0**	**1**	**1**	**2**
1991-92	**Boston**	**NHL**	**60**	**25**	**23**	**48**	**46**	**8**	**0**	**1**	**1**	**6**
1992-93	**Washington**	**NHL**	**68**	**11**	**17**	**28**	**65**	**6**	**1**	**4**	**5**	**6**
1993-94	**New Jersey**	**NHL**	**76**	**10**	**23**	**33**	**51**	**20**	**1**	**7**	**8**	**20**
1994-95	**New Jersey**	**NHL**	**41**	**5**	**11**	**16**	**19**	**17**	**1**	**4**	**5**	**6** ♦
1995-96	**New Jersey**	**NHL**	**52**	**5**	**5**	**10**	**14**	....	....	....	....	....
	NHL Totals		**994**	**305**	**376**	**681**	**847**	**117**	**19**	**36**	**55**	**132**

Played in NHL All-Star Game (1985)

Traded to **NY Rangers** by **Washington** with Washington's second round choice (Jason Prosofsky) in 1989 Entry Draft for Bob Crawford, Kelly Miller and Mike Ridley, January 1, 1987. Traded to **Los Angeles** by **NY Rangers** with Tom Laidlaw for Jeff Crossman, Marcel Dionne and Los Angeles' third round choice (later traded to Minnesota — Minnesota selected Murray Garbutt) in 1989 Entry Draft. Traded to **Boston** by **Los Angeles** for Steve Kasper, January 23, 1989. Signed as a free agent by **Washington**, June 30, 1992. Signed as a free agent by **New Jersey**, September 30, 1993.

CARSON, JIMMY

Center. Shoots right. 6'1", 200 lbs. Born, Southfield, MI, July 20, 1968.
(Los Angeles' 1st choice, 2nd overall, in 1986 Entry Draft).

			Regular Season					Playoffs				
Season	Club	Lea	GP	G	A	TP	PIM	GP	G	A	TP	PIM
1984-85	Verdun	QMJHL	68	44	72	116	12	14	9	17	26	12
1985-86a	Verdun	QMJHL	69	70	83	153	46	5	2	6	8	0
1986-87b	Los Angeles	NHL	80	37	42	79	22	5	1	2	3	6
1987-88	Los Angeles	NHL	80	55	52	107	45	5	5	3	8	4
1988-89	Edmonton	NHL	80	49	51	100	36	7	2	1	3	6
1989-90	Edmonton	NHL	4	1	2	3	0	....	....	....	....	....
	Detroit	NHL	44	20	16	36	8	....	....	....	....	....
1990-91	Detroit	NHL	64	21	25	46	28	7	2	1	3	4
1991-92	Detroit	NHL	80	34	35	69	30	11	2	3	5	0
1992-93	Detroit	NHL	52	25	26	51	18	....	....	....	....	....
	Los Angeles	NHL	34	12	10	22	14	18	5	4	9	2
1993-94	Los Angeles	NHL	25	4	7	11	2	....	....	....	....	....
	Vancouver	NHL	34	7	10	17	22	2	0	1	1	0
1994-95	Hartford	NHL	38	9	10	19	29	....	....	....	....	....
1995-96	Hartford	NHL	11	1	0	1	0	....	....	....	....	....
	Lausanne	Switz.	13	3	4	7	14	....	....	....	....	....
	NHL Totals		626	275	286	561	254	55	17	15	32	22

a QMJHL Second All-Star Team (1986)
b Named to NHL All-Rookie Team (1987)

Played in NHL All-Star Game (1989)

Traded to **Edmonton** by **Los Angeles** with Martin Gelinas, Los Angeles' first round choices in 1989 (later traded to New Jersey — New Jersey selected Jason Miller), 1991 (Martin Rucinsky) and 1993 (Nick Stajduhar) Entry Drafts and cash for Wayne Gretzky, Mike Krushelnyski and Marty McSorley, August 9, 1988. Traded to **Detroit** by **Edmonton** with Kevin McClelland and Edmonton's fifth round choice (later traded to Montreal — Montreal selected Brad Layzell) in 1991 Entry Draft for Petr Klima, Joe Murphy, Adam Graves and Jeff Sharples, November 2, 1989. Traded to **Los Angeles** by **Detroit** with Marc Potvin and Gary Shuchuk for Paul Coffey, Sylvain Couturier and Jim Hiller, January 29, 1993. Traded to **Vancouver** by **Los Angeles** for Dixon Ward and a conditional draft choice in 1995 Entry Draft, January 8, 1994. Signed as a free agent by **Hartford**, July 15, 1994.

CARTER, ANSON — WSH.

Center. Shoots right. 6'1", 175 lbs. Born, Toronto, Ont., June 6, 1974.
(Quebec's 10th choice, 220th overall, in 1992 Entry Draft).

			Regular Season					Playoffs				
Season	Club	Lea	GP	G	A	TP	PIM	GP	G	A	TP	PIM
1992-93	Michigan State	CCHA	34	15	7	22	20	....	....	....	....	....
1993-94a	Michigan State	CCHA	39	30	24	54	36	....	....	....	....	....
1994-95ab	Michigan State	CCHA	39	34	17	51	40	....	....	....	....	....
1995-96c	Michigan State	CCHA	42	23	20	43	36	....	....	....	....	....

a CCHA First All-Star Team (1994, 1995)
b NCAA West Second All-American Team (1995)
c CCHA Second All-Star Team (1996)

Traded to **Washington** by **Colorado** for Washington's fourth round choice (Ben Storey) in 1996 Entry Draft, April 3, 1996.

CASSELMAN, MIKE — FLA.

Center. Shoots left. 5'11", 190 lbs. Born, Morrisburg, Ont., August 23, 1968.
(Detroit's 1st choice, 3rd overall, in 1990 Supplemental Draft).

			Regular Season					Playoffs				
Season	Club	Lea	GP	G	A	TP	PIM	GP	G	A	TP	PIM
1987-88	Clarkson	ECAC	24	4	1	5	....	....	....	....	....	....
1988-89	Clarkson	ECAC	31	3	14	17	....	....	....	....	....	....
1989-90	Clarkson	ECAC	34	22	21	43	69	....	....	....	....	....
1990-91	Clarkson	ECAC	40	19	35	54	44	....	....	....	....	....
1991-92a	Toledo	ECHL	61	39	60	99	83	5	0	1	1	6
	Adirondack	AHL	1	0	0	0	0	....	....	....	....	....
1992-93	Adirondack	AHL	60	12	19	31	27	8	3	3	6	0
	Toledo	ECHL	3	0	1	1	2	....	....	....	....	....
1993-94	Adirondack	AHL	77	17	38	55	34	12	2	4	6	10
1994-95	Adirondack	AHL	60	17	43	60	42	4	0	0	0	2
1995-96	Florida	NHL	3	0	0	0	0	....	....	....	....	....
	Carolina	AHL	70	34	68	102	46	....	....	....	....	....
	NHL Totals		3	0	0	0	0	....	....	....	....	....

a ECHL Second All-Star Team (1992)

Signed as a free agent by **Florida**, October 31, 1995.

CASSELS, ANDREW — (KAS-uhls) HFD.

Center. Shoots left. 5'11", 177 lbs. Born, Bramalea, Ont., July 23, 1969.
(Montreal's 1st choice, 17th overall, in 1987 Entry Draft).

			Regular Season					Playoffs				
Season	Club	Lea	GP	G	A	TP	PIM	GP	G	A	TP	PIM
1986-87	Ottawa	OHL	66	26	66	92	28	11	5	9	14	7
1987-88a	Ottawa	OHL	61	48	*103	*151	39	16	8	*24	*32	13
1988-89a	Ottawa	OHL	56	37	97	134	66	12	5	10	15	10
1989-90	Montreal	NHL	6	2	0	2	2	....	....	....	....	....
	Sherbrooke	AHL	55	22	45	67	25	12	2	11	13	6
1990-91	Montreal	NHL	54	6	19	25	20	8	0	2	2	2
1991-92	Hartford	NHL	67	11	30	41	18	7	2	4	6	6
1992-93	Hartford	NHL	84	21	64	85	62	....	....	....	....	....
1993-94	Hartford	NHL	79	16	42	58	37	....	....	....	....	....
1994-95	Hartford	NHL	46	7	30	37	18	....	....	....	....	....
1995-96	Hartford	NHL	81	20	43	63	39	....	....	....	....	....
	NHL Totals		417	83	228	311	196	15	2	6	8	8

a OHL First All-Star Team (1988,1989)

Traded to **Hartford** by **Montreal** for Hartford's second round choice (Valeri Bure) in 1992 Entry Draft, September 17, 1991.

CASSIDY, BRUCE

Defense. Shoots left. 5'11", 176 lbs. Born, Ottawa, Ont., May 20, 1965.
(Chicago's 1st choice, 18th overall, in 1983 Entry Draft).

			Regular Season					Playoffs				
Season	Club	Lea	GP	G	A	TP	PIM	GP	G	A	TP	PIM
1982-83	Ottawa	OHL	70	25	86	111	33	9	3	9	12	10
1983-84	Chicago	NHL	1	0	0	0	0	....	....	....	....	....
a	Ottawa	OHL	67	27	68	95	58	13	6	16	22	6
1984-85	Ottawa	OHL	28	13	27	40	15	....	....	....	....	....
1985-86	Chicago	NHL	1	0	0	0	0	....	....	....	....	....
	Nova Scotia	AHL	4	0	0	0	0	....	....	....	....	....
1986-87	Chicago	NHL	2	0	0	0	0	....	....	....	....	....
	Nova Scotia	AHL	19	2	8	10	4	....	....	....	....	....
	Cdn. Olympic	....	12	3	6	9	4	....	....	....	....	....
	Saginaw	IHL	10	2	13	15	6	2	1	1	2	0
1987-88	Chicago	NHL	21	3	10	13	6	....	....	....	....	....
	Saginaw	IHL	60	9	37	46	59	10	2	3	5	19
1988-89	Chicago	NHL	9	0	2	2	4	1	0	0	0	0
	Saginaw	IHL	72	16	64	80	80	6	0	2	2	6
1989-90	Chicago	NHL	2	1	1	2	0	....	....	....	....	....
b	Indianapolis	IHL	75	11	46	57	56	14	1	10	11	20
1990-91	Alleghe	Italy	36	23	52	75	20	10	7	8	15	2
1992-93	Alleghe	Italy	36	24	47	71	....	8	5	9	14	....
1993-94	Kaufbeuren	Ger.	33	9	12	21	....	4	1	2	3	....
1994-95	Indianapolis	IHL	29	2	13	15	16	....	....	....	....	....
1995-96	Indianapolis	IHL	56	5	16	21	46	5	1	0	1	4
	NHL Totals		36	4	13	17	10	1	0	0	0	0

a OHL Second All-Star Team (1984)
b IHL First All-Star Team (1989, 1990)

Signed as a free agent by **Chicago**, July 28, 1994.

CAVA, PETER — TOR.

Center. Shoots left. 5'11", 175 lbs. Born, Thunder Bay, Ont., February 14, 1978.
(Toronto's 7th choice, 110th overall, in 1996 Entry Draft).

			Regular Season					Playoffs				
Season	Club	Lea	GP	G	A	TP	PIM	GP	G	A	TP	PIM
1995-96	S.S. Marie	OHL	40	14	17	31	44	4	1	1	2	4

CAVALLINI, GINO

Left wing. Shoots left. 6'1", 215 lbs. Born, Toronto, Ont., November 24, 1962.

			Regular Season					Playoffs				
Season	Club	Lea	GP	G	A	TP	PIM	GP	G	A	TP	PIM
1982-83	Bowling Green	CCHA	40	8	16	24	52	....	....	....	....	....
1983-84	Bowling Green	CCHA	43	25	23	48	16	....	....	....	....	....
1984-85	Calgary	NHL	27	6	10	16	14	3	0	0	0	4
	Moncton	AHL	51	29	19	48	28	....	....	....	....	....
1985-86	Calgary	NHL	27	7	7	14	26	....	....	....	....	....
	Moncton	AHL	4	3	2	5	7	....	....	....	....	....
	St. Louis	NHL	30	6	5	11	36	17	4	5	9	10
1986-87	St. Louis	NHL	80	18	26	44	54	6	3	1	4	2
1987-88	St. Louis	NHL	64	15	17	32	62	10	5	5	10	19
1988-89	St. Louis	NHL	74	20	23	43	79	9	0	2	2	17
1989-90	St. Louis	NHL	80	15	15	30	77	12	1	3	4	12
1990-91	St. Louis	NHL	78	8	27	35	81	13	1	3	4	2
1991-92	St. Louis	NHL	48	9	7	16	40	....	....	....	....	....
	Quebec	NHL	18	1	7	8	4	....	....	....	....	....
1992-93	Quebec	NHL	67	9	15	24	34	4	0	0	0	0
1993-94	Milwaukee	IHL	78	43	35	78	64	4	3	4	7	6
1994-95a	Milwaukee	IHL	80	53	35	88	54	15	7	2	9	10
1995-96	Milwaukee	IHL	82	43	39	82	20	5	3	1	4	2
	NHL Totals		593	114	159	273	507	74	14	19	33	66

a IHL Second All-Star Team (1995)

Signed as a free agent by **Calgary**, May 16, 1984. Traded to **St. Louis** by **Calgary** with Eddy Beers and Charles Bourgeois for Joe Mullen, Terry Johnson and Rik Wilson, February 1, 1986. Claimed on waivers by **Quebec** from **St. Louis**, February 27, 1992.

CAVALLINI, PAUL

Defense. Shoots left. 6'1", 202 lbs. Born, Toronto, Ont., October 13, 1965.
(Washington's 9th choice, 205th overall, in 1984 Entry Draft).

			Regular Season					Playoffs				
Season	Club	Lea	GP	G	A	TP	PIM	GP	G	A	TP	PIM
1984-85	Providence	H.E.	37	4	10	14	52	....	....	....	....	....
1985-86	Cdn. National	....	52	1	11	12	95	....	....	....	....	....
	Binghamton	AHL	15	3	4	7	20	6	0	2	2	56
1986-87	Washington	NHL	6	0	2	2	8	....	....	....	....	....
	Binghamton	AHL	66	12	24	36	188	13	2	7	9	35
1987-88	Washington	NHL	24	2	3	5	66	....	....	....	....	....
	St. Louis	NHL	48	4	7	11	86	10	1	6	7	26
1988-89	St. Louis	NHL	65	4	20	24	128	10	2	2	4	14
1989-90a	St. Louis	NHL	80	8	39	47	106	12	2	3	5	20
1990-91	St. Louis	NHL	67	10	25	35	89	13	2	3	5	20
1991-92	St. Louis	NHL	66	10	25	35	95	4	0	1	1	6
1992-93	St. Louis	NHL	11	1	4	5	10	....	....	....	....	....
	Washington	NHL	71	5	8	13	46	6	0	2	2	18
1993-94	Dallas	NHL	74	11	33	44	82	9	1	8	9	4
1994-95	Dallas	NHL	44	1	11	12	28	5	0	2	2	6
1995-96	Dallas	NHL	8	0	0	0	6	....	....	....	....	....
	NHL Totals		564	56	177	233	750	69	8	27	35	114

a Won Alka-Seltzer Plus Award (1990)

Played in NHL All-Star Game (1990)

Traded to **St. Louis** by **Washington** for Montreal's second round choice (previously acquired by St. Louis — Washington selected Wade Bartley) in 1988 Entry Draft, December 11, 1987. Traded to **Washington** by **St. Louis** for Kevin Miller, November 2, 1992. Traded to **Dallas** by **Washington** for future considerations (Enrico Ciccone, June 25, 1993), June 20, 1993.

CERVEN, MARTIN — EDM.

Center. Shoots left. 6'4", 200 lbs. Born, Trencin, Czech., March 7, 1977.
(Edmonton's 6th choice, 161st overall, in 1995 Entry Draft).

			Regular Season					Playoffs				
Season	Club	Lea	GP	G	A	TP	PIM	GP	G	A	TP	PIM
1994-95	Dukla Trencin	Slo. Jr.	22	8	3	11	....	....	....	....	....	....
1995-96	Spokane	WHL	40	9	9	18	42	....	....	....	....	....
	Seattle	WHL	27	6	14	20	10	5	1	2	3	0

CHAMBERS, SHAWN — N.J.

Defense. Shoots left. 6'2", 200 lbs. Born, Sterling Hts., MI, October 11, 1966.
(Minnesota's 1st choice, 4th overall, in 1987 Supplemental Draft).

			Regular Season					Playoffs				
Season	**Club**	**Lea**	**GP**	**G**	**A**	**TP**	**PIM**	**GP**	**G**	**A**	**TP**	**PIM**
1985-86	Alaska-Fair.	G.N.	25	15	21	36	34	....	....	....	....	....
1986-87	Alaska-Fair.	G.N.	28	8	29	37	84	....	....	....	....	....
	Seattle	WHL	28	8	25	33	58	....	....	....	....	....
	Fort Wayne	IHL	12	2	6	8	0	10	1	4	5	5
1987-88	**Minnesota**	**NHL**	**19**	**1**	**7**	**8**	**21**	....	....	....	....	....
	Kalamazoo	IHL	19	1	6	7	22	....	....	....	....	....
1988-89	**Minnesota**	**NHL**	**72**	**5**	**19**	**24**	**80**	**3**	**0**	**2**	**2**	**0**
1989-90	**Minnesota**	**NHL**	**78**	**8**	**18**	**26**	**81**	**7**	**2**	**1**	**3**	**10**
1990-91	**Minnesota**	**NHL**	**29**	**1**	**3**	**4**	**24**	**23**	**0**	**7**	**7**	**16**
	Kalamazoo	IHL	3	1	1	2	0	....	....	....	....	....
1991-92	**Washington**	**NHL**	**2**	**0**	**0**	**0**	**2**	....	....	....	....	....
	Baltimore	AHL	5	2	3	5	9	....	....	....	....	....
1992-93	**Tampa Bay**	**NHL**	**55**	**10**	**29**	**39**	**36**	....	....	....	....	....
	Atlanta	IHL	6	0	2	2	18	....	....	....	....	....
1993-94	**Tampa Bay**	**NHL**	**66**	**11**	**23**	**34**	**23**	....	....	....	....	....
1994-95	**Tampa Bay**	**NHL**	**24**	**2**	**12**	**14**	**6**	....	....	....	....	....
	New Jersey	**NHL**	**21**	**2**	**5**	**7**	**6**	**20**	**4**	**5**	**9**	**2** ♦
1995-96	**New Jersey**	**NHL**	**64**	**2**	**21**	**23**	**18**	....	....	....	....	....
	NHL Totals		**430**	**42**	**137**	**179**	**297**	**53**	**6**	**15**	**21**	**28**

Traded to **Washington** by **Minnesota** for Steve Maltais and Trent Klatt, June 21, 1991. Claimed by **Tampa Bay** from **Washington** in Expansion Draft, June 18, 1992. Traded to **New Jersey** by **Tampa Bay** with Danton Cole for Alexander Semak and Ben Hankinson, March 14, 1995.

CHARA, ZDENO — NYI

Defense. Shoots left. 6'8", 231 lbs. Born, Trencin, Czech., March 18, 1977.
(NY Islanders' 3rd choice, 56th overall, in 1996 Entry Draft).

			Regular Season					Playoffs				
Season	**Club**	**Lea**	**GP**	**G**	**A**	**TP**	**PIM**	**GP**	**G**	**A**	**TP**	**PIM**
1994-95	Trencin	Slo. Jr.	2	0	0	0	0	....	....	....	....	....
	Trencin	Slo. Jr. B	30	22	22	44	113	....	....	....	....	....
1995-96	Trencin	Slo. Jr.	22	1	13	14	80	....	....	....	....	....
	Piestany	Slo. 2	10	1	3	4	10	....	....	....	....	....
	Sparta	Cz. Jr.	15	1	2	3	42	....	....	....	....	....
	Sparta	Czech.	1	0	0	0	0	....	....	....	....	....

CHARBONNEAU, JOSE — (SHAHR-buh-noh, JOH-see)

Right wing. Shoots right. 6', 195 lbs. Born, Ferme-Neuve, Que., November 21, 1966.
(Montreal's 1st choice, 12th overall, in 1985 Entry Draft).

			Regular Season					Playoffs				
Season	**Club**	**Lea**	**GP**	**G**	**A**	**TP**	**PIM**	**GP**	**G**	**A**	**TP**	**PIM**
1983-84	Drummondville	QMJHL	65	31	59	90	110	....	....	....	....	....
1984-85	Drummondville	QMJHL	46	34	40	74	91	12	5	10	15	20
1985-86	Drummondville	QMJHL	57	44	45	89	158	23	16	20	36	40
1986-87	Sherbrooke	AHL	72	14	27	41	94	16	5	12	17	17
1987-88	**Montreal**	**NHL**	**16**	**0**	**2**	**2**	**6**	**8**	**0**	**0**	**0**	**4**
	Sherbrooke	AHL	55	30	35	65	108	....	....	....	....	....
1988-89	**Montreal**	**NHL**	**9**	**1**	**3**	**4**	**6**	....	....	....	....	....
	Sherbrooke	AHL	33	13	15	28	95	....	....	....	....	....
	Vancouver	**NHL**	**13**	**0**	**1**	**1**	**6**	....	....	....	....	....
	Milwaukee	IHL	13	8	5	13	46	10	3	2	5	23
1989-90	Milwaukee	IHL	65	23	38	61	137	5	0	1	1	8
1990-91	Cdn. National	....	56	22	29	51	54	....	....	....	....	....
1991-92						DID NOT PLAY						
1992-93	Cdn. National	....	1	0	0	0	0	....	....	....	....	....
1993-94	**Vancouver**	**NHL**	**30**	**7**	**7**	**14**	**49**	**3**	**1**	**0**	**1**	**4**
	Hamilton	AHL	7	3	2	5	8	....	....	....	....	....
1994-95	**Vancouver**	**NHL**	**3**	**1**	**0**	**1**	**0**	....	....	....	....	....
	Las Vegas	IHL	27	8	12	20	102	9	1	1	2	71
1995-96	Landshut	Ger.	47	32	24	56	102	11	10	6	16	28
	NHL Totals		**71**	**9**	**13**	**22**	**67**	**11**	**1**	**0**	**1**	**8**

Traded to **Vancouver** by **Montreal** for Dan Woodley, January 25, 1989. Signed as a free agent by **Vancouver**, October 3, 1993.

CHARRON, ERIC — WSH.

Defense. Shoots left. 6'3", 192 lbs. Born, Verdun, Que., January 14, 1970.
(Montreal's 1st choice, 20th overall, in 1988 Entry Draft).

			Regular Season					Playoffs				
Season	**Club**	**Lea**	**GP**	**G**	**A**	**TP**	**PIM**	**GP**	**G**	**A**	**TP**	**PIM**
1987-88	Trois-Rivières	QMJHL	67	3	13	16	135	....	....	....	....	....
1988-89	Trois-Rivières	QMJHL	38	2	16	18	111	....	....	....	....	....
	Verdun	QMJHL	28	2	15	17	66	....	....	....	....	....
	Sherbrooke	AHL	1	0	0	0	0	....	....	....	....	....
1989-90	St-Hyacinthe	QMJHL	68	13	38	51	152	11	3	4	7	67
	Sherbrooke	AHL	....	....	....	....	....	2	0	0	0	0
1990-91	Fredericton	AHL	71	1	11	12	108	2	1	0	1	29
1991-92	Fredericton	AHL	59	2	11	13	98	6	1	0	1	4
1992-93	**Montreal**	**NHL**	**3**	**0**	**0**	**0**	**2**	....	....	....	....	....
	Fredericton	AHL	54	3	13	16	93	....	....	....	....	....
	Atlanta	IHL	11	0	2	2	12	3	0	1	1	6
1993-94	**Tampa Bay**	**NHL**	**4**	**0**	**0**	**0**	**2**	....	....	....	....	....
	Atlanta	IHL	66	5	18	23	144	14	1	4	5	28
1994-95	**Tampa Bay**	**NHL**	**45**	**1**	**4**	**5**	**26**	....	....	....	....	....
1995-96	**Tampa Bay**	**NHL**	**14**	**0**	**0**	**0**	**18**	....	....	....	....	....
	Washington	**NHL**	**4**	**0**	**1**	**1**	**4**	**6**	**0**	**0**	**0**	**8**
	Portland	AHL	45	0	8	8	88	20	1	1	2	33
	NHL Totals		**70**	**1**	**5**	**6**	**52**	**6**	**0**	**0**	**0**	**8**

Traded to **Tampa Bay** by **Montreal** with Alain Cote and future considerations (Donald Dufresne, June 18, 1993) for Rob Ramage, March 20, 1993. Traded to **Washington** by **Tampa Bay** for a conditional draft choice in 1997 Entry Draft, November 16, 1995.

CHASE, DON

Center. Shoots right. 5'11", 190 lbs. Born, Springfield, MA, March 17, 1974.
(Montreal's 7th choice, 116th overall, in 1992 Entry Draft).

			Regular Season					Playoffs				
Season	**Club**	**Lea**	**GP**	**G**	**A**	**TP**	**PIM**	**GP**	**G**	**A**	**TP**	**PIM**
1992-93	Boston College	H.E.	38	7	5	12	48	....	....	....	....	....
1993-94	Boston College	H.E.	35	14	13	27	58	....	....	....	....	....
1994-95	Boston College	H.E.	35	19	12	31	74	....	....	....	....	....
1995-96	Boston College	H.E.	35	12	15	27	87	....	....	....	....	....
	Fredericton	AHL	7	1	1	2	2	....	....	....	....	....

CHASE, KELLY — HFD.

Right wing. Shoots right. 5'11", 193 lbs. Born, Porcupine Plain, Sask., October 25, 1967.

			Regular Season					Playoffs				
Season	**Club**	**Lea**	**GP**	**G**	**A**	**TP**	**PIM**	**GP**	**G**	**A**	**TP**	**PIM**
1985-86	Saskatoon	WHL	57	7	18	25	172	10	3	4	7	37
1986-87	Saskatoon	WHL	68	17	29	46	285	11	2	8	10	37
1987-88	Saskatoon	WHL	70	21	34	55	*343	9	3	5	8	32
1988-89	Peoria	IHL	38	14	7	21	278	....	....	....	....	....
1989-90	**St. Louis**	**NHL**	**43**	**1**	**3**	**4**	**244**	**9**	**1**	**0**	**1**	**46**
	Peoria	IHL	10	1	2	3	76	....	....	....	....	....
1990-91	**St. Louis**	**NHL**	**2**	**1**	**0**	**1**	**15**	**6**	**0**	**0**	**0**	**18**
	Peoria	IHL	61	20	34	54	406	10	4	3	7	61
1991-92	**St. Louis**	**NHL**	**46**	**1**	**2**	**3**	**264**	**1**	**0**	**0**	**0**	**7**
1992-93	**St. Louis**	**NHL**	**49**	**2**	**5**	**7**	**204**	....	....	....	....	....
1993-94	**St. Louis**	**NHL**	**68**	**2**	**5**	**7**	**278**	**4**	**0**	**1**	**1**	**6**
1994-95	**Hartford**	**NHL**	**28**	**0**	**4**	**4**	**141**	....	....	....	....	....
1995-96	**Hartford**	**NHL**	**55**	**2**	**4**	**6**	**230**	....	....	....	....	....
	NHL Totals		**291**	**9**	**23**	**32**	**1376**	**20**	**1**	**1**	**2**	**77**

Signed as a free agent by **St. Louis**, February 23, 1988. Claimed by **Hartford** from **St. Louis** in NHL Waiver Draft, January 18, 1995.

CHASSE, DENIS — (shah-SAY)

Right wing. Shoots right. 6'2", 200 lbs. Born, Montreal, Que., February 7, 1970.

			Regular Season					Playoffs				
Season	**Club**	**Lea**	**GP**	**G**	**A**	**TP**	**PIM**	**GP**	**G**	**A**	**TP**	**PIM**
1987-88	St-Jean	QMJHL	13	0	1	1	2	1	0	0	0	0
1988-89	Verdun	QMJHL	38	12	12	24	61	....	....	....	....	....
	Drummondville	QMJHL	30	15	16	31	77	3	0	2	2	28
1989-90	Drummondville	QMJHL	34	14	29	43	85	....	....	....	....	....
	Chicoutimi	QMJHL	33	19	27	46	105	7	7	4	11	50
1990-91	Drummondville	QMJHL	62	47	54	101	246	13	9	11	20	56
1991-92	Halifax	AHL	73	26	35	61	254	....	....	....	....	....
1992-93	Halifax	AHL	75	35	41	76	242	....	....	....	....	....
1993-94	Cornwall	AHL	48	27	39	66	194	....	....	....	....	....
	St. Louis	**NHL**	**3**	**0**	**1**	**1**	**15**	....	....	....	....	....
1994-95	**St. Louis**	**NHL**	**47**	**7**	**9**	**16**	**133**	**7**	**1**	**7**	**8**	**23**
1995-96	**St. Louis**	**NHL**	**42**	**3**	**0**	**3**	**108**	....	....	....	....	....
	Worcester	AHL	3	0	0	0	6	....	....	....	....	....
	Washington	**NHL**	**3**	**0**	**0**	**0**	**5**	....	....	....	....	....
	Winnipeg	**NHL**	**15**	**0**	**0**	**0**	**12**	....	....	....	....	....
	NHL Totals		**110**	**10**	**10**	**20**	**273**	**7**	**1**	**7**	**8**	**23**

Signed as a free agent by **Quebec**, May 14, 1991. Traded to **St. Louis** by **Quebec** with Steve Duchesne for Garth Butcher, Ron Sutter and Bob Bassen, January 23, 1994. Traded to **Washington** by **St. Louis** for Rob Pearson, January 29, 1996. Traded to **Winnipeg** by **Washington** for Stewart Malgunas, February 15, 1996.

CHEBATURKIN, VLADIMIR — NYI

Defense. Shoots left. 6'2", 213 lbs. Born, Tyumen, USSR, April 23, 1975.
(NY Islanders' 3rd choice, 66th overall, in 1993 Entry Draft).

			Regular Season					Playoffs				
Season	**Club**	**Lea**	**GP**	**G**	**A**	**TP**	**PIM**	**GP**	**G**	**A**	**TP**	**PIM**
1993-94	Elektrostal	CIS 2	42	4	4	8	38	....	....	....	....	....
1994-95	Elektrostal	CIS	52	2	6	8	90	....	....	....	....	....
1995-96	Elektrostal	CIS	44	1	6	7	30	1	0	0	0	0

CHECCO, NICHOLAS — (CHEH-koh) COL.

Center. Shoots left. 5'11", 185 lbs. Born, Minneapolis, MN, November 18, 1974.
(Quebec's 7th choice, 137th overall, in 1993 Entry Draft).

			Regular Season					Playoffs				
Season	**Club**	**Lea**	**GP**	**G**	**A**	**TP**	**PIM**	**GP**	**G**	**A**	**TP**	**PIM**
1993-94	U. Minnesota	WCHA	41	7	5	12	28	....	....	....	....	....
1994-95	U. Minnesota	WCHA	43	14	11	25	46	....	....	....	....	....
1995-96	U. Minnesota	WCHA	41	8	11	19	34	....	....	....	....	....

CHELIOS, CHRIS — (CHELL-EE-ohs) CHI.

Defense. Shoots right. 6'1", 186 lbs. Born, Chicago, IL, January 25, 1962.
(Montreal's 5th choice, 40th overall, in 1981 Entry Draft).

			Regular Season					Playoffs				
Season	**Club**	**Lea**	**GP**	**G**	**A**	**TP**	**PIM**	**GP**	**G**	**A**	**TP**	**PIM**
1981-82	U. Wisconsin	WCHA	43	6	43	49	50	....	....	....	....	....
1982-83ab	U. Wisconsin	WCHA	26	9	17	26	50	....	....	....	....	....
1983-84	U.S. National	....	60	14	35	49	58	....	....	....	....	....
	U.S. Olympic	....	6	0	4	4	8	....	....	....	....	....
	Montreal	**NHL**	**12**	**0**	**2**	**2**	**12**	**15**	**1**	**9**	**10**	**17**
1984-85c	**Montreal**	**NHL**	**74**	**9**	**55**	**64**	**87**	**9**	**2**	**8**	**10**	**17**
1985-86	**Montreal**	**NHL**	**41**	**8**	**26**	**34**	**67**	**20**	**2**	**9**	**11**	**49** ♦
1986-87	**Montreal**	**NHL**	**71**	**11**	**33**	**44**	**124**	**17**	**4**	**9**	**13**	**38**
1987-88	**Montreal**	**NHL**	**71**	**20**	**41**	**61**	**172**	**11**	**3**	**1**	**4**	**29**
1988-89de	**Montreal**	**NHL**	**80**	**15**	**58**	**73**	**185**	**21**	**4**	**15**	**19**	**28**
1989-90	**Montreal**	**NHL**	**53**	**9**	**22**	**31**	**136**	**5**	**0**	**1**	**1**	**8**
1990-91f	**Chicago**	**NHL**	**77**	**12**	**52**	**64**	**192**	**6**	**1**	**7**	**8**	**46**
1991-92	**Chicago**	**NHL**	**80**	**9**	**47**	**56**	**245**	**18**	**6**	**15**	**21**	**37**
1992-93de	**Chicago**	**NHL**	**84**	**15**	**58**	**73**	**282**	**4**	**0**	**2**	**2**	**14**
1993-94	**Chicago**	**NHL**	**76**	**16**	**44**	**60**	**212**	**6**	**1**	**1**	**2**	**8**
1994-95	Biel	Switz.	3	0	3	3	4	....	....	....	....	....
d	**Chicago**	**NHL**	**48**	**5**	**33**	**38**	**72**	**16**	**4**	**7**	**11**	**12**
1995-96de	**Chicago**	**NHL**	**81**	**14**	**58**	**72**	**140**	**9**	**0**	**3**	**3**	**8**
	NHL Totals		**848**	**143**	**529**	**672**	**1926**	**157**	**28**	**87**	**115**	**311**

a WCHA Second All-Star Team (1983)
b NCAA All-Tournament Team (1983)
c NHL All-Rookie Team (1985)
d NHL First All-Star Team (1989, 1993, 1995, 1996)
e Won James Norris Memorial Trophy (1989, 1993, 1996)
f NHL Second All-Star Team (1991)

Played in NHL All-Star Game (1985, 1990-94, 1996)

Traded to **Chicago** by **Montreal** with Montreal's second round choice (Michael Pomichter) in 1991 Entry Draft for Denis Savard, June 29, 1990.

CHEREDARYK, STEVE — PHO.

Defense. Shoots left. 6'2", 197 lbs. Born, Calgary, Alta., November 20, 1975.
(Winnipeg's 4th choice, 82nd overall, in 1994 Entry Draft).

			Regular Season					Playoffs				
Season	**Club**	**Lea**	**GP**	**G**	**A**	**TP**	**PIM**	**GP**	**G**	**A**	**TP**	**PIM**
1992-93	Medicine Hat	WHL	67	1	9	10	88	10	0	1	1	16
1993-94	Medicine Hat	WHL	72	3	35	38	151	3	0	1	1	9
1994-95	Medicine Hat	WHL	70	3	26	29	193	5	0	1	1	13
	Springfield	AHL	3	0	1	1	0	....	....	....	....	....
1995-96	Springfield	AHL	32	0	1	1	36	....	....	....	....	....
	Knoxville	ECHL	13	0	10	10	72	6	2	4	6	12

CHERVYAKOV, DENIS (CHAIR-vuh-kahf)

Defense. Shoots left. 6', 185 lbs. Born, Leningrad, USSR, April 20, 1970.
(Boston's 9th choice, 256th overall, in 1992 Entry Draft).

			Regular Season					Playoffs				
Season	Club	Lea	GP	G	A	TP	PIM	GP	G	A	TP	PIM
1990-91	Leningrad	USSR	28	2	1	3	40					
1991-92	Riga	CIS	14	0	1	1	12					
1992-93	**Boston**	**NHL**	**2**	**0**	**0**	**0**	**2**					
	Providence	AHL	48	4	12	16	99					
	Atlanta	IHL	1	0	0	0	0					
1993-94	Providence	AHL	58	2	16	18	128					
1994-95	Providence	AHL	65	1	18	19	130	10	0	2	2	14
1995-96	Providence	AHL	64	3	7	10	58	4	1	0	1	21
	NHL Totals		**2**	**0**	**0**	**0**	**2**					

CHIASSON, STEVE (CHAY-sahn) CGY.

Defense. Shoots left. 6'1", 205 lbs. Born, Barrie, Ont., April 14, 1967.
(Detroit's 3rd choice, 50th overall, in 1985 Entry Draft).

			Regular Season					Playoffs				
Season	Club	Lea	GP	G	A	TP	PIM	GP	G	A	TP	PIM
1984-85	Guelph	OHL	61	8	22	30	139					
1985-86a	Guelph	OHL	54	12	30	42	126	18	10	10	20	37
1986-87	**Detroit**	**NHL**	**45**	**1**	**4**	**5**	**73**	**2**	**0**	**0**	**0**	**19**
1987-88	**Detroit**	**NHL**	**29**	**2**	**9**	**11**	**57**	**9**	**2**	**2**	**4**	**31**
	Adirondack	AHL	23	6	11	17	58					
1988-89	**Detroit**	**NHL**	**65**	**12**	**35**	**47**	**149**	**5**	**2**	**1**	**3**	**6**
1989-90	**Detroit**	**NHL**	**67**	**14**	**28**	**42**	**114**					
1990-91	**Detroit**	**NHL**	**42**	**3**	**17**	**20**	**80**	**5**	**3**	**1**	**4**	**19**
1991-92	**Detroit**	**NHL**	**62**	**10**	**24**	**34**	**136**	**11**	**1**	**5**	**6**	**12**
1992-93	**Detroit**	**NHL**	**79**	**12**	**50**	**62**	**155**	**7**	**2**	**2**	**4**	**19**
1993-94	**Detroit**	**NHL**	**82**	**13**	**33**	**46**	**122**	**7**	**2**	**3**	**5**	**2**
1994-95	**Calgary**	**NHL**	**45**	**2**	**23**	**25**	**39**	**7**	**1**	**2**	**3**	**9**
1995-96	**Calgary**	**NHL**	**76**	**8**	**25**	**33**	**62**	**4**	**2**	**1**	**3**	**0**
	NHL Totals		**592**	**77**	**248**	**325**	**987**	**57**	**15**	**17**	**32**	**117**

a Won Stafford Smythe Memorial Trophy (Memorial Cup Tournament MVP) (1986)

Played in NHL All-Star Game (1993)

Traded to **Calgary** by **Detroit** for Mike Vernon, June 29, 1994.

CHORSKE, TOM (CHOHR-skee) OTT.

Right wing. Shoots right. 6'1", 205 lbs. Born, Minneapolis, MN, September 18, 1966.
(Montreal's 2nd choice, 16th overall, in 1985 Entry Draft).

			Regular Season					Playoffs				
Season	Club	Lea	GP	G	A	TP	PIM	GP	G	A	TP	PIM
1985-86	U. Minnesota	WCHA	39	6	4	10	16					
1986-87	U. Minnesota	WCHA	47	20	22	42	20					
1987-88	U.S. National	....	36	9	16	25	24					
1988-89a	U. Minnesota	WCHA	37	25	24	49	28					
1989-90	**Montreal**	**NHL**	**14**	**3**	**1**	**4**	**2**					
	Sherbrooke	AHL	59	22	24	46	54	12	4	4	8	8
1990-91	**Montreal**	**NHL**	**57**	**9**	**11**	**20**	**32**					
1991-92	**New Jersey**	**NHL**	**76**	**19**	**17**	**36**	**32**	**7**	**0**	**3**	**3**	**4**
1992-93	**New Jersey**	**NHL**	**50**	**7**	**12**	**19**	**25**	**1**	**0**	**0**	**0**	**0**
	Utica	AHL	6	1	4	5	2					
1993-94	**New Jersey**	**NHL**	**76**	**21**	**20**	**41**	**32**	**20**	**4**	**3**	**7**	**0**
1994-95	Milan Devils	Italy	7	11	5	16	6					
	New Jersey	**NHL**	**42**	**10**	**8**	**18**	**16**	**17**	**1**	**5**	**6**	**4 ♦**
1995-96	**Ottawa**	**NHL**	**72**	**15**	**14**	**29**	**21**					
	NHL Totals		**387**	**84**	**83**	**167**	**160**	**45**	**5**	**11**	**16**	**8**

a WCHA First All-Star Team (1989)

Traded to **New Jersey** by **Montreal** with Stephane Richer for Kirk Muller and Roland Melanson, September 20, 1991. Claimed on waivers by **Ottawa** from **New Jersey**, October 5, 1995.

CHOUINARD, MARC ANA.

Center. Shoots right. 6'5", 187 lbs. Born, Charlesbourg, Ont., May 5, 1977.
(Winnipeg's 2nd choice, 32nd overall, in 1995 Entry Draft).

			Regular Season					Playoffs				
Season	Club	Lea	GP	G	A	TP	PIM	GP	G	A	TP	PIM
1993-94	Beauport	QMJHL	62	11	19	30	23	13	2	5	7	2
1994-95	Beauport	QMJHL	68	24	40	64	32	18	1	6	7	4
1995-96	Beauport	QMJHL	30	14	21	35	19					
	Halifax	QMJHL	24	6	12	18	17	6	2	1	3	2

Traded to **Anaheim** by **Winnipeg** with Teemu Selanne and Winnipeg's fourth round choice (later traded to Toronto — later traded to Montreal — Montreal selected Kim Staal) in 1996 Entry Draft for Chad Kilger, Oleg Tverdovsky and Anaheim's third round choice (Per-Anton Ludstrom) in 1996 Entry Draft, February 7, 1996.

CHRISTIAN, DAVE

Right wing. Shoots right. 5'11", 175 lbs. Born, Warroad, MN, May 12, 1959.
(Winnipeg's 2nd choice, 40th overall, in 1979 Entry Draft).

			Regular Season					Playoffs				
Season	Club	Lea	GP	G	A	TP	PIM	GP	G	A	TP	PIM
1977-78	North Dakota	WCHA	38	8	16	24	14					
1978-79	North Dakota	WCHA	40	22	24	46	22					
1979-80	U.S. National	....	59	10	20	30	26					
	U.S. Olympic	....	7	0	8	8	6					
	Winnipeg	**NHL**	**15**	**8**	**10**	**18**	**2**					
1980-81	**Winnipeg**	**NHL**	**80**	**28**	**43**	**71**	**22**					
1981-82	**Winnipeg**	**NHL**	**80**	**25**	**51**	**76**	**28**	**4**	**0**	**1**	**1**	**2**
1982-83	**Winnipeg**	**NHL**	**55**	**18**	**26**	**44**	**23**	**3**	**0**	**0**	**0**	**0**
1983-84	**Washington**	**NHL**	**80**	**29**	**52**	**81**	**28**	**8**	**5**	**4**	**9**	**5**
1984-85	**Washington**	**NHL**	**80**	**26**	**43**	**69**	**14**	**5**	**1**	**1**	**2**	**0**
1985-86	**Washington**	**NHL**	**80**	**41**	**42**	**83**	**15**	**9**	**4**	**4**	**8**	**0**
1986-87	**Washington**	**NHL**	**76**	**23**	**27**	**50**	**8**	**7**	**1**	**3**	**4**	**6**
1987-88	**Washington**	**NHL**	**80**	**37**	**21**	**58**	**26**	**14**	**5**	**6**	**11**	**6**
1988-89	**Washington**	**NHL**	**80**	**34**	**31**	**65**	**12**	**6**	**1**	**1**	**2**	**0**
1989-90	**Washington**	**NHL**	**28**	**3**	**8**	**11**	**4**					
	Boston	**NHL**	**50**	**12**	**17**	**29**	**8**	**21**	**4**	**1**	**5**	**4**
1990-91	**Boston**	**NHL**	**78**	**32**	**21**	**53**	**41**	**19**	**8**	**4**	**12**	**4**
1991-92	**St. Louis**	**NHL**	**78**	**20**	**24**	**44**	**41**	**4**	**3**	**0**	**3**	**0**
1992-93	**Chicago**	**NHL**	**60**	**4**	**14**	**18**	**12**	**1**	**0**	**0**	**0**	**0**
1993-94	**Chicago**	**NHL**	**9**	**0**	**3**	**3**	**0**	**1**	**0**	**0**	**0**	**0**
	Indianapolis	IHL	40	8	18	26	6					
1994-95	Minnesota	IHL	81	38	42	80	16	3	0	1	1	0
1995-96	Minnesota	IHL	69	21	25	46	8					
	NHL Totals		**1009**	**340**	**433**	**773**	**284**	**102**	**32**	**25**	**57**	**27**

Played in NHL All-Star Game (1991)

Traded to **Washington** by **Winnipeg** for Washington's first round choice (Bob Dollas) in the 1983 Entry Draft, June 8, 1983. Traded to **Boston** by **Washington** for Bob Joyce, December 13, 1989. Acquired by **St. Louis** from **Boston** with Boston's third round choice (Vitali Prokhorov) in 1992 Entry Draft and Boston's seventh round choice (Lance Burns) in 1992 Entry Draft as compensation for Boston's free agent signings of Glen Featherstone and Dave Thomlinson, July 30, 1991. Claimed by **Chicago** from **St. Louis** in NHL Waiver Draft, October 4, 1992.

CHRISTIAN, JEFF PIT.

Left wing. Shoots left. 6'2", 210 lbs. Born, Burlington, Ont., July 30, 1970.
(New Jersey's 2nd choice, 23rd overall, in 1988 Entry Draft).

			Regular Season					Playoffs				
Season	Club	Lea	GP	G	A	TP	PIM	GP	G	A	TP	PIM
1987-88	London	OHL	64	15	29	44	154	9	1	5	6	27
1988-89	London	OHL	60	27	30	57	221	20	3	4	7	56
1989-90	London	OHL	18	14	7	21	64					
	Owen Sound	OHL	37	19	26	45	145	10	6	7	13	43
1990-91	Utica	AHL	80	24	42	66	165					
1991-92	**New Jersey**	**NHL**	**2**	**0**	**0**	**0**	**2**					
	Utica	AHL	76	27	24	51	198	4	0	0	0	16
1992-93	Utica	AHL	22	4	6	10	39					
	Hamilton	AHL	11	2	5	7	35					
	Cincinnati	IHL	36	5	12	17	113					
1993-94	Albany	AHL	76	34	43	77	227	5	1	2	3	19
1994-95	**Pittsburgh**	**NHL**	**1**	**0**	**0**	**0**	**0**					
	Cleveland	IHL	56	13	24	37	126	2	0	1	1	8
1995-96	**Pittsburgh**	**NHL**	**3**	**0**	**0**	**0**	**2**					
	Cleveland	IHL	66	23	32	55	131	3	0	1	1	8
	NHL Totals		**6**	**0**	**0**	**0**	**4**					

Signed as a free agent by **Pittsburgh**, August 2, 1994.

CHRISTIE, RYAN DAL.

Left wing. Shoots left. 6'2", 175 lbs. Born, Beamsville, Ont., July 3, 1978.
(Dallas' 4th choice, 112th overall, in 1996 Entry Draft).

			Regular Season					Playoffs				
Season	Club	Lea	GP	G	A	TP	PIM	GP	G	A	TP	PIM
1994-95	St. Catharines	Jr. B	40	10	11	21	96					
1995-96	Owen Sound	OHL	66	29	17	46	93	6	1	1	2	0

CHURCH, BRAD WSH.

Left wing. Shoots left. 6'1", 210 lbs. Born, Dauphin, Man., November 14, 1976.
(Washington's 1st choice, 17th overall, in 1995 Entry Draft).

			Regular Season					Playoffs				
Season	Club	Lea	GP	G	A	TP	PIM	GP	G	A	TP	PIM
1993-94	Prince Albert	WHL	71	33	20	53	197					
1994-95	Prince Albert	WHL	62	26	24	50	184	15	6	9	15	32
1995-96	Prince Albert	WHL	69	42	46	88	123	18	15	*20	*35	74

CHURLA, SHANE NYR

Right wing. Shoots right. 6'1", 200 lbs. Born, Fernie, B.C., June 24, 1965.
(Hartford's 4th choice, 110th overall, in 1985 Entry Draft).

			Regular Season					Playoffs				
Season	Club	Lea	GP	G	A	TP	PIM	GP	G	A	TP	PIM
1983-84	Medicine Hat	WHL	48	3	7	10	115	14	1	5	6	41
1984-85	Medicine Hat	WHL	70	14	20	34	370	9	1	0	1	55
1985-86	Binghamton	AHL	52	4	10	14	306	3	0	0	0	22
1986-87	**Hartford**	**NHL**	**20**	**0**	**1**	**1**	**78**	**2**	**0**	**0**	**0**	**42**
	Binghamton	AHL	24	1	5	6	249					
1987-88	**Hartford**	**NHL**	**2**	**0**	**0**	**0**	**14**					
	Binghamton	AHL	25	5	8	13	168					
	Calgary	**NHL**	**29**	**1**	**5**	**6**	**132**	**7**	**0**	**1**	**1**	**17**
1988-89	**Calgary**	**NHL**	**5**	**0**	**0**	**0**	**25**					
	Salt Lake	IHL	32	3	13	16	278					
	Minnesota	**NHL**	**13**	**1**	**0**	**1**	**54**					
1989-90	**Minnesota**	**NHL**	**53**	**2**	**3**	**5**	**292**	**7**	**0**	**0**	**0**	**44**
1990-91	**Minnesota**	**NHL**	**40**	**2**	**2**	**4**	**286**	**22**	**2**	**1**	**3**	**90**
1991-92	**Minnesota**	**NHL**	**57**	**4**	**1**	**5**	**278**					
1992-93	**Minnesota**	**NHL**	**73**	**5**	**16**	**21**	**286**					
1993-94	**Dallas**	**NHL**	**69**	**6**	**7**	**13**	**333**	**9**	**1**	**3**	**4**	**35**
1994-95	**Dallas**	**NHL**	**27**	**1**	**3**	**4**	**186**	**5**	**0**	**0**	**0**	**20**
1995-96	**Dallas**	**NHL**	**34**	**3**	**4**	**7**	**168**					
	Los Angeles	**NHL**	**11**	**1**	**2**	**3**	**37**					
	NY Rangers	**NHL**	**10**	**0**	**0**	**0**	**26**	**11**	**2**	**2**	**4**	**14**
	NHL Totals		**443**	**26**	**44**	**70**	**2195**	**63**	**5**	**7**	**12**	**262**

Traded to **Calgary** by **Hartford** with Dana Murzyn for Neil Sheehy, Carey Wilson, and the rights to Lane MacDonald, January 3, 1988. Traded to **Minnesota** by **Calgary** with Perry Berezan for Brian MacLellan and Minnesota's fourth round choice (Robert Reichel) in 1989 Entry Draft, March 4, 1989. Claimed by **San Jose** from **Minnesota** in Dispersal Draft, May 30, 1991. Traded to **Minnesota** by **San Jose** for Kelly Kisio, June 3, 1991. Traded to **Los Angeles** by **Dallas** with Doug Zmolek for Darryl Sydor and Los Angeles' fifth round choice (Ryan Christie) in 1996 Entry Draft, February 17, 1996. Traded to **NY Rangers** by **Los Angeles** with Marty McSorley and Jari Kurri for Ray Ferraro, Ian Laperriere, Mattias Norstrom, Nathan Lafayette and NY Rangers' fourth round choice in 1997 Entry Draft, March 14, 1996.

CHYNOWETH, DEAN (shih-NOWTH) BOS.

Defense. Shoots right. 6'1", 190 lbs. Born, Calgary, Alta., October 30, 1968.
(NY Islanders' 1st choice, 13th overall, in 1987 Entry Draft).

			Regular Season					Playoffs				
Season	Club	Lea	GP	G	A	TP	PIM	GP	G	A	TP	PIM
1985-86	Medicine Hat	WHL	69	3	12	15	208	17	3	2	5	52
1986-87	Medicine Hat	WHL	67	3	18	21	285	13	4	2	6	28
1987-88	Medicine Hat	WHL	64	1	21	22	274	16	0	6	6	*87
1988-89	**NY Islanders**	**NHL**	**6**	**0**	**0**	**0**	**48**	....	....	....	....	....
1989-90	**NY Islanders**	**NHL**	**20**	**0**	**2**	**2**	**39**	....	....	....	....	....
	Springfield	AHL	40	0	7	7	98	17	0	4	4	36
1990-91	**NY Islanders**	**NHL**	**25**	**1**	**1**	**2**	**59**	....	....	....	....	....
	Capital Dist.	AHL	44	1	5	6	176	....	....	....	....	....
1991-92	**NY Islanders**	**NHL**	**11**	**1**	**0**	**1**	**23**	....	....	....	....	....
	Capital Dist.	AHL	43	4	6	10	164	6	1	1	2	39
1992-93	Capital Dist.	AHL	52	3	10	13	197	4	0	1	1	9
1993-94	**NY Islanders**	**NHL**	**39**	**0**	**4**	**4**	**122**	**2**	**0**	**0**	**0**	**2**
	Salt Lake	IHL	5	0	1	1	33	....	....	....	....	....
1994-95	**NY Islanders**	**NHL**	**32**	**0**	**2**	**2**	**77**	....	....	....	....	....
1995-96	**NY Islanders**	**NHL**	**14**	**0**	**1**	**1**	**40**	....	....	....	....	....
	Boston	**NHL**	**35**	**2**	**5**	**7**	**88**	**4**	**0**	**0**	**0**	**24**
	NHL Totals		**182**	**4**	**15**	**19**	**496**	**6**	**0**	**0**	**0**	**26**

Traded to **Boston** by **NY Islanders** for Boston's fifth round choice (Petr Sachl) in 1996 Entry Draft, December 9, 1995.

CHYZOWSKI, DAVID (chih-ZOW-skee)

Left wing. Shoots left. 6'1", 190 lbs. Born, Edmonton, Alta., July 11, 1971.
(NY Islanders' 1st choice, 2nd overall, in 1989 Entry Draft).

			Regular Season					Playoffs				
Season	Club	Lea	GP	G	A	TP	PIM	GP	G	A	TP	PIM
1987-88	Kamloops	WHL	66	16	17	33	117	18	2	4	6	26
1988-89a	Kamloops	WHL	68	56	48	104	139	16	15	13	28	32
1989-90	**NY Islanders**	**NHL**	**34**	**8**	**6**	**14**	**45**	....	....	....	....	....
	Springfield	AHL	4	0	0	0	7	....	....	....	....	....
	Kamloops	WHL	4	5	2	7	17	17	11	6	17	46
1990-91	**NY Islanders**	**NHL**	**56**	**5**	**9**	**14**	**61**	....	....	....	....	....
	Capital Dist.	AHL	7	3	6	9	22	....	....	....	....	....
1991-92	**NY Islanders**	**NHL**	**12**	**1**	**1**	**2**	**17**	....	....	....	....	....
	Capital Dist.	AHL	55	15	18	33	121	6	1	1	2	23
1992-93	Capital Dist.	AHL	66	15	21	36	177	3	2	0	2	0
1993-94	**NY Islanders**	**NHL**	**3**	**1**	**0**	**1**	**4**	**2**	**0**	**0**	**0**	**0**
	Salt Lake	IHL	66	27	13	40	151	....	....	....	....	....
1994-95	**NY Islanders**	**NHL**	**13**	**0**	**0**	**0**	**11**	....	....	....	....	....
	Kalamazoo	IHL	4	0	4	4	8	16	9	5	14	27
1995-96	Adirondack	AHL	80	44	39	83	160	3	0	0	0	6
	NHL Totals		**118**	**15**	**16**	**31**	**138**	**2**	**0**	**0**	**0**	**0**

a WHL West All-Star Team (1989)

Signed as a free agent by **Detroit**, August 29, 1995.

CIAVAGLIA, PETER (see-a-VIHG-lee-a)

Center. Shoots left. 5'10", 173 lbs. Born, Albany, NY, July 15, 1969.
(Calgary's 8th choice, 145th overall, in 1987 Entry Draft).

			Regular Season					Playoffs				
Season	Club	Lea	GP	G	A	TP	PIM	GP	G	A	TP	PIM
1987-88	Harvard	ECAC	30	10	23	33	16	....	....	....	....	....
1988-89a	Harvard	ECAC	34	15	48	63	36	....	....	....	....	....
1989-90	Harvard	ECAC	28	17	18	35	22	....	....	....	....	....
1990-91ab	Harvard	ECAC	27	24	*38	*62	2	....	....	....	....	....
1991-92	**Buffalo**	**NHL**	**2**	**0**	**0**	**0**	**0**	....	....	....	....	....
	Rochester	AHL	77	37	61	98	16	6	2	5	7	6
1992-93	**Buffalo**	**NHL**	**3**	**0**	**0**	**0**	**0**	....	....	....	....	....
	Rochester	AHL	64	35	67	102	32	17	9	16	25	12
1993-94	Leksand	Swe.	39	14	18	32	34	4	1	2	3	0
	U.S. National	....	18	2	9	11	6	....	....	....	....	....
	U.S. Olympic	....	8	2	4	6	0	....	....	....	....	....
1994-95	Detroit	IHL	73	22	59	81	83	5	1	1	2	6
1995-96	Detroit	IHL	75	22	56	78	38	12	6	11	17	12
	NHL Totals		**5**	**0**	**0**	**0**	**0**	....	....	....	....	....

a ECAC Second All-Star Team (1989, 1991)
b NCAA East Second All-American Team (1991)

Signed as a free agent by **Buffalo**, August 30, 1991.

CICCARELLI, DINO (sih-sih-REHL-ee) T.B.

Right wing. Shoots right. 5'10", 185 lbs. Born, Sarnia, Ont., February 8, 1960.

			Regular Season					Playoffs				
Season	Club	Lea	GP	G	A	TP	PIM	GP	G	A	TP	PIM
1977-78a	London	OHA	68	72	70	142	49	9	6	10	16	6
1978-79	London	OHA	30	8	11	19	35	7	3	5	8	0
1979-80	London	OHA	62	50	53	103	72	5	2	6	8	15
1980-81	**Minnesota**	**NHL**	**32**	**18**	**12**	**30**	**29**	**19**	**14**	**7**	**21**	**25**
	Oklahoma City	CHL	48	32	25	57	45	....	....	....	....	....
1981-82	**Minnesota**	**NHL**	**76**	**55**	**51**	**106**	**138**	**4**	**3**	**1**	**4**	**2**
1982-83	**Minnesota**	**NHL**	**77**	**37**	**38**	**75**	**94**	**9**	**4**	**6**	**10**	**11**
1983-84	**Minnesota**	**NHL**	**79**	**38**	**33**	**71**	**58**	**16**	**4**	**5**	**9**	**27**
1984-85	**Minnesota**	**NHL**	**51**	**15**	**17**	**32**	**41**	**9**	**3**	**3**	**6**	**8**
1985-86	**Minnesota**	**NHL**	**75**	**44**	**45**	**89**	**51**	**5**	**0**	**1**	**1**	**6**
1986-87	**Minnesota**	**NHL**	**80**	**52**	**51**	**103**	**88**	....	....	....	....	....
1987-88	**Minnesota**	**NHL**	**67**	**41**	**45**	**86**	**79**	....	....	....	....	....
1988-89	**Minnesota**	**NHL**	**65**	**32**	**27**	**59**	**64**	....	....	....	....	....
	Washington	**NHL**	**11**	**12**	**3**	**15**	**12**	**6**	**3**	**3**	**6**	**12**
1989-90	**Washington**	**NHL**	**80**	**41**	**38**	**79**	**122**	**8**	**8**	**3**	**11**	**6**
1990-91	**Washington**	**NHL**	**54**	**21**	**18**	**39**	**66**	**11**	**5**	**4**	**9**	**22**
1991-92	**Washington**	**NHL**	**78**	**38**	**38**	**76**	**78**	**7**	**5**	**4**	**9**	**14**
1992-93	**Detroit**	**NHL**	**82**	**41**	**56**	**97**	**81**	**7**	**4**	**2**	**6**	**16**
1993-94	**Detroit**	**NHL**	**66**	**28**	**29**	**57**	**73**	**7**	**5**	**2**	**7**	**14**
1994-95	**Detroit**	**NHL**	**42**	**16**	**27**	**43**	**39**	**16**	**9**	**2**	**11**	**22**
1995-96	**Detroit**	**NHL**	**64**	**22**	**21**	**43**	**99**	**17**	**6**	**2**	**8**	**26**
	NHL Totals		**1079**	**551**	**549**	**1100**	**1212**	**141**	**73**	**45**	**118**	**211**

a OHA Second All-Star Team (1978)

Played in NHL All-Star Game (1982, 1983, 1989)

Signed as a free agent by **Minnesota**, September 28, 1979. Traded to **Washington** by **Minnesota** with Bob Rouse for Mike Gartner and Larry Murphy, March 7, 1989. Traded to **Detroit** by **Washington** for Kevin Miller, June 20, 1992. Traded to **Tampa Bay** by **Detroit** for a conditional choice in 1998 Entry Draft, August 28, 1996.

CICCONE, ENRICO (CHIH-koh-nee) CHI.

Defense. Shoots left. 6'5", 220 lbs. Born, Montreal, Que., April 10, 1970.
(Minnesota's 5th choice, 92nd overall, in 1990 Entry Draft).

			Regular Season					Playoffs				
Season	Club	Lea	GP	G	A	TP	PIM	GP	G	A	TP	PIM
1987-88	Shawinigan	QMJHL	61	2	12	14	324	....	....	....	....	....
1988-89	Shawinigan	QMJHL	34	7	11	18	132	....	....	....	....	....
	Trois-Rivières	QMJHL	24	0	7	7	153	....	....	....	....	....
1989-90	Trois-Rivières	QMJHL	40	4	24	28	227	3	0	0	0	15
1990-91	Kalamazoo	IHL	57	4	9	13	384	4	0	1	1	32
1991-92	**Minnesota**	**NHL**	**11**	**0**	**0**	**0**	**48**	....	....	....	....	....
	Kalamazoo	IHL	53	4	16	20	406	10	0	1	1	58
1992-93	**Minnesota**	**NHL**	**31**	**0**	**1**	**1**	**115**	....	....	....	....	....
	Kalamazoo	IHL	13	1	3	4	50	....	....	....	....	....
	Hamilton	AHL	6	1	3	4	44	....	....	....	....	....
1993-94	**Washington**	**NHL**	**46**	**1**	**1**	**2**	**174**	....	....	....	....	....
	Portland	AHL	6	0	0	0	27	....	....	....	....	....
	Tampa Bay	**NHL**	**11**	**0**	**1**	**1**	**52**	....	....	....	....	....
1994-95	**Tampa Bay**	**NHL**	**41**	**2**	**4**	**6**	***225**	....	....	....	....	....
1995-96	**Tampa Bay**	**NHL**	**55**	**2**	**3**	**5**	**258**	....	....	....	....	....
	Chicago	**NHL**	**11**	**0**	**1**	**1**	**48**	**9**	**1**	**0**	**1**	**30**
	NHL Totals		**206**	**5**	**11**	**16**	**920**	**9**	**1**	**0**	**1**	**30**

Traded to **Washington** by **Dallas** to complete June 20, 1993 trade which sent Paul Cavallini to Dallas for future considerations, June 25, 1993. Traded to **Tampa Bay** by **Washington** with Washington's third round choice (later traded to Anaheim — Anaheim selected Craig Reichert) in 1994 Entry Draft and the return of future draft choices transferred in the Pat Elynuik trade for Joe Reekie, March 21, 1994. Traded to **Chicago** by **Tampa Bay** with Tampa Bay's second round choice (Jeff Paul) in 1996 Entry Draft for Patrick Poulin, Igor Ulanov and Chicago's second round choice (later traded to New Jersey — New Jersey selected Pierre Dagenais) in 1996 Entry Draft, March 20, 1996.

CIERNY, JOZEF (chee-ER-nee)

Left wing. Shoots left. 6'2", 185 lbs. Born, Zvolen, Czech., May 13, 1974.
(Buffalo's 2nd choice, 35th overall, in 1992 Entry Draft).

			Regular Season					Playoffs				
Season	Club	Lea	GP	G	A	TP	PIM	GP	G	A	TP	PIM
1991-92	ZTK Zvolen	Czech.2	26	10	3	13	8	....	....	....	....	....
1992-93	Rochester	AHL	54	27	27	54	36	....	....	....	....	....
1993-94	**Edmonton**	**NHL**	**1**	**0**	**0**	**0**	**0**	....	....	....	....	....
	Cape Breton	AHL	73	30	27	57	88	4	1	1	2	4
1994-95	Cape Breton	AHL	73	28	24	52	58	....	....	....	....	....
1995-96	Detroit	IHL	20	2	5	7	16	....	....	....	....	....
	Los Angeles	IHL	43	23	16	39	36	....	....	....	....	....
	NHL Totals		**1**	**0**	**0**	**0**	**0**	....	....	....	....	....

Traded to **Edmonton** by **Buffalo** with Buffalo's fourth round choice (Jussi Tarvainen) in 1994 Entry Draft for Craig Simpson, September 1, 1993.

CIGER, ZDENO (SEE-gur) EDM.

Left wing. Shoots left. 6'1", 190 lbs. Born, Martin, Czech., October 19, 1969.
(New Jersey's 3rd choice, 54th overall, in 1988 Entry Draft).

			Regular Season					Playoffs				
Season	Club	Lea	GP	G	A	TP	PIM	GP	G	A	TP	PIM
1987-88	Dukla Trencin	Czech.	8	3	4	7	2	....	....	....	....	....
1988-89	Dukla Trencin	Czech.	43	18	13	31	18	....	....	....	....	....
1989-90	Dukla Trencin	Czech.	53	18	28	46	....	....	....	....	....	....
1990-91	**New Jersey**	**NHL**	**45**	**8**	**17**	**25**	**8**	**6**	**0**	**2**	**2**	**4**
	Utica	AHL	8	5	4	9	2	....	....	....	....	....
1991-92	**New Jersey**	**NHL**	**20**	**6**	**5**	**11**	**10**	**7**	**2**	**4**	**6**	**0**
1992-93	**New Jersey**	**NHL**	**27**	**4**	**8**	**12**	**2**	....	....	....	....	....
	Edmonton	**NHL**	**37**	**9**	**15**	**24**	**6**	....	....	....	....	....
1993-94	**Edmonton**	**NHL**	**84**	**22**	**35**	**57**	**8**	....	....	....	....	....
1994-95	Dukla Trencin	Slov.	34	23	25	48	8	9	2	9	11	2
	Edmonton	**NHL**	**5**	**2**	**2**	**4**	**0**	....	....	....	....	....
1995-96	**Edmonton**	**NHL**	**78**	**31**	**39**	**70**	**41**	....	....	....	....	....
	NHL Totals		**296**	**82**	**121**	**203**	**75**	**13**	**2**	**6**	**8**	**4**

Traded to **Edmonton** by **New Jersey** with Kevin Todd for Bernie Nicholls, January 13, 1993.

CIRELLA, JOE (suh-REHL-uh)

Defense. Shoots right. 6'3", 210 lbs. Born, Hamilton, Ont., May 9, 1963.
(Colorado's 1st choice, 5th overall, in 1981 Entry Draft).

			Regular Season					Playoffs				
Season	Club	Lea	GP	G	A	TP	PIM	GP	G	A	TP	PIM
1980-81	Oshawa	OHA	56	5	31	36	220	11	0	2	2	41
1981-82	**Colorado**	**NHL**	**65**	**7**	**12**	**19**	**52**	....	....	....	....	....
	Oshawa	OHL	3	0	1	1	0	11	7	10	17	32
1982-83	**New Jersey**	**NHL**	**2**	**0**	**1**	**1**	**4**	....	....	....	....	....
a	Oshawa	OHL	56	13	55	68	110	17	4	16	20	37
1983-84	**New Jersey**	**NHL**	**79**	**11**	**33**	**44**	**137**	....	....	....	....	....
1984-85	**New Jersey**	**NHL**	**66**	**6**	**18**	**24**	**141**	....	....	....	....	....
1985-86	**New Jersey**	**NHL**	**66**	**6**	**23**	**29**	**147**	....	....	....	....	....
1986-87	**New Jersey**	**NHL**	**65**	**9**	**22**	**31**	**111**	....	....	....	....	....
1987-88	**New Jersey**	**NHL**	**80**	**8**	**31**	**39**	**191**	**19**	**0**	**7**	**7**	**49**
1988-89	**New Jersey**	**NHL**	**80**	**3**	**19**	**22**	**155**	....	....	....	....	....
1989-90	**Quebec**	**NHL**	**56**	**4**	**14**	**18**	**67**	....	....	....	....	....
1990-91	**Quebec**	**NHL**	**39**	**2**	**10**	**12**	**59**	....	....	....	....	....
	NY Rangers	**NHL**	**19**	**1**	**0**	**1**	**52**	**6**	**0**	**2**	**2**	**26**
1991-92	**NY Rangers**	**NHL**	**67**	**3**	**12**	**15**	**121**	**13**	**0**	**4**	**4**	**23**
1992-93	**NY Rangers**	**NHL**	**55**	**3**	**6**	**9**	**85**	....	....	....	....	....
1993-94	**Florida**	**NHL**	**63**	**1**	**9**	**10**	**99**	....	....	....	....	....
1994-95	**Florida**	**NHL**	**20**	**0**	**1**	**1**	**21**	....	....	....	....	....
1995-96	**Ottawa**	**NHL**	**6**	**0**	**0**	**0**	**4**	....	....	....	....	....
	Milwaukee	IHL	40	1	8	9	65	5	0	1	1	20
	NHL Totals		**828**	**64**	**211**	**275**	**1446**	**38**	**0**	**13**	**13**	**98**

a OHL First All-Star Team (1983)

Played in NHL All-Star Game (1984)

Traded to **Quebec** by **New Jersey** with Claude Loiselle and New Jersey's eighth round choice (Alexander Karpovtsev) in 1990 Entry Draft for Walt Poddubny and Quebec's fourth round choice (Mike Bodnarchuk) in 1990 Entry Draft, June 17, 1989. Traded to **NY Rangers** by **Quebec** for Aaron Miller and NY Rangers' fifth round choice (Bill Lindsay) in 1991 Entry Draft, January 17, 1991. Claimed by **Florida** from **NY Rangers** in Expansion Draft, June 24, 1993. Signed as a free agent by **Ottawa**, October 10, 1995.

CIRJAK, JOHN COL.

Center. Shoots right. 6'2", 180 lbs. Born, Vancouver, B.C., February 10, 1977.
(Colorado's 6th choice, 155th overall, in 1995 Entry Draft).

			Regular Season					Playoffs				
Season	Club	Lea	GP	G	A	TP	PIM	GP	G	A	TP	PIM
1993-94	Spokane	WHL	44	2	5	7	22	3	0	0	0	0
1994-95	Spokane	WHL	69	21	37	58	58	11	4	11	15	11
1995-96	Spokane	WHL	68	23	40	63	67	18	3	11	14	6

CISAR, MARIAN (SIH-sahr) L.A.

Right wing. Shoots right. 6', 176 lbs. Born, Bratislava, Czech., February 25, 1978.
(Los Angeles' 2nd choice, 37th overall, in 1996 Entry Draft).

			Regular Season					Playoffs				
Season	Club	Lea	GP	G	A	TP	PIM	GP	G	A	TP	PIM
1994-95	Bratislava	Slo. Jr.	38	42	28	70	16	....	....	....	....	....
1995-96	Bratislava	Slo. Jr.	16	26	17	43	2	....	....	....	....	....
	Bratislava	Slovak	13	3	3	6	0	6	3	0	3	0

CLARK, BRETT MTL.

Defense. Shoots left. 6', 175 lbs. Born, Moosomin, Sask., December 23, 1976.
(Montreal's 7th choice, 154th overall, in 1996 Entry Draft).

			Regular Season					Playoffs				
Season	Club	Lea	GP	G	A	TP	PIM	GP	G	A	TP	PIM
1994-95	Melville	Jr. A	62	19	32	51	77	....	....	....	....	....
1995-96	Maine	H.E.	39	7	31	38	22	....	....	....	....	....

CLARK, CHRIS CGY.

Right wing. Shoots right. 6', 190 lbs. Born, Manchester, CT, March 8, 1976.
(Calgary's 3rd choice, 77th overall, in 1994 Entry Draft).

			Regular Season					Playoffs				
Season	Club	Lea	GP	G	A	TP	PIM	GP	G	A	TP	PIM
1994-95	Clarkson	ECAC	32	12	11	23	92	....	....	....	....	....
1995-96	Clarkson	ECAC	38	10	8	18	108	....	....	....	....	....

CLARK, JASON VAN.

Center. Shoots left. 6'1", 185 lbs. Born, Belmont, Ont., May 6, 1972.
(Vancouver's 8th choice, 141st overall, in 1992 Entry Draft).

			Regular Season					Playoffs				
Season	Club	Lea	GP	G	A	TP	PIM	GP	G	A	TP	PIM
1992-93	Bowling Green	CCHA	40	10	17	27	42	....	....	....	....	....
1993-94	Bowling Green	CCHA	37	10	18	28	39	....	....	....	....	....
1994-95	Bowling Green	CCHA	37	17	22	39	50	....	....	....	....	....
1995-96	Bowling Green	CCHA	41	15	28	43	50	....	....	....	....	....

CLARK, WENDEL TOR.

Left wing. Shoots left. 5'11", 194 lbs. Born, Kelvington, Sask., October 25, 1966.
(Toronto's 1st choice, 1st overall, in 1985 Entry Draft).

			Regular Season					Playoffs				
Season	Club	Lea	GP	G	A	TP	PIM	GP	G	A	TP	PIM
1983-84	Saskatoon	WHL	72	23	45	68	225	....	....	....	....	....
1984-85a	Saskatoon	WHL	64	32	55	87	253	3	3	3	6	7
1985-86b	**Toronto**	**NHL**	**66**	**34**	**11**	**45**	**227**	**10**	**5**	**1**	**6**	**47**
1986-87	**Toronto**	**NHL**	**80**	**37**	**23**	**60**	**271**	**13**	**6**	**5**	**11**	**38**
1987-88	**Toronto**	**NHL**	**28**	**12**	**11**	**23**	**80**	....	....	....	....	....
1988-89	**Toronto**	**NHL**	**15**	**7**	**4**	**11**	**66**	....	....	....	....	....
1989-90	**Toronto**	**NHL**	**38**	**18**	**8**	**26**	**116**	**5**	**1**	**1**	**2**	**19**
1990-91	**Toronto**	**NHL**	**63**	**18**	**16**	**34**	**152**	....	....	....	....	....
1991-92	**Toronto**	**NHL**	**43**	**19**	**21**	**40**	**123**	....	....	....	....	....
1992-93	**Toronto**	**NHL**	**66**	**17**	**22**	**39**	**193**	**21**	**10**	**10**	**20**	**51**
1993-94	**Toronto**	**NHL**	**64**	**46**	**30**	**76**	**115**	**18**	**9**	**7**	**16**	**24**
1994-95	**Quebec**	**NHL**	**37**	**12**	**18**	**30**	**45**	**6**	**1**	**2**	**3**	**6**
1995-96	**NY Islanders**	**NHL**	**58**	**24**	**19**	**43**	**60**	....	....	....	....	....
	Toronto	**NHL**	**13**	**8**	**7**	**15**	**16**	**6**	**2**	**2**	**4**	**2**
	NHL Totals		**571**	**252**	**190**	**442**	**1464**	**79**	**34**	**28**	**62**	**187**

a WHL East First All-Star Team (1985)
b NHL All-Rookie Team (1986)

Played in NHL All-Star Game (1986)

Traded to **Quebec** by **Toronto** with Sylvain Lefebvre, Landon Wilson and Toronto's first round choice (Jeffrey Kealty) in 1994 Entry Draft for Mats Sundin, Garth Butcher, Todd Warriner and Philadelphia's first round choice (previously acquired by Quebec — later traded to Washington — Washington selected Nolan Baumgartner) in 1994 Entry Draft, June 28, 1994. Traded to **NY Islanders** by **Colorado** for Claude Lemieux, October 3, 1995. Traded to **Toronto** by **NY Islanders** with Mathieu Schneider and D.J. Smith for Darby Hendrickson, Sean Haggerty, Kenny Jonsson and Toronto's first round choice in 1997 Entry Draft, March 13, 1996.

CLIFFORD, BRIAN PIT.

Center. Shoots right. 6', 185 lbs. Born, Buffalo, NY, June 18, 1973.
(Pittsburgh's 6th choice, 126th overall, in 1991 Entry Draft).

			Regular Season					Playoffs				
Season	Club	Lea	GP	G	A	TP	PIM	GP	G	A	TP	PIM
1992-93	Michigan State	CCHA	34	15	7	22	20	....	....	....	....	....
1993-94	Michigan State	CCHA	35	6	4	10	22	....	....	....	....	....
1994-95	Michigan State	CCHA	17	2	5	7	8	....	....	....	....	....
1995-96	Michigan State	CCHA	18	1	1	2	6	....	....	....	....	....

CLOUTIER, COLIN (clootz-YAY) T.B.

Center. Shoots left. 6'3", 224 lbs. Born, Winnipeg, Man., January 27, 1976.
(Tampa Bay's 2nd choice, 34th overall, in 1994 Entry Draft).

			Regular Season					Playoffs				
Season	Club	Lea	GP	G	A	TP	PIM	GP	G	A	TP	PIM
1992-93	Brandon	WHL	60	11	15	26	138	4	0	0	0	18
1993-94	Brandon	WHL	30	10	13	23	102	11	2	5	7	23
1994-95	Brandon	WHL	47	16	27	43	170	16	5	6	11	47
1995-96	Brandon	WHL	39	9	19	28	84	....	....	....	....	....
	Lethbridge	WHL	14	5	10	15	39	3	2	2	4	19

CLOUTIER, FRANCOIS (clootz-YAY) FLA.

Left wing. Shoots left. 6'2", 206 lbs. Born, Sherbrooke, Que., April 28, 1977.
(Florida's 6th choice, 114th overall, in 1995 Entry Draft).

			Regular Season					Playoffs				
Season	Club	Lea	GP	G	A	TP	PIM	GP	G	A	TP	PIM
1993-94	Hull	QMJHL	7	0	0	0	2	....	....	....	....	....
1994-95	Hull	QMJHL	58	15	5	20	70	17	2	4	6	36
1995-96	Hull	QMJHL	46	13	19	32	150	18	0	5	5	40

CLOUTIER, SYLVAIN (clootz-YAY) DET.

Center. Shoots left. 6', 195 lbs. Born, Mont-Laurier, Que., February 13, 1974.
(Detroit's 3rd choice, 70th overall, in 1992 Entry Draft).

			Regular Season					Playoffs				
Season	Club	Lea	GP	G	A	TP	PIM	GP	G	A	TP	PIM
1991-92	Guelph	OHL	62	35	31	66	74	....	....	....	....	....
1992-93	Guelph	OHL	44	26	29	55	78	5	0	5	5	14
1993-94	Guelph	OHL	66	45	71	116	127	9	7	9	16	32
	Adirondack	AHL	2	0	2	2	2	....	....	....	....	....
1994-95	Adirondack	AHL	71	7	26	33	144	....	....	....	....	....
1995-96	Adirondack	AHL	65	11	17	28	118	3	0	0	0	4
	Toledo	ECHL	6	4	2	6	4	....	....	....	....	....

COFFEY, PAUL DET.

Defense. Shoots left. 6', 190 lbs. Born, Weston, Ont., June 1, 1961.
(Edmonton's 1st choice, 6th overall, in the 1980 Draft).

			Regular Season					Playoffs				
Season	Club	Lea	GP	G	A	TP	PIM	GP	G	A	TP	PIM
1978-79	S.S. Marie	OHA	68	17	72	89	103	....	....	....	....	....
1979-80a	S.S. Marie	OHA	23	10	21	31	63	....	....	....	....	....
	Kitchener	OHA	52	19	52	71	130	....	....	....	....	....
1980-81	**Edmonton**	**NHL**	**74**	**9**	**23**	**32**	**130**	**9**	**4**	**3**	**7**	**22**
1981-82b	**Edmonton**	**NHL**	**80**	**29**	**60**	**89**	**106**	**5**	**1**	**1**	**2**	**6**
1982-83b	**Edmonton**	**NHL**	**80**	**29**	**67**	**96**	**87**	**16**	**7**	**7**	**14**	**14**
1983-84b	**Edmonton**	**NHL**	**80**	**40**	**86**	**126**	**104**	**19**	**8**	**14**	**22**	**21** ♦
1984-85cd	**Edmonton**	**NHL**	**80**	**37**	**84**	**121**	**97**	**18**	**12**	**25**	**37**	**44** ♦
1985-86cd	**Edmonton**	**NHL**	**79**	**48**	**90**	**138**	**120**	**10**	**1**	**9**	**10**	**30**
1986-87	**Edmonton**	**NHL**	**59**	**17**	**50**	**67**	**49**	**17**	**3**	**8**	**11**	**30** ♦
1987-88	**Pittsburgh**	**NHL**	**46**	**15**	**52**	**67**	**93**	....	....	....	....	....
1988-89d	**Pittsburgh**	**NHL**	**75**	**30**	**83**	**113**	**195**	**11**	**2**	**13**	**15**	**31**
1989-90b	**Pittsburgh**	**NHL**	**80**	**29**	**74**	**103**	**95**	....	....	....	....	....
1990-91	**Pittsburgh**	**NHL**	**76**	**24**	**69**	**93**	**128**	**12**	**2**	**9**	**11**	**6** ♦
1991-92	**Pittsburgh**	**NHL**	**54**	**10**	**54**	**64**	**62**	....	....	....	....	....
	Los Angeles	**NHL**	**10**	**1**	**4**	**5**	**25**	**6**	**4**	**3**	**7**	**2**
1992-93	**Los Angeles**	**NHL**	**50**	**8**	**49**	**57**	**50**	....	....	....	....	....
	Detroit	**NHL**	**30**	**4**	**26**	**30**	**27**	**7**	**2**	**9**	**11**	**2**
1993-94	**Detroit**	**NHL**	**80**	**14**	**63**	**77**	**106**	**7**	**1**	**6**	**7**	**8**
1994-95cd	**Detroit**	**NHL**	**45**	**14**	**44**	**58**	**72**	**18**	**6**	**12**	**18**	**10**
1995-96	**Detroit**	**NHL**	**76**	**14**	**60**	**74**	**90**	**17**	**5**	**9**	**14**	**30**
	NHL Totals		**1154**	**372**	**1038**	**1410**	**1636**	**172**	**58**	**128**	**186**	**256**

a OHA Second All-Star Team (1980)
b NHL Second All-Star Team (1982, 1983, 1984, 1990)
c Won James Norris Memorial Trophy (1985, 1986, 1995)
d NHL First All-Star Team (1985, 1986, 1989, 1995)

Played in NHL All-Star Game (1982-86, 1988-94, 1996)

Traded to **Pittsburgh** by **Edmonton** with Dave Hunter and Wayne Van Dorp for Craig Simpson, Dave Hannan, Moe Mantha and Chris Joseph, November 24, 1987. Traded to **Los Angeles** by **Pittsburgh** for Brian Benning, Jeff Chychrun and Los Angeles' first round choice (later traded to Philadelphia — Philadelphia selected Jason Bowen) in 1992 Entry Draft, February 19, 1992. Traded to **Detroit** by **Los Angeles** with Sylvain Couturier and Jim Hiller for Jimmy Carson, Marc Potvin and Gary Shuchuk, January 29, 1993.

COLE, DANTON

Center/Right wing. Shoots right. 5'11", 185 lbs. Born, Pontiac, MI, January 10, 1967.
(Winnipeg's 6th choice, 123rd overall, in 1985 Entry Draft).

			Regular Season					Playoffs				
Season	Club	Lea	GP	G	A	TP	PIM	GP	G	A	TP	PIM
1985-86	Michigan State	CCHA	43	11	10	21	22	....	....	....	....	....
1986-87	Michigan State	CCHA	44	9	15	24	16	....	....	....	....	....
1987-88	Michigan State	CCHA	46	20	36	56	38	....	....	....	....	....
1988-89	Michigan State	CCHA	47	29	33	62	46	....	....	....	....	....
1989-90	**Winnipeg**	**NHL**	**2**	**1**	**1**	**2**	**0**	....	....	....	....	....
	Moncton	AHL	80	31	42	73	18	....	....	....	....	....
1990-91	**Winnipeg**	**NHL**	**66**	**13**	**11**	**24**	**24**	....	....	....	....	....
	Moncton	AHL	3	1	1	2	0	....	....	....	....	....
1991-92	**Winnipeg**	**NHL**	**52**	**7**	**5**	**12**	**32**	....	....	....	....	....
1992-93	**Tampa Bay**	**NHL**	**67**	**12**	**15**	**27**	**23**	....	....	....	....	....
	Atlanta	IHL	1	1	0	1	2	....	....	....	....	....
1993-94	**Tampa Bay**	**NHL**	**81**	**20**	**23**	**43**	**32**	....	....	....	....	....
1994-95	**Tampa Bay**	**NHL**	**26**	**3**	**3**	**6**	**6**	....	....	....	....	....
	New Jersey	**NHL**	**12**	**1**	**2**	**3**	**8**	**1**	**0**	**0**	**0**	**0** ♦
1995-96	**NY Islanders**	**NHL**	**10**	**1**	**0**	**1**	**0**	....	....	....	....	....
	Utah	IHL	34	28	15	43	22	....	....	....	....	....
	Chicago	**NHL**	**2**	**0**	**0**	**0**	**0**	....	....	....	....	....
	Indianapolis	IHL	32	9	13	22	20	5	1	5	6	8
	NHL Totals		**318**	**58**	**60**	**118**	**125**	**1**	**0**	**0**	**0**	**0**

Traded to **Tampa Bay** by **Winnipeg** for future considerations, June 19, 1992. Traded to **New Jersey** by **Tampa Bay** with Shawn Chambers for Alexander Semak and Ben Hankinson, March 14, 1995. Signed as a free agent by **NY Islanders**, August 26, 1995. Traded to **Chicago** by **NY Islanders** for Bob Halkidis, February 2, 1996.

COLEMAN, JON DET.

Defense. Shoots right. 6'1", 190 lbs. Born, Boston, MA, March 9, 1975.
(Detroit's 2nd choice, 48th overall, in 1993 Entry Draft).

			Regular Season					Playoffs				
Season	Club	Lea	GP	G	A	TP	PIM	GP	G	A	TP	PIM
1993-94	Boston U.	H.E.	29	1	14	15	26	....	....	....	....	....
1994-95	Boston U.	H.E.	40	5	23	28	42	....	....	....	....	....
1995-96ab	Boston U.	H.E.	40	7	31	38	58	....	....	....	....	....

a Hockey East All-Star Team (1996)
b NCAA East Second All-American Team (1996)

COLES, BRUCE PHI.

Left wing. Shoots left. 5'9", 183 lbs. Born, Montreal, Que., January 12, 1968.
(Montreal's 1st choice, 23rd overall, in 1990 Supplemental Draft).

			Regular Season					Playoffs				
Season	Club	Lea	GP	G	A	TP	PIM	GP	G	A	TP	PIM
1987-89	RPI	ECAC	32	16	23	39	48	....	....	....	....	....
1988-89	RPI	ECAC	27	8	14	22	66	....	....	....	....	....
1989-90	RPI	ECAC	34	*28	24	52	142	....	....	....	....	....
1990-91	RPI	ECAC	31	23	29	52	145	....	....	....	....	....
1991-92	Winston-Salem	ECHL	16	2	6	8	37	....	....	....	....	....
	Johnstown	ECHL	43	32	45	77	113	6	3	1	4	12
1992-93	Johnstown	ECHL	28	28	26	54	61	5	1	3	4	29
	Cdn. National	....	27	9	22	31	20	....	....	....	....	....
1993-94	Johnstown	ECHL	24	23	20	43	56	3	0	1	1	10
1994-95	Johnstown	ECHL	29	20	25	45	56	....	....	....	....	....
	Hershey	AHL	51	16	25	41	73	6	1	5	6	14
1995-96	Hershey	AHL	68	23	29	52	75	5	2	2	4	6

Signed as a free agent by **Philadelphia**, May 31, 1995

CONACHER, PAT (KAH-nuh-kuhr)

Left wing. Shoots left. 5'8", 190 lbs. Born, Edmonton, Alta., May 1, 1959.
(NY Rangers' 3rd choice, 76th overall, in 1979 Entry Draft).

			Regular Season					Playoffs				
Season	Club	Lea	GP	G	A	TP	PIM	GP	G	A	TP	PIM
1977-78	Billings	WHL	72	31	44	75	105	20	15	14	29	22
1978-79	Billings	WHL	39	25	37	62	50	....	....	....	....	....
	Saskatoon	WHL	33	15	32	47	37	....	....	....	....	....
1979-80	NY Rangers	NHL	17	0	5	5	4	3	0	1	1	2
	New Haven	AHL	53	11	14	25	43	7	1	1	2	4
1980-81			DID NOT PLAY									
1981-82	Springfield	AHL	77	23	22	45	38	....	....	....	....	....
1982-83	NY Rangers	NHL	5	0	1	1	4	....	....	....	....	....
	Tulsa	CHL	63	29	28	57	44	....	....	....	....	....
1983-84	Edmonton	NHL	45	2	8	10	31	3	1	0	1	2 ♦
	Moncton	AHL	28	7	16	23	30	....	....	....	....	....
1984-85	Nova Scotia	AHL	68	20	45	65	44	6	3	2	5	0
1985-86	New Jersey	NHL	2	0	2	2	2	....	....	....	....	....
	Maine	AHL	69	15	30	45	83	5	1	1	2	11
1986-87	Maine	AHL	56	12	14	26	47	....	....	....	....	....
1987-88	New Jersey	NHL	24	2	5	7	12	17	2	2	4	14
	Utica	AHL	47	14	33	47	32	....	....	....	....	....
1988-89	New Jersey	NHL	55	7	5	12	14	....	....	....	....	....
1989-90	New Jersey	NHL	19	3	3	6	4	5	1	0	1	10
	Utica	AHL	57	13	36	49	53	....	....	....	....	....
1990-91	New Jersey	NHL	49	5	11	16	27	7	0	2	2	2
	Utica	AHL	4	0	1	1	6	....	....	....	....	....
1991-92	New Jersey	NHL	44	7	3	10	16	7	1	1	2	4
1992-93	Los Angeles	NHL	81	9	8	17	20	24	6	4	10	6
1993-94	Los Angeles	NHL	77	15	13	28	71	....	....	....	....	....
1994-95	Los Angeles	NHL	48	7	9	16	12	....	....	....	....	....
1995-96	Los Angeles	NHL	35	5	2	7	18	....	....	....	....	....
	Calgary	NHL	7	0	0	0	0	....	....	....	....	....
	NY Islanders	NHL	13	1	1	2	0	....	....	....	....	....
	NHL Totals		521	63	76	139	235	66	11	10	21	40

Signed as a free agent by **Edmonton**, October 4, 1983. Signed as a free agent by **New Jersey**, August 14, 1985. Traded to **Los Angeles** by **New Jersey** for future considerations, September 3, 1992. Traded to **Calgary** by **Los Angeles** for Craig Ferguson, February 10, 1996. Traded to **NY Islanders** by **Calgary** with Calgary's sixth round choice in 1997 Entry Draft for Bob Sweeney, March 20, 1996.

CONN, ROB

Left/Right wing. Shoots right. 6'2", 200 lbs. Born, Calgary, Alta., September 3, 1968.

			Regular Season					Playoffs				
Season	Club	Lea	GP	G	A	TP	PIM	GP	G	A	TP	PIM
1988-89	Alaska-Anch.	G.N.	33	21	17	38	46	....	....	....	....	....
1989-90	Alaska-Anch.	G.N.	34	27	21	48	46	....	....	....	....	....
1990-91	Alaska-Anch.	G.N.	43	28	32	60	53	....	....	....	....	....
1991-92	Chicago	NHL	2	0	0	0	2	....	....	....	....	....
	Indianapolis	IHL	72	19	16	35	100	....	....	....	....	....
1992-93	Indianapolis	IHL	75	13	14	27	81	5	0	1	1	6
1993-94	Indianapolis	IHL	51	16	11	27	46	....	....	....	....	....
1994-95	Indianapolis	IHL	10	4	4	8	11	....	....	....	....	....
	Albany	AHL	68	35	32	67	76	14	4	6	10	16
1995-96	Buffalo	NHL	28	2	5	7	18	....	....	....	....	....
	Rochester	AHL	36	22	15	37	40	19	7	6	13	10
	NHL Totals		30	2	5	7	20	....	....	....	....	....

Signed as a free agent by **Chicago**, July 31, 1991. Traded to **New Jersey** by **Chicago** for Dean Malkoc, January 30, 1995. Claimed by **Buffalo** from **New Jersey** in NHL Waiver Draft, October 2, 1995.

CONROY, AL

Center. Shoots right. 5'8", 170 lbs. Born, Calgary, Alta., January 17, 1966.

			Regular Season					Playoffs				
Season	Club	Lea	GP	G	A	TP	PIM	GP	G	A	TP	PIM
1986-87	Rapperswill	Switz.	36	30	32	62	0	....	....	....	....	....
	Rochester	AHL	13	4	4	8	40	13	1	3	4	50
1987-88	Varese	Italy	36	25	39	64	....	....	....	....	....	....
	Adirondack	AHL	13	5	8	13	20	11	1	3	4	41
1988-89	Dortmund	W. Ger.	46	53	78	131	....	....	....	....	....	....
1989-90	Adirondack	AHL	77	23	33	56	147	5	0	0	0	20
1990-91	Adirondack	AHL	80	26	39	65	172	2	1	1	2	0
1991-92	Philadelphia	NHL	31	2	9	11	74	....	....	....	....	....
	Hershey	AHL	47	17	28	45	90	6	4	2	6	12
1992-93	Philadelphia	NHL	21	3	2	5	17	....	....	....	....	....
	Hershey	AHL	60	28	32	60	130	....	....	....	....	....
1993-94	Philadelphia	NHL	62	4	3	7	65	....	....	....	....	....
1994-95	Detroit	IHL	71	18	40	58	151	....	....	....	....	....
	Houston	IHL	9	3	4	7	17	4	1	2	3	8
1995-96	Houston	IHL	82	24	38	62	134	....	....	....	....	....
	NHL Totals		114	9	14	23	156	....	....	....	....	....

Signed as a free agent by **Detroit**, August 16, 1989. Signed as a free agent by **Philadelphia**, August 21, 1991.

CONROY, CRAIG — MTL.

Center. Shoots right. 6'2", 198 lbs. Born, Potsdam, NY, September 4, 1971.
(Montreal's 7th choice, 123rd overall, in 1990 Entry Draft).

			Regular Season					Playoffs				
Season	Club	Lea	GP	G	A	TP	PIM	GP	G	A	TP	PIM
1990-91	Clarkson	ECAC	40	8	21	29	24	....	....	....	....	....
1991-92	Clarkson	ECAC	31	19	17	36	36	....	....	....	....	....
1992-93	Clarkson	ECAC	35	10	23	33	26	....	....	....	....	....
1993-94abc	Clarkson	ECAC	34	26	*40	*66	46	....	....	....	....	....
1994-95	Fredericton	AHL	55	26	18	44	29	11	7	3	10	6
	Montreal	NHL	6	1	0	1	0	....	....	....	....	....
1995-96	Montreal	NHL	7	0	0	0	2	....	....	....	....	....
	Fredericton	AHL	67	31	38	69	65	10	5	7	12	6
	NHL Totals		13	1	0	1	2	....	....	....	....	....

a ECAC First All-Star Team (1994)
b NCAA East First All-American Team (1994)
c NCAA Final Four All-Tournament Team (1994)

CONVERY, BRANDON — TOR.

Center. Shoots right. 6'1", 182 lbs. Born, Kingston, Ont., February 4, 1974.
(Toronto's 1st choice, 8th overall, in 1992 Entry Draft).

			Regular Season					Playoffs				
Season	Club	Lea	GP	G	A	TP	PIM	GP	G	A	TP	PIM
1990-91	Sudbury	OHL	56	26	22	48	18	5	1	1	2	2
1991-92	Sudbury	OHL	44	40	26	66	44	5	3	2	5	4
1992-93	Sudbury	OHL	7	7	9	16	6	....	....	....	....	....
	Niagara Falls	OHL	51	38	39	77	24	4	1	3	4	4
	St. John's	AHL	3	0	0	0	0	5	0	1	1	0
1993-94	Niagara Falls	OHL	29	24	29	53	30	....	....	....	....	....
	Belleville	OHL	23	16	19	35	22	12	4	10	14	13
	St. John's	AHL	....	....	....	....	....	1	0	0	0	0
1994-95	St. John's	AHL	76	34	37	71	43	5	2	2	4	4
1995-96	Toronto	NHL	11	5	2	7	4	5	0	0	0	2
	St. John's	AHL	57	22	23	45	28	....	....	....	....	....
	NHL Totals		11	5	2	7	4	5	0	0	0	2

COOPER, DAVID

Defense. Shoots left. 6'2", 204 lbs. Born, Ottawa, Ont., November 2, 1973.
(Buffalo's 1st choice, 11th overall, in 1992 Entry Draft).

			Regular Season					Playoffs				
Season	Club	Lea	GP	G	A	TP	PIM	GP	G	A	TP	PIM
1989-90	Medicine Hat	WHL	61	4	11	15	65	3	0	2	2	2
1990-91	Medicine Hat	WHL	64	12	31	43	66	11	1	3	4	23
1991-92a	Medicine Hat	WHL	72	17	47	64	176	4	1	4	5	8
1992-93	Medicine Hat	WHL	63	15	50	65	88	10	2	2	4	32
	Rochester	AHL	....	....	....	....	....	2	0	0	0	2
1993-94	Rochester	AHL	68	10	25	35	82	4	1	1	2	2
1994-95	Rochester	AHL	21	2	4	6	48	....	....	....	....	....
	S. Carolina	ECHL	39	9	19	28	90	9	3	8	11	24
1995-96	Rochester	AHL	67	9	18	27	79	8	0	1	1	12

a WHL East First All-Star Team (1992)

COPELAND, ADAM — EDM.

Right wing. Shoots right. 6'1", 185 lbs. Born, St. Catharines, Ont., June 5, 1976.
(Edmonton's 6th choice, 79th overall, in 1994 Entry Draft).

			Regular Season					Playoffs				
Season	Club	Lea	GP	G	A	TP	PIM	GP	G	A	TP	PIM
1994-95	Miami-Ohio	CCHA	39	6	4	10	28	....	....	....	....	....
1995-96	Miami-Ohio	CCHA	36	10	4	14	38	....	....	....	....	....

CORBET, RENE (cohr-BAY, ruh-NAY) — COL.

Left wing. Shoots left. 6', 187 lbs. Born, Victoriaville, Que., June 25, 1973.
(Quebec's 2nd choice, 24th overall, in 1991 Entry Draft).

			Regular Season					Playoffs				
Season	Club	Lea	GP	G	A	TP	PIM	GP	G	A	TP	PIM
1990-91	Drummondville	QMJHL	45	25	40	65	34	14	11	6	17	15
1991-92	Drummondville	QMJHL	56	46	50	96	90	4	1	2	3	17
1992-93ab	Drummondville	QMJHL	63	*79	69	*148	143	10	7	13	20	16
1993-94	Quebec	NHL	9	1	1	2	0	....	....	....	....	....
c	Cornwall	AHL	68	37	40	77	56	13	7	2	9	18
1994-95	Cornwall	AHL	65	33	24	57	79	12	2	8	10	27
	Quebec	NHL	8	0	3	3	2	2	0	1	1	0
1995-96	Colorado	NHL	33	3	6	9	33	8	3	2	5	2 ♦
	Cornwall	AHL	9	5	6	11	10	....	....	....	....	....
	NHL Totals		50	4	10	14	35	10	3	3	6	2

a QMJHL First All-Star Team (1993)
b Canadian Major Junior First All-Star Team (1993)
c Won Dudley "Red" Garrett Memorial Trophy (Top Rookie - AHL) (1994)

CORCORAN, BRIAN — ANA.

Defense. Shoots left. 6'2", 247 lbs. Born, Baldwinsville, NY, April 23, 1972.

			Regular Season					Playoffs				
Season	Club	Lea	GP	G	A	TP	PIM	GP	G	A	TP	PIM
1993-94	U. Mass.	NCAA	15	1	7	8	24	....	....	....	....	....
1994-95	U. Mass.	H.E.	20	3	3	6	40	....	....	....	....	....
1995-96	Raleigh	ECHL	56	3	13	16	165	....	....	....	....	....
	Baltimore	AHL	18	0	2	2	24	6	0	0	0	4

Signed as a free agent by **Anaheim**, March 29, 1995.

CORKUM, BOB — PHI.

Center. Shoots right. 6'2", 210 lbs. Born, Salisbury, MA, December 18, 1967.
(Buffalo's 3rd choice, 47th overall, in 1986 Entry Draft).

			Regular Season					Playoffs				
Season	Club	Lea	GP	G	A	TP	PIM	GP	G	A	TP	PIM
1985-86	U. of Maine	H.E.	39	7	26	33	53	....	....	....	....	....
1986-87	U. of Maine	H.E.	35	18	11	29	24	....	....	....	....	....
1987-88	U. of Maine	H.E.	40	14	18	32	64	....	....	....	....	....
1988-89	U. of Maine	H.E.	45	17	31	48	64	....	....	....	....	....
1989-90	Buffalo	NHL	8	2	0	2	4	5	1	0	1	4
	Rochester	AHL	43	8	11	19	45	12	2	5	7	16
1990-91	Rochester	AHL	69	13	21	34	77	15	4	4	8	4
1991-92	Buffalo	NHL	20	2	4	6	21	4	1	0	1	0
	Rochester	AHL	52	16	12	28	47	8	0	6	6	8
1992-93	Buffalo	NHL	68	6	4	10	38	5	0	0	0	2
1993-94	Anaheim	NHL	76	23	28	51	18	....	....	....	....	....
1994-95	Anaheim	NHL	44	10	9	19	25	....	....	....	....	....
1995-96	Anaheim	NHL	48	5	7	12	26	....	....	....	....	....
	Philadelphia	NHL	28	4	3	7	8	12	1	2	3	6
	NHL Totals		292	52	55	107	140	26	3	2	5	12

Claimed by **Anaheim** from **Buffalo** in Expansion Draft, June 24, 1993. Traded to **Philadelphia** by **Anaheim** for Chris Herperger and Winnipeg's seventh round choice (previously acquired by Philadelphia) in 1997 Entry Draft, February 6, 1996.

CORNFORTH, MARK — BOS.

Defense. Shoots left. 6'1", 193 lbs. Born, Montreal, Que., November 13, 1972.

			Regular Season					Playoffs				
Season	Club	Lea	GP	G	A	TP	PIM	GP	G	A	TP	PIM
1991-92	Merrimack	H.E.	23	1	9	10	20	....	....	....	....	....
1992-93	Merrimack	H.E.	36	3	18	21	27	....	....	....	....	....
1993-94	Merrimack	H.E.	37	5	13	18	29	....	....	....	....	....
1994-95	Merrimack	H.E.	30	8	20	28	43	....	....	....	....	....
	Syracuse	AHL	2	0	1	1	2	....	....	....	....	....
1995-96	Boston	NHL	6	0	0	0	4	....	....	....	....	....
	Providence	AHL	65	5	10	15	117	4	0	0	0	4
	NHL Totals		6	0	0	0	4	....	....	....	....	....

Signed as a free agent by **Boston**, October 6, 1995.

CORRIVEAU, YVON (KOHR-ih-voh, IGH-vihn)

Left wing. Shoots left. 6'1", 195 lbs. Born, Welland, Ont., February 8, 1967.
(Washington's 1st choice, 19th overall, in 1985 Entry Draft).

			Regular Season					Playoffs				
Season	Club	Lea	GP	G	A	TP	PIM	GP	G	A	TP	PIM
1984-85	Toronto	OHL	59	23	28	51	65	3	0	0	0	5
1985-86	Washington	NHL	2	0	0	0	0	4	0	3	3	2
	Toronto	OHL	59	54	36	90	75	4	1	1	2	0
1986-87	Washington	NHL	17	1	1	2	24					
	Toronto	OHL	23	14	19	33	23					
	Binghamton	AHL	7	0	0	0	2	8	0	1	1	0
1987-88	Washington	NHL	44	10	9	19	84	13	1	2	3	30
	Binghamton	AHL	35	15	14	29	64					
1988-89	Washington	NHL	33	3	2	5	62	1	0	0	0	0
	Baltimore	AHL	33	16	23	39	65					
1989-90	Washington	NHL	50	9	6	15	50					
	Hartford	NHL	13	4	1	5	22	4	1	0	1	0
1990-91	Hartford	NHL	23	1	1	2	18					
	Springfield	AHL	44	17	25	42	10	18	*10	6	16	31
1991-92	Hartford	NHL	38	12	8	20	36	7	3	2	5	18
	Springfield	AHL	39	26	15	41	40					
1992-93	San Jose	NHL	20	3	7	10	0					
	Hartford	NHL	37	5	5	10	14					
1993-94	Hartford	NHL	3	0	0	0	0					
	Springfield	AHL	71	42	39	81	53	6	7	3	10	20
1994-95	Minnesota	IHL	62	18	24	42	26	3	1	1	2	0
1995-96	Minnesota	IHL	60	21	22	43	40					
	Detroit	IHL	14	5	6	11	12	4	0	1	1	6
	NHL Totals		**280**	**48**	**40**	**88**	**310**	**29**	**5**	**7**	**12**	**50**

Traded to **Hartford** by **Washington** for Mike Liut, March 6, 1990. Traded to **Washington** by **Hartford** to complete June 15, 1992 deal in which Mark Hunter and future considerations were traded to Washington for Nick Kypreos, August 20, 1992. Claimed by **San Jose** from **Washington** in NHL Waiver Draft, October 4, 1992. Traded to **Hartford** by **San Jose** to complete October 9, 1992 trade in which Michel Picard was traded to San Jose for future considerations, January 21, 1993.

CORSON, SHAYNE — ST.L.

Left wing. Shoots left. 6'1", 200 lbs. Born, Midland, Ont., August 13, 1966.
(Montreal's 2nd choice, 8th overall, in 1984 Entry Draft).

			Regular Season					Playoffs				
Season	Club	Lea	GP	G	A	TP	PIM	GP	G	A	TP	PIM
1983-84	Brantford	OHL	66	25	46	71	165	6	4	1	5	26
1984-85	Hamilton	OHL	54	27	63	90	154	11	3	7	10	19
1985-86	Montreal	NHL	3	0	0	0	2					
	Hamilton	OHL	47	41	57	98	153					
1986-87	Montreal	NHL	55	12	11	23	144	17	6	5	11	30
1987-88	Montreal	NHL	71	12	27	39	152	3	1	0	1	12
1988-89	Montreal	NHL	80	26	24	50	193	21	4	5	9	65
1989-90	Montreal	NHL	76	31	44	75	144	11	2	8	10	20
1990-91	Montreal	NHL	71	23	24	47	138	13	9	6	15	36
1991-92	Montreal	NHL	64	17	36	53	118	10	2	5	7	15
1992-93	Edmonton	NHL	80	16	31	47	209					
1993-94	Edmonton	NHL	64	25	29	54	118					
1994-95	Edmonton	NHL	48	12	24	36	86					
1995-96	St. Louis	NHL	77	18	28	46	192	13	8	6	14	22
	NHL Totals		**689**	**192**	**278**	**470**	**1496**	**88**	**32**	**35**	**67**	**200**

Played in NHL All-Star Game (1990, 1994)

Traded to **Edmonton** by **Montreal** with Brent Gilchrist and Vladimir Vujtek for Vincent Damphousse and Edmonton's fourth round choice (Adam Wiesel) in 1993 Entry Draft, August 27, 1992. Signed as a free agent by **St. Louis**, July 28, 1995.

CORT, JOEL — WSH.

Defense. Shoots left. 6'3", 227 lbs. Born, Hamilton, Ont., April 30, 1977.
(Washington's 7th choice, 124th overall, in 1995 Entry Draft).

			Regular Season					Playoffs				
Season	Club	Lea	GP	G	A	TP	PIM	GP	G	A	TP	PIM
1994-95	Guelph	OHL	29	1	3	4	20					
1995-96	Guelph	OHL	60	1	4	5	65	16	1	2	3	10

COTE, PATRICK — DAL.

Left wing. Shoots left. 6'3", 199 lbs. Born, Lasalle, Que., January 24, 1975.
(Dallas' 2nd choice, 37th overall, in 1995 Entry Draft).

			Regular Season					Playoffs				
Season	Club	Lea	GP	G	A	TP	PIM	GP	G	A	TP	PIM
1993-94	Beauport	QMJHL	48	2	4	6	230	12	1	0	1	61
1994-95	Beauport	QMJHL	56	20	20	40	314	17	8	8	16	115
1995-96	Dallas	NHL	2	0	0	0	5					
	Michigan	IHL	57	4	6	10	239	3	0	0	0	2
	NHL Totals		**2**	**0**	**0**	**0**	**5**					

COTE, SYLVAIN (KOH-tay) — WSH.

Defense. Shoots right. 6', 190 lbs. Born, Quebec City, Que., January 19, 1966.
(Hartford's 1st choice, 11th overall, in 1984 Entry Draft).

			Regular Season					Playoffs				
Season	Club	Lea	GP	G	A	TP	PIM	GP	G	A	TP	PIM
1982-83	Quebec	QMJHL	66	10	24	34	50					
1983-84	Quebec	QMJHL	66	15	50	65	89	5	1	1	2	0
1984-85	Hartford	NHL	67	3	9	12	17					
1985-86	Hartford	NHL	2	0	0	0	0					
a	Hull	QMJHL	26	10	33	43	14	13	6	*28	34	22
	Binghamton	AHL	12	2	4	6	0					
1986-87	Hartford	NHL	67	2	8	10	20	2	0	2	2	2
1987-88	Hartford	NHL	67	7	21	28	30	6	1	1	2	4
1988-89	Hartford	NHL	78	8	9	17	49	3	0	1	1	4
1989-90	Hartford	NHL	28	4	2	6	14	5	0	0	0	2
1990-91	Hartford	NHL	73	7	12	19	17	6	0	2	2	2
1991-92	Washington	NHL	78	11	29	40	31	7	1	2	3	4
1992-93	Washington	NHL	77	21	29	50	34	6	1	1	2	4
1993-94	Washington	NHL	84	16	35	51	66	9	1	8	9	6
1994-95	Washington	NHL	47	5	14	19	53	7	1	3	4	2
1995-96	Washington	NHL	81	5	33	38	40	6	2	0	2	12
	NHL Totals		**749**	**89**	**201**	**290**	**371**	**57**	**7**	**20**	**27**	**42**

a QMJHL First All-Star Team (1986).

Traded to **Washington** by **Hartford** for Washington's second round choice (Andrei Nikolishin) in 1992 Entry Draft, September 8, 1991.

COURTNALL, GEOFF — ST.L.

Left wing. Shoots left. 6'1", 195 lbs. Born, Duncan, B.C., August 18, 1962.

			Regular Season					Playoffs				
Season	Club	Lea	GP	G	A	TP	PIM	GP	G	A	TP	PIM
1980-81	Victoria	WHL	11	3	4	7	6	15	2	1	3	7
1981-82	Victoria	WHL	72	35	57	90	100	4	1	0	1	2
1982-83	Victoria	WHL	71	41	73	114	186	12	6	7	13	42
1983-84	Boston	NHL	4	0	0	0	0					
	Hershey	AHL	74	14	12	26	51					
1984-85	Boston	NHL	64	12	16	28	82	5	0	2	2	7
	Hershey	AHL	9	8	4	12	4					
1985-86	Boston	NHL	64	21	16	37	61	3	0	0	0	2
	Moncton	AHL	12	8	8	16	6					
1986-87	Boston	NHL	65	13	23	36	117	1	0	0	0	0
1987-88	Boston	NHL	62	32	26	58	108					
	Edmonton	NHL	12	4	4	8	15	19	0	3	3	23 ♦
1988-89	Washington	NHL	79	42	38	80	112	6	2	5	7	12
1989-90	Washington	NHL	80	35	39	74	104	15	4	9	13	32
1990-91	St. Louis	NHL	66	27	30	57	56					
	Vancouver	NHL	11	6	2	8	8	6	3	5	8	4
1991-92	Vancouver	NHL	70	23	34	57	116	12	6	8	14	20
1992-93	Vancouver	NHL	84	31	46	77	167	12	4	10	14	12
1993-94	Vancouver	NHL	82	26	44	70	123	24	9	10	19	51
1994-95	Vancouver	NHL	45	16	18	34	81	11	4	2	6	34
1995-96	St. Louis	NHL	69	24	16	40	101	13	0	3	3	14
	NHL Totals		**857**	**312**	**352**	**664**	**1251**	**127**	**32**	**57**	**89**	**211**

Signed as a free agent by **Boston**, July 6, 1983. Traded to **Edmonton** by **Boston** with Bill Ranford and future considerations for Andy Moog, March 8, 1988. Rights traded to **Washington** by **Edmonton** for Greg C. Adams, July 22, 1988. Traded to **St. Louis** by **Washington** for Peter Zezel and Mike Lalor, July 13, 1990. Traded to **Vancouver** by **St. Louis** with Robert Dirk, Sergio Momesso, Cliff Ronning and St. Louis' fifth round choice (Brian Loney) in 1992 Entry Draft for Dan Quinn and Garth Butcher, March 5, 1991. Signed as a free agent by **St. Louis**, July 14, 1995.

COURTNALL, RUSS — VAN.

Right wing. Shoots right. 5'11", 185 lbs. Born, Duncan, B.C., June 2, 1965.
(Toronto's 1st choice, 7th overall, in 1983 Entry Draft).

			Regular Season					Playoffs				
Season	Club	Lea	GP	G	A	TP	PIM	GP	G	A	TP	PIM
1982-83	Victoria	WHL	60	36	61	97	33	12	11	7	18	6
1983-84	Victoria	WHL	32	29	37	66	63					
	Cdn. National	....	16	4	7	11	10					
	Cdn. Olympic	....	7	1	3	4	2					
	Toronto	NHL	14	3	9	12	6					
1984-85	Toronto	NHL	69	12	10	22	44					
1985-86	Toronto	NHL	73	22	38	60	52	10	3	6	9	8
1986-87	Toronto	NHL	79	29	44	73	90	13	3	4	7	11
1987-88	Toronto	NHL	65	23	26	49	47	6	2	1	3	0
1988-89	Toronto	NHL	9	1	1	2	4					
	Montreal	NHL	64	22	17	39	15	21	8	5	13	18
1989-90	Montreal	NHL	80	27	32	59	27	11	5	1	6	10
1990-91	Montreal	NHL	79	26	50	76	29	13	8	3	11	7
1991-92	Montreal	NHL	27	7	14	21	6	10	1	1	2	4
1992-93	Minnesota	NHL	84	36	43	79	49					
1993-94	Dallas	NHL	84	23	57	80	59	9	1	8	9	0
1994-95	Dallas	NHL	32	7	10	17	13					
	Vancouver	NHL	13	4	14	18	4	11	4	8	12	21
1995-96	Vancouver	NHL	81	26	39	65	40	6	1	3	4	2
	NHL Totals		**853**	**268**	**404**	**672**	**485**	**110**	**36**	**40**	**76**	**81**

Played in NHL All-Star Game (1994)

Traded to **Montreal** by **Toronto** for John Kordic and Montreal's sixth round choice (Michael Doers) in 1989 Entry Draft, November 7, 1988. Traded to **Minnesota** by **Montreal** for Brian Bellows, August 31, 1992. Traded to **Vancouver** by **Dallas** for Greg Adams, Dan Kesa and Vancouver's fifth round choice (later traded to Los Angeles — Los Angeles selected Jason Morgan) in 1995 Entry Draft, April 7, 1995.

COURVILLE, LARRY — VAN.

Left wing. Shoots left. 6'1", 180 lbs. Born, Timmins, Ont., April 2, 1975.
(Winnipeg's 6th choice, 119th overall, in 1993 Entry Draft).

			Regular Season					Playoffs				
Season	Club	Lea	GP	G	A	TP	PIM	GP	G	A	TP	PIM
1991-92	Cornwall	OHL	60	8	12	20	80	6	0	0	0	8
1992-93	Newmarket	OHL	64	21	18	39	181	7	0	6	6	14
1993-94	Newmarket	OHL	39	20	19	39	134					
	Moncton	AHL	8	2	0	2	37	10	2	2	4	27
1994-95a	Sarnia	OHL	16	9	9	18	58					
	Oshawa	OHL	28	25	30	55	72	7	4	10	14	10
1995-96	Vancouver	NHL	3	1	0	1	0					
	Syracuse	AHL	71	17	32	49	127	14	5	3	8	10
	NHL Totals		**3**	**1**	**0**	**1**	**0**					

a OHL Second All-Star Team (1995)

Re-entered NHL Entry Draft, **Vancouver's** 2nd choice, 61st overall in 1995 Entry Draft.

COUTURIER, SYLVAIN (koo-TOOR-ee-yah, SIHL-vay)

Center. Shoots left. 6'2", 205 lbs. Born, Greenfield Park, Que., April 23, 1968.
(Los Angeles' 3rd choice, 65th overall, in 1986 Entry Draft).

			Regular Season					Playoffs				
Season	Club	Lea	GP	G	A	TP	PIM	GP	G	A	TP	PIM
1985-86	Laval	QMJHL	68	21	37	58	64	14	1	7	8	28
1986-87	Laval	QMJHL	67	39	51	90	77	13	12	14	26	19
1987-88	Laval	QMJHL	67	70	67	137	115					
1988-89	Los Angeles	NHL	16	1	3	4	2					
	New Haven	AHL	44	18	20	38	33	10	2	2	4	11
1989-90	New Haven	AHL	50	9	8	17	47					
1990-91	Los Angeles	NHL	3	0	1	1	0					
	Phoenix	IHL	66	50	37	87	49	10	8	2	10	10
1991-92	Los Angeles	NHL	14	3	1	4	2					
	Phoenix	IHL	39	19	20	39	68					
1992-93	Phoenix	IHL	38	23	16	39	63					
	Adirondack	AHL	29	17	17	34	12	11	3	5	8	10
	Fort Wayne	IHL						4	2	3	5	2
1993-94	Milwaukee	IHL	80	41	51	92	123	4	1	2	3	2
1994-95	Milwaukee	IHL	77	31	41	72	77	15	1	4	5	10
1995-96	Milwaukee	IHL	82	33	52	85	60	5	1	0	1	2
	NHL Totals		**33**	**4**	**5**	**9**	**4**					

Traded to **Detroit** by **Los Angeles** with Paul Coffey and Jim Hiller for Jimmy Carson, Marc Potvin and Gary Shuchuk, January 29, 1993.

COWIE, ROB

Defense. Shoots left. 6', 195 lbs. Born, Toronto, Ont., November 3, 1967.

			Regular Season					Playoffs				
Season	Club	Lea	GP	G	A	TP	PIM	GP	G	A	TP	PIM
1987-88	Northeastern	H.E.	36	7	8	15	38	....	....	....	....	....
1988-89a	Northeastern	H.E.	36	7	34	41	60	....	....	....	....	....
1989-90bc	Northeastern	H.E.	34	14	31	45	54	....	....	....	....	....
1990-91a	Northeastern	H.E.	33	18	23	41	56	....	....	....	....	....
1991-92	Moncton	AHL	64	11	30	41	89	5	1	1	2	0
1992-93	Moncton	AHL	67	12	20	32	91	5	3	5	8	2
1993-94d	Springfield	AHL	78	17	57	74	124	6	3	6	9	4
1994-95	Phoenix	IHL	51	14	33	47	71	....	....	....	....	....
	Los Angeles	**NHL**	**32**	**2**	**7**	**9**	**20**	....	....	....	....	....
1995-96	**Los Angeles**	**NHL**	**46**	**5**	**5**	**10**	**32**	....	....	....	....	....
	Phoenix	IHL	22	2	17	19	48	4	1	3	4	0
	NHL Totals		**78**	**7**	**12**	**19**	**52**	....	....	....	....	....

a Hockey East Second All-Star Team (1989,1991)
b Hockey East First All-Star Team (1990)
c NCAA East First All-American Team (1990)
d AHL Second All-Star Team (1994)

Signed as a free agent by **Winnipeg**, July 4, 1991. Signed as a free agent by **Hartford**, August 9, 1993. Signed as a free agent by **Los Angeles**, July 8,1994.

CRAIG, MIKE — TOR.

Right wing. Shoots right. 6'1", 180 lbs. Born, St. Mary's, Ont., June 6, 1971.
(Minnesota's 2nd choice, 28th overall, in 1989 Entry Draft).

			Regular Season					Playoffs				
Season	Club	Lea	GP	G	A	TP	PIM	GP	G	A	TP	PIM
1987-88	Oshawa	OHL	61	6	10	16	39	7	7	0	1	11
1988-89	Oshawa	OHL	63	36	36	72	34	6	3	1	4	6
1989-90	Oshawa	OHL	43	36	40	76	85	17	10	16	26	46
1990-91	**Minnesota**	**NHL**	**39**	**8**	**4**	**12**	**32**	**10**	**1**	**1**	**2**	**20**
1991-92	**Minnesota**	**NHL**	**67**	**15**	**16**	**31**	**155**	**4**	**1**	**0**	**1**	**7**
1992-93	**Minnesota**	**NHL**	**70**	**15**	**23**	**38**	**106**	....	....	....	....	....
1993-94	**Dallas**	**NHL**	**72**	**13**	**24**	**37**	**139**	**4**	**0**	**0**	**0**	**2**
1994-95	**Toronto**	**NHL**	**37**	**5**	**5**	**10**	**12**	**2**	**0**	**1**	**1**	**2**
1995-96	**Toronto**	**NHL**	**70**	**8**	**12**	**20**	**42**	**6**	**0**	**0**	**0**	**18**
	NHL Totals		**355**	**64**	**84**	**148**	**486**	**26**	**2**	**2**	**4**	**49**

Signed as a free agent by **Toronto**, July 29, 1994.

CRAIGHEAD, JOHN — TOR.

Right wing. Shoots right. 6', 195 lbs. Born, Vancouver, B.C., November 23, 1971.

			Regular Season					Playoffs				
Season	Club	Lea	GP	G	A	TP	PIM	GP	G	A	TP	PIM
1990-91	Br. Columbia	Jr. A	25	21	23	44	120	....	....	....	....	....
1991-92	W. Palm Beach	SHL	39	12	17	29	160	....	....	....	....	....
1992-93						UNAVAILABLE						
1993-94	Huntington	ECHL	9	4	2	6	44	....	....	....	....	....
	Richmond	ECHL	28	18	12	30	89	....	....	....	....	....
1994-95	Detroit	IHL	44	5	7	12	285	3	0	1	1	4
1995-96	Detroit	IHL	63	7	9	16	368	10	2	3	5	28

Signed as a free agent by **Toronto**, July 22, 1996.

CRAIGWELL, DALE

Center. Shoots left. 5'11", 180 lbs. Born, Toronto, Ont., April 24, 1971.
(San Jose's 11th choice, 199th overall, in 1991 Entry Draft).

			Regular Season					Playoffs				
Season	Club	Lea	GP	G	A	TP	PIM	GP	G	A	TP	PIM
1988-89	Oshawa	OHL	55	9	14	23	15	....	....	....	....	....
1989-90	Oshawa	OHL	64	22	41	63	39	17	7	7	14	11
1990-91	Oshawa	OHL	56	27	68	95	34	16	7	16	23	9
1991-92	**San Jose**	**NHL**	**32**	**5**	**11**	**16**	**8**	....	....	....	....	....
	Kansas City	IHL	48	6	19	25	29	12	4	7	11	4
1992-93	**San Jose**	**NHL**	**8**	**3**	**1**	**4**	**4**	....	....	....	....	....
	Kansas City	IHL	60	15	38	53	24	12	*7	5	12	2
1993-94	**San Jose**	**NHL**	**58**	**3**	**6**	**9**	**16**	....	....	....	....	....
	Kansas City	IHL	5	3	1	4	0	....	....	....	....	....
1994-95						DID NOT PLAY – INJURED						
1995-96	San Francisco	IHL	75	11	49	60	38	4	2	0	2	0
	NHL Totals		**98**	**11**	**18**	**29**	**28**	....	....	....	....	....

CRAVEN, MURRAY — CHI.

Left wing. Shoots left. 6'2", 185 lbs. Born, Medicine Hat, Alta., July 20, 1964.
(Detroit's 1st choice, 17th overall, in 1982 Entry Draft).

			Regular Season					Playoffs				
Season	Club	Lea	GP	G	A	TP	PIM	GP	G	A	TP	PIM
1980-81	Medicine Hat	WHL	69	5	10	15	18	5	0	0	0	2
1981-82	Medicine Hat	WHL	72	35	46	81	49	....	....	....	....	....
1982-83	**Detroit**	**NHL**	**31**	**4**	**7**	**11**	**6**	....	....	....	....	....
	Medicine Hat	WHL	28	17	29	46	35	....	....	....	....	....
1983-84	**Detroit**	**NHL**	**15**	**0**	**4**	**4**	**6**	....	....	....	....	....
	Medicine Hat	WHL	48	38	56	94	53	4	5	3	8	4
1984-85	**Philadelphia**	**NHL**	**80**	**26**	**35**	**61**	**30**	**19**	**4**	**6**	**10**	**11**
1985-86	**Philadelphia**	**NHL**	**78**	**21**	**33**	**54**	**34**	**5**	**0**	**3**	**3**	**4**
1986-87	**Philadelphia**	**NHL**	**77**	**19**	**30**	**49**	**38**	**12**	**3**	**1**	**4**	**9**
1987-88	**Philadelphia**	**NHL**	**72**	**30**	**46**	**76**	**58**	**7**	**2**	**5**	**7**	**4**
1988-89	**Philadelphia**	**NHL**	**51**	**9**	**28**	**37**	**52**	**1**	**0**	**0**	**0**	**0**
1989-90	**Philadelphia**	**NHL**	**76**	**25**	**50**	**75**	**42**	....	....	....	....	....
1990-91	**Philadelphia**	**NHL**	**77**	**19**	**47**	**66**	**53**	....	....	....	....	....
1991-92	**Philadelphia**	**NHL**	**12**	**3**	**3**	**6**	**8**	....	....	....	....	....
	Hartford	**NHL**	**61**	**24**	**30**	**54**	**38**	**7**	**3**	**3**	**6**	**6**
1992-93	**Hartford**	**NHL**	**67**	**25**	**42**	**67**	**20**	....	....	....	....	....
	Vancouver	**NHL**	**10**	**0**	**10**	**10**	**12**	**12**	**4**	**6**	**10**	**4**
1993-94	**Vancouver**	**NHL**	**78**	**15**	**40**	**55**	**30**	**22**	**4**	**9**	**13**	**18**
1994-95	**Chicago**	**NHL**	**16**	**4**	**3**	**7**	**2**	**16**	**5**	**5**	**10**	**4**
1995-96	**Chicago**	**NHL**	**66**	**18**	**29**	**47**	**36**	**9**	**1**	**4**	**5**	**2**
	NHL Totals		**867**	**242**	**437**	**679**	**465**	**110**	**26**	**42**	**68**	**62**

Traded to **Philadelphia** by **Detroit** with Joe Paterson for Darryl Sittler, October 10, 1984. Traded to **Hartford** by **Philadelphia** with Philadelphia's fourth round choice (Kevin Smyth) in 1992 Entry Draft for Kevin Dineen, November 13, 1991. Traded to **Vancouver** by **Hartford** with Vancouver's fifth round choice (previously acquired by Hartford — Vancouver selected Scott Walker) in 1993 Entry Draft for Robert Kron, Vancouver's third round choice (Marek Malik) in 1993 Entry Draft and future considerations (Jim Sandlak, May 17, 1993), March 22, 1993. Traded to **Chicago** by **Vancouver** for Christian Ruutu, March 10, 1995.

CRAWFORD, GLENN — N.J.

Center. Shoots left. 5'11", 175 lbs. Born, Orillia, Ont., February 27, 1978.
(New Jersey's 9th choice, 118th overall, in 1996 Entry Draft).

			Regular Season					Playoffs				
Season	Club	Lea	GP	G	A	TP	PIM	GP	G	A	TP	PIM
1994-95	Windsor	OHL	61	5	11	16	17	10	2	5	7	8
1995-96	Windsor	OHL	65	26	33	59	44	7	4	4	8	6

CREIGHTON, ADAM — (KRAY-ton) — ST.L.

Center. Shoots left. 6'5", 220 lbs. Born, Burlington, Ont., June 2, 1965.
(Buffalo's 3rd choice, 11th overall, in 1983 Entry Draft).

			Regular Season					Playoffs				
Season	Club	Lea	GP	G	A	TP	PIM	GP	G	A	TP	PIM
1981-82	Ottawa	OHL	60	15	27	42	73	17	7	1	8	40
1982-83	Ottawa	OHL	68	44	46	90	88	9	0	2	2	12
1983-84	**Buffalo**	**NHL**	**7**	**2**	**2**	**4**	**4**	....	....	....	....	....
a	Ottawa	OHL	56	42	49	91	79	13	16	11	27	28
1984-85	**Buffalo**	**NHL**	**30**	**2**	**8**	**10**	**33**	....	....	....	....	....
	Rochester	AHL	6	5	3	8	2	5	2	1	3	20
	Ottawa	OHL	10	4	14	18	23	5	6	2	8	11
1985-86	**Buffalo**	**NHL**	**19**	**1**	**1**	**2**	**2**	....	....	....	....	....
	Rochester	AHL	32	17	21	38	27	....	....	....	....	....
1986-87	**Buffalo**	**NHL**	**56**	**18**	**22**	**40**	**26**	....	....	....	....	....
1987-88	**Buffalo**	**NHL**	**36**	**10**	**17**	**27**	**87**	....	....	....	....	....
1988-89	**Buffalo**	**NHL**	**24**	**7**	**10**	**17**	**44**	....	....	....	....	....
	Chicago	**NHL**	**43**	**15**	**14**	**29**	**92**	**15**	**5**	**6**	**11**	**44**
1989-90	**Chicago**	**NHL**	**80**	**34**	**36**	**70**	**224**	**20**	**3**	**6**	**9**	**59**
1990-91	**Chicago**	**NHL**	**72**	**22**	**29**	**51**	**135**	**6**	**0**	**1**	**1**	**10**
1991-92	**Chicago**	**NHL**	**11**	**6**	**6**	**12**	**16**	....	....	....	....	....
	NY Islanders	**NHL**	**66**	**15**	**9**	**24**	**102**	....	....	....	....	....
1992-93	**Tampa Bay**	**NHL**	**83**	**19**	**20**	**39**	**110**	....	....	....	....	....
1993-94	**Tampa Bay**	**NHL**	**53**	**10**	**10**	**20**	**37**	....	....	....	....	....
1994-95	**St. Louis**	**NHL**	**48**	**14**	**20**	**34**	**74**	**7**	**2**	**0**	**2**	**16**
1995-96	**St. Louis**	**NHL**	**61**	**11**	**10**	**21**	**78**	**13**	**1**	**1**	**2**	**8**
	NHL Totals		**689**	**186**	**214**	**400**	**1064**	**61**	**11**	**14**	**25**	**137**

a Won Stafford Smythe Memorial Trophy (Memorial Cup Tournament MVP) (1984)

Traded to **Chicago** by **Buffalo** for Rick Vaive, December 26, 1988. Traded to **NY Islanders** by **Chicago** with Steve Thomas for Brent Sutter and Brad Lauer, October 25, 1991. Claimed by **Tampa Bay** from **NY Islanders** in NHL Waiver Draft, October 4, 1992. Traded to **St. Louis** by **Tampa Bay** for Tom Tilley, October 6, 1994.

CREURER, TROY — (KRUH-yuhr) — VAN.

Defense. Shoots left. 6'1", 185 lbs. Born, Weyburn, Sask., May 2, 1975.
(Vancouver's 5th choice, 158th overall, in 1993 Entry Draft).

			Regular Season					Playoffs				
Season	Club	Lea	GP	G	A	TP	PIM	GP	G	A	TP	PIM
1993-94	St. Lawrence	ECAC	31	5	10	15	22	....	....	....	....	....
1994-95	St. Lawrence	ECAC	33	1	11	12	30	....	....	....	....	....
1995-96	St. Lawrence	ECAC	35	2	15	17	24	....	....	....	....	....

CRONAN, EARL — MTL.

Left wing. Shoots left. 6'1", 195 lbs. Born, Warwick, RI, January 2, 1973.
(Montreal's 11th choice, 212th overall, in 1992 Entry Draft).

			Regular Season					Playoffs				
Season	Club	Lea	GP	G	A	TP	PIM	GP	G	A	TP	PIM
1992-93	Colgate	ECAC	33	8	9	17	40	....	....	....	....	....
1993-94	Colgate	ECAC	32	14	17	31	80	....	....	....	....	....
1994-95	Colgate	ECAC	37	21	20	41	81	....	....	....	....	....
1995-96	Colgate	ECAC	32	9	12	21	28	....	....	....	....	....

CRONIN, SHAWN

Defense. Shoots left. 6'2", 225 lbs. Born, Joliet, IL, August 20, 1963.

			Regular Season					Playoffs				
Season	Club	Lea	GP	G	A	TP	PIM	GP	G	A	TP	PIM
1982-83	Ill.-Chicago	CCHA	36	1	5	6	52	....	....	....	....	....
1983-84	Ill.-Chicago	CCHA	32	0	4	4	41	....	....	....	....	....
1984-85	Ill.-Chicago	CCHA	31	2	6	8	52	....	....	....	....	....
1985-86	Ill.-Chicago	CCHA	35	3	8	11	70	....	....	....	....	....
1986-87	Salt Lake	IHL	53	8	16	24	118	....	....	....	....	....
	Binghamton	AHL	12	0	1	1	60	10	0	0	0	41
1987-88	Binghamton	AHL	65	3	8	11	212	4	0	0	0	15
1988-89	**Washington**	**NHL**	**1**	**0**	**0**	**0**	**0**	....	....	....	....	....
	Baltimore	AHL	75	3	9	12	267	....	....	....	....	....
1989-90	**Winnipeg**	**NHL**	**61**	**0**	**4**	**4**	**243**	**5**	**0**	**0**	**0**	**7**
1990-91	**Winnipeg**	**NHL**	**67**	**1**	**5**	**6**	**189**	....	....	....	....	....
1991-92	**Winnipeg**	**NHL**	**65**	**0**	**4**	**4**	**271**	**4**	**0**	**0**	**0**	**6**
1992-93	**Philadelphia**	**NHL**	**35**	**2**	**1**	**3**	**37**	....	....	....	....	....
	Hershey	AHL	7	0	1	1	12	....	....	....	....	....
1993-94	**San Jose**	**NHL**	**34**	**0**	**2**	**2**	**76**	**14**	**1**	**0**	**1**	**20**
1994-95	**San Jose**	**NHL**	**29**	**0**	**2**	**2**	**61**	**9**	**0**	**0**	**0**	**5**
1995-96	Fort Wayne	IHL	48	0	1	1	120	5	0	0	0	8
	NHL Totals		**292**	**3**	**18**	**21**	**877**	**32**	**1**	**0**	**1**	**38**

Signed as a free agent by **Hartford**, March, 1986. Signed as a free agent by **Washington**, June 6, 1988. Signed as a free agent by **Philadelphia**, June 12, 1989. Traded to **Winnipeg** by **Philadelphia** for future considerations (Keith Acton and Pete Peeters were traded to Philadelphia for Toronto's fifth round choice (previously acquired by Philadelphia — Winnipeg selected Juha Ylonen), October 3, 1989), July 21, 1989. Traded to **Quebec** by **Winnipeg** for Dan Lambert, August 25, 1992. Claimed by **Philadelphia** from **Quebec** in NHL Waiver Draft, October 4, 1992. Traded to **San Jose** by **Philadelphia** for cash, August 5, 1993.

CROSS, CORY — T.B.

Defense. Shoots left. 6'5", 212 lbs. Born, Lloydminster, Alta., January 3, 1971.
(Tampa Bay's 1st choice, 1st overall, in 1992 Supplemental Draft).

			Regular Season					Playoffs				
Season	Club	Lea	GP	G	A	TP	PIM	GP	G	A	TP	PIM
1989-90	U. of Alberta	CWUAA				UNAVAILABLE						
1990-91	U. of Alberta	CWUAA	20	2	5	7	16	....	....	....	....	....
1991-92	U. of Alberta	CWUAA	41	4	11	15	82	....	....	....	....	....
1992-93	U. of Alberta	CWUAA	43	11	28	39	105	....	....	....	....	....
	Atlanta	IHL	7	0	1	1	2	4	0	0	0	6
1993-94	**Tampa Bay**	**NHL**	**5**	**0**	**0**	**0**	**6**	....	....	....	....	....
	Atlanta	IHL	70	4	14	18	72	9	1	2	3	14
1994-95	Atlanta	IHL	41	5	10	15	67	....	....	....	....	....
	Tampa Bay	**NHL**	**43**	**1**	**5**	**6**	**41**	....	....	....	....	....
1995-96	**Tampa Bay**	**NHL**	**75**	**2**	**14**	**16**	**66**	**6**	**0**	**0**	**0**	**22**
	NHL Totals		**123**	**3**	**19**	**22**	**113**	**6**	**0**	**0**	**0**	**22**

CROWDER, TROY

Right wing. Shoots right. 6'4", 220 lbs. Born, Sudbury, Ont., May 3, 1968.
(New Jersey's 6th choice, 108th overall, in 1986 Entry Draft).

			Regular Season					Playoffs				
Season	Club	Lea	GP	G	A	TP	PIM	GP	G	A	TP	PIM
1985-86	Hamilton	OHL	56	4	4	8	178	....	....	....	....	....
1986-87	Belleville	OHL	21	5	5	10	52	....	....	....	....	....
	North Bay	OHL	35	6	11	17	90	23	3	9	12	99
1987-88	North Bay	OHL	9	1	2	3	44	....	....	....	....	....
	Belleville	OHL	46	12	27	39	103	6	2	3	5	24
	Utica	AHL	3	0	0	0	36	....	....	....	....	....
	New Jersey	**NHL**	....	....	....	....	....	**1**	**0**	**0**	**0**	**12**
1988-89	Utica	AHL	62	6	4	10	152	2	0	0	0	25
1989-90	**New Jersey**	**NHL**	**10**	**0**	**0**	**0**	**23**	**2**	**0**	**0**	**0**	**10**
	Nashville	ECHL	3	0	0	0	15	....	....	....	....	....
1990-91	**New Jersey**	**NHL**	**59**	**6**	**3**	**9**	**182**	....	....	....	....	....
1991-92	**Detroit**	**NHL**	**7**	**0**	**0**	**0**	**35**	**1**	**0**	**0**	**0**	**0**
1992-93			DID NOT PLAY – INJURED									
1993-94			DID NOT PLAY – INJURED									
1994-95	**Los Angeles**	**NHL**	**29**	**1**	**2**	**3**	**99**	....	....	....	....	....
1995-96	**Los Angeles**	**NHL**	**15**	**1**	**0**	**1**	**42**	....	....	....	....	....
	NHL Totals		**120**	**8**	**5**	**13**	**381**	**4**	**0**	**0**	**0**	**22**

Signed as a free agent by **Detroit**, August 27, 1991. Signed as a free agent by **Los Angeles**, August 31, 1994.

CROWE, PHILIP — OTT.

Left wing. Shoots left. 6'2", 220 lbs. Born, Nanton, Alta., April 14, 1970.

			Regular Season					Playoffs				
Season	Club	Lea	GP	G	A	TP	PIM	GP	G	A	TP	PIM
1991-92	Adirondack	AHL	6	1	0	1	29	....	....	....	....	....
	Columbus	ECHL	32	4	7	11	145	....	....	....	....	....
	Toledo	ECHL	2	0	0	0	0	5	0	0	0	58
1992-93	Phoenix	IHL	53	3	3	6	190	....	....	....	....	....
1993-94	Fort Wayne	IHL	5	0	1	1	26	....	....	....	....	....
	Phoenix	IHL	2	0	0	0	0	....	....	....	....	....
	Los Angeles	**NHL**	**31**	**0**	**2**	**2**	**77**	....	....	....	....	....
1994-95	Hershey	AHL	46	11	6	17	132	6	0	1	1	19
1995-96	**Philadelphia**	**NHL**	**16**	**1**	**1**	**2**	**28**	....	....	....	....	....
	Hershey	AHL	39	6	8	14	105	5	1	2	3	19
	NHL Totals		**47**	**1**	**3**	**4**	**105**	....	....	....	....	....

Signed as a free agent by **Los Angeles**, November 8, 1993. Signed as a free agent by **Philadelphia**, July 19, 1994. Signed as a free agent by **Ottawa**, August, 1996.

CROWLEY, MIKE — ANA.

Defense. Shoots left. 5'11", 175 lbs. Born, Bloomington, MN, July 4, 1975.
(Philadelphia's 5th choice, 140th overall, in 1993 Entry Draft).

			Regular Season					Playoffs				
Season	Club	Lea	GP	G	A	TP	PIM	GP	G	A	TP	PIM
1994-95	U. Minnesota	WCHA	41	11	27	38	60	....	....	....	....	....
1995-96ab	U. Minnesota	WCHA	42	17	46	63	28	....	....	....	....	....

a WCHA First All-Star Team (1996)
b NCAA West First All-American Team (1996)

Traded to **Anaheim** by **Philadelphia** with Anatoli Semenov for Brian Wesenberg, March 19, 1996.

CROWLEY, TED

Defense. Shoots right. 6'2", 188 lbs. Born, Concord, MA, May 3, 1970.
(Toronto's 4th choice, 69th overall, in 1988 Entry Draft).

			Regular Season					Playoffs				
Season	Club	Lea	GP	G	A	TP	PIM	GP	G	A	TP	PIM
1989-90	Boston College	H.E.	39	7	24	31	34	....	....	....	....	....
1990-91ab	Boston College	H.E.	39	12	24	36	61	....	....	....	....	....
1991-92	U.S. National	....	42	6	7	13	65	....	....	....	....	....
	St. John's	AHL	29	5	4	9	33	10	3	1	4	11
1992-93	St. John's	AHL	79	19	38	57	41	9	2	2	4	4
1993-94	U.S. National	....	48	9	13	22	80	....	....	....	....	....
	U.S. Olympic	....	8	0	2	2	8	....	....	....	....	....
	Hartford	**NHL**	**21**	**1**	**2**	**3**	**10**	....	....	....	....	....
1994-95	Chicago	IHL	53	8	23	31	68	....	....	....	....	....
	Houston	IHL	23	4	9	13	35	3	0	1	1	0
1995-96	Providence	AHL	72	12	30	42	47	4	1	2	3	2
	NHL Totals		**21**	**1**	**2**	**3**	**10**	....	....	....	....	....

a Hockey East First All-Star Team (1991)
b NCAA East Second All-American Team (1991)

Traded to **Hartford** by **Toronto** for Mark Greig and Hartford's sixth round choice (later traded to NY Rangers — NY Rangers selected Yuri Litvinov) in 1994 Entry Draft, January 25, 1994. Signed as a free agent by **Boston**, August 9, 1995.

CROZIER, GREG — PIT.

Left wing. Shoots left. 6'4", 200 lbs. Born, Calgary, Alta., July 6, 1976.
(Pittsburgh's 4th choice, 73rd overall, in 1994 Entry Draft).

			Regular Season					Playoffs				
Season	Club	Lea	GP	G	A	TP	PIM	GP	G	A	TP	PIM
1994-95	Lawrence	HS	31	45	32	77	22	....	....	....	....	....
1995-96	U. of Michigan	CCHA	42	14	10	24	46	....	....	....	....	....

CULL, TRENT — TOR.

Defense. Shoots left. 6'3", 210 lbs. Born, Brampton, Ont., September 27, 1973.

			Regular Season					Playoffs				
Season	Club	Lea	GP	G	A	TP	PIM	GP	G	A	TP	PIM
1989-90	Owen Sound	OHL	57	0	5	5	53	12	0	2	2	11
1990-91	Owen Sound	OHL	24	1	2	3	19	....	....	....	....	....
	Windsor	OHL	33	1	6	7	34	11	0	0	0	8
1991-92	Windsor	OHL	32	0	6	6	66	....	....	....	....	....
	Kingston	OHL	18	0	0	0	31	....	....	....	....	....
1992-93	Kingston	OHL	60	11	28	39	144	16	2	8	10	37
1993-94	Kingston	OHL	50	2	30	32	147	6	0	1	1	6
1994-95	St. John's	AHL	43	0	1	1	53	....	....	....	....	....
1995-96	St. John's	AHL	46	2	1	3	118	4	0	0	0	6

Signed as a free agent by **Toronto**, June 4, 1994.

CULLEN, JOHN — T.B.

Center. Shoots right. 5'10", 180 lbs. Born, Puslinch, Ont., August 2, 1964.
(Buffalo's 2nd choice, 10th overall, in 1986 Supplemental Draft).

			Regular Season					Playoffs				
Season	Club	Lea	GP	G	A	TP	PIM	GP	G	A	TP	PIM
1983-84	Boston U.	ECAC	40	23	33	56	28	....	....	....	....	....
1984-85a	Boston U.	H.E.	41	27	32	59	46	....	....	....	....	....
1985-86ab	Boston U.	H.E.	43	25	49	74	54	....	....	....	....	....
1986-87c	Boston U.	H.E.	36	23	29	52	35	....	....	....	....	....
1987-88defg	Flint	IHL	81	48	*109	*157	113	16	11	*15	26	16
1988-89	**Pittsburgh**	**NHL**	**79**	**12**	**37**	**49**	**112**	**11**	**3**	**6**	**9**	**28**
1989-90	**Pittsburgh**	**NHL**	**72**	**32**	**60**	**92**	**138**	....	....	....	....	....
1990-91	**Pittsburgh**	**NHL**	**65**	**31**	**63**	**94**	**83**	....	....	....	....	....
	Hartford	**NHL**	**13**	**8**	**8**	**16**	**18**	**6**	**2**	**7**	**9**	**10**
1991-92	**Hartford**	**NHL**	**77**	**26**	**51**	**77**	**141**	**7**	**2**	**1**	**3**	**12**
1992-93	**Hartford**	**NHL**	**19**	**5**	**4**	**9**	**58**	....	....	....	....	....
	Toronto	**NHL**	**47**	**13**	**28**	**41**	**53**	**12**	**2**	**3**	**5**	**0**
1993-94	**Toronto**	**NHL**	**53**	**13**	**17**	**30**	**67**	**3**	**0**	**0**	**0**	**0**
1994-95	**Pittsburgh**	**NHL**	**46**	**13**	**24**	**37**	**66**	**9**	**0**	**2**	**2**	**8**
1995-96	**Tampa Bay**	**NHL**	**76**	**16**	**34**	**50**	**65**	**5**	**3**	**3**	**6**	**0**
	NHL Totals		**547**	**169**	**326**	**495**	**801**	**53**	**12**	**22**	**34**	**58**

a Hockey East First All-Star Team (1985, 1986)
b NCAA East Second All-American Team (1986)
c Hockey East Second All-Star Team (1987)
d IHL First All-Star Team (1988)
e Won James Gatschene Memorial Trophy (MVP - IHL) (1988)
f Shared Garry F. Longman Memorial Trophy (Top Rookie - IHL) with Ed Belfour (1988)
g Won Leo P. Lamoureux Memorial Trophy (Top Scorer - IHL) (1988)

Played in NHL All-Star Game (1991, 1992)

Signed as a free agent by **Pittsburgh**, June 21, 1988. Traded to **Hartford** by **Pittsburgh** with Jeff Parker and Zarley Zalapski for Ron Francis, Grant Jennings and Ulf Samuelsson, March 4, 1991. Traded to **Toronto** by **Hartford** for future considerations, November 24, 1992. Signed as a free agent by **Pittsburgh**, August 3, 1994. Signed as a free agent by **Tampa Bay**, September 11, 1995.

CULLEN, MATT — ANA.

Center. Shoots left. 6'1", 182 lbs. Born, Virginia, MN, November 2, 1976.
(Anaheim's 2nd choice, 35th overall, in 1996 Entry Draft).

			Regular Season					Playoffs				
Season	Club	Lea	GP	G	A	TP	PIM	GP	G	A	TP	PIM
1994-95	Moorhead	HS	28	47	42	89	78	....	....	....	....	....
1995-96	St. Cloud	WCHA	39	12	29	41	28	....	....	....	....	....

CULLEN, THOMAS — N.J.

Defense. Shoots left. 6'1", 205 lbs. Born, Mississauga, Ont., July 14, 1975.
(New Jersey's 8th choice, 195th overall, in 1993 Entry Draft).

			Regular Season					Playoffs				
Season	Club	Lea	GP	G	A	TP	PIM	GP	G	A	TP	PIM
1993-94	St. Lawrence	ECAC	23	1	3	4	32	....	....	....	....	....
1994-95	St. Lawrence	ECAC	32	9	19	28	67	....	....	....	....	....
1995-96	St. Lawrence	ECAC	34	6	9	15	84	....	....	....	....	....

CULLIMORE, JASSEN — VAN.

Defense. Shoots left. 6'5", 225 lbs. Born, Simcoe, Ont., December 4, 1972.
(Vancouver's 2nd choice, 29th overall, in 1991 Entry Draft).

			Regular Season					Playoffs				
Season	Club	Lea	GP	G	A	TP	PIM	GP	G	A	TP	PIM
1989-90	Peterborough	OHL	59	2	6	8	61	11	0	2	2	8
1990-91	Peterborough	OHL	62	8	16	24	74	4	1	0	1	7
1991-92a	Peterborough	OHL	54	9	37	46	65	10	3	6	9	8
1992-93	Hamilton	AHL	56	5	7	12	60	....	....	....	....	....
1993-94	Hamilton	AHL	71	8	20	28	86	3	0	1	1	2
1994-95	Syracuse	AHL	33	2	7	9	66	....	....	....	....	....
	Vancouver	**NHL**	**34**	**1**	**2**	**3**	**39**	**11**	**0**	**0**	**0**	**12**
1995-96	**Vancouver**	**NHL**	**27**	**1**	**1**	**2**	**21**	....	....	....	....	....
	NHL Totals		**61**	**2**	**3**	**5**	**60**	**11**	**0**	**0**	**0**	**12**

a OHL Second All-Star Team (1992)

CUMMINS, JIM — CHI.

Right wing. Shoots right. 6'2", 203 lbs. Born, Dearborn, MI, May 17, 1970.
(NY Rangers' 5th choice, 67th overall, in 1989 Entry Draft).

			Regular Season					Playoffs				
Season	Club	Lea	GP	G	A	TP	PIM	GP	G	A	TP	PIM
1988-89	Michigan State	CCHA	30	3	8	11	98	....	....	....	....	....
1989-90	Michigan State	CCHA	41	8	7	15	94	....	....	....	....	....
1990-91	Michigan State	CCHA	34	9	6	15	110	....	....	....	....	....
1991-92	**Detroit**	**NHL**	**1**	**0**	**0**	**0**	**7**	....	....	....	....	....
	Adirondack	AHL	65	7	13	20	338	5	0	0	0	19
1992-93	**Detroit**	**NHL**	**7**	**1**	**1**	**2**	**58**	....	....	....	....	....
	Adirondack	AHL	43	16	4	20	179	9	3	1	4	4
1993-94	**Philadelphia**	**NHL**	**22**	**1**	**2**	**3**	**71**	....	....	....	....	....
	Hershey	AHL	17	6	6	12	70	....	....	....	....	....
	Tampa Bay	**NHL**	**4**	**0**	**0**	**0**	**13**	....	....	....	....	....
	Atlanta	IHL	7	4	5	9	14	13	1	2	3	90
1994-95	**Tampa Bay**	**NHL**	**10**	**1**	**0**	**1**	**41**	....	....	....	....	....
	Chicago	**NHL**	**27**	**3**	**1**	**4**	**117**	**14**	**1**	**1**	**2**	**4**
1995-96	**Chicago**	**NHL**	**52**	**2**	**4**	**6**	**180**	**10**	**0**	**0**	**0**	**2**
	NHL Totals		**123**	**8**	**8**	**16**	**487**	**24**	**1**	**1**	**2**	**6**

Traded to **Detroit** by **NY Rangers** with Kevin Miller and Dennis Vial for Joey Kocur and Per Djoos, March 5, 1991. Traded to **Philadelphia** by **Detroit** with Philadelphia's fourth round choice (previously acquired by Detroit — later traded to Boston — Boston selected Charles Paquette) in 1993 Entry Draft for Greg Johnson and Philadelphia's fifth round choice (Frederic Deschenes) in 1994 Entry Draft, June 20, 1993. Traded to **Tampa Bay** by **Philadelphia** with Philadelphia's fourth round choice in 1995 Entry Draft for Rob DiMaio, March 18, 1994. Traded to **Chicago** by **Tampa Bay** with Tom Tilley and Jeff Buchanan for Paul Ysebaert and Rich Sutter, February 22, 1995.

CUNNEYWORTH, RANDY — OTT.

Left wing. Shoots left. 6', 180 lbs. Born, Etobicoke, Ont., May 10, 1961.
(Buffalo's 9th choice, 167th overall, in 1980 Entry Draft).

			Regular Season					Playoffs				
Season	Club	Lea	GP	G	A	TP	PIM	GP	G	A	TP	PIM
1979-80	Ottawa	OHA	63	16	25	41	145	11	0	1	1	13
1980-81	**Buffalo**	**NHL**	**1**	**0**	**0**	**0**	**2**	....	....	....	....	....
	Rochester	AHL	1	0	1	1	2	....	....	....	....	....
	Ottawa	OHA	67	54	74	128	240	15	5	8	13	35
1981-82	**Buffalo**	**NHL**	**20**	**2**	**4**	**6**	**47**	....	....	....	....	....
	Rochester	AHL	57	12	15	27	86	9	4	0	4	30
1982-83	Rochester	AHL	78	23	33	56	111	16	4	4	8	35
1983-84	Rochester	AHL	54	18	17	35	85	17	5	5	10	55
1984-85	Rochester	AHL	72	30	38	68	148	5	2	1	3	16
1985-86	**Pittsburgh**	**NHL**	**75**	**15**	**30**	**45**	**74**	....	....	....	....	....
1986-87	**Pittsburgh**	**NHL**	**79**	**26**	**27**	**53**	**142**	....	....	....	....	....
1987-88	**Pittsburgh**	**NHL**	**71**	**35**	**39**	**74**	**141**	....	....	....	....	....
1988-89	**Pittsburgh**	**NHL**	**70**	**25**	**19**	**44**	**156**	**11**	**3**	**5**	**8**	**26**
1989-90	**Winnipeg**	**NHL**	**28**	**5**	**6**	**11**	**34**	....	....	....	....	....
	Hartford	**NHL**	**43**	**9**	**9**	**18**	**41**	**4**	**0**	**0**	**0**	**2**
1990-91	**Hartford**	**NHL**	**32**	**9**	**5**	**14**	**49**	**1**	**0**	**0**	**0**	**0**
	Springfield	AHL	2	0	0	0	5	....	....	....	....	....
1991-92	**Hartford**	**NHL**	**39**	**7**	**10**	**17**	**71**	**7**	**3**	**0**	**3**	**9**
1992-93	**Hartford**	**NHL**	**39**	**5**	**4**	**9**	**63**	....	....	....	....	....
1993-94	**Hartford**	**NHL**	**63**	**9**	**8**	**17**	**87**	....	....	....	....	....
	Chicago	**NHL**	**16**	**4**	**3**	**7**	**13**	**6**	**0**	**0**	**0**	**8**
1994-95	**Ottawa**	**NHL**	**48**	**5**	**5**	**10**	**68**	....	....	....	....	....
1995-96	**Ottawa**	**NHL**	**81**	**17**	**19**	**36**	**130**	....	....	....	....	....
	NHL Totals		**705**	**173**	**188**	**361**	**1118**	**29**	**6**	**5**	**11**	**45**

Traded to **Pittsburgh** by **Buffalo** with Mike Moller for Pat Hughes, October 4, 1985. Traded to **Winnipeg** by **Pittsburgh** with Rick Tabaracci and Dave McLlwain for Jim Kyte, Andrew McBain and Randy Gilhen, June 17, 1989. Traded to **Hartford** by **Winnipeg** for Paul MacDermid, December 13, 1989. Traded to **Chicago** by **Hartford** with Gary Suter and Hartford's third round choice (later traded to Vancouver — Vancouver selected Larry Courville) in 1995 Entry Draft for Frantisek Kucera and Jocelyn Lemieux, March 11, 1994. Signed as a free agent by **Ottawa**, July 15, 1994.

CURRAN, BRIAN

Defense. Shoots left. 6'5", 220 lbs. Born, Toronto, Ont., November 5, 1963.
(Boston's 2nd choice, 22nd overall, in 1982 Entry Draft).

			Regular Season					Playoffs				
Season	Club	Lea	GP	G	A	TP	PIM	GP	G	A	TP	PIM
1980-81	Portland	WHL	59	2	28	30	275	7	0	1	1	13
1981-82	Portland	WHL	51	2	16	18	132	14	1	7	8	63
1982-83	Portland	WHL	56	1	30	31	187	14	1	3	4	57
1983-84	**Boston**	**NHL**	**16**	**1**	**1**	**2**	**57**	**3**	**0**	**0**	**0**	**7**
	Hershey	AHL	23	0	2	2	94	....	....	....	....	....
1984-85	**Boston**	**NHL**	**56**	**0**	**1**	**1**	**158**	....	....	....	....	....
	Hershey	AHL	4	0	0	0	19	....	....	....	....	....
1985-86	**Boston**	**NHL**	**43**	**2**	**5**	**7**	**192**	**2**	**0**	**0**	**0**	**4**
1986-87	**NY Islanders**	**NHL**	**68**	**0**	**10**	**10**	**356**	**8**	**0**	**0**	**0**	**51**
1987-88	**NY Islanders**	**NHL**	**22**	**0**	**1**	**1**	**68**	....	....	....	....	....
	Springfield	AHL	8	1	0	1	43	....	....	....	....	....
	Toronto	**NHL**	**7**	**0**	**1**	**1**	**19**	**6**	**0**	**0**	**0**	**41**
1988-89	**Toronto**	**NHL**	**47**	**1**	**4**	**5**	**185**	....	....	....	....	....
1989-90	**Toronto**	**NHL**	**72**	**2**	**9**	**11**	**301**	**5**	**0**	**1**	**1**	**19**
1990-91	**Toronto**	**NHL**	**4**	**0**	**0**	**0**	**7**	....	....	....	....	....
	Newmarket	AHL	6	0	1	1	32	....	....	....	....	....
	Buffalo	**NHL**	**17**	**0**	**1**	**1**	**43**	....	....	....	....	....
	Rochester	AHL	10	0	0	0	36	....	....	....	....	....
1991-92	**Buffalo**	**NHL**	**3**	**0**	**0**	**0**	**14**	....	....	....	....	....
	Rochester	AHL	36	0	3	3	122	....	....	....	....	....
1992-93	Cape Breton	AHL	61	2	24	26	223	12	0	3	3	12
1993-94	**Washington**	**NHL**	**26**	**1**	**0**	**1**	**61**	....	....	....	....	....
	Portland	AHL	46	1	6	7	247	15	0	1	1	59
1994-95	Portland	AHL	59	2	10	12	328	7	0	0	0	24
1995-96	Portland	AHL	34	1	2	3	122	....	....	....	....	....
	Michigan	IHL	18	0	5	5	55	10	0	4	4	38
	NHL Totals		**381**	**7**	**33**	**40**	**1461**	**24**	**0**	**1**	**1**	**122**

Signed as a free agent by **NY Islanders**, August 29, 1987. Traded to **Toronto** by **NY Islanders** for Toronto's sixth round choice (Pavel Gross) in 1988 Entry Draft, March 8, 1988. Traded to **Buffalo** by **Toronto** with Lou Franceschetti for Mike Foligno and Buffalo's eighth round choice (Thomas Kucharcik) in 1991 Entry Draft, December 17, 1990. Signed as a free agent by **Edmonton**, October 27, 1992. Signed as a free agent by **Washington**, October 21, 1993.

CURRIE, DAN

Left wing. Shoots left. 6'2", 195 lbs. Born, Burlington, Ont., March 15, 1968.
(Edmonton's 4th choice, 84th overall, in 1986 Entry Draft).

			Regular Season					Playoffs				
Season	Club	Lea	GP	G	A	TP	PIM	GP	G	A	TP	PIM
1985-86	S.S. Marie	OHL	66	21	24	45	37	....	....	....	....	....
1986-87	S.S. Marie	OHL	66	31	52	83	53	4	2	1	3	2
1987-88	Nova Scotia	AHL	3	4	2	6	0	5	4	3	7	0
	S.S. Marie	OHL	57	50	59	109	53	6	3	9	12	4
1988-89	Cape Breton	AHL	77	29	36	65	29	....	....	....	....	....
1989-90	Cape Breton	AHL	77	36	40	76	28	6	4	4	8	0
1990-91	**Edmonton**	**NHL**	**5**	**0**	**0**	**0**	**0**	....	....	....	....	....
	Cape Breton	AHL	71	47	45	92	51	4	3	1	4	8
1991-92	**Edmonton**	**NHL**	**7**	**1**	**0**	**1**	**0**	....	....	....	....	....
a	Cape Breton	AHL	66	*50	42	92	39	5	4	5	9	4
1992-93	**Edmonton**	**NHL**	**5**	**0**	**0**	**0**	**4**	....	....	....	....	....
b	Cape Breton	AHL	75	57	41	98	73	16	7	4	11	29
1993-94	**Los Angeles**	**NHL**	**5**	**1**	**1**	**2**	**0**	....	....	....	....	....
	Phoenix	IHL	74	37	49	86	96	....	....	....	....	....
1994-95	Phoenix	IHL	16	2	6	8	8	....	....	....	....	....
	Minnesota	IHL	54	18	35	53	34	3	0	0	0	2
1995-96	Chicago	IHL	79	39	34	73	53	9	5	4	9	12
	NHL Totals		**22**	**2**	**1**	**3**	**4**	....	....	....	....	....

a AHL Second All-Star Team (1992)
b AHL First All-Star Team (1993)

Signed as a free agent by **Los Angeles**, July 16, 1993.

CURTIN, LUKE — COL.

Left wing. Shoots left. 6'2", 190 lbs. Born, St. Paul, MN, September 23, 1977.
(Colorado's 6th choice, 134th overall, in 1996 Entry Draft).

			Regular Season					Playoffs				
Season	Club	Lea	GP	G	A	TP	PIM	GP	G	A	TP	PIM
1994-95	Langley	Jr. A	59	26	47	73	49	....	....	....	....	....
1995-96	Kelowna	WHL	69	21	26	47	39	6	3	2	5	6

CZERKAWSKI, MARIUSZ (chehr-KAWV-skee) — EDM.

Right wing. Shoots right. 6', 195 lbs. Born, Radomsko, Poland, April 13, 1972.
(Boston's 5th choice, 106th overall, in 1991 Entry Draft).

			Regular Season					Playoffs				
Season	Club	Lea	GP	G	A	TP	PIM	GP	G	A	TP	PIM
1990-91	GKS Tychy	Poland	24	25	15	40	....	....	....	....	....	....
1991-92	Djurgarden	Swe.	39	8	5	13	4	3	0	0	0	2
1992-93	Hammarby	Swe. 2	32	39	30	69	74	....	....	....	....	....
1993-94	Djurgarden	Swe.	39	13	21	34	20	6	3	1	4	2
	Boston	**NHL**	**4**	**2**	**1**	**3**	**0**	**13**	**3**	**3**	**6**	**4**
1994-95	Kiekko-Espoo	Fin.	7	9	3	12	10	....	....	....	....	....
	Boston	**NHL**	**47**	**12**	**14**	**26**	**31**	**5**	**1**	**0**	**1**	**0**
1995-96	**Boston**	**NHL**	**33**	**5**	**6**	**11**	**10**	....	....	....	....	....
	Edmonton	**NHL**	**37**	**12**	**17**	**29**	**8**	....	....	....	....	....
	NHL Totals		**121**	**31**	**38**	**69**	**49**	**18**	**4**	**3**	**7**	**4**

Traded to **Edmonton** by **Boston** with Sean Brown and Boston's first round choice (Matthieu Descoteaux) in 1996 Entry Draft for Bill Ranford, January 11, 1996.

DACKELL, ANDREAS — OTT.

Right wing. Shoots right. 5'10", 191 lbs. Born, Gavle, Sweden, December 29, 1972.
(Ottawa's 3rd choice, 136th overall, in 1996 Entry Draft).

			Regular Season					Playoffs				
Season	Club	Lea	GP	G	A	TP	PIM	GP	G	A	TP	PIM
1990-91	Brynas	Swe.	3	0	1	1	2	....	....	....	....	....
1991-92	Brynas	Swe.	4	0	0	0	2	2	0	1	1	4
1992-93	Brynas	Swe.	40	12	15	27	12	10	4	5	9	2
1993-94	Brynas	Swe.	38	12	17	29	47	7	2	2	4	8
1994-95	Brynas	Swe.	39	17	16	33	34	14	3	3	6	14
1995-96	Brynas	Swe.	22	6	6	12	8	....	....	....	....	....

DAGENAIS, PIERRE (da-ZHUH-nay) — N.J.

Left wing. Shoots left. 6'3", 185 lbs. Born, Blainville, Que., March 4, 1978.
(New Jersey's 4th choice, 47th overall, in 1996 Entry Draft).

			Regular Season					Playoffs				
Season	Club	Lea	GP	G	A	TP	PIM	GP	G	A	TP	PIM
1994-95	Regents	Midget	34	28	14	42	68	....	....	....	....	....
1995-96	Moncton	QMJHL	67	43	25	68	59	....	....	....	....	....

DAHL, KEVIN (DAHL)

Defense. Shoots right. 5'11", 190 lbs. Born, Regina, Sask., December 30, 1968.
(Montreal's 12th choice, 230th overall, in 1988 Entry Draft).

			Regular Season					Playoffs				
Season	Club	Lea	GP	G	A	TP	PIM	GP	G	A	TP	PIM
1986-87	Bowling Green	CCHA	32	2	6	8	54	....	....	....	....	....
1987-88	Bowling Green	CCHA	44	2	23	25	78	....	....	....	....	....
1988-89	Bowling Green	CCHA	46	9	26	35	51	....	....	....	....	....
1989-90	Bowling Green	CCHA	43	8	22	30	74	....	....	....	....	....
1990-91	Fredericton	AHL	32	1	15	16	45	9	0	1	1	11
	Winston-Salem	ECHL	36	7	17	24	58	....	....	....	....	....
1991-92	Cdn. National	....	45	2	15	17	44	....	....	....	....	....
	Cdn. Olympic	....	8	2	0	2	6	....	....	....	....	....
	Salt Lake	IHL	13	0	2	2	12	5	0	0	0	13
1992-93	**Calgary**	**NHL**	**61**	**2**	**9**	**11**	**56**	**6**	**0**	**2**	**2**	**8**
1993-94	**Calgary**	**NHL**	**33**	**0**	**3**	**3**	**23**	**6**	**0**	**0**	**0**	**4**
	Saint John	AHL	2	0	0	0	0	....	....	....	....	....
1994-95	**Calgary**	**NHL**	**34**	**4**	**8**	**12**	**38**	**3**	**0**	**0**	**0**	**0**
1995-96	**Calgary**	**NHL**	**32**	**1**	**1**	**2**	**26**	**1**	**0**	**0**	**0**	**0**
	Saint John	AHL	23	4	11	15	37	....	....	....	....	....
	NHL Totals		**160**	**7**	**21**	**28**	**143**	**16**	**0**	**2**	**2**	**12**

Signed as a free agent by **Calgary**, July 27, 1991.

DAHLEN, ULF (DAH-lehn) — S.J.

Right wing. Shoots left. 6'2", 195 lbs. Born, Ostersund, Sweden, January 12, 1967.
(NY Rangers' 1st choice, 7th overall, in 1985 Entry Draft).

			Regular Season					Playoffs				
Season	Club	Lea	GP	G	A	TP	PIM	GP	G	A	TP	PIM
1983-84	Ostersund	Swe. 2	36	15	11	26	10	....	....	....	....	....
1984-85	Ostersund	Swe. 2	36	33	26	59	20	....	....	....	....	....
1985-86	Bjorkloven	Swe.	22	4	3	7	8	....	....	....	....	....
1986-87	Bjorkloven	Swe.	31	9	12	21	20	6	6	2	8	4
1987-88	**NY Rangers**	**NHL**	**70**	**29**	**23**	**52**	**26**	....	....	....	....	....
	Colorado	IHL	2	2	2	4	0	....	....	....	....	....
1988-89	**NY Rangers**	**NHL**	**56**	**24**	**19**	**43**	**50**	**4**	**0**	**0**	**0**	**0**
1989-90	**NY Rangers**	**NHL**	**63**	**18**	**18**	**36**	**30**	....	....	....	....	....
	Minnesota	**NHL**	**13**	**2**	**4**	**6**	**0**	**7**	**1**	**4**	**5**	**2**
1990-91	**Minnesota**	**NHL**	**66**	**21**	**18**	**39**	**6**	**15**	**2**	**6**	**8**	**4**
1991-92	**Minnesota**	**NHL**	**79**	**36**	**30**	**66**	**10**	**7**	**0**	**3**	**3**	**2**
1992-93	**Minnesota**	**NHL**	**83**	**35**	**39**	**74**	**6**	....	....	....	....	....
1993-94	**Dallas**	**NHL**	**65**	**19**	**38**	**57**	**10**	....	....	....	....	....
	San Jose	**NHL**	**13**	**6**	**6**	**12**	**0**	**14**	**6**	**2**	**8**	**0**
1994-95	**San Jose**	**NHL**	**46**	**11**	**23**	**34**	**11**	**11**	**5**	**4**	**9**	**0**
1995-96	**San Jose**	**NHL**	**59**	**16**	**12**	**28**	**27**	....	....	....	....	....
	NHL Totals		**613**	**217**	**230**	**447**	**176**	**58**	**14**	**19**	**33**	**8**

Traded to **Minnesota** by **NY Rangers** with Los Angeles' fourth round choice (previously acquired by NY Rangers — Minnesota selected Cal McGowan) in 1990 Entry Draft and future considerations for Mike Gartner, March 6, 1990. Traded to **San Jose** by **Dallas** with Dallas' seventh round choice (Brad Mehalko) in 1995 Entry Draft for Doug Zmolek, Mike Lalor and cash, March 19, 1994.

DAHLQUIST, CHRIS (DAHL-kwist)

Defense. Shoots left. 6'1", 195 lbs. Born, Fridley, MN, December 14, 1962.

			Regular Season					Playoffs				
Season	Club	Lea	GP	G	A	TP	PIM	GP	G	A	TP	PIM
1981-82	Lake Superior	CCHA	39	4	10	14	62	....	....	....	....	....
1982-83	Lake Superior	CCHA	35	0	12	12	63	....	....	....	....	....
1983-84	Lake Superior	CCHA	40	4	19	23	76	....	....	....	....	....
1984-85	Lake Superior	CCHA	32	4	10	14	18	....	....	....	....	....
1985-86	Pittsburgh	NHL	5	1	2	3	2	....	....	....	....	....
	Baltimore	AHL	65	4	21	25	64	....	....	....	....	....
1986-87	Pittsburgh	NHL	19	0	1	1	20	....	....	....	....	....
	Baltimore	AHL	51	1	16	17	50	....	....	....	....	....
1987-88	Pittsburgh	NHL	44	3	6	9	69	....	....	....	....	....
1988-89	Pittsburgh	NHL	43	1	5	6	42	2	0	0	0	0
	Muskegon	IHL	10	3	6	9	14	....	....	....	....	....
1989-90	Pittsburgh	NHL	62	4	10	14	56	....	....	....	....	....
	Muskegon	IHL	6	1	1	2	8	....	....	....	....	....
1990-91	Pittsburgh	NHL	22	1	2	3	30	....	....	....	....	....
	Minnesota	NHL	42	2	6	8	33	23	1	6	7	20
1991-92	Minnesota	NHL	74	1	13	14	68	7	0	0	0	6
1992-93	Calgary	NHL	74	3	7	10	66	6	3	1	4	4
1993-94	Calgary	NHL	77	1	11	12	52	1	0	0	0	0
1994-95	Ottawa	NHL	46	1	7	8	36	....	....	....	....	....
1995-96	Ottawa	NHL	24	1	1	2	14	....	....	....	....	....
	Cincinnati	IHL	38	4	8	12	50	2	1	3	4	0
	NHL Totals		532	19	71	90	488	39	4	7	11	30

Signed as a free agent by **Pittsburgh**, May 7, 1985. Traded to **Minnesota** by **Pittsburgh** with Jim Johnson for Larry Murphy and Peter Taglianetti, December 11, 1990. Claimed by **Calgary** from **Minnesota** in NHL Waiver Draft, October 4, 1992. Signed as a free agent by **Ottawa**, July 4, 1994.

DAIGLE, ALEXANDRE (DAYG) OTT.

Center. Shoots left. 6', 185 lbs. Born, Montreal, Que., February 7, 1975.
(Ottawa's 1st choice, 1st overall, in 1993 Entry Draft).

			Regular Season					Playoffs				
Season	Club	Lea	GP	G	A	TP	PIM	GP	G	A	TP	PIM
1991-92ab	Victoriaville	QMJHL	66	35	75	110	63	....	....	....	....	....
1992-93c	Victoriaville	QMJHL	53	45	92	137	85	6	5	6	11	4
1993-94	Ottawa	NHL	84	20	31	51	40	....	....	....	....	....
1994-95	Victoriaville	QMJHL	18	14	20	34	16	....	....	....	....	....
	Ottawa	NHL	47	16	21	37	14	....	....	....	....	....
1995-96	Ottawa	NHL	50	5	12	17	24	....	....	....	....	....
	NHL Totals		181	41	64	105	78	....	....	....	....	....

a QMJHL Second All-Star Team (1992)
b Canadian Major Junior Rookie of the Year (1992)
c QMJHL First All-Star Team (1993)

DAIGNEAULT, JEAN-JACQUES (J.J.) (DAYN-yoh) PIT.

Defense. Shoots left. 5'10", 186 lbs. Born, Montreal, Que., October 12, 1965.
(Vancouver's 1st choice, 10th overall, in 1984 Entry Draft).

			Regular Season					Playoffs				
Season	Club	Lea	GP	G	A	TP	PIM	GP	G	A	TP	PIM
1981-82	Laval	QMJHL	64	4	25	29	41	18	1	3	4	2
1982-83a	Longueuil	QMJHL	70	26	58	84	58	15	4	11	15	35
1983-84	Cdn. National	....	55	5	14	19	40	....	....	....	....	....
	Cdn. Olympic	....	7	1	1	2	0	....	....	....	....	....
	Longueuil	QMJHL	10	2	11	13	6	14	3	13	16	30
1984-85	Vancouver	NHL	67	4	23	27	69	....	....	....	....	....
1985-86	Vancouver	NHL	64	5	23	28	45	3	0	2	2	0
1986-87	Philadelphia	NHL	77	6	16	22	56	9	1	0	1	0
1987-88	Philadelphia	NHL	28	2	2	4	12	....	....	....	....	....
	Hershey	AHL	10	1	5	6	8	....	....	....	....	....
1988-89	Hershey	AHL	12	0	10	10	13	....	....	....	....	....
	Sherbrooke	AHL	63	10	33	43	48	6	1	3	4	2
1989-90	Montreal	NHL	36	2	10	12	14	9	0	0	0	2
	Sherbrooke	AHL	28	8	19	27	18	....	....	....	....	....
1990-91	Montreal	NHL	51	3	16	19	31	5	0	1	1	0
1991-92	Montreal	NHL	79	4	14	18	36	11	0	3	3	4
1992-93	Montreal	NHL	66	8	10	18	57	20	1	3	4	22 ♦
1993-94	Montreal	NHL	68	2	12	14	73	7	0	1	1	12
1994-95	Montreal	NHL	45	3	5	8	40	....	....	....	....	....
1995-96	Montreal	NHL	7	0	1	1	6	....	....	....	....	....
	St. Louis	NHL	37	1	3	4	24	....	....	....	....	....
	Worcester	IHL	9	1	10	11	10	....	....	....	....	....
	Pittsburgh	NHL	13	3	3	6	23	17	1	9	10	36
	NHL Totals		638	43	138	181	486	81	3	19	22	76

a QMJHL First All-Star Team (1983)

Traded to **Philadelphia** by **Vancouver** with Vancouver's second round choice (Kent Hawley) in 1986 Entry Draft for Dave Richter, Rich Sutter and Vancouver's third round choice (previously acquired by Philadelphia — Vancouver selected Don Gibson) in 1986 Entry Draft, June 6, 1986. Traded to **Montreal** by **Philadelphia** for Scott Sandelin, November 7, 1988. Traded to **St. Louis** by **Montreal** for Pat Jablonski, November 7, 1995. Traded to **Pittsburgh** by **St. Louis** for Pittsburgh's sixth round choice (Stephen Wagner) in 1996 Entry Draft, March 20, 1996.

DALE, ANDREW L.A.

Center. Shoots left. 6'1", 196 lbs. Born, Sudbury, Ont., February 16, 1976.
(Los Angeles' 6th choice, 189th overall, in 1994 Entry Draft).

			Regular Season					Playoffs				
Season	Club	Lea	GP	G	A	TP	PIM	GP	G	A	TP	PIM
1993-94	Sudbury	OHL	53	8	13	21	21	9	0	3	3	4
1994-95	Sudbury	OHL	65	21	30	51	99	18	2	9	11	37
1995-96	Sudbury	OHL	40	32	24	56	47	....	....	....	....	....
	Kitchener	OHL	24	12	21	33	28	12	5	5	10	25

DALGARNO, BRAD

Right wing. Shoots right. 6'3", 215 lbs. Born, Vancouver, B.C., August 11, 1967.
(NY Islanders' 1st choice, 6th overall, in 1985 Entry Draft).

			Regular Season					Playoffs				
Season	Club	Lea	GP	G	A	TP	PIM	GP	G	A	TP	PIM
1984-85	Hamilton	OHA	66	23	30	53	86	....	....	....	....	....
1985-86	NY Islanders	NHL	2	1	0	1	0	....	....	....	....	....
	Hamilton	OHL	54	22	43	65	79	....	....	....	....	....
1986-87	Hamilton	OHL	60	27	32	59	100	....	....	....	....	....
	NY Islanders	NHL	....	....	....	....	....	1	0	1	1	0
1987-88	NY Islanders	NHL	38	2	8	10	58	4	0	0	0	19
	Springfield	AHL	39	13	11	24	76	....	....	....	....	....
1988-89	NY Islanders	NHL	55	11	10	21	86	....	....	....	....	....
1989-90					DID NOT PLAY							
1990-91	NY Islanders	NHL	41	3	12	15	24	....	....	....	....	....
	Capital Dist.	AHL	27	6	14	20	26	....	....	....	....	....
1991-92	NY Islanders	NHL	15	2	1	3	12	....	....	....	....	....
	Capital Dist.	AHL	14	7	8	15	34	....	....	....	....	....
1992-93	NY Islanders	NHL	57	15	17	32	62	18	2	2	4	14
	Capital Dist.	AHL	19	10	4	14	16	....	....	....	....	....
1993-94	NY Islanders	NHL	73	11	19	30	62	4	0	1	1	4
1994-95	NY Islanders	NHL	22	3	2	5	14	....	....	....	....	....
1995-96	NY Islanders	NHL	18	1	2	3	14	....	....	....	....	....
	NHL Totals		321	49	71	120	332	27	2	4	6	37

DAMPHOUSSE, VINCENT (DAHM-fooz) MTL.

Center. Shoots left. 6'1", 195 lbs. Born, Montreal, Que., December 17, 1967.
(Toronto's 1st choice, 6th overall, in 1986 Entry Draft).

			Regular Season					Playoffs				
Season	Club	Lea	GP	G	A	TP	PIM	GP	G	A	TP	PIM
1983-84	Laval	QMJHL	66	29	36	65	25	....	....	....	....	....
1984-85	Laval	QMJHL	68	35	68	103	62	....	....	....	....	....
1985-86a	Laval	QMJHL	69	45	110	155	70	14	9	27	36	12
1986-87	Toronto	NHL	80	21	25	46	26	12	1	5	6	8
1987-88	Toronto	NHL	75	12	36	48	40	6	0	1	1	10
1988-89	Toronto	NHL	80	26	42	68	75	....	....	....	....	....
1989-90	Toronto	NHL	80	33	61	94	56	5	0	2	2	2
1990-91	Toronto	NHL	79	26	47	73	65	....	....	....	....	....
1991-92	Edmonton	NHL	80	38	51	89	53	16	6	8	14	8
1992-93	Montreal	NHL	84	39	58	97	98	20	11	12	23	16 ♦
1993-94	Montreal	NHL	84	40	51	91	75	7	1	2	3	8
1994-95	Ratingen	Ger.	11	5	7	12	24	....	....	....	....	....
	Montreal	NHL	48	10	30	40	42	....	....	....	....	....
1995-96	Montreal	NHL	80	38	56	94	158	6	4	4	8	0
	NHL Totals		770	283	457	740	688	72	23	34	57	52

a QMJHL Second All-Star Team (1986)

Played in NHL All-Star Game (1991, 1992)

Traded to **Edmonton** by **Toronto** with Peter Ing, Scott Thornton, Luke Richardson, future considerations and cash for Grant Fuhr, Glenn Anderson and Craig Berube, September 19, 1991. Traded to **Montreal** by **Edmonton** with Edmonton's fourth round choice (Adam Wiesel) in 1993 Entry Draft for Shayne Corson, Brent Gilchrist and Vladimir Vujtek, August 27, 1992.

DANDENAULT, MATHIEU (DAHN-deh-noh) DET.

Right wing. Shoots right. 6', 174 lbs. Born, Sherbrooke, Que., February 3, 1976.
(Detroit's 2nd choice, 49th overall, in 1994 Entry Draft).

			Regular Season					Playoffs				
Season	Club	Lea	GP	G	A	TP	PIM	GP	G	A	TP	PIM
1993-94	Sherbrooke	QMJHL	67	17	36	53	67	12	4	10	14	12
1994-95	Sherbrooke	QMJHL	67	37	70	107	76	7	1	7	8	10
1995-96	Detroit	NHL	34	5	7	12	6	....	....	....	....	....
	Adirondack	AHL	4	0	0	0	0	....	....	....	....	....
	NHL Totals		34	5	7	12	6	....	....	....	....	....

DANEYKO, KEN (DAN-ee-KOH) N.J.

Defense. Shoots left. 6', 210 lbs. Born, Windsor, Ont., April 17, 1964.
(New Jersey's 2nd choice, 18th overall, in 1982 Entry Draft).

			Regular Season					Playoffs				
Season	Club	Lea	GP	G	A	TP	PIM	GP	G	A	TP	PIM
1980-81	Spokane	WHL	62	6	13	19	140	4	0	0	0	6
1981-82	Spokane	WHL	26	1	11	12	147	....	....	....	....	....
	Seattle	WHL	38	1	22	23	151	14	1	9	10	49
1982-83	Seattle	WHL	69	17	43	60	150	4	1	3	4	14
1983-84	New Jersey	NHL	11	1	4	5	17	....	....	....	....	....
	Kamloops	WH	19	6	28	34	52	17	4	9	13	28
1984-85	New Jersey	NHL	1	0	0	0	10	....	....	....	....	....
	Maine	AHL	80	4	9	13	206	11	1	3	4	36
1985-86	New Jersey	NHL	44	0	10	10	100	....	....	....	....	....
	Maine	AHL	21	3	2	5	75	....	....	....	....	....
1986-87	New Jersey	NHL	79	2	12	14	183	....	....	....	....	....
1987-88	New Jersey	NHL	80	5	7	12	239	20	1	6	7	83
1988-89	New Jersey	NHL	80	5	5	10	283	....	....	....	....	....
1989-90	New Jersey	NHL	74	6	15	21	216	6	2	0	2	21
1990-91	New Jersey	NHL	80	4	16	20	249	7	0	1	1	10
1991-92	New Jersey	NHL	80	1	7	8	170	7	0	3	3	16
1992-93	New Jersey	NHL	84	2	11	13	236	5	0	0	0	8
1993-94	New Jersey	NHL	78	1	9	10	176	20	0	1	1	45
1994-95	New Jersey	NHL	25	1	2	3	54	20	1	0	1	22 ♦
1995-96	New Jersey	NHL	80	2	4	6	115	....	....	....	....	....
	NHL Totals		796	30	102	132	2048	85	4	11	15	205

DANIELS, JEFF — HFD.

Left wing. Shoots left. 6'1", 200 lbs. Born, Oshawa, Ont., June 24, 1968.
(Pittsburgh's 6th choice, 109th overall, in 1986 Entry Draft).

			Regular Season					Playoffs				
Season	Club	Lea	GP	G	A	TP	PIM	GP	G	A	TP	PIM
1984-85	Oshawa	OHL	59	7	11	18	16	....	....	....	....	....
1985-86	Oshawa	OHL	62	13	19	32	23	6	0	1	1	0
1986-87	Oshawa	OHL	54	14	9	23	22	15	3	2	5	5
1987-88	Oshawa	OHL	64	29	39	68	59	4	2	3	5	0
1988-89	Muskegon	IHL	58	21	21	42	58	11	3	5	8	11
1989-90	Muskegon	IHL	80	30	47	77	39	6	1	1	2	7
1990-91	**Pittsburgh**	**NHL**	**11**	**0**	**2**	**2**	**2**	....	....	....	....	....
	Muskegon	IHL	62	23	29	52	18	5	1	3	4	2
1991-92	**Pittsburgh**	**NHL**	**2**	**0**	**0**	**0**	**0**	....	....	....	....	....
	Muskegon	IHL	44	19	16	35	38	10	5	4	9	9
1992-93	**Pittsburgh**	**NHL**	**58**	**5**	**4**	**9**	**14**	**12**	**3**	**2**	**5**	**0**
	Cleveland	IHL	3	2	1	3	0	....	....	....	....	....
1993-94	**Pittsburgh**	**NHL**	**63**	**3**	**5**	**8**	**20**	....	....	....	....	....
	Florida	**NHL**	**7**	**0**	**0**	**0**	**0**	....	....	....	....	....
1994-95	**Florida**	**NHL**	**3**	**0**	**0**	**0**	**0**	....	....	....	....	....
	Detroit	IHL	25	8	12	20	6	5	1	0	1	0
1995-96	Springfield	AHL	72	22	20	42	32	10	3	0	3	2
	NHL Totals		**144**	**8**	**11**	**19**	**36**	**12**	**3**	**2**	**5**	**0**

Traded to **Florida** by **Pittsburgh** for Greg Hawgood, March 19, 1994. Signed as a free agent by **Hartford**, August 18, 1995.

DANIELS, SCOTT — PHI.

Left wing. Shoots left. 6'3", 200 lbs. Born, Prince Albert, Sask., September 19, 1969.
(Hartford's 6th choice, 136th overall, in 1989 Entry Draft).

			Regular Season					Playoffs				
Season	Club	Lea	GP	G	A	TP	PIM	GP	G	A	TP	PIM
1986-87	Kamloops	WHL	43	6	4	10	68	....	....	....	....	....
	N. Westminster	WHL	19	4	7	11	30	....	....	....	....	....
1987-88	N. Westminster	WHL	37	6	11	17	157	....	....	....	....	....
	Regina	WHL	19	2	3	5	83	....	....	....	....	....
1988-89	Regina	WHL	64	21	26	47	241	....	....	....	....	....
1989-90	Regina	WHL	52	28	31	59	171	....	....	....	....	....
1990-91	Springfield	AHL	40	2	6	8	121	....	....	....	....	....
	Louisville	ECHL	9	5	3	8	34	1	0	2	2	0
1991-92	Springfield	AHL	54	7	15	22	213	10	0	0	0	32
1992-93	**Hartford**	**NHL**	**1**	**0**	**0**	**0**	**19**	....	....	....	....	....
	Springfield	AHL	60	11	12	23	181	12	2	7	9	12
1993-94	Springfield	AHL	52	9	11	20	185	6	0	1	1	53
1994-95	Springfield	AHL	48	9	5	14	277	....	....	....	....	....
	Hartford	**NHL**	**12**	**0**	**2**	**2**	**55**	....	....	....	....	....
1995-96	**Hartford**	**NHL**	**53**	**3**	**4**	**7**	**254**	....	....	....	....	....
	Springfield	AHL	6	4	1	5	17	....	....	....	....	....
	NHL Totals		**66**	**3**	**6**	**9**	**328**	....	....	....	....	....

Signed as a free agent by **Philadelphia**, June 27, 1996.

DARBY, CRAIG — PHI.

Center. Shoots right. 6'3", 200 lbs. Born, Oneida, NY, September 26, 1972.
(Montreal's 3rd choice, 43rd overall, in 1991 Entry Draft).

			Regular Season					Playoffs				
Season	Club	Lea	GP	G	A	TP	PIM	GP	G	A	TP	PIM
1991-92	Providence	H.E.	35	17	24	41	47	....	....	....	....	....
1992-93	Providence	H.E.	35	11	21	32	62	....	....	....	....	....
1993-94	Fredericton	AHL	66	23	33	56	51	....	....	....	....	....
1994-95	Fredericton	AHL	64	21	47	68	82	....	....	....	....	....
	Montreal	**NHL**	**10**	**0**	**2**	**2**	**0**	....	....	....	....	....
	NY Islanders	**NHL**	**3**	**0**	**0**	**0**	**0**	....	....	....	....	....
1995-96	**NY Islanders**	**NHL**	**10**	**0**	**2**	**2**	**0**	....	....	....	....	....
	Worcester	AHL	68	22	28	50	47	4	1	1	2	2
	NHL Totals		**23**	**0**	**4**	**4**	**0**	....	....	....	....	....

Traded to **NY Islanders** by **Montreal** with Kirk Muller and Mathieu Schneider for Pierre Turgeon and Vladimir Malakhov, April 5, 1995. Claimed on waivers by **Philadelphia** from **NY Islanders**, June 4, 1996.

DARLING, DION — MTL.

Defense. Shoots left. 6'3", 205 lbs. Born, Edmonton, Alta., October 22, 1974.
(Montreal's 7th choice, 125th overall, in 1993 Entry Draft).

			Regular Season					Playoffs				
Season	Club	Lea	GP	G	A	TP	PIM	GP	G	A	TP	PIM
1991-92	St. Albert	AJHL	29	5	15	20	101	....	....	....	....	....
1992-93	Spokane	WHL	69	1	4	5	168	9	0	1	1	14
1993-94	Spokane	WHL	45	1	8	9	190	....	....	....	....	....
	Moose Jaw	WHL	23	4	6	10	96	....	....	....	....	....
	Wheeling	ECHL	3	0	1	1	7	9	0	1	1	14
1994-95	Fredericton	AHL	51	0	2	2	153	....	....	....	....	....
	Wheeling	ECHL	4	0	0	0	24	....	....	....	....	....
1995-96	Fredericton	AHL	74	3	2	5	215	6	0	0	0	5

DAVIDSON, MATT — BUF.

Right wing. Shoots right. 6'2", 190 lbs. Born, Flin Flon, Man., August 9, 1977.
(Buffalo's 5th choice, 94th overall, in 1995 Entry Draft).

			Regular Season					Playoffs				
Season	Club	Lea	GP	G	A	TP	PIM	GP	G	A	TP	PIM
1993-94	Portland	WHL	59	4	12	16	18	10	0	0	0	4
1994-95	Portland	WHL	72	17	20	37	51	9	1	3	4	0
1995-96	Portland	WHL	70	24	26	50	96	7	2	2	4	2

DAVIDSSON, JOHAN — (DAH-vihd-suhn) — ANA.

Center. Shoots right. 5'11", 170 lbs. Born, Jonkoping, Sweden, January 6, 1976.
(Anaheim's 2nd choice, 28th overall, in 1994 Entry Draft).

			Regular Season					Playoffs				
Season	Club	Lea	GP	G	A	TP	PIM	GP	G	A	TP	PIM
1992-93	HV-71	Swe.	8	1	0	1	0	....	....	....	....	....
1993-94	HV-71	Swe.	38	2	5	7	4	....	....	....	....	....
1994-95	HV-71	Swe.	37	4	7	11	20	13	3	2	5	0
1995-96	HV-71	Swe.	39	7	11	18	20	4	0	2	2	0

DAVIS, JUSTIN — WSH.

Right wing. Shoots right. 6'2", 175 lbs. Born, Burlington, Ont., March 1, 1978.
(Washington's 7th choice, 85th overall, in 1996 Entry Draft).

			Regular Season					Playoffs				
Season	Club	Lea	GP	G	A	TP	PIM	GP	G	A	TP	PIM
1995-96	Kingston	OHL	64	30	18	48	20	6	2	3	5	0

DAVIS, RYAN — BUF.

Right wing. Shoots right. 6'2", 165 lbs. Born, Hamilton, Ont., February 16, 1978.
(Buffalo's 8th choice, 142nd overall, in 1996 Entry Draft).

			Regular Season					Playoffs				
Season	Club	Lea	GP	G	A	TP	PIM	GP	G	A	TP	PIM
1995-96	Owen Sound	OHL	60	11	9	20	62	5	1	0	1	5

DAWE, JASON — (DAW) — BUF.

Left wing. Shoots left. 5'10", 195 lbs. Born, North York, Ont., May 29, 1973.
(Buffalo's 2nd choice, 35th overall, in 1991 Entry Draft).

			Regular Season					Playoffs				
Season	Club	Lea	GP	G	A	TP	PIM	GP	G	A	TP	PIM
1989-90	Peterborough	OHL	50	15	18	33	19	12	4	7	11	4
1990-91	Peterborough	OHL	66	43	27	70	43	4	3	1	4	0
1991-92	Peterborough	OHL	66	53	55	108	55	4	5	0	5	0
1992-93abc	Peterborough	OHL	59	58	68	126	80	21	18	33	51	18
	Rochester	AHL	....	....	....	....	....	3	1	0	1	0
1993-94	**Buffalo**	**NHL**	**32**	**6**	**7**	**13**	**12**	**6**	**0**	**1**	**1**	**6**
	Rochester	AHL	48	22	14	36	44	....	....	....	....	....
1994-95	Rochester	AHL	44	27	19	46	24	....	....	....	....	....
	Buffalo	**NHL**	**42**	**7**	**4**	**11**	**19**	**5**	**2**	**1**	**3**	**6**
1995-96	**Buffalo**	**NHL**	**67**	**25**	**25**	**50**	**33**	....	....	....	....	....
	Rochester	AHL	7	5	4	9	2	....	....	....	....	....
	NHL Totals		**141**	**38**	**36**	**74**	**64**	**11**	**2**	**2**	**4**	**12**

a OHL First All-Star Team (1993)
b Canadian Major Junior Second All-Star Team (1993)
c Won George Parsons Trophy (Memorial Cup Tournament Most Sportsmanlike Player) (1993)

DAY, JOE — ANA.

Center. Shoots left. 5'11", 180 lbs. Born, Chicago, IL, May 11, 1968.
(Hartford's 8th choice, 186th overall, in 1987 Entry Draft).

			Regular Season					Playoffs				
Season	Club	Lea	GP	G	A	TP	PIM	GP	G	A	TP	PIM
1986-87	St. Lawrence	ECAC	33	9	11	20	25	....	....	....	....	....
1987-88	St. Lawrence	ECAC	30	21	16	37	36	....	....	....	....	....
1988-89	St. Lawrence	ECAC	36	21	27	48	44	....	....	....	....	....
1989-90a	St. Lawrence	ECAC	32	19	26	45	30	....	....	....	....	....
1990-91	Springfield	AHL	75	24	29	53	82	18	5	5	10	27
1991-92	**Hartford**	**NHL**	**24**	**0**	**3**	**3**	**10**	....	....	....	....	....
	Springfield	AHL	50	33	25	58	92	....	....	....	....	....
1992-93	**Hartford**	**NHL**	**24**	**1**	**7**	**8**	**47**	....	....	....	....	....
	Springfield	AHL	33	15	20	35	118	15	0	8	8	40
1993-94	**NY Islanders**	**NHL**	**24**	**0**	**0**	**0**	**30**	....	....	....	....	....
	Salt Lake	IHL	33	16	10	26	153	....	....	....	....	....
1994-95	Detroit	IHL	32	16	10	26	126	5	0	2	2	21
1995-96	Detroit	IHL	53	19	19	38	105	....	....	....	....	....
	Las Vegas	IHL	29	11	17	28	70	15	7	3	10	46
	NHL Totals		**72**	**1**	**10**	**11**	**87**	....	....	....	....	....

a ECAC Second All-Star Team (1990)

Signed as a free agent by **NY Islanders**, August 24, 1993. Signed as a free agent by **Anaheim**, August 19, 1996.

DAZE, ERIC — (dah-ZAY) — CHI.

Left wing. Shoots left. 6'4", 215 lbs. Born, Montreal, Que., July 2, 1975.
(Chicago's 5th choice, 90th overall, in 1993 Entry Draft).

			Regular Season					Playoffs				
Season	Club	Lea	GP	G	A	TP	PIM	GP	G	A	TP	PIM
1992-93	Beauport	QMJHL	68	19	36	55	24	....	....	....	....	....
1993-94a	Beauport	QMJHL	66	59	48	107	31	15	16	8	24	2
1994-95ab	Beauport	QMJHL	57	54	45	99	20	16	9	12	21	23
	Chicago	**NHL**	**4**	**1**	**1**	**2**	**2**	**16**	**0**	**1**	**1**	**4**
1995-96c	**Chicago**	**NHL**	**80**	**30**	**23**	**53**	**18**	**10**	**3**	**5**	**8**	**0**
	NHL Totals		**84**	**31**	**24**	**55**	**20**	**26**	**3**	**6**	**9**	**4**

a QMJHL First All-Star Team (1994, 1995)
b Canadian Major Junior Most Sportsmanlike Player of the Year (1995)
c NHL All-Rookie Team (1996)

DEADMARSH, ADAM — COL.

Center. Shoots right. 6', 195 lbs. Born, Trail, B.C., May 10, 1975.
(Quebec's 2nd choice, 14th overall, in 1993 Entry Draft).

			Regular Season					Playoffs				
Season	Club	Lea	GP	G	A	TP	PIM	GP	G	A	TP	PIM
1991-92	Portland	WHL	68	30	30	60	81	6	3	3	6	13
1992-93	Portland	WHL	58	33	36	69	126	16	7	8	15	29
1993-94	Portland	WHL	65	43	56	99	212	10	9	8	17	33
1994-95	Portland	WHL	29	28	20	48	129	....	....	....	....	....
	Quebec	**NHL**	**48**	**9**	**8**	**17**	**56**	**6**	**0**	**1**	**1**	**0**
1995-96	**Colorado**	**NHL**	**78**	**21**	**27**	**48**	**142**	**22**	**5**	**12**	**17**	**25** ♦
	NHL Totals		**126**	**30**	**35**	**65**	**198**	**28**	**5**	**13**	**18**	**25**

DEAN, KEVIN — N.J.

Defense. Shoots left. 6'2", 195 lbs. Born, Madison, WI, April 1, 1969.
(New Jersey's 4th choice, 86th overall, in 1987 Entry Draft).

			Regular Season					Playoffs				
Season	Club	Lea	GP	G	A	TP	PIM	GP	G	A	TP	PIM
1987-88	N. Hampshire	H.E.	27	1	6	7	34	....	....	....	....	....
1988-89	N. Hampshire	H.E.	34	1	12	13	28	....	....	....	....	....
1989-90	N. Hampshire	H.E.	39	2	6	8	42	....	....	....	....	....
1990-91	N. Hampshire	H.E.	31	10	12	22	22	....	....	....	....	....
	Utica	AHL	7	0	1	1	2	....	....	....	....	....
1991-92	Utica	AHL	23	0	3	3	6	....	....	....	....	....
	Cincinnati	ECHL	30	3	22	25	43	9	1	6	7	8
1992-93	Cincinnati	IHL	13	2	1	3	15	....	....	....	....	....
	Utica	AHL	57	2	16	18	76	5	1	0	1	8
1993-94	Albany	AHL	70	9	33	42	92	5	0	2	2	7
1994-95a	Albany	AHL	68	5	37	42	66	8	0	4	4	4
	New Jersey	**NHL**	**17**	**0**	**1**	**1**	**4**	**3**	**0**	**2**	**2**	**0** ♦
1995-96	**New Jersey**	**NHL**	**41**	**0**	**6**	**6**	**28**	....	....	....	....	....
	Albany	AHL	1	1	0	1	2	....	....	....	....	....
	NHL Totals		**58**	**0**	**7**	**7**	**32**	**3**	**0**	**2**	**2**	**0**

a AHL First All-Star Team (1995)

DEBRUSK, LOUIE (dah-BRUHSK) EDM.

Left wing. Shoots left. 6'2", 215 lbs. Born, Cambridge, Ont., March 19, 1971.
(NY Rangers' 4th choice, 49th overall, in 1989 Entry Draft).

			Regular Season					Playoffs				
Season	Club	Lea	GP	G	A	TP	PIM	GP	G	A	TP	PIM
1988-89	London	OHL	59	11	11	22	149	19	1	1	2	43
1989-90	London	OHL	61	21	19	40	198	6	2	2	4	24
1990-91	London	OHL	61	31	33	64	*223	7	2	2	4	14
	Binghamton	AHL	2	0	0	0	7	2	0	0	0	9
1991-92	**Edmonton**	**NHL**	**25**	**2**	**1**	**3**	**124**	....	....	....	....	....
	Cape Breton	AHL	28	2	2	4	73	....	....	....	....	....
1992-93	**Edmonton**	**NHL**	**51**	**8**	**2**	**10**	**205**	....	....	....	....	....
1993-94	**Edmonton**	**NHL**	**48**	**4**	**6**	**10**	**185**	....	....	....	....	....
	Cape Breton	AHL	5	3	1	4	58	....	....	....	....	....
1994-95	**Edmonton**	**NHL**	**34**	**2**	**0**	**2**	**93**	....	....	....	....	....
1995-96	**Edmonton**	**NHL**	**38**	**1**	**3**	**4**	**96**	....	....	....	....	....
	NHL Totals		**196**	**17**	**12**	**29**	**703**	....	....	....	....	....

Traded to **Edmonton** by **NY Rangers** with Bernie Nicholls and Steven Rice for Mark Messier and future considerations, October 4, 1991.

DECIANTIS, ROB PHO.

Center. Shoots left. 6', 175 lbs. Born, Toronto, Ont., June 11, 1977.
(Winnipeg's 11th choice, 214th overall, in 1995 Entry Draft).

			Regular Season					Playoffs				
Season	Club	Lea	GP	G	A	TP	PIM	GP	G	A	TP	PIM
1994-95	Kitchener	OHL	63	19	24	43	26	5	4	3	7	2
1995-96	Kitchener	OHL	33	27	36	63	37	10	4	6	10	16

DEEKS, ALAIN ANA.

Defense. Shoots right. 6'5", 230 lbs. Born, Hawkesbury, Ont., April 15, 1969.

			Regular Season					Playoffs				
Season	Club	Lea	GP	G	A	TP	PIM	GP	G	A	TP	PIM
1991-92	Columbus	ECHL	46	15	24	39	73	....	....	....	....	....
1992-93	Hamilton	AHL	18	0	6	6	6	....	....	....	....	....
	New Haven	AHL	1	0	0	0	0	....	....	....	....	....
	Columbus	ECHL	23	5	11	16	34	....	....	....	....	....
1993-94	P.E.I.	AHL	35	1	3	4	36	....	....	....	....	....
	Thunder Bay	ColHL	22	1	5	6	16	9	3	6	9	13
1994-95	Knoxville	ECHL	58	15	13	28	150	1	0	0	0	0
	Las Vegas	IHL	13	1	2	3	27	5	1	1	2	6
1995-96	Baltimore	AHL	35	1	1	2	21	....	....	....	....	....

Signed as a free agent by **Ottawa**, July 2, 1993. Signed as a free agent by **Anaheim**, July 10, 1995.

DELISLE, JONATHAN MTL.

Right wing. Shoots right. 5'10", 186 lbs. Born, Ste-Anne-des-Plaines, Que., June 30, 1977.
(Montreal's 4th choice, 86th overall, in 1995 Entry Draft).

			Regular Season					Playoffs				
Season	Club	Lea	GP	G	A	TP	PIM	GP	G	A	TP	PIM
1993-94	Verdun	QMJHL	61	16	17	33	130	4	0	1	1	14
1994-95	Hull	QMJHL	60	21	38	59	218	19	11	8	19	43
1995-96	Hull	QMJHL	62	31	57	88	193	18	6	13	19	64

DELISLE, XAVIER T.B.

Center. Shoots right. 5'11", 182 lbs. Born, Quebec City, Que., May 24, 1977.
(Tampa Bay's 5th choice, 157th overall, in 1996 Entry Draft).

			Regular Season					Playoffs				
Season	Club	Lea	GP	G	A	TP	PIM	GP	G	A	TP	PIM
1994-95	Granby	QMJHL	72	18	36	54	48	13	2	6	8	4
1995-96ab	Granby	QMJHL	67	45	75	120	45	20	13	*27	*40	12

a QMJHL Second All-Star Team (1996)
b Memorial Cup All-Star Team (1996)

DEMARTINIS, LUCIO TOR.

Left wing. Shoots left. 6'2", 182 lbs. Born, Montreal, Que., July 31, 1978.
(Toronto's 11th choice, 151st overall, in 1996 Entry Draft).

			Regular Season					Playoffs				
Season	Club	Lea	GP	G	A	TP	PIM	GP	G	A	TP	PIM
1995-96	Shawinigan	QMJHL	57	10	4	14	91	....	....	....	....	....

DEMITRA, PAVOL (deh-MIHT-rah) OTT.

Left wing. Shoots left. 6', 189 lbs. Born, Dubnica, Czech., November 29, 1974.
(Ottawa's 9th choice, 227th overall, in 1993 Entry Draft).

			Regular Season					Playoffs				
Season	Club	Lea	GP	G	A	TP	PIM	GP	G	A	TP	PIM
1991-92	Spartak Dubnica	Czech. 2	28	13	10	23	12	....	....	....	....	....
1992-93	Dukla Trencin	Czech.	46	10	18	28	....	....	....	....	....	....
	CAPEH Dubnica	Czech. 2	4	3	0	3	....	....	....	....	....	....
1993-94	**Ottawa**	**NHL**	**12**	**1**	**1**	**2**	**4**	....	....	....	....	....
	P.E.I.	AHL	41	18	23	41	8	....	....	....	....	....
1994-95	P.E.I.	AHL	61	26	48	74	23	5	0	7	7	0
	Ottawa	**NHL**	**16**	**4**	**3**	**7**	**0**	....	....	....	....	....
1995-96	**Ottawa**	**NHL**	**31**	**7**	**10**	**17**	**6**	....	....	....	....	....
	P.E.I.	AHL	48	28	53	81	44	....	....	....	....	....
	NHL Totals		**59**	**12**	**14**	**26**	**10**	....	....	....	....	....

DEMPSEY, NATHAN TOR.

Left wing. Shoots left. 6', 170 lbs. Born, Spruce Grove, Alta., July 14, 1974.
(Toronto's 11th choice, 148th overall, in 1992 Entry Draft).

			Regular Season					Playoffs				
Season	Club	Lea	GP	G	A	TP	PIM	GP	G	A	TP	PIM
1991-92	Regina	WHL	70	4	22	26	72	....	....	....	....	....
1992-93	Regina	WHL	72	12	29	41	95	13	3	8	11	14
	St. John's	AHL	....	....	....	....	....	2	0	0	0	0
1993-94a	Regina	WHL	56	14	36	50	100	4	0	0	0	4
1994-95	St. John's	AHL	74	7	30	37	91	5	1	0	1	11
1995-96	St. John's	AHL	73	5	15	20	103	4	1	0	1	9

a WHL East Second All-Star Team (1994)

DESCOTEAUX, MATTHIEU (DAY-koh-toh) EDM.

Defense. Shoots left. 6'3", 190 lbs. Born, Pierreville, Que., September 23, 1977.
(Edmonton's 2nd choice, 19th overall, in 1996 Entry Draft).

			Regular Season					Playoffs				
Season	Club	Lea	GP	G	A	TP	PIM	GP	G	A	TP	PIM
1994-95	Shawinigan	QMJHL	50	3	2	5	28	15	1	1	2	19
1995-96	Shawinigan	QMJHL	69	2	13	15	129	6	0	0	0	6

DESJARDINS, ERIC (deh-ZHAHR-dai) PHI.

Defense. Shoots right. 6'1", 200 lbs. Born, Rouyn, Que., June 14, 1969.
(Montreal's 3rd choice, 38th overall, in 1987 Entry Draft).

			Regular Season					Playoffs				
Season	Club	Lea	GP	G	A	TP	PIM	GP	G	A	TP	PIM
1986-87a	Granby	QMJHL	66	14	24	38	178	8	3	2	5	10
1987-88	Sherbrooke	AHL	3	0	0	0	6	4	0	2	2	2
b	Granby	QMJHL	62	18	49	67	138	5	0	3	3	10
1988-89	**Montreal**	**NHL**	**36**	**2**	**12**	**14**	**26**	**14**	**1**	**1**	**2**	**6**
1989-90	**Montreal**	**NHL**	**55**	**3**	**13**	**16**	**51**	**6**	**0**	**0**	**0**	**10**
1990-91	**Montreal**	**NHL**	**62**	**7**	**18**	**25**	**27**	**13**	**1**	**4**	**5**	**8**
1991-92	**Montreal**	**NHL**	**77**	**6**	**32**	**38**	**50**	**11**	**3**	**3**	**6**	**4**
1992-93	**Montreal**	**NHL**	**82**	**13**	**32**	**45**	**98**	**20**	**4**	**10**	**14**	**23** ♦
1993-94	**Montreal**	**NHL**	**84**	**12**	**23**	**35**	**97**	**7**	**0**	**2**	**2**	**4**
1994-95	**Montreal**	**NHL**	**9**	**0**	**6**	**6**	**2**	....	....	....	....	....
	Philadelphia	**NHL**	**34**	**5**	**18**	**23**	**12**	**15**	**4**	**4**	**8**	**10**
1995-96	**Philadelphia**	**NHL**	**80**	**7**	**40**	**47**	**45**	**12**	**0**	**6**	**6**	**2**
	NHL Totals		**519**	**55**	**194**	**249**	**408**	**98**	**13**	**30**	**43**	**67**

a QMJHL Second All-Star Team (1987)
b QMJHL First All-Star Team (1988)

Played in NHL All-Star Game (1992, 1996)

Traded to **Philadelphia** by **Montreal** with Gilbert Dionne and John LeClair for Mark Recchi and Philadelphia's third round choice (Martin Hohenberger) in 1995 Entry Draft, February 9, 1995.

DEULING, JARRETT NYI

Left wing. Shoots left. 6', 202 lbs. Born, Vernon, B.C., March 4, 1974.
(NY Islanders' 2nd choice, 56th overall, in 1992 Entry Draft).

			Regular Season					Playoffs				
Season	Club	Lea	GP	G	A	TP	PIM	GP	G	A	TP	PIM
1990-91	Kamloops	WHL	48	4	12	16	43	12	5	2	7	7
1991-92	Kamloops	WHL	68	28	26	54	79	17	10	6	16	18
1992-93	Kamloops	WHL	68	31	32	63	93	13	6	7	13	14
1993-94	Kamloops	WHL	70	44	59	103	171	18	*13	8	21	43
1994-95	Worcester	AHL	63	11	8	19	37	....	....	....	....	....
1995-96	**NY Islanders**	**NHL**	**14**	**0**	**1**	**1**	**11**	....	....	....	....	....
	Worcester	AHL	57	16	7	23	57	4	1	2	3	2
	NHL Totals		**14**	**0**	**1**	**1**	**11**	....	....	....	....	....

DEVEREAUX, BOYD EDM.

Center. Shoots left. 6', 175 lbs. Born, Seaforth, Ont., April 16, 1978.
(Edmonton's 1st choice, 6th overall, in 1996 Entry Draft).

			Regular Season					Playoffs				
Season	Club	Lea	GP	G	A	TP	PIM	GP	G	A	TP	PIM
1994-95	Stratford	Jr. B	45	31	74	105	21	....	....	....	....	....
1995-96	Kitchener	OHL	66	20	38	58	35	12	3	7	10	4

de VRIES, GREG EDM.

Defense. Shoots left. 6'3", 218 lbs. Born, Sundridge, Ont., January 4, 1973.

			Regular Season					Playoffs				
Season	Club	Lea	GP	G	A	TP	PIM	GP	G	A	TP	PIM
1991-92	Bowling Green	CCHA	24	0	3	3	20	....	....	....	....	....
1992-93	Niagara Falls	OHL	62	3	23	26	86	4	0	1	1	6
1993-94	Niagara Falls	OHL	64	5	40	45	135	....	....	....	....	....
	Cape Breton	AHL	9	0	0	0	11	1	0	0	0	0
1994-95	Cape Breton	AHL	77	5	19	24	68	....	....	....	....	....
1995-96	**Edmonton**	**NHL**	**13**	**1**	**1**	**2**	**12**	....	....	....	....	....
	Cape Breton	AHL	58	9	30	39	174	....	....	....	....	....
	NHL Totals		**13**	**1**	**1**	**2**	**12**	....	....	....	....	....

Signed as a free agent by **Edmonton**, March 20, 1994.

DEWOLF, JOSHUA N.J.

Defense. Shoots left. 6'2", 190 lbs. Born, Bloomington, MN, July 25, 1977.
(New Jersey's 3rd choice, 41st overall, in 1996 Entry Draft).

			Regular Season					Playoffs				
Season	Club	Lea	GP	G	A	TP	PIM	GP	G	A	TP	PIM
1994-95	Bloom.-Jeff.	HS	28	6	22	28	52	....	....	....	....	....
1995-96	Twin Cities	Jr. A	40	11	15	26	38	....	....	....	....	....

DEYELL, MARK TOR.

Center. Shoots right. 6', 180 lbs. Born, Regina, Sask., March 26, 1976.
(Toronto's 4th choice, 126th overall, in 1994 Entry Draft).

			Regular Season					Playoffs				
Season	Club	Lea	GP	G	A	TP	PIM	GP	G	A	TP	PIM
1993-94	Saskatoon	WHL	66	17	36	53	52	16	5	2	7	20
1994-95	Saskatoon	WHL	70	34	68	102	56	10	2	5	7	14
1995-96a	Saskatoon	WHL	69	61	*98	*159	122	4	0	5	5	8

a WHL East First All-Star Team (1996)

DHADPHALE, ANIKET (dahd-FAH-lee, AN-ih-keht) S.J.

Center. Shoots left. 6'3", 185 lbs. Born, Ann Arbor, MI, April 26, 1976.
(San Jose's 11th choice, 245th overall, in 1994 Entry Draft).

			Regular Season					Playoffs				
Season	Club	Lea	GP	G	A	TP	PIM	GP	G	A	TP	PIM
1994-95	Stratford	Jr. B	46	31	33	64	74	....	....	....	....	....
1995-96	Notre Dame	CCHA	34	13	7	20	34	....	....	....	....	....

DIDUCK, GERALD (DIH-duhk) HFD.

Defense. Shoots right. 6'2", 217 lbs. Born, Edmonton, Alta., April 6, 1965.
(NY Islanders' 2nd choice, 16th overall, in 1983 Entry Draft).

			Regular Season					Playoffs				
Season	Club	Lea	GP	G	A	TP	PIM	GP	G	A	TP	PIM
1981-82	Lethbridge	WHL	71	1	15	16	81	12	0	3	3	27
1982-83	Lethbridge	WHL	67	8	16	24	151	20	3	12	15	49
1983-84	Lethbridge	WHL	65	10	24	34	133	5	1	4	5	27
	Indianapolis	IHL	....	....	....	....	....	10	1	6	7	19
1984-85	NY Islanders	NHL	65	2	8	10	80	....	....	....	....	....
1985-86	NY Islanders	NHL	10	1	2	3	2	....	....	....	....	....
	Springfield	AHL	61	6	14	20	173	....	....	....	....	....
1986-87	NY Islanders	NHL	30	2	3	5	67	14	0	1	1	35
	Springfield	AHL	45	6	8	14	120	....	....	....	....	....
1987-88	NY Islanders	NHL	68	7	12	19	113	6	1	0	1	42
1988-89	NY Islanders	NHL	65	11	21	32	155	....	....	....	....	....
1989-90	NY Islanders	NHL	76	3	17	20	163	5	0	0	0	12
1990-91	Montreal	NHL	32	1	2	3	39	....	....	....	....	....
	Vancouver	NHL	31	3	7	10	66	6	1	0	1	11
1991-92	Vancouver	NHL	77	6	21	27	229	5	0	0	0	10
1992-93	Vancouver	NHL	80	6	14	20	171	12	4	2	6	12
1993-94	Vancouver	NHL	55	1	10	11	72	24	1	7	8	22
1994-95	Vancouver	NHL	22	1	3	4	15	....	....	....	....	....
	Chicago	NHL	13	1	0	1	48	16	1	3	4	22
1995-96	Hartford	NHL	79	1	9	10	88	....	....	....	....	....
	NHL Totals		**703**	**46**	**129**	**175**	**1308**	**88**	**8**	**13**	**21**	**166**

Traded to **Montreal** by **NY Islanders** for Craig Ludwig, September 4, 1990. Traded to **Vancouver** by **Montreal** for Vancouver's fourth round choice (Vladimir Vujtek) in 1991 Entry Draft, January 12, 1991. Traded to **Chicago** by **Vancouver** for Bogdan Savenko and Hartford's third round choice (previously acquired by Chicago — Vancouver selected Larry Courville) in 1995 Entry Draft, April 7, 1995. Signed as a free agent by **Hartford**, August 24, 1995.

DILLABOUGH, TRAVIS L.A.

Center. Shoots left. 6', 175 lbs. Born, Peterborough, Ont., June 20, 1975.
(Los Angeles' 9th choice, 198th overall, in 1993 Entry Draft).

			Regular Season					Playoffs				
Season	Club	Lea	GP	G	A	TP	PIM	GP	G	A	TP	PIM
1993-94	Providence	H.E.	33	4	8	12	42	....	....	....	....	....
1994-95	Providence	H.E.	37	3	11	14	48	....	....	....	....	....
1995-96	Providence	H.E.	37	11	11	22	60	....	....	....	....	....

DiMAIO, ROB (duh-MIGH-oh) PHI.

Center. Shoots right. 5'10", 190 lbs. Born, Calgary, Alta., February 19, 1968.
(NY Islanders' 6th choice, 118th overall, in 1987 Entry Draft).

			Regular Season					Playoffs				
Season	Club	Lea	GP	G	A	TP	PIM	GP	G	A	TP	PIM
1986-87	Medicine Hat	WHL	70	27	43	70	130	20	7	11	18	46
1987-88a	Medicine Hat	WHL	54	47	43	90	120	14	12	19	*31	59
1988-89	NY Islanders	NHL	16	1	0	1	30	....	....	....	....	....
	Springfield	AHL	40	13	18	31	67	....	....	....	....	....
1989-90	NY Islanders	NHL	7	0	0	0	2	1	1	0	1	4
	Springfield	AHL	54	25	27	52	69	16	4	7	11	45
1990-91	NY Islanders	NHL	1	0	0	0	0	....	....	....	....	....
	Capital Dist.	AHL	12	3	4	7	22	....	....	....	....	....
1991-92	NY Islanders	NHL	50	5	2	7	43	....	....	....	....	....
1992-93	Tampa Bay	NHL	54	9	15	24	62	....	....	....	....	....
1993-94	Tampa Bay	NHL	39	8	7	15	40	....	....	....	....	....
	Philadelphia	NHL	14	3	5	8	6	....	....	....	....	....
1994-95	Philadelphia	NHL	36	3	1	4	53	15	2	4	6	4
1995-96	Philadelphia	NHL	59	6	15	21	58	3	0	0	0	0
	NHL Totals		**276**	**35**	**45**	**80**	**294**	**19**	**3**	**4**	**7**	**8**

a Won Stafford Smythe Memorial Trophy (Memorial Cup Tournament MVP) (1988)

Claimed by **Tampa Bay** from **NY Islanders** in Expansion Draft, June 18, 1992. Traded to **Philadelphia** by **Tampa Bay** for Jim Cummins and Philadelphia's fourth round choice in 1995 Entry Draft, March 18, 1994.

DINEEN, GORD

Defense. Shoots right. 6', 195 lbs. Born, Quebec City, Que., September 21, 1962.
(NY Islanders' 2nd choice, 42nd overall, in 1981 Entry Draft).

			Regular Season					Playoffs				
Season	Club	Lea	GP	G	A	TP	PIM	GP	G	A	TP	PIM
1980-81	S.S. Marie	OHA	68	4	26	30	158	19	1	7	8	58
1981-82	S.S. Marie	OHL	68	9	45	54	185	13	1	2	3	52
1982-83	NY Islanders	NHL	2	0	0	0	4	....	....	....	....	....
abc	Indianapolis	CHL	73	10	47	57	78	13	2	10	12	29
1983-84	NY Islanders	NHL	43	1	11	12	32	9	1	1	2	28
	Indianapolis	CHL	26	4	13	17	63	....	....	....	....	....
1984-85	NY Islanders	NHL	48	1	12	13	89	10	0	0	0	26
	Springfield	AHL	25	1	8	9	46	....	....	....	....	....
1985-86	NY Islanders	NHL	57	1	8	9	81	3	0	0	0	2
	Springfield	AHL	11	2	3	5	20	....	....	....	....	....
1986-87	NY Islanders	NHL	71	4	10	14	110	7	0	4	4	4
1987-88	NY Islanders	NHL	57	4	12	16	62	....	....	....	....	....
	Minnesota	NHL	13	1	1	2	21	....	....	....	....	....
1988-89	Minnesota	NHL	2	0	1	1	2	....	....	....	....	....
	Kalamazoo	IHL	25	2	6	8	49	....	....	....	....	....
	Pittsburgh	NHL	38	1	2	3	42	11	0	2	2	8
1989-90	Pittsburgh	NHL	69	1	8	9	125	....	....	....	....	....
1990-91	Pittsburgh	NHL	9	0	0	0	4	....	....	....	....	....
	Muskegon	IHL	40	1	14	15	57	5	0	2	2	0
1991-92	Pittsburgh	NHL	1	0	0	0	0	....	....	....	....	....
d	Muskegon	IHL	79	8	37	45	83	14	2	4	6	33
1992-93	Ottawa	NHL	32	2	4	6	30	....	....	....	....	....
	San Diego	IHL	41	6	23	29	36	....	....	....	....	....
1993-94	Ottawa	NHL	77	0	21	21	89	....	....	....	....	....
	San Diego	IHL	3	0	0	0	2	....	....	....	....	....
1994-95	Denver	IHL	68	5	27	32	75	17	1	6	7	8
	NY Islanders	NHL	9	0	0	0	2	....	....	....	....	....
1995-96	Utah	IHL	82	1	17	18	89	22	0	3	3	14
	NHL Totals		**528**	**16**	**90**	**106**	**693**	**40**	**1**	**7**	**8**	**68**

a CHL First All-Star Team (1983)
b Won Bob Gassoff Trophy (CHL's Most Improved Defenseman) (1983)
c Won Bobby Orr Trophy (CHL's Top Defenseman) (1983)
d IHL First All-Star Team (1992)

Traded to **Minnesota** by **NY Islanders** for Chris Pryor and future considerations, March 8, 1988. Traded to **Pittsburgh** by **Minnesota** with Scott Bjugstad for Ville Siren and Steve Gotaas, December 17, 1988. Signed as a free agent by **Ottawa**, August 31, 1992. Signed as a free agent by **NY Islanders**, July 26, 1994.

DINEEN, KEVIN HFD.

Right wing. Shoots right. 5'11", 190 lbs. Born, Quebec City, Que., October 28, 1963.
(Hartford's 3rd choice, 56th overall, in 1982 Entry Draft).

			Regular Season					Playoffs				
Season	Club	Lea	GP	G	A	TP	PIM	GP	G	A	TP	PIM
1981-82	U. of Denver	WCHA	26	10	10	20	70	....	....	....	....	....
1982-83	U. of Denver	WCHA	36	16	13	29	108	....	....	....	....	....
1983-84	Cdn. National	....	52	5	11	16	2	....	....	....	....	....
	Cdn Olympic	....	7	0	0	0	0	....	....	....	....	....
1984-85	Hartford	NHL	57	25	16	41	120	....	....	....	....	....
	Binghamton	AHL	25	15	8	23	41	....	....	....	....	....
1985-86	Hartford	NHL	57	33	35	68	124	10	6	7	13	18
1986-87	Hartford	NHL	78	40	39	79	110	6	2	1	3	31
1987-88	Hartford	NHL	74	25	25	50	217	6	4	4	8	8
1988-89	Hartford	NHL	79	45	44	89	167	4	1	0	1	10
1989-90	Hartford	NHL	67	25	41	66	164	6	3	2	5	18
1990-91a	Hartford	NHL	61	17	30	47	104	6	1	0	1	16
1991-92	Hartford	NHL	16	4	2	6	23	....	....	....	....	....
	Philadelphia	NHL	64	26	30	56	130	....	....	....	....	....
1992-93	Philadelphia	NHL	83	35	28	63	201	....	....	....	....	....
1993-94	Philadelphia	NHL	71	19	23	42	113	....	....	....	....	....
1994-95	Houston	IHL	17	6	4	10	42	....	....	....	....	....
	Philadelphia	NHL	40	8	5	13	39	15	6	4	10	18
1995-96	Philadelphia	NHL	26	0	2	2	50	....	....	....	....	....
	Hartford	NHL	20	2	7	9	67	....	....	....	....	....
	NHL Totals		**793**	**304**	**327**	**631**	**1629**	**53**	**23**	**18**	**41**	**119**

a Won Bud Light/NHL Man of the Year Award (1991)

Played in NHL All-Star Game (1988, 1989)

Traded to **Philadelphia** by **Hartford** for Murray Craven and Philadelphia's fourth round choice (Kevin Smyth) in 1992 Entry Draft, November 13, 1991. Traded to **Hartford** by **Philadelphia** for a conditional choice in 1997 Entry Draft, December 28, 1995.

DINGMAN, CHRIS CGY.

Left wing. Shoots left. 6'4", 225 lbs. Born, Edmonton, Alta., July 6, 1976.
(Calgary's 1st choice, 19th overall, in 1994 Entry Draft).

			Regular Season					Playoffs				
Season	Club	Lea	GP	G	A	TP	PIM	GP	G	A	TP	PIM
1992-93	Brandon	WHL	50	10	17	27	64	4	0	0	0	0
1993-94	Brandon	WHL	45	21	20	41	77	13	1	7	8	39
1994-95	Brandon	WHL	66	40	43	83	201	3	1	0	1	9
1995-96	Brandon	WHL	40	16	29	45	109	19	12	11	23	60
	Saint John	AHL	....	....	....	....	....	1	0	0	0	0

DIONNE, GILBERT (dee-AHN, ZHIHL-bair) FLA.

Left wing. Shoots left. 6', 194 lbs. Born, Drummondville, Que., September 19, 1970.
(Montreal's 5th choice, 81st overall, in 1990 Entry Draft).

			Regular Season					Playoffs				
Season	Club	Lea	GP	G	A	TP	PIM	GP	G	A	TP	PIM
1988-89	Kitchener	OHL	66	11	33	44	13	5	1	1	2	4
1989-90	Kitchener	OHL	64	48	57	105	85	17	13	10	23	22
1990-91	Montreal	NHL	2	0	0	0	0	....	....	....	....	....
	Fredericton	AHL	77	40	47	87	62	9	6	5	11	8
1991-92a	Montreal	NHL	39	21	13	34	10	11	3	4	7	10
	Fredericton	AHL	29	19	27	46	20	....	....	....	....	....
1992-93	Montreal	NHL	75	20	28	48	63	20	6	6	12	20 ♦
	Fredericton	AHL	3	4	3	7	0	....	....	....	....	....
1993-94	Montreal	NHL	74	19	26	45	31	5	1	2	3	0
1994-95	Montreal	NHL	6	0	3	3	2	....	....	....	....	....
	Philadelphia	NHL	20	0	6	6	2	3	0	0	0	4
1995-96	Philadelphia	NHL	2	0	1	1	0	....	....	....	....	....
	Florida	NHL	5	1	2	3	0	....	....	....	....	....
b	Carolina	AHL	55	43	58	101	29	....	....	....	....	....
	NHL Totals		**223**	**61**	**79**	**140**	**108**	**39**	**10**	**12**	**22**	**34**

a NHL/Upper Deck All-Rookie Team (1992)
b AHL Second All-Star Team (1996)

Traded to **Philadelphia** by **Montreal** with Eric Desjardins and John LeClair for Mark Recchi and Philadelphia's third round choice (Martin Hohenberger) in 1995 Entry draft, February 9, 1995. Signed as a free agent by **Florida**, January 29, 1996.

DI PIETRO, PAUL (dee-pee-AY-troh) L.A.

Center. Shoots right. 5'9", 181 lbs. Born, Sault Ste. Marie, Ont., September 8, 1970.
(Montreal's 6th choice, 102nd overall, in 1990 Entry Draft).

			Regular Season					Playoffs				
Season	Club	Lea	GP	G	A	TP	PIM	GP	G	A	TP	PIM
1986-87	Sudbury	OHL	49	5	11	16	13	....	....	....	....	....
1987-88	Sudbury	OHL	63	25	42	67	27	....	....	....	....	....
1988-89	Sudbury	OHL	57	31	48	79	27	....	....	....	....	....
1989-90	Sudbury	OHL	66	56	63	119	57	7	3	6	9	7
1990-91	Fredericton	AHL	78	39	31	70	38	9	5	6	11	2
1991-92	Montreal	NHL	33	4	6	10	25	....	....	....	....	....
	Fredericton	AHL	43	26	31	57	52	7	3	4	7	8
1992-93	Montreal	NHL	29	4	13	17	14	17	8	5	13	8 ♦
	Fredericton	AHL	26	8	16	24	16	....	....	....	....	....
1993-94	Montreal	NHL	70	13	20	33	37	7	2	4	6	2
1994-95	Montreal	NHL	22	4	5	9	4	....	....	....	....	....
	Toronto	NHL	12	1	1	2	6	7	1	1	2	0
1995-96	Toronto	NHL	20	4	4	8	4	....	....	....	....	....
	St. John's	AHL	2	2	2	4	0	....	....	....	....	....
	Houston	IHL	36	18	23	41	44	....	....	....	....	....
	Las Vegas	IHL	13	5	6	11	10	13	4	8	12	16
	NHL Totals		**186**	**30**	**49**	**79**	**90**	**31**	**11**	**10**	**21**	**10**

Traded to **Toronto** by **Montreal** for a conditional fourth round draft choice, April 6, 1995. Signed as a free agent by **Los Angeles**, July 23, 1996.

DIRK, ROBERT

Defense. Shoots left. 6'4", 210 lbs. Born, Regina, Sask., August 20, 1966.
(St. Louis' 4th choice, 53rd overall, in 1984 Entry Draft).

			Regular Season					Playoffs				
Season	Club	Lea	GP	G	A	TP	PIM	GP	G	A	TP	PIM
1982-83	Regina	WHL	1	0	0	0	0	....	....	....	....	....
1983-84	Regina	WHL	62	2	10	12	64	23	1	12	13	24
1984-85	Regina	WHL	69	10	34	44	97	8	0	0	0	4
1985-86	Regina	WHL	72	19	60	79	140	10	3	5	8	8
1986-87	Peoria	IHL	76	5	17	22	155	....	....	....	....	....
1987-88	**St. Louis**	**NHL**	**7**	**0**	**1**	**1**	**16**	**6**	**0**	**1**	**1**	**2**
	Peoria	IHL	54	4	21	25	126	....	....	....	....	....
1988-89	**St. Louis**	**NHL**	**9**	**0**	**1**	**1**	**11**	....	....	....	....	....
	Peoria	IHL	22	0	2	2	54	....	....	....	....	....
1989-90	**St. Louis**	**NHL**	**37**	**1**	**1**	**2**	**128**	**3**	**0**	**0**	**0**	**0**
	Peoria	IHL	24	1	2	3	79	....	....	....	....	....
1990-91	**St. Louis**	**NHL**	**41**	**1**	**3**	**4**	**100**	....	....	....	....	....
	Peoria	IHL	3	0	0	0	2	....	....	....	....	....
	Vancouver	**NHL**	**11**	**1**	**0**	**1**	**20**	**6**	**0**	**0**	**0**	**13**
1991-92	**Vancouver**	**NHL**	**72**	**2**	**7**	**9**	**126**	**13**	**0**	**0**	**0**	**20**
1992-93	**Vancouver**	**NHL**	**69**	**4**	**8**	**12**	**150**	**9**	**0**	**0**	**0**	**6**
1993-94	**Vancouver**	**NHL**	**65**	**2**	**3**	**5**	**105**	....	....	....	....	....
	Chicago	**NHL**	**6**	**0**	**0**	**0**	**26**	**2**	**0**	**0**	**0**	**15**
1994-95	**Anaheim**	**NHL**	**38**	**1**	**3**	**4**	**56**	....	....	....	....	....
1995-96	**Anaheim**	**NHL**	**44**	**1**	**2**	**3**	**42**	....	....	....	....	....
	Montreal	**NHL**	**3**	**0**	**0**	**0**	**6**	....	....	....	....	....
	NHL Totals		**402**	**13**	**29**	**42**	**786**	**39**	**0**	**1**	**1**	**56**

Traded to **Vancouver** by **St. Louis** with Geoff Courtnall, Sergio Momesso, Cliff Ronning and St. Louis' fifth round choice (Brian Loney) in 1992 Entry Draft for Dan Quinn and Garth Butcher, March 5, 1991. Traded to **Chicago** by **Vancouver** for Chicago's fourth round choice (Mike Dubinsky) in 1994 Entry Draft, March 21, 1994. Traded to **Anaheim** by **Chicago** for Tampa Bay's fourth round choice (previously acquired by Anaheim — Chicago selected Chris Van Dyk) in 1995 Entry Draft, July 12, 1994. Traded to **Montreal** by **Anaheim** for Jim Campbell, January 21, 1996.

DOAN, SHANE — PHO.

Right wing. Shoots right. 6'1", 215 lbs. Born, Halkirk, Alta., October 10, 1976.
(Winnipeg's 1st choice, 7th overall, in 1995 Entry Draft).

			Regular Season					Playoffs				
Season	Club	Lea	GP	G	A	TP	PIM	GP	G	A	TP	PIM
1992-93	Kamloops	WHL	51	7	12	19	65	13	0	1	1	8
1993-94	Kamloops	WHL	52	24	24	48	88	....	....	....	....	....
1994-95ab	Kamloops	WHL	71	37	57	94	106	21	6	10	16	16
1995-96	**Winnipeg**	**NHL**	**74**	**7**	**10**	**17**	**101**	**6**	**0**	**0**	**0**	**6**
	NHL Totals		**74**	**7**	**10**	**17**	**101**	**6**	**0**	**0**	**0**	**6**

a Memorial Cup All-Star Team (1995)
b Won Stafford Smythe Memorial Trophy (Memorial Cup Tournament MVP) (1995)

DOIG, JASON — PHO.

Defense. Shoots right. 6'3", 216 lbs. Born, Montreal, Que., January 29, 1977.
(Winnipeg's 3rd choice, 34th overall, in 1995 Entry Draft).

			Regular Season					Playoffs				
Season	Club	Lea	GP	G	A	TP	PIM	GP	G	A	TP	PIM
1993-94	St-Jean	QMJHL	63	8	17	25	65	5	0	2	2	2
1994-95	Laval	QMJHL	55	13	42	55	259	20	4	13	17	39
1995-96	**Winnipeg**	**NHL**	**15**	**1**	**1**	**2**	**28**	....	....	....	....	....
	Laval	QMJHL	5	3	6	9	20	....	....	....	....	....
a	Granby	QMJHL	24	4	30	34	91	20	10	22	32	*110
	Springfield	AHL	5	0	0	0	28	....	....	....	....	....
	NHL Totals		**15**	**1**	**1**	**2**	**28**	....	....	....	....	....

a Memorial Cup All-Star Team (1996)

DOLLAS, BOBBY — ANA.

Defense. Shoots left. 6'2", 212 lbs. Born, Montreal, Que., January 31, 1965.
(Winnipeg's 2nd choice, 14th overall, in 1983 Entry Draft).

			Regular Season					Playoffs				
Season	Club	Lea	GP	G	A	TP	PIM	GP	G	A	TP	PIM
1982-83a	Laval	QMJHL	63	16	45	61	144	11	5	5	10	23
1983-84	**Winnipeg**	**NHL**	**1**	**0**	**0**	**0**	**0**	....	....	....	....	....
	Laval	QMJHL	54	12	33	45	80	14	1	8	9	23
1984-85	**Winnipeg**	**NHL**	**9**	**0**	**0**	**0**	**0**	....	....	....	....	....
	Sherbrooke	AHL	8	1	3	4	4	17	3	6	9	17
1985-86	**Winnipeg**	**NHL**	**46**	**0**	**5**	**5**	**66**	**3**	**0**	**0**	**0**	**2**
	Sherbrooke	AHL	25	4	7	11	29	....	....	....	....	....
1986-87	Sherbrooke	AHL	75	6	18	24	87	16	2	4	6	13
1987-88	**Quebec**	**NHL**	**9**	**0**	**0**	**0**	**2**	....	....	....	....	....
	Moncton	AHL	26	4	10	14	20	....	....	....	....	....
	Fredericton	AHL	33	4	8	12	27	15	2	2	4	24
1988-89	**Quebec**	**NHL**	**16**	**0**	**3**	**3**	**16**	....	....	....	....	....
	Halifax	AHL	57	5	19	24	65	4	1	0	1	14
1989-90	Cdn. National	....	68	8	29	37	60	....	....	....	....	....
1990-91	**Detroit**	**NHL**	**56**	**3**	**5**	**8**	**20**	**7**	**1**	**0**	**1**	**13**
1991-92	**Detroit**	**NHL**	**27**	**3**	**1**	**4**	**20**	**2**	**0**	**1**	**1**	**0**
	Adirondack	AHL	19	1	6	7	33	18	7	4	11	22
1992-93	**Detroit**	**NHL**	**6**	**0**	**0**	**0**	**2**	....	....	....	....	....
c	Adirondack	AHL	64	7	36	43	54	11	3	8	11	8
1993-94	**Anaheim**	**NHL**	**77**	**9**	**11**	**20**	**55**	....	....	....	....	....
1994-95	**Anaheim**	**NHL**	**45**	**7**	**13**	**20**	**12**	....	....	....	....	....
1995-96	**Anaheim**	**NHL**	**82**	**8**	**22**	**30**	**64**	....	....	....	....	....
	NHL Totals		**374**	**30**	**60**	**90**	**257**	**12**	**1**	**1**	**2**	**15**

a QMJHL Second All-Star Team (1983)
b Won Eddie Shore Plaque (AHL's Outstanding Defenseman) (1993)
c AHL First All-Star Team (1993)

Traded to **Quebec** by **Winnipeg** for Stu Kulak, December 17, 1987. Signed as a free agent by **Detroit**, October 18, 1990. Claimed by **Anaheim** from **Detroit** in Expansion Draft, June 24, 1993.

DOMENICHELLI, HNAT — HFD.

Center. Shoots left. 6', 175 lbs. Born, Edmonton, Alta., February 17, 1976.
(Hartford's 2nd choice, 83rd overall, in 1994 Entry Draft).

			Regular Season					Playoffs				
Season	Club	Lea	GP	G	A	TP	PIM	GP	G	A	TP	PIM
1992-93	Kamloops	WHL	45	12	8	20	15	11	1	1	2	2
1993-94	Kamloops	WHL	69	27	40	67	31	19	10	12	22	0
1994-95a	Kamloops	WHL	72	52	62	114	34	19	9	9	18	9
1995-96bc	Kamloops	WHL	62	59	89	148	37	16	7	9	16	29

a WHL West Second All-Star Team (1995)
b WHL West First All-Star Team (1996)
c Canadian Major Junior First All-Star Team (1996)

DOMI, TIE — (DOH-mee) TOR.

Right wing. Shoots right. 5'10", 200 lbs. Born, Windsor, Ont., November 1, 1969.
(Toronto's 2nd choice, 27th overall, in 1988 Entry Draft).

			Regular Season					Playoffs				
Season	Club	Lea	GP	G	A	TP	PIM	GP	G	A	TP	PIM
1986-87	Peterborough	OHL	18	1	1	2	79	....	....	....	....	....
1987-88	Peterborough	OHL	60	22	21	43	292	12	3	9	12	24
1988-89	Peterborough	OHL	43	14	16	30	175	17	10	9	19	70
1989-90	**Toronto**	**NHL**	**2**	**0**	**0**	**0**	**42**	....	....	....	....	....
	Newmarket	AHL	57	14	11	25	285	....	....	....	....	....
1990-91	**NY Rangers**	**NHL**	**28**	**1**	**0**	**1**	**185**	....	....	....	....	....
	Binghamton	AHL	25	11	6	17	219	7	3	2	5	16
1991-92	**NY Rangers**	**NHL**	**42**	**2**	**4**	**6**	**246**	**6**	**1**	**1**	**2**	**32**
1992-93	**NY Rangers**	**NHL**	**12**	**2**	**0**	**2**	**95**	....	....	....	....	....
	Winnipeg	**NHL**	**49**	**3**	**10**	**13**	**249**	**6**	**1**	**0**	**1**	**23**
1993-94	**Winnipeg**	**NHL**	**81**	**8**	**11**	**19**	***347**	....	....	....	....	....
1994-95	**Winnipeg**	**NHL**	**31**	**4**	**4**	**8**	**128**	....	....	....	....	....
	Toronto	**NHL**	**9**	**0**	**1**	**1**	**31**	**7**	**1**	**0**	**1**	**0**
1995-96	**Toronto**	**NHL**	**72**	**7**	**6**	**13**	**297**	**6**	**0**	**2**	**2**	**4**
	NHL Totals		**326**	**27**	**36**	**63**	**1620**	**25**	**3**	**3**	**6**	**59**

Traded to **NY Rangers** by **Toronto** with Mark LaForest for Greg Johnston, June 28, 1990. Traded to **Winnipeg** by **NY Rangers** with Kris King for Ed Olczyk, December 28, 1992. Traded to **Toronto** by **Winnipeg** for Mike Eastwood and Toronto's third round choice (Brad Isbister) in 1995 Entry Draft, April 7, 1995.

DONATO, TED — (duh-NAH-toh) BOS.

Left wing. Shoots left. 5'10", 181 lbs. Born, Boston, MA, April 28, 1969.
(Boston's 6th choice, 98th overall, in 1987 Entry Draft).

			Regular Season					Playoffs				
Season	Club	Lea	GP	G	A	TP	PIM	GP	G	A	TP	PIM
1987-88	Harvard	ECAC	28	12	14	26	24	....	....	....	....	....
1988-89	Harvard	ECAC	34	14	37	51	30	....	....	....	....	....
1989-90	Harvard	ECAC	16	5	6	11	34	....	....	....	....	....
1990-91a	Harvard	ECAC	27	19	*37	56	26	....	....	....	....	....
1991-92	U.S. National	....	52	11	22	33	24	....	....	....	....	....
	U.S. Olympic	....	8	4	3	7	8	....	....	....	....	....
	Boston	**NHL**	**10**	**1**	**2**	**3**	**8**	**15**	**3**	**4**	**7**	**4**
1992-93	**Boston**	**NHL**	**82**	**15**	**20**	**35**	**61**	**4**	**0**	**1**	**1**	....
1993-94	**Boston**	**NHL**	**84**	**22**	**32**	**54**	**59**	**13**	**4**	**2**	**6**	**10**
1994-95	TuTo	Fin.	14	5	5	10	47	....	....	....	....	....
	Boston	**NHL**	**47**	**10**	**10**	**20**	**10**	**5**	**0**	**0**	**0**	**4**
1995-96	**Boston**	**NHL**	**82**	**23**	**26**	**49**	**46**	**5**	**1**	**2**	**3**	**2**
	NHL Totals		**305**	**71**	**90**	**161**	**184**	**42**	**8**	**9**	**17**	**20**

a ECAC First All-Star Team (1991)

DONNELLY, GORD

Defense. Shoots right. 6'1", 202 lbs. Born, Montreal, Que., April 5, 1962.
(St. Louis' 3rd choice, 62nd overall, in 1981 Entry Draft).

			Regular Season					Playoffs				
Season	Club	Lea	GP	G	A	TP	PIM	GP	G	A	TP	PIM
1980-81	Sherbrooke	QMJHL	67	15	23	38	252	14	1	2	3	35
1981-82	Sherbrooke	QMJHL	60	8	41	49	250	22	2	7	9	106
1982-83	Salt Lake	CHL	67	3	12	15	222	6	1	1	2	8
1983-84	**Quebec**	**NHL**	**38**	**0**	**5**	**5**	**60**	....	....	....	....	....
	Fredericton	AHL	30	2	3	5	146	7	1	1	2	43
1984-85	**Quebec**	**NHL**	**22**	**0**	**0**	**0**	**33**	....	....	....	....	....
	Fredericton	AHL	42	1	5	6	134	6	0	1	1	25
1985-86	**Quebec**	**NHL**	**36**	**2**	**2**	**4**	**85**	**1**	**0**	**0**	**0**	**0**
	Fredericton	AHL	38	3	5	8	103	5	0	0	0	33
1986-87	**Quebec**	**NHL**	**38**	**0**	**2**	**2**	**143**	**13**	**0**	**0**	**0**	**53**
1987-88	**Quebec**	**NHL**	**63**	**4**	**3**	**7**	**301**	....	....	....	....	....
1988-89	**Quebec**	**NHL**	**16**	**4**	**0**	**4**	**46**	....	....	....	....	....
	Winnipeg	**NHL**	**57**	**6**	**10**	**16**	**228**	....	....	....	....	....
1989-90	**Winnipeg**	**NHL**	**55**	**3**	**3**	**6**	**222**	**6**	**0**	**1**	**1**	**8**
1990-91	**Winnipeg**	**NHL**	**57**	**3**	**4**	**7**	**265**	....	....	....	....	....
1991-92	**Winnipeg**	**NHL**	**4**	**0**	**0**	**0**	**11**	....	....	....	....	....
	Buffalo	**NHL**	**67**	**2**	**3**	**5**	**305**	**6**	**0**	**1**	**1**	**0**
1992-93	**Buffalo**	**NHL**	**60**	**3**	**8**	**11**	**221**	....	....	....	....	....
1993-94	**Buffalo**	**NHL**	**7**	**0**	**0**	**0**	**31**	....	....	....	....	....
	Dallas	**NHL**	**18**	**0**	**1**	**1**	**66**	....	....	....	....	....
1994-95	Kalamazoo	IHL	7	2	2	4	18	....	....	....	....	....
	Dallas	**NHL**	**16**	**1**	**0**	**1**	**52**	....	....	....	....	....
1995-96	Houston	IHL	73	3	4	7	333	....	....	....	....	....
	NHL Totals		**554**	**28**	**41**	**69**	**2069**	**26**	**0**	**2**	**2**	**61**

Rights transferred to **Quebec** by **St. Louis** with rights to Claude Julien when St. Louis signed Jacques Demers as coach, August 19, 1983. Traded to **Winnipeg** by **Quebec** for Mario Marois, December 6, 1988. Traded to **Buffalo** by **Winnipeg** with Dave McLlwain, Winnipeg's fifth round choice (Yuri Khmylev) in 1992 Entry Draft and future considerations for Darrin Shannon, Mike Hartman and Dean Kennedy, October 11, 1991. Traded to **Dallas** by **Buffalo** for James Black and Dallas' seventh round choice (Steve Webb) in 1994 Entry Draft, December 15, 1993.

DONNELLY, MIKE — NYI

Left wing. Shoots left. 5'11", 185 lbs. Born, Detroit, MI, October 10, 1963.

			Regular Season					Playoffs				
Season	Club	Lea	GP	G	A	TP	PIM	GP	G	A	TP	PIM
1982-83	Michigan State	CCHA	24	7	13	20	8					
1983-84	Michigan State	CCHA	44	18	14	32	40					
1984-85	Michigan State	CCHA	44	26	21	47	48					
1985-86ab	Michigan State	CCHA	44	*59	38	97	65					
1986-87	NY Rangers	NHL	5	1	1	2	0					
	New Haven	AHL	58	27	34	61	52	7	2	0	2	9
1987-88	NY Rangers	NHL	17	2	2	4	8					
	Colorado	IHL	8	7	11	18	15					
	Buffalo	NHL	40	6	8	14	44					
1988-89	Buffalo	NHL	22	4	6	10	10					
	Rochester	AHL	53	32	37	69	53					
1989-90	Buffalo	NHL	12	1	2	3	8					
	Rochester	AHL	68	43	55	98	71	16	*12	7	19	9
1990-91	Los Angeles	NHL	53	7	5	12	41	12	5	4	9	6
	New Haven	AHL	18	10	6	16	2					
1991-92	Los Angeles	NHL	80	29	16	45	20	6	1	0	1	4
1992-93	Los Angeles	NHL	84	29	40	69	45	24	6	7	13	14
1993-94	Los Angeles	NHL	81	21	21	42	34					
1994-95	Los Angeles	NHL	9	1	1	2	4					
	Dallas	NHL	35	11	14	25	29	5	0	1	1	6
1995-96	Dallas	NHL	24	2	5	7	10					
	Michigan	IHL	21	8	15	23	20	8	3	0	3	10
	NHL Totals		462	114	121	235	253	47	12	12	24	30

a CCHA First All-Star Team (1986)
b NCAA West First All-American Team (1986)

Signed as a free agent by **NY Rangers**, August 15, 1986. Traded to **Buffalo** by **NY Rangers** with Rangers' fifth round choice (Alexander Mogilny) in 1988 Entry Draft for Paul Cyr and Buffalo's tenth round choice (Eric Fenton) in 1988 Entry Draft, December 31, 1987. Traded to **Los Angeles** by **Buffalo** for Mikko Makela, September 30, 1990. Traded to **Dallas** by **Los Angeles** with Los Angeles' seventh round choice in 1996 Entry Draft for Dallas' fourth round choice (later traded to Washington — Washington selected Justin Davis) in 1996 Entry Draft, February 17, 1995. Signed as a free agent by **NY Islanders**, August 19, 1996.

DONOVAN, SHEAN — S.J.

Right wing. Shoots right. 6'2", 190 lbs. Born, Timmins, Ont., January 22, 1975.
(San Jose's 2nd choice, 28th overall, in 1993 Entry Draft).

			Regular Season					Playoffs				
Season	Club	Lea	GP	G	A	TP	PIM	GP	G	A	TP	PIM
1991-92	Ottawa	OHL	58	11	8	19	14	11	1	0	1	5
1992-93	Ottawa	OHL	66	29	23	52	33					
1993-94	Ottawa	OHL	62	35	49	84	63	17	10	11	21	14
1994-95	Ottawa	OHL	29	22	19	41	41					
	San Jose	NHL	14	0	0	0	6	7	0	1	1	6
	Kansas City	IHL	5	0	2	2	7	14	5	3	8	23
1995-96	San Jose	NHL	74	13	8	21	39					
	Kansas City	IHL	4	0	0	0	8	5	0	0	0	8
	NHL Totals		88	13	8	21	45	7	0	1	1	6

DOURIS, PETER (DOOR-ihs)

Right wing. Shoots right. 6'1", 195 lbs. Born, Toronto, Ont., February 19, 1966.
(Winnipeg's 1st choice, 30th overall, in 1984 Entry Draft).

			Regular Season					Playoffs				
Season	Club	Lea	GP	G	A	TP	PIM	GP	G	A	TP	PIM
1983-84	N. Hampshire	ECAC	37	19	15	34	14					
1984-85	N. Hampshire	H.E.	42	27	24	51	34					
1985-86	Winnipeg	NHL	11	0	0	0	0					
	Cdn. Olympic	....	33	16	7	23	18					
1986-87	Winnipeg	NHL	6	0	0	0	0					
	Sherbrooke	AHL	62	14	28	42	24	17	7	*15	*22	16
1987-88	Winnipeg	NHL	4	0	2	2	0	1	0	0	0	0
	Moncton	AHL	73	42	37	79	53					
1988-89	Peoria	IHL	81	28	41	69	32	4	1	2	3	0
1989-90	Boston	NHL	36	5	6	11	15	8	0	1	1	8
	Maine	AHL	38	17	20	37	14					
1990-91	Boston	NHL	39	5	2	7	9	7	0	1	1	6
	Maine	AHL	35	16	15	31	9	2	3	0	3	2
1991-92	Boston	NHL	54	10	13	23	10	7	2	3	5	0
	Maine	AHL	12	4	3	7	2					
1992-93	Boston	NHL	19	4	4	8	4	4	1	0	1	0
	Providence	AHL	50	29	26	55	12					
1993-94	Anaheim	NHL	74	12	22	34	21					
1994-95	Anaheim	NHL	46	10	11	21	12					
1995-96	Anaheim	NHL	31	8	7	15	9					
	NHL Totals		320	54	67	121	80	27	3	5	8	14

Traded to **St. Louis** by **Winnipeg** for Kent Carlson and St. Louis' twelfth round choice (Sergei Kharin) in 1989 Entry Draft and St. Louis' fourth round choice (Scott Levins) in 1990 Entry Draft, September 29, 1988. Signed as a free agent by **Boston**, June 27, 1989. Signed as a free agent by **Anaheim**, July 22, 1993.

DOWD, JIM — VAN.

Center. Shoots right. 6'1", 190 lbs. Born, Brick, NJ, December 25, 1968.
(New Jersey's 7th choice, 149th overall, in 1987 Entry Draft).

			Regular Season					Playoffs				
Season	Club	Lea	GP	G	A	TP	PIM	GP	G	A	TP	PIM
1987-88	Lake Superior	CCHA	45	18	27	45	16					
1988-89	Lake Superior	CCHA	46	24	35	59	40					
1989-90ab	Lake Superior	CCHA	46	25	*67	92	30					
1990-91cd	Lake Superior	CCHA	44	24	*54	*78	53					
1991-92	New Jersey	NHL	1	0	0	0	0					
	Utica	AHL	78	17	42	59	47	4	2	2	4	4
1992-93	New Jersey	NHL	1	0	0	0	0					
	Utica	AHL	78	27	45	72	62	5	1	7	8	10
1993-94	New Jersey	NHL	15	5	10	15	0	19	2	6	8	8
	Albany	AHL	58	26	37	63	76					
1994-95	New Jersey	NHL	10	1	4	5	0	11	2	1	3	8 ♦
1995-96	New Jersey	NHL	28	4	9	13	17					
	Vancouver	NHL	38	1	6	7	6	1	0	0	0	0
	NHL Totals		93	11	29	40	23	31	4	7	11	16

a CCHA Second All-Star Team (1990)
b NCAA West Second All-American Team (1990)
c CCHA First All-Star Team (1991)
d NCAA West First All-American Team (1991)

Traded to **Hartford** by **New Jersey** with New Jersey's second round choice in 1997 Entry Draft for Jocelyn Lemieux and Hartford's second round choice in 1998 Entry Draft, December 19, 1995. Traded to **Vancouver** by **Hartford** with Frantisek Kucera and Hartford's second round choice in 1997 Entry Draft for Jeff Brown and Vancouver's third round choice in 1998 Entry Draft, December 19, 1995.

DOYLE, JASON — BOS.

Right wing. Shoots right. 6'1", 200 lbs. Born, Toronto, Ont., May 15, 1978.
(Boston's 4th choice, 80th overall, in 1996 Entry Draft).

			Regular Season					Playoffs				
Season	Club	Lea	GP	G	A	TP	PIM	GP	G	A	TP	PIM
1994-95	London	OHL	45	4	10	14	7	4	1	1	2	0
1995-96	London	OHL	21	11	5	16	24					
	S.S. Marie	OHL	44	17	17	34	30	4	1	1	2	6

DOYLE, TREVOR — FLA.

Defense. Shoots right. 6'3", 212 lbs. Born, Ottawa, Ont., January 1, 1974.
(Florida's 9th choice, 161st overall, in 1993 Entry Draft).

			Regular Season					Playoffs				
Season	Club	Lea	GP	G	A	TP	PIM	GP	G	A	TP	PIM
1991-92	Kingston	OHL	26	0	1	1	19					
1992-93	Kingston	OHL	62	1	8	9	148	16	2	3	5	25
1993-94	Kingston	OHL	53	2	12	14	246	3	0	0	0	4
1994-95	Cincinnati	IHL	52	0	3	3	139	6	0	0	0	13
1995-96	Carolina	AHL	48	1	2	3	117					

DRAKE, DALLAS — PHO.

Center. Shoots left. 6', 180 lbs. Born, Trail, B.C., February 4, 1969.
(Detroit's 6th choice, 116th overall, in 1989 Entry Draft).

			Regular Season					Playoffs				
Season	Club	Lea	GP	G	A	TP	PIM	GP	G	A	TP	PIM
1988-89	N. Michigan	WCHA	38	17	22	39	22					
1989-90	N. Michigan	WCHA	46	13	24	37	42					
1990-91	N. Michigan	WCHA	44	22	36	58	89					
1991-92ab	N. Michigan	WCHA	38	*39	41	*80	46					
1992-93	Detroit	NHL	72	18	26	44	93	7	3	3	6	6
1993-94	Detroit	NHL	47	10	22	32	37					
	Adirondack	AHL	1	2	0	2	0					
	Winnipeg	NHL	15	3	5	8	12					
1994-95	Winnipeg	NHL	43	8	18	26	30					
1995-96	Winnipeg	NHL	69	19	20	39	36	3	0	0	0	0
	NHL Totals		246	58	91	149	208	10	3	3	6	6

a WCHA First All-Star Team (1992)
b NCAA West First All-American Team (1992)

Traded to **Winnipeg** by **Detroit** with Tim Cheveldae for Bob Essensa and Sergei Bautin, March 8, 1994.

DRAPEAU, ETIENNE — MTL.

Center. Shoots left. 6'1", 181 lbs. Born, Quebec City, Que., January 10, 1978.
(Montreal's 5th choice, 99th overall, in 1996 Entry Draft).

			Regular Season					Playoffs				
Season	Club	Lea	GP	G	A	TP	PIM	GP	G	A	TP	PIM
1994-95	Halifax	QMJHL	63	26	35	61	121	7	2	2	4	20
1995-96	Halifax	QMJHL	42	10	25	35	98					
	Beauport	QMJHL	28	8	12	20	37	20	8	7	15	66

DRAPER, KRIS — DET.

Center. Shoots left. 5'11", 185 lbs. Born, Toronto, Ont., May 24, 1971.
(Winnipeg's 4th choice, 62nd overall, in 1989 Entry Draft).

			Regular Season					Playoffs				
Season	Club	Lea	GP	G	A	TP	PIM	GP	G	A	TP	PIM
1988-89	Cdn. National	....	60	11	15	26	16					
1989-90	Cdn. National	....	61	12	22	34	44					
1990-91	Winnipeg	NHL	3	1	0	1	5					
	Ottawa	OHL	39	19	42	61	35	17	8	11	19	20
	Moncton	AHL	7	2	1	3	2					
1991-92	Winnipeg	NHL	10	2	0	2	2	2	0	0	0	0
	Moncton	AHL	61	11	18	29	113	4	0	1	1	6
1992-93	Winnipeg	NHL	7	0	0	0	2					
	Moncton	AHL	67	12	23	35	40	5	2	2	4	18
1993-94	Detroit	NHL	39	5	8	13	31	7	2	2	4	4
	Adirondack	AHL	46	20	23	43	49					
1994-95	Detroit	NHL	36	2	6	8	22	18	4	1	5	12
1995-96	Detroit	NHL	52	7	9	16	32	18	4	2	6	18
	NHL Totals		147	17	23	40	94	45	10	5	15	34

Traded to **Detroit** by **Winnipeg** for future considerations, June 30, 1993.

DRIVER, BRUCE — NYR

Defense. Shoots left. 6', 185 lbs. Born, Toronto, Ont., April 29, 1962.
(Colorado's 6th choice, 108th overall, in 1981 Entry Draft).

			Regular Season					Playoffs				
Season	Club	Lea	GP	G	A	TP	PIM	GP	G	A	TP	PIM
1980-81	U. Wisconsin	WCHA	42	5	15	20	42					
1981-82ab	U. Wisconsin	WCHA	46	7	37	44	84					
1982-83c	U. Wisconsin	WCHA	49	19	42	61	100					
1983-84	Cdn. National	....	61	11	17	28	44					
	Cdn. Olympic	....	7	3	1	4	10					
	New Jersey	NHL	4	0	2	2	0					
	Maine	AHL	12	2	6	8	15	16	0	10	10	8
1984-85	New Jersey	NHL	67	9	23	32	36					
1985-86	New Jersey	NHL	40	3	15	18	32					
	Maine	AHL	15	4	7	11	16					
1986-87	New Jersey	NHL	74	6	28	34	36					
1987-88	New Jersey	NHL	74	15	40	55	68	20	3	7	10	14
1988-89	New Jersey	NHL	27	1	15	16	24					
1989-90	New Jersey	NHL	75	7	46	53	63	6	1	5	6	6
1990-91	New Jersey	NHL	73	9	36	45	62	7	1	2	3	12
1991-92	New Jersey	NHL	78	7	35	42	66	7	0	4	4	2
1992-93	New Jersey	NHL	83	14	40	54	66	5	1	3	4	4
1993-94	New Jersey	NHL	66	8	24	32	63	20	3	5	8	12
1994-95	New Jersey	NHL	41	4	12	16	18	17	1	6	7	8 ♦
1995-96	NY Rangers	NHL	66	3	34	37	42	11	0	7	7	4
	NHL Totals		768	86	350	436	576	93	10	39	49	62

a WCHA First All-Star Team (1982)
b NCAA All-Tournament Team (1982)
c WCHA Second All-Star Team (1983)

Signed as a free agent by **NY Rangers**, September 28, 1995.

DROLET, JIMMY — MTL.

Defense. Shoots left. 6'1", 180 lbs. Born, Vanier, Que., February 19, 1976.
(Montreal's 7th choice, 122nd overall, in 1994 Entry Draft).

			Regular Season					Playoffs				
Season	Club	Lea	GP	G	A	TP	PIM	GP	G	A	TP	PIM
1993-94	St-Hyacinthe	QMJHL	72	10	46	56	93	7	1	7	8	10
1994-95	St-Hyacinthe	QMJHL	68	9	27	36	126	5	0	2	2	12
1995-96	St-Hyacinthe	QMJHL	33	4	27	31	65	....	....	....	....	....
	Granby	QMJHL	29	4	26	30	70	21	7	18	25	28

DROPPA, IVAN — CHI.

Defense. Shoots left. 6'2", 209 lbs. Born, Liptovsky Mikulas, Czech., February 1, 1972.
(Chicago's 2nd choice, 37th overall, in 1990 Entry Draft).

			Regular Season					Playoffs				
Season	Club	Lea	GP	G	A	TP	PIM	GP	G	A	TP	PIM
1990-91	VSZ Kosice	Czech.	54	1	7	8	12	....	....	....	....	....
1991-92	VSZ Kosice	Czech.	43	4	9	13	24	....	....	....	....	....
1992-93	Indianapolis	IHL	77	14	29	43	92	5	0	1	1	2
1993-94	Chicago	NHL	12	0	1	1	12	....	....	....	....	....
	Indianapolis	IHL	55	9	10	19	71	....	....	....	....	....
1994-95	Indianapolis	IHL	67	5	28	33	91	....	....	....	....	....
1995-96	Chicago	NHL	7	0	0	0	2	....	....	....	....	....
	Indianapolis	IHL	72	6	30	36	71	3	0	1	1	2
	NHL Totals		19	0	1	1	14	....	....	....	....	....

DRUCE, JOHN — PHI.

Right wing. Shoots right. 6'2", 195 lbs. Born, Peterborough, Ont., February 23, 1966.
(Washington's 2nd choice, 40th overall, in 1985 Entry Draft).

			Regular Season					Playoffs				
Season	Club	Lea	GP	G	A	TP	PIM	GP	G	A	TP	PIM
1984-85	Peterborough	OHL	54	12	14	26	90	17	6	2	8	21
1985-86	Peterborough	OHL	49	22	24	46	84	16	0	5	5	34
1986-87	Binghamton	AHL	77	13	9	22	131	12	0	3	3	28
1987-88	Binghamton	AHL	68	32	29	61	82	1	0	0	0	0
1988-89	Washington	NHL	48	8	7	15	62	1	0	0	0	0
	Baltimore	AHL	16	2	11	13	10	....	....	....	....	....
1989-90	Washington	NHL	45	8	3	11	52	15	14	3	17	23
	Baltimore	AHL	26	15	16	31	38	....	....	....	....	....
1990-91	Washington	NHL	80	22	36	58	46	11	1	1	2	7
1991-92	Washington	NHL	67	19	18	37	39	7	1	0	1	2
1992-93	Winnipeg	NHL	50	6	14	20	37	2	0	0	0	0
1993-94	Los Angeles	NHL	55	14	17	31	50	....	....	....	....	....
	Phoenix	IHL	8	5	6	11	9	....	....	....	....	....
1994-95	Los Angeles	NHL	43	15	5	20	20	....	....	....	....	....
1995-96	Los Angeles	NHL	64	9	12	21	14	....	....	....	....	....
	Philadelphia	NHL	13	4	4	8	13	2	0	2	2	2
	NHL Totals		465	105	116	221	333	38	16	6	22	34

Traded to **Winnipeg** by **Washington** with Toronto's fourth round choice (previously acquired by Washington — later traded to Detroit — Detroit selected John Jakopin) in 1993 Entry Draft for Pat Elynuik, October 1, 1992. Signed as a free agent by Los Angeles, August 2, 1993. Traded to **Philadelphia** by **Los Angeles** with Los Angeles' seventh round choice in 1997 Entry Draft for Los Angeles' fourth round choice (previously acquired by Philadelphia — Los Angeles selected Mikael Simons) in 1996 Entry Draft, March 19, 1996.

DRURY, CHRIS — COL.

Center. Shoots right. 5'10", 180 lbs. Born, Trumbull, CT, August 20, 1976.
(Quebec's 5th choice, 72nd overall, in 1994 Entry Draft).

			Regular Season					Playoffs				
Season	Club	Lea	GP	G	A	TP	PIM	GP	G	A	TP	PIM
1994-95	Boston U.	H.E.	39	12	15	27	38	....	....	....	....	....
1995-96ab	Boston U.	H.E.	37	35	33	*68	46	....	....	....	....	....

a Hockey East All-Star Team (1996)
b NCAA East Second All-American Team (1996)

DRURY, TED — (DROO-ree) OTT.

Center. Shoots left. 6', 185 lbs. Born, Boston, MA, September 13, 1971.
(Calgary's 2nd choice, 42nd overall, in 1989 Entry Draft).

			Regular Season					Playoffs				
Season	Club	Lea	GP	G	A	TP	PIM	GP	G	A	TP	PIM
1989-90	Harvard	ECAC	17	9	13	22	10	....	....	....	....	....
1990-91	Harvard	ECAC	25	18	18	36	22	....	....	....	....	....
1991-92	U.S. National	....	53	11	23	34	30	....	....	....	....	....
	U.S. Olympic	....	7	1	1	2	0	....	....	....	....	....
1992-93ab	Harvard	ECAC	31	22	*41	*63	28	....	....	....	....	....
1993-94	Calgary	NHL	34	5	7	12	26	....	....	....	....	....
	U.S. National	....	11	1	4	5	11	....	....	....	....	....
	U.S. Olympic	....	7	1	2	3	2	....	....	....	....	....
	Hartford	NHL	16	1	5	6	10	....	....	....	....	....
1994-95	Hartford	NHL	34	3	6	9	21	....	....	....	....	....
	Springfield	AHL	2	0	1	1	0	....	....	....	....	....
1995-96	Ottawa	NHL	42	9	7	16	54	....	....	....	....	....
	NHL Totals		126	18	25	43	111	....	....	....	....	....

a ECAC First All-Star Team (1993)
b NCAA East First All-America Team (1993)

Traded to **Hartford** by **Calgary** with Gary Suter and Paul Ranheim for James Patrick, Zarley Zalapski and Michael Nylander, March 10, 1994. Claimed by **Ottawa** from **Hartford** in NHL Waiver Draft, October 2, 1995.

DUBE, CHRISTIAN — (doo-BAY) NYR

Center. Shoots right. 5'11", 170 lbs. Born, Sherbrooke, Que., April 25, 1977.
(NY Rangers' 1st choice, 39th overall, in 1995 Entry Draft).

			Regular Season					Playoffs				
Season	Club	Lea	GP	G	A	TP	PIM	GP	G	A	TP	PIM
1993-94	Sherbrooke	QMJHL	72	31	41	72	22	11	3	2	5	8
1994-95	Sherbrooke	QMJHL	71	36	65	101	43	7	1	7	8	8
1995-96abc	Sherbrooke	QMJHL	62	52	93	145	105	7	5	5	10	6

a QMJHL First All-Star Team (1996)
b Canadian Major Junior First All-Star Team (1996)
c Canadian Major Junior Player of the Year (1996)

DUBE, YANNICK — (doo-BAY)

Center. Shoots right. 5'9", 170 lbs. Born, Gaspé, Que., June 14, 1974.
(Vancouver's 6th choice, 117th overall, in 1994 Entry Draft).

			Regular Season					Playoffs				
Season	Club	Lea	GP	G	A	TP	PIM	GP	G	A	TP	PIM
1991-92	Laval	QMJHL	65	14	19	33	8	10	0	2	2	2
1992-93	Laval	QMJHL	68	45	38	83	25	13	6	7	13	6
1993-94abcd	Laval	QMJHL	64	*66	75	*141	30	21	12	18	30	8
1994-95	Cdn. National	....	24	4	6	10	16	....	....	....	....	....
	Syracuse	AHL	39	10	11	21	8	....	....	....	....	....
	Laval	QMJHL	1	0	1	1	0	16	11	3	14	12
1995-96	P.E.I.	AHL	4	0	1	1	0	....	....	....	....	....
	Cornwall	AHL	61	17	20	37	10	3	0	1	1	0

a QMJHL First All-Star Team (1994)
b Canadian Major Junior Second All-Star Team (1994)
c Canadian Major Junior Most Sportsmanlike Player of the Year (1994)
d Won George Parsons Trophy (Memorial Cup Tournament Most Sportsmanlike Player) (1994)

DUBINSKY, STEVE — CHI.

Center. Shoots left. 6', 190 lbs. Born, Montreal, Que., July 9, 1970.
(Chicago's 9th choice, 226th overall, in 1990 Entry Draft).

			Regular Season					Playoffs				
Season	Club	Lea	GP	G	A	TP	PIM	GP	G	A	TP	PIM
1989-90	Clarkson	ECAC	35	7	10	17	24	....	....	....	....	....
1990-91	Clarkson	ECAC	39	13	23	36	26	....	....	....	....	....
1991-92	Clarkson	ECAC	32	20	31	51	40	....	....	....	....	....
1992-93	Clarkson	ECAC	35	18	26	44	58	....	....	....	....	....
1993-94	Chicago	NHL	27	2	6	8	16	6	0	0	0	10
	Indianapolis	IHL	54	15	25	40	63	....	....	....	....	....
1994-95	Indianapolis	IHL	62	16	11	27	29	....	....	....	....	....
	Chicago	NHL	16	0	0	0	8	....	....	....	....	....
1995-96	Chicago	NHL	43	2	3	5	14	....	....	....	....	....
	Indianapolis	IHL	16	8	8	16	10	....	....	....	....	....
	NHL Totals		86	4	9	13	38	6	0	0	0	10

DUCHESNE, STEVE — (doo-SHAYN) OTT.

Defense. Shoots left. 5'11", 195 lbs. Born, Sept-Iles, Que., June 30, 1965.

			Regular Season					Playoffs				
Season	Club	Lea	GP	G	A	TP	PIM	GP	G	A	TP	PIM
1983-84	Drummondville	QMJHL	67	1	34	35	79	....	....	....	....	....
1984-85a	Drummondville	QMJHL	65	22	54	76	94	5	4	7	11	8
1985-86	New Haven	AHL	75	14	35	49	76	5	0	2	2	9
1986-87b	Los Angeles	NHL	75	13	25	38	74	5	2	2	4	4
1987-88	Los Angeles	NHL	71	16	39	55	109	5	1	3	4	14
1988-89	Los Angeles	NHL	79	25	50	75	92	11	4	4	8	12
1989-90	Los Angeles	NHL	79	20	42	62	36	10	2	9	11	6
1990-91	Los Angeles	NHL	78	21	41	62	66	12	4	8	12	8
1991-92	Philadelphia	NHL	78	18	38	56	86	....	....	....	....	....
1992-93	Quebec	NHL	82	20	62	82	57	6	0	5	5	6
1993-94	St. Louis	NHL	36	12	19	31	14	4	0	2	2	2
1994-95	St. Louis	NHL	47	12	26	38	36	7	0	4	4	2
1995-96	Ottawa	NHL	62	12	24	36	42	....	....	....	....	....
	NHL Totals		687	169	366	535	612	60	13	37	50	54

a QMJHL First All-Star Team (1985)
b NHL All-Rookie Team (1987)

Played in NHL All-Star Game (1989, 1990, 1993)

Signed as a free agent by **Los Angeles,** October 1, 1984. Traded to **Philadelphia** by **Los Angeles** with Steve Kasper and Los Angeles' fourth round choice (Aris Brimanis) in 1991 Entry Draft for Jari Kurri and Jeff Chychrun, May 30, 1991. Traded to **Quebec** by **Philadelphia** with Peter Forsberg, Kerry Huffman, Mike Ricci, Ron Hextall, Chris Simon, Philadelphia's first round choice in the 1993 (Jocelyn Thibault) and 1994 (later traded to Toronto — later traded to Washington — Washington selected Nolan Baumgartner) Entry Drafts and cash for Eric Lindros, June 30, 1992. Traded to **St. Louis** by **Quebec** with Denis Chasse for Garth Butcher, Ron Sutter and Bob Bassen, January 23, 1994. Traded to **Ottawa** by **St. Louis** for Ottawa's second round choice (later traded to Buffalo — Buffalo selected Cory Sarich) in 1996 Entry Draft, August 5, 1995.

DUERDEN, DAVE — FLA.

Left wing. Shoots left. 6'2", 201 lbs. Born, Oshawa, Ont., April 11, 1977.
(Florida's 4th choice, 80th overall, in 1995 Entry Draft).

			Regular Season					Playoffs				
Season	Club	Lea	GP	G	A	TP	PIM	GP	G	A	TP	PIM
1994-95	Peterborough	OHL	66	20	33	53	21	11	6	2	8	6
1995-96	Peterborough	OHL	66	35	35	70	47	24	14	13	27	16

DUFRESNE, DONALD — (doo-FRAYN, DOH-nal)

Defense. Shoots right. 6'1", 206 lbs. Born, Quebec City, Que., April 10, 1967.
(Montreal's 8th choice, 117th overall, in 1985 Entry Draft).

			Regular Season					Playoffs				
Season	Club	Lea	GP	G	A	TP	PIM	GP	G	A	TP	PIM
1983-84	Trois-Rivières	QMJHL	67	7	12	19	97	....	....	....	....	....
1984-85	Trois-Rivières	QMJHL	65	5	30	35	112	7	1	3	4	12
1985-86a	Trois-Rivières	QMJHL	63	8	32	40	160	1	0	0	0	0
1986-87a	Trois-Rivières	QMJHL	51	5	21	26	79	....	....	....	....	....
	Longueuil	QMJHL	16	0	8	8	18	20	1	8	9	38
1987-88	Sherbrooke	AHL	47	1	8	9	107	6	1	0	1	34
1988-89	Montreal	NHL	13	0	1	1	43	6	1	1	2	4
	Sherbrooke	AHL	47	0	12	12	170	....	....	....	....	....
1989-90	Montreal	NHL	18	0	4	4	23	10	0	1	1	18
	Sherbrooke	AHL	38	2	11	13	104	....	....	....	....	....
1990-91	Montreal	NHL	53	2	13	15	55	10	0	1	1	21
	Fredericton	AHL	10	1	4	5	35	1	0	0	0	0
1991-92	Montreal	NHL	3	0	0	0	2	....	....	....	....	....
	Fredericton	AHL	31	8	12	20	60	7	0	0	0	10
1992-93	Montreal	NHL	32	1	2	3	32	2	0	0	0	0 ♦
1993-94	Tampa Bay	NHL	51	2	6	8	48	....	....	....	....	....
	Los Angeles	NHL	9	0	0	0	10	....	....	....	....	....
1994-95	St. Louis	NHL	22	0	3	3	10	3	0	0	0	4
1995-96	St. Louis	NHL	3	0	0	0	4	....	....	....	....	....
	Worcester	AHL	13	1	1	2	14	....	....	....	....	....
	Edmonton	NHL	42	1	6	7	16	....	....	....	....	....
	NHL Totals		246	6	35	41	243	31	1	3	4	47

a QMJHL Second All-Star Team (1986, 1987)

Traded to **Tampa Bay** by **Montreal** to complete March 20, 1993 trade in which Rob Ramage was traded to Montreal for Eric Charron, Alain Cote and future considerations, June 20, 1993. Traded to **Los Angeles** by **Tampa Bay** for Los Angeles' sixth round choice (Daniel Juden) in 1994 Entry Draft, March 19, 1994. Claimed by **St. Louis** from **Los Angeles** in NHL Waiver Draft, January 18, 1995. Traded to **Edmonton** by **St. Louis** with Jeff Norton for Igor Kravchuk and Ken Sutton, January 4, 1996.

DUMONT, JEAN-PIERRE — NYI

Right wing. Shoots left. 6'1", 187 lbs. Born, Montreal, Que., April 1, 1978.
(NY Islanders' 1st choice, 3rd overall, in 1996 Entry Draft).

			Regular Season					Playoffs				
Season	Club	Lea	GP	G	A	TP	PIM	GP	G	A	TP	PIM
1993-94	Val d'Or	QMJHL	25	9	11	20	10	....	....	....	....	....
1994-95	Val d'Or	QMJHL	48	5	14	19	24	....	....	....	....	....
1995-96	Val d'Or	QMJHL	66	48	57	105	109	13	12	8	20	22

DUNCANSON, CRAIG

Left wing. Shoots left. 6', 190 lbs. Born, Sudbury, Ont., March 17, 1967.
(Los Angeles' 1st choice, 9th overall, in 1985 Entry Draft).

			Regular Season					Playoffs				
Season	Club	Lea	GP	G	A	TP	PIM	GP	G	A	TP	PIM
1983-84	Sudbury	OHL	62	38	38	76	176	....	....	....	....	....
1984-85	Sudbury	OHL	53	35	28	63	129	....	....	....	....	....
1985-86	**Los Angeles**	**NHL**	**2**	**0**	**1**	**1**	**0**	....	....	....	....	....
	Sudbury	OHL	21	12	17	29	55	....	....	....	....	....
	Cornwall	OHL	40	31	50	81	135	6	4	7	11	2
	New Haven	AHL	....	....	....	....	....	2	0	0	0	5
1986-87	**Los Angeles**	**NHL**	**2**	**0**	**0**	**0**	**24**	....	....	....	....	....
	Cornwall	OHL	52	22	45	67	88	5	4	3	7	20
1987-88	**Los Angeles**	**NHL**	**9**	**0**	**0**	**0**	**12**	....	....	....	....	....
	New Haven	AHL	57	15	25	40	170	....	....	....	....	....
1988-89	**Los Angeles**	**NHL**	**5**	**0**	**0**	**0**	**0**	....	....	....	....	....
	New Haven	AHL	69	25	39	64	200	17	4	8	12	60
1989-90	**Los Angeles**	**NHL**	**10**	**3**	**2**	**5**	**9**	....	....	....	....	....
	New Haven	AHL	51	17	30	47	152	....	....	....	....	....
1990-91	**Winnipeg**	**NHL**	**7**	**2**	**0**	**2**	**16**	....	....	....	....	....
	Moncton	AHL	58	16	34	50	107	9	3	11	14	31
1991-92	Baltimore	AHL	46	20	26	46	98	....	....	....	....	....
	Moncton	AHL	19	12	9	21	6	11	6	4	10	10
1992-93	**NY Rangers**	**NHL**	**3**	**0**	**1**	**1**	**0**	....	....	....	....	....
	Binghamton	AHL	69	35	59	94	126	14	7	5	12	9
1993-94	Binghamton	AHL	70	25	44	69	83	....	....	....	....	....
1994-95	Binghamton	AHL	62	21	43	64	105	11	4	4	8	16
1995-96	Orlando	IHL	79	19	24	43	123	22	3	10	13	16
	NHL Totals		**38**	**5**	**4**	**9**	**61**	....	....	....	....	....

Traded to **Minnesota** by **Los Angeles** for Daniel Berthiaume, September 6, 1990. Traded to **Winnipeg** by **Minnesota** for Brian Hunt, September 6, 1990. Traded to **Washington** by **Winnipeg** with Brent Hughes and Simon Wheeldon for Bob Joyce, Tyler Larter and Kent Paynter, May 21, 1991. Signed as a free agent by **NY Rangers**, September 4, 1992.

DUPAUL, COSMO — OTT.

Center. Shoots left. 6', 186 lbs. Born, Pointe-Claire, Que., April 11, 1975.
(Ottawa's 4th choice, 91st overall, in 1993 Entry Draft).

			Regular Season					Playoffs				
Season	Club	Lea	GP	G	A	TP	PIM	GP	G	A	TP	PIM
1992-93	Victoriaville	QMJHL	67	23	35	58	16	6	1	3	4	2
1993-94	Victoriaville	QMJHL	66	26	46	72	32	5	2	2	4	6
1994-95	Victoriaville	QMJHL	71	29	44	73	60	4	3	4	7	6
	P.E.I.	AHL	3	0	1	1	2	1	0	0	0	0
1995-96	Thunder Bay	ColHL	63	25	32	57	20	19	5	11	16	4
	P.E.I.	AHL	8	1	1	2	2	....	....	....	....	....

DUPRE, YANICK — (doo-PRAY, YAH-nihk) — PHI.

Left wing. Shoots left. 6', 189 lbs. Born, Montreal, Que., November 20, 1972.
(Philadelphia's 2nd choice, 50th overall, in 1991 Entry Draft).

			Regular Season					Playoffs				
Season	Club	Lea	GP	G	A	TP	PIM	GP	G	A	TP	PIM
1989-90	Chicoutimi	QMJHL	24	5	9	14	27	....	....	....	....	....
	Drummondville	QMJHL	29	10	10	20	42	....	....	....	....	....
1990-91	Drummondville	QMJHL	58	29	38	67	87	11	8	5	13	33
1991-92	**Philadelphia**	**NHL**	**1**	**0**	**0**	**0**	**0**	....	....	....	....	....
	Drummondville	QMJHL	28	19	17	36	48	....	....	....	....	....
	Verdun	QMJHL	12	7	14	21	21	19	9	9	18	20
1992-93	Hershey	AHL	63	13	24	37	22	....	....	....	....	....
1993-94	Hershey	AHL	51	22	20	42	42	8	1	3	4	2
1994-95	Hershey	AHL	41	15	19	34	35	....	....	....	....	....
	Philadelphia	**NHL**	**22**	**0**	**0**	**0**	**8**	....	....	....	....	....
1995-96	**Philadelphia**	**NHL**	**12**	**2**	**0**	**2**	**8**	....	....	....	....	....
	Hershey	AHL	52	20	36	56	81	....	....	....	....	....
	NHL Totals		**35**	**2**	**0**	**2**	**16**	....	....	....	....	....

DUTHIE, RYAN

Center. Shoots right. 5'10", 180 lbs. Born, Red Deer, Alta., September 2, 1974.
(NY Islanders' 4th choice, 105th overall, in 1992 Entry Draft).

			Regular Season					Playoffs				
Season	Club	Lea	GP	G	A	TP	PIM	GP	G	A	TP	PIM
1991-92	Spokane	WHL	67	23	37	60	119	10	5	10	15	18
1992-93	Spokane	WHL	60	26	58	84	122	9	7	2	9	8
1993-94a	Spokane	WHL	71	57	69	126	111	3	3	5	8	11
1994-95	Saint John	AHL	72	18	21	39	70	2	0	0	0	0
1995-96	Adirondack	AHL	52	16	21	37	36	3	1	0	1	2

a WHL West First All-Star Team (1994)

Re-entered NHL Entry Draft. **Calgary's** 4th choice, 91st overall in 1994 Entry Draft.

DUTIAUME, MARK — BUF.

Left wing. Shoots left. 6', 200 lbs. Born, Winnipeg, Man., January 31, 1977.
(Buffalo's 3rd choice, 42nd overall, in 1995 Entry Draft).

			Regular Season					Playoffs				
Season	Club	Lea	GP	G	A	TP	PIM	GP	G	A	TP	PIM
1993-94	Tri-City	WHL	3	2	0	2	0	....	....	....	....	....
	Brandon	WHL	55	4	7	11	43	12	0	2	2	6
1994-95	Brandon	WHL	62	23	21	44	80	17	1	2	3	33
1995-96	Brandon	WHL	7	0	4	4	6	9	2	1	3	12

DVORAK, RADEK — (duh-VOHR-ak) — FLA.

Left wing. Shoots right. 6'2", 187 lbs. Born, Tabor, Czech., March 9, 1977.
(Florida's 1st choice, 10th overall, in 1995 Entry Draft).

			Regular Season					Playoffs				
Season	Club	Lea	GP	G	A	TP	PIM	GP	G	A	TP	PIM
1993-94	Budejovice	Czech.	8	0	0	0	0	....	....	....	....	....
1994-95	Budejovice	Czech.	10	3	5	8	2	9	5	1	6	....
1995-96	**Florida**	**NHL**	**77**	**13**	**14**	**27**	**20**	**16**	**1**	**3**	**4**	**0**
	NHL Totals		**77**	**13**	**14**	**27**	**20**	**16**	**1**	**3**	**4**	**0**

DWYER, GORDIE — ST.L.

Left wing. Shoots left. 6'2", 190 lbs. Born, Dalhousie, NB, January 25, 1978.
(St. Louis' 2nd choice, 67th overall, in 1996 Entry Draft).

			Regular Season					Playoffs				
Season	Club	Lea	GP	G	A	TP	PIM	GP	G	A	TP	PIM
1994-95	Hull	QMJHL	57	3	7	10	204	17	1	3	4	54
1995-96	Hull	QMJHL	25	5	9	14	199	....	....	....	....	....
	Laval	QMJHL	22	5	17	22	72	....	....	....	....	....
	Beauport	QMJHL	22	4	9	13	87	20	3	5	8	104

DYKHUIS, KARL — (DIGH-kowz) — PHI.

Defense. Shoots left. 6'3", 205 lbs. Born, Sept-Iles, Que., July 8, 1972.
(Chicago's 1st choice, 16th overall, in 1990 Entry Draft).

			Regular Season					Playoffs				
Season	Club	Lea	GP	G	A	TP	PIM	GP	G	A	TP	PIM
1988-89	Hull	QMJHL	63	2	29	31	59	9	1	9	10	6
1989-90a	Hull	QMJHL	69	10	46	56	119	11	2	5	7	2
1990-91	Cdn. National	....	37	2	9	11	16	....	....	....	....	....
	Longueuil	QMJHL	3	1	4	4	6	8	2	5	7	6
1991-92	**Chicago**	**NHL**	**6**	**1**	**3**	**4**	**4**	....	....	....	....	....
	Cdn. National	....	19	1	2	3	16	....	....	....	....	....
	Verdun	QMJHL	29	5	19	24	55	17	0	12	12	14
1992-93	**Chicago**	**NHL**	**12**	**0**	**5**	**5**	**0**	....	....	....	....	....
	Indianapolis	IHL	59	5	18	23	76	5	1	1	2	8
1993-94	Indianapolis	IHL	73	7	25	32	132	....	....	....	....	....
1994-95	Indianapolis	IHL	52	2	21	23	63	....	....	....	....	....
	Hershey	AHL	1	0	0	0	0	....	....	....	....	....
	Philadelphia	**NHL**	**33**	**2**	**6**	**8**	**37**	**15**	**4**	**4**	**8**	**14**
1995-96	**Philadelphia**	**NHL**	**82**	**5**	**15**	**20**	**101**	**12**	**2**	**2**	**4**	**22**
	NHL Totals		**133**	**8**	**29**	**37**	**142**	**27**	**6**	**6**	**12**	**36**

a QMJHL First All-Star Team (1990)

Traded to **Philadelphia** by **Chicago** for Bob Wilkie and a possible conditional choice in 1997 Entry Draft, February 16, 1995.

DZIEDZIC, JOE — (zehd-ZIHK) — PIT.

Left wing. Shoots left. 6'3", 227 lbs. Born, Minneapolis, MN, December 18, 1971.
(Pittsburgh's 2nd choice, 61st overall, in 1990 Entry Draft).

			Regular Season					Playoffs				
Season	Club	Lea	GP	G	A	TP	PIM	GP	G	A	TP	PIM
1990-91	U. Minnesota	WCHA	20	6	4	10	26	....	....	....	....	....
1991-92	U. Minnesota	WCHA	34	8	9	17	68	....	....	....	....	....
1992-93	U. Minnesota	WCHA	41	11	14	25	62	....	....	....	....	....
1993-94	U. Minnesota	WCHA	18	7	10	17	48	....	....	....	....	....
1994-95	Cleveland	IHL	68	15	15	30	74	4	1	0	1	10
1995-96	**Pittsburgh**	**NHL**	**69**	**5**	**5**	**10**	**68**	**16**	**1**	**2**	**3**	**19**
	NHL Totals		**69**	**5**	**5**	**10**	**68**	**16**	**1**	**2**	**3**	**19**

EAGLES, MIKE — WSH.

Center/Left wing. Shoots left. 5'10", 190 lbs. Born, Sussex, N.B., March 7, 1963.
(Quebec's 5th choice, 116th overall, in 1981 Entry Draft).

			Regular Season					Playoffs				
Season	Club	Lea	GP	G	A	TP	PIM	GP	G	A	TP	PIM
1980-81	Kitchener	OHA	56	11	27	38	64	18	4	2	6	36
1981-82	Kitchener	OHL	62	26	40	66	148	15	3	11	14	27
1982-83	**Quebec**	**NHL**	**2**	**0**	**0**	**0**	**2**	....	....	....	....	....
	Kitchener	OHL	58	26	36	62	133	12	5	7	12	27
1983-84	Fredericton	AHL	68	13	29	42	85	4	0	0	0	5
1984-85	Fredericton	AHL	36	4	20	24	80	3	0	0	0	2
1985-86	**Quebec**	**NHL**	**73**	**11**	**12**	**23**	**49**	**3**	**0**	**0**	**0**	**2**
1986-87	**Quebec**	**NHL**	**73**	**13**	**19**	**32**	**55**	**4**	**1**	**0**	**1**	**10**
1987-88	**Quebec**	**NHL**	**76**	**10**	**10**	**20**	**74**	....	....	....	....	....
1988-89	**Chicago**	**NHL**	**47**	**5**	**11**	**16**	**44**	....	....	....	....	....
1989-90	**Chicago**	**NHL**	**23**	**1**	**2**	**3**	**34**	....	....	....	....	....
	Indianapolis	IHL	24	11	13	24	47	13	*10	10	20	34
1990-91	**Winnipeg**	**NHL**	**44**	**0**	**9**	**9**	**79**	....	....	....	....	....
	Indianapolis	IHL	25	15	14	29	47	....	....	....	....	....
1991-92	**Winnipeg**	**NHL**	**65**	**7**	**10**	**17**	**118**	**7**	**0**	**0**	**0**	**8**
1992-93	**Winnipeg**	**NHL**	**84**	**8**	**18**	**26**	**131**	**5**	**0**	**1**	**1**	**6**
1993-94	**Winnipeg**	**NHL**	**73**	**4**	**8**	**12**	**96**	....	....	....	....	....
1994-95	**Winnipeg**	**NHL**	**27**	**2**	**1**	**3**	**40**	....	....	....	....	....
	Washington	**NHL**	**13**	**1**	**3**	**4**	**8**	**7**	**0**	**2**	**2**	**4**
1995-96	**Washington**	**NHL**	**70**	**4**	**7**	**11**	**75**	**6**	**1**	**1**	**2**	**2**
	NHL Totals		**670**	**66**	**110**	**176**	**805**	**32**	**2**	**4**	**6**	**32**

Traded to **Chicago** by **Quebec** for Bob Mason, July 5, 1988. Traded to **Winnipeg** by **Chicago** for Winnipeg's fourth round choice (Igor Kravchuk) in 1991 Entry Draft, December 14, 1990. Traded to **Washington** by **Winnipeg** with Igor Ulanov for Washington's third (later traded to Dallas — Dallas selected Sergei Gusev) and fifth (Brian Elder) round choices in 1995 Entry Draft, April 7, 1995.

EAKINS, DALLAS — (EE-kins) — PHO.

Defense. Shoots left. 6'2", 195 lbs. Born, Dade City, FL, February 27, 1967.
(Washington's 11th choice, 208th overall, in 1985 Entry Draft).

			Regular Season					Playoffs				
Season	Club	Lea	GP	G	A	TP	PIM	GP	G	A	TP	PIM
1984-85	Peterborough	OHL	48	0	8	8	96	7	0	0	0	18
1985-86	Peterborough	OHL	60	6	16	22	134	16	0	1	1	30
1986-87	Peterborough	OHL	54	3	11	14	145	12	1	4	5	37
1987-88	Peterborough	OHL	64	11	27	38	129	12	3	12	15	16
1988-89	Baltimore	AHL	62	0	10	10	139	....	....	....	....	....
1989-90	Moncton	AHL	75	2	11	13	189	....	....	....	....	....
1990-91	Moncton	AHL	75	1	12	13	132	9	0	1	1	44
1991-92	Moncton	AHL	67	3	13	16	136	11	2	1	3	16
1992-93	**Winnipeg**	**NHL**	**14**	**0**	**2**	**2**	**38**	....	....	....	....	....
	Moncton	AHL	55	4	6	10	132	....	....	....	....	....
1993-94	**Florida**	**NHL**	**1**	**0**	**0**	**0**	**0**	....	....	....	....	....
	Cincinnati	IHL	80	1	18	19	143	8	0	1	1	41
1994-95	Cincinnati	IHL	59	6	12	18	69	....	....	....	....	....
	Florida	**NHL**	**17**	**0**	**1**	**1**	**35**	....	....	....	....	....
1995-96	**St. Louis**	**NHL**	**16**	**0**	**1**	**1**	**34**	....	....	....	....	....
	Worcester	AHL	4	0	0	0	12	....	....	....	....	....
	Winnipeg	**NHL**	**2**	**0**	**0**	**0**	**0**	....	....	....	....	....
	NHL Totals		**50**	**0**	**4**	**4**	**107**	....	....	....	....	....

Signed as a free agent by **Winnipeg**, October 17, 1989. Signed as a free agent by **Florida**, July 8, 1993. Traded to **St. Louis** by **Florida** for St. Louis' fourth round choice in 1997 Entry Draft, September 28, 1995. Claimed on waivers by **Winnipeg** from **St. Louis**, March 20, 1996.

EASTWOOD, MIKE — PHO.

Center. Shoots right. 6'3", 205 lbs. Born, Ottawa, Ont., July 1, 1967.
(Toronto's 5th choice, 91st overall, in 1987 Entry Draft).

			Regular Season					Playoffs				
Season	Club	Lea	GP	G	A	TP	PIM	GP	G	A	TP	PIM
1987-88	W. Michigan	CCHA	42	5	8	13	14	....	....	....	....	....
1988-89	W. Michigan	CCHA	40	10	13	23	87	....	....	....	....	....
1989-90	W. Michigan	CCHA	40	25	27	52	36	....	....	....	....	....
1990-91a	W. Michigan	CCHA	42	29	32	61	84	....	....	....	....	....
1991-92	**Toronto**	**NHL**	**9**	**0**	**2**	**2**	**4**	....	....	....	....	....
	St. John's	AHL	61	18	25	43	28	16	9	10	19	16
1992-93	**Toronto**	**NHL**	**12**	**1**	**6**	**7**	**21**	**10**	**1**	**2**	**3**	**8**
	St. John's	AHL	60	24	35	59	32	....	....	....	....	....
1993-94	**Toronto**	**NHL**	**54**	**8**	**10**	**18**	**28**	**18**	**3**	**2**	**5**	**12**
1994-95	**Toronto**	**NHL**	**36**	**5**	**5**	**10**	**32**	....	....	....	....	....
	Winnipeg	**NHL**	**13**	**3**	**6**	**9**	**4**	....	....	....	....	....
1995-96	**Winnipeg**	**NHL**	**80**	**14**	**14**	**28**	**20**	**6**	**0**	**1**	**1**	**2**
	NHL Totals		**204**	**31**	**43**	**74**	**109**	**34**	**4**	**5**	**9**	**22**

a CCHA Second All-Star Team (1991)

Traded to **Winnipeg** by **Toronto** with Toronto's third round choice (Brad Isbister) in 1995 Entry Draft for Tie Domi, April 7, 1995.

EGELAND, ALLAN — T.B.

Center. Shoots left. 6', 184 lbs. Born, Lethbridge, Alta., January 31, 1973.
(Tampa Bay's 3rd choice, 55th overall, in 1993 Entry Draft).

			Regular Season					Playoffs				
Season	Club	Lea	GP	G	A	TP	PIM	GP	G	A	TP	PIM
1990-91	Lethbridge	WHL	67	2	16	18	57	9	0	0	0	0
1991-92	Tacoma	WHL	72	35	39	74	135	4	0	1	1	18
1992-93a	Tacoma	WHL	71	56	57	113	119	7	9	7	16	18
1993-94b	Tacoma	WHL	70	47	76	123	204	8	5	3	8	26
1994-95	Atlanta	IHL	60	8	16	24	112	5	0	1	1	16
1995-96	**Tampa Bay**	**NHL**	**5**	**0**	**0**	**0**	**2**	....	....	....	....	....
	Atlanta	IHL	68	22	22	44	182	3	0	1	1	0
	NHL Totals		**5**	**0**	**0**	**0**	**2**	....	....	....	....	....

a WHL West First All-Star Team (1993)
b WHL West Second All-Star Team (1994)

EISENHUT, NEIL — (IGHS-ihn-huht)

Center. Shoots left. 6'1", 190 lbs. Born, Osoyoos, B.C., February 9, 1967.
(Vancouver's 11th choice, 238th overall, in 1987 Entry Draft).

			Regular Season					Playoffs				
Season	Club	Lea	GP	G	A	TP	PIM	GP	G	A	TP	PIM
1987-88	North Dakota	WCHA	42	12	20	32	14	....	....	....	....	....
1988-89	North Dakota	WCHA	41	22	16	38	20	....	....	....	....	....
1989-90	North Dakota	WCHA	45	22	32	54	46	....	....	....	....	....
1990-91	North Dakota	WCHA	20	9	15	24	10	....	....	....	....	....
1991-92	Milwaukee	IHL	76	13	23	36	26	2	1	2	3	0
1992-93	Hamilton	AHL	72	22	40	62	41	....	....	....	....	....
1993-94	**Vancouver**	**NHL**	**13**	**1**	**3**	**4**	**21**	....	....	....	....	....
	Hamilton	AHL	60	17	36	53	30	4	1	4	5	0
1994-95	Saint John	AHL	75	16	39	55	30	5	1	1	2	6
	Calgary	**NHL**	**3**	**0**	**0**	**0**	**0**	....	....	....	....	....
1995-96	Orlando	IHL	59	10	18	28	30	....	....	....	....	....
	Binghamton	AHL	10	3	3	6	2	4	3	2	5	0
	NHL Totals		**16**	**1**	**3**	**4**	**21**	....	....	....	....	....

Signed as a free agent by **Calgary**, June 16, 1994.

EKLUND, PER — DET.

Left wing. Shoots left. 5'11", 196 lbs. Born, Sollentuna, Sweden, July 9, 1970.
(Detroit's 8th choice, 182nd overall, in 1995 Entry Draft).

			Regular Season					Playoffs				
Season	Club	Lea	GP	G	A	TP	PIM	GP	G	A	TP	PIM
1991-92	Vasby	Swe. 2	29	13	24	37	26	....	....	....	....	....
1992-93	Huddinge	Swe. 2	36	22	23	45	14	....	....	....	....	....
1993-94	Huddinge	Swe. 2	35	20	11	31	40	....	....	....	....	....
1994-95	Djurgarden	Swe.	40	19	10	29	20	3	1	1	2	4
1995-96	Djurgarden	Swe.	39	17	10	27	10	1	0	0	0	0

EKMAN, NILS — (EHK-mahn) CGY.

Left wing. Shoots left. 5'11", 175 lbs. Born, Stockholm, Sweden, March 11, 1976.
(Calgary's 6th choice, 107th overall, in 1994 Entry Draft).

			Regular Season					Playoffs				
Season	Club	Lea	GP	G	A	TP	PIM	GP	G	A	TP	PIM
1993-94	Hammarby	Swe. 2	18	7	2	9	4	....	....	....	....	....
1994-95	Hammarby	Swe. 2	29	10	7	17	18	....	....	....	....	....
1995-96	Hammarby	Swe. 2	26	9	7	16	53	1	0	0	0	0

ELFRING, CALVIN — COL.

Defense. Shoots left. 6', 170 lbs. Born, Lethbridge, Alta., April 23, 1976.
(Quebec's 9th choice, 165th overall, in 1994 Entry Draft).

			Regular Season					Playoffs				
Season	Club	Lea	GP	G	A	TP	PIM	GP	G	A	TP	PIM
1994-95	Colorado	WCHA	43	3	23	26	34	....	....	....	....	....
1995-96	Colorado	WCHA	42	10	24	34	32	....	....	....	....	....

ELIAS, PATRIK — (EH-lih-ahsh) N.J.

Left wing. Shoots left. 6', 175 lbs. Born, Trebic, Czech., April 13, 1976.
(New Jersey's 2nd choice, 51st overall, in 1994 Entry Draft).

			Regular Season					Playoffs				
Season	Club	Lea	GP	G	A	TP	PIM	GP	G	A	TP	PIM
1992-93	Kladno	Czech.	2	0	0	0	....	....	....	....	....	....
1993-94	Kladno	Czech.	15	1	2	3	....	11	2	2	4	....
1994-95	Kladno	Czech.	28	4	3	7	37	7	1	2	3	12
1995-96	**New Jersey**	**NHL**	**1**	**0**	**0**	**0**	**0**	....	....	....	....	....
	Albany	AHL	74	27	36	63	83	4	1	1	2	2
	NHL Totals		**1**	**0**	**0**	**0**	**0**	....	....	....	....	....

ELICK, MICKEY — NYR

Defense. Shoots left. 6'1", 180 lbs. Born, Calgary, Alta., March 17, 1974.
(NY Rangers' 8th choice, 192nd overall, in 1992 Entry Draft).

			Regular Season					Playoffs				
Season	Club	Lea	GP	G	A	TP	PIM	GP	G	A	TP	PIM
1992-93	U. Wisconsin	WCHA	33	1	6	7	24	....	....	....	....	....
1993-94	U. Wisconsin	WCHA	42	7	12	19	54	....	....	....	....	....
1994-95	U. Wisconsin	WCHA	43	5	24	29	52	....	....	....	....	....
1995-96	U. Wisconsin	WCHA	39	14	26	40	60	....	....	....	....	....

ELIK, TODD — (EHL-ihk) BOS.

Center. Shoots left. 6'2", 195 lbs. Born, Brampton, Ont., April 15, 1966.

			Regular Season					Playoffs				
Season	Club	Lea	GP	G	A	TP	PIM	GP	G	A	TP	PIM
1984-85	Kingston	OHL	34	14	11	25	6	....	....	....	....	....
	North Bay	OHL	23	4	6	10	2	4	2	0	2	0
1985-86	North Bay	OHL	40	12	34	46	20	10	7	6	13	0
1986-87	U. of Regina	CWUAA	27	26	34	60	137	....	....	....	....	....
	Cdn. National	....	1	0	0	0	0	....	....	....	....	....
1987-88	Colorado	IHL	81	44	56	100	83	12	8	12	20	9
1988-89	Denver	IHL	28	20	15	35	22	....	....	....	....	....
	New Haven	AHL	43	11	25	36	31	17	10	12	22	44
1989-90	**Los Angeles**	**NHL**	**48**	**10**	**23**	**33**	**41**	**10**	**3**	**9**	**12**	**10**
	New Haven	AHL	32	20	23	43	42	....	....	....	....	....
1990-91	**Los Angeles**	**NHL**	**74**	**21**	**37**	**58**	**58**	**12**	**2**	**7**	**9**	**6**
1991-92	**Minnesota**	**NHL**	**62**	**14**	**32**	**46**	**125**	**5**	**1**	**1**	**2**	**2**
1992-93	**Minnesota**	**NHL**	**46**	**13**	**18**	**31**	**48**	....	....	....	....	....
	Edmonton	**NHL**	**14**	**1**	**9**	**10**	**8**	....	....	....	....	....
1993-94	**Edmonton**	**NHL**	**4**	**0**	**0**	**0**	**6**	....	....	....	....	....
	San Jose	**NHL**	**75**	**25**	**41**	**66**	**89**	**14**	**5**	**5**	**10**	**12**
1994-95	**San Jose**	**NHL**	**22**	**7**	**10**	**17**	**18**	....	....	....	....	....
	St. Louis	**NHL**	**13**	**2**	**4**	**6**	**4**	**7**	**4**	**3**	**7**	**2**
1995-96	**Boston**	**NHL**	**59**	**13**	**33**	**46**	**40**	**4**	**0**	**2**	**2**	**16**
	Providence	AHL	7	2	7	9	10	....	....	....	....	....
	NHL Totals		**417**	**106**	**207**	**313**	**437**	**52**	**15**	**27**	**42**	**48**

Signed as a free agent by **NY Rangers**, February 26, 1988. Traded to **Los Angeles** by **NY Rangers** with Igor Liba, Michael Boyce and future considerations for Dean Kennedy and Denis Larocque, December 12, 1988. Traded to **Minnesota** by **Los Angeles** for Randy Gilhen, Charlie Huddy, Jim Thomson and NY Rangers' fourth round choice (previously acquired by Minnesota — Los Angeles selected Alexei Zhitnik) in 1991 Entry Draft, June 22, 1991. Traded to **Edmonton** by **Minnesota** for Brent Gilchrist, March 5, 1993. Claimed on waivers by **San Jose** from **Edmonton**, October 26, 1993. Traded to **St. Louis** by **San Jose** for Kevin Miller, March 23, 1995. Signed as a free agent by **Boston**, August 8, 1995.

ELLETT, DAVE — TOR.

Defense. Shoots left. 6'2", 205 lbs. Born, Cleveland, OH, March 30, 1964.
(Winnipeg's 3rd choice, 75th overall, in 1982 Entry Draft).

			Regular Season					Playoffs				
Season	Club	Lea	GP	G	A	TP	PIM	GP	G	A	TP	PIM
1982-83	Bowling Green	CCHA	40	4	13	17	34	....	....	....	....	....
1983-84ab	Bowling Green	CCHA	43	15	39	54	96	....	....	....	....	....
1984-85	**Winnipeg**	**NHL**	**80**	**11**	**27**	**38**	**85**	**8**	**1**	**5**	**6**	**4**
1985-86	**Winnipeg**	**NHL**	**80**	**15**	**31**	**46**	**96**	**3**	**0**	**1**	**1**	**0**
1986-87	**Winnipeg**	**NHL**	**78**	**13**	**31**	**44**	**53**	**10**	**0**	**8**	**8**	**2**
1987-88	**Winnipeg**	**NHL**	**68**	**13**	**45**	**58**	**106**	**5**	**1**	**2**	**3**	**10**
1988-89	**Winnipeg**	**NHL**	**75**	**22**	**34**	**56**	**62**	....	....	....	....	....
1989-90	**Winnipeg**	**NHL**	**77**	**17**	**29**	**46**	**96**	**7**	**2**	**0**	**2**	**6**
1990-91	**Winnipeg**	**NHL**	**17**	**4**	**7**	**11**	**6**	....	....	....	....	....
	Toronto	**NHL**	**60**	**8**	**30**	**38**	**69**	....	....	....	....	....
1991-92	**Toronto**	**NHL**	**79**	**18**	**33**	**51**	**95**	....	....	....	....	....
1992-93	**Toronto**	**NHL**	**70**	**6**	**34**	**40**	**46**	**21**	**4**	**8**	**12**	**8**
1993-94	**Toronto**	**NHL**	**68**	**7**	**36**	**43**	**42**	**18**	**3**	**15**	**18**	**31**
1994-95	**Toronto**	**NHL**	**33**	**5**	**10**	**15**	**26**	**7**	**0**	**2**	**2**	**0**
1995-96	**Toronto**	**NHL**	**80**	**3**	**19**	**22**	**59**	**6**	**0**	**0**	**0**	**4**
	NHL Totals		**865**	**142**	**366**	**508**	**841**	**85**	**11**	**41**	**52**	**65**

a CCHA Second All-Star Team (1984)
b Named to NCAA All-Tournament Team (1984)

Played in NHL All-Star Game (1989, 1992)

Traded to **Toronto** by **Winnipeg** with Paul Fenton for Ed Olczyk and Mark Osborne, November 10, 1990.

ELOMO, MIIKA — (eh-LOH-moh, MEE-ka) WSH.

Left wing. Shoots left. 6', 180 lbs. Born, Turku, Finland, April 21, 1977.
(Washington's 2nd choice, 23rd overall, in 1995 Entry Draft).

			Regular Season					Playoffs				
Season	Club	Lea	GP	G	A	TP	PIM	GP	G	A	TP	PIM
1994-95	Kiekko-67	Fin. 2	14	9	2	11	39	....	....	....	....	....
	TPS	Fin. Jr.	14	3	8	11	24	....	....	....	....	....
1995-96	TPS	Fin. Jr.	6	0	2	2	18	....	....	....	....	....
	Kiekko-67	Fin. 2	21	9	6	15	100	....	....	....	....	....
	TPS	Fin.	10	1	1	2	8	3	0	0	0	2

ELYNUIK, PAT — (EL-ih-NYUK) DAL.

Right wing. Shoots right. 6', 185 lbs. Born, Foam Lake, Sask., October 30, 1967.
(Winnipeg's 1st choice, 8th overall, in 1986 Entry Draft).

			Regular Season					Playoffs				
Season	Club	Lea	GP	G	A	TP	PIM	GP	G	A	TP	PIM
1984-85	Prince Albert	WHL	70	23	20	43	54	13	9	3	12	7
1985-86a	Prince Albert	WHL	68	53	53	106	62	20	7	9	16	17
1986-87a	Prince Albert	WHL	64	51	62	113	40	8	5	5	10	12
1987-88	**Winnipeg**	**NHL**	**13**	**1**	**3**	**4**	**12**	....	....	....	....	....
	Moncton	AHL	30	11	18	29	35	....	....	....	....	....
1988-89	**Winnipeg**	**NHL**	**56**	**26**	**25**	**51**	**29**	....	....	....	....	....
	Moncton	AHL	7	8	2	10	2	....	....	....	....	....
1989-90	**Winnipeg**	**NHL**	**80**	**32**	**42**	**74**	**83**	**7**	**2**	**4**	**6**	**2**
1990-91	**Winnipeg**	**NHL**	**80**	**31**	**34**	**65**	**73**	....	....	....	....	....
1991-92	**Winnipeg**	**NHL**	**60**	**25**	**25**	**50**	**65**	**7**	**2**	**2**	**4**	**4**
1992-93	**Washington**	**NHL**	**80**	**22**	**35**	**57**	**66**	**6**	**2**	**3**	**5**	**19**
1993-94	**Washington**	**NHL**	**4**	**1**	**1**	**2**	**0**	....	....	....	....	....
	Tampa Bay	**NHL**	**63**	**12**	**14**	**26**	**64**	....	....	....	....	....
1994-95	**Ottawa**	**NHL**	**41**	**3**	**7**	**10**	**51**	....	....	....	....	....
1995-96	**Ottawa**	**NHL**	**29**	**1**	**2**	**3**	**16**	....	....	....	....	....
	Fort Wayne	IHL	42	22	28	50	43	....	....	....	....	....
	NHL Totals		**506**	**154**	**188**	**342**	**459**	**20**	**6**	**9**	**15**	**25**

a WHL East All-Star Team (1986, 1987)

Traded to **Washington** by **Winnipeg** for John Druce and Toronto's fourth round choice (previously acquired by Washington — later traded to Detroit — Detroit selected John Jakopin) in 1993 Entry Draft, October 1, 1992. Signed as a free agent by **Ottawa**, June 22, 1994. Traded to **Tampa Bay** by **Washington** for future draft choices, October 22, 1993. Signed as a free agent by **Ottawa**, June 21, 1994. Signed as a free agent by **Dallas**, August 6, 1996.

EMERSON, NELSON — HFD.

Right wing. Shoots right. 5'11", 175 lbs. Born, Hamilton, Ont., August 17, 1967.
(St. Louis' 2nd choice, 44th overall, in 1985 Entry Draft).

			Regular Season					Playoffs				
Season	Club	Lea	GP	G	A	TP	PIM	GP	G	A	TP	PIM
1986-87	Bowling Green	CCHA	45	26	35	61	28	....	....	....	....	....
1987-88ab	Bowling Green	CCHA	45	34	49	83	54	....	....	....	....	....
1988-89c	Bowling Green	CCHA	44	22	46	68	46	....	....	....	....	....
1989-90bd	Bowling Green	CCHA	44	30	52	82	42	....	....	....	....	....
	Peoria	IHL	3	1	1	2	0	....	....	....	....	....
1990-91	**St. Louis**	**NHL**	**4**	**0**	**3**	**3**	**2**	....	....	....	....	....
ef	Peoria	IHL	73	36	79	115	91	17	9	12	21	16
1991-92	**St. Louis**	**NHL**	**79**	**23**	**36**	**59**	**66**	**6**	**3**	**3**	**6**	**21**
1992-93	**St. Louis**	**NHL**	**82**	**22**	**51**	**73**	**62**	**11**	**1**	**6**	**7**	**6**
1993-94	**Winnipeg**	**NHL**	**83**	**33**	**41**	**74**	**80**	....	....	....	....	....
1994-95	**Winnipeg**	**NHL**	**48**	**14**	**23**	**37**	**26**	....	....	....	....	....
1995-96	**Hartford**	**NHL**	**81**	**29**	**29**	**58**	**78**	....	....	....	....	....
	NHL Totals		**377**	**121**	**183**	**304**	**314**	**17**	**4**	**9**	**13**	**27**

a NCAA West Second All-American Team (1988)
b CCHA First All-Star Team (1988, 1990)
c CCHA Second All-Star Team (1989)
d NCAA West First All-American Team (1990)
e IHL First All-Star Team (1991)
f Won Garry F. Longman Memorial Trophy (Top Rookie - IHL) (1991)

Traded to **Winnipeg** by **St. Louis** with Stephane Quintal for Phil Housley, September 24, 1993. Traded to **Hartford** by **Winnipeg** for Darren Turcotte, October 6, 1995.

EMMA, DAVID

Center. Shoots left. 5'11", 180 lbs. Born, Cranston, RI, January 14, 1969.
(New Jersey's 6th choice, 110th overall, in 1989 Entry Draft).

			Regular Season					Playoffs				
Season	Club	Lea	GP	G	A	TP	PIM	GP	G	A	TP	PIM
1987-88	Boston College	H.E.	30	19	16	35	30	....	....	....	....	....
1988-89	Boston College	H.E.	36	20	31	51	36	....	....	....	....	....
1989-90ab	Boston College	H.E.	42	38	34	*72	46	....	....	....	....	....
1990-91abcd	Boston College	H.E.	39	*35	46	*81	44	....	....	....	....	....
1991-92	U.S. National	....	55	15	16	31	32	....	....	....	....	....
	U.S. Olympic	....	6	0	1	1	6	....	....	....	....	....
	Utica	AHL	15	4	7	11	12	4	1	1	2	2
1992-93	**New Jersey**	**NHL**	**2**	**0**	**0**	**0**	**0**	....	....	....	....	....
	Utica	AHL	61	21	40	61	47	5	2	1	3	6
1993-94	**New Jersey**	**NHL**	**15**	**5**	**5**	**10**	**2**	....	....	....	....	....
	Albany	AHL	56	26	29	55	53	5	1	2	3	8
1994-95	**New Jersey**	**NHL**	**6**	**0**	**1**	**1**	**0**	....	....	....	....	....
	Albany	AHL	1	0	0	0	0	....	....	....	....	....
1995-96	Detroit	IHL	79	30	32	62	75	11	5	2	7	2
	NHL Totals		**23**	**5**	**6**	**11**	**2**	....	....	....	....	....

a Hockey East First All-Star Team (1990, 1991)
b NCAA East First All-American Team (1990, 1991)
c Hockey East Player of the Year (1991)
d Won Hobey Baker Memorial Award (Top U.S. Collegiate Player) (1991)

EMMONS, JOHN — CGY.

Center. Shoots left. 6', 185 lbs. Born, San Jose, CA, August 17, 1974.
(Calgary's 7th choice, 122nd overall, in 1993 Entry Draft).

			Regular Season					Playoffs				
Season	Club	Lea	GP	G	A	TP	PIM	GP	G	A	TP	PIM
1992-93	Yale	ECAC	28	3	5	8	66	....	....	....	....	....
1993-94	Yale	ECAC	25	5	12	17	66	....	....	....	....	....
1994-95	Yale	ECAC	28	4	16	20	57	....	....	....	....	....
1995-96	Yale	ECAC	31	8	20	28	124	....	....	....	....	....

ENGBLOM, DAVID — DET.

Center. Shoots left. 6'1", 183 lbs. Born, Vallentuna, Sweden, June 2, 1977.
(Detroit's 10th choice, 234th overall, in 1995 Entry Draft).

			Regular Season					Playoffs				
Season	Club	Lea	GP	G	A	TP	PIM	GP	G	A	TP	PIM
1993-94	Vallentuna	Swe. 2	27	0	0	0	4	....	....	....	....	....
1994-95	Vallentuna	Swe. 2	32	1	4	5	12	....	....	....	....	....
1995-96	AIK	Swe.	39	0	4	4	6	....	....	....	....	....

ENGLEHART, BRAD — ANA.

Center. Shoots left. 5'11", 180 lbs. Born, Woodstock, N.B., September 16, 1975.
(Anaheim's 8th choice, 184th overall, in 1994 Entry Draft).

			Regular Season					Playoffs				
Season	Club	Lea	GP	G	A	TP	PIM	GP	G	A	TP	PIM
1994-95	U. Wisconsin	WCHA	29	6	6	12	42	....	....	....	....	....
1995-96	U. Wisconsin	WCHA	39	6	7	13	67	....	....	....	....	....

EPANCHINTSEV, VADIM (yeh-pahn-CHIHN-tsehv) — T.B.

Center. Shoots left. 5'9", 165 lbs. Born, Orsk, USSR, March 16, 1976.
(Tampa Bay's 3rd choice, 55th overall, in 1994 Entry Draft).

			Regular Season					Playoffs				
Season	Club	Lea	GP	G	A	TP	PIM	GP	G	A	TP	PIM
1993-94	Spartak	CIS	46	6	5	11	16	3	0	1	1	0
1994-95	Spartak	CIS	43	4	8	12	24	....	....	....	....	....
1995-96	Spartak	CIS	51	20	12	32	28	4	0	2	2	4

ERIKSSON, ANDERS — DET.

Defense. Shoots left. 6'3", 218 lbs. Born, Bollnas, Sweden, January 9, 1975.
(Detroit's 1st choice, 22nd overall, in 1993 Entry Draft).

			Regular Season					Playoffs				
Season	Club	Lea	GP	G	A	TP	PIM	GP	G	A	TP	PIM
1992-93	MoDo	Swe.	20	0	2	2	2	1	0	0	0	0
1993-94	MoDo	Swe.	38	2	8	10	42	11	0	0	0	8
1994-95	MoDo	Swe.	39	3	6	9	54	....	....	....	....	....
1995-96	**Detroit**	**NHL**	**1**	**0**	**0**	**0**	**2**	**3**	**0**	**0**	**0**	**0**
	Adirondack	AHL	75	6	36	42	64	3	0	0	0	0
	NHL Totals		**1**	**0**	**0**	**0**	**2**	**3**	**0**	**0**	**0**	**0**

ERREY, BOB (AIRY) — DET.

Left wing. Shoots left. 5'10", 185 lbs. Born, Montreal, Que., September 21, 1964.
(Pittsburgh's 1st choice, 15th overall, in 1983 Entry Draft).

			Regular Season					Playoffs				
Season	Club	Lea	GP	G	A	TP	PIM	GP	G	A	TP	PIM
1981-82	Peterborough	OHL	68	29	31	60	39	9	3	1	4	9
1982-83a	Peterborough	OHL	67	53	47	100	74	4	1	3	4	7
1983-84	**Pittsburgh**	**NHL**	**65**	**9**	**13**	**22**	**29**	....	....	....	....	....
1984-85	**Pittsburgh**	**NHL**	**16**	**0**	**2**	**2**	**7**	....	....	....	....	....
	Baltimore	AHL	59	17	24	41	14	8	3	4	7	11
1985-86	**Pittsburgh**	**NHL**	**37**	**11**	**6**	**17**	**8**	....	....	....	....	....
	Baltimore	AHL	18	8	7	15	28	....	....	....	....	....
1986-87	**Pittsburgh**	**NHL**	**72**	**16**	**18**	**34**	**46**	....	....	....	....	....
1987-88	**Pittsburgh**	**NHL**	**17**	**3**	**6**	**9**	**18**	....	....	....	....	....
1988-89	**Pittsburgh**	**NHL**	**76**	**26**	**32**	**58**	**124**	**11**	**1**	**2**	**3**	**12**
1989-90	**Pittsburgh**	**NHL**	**78**	**20**	**19**	**39**	**109**	....	....	....	....	....
1990-91	**Pittsburgh**	**NHL**	**79**	**20**	**22**	**42**	**115**	**24**	**5**	**2**	**7**	**29** ♦
1991-92	**Pittsburgh**	**NHL**	**78**	**19**	**16**	**35**	**119**	**14**	**3**	**0**	**3**	**10** ♦
1992-93	**Pittsburgh**	**NHL**	**54**	**8**	**6**	**14**	**76**	....	....	....	....	....
	Buffalo	**NHL**	**8**	**1**	**3**	**4**	**4**	**4**	**0**	**1**	**1**	**10**
1993-94	**San Jose**	**NHL**	**64**	**12**	**18**	**30**	**126**	**14**	**3**	**2**	**5**	**10**
1994-95	**San Jose**	**NHL**	**13**	**2**	**2**	**4**	**27**	....	....	....	....	....
	Detroit	**NHL**	**30**	**6**	**11**	**17**	**31**	**18**	**1**	**5**	**6**	**30**
1995-96	**Detroit**	**NHL**	**71**	**11**	**21**	**32**	**66**	**14**	**0**	**4**	**4**	**8**
	NHL Totals		**758**	**164**	**195**	**359**	**905**	**99**	**13**	**16**	**29**	**109**

a OHL First All-Star Team (1983)

Traded to **Buffalo** by **Pittsburgh** for Mike Ramsey, March 22, 1993. Signed as a free agent by **San Jose**, August 17, 1993. Traded to **Detroit** by **San Jose** for Detroit's fifth round choice (Michal Bros) in 1995 Entry Draft, February 27, 1995.

ESAU, LEONARD (EE-saw)

Defense. Shoots right. 6'3", 190 lbs. Born, Meadow Lake, Sask., June 3, 1968.
(Toronto's 5th choice, 86th overall, in 1988 Entry Draft).

			Regular Season					Playoffs				
Season	Club	Lea	GP	G	A	TP	PIM	GP	G	A	TP	PIM
1988-89	St. Cloud	NCAA	35	12	27	39	69	....	....	....	....	....
1989-90	St. Cloud	NCAA	29	8	11	19	83	....	....	....	....	....
1990-91	Newmarket	AHL	76	4	14	18	28	....	....	....	....	....
1991-92	**Toronto**	**NHL**	**2**	**0**	**0**	**0**	**0**	....	....	....	....	....
	St. John's	AHL	78	9	29	38	68	13	0	2	2	14
1992-93	**Quebec**	**NHL**	**4**	**0**	**1**	**1**	**2**	....	....	....	....	....
	Halifax	AHL	75	11	31	42	79	....	....	....	....	....
1993-94	**Calgary**	**NHL**	**6**	**0**	**3**	**3**	**7**	....	....	....	....	....
	Saint John	AHL	75	12	36	48	129	7	2	2	4	6
1994-95	Saint John	AHL	54	13	27	40	73	5	0	2	2	0
	Edmonton	**NHL**	**14**	**0**	**6**	**6**	**15**	....	....	....	....	....
	Calgary	**NHL**	**1**	**0**	**0**	**0**	**0**	....	....	....	....	....
1995-96	Cincinnati	IHL	82	15	21	36	150	17	5	6	11	26
	NHL Totals		**27**	**0**	**10**	**10**	**24**	....	....	....	....	....

Traded to **Quebec** by **Toronto** for Ken McRae, July 21, 1992. Signed as a free agent by **Calgary**, September 6, 1993. Claimed by **Edmonton** from **Calgary** in NHL Waiver Draft, January 18, 1995. Claimed on waivers by **Calgary** from **Edmonton**, March 7, 1995. Signed as a free agent by **Florida**, August 31, 1995.

ESBJORS, JOACIM (ehs-BEE-yuhrs, yoh-AH-kihm) — HFD.

Defense. Shoots left. 6'1", 194 lbs. Born, Goteborg, Sweden, July 4, 1970.
(Hartford's 11th choice, 249th overall, in 1992 Entry Draft).

			Regular Season					Playoffs				
Season	Club	Lea	GP	G	A	TP	PIM	GP	G	A	TP	PIM
1989-90	V. Frolunda	Swe.	24	0	4	4	23	....	....	....	....	....
1990-91	V. Frolunda	Swe.	22	1	5	6	16	....	....	....	....	....
1991-92	V. Frolunda	Swe.	40	9	9	18	22	3	1	0	1	2
1992-93	V. Frolunda	Swe.	20	1	6	7	26	....	....	....	....	....
1993-94	V. Frolunda	Swe.	38	4	7	11	44	4	0	0	0	2
1994-95	V. Frolunda	Swe.	22	1	4	5	22	....	....	....	....	....
1995-96	V. Frolunda	Swe.	38	3	4	7	39	13	2	0	2	8

EVASON, DEAN (EH-vih-suhn)

Center. Shoots right. 5'10", 180 lbs. Born, Flin Flon, Man., August 22, 1964.
(Washington's 3rd choice, 89th overall, in 1982 Entry Draft).

			Regular Season					Playoffs				
Season	Club	Lea	GP	G	A	TP	PIM	GP	G	A	TP	PIM
1980-81	Spokane	WHL	3	1	1	2	0	....	....	....	....	....
1981-82	Spokane	WHL	26	8	14	22	65	....	....	....	....	....
	Kamloops	WHL	44	21	55	76	47	4	2	1	3	0
1982-83	Kamloops	WHL	70	71	93	164	102	7	5	7	12	18
1983-84	**Washington**	**NHL**	**2**	**0**	**0**	**0**	**2**	....	....	....	....	....
a	Kamloops	WHL	57	49	88	137	89	17	*21	20	41	33
1984-85	**Washington**	**NHL**	**15**	**3**	**4**	**7**	**2**	....	....	....	....	....
	Hartford	**NHL**	**2**	**0**	**0**	**0**	**0**	....	....	....	....	....
	Binghamton	AHL	65	27	49	76	38	8	3	5	8	9
1985-86	**Hartford**	**NHL**	**55**	**20**	**28**	**48**	**65**	**10**	**1**	**4**	**5**	**10**
	Binghamton	AHL	26	9	17	26	29	....	....	....	....	....
1986-87	**Hartford**	**NHL**	**80**	**22**	**37**	**59**	**67**	**5**	**3**	**2**	**5**	**35**
1987-88	**Hartford**	**NHL**	**77**	**10**	**18**	**28**	**115**	**6**	**1**	**1**	**2**	**2**
1988-89	**Hartford**	**NHL**	**67**	**11**	**17**	**28**	**60**	**4**	**1**	**2**	**3**	**10**
1989-90	**Hartford**	**NHL**	**78**	**18**	**25**	**43**	**138**	**7**	**2**	**2**	**4**	**22**
1990-91	**Hartford**	**NHL**	**75**	**6**	**23**	**29**	**170**	**6**	**0**	**4**	**4**	**29**
1991-92	**San Jose**	**NHL**	**74**	**11**	**15**	**26**	**99**	....	....	....	....	....
1992-93	**San Jose**	**NHL**	**84**	**12**	**19**	**31**	**132**	....	....	....	....	....
1993-94	**Dallas**	**NHL**	**80**	**11**	**33**	**44**	**66**	**9**	**0**	**2**	**2**	**12**
1994-95	**Dallas**	**NHL**	**47**	**8**	**7**	**15**	**48**	**5**	**1**	**2**	**3**	**12**
1995-96	**Calgary**	**NHL**	**67**	**7**	**7**	**14**	**38**	**3**	**0**	**1**	**1**	**0**
	NHL Totals		**803**	**139**	**233**	**372**	**1002**	**55**	**9**	**20**	**29**	**132**

a WHL First All-Star Team, West Division (1984)

Traded to **Hartford** by **Washington** with Peter Sidorkiewicz for David Jensen, March 12, 1985. Traded to **San Jose** by **Hartford** for Dan Keczmer, October 2, 1991. Traded to **Dallas** by **San Jose** for San Jose's sixth round choice (previously acquired by Dallas — San Jose selected Petri Varis) in 1993 Entry Draft, June 26, 1993. Signed as a free agent by **Calgary**, August 1, 1995.

EWEN, TODD (YOO-ihn) S.J.

Right wing. Shoots right. 6'2", 220 lbs. Born, Saskatoon, Sask., March 22, 1966.
(Edmonton's 9th choice, 168th overall, in 1984 Entry Draft).

			Regular Season					Playoffs				
Season	**Club**	**Lea**	**GP**	**G**	**A**	**TP**	**PIM**	**GP**	**G**	**A**	**TP**	**PIM**
1982-83	Kamloops	WHL	3	0	0	0	2	2	0	0	0	0
1983-84	N. Westminster	WHL	68	11	13	24	176	7	2	1	3	15
1984-85	N. Westminster	WHL	56	11	20	31	304	10	1	8	9	60
1985-86	N. Westminster	WHL	60	28	24	52	289	....	....	....	....	....
	Maine	AHL	....	....	....	....	....	3	0	0	0	7
1986-87	**St. Louis**	**NHL**	**23**	**2**	**0**	**2**	**84**	**4**	**0**	**0**	**0**	**23**
	Peoria	IHL	16	3	3	6	110	....	....	....	....	....
1987-88	**St. Louis**	**NHL**	**64**	**4**	**2**	**6**	**227**	**6**	**0**	**0**	**0**	**21**
1988-89	**St. Louis**	**NHL**	**34**	**4**	**5**	**9**	**171**	**2**	**0**	**0**	**0**	**21**
1989-90	**St. Louis**	**NHL**	**3**	**0**	**0**	**0**	**11**	....	....	....	....	....
	Peoria	IHL	2	0	0	0	12	....	....	....	....	....
	Montreal	**NHL**	**41**	**4**	**6**	**10**	**158**	**10**	**0**	**0**	**0**	**4**
1990-91	**Montreal**	**NHL**	**28**	**3**	**2**	**5**	**128**	....	....	....	....	....
1991-92	**Montreal**	**NHL**	**46**	**1**	**2**	**3**	**130**	**3**	**0**	**0**	**0**	**18**
1992-93	**Montreal**	**NHL**	**75**	**5**	**9**	**14**	**193**	**1**	**0**	**0**	**0**	**0** ♦
1993-94	**Anaheim**	**NHL**	**76**	**9**	**9**	**18**	**272**	....	....	....	....	....
1994-95	**Anaheim**	**NHL**	**24**	**0**	**0**	**0**	**90**	....	....	....	....	....
1995-96	**Anaheim**	**NHL**	**53**	**4**	**3**	**7**	**285**	....	....	....	....	....
	NHL Totals		**467**	**36**	**38**	**74**	**1749**	**26**	**0**	**0**	**0**	**87**

Traded to **St. Louis** by **Edmonton** for Shawn Evans, October 15, 1986. Traded to **Montreal** by **St. Louis** for future considerations, December 12, 1989. Traded to **Anaheim** by **Montreal** with Patrik Carnback for Anaheim's third round choice (Chris Murray) in 1994 Entry Draft, August 10, 1993. Signed as a free agent by **San Jose**, July 25, 1996.

FAFARD, DOMINIC EDM.

Defense. Shoots right. 6'5", 230 lbs. Born, Longueuil, Que., July 13, 1974.

			Regular Season					Playoffs				
Season	**Club**	**Lea**	**GP**	**G**	**A**	**TP**	**PIM**	**GP**	**G**	**A**	**TP**	**PIM**
1993-94	Victoriaville	QMJHL	72	6	32	38	70	5	0	1	1	6
1994-95	Wheeling	ECHL	39	2	8	10	44	....	....	....	....	....
	Cape Breton	AHL	1	0	0	0	0	....	....	....	....	....
	S. Carolina	ECHL	7	0	1	1	4	8	1	0	1	6
1995-96	Wheeling	ECHL	2	0	0	0	0	....	....	....	....	....
	Raleigh	ECHL	4	0	1	1	2	....	....	....	....	....
	Oklahoma City	CHL	56	6	26	32	77	13	0	3	3	10

Signed as a free agent by **Edmonton**, September 30, 1994.

FAIR, QUINN L.A.

Defense. Shoots right. 6'1", 210 lbs. Born, Campbell River, B.C., May 23, 1973.
(Los Angeles' 1st choice, 7th overall, in 1994 Supplemental Draft).

			Regular Season					Playoffs				
Season	**Club**	**Lea**	**GP**	**G**	**A**	**TP**	**PIM**	**GP**	**G**	**A**	**TP**	**PIM**
1992-93	Kent State	CCHA	37	6	6	12	77	....	....	....	....	....
1993-94	Kent State	CCHA	39	11	13	24	92	....	....	....	....	....
1994-95	Bowling Green	CCHA	37	4	7	11	62	....	....	....	....	....
1995-96	Bowling Green	CCHA	40	6	21	27	76	....	....	....	....	....

FAIRCHILD, KELLY TOR.

Center. Shoots left. 5'11", 180 lbs. Born, Hibbing, MN, April 9, 1973.
(Los Angeles' 7th choice, 152nd overall, in 1991 Entry Draft).

			Regular Season					Playoffs				
Season	**Club**	**Lea**	**GP**	**G**	**A**	**TP**	**PIM**	**GP**	**G**	**A**	**TP**	**PIM**
1991-92	U. Wisconsin	WCHA	37	11	10	21	45	....	....	....	....	....
1992-93	U. Wisconsin	WCHA	42	25	29	54	54	....	....	....	....	....
1993-94a	U. Wisconsin	WCHA	42	20	44	*64	81	....	....	....	....	....
1994-95	St. John's	AHL	53	27	23	50	51	4	0	2	2	4
1995-96	**Toronto**	**NHL**	**1**	**0**	**1**	**1**	**2**	....	....	....	....	....
	St. John's	AHL	78	29	49	78	85	2	0	1	1	4
	NHL Totals		**1**	**0**	**1**	**1**	**2**	....	....	....	....	....

a WCHA First All-Star Team (1994)

Traded to **Toronto** by **Los Angeles** with Dixon Ward, Guy Leveque and Shayne Toporowski for Eric Lacroix, Chris Snell and Toronto's fourth round choice (Eric Belanger) in 1996 Entry Draft, October 3, 1994.

FALLOON, PAT (fah-LOON) PHI.

Right wing. Shoots right. 5'11", 190 lbs. Born, Foxwarren, Man., September 22, 1972.
(San Jose's 1st choice, 2nd overall, in 1991 Entry Draft).

			Regular Season					Playoffs				
Season	**Club**	**Lea**	**GP**	**G**	**A**	**TP**	**PIM**	**GP**	**G**	**A**	**TP**	**PIM**
1988-89	Spokane	WHL	72	22	56	78	41	....	....	....	....	....
1989-90	Spokane	WHL	71	60	64	124	48	6	5	8	13	4
1990-91abcd	Spokane	WHL	61	64	74	138	33	15	10	14	24	10
1991-92	**San Jose**	**NHL**	**79**	**25**	**34**	**59**	**16**	....	....	....	....	....
1992-93	**San Jose**	**NHL**	**41**	**14**	**14**	**28**	**12**	....	....	....	....	....
1993-94	**San Jose**	**NHL**	**83**	**22**	**31**	**53**	**18**	**14**	**1**	**2**	**3**	**6**
1994-95	**San Jose**	**NHL**	**46**	**12**	**7**	**19**	**25**	**11**	**3**	**1**	**4**	**0**
1995-96	**San Jose**	**NHL**	**9**	**3**	**0**	**3**	**4**	....	....	....	....	....
	Philadelphia	**NHL**	**62**	**22**	**26**	**48**	**6**	**12**	**3**	**2**	**5**	**2**
	NHL Totals		**320**	**98**	**112**	**210**	**81**	**37**	**7**	**5**	**12**	**8**

a WHL West First All-Star Team (1991)
b Canadian Major Junior Most Sportsmanlike Player of the Year (1991)
c Memorial Cup All-Star Team (1991)
d Won Stafford Smythe Memorial Trophy (Memorial Cup Tournament MVP) (1991)

Traded to **Philadelphia** by **San Jose** for Martin Spanhel, Philadelphia's first round choice (later traded to Phoenix — Phoenix selected Daniel Briere) in 1996 Entry Draft and Philadelphia's fourth round choice (later traded to Buffalo — Buffalo selected Mike Martone), in 1996 Entry Draft, November 16, 1995.

FAUST, ANDRE

Center. Shoots left. 5'11", 191 lbs. Born, Joliette, Que., October 7, 1969.
(New Jersey's 8th choice, 173rd overall, in 1989 Entry Draft).

			Regular Season					Playoffs				
Season	**Club**	**Lea**	**GP**	**G**	**A**	**TP**	**PIM**	**GP**	**G**	**A**	**TP**	**PIM**
1988-89	Princeton	ECAC	27	15	24	39	28	....	....	....	....	....
1989-90a	Princeton	ECAC	22	9	28	37	20	....	....	....	....	....
1990-91	Princeton	ECAC	26	15	22	37	51	....	....	....	....	....
1991-92a	Princeton	ECAC	27	14	21	35	38	....	....	....	....	....
1992-93	**Philadelphia**	**NHL**	**10**	**2**	**2**	**4**	**4**	....	....	....	....	....
	Hershey	AHL	62	26	25	51	71	....	....	....	....	....
1993-94	**Philadelphia**	**NHL**	**37**	**8**	**5**	**13**	**10**	....	....	....	....	....
	Hershey	AHL	13	6	7	13	10	10	4	3	7	26
1994-95	Hershey	AHL	55	12	28	40	72	6	1	5	6	12
1995-96	Springfield	AHL	50	19	19	38	40	10	5	2	7	6
	NHL Totals		**47**	**10**	**7**	**17**	**14**	....	....	....	....	....

a ECAC Second All-Star Team (1990, 1992)

Signed as a free agent by **Philadelphia**, October 5, 1992. Traded to **Winnipeg** by **Philadelphia** for Winnipeg's seventh round choice in 1997 Entry Draft, September 20, 1995.

FEATHERSTONE, GLEN HFD.

Defense. Shoots left. 6'4", 209 lbs. Born, Toronto, Ont., July 8, 1968.
(St. Louis' 4th choice, 73rd overall, in 1986 Entry Draft).

			Regular Season					Playoffs				
Season	**Club**	**Lea**	**GP**	**G**	**A**	**TP**	**PIM**	**GP**	**G**	**A**	**TP**	**PIM**
1985-86	Windsor	OHL	49	0	6	6	135	14	1	1	2	23
1986-87	Windsor	OHL	47	6	11	17	154	14	2	6	8	19
1987-88	Windsor	OHL	53	7	27	34	201	12	6	9	15	47
1988-89	**St. Louis**	**NHL**	**18**	**0**	**2**	**2**	**22**	**6**	**0**	**0**	**0**	**25**
	Peoria	IHL	37	5	19	24	97	....	....	....	....	....
1989-90	**St. Louis**	**NHL**	**58**	**0**	**12**	**12**	**145**	**12**	**0**	**2**	**2**	**47**
	Peoria	IHL	15	1	4	5	43	....	....	....	....	....
1990-91	**St. Louis**	**NHL**	**68**	**5**	**15**	**20**	**204**	**9**	**0**	**0**	**0**	**31**
1991-92	**Boston**	**NHL**	**7**	**1**	**0**	**1**	**20**	....	....	....	....	....
1992-93	**Boston**	**NHL**	**34**	**5**	**5**	**10**	**102**	....	....	....	....	....
	Providence	AHL	8	3	4	7	60	....	....	....	....	....
1993-94	**Boston**	**NHL**	**58**	**1**	**8**	**9**	**152**	**1**	**0**	**0**	**0**	**0**
1994-95	**NY Rangers**	**NHL**	**6**	**1**	**0**	**1**	**18**	....	....	....	....	....
	Hartford	**NHL**	**13**	**1**	**1**	**2**	**32**	....	....	....	....	....
1995-96	**Hartford**	**NHL**	**68**	**2**	**10**	**12**	**138**	....	....	....	....	....
	NHL Totals		**330**	**16**	**53**	**69**	**833**	**28**	**0**	**2**	**2**	**103**

Signed as a free agent by **Boston**, July 25, 1991. Traded to **NY Rangers** by **Boston** for Daniel Lacroix, August 19, 1994. Traded to **Hartford** by **NY Rangers** with Michael Stewart, NY Rangers' first round choice (Jean-Sebastien Giguere) in 1995 Entry Draft and fourth round choice (Steve Wasylko) in 1996 Entry Draft for Pat Verbeek, March 23, 1995.

FEDOROV, SERGEI (FEH-duh-rahf) DET.

Center. Shoots left. 6'1", 200 lbs. Born, Pskov, USSR, December 13, 1969.
(Detroit's 4th choice, 74th overall, in 1989 Entry Draft).

			Regular Season					Playoffs				
Season	**Club**	**Lea**	**GP**	**G**	**A**	**TP**	**PIM**	**GP**	**G**	**A**	**TP**	**PIM**
1986-87	CSKA	USSR	29	6	6	12	12	....	....	....	....	....
1987-88	CSKA	USSR	48	7	9	16	20	....	....	....	....	....
1988-89	CSKA	USSR	44	9	8	17	35	....	....	....	....	....
1989-90	CSKA	USSR	48	19	10	29	22	....	....	....	....	....
1990-91a	**Detroit**	**NHL**	**77**	**31**	**48**	**79**	**66**	**7**	**1**	**5**	**6**	**4**
1991-92	**Detroit**	**NHL**	**80**	**32**	**54**	**86**	**72**	**11**	**5**	**5**	**10**	**8**
1992-93	**Detroit**	**NHL**	**73**	**34**	**53**	**87**	**72**	**7**	**3**	**6**	**9**	**23**
1993-94bcde	**Detroit**	**NHL**	**82**	**56**	**64**	**120**	**34**	**7**	**1**	**7**	**8**	**6**
1994-95	**Detroit**	**NHL**	**42**	**20**	**30**	**50**	**24**	**17**	**7**	***17**	***24**	**6**
1995-96c	**Detroit**	**NHL**	**78**	**39**	**68**	**107**	**48**	**19**	**2**	***18**	**20**	**10**
	NHL Totals		**432**	**212**	**317**	**529**	**316**	**68**	**19**	**58**	**77**	**57**

a NHL/Upper Deck All-Rookie Team (1991)
b NHL First All-Star Team (1994)
c Won Frank J. Selke Trophy (1994, 1996)
d Won Lester B. Pearson Award (1994)
e Won Hart Trophy (1994)

Played in NHL All-Star Game (1992, 1994, 1996)

FEDOTOV, SERGEI HFD.

Defense. Shoots left. 6'1", 185 lbs. Born, Moscow, USSR, January 24, 1977.
(Hartford's 2nd choice, 35th overall, in 1995 Entry Draft).

			Regular Season					Playoffs				
Season	**Club**	**Lea**	**GP**	**G**	**A**	**TP**	**PIM**	**GP**	**G**	**A**	**TP**	**PIM**
1994-95	Moscow D'amo	CIS	8	0	0	0	2	....	....	....	....	....
1995-96	Magnitogorsk	CIS	7	0	0	0	2	....	....	....	....	....
	Moscow D'amo	CIS	4	0	0	0	24	....	....	....	....	....
	Saratov	CIS	41	4	8	12	30	....	....	....	....	....

FEDYK, BRENT (FEH-dihk) DAL.

Left wing. Shoots right. 6', 194 lbs. Born, Yorkton, Sask., March 8, 1967.
(Detroit's 1st choice, 8th overall, in 1985 Entry Draft).

			Regular Season					Playoffs				
Season	**Club**	**Lea**	**GP**	**G**	**A**	**TP**	**PIM**	**GP**	**G**	**A**	**TP**	**PIM**
1983-84	Regina	WHL	63	15	28	43	30	23	8	7	15	6
1984-85	Regina	WHL	66	35	35	70	48	8	5	4	9	0
1985-86	Regina	WHL	50	43	34	77	47	5	0	1	1	0
1986-87	Regina	WHL	12	9	6	15	9	....	....	....	....	....
	Seattle	WHL	13	5	11	16	9	....	....	....	....	....
	Portland	WHL	11	5	4	9	6	14	5	6	11	0
1987-88	**Detroit**	**NHL**	**2**	**0**	**1**	**1**	**2**	....	....	....	....	....
	Adirondack	AHL	34	9	11	20	22	5	0	2	2	6
1988-89	**Detroit**	**NHL**	**5**	**2**	**0**	**2**	**0**	....	....	....	....	....
	Adirondack	AHL	66	40	28	68	33	15	7	8	15	23
1989-90	**Detroit**	**NHL**	**27**	**1**	**4**	**5**	**6**	....	....	....	....	....
	Adirondack	AHL	33	14	15	29	24	6	2	1	3	4
1990-91	**Detroit**	**NHL**	**67**	**16**	**19**	**35**	**38**	**6**	**1**	**0**	**1**	**2**
1991-92	**Detroit**	**NHL**	**61**	**5**	**8**	**13**	**42**	**1**	**0**	**0**	**0**	**2**
	Adirondack	AHL	1	0	2	2	0	....	....	....	....	....
1992-93	**Philadelphia**	**NHL**	**74**	**21**	**38**	**59**	**48**	....	....	....	....	....
1993-94	**Philadelphia**	**NHL**	**72**	**20**	**18**	**38**	**74**	....	....	....	....	....
1994-95	**Philadelphia**	**NHL**	**30**	**8**	**4**	**12**	**14**	**9**	**2**	**2**	**4**	**8**
1995-96	**Philadelphia**	**NHL**	**24**	**10**	**5**	**15**	**24**	....	....	....	....	....
	Dallas	**NHL**	**41**	**10**	**9**	**19**	**30**	....	....	....	....	....
	NHL Totals		**403**	**93**	**106**	**199**	**278**	**16**	**3**	**2**	**5**	**12**

Traded to **Philadelphia** by **Detroit** for Philadelphia's fourth round choice (later traded to Boston — Boston selected Charles Paquette) in 1993 Entry Draft, October 1, 1992. Traded to **Dallas** by **Philadelphia** for Trent Klatt, December 13, 1995.

FELSNER, DENNY

Left wing. Shoots left. 6', 195 lbs. Born, Warren, MI, April 29, 1970.
(St. Louis' 3rd choice, 55th overall, in 1989 Entry Draft).

				Regular Season					Playoffs			
Season	Club	Lea	GP	G	A	TP	PIM	GP	G	A	TP	PIM
1988-89	U. of Michigan	CCHA	39	30	19	49	22	.....				
1989-90	U. of Michigan	CCHA	33	27	16	43	24	.....				
1990-91ab	U. of Michigan	CCHA	46	*40	35	75	58	.....				
1991-92ac	U. of Michigan	CCHA	44	42	52	94	46	.....				
	St. Louis	**NHL**	3	0	1	1	0	1	0	0	0	0
1992-93	**St. Louis**	**NHL**	6	0	3	3	2	9	2	3	5	2
	Peoria	IHL	29	14	21	35	8	.....				
1993-94	**St. Louis**	**NHL**	6	1	0	1	2	.....				
	Peoria	IHL	6	8	3	11	14	.....				
1994-95	Peoria	IHL	25	10	12	22	14	8	2	3	5	0
	St. Louis	**NHL**	3	0	0	0	2	.....				
1995-96	Syracuse	AHL	66	23	34	57	22	14	5	12	17	0
	NHL Totals		18	1	4	5	6	10	2	3	5	2

a CCHA First All-Star Team (1991, 1992)
b NCAA West Second All-American Team (1991)
c NCAA West First All-American Team (1992)
Signed as a free agent by **Vancouver**, August 31, 1995.

FERGUSON, CRAIG   FLA.

Right wing. Shoots left. 5'11", 190 lbs. Born, Castro Valley, CA, April 8, 1970.
(Montreal's 7th choice, 146th overall, in 1989 Entry Draft).

				Regular Season					Playoffs			
Season	Club	Lea	GP	G	A	TP	PIM	GP	G	A	TP	PIM
1988-89	Yale	ECAC	24	11	6	17	20	.....				
1989-90	Yale	ECAC	28	6	13	19	36	.....				
1990-91	Yale	ECAC	29	11	10	21	34	.....				
1991-92	Yale	ECAC	27	9	16	25	26	.....				
1992-93	Fredericton	AHL	55	15	13	28	20	5	0	1	1	2
	Wheeling	ECHL	9	6	5	11	24	.....				
1993-94	**Montreal**	**NHL**	2	0	1	1	0	.....				
	Fredericton	AHL	57	29	32	61	60	.....				
1994-95	Fredericton	AHL	80	27	35	62	62	17	6	2	8	6
	Montreal	**NHL**	1	0	0	0	0	.....				
1995-96	**Montreal**	**NHL**	10	1	0	1	2	.....				
	Calgary	**NHL**	8	0	0	0	4	.....				
	Saint John	AHL	18	5	13	18	8	.....				
	Phoenix	IHL	31	6	9	15	25	4	0	2	2	6
	NHL Totals		21	1	1	2	6	.....				

Traded to **Calgary** by **Montreal** with Yves Sarault for a conditional choice in 1997 Entry Draft, November 26, 1995. Traded to **Los Angeles** by **Calgary** for Pat Conacher, February 10, 1996. Signed as a free agent by **Florida**, July 24, 1996.

FERGUSON, SCOTT   EDM.

Defense. Shoots left. 6'1", 195 lbs. Born, Camrose, Alta., January 6, 1973.

				Regular Season					Playoffs			
Season	Club	Lea	GP	G	A	TP	PIM	GP	G	A	TP	PIM
1990-91	Kamloops	WHL	4	0	0	0	0	.....				
1991-92	Kamloops	WHL	62	4	10	14	138	12	0	2	2	21
1992-93	Kamloops	WHL	71	4	19	23	206	13	0	2	2	24
1993-94a	Kamloops	WHL	68	5	49	54	180	19	5	11	16	48
1994-95	Cape Breton	AHL	58	4	6	10	103	.....				
	Wheeling	ECHL	5	1	5	6	16	.....				
1995-96	Cape Breton	AHL	80	5	16	21	196	.....				

a WHL West Second All-Star Team (1994)
Signed as a free agent by **Edmonton**, June 2, 1994.

FERNER, MARK

Defense. Shoots left. 6', 193 lbs. Born, Regina, Sask., September 5, 1965.
(Buffalo's 12th choice, 194th overall, in 1983 Entry Draft).

				Regular Season					Playoffs			
Season	Club	Lea	GP	G	A	TP	PIM	GP	G	A	TP	PIM
1982-83	Kamloops	WHL	69	6	15	21	81	7	0	0	0	7
1983-84	Kamloops	WHL	72	9	30	39	169	14	1	8	9	20
1984-85a	Kamloops	WHL	69	15	39	54	91	15	4	9	13	21
1985-86	Rochester	AHL	63	3	14	17	87	.....				
1986-87	**Buffalo**	**NHL**	13	0	3	3	9	.....				
	Rochester	AHL	54	0	12	12	157	.....				
1987-88	Rochester	AHL	69	1	25	26	165	7	1	4	5	31
1988-89	**Buffalo**	**NHL**	2	0	0	0	2	.....				
	Rochester	AHL	55	0	18	18	97	.....				
1989-90	**Washington**	**NHL**	2	0	0	0	0	.....				
	Baltimore	AHL	74	7	28	35	76	11	1	2	3	21
1990-91	**Washington**	**NHL**	7	0	1	1	4	.....				
b	Baltimore	AHL	61	14	40	54	38	6	1	4	5	24
1991-92	Baltimore	AHL	57	7	38	45	67	.....				
	St. John's	AHL	15	1	8	9	6	14	2	14	16	38
1992-93	New Haven	AHL	34	5	7	12	69	.....				
	San Diego	IHL	26	0	15	15	34	11	1	2	3	8
1993-94	**Anaheim**	**NHL**	50	3	5	8	30	.....				
1994-95	San Diego	IHL	46	3	12	15	51	.....				
	Anaheim	**NHL**	14	0	1	1	6	.....				
	Detroit	**NHL**	3	0	0	0	0	.....				
	Adirondack	AHL	3	0	0	0	2	1	0	0	0	0
1995-96	Orlando	IHL	43	4	18	22	37	23	4	10	14	8
	NHL Totals		91	3	10	13	51	.....				

a WHL West First All-Star Team (1985)
b AHL Second All-Star Team (1991)

Traded to **Washington** by **Buffalo** for Scott McCrory, June 1, 1989. Traded to **Toronto** by **Washington** for future considerations, February 27, 1992. Signed as a free agent by **Ottawa**, August 6, 1992. Claimed by **Anaheim** from **Ottawa** in Expansion Draft, June 24, 1993. Traded to **Detroit** by **Anaheim** with Stu Grimson and Anaheim's sixth round choice (Magnus Nilsson) in 1996 Entry Draft for Mike Sillinger and Jason York, April 4, 1995.

FERRARO, CHRIS   NYR

Right wing. Shoots right. 5'10", 175 lbs. Born, Port Jefferson, NY, January 24, 1973.
(NY Rangers' 4th choice, 85th overall, in 1992 Entry Draft).

				Regular Season					Playoffs			
Season	Club	Lea	GP	G	A	TP	PIM	GP	G	A	TP	PIM
1992-93	U. of Maine	H.E.	39	25	26	51	46	.....				
1993-94	U. of Maine	H.E.	4	0	1	1	8	.....				
	U.S. National	.....	48	8	34	42	58	.....				
1994-95	Atlanta	IHL	54	13	14	27	72	.....				
	Binghamton	AHL	13	6	4	10	38	10	2	3	5	16
1995-96	**NY Rangers**	**NHL**	2	1	0	1	0	.....				
	Binghamton	AHL	77	32	67	99	208	4	4	2	6	13
	NHL Totals		2	1	0	1	0	.....				

FERRARO, PETER   NYR

Center. Shoots right. 5'10", 175 lbs. Born, Port Jefferson, NY, January 24, 1973.
(NY Rangers' 1st choice, 24th overall, in 1992 Entry Draft).

				Regular Season					Playoffs			
Season	Club	Lea	GP	G	A	TP	PIM	GP	G	A	TP	PIM
1992-93	U. of Maine	H.E.	36	18	32	50	106	.....				
1993-94	U. of Maine	H.E.	4	3	6	9	16	.....				
	U.S. National	.....	60	30	34	64	87	.....				
	U.S. Olympic	.....	8	6	0	6	6	.....				
1994-95	Atlanta	IHL	61	15	24	39	118	.....				
	Binghamton	AHL	12	2	6	8	67	11	4	3	7	51
1995-96	**NY Rangers**	**NHL**	5	0	1	1	0	.....				
a	Binghamton	AHL	68	48	53	101	157	4	1	6	7	22
	NHL Totals		5	0	1	1	0	.....				

a AHL First All-Star Team (1996)

FERRARO, RAY   L.A.

Center. Shoots left. 5'10", 185 lbs. Born, Trail, B.C., August 23, 1964.
(Hartford's 5th choice, 88th overall, in 1982 Entry Draft).

				Regular Season					Playoffs			
Season	Club	Lea	GP	G	A	TP	PIM	GP	G	A	TP	PIM
1982-83	Portland	WHL	50	41	49	90	39	14	14	10	24	13
1983-84a	Brandon	WHL	72	*108	84	*192	84	11	13	15	28	20
1984-85	**Hartford**	**NHL**	44	11	17	28	40	.....				
	Binghamton	AHL	37	20	13	33	29	.....				
1985-86	**Hartford**	**NHL**	76	30	47	77	57	10	3	6	9	4
1986-87	**Hartford**	**NHL**	80	27	32	59	42	6	1	1	2	8
1987-88	**Hartford**	**NHL**	68	21	29	50	81	6	1	1	2	6
1988-89	**Hartford**	**NHL**	80	41	35	76	86	4	2	0	2	4
1989-90	**Hartford**	**NHL**	79	25	29	54	109	7	0	3	3	2
1990-91	**Hartford**	**NHL**	15	2	5	7	18	.....				
	NY Islanders	**NHL**	61	19	16	35	52	.....				
1991-92	**NY Islanders**	**NHL**	80	40	40	80	92	.....				
1992-93	**NY Islanders**	**NHL**	46	14	13	27	40	18	13	7	20	18
	Capital Dist.	AHL	1	0	2	2	2	.....				
1993-94	**NY Islanders**	**NHL**	82	21	32	53	83	4	1	0	1	6
1994-95	**NY Islanders**	**NHL**	47	22	21	43	30	.....				
1995-96	**NY Rangers**	**NHL**	65	25	29	54	82	.....				
	Los Angeles	**NHL**	11	4	2	6	10	.....				
	NHL Totals		834	302	347	649	822	55	21	18	39	48

a WHL First All-Star Team (1984)
Played in NHL All-Star Game (1992)

Traded to **NY Islanders** by **Hartford** for Doug Crossman, November 13, 1990. Signed as a free agent by **NY Rangers**, August 9, 1995. Traded to **Los Angeles** by **NY Rangers** with Ian Laperriere, Mattias Norstrom, Nathan Lafayette and NY Rangers' fourth round choice in 1997 Entry Draft for Marty McSorley, Jari Kurri and Shane Churla, March 14, 1996.

FETISOV, VIACHESLAV   (feh-TEE-sahf) DET.

Defense. Shoots left. 6'1", 220 lbs. Born, Moscow, USSR, April 20, 1958.
(New Jersey's 6th choice, 150th overall, in 1983 Entry Draft).

				Regular Season					Playoffs			
Season	Club	Lea	GP	G	A	TP	PIM	GP	G	A	TP	PIM
1974-75	CSKA	USSR	1	0	0	0	0	.....				
1976-77	CSKA	USSR	28	3	4	7	14	.....				
1977-78a	CSKA	USSR	35	9	18	27	46	.....				
1978-79	CSKA	USSR	29	10	19	29	40	.....				
1979-80	CSKA	USSR	37	10	14	24	46	.....				
1980-81	CSKA	USSR	48	13	16	29	44	.....				
1981-82ac	CSKA	USSR	46	15	26	41	20	.....				
1982-83a	CSKA	USSR	43	6	17	23	46	.....				
1983-84ab	CSKA	USSR	44	19	30	49	38	.....				
1984-85a	CSKA	USSR	20	13	12	25	6	.....				
1985-86abc	CSKA	USSR	40	15	19	34	12	.....				
1986-87ab	CSKA	USSR	39	13	20	33	18	.....				
1987-88ab	CSKA	USSR	46	18	17	35	26	.....				
1988-89	CSKA	USSR	23	9	8	17	18	.....				
1989-90	**New Jersey**	**NHL**	72	8	34	42	52	6	0	2	2	10
1990-91	**New Jersey**	**NHL**	67	3	16	19	62	7	0	0	0	17
	Utica	AHL	1	1	1	2	0	.....				
1991-92	**New Jersey**	**NHL**	70	3	23	26	108	6	0	3	3	8
1992-93	**New Jersey**	**NHL**	76	4	23	27	158	5	0	2	2	4
1993-94	**New Jersey**	**NHL**	52	1	14	15	30	14	1	0	1	8
1994-95	**New Jersey**	**NHL**	4	0	1	1	0	.....				
1994-95	Spartak	CIS	1	0	1	1	4	.....				
	Detroit	**NHL**	14	3	11	14	2	18	0	8	8	14
1995-96	**Detroit**	**NHL**	69	7	35	42	96	19	1	4	5	34
	NHL Totals		424	29	157	186	508	75	2	19	21	95

a Soviet National League All-Star Team (1979, 1980, 1982-88)
b Leningradskaya-Pravda Trophy (Top Scoring Defenseman) (1984, 1986-88)
c Soviet Player of the Year (1982, 1986, 1988)

Traded to **Detroit** by **New Jersey** for Detroit's third round choice (David Gosselin) in 1995 Entry Draft, April 3, 1995.

FILATOV, ANATOLI   (fih-LAH-tohv) S.J.

Right wing. Shoots right. 5'10", 195 lbs. Born, Kamenogorsk, USSR, April 28, 1975.
(San Jose's 9th choice, 158th overall, in 1993 Entry Draft).

				Regular Season					Playoffs			
Season	Club	Lea	GP	G	A	TP	PIM	GP	G	A	TP	PIM
1992-93	Kamenogorsk	CIS	17	4	0	4	14	.....				
1993-94	Kamenogorsk	CIS	20	3	3	6	22	.....				
1994-95	Kamenogorsk	CIS	33	6	6	12	30	.....				
	Niagara Falls	OHL	12	2	3	5	6	.....				
1995-96	Kamenogorsk	CIS	48	9	15	24	78	.....				

FINLEY, JEFF   PHO.

Defense. Shoots left. 6'2", 204 lbs.   Born, Edmonton, Alta., April 14, 1967.
(NY Islanders' 4th choice, 55th overall, in 1985 Entry Draft).

				Regular Season					Playoffs			
Season	Club	Lea	GP	G	A	TP	PIM	GP	G	A	TP	PIM
1983-84	Portland	WHL	5	0	0	0	5	5	0	1	1	4
1984-85	Portland	WHL	69	6	44	50	57	6	1	2	3	2
1985-86	Portland	WHL	70	11	59	70	83	15	1	7	8	16
1986-87	Portland	WHL	72	13	53	66	113	20	1	*21	22	27
1987-88	**NY Islanders**	**NHL**	**10**	**0**	**5**	**5**	**15**	**1**	**0**	**0**	**0**	**2**
	Springfield	AHL	52	5	18	23	50	....	....	....	....	....
1988-89	**NY Islanders**	**NHL**	**4**	**0**	**0**	**0**	**6**	....	....	....	....	....
	Springfield	AHL	65	3	16	19	55	....	....	....	....	....
1989-90	**NY Islanders**	**NHL**	**11**	**0**	**1**	**1**	**0**	**5**	**0**	**2**	**2**	**2**
	Springfield	AHL	57	1	15	16	41	13	1	4	5	23
1990-91	**NY Islanders**	**NHL**	**11**	**0**	**0**	**0**	**4**	....	....	....	....	....
	Capital Dist.	AHL	67	10	34	44	34	....	....	....	....	....
1991-92	**NY Islanders**	**NHL**	**51**	**1**	**10**	**11**	**26**	....	....	....	....	....
	Capital Dist.	AHL	20	1	9	10	6	....	....	....	....	....
1992-93	Capital Dist.	AHL	61	6	29	35	34	4	0	1	1	0
1993-94	**Philadelphia**	**NHL**	**55**	**1**	**8**	**9**	**24**	....	....	....	....	....
1994-95	Hershey	AHL	36	2	9	11	33	6	0	1	1	8
1995-96	**Winnipeg**	**NHL**	**65**	**1**	**5**	**6**	**81**	**6**	**0**	**0**	**0**	**4**
	Springfield	AHL	14	3	12	15	22	....	....	....	....	....
	NHL Totals		**207**	**3**	**29**	**32**	**156**	**12**	**0**	**2**	**2**	**8**

Traded to **Ottawa** by **NY Islanders** for Chris Luongo, June 30, 1993. Signed as a free agent by **Philadelphia**, July 30, 1993. Traded to **Winnipeg** by **Philadelphia** for Russ Romaniuk, June 27, 1995.

FINN, STEVEN   L.A.

Defense. Shoots left. 6', 200 lbs.   Born, Laval, Que., August 20, 1966.
(Quebec's 3rd choice, 57th overall, in 1984 Entry Draft).

				Regular Season					Playoffs			
Season	Club	Lea	GP	G	A	TP	PIM	GP	G	A	TP	PIM
1982-83	Laval	QMJHL	69	7	30	37	108	6	0	2	2	6
1983-84	Laval	QMJHL	68	7	39	46	159	14	1	6	7	27
1984-85a	Laval	QMJHL	61	20	33	53	169	....	....	....	....	....
	Fredericton	AHL	4	0	0	0	14	6	1	1	2	4
1985-86	**Quebec**	**NHL**	**17**	**0**	**1**	**1**	**28**	....	....	....	....	....
	Laval	QMJHL	29	4	15	19	111	14	6	16	22	57
1986-87	**Quebec**	**NHL**	**36**	**2**	**5**	**7**	**40**	**13**	**0**	**2**	**2**	**29**
	Fredericton	AHL	38	7	19	26	73	....	....	....	....	....
1987-88	**Quebec**	**NHL**	**75**	**3**	**7**	**10**	**198**	....	....	....	....	....
1988-89	**Quebec**	**NHL**	**77**	**2**	**6**	**8**	**235**	....	....	....	....	....
1989-90	**Quebec**	**NHL**	**64**	**3**	**9**	**12**	**208**	....	....	....	....	....
1990-91	**Quebec**	**NHL**	**71**	**6**	**13**	**19**	**228**	....	....	....	....	....
1991-92	**Quebec**	**NHL**	**65**	**4**	**7**	**11**	**194**	....	....	....	....	....
1992-93	**Quebec**	**NHL**	**80**	**5**	**9**	**14**	**160**	**6**	**0**	**1**	**1**	**8**
1993-94	**Quebec**	**NHL**	**80**	**4**	**13**	**17**	**159**	....	....	....	....	....
1994-95	**Quebec**	**NHL**	**40**	**0**	**3**	**3**	**64**	**4**	**0**	**1**	**1**	**2**
1995-96	**Tampa Bay**	**NHL**	**16**	**0**	**0**	**0**	**24**	....	....	....	....	....
	Los Angeles	**NHL**	**50**	**3**	**2**	**5**	**102**	....	....	....	....	....
	NHL Totals		**671**	**32**	**75**	**107**	**1640**	**23**	**0**	**4**	**4**	**39**

a   QMJHL Second All-Star Team (1985)

Traded to **Tampa Bay** by **Colorado** for Tampa Bay's fourth round choice in 1997 Entry Draft, October 5, 1995. Traded to **Los Angeles** by **Tampa Bay** for Michel Petit, November 13, 1995.

FINNSTROM, JOHAN   (FIHN-struhm)   CGY.

Defense. Shoots left. 6'3", 205 lbs.   Born, Broby, Sweden, March 27, 1976.
(Calgary's 5th choice, 97th overall, in 1994 Entry Draft).

				Regular Season					Playoffs			
Season	Club	Lea	GP	G	A	TP	PIM	GP	G	A	TP	PIM
1993-94	Rogle	Swe.	7	1	1	2	2	....	....	....	....	....
1994-95	Rogle	Swe.	19	0	0	0	10	....	....	....	....	....
1995-96	Rogle	Swe.	18	0	0	0	10	....	....	....	....	....

FIORENTINO, PETER   NYR

Defense. Shoots right. 6'1", 205 lbs.   Born, Niagara Falls, Ont., December 22, 1968.
(NY Rangers' 11th choice, 215th overall, in 1988 Entry Draft).

				Regular Season					Playoffs			
Season	Club	Lea	GP	G	A	TP	PIM	GP	G	A	TP	PIM
1985-86	S.S. Marie	OHL	58	1	6	7	87	....	....	....	....	....
1986-87	S.S. Marie	OHL	64	1	12	13	187	....	....	....	....	....
1987-88	S.S. Marie	OHL	65	5	27	32	252	6	2	2	4	21
1988-89	S.S. Marie	OHL	55	5	24	29	220	....	....	....	....	....
	Denver	IHL	10	0	0	0	39	4	0	0	0	24
1989-90	Flint	IHL	64	2	7	9	302	....	....	....	....	....
1990-91	Binghamton	AHL	55	2	11	13	361	1	0	0	0	0
1991-92	**NY Rangers**	**NHL**	**1**	**0**	**0**	**0**	**0**	....	....	....	....	....
	Binghamton	AHL	70	2	11	13	340	5	0	1	1	24
1992-93	Binghamton	AHL	64	9	5	14	286	13	0	3	3	22
1993-94	Binghamton	AHL	68	7	15	22	220	....	....	....	....	....
1994-95	Binghamton	AHL	66	9	16	25	183	2	0	1	1	11
1995-96	Las Vegas	IHL	54	5	7	12	192	....	....	....	....	....
	Indianapolis	IHL	10	0	0	0	27	5	0	0	0	2
	NHL Totals		**1**	**0**	**0**	**0**	**0**	....	....	....	....	....

FISHER, CRAIG   NYI

Center. Shoots left. 6'3", 180 lbs.   Born, Oshawa, Ont., June 30, 1970.
(Philadelphia's 3rd choice, 56th overall, in 1988 Entry Draft).

				Regular Season					Playoffs			
Season	Club	Lea	GP	G	A	TP	PIM	GP	G	A	TP	PIM
1988-89	Miami-Ohio	CCHA	37	22	20	42	37	....	....	....	....	....
1989-90a	Miami-Ohio	CCHA	39	37	29	66	38	....	....	....	....	....
	Philadelphia	**NHL**	**2**	**0**	**0**	**0**	**0**	....	....	....	....	....
1990-91	**Philadelphia**	**NHL**	**2**	**0**	**0**	**0**	**0**	....	....	....	....	....
	Hershey	AHL	77	43	36	79	46	7	5	3	8	2
1991-92	Cape Breton	AHL	60	20	25	45	28	1	0	0	0	0
1992-93	Cape Breton	AHL	75	32	29	61	74	1	0	0	0	2
1993-94	Cape Breton	AHL	16	5	5	10	11	....	....	....	....	....
	Winnipeg	**NHL**	**4**	**0**	**0**	**0**	**2**	....	....	....	....	....
	Moncton	AHL	46	26	35	61	36	21	11	11	22	28
1994-95	Indianapolis	IHL	77	53	40	93	65	....	....	....	....	....
1995-96b	Orlando	IHL	82	*74	56	130	81	14	10	7	17	6
	NHL Totals		**8**	**0**	**0**	**0**	**2**	....	....	....	....	....

a   CCHA First All-Star Team (1990)
b   IHL First All-Star Team (1996)

Traded to **Edmonton** by **Philadelphia** with Scott Mellanby and Craig Berube for Dave Brown, Corey Foster and Jari Kurri, May 30, 1991. Traded to **Winnipeg** by **Edmonton** for cash, December 9, 1993. Signed as a free agent by **Chicago**, June 9, 1994. Signed as a free agent by **NY Islanders**, July 29, 1996.

FITZGERALD, RUSTY   PIT.

Center. Shoots left. 6', 210 lbs.   Born, Minneapolis, MN, October 4, 1972.
(Pittsburgh's 2nd choice, 38th overall, in 1991 Entry Draft).

				Regular Season					Playoffs			
Season	Club	Lea	GP	G	A	TP	PIM	GP	G	A	TP	PIM
1991-92	Minn.-Duluth	WCHA	37	9	11	20	40	....	....	....	....	....
1992-93	Minn.-Duluth	WCHA	39	24	23	47	48	....	....	....	....	....
1993-94	Minn.-Duluth	WCHA	37	11	25	36	59	....	....	....	....	....
1994-95	Minn.-Duluth	WCHA	34	16	22	38	50	....	....	....	....	....
	Cleveland	IHL	2	0	1	1	0	3	3	0	3	6
	Pittsburgh	**NHL**	**4**	**1**	**0**	**1**	**0**	**5**	**0**	**0**	**0**	**4**
1995-96	**Pittsburgh**	**NHL**	**21**	**1**	**2**	**3**	**12**	....	....	....	....	....
	Cleveland	IHL	46	17	19	36	90	1	0	0	0	2
	NHL Totals		**25**	**2**	**2**	**4**	**12**	**5**	**0**	**0**	**0**	**4**

FITZGERALD, TOM   FLA.

Right wing/Center. Shoots right. 6'1", 191 lbs.   Born, Melrose, MA, August 28, 1968.
(NY Islanders' 1st choice, 17th overall, in 1986 Entry Draft).

				Regular Season					Playoffs			
Season	Club	Lea	GP	G	A	TP	PIM	GP	G	A	TP	PIM
1986-87	Providence	H.E.	27	8	14	22	22	....	....	....	....	....
1987-88	Providence	H.E.	36	19	15	34	50	....	....	....	....	....
1988-89	**NY Islanders**	**NHL**	**23**	**3**	**5**	**8**	**10**	....	....	....	....	....
	Springfield	AHL	61	24	18	42	43	....	....	....	....	....
1989-90	**NY Islanders**	**NHL**	**19**	**2**	**5**	**7**	**4**	**4**	**1**	**0**	**1**	**4**
	Springfield	AHL	53	30	23	53	32	14	2	9	11	13
1990-91	**NY Islanders**	**NHL**	**41**	**5**	**5**	**10**	**24**	....	....	....	....	....
	Capital Dist.	AHL	27	7	7	14	50	....	....	....	....	....
1991-92	**NY Islanders**	**NHL**	**45**	**6**	**11**	**17**	**28**	....	....	....	....	....
	Capital Dist.	AHL	4	1	1	2	4	....	....	....	....	....
1992-93	**NY Islanders**	**NHL**	**77**	**9**	**18**	**27**	**34**	**18**	**2**	**5**	**7**	**18**
1993-94	**Florida**	**NHL**	**83**	**18**	**14**	**32**	**54**	....	....	....	....	....
1994-95	**Florida**	**NHL**	**48**	**3**	**13**	**16**	**31**	....	....	....	....	....
1995-96	**Florida**	**NHL**	**82**	**13**	**21**	**34**	**75**	**22**	**4**	**4**	**8**	**34**
	NHL Totals		**418**	**59**	**92**	**151**	**260**	**44**	**7**	**9**	**16**	**56**

Claimed by **Florida** from **NY Islanders** in Expansion Draft, June 24, 1993.

FITZPATRICK, RORY   MTL.

Defense. Shoots right. 6'1", 205 lbs.   Born, Rochester, NY, January 11, 1975.
(Montreal's 2nd choice, 47th overall, in 1993 Entry Draft).

				Regular Season					Playoffs			
Season	Club	Lea	GP	G	A	TP	PIM	GP	G	A	TP	PIM
1992-93	Sudbury	OHL	58	4	20	24	68	14	0	0	0	17
1993-94	Sudbury	OHL	65	12	34	46	112	10	2	5	7	10
1994-95	Sudbury	OHL	56	12	36	48	72	18	3	15	18	21
	Fredericton	AHL	....	....	....	....	....	10	1	2	3	5
1995-96	**Montreal**	**NHL**	**42**	**0**	**2**	**2**	**18**	**6**	**1**	**1**	**2**	**0**
	Fredericton	AHL	18	4	6	10	36	....	....	....	....	....
	NHL Totals		**42**	**0**	**2**	**2**	**18**	**6**	**1**	**1**	**2**	**0**

FLATLEY, PAT   (FLAT-lee)

Right wing. Shoots right. 6'2", 197 lbs.   Born, Toronto, Ont., October 3, 1963.
(NY Islanders' 1st choice, 21st overall, in 1982 Entry Draft).

				Regular Season					Playoffs			
Season	Club	Lea	GP	G	A	TP	PIM	GP	G	A	TP	PIM
1981-82	U. Wisconsin	WCHA	17	10	9	19	40	....	....	....	....	....
1982-83ab	U. Wisconsin	WCHA	26	17	24	41	48	....	....	....	....	....
1983-84	Cdn. National		57	31	17	48	136	....	....	....	....	....
	Cdn. Olympic		7	3	3	6	70	....	....	....	....	....
	NY Islanders	**NHL**	**16**	**2**	**7**	**9**	**6**	**21**	**9**	**6**	**15**	**14**
1984-85	**NY Islanders**	**NHL**	**78**	**20**	**31**	**51**	**106**	**4**	**1**	**0**	**1**	**6**
1985-86	**NY Islanders**	**NHL**	**73**	**18**	**34**	**52**	**66**	**3**	**0**	**0**	**0**	**21**
1986-87	**NY Islanders**	**NHL**	**63**	**16**	**35**	**51**	**81**	**11**	**3**	**2**	**5**	**6**
1987-88	**NY Islanders**	**NHL**	**40**	**9**	**15**	**24**	**28**	....	....	....	....	....
1988-89	**NY Islanders**	**NHL**	**41**	**10**	**15**	**25**	**31**	....	....	....	....	....
	Springfield	AHL	2	1	1	2	2	....	....	....	....	....
1989-90	**NY Islanders**	**NHL**	**62**	**17**	**32**	**49**	**101**	**5**	**3**	**0**	**3**	**2**
1990-91	**NY Islanders**	**NHL**	**56**	**20**	**25**	**45**	**74**	....	....	....	....	....
1991-92	**NY Islanders**	**NHL**	**38**	**8**	**28**	**36**	**31**	....	....	....	....	....
1992-93	**NY Islanders**	**NHL**	**80**	**13**	**47**	**60**	**63**	**15**	**2**	**7**	**9**	**12**
1993-94	**NY Islanders**	**NHL**	**64**	**12**	**30**	**42**	**40**	....	....	....	....	....
1994-95	**NY Islanders**	**NHL**	**45**	**7**	**20**	**27**	**12**	....	....	....	....	....
1995-96	**NY Islanders**	**NHL**	**56**	**8**	**9**	**17**	**21**	....	....	....	....	....
	NHL Totals		**712**	**160**	**328**	**488**	**660**	**59**	**18**	**15**	**33**	**61**

a   WCHA First All-Star Team (1983)
b   Named to NCAA All-Tournament Team (1983)

FLEMING, GERRY   MTL.

Left wing. Shoots left. 6'5", 253 lbs.   Born, Montreal, Que., October 16, 1967.

				Regular Season					Playoffs			
Season	Club	Lea	GP	G	A	TP	PIM	GP	G	A	TP	PIM
1990-91	U.P.E.I.	AUAA				UNAVAILABLE						
1991-92	Charlottetown	Sr.				UNAVAILABLE						
	Fredericton	AHL	37	4	6	10	133	1	0	0	0	7
1992-93	Fredericton	AHL	64	9	17	26	262	5	1	2	3	14
1993-94	**Montreal**	**NHL**	**5**	**0**	**0**	**0**	**25**	....	....	....	....	....
	Fredericton	AHL	46	6	16	22	188	....	....	....	....	....
1994-95	Fredericton	AHL	16	3	3	6	60	10	2	0	2	67
	Montreal	**NHL**	**6**	**0**	**0**	**0**	**17**	....	....	....	....	....
1995-96	Fredericton	AHL	40	8	9	17	127	10	3	1	4	19
	NHL Totals		**11**	**0**	**0**	**0**	**42**	....	....	....	....	....

Signed as a free agent by **Montreal**, February 17, 1992.

FLEURY, THEOREN (FLUH-ree, THAIR-ihn) CGY.

Right wing. Shoots right. 5'6", 160 lbs. Born, Oxbow, Sask., June 29, 1968.
(Calgary's 9th choice, 166th overall, in 1987 Entry Draft).

			Regular Season					Playoffs				
Season	Club	Lea	GP	G	A	TP	PIM	GP	G	A	TP	PIM
1984-85	Moose Jaw	WHL	71	29	46	75	82	....	....	....	....	....
1985-86	Moose Jaw	WHL	72	43	65	108	124	....	....	....	....	....
1986-87	Moose Jaw	WHL	66	61	68	129	110	9	7	9	16	34
1987-88	Moose Jaw	WHL	65	68	92	*160	235	....	....	....	....	....
	Salt Lake	IHL	2	3	4	7	7	8	11	5	16	16
1988-89	Calgary	NHL	36	14	20	34	46	22	5	6	11	24 ♦
	Salt Lake	IHL	40	37	37	74	81	....	....	....	....	....
1989-90	Calgary	NHL	80	31	35	66	157	6	2	3	5	10
1990-91a	Calgary	NHL	79	51	53	104	136	7	2	5	7	14
1991-92	Calgary	NHL	80	33	40	73	133	....	....	....	....	....
1992-93	Calgary	NHL	83	34	66	100	88	6	5	7	12	27
1993-94	Calgary	NHL	83	40	45	85	186	7	6	4	10	5
1994-95	Tappara	Fin.	10	8	9	17	22	....	....	....	....	....
b	Calgary	NHL	47	29	29	58	112	7	7	7	14	2
1995-96	Calgary	NHL	80	46	50	96	112	4	2	1	3	14
	NHL Totals		568	278	338	616	970	59	29	33	62	96

a Co-winner of Alka-Seltzer Plus Award with Marty McSorley (1991)
b NHL Second All-Star Team (1995)

Played in NHL All-Star Game (1991, 1992, 1996)

FLICHEL, MARTY (FLICK-ehl) DAL.

Right wing. Shoots left. 5'11", 175 lbs. Born, Hodgeville, Sask., March 6, 1976.
(Dallas' 6th choice, 228th overall, in 1994 Entry Draft).

			Regular Season					Playoffs				
Season	Club	Lea	GP	G	A	TP	PIM	GP	G	A	TP	PIM
1992-93	Tacoma	WHL	61	21	20	41	19	7	0	0	0	8
1993-94	Tacoma	WHL	72	27	48	75	69	8	1	4	5	13
1994-95	Tacoma	WHL	67	25	53	78	81	4	2	3	5	8
1995-96	Kelowna	WHL	69	28	79	107	107	6	1	6	7	10

FLINTON, ERIC NYR

Left wing. Shoots left. 6'2", 200 lbs. Born, William Lake, B.C., February 2, 1972.
(Ottawa's 1st choice, 1st overall, in 1993 Supplemental Draft).

			Regular Season					Playoffs				
Season	Club	Lea	GP	G	A	TP	PIM	GP	G	A	TP	PIM
1991-92	N. Hampshire	H.E.	36	6	4	10	10	....	....	....	....	....
1992-93	N. Hampshire	H.E.	37	18	18	36	14	....	....	....	....	....
1993-94	N. Hampshire	H.E.	40	16	25	41	36	....	....	....	....	....
1994-95a	N. Hampshire	H.E.	36	22	23	45	44	....	....	....	....	....
1995-96	Charlotte	ECHL	69	20	26	46	29	16	5	8	13	4

a Hockey East Second All-Star Team (1995)

Signed as a free agent by **NY Rangers**, September 12, 1995.

FOCHT, DAN (FOHKT) PHO.

Defense. Shoots left. 6'6", 226 lbs. Born, Regina, Sask., December 31, 1977.
(Phoenix's 1st choice, 11th overall, in 1996 Entry Draft).

			Regular Season					Playoffs				
Season	Club	Lea	GP	G	A	TP	PIM	GP	G	A	TP	PIM
1994-95	Saskatoon	Midget	33	6	12	18	98	....	....	....	....	....
1995-96	Tri-City	WHL	63	6	12	18	161	11	1	1	2	23

FOGARTY, BRYAN

Defense. Shoots left. 6'2", 206 lbs. Born, Brantford, Ont., June 11, 1969.
(Quebec's 1st choice, 9th overall, in 1987 Entry Draft).

			Regular Season					Playoffs				
Season	Club	Lea	GP	G	A	TP	PIM	GP	G	A	TP	PIM
1985-86	Kingston	OHL	47	2	19	21	14	10	1	3	4	4
1986-87a	Kingston	OHL	56	20	50	70	46	12	2	3	5	5
1987-88	Kingston	OHL	48	11	36	47	50	....	....	....	....	....
1988-89abc	Niagara Falls	OHL	60	47	*108	*155	88	17	10	22	32	36
1989-90	Quebec	NHL	45	4	10	14	31	....	....	....	....	....
	Halifax	AHL	22	5	14	19	6	6	2	4	6	0
1990-91	Quebec	NHL	45	9	22	31	24	....	....	....	....	....
	Halifax	AHL	5	0	2	2	0	....	....	....	....	....
1991-92	Quebec	NHL	20	3	12	15	16	....	....	....	....	....
	Halifax	AHL	2	0	0	0	2	....	....	....	....	....
	New Haven	AHL	4	0	1	1	6	....	....	....	....	....
	Muskegon	IHL	8	2	4	6	30	....	....	....	....	....
1992-93	Pittsburgh	NHL	12	0	4	4	4	....	....	....	....	....
	Cleveland	IHL	15	2	5	7	8	3	0	1	1	17
1993-94	Atlanta	IHL	8	1	5	6	4	....	....	....	....	....
	Las Vegas	IHL	33	3	16	19	38	....	....	....	....	....
	Kansas City	IHL	3	2	1	3	2	....	....	....	....	....
	Montreal	NHL	13	1	2	3	10	....	....	....	....	....
1994-95	Montreal	NHL	21	5	2	7	34	....	....	....	....	....
1995-96	Minnesota	IHL	17	3	12	15	24	....	....	....	....	....
	Detroit	IHL	18	1	5	6	14	....	....	....	....	....
	Davos	Switz.	....	....	....	....	....	3	1	1	2	0
	NHL Totals		156	22	52	74	119	....	....	....	....	....

a OHL First All-Star Team (1987, 1989)
b Canadian Major Junior Player of the Year (1989)
c Canadian Major Junior Defenseman of the Year (1989)

Traded to **Pittsburgh** by **Quebec** for Scott Young, March 10, 1992. Signed as a free agent by **Tampa Bay**, September 28, 1993. Signed as a free agent by **Montreal**, February 25, 1994. Signed as a free agent by **Buffalo**, September 8, 1995.

FOOTE, ADAM COL.

Defense. Shoots right. 6'1", 202 lbs. Born, Toronto, Ont., July 10, 1971.
(Quebec's 2nd choice, 22nd overall, in 1989 Entry Draft).

			Regular Season					Playoffs				
Season	Club	Lea	GP	G	A	TP	PIM	GP	G	A	TP	PIM
1988-89	S.S. Marie	OHL	66	7	32	39	120	....	....	....	....	....
1989-90	S.S. Marie	OHL	61	12	43	55	199	....	....	....	....	....
1990-91a	S.S. Marie	OHL	59	18	51	69	93	14	5	12	17	28
1991-92	Quebec	NHL	46	2	5	7	44	....	....	....	....	....
	Halifax	AHL	6	0	1	1	2	....	....	....	....	....
1992-93	Quebec	NHL	81	4	12	16	168	6	0	1	1	2
1993-94	Quebec	NHL	45	2	6	8	67	....	....	....	....	....
1994-95	Quebec	NHL	35	0	7	7	52	6	0	1	1	14
1995-96	Colorado	NHL	73	5	11	16	88	22	1	3	4	36 ♦
	NHL Totals		280	13	41	54	419	34	1	5	6	52

a OHL First All-Star Team (1991)

FORBES, COLIN PHI.

Left wing. Shoots left. 6'3", 205 lbs. Born, New Westminster, B.C., February 16, 1976.
(Philadelphia's 5th choice, 166th overall, in 1994 Entry Draft).

			Regular Season					Playoffs				
Season	Club	Lea	GP	G	A	TP	PIM	GP	G	A	TP	PIM
1993-94	Sherwood Park	AJHL	47	18	22	40	76	....	....	....	....	....
1994-95	Portland	WHL	72	24	31	55	108	9	1	3	4	10
1995-96	Portland	WHL	72	33	44	77	137	7	2	5	7	14
	Hershey	AHL	2	1	0	1	2	4	0	2	2	2

FORSANDER, JOHAN DET.

Left wing. Shoots left. 6'1", 174 lbs. Born, Jonkoping, Sweden, April 28, 1978.
(Detroit's 3rd choice, 108th overall, in 1996 Entry Draft).

			Regular Season					Playoffs				
Season	Club	Lea	GP	G	A	TP	PIM	GP	G	A	TP	PIM
1994-95	HV 71	Swe. Jr.	25	2	2	4	6	....	....	....	....	....
1995-96	HV 71	Swe. Jr.	27	15	8	23	12	....	....	....	....	....
	HV 71	Swe.	6	0	0	0	0	3	0	0	0	2

FORSBERG, PETER (FOHRS-buhrg) COL.

Center. Shoots left. 6', 190 lbs. Born, Ornskoldsvik, Sweden, July 20, 1973.
(Philadelphia's 1st choice, 6th overall, in 1991 Entry Draft).

			Regular Season					Playoffs				
Season	Club	Lea	GP	G	A	TP	PIM	GP	G	A	TP	PIM
1990-91	MoDo	Swe.	23	7	10	17	22	....	....	....	....	....
1991-92	MoDo	Swe.	39	9	18	27	78	....	....	....	....	....
1992-93	MoDo	Swe.	39	23	24	47	92	3	4	1	5	0
1993-94	MoDo	Swe.	39	18	26	44	82	11	9	7	16	14
1994-95	MoDo	Swe.	11	5	9	14	20	....	....	....	....	....
ab	Quebec	NHL	47	15	35	50	16	6	2	4	6	4
1995-96	Colorado	NHL	82	30	86	116	47	22	10	11	21	18 ♦
	NHL Totals		129	45	121	166	63	28	12	15	27	22

a NHL/Upper Deck All-Rookie Team (1995)
b Won Calder Memorial Trophy (1995)

Played in NHL All-Star Game (1996)

Traded to **Quebec** by **Philadelphia** with Steve Duchesne, Kerry Huffman, Mike Ricci, Ron Hextall, Chris Simon, Philadelphia's first round choice in the 1993 (Jocelyn Thibault) and 1994 (later traded to Toronto — later traded to Washington — Washington selected Nolan Baumgartner) Entry Drafts and cash for Eric Lindros, June 30, 1992.

FOSTER, COREY PIT.

Defense. Shoots left. 6'3", 204 lbs. Born, Ottawa, Ont., October 27, 1969.
(New Jersey's 1st choice, 12th overall, in 1988 Entry Draft).

			Regular Season					Playoffs				
Season	Club	Lea	GP	G	A	TP	PIM	GP	G	A	TP	PIM
1986-87	Peterborough	OHL	30	3	4	7	4	1	0	0	0	0
1987-88	Peterborough	OHL	66	13	31	44	58	11	5	9	14	13
1988-89	New Jersey	NHL	2	0	0	0	0	....	....	....	....	....
	Peterborough	OHL	55	14	42	56	42	17	1	17	18	12
1989-90	Cape Breton	AHL	54	7	17	24	32	1	0	0	0	0
1990-91	Cape Breton	AHL	67	14	11	25	51	4	2	4	6	4
1991-92	Philadelphia	NHL	25	3	4	7	20	....	....	....	....	....
	Hershey	AHL	19	5	9	14	26	6	1	1	2	5
1992-93	Hershey	AHL	80	9	25	34	102	....	....	....	....	....
1993-94	Hershey	AHL	66	21	37	58	96	9	2	5	7	10
1994-95	P.E.I.	AHL	78	13	34	47	61	11	2	5	7	12
1995-96	Pittsburgh	NHL	11	2	2	4	2	3	0	0	0	4
	Cleveland	IHL	61	10	36	46	93	....	....	....	....	....
	NHL Totals		38	5	6	11	22	3	0	0	0	4

Traded to **Edmonton** by **New Jersey** for Edmonton's first round choice (Jason Miller) in 1989 Entry Draft, June 17, 1989. Traded to **Philadelphia** by **Edmonton** with Dave Brown and Jari Kurri for Craig Fisher, Scott Mellanby and Craig Berube, May 30, 1991. Signed as a free agent by **Ottawa**, June 20, 1994. Signed as a free agent by **Pittsburgh**, August 7, 1995.

FRANCIS, RON PIT.

Center. Shoots left. 6'2", 200 lbs. Born, Sault Ste. Marie, Ont., March 1, 1963.
(Hartford's 1st choice, 4th overall, in 1981 Entry Draft).

			Regular Season					Playoffs				
Season	Club	Lea	GP	G	A	TP	PIM	GP	G	A	TP	PIM
1980-81	S.S. Marie	OHA	64	26	43	69	33	19	7	8	15	34
1981-82	Hartford	NHL	59	25	43	68	51	....	....	....	....	....
	S.S. Marie	OHL	25	18	30	48	46	....	....	....	....	....
1982-83	Hartford	NHL	79	31	59	90	60	....	....	....	....	....
1983-84	Hartford	NHL	72	23	60	83	45	....	....	....	....	....
1984-85	Hartford	NHL	80	24	57	81	66	....	....	....	....	....
1985-86	Hartford	NHL	53	24	53	77	24	10	1	2	3	4
1986-87	Hartford	NHL	75	30	63	93	45	6	2	2	4	6
1987-88	Hartford	NHL	80	25	50	75	87	6	2	5	7	2
1988-89	Hartford	NHL	69	29	48	77	36	4	0	2	2	0
1989-90	Hartford	NHL	80	32	69	101	73	7	3	3	6	8
1990-91	Hartford	NHL	67	21	55	76	51	....	....	....	....	....
	Pittsburgh	NHL	14	2	9	11	21	24	7	10	17	24 ♦
1991-92	Pittsburgh	NHL	70	21	33	54	30	21	8	*19	27	6 ♦
1992-93	Pittsburgh	NHL	84	24	76	100	68	12	6	11	17	19
1993-94	Pittsburgh	NHL	82	27	66	93	62	6	0	2	2	6
1994-95abc	Pittsburgh	NHL	44	11	*48	59	18	12	6	13	19	4
1995-96	Pittsburgh	NHL	77	27	*92	119	56	11	3	6	9	4
	NHL Totals		1085	376	881	1257	793	119	38	75	113	83

a Won Alka-Seltzer Plus Award (1995)
b Won Frank J. Selke Trophy (1995)
c Won Lady Byng Trophy (1995)

Played in NHL All-Star Game (1983, 1985, 1990, 1996)

Traded to **Pittsburgh** by **Hartford** with Grant Jennings and Ulf Samuelsson for John Cullen, Jeff Parker and Zarley Zalapski, March 4, 1991.

FRASER, IAIN — S.J.

Center. Shoots left. 5'10", 175 lbs. Born, Scarborough, Ont., August 10, 1969.
(NY Islanders' 12th choice, 233rd overall, in 1989 Entry Draft).

			Regular Season					Playoffs				
Season	Club	Lea	GP	G	A	TP	PIM	GP	G	A	TP	PIM
1986-87	Oshawa	OHL	5	1	2	3	0	....	....	....	....	....
1987-88	Oshawa	OHL	16	4	4	8	22	6	2	3	5	2
1988-89	Oshawa	OHL	62	33	57	90	87	6	2	8	10	12
1989-90ab	Oshawa	OHL	56	40	65	105	75	17	10	*22	32	8
1990-91	Capital Dist.	AHL	32	5	13	18	16	....	....	....	....	....
	Richmond	ECHL	3	1	1	2	0	....	....	....	....	....
1991-92	Capital Dist.	AHL	45	9	11	20	24	....	....	....	....	....
1992-93	**NY Islanders**	**NHL**	**7**	**2**	**2**	**4**	**2**	....	....	....	....	....
c	Capital Dist.	AHL	74	41	69	110	16	4	0	1	1	0
1993-94	**Quebec**	**NHL**	**60**	**17**	**20**	**37**	**23**	....	....	....	....	....
1994-95	**Dallas**	**NHL**	**4**	**0**	**0**	**0**	**0**	....	....	....	....	....
	Edmonton	**NHL**	**9**	**3**	**0**	**3**	**0**	....	....	....	....	....
	Denver	IHL	1	0	0	0	0	....	....	....	....	....
1995-96	**Winnipeg**	**NHL**	**12**	**1**	**1**	**2**	**4**	**4**	**0**	**0**	**0**	**0**
	Springfield	AHL	53	24	47	71	27	6	0	6	6	2
	NHL Totals		**92**	**23**	**23**	**46**	**29**	**4**	**0**	**0**	**0**	**0**

a Memorial Cup All-Star Team (1990)
b Won Stafford Smythe Memorial Trophy (Memorial Cup Tournament MVP) (1990)
c AHL Second All-Star Team (1993)

Signed as a free agent by **Quebec**, August 3, 1993. Traded to **Dallas** by **Quebec** for Dallas' seventh round choice (Dan Hinote) in 1996 Entry Draft, January 31, 1995. Claimed on waivers by **Edmonton** from **Dallas**, March 3, 1995. Signed as a free agent by **Winnipeg**, October 11, 1995. Signed as a free agent by **San Jose**, August 26, 1996.

FRASER, SCOTT — MTL.

Center. Shoots right. 6'1", 178 lbs. Born, Moncton, N.B., May 3, 1972.
(Montreal's 12th choice, 193rd overall, in 1991 Entry Draft).

			Regular Season					Playoffs				
Season	Club	Lea	GP	G	A	TP	PIM	GP	G	A	TP	PIM
1990-91	Dartmouth	ECAC	24	10	10	20	30	....	....	....	....	....
1991-92	Dartmouth	ECAC	24	11	7	18	60	....	....	....	....	....
1992-93	Cdn. National	....	5	1	0	1	0	....	....	....	....	....
a	Dartmouth	ECAC	26	21	23	44	13	....	....	....	....	....
1993-94	Dartmouth	ECAC	24	17	13	30	34	....	....	....	....	....
	Cdn. National	....	4	0	1	1	4	....	....	....	....	....
1994-95	Fredericton	AHL	65	23	25	48	36	16	3	5	8	14
	Wheeling	ECHL	8	4	2	6	8	....	....	....	....	....
1995-96	**Montreal**	**NHL**	**15**	**2**	**0**	**2**	**4**	....	....	....	....	....
	Fredericton	AHL	58	37	37	74	43	10	9	7	16	2
	NHL Totals		**15**	**2**	**0**	**2**	**4**	....	....	....	....	....

a ECAC Second All-Star Team (1993)

FREER, MARK — (FRIHR)

Center. Shoots left. 5'10", 180 lbs. Born, Peterborough, Ont., July 14, 1968.

			Regular Season					Playoffs				
Season	Club	Lea	GP	G	A	TP	PIM	GP	G	A	TP	PIM
1985-86	Peterborough	OHL	65	16	28	44	24	14	3	4	7	13
1986-87	**Philadelphia**	**NHL**	**1**	**0**	**1**	**1**	**0**	....	....	....	....	....
	Peterborough	OHL	65	39	43	82	44	12	2	6	8	5
1987-88	**Philadelphia**	**NHL**	**1**	**0**	**0**	**0**	**0**	....	....	....	....	....
	Peterborough	OHL	63	38	70	108	63	12	5	12	17	4
1988-89	**Philadelphia**	**NHL**	**5**	**0**	**1**	**1**	**0**	....	....	....	....	....
	Hershey	AHL	75	30	49	79	77	12	4	6	10	2
1989-90	**Philadelphia**	**NHL**	**2**	**0**	**0**	**0**	**0**	....	....	....	....	....
	Hershey	AHL	65	28	36	64	31	....	....	....	....	....
1990-91	Hershey	AHL	77	18	44	62	45	7	1	3	4	17
1991-92	**Philadelphia**	**NHL**	**50**	**6**	**7**	**13**	**18**	....	....	....	....	....
	Hershey	AHL	31	13	11	24	38	6	0	3	3	2
1992-93	**Ottawa**	**NHL**	**63**	**10**	**14**	**24**	**39**	....	....	....	....	....
1993-94	**Calgary**	**NHL**	**2**	**0**	**0**	**0**	**4**	....	....	....	....	....
	Saint John	AHL	77	33	53	86	45	7	2	4	6	16
1994-95	Houston	IHL	80	38	42	80	54	4	0	1	1	4
1995-96	Houston	IHL	80	22	31	53	67	....	....	....	....	....
	NHL Totals		**124**	**16**	**23**	**39**	**61**	....	....	....	....	....

Signed as a free agent by **Philadelphia**, October 7, 1986. Claimed by **Ottawa** from **Philadelphia** in Expansion Draft, June 18, 1992. Signed as a free agent by **Calgary**, August 10, 1993.

FRIEDMAN, DOUG

Left wing. Shoots left. 6'1", 189 lbs. Born, Cape Elizabeth, ME, September 1, 1971.
(Quebec's 11th choice, 222nd overall, in 1991 Entry Draft).

			Regular Season					Playoffs				
Season	Club	Lea	GP	G	A	TP	PIM	GP	G	A	TP	PIM
1990-91	Boston U.	H.E.	36	6	6	12	37	....	....	....	....	....
1991-92	Boston U.	H.E.	34	11	8	19	42	....	....	....	....	....
1992-93	Boston U.	H.E.	38	17	24	41	62	....	....	....	....	....
1993-94	Boston U.	H.E.	41	9	23	32	110	....	....	....	....	....
1994-95	Cornwall	AHL	55	6	9	15	56	3	0	0	0	0
1995-96	Cornwall	AHL	80	12	22	34	178	8	1	1	2	17

FRIESEN, JEFF — (FREE-zuhn) S.J.

Center. Shoots left. 6', 185 lbs. Born, Meadow Lake, Sask., August 5, 1976.
(San Jose's 1st choice, 11th overall, in 1994 Entry Draft).

			Regular Season					Playoffs				
Season	Club	Lea	GP	G	A	TP	PIM	GP	G	A	TP	PIM
1991-92	Regina	WHL	4	3	1	4	2	....	....	....	....	....
1992-93	Regina	WHL	70	45	38	83	23	13	7	10	17	8
1993-94	Regina	WHL	66	51	67	118	48	4	3	2	5	2
1994-95	Regina	WHL	25	21	23	44	22	....	....	....	....	....
a	**San Jose**	**NHL**	**48**	**15**	**10**	**25**	**14**	**11**	**1**	**5**	**6**	**4**
1995-96	**San Jose**	**NHL**	**79**	**15**	**31**	**46**	**42**	....	....	....	....	....
	NHL Totals		**127**	**30**	**41**	**71**	**56**	**11**	**1**	**5**	**6**	**4**

a NHL/Upper Deck All-Rookie Team (1995)

FRYLEN, EDVIN — (FRYUH-lehn) ST.L.

Defense. Shoots left. 6', 211 lbs. Born, Jarfalla, Sweden, December 23, 1975.
(St. Louis' 3rd choice, 120th overall, in 1994 Entry Draft).

			Regular Season					Playoffs				
Season	Club	Lea	GP	G	A	TP	PIM	GP	G	A	TP	PIM
1991-92	Vasteras	Swe.	2	0	0	0	0	....	....	....	....	....
1992-93	Vasteras	Swe.	29	0	2	2	14	3	0	0	0	0
1993-94	Vasteras	Swe.	32	1	0	1	26	....	....	....	....	....
1994-95	Vasteras	Swe.	25	2	1	3	14	4	0	0	0	4
1995-96	Vasteras	Swe.	39	8	5	13	16	....	....	....	....	....

GAFFNEY, MIKE — OTT.

Defense. Shoots right. 6'1", 202 lbs. Born, Worchester, MA, June 19, 1976.
(Ottawa's 4th choice, 131st overall, in 1994 Entry Draft).

			Regular Season					Playoffs				
Season	Club	Lea	GP	G	A	TP	PIM	GP	G	A	TP	PIM
1994-95	Massachusetts	H.E.	33	1	4	5	38	....	....	....	....	....
1995-96	Massachusetts	H.E.	33	0	6	6	41	....	....	....	....	....

GAGNER, DAVE — (GAH-nyay) CGY.

Center. Shoots left. 5'10", 180 lbs. Born, Chatham, Ont., December 11, 1964.
(NY Rangers' 1st choice, 12th overall, in 1983 Entry Draft).

			Regular Season					Playoffs				
Season	Club	Lea	GP	G	A	TP	PIM	GP	G	A	TP	PIM
1981-82	Brantford	OHL	68	30	46	76	31	11	3	6	9	6
1982-83a	Brantford	OHL	70	55	66	121	57	8	5	5	10	4
1983-84	Cdn. National	....	50	19	18	37	26	....	....	....	....	....
	Cdn. Olympic	....	7	5	2	7	6	....	....	....	....	....
	Brantford	OHL	12	7	13	20	4	6	0	4	4	6
1984-85	**NY Rangers**	**NHL**	**38**	**6**	**6**	**12**	**16**	....	....	....	....	....
	New Haven	AHL	38	13	20	33	23	....	....	....	....	....
1985-86	**NY Rangers**	**NHL**	**32**	**4**	**6**	**10**	**19**	....	....	....	....	....
	New Haven	AHL	16	10	11	21	11	4	1	2	3	2
1986-87	**NY Rangers**	**NHL**	**10**	**1**	**4**	**5**	**12**	....	....	....	....	....
	New Haven	AHL	56	22	41	63	50	7	1	5	6	18
1987-88	**Minnesota**	**NHL**	**51**	**8**	**11**	**19**	**55**	....	....	....	....	....
	Kalamazoo	IHL	14	16	10	26	26	....	....	....	....	....
1988-89	**Minnesota**	**NHL**	**75**	**35**	**43**	**78**	**104**	....	....	....	....	....
	Kalamazoo	IHL	1	0	1	1	4	....	....	....	....	....
1989-90	**Minnesota**	**NHL**	**79**	**40**	**38**	**78**	**54**	**7**	**2**	**3**	**5**	**16**
1990-91	**Minnesota**	**NHL**	**73**	**40**	**42**	**82**	**114**	**23**	**12**	**15**	**27**	**28**
1991-92	**Minnesota**	**NHL**	**78**	**31**	**40**	**71**	**107**	**7**	**2**	**4**	**6**	**8**
1992-93	**Minnesota**	**NHL**	**84**	**33**	**43**	**76**	**143**	....	....	....	....	....
1993-94	**Dallas**	**NHL**	**76**	**32**	**29**	**61**	**83**	**9**	**5**	**1**	**6**	**2**
1994-95	Courmaosta	Italy	3	0	0	0	0	....	....	....	....	....
	Courmaosta	Euro.	1	0	4	4	0	....	....	....	....	....
	Dallas	**NHL**	**48**	**14**	**28**	**42**	**42**	**5**	**1**	**1**	**2**	**4**
1995-96	**Dallas**	**NHL**	**45**	**14**	**13**	**27**	**44**	....	....	....	....	....
	Toronto	**NHL**	**28**	**7**	**15**	**22**	**59**	**6**	**0**	**2**	**2**	**6**
	NHL Totals		**717**	**265**	**318**	**583**	**852**	**57**	**22**	**26**	**48**	**64**

a OHL Second All-Star Team (1983)

Played in NHL All-Star Game (1991)

Traded to **Minnesota** by **NY Rangers** with Jay Caulfield for Jari Gronstrand and Paul Boutilier, October 8, 1987. Traded to **Toronto** by **Dallas** with Dallas' sixth round choice (Dmitriy Yakushin) in 1996 Entry Draft for Benoit Hogue and Randy Wood, January 29, 1996. Traded to **Calgary** by **Toronto** for Calgary's third round choice (Mike Lankshear) in 1996 Entry Draft, June 22, 1996.

GALANOV, MAXIM — NYR

Defense. Shoots left. 6'1", 175 lbs. Born, Krasnoyarsk, USSR, March 13, 1974.
(NY Rangers' 3rd choice, 61st overall, in 1993 Entry Draft).

			Regular Season					Playoffs				
Season	Club	Lea	GP	G	A	TP	PIM	GP	G	A	TP	PIM
1992-93	Togliatti	CIS	41	4	2	6	12	10	1	1	2	12
1993-94	Togliatti	CIS	7	1	0	1	4	12	1	0	1	8
1994-95	Togliatti	CIS	45	5	6	11	54	9	0	1	1	12
1995-96	Binghamton	AHL	72	17	36	53	24	4	1	1	2	0

GALLANT, CHESTER — PHI.

Right wing. Shoots right. 6'1", 184 lbs. Born, Thunder Bay, Ont., December 22, 1977.
(Philadelphia's 2nd choice, 64th overall, in 1996 Entry Draft).

			Regular Season					Playoffs				
Season	Club	Lea	GP	G	A	TP	PIM	GP	G	A	TP	PIM
1994-95	Sudbury	OHL	37	3	5	8	63	....	....	....	....	....
	Niagara Falls	OHL	26	3	5	8	70	6	1	0	1	19
1995-96	Niagara Falls	OHL	66	10	20	30	178	10	2	0	2	18

GALLEY, GARRY — BUF.

Defense. Shoots left. 6', 204 lbs. Born, Montreal, Que., April 16, 1963.
(Los Angeles' 4th choice, 100th overall, in 1983 Entry Draft).

			Regular Season					Playoffs				
Season	Club	Lea	GP	G	A	TP	PIM	GP	G	A	TP	PIM
1981-82	Bowling Green	CCHA	42	3	36	39	48	....	....	....	....	....
1982-83	Bowling Green	CCHA	40	17	29	46	40	....	....	....	....	....
1983-84ab	Bowling Green	CCHA	44	15	52	67	61	....	....	....	....	....
1984-85	**Los Angeles**	**NHL**	**78**	**8**	**30**	**38**	**82**	**3**	**1**	**0**	**1**	**2**
1985-86	**Los Angeles**	**NHL**	**49**	**9**	**13**	**22**	**46**	....	....	....	....	....
	New Haven	AHL	4	2	6	8	6	....	....	....	....	....
1986-87	**Los Angeles**	**NHL**	**30**	**5**	**11**	**16**	**57**	....	....	....	....	....
	Washington	**NHL**	**18**	**1**	**10**	**11**	**10**	**2**	**0**	**0**	**0**	**0**
1987-88	**Washington**	**NHL**	**58**	**7**	**23**	**30**	**44**	**13**	**2**	**4**	**6**	**13**
1988-89	**Boston**	**NHL**	**78**	**8**	**21**	**29**	**80**	**9**	**0**	**1**	**1**	**33**
1989-90	**Boston**	**NHL**	**71**	**8**	**27**	**35**	**75**	**21**	**3**	**3**	**6**	**34**
1990-91	**Boston**	**NHL**	**70**	**6**	**21**	**27**	**84**	**16**	**1**	**5**	**6**	**17**
1991-92	**Boston**	**NHL**	**38**	**2**	**12**	**14**	**83**	....	....	....	....	....
	Philadelphia	**NHL**	**39**	**3**	**15**	**18**	**34**	....	....	....	....	....
1992-93	**Philadelphia**	**NHL**	**83**	**13**	**49**	**62**	**115**	....	....	....	....	....
1993-94	**Philadelphia**	**NHL**	**81**	**10**	**60**	**70**	**91**	....	....	....	....	....
1994-95	**Philadelphia**	**NHL**	**33**	**2**	**20**	**22**	**20**	....	....	....	....	....
	Buffalo	**NHL**	**14**	**1**	**9**	**10**	**10**	**5**	**0**	**3**	**3**	**4**
1995-96	**Buffalo**	**NHL**	**78**	**10**	**44**	**54**	**81**	....	....	....	....	....
	NHL Totals		**818**	**93**	**365**	**458**	**912**	**69**	**7**	**16**	**23**	**103**

a CCHA First All-Star Team (1984)
b NCAA All-American (1984)

Played in NHL All-Star Game (1991, 1994)

Traded to **Washington** by **Los Angeles** for Al Jensen, February 14, 1987. Signed as a free agent by **Boston**, July 8, 1988. Traded to **Philadelphia** by **Boston** with Wes Walz and Boston's third round choice (Milos Holan) in 1993 Entry Draft for Gord Murphy, Brian Dobbin, Philadelphia's third round choice (Sergei Zholtok) in 1992 Entry Draft and Philadelphia's fourth round choice (Charles Paquette) in 1993 Entry Draft, January 2, 1992. Traded to **Buffalo** by **Philadelphia** for Petr Svoboda, April 7, 1995.

GARANIN, YEVGENY — PHO.

Center. Shoots left. 6'4", 191 lbs. Born, Voskresensk, USSR, August 3, 1973.
(Winnipeg's 9th choice, 228th overall, in 1992 Entry Draft).

			Regular Season					Playoffs				
Season	Club	Lea	GP	G	A	TP	PIM	GP	G	A	TP	PIM
1991-92	Khimik	CIS	1	1	0	1	0	....	....	....	....	....
1992-93	Khimik	CIS	34	5	4	9	10	1	0	0	0	2
1993-94	Khimik	CIS	46	6	4	10	12	3	0	0	0	0
1994-95	Khimik	CIS	50	19	8	27	6	2	0	0	0	0
1995-96	Khimik	CIS	50	14	12	26	12	....	....	....	....	....

GARDINER, BRUCE — OTT.

Center. Shoots right. 6'1", 185 lbs. Born, Barrie, Ont., February 11, 1971.
(St. Louis' 6th choice, 131st overall, in 1991 Entry Draft).

			Regular Season					Playoffs				
Season	Club	Lea	GP	G	A	TP	PIM	GP	G	A	TP	PIM
1990-91	Colgate	ECAC	27	4	9	13	72	....	....	....	....	....
1991-92	Colgate	ECAC	23	7	8	15	77	....	....	....	....	....
1992-93	Colgate	ECAC	33	17	12	29	64	....	....	....	....	....
1993-94a	Colgate	ECAC	33	23	23	46	68	....	....	....	....	....
	Peoria	IHL	3	0	0	0	0	....	....	....	....	....
1994-95	P.E.I.	AHL	72	17	20	37	132	7	4	1	5	4
1995-96	P.E.I.	AHL	38	11	13	24	87	5	2	4	6	4

a ECAC Second All-Star Team (1994)

Signed as a free agent by **Ottawa**, June 14, 1994.

GARPENLOV, JOHAN — (GAHR-pehn-LAHV, YOH-hahn) — FLA.

Left wing. Shoots left. 5'11", 184 lbs. Born, Stockholm, Sweden, March 21, 1968.
(Detroit's 5th choice, 85th overall, in 1986 Entry Draft).

			Regular Season					Playoffs				
Season	Club	Lea	GP	G	A	TP	PIM	GP	G	A	TP	PIM
1986-87	Djurgarden	Swe.	29	5	8	13	22	2	0	0	0	0
1987-88	Djurgarden	Swe.	30	7	10	17	12	3	1	3	4	4
1988-89	Djurgarden	Swe.	36	12	19	31	20	8	3	4	7	10
1989-90	Djurgarden	Swe.	39	20	13	33	35	8	2	4	6	4
1990-91	**Detroit**	**NHL**	**71**	**18**	**22**	**40**	**18**	**6**	**0**	**1**	**1**	**4**
1991-92	**Detroit**	**NHL**	**16**	**1**	**1**	**2**	**4**	....	....	....	....	....
	Adirondack	AHL	9	3	3	6	6	....	....	....	....	....
	San Jose	**NHL**	**12**	**5**	**6**	**11**	**4**	....	....	....	....	....
1992-93	**San Jose**	**NHL**	**79**	**22**	**44**	**66**	**56**	....	....	....	....	....
1993-94	**San Jose**	**NHL**	**80**	**18**	**35**	**53**	**28**	**14**	**4**	**6**	**10**	**6**
1994-95	**San Jose**	**NHL**	**13**	**1**	**1**	**2**	**2**	....	....	....	....	....
	Florida	**NHL**	**27**	**3**	**9**	**12**	**0**	....	....	....	....	....
1995-96	**Florida**	**NHL**	**82**	**23**	**28**	**51**	**36**	**20**	**4**	**2**	**6**	**8**
	NHL Totals		**380**	**91**	**146**	**237**	**148**	**40**	**8**	**9**	**17**	**18**

Traded to **San Jose** by **Detroit** for Bob McGill and Vancouver's eighth round choice (previously acquired by Detroit — San Jose selected C.J. Denomme) in 1992 Entry Draft, March 9, 1992. Traded to **Florida** by **San Jose** for a conditional choice in 1998 Entry Draft, March 3, 1995.

GARTNER, MIKE — PHO.

Right wing. Shoots right. 6', 187 lbs. Born, Ottawa, Ont., October 29, 1959.
(Washington's 1st choice, 4th overall, in 1979 Entry Draft).

			Regular Season					Playoffs				
Season	Club	Lea	GP	G	A	TP	PIM	GP	G	A	TP	PIM
1976-77	Niagara Falls	OHA	62	33	42	75	125	....	....	....	....	....
1977-78a	Niagara Falls	OHA	64	41	49	90	56	....	....	....	....	....
1978-79	Cincinnati	WHA	78	27	25	52	123	3	0	2	2	2
1979-80	**Washington**	**NHL**	**77**	**36**	**32**	**68**	**66**	....	....	....	....	....
1980-81	**Washington**	**NHL**	**80**	**48**	**46**	**94**	**100**	....	....	....	....	....
1981-82	**Washington**	**NHL**	**80**	**35**	**45**	**80**	**121**	....	....	....	....	....
1982-83	**Washington**	**NHL**	**73**	**38**	**38**	**76**	**54**	**4**	**0**	**0**	**0**	**4**
1983-84	**Washington**	**NHL**	**80**	**40**	**45**	**85**	**90**	**8**	**3**	**7**	**10**	**16**
1984-85	**Washington**	**NHL**	**80**	**50**	**52**	**102**	**71**	**5**	**4**	**3**	**7**	**9**
1985-86	**Washington**	**NHL**	**74**	**35**	**40**	**75**	**63**	**9**	**2**	**10**	**12**	**4**
1986-87	**Washington**	**NHL**	**78**	**41**	**32**	**73**	**61**	**7**	**4**	**3**	**7**	**14**
1987-88	**Washington**	**NHL**	**80**	**48**	**33**	**81**	**73**	**14**	**3**	**4**	**7**	**14**
1988-89	**Washington**	**NHL**	**56**	**26**	**29**	**55**	**71**	....	....	....	....	....
	Minnesota	**NHL**	**13**	**7**	**7**	**14**	**2**	**5**	**0**	**0**	**0**	**6**
1989-90	**Minnesota**	**NHL**	**67**	**34**	**36**	**70**	**32**	....	....	....	....	....
	NY Rangers	**NHL**	**12**	**11**	**5**	**16**	**6**	**10**	**5**	**3**	**8**	**12**
1990-91	**NY Rangers**	**NHL**	**79**	**49**	**20**	**69**	**53**	**6**	**1**	**1**	**2**	**0**
1991-92	**NY Rangers**	**NHL**	**76**	**40**	**41**	**81**	**55**	**13**	**8**	**8**	**16**	**4**
1992-93	**NY Rangers**	**NHL**	**84**	**45**	**23**	**68**	**59**	....	....	....	....	....
1993-94	**NY Rangers**	**NHL**	**71**	**28**	**24**	**52**	**58**	....	....	....	....	....
	Toronto	**NHL**	**10**	**6**	**6**	**12**	**4**	**18**	**5**	**6**	**11**	**14**
1994-95	**Toronto**	**NHL**	**38**	**12**	**8**	**20**	**6**	**5**	**2**	**2**	**4**	**2**
1995-96	**Toronto**	**NHL**	**82**	**35**	**19**	**54**	**52**	**6**	**4**	**1**	**5**	**4**
	NHL Totals		**1290**	**664**	**581**	**1245**	**1097**	**110**	**41**	**48**	**89**	**103**

a OHA First All-Star Team (1978)

Played in NHL All-Star Game (1981, 1985, 1986, 1988, 1990, 1993, 1996)

Traded to **Minnesota** by **Washington** with Larry Murphy for Dino Ciccarelli and Bob Rouse, March 7, 1989. Traded to **NY Rangers** by **Minnesota** for Ulf Dahlen, Los Angeles' fourth round choice (previously acquired by NY Rangers — Minnesota selected Cal McGowan) in 1990 Entry Draft and future considerations, March 6, 1990. Traded to **Toronto** by **NY Rangers** for Glenn Anderson, the rights to Scott Malone and Toronto's fourth round choice (Alexander Korobolin) in 1994 Entry Draft, March 21, 1994. Traded to **Phoenix** by **Toronto** for Chicago's fourth round choice (previously acquired by Phoenix — Toronto selected Vladimir Antipov) in 1996 Entry Draft, June 22, 1996.

GASKINS, JON — EDM.

Defense. Shoots left. 6'3", 205 lbs. Born, Dallas, TX, January 11, 1976.
(Edmonton's 8th choice, 110th overall, in 1994 Entry Draft).

			Regular Season					Playoffs				
Season	Club	Lea	GP	G	A	TP	PIM	GP	G	A	TP	PIM
1994-95	Michigan State	CCHA	28	1	5	6	18	....	....	....	....	....
1995-96	Michigan State	CCHA	17	0	1	1	4	....	....	....	....	....

GAUDREAU, ROB — (GUH-droh)

Right wing. Shoots right. 5'11", 185 lbs. Born, Lincoln, RI, January 20, 1970.
(Pittsburgh's 8th choice, 172nd overall, in 1988 Entry Draft).

			Regular Season					Playoffs				
Season	Club	Lea	GP	G	A	TP	PIM	GP	G	A	TP	PIM
1988-89	Providence	H.E.	42	28	29	57	32	....	....	....	....	....
1989-90	Providence	H.E.	32	20	18	38	12	....	....	....	....	....
1990-91a	Providence	H.E.	36	34	27	61	20	....	....	....	....	....
1991-92bc	Providence	H.E.	36	21	34	55	22	....	....	....	....	....
1992-93	**San Jose**	**NHL**	**59**	**23**	**20**	**43**	**18**	....	....	....	....	....
	Kansas City	IHL	19	8	6	14	6	....	....	....	....	....
1993-94	**San Jose**	**NHL**	**84**	**15**	**20**	**35**	**28**	**14**	**2**	**0**	**2**	**0**
1994-95	**Ottawa**	**NHL**	**36**	**5**	**9**	**14**	**8**	....	....	....	....	....
1995-96	**Ottawa**	**NHL**	**52**	**8**	**5**	**13**	**15**	....	....	....	....	....
	P.E.I.	AHL	3	2	0	2	4	....	....	....	....	....
	NHL Totals		**231**	**51**	**54**	**105**	**69**	**14**	**2**	**0**	**2**	**0**

a Hockey East Second All-Star Team (1991)
b NCAA East Second All-American Team (1992)
c Hockey East First All-Star Team (1992)

Rights traded to **Minnesota** by **Pittsburgh** for Richard Zemlak, November 1, 1988. Claimed by **San Jose** from **Minnesota** in Dispersal Draft, May 30, 1991. Claimed by **Ottawa** from **San Jose** in NHL Waiver Draft, January 18, 1995.

GAUTHIER, DANIEL — (GOH-tyay)

Left wing. Shoots left. 6'1", 190 lbs. Born, Charlemagne, Que., May 17, 1970.
(Pittsburgh's 3rd choice, 62nd overall, in 1988 Entry Draft).

			Regular Season					Playoffs				
Season	Club	Lea	GP	G	A	TP	PIM	GP	G	A	TP	PIM
1986-87	Longueuil	QMJHL	64	23	22	45	23	18	4	5	9	15
1987-88	Victoriaville	QMJHL	66	43	47	90	53	5	2	1	3	0
1988-89	Victoriaville	QMJHL	64	41	75	116	84	16	12	17	29	30
1989-90	Victoriaville	QMJHL	62	45	69	114	32	16	8	*19	27	16
1990-91	Albany	IHL	1	1	0	1	0	....	....	....	....	....
ab	Knoxville	ECHL	61	41	*93	134	40	2	0	4	4	4
1991-92	Muskegon	IHL	68	19	18	37	28	9	3	6	9	8
1992-93	Cleveland	IHL	80	40	66	106	88	4	2	2	4	14
1993-94	Cincinnati	IHL	74	30	34	64	101	10	2	3	5	14
1994-95	Indianapolis	IHL	66	22	50	72	53	....	....	....	....	....
	Chicago	**NHL**	**5**	**0**	**0**	**0**	**0**	....	....	....	....	....
1995-96	Indianapolis	IHL	70	28	39	67	44	....	....	....	....	....
	Peoria	IHL	10	3	5	8	10	11	4	6	10	6
	NHL Totals		**5**	**0**	**0**	**0**	**0**	....	....	....	....	....

a ECHL First All-Star Team (1991)
b ECHL Rookie of the Year (1991)

Signed as a free agent by **Florida**, July 14, 1993. Signed as a free agent by **Chicago**, June 14, 1994.

GAUTHIER, DENIS — (GOH-tyay) — CGY.

Defense. Shoots left. 6'2", 195 lbs. Born, Montreal, Que., October 1, 1976.
(Calgary's 1st choice, 20th overall, in 1995 Entry Draft).

			Regular Season					Playoffs				
Season	Club	Lea	GP	G	A	TP	PIM	GP	G	A	TP	PIM
1992-93	Drummondville	QMJHL	60	1	7	8	136	10	0	5	5	40
1993-94	Drummondville	QMJHL	60	0	7	7	176	9	2	0	2	41
1994-95	Drummondville	QMJHL	64	9	31	40	190	4	0	5	5	12
1995-96ab	Drummondville	QMJHL	53	25	49	74	140	6	4	4	8	32
	Saint John	AHL	5	2	0	2	8	16	1	6	7	20

a QMJHL First All-Star Team (1996)
b Canadian Major Junior First All-Star Team (1996)

GAVEY, AARON — T.B.

Center. Shoots left. 6'1", 194 lbs. Born, Sudbury, Ont., February 22, 1974.
(Tampa Bay's 4th choice, 74th overall, in 1992 Entry Draft).

			Regular Season					Playoffs				
Season	Club	Lea	GP	G	A	TP	PIM	GP	G	A	TP	PIM
1991-92	S.S. Marie	OHL	48	7	11	18	27	19	5	1	6	10
1992-93	S.S. Marie	OHL	62	45	39	84	116	18	5	9	14	36
1993-94	S.S. Marie	OHL	60	42	60	102	116	14	11	10	21	22
1994-95	Atlanta	IHL	66	18	17	35	85	5	0	1	1	9
1995-96	**Tampa Bay**	**NHL**	**73**	**8**	**4**	**12**	**56**	**6**	**0**	**0**	**0**	**4**
	NHL Totals		**73**	**8**	**4**	**12**	**56**	**6**	**0**	**0**	**0**	**4**

GELINAS, MARTIN — (ZHEHL-in-nuh, MAHR-ta) — VAN.

Left wing. Shoots left. 5'11", 195 lbs. Born, Shawinigan, Que., June 5, 1970.
(Los Angeles' 1st choice, 7th overall, in 1988 Entry Draft).

			Regular Season					Playoffs				
Season	Club	Lea	GP	G	A	TP	PIM	GP	G	A	TP	PIM
1987-88a	Hull	QMJHL	65	63	68	131	74	17	15	18	33	32
1988-89	**Edmonton**	**NHL**	**6**	**1**	**2**	**3**	**0**	....	....	....	....	....
	Hull	QMJHL	41	38	39	77	31	9	5	4	9	14
1989-90	**Edmonton**	**NHL**	**46**	**17**	**8**	**25**	**30**	**20**	**2**	**3**	**5**	**6 ♦**
1990-91	**Edmonton**	**NHL**	**73**	**20**	**20**	**40**	**34**	**18**	**3**	**6**	**9**	**25**
1991-92	**Edmonton**	**NHL**	**68**	**11**	**18**	**29**	**62**	**15**	**1**	**3**	**4**	**10**
1992-93	**Edmonton**	**NHL**	**65**	**11**	**12**	**23**	**30**	....	....	....	....	....
1993-94	**Quebec**	**NHL**	**31**	**6**	**6**	**12**	**8**	....	....	....	....	....
	Vancouver	**NHL**	**33**	**8**	**8**	**16**	**26**	**24**	**5**	**4**	**9**	**14**
1994-95	**Vancouver**	**NHL**	**46**	**13**	**10**	**23**	**36**	**3**	**0**	**1**	**1**	**0**
1995-96	**Vancouver**	**NHL**	**81**	**30**	**26**	**56**	**59**	**6**	**1**	**1**	**2**	**12**
	NHL Totals		**449**	**117**	**110**	**227**	**285**	**86**	**12**	**18**	**30**	**67**

a Won George Parsons Trophy (Memorial Cup Tournament Most Sportsmanlike Player) (1988)

Traded to **Edmonton** by **Los Angeles** with Jimmy Carson and Los Angeles' first round choices in 1989, (acquired by New Jersey — New Jersey selected Jason Miller), 1991 (Martin Rucinsky) and 1993 (Nick Stajduhar) Entry Drafts and cash for Wayne Gretzky, Mike Krushelnyski and Marty McSorley, August 9, 1988. Traded to **Quebec** by **Edmonton** with Edmonton's sixth round choice (Nicholas Checco) in 1993 Entry Draft for Scott Pearson, June 20, 1993. Claimed on waivers by **Vancouver** from **Quebec**, January 15, 1994.

GENDRON, MARTIN — (ZHEHN-drawn) — WSH.

Right wing. Shoots right. 5'9", 190 lbs. Born, Valleyfield, Que., February 15, 1974.
(Washington's 4th choice, 71st overall, in 1992 Entry Draft).

			Regular Season					Playoffs				
Season	Club	Lea	GP	G	A	TP	PIM	GP	G	A	TP	PIM
1990-91	St-Hyacinthe	QMJHL	55	34	23	57	33	4	1	2	3	0
1991-92a	St-Hyacinthe	QMJHL	69	*71	66	137	45	6	7	4	11	14
1992-93bc	St-Hyacinthe	QMJHL	63	73	61	134	44	....	....	....	....	....
	Baltimore	AHL	10	1	2	3	2	3	0	0	0	0
1993-94	Cdn. National	....	19	4	5	9	2	....	....	....	....	....
	Hull	QMJHL	37	39	36	75	18	20	*21	17	38	8
1994-95	Portland	AHL	72	36	32	68	54	4	5	1	6	2
	Washington	**NHL**	**8**	**2**	**1**	**3**	**2**	....	....	....	....	....
1995-96	**Washington**	**NHL**	**20**	**2**	**1**	**3**	**8**	....	....	....	....	....
	Portland	AHL	48	38	29	67	39	22	*15	18	33	8
	NHL Totals		**28**	**4**	**2**	**6**	**10**	....	....	....	....	....

a QMJHL First All-Star Team (1992)
b QMJHL Second All-Star Team (1993)
c Canadian Major Junior First All-Star Team (1993)

GEORGE, CHRIS — COL.

Right wing. Shoots right. 5'11", 175 lbs. Born, Toronto, Ont., May 9, 1976.
(Colorado's 9th choice, 228th overall, in 1995 Entry Draft).

			Regular Season					Playoffs				
Season	Club	Lea	GP	G	A	TP	PIM	GP	G	A	TP	PIM
1994-95	Sarnia	OHL	41	1	3	4	102	4	0	0	0	12
1995-96	Sarnia	OHL	13	0	0	0	48	....	....	....	....	....
	Barrie	OHL	42	12	8	20	118	7	0	1	1	20

GERIS, DAVE — FLA.

Defense. Shoots left. 6'5", 240 lbs. Born, North Bay, Ont., June 7, 1976.
(Florida's 6th choice, 105th overall, in 1994 Entry Draft).

			Regular Season					Playoffs				
Season	Club	Lea	GP	G	A	TP	PIM	GP	G	A	TP	PIM
1993-94	Windsor	OHL	63	0	6	6	121	3	0	0	0	6
1994-95	Windsor	OHL	65	5	11	16	135	10	1	6	7	21
1995-96	Windsor	OHL	64	8	20	28	205	7	1	0	1	20

GERNANDER, KEN — NYR

Center. Shoots left. 5'10", 180 lbs. Born, Coleraine, MN, June 30, 1969.
(Winnipeg's 4th choice, 96th overall, in 1987 Entry Draft).

			Regular Season					Playoffs				
Season	Club	Lea	GP	G	A	TP	PIM	GP	G	A	TP	PIM
1987-88	U. Minnesota	WCHA	44	14	14	28	14	....	....	....	....	....
1988-89	U. Minnesota	WCHA	44	9	11	20	2	....	....	....	....	....
1989-90	U. Minnesota	WCHA	44	32	17	49	24	....	....	....	....	....
1990-91	U. Minnesota	WCHA	44	23	20	43	24	....	....	....	....	....
1991-92	Fort Wayne	IHL	13	7	6	13	2	....	....	....	....	....
	Moncton	AHL	43	8	18	26	9	8	1	1	2	2
1992-93	Moncton	AHL	71	18	29	47	20	5	1	4	5	0
1993-94	Moncton	AHL	71	22	25	47	12	19	6	1	7	0
1994-95	Binghamton	AHL	80	28	25	53	24	11	2	2	4	6
1995-96	**NY Rangers**	**NHL**	**10**	**2**	**3**	**5**	**4**	**6**	**0**	**0**	**0**	**0**
a	Binghamton	AHL	63	44	29	73	38	....	....	....	....	....
	NHL Totals		**10**	**2**	**3**	**5**	**4**	**6**	**0**	**0**	**0**	**0**

a Won Fred Hunt Memorial Trophy (Sportsmanship - AHL) (1996)

Signed as a free agent by **NY Rangers**, July 4, 1994.

GILBERT, GREG

Left wing. Shoots left. 6'1", 191 lbs. Born, Mississauga, Ont., January 22, 1962.
(NY Islanders' 5th choice, 80th overall, in 1980 Entry Draft).

			Regular Season					Playoffs				
Season	Club	Lea	GP	G	A	TP	PIM	GP	G	A	TP	PIM
1979-80	Toronto	OHA	68	10	11	21	35	....	....	....	....	....
1980-81	Toronto	OHA	64	30	37	67	73	5	2	6	8	16
1981-82	**NY Islanders**	**NHL**	**1**	**1**	**0**	**1**	**0**	**4**	**1**	**1**	**2**	**2 ♦**
	Toronto	OHL	65	41	67	108	119	10	4	12	16	23
1982-83	**NY Islanders**	**NHL**	**45**	**8**	**11**	**19**	**30**	**10**	**1**	**0**	**1**	**14 ♦**
	Indianapolis	CHL	24	11	16	27	23	....	....	....	....	....
1983-84	**NY Islanders**	**NHL**	**79**	**31**	**35**	**66**	**59**	**21**	**5**	**7**	**12**	**39**
1984-85	**NY Islanders**	**NHL**	**58**	**13**	**25**	**38**	**36**	....	....	....	....	....
1985-86	**NY Islanders**	**NHL**	**60**	**9**	**19**	**28**	**82**	**2**	**0**	**0**	**0**	**9**
	Springfield	AHL	2	0	0	0	2	....	....	....	....	....
1986-87	**NY Islanders**	**NHL**	**51**	**6**	**7**	**13**	**26**	**10**	**2**	**2**	**4**	**6**
1987-88	**NY Islanders**	**NHL**	**76**	**17**	**28**	**45**	**46**	**4**	**0**	**0**	**0**	**6**
1988-89	**NY Islanders**	**NHL**	**55**	**8**	**13**	**21**	**45**	....	....	....	....	....
	Chicago	**NHL**	**4**	**0**	**0**	**0**	**0**	**15**	**1**	**5**	**6**	**20**
1989-90	**Chicago**	**NHL**	**70**	**12**	**25**	**37**	**54**	**19**	**5**	**8**	**13**	**34**
1990-91	**Chicago**	**NHL**	**72**	**10**	**15**	**25**	**58**	**5**	**0**	**1**	**1**	**2**
1991-92	**Chicago**	**NHL**	**50**	**7**	**5**	**12**	**35**	**10**	**1**	**3**	**4**	**16**
1992-93	**Chicago**	**NHL**	**77**	**13**	**19**	**32**	**57**	**3**	**0**	**0**	**0**	**0**
1993-94	**NY Rangers**	**NHL**	**76**	**4**	**11**	**15**	**29**	**23**	**1**	**3**	**4**	**8 ♦**
1994-95	**St. Louis**	**NHL**	**46**	**11**	**14**	**25**	**11**	**7**	**0**	**3**	**3**	**6**
1995-96	**St. Louis**	**NHL**	**17**	**0**	**1**	**1**	**8**	....	....	....	....	....
	NHL Totals		**837**	**150**	**228**	**378**	**576**	**133**	**17**	**33**	**50**	**162**

Traded to **Chicago** by **NY Islanders** for Chicago's fifth round choice (Steve Young) in 1989 Entry Draft, March 7, 1989. Signed as a free agent by **NY Rangers**, July 29, 1993. Claimed by **St. Louis** from **NY Rangers** in NHL Waiver Draft, January 18, 1995.

GILCHRIST, BRENT — DAL.

Left wing. Shoots left. 5'11", 180 lbs. Born, Moose Jaw, Sask., April 3, 1967.
(Montreal's 6th choice, 79th overall, in 1985 Entry Draft).

			Regular Season					Playoffs				
Season	Club	Lea	GP	G	A	TP	PIM	GP	G	A	TP	PIM
1983-84	Kelowna	WHL	69	16	11	27	16	....	....	....	....	....
1984-85	Kelowna	WHL	51	35	38	73	58	6	5	2	7	8
1985-86	Spokane	WHL	52	45	45	90	57	9	6	7	13	19
1986-87	Spokane	WHL	46	45	55	100	71	5	2	7	9	6
	Sherbrooke	AHL	....	....	....	....	....	10	2	7	9	2
1987-88	Sherbrooke	AHL	77	26	48	74	83	6	1	3	4	6
1988-89	**Montreal**	**NHL**	**49**	**8**	**16**	**24**	**16**	**9**	**1**	**1**	**2**	**10**
	Sherbrooke	AHL	7	6	5	11	7	....	....	....	....	....
1989-90	**Montreal**	**NHL**	**57**	**9**	**15**	**24**	**28**	**8**	**2**	**0**	**2**	**2**
1990-91	**Montreal**	**NHL**	**51**	**6**	**9**	**15**	**10**	**13**	**5**	**3**	**8**	**6**
1991-92	**Montreal**	**NHL**	**79**	**23**	**27**	**50**	**57**	**11**	**2**	**4**	**6**	**6**
1992-93	**Edmonton**	**NHL**	**60**	**10**	**10**	**20**	**47**	....	....	....	....	....
	Minnesota	**NHL**	**8**	**0**	**1**	**1**	**2**	....	....	....	....	....
1993-94	**Dallas**	**NHL**	**76**	**17**	**14**	**31**	**31**	**9**	**3**	**1**	**4**	**2**
1994-95	**Dallas**	**NHL**	**32**	**9**	**4**	**13**	**16**	**5**	**0**	**1**	**1**	**2**
1995-96	**Dallas**	**NHL**	**77**	**20**	**22**	**42**	**36**	....	....	....	....	....
	NHL Totals		**489**	**102**	**118**	**220**	**243**	**55**	**13**	**10**	**23**	**28**

Traded to **Edmonton** by **Montreal** with Shayne Corson and Vladimir Vujtek for Vincent Damphousse and Edmonton's fourth round choice (Adam Wiesel) in 1993 Entry Draft, August 27, 1992. Traded to **Minnesota** by **Edmonton** for Todd Elik, March 5, 1993.

GILHEN, RANDY (GIHL-uhn)

Center. Shoots left. 6', 190 lbs. Born, Zweibrucken, W. Germany, June 13, 1963.
(Hartford's 6th choice, 109th overall, in 1982 Entry Draft).

			Regular Season					Playoffs				
Season	Club	Lea	GP	G	A	TP	PIM	GP	G	A	TP	PIM
1980-81	Saskatoon	WHL	68	10	5	15	154	....	....	....	....	....
1981-82	Saskatoon	WHL	25	15	9	24	45	....	....	....	....	....
	Winnipeg	WHL	36	26	28	54	42	....	....	....	....	....
1982-83	**Hartford**	**NHL**	**2**	**0**	**1**	**1**	**0**	....	....	....	....	....
	Winnipeg	WHL	71	57	44	101	84	3	2	2	4	0
1983-84	Binghamton	AHL	73	8	12	20	72	....	....	....	....	....
1984-85	Salt Lake	IHL	57	20	20	40	28	....	....	....	....	....
	Binghamton	AHL	18	3	3	6	9	8	4	1	5	16
1985-86	Fort Wayne	IHL	82	44	40	84	48	15	10	8	18	6
1986-87	**Winnipeg**	**NHL**	**2**	**0**	**0**	**0**	**0**	....	....	....	....	....
	Sherbrooke	AHL	75	36	29	65	44	17	7	13	20	10
1987-88	**Winnipeg**	**NHL**	**13**	**3**	**2**	**5**	**15**	**4**	**1**	**0**	**1**	**10**
	Moncton	AHL	68	40	47	87	51	....	....	....	....	....
1988-89	**Winnipeg**	**NHL**	**64**	**5**	**3**	**8**	**38**	....	....	....	....	....
1989-90	**Pittsburgh**	**NHL**	**61**	**5**	**11**	**16**	**54**	....	....	....	....	....
1990-91	**Pittsburgh**	**NHL**	**72**	**15**	**10**	**25**	**51**	**16**	**1**	**0**	**1**	**14 ♦**
1991-92	**Los Angeles**	**NHL**	**33**	**3**	**6**	**9**	**14**	....	....	....	....	....
	NY Rangers	**NHL**	**40**	**7**	**7**	**14**	**14**	**13**	**1**	**2**	**3**	**2**
1992-93	**NY Rangers**	**NHL**	**33**	**3**	**2**	**5**	**8**	....	....	....	....	....
	Tampa Bay	**NHL**	**11**	**0**	**2**	**2**	**6**	....	....	....	....	....
1993-94	**Florida**	**NHL**	**20**	**4**	**4**	**8**	**16**	....	....	....	....	....
	Winnipeg	**NHL**	**40**	**3**	**3**	**6**	**34**	....	....	....	....	....
1994-95	**Winnipeg**	**NHL**	**44**	**5**	**6**	**11**	**52**	....	....	....	....	....
1995-96	**Winnipeg**	**NHL**	**22**	**2**	**3**	**5**	**12**	....	....	....	....	....
	NHL Totals		**457**	**55**	**60**	**115**	**314**	**33**	**3**	**2**	**5**	**26**

Signed as a free agent by **Winnipeg**, November 8, 1985. Traded to **Pittsburgh** by **Winnipeg** with Jim Kyte and Andrew McBain for Randy Cunneyworth, Rick Tabaracci and Dave McLlwain, June 17, 1989. Claimed by **Minnesota** from **Pittsburgh** in Expansion Draft, May 30, 1991. Traded to **Los Angeles** by **Minnesota** with Charlie Huddy, Jim Thomson and NY Rangers' fourth round choice (previously acquired by Minnesota — Los Angeles selected Alexei Zhitnik) in 1991 Entry Draft for Todd Elik, June 22, 1991. Traded to **NY Rangers** by **Los Angeles** for Corey Millen, December 23, 1991. Traded to **Tampa Bay** by **NY Rangers** for Mike Hartman, March 22, 1993. Claimed by **Florida** from **Tampa Bay** in Expansion Draft, June 24, 1993. Traded to **Winnipeg** by **Florida** for Stu Barnes and St. Louis' sixth round choice (previously acquired by Winnipeg — later traded to Edmonton — later traded to Winnipeg — Winnipeg selected Chris Kibermanis), November 25, 1993.

GILL, HAL — BOS.

Defense. Shoots left. 6'6", 200 lbs. Born, Concord, MA, April 6, 1975.
(Boston's 8th choice, 207th overall, in 1993 Entry Draft).

			Regular Season					Playoffs				
Season	Club	Lea	GP	G	A	TP	PIM	GP	G	A	TP	PIM
1993-94	Providence	H.E.	31	1	2	3	26	....	....	....	....	....
1994-95	Providence	H.E.	26	1	3	4	22	....	....	....	....	....
1995-96	Providence	H.E.	39	5	12	17	54	....	....	....	....	....

GILL, TODD (GIHL) — S.J.

Defense. Shoots left. 6', 180 lbs. Born, Cardinal, Ont., November 9, 1965.
(Toronto's 2nd choice, 25th overall, in 1984 Entry Draft).

			Regular Season					Playoffs				
Season	Club	Lea	GP	G	A	TP	PIM	GP	G	A	TP	PIM
1982-83	Windsor	OHL	70	12	24	36	108	3	0	0	0	11
1983-84	Windsor	OHL	68	9	48	57	184	3	1	1	2	10
1984-85	**Toronto**	**NHL**	**10**	**1**	**0**	**1**	**13**	....	....	....	....	....
	Windsor	OHL	53	17	40	57	148	4	0	1	1	14
1985-86	**Toronto**	**NHL**	**15**	**1**	**2**	**3**	**28**	**1**	**0**	**0**	**0**	**0**
	St. Catharines	AHL	58	8	25	33	90	10	1	6	7	17
1986-87	**Toronto**	**NHL**	**61**	**4**	**27**	**31**	**92**	**13**	**2**	**2**	**4**	**42**
	Newmarket	AHL	11	1	8	9	33	....	....	....	....	....
1987-88	**Toronto**	**NHL**	**65**	**8**	**17**	**25**	**131**	**6**	**1**	**3**	**4**	**20**
	Newmarket	AHL	2	0	1	1	2	....	....	....	....	....
1988-89	**Toronto**	**NHL**	**59**	**11**	**14**	**25**	**72**	....	....	....	....	....
1989-90	**Toronto**	**NHL**	**48**	**1**	**14**	**15**	**92**	**5**	**0**	**3**	**3**	**16**
1990-91	**Toronto**	**NHL**	**72**	**2**	**22**	**24**	**113**	....	....	....	....	....
1991-92	**Toronto**	**NHL**	**74**	**2**	**15**	**17**	**91**	....	....	....	....	....
1992-93	**Toronto**	**NHL**	**69**	**11**	**32**	**43**	**66**	**21**	**1**	**10**	**11**	**26**
1993-94	**Toronto**	**NHL**	**45**	**4**	**24**	**28**	**44**	**18**	**1**	**5**	**6**	**37**
1994-95	**Toronto**	**NHL**	**47**	**7**	**25**	**32**	**64**	**7**	**0**	**3**	**3**	**6**
1995-96	**Toronto**	**NHL**	**74**	**7**	**18**	**25**	**116**	**6**	**0**	**0**	**0**	**24**
	NHL Totals		**639**	**59**	**210**	**269**	**922**	**77**	**5**	**26**	**31**	**171**

Traded to **San Jose** by **Toronto** for Jamie Baker and San Jose's fifth round choice (Peter Cava) in 1996 Entry Draft, June 14, 1996.

GILLAM, SEAN — DET.

Defense. Shoots right. 6'2", 187 lbs. Born, Lethbridge, Alta., May 7, 1976.
(Detroit's 3rd choice, 75th overall, in 1994 Entry Draft).

			Regular Season					Playoffs				
Season	Club	Lea	GP	G	A	TP	PIM	GP	G	A	TP	PIM
1992-93	Spokane	WHL	70	6	27	33	121	10	0	2	2	10
1993-94	Spokane	WHL	70	7	17	24	106	3	0	0	0	6
1994-95a	Spokane	WHL	72	16	40	56	192	11	0	3	3	33
1995-96a	Spokane	WHL	69	11	58	69	123	18	2	12	14	26

a WHL West Second All-Star Team (1995, 1996)

GILLIS, RYAN — CGY.

Defense. Shoots left. 6'1", 195 lbs. Born, Salisbury, NB, December 31, 1976.
(Calgary's 6th choice, 176th overall, in 1995 Entry Draft).

			Regular Season					Playoffs				
Season	Club	Lea	GP	G	A	TP	PIM	GP	G	A	TP	PIM
1992-93	North Bay	OHL	50	1	2	3	17	5	0	0	0	0
1993-94	North Bay	OHL	49	2	9	11	47	18	0	0	0	8
1994-95	North Bay	OHL	65	4	31	35	58	6	0	3	3	6
1995-96	North Bay	OHL	64	8	34	42	100	....	....	....	....	....

GILMOUR, DOUG — TOR.

Center. Shoots left. 5'11", 172 lbs. Born, Kingston, Ont., June 25, 1963.
(St. Louis' 4th choice, 134th overall, in 1982 Entry Draft).

			Regular Season					Playoffs				
Season	Club	Lea	GP	G	A	TP	PIM	GP	G	A	TP	PIM
1981-82	Cornwall	OHL	67	46	73	119	42	5	6	9	15	2
1982-83a	Cornwall	OHL	68	70	*107	*177	62	8	8	10	18	16
1983-84	**St. Louis**	**NHL**	**80**	**25**	**28**	**53**	**57**	**11**	**2**	**9**	**11**	**10**
1984-85	**St. Louis**	**NHL**	**78**	**21**	**36**	**57**	**49**	**3**	**1**	**1**	**2**	**2**
1985-86	**St. Louis**	**NHL**	**74**	**25**	**28**	**53**	**41**	**19**	**9**	**12**	***21**	**25**
1986-87	**St. Louis**	**NHL**	**80**	**42**	**63**	**105**	**58**	**6**	**2**	**2**	**4**	**16**
1987-88	**St. Louis**	**NHL**	**72**	**36**	**50**	**86**	**59**	**10**	**3**	**14**	**17**	**18**
1988-89	**Calgary**	**NHL**	**72**	**26**	**59**	**85**	**44**	**22**	**11**	**11**	**22**	**20 ♦**
1989-90	**Calgary**	**NHL**	**78**	**24**	**67**	**91**	**54**	**6**	**3**	**1**	**4**	**8**
1990-91	**Calgary**	**NHL**	**78**	**20**	**61**	**81**	**144**	**7**	**1**	**1**	**2**	**0**
1991-92	**Calgary**	**NHL**	**38**	**11**	**27**	**38**	**46**	....	....	....	....	....
	Toronto	**NHL**	**40**	**15**	**34**	**49**	**32**	....	....	....	....	....
1992-93b	**Toronto**	**NHL**	**83**	**32**	**95**	**127**	**100**	**21**	**10**	***25**	**35**	**30**
1993-94	**Toronto**	**NHL**	**83**	**27**	**84**	**111**	**105**	**18**	**6**	**22**	**28**	**42**
1994-95	Rapperswil	Switz.	9	2	13	15	16	....	....	....	....	....
	Toronto	**NHL**	**44**	**10**	**23**	**33**	**26**	**7**	**0**	**6**	**6**	**6**
1995-96	**Toronto**	**NHL**	**81**	**32**	**40**	**72**	**77**	**6**	**1**	**7**	**8**	**12**
	NHL Totals		**981**	**346**	**695**	**1041**	**892**	**136**	**49**	**111**	**160**	**189**

a OHL First All-Star Team (1983)
b Won Frank J. Selke Trophy (1993)

Played in NHL All-Star Game (1993, 1994)

Traded to **Calgary** by **St. Louis** with Mark Hunter, Steve Bozek and Michael Dark for Mike Bullard, Craig Coxe and Tim Corkery, September 6, 1988. Traded to **Toronto** by **Calgary** with Jamie Macoun, Ric Nattress, Kent Manderville and Rick Wamsley for Gary Leeman, Alexander Godynyuk, Jeff Reese, Michel Petit and Craig Berube, January 2, 1992.

GIRARD, RICK — VAN.

Center. Shoots left. 5'11", 175 lbs. Born, Edmonton, Alta., May 1, 1974.
(Vancouver's 2nd choice, 46th overall, in 1993 Entry Draft).

			Regular Season					Playoffs				
Season	Club	Lea	GP	G	A	TP	PIM	GP	G	A	TP	PIM
1991-92	Swift Current	WHL	45	14	17	31	6	8	2	0	2	2
1992-93ab	Swift Current	WHL	72	71	70	141	25	17	9	17	26	10
1993-94a	Swift Current	WHL	58	40	49	89	43	7	1	8	9	6
	Hamilton	AHL	1	1	1	2	0	....	....	....	....	....
1994-95	Syracuse	AHL	26	10	13	23	22	....	....	....	....	....
1995-96	Syracuse	AHL	67	15	21	36	32	16	9	8	17	16

a WHL East First All-Star Team (1993, 1994)
b Canadian Major Junior Sportsmanlike Player of the Year (1993)

GIROUX, RAYMOND — (jih-ROO) — PHI.

Defense. Shoots left. 6', 180 lbs. Born, North Bay, Ont., July 20, 1976.
(Philadelphia's 7th choice, 202nd overall, in 1994 Entry Draft).

			Regular Season					Playoffs				
Season	Club	Lea	GP	G	A	TP	PIM	GP	G	A	TP	PIM
1994-95	Yale	ECAC	27	1	3	4	8	....	....	....	....	....
1995-96	Yale	ECAC	30	3	16	19	36	....	....	....	....	....

GLYNN, BRIAN — (GLIHN) — HFD.

Defense. Shoots left. 6'4", 218 lbs. Born, Iserlohn, West Germany, November 23, 1967.
(Calgary's 2nd choice, 37th overall, in 1986 Entry Draft).

			Regular Season					Playoffs				
Season	Club	Lea	GP	G	A	TP	PIM	GP	G	A	TP	PIM
1984-85	Saskatoon	WHL	12	1	0	1	2	3	0	0	0	0
1985-86	Saskatoon	WHL	66	7	25	32	131	13	0	3	3	30
1986-87	Saskatoon	WHL	44	2	26	28	163	11	1	3	4	19
1987-88	**Calgary**	**NHL**	**67**	**5**	**14**	**19**	**87**	**1**	**0**	**0**	**0**	**0**
1988-89	**Calgary**	**NHL**	**9**	**0**	**1**	**1**	**19**	....	....	....	....	....
	Salt Lake	IHL	31	3	10	13	105	14	3	7	10	31
1989-90	**Calgary**	**NHL**	**1**	**0**	**0**	**0**	**0**	....	....	....	....	....
ab	Salt Lake	IHL	80	17	44	61	164	....	....	....	....	....
1990-91	Salt Lake	IHL	8	1	3	4	18	....	....	....	....	....
	Minnesota	**NHL**	**66**	**8**	**11**	**19**	**83**	**23**	**2**	**6**	**8**	**18**
1991-92	**Minnesota**	**NHL**	**37**	**2**	**12**	**14**	**24**	....	....	....	....	....
	Edmonton	**NHL**	**25**	**2**	**6**	**8**	**6**	**16**	**4**	**1**	**5**	**12**
1992-93	**Edmonton**	**NHL**	**64**	**4**	**12**	**16**	**60**	....	....	....	....	....
1993-94	**Ottawa**	**NHL**	**48**	**2**	**13**	**15**	**41**	....	....	....	....	....
	Vancouver	**NHL**	**16**	**0**	**0**	**0**	**12**	**17**	**0**	**3**	**3**	**10**
1994-95	**Hartford**	**NHL**	**43**	**1**	**6**	**7**	**32**	....	....	....	....	....
1995-96	**Hartford**	**NHL**	**54**	**0**	**4**	**4**	**44**	....	....	....	....	....
	NHL Totals		**430**	**24**	**79**	**103**	**408**	**57**	**6**	**10**	**16**	**40**

a IHL First All-Star Team (1990)
b Won Governors' Trophy (Outstanding Defenseman - IHL) (1990)

Traded to **Minnesota** by **Calgary** for Frantisek Musil, October 26, 1990. Traded to **Edmonton** by **Minnesota** for David Shaw, January 21, 1992. Traded to **Ottawa** by **Edmonton** for Ottawa's eighth round choice (Rob Quinn) in 1994 Entry Draft, September 15, 1993. Claimed on waivers by **Vancouver** from **Ottawa**, February 5, 1994. Claimed by **Hartford** from **Vancouver** in NHL Waiver Draft, January 18, 1995.

GODYNYUK, ALEXANDER — (goh-dih-NYOOK) — HFD.

Defense. Shoots left. 6', 207 lbs. Born, Kiev, Ukraine, January 27, 1970.
(Toronto's 5th choice, 115th overall, in 1990 Entry Draft).

			Regular Season					Playoffs				
Season	Club	Lea	GP	G	A	TP	PIM	GP	G	A	TP	PIM
1986-87	Sokol Kiev	USSR	9	0	1	1	2	....	....	....	....	....
1987-88	Sokol Kiev	USSR	2	0	0	0	2	....	....	....	....	....
1988-89	Sokol Kiev	USSR	30	3	3	6	12	....	....	....	....	....
1989-90	Sokol Kiev	USSR	37	3	2	5	31	....	....	....	....	....
1990-91	Sokol Kiev	USSR	19	3	1	4	20	....	....	....	....	....
	Toronto	**NHL**	**18**	**0**	**3**	**3**	**16**	....	....	....	....	....
	Newmarket	AHL	11	0	1	1	29	....	....	....	....	....
1991-92	**Toronto**	**NHL**	**31**	**3**	**6**	**9**	**59**	....	....	....	....	....
	Calgary	**NHL**	**6**	**0**	**1**	**1**	**4**	....	....	....	....	....
	Salt Lake	IHL	17	2	1	3	24	....	....	....	....	....
1992-93	**Calgary**	**NHL**	**27**	**3**	**4**	**7**	**19**	....	....	....	....	....
1993-94	**Florida**	**NHL**	**26**	**0**	**10**	**10**	**35**	....	....	....	....	....
	Hartford	**NHL**	**43**	**3**	**9**	**12**	**40**	....	....	....	....	....
1994-95	**Hartford**	**NHL**	**14**	**0**	**0**	**0**	**8**	....	....	....	....	....
1995-96	**Hartford**	**NHL**	**3**	**0**	**0**	**0**	**2**	....	....	....	....	....
	Springfield	AHL	14	1	3	4	19	....	....	....	....	....
	Detroit	IHL	7	0	3	3	12	....	....	....	....	....
	Minnesota	IHL	45	9	17	26	81	....	....	....	....	....
	NHL Totals		**168**	**9**	**33**	**42**	**183**	....	....	....	....	....

Traded to **Calgary** by **Toronto** with Craig Berube, Gary Leeman, Michel Petit and Jeff Reese for Doug Gilmour, Jamie Macoun, Ric Nattress, Rick Wamsley and Kent Manderville, January 2, 1992. Claimed by **Florida** from **Calgary** in Expansion Draft, June 24, 1993. Traded to **Hartford** by **Florida** for Jim McKenzie, December 16, 1993.

GOLDEN, RYAN — BOS.

Center. Shoots left. 6'3", 197 lbs. Born, Boston, MA, October 15, 1974.
(Boston's 7th choice, 181st overall, in 1993 Entry Draft).

			Regular Season					Playoffs				
Season	Club	Lea	GP	G	A	TP	PIM	GP	G	A	TP	PIM
1993-94	Lowell	H.E.	14	0	3	3	12	....	....	....	....	....
1994-95	Lowell	H.E.	10	0	0	0	10	....	....	....	....	....
1995-96	Lowell	H.E.	21	1	1	2	30	....	....	....	....	....

GOLOKHVASTOV, KONSTANTIN — T.B.

Right wing. Shoots right. 6'1", 185 lbs. Born, Dneprodzerzinsk, USSR, February 6, 1977.
(Tampa Bay's 4th choice, 108th overall, in 1995 Entry Draft).

			Regular Season					Playoffs				
Season	Club	Lea	GP	G	A	TP	PIM	GP	G	A	TP	PIM
1994-95	Moscow D'amo	CIS	6	0	0	0	2	....	....	....	....	....
1995-96	Nizhnekamsk	CIS	21	6	1	7	2	....	....	....	....	....

GOLUBOVSKY, YAN — (goh-luh-BOHV-skee) — DET.

Defense. Shoots right. 6'3", 183 lbs. Born, Novosibirsk, USSR, March 9, 1976.
(Detroit's 1st choice, 23rd overall, in 1994 Entry Draft).

			Regular Season					Playoffs				
Season	Club	Lea	GP	G	A	TP	PIM	GP	G	A	TP	PIM
1993-94	Mosc. D'amo 2	CIS 3				UNAVAILABLE						
	Russian Pen's	IHL	8	0	0	0	23	....	....	....	....	....
1994-95	Adirondack	AHL	57	4	2	6	39	....	....	....	....	....
1995-96	Adirondack	AHL	71	5	16	21	97	3	0	0	0	2

GONCHAR, SERGEI — (gohn-CHAR) — WSH.

Defense. Shoots left. 6'2", 212 lbs. Born, Chelyabinsk, USSR, April 13, 1974.
(Washington's 1st choice, 14th overall, in 1992 Entry Draft).

			Regular Season					Playoffs				
Season	Club	Lea	GP	G	A	TP	PIM	GP	G	A	TP	PIM
1991-92	Chelyabinsk	CIS	31	1	0	1	6	....	....	....	....	....
1992-93	Moscow D'amo	CIS	31	1	3	4	70	10	0	0	0	12
1993-94	Moscow D'amo	CIS	44	4	5	9	36	10	0	3	3	14
	Portland	AHL	....	....	....	....	....	2	0	0	0	0
1994-95	Portland	AHL	61	10	32	42	67	....	....	....	....	....
	Washington	**NHL**	**31**	**2**	**5**	**7**	**22**	**7**	**2**	**2**	**4**	**2**
1995-96	**Washington**	**NHL**	**78**	**15**	**26**	**41**	**60**	**6**	**2**	**4**	**6**	**4**
	NHL Totals		**109**	**17**	**31**	**48**	**82**	**13**	**4**	**6**	**10**	**6**

GONEAU, DANIEL — (guh-NOH) — NYR

Left wing. Shoots left. 6'1", 196 lbs. Born, Montreal, Que., January 16, 1976.
(Boston's 2nd choice, 47th overall, in 1994 Entry Draft).

			Regular Season					Playoffs				
Season	Club	Lea	GP	G	A	TP	PIM	GP	G	A	TP	PIM
1992-93	Laval	QMJHL	62	16	25	41	44	13	0	4	4	4
1993-94	Laval	QMJHL	68	29	57	86	81	19	8	21	29	45
1994-95	Laval	QMJHL	56	16	31	47	78	20	5	10	15	33
1995-96a	Granby	QMJHL	67	54	51	105	115	21	11	22	33	40

a QMJHL First All-Star Team (1996)

Re-entered NHL Entry Draft, **NY Rangers'** 2nd choice, 48th overall in 1996 Entry Draft.

GORBACHEV, SERGEI — DAL.

Right wing. Shoots left. 6'1", 185 lbs. Born, Saratov, USSR, October 24, 1975.
(San Jose's 7th choice, 167th overall, in 1994 Entry Draft).

			Regular Season					Playoffs				
Season	Club	Lea	GP	G	A	TP	PIM	GP	G	A	TP	PIM
1993-94	Moscow D'amo	CIS 2	2	0	0	0	0	....	....	....	....	....
1994-95	Moscow D'amo	CIS	4	0	1	1	2	....	....	....	....	....
1995-96	Saratov	CIS				DID NOT PLAY						

Traded to **Dallas** by **San Jose** for Dallas' fifth round choice in 1998 Entry Draft, August 15, 1996.

GORDIOUK, VIKTOR — (gohr-dee-YOOK)

Left wing. Shoots right. 5'10", 176 lbs. Born, Odintsovo, USSR, April 11, 1970.
(Buffalo's 6th choice, 142nd overall, in 1990 Entry Draft).

			Regular Season					Playoffs				
Season	Club	Lea	GP	G	A	TP	PIM	GP	G	A	TP	PIM
1986-87	Soviet Wings	USSR	2	0	0	0	0	....	....	....	....	....
1987-88	Soviet Wings	USSR	26	2	2	4	6	....	....	....	....	....
1988-89	Soviet Wings	USSR	41	5	1	6	10	....	....	....	....	....
1989-90	Soviet Wings	USSR	48	11	4	15	24	....	....	....	....	....
1990-91	Soviet Wings	USSR	46	12	10	22	22	....	....	....	....	....
1991-92	Soviet Wings	CIS	42	16	7	23	24	....	....	....	....	....
1992-93	**Buffalo**	**NHL**	**16**	**3**	**6**	**9**	**0**	....	....	....	....	....
	Rochester	AHL	35	11	14	25	8	17	9	9	18	4
1993-94	Rochester	AHL	74	28	39	67	26	4	3	0	3	2
1994-95	Rochester	AHL	63	31	30	61	36	3	0	2	2	0
	Buffalo	**NHL**	**10**	**0**	**2**	**2**	**0**	....	....	....	....	....
1995-96	Los Angeles	IHL	68	17	44	61	53	....	....	....	....	....
	Utah	IHL	13	4	4	8	6	22	4	6	10	14
	NHL Totals		**26**	**3**	**8**	**11**	**0**	....	....	....	....	....

GORDON, RHETT — PHO.

Right wing. Shoots right. 5'11", 175 lbs. Born, Regina, Sask., August 26, 1976.

			Regular Season					Playoffs				
Season	Club	Lea	GP	G	A	TP	PIM	GP	G	A	TP	PIM
1992-93	Regina	WHL	2	1	0	1	2	4	0	0	0	0
1993-94	Regina	WHL	60	19	28	47	14	4	0	0	0	7
1994-95	Regina	WHL	71	36	43	79	64	4	2	2	4	0
1995-96a	Regina	WHL	66	53	50	103	68	11	9	4	13	10
	Springfield	AHL	2	0	0	0	2	1	0	0	0	0

a WHL West First All-Star Team (1996)

Signed as a free agent by **Winnipeg**, September 29, 1994.

GORDON, ROBB — VAN.

Center. Shoots right. 5'11", 170 lbs. Born, Murrayville, B.C., January 13, 1976.
(Vancouver's 2nd choice, 39th overall, in 1994 Entry Draft).

			Regular Season					Playoffs				
Season	Club	Lea	GP	G	A	TP	PIM	GP	G	A	TP	PIM
1994-95	U. of Michigan	CCHA	39	15	26	41	72	....	....	....	....	....
1995-96	Kelowna	WHL	58	51	63	114	84	6	3	6	9	19

GORENKO, DMITRI (goh-REHN-koh) HFD.

Left wing. Shoots left. 6', 165 lbs. Born, Barnaul, USSR, February 13, 1975.
(Hartford's 6th choice, 214th overall, in 1993 Entry Draft).

			Regular Season					Playoffs				
Season	Club	Lea	GP	G	A	TP	PIM	GP	G	A	TP	PIM
1991-92	CSKA	CIS	14	0	1	1	6	....	....	....	....	....
1992-93	CSKA	CIS	42	3	0	3	20	....	....	....	....	....
1993-94	CSKA	CIS	40	5	1	6	28	3	1	0	1	2
1994-95	CSKA	CIS	33	5	2	7	35	....	....	....	....	....
1995-96	Omsk	CIS	37	4	2	6	14	3	0	1	1	0

GOROKHOV, ILJA NYR

Defense. Shoots right. 6', 185 lbs. Born, Yaroslavl, USSR, August 23, 1977.
(NY Rangers' 8th choice, 195th overall, in 1995 Entry Draft).

			Regular Season					Playoffs				
Season	Club	Lea	GP	G	A	TP	PIM	GP	G	A	TP	PIM
1994-95	Yaroslavl	CIS	1	0	0	0	0	....	....	....	....	....
1995-96	Yaroslavl	CIS	43	0	3	3	10	2	0	0	0	0

GOSSELIN, DAVID N.J.

Right wing. Shoots right. 6', 175 lbs. Born, Levis, Que., June 22, 1977.
(New Jersey's 4th choice, 78th overall, in 1995 Entry Draft).

			Regular Season					Playoffs				
Season	Club	Lea	GP	G	A	TP	PIM	GP	G	A	TP	PIM
1994-95	Sherbrooke	QMJHL	58	8	8	16	36	7	0	0	0	2
1995-96	Sherbrooke	QMJHL	55	24	24	48	147	7	2	2	4	4

GOVEDARIS, CHRIS (goh-va-DAIR-us)

Left wing. Shoots left. 6', 200 lbs. Born, Toronto, Ont., February 2, 1970.
(Hartford's 1st choice, 11th overall, in 1988 Entry Draft).

			Regular Season					Playoffs				
Season	Club	Lea	GP	G	A	TP	PIM	GP	G	A	TP	PIM
1986-87	Toronto	OHL	64	36	28	64	148	....	....	....	....	....
1987-88	Toronto	OHL	62	42	38	80	118	4	2	1	3	10
1988-89	Toronto	OHL	49	41	38	79	117	6	2	3	5	0
1989-90	**Hartford**	**NHL**	**12**	**0**	**1**	**1**	**6**	**2**	**0**	**0**	**0**	**2**
	Binghamton	AHL	14	3	3	6	4	....	....	....	....	....
	Hamilton	OHL	23	11	21	32	53	....	....	....	....	....
1990-91	**Hartford**	**NHL**	**14**	**1**	**3**	**4**	**4**	....	....	....	....	....
	Springfield	AHL	56	26	36	62	133	9	2	5	7	36
1991-92	Springfield	AHL	43	14	25	39	55	11	3	2	5	25
1992-93	**Hartford**	**NHL**	**7**	**1**	**0**	**1**	**0**	....	....	....	....	....
	Springfield	AHL	65	31	24	55	58	15	7	4	11	18
1993-94	**Toronto**	**NHL**	**12**	**2**	**2**	**4**	**14**	**2**	**0**	**0**	**0**	**0**
	St. John's	AHL	62	35	35	70	76	11	6	5	11	22
1994-95	Milwaukee	IHL	54	34	25	59	71	....	....	....	....	....
	Adirondack	AHL	24	19	11	30	34	4	2	1	3	10
1995-96	Minnesota	IHL	81	31	36	67	133	....	....	....	....	....
	NHL Totals		**45**	**4**	**6**	**10**	**24**	**4**	**0**	**0**	**0**	**2**

Signed as a free agent by **Toronto**, September 16, 1993. Signed as a free agent by **Winnipeg**, August 14, 1995.

GRACHEV, VLADIMIR NYI

Left wing. Shoots left. 6', 178 lbs. Born, Moscow, USSR, January 28, 1973.
(NY Islanders' 6th choice, 152nd overall, in 1992 Entry Draft).

			Regular Season					Playoffs				
Season	Club	Lea	GP	G	A	TP	PIM	GP	G	A	TP	PIM
1991-92	Mosc. D'amo 2	CIS 3	62	13	3	16	26	....	....	....	....	....
1992-93	Moscow D'amo	CIS	33	2	1	3	26	7	0	0	0	2
1993-94	Moscow D'amo	CIS	36	4	3	7	10	6	0	0	0	4
1994-95	Moscow D'amo	CIS	48	13	8	21	20	14	7	2	9	10
1995-96	Moscow D'amo	CIS	44	5	9	14	16	11	2	1	3	2

GRANATO, TONY S.J.

Left wing. Shoots right. 5'10", 185 lbs. Born, Downers Grove, IL, July 25, 1964.
(NY Rangers' 5th choice, 120th overall, in 1982 Entry Draft).

			Regular Season					Playoffs				
Season	Club	Lea	GP	G	A	TP	PIM	GP	G	A	TP	PIM
1983-84	U. Wisconsin	WCHA	35	14	17	31	48	....	....	....	....	....
1984-85	U. Wisconsin	WCHA	42	33	34	67	94	....	....	....	....	....
1985-86	U. Wisconsin	WCHA	33	25	24	49	36	....	....	....	....	....
1986-87ab	U. Wisconsin	WCHA	42	28	45	73	64	....	....	....	....	....
1987-88	U.S. National	....	49	40	31	71	55	....	....	....	....	....
	U.S. Olympic	....	6	1	7	8	4	....	....	....	....	....
	Colorado	IHL	22	13	14	27	36	8	9	4	13	16
1988-89c	**NY Rangers**	**NHL**	**78**	**36**	**27**	**63**	**140**	**4**	**1**	**1**	**2**	**21**
1989-90	**NY Rangers**	**NHL**	**37**	**7**	**18**	**25**	**77**	....	....	....	....	....
	Los Angeles	**NHL**	**19**	**5**	**6**	**11**	**45**	**10**	**5**	**4**	**9**	**12**
1990-91	**Los Angeles**	**NHL**	**68**	**30**	**34**	**64**	**154**	**12**	**1**	**4**	**5**	**28**
1991-92	**Los Angeles**	**NHL**	**80**	**39**	**29**	**68**	**187**	**6**	**1**	**5**	**6**	**10**
1992-93	**Los Angeles**	**NHL**	**81**	**37**	**45**	**82**	**171**	**24**	**6**	**11**	**17**	**50**
1993-94	**Los Angeles**	**NHL**	**50**	**7**	**14**	**21**	**150**	....	....	....	....	....
1994-95	**Los Angeles**	**NHL**	**33**	**13**	**11**	**24**	**68**	....	....	....	....	....
1995-96	**Los Angeles**	**NHL**	**49**	**17**	**18**	**35**	**46**	....	....	....	....	....
	NHL Totals		**495**	**191**	**202**	**393**	**1038**	**56**	**14**	**25**	**39**	**121**

a WCHA Second All-Star Team (1987)
b NCAA West Second All-American Team (1987)
c NHL All-Rookie Team (1989)

Traded to **Los Angeles** by **NY Rangers** with Tomas Sandstrom for Bernie Nicholls, January 20, 1990. Signed as a free agent by **San Jose**, August 14, 1996.

GRAND PIERRE, JEAN-LUC BUF.

Defense. Shoots left. 6'2", 197 lbs. Born, Montreal, Que., February 2, 1977.
(St. Louis' 5th choice, 179th overall, in 1995 Entry Draft).

			Regular Season					Playoffs				
Season	Club	Lea	GP	G	A	TP	PIM	GP	G	A	TP	PIM
1994-95	Val d'Or	QMJHL	59	10	13	23	126	....	....	....	....	....
1995-96	Val d'Or	QMJHL	67	13	21	34	209	13	1	4	5	47

Traded to **Buffalo** by **St. Louis** with Ottawa's second round choice (previously acquired by St. Louis — Buffalo selected Cory Sarich) in 1996 Entry Draft and St. Louis' third round choice in 1997 Entry Draft for Yuri Khmylev and Buffalo's eighth round choice (Andrei Podkonicky) in 1996 Entry Draft, March 20, 1996.

GRATTON, BENOIT WSH.

Left wing. Shoots left. 5'10", 163 lbs. Born, Montreal, Que., December 28, 1976.
(Washington's 6th choice, 105th overall, in 1995 Entry Draft).

			Regular Season					Playoffs				
Season	Club	Lea	GP	G	A	TP	PIM	GP	G	A	TP	PIM
1993-94	Laval	QMJHL	51	9	14	23	70	20	2	1	3	19
1994-95	Laval	QMJHL	71	30	58	88	199	20	8	*21	29	42
1995-96	Laval	QMJHL	38	21	39	60	130	....	....	....	....	....
	Granby	QMJHL	27	12	46	58	97	21	13	26	39	68

GRATTON, CHRIS T.B.

Center. Shoots left. 6'4", 218 lbs. Born, Brantford, Ont., July 5, 1975.
(Tampa Bay's 1st choice, 3rd overall, in 1993 Entry Draft).

			Regular Season					Playoffs				
Season	Club	Lea	GP	G	A	TP	PIM	GP	G	A	TP	PIM
1991-92	Kingston	OHL	62	27	29	66	37	....	....	....	....	....
1992-93	Kingston	OHL	58	55	54	109	125	16	11	18	29	42
1993-94	**Tampa Bay**	**NHL**	**84**	**13**	**29**	**42**	**123**	....	....	....	....	....
1994-95	**Tampa Bay**	**NHL**	**46**	**7**	**20**	**27**	**89**	....	....	....	....	....
1995-96	**Tampa Bay**	**NHL**	**82**	**17**	**21**	**38**	**105**	**6**	**0**	**2**	**2**	**27**
	NHL Totals		**212**	**37**	**70**	**107**	**317**	**6**	**0**	**2**	**2**	**27**

GRAVES, ADAM NYR

Center. Shoots left. 6', 205 lbs. Born, Toronto, Ont., April 12, 1968.
(Detroit's 2nd choice, 22nd overall, in 1986 Entry Draft).

			Regular Season					Playoffs				
Season	Club	Lea	GP	G	A	TP	PIM	GP	G	A	TP	PIM
1985-86	Windsor	OHL	62	27	37	64	35	16	5	11	16	10
1986-87	Windsor	OHL	66	45	55	100	70	14	9	8	17	32
	Adirondack	AHL	....	....	....	....	....	5	0	1	1	0
1987-88	**Detroit**	**NHL**	**9**	**0**	**1**	**1**	**8**	....	....	....	....	....
	Windsor	OHL	37	28	32	60	107	12	14	18	*32	16
1988-89	**Detroit**	**NHL**	**56**	**7**	**5**	**12**	**60**	**5**	**0**	**0**	**0**	**4**
	Adirondack	AHL	14	10	11	21	28	14	11	7	18	17
1989-90	**Detroit**	**NHL**	**13**	**0**	**1**	**1**	**13**	....	....	....	....	....
	Edmonton	**NHL**	**63**	**9**	**12**	**21**	**123**	**22**	**5**	**6**	**11**	**17** ♦
1990-91	**Edmonton**	**NHL**	**76**	**7**	**18**	**25**	**127**	**18**	**2**	**4**	**6**	**22**
1991-92	**NY Rangers**	**NHL**	**80**	**26**	**33**	**59**	**139**	**10**	**5**	**3**	**8**	**22**
1992-93	**NY Rangers**	**NHL**	**84**	**36**	**29**	**65**	**148**	....	....	....	....	....
1993-94ab	**NY Rangers**	**NHL**	**84**	**52**	**27**	**79**	**127**	**23**	**10**	**7**	**17**	**24** ♦
1994-95	**NY Rangers**	**NHL**	**47**	**17**	**14**	**31**	**51**	**10**	**4**	**4**	**8**	**8**
1995-96	**NY Rangers**	**NHL**	**82**	**22**	**36**	**58**	**100**	**10**	**7**	**1**	**8**	**4**
	NHL Totals		**594**	**176**	**176**	**352**	**896**	**98**	**33**	**25**	**58**	**101**

a NHL Second All-Star Team (1994)
b Won King Clancy Memorial Trophy (1994)

Played in NHL All-Star Game (1994)

Traded to **Edmonton** by **Detroit** with Petr Klima, Joe Murphy and Jeff Sharples for Jimmy Carson, Kevin McClelland and Edmonton's fifth round choice (later traded to Montreal — Montreal selected Brad Layzell) in 1991 Entry Draft, November 2, 1989. Signed as a free agent by **NY Rangers**, September 3, 1991.

GREEN, JOSH L.A.

Left wing. Shoots left. 6'3", 197 lbs. Born, Camrose, Alta., November 16, 1977.
(Los Angeles' 1st choice, 30th overall, in 1996 Entry Draft).

			Regular Season					Playoffs				
Season	Club	Lea	GP	G	A	TP	PIM	GP	G	A	TP	PIM
1993-94	Medicine Hat	WHL	63	22	22	44	43	3	0	0	0	4
1994-95	Medicine Hat	WHL	68	32	23	55	64	5	5	1	6	2
1995-96	Medicine Hat	WHL	46	18	25	43	55	5	2	2	4	4

GREEN, TRAVIS NYI

Center. Shoots right. 6'1", 193 lbs. Born, Castlegar, B.C., December 20, 1970.
(NY Islanders' 2nd choice, 23rd overall, in 1989 Entry Draft).

			Regular Season					Playoffs				
Season	Club	Lea	GP	G	A	TP	PIM	GP	G	A	TP	PIM
1986-87	Spokane	WHL	64	8	17	25	27	3	0	0	0	0
1987-88	Spokane	WHL	72	33	54	87	42	15	10	10	20	13
1988-89	Spokane	WHL	75	51	51	102	79	....	....	....	....	....
1989-90	Spokane	WHL	50	45	44	89	80	....	....	....	....	....
	Medicine Hat	WHL	25	15	24	39	19	3	0	0	0	2
1990-91	Capital Dist.	AHL	73	21	34	55	26	....	....	....	....	....
1991-92	Capital Dist.	AHL	71	23	27	50	10	7	0	4	4	21
1992-93	**NY Islanders**	**NHL**	**61**	**7**	**18**	**25**	**43**	**12**	**3**	**1**	**4**	**6**
	Capital Dist.	AHL	20	12	11	23	39	....	....	....	....	....
1993-94	**NY Islanders**	**NHL**	**83**	**18**	**22**	**40**	**44**	**4**	**0**	**0**	**0**	**2**
1994-95	**NY Islanders**	**NHL**	**42**	**5**	**7**	**12**	**25**	....	....	....	....	....
1995-96	**NY Islanders**	**NHL**	**69**	**25**	**45**	**70**	**42**	....	....	....	....	....
	NHL Totals		**255**	**55**	**92**	**147**	**154**	**16**	**3**	**1**	**4**	**8**

GREENLAW, JEFF

Left wing. Shoots left. 6'1", 230 lbs. Born, Toronto, Ont., February 28, 1968.
(Washington's 1st choice, 19th overall, in 1986 Entry Draft).

			Regular Season					Playoffs				
Season	Club	Lea	GP	G	A	TP	PIM	GP	G	A	TP	PIM
1985-86	Cdn. Olympic	....	57	3	16	19	81	....	....	....	....	....
1986-87	**Washington**	**NHL**	**22**	**0**	**3**	**3**	**44**	....	....	....	....	....
	Binghamton	AHL	4	0	2	2	0	....	....	....	....	....
1987-88	Binghamton	AHL	56	8	7	15	142	1	0	0	0	2
	Washington	**NHL**	....	....	....	....	....	**1**	**0**	**0**	**0**	**19**
1988-89	Baltimore	AHL	55	12	15	27	115	....	....	....	....	....
1989-90	Baltimore	AHL	10	3	2	5	26	7	1	0	1	13
1990-91	**Washington**	**NHL**	**10**	**2**	**0**	**2**	**10**	**1**	**0**	**0**	**0**	**2**
	Baltimore	AHL	50	17	17	34	93	3	1	1	2	2
1991-92	**Washington**	**NHL**	**5**	**0**	**1**	**1**	**34**	....	....	....	....	....
	Baltimore	AHL	37	6	8	14	57	....	....	....	....	....
1992-93	**Washington**	**NHL**	**16**	**1**	**1**	**2**	**18**	....	....	....	....	....
	Baltimore	AHL	49	12	14	26	66	7	3	1	4	0
1993-94	**Florida**	**NHL**	**4**	**0**	**1**	**1**	**2**	....	....	....	....	....
	Cincinnati	IHL	55	14	15	29	85	11	2	2	4	28
1994-95	Cincinnati	IHL	67	10	21	31	117	10	2	0	2	22
1995-96	Cincinnati	IHL	64	17	15	32	112	17	2	4	6	36
	NHL Totals		**57**	**3**	**6**	**9**	**108**	**2**	**0**	**0**	**0**	**21**

Signed as a free agent by **Florida**, July 14, 1993.

GREIG, MARK (GREG)

Right wing. Shoots right. 5'11", 190 lbs. Born, High River, Alta., January 25, 1970.
(Hartford's 1st choice, 15th overall, in 1990 Entry Draft).

			Regular Season					Playoffs				
Season	Club	Lea	GP	G	A	TP	PIM	GP	G	A	TP	PIM
1987-88	Lethbridge	WHL	65	9	18	27	38	....	....	....	....	....
1988-89	Lethbridge	WHL	71	36	72	108	113	8	5	5	10	16
1989-90a	Lethbridge	WHL	65	55	80	135	149	18	11	21	32	35
1990-91	**Hartford**	**NHL**	**4**	**0**	**0**	**0**	**0**	....	....	....	....	....
	Springfield	AHL	73	32	55	87	73	17	2	6	8	22
1991-92	**Hartford**	**NHL**	**17**	**0**	**5**	**5**	**6**	....	....	....	....	....
	Springfield	AHL	50	20	27	47	38	9	1	1	2	20
1992-93	**Hartford**	**NHL**	**22**	**1**	**7**	**8**	**27**	....	....	....	....	....
	Springfield	AHL	55	20	38	58	86	....	....	....	....	....
1993-94	**Hartford**	**NHL**	**31**	**4**	**5**	**9**	**31**	....	....	....	....	....
	Springfield	AHL	4	0	4	4	21	....	....	....	....	....
	Toronto	**NHL**	**13**	**2**	**2**	**4**	**10**	....	....	....	....	....
	St. John's	AHL	9	4	6	10	0	11	4	2	6	26
1994-95	Saint John	AHL	67	31	50	81	82	2	0	1	1	0
	Calgary	**NHL**	**8**	**1**	**1**	**2**	**2**	....	....	....	....	....
1995-96	Atlanta	IHL	71	25	48	73	104	3	2	1	3	4
	NHL Totals		**95**	**8**	**20**	**28**	**76**	....	....	....	....	....

a WHL East First All-Star Team (1990)

Traded to **Toronto** by **Hartford** with Hartford's sixth round choice (later traded to NY Rangers — NY Rangers selected Yuri Litvinov) in 1994 Entry Draft for Ted Crowley, January 25, 1994. Signed as a free agent by **Calgary**, August 9, 1994.

GRETZKY, BRENT (GRETZ-kee)

Center. Shoots left. 5'10", 160 lbs. Born, Brantford, Ont., February 20, 1972.
(Tampa Bay's 3rd choice, 49th overall, in 1992 Entry Draft).

			Regular Season					Playoffs				
Season	Club	Lea	GP	G	A	TP	PIM	GP	G	A	TP	PIM
1989-90	Belleville	OHL	66	15	32	47	30	11	0	0	0	0
1990-91	Belleville	OHL	66	26	56	82	25	6	3	3	6	2
1991-92	Belleville	OHL	62	43	78	121	37	....	....	....	....	....
1992-93	Atlanta	IHL	77	20	34	54	84	9	3	2	5	8
1993-94	**Tampa Bay**	**NHL**	**10**	**1**	**2**	**3**	**2**	....	....	....	....	....
	Atlanta	IHL	54	17	23	40	30	14	1	1	2	2
1994-95	Atlanta	IHL	67	19	32	51	42	5	4	1	5	4
	Tampa Bay	**NHL**	**3**	**0**	**1**	**1**	**0**	....	....	....	....	....
1995-96	St. John's	AHL	68	13	28	41	40	4	0	6	6	0
	NHL Totals		**13**	**1**	**3**	**4**	**2**	....	....	....	....	....

Signed as a free agent by **Toronto**, September 20, 1995.

GRETZKY, WAYNE (GRETZ-kee) NYR

Center. Shoots left. 6', 180 lbs. Born, Brantford, Ont., January 26, 1961.

			Regular Season					Playoffs				
Season	Club	Lea	GP	G	A	TP	PIM	GP	G	A	TP	PIM
1976-77	Peterborough	OHA	3	0	3	3	0	....	....	....	....	....
1977-78a	S.S. Marie	OHA	64	70	112	182	14	13	6	20	26	0
1978-79	Indianapolis	WHA	8	3	3	6	0	....	....	....	....	....
bc	Edmonton	WHA	72	43	61	104	19	13	*10	10	*20	2
1979-80def	**Edmonton**	**NHL**	**79**	**51**	***86**	***137**	**21**	**3**	**2**	**1**	**3**	**0**
1980-81 dghij	**Edmonton**	**NHL**	**80**	**55**	***109**	***164**	**28**	**9**	**7**	**14**	**21**	**4**
1981-82 dghijklp	**Edmonton**	**NHL**	**80**	***92**	***120**	***212**	**26**	**5**	**5**	**7**	**12**	**8**
1982-83 dghilmn	**Edmonton**	**NHL**	**80**	***71**	***125**	***196**	**59**	**16**	**12**	***26**	***38**	**4**
1983-84 dghlp	**Edmonton**	**NHL**	**74**	***87**	***118**	***205**	**39**	**19**	**13**	***22**	***35**	**12 ♦**
1984-85 dghilmnopq	**Edmonton**	**NHL**	**80**	***73**	***135**	***208**	**52**	**18**	**17**	***30**	***47**	**4 ♦**
1985-86 dghijq	**Edmonton**	**NHL**	**80**	**52**	***163**	***215**	**46**	**10**	**8**	**11**	**19**	**2**
1986-87 dghlpq	**Edmonton**	**NHL**	**79**	***62**	***121**	***183**	**28**	**21**	**5**	***29**	***34**	**6 ♦**
1987-88fmo	**Edmonton**	**NHL**	**64**	**40**	***109**	**149**	**24**	**19**	**12**	***31**	***43**	**16 ♦**
1988-89dfr	**Los Angeles**	**NHL**	**78**	**54**	***114**	**168**	**26**	**11**	**5**	**17**	**22**	**0**
1989-90fh	**Los Angeles**	**NHL**	**73**	**40**	***102**	***142**	**42**	**7**	**3**	**7**	**10**	**0**
1990-91egh	**Los Angeles**	**NHL**	**78**	**41**	***122**	***163**	**16**	**12**	**4**	**11**	**15**	**2**
1991-92e	**Los Angeles**	**NHL**	**74**	**31**	***90**	**121**	**34**	**6**	**2**	**5**	**7**	**2**
1992-93	**Los Angeles**	**NHL**	**45**	**16**	**49**	**65**	**6**	**24**	***15**	***25**	***40**	**4**
1993-94efh	**Los Angeles**	**NHL**	**81**	**38**	***92**	***130**	**20**	....	....	....	....	....
1994-95	**Los Angeles**	**NHL**	**48**	**11**	**37**	**48**	**6**	....	....	....	....	....
1995-96	**Los Angeles**	**NHL**	**62**	**15**	**66**	**81**	**32**	....	....	....	....	....
	St. Louis	**NHL**	**18**	**8**	**13**	**21**	**2**	**13**	**2**	**14**	**16**	**0**
	NHL Totals		**1253**	***837**	***1771**	***2608**	**507**	**193**	***112**	***250**	***362**	**64**

a OHA Second All-Star Team (1978)
b WHA Second All-Star Team (1979)
c Named WHA's Rookie of the Year (1979)
d Won Hart Trophy (1980, 1981, 1982, 1983, 1984, 1985, 1986, 1987, 1989)
e Won Lady Byng Trophy (1980, 1991, 1992, 1994)
f NHL Second All-Star Team (1980, 1988, 1989, 1990, 1994)
g NHL First All-Star Team (1981, 1982, 1983, 1984, 1985, 1986, 1987, 1991)
h Won Art Ross Trophy (1981, 1982, 1983, 1984, 1985, 1986, 1987, 1990, 1991, 1994)
i NHL record for assists in regular season (1981, 1982, 1983, 1985, 1986)
j NHL record for points in regular season (1981, 1982, 1986)
k NHL record for goals in regular season (1982)
l Won Lester B. Pearson Award (1982, 1983, 1984, 1985, 1987)
m NHL record for assists in one playoff year (1983, 1985, 1988)
n NHL record for points in one playoff year (1983, 1985)
o Won Conn Smythe Trophy (1985, 1988)
p NHL Plus/Minus Leader (1982, 1984, 1985, 1987)
q Selected Chrysler-Dodge/NHL Performer of the Year (1985, 1986, 1987)
r Won Dodge Performance of the Year Award (1989)

Played in NHL All-Star Game (1980-1986, 1988-94, 1996)

Reclaimed by **Edmonton** as an under-age junior prior to Expansion Draft, June 9, 1979. Claimed as priority selection by **Edmonton**, June 9, 1979. Traded to **Los Angeles** by **Edmonton** with Mike Krushelnyski and Marty McSorley for Jimmy Carson, Martin Gelinas, Los Angeles' first round choices in 1989 (acquired by New Jersey — New Jersey selected Jason Miller), 1991 (Martin Rucinsky) and 1993 (Nick Stajduhar) Entry Drafts and cash, August 9, 1988. Traded to **St. Louis** by **Los Angeles** for Craig Johnson, Patrice Tardif, Roman Vopat, St. Louis fifth round choice (Peter Hogan) in 1996 Entry Draft and first round choice in 1997 Entry Draft, February 27, 1996. Signed as a free agent by **NY Rangers**, July 21, 1996.

GRIER, MICHAEL EDM.

Right wing. Shoots right. 6'1", 232 lbs. Born, Detroit, MI, January 5, 1975.
(St. Louis' 7th choice, 219th overall, in 1993 Entry Draft).

			Regular Season					Playoffs				
Season	Club	Lea	GP	G	A	TP	PIM	GP	G	A	TP	PIM
1993-94	Boston U.	H.E.	39	9	9	18	56	....	....	....	....	....
1994-95ab	Boston U.	H.E.	37	*29	26	55	85	....	....	....	....	....
1995-96	Boston U.	H.E.	38	21	25	46	82	....	....	....	....	....

a Hockey East First All-Star Team (1995)
b NCAA East First All-American Team (1995)

Rights traded to **Edmonton** by **St. Louis** with Curtis Joseph for St. Louis' first round choices (previously acquired by Edmonton) in 1996 (Marty Reasoner) and 1997 Entry Drafts, August 4, 1995.

GRIEVE, BRENT L.A.

Left wing. Shoots left. 6'1", 202 lbs. Born, Oshawa, Ont., May 9, 1969.
(NY Islanders' 4th choice, 65th overall, in 1989 Entry Draft).

			Regular Season					Playoffs				
Season	Club	Lea	GP	G	A	TP	PIM	GP	G	A	TP	PIM
1986-87	Oshawa	OHL	60	9	19	28	102	24	3	8	11	22
1987-88	Oshawa	OHL	55	19	20	39	122	7	0	1	1	8
1988-89	Oshawa	OHL	49	34	33	67	105	6	4	3	7	4
1989-90	Oshawa	OHL	62	46	47	93	125	17	10	10	20	26
1990-91	Capital Dist.	AHL	61	14	13	27	80	....	....	....	....	....
	Kansas City	IHL	5	2	2	4	2	....	....	....	....	....
1991-92	Capital Dist.	AHL	74	34	32	66	84	7	3	1	4	16
1992-93	Capital Dist.	AHL	79	34	28	62	122	4	1	1	2	10
1993-94	**NY Islanders**	**NHL**	**3**	**0**	**0**	**0**	**7**	....	....	....	....	....
	Salt Lake	IHL	22	9	5	14	30	....	....	....	....	....
	Edmonton	**NHL**	**24**	**13**	**5**	**18**	**14**	....	....	....	....	....
	Cape Breton	AHL	20	10	11	21	14	4	2	4	6	16
1994-95	**Chicago**	**NHL**	**24**	**1**	**5**	**6**	**23**	....	....	....	....	....
1995-96	**Chicago**	**NHL**	**28**	**2**	**4**	**6**	**28**	....	....	....	....	....
	Indianapolis	IHL	24	9	10	19	16	....	....	....	....	....
	Phoenix	IHL	13	8	11	19	14	4	2	1	3	18
	NHL Totals		**79**	**16**	**14**	**30**	**72**	....	....	....	....	....

Traded to **Edmonton**, by **NY Islanders** for Marc Laforge, December 15, 1993. Signed as a free agent by **Chicago**, July 7, 1994. Signed as a free agent by **Los Angeles**, August 2, 1996.

GRILLO, DEAN S.J.

Right wing. Shoots right. 6'2", 210 lbs. Born, Bemidji, MN, December 8, 1972.
(San Jose's 9th choice, 155th overall, in 1991 Entry Draft).

			Regular Season					Playoffs				
Season	Club	Lea	GP	G	A	TP	PIM	GP	G	A	TP	PIM
1992-93	North Dakota	WCHA	29	7	4	11	14	....	....	....	....	....
1993-94	North Dakota	WCHA	38	11	14	25	14	....	....	....	....	....
1994-95	Kansas City	IHL	72	15	21	36	24	18	3	5	8	18
1995-96	Kansas City	IHL	65	9	10	19	26	5	0	0	0	2

GRIMSON, STU DET.

Left wing. Shoots left. 6'5", 227 lbs. Born, Kamloops, B.C., May 20, 1965.
(Detroit's 11th choice, 186th overall, in 1983 Entry Draft).

			Regular Season					Playoffs				
Season	Club	Lea	GP	G	A	TP	PIM	GP	G	A	TP	PIM
1982-83	Regina	WHL	48	0	1	1	105	5	0	0	0	14
1983-84	Regina	WHL	63	8	8	16	131	21	0	1	1	29
1984-85	Regina	WHL	71	24	32	56	248	8	1	2	3	14
1985-86	U. Manitoba	CWUAA	12	7	4	11	113	3	1	1	2	20
1986-87	U. Manitoba	CWUAA	29	8	8	16	67	14	4	2	6	28
1987-88	Salt Lake	IHL	38	9	5	14	268	....	....	....	....	....
1988-89	**Calgary**	**NHL**	**1**	**0**	**0**	**0**	**5**	....	....	....	....	....
	Salt Lake	IHL	72	9	18	27	397	14	2	3	5	86
1989-90	**Calgary**	**NHL**	**3**	**0**	**0**	**0**	**17**	....	....	....	....	....
	Salt Lake	IHL	62	8	8	16	319	4	0	0	0	8
1990-91	**Chicago**	**NHL**	**35**	**0**	**1**	**1**	**183**	**5**	**0**	**0**	**0**	**46**
1991-92	**Chicago**	**NHL**	**54**	**2**	**2**	**4**	**234**	**14**	**0**	**1**	**1**	**10**
	Indianapolis	IHL	5	1	1	2	17	....	....	....	....	....
1992-93	**Chicago**	**NHL**	**78**	**1**	**1**	**2**	**193**	**2**	**0**	**0**	**0**	**4**
1993-94	**Anaheim**	**NHL**	**77**	**1**	**5**	**6**	**199**	....	....	....	....	....
1994-95	**Anaheim**	**NHL**	**31**	**0**	**1**	**1**	**110**	....	....	....	....	....
	Detroit	**NHL**	**11**	**0**	**0**	**0**	**37**	**11**	**1**	**0**	**1**	**26**
1995-96	**Detroit**	**NHL**	**56**	**0**	**1**	**1**	**128**	**2**	**0**	**0**	**0**	**0**
	NHL Totals		**346**	**4**	**11**	**15**	**1106**	**34**	**1**	**1**	**2**	**86**

Re-entered NHL Entry Draft. **Calgary's** 8th choice, 143rd overall, in 1985 Entry Draft.

Claimed on conditional waivers by **Chicago** from **Calgary**, October 1, 1990. Claimed by **Anaheim** from **Chicago** in Expansion Draft, June 24, 1993. Traded to **Detroit** by **Anaheim** with Mark Ferner and Anaheim's sixth round choice (Magnus Nilsson) in 1996 Entry Draft for Mike Sillinger and Jason York, April 4, 1995.

GROLEAU, FRANCOIS MTL.

Defense. Shoots left. 6', 200 lbs. Born, Longueuil, Que., January 23, 1973.
(Calgary's 2nd choice, 41st overall, in 1991 Entry Draft).

			Regular Season					Playoffs				
Season	Club	Lea	GP	G	A	TP	PIM	GP	G	A	TP	PIM
1989-90a	Shawinigan	QMJHL	65	11	54	65	80	6	0	1	1	12
1990-91	Shawinigan	QMJHL	70	9	60	69	70	6	0	3	3	2
1991-92b	Shawinigan	QMJHL	65	8	70	78	74	10	5	15	20	8
1992-93	St-Jean	QMJHL	48	7	38	45	66	4	0	1	1	14
1993-94	Saint John	AHL	73	8	14	22	49	7	0	1	1	2
1994-95	Saint John	AHL	65	6	34	40	28	....	....	....	....	....
	Cornwall	AHL	8	1	2	3	7	14	2	7	9	16
1995-96	**Montreal**	**NHL**	**2**	**0**	**1**	**1**	**2**	....	....	....	....	....
	San Francisco	IHL	63	6	26	32	60	....	....	....	....	....
	Fredericton	AHL	12	3	5	8	10	10	1	6	7	14
	NHL Totals		**2**	**0**	**1**	**1**	**2**	....	....	....	....	....

a QMJHL Second All-Star Team (1990)
b QMJHL First All-Star Team (1992)

Traded to **Quebec** by **Calgary** for Ed Ward, March 23, 1995. Signed as a free agent by **Montreal**, June 17, 1995.

GRONMAN, TUOMAS (GROHN-mahn) CHI.

Defense. Shoots right. 6'3", 198 lbs. Born, Viitasaari, Finland, March 22, 1974.
(Quebec's 3rd choice, 29th overall, in 1992 Entry Draft).

			Regular Season					Playoffs				
Season	Club	Lea	GP	G	A	TP	PIM	GP	G	A	TP	PIM
1991-92	Tacoma	WHL	61	5	18	23	102	4	0	1	1	2
1992-93	Lukko	Fin.	45	2	11	13	46	3	1	0	1	2
1993-94	Lukko	Fin.	44	4	12	16	60	9	0	1	1	14
1994-95	TPS	Fin.	47	4	20	24	66	13	2	2	4	43
1995-96	TPS	Fin.	32	5	7	12	85	11	1	4	5	16

Rights traded to **Chicago** by **Colorado** for Chicago's second round choice in 1998 Entry Draft, July 10, 1996.

GRONVALL, JANNE

(GROHN-vahl, YAH-neh)

Defense. Shoots left. 6'3", 195 lbs.   Born, Rauma, Finland, July 17, 1973.
(Toronto's 5th choice, 101st overall, in 1992 Entry Draft).

				Regular Season					Playoffs			
Season	Club	Lea	GP	G	A	TP	PIM	GP	G	A	TP	PIM
1989-90	Lukko	Fin.	5	0	0	0	0	....	....	....	....	....
1990-91	Lukko	Fin.	40	2	8	10	30	....	....	....	....	....
1991-92	Lukko	Fin.	42	2	6	8	40	2	0	0	0	2
1992-93	Tappara	Fin.	46	1	7	8	54	....	....	....	....	....
1993-94	Tappara	Fin.	47	2	9	11	54	10	0	4	4	31
	St. John's	AHL	....	....	....	....	....	9	0	0	0	2
1994-95	St. John's	AHL	76	8	29	37	75	5	0	0	0	0
1995-96	St. John's	AHL	76	4	31	35	82	2	1	0	1	2

GROSEK, MICHAL

BUF.

Left wing. Shoots right. 6'2", 196 lbs.   Born, Vyskov, Czech., June 1, 1975.
(Winnipeg's 7th choice, 145th overall, in 1993 Entry Draft).

				Regular Season					Playoffs			
Season	Club	Lea	GP	G	A	TP	PIM	GP	G	A	TP	PIM
1992-93	ZPS Zlin	Czech.	17	1	3	4	....	....	....	....	....	....
1993-94	Winnipeg	NHL	3	1	0	1	0	....	....	....	....	....
	Tacoma	WHL	30	25	20	45	106	7	2	2	4	30
	Moncton	AHL	20	1	2	3	47	2	0	0	0	0
1994-95	Springfield	AHL	45	10	22	32	98	....	....	....	....	....
	Winnipeg	NHL	24	2	2	4	21	....	....	....	....	....
1995-96	Winnipeg	NHL	1	0	0	0	0	....	....	....	....	....
	Buffalo	NHL	22	6	4	10	31	....	....	....	....	....
	Springfield	AHL	39	16	19	35	68	....	....	....	....	....
	NHL Totals		50	9	6	15	52	....	....	....	....	....

Traded to **Buffalo** by **Winnipeg** with Darryl Shannon for Craig Muni, February 15, 1996.

GRUDEN, JOHN

BOS.

Defense. Shoots left. 6', 190 lbs.   Born, Virginia, MN, June 4, 1970.
(Boston's 7th choice, 168th overall, in 1990 Entry Draft).

				Regular Season					Playoffs			
Season	Club	Lea	GP	G	A	TP	PIM	GP	G	A	TP	PIM
1990-91	Ferris State	CCHA	37	4	11	15	27	....	....	....	....	....
1991-92	Ferris State	CCHA	37	9	14	23	24	....	....	....	....	....
1992-93	Ferris State	CCHA	41	16	14	30	58	....	....	....	....	....
1993-94ab	Ferris State	CCHA	38	11	25	36	52	....	....	....	....	....
	Boston	NHL	7	0	1	1	2	....	....	....	....	....
1994-95	Boston	NHL	38	0	6	6	22	....	....	....	....	....
	Providence	AHL	1	0	1	1	0	....	....	....	....	....
1995-96	Boston	NHL	14	0	0	0	4	3	0	1	1	0
	Providence	AHL	39	5	19	24	29	....	....	....	....	....
	NHL Totals		59	0	7	7	28	3	0	1	1	0

a CCHA First All-Star Team (1994)
b NCAA West First All-American Team (1994)

GUERARD, DANIEL

OTT.

Right wing. Shoots right. 6'4", 215 lbs.   Born, LaSalle, Que., April 9, 1974.
(Ottawa's 5th choice, 98th overall, in 1992 Entry Draft).

				Regular Season					Playoffs			
Season	Club	Lea	GP	G	A	TP	PIM	GP	G	A	TP	PIM
1991-92	Victoriaville	QMJHL	31	5	16	21	66	....	....	....	....	....
1992-93	Verdun	QMJHL	58	31	26	57	131	4	1	1	2	17
	New Haven	AHL	2	2	1	3	0	....	....	....	....	....
1993-94	Verdun	QMJHL	53	31	34	65	169	4	3	1	4	4
	P.E.I.	AHL	3	0	0	0	17	....	....	....	....	....
1994-95	P.E.I.	AHL	68	20	22	42	95	6	0	1	1	16
	Ottawa	NHL	2	0	0	0	0	....	....	....	....	....
1995-96	P.E.I.	AHL	42	3	7	10	56	....	....	....	....	....
	NHL Totals		2	0	0	0	0	....	....	....	....	....

GUERIN, BILL

(GAIR-ihn)   N.J.

Right wing. Shoots right. 6'2", 200 lbs.   Born, Wilbraham, MA, November 9, 1970.
(New Jersey's 1st choice, 5th overall, in 1989 Entry Draft).

				Regular Season					Playoffs			
Season	Club	Lea	GP	G	A	TP	PIM	GP	G	A	TP	PIM
1989-90	Boston College	H.E.	39	14	11	25	54	....	....	....	....	....
1990-91	Boston College	H.E.	38	26	19	45	102	....	....	....	....	....
	U.S. National		46	12	15	27	67	....	....	....	....	....
1991-92	New Jersey	NHL	5	0	1	1	9	6	3	0	3	4
	Utica	AHL	22	13	10	23	6	4	1	3	4	14
1992-93	New Jersey	NHL	65	14	20	34	63	5	1	1	2	4
	Utica	AHL	18	10	7	17	47	....	....	....	....	....
1993-94	New Jersey	NHL	81	25	19	44	101	17	2	1	3	35
1994-95	New Jersey	NHL	48	12	13	25	72	20	3	8	11	30 ♦
1995-96	New Jersey	NHL	80	23	30	53	116	....	....	....	....	....
	NHL Totals		279	74	83	157	361	48	9	10	19	73

GUNKO, YURI

ST.L.

Defense. Shoots left. 6'1", 187 lbs.   Born, Kiev, USSR, February 28, 1972.
(St. Louis' 11th choice, 230th overall, in 1992 Entry Draft).

				Regular Season					Playoffs			
Season	Club	Lea	GP	G	A	TP	PIM	GP	G	A	TP	PIM
1990-91	Sokol Kiev	USSR	14	0	0	0	8	....	....	....	....	....
1991-92	Sokol Kiev	CIS	22	1	0	1	16	....	....	....	....	....
1992-93	Sokol Kiev	CIS	40	2	3	5	28	....	....	....	....	....
1993-94	Sokol Kiev	CIS	42	0	8	8	28	....	....	....	....	....
1994-95	Sokol Kiev	CIS	25	4	0	4	18	....	....	....	....	....
1995-96	Kazan	CIS	41	1	2	3	22	5	1	0	1	4

GUOLLA, STEPHEN

S.J.

Left wing. Shoots left. 6', 180 lbs.   Born, Scarborough, Ont., March 15, 1973.
(Ottawa's 1st choice, 3rd overall, in 1994 Supplemental Draft).

				Regular Season					Playoffs			
Season	Club	Lea	GP	G	A	TP	PIM	GP	G	A	TP	PIM
1991-92	Michigan State	CCHA	33	4	9	13	8	....	....	....	....	....
1992-93	Michigan State	CCHA	39	19	35	54	6	....	....	....	....	....
1993-94ab	Michigan State	CCHA	41	23	46	69	16	....	....	....	....	....
1994-95	Michigan State	CCHA	40	16	35	51	16	....	....	....	....	....
1995-96	P.E.I.	AHL	72	32	48	80	28	3	0	0	0	0

a CCHA Second All-Star Team (1994)
b NCAA West Second All-American Team (1994)

Signed as a free agent by **San Jose**, August 22, 1996.

GUREN, MILOSLAV

MTL.

Defense. Shoots left. 6'2", 205 lbs.   Born, Uherske. Hradiste, Czech., September 24, 1976.
(Montreal's 2nd choice, 60th overall, in 1995 Entry Draft).

				Regular Season					Playoffs			
Season	Club	Lea	GP	G	A	TP	PIM	GP	G	A	TP	PIM
1993-94	ZPS Zlin	Czech.	22	1	5	6	....	3	0	0	0	....
1994-95	ZPS Zlin	Czech.	32	3	7	10	10	12	1	0	1	6
1995-96	ZPS Zlin	Czech.	28	1	2	3	....	7	1	0	1	....

GUSAROV, ALEXEI

(goo-SAH-rahf)   COL.

Defense. Shoots left. 6'3", 185 lbs.   Born, Leningrad, USSR, July 8, 1964.
(Quebec's 11th choice, 213th overall, in 1988 Entry Draft).

				Regular Season					Playoffs			
Season	Club	Lea	GP	G	A	TP	PIM	GP	G	A	TP	PIM
1981-82	SKA Leningrad	USSR	20	1	2	3	16	....	....	....	....	....
1982-83	SKA Leningrad	USSR	42	2	1	3	32	....	....	....	....	....
1983-84	SKA Leningrad	USSR	43	2	3	5	32	....	....	....	....	....
1984-85	CSKA	USSR	36	3	2	5	26	....	....	....	....	....
1985-86	CSKA	USSR	40	3	5	8	30	....	....	....	....	....
1986-87	CSKA	USSR	38	4	7	11	24	....	....	....	....	....
1987-88	CSKA	USSR	39	3	2	5	28	....	....	....	....	....
1988-89	CSKA	USSR	42	5	4	9	37	....	....	....	....	....
1989-90	CSKA	USSR	42	4	7	11	42	....	....	....	....	....
1990-91	CSKA	USSR	15	0	0	0	12	....	....	....	....	....
	Quebec	NHL	36	3	9	12	12	....	....	....	....	....
	Halifax	AHL	2	0	3	3	2	....	....	....	....	....
1991-92	Quebec	NHL	68	5	18	23	22	....	....	....	....	....
	Halifax	AHL	3	0	0	0	0	....	....	....	....	....
1992-93	Quebec	NHL	79	8	22	30	57	5	0	1	1	0
1993-94	Quebec	NHL	76	5	20	25	38	....	....	....	....	....
1994-95	Quebec	NHL	14	1	2	3	6	....	....	....	....	....
1995-96	Colorado	NHL	65	5	15	20	56	21	0	9	9	12 ♦
	NHL Totals		338	27	86	113	191	26	0	10	10	12

GUSEV, SERGEY

DAL.

Defense. Shoots left. 6'1", 195 lbs.   Born, Nizhny Tagil, USSR, July 31, 1975.
(Dallas' 4th choice, 69th overall, in 1995 Entry Draft).

				Regular Season					Playoffs			
Season	Club	Lea	GP	G	A	TP	PIM	GP	G	A	TP	PIM
1994-95	CSK Samara	CIS	50	3	5	8	58	....	....	....	....	....
1995-96	Michigan	IHL	73	11	17	28	76	....	....	....	....	....

GUSMANOV, RAVIL

CHI.

Left wing. Shoots left. 6'3", 185 lbs.   Born, Naberezhnye Chelny, USSR, July 25, 1972.
(Winnipeg's 5th choice, 93rd overall, in 1993 Entry Draft).

				Regular Season					Playoffs			
Season	Club	Lea	GP	G	A	TP	PIM	GP	G	A	TP	PIM
1990-91	Chelyabinsk	USSR	15	0	0	0	10	....	....	....	....	....
1991-92	Chelyabinsk	CIS	38	4	4	8	20	....	....	....	....	....
1992-93	Chelyabinsk	CIS	39	15	8	23	30	8	4	0	4	2
1993-94	Chelyabinsk	CIS	43	18	9	27	51	6	4	3	7	10
1994-95	Springfield	AHL	72	18	15	33	14	....	....	....	....	....
1995-96	Winnipeg	NHL	4	0	0	0	0	....	....	....	....	....
	Springfield	AHL	60	36	32	68	20	....	....	....	....	....
	Indianapolis	IHL	11	6	10	16	4	5	2	3	5	4
	NHL Totals		4	0	0	0	0	....	....	....	....	....

Traded to **Chicago** by **Winnipeg** for Chicago's fourth round choice (later traded to Toronto — Toronto selected Vladimir Antipov) in 1996 Entry Draft, March 20, 1996.

GUSTAFSSON, PER

FLA.

Defense. Shoots left. 6'2", 190 lbs.   Born, Osterham, Sweden, June 6, 1970.
(Florida's 10th choice, 261st overall, in 1994 Entry Draft).

				Regular Season					Playoffs			
Season	Club	Lea	GP	G	A	TP	PIM	GP	G	A	TP	PIM
1993-94	HV-71	Swe.	34	9	7	16	10	....	....	....	....	....
1994-95	HV-71	Swe.	38	10	6	16	14	13	7	5	12	8
1995-96	HV-71	Swe.	34	8	13	21	12	4	3	1	4	2

GUZIOR, RUSSELL

MTL.

Center. Shoots right. 5'10", 165 lbs.   Born, Chicago, IL, January 12, 1974.
(Montreal's 13th choice, 281st overall, in 1993 Entry Draft).

				Regular Season					Playoffs			
Season	Club	Lea	GP	G	A	TP	PIM	GP	G	A	TP	PIM
1993-94	Providence	H.E.	34	9	13	22	8	....	....	....	....	....
1994-95	Providence	H.E.	9	1	7	8	10	....	....	....	....	....
1995-96	Providence	H.E.	38	20	17	37	24	....	....	....	....	....

HAGGERTY, RYAN

EDM.

Left wing. Shoots left. 6'1", 195 lbs.   Born, Rye, NY, May 2, 1973.
(Edmonton's 6th choice, 93rd overall, in 1991 Entry Draft).

				Regular Season					Playoffs			
Season	Club	Lea	GP	G	A	TP	PIM	GP	G	A	TP	PIM
1991-92	Boston College	H.E.	34	12	5	17	16	....	....	....	....	....
1992-93	Boston College	H.E.	32	6	5	11	12	....	....	....	....	....
1993-94	Boston College	H.E.	36	17	23	40	16	....	....	....	....	....
1994-95	Boston College	H.E.	35	23	22	45	20	....	....	....	....	....
1995-96	Cape Breton	AHL	29	5	6	11	12	....	....	....	....	....
	Wheeling	ECHL	4	0	2	2	0	....	....	....	....	....

HAGGERTY, SEAN

NYI

Left wing. Shoots left. 6'1", 186 lbs.   Born, Rye, NY, February 11, 1976.
(Toronto's 2nd choice, 48th overall, in 1994 Entry Draft).

				Regular Season					Playoffs			
Season	Club	Lea	GP	G	A	TP	PIM	GP	G	A	TP	PIM
1993-94	Detroit	OHL	60	31	32	63	21	17	9	10	19	11
1994-95a	Detroit	OHL	61	40	49	89	37	21	13	24	37	18
1995-96	Toronto	NHL	1	0	0	0	0	....	....	....	....	....
b	Detroit	OHL	66	*60	51	111	78	17	15	9	24	30
	Worcester	AHL	....	....	....	....	....	1	0	0	0	2
	NHL Totals		1	0	0	0	0	....	....	....	....	....

a Memorial Cup All-Star Team (1995)
b OHL Second All-Star Team (1996)

Traded to **NY Islanders** by **Toronto** with Darby Hendrickson, Kenny Jonsson and Toronto's first round choice in 1997 Entry Draft for Wendel Clark, Mathieu Schneider and D.J. Smith, March 13, 1996.

HAJT, CHRIS (HIGHT) EDM.

Defense. Shoots left. 6'3", 206 lbs. Born, Saskatoon, Sask., July 5, 1978.
(Edmonton's 3rd choice, 32nd overall, in 1996 Entry Draft).

			Regular Season					Playoffs				
Season	Club	Lea	GP	G	A	TP	PIM	GP	G	A	TP	PIM
1994-95	Guelph	OHL	57	1	7	8	35	14	0	2	2	9
1995-96	Guelph	OHL	63	8	27	35	69	16	0	6	6	13

HAKANEN, TIMO S.J.

Center. Shoots left. 6'2", 190 lbs. Born, Pori, Finland, March 26, 1977.
(San Jose's 7th choice, 140th overall, in 1995 Entry Draft).

			Regular Season					Playoffs				
Season	Club	Lea	GP	G	A	TP	PIM	GP	G	A	TP	PIM
1994-95	Assat	Fin. Jr.	36	23	21	44	6	5	0	0	0	0
1995-96	Assat	Fin. Jr.	28	8	24	32	6	....	....	....	....	....
	Assat	Fin.	12	0	2	2	0	3	0	0	0	0

HAKANSSON, JONAS PHI.

Left wing. Shoots right. 6'1", 202 lbs. Born, Malmo, Sweden, January 4, 1974.
(Philadelphia's 8th choice, 199th overall, in 1992 Entry Draft).

			Regular Season					Playoffs				
Season	Club	Lea	GP	G	A	TP	PIM	GP	G	A	TP	PIM
1990-91	Malmo	Swe.	8	0	0	0	0	1	0	0	0	0
1991-92	Malmo	Swe. Jr.			UNAVAILABLE							
1992-93	Malmo	Swe.	11	0	0	0	0	....	....	....	....	....
1993-94	Pantern	Swe. 2	26	9	5	14	20	....	....	....	....	....
1994-95	Pantern	Swe. 2	26	2	2	4	10	....	....	....	....	....
1995-96	Pantern	Swe. 2	30	7	6	13	14	....	....	....	....	....

HAKANSSON, MIKAEL TOR.

Center. Shoots left. 6'1", 196 lbs. Born, Stockholm, Sweden, May 31, 1974.
(Toronto's 7th choice, 125th overall, in 1992 Entry Draft).

			Regular Season					Playoffs				
Season	Club	Lea	GP	G	A	TP	PIM	GP	G	A	TP	PIM
1990-91	Nacka	Swe. 2	27	2	5	7	6	....	....	....	....	....
1991-92	Nacka	Swe. 2	29	3	15	18	24	....	....	....	....	....
1992-93	Djurgarden	Swe.	40	0	1	1	6	3	0	0	0	0
1993-94	Djurgarden	Swe.	37	3	3	6	12	4	0	0	0	0
1994-95	MoDo	Swe.	37	3	7	10	16	....	....	....	....	....
1995-96	MoDo	Swe.	40	8	4	12	18	8	2	0	2	0

HALFNIGHT, ASHLIN HFD.

Defense. Shoots left. 6', 180 lbs. Born, Toronto, Ont., March 14, 1975.
(Hartford's 5th choice, 213th overall, in 1994 Entry Draft).

			Regular Season					Playoffs				
Season	Club	Lea	GP	G	A	TP	PIM	GP	G	A	TP	PIM
1992-93	Cdn. National	....	3	1	0	1	2	....	....	....	....	....
1993-94	Harvard	ECAC	30	2	8	10	24	....	....	....	....	....
1994-95	Harvard	ECAC	24	5	15	20	42	....	....	....	....	....
1995-96	Harvard	ECAC	30	2	10	12	12	....	....	....	....	....

HALKIDIS, BOB (hal-KEE-dihs) FLA.

Defense. Shoots left. 5'11", 205 lbs. Born, Toronto, Ont., March 5, 1966.
(Buffalo's 4th choice, 81st overall, in 1984 Entry Draft).

			Regular Season					Playoffs				
Season	Club	Lea	GP	G	A	TP	PIM	GP	G	A	TP	PIM
1983-84	London	OHL	51	9	22	31	123	8	0	2	2	27
1984-85a	London	OHL	62	14	50	64	154	8	3	6	9	22
	Buffalo	**NHL**	....	....	....	....	....	**4**	**0**	**0**	**0**	**19**
1985-86	**Buffalo**	**NHL**	**37**	**1**	**9**	**10**	**115**	....	....	....	....	....
1986-87	**Buffalo**	**NHL**	**6**	**1**	**1**	**2**	**19**	....	....	....	....	....
	Rochester	AHL	59	1	8	9	144	8	0	0	0	43
1987-88	**Buffalo**	**NHL**	**30**	**0**	**3**	**3**	**115**	**4**	**0**	**0**	**0**	**22**
	Rochester	AHL	15	2	5	7	50	....	....	....	....	....
1988-89	**Buffalo**	**NHL**	**16**	**0**	**1**	**1**	**66**	....	....	....	....	....
	Rochester	AHL	16	0	6	6	64	....	....	....	....	....
1989-90	Rochester	AHL	18	1	13	14	70	....	....	....	....	....
	Los Angeles	**NHL**	**20**	**0**	**4**	**4**	**56**	**8**	**0**	**1**	**1**	**8**
	New Haven	AHL	30	3	17	20	67	....	....	....	....	....
1990-91	**Los Angeles**	**NHL**	**34**	**1**	**3**	**4**	**133**	**3**	**0**	**0**	**0**	**0**
	New Haven	AHL	7	1	3	4	10	....	....	....	....	....
	Phoenix	IHL	4	1	5	6	6	....	....	....	....	....
1991-92	**Toronto**	**NHL**	**46**	**3**	**3**	**6**	**145**	....	....	....	....	....
1992-93	St. John's	AHL	29	2	13	15	61	....	....	....	....	....
	Milwaukee	IHL	26	0	9	9	79	5	0	1	1	27
1993-94	**Detroit**	**NHL**	**28**	**1**	**4**	**5**	**93**	**1**	**0**	**0**	**0**	**2**
	Adirondack	AHL	15	0	6	6	46	....	....	....	....	....
1994-95	**Detroit**	**NHL**	**4**	**0**	**1**	**1**	**6**	....	....	....	....	....
	Tampa Bay	**NHL**	**27**	**1**	**3**	**4**	**40**	....	....	....	....	....
1995-96	**Tampa Bay**	**NHL**	**3**	**0**	**0**	**0**	**7**	....	....	....	....	....
	Atlanta	IHL	21	1	7	8	62	....	....	....	....	....
	NY Islanders	**NHL**	**5**	**0**	**0**	**0**	**30**	....	....	....	....	....
	Utah	IHL	27	0	7	7	72	12	1	1	2	36
	NHL Totals		**256**	**8**	**32**	**40**	**825**	**20**	**0**	**1**	**1**	**51**

a OHL First All-Star Team (1985)

Traded to **Los Angeles** by **Buffalo** with future considerations for Dale DeGray and future considerations, November 24, 1989. Signed as a free agent by **Toronto**, July 24, 1991. Signed as a free agent by **Detroit**, September 2, 1993. Claimed on waivers by **Tampa Bay** from **Detroit**, February 10, 1995. Claimed on waivers by **Chicago** from **Tampa Bay**, December 6, 1995. Traded to **NY Islanders** by **Chicago** for Danton Cole, February 2, 1996. Signed as a free agent by **Florida**, July 25, 1996.

HALKO, STEVEN HFD.

Defense. Shoots right. 6'1", 183 lbs. Born, Etobicoke, Ont., March 8, 1974.
(Hartford's 10th choice, 225th overall, in 1992 Entry Draft).

			Regular Season					Playoffs				
Season	Club	Lea	GP	G	A	TP	PIM	GP	G	A	TP	PIM
1992-93	U. of Michigan	CCHA	39	1	12	13	12	....	....	....	....	....
1993-94	U. of Michigan	CCHA	41	2	13	15	32	....	....	....	....	....
1994-95a	U. of Michigan	CCHA	39	2	14	16	20	....	....	....	....	....
1995-96a	U. of Michigan	CCHA	43	4	16	20	32	....	....	....	....	....

a CCHA Second All-Star Team (1995, 1996)

HALL, TODD HFD.

Defense. Shoots left. 6'1", 212 lbs. Born, Hamden, CT, January 22, 1973.
(Hartford's 3rd choice, 53rd overall, in 1991 Entry Draft).

			Regular Season					Playoffs				
Season	Club	Lea	GP	G	A	TP	PIM	GP	G	A	TP	PIM
1991-92	Boston College	H.E.	33	2	10	12	14	....	....	....	....	....
1992-93	Boston College	H.E.	34	2	10	12	22	....	....	....	....	....
1993-94	N. Hampshire	H.E.			DID NOT PLAY							
1994-95	N. Hampshire	H.E.	36	8	18	26	16	....	....	....	....	....
1995-96a	N. Hampshire	H.E.	31	4	26	30	10	....	....	....	....	....

a Hockey East All-Star Team (1996)

HALLER, KEVIN (HAHL-ehr) PHI.

Defense. Shoots left. 6'2", 195 lbs. Born, Trochu, Alta., December 5, 1970.
(Buffalo's 1st choice, 14th overall, in 1989 Entry Draft).

			Regular Season					Playoffs				
Season	Club	Lea	GP	G	A	TP	PIM	GP	G	A	TP	PIM
1988-89	Regina	WHL	72	10	31	41	99	....	....	....	....	....
1989-90	**Buffalo**	**NHL**	**2**	**0**	**0**	**0**	**0**	....	....	....	....	....
a	Regina	WHL	58	16	37	53	93	11	2	9	11	16
1990-91	**Buffalo**	**NHL**	**21**	**1**	**8**	**9**	**20**	**6**	**1**	**4**	**5**	**10**
	Rochester	AHL	52	2	8	10	53	10	2	1	3	6
1991-92	**Buffalo**	**NHL**	**58**	**6**	**15**	**21**	**75**	....	....	....	....	....
	Rochester	AHL	4	0	0	0	18	....	....	....	....	....
	Montreal	**NHL**	**8**	**2**	**2**	**4**	**17**	**9**	**0**	**0**	**0**	**6**
1992-93	**Montreal**	**NHL**	**73**	**11**	**14**	**25**	**117**	**17**	**1**	**6**	**7**	**16** ♦
1993-94	**Montreal**	**NHL**	**68**	**4**	**9**	**13**	**118**	**7**	**1**	**1**	**2**	**19**
1994-95	**Philadelphia**	**NHL**	**36**	**2**	**8**	**10**	**48**	**15**	**4**	**4**	**8**	**10**
1995-96	**Philadelphia**	**NHL**	**69**	**5**	**9**	**14**	**92**	**6**	**0**	**1**	**1**	**8**
	NHL Totals		**335**	**31**	**65**	**96**	**487**	**60**	**7**	**16**	**23**	**69**

a WHL East First All-Star Team (1990)

Traded to **Montreal** by **Buffalo** for Petr Svoboda, March 10, 1992. Traded to **Philadelphia** by **Montreal** for Yves Racine, June 29, 1994.

HAMEL, DENIS BUF.

Left wing. Shoots left. 6'2", 200 lbs. Born, Lachute, Que., May 10, 1977.
(St. Louis' 5th choice, 153rd overall, in 1995 Entry Draft).

			Regular Season					Playoffs				
Season	Club	Lea	GP	G	A	TP	PIM	GP	G	A	TP	PIM
1994-95	Chicoutimi	QMJHL	66	15	12	27	155	12	2	0	2	27
1995-96	Chicoutimi	QMJHL	65	40	49	89	199	17	10	14	24	64

Traded to **Buffalo** by **St. Louis** for Charlie Huddy and Buffalo's seventh round choice (Daniel Corso) in 1996 Entry Draft, March 19, 1996.

HAMILTON, HUGH HFD.

Defense. Shoots left. 6'1", 175 lbs. Born, Saskatoon, Sask., February 11, 1977.
(Hartford's 5th choice, 113th overall, in 1995 Entry Draft).

			Regular Season					Playoffs				
Season	Club	Lea	GP	G	A	TP	PIM	GP	G	A	TP	PIM
1993-94	Spokane	WHL	64	5	9	14	70	3	0	0	0	0
1994-95	Spokane	WHL	60	5	28	33	102	11	3	5	8	16
1995-96	Spokane	WHL	72	11	49	60	92	18	3	5	8	26

HAMR, RADEK (HAM-uhr, RA-dehk)

Defense. Shoots left. 5'11", 175 lbs. Born, Usti-Nad-Labem, Czech., June 15, 1974.
(Ottawa's 4th choice, 73rd overall, in 1992 Entry Draft).

			Regular Season					Playoffs				
Season	Club	Lea	GP	G	A	TP	PIM	GP	G	A	TP	PIM
1991-92	Sparta Praha	Czech.	3	0	0	0	....	....	....	....	....	....
1992-93	**Ottawa**	**NHL**	**4**	**0**	**0**	**0**	**0**	....	....	....	....	....
	New Haven	AHL	59	4	21	25	18	....	....	....	....	....
1993-94	**Ottawa**	**NHL**	**7**	**0**	**0**	**0**	**0**	....	....	....	....	....
	P.E.I.	AHL	69	10	26	36	44	....	....	....	....	....
1994-95	P.E.I.	AHL	7	0	1	1	2	....	....	....	....	....
	Fort Wayne	IHL	58	3	13	16	14	1	0	0	0	0
1995-96	Sparta Praha	Czech.	30	2	3	5	....	4	0	0	0	....
	NHL Totals		**11**	**0**	**0**	**0**	**0**	....	....	....	....	....

HAMRLIK, MARTIN (HAHM-reh-lik)

Defense. Shoots right. 5'11", 185 lbs. Born, Gottwaldov, Czech., May 6, 1973.
(Hartford's 2nd choice, 31st overall, in 1991 Entry Draft).

			Regular Season					Playoffs				
Season	Club	Lea	GP	G	A	TP	PIM	GP	G	A	TP	PIM
1989-90	TJ Zlin	Czech.	11	2	0	2	....	....	....	....	....	....
1990-91	TJ Zlin	Czech.	50	8	14	22	44	....	....	....	....	....
1991-92	ZPS Zlin	Czech.	4	0	2	2	23	....	....	....	....	....
1992-93	Ottawa	OHL	26	4	11	15	41	....	....	....	....	....
	Springfield	AHL	8	1	3	4	16	....	....	....	....	....
1993-94	Springfield	AHL	1	0	0	0	0	....	....	....	....	....
	Peoria	IHL	47	1	11	12	61	6	0	1	1	2
1994-95	Peoria	IHL	77	5	13	18	120	3	0	0	0	2
1995-96	Peoria	IHL	65	6	25	31	91	....	....	....	....	....

Traded to **St. Louis** by **Hartford** for cash, November 12, 1993.

HAMRLIK, ROMAN (HAHM-reh-lik) T.B.

Defense. Shoots left. 6'2", 202 lbs. Born, Gottwaldov, Czech., April 12, 1974.
(Tampa Bay's 1st choice, 1st overall, in 1992 Entry Draft).

			Regular Season					Playoffs				
Season	Club	Lea	GP	G	A	TP	PIM	GP	G	A	TP	PIM
1990-91	TJ Zlin	Czech.	14	2	2	4	18	....	....	....	....	....
1991-92	ZPS Zlin	Czech.	34	5	5	10	50	....	....	....	....	....
1992-93	**Tampa Bay**	**NHL**	**67**	**6**	**15**	**21**	**71**	....	....	....	....	....
	Atlanta	IHL	2	1	1	2	2	....	....	....	....	....
1993-94	**Tampa Bay**	**NHL**	**64**	**3**	**18**	**21**	**135**	....	....	....	....	....
1994-95	ZPS Zlin	Czech.	2	1	0	1	10	....	....	....	....	....
	Tampa Bay	**NHL**	**48**	**12**	**11**	**23**	**86**	....	....	....	....	....
1995-96	**Tampa Bay**	**NHL**	**82**	**16**	**49**	**65**	**103**	**5**	**0**	**1**	**1**	**4**
	NHL Totals		**261**	**37**	**93**	**130**	**395**	**5**	**0**	**1**	**1**	**4**

Played in NHL All-Star Game (1996)

HANDZUS, MICHAL ST.L.

Center. Shoots left. 6'3", 191 lbs. Born, Banska Bystrica, Czech., March 11, 1977.
(St. Louis' 3rd choice, 101st overall, in 1995 Entry Draft).

			Regular Season					Playoffs				
Season	Club	Lea	GP	G	A	TP	PIM	GP	G	A	TP	PIM
1994-95	B. Bystrica	Slov. 2	22	15	14	29	10	....	....	....	....	....
1995-96	B. Bystrica	Slovak	19	3	1	4	8	....	....	....	....	....

HANKINSON, BEN

Right wing. Shoots right. 6'2", 210 lbs. Born, Edina, MN, May 1, 1969.
(New Jersey's 5th choice, 107th overall, in 1987 Entry Draft).

			Regular Season					Playoffs				
Season	Club	Lea	GP	G	A	TP	PIM	GP	G	A	TP	PIM
1987-88	U. Minnesota	WCHA	24	4	7	11	36	....	....	....	....	....
1988-89	U. Minnesota	WCHA	43	7	11	18	115	....	....	....	....	....
1989-90a	U. Minnesota	WCHA	46	25	41	66	34	....	....	....	....	....
1990-91	U. Minnesota	WCHA	43	19	21	40	133	....	....	....	....	....
1991-92	Utica	AHL	77	17	16	33	186	4	3	1	4	2
1992-93	**New Jersey**	**NHL**	**4**	**2**	**1**	**3**	**9**	....	....	....	....	....
	Utica	AHL	75	35	27	62	145	5	2	2	4	6
1993-94	**New Jersey**	**NHL**	**13**	**1**	**0**	**1**	**23**	**2**	**1**	**0**	**1**	**4**
	Albany	AHL	29	9	14	23	80	5	3	1	4	6
1994-95	**New Jersey**	**NHL**	**8**	**0**	**0**	**0**	**7**	....	....	....	....	....
	Albany	AHL	1	1	0	1	6	....	....	....	....	....
	Tampa Bay	**NHL**	**18**	**0**	**2**	**2**	**6**	....	....	....	....	....
1995-96	Adirondack	AHL	75	25	21	46	210	3	0	0	0	8
	NHL Totals		**43**	**3**	**3**	**6**	**45**	**2**	**1**	**0**	**1**	**4**

a WCHA First All-Star Team (1990)

Traded to **Tampa Bay** by **New Jersey** with Alexander Semak for Shawn Chambers and Danton Cole, March 14, 1995. Traded to **Detroit** by **Tampa Bay** with Marc Bergevin for Shawn Burr and Detroit's third round choice (later traded to Boston — Boston selected Jason Doyle) in 1996 Entry Draft, August 17, 1995.

HANKINSON, CASEY — CHI.

Left wing. Shoots left. 6'1", 187 lbs. Born, Edina, MN, May 8, 1976.
(Chicago's 9th choice, 201st overall, in 1995 Entry Draft).

			Regular Season					Playoffs				
Season	Club	Lea	GP	G	A	TP	PIM	GP	G	A	TP	PIM
1994-95	U. Minnesota	WCHA	33	7	1	8	86	....	....	....	....	....
1995-96	U. Minnesota	WCHA	39	16	19	35	101	....	....	....	....	....

HANNAN, DAVE — OTT.

Center. Shoots left. 5'10", 180 lbs. Born, Sudbury, Ont., November 26, 1961.
(Pittsburgh's 9th choice, 196th overall, in 1981 Entry Draft).

			Regular Season					Playoffs				
Season	Club	Lea	GP	G	A	TP	PIM	GP	G	A	TP	PIM
1979-80	S.S. Marie	OHA	28	11	10	21	31	....	....	....	....	....
	Brantford	OHA	25	5	10	15	26	....	....	....	....	....
1980-81	Brantford	OHA	56	46	35	81	155	6	2	4	6	20
1981-82	**Pittsburgh**	**NHL**	**1**	**0**	**0**	**0**	**0**	....	....	....	....	....
	Erie	AHL	76	33	37	70	129	....	....	....	....	....
1982-83	**Pittsburgh**	**NHL**	**74**	**11**	**22**	**33**	**127**	....	....	....	....	....
	Baltimore	AHL	5	2	2	4	13	....	....	....	....	....
1983-84	**Pittsburgh**	**NHL**	**24**	**2**	**3**	**5**	**33**	....	....	....	....	....
	Baltimore	AHL	47	18	24	42	98	10	2	6	8	27
1984-85	**Pittsburgh**	**NHL**	**30**	**6**	**7**	**13**	**43**	....	....	....	....	....
	Baltimore	AHL	49	20	25	45	91	....	....	....	....	....
1985-86	**Pittsburgh**	**NHL**	**75**	**17**	**18**	**35**	**91**	....	....	....	....	....
1986-87	**Pittsburgh**	**NHL**	**58**	**10**	**15**	**25**	**56**	....	....	....	....	....
1987-88	**Pittsburgh**	**NHL**	**21**	**4**	**3**	**7**	**23**	....	....	....	....	....
	Edmonton	**NHL**	**51**	**9**	**11**	**20**	**43**	**12**	**1**	**1**	**2**	**8** ♦
1988-89	**Pittsburgh**	**NHL**	**72**	**10**	**20**	**30**	**157**	**8**	**0**	**1**	**1**	**4**
1989-90	**Toronto**	**NHL**	**39**	**6**	**9**	**15**	**55**	**3**	**1**	**0**	**1**	**4**
1990-91	**Toronto**	**NHL**	**74**	**11**	**23**	**34**	**82**	....	....	....	....	....
1991-92	**Toronto**	**NHL**	**35**	**2**	**2**	**4**	**16**	....	....	....	....	....
	Cdn. National	....	3	0	0	0	2	....	....	....	....	....
	Cdn. Olympic	....	8	3	5	8	8	....	....	....	....	....
	Buffalo	**NHL**	**12**	**2**	**4**	**6**	**48**	**7**	**2**	**0**	**2**	**2**
1992-93	**Buffalo**	**NHL**	**55**	**5**	**15**	**20**	**43**	**8**	**1**	**1**	**2**	**18**
1993-94	**Buffalo**	**NHL**	**83**	**6**	**15**	**21**	**53**	**7**	**1**	**0**	**1**	**6**
1994-95	**Buffalo**	**NHL**	**42**	**4**	**12**	**16**	**32**	**5**	**0**	**2**	**2**	**2**
1995-96	**Buffalo**	**NHL**	**57**	**6**	**10**	**16**	**30**	....	....	....	....	....
	Colorado	**NHL**	**4**	**1**	**0**	**1**	**2**	**13**	**0**	**2**	**2**	**2** ♦
	NHL Totals		**807**	**112**	**189**	**301**	**934**	**63**	**6**	**7**	**13**	**46**

Traded to **Edmonton** by **Pittsburgh** with Craig Simpson, Moe Mantha and Chris Joseph for Paul Coffey, Dave Hunter and Wayne Van Dorp, November 24, 1987. Claimed by **Pittsburgh** from **Edmonton** in NHL Waiver Draft, October 3, 1988. Claimed by **Toronto** from **Pittsburgh** in NHL Waiver Draft, October 2, 1989. Traded to **Buffalo** by **Toronto** for Minnesota's fifth round choice (previously acquired by Buffalo — Toronto selected Chris Deruiter) in 1992 Entry Draft, March 10, 1992. Traded to **Colorado** by **Buffalo** for Colorado's sixth round choice (Darren Mortier) in 1996 Entry Draft, March 20, 1996. Signed as a free agent by **Ottawa**, August 28, 1996.

HANSEN, TAVIS — PHO.

Center. Shoots right. 6'1", 180 lbs. Born, Prince Albert, Sask., June 17, 1975.
(Winnipeg's 3rd choice, 58th overall, in 1994 Entry Draft).

			Regular Season					Playoffs				
Season	Club	Lea	GP	G	A	TP	PIM	GP	G	A	TP	PIM
1993-94	Tacoma	WHL	71	23	31	54	122	8	1	3	4	17
1994-95	Tacoma	WHL	71	32	41	73	142	4	1	1	2	8
	Winnipeg	**NHL**	**1**	**0**	**0**	**0**	**0**	....	....	....	....	....
1995-96	Springfield	AHL	67	6	16	22	85	5	1	2	3	2
	NHL Totals		**1**	**0**	**0**	**0**	**0**	....	....	....	....	....

HARBERTS, TIMOTHY — PIT.

Center. Shoots right. 6'1", 185 lbs. Born, Edina, MN, May 20, 1975.
(Pittsburgh's 9th choice, 234th overall, in 1993 Entry Draft).

			Regular Season					Playoffs				
Season	Club	Lea	GP	G	A	TP	PIM	GP	G	A	TP	PIM
1993-94	Notre Dame	CCHA	36	10	12	22	19	....	....	....	....	....
1994-95	Notre Dame	CCHA	37	21	13	34	4	....	....	....	....	....
1995-96	Notre Dame	CCHA	35	8	17	25	10	....	....	....	....	....

HARDING, MIKE — HFD.

Right wing. Shoots right. 6'4", 225 lbs. Born, Edmonton, Alta., February 24, 1971.
(Hartford's 6th choice, 119th overall, in 1991 Entry Draft).

			Regular Season					Playoffs				
Season	Club	Lea	GP	G	A	TP	PIM	GP	G	A	TP	PIM
1991-92	N. Michigan	WCHA	28	6	8	14	46	....	....	....	....	....
1992-93	N. Michigan	WCHA	39	17	18	35	66	....	....	....	....	....
1993-94a	N. Michigan	WCHA	38	24	25	49	66	....	....	....	....	....
1994-95	N. Michigan	WCHA	40	16	22	38	68	....	....	....	....	....
1995-96	Springfield	AHL	42	5	3	8	50	....	....	....	....	....
	Richmond	ECHL	19	4	4	8	40	....	....	....	....	....

a WCHA Second All-Star Team (1994)

HARKINS, BRETT

Left wing. Shoots left. 6'1", 185 lbs. Born, North Ridgeville, OH, July 2, 1970.
(NY Islanders' 9th choice, 133rd overall, in 1989 Entry Draft).

			Regular Season					Playoffs				
Season	Club	Lea	GP	G	A	TP	PIM	GP	G	A	TP	PIM
1989-90	Bowling Green	CCHA	41	11	43	54	45	....	....	....	....	....
1990-91	Bowling Green	CCHA	40	22	38	60	30	....	....	....	....	....
1991-92	Bowling Green	CCHA	34	8	39	47	32	....	....	....	....	....
1992-93	Bowling Green	CCHA	35	19	28	47	28	....	....	....	....	....
1993-94	Adirondack	AHL	80	22	47	69	23	10	1	5	6	4
1994-95	Providence	AHL	80	23	*69	92	32	13	8	14	22	4
	Boston	**NHL**	**1**	**0**	**1**	**1**	**0**	....	....	....	....	....
1995-96	**Florida**	**NHL**	**8**	**0**	**3**	**3**	**6**	....	....	....	....	....
	Carolina	AHL	55	23	*71	94	44	....	....	....	....	....
	NHL Totals		**9**	**0**	**4**	**4**	**6**	....	....	....	....	....

Signed as a free agent by **Boston**, July 1, 1994. Signed as a free agent by **Florida**, July 24, 1995.

HARKINS, TODD — FLA.

Center. Shoots right. 6'3", 210 lbs. Born, Cleveland, OH, October 8, 1968.
(Calgary's 2nd choice, 42nd overall, in 1988 Entry Draft).

			Regular Season					Playoffs				
Season	Club	Lea	GP	G	A	TP	PIM	GP	G	A	TP	PIM
1987-88	Miami-Ohio	CCHA	34	9	7	16	133	....	....	....	....	....
1988-89	Miami-Ohio	CCHA	36	8	7	15	77	....	....	....	....	....
1989-90	Miami-Ohio	CCHA	40	27	17	44	78	....	....	....	....	....
1990-91	Salt Lake	IHL	79	15	27	42	113	3	0	0	0	0
1991-92	**Calgary**	**NHL**	**5**	**0**	**0**	**0**	**7**	....	....	....	....	....
	Salt Lake	IHL	72	32	30	62	67	5	1	1	2	6
1992-93	**Calgary**	**NHL**	**15**	**2**	**3**	**5**	**22**	....	....	....	....	....
	Salt Lake	IHL	53	13	21	34	90	....	....	....	....	....
1993-94	Saint John	AHL	38	13	9	22	64	....	....	....	....	....
	Hartford	**NHL**	**28**	**1**	**0**	**1**	**49**	....	....	....	....	....
	Springfield	AHL	1	0	3	3	0	....	....	....	....	....
1994-95	Chicago	IHL	52	18	25	43	136	....	....	....	....	....
	Houston	IHL	25	9	10	19	77	4	1	1	2	28
1995-96	Carolina	AHL	69	27	28	55	172	....	....	....	....	....
	NHL Totals		**48**	**3**	**3**	**6**	**78**	....	....	....	....	....

Traded to **Hartford** by **Calgary** for Scott Morrow, January 24, 1994. Signed as a free agent by **Florida**, June 6, 1995.

HARLOCK, DAVID

Defense. Shoots left. 6'2", 205 lbs. Born, Toronto, Ont., March 16, 1971.
(New Jersey's 2nd choice, 24th overall, in 1990 Entry Draft).

			Regular Season					Playoffs				
Season	Club	Lea	GP	G	A	TP	PIM	GP	G	A	TP	PIM
1989-90	U. of Michigan	CCHA	42	2	13	15	44	....	....	....	....	....
1990-91	U. of Michigan	CCHA	39	2	8	10	70	....	....	....	....	....
1991-92	U. of Michigan	CCHA	44	1	6	7	80	....	....	....	....	....
1992-93	U. of Michigan	CCHA	38	3	9	12	58	....	....	....	....	....
	Cdn. National	....	4	0	0	0	2	....	....	....	....	....
1993-94	Cdn. National	....	41	0	3	3	28	....	....	....	....	....
	Cdn. Olympic	....	8	0	0	0	8	....	....	....	....	....
	Toronto	**NHL**	**6**	**0**	**0**	**0**	**0**	....	....	....	....	....
	St. John's	AHL	10	0	3	3	2	9	0	0	0	6
1994-95	St. John's	AHL	58	0	6	6	44	5	0	0	0	0
	Toronto	**NHL**	**1**	**0**	**0**	**0**	**0**	....	....	....	....	....
1995-96	**Toronto**	**NHL**	**1**	**0**	**0**	**0**	**0**	....	....	....	....	....
	St. John's	AHL	77	0	12	12	92	4	0	1	1	2
	NHL Totals		**8**	**0**	**0**	**0**	**0**	....	....	....	....	....

Signed as a free agent by **Toronto**, August 20, 1993.

HARLTON, TYLER — ST.L.

Defense. Shoots left. 6'3", 201 lbs. Born, Pense, Sask., January 11, 1976.
(St. Louis' 2nd choice, 94th overall, in 1994 Entry Draft).

			Regular Season					Playoffs				
Season	Club	Lea	GP	G	A	TP	PIM	GP	G	A	TP	PIM
1994-95	Michigan State	CCHA	39	1	3	4	55	....	....	....	....	....
1995-96	Michigan State	CCHA	39	1	6	7	51	....	....	....	....	....

HART, GREG — MTL.

Right wing. Shoots right. 5'11", 202 lbs. Born, Kamloops, B.C., January 14, 1977.
(Montreal's 8th choice, 190th overall, in 1995 Entry Draft).

			Regular Season					Playoffs				
Season	Club	Lea	GP	G	A	TP	PIM	GP	G	A	TP	PIM
1993-94	Kamloops	WHL	48	5	4	9	16	8	0	0	0	2
1994-95	Kamloops	WHL	60	6	9	15	9	14	3	2	5	0
1995-96	Kamloops	WHL	17	5	2	7	6	....	....	....	....	....

HARTMAN, MIKE

Left wing. Shoots left. 6', 190 lbs. Born, Detroit, MI, February 7, 1967.
(Buffalo's 8th choice, 131st overall, in 1986 Entry Draft).

			Regular Season					Playoffs				
Season	Club	Lea	GP	G	A	TP	PIM	GP	G	A	TP	PIM
1984-85	Belleville	OHL	49	13	12	25	119	....	....	....	....	....
1985-86	Belleville	OHL	4	2	1	3	5	....	....	....	....	....
	North Bay	OHL	53	19	16	35	205	10	2	4	6	34
1986-87	**Buffalo**	**NHL**	**17**	**3**	**3**	**6**	**69**	....	....	....	....	....
	North Bay	OHL	32	15	24	39	144	19	7	8	15	88
1987-88	**Buffalo**	**NHL**	**18**	**3**	**1**	**4**	**90**	**6**	**0**	**0**	**0**	**35**
	Rochester	AHL	57	13	14	27	283	4	1	0	1	22
1988-89	**Buffalo**	**NHL**	**70**	**8**	**9**	**17**	**316**	**5**	**0**	**0**	**0**	**34**
1989-90	**Buffalo**	**NHL**	**60**	**11**	**10**	**21**	**211**	**6**	**0**	**0**	**0**	**18**
1990-91	**Buffalo**	**NHL**	**60**	**9**	**3**	**12**	**204**	**2**	**0**	**0**	**0**	**17**
1991-92	**Winnipeg**	**NHL**	**75**	**4**	**4**	**8**	**264**	**2**	**0**	**0**	**0**	**2**
1992-93	**Tampa Bay**	**NHL**	**58**	**4**	**4**	**8**	**154**	....	....	....	....	....
	NY Rangers	**NHL**	**3**	**0**	**0**	**0**	**6**	....	....	....	....	....
1993-94	**NY Rangers**	**NHL**	**35**	**1**	**1**	**2**	**70**	....	....	....	....	.... ♦
1994-95	**NY Rangers**	**NHL**	**1**	**0**	**0**	**0**	**4**	....	....	....	....	....
	Detroit	IHL	6	1	0	1	52	1	0	0	0	0
1995-96	Orlando	IHL	77	14	10	24	243	21	2	2	4	31
	NHL Totals		**397**	**43**	**35**	**78**	**1388**	**21**	**0**	**0**	**0**	**106**

Traded to **Winnipeg** by **Buffalo** with Darrin Shannon and Dean Kennedy for Dave McLlwain, Gord Donnelly, Winnipeg's fifth round choice (Yuri Khmylev) in 1992 Entry Draft and future considerations, October 11, 1991. Claimed by **Tampa Bay** from **Winnipeg** in Expansion Draft, June 18, 1992. Traded to **NY Rangers** by **Tampa Bay** for Randy Gilhen, March 22, 1993.

HARVEY, TODD — DAL.

Center. Shoots right. 6', 195 lbs. Born, Hamilton, Ont., February 17, 1975.
(Dallas' 1st choice, 9th overall, in 1993 Entry Draft).

			Regular Season					Playoffs				
Season	Club	Lea	GP	G	A	TP	PIM	GP	G	A	TP	PIM
1991-92	Detroit	OHL	58	21	43	64	141	7	3	5	8	30
1992-93	Detroit	OHL	55	50	50	100	83	15	9	12	21	39
1993-94	Detroit	OHL	49	34	51	85	75	17	10	12	22	26
1994-95	Detroit	OHL	11	8	14	22	12	....	....	....	....	....
	Dallas	**NHL**	**40**	**11**	**9**	**20**	**67**	**5**	**0**	**0**	**0**	**8**
1995-96	**Dallas**	**NHL**	**69**	**9**	**20**	**29**	**136**	....	....	....	....	....
	Michigan	IHL	5	1	3	4	8	....	....	....	....	....
	NHL Totals		**109**	**20**	**29**	**49**	**203**	**5**	**0**	**0**	**0**	**8**

HATCHER, DERIAN — DAL.

Defense. Shoots left. 6'5", 225 lbs. Born, Sterling Heights, MI, June 4, 1972.
(Minnesota's 1st choice, 8th overall, in 1990 Entry Draft).

			Regular Season					Playoffs				
Season	Club	Lea	GP	G	A	TP	PIM	GP	G	A	TP	PIM
1989-90	North Bay	OHL	64	14	38	52	81	5	2	3	5	8
1990-91	North Bay	OHL	64	13	49	62	163	10	2	10	12	28
1991-92	**Minnesota**	**NHL**	**43**	**8**	**4**	**12**	**88**	**5**	**0**	**2**	**2**	**8**
1992-93	**Minnesota**	**NHL**	**67**	**4**	**15**	**19**	**178**	....	....	....	....	....
	Kalamazoo	IHL	2	1	2	3	21	....	....	....	....	....
1993-94	**Dallas**	**NHL**	**83**	**12**	**19**	**31**	**211**	**9**	**0**	**2**	**2**	**14**
1994-95	**Dallas**	**NHL**	**43**	**5**	**11**	**16**	**105**	....	....	....	....	....
1995-96	**Dallas**	**NHL**	**79**	**8**	**23**	**31**	**129**	....	....	....	....	....
	NHL Totals		**315**	**37**	**72**	**109**	**711**	**14**	**0**	**4**	**4**	**22**

HATCHER, KEVIN — PIT.

Defense. Shoots right. 6'4", 225 lbs. Born, Detroit, MI, September 9, 1966.
(Washington's 1st choice, 17th overall, in 1984 Entry Draft).

			Regular Season					Playoffs				
Season	Club	Lea	GP	G	A	TP	PIM	GP	G	A	TP	PIM
1983-84	North Bay	OHL	67	10	39	49	61	4	2	2	4	11
1984-85	**Washington**	**NHL**	**2**	**1**	**0**	**1**	**0**	**1**	**0**	**0**	**0**	**0**
a	North Bay	OHL	58	26	37	63	75	8	3	8	11	9
1985-86	**Washington**	**NHL**	**79**	**9**	**10**	**19**	**119**	**9**	**1**	**1**	**2**	**19**
1986-87	**Washington**	**NHL**	**78**	**8**	**16**	**24**	**144**	**7**	**1**	**0**	**1**	**20**
1987-88	**Washington**	**NHL**	**71**	**14**	**27**	**41**	**137**	**14**	**5**	**7**	**12**	**55**
1988-89	**Washington**	**NHL**	**62**	**13**	**27**	**40**	**101**	**6**	**1**	**4**	**5**	**20**
1989-90	**Washington**	**NHL**	**80**	**13**	**41**	**54**	**102**	**11**	**0**	**8**	**8**	**32**
1990-91	**Washington**	**NHL**	**79**	**24**	**50**	**74**	**69**	**11**	**3**	**3**	**6**	**8**
1991-92	**Washington**	**NHL**	**79**	**17**	**37**	**54**	**105**	**7**	**2**	**4**	**6**	**19**
1992-93	**Washington**	**NHL**	**83**	**34**	**45**	**79**	**114**	**6**	**0**	**1**	**1**	**14**
1993-94	**Washington**	**NHL**	**72**	**16**	**24**	**40**	**108**	**11**	**3**	**4**	**7**	**37**
1994-95	**Dallas**	**NHL**	**47**	**10**	**19**	**29**	**66**	**5**	**2**	**1**	**3**	**2**
1995-96	**Dallas**	**NHL**	**74**	**15**	**26**	**41**	**58**	....	....	....	....	....
	NHL Totals		**806**	**174**	**322**	**496**	**1123**	**88**	**18**	**33**	**51**	**226**

a OHL Second All-Star Team (1985)

Played in NHL All-Star Game (1990, 1991, 1992, 1996)

Traded to **Dallas** by **Washington** for Mark Tinordi and Rick Mrozik, January 18, 1995. Traded to **Pittsburgh** by **Dallas** for Sergei Zubov, June 22, 1996.

HAUER, BRETT — EDM.

Defense. Shoots right. 6'2", 200 lbs. Born, Richfield, MN, July 11, 1971.
(Vancouver's 3rd choice, 71st overall, in 1989 Entry Draft).

			Regular Season					Playoffs				
Season	Club	Lea	GP	G	A	TP	PIM	GP	G	A	TP	PIM
1989-90	Minn.-Duluth	WCHA	37	2	6	8	44	....	....	....	....	....
1990-91	Minn.-Duluth	WCHA	30	1	7	8	54	....	....	....	....	....
1991-92	Minn.-Duluth	WCHA	33	8	14	22	40	....	....	....	....	....
1992-93ab	Minn. Duluth	WCHA	40	10	46	56	52	....	....	....	....	....
1993-94	U.S. National	....	57	6	14	20	88	....	....	....	....	....
	U.S. Olympic	....	8	0	0	0	10	....	....	....	....	....
	Las Vegas	IHL	21	0	7	7	8	1	0	0	0	0
1994-95	AIK	Swe.	37	1	3	4	38	....	....	....	....	....
1995-96	**Edmonton**	**NHL**	**29**	**4**	**2**	**6**	**30**	....	....	....	....	....
	Cape Breton	AHL	17	3	5	8	29	....	....	....	....	....
	NHL Totals		**29**	**4**	**2**	**6**	**30**	....	....	....	....	....

a WCHA First All-Star Team (1993)
b NCAA West First All-American Team (1993)

Traded to **Edmonton** by **Vancouver** for a conditional draft choice, August 24, 1995.

HAWERCHUK, DALE (HOW-uhr-CHUHK) — PHI.

Center. Shoots left. 5'11", 190 lbs. Born, Toronto, Ont., April 4, 1963.
(Winnipeg's 1st choice, 1st overall, in 1981 Entry Draft).

			Regular Season					Playoffs				
Season	Club	Lea	GP	G	A	TP	PIM	GP	G	A	TP	PIM
1979-80a	Cornwall	QJHL	72	37	66	103	21	18	20	25	45	0
1980-81bcd	Cornwall	QJHL	72	81	102	183	69	19	15	20	35	8
1981-82e	**Winnipeg**	**NHL**	**80**	**45**	**58**	**103**	**47**	**4**	**1**	**7**	**8**	**5**
1982-83	**Winnipeg**	**NHL**	**79**	**40**	**51**	**91**	**31**	**3**	**1**	**4**	**5**	**8**
1983-84	**Winnipeg**	**NHL**	**80**	**37**	**65**	**102**	**73**	**3**	**1**	**1**	**2**	**0**
1984-85f	**Winnipeg**	**NHL**	**80**	**53**	**77**	**130**	**74**	**3**	**2**	**1**	**3**	**4**
1985-86	**Winnipeg**	**NHL**	**80**	**46**	**59**	**105**	**44**	**3**	**0**	**3**	**3**	**0**
1986-87	**Winnipeg**	**NHL**	**80**	**47**	**53**	**100**	**52**	**10**	**5**	**8**	**13**	**4**
1987-88	**Winnipeg**	**NHL**	**80**	**44**	**77**	**121**	**59**	**5**	**3**	**4**	**7**	**16**
1988-89	**Winnipeg**	**NHL**	**75**	**41**	**55**	**96**	**28**	....	....	....	....	....
1989-90	**Winnipeg**	**NHL**	**79**	**26**	**55**	**81**	**60**	**7**	**3**	**5**	**8**	**2**
1990-91	**Buffalo**	**NHL**	**80**	**31**	**58**	**89**	**32**	**6**	**2**	**4**	**6**	**10**
1991-92	**Buffalo**	**NHL**	**77**	**23**	**75**	**98**	**27**	**7**	**2**	**5**	**7**	**0**
1992-93	**Buffalo**	**NHL**	**81**	**16**	**80**	**96**	**52**	**8**	**5**	**9**	**14**	**2**
1993-94	**Buffalo**	**NHL**	**81**	**35**	**51**	**86**	**91**	**7**	**0**	**7**	**7**	**4**
1994-95	**Buffalo**	**NHL**	**23**	**5**	**11**	**16**	**2**	**2**	**0**	**0**	**0**	**0**
1995-96	**St. Louis**	**NHL**	**66**	**13**	**28**	**41**	**22**	....	....	....	....	....
	Philadelphia	**NHL**	**16**	**4**	**16**	**20**	**4**	**12**	**3**	**6**	**9**	**12**
	NHL Totals		**1137**	**506**	**869**	**1375**	**698**	**80**	**28**	**64**	**92**	**67**

a Won George Parsons Trophy (Memorial Cup Tournament Most Sportsmanlike Player) (1980)
b QMJHL First All-Star Team (1981)
c Canadian Major Junior Player of the Year (1981)
d Won Stafford Smythe Memorial Trophy (Memorial Cup Tournament MVP) (1981)
e Won Calder Memorial Trophy (1982)
f NHL Second All-Star Team (1985)

Played in NHL All-Star Game (1982, 1985, 1986, 1988)

Traded to **Buffalo** by **Winnipeg** with Winnipeg's first round choice (Brad May) in 1990 Entry Draft and future considerations for Phil Housley, Scott Arniel, Jeff Parker and Buffalo's first round choice (Keith Tkachuk) in 1990 Entry Draft, June 16, 1990. Signed as a free agent by **St. Louis**, September 8, 1995. Traded to **Philadelphia** by **St. Louis** for Craig MacTavish, March 15, 1996.

HAWGOOD, GREG (HAW-guhd)

Defense. Shoots left. 5'10", 190 lbs. Born, Edmonton, Alta., August 10, 1968.
(Boston's 9th choice, 202nd overall, in 1986 Entry Draft).

			Regular Season					Playoffs				
Season	Club	Lea	GP	G	A	TP	PIM	GP	G	A	TP	PIM
1983-84	Kamloops	WHL	49	10	23	33	39	....	....	....	....	....
1984-85	Kamloops	WHL	66	25	40	65	72	....	....	....	....	....
1985-86a	Kamloops	WHL	71	34	85	119	86	16	9	22	31	16
1986-87a	Kamloops	WHL	61	30	93	123	139	....	....	....	....	....
1987-88	**Boston**	**NHL**	**1**	**0**	**0**	**0**	**0**	**3**	**1**	**0**	**1**	**0**
ab	Kamloops	WHL	63	48	85	133	142	16	10	16	26	33
1988-89	**Boston**	**NHL**	**56**	**16**	**24**	**40**	**84**	**10**	**0**	**2**	**2**	**2**
	Maine	AHL	21	2	9	11	41	....	....	....	....	....
1989-90	**Boston**	**NHL**	**77**	**11**	**27**	**38**	**76**	**15**	**1**	**3**	**4**	**12**
1990-91	Asiago	Italy	2	3	0	3	9	....	....	....	....	....
	Edmonton	**NHL**	**6**	**0**	**1**	**1**	**6**	....	....	....	....	....
	Maine	AHL	5	0	1	1	13	....	....	....	....	....
	Cape Breton	AHL	55	10	32	42	73	4	0	3	3	23
1991-92	**Edmonton**	**NHL**	**20**	**2**	**11**	**13**	**22**	**13**	**0**	**3**	**3**	**23**
cd	Cape Breton	AHL	56	20	55	75	26	3	2	2	4	0
1992-93	**Edmonton**	**NHL**	**29**	**5**	**13**	**18**	**35**	....	....	....	....	....
	Philadelphia	**NHL**	**40**	**6**	**22**	**28**	**39**	....	....	....	....	....
1993-94	**Philadelphia**	**NHL**	**19**	**3**	**12**	**15**	**19**	....	....	....	....	....
	Florida	**NHL**	**33**	**2**	**14**	**16**	**9**	....	....	....	....	....
	Pittsburgh	**NHL**	**12**	**1**	**2**	**3**	**8**	**1**	**0**	**0**	**0**	**0**
1994-95	**Pittsburgh**	**NHL**	**21**	**1**	**4**	**5**	**25**	....	....	....	....	....
	Cleveland	IHL	....	....	....	....	....	3	1	0	1	4
1995-96ef	Las Vegas	IHL	78	20	65	85	101	15	5	11	16	24
	NHL Totals		**314**	**47**	**130**	**177**	**323**	**42**	**2**	**8**	**10**	**37**

a WHL West All-Star Team (1986, 1987, 1988)
b Canadian Major Junior Defenseman of the Year (1988)
c AHL First All-Star Team (1992)
d Won Eddie Shore Plaque (Top Defenseman - AHL) (1992)
e IHL First All-Star Team (1996)
f Won Governors' Trophy (Top Defenseman - IHL) (1996)

Traded to **Edmonton** by **Boston** for Vladimir Ruzicka, October 22, 1990. Traded to **Philadelphia** by **Edmonton** with Josef Beranek for Brian Benning, January 16, 1993. Traded to **Florida** by **Philadelphia** for cash, November 30, 1993. Traded to **Pittsburgh** by **Florida** for Jeff Daniels, March 19, 1994.

HAWKINS, TODD

Left/Right wing. Shoots right. 6'1", 195 lbs. Born, Kingston, Ont., August 2, 1966.
(Vancouver's 10th choice, 217th overall, in 1986 Entry Draft).

			Regular Season					Playoffs				
Season	Club	Lea	GP	G	A	TP	PIM	GP	G	A	TP	PIM
1984-85	Belleville	OHL	58	7	16	23	117	12	1	0	1	10
1985-86	Belleville	OHL	60	14	13	27	172	24	9	7	16	60
1986-87	Belleville	OHL	60	47	40	87	187	6	3	5	8	16
1987-88	Flint	IHL	50	13	13	26	337	16	3	5	8	*174
	Fredericton	AHL	2	0	4	4	11	....	....	....	....	....
1988-89	**Vancouver**	**NHL**	**4**	**0**	**0**	**0**	**9**	....	....	....	....	....
	Milwaukee	IHL	63	12	14	26	307	9	1	0	1	33
1989-90	**Vancouver**	**NHL**	**4**	**0**	**0**	**0**	**6**	....	....	....	....	....
	Milwaukee	IHL	61	23	17	40	273	5	4	1	5	19
1990-91	Newmarket	AHL	22	2	5	7	66	....	....	....	....	....
	Milwaukee	IHL	39	9	11	20	134	....	....	....	....	....
1991-92	**Toronto**	**NHL**	**2**	**0**	**0**	**0**	**0**	....	....	....	....	....
	St. John's	AHL	66	30	27	57	139	7	1	0	1	10
1992-93	St. John's	AHL	72	21	41	62	103	9	1	3	4	10
1993-94	Cleveland	IHL	76	19	14	33	115	....	....	....	....	....
1994-95	Cleveland	IHL	4	2	0	2	29	....	....	....	....	....
	Minnesota	IHL	47	10	8	18	95	3	0	1	1	12
1995-96	Cincinnati	IHL	73	16	12	28	65	17	7	4	11	32
	NHL Totals		**10**	**0**	**0**	**0**	**15**	....	....	....	....	....

Traded to **Toronto** by **Vancouver** for Brian Blad, January 22, 1991. Signed as a free agent by **Pittsburgh**, August 20, 1993.

HAY, DWAYNE — WSH.

Left wing. Shoots left. 6'1", 183 lbs. Born, London, Ont., February 11, 1977.
(Washington's 3rd choice, 43rd overall, in 1995 Entry Draft).

			Regular Season					Playoffs				
Season	Club	Lea	GP	G	A	TP	PIM	GP	G	A	TP	PIM
1994-95	Guelph	OHL	65	26	28	54	37	14	5	7	12	6
1995-96	Guelph	OHL	60	28	30	58	49	16	4	9	13	18

HEALEY, PAUL — PHI.

Right wing. Shoots right. 6'2", 196 lbs. Born, Edmonton, Alta., March 20, 1975.
(Philadelphia's 7th choice, 192nd overall, in 1993 Entry Draft).

			Regular Season					Playoffs				
Season	Club	Lea	GP	G	A	TP	PIM	GP	G	A	TP	PIM
1992-93	Prince Albert	WHL	72	12	20	32	66	....	....	....	....	....
1993-94	Prince Albert	WHL	63	23	26	49	70	....	....	....	....	....
1994-95a	Prince Albert	WHL	71	43	50	93	67	12	3	4	7	2
1995-96	Hershey	AHL	60	7	15	22	35	....	....	....	....	....

a WHL East Second All-Star Team (1995)

HECHT, JOCHEN — ST.L.

Center. Shoots left. 6'1", 180 lbs. Born, Mannheim, Germany, June 21, 1977.
(St. Louis' 1st choice, 49th overall, in 1995 Entry Draft).

			Regular Season					Playoffs				
Season	Club	Lea	GP	G	A	TP	PIM	GP	G	A	TP	PIM
1994-95	Mannheim	Ger.	43	11	12	23	68	10	5	4	9	12
1995-96	Mannheim	Ger.	44	12	16	28	68	8	3	2	5	6

HEDICAN, BRET — VAN.

Defense. Shoots left. 6'2", 195 lbs. Born, St. Paul, MN, August 10, 1970.
(St. Louis' 10th choice, 198th overall, in 1988 Entry Draft).

			Regular Season					Playoffs				
Season	Club	Lea	GP	G	A	TP	PIM	GP	G	A	TP	PIM
1988-89	St. Cloud	NCAA	28	5	3	8	28	....	....	....	....	....
1989-90	St. Cloud	NCAA	36	4	17	21	37	....	....	....	....	....
1990-91a	St. Cloud	WCHA	41	21	26	47	26	....	....	....	....	....
1991-92	U.S. National	....	54	1	8	9	59	....	....	....	....	....
	U.S. Olympic	....	8	0	0	0	4	....	....	....	....	....
	St. Louis	NHL	4	1	0	1	0	5	0	0	0	0
1992-93	St. Louis	NHL	42	0	8	8	30	10	0	0	0	14
	Peoria	IHL	19	0	8	8	10	....	....	....	....	....
1993-94	St. Louis	NHL	61	0	11	11	64	....	....	....	....	....
	Vancouver	NHL	8	0	1	1	0	24	1	6	7	16
1994-95	Vancouver	NHL	45	2	11	13	34	11	0	2	2	6
1995-96	Vancouver	NHL	77	6	23	29	83	6	0	1	1	10
	NHL Totals		237	9	54	63	211	56	1	9	10	46

a WCHA First All-Star Team (1991)

Traded to **Vancouver** by **St. Louis** with Jeff Brown and Nathan Lafayette for Craig Janney, March 21, 1994.

HEINZE, STEPHEN — (HIGHNS) BOS.

Right wing. Shoots right. 5'11", 193 lbs. Born, Lawrence, MA, January 30, 1970.
(Boston's 2nd choice, 60th overall, in 1988 Entry Draft).

			Regular Season					Playoffs				
Season	Club	Lea	GP	G	A	TP	PIM	GP	G	A	TP	PIM
1988-89	Boston College	H.E.	36	26	23	49	26	....	....	....	....	....
1989-90ab	Boston College	H.E.	40	27	36	63	41	....	....	....	....	....
1990-91	Boston College	H.E.	35	21	26	47	35	....	....	....	....	....
1991-92	U.S. National	....	49	18	15	33	38	....	....	....	....	....
	U.S. Olympic	....	8	1	3	4	8	....	....	....	....	....
	Boston	NHL	14	3	4	7	6	7	0	3	3	17
1992-93	Boston	NHL	73	18	13	31	24	4	1	1	2	2
1993-94	Boston	NHL	77	10	11	21	32	13	2	3	5	7
1994-95	Boston	NHL	36	7	9	16	23	5	0	0	0	0
1995-96	Boston	NHL	76	16	12	28	43	5	1	1	2	4
	NHL Totals		276	54	49	103	128	34	4	8	12	30

a Hockey East First All-Star Team (1990)
b NCAA East First All-American Team (1990)

HEJDUK, MILAN — (HEHI-duhk) COL.

Right wing. Shoots right. 5'11", 163 lbs. Born, Usti-nad-Labem, Czech., February 14, 1976.
(Quebec's 6th choice, 87th overall, in 1994 Entry Draft).

			Regular Season					Playoffs				
Season	Club	Lea	GP	G	A	TP	PIM	GP	G	A	TP	PIM
1993-94	Pardubice	Czech.	22	6	3	9	....	10	5	1	6	....
1994-95	Pardubice	Czech.	43	11	13	24	6	6	3	1	4	0
1995-96	Pardubice	Czech.	37	13	7	20	....	....	....	....	....	....

HELENIUS, SAMI — CGY.

Defense. Shoots left. 6'5", 225 lbs. Born, Helsinki, Finland, January 22, 1974.
(Calgary's 5th choice, 102nd overall, in 1992 Entry Draft).

			Regular Season					Playoffs				
Season	Club	Lea	GP	G	A	TP	PIM	GP	G	A	TP	PIM
1992-93	Jokerit	Fin.	1	0	0	0	0	....	....	....	....	....
1993-94	Reipas	Fin.	37	2	3	5	46	....	....	....	....	....
1994-95	Saint John	AHL	69	2	5	7	217	....	....	....	....	....
1995-96	Saint John	AHL	68	0	3	3	231	10	0	0	0	9

HELMER, BRYAN — N.J.

Defense. Shoots right. 6'1", 200 lbs. Born, Sault Ste. Marie, Ont., July 15, 1972.

			Regular Season					Playoffs				
Season	Club	Lea	GP	G	A	TP	PIM	GP	G	A	TP	PIM
1993-94	Albany	AHL	65	4	19	23	79	5	0	0	0	9
1994-95	Albany	AHL	77	7	36	43	101	7	1	0	1	0
1995-96	Albany	AHL	80	14	30	44	107	4	2	0	2	6

Signed as a free agent by **New Jersey**, July 10, 1994.

HEMENWAY, KEN — PHI.

Defense. Shoots right. 6'1", 187 lbs. Born, Boston, MA, August 1, 1975.
(Philadelphia's 11th choice, 270th overall, in 1993 Entry Draft).

			Regular Season					Playoffs				
Season	Club	Lea	GP	G	A	TP	PIM	GP	G	A	TP	PIM
1994-95	Boston College	H.E.	32	4	6	10	24	....	....	....	....	....
1995-96	Boston College	H.E.	36	12	13	25	26	....	....	....	....	....

HENDRICKSON, DANIEL — WSH.

Right wing. Shoots right. 5'10", 180 lbs. Born, Minneapolis, MN, December 26, 1974.
(Washington's 5th choice, 173rd overall, in 1993 Entry Draft).

			Regular Season					Playoffs				
Season	Club	Lea	GP	G	A	TP	PIM	GP	G	A	TP	PIM
1993-94	U. Minnesota	WCHA	39	3	2	5	60	....	....	....	....	....
1994-95	U. Minnesota	WCHA	40	4	13	17	69	....	....	....	....	....
1995-96	U. Minnesota	WCHA	23	2	3	5	29	....	....	....	....	....

HENDRICKSON, DARBY — NYI

Center. Shoots left. 6', 185 lbs. Born, Richfield, MN, August 28, 1972.
(Toronto's 3rd choice, 73rd overall, in 1990 Entry Draft).

			Regular Season					Playoffs				
Season	Club	Lea	GP	G	A	TP	PIM	GP	G	A	TP	PIM
1991-92	U. Minnesota	WCHA	41	25	28	53	61	....	....	....	....	....
1992-93	U. Minnesota	WCHA	31	12	15	27	35	....	....	....	....	....
1993-94	U.S. National	....	59	12	16	28	30	....	....	....	....	....
	U.S. Olympic	....	8	0	0	0	6	....	....	....	....	....
	St. John's	AHL	6	4	1	5	4	3	1	1	2	0
	Toronto	NHL	....	....	....	....	....	2	0	0	0	0
1994-95	St. John's	AHL	59	16	20	36	48	....	....	....	....	....
	Toronto	NHL	8	0	1	1	4	....	....	....	....	....
1995-96	Toronto	NHL	46	6	6	12	47	....	....	....	....	....
	NY Islanders	NHL	16	1	4	5	33	....	....	....	....	....
	NHL Totals		70	7	11	18	84	2	0	0	0	0

Traded to **NY Islanders** by **Toronto** with Sean Haggerty, Kenny Jonsson and Toronto's first round choice in 1997 Entry Draft for Wendel Clark, Mathieu Schneider and D.J. Smith, March 13, 1996.

HERBERS, IAN

Defense. Shoots left. 6'4", 225 lbs. Born, Jasper, Alta., July 18, 1967.
(Buffalo's 11th choice, 190th overall, in 1987 Entry Draft).

			Regular Season					Playoffs				
Season	Club	Lea	GP	G	A	TP	PIM	GP	G	A	TP	PIM
1984-85	Kelowna	WHL	68	3	14	17	120	6	0	1	1	9
1985-86	Spokane	WHL	29	1	6	7	85	....	....	....	....	....
	Lethbridge	WHL	32	1	4	5	109	10	1	0	1	37
1986-87	Swift Current	WHL	72	5	8	13	230	4	1	1	2	12
1987-88	Swift Current	WHL	56	5	14	19	238	4	0	2	2	4
1988-89	U. of Alberta	CWUAA	47	4	22	26	137	....	....	....	....	....
1989-90	U. of Alberta	CWUAA	45	5	31	36	83	....	....	....	....	....
1990-91a	U. of Alberta	CWUAA	45	6	24	30	87	....	....	....	....	....
1991-92a	U. of Alberta	CWUAA	43	14	34	48	86	....	....	....	....	....
1992-93	Cape Breton	AHL	77	7	15	22	129	10	0	1	1	16
1993-94	Edmonton	NHL	22	0	2	2	32	....	....	....	....	....
	Cape Breton	AHL	53	7	16	23	122	5	0	3	3	12
1994-95	Cape Breton	AHL	36	1	11	12	104	....	....	....	....	....
	Detroit	IHL	37	1	5	6	46	5	1	1	2	6
1995-96	Detroit	IHL	73	3	11	14	140	12	3	5	8	29
	NHL Totals		22	0	2	2	32	....	....	....	....	....

a CIAU All-Canadian Team (1991, 1992)

Signed as a free agent by **Edmonton**, September 9, 1992.

HERPERGER, CHRIS — ANA.

Left wing. Shoots left. 6', 190 lbs. Born, Esterhazy, Sask., February 24, 1974.
(Philadelphia's 10th choice, 223rd overall, in 1992 Entry Draft).

			Regular Season					Playoffs				
Season	Club	Lea	GP	G	A	TP	PIM	GP	G	A	TP	PIM
1990-91	Swift Current	WHL	10	0	1	1	5	....	....	....	....	....
1991-92	Swift Current	WHL	72	14	19	33	44	8	0	1	1	9
1992-93	Swift Current	WHL	20	9	7	16	31	....	....	....	....	....
	Seattle	WHL	46	20	11	31	30	5	1	1	2	6
1993-94	Seattle	WHL	71	44	51	95	110	9	12	10	22	12
1994-95a	Seattle	WHL	59	49	52	101	106	4	4	0	4	6
	Hershey	AHL	4	0	0	0	0	....	....	....	....	....
1995-96	Hershey	AHL	46	8	12	20	36	....	....	....	....	....
	Baltimore	AHL	21	2	3	5	17	9	2	3	5	6

a WHL West Second All-Star Team (1995)

Traded to **Anaheim** by **Philadelphia** with Winnipeg's seventh round choice (previously acquired by Philadelphia) in 1997 Entry Draft for Bob Corkum, February 6, 1996.

HERR, MATT — WSH.

Center. Shoots left. 6'1", 180 lbs. Born, Hackensack, NJ, May 26, 1976.
(Washington's 4th choice, 93rd overall, in 1994 Entry Draft).

			Regular Season					Playoffs				
Season	Club	Lea	GP	G	A	TP	PIM	GP	G	A	TP	PIM
1994-95	U. of Michigan	CCHA	37	11	8	19	51	....	....	....	....	....
1995-96	U. of Michigan	CCHA	40	18	13	31	55	....	....	....	....	....

HERTER, JASON

Defense. Shoots right. 6'1", 190 lbs. Born, Hafford, Sask., October 2, 1970.
(Vancouver's 1st choice, 8th overall, in 1989 Entry Draft).

			Regular Season					Playoffs				
Season	Club	Lea	GP	G	A	TP	PIM	GP	G	A	TP	PIM
1988-89	North Dakota	WCHA	41	8	24	32	62	....	....	....	....	....
1989-90a	North Dakota	WCHA	38	11	39	50	40	....	....	....	....	....
1990-91a	North Dakota	WCHA	39	11	26	37	52	....	....	....	....	....
1991-92	Milwaukee	IHL	56	7	18	25	34	1	0	0	0	2
1992-93	Hamilton	AHL	70	7	16	23	68	....	....	....	....	....
1993-94	Kalamazoo	IHL	68	14	28	42	92	5	3	0	3	14
1994-95	Kalamazoo	IHL	60	12	20	32	70	16	2	8	10	10
1995-96	NY Islanders	NHL	1	0	1	1	0	....	....	....	....	....
	Utah	IHL	74	14	31	45	58	20	4	10	14	8
	NHL Totals		1	0	1	1	0	....	....	....	....	....

a WCHA Second All-Star Team (1990, 1991)

Signed as a free agent by **Dallas**, August 6, 1993. Traded to **NY Islanders** by **Dallas** for cash, September 21, 1995.

HEWARD, JAMIE — TOR.

Defense. Shoots right. 6'2", 207 lbs. Born, Regina, Sask., March 30, 1971.
(Pittsburgh's 1st choice, 16th overall, in 1989 Entry Draft).

			Regular Season					Playoffs				
Season	Club	Lea	GP	G	A	TP	PIM	GP	G	A	TP	PIM
1987-88	Regina	WHL	68	10	17	27	17	4	1	1	2	2
1988-89	Regina	WHL	52	31	28	59	29	....	....	....	....	....
1989-90	Regina	WHL	72	14	44	58	42	11	2	2	4	10
1990-91a	Regina	WHL	71	23	61	84	41	8	2	9	11	6
1991-92	Muskegon	IHL	54	6	21	27	37	14	1	4	5	4
1992-93	Cleveland	IHL	58	9	18	27	64	....	....	....	....	....
1993-94	Cleveland	IHL	73	8	16	24	72	....	....	....	....	....
1994-95	Cdn. National	....	51	11	35	46	32	....	....	....	....	....
1995-96	Toronto	NHL	5	0	0	0	0	....	....	....	....	....
b	St. John's	AHL	73	22	34	56	33	3	1	1	2	6
	NHL Totals		5	0	0	0	0	....	....	....	....	....

a WHL East First All-Star Team (1991)
b AHL First All-Star Team (1996)

Signed as a free agent by **Toronto**, May 4, 1995.

HICKS, ALEX — ANA.

Left wing. Shoots left. 6'1", 195 lbs. Born, Calgary, Alta., September 4, 1969.

			Regular Season					Playoffs				
Season	Club	Lea	GP	G	A	TP	PIM	GP	G	A	TP	PIM
1992-93	Toledo	ECHL	50	26	34	60	100	16	5	10	15	79
1993-94	Toledo	ECHL	60	31	49	80	240	14	10	10	20	56
1994-95	Las Vegas	IHL	79	24	42	66	212	9	2	4	6	47
1995-96	Anaheim	NHL	64	10	11	21	37	....	....	....	....	....
	Baltimore	AHL	13	2	10	12	23	....	....	....	....	....
	NHL Totals		64	10	11	21	37	....	....	....	....	....

Signed as a free agent by **Anaheim**, August 17, 1995.

HIGGINS, MATT — MTL.

Left wing. Shoots left. 6'1", 170 lbs. Born, Calgary, Alta., October 29, 1977.
(Montreal's 1st choice, 18th overall, in 1996 Entry Draft).

			Regular Season					Playoffs				
Season	Club	Lea	GP	G	A	TP	PIM	GP	G	A	TP	PIM
1993-94	Moose Jaw	WHL	64	6	10	16	10	....	....	....	....	....
1994-95	Moose Jaw	WHL	72	36	34	70	26	10	1	2	3	2
1995-96	Moose Jaw	WHL	67	30	33	63	43	....	....	....	....	....

HILL, SEAN (HIHL, SHAWN) OTT.

Defense. Shoots right. 6', 195 lbs. Born, Duluth, MN, February 14, 1970.
(Montreal's 9th choice, 167th overall, in 1988 Entry Draft).

			Regular Season					Playoffs				
Season	Club	Lea	GP	G	A	TP	PIM	GP	G	A	TP	PIM
1988-89	U. Wisconsin	WCHA	45	2	23	25	69	....	....	....	....	....
1989-90a	U. Wisconsin	WCHA	42	14	39	53	78	....	....	....	....	....
1990-91ab	U. Wisconsin	WCHA	37	19	32	51	122	....	....	....	....	....
	Montreal	**NHL**	....	....	....	....	....	**1**	**0**	**0**	**0**	**0**
	Fredericton	AHL	....	....	....	....	....	3	0	2	2	2
1991-92	Fredericton	AHL	42	7	20	27	65	7	1	3	4	6
	U.S. National	....	12	4	3	7	16	....	....	....	....	....
	U.S. Olympic	....	8	2	0	2	6	....	....	....	....	....
	Montreal	**NHL**	....	....	....	....	....	**4**	**1**	**0**	**1**	**2**
1992-93	**Montreal**	**NHL**	**31**	**2**	**6**	**8**	**54**	**3**	**0**	**0**	**0**	**4** ♦
	Fredericton	AHL	6	1	3	4	10	....	....	....	....	....
1993-94	**Anaheim**	**NHL**	**68**	**7**	**20**	**27**	**78**	....	....	....	....	....
1994-95	**Ottawa**	**NHL**	**45**	**1**	**14**	**15**	**30**	....	....	....	....	....
1995-96	**Ottawa**	**NHL**	**80**	**7**	**14**	**21**	**94**	....	....	....	....	....
	NHL Totals		**224**	**17**	**54**	**71**	**256**	**8**	**1**	**0**	**1**	**6**

a WCHA Second All-Star Team (1990, 1991)
b NCAA West Second All-American Team (1991)

Claimed by **Anaheim** from **Montreal** in Expansion Draft, June 24, 1993. Traded to **Ottawa** by **Anaheim** with Anaheim's ninth round choice (Frederic Cassivi) in 1994 Entry Draft for Ottawa's third round choice (later traded to Tampa Bay — Tampa Bay selected Vadim Epanchintsev) in 1994 Entry Draft, June 29, 1994.

HILLER, JIM

Right wing. Shoots right. 6', 190 lbs. Born, Port Alberni, B.C., May 15, 1969.
(Los Angeles' 10th choice, 207th overall, in 1989 Entry Draft).

			Regular Season					Playoffs				
Season	Club	Lea	GP	G	A	TP	PIM	GP	G	A	TP	PIM
1989-90	N. Michigan	WCHA	39	23	33	56	52	....	....	....	....	....
1990-91	N. Michigan	WCHA	43	22	41	63	59	....	....	....	....	....
1991-92ab	N. Michigan	WCHA	39	28	52	80	115	....	....	....	....	....
1992-93	**Los Angeles**	**NHL**	**40**	**6**	**6**	**12**	**90**	....	....	....	....	....
	Phoenix	IHL	3	0	2	2	2	....	....	....	....	....
	Detroit	**NHL**	**21**	**2**	**6**	**8**	**19**	**2**	**0**	**0**	**0**	**4**
1993-94	**NY Rangers**	**NHL**	**2**	**0**	**0**	**0**	**7**	....	....	....	....	....
	Binghamton	AHL	67	27	34	61	61	....	....	....	....	....
1994-95	Binghamton	AHL	49	15	13	28	44	....	....	....	....	....
	Atlanta	IHL	17	5	10	15	28	5	0	3	3	8
1995-96	Cdn. National	....	53	17	26	43	68	....	....	....	....	....
	NHL Totals		**63**	**8**	**12**	**20**	**116**	**2**	**0**	**0**	**0**	**4**

a NCAA West Second All-American Team (1992)
b WCHA Second All-Star Team (1992)

Traded to **Detroit** by **Los Angeles** with Paul Coffey and Sylvain Couturier for Jimmy Carson, Marc Potvin and Gary Shuchuk, January 29, 1993. Claimed on waivers by **NY Rangers** from **Detroit**, October 12, 1993.

HILTON, KEVIN DET.

Center. Shoots left. 5'11", 170 lbs. Born, Trenton, MI, January 5, 1975.
(Detroit's 3rd choice, 74th overall, in 1993 Entry Draft).

			Regular Season					Playoffs				
Season	Club	Lea	GP	G	A	TP	PIM	GP	G	A	TP	PIM
1992-93	U. of Michigan	CCHA	36	16	15	31	8	....	....	....	....	....
1993-94	U. of Michigan	CCHA	39	11	12	23	16	....	....	....	....	....
1994-95	U. of Michigan	CCHA	37	20	31	51	14	....	....	....	....	....
1995-96ab	U. of Michigan	CCHA	43	10	*51	61	8	....	....	....	....	....

a CCHA First All-Star Team (1996)
b NCAA West Second All-American Team (1996)

HIRVONEN, TOMI COL.

Center. Shoots left. 5'11", 180 lbs. Born, Tampere, Finland, January 11, 1977.
(Colorado's 8th choice, 207th overall, in 1995 Entry Draft).

			Regular Season					Playoffs				
Season	Club	Lea	GP	G	A	TP	PIM	GP	G	A	TP	PIM
1994-95	Ilves	Fin. Jr.	28	9	13	22	30	8	4	2	6	14
1995-96	Ilves	Fin. Jr.	12	7	12	19	45	....	....	....	....	....
	Koo-Vee	Fin. 2	7	4	1	5	26	....	....	....	....	....
	Ilves	Fin.	28	1	0	1	24	....	....	....	....	....

HLAVAC, JAN NYI

Left wing. Shoots left. 6', 183 lbs. Born, Prague, Czech., September 20, 1976.
(NY Islanders' 2nd choice, 28th overall, in 1995 Entry Draft).

			Regular Season					Playoffs				
Season	Club	Lea	GP	G	A	TP	PIM	GP	G	A	TP	PIM
1993-94	HC Sparta	Czech.	9	1	1	2	....	....	....	....	....	....
1994-95	HC Sparta	Czech.	38	7	6	13	18	5	0	2	2	0
1995-96	HC Sparta	Czech.	34	8	5	13	....	12	1	2	3	....

HLUSHKO, TODD (huh-LUSH-koh) CGY.

Center. Shoots left. 5'11", 185 lbs. Born, Toronto, Ont., February 7, 1970.
(Washington's 14th choice, 240th overall, in 1989 Entry Draft).

			Regular Season					Playoffs				
Season	Club	Lea	GP	G	A	TP	PIM	GP	G	A	TP	PIM
1988-89	Guelph	OHL	66	28	18	46	71	7	5	3	8	18
1989-90	Owen Sound	OHL	25	9	17	26	31	....	....	....	....	....
	London	OHL	40	27	17	44	39	6	2	4	6	10
1990-91	Baltimore	AHL	66	9	14	23	55	....	....	....	....	....
1991-92	Baltimore	AHL	74	16	35	51	113	....	....	....	....	....
1992-93	Cdn. National	....	58	22	26	48	10	....	....	....	....	....
1993-94	Cdn. National	....	55	22	6	28	61	....	....	....	....	....
	Cdn. Olympic	....	8	5	0	5	6	....	....	....	....	....
	Philadelphia	**NHL**	**2**	**1**	**0**	**1**	**0**	....	....	....	....	....
	Hershey	AHL	9	6	0	6	4	6	2	1	3	4
1994-95	Saint John	AHL	46	22	10	32	36	4	2	2	4	22
	Calgary	**NHL**	**2**	**0**	**1**	**1**	**2**	**1**	**0**	**0**	**0**	**2**
1995-96	**Calgary**	**NHL**	**4**	**0**	**0**	**0**	**6**	....	....	....	....	....
	Saint John	AHL	35	14	13	27	70	16	8	1	9	26
	NHL Totals		**8**	**1**	**1**	**2**	**8**	**1**	**0**	**0**	**0**	**2**

Signed as a free agent by **Philadelphia**, March 7, 1994. Signed as a free agent by **Calgary**, June 17, 1994.

HOCKING, JUSTIN OTT.

Right wing. Shoots right. 6'4", 205 lbs. Born, Stettler, Alta., January 9, 1974.
(Los Angeles' 1st choice, 39th overall, in 1992 Entry Draft).

			Regular Season					Playoffs				
Season	Club	Lea	GP	G	A	TP	PIM	GP	G	A	TP	PIM
1991-92	Spokane	WHL	71	4	6	10	309	10	0	3	3	28
1992-93	Spokane	WHL	16	0	1	1	75	....	....	....	....	....
	Medicine Hat	WHL	54	1	9	10	119	10	0	1	1	13
1993-94	**Los Angeles**	**NHL**	**1**	**0**	**0**	**0**	**0**	....	....	....	....	....
a	Medicine Hat	WHL	68	7	26	33	236	3	0	0	0	6
	Phoenix	IHL	3	0	0	0	15	....	....	....	....	....
1994-95	Syracuse	AHL	7	0	0	0	24	....	....	....	....	....
	Portland	AHL	9	0	1	1	34	....	....	....	....	....
	Knoxville	ECHL	20	0	6	6	70	4	0	0	0	26
	Phoenix	IHL	20	1	1	2	50	1	0	0	0	0
1995-96	P.E.I.	AHL	74	4	8	12	251	4	0	2	2	5
	NHL Totals		**1**	**0**	**0**	**0**	**0**	....	....	....	....	....

a WHL East Second All-Star Team (1994)

Claimed by **Ottawa** from **Los Angeles** in NHL Waiver Draft, October 2, 1995.

HOGAN, PETER L.A.

Defense. Shoots right. 6'2", 167 lbs. Born, Oshawa, Ont., January 10, 1978.
(Los Angeles' 7th choice, 123rd overall, in 1996 Entry Draft).

			Regular Season					Playoffs				
Season	Club	Lea	GP	G	A	TP	PIM	GP	G	A	TP	PIM
1994-95	Wexford	Midget	36	5	16	21	....	....	....	....	....	....
1995-96	Oshawa	OHL	66	3	25	28	54	5	2	0	2	2

HOGARDH, PETER NYI

Center. Shoots left. 5'10", 183 lbs. Born, Snotorp, Sweden, May 25, 1976.
(NY Islanders' 9th choice, 203rd overall, in 1994 Entry Draft).

			Regular Season					Playoffs				
Season	Club	Lea	GP	G	A	TP	PIM	GP	G	A	TP	PIM
1993-94	V. Frolunda	Swe.	16	1	0	1	2	....	....	....	....	....
1994-95	V. Frolunda	Swe.	4	0	0	0	0	....	....	....	....	....
	V. Frolunda	Swe. 2	13	1	4	5	4	....	....	....	....	....
1995-96	V. Frolunda	Swe.	27	0	2	2	6	....	....	....	....	....

HOGUE, BENOIT (HOHG) DAL.

Center. Shoots left. 5'10", 194 lbs. Born, Repentigny, Que., October 28, 1966.
(Buffalo's 2nd choice, 35th overall, in 1985 Entry Draft).

			Regular Season					Playoffs				
Season	Club	Lea	GP	G	A	TP	PIM	GP	G	A	TP	PIM
1983-84	St-Jean	QMJHL	59	14	11	25	42	....	....	....	....	....
1984-85	St-Jean	QMJHL	63	46	44	90	92	....	....	....	....	....
1985-86	St-Jean	QMJHL	65	54	54	108	115	9	6	4	10	26
1986-87	Rochester	AHL	52	14	20	34	52	12	5	4	9	8
1987-88	**Buffalo**	**NHL**	**3**	**1**	**1**	**2**	**0**	....	....	....	....	....
	Rochester	AHL	62	24	31	55	141	7	6	1	7	46
1988-89	**Buffalo**	**NHL**	**69**	**14**	**30**	**44**	**120**	**5**	**0**	**0**	**0**	**17**
1989-90	**Buffalo**	**NHL**	**45**	**11**	**7**	**18**	**79**	**3**	**0**	**0**	**0**	**10**
1990-91	**Buffalo**	**NHL**	**76**	**19**	**28**	**47**	**76**	**5**	**3**	**1**	**4**	**10**
1991-92	**Buffalo**	**NHL**	**3**	**0**	**1**	**1**	**0**	....	....	....	....	....
	NY Islanders	**NHL**	**72**	**30**	**45**	**75**	**67**	....	....	....	....	....
1992-93	**NY Islanders**	**NHL**	**70**	**33**	**42**	**75**	**108**	**18**	**6**	**6**	**12**	**31**
1993-94	**NY Islanders**	**NHL**	**83**	**36**	**33**	**69**	**73**	**4**	**0**	**1**	**1**	**4**
1994-95	**NY Islanders**	**NHL**	**33**	**6**	**4**	**10**	**34**	....	....	....	....	....
	Toronto	**NHL**	**12**	**3**	**3**	**6**	**0**	**7**	**0**	**0**	**0**	**6**
1995-96	**Toronto**	**NHL**	**44**	**12**	**25**	**37**	**68**	....	....	....	....	....
	Dallas	**NHL**	**34**	**7**	**20**	**27**	**36**	....	....	....	....	....
	NHL Totals		**544**	**172**	**239**	**411**	**661**	**42**	**9**	**8**	**17**	**78**

Traded to **NY Islanders** by **Buffalo** with Pierre Turgeon, Uwe Krupp and Dave McLlwain for Pat Lafontaine, Randy Hillier, Randy Wood and NY Islanders' fourth round choice (Dean Melanson) in 1992 Entry Draft, October 25, 1991. Traded to **Toronto** by **NY Islanders** with NY Islanders' third round choice (Brian Pepperall) in 1995 Entry Draft and fifth round choice (Brandon Sugden) in 1996 Entry Draft for Eric Fichaud, April 6, 1995. Traded to **Dallas** by **Toronto** with Randy Wood for Dave Gagner and Dallas' sixth round choice (Dmitriy Yakushin) in 1996 Entry Draft, January 29, 1996.

HOHENBERGER, MARTIN MTL.

Left wing. Shoots left. 6', 195 lbs. Born, Villach, Austria, January 29, 1977.
(Montreal's 3rd choice, 74th overall, in 1995 Entry Draft).

			Regular Season					Playoffs				
Season	Club	Lea	GP	G	A	TP	PIM	GP	G	A	TP	PIM
1993-94	Victoria	WHL	61	3	13	16	82	....	....	....	....	....
1994-95	Prince George	WHL	47	10	21	31	81	....	....	....	....	....
1995-96	Prince George	WHL	37	10	19	29	19	....	....	....	....	....
	Lethbridge	WHL	20	5	1	6	21	4	0	3	3	4

HOLAN, MILOS ANA.

Defense. Shoots left. 5'11", 191 lbs. Born, Bilovec, Czech., April 22, 1971.
(Philadelphia's 3rd choice, 77th overall, in 1993 Entry Draft).

			Regular Season					Playoffs				
Season	Club	Lea	GP	G	A	TP	PIM	GP	G	A	TP	PIM
1988-89	TJ Vitkovice	Czech.	7	0	0	0	0	....	....	....	....	....
1989-90	TJ Vitkovice	Czech.	50	8	8	16	....	....	....	....	....	....
1990-91	Dukla Trencin	Czech.	53	6	13	19	....	....	....	....	....	....
1991-92	Dukla Trencin	Czech.	51	13	22	35	32	....	....	....	....	....
1992-93a	TJ Vitkovice	Czech.	53	35	33	68	....	....	....	....	....	....
1993-94	**Philadelphia**	**NHL**	**8**	**1**	**1**	**2**	**4**	....	....	....	....	....
	Hershey	AHL	27	7	22	29	16	....	....	....	....	....
1994-95	Hershey	AHL	55	22	27	49	75	....	....	....	....	....
	Anaheim	**NHL**	**25**	**2**	**8**	**10**	**14**	....	....	....	....	....
1995-96	**Anaheim**	**NHL**	**16**	**2**	**2**	**4**	**24**	....	....	....	....	....
	NHL Totals		**49**	**5**	**11**	**16**	**42**	....	....	....	....	....

a Czechoslovakian Player of the Year (1993)

Traded to **Anaheim** by **Philadelphia** for Anatoli Semenov, March 8, 1995.

HOLDEN, JOSH VAN.

Center. Shoots left. 5'11", 167 lbs. Born, Calgary, Alta., January 18, 1978.
(Vancouver's 1st choice, 12th overall, in 1996 Entry Draft).

			Regular Season					Playoffs				
Season	Club	Lea	GP	G	A	TP	PIM	GP	G	A	TP	PIM
1994-95	Regina	WHL	62	20	23	43	45	4	3	1	4	0
1995-96	Regina	WHL	70	57	55	112	105	11	4	5	9	23

HOLIK, BOBBY (HOH-leek) N.J.

Left wing. Shoots right. 6'3", 220 lbs. Born, Jihlava, Czech., January 1, 1971.
(Hartford's 1st choice, 10th overall, in 1989 Entry Draft).

			Regular Season					Playoffs				
Season	Club	Lea	GP	G	A	TP	PIM	GP	G	A	TP	PIM
1987-88	Dukla Jihlava	Czech.	31	5	9	14	16	....	....	....	....	....
1988-89	Dukla Jihlava	Czech.	24	7	10	17	32	....	....	....	....	....
1989-90	Dukla Jihlava	Czech.	42	15	26	41	....	....	....	....	....	....
1990-91	**Hartford**	**NHL**	**78**	**21**	**22**	**43**	**113**	**6**	**0**	**0**	**0**	**7**
1991-92	**Hartford**	**NHL**	**76**	**21**	**24**	**45**	**44**	**7**	**0**	**1**	**1**	**6**
1992-93	**New Jersey**	**NHL**	**61**	**20**	**19**	**39**	**76**	**5**	**1**	**1**	**2**	**6**
	Utica	AHL	1	0	0	0	2	....	....	....	....	....
1993-94	**New Jersey**	**NHL**	**70**	**13**	**20**	**33**	**72**	**20**	**0**	**3**	**3**	**6**
1994-95	**New Jersey**	**NHL**	**48**	**10**	**10**	**20**	**18**	**20**	**4**	**4**	**8**	**22** ♦
1995-96	**New Jersey**	**NHL**	**63**	**13**	**17**	**30**	**58**	....	....	....	....	....
	NHL Totals		**396**	**98**	**112**	**210**	**381**	**58**	**5**	**9**	**14**	**47**

Traded to **New Jersey** by **Hartford** with Hartford's second round choice (Jay Pandolfo) in 1993 Entry Draft and future considerations for Sean Burke and Eric Weinrich, August 28, 1992.

HOLLAND, JASON NYI

Defense. Shoots right. 6'2", 193 lbs. Born, Morinville, Alta., April 30, 1976.
(NY Islanders' 2nd choice, 38th overall, in 1994 Entry Draft).

			Regular Season					Playoffs				
Season	Club	Lea	GP	G	A	TP	PIM	GP	G	A	TP	PIM
1993-94	Kamloops	WHL	59	14	15	29	80	18	2	3	5	4
1994-95	Kamloops	WHL	71	9	32	41	65	21	2	7	9	9
1995-96a	Kamloops	WHL	63	24	33	57	98	16	4	9	13	22

a WHL West First All-Star Team (1996)

HOLLINGER, TERRY BUF.

Defense. Shoots left. 6'1", 200 lbs. Born, Regina, Sask., February 24, 1971.
(St. Louis' 7th choice, 153rd overall, in 1991 Entry Draft).

			Regular Season					Playoffs				
Season	Club	Lea	GP	G	A	TP	PIM	GP	G	A	TP	PIM
1990-91	Regina	WHL	8	1	6	7	6	....	....	....	....	....
	Lethbridge	WHL	62	9	32	41	113	16	3	14	17	22
1991-92	Lethbridge	WHL	65	23	62	85	155	5	1	2	3	13
	Peoria	IHL	1	0	2	2	0	5	0	1	1	0
1992-93	Peoria	IHL	72	2	28	30	67	4	1	1	2	0
1993-94	**St. Louis**	**NHL**	**2**	**0**	**0**	**0**	**0**	....	....	....	....	....
	Peoria	IHL	78	12	31	43	96	6	0	3	3	31
1994-95	Peoria	IHL	69	7	25	32	137	4	2	4	6	8
	St. Louis	**NHL**	**5**	**0**	**0**	**0**	**2**	....	....	....	....	....
1995-96a	Rochester	AHL	62	5	50	55	71	19	3	11	14	12
	NHL Totals		**7**	**0**	**0**	**0**	**2**	....	....	....	....	....

a AHL Second All-Star Team (1996)

Signed as a free agent by **Buffalo**, August 23, 1995.

HOLMSTROM, TOMAS DET.

Left wing. Shoots left. 6', 200 lbs. Born, Pitea, Sweden, January 23, 1973.
(Detroit's 9th choice, 257th overall, in 1994 Entry Draft).

			Regular Season					Playoffs				
Season	Club	Lea	GP	G	A	TP	PIM	GP	G	A	TP	PIM
1994-95	Lulea	Swe.	40	14	14	28	56	....	....	....	....	....
1995-96	Lulea	Swe.	34	12	11	23	78	11	6	2	8	22

HOLZINGER, BRIAN BUF.

Center. Shoots right. 5'11", 180 lbs. Born, Parma, OH, October 10, 1972.
(Buffalo's 7th choice, 124th overall, in 1991 Entry Draft).

			Regular Season					Playoffs				
Season	Club	Lea	GP	G	A	TP	PIM	GP	G	A	TP	PIM
1991-92	Bowling Green	CCHA	30	14	8	22	36	....	....	....	....	....
1992-93a	Bowling Green	CCHA	41	31	26	57	44	....	....	....	....	....
1993-94	Bowling Green	CCHA	38	22	15	37	24	....	....	....	....	....
1994-95bcd	Bowling Green	CCHA	38	35	33	68	42	....	....	....	....	....
	Buffalo	**NHL**	**4**	**0**	**3**	**3**	**0**	**4**	**2**	**1**	**3**	**2**
1995-96	**Buffalo**	**NHL**	**58**	**10**	**10**	**20**	**37**	....	....	....	....	....
	Rochester	AHL	17	10	11	21	14	19	10	14	24	10
	NHL Totals		**62**	**10**	**13**	**23**	**37**	**4**	**2**	**1**	**3**	**2**

a CCHA Second All-Star Team (1993)
b CCHA First All-Star Team (1995)
c NCAA West First All-American Team (1995)
d Won Hobey Baker Memorial Award (Top U.S. Collegiate Player) (1995)

HORACEK, TONY (HOHR-uh-chehk) PHI.

Left wing. Shoots left. 6'4", 210 lbs. Born, Vancouver, B.C., February 3, 1967.
(Philadelphia's 8th choice, 147th overall, in 1985 Entry Draft).

			Regular Season					Playoffs				
Season	Club	Lea	GP	G	A	TP	PIM	GP	G	A	TP	PIM
1984-85	Kelowna	WHL	67	9	18	27	114	6	0	1	1	11
1985-86	Spokane	WHL	64	19	28	47	129	9	4	5	9	29
1986-87	Spokane	WHL	64	23	37	60	177	5	1	3	4	18
	Hershey	AHL	....	....	....	....	....	1	0	0	0	0
1987-88	Hershey	AHL	1	0	0	0	0	....	....	....	....	....
	Spokane	WHL	24	17	23	40	63	....	....	....	....	....
	Kamloops	WHL	26	14	17	31	51	18	6	4	10	73
1988-89	Hershey	AHL	10	0	0	0	38	....	....	....	....	....
	Indianapolis	IHL	43	11	13	24	138	....	....	....	....	....
1989-90	**Philadelphia**	**NHL**	**48**	**5**	**5**	**10**	**117**	....	....	....	....	....
	Hershey	AHL	12	0	5	5	25	....	....	....	....	....
1990-91	**Philadelphia**	**NHL**	**34**	**3**	**6**	**9**	**49**	....	....	....	....	....
	Hershey	AHL	19	5	3	8	35	4	2	0	2	14
1991-92	**Philadelphia**	**NHL**	**34**	**1**	**3**	**4**	**51**	....	....	....	....	....
	Chicago	**NHL**	**12**	**1**	**4**	**5**	**21**	**2**	**1**	**0**	**1**	**2**
1992-93	Indianapolis	IHL	6	1	1	2	28	5	3	2	5	18
1993-94	**Chicago**	**NHL**	**7**	**0**	**0**	**0**	**53**	....	....	....	....	....
	Indianapolis	IHL	29	6	7	13	63	....	....	....	....	....
1994-95	Indianapolis	IHL	51	7	19	26	201	....	....	....	....	....
	Chicago	**NHL**	**19**	**0**	**1**	**1**	**25**	....	....	....	....	....
1995-96	Hershey	AHL	34	4	9	13	75	5	1	1	2	4
	NHL Totals		**154**	**10**	**19**	**29**	**316**	**2**	**1**	**0**	**1**	**2**

Traded to **Chicago** by **Philadelphia** for Ryan McGill, February 7, 1992. Signed as a free agent by **Philadelphia**, July 17, 1995.

HOUDA, DOUG (HOO-duh) BUF.

Defense. Shoots right. 6'2", 190 lbs. Born, Blairmore, Alta., June 3, 1966.
(Detroit's 2nd choice, 28th overall, in 1984 Entry Draft).

			Regular Season					Playoffs				
Season	Club	Lea	GP	G	A	TP	PIM	GP	G	A	TP	PIM
1982-83	Calgary	WHL	71	5	23	28	99	16	1	3	4	44
1983-84	Calgary	WHL	69	6	30	36	195	4	0	0	0	7
1984-85a	Calgary	WHL	65	20	54	74	182	8	3	4	7	29
1985-86	**Detroit**	**NHL**	**6**	**0**	**0**	**0**	**4**	....	....	....	....	....
	Calgary	WHL	16	4	10	14	60	....	....	....	....	....
	Medicine Hat	WHL	35	9	23	32	80	25	4	19	23	64
1986-87	Adirondack	AHL	77	6	23	29	142	11	1	8	9	50
1987-88	**Detroit**	**NHL**	**11**	**1**	**1**	**2**	**10**	....	....	....	....	....
b	Adirondack	AHL	71	10	32	42	169	11	0	3	3	44
1988-89	**Detroit**	**NHL**	**57**	**2**	**11**	**13**	**67**	**6**	**0**	**1**	**1**	**0**
	Adirondack	AHL	7	0	3	3	8	....	....	....	....	....
1989-90	**Detroit**	**NHL**	**73**	**2**	**9**	**11**	**127**	....	....	....	....	....
1990-91	**Detroit**	**NHL**	**22**	**0**	**4**	**4**	**43**	....	....	....	....	....
	Adirondack	AHL	38	9	17	26	67	....	....	....	....	....
	Hartford	**NHL**	**19**	**1**	**2**	**3**	**41**	**6**	**0**	**0**	**0**	**8**
1991-92	**Hartford**	**NHL**	**56**	**3**	**6**	**9**	**125**	**6**	**0**	**2**	**2**	**13**
1992-93	**Hartford**	**NHL**	**60**	**2**	**6**	**8**	**167**	....	....	....	....	....
1993-94	**Hartford**	**NHL**	**7**	**0**	**0**	**0**	**23**	....	....	....	....	....
	Los Angeles	**NHL**	**54**	**2**	**6**	**8**	**165**	....	....	....	....	....
1994-95	**Buffalo**	**NHL**	**28**	**1**	**2**	**3**	**68**	....	....	....	....	....
1995-96	**Buffalo**	**NHL**	**38**	**1**	**3**	**4**	**52**	....	....	....	....	....
	Rochester	AHL	21	1	6	7	41	19	3	5	8	30
	NHL Totals		**431**	**15**	**50**	**65**	**892**	**18**	**0**	**3**	**3**	**21**

a WHL East Second All-Star Team (1985)
b AHL First All-Star Team (1988)

Traded to **Hartford** by **Detroit** for Doug Crossman, February 20, 1991. Traded to **Los Angeles** by **Hartford** for Marc Potvin, November 3, 1993. Traded to **Buffalo** by **Los Angeles** for Sean O'Donnell, July 26, 1994.

HOUDE, ERIC MTL.

Center. Shoots left. 5'11", 190 lbs. Born, Montreal, Que., December 19, 1976.
(Montreal's 9th choice, 216th overall, in 1995 Entry Draft).

			Regular Season					Playoffs				
Season	Club	Lea	GP	G	A	TP	PIM	GP	G	A	TP	PIM
1993-94	St-Jean	QMJHL	71	16	16	32	14	5	1	1	2	4
1994-95	St-Jean	QMJHL	40	10	13	23	23	....	....	....	....	....
	Halifax	QMJHL	28	13	23	36	8	3	2	1	3	4
1995-96	Halifax	QMJHL	69	40	48	88	35	6	3	4	7	2

HOUGH, MIKE (HUHF) FLA.

Left wing. Shoots left. 6'1", 197 lbs. Born, Montreal, Que., February 6, 1963.
(Quebec's 7th choice, 181st overall, in 1982 Entry Draft).

			Regular Season					Playoffs				
Season	Club	Lea	GP	G	A	TP	PIM	GP	G	A	TP	PIM
1981-82	Kitchener	OHL	58	14	24	38	172	14	4	1	5	16
1982-83	Kitchener	OHL	61	17	27	44	156	12	5	4	9	30
1983-84	Fredericton	AHL	69	11	16	27	142	1	0	0	0	7
1984-85	Fredericton	AHL	76	21	27	48	49	6	1	1	2	2
1985-86	Fredericton	AHL	74	21	33	54	68	6	0	3	3	8
1986-87	**Quebec**	**NHL**	**56**	**6**	**8**	**14**	**79**	**9**	**0**	**3**	**3**	**26**
	Fredericton	AHL	10	1	3	4	20	....	....	....	....	....
1987-88	**Quebec**	**NHL**	**17**	**3**	**2**	**5**	**2**	....	....	....	....	....
	Fredericton	AHL	46	16	25	41	133	15	4	8	12	55
1988-89	**Quebec**	**NHL**	**46**	**9**	**10**	**19**	**39**	....	....	....	....	....
	Halifax	AHL	22	11	10	21	87	....	....	....	....	....
1989-90	**Quebec**	**NHL**	**43**	**13**	**13**	**26**	**84**	....	....	....	....	....
1990-91	**Quebec**	**NHL**	**63**	**13**	**20**	**33**	**111**	....	....	....	....	....
1991-92	**Quebec**	**NHL**	**61**	**16**	**22**	**38**	**77**	....	....	....	....	....
1992-93	**Quebec**	**NHL**	**77**	**8**	**22**	**30**	**69**	**6**	**0**	**1**	**1**	**2**
1993-94	**Florida**	**NHL**	**78**	**6**	**23**	**29**	**62**	....	....	....	....	....
1994-95	**Florida**	**NHL**	**48**	**6**	**7**	**13**	**38**	....	....	....	....	....
1995-96	**Florida**	**NHL**	**64**	**7**	**16**	**23**	**37**	**22**	**4**	**1**	**5**	**8**
	NHL Totals		**553**	**87**	**143**	**230**	**598**	**37**	**4**	**5**	**9**	**36**

Traded to **Washington** by **Quebec** for Reggie Savage and Paul MacDermid, June 20, 1993. Claimed by **Florida** from **Washington** in Expansion Draft, June 24, 1993.

HOULDER, BILL (HOHL-duhr) T.B.

Defense. Shoots left. 6'3", 211 lbs. Born, Thunder Bay, Ont., March 11, 1967.
(Washington's 4th choice, 82nd overall, in 1985 Entry Draft).

			Regular Season					Playoffs				
Season	Club	Lea	GP	G	A	TP	PIM	GP	G	A	TP	PIM
1984-85	North Bay	OHL	66	4	20	24	37	8	0	0	0	2
1985-86	North Bay	OHL	59	5	30	35	97	10	1	6	7	12
1986-87	North Bay	OHL	62	17	51	68	68	22	4	19	23	20
1987-88	**Washington**	**NHL**	**30**	**1**	**2**	**3**	**10**	....	....	....	....	....
	Fort Wayne	IHL	43	10	14	24	32	....	....	....	....	....
1988-89	**Washington**	**NHL**	**8**	**0**	**3**	**3**	**4**	....	....	....	....	....
	Baltimore	AHL	65	10	36	46	50	....	....	....	....	....
1989-90	**Washington**	**NHL**	**41**	**1**	**11**	**12**	**28**	....	....	....	....	....
	Baltimore	AHL	26	3	7	10	12	7	0	2	2	2
1990-91	**Buffalo**	**NHL**	**7**	**0**	**2**	**2**	**4**	....	....	....	....	....
a	Rochester	AHL	69	13	53	66	28	15	5	13	18	4
1991-92	**Buffalo**	**NHL**	**10**	**1**	**0**	**1**	**8**	....	....	....	....	....
	Rochester	AHL	42	8	26	34	16	16	5	6	11	4
1992-93	**Buffalo**	**NHL**	**15**	**3**	**5**	**8**	**6**	**8**	**0**	**2**	**2**	**4**
bc	San Diego	IHL	64	24	48	72	39	....	....	....	....	....
1993-94	**Anaheim**	**NHL**	**80**	**14**	**25**	**39**	**40**	....	....	....	....	....
1994-95	**St. Louis**	**NHL**	**41**	**5**	**13**	**18**	**20**	**4**	**1**	**1**	**2**	**0**
1995-96	**Tampa Bay**	**NHL**	**61**	**5**	**23**	**28**	**22**	**6**	**0**	**1**	**1**	**4**
	NHL Totals		**293**	**30**	**84**	**114**	**142**	**18**	**1**	**4**	**5**	**8**

a AHL First All-Star Team (1991)
b Won Governor's Trophy (Outstanding Defenseman - IHL) (1993)
c IHL First All-Star Team (1993)

Traded to **Buffalo** by **Washington** for Shawn Anderson, September 30, 1990. Claimed by **Anaheim** from **Buffalo** in Expansion Draft, June 24, 1993. Traded to **St. Louis** by **Anaheim** for Jason Marshall, August 29, 1994. Signed as a free agent by **Tampa Bay**, July 26, 1995.

HOULE, JEAN-FRANCOIS MTL.

Left wing. Shoots left. 5'9", 175 lbs. Born, Charlesbourg, Que., January 14, 1975.
(Montreal's 5th choice, 99th overall, in 1993 Entry Draft).

			Regular Season					Playoffs				
Season	Club	Lea	GP	G	A	TP	PIM	GP	G	A	TP	PIM
1993-94	Clarkson	ECAC	34	6	19	25	20	....	....	....	....	....
1994-95	Clarkson	ECAC	34	8	11	19	42	....	....	....	....	....
1995-96	Clarkson	ECAC	38	14	15	29	46	....	....	....	....	....

HOUSE, BOBBY — N.J.

Right wing. Shoots right. 6'1", 200 lbs. Born, Whitehorse, Yukon, January 7, 1973.
(Chicago's 4th choice, 66th overall, in 1991 Entry Draft).

			Regular Season					Playoffs				
Season	Club	Lea	GP	G	A	TP	PIM	GP	G	A	TP	PIM
1989-90	Spokane	WHL	64	18	16	34	74	5	0	0	0	6
1990-91	Spokane	WHL	38	11	19	30	63	....	....	....	....	....
	Brandon	WHL	23	18	7	25	14	....	....	....	....	....
1991-92	Brandon	WHL	71	35	42	77	133	....	....	....	....	....
1992-93a	Brandon	WHL	61	57	39	96	87	4	2	2	4	0
1993-94	Indianapolis	IHL	42	10	8	18	51	....	....	....	....	....
	Flint	ColHL	4	3	3	6	0	....	....	....	....	....
1994-95	Columbus	ECHL	9	11	6	17	2	....	....	....	....	....
	Indianapolis	IHL	26	2	3	5	26	....	....	....	....	....
	Albany	AHL	26	4	7	11	12	8	1	1	2	0
1995-96	Albany	AHL	77	37	49	86	57	4	0	0	0	4

a WHL East Second All-Star Team (1993)

Traded to **New Jersey** by **Chicago** for cash, May 21, 1996.

HOUSLEY, PHIL — (HOWZ-lee) WSH.

Defense. Shoots left. 5'10", 185 lbs. Born, St. Paul, MN, March 9, 1964.
(Buffalo's 1st choice, 6th overall, in 1982 Entry Draft).

			Regular Season					Playoffs				
Season	Club	Lea	GP	G	A	TP	PIM	GP	G	A	TP	PIM
1981-82	South St. Paul	HS	22	31	34	65	18	....	....	....	....	....
1982-83a	**Buffalo**	**NHL**	**77**	**19**	**47**	**66**	**39**	**10**	**3**	**4**	**7**	**2**
1983-84	**Buffalo**	**NHL**	**75**	**31**	**46**	**77**	**33**	**3**	**0**	**0**	**0**	**6**
1984-85	**Buffalo**	**NHL**	**73**	**16**	**53**	**69**	**28**	**5**	**3**	**2**	**5**	**2**
1985-86	**Buffalo**	**NHL**	**79**	**15**	**47**	**62**	**54**	....	....	....	....	....
1986-87	**Buffalo**	**NHL**	**78**	**21**	**46**	**67**	**57**	....	....	....	....	....
1987-88	**Buffalo**	**NHL**	**74**	**29**	**37**	**66**	**96**	**6**	**2**	**4**	**6**	**6**
1988-89	**Buffalo**	**NHL**	**72**	**26**	**44**	**70**	**47**	**5**	**1**	**3**	**4**	**2**
1989-90	**Buffalo**	**NHL**	**80**	**21**	**60**	**81**	**32**	**6**	**1**	**4**	**5**	**4**
1990-91	**Winnipeg**	**NHL**	**78**	**23**	**53**	**76**	**24**	....	....	....	....	....
1991-92b	**Winnipeg**	**NHL**	**74**	**23**	**63**	**86**	**92**	**7**	**1**	**4**	**5**	**0**
1992-93	**Winnipeg**	**NHL**	**80**	**18**	**79**	**97**	**52**	**6**	**0**	**7**	**7**	**2**
1993-94	**St. Louis**	**NHL**	**26**	**7**	**15**	**22**	**12**	**4**	**2**	**1**	**3**	**4**
1994-95	Grasshoppers	Switz. 2	10	6	8	14	34	....	....	....	....	....
	Calgary	**NHL**	**43**	**8**	**35**	**43**	**18**	**7**	**0**	**9**	**9**	**0**
1995-96	**Calgary**	**NHL**	**59**	**16**	**36**	**52**	**22**	....	....	....	....	....
	New Jersey	**NHL**	**22**	**1**	**15**	**16**	**8**	....	....	....	....	....
	NHL Totals		**990**	**274**	**676**	**950**	**614**	**59**	**13**	**38**	**51**	**28**

a NHL All-Rookie Team (1983)
b NHL Second All-Star Team (1992)

Played in NHL All-Star Game (1984, 1989-93)

Traded to **Winnipeg** by **Buffalo** with Scott Arniel, Jeff Parker and Buffalo's first round choice (Keith Tkachuk) in 1990 Entry Draft for Dale Hawerchuk, Winnipeg's first round choice (Brad May) in 1990 Entry Draft and future considerations, June 16, 1990. Traded to **St. Louis** by **Winnipeg** for Nelson Emerson and Stephane Quintal, September 24, 1993. Traded to **Calgary** by **St. Louis** with St. Louis' second round choice (Steve Begin) in 1996 Entry Draft and second round choice in 1997 Entry Draft for Al MacInnis and Calgary's fourth round choice in 1997 Entry Draft, July 4, 1994. Traded to **New Jersey** by **Calgary** with Dan Keczmer for Tommy Albelin, Cale Hulse and Jocelyn Lemieux, February 26, 1996. Signed as a free agent by **Washington**, July 22, 1996.

HRDINA, JAN — PIT.

Center. Shoots right. 6', 190 lbs. Born, Hradec Kralove, Czech., February 5, 1976.
(Pittsburgh's 4th choice, 128th overall, in 1995 Entry Draft).

			Regular Season					Playoffs				
Season	Club	Lea	GP	G	A	TP	PIM	GP	G	A	TP	PIM
1993-94	Stadion	Czech.	23	1	5	6	....	4	0	1	1	....
1994-95	Seattle	WHL	69	41	59	100	79	4	0	1	1	8
1995-96	Seattle	WHL	30	19	28	47	37	....	....	....	....	....
	Spokane	WHL	18	10	16	26	25	18	5	14	19	49

HRKAC, TONY — (HUHR-kuhz)

Center. Shoots left. 5'11", 170 lbs. Born, Thunder Bay, Ont., July 7, 1966.
(St. Louis' 2nd choice, 32nd overall, in 1984 Entry Draft).

			Regular Season					Playoffs				
Season	Club	Lea	GP	G	A	TP	PIM	GP	G	A	TP	PIM
1984-85	North Dakota	WCHA	36	18	36	54	16	....	....	....	....	....
1985-86	Cdn. Olympic	....	62	19	30	49	36	....	....	....	....	....
1986-87abcd	North Dakota	WCHA	48	46	79	125	48	....	....	....	....	....
	St. Louis	**NHL**	....	....	....	....	....	**3**	**0**	**0**	**0**	**0**
1987-88	**St. Louis**	**NHL**	**67**	**11**	**37**	**48**	**22**	**10**	**6**	**1**	**7**	**4**
1988-89	**St. Louis**	**NHL**	**70**	**17**	**28**	**45**	**8**	**4**	**1**	**1**	**2**	**0**
1989-90	**St. Louis**	**NHL**	**28**	**5**	**12**	**17**	**8**	....	....	....	....	....
	Quebec	**NHL**	**22**	**4**	**8**	**12**	**2**	....	....	....	....	....
	Halifax	AHL	20	12	21	33	4	6	5	9	14	4
1990-91	**Quebec**	**NHL**	**70**	**16**	**32**	**48**	**16**	....	....	....	....	....
	Halifax	AHL	3	4	1	5	2	....	....	....	....	....
1991-92	**San Jose**	**NHL**	**22**	**2**	**10**	**12**	**4**	....	....	....	....	....
	Chicago	**NHL**	**18**	**1**	**2**	**3**	**6**	**3**	**0**	**0**	**0**	**2**
1992-93efg	Indianapolis	IHL	80	45	*87	*132	70	5	0	2	2	2
1993-94	**St. Louis**	**NHL**	**36**	**6**	**5**	**11**	**8**	**4**	**0**	**0**	**0**	**0**
	Peoria	IHL	45	30	51	81	25	1	1	2	3	0
1994-95	Milwaukee	IHL	71	24	67	91	26	15	4	9	13	16
1995-96	Milwaukee	IHL	43	14	28	42	18	5	1	3	4	4
	NHL Totals		**333**	**62**	**134**	**196**	**74**	**24**	**7**	**2**	**9**	**6**

a WCHA First All-Star Team (1987)
b NCAA West First All-American Team (1987)
c NCAA All-Tournament Team, Tournament MVP (1987)
d Won 1987 Hobey Baker Memorial Award (Top U.S. Collegiate Player) (1987)
e Won James Gatschene Memorial Trophy (MVP - IHL) (1993)
f Won Leo P. Lamoureux Memorial Trophy (Leading Scorer - IHL) (1993)
g IHL First All-Star Team (1993)

Traded to **Quebec** by **St. Louis** with Greg Millen for Jeff Brown, December 13, 1989. Traded to **San Jose** by **Quebec** for Greg Paslawski, May 31, 1991. Traded to **Chicago** by **San Jose** for future considerations, February 7, 1992. Signed as a free agent by **St. Louis**, July 30, 1993.

HRUSKA, DAVID — OTT.

Right wing. Shoots right. 6', 189 lbs. Born, Sokolov, Czech., January 8, 1977.
(Ottawa's 6th choice, 131st overall, in 1995 Entry Draft).

			Regular Season					Playoffs				
Season	Club	Lea	GP	G	A	TP	PIM	GP	G	A	TP	PIM
1995-96	Red Deer	WHL	28	14	14	28	6	....	....	....	....	....
	Vsetin	Czech.	5	1	0	1	....	1	0	0	0	....

HUARD, BILL — (HYOO-ahrd) DAL.

Left wing. Shoots left. 6'1", 215 lbs. Born, Welland, Ont., June 24, 1967.

			Regular Season					Playoffs				
Season	Club	Lea	GP	G	A	TP	PIM	GP	G	A	TP	PIM
1986-87	Peterborough	OHL	61	14	11	25	61	12	5	2	7	19
1987-88	Peterborough	OHL	66	28	33	61	132	12	7	8	15	33
1988-89	Carolina	ECHL	40	27	21	48	177	10	7	2	9	70
1989-90	Utica	AHL	27	1	7	8	67	5	0	1	1	33
	Nashville	ECHL	34	24	27	51	212	....	....	....	....	....
1990-91	Utica	AHL	72	11	16	27	359	....	....	....	....	....
1991-92	Utica	AHL	62	9	11	20	233	4	1	1	2	4
1992-93	**Boston**	**NHL**	**2**	**0**	**0**	**0**	**0**	....	....	....	....	....
	Providence	AHL	72	18	19	37	302	6	3	0	3	9
1993-94	**Ottawa**	**NHL**	**63**	**2**	**2**	**4**	**162**	....	....	....	....	....
1994-95	**Ottawa**	**NHL**	**26**	**1**	**1**	**2**	**64**	....	....	....	....	....
	Quebec	**NHL**	**7**	**2**	**2**	**4**	**13**	**1**	**0**	**0**	**0**	**0**
1995-96	**Dallas**	**NHL**	**51**	**6**	**6**	**12**	**176**	....	....	....	....	....
	Michigan	IHL	12	1	1	2	74	....	....	....	....	....
	NHL Totals		**149**	**11**	**11**	**22**	**415**	**1**	**0**	**0**	**0**	**0**

Signed as a free agent by **New Jersey**, October 1, 1989. Signed as a free agent by **Boston**, December 4, 1992. Signed as a free agent by **Ottawa**, June 30, 1993. Traded to **Quebec** by **Ottawa** for Mika Stromberg and Colorado's fourth round choice (Kevin Boyd) in 1995 Entry Draft, April 7, 1995. Claimed by **Dallas** from **Colorado** in NHL Waiver Draft, October 2, 1995.

HUDDY, CHARLIE — (HUH-dee)

Defense. Shoots left. 6', 210 lbs. Born, Oshawa, Ont., June 2, 1959.

			Regular Season					Playoffs				
Season	Club	Lea	GP	G	A	TP	PIM	GP	G	A	TP	PIM
1977-78	Oshawa	OHA	59	17	18	35	81	6	2	1	3	10
1978-79	Oshawa	OHA	64	20	38	58	108	5	3	4	7	12
1979-80	Houston	CHL	79	14	34	48	46	6	1	0	1	2
1980-81	**Edmonton**	**NHL**	**12**	**2**	**5**	**7**	**6**	....	....	....	....	....
	Wichita	CHL	47	8	36	44	71	17	3	11	14	10
1981-82	**Edmonton**	**NHL**	**41**	**4**	**11**	**15**	**46**	**5**	**1**	**2**	**3**	**14**
	Wichita	CHL	32	7	19	26	51	....	....	....	....	....
1982-83a	**Edmonton**	**NHL**	**76**	**20**	**37**	**57**	**58**	**15**	**1**	**6**	**7**	**10**
1983-84	**Edmonton**	**NHL**	**75**	**8**	**34**	**42**	**43**	**12**	**1**	**9**	**10**	**8** ♦
1984-85	**Edmonton**	**NHL**	**80**	**7**	**44**	**51**	**46**	**18**	**3**	**17**	**20**	**17** ♦
1985-86	**Edmonton**	**NHL**	**76**	**6**	**35**	**41**	**55**	**7**	**0**	**2**	**2**	**0**
1986-87	**Edmonton**	**NHL**	**58**	**4**	**15**	**19**	**35**	**21**	**1**	**7**	**8**	**21** ♦
1987-88	**Edmonton**	**NHL**	**77**	**13**	**28**	**41**	**71**	**13**	**4**	**5**	**9**	**10** ♦
1988-89	**Edmonton**	**NHL**	**76**	**11**	**33**	**44**	**52**	**7**	**2**	**0**	**2**	**4**
1989-90	**Edmonton**	**NHL**	**70**	**1**	**23**	**24**	**56**	**22**	**0**	**6**	**6**	**11** ♦
1990-91	**Edmonton**	**NHL**	**53**	**5**	**22**	**27**	**32**	**18**	**3**	**7**	**10**	**10**
1991-92	**Los Angeles**	**NHL**	**56**	**4**	**19**	**23**	**43**	**6**	**1**	**1**	**2**	**10**
1992-93	**Los Angeles**	**NHL**	**82**	**2**	**25**	**27**	**64**	**23**	**1**	**4**	**5**	**12**
1993-94	**Los Angeles**	**NHL**	**79**	**5**	**13**	**18**	**71**	....	....	....	....	....
1994-95	**Los Angeles**	**NHL**	**9**	**0**	**1**	**1**	**6**	....	....	....	....	....
	Buffalo	**NHL**	**32**	**2**	**4**	**6**	**36**	**3**	**0**	**0**	**0**	**0**
1995-96	**Buffalo**	**NHL**	**52**	**5**	**5**	**10**	**59**	....	....	....	....	....
	St. Louis	**NHL**	**12**	**0**	**0**	**0**	**6**	**13**	**1**	**0**	**1**	**8**
	NHL Totals		**1016**	**99**	**354**	**453**	**785**	**183**	**19**	**66**	**85**	**135**

a NHL Plus/Minus Leader (1983)

Signed as a free agent by **Edmonton**, September 14, 1979. Claimed by **Minnesota** from **Edmonton** in Expansion Draft, May 30, 1991. Traded to **Los Angeles** by **Minnesota** with Randy Gilhen, Jim Thomson and NY Rangers' fourth round choice (previously acquired by Minnesota — Los Angeles selected Alexei Zhitnik) in 1991 Entry Draft for Todd Elik, June 22, 1991. Traded to **Buffalo** by **Los Angeles** with Alexei Zhitnik, Robb Stauber and Los Angeles' fifth round choice (Marian Menhart) in 1995 Entry Draft for Philippe Boucher, Denis Tsygurov and Grant Fuhr, February 14, 1995. Traded to **St. Louis** by **Buffalo** with Buffalo's seventh round choice (Daniel Corso) in 1996 Entry Draft for Denis Hamel, March 19, 1996.

HUDSON, MIKE — ST.L.

Center/Left wing. Shoots left. 6'1", 205 lbs. Born, Guelph, Ont., February 6, 1967.
(Chicago's 6th choice, 140th overall, in 1986 Entry Draft).

			Regular Season					Playoffs				
Season	Club	Lea	GP	G	A	TP	PIM	GP	G	A	TP	PIM
1984-85	Hamilton	OHL	50	10	12	22	13	....	....	....	....	....
1985-86	Hamilton	OHL	7	3	2	5	4	....	....	....	....	....
	Sudbury	OHL	59	35	42	77	20	4	2	5	7	7
1986-87	Sudbury	OHL	63	40	57	97	18	....	....	....	....	....
1987-88	Saginaw	IHL	75	18	30	48	44	10	2	3	5	20
1988-89	**Chicago**	**NHL**	**41**	**7**	**16**	**23**	**20**	**10**	**1**	**2**	**3**	**18**
	Saginaw	IHL	30	15	17	32	10	....	....	....	....	....
1989-90	**Chicago**	**NHL**	**49**	**9**	**12**	**21**	**56**	**4**	**0**	**0**	**0**	**2**
1990-91	**Chicago**	**NHL**	**55**	**7**	**9**	**16**	**62**	**6**	**0**	**2**	**2**	**8**
	Indianapolis	IHL	3	1	2	3	0	....	....	....	....	....
1991-92	**Chicago**	**NHL**	**76**	**14**	**15**	**29**	**92**	**16**	**3**	**5**	**8**	**26**
1992-93	**Chicago**	**NHL**	**36**	**1**	**6**	**7**	**44**	....	....	....	....	....
	Edmonton	**NHL**	**5**	**0**	**1**	**1**	**2**	....	....	....	....	....
1993-94	**NY Rangers**	**NHL**	**48**	**4**	**7**	**11**	**47**	....	....	....	....	.... ♦
1994-95	**Pittsburgh**	**NHL**	**40**	**2**	**9**	**11**	**34**	**11**	**0**	**0**	**0**	**6**
1995-96	**Toronto**	**NHL**	**27**	**2**	**0**	**2**	**29**	....	....	....	....	....
	St. Louis	**NHL**	**32**	**3**	**12**	**15**	**26**	**2**	**0**	**1**	**1**	**4**
	NHL Totals		**409**	**49**	**87**	**136**	**412**	**49**	**4**	**10**	**14**	**64**

Traded to **Edmonton** by **Chicago** for Craig Muni, March 22, 1993. Claimed by **NY Rangers** from **Edmonton** in NHL Waiver Draft, October 3, 1993. Claimed by **Pittsburgh** from **NY Rangers** in NHL Waiver Draft, January 18, 1995. Signed as a free agent by **Toronto**, September 22, 1995. Claimed on waivers by **St. Louis** from **Toronto**, January 4, 1996.

HUFFMAN, KERRY

Defense. Shoots left. 6'2", 200 lbs. Born, Peterborough, Ont., January 3, 1968.
(Philadelphia's 1st choice, 20th overall, in 1986 Entry Draft).

			Regular Season					Playoffs				
Season	Club	Lea	GP	G	A	TP	PIM	GP	G	A	TP	PIM
1985-86a	Guelph	OHL	56	3	24	27	35	20	1	10	11	10
1986-87	**Philadelphia**	**NHL**	**9**	**0**	**0**	**0**	**2**	....	....	....	....	....
	Hershey	AHL	3	0	1	1	0	4	0	0	0	0
b	Guelph	OHL	44	4	31	35	20	5	0	2	2	8
1987-88	**Philadelphia**	**NHL**	**52**	**6**	**17**	**23**	**34**	**2**	**0**	**0**	**0**	**0**
1988-89	**Philadelphia**	**NHL**	**29**	**0**	**11**	**11**	**31**	....	....	....	....	....
	Hershey	AHL	29	2	13	15	16	....	....	....	....	....
1989-90	**Philadelphia**	**NHL**	**43**	**1**	**12**	**13**	**34**	....	....	....	....	....
1990-91	**Philadelphia**	**NHL**	**10**	**1**	**2**	**3**	**10**	....	....	....	....	....
	Hershey	AHL	45	5	29	34	20	7	1	2	3	0
1991-92	**Philadelphia**	**NHL**	**60**	**14**	**18**	**32**	**41**	....	....	....	....	....
1992-93	**Quebec**	**NHL**	**52**	**4**	**18**	**22**	**54**	**3**	**0**	**0**	**0**	**0**
1993-94	**Quebec**	**NHL**	**28**	**0**	**6**	**6**	**28**	....	....	....	....	....
	Ottawa	**NHL**	**34**	**4**	**8**	**12**	**12**	....	....	....	....	....
1994-95	**Ottawa**	**NHL**	**37**	**2**	**4**	**6**	**46**	....	....	....	....	....
1995-96	**Ottawa**	**NHL**	**43**	**4**	**11**	**15**	**63**	....	....	....	....	....
	Philadelphia	**NHL**	**4**	**1**	**1**	**2**	**6**	**6**	**0**	**0**	**0**	**2**
	NHL Totals		**401**	**37**	**108**	**145**	**361**	**11**	**0**	**0**	**0**	**2**

a Won George Parsons Trophy (Memorial Cup Tournament Most Sportsmanlike Player) (1986)
b OHL First All-Star Team (1987)

Traded to **Quebec** by **Philadelphia** with Peter Forsberg, Steve Duchesne, Mike Ricci, Ron Hextall, Chris Simon, Philadelphia's first round choice in the 1993 (Jocelyn Thibault) and 1994 (later traded to Toronto — later traded to Washington — Washington selected Nolan Baumgartner) — Entry Drafts and cash for Eric Lindros, June 30, 1992. Claimed on waivers by **Ottawa** from **Quebec**, January 15, 1994. Traded to **Philadelphia** by **Ottawa** for future considerations, March 19, 1996.

HUGHES, BRENT — NYI

Left wing. Shoots left. 5'11", 195 lbs. Born, New Westminster, B.C., April 5, 1966.

			Regular Season					Playoffs				
Season	Club	Lea	GP	G	A	TP	PIM	GP	G	A	TP	PIM
1983-84	N. Westminster	WHL	67	21	18	39	133	9	2	2	4	27
1984-85	N. Westminster	WHL	64	25	32	57	135	11	2	1	3	37
1985-86	N. Westminster	WHL	71	28	52	80	180	....	....	....	....	....
1986-87	N. Westminster	WHL	8	5	4	9	22	....	....	....	....	....
	Victoria	WHL	61	38	61	99	146	5	4	1	5	8
1987-88	Moncton	AHL	73	13	19	32	206	....	....	....	....	....
1988-89	**Winnipeg**	**NHL**	**28**	**3**	**2**	**5**	**82**	....	....	....	....	....
	Moncton	AHL	54	34	34	68	286	10	9	4	13	40
1989-90	**Winnipeg**	**NHL**	**11**	**1**	**2**	**3**	**33**	....	....	....	....	....
	Moncton	AHL	65	31	29	60	277	....	....	....	....	....
1990-91	Moncton	AHL	63	21	22	43	144	3	0	0	0	7
1991-92	Baltimore	AHL	55	25	29	54	190	....	....	....	....	....
	Boston	**NHL**	**8**	**1**	**1**	**2**	**38**	**10**	**2**	**0**	**2**	**20**
	Maine	AHL	12	6	4	10	34	....	....	....	....	....
1992-93	**Boston**	**NHL**	**62**	**5**	**4**	**9**	**191**	**1**	**0**	**0**	**0**	**2**
1993-94	**Boston**	**NHL**	**77**	**13**	**11**	**24**	**143**	**13**	**2**	**1**	**3**	**27**
	Providence	AHL	6	2	5	7	4	....	....	....	....	....
1994-95	**Boston**	**NHL**	**44**	**6**	**6**	**12**	**139**	**5**	**0**	**0**	**0**	**4**
1995-96	**Buffalo**	**NHL**	**76**	**5**	**10**	**15**	**148**	....	....	....	....	....
	NHL Totals		**306**	**34**	**36**	**70**	**774**	**29**	**4**	**1**	**5**	**53**

Signed as a free agent by **Winnipeg**, June 13, 1988. Traded to **Washington** by **Winnipeg** with Craig Duncanson and Simon Wheeldon for Bob Joyce, Tyler Larter and Kent Paynter, May 21, 1991. Traded to **Boston** by **Washington** with future considerations for John Byce and Dennis Smith, February 24, 1992. Claimed By **Buffalo** from **Boston** in NHL Waiver Draft, October 2, 1995. Signed as a free agent by **NY Islanders**, August 9, 1996.

HUGHES, RYAN

Center. Shoots left. 6'2", 196 lbs. Born, Montreal, Que., January 17, 1972.
(Quebec's 2nd choice, 22nd overall, in 1990 Entry Draft).

			Regular Season					Playoffs				
Season	Club	Lea	GP	G	A	TP	PIM	GP	G	A	TP	PIM
1989-90	Cornell	ECAC	27	7	16	23	35	....	....	....	....	....
1990-91	Cornell	ECAC	32	18	34	52	28	....	....	....	....	....
1991-92	Cornell	ECAC	27	8	13	21	36	....	....	....	....	....
1992-93	Cornell	ECAC	26	8	14	22	30	....	....	....	....	....
1993-94	Cornwall	AHL	54	17	12	29	24	13	2	4	6	6
1994-95	Cornwall	AHL	72	15	24	39	48	14	0	7	7	10
1995-96	**Boston**	**NHL**	**3**	**0**	**0**	**0**	**0**	....	....	....	....	....
	Providence	AHL	78	22	52	74	89	4	1	2	3	20
	NHL Totals		**3**	**0**	**0**	**0**	**0**	....	....	....	....	....

Signed as a free agent by **Boston**, October 6, 1995.

HULBIG, JOE — EDM.

Left wing. Shoots left. 6'3", 215 lbs. Born, Norwood, MA, September 29, 1973.
(Edmonton's 1st choice, 13th overall, in 1992 Entry Draft).

			Regular Season					Playoffs				
Season	Club	Lea	GP	G	A	TP	PIM	GP	G	A	TP	PIM
1992-93	Providence	H.E.	26	3	13	16	22	....	....	....	....	....
1993-94	Providence	H.E.	28	6	4	10	36	....	....	....	....	....
1994-95	Providence	H.E.	37	14	21	35	36	....	....	....	....	....
1995-96	Providence	H.E.	31	14	22	36	56	....	....	....	....	....

HULL, BRETT — ST.L.

Right wing. Shoots right. 5'10", 201 lbs. Born, Belleville, Ont., August 9, 1964.
(Calgary's 6th choice, 117th overall, in 1984 Entry Draft).

			Regular Season					Playoffs				
Season	Club	Lea	GP	G	A	TP	PIM	GP	G	A	TP	PIM
1984-85	Minn.-Duluth	WCHA	48	32	28	60	24	....	....	....	....	....
1985-86a	Minn.-Duluth	WCHA	42	52	32	84	46	....	....	....	....	....
	Calgary	**NHL**	....	....	....	....	....	**2**	**0**	**0**	**0**	**0**
1986-87	**Calgary**	**NHL**	**5**	**1**	**0**	**1**	**0**	**4**	**2**	**1**	**3**	**0**
bc	Moncton	AHL	67	50	42	92	16	3	2	2	4	2
1987-88	**Calgary**	**NHL**	**52**	**26**	**24**	**50**	**12**	....	....	....	....	....
	St. Louis	**NHL**	**13**	**6**	**8**	**14**	**4**	**10**	**7**	**2**	**9**	**4**
1988-89	**St. Louis**	**NHL**	**78**	**41**	**43**	**84**	**33**	**10**	**5**	**5**	**10**	**6**
1989-90def	**St. Louis**	**NHL**	**80**	***72**	**41**	**113**	**24**	**12**	**13**	**8**	**21**	**17**
1990-91 dfghi	**St. Louis**	**NHL**	**78**	***86**	**45**	**131**	**22**	**13**	**11**	**8**	**19**	**4**
1991-92d	**St. Louis**	**NHL**	**73**	***70**	**39**	**109**	**48**	**6**	**4**	**4**	**8**	**4**
1992-93	**St. Louis**	**NHL**	**80**	**54**	**47**	**101**	**41**	**11**	**8**	**5**	**13**	**2**
1993-94	**St. Louis**	**NHL**	**81**	**57**	**40**	**97**	**38**	**4**	**2**	**1**	**3**	**0**
1994-95	**St. Louis**	**NHL**	**48**	**29**	**21**	**50**	**10**	**7**	**6**	**2**	**8**	**0**
1995-96	**St. Louis**	**NHL**	**70**	**43**	**40**	**83**	**30**	**13**	**6**	**5**	**11**	**10**
	NHL Totals		**658**	**485**	**348**	**833**	**262**	**92**	**64**	**41**	**105**	**47**

a WCHA First All-Star Team (1986)
b AHL First All-Star Team (1987)
c Won Dudley "Red" Garrett Memorial Trophy (Top Rookie - AHL) (1987)
d NHL First All-Star Team (1990, 1991, 1992)
e Won Lady Byng Trophy (1990)
f Won Dodge Ram Tough Award (1990, 1991)
g Won Hart Memorial Trophy (1991)
h Won Lester B. Pearson Award (1991)
i Won ProSet/NHL Player of the Year Award (1991)

Played in NHL All-Star Game (1989, 1990, 1992-94, 1996)

Traded to **St. Louis** by **Calgary** with Steve Bozek for Rob Ramage and Rick Wamsley, March 7, 1988.

HULL, JODY — FLA.

Right wing. Shoots right. 6'2", 195 lbs. Born, Cambridge, Ont., February 2, 1969.
(Hartford's 1st choice, 18th overall, in 1987 Entry Draft).

			Regular Season					Playoffs				
Season	Club	Lea	GP	G	A	TP	PIM	GP	G	A	TP	PIM
1985-86	Peterborough	OHL	61	20	22	42	29	16	1	5	6	4
1986-87	Peterborough	OHL	49	18	34	52	22	12	4	9	13	14
1987-88a	Peterborough	OHL	60	50	44	94	33	12	10	8	18	8
1988-89	**Hartford**	**NHL**	**60**	**16**	**18**	**34**	**10**	**1**	**0**	**0**	**0**	**2**
1989-90	**Hartford**	**NHL**	**38**	**7**	**10**	**17**	**21**	**5**	**0**	**1**	**1**	**2**
	Binghamton	AHL	21	7	10	17	6	....	....	....	....	....
1990-91	**NY Rangers**	**NHL**	**47**	**5**	**8**	**13**	**10**	....	....	....	....	....
1991-92	**NY Rangers**	**NHL**	**3**	**0**	**0**	**0**	**2**	....	....	....	....	....
	Binghamton	AHL	69	34	31	65	28	11	5	2	7	4
1992-93	**Ottawa**	**NHL**	**69**	**13**	**21**	**34**	**14**	....	....	....	....	....
1993-94	**Florida**	**NHL**	**69**	**13**	**13**	**26**	**8**	....	....	....	....	....
1994-95	**Florida**	**NHL**	**46**	**11**	**8**	**19**	**8**	....	....	....	....	....
1995-96	**Florida**	**NHL**	**78**	**20**	**17**	**37**	**25**	**14**	**3**	**2**	**5**	**0**
	NHL Totals		**410**	**85**	**95**	**180**	**98**	**20**	**3**	**3**	**6**	**4**

a OHL Second All-Star Team (1988)

Traded to **NY Rangers** by **Hartford** for Carey Wilson and NY Rangers' third round choice (Mikael Nylander) in the 1991 Entry Draft, July 9, 1990. Traded to **Ottawa** by **NY Rangers** for future considerations, July 28, 1992. Signed as a free agent by **Florida**, August 10, 1993.

HULSE, CALE — CGY.

Defense. Shoots right. 6'3", 210 lbs. Born, Edmonton, Alta., November 10, 1973.
(New Jersey's 3rd choice, 66th overall, in 1992 Entry Draft).

			Regular Season					Playoffs				
Season	Club	Lea	GP	G	A	TP	PIM	GP	G	A	TP	PIM
1991-92	Portland	WHL	70	4	18	22	250	6	0	2	2	27
1992-93	Portland	WHL	72	10	26	36	284	16	4	4	8	65
1993-94	Albany	AHL	79	7	14	21	186	5	0	3	3	11
1994-95	Albany	AHL	77	5	13	18	215	12	1	1	2	17
1995-96	**New Jersey**	**NHL**	**8**	**0**	**0**	**0**	**15**	....	....	....	....	....
	Albany	AHL	42	4	23	27	107	....	....	....	....	....
	Calgary	**NHL**	**3**	**0**	**0**	**0**	**5**	**1**	**0**	**0**	**0**	**0**
	Saint John	AHL	13	2	7	9	39	....	....	....	....	....
	NHL Totals		**11**	**0**	**0**	**0**	**20**	**1**	**0**	**0**	**0**	**0**

Traded to **Calgary** by **New Jersey** with Tommy Albelin and Jocelyn Lemieux for Phil Housley and Dan Keczmer, February 26, 1996.

HULST, KENT — WSH.

Center. Shoots left. 6', 180 lbs. Born, St. Thomas, Ont., April 8, 1968.
(Toronto's 4th choice, 69th overall, in 1986 Entry Draft).

			Regular Season					Playoffs				
Season	Club	Lea	GP	G	A	TP	PIM	GP	G	A	TP	PIM
1985-86	Belleville	OHL	43	6	17	23	20	....	....	....	....	....
	Windsor	OHL	17	6	10	16	9	....	....	....	....	....
1986-87	Windsor	OHL	37	18	20	38	49	....	....	....	....	....
	Belleville	OHL	27	13	10	23	17	6	1	1	2	0
1987-88	Belleville	OHL	66	42	43	85	48	6	3	1	4	7
1988-89	Belleville	OHL	45	21	41	62	43	....	....	....	....	....
	Flint	IHL	7	0	1	1	4	....	....	....	....	....
	Newmarket	AHL	....	....	....	....	....	2	1	1	2	2
1989-90	Newmarket	AHL	80	26	34	60	29	....	....	....	....	....
1990-91	Newmarket	AHL	79	28	37	65	57	....	....	....	....	....
1991-92	New Haven	AHL	80	21	39	60	59	5	2	2	4	0
1992-93	Lyss	Switz.	30	10	20	30	....	....	....	....	....	....
1993-94	Portland	AHL	72	34	33	67	68	17	4	6	10	14
1994-95	Portland	AHL	29	10	17	27	80	7	3	1	4	2
1995-96	Portland	AHL	75	25	47	72	122	24	11	16	27	30

Signed as a free agent by **Washington**, August, 1996.

HUNT, GORDON — DET.

Center. Shoots left. 6'5", 200 lbs. Born, Greenwich, CT, July 15, 1975.
(Detroit's 12th choice, 282nd overall, in 1993 Entry Draft).

			Regular Season					Playoffs				
Season	Club	Lea	GP	G	A	TP	PIM	GP	G	A	TP	PIM
1993-94	Ferris State	CCHA	37	2	3	5	42	....	....	....	....	....
1994-95	Ferris State	CCHA	29	8	7	15	47	....	....	....	....	....
1995-96	Ferris State	CCHA	35	12	11	23	62	....	....	....	....	....

HUNTER, DALE — WSH.

Center. Shoots left. 5'10", 198 lbs. Born, Petrolia, Ont., July 31, 1960.
(Quebec's 2nd choice, 41st overall, in 1979 Entry Draft).

			Regular Season					Playoffs				
Season	Club	Lea	GP	G	A	TP	PIM	GP	G	A	TP	PIM
1977-78	Kitchener	OHA	68	22	42	64	115	....	....	....	....	....
1978-79	Sudbury	OHA	59	42	68	110	188	10	4	12	16	47
1979-80	Sudbury	OHA	61	34	51	85	189	9	6	9	15	45
1980-81	Quebec	NHL	80	19	44	63	226	5	4	2	6	34
1981-82	Quebec	NHL	80	22	50	72	272	16	3	7	10	52
1982-83	Quebec	NHL	80	17	46	63	206	4	2	1	3	24
1983-84	Quebec	NHL	77	24	55	79	232	9	2	3	5	41
1984-85	Quebec	NHL	80	20	52	72	209	17	4	6	10	*97
1985-86	Quebec	NHL	80	28	42	70	265	3	0	0	0	15
1986-87	Quebec	NHL	46	10	29	39	135	13	1	7	8	56
1987-88	Washington	NHL	79	22	37	59	240	14	7	5	12	98
1988-89	Washington	NHL	80	20	37	57	219	6	0	4	4	29
1989-90	Washington	NHL	80	23	39	62	233	15	4	8	12	61
1990-91	Washington	NHL	76	16	30	46	234	11	1	9	10	41
1991-92	Washington	NHL	80	28	50	78	205	7	1	4	5	16
1992-93	Washington	NHL	84	20	59	79	198	6	7	1	8	35
1993-94	Washington	NHL	52	9	29	38	131	7	0	3	3	14
1994-95	Washington	NHL	45	8	15	23	101	7	4	4	8	24
1995-96	Washington	NHL	82	13	24	37	112	6	1	5	6	24
	NHL Totals		1181	299	638	937	3218	146	41	69	110	661

Traded to **Washington** by **Quebec** with Clint Malarchuk for Gaetan Duchesne, Alan Haworth, and Washington's first round choice (Joe Sakic) in 1987 Entry Draft, June 13, 1987.

HUNTER, TIM — S.J.

Right wing. Shoots right. 6'2", 202 lbs. Born, Calgary, Alta., September 10, 1960.
(Atlanta's 4th choice, 54th overall, in 1979 Entry Draft).

			Regular Season					Playoffs				
Season	Club	Lea	GP	G	A	TP	PIM	GP	G	A	TP	PIM
1979-80	Seattle	WHL	72	14	53	67	311	12	1	2	3	41
1980-81	Birmingham	CHL	58	3	5	8	*236	....	....	....	....	....
	Nova Scotia	AHL	17	0	0	0	62	6	0	1	1	45
1981-82	Calgary	NHL	2	0	0	0	9	....	....	....	....	....
	Oklahoma City	CHL	55	4	12	16	222	....	....	....	....	....
1982-83	Calgary	NHL	16	1	0	1	54	9	1	0	1	*70
	Colorado	CHL	46	5	12	17	225	....	....	....	....	....
1983-84	Calgary	NHL	43	4	4	8	130	7	0	0	0	21
1984-85	Calgary	NHL	71	11	11	22	259	4	0	0	0	24
1985-86	Calgary	NHL	66	8	7	15	291	19	0	3	3	108
1986-87	Calgary	NHL	73	6	15	21	*361	6	0	0	0	51
1987-88	Calgary	NHL	68	8	5	13	337	9	4	0	4	32
1988-89	Calgary	NHL	75	3	9	12	*375	19	0	4	4	32 ♦
1989-90	Calgary	NHL	67	2	3	5	279	6	0	0	0	4
1990-91	Calgary	NHL	34	5	2	7	143	7	0	0	0	10
1991-92	Calgary	NHL	30	1	3	4	167	....	....	....	....	....
1992-93	Quebec	NHL	48	5	3	8	94	....	....	....	....	....
	Vancouver	NHL	26	0	4	4	99	11	0	0	0	26
1993-94	Vancouver	NHL	56	3	4	7	171	24	0	0	0	26
1994-95	Vancouver	NHL	34	3	2	5	120	11	0	0	0	22
1995-96	Vancouver	NHL	60	2	0	2	122	....	....	....	....	....
	NHL Totals		769	62	72	134	3011	132	5	7	12	426

Claimed by **Tampa Bay** from **Calgary** in Expansion Draft, June 18, 1992. Traded to **Quebec** by **Tampa Bay** for future considerations (Martin Simard, September 14, 1992), June 19, 1992. Claimed on waivers by **Vancouver** from **Quebec**, February 12, 1993. Signed as a free agent by **San Jose**, July 23, 1996.

HURLBUT, MIKE

Defense. Shoots left. 6'2", 200 lbs. Born, Massena, NY, October 7, 1966.
(NY Rangers' 1st choice, 5th overall, in 1988 Supplemental Draft).

			Regular Season					Playoffs				
Season	Club	Lea	GP	G	A	TP	PIM	GP	G	A	TP	PIM
1985-86	St. Lawrence	ECAC	25	2	10	12	40	....	....	....	....	....
1986-87	St. Lawrence	ECAC	35	8	15	23	44	....	....	....	....	....
1987-88	St. Lawrence	ECAC	38	6	12	18	18	....	....	....	....	....
1988-89ab	St. Lawrence	ECAC	36	8	25	33	30	....	....	....	....	....
	Denver	IHL	8	0	2	2	13	4	1	2	3	2
1989-90	Flint	IHL	74	3	34	37	38	3	0	1	1	2
1990-91	San Diego	IHL	2	1	0	1	0	....	....	....	....	....
	Binghamton	AHL	33	2	11	13	27	3	0	1	1	0
1991-92	Binghamton	AHL	79	16	39	55	64	11	2	7	9	8
1992-93	NY Rangers	NHL	23	1	8	9	16	....	....	....	....	....
	Binghamton	AHL	45	11	25	36	46	14	2	5	7	12
1993-94	Quebec	NHL	1	0	0	0	0	....	....	....	....	....
	Cornwall	AHL	77	13	33	46	100	13	3	7	10	12
1994-95c	Cornwall	AHL	74	11	49	60	69	3	1	0	1	15
1995-96	Minnesota	IHL	22	1	4	5	22	....	....	....	....	....
	Houston	IHL	38	3	12	15	33	....	....	....	....	....
	NHL Totals		24	1	8	9	16	....	....	....	....	....

a ECAC First All-Star Team (1989)
b NCAA East First All-American Team (1989)
c AHL Second All-Star Team (1995)

Traded to **Quebec** by **NY Rangers** for Alexander Karpovtsev, September 7, 1993.

HURLEY, MIKE — DAL.

Right wing. Shoots right. 5'11", 173 lbs. Born, Charlottetown, P.E.I., November 17, 1977.
(Dallas' 3rd choice, 90th overall, in 1996 Entry Draft).

			Regular Season					Playoffs				
Season	Club	Lea	GP	G	A	TP	PIM	GP	G	A	TP	PIM
1994-95	Tri-City	WHL	47	2	4	6	10	10	0	1	1	0
1995-96	Tri-City	WHL	65	32	13	45	34	11	0	3	3	6

HUSCROFT, JAMIE — CGY.

Defense. Shoots right. 6'2", 200 lbs. Born, Creston, B.C., January 9, 1967.
(New Jersey's 9th choice, 171st overall, in 1985 Entry Draft).

			Regular Season					Playoffs				
Season	Club	Lea	GP	G	A	TP	PIM	GP	G	A	TP	PIM
1983-84	Seattle	WHL	63	0	12	12	77	5	0	0	0	15
1984-85	Seattle	WHL	69	3	13	16	273	....	....	....	....	....
1985-86	Seattle	WHL	66	6	20	26	394	5	0	1	1	18
1986-87	Seattle	WHL	21	1	18	19	99	....	....	....	....	....
	Medicine Hat	WHL	35	4	21	25	170	20	0	3	3	*125
1987-88	Utica	AHL	71	5	7	12	316	....	....	....	....	....
	Flint	IHL	3	1	0	1	2	16	0	1	1	110
1988-89	New Jersey	NHL	15	0	2	2	51	....	....	....	....	....
	Utica	AHL	41	2	10	12	215	5	0	0	0	40
1989-90	New Jersey	NHL	42	2	3	5	149	5	0	0	0	16
	Utica	AHL	22	3	6	9	122	....	....	....	....	....
1990-91	New Jersey	NHL	8	0	1	1	27	3	0	0	0	6
	Utica	AHL	59	3	15	18	339	....	....	....	....	....
1991-92	Utica	AHL	50	4	7	11	224	....	....	....	....	....
1992-93	Providence	AHL	69	2	15	17	257	2	0	1	1	6
1993-94	Boston	NHL	36	0	1	1	144	4	0	0	0	9
	Providence	AHL	32	1	10	11	157	....	....	....	....	....
1994-95	Boston	NHL	34	0	6	6	103	5	0	0	0	11
1995-96	Calgary	NHL	70	3	9	12	162	4	0	1	1	4
	NHL Totals		205	5	22	27	636	21	0	1	1	46

Signed as a free agent by **Boston**, July 23, 1992. Signed as a free agent by **Calgary**, August 22, 1995.

HUSKA, RYAN (HUHS-kuh) — CHI.

Left wing. Shoots left. 6'2", 194 lbs. Born, Cranbrook, B.C., July 2, 1975.
(Chicago's 4th choice, 76th overall, in 1993 Entry Draft).

			Regular Season					Playoffs				
Season	Club	Lea	GP	G	A	TP	PIM	GP	G	A	TP	PIM
1991-92	Kamloops	WHL	44	4	5	9	23	6	0	1	1	0
1992-93	Kamloops	WHL	68	17	15	32	50	13	2	6	8	4
1993-94	Kamloops	WHL	69	23	31	54	66	19	9	5	14	23
1994-95	Kamloops	WHL	66	27	40	67	78	17	7	8	15	12
1995-96	Indianapolis	IHL	28	2	3	5	15	5	1	1	2	27

HYMOVITZ, DAVID — CHI.

Left wing. Shoots left. 5'11", 170 lbs. Born, Boston, MA, May 30, 1974.
(Chicago's 9th choice, 209th overall, in 1992 Entry Draft).

			Regular Season					Playoffs				
Season	Club	Lea	GP	G	A	TP	PIM	GP	G	A	TP	PIM
1992-93	Boston College	H.E.	37	7	6	13	6	....	....	....	....	....
1993-94	Boston College	H.E.	36	18	14	32	18	....	....	....	....	....
1994-95	Boston College	H.E.	35	21	19	40	22	....	....	....	....	....
1995-96a	Boston College	H.E.	35	26	18	44	32	....	....	....	....	....

a Hockey East All-Star Team (1996)

IAFRATE, AL (IGH-uh-FRAY-tee) — S.J.

Defense. Shoots left. 6'3", 235 lbs. Born, Dearborn, MI, March 21, 1966.
(Toronto's 1st choice, 4th overall, in 1984 Entry Draft).

			Regular Season					Playoffs				
Season	Club	Lea	GP	G	A	TP	PIM	GP	G	A	TP	PIM
1983-84a	U.S. National	....	55	4	17	21	26	....	....	....	....	....
	U.S. Olympic	....	6	0	0	0	2	....	....	....	....	....
	Belleville	OHL	10	2	4	6	2	3	0	1	1	5
1984-85	Toronto	NHL	68	5	16	21	51	....	....	....	....	....
1985-86	Toronto	NHL	65	8	25	33	40	10	0	3	3	4
1986-87	Toronto	NHL	80	9	21	30	55	13	1	3	4	11
1987-88	Toronto	NHL	77	22	30	52	80	6	3	4	7	6
1988-89	Toronto	NHL	65	13	20	33	72	....	....	....	....	....
1989-90	Toronto	NHL	75	21	42	63	135	....	....	....	....	....
1990-91	Toronto	NHL	42	3	15	18	113	....	....	....	....	....
	Washington	NHL	30	6	8	14	124	10	1	3	4	22
1991-92	Washington	NHL	78	17	34	51	180	7	4	2	6	14
1992-93a	Washington	NHL	81	25	41	66	169	6	6	0	6	4
1993-94	Washington	NHL	67	10	35	45	143	....	....	....	....	....
	Boston	NHL	12	5	8	13	20	13	3	1	4	6
1994-95			DID NOT PLAY – INJURED									
1995-96			DID NOT PLAY – INJURED									
	NHL Totals		740	144	295	439	1182	65	18	16	34	67

a NHL Second All-Star Team (1993)

Played in NHL All-Star Game (1988, 1990, 1993, 1994)

Traded to **Washington** by **Toronto** for Peter Zezel and Bob Rouse, January 16, 1991. Traded to **Boston** by **Washington** for Joe Juneau, March 21, 1994. Traded to **San Jose** by **Boston** for Jeff Odgers and Pittsburgh's fifth round choice (previously acquired by San Jose – Boston selected Elias Abrahamsson) in 1996 Entry Draft, June 21, 1996.

IGINLA, JAROME (ih-GIHN-lah, jah-ROHM) — CGY.

Right wing. Shoots right. 6'1", 193 lbs. Born, Edmonton, Alta., July 1, 1977.
(Dallas' 1st choice, 11th overall, in 1995 Entry Draft).

			Regular Season					Playoffs				
Season	Club	Lea	GP	G	A	TP	PIM	GP	G	A	TP	PIM
1993-94	Kamloops	WHL	48	6	23	39	33	19	3	6	9	10
1994-95a	Kamloops	WHL	72	33	38	71	111	21	7	11	18	34
1995-96bc	Kamloops	WHL	63	63	73	136	120	16	16	13	29	44
	Calgary	NHL	....	....	....	....	....	2	1	1	2	0
	NHL Totals		....	....	....	....	....	2	1	1	2	0

a Won George Parsons Trophy (Memorial Cup Tournament Most Sportsmanlike Player) (1995)
b WHL West First All-Star Team (1996)
c Canadian Major Junior First All-Star Team (1996)

Traded to **Calgary** by **Dallas** with Corey Millen for Joe Nieuwendyk, December 19, 1995.

IGNATOV, NIKOLAI — T.B.

Defense. Shoots left. 6'2", 200 lbs. Born, Moscow, USSR, April 22, 1978.
(Tampa Bay's 4th choice, 152nd overall, in 1996 Entry Draft).

			Regular Season					Playoffs				
Season	Club	Lea	GP	G	A	TP	PIM	GP	G	A	TP	PIM
1995-96	CSKA 2	CIS 2	UNAVAILABLE									

INTRANUOVO, RALPH (ihn-trah-NOO-voh) EDM.

Center. Shoots left. 5'8", 185 lbs. Born, East York, Ont., December 11, 1973.
(Edmonton's 5th choice, 96th overall, in 1992 Entry Draft).

			Regular Season					Playoffs				
Season	Club	Lea	GP	G	A	TP	PIM	GP	G	A	TP	PIM
1990-91	S.S. Marie	OHL	63	25	42	67	22	14	7	13	20	17
1991-92	S.S. Marie	OHL	65	50	63	113	44	18	10	14	24	12
1992-93ab	S.S. Marie	OHL	54	31	47	78	61	18	10	16	26	30
1993-94	Cape Breton	AHL	66	21	31	52	39	4	1	2	3	2
1994-95c	Cape Breton	AHL	70	46	47	93	62	....	....	....	....	....
	Edmonton	**NHL**	**1**	**0**	**1**	**1**	**0**	....	....	....	....	....
1995-96	**Edmonton**	**NHL**	**13**	**1**	**2**	**3**	**4**	....	....	....	....	....
	Cape Breton	AHL	52	34	39	73	84	....	....	....	....	....
	NHL Totals		**14**	**1**	**3**	**4**	**4**	....	....	....	....	....

a Won Stafford Smythe Memorial Trophy (Memorial Cup Tournament MVP) (1993)
b Memorial Cup All-Star Team (1993)
c AHL Second All-Star Team (1995)

IRVING, JOEL MTL.

Center. Shoots right. 6'3", 190 lbs. Born, Lumsden, Sask., January 2, 1976.
(Montreal's 8th choice, 148th overall, in 1994 Entry Draft).

			Regular Season					Playoffs				
Season	Club	Lea	GP	G	A	TP	PIM	GP	G	A	TP	PIM
1994-95	W. Michigan	CCHA	30	2	3	5	20	....	....	....	....	....
1995-96	W. Michigan	CCHA	39	7	6	13	58	....	....	....	....	....

ISBISTER, BRAD PHO.

Right wing. Shoots right. 6'2", 198 lbs. Born, Edmonton, Alta., May 7, 1977.
(Winnipeg's 4th choice, 67th overall, in 1995 Entry Draft).

			Regular Season					Playoffs				
Season	Club	Lea	GP	G	A	TP	PIM	GP	G	A	TP	PIM
1993-94	Portland	WHL	64	7	10	17	45	....	....	....	....	....
1994-95	Portland	WHL	67	16	20	36	123	....	....	....	....	....
1995-96	Portland	WHL	71	45	44	89	184	7	2	4	6	20

JACKMAN, RICHARD DAL.

Defense. Shoots right. 6'2", 180 lbs. Born, Toronto, Ont., June 28, 1978.
(Dallas' 1st choice, 5th overall, in 1996 Entry Draft).

			Regular Season					Playoffs				
Season	Club	Lea	GP	G	A	TP	PIM	GP	G	A	TP	PIM
1995-96	S.S. Marie	OHL	66	13	29	42	97	4	1	0	1	15

JACKSON, DANE BUF.

Right wing. Shoots right. 6'1", 200 lbs. Born, Castlegar, B.C., May 17, 1970.
(Vancouver's 3rd choice, 44th overall, in 1988 Entry Draft).

			Regular Season					Playoffs				
Season	Club	Lea	GP	G	A	TP	PIM	GP	G	A	TP	PIM
1988-89	North Dakota	WCHA	30	4	5	9	33	....	....	....	....	....
1989-90	North Dakota	WCHA	44	15	11	26	56	....	....	....	....	....
1990-91	North Dakota	WCHA	37	17	9	26	79	....	....	....	....	....
1991-92	North Dakota	WCHA	39	23	19	42	81	....	....	....	....	....
1992-93	Hamilton	AHL	68	23	20	43	59	....	....	....	....	....
1993-94	**Vancouver**	**NHL**	**12**	**5**	**1**	**6**	**9**	....	....	....	....	....
	Hamilton	AHL	60	25	35	60	75	4	2	2	4	16
1994-95	Syracuse	AHL	78	30	28	58	162	....	....	....	....	....
	Vancouver	**NHL**	**3**	**1**	**0**	**1**	**4**	**6**	**0**	**0**	**0**	**10**
1995-96	**Buffalo**	**NHL**	**22**	**5**	**4**	**9**	**41**	....	....	....	....	....
	Rochester	AHL	50	27	19	46	132	19	4	6	10	53
	NHL Totals		**37**	**11**	**5**	**16**	**54**	**6**	**0**	**0**	**0**	**10**

Signed as a free agent by **Buffalo**, September 20, 1995.

JACQUES, ALEXANDRE DET.

Center. Shoots right. 5'11", 165 lbs. Born, Laval, Que., September 27, 1977.
(Detroit's 6th choice, 162nd overall, in 1996 Entry Draft).

			Regular Season					Playoffs				
Season	Club	Lea	GP	G	A	TP	PIM	GP	G	A	TP	PIM
1994-95	Shawinigan	QMJHL	71	9	8	17	18	14	8	5	13	8
1995-96	Shawinigan	QMJHL	60	25	32	57	57	6	3	2	5	2

JAGR, JAROMIR (YAH-guhr) PIT.

Right wing. Shoots left. 6'2", 216 lbs. Born, Kladno, Czech., February 15, 1972.
(Pittsburgh's 1st choice, 5th overall, in 1990 Entry Draft).

			Regular Season					Playoffs				
Season	Club	Lea	GP	G	A	TP	PIM	GP	G	A	TP	PIM
1988-89	Kladno	Czech.	39	8	10	18	4	....	....	....	....	....
1989-90	Kladno	Czech.	51	30	29	59	....	....	....	....	....	....
1990-91a	**Pittsburgh**	**NHL**	**80**	**27**	**30**	**57**	**42**	**24**	**3**	**10**	**13**	**6 ♦**
1991-92	**Pittsburgh**	**NHL**	**70**	**32**	**37**	**69**	**34**	**21**	**11**	**13**	**24**	**6 ♦**
1992-93	**Pittsburgh**	**NHL**	**81**	**34**	**60**	**94**	**61**	**12**	**5**	**4**	**9**	**23**
1993-94	**Pittsburgh**	**NHL**	**80**	**32**	**67**	**99**	**61**	**6**	**2**	**4**	**6**	**16**
1994-95	Kladno	Czech.	11	8	14	22	10	....	....	....	....	....
	Bolzano	Euro.	5	8	8	16	4	....	....	....	....	....
	Bolzano	Italy	1	0	0	0	0	....	....	....	....	....
	Schalke	Ger. 2	1	1	10	11	0	....	....	....	....	....
bc	**Pittsburgh**	**NHL**	**48**	**32**	**38**	***70**	**37**	**12**	**10**	**5**	**15**	**6**
1995-96b	**Pittsburgh**	**NHL**	**82**	**62**	**87**	**149**	**96**	**18**	**11**	**12**	**23**	**18**
	NHL Totals		**441**	**219**	**319**	**538**	**331**	**93**	**42**	**48**	**90**	**75**

a NHL/Upper Deck All-Rookie Team (1991)
b NHL First All-Star Team (1995, 1996)
c Won Art Ross Trophy (1995)

Played in NHL All-Star Game (1992, 1993, 1996)

JAKOPIN, JOHN DET.

Defense. Shoots right. 6'5", 220 lbs. Born, Toronto, Ont., May 16, 1975.
(Detroit's 4th choice, 97th overall, in 1993 Entry Draft).

			Regular Season					Playoffs				
Season	Club	Lea	GP	G	A	TP	PIM	GP	G	A	TP	PIM
1993-94	Merrimack	H.E.	36	2	8	10	64	....	....	....	....	....
1994-95	Merrimack	H.E.	37	4	10	14	42	....	....	....	....	....
1995-96	Merrimack	H.E.	32	10	15	25	68	....	....	....	....	....

JANDERA, LUBOMIR CHI.

Defense. Shoots left. 5'11", 180 lbs. Born, Chomutov, Czech., April 21, 1976.
(Chicago's 9th choice, 222nd overall, in 1994 Entry Draft).

			Regular Season					Playoffs				
Season	Club	Lea	GP	G	A	TP	PIM	GP	G	A	TP	PIM
1994-95	Pardubice	Czech.	5	0	0	0	0	3	0	0	0	0
1995-96	Decin	Czech. 2	20	4	5	9	....	....	....	....	....	....

JANNEY, CRAIG PHO.

Center. Shoots left. 6'1", 190 lbs. Born, Hartford, CT, September 26, 1967.
(Boston's 1st choice, 13th overall, in 1986 Entry Draft).

			Regular Season					Playoffs				
Season	Club	Lea	GP	G	A	TP	PIM	GP	G	A	TP	PIM
1985-86	Boston College	H.E.	34	13	14	27	8	....	....	....	....	....
1986-87ab	Boston College	H.E.	37	26	55	81	6	....	....	....	....	....
1987-88	U.S. National	....	52	26	44	70	6	....	....	....	....	....
	U.S. Olympic	....	5	3	1	4	2	....	....	....	....	....
	Boston	**NHL**	**15**	**7**	**9**	**16**	**0**	**23**	**6**	**10**	**16**	**11**
1988-89	**Boston**	**NHL**	**62**	**16**	**46**	**62**	**12**	**10**	**4**	**9**	**13**	**21**
1989-90	**Boston**	**NHL**	**55**	**24**	**38**	**62**	**4**	**18**	**3**	**19**	**22**	**2**
1990-91	**Boston**	**NHL**	**77**	**26**	**66**	**92**	**8**	**18**	**4**	**18**	**22**	**11**
1991-92	**Boston**	**NHL**	**53**	**12**	**39**	**51**	**20**	....	....	....	....	....
	St. Louis	**NHL**	**25**	**6**	**30**	**36**	**2**	**6**	**0**	**6**	**6**	**0**
1992-93	**St. Louis**	**NHL**	**84**	**24**	**82**	**106**	**12**	**11**	**2**	**9**	**11**	**0**
1993-94	**St. Louis**	**NHL**	**69**	**16**	**68**	**84**	**24**	**4**	**1**	**3**	**4**	**0**
1994-95	**St. Louis**	**NHL**	**8**	**2**	**5**	**7**	**0**	....	....	....	....	....
	San Jose	**NHL**	**27**	**5**	**15**	**20**	**10**	**11**	**3**	**4**	**7**	**4**
1995-96	**San Jose**	**NHL**	**71**	**13**	**49**	**62**	**26**	....	....	....	....	....
	Winnipeg	**NHL**	**13**	**7**	**13**	**20**	**0**	**6**	**1**	**2**	**3**	**0**
	NHL Totals		**559**	**158**	**460**	**618**	**118**	**107**	**24**	**80**	**104**	**49**

a Hockey East First All-Star Team (1987)
b NCAA East First All-American Team (1987)

Traded to **St. Louis** by **Boston** with Stephane Quintal for Adam Oates, February 7, 1992. Acquired by **Vancouver** from **St. Louis** with St. Louis' second round choice (Dave Scathard) in 1994 Entry Draft as compensation for St. Louis' signing of free agent Petr Nedved, March 14, 1994. Traded to **St. Louis** by **Vancouver** for Jeff Brown, Bret Hedican and Nathan Lafayette, March 21, 1994. Traded to **San Jose** by **St. Louis** with cash for Jeff Norton and a conditional choice in 1997 Entry Draft, March 6, 1995. Traded to **Winnipeg** by **San Jose** for Darren Turcotte and Dallas' second round choice (previously acquired by Winnipeg — later traded to Chicago — Chicago selected Remi Royer) in 1996 Entry Draft, March 18, 1996.

JANSSENS, MARK HFD.

Center. Shoots left. 6'3", 212 lbs. Born, Surrey, B.C., May 19, 1968.
(NY Rangers' 4th choice, 72nd overall, in 1986 Entry Draft).

			Regular Season					Playoffs				
Season	Club	Lea	GP	G	A	TP	PIM	GP	G	A	TP	PIM
1984-85	Regina	WHL	70	8	22	30	51	....	....	....	....	....
1985-86	Regina	WHL	71	25	38	63	146	9	0	2	2	17
1986-87	Regina	WHL	68	24	38	62	209	3	0	1	1	14
1987-88	**NY Rangers**	**NHL**	**1**	**0**	**0**	**0**	**0**	....	....	....	....	....
	Colorado	IHL	6	2	2	4	24	12	3	2	5	20
	Regina	WHL	71	39	51	90	202	4	3	4	7	6
1988-89	**NY Rangers**	**NHL**	**5**	**0**	**0**	**0**	**0**	....	....	....	....	....
	Denver	IHL	38	19	19	38	104	4	3	0	3	18
1989-90	**NY Rangers**	**NHL**	**80**	**5**	**8**	**13**	**161**	**9**	**2**	**1**	**3**	**10**
1990-91	**NY Rangers**	**NHL**	**67**	**9**	**7**	**16**	**172**	**6**	**3**	**0**	**3**	**6**
1991-92	**NY Rangers**	**NHL**	**4**	**0**	**0**	**0**	**5**	....	....	....	....	....
	Binghamton	AHL	55	10	23	33	109	....	....	....	....	....
	Minnesota	**NHL**	**3**	**0**	**0**	**0**	**0**	....	....	....	....	....
	Kalamazoo	IHL	2	0	0	0	2	11	1	2	3	22
1992-93	**Hartford**	**NHL**	**76**	**12**	**17**	**29**	**237**	....	....	....	....	....
1993-94	**Hartford**	**NHL**	**84**	**2**	**10**	**12**	**137**	....	....	....	....	....
1994-95	**Hartford**	**NHL**	**46**	**2**	**5**	**7**	**93**	....	....	....	....	....
1995-96	**Hartford**	**NHL**	**81**	**2**	**7**	**9**	**155**	....	....	....	....	....
	NHL Totals		**447**	**32**	**54**	**86**	**960**	**15**	**5**	**1**	**6**	**16**

Traded to **Minnesota** by **NY Rangers** for Mario Thyer and Minnesota's third round choice (Maxim Galanov) in 1993 Entry Draft, March 10, 1992. Traded to **Hartford** by **Minnesota** for James Black, September 3, 1992.

JENNINGS, GRANT

Defense. Shoots left. 6'3", 210 lbs. Born, Hudson Bay, Sask., May 5, 1965.

			Regular Season					Playoffs				
Season	Club	Lea	GP	G	A	TP	PIM	GP	G	A	TP	PIM
1983-84	Saskatoon	WHL	64	5	13	18	102	....	....	....	....	....
1984-85	Saskatoon	WHL	47	10	24	34	134	2	1	0	1	2
1985-86	Binghamton	AHL	51	0	4	4	109	....	....	....	....	....
1986-87	Fort Wayne	IHL	3	0	0	0	0	....	....	....	....	....
	Binghamton	AHL	47	1	5	6	125	13	0	2	2	17
1987-88	**Washington**	**NHL**	....	....	....	....	....	**1**	**0**	**0**	**0**	**0**
	Binghamton	AHL	56	2	12	14	195	3	1	0	1	15
1988-89	**Hartford**	**NHL**	**55**	**3**	**10**	**13**	**159**	**4**	**1**	**0**	**1**	**17**
	Binghamton	AHL	2	0	0	0	2	....	....	....	....	....
1989-90	**Hartford**	**NHL**	**64**	**3**	**6**	**9**	**171**	**7**	**0**	**0**	**0**	**13**
1990-91	**Hartford**	**NHL**	**44**	**1**	**4**	**5**	**82**	....	....	....	....	....
	Pittsburgh	**NHL**	**13**	**1**	**3**	**4**	**26**	**13**	**1**	**1**	**2**	**16 ♦**
1991-92	**Pittsburgh**	**NHL**	**53**	**4**	**5**	**9**	**104**	**10**	**0**	**0**	**0**	**12 ♦**
1992-93	**Pittsburgh**	**NHL**	**58**	**0**	**5**	**5**	**65**	**12**	**0**	**0**	**0**	**8**
1993-94	**Pittsburgh**	**NHL**	**61**	**2**	**4**	**6**	**126**	**3**	**0**	**0**	**0**	**2**
1994-95	**Pittsburgh**	**NHL**	**25**	**0**	**4**	**4**	**36**	....	....	....	....	....
	Toronto	**NHL**	**10**	**0**	**2**	**2**	**7**	**4**	**0**	**0**	**0**	**0**
1995-96	**Buffalo**	**NHL**	**6**	**0**	**0**	**0**	**28**	....	....	....	....	....
	Rochester	AHL	9	0	1	1	28	....	....	....	....	....
	Atlanta	IHL	3	0	0	0	19	3	0	0	0	20
	NHL Totals		**389**	**14**	**43**	**57**	**804**	**54**	**2**	**1**	**3**	**68**

Signed as a free agent by **Washington**, June 25, 1985. Traded to **Hartford** by **Washington** with Ed Kastelic for Mike Millar and Neil Sheehy, July 6, 1988. Traded to **Pittsburgh** by **Hartford** with Ron Francis and Ulf Samuelsson for John Cullen, Jeff Parker and Zarley Zalapski, March 4, 1991. Traded to **Toronto** by **Pittsburgh** for Drake Berehowsky, April 7, 1995. Signed as a free agent by **Bufalo**, September 20, 1995.

JINDRICH, ROBERT S.J.

Defense. Shoots left. 5'11", 185 lbs. Born, Sokolov, Czech., October 14, 1976.
(San Jose's 10th choice, 168th overall, in 1995 Entry Draft).

			Regular Season					Playoffs				
Season	Club	Lea	GP	G	A	TP	PIM	GP	G	A	TP	PIM
1993-94	Plzen	Czech.	18	0	2	2	....	....	....	....	....	....
1994-95	Plzen	Czech.	11	1	0	1	4	....	....	....	....	....
1995-96	Plzen	Czech.	37	1	3	4	....	3	0	0	0	....

JINMAN, LEE DAL.

Center. Shoots right. 5'10", 160 lbs. Born, Toronto, Ont., January 10, 1976.
(Dallas' 2nd choice, 46th overall, in 1994 Entry Draft).

			Regular Season					Playoffs				
Season	Club	Lea	GP	G	A	TP	PIM	GP	G	A	TP	PIM
1993-94	North Bay	OHL	66	31	66	97	33	18	*18	19	37	8
1994-95	North Bay	OHL	63	39	65	104	41	6	5	5	10	4
1995-96	North Bay	OHL	38	19	33	52	23	....	....	....	....	....
	Detroit	OHL	26	10	35	45	26	17	6	15	21	16

JOBIN, FREDERIC — WSH.

Defense. Shoots left. 6', 210 lbs. Born, Montreal, Que., January 28, 1977.
(Washington's 8th choice, 147th overall, in 1995 Entry Draft).

			Regular Season					Playoffs				
Season	Club	Lea	GP	G	A	TP	PIM	GP	G	A	TP	PIM
1993-94	Laval	QMJHL	67	4	11	15	150	21	2	1	3	40
1994-95	Laval	QMJHL	70	0	13	13	285	20	1	1	2	106
1995-96	Granby	QMJHL	40	4	8	12	239	....	....	....	....	....
	Laval	QMJHL	27	1	9	10	82	....	....	....	....	....

JOHANSSON, ANDREAS — NYI

Center. Shoots left. 6', 205 lbs. Born, Hofors, Sweden, May 19, 1973.
(NY Islanders' 7th choice, 136th overall, in 1991 Entry Draft).

			Regular Season					Playoffs				
Season	Club	Lea	GP	G	A	TP	PIM	GP	G	A	TP	PIM
1990-91	Falun	Swe. 2	31	12	10	22	38	....	....	....	....	....
1991-92	Farjestad	Swe.	30	3	1	4	10	6	0	0	0	4
1992-93	Farjestad	Swe.	38	4	7	11	38	2	0	0	0	0
1993-94	Farjestad	Swe.	20	3	6	9	6	....	....	....	....	....
1994-95	Farjestad	Swe.	36	9	10	19	42	4	0	0	0	10
1995-96	**NY Islanders**	**NHL**	**3**	**0**	**1**	**1**	**0**	....	....	....	....	....
	Worcester	AHL	29	5	5	10	32	....	....	....	....	....
	Utah	IHL	22	4	13	17	28	12	0	5	5	6
	NHL Totals		**3**	**0**	**1**	**1**	**0**	....	....	....	....	....

JOHANSSON, CALLE (yo-HAHN-sehn, KAL-ee) — WSH.

Defense. Shoots left. 5'11", 200 lbs. Born, Goteborg, Sweden, February 14, 1967.
(Buffalo's 1st choice, 14th overall, in 1985 Entry Draft).

			Regular Season					Playoffs				
Season	Club	Lea	GP	G	A	TP	PIM	GP	G	A	TP	PIM
1983-84	V. Frolunda	Swe.	28	4	4	8	10	....	....	....	....	....
1984-85	V. Frolunda	Swe.2	25	8	13	21	16	6	1	2	3	4
1985-86	Bjorkloven	Swe.	17	1	2	3	4	....	....	....	....	....
1986-87	Bjorkloven	Swe.	30	2	13	15	20	6	1	3	4	6
1987-88a	**Buffalo**	**NHL**	**71**	**4**	**38**	**42**	**37**	**6**	**0**	**1**	**1**	**0**
1988-89	**Buffalo**	**NHL**	**47**	**2**	**11**	**13**	**33**	....	....	....	....	....
	Washington	**NHL**	**12**	**1**	**7**	**8**	**4**	**6**	**1**	**2**	**3**	**0**
1989-90	**Washington**	**NHL**	**70**	**8**	**31**	**39**	**25**	**15**	**1**	**6**	**7**	**4**
1990-91	**Washington**	**NHL**	**80**	**11**	**41**	**52**	**23**	**10**	**2**	**7**	**9**	**8**
1991-92	**Washington**	**NHL**	**80**	**14**	**42**	**56**	**49**	**7**	**0**	**5**	**5**	**4**
1992-93	**Washington**	**NHL**	**77**	**7**	**38**	**45**	**56**	**6**	**0**	**5**	**5**	**4**
1993-94	**Washington**	**NHL**	**84**	**9**	**33**	**42**	**59**	**6**	**1**	**3**	**4**	**4**
1994-95	Kloten	Switz.	5	1	2	3	8	....	....	....	....	....
	Washington	**NHL**	**46**	**5**	**26**	**31**	**35**	**7**	**3**	**1**	**4**	**0**
1995-96	**Washington**	**NHL**	**78**	**10**	**25**	**35**	**50**	....	....	....	....	....
	NHL Totals		**645**	**71**	**292**	**363**	**371**	**63**	**8**	**30**	**38**	**24**

a NHL All-Rookie Team (1988)

Traded to **Washington** by **Buffalo** with Buffalo's second round choice (Byron Dafoe) in 1989 Entry Draft for Clint Malarchuk, Grant Ledyard and Washington's sixth round choice (Brian Holzinger) in 1991 Entry Draft, March 7, 1989.

JOHANSSON, DANIEL (YOOH-hahn-suhn) — NYI

Defense. Shoots right. 5'11", 180 lbs. Born, Glimakra, Sweden, September 10, 1974.
(NY Islanders' 9th choice, 222nd overall, in 1993 Entry Draft).

			Regular Season					Playoffs				
Season	Club	Lea	GP	G	A	TP	PIM	GP	G	A	TP	PIM
1991-92	Rogle	Swe. 2	33	4	9	13	30	....	....	....	....	....
1992-93	Rogle	Swe.	28	2	4	6	20	....	....	....	....	....
1993-94	Rogle	Swe.	37	5	10	15	34	3	0	0	0	0
1994-95	Rogle	Swe.	22	4	2	6	16	....	....	....	....	....
1995-96	HV-71	Swe.	40	3	5	8	24	4	0	1	1	0

JOHANSSON, MATHIAS — CGY.

Center. Shoots left. 6'2", 190 lbs. Born, Oskarshamn, Sweden, February 22, 1974.
(Calgary's 3rd choice, 54th overall, in 1992 Entry Draft).

			Regular Season					Playoffs				
Season	Club	Lea	GP	G	A	TP	PIM	GP	G	A	TP	PIM
1990-91	Farjestad	Swe.	3	0	0	0	0	....	....	....	....	....
1991-92	Farjestad	Swe.	16	0	0	0	2	1	0	0	0	0
1992-93	Farjestad	Swe.	11	2	1	3	4	3	0	0	0	0
1993-94	Farjestad	Swe.	16	2	1	3	4	....	....	....	....	....
1994-95	Farjestad	Swe.	40	7	8	15	30	4	4	3	7	2
1995-96	Farjestad	Swe.	40	8	21	29	10	8	2	1	3	4

JOHANSSON, ROGER (yo-HAHN-suhn)

Defense. Shoots left. 6'1", 190 lbs. Born, Ljungby, Sweden, April 17, 1967.
(Calgary's 5th choice, 80th overall, in 1985 Entry Draft).

			Regular Season					Playoffs				
Season	Club	Lea	GP	G	A	TP	PIM	GP	G	A	TP	PIM
1983-84	Troja	Swe. 2	11	2	2	4	12	....	....	....	....	....
1984-85	Troja	Swe. 2	30	1	6	7	20	9	0	4	4	8
1985-86	Troja	Swe. 2	32	5	16	21	42	....	....	....	....	....
1986-87	Farjestad	Swe.	31	6	11	17	20	7	1	1	2	8
1987-88	Farjestad	Swe.	24	3	11	14	20	9	1	6	7	12
1988-89	Farjestad	Swe.	40	5	15	20	38	....	....	....	....	....
1989-90	**Calgary**	**NHL**	**35**	**0**	**5**	**5**	**48**	....	....	....	....	....
1990-91	**Calgary**	**NHL**	**38**	**4**	**13**	**17**	**47**	....	....	....	....	....
1991-92	Leksand	Swe.	22	3	9	12	42	....	....	....	....	....
1992-93	**Calgary**	**NHL**	**77**	**4**	**16**	**20**	**62**	**5**	**0**	**1**	**1**	**2**
1993-94	Leksand	Swe.	38	6	15	21	56	4	0	1	1	0
1994-95	Leksand	Swe.	7	0	0	0	14	....	....	....	....	....
	Chicago	**NHL**	**11**	**1**	**0**	**1**	**6**	....	....	....	....	....
1995-96	Farjestad	Swe.	34	3	4	7	46	8	3	1	4	16
	NHL Totals		**161**	**9**	**34**	**43**	**163**	**5**	**0**	**1**	**1**	**2**

Claimed by **Chicago** from **Calgary** in NHL Waiver Draft, January 18, 1995.

JOHNSON, ANDY — CHI.

Defense. Shoots left. 6'3", 188 lbs. Born, Fredericton, N.B., March 6, 1978.
(Chicago's 4th choice, 130th overall, in 1996 Entry Draft).

			Regular Season					Playoffs				
Season	Club	Lea	GP	G	A	TP	PIM	GP	G	A	TP	PIM
1995-96	Peterborough	OHL	54	0	4	4	57	22	0	6	6	21

JOHNSON, CLINT — PIT.

Left wing. Shoots left. 6'2", 200 lbs. Born, Duluth, MN, April 7, 1976.
(Pittsburgh's 7th choice, 128th overall, in 1994 Entry Draft).

			Regular Season					Playoffs				
Season	Club	Lea	GP	G	A	TP	PIM	GP	G	A	TP	PIM
1994-95	St. Paul	USHL	14	0	3	3	8	....	....	....	....	....
1995-96	U. Minnesota	WCHA	1	0	0	0	0	....	....	....	....	....

JOHNSON, CRAIG — L.A.

Left wing/Center. Shoots left. 6'2", 197 lbs. Born, St. Paul, MN, March 8, 1972.
(St. Louis' 1st choice, 33rd overall, in 1990 Entry Draft).

			Regular Season					Playoffs				
Season	Club	Lea	GP	G	A	TP	PIM	GP	G	A	TP	PIM
1990-91	U. Minnesota	WCHA	33	13	18	31	34	....	....	....	....	....
1991-92	U. Minnesota	WCHA	41	17	38	55	66	....	....	....	....	....
1992-93	U. Minnesota	WCHA	42	22	24	46	70	....	....	....	....	....
1993-94	U.S. National	....	54	25	26	51	64	....	....	....	....	....
	U.S. Olympic	....	8	0	4	4	4	....	....	....	....	....
1994-95	Peoria	IHL	16	2	6	8	25	9	0	4	4	10
	St. Louis	**NHL**	**15**	**3**	**3**	**6**	**6**	**1**	**0**	**0**	**0**	**2**
1995-96	**St. Louis**	**NHL**	**49**	**8**	**7**	**15**	**30**	....	....	....	....	....
	Worcester	AHL	5	3	0	3	2	....	....	....	....	....
	Los Angeles	**NHL**	**11**	**5**	**4**	**9**	**6**	....	....	....	....	....
	NHL Totals		**75**	**16**	**14**	**30**	**42**	**1**	**0**	**0**	**0**	**2**

Traded to **Los Angeles** by **St. Louis** with Patrice Tardif, Roman Vopat, St. Louis fifth round choice (Peter Hogan) in 1996 Entry Draft and first round choice in 1997 Entry Draft for Wayne Gretzky, February 27, 1996.

JOHNSON, GREG — DET.

Center. Shoots left. 5'10", 185 lbs. Born, Thunder Bay, Ont., March 16, 1971.
(Philadelphia's 1st choice, 33rd overall, in 1989 Entry Draft).

			Regular Season					Playoffs				
Season	Club	Lea	GP	G	A	TP	PIM	GP	G	A	TP	PIM
1989-90	North Dakota	WCHA	44	17	38	55	11	....	....	....	....	....
1990-91ab	North Dakota	WCHA	38	18	*61	79	6	....	....	....	....	....
1991-92ac	North Dakota	WCHA	39	20	*54	74	8	....	....	....	....	....
1992-93ab	North Dakota	WCHA	34	19	45	64	18	....	....	....	....	....
	Cdn. National	....	23	6	14	20	2	....	....	....	....	....
1993-94	**Detroit**	**NHL**	**52**	**6**	**11**	**17**	**22**	**7**	**2**	**2**	**4**	**2**
	Cdn. National	....	6	2	6	8	4	....	....	....	....	....
	Cdn. Olympic	....	8	0	3	3	0	....	....	....	....	....
	Adirondack	AHL	3	2	4	6	0	4	0	4	4	2
1994-95	**Detroit**	**NHL**	**22**	**3**	**5**	**8**	**14**	**1**	**0**	**0**	**0**	**0**
1995-96	**Detroit**	**NHL**	**60**	**18**	**22**	**40**	**30**	**13**	**3**	**1**	**4**	**8**
	NHL Totals		**134**	**27**	**38**	**65**	**66**	**21**	**5**	**3**	**8**	**10**

a WCHA First All-Star Team (1991, 1993)
b NCAA West First All-American Team (1991, 1993)
c NCAA West Second All-American Team (1992)

Traded to **Detroit** by **Philadelphia** with Philadelphia's fifth round choice (Frederic Deschenes) in 1994 Entry Draft for Jim Cummins and Philadelphia's fourth round choice (previously acquired by Detroit — later traded to Boston — Boston selected Charles Paquette) in 1993 Entry Draft, June 20, 1993.

JOHNSON, JIM — PHO.

Defense. Shoots left. 6'1", 190 lbs. Born, New Hope, MN, August 9, 1962.

			Regular Season					Playoffs				
Season	Club	Lea	GP	G	A	TP	PIM	GP	G	A	TP	PIM
1981-82	Minn.-Duluth	WCHA	40	0	10	10	62	....	....	....	....	....
1982-83	Minn.-Duluth	WCHA	44	3	18	21	118	....	....	....	....	....
1983-84	Minn.-Duluth	WCHA	43	3	13	16	116	....	....	....	....	....
1984-85	Minn.-Duluth	WCHA	47	7	29	36	49	....	....	....	....	....
1985-86	**Pittsburgh**	**NHL**	**80**	**3**	**26**	**29**	**115**	....	....	....	....	....
1986-87	**Pittsburgh**	**NHL**	**80**	**5**	**25**	**30**	**116**	....	....	....	....	....
1987-88	**Pittsburgh**	**NHL**	**55**	**1**	**12**	**13**	**87**	....	....	....	....	....
1988-89	**Pittsburgh**	**NHL**	**76**	**2**	**14**	**16**	**163**	**11**	**0**	**5**	**5**	**44**
1989-90	**Pittsburgh**	**NHL**	**75**	**3**	**13**	**16**	**154**	....	....	....	....	....
1990-91	**Pittsburgh**	**NHL**	**24**	**0**	**5**	**5**	**23**	....	....	....	....	....
	Minnesota	**NHL**	**44**	**1**	**9**	**10**	**100**	**14**	**0**	**1**	**1**	**52**
1991-92	**Minnesota**	**NHL**	**71**	**4**	**10**	**14**	**102**	**7**	**1**	**3**	**4**	**18**
1992-93	**Minnesota**	**NHL**	**79**	**3**	**20**	**23**	**105**	....	....	....	....	....
1993-94	**Dallas**	**NHL**	**53**	**0**	**7**	**7**	**51**	....	....	....	....	....
	Washington	**NHL**	**8**	**0**	**0**	**0**	**12**	....	....	....	....	....
1994-95	**Washington**	**NHL**	**47**	**0**	**13**	**13**	**43**	**7**	**0**	**2**	**2**	**8**
1995-96	**Washington**	**NHL**	**66**	**2**	**4**	**6**	**34**	**6**	**0**	**0**	**0**	**6**
	NHL Totals		**758**	**24**	**158**	**182**	**1105**	**45**	**1**	**11**	**12**	**128**

Signed as a free agent by **Pittsburgh**, June 9, 1985. Traded to **Minnesota** by **Pittsburgh** with Chris Dahlquist for Larry Murphy and Peter Taglianetti, December 11, 1990. Traded to **Washington** by **Dallas** for Alan May and Washington's seventh round choice (Jeff Dewar) in 1995 Entry Draft, March 21, 1994. Signed as a free agent by **Phoenix**, July 6, 1996.

JOHNSON, MATT — L.A.

Left wing. Shoots left. 6'5", 230 lbs. Born, Welland, Ont., November 23, 1975.
(Los Angeles' 2nd choice, 33rd overall, in 1994 Entry Draft).

			Regular Season					Playoffs				
Season	Club	Lea	GP	G	A	TP	PIM	GP	G	A	TP	PIM
1992-93	Peterborough	OHL	66	8	17	25	211	16	1	1	2	56
1993-94	Peterborough	OHL	50	13	24	37	233	....	....	....	....	....
1994-95	Peterborough	OHL	14	1	2	3	43	....	....	....	....	....
	Los Angeles	**NHL**	**14**	**1**	**0**	**1**	**102**	....	....	....	....	....
1995-96	**Los Angeles**	**NHL**	**1**	**0**	**0**	**0**	**5**	....	....	....	....	....
	Phoenix	IHL	29	4	4	8	87	....	....	....	....	....
	NHL Totals		**15**	**1**	**0**	**1**	**107**	....	....	....	....	....

JOHNSON, RYAN — FLA.

Center. Shoots left. 6'2", 185 lbs. Born, Thunder Bay, Ont., June 14, 1976.
(Florida's 4th choice, 36th overall, in 1994 Entry Draft).

			Regular Season					Playoffs				
Season	Club	Lea	GP	G	A	TP	PIM	GP	G	A	TP	PIM
1994-95	North Dakota	WCHA	38	6	22	28	39	....	....	....	....	....
1995-96	North Dakota	WCHA	21	2	17	19	14	....	....	....	....	....
	Cdn. National	....	28	5	12	17	14	....	....	....	....	....

JOHNSSON, KIM — NYR

Defense. Shoots left. 6'1", 175 lbs. Born, Malmo, Sweden, March 16, 1976.
(NY Rangers' 15th choice, 286th overall, in 1994 Entry Draft).

			Regular Season					Playoffs				
Season	Club	Lea	GP	G	A	TP	PIM	GP	G	A	TP	PIM
1993-94	Malmo	Swe.	2	0	0	0	0	....	....	....	....	....
1994-95	Malmo	Swe.	13	0	0	0	4	....	....	....	....	....
1995-96	Malmo	Swe.	38	2	0	2	30	4	0	1	1	8

JOMPHE, JEAN-FRANCOIS (zhohm-PHEE) ANA.

Center. Shoots left. 6'1", 195 lbs. Born, Harve' St. Pierre, Que., December 28, 1972.

			Regular Season					Playoffs				
Season	Club	Lea	GP	G	A	TP	PIM	GP	G	A	TP	PIM
1990-91	Shawinigan	QMJHL	42	17	22	39	14	6	2	1	3	2
1991-92	Shawinigan	QMJHL	44	28	33	61	69	10	6	10	16	10
1992-93	Sherbrooke	QMJHL	60	43	43	86	86	15	10	13	23	18
1993-94	San Diego	IHL	29	2	3	5	12	....	....	....	....	....
	Greensboro	ECHL	25	9	9	18	41	1	1	0	1	0
1994-95	Cdn. National	....	52	33	25	58	85	....	....	....	....	....
1995-96	**Anaheim**	**NHL**	**31**	**2**	**12**	**14**	**39**	....	....	....	....	....
	Baltimore	AHL	47	21	34	55	75	....	....	....	....	....
	NHL Totals		**31**	**2**	**12**	**14**	**39**	....	....	....	....	....

Signed as a free agent by **Anaheim**, September 7, 1993

JONES, BRAD

Left wing. Shoots left. 6', 195 lbs. Born, Sterling Heights, MI, June 26, 1965.
(Winnipeg's 8th choice, 156th overall, in 1984 Entry Draft).

			Regular Season					Playoffs				
Season	Club	Lea	GP	G	A	TP	PIM	GP	G	A	TP	PIM
1983-84	U. of Michigan	CCHA	37	8	26	34	32	....	....	....	....	....
1984-85	U. of Michigan	CCHA	34	21	27	48	66	....	....	....	....	....
1985-86a	U. of Michigan	CCHA	36	28	39	67	40	....	....	....	....	....
1986-87bc	U. of Michigan	CCHA	40	32	46	78	64	....	....	....	....	....
	Winnipeg	**NHL**	**4**	**1**	**0**	**1**	**0**	....	....	....	....	....
1987-88	**Winnipeg**	**NHL**	**19**	**2**	**5**	**7**	**15**	**1**	**0**	**0**	**0**	**0**
	U.S. National	....	50	27	23	50	59	....	....	....	....	....
1988-89	**Winnipeg**	**NHL**	**22**	**6**	**5**	**11**	**6**	....	....	....	....	....
	Moncton	AHL	44	20	19	39	62	7	0	1	1	22
1989-90	**Winnipeg**	**NHL**	**2**	**0**	**0**	**0**	**0**	....	....	....	....	....
	Moncton	AHL	15	5	6	11	47	....	....	....	....	....
	New Haven	AHL	36	8	11	19	71	....	....	....	....	....
1990-91	**Los Angeles**	**NHL**	**53**	**9**	**11**	**20**	**57**	**8**	**1**	**1**	**2**	**2**
1991-92	**Philadelphia**	**NHL**	**48**	**7**	**10**	**17**	**44**	....	....	....	....	....
1992-93	Ilves	Fin.	26	10	7	17	62	....	....	....	....	....
	New Haven	AHL	4	2	1	3	6	....	....	....	....	....
1993-94						UNAVAILABLE						
1994-95	Springfield	AHL	61	23	22	45	47	....	....	....	....	....
1995-96	Binghamton	AHL	62	25	27	52	36	4	1	1	2	0
	NHL Totals		**148**	**25**	**31**	**56**	**122**	**9**	**1**	**1**	**2**	**2**

a CCHA Second All-Star Team (1986)
b CCHA First All-Star Team (1987)
c NCAA West Second All-American Team (1987)

Traded to **Los Angeles** by **Winnipeg** for Phil Sykes, December 1, 1989. Signed as a free agent by **Philadelphia**, August 6, 1991. Signed as a free agent by **NY Rangers**, August 22, 1995.

JONES, KEITH WSH.

Right wing. Shoots left. 6'2", 200 lbs. Born, Brantford, Ont., November 8, 1968.
(Washington's 7th choice, 141st overall, in 1988 Entry Draft).

			Regular Season					Playoffs				
Season	Club	Lea	GP	G	A	TP	PIM	GP	G	A	TP	PIM
1988-89	W. Michigan	CCHA	37	9	12	21	51	....	....	....	....	....
1989-90	W. Michigan	CCHA	40	19	18	37	82	....	....	....	....	....
1990-91	W. Michigan	CCHA	41	30	19	49	106	....	....	....	....	....
1991-92a	W. Michigan	CCHA	35	25	31	56	77	....	....	....	....	....
	Baltimore	AHL	6	2	4	6	0	....	....	....	....	....
1992-93	**Washington**	**NHL**	**71**	**12**	**14**	**26**	**124**	**6**	**0**	**0**	**0**	**10**
	Baltimore	AHL	8	7	3	10	4	....	....	....	....	....
1993-94	**Washington**	**NHL**	**68**	**16**	**19**	**35**	**149**	**11**	**0**	**1**	**1**	**36**
	Portland	AHL	6	5	7	12	4	....	....	....	....	....
1994-95	**Washington**	**NHL**	**40**	**14**	**6**	**20**	**65**	**7**	**4**	**4**	**8**	**22**
1995-96	**Washington**	**NHL**	**68**	**18**	**23**	**41**	**103**	**2**	**0**	**0**	**0**	**7**
	NHL Totals		**247**	**60**	**62**	**122**	**441**	**26**	**4**	**5**	**9**	**75**

a CCHA First All-Star Team (1992)

JONSSON, HANS (YOOHN-suhn) PIT.

Defense. Shoots left. 6'1", 183 lbs. Born, Jarved, Sweden, August 2, 1973.
(Pittsburgh's 11th choice, 286th overall, in 1993 Entry Draft).

			Regular Season					Playoffs				
Season	Club	Lea	GP	G	A	TP	PIM	GP	G	A	TP	PIM
1991-92	MoDo	Swe.	6	0	1	1	4	....	....	....	....	....
1992-93	MoDo	Swe.	40	2	2	4	24	3	0	1	1	2
1993-94	MoDo	Swe.	23	4	1	5	18	10	0	1	1	12
1994-95	MoDo	Swe.	39	4	6	10	30	....	....	....	....	....
1995-96	MoDo	Swe.	36	10	6	16	30	8	2	1	3	24

JONSSON, JORGEN CGY.

Left wing. Shoots left. 6', 185 lbs. Born, Angelholm, Sweden, September 29, 1972.
(Calgary's 11th choice, 227th overall, in 1994 Entry Draft).

			Regular Season					Playoffs				
Season	Club	Lea	GP	G	A	TP	PIM	GP	G	A	TP	PIM
1992-93	Rogle	Swe.	40	17	11	28	28	....	....	....	....	....
1993-94	Rogle	Swe.	40	17	14	31	46	....	....	....	....	....
1994-95	Rogle	Swe.	22	4	6	10	18	....	....	....	....	....
1995-96	Farjestad	Swe.	39	11	15	26	36	8	0	4	4	6

JONSSON, KENNY (YAHN-suhn) NYI

Defense. Shoots left. 6'3", 195 lbs. Born, Angelholm, Sweden, October 6, 1974.
(Toronto's 1st choice, 12th overall, in 1993 Entry Draft).

			Regular Season					Playoffs				
Season	Club	Lea	GP	G	A	TP	PIM	GP	G	A	TP	PIM
1991-92	Rogle	Swe. 2	30	4	11	15	24	....	....	....	....	....
1992-93a	Rogle	Swe.	39	3	10	13	42	....	....	....	....	....
1993-94	Rogle	Swe.	36	4	13	17	40	3	1	1	2	2
1994-95	Rogle	Swe.	8	3	1	4	20	....	....	....	....	....
	St. John's	AHL	10	2	5	7	2	....	....	....	....	....
b	**Toronto**	**NHL**	**39**	**2**	**7**	**9**	**16**	**4**	**0**	**0**	**0**	**0**
1995-96	**Toronto**	**NHL**	**50**	**4**	**22**	**26**	**22**	....	....	....	....	....
	NY Islanders	**NHL**	**16**	**0**	**4**	**4**	**10**	....	....	....	....	....
	NHL Totals		**105**	**6**	**33**	**39**	**48**	**4**	**0**	**0**	**0**	**0**

a Swedish Rookie of the Year (1993)
b NHL/Upper Deck All-Rookie Team (1995)

Traded to **NY Islanders** by **Toronto** with Sean Haggerty, Darby Hendrickson and Toronto's first round choice in 1997 Entry Draft for Wendel Clark, Mathieu Schneider and D.J. Smith, March 13, 1996.

JOSEPH, CHRIS PIT.

Defense. Shoots right. 6'2", 202 lbs. Born, Burnaby, B.C., September 10, 1969.
(Pittsburgh's 1st choice, 5th overall, in 1987 Entry Draft).

			Regular Season					Playoffs				
Season	Club	Lea	GP	G	A	TP	PIM	GP	G	A	TP	PIM
1985-86	Seattle	WHL	72	4	8	12	50	5	0	3	3	12
1986-87	Seattle	WHL	67	13	45	58	155	....	....	....	....	....
1987-88	**Pittsburgh**	**NHL**	**17**	**0**	**4**	**4**	**12**	....	....	....	....	....
	Seattle	WHL	23	5	14	19	49	....	....	....	....	....
	Edmonton	**NHL**	**7**	**0**	**4**	**4**	**6**	....	....	....	....	....
	Nova Scotia	AHL	8	0	2	2	8	4	0	0	0	9
1988-89	**Edmonton**	**NHL**	**44**	**4**	**5**	**9**	**54**	....	....	....	....	....
	Cape Breton	AHL	5	1	1	2	18	....	....	....	....	....
1989-90	**Edmonton**	**NHL**	**4**	**0**	**2**	**2**	**2**	....	....	....	....	....
	Cape Breton	AHL	61	10	20	30	69	6	2	1	3	4
1990-91	**Edmonton**	**NHL**	**49**	**5**	**17**	**22**	**59**	....	....	....	....	....
1991-92	**Edmonton**	**NHL**	**7**	**0**	**0**	**0**	**8**	**5**	**1**	**3**	**4**	**2**
	Cape Breton	AHL	63	14	29	43	72	5	0	2	2	8
1992-93	**Edmonton**	**NHL**	**33**	**2**	**10**	**12**	**48**	....	....	....	....	....
1993-94	**Edmonton**	**NHL**	**10**	**1**	**1**	**2**	**28**	....	....	....	....	....
	Tampa Bay	**NHL**	**66**	**10**	**19**	**29**	**108**	....	....	....	....	....
1994-95	**Pittsburgh**	**NHL**	**33**	**5**	**10**	**15**	**46**	**10**	**1**	**1**	**2**	**12**
1995-96	**Pittsburgh**	**NHL**	**70**	**5**	**14**	**19**	**71**	**15**	**1**	**0**	**1**	**8**
	NHL Totals		**340**	**32**	**86**	**118**	**442**	**30**	**3**	**4**	**7**	**22**

Traded to **Edmonton** by **Pittsburgh** with Craig Simpson, Dave Hannan and Moe Mantha for Paul Coffey, Dave Hunter and Wayne Van Dorp, November 24, 1987. Traded to **Tampa Bay** by **Edmonton** for Bob Beers, November 11, 1993. Claimed by **Pittsburgh** from **Tampa Bay** in NHL Waiver Draft, January 18, 1995.

JOVANOVSKI, ED (joh-van-OHV-skee) FLA.

Defense. Shoots left. 6'2", 205 lbs. Born, Windsor, Ont., June 26, 1976.
(Florida's 1st choice, 1st overall, in 1994 Entry Draft).

			Regular Season					Playoffs				
Season	Club	Lea	GP	G	A	TP	PIM	GP	G	A	TP	PIM
1993-94a	Windsor	OHL	62	15	36	51	221	4	0	0	0	15
1994-95b	Windsor	OHL	50	23	42	65	198	9	2	7	9	39
1995-96c	**Florida**	**NHL**	**70**	**10**	**11**	**21**	**137**	**22**	**1**	**8**	**9**	**52**
	NHL Totals		**70**	**10**	**11**	**21**	**137**	**22**	**1**	**8**	**9**	**52**

a OHL Second All-Star Team (1994)
b OHL First All-Star Team (1995)
c NHL All-Rookie Team (1996)

JUDEN, DANIEL T.B.

Right wing. Shoots right. 6'3", 190 lbs. Born, Beverly, MA, April 17, 1976.
(Tampa Bay's 5th choice, 137th overall, in 1994 Entry Draft).

			Regular Season					Playoffs				
Season	Club	Lea	GP	G	A	TP	PIM	GP	G	A	TP	PIM
1994-95	Massachusetts	H.E.	3	0	0	0	0	....	....	....	....	....
1995-96	Massachusetts	H.E.	32	3	1	4	16	....	....	....	....	....

JUHLIN, PATRIK (ew-LEEN) PHI.

Left wing. Shoots left. 6', 194 lbs. Born, Huddinge, Sweden, April 24, 1970.
(Philadelphia's 2nd choice, 34th overall, in 1989 Entry Draft).

			Regular Season					Playoffs				
Season	Club	Lea	GP	G	A	TP	PIM	GP	G	A	TP	PIM
1988-89	Vasteras	Swe. 2	30	29	13	42	....	....	....	....	....	....
1989-90	Vasteras	Swe.	35	10	13	23	18	2	0	0	0	0
1990-91	Vasteras	Swe.	40	13	9	22	24	4	3	1	4	0
1991-92	Vasteras	Swe.	39	15	12	27	40	....	....	....	....	....
1992-93	Vasteras	Swe.	34	14	12	26	22	3	0	1	1	2
1993-94	Vasteras	Swe.	40	15	16	31	20	4	1	1	2	2
1994-95	Vasteras	Swe.	11	5	9	14	8	....	....	....	....	....
	Philadelphia	**NHL**	**42**	**4**	**3**	**7**	**6**	**13**	**1**	**0**	**1**	**2**
1995-96	**Philadelphia**	**NHL**	**14**	**3**	**3**	**6**	**17**	....	....	....	....	....
	Hershey	AHL	14	5	2	7	8	1	0	0	0	0
	NHL Totals		**56**	**7**	**6**	**13**	**23**	**13**	**1**	**0**	**1**	**2**

JUNEAU, JOE (ZHOO-noh, ZHOH-ay) WSH.

Center/Left Wing. Shoots right. 6', 195 lbs. Born, Pont-Rouge, Que., January 5, 1968.
(Boston's 3rd choice, 81st overall, in 1988 Entry Draft).

			Regular Season					Playoffs				
Season	Club	Lea	GP	G	A	TP	PIM	GP	G	A	TP	PIM
1987-88	RPI	ECAC	31	16	29	45	18	....	....	....	....	....
1988-89	RPI	ECAC	30	12	23	35	40	....	....	....	....	....
1989-90a	RPI	ECAC	34	18	*52	*70	31	....	....	....	....	....
	Cdn. National	....	3	0	2	2	4	....	....	....	....	....
1990-91bc	RPI	ECAC	29	23	40	63	68	....	....	....	....	....
	Cdn. National	....	7	2	3	5	0	....	....	....	....	....
1991-92	Cdn. National	....	60	20	49	69	35	....	....	....	....	....
	Cdn. Olympic	....	8	6	9	15	4	....	....	....	....	....
	Boston	**NHL**	**14**	**5**	**14**	**19**	**4**	**15**	**4**	**8**	**12**	**21**
1992-93d	**Boston**	**NHL**	**84**	**32**	**70**	**102**	**33**	**4**	**2**	**4**	**6**	**6**
1993-94	**Boston**	**NHL**	**63**	**14**	**58**	**72**	**35**	....	....	....	....	....
	Washington	**NHL**	**11**	**5**	**8**	**13**	**6**	**11**	**4**	**5**	**9**	**6**
1994-95	**Washington**	**NHL**	**44**	**5**	**38**	**43**	**8**	**7**	**2**	**6**	**8**	**2**
1995-96	**Washington**	**NHL**	**80**	**14**	**50**	**64**	**30**	**5**	**0**	**7**	**7**	**6**
	NHL Totals		**296**	**75**	**238**	**313**	**116**	**42**	**12**	**30**	**42**	**41**

a NCAA East First All-American Team (1990)
b ECAC Second All-Star Team (1991)
c NCAA East Second All-American Team (1991)
d NHL/Upper Deck All-Rookie Team (1993)

Traded to **Washington** by **Boston** for Al Iafrate, March 21, 1994.

JUNKER, STEVE

Left wing. Shoots left. 6', 184 lbs. Born, Castlegar, B.C., June 26, 1972.
(NY Islanders' 5th choice, 92nd overall, in 1991 Entry Draft).

			Regular Season					Playoffs				
Season	Club	Lea	GP	G	A	TP	PIM	GP	G	A	TP	PIM
1990-91	Spokane	WHL	71	39	38	77	86	15	5	13	18	6
1991-92	Spokane	WHL	58	28	32	60	110	10	6	7	13	18
1992-93	Capital Dist.	AHL	79	16	31	47	20	4	0	0	0	0
	NY Islanders	**NHL**	....	....	....	....	....	**3**	**0**	**1**	**1**	**0**
1993-94	**NY Islanders**	**NHL**	**5**	**0**	**0**	**0**	**0**	....	....	....	....	....
	Salt Lake	IHL	71	9	14	23	36	....	....	....	....	....
1994-95	Denver	IHL	72	13	16	29	37	11	3	4	7	4
1995-96	Rochester	AHL	29	5	2	7	31	....	....	....	....	....
	Detroit	IHL	22	4	5	9	14	....	....	....	....	....
	Los Angeles	IHL	7	0	3	3	4	....	....	....	....	....
	NHL Totals		**5**	**0**	**0**	**0**	**0**	**3**	**0**	**1**	**1**	**0**

KACIR, MARIAN — T.B.

Right wing. Shoots left. 6'1", 195 lbs. Born, Hodonin, Czech., September 29, 1974.
(Tampa Bay's 4th choice, 81st overall, in 1993 Entry Draft).

			Regular Season					Playoffs				
Season	**Club**	**Lea**	**GP**	**G**	**A**	**TP**	**PIM**	**GP**	**G**	**A**	**TP**	**PIM**
1992-93	Owen Sound	OHL	56	20	36	56	8	8	3	5	8	4
1993-94	Owen Sound	OHL	66	23	64	87	26	9	5	4	9	2
1994-95	Charlotte	ECHL	5	2	3	5	2	....	....	....	....	....
	Nashville	ECHL	9	1	7	8	2	4	1	2	3	6
	Chicago	IHL	29	4	6	10	6	....	....	....	....	....
1995-96	Nashville	ECHL	36	22	33	55	6	....	....	....	....	....
	Atlanta	IHL	2	0	0	0	0	....	....	....	....	....

KALLIO, TOMI — COL.

Left wing. Shoots left. 6'1", 176 lbs. Born, Turku, Finland, January 27, 1977.
(Colorado's 4th choice, 81st overall, in 1995 Entry Draft).

			Regular Season					Playoffs				
Season	**Club**	**Lea**	**GP**	**G**	**A**	**TP**	**PIM**	**GP**	**G**	**A**	**TP**	**PIM**
1994-95	TPS	Fin. Jr.	14	5	12	17	24	....	....	....	....	....
	Kiekko-67	Fin. 2	25	8	5	13	16	7	3	1	4	6
1995-96	TPS	Fin. Jr.	8	8	3	11	14	....	....	....	....	....
	Kiekko-67	Fin. 2	29	10	11	21	28	....	....	....	....	....
	TPS	Fin.	8	2	3	5	10	4	0	0	0	2

KALMIKOV, KONSTANTIN — TOR.

Left wing. Shoots right. 6'4", 205 lbs. Born, Kharkov, USSR, June 14, 1978.
(Toronto's 4th choice, 68th overall, in 1996 Entry Draft).

			Regular Season					Playoffs				
Season	**Club**	**Lea**	**GP**	**G**	**A**	**TP**	**PIM**	**GP**	**G**	**A**	**TP**	**PIM**
1994-95	Druzhba-78	Midget	65	51	55	106	45	....	....	....	....	....
1995-96	Flint	ColHL	38	4	12	16	16	....	....	....	....	....
	Detroit	ColHL	5	0	1	1	0	....	....	....	....	....

KAMENSKY, VALERI — (kah-MEHN-skee) — COL.

Left wing. Shoots right. 6'2", 198 lbs. Born, Voskresensk, USSR, April 18, 1966.
(Quebec's 8th choice, 129th overall, in 1988 Entry Draft).

			Regular Season					Playoffs				
Season	**Club**	**Lea**	**GP**	**G**	**A**	**TP**	**PIM**	**GP**	**G**	**A**	**TP**	**PIM**
1982-83	Khimik	USSR	5	0	0	0	0	....	....	....	....	....
1983-84	Khimik	USSR	20	2	2	4	6	....	....	....	....	....
1984-85	Khimik	USSR	45	9	3	12	24	....	....	....	....	....
1985-86	CSKA	USSR	40	15	9	24	8	....	....	....	....	....
1986-87	CSKA	USSR	37	13	8	21	16	....	....	....	....	....
1987-88	CSKA	USSR	51	26	20	46	40	....	....	....	....	....
1988-89	CSKA	USSR	40	18	10	28	30	....	....	....	....	....
1989-90	CSKA	USSR	45	19	18	37	40	....	....	....	....	....
1990-91	CSKA	USSR	46	20	26	46	66	....	....	....	....	....
1991-92	**Quebec**	**NHL**	**23**	**7**	**14**	**21**	**14**	....	....	....	....	....
1992-93	**Quebec**	**NHL**	**32**	**15**	**22**	**37**	**14**	**6**	**0**	**1**	**1**	**6**
1993-94	**Quebec**	**NHL**	**76**	**28**	**37**	**65**	**42**	....	....	....	....	....
1994-95	Ambri	Switz.	12	13	6	19	2	....	....	....	....	....
	Quebec	**NHL**	**40**	**10**	**20**	**30**	**22**	**2**	**1**	**0**	**1**	**0**
1995-96	**Colorado**	**NHL**	**81**	**38**	**47**	**85**	**85**	**22**	**10**	**12**	**22**	**28** ◆
	NHL Totals		**252**	**98**	**140**	**238**	**177**	**30**	**11**	**13**	**24**	**34**

KAMINSKI, KEVIN — (kah-MIN-skee) — WSH.

Center. Shoots left. 5'10", 190 lbs. Born, Churchbridge, Sask., March 13, 1969.
(Minnesota's 3rd choice, 48th overall, in 1987 Entry Draft).

			Regular Season					Playoffs				
Season	**Club**	**Lea**	**GP**	**G**	**A**	**TP**	**PIM**	**GP**	**G**	**A**	**TP**	**PIM**
1986-87	Saskatoon	WHL	67	26	44	70	325	11	5	6	11	45
1987-88	Saskatoon	WHL	55	38	61	99	247	10	5	7	12	37
1988-89	**Minnesota**	**NHL**	**1**	**0**	**0**	**0**	**0**	....	....	....	....	....
	Saskatoon	WHL	52	25	43	68	199	8	4	9	13	25
1989-90	**Quebec**	**NHL**	**1**	**0**	**0**	**0**	**0**	....	....	....	....	....
	Halifax	AHL	19	3	4	7	128	2	0	0	0	5
1990-91	Halifax	AHL	7	1	0	1	44	....	....	....	....	....
	Fort Wayne	IHL	56	9	15	24	*455	19	4	2	6	*169
1991-92	**Quebec**	**NHL**	**5**	**0**	**0**	**0**	**45**	....	....	....	....	....
	Halifax	AHL	63	18	27	45	329	....	....	....	....	....
1992-93	Halifax	AHL	79	27	37	64	*345	....	....	....	....	....
1993-94	**Washington**	**NHL**	**13**	**0**	**5**	**5**	**87**	....	....	....	....	....
	Portland	AHL	39	10	22	32	263	16	4	5	9	*91
1994-95	Portland	AHL	34	15	20	35	292	....	....	....	....	....
	Washington	**NHL**	**27**	**1**	**1**	**2**	**102**	**5**	**0**	**0**	**0**	**36**
1995-96	**Washington**	**NHL**	**54**	**1**	**2**	**3**	**164**	**3**	**0**	**0**	**0**	**16**
	NHL Totals		**101**	**2**	**8**	**10**	**398**	**8**	**0**	**0**	**0**	**52**

Traded to **Quebec** by **Minnesota** for Gaetan Duchesne, June 19, 1989. Traded to **Washington** by **Quebec** for Mark Matier, June 15, 1993.

KAMINSKY, YAN — (kah-MEHN-skee)

Right wing. Shoots left. 6'1", 176 lbs. Born, Penza, USSR, July 28, 1971.
(Winnipeg's 4th choice, 99th overall, in 1991 Entry Draft).

			Regular Season					Playoffs				
Season	**Club**	**Lea**	**GP**	**G**	**A**	**TP**	**PIM**	**GP**	**G**	**A**	**TP**	**PIM**
1989-90	Moscow D'amo	USSR	6	1	0	1	4	....	....	....	....	....
1990-91	Moscow D'amo	USSR	25	10	5	15	2	....	....	....	....	....
1991-92	Moscow D'amo	CIS	42	9	7	16	22	....	....	....	....	....
1992-93	Moscow D'amo	CIS	39	15	14	29	12	10	2	5	7	8
1993-94	**Winnipeg**	**NHL**	**1**	**0**	**0**	**0**	**0**	....	....	....	....	....
	Moncton	AHL	33	9	13	22	6	....	....	....	....	....
	NY Islanders	**NHL**	**23**	**2**	**1**	**3**	**4**	**2**	**0**	**0**	**0**	**4**
1994-95	Denver	IHL	38	17	16	33	14	15	6	6	12	0
	NY Islanders	**NHL**	**2**	**1**	**1**	**2**	**0**	....	....	....	....	....
1995-96	Utah	IHL	16	3	3	6	8	21	3	5	8	4
	NHL Totals		**26**	**3**	**2**	**5**	**4**	**2**	**0**	**0**	**0**	**4**

Traded to **NY Islanders** by **Winnipeg** for Wayne McBean, February 1, 1994.

KANE, BOYD — PIT.

Left wing. Shoots left. 6'1", 207 lbs. Born, Swift Current, Sask., April 18, 1978.
(Pittsburgh's 3rd choice, 72nd overall, in 1996 Entry Draft).

			Regular Season					Playoffs				
Season	**Club**	**Lea**	**GP**	**G**	**A**	**TP**	**PIM**	**GP**	**G**	**A**	**TP**	**PIM**
1995-96	Regina	WHL	72	21	42	63	155	11	5	7	12	12

KAPANEN, SAMI — HFD.

Left wing. Shoots left. 5'10", 170 lbs. Born, Vantaa, Finland, June 14, 1973.
(Hartford's 4th choice, 87th overall, in 1995 Entry Draft).

			Regular Season					Playoffs				
Season	**Club**	**Lea**	**GP**	**G**	**A**	**TP**	**PIM**	**GP**	**G**	**A**	**TP**	**PIM**
1990-91	KalPa	Fin.	14	1	2	3	2	8	2	1	3	2
1991-92	KalPa	Fin.	42	15	10	25	8	....	....	....	....	....
1992-93	KalPa	Fin.	37	4	17	21	12	....	....	....	....	....
1993-94	KalPa	Fin.	48	23	32	55	16	....	....	....	....	....
1994-95	HIFK	Fin.	49	14	28	42	42	3	0	0	0	0
1995-96	**Hartford**	**NHL**	**35**	**5**	**4**	**9**	**6**	....	....	....	....	....
	Springfield	AHL	28	14	17	31	4	3	1	2	3	0
	NHL Totals		**35**	**5**	**4**	**9**	**6**	....	....	....	....	....

KARABIN, LADISLAV — (kar-ah-BIN)

Left wing. Shoots left. 6'1", 189 lbs. Born, Spisska Nova Ves, Czech., February 16, 1970.
(Pittsburgh's 11th choice, 173rd overall, in 1990 Entry Draft).

			Regular Season					Playoffs				
Season	**Club**	**Lea**	**GP**	**G**	**A**	**TP**	**PIM**	**GP**	**G**	**A**	**TP**	**PIM**
1988-89	Bratislava	Czech.	31	7	2	9	10	....	....	....	....	....
1989-90	Bratislava	Czech. 2				UNAVAILABLE						
1990-91	Bratislava	Czech.	49	21	7	28	57	....	....	....	....	....
1991-92	Bratislava	Czech.	27	4	8	12	10	....	....	....	....	....
1992-93	Bratislava	Czech.	39	21	23	44	....	....	....	....	....	....
1993-94	**Pittsburgh**	**NHL**	**9**	**0**	**0**	**0**	**2**	....	....	....	....	....
	Cleveland	IHL	58	13	26	39	48	....	....	....	....	....
1994-95	Cleveland	IHL	47	15	25	40	26	4	0	0	0	2
1995-96	Rochester	AHL	21	3	5	8	18	....	....	....	....	....
	Los Angeles	IHL	32	6	8	14	58	....	....	....	....	....
	NHL Totals		**9**	**0**	**0**	**0**	**2**	....	....	....	....	....

Signed as a free agent by **Buffalo**, September 20, 1995.

KARALAHTI, JERE — L.A.

Defense. Shoots right. 6'2", 185 lbs. Born, Helsinki, Finland, March 25, 1975.
(Los Angeles' 7th choice, 146th overall, in 1993 Entry Draft).

			Regular Season					Playoffs				
Season	**Club**	**Lea**	**GP**	**G**	**A**	**TP**	**PIM**	**GP**	**G**	**A**	**TP**	**PIM**
1993-94	HIFK	Fin.	46	1	10	11	36	3	0	0	0	6
1994-95	HIFK	Fin.	37	1	7	8	42	3	0	0	0	0
1995-96	HIFK	Fin.	36	4	6	10	102	3	0	0	0	4

KARAMNOV, VITALI — (kuh-RAHM-nov)

Left wing. Shoots left. 6'2", 185 lbs. Born, Moscow, USSR, July 6, 1968.
(St. Louis' 2nd choice, 62nd overall, in 1992 Entry Draft).

			Regular Season					Playoffs				
Season	**Club**	**Lea**	**GP**	**G**	**A**	**TP**	**PIM**	**GP**	**G**	**A**	**TP**	**PIM**
1986-87	Moscow D'amo	USSR	4	0	0	0	0	....	....	....	....	....
1987-88	Moscow D'amo	USSR	2	0	1	1	0	....	....	....	....	....
1988-89	D'amo Kharkov	USSR	23	4	1	5	19	....	....	....	....	....
1989-90	Torpedo Yaro.	USSR	47	6	7	13	32	....	....	....	....	....
1990-91	Torpedo Yaro.	USSR	45	14	7	21	30	....	....	....	....	....
1991-92	Moscow D'amo	CIS	40	13	19	32	25	....	....	....	....	....
1992-93	**St. Louis**	**NHL**	**7**	**0**	**1**	**1**	**0**	....	....	....	....	....
	Peoria	IHL	23	8	12	20	47	....	....	....	....	....
1993-94	**St. Louis**	**NHL**	**59**	**9**	**12**	**21**	**51**	....	....	....	....	....
	Peoria	IHL	3	0	1	1	2	1	0	1	1	0
1994-95	Peoria	IHL	15	6	9	15	7	....	....	....	....	....
	St. Louis	**NHL**	**26**	**3**	**7**	**10**	**14**	**2**	**0**	**0**	**0**	**2**
1995-96	JyP HT	Fin.	24	8	7	15	36	....	....	....	....	....
	NHL Totals		**92**	**12**	**20**	**32**	**65**	**2**	**0**	**0**	**0**	**2**

KARIYA, PAUL — (kah-REE-ah) — ANA.

Left wing. Shoots left. 5'11", 175 lbs. Born, Vancouver, B.C., October 16, 1974.
(Anaheim's 1st choice, 4th overall, in 1993 Entry Draft).

			Regular Season					Playoffs				
Season	**Club**	**Lea**	**GP**	**G**	**A**	**TP**	**PIM**	**GP**	**G**	**A**	**TP**	**PIM**
1992-93abcd	U. of Maine	H.E.	36	24	*69	*93	12	....	....	....	....	....
1993-94	U. of Maine	H.E.	12	8	16	24	4	....	....	....	....	....
	Cdn. National	....	23	7	34	41	2	....	....	....	....	....
	Cdn. Olympic	....	8	3	4	7	2	....	....	....	....	....
1994-95e	**Anaheim**	**NHL**	**47**	**18**	**21**	**39**	**4**	....	....	....	....	....
1995-96fg	**Anaheim**	**NHL**	**82**	**50**	**58**	**108**	**20**	....	....	....	....	....
	NHL Totals		**129**	**68**	**79**	**147**	**24**	....	....	....	....	....

a Hockey East First All-Star Team (1993)
b NCAA East First All-American Team (1993)
c NCAA Final Four All-Tournament Team (1993)
d Won Hobey Baker Memorial Award (Top U.S. Collegiate Player) (1993)
e NHL/Upper Deck All-Rookie Team (1995)
f NHL First All-Star Team (1996)
g Won Lady Byng Trophy (1996)

Played in NHL All-Star Game (1996)

KARLSSON, ANDREAS — CGY.

Center. Shoots left. 6'2", 180 lbs. Born, Leksand, Sweden, August 19, 1975.
(Calgary's 8th choice, 148th overall, in 1993 Entry Draft).

			Regular Season					Playoffs				
Season	**Club**	**Lea**	**GP**	**G**	**A**	**TP**	**PIM**	**GP**	**G**	**A**	**TP**	**PIM**
1992-93	Leksand	Swe.	13	0	0	0	6	....	....	....	....	....
1993-94	Leksand	Swe.	21	0	0	0	10	3	0	0	0	0
1994-95	Leksand	Swe.	24	7	8	15	0	4	0	1	1	0
1995-96	Leksand	Swe.	40	10	13	23	10	5	2	1	3	4

KARPA, DAVE — ANA.

Defense. Shoots right. 6'1", 202 lbs. Born, Regina, Sask., May 7, 1971.
(Quebec's 4th choice, 68th overall, in 1991 Entry Draft).

			Regular Season					Playoffs				
Season	Club	Lea	GP	G	A	TP	PIM	GP	G	A	TP	PIM
1990-91	Ferris State	CCHA	41	6	19	25	109	....	....	....	....	....
1991-92	Ferris State	CCHA	34	7	12	19	124	....	....	....	....	....
	Quebec	NHL	4	0	0	0	14	....	....	....	....	....
	Halifax	AHL	2	0	0	0	4	....	....	....	....	....
1992-93	Quebec	NHL	12	0	1	1	13	3	0	0	0	0
	Halifax	AHL	71	4	27	31	167	....	....	....	....	....
1993-94	Quebec	NHL	60	5	12	17	148	....	....	....	....	....
	Cornwall	AHL	1	0	0	0	0	12	2	2	4	27
1994-95	Quebec	NHL	2	0	0	0	0	....	....	....	....	....
	Cornwall	AHL	6	0	2	2	19	....	....	....	....	....
	Anaheim	NHL	26	1	5	6	91	....	....	....	....	....
1995-96	Anaheim	NHL	72	3	16	19	270	....	....	....	....	....
	NHL Totals		176	9	34	43	536	3	0	0	0	0

Traded to **Anaheim** by **Quebec** for Anaheim's fourth round choice in 1997 Entry Draft, March 9, 1995.

KARPOV, VALERI — (KAHR-pahf) ANA.

Right wing. Shoots left. 5'10", 176 lbs. Born, Chelyabinsk, USSR, August 5, 1971.
(Anaheim's 3rd choice, 56th overall, in 1993 Entry Draft).

			Regular Season					Playoffs				
Season	Club	Lea	GP	G	A	TP	PIM	GP	G	A	TP	PIM
1988-89	Chelyabinsk	USSR	5	0	0	0	0	....	....	....	....	....
1989-90	Chelyabinsk	USSR	24	1	2	3	6	....	....	....	....	....
1990-91	Chelyabinsk	USSR	25	8	4	12	15	....	....	....	....	....
1991-92	Chelyabinsk	CIS	44	16	10	26	34	....	....	....	....	....
1992-93	CSKA	CIS	9	2	6	8	0	....	....	....	....	....
a	Chelyabinsk	CIS	29	10	15	25	6	8	0	1	1	10
1993-94	Chelyabinsk	CIS	32	13	16	29	....	6	2	5	7	2
1994-95	Chelyabinsk	CIS	10	6	8	14	8	....	....	....	....	....
	Anaheim	NHL	30	4	7	11	6	....	....	....	....	....
	San Diego	IHL	5	3	3	6	0	....	....	....	....	....
1995-96	Anaheim	NHL	37	9	8	17	10	....	....	....	....	....
	NHL Totals		67	13	15	28	16	....	....	....	....	....

a CIS All-Star Team (1993)

KARPOVTSEV, ALEXANDER — (kar-POHV-tzehv) NYR

Defense. Shoots right. 6'1", 200 lbs. Born, Moscow, USSR, April 7, 1970.
(Quebec's 7th choice, 158th overall, in 1990 Entry Draft).

			Regular Season					Playoffs				
Season	Club	Lea	GP	G	A	TP	PIM	GP	G	A	TP	PIM
1987-88	Moscow D'amo	USSR	2	0	1	1	10	....	....	....	....	....
1989-90	Moscow D'amo	USSR	35	1	1	2	27	....	....	....	....	....
1990-91	Moscow D'amo	USSR	40	0	5	5	15	....	....	....	....	....
1991-92	Moscow D'amo	CIS	35	4	2	6	26	....	....	....	....	....
1992-93	Moscow D'amo	CIS	36	3	11	14	100	7	2	1	3	0
1993-94	NY Rangers	NHL	67	3	15	18	58	17	0	4	4	12 ♦
1994-95	Moscow D'amo	CIS	13	0	2	2	10	....	....	....	....	....
	NY Rangers	NHL	47	4	8	12	30	8	1	0	1	0
1995-96	NY Rangers	NHL	40	2	16	18	26	6	0	1	1	4
	NHL Totals		154	9	39	48	114	31	1	5	6	16

Traded to **NY Rangers** by **Quebec** for Mike Hurlbut, September 7, 1993.

KASATONOV, ALEXEI — (kah-sah-TOH-nahf)

Defense. Shoots left. 6'1", 215 lbs. Born, Leningrad, USSR, October 14, 1959.
(New Jersey's 10th choice, 225th overall, in 1983 Entry Draft).

			Regular Season					Playoffs				
Season	Club	Lea	GP	G	A	TP	PIM	GP	G	A	TP	PIM
1976-77	SKA Leningrad	USSR	7	0	0	0	0	....	....	....	....	....
1977-78	SKA Leningrad	USSR	35	4	7	11	15	....	....	....	....	....
1978-79	CSKA	USSR	40	5	14	19	30	....	....	....	....	....
1979-80a	CSKA	USSR	37	5	8	13	26	....	....	....	....	....
1980-81a	CSKA	USSR	47	10	12	22	38	....	....	....	....	....
1981-82a	CSKA	USSR	46	12	27	39	45	....	....	....	....	....
1982-83a	CSKA	USSR	44	12	19	31	37	....	....	....	....	....
1983-84a	CSKA	USSR	39	12	24	36	20	....	....	....	....	....
1984-85a	CSKA	USSR	40	18	18	36	26	....	....	....	....	....
1985-86a	CSKA	USSR	40	6	17	23	27	....	....	....	....	....
1986-87a	CSKA	USSR	40	13	17	30	16	....	....	....	....	....
1987-88a	CSKA	USSR	43	8	12	20	8	....	....	....	....	....
1988-89	CSKA	USSR	41	8	14	22	8	....	....	....	....	....
1989-90	CSKA	USSR	30	6	7	13	16	....	....	....	....	....
	New Jersey	NHL	39	6	15	21	16	6	0	3	3	14
	Utica	AHL	3	0	2	2	7	....	....	....	....	....
1990-91	New Jersey	NHL	78	10	31	41	76	7	1	3	4	10
1991-92	New Jersey	NHL	76	12	28	40	70	7	1	1	2	12
1992-93	New Jersey	NHL	64	3	14	17	57	4	0	0	0	0
1993-94	Anaheim	NHL	55	4	18	22	43	....	....	....	....	....
	St. Louis	NHL	8	0	2	2	19	4	2	0	2	2
1994-95	CSKA	CIS	9	2	3	5	6	....	....	....	....	....
	Boston	NHL	44	2	14	16	33	5	0	0	0	2
1995-96	Boston	NHL	19	1	0	1	12	....	....	....	....	....
	Providence	AHL	16	3	6	9	10	....	....	....	....	....
	NHL Totals		383	38	122	160	326	33	4	7	11	40

a Soviet National League All-Star Team (1980-88)

Played in NHL All-Star Game (1994)

Claimed by **Anaheim** from **New Jersey** in Expansion Draft, June 24, 1993. Traded to **St. Louis** by **Anaheim** for Maxim Bets and St. Louis' sixth round choice (later traded back to St. Louis — St. Louis selected Denis Hamel) in 1995 Entry Draft, March 21, 1994. Signed as a free agent by **Boston**, June 22, 1994.

KASMINSKI, ERIK — OTT.

Right wing. Shoots right. 6'3", 205 lbs. Born, Hudson, OH, March 23, 1976.
(Ottawa's 9th choice, 231st overall, in 1995 Entry Draft).

			Regular Season					Playoffs				
Season	Club	Lea	GP	G	A	TP	PIM	GP	G	A	TP	PIM
1994-95	Cleveland	Jr. B	42	34	33	67	99	....	....	....	....	....
1995-96	Northeastern	H.E.	34	5	8	13	30	....	....	....	....	....

KASPARAITIS, DARIUS — (KAZ-puhr-IGH-tihz) NYI

Defense. Shoots left. 5'10", 205 lbs. Born, Elektrenai, USSR, October 16, 1972.
(NY Islanders' 1st choice, 5th overall, in 1992 Entry Draft).

			Regular Season					Playoffs				
Season	Club	Lea	GP	G	A	TP	PIM	GP	G	A	TP	PIM
1988-89	Moscow D'amo	USSR	3	0	0	0	0	....	....	....	....	....
1989-90	Moscow D'amo	USSR	1	0	0	0	0	....	....	....	....	....
1990-91	Moscow D'amo	USSR	17	0	1	1	10	....	....	....	....	....
1991-92	Moscow D'amo	CIS	31	2	10	12	14	....	....	....	....	....
1992-93	Moscow D'amo	CIS	7	1	3	4	8	....	....	....	....	....
	NY Islanders	NHL	79	4	17	21	166	18	0	5	5	31
1993-94	NY Islanders	NHL	76	1	10	11	142	4	0	0	0	8
1994-95	NY Islanders	NHL	13	0	1	1	22	....	....	....	....	....
1995-96	NY Islanders	NHL	46	1	7	8	93	....	....	....	....	....
	NHL Totals		214	6	35	41	423	22	0	5	5	39

KAZAKEVICH, MIKHAIL — PIT.

Left wing. Shoots left. 6'1", 187 lbs. Born, Murmansk, USSR, January 14, 1976.
(Pittsburgh's 13th choice, 258th overall, in 1994 Entry Draft).

			Regular Season					Playoffs				
Season	Club	Lea	GP	G	A	TP	PIM	GP	G	A	TP	PIM
1992-93	Yaroslavl	CIS	7	0	1	1	0	3	0	0	0	0
1993-94	Yaroslavl	CIS	4	0	0	0	2	....	....	....	....	....
1994-95	Yaroslavl	CIS	11	1	3	4	2	....	....	....	....	....
1995-96	Moncton	QMJHL	41	7	13	20	16	....	....	....	....	....
	Shawinigan	QMJHL	14	1	3	4	8	4	0	1	1	2

KEALTY, JEFF — COL.

Defense. Shoots left. 6'4", 175 lbs. Born, Boston, MA, April 9, 1976.
(Quebec's 2nd choice, 22nd overall, in 1994 Entry Draft).

			Regular Season					Playoffs				
Season	Club	Lea	GP	G	A	TP	PIM	GP	G	A	TP	PIM
1994-95	Boston U.	H.E.	25	0	5	5	29	....	....	....	....	....
1995-96	Boston U.	H.E.	35	4	14	18	38	....	....	....	....	....

KEANE, MIKE — COL.

Right wing. Shoots right. 5'10", 185 lbs. Born, Winnipeg, Man., May 29, 1967.

			Regular Season					Playoffs				
Season	Club	Lea	GP	G	A	TP	PIM	GP	G	A	TP	PIM
1984-85	Moose Jaw	WHL	65	17	26	43	141	....	....	....	....	....
1985-86	Moose Jaw	WHL	67	34	49	83	162	13	6	8	14	9
1986-87	Moose Jaw	WHL	53	25	45	70	107	9	3	9	12	11
	Sherbrooke	AHL	....	....	....	....	....	9	2	2	4	16
1987-88	Sherbrooke	AHL	78	25	43	68	70	6	1	1	2	18
1988-89	Montreal	NHL	69	16	19	35	69	21	4	3	7	17
1989-90	Montreal	NHL	74	9	15	24	78	11	0	1	1	8
1990-91	Montreal	NHL	73	13	23	36	50	12	3	2	5	6
1991-92	Montreal	NHL	67	11	30	41	64	8	1	1	2	16
1992-93	Montreal	NHL	77	15	45	60	95	19	2	13	15	6 ♦
1993-94	Montreal	NHL	80	16	30	46	119	6	3	1	4	4
1994-95	Montreal	NHL	48	10	10	20	15	....	....	....	....	....
1995-96	Montreal	NHL	18	0	7	7	6	....	....	....	....	....
	Colorado	NHL	55	10	10	20	40	22	3	2	5	16 ♦
	NHL Totals		561	100	189	289	536	99	16	23	39	73

Signed as a free agent by **Montreal**, September 25, 1985. Traded to **Colorado** by **Montreal** with Patrick Roy for Andrei Kovalenko, Martin Rucinsky and Jocelyn Thibault, December 6, 1995.

KECZMER, DAN — (KEHS-muhr) DAL.

Defense. Shoots left. 6'1", 190 lbs. Born, Mt. Clemens, MI, May 25, 1968.
(Minnesota's 11th choice, 201st overall, in 1986 Entry Draft).

			Regular Season					Playoffs				
Season	Club	Lea	GP	G	A	TP	PIM	GP	G	A	TP	PIM
1986-87	Lake Superior	CCHA	38	3	5	8	26	....	....	....	....	....
1987-88	Lake Superior	CCHA	41	2	15	17	34	....	....	....	....	....
1988-89	Lake Superior	CCHA	46	3	26	29	68	....	....	....	....	....
1989-90a	Lake Superior	CCHA	43	13	23	36	48	....	....	....	....	....
1990-91	Minnesota	NHL	9	0	1	1	6	....	....	....	....	....
	Kalamazoo	IHL	60	4	20	24	60	9	1	2	3	10
1991-92	U.S. National	....	51	3	11	14	56	....	....	....	....	....
	Hartford	NHL	1	0	0	0	0	....	....	....	....	....
	Springfield	AHL	18	3	4	7	10	4	0	0	0	6
1992-93	Hartford	NHL	23	4	4	8	28	....	....	....	....	....
	Springfield	AHL	37	1	13	14	38	12	0	4	4	14
1993-94	Hartford	NHL	12	0	1	1	12	....	....	....	....	....
	Springfield	AHL	7	0	1	1	4	....	....	....	....	....
	Calgary	NHL	57	1	20	21	48	3	0	0	0	4
1994-95	Calgary	NHL	28	2	3	5	10	7	0	1	1	2
1995-96	Calgary	NHL	13	0	0	0	14	....	....	....	....	....
	Saint John	AHL	22	3	11	14	14	....	....	....	....	....
	Albany	AHL	17	0	4	4	4	1	0	0	0	0
	NHL Totals		143	7	29	36	118	10	0	1	1	6

a CCHA Second All-Star Team (1990)

Claimed by **San Jose** from **Minnesota** in Dispersal Draft, May 30, 1991. Traded to **Hartford** by **San Jose** for Dean Evason, October 2, 1991. Traded to **Calgary** by **Hartford** for Jeff Reese, November 19, 1993. Traded to **New Jersey** by **Calgary** with Phil Housley for Tommy Albelin, Cale Hulse and Jocelyn Lemieux, February 26, 1996. Signed as a free agent by **Dallas**, August 19, 1996.

KELLEHER, CHRIS — PIT.

Defense. Shoots left. 6'1", 215 lbs. Born, Cambridge, MA, March 23, 1975.
(Pittsburgh's 5th choice, 130th overall, in 1993 Entry Draft).

			Regular Season					Playoffs				
Season	Club	Lea	GP	G	A	TP	PIM	GP	G	A	TP	PIM
1994-95	Boston U.	H.E.	35	3	17	20	62	....	....	....	....	....
1995-96	Boston U.	H.E.	37	7	18	25	43	....	....	....	....	....

KELLY, STEVE — EDM.

Center. Shoots left. 6'1", 190 lbs. Born, Vancouver, B.C., October 26, 1976.
(Edmonton's 1st choice, 6th overall, in 1995 Entry Draft).

			Regular Season					Playoffs				
Season	Club	Lea	GP	G	A	TP	PIM	GP	G	A	TP	PIM
1992-93	Prince Albert	WHL	65	11	9	20	75	....	....	....	....	....
1993-94	Prince Albert	WHL	65	19	42	61	106	....	....	....	....	....
1994-95	Prince Albert	WHL	68	31	41	72	153	15	7	9	16	35
1995-96	Prince Albert	WHL	70	27	74	101	203	18	13	18	31	47

KELMAN, TODD — ST.L.

Defense. Shoots left. 6'1", 190 lbs. Born, Calgary, Alta., January 5, 1975.
(St. Louis' 4th choice, 141st overall, in 1993 Entry Draft).

			Regular Season					Playoffs				
Season	Club	Lea	GP	G	A	TP	PIM	GP	G	A	TP	PIM
1993-94	Bowling Green	CCHA	18	0	2	2	12					
1994-95	Bowling Green	CCHA	37	2	5	7	20					
1995-96	Bowling Green	CCHA	32	1	5	6	40					

KENADY, CHRIS — ST.L.

Right wing. Shoots right. 6'2", 195 lbs. Born, Mound, MN, April 10, 1973.
(St. Louis' 8th choice, 175th overall, in 1991 Entry Draft).

			Regular Season					Playoffs				
Season	Club	Lea	GP	G	A	TP	PIM	GP	G	A	TP	PIM
1991-92	U. of Denver	WCHA	36	8	5	13	56					
1992-93	U. of Denver	WCHA	38	8	16	24	95					
1993-94	U. of Denver	WCHA	37	14	11	25	125					
1994-95	U. of Denver	WCHA	39	21	17	38	113					
1995-96	Worcester	AHL	43	9	10	19	58	2	0	0	0	0

KENNEDY, MIKE — DAL.

Center. Shoots right. 6'1", 195 lbs. Born, Vancouver, B.C., April 13, 1972.
(Minnesota's 5th choice, 97th overall, in 1991 Entry Draft).

			Regular Season					Playoffs				
Season	Club	Lea	GP	G	A	TP	PIM	GP	G	A	TP	PIM
1989-90	U.B.C.	CIAU	9	5	7	12	0					
1990-91	U.B.C.	CIAU	28	17	17	34	18					
1991-92a	Seattle	WHL	71	42	47	89	134	15	11	6	17	20
1992-93	Kalamazoo	IHL	77	21	30	51	39					
1993-94	Kalamazoo	IHL	63	20	18	38	42	3	1	2	3	2
1994-95	Kalamazoo	IHL	42	20	28	48	29					
	Dallas	**NHL**	**44**	**6**	**12**	**18**	**33**	**5**	**0**	**0**	**0**	**9**
1995-96	**Dallas**	**NHL**	**61**	**9**	**17**	**26**	**48**					
	NHL Totals		**105**	**15**	**29**	**44**	**81**	**5**	**0**	**0**	**0**	**9**

a WHL West Second All-Star Team (1982)

KENNEDY, SHELDON — BOS.

Right wing. Shoots right. 5'10", 180 lbs. Born, Elkhorn, Man., June 15, 1969.
(Detroit's 5th choice, 80th overall, in 1988 Entry Draft).

			Regular Season					Playoffs				
Season	Club	Lea	GP	G	A	TP	PIM	GP	G	A	TP	PIM
1986-87	Swift Current	WHL	49	23	41	64	43	4	0	3	3	4
1987-88	Swift Current	WHL	59	53	64	117	45	10	8	9	17	12
1988-89a	Swift Current	WHL	51	58	48	106	92	12	9	15	24	22
1989-90	**Detroit**	**NHL**	**20**	**2**	**7**	**9**	**10**					
	Adirondack	AHL	26	11	15	26	35					
1990-91	**Detroit**	**NHL**	**7**	**1**	**0**	**1**	**12**					
	Adirondack	AHL	11	1	3	4	8					
1991-92	**Detroit**	**NHL**	**27**	**3**	**8**	**11**	**24**					
	Adirondack	AHL	46	25	24	49	56	16	5	9	14	12
1992-93	**Detroit**	**NHL**	**68**	**19**	**11**	**30**	**46**	**7**	**1**	**1**	**2**	**2**
1993-94	**Detroit**	**NHL**	**61**	**6**	**7**	**13**	**30**	**7**	**1**	**2**	**3**	**0**
1994-95	**Calgary**	**NHL**	**30**	**7**	**8**	**15**	**45**	**7**	**3**	**1**	**4**	**16**
1995-96	**Calgary**	**NHL**	**41**	**3**	**7**	**10**	**36**	**3**	**1**	**0**	**1**	**2**
	Saint John	AHL	3	4	0	4	8					
	NHL Totals		**254**	**41**	**48**	**89**	**203**	**24**	**6**	**4**	**10**	**20**

a Memorial Cup All-Star Team (1989)

Traded to **Winnipeg** by **Detroit** for Winnipeg's third round choice (Darryl Laplante) in 1995 Entry Draft, May 25, 1994. Claimed by **Calgary** from **Winnipeg** in NHL Waiver Draft, January 18, 1995. Signed as free agent by **Boston**, August 7, 1996.

KENNEY, JAY — OTT.

Defense. Shoots left. 6'2", 190 lbs. Born, New York, NY, September 21, 1973.
(Ottawa's 8th choice, 169th overall, in 1992 Entry Draft).

			Regular Season					Playoffs				
Season	Club	Lea	GP	G	A	TP	PIM	GP	G	A	TP	PIM
1992-93	Providence	H.E.	24	1	8	9	10					
1993-94	Providence	H.E.	21	2	7	9	8					
1994-95	Providence	H.E.	35	4	12	16	12					
1995-96	Providence	H.E.	38	3	9	12	16					

KENNY, SHANE — PHI.

Defense. Shoots left. 6'2", 230 lbs. Born, Oromocto, N.B., March 1, 1977.
(Philadelphia's 2nd choice, 48th overall, in 1995 Entry Draft).

			Regular Season					Playoffs				
Season	Club	Lea	GP	G	A	TP	PIM	GP	G	A	TP	PIM
1993-94	Owen Sound	OHL	54	4	9	13	138	2	0	0	0	6
1994-95	Owen Sound	OHL	65	13	19	32	134	9	0	2	2	8
1995-96	Owen Sound	OHL	60	12	27	39	149	6	1	7	8	14

KESA, DAN (KEH-suh) — HFD.

Right wing. Shoots right. 6', 198 lbs. Born, Vancouver, B.C., November 23, 1971.
(Vancouver's 5th choice, 95th overall, in 1991 Entry Draft).

			Regular Season					Playoffs				
Season	Club	Lea	GP	G	A	TP	PIM	GP	G	A	TP	PIM
1990-91	Prince Albert	WHL	69	30	23	53	116	3	1	1	2	0
1991-92	Prince Albert	WHL	62	46	51	97	201	10	9	10	19	27
1992-93	Hamilton	AHL	62	16	24	40	76					
1993-94	**Vancouver**	**NHL**	**19**	**2**	**4**	**6**	**18**					
	Hamilton	AHL	53	37	33	70	33	4	1	4	5	4
1994-95	Syracuse	AHL	70	34	44	78	81					
1995-96	**Dallas**	**NHL**	**3**	**0**	**0**	**0**	**0**					
	Michigan	IHL	15	4	11	15	33					
	Springfield	AHL	22	10	5	15	13					
	Detroit	IHL	27	9	6	15	22	12	6	4	10	4
	NHL Totals		**22**	**2**	**4**	**6**	**18**					

Traded by **Dallas** by **Vancouver** with Greg Adams and Vancouver's fifth round choice (later traded to Los Angeles — Los Angeles selected Jason Morgan) in 1995 Entry Draft for Russ Courtnall, April 7, 1995. Traded to **Hartford** by **Dallas** with a conditional draft choice in 1997 Entry Draft for Robert Petrovicky, November 29, 1995.

KHARLAMOV, ALEXANDER (khahr-LAH-mohv) — WSH.

Center. Shoots left. 5'10", 180 lbs. Born, Moscow, USSR, September 23, 1975.
(Washington's 2nd choice, 15th overall, in 1994 Entry Draft).

			Regular Season					Playoffs				
Season	Club	Lea	GP	G	A	TP	PIM	GP	G	A	TP	PIM
1992-93	CSKA	CIS	42	8	4	12	12					
1993-94	CSKA	CIS	46	8	8	16	26	3	1	0	1	2
	Russian Pen's	IHL	12	2	2	4	4					
1994-95	CSKA	CIS	45	8	4	12	12					
1995-96	Portland	AHL	65	14	18	32	35	14	2	3	5	8

KHMYLEV, YURI (kheh-meh-LUHV) — ST.L.

Left wing. Shoots right. 6'1", 189 lbs. Born, Moscow, USSR, August 9, 1964.
(Buffalo's 7th choice, 108th overall, in 1992 Entry Draft).

			Regular Season					Playoffs				
Season	Club	Lea	GP	G	A	TP	PIM	GP	G	A	TP	PIM
1981-82	Soviet Wings	USSR	8	2	2	4	2					
1982-83	Soviet Wings	USSR	51	9	7	16	14					
1983-84	Soviet Wings	USSR	43	7	8	15	10					
1984-85	Soviet Wings	USSR	30	11	4	15	24					
1985-86	Soviet Wings	USSR	40	24	9	33	22					
1986-87	Soviet Wings	USSR	40	15	15	30	48					
1987-88	Soviet Wings	USSR	48	21	8	29	46					
1988-89	Soviet Wings	USSR	44	16	18	34	38					
1989-90	Soviet Wings	USSR	44	14	13	27	30					
1990-91	Soviet Wings	USSR	45	25	14	39	26					
1991-92	Soviet Wings	CIS	42	19	17	36	20					
1992-93	**Buffalo**	**NHL**	**68**	**20**	**19**	**39**	**28**	**8**	**4**	**3**	**7**	**4**
1993-94	**Buffalo**	**NHL**	**72**	**27**	**31**	**58**	**49**	**7**	**3**	**1**	**4**	**8**
1994-95	Soviet Wings	IHL	11	2	2	4	4					
	Buffalo	**NHL**	**48**	**8**	**17**	**25**	**14**	**5**	**0**	**1**	**1**	**8**
1995-96	**Buffalo**	**NHL**	**66**	**8**	**20**	**28**	**40**					
	St. Louis	**NHL**	**7**	**0**	**1**	**1**	**0**	**6**	**1**	**1**	**2**	**4**
	NHL Totals		**261**	**63**	**88**	**151**	**131**	**26**	**8**	**6**	**14**	**24**

Traded to **St. Louis** by **Buffalo** with Buffalo's eighth round choice (Andrei Podkonicky) in 1996 Entry Draft for Jean-Luc Grand Pierre, Ottawa's second round choice (previously acquired by St. Louis — Buffalo selected Cory Sarich) in 1996 Entry Draft and St. Louis' third round choice in 1997 Entry Draft, March 20, 1996.

KHRISTICH, DIMITRI (KRIH-stihch) — L.A.

Left wing/Center. Shoots right. 6'2", 195 lbs. Born, Kiev, USSR, July 23, 1969.
(Washington's 6th choice, 120th overall, in 1988 Entry Draft).

			Regular Season					Playoffs				
Season	Club	Lea	GP	G	A	TP	PIM	GP	G	A	TP	PIM
1985-86	Sokol Kiev	USSR	4	0	0	0	0					
1986-87	Sokol Kiev	USSR	20	3	0	3	4					
1987-88	Sokol Kiev	USSR	37	9	1	10	18					
1988-89	Sokol Kiev	USSR	42	17	10	27	15					
1989-90	Sokol Kiev	USSR	47	14	22	36	32					
1990-91	Sokol Kiev	USSR	28	10	12	22	20					
	Washington	**NHL**	**40**	**13**	**14**	**27**	**21**	**11**	**1**	**3**	**4**	**6**
	Baltimore	AHL	3	0	0	0	0					
1991-92	**Washington**	**NHL**	**80**	**36**	**37**	**73**	**35**	**7**	**3**	**2**	**5**	**15**
1992-93	**Washington**	**NHL**	**64**	**31**	**35**	**66**	**28**	**6**	**2**	**5**	**7**	**2**
1993-94	**Washington**	**NHL**	**83**	**29**	**29**	**58**	**73**	**11**	**2**	**3**	**5**	**10**
1994-95	**Washington**	**NHL**	**48**	**12**	**14**	**26**	**41**	**7**	**1**	**4**	**5**	**0**
1995-96	**Los Angeles**	**NHL**	**76**	**27**	**37**	**64**	**44**					
	NHL Totals		**391**	**148**	**166**	**314**	**242**	**42**	**9**	**17**	**26**	**33**

Traded to **Los Angeles** by **Washington** with Byron Dafoe for Los Angeles' first round choice (Alexander Volchkov) and Dallas' fourth round choice (previously acquired by Los Angeles – Washington selected Justin Davis) in 1996 Entry Draft, July 8, 1995.

KILGER, CHAD (KIHL-guhr) — PHO.

Center. Shoots left. 6'3", 204 lbs. Born, Cornwall, Ont., November 27, 1976.
(Anaheim's 1st choice, 4th overall, in 1995 Entry Draft).

			Regular Season					Playoffs				
Season	Club	Lea	GP	G	A	TP	PIM	GP	G	A	TP	PIM
1993-94	Kingston	OHL	66	17	35	52	23	6	7	2	9	8
1994-95	Kingston	OHL	65	42	53	95	95	6	5	2	7	10
1995-96	**Anaheim**	**NHL**	**45**	**5**	**7**	**12**	**22**					
	Winnipeg	**NHL**	**29**	**2**	**3**	**5**	**12**	**4**	**1**	**0**	**1**	**0**
	NHL Totals		**74**	**7**	**10**	**17**	**34**	**4**	**1**	**0**	**1**	**0**

Traded to **Winnipeg** by **Anaheim** with Oleg Tverdovsky and Anaheim's third round choice (Per-Anton Lundstrom) in 1996 Entry Draft for Teemu Selanne, Marc Chouinard and Winnipeg's fourth round choice (later traded to Toronto — later traded to Montreal — Montreal selected Kim Staal) in 1996 Entry Draft, February 7, 1996.

KIMBLE, DARIN

Right wing. Shoots right. 6'2", 210 lbs. Born, Lucky Lake, Sask., November 22, 1968.
(Quebec's 5th choice, 66th overall, in 1988 Entry Draft).

			Regular Season					Playoffs				
Season	Club	Lea	GP	G	A	TP	PIM	GP	G	A	TP	PIM
1985-86	Calgary	WHL	37	14	8	22	93					
	N. Westminster	WHL	11	1	1	2	22					
	Brandon	WHL	15	1	6	7	39					
1986-87	Prince Albert	WHL	68	17	13	30	190					
1987-88	Prince Albert	WHL	67	35	36	71	307	10	3	2	5	4
1988-89	**Quebec**	**NHL**	**26**	**3**	**1**	**4**	**149**					
	Halifax	AHL	39	8	6	14	188					
1989-90	**Quebec**	**NHL**	**44**	**5**	**5**	**10**	**185**					
	Halifax	AHL	18	6	6	12	37	6	1	1	2	61
1990-91	**Quebec**	**NHL**	**35**	**2**	**5**	**7**	**114**					
	Halifax	AHL	7	1	4	5	20					
	St. Louis	**NHL**	**26**	**1**	**1**	**2**	**128**	**13**	**0**	**0**	**0**	**38**
1991-92	**St. Louis**	**NHL**	**46**	**1**	**3**	**4**	**166**	**5**	**0**	**0**	**0**	**7**
1992-93	**Boston**	**NHL**	**55**	**7**	**3**	**10**	**177**	**4**	**0**	**0**	**0**	**2**
	Providence	AHL	12	1	4	5	34					
1993-94	**Chicago**	**NHL**	**65**	**4**	**2**	**6**	**133**	**1**	**0**	**0**	**0**	**5**
1994-95	**Chicago**	**NHL**	**14**	**0**	**0**	**0**	**30**					
1995-96	Indianapolis	IHL	9	1	0	1	15					
	Albany	AHL	60	4	15	19	144	3	0	0	0	2
	NHL Totals		**311**	**23**	**20**	**43**	**1082**	**23**	**0**	**0**	**0**	**52**

Traded to **St. Louis** by **Quebec** for Herb Raglan, Tony Twist and Andy Rymsha, February 4, 1991. Traded to **Tampa Bay** by **St. Louis** with Pat Jablonski and Steve Tuttle for future considerations, June 19, 1992. Traded to **Boston** by **Tampa Bay** with future considerations for Ken Hodge and Matt Hervey, September 4, 1992. Signed as a free agent by **Florida**, July 9, 1993. Traded to **Chicago** by **Florida** for Keith Brown, September 30, 1993. Traded to **New Jersey** by **Chicago** for Michael Vukonich and Bill H. Armstrong, November 1, 1995.

KING, DEREK **NYI**

Left wing. Shoots left. 6', 212 lbs. Born, Hamilton, Ont., February 11, 1967.
(NY Islanders' 2nd choice, 13th overall, in 1985 Entry Draft).

			Regular Season					Playoffs				
Season	**Club**	**Lea**	**GP**	**G**	**A**	**TP**	**PIM**	**GP**	**G**	**A**	**TP**	**PIM**
1984-85	S.S. Marie	OHL	63	35	38	73	106	16	3	13	16	11
1985-86	S.S. Marie	OHL	25	12	17	29	33	....	....	....	....	....
	Oshawa	OHL	19	8	13	21	15	6	3	2	5	13
1986-87	**NY Islanders**	**NHL**	**2**	**0**	**0**	**0**	**0**	....	....	....	....	....
a	Oshawa	OHL	57	53	53	106	74	17	14	10	24	40
1987-88	**NY Islanders**	**NHL**	**55**	**12**	**24**	**36**	**30**	**5**	**0**	**2**	**2**	**2**
	Springfield	AHL	10	7	6	13	6	....	....	....	....	....
1988-89	**NY Islanders**	**NHL**	**60**	**14**	**29**	**43**	**14**	....	....	....	....	....
	Springfield	AHL	4	4	0	4	0	....	....	....	....	....
1989-90	**NY Islanders**	**NHL**	**46**	**13**	**27**	**40**	**20**	**4**	**0**	**0**	**0**	**4**
	Springfield	AHL	21	11	12	23	33	....	....	....	....	....
1990-91	**NY Islanders**	**NHL**	**66**	**19**	**26**	**45**	**44**	....	....	....	....	....
1991-92	**NY Islanders**	**NHL**	**80**	**40**	**38**	**78**	**46**	....	....	....	....	....
1992-93	**NY Islanders**	**NHL**	**77**	**38**	**38**	**76**	**47**	**18**	**3**	**11**	**14**	**14**
1993-94	**NY Islanders**	**NHL**	**78**	**30**	**40**	**70**	**59**	**4**	**0**	**1**	**1**	**0**
1994-95	**NY Islanders**	**NHL**	**43**	**10**	**16**	**26**	**41**	....	....	....	....	....
1995-96	**NY Islanders**	**NHL**	**61**	**12**	**20**	**32**	**23**	....	....	....	....	....
	NHL Totals		**568**	**188**	**258**	**446**	**324**	**31**	**3**	**14**	**17**	**20**

a OHL First All-Star Team (1987)

KING, KRIS **PHO.**

Left wing. Shoots left. 5'11", 208 lbs. Born, Bracebridge, Ont., February 18, 1966.
(Washington's 4th choice, 80th overall, in 1984 Entry Draft).

			Regular Season					Playoffs				
Season	**Club**	**Lea**	**GP**	**G**	**A**	**TP**	**PIM**	**GP**	**G**	**A**	**TP**	**PIM**
1983-84	Peterborough	OHL	62	13	18	31	168	8	3	3	6	14
1984-85	Peterborough	OHL	61	18	35	53	222	16	2	8	10	28
1985-86	Peterborough	OHL	58	19	40	59	254	8	4	0	4	21
1986-87	Binghamton	AHL	7	0	0	0	18	....	....	....	....	....
	Peterborough	OHL	46	23	33	56	160	12	5	8	13	41
1987-88	**Detroit**	**NHL**	**3**	**1**	**0**	**1**	**2**	....	....	....	....	....
	Adirondack	AHL	76	21	32	53	337	10	4	4	8	53
1988-89	**Detroit**	**NHL**	**55**	**2**	**3**	**5**	**168**	**2**	**0**	**0**	**0**	**2**
1989-90	**NY Rangers**	**NHL**	**68**	**6**	**7**	**13**	**286**	**10**	**0**	**1**	**1**	**38**
1990-91	**NY Rangers**	**NHL**	**72**	**11**	**14**	**25**	**154**	**6**	**2**	**0**	**2**	**36**
1991-92	**NY Rangers**	**NHL**	**79**	**10**	**9**	**19**	**224**	**13**	**4**	**1**	**5**	**14**
1992-93	**NY Rangers**	**NHL**	**30**	**0**	**3**	**3**	**67**	....	....	....	....	....
	Winnipeg	**NHL**	**48**	**8**	**8**	**16**	**136**	**6**	**1**	**1**	**2**	**4**
1993-94	**Winnipeg**	**NHL**	**83**	**4**	**8**	**12**	**205**	....	....	....	....	....
1994-95	**Winnipeg**	**NHL**	**48**	**4**	**2**	**6**	**85**	....	....	....	....	....
1995-96a	**Winnipeg**	**NHL**	**81**	**9**	**11**	**20**	**151**	**5**	**0**	**1**	**1**	**4**
	NHL Totals		**567**	**55**	**65**	**120**	**1478**	**42**	**7**	**4**	**11**	**98**

a Won King Clancy Memorial Trophy (1996)

Signed as a free agent by **Detroit**, March 23, 1987. Traded to **NY Rangers** by **Detroit** for Chris McRae and Detroit's fifth round choice (previously acquired by NY Rangers — Detroit selected Tony Burns) in 1990 Entry Draft, September 7, 1989. Traded to **Winnipeg** by **NY Rangers** with Tie Domi for Ed Olczyk, December 28, 1992.

KING, STEVEN **PHI.**

Right wing. Shoots right. 6', 195 lbs. Born, Greenwich, RI, July 22, 1969.
(NY Rangers' 1st choice, 21st overall, in 1991 Supplemental Draft).

			Regular Season					Playoffs				
Season	**Club**	**Lea**	**GP**	**G**	**A**	**TP**	**PIM**	**GP**	**G**	**A**	**TP**	**PIM**
1989-90	Brown	ECAC	27	19	8	27	53	....	....	....	....	....
1990-91	Brown	ECAC	27	19	15	34	76	....	....	....	....	....
1991-92	Binghamton	AHL	66	27	15	42	56	10	2	0	2	14
1992-93	**NY Rangers**	**NHL**	**24**	**7**	**5**	**12**	**16**	....	....	....	....	....
	Binghamton	AHL	53	35	33	68	100	14	7	9	16	26
1993-94	**Anaheim**	**NHL**	**36**	**8**	**3**	**11**	**44**	....	....	....	....	....
1994-95			DID NOT PLAY – INJURED									
1995-96	**Anaheim**	**NHL**	**7**	**2**	**0**	**2**	**15**	....	....	....	....	....
	Baltimore	AHL	68	40	21	61	95	12	7	5	12	20
	NHL Totals		**67**	**17**	**8**	**25**	**75**	....	....	....	....	....

Claimed by **Anaheim** from **NY Rangers** in Expansion Draft, June 24, 1993. Signed as a free agent by **Philadelphia**, July 31, 1996.

KINNEAR, GEORDIE **N.J.**

Defense. Shoots left. 6'1", 200 lbs. Born, Simcoe, Ont., July 9, 1973.
(New Jersey's 7th choice, 162nd overall, in 1992 Entry Draft).

			Regular Season					Playoffs				
Season	**Club**	**Lea**	**GP**	**G**	**A**	**TP**	**PIM**	**GP**	**G**	**A**	**TP**	**PIM**
1990-91	Peterborough	OHL	37	1	0	1	76	2	0	0	0	10
1991-92	Peterborough	OHL	63	5	16	21	195	10	0	2	2	36
1992-93	Peterborough	OHL	58	6	22	28	161	19	1	5	6	43
1993-94	Albany	AHL	59	3	12	15	197	5	0	0	0	21
1994-95	Albany	AHL	68	5	11	16	136	9	1	1	2	7
1995-96	Albany	AHL	73	4	7	11	170	4	0	1	1	2

KIPRUSOFF, MARKO (KIHP-ruh-sohf)

Defense. Shoots left. 6', 195 lbs. Born, Turku, Finland, June 6, 1972.
(Montreal's 4th choice, 70th overall, in 1994 Entry Draft).

			Regular Season					Playoffs				
Season	**Club**	**Lea**	**GP**	**G**	**A**	**TP**	**PIM**	**GP**	**G**	**A**	**TP**	**PIM**
1990-91	TPS	Fin.	3	0	0	0	0	....	....	....	....	....
1991-92	TPS	Fin.	23	0	2	2	0	....	....	....	....	....
	HPK	Fin.	3	0	0	0	0	....	....	....	....	....
1992-93	TPS	Fin.	43	3	7	10	14	12	2	3	5	6
1993-94	TPS	Fin.	48	5	19	24	8	11	0	6	6	4
1994-95	TPS	Fin.	50	10	21	31	16	13	0	9	9	2
1995-96	**Montreal**	**NHL**	**24**	**0**	**4**	**4**	**8**	....	....	....	....	....
	Fredericton	AHL	28	4	10	14	2	10	2	5	7	2
	NHL Totals		**24**	**0**	**4**	**4**	**8**	....	....	....	....	....

KIRTON, SCOTT **BOS.**

Right wing. Shoots right. 6'4", 215 lbs. Born, Penetanguishene, Ont., October 4, 1971.
(Chicago's 7th choice, 154th overall, in 1991 Entry Draft).

			Regular Season					Playoffs				
Season	**Club**	**Lea**	**GP**	**G**	**A**	**TP**	**PIM**	**GP**	**G**	**A**	**TP**	**PIM**
1991-92	North Dakota	WCHA	37	5	6	11	68	....	....	....	....	....
1992-93	North Dakota	WCHA	30	4	16	20	100	....	....	....	....	....
1993-94	North Dakota	WCHA	37	3	6	9	49	....	....	....	....	....
1994-95	North Dakota	WCHA	37	8	20	28	65	....	....	....	....	....
1995-96	Providence	AHL	2	0	1	1	0	....	....	....	....	....
	Charlotte	ECHL	56	17	19	36	176	16	4	6	10	50

Signed as a free agent by **Boston**, August 25, 1995.

KLATT, TRENT (KLAT) **PHI.**

Right wing. Shoots right. 6'1", 205 lbs. Born, Robbinsdale, MN, January 30, 1971.
(Washington's 5th choice, 82nd overall, in 1989 Entry Draft).

			Regular Season					Playoffs				
Season	**Club**	**Lea**	**GP**	**G**	**A**	**TP**	**PIM**	**GP**	**G**	**A**	**TP**	**PIM**
1989-90	U. Minnesota	WCHA	38	22	14	36	16	....	....	....	....	....
1990-91	U. Minnesota	WCHA	39	16	28	44	58	....	....	....	....	....
1991-92	U. Minnesota	WCHA	41	27	36	63	76	....	....	....	....	....
	Minnesota	**NHL**	**1**	**0**	**0**	**0**	**0**	**6**	**0**	**0**	**0**	**2**
1992-93	**Minnesota**	**NHL**	**47**	**4**	**19**	**23**	**38**	....	....	....	....	....
	Kalamazoo	IHL	31	8	11	19	18	....	....	....	....	....
1993-94	**Dallas**	**NHL**	**61**	**14**	**24**	**38**	**30**	**9**	**2**	**1**	**3**	**4**
	Kalamazoo	IHL	6	3	2	5	4	....	....	....	....	....
1994-95	**Dallas**	**NHL**	**47**	**12**	**10**	**22**	**26**	**5**	**1**	**0**	**1**	**0**
1995-96	**Dallas**	**NHL**	**22**	**4**	**4**	**8**	**23**	....	....	....	....	....
	Michigan	IHL	2	1	2	3	5	....	....	....	....	....
	Philadelphia	**NHL**	**49**	**3**	**8**	**11**	**21**	**12**	**4**	**1**	**5**	**0**
	NHL Totals		**227**	**37**	**65**	**102**	**138**	**32**	**7**	**2**	**9**	**6**

Traded to **Philadelphia** by **Dallas** for Brent Fedyk, December 13, 1995.

KLEE, KEN **WSH.**

Right wing. Shoots right. 6'1", 205 lbs. Born, Indianapolis, IN, April 24, 1971.
(Washington's 11th choice, 177th overall, in 1990 Entry Draft).

			Regular Season					Playoffs				
Season	**Club**	**Lea**	**GP**	**G**	**A**	**TP**	**PIM**	**GP**	**G**	**A**	**TP**	**PIM**
1989-90	Bowling Green	CCHA	39	0	5	5	52	....	....	....	....	....
1990-91	Bowling Green	CCHA	37	7	28	35	50	....	....	....	....	....
1991-92	Bowling Green	CCHA	10	0	1	1	14	....	....	....	....	....
1992-93	Baltimore	AHL	77	4	14	18	93	7	0	1	1	15
1993-94	Portland	AHL	65	2	9	11	87	17	1	2	3	14
1994-95	Portland	AHL	49	5	7	12	89	....	....	....	....	....
	Washington	**NHL**	**23**	**3**	**1**	**4**	**41**	**7**	**0**	**0**	**0**	**4**
1995-96	**Washington**	**NHL**	**66**	**8**	**3**	**11**	**60**	**1**	**0**	**0**	**0**	**0**
	NHL Totals		**89**	**11**	**4**	**15**	**101**	**8**	**0**	**0**	**0**	**4**

KLEMM, JON **COL.**

Defense. Shoots right. 6'3", 200 lbs. Born, Cranbrook, B.C., January 8, 1970.

			Regular Season					Playoffs				
Season	**Club**	**Lea**	**GP**	**G**	**A**	**TP**	**PIM**	**GP**	**G**	**A**	**TP**	**PIM**
1988-89	Seattle	WHL	2	1	1	2	0	....	....	....	....	....
	Spokane	WHL	66	6	34	40	42	....	....	....	....	....
1989-90	Spokane	WHL	66	3	28	31	100	6	1	1	2	5
1990-91	Spokane	WHL	72	7	58	65	65	15	3	6	9	8
1991-92	**Quebec**	**NHL**	**4**	**0**	**1**	**1**	**0**	....	....	....	....	....
	Halifax	AHL	70	6	13	19	40	....	....	....	....	....
1992-93	Halifax	AHL	80	3	20	23	32	....	....	....	....	....
1993-94	**Quebec**	**NHL**	**7**	**0**	**0**	**0**	**4**	....	....	....	....	....
	Cornwall	AHL	66	4	26	30	78	13	1	2	3	6
1994-95	Cornwall	AHL	65	6	13	19	84	....	....	....	....	....
	Quebec	**NHL**	**4**	**1**	**0**	**1**	**2**	....	....	....	....	....
1995-96	**Colorado**	**NHL**	**56**	**3**	**12**	**15**	**20**	**15**	**2**	**1**	**3**	**0** ♦
	NHL Totals		**71**	**4**	**13**	**17**	**26**	**15**	**2**	**1**	**3**	**0**

Signed as a free agent by **Calgary**, September 11, 1984. Signed as a free agent by **Philadelphia**, July 20, 1995.

KLEVAKIN, DIMITRI (kleh-VAH-kihn) **T.B.**

Right wing. Shoots left. 5'11", 163 lbs. Born, Angarsk, USSR, February 20, 1976.
(Tampa Bay's 4th choice, 86th overall, in 1994 Entry Draft).

			Regular Season					Playoffs				
Season	**Club**	**Lea**	**GP**	**G**	**A**	**TP**	**PIM**	**GP**	**G**	**A**	**TP**	**PIM**
1992-93	Spartak	CIS	8	1	1	2	0	....	....	....	....	....
1993-94	Spartak	CIS	42	6	3	9	6	4	1	0	1	0
1994-95	Spartak	CIS	52	12	10	22	4	....	....	....	....	....
1995-96	Spartak	CIS	49	8	15	23	54	5	3	0	3	0

KLIMA, PETR (KLEE-muh) **L.A.**

Right/Left wing. Shoots right. 6', 190 lbs. Born, Chomutov, Czech., December 23, 1964.
(Detroit's 5th choice, 86th overall, in 1983 Entry Draft).

			Regular Season					Playoffs				
Season	**Club**	**Lea**	**GP**	**G**	**A**	**TP**	**PIM**	**GP**	**G**	**A**	**TP**	**PIM**
1981-82	Litvinov	Czech.	18	7	3	10	8	....	....	....	....	....
1982-83	Litvinov	Czech.	44	19	17	36	74	....	....	....	....	....
1983-84	Dukla Jihlava	Czech.	41	20	16	36	46	....	....	....	....	....
1984-85	Dukla Jihlava	Czech.	35	23	22	45	76	....	....	....	....	....
1985-86	**Detroit**	**NHL**	**74**	**32**	**24**	**56**	**16**	....	....	....	....	....
1986-87	**Detroit**	**NHL**	**77**	**30**	**23**	**53**	**42**	**13**	**1**	**2**	**3**	**4**
1987-88	**Detroit**	**NHL**	**78**	**37**	**25**	**62**	**46**	**12**	**10**	**8**	**18**	**10**
1988-89	**Detroit**	**NHL**	**51**	**25**	**16**	**41**	**44**	**6**	**2**	**4**	**6**	**19**
	Adirondack	AHL	5	5	1	6	4	....	....	....	....	....
1989-90	**Detroit**	**NHL**	**13**	**5**	**5**	**10**	**6**	....	....	....	....	....
	Edmonton	**NHL**	**63**	**25**	**28**	**53**	**66**	**21**	**5**	**0**	**5**	**8** ♦
1990-91	**Edmonton**	**NHL**	**70**	**40**	**28**	**68**	**113**	**18**	**7**	**6**	**13**	**16**
1991-92	**Edmonton**	**NHL**	**57**	**21**	**13**	**34**	**52**	**15**	**1**	**4**	**5**	**8**
1992-93	**Edmonton**	**NHL**	**68**	**32**	**16**	**48**	**100**	....	....	....	....	....
1993-94	**Tampa Bay**	**NHL**	**75**	**28**	**27**	**55**	**76**	....	....	....	....	....
1994-95	Wolfsburg	Ger. 2	12	27	11	38	28	....	....	....	....	....
	ZPS Zlin	Czech.	1	1	0	1	0	....	....	....	....	....
	Tampa Bay	**NHL**	**47**	**13**	**13**	**26**	**26**	....	....	....	....	....
1995-96	**Tampa Bay**	**NHL**	**67**	**22**	**30**	**52**	**68**	**4**	**2**	**0**	**2**	**14**
	NHL Totals		**740**	**310**	**248**	**558**	**655**	**89**	**28**	**24**	**52**	**79**

Traded to **Edmonton** by **Detroit** with Joe Murphy, Adam Graves and Jeff Sharples for Jimmy Carson, Kevin McClelland and Edmonton's fifth round choice (later traded to Montreal — Montreal selected Brad Layzell) in 1991 Entry Draft, November 2, 1989. Traded to **Tampa Bay** by **Edmonton** for Tampa Bay's third round choice (Brad Symes) in 1994 Entry Draft, June 16, 1993. Traded to **Los Angeles** by **Tampa Bay** for a conditional choice in 1997 Entry Draft, August 22, 1996.

KLIMENTIEV, SERGEI (klih-MEHN-tyehv) **BUF.**

Defense. Shoots left. 5'11", 200 lbs. Born, Kiev, USSR, April 5, 1975.
(Buffalo's 4th choice, 121st overall, in 1994 Entry Draft).

			Regular Season					Playoffs				
Season	**Club**	**Lea**	**GP**	**G**	**A**	**TP**	**PIM**	**GP**	**G**	**A**	**TP**	**PIM**
1991-92	SVSM Kiev	CIS 3	42	4	15	19	....					
1992-93	Sokol Kiev	CIS	3	0	0	0	4	1	0	0	0	0
1993-94	Medicine Hat	WHL	72	16	26	42	165	3	0	0	0	4
1994-95	Medicine Hat	WHL	71	19	45	64	146	5	4	2	6	14
	Rochester	AHL	7	0	0	0	8	1	0	0	0	0
1995-96	Rochester	AHL	70	7	29	36	74	19	2	8	10	16

KLIMOVICH, SERGEI (klee-MOH-vich) CHI.

Center. Shoots right. 6'3", 189 lbs. Born, Novosibirsk, USSR, March 8, 1974.
(Chicago's 3rd choice, 41st overall, in 1992 Entry Draft).

			Regular Season					Playoffs				
Season	Club	Lea	GP	G	A	TP	PIM	GP	G	A	TP	PIM
1991-92	Moscow D'amo	CIS	3	0	0	0	0	....	....	....	....	....
1992-93	Moscow D'amo	CIS	30	4	1	5	14	10	1	0	1	2
1993-94	Moscow D'amo	CIS	39	7	4	11	14	12	2	3	5	6
1994-95	Moscow D'amo	CIS	4	1	0	1	2	....	....	....	....	....
	Indianapolis	IHL	71	14	30	44	20	....	....	....	....	....
1995-96	Indianapolis	IHL	68	17	21	38	28	5	1	1	2	6

KNIPSCHEER, FRED (kuh-NIHP-sheer)

Center. Shoots left. 5'11", 185 lbs. Born, Ft. Wayne, IN, September 3, 1969.

			Regular Season					Playoffs				
Season	Club	Lea	GP	G	A	TP	PIM	GP	G	A	TP	PIM
1990-91	St. Cloud	WCHA	40	9	10	19	57	....	....	....	....	....
1991-92	St. Cloud	WCHA	33	15	17	32	48	....	....	....	....	....
1992-93ab	St. Cloud	WCHA	36	34	26	60	68	....	....	....	....	....
1993-94	**Boston**	**NHL**	**11**	**3**	**2**	**5**	**14**	**12**	**2**	**1**	**3**	**6**
	Providence	AHL	62	26	13	39	50	....	....	....	....	....
1994-95	Providence	AHL	71	29	34	63	81	....	....	....	....	....
	Boston	**NHL**	**16**	**3**	**1**	**4**	**2**	**4**	**0**	**0**	**0**	**0**
1995-96	**St. Louis**	**NHL**	**1**	**0**	**0**	**0**	**2**	....	....	....	....	....
	Worcester	AHL	68	36	37	73	93	3	0	0	0	2
	NHL Totals		**28**	**6**	**3**	**9**	**18**	**16**	**2**	**1**	**3**	**6**

a WCHA First All-Star Team (1993)
b NCAA West Second All-American Team (1993)

Signed as a free agent by **Boston**, April 30, 1993. Traded to **St. Louis** by **Boston** for Rick Zombo, October 2, 1995.

KNUBLE, MICHAEL (NOO-buhl) DET.

Right wing. Shoots right. 6'3", 208 lbs. Born, Toronto, Ont., July 4, 1972.
(Detroit's 4th choice, 76th overall, in 1991 Entry Draft).

			Regular Season					Playoffs				
Season	Club	Lea	GP	G	A	TP	PIM	GP	G	A	TP	PIM
1991-92	U. of Michigan	CCHA	43	7	8	15	48	....	....	....	....	....
1992-93	U. of Michigan	CCHA	39	26	16	42	57	....	....	....	....	....
1993-94a	U. of Michigan	CCHA	41	32	26	58	71	....	....	....	....	....
1994-95ab	U. of Michigan	CCHA	34	*38	22	60	62	....	....	....	....	....
	Adirondack	AHL	....	....	....	....	....	3	0	0	0	0
1995-96	Adirondack	AHL	80	22	23	45	59	3	1	0	1	0

a CCHA Second All-Star Team (1994, 1995)
b NCAA West Second All-American Team (1995)

KNUTSEN, ESPEN (kuh-NOOT-suhn) HFD.

Center. Shoots left. 5'11", 172 lbs. Born, Oslo, Norway, January 12, 1972.
(Hartford's 9th choice, 204th overall, in 1990 Entry Draft).

			Regular Season					Playoffs				
Season	Club	Lea	GP	G	A	TP	PIM	GP	G	A	TP	PIM
1989-90	Valerengen	Nor.	34	22	26	48	....	....	....	....	....	....
1990-91	Valerengen	Nor.	31	30	24	54	42	5	3	4	7	....
1991-92	Valerengen	Nor.	30	28	26	54	37	8	7	8	15	....
1992-93	Valerengen	Nor.	13	11	13	24	4	....	....	....	....	....
1993-94	Valerengen	Nor.	38	32	26	58	20	....	....	....	....	....
1994-95	Djurgarden	Swe.	30	6	14	20	18	3	0	1	1	0
1995-96	Djurgarden	Swe.	32	10	23	33	50	4	1	0	1	2

KOCUR, JOE (KOH-suhr)

Right wing. Shoots right. 6', 205 lbs. Born, Calgary, Alta., December 21, 1964.
(Detroit's 6th choice, 88th overall, in 1983 Entry Draft).

			Regular Season					Playoffs				
Season	Club	Lea	GP	G	A	TP	PIM	GP	G	A	TP	PIM
1982-83	Saskatoon	WHL	62	23	17	40	289	6	2	3	5	25
1983-84	Saskatoon	WHL	69	40	41	81	258	....	....	....	....	....
	Adirondack	AHL	....	....	....	....	....	5	0	0	0	20
1984-85	**Detroit**	**NHL**	**17**	**1**	**0**	**1**	**64**	**3**	**1**	**0**	**1**	**5**
	Adirondack	AHL	47	12	7	19	171	....	....	....	....	....
1985-86	**Detroit**	**NHL**	**59**	**9**	**6**	**15**	***377**	....	....	....	....	....
	Adirondack	AHL	9	6	2	8	34	....	....	....	....	....
1986-87	**Detroit**	**NHL**	**77**	**9**	**9**	**18**	**276**	**16**	**2**	**3**	**5**	**71**
1987-88	**Detroit**	**NHL**	**63**	**7**	**7**	**14**	**263**	**10**	**0**	**1**	**1**	**13**
1988-89	**Detroit**	**NHL**	**60**	**9**	**9**	**18**	**213**	**3**	**0**	**1**	**1**	**6**
1989-90	**Detroit**	**NHL**	**71**	**16**	**20**	**36**	**268**	....	....	....	....	....
1990-91	**Detroit**	**NHL**	**52**	**5**	**4**	**9**	**253**	....	....	....	....	....
	NY Rangers	**NHL**	**5**	**0**	**0**	**0**	**36**	**6**	**0**	**2**	**2**	**21**
1991-92	**NY Rangers**	**NHL**	**51**	**7**	**4**	**11**	**121**	**12**	**1**	**1**	**2**	**38**
1992-93	**NY Rangers**	**NHL**	**65**	**3**	**6**	**9**	**131**	....	....	....	....	....
1993-94	**NY Rangers**	**NHL**	**71**	**2**	**1**	**3**	**129**	**20**	**1**	**1**	**2**	**17** ♦
1994-95	**NY Rangers**	**NHL**	**48**	**1**	**2**	**3**	**71**	**10**	**0**	**0**	**0**	**8**
1995-96	**NY Rangers**	**NHL**	**38**	**1**	**2**	**3**	**49**	....	....	....	....	....
	Vancouver	**NHL**	**7**	**0**	**1**	**1**	**19**	**1**	**0**	**0**	**0**	**0**
	NHL Totals		**684**	**70**	**71**	**141**	**2270**	**81**	**5**	**9**	**14**	**179**

Traded to **NY Rangers** by **Detroit** with Per Djoos for Kevin Miller, Jim Cummins and Dennis Vial, March 5, 1991. Traded to **Vancouver** by **NY Rangers** for Kay Whitmore, March 20, 1996.

KOHN, LADISLAV (KOHN) CGY.

Right wing. Shoots left. 5'10", 180 lbs. Born, Uherske Hradiste, Czech., March 4, 1975.
(Calgary's 9th choice, 175th overall, in 1994 Entry Draft).

			Regular Season					Playoffs				
Season	Club	Lea	GP	G	A	TP	PIM	GP	G	A	TP	PIM
1993-94	Brandon	WHL	2	0	0	0	0	....	....	....	....	....
	Swift Current	WHL	69	33	35	68	68	7	5	4	9	8
1994-95	Swift Current	WHL	65	32	60	92	122	6	2	6	8	14
	Saint John	AHL	1	0	0	0	0	....	....	....	....	....
1995-96	**Calgary**	**NHL**	**5**	**1**	**0**	**1**	**2**	....	....	....	....	....
	Saint John	AHL	73	28	45	73	97	16	6	5	11	12
	NHL Totals		**5**	**1**	**0**	**1**	**2**	....	....	....	....	....

KOIVU, SAKU (KOY-voo, SA-koo) MTL.

Center. Shoots left. 5'9", 175 lbs. Born, Turku, Finland, November 23, 1974.
(Montreal's 1st choice, 21st overall, in 1993 Entry Draft).

			Regular Season					Playoffs				
Season	Club	Lea	GP	G	A	TP	PIM	GP	G	A	TP	PIM
1992-93	TPS	Fin.	46	3	7	10	28	11	3	2	5	2
1993-94	TPS	Fin.	47	23	30	53	42	11	4	8	12	16
1994-95	TPS	Fin.	45	27	47	74	73	13	7	10	17	16
1995-96	**Montreal**	**NHL**	**82**	**20**	**25**	**45**	**40**	**6**	**3**	**1**	**4**	**8**
	NHL Totals		**82**	**20**	**25**	**45**	**40**	**6**	**3**	**1**	**4**	**8**

KOLESAR, MARK (kohl-UH-sahr) TOR.

Left wing. Shoots right. 6'1", 188 lbs. Born, Brampton, Ont., January 23, 1973.

			Regular Season					Playoffs				
Season	Club	Lea	GP	G	A	TP	PIM	GP	G	A	TP	PIM
1991-92	Brandon	WHL	56	6	7	13	36	....	....	....	....	....
1992-93	Brandon	WHL	68	27	33	60	110	4	0	0	0	4
1993-94	Brandon	WHL	59	29	37	66	131	14	8	3	11	48
1994-95	St. John's	AHL	65	12	18	30	62	5	1	0	1	2
1995-96	**Toronto**	**NHL**	**21**	**2**	**2**	**4**	**14**	**3**	**1**	**0**	**1**	**2**
	St. John's	AHL	52	22	13	35	47	....	....	....	....	....
	NHL Totals		**21**	**2**	**2**	**4**	**14**	**3**	**1**	**0**	**1**	**2**

Signed as a free agent by **Toronto**, May 24, 1994.

KOLKUNOV, ALEXEI PIT.

Center. Shoots right. 6', 185 lbs. Born, Belgorod, USSR, February 3, 1977.
(Pittsburgh's 5th choice, 154th overall, in 1995 Entry Draft).

			Regular Season					Playoffs				
Season	Club	Lea	GP	G	A	TP	PIM	GP	G	A	TP	PIM
1994-95	Soviet Wings	CIS	7	0	0	0	0	4	1	0	1	0
1995-96	Soviet Wings	CIS	43	9	3	12	35	....	....	....	....	....

KOMARNISKI, ZENITH VAN.

Defense. Shoots left. 5'11", 190 lbs. Born, Edmonton, Alta., August 13, 1978.
(Vancouver's 2nd choice, 75th overall, in 1996 Entry Draft).

			Regular Season					Playoffs				
Season	Club	Lea	GP	G	A	TP	PIM	GP	G	A	TP	PIM
1994-95	Tri-City	WHL	66	5	19	24	110	17	1	2	3	47
1995-96	Tri-City	WHL	42	5	21	26	85	....	....	....	....	....

KONDRASHKIN, SERGEI (kohn-DRAHSH-kihn) NYR

Right wing. Shoots left. 6', 192 lbs. Born, Cherepovets, USSR, April 2, 1975.
(NY Rangers' 7th choice, 162nd overall, in 1993 Entry Draft).

			Regular Season					Playoffs				
Season	Club	Lea	GP	G	A	TP	PIM	GP	G	A	TP	PIM
1992-93	Cherepovets	CIS	41	7	3	10	8	....	....	....	....	....
1993-94	Cherepovets	CIS	41	7	2	9	26	....	....	....	....	....
1994-95	Cherepovets	CIS	51	7	2	9	22	....	....	....	....	....
1995-96	Cherepovets	CIS	28	2	1	3	8	3	1	0	1	2

KONOWALCHUK, STEVE (kahn-uh-WAHL-chuhk) WSH.

Center. Shoots left. 6'1", 195 lbs. Born, Salt Lake City, UT, November 11, 1972.
(Washington's 5th choice, 58th overall, in 1991 Entry Draft).

			Regular Season					Playoffs				
Season	Club	Lea	GP	G	A	TP	PIM	GP	G	A	TP	PIM
1990-91	Portland	WHL	72	43	49	92	78	....	....	....	....	....
1991-92	**Washington**	**NHL**	**1**	**0**	**0**	**0**	**0**	....	....	....	....	....
	Baltimore	AHL	3	1	1	2	0	....	....	....	....	....
a	Portland	WHL	64	51	53	104	95	6	3	6	9	12
1992-93	**Washington**	**NHL**	**36**	**4**	**7**	**11**	**16**	**2**	**0**	**1**	**1**	**0**
	Baltimore	AHL	37	18	28	46	74	....	....	....	....	....
1993-94	**Washington**	**NHL**	**62**	**12**	**14**	**26**	**33**	**11**	**0**	**1**	**1**	**10**
	Portland	AHL	8	11	4	15	4	....	....	....	....	....
1994-95	**Washington**	**NHL**	**46**	**11**	**14**	**25**	**44**	**7**	**2**	**5**	**7**	**12**
1995-96	**Washington**	**NHL**	**70**	**23**	**22**	**45**	**92**	**2**	**0**	**2**	**2**	**0**
	NHL Totals		**215**	**50**	**57**	**107**	**185**	**22**	**2**	**9**	**11**	**22**

a WHL First All-Star Team (1992)

KONSTANTINOV, VLADIMIR (kohn-stahn-TEE-nahf) DET.

Defense. Shoots right. 5'11", 190 lbs. Born, Murmansk, USSR, March 19, 1967.
(Detroit's 12th choice, 221st overall, in 1989 Entry Draft).

			Regular Season					Playoffs				
Season	Club	Lea	GP	G	A	TP	PIM	GP	G	A	TP	PIM
1984-85	CSKA	USSR	40	1	4	5	10	....	....	....	....	....
1985-86	CSKA	USSR	26	4	3	7	12	....	....	....	....	....
1986-87	CSKA	USSR	35	2	2	4	19	....	....	....	....	....
1987-88	CSKA	USSR	50	3	6	9	32	....	....	....	....	....
1988-89	CSKA	USSR	37	7	8	15	20	....	....	....	....	....
1989-90	CSKA	USSR	47	14	14	28	44	....	....	....	....	....
1990-91	CSKA	USSR	45	5	12	17	42	....	....	....	....	....
1991-92a	**Detroit**	**NHL**	**79**	**8**	**26**	**34**	**172**	**11**	**0**	**1**	**1**	**16**
1992-93	**Detroit**	**NHL**	**82**	**5**	**17**	**22**	**137**	**7**	**0**	**1**	**1**	**8**
1993-94	**Detroit**	**NHL**	**80**	**12**	**21**	**33**	**138**	**7**	**0**	**2**	**2**	**4**
1994-95	Wedemark	Ger. 2	15	13	17	30	51	....	....	....	....	....
	Detroit	**NHL**	**47**	**3**	**11**	**14**	**101**	**18**	**1**	**1**	**2**	**22**
1995-96bc	**Detroit**	**NHL**	**81**	**14**	**20**	**34**	**139**	**19**	**4**	**5**	**9**	**28**
	NHL Totals		**369**	**42**	**95**	**137**	**687**	**62**	**5**	**10**	**15**	**78**

a NHL/Upper Deck All-Rookie Team (1992)
b NHL Second All-Star Team (1996)
c Won Alka-Seltzer Plus Award (1996)

KONTOS, CHRIS
(KONN-tohs)

Left wing/Center. Shoots left. 6'1", 195 lbs.　Born, Toronto, Ont., December 10, 1963.
(NY Rangers' 1st choice, 15th overall, in 1982 Entry Draft).

			Regular Season					Playoffs				
Season	Club	Lea	GP	G	A	TP	PIM	GP	G	A	TP	PIM
1980-81	Sudbury	OHA	57	17	27	44	36	....	....	....	....	....
1981-82	Sudbury	OHL	12	6	6	12	18	....	....	....	....	....
	Toronto	OHL	59	36	56	92	68	10	7	9	16	2
1982-83	**NY Rangers**	**NHL**	**44**	**8**	**7**	**15**	**33**	....	....	....	....	....
	Toronto	OHL	28	21	33	54	23	....	....	....	....	....
1983-84	**NY Rangers**	**NHL**	**6**	**0**	**1**	**1**	**8**	....	....	....	....	....
	Tulsa	CHL	21	5	13	18	8	....	....	....	....	....
1984-85	**NY Rangers**	**NHL**	**28**	**4**	**8**	**12**	**24**	....	....	....	....	....
	New Haven	AHL	48	19	24	43	30	....	....	....	....	....
1985-86	Ilves	Fin.	36	16	15	31	30	....	....	....	....	....
	New Haven	AHL	21	8	15	23	12	5	4	2	6	4
1986-87	**Pittsburgh**	**NHL**	**31**	**8**	**9**	**17**	**6**	....	....	....	....	....
	New Haven	AHL	36	14	17	31	29	....	....	....	....	....
1987-88	**Pittsburgh**	**NHL**	**36**	**1**	**7**	**8**	**12**	....	....	....	....	....
	Muskegon	IHL	10	3	6	9	8	....	....	....	....	....
	Los Angeles	**NHL**	**6**	**2**	**10**	**12**	**2**	**4**	**1**	**0**	**1**	**4**
	New Haven	AHL	16	8	16	24	4	....	....	....	....	....
1988-89	EHC Kloten	Swiss	36	33	22	55	....	6	6	2	8	....
	Los Angeles	**NHL**	**7**	**2**	**1**	**3**	**2**	**11**	**9**	**0**	**9**	**8**
1989-90	**Los Angeles**	**NHL**	**6**	**2**	**2**	**4**	**4**	**5**	**1**	**0**	**1**	**0**
	New Haven	AHL	42	10	20	30	25	....	....	....	....	....
1990-91	Phoenix	IHL	69	26	36	62	19	11	9	12	21	0
1991-92	Cdn. National	....	26	10	10	20	4	....	....	....	....	....
1992-93	**Tampa Bay**	**NHL**	**66**	**27**	**24**	**51**	**12**	....	....	....	....	....
1993-94	Cdn. National	....	35	16	16	32	12	....	....	....	....	....
	Cdn. Olympic	....	8	3	1	4	2	....	....	....	....	....
1994-95	Skelleftea	Swe.	36	21	27	48	30	5	2	3	5	4
	Cdn. National	....	3	0	1	1	4	....	....	....	....	....
1995-96	Cincinnati	IHL	81	26	44	70	13	17	5	8	13	0
	NHL Totals		**230**	**54**	**69**	**123**	**103**	**20**	**11**	**0**	**11**	**12**

Traded to **Pittsburgh** by **NY Rangers** for Ron Duguay, January 21, 1987. Traded to **Los Angeles** by **Pittsburgh** with Pittsburgh's sixth round choice (Micah Aivazoff) in 1988 Entry Draft for Bryan Erickson, February 5, 1988. Signed as a free agent by **Tampa Bay**, July 21, 1992. Signed as a free agent by **Florida**, July 7, 1995.

KORDIC, DAN
PHI.

Left wing. Shoots left. 6'5", 234 lbs.　Born, Edmonton, Alta., April 18, 1971.
(Philadelphia's 9th choice, 88th overall, in 1990 Entry Draft).

			Regular Season					Playoffs				
Season	Club	Lea	GP	G	A	TP	PIM	GP	G	A	TP	PIM
1987-88	Medicine Hat	WHL	63	1	5	6	75	....	....	....	....	....
1988-89	Medicine Hat	WHL	70	1	13	14	190	....	....	....	....	....
1989-90	Medicine Hat	WHL	59	4	12	16	182	3	0	0	0	9
1990-91	Medicine Hat	WHL	67	8	15	23	150	12	2	6	8	42
1991-92	**Philadelphia**	**NHL**	**46**	**1**	**3**	**4**	**126**	....	....	....	....	....
1992-93	Hershey	AHL	14	0	2	2	17	....	....	....	....	....
1993-94	**Philadelphia**	**NHL**	**4**	**0**	**0**	**0**	**5**	....	....	....	....	....
	Hershey	AHL	64	0	4	4	164	11	0	3	3	26
1994-95	Hershey	AHL	37	0	2	2	121	6	0	1	1	21
1995-96	**Philadelphia**	**NHL**	**9**	**1**	**0**	**1**	**31**	....	....	....	....	....
	Hershey	AHL	52	2	6	8	101	....	....	....	....	....
	NHL Totals		**59**	**2**	**3**	**5**	**162**					

KOROBOLIN, ALEXANDER
(koh-roh-BOH-lihn)　NYR

Defense. Shoots left. 6'2", 189 lbs.　Born, Chelyabinsk, USSR, March 12, 1976.
(NY Rangers' 4th choice, 100th overall, in 1994 Entry Draft).

			Regular Season					Playoffs				
Season	Club	Lea	GP	G	A	TP	PIM	GP	G	A	TP	PIM
1993-94	Chelyabinsk	CIS	32	0	0	0	30	....	....	....	....	....
1994-95	Chelyabinsk	CIS 2				UNAVAILABLE						
1995-96	Chelyabinsk	CIS 2				UNAVAILABLE						

KOROLEV, IGOR
(koh-roh-LEHV)　PHO.

Right wing. Shoots left. 6'1", 187 lbs.　Born, Moscow, USSR, September 6, 1970.
(St. Louis' 1st choice, 38th overall, in 1992 Entry Draft).

			Regular Season					Playoffs				
Season	Club	Lea	GP	G	A	TP	PIM	GP	G	A	TP	PIM
1988-89	Moscow D'amo	USSR	1	0	0	0	2	....	....	....	....	....
1989-90	Moscow D'amo	USSR	17	3	2	5	2	....	....	....	....	....
1990-91	Moscow D'amo	USSR	38	12	4	16	12	....	....	....	....	....
1991-92	Moscow D'amo	CIS	39	15	12	27	16	....	....	....	....	....
1992-93	Moscow D'amo	CIS	5	1	2	3	4	....	....	....	....	....
	St. Louis	**NHL**	**74**	**4**	**23**	**27**	**20**	**3**	**0**	**0**	**0**	**0**
1993-94	**St. Louis**	**NHL**	**73**	**6**	**10**	**16**	**40**	**2**	**0**	**0**	**0**	**0**
1994-95	Moscow D'amo	CIS	13	4	6	10	18	....	....	....	....	....
	Winnipeg	**NHL**	**45**	**8**	**22**	**30**	**10**	....	....	....	....	....
1995-96	**Winnipeg**	**NHL**	**73**	**22**	**29**	**51**	**42**	**6**	**0**	**3**	**3**	**0**
	NHL Totals		**265**	**40**	**84**	**124**	**112**	**11**	**0**	**3**	**3**	**0**

Claimed by **Winnipeg** from **St. Louis** in NHL Waiver Draft, January 18, 1995.

KOROLYUK, ALEXANDER
(koh-roh-LYUHK)　S.J.

Right wing. Shoots left. 5'9", 170 lbs.　Born, Moscow, USSR, January 15, 1976.
(San Jose's 6th choice, 141st overall, in 1994 Entry Draft).

			Regular Season					Playoffs				
Season	Club	Lea	GP	G	A	TP	PIM	GP	G	A	TP	PIM
1993-94	Soviet Wings	CIS	22	4	4	8	20	3	1	0	1	4
1994-95	Soviet Wings	CIS	52	16	13	29	62	4	1	2	3	4
1995-96	Soviet Wings	CIS	50	30	19	49	77	....	....	....	....	....

KOVALENKO, ANDREI
(koh-vah-LEHN-koh)　MTL.

Right wing. Shoots left. 5'10", 215 lbs.　Born, Balakovo, USSR, June 7, 1970.
(Quebec's 6th choice, 148th overall, in 1990 Entry Draft).

			Regular Season					Playoffs				
Season	Club	Lea	GP	G	A	TP	PIM	GP	G	A	TP	PIM
1988-89	CSKA	USSR	10	1	0	1	0	....	....	....	....	....
1989-90	CSKA	USSR	48	8	5	13	20	....	....	....	....	....
1990-91	CSKA	USSR	45	13	8	21	26	....	....	....	....	....
1991-92	CSKA	CIS	44	19	13	32	32	....	....	....	....	....
1992-93	CSKA	CIS	3	3	1	4	4	....	....	....	....	....
	Quebec	**NHL**	**81**	**27**	**41**	**68**	**57**	**4**	**1**	**0**	**1**	**2**
1993-94	**Quebec**	**NHL**	**58**	**16**	**17**	**33**	**46**	....	....	....	....	....
1994-95	Togliatti	CIS	11	9	2	11	14	....	....	....	....	....
	Quebec	**NHL**	**45**	**14**	**10**	**24**	**31**	**6**	**0**	**1**	**1**	**2**
1995-96	**Colorado**	**NHL**	**26**	**11**	**11**	**22**	**16**	....	....	....	....	....
	Montreal	**NHL**	**51**	**17**	**17**	**34**	**33**	**6**	**0**	**0**	**0**	**6**
	NHL Totals		**261**	**85**	**96**	**181**	**183**	**16**	**1**	**1**	**2**	**10**

Traded to **Montreal** by **Colorado** with Martin Rucinsky and Jocelyn Thibault for Patrick Roy and Mike Keane, December 6, 1995.

KOVALEV, ALEXEI
(koh-VAH-lehv)　NYR

Right wing. Shoots left. 6', 205 lbs.　Born, Togliatti, USSR, February 24, 1973.
(NY Rangers' 1st choice, 15th overall, in 1991 Entry Draft).

			Regular Season					Playoffs				
Season	Club	Lea	GP	G	A	TP	PIM	GP	G	A	TP	PIM
1989-90	Moscow D'amo	USSR	1	0	0	0	0	....	....	....	....	....
1990-91	Moscow D'amo	USSR	18	1	2	3	4	....	....	....	....	....
1991-92	Moscow D'amo	CIS	33	16	9	25	20	....	....	....	....	....
1992-93	**NY Rangers**	**NHL**	**65**	**20**	**18**	**38**	**79**	....	....	....	....	....
	Binghamton	AHL	13	13	11	24	35	9	3	5	8	14
1993-94	**NY Rangers**	**NHL**	**76**	**23**	**33**	**56**	**154**	**23**	**9**	**12**	**21**	**18 ◆**
1994-95	Togliatti	CIS	12	8	8	16	49	....	....	....	....	....
	NY Rangers	**NHL**	**48**	**13**	**15**	**28**	**30**	**10**	**4**	**7**	**11**	**10**
1995-96	**NY Rangers**	**NHL**	**81**	**24**	**34**	**58**	**98**	**11**	**3**	**4**	**7**	**14**
	NHL Totals		**270**	**80**	**100**	**180**	**361**	**44**	**16**	**23**	**39**	**42**

KOVESHNIKOV, ANATOLI
DAL.

Right wing. Shoots left. 6'2", 187 lbs.　Born, Kiev, USSR, May 31, 1973.
(Dallas' 8th choice, 193rd overall, in 1995 Entry Draft).

			Regular Season					Playoffs				
Season	Club	Lea	GP	G	A	TP	PIM	GP	G	A	TP	PIM
1992-93	Sokol Kiev	CIS	23	1	0	1	4	3	0	0	0	0
1993-94	Sokol Kiev	CIS	34	2	2	4	16	....	....	....	....	....
1994-95	Sokol Kiev	CIS	51	8	0	8	10	....	....	....	....	....
1995-96	Sokol Kiev	CIS	36	4	2	6	45	....	....	....	....	....
	Lada Togliatti	CIS	9	0	1	1	6	4	1	0	1	2

KOZLOV, VIKTOR
(KAHS-lahf)　S.J.

Left wing. Shoots right. 6'5", 225 lbs.　Born, Togliatti, USSR, February 14, 1975.
(San Jose's 1st choice, 6th overall, in 1993 Entry Draft).

			Regular Season					Playoffs				
Season	Club	Lea	GP	G	A	TP	PIM	GP	G	A	TP	PIM
1990-91	Togliatti	USSR 2	2	2	0	2	0	....	....	....	....	....
1991-92	Togliatti	CIS	3	0	0	0	0	....	....	....	....	....
1992-93	Moscow D'amo	CIS	30	6	5	11	4	10	3	0	3	0
1993-94	Moscow D'amo	CIS	42	16	9	25	14	7	3	2	5	0
1994-95	Moscow D'amo	CIS	3	1	1	2	2	....	....	....	....	....
	San Jose	**NHL**	**16**	**2**	**0**	**2**	**2**	....	....	....	....	....
	Kansas City	IHL	4	1	1	2	0	13	4	5	9	12
1995-96	**San Jose**	**NHL**	**62**	**6**	**13**	**19**	**6**	....	....	....	....	....
	Kansas City	IHL	15	4	7	11	12	....	....	....	....	....
	NHL Totals		**78**	**8**	**13**	**21**	**8**					

KOZLOV, VYACHESLAV
(KAHS-lahf, VYACH-ih-slav)　DET.

Center. Shoots left. 5'10", 180 lbs.　Born, Voskresensk, USSR, May 3, 1972.
(Detroit's 2nd choice, 45th overall, in 1990 Entry Draft).

			Regular Season					Playoffs				
Season	Club	Lea	GP	G	A	TP	PIM	GP	G	A	TP	PIM
1987-88	Khimik	USSR	2	0	0	0	0	....	....	....	....	....
1988-89	Khimik	USSR	14	0	1	1	2	....	....	....	....	....
1989-90	Khimik	USSR	45	14	12	26	38	....	....	....	....	....
1990-91	Khimik	USSR	45	11	13	24	46	....	....	....	....	....
1991-92	CSKA	CIS	11	6	5	11	12	....	....	....	....	....
	Detroit	**NHL**	**7**	**0**	**2**	**2**	**2**	....	....	....	....	....
1992-93	**Detroit**	**NHL**	**17**	**4**	**1**	**5**	**14**	**4**	**0**	**2**	**2**	**2**
	Adirondack	AHL	45	23	36	59	54	4	1	1	2	4
1993-94	**Detroit**	**NHL**	**77**	**34**	**39**	**73**	**50**	**7**	**2**	**5**	**7**	**12**
	Adirondack	AHL	3	0	1	1	15	....	....	....	....	....
1994-95	CSKA	CIS	10	3	4	7	14	....	....	....	....	....
	Detroit	**NHL**	**46**	**13**	**20**	**33**	**45**	**18**	**9**	**7**	**16**	**10**
1995-96	**Detroit**	**NHL**	**82**	**36**	**37**	**73**	**70**	**19**	**5**	**7**	**12**	**10**
	NHL Totals		**229**	**87**	**99**	**186**	**181**	**48**	**16**	**21**	**37**	**34**

KRAFT, RYAN
S.J.

Center. Shoots left. 5'9", 181 lbs.　Born, Bottineau, ND, November 7, 1975.
(San Jose's 11th choice, 194th overall, in 1995 Entry Draft).

			Regular Season					Playoffs				
Season	Club	Lea	GP	G	A	TP	PIM	GP	G	A	TP	PIM
1994-95	U. Minnesota	WCHA	44	13	33	46	44	....	....	....	....	....
1995-96	U. Minnesota	WCHA	41	13	24	37	24	....	....	....	....	....

KRALL, JUSTIN
DET.

Defense. Shoots left. 6'2", 170 lbs.　Born, Toledo, OH, February 20, 1974.
(Detroit's 8th choice, 183rd overall, in 1992 Entry Draft).

			Regular Season					Playoffs				
Season	Club	Lea	GP	G	A	TP	PIM	GP	G	A	TP	PIM
1992-93	Miami-Ohio	CCHA	39	5	6	11	26	....	....	....	....	....
1993-94	Miami-Ohio	CCHA	38	1	4	6	32	....	....	....	....	....
1994-95	Miami-Ohio	CCHA	38	1	9	10	38	....	....	....	....	....
1995-96	Miami-Ohio	CCHA	34	2	8	10	31	....	....	....	....	....

KRAVCHUK, IGOR (krahv-CHOOK) ST.L.

Defense. Shoots left. 6'1", 200 lbs. Born, Ufa, USSR, September 13, 1966.
(Chicago's 5th choice, 71st overall, in 1991 Entry Draft).

			Regular Season					Playoffs				
Season	**Club**	**Lea**	**GP**	**G**	**A**	**TP**	**PIM**	**GP**	**G**	**A**	**TP**	**PIM**
1982-83	Yulayev	USSR	10	0	0	0	0	....	....	....	....	....
	Yulayev	USSR 2	....	....	....	....	....	....	....	....	....	....
1984-85	Yulayev	USSR 2	50	3	2	5	22	....	....	....	....	....
1985-86	Yulayev	USSR	21	2	2	4	6	....	....	....	....	....
1986-87	Yulayev	USSR	22	0	1	1	8	....	....	....	....	....
1987-88	CSKA	USSR	48	1	8	9	12	....	....	....	....	....
1988-89	CSKA	USSR	22	3	3	6	2	....	....	....	....	....
1989-90	CSKA	USSR	48	1	3	4	16	....	....	....	....	....
1990-91	CSKA	USSR	41	6	5	11	16	....	....	....	....	....
1991-92	CSKA	CIS	30	3	8	11	6	....	....	....	....	....
	Chicago	**NHL**	**18**	**1**	**8**	**9**	**4**	**18**	**2**	**6**	**8**	**8**
1992-93	**Chicago**	**NHL**	**38**	**6**	**9**	**15**	**30**	....	....	....	....	....
	Edmonton	**NHL**	**17**	**4**	**8**	**12**	**2**	....	....	....	....	....
1993-94	**Edmonton**	**NHL**	**81**	**12**	**38**	**50**	**16**	....	....	....	....	....
1994-95	**Edmonton**	**NHL**	**36**	**7**	**11**	**18**	**29**	....	....	....	....	....
1995-96	**Edmonton**	**NHL**	**26**	**4**	**4**	**8**	**10**	....	....	....	....	....
	St. Louis	**NHL**	**40**	**3**	**12**	**15**	**24**	**10**	**1**	**5**	**6**	**4**
	NHL Totals		**256**	**37**	**90**	**127**	**115**	**28**	**3**	**11**	**14**	**12**

Traded to **Edmonton** by **Chicago** with Dean McAmmond for Joe Murphy, February 24, 1993. Traded to **St. Louis** by **Edmonton** with Ken Sutton for Jeff Norton and Donald Dufresne, January 4, 1996.

KRIVCHENKOV, ALEXEI (krihv-chehn-KOHV) PIT.

Defense. Shoots left. 6', 190 lbs. Born, Novosibirsk, USSR, June 11, 1974.
(Pittsburgh's 5th choice, 76th overall, in 1994 Entry Draft).

			Regular Season					Playoffs				
Season	**Club**	**Lea**	**GP**	**G**	**A**	**TP**	**PIM**	**GP**	**G**	**A**	**TP**	**PIM**
1993-94	Sibir Novosibirsk	CIS 2	37	1	3	4	48	....	....	....	....	....
	CSKA	CIS	4	0	0	0	2	3	0	0	0	0
1994-95	CSKA	CIS	46	1	4	5	43	2	0	0	0	0
1995-96	Hampton Rds.	ECHL	16	3	3	6	28	....	....	....	....	....
	Cleveland	IHL	37	1	4	5	30	....	....	....	....	....

KRIVOKRASOV, SERGEI (krih-vuh-KRA-sahf) CHI.

Right wing. Shoots left. 5'11", 185 lbs. Born, Angarsk, USSR, April 15, 1974.
(Chicago's 1st choice, 12th overall, in 1992 Entry Draft).

			Regular Season					Playoffs				
Season	**Club**	**Lea**	**GP**	**G**	**A**	**TP**	**PIM**	**GP**	**G**	**A**	**TP**	**PIM**
1990-91	CSKA	USSR	41	4	0	4	8	....	....	....	....	....
1991-92	CSKA	CIS	42	10	8	18	35	....	....	....	....	....
1992-93	**Chicago**	**NHL**	**4**	**0**	**0**	**0**	**2**	....	....	....	....	....
	Indianapolis	IHL	78	36	33	69	157	5	3	1	4	2
1993-94	**Chicago**	**NHL**	**9**	**1**	**0**	**1**	**4**	....	....	....	....	....
	Indianapolis	IHL	53	19	26	45	145	....	....	....	....	....
1994-95	Indianapolis	IHL	29	12	15	27	41	....	....	....	....	....
	Chicago	**NHL**	**41**	**12**	**7**	**19**	**33**	**10**	**0**	**0**	**0**	**8**
1995-96	**Chicago**	**NHL**	**46**	**6**	**10**	**16**	**32**	**5**	**1**	**0**	**1**	**2**
	Indianapolis	IHL	9	4	5	9	28	....	....	....	....	....
	NHL Totals		**100**	**19**	**17**	**36**	**71**	**15**	**1**	**0**	**1**	**10**

KRIZ, PAVEL (KRIHZH) CHI.

Defense. Shoots right. 6'1", 205 lbs. Born, Nymburk, Czech., January 2, 1977.
(Chicago's 5th choice, 97th overall, in 1995 Entry Draft).

			Regular Season					Playoffs				
Season	**Club**	**Lea**	**GP**	**G**	**A**	**TP**	**PIM**	**GP**	**G**	**A**	**TP**	**PIM**
1994-95	Tri-City	WHL	68	6	34	40	47	17	5	12	17	6
1995-96	Saskatoon	WHL	71	11	52	63	96	4	0	2	2	0

KRON, ROBERT (KROHN) HFD.

Left wing. Shoots left. 5'11", 185 lbs. Born, Brno, Czech., February 27, 1967.
(Vancouver's 5th choice, 88th overall, in 1985 Entry Draft).

			Regular Season					Playoffs				
Season	**Club**	**Lea**	**GP**	**G**	**A**	**TP**	**PIM**	**GP**	**G**	**A**	**TP**	**PIM**
1983-84	Ingstav Brno	Czech.2	3	0	1	1	0	....	....	....	....	....
1984-85	Zetor Brno	Czech.	40	6	8	14	6	....	....	....	....	....
1985-86	Zetor Brno	Czech.	44	5	6	11	....	....	....	....	....	....
1986-87	Zetor Brno	Czech.	34	18	11	29	10	....	....	....	....	....
1987-88	Zetor Brno	Czech.	44	14	7	21	30	....	....	....	....	....
1988-89	Dukla Trencin	Czech.	43	28	19	47	26	....	....	....	....	....
1989-90	Dukla Trencin	Czech.	39	22	22	44	....	....	....	....	....	....
1990-91	**Vancouver**	**NHL**	**76**	**12**	**20**	**32**	**21**	....	....	....	....	....
1991-92	**Vancouver**	**NHL**	**36**	**2**	**2**	**4**	**2**	**11**	**1**	**2**	**3**	**2**
1992-93	**Vancouver**	**NHL**	**32**	**10**	**11**	**21**	**14**	....	....	....	....	....
	Hartford	**NHL**	**13**	**4**	**2**	**6**	**4**	....	....	....	....	....
1993-94	**Hartford**	**NHL**	**77**	**24**	**26**	**50**	**8**	....	....	....	....	....
1994-95	**Hartford**	**NHL**	**37**	**10**	**8**	**18**	**10**	....	....	....	....	....
1995-96	**Hartford**	**NHL**	**77**	**22**	**28**	**50**	**6**	....	....	....	....	....
	NHL Totals		**348**	**84**	**97**	**181**	**65**	**11**	**1**	**2**	**3**	**2**

Traded to **Hartford** by **Vancouver** with Vancouver's third round choice (Marek Malik) in 1993 Entry Draft and future considerations (Jim Sandlak, May 17, 1993) for Murray Craven and Vancouver's fifth round choice (previously acquired by Hartford — Vancouver selected Scott Walker) in 1993 Entry Draft, March 22, 1993.

KROPAC, RADOSLAV (KRO-pahch) NYR

Right wing. Shoots left. 6', 187 lbs. Born, Bratislava, Czech., April 5, 1975.
(NY Rangers' 13th choice, 260th overall, in 1994 Entry Draft).

			Regular Season					Playoffs				
Season	**Club**	**Lea**	**GP**	**G**	**A**	**TP**	**PIM**	**GP**	**G**	**A**	**TP**	**PIM**
1993-94	Bratislava	Slovak	33	7	6	13	12	....	....	....	....	....
1994-95	Bratislava	Slovak	35	17	8	25	38	....	....	....	....	....
1995-96	Bratislava	Slovak	31	5	9	14	8	13	4	3	7	....

KROUPA, VLASTIMIL (KROO-pah, VLAS-tuh-meel) S.J.

Defense. Shoots left. 6'3", 210 lbs. Born, Most, Czech., April 27, 1975.
(San Jose's 3rd choice, 45th overall, in 1993 Entry Draft).

			Regular Season					Playoffs				
Season	**Club**	**Lea**	**GP**	**G**	**A**	**TP**	**PIM**	**GP**	**G**	**A**	**TP**	**PIM**
1992-93	Litvinov	Czech.	9	0	1	1	....	....	....	....	....	....
1993-94	**San Jose**	**NHL**	**27**	**1**	**3**	**4**	**20**	**14**	**1**	**2**	**3**	**21**
	Kansas City	IHL	39	3	12	15	12	....	....	....	....	....
1994-95	Kansas City	IHL	51	4	8	12	49	12	2	4	6	22
	San Jose	**NHL**	**14**	**0**	**2**	**2**	**16**	**6**	**0**	**0**	**0**	**4**
1995-96	**San Jose**	**NHL**	**27**	**1**	**7**	**8**	**18**	....	....	....	....	....
	Kansas City	IHL	39	5	22	27	44	5	0	1	1	6
	NHL Totals		**68**	**2**	**12**	**14**	**54**	**20**	**1**	**2**	**3**	**25**

KRUPP, UWE (KROOP, OO-VAY) COL.

Defense. Shoots right. 6'6", 235 lbs. Born, Cologne, West Germany, June 24, 1965.
(Buffalo's 13th choice, 214th overall, in 1983 Entry Draft).

			Regular Season					Playoffs				
Season	**Club**	**Lea**	**GP**	**G**	**A**	**TP**	**PIM**	**GP**	**G**	**A**	**TP**	**PIM**
1982-83	Koln	W.Ger.	11	0	0	0	0	....	....	....	....	....
1983-84	Koln	W.Ger.	26	0	4	4	22	....	....	....	....	....
1984-85	Koln	W.Ger.	39	11	8	19	36	....	....	....	....	....
1985-86	Koln	W.Ger.	45	10	21	31	83	....	....	....	....	....
1986-87	**Buffalo**	**NHL**	**26**	**1**	**4**	**5**	**23**	....	....	....	....	....
	Rochester	AHL	42	3	19	22	50	17	1	11	12	16
1987-88	**Buffalo**	**NHL**	**75**	**2**	**9**	**11**	**151**	**6**	**0**	**0**	**0**	**15**
1988-89	**Buffalo**	**NHL**	**70**	**5**	**13**	**18**	**55**	**5**	**0**	**1**	**1**	**4**
1989-90	**Buffalo**	**NHL**	**74**	**3**	**20**	**23**	**85**	**6**	**0**	**0**	**0**	**4**
1990-91	**Buffalo**	**NHL**	**74**	**12**	**32**	**44**	**66**	**6**	**1**	**1**	**2**	**6**
1991-92	**Buffalo**	**NHL**	**8**	**2**	**0**	**2**	**6**	....	....	....	....	....
	NY Islanders	**NHL**	**59**	**6**	**29**	**35**	**43**	....	....	....	....	....
1992-93	**NY Islanders**	**NHL**	**80**	**9**	**29**	**38**	**67**	**18**	**1**	**5**	**6**	**12**
1993-94	**NY Islanders**	**NHL**	**41**	**7**	**14**	**21**	**30**	**4**	**0**	**1**	**1**	**4**
1994-95	Landshut	Ger.	5	1	2	3	6	....	....	....	....	....
	Quebec	**NHL**	**44**	**6**	**17**	**23**	**20**	**5**	**0**	**2**	**2**	**2**
1995-96	**Colorado**	**NHL**	**6**	**0**	**3**	**3**	**4**	**22**	**4**	**12**	**16**	**33** ♦
	NHL Totals		**557**	**53**	**170**	**223**	**550**	**72**	**6**	**22**	**28**	**80**

Played in NHL All-Star Game (1991)

Traded to **NY Islanders** by **Buffalo** with Pierre Turgeon, Benoit Hogue and Dave McLlwain for Pat Lafontaine, Randy Hillier, Randy Wood and NY Islanders' fourth round choice (Dean Melanson) in 1992 Entry Draft, October 25, 1991. Traded to **Quebec** by **NY Islanders** with NY Islanders' first round choice (Wade Belak) in 1994 Entry Draft for Ron Sutter and Quebec's first round choice (Brett Lindros) in 1994 Entry Draft, June 28, 1994.

KRUPPKE, GORD (KRUHP-kee)

Defense. Shoots right. 6'1", 215 lbs. Born, Slave Lake, Alta., April 2, 1969.
(Detroit's 2nd choice, 32nd overall, in 1987 Entry Draft).

			Regular Season					Playoffs				
Season	**Club**	**Lea**	**GP**	**G**	**A**	**TP**	**PIM**	**GP**	**G**	**A**	**TP**	**PIM**
1985-86	Prince Albert	WHL	62	1	8	9	81	20	4	4	8	22
1986-87	Prince Albert	WHL	49	2	10	12	129	8	0	0	0	9
1987-88	Prince Albert	WHL	54	8	8	16	113	10	0	0	0	46
1988-89	Prince Albert	WHL	62	6	26	32	254	3	0	0	0	11
1989-90	Adirondack	AHL	59	2	12	14	103	....	....	....	....	....
1990-91	**Detroit**	**NHL**	**4**	**0**	**0**	**0**	**0**	....	....	....	....	....
	Adirondack	AHL	45	1	8	9	153	....	....	....	....	....
1991-92	Adirondack	AHL	65	3	9	12	208	16	0	1	1	52
1992-93	**Detroit**	**NHL**	**10**	**0**	**0**	**0**	**20**	....	....	....	....	....
	Adirondack	AHL	41	2	12	14	197	9	1	2	3	20
1993-94	**Detroit**	**NHL**	**9**	**0**	**0**	**0**	**12**	....	....	....	....	....
	Adirondack	AHL	54	2	9	11	210	12	1	3	4	32
1994-95	Adirondack	AHL	48	2	9	11	157	....	....	....	....	....
	St. John's	AHL	3	0	1	1	6	....	....	....	....	....
1995-96	Houston	IHL	50	0	4	4	119	....	....	....	....	....
	NHL Totals		**23**	**0**	**0**	**0**	**32**	....	....	....	....	....

Traded to **Toronto** by **Detroit** for other considerations, April 7, 1995.

KRUSE, PAUL (KROOZ) CGY.

Left wing. Shoots left. 6', 202 lbs. Born, Merritt, B.C., March 15, 1970.
(Calgary's 6th choice, 83rd overall, in 1990 Entry Draft).

			Regular Season					Playoffs				
Season	**Club**	**Lea**	**GP**	**G**	**A**	**TP**	**PIM**	**GP**	**G**	**A**	**TP**	**PIM**
1988-89	Kamloops	WHL	68	8	15	23	209	....	....	....	....	....
1989-90	Kamloops	WHL	67	22	23	45	291	17	3	5	8	79
1990-91	**Calgary**	**NHL**	**1**	**0**	**0**	**0**	**7**	....	....	....	....	....
	Salt Lake	IHL	83	24	20	44	313	4	1	1	2	4
1991-92	**Calgary**	**NHL**	**16**	**3**	**1**	**4**	**65**	....	....	....	....	....
	Salt Lake	IHL	57	14	15	29	267	5	1	2	3	19
1992-93	**Calgary**	**NHL**	**27**	**2**	**3**	**5**	**41**	....	....	....	....	....
	Salt Lake	IHL	35	1	4	5	206	....	....	....	....	....
1993-94	**Calgary**	**NHL**	**68**	**3**	**8**	**11**	**185**	**7**	**0**	**0**	**0**	**14**
1994-95	**Calgary**	**NHL**	**45**	**11**	**5**	**16**	**141**	**7**	**4**	**2**	**6**	**10**
1995-96	**Calgary**	**NHL**	**75**	**3**	**12**	**15**	**145**	**3**	**0**	**0**	**0**	**4**
	NHL Totals		**232**	**22**	**29**	**51**	**584**	**17**	**4**	**2**	**6**	**28**

KRYGIER, TODD (KREE-guhr) WSH.

Left wing. Shoots left. 6', 185 lbs. Born, Chicago Heights, MI, October 12, 1965.
(Hartford's 1st choice, 16th overall, in 1988 Supplemental Draft).

			Regular Season					Playoffs				
Season	**Club**	**Lea**	**GP**	**G**	**A**	**TP**	**PIM**	**GP**	**G**	**A**	**TP**	**PIM**
1984-85	U. Connecticut	NCAA	14	14	11	25	12	....	....	....	....	....
1985-86	U. Connecticut	NCAA	32	29	27	56	46	....	....	....	....	....
1986-87	U. Connecticut	NCAA	28	24	24	48	44	....	....	....	....	....
1987-88	U. Connecticut	NCAA	27	32	39	71	28	....	....	....	....	....
	New Haven	AHL	13	1	5	6	34	....	....	....	....	....
1988-89	Binghamton	AHL	76	26	42	68	77	....	....	....	....	....
1989-90	**Hartford**	**NHL**	**58**	**18**	**12**	**30**	**52**	**7**	**2**	**1**	**3**	**4**
	Binghamton	AHL	12	1	9	10	16	....	....	....	....	....
1990-91	**Hartford**	**NHL**	**72**	**13**	**17**	**30**	**95**	**6**	**0**	**2**	**2**	**0**
1991-92	**Washington**	**NHL**	**67**	**13**	**17**	**30**	**107**	**5**	**2**	**1**	**3**	**4**
1992-93	**Washington**	**NHL**	**77**	**11**	**12**	**23**	**60**	**6**	**1**	**1**	**2**	**4**
1993-94	**Washington**	**NHL**	**66**	**12**	**18**	**30**	**60**	**5**	**2**	**0**	**2**	**10**
1994-95	**Anaheim**	**NHL**	**35**	**11**	**11**	**22**	**10**	....	....	....	....	....
1995-96	**Anaheim**	**NHL**	**60**	**9**	**28**	**37**	**70**	....	....	....	....	....
	Washington	**NHL**	**16**	**6**	**5**	**11**	**12**	**6**	**2**	**0**	**2**	**12**
	NHL Totals		**451**	**93**	**120**	**213**	**466**	**35**	**9**	**5**	**14**	**34**

Traded to **Washington** by **Hartford** for future considerations (Washington's fourth round choice — later traded to Calgary — Calgary selected Jason Smith in 1993 Entry Draft), October 3, 1991. Traded to **Anaheim** by **Washington** for Anaheim's fourth round choice (later traded to Dallas — Dallas selected Mike Hurley) in 1996 Entry Draft, February 2, 1995. Traded to **Washington** by **Anaheim** for Mike Torchia, March 8, 1996.

KUBA, FILIP FLA.

Defense. Shoots left. 6'3", 202 lbs. Born, Ostrava, Czech., December 29, 1976.
(Florida's 8th choice, 192nd overall, in 1995 Entry Draft).

			Regular Season					Playoffs				
Season	**Club**	**Lea**	**GP**	**G**	**A**	**TP**	**PIM**	**GP**	**G**	**A**	**TP**	**PIM**
1994-95	Vitkovice	Czech. Jr.	35	10	15	25	....	....	....	....	....	....
	Vitkovice	Czech.	....	....	....	....	....	4	0	0	0	2
1995-96	Vitkovice	Czech.	19	0	1	1	....	....	....	....	....	....

KUCERA, FRANTISEK (koo-CHAIR-uh) VAN.

Defense. Shoots right. 6'2", 205 lbs. Born, Prague, Czech., February 3, 1968.
(Chicago's 3rd choice, 77th overall, in 1986 Entry Draft).

			Regular Season					Playoffs				
Season	Club	Lea	GP	G	A	TP	PIM	GP	G	A	TP	PIM
1985-86	Sparta Praha	Czech.	15	0	0	0	....	....	....	....	....	....
1986-87	Sparta Praha	Czech.	40	5	2	7	14	....	....	....	....	....
1987-88	Sparta Praha	Czech.	46	7	2	9	30	....	....	....	....	....
1988-89	Dukla Jihlava	Czech.	45	10	9	19	28	....	....	....	....	....
1989-90	Dukla Jihlava	Czech.	43	9	10	19	....	....	....	....	....	....
1990-91	**Chicago**	**NHL**	**40**	**2**	**12**	**14**	**32**	....	....	....	....	....
	Indianapolis	IHL	35	8	19	27	23	7	0	1	1	15
1991-92	**Chicago**	**NHL**	**61**	**3**	**10**	**13**	**36**	**6**	**0**	**0**	**0**	**0**
	Indianapolis	IHL	7	1	2	3	4	....	....	....	....	....
1992-93	**Chicago**	**NHL**	**71**	**5**	**14**	**19**	**59**	....	....	....	....	....
1993-94	**Chicago**	**NHL**	**60**	**4**	**13**	**17**	**34**	....	....	....	....	....
	Hartford	**NHL**	**16**	**1**	**3**	**4**	**14**	....	....	....	....	....
1994-95	Sparta Praha	Czech.	16	1	2	3	14	....	....	....	....	....
	Hartford	**NHL**	**48**	**3**	**17**	**20**	**30**	....	....	....	....	....
1995-96	**Hartford**	**NHL**	**30**	**2**	**6**	**8**	**10**	....	....	....	....	....
	Vancouver	**NHL**	**24**	**1**	**0**	**1**	**10**	**6**	**0**	**1**	**1**	**0**
	NHL Totals		**350**	**21**	**75**	**96**	**225**	**12**	**0**	**1**	**1**	**0**

Traded to **Hartford** by **Chicago** with Jocelyn Lemieux for Gary Suter, Randy Cunneyworth and Hartford's third round choice (later traded to Vancouver — Vancouver selected Larry Courville) in 1995 Entry Draft, March 11, 1994. Traded to **Vancouver** by **Hartford** with Jim Dowd and Hartford's second round choice in 1997 Entry Draft for Jeff Brown and Vancouver's third round choice in 1998 Entry Draft, December 19, 1995.

KUCHARCIK, TOMAS (koo-HAHR-chihk) TOR.

Center. Shoots left. 6'2", 200 lbs. Born, Vlasim, Czech., May 10, 1970.
(Toronto's 11th choice, 167th overall, in 1991 Entry Draft).

			Regular Season					Playoffs				
Season	Club	Lea	GP	G	A	TP	PIM	GP	G	A	TP	PIM
1990-91	Dukla Jihlava	Czech.	30	10	6	16	6	....	....	....	....	....
1991-92	Dukla Jihlava	Czech.	45	16	23	39	24	....	....	....	....	....
1992-93	Dukla Jihlava	Czech.	39	17	20	37	....	....	....	....	....	....
1993-94	Skoda Plzen	Czech.	32	10	10	20	0	....	....	....	....	....
	St. John's	AHL	8	2	3	5	4	10	3	4	7	2
1994-95	Plzen	Czech.	40	14	4	18	22	3	0	0	0	14
1995-96	ZPS Plzen	Czech.	17	5	6	11	....	....	....	....	....	....
	Slavia Praha	Czech.	23	5	6	11	....	7	3	2	5	....

KUDASHOV, ALEXEI (koo-dah-SHOV)

Center. Shoots right. 6', 183 lbs. Born, Elektrostal, USSR, July 21, 1971.
(Toronto's 3rd choice, 102nd overall, in 1991 Entry Draft).

			Regular Season					Playoffs				
Season	Club	Lea	GP	G	A	TP	PIM	GP	G	A	TP	PIM
1989-90	Soviet Wings	USSR	45	0	5	5	14	....	....	....	....	....
1990-91	Soviet Wings	USSR	45	9	5	14	10	....	....	....	....	....
1991-92	Soviet Wings	CIS	42	9	16	25	14	....	....	....	....	....
1992-93	Soviet Wings	CIS	41	8	20	28	24	7	1	3	4	4
1993-94	Soviet Wings	CIS	1	2	0	2	0	....	....	....	....	....
	Toronto	**NHL**	**25**	**1**	**0**	**1**	**4**	....	....	....	....	....
	Rus. Olympic	....	8	1	2	3	4	....	....	....	....	....
	St. John's	AHL	27	7	15	22	21	....	....	....	....	....
1994-95	St. John's	AHL	75	25	54	79	17	5	1	4	5	2
1995-96	Carolina	AHL	33	7	22	29	18	....	....	....	....	....
	Dusseldorf	Ger.	9	7	8	15	4	13	5	5	10	14
	NHL Totals		**25**	**1**	**0**	**1**	**4**	....	....	....	....	....

Signed as a free agent by **Florida**, September 10, 1995.

KUDELSKI, BOB

Right wing. Shoots right. 6'1", 205 lbs. Born, Springfield, MA, March 3, 1964.
(Los Angeles' 1st choice, 2nd overall, in 1986 Supplemental Draft).

			Regular Season					Playoffs				
Season	Club	Lea	GP	G	A	TP	PIM	GP	G	A	TP	PIM
1983-84	Yale	ECAC	21	14	12	26	12	....	....	....	....	....
1984-85	Yale	ECAC	32	21	23	44	38	....	....	....	....	....
1985-86	Yale	ECAC	31	18	23	41	48	....	....	....	....	....
1986-87a	Yale	ECAC	30	25	22	47	34	....	....	....	....	....
1987-88	**Los Angeles**	**NHL**	**26**	**0**	**1**	**1**	**8**	....	....	....	....	....
	New Haven	AHL	50	15	19	34	41	....	....	....	....	....
1988-89	**Los Angeles**	**NHL**	**14**	**1**	**3**	**4**	**17**	....	....	....	....	....
	New Haven	AHL	60	32	19	51	43	17	8	5	13	12
1989-90	**Los Angeles**	**NHL**	**62**	**23**	**13**	**36**	**49**	**8**	**1**	**2**	**3**	**2**
1990-91	**Los Angeles**	**NHL**	**72**	**23**	**13**	**36**	**46**	**8**	**3**	**2**	**5**	**2**
1991-92	**Los Angeles**	**NHL**	**80**	**22**	**21**	**43**	**42**	**6**	**0**	**0**	**0**	**0**
1992-93	**Los Angeles**	**NHL**	**15**	**3**	**3**	**6**	**8**	....	....	....	....	....
	Ottawa	**NHL**	**48**	**21**	**14**	**35**	**22**	....	....	....	....	....
1993-94	**Ottawa**	**NHL**	**42**	**26**	**15**	**41**	**14**	....	....	....	....	....
	Florida	**NHL**	**44**	**14**	**15**	**29**	**10**	....	....	....	....	....
1994-95	**Florida**	**NHL**	**26**	**6**	**3**	**9**	**2**	....	....	....	....	....
1995-96	**Florida**	**NHL**	**13**	**0**	**1**	**1**	**0**	....	....	....	....	....
	Carolina	AHL	4	1	0	1	0	....	....	....	....	....
	NHL Totals		**442**	**139**	**102**	**241**	**218**	**22**	**4**	**4**	**8**	**4**

a ECAC First All-Star Team (1987)

Played in NHL All-Star Game (1994)

Traded to **Ottawa** by **Los Angeles** with Shawn McCosh for Marc Fortier and Jim Thomson, December 19, 1992. Traded to **Florida** by **Ottawa** for Evgeny Davydov, Scott Levins and Florida's sixth round choice (Mike Gaffney) in 1994 Entry Draft and Dallas' fourth round choice (previously acquired by Florida — Ottawa selected Kevin Bolibruck) in 1995 Entry Draft, January 6, 1994.

KUDRNA, JAROSLAV S.J.

Left wing. Shoots left. 6', 180 lbs. Born, Hradec Kralove, Czech., December 5, 1975.
(San Jose's 8th choice, 142nd overall, in 1995 Entry Draft).

			Regular Season					Playoffs				
Season	Club	Lea	GP	G	A	TP	PIM	GP	G	A	TP	PIM
1993-94	Hrad. Kralove	Czech.	5	0	0	0	0	2	0	1	1	....
1994-95	Penticton	BCJHL	58	60	55	115	148	....	....	....	....	....
1995-96	Pardubice	Czech.	38	14	15	29	....	....	....	....	....	....

KUKI, ARTO (KUH-kee) MTL.

Center. Shoots left. 6'3", 205 lbs. Born, Espoo, Finland, February 22, 1976.
(Montreal's 6th choice, 96th overall, in 1994 Entry Draft).

			Regular Season					Playoffs				
Season	Club	Lea	GP	G	A	TP	PIM	GP	G	A	TP	PIM
1994-95	Kiekko-Espoo	Fin.	4	0	1	1	0	....	....	....	....	....
1995-96	Kiekko-Espoo	Fin.	47	6	3	9	16	....	....	....	....	....

KURRI, JARI (KUHR-ree, YAH-ree) ANA.

Right wing. Shoots right. 6'1", 195 lbs. Born, Helsinki, Finland, May 18, 1960.
(Edmonton's 3rd choice, 69th overall, in 1980 Entry Draft).

			Regular Season					Playoffs				
Season	Club	Lea	GP	G	A	TP	PIM	GP	G	A	TP	PIM
1977-78	Jokerit	Fin.	29	2	9	11	12	....	....	....	....	....
1978-79	Jokerit	Fin.	33	16	14	30	12	....	....	....	....	....
1979-80	Jokerit	Fin.	33	23	16	39	22	6	7	2	9	13
1980-81	**Edmonton**	**NHL**	**75**	**32**	**43**	**75**	**40**	**9**	**5**	**7**	**12**	**4**
1981-82	**Edmonton**	**NHL**	**71**	**32**	**54**	**86**	**32**	**5**	**2**	**5**	**7**	**10**
1982-83	**Edmonton**	**NHL**	**80**	**45**	**59**	**104**	**22**	**16**	**8**	**15**	**23**	**8**
1983-84a	**Edmonton**	**NHL**	**64**	**52**	**61**	**113**	**14**	**19**	***14**	**14**	**28**	**13 ♦**
1984-85bc	**Edmonton**	**NHL**	**73**	**71**	**64**	**135**	**30**	**18**	***19**	**12**	**31**	**6 ♦**
1985-86a	**Edmonton**	**NHL**	**78**	***68**	**63**	**131**	**22**	**10**	**2**	**10**	**12**	**4**
1986-87c	**Edmonton**	**NHL**	**79**	**54**	**54**	**108**	**41**	**21**	***15**	**10**	**25**	**20 ♦**
1987-88	**Edmonton**	**NHL**	**80**	**43**	**53**	**96**	**30**	**19**	***14**	**17**	**31**	**12 ♦**
1988-89a	**Edmonton**	**NHL**	**76**	**44**	**58**	**102**	**69**	**7**	**3**	**5**	**8**	**6**
1989-90	**Edmonton**	**NHL**	**78**	**33**	**60**	**93**	**48**	**22**	**10**	**15**	**25**	**18 ♦**
1990-91	Milan Devils	Italy	30	27	48	75	6	10	10	12	22	2
1991-92	**Los Angeles**	**NHL**	**73**	**23**	**37**	**60**	**24**	**4**	**1**	**2**	**3**	**4**
1992-93	**Los Angeles**	**NHL**	**82**	**27**	**60**	**87**	**38**	**24**	**9**	**8**	**17**	**12**
1993-94	**Los Angeles**	**NHL**	**81**	**31**	**46**	**77**	**48**	....	....	....	....	....
1994-95	Jokerit	Fin.	20	10	9	19	10	....	....	....	....	....
	Los Angeles	**NHL**	**38**	**10**	**19**	**29**	**24**	....	....	....	....	....
1995-96	**Los Angeles**	**NHL**	**57**	**17**	**23**	**40**	**37**	....	....	....	....	....
	NY Rangers	**NHL**	**14**	**1**	**4**	**5**	**2**	**11**	**3**	**5**	**8**	**2**
	NHL Totals		**1099**	**583**	**758**	**1341**	**521**	**185**	**105**	**125**	**230**	**119**

a NHL Second All-Star Team (1984, 1986, 1989)
b Won Lady Byng Memorial Trophy (1985)
c NHL First All-Star Team (1985, 1987)

Played in NHL All-Star Game (1983, 1985, 1986, 1988-90, 1993)

Traded to **Philadelphia** by **Edmonton** with Dave Brown and Corey Foster for Craig Fisher, Scott Mellanby and Craig Berube, May 30, 1991. Traded to **Los Angeles** by **Philadelphia** with Jeff Chychrun for Steve Duchesne, Steve Kasper and Los Angeles' fourth round choice (Aris Brimanis) in 1991 Entry Draft, May 30, 1991. Traded to **NY Rangers** by **Los Angeles** with Marty McSorley and Shane Churla for Ray Ferraro, Ian Laperriere, Mattias Norstrom, Nathan Lafayette and NY Rangers' fourth round choice in 1997 Entry Draft, March 14, 1996. Signed as a free agent by **Anaheim**, August 14, 1996.

KURTZ, JUSTIN PHO.

Defense. Shoots left. 6', 188 lbs. Born, Winnipeg, Man., January 14, 1977.
(Winnipeg's 5th choice, 84th overall, in 1995 Entry Draft).

			Regular Season					Playoffs				
Season	Club	Lea	GP	G	A	TP	PIM	GP	G	A	TP	PIM
1993-94	Brandon	WHL	63	3	13	16	37	14	1	3	4	24
1994-95	Brandon	WHL	65	8	34	42	75	18	2	2	4	26
1995-96a	Brandon	WHL	53	19	55	74	107	18	4	6	10	37

a WHL East Second All-Star Team (1996)

KUSTER, HENRY (KOO-stuhr) BOS.

Right wing. Shoots right. 6', 195 lbs. Born, Edmonton, Alta., November 11, 1977.
(Boston's 2nd choice, 45th overall, in 1996 Entry Draft).

			Regular Season					Playoffs				
Season	Club	Lea	GP	G	A	TP	PIM	GP	G	A	TP	PIM
1993-94	Medicine Hat	WHL	67	14	27	41	26	3	0	0	0	2
1994-95	Medicine Hat	WHL	71	28	26	54	61	5	1	3	4	6
1995-96	Medicine Hat	WHL	72	35	43	78	54	1	0	0	0	0

KUZNETSOV, MAXIM (kooz-NEHT-zahv) DET.

Defense. Shoots left. 6'5", 198 lbs. Born, Pavlodar, USSR, March 24, 1977.
(Detroit's 1st choice, 26th overall, in 1995 Entry Draft).

			Regular Season					Playoffs				
Season	Club	Lea	GP	G	A	TP	PIM	GP	G	A	TP	PIM
1994-95	Moscow D'amo	CIS	11	0	0	0	8	....	....	....	....	....
1995-96	Moscow D'amo	CIS	9	1	1	2	22	4	0	0	0	0

KVASHA, OLEG (kuh-VAH-shah) FLA.

Left wing. Shoots right. 6'5", 205 lbs. Born, Moscow, USSR, July 26, 1978.
(Florida's 3rd choice, 65th overall, in 1996 Entry Draft).

			Regular Season					Playoffs				
Season	Club	Lea	GP	G	A	TP	PIM	GP	G	A	TP	PIM
1995-96	CSKA	CIS	38	2	3	5	14	2	0	0	0	0

KYPREOS, NICK (KIH-pree-ohz) TOR.

Left wing. Shoots left. 6', 205 lbs. Born, Toronto, Ont., June 4, 1966.

			Regular Season					Playoffs				
Season	Club	Lea	GP	G	A	TP	PIM	GP	G	A	TP	PIM
1983-84	North Bay	OHL	51	12	11	23	36	4	3	2	5	9
1984-85	North Bay	OHL	64	41	36	77	71	8	2	2	4	15
1985-86a	North Bay	OHL	64	62	35	97	112	....	....	....	....	....
1986-87	Hershey	AHL	10	0	1	1	4	....	....	....	....	....
b	North Bay	OHL	46	49	41	90	54	24	11	5	16	78
1987-88	Hershey	AHL	71	24	20	44	101	12	0	2	2	17
1988-89	Hershey	AHL	28	12	15	27	19	12	4	5	9	11
1989-90	**Washington**	**NHL**	**31**	**5**	**4**	**9**	**82**	**7**	**1**	**0**	**1**	**15**
	Baltimore	AHL	14	6	5	11	6	7	4	1	5	17
1990-91	**Washington**	**NHL**	**79**	**9**	**9**	**18**	**196**	**9**	**0**	**1**	**1**	**38**
1991-92	**Washington**	**NHL**	**65**	**4**	**6**	**10**	**206**	....	....	....	....	....
1992-93	**Hartford**	**NHL**	**75**	**17**	**10**	**27**	**325**	....	....	....	....	....
1993-94	**Hartford**	**NHL**	**10**	**0**	**0**	**0**	**37**	....	....	....	....	....
	NY Rangers	**NHL**	**46**	**3**	**5**	**8**	**102**	**3**	**0**	**0**	**0**	**2 ♦**
1994-95	**NY Rangers**	**NHL**	**40**	**1**	**3**	**4**	**93**	**10**	**0**	**2**	**2**	**6**
1995-96	**NY Rangers**	**NHL**	**42**	**3**	**4**	**7**	**77**	....	....	....	....	....
	Toronto	**NHL**	**19**	**1**	**1**	**2**	**30**	**5**	**0**	**0**	**0**	**4**
	NHL Totals		**407**	**43**	**42**	**85**	**1148**	**34**	**1**	**3**	**4**	**65**

a OHL First All-Star Team (1986)
b OHL Second All-Star Team (1987)

Signed as a free agent by **Philadelphia,** September 30, 1984. Claimed by **Washington** from **Philadelphia** in NHL Waiver Draft, October 2, 1989. Traded to **Hartford** by **Washington** for Mark Hunter and future considerations (Yvon Corriveau, August 20, 1992), June 15, 1992. Traded to **NY Rangers** by **Hartford** with Steve Larmer, Barry Richter and Hartford's sixth round choice (Yuri Litvinov) in 1994 Entry Draft for Darren Turcotte and James Patrick, November 2, 1993. Traded to **Toronto** by **NY Rangers** for Bill Berg, February 29, 1996.

KYTE, JIM (KITE)

Defense. Shoots left. 6'5", 210 lbs. Born, Ottawa, Ont., March 21, 1964.
(Winnipeg's 1st choice, 12th overall, in 1982 Entry Draft).

			Regular Season					Playoffs				
Season	Club	Lea	GP	G	A	TP	PIM	GP	G	A	TP	PIM
1981-82	Cornwall	OHL	52	4	13	17	148	5	0	0	0	10
1982-83	Winnipeg	NHL	2	0	0	0	0	....	....	....	....	....
	Cornwall	OHL	65	6	30	36	195	8	0	2	2	24
1983-84	Winnipeg	NHL	58	1	2	3	55	3	0	0	0	11
1984-85	Winnipeg	NHL	71	0	3	3	111	8	0	0	0	14
1985-86	Winnipeg	NHL	71	1	3	4	126	3	0	0	0	12
1986-87	Winnipeg	NHL	72	5	5	10	162	10	0	4	4	36
1987-88	Winnipeg	NHL	51	1	3	4	128	....	....	....	....	....
1988-89	Winnipeg	NHL	74	3	9	12	190	....	....	....	....	....
1989-90	Pittsburgh	NHL	56	3	1	4	125	....	....	....	....	....
1990-91	Pittsburgh	NHL	1	0	0	0	2	....	....	....	....	....
	Muskegon	IHL	25	2	5	7	157	....	....	....	....	....
	Calgary	NHL	42	0	9	9	153	7	0	0	0	7
1991-92	Calgary	NHL	21	0	1	1	107	....	....	....	....	....
	Salt Lake	IHL	6	0	1	1	9	....	....	....	....	....
1992-93	Ottawa	NHL	4	0	1	1	4	....	....	....	....	....
	New Haven	AHL	63	6	18	24	163	....	....	....	....	....
1993-94	Las Vegas	IHL	75	2	16	18	246	4	0	1	1	51
1994-95	Las Vegas	IHL	76	3	17	20	195	....	....	....	....	....
	San Jose	NHL	18	2	5	7	33	11	0	2	2	14
1995-96	San Jose	NHL	57	1	7	8	146	....	....	....	....	....
	NHL Totals		598	17	49	66	1342	42	0	6	6	94

Traded to **Pittsburgh** by **Winnipeg** with Andrew McBain and Randy Gilhen for Randy Cunneyworth, Rick Tabaracci and Dave McLlwain, June 17, 1989. Traded to **Calgary** by **Pittsburgh** for Jiri Hrdina, December 13, 1990. Signed as a free agent by **Ottawa**, September 10, 1992. Signed as a free agent by **San Jose**, March 31, 1995.

LABELLE, MARC DAL.

Left wing. Shoots left. 6'1", 215 lbs. Born, Maniwaki, Que., December 20, 1969.

			Regular Season					Playoffs				
Season	Club	Lea	GP	G	A	TP	PIM	GP	G	A	TP	PIM
1987-88	Victoriaville	QMJHL	63	11	14	25	236	5	2	4	6	20
1988-89	Victoriaville	QMJHL	62	9	26	35	202	15	6	3	9	30
1989-90	Victoriaville	QMJHL	56	18	21	39	192	16	4	8	12	42
1990-91	Fredericton	AHL	25	1	4	5	95	4	0	2	2	25
	Richmond	ECHL	5	1	1	2	37	....	....	....	....	....
1991-92	Fredericton	AHL	62	7	10	17	238	3	0	0	0	6
1992-93	San Diego	IHL	5	0	2	2	5	....	....	....	....	....
	New Haven	AHL	31	5	4	9	124	....	....	....	....	....
1993-94	Cincinnati	IHL	37	2	1	3	133	4	0	1	1	6
1994-95	Cincinnati	IHL	54	3	4	7	173	8	0	0	0	7
1995-96	Cincinnati	IHL	57	6	11	17	218	....	....	....	....	....
	Milwaukee	IHL	20	5	3	8	50	5	1	1	2	4

Signed as a free agent by **Montreal**, January 21, 1991. Signed as a free agent by **Ottawa**, July 30, 1992. Claimed by **Florida** from **Ottawa** in Expansion Draft, June 24, 1993. Signed as a free agent by **Dallas**, April 15, 1996.

LABRAATEN, JAN CGY.

Left wing. Shoots right. 6'2", 198 lbs. Born, Karlstad, Sweden, February 17, 1977.
(Calgary's 4th choice, 98th overall, in 1995 Entry Draft).

			Regular Season					Playoffs				
Season	Club	Lea	GP	G	A	TP	PIM	GP	G	A	TP	PIM
1994-95	Farjestad	Swe. Jr.	25	10	6	16	20	....	....	....	....	....
	Farjestad	Swe.	2	0	1	1	2	1	0	0	0	0
1995-96	Farjestad	Swe.	4	0	0	0	0	....	....	....	....	....

LACHANCE, BOB ST.L.

Right wing. Shoots right. 5'11", 180 lbs. Born, Northampton, MA, February 1, 1974.
(St. Louis' 5th choice, 134th overall, in 1992 Entry Draft).

			Regular Season					Playoffs				
Season	Club	Lea	GP	G	A	TP	PIM	GP	G	A	TP	PIM
1992-93	Boston U.	H.E.	33	4	10	14	24	....	....	....	....	....
1993-94	Boston U.	H.E.	32	13	19	32	42	....	....	....	....	....
1994-95	Boston U.	H.E.	37	12	29	41	51	....	....	....	....	....
1995-96	Boston U.	H.E.	39	15	37	52	67	....	....	....	....	....
	Worcester	AHL	7	1	0	1	6	....	....	....	....	....

LACHANCE, SCOTT NYI

Defense. Shoots left. 6'1", 196 lbs. Born, Charlottesville, VA, October 22, 1972.
(NY Islanders' 1st choice, 4th overall, in 1991 Entry Draft).

			Regular Season					Playoffs				
Season	Club	Lea	GP	G	A	TP	PIM	GP	G	A	TP	PIM
1990-91	Boston U.	H.E.	31	5	19	24	48	....	....	....	....	....
1991-92	U.S. National	....	36	1	10	11	34	....	....	....	....	....
	U.S. Olympic	....	8	0	1	1	6	....	....	....	....	....
	NY Islanders	NHL	17	1	4	5	9	....	....	....	....	....
1992-93	NY Islanders	NHL	75	7	17	24	67	....	....	....	....	....
1993-94	NY Islanders	NHL	74	3	11	14	70	3	0	0	0	0
1994-95	NY Islanders	NHL	26	6	7	13	26	....	....	....	....	....
1995-96	NY Islanders	NHL	55	3	10	13	54	....	....	....	....	....
	NHL Totals		247	20	49	69	226	3	0	0	0	0

LACOUTURE, DAN (la-koo-TUHR) NYI

Left wing. Shoots left. 6'2", 201 lbs. Born, Hyannis, MA, April 18, 1977.
(NY Islanders' 2nd choice, 29th overall, in 1996 Entry Draft).

			Regular Season					Playoffs				
Season	Club	Lea	GP	G	A	TP	PIM	GP	G	A	TP	PIM
1994-95	Springfield	Jr. B	49	37	39	76	100	....	....	....	....	....
1995-96	Jr. Whalers	Jr. B	42	36	48	84	102	....	....	....	....	....

LACROIX, DANIEL (luh-KWAH) PHI.

Left wing. Shoots left. 6'2", 205 lbs. Born, Montreal, Que., March 11, 1969.
(NY Rangers' 2nd choice, 31st overall, in 1987 Entry Draft).

			Regular Season					Playoffs				
Season	Club	Lea	GP	G	A	TP	PIM	GP	G	A	TP	PIM
1986-87	Granby	QMJHL	54	9	16	25	311	8	1	2	3	22
1987-88	Granby	QMJHL	58	24	50	74	468	5	0	4	4	12
1988-89	Granby	QMJHL	70	45	49	94	320	4	1	1	2	57
	Denver	IHL	2	0	1	1	0	2	0	1	1	0
1989-90	Flint	IHL	61	12	16	28	128	4	2	0	2	24
1990-91	Binghamton	AHL	54	7	12	19	237	5	1	0	1	24
1991-92	Binghamton	AHL	52	12	20	32	149	11	2	4	6	28
1992-93	Binghamton	AHL	73	21	22	43	255	....	....	....	....	....
1993-94	NY Rangers	NHL	4	0	0	0	0	....	....	....	....	....
	Binghamton	AHL	59	20	23	43	278	....	....	....	....	....
1994-95	Providence	AHL	40	15	11	26	266	....	....	....	....	....
	Boston	NHL	23	1	0	1	38	....	....	....	....	....
	NY Rangers	NHL	1	0	0	0	0	....	....	....	....	....
1995-96	NY Rangers	NHL	25	2	2	4	30	....	....	....	....	....
	Binghamton	AHL	26	12	15	27	155	....	....	....	....	....
	NHL Totals		53	3	2	5	68	....	....	....	....	....

Traded to **Boston** by **NY Rangers** for Glen Featherstone, August 19, 1994. Claimed on waivers by **NY Rangers** from **Boston**, March 23, 1995. Signed as a free agent by **Philadelphia**, July 18, 1996.

LACROIX, ERIC (luh-KWAH) COL.

Left wing. Shoots left. 6'1", 205 lbs. Born, Montreal, Que., July 15, 1971.
(Toronto's 6th choice, 136th overall, in 1990 Entry Draft).

			Regular Season					Playoffs				
Season	Club	Lea	GP	G	A	TP	PIM	GP	G	A	TP	PIM
1990-91	St. Lawrence	ECAC	35	13	11	24	35	....	....	....	....	....
1991-92	St. Lawrence	ECAC	34	11	20	31	40	....	....	....	....	....
1992-93	St. John's	AHL	76	15	19	34	59	9	5	3	8	4
1993-94	Toronto	NHL	3	0	0	0	2	2	0	0	0	0
	St. John's	AHL	59	17	22	39	69	11	5	3	8	6
1994-95	St. John's	AHL	1	0	0	0	2	....	....	....	....	....
	Phoenix	IHL	25	7	1	8	31	....	....	....	....	....
	Los Angeles	NHL	45	9	7	16	54	....	....	....	....	....
1995-96	Los Angeles	NHL	72	16	16	32	110	....	....	....	....	....
	NHL Totals		120	25	23	48	166	2	0	0	0	0

Traded to **Los Angeles** by **Toronto** with Chris Snell and Toronto's fourth round choice (Eric Belanger) in 1996 Entry Draft for Dixon Ward, Guy Leveque, Kelly Fairchild and Shayne Toporowski, October 3, 1994. Traded to **Colorado** by **Los Angeles** with Los Angeles' first round choice in 1998 Entry Draft for Stephane Fiset and Colorado's first round choice in 1998 Entry Draft, June 20, 1996.

LADOUCEUR, RANDY (LAD-uh-SOOR)

Defense. Shoots left. 6'2", 220 lbs. Born, Brockville, Ont., June 30, 1960.

			Regular Season					Playoffs				
Season	Club	Lea	GP	G	A	TP	PIM	GP	G	A	TP	PIM
1978-79	Brantford	OHA	64	3	17	20	141	....	....	....	....	....
1979-80	Brantford	OHA	37	6	15	21	125	8	0	5	5	18
1980-81	Kalamazoo	IHL	80	7	30	37	52	8	1	3	4	10
1981-82	Adirondack	AHL	78	4	28	32	78	5	1	1	2	6
1982-83	Detroit	NHL	27	0	4	4	16	....	....	....	....	....
	Adirondack	AHL	48	11	21	32	54	....	....	....	....	....
1983-84	Detroit	NHL	71	3	17	20	58	4	1	0	1	6
	Adirondack	AHL	11	3	5	8	12	....	....	....	....	....
1984-85	Detroit	NHL	80	3	27	30	108	3	1	0	1	0
1985-86	Detroit	NHL	78	5	13	18	196	....	....	....	....	....
1986-87	Detroit	NHL	34	3	6	9	70	....	....	....	....	....
	Hartford	NHL	36	2	3	5	51	6	0	2	2	12
1987-88	Hartford	NHL	67	1	7	8	91	6	1	1	2	4
1988-89	Hartford	NHL	75	2	5	7	95	1	0	0	0	10
1989-90	Hartford	NHL	71	3	12	15	126	7	1	0	1	10
1990-91	Hartford	NHL	67	1	3	4	118	6	1	4	5	6
1991-92	Hartford	NHL	74	1	9	10	127	7	0	1	1	11
1992-93	Hartford	NHL	62	2	4	6	109	....	....	....	....	....
1993-94	Anaheim	NHL	81	1	9	10	74	....	....	....	....	....
1994-95	Anaheim	NHL	44	2	4	6	36	....	....	....	....	....
1995-96	Anaheim	NHL	63	1	3	4	47	....	....	....	....	....
	NHL Totals		930	30	126	156	1322	40	5	8	13	59

Signed as a free agent by **Detroit**, November 1, 1979. Traded to **Hartford** by **Detroit** for Dave Barr, January 12, 1987. Claimed by **Anaheim** from **Hartford** in Expansion Draft, June 24, 1993.

LAFAYETTE, NATHAN (LAH-fay-eht) L.A.

Center. Shoots right. 6'1", 200 lbs. Born, New Westminster, B.C., February 17, 1973.
(St. Louis' 3rd choice, 65th overall, in 1991 Entry Draft).

			Regular Season					Playoffs				
Season	Club	Lea	GP	G	A	TP	PIM	GP	G	A	TP	PIM
1989-90	Kingston	OHL	53	6	8	14	14	7	0	1	1	0
1990-91	Kingston	OHL	35	13	13	26	10	....	....	....	....	....
	Cornwall	OHL	28	16	22	38	25	....	....	....	....	....
1991-92a	Cornwall	OHL	66	28	45	73	26	6	2	5	7	15
1992-93	Newmarket	OHL	58	49	38	87	26	7	4	5	9	19
1993-94	St. Louis	NHL	38	2	3	5	14	....	....	....	....	....
	Peoria	IHL	27	13	11	24	20	....	....	....	....	....
	Vancouver	NHL	11	1	1	2	4	20	2	7	9	4
1994-95	Syracuse	AHL	27	9	9	18	10	....	....	....	....	....
	Vancouver	NHL	27	4	4	8	2	....	....	....	....	....
	NY Rangers	NHL	12	0	0	0	0	8	0	0	0	2
1995-96	NY Rangers	NHL	5	0	0	0	2	....	....	....	....	....
	Binghamton	AHL	57	21	27	48	32	....	....	....	....	....
	Los Angeles	NHL	12	2	4	6	6	....	....	....	....	....
	NHL Totals		105	9	12	21	28	28	2	7	9	6

a Canadian Major Junior Scholastic Player of the Year (1992)

Traded to **Vancouver** by **St. Louis** with Jeff Brown and Bret Hedican for Craig Janney, March 21, 1994. Traded to **NY Rangers** by **Vancouver** for Corey Hirsch, April 7, 1995. Traded to **Los Angeles** by **NY Rangers** with Ray Ferraro, Mattias Norstrom, Ian Laperriere and NY Rangers' fourth round choice in 1997 Entry Draft for Marty McSorley, Jari Kurri and Shane Churla, March 14, 1996.

LAFLAMME, CHRISTIAN (lah-FLAM) CHI.

Defense. Shoots right. 6'1", 195 lbs. Born, St. Charles, Que., November 24, 1976.
(Chicago's 2nd choice, 45th overall, in 1995 Entry Draft).

			Regular Season					Playoffs				
Season	Club	Lea	GP	G	A	TP	PIM	GP	G	A	TP	PIM
1992-93	Verdun	QMJHL	69	2	17	19	85	3	0	2	2	6
1993-94	Verdun	QMJHL	72	4	34	38	85	4	0	3	3	4
1994-95a	Beauport	QMJHL	67	6	41	47	82	8	1	4	5	6
1995-96	Beauport	QMJHL	41	13	23	36	63	20	7	17	24	32

a QMJHL Second All-Star Team (1995)

LaFONTAINE, PAT (luh-FAHN-tayn) BUF.

Center. Shoots right. 5'10", 180 lbs. Born, St. Louis, MO, February 22, 1965.
(NY Islanders' 1st choice, 3rd overall, in 1983 Entry Draft).

			Regular Season					Playoffs				
Season	Club	Lea	GP	G	A	TP	PIM	GP	G	A	TP	PIM
1982-83ab	Verdun	QMJHL	70	*104	*130	*234	10	15	11	*24	*35	4
1983-84	U.S. National	....	58	56	55	111	22	....	....	....	....	....
	U.S. Olympic	....	6	5	5	10	0	....	....	....	....	....
	NY Islanders	NHL	15	13	6	19	6	16	3	6	9	8
1984-85	NY Islanders	NHL	67	19	35	54	32	9	1	2	3	4
1985-86	NY Islanders	NHL	65	30	23	53	43	3	1	0	1	0
1986-87	NY Islanders	NHL	80	38	32	70	70	14	5	7	12	10
1987-88	NY Islanders	NHL	75	47	45	92	52	6	4	5	9	8
1988-89	NY Islanders	NHL	79	45	43	88	26	....	....	....	....	....
1989-90c	NY Islanders	NHL	74	54	51	105	38	2	0	1	1	0
1990-91	NY Islanders	NHL	75	41	44	85	42	....	....	....	....	....
1991-92	Buffalo	NHL	57	46	47	93	98	7	8	3	11	4
1992-93d	Buffalo	NHL	84	53	95	148	63	7	2	10	12	0
1993-94	Buffalo	NHL	16	5	13	18	2	....	....	....	....	....
1994-95e	Buffalo	NHL	22	12	15	27	4	5	2	2	4	2
1995-96	Buffalo	NHL	76	40	51	91	36	....	....	....	....	....
	NHL Totals		785	443	500	943	512	69	26	36	62	36

a QMJHL First All-Star Team (1983)
b Canadian Major Junior Player of the Year (1983)
c Won Dodge Performer of the Year Award (1990)
d NHL Second All-Star Team (1993)
e Won Bill Masterton Memorial Trophy (1995)

Played in NHL All-Star Game (1988-91, 1993)

Traded to **Buffalo** by **NY Islanders** with Randy Hillier, Randy Wood and NY Islanders' fourth round choice (Dean Melanson) in 1992 Entry Draft for Pierre Turgeon, Uwe Krupp, Benoit Hogue and Dave McLlwain, October 25, 1991.

LAHEY, MATTHEW WSH.

Left wing. Shoots left. 6'1", 216 lbs. Born, Ottawa, Ont., October 12, 1977.
(Washington's 8th choice, 126th overall, in 1996 Entry Draft).

			Regular Season					Playoffs				
Season	Club	Lea	GP	G	A	TP	PIM	GP	G	A	TP	PIM
1994-95	Peterborough	OHL	63	6	6	12	87	11	1	1	2	18
1995-96	Peterborough	OHL	60	20	15	35	117	24	4	5	9	38

LALOR, MIKE (LAH-luhr) DAL.

Defense. Shoots left. 6', 200 lbs. Born, Buffalo, NY, March 8, 1963.

			Regular Season					Playoffs				
Season	Club	Lea	GP	G	A	TP	PIM	GP	G	A	TP	PIM
1981-82	Brantford	OHL	64	3	13	16	114	11	0	6	6	11
1982-83	Brantford	OHL	65	10	30	40	113	8	1	3	4	20
1983-84	Nova Scotia	AHL	67	5	11	16	80	12	0	2	2	13
1984-85	Sherbrooke	AHL	79	9	23	32	114	17	3	5	8	36
1985-86	Montreal	NHL	62	3	5	8	56	17	1	2	3	29 ♦
1986-87	Montreal	NHL	57	0	10	10	47	13	2	1	3	29
1987-88	Montreal	NHL	66	1	10	11	113	11	0	0	0	11
1988-89	Montreal	NHL	12	1	4	5	15	....	....	....	....	....
	St. Louis	NHL	36	1	14	15	54	10	1	1	2	14
1989-90	St. Louis	NHL	78	0	16	16	81	12	0	2	2	31
1990-91	Washington	NHL	68	1	5	6	61	10	1	2	3	22
1991-92	Washington	NHL	64	5	7	12	64	....	....	....	....	....
	Winnipeg	NHL	15	2	3	5	14	7	0	0	0	19
1992-93	Winnipeg	NHL	64	1	8	9	76	4	0	2	2	4
1993-94	San Jose	NHL	23	0	2	2	8	....	....	....	....	....
	Dallas	NHL	12	0	1	1	6	5	0	0	0	6
1994-95	Dallas	NHL	12	0	0	0	9	3	0	0	0	2
	Kalamazoo	IHL	5	0	1	1	11	....	....	....	....	....
1995-96	Dallas	NHL	63	1	2	3	31	....	....	....	....	....
	San Francisco	IHL	12	2	2	4	6	....	....	....	....	....
	NHL Totals		632	16	87	103	635	92	5	10	15	167

Signed as a free agent by **Montreal**, September, 1983. Traded to **St. Louis** by **Montreal** with Montreal's first round choice (later traded to Vancouver — Vancouver selected Shawn Antoski) in 1990 Entry Draft for St. Louis' first round choice (Turner Stevenson) in 1990 Entry Draft, January 16, 1989. Traded to **Washington** by **St. Louis** with Peter Zezel for Geoff Courtnall, July 13, 1990. Traded to **Winnipeg** by **Washington** for Paul MacDermid, March 2, 1992. Signed as a free agent by **San Jose**, August 13, 1993. Traded to **Dallas** by **San Jose** with Doug Zmolek and cash for Ulf Dahlen and Dallas' seventh round choice (Brad Mehalko) in 1995 Entry Draft, March 19, 1994.

LAMARCHE, MARTIN OTT.

Left wing. Shoots left. 6'1", 206 lbs. Born, Ste-Justine, Que., October 2, 1975.

			Regular Season					Playoffs				
Season	Club	Lea	GP	G	A	TP	PIM	GP	G	A	TP	PIM
1991-92	Chicoutimi	QMJHL	62	2	6	8	62	4	0	0	0	0
1992-93	St-Jean	QMJHL	51	2	5	7	134	2	0	0	0	0
1993-94	Sherbrooke	QMJHL	53	10	20	30	121	10	2	1	3	44
1994-95	Shawinigan	QMJHL	58	20	29	49	353	14	3	10	13	65
1995-96	P.E.I.	AHL	30	0	1	1	88	....	....	....	....	....

Signed as a free agent by **Ottawa**, March 3, 1995.

LAMB, MARK

Center. Shoots left. 5'9", 180 lbs. Born, Ponteix, Sask., August 3, 1964.
(Calgary's 5th choice, 72nd overall, in 1982 Entry Draft).

			Regular Season					Playoffs				
Season	Club	Lea	GP	G	A	TP	PIM	GP	G	A	TP	PIM
1981-82	Billings	WHL	72	45	56	101	46	5	4	6	10	4
1982-83	Nanaimo	WHL	30	14	37	51	16	....	....	....	....	....
	Medicine Hat	WHL	46	22	43	65	33	5	3	2	5	4
	Colorado	CHL	....	....	....	....	....	6	0	2	2	0
1983-84a	Medicine Hat	WHL	72	59	77	136	30	14	12	11	23	6
1984-85	Moncton	AHL	80	23	49	72	53	....	....	....	....	....
1985-86	Calgary	NHL	1	0	0	0	0	....	....	....	....	....
	Moncton	AHL	79	26	50	76	51	10	2	6	8	17
1986-87	Detroit	NHL	22	2	1	3	8	11	0	0	0	11
	Adirondack	AHL	49	14	36	50	45	....	....	....	....	....
1987-88	Edmonton	NHL	2	0	0	0	0	....	....	....	....	....
	Nova Scotia	AHL	69	27	61	88	45	5	0	5	5	6
1988-89	Edmonton	NHL	20	2	8	10	14	6	0	2	2	8
	Cape Breton	AHL	54	33	49	82	29	....	....	....	....	....
1989-90	Edmonton	NHL	58	12	16	28	42	22	6	11	17	2 ♦
1990-91	Edmonton	NHL	37	4	8	12	25	15	0	5	5	20
1991-92	Edmonton	NHL	59	6	22	28	46	16	1	1	2	10
1992-93	Ottawa	NHL	71	7	19	26	64	....	....	....	....	....
1993-94	Ottawa	NHL	66	11	18	29	56	....	....	....	....	....
	Philadelphia	NHL	19	1	6	7	16	....	....	....	....	....
1994-95	Philadelphia	NHL	8	0	2	2	2	....	....	....	....	....
	Montreal	NHL	39	1	0	1	18	....	....	....	....	....
1995-96	Montreal	NHL	1	0	0	0	0	....	....	....	....	....
	Houston	IHL	67	17	60	77	65	....	....	....	....	....
	NHL Totals		403	46	100	146	291	70	7	19	26	51

a WHL East First All-Star Team (1984)

Signed as a free agent by **Detroit**, July 28, 1986. Claimed by **Edmonton** from **Detroit** in NHL Waiver Draft, October 5, 1987. Claimed by **Ottawa** from **Edmonton** in Expansion Draft, June 18, 1992. Traded to **Philadelphia** by **Ottawa** for Claude Boivin and Kirk Daubenspeck, March 5, 1994. Traded to **Montreal** by **Philadelphia** for cash, February 10, 1995.

LAMBERT, DAN (lahm-BAIR)

Defense. Shoots left. 5'8", 177 lbs. Born, St. Boniface, Man., January 12, 1970.
(Quebec's 8th choice, 106th overall, in 1989 Entry Draft).

			Regular Season					Playoffs				
Season	Club	Lea	GP	G	A	TP	PIM	GP	G	A	TP	PIM
1986-87	Swift Current	WHL	68	13	53	66	95	4	1	1	2	9
1987-88	Swift Current	WHL	69	20	63	83	120	10	2	10	12	45
1988-89abc	Swift Current	WHL	57	25	77	102	158	12	9	19	28	12
1989-90a	Swift Current	WHL	50	17	51	68	119	4	2	3	5	12
1990-91	Quebec	NHL	1	0	0	0	0	....	....	....	....	....
	Halifax	AHL	30	7	13	20	20	....	....	....	....	....
	Fort Wayne	IHL	49	10	27	37	65	19	4	10	14	20
1991-92	Quebec	NHL	28	6	9	15	22	....	....	....	....	....
	Halifax	AHL	47	3	28	31	33	....	....	....	....	....
1992-93	Moncton	AHL	73	11	30	41	100	5	1	2	3	2
1993-94	HIFK	Fin.	13	1	2	3	8	....	....	....	....	....
	Fort Wayne	IHL	62	10	27	37	138	18	3	12	15	20
1994-95	San Diego	IHL	70	6	19	25	95	5	0	5	5	10
1995-96d	Los Angeles	IHL	81	22	65	87	121	....	....	....	....	....
	NHL Totals		29	6	9	15	22	....	....	....	....	....

a WHL East First All-Star Team (1989, 1990)
b Memorial Cup All-Star Team (1989)
c Won Stafford Smythe Memorial Trophy (Memorial Cup Tournament MVP) (1989)
d IHL Second All-Star Team (1996)

Traded to **Winnipeg** by **Quebec** for Shawn Cronin, August 25, 1992.

LAMBERT, DENNY (lahm-BAIR) OTT.

Left wing. Shoots left. 5'11", 200 lbs. Born, Wawa, Ont., January 7, 1970.

			Regular Season					Playoffs				
Season	Club	Lea	GP	G	A	TP	PIM	GP	G	A	TP	PIM
1988-89	S.S. Marie	OHL	61	14	15	29	2032	....	....	....	....	....
1989-90	S.S. Marie	OHL	61	23	29	52	276	....	....	....	....	....
1990-91	S.S. Marie	OHL	59	28	39	67	169	14	7	9	16	48
1991-92	San Diego	IHL	71	17	14	31	229	3	0	0	0	10
	St. Thomas	ColHL	5	2	6	8	9	....	....	....	....	....
1992-93	San Diego	IHL	56	18	12	30	277	14	1	1	2	44
1993-94	San Diego	IHL	79	13	14	27	314	6	1	0	1	55
1994-95	San Diego	IHL	75	25	35	60	222	....	....	....	....	....
	Anaheim	NHL	13	1	3	4	4	....	....	....	....	....
1995-96	Anaheim	NHL	33	0	8	8	55	....	....	....	....	....
	Baltimore	AHL	44	14	28	42	126	12	3	9	12	39
	NHL Totals		46	1	11	12	59	....	....	....	....	....

Signed as a free agent by **Anaheim**, August 16, 1993. Signed as a free agent by **Ottawa**, July 29, 1996.

LANE, CHRIS BOS.

Defense. Shoots right. 6'1", 183 lbs. Born, Edmonton, Alta., February 16, 1978.
(Boston's 7th choice, 155th overall, in 1996 Entry Draft).

			Regular Season					Playoffs				
Season	Club	Lea	GP	G	A	TP	PIM	GP	G	A	TP	PIM
1995-96	Spokane	WHL	50	1	2	3	40	17	0	1	1	4

LANG, ROBERT (LUHNG) L.A.

Center. Shoots right. 6'2", 200 lbs. Born, Teplice, Czech., December 19, 1970.
(Los Angeles' 6th choice, 133rd overall, in 1990 Entry Draft).

			Regular Season					Playoffs				
Season	Club	Lea	GP	G	A	TP	PIM	GP	G	A	TP	PIM
1988-89	Litvinov	Czech.	7	3	2	5	0	....	....	....	....	....
1989-90	Litvinov	Czech.	39	11	10	21	....	....	....	....	....	....
1990-91	Litvinov	Czech.	56	26	26	52	38	....	....	....	....	....
1991-92	Litvinov	Czech.	43	12	31	43	34	....	....	....	....	....
1992-93	Los Angeles	NHL	11	0	5	5	2	....	....	....	....	....
	Phoenix	IHL	38	9	21	30	20	....	....	....	....	....
1993-94	Los Angeles	NHL	32	9	10	19	10	....	....	....	....	....
	Phoenix	IHL	44	11	24	35	34	....	....	....	....	....
1994-95	Litvinov	Czech.	16	4	19	23	28	....	....	....	....	....
	Los Angeles	NHL	36	4	8	12	4	....	....	....	....	....
1995-96	Los Angeles	NHL	68	6	16	22	10	....	....	....	....	....
	NHL Totals		147	19	39	58	26	....	....	....	....	....

LANGDON, DARREN — NYR

Left wing. Shoots left. 6'1", 205 lbs. Born, Deer Lake, Nfld., January 8, 1971.

			Regular Season					Playoffs				
Season	Club	Lea	GP	G	A	TP	PIM	GP	G	A	TP	PIM
1991-92	Summerside	MJHL	44	34	49	83	441	....	....	....	....	....
1992-93	Binghamton	AHL	18	3	4	7	115	8	0	1	1	14
	Dayton	ECHL	54	23	22	45	429	3	0	1	1	40
1993-94	Binghamton	AHL	54	2	7	9	327	....	....	....	....	....
1994-95	Binghamton	AHL	55	6	14	20	296	11	1	3	4	*84
	NY Rangers	**NHL**	**18**	**1**	**1**	**2**	**62**	....	....	....	....	....
1995-96	**NY Rangers**	**NHL**	**64**	**7**	**4**	**11**	**175**	**2**	**0**	**0**	**0**	**0**
	Binghamton	AHL	1	0	0	0	12	....	....	....	....	....
	NHL Totals		**82**	**8**	**5**	**13**	**237**	**2**	**0**	**0**	**0**	**0**

Signed as a free agent by **NY Rangers**, August 16, 1993.

LANGENBRUNNER, JAMIE (lan-gehn-BROO-nuhr) — DAL.

Center. Shoots right. 5'11", 190 lbs. Born, Duluth, MN, July 24, 1975.
(Dallas' 2nd choice, 35th overall, in 1993 Entry Draft).

			Regular Season					Playoffs				
Season	Club	Lea	GP	G	A	TP	PIM	GP	G	A	TP	PIM
1993-94	Peterborough	OHL	62	33	58	91	53	7	4	6	10	2
1994-95	Peterborough	OHL	62	42	57	99	84	11	8	14	22	12
	Dallas	**NHL**	**2**	**0**	**0**	**0**	**2**	....	....	....	....	....
	Kalamazoo	IHL	....	....	....	....	....	11	1	3	4	2
1995-96	**Dallas**	**NHL**	**12**	**2**	**2**	**4**	**6**	....	....	....	....	....
	Michigan	IHL	59	25	40	65	129	10	3	10	13	8
	NHL Totals		**14**	**2**	**2**	**4**	**8**	....	....	....	....	....

LANGKOW, DAYMOND (LAING-kow) — T.B.

Center. Shoots left. 5'11", 175 lbs. Born, Edmonton, Alta, September 27, 1976.
(Tampa Bay's 1st choice, 5th overall, in 1995 Entry Draft).

			Regular Season					Playoffs				
Season	Club	Lea	GP	G	A	TP	PIM	GP	G	A	TP	PIM
1992-93	Tri-City	WHL	64	22	42	64	100	4	1	0	1	4
1993-94	Tri-City	WHL	61	40	43	83	174	4	2	2	4	15
1994-95ab	Tri-City	WHL	72	*67	73	*140	142	17	12	15	27	52
1995-96c	Tri-City	WHL	48	30	61	91	103	11	14	13	27	20
	Tampa Bay	**NHL**	**4**	**0**	**1**	**1**	**0**	....	....	....	....	....
	NHL Totals		**4**	**0**	**1**	**1**	**0**	....	....	....	....	....

a WHL West First All-Star Team (1995)
b Canadian Major Junior First All-Star Team (1995)
c WHL West Second All-Star Team (1996)

LANK, JEFF — PHI.

Defense. Shoots left. 6'3", 205 lbs. Born, Indian Head, Sask., March 1, 1975.
(Montreal's 6th choice, 113th overall, in 1993 Entry Draft).

			Regular Season					Playoffs				
Season	Club	Lea	GP	G	A	TP	PIM	GP	G	A	TP	PIM
1991-92	Prince Albert	WHL	56	2	8	10	26	9	0	0	0	2
1992-93	Prince Albert	WHL	63	1	11	12	60	....	....	....	....	....
1993-94	Prince Albert	WHL	72	9	38	47	62	....	....	....	....	....
1994-95	Prince Albert	WHL	68	12	25	37	60	13	2	10	12	8
1995-96	Hershey	AHL	72	7	13	20	70	5	0	0	0	8

Re-entered NHL Entry Draft, **Philadelphia's** 9th choice, 230th overall in 1995 Entry Draft.

LANKSHEAR, MIKE — TOR.

Defense. Shoots left. 6'2", 185 lbs. Born, Calgary, Alta., September 8, 1978.
(Toronto's 3rd choice, 66th overall, in 1996 Entry Draft).

			Regular Season					Playoffs				
Season	Club	Lea	GP	G	A	TP	PIM	GP	G	A	TP	PIM
1994-95	Burlington	Jr. A	40	6	18	24	43	....	....	....	....	....
1995-96	Guelph	OHL	63	8	20	28	73	15	2	6	8	19

LAPERRIERE, DANIEL (luh-PAIR-ee-YAIR) — WSH.

Defense. Shoots left. 6'1", 195 lbs. Born, Laval, Que., March 28, 1969.
(St. Louis' 4th choice, 93rd overall, in 1989 Entry Draft).

			Regular Season					Playoffs				
Season	Club	Lea	GP	G	A	TP	PIM	GP	G	A	TP	PIM
1988-89	St. Lawrence	ECAC	28	0	7	7	10	....	....	....	....	....
1989-90	St. Lawrence	ECAC	31	6	19	25	16	....	....	....	....	....
1990-91a	St. Lawrence	ECAC	34	7	31	38	18	....	....	....	....	....
1991-92bc	St. Lawrence	ECAC	32	8	*45	53	36	....	....	....	....	....
1992-93	**St. Louis**	**NHL**	**5**	**0**	**1**	**1**	**0**	....	....	....	....	....
	Peoria	IHL	54	4	20	24	28	....	....	....	....	....
1993-94	**St. Louis**	**NHL**	**20**	**1**	**3**	**4**	**8**	....	....	....	....	....
	Peoria	IHL	56	10	37	47	16	6	0	2	2	2
1994-95	Peoria	IHL	65	19	33	52	42	....	....	....	....	....
	St. Louis	**NHL**	**4**	**0**	**0**	**0**	**15**	....	....	....	....	....
	Ottawa	**NHL**	**13**	**1**	**1**	**2**	**0**	....	....	....	....	....
1995-96	**Ottawa**	**NHL**	**6**	**0**	**0**	**0**	**4**	....	....	....	....	....
	P.E.I.	AHL	15	2	7	9	4	....	....	....	....	....
	Atlanta	IHL	15	4	9	13	4	....	....	....	....	....
	Kansas City	IHL	23	2	6	8	11	5	0	1	1	0
	NHL Totals		**48**	**2**	**5**	**7**	**27**	....	....	....	....	....

a ECAC Second All-Star Team (1991)
b ECAC First All-Star Team (1992)
c NCAA East First All-American Team (1992)

Traded to **Ottawa** by **St. Louis** with St. Louis' ninth round choice (Erik Kasminski) in 1995 Entry Draft for Ottawa's ninth round choice (Libor Zabransy) in 1995 Entry Draft, April 7, 1995. Signed as a free agent by **Washington**, July 12, 1996.

LAPERRIERE, IAN (luh-PAIR-ee-YAIR, EE-ihn) — L.A.

Center. Shoots right. 6'1", 195 lbs. Born, Montreal, Que., January 19, 1974.
(St. Louis' 6th choice, 158th overall, in 1992 Entry Draft).

			Regular Season					Playoffs				
Season	Club	Lea	GP	G	A	TP	PIM	GP	G	A	TP	PIM
1990-91	Drummondville	QMJHL	65	19	29	48	117	14	2	9	11	48
1991-92	Drummondville	QMJHL	70	28	49	77	160	4	2	2	4	9
1992-93a	Drummondville	QMJHL	60	44	*96	140	188	10	6	13	19	20
1993-94	**St. Louis**	**NHL**	**1**	**0**	**0**	**0**	**0**	....	....	....	....	....
	Drummondville	QMJHL	62	41	72	113	150	9	4	6	10	35
	Peoria	IHL	....	....	....	....	....	5	1	3	4	2
1994-95	Peoria	IHL	51	16	32	48	111	....	....	....	....	....
	St. Louis	**NHL**	**37**	**13**	**14**	**27**	**85**	**7**	**0**	**4**	**4**	**21**
1995-96	**St. Louis**	**NHL**	**33**	**3**	**6**	**9**	**87**	....	....	....	....	....
	Worcester	AHL	3	2	1	3	22	....	....	....	....	....
	NY Rangers	**NHL**	**28**	**1**	**2**	**3**	**53**	....	....	....	....	....
	Los Angeles	**NHL**	**10**	**2**	**3**	**5**	**15**	....	....	....	....	....
	NHL Totals		**109**	**19**	**25**	**44**	**240**	**7**	**0**	**4**	**4**	**21**

a QMJHL Second All-Star Team (1993)

Traded to **NY Rangers** by **St. Louis** for Stephane Matteau, December 28, 1995. Traded to **Los Angeles** by **NY Rangers** with Ray Ferraro, Mattias Norstrom, Nathan Lafayette and NY Rangers' fourth round choice in 1997 Entry Draft for Marty McSorley, Jari Kurri and Shane Churla, March 14, 1996.

LAPLANTE, DARRYL — DET.

Center. Shoots left. 6'1", 185 lbs. Born, Calgary, Alta., March 28, 1977.
(Detroit's 3rd choice, 58th overall, in 1995 Entry Draft).

			Regular Season					Playoffs				
Season	Club	Lea	GP	G	A	TP	PIM	GP	G	A	TP	PIM
1994-95	Moose Jaw	WHL	71	22	24	46	66	10	2	2	4	7
1995-96	Moose Jaw	WHL	72	42	40	82	76	....	....	....	....	....

LAPLANTE, MIKE — ANA.

Defense. Shoots left. 6'2", 190 lbs. Born, Calgary, Alta., July 12, 1975.
(Anaheim's 6th choice, 159th overall, in 1995 Entry Draft).

			Regular Season					Playoffs				
Season	Club	Lea	GP	G	A	TP	PIM	GP	G	A	TP	PIM
1994-95	Calgary	Jr. A	54	6	28	34	262	....	....	....	....	....
	North Bay	OHL	2	0	0	0	0	....	....	....	....	....
1995-96	North Bay	OHL	1	0	0	0	0	....	....	....	....	....
	U. Wisconsin	WCHA	33	0	10	10	66	....	....	....	....	....

LAPOINTE, CLAUDE (luh-PWAH, KLOHD) — NYI

Center. Shoots left. 5'9", 181 lbs. Born, Lachine, Que., October 11, 1968.
(Quebec's 12th choice, 234th overall, in 1988 Entry Draft).

			Regular Season					Playoffs				
Season	Club	Lea	GP	G	A	TP	PIM	GP	G	A	TP	PIM
1986-87	Trois-Rivières	QMJHL	70	47	57	104	123	....	....	....	....	....
1987-88	Laval	QMJHL	69	37	83	120	143	13	2	17	19	53
1988-89	Laval	QMJHL	63	32	72	104	158	17	5	14	19	66
1989-90	Halifax	AHL	63	18	19	37	51	6	1	1	2	34
1990-91	**Quebec**	**NHL**	**13**	**2**	**2**	**4**	**4**	....	....	....	....	....
	Halifax	AHL	43	17	17	34	46	....	....	....	....	....
1991-92	**Quebec**	**NHL**	**78**	**13**	**20**	**33**	**86**	....	....	....	....	....
1992-93	**Quebec**	**NHL**	**74**	**10**	**26**	**36**	**98**	**6**	**2**	**4**	**6**	**8**
1993-94	**Quebec**	**NHL**	**59**	**11**	**17**	**28**	**70**	....	....	....	....	....
1994-95	**Quebec**	**NHL**	**29**	**4**	**8**	**12**	**41**	**5**	**0**	**0**	**0**	**8**
1995-96	**Colorado**	**NHL**	**3**	**0**	**0**	**0**	**0**	....	....	....	....	....
	Calgary	**NHL**	**32**	**4**	**5**	**9**	**20**	**2**	**0**	**0**	**0**	**0**
	Saint John	AHL	12	5	3	8	10	....	....	....	....	....
	NHL Totals		**288**	**44**	**78**	**122**	**319**	**13**	**2**	**4**	**6**	**16**

Traded to **Calgary** by **Colorado** for Calgary's seventh round choice (Samuel Pahlsson) in 1996 Entry Draft, November 1, 1995. Signed as a free agent by **NY Islanders**, August 14, 1996.

LAPOINTE, MARTIN (luh-POYNT, MAHR-tai) — DET.

Right wing. Shoots right. 5'11", 200 lbs. Born, Ville Ste. Pierre, Que., September 12, 1973.
(Detroit's 1st choice, 10th overall, in 1991 Entry Draft).

			Regular Season					Playoffs				
Season	Club	Lea	GP	G	A	TP	PIM	GP	G	A	TP	PIM
1989-90a	Laval	QMJHL	65	42	54	96	77	14	8	17	25	54
1990-91b	Laval	QMJHL	64	44	54	98	66	13	7	14	21	26
1991-92	**Detroit**	**NHL**	**4**	**0**	**1**	**1**	**5**	**3**	**0**	**1**	**1**	**4**
	Laval	QMJHL	31	25	30	55	84	10	4	10	14	32
	Adirondack	AHL	....	....	....	....	....	8	2	2	4	4
1992-93	**Detroit**	**NHL**	**3**	**0**	**0**	**0**	**0**	....	....	....	....	....
ac	Laval	QMJHL	35	38	51	89	41	13	*13	*17	*30	22
	Adirondack	AHL	8	1	2	3	9	....	....	....	....	....
1993-94	**Detroit**	**NHL**	**50**	**8**	**8**	**16**	**55**	**4**	**0**	**0**	**0**	**6**
	Adirondack	AHL	28	25	21	46	47	4	1	1	2	8
1994-95	Adirondack	AHL	39	29	16	45	80	....	....	....	....	....
	Detroit	**NHL**	**39**	**4**	**6**	**10**	**73**	**2**	**0**	**1**	**1**	**8**
1995-96	**Detroit**	**NHL**	**58**	**6**	**3**	**9**	**93**	**11**	**1**	**2**	**3**	**12**
	NHL Totals		**154**	**18**	**18**	**36**	**226**	**20**	**1**	**4**	**5**	**30**

a QMJHL First All-Star Team (1990, 1993)
b QMJHL Second All-Star Team (1991)
c Memorial Cup All-Star Team (1993)

LAPORTE, ALEXANDRE — T.B.

Defense. Shoots right. 6'3", 210 lbs. Born, Cowansville, Que., May 1, 1975.
(Tampa Bay's 9th choice, 211th overall, in 1993 Entry Draft).

			Regular Season					Playoffs				
Season	Club	Lea	GP	G	A	TP	PIM	GP	G	A	TP	PIM
1991-92	Victoriaville	QMJHL	44	1	4	5	43	....	....	....	....	....
1992-93	Victoriaville	QMJHL	56	1	3	4	30	6	0	0	0	2
1993-94	Victoriaville	QMJHL	56	3	9	12	68	5	1	0	1	2
1994-95	St-Hyacinthe	QMJHL	38	3	6	9	70	....	....	....	....	....
	Drummondville	QMJHL	23	0	6	6	28	4	0	1	1	0
1995-96	Nashville	ECHL	38	2	9	11	60	5	0	0	0	8
	Atlanta	IHL	14	0	1	1	5	....	....	....	....	....

LARAQUE, GEORGES — EDM.

Right wing. Shoots right. 6'3", 235 lbs. Born, Montreal, Que., December 7, 1976.
(Edmonton's 2nd choice, 31st overall, in 1995 Entry Draft).

			Regular Season					Playoffs				
Season	Club	Lea	GP	G	A	TP	PIM	GP	G	A	TP	PIM
1993-94	St-Jean	QMJHL	70	11	11	22	142	4	0	0	0	7
1994-95	St-Jean	QMJHL	62	19	22	41	259	7	1	1	2	42
1995-96	Laval	QMJHL	11	8	13	21	76	....	....	....	....	....
	St-Hyacinthe	QMJHL	8	3	4	7	59	....	....	....	....	....
	Granby	QMJHL	22	9	7	16	125	18	7	6	13	104

LARIONOV, IGOR (LAIR-ee-AH-nohv) DET.

Center. Shoots left. 5'9", 170 lbs. Born, Voskresensk, USSR, December 3, 1960.
(Vancouver's 11th choice, 214th overall, in 1985 Entry Draft).

			Regular Season					Playoffs				
Season	Club	Lea	GP	G	A	TP	PIM	GP	G	A	TP	PIM
1977-78	Khimik	USSR	6	3	0	3	4	....	....	....	....	....
1978-79	Khimik	USSR	32	3	4	7	12	....	....	....	....	....
1979-80	Khimik	USSR	42	11	7	18	24	....	....	....	....	....
1980-81	Khimik	USSR	43	22	23	45	36	....	....	....	....	....
1981-82	CSKA	USSR	46	31	22	53	6	....	....	....	....	....
1982-83a	CSKA	USSR	44	20	19	39	20	....	....	....	....	....
1983-84	CSKA	USSR	43	15	26	41	30	....	....	....	....	....
1984-85	CSKA	USSR	40	18	28	46	20	....	....	....	....	....
1985-86a	CSKA	USSR	40	21	31	52	33	....	....	....	....	....
1986-87a	CSKA	USSR	39	20	26	46	34	....	....	....	....	....
1987-88ab	CSKA	USSR	51	25	32	57	54	....	....	....	....	....
1988-89	CSKA	USSR	31	15	12	27	22	....	....	....	....	....
1989-90	**Vancouver**	**NHL**	**74**	**17**	**27**	**44**	**20**	....	....	....	....	....
1990-91	**Vancouver**	**NHL**	**64**	**13**	**21**	**34**	**14**	**6**	**1**	**0**	**1**	**6**
1991-92	**Vancouver**	**NHL**	**72**	**21**	**44**	**65**	**54**	**13**	**3**	**7**	**10**	**4**
1992-93	Lugano	Switz.	24	10	19	29	44	....	....	....	....	....
1993-94	**San Jose**	**NHL**	**60**	**18**	**38**	**56**	**40**	**14**	**5**	**13**	**18**	**10**
1994-95	**San Jose**	**NHL**	**33**	**4**	**20**	**24**	**14**	**11**	**1**	**8**	**9**	**2**
1995-96	**San Jose**	**NHL**	**4**	**1**	**1**	**2**	**0**	....	....	....	....	....
	Detroit	**NHL**	**69**	**21**	**50**	**71**	**34**	**19**	**6**	**7**	**13**	**6**
	NHL Totals		**376**	**95**	**201**	**296**	**176**	**63**	**16**	**35**	**51**	**28**

a Soviet National League All-Star (1983, 1986-88)
b Soviet Player of the Year (1988)

Claimed by **San Jose** from **Vancouver** in NHL Waiver Draft, October 4, 1992. Traded to **Detroit** by **San Jose** with a conditional draft choice in 1998 Entry Draft for Ray Sheppard, October 24, 1995.

LAROCQUE, MARIO (luh-RAWK) T.B.

Defense. Shoots left. 6'2", 182 lbs. Born, Montreal, Que., April 24, 1978.
(Tampa Bay's 1st choice, 16th overall, in 1996 Entry Draft).

			Regular Season					Playoffs				
Season	Club	Lea	GP	G	A	TP	PIM	GP	G	A	TP	PIM
1994-95	Bourassa	Midget	43	0	6	6	153	....	....	....	....	....
1995-96	Hull	QMJHL	68	7	19	26	196	14	2	5	7	16

LAROSE, BENOIT L.A.

Defense. Shoots left. 6'5", 195 lbs. Born, St-Jerome, Que., May 17, 1977.
(Los Angeles' 7th choice, 157th overall, in 1995 Entry Draft).

			Regular Season					Playoffs				
Season	Club	Lea	GP	G	A	TP	PIM	GP	G	A	TP	PIM
1993-94	Victoriaville	QMJHL	65	0	5	5	69	5	0	0	0	2
1994-95	Victoriaville	QMJHL	23	0	3	3	99	....	....	....	....	....
	Sherbrooke	QMJHL	28	0	0	0	32	3	0	0	0	0
1995-96	Sherbrooke	QMJHL	62	0	6	6	215	7	1	0	1	12

LAROSE, GUY (luh-ROHS)

Center. Shoots left. 5'9", 180 lbs. Born, Hull, Que., August 31, 1967.
(Buffalo's 11th choice, 224th overall, in 1985 Entry Draft).

			Regular Season					Playoffs				
Season	Club	Lea	GP	G	A	TP	PIM	GP	G	A	TP	PIM
1984-85	Guelph	OHL	58	30	30	60	63	....	....	....	....	....
1985-86	Guelph	OHL	37	12	36	48	55	....	....	....	....	....
	Ottawa	OHL	28	19	25	44	63	....	....	....	....	....
1986-87	Ottawa	OHL	66	28	49	77	77	11	2	8	10	27
1987-88	Moncton	AHL	77	22	31	53	127	....	....	....	....	....
1988-89	**Winnipeg**	**NHL**	**3**	**0**	**1**	**1**	**6**	....	....	....	....	....
	Moncton	AHL	72	32	27	59	176	10	4	4	8	37
1989-90	Moncton	AHL	79	44	26	70	232	....	....	....	....	....
1990-91	**Winnipeg**	**NHL**	**7**	**0**	**0**	**0**	**8**	....	....	....	....	....
	Moncton	AHL	35	14	10	24	60	....	....	....	....	....
	Binghamton	AHL	34	21	15	36	48	10	8	5	13	37
1991-92	Binghamton	AHL	30	10	11	21	36	....	....	....	....	....
	Toronto	**NHL**	**34**	**9**	**5**	**14**	**27**	....	....	....	....	....
	St. John's	AHL	15	7	7	14	26	....	....	....	....	....
1992-93	**Toronto**	**NHL**	**9**	**0**	**0**	**0**	**8**	....	....	....	....	....
	St. John's	AHL	5	0	1	1	8	9	5	2	7	6
1993-94	**Toronto**	**NHL**	**10**	**1**	**2**	**3**	**10**	....	....	....	....	....
	St. John's	AHL	23	13	16	29	41	....	....	....	....	....
	Calgary	**NHL**	**7**	**0**	**1**	**1**	**4**	....	....	....	....	....
	Saint John	AHL	15	11	11	22	20	7	3	2	5	22
1994-95	Providence	AHL	68	25	33	58	93	12	4	6	10	22
	Boston	**NHL**	....	....	....	....	....	**4**	**0**	**0**	**0**	**0**
1995-96	Detroit	IHL	50	28	15	43	53	....	....	....	....	....
	Las Vegas	IHL	25	10	22	32	54	15	3	6	9	14
	NHL Totals		**70**	**10**	**9**	**19**	**63**	**4**	**0**	**0**	**0**	**0**

Signed as a free agent by **Winnipeg**, July 16, 1987. Traded to **NY Rangers** by **Winnipeg** for Rudy Poeschek, January 22, 1991. Traded to **Toronto** by **NY Rangers** for Mike Stevens, December 26, 1991. Claimed on waivers by **Calgary** from **Toronto**, January 1, 1994. Signed as a free agent by **Boston**, July 11, 1994.

LAROUCHE, STEVE (luh-ROOSH)

Center. Shoots right. 6', 180 lbs. Born, Rouyn, Que., April 14, 1971.
(Montreal's 3rd choice, 41st overall, in 1989 Entry Draft).

			Regular Season					Playoffs				
Season	Club	Lea	GP	G	A	TP	PIM	GP	G	A	TP	PIM
1987-88	Trois-Rivières	QMJHL	66	11	29	40	25	....	....	....	....	....
1988-89	Trois-Rivières	QMJHL	70	51	102	153	53	4	4	2	6	6
1989-90a	Trois-Rivières	QMJHL	60	55	90	145	40	7	3	5	8	8
	Cdn. National	....	1	1	0	1	0	....	....	....	....	....
1990-91	Chicoutimi	QMJHL	45	35	41	76	64	17	*13	*20	*33	20
1991-92	Fredericton	AHL	74	21	35	56	41	7	1	0	1	0
1992-93	Fredericton	AHL	77	27	65	92	52	5	2	5	7	6
1993-94	Atlanta	IHL	80	43	53	96	73	14	*16	10	*26	16
1994-95bcd	P.E.I.	AHL	70	*53	48	101	54	2	1	0	1	0
	Ottawa	**NHL**	**18**	**8**	**7**	**15**	**6**	....	....	....	....	....
1995-96	**NY Rangers**	**NHL**	**1**	**0**	**0**	**0**	**0**	....	....	....	....	....
	Binghamton	AHL	39	20	46	66	47	....	....	....	....	....
	Los Angeles	**NHL**	**7**	**1**	**2**	**3**	**4**	....	....	....	....	....
	Phoenix	IHL	33	19	17	36	14	4	0	1	1	8
	NHL Totals		**26**	**9**	**9**	**18**	**10**	....	....	....	....	....

a QMJHL Second All-Star Team (1990)
b AHL First All-Star Team (1995)
c Won Fred Hunt Memorial Trophy (Sportsmanship - AHL) (1995)
d Won Les Cunningham Plaque (MVP - AHL) (1995)

Signed as a free agent by **Ottawa**, September 11, 1994. Traded to **NY Rangers** by **Ottawa** for Jean-Yves Roy, October 5, 1995. Traded to **Los Angeles** by **NY Rangers** for Chris Snell, January 14, 1996.

LARSEN, BRAD COL.

Left wing. Shoots left. 5'11", 212 lbs. Born, Nakusp, B.C., January 28, 1977.
(Ottawa's 3rd choice, 53rd overall, in 1995 Entry Draft).

			Regular Season					Playoffs				
Season	Club	Lea	GP	G	A	TP	PIM	GP	G	A	TP	PIM
1993-94	Swift Current	WHL	64	15	18	33	32	7	1	2	3	4
1994-95	Swift Current	WHL	62	24	33	57	73	6	0	1	1	2
1995-96	Swift Current	WHL	51	30	47	77	67	6	3	2	5	13

Traded to **Colorado** by **Ottawa** for Janne Laukkanen, January 26, 1996.

LAUER, BRAD (LAU-er) PIT.

Left wing. Shoots left. 6', 195 lbs. Born, Humboldt, Sask., October 27, 1966.
(NY Islanders' 3rd choice, 34th overall, in 1985 Entry Draft).

			Regular Season					Playoffs				
Season	Club	Lea	GP	G	A	TP	PIM	GP	G	A	TP	PIM
1983-84	Regina	WHL	60	5	7	12	51	16	0	1	1	24
1984-85	Regina	WHL	72	33	46	79	57	8	6	6	12	9
1985-86	Regina	WHL	57	36	38	74	69	10	4	5	9	2
1986-87	**NY Islanders**	**NHL**	**61**	**7**	**14**	**21**	**65**	**6**	**2**	**0**	**2**	**4**
1987-88	**NY Islanders**	**NHL**	**69**	**17**	**18**	**35**	**67**	**5**	**3**	**1**	**4**	**4**
1988-89	**NY Islanders**	**NHL**	**14**	**3**	**2**	**5**	**2**	....	....	....	....	....
	Springfield	AHL	8	1	5	6	0	....	....	....	....	....
1989-90	**NY Islanders**	**NHL**	**63**	**6**	**18**	**24**	**19**	**4**	**0**	**2**	**2**	**10**
	Springfield	AHL	7	4	2	6	0	....	....	....	....	....
1990-91	**NY Islanders**	**NHL**	**44**	**4**	**8**	**12**	**45**	....	....	....	....	....
	Capital Dist.	AHL	11	5	11	16	14	....	....	....	....	....
1991-92	**NY Islanders**	**NHL**	**8**	**1**	**0**	**1**	**2**	....	....	....	....	....
	Chicago	**NHL**	**6**	**0**	**0**	**0**	**4**	**7**	**1**	**1**	**2**	**2**
	Indianapolis	IHL	57	24	30	54	46	....	....	....	....	....
1992-93	**Chicago**	**NHL**	**7**	**0**	**1**	**1**	**2**	....	....	....	....	....
a	Indianapolis	IHL	62	*50	41	91	80	5	3	1	4	6
1993-94	**Ottawa**	**NHL**	**30**	**2**	**5**	**7**	**6**	....	....	....	....	....
	Las Vegas	IHL	32	21	21	42	30	4	1	0	1	2
1994-95	Cleveland	IHL	51	32	27	59	48	4	4	2	6	6
1995-96	**Pittsburgh**	**NHL**	**21**	**4**	**1**	**5**	**6**	**12**	**1**	**1**	**2**	**4**
	Cleveland	IHL	53	25	27	52	44	....	....	....	....	....
	NHL Totals		**323**	**44**	**67**	**111**	**218**	**34**	**7**	**5**	**12**	**24**

a IHL First All-Star Team (1993)

Traded to **Chicago** by **NY Islanders** with Brent Sutter for Adam Creighton and Steve Thomas, October 25, 1991. Signed as a free agent by **Ottawa**, January 3, 1994. Signed as a free agent by **Pittsburgh**, August 10, 1995.

LAUKKANEN, JANNE (LOW-kah-nehn) OTT.

Defense. Shoots left. 6', 180 lbs. Born, Lahti, Finland, March 19, 1970.
(Quebec's 8th choice, 156th overall, in 1991 Entry Draft).

			Regular Season					Playoffs				
Season	Club	Lea	GP	G	A	TP	PIM	GP	G	A	TP	PIM
1990-91	Reipas	Fin.	44	8	14	22	56	....	....	....	....	....
1991-92	HPK	Fin.	43	5	14	19	62	....	....	....	....	....
1992-93	HPK	Fin.	47	8	21	29	76	12	1	4	5	10
1993-94	HPK	Fin.	48	5	24	29	46	....	....	....	....	....
1994-95	Cornwall	AHL	55	8	26	34	41	....	....	....	....	....
	Quebec	**NHL**	**11**	**0**	**3**	**3**	**4**	**6**	**1**	**0**	**1**	**2**
1995-96	**Colorado**	**NHL**	**3**	**1**	**0**	**1**	**0**	....	....	....	....	....
	Cornwall	AHL	35	7	20	27	60	....	....	....	....	....
	Ottawa	**NHL**	**20**	**0**	**2**	**2**	**14**	....	....	....	....	....
	NHL Totals		**34**	**1**	**5**	**6**	**18**	**6**	**1**	**0**	**1**	**2**

Traded to **Ottawa** by **Colorado** for Brad Larsen, January 26, 1996.

LAUS, PAUL (LOWZ) FLA.

Defense. Shoots right. 6'1", 216 lbs. Born, Beamsville, Ont., September 26, 1970.
(Pittsburgh's 2nd choice, 37th overall, in 1989 Entry Draft).

			Regular Season					Playoffs				
Season	Club	Lea	GP	G	A	TP	PIM	GP	G	A	TP	PIM
1987-88	Hamilton	OHL	56	1	9	10	171	14	0	0	0	28
1988-89	Niagara Falls	OHL	49	1	10	11	225	15	0	5	5	56
1989-90	Niagara Falls	OHL	60	13	35	48	231	16	6	16	22	71
1990-91	Albany	IHL	7	0	0	0	7	....	....	....	....	....
	Knoxville	ECHL	20	6	12	18	83	....	....	....	....	....
	Muskegon	IHL	35	3	4	7	103	4	0	0	0	13
1991-92	Muskegon	IHL	75	0	21	21	248	14	2	5	7	70
1992-93	Cleveland	IHL	76	8	18	26	427	4	1	0	1	27
1993-94	**Florida**	**NHL**	**39**	**2**	**0**	**2**	**109**	....	....	....	....	....
1994-95	**Florida**	**NHL**	**37**	**0**	**7**	**7**	**138**	....	....	....	....	....
1995-96	**Florida**	**NHL**	**78**	**3**	**6**	**9**	**236**	**21**	**2**	**6**	**8**	***62**
	NHL Totals		**154**	**5**	**13**	**18**	**483**	**21**	**2**	**6**	**8**	**62**

Claimed by **Florida** from **Pittsburgh** in Expansion Draft, June 24, 1993.

LAVIGNE, ERIC (luh-VEEN)

Defense. Shoots left. 6'3", 195 lbs. Born, Victoriaville, Que., November 4, 1972.
(Washington's 3rd choice, 25th overall, in 1991 Entry Draft).

			Regular Season					Playoffs				
Season	Club	Lea	GP	G	A	TP	PIM	GP	G	A	TP	PIM
1989-90	Hull	QMJHL	69	7	11	18	203	11	0	0	0	32
1990-91	Hull	QMJHL	66	11	11	22	153	4	0	1	1	16
1991-92	Hull	QMJHL	46	4	17	21	101	6	0	0	0	32
1992-93	Hull	QMJHL	59	7	20	27	221	10	2	4	6	47
1993-94	Phoenix	IHL	62	3	11	14	168	....	....	....	....	....
1994-95	Phoenix	IHL	69	4	10	14	233	....	....	....	....	....
	Los Angeles	**NHL**	**1**	**0**	**0**	**0**	**0**	....	....	....	....	....
	Detroit	IHL	1	0	0	0	2	5	0	0	0	26
1995-96	P.E.I.	AHL	72	5	13	18	154	2	0	0	0	6
	NHL Totals		**1**	**0**	**0**	**0**	**0**	....	....	....	....	....

Signed as a free agent by **Los Angeles**, October 13, 1993. Signed as a free agent by **Ottawa**, August 9, 1995.

LAWRENCE, MARK — DAL.

Right wing. Shoots right. 6'4", 215 lbs. Born, Burlington, Ont., January 27, 1972.
(Minnesota's 6th choice, 118th overall, in 1991 Entry Draft).

			Regular Season					Playoffs				
Season	Club	Lea	GP	G	A	TP	PIM	GP	G	A	TP	PIM
1988-89	Niagara Falls	OHL	63	9	27	36	142	....	....	....	....	....
1989-90	Niagara Falls	OHL	54	15	18	33	123	16	2	5	7	42
1990-91	Detroit	OHL	66	27	38	65	53	....	....	....	....	....
1991-92	Detroit	OHL	28	19	26	45	54	....	....	....	....	....
	North Bay	OHL	24	13	14	27	21	21	*23	12	35	36
1992-93	Dayton	ECHL	20	8	14	22	46	....	....	....	....	....
	Kalamazoo	IHL	57	22	13	35	47	....	....	....	....	....
1993-94	Kalamazoo	IHL	64	17	20	37	90	....	....	....	....	....
1994-95	Kalamazoo	IHL	77	21	29	50	92	16	3	7	10	28
	Dallas	**NHL**	2	0	0	0	0	....	....	....	....	....
1995-96	**Dallas**	**NHL**	13	0	1	1	17	....	....	....	....	....
	Michigan	IHL	55	15	14	29	92	10	3	4	7	30
	NHL Totals		**15**	**0**	**1**	**1**	**17**	....	....	....	....	....

LAZARENKO, ALEXEI (la-zah-REHN-koh) — NYR

Left wing. Shoots left. 5'11", 176 lbs. Born, Moscow, USSR, January 3, 1976.
(NY Rangers' 9th choice, 182nd overall, in 1994 Entry Draft).

			Regular Season					Playoffs				
Season	Club	Lea	GP	G	A	TP	PIM	GP	G	A	TP	PIM
1994-95	CSKA-2	CIS	5	0	0	0	0	....	....	....	....	....
1995-96	Chicoutimi	QMJHL	57	24	30	54	125	12	6	2	8	16

LEACH, JAMIE

Right wing. Shoots right. 6'1", 205 lbs. Born, Winnipeg, Man., August 25, 1969.
(Pittsburgh's 3rd choice, 47th overall, in 1987 Entry Draft).

			Regular Season					Playoffs				
Season	Club	Lea	GP	G	A	TP	PIM	GP	G	A	TP	PIM
1985-86	N. Westminster	WHL	58	8	7	15	20	....	....	....	....	....
1986-87	Hamilton	OHL	64	12	19	31	67	....	....	....	....	....
1987-88	Hamilton	OHL	64	24	19	43	79	14	6	7	13	12
1988-89	Niagara Falls	OHL	58	45	62	107	47	17	9	11	20	25
1989-90	**Pittsburgh**	**NHL**	10	0	3	3	0	....	....	....	....	....
	Muskegon	IHL	72	22	36	58	39	15	9	4	13	14
1990-91	**Pittsburgh**	**NHL**	7	2	0	2	0	....	....	....	....	....
	Muskegon	IHL	43	33	22	55	26	....	....	....	....	....
1991-92	**Pittsburgh**	**NHL**	38	5	4	9	8	....	....	....	....	....
	Muskegon	IHL	3	1	1	2	2	....	....	....	....	....
1992-93	**Pittsburgh**	**NHL**	5	0	0	0	2	....	....	....	....	....
	Cleveland	IHL	9	5	3	8	2	4	1	2	3	0
	Hartford	**NHL**	19	3	2	5	2	....	....	....	....	....
	Springfield	AHL	29	13	15	28	33	....	....	....	....	....
1993-94	**Florida**	**NHL**	2	1	0	1	0	....	....	....	....	....
	Cincinnati	IHL	74	15	19	34	64	11	1	0	1	4
1994-95	Cdn. National	....	41	12	26	38	26	....	....	....	....	....
	Cincinnati	IHL	11	0	2	2	9	....	....	....	....	....
	San Diego	IHL	....	....	....	....	....	4	0	0	0	0
1995-96	Rochester	AHL	47	12	14	26	52	2	0	0	0	0
	S. Carolina	ECHL	5	6	1	7	4	....	....	....	....	....
	NHL Totals		**81**	**11**	**9**	**20**	**12**	....	....	....	....	....

Claimed on waivers by **Hartford** from **Pittsburgh**, November 21, 1992. Signed as a free agent by **Florida**, August 31, 1993. Signed as a free agent by **Buffalo**, August 31, 1995.

LEACH, STEPHEN — ST.L.

Right wing. Shoots right. 5'11", 197 lbs. Born, Cambridge, MA, January 16, 1966.
(Washington's 2nd choice, 34th overall, in 1984 Entry Draft).

			Regular Season					Playoffs				
Season	Club	Lea	GP	G	A	TP	PIM	GP	G	A	TP	PIM
1984-85	N. Hampshire	H.E.	41	12	25	37	53	....	....	....	....	....
1985-86	**Washington**	**NHL**	11	1	1	2	2	6	0	1	1	0
	N. Hampshire	H.E.	25	22	6	28	30	....	....	....	....	....
1986-87	**Washington**	**NHL**	15	1	0	1	6	....	....	....	....	....
	Binghamton	AHL	54	18	21	39	39	13	3	1	4	6
1987-88	**Washington**	**NHL**	8	1	1	2	17	9	2	1	3	0
	U.S. National	....	49	26	20	46	30	....	....	....	....	....
	U.S. Olympic	....	6	1	2	3	0	....	....	....	....	....
1988-89	**Washington**	**NHL**	74	11	19	30	94	6	1	0	1	12
1989-90	**Washington**	**NHL**	70	18	14	32	104	14	2	2	4	8
1990-91	**Washington**	**NHL**	68	11	19	30	99	9	1	2	3	8
1991-92	**Boston**	**NHL**	78	31	29	60	147	15	4	0	4	10
1992-93	**Boston**	**NHL**	79	26	25	51	126	4	1	1	2	2
1993-94	**Boston**	**NHL**	42	5	10	15	74	5	0	1	1	2
1994-95	**Boston**	**NHL**	35	5	6	11	68	....	....	....	....	....
1995-96	**Boston**	**NHL**	59	9	13	22	86	....	....	....	....	....
	St. Louis	**NHL**	14	2	4	6	22	11	3	2	5	10
	NHL Totals		**553**	**121**	**141**	**262**	**845**	**79**	**14**	**10**	**24**	**52**

Traded to **Boston** by **Washington** for Randy Burridge, June 21, 1991. Traded to **St. Louis** by **Boston** for Kevin Sawyer and Steve Staios, March 8, 1996.

LEBEAU, STEPHAN (leh-BOH)

Center. Shoots right. 5'10", 173 lbs. Born, St. Jerome, Que., February 28, 1968.

			Regular Season					Playoffs				
Season	Club	Lea	GP	G	A	TP	PIM	GP	G	A	TP	PIM
1984-85	Shawinigan	QMJHL	66	41	38	79	18	9	4	5	9	4
1985-86	Shawinigan	QMJHL	72	69	77	146	22	5	4	2	6	4
1986-87a	Shawinigan	QMJHL	65	77	90	167	60	14	9	20	29	20
1987-88a	Shawinigan	QMJHL	67	*94	94	188	66	11	17	9	26	10
	Sherbrooke	AHL	....	....	....	....	....	1	0	1	1	0
1988-89	**Montreal**	**NHL**	1	0	1	1	2	....	....	....	....	....
bcde	Sherbrooke	AHL	78	*70	64	*134	47	6	1	4	5	8
1989-90	**Montreal**	**NHL**	57	15	20	35	11	2	3	0	3	0
1990-91	**Montreal**	**NHL**	73	22	31	53	24	7	2	1	3	2
1991-92	**Montreal**	**NHL**	77	27	31	58	14	8	1	3	4	4
1992-93	**Montreal**	**NHL**	71	31	49	80	20	13	3	3	6	6 ♦
1993-94	**Montreal**	**NHL**	34	9	7	16	8	....	....	....	....	....
	Anaheim	**NHL**	22	6	4	10	14	....	....	....	....	....
1994-95	**Anaheim**	**NHL**	38	8	16	24	12	....	....	....	....	....
1995-96	Lugano	Switz.	36	25	28	53	10	4	2	2	4	0
	NHL Totals		**373**	**118**	**159**	**277**	**105**	**30**	**9**	**7**	**16**	**12**

a QMJHL Second All-Star Team (1987, 1988)
b AHL First All-Star Team (1989)
c Won Dudley "Red" Garrett Memorial Trophy (Top Rookie - AHL) (1989)
d Won John B. Sollenberger Trophy (Top Scorer - AHL) (1989)
e Won Les Cunningham Plaque (MVP - AHL) (1989)

Signed as a free agent by **Montreal**, September 27, 1986. Traded to **Anaheim** by **Montreal** for Ron Tugnutt, February 20, 1994.

LEBLANC, JOHN (leh-BLAHNK)

Right wing. Shoots left. 6'1", 190 lbs. Born, Campbellton, N.B., January 21, 1964.

			Regular Season					Playoffs				
Season	Club	Lea	GP	G	A	TP	PIM	GP	G	A	TP	PIM
1983-84	Hull	QMJHL	69	39	35	74	32	....	....	....	....	....
1984-85	New Brunswick	AUAA	24	25	34	59	32	....	....	....	....	....
1985-86a	New Brunswick	AUAA	24	38	28	66	35	....	....	....	....	....
1986-87	**Vancouver**	**NHL**	2	1	0	1	0	....	....	....	....	....
	Fredericton	AHL	75	40	30	70	27	....	....	....	....	....
1987-88	**Vancouver**	**NHL**	41	12	10	22	18	....	....	....	....	....
	Fredericton	AHL	35	26	25	51	54	15	6	7	13	34
1988-89	Milwaukee	IHL	61	39	31	70	42	....	....	....	....	....
	Edmonton	**NHL**	2	1	0	1	0	1	0	0	0	0
	Cape Breton	AHL	3	4	0	4	0	....	....	....	....	....
1989-90	Cape Breton	AHL	77	*54	34	88	50	6	4	0	4	4
1990-91			DID NOT PLAY									
1991-92	**Winnipeg**	**NHL**	16	6	1	7	6	....	....	....	....	....
	Moncton	AHL	56	31	22	53	24	10	3	2	5	8
1992-93	**Winnipeg**	**NHL**	3	0	0	0	2	....	....	....	....	....
	Moncton	AHL	77	48	40	88	29	5	2	1	3	6
1993-94	**Winnipeg**	**NHL**	17	6	2	8	2	....	....	....	....	....
	Moncton	AHL	41	25	26	51	38	20	3	6	9	6
1994-95	Springfield	AHL	65	39	34	73	32	....	....	....	....	....
	Winnipeg	**NHL**	2	0	0	0	0	....	....	....	....	....
1995-96	Orlando	IHL	60	22	24	46	20	....	....	....	....	....
	Fort Wayne	IHL	16	12	11	23	4	5	0	2	2	14
	NHL Totals		**83**	**26**	**13**	**39**	**28**	**1**	**0**	**0**	**0**	**0**

a Canadian University Player of the Year (1986)

Signed as a free agent by **Vancouver**, April 12, 1986. Traded to **Edmonton** by **Vancouver** with Vancouver's fifth round choice (Peter White) in 1989 Entry Draft for Doug Smith and Gregory C. Adams, March 7, 1989. Traded to **Winnipeg** by **Edmonton** with Edmonton's tenth round choice (Teemu Numminen) in 1992 Entry Draft for Winnipeg's fifth round choice (Ryan Haggerty) in 1991 Entry Draft, June 12, 1991.

LeBOUTILLIER, PETER — ANA.

Right wing. Shoots right. 6'1", 198 lbs. Born, Minnedosa, Man., January 11, 1975.
(NY Islanders' 6th choice, 144th overall, in 1993 Entry Draft).

			Regular Season					Playoffs				
Season	Club	Lea	GP	G	A	TP	PIM	GP	G	A	TP	PIM
1992-93	Red Deer	WHL	67	8	26	34	284	2	0	1	1	5
1993-94	Red Deer	WHL	66	19	20	39	300	2	0	1	1	4
1994-95	Red Deer	WHL	59	27	16	43	159	....	....	....	....	....
1995-96	Baltimore	AHL	68	7	9	16	228	11	0	0	0	33

Re-entered NHL Entry Draft, **Anaheim's** 5th choice, 133rd overall, in 1995 Entry Draft.

LeCLAIR, JOHN (luh-KLAIR) — PHI.

Left wing. Shoots left. 6'3", 226 lbs. Born, St. Albans, VT, July 5, 1969.
(Montreal's 2nd choice, 33rd overall, in 1987 Entry Draft).

			Regular Season					Playoffs				
Season	Club	Lea	GP	G	A	TP	PIM	GP	G	A	TP	PIM
1987-88	U. of Vermont	ECAC	31	12	22	34	62	....	....	....	....	....
1988-89	U. of Vermont	ECAC	18	9	12	21	40	....	....	....	....	....
1989-90	U. of Vermont	ECAC	10	10	6	16	38	....	....	....	....	....
1990-91a	U. of Vermont	ECAC	33	25	20	45	58	....	....	....	....	....
	Montreal	**NHL**	10	2	5	7	2	3	0	0	0	0
1991-92	**Montreal**	**NHL**	59	8	11	19	14	8	1	1	2	4
	Fredericton	AHL	8	7	7	14	10	2	0	0	0	4
1992-93	**Montreal**	**NHL**	72	19	25	44	33	20	4	6	10	14 ♦
1993-94	**Montreal**	**NHL**	74	19	24	43	32	7	2	1	3	8
1994-95b	**Montreal**	**NHL**	9	1	4	5	10	....	....	....	....	....
	Philadelphia	**NHL**	37	25	24	49	20	15	5	7	12	4
1995-96c	**Philadelphia**	**NHL**	82	51	46	97	64	11	6	5	11	6
	NHL Totals		**343**	**125**	**139**	**264**	**175**	**64**	**18**	**20**	**38**	**36**

a ECAC Second All-Star Team (1991)
b NHL First All-Star Team (1995)
c NHL Second All-Star Team (1996)

Played in NHL All-Star Game (1996)

Traded to **Philadelphia** by **Montreal** with Eric Desjardins and Gilbert Dionne for Mark Recchi and Philadelphia's third round choice (Martin Hohenberger) in 1995 Entry Draft, February 9, 1995.

LECLERC, MIKE — ANA.

Left wing. Shoots left. 6'1", 205 lbs. Born, Winnipeg, Man., November 10, 1976.
(Anaheim's 3rd choice, 55th overall, in 1995 Entry Draft).

			Regular Season					Playoffs				
Season	Club	Lea	GP	G	A	TP	PIM	GP	G	A	TP	PIM
1992-93	Victoria	WHL	70	4	11	15	118	....	....	....	....	....
1993-94	Victoria	WHL	68	29	11	40	112	....	....	....	....	....
1994-95	Prince George	WHL	43	20	36	56	78	....	....	....	....	....
	Brandon	WHL	23	5	8	13	50	18	10	6	16	33
1995-96a	Brandon	WHL	71	58	53	111	161	19	6	19	25	25

a WHL East Second All-Star Team (1996)

LECOMPTE, ERIC (luh-COMP) — CHI.

Left wing. Shoots left. 6'4", 190 lbs. Born, Montreal, Que., April 4, 1975.
(Chicago's 1st choice, 24th overall, in 1993 Entry Draft).

			Regular Season					Playoffs				
Season	Club	Lea	GP	G	A	TP	PIM	GP	G	A	TP	PIM
1991-92	Hull	QMJHL	60	16	17	33	138	6	1	0	1	4
1992-93	Hull	QMJHL	66	33	38	71	149	10	4	4	8	52
1993-94	Hull	QMJHL	62	39	49	88	171	20	10	10	20	68
1994-95	Hull	QMJHL	12	11	9	20	58	....	....	....	....	....
	St-Jean	QMJHL	18	9	10	19	54	....	....	....	....	....
	Sherbrooke	QMJHL	34	22	29	51	111	4	2	2	4	4
	Indianapolis	IHL	3	2	0	2	2	....	....	....	....	....
1995-96	Indianapolis	IHL	79	24	20	44	131	....	....	....	....	....

LEDYARD, GRANT — DAL.

Defense. Shoots left. 6'2", 195 lbs. Born, Winnipeg, Man., November 19, 1961.

			Regular Season					Playoffs				
Season	Club	Lea	GP	G	A	TP	PIM	GP	G	A	TP	PIM
1980-81	Saskatoon	WHL	71	9	28	37	148	....	....	....	....	....
1981-82	Fort Garry	MJHL	63	25	45	70	150	....	....	....	....	....
1982-83	Tulsa	CHL	80	13	29	42	115	....	....	....	....	....
1983-84a	Tulsa	CHL	58	9	17	26	71	9	5	4	9	10
1984-85	**NY Rangers**	**NHL**	**42**	**8**	**12**	**20**	**53**	**3**	**0**	**2**	**2**	**4**
	New Haven	AHL	36	6	20	26	18	....	....	....	....	....
1985-86	**NY Rangers**	**NHL**	**27**	**2**	**9**	**11**	**20**	....	....	....	....	....
	Los Angeles	**NHL**	**52**	**7**	**18**	**25**	**78**	....	....	....	....	....
1986-87	**Los Angeles**	**NHL**	**67**	**14**	**23**	**37**	**93**	**5**	**0**	**0**	**0**	**10**
1987-88	**Los Angeles**	**NHL**	**23**	**1**	**7**	**8**	**52**	....	....	....	....	....
	New Haven	AHL	3	2	1	3	4	....	....	....	....	....
	Washington	**NHL**	**21**	**4**	**3**	**7**	**14**	**14**	**1**	**0**	**1**	**30**
1988-89	**Washington**	**NHL**	**61**	**3**	**11**	**14**	**43**	....	....	....	....	....
	Buffalo	**NHL**	**13**	**1**	**5**	**6**	**8**	**5**	**1**	**2**	**3**	**2**
1989-90	**Buffalo**	**NHL**	**67**	**2**	**13**	**15**	**37**	....	....	....	....	....
1990-91	**Buffalo**	**NHL**	**60**	**8**	**23**	**31**	**46**	**6**	**3**	**3**	**6**	**10**
1991-92	**Buffalo**	**NHL**	**50**	**5**	**16**	**21**	**45**	....	....	....	....	....
1992-93	**Buffalo**	**NHL**	**50**	**2**	**14**	**16**	**45**	**8**	**0**	**0**	**0**	**8**
	Rochester	AHL	5	0	2	2	8	....	....	....	....	....
1993-94	**Dallas**	**NHL**	**84**	**9**	**37**	**46**	**42**	**9**	**1**	**2**	**3**	**6**
1994-95	**Dallas**	**NHL**	**38**	**5**	**13**	**18**	**20**	**3**	**0**	**0**	**0**	**2**
1995-96	**Dallas**	**NHL**	**73**	**5**	**19**	**24**	**20**	....	....	....	....	....
	NHL Totals		**728**	**76**	**223**	**299**	**616**	**53**	**6**	**9**	**15**	**72**

a Won Bob Gassoff Trophy (CHL's Most Improved Defenseman) (1984)

Signed as a free agent by **NY Rangers**, July 7, 1982. Traded to **Los Angeles** by **NY Rangers** with Roland Melanson for Los Angeles' fourth round choice (Mike Sullivan) in 1987 Entry Draft and Brian MacLellan, December 7, 1985. Traded to **Washington** by **Los Angeles** for Craig Laughlin, February 9, 1988. Traded to **Buffalo** by **Washington** with Clint Malarchuk and Washington's sixth round choice (Brian Holzinger) in 1991 Entry Draft for Calle Johansson and Buffalo's second round choice (Byron Dafoe) in 1989 Entry Draft, March 7, 1989. Signed as a free agent by **Dallas**, August 12, 1993.

LEETCH, BRIAN — NYR

Defense. Shoots left. 5'11", 190 lbs. Born, Corpus Christi, TX, March 3, 1968.
(NY Rangers' 1st choice, 9th overall, in 1986 Entry Draft).

			Regular Season					Playoffs				
Season	Club	Lea	GP	G	A	TP	PIM	GP	G	A	TP	PIM
1986-87ab	Boston College	H.E.	37	9	38	47	10	....	....	....	....	....
1987-88	U.S. National	....	50	13	61	74	38	....	....	....	....	....
	U.S. Olympic	....	6	1	5	6	4	....	....	....	....	....
	NY Rangers	**NHL**	**17**	**2**	**12**	**14**	**0**	....	....	....	....	....
1988-89cd	**NY Rangers**	**NHL**	**68**	**23**	**48**	**71**	**50**	**4**	**3**	**2**	**5**	**2**
1989-90	**NY Rangers**	**NHL**	**72**	**11**	**45**	**56**	**26**	....	....	....	....	....
1990-91e	**NY Rangers**	**NHL**	**80**	**16**	**72**	**88**	**42**	**6**	**1**	**3**	**4**	**0**
1991-92fg	**NY Rangers**	**NHL**	**80**	**22**	**80**	**102**	**26**	**13**	**4**	**11**	**15**	**4**
1992-93	**NY Rangers**	**NHL**	**36**	**6**	**30**	**36**	**26**	....	....	....	....	....
1993-94eh	**NY Rangers**	**NHL**	**84**	**23**	**56**	**79**	**67**	**23**	**11**	***23**	***34**	**6 ♦**
1994-95	**NY Rangers**	**NHL**	**48**	**9**	**32**	**41**	**18**	**10**	**6**	**8**	**14**	**8**
1995-96e	**NY Rangers**	**NHL**	**82**	**15**	**70**	**85**	**30**	**11**	**1**	**6**	**7**	**4**
	NHL Totals		**567**	**127**	**445**	**572**	**285**	**67**	**26**	**53**	**79**	**24**

a Hockey East First All-Star Team (1987)
b NCAA East First All-American Team (1987)
c NHL All-Rookie Team (1989)
d Won Calder Memorial Trophy (1989)
e NHL Second All-Star Team (1991, 1994, 1996)
f Won James Norris Memorial Trophy (1992)
g NHL First All-Star Team (1992)
h Won Conn Smythe Trophy (1994)

Played in NHL All-Star Game (1990-92, 1994, 1996)

LEFEBVRE, CHRISTIAN (luh-FAHV) — CGY.

Defense. Shoots left. 6'5", 212 lbs. Born, Montreal, Que., March 3, 1978.
(Calgary's 6th choice, 94th overall, in 1996 Entry Draft).

			Regular Season					Playoffs				
Season	Club	Lea	GP	G	A	TP	PIM	GP	G	A	TP	PIM
1994-95	Granby	QMJHL	24	1	1	2	11	4	0	0	0	0
1995-96	Granby	QMJHL	36	4	6	10	41	20	2	2	4	30

LEFEBVRE, SYLVAIN (luh-FAYV) — COL.

Defense. Shoots left. 6'2", 205 lbs. Born, Richmond, Que., October 14, 1967.

			Regular Season					Playoffs				
Season	Club	Lea	GP	G	A	TP	PIM	GP	G	A	TP	PIM
1984-85	Laval	QMJHL	66	7	5	12	31	....	....	....	....	....
1985-86	Laval	QMJHL	71	8	17	25	48	14	1	0	1	25
1986-87	Laval	QMJHL	70	10	36	46	44	15	1	6	7	12
1987-88	Sherbrooke	AHL	79	3	24	27	73	6	2	3	5	4
1988-89a	Sherbrooke	AHL	77	15	32	47	119	6	1	3	4	4
1989-90	**Montreal**	**NHL**	**68**	**3**	**10**	**13**	**61**	**6**	**0**	**0**	**0**	**2**
1990-91	**Montreal**	**NHL**	**63**	**5**	**18**	**23**	**30**	**11**	**1**	**0**	**1**	**6**
1991-92	**Montreal**	**NHL**	**69**	**3**	**14**	**17**	**91**	**2**	**0**	**0**	**0**	**2**
1992-93	**Toronto**	**NHL**	**81**	**2**	**12**	**14**	**90**	**21**	**3**	**3**	**6**	**20**
1993-94	**Toronto**	**NHL**	**84**	**2**	**9**	**11**	**79**	**18**	**0**	**3**	**3**	**16**
1994-95	**Quebec**	**NHL**	**48**	**2**	**11**	**13**	**17**	**6**	**0**	**2**	**2**	**2**
1995-96	**Colorado**	**NHL**	**75**	**5**	**11**	**16**	**49**	**22**	**0**	**5**	**5**	**12 ♦**
	NHL Totals		**488**	**22**	**85**	**107**	**417**	**86**	**4**	**13**	**17**	**60**

a AHL Second All-Star Team (1989)

Signed as a free agent by **Montreal**, September 24, 1986. Traded to **Toronto** by **Montreal** for Toronto's third round choice (Martin Belanger) in 1994 Entry Draft, August 20, 1992. Traded to **Quebec** by **Toronto** with Wendel Clark, Landon Wilson and Toronto's first round choice (Jeffrey Kealty) in 1994 Entry Draft for Mats Sundin, Garth Butcher, Todd Warriner and Philadelphia's first round choice (previously acquired by Quebec — later traded to Washington — Washington selected Nolan Baumgartner) in 1994 Entry Draft, June 28, 1994.

LEGG, MIKE — N.J.

Right wing. Shoots right. 5'11", 165 lbs. Born, London, Ont., May 25, 1975.
(New Jersey's 11th choice, 273rd overall, in 1993 Entry Draft).

			Regular Season					Playoffs				
Season	Club	Lea	GP	G	A	TP	PIM	GP	G	A	TP	PIM
1993-94	U. of Michigan	CCHA	37	10	13	23	20	....	....	....	....	....
1994-95	U. of Michigan	CCHA	39	14	23	37	22	....	....	....	....	....
1995-96	U. of Michigan	CCHA	42	15	25	40	24	....	....	....	....	....

LEHTERA, TERO — FLA.

Left wing. Shoots right. 6', 185 lbs. Born, Espoo, Finland, April 21, 1972.
(Florida's 9th choice, 235th overall, in 1994 Entry Draft).

			Regular Season					Playoffs				
Season	Club	Lea	GP	G	A	TP	PIM	GP	G	A	TP	PIM
1993-94	Espoo	Fin.	48	19	27	46	2	....	....	....	....	....
1994-95	Malmo	Swe.	37	12	11	23	10	9	0	1	1	0
1995-96	Jokerit	Fin.	48	11	12	23	27	11	2	5	7	2

LEHTINEN, JERE (lehkh-TIH-nehn) — DAL.

Right wing. Shoots right. 6', 192 lbs. Born, Espoo, Finland, June 24, 1973.
(Minnesota's 3rd choice, 88th overall, in 1992 Entry Draft).

			Regular Season					Playoffs				
Season	Club	Lea	GP	G	A	TP	PIM	GP	G	A	TP	PIM
1990-91	Espoo	Fin. 2	32	15	9	24	12	....	....	....	....	....
1991-92	Espoo	Fin. 2	43	32	17	49	6	....	....	....	....	....
1992-93	Kiekko-Espoo	Fin.	45	13	14	27	6	....	....	....	....	....
1993-94	TPS	Fin.	42	19	20	39	6	11	11	2	13	2
1994-95	TPS	Fin.	39	19	23	42	33	13	8	6	14	4
1995-96	**Dallas**	**NHL**	**57**	**6**	**22**	**28**	**16**	....	....	....	....	....
	Michigan	IHL	1	1	0	1	0	....	....	....	....	....
	NHL Totals		**57**	**6**	**22**	**28**	**16**	....	....	....	....	....

LEMIEUX, CLAUDE (lehm-YOO) — COL.

Right wing. Shoots right. 6'1", 215 lbs. Born, Buckingham, Que., July 16, 1965.
(Montreal's 2nd choice, 26th overall, in 1983 Entry Draft).

			Regular Season					Playoffs				
Season	Club	Lea	GP	G	A	TP	PIM	GP	G	A	TP	PIM
1982-83	Trois-Rivières	QMJHL	62	28	38	66	187	4	1	0	1	30
1983-84	**Montreal**	**NHL**	**8**	**1**	**1**	**2**	**12**	....	....	....	....	....
	Verdun	QMJHL	51	41	45	86	225	9	8	12	20	63
	Nova Scotia	AHL	....	....	....	....	....	2	1	0	1	0
1984-85	**Montreal**	**NHL**	**1**	**0**	**1**	**1**	**7**	....	....	....	....	....
a	Verdun	QMJHL	52	58	66	124	152	14	23	17	40	38
1985-86	**Montreal**	**NHL**	**10**	**1**	**2**	**3**	**22**	**20**	**10**	**6**	**16**	**68 ♦**
	Sherbrooke	AHL	58	21	32	53	145	....	....	....	....	....
1986-87	**Montreal**	**NHL**	**76**	**27**	**26**	**53**	**156**	**17**	**4**	**9**	**13**	**41**
1987-88	**Montreal**	**NHL**	**78**	**31**	**30**	**61**	**137**	**11**	**3**	**2**	**5**	**20**
1988-89	**Montreal**	**NHL**	**69**	**29**	**22**	**51**	**136**	**18**	**4**	**3**	**7**	**58**
1989-90	**Montreal**	**NHL**	**39**	**8**	**10**	**18**	**106**	**11**	**1**	**3**	**4**	**38**
1990-91	**New Jersey**	**NHL**	**78**	**30**	**17**	**47**	**105**	**7**	**4**	**0**	**4**	**34**
1991-92	**New Jersey**	**NHL**	**74**	**41**	**27**	**68**	**109**	**7**	**4**	**3**	**7**	**26**
1992-93	**New Jersey**	**NHL**	**77**	**30**	**51**	**81**	**155**	**5**	**2**	**0**	**2**	**19**
1993-94	**New Jersey**	**NHL**	**79**	**18**	**26**	**44**	**86**	**20**	**7**	**11**	**18**	**44**
1994-95b	**New Jersey**	**NHL**	**45**	**6**	**13**	**19**	**86**	**20**	***13**	**3**	**16**	**20 ♦**
1995-96	**Colorado**	**NHL**	**79**	**39**	**32**	**71**	**117**	**19**	**5**	**7**	**12**	**55 ♦**
	NHL Totals		**713**	**261**	**258**	**519**	**1234**	**155**	**57**	**47**	**104**	**423**

a QMJHL First All-Star Team (1985)
b Won Conn Smythe Trophy (1995)

Traded to **New Jersey** by **Montreal** for Sylvain Turgeon, September 4, 1990. Traded to **NY Islanders** by **New Jersey** for Steve Thomas, October 3, 1995. Traded to **Colorado** by **NY Islanders** for Wendel Clark, October 3, 1995.

LEMIEUX, JOCELYN (lehm-YOO)

Right wing. Shoots left. 5'10", 200 lbs. Born, Mont-Laurier, Que., November 18, 1967.
(St. Louis' 1st choice, 10th overall, in 1986 Entry Draft).

			Regular Season					Playoffs				
Season	Club	Lea	GP	G	A	TP	PIM	GP	G	A	TP	PIM
1984-85	Laval	QMJHL	68	13	19	32	92	....	....	....	....	....
1985-86a	Laval	QMJHL	71	57	68	125	131	14	9	15	24	37
1986-87	**St. Louis**	**NHL**	**53**	**10**	**8**	**18**	**94**	**5**	**0**	**1**	**1**	**6**
1987-88	**St. Louis**	**NHL**	**23**	**1**	**0**	**1**	**42**	**5**	**0**	**0**	**0**	**15**
	Peoria	IHL	8	0	5	5	35	....	....	....	....	....
1988-89	**Montreal**	**NHL**	**1**	**0**	**1**	**1**	**0**	....	....	....	....	....
	Sherbrooke	AHL	73	25	28	53	134	4	3	1	4	6
1989-90	**Montreal**	**NHL**	**34**	**4**	**2**	**6**	**61**	....	....	....	....	....
	Chicago	**NHL**	**39**	**10**	**11**	**21**	**47**	**18**	**1**	**8**	**9**	**28**
1990-91	**Chicago**	**NHL**	**67**	**6**	**7**	**13**	**119**	**4**	**0**	**0**	**0**	**0**
1991-92	**Chicago**	**NHL**	**78**	**6**	**10**	**16**	**80**	**18**	**3**	**1**	**4**	**33**
1992-93	**Chicago**	**NHL**	**81**	**10**	**21**	**31**	**111**	**4**	**1**	**0**	**1**	**2**
1993-94	**Chicago**	**NHL**	**66**	**12**	**8**	**20**	**63**	....	....	....	....	....
	Hartford	**NHL**	**16**	**6**	**1**	**7**	**19**	....	....	....	....	....
1994-95	**Hartford**	**NHL**	**41**	**6**	**5**	**11**	**32**	....	....	....	....	....
1995-96	**Hartford**	**NHL**	**29**	**1**	**2**	**3**	**31**	....	....	....	....	....
	New Jersey	**NHL**	**18**	**0**	**1**	**1**	**4**	....	....	....	....	....
	Calgary	**NHL**	**20**	**4**	**4**	**8**	**10**	**4**	**0**	**0**	**0**	**0**
	NHL Totals		**566**	**76**	**81**	**157**	**713**	**58**	**5**	**10**	**15**	**84**

a QMJHL First All-Star Team (1986)

Traded to **Montreal** by **St. Louis** with Darrell May and St. Louis' second round choice (Patrice Brisebois) in the 1989 Entry Draft for Sergio Momesso and Vincent Riendeau, August 9, 1988. Traded to **Chicago** by **Montreal** for Chicago's third round choice (Charles Poulin) in 1990 Entry Draft, January 5, 1990. Traded to **Hartford** by **Chicago** with Frantisek Kucera for Gary Suter, Randy Cunneyworth and Hartford's third round choice (later traded to Vancouver — Vancouver selected Larry Courville) in 1995 Entry Draft, March 11, 1994. Traded to **New Jersey** by **Hartford** with Hartford's second round choice in 1998 Entry Draft for Jim Dowd and New Jersey's second round choice in 1997 Entry Draft, December 19, 1995. Traded to **Calgary** by **New Jersey** with Tommy Albelin and Cale Hulse for Phil Housley and Dan Keczmer, February 26, 1996.

LEMIEUX, MARIO (lehm-YOO) PIT.

Center. Shoots right. 6'4", 225 lbs. Born, Montreal, Que., October 5, 1965.
(Pittsburgh's 1st choice, 1st overall, in 1984 Entry Draft).

			Regular Season					Playoffs				
Season	Club	Lea	GP	G	A	TP	PIM	GP	G	A	TP	PIM
1981-82	Laval	QMJHL	64	30	66	96	22	18	5	9	14	31
1982-83a	Laval	QMJHL	66	84	100	184	76	12	14	18	32	18
1983-84bc	Laval	QMJHL	70	*133	*149	*282	92	14	*29	*23	*52	29
1984-85de	**Pittsburgh**	**NHL**	**73**	**43**	**57**	**100**	**54**	....	....	....	....	....
1985-86fg	**Pittsburgh**	**NHL**	**79**	**48**	**93**	**141**	**43**	....	....	....	....	....
1986-87f	**Pittsburgh**	**NHL**	**63**	**54**	**53**	**107**	**57**	....	....	....	....	....
1987-88 ghijkl	**Pittsburgh**	**NHL**	**77**	***70**	**98**	***168**	**92**	....	....	....	....	....
1988-89ijlm	**Pittsburgh**	**NHL**	**76**	***85**	***114**	***199**	**100**	**11**	**12**	**7**	**19**	**16**
1989-90	**Pittsburgh**	**NHL**	**59**	**45**	**78**	**123**	**78**	....	....	....	....	....
1990-91n	**Pittsburgh**	**NHL**	**26**	**19**	**26**	**45**	**30**	**23**	**16**	***28**	***44**	**16** ♦
1991-92fino	**Pittsburgh**	**NHL**	**64**	**44**	**87**	***131**	**94**	**15**	***16**	**18**	***34**	**2** ♦
1992-93 ghijpq	**Pittsburgh**	**NHL**	**60**	**69**	**91**	***160**	**38**	**11**	**8**	**10**	**18**	**10**
1993-94	**Pittsburgh**	**NHL**	**22**	**17**	**20**	**37**	**32**	**6**	**4**	**3**	**7**	**2**
1994-95			DID NOT PLAY									
1995-96ghij	**Pittsburgh**	**NHL**	**70**	***69**	***92**	***161**	**54**	**18**	**11**	**16**	**27**	**33**
	NHL Totals		**669**	**563**	**809**	**1372**	**672**	**84**	**67**	**82**	**149**	**79**

a QMJHL Second All-Star Team (1983)
b QMJHL First All-Star Team (1984)
c Canadian Major Junior Player of the Year (1984)
d Won Calder Memorial Trophy (1985)
e NHL All-Rookie Team (1985)
f NHL Second All-Star Team (1986, 1987, 1992)
g Won Lester B. Pearson Award (1986, 1988, 1993, 1996)
h Won Hart Trophy (1988, 1993, 1996)
i Won Art Ross Trophy (1988, 1989, 1992, 1993, 1996)
j NHL First All-Star Team (1988, 1989, 1993, 1996)
k Won Dodge Performance of the Year Award (1988)
l Won Dodge Performer of the Year Award (1988, 1989)
m Won Dodge Ram Tough Award (1989)
n Won Conn Smythe Trophy (1991, 1992)
o Won ProSet/NHL Player of the Year Award (1992)
p Won Bill Masterton Memorial Trophy (1993)
q Won Alka-Seltzer Plus Award (1993)

Played in NHL All-Star Game (1985, 1986, 1988-90, 1992, 1996)

LEPLER, PAUL MTL.

Defense. Shoots left. 6'3", 190 lbs. Born, Granite Falls, MN, November 26, 1972.
(Montreal's 14th choice, 237th overall, in 1991 Entry Draft).

			Regular Season					Playoffs				
Season	Club	Lea	GP	G	A	TP	PIM	GP	G	A	TP	PIM
1992-93	St. Cloud	WCHA	26	2	4	6	16	....	....	....	....	....
1993-94	St. Cloud	WCHA	35	1	4	5	48	....	....	....	....	....
1994-95	St. Cloud	WCHA	38	3	3	6	68	....	....	....	....	....
1995-96	St. Cloud	WCHA	26	1	5	6	66	....	....	....	....	....

LEROUX, FRANCOIS (leh-ROO) PIT.

Defense. Shoots left. 6'5", 235 lbs. Born, Ste.-Adele, Que., April 18, 1970.
(Edmonton's 1st choice, 19th overall, in 1988 Entry Draft).

			Regular Season					Playoffs				
Season	Club	Lea	GP	G	A	TP	PIM	GP	G	A	TP	PIM
1987-88	St-Jean	QMJHL	58	3	8	11	143	7	2	0	2	21
1988-89	**Edmonton**	**NHL**	**2**	**0**	**0**	**0**	**0**	....	....	....	....	....
	St-Jean	QMJHL	57	8	34	42	185	....	....	....	....	....
1989-90	**Edmonton**	**NHL**	**3**	**0**	**1**	**1**	**0**	....	....	....	....	....
	Victoriaville	QMJHL	54	4	33	37	169	....	....	....	....	....
1990-91	**Edmonton**	**NHL**	**1**	**0**	**2**	**2**	**0**	....	....	....	....	....
	Cape Breton	AHL	71	2	7	9	124	4	0	1	1	19
1991-92	**Edmonton**	**NHL**	**4**	**0**	**0**	**0**	**7**	....	....	....	....	....
	Cape Breton	AHL	61	7	22	29	114	5	0	0	0	8
1992-93	**Edmonton**	**NHL**	**1**	**0**	**0**	**0**	**4**	....	....	....	....	....
	Cape Breton	AHL	55	10	24	34	139	16	0	5	5	29
1993-94	**Ottawa**	**NHL**	**23**	**0**	**1**	**1**	**70**	....	....	....	....	....
	P.E.I.	AHL	25	4	6	10	52	....	....	....	....	....
1994-95	P.E.I.	AHL	45	4	14	18	137	....	....	....	....	....
	Pittsburgh	**NHL**	**40**	**0**	**2**	**2**	**114**	**12**	**0**	**2**	**2**	**14**
1995-96	**Pittsburgh**	**NHL**	**66**	**2**	**9**	**11**	**161**	**18**	**1**	**1**	**2**	**20**
	NHL Totals		**140**	**2**	**15**	**17**	**356**	**30**	**1**	**3**	**4**	**34**

Claimed on waivers by **Ottawa** from **Edmonton**, October 6, 1993. Claimed by **Pittsburgh** from **Ottawa** in NHL Waiver Draft, January 18, 1995.

LEROUX, JEAN-YVES (leh-ROO) CHI.

Left wing. Shoots left. 6'2", 193 lbs. Born, Montreal, Que., June 24, 1976.
(Chicago's 2nd choice, 40th overall, in 1994 Entry Draft).

			Regular Season					Playoffs				
Season	Club	Lea	GP	G	A	TP	PIM	GP	G	A	TP	PIM
1992-93	Beauport	QMJHL	62	20	25	45	33	....	....	....	....	....
1993-94a	Beauport	QMJHL	45	14	25	39	43	15	7	6	13	33
1994-95	Beauport	QMJHL	59	19	33	52	125	17	4	6	10	39
1995-96	Beauport	QMJHL	54	41	41	82	176	20	5	18	23	20

a QMJHL Second All-Star Team (1994)

LESCHYSHYN, CURTIS (luh-SIH-shuhn) COL.

Defense. Shoots left. 6'1", 205 lbs. Born, Thompson, Man., September 21, 1969.
(Quebec's 1st choice, 3rd overall, in 1988 Entry Draft).

			Regular Season					Playoffs				
Season	Club	Lea	GP	G	A	TP	PIM	GP	G	A	TP	PIM
1986-87	Saskatoon	WHL	70	14	26	40	107	11	1	5	6	14
1987-88	Saskatoon	WHL	56	14	41	55	86	10	2	5	7	16
1988-89	**Quebec**	**NHL**	**71**	**4**	**9**	**13**	**71**	....	....	....	....	....
1989-90	**Quebec**	**NHL**	**68**	**2**	**6**	**8**	**44**	....	....	....	....	....
1990-91	**Quebec**	**NHL**	**55**	**3**	**7**	**10**	**49**	....	....	....	....	....
1991-92	**Quebec**	**NHL**	**42**	**5**	**12**	**17**	**42**	....	....	....	....	....
	Halifax	AHL	6	0	2	2	4	....	....	....	....	....
1992-93	**Quebec**	**NHL**	**82**	**9**	**23**	**32**	**61**	**6**	**1**	**1**	**2**	**6**
1993-94	**Quebec**	**NHL**	**72**	**5**	**17**	**22**	**65**	....	....	....	....	....
1994-95	**Quebec**	**NHL**	**44**	**2**	**13**	**15**	**20**	**3**	**0**	**1**	**1**	**4**
1995-96	**Colorado**	**NHL**	**77**	**4**	**15**	**19**	**73**	**17**	**1**	**2**	**3**	**8** ♦
	NHL Totals		**511**	**34**	**102**	**136**	**425**	**26**	**2**	**4**	**6**	**18**

LETANG, ALAN MTL.

Defense. Shoots left. 6', 185 lbs. Born, Renfrew, Ont., September 4, 1975.
(Montreal's 10th choice, 203rd overall, in 1993 Entry Draft).

			Regular Season					Playoffs				
Season	Club	Lea	GP	G	A	TP	PIM	GP	G	A	TP	PIM
1991-92	Cornwall	OHL	47	1	4	5	16	6	0	0	0	2
1992-93	Newmarket	OHL	66	1	25	26	14	6	0	3	3	2
1993-94	Newmarket	OHL	58	3	21	24	30	....	....	....	....	....
1994-95	Sarnia	OHL	62	5	36	41	35	4	2	2	4	6
1995-96	Fredericton	AHL	71	0	26	26	40	10	0	3	3	4

LEVEQUE, GUY (luv-VEHK)

Center. Shoots right. 5'11", 180 lbs. Born, Kingston, Ont., December 28, 1972.
(Los Angeles' 1st choice, 42nd overall, in 1991 Entry Draft).

			Regular Season					Playoffs				
Season	Club	Lea	GP	G	A	TP	PIM	GP	G	A	TP	PIM
1989-90	Cornwall	OHL	62	10	15	25	30	3	0	0	0	4
1990-91	Cornwall	OHL	66	41	56	97	34	....	....	....	....	....
1991-92	Cornwall	OHL	37	23	36	59	40	6	3	5	8	2
1992-93	**Los Angeles**	**NHL**	**12**	**2**	**1**	**3**	**19**	....	....	....	....	....
	Phoenix	IHL	56	27	30	57	71	....	....	....	....	....
1993-94	**Los Angeles**	**NHL**	**5**	**0**	**1**	**1**	**2**	....	....	....	....	....
	Phoenix	IHL	39	10	16	26	47	....	....	....	....	....
1994-95	Cdn. National	....	31	17	17	34	14	....	....	....	....	....
	Phoenix	IHL	2	0	0	0	15	....	....	....	....	....
	St. John's	AHL	37	8	14	22	31	3	0	0	0	0
1995-96	Minnesota	IHL	12	1	4	5	2	....	....	....	....	....
	NHL Totals		**17**	**2**	**2**	**4**	**21**	....	....	....	....	....

Traded to **Toronto** by **Los Angeles** with Dixon Ward, Kelly Fairchild and Shayne Toporowski for Eric Lacroix, Chris Snell and Toronto's fourth round choice (Eric Belanger) in 1996 Entry Draft, October 3, 1994.

LEVINS, SCOTT

Center/Right wing. Shoots right. 6'4", 210 lbs. Born, Spokane, WA, January 30, 1970.
(Winnipeg's 4th choice, 75th overall, in 1990 Entry Draft).

			Regular Season					Playoffs				
Season	Club	Lea	GP	G	A	TP	PIM	GP	G	A	TP	PIM
1989-90a	Tri-Cities	WHL	71	25	37	62	132	6	2	3	5	18
1990-91	Moncton	AHL	74	12	26	38	133	4	0	0	0	4
1991-92	Moncton	AHL	69	15	18	33	271	11	3	4	7	30
1992-93	**Winnipeg**	**NHL**	**9**	**0**	**1**	**1**	**18**	....	....	....	....	....
	Moncton	AHL	54	22	26	48	158	5	1	3	4	14
1993-94	**Florida**	**NHL**	**29**	**5**	**6**	**11**	**69**	....	....	....	....	....
	Ottawa	**NHL**	**33**	**3**	**5**	**8**	**93**	....	....	....	....	....
1994-95	**Ottawa**	**NHL**	**24**	**5**	**6**	**11**	**51**	....	....	....	....	....
	P.E.I.	AHL	6	0	4	4	14	....	....	....	....	....
1995-96	**Ottawa**	**NHL**	**27**	**0**	**2**	**2**	**80**	....	....	....	....	....
	Detroit	IHL	9	0	0	0	9	....	....	....	....	....
	NHL Totals		**122**	**13**	**20**	**33**	**311**	....	....	....	....	....

a WHL West Second All-Star Team (1990)

Claimed by **Florida** from **Winnipeg** in Expansion Draft, June 24, 1993. Traded to **Ottawa** by **Florida** with Evgeny Davydov, Florida's sixth round choice (Mike Gaffney) in 1994 Entry Draft and Dallas' fourth round choice (previously acquired by Florida — Ottawa selected Kevin Bolibruck) in 1995 Entry Draft for Bob Kudelski, January 6, 1994.

LIDSTER, DOUG NYR

Defense. Shoots right. 6'1", 190 lbs. Born, Kamloops, B.C., October 18, 1960.
(Vancouver's 6th choice, 133rd overall, in 1980 Entry Draft).

			Regular Season					Playoffs				
Season	Club	Lea	GP	G	A	TP	PIM	GP	G	A	TP	PIM
1977-78	Seattle	WHL	2	0	0	0	0	....	....	....	....	....
1978-79	Kamloops	BCJHL	59	36	47	83	50	....	....	....	....	....
1979-80	Colorado	WCHA	39	18	25	43	52	....	....	....	....	....
1980-81	Colorado	WCHA	36	10	30	40	54	....	....	....	....	....
1981-82	Colorado	WCHA	36	13	22	35	32	....	....	....	....	....
1982-83	Colorado	WCHA	34	15	41	56	30	....	....	....	....	....
1983-84	Cdn. National	....	59	6	20	26	28	....	....	....	....	....
	Cdn. Olympic	....	7	0	2	2	2	....	....	....	....	....
	Vancouver	**NHL**	**8**	**0**	**0**	**0**	**4**	**2**	**0**	**1**	**1**	**0**
1984-85	**Vancouver**	**NHL**	**78**	**6**	**24**	**30**	**55**	....	....	....	....	....
1985-86	**Vancouver**	**NHL**	**78**	**12**	**16**	**28**	**56**	**3**	**0**	**1**	**1**	**2**
1986-87	**Vancouver**	**NHL**	**80**	**12**	**51**	**63**	**40**	....	....	....	....	....
1987-88	**Vancouver**	**NHL**	**64**	**4**	**32**	**36**	**105**	....	....	....	....	....
1988-89	**Vancouver**	**NHL**	**63**	**5**	**17**	**22**	**78**	**7**	**1**	**1**	**2**	**9**
1989-90	**Vancouver**	**NHL**	**80**	**8**	**28**	**36**	**36**	....	....	....	....	....
1990-91	**Vancouver**	**NHL**	**78**	**6**	**32**	**38**	**77**	**6**	**0**	**2**	**2**	**6**
1991-92	**Vancouver**	**NHL**	**66**	**6**	**23**	**29**	**39**	**11**	**1**	**2**	**3**	**11**
1992-93	**Vancouver**	**NHL**	**71**	**6**	**19**	**25**	**36**	**12**	**0**	**3**	**3**	**8**
1993-94	**NY Rangers**	**NHL**	**34**	**0**	**2**	**2**	**33**	**9**	**2**	**0**	**2**	**10** ♦
1994-95	**St. Louis**	**NHL**	**37**	**2**	**7**	**9**	**12**	**4**	**0**	**0**	**0**	**2**
1995-96	**NY Rangers**	**NHL**	**59**	**5**	**9**	**14**	**50**	**7**	**1**	**0**	**1**	**6**
	NHL Totals		**796**	**72**	**260**	**332**	**621**	**61**	**5**	**10**	**15**	**54**

Traded to **NY Rangers** by **Vancouver** to complete June 20, 1993 trade which sent John Vanbiesbrouck to Vancouver for future considerations, June 25, 1993. Traded to **St. Louis** by **NY Rangers** with Esa Tikkanen for Petr Nedved, July 24, 1994. Traded to **NY Rangers** by **St. Louis** for Jay Wells, July 28, 1995.

LIDSTROM, NICKLAS (LID-struhm) DET.

Defense. Shoots left. 6'2", 185 lbs. Born, Vasteras, Sweden, April 28, 1970.
(Detroit's 3rd choice, 53rd overall, in 1989 Entry Draft).

			Regular Season					Playoffs				
Season	Club	Lea	GP	G	A	TP	PIM	GP	G	A	TP	PIM
1987-88	Vasteras	Swe. 2	3	0	0	0	....	....	....	....	....	....
1988-89	Vasteras	Swe.	19	0	2	2	4	....	....	....	....	....
1989-90	Vasteras	Swe.	39	8	8	16	14	2	0	1	1	2
1990-91	Vasteras	Swe.	38	4	19	23	2	4	0	0	0	4
1991-92a	**Detroit**	**NHL**	**80**	**11**	**49**	**60**	**22**	**11**	**1**	**2**	**3**	**0**
1992-93	**Detroit**	**NHL**	**84**	**7**	**34**	**41**	**28**	**7**	**1**	**0**	**1**	**0**
1993-94	**Detroit**	**NHL**	**84**	**10**	**46**	**56**	**26**	**7**	**3**	**2**	**5**	**0**
1994-95	Vasteras	Swe.	13	2	10	12	4	....	....	....	....	....
	Detroit	**NHL**	**43**	**10**	**16**	**26**	**6**	**18**	**4**	**12**	**16**	**8**
1995-96	**Detroit**	**NHL**	**81**	**17**	**50**	**67**	**20**	**19**	**5**	**9**	**14**	**10**
	NHL Totals		**372**	**55**	**195**	**250**	**102**	**62**	**14**	**25**	**39**	**18**

a NHL/Upper Deck All-Rookie Team (1992)

Played in NHL All-Star Game (1996)

LILLEY, JOHN

Right wing. Shoots right. 5'9", 170 lbs.   Born, Wakefield, MA, August 3, 1972.
(Winnipeg's 8th choice, 140th overall, in 1990 Entry Draft).

			Regular Season					Playoffs				
Season	Club	Lea	GP	G	A	TP	PIM	GP	G	A	TP	PIM
1991-92	Boston U.	H.E.	23	9	9	18	43	....	....	....	....	....
1992-93	Boston U.	H.E.	4	0	1	1	13	....	....	....	....	....
	Seattle	WHL	45	22	28	50	55	5	1	3	4	9
1993-94	U.S. National	....	58	27	23	50	117	....	....	....	....	....
	U.S. Olympic	....	8	3	1	4	4	....	....	....	....	....
	Anaheim	**NHL**	**13**	**1**	**6**	**7**	**8**	....	....	....	....	....
	San Diego	IHL	2	2	1	3	0	....	....	....	....	....
1994-95	San Diego	IHL	45	9	15	24	71	2	0	0	0	2
	Anaheim	**NHL**	**9**	**2**	**2**	**4**	**5**	....	....	....	....	....
1995-96	**Anaheim**	**NHL**	**1**	**0**	**0**	**0**	**0**	....	....	....	....	....
	Baltimore	AHL	12	2	4	6	34	....	....	....	....	....
	Los Angeles	IHL	64	12	20	32	112	....	....	....	....	....
	NHL Totals		**23**	**3**	**8**	**11**	**13**					

Signed as a free agent by **Anaheim**, March 9, 1994.

LIND, JUHA   DAL.

Center. Shoots left. 5'11", 160 lbs.   Born, Helsinki, Finland, January 2, 1974.
(Minnesota's 6th choice, 178th overall, in 1992 Entry Draft).

			Regular Season					Playoffs				
Season	Club	Lea	GP	G	A	TP	PIM	GP	G	A	TP	PIM
1991-92	Jokerit Jrs.	Fin.	28	16	24	40	10	....	....	....	....	....
1992-93	Vantaa	Fin. 2	25	8	12	20	8	....	....	....	....	....
	Jokerit	Fin.	6	0	0	0	2	1	0	0	0	0
1993-94	Jokerit	Fin.	47	17	11	28	37	11	2	5	7	4
1994-95	Jokerit	Fin.	50	10	8	18	12	11	1	2	3	6
1995-96	Jokerit	Fin.	50	15	22	37	32	11	4	5	9	4

LINDEN, JAMIE   FLA.

Right wing. Shoots right. 6'3", 185 lbs.   Born, Medicine Hat, Alta., July 19, 1972.

			Regular Season					Playoffs				
Season	Club	Lea	GP	G	A	TP	PIM	GP	G	A	TP	PIM
1988-89	Portland	WHL	1	0	1	1	0	....	....	....	....	....
1989-90	Portland	WHL	67	5	7	12	124	....	....	....	....	....
1990-91	Portland	WHL	2	0	1	1	6	....	....	....	....	....
	Prince Albert	WHL	64	9	12	21	114	3	0	0	0	0
1992-93	Spokane	WHL	15	3	1	4	58	....	....	....	....	....
	Medicine Hat	WHL	50	9	9	18	147	10	1	6	7	15
1993-94	Cincinnati	IHL	47	1	5	6	55	2	0	0	0	2
	Birmingham	ECHL	16	3	7	10	38	....	....	....	....	....
1994-95	Cincinnati	IHL	51	3	6	9	173	....	....	....	....	....
	Florida	**NHL**	**4**	**0**	**0**	**0**	**17**	....	....	....	....	....
1995-96	Carolina	AHL	50	4	8	12	92	....	....	....	....	....
	NHL Totals		**4**	**0**	**0**	**0**	**17**					

Signed as a free agent by **Florida**, October 4, 1993.

LINDEN, TREVOR   VAN.

Center/Right wing. Shoots right. 6'4", 210 lbs.   Born, Medicine Hat, Alta., April 11, 1970.
(Vancouver's 1st choice, 2nd overall, in 1988 Entry Draft).

			Regular Season					Playoffs				
Season	Club	Lea	GP	G	A	TP	PIM	GP	G	A	TP	PIM
1986-87	Medicine Hat	WHL	72	14	22	36	59	20	5	4	9	17
1987-88	Medicine Hat	WHL	67	46	64	110	76	16	*13	12	25	19
1988-89a	**Vancouver**	**NHL**	**80**	**30**	**29**	**59**	**41**	**7**	**3**	**4**	**7**	**8**
1989-90	**Vancouver**	**NHL**	**73**	**21**	**30**	**51**	**43**	....	....	....	....	....
1990-91	**Vancouver**	**NHL**	**80**	**33**	**37**	**70**	**65**	**6**	**0**	**7**	**7**	**2**
1991-92	**Vancouver**	**NHL**	**80**	**31**	**44**	**75**	**101**	**13**	**4**	**8**	**12**	**6**
1992-93	**Vancouver**	**NHL**	**84**	**33**	**39**	**72**	**64**	**12**	**5**	**8**	**13**	**16**
1993-94	**Vancouver**	**NHL**	**84**	**32**	**29**	**61**	**73**	**24**	**12**	**13**	**25**	**18**
1994-95	**Vancouver**	**NHL**	**48**	**18**	**22**	**40**	**40**	**11**	**2**	**6**	**8**	**12**
1995-96	**Vancouver**	**NHL**	**82**	**33**	**47**	**80**	**42**	**6**	**4**	**4**	**8**	**6**
	NHL Totals		**611**	**231**	**277**	**508**	**469**	**79**	**30**	**50**	**80**	**68**

a   NHL All-Rookie Team (1989)
Played in NHL All-Star Game (1991, 1992)

LINDGREN, MATS   EDM.

Center. Shoots left. 6'2", 200 lbs.   Born, Skelleftea, Sweden, October 1, 1974.
(Winnipeg's 1st choice, 15th overall, in 1993 Entry Draft).

			Regular Season					Playoffs				
Season	Club	Lea	GP	G	A	TP	PIM	GP	G	A	TP	PIM
1991-92	Skelleftea	Swe. 2	29	14	8	22	14	....	....	....	....	....
1992-93	Skelleftea	Swe. 2	32	20	14	34	18	....	....	....	....	....
1993-94	Farjestad	Swe.	22	11	6	17	26	....	....	....	....	....
1994-95	Farjestad	Swe.	37	17	15	32	20	3	0	0	0	4
1995-96	Cape Breton	AHL	13	7	5	12	6	....	....	....	....	....

Traded to **Edmonton** by **Winnipeg** with Boris Mironov, Winnipeg's first round choice (Jason Bonsignore) in 1994 Entry Draft and Florida's fourth round choice (previously acquired by Winnipeg — Edmonton selected Adam Copeland) in 1994 Entry Draft for Dave Manson and St. Louis' sixth round choice (previously acquired by Edmonton — Winnipeg selected Chris Kibermanis) in 1994 Entry Draft, March 15, 1994.

LINDQVIST, FREDRIK   N.J.

Center. Shoots left. 5'11", 176 lbs.   Born, Sodertalje, Sweden, June 21, 1973.
(New Jersey's 4th choice, 55th overall, in 1991 Entry Draft).

			Regular Season					Playoffs				
Season	Club	Lea	GP	G	A	TP	PIM	GP	G	A	TP	PIM
1989-90	Huddinge	Swe. 2	2	0	0	0	0	....	....	....	....	....
1990-91	Djurgarden	Swe.	28	6	4	10	0	7	1	0	1	2
1991-92	Djurgarden	Swe.	39	9	6	15	14	10	1	1	2	2
1992-93	Djurgarden	Swe.	39	9	11	20	8	4	1	2	3	2
1993-94	Djurgarden	Swe.	25	5	8	13	8	6	2	1	3	2
1994-95	Djurgarden	Swe.	40	11	16	27	14	3	0	0	0	2
1995-96	Djurgarden	Swe.	33	12	19	31	16	1	0	0	0	0

LINDROS, BRETT   (LIHND-rahz)

Right wing. Shoots right. 6'4", 215 lbs.   Born, London, Ont., December 2, 1975.
(NY Islanders' 1st choice, 9th overall, in 1994 Entry Draft).

			Regular Season					Playoffs				
Season	Club	Lea	GP	G	A	TP	PIM	GP	G	A	TP	PIM
1992-93	Kingston	OHL	31	11	11	22	162	....	....	....	....	....
	Cdn. National	....	11	1	6	7	33	....	....	....	....	....
1993-94	Cdn. National	....	44	7	7	14	118	....	....	....	....	....
	Kingston	OHL	15	4	6	10	94	3	0	0	0	18
1994-95	Kingston	OHL	26	24	23	47	63	....	....	....	....	....
	NY Islanders	**NHL**	**33**	**1**	**3**	**4**	**100**	....	....	....	....	....
1995-96	**NY Islanders**	**NHL**	**18**	**1**	**2**	**3**	**47**	....	....	....	....	....
	NHL Totals		**51**	**2**	**5**	**7**	**147**					

LINDROS, ERIC   (LIHND-rahz)   PHI.

Center. Shoots right. 6'4", 236 lbs.   Born, London, Ont., February 28, 1973.
(Quebec's 1st choice, 1st overall, in 1991 Entry Draft).

			Regular Season					Playoffs				
Season	Club	Lea	GP	G	A	TP	PIM	GP	G	A	TP	PIM
1988-89	Cdn. National	....	2	1	0	1	0	....	....	....	....	....
1989-90	Det. Comp.	USHL	14	23	29	52	123	....	....	....	....	....
	Cdn. National	....	3	1	0	1	4	....	....	....	....	....
a	Oshawa	OHL	25	17	19	36	61	17	18	18	36	76
1990-91bc	Oshawa	OHL	57	*71	78	*149	189	16	*18	20	*38	*93
1991-92	Oshawa	OHL	13	9	22	31	54	....	....	....	....	....
	Cdn. National	....	24	19	16	35	34	....	....	....	....	....
	Cdn. Olympic	....	8	5	6	11	6	....	....	....	....	....
1992-93d	**Philadelphia**	**NHL**	**61**	**41**	**34**	**75**	**147**	....	....	....	....	....
1993-94	**Philadelphia**	**NHL**	**65**	**44**	**53**	**97**	**103**	....	....	....	....	....
1994-95efg	**Philadelphia**	**NHL**	**46**	**29**	**41**	***70**	**60**	**12**	**4**	**11**	**15**	**18**
1995-96h	**Philadelphia**	**NHL**	**73**	**47**	**68**	**115**	**163**	**12**	**6**	**6**	**12**	**43**
	NHL Totals		**245**	**161**	**196**	**357**	**473**	**24**	**10**	**17**	**27**	**61**

a   Memorial Cup All-Star Team (1990)
b   OHL First All-Star Team (1991)
c   Canadian Major Junior Player of the Year (1991)
d   NHL/Upper Deck All-Rookie Team (1993)
e   NHL First All-Star Team (1995)
f   Won Lester B. Pearson Award (1995)
g   Won Hart Trophy (1995)
h   NHL Second All-Star Team (1996)
Played in NHL All-Star Game (1994, 1996)

Traded to **Philadelphia** by **Quebec** for Peter Forsberg, Steve Duchesne, Kerry Huffman, Mike Ricci, Ron Hextall, Chris Simon, Philadelphia's first round choice in the 1993 (Jocelyn Thibault) and 1994 (later traded to Toronto — later traded to Washington — Washington selected Nolan Baumgartner) Entry Drafts and cash, June 30, 1992.

LINDSAY, BILL   FLA.

Left wing. Shoots left. 5'11", 190 lbs.   Born, Big Fork, MT, May 17, 1971.
(Quebec's 6th choice, 103rd overall, in 1991 Entry Draft).

			Regular Season					Playoffs				
Season	Club	Lea	GP	G	A	TP	PIM	GP	G	A	TP	PIM
1990-91	Tri-Cities	WHL	63	46	47	93	151	5	3	6	9	10
1991-92	**Quebec**	**NHL**	**23**	**2**	**4**	**6**	**14**	....	....	....	....	....
a	Tri-Cities	WHL	42	34	59	93	111	3	2	3	5	16
1992-93	**Quebec**	**NHL**	**44**	**4**	**9**	**13**	**16**	....	....	....	....	....
	Halifax	AHL	20	11	13	24	18	....	....	....	....	....
1993-94	**Florida**	**NHL**	**84**	**6**	**6**	**12**	**97**	....	....	....	....	....
1994-95	**Florida**	**NHL**	**48**	**10**	**9**	**19**	**46**	....	....	....	....	....
1995-96	**Florida**	**NHL**	**73**	**12**	**22**	**34**	**57**	**22**	**5**	**5**	**10**	**18**
	NHL Totals		**272**	**34**	**50**	**84**	**230**	**22**	**5**	**5**	**10**	**18**

a   WHL West Second All-Star Team (1992)
Claimed by **Florida** from **Quebec** in Expansion Draft, June 24, 1993.

LING, DAVID   CGY.

Right wing. Shoots right. 5'9", 185 lbs.   Born, Halifax, N.S., January 9, 1975.
(Quebec's 9th choice, 179th overall, in 1993 Entry Draft).

			Regular Season					Playoffs				
Season	Club	Lea	GP	G	A	TP	PIM	GP	G	A	TP	PIM
1992-93	Kingston	OHL	64	17	46	63	275	16	3	12	15	*72
1993-94	Kingston	OHL	61	37	40	77	*254	6	4	2	6	16
1994-95abc	Kingston	OHL	62	*61	74	135	136	6	7	8	15	12
1995-96	Saint John	AHL	75	24	32	56	179	9	0	5	5	12

a   OHL First All-Star Team (1995)
b   Canadian Major Junior First All-Star Team (1995)
c   Canadian Junior Player of the Year (1995)

Traded to **Calgary** by **Colorado** with Colorado's ninth round choice (Steve Shirreffs) in 1995 Entry Draft for Calgary's ninth round choice (Chris George) in 1995 Entry Draft, July 7, 1995.

LINNA, KAJ

Defense. Shoots left. 6'2", 210 lbs.   Born, Helsinki, Finland, January 24, 1971.
(Ottawa's 7th choice, 183rd overall, in 1995 Entry Draft).

			Regular Season					Playoffs				
Season	Club	Lea	GP	G	A	TP	PIM	GP	G	A	TP	PIM
1990-91	Karhu-Kissat	Fin. 2	40	2	8	10	8	....	....	....	....	....
1991-92	Boston U.	H.E.	32	7	14	21	42	....	....	....	....	....
1992-93	Boston U.	H.E.	36	2	27	29	71	....	....	....	....	....
1993-94	Boston U.	H.E.	34	4	13	17	26	....	....	....	....	....
1994-95	Boston U.	H.E.	36	7	20	27	26	....	....	....	....	....
1995-96	P.E.I.	AHL	67	6	24	30	32	5	1	2	3	4

LINTNER, RICHARD   PHO.

Defense. Shoots right. 6'3", 194 lbs.   Born, Trencin, Czech., November 15, 1977.
(Phoenix's 4th choice, 119th overall, in 1996 Entry Draft).

			Regular Season					Playoffs				
Season	Club	Lea	GP	G	A	TP	PIM	GP	G	A	TP	PIM
1994-95	Dukla Trencin	Slo. Jr.	42	12	13	25	20	....	....	....	....	....
1995-96	Dukla Trencin	Slo. Jr.	30	15	17	32	210	....	....	....	....	....
	Dukla Trencin	Slovak	2	0	0	0	0	....	....	....	....	....

LIPIANSKY, JAN   (LIH-pyahn-skee)   PHI.

Left wing. Shoots left. 6'2", 187 lbs.   Born, Bratislava, Czech., July 23, 1974.
(Philadelphia's 10th choice, 270th overall, in 1994 Entry Draft).

			Regular Season					Playoffs				
Season	Club	Lea	GP	G	A	TP	PIM	GP	G	A	TP	PIM
1993-94	Bratislava	Slovak	32	11	5	16	12	....	....	....	....	....
1994-95	Hershey	AHL	7	0	0	0	2	....	....	....	....	....
	Bratislava	Slovak	12	8	7	15	4	8	0	2	2	6
1995-96	Bratislava	Slovak	33	14	6	20	8	13	5	4	9	

LIPUMA, CHRIS (lih-POO-muh) S.J.

Defense. Shoots left. 6', 183 lbs. Born, Bridgeview, IL, March 23, 1971.

			Regular Season					Playoffs				
Season	Club	Lea	GP	G	A	TP	PIM	GP	G	A	TP	PIM
1990-91	Kitchener	OHL	61	6	30	36	145	4	0	1	1	4
1991-92	Kitchener	OHL	61	13	59	72	115	14	4	9	13	34
1992-93	**Tampa Bay**	**NHL**	**15**	**0**	**5**	**5**	**34**	....	....	....	....	....
	Atlanta	IHL	66	4	14	18	379	9	1	1	2	35
1993-94	**Tampa Bay**	**NHL**	**27**	**0**	**4**	**4**	**77**	....	....	....	....	....
	Atlanta	IHL	42	2	10	12	254	11	1	1	2	28
1994-95	Atlanta	IHL	41	5	12	17	191	....	....	....	....	....
	Tampa Bay	**NHL**	**1**	**0**	**0**	**0**	**0**	....	....	....	....	....
	Nashville	ECHL	1	0	0	0	0	....	....	....	....	....
1995-96	**Tampa Bay**	**NHL**	**21**	**0**	**0**	**0**	**13**	....	....	....	....	....
	Atlanta	IHL	48	5	11	16	146	....	....	....	....	....
	NHL Totals		**64**	**0**	**9**	**9**	**124**	....	....	....	....	....

Signed as a free agent by **Tampa Bay**, June 29, 1992. Signed as a free agent by **San Jose**, August 26, 1996.

LITVINOV, YURI (liht-VIH-nohv) NYR

Center. Shoots right. 5'10", 176 lbs. Born, Donetsk, USSR, April 11, 1976.
(NY Rangers' 7th choice, 135th overall, in 1994 Entry Draft).

			Regular Season					Playoffs				
Season	Club	Lea	GP	G	A	TP	PIM	GP	G	A	TP	PIM
1993-94	Soviet Wings	CIS	42	5	6	11	34	....	....	....	....	....
1994-95	Soviet Wings	CIS	6	0	0	0	8	....	....	....	....	....
1995-96	Soviet Wings	CIS	8	0	1	1	4	....	....	....	....	....

LOACH, LONNIE (LOHCH)

Left wing. Shoots left. 5'10", 181 lbs. Born, New Liskeard, Ont., April 14, 1968.
(Chicago's 4th choice, 98th overall, in 1986 Entry Draft).

			Regular Season					Playoffs				
Season	Club	Lea	GP	G	A	TP	PIM	GP	G	A	TP	PIM
1985-86	Guelph	OHL	65	41	42	83	63	20	7	8	15	16
1986-87	Guelph	OHL	56	31	24	55	42	5	2	1	3	2
1987-88	Guelph	OHL	66	43	49	92	75	....	....	....	....	....
1988-89	Flint	IHL	41	22	26	48	30	....	....	....	....	....
	Saginaw	IHL	32	7	6	13	27	....	....	....	....	....
1989-90	Indianapolis	IHL	3	0	0	0	0	....	....	....	....	....
	Cdn. National	....	9	3	1	4	2	....	....	....	....	....
	Fort Wayne	IHL	54	15	33	48	40	5	4	2	6	15
1990-91ab	Fort Wayne	IHL	81	55	76	*131	45	19	5	11	16	13
1991-92	Adirondack	AHL	67	37	49	86	69	19	*13	4	17	10
1992-93	**Ottawa**	**NHL**	**3**	**0**	**0**	**0**	**0**	....	....	....	....	....
	Los Angeles	**NHL**	**50**	**10**	**13**	**23**	**27**	**1**	**0**	**0**	**0**	**0**
	Phoenix	IHL	4	2	3	5	10	....	....	....	....	....
1993-94	**Anaheim**	**NHL**	**3**	**0**	**0**	**0**	**2**	....	....	....	....	....
	San Diego	IHL	74	42	49	91	65	9	4	10	14	6
1994-95	San Diego	IHL	13	3	10	13	21	....	....	....	....	....
	Detroit	IHL	64	32	43	75	45	3	2	1	3	2
1995-96	Detroit	IHL	79	35	51	86	75	11	1	5	6	8
	NHL Totals		**56**	**10**	**13**	**23**	**29**	**1**	**0**	**0**	**0**	**0**

a IHL Second All-Star Team (1991)
b Won Leo P. Lamoureux Memorial Trophy (Leading Scorer - IHL) (1991)

Signed as a free agent by **Detroit**, June 7, 1991. Claimed by **Ottawa** from **Detroit** in Expansion Draft, June 18, 1992. Claimed on waivers by **Los Angeles** from **Ottawa**, October 21, 1992. Claimed by **Anaheim** from **Los Angeles** in Expansion Draft, June 24, 1993.

LOEWEN, DARCY (LOH-wihn)

Left wing. Shoots left. 5'10", 185 lbs. Born, Calgary, Alta., February 26, 1969.
(Buffalo's 2nd choice, 55th overall, in 1988 Entry Draft).

			Regular Season					Playoffs				
Season	Club	Lea	GP	G	A	TP	PIM	GP	G	A	TP	PIM
1986-87	Spokane	WHL	68	15	25	40	129	5	0	0	0	16
1987-88	Spokane	WHL	72	30	44	74	231	15	7	5	12	54
1988-89	Spokane	WHL	60	31	27	58	194	....	....	....	....	....
	Cdn. National	....	2	0	0	0	0	....	....	....	....	....
1989-90	**Buffalo**	**NHL**	**4**	**0**	**0**	**0**	**4**	....	....	....	....	....
	Rochester	AHL	50	7	11	18	193	5	1	0	1	6
1990-91	**Buffalo**	**NHL**	**6**	**0**	**0**	**0**	**8**	....	....	....	....	....
	Rochester	AHL	71	13	15	28	130	15	1	5	6	14
1991-92	**Buffalo**	**NHL**	**2**	**0**	**0**	**0**	**2**	....	....	....	....	....
	Rochester	AHL	73	11	20	31	193	4	0	1	1	8
1992-93	**Ottawa**	**NHL**	**79**	**4**	**5**	**9**	**145**	....	....	....	....	....
1993-94	**Ottawa**	**NHL**	**44**	**0**	**3**	**3**	**52**	....	....	....	....	....
1994-95	Las Vegas	IHL	64	9	21	30	183	7	1	1	2	16
1995-96	Las Vegas	IHL	72	14	23	37	198	....	....	....	....	....
	NHL Totals		**135**	**4**	**8**	**12**	**211**	....	....	....	....	....

Claimed by **Ottawa** from **Buffalo** in Expansion Draft, June 18, 1992.

LONEY, BRIAN (LOH-nee) VAN.

Right wing. Shoots right. 6'2", 200 lbs. Born, Winnipeg, Man., August 9, 1972.
(Vancouver's 6th choice, 110th overall, in 1992 Entry Draft).

			Regular Season					Playoffs				
Season	Club	Lea	GP	G	A	TP	PIM	GP	G	A	TP	PIM
1991-92	Ohio State	CCHA	37	21	34	55	109	....	....	....	....	....
1992-93	Red Deer	WHL	66	39	36	75	147	4	1	1	2	19
	Cdn. National	....	1	0	1	1	0	....	....	....	....	....
	Hamilton	AHL	3	0	2	2	0	....	....	....	....	....
1993-94	Hamilton	AHL	67	18	16	34	76	4	0	0	0	8
1994-95	Syracuse	AHL	67	23	17	40	98	....	....	....	....	....
1995-96	**Vancouver**	**NHL**	**12**	**2**	**3**	**5**	**6**	....	....	....	....	....
	Syracuse	AHL	48	34	17	51	157	14	3	8	11	20
	NHL Totals		**12**	**2**	**3**	**5**	**6**	....	....	....	....	....

LONG, ANDREW FLA.

Right wing. Shoots right. 6'2", 181 lbs. Born, Toronto, Ont., August 10, 1978.
(Florida's 5th choice, 129th overall, in 1996 Entry Draft).

			Regular Season					Playoffs				
Season	Club	Lea	GP	G	A	TP	PIM	GP	G	A	TP	PIM
1995-96	Guelph	OHL	48	8	10	18	16	10	0	1	1	4

LOVEN, FREDERIK PHO.

Center. Shoots left. 6'2", 187 lbs. Born, Stockholm, Sweden, March 14, 1977.
(Winnipeg's 10th choice, 189th overall, in 1995 Entry Draft).

			Regular Season					Playoffs				
Season	Club	Lea	GP	G	A	TP	PIM	GP	G	A	TP	PIM
1994-94	Djurgarden	Swe. Jr.	29	6	10	16	14	....	....	....	....	....
1995-96	Djurgarden	Swe.	4	0	0	0	0	4	0	0	0	0

LOWE, KEVIN (LOH) NYR

Defense. Shoots left. 6'2", 190 lbs. Born, Lachute, Que., April 15, 1959.
(Edmonton's 1st choice, 21st overall, in 1979 Entry Draft).

			Regular Season					Playoffs				
Season	Club	Lea	GP	G	A	TP	PIM	GP	G	A	TP	PIM
1977-78	Quebec	QJHL	64	13	52	65	86	4	1	2	3	6
1978-79a	Quebec	QJHL	68	26	60	86	120	6	1	7	8	36
1979-80	Edmonton	NHL	64	2	19	21	70	3	0	1	1	0
1980-81	Edmonton	NHL	79	10	24	34	94	9	0	2	2	11
1981-82	Edmonton	NHL	80	9	31	40	63	5	0	3	3	0
1982-83	Edmonton	NHL	80	6	34	40	43	16	1	8	9	10
1983-84	Edmonton	NHL	80	4	42	46	59	19	3	7	10	16 ♦
1984-85	Edmonton	NHL	80	4	21	25	104	16	0	5	5	8 ♦
1985-86	Edmonton	NHL	74	2	16	18	90	10	1	3	4	15
1986-87	Edmonton	NHL	77	8	29	37	94	21	2	4	6	22 ♦
1987-88	Edmonton	NHL	70	9	15	24	89	19	0	2	2	26 ♦
1988-89	Edmonton	NHL	76	7	18	25	98	7	1	2	3	4
1989-90bc	Edmonton	NHL	78	7	26	33	140	20	0	2	2	10 ♦
1990-91	Edmonton	NHL	73	3	13	16	113	14	1	1	2	14
1991-92	Edmonton	NHL	55	2	8	10	107	11	0	3	3	16
1992-93	NY Rangers	NHL	49	3	12	15	58	....	....	....	....	....
1993-94	NY Rangers	NHL	71	5	14	19	70	22	1	0	1	20 ♦
1994-95	NY Rangers	NHL	44	1	7	8	58	10	0	1	1	12
1995-96	NY Rangers	NHL	53	1	5	6	76	10	0	4	4	4
	NHL Totals		**1183**	**83**	**334**	**417**	**1426**	**212**	**10**	**48**	**58**	**188**

a QMJHL Second All-Star Team (1979)
b Won Bud Man of the Year Award (1990)
c Won King Clancy Memorial Trophy (1990)

Played in NHL All-Star Game (1984-86, 1988-90, 1993)

Traded to **NY Rangers** by **Edmonton** for Roman Oksyuta and NY Rangers' third round choice (Alexander Kerch) in 1993 Entry Draft, December 11, 1992.

LOWRY, DAVE FLA.

Left wing. Shoots left. 6'1", 200 lbs. Born, Sudbury, Ont., February 14, 1965.
(Vancouver's 6th choice, 110th overall, in 1983 Entry Draft).

			Regular Season					Playoffs				
Season	Club	Lea	GP	G	A	TP	PIM	GP	G	A	TP	PIM
1982-83	London	OHL	42	11	16	27	48	3	0	0	0	14
1983-84	London	OHL	66	29	47	76	125	8	6	6	12	41
1984-85a	London	OHL	61	60	60	120	94	8	6	5	11	10
1985-86	Vancouver	NHL	73	10	8	18	143	3	0	0	0	0
1986-87	Vancouver	NHL	70	8	10	18	176	....	....	....	....	....
1987-88	Vancouver	NHL	22	1	3	4	38	....	....	....	....	....
	Fredericton	AHL	46	18	27	45	59	14	7	3	10	72
1988-89	St. Louis	NHL	21	3	3	6	11	10	0	5	5	4
	Peoria	IHL	58	31	35	66	45	....	....	....	....	....
1989-90	St. Louis	NHL	78	19	6	25	75	12	2	1	3	39
1990-91	St. Louis	NHL	79	19	21	40	168	13	1	4	5	35
1991-92	St. Louis	NHL	75	7	13	20	77	6	0	1	1	20
1992-93	St. Louis	NHL	58	5	8	13	101	11	2	0	2	14
1993-94	Florida	NHL	80	15	22	37	64	....	....	....	....	....
1994-95	Florida	NHL	45	10	10	20	25	....	....	....	....	....
1995-96	Florida	NHL	63	10	14	24	36	22	10	7	17	39
	NHL Totals		**664**	**107**	**118**	**225**	**914**	**77**	**15**	**18**	**33**	**151**

a OHL First All-Star Team (1985)

Traded to **St. Louis** by **Vancouver** for Ernie Vargas, September 29, 1988. Claimed by **Florida** from **St. Louis** in Expansion Draft, June 24, 1993.

LUCHINKIN, SERGEI DAL.

Right wing. Shoots left. 5'11", 172 lbs. Born, Dmitrov, USSR, October 16, 1976.
(Dallas' 9th choice, 202nd overall, in 1995 Entry Draft).

			Regular Season					Playoffs				
Season	Club	Lea	GP	G	A	TP	PIM	GP	G	A	TP	PIM
1994-95	Moscow D'amo	CIS	6	1	0	1	4	....	....	....	....	....
1995-96	Moscow D'amo	CIS	21	6	2	8	14	10	0	1	1	6

LUDWIG, CRAIG DAL.

Defense. Shoots left. 6'3", 220 lbs. Born, Rhinelander, WI, March 15, 1961.
(Montreal's 5th choice, 61st overall, in 1980 Entry Draft).

			Regular Season					Playoffs				
Season	Club	Lea	GP	G	A	TP	PIM	GP	G	A	TP	PIM
1979-80	North Dakota	WCHA	33	1	8	9	32	....	....	....	....	....
1980-81	North Dakota	WCHA	34	4	8	12	48	....	....	....	....	....
1981-82	North Dakota	WCHA	37	4	17	21	42	....	....	....	....	....
1982-83	Montreal	NHL	80	0	25	25	59	3	0	0	0	2
1983-84	Montreal	NHL	80	7	18	25	52	15	0	3	3	23
1984-85	Montreal	NHL	72	5	14	19	90	12	0	2	2	6
1985-86	Montreal	NHL	69	2	4	6	63	20	0	1	1	48 ♦
1986-87	Montreal	NHL	75	4	12	16	105	17	2	3	5	30
1987-88	Montreal	NHL	74	4	10	14	69	11	1	1	2	6
1988-89	Montreal	NHL	74	3	13	16	73	21	0	2	2	24
1989-90	Montreal	NHL	73	1	15	16	108	11	0	1	1	16
1990-91	NY Islanders	NHL	75	1	8	9	77	....	....	....	....	....
1991-92	Minnesota	NHL	73	2	9	11	54	7	0	1	1	19
1992-93	Minnesota	NHL	78	1	10	11	153	....	....	....	....	....
1993-94	Dallas	NHL	84	1	13	14	123	9	0	3	3	8
1994-95	Dallas	NHL	47	2	7	9	61	4	0	1	1	2
1995-96	Dallas	NHL	65	1	2	3	70	....	....	....	....	....
	NHL Totals		**1019**	**34**	**160**	**194**	**1157**	**130**	**3**	**18**	**21**	**184**

Traded to **NY Islanders** by **Montreal** for Gerald Diduck, September 4, 1990. Traded to **Minnesota** by **NY Islanders** for Tom Kurvers, June 22, 1991.

LUHNING, WARREN NYI

Right wing. Shoots right. 6'2", 185 lbs. Born, Edmonton, Alta., July 3, 1975.
(NY Islanders' 4th choice, 92nd overall, in 1993 Entry Draft).

			Regular Season					Playoffs				
Season	Club	Lea	GP	G	A	TP	PIM	GP	G	A	TP	PIM
1993-94	U. of Michigan	CCHA	38	13	6	19	83	....	....	....	....	....
1994-95	U. of Michigan	CCHA	36	17	23	40	80	....	....	....	....	....
1995-96	U. of Michigan	CCHA	40	20	32	52	123	....	....	....	....	....

LUKOWICH, BRAD (loo-KUH-wihch) DAL.

Defense. Shoots left. 6'1", 170 lbs. Born, Cranbrook, B.C., August 12, 1976.
(NY Islanders' 4th choice, 90th overall, in 1994 Entry Draft).

			Regular Season					Playoffs				
Season	Club	Lea	GP	G	A	TP	PIM	GP	G	A	TP	PIM
1992-93	Kamloops	WHL	1	0	0	0	0	....	....	....	....	....
1993-94	Kamloops	WHL	42	5	11	16	166	16	0	1	1	35
1994-95	Kamloops	WHL	63	10	35	45	125	18	0	7	7	21
1995-96	Kamloops	WHL	65	14	55	69	114	13	2	10	12	29

Traded to **Dallas** by **NY Islanders** for Dallas' third round choice in 1997 Entry Draft, June 1, 1996.

LUMME, JYRKI (LOO-mee, YUHR-kee) VAN.

Defense. Shoots left. 6'1", 205 lbs. Born, Tampere, Finland, July 16, 1966.
(Montreal's 3rd choice, 57th overall, in 1986 Entry Draft).

			Regular Season					Playoffs				
Season	Club	Lea	GP	G	A	TP	PIM	GP	G	A	TP	PIM
1984-85	KooVee	Fin. 3	30	6	4	10	44	....	....	....	....	....
1985-86	Ilves	Fin.	31	1	4	5	4	....	....	....	....	....
1986-87	Ilves	Fin.	43	12	12	24	52	4	0	1	1	2
1987-88	Ilves	Fin.	43	8	22	30	75	....	....	....	....	....
1988-89	**Montreal**	**NHL**	**21**	**1**	**3**	**4**	**10**	....	....	....	....	....
	Sherbrooke	AHL	26	4	11	15	10	6	1	3	4	4
1989-90	**Montreal**	**NHL**	**54**	**1**	**19**	**20**	**41**	....	....	....	....	....
	Vancouver	**NHL**	**11**	**3**	**7**	**10**	**8**	....	....	....	....	....
1990-91	**Vancouver**	**NHL**	**80**	**5**	**27**	**32**	**59**	**6**	**2**	**3**	**5**	**0**
1991-92	**Vancouver**	**NHL**	**75**	**12**	**32**	**44**	**65**	**13**	**2**	**3**	**5**	**4**
1992-93	**Vancouver**	**NHL**	**74**	**8**	**36**	**44**	**55**	**12**	**0**	**5**	**5**	**6**
1993-94	**Vancouver**	**NHL**	**83**	**13**	**42**	**55**	**50**	**24**	**2**	**11**	**13**	**16**
1994-95	Ilves	Fin.	12	4	4	8	24	....	....	....	....	....
	Vancouver	**NHL**	**36**	**5**	**12**	**17**	**26**	**11**	**2**	**6**	**8**	**8**
1995-96	**Vancouver**	**NHL**	**80**	**17**	**37**	**54**	**50**	**6**	**1**	**3**	**4**	**2**
	NHL Totals		**514**	**65**	**215**	**280**	**364**	**72**	**9**	**31**	**40**	**36**

Traded to **Vancouver** by **Montreal** for St. Louis' second round choice (previously acquired by Vancouver — Montreal selected Craig Darby) in 1991 Entry Draft, March 6, 1990.

LUNDSTROM, PER-ANTON PHO.

Defense. Shoots left. 6'2", 185 lbs. Born, Umea, Sweden, September 29, 1977.
(Phoenix's 3rd choice, 62nd overall, in 1996 Entry Draft).

			Regular Season					Playoffs				
Season	Club	Lea	GP	G	A	TP	PIM	GP	G	A	TP	PIM
1994-95	MoDo	Swe. Jr.	20	3	4	7	18	....	....	....	....	....
1995-96	MoDo	Swe. Jr.	25	3	3	6	28	2	1	0	1	4
	MoDo	Swe.	19	1	1	2	29	4	0	0	0	2

LUONGO, CHRIS (loo-WAHN-goh) NYI

Defense. Shoots right. 5'10", 206 lbs. Born, Detroit, MI, March 17, 1967.
(Detroit's 5th choice, 92nd overall, in 1985 Entry Draft).

			Regular Season					Playoffs				
Season	Club	Lea	GP	G	A	TP	PIM	GP	G	A	TP	PIM
1985-86	Michigan State	CCHA	38	1	5	6	29	....	....	....	....	....
1986-87a	Michigan State	CCHA	27	4	16	20	38	....	....	....	....	....
1987-88	Michigan State	CCHA	45	3	15	18	49	....	....	....	....	....
1988-89b	Michigan State	CCHA	47	4	21	25	42	....	....	....	....	....
1989-90	Adirondack	AHL	53	9	14	23	37	3	0	0	0	0
	Phoenix	IHL	23	5	9	14	41	....	....	....	....	....
1990-91	**Detroit**	**NHL**	**4**	**0**	**1**	**1**	**4**	....	....	....	....	....
	Adirondack	AHL	76	14	25	39	71	2	0	0	0	7
1991-92	Adirondack	AHL	80	6	20	26	60	19	3	5	8	10
1992-93	**Ottawa**	**NHL**	**76**	**3**	**9**	**12**	**68**	....	....	....	....	....
	New Haven	AHL	7	0	2	2	2	....	....	....	....	....
1993-94	**NY Islanders**	**NHL**	**17**	**1**	**3**	**4**	**13**	....	....	....	....	....
	Salt Lake	IHL	51	9	31	40	54	....	....	....	....	....
1994-95	Denver	IHL	41	1	14	15	26	....	....	....	....	....
	NY Islanders	**NHL**	**47**	**1**	**3**	**4**	**36**	....	....	....	....	....
1995-96	**NY Islanders**	**NHL**	**74**	**3**	**7**	**10**	**55**	....	....	....	....	....
	NHL Totals		**218**	**8**	**23**	**31**	**176**	....	....	....	....	....

a Named to NCAA All-Tournament Team (1987)
b CCHA Second All-Star Team (1989)

Signed as a free agent by **Ottawa**, September 9, 1992. Traded to **NY Islanders** by **Ottawa** for Jeff Finley, June 30, 1993.

LYDMAN, TONI CGY.

Defense. Shoots left. 6'1", 183 lbs. Born, Lahti, Finland, September 25, 1977.
(Calgary's 5th choice, 89th overall, in 1996 Entry Draft).

			Regular Season					Playoffs				
Season	Club	Lea	GP	G	A	TP	PIM	GP	G	A	TP	PIM
1994-95	Reipas	Fin. Jr.	26	6	4	10	10	....	....	....	....	....
1995-96	Reipas	Fin. Jr.	9	2	2	4	6	....	....	....	....	....
	Reipas	Fin. 2	39	5	2	7	30	3	0	1	1	0

MacDONALD, CRAIG HFD.

Center. Shoots left. 6'2", 180 lbs. Born, Antigonish, N.S., April 7, 1977.
(Hartford's 3rd choice, 88th overall, in 1996 Entry Draft).

			Regular Season					Playoffs				
Season	Club	Lea	GP	G	A	TP	PIM	GP	G	A	TP	PIM
1994-95	Lawrence Aca.	HS	30	25	52	77	10	....	....	....	....	....
1995-96	Harvard	ECAC	34	7	10	17	10	....	....	....	....	....

MacDONALD, DOUG

Left wing. Shoots left. 6', 192 lbs. Born, Assiniboia, Sask., February 8, 1969.
(Buffalo's 3rd choice, 77th overall, in 1989 Entry Draft).

			Regular Season					Playoffs				
Season	Club	Lea	GP	G	A	TP	PIM	GP	G	A	TP	PIM
1988-89	U. Wisconsin	WCHA	44	23	25	48	50	....	....	....	....	....
1989-90	U. Wisconsin	WCHA	44	16	35	51	52	....	....	....	....	....
1990-91	U. Wisconsin	WCHA	31	20	26	46	50	....	....	....	....	....
1991-92	U. Wisconsin	WCHA	29	14	25	39	58	....	....	....	....	....
1992-93	**Buffalo**	**NHL**	**5**	**1**	**0**	**1**	**2**	....	....	....	....	....
	Rochester	AHL	64	25	33	58	58	7	0	2	2	4
1993-94	**Buffalo**	**NHL**	**4**	**0**	**0**	**0**	**0**	....	....	....	....	....
	Rochester	AHL	63	25	19	44	46	4	1	1	2	8
1994-95	Rochester	AHL	58	21	25	46	73	5	0	1	1	0
	Buffalo	**NHL**	**2**	**0**	**0**	**0**	**0**	....	....	....	....	....
1995-96	Cincinnati	IHL	71	19	40	59	66	15	1	3	4	14
	NHL Totals		**11**	**1**	**0**	**1**	**2**	....	....	....	....	....

MacDONALD, JASON DET.

Right wing. Shoots right. 6', 195 lbs. Born, Charlottetown, P.E.I., April 1, 1974.
(Detroit's 5th choice, 142nd overall, in 1992 Entry Draft).

			Regular Season					Playoffs				
Season	Club	Lea	GP	G	A	TP	PIM	GP	G	A	TP	PIM
1990-91	North Bay	OHL	57	12	15	27	126	10	3	3	6	15
1991-92	North Bay	OHL	17	5	8	13	50	....	....	....	....	....
	Owen Sound	OHL	42	17	19	36	129	5	0	3	3	16
1992-93	Owen Sound	OHL	56	46	43	89	197	8	6	5	11	28
1993-94a	Owen Sound	OHL	66	55	61	116	177	9	7	11	18	36
	Adirondack	AHL	....	....	....	....	....	1	0	0	0	0
1994-95	Adirondack	AHL	68	14	21	35	238	4	0	0	0	2
1995-96	Adirondack	AHL	43	9	13	22	99	....	....	....	....	....
	Toledo	ECHL	9	5	5	10	26	9	3	1	4	39

a OHL Second All-Star Team (1994)

MacINNIS, AL ST.L.

Defense. Shoots right. 6'2", 196 lbs. Born, Inverness, N.S., July 11, 1963.
(Calgary's 1st choice, 15th overall, in 1981 Entry Draft).

			Regular Season					Playoffs				
Season	Club	Lea	GP	G	A	TP	PIM	GP	G	A	TP	PIM
1980-81	Kitchener	OHA	47	11	28	39	59	18	4	12	16	20
1981-82	**Calgary**	**NHL**	**2**	**0**	**0**	**0**	**0**	....	....	....	....	....
a	Kitchener	OHL	59	25	50	75	145	15	5	10	15	44
1982-83	**Calgary**	**NHL**	**14**	**1**	**3**	**4**	**9**	....	....	....	....	....
a	Kitchener	OHL	51	38	46	84	67	8	3	8	11	9
1983-84	**Calgary**	**NHL**	**51**	**11**	**34**	**45**	**42**	**11**	**2**	**12**	**14**	**13**
	Colorado	CHL	19	5	14	19	22	....	....	....	....	....
1984-85	**Calgary**	**NHL**	**67**	**14**	**52**	**66**	**75**	**4**	**1**	**2**	**3**	**8**
1985-86	**Calgary**	**NHL**	**77**	**11**	**57**	**68**	**76**	**21**	**4**	***15**	**19**	**30**
1986-87b	**Calgary**	**NHL**	**79**	**20**	**56**	**76**	**97**	**4**	**1**	**0**	**1**	**0**
1987-88	**Calgary**	**NHL**	**80**	**25**	**58**	**83**	**114**	**7**	**3**	**6**	**9**	**18**
1988-89bc	**Calgary**	**NHL**	**79**	**16**	**58**	**74**	**126**	**22**	**7**	***24**	***31**	**46** ♦
1989-90d	**Calgary**	**NHL**	**79**	**28**	**62**	**90**	**82**	**6**	**2**	**3**	**5**	**8**
1990-91d	**Calgary**	**NHL**	**78**	**28**	**75**	**103**	**90**	**7**	**2**	**3**	**5**	**8**
1991-92	**Calgary**	**NHL**	**72**	**20**	**57**	**77**	**83**	....	....	....	....	....
1992-93	**Calgary**	**NHL**	**50**	**11**	**43**	**54**	**61**	**6**	**1**	**6**	**7**	**10**
1993-94b	**Calgary**	**NHL**	**75**	**28**	**54**	**82**	**95**	**7**	**2**	**6**	**8**	**12**
1994-95	**St. Louis**	**NHL**	**32**	**8**	**20**	**28**	**43**	**7**	**1**	**5**	**6**	**10**
1995-96	**St. Louis**	**NHL**	**82**	**17**	**44**	**61**	**88**	**13**	**3**	**4**	**7**	**20**
	NHL Totals		**917**	**238**	**673**	**911**	**1081**	**115**	**29**	**86**	**115**	**183**

a OHL First All-Star Team (1982, 1983)
b NHL Second All-Star Team (1987, 1989, 1994)
c Won Conn Smythe Trophy (1989)
d NHL First All-Star Team (1990, 1991)

Played in NHL All-Star Game (1985, 1988, 1990-92, 1994, 1996)

Traded to **St. Louis** by **Calgary** with Calgary's fourth round choice in 1997 Entry Draft for Phil Housley, St. Louis' second round choice (Steve Begin) in 1996 Entry Draft and second round choice in 1997 Entry Draft, July 4, 1994.

MacINTYRE, ANDY CHI.

Left wing. Shoots left. 6'1", 190 lbs. Born, Thunder Bay, Ont., April 16, 1974.
(Chicago's 4th choice, 89th overall, in 1992 Entry Draft).

			Regular Season					Playoffs				
Season	Club	Lea	GP	G	A	TP	PIM	GP	G	A	TP	PIM
1990-91	Seattle	WHL	71	16	13	29	52	4	0	0	0	2
1991-92	Seattle	WHL	12	6	2	8	18	....	....	....	....	....
	Saskatoon	WHL	55	22	13	35	66	22	10	2	12	17
1992-93	Saskatoon	WHL	72	35	29	64	82	9	3	2	5	2
1993-94a	Saskatoon	WHL	72	54	35	89	58	16	6	6	12	16
1994-95	Indianapolis	IHL	51	9	8	17	17	....	....	....	....	....
	Columbus	ECHL	22	7	8	15	5	....	....	....	....	....
1995-96	Indianapolis	IHL	21	2	7	9	11	....	....	....	....	....
	Columbus	ECHL	27	5	7	12	31	2	0	1	1	0

a WHL East Second All-Star Team (1994)

MACIVER, NORM (mac-IGH-ver) PHO.

Defense. Shoots left. 5'11", 180 lbs. Born, Thunder Bay, Ont., September 8, 1964.

			Regular Season					Playoffs				
Season	Club	Lea	GP	G	A	TP	PIM	GP	G	A	TP	PIM
1982-83	Minn.-Duluth	WCHA	45	1	26	27	40	6	0	2	2	2
1983-84a	Minn.-Duluth	WCHA	31	13	28	41	28	8	1	10	11	8
1984-85bc	Minn.-Duluth	WCHA	47	14	47	61	63	10	3	3	6	6
1985-86bc	Minn.-Duluth	WCHA	42	11	51	62	36	4	2	3	5	2
1986-87	**NY Rangers**	**NHL**	**3**	**0**	**1**	**1**	**0**	....	....	....	....	....
	New Haven	AHL	71	6	30	36	73	7	0	0	0	9
1987-88	**NY Rangers**	**NHL**	**37**	**9**	**15**	**24**	**14**	....	....	....	....	....
	Colorado	IHL	27	6	20	26	22	....	....	....	....	....
1988-89	**NY Rangers**	**NHL**	**26**	**0**	**10**	**10**	**14**	....	....	....	....	....
	Hartford	**NHL**	**37**	**1**	**22**	**23**	**24**	**1**	**0**	**0**	**0**	**2**
1989-90	Binghamton	AHL	2	0	0	0	0	....	....	....	....	....
	Edmonton	**NHL**	**1**	**0**	**0**	**0**	**0**	....	....	....	....	....
	Cape Breton	AHL	68	13	37	50	55	6	0	7	7	10
1990-91	**Edmonton**	**NHL**	**21**	**2**	**5**	**7**	**14**	**18**	**0**	**4**	**4**	**8**
de	Cape Breton	AHL	56	13	46	59	60	....	....	....	....	....
1991-92	**Edmonton**	**NHL**	**57**	**6**	**34**	**40**	**38**	**13**	**1**	**2**	**3**	**10**
1992-93	**Ottawa**	**NHL**	**80**	**17**	**46**	**63**	**84**	....	....	....	....	....
1993-94	**Ottawa**	**NHL**	**53**	**3**	**20**	**23**	**26**	....	....	....	....	....
1994-95	**Ottawa**	**NHL**	**28**	**4**	**7**	**11**	**10**	....	....	....	....	....
	Pittsburgh	**NHL**	**13**	**0**	**9**	**9**	**6**	**12**	**1**	**4**	**5**	**8**
1995-96	**Pittsburgh**	**NHL**	**32**	**2**	**21**	**23**	**32**	....	....	....	....	....
	Winnipeg	**NHL**	**39**	**5**	**25**	**30**	**26**	**6**	**1**	**0**	**1**	**2**
	NHL Totals		**427**	**49**	**215**	**264**	**288**	**50**	**3**	**10**	**13**	**30**

a WCHA Second All-Star Team (1984)
b WCHA First All-Star Team (1985, 1986)
c NCAA West First All-American Team (1985, 1986)
d AHL First All-Star Team (1991)
e Won Eddie Shore Plaque (Top Defenseman - AHL) (1991)

Signed as a free agent by **NY Rangers**, September 8, 1986. Traded to **Hartford** by **NY Rangers** with Brian Lawton and Don Maloney for Carey Wilson and Hartford's fifth round choice (Lubos Rob) in 1990 Entry Draft, December 26, 1988. Traded to **Edmonton** by **Hartford** for Jim Ennis, October 10, 1989. Claimed by **Ottawa** from **Edmonton** in NHL Waiver Draft, October 4, 1992. Traded to **Pittsburgh** by **Ottawa** with Troy Murray for Martin Straka, April 7, 1995. Traded to **Winnipeg** by **Pittsburgh** for Neil Wilkinson, December 28, 1995.

MACKINNON, STEPHEN OTT.

Left wing. Shoots left. 6'4", 200 lbs. Born, Lowell, MA, August 20, 1976.
(Ottawa's 9th choice, 237th overall, in 1994 Entry Draft).

			Regular Season					Playoffs				
Season	Club	Lea	GP	G	A	TP	PIM	GP	G	A	TP	PIM
1994-95	Cushing	HS	25	26	29	55	....	....	....	....	....	....
1995-96	Massachusetts	H.E.	18	1	0	1	61	....	....	....	....	....

MacLEAN, DONALD L.A.

Center. Shoots left. 6'2", 174 lbs. Born, Sydney, N.S., January 14, 1977.
(Los Angeles' 2nd choice, 33rd overall, in 1995 Entry Draft).

			Regular Season					Playoffs				
Season	Club	Lea	GP	G	A	TP	PIM	GP	G	A	TP	PIM
1994-95	Beauport	QMJHL	64	15	27	42	37	17	4	4	8	6
1995-96	Beauport	QMJHL	1	0	1	1	0	....	....	....	....	....
	Laval	QMJHL	21	17	11	28	29	....	....	....	....	....
	Hull	QMJHL	39	26	34	60	44	17	6	7	13	14

MacLEAN, JOHN — N.J.

Right wing. Shoots right. 6', 200 lbs. Born, Oshawa, Ont., November 20, 1964.
(New Jersey's 1st choice, 6th overall, in 1983 Entry Draft).

			Regular Season					Playoffs				
Season	Club	Lea	GP	G	A	TP	PIM	GP	G	A	TP	PIM
1981-82	Oshawa	OHL	67	17	22	39	197	12	3	6	9	63
1982-83	Oshawa	OHL	66	47	51	98	138	17	*18	20	*38	35
1983-84	New Jersey	NHL	23	1	0	1	10	....	....	....	....	....
	Oshawa	OHL	30	23	36	59	58	7	2	5	7	18
1984-85	New Jersey	NHL	61	13	20	33	44	....	....	....	....	....
1985-86	New Jersey	NHL	74	21	36	57	112	....	....	....	....	....
1986-87	New Jersey	NHL	80	31	36	67	120	....	....	....	....	....
1987-88	New Jersey	NHL	76	23	16	39	147	20	7	11	18	60
1988-89	New Jersey	NHL	74	42	45	87	122	....	....	....	....	....
1989-90	New Jersey	NHL	80	41	38	79	80	6	4	1	5	12
1990-91	New Jersey	NHL	78	45	33	78	150	7	5	3	8	20
1991-92			DID NOT PLAY – INJURED									
1992-93	New Jersey	NHL	80	24	24	48	102	5	0	1	1	10
1993-94	New Jersey	NHL	80	37	33	70	95	20	6	10	16	22
1994-95	New Jersey	NHL	46	17	12	29	32	20	5	13	18	14 ♦
1995-96	New Jersey	NHL	76	20	28	48	91	....	....	....	....	....
	NHL Totals		828	315	321	636	1105	78	27	39	66	138

Played in NHL All-Star Game (1989, 1991)

MacLEOD, PAT

Defense. Shoots left. 5'11", 190 lbs. Born, Melfort, Sask., June 15, 1969.
(Minnesota's 5th choice, 87th overall, in 1989 Entry Draft).

			Regular Season					Playoffs				
Season	Club	Lea	GP	G	A	TP	PIM	GP	G	A	TP	PIM
1987-88	Kamloops	WHL	50	13	33	46	27	18	2	7	9	6
1988-89	Kamloops	WHL	37	11	34	45	14	15	7	18	25	24
1989-90	Kalamazoo	IHL	82	9	38	47	27	10	1	6	7	2
1990-91	Minnesota	NHL	1	0	1	1	0	....	....	....	....	....
	Kalamazoo	IHL	59	10	30	40	16	11	1	2	3	5
1991-92	San Jose	NHL	37	5	11	16	4	....	....	....	....	....
	Kansas City	IHL	45	9	21	30	19	11	1	4	5	4
1992-93	San Jose	NHL	13	0	1	1	10	....	....	....	....	....
	Kansas City	IHL	18	8	8	16	14	10	2	4	6	7
1993-94a	Milwaukee	IHL	73	21	52	73	18	3	1	2	3	0
1994-95	Milwaukee	IHL	69	11	36	47	16	15	3	6	9	8
1995-96	Dallas	NHL	2	0	0	0	0	....	....	....	....	....
	Michigan	IHL	50	3	23	26	18	7	0	3	3	0
	NHL Totals		53	5	13	18	14	....	....	....	....	....

a IHL First All-Star Team (1994)

Claimed by **San Jose** from **Minnesota** in Dispersal Draft, May 30, 1991. Signed as a free agent by **Dallas**, July 31, 1995.

MACNEIL, IAN — HFD.

Center. Shoots left. 6'2", 171 lbs. Born, Halifax, N.S., April 27, 1977.
(Hartford's 3rd choice, 85th overall, in 1995 Entry Draft).

			Regular Season					Playoffs				
Season	Club	Lea	GP	G	A	TP	PIM	GP	G	A	TP	PIM
1994-95	Oshawa	OHL	60	7	21	28	62	7	0	2	2	0
1995-96	Oshawa	OHL	49	15	17	32	54	5	1	2	3	8

MacNEVIN, JOSH — N.J.

Defense. Shoots right. 6'2", 185 lbs. Born, Calgary, Alta., July 14, 1977.
(New Jersey's 8th choice, 101st overall, in 1996 Entry Draft).

			Regular Season					Playoffs				
Season	Club	Lea	GP	G	A	TP	PIM	GP	G	A	TP	PIM
1995-96	Vernon	Jr. A	51	13	45	58	54	....	....	....	....	....

MACOUN, JAMIE (muh-KOW-uhn) — TOR.

Defense. Shoots left. 6'2", 200 lbs. Born, Newmarket, Ont., August 17, 1961.

			Regular Season					Playoffs				
Season	Club	Lea	GP	G	A	TP	PIM	GP	G	A	TP	PIM
1980-81	Ohio State	CCHA	38	9	20	29	83	....	....	....	....	....
1981-82	Ohio State	CCHA	25	2	18	20	89	....	....	....	....	....
1982-83	Ohio State	CCHA	19	6	21	27	54	....	....	....	....	....
	Calgary	NHL	22	1	4	5	25	9	0	2	2	8
1983-84a	Calgary	NHL	72	9	23	32	97	11	1	0	1	0
1984-85	Calgary	NHL	70	9	30	39	67	4	1	0	1	4
1985-86	Calgary	NHL	77	11	21	32	81	22	1	6	7	23
1986-87	Calgary	NHL	79	7	33	40	111	3	0	1	1	8
1987-88			DID NOT PLAY – INJURED									
1988-89	Calgary	NHL	72	8	19	27	76	22	3	6	9	30 ♦
1989-90	Calgary	NHL	78	8	27	35	70	6	0	3	3	10
1990-91	Calgary	NHL	79	7	15	22	84	7	0	1	1	4
1991-92	Calgary	NHL	37	2	12	14	53	....	....	....	....	....
	Toronto	NHL	39	3	13	16	18	....	....	....	....	....
1992-93	Toronto	NHL	77	4	15	19	55	21	0	6	6	36
1993-94	Toronto	NHL	82	3	27	30	115	18	1	1	2	12
1994-95	Toronto	NHL	46	2	8	10	75	7	1	2	3	8
1995-96	Toronto	NHL	82	0	8	8	87	6	0	2	2	8
	NHL Totals		912	74	255	329	1014	136	8	30	38	151

a NHL All-Rookie Team (1984)

Signed as a free agent by **Calgary**, January 30, 1983. Traded to **Toronto** by **Calgary** with Doug Gilmour, Ric Natress, Kent Manderville and Rick Wamsley for Gary Leeman, Alexander Godynyuk, Jeff Reese, Michel Petit and Craig Berube, January 2, 1992.

MacTAVISH, CRAIG — ST.L.

Center. Shoots left. 6'1", 195 lbs. Born, London, Ont., August 15, 1958.
(Boston's 9th choice, 153rd overall, in 1978 Amateur Draft).

			Regular Season					Playoffs				
Season	Club	Lea	GP	G	A	TP	PIM	GP	G	A	TP	PIM
1978-79	Lowell	ECAC	....	....	....	....	....	....	....	....	....	....
1979-80	Boston	NHL	46	11	17	28	8	10	2	3	5	7
	Binghamton	AHL	34	17	15	32	29	....	....	....	....	....
1980-81	Boston	NHL	24	3	5	8	13	....	....	....	....	....
	Springfield	AHL	53	19	24	43	81	7	5	4	9	8
1981-82	Boston	NHL	2	0	1	1	0	....	....	....	....	....
	Erie	AHL	72	23	32	55	37	....	....	....	....	....
1982-83	Boston	NHL	75	10	20	30	18	17	3	1	4	18
1983-84	Boston	NHL	70	20	23	43	35	1	0	0	0	0
1984-85			DID NOT PLAY									
1985-86	Edmonton	NHL	74	23	24	47	70	10	4	4	8	11
1986-87	Edmonton	NHL	79	20	19	39	55	21	1	9	10	16 ♦
1987-88	Edmonton	NHL	80	15	17	32	47	19	0	1	1	31 ♦
1988-89	Edmonton	NHL	80	21	31	52	55	7	0	1	1	8
1989-90	Edmonton	NHL	80	21	22	43	89	22	2	6	8	29 ♦
1990-91	Edmonton	NHL	80	17	15	32	76	18	3	3	6	20
1991-92	Edmonton	NHL	80	12	18	30	98	16	3	0	3	28
1992-93	Edmonton	NHL	82	10	20	30	110	....	....	....	....	....
1993-94	Edmonton	NHL	66	16	10	26	80	....	....	....	....	....
	NY Rangers	NHL	12	4	2	6	11	23	1	4	5	22 ♦
1994-95	Philadelphia	NHL	45	3	9	12	23	15	1	4	5	20
1995-96	Philadelphia	NHL	55	5	8	13	62	....	....	....	....	....
	St. Louis	NHL	13	0	1	1	8	13	0	2	2	6
	NHL Totals		1043	211	262	473	858	192	20	38	58	216

Played in NHL All-Star Game (1996)

Signed as a free agent by **Edmonton,** February 1, 1985. Traded to **NY Rangers** by **Edmonton** for Todd Marchant, March 21, 1994. Signed as a free agent by **Philadelphia**, July 6, 1994. Traded to **St. Louis** by **Philadelphia** for Dale Hawerchuk, March 15, 1996.

MacWILLIAM, MIKE

Left wing. Shoots left. 6'4", 230 lbs. Born, Burnaby, B.C., February 14, 1967.

			Regular Season					Playoffs				
Season	Club	Lea	GP	G	A	TP	PIM	GP	G	A	TP	PIM
1985-86	Medicine Hat	WHL	52	8	6	14	98	....	....	....	....	....
1986-87	Medicine Hat	WHL	44	7	17	24	134	19	1	0	1	35
1987-88	N. Westminster	WHL	DID NOT PLAY – INJURED									
1988-89	Milwaukee	IHL	6	1	1	2	28	....	....	....	....	....
	Flint	IHL	18	0	0	0	92	....	....	....	....	....
1989-90			DID NOT PLAY – INJURED									
1990-91	Adirondack	AHL	8	0	0	0	32	....	....	....	....	....
	Greensboro	ECHL	15	2	7	9	209	....	....	....	....	....
1991-92	St. John's	AHL	44	7	8	15	301	2	0	0	0	8
	Greensboro	ECHL	8	2	5	7	94	....	....	....	....	....
1992-93	Greensboro	ECHL	12	5	5	10	137	....	....	....	....	....
1993-94	Tulsa	CHL	39	16	12	28	326	....	....	....	....	....
1994-95	Denver	IHL	30	5	6	11	218	12	2	2	4	56
1995-96	NY Islanders	NHL	6	0	0	0	14	....	....	....	....	....
	Utah	IHL	53	8	16	24	317	6	0	2	2	53
	NHL Totals		6	0	0	0	14	....	....	....	....	....

Signed as a free agnt by **Philadelphia**, October 7, 1986. Signed as a free agent by **Toronto**, July 30, 1991. Signed as a free agent by **NY Islanders**, July 25, 1995.

MADER, MIKE — PHO.

Defense. Shoots right. 6'2", 180 lbs. Born, Manchester, CT, November 7, 1975.
(Winnipeg's 10th choice, 238th overall, in 1994 Entry Draft).

			Regular Season					Playoffs				
Season	Club	Lea	GP	G	A	TP	PIM	GP	G	A	TP	PIM
1994-95	Providence	H.E.	29	1	5	6	26	....	....	....	....	....
1995-96	Providence	H.E.	37	3	6	9	33	....	....	....	....	....

MAGUIRE, DEREK — MTL.

Defense. Shoots right. 5'10", 210 lbs. Born, Rochester, NY, December 9, 1971.
(Montreal's 10th choice, 186th overall, in 1990 Entry Draft).

			Regular Season					Playoffs				
Season	Club	Lea	GP	G	A	TP	PIM	GP	G	A	TP	PIM
1990-91	Harvard	ECAC	25	3	14	17	12	....	....	....	....	....
1991-92	Harvard	ECAC	25	1	16	17	16	....	....	....	....	....
1992-93	Harvard	ECAC	16	3	9	12	10	....	....	....	....	....
1993-94abc	Harvard	ECAC	31	6	32	38	14	....	....	....	....	....
1994-95	Fredericton	AHL	52	6	14	20	19	17	0	4	4	4
1995-96	Fredericton	AHL	4	0	2	2	2	3	0	1	1	0

a ECAC Second All-Star Team (1994)
b NCAA East Second All-American Team (1994)
c NCAA Final Four All-Tournament Team (1994)

MAJOR, MARK — DET.

Left wing. Shoots left. 6'3", 223 lbs. Born, Toronto, Ont., March 20, 1970.
(Pittsburgh's 2nd choice, 25th overall, in 1988 Entry Draft).

			Regular Season					Playoffs				
Season	Club	Lea	GP	G	A	TP	PIM	GP	G	A	TP	PIM
1987-88	North Bay	OHL	57	16	17	33	272	4	0	2	2	8
1988-89	North Bay	OHL	11	3	2	5	58	....	....	....	....	....
	Kingston	OHL	53	22	29	51	193	....	....	....	....	....
1989-90	Kingston	OHL	62	29	32	61	168	6	3	3	6	12
1990-91	Muskegon	IHL	60	8	10	18	160	5	0	0	0	0
1991-92	Muskegon	IHL	80	13	18	31	302	12	1	3	4	29
1992-93	Cleveland	IHL	82	13	15	28	155	3	0	0	0	0
1993-94	Providence	AHL	61	17	9	26	176	....	....	....	....	....
1994-95	Detroit	IHL	78	17	19	36	229	5	0	1	1	23
1995-96	Adirondack	AHL	78	10	19	29	234	3	0	0	0	21

Signed as a free agent by **Boston**, July 22, 1993. Signed as a free agent by **Detroit**, June 26, 1995.

MAKINEN, MARKO (mya-KIH-nehn) — S.J.

Right wing. Shoots right. 6'4", 198 lbs. Born, Turku, Finland, March 31, 1977.
(San Jose's 3rd choice, 64th overall, in 1995 Entry Draft).

			Regular Season					Playoffs				
Season	Club	Lea	GP	G	A	TP	PIM	GP	G	A	TP	PIM
1994-95	TPS	Fin. Jr.	26	7	1	8	34	....	....	....	....	....
	Kiekko-67	Fin. 2	4	0	0	0	6	....	....	....	....	....
1995-96	TPS	Fin. Jr.	11	5	1	6	28	....	....	....	....	....
	Kiekko-67	Fin. Jr.	4	4	2	6	12	....	....	....	....	....
	Kiekko-67	Fin. 2	21	6	2	8	98	6	2	2	4	6

MALAKHOV, VLADIMIR (mah-LAH-kahf) MTL.

Defense. Shoots left. 6'3", 220 lbs. Born, Sverdlovsk, USSR, August 30, 1968.
(NY Islanders' 12th choice, 191st overall, in 1989 Entry Draft).

			Regular Season					Playoffs				
Season	Club	Lea	GP	G	A	TP	PIM	GP	G	A	TP	PIM
1986-87	Spartak	USSR	22	0	1	1	12	....	....	....	....	....
1987-88	Spartak	USSR	28	2	2	4	26	....	....	....	....	....
1988-89	CSKA	USSR	34	6	2	8	16	....	....	....	....	....
1989-90	CSKA	USSR	48	2	10	12	34	....	....	....	....	....
1990-91	CSKA	USSR	46	5	13	18	22	....	....	....	....	....
1991-92	CSKA	CIS	40	1	9	10	12	....	....	....	....	....
1992-93a	**NY Islanders**	**NHL**	**64**	**14**	**38**	**52**	**59**	**17**	**3**	**6**	**9**	**12**
	Capital Dist.	AHL	3	2	1	3	11	....	....	....	....	....
1993-94	**NY Islanders**	**NHL**	**76**	**10**	**47**	**57**	**80**	**4**	**0**	**0**	**0**	**6**
1994-95	**NY Islanders**	**NHL**	**26**	**3**	**13**	**16**	**32**	....	....	....	....	....
	Montreal	**NHL**	**14**	**1**	**4**	**5**	**14**	....	....	....	....	....
1995-96	**Montreal**	**NHL**	**61**	**5**	**23**	**28**	**79**	....	....	....	....	....
	NHL Totals		**241**	**33**	**125**	**158**	**264**	**21**	**3**	**6**	**9**	**18**

a NHL/Upper Deck All-Rookie Team (1993)

Traded to **Montreal** by **NY Islanders** with Pierre Turgeon for Kirk Muller, Mathieu Schneider and Craig Darby, April 5, 1995.

MALGUNAS, STEWART (mal-GOO-nuhs) WSH.

Defense. Shoots left. 6', 200 lbs. Born, Prince George, B.C., April 21, 1970.
(Detroit's 3rd choice, 66th overall, in 1990 Entry Draft).

			Regular Season					Playoffs				
Season	Club	Lea	GP	G	A	TP	PIM	GP	G	A	TP	PIM
1987-88	N. Westminster	WHL	6	0	0	0	0	....	....	....	....	....
1988-89	Seattle	WHL	72	11	41	52	51	....	....	....	....	....
1989-90a	Seattle	WHL	63	15	48	63	116	13	2	9	11	32
1990-91	Adirondack	AHL	78	5	19	24	70	2	0	0	0	4
1991-92	Adirondack	AHL	69	4	28	32	82	18	2	6	8	28
1992-93	Adirondack	AHL	45	3	12	15	39	11	3	3	6	8
1993-94	**Philadelphia**	**NHL**	**67**	**1**	**3**	**4**	**86**	....	....	....	....	....
1994-95	**Philadelphia**	**NHL**	**4**	**0**	**0**	**0**	**4**	....	....	....	....	....
	Hershey	AHL	32	3	5	8	28	6	2	1	3	31
1995-96	**Winnipeg**	**NHL**	**29**	**0**	**1**	**1**	**32**	....	....	....	....	....
	Washington	**NHL**	**1**	**0**	**0**	**0**	**0**	....	....	....	....	....
	Portland	AHL	16	2	5	7	18	13	1	3	4	19
	NHL Totals		**101**	**1**	**4**	**5**	**122**	....	....	....	....	....

a WHL West First All-Star Team (1990)

Traded to **Philadelphia** by **Detroit** for Philadelphia's fifth round choice (David Arsenault) in 1995 Entry Draft, September 9, 1993. Signed as a free agent by **Winnipeg**, August 9, 1995. Traded to **Washington** by **Winnipeg** for Denis Chasse, February 15, 1996.

MALIK, MAREK (MAW-leck) HFD.

Defense. Shoots left. 6'5", 190 lbs. Born, Ostrava, Czech., June 24, 1975.
(Hartford's 2nd choice, 72nd overall, in 1993 Entry Draft).

			Regular Season					Playoffs				
Season	Club	Lea	GP	G	A	TP	PIM	GP	G	A	TP	PIM
1992-93	TJ Vitkovice Jr.	Czech.	20	5	10	15	16	....	....	....	....	....
1993-94	TJ Vitkovice	Czech.	38	3	3	6	0	3	0	1	1	0
1994-95	Springfield	AHL	58	11	30	41	91	....	....	....	....	....
	Hartford	**NHL**	**1**	**0**	**1**	**1**	**0**	....	....	....	....	....
1995-96	**Hartford**	**NHL**	**7**	**0**	**0**	**0**	**4**	....	....	....	....	....
	Springfield	AHL	68	8	14	22	135	8	1	3	4	20
	NHL Totals		**8**	**0**	**1**	**1**	**4**					

MALKOC, DEAN (mal-KAWK) VAN.

Defense. Shoots left. 6'3", 200 lbs. Born, Vancouver, B.C., January 26, 1970.
(New Jersey's 7th choice, 95th overall, in 1990 Entry Draft).

			Regular Season					Playoffs				
Season	Club	Lea	GP	G	A	TP	PIM	GP	G	A	TP	PIM
1989-90	Kamloops	WHL	48	3	18	21	209	17	0	3	3	56
1990-91	Kamloops	WHL	8	1	4	5	47	....	....	....	....	....
	Swift Current	WHL	56	10	23	33	248	3	0	2	2	5
	Utica	AHL	1	0	0	0	0	....	....	....	....	....
1991-92	Utica	AHL	66	1	11	12	274	4	0	2	2	6
1992-93	Utica	AHL	73	5	19	24	255	5	0	1	1	8
1993-94	Albany	AHL	79	0	9	9	296	5	0	0	0	21
1994-95	Albany	AHL	9	0	1	1	52	....	....	....	....	....
	Indianapolis	IHL	62	1	3	4	193	....	....	....	....	....
1995-96	**Vancouver**	**NHL**	**41**	**0**	**2**	**2**	**136**	....	....	....	....	....
	NHL Totals		**41**	**0**	**2**	**2**	**136**	....	....	....	....	....

Traded to **Chicago** by **New Jersey** for Rob Conn, January 30, 1995. Signed as a free agent by **Vancouver**, September 8, 1995.

MALLETTE, TROY (muh-LEHT) BOS.

Left wing. Shoots left. 6'2", 210 lbs. Born, Sudbury, Ont., February 25, 1970.
(NY Rangers' 1st choice, 22nd overall, in 1988 Entry Draft).

			Regular Season					Playoffs				
Season	Club	Lea	GP	G	A	TP	PIM	GP	G	A	TP	PIM
1986-87	S.S. Marie	OHL	65	20	25	45	157	4	0	2	2	12
1987-88	S.S. Marie	OHL	62	18	30	48	186	6	1	3	4	12
1988-89	S.S. Marie	OHL	64	39	37	76	172	....	....	....	....	....
1989-90	**NY Rangers**	**NHL**	**79**	**13**	**16**	**29**	**305**	**10**	**2**	**2**	**4**	**81**
1990-91	**NY Rangers**	**NHL**	**71**	**12**	**10**	**22**	**252**	**5**	**0**	**0**	**0**	**18**
1991-92	**Edmonton**	**NHL**	**15**	**1**	**3**	**4**	**36**	....	....	....	....	....
	New Jersey	**NHL**	**17**	**3**	**4**	**7**	**43**	....	....	....	....	....
1992-93	**New Jersey**	**NHL**	**34**	**4**	**3**	**7**	**56**	....	....	....	....	....
	Utica	AHL	5	3	3	6	17	....	....	....	....	....
1993-94	**Ottawa**	**NHL**	**82**	**7**	**16**	**23**	**166**	....	....	....	....	....
1994-95	**Ottawa**	**NHL**	**23**	**3**	**5**	**8**	**35**	....	....	....	....	....
	P.E.I.	AHL	5	1	5	6	9	....	....	....	....	....
1995-96	**Ottawa**	**NHL**	**64**	**2**	**3**	**5**	**171**	....	....	....	....	....
	NHL Totals		**385**	**45**	**60**	**105**	**1064**	**15**	**2**	**2**	**4**	**99**

Acquired by **Edmonton** from **NY Rangers** as compensation for NY Rangers' signing of free agent Adam Graves, September 12, 1991. Traded to **New Jersey** by **Edmonton** for David Maley, January 12, 1992. Traded to **Ottawa** by **New Jersey** with Craig Billington and New Jersey's fourth round choice (Cosmo Dupaul) in 1993 Entry Draft for Peter Sidorkiewicz and future considerations (Mike Peluso, June 26, 1993), June 20, 1993. Signed as a free agent by **Boston**, July 24, 1996.

MALONE, SCOTT NYR

Defense. Shoots left. 6', 195 lbs. Born, Boston, MA, January 16, 1971.
(Toronto's 10th choice, 220th overall, in 1990 Entry Draft).

			Regular Season					Playoffs				
Season	Club	Lea	GP	G	A	TP	PIM	GP	G	A	TP	PIM
1991-92	N. Hampshire	H.E.	27	0	4	4	52	....	....	....	....	....
1992-93	N. Hampshire	H.E.	36	5	6	11	96	....	....	....	....	....
1993-94a	N. Hampshire	H.E.	40	14	6	20	*162	....	....	....	....	....
1994-95	Birmingham	ECHL	8	1	4	5	36	....	....	....	....	....
	Binghamton	AHL	48	3	14	17	85	11	0	2	2	12
1995-96	Binghamton	AHL	58	3	13	16	94	4	0	0	0	21

a Hockey East Second All-Star Team (1994)

Rights traded to **NY Rangers** by **Toronto** with Glenn Anderson and Toronto's fourth round choice (Alexander Korobolin) in 1994 Entry Draft for Mike Gartner, March 21, 1994.

MALTAIS, STEVE (MAHL-tay)

Left wing. Shoots left. 6'2", 205 lbs. Born, Arvida, Que., January 25, 1969.
(Washington's 2nd choice, 57th overall, in 1987 Entry Draft).

			Regular Season					Playoffs				
Season	Club	Lea	GP	G	A	TP	PIM	GP	G	A	TP	PIM
1986-87	Cornwall	OHL	65	32	12	44	29	5	0	0	0	2
1987-88	Cornwall	OHL	59	39	46	85	30	11	9	6	15	33
1988-89	Cornwall	OHL	58	53	70	123	67	18	14	16	30	16
	Fort Wayne	IHL	....	....	....	....	....	4	2	1	3	0
1989-90	**Washington**	**NHL**	**8**	**0**	**0**	**0**	**2**	**1**	**0**	**0**	**0**	**0**
	Baltimore	AHL	67	29	37	66	54	12	6	10	16	6
1990-91	**Washington**	**NHL**	**7**	**0**	**0**	**0**	**2**	....	....	....	....	....
	Baltimore	AHL	73	36	43	79	97	6	1	4	5	10
1991-92	**Minnesota**	**NHL**	**12**	**2**	**1**	**3**	**2**	....	....	....	....	....
	Kalamazoo	IHL	48	25	31	56	51	....	....	....	....	....
	Halifax	AHL	10	3	3	6	0	....	....	....	....	....
1992-93	**Tampa Bay**	**NHL**	**63**	**7**	**13**	**20**	**35**	....	....	....	....	....
	Atlanta	IHL	16	14	10	24	22	....	....	....	....	....
1993-94	**Detroit**	**NHL**	**4**	**0**	**1**	**1**	**0**	....	....	....	....	....
	Adirondack	AHL	73	35	49	84	79	12	5	11	16	14
1994-95a	Chicago	IHL	79	*57	40	97	145	3	1	1	2	0
1995-96b	Chicago	IHL	81	56	66	122	161	9	7	7	14	20
	NHL Totals		**94**	**9**	**15**	**24**	**41**	**1**	**0**	**0**	**0**	**0**

a IHL First All-Star Team (1995)
b IHL Second All-Star Team (1996)

Traded to **Minnesota** by **Washington** with Trent Klatt for Shawn Chambers, June 21, 1991. Traded to **Quebec** by **Minnesota** for Kip Miller, March 8, 1992. Claimed by **Tampa Bay** from **Quebec** in Expansion Draft, June 18, 1992. Traded to **Detroit** by **Tampa Bay** for Dennis Vial, June 8, 1993.

MALTBY, KIRK DET.

Right wing. Shoots right. 6', 180 lbs. Born, Guelph, Ont., December 22, 1972.
(Edmonton's 4th choice, 65th overall, in 1992 Entry Draft).

			Regular Season					Playoffs				
Season	Club	Lea	GP	G	A	TP	PIM	GP	G	A	TP	PIM
1989-90	Owen Sound	OHL	61	12	15	27	90	12	1	6	7	15
1990-91	Owen Sound	OHL	66	34	32	66	100	....	....	....	....	....
1991-92	Owen Sound	OHL	66	50	41	91	99	5	3	3	6	18
1992-93	Cape Breton	AHL	73	22	23	45	130	16	3	3	6	45
1993-94	**Edmonton**	**NHL**	**68**	**11**	**8**	**19**	**74**	....	....	....	....	....
1994-95	**Edmonton**	**NHL**	**47**	**8**	**3**	**11**	**49**	....	....	....	....	....
1995-96	**Edmonton**	**NHL**	**49**	**2**	**6**	**8**	**61**	....	....	....	....	....
	Cape Breton	AHL	4	1	2	3	6	....	....	....	....	....
	Detroit	**NHL**	**6**	**1**	**0**	**1**	**6**	**8**	**0**	**1**	**1**	**4**
	NHL Totals		**170**	**22**	**17**	**39**	**190**	**8**	**0**	**1**	**1**	**4**

Traded to **Detroit** by **Edmonton** for Dan McGillis, March 20, 1996.

MANDERVILLE, KENT

Left wing. Shoots left. 6'3", 210 lbs. Born, Edmonton, Alta., April 12, 1971.
(Calgary's 1st choice, 24th overall, in 1989 Entry Draft).

			Regular Season					Playoffs				
Season	Club	Lea	GP	G	A	TP	PIM	GP	G	A	TP	PIM
1989-90	Cornell	ECAC	26	11	15	26	28	....	....	....	....	....
1990-91	Cornell	ECAC	28	17	14	31	60	....	....	....	....	....
	Cdn. National	....	3	1	2	3	0	....	....	....	....	....
1991-92	Cdn. National	....	63	16	24	40	78	....	....	....	....	....
	Cdn. Olympic	....	8	1	2	3	0	....	....	....	....	....
	Toronto	**NHL**	**15**	**0**	**4**	**4**	**0**	....	....	....	....	....
	St. John's	AHL	....	....	....	....	....	12	5	9	14	14
1992-93	**Toronto**	**NHL**	**18**	**1**	**1**	**2**	**17**	**18**	**1**	**0**	**1**	**8**
	St. John's	AHL	56	19	28	47	86	2	0	2	2	0
1993-94	**Toronto**	**NHL**	**67**	**7**	**9**	**16**	**63**	**12**	**1**	**0**	**1**	**4**
1994-95	**Toronto**	**NHL**	**36**	**0**	**1**	**1**	**22**	**7**	**0**	**0**	**0**	**6**
1995-96	**Edmonton**	**NHL**	**37**	**3**	**5**	**8**	**38**	....	....	....	....	....
	St. John's	AHL	27	16	12	28	26	....	....	....	....	....
	NHL Totals		**173**	**11**	**20**	**31**	**140**	**37**	**2**	**0**	**2**	**18**

Traded to **Toronto** by **Calgary** with Doug Gilmour, Jamie Macoun, Rick Wamsley and Ric Nattress for Gary Leeman, Alexander Godynyuk, Jeff Reese, Michel Petit and Craig Berube, January 2, 1992. Traded to **Edmonton** by **Toronto** for Peter White and Edmonton's fourth round choice (Jason Sessa) in 1996 Entry Draft, December 4, 1995.

MANELUK, MIKE OTT.

Left wing. Shoots right. 5'11", 188 lbs. Born, Winnipeg, Man., October 1, 1973.

			Regular Season					Playoffs				
Season	Club	Lea	GP	G	A	TP	PIM	GP	G	A	TP	PIM
1991-92	Brandon	WHL	68	23	30	53	102	....	....	....	....	....
1992-93	Brandon	WHL	72	36	51	87	75	4	2	1	3	2
1993-94	Brandon	WHL	63	50	47	97	112	13	11	3	14	23
	San Diego	IHL	....	....	....	....	....	1	0	0	0	0
1994-95	Cdn. National	....	44	36	24	60	34	....	....	....	....	....
	San Diego	IHL	10	0	1	1	4	....	....	....	....	....
1995-96	Baltimore	AHL	74	33	38	71	73	6	4	3	7	14

Signed as a free agent by **Anaheim**, January 28, 1994. Traded to **Ottawa** by **Anaheim** for Kevin Brown, July 1, 1996.

MANLOW, ERIC CHI.

Center. Shoots left. 6', 190 lbs. Born, Belleville, Ont., April 7, 1975.
(Chicago's 2nd choice, 50th overall, in 1993 Entry Draft).

			Regular Season					Playoffs				
Season	Club	Lea	GP	G	A	TP	PIM	GP	G	A	TP	PIM
1991-92	Kitchener	OHL	59	26	21	47	31	14	2	5	7	10
1992-93	Kitchener	OHL	53	12	20	32	17	4	0	1	1	2
1993-94	Kitchener	OHL	49	28	32	60	25	3	0	1	1	4
1994-95	Kitchener	OHL	44	25	29	54	26	....	....	....	....	....
	Detroit	OHL	16	4	16	20	11	21	11	10	21	18
1995-96	Indianapolis	IHL	75	6	11	17	32	4	0	1	1	4

MANN, CAMERON BOS.

Right wing. Shoots right. 6', 190 lbs.   Born, Thompson, Man., April 20, 1977.
(Boston's 5th choice, 99th overall, in 1995 Entry Draft).

			Regular Season					Playoffs				
Season	Club	Lea	GP	G	A	TP	PIM	GP	G	A	TP	PIM
1994-95	Peterborough	OHL	64	19	24	43	40	11	3	8	11	4
1995-96abc	Peterborough	OHL	66	42	60	102	108	24	*27	16	*43	33

a OHL First All-Star Team (1996)
b Memorial Cup All-Star Team (1996)
c Won Stafford Smythe Memorial Trophy (Memorial Cup Tournament MVP) (1996)

MANSON, DAVE PHO.

Defense. Shoots left. 6'2", 202 lbs.   Born, Prince Albert, Sask., January 27, 1967.
(Chicago's 1st choice, 11th overall, in 1985 Entry Draft).

			Regular Season					Playoffs				
Season	Club	Lea	GP	G	A	TP	PIM	GP	G	A	TP	PIM
1983-84	Prince Albert	WHL	70	2	7	9	233	5	0	0	0	4
1984-85	Prince Albert	WHL	72	8	30	38	247	13	1	0	1	34
1985-86	Prince Albert	WHL	70	14	34	48	177	20	1	8	9	63
1986-87	Chicago	NHL	63	1	8	9	146	3	0	0	0	10
1987-88	Chicago	NHL	54	1	6	7	185	5	0	0	0	27
	Saginaw	IHL	6	0	3	3	37	....	....	....	....	....
1988-89	Chicago	NHL	79	18	36	54	352	16	0	8	8	84
1989-90	Chicago	NHL	59	5	23	28	301	20	2	4	6	46
1990-91	Chicago	NHL	75	14	15	29	191	6	0	1	1	36
1991-92	Edmonton	NHL	79	15	32	47	220	16	3	9	12	44
1992-93	Edmonton	NHL	83	15	30	45	210	....	....	....	....	....
1993-94	Edmonton	NHL	57	3	13	16	140	....	....	....	....	....
	Winnipeg	NHL	13	1	4	5	51	....	....	....	....	....
1994-95	Winnipeg	NHL	44	3	15	18	139	....	....	....	....	....
1995-96	Winnipeg	NHL	82	7	23	30	205	6	2	1	3	30
	NHL Totals		688	83	205	288	2140	72	7	23	30	277

Played in NHL All-Star Game (1989, 1993)

Traded to **Edmonton** by **Chicago** with Chicago's third round choice (Kirk Maltby) in 1992 Entry Draft for Steve Smith, October 2, 1991. Traded to **Winnipeg** by **Edmonton** with St. Louis' sixth round choice (previously acquired by Edmonton — Winnipeg selected Chris Kibermanis) in 1994 Entry Draft for Boris Mironov, Mats Lindgren, Winnipeg's first round choice (Jason Bonsignore) in 1994 Entry Draft and Florida's fourth round choice (previously acquired by Winnipeg — Edmonton selected Adam Copeland) in 1994 Entry Draft, March 15, 1994.

MARA, ROB CHI.

Right wing. Shoots right. 6'1", 175 lbs.   Born, Boston, MA, September 25, 1975.
(Chicago's 11th choice, 263rd overall, in 1994 Entry Draft).

			Regular Season					Playoffs				
Season	Club	Lea	GP	G	A	TP	PIM	GP	G	A	TP	PIM
1994-95	Colgate	ECAC	33	6	8	14	33	....	....	....	....	....
1995-96	Colgate	ECAC	33	8	6	14	36	....	....	....	....	....

MARCHANT, TERRY (mahr-SHAHNT) EDM.

Left wing. Shoots left. 6'2", 205 lbs.   Born, Buffalo, NY, February 24, 1976.
(Edmonton's 9th choice, 136th overall, in 1994 Entry Draft).

			Regular Season					Playoffs				
Season	Club	Lea	GP	G	A	TP	PIM	GP	G	A	TP	PIM
1994-95	Lake Superior	CCHA	23	2	5	7	12	....	....	....	....	....
1995-96	Lake Superior	CCHA	36	8	5	13	15	....	....	....	....	....

MARCHANT, TODD (mahr-SHAHNT) EDM.

Center. Shoots left. 5'10", 175 lbs.   Born, Buffalo, NY, August 12, 1973.
(NY Rangers' 8th choice, 164th overall, in 1993 Entry Draft).

			Regular Season					Playoffs				
Season	Club	Lea	GP	G	A	TP	PIM	GP	G	A	TP	PIM
1991-92	Clarkson	ECAC	32	20	12	32	32	....	....	....	....	....
1992-93a	Clarkson	ECAC	33	18	28	46	38	....	....	....	....	....
1993-94	U.S. National	....	59	28	39	67	48	....	....	....	....	....
	U.S. Olympic	....	8	1	1	2	6	....	....	....	....	....
	NY Rangers	NHL	1	0	0	0	0	....	....	....	....	....
	Binghamton	AHL	8	2	7	9	6	....	....	....	....	....
	Edmonton	NHL	3	0	1	1	2	....	....	....	....	....
	Cape Breton	AHL	3	1	4	5	2	5	1	1	2	0
1994-95	Cape Breton	AHL	38	22	25	47	25	....	....	....	....	....
	Edmonton	NHL	45	13	14	27	32	....	....	....	....	....
1995-96	Edmonton	NHL	81	19	19	38	66	....	....	....	....	....
	NHL Totals		130	32	34	66	100	....	....	....	....	....

a ECAC Second All-Star Team (1993)

Traded to **Edmonton** by **NY Rangers** for Craig MacTavish, March 21, 1994.

MARCHMENT, BRYAN EDM.

Defense. Shoots left. 6'1", 205 lbs.   Born, Scarborough, Ont., May 1, 1969.
(Winnipeg's 1st choice, 16th overall, in 1987 Entry Draft).

			Regular Season					Playoffs				
Season	Club	Lea	GP	G	A	TP	PIM	GP	G	A	TP	PIM
1985-86	Belleville	OHL	57	5	15	20	225	21	0	7	7	83
1986-87	Belleville	OHL	52	6	38	44	238	6	0	4	4	17
1987-88	Belleville	OHL	56	7	51	58	200	6	1	3	4	19
1988-89	Winnipeg	NHL	2	0	0	0	2	....	....	....	....	....
a	Belleville	OHL	43	14	36	50	118	5	0	1	1	12
1989-90	Winnipeg	NHL	7	0	2	2	28	....	....	....	....	....
	Moncton	AHL	56	4	19	23	217	....	....	....	....	....
1990-91	Winnipeg	NHL	28	2	2	4	91	....	....	....	....	....
	Moncton	AHL	33	2	11	13	101	....	....	....	....	....
1991-92	Chicago	NHL	58	5	10	15	168	16	1	0	1	36
1992-93	Chicago	NHL	78	5	15	20	313	4	0	0	0	12
1993-94	Chicago	NHL	13	1	4	5	42	....	....	....	....	....
	Hartford	NHL	42	3	7	10	124	....	....	....	....	....
1994-95	Edmonton	NHL	40	1	5	6	184	....	....	....	....	....
1995-96	Edmonton	NHL	78	3	15	18	202	....	....	....	....	....
	NHL Totals		346	20	60	80	1154	20	1	0	1	48

a OHL Second All-Star Team (1989)

Traded to **Chicago** by **Winnipeg** with Chris Norton for Troy Murray and Warren Rychel, July 22, 1991. Traded to **Hartford** by **Chicago** with Steve Larmer for Eric Weinrich and Patrick Poulin, November 2, 1993. Acquired by **Edmonton** from **Hartford** as compensation for Hartford's signing of free agent Steven Rice, August 30, 1994.

MARHA, JOSEF (MAHR-hah) COL.

Center. Shoots left. 6', 176 lbs.   Born, Havlickuv Brod, Czech., June 2, 1976.
(Quebec's 3rd choice, 35th overall, in 1994 Entry Draft).

			Regular Season					Playoffs				
Season	Club	Lea	GP	G	A	TP	PIM	GP	G	A	TP	PIM
1992-93	Dukla Jihlava	Czech.	7	2	2	4	....	....	....	....	....	....
1993-94	Dukla Jihlava	Czech.	41	7	2	9	....	3	0	1	1	....
1994-95	Dukla Jihlava	Czech.	35	3	7	10	6	....	....	....	....	....
1995-96	Colorado	NHL	2	0	1	1	0	....	....	....	....	....
	Cornwall	AHL	74	18	30	48	30	8	1	2	3	10
	NHL Totals		2	0	1	1	0	....	....	....	....	....

MARINUCCI, CHRIS (mair-ihn-OO-chee) NYI

Center. Shoots left. 6', 188 lbs.   Born, Grand Rapids, MN, December 29, 1971.
(NY Islanders' 4th choice, 90th overall, in 1990 Entry Draft).

			Regular Season					Playoffs				
Season	Club	Lea	GP	G	A	TP	PIM	GP	G	A	TP	PIM
1990-91	Minn.-Duluth	WCHA	36	6	10	16	20	....	....	....	....	....
1991-92	Minn.-Duluth	WCHA	37	6	13	19	41	....	....	....	....	....
1992-93a	Minn. Duluth	WCHA	40	35	42	77	52	....	....	....	....	....
1993-94bcd	Minn. Duluth	WCHA	38	*30	31	61	65	....	....	....	....	....
1994-95	Denver	IHL	74	29	40	69	42	14	3	4	7	12
	NY Islanders	NHL	12	1	4	5	2	....	....	....	....	....
1995-96	Utah	IHL	8	3	5	8	8	....	....	....	....	....
	NHL Totals		12	1	4	5	2	....	....	....	....	....

a WCHA Second All-Star Team (1993)
b WCHA First All-Star Team (1994)
c NCAA West First All-American Team (1994)
d Won Hobey Baker Memorial Award (Top U.S. Collegiate Player) (1994)

MARK, GORDON

Defense. Shoots right. 6'4", 218 lbs.   Born, Edmonton, Alta., September 10, 1964.
(New Jersey's 4th choice, 108th overall, in 1983 Entry Draft).

			Regular Season					Playoffs				
Season	Club	Lea	GP	G	A	TP	PIM	GP	G	A	TP	PIM
1982-83	Kamloops	WHL	71	12	20	32	135	7	1	1	2	8
1983-84	Kamloops	WHL	67	12	30	42	202	17	2	6	8	27
1984-85	Kamloops	WHL	32	11	23	34	68	7	1	2	3	10
1985-86	Maine	AHL	77	9	13	22	134	5	0	1	1	9
1986-87	New Jersey	NHL	36	3	5	8	82	....	....	....	....	....
	Maine	AHL	29	4	10	14	66	....	....	....	....	....
1987-88	New Jersey	NHL	19	0	2	2	27	....	....	....	....	....
	Utica	AHL	50	5	21	26	96	....	....	....	....	....
1988-89	Stony Plain	Sr.			UNAVAILABLE			....	....	....	....	....
1989-90	Stony Plain	Sr.			UNAVAILABLE			....	....	....	....	....
1990-91	Stony Plain	Sr.			UNAVAILABLE			....	....	....	....	....
1991-92	Stony Plain	Sr.			UNAVAILABLE			....	....	....	....	....
1992-93	Cape Breton	AHL	60	3	21	24	78	16	1	7	8	20
1993-94	Cape Breton	AHL	49	11	20	31	116	5	0	2	2	26
	Edmonton	NHL	12	0	1	1	43	....	....	....	....	....
1994-95	Edmonton	NHL	18	0	2	2	35	....	....	....	....	....
1995-96	Las Vegas	IHL	60	2	7	9	98	1	0	0	0	0
	NHL Totals		85	3	10	13	187	....	....	....	....	....

Signed as a free agent by **Edmonton**, February 1, 1994.

MARKKANEN, MIKKO S.J.

Right wing. Shoots right. 5'9", 169 lbs.   Born, Turku, Finland, January 9, 1977.
(San Jose's 12th choice, 220th overall, in 1995 Entry Draft).

			Regular Season					Playoffs				
Season	Club	Lea	GP	G	A	TP	PIM	GP	G	A	TP	PIM
1994-95	TPS	Fin. Jr.	32	10	8	18	28	....	....	....	....	....
	Kiekko-67	Fin. 2	1	0	1	1	0	....	....	....	....	....
1995-96	TPS	Fin. Jr.	7	2	3	5	16	....	....	....	....	....
	Kiekko-67	Fin. 2	38	9	11	20	34	6	1	1	2	6

MARKOV, DANIIL TOR.

Defense. Shoots left. 5'11", 176 lbs.   Born, Moscow, USSR, July 11, 1976.
(Toronto's 7th choice, 223rd overall, in 1995 Entry Draft).

			Regular Season					Playoffs				
Season	Club	Lea	GP	G	A	TP	PIM	GP	G	A	TP	PIM
1993-94	Spartak	CIS	13	1	0	1	6	1	0	0	0	0
1994-95	Spartak	CIS	39	0	1	1	36	....	....	....	....	....
1995-96	Spartak	CIS	38	2	0	2	12	2	0	0	0	2

MARLEAU, DOMINIC (mahr-LOH) DAL.

Defense. Shoots right. 6'2", 195 lbs.   Born, Lasalle, Que., February 11, 1977.
(Dallas' 6th choice, 141st overall, in 1995 Entry Draft).

			Regular Season					Playoffs				
Season	Club	Lea	GP	G	A	TP	PIM	GP	G	A	TP	PIM
1993-94	Victoriaville	QMJHL	67	2	10	12	45	5	0	1	1	4
1994-95	Victoriaville	QMJHL	63	3	13	16	78	3	0	0	0	11
1995-96	Victoriaville	QMJHL	6	0	2	2	7	....	....	....	....	....
	Laval	QMJHL	27	0	6	6	41	....	....	....	....	....
	Beauport	QMJHL	18	2	3	5	22	19	0	3	3	6

MAROIS, DANIEL (mair-WAH) TOR.

Right wing. Shoots right. 6', 190 lbs. Born, Montreal, Que., October 3, 1968.
(Toronto's 2nd choice, 28th overall, in 1987 Entry Draft).

			Regular Season					Playoffs				
Season	Club	Lea	GP	G	A	TP	PIM	GP	G	A	TP	PIM
1985-86	Verdun	QMJHL	58	42	35	77	110	5	4	2	6	6
1986-87	Chicoutimi	QMJHL	40	22	26	48	143	16	7	14	21	25
1987-88	Verdun	QMJHL	67	52	36	88	153	....	....	....	....	....
	Newmarket	AHL	8	4	4	8	4	....	....	....	....	....
	Toronto	**NHL**	....	....	....	....	....	**3**	**1**	**0**	**1**	**0**
1988-89	**Toronto**	**NHL**	**76**	**31**	**23**	**54**	**76**	....	....	....	....	....
1989-90	**Toronto**	**NHL**	**68**	**39**	**37**	**76**	**82**	**5**	**2**	**2**	**4**	**12**
1990-91	**Toronto**	**NHL**	**78**	**21**	**9**	**30**	**112**	....	....	....	....	....
1991-92	**Toronto**	**NHL**	**63**	**15**	**11**	**26**	**76**	....	....	....	....	....
	NY Islanders	**NHL**	**12**	**2**	**5**	**7**	**18**	....	....	....	....	....
1992-93	**NY Islanders**	**NHL**	**28**	**2**	**5**	**7**	**35**	....	....	....	....	....
	Capital Dist.	AHL	4	2	0	2	0	....	....	....	....	....
1993-94	**Boston**	**NHL**	**22**	**7**	**3**	**10**	**18**	**11**	**0**	**1**	**1**	**16**
	Providence	AHL	6	1	2	3	6	....	....	....	....	....
1994-95			DID NOT PLAY – INJURED									
1995-96	**Dallas**	**NHL**	**3**	**0**	**0**	**0**	**2**	....	....	....	....	....
	Michigan	IHL	61	28	28	56	105	....	....	....	....	....
	Minnesota	IHL	13	4	3	7	20	....	....	....	....	....
	NHL Totals		**350**	**117**	**93**	**210**	**419**	**19**	**3**	**3**	**6**	**28**

Traded to **NY Islanders** by **Toronto** with Claude Loiselle for Ken Baumgartner and Dave McLlwain, March 10, 1992. Traded to **Boston** by **NY Islanders** for Boston's eighth round choice (Peter Hogardh) in 1994 Entry Draft, March 18, 1993. Signed as a free agent by **Dallas**, January 26, 1995. Signed as a free agent by **Toronto**, August 22, 1996.

MARSHALL, BOBBY ANA.

Defense. Shoots left. 6'1", 190 lbs. Born, North York, Ont., April 11, 1972.
(Calgary's 6th choice, 129th overall, in 1991 Entry Draft).

			Regular Season					Playoffs				
Season	Club	Lea	GP	G	A	TP	PIM	GP	G	A	TP	PIM
1990-91	Miami-Ohio	CCHA	37	3	15	18	44	....	....	....	....	....
1991-92	Miami-Ohio	CCHA	40	5	20	25	48	....	....	....	....	....
1992-93ab	Miami-Ohio	CCHA	40	2	43	45	40	....	....	....	....	....
1993-94a	Miami-Ohio	CCHA	38	3	24	27	76	....	....	....	....	....
1994-95	Saint John	AHL	77	7	24	31	62	5	0	0	0	4
1995-96	Saint John	AHL	10	0	5	5	8	....	....	....	....	....
	Baltimore	AHL	67	3	28	31	38	12	2	8	10	8

a CCHA Second All-Star Team (1993, 1994)
b NCAA West Second All-American Team (1993)

Traded to **Anaheim** by **Calgary** for Jarrod Skalde, October 30, 1995.

MARSHALL, GRANT DAL.

Right wing. Shoots right. 6'1", 193 lbs. Born, Mississauga, Ont., June 9, 1973.
(Toronto's 2nd choice, 23rd overall, in 1992 Entry Draft).

			Regular Season					Playoffs				
Season	Club	Lea	GP	G	A	TP	PIM	GP	G	A	TP	PIM
1990-91	Ottawa	OHL	26	6	11	17	25	1	0	0	0	0
1991-92	Ottawa	OHL	61	32	51	83	132	11	6	11	17	11
1992-93	Ottawa	OHL	30	14	29	43	83	....	....	....	....	....
	Newmarket	OHL	31	11	25	36	89	7	4	7	11	20
	St. John's	AHL	2	0	0	0	0	2	0	0	0	2
1993-94	St. John's	AHL	67	11	29	40	155	11	1	5	6	17
1994-95	Kalamazoo	IHL	61	17	29	46	96	16	9	3	12	27
	Dallas	**NHL**	**2**	**0**	**1**	**1**	**0**	....	....	....	....	....
1995-96	**Dallas**	**NHL**	**70**	**9**	**19**	**28**	**111**	....	....	....	....	....
	NHL Totals		**72**	**9**	**20**	**29**	**111**	....	....	....	....	....

Acquired by **Dallas** from **Toronto** with Peter Zezel as compensation for Toronto's signing of free agent Mike Craig, August 10, 1994.

MARSHALL, JASON ANA.

Defense. Shoots right. 6'2", 195 lbs. Born, Cranbrook, B.C., February 22, 1971.
(St. Louis' 1st choice, 9th overall, in 1989 Entry Draft).

			Regular Season					Playoffs				
Season	Club	Lea	GP	G	A	TP	PIM	GP	G	A	TP	PIM
1988-89	Cdn. National	....	2	0	1	1	0	....	....	....	....	....
1989-90	Cdn. National	....	73	1	11	12	57	....	....	....	....	....
1990-91	Tri-Cities	WHL	59	10	34	44	236	7	1	2	3	20
	Peoria	IHL	....	....	....	....	....	18	0	1	1	48
1991-92	**St. Louis**	**NHL**	**2**	**1**	**0**	**1**	**4**	....	....	....	....	....
	Peoria	IHL	78	4	18	22	178	10	0	1	1	16
1992-93	Peoria	IHL	77	4	16	20	229	4	0	0	0	20
1993-94	Cdn. National	....	41	3	10	13	60	....	....	....	....	....
	Peoria	IHL	20	1	1	2	72	3	2	0	2	2
1994-95	San Diego	IHL	80	7	18	25	218	5	0	1	1	8
	Anaheim	**NHL**	**1**	**0**	**0**	**0**	**0**	....	....	....	....	....
1995-96	**Anaheim**	**NHL**	**24**	**0**	**1**	**1**	**42**	....	....	....	....	....
	Baltimore	AHL	57	1	13	14	150	....	....	....	....	....
	NHL Totals		**27**	**1**	**1**	**2**	**46**	....	....	....	....	....

Traded to **Anaheim** by **St. Louis** for Bill Houlder, August 29, 1994.

MARTIN, CRAIG FLA.

Right wing. Shoots right. 6'2", 215 lbs. Born, Amherst, N.S., January 21, 1971.
(Winnipeg's 6th choice, 98th overall, in 1990 Entry Draft).

			Regular Season					Playoffs				
Season	Club	Lea	GP	G	A	TP	PIM	GP	G	A	TP	PIM
1989-90	Hull	QMJHL	66	14	31	45	299	11	2	1	3	65
1990-91	Hull	QMJHL	18	5	6	11	87	....	....	....	....	....
	St-Hyacinthe	QMJHL	36	8	9	17	166	....	....	....	....	....
1991-92	Moncton	AHL	11	1	1	2	70	....	....	....	....	....
	Fort Wayne	IHL	24	0	0	0	115	....	....	....	....	....
1992-93	Moncton	AHL	64	5	13	18	198	5	0	1	1	22
1993-94	Adirondack	AHL	76	15	24	39	297	12	2	2	4	63
1994-95	**Winnipeg**	**NHL**	**20**	**0**	**1**	**1**	**19**	....	....	....	....	....
	Springfield	AHL	6	0	1	1	21	....	....	....	....	....
1995-96	Springfield	AHL	48	6	5	11	245	8	0	1	1	34
	NHL Totals		**20**	**0**	**1**	**1**	**19**	....	....	....	....	....

Signed as a free agent by **Detroit**, July 28, 1993. Signed as a free agent by **Florida**, August 1, 1996.

MARTIN, JUSTIN L.A.

Right wing. Shoots right. 6'3", 210 lbs. Born, Syracuse, NY, May 1, 1975.
(Los Angeles' 8th choice, 172nd overall, in 1993 Entry Draft).

			Regular Season					Playoffs				
Season	Club	Lea	GP	G	A	TP	PIM	GP	G	A	TP	PIM
1994-95	Vermont	ECAC	23	4	2	6	20	....	....	....	....	....
1995-96	Vermont	ECAC	28	1	0	1	20	....	....	....	....	....

MARTIN, MATT TOR.

Defense. Shoots left. 6'3", 205 lbs. Born, Hamden, CT, April 30, 1971.
(Toronto's 4th choice, 66th overall, in 1989 Entry Draft).

			Regular Season					Playoffs				
Season	Club	Lea	GP	G	A	TP	PIM	GP	G	A	TP	PIM
1990-91	U. of Maine	H.E.	35	3	12	15	48	....	....	....	....	....
1991-92	U. of Maine	H.E.	30	4	14	18	46	....	....	....	....	....
1992-93	U. of Maine	H.E.	44	6	26	32	88	....	....	....	....	....
	St. John's	AHL	2	0	0	0	2	9	1	5	6	4
1993-94	U.S. National	....	39	7	8	15	127	....	....	....	....	....
	U.S. Olympic	....	8	0	2	2	8	....	....	....	....	....
	Toronto	**NHL**	**12**	**0**	**1**	**1**	**6**	....	....	....	....	....
	St. John's	AHL	12	1	5	6	9	11	1	5	6	33
1994-95	St. John's	AHL	49	2	16	18	54	....	....	....	....	....
	Toronto	**NHL**	**15**	**0**	**0**	**0**	**13**	....	....	....	....	....
1995-96	**Toronto**	**NHL**	**13**	**0**	**0**	**0**	**14**	....	....	....	....	....
	NHL Totals		**40**	**0**	**1**	**1**	**33**	....	....	....	....	....

MARTIN, MIKE NYR

Defense. Shoots right. 6'2", 204 lbs. Born, Stratford, Ont., October 27, 1976.
(NY Rangers' 2nd choice, 65th overall, in 1995 Entry Draft).

			Regular Season					Playoffs				
Season	Club	Lea	GP	G	A	TP	PIM	GP	G	A	TP	PIM
1992-93	Windsor	OHL	61	2	7	9	80	....	....	....	....	....
1993-94	Windsor	OHL	64	2	29	31	94	4	1	2	3	4
1994-95	Windsor	OHL	53	9	28	37	79	10	1	3	4	21
1995-96	Windsor	OHL	65	19	48	67	128	7	0	6	6	14

MARTINI, DARCY

Defense. Shoots left. 6'4", 220 lbs. Born, Castlegar, B.C., January 30, 1969.
(Edmonton's 8th choice, 162nd overall, in 1989 Entry Draft).

			Regular Season					Playoffs				
Season	Club	Lea	GP	G	A	TP	PIM	GP	G	A	TP	PIM
1988-89	Michigan Tech	WCHA	35	1	2	3	103	....	....	....	....	....
1989-90	Michigan Tech	WCHA	36	3	6	9	151	....	....	....	....	....
1990-91	Michigan Tech	WCHA	34	10	13	23	*184	....	....	....	....	....
1991-92	Michigan Tech	WCHA	17	5	13	18	58	....	....	....	....	....
1992-93	Cape Breton	AHL	47	1	6	7	36	2	0	1	1	0
	Wheeling	ECHL	6	0	2	2	2	....	....	....	....	....
1993-94	**Edmonton**	**NHL**	**2**	**0**	**0**	**0**	**0**	....	....	....	....	....
	Cape Breton	AHL	65	18	38	56	131	5	1	3	4	26
1994-95	Cape Breton	AHL	31	2	13	15	75	....	....	....	....	....
	Portland	AHL	22	3	6	9	28	....	....	....	....	....
	Minnesota	IHL	10	3	1	4	10	1	0	0	0	2
1995-96	Los Angeles	IHL	49	15	31	46	50	....	....	....	....	....
	San Francisco	IHL	17	3	4	7	10	4	0	2	2	2
	NHL Totals		**2**	**0**	**0**	**0**	**0**	....	....	....	....	....

MARTINS, STEVE HFD.

Center. Shoots left. 5'9", 175 lbs. Born, Gatineau, Que., April 13, 1972.
(Hartford's 1st choice, 5th overall, in 1994 Supplemental Draft).

			Regular Season					Playoffs				
Season	Club	Lea	GP	G	A	TP	PIM	GP	G	A	TP	PIM
1991-92	Harvard	ECAC	20	13	14	27	26	....	....	....	....	....
1992-93	Harvard	ECAC	18	6	8	14	40	....	....	....	....	....
1993-94abc	Harvard	ECAC	32	25	35	60	*93	....	....	....	....	....
1994-95	Harvard	ECAC	28	15	23	38	93	....	....	....	....	....
1995-96	**Hartford**	**NHL**	**23**	**1**	**3**	**4**	**8**	....	....	....	....	....
	Springfield	AHL	30	9	20	29	10	....	....	....	....	....
	NHL Totals		**23**	**1**	**3**	**4**	**8**	....	....	....	....	....

a ECAC First All-Star Team (1994)
b NCAA East First All-American Team (1994)
c NCAA Final Four All-Tournament Team (1994)

MARTONE, MIKE BUF.

Defense. Shoots right. 6'1", 200 lbs. Born, Sault Ste. Marie, Ont., September 26, 1977.
(Buffalo's 6th choice, 106th overall, in 1996 Entry Draft).

			Regular Season					Playoffs				
Season	Club	Lea	GP	G	A	TP	PIM	GP	G	A	TP	PIM
1994-95	Peterborough	OHL	62	3	9	12	99	10	0	2	2	4
1995-96	Peterborough	OHL	64	3	12	15	127	24	7	5	12	37

MASON, WES N.J.

Left wing. Shoots left. 6'2", 180 lbs. Born, Windsor, Ont., December 12, 1977.
(New Jersey's 2nd choice, 38th overall, in 1996 Entry Draft).

			Regular Season					Playoffs				
Season	Club	Lea	GP	G	A	TP	PIM	GP	G	A	TP	PIM
1994-95	Sarnia	OHL	38	1	8	9	50	2	0	0	0	9
1995-96	Sarnia	OHL	63	23	45	68	97	10	3	2	5	16

MASTAD, MILT (MIHZ-tahd) BOS.

Defense. Shoots left. 6'3", 205 lbs. Born, Regina, Sask., March 5, 1975.
(Boston's 6th choice, 155th overall, in 1993 Entry Draft).

			Regular Season					Playoffs				
Season	Club	Lea	GP	G	A	TP	PIM	GP	G	A	TP	PIM
1992-93	Seattle	WHL	60	1	1	2	123	5	0	1	1	14
1993-94	Seattle	WHL	29	1	3	4	59	....	....	....	....	....
	Moose Jaw	WHL	41	2	8	10	74	....	....	....	....	....
1994-95	Moose Jaw	WHL	68	1	8	9	155	5	0	0	0	6
1995-96	Providence	AHL	18	0	2	2	52	....	....	....	....	....

MATSOS, DAVID T.B.

Left wing. Shoots left. 6'1", 201 lbs. Born, Burlington, Ont., November 12, 1973.

			Regular Season					Playoffs				
Season	Club	Lea	GP	G	A	TP	PIM	GP	G	A	TP	PIM
1989-90	S.S. Marie	OHL	53	2	5	7	31	....	....	....	....	....
1990-91	S.S. Marie	OHL	60	10	16	26	41	14	2	5	7	10
1991-92	S.S. Marie	OHL	61	23	22	45	34	19	4	5	9	6
1992-93	S.S. Marie	OHL	62	36	27	63	44	16	3	8	11	18
1993-94	Western Ont.	OUAA	37	25	16	41	26	....	....	....	....	....
1994-95	Western Ont.	OUAA	33	15	16	31	25	....	....	....	....	....
1995-96	Cdn. National	....	43	18	15	33	37	....	....	....	....	....

Signed as a free agent by **Tampa Bay**, May 1, 1996.

MATTE, CHRISTIAN — COL.

Right wing. Shoots right. 5'11", 166 lbs. Born, Hull, Que., January 20, 1975.
(Quebec's 8th choice, 153rd overall, in 1993 Entry Draft).

			Regular Season					Playoffs				
Season	Club	Lea	GP	G	A	TP	PIM	GP	G	A	TP	PIM
1992-93	Granby	QMJHL	68	17	36	53	59	....	....	....	....	....
1993-94a	Granby	QMJHL	59	50	47	97	103	7	5	5	10	12
	Cornwall	AHL	1	0	0	0	0	....	....	....	....	....
1994-95	Granby	QMJHL	66	50	66	116	86	13	11	7	18	12
	Cornwall	AHL	....	....	....	....	....	3	0	1	1	2
1995-96	Cornwall	AHL	64	20	32	52	51	7	1	1	2	6

a QMJHL Second All-Star Team (1994)

MATTEAU, STEPHANE (mah-TOH) — ST.L.

Left wing. Shoots left. 6'3", 210 lbs. Born, Rouyn-Noranda, Que., September 2, 1969.
(Calgary's 2nd choice, 25th overall, in 1987 Entry Draft).

			Regular Season					Playoffs				
Season	Club	Lea	GP	G	A	TP	PIM	GP	G	A	TP	PIM
1985-86	Hull	QMJHL	60	6	8	14	19	4	0	0	0	0
1986-87	Hull	QMJHL	69	27	48	75	113	8	3	7	10	8
1987-88	Hull	QMJHL	57	17	40	57	179	18	5	14	19	94
1988-89	Hull	QMJHL	59	44	45	89	202	9	8	6	14	30
	Salt Lake	IHL	....	....	....	....	....	9	0	4	4	13
1989-90	Salt Lake	IHL	81	23	35	58	130	10	6	3	9	38
1990-91	**Calgary**	**NHL**	**78**	**15**	**19**	**34**	**93**	**5**	**0**	**1**	**1**	**0**
1991-92	**Calgary**	**NHL**	**4**	**1**	**0**	**1**	**19**	....	....	....	....	....
	Chicago	**NHL**	**20**	**5**	**8**	**13**	**45**	**18**	**4**	**6**	**10**	**24**
1992-93	**Chicago**	**NHL**	**79**	**15**	**18**	**33**	**98**	**3**	**0**	**1**	**1**	**2**
1993-94	**Chicago**	**NHL**	**65**	**15**	**16**	**31**	**55**	....	....	....	....	....
	NY Rangers	**NHL**	**12**	**4**	**3**	**7**	**2**	**23**	**6**	**3**	**9**	**20** ♦
1994-95	**NY Rangers**	**NHL**	**41**	**3**	**5**	**8**	**25**	**9**	**0**	**1**	**1**	**10**
1995-96	**NY Rangers**	**NHL**	**32**	**4**	**2**	**6**	**22**	....	....	....	....	....
	St. Louis	**NHL**	**46**	**7**	**13**	**20**	**65**	**11**	**0**	**2**	**2**	**8**
	NHL Totals		**377**	**69**	**84**	**153**	**424**	**69**	**10**	**14**	**24**	**64**

Traded to **Chicago** by **Calgary** for Trent Yawney, December 16, 1991. Traded to **NY Rangers** by **Chicago** with Brian Noonan for Tony Amonte and the rights to Matt Oates, March 21, 1994. Traded to **St. Louis** by **NY Rangers** for Ian Laperriere, December 28, 1995.

MATTSSON, JESPER — CGY.

Center. Shoots right. 6', 185 lbs. Born, Malmo, Sweden, May 13, 1975.
(Calgary's 1st choice, 18th overall, in 1993 Entry Draft).

			Regular Season					Playoffs				
Season	Club	Lea	GP	G	A	TP	PIM	GP	G	A	TP	PIM
1991-92	Malmo	Swe.	24	0	1	1	2	....	....	....	....	....
1992-93	Malmo	Swe.	40	9	8	17	14	5	0	0	0	0
1993-94	Malmo	Swe.	40	3	6	9	14	9	1	2	3	2
1994-95	Malmo	Swe.	37	9	6	15	18	9	2	0	2	18
1995-96	Saint John	AHL	73	12	26	38	18	9	1	1	2	2

MATVICHUK, RICHARD (MAT-vih-chuhk) — DAL.

Defense. Shoots left. 6'2", 200 lbs. Born, Edmonton, Alta., February 5, 1973.
(Minnesota's 1st choice, 8th overall, in 1991 Entry Draft).

			Regular Season					Playoffs				
Season	Club	Lea	GP	G	A	TP	PIM	GP	G	A	TP	PIM
1989-90	Saskatoon	WHL	56	8	24	32	126	10	2	8	10	16
1990-91	Saskatoon	WHL	68	13	36	49	117	....	....	....	....	....
1991-92a	Saskatoon	WHL	58	14	40	54	126	22	1	9	10	61
1992-93	**Minnesota**	**NHL**	**53**	**2**	**3**	**5**	**26**	....	....	....	....	....
	Kalamazoo	IHL	3	0	1	1	6	....	....	....	....	....
1993-94	**Dallas**	**NHL**	**25**	**0**	**3**	**3**	**22**	**7**	**1**	**1**	**2**	**12**
	Kalamazoo	IHL	43	8	17	25	84	....	....	....	....	....
1994-95	**Dallas**	**NHL**	**14**	**0**	**2**	**2**	**14**	**5**	**0**	**2**	**2**	**4**
	Kalamazoo	IHL	17	0	6	6	16	....	....	....	....	....
1995-96	**Dallas**	**NHL**	**73**	**6**	**16**	**22**	**71**	....	....	....	....	....
	NHL Totals		**165**	**8**	**24**	**32**	**133**	**12**	**1**	**3**	**4**	**16**

a WHL East First All-Star Team (1992)

MAUDIE, BOB — NYR

Center. Shoots left. 5'11", 180 lbs. Born, Cranbrook, B.C., September 17, 1976.
(NY Rangers' 9th choice, 221st overall, in 1995 Entry Draft).

			Regular Season					Playoffs				
Season	Club	Lea	GP	G	A	TP	PIM	GP	G	A	TP	PIM
1992-93	Kamloops	WHL	38	1	5	6	24	3	0	0	0	0
1993-94	Kamloops	WHL	65	11	13	24	29	19	1	1	2	2
1994-95	Kamloops	WHL	67	9	29	38	34	21	1	2	3	8
1995-96	Kamloops	WHL	67	39	62	101	77	16	8	11	19	16

MAY, ALAN

Right wing. Shoots right. 6'1", 200 lbs. Born, Swan Hills, Alta., January 14, 1965.

			Regular Season					Playoffs				
Season	Club	Lea	GP	G	A	TP	PIM	GP	G	A	TP	PIM
1985-86	Medicine Hat	WHL	6	1	0	1	25	....	....	....	....	....
	N. Westminster	WHL	32	8	9	17	81	....	....	....	....	....
1986-87	Springfield	AHL	4	0	2	2	11	....	....	....	....	....
	Carolina	ACHL	42	23	14	37	310	5	2	2	4	57
1987-88	**Boston**	**NHL**	**3**	**0**	**0**	**0**	**15**	....	....	....	....	....
	Maine	AHL	61	14	11	25	257	....	....	....	....	....
	Nova Scotia	AHL	13	4	1	5	54	4	0	0	0	51
1988-89	**Edmonton**	**NHL**	**3**	**1**	**0**	**1**	**7**	....	....	....	....	....
	Cape Breton	AHL	50	12	13	25	214	....	....	....	....	....
	New Haven	AHL	12	2	8	10	99	16	6	3	9	*105
1989-90	**Washington**	**NHL**	**77**	**7**	**10**	**17**	**339**	**15**	**0**	**0**	**0**	**37**
1990-91	**Washington**	**NHL**	**67**	**4**	**6**	**10**	**264**	**11**	**1**	**1**	**2**	**37**
1991-92	**Washington**	**NHL**	**75**	**6**	**9**	**15**	**221**	**7**	**0**	**0**	**0**	**0**
1992-93	**Washington**	**NHL**	**83**	**6**	**10**	**16**	**268**	**6**	**0**	**1**	**1**	**6**
1993-94	**Washington**	**NHL**	**43**	**4**	**7**	**11**	**97**	....	....	....	....	....
	Dallas	**NHL**	**8**	**1**	**0**	**1**	**18**	**1**	**0**	**0**	**0**	**0**
1994-95	**Dallas**	**NHL**	**27**	**1**	**1**	**2**	**106**	....	....	....	....	....
	Calgary	**NHL**	**7**	**1**	**2**	**3**	**13**	....	....	....	....	....
1995-96	Orlando	IHL	4	0	0	0	11	....	....	....	....	....
	Utah	IHL	53	13	12	25	108	14	1	2	3	14
	NHL Totals		**393**	**31**	**45**	**76**	**1348**	**40**	**1**	**2**	**3**	**80**

Signed as a free agent by **Boston**, October 30, 1987. Traded to **Edmonton** by **Boston** for Moe Lemay, March 8, 1988. Traded to **Los Angeles** by **Edmonton** with Jim Wiemer for Brian Wilks and John English, March 7, 1989. Traded to **Washington** by **Los Angeles** for Washington's fifth round choice (Thomas Newman) in 1989 Entry Draft, June 17, 1989. Traded to **Dallas** by **Washington** with Washington's seventh round choice (Jeff Dewar) in 1995 Entry Draft for Jim Johnson, March 21, 1994. Traded to **Calgary** by **Dallas** for Calgary's eighth round choice (Sergei Luchinkin) in 1995 Entry Draft, April 7, 1995.

MAY, BRAD — BUF.

Left wing. Shoots left. 6'1", 210 lbs. Born, Toronto, Ont., November 29, 1971.
(Buffalo's 1st choice, 14th overall, in 1990 Entry Draft).

			Regular Season					Playoffs				
Season	Club	Lea	GP	G	A	TP	PIM	GP	G	A	TP	PIM
1988-89	Niagara Falls	OHL	65	8	14	22	304	17	0	1	1	55
1989-90a	Niagara Falls	OHL	61	32	58	90	223	16	9	13	22	64
1990-91a	Niagara Falls	OHL	34	37	32	69	93	14	11	14	25	53
1991-92	**Buffalo**	**NHL**	**69**	**11**	**6**	**17**	**309**	**7**	**1**	**4**	**5**	**2**
1992-93	**Buffalo**	**NHL**	**82**	**13**	**13**	**26**	**242**	**8**	**1**	**1**	**2**	**14**
1993-94	**Buffalo**	**NHL**	**84**	**18**	**27**	**45**	**171**	**7**	**0**	**2**	**2**	**9**
1994-95	**Buffalo**	**NHL**	**33**	**3**	**3**	**6**	**87**	**4**	**0**	**0**	**0**	**2**
1995-96	**Buffalo**	**NHL**	**79**	**15**	**29**	**44**	**295**	....	....	....	....	....
	NHL Totals		**347**	**60**	**78**	**138**	**1104**	**26**	**2**	**7**	**9**	**27**

a OHL Second All-Star Team (1990, 1991)

MAYER, DEREK

Defense. Shoots right. 6', 200 lbs. Born, Rossland, B.C., May 21, 1967.
(Detroit's 3rd choice, 43rd overall, in 1986 Entry Draft).

			Regular Season					Playoffs				
Season	Club	Lea	GP	G	A	TP	PIM	GP	G	A	TP	PIM
1985-86	Denver	WCHA	44	2	7	9	42	....	....	....	....	....
1986-87	Denver	WCHA	38	5	17	22	87	....	....	....	....	....
1987-88	Denver	WCHA	34	5	16	21	82	....	....	....	....	....
1988-89	Cdn. National	....	58	3	13	16	81	....	....	....	....	....
1989-90	Adirondack	AHL	62	4	26	30	56	5	0	6	6	4
1990-91	San Diego	IHL	31	9	24	33	31	....	....	....	....	....
	Adirondack	AHL	21	4	9	13	20	2	0	1	1	0
1991-92	Adirondack	AHL	25	4	11	15	31	....	....	....	....	....
	San Diego	IHL	30	7	16	23	47	4	0	0	0	20
1992-93	Cdn. National	....	64	12	28	40	108	....	....	....	....	....
1993-94	Cdn. National	....	49	4	15	19	61	....	....	....	....	....
	Cdn. Olympic	....	8	1	2	3	18	....	....	....	....	....
	Ottawa	**NHL**	**17**	**2**	**2**	**4**	**8**	....	....	....	....	....
1994-95	Atlanta	IHL	55	7	17	24	77	5	1	1	2	10
1995-96	Cdn. National	....	12	1	4	5	25	....	....	....	....	....
	Tappara	Fin.	50	17	8	25	96	4	3	4	7	18
	NHL Totals		**17**	**2**	**2**	**4**	**8**	....	....	....	....	....

Signed as a free agent by **Ottawa**, March 4, 1994.

MAYERS, JAMAL — ST.L.

Center. Shoots right. 6', 190 lbs. Born, Toronto, Ont., October 24, 1974.
(St. Louis' 3rd choice, 89th overall, in 1993 Entry Draft).

			Regular Season					Playoffs				
Season	Club	Lea	GP	G	A	TP	PIM	GP	G	A	TP	PIM
1992-93	W. Michigan	CCHA	38	8	17	25	26	....	....	....	....	....
1993-94	W. Michigan	CCHA	40	17	32	49	40	....	....	....	....	....
1994-95	W. Michigan	CCHA	39	13	32	45	40	....	....	....	....	....
1995-96	W. Michigan	CCHA	38	17	22	39	75	....	....	....	....	....

McALLISTER, CHRIS — VAN.

Defense. Shoots left. 6'7", 238 lbs. Born, Saskatoon, Sask., June 16, 1975.
(Vancouver's 2nd choice, 40th overall, in 1995 Entry Draft).

			Regular Season					Playoffs				
Season	Club	Lea	GP	G	A	TP	PIM	GP	G	A	TP	PIM
1993-94	Saskatoon	WHL	2	0	0	0	5	....	....	....	....	....
1994-95	Saskatoon	WHL	65	2	8	10	134	10	0	0	0	28
1995-96	Syracuse	AHL	68	0	2	2	142	16	0	0	0	34

McALPINE, CHRIS — N.J.

Defense. Shoots right. 6', 210 lbs. Born, Roseville, MN, December 1, 1971.
(New Jersey's 10th choice, 137th overall, in 1990 Entry Draft).

			Regular Season					Playoffs				
Season	Club	Lea	GP	G	A	TP	PIM	GP	G	A	TP	PIM
1990-91	U. Minnesota	WCHA	38	7	9	16	112	....	....	....	....	....
1991-92	U. Minnesota	WCHA	39	3	9	12	126	....	....	....	....	....
1992-93	U. Minnesota	WCHA	41	14	9	23	82	....	....	....	....	....
1993-94ab	U. Minnesota	WCHA	36	12	18	30	121	....	....	....	....	....
1994-95	Albany	AHL	48	4	18	22	49	....	....	....	....	....
	New Jersey	**NHL**	**24**	**0**	**3**	**3**	**17**	....	....	....	....	.... ♦
1995-96	Albany	AHL	57	5	14	19	72	4	0	0	0	13
	NHL Totals		**24**	**0**	**3**	**3**	**17**	....	....	....	....	....

a WCHA First All-Star Team (1994)
b NCAA West Second All-American Team (1994)

McAMMOND, DEAN — EDM.

Center. Shoots left. 5'11", 185 lbs. Born, Grand Cache, Alta., June 15, 1973.
(Chicago's 1st choice, 22nd overall, in 1991 Entry Draft).

			Regular Season					Playoffs				
Season	Club	Lea	GP	G	A	TP	PIM	GP	G	A	TP	PIM
1989-90	Prince Albert	WHL	53	11	11	22	49	14	2	3	5	18
1990-91	Prince Albert	WHL	71	33	35	68	108	2	0	1	1	6
1991-92	**Chicago**	**NHL**	**5**	**0**	**2**	**2**	**0**	**3**	**0**	**0**	**0**	**2**
	Prince Albert	WHL	63	37	54	91	189	10	12	11	23	26
1992-93	Prince Albert	WHL	30	19	29	48	44	....	....	....	....	....
	Swift Current	WHL	18	10	13	23	24	17	*16	19	35	20
1993-94	**Edmonton**	**NHL**	**45**	**6**	**21**	**27**	**16**	....	....	....	....	....
	Cape Breton	AHL	28	9	12	21	38	....	....	....	....	....
1994-95	**Edmonton**	**NHL**	**6**	**0**	**0**	**0**	**0**	....	....	....	....	....
1995-96	**Edmonton**	**NHL**	**53**	**15**	**15**	**30**	**23**	....	....	....	....	....
	Cape Breton	AHL	22	9	15	24	55	....	....	....	....	....
	NHL Totals		**109**	**21**	**38**	**59**	**39**	**3**	**0**	**0**	**0**	**2**

Traded to **Edmonton** by **Chicago** with Igor Kravchuk for Joe Murphy, February 24, 1993.

McBAIN, JASON — HFD.

Defense. Shoots left. 6'2", 180 lbs. Born, Ilion, NY, April 12, 1974.
(Hartford's 5th choice, 81st overall, in 1992 Entry Draft).

			Regular Season					Playoffs				
Season	Club	Lea	GP	G	A	TP	PIM	GP	G	A	TP	PIM
1990-91	Lethbridge	WHL	52	2	7	9	39	1	0	0	0	0
1991-92	Lethbridge	WHL	13	0	1	1	12	....	....	....	....	....
	Portland	WHL	54	9	23	32	95	6	1	0	1	13
1992-93	Portland	WHL	71	9	35	44	76	16	2	12	14	14
1993-94	Portland	WHL	63	15	51	66	86	10	2	7	9	14
1994-95	Springfield	AHL	77	16	28	44	92	....	....	....	....	....
1995-96	**Hartford**	**NHL**	**3**	**0**	**0**	**0**	**0**	....	....	....	....	....
	Springfield	AHL	73	11	33	44	43	8	1	1	2	2
	NHL Totals		**3**	**0**	**0**	**0**	**0**	....	....	....	....	....

McBAIN, MIKE — T.B.

Defense. Shoots left. 6'1", 191 lbs. Born, Kimberley, B.C., January 12, 1977.
(Tampa Bay's 2nd choice, 30th overall, in 1995 Entry Draft).

			Regular Season					Playoffs				
Season	Club	Lea	GP	G	A	TP	PIM	GP	G	A	TP	PIM
1993-94	Red Deer	WHL	58	4	13	17	41	4	0	0	0	0
1994-95	Red Deer	WHL	68	6	28	34	55	....	....	....	....	....
1995-96	Red Deer	WHL	68	7	34	41	68	10	1	7	8	10

McCABE, BRYAN — NYI

Defense. Shoots left. 6'1", 204 lbs. Born, St. Catharines, Ont., June 8, 1975.
(NY Islanders' 2nd choice, 40th overall, in 1993 Entry Draft).

			Regular Season					Playoffs				
Season	Club	Lea	GP	G	A	TP	PIM	GP	G	A	TP	PIM
1991-92	Medicine Hat	WHL	68	6	24	30	157	4	0	0	0	6
1992-93	Medicine Hat	WHL	14	0	13	13	83	....	....	....	....	....
a	Spokane	WHL	46	3	44	47	134	6	1	5	6	28
1993-94	Spokane	WHL	64	22	62	84	218	3	0	4	4	4
1994-95	Spokane	WHL	42	14	39	53	115	....	....	....	....	....
bc	Brandon	WHL	20	6	10	16	38	18	4	13	17	59
1995-96	**NY Islanders**	**NHL**	**82**	**7**	**16**	**23**	**156**	....	....	....	....	....
	NHL Totals		**82**	**7**	**16**	**23**	**156**	....	....	....	....	....

a WHL West Second All-Star Team (1993)
b WHL East First All-Star Team (1995)
c Memorial Cup All-Star Team (1995)

McCABE, SCOTT — N.J.

Defense. Shoots left. 6'4", 189 lbs. Born, St. Clair Shores, MI, May 28, 1974.
(New Jersey's 4th choice, 94th overall, in 1992 Entry Draft).

			Regular Season					Playoffs				
Season	Club	Lea	GP	G	A	TP	PIM	GP	G	A	TP	PIM
1992-93	Lake Superior	CCHA	DID NOT PLAY									
1993-94	Lake Superior	CCHA	18	3	5	8	14	....	....	....	....	....
1994-95	Lake Superior	CCHA	6	0	0	0	7	....	....	....	....	....
1995-96	Lake Superior	CCHA	16	0	6	6	8	....	....	....	....	....

McCAMBRIDGE, KEITH — CGY.

Defense. Shoots left. 6'2", 205 lbs. Born, Thompson, Man., February 1, 1974.
(Calgary's 10th choice, 201st overall, in 1994 Entry Draft).

			Regular Season					Playoffs				
Season	Club	Lea	GP	G	A	TP	PIM	GP	G	A	TP	PIM
1991-92	Swift Current	WHL	72	1	4	5	84	8	0	0	0	2
1992-93	Swift Current	WHL	70	0	6	6	87	17	0	1	1	27
1993-94	Swift Current	WHL	71	0	10	10	179	7	0	0	0	4
1994-95	Swift Current	WHL	48	5	7	12	120	....	....	....	....	....
	Kamloops	WHL	21	0	6	6	90	21	0	5	5	49
1995-96	Saint John	AHL	48	1	3	4	89	16	0	0	0	6

McCANN, SEAN — FLA.

Defense. Shoots right. 6', 195 lbs. Born, North York, Ont., September 18, 1971.
(Florida's 1st choice, 1st overall, in 1994 Supplemental Draft).

			Regular Season					Playoffs				
Season	Club	Lea	GP	G	A	TP	PIM	GP	G	A	TP	PIM
1990-91	Harvard	ECAC	28	2	9	11	88	....	....	....	....	....
1991-92	Harvard	ECAC	27	4	10	14	51	....	....	....	....	....
1992-93	Harvard	ECAC	31	4	5	9	38	....	....	....	....	....
1993-94abcd	Harvard	ECAC	33	22	17	39	82	....	....	....	....	....
1994-95	Cincinnati	IHL	76	10	12	22	58	10	0	2	2	8
1995-96	Carolina	AHL	80	14	33	47	61	....	....	....	....	....

a ECAC First All-Star Team (1994)
b NCAA East First All-American Team (1994)
c NCAA Final Four All-Tournament Team (1994)
d NCAA Final Four Tournament Most Valuable Player (1994)

McCARTHY, SANDY — CGY.

Right wing. Shoots right. 6'3", 225 lbs. Born, Toronto, Ont., June 15, 1972.
(Calgary's 3rd choice, 52nd overall, in 1991 Entry Draft).

			Regular Season					Playoffs				
Season	Club	Lea	GP	G	A	TP	PIM	GP	G	A	TP	PIM
1989-90	Laval	QMJHL	65	10	11	21	269	14	3	3	6	60
1990-91	Laval	QMJHL	68	21	19	40	297	13	6	5	11	67
1991-92	Laval	QMJHL	62	39	51	90	326	8	4	5	9	81
1992-93	Salt Lake	IHL	77	18	20	38	220	....	....	....	....	....
1993-94	**Calgary**	**NHL**	**79**	**5**	**5**	**10**	**173**	**7**	**0**	**0**	**0**	**34**
1994-95	**Calgary**	**NHL**	**37**	**5**	**3**	**8**	**101**	**6**	**0**	**1**	**1**	**17**
1995-96	**Calgary**	**NHL**	**75**	**9**	**7**	**16**	**173**	**4**	**0**	**0**	**0**	**10**
	NHL Totals		**191**	**19**	**15**	**34**	**447**	**17**	**0**	**1**	**1**	**61**

McCARTY, DARREN — DET.

Right wing. Shoots right. 6'1", 210 lbs. Born, Burnaby, B.C., April 1, 1972.
(Detroit's 2nd choice, 46th overall, in 1992 Entry Draft).

			Regular Season					Playoffs				
Season	Club	Lea	GP	G	A	TP	PIM	GP	G	A	TP	PIM
1990-91	Belleville	OHL	60	30	37	67	151	6	2	2	4	13
1991-92a	Belleville	OHL	65	*55	72	127	177	5	1	4	5	13
1992-93	Adirondack	AHL	73	17	19	36	278	11	0	1	1	33
1993-94	**Detroit**	**NHL**	**67**	**9**	**17**	**26**	**181**	**7**	**2**	**2**	**4**	**8**
1994-95	**Detroit**	**NHL**	**31**	**5**	**8**	**13**	**88**	**18**	**3**	**2**	**5**	**14**
1995-96	**Detroit**	**NHL**	**63**	**15**	**14**	**29**	**158**	**19**	**3**	**2**	**5**	**20**
	NHL Totals		**161**	**29**	**39**	**68**	**427**	**44**	**8**	**6**	**14**	**42**

a OHL First All-Star Team (1992)

McCAULEY, ALYN — N.J.

Center. Shoots left. 5'11", 185 lbs. Born, Brockville, Ont., May 29, 1977.
(New Jersey's 5th choice, 79th overall, in 1995 Entry Draft).

			Regular Season					Playoffs				
Season	Club	Lea	GP	G	A	TP	PIM	GP	G	A	TP	PIM
1993-94	Ottawa	OHL	38	13	23	36	10	13	5	14	19	4
1994-95	Ottawa	OHL	65	16	38	54	20	....	....	....	....	....
1995-96	Ottawa	OHL	55	34	48	82	24	2	0	0	0	0

McCAULEY, BILL — BOS.

Center. Shoots left. 6'1", 195 lbs. Born, Detroit, MI, April 20, 1975.
(Florida's 6th choice, 83rd overall, in 1993 Entry Draft).

			Regular Season					Playoffs				
Season	Club	Lea	GP	G	A	TP	PIM	GP	G	A	TP	PIM
1992-93	Detroit	OHL	65	13	37	50	24	15	1	4	5	6
1993-94	Detroit	OHL	59	18	39	57	51	16	4	7	11	25
1994-95	Detroit	OHL	66	41	61	102	43	21	12	*27	*39	12
1995-96	Providence	AHL	62	11	17	28	71	....	....	....	....	....

Re-entered NHL Entry Draft, **Boston's** 4th choice, 73rd overall in 1995 Entry Draft.

McCLEARY, TRENT — BOS.

Right wing. Shoots right. 6', 180 lbs. Born, Swift Current, Sask., October 10, 1972.

			Regular Season					Playoffs				
Season	Club	Lea	GP	G	A	TP	PIM	GP	G	A	TP	PIM
1991-92	Swift Current	WHL	72	23	22	45	240	8	1	2	3	16
1992-93	Swift Current	WHL	63	17	33	50	138	17	5	4	9	16
	New Haven	AHL	2	1	0	1	6	....	....	....	....	....
1993-94	P.E.I.	AHL	4	0	0	0	6	....	....	....	....	....
	Thunder Bay	ColHL	51	23	17	40	123	9	2	11	13	15
1994-95	P.E.I.	AHL	51	9	20	29	60	9	2	3	5	26
1995-96	**Ottawa**	**NHL**	**75**	**4**	**10**	**14**	**68**	....	....	....	....	....
	NHL Totals		**75**	**4**	**10**	**14**	**68**	....	....	....	....	....

Signed as a free agent by **Ottawa**, October 9, 1992. Traded to **Boston** by **Ottawa** with Ottawa's third round choice (Eric Naud) in 1996 Entry Draft for Shawn McEachern, June 22, 1996.

McCOSH, SHAWN — PHI.

Center. Shoots right. 6', 188 lbs. Born, Oshawa, Ont., June 5, 1969.
(Detroit's 5th choice, 95th overall, in 1989 Entry Draft).

			Regular Season					Playoffs				
Season	Club	Lea	GP	G	A	TP	PIM	GP	G	A	TP	PIM
1986-87	Hamilton	OHL	50	11	17	28	49	6	1	0	1	2
1987-88	Hamilton	OHL	64	17	36	53	96	14	6	8	14	14
1988-89	Niagara Falls	OHL	56	41	62	103	75	14	4	13	17	23
1989-90	Niagara Falls	OHL	9	6	10	16	24	....	....	....	....	....
	Hamilton	OHL	39	24	28	52	65	....	....	....	....	....
1990-91	New Haven	AHL	66	16	21	37	104	....	....	....	....	....
1991-92	**Los Angeles**	**NHL**	**4**	**0**	**0**	**0**	**4**	....	....	....	....	....
	Phoenix	IHL	71	21	32	53	118	....	....	....	....	....
	New Haven	AHL	....	....	....	....	....	5	0	1	1	0
1992-93	New Haven	AHL	46	22	32	54	54	....	....	....	....	....
	Phoenix	IHL	22	9	8	17	36	....	....	....	....	....
1993-94	Binghamton	AHL	75	31	44	75	68	....	....	....	....	....
1994-95	Binghamton	AHL	67	23	60	83	73	8	3	9	12	6
	NY Rangers	**NHL**	**5**	**1**	**0**	**1**	**2**	....	....	....	....	....
1995-96	Hershey	AHL	71	31	52	83	82	5	1	5	6	8
	NHL Totals		**9**	**1**	**0**	**1**	**6**	....	....	....	....	....

Traded to **Los Angeles** by **Detroit** for Los Angeles' eighth round choice (Justin Krall) in 1992 Entry Draft, August 15, 1990. Traded to **Ottawa** by **Los Angeles** with Bob Kudelski for Marc Fortier and Jim Thomson, December 19, 1992. Signed as a free agent by **NY Rangers**, July 30, 1993. Signed as a free agent by **Philadelphia**, July 31, 1995.

McCRIMMON, BRAD — PHO.

Defense. Shoots left. 5'11", 197 lbs. Born, Dodsland, Sask., March 29, 1959.
(Boston's 2nd choice, 15th overall, in 1979 Entry Draft).

			Regular Season					Playoffs				
Season	Club	Lea	GP	G	A	TP	PIM	GP	G	A	TP	PIM
1977-78a	Brandon	WHL	65	19	78	97	245	8	2	11	13	20
1978-79a	Brandon	WHL	66	24	74	98	139	22	9	19	28	34
1979-80	**Boston**	**NHL**	**72**	**5**	**11**	**16**	**94**	**10**	**1**	**1**	**2**	**28**
1980-81	**Boston**	**NHL**	**78**	**11**	**18**	**29**	**148**	**3**	**0**	**1**	**1**	**2**
1981-82	**Boston**	**NHL**	**78**	**1**	**8**	**9**	**83**	**2**	**0**	**0**	**0**	**2**
1982-83	**Philadelphia**	**NHL**	**79**	**4**	**21**	**25**	**61**	**3**	**0**	**0**	**0**	**4**
1983-84	**Philadelphia**	**NHL**	**71**	**0**	**24**	**24**	**76**	**1**	**0**	**0**	**0**	**4**
1984-85	**Philadelphia**	**NHL**	**66**	**8**	**35**	**43**	**81**	**11**	**2**	**1**	**3**	**15**
1985-86	**Philadelphia**	**NHL**	**80**	**13**	**43**	**56**	**85**	**5**	**2**	**0**	**2**	**2**
1986-87	**Philadelphia**	**NHL**	**71**	**10**	**29**	**39**	**52**	**26**	**3**	**5**	**8**	**30**
1987-88bc	**Calgary**	**NHL**	**80**	**7**	**35**	**42**	**98**	**9**	**2**	**3**	**5**	**22**
1988-89	**Calgary**	**NHL**	**72**	**5**	**17**	**22**	**96**	**22**	**0**	**3**	**3**	**30 ♦**
1989-90	**Calgary**	**NHL**	**79**	**4**	**15**	**19**	**78**	**6**	**0**	**2**	**2**	**8**
1990-91	**Detroit**	**NHL**	**64**	**0**	**13**	**13**	**81**	**7**	**1**	**1**	**2**	**21**
1991-92	**Detroit**	**NHL**	**79**	**7**	**22**	**29**	**118**	**11**	**0**	**1**	**1**	**8**
1992-93	**Detroit**	**NHL**	**60**	**1**	**14**	**15**	**71**	....	....	....	....	....
1993-94	**Hartford**	**NHL**	**65**	**1**	**5**	**6**	**72**	....	....	....	....	....
1994-95	**Hartford**	**NHL**	**33**	**0**	**1**	**1**	**42**	....	....	....	....	....
1995-96	**Hartford**	**NHL**	**58**	**3**	**6**	**9**	**62**	....	....	....	....	....
	NHL Totals		**1185**	**80**	**317**	**397**	**1398**	**116**	**11**	**18**	**29**	**176**

a WHL First All-Star Team (1978, 1979)
b NHL Second All-Star Team (1988)
c NHL Plus/Minus Leader (1988)

Played in NHL All-Star Game (1988)

Traded to **Philadelphia** by **Boston** for Pete Peeters, June 9, 1982. Traded to **Calgary** by **Philadelphia** for Calgary's third round choice (Dominic Roussel) in 1988 Entry Draft and first round choice (later traded to Toronto — Toronto selected Steve Bancroft) in 1989 Entry Draft, August 26, 1987. Traded to **Detroit** by **Calgary** for Detroit's second round choice (later traded to New Jersey — New Jersey selected David Harlock) in 1990 Entry Draft, June 15, 1990. Traded to **Hartford** by **Detroit** for Detroit's sixth round choice (previously acquired by Hartford — Detroit selected Tim Spitzig) in 1993 Entry Draft, June 1, 1993. Signed as a free agent by **Phoenix**, July 16, 1996.

McDONOUGH, HUBIE (mihk-DUN-uh)

Center. Shoots left. 5'9", 180 lbs. Born, Manchester, NH, July 8, 1963.

			Regular Season					Playoffs				
Season	Club	Lea	GP	G	A	TP	PIM	GP	G	A	TP	PIM
1986-87	Flint	IHL	82	27	52	79	59	6	3	2	5	0
1987-88	New Haven	AHL	78	30	29	59	43	....	....	....	....	....
1988-89	Los Angeles	NHL	4	0	1	1	0	....	....	....	....	....
	New Haven	AHL	74	37	55	92	41	17	10	*21	*31	6
1989-90	Los Angeles	NHL	22	3	4	7	10	....	....	....	....	....
	NY Islanders	NHL	54	18	11	29	26	5	1	0	1	4
1990-91	NY Islanders	NHL	52	6	6	12	10	....	....	....	....	....
	Capital Dist.	AHL	17	9	9	18	4	....	....	....	....	....
1991-92	NY Islanders	NHL	33	7	2	9	15	....	....	....	....	....
	Capital Dist.	AHL	21	11	18	29	14	....	....	....	....	....
1992-93	San Jose	NHL	30	6	2	8	6	....	....	....	....	....
a	San Diego	IHL	48	26	49	75	26	14	4	7	11	6
1993-94	San Diego	IHL	69	31	48	79	61	8	0	7	7	6
1994-95a	San Diego	IHL	80	43	55	98	10	5	0	1	1	4
1995-96	Los Angeles	IHL	11	11	9	20	10	....	....	....	....	....
	Orlando	IHL	58	26	32	58	40	23	7	11	18	10
	NHL Totals		195	40	26	66	67	5	1	0	1	4

a IHL Second All-Star Team (1993, 1995)

Signed as a free agent by **Los Angeles**, April 18, 1988. Traded to **NY Islanders** by **Los Angeles** with Ken Baumgartner for Mikko Makela, November 29, 1989. Traded to **San Jose** by **NY Islanders** for cash, August 28, 1992.

McEACHERN, SHAWN (muh-GEH-kruhn) OTT.

Center. Shoots left. 5'11", 195 lbs. Born, Waltham, MA, February 28, 1969.
(Pittsburgh's 6th choice, 110th overall, in 1987 Entry Draft).

			Regular Season					Playoffs				
Season	Club	Lea	GP	G	A	TP	PIM	GP	G	A	TP	PIM
1988-89	Boston U.	H.E.	36	20	28	48	32	....	....	....	....	....
1989-90a	Boston U.	H.E.	43	25	31	56	78	....	....	....	....	....
1990-91bc	Boston U.	H.E.	41	34	48	82	43	....	....	....	....	....
1991-92	U.S. National	....	57	26	23	49	38	....	....	....	....	....
	U.S. Olympic	....	8	1	0	1	10	....	....	....	....	....
	Pittsburgh	NHL	15	0	4	4	0	19	2	7	9	4 ♦
1992-93	Pittsburgh	NHL	84	28	33	61	46	12	3	2	5	10
1993-94	Los Angeles	NHL	49	8	13	21	24	....	....	....	....	....
	Pittsburgh	NHL	27	12	9	21	10	6	1	0	1	2
1994-95	Kiekko-Espoo	Fin.	8	1	3	4	6	....	....	....	....	....
	Pittsburgh	NHL	44	13	13	26	22	11	0	2	2	8
1995-96	Boston	NHL	82	24	29	53	34	5	2	1	3	8
	NHL Totals		301	85	101	186	136	53	8	12	20	32

a Hockey East Second All-Star Team (1990)
b Hockey East First All-Star Team (1991)
c NCAA East First All-American Team (1991)

Traded to **Los Angeles** by **Pittsburgh** for Marty McSorley, August 27, 1993. Traded to **Pittsburgh** by **Los Angeles** with Tomas Sandstrom for Marty McSorley and Jim Paek, February 16, 1994. Traded to **Boston** by **Pittsburgh** with Kevin Stevens for Glen Murray, Bryan Smolinski and Boston's third round choice (Boyd Kane) in 1996 Entry Draft, August 2, 1995. Traded to **Ottawa** by **Boston** for Trent McCleary and Ottawa's third round choice (Eric Naud) in 1996 Entry Draft, June 22, 1996.

McGILLIS, DANIEL EDM.

Defense. Shoots left. 6'2", 220 lbs. Born, Hawkesbury, Ont., July 1, 1972.
(Detroit's 10th choice, 238th overall, in 1992 Entry Draft).

			Regular Season					Playoffs				
Season	Club	Lea	GP	G	A	TP	PIM	GP	G	A	TP	PIM
1992-93	Northeastern	H.E.	35	5	12	17	42	....	....	....	....	....
1993-94	Northeastern	H.E.	38	4	25	29	82	....	....	....	....	....
1994-95a	Northeastern	H.E.	34	9	22	31	70	....	....	....	....	....
1995-96bc	Northeastern	H.E.	34	12	24	36	50	....	....	....	....	....

a Hockey East Second All-Star Team (1995)
b Hockey East All-Star Team (1996)
c NCAA East First All-American Team (1996)

Traded to **Edmonton** by **Detroit** for Kirk Maltby, March 20, 1996.

McINNIS, MARTY NYI

Center. Shoots right. 5'11", 183 lbs. Born, Hingham, MA., June 2, 1970.
(NY Islanders' 10th choice, 163rd overall, in 1988 Entry Draft).

			Regular Season					Playoffs				
Season	Club	Lea	GP	G	A	TP	PIM	GP	G	A	TP	PIM
1988-89	Boston College	H.E.	39	13	19	32	8	....	....	....	....	....
1989-90	Boston College	H.E.	41	24	29	53	43	....	....	....	....	....
1990-91	Boston College	H.E.	38	21	36	57	40	....	....	....	....	....
1991-92	U.S. National	....	54	15	19	34	20	....	....	....	....	....
	U.S. Olympic	....	8	6	2	8	4	....	....	....	....	....
	NY Islanders	NHL	15	3	5	8	0	....	....	....	....	....
1992-93	NY Islanders	NHL	56	10	20	30	24	3	0	1	1	0
	Capital Dist.	AHL	10	4	12	16	2	....	....	....	....	....
1993-94	NY Islanders	NHL	81	25	31	56	24	4	0	0	0	0
1994-95	NY Islanders	NHL	41	9	7	16	8	....	....	....	....	....
1995-96	NY Islanders	NHL	74	12	34	46	39	....	....	....	....	....
	NHL Totals		267	59	97	156	95	7	0	1	1	0

McINTYRE, JOHN VAN.

Center. Shoots left. 6'1", 190 lbs. Born, Ravenswood, Ont., April 29, 1969.
(Toronto's 3rd choice, 49th overall, in 1987 Entry Draft).

			Regular Season					Playoffs				
Season	Club	Lea	GP	G	A	TP	PIM	GP	G	A	TP	PIM
1985-86	Guelph	OHL	30	4	6	10	25	20	1	5	6	31
1986-87	Guelph	OHL	47	8	22	30	95	....	....	....	....	....
1987-88	Guelph	OHL	39	24	18	42	109	....	....	....	....	....
1988-89	Guelph	OHL	52	30	26	56	129	7	5	4	9	25
	Newmarket	AHL	3	0	2	2	7	5	1	1	2	20
1989-90	Toronto	NHL	59	5	12	17	117	2	0	0	0	2
	Newmarket	AHL	6	2	2	4	12	....	....	....	....	....
1990-91	Toronto	NHL	13	0	3	3	25	....	....	....	....	....
	Los Angeles	NHL	56	8	5	13	115	12	0	1	1	24
1991-92	Los Angeles	NHL	73	5	19	24	100	6	0	4	4	12
1992-93	Los Angeles	NHL	49	2	5	7	80	....	....	....	....	....
	NY Rangers	NHL	11	1	0	1	4	....	....	....	....	....
1993-94	Vancouver	NHL	62	3	6	9	38	24	0	1	1	16
1994-95	Vancouver	NHL	28	0	4	4	37	....	....	....	....	....
1995-96	Syracuse	AHL	53	13	14	27	78	....	....	....	....	....
	NHL Totals		351	24	54	78	516	44	0	6	6	54

Traded to **Los Angeles** by **Toronto** for Mike Krushelnyski, November 9, 1990. Traded to **NY Rangers** by **Los Angeles** for Mark Hardy and Ottawa's fifth round choice (previously acquired by NY Rangers — Los Angeles selected Frederick Beaubien) in 1993 Entry Draft, March 22, 1993. Claimed by **Vancouver** from **NY Rangers** in NHL Waiver Draft, October 3, 1993.

McKAY, KEVIN CHI.

Defense. Shoots left. 6'3", 198 lbs. Born, North Battleford, Sask., January 4, 1977.
(Chicago's 3rd choice, 71st overall, in 1995 Entry Draft).

			Regular Season					Playoffs				
Season	Club	Lea	GP	G	A	TP	PIM	GP	G	A	TP	PIM
1993-94	Moose Jaw	WHL	6	0	0	0	2	....	....	....	....	....
1994-95	Moose Jaw	WHL	56	1	11	12	93	10	0	2	2	13
1995-96	Moose Jaw	WHL	44	2	12	14	144	....	....	....	....	....

McKAY, RANDY N.J.

Right wing. Shoots right. 6'1", 205 lbs. Born, Montreal, Que., January 25, 1967.
(Detroit's 6th choice, 113th overall, in 1985 Entry Draft).

			Regular Season					Playoffs				
Season	Club	Lea	GP	G	A	TP	PIM	GP	G	A	TP	PIM
1984-85	Michigan Tech	WCHA	25	4	5	9	32	....	....	....	....	....
1985-86	Michigan Tech	WCHA	40	12	22	34	46	....	....	....	....	....
1986-87	Michigan Tech	WCHA	39	5	11	16	46	....	....	....	....	....
1987-88	Michigan Tech	WCHA	41	17	24	41	70	....	....	....	....	....
	Adirondack	AHL	10	0	3	3	12	6	0	4	4	0
1988-89	Detroit	NHL	3	0	0	0	0	2	0	0	0	2
	Adirondack	AHL	58	29	34	63	170	14	4	7	11	60
1989-90	Detroit	NHL	33	3	6	9	51	....	....	....	....	....
	Adirondack	AHL	36	16	23	39	99	6	3	0	3	35
1990-91	Detroit	NHL	47	1	7	8	183	5	0	1	1	41
1991-92	New Jersey	NHL	80	17	16	33	246	7	1	3	4	10
1992-93	New Jersey	NHL	73	11	11	22	206	5	0	0	0	16
1993-94	New Jersey	NHL	78	12	15	27	244	20	1	2	3	24
1994-95	New Jersey	NHL	33	5	7	12	44	19	8	4	12	11 ♦
1995-96	New Jersey	NHL	76	11	10	21	145	....	....	....	....	....
	NHL Totals		423	60	72	132	1119	58	10	10	20	104

Acquired by **New Jersey** from **Detroit** with Dave Barr as compensation for Detroit's signing of free agent Troy Crowder, September 9, 1991.

McKEE, JAY BUF.

Defense. Shoots left. 6'3", 195 lbs. Born, Kingston, Ont., September 8, 1977.
(Buffalo's 1st choice, 14th overall, in 1995 Entry Draft).

			Regular Season					Playoffs				
Season	Club	Lea	GP	G	A	TP	PIM	GP	G	A	TP	PIM
1993-94	Sudbury	OHL	51	0	1	1	51	3	0	0	0	0
1994-95	Niagara Falls	OHL	65	9	19	28	151	6	2	3	5	10
1995-96	Buffalo	NHL	1	0	1	1	2	....	....	....	....	....
a	Niagara Falls	OHL	64	5	41	46	129	10	1	5	6	16
	Rochester	AHL	4	0	1	1	15	....	....	....	....	....
	NHL Totals		1	0	1	1	2	....	....	....	....	....

a OHL Second All-Star Team (1996)

McKENNA, STEVE L.A.

Defense. Shoots left. 6'8", 247 lbs. Born, Toronto, Ont., August 21, 1973.

			Regular Season					Playoffs				
Season	Club	Lea	GP	G	A	TP	PIM	GP	G	A	TP	PIM
1993-94	Merrimack	H.E.	37	1	2	3	74	....	....	....	....	....
1994-95	Merrimack	H.E.	37	1	9	10	74	....	....	....	....	....
1995-96	Merrimack	H.E.	33	3	11	14	67	....	....	....	....	....

Signed as a free agent by **Los Angeles**, May 23, 1996.

McKENZIE, JIM PHO.

Left wing/Defense. Shoots left. 6'3", 205 lbs. Born, Gull Lake, Sask., November 3, 1969.
(Hartford's 3rd choice, 73rd overall, in 1989 Entry Draft).

			Regular Season					Playoffs				
Season	Club	Lea	GP	G	A	TP	PIM	GP	G	A	TP	PIM
1985-86	Moose Jaw	WHL	3	0	2	2	0	....	....	....	....	....
1986-87	Moose Jaw	WHL	65	5	3	8	125	9	0	0	0	7
1987-88	Moose Jaw	WHL	62	1	17	18	134	....	....	....	....	....
1988-89	Victoria	WHL	67	15	27	42	176	8	1	4	5	30
1989-90	Hartford	NHL	5	0	0	0	4	....	....	....	....	....
	Binghamton	AHL	56	4	12	16	149	....	....	....	....	....
1990-91	Hartford	NHL	41	4	3	7	108	6	0	0	0	8
	Springfield	AHL	24	3	4	7	102	....	....	....	....	....
1991-92	Hartford	NHL	67	5	1	6	87	....	....	....	....	....
1992-93	Hartford	NHL	64	3	6	9	202	....	....	....	....	....
1993-94	Hartford	NHL	26	1	2	3	67	....	....	....	....	....
	Dallas	NHL	34	2	3	5	63	....	....	....	....	....
	Pittsburgh	NHL	11	0	0	0	16	3	0	0	0	0
1994-95	Pittsburgh	NHL	39	2	1	3	63	5	0	0	0	4
1995-96	Winnipeg	NHL	73	4	2	6	202	1	0	0	0	2
	NHL Totals		360	21	18	39	812	15	0	0	0	14

Traded to **Florida** by **Hartford** for Alexander Godynyuk, December 16, 1993. Traded to **Dallas** by **Florida** for Dallas' fourth round choice (later traded to Ottawa — Ottawa selected Kevin Bolibruck) in 1995 Entry Draft, December 16, 1993. Traded to **Pittsburgh** by **Dallas** for Mike Needham, March 21, 1994. Signed as a free agent by **NY Islanders**, August 2, 1995. Claimed by **Winnipeg** from **NY Islanders** in NHL Waiver Draft, October 2, 1995.

McKIM, ANDREW

Center. Shoots right. 5'8", 175 lbs. Born, St. John, N.B., July 6, 1970.

			Regular Season					Playoffs				
Season	Club	Lea	GP	G	A	TP	PIM	GP	G	A	TP	PIM
1988-89	Verdun	QMJHL	68	50	56	106	36	....	....	....	....	....
1989-90a	Hull	QMJHL	70	66	84	130	44	11	8	10	18	8
1990-91	Salt Lake	IHL	74	30	30	60	48	4	0	2	2	6
1991-92	St. John's	AHL	79	43	50	93	79	16	11	12	23	4
1992-93	Boston	NHL	7	1	3	4	0	....	....	....	....	....
	Providence	AHL	61	23	46	69	64	6	2	2	4	0
1993-94	Boston	NHL	29	0	1	1	4	....	....	....	....	....
	Providence	AHL	46	13	24	37	49	....	....	....	....	....
1994-95	Adirondack	AHL	77	39	55	94	22	4	3	3	6	0
	Detroit	NHL	2	0	0	0	2	....	....	....	....	....
1995-96	Cdn. National	....	10	7	7	14	6	....	....	....	....	....
	NHL Totals		38	1	4	5	6	....	....	....	....	....

a QMJHL First All-Star Team (1990)

Signed as a free agent by **Calgary**, October 5, 1990. Signed as a free agent by **Boston**, July 23, 1992. Signed as a free agent by **Detroit**, August 31, 1994.

McLAREN, KYLE — BOS.

Defense. Shoots left. 6'4", 210 lbs.   Born, Humbolt, Sask., June 18, 1977.
(Boston's 1st choice, 9th overall, in 1995 Entry Draft).

			Regular Season					Playoffs				
Season	Club	Lea	GP	G	A	TP	PIM	GP	G	A	TP	PIM
1993-94	Tacoma	WHL	62	1	9	10	53	6	1	4	5	6
1994-95	Tacoma	WHL	47	13	19	32	68	4	1	1	2	4
1995-96a	**Boston**	**NHL**	74	5	12	17	73	5	0	0	0	14
	NHL Totals		74	5	12	17	73	5	0	0	0	14

a NHL All-Rookie Team (1996)

McLAREN, STEVE — CHI.

Defense. Shoots left. 6', 194 lbs.   Born, Owen Sound, Ont., February 3, 1975.
(Chicago's 3rd choice, 85th overall, in 1994 Entry Draft).

			Regular Season					Playoffs				
Season	Club	Lea	GP	G	A	TP	PIM	GP	G	A	TP	PIM
1993-94	North Bay	OHL	55	2	15	17	130	18	0	3	3	50
1994-95	North Bay	OHL	27	3	10	13	119	6	2	1	3	23
1995-96	Indianapolis	IHL	54	1	2	3	170	3	0	0	0	2

McLAUGHLIN, PETER — PIT.

Defense. Shoots left. 6'3", 190 lbs.   Born, Norwood, MA, June 29, 1973.
(Pittsburgh's 8th choice, 170th overall, in 1991 Entry Draft).

			Regular Season					Playoffs				
Season	Club	Lea	GP	G	A	TP	PIM	GP	G	A	TP	PIM
1992-93	Harvard	ECAC	31	2	6	8	28	....	....	....	....	....
1993-94	Harvard	ECAC	33	0	7	7	32	....	....	....	....	....
1994-95	Harvard	ECAC	30	1	6	7	44	....	....	....	....	....
1995-96	Harvard	ECAC	31	2	6	8	24	....	....	....	....	....

McLLWAIN, DAVE   (MA-kuhl-WAYN) — NYI

Center/Right wing. Shoots left. 6', 185 lbs.   Born, Seaforth, Ont., January 9, 1967.
(Pittsburgh's 9th choice, 172nd overall, in 1986 Entry Draft).

			Regular Season					Playoffs				
Season	Club	Lea	GP	G	A	TP	PIM	GP	G	A	TP	PIM
1984-85	Kitchener	OHL	61	13	21	34	29	....	....	....	....	....
1985-86	Kitchener	OHL	13	7	7	14	12	....	....	....	....	....
	North Bay	OHL	51	30	28	58	25	10	4	4	8	2
1986-87a	North Bay	OHL	60	46	73	119	35	24	7	18	25	40
1987-88	**Pittsburgh**	**NHL**	66	11	8	19	40	....	....	....	....	....
	Muskegon	IHL	9	4	6	10	23	6	2	3	5	8
1988-89	**Pittsburgh**	**NHL**	24	1	2	3	4	3	0	1	1	0
	Muskegon	IHL	46	37	35	72	51	7	8	2	10	6
1989-90	**Winnipeg**	**NHL**	80	25	26	51	60	7	0	1	1	2
1990-91	**Winnipeg**	**NHL**	60	14	11	25	46	....	....	....	....	....
1991-92	**Winnipeg**	**NHL**	3	1	1	2	2	....	....	....	....	....
	Buffalo	**NHL**	5	0	0	0	2	....	....	....	....	....
	NY Islanders	**NHL**	54	8	15	23	28	....	....	....	....	....
	Toronto	**NHL**	11	1	2	3	4	....	....	....	....	....
1992-93	**Toronto**	**NHL**	66	14	4	18	30	4	0	0	0	0
1993-94	**Ottawa**	**NHL**	66	17	26	43	48	....	....	....	....	....
1994-95	**Ottawa**	**NHL**	43	5	6	11	22	....	....	....	....	....
1995-96	**Ottawa**	**NHL**	1	0	1	1	2	....	....	....	....	....
	Cleveland	IHL	60	30	45	75	80	....	....	....	....	....
	Pittsburgh	**NHL**	18	2	4	6	4	6	0	0	0	0
	NHL Totals		497	99	106	205	292	20	0	2	2	2

a OHL Second All-Star Team (1987)

Traded to **Winnipeg** by **Pittsburgh** with Randy Cunneyworth and Rick Tabaracci for Jim Kyte, Andrew McBain and Randy Gilhen, June 17, 1989. Traded to **Buffalo** by **Winnipeg** with Gord Donnelly, Winnipeg's fifth round choice (Yuri Khmylev) in 1992 Entry Draft and future considerations for Darrin Shannon, Mike Hartman and Dean Kennedy, October 11, 1991. Traded to **NY Islanders** by **Buffalo** with Pierre Turgeon, Uwe Krupp and Benoit Hogue for Pat Lafontaine, Randy Hillier, Randy Wood and NY Islanders' fourth round choice (Dean Melanson) in 1992 Entry Draft, October 25, 1991. Traded to **Toronto** by **NY Islanders** with Ken Baumgartner for Daniel Marois and Claude Loiselle, March 10, 1992. Claimed by **Ottawa** from **Toronto** in NHL Waiver Draft, October 3, 1993. Traded to **Pittsburgh** by **Ottawa** for Pittsburgh's eighth round choice (Erich Goldmann) in 1996 Entry Draft, March 1, 1996. Signed as a free agent by **NY Islanders**, July 29, 1996.

McMAHON, MARK — HFD.

Defense. Shoots left. 6'1", 179 lbs.   Born, Geralton, Ont., February 10, 1978.
(Hartford's 5th choice, 116th overall, in 1996 Entry Draft).

			Regular Season					Playoffs				
Season	Club	Lea	GP	G	A	TP	PIM	GP	G	A	TP	PIM
1994-95	Elmira	Jr. B	41	3	10	13	91	....	....	....	....	....
1995-96	Kitchener	OHL	55	1	8	9	105	5	0	1	1	17

McNEIL, SHAWN — WSH.

Center. Shoots left. 5'11", 175 lbs.   Born, Pembroke, Ont., March 17, 1978.
(Washington's 6th choice, 78th overall, in 1996 Entry Draft).

			Regular Season					Playoffs				
Season	Club	Lea	GP	G	A	TP	PIM	GP	G	A	TP	PIM
1993-94	Kamloops	WHL	1	0	0	0	0	....	....	....	....	....
1994-95	Kamloops	WHL	43	4	3	7	11	9	0	1	1	0
1995-96	Kamloops	WHL	67	15	30	45	24	16	4	12	16	17

McRAE, BASIL   (muh-KRAY, BA-zihl) — ST.L.

Left wing. Shoots left. 6'2", 210 lbs.   Born, Beaverton, Ont., January 5, 1961.
(Quebec's 3rd choice, 87th overall, in 1980 Entry Draft).

			Regular Season					Playoffs				
Season	Club	Lea	GP	G	A	TP	PIM	GP	G	A	TP	PIM
1979-80	London	OHA	67	24	36	60	116	5	0	0	0	18
1980-81	London	OHA	65	29	23	52	266	....	....	....	....	....
1981-82	**Quebec**	**NHL**	20	4	3	7	69	9	1	0	1	34
	Fredericton	AHL	47	11	15	26	175	....	....	....	....	....
1982-83	**Quebec**	**NHL**	22	1	1	2	59	....	....	....	....	....
	Fredericton	AHL	53	22	19	41	146	12	1	5	6	75
1983-84	**Toronto**	**NHL**	3	0	0	0	19	....	....	....	....	....
	St. Catharines	AHL	78	14	25	39	187	6	0	0	0	40
1984-85	**Toronto**	**NHL**	1	0	0	0	0	....	....	....	....	....
	St. Catharines	AHL	72	30	25	55	186	....	....	....	....	....
1985-86	**Detroit**	**NHL**	4	0	0	0	5	....	....	....	....	....
	Adirondack	AHL	69	22	30	52	259	17	5	4	9	101
1986-87	**Detroit**	**NHL**	36	2	2	4	193	....	....	....	....	....
	Quebec	**NHL**	33	9	5	14	149	13	3	1	4	*99
1987-88	**Minnesota**	**NHL**	80	5	11	16	382	....	....	....	....	....
1988-89	**Minnesota**	**NHL**	78	12	19	31	365	5	0	0	0	58
1989-90	**Minnesota**	**NHL**	66	9	17	26	*351	7	1	0	1	24
1990-91	**Minnesota**	**NHL**	40	1	3	4	224	22	1	1	2	*94
1991-92	**Minnesota**	**NHL**	59	5	8	13	245	....	....	....	....	....
1992-93	**Tampa Bay**	**NHL**	14	2	3	5	71	....	....	....	....	....
	St. Louis	**NHL**	33	1	3	4	98	11	0	1	1	24
1993-94	**St. Louis**	**NHL**	40	1	2	3	103	2	0	0	0	12
1994-95	**St. Louis**	**NHL**	21	0	5	5	72	7	2	1	3	4
	Peoria	IHL	2	0	0	0	12	....	....	....	....	....
1995-96	**St. Louis**	**NHL**	18	1	1	2	40	2	0	0	0	0
	NHL Totals		568	53	83	136	2445	78	8	4	12	349

Traded to **Toronto** by **Quebec** for Richard Turmel, August 12, 1983. Signed as a free agent by **Detroit**, July 17, 1985. Traded to **Quebec** by **Detroit** with John Ogrodnick and Doug Shedden for Brent Ashton, Gilbert Delorme and Mark Kumpel, January 17, 1987. Signed as a free agent by **Minnesota**, June 29, 1987. Claimed by **Tampa Bay** from **Minnesota** in Expansion Draft, June 18, 1992. Traded to **St. Louis** by **Tampa Bay** with Doug Crossman and Tampa Bay's fourth round choice (Andrei Petrakov) in 1996 Entry Draft for Jason Ruff and future considerations, January 28, 1993.

McRAE, KEN — L.A.

Center. Shoots right. 6'1", 195 lbs.   Born, Winchester, Ont., April 23, 1968.
(Quebec's 1st choice, 18th overall, in 1986 Entry Draft).

			Regular Season					Playoffs				
Season	Club	Lea	GP	G	A	TP	PIM	GP	G	A	TP	PIM
1985-86	Sudbury	OHL	66	25	49	74	127	4	2	1	3	12
1986-87	Sudbury	OHL	21	12	15	27	40	....	....	....	....	....
	Hamilton	OHL	20	7	12	19	25	7	1	1	2	12
1987-88	**Quebec**	**NHL**	1	0	0	0	0	....	....	....	....	....
	Hamilton	OHL	62	30	55	85	158	14	13	9	22	35
	Fredericton	AHL	....	....	....	....	....	3	0	0	0	8
1988-89	**Quebec**	**NHL**	37	6	11	17	68	....	....	....	....	....
	Halifax	AHL	41	20	21	41	87	....	....	....	....	....
1989-90	**Quebec**	**NHL**	66	7	8	15	191	....	....	....	....	....
1990-91	**Quebec**	**NHL**	12	0	0	0	36	....	....	....	....	....
	Halifax	AHL	60	10	36	46	193	....	....	....	....	....
1991-92	**Quebec**	**NHL**	10	0	1	1	31	....	....	....	....	....
	Halifax	AHL	52	30	41	71	184	....	....	....	....	....
1992-93	**Toronto**	**NHL**	2	0	0	0	2	....	....	....	....	....
	St. John's	AHL	64	30	44	74	135	9	6	6	12	27
1993-94	**Toronto**	**NHL**	9	1	1	2	36	6	0	0	0	4
	St. John's	AHL	65	23	41	64	200	....	....	....	....	....
1994-95	Detroit	IHL	24	4	9	13	38	....	....	....	....	....
	Phoenix	IHL	2	2	0	2	0	9	3	8	11	21
1995-96	Phoenix	IHL	45	11	14	25	102	4	1	1	2	24
	NHL Totals		137	14	21	35	364	6	0	0	0	4

Traded to **Toronto** by **Quebec** for Len Esau, July 21, 1992. Signed as a free agent by **Edmonton**, September 9, 1994. Signed as a free agent by **Los Angeles**, September 12, 1995.

McSORLEY, MARTY — S.J.

Defense. Shoots right. 6'1", 225 lbs.   Born, Hamilton, Ont., May 18, 1963.

			Regular Season					Playoffs				
Season	Club	Lea	GP	G	A	TP	PIM	GP	G	A	TP	PIM
1981-82	Belleville	OHL	58	6	13	19	234	....	....	....	....	....
1982-83	Belleville	OHL	70	10	41	51	183	4	0	0	0	7
	Baltimore	AHL	2	0	0	0	22	....	....	....	....	....
1983-84	**Pittsburgh**	**NHL**	72	2	7	9	224	....	....	....	....	....
1984-85	**Pittsburgh**	**NHL**	15	0	0	0	15	....	....	....	....	....
	Baltimore	AHL	58	6	24	30	154	14	0	7	7	47
1985-86	**Edmonton**	**NHL**	59	11	12	23	265	8	0	2	2	50
	Nova Scotia	AHL	9	2	4	6	34	....	....	....	....	....
1986-87	**Edmonton**	**NHL**	41	2	4	6	159	21	4	3	7	65 ♦
	Nova Scotia	AHL	7	2	2	4	48	....	....	....	....	....
1987-88	**Edmonton**	**NHL**	60	9	17	26	223	16	0	3	3	67 ♦
1988-89	**Los Angeles**	**NHL**	66	10	17	27	350	11	0	2	2	33
1989-90	**Los Angeles**	**NHL**	75	15	21	36	322	10	1	3	4	18
1990-91a	**Los Angeles**	**NHL**	61	7	32	39	221	12	0	0	0	58
1991-92	**Los Angeles**	**NHL**	71	7	22	29	268	6	1	0	1	21
1992-93	**Los Angeles**	**NHL**	81	15	26	41	*399	24	4	6	10	*60
1993-94	**Pittsburgh**	**NHL**	47	3	18	21	139	....	....	....	....	....
	Los Angeles	**NHL**	18	4	6	10	55	....	....	....	....	....
1994-95	**Los Angeles**	**NHL**	41	3	18	21	83	....	....	....	....	....
1995-96	**Los Angeles**	**NHL**	59	10	21	31	148	....	....	....	....	....
	NY Rangers	**NHL**	9	0	2	2	21	4	0	0	0	0
	NHL Totals		775	98	223	321	2892	112	10	19	29	372

a Co-winner of Alka-Seltzer Plus Award with Theoren Fleury (1991)

Signed as a free agent by **Pittsburgh**, July 30, 1982. Traded to **Edmonton** by **Pittsburgh** with Tim Hrynewich and future considerations (Craig Muni, October 6, 1986) for Gilles Meloche, September 12, 1985. Traded to **Los Angeles** by **Edmonton** with Wayne Gretzky and Mike Krushelnyski for Jimmy Carson, Martin Gelinas, Los Angeles' first round choices in 1989 (acquired by New Jersey — New Jersey selected Jason Miller), 1991 (Martin Rucinsky) and 1993 (Nick Stajduhar) Entry Drafts and cash, August 9, 1988. Traded to **Pittsburgh** by **Los Angeles**, for Shawn McEachern, August 27, 1993. Traded to **Los Angeles** by **Pittsburgh** with Jim Paek for Tomas Sandstrom and Shawn McEachern, February 16, 1994. Traded to **NY Rangers** by **Los Angeles** with Jari Kurri and Shane Churla for Ray Ferraro, Ian Laperriere, Mattias Norstrom, Nathan Lafayette and NY Rangers' fourth round choice in 1997 Entry Draft, March 14, 1996. Traded to **San Jose** by **NY Rangers** for Jayson More, Brian Swanson and a conditional choice in 1998 Entry Draft, August 20, 1996.

McSWEEN, DON

Defense. Shoots left. 5'11", 197 lbs.   Born, Detroit, MI, June 9, 1964.
(Buffalo's 10th choice, 154th overall, in 1983 Entry Draft.)

				Regular Season					Playoffs				
Season	Club	Lea	GP	G	A	TP	PIM	GP	G	A	TP	PIM
1983-84	Michigan State	CCHA	46	10	26	36	30	....	....	....	....	....
1984-85	Michigan State	CCHA	44	2	23	25	52	....	....	....	....	....
1985-86a	Michigan State	CCHA	45	9	29	38	18	....	....	....	....	....
1986-87abc	Michigan State	CCHA	45	7	23	30	34	....	....	....	....	....
1987-88	**Buffalo**	**NHL**	**5**	**0**	**1**	**1**	**6**	....	....	....	....	....
	Rochester	AHL	63	9	29	38	108	6	0	1	1	15
1988-89	Rochester	AHL	66	7	22	29	45	....	....	....	....	....
1989-90	**Buffalo**	**NHL**	**4**	**0**	**0**	**0**	**6**	....	....	....	....	....
d	Rochester	AHL	70	16	43	59	43	17	3	10	13	12
1990-91	Rochester	AHL	74	7	44	51	57	15	2	5	7	8
1991-92	Rochester	AHL	75	6	32	38	60	16	5	6	11	18
1992-93	San Diego	IHL	80	15	40	55	85	14	1	2	3	10
1993-94	San Diego	IHL	38	5	13	18	36	....	....	....	....	....
	Anaheim	**NHL**	**32**	**3**	**9**	**12**	**39**	....	....	....	....	....
1994-95	**Anaheim**	**NHL**	**2**	**0**	**0**	**0**	**0**	....	....	....	....	....
1995-96	**Anaheim**	**NHL**	**4**	**0**	**0**	**0**	**4**	....	....	....	....	....
	Baltimore	AHL	12	1	9	10	2	....	....	....	....	....
	NHL Totals		**47**	**3**	**10**	**13**	**55**	....	....	....	....	....

a   CCHA First All-Star Team (1986, 1987)
b   NCAA West Second All-American Team (1987)
c   Named to NCAA All-Tournament Team (1987)
d   AHL First All-Star Team (1990)

Signed as a free agent by **Anaheim**, January 12, 1994.

MEHALKO, BRAD   S.J.

Right wing. Shoots right. 5'11", 182 lbs.   Born, Lethbridge, Alta., January 4, 1977.
(San Jose's 9th choice, 167th overall, in 1995 Entry Draft.)

				Regular Season					Playoffs				
Season	Club	Lea	GP	G	A	TP	PIM	GP	G	A	TP	PIM
1993-94	Lethbridge	WHL	62	9	9	18	48	9	0	1	1	9
1994-95	Lethbridge	WHL	52	11	15	26	83	....	....	....	....	....
1995-96	Lethbridge	WHL	48	15	37	52	97	....	....	....	....	....
	Prince George	WHL	23	6	15	21	30	....	....	....	....	....

MEKESHKIN, DIMITRI   (meh-KEHSH-kihn)   WSH.

Defense. Shoots left. 6'2", 186 lbs.   Born, Izhevsk, USSR, January 29, 1976.
(Washington's 6th choice, 145th overall, in 1994 Entry Draft.)

				Regular Season					Playoffs				
Season	Club	Lea	GP	G	A	TP	PIM	GP	G	A	TP	PIM
1993-94	Avangard Omsk	CIS	21	0	0	0	14	3	0	0	0	2
1994-95	Avangard Omsk	CIS	16	0	2	2	4	....	....	....	....	....
1995-96	Avangard Omsk	CIS 2				UNAVAILABLE						

MELANSON, DEAN   (meh-LAHN-suhn)

Defense. Shoots right. 5'11", 211 lbs.   Born, Antigonish, N.S., November 19, 1973.
(Buffalo's 4th choice, 80th overall, in 1992 Entry Draft.)

				Regular Season					Playoffs				
Season	Club	Lea	GP	G	A	TP	PIM	GP	G	A	TP	PIM
1990-91	St-Hyacinthe	QMJHL	69	10	17	27	110	4	0	1	1	2
1991-92	St-Hyacinthe	QMJHL	42	8	19	27	158	6	1	2	3	25
1992-93	Rochester	AHL	8	0	1	1	6	14	1	6	7	18
	St. Hyacinthe	QMJHL	57	13	29	42	253	....	....	....	....	....
1993-94	Rochester	AHL	80	1	21	22	138	4	0	1	1	2
1994-95	Rochester	AHL	43	4	7	11	84	....	....	....	....	....
	Buffalo	**NHL**	**5**	**0**	**0**	**0**	**4**	....	....	....	....	....
1995-96	Rochester	AHL	70	3	13	16	204	14	3	3	6	22
	NHL Totals		**5**	**0**	**0**	**0**	**4**	....	....	....	....	....

MELENOVSKY, MAREK   TOR.

Center. Shoots left. 5'9", 176 lbs.   Born, Humpolec, Czech., March 30, 1977.
(Toronto's 5th choice, 171st overall, in 1995 Entry Draft.)

				Regular Season					Playoffs				
Season	Club	Lea	GP	G	A	TP	PIM	GP	G	A	TP	PIM
1993-94	Dukla Jihlava	Czech.	1	0	0	0	....	....	....	....	....	....
1994-95	Dukla Jihlava	Czech. Jr	28	23	11	34	....	....	....	....	....	....
	Dukla Jihlava	Czech.	3	0	0	0	0	5	1	3	4	0
1995-96	Dukla Jihlava	Czech.	33	3	3	6	....	5	1	2	3	....

MELLANBY, SCOTT   FLA.

Right wing. Shoots right. 6'1", 199 lbs.   Born, Montreal, Que., June 11, 1966.
(Philadelphia's 2nd choice, 27th overall, in 1984 Entry Draft.)

				Regular Season					Playoffs				
Season	Club	Lea	GP	G	A	TP	PIM	GP	G	A	TP	PIM
1984-85	U. Wisconsin	WCHA	40	14	24	38	60	....	....	....	....	....
1985-86	U. Wisconsin	WCHA	32	21	23	44	89	....	....	....	....	....
	Philadelphia	**NHL**	**2**	**0**	**0**	**0**	**0**	....	....	....	....	....
1986-87	**Philadelphia**	**NHL**	71	11	21	32	94	24	5	5	10	46
1987-88	**Philadelphia**	**NHL**	75	25	26	51	185	7	0	1	1	16
1988-89	**Philadelphia**	**NHL**	76	21	29	50	183	19	4	5	9	28
1989-90	**Philadelphia**	**NHL**	57	6	17	23	77	....	....	....	....	....
1990-91	**Philadelphia**	**NHL**	74	20	21	41	155	....	....	....	....	....
1991-92	**Edmonton**	**NHL**	80	23	27	50	197	16	2	1	3	29
1992-93	**Edmonton**	**NHL**	69	15	17	32	147	....	....	....	....	....
1993-94	**Florida**	**NHL**	80	30	30	60	149	....	....	....	....	....
1994-95	**Florida**	**NHL**	48	13	12	25	90	....	....	....	....	....
1995-96	**Florida**	**NHL**	79	32	38	70	160	22	3	6	9	44
	NHL Totals		**711**	**196**	**238**	**434**	**1437**	**88**	**14**	**18**	**32**	**163**

Played in NHL All-Star Game (1996)

Traded to **Edmonton** by **Philadelphia** with Craig Fisher and Craig Berube for Dave Brown, Corey Foster and Jari Kurri, May 30, 1991. Claimed by **Florida** from **Edmonton** in Expansion Draft, June 24, 1993.

MELYAKOV, IGOR   (mehl-yuh-KAHF)   L.A.

Left wing. Shoots left. 5'10", 176 lbs.   Born, Lipetsk, USSR, December 23, 1976.
(Los Angeles' 6th choice, 137th overall, in 1995 Entry Draft.)

				Regular Season					Playoffs				
Season	Club	Lea	GP	G	A	TP	PIM	GP	G	A	TP	PIM
1993-94	Yaroslavl	CIS	39	4	3	7	10	4	0	0	0	0
1994-95	Yaroslavl	CIS	50	6	8	14	34	4	0	1	1	0
1995-96	Yaroslavl	CIS	39	5	1	6	6	3	0	0	0	2

MENHART, MARIAN   BUF.

Defense. Shoots left. 6'3", 220 lbs.   Born, Most, Czech., February 14, 1977.
(Buffalo's 6th choice, 111th overall, in 1995 Entry Draft.)

				Regular Season					Playoffs				
Season	Club	Lea	GP	G	A	TP	PIM	GP	G	A	TP	PIM
1994-95	Litvinov	Czech. Jr.	36	15	19	34	....	....	....	....	....	....
1995-96	Prince Albert	WHL	62	1	14	15	65	18	1	1	2	14

MESSIER, JOBY   (MEHS-see-ay)

Defense. Shoots right. 6', 200 lbs.   Born, Regina, Sask., March 2, 1970.
(NY Rangers' 7th choice, 118th overall, in 1989 Entry Draft.)

				Regular Season					Playoffs				
Season	Club	Lea	GP	G	A	TP	PIM	GP	G	A	TP	PIM
1988-89	Michigan State	CCHA	39	2	10	12	66	....	....	....	....	....
1989-90	Michigan State	CCHA	42	1	11	12	58	....	....	....	....	....
1990-91	Michigan State	CCHA	39	5	11	16	71	....	....	....	....	....
1991-92ab	Michigan State	CCHA	41	13	15	28	81	....	....	....	....	....
1992-93	**NY Rangers**	**NHL**	**11**	**0**	**0**	**0**	**6**	....	....	....	....	....
	Binghamton	AHL	60	5	16	21	63	14	1	1	2	6
1993-94	**NY Rangers**	**NHL**	**4**	**0**	**2**	**2**	**0**	....	....	....	....	....
	Binghamton	AHL	42	6	14	20	58	....	....	....	....	....
1994-95	Binghamton	AHL	25	2	9	11	36	1	0	0	0	0
	NY Rangers	**NHL**	**10**	**0**	**2**	**2**	**18**	....	....	....	....	....
1995-96	Utah	IHL			DID NOT PLAY – INJURED							
	NHL Totals		**25**	**0**	**4**	**4**	**24**	....	....	....	....	....

a   CCHA First All-Star Team (1992)
b   NCAA West First All-American Team (1992)

Signed as a free agent by **NY Islanders**, September 26, 1995.

MESSIER, MARK   (MEHS-see-ay)   NYR

Center. Shoots left. 6'1", 205 lbs.   Born, Edmonton, Alta., January 18, 1961.
(Edmonton's 2nd choice, 48th overall, in 1979 Entry Draft.)

				Regular Season					Playoffs				
Season	Club	Lea	GP	G	A	TP	PIM	GP	G	A	TP	PIM
1977-78	Portland	WHL	....	....	....	....	....	7	4	1	5	2
1978-79	Indianapolis	WHA	5	0	0	0	0	....	....	....	....	....
	Cincinnati	WHA	47	1	10	11	58	....	....	....	....	....
1979-80	**Edmonton**	**NHL**	**75**	**12**	**21**	**33**	**120**	**3**	**1**	**2**	**3**	**2**
	Houston	CHL	4	0	3	3	4	....	....	....	....	....
1980-81	**Edmonton**	**NHL**	72	23	40	63	102	9	2	5	7	13
1981-82a	**Edmonton**	**NHL**	78	50	38	88	119	5	1	2	3	8
1982-83a	**Edmonton**	**NHL**	77	48	58	106	72	15	15	6	21	14
1983-84bc	**Edmonton**	**NHL**	73	37	64	101	165	19	8	18	26	19 ♦
1984-85	**Edmonton**	**NHL**	55	23	31	54	57	18	12	13	25	12 ♦
1985-86	**Edmonton**	**NHL**	63	35	49	84	68	10	4	6	10	18
1986-87	**Edmonton**	**NHL**	77	37	70	107	73	21	12	16	28	16 ♦
1987-88	**Edmonton**	**NHL**	77	37	74	111	103	19	11	23	34	29 ♦
1988-89	**Edmonton**	**NHL**	72	33	61	94	130	7	1	11	12	8
1989-90ade	**Edmonton**	**NHL**	79	45	84	129	79	22	9	*22	31	20 ♦
1990-91	**Edmonton**	**NHL**	53	12	52	64	34	18	4	11	15	16
1991-92ade	**NY Rangers**	**NHL**	79	35	72	107	76	11	7	7	14	6
1992-93	**NY Rangers**	**NHL**	75	25	66	91	72	....	....	....	....	....
1993-94	**NY Rangers**	**NHL**	76	26	58	84	76	23	12	18	30	33 ♦
1994-95	**NY Rangers**	**NHL**	46	14	39	53	40	10	3	10	13	8
1995-96	**NY Rangers**	**NHL**	74	47	52	99	122	11	4	7	11	16
	NHL Totals		**1201**	**539**	**929**	**1468**	**1508**	**221**	**106**	**177**	**283**	**238**

a   NHL First All-Star Team (1982, 1983, 1990, 1992)
b   NHL Second All-Star Team (1984)
c   Won Conn Smythe Trophy (1984)
d   Won Hart Trophy (1990, 1992)
e   Won Lester B. Pearson Award (1990, 1992)

Played in NHL All-Star Game (1982-86, 1988-92, 1994, 1996)

Traded to **NY Rangers** by **Edmonton** with future considerations for Bernie Nicholls, Steven Rice and Louie DeBrusk, October 4, 1991.

METHOT, FRANCOIS   BUF.

Center. Shoots right. 6', 171 lbs.   Born, Montreal, Que., April 26, 1978.
(Buffalo's 4th choice, 54th overall, in 1996 Entry Draft.)

				Regular Season					Playoffs				
Season	Club	Lea	GP	G	A	TP	PIM	GP	G	A	TP	PIM
1994-95	St-Hyacinthe	QMJHL	60	14	38	52	22	5	0	1	1	0
1995-96	St-Hyacinthe	QMJHL	68	32	62	94	22	12	6	6	12	4

MIETTINEN, TOMMI   (mih-EHT-tih-nehn)   ANA.

Center. Shoots left. 5'10", 165 lbs.   Born, Kuopio, Finland, December 3, 1975.
(Anaheim's 9th choice, 236th overall, in 1994 Entry Draft.)

				Regular Season					Playoffs				
Season	Club	Lea	GP	G	A	TP	PIM	GP	G	A	TP	PIM
1992-93	KalPa	Fin.	14	0	0	0	0	....	....	....	....	....
1993-94	KalPa	Fin.	47	5	7	12	14	....	....	....	....	....
1994-95	KalPa	Fin.	48	13	16	29	26	....	....	....	....	....
1995-96	TPS	Fin.	36	3	10	13	10	10	2	1	3	29

MIKESCH, JEFF   DET.

Center. Shoots left. 6', 175 lbs.   Born, Hancook, MI, April 11, 1975.
(Detroit's 8th choice, 231st overall, in 1994 Entry Draft.)

				Regular Season					Playoffs				
Season	Club	Lea	GP	G	A	TP	PIM	GP	G	A	TP	PIM
1993-94	Michigan Tech	WCHA	41	9	4	13	80	....	....	....	....	....
1994-95	Michigan Tech	WCHA	36	9	8	17	83	....	....	....	....	....
1995-96	Michigan Tech	WCHA	41	13	13	26	66	....	....	....	....	....

MIKULCHIK, OLEG (mih-KOOL-chihk, OH-lehg) ANA.

Defense. Shoots right. 6'2", 200 lbs. Born, Minsk, USSR, June 27, 1964.

			Regular Season					Playoffs				
Season	Club	Lea	GP	G	A	TP	PIM	GP	G	A	TP	PIM
1983-84	Moscow D'amo	USSR	17	0	0	0	6	....	....	....	....	....
1984-85	Moscow D'amo	USSR	30	1	3	4	26	....	....	....	....	....
1985-86	Moscow D'amo	USSR	40	0	1	1	36	....	....	....	....	....
1986-87	Moscow D'amo	USSR	39	5	3	8	34	....	....	....	....	....
1987-88	Moscow D'amo	USSR	48	7	8	15	63	....	....	....	....	....
1988-89	Moscow D'amo	USSR	43	4	7	11	52	....	....	....	....	....
1989-90	Moscow D'amo	USSR	32	1	3	4	31	....	....	....	....	....
1990-91	Moscow D'amo	USSR	36	2	6	8	40	....	....	....	....	....
1991-92	Khimik	CIS	15	3	2	5	20	....	....	....	....	....
	New Haven	AHL	30	3	3	6	63	4	1	3	4	6
1992-93	Moncton	AHL	75	6	20	26	159	5	0	0	0	4
1993-94	**Winnipeg**	**NHL**	**4**	**0**	**1**	**1**	**17**	....	....	....	....	....
	Moncton	AHL	67	9	38	47	121	21	2	10	12	18
1994-95	Springfield	AHL	50	5	16	21	59	....	....	....	....	....
	Winnipeg	**NHL**	**25**	**0**	**2**	**2**	**12**	....	....	....	....	....
1995-96	**Anaheim**	**NHL**	**8**	**0**	**0**	**0**	**4**	....	....	....	....	....
	Baltimore	AHL	19	1	7	8	46	12	2	3	5	22
	NHL Totals		**37**	**0**	**3**	**3**	**33**	....	....	....	....	....

Signed as a free agent by **Winnipeg**, July 26, 1993. Signed as a free agent by **Anaheim**, August 8, 1995.

MILLAR, CRAIG BUF.

Defense. Shoots left. 6'2", 200 lbs. Born, Winnipeg, Man., July 12, 1976.
(Buffalo's 10th choice, 225th overall, in 1994 Entry Draft).

			Regular Season					Playoffs				
Season	Club	Lea	GP	G	A	TP	PIM	GP	G	A	TP	PIM
1992-93	Swift Current	WHL	43	2	1	3	8	....	....	....	....	....
1993-94	Swift Current	WHL	66	2	9	11	53	7	0	3	3	4
1994-95	Swift Current	WHL	72	8	42	50	80	6	1	1	2	10
1995-96a	Swift Current	WHL	72	31	46	77	151	6	1	0	1	22

a WHL East First All-Star Team (1996)

MILLEN, COREY CGY.

Center. Shoots right. 5'7", 170 lbs. Born, Cloquet, MN, March 30, 1964.
(NY Rangers' 3rd choice, 57th overall, in 1982 Entry Draft).

			Regular Season					Playoffs				
Season	Club	Lea	GP	G	A	TP	PIM	GP	G	A	TP	PIM
1982-83	U. Minnesota	WCHA	21	14	15	29	18	....	....	....	....	....
1983-84	U.S. National	....	45	15	11	26	10	....	....	....	....	....
	U.S. Olympic	....	6	0	0	0	2	....	....	....	....	....
1984-85	U. Minnesota	WCHA	38	28	36	64	60	....	....	....	....	....
1985-86ab	U. Minnesota	WCHA	48	41	42	83	64	....	....	....	....	....
1986-87bc	U. Minnesota	WCHA	42	36	29	65	62	....	....	....	....	....
1987-88	U.S. National	....	47	41	43	84	26	....	....	....	....	....
	U.S. Olympic	....	6	6	5	11	4	....	....	....	....	....
1988-89	Ambri	Switz.	36	32	22	54	18	6	4	3	7	0
1989-90	**NY Rangers**	**NHL**	**4**	**0**	**0**	**0**	**2**	....	....	....	....	....
	Flint	IHL	11	4	5	9	2	....	....	....	....	....
1990-91	**NY Rangers**	**NHL**	**4**	**3**	**1**	**4**	**0**	**6**	**1**	**2**	**3**	**0**
	Binghamton	AHL	40	19	37	56	68	6	0	7	7	6
1991-92	**NY Rangers**	**NHL**	**11**	**1**	**4**	**5**	**10**	....	....	....	....	....
	Binghamton	AHL	15	8	7	15	44	....	....	....	....	....
	Los Angeles	**NHL**	**46**	**20**	**21**	**41**	**44**	**6**	**0**	**1**	**1**	**6**
1992-93	**Los Angeles**	**NHL**	**42**	**23**	**16**	**39**	**42**	**23**	**2**	**4**	**6**	**12**
1993-94	**New Jersey**	**NHL**	**78**	**20**	**30**	**50**	**52**	**7**	**1**	**0**	**1**	**2**
1994-95	**New Jersey**	**NHL**	**17**	**2**	**3**	**5**	**8**	....	....	....	....	....
	Dallas	**NHL**	**28**	**3**	**15**	**18**	**28**	**5**	**1**	**0**	**1**	**2**
1995-96	**Dallas**	**NHL**	**13**	**3**	**4**	**7**	**8**	....	....	....	....	....
	Michigan	IHL	11	8	11	19	14	....	....	....	....	....
	Calgary	**NHL**	**31**	**4**	**10**	**14**	**10**	....	....	....	....	....
	NHL Totals		**274**	**79**	**104**	**183**	**204**	**47**	**5**	**7**	**12**	**22**

a NCAA West Second All-American Team (1986)
b WCHA Second All-Star Team (1986, 1987)
c Named to NCAA All-Tournament Team (1987)

Traded to **Los Angeles** by **NY Rangers** for Randy Gilhen, December 23, 1991. Traded to **New Jersey** by **Los Angeles** for New Jersey's fifth round choice (Jason Saal) in 1993 Entry Draft, June 26, 1993. Traded to **Dallas** by **New Jersey** for Neal Broten, February 27, 1995. Traded to **Calgary** by **Dallas** with Jarome Iginla for Joe Nieuwendyk, December 19, 1995.

MILLER, AARON COL.

Defense. Shoots right. 6'3", 197 lbs. Born, Buffalo, NY, August 11, 1971.
(NY Rangers' 6th choice, 88th overall, in 1989 Entry Draft).

			Regular Season					Playoffs				
Season	Club	Lea	GP	G	A	TP	PIM	GP	G	A	TP	PIM
1989-90	U. of Vermont	ECAC	31	1	15	16	24	....	....	....	....	....
1990-91	U. of Vermont	ECAC	30	3	7	10	22	....	....	....	....	....
1991-92	U. of Vermont	ECAC	31	3	16	19	28	....	....	....	....	....
1992-93ab	U. of Vermont	ECAC	30	4	13	17	16	....	....	....	....	....
1993-94	**Quebec**	**NHL**	**1**	**0**	**0**	**0**	**0**	....	....	....	....	....
	Cornwall	AHL	64	4	10	14	49	13	0	2	2	10
1994-95	Cornwall	AHL	76	4	18	22	69	....	....	....	....	....
	Quebec	**NHL**	**9**	**0**	**3**	**3**	**6**	....	....	....	....	....
1995-96	**Colorado**	**NHL**	**5**	**0**	**0**	**0**	**0**	....	....	....	....	....
	Cornwall	AHL	62	4	23	27	77	8	0	1	1	6
	NHL Totals		**15**	**0**	**3**	**3**	**6**	....	....	....	....	....

a ECAC First All-Star Team (1993)
b NCAA East Second All-American Team (1993)

Traded to **Quebec** by **NY Rangers** with NY Rangers' fifth round choice (Bill Lindsay) in 1991 Entry Draft for Joe Cirella, January 17, 1991.

MILLER, JASON

Left wing. Shoots left. 6'1", 190 lbs. Born, Edmonton, Alta., March 1, 1971.
(New Jersey's 2nd choice, 18th overall, in 1989 Entry Draft).

			Regular Season					Playoffs				
Season	Club	Lea	GP	G	A	TP	PIM	GP	G	A	TP	PIM
1987-88	Medicine Hat	WHL	71	11	18	29	28	15	0	1	1	2
1988-89	Medicine Hat	WHL	72	51	55	106	44	3	1	2	3	2
1989-90	Medicine Hat	WHL	66	43	56	99	40	3	3	2	5	0
1990-91	**New Jersey**	**NHL**	**1**	**0**	**0**	**0**	**0**	....	....	....	....	....
a	Medicine Hat	WHL	66	60	76	136	31	12	9	10	19	8
1991-92	**New Jersey**	**NHL**	**3**	**0**	**0**	**0**	**0**	....	....	....	....	....
	Utica	AHL	71	23	32	55	31	4	1	3	4	0
1992-93	**New Jersey**	**NHL**	**2**	**0**	**0**	**0**	**0**	....	....	....	....	....
	Utica	AHL	72	28	42	70	43	5	4	4	8	2
1993-94	Albany	AHL	77	22	53	75	65	5	1	1	2	4
1994-95	Adirondack	AHL	77	32	33	65	39	4	1	0	1	0
1995-96	HPK	Fin.	22	4	6	10	10	....	....	....	....	....
	Kaufbeuren	Ger.	3	1	1	2	0	....	....	....	....	....
	Peoria	IHL	39	16	22	38	6	11	1	2	3	4
	NHL Totals		**6**	**0**	**0**	**0**	**0**	....	....	....	....	....

a WHL East Second All-Star Team (1991)

Signed as a free agent by **Detroit**, August 26, 1994.

MILLER, KELLY WSH.

Left wing. Shoots left. 5'11", 197 lbs. Born, Lansing, MI, March 3, 1963.
(NY Rangers' 9th choice, 183rd overall, in 1982 Entry Draft).

			Regular Season					Playoffs				
Season	Club	Lea	GP	G	A	TP	PIM	GP	G	A	TP	PIM
1981-82	Michigan State	CCHA	38	11	18	29	17	....	....	....	....	....
1982-83	Michigan State	CCHA	36	16	19	35	12	....	....	....	....	....
1983-84	Michigan State	CCHA	46	28	21	49	12	....	....	....	....	....
1984-85ab	Michigan State	CCHA	43	27	23	50	21	....	....	....	....	....
	NY Rangers	**NHL**	**5**	**0**	**2**	**2**	**2**	**3**	**0**	**0**	**0**	**2**
1985-86	**NY Rangers**	**NHL**	**74**	**13**	**20**	**33**	**52**	**16**	**3**	**4**	**7**	**4**
1986-87	**NY Rangers**	**NHL**	**38**	**6**	**14**	**20**	**22**	....	....	....	....	....
	Washington	**NHL**	**39**	**10**	**12**	**22**	**26**	**7**	**2**	**2**	**4**	**0**
1987-88	**Washington**	**NHL**	**80**	**9**	**23**	**32**	**35**	**14**	**4**	**4**	**8**	**10**
1988-89	**Washington**	**NHL**	**78**	**19**	**21**	**40**	**45**	**6**	**1**	**0**	**1**	**2**
1989-90	**Washington**	**NHL**	**80**	**18**	**22**	**40**	**49**	**15**	**3**	**5**	**8**	**23**
1990-91	**Washington**	**NHL**	**80**	**24**	**26**	**50**	**29**	**11**	**4**	**2**	**6**	**6**
1991-92	**Washington**	**NHL**	**78**	**14**	**38**	**52**	**49**	**7**	**1**	**2**	**3**	**4**
1992-93	**Washington**	**NHL**	**84**	**18**	**27**	**45**	**32**	**6**	**0**	**3**	**3**	**2**
1993-94	**Washington**	**NHL**	**84**	**14**	**25**	**39**	**32**	**11**	**2**	**7**	**9**	**0**
1994-95	**Washington**	**NHL**	**48**	**10**	**13**	**23**	**6**	**7**	**0**	**3**	**3**	**4**
1995-96	**Washington**	**NHL**	**74**	**7**	**13**	**20**	**30**	**6**	**0**	**1**	**1**	**4**
	NHL Totals		**842**	**162**	**256**	**418**	**409**	**109**	**20**	**33**	**53**	**61**

a CCHA First All-Star Team (1985)
b NCAA West First All-American Team (1985)

Traded to **Washington** by **NY Rangers** with Bob Crawford and Mike Ridley for Bob Carpenter and Washington's second round choice (Jason Prosofsky) in 1989 Entry Draft, January 1, 1987.

MILLER, KEVIN CHI.

Center. Shoots right. 5'11", 190 lbs. Born, Lansing, MI, September 2, 1965.
(NY Rangers' 10th choice, 202nd overall, in 1984 Entry Draft).

			Regular Season					Playoffs				
Season	Club	Lea	GP	G	A	TP	PIM	GP	G	A	TP	PIM
1984-85	Michigan State	CCHA	44	11	29	40	84	....	....	....	....	....
1985-86	Michigan State	CCHA	45	19	52	71	112	....	....	....	....	....
1986-87	Michigan State	CCHA	42	25	56	81	63	....	....	....	....	....
1987-88	Michigan State	CCHA	9	6	3	9	18	....	....	....	....	....
	U.S. National	....	48	31	32	63	33	....	....	....	....	....
	U.S. Olympic	....	5	1	3	4	4	....	....	....	....	....
1988-89	**NY Rangers**	**NHL**	**24**	**3**	**5**	**8**	**2**	....	....	....	....	....
	Denver	IHL	55	29	47	76	19	4	2	1	3	2
1989-90	**NY Rangers**	**NHL**	**16**	**0**	**5**	**5**	**2**	**1**	**0**	**0**	**0**	**0**
	Flint	IHL	48	19	23	42	41	....	....	....	....	....
1990-91	**NY Rangers**	**NHL**	**63**	**17**	**27**	**44**	**63**	....	....	....	....	....
	Detroit	**NHL**	**11**	**5**	**2**	**7**	**4**	**7**	**3**	**2**	**5**	**20**
1991-92	**Detroit**	**NHL**	**80**	**20**	**26**	**46**	**53**	**9**	**0**	**2**	**2**	**4**
1992-93	**Washington**	**NHL**	**10**	**0**	**3**	**3**	**35**	....	....	....	....	....
	St. Louis	**NHL**	**72**	**24**	**22**	**46**	**65**	**10**	**0**	**3**	**3**	**11**
1993-94	**St. Louis**	**NHL**	**75**	**23**	**25**	**48**	**83**	**3**	**1**	**0**	**1**	**4**
1994-95	**St. Louis**	**NHL**	**15**	**2**	**5**	**7**	**0**	....	....	....	....	....
	San Jose	**NHL**	**21**	**6**	**7**	**13**	**13**	**6**	**0**	**0**	**0**	**2**
1995-96	**San Jose**	**NHL**	**68**	**22**	**20**	**42**	**41**	....	....	....	....	....
	Pittsburgh	**NHL**	**13**	**6**	**5**	**11**	**4**	**18**	**3**	**2**	**5**	**8**
	NHL Totals		**468**	**128**	**152**	**280**	**365**	**54**	**7**	**9**	**16**	**49**

Traded to **Detroit** by **NY Rangers** with Jim Cummins and Dennis Vial for Joey Kocur and Per Djoos, March 5, 1991. Traded to **Washington** by **Detroit** for Dino Ciccarelli, June 20, 1992. Traded to **St. Louis** by **Washington** for Paul Cavallini, November 2, 1992. Traded to **San Jose** by **St. Louis** for Todd Elik, March 23, 1995. Traded to **Pittsburgh** by **San Jose** for Pittsburgh's fifth round choice (later traded to Boston — Boston selected Elias Abrahamsson) in 1996 Entry Draft and future considerations, March 20, 1996. Signed as a free agent by **Chicago**, July 18, 1996.

MILLER, KIP CHI.

Center. Shoots left. 5'10", 190 lbs. Born, Lansing, MI, June 11, 1969.
(Quebec's 4th choice, 72nd overall, in 1987 Entry Draft).

			Regular Season					Playoffs				
Season	Club	Lea	GP	G	A	TP	PIM	GP	G	A	TP	PIM
1986-87	Michigan State	CCHA	41	20	19	39	92	....	....	....	....	....
1987-88	Michigan State	CCHA	39	16	25	41	51	....	....	....	....	....
1988-89ab	Michigan State	CCHA	47	32	45	77	94	....	....	....	....	....
1989-90abc	Michigan State	CCHA	45	*48	53	*101	60	....	....	....	....	....
1990-91	**Quebec**	**NHL**	**13**	**4**	**3**	**7**	**7**	....	....	....	....	....
	Halifax	AHL	66	36	33	69	40	....	....	....	....	....
1991-92	**Quebec**	**NHL**	**36**	**5**	**10**	**15**	**12**	....	....	....	....	....
	Halifax	AHL	24	9	17	26	8	....	....	....	....	....
	Minnesota	**NHL**	**3**	**1**	**2**	**3**	**2**	....	....	....	....	....
	Kalamazoo	IHL	6	1	8	9	4	12	3	9	12	12
1992-93	Kalamazoo	IHL	61	17	39	56	59	....	....	....	....	....
1993-94	**San Jose**	**NHL**	**11**	**2**	**2**	**4**	**6**	....	....	....	....	....
	Kansas City	IHL	71	38	54	92	51	....	....	....	....	....
1994-95	Denver	IHL	71	46	60	106	54	17	*15	14	29	8
	NY Islanders	**NHL**	**8**	**0**	**1**	**1**	**0**	....	....	....	....	....
1995-96	**Chicago**	**NHL**	**10**	**1**	**4**	**5**	**2**	....	....	....	....	....
	Indianapolis	IHL	73	32	59	91	46	5	2	6	8	2
	NHL Totals		**81**	**13**	**22**	**35**	**29**	....	....	....	....	....

a CCHA First All-Star Team (1989, 1990)
b NCAA West First All-American Team (1989, 1990)
c Won Hobey Baker Memorial Award (Top U.S. Collegiate Player) (1990)

Traded to **Minnesota** by **Quebec** for Steve Maltais, March 8, 1992. Signed as a free agent by **San Jose**, August 10, 1993. Signed as a free agent by **NY Islanders**, July 7, 1994. Signed as a free agent by **Chicago**, July 21, 1995.

MILLER, TODD — NYI

Center. Shoots right. 6', 174 lbs. Born, Elliot Lake, Ont., May 24, 1978.
(NY Islanders' 7th choice, 138th overall, in 1996 Entry Draft).

			Regular Season					Playoffs				
Season	Club	Lea	GP	G	A	TP	PIM	GP	G	A	TP	PIM
1995-96	Sarnia	OHL	62	12	16	28	44	1	0	0	0	0

MILLS, CRAIG — CHI.

Right wing. Shoots right. 5'11", 174 lbs. Born, Toronto, Ont., August 27, 1976.
(Winnipeg's 5th choice, 108th overall, in 1994 Entry Draft).

			Regular Season					Playoffs				
Season	Club	Lea	GP	G	A	TP	PIM	GP	G	A	TP	PIM
1993-94	Belleville	OHL	63	15	18	33	88	12	2	1	3	11
1994-95	Belleville	OHL	62	39	41	80	104	13	7	9	16	8
1995-96	**Winnipeg**	**NHL**	**4**	**0**	**2**	**2**	**0**	**1**	**0**	**0**	**0**	**0**
	Belleville	OHL	48	10	19	29	113	14	4	5	9	32
	Springfield	AHL	....	....	....	....	....	2	0	0	0	0
	NHL Totals		**4**	**0**	**2**	**2**	**0**	**1**	**0**	**0**	**0**	**0**

Traded to **Chicago** by **Phoenix** with Alexei Zhamnov and Phoenix's first round choice in 1998 Entry Draft for Jeremy Roenick, August 16, 1996.

MIRONOV, BORIS (mih-RAH-nahf) — EDM.

Defense. Shoots right. 6'3", 220 lbs. Born, Moscow, USSR, March 21, 1972.
(Winnipeg's 2nd choice, 27th overall, in 1992 Entry Draft).

			Regular Season					Playoffs				
Season	Club	Lea	GP	G	A	TP	PIM	GP	G	A	TP	PIM
1988-89	CSKA	USSR	1	0	0	0	0	....	....	....	....	....
1989-90	CSKA	USSR	7	0	0	0	0	....	....	....	....	....
1990-91	CSKA	USSR	36	1	5	6	16	....	....	....	....	....
1991-92	CSKA	CIS	36	2	1	3	22	....	....	....	....	....
1992-93	CSKA	CIS	19	0	5	5	20	....	....	....	....	....
1993-94a	**Winnipeg**	**NHL**	**65**	**7**	**22**	**29**	**96**	....	....	....	....	....
	Edmonton	**NHL**	**14**	**0**	**2**	**2**	**14**	....	....	....	....	....
1994-95	**Edmonton**	**NHL**	**29**	**1**	**7**	**8**	**40**	....	....	....	....	....
	Cape Breton	AHL	4	2	5	7	23	....	....	....	....	....
1995-96	**Edmonton**	**NHL**	**78**	**8**	**24**	**32**	**101**	....	....	....	....	....
	NHL Totals		**186**	**16**	**55**	**71**	**251**	....	....	....	....	....

a NHL/Upper Deck All-Rookie Team (1994)

Traded to **Edmonton** by **Winnipeg** with Mats Lindgren, Winnipeg's first round choice (Jason Bonsignore) in 1994 Entry Draft and Florida's fourth round choice (previously acquired by Winnipeg — Edmonton selected Adam Copeland) in 1994 Entry Draft for Dave Manson and St. Louis' sixth round choice (previously acquired by Edmonton — Winnipeg selected Chris Kibermanis) in 1994 Entry Draft, March 15, 1994.

MIRONOV, DMITRI (mih-RAWN-ohv) — PIT.

Defense. Shoots right. 6'2", 214 lbs. Born, Moscow, USSR, December 25, 1965.
(Toronto's 9th choice, 160th overall, in 1991 Entry Draft).

			Regular Season					Playoffs				
Season	Club	Lea	GP	G	A	TP	PIM	GP	G	A	TP	PIM
1985-86	CSKA	USSR	9	0	1	1	8	....	....	....	....	....
1986-87	CSKA	USSR	20	1	3	4	10	....	....	....	....	....
1987-88	Soviet Wings	USSR	44	12	6	18	30	....	....	....	....	....
1988-89	Soviet Wings	USSR	44	5	6	11	44	....	....	....	....	....
1989-90	Soviet Wings	USSR	45	4	11	15	34	....	....	....	....	....
1990-91	Soviet Wings	USSR	45	16	12	28	22	....	....	....	....	....
1991-92	Soviet Wings	CIS	35	15	16	31	62	....	....	....	....	....
	Toronto	**NHL**	**7**	**1**	**0**	**1**	**0**	....	....	....	....	....
1992-93	**Toronto**	**NHL**	**59**	**7**	**24**	**31**	**40**	**14**	**1**	**2**	**3**	**2**
1993-94	**Toronto**	**NHL**	**76**	**9**	**27**	**36**	**78**	**18**	**6**	**9**	**15**	**6**
1994-95	**Toronto**	**NHL**	**33**	**5**	**12**	**17**	**28**	**6**	**2**	**1**	**3**	**2**
1995-96	**Pittsburgh**	**NHL**	**72**	**3**	**31**	**34**	**88**	**15**	**0**	**1**	**1**	**10**
	NHL Totals		**247**	**25**	**94**	**119**	**234**	**53**	**9**	**13**	**22**	**20**

Traded to **Pittsburgh** by **Toronto** with Toronto's second round choice (later traded to New Jersey — New Jersey selected Joshua Dewolf) in 1996 Entry Draft for Larry Murphy, July 8, 1995.

MITCHELL, JEFF — DAL.

Center/Right wing. Shoots right. 6'1", 190 lbs. Born, Wayne, MI, May 16, 1975.
(Los Angeles' 2nd choice, 68th overall, in 1993 Entry Draft).

			Regular Season					Playoffs				
Season	Club	Lea	GP	G	A	TP	PIM	GP	G	A	TP	PIM
1992-93	Detroit	OHL	62	10	15	25	100	15	3	3	6	16
1993-94	Detroit	OHL	59	25	18	43	99	17	3	5	8	22
1994-95	Detroit	OHL	61	30	30	60	121	21	9	12	21	48
1995-96	Michigan	IHL	50	5	4	9	119	....	....	....	....	....

Rights traded to **Dallas** by **Los Angeles** for Vancouver's fifth round choice (previously acquired by Dallas — Los Angeles selected Jason Morgan) in 1995 Entry Draft, June 7, 1995.

MODANO, MIKE — DAL.

Center. Shoots left. 6'3", 200 lbs. Born, Livonia, MI, June 7, 1970.
(Minnesota's 1st choice, 1st overall, in 1988 Entry Draft).

			Regular Season					Playoffs				
Season	Club	Lea	GP	G	A	TP	PIM	GP	G	A	TP	PIM
1986-87	Prince Albert	WHL	70	32	30	62	96	8	1	4	5	4
1987-88	Prince Albert	WHL	65	47	80	127	80	9	7	11	18	18
1988-89a	Prince Albert	WHL	41	39	66	105	74	....	....	....	....	....
	Minnesota	**NHL**	....	....	....	....	....	**2**	**0**	**0**	**0**	**0**
1989-90b	**Minnesota**	**NHL**	**80**	**29**	**46**	**75**	**63**	**7**	**1**	**1**	**2**	**12**
1990-91	**Minnesota**	**NHL**	**79**	**28**	**36**	**64**	**65**	**23**	**8**	**12**	**20**	**16**
1991-92	**Minnesota**	**NHL**	**76**	**33**	**44**	**77**	**46**	**7**	**3**	**2**	**5**	**4**
1992-93	**Minnesota**	**NHL**	**82**	**33**	**60**	**93**	**83**	....	....	....	....	....
1993-94	**Dallas**	**NHL**	**76**	**50**	**43**	**93**	**54**	**9**	**7**	**3**	**10**	**16**
1994-95	**Dallas**	**NHL**	**30**	**12**	**17**	**29**	**8**	....	....	....	....	....
1995-96	**Dallas**	**NHL**	**78**	**36**	**45**	**81**	**63**	....	....	....	....	....
	NHL Totals		**501**	**221**	**291**	**512**	**382**	**48**	**19**	**18**	**37**	**48**

a WHL East All-Star Team (1989)
b NHL All-Rookie Team (1990)

Played in NHL All-Star Game (1993)

MODIN, FREDRIK (muh-DEEN) — TOR.

Left wing. Shoots left. 6'3", 202 lbs. Born, Sundsvall, Sweden, October 8, 1974.
(Toronto's 3rd choice, 64th overall, in 1994 Entry Draft).

			Regular Season					Playoffs				
Season	Club	Lea	GP	G	A	TP	PIM	GP	G	A	TP	PIM
1991-92	Sundsvall	Swe. 2	11	1	0	1	0	....	....	....	....	....
1992-93	Sundsvall	Swe. 2	30	5	7	12	12	....	....	....	....	....
1993-94	Sundsvall	Swe. 2	30	16	15	31	36	....	....	....	....	....
1994-95	Brynas	Swe.	38	9	10	19	33	14	4	4	8	6
1995-96	Brynas	Swe.	22	4	8	12	22	....	....	....	....	....

MODRY, JAROSLAV (MOHD-ree) — L.A.

Defense. Shoots left. 6'2", 195 lbs. Born, Ceske-Budejovice, Czech., February 27, 1971.
(New Jersey's 11th choice, 179th overall, in 1990 Entry Draft).

			Regular Season					Playoffs				
Season	Club	Lea	GP	G	A	TP	PIM	GP	G	A	TP	PIM
1987-88	Budejovice	Czech.	3	0	0	0	0	....	....	....	....	....
1988-89	Budejovice	Czech.	28	0	1	1	8	....	....	....	....	....
1989-90	Budejovice	Czech.	41	2	2	4	....	....	....	....	....	....
1990-91	Dukla Trencin	Czech.	33	1	9	10	6	....	....	....	....	....
1991-92	Dukla Trencin	Czech.	18	0	4	4	6	....	....	....	....	....
	Budejovice	Czech. 2	14	4	10	14	....	....	....	....	....	....
1992-93	Utica	AHL	80	7	35	42	62	5	0	2	2	2
1993-94	**New Jersey**	**NHL**	**41**	**2**	**15**	**17**	**18**	....	....	....	....	....
	Albany	AHL	19	1	5	6	25	....	....	....	....	....
1994-95	Budejovice	Czech.	19	1	3	4	30	....	....	....	....	....
	New Jersey	**NHL**	**11**	**0**	**0**	**0**	**0**	....	....	....	....	....
	Albany	AHL	18	5	6	11	14	14	3	3	6	4
1995-96	**Ottawa**	**NHL**	**64**	**4**	**14**	**18**	**38**	....	....	....	....	....
	Los Angeles	**NHL**	**9**	**0**	**3**	**3**	**6**	....	....	....	....	....
	NHL Totals		**125**	**6**	**32**	**38**	**62**	....	....	....	....	....

Traded to **Ottawa** by **New Jersey** for Ottawa's fourth round choice (Alyn McCauley) in 1995 Entry Draft, July 8, 1995. Traded to **Los Angeles** by **Ottawa** with Ottawa's eighth round choice (Stephen Valiquette) in 1996 Entry Draft for Kevin Brown, March 20, 1996.

MOGER, SANDY (MOH-guhr) — BOS.

Center. Shoots right. 6'3", 208 lbs. Born, 100 Mile House, B.C., March 21, 1969.
(Vancouver's 7th choice, 176th overall, in 1989 Entry Draft).

			Regular Season					Playoffs				
Season	Club	Lea	GP	G	A	TP	PIM	GP	G	A	TP	PIM
1988-89	Lake Superior	CCHA	21	3	5	8	26	....	....	....	....	....
1989-90	Lake Superior	CCHA	46	17	15	32	76	....	....	....	....	....
1990-91	Lake Superior	CCHA	45	27	21	48	*172	....	....	....	....	....
1991-92a	Lake Superior	CCHA	38	24	24	48	93	....	....	....	....	....
1992-93	Hamilton	AHL	78	23	26	49	57	....	....	....	....	....
1993-94	Hamilton	AHL	29	9	8	17	41	....	....	....	....	....
1994-95	Providence	AHL	63	32	29	61	105	....	....	....	....	....
	Boston	**NHL**	**18**	**2**	**6**	**8**	**6**	....	....	....	....	....
1995-96	**Boston**	**NHL**	**80**	**15**	**14**	**29**	**65**	**5**	**2**	**2**	**4**	**12**
	NHL Totals		**98**	**17**	**20**	**37**	**71**	**5**	**2**	**2**	**4**	**12**

a CCHA Second All-Star Team (1992)

Signed as a free agent by **Boston**, June 22, 1994.

MOGILNY, ALEXANDER (moh-GIHL-nee) — VAN.

Right wing. Shoots left. 5'11", 187 lbs. Born, Khabarovsk, USSR, February 18, 1969.
(Buffalo's 4th choice, 89th overall, in 1988 Entry Draft).

			Regular Season					Playoffs				
Season	Club	Lea	GP	G	A	TP	PIM	GP	G	A	TP	PIM
1986-87	CSKA	USSR	28	15	1	16	4	....	....	....	....	....
1987-88	CSKA	USSR	39	12	8	20	14	....	....	....	....	....
1988-89	CSKA	USSR	31	11	11	22	24	....	....	....	....	....
1989-90	**Buffalo**	**NHL**	**65**	**15**	**28**	**43**	**16**	**4**	**0**	**1**	**1**	**2**
1990-91	**Buffalo**	**NHL**	**62**	**30**	**34**	**64**	**16**	**6**	**0**	**6**	**6**	**2**
1991-92	**Buffalo**	**NHL**	**67**	**39**	**45**	**84**	**73**	**2**	**0**	**2**	**2**	**0**
1992-93a	**Buffalo**	**NHL**	**77**	***76**	**51**	**127**	**40**	**7**	**7**	**3**	**10**	**6**
1993-94	**Buffalo**	**NHL**	**66**	**32**	**47**	**79**	**22**	**7**	**4**	**2**	**6**	**6**
1994-95	Spartak	CIS	1	0	1	1	0	....	....	....	....	....
	Buffalo	**NHL**	**44**	**19**	**28**	**47**	**36**	**5**	**3**	**2**	**5**	**2**
1995-96a	**Vancouver**	**NHL**	**79**	**55**	**52**	**107**	**16**	**6**	**1**	**8**	**9**	**8**
	NHL Totals		**460**	**266**	**285**	**551**	**219**	**37**	**15**	**24**	**39**	**26**

a NHL Second All-Star Team (1993, 1996)

Played in NHL All-Star Game (1992-94, 1996)

Traded to **Vancouver** by **Buffalo** with Buffalo's fifth round choice (Todd Norman) in 1995 Entry Draft for Mike Peca, Mike Wilson and Vancouver's first round choice (Jay McKee) in 1995 Entry Draft, July 8, 1995.

MOMESSO, SERGIO (moh-MESS-oh) — NYR

Left wing. Shoots left. 6'3", 215 lbs. Born, Montreal, Que., September 4, 1965.
(Montreal's 3rd choice, 27th overall, in 1983 Entry Draft).

			Regular Season					Playoffs				
Season	Club	Lea	GP	G	A	TP	PIM	GP	G	A	TP	PIM
1982-83	Shawinigan	QMJHL	70	27	42	69	93	10	5	4	9	55
1983-84	**Montreal**	**NHL**	**1**	**0**	**0**	**0**	**0**	....	....	....	....	....
	Shawinigan	QMJHL	68	42	88	130	235	6	4	4	8	13
	Nova Scotia	AHL	....	....	....	....	....	8	0	2	2	4
1984-85a	Shawinigan	QMJHL	64	56	90	146	216	8	7	8	15	17
1985-86	**Montreal**	**NHL**	**24**	**8**	**7**	**15**	**46**	....	....	....	....	....
1986-87	**Montreal**	**NHL**	**59**	**14**	**17**	**31**	**96**	**11**	**1**	**3**	**4**	**31**
	Sherbrooke	AHL	6	1	6	7	10	....	....	....	....	....
1987-88	**Montreal**	**NHL**	**53**	**7**	**14**	**21**	**101**	**6**	**0**	**2**	**2**	**16**
1988-89	**St. Louis**	**NHL**	**53**	**9**	**17**	**26**	**139**	**10**	**2**	**5**	**7**	**24**
1989-90	**St. Louis**	**NHL**	**79**	**24**	**32**	**56**	**199**	**12**	**3**	**2**	**5**	**63**
1990-91	**St. Louis**	**NHL**	**59**	**10**	**18**	**28**	**131**	....	....	....	....	....
	Vancouver	**NHL**	**11**	**6**	**2**	**8**	**43**	**6**	**0**	**3**	**3**	**25**
1991-92	**Vancouver**	**NHL**	**58**	**20**	**23**	**43**	**198**	**13**	**0**	**5**	**5**	**30**
1992-93	**Vancouver**	**NHL**	**84**	**18**	**20**	**38**	**200**	**12**	**3**	**0**	**3**	**30**
1993-94	**Vancouver**	**NHL**	**68**	**14**	**13**	**27**	**149**	**24**	**3**	**4**	**7**	**56**
1994-95	Milan Devils	Euro.	2	2	3	5	0	....	....	....	....	....
	Milan Devils	Italy	2	1	4	5	2	....	....	....	....	....
	Vancouver	**NHL**	**48**	**10**	**15**	**25**	**65**	**11**	**3**	**1**	**4**	**16**
1995-96	**Toronto**	**NHL**	**54**	**7**	**8**	**15**	**112**	....	....	....	....	....
	NY Rangers	**NHL**	**19**	**4**	**4**	**8**	**30**	**11**	**3**	**1**	**4**	**14**
	NHL Totals		**670**	**151**	**190**	**341**	**1509**	**116**	**18**	**26**	**44**	**305**

a QMJHL First All-Star Team (1985)

Traded to **St. Louis** by **Montreal** with Vincent Riendeau for Jocelyn Lemieux, Darrell May and St. Louis' second round choice (Patrice Brisebois) in the 1989 Entry Draft, August 9, 1988. Traded to **Vancouver** by **St. Louis** with Geoff Courtnall, Robert Dirk, Cliff Ronning and St. Louis' fifth round choice (Brian Loney) in 1992 Entry Draft for Dan Quinn and Garth Butcher, March 5, 1991. Traded to **Toronto** by **Vancouver** for Mike Ridley, July 8, 1995. Traded by **NY Rangers** by **Toronto** for Wayne Presley, February 29, 1996.

MONTGOMERY, JIM

Center. Shoots right. 5'10", 185 lbs. Born, Montreal, Que., June 30, 1969.

			Regular Season					Playoffs				
Season	Club	Lea	GP	G	A	TP	PIM	GP	G	A	TP	PIM
1989-90	U. of Maine	H.E.	45	26	34	60	35	....	....	....	....	....
1990-91	U. of Maine	H.E.	43	24	*57	81	44	....	....	....	....	....
1991-92a	U. of Maine	H.E.	37	21	44	65	46	....	....	....	....	....
1992-93bcde	U. of Maine	H.E.	45	32	63	95	40	....	....	....	....	....
1993-94	**St. Louis**	**NHL**	**67**	**6**	**14**	**20**	**44**	....	....	....	....	....
	Peoria	IHL	12	7	8	15	10	....	....	....	....	....
1994-95	**Montreal**	**NHL**	**5**	**0**	**0**	**0**	**2**	....	....	....	....	....
	Philadelphia	**NHL**	**8**	**1**	**1**	**2**	**6**	**7**	**1**	**0**	**1**	**2**
	Hershey	AHL	16	8	6	14	14	6	3	2	5	25
1995-96	**Philadelphia**	**NHL**	**5**	**1**	**2**	**3**	**9**	**1**	**0**	**0**	**0**	**0**
f	Hershey	AHL	78	34	*71	105	95	4	3	2	5	6
	NHL Totals		**85**	**8**	**17**	**25**	**61**	**8**	**1**	**0**	**1**	**2**

a Hockey East Second All-Star Team (1992)
b Hockey East First All-Star Team (1993)
c NCAA East Second All-American Team (1993)
d NCAA Final Four All-Tournament Team (1993)
e NCAA Final Four Tournament Most Valuable Player (1993)
f AHL Second All-Star Team (1996)

Signed as a free agent by **St. Louis**, June 2, 1993. Traded to **Montreal** by **St. Louis** for Guy Carbonneau, August 19, 1994. Claimed on waivers by **Philadelphia** from **Montreal**, February 10, 1995.

MONTREUIL, ERIC — FLA.

Center. Shoots left. 6'1", 177 lbs. Born, Verdun, Que., May 18, 1975.
(Florida's 13th choice, 265th overall, in 1993 Draft).

			Regular Season					Playoffs				
Season	Club	Lea	GP	G	A	TP	PIM	GP	G	A	TP	PIM
1992-93	Chicoutimi	QMJHL	70	19	13	32	98	4	0	1	1	2
1993-94	Beauport	QMJHL	67	31	40	71	122	15	4	8	12	39
1994-95	Beauport	QMJHL	70	21	39	60	186	18	5	10	15	72
1995-96	Carolina	AHL	66	7	8	15	81	....	....	....	....	....

MOORE, BARRIE — BUF.

Left wing. Shoots left. 5'11", 175 lbs. Born, London, Ont., May 22, 1975.
(Buffalo's 7th choice, 220th overall, in 1993 Entry Draft).

			Regular Season					Playoffs				
Season	Club	Lea	GP	G	A	TP	PIM	GP	G	A	TP	PIM
1991-92	Sudbury	OHL	62	15	38	53	57	11	0	7	7	12
1992-93	Sudbury	OHL	57	13	26	39	71	14	4	3	7	19
1993-94	Sudbury	OHL	65	36	49	85	69	10	3	5	8	14
1994-95	Sudbury	OHL	60	47	42	89	67	18	*15	14	29	24
1995-96	**Buffalo**	**NHL**	**3**	**0**	**0**	**0**	**0**	....	....	....	....	....
	Rochester	AHL	64	26	30	56	40	18	3	6	9	18
	NHL Totals		**3**	**0**	**0**	**0**	**0**	....	....	....	....	....

MORAN, IAN — PIT.

Defense. Shoots right. 5'11", 195 lbs. Born, Cleveland, OH, August 24, 1972.
(Pittsburgh's 6th choice, 107th overall, in 1990 Entry Draft).

			Regular Season					Playoffs				
Season	Club	Lea	GP	G	A	TP	PIM	GP	G	A	TP	PIM
1991-92	Boston College	H.E.	30	2	16	18	44	....	....	....	....	....
1992-93	Boston College	H.E.	31	8	12	20	32	....	....	....	....	....
1993-94	U.S. National	....	50	8	15	23	69	....	....	....	....	....
	Cleveland	IHL	33	5	13	18	39	....	....	....	....	....
1994-95	Cleveland	IHL	64	7	31	38	94	4	0	1	1	2
	Pittsburgh	**NHL**	....	....	....	....	....	**8**	**0**	**0**	**0**	**0**
1995-96	**Pittsburgh**	**NHL**	**51**	**1**	**1**	**2**	**47**	....	....	....	....	....
	NHL Totals		**51**	**1**	**1**	**2**	**47**	**8**	**0**	**0**	**0**	**0**

MORE, JAYSON — (MOHR) NYR

Defense. Shoots right. 6'2", 210 lbs. Born, Souris, Man., January 12, 1969.
(NY Rangers' 1st choice, 10th overall, in 1987 Entry Draft).

			Regular Season					Playoffs				
Season	Club	Lea	GP	G	A	TP	PIM	GP	G	A	TP	PIM
1984-85	Lethbridge	WHL	71	3	9	12	101	4	1	0	1	7
1985-86	Lethbridge	WHL	61	7	18	25	155	9	0	2	2	36
1986-87	Brandon	WHL	21	4	6	10	62	....	....	....	....	....
	N. Westminster	WHL	43	4	23	27	155	....	....	....	....	....
1987-88a	N. Westminster	WHL	70	13	47	60	270	5	0	2	2	26
1988-89	**NY Rangers**	**NHL**	**1**	**0**	**0**	**0**	**0**	....	....	....	....	....
	Denver	IHL	62	7	15	22	138	3	0	1	1	26
1989-90	Flint	IHL	9	1	5	6	41	....	....	....	....	....
	Minnesota	**NHL**	**5**	**0**	**0**	**0**	**16**	....	....	....	....	....
	Kalamazoo	IHL	64	9	25	34	316	10	0	3	3	13
1990-91	Kalamazoo	IHL	10	0	5	5	46	....	....	....	....	....
	Fredericton	AHL	57	7	17	24	152	9	1	1	2	34
1991-92	**San Jose**	**NHL**	**46**	**4**	**13**	**17**	**85**	....	....	....	....	....
	Kansas City	IHL	2	0	2	2	4	....	....	....	....	....
1992-93	**San Jose**	**NHL**	**73**	**5**	**6**	**11**	**179**	....	....	....	....	....
1993-94	**San Jose**	**NHL**	**49**	**1**	**6**	**7**	**63**	**13**	**0**	**2**	**2**	**32**
	Kansas City	IHL	2	1	0	1	25	....	....	....	....	....
1994-95	**San Jose**	**NHL**	**45**	**0**	**6**	**6**	**71**	**11**	**0**	**4**	**4**	**6**
1995-96	**San Jose**	**NHL**	**74**	**2**	**7**	**9**	**147**	....	....	....	....	....
	NHL Totals		**293**	**12**	**38**	**50**	**561**	**24**	**0**	**6**	**6**	**38**

a WHL All-Star Team (1988)

Traded to **Minnesota** by **NY Rangers** for Dave Archibald, November 1, 1989. Traded to **Montreal** by **Minnesota** for Brian Hayward, November 7, 1990. Claimed by **San Jose** from **Montreal** in Expansion Draft, May 30, 1991. Traded to **NY Rangers** by **San Jose** with Brian Swanson and a conditional choice in 1998 Entry Draft for Marty McSorley, August 20, 1996.

MOREAU, ETHAN — CHI.

Left wing. Shoots left. 6'2", 205 lbs. Born, Huntsville, Ont., September 22, 1975.
(Chicago's 1st choice, 14th overall, in 1994 Entry Draft).

			Regular Season					Playoffs				
Season	Club	Lea	GP	G	A	TP	PIM	GP	G	A	TP	PIM
1991-92	Niagara Falls	OHL	62	20	35	55	39	17	4	6	10	4
1992-93	Niagara Falls	OHL	65	32	41	73	69	4	0	3	3	4
1993-94	Niagara Falls	OHL	59	44	54	98	100	....	....	....	....	....
1994-95	Niagara Falls	OHL	39	25	41	66	69	....	....	....	....	....
	Sudbury	OHL	23	13	17	30	22	18	6	12	18	26
1995-96	**Chicago**	**NHL**	**8**	**0**	**1**	**1**	**4**	....	....	....	....	....
	Indianapolis	IHL	71	21	20	41	126	5	4	0	4	8
	NHL Totals		**8**	**0**	**1**	**1**	**4**					

MORGAN, JASON — L.A.

Center. Shoots left. 6'1", 185 lbs. Born, St. John's, Nfld., October 9, 1976.
(Los Angeles' 5th choice, 118th overall, in 1995 Entry Draft).

			Regular Season					Playoffs				
Season	Club	Lea	GP	G	A	TP	PIM	GP	G	A	TP	PIM
1993-94	Kitchener	OHL	65	6	15	21	16	5	1	0	1	0
1994-95	Kitchener	OHL	35	3	15	18	25	....	....	....	....	....
	Kingston	OHL	20	0	3	3	14	6	0	2	2	0
1995-96	Kingston	OHL	66	16	38	54	50	6	1	2	3	0

MORIN, STEPHANE — (moh-RAI)

Center. Shoots left. 6', 174 lbs. Born, Montreal, Que., March 27, 1969.
(Quebec's 3rd choice, 43rd overall, in 1989 Entry Draft).

			Regular Season					Playoffs				
Season	Club	Lea	GP	G	A	TP	PIM	GP	G	A	TP	PIM
1986-87	Shawinigan	QMJHL	65	9	14	23	28	....	....	....	....	....
1987-88	Chicoutimi	QMJHL	68	38	45	83	18	6	3	8	11	2
1988-89a	Chicoutimi	QMJHL	70	77	*109	*186	71	....	....	....	....	....
1989-90	**Quebec**	**NHL**	**6**	**0**	**2**	**2**	**2**	....	....	....	....	....
	Halifax	AHL	65	28	32	60	60	6	3	4	7	6
1990-91	**Quebec**	**NHL**	**48**	**13**	**27**	**40**	**30**	....	....	....	....	....
	Halifax	AHL	17	8	14	22	18	....	....	....	....	....
1991-92	**Quebec**	**NHL**	**30**	**2**	**8**	**10**	**14**	....	....	....	....	....
	Halifax	AHL	30	17	13	30	29	....	....	....	....	....
1992-93	**Vancouver**	**NHL**	**1**	**0**	**1**	**1**	**0**	....	....	....	....	....
	Hamilton	AHL	70	31	54	85	49	....	....	....	....	....
1993-94	**Vancouver**	**NHL**	**5**	**1**	**1**	**2**	**6**	....	....	....	....	....
b	Hamilton	AHL	69	38	71	109	48	4	3	2	5	4
1994-95cd	Minnesota	IHL	81	33	*81	*114	53	2	0	1	1	0
1995-96	Minnesota	IHL	80	27	51	78	75	....	....	....	....	....
	NHL Totals		**90**	**16**	**39**	**55**	**52**	....	....	....	....	....

a QMJHL First All-Star Team (1989)
b AHL Second All-Star Team (1994)
c IHL First All-Star Team (1995)
d Won Leo P. Lamoureux Memorial Trophy (Top Scorer - IHL) (1995)

Signed as a free agent by **Vancouver**, October 5, 1992.

MORO, MARC — OTT.

Defense. Shoots left. 6'1", 209 lbs. Born, Toronto, Ont., July 17, 1977.
(Ottawa's 2nd choice, 27th overall, in 1995 Entry Draft).

			Regular Season					Playoffs				
Season	Club	Lea	GP	G	A	TP	PIM	GP	G	A	TP	PIM
1993-94	Kingston	OHL	43	0	3	3	81	....	....	....	....	....
1994-95	Kingston	OHL	64	4	12	16	255	6	0	0	0	23
1995-96	Kingston	OHL	66	4	17	21	261	6	0	0	0	12
	P.E.I.	AHL	2	0	0	0	7	2	0	0	0	4

MOROZOV, ALEXEI — (moh-ROH-zohv) PIT.

Right wing. Shoots left. 6'1", 178 lbs. Born, Moscow, USSR, February 16, 1977.
(Pittsburgh's 1st choice, 24th overall, in 1995 Entry Draft).

			Regular Season					Playoffs				
Season	Club	Lea	GP	G	A	TP	PIM	GP	G	A	TP	PIM
1993-94	Soviet Wings	CIS	7	0	0	0	0	3	0	0	0	2
1994-95	Soviet Wings	CIS	48	15	12	27	53	4	0	3	3	0
1995-96	Soviet Wings	CIS	47	13	9	22	26	....	....	....	....	....

MOROZOV, VALENTIN — (moh-ROH-zohv) PIT.

Center. Shoots left. 5'11", 176 lbs. Born, Moscow, USSR, June 1, 1975.
(Pittsburgh's 8th choice, 154th overall, in 1994 Entry Draft).

			Regular Season					Playoffs				
Season	Club	Lea	GP	G	A	TP	PIM	GP	G	A	TP	PIM
1992-93	CSKA	CIS	17	0	0	0	6	....	....	....	....	....
1993-94	CSKA	CIS	18	4	1	5	8	3	0	1	1	0
1994-95	CSKA	CIS	47	9	4	13	10	2	2	0	2	0
1995-96	CSKA	CIS	51	30	11	41	28	3	1	0	1	2

MORRIS, DEREK — CGY.

Defense. Shoots right. 5'11", 180 lbs. Born, Edmonton, Alta., August 24, 1978.
(Calgary's 1st choice, 13th overall, in 1996 Entry Draft).

			Regular Season					Playoffs				
Season	Club	Lea	GP	G	A	TP	PIM	GP	G	A	TP	PIM
1994-95	Red Deer	Midget	31	6	35	41	74	....	....	....	....	....
1995-96	Regina	WHL	67	8	44	52	70	11	1	7	8	26

MORRISON, BRENDAN — N.J.

Center. Shoots left. 5'11", 170 lbs. Born, N. Vancouver, B.C., August 12, 1975.
(New Jersey's 3rd choice, 39th overall, in 1993 Entry Draft).

			Regular Season					Playoffs				
Season	Club	Lea	GP	G	A	TP	PIM	GP	G	A	TP	PIM
1993-94	U. of Michigan	CCHA	38	20	28	48	24	....	....	....	....	....
1994-95ab	U. of Michigan	CCHA	39	23	*53	*76	42	....	....	....	....	....
1995-96ab	U. of Michigan	CCHA	35	28	44	*72	41	....	....	....	....	....

a CCHA First All-Star Team (1995, 1996)
b NCAA West First All-American Team (1995, 1996)

MORROW, SCOTT

Left wing. Shoots left. 6'1", 185 lbs. Born, Chicago, IL, June 18, 1969.
(Hartford's 4th choice, 95th overall, in 1988 Entry Draft).

			Regular Season					Playoffs				
Season	Club	Lea	GP	G	A	TP	PIM	GP	G	A	TP	PIM
1988-89	N. Hampshire	H.E.	19	6	7	13	14	....	....	....	....	....
1989-90	N. Hampshire	H.E.	29	10	11	21	35	....	....	....	....	....
1990-91	N. Hampshire	H.E.	31	11	11	22	52	....	....	....	....	....
1991-92a	N. Hampshire	H.E.	35	30	23	53	65	....	....	....	....	....
	Springfield	AHL	2	0	1	1	0	5	0	0	0	9
1992-93	Springfield	AHL	70	22	29	51	80	15	6	9	15	21
1993-94	Springfield	AHL	30	12	15	27	28	....	....	....	....	....
	Saint John	AHL	8	2	2	4	0	7	2	1	3	10
1994-95	Saint John	AHL	64	18	21	39	105	5	2	0	2	4
	Calgary	**NHL**	**4**	**0**	**0**	**0**	**0**	....	....	....	....	....
1995-96	Hershey	AHL	79	48	45	93	110	5	2	2	4	6
	NHL Totals		**4**	**0**	**0**	**0**	**0**	....	....	....	....	....

a Hockey East Second All-Star Team (1992)

Traded to **Calgary** by **Hartford** for Todd Harkins, January 24, 1994. Signed as a free agent by **Philadelphia**, July 31, 1995.

MORTIER, DARREN   BUF.

Center. Shoots right. 6'1", 175 lbs.   Born, Sarnia, Ont., May 4, 1977.
(Buffalo's 9th choice, 161st overall, in 1996 Entry Draft).

			Regular Season					Playoffs				
Season	Club	Lea	GP	G	A	TP	PIM	GP	G	A	TP	PIM
1994-95	Sarnia	OHL	42	10	5	15	6	2	0	0	0	9
1995-96	Sarnia	OHL	63	20	22	42	26	10	1	6	7	0

MOSER, JAY   BOS.

Defense. Shoots left. 6'2", 170 lbs.   Born, Cottage Grove, MN, December 26, 1972.
(Boston's 7th choice, 172nd overall, in 1991 Entry Draft).

			Regular Season					Playoffs				
Season	Club	Lea	GP	G	A	TP	PIM	GP	G	A	TP	PIM
1991-92	St. Cloud	WCHA	35	3	9	12	40	....	....	....	....	....
1992-93	St. Cloud	WCHA	33	2	9	11	77	....	....	....	....	....
1993-94					DID NOT PLAY							
1994-95	U. Minnesota	WCHA	13	1	5	6	29	....	....	....	....	....
1995-96	U. Minnesota	WCHA	21	10	9	19	18	....	....	....	....	....

MROZIK, RICK   (muh-ROH-zihk)   WSH.

Defense. Shoots left. 6'2", 185 lbs.   Born, Duluth, MN, January 2, 1975.
(Dallas' 4th choice, 136th overall, in 1993 Entry Draft).

			Regular Season					Playoffs				
Season	Club	Lea	GP	G	A	TP	PIM	GP	G	A	TP	PIM
1993-94	Minn.-Duluth	WCHA	38	2	9	11	38	....	....	....	....	....
1994-95	Minn.-Duluth	WCHA	3	0	0	0	2	....	....	....	....	....
1995-96	Minn. Duluth	WCHA	35	3	19	22	63	....	....	....	....	....

Traded to **Washington** by **Dallas** with Mark Tinordi for Kevin Hatcher, January 18, 1995.

MUCKALT, BILL   VAN.

Center. Shoots right. 6', 180 lbs.   Born, Williams Lake, B.C., July 15, 1974.
(Vancouver's 9th choice, 221st overall, in 1994 Entry Draft).

			Regular Season					Playoffs				
Season	Club	Lea	GP	G	A	TP	PIM	GP	G	A	TP	PIM
1994-95	U. of Michigan	CCHA	39	19	18	37	42	....	....	....	....	....
1995-96	U. of Michigan	CCHA	41	28	30	58	34	....	....	....	....	....

MUELLER, BRIAN   HFD.

Defense. Shoots left. 5'11", 225 lbs.   Born, Liverpool, NY, June 2, 1972.
(Hartford's 7th choice, 141st overall, in 1991 Entry Draft).

			Regular Season					Playoffs				
Season	Club	Lea	GP	G	A	TP	PIM	GP	G	A	TP	PIM
1991-92	Clarkson	ECAC	28	4	13	17	30	....	....	....	....	....
1992-93	Clarkson	ECAC	32	6	23	29	12	....	....	....	....	....
1993-94ab	Clarkson	ECAC	34	17	39	56	60	....	....	....	....	....
1994-95a	Clarkson	ECAC	36	12	42	54	56	....	....	....	....	....
1995-96	Springfield	AHL	51	7	12	19	49	2	0	0	0	0
	Richmond	ECHL	3	1	1	2	2	3	0	2	2	0

a   ECAC First All-Star Team (1994, 1995)
b   NCAA East First All-American Team (1994)

MUIR, BRYAN   EDM.

Defense. Shoots left. 6'4", 220 lbs.   Born, Winnipeg, Man., June 8, 1973.

			Regular Season					Playoffs				
Season	Club	Lea	GP	G	A	TP	PIM	GP	G	A	TP	PIM
1992-93	N. Hampshire	H.E.	26	1	2	3	24	....	....	....	....	....
1993-94	N. Hampshire	H.E.	40	0	4	4	48	....	....	....	....	....
1994-95	N. Hampshire	H.E.	28	9	9	18	46	....	....	....	....	....
1995-96	Cdn. National	....	42	6	12	18	38	....	....	....	....	....
	Edmonton	**NHL**	5	0	0	0	6	....	....	....	....	....
	NHL Totals		**5**	**0**	**0**	**0**	**6**	....	....	....	....	....

Signed as a free agent by **Edmonton**, April 30, 1996.

MULHERN, RYAN   CGY.

Center. Shoots right. 6'1", 180 lbs.   Born, Philadelphia, PA, January 11, 1973.
(Calgary's 8th choice, 174th overall, in 1992 Entry Draft).

			Regular Season					Playoffs				
Season	Club	Lea	GP	G	A	TP	PIM	GP	G	A	TP	PIM
1992-93	Brown	ECAC	31	15	9	24	46	....	....	....	....	....
1993-94	Brown	ECAC	27	18	17	35	48	....	....	....	....	....
1994-95	Brown	ECAC	30	18	16	34	*108	....	....	....	....	....
1995-96	Brown	ECAC	32	10	16	26	78	....	....	....	....	....

MULLEN, JOE

Right wing. Shoots right. 5'9", 180 lbs.   Born, New York, NY, February 26, 1957.

			Regular Season					Playoffs				
Season	Club	Lea	GP	G	A	TP	PIM	GP	G	A	TP	PIM
1977-78a	Boston College	ECAC	34	34	34	68	12	....	....	....	....	....
1978-79a	Boston College	ECAC	25	32	24	56	8	....	....	....	....	....
1979-80bc	Salt Lake	CHL	75	40	32	72	21	13	*9	11	20	0
	St. Louis	**NHL**	1	0	0	0	0	....	....	....	....	....
1980-81de	Salt Lake	CHL	80	59	58	*117	8	17	11	9	20	0
1981-82	**St. Louis**	**NHL**	45	25	34	59	4	10	7	11	18	4
	Salt Lake	CHL	27	21	27	48	12	....	....	....	....	....
1982-83	**St. Louis**	**NHL**	49	17	30	47	6	....	....	....	....	....
1983-84	**St. Louis**	**NHL**	80	41	44	85	19	6	2	0	2	0
1984-85	**St. Louis**	**NHL**	79	40	52	92	6	3	0	0	0	0
1985-86	**St. Louis**	**NHL**	48	28	24	52	10	....	....	....	....	....
	Calgary	**NHL**	29	16	22	38	11	21	*12	7	19	4
1986-87f	**Calgary**	**NHL**	79	47	40	87	14	6	2	1	3	0
1987-88	**Calgary**	**NHL**	80	40	44	84	30	7	2	4	6	10
1988-89fgh	**Calgary**	**NHL**	79	51	59	110	16	21	*16	8	24	4 ♦
1989-90	**Calgary**	**NHL**	78	36	33	69	24	6	3	0	3	0
1990-91	**Pittsburgh**	**NHL**	47	17	22	39	6	22	8	9	17	4 ♦
1991-92	**Pittsburgh**	**NHL**	77	42	45	87	30	9	3	1	4	4 ♦
1992-93	**Pittsburgh**	**NHL**	72	33	37	70	14	12	4	2	6	6
1993-94	**Pittsburgh**	**NHL**	84	38	32	70	41	6	1	0	1	2
1994-95	**Pittsburgh**	**NHL**	45	16	21	37	6	12	0	3	3	4
1995-96	**Boston**	**NHL**	37	8	7	15	0	....	....	....	....	....
	NHL Totals		**1008**	**495**	**546**	**1041**	**237**	**142**	**60**	**46**	**106**	**42**

a   ECAC First All-Star Team (1978, 1979)
b   CHL Second All-Star Team (1980)
c   Won Ken McKenzie Trophy (CHL's Top Rookie) (1980)
d   CHL First All-Star Team (1981)
e   Won Tommy Ivan Trophy (CHL's Most Valuable Player) (1981)
f   Won Lady Byng Trophy (1987, 1989)
g   NHL First All-Star Team (1989)
h   NHL Plus/Minus Leader (1989)
Played in NHL All-Star Game (1989, 1990, 1994)

Signed as a free agent by **St. Louis**, August 16, 1979. Traded to **Calgary** by **St. Louis** with Terry Johnson and Rik Wilson for Ed Beers, Charles Bourgeois and Gino Cavallini, February 1, 1986. Traded to **Pittsburgh** by **Calgary** for Pittsburgh's second round choice (Nicolas Perreault) in 1990 Entry Draft, June 16, 1990. Signed as a free agent by **Boston**, September 13, 1995.

MULLER, KIRK   TOR.

Left wing. Shoots left. 6', 205 lbs.   Born, Kingston, Ont., February 8, 1966.
(New Jersey's 1st choice, 2nd overall, in 1984 Entry Draft).

			Regular Season					Playoffs				
Season	Club	Lea	GP	G	A	TP	PIM	GP	G	A	TP	PIM
1981-82	Kingston	OHL	67	12	39	51	27	4	5	1	6	4
1982-83	Guelph	OHL	66	52	60	112	41	....	....	....	....	....
1983-84	Guelph	OHL	49	31	63	94	27	....	....	....	....	....
	Cdn. National	....	15	2	2	4	6	....	....	....	....	....
	Cdn. Olympic	....	6	2	1	3	0	....	....	....	....	....
1984-85	**New Jersey**	**NHL**	80	17	37	54	69	....	....	....	....	....
1985-86	**New Jersey**	**NHL**	77	25	41	66	45	....	....	....	....	....
1986-87	**New Jersey**	**NHL**	79	26	50	76	75	....	....	....	....	....
1987-88	**New Jersey**	**NHL**	80	37	57	94	114	20	4	8	12	37
1988-89	**New Jersey**	**NHL**	80	31	43	74	119	....	....	....	....	....
1989-90	**New Jersey**	**NHL**	80	30	56	86	74	6	1	3	4	11
1990-91	**New Jersey**	**NHL**	80	19	51	70	76	7	0	2	2	10
1991-92	**Montreal**	**NHL**	78	36	41	77	86	11	4	3	7	31
1992-93	**Montreal**	**NHL**	80	37	57	94	77	20	10	7	17	18 ♦
1993-94	**Montreal**	**NHL**	76	23	34	57	96	7	6	2	8	4
1994-95	**Montreal**	**NHL**	33	8	11	19	33	....	....	....	....	....
	NY Islanders	**NHL**	12	3	5	8	14	....	....	....	....	....
1995-96	**NY Islanders**	**NHL**	15	4	3	7	15	....	....	....	....	....
	Toronto	**NHL**	36	9	16	25	42	6	3	2	5	0
	NHL Totals		**886**	**305**	**502**	**807**	**935**	**77**	**28**	**27**	**55**	**111**

Played in NHL All-Star Game (1985, 1986, 1988, 1990, 1992, 1993)

Traded to **Montreal** by **New Jersey** with Roland Melanson for Stephane Richer and Tom Chorske, September 20, 1991. Traded to **NY Islanders** by **Montreal** with Mathieu Schneider and Craig Darby for Pierre Turgeon and Vladimir Malakhov, April 5, 1995. Traded to **Toronto** by **NY Islanders** with Don Beaupre for future considerations, January 23, 1996.

MULLER, MIKE

Defense. Shoots left. 6'2", 205 lbs.   Born, Fairview, MN, September 18, 1971.
(Winnipeg's 2nd choice, 35th overall, in 1990 Entry Draft).

			Regular Season					Playoffs				
Season	Club	Lea	GP	G	A	TP	PIM	GP	G	A	TP	PIM
1990-91	U. Minnesota	WCHA	33	4	4	8	44	....	....	....	....	....
1991-92	U. Minnesota	WCHA	41	4	12	16	52	....	....	....	....	....
1992-93	Moscow D'amo	CIS	11	1	0	1	8	....	....	....	....	....
1993-94	Moncton	AHL	61	2	14	16	88	....	....	....	....	....
1994-95	Springfield	AHL	64	2	5	7	61	....	....	....	....	....
1995-96	Minnesota	IHL	53	3	7	10	72	....	....	....	....	....

MULLIN, KORY   TOR.

Defense. Shoots left. 6'2", 185 lbs.   Born, Lethbridge, Alta., May 24, 1975.

			Regular Season					Playoffs				
Season	Club	Lea	GP	G	A	TP	PIM	GP	G	A	TP	PIM
1991-92	Tri-City	WHL	49	2	5	7	82	5	1	0	1	6
1992-93	Tri-City	WHL	68	2	10	12	95	4	0	0	0	11
1993-94	Tri-City	WHL	6	0	5	5	11	....	....	....	....	....
	Tacoma	WHL	59	3	11	14	86	8	0	0	0	0
1994-95	Lethbridge	WHL	48	6	21	27	72	....	....	....	....	....
1995-96	Brantford	ColHL	1	0	0	0	0	....	....	....	....	....
	St. John's	AHL	55	6	4	10	73	2	0	1	1	0

Signed as a free agent by **Toronto**, September 23, 1993.

MUNI, CRAIG (MYOO-ne)

Defense. Shoots left. 6'3", 208 lbs. Born, Toronto, Ont., July 19, 1962.
(Toronto's 1st choice, 25th overall, in 1980 Entry Draft).

			Regular Season					Playoffs				
Season	Club	Lea	GP	G	A	TP	PIM	GP	G	A	TP	PIM
1980-81	Kingston	OHA	38	2	14	16	65	....	....	....	....	....
	Windsor	OHA	25	5	11	16	41	11	1	4	5	14
	New Brunswick	AHL	....	....	....	....	....	2	0	1	1	10
1981-82	Toronto	NHL	3	0	0	0	2	....	....	....	....	....
	Windsor	OHL	49	5	32	37	92	9	2	3	5	16
	Cincinnati	CHL	....	....	....	....	....	3	0	2	2	2
1982-83	Toronto	NHL	2	0	1	1	0	....	....	....	....	....
	St. Catharines	AHL	64	6	32	38	52	....	....	....	....	....
1983-84	St. Catharines	AHL	64	4	16	20	79	7	0	1	1	0
1984-85	Toronto	NHL	8	0	0	0	0	....	....	....	....	....
	St. Catharines	AHL	68	7	17	24	54	....	....	....	....	....
1985-86	Toronto	NHL	6	0	1	1	4	....	....	....	....	....
	St. Catharines	AHL	73	3	34	37	91	13	0	5	5	16
1986-87	Edmonton	NHL	79	7	22	29	85	14	0	2	2	17 ♦
1987-88	Edmonton	NHL	72	4	15	19	77	19	0	4	4	31 ♦
1988-89	Edmonton	NHL	69	5	13	18	71	7	0	3	3	8
1989-90	Edmonton	NHL	71	5	12	17	81	22	0	3	3	16 ♦
1990-91	Edmonton	NHL	76	1	9	10	77	18	0	3	3	20
1991-92	Edmonton	NHL	54	2	5	7	34	3	0	0	0	2
1992-93	Edmonton	NHL	72	0	11	11	67	....	....	....	....	....
	Chicago	NHL	9	0	0	0	8	4	0	0	0	2
1993-94	Chicago	NHL	9	0	4	4	4	....	....	....	....	....
	Buffalo	NHL	73	2	8	10	62	7	0	0	0	4
1994-95	Buffalo	NHL	40	0	6	6	36	5	0	1	1	2
1995-96	Buffalo	NHL	47	0	4	4	69	....	....	....	....	....
	Winnipeg	NHL	25	1	3	4	37	6	0	1	1	2
	NHL Totals		715	27	114	141	714	105	0	17	17	104

Signed as a free agent by **Edmonton,** August 18, 1986. Sold to **Buffalo** by **Edmonton,** October 2, 1986. Traded to **Pittsburgh** by **Buffalo** for future considerations, October 3, 1986. Traded to **Edmonton** by **Pittsburgh** to complete September 11, 1985 trade which sent Gilles Meloche to Pittsburgh for Tim Hrynewich, Marty McSorley and future considerations, October 6, 1986. Traded to **Chicago** by **Edmonton** for Mike Hudson, March 22, 1993. Traded to **Buffalo** by **Chicago** with Chicago's fifth round choice (Daniel Bienvenue) in 1995 Entry Draft for Keith Carney and Buffalo's sixth round choice (Marc Magliarditi) in 1995 Entry Draft, October 27, 1993. Traded to **Winnipeg** by **Buffalo** for Darryl Shannon and Michael Grosek, February 15, 1996.

MURPHY, BURKE CGY.

Left wing. Shoots left. 6', 180 lbs. Born, Gloucester, Ont., June 5, 1973.
(Calgary's 11th choice, 278th overall, in 1993 Entry Draft).

			Regular Season					Playoffs				
Season	Club	Lea	GP	G	A	TP	PIM	GP	G	A	TP	PIM
1992-93	St. Lawrence	ECAC	32	19	10	29	32	....	....	....	....	....
1993-94	St. Lawrence	ECAC	30	20	17	37	42	....	....	....	....	....
1994-95a	St. Lawrence	ECAC	33	27	23	50	61	....	....	....	....	....
1995-96bc	St. Lawrence	ECAC	35	*33	25	58	37	....	....	....	....	....

a ECAC Second All-Star Team (1995)
b ECAC First All-Star Team (1996)
c NCAA East Second All-American Team (1996)

MURPHY, CORY T.B.

Defense. Shoots left. 6'2", 202 lbs. Born, Perth, Ont., October 22, 1976.
(Tampa Bay's 6th choice, 160th overall, in 1995 Entry Draft).

			Regular Season					Playoffs				
Season	Club	Lea	GP	G	A	TP	PIM	GP	G	A	TP	PIM
1992-93	Ottawa	OHL	66	3	6	9	22	....	....	....	....	....
1993-94	Ottawa	OHL	57	2	13	15	68	10	3	0	3	4
1994-95	Ottawa	OHL	20	2	2	4	33	....	....	....	....	....
	S.S. Marie	OHL	11	0	4	4	18	....	....	....	....	....
1995-96	S.S. Marie	OHL	52	1	16	17	109	4	0	1	1	11

MURPHY, GORD FLA.

Defense. Shoots right. 6'2", 191 lbs. Born, Willowdale, Ont., March 23, 1967.
(Philadelphia's 10th choice, 189th overall, in 1985 Entry Draft).

			Regular Season					Playoffs				
Season	Club	Lea	GP	G	A	TP	PIM	GP	G	A	TP	PIM
1984-85	Oshawa	OHL	59	3	12	15	25	....	....	....	....	....
1985-86	Oshawa	OHL	64	7	15	22	56	6	1	1	2	6
1986-87	Oshawa	OHL	56	7	30	37	95	24	6	16	22	22
1987-88	Hershey	AHL	62	8	20	28	44	12	0	8	8	12
1988-89	Philadelphia	NHL	75	4	31	35	68	19	2	7	9	13
1989-90	Philadelphia	NHL	75	14	27	41	95	....	....	....	....	....
1990-91	Philadelphia	NHL	80	11	31	42	58	....	....	....	....	....
1991-92	Philadelphia	NHL	31	2	8	10	33	....	....	....	....	....
	Boston	NHL	42	3	6	9	51	15	1	0	1	12
1992-93	Boston	NHL	49	5	12	17	62	....	....	....	....	....
	Providence	AHL	2	1	3	4	2	....	....	....	....	....
1993-94	Florida	NHL	84	14	29	43	71	....	....	....	....	....
1994-95	Florida	NHL	46	6	16	22	24	....	....	....	....	....
1995-96	Florida	NHL	70	8	22	30	30	14	0	4	4	6
	NHL Totals		552	67	182	249	492	48	3	11	14	31

Traded to **Boston** by **Philadelphia** with Brian Dobbin, Philadelphia's third round choice (Sergei Zholtok) in 1992 Entry Draft and Philadelphia's fourth round choice (Charles Paquette) in 1993 Entry Draft, for Garry Galley, Wes Walz and Boston's third round choice (Milos Holan) in 1993 Entry Draft, January 2, 1992. Traded to **Dallas** by **Boston** for future considerations (Jon Casey traded to Boston for Andy Moog, June 25, 1993), June 20, 1993. Claimed by **Florida** from **Dallas** in Expansion Draft, June 24, 1993.

MURPHY, JOE ST.L.

Right wing. Shoots left. 6'1", 190 lbs. Born, London, Ont., October 16, 1967.
(Detroit's 1st choice, 1st overall, in 1986 Entry Draft).

			Regular Season					Playoffs				
Season	Club	Lea	GP	G	A	TP	PIM	GP	G	A	TP	PIM
1985-86	Michigan State	CCHA	35	24	37	61	50	....	....	....	....	....
	Cdn. National	....	8	3	3	6	2	....	....	....	....	....
1986-87	Detroit	NHL	5	0	1	1	2	....	....	....	....	....
	Adirondack	AHL	71	21	38	59	61	10	2	1	3	33
1987-88	Detroit	NHL	50	10	9	19	37	8	0	1	1	6
	Adirondack	AHL	6	5	6	11	4	....	....	....	....	....
1988-89	Detroit	NHL	26	1	7	8	28	....	....	....	....	....
	Adirondack	AHL	47	31	35	66	66	16	6	11	17	17
1989-90	Detroit	NHL	9	3	1	4	4	....	....	....	....	....
	Edmonton	NHL	62	7	18	25	56	22	6	8	14	16 ♦
1990-91	Edmonton	NHL	80	27	35	62	35	15	2	5	7	14
1991-92	Edmonton	NHL	80	35	47	82	52	16	8	16	24	12
1992-93	Chicago	NHL	19	7	10	17	18	4	0	0	0	8
1993-94	Chicago	NHL	81	31	39	70	111	6	1	3	4	25
1994-95	Chicago	NHL	40	23	18	41	89	16	9	3	12	29
1995-96	Chicago	NHL	70	22	29	51	86	10	6	2	8	33
	NHL Totals		522	166	214	380	518	97	32	38	70	143

Traded to **Edmonton** by **Detroit** with Petr Klima, Adam Graves and Jeff Sharples for Jimmy Carson, Kevin McClelland and Edmonton's fifth round choice (later traded to Montreal — Montreal selected Brad Layzell) in 1991 Entry Draft, November 2, 1989. Traded to **Chicago** by **Edmonton** for Igor Kravchuk and Dean McAmmond, February 24, 1993. Signed as a free agent by **St. Louis,** July 8, 1996.

MURPHY, LARRY TOR.

Defense. Shoots right. 6'2", 210 lbs. Born, Scarborough, Ont., March 8, 1961.
(Los Angeles' 1st choice, 4th overall, in 1980 Entry Draft).

			Regular Season					Playoffs				
Season	Club	Lea	GP	G	A	TP	PIM	GP	G	A	TP	PIM
1978-79	Peterborough	OHA	66	6	21	27	82	19	1	9	10	42
1979-80a	Peterborough	OHA	68	21	68	89	88	14	4	13	17	20
1980-81	Los Angeles	NHL	80	16	60	76	79	4	3	0	3	2
1981-82	Los Angeles	NHL	79	22	44	66	95	10	2	8	10	12
1982-83	Los Angeles	NHL	77	14	48	62	81	....	....	....	....	....
1983-84	Los Angeles	NHL	6	0	3	3	0	....	....	....	....	....
	Washington	NHL	72	13	33	46	50	8	0	3	3	6
1984-85	Washington	NHL	79	13	42	55	51	5	2	3	5	0
1985-86	Washington	NHL	78	21	44	65	50	9	1	5	6	6
1986-87b	Washington	NHL	80	23	58	81	39	7	2	2	4	6
1987-88	Washington	NHL	79	8	53	61	72	13	4	4	8	33
1988-89	Washington	NHL	65	7	29	36	70	....	....	....	....	....
	Minnesota	NHL	13	4	6	10	12	5	0	2	2	8
1989-90	Minnesota	NHL	77	10	58	68	44	7	1	2	3	31
1990-91	Minnesota	NHL	31	4	11	15	38	....	....	....	....	....
	Pittsburgh	NHL	44	5	23	28	30	23	5	18	23	44 ♦
1991-92	Pittsburgh	NHL	77	21	56	77	48	21	6	10	16	19 ♦
1992-93b	Pittsburgh	NHL	83	22	63	85	73	12	2	11	13	10
1993-94	Pittsburgh	NHL	84	17	56	73	44	6	0	5	5	0
1994-95b	Pittsburgh	NHL	48	13	25	38	18	12	2	13	15	0
1995-96	Toronto	NHL	82	12	49	61	34	6	0	2	2	4
	NHL Totals		1234	245	761	1006	928	148	30	88	118	181

a OHA First All-Star Team (1980)
b NHL Second All-Star Team (1987, 1993, 1995)

Played in NHL All-Star Game (1994, 1996)

Traded to **Washington** by **Los Angeles** for Ken Houston and Brian Engblom, October 18, 1983. Traded to **Minnesota** by **Washington** with Mike Gartner for Dino Ciccarelli and Bob Rouse, March 7, 1989. Traded to **Pittsburgh** by **Minnesota** with Peter Taglianetti for Chris Dahlquist and Jim Johnson, December 11, 1990. Traded to **Toronto** by **Pittsburgh** for Dmitri Mironov and Toronto's second round choice (later traded to New Jersey — New Jersey selected Joshua Dewolf) in 1996 Entry Draft, July 8, 1995.

MURPHY, MARK TOR.

Left wing. Shoots left. 5'11", 200 lbs. Born, Stoughton, MA, August 6, 1976.
(Toronto's 6th choice, 197th overall, in 1995 Entry Draft).

			Regular Season					Playoffs				
Season	Club	Lea	GP	G	A	TP	PIM	GP	G	A	TP	PIM
1994-95	Stratford	Jr. B	47	52	56	108	64	....	....	....	....	....
1995-96	Stratford	Jr. B	1	0	0	0	0	....	....	....	....	....

MURRAY, CHRIS MTL.

Right wing. Shoots right. 6'2", 209 lbs. Born, Port Hardy, B.C., October 25, 1974.
(Montreal's 3rd choice, 54th overall, in 1994 Entry Draft).

			Regular Season					Playoffs				
Season	Club	Lea	GP	G	A	TP	PIM	GP	G	A	TP	PIM
1991-92	Kamloops	WHL	33	1	1	2	218	5	0	0	0	10
1992-93	Kamloops	WHL	62	6	10	16	217	13	0	4	4	34
1993-94	Kamloops	WHL	59	14	16	30	260	15	4	2	6	*107
1994-95	Fredericton	AHL	55	6	12	18	234	12	1	1	2	50
	Montreal	NHL	3	0	0	0	4	....	....	....	....	....
1995-96	Montreal	NHL	48	3	4	7	163	4	0	0	0	4
	Fredericton	AHL	30	13	13	26	217	....	....	....	....	....
	NHL Totals		51	3	4	7	167	4	0	0	0	4

MURRAY, GLEN PIT.

Right wing. Shoots right. 6'2", 220 lbs. Born, Halifax, N.S., November 1, 1972.
(Boston's 1st choice, 18th overall, in 1991 Entry Draft).

			Regular Season					Playoffs				
Season	Club	Lea	GP	G	A	TP	PIM	GP	G	A	TP	PIM
1989-90	Sudbury	OHL	62	8	28	36	17	7	0	0	0	4
1990-91	Sudbury	OHL	66	27	38	65	82	5	8	4	12	10
1991-92	Boston	NHL	5	3	1	4	0	15	4	2	6	10
	Sudbury	OHL	54	37	47	84	93	11	7	4	11	18
1992-93	Boston	NHL	27	3	4	7	8	....	....	....	....	....
	Providence	AHL	48	30	26	56	42	6	1	4	5	4
1993-94	Boston	NHL	81	18	13	31	48	13	4	5	9	14
1994-95	Boston	NHL	35	5	2	7	46	2	0	0	0	2
1995-96	Pittsburgh	NHL	69	14	15	29	57	18	2	6	8	10
	NHL Totals		217	43	35	78	159	48	10	13	23	36

Traded to **Pittsburgh** by **Boston** with Bryan Smolinski and Boston's third round choice (Boyd Kane) in 1996 Entry Draft for Kevin Stevens and Shawn McEachern, August 2, 1995.

MURRAY, MARTY — CGY.

Center. Shoots left. 5'9", 175 lbs. Born, Deloraine, Man., February 16, 1975.
(Calgary's 5th choice, 96th overall, in 1993 Entry Draft).

			Regular Season					Playoffs				
Season	Club	Lea	GP	G	A	TP	PIM	GP	G	A	TP	PIM
1991-92	Brandon	WHL	68	20	36	56	22	....	....	....	....	....
1992-93	Brandon	WHL	67	29	65	94	50	4	1	3	4	0
1993-94ab	Brandon	WHL	64	43	71	114	33	14	6	14	20	14
1994-95a	Brandon	WHL	65	40	*88	128	53	18	9	*20	29	16
1995-96	**Calgary**	**NHL**	**15**	**3**	**3**	**6**	**0**	....	....	....	....	....
	Saint John	AHL	58	25	31	56	20	14	2	4	6	4
	NHL Totals		**15**	**3**	**3**	**6**	**0**	....	....	....	....	....

a WHL East First All-Star Team (1994, 1995)
b Canadian Major Junior Second All-Star Team (1994)

MURRAY, MIKE — CGY.

Right wing. Shoots right. 6'1", 200 lbs. Born, Cumberland, RI, April 18, 1971.
(Calgary's 10th choice, 188th overall, in 1990 Entry Draft).

			Regular Season					Playoffs				
Season	Club	Lea	GP	G	A	TP	PIM	GP	G	A	TP	PIM
1990-91	Lowell	H.E.	30	5	8	13	18	....	....	....	....	....
1991-92	Lowell	H.E.	31	22	15	37	40	....	....	....	....	....
1992-93a	Lowell	H.E.	39	23	33	56	78	....	....	....	....	....
1993-94	Lowell	H.E.	35	17	11	28	92	....	....	....	....	....
1994-95	Saint John	AHL	65	8	27	35	53	4	0	0	0	6
1995-96	Dayton	ECHL	21	17	10	27	28	....	....	....	....	....
	Saint John	AHL	32	7	11	18	77	....	....	....	....	....

a Hockey East Second All-Star Team (1993)

MURRAY, REM — EDM.

Left wing. Shoots left. 6'1", 183 lbs. Born, Stratford, Ont., October 9, 1972.
(Los Angeles' 5th choice, 135th overall, in 1992 Entry Draft).

			Regular Season					Playoffs				
Season	Club	Lea	GP	G	A	TP	PIM	GP	G	A	TP	PIM
1991-92	Michigan State	CCHA	41	12	36	48	16	....	....	....	....	....
1992-93	Michigan State	CCHA	40	22	35	57	24	....	....	....	....	....
1993-94	Michigan State	CCHA	41	16	38	54	18	....	....	....	....	....
1994-95a	Michigan State	CCHA	40	20	36	56	21	....	....	....	....	....
1995-96	Cape Breton	AHL	79	31	59	90	40	....	....	....	....	....

a CCHA Second All-Star Team (1995)

Signed as a free agent by **Edmonton**, September 19, 1995.

MURRAY, ROB — PHO.

Center. Shoots right. 6'1", 180 lbs. Born, Toronto, Ont., April 4, 1967.
(Washington's 3rd choice, 61st overall, in 1985 Entry Draft).

			Regular Season					Playoffs				
Season	Club	Lea	GP	G	A	TP	PIM	GP	G	A	TP	PIM
1984-85	Peterborough	OHL	63	12	9	21	155	17	2	7	9	45
1985-86	Peterborough	OHL	52	14	18	32	125	16	1	2	3	50
1986-87	Peterborough	OHL	62	17	37	54	204	3	1	4	5	8
1987-88	Fort Wayne	IHL	80	12	21	33	139	6	0	2	2	16
1988-89	Baltimore	AHL	80	11	23	34	235	....	....	....	....	....
1989-90	**Washington**	**NHL**	**41**	**2**	**7**	**9**	**58**	**9**	**0**	**0**	**0**	**18**
	Baltimore	AHL	23	5	4	9	63	....	....	....	....	....
1990-91	**Washington**	**NHL**	**17**	**0**	**3**	**3**	**19**	....	....	....	....	....
	Baltimore	AHL	48	6	20	26	177	4	0	0	0	12
1991-92	**Winnipeg**	**NHL**	**9**	**0**	**1**	**1**	**18**	....	....	....	....	....
	Moncton	AHL	60	16	15	31	247	8	0	1	1	56
1992-93	**Winnipeg**	**NHL**	**10**	**1**	**0**	**1**	**6**	....	....	....	....	....
	Moncton	AHL	56	16	21	37	147	3	0	0	0	6
1993-94	**Winnipeg**	**NHL**	**6**	**0**	**0**	**0**	**2**	....	....	....	....	....
	Moncton	AHL	69	25	32	57	280	21	2	3	5	60
1994-95	Springfield	AHL	78	16	38	54	373	....	....	....	....	....
	Winnipeg	**NHL**	**10**	**0**	**2**	**2**	**2**	....	....	....	....	....
1995-96	**Winnipeg**	**NHL**	**1**	**0**	**0**	**0**	**2**	....	....	....	....	....
	Springfield	AHL	74	10	28	38	263	10	1	6	7	32
	NHL Totals		**94**	**3**	**13**	**16**	**107**	**9**	**0**	**0**	**0**	**18**

Claimed by **Minnesota** from **Washington** in Expansion Draft, May 30, 1991. Traded to **Winnipeg** by **Minnesota** with future considerations for Winnipeg's seventh round choice (Geoff Finch) in 1991 Entry Draft and future considerations, May 31, 1991.

MURRAY, TROY

Center. Shoots right. 6'1", 195 lbs. Born, Calgary, Alta., July 31, 1962.
(Chicago's 6th choice, 57th overall, in 1980 Entry Draft).

			Regular Season					Playoffs				
Season	Club	Lea	GP	G	A	TP	PIM	GP	G	A	TP	PIM
1980-81a	North Dakota	WCHA	38	33	45	78	28	....	....	....	....	....
1981-82a	North Dakota	WCHA	26	13	17	30	62	....	....	....	....	....
	Chicago	**NHL**	**1**	**0**	**0**	**0**	**0**	**7**	**1**	**0**	**1**	**5**
1982-83	**Chicago**	**NHL**	**54**	**8**	**8**	**16**	**27**	**2**	**0**	**0**	**0**	**0**
1983-84	**Chicago**	**NHL**	**61**	**15**	**15**	**30**	**45**	**5**	**1**	**0**	**1**	**7**
1984-85	**Chicago**	**NHL**	**80**	**26**	**40**	**66**	**82**	**15**	**5**	**14**	**19**	**24**
1985-86b	**Chicago**	**NHL**	**80**	**45**	**54**	**99**	**94**	**2**	**0**	**0**	**0**	**2**
1986-87	**Chicago**	**NHL**	**77**	**28**	**43**	**71**	**59**	**4**	**0**	**0**	**0**	**5**
1987-88	**Chicago**	**NHL**	**79**	**22**	**36**	**58**	**96**	**5**	**1**	**0**	**1**	**8**
1988-89	**Chicago**	**NHL**	**79**	**21**	**30**	**51**	**113**	**16**	**3**	**6**	**9**	**25**
1989-90	**Chicago**	**NHL**	**68**	**17**	**38**	**55**	**86**	**20**	**4**	**4**	**8**	**22**
1990-91	**Chicago**	**NHL**	**75**	**14**	**23**	**37**	**74**	**6**	**0**	**1**	**1**	**12**
1991-92	**Winnipeg**	**NHL**	**74**	**17**	**30**	**47**	**69**	**7**	**0**	**0**	**0**	**2**
1992-93	**Winnipeg**	**NHL**	**29**	**3**	**4**	**7**	**34**	....	....	....	....	....
	Chicago	**NHL**	**22**	**1**	**3**	**4**	**25**	**4**	**0**	**0**	**0**	**2**
1993-94	**Chicago**	**NHL**	**12**	**0**	**1**	**1**	**6**	....	....	....	....	....
	Indianapolis	IHL	8	3	3	6	12	....	....	....	....	....
	Ottawa	**NHL**	**15**	**2**	**3**	**5**	**4**	....	....	....	....	....
1994-95	**Ottawa**	**NHL**	**33**	**4**	**10**	**14**	**16**	....	....	....	....	....
	Pittsburgh	**NHL**	**13**	**0**	**2**	**2**	**23**	**12**	**2**	**1**	**3**	**12**
1995-96	**Colorado**	**NHL**	**63**	**7**	**14**	**21**	**22**	**8**	**0**	**0**	**0**	**19 ♦**
	NHL Totals		**915**	**230**	**354**	**584**	**875**	**113**	**17**	**26**	**43**	**145**

a WCHA Second All-Star Team (1981, 1982)
b Won Frank J. Selke Memorial Trophy (1986)

Traded to **Winnipeg** by **Chicago** with Warren Rychel for Bryan Marchment and Chris Norton, July 22, 1991. Traded to **Chicago** by **Winnipeg** for Steve Bancroft and future considerations, February 21, 1993. Traded to **Ottawa** by **Chicago** with Chicago's eleventh round choice (Antti Tormanen) in 1994 Entry Draft for Ottawa's eleventh round choice (Rob Mara) in 1994 Entry Draft, March 11, 1994. Traded to **Pittsburgh** by **Ottawa** with Norm Maciver for Martin Straka, April 7, 1995. Signed as a free agent by **Colorado**, August 7, 1995.

MURZYN, DANA (MUHR-zihn) — VAN.

Defense. Shoots left. 6'2", 200 lbs. Born, Calgary, Alta., December 9, 1966.
(Hartford's 1st choice, 5th overall, in 1985 Entry Draft).

			Regular Season					Playoffs				
Season	Club	Lea	GP	G	A	TP	PIM	GP	G	A	TP	PIM
1983-84	Calgary	WHL	65	11	20	31	135	2	0	0	0	10
1984-85a	Calgary	WHL	72	32	60	92	233	8	1	11	12	16
1985-86b	**Hartford**	**NHL**	**78**	**3**	**23**	**26**	**125**	**4**	**0**	**0**	**0**	**10**
1986-87	**Hartford**	**NHL**	**74**	**9**	**19**	**28**	**95**	**6**	**2**	**1**	**3**	**29**
1987-88	**Hartford**	**NHL**	**33**	**1**	**6**	**7**	**45**	....	....	....	....	....
	Calgary	**NHL**	**41**	**6**	**5**	**11**	**94**	**5**	**2**	**0**	**2**	**13**
1988-89	**Calgary**	**NHL**	**63**	**3**	**19**	**22**	**142**	**21**	**0**	**3**	**3**	**20 ♦**
1989-90	**Calgary**	**NHL**	**78**	**7**	**13**	**20**	**140**	**6**	**2**	**2**	**4**	**2**
1990-91	**Calgary**	**NHL**	**19**	**0**	**2**	**2**	**30**	....	....	....	....	....
	Vancouver	**NHL**	**10**	**1**	**0**	**1**	**8**	**6**	**0**	**1**	**1**	**8**
1991-92	**Vancouver**	**NHL**	**70**	**3**	**11**	**14**	**147**	**1**	**0**	**0**	**0**	**15**
1992-93	**Vancouver**	**NHL**	**79**	**5**	**11**	**16**	**196**	**12**	**3**	**2**	**5**	**18**
1993-94	**Vancouver**	**NHL**	**80**	**6**	**14**	**20**	**109**	**7**	**0**	**0**	**0**	**4**
1994-95	**Vancouver**	**NHL**	**40**	**0**	**8**	**8**	**129**	**8**	**0**	**1**	**1**	**22**
1995-96	**Vancouver**	**NHL**	**69**	**2**	**10**	**12**	**130**	**6**	**0**	**0**	**0**	**25**
	NHL Totals		**734**	**46**	**141**	**187**	**1390**	**82**	**9**	**10**	**19**	**166**

a WHL East First All-Star Team, (1985)
b NHL All-Rookie Team (1986)

Traded to **Calgary** by **Hartford** with Shane Churla for Neil Sheehy, Carey Wilson and the rights to Lane MacDonald, January 3, 1988. Traded to **Vancouver** by **Calgary** for Ron Stern, Kevan Guy and future considerations, March 5, 1991.

MUSIL, FRANK (moo-SIHL) — OTT.

Defense. Shoots left. 6'3", 215 lbs. Born, Pardubice, Czech., December 17, 1964.
(Minnesota's 3rd choice, 38th overall, in 1983 Entry Draft).

			Regular Season					Playoffs				
Season	Club	Lea	GP	G	A	TP	PIM	GP	G	A	TP	PIM
1980-81	Pardubice	Czech.	2	0	0	0	0	....	....	....	....	....
1981-82	Pardubice	Czech.	35	1	3	4	34	....	....	....	....	....
1982-83	Pardubice	Czech.	33	1	2	3	44	....	....	....	....	....
1983-84	Pardubice	Czech.	37	4	8	12	72	....	....	....	....	....
1984-85	Dukla Jihlava	Czech.	44	4	6	10	76	....	....	....	....	....
1985-86	Dukla Jihlava	Czech.	34	4	7	11	42	....	....	....	....	....
1986-87	**Minnesota**	**NHL**	**72**	**2**	**9**	**11**	**148**	....	....	....	....	....
1987-88	**Minnesota**	**NHL**	**80**	**9**	**8**	**17**	**213**	....	....	....	....	....
1988-89	**Minnesota**	**NHL**	**55**	**1**	**19**	**20**	**54**	**5**	**1**	**1**	**2**	**4**
1989-90	**Minnesota**	**NHL**	**56**	**2**	**8**	**10**	**109**	**4**	**0**	**0**	**0**	**14**
1990-91	**Minnesota**	**NHL**	**8**	**0**	**2**	**2**	**23**	....	....	....	....	....
	Calgary	**NHL**	**67**	**7**	**14**	**21**	**160**	**7**	**0**	**0**	**0**	**10**
1991-92	**Calgary**	**NHL**	**78**	**4**	**8**	**12**	**103**	....	....	....	....	....
1992-93	**Calgary**	**NHL**	**80**	**6**	**10**	**16**	**131**	**6**	**1**	**1**	**2**	**7**
1993-94	**Calgary**	**NHL**	**75**	**1**	**8**	**9**	**50**	**7**	**0**	**1**	**1**	**4**
1994-95	Sparta Praha	Czech.	19	1	4	5	50	....	....	....	....	....
	Saxonia	Ger.	1	0	0	0	2	....	....	....	....	....
	Calgary	**NHL**	**35**	**0**	**5**	**5**	**61**	**5**	**0**	**1**	**1**	**0**
1995-96	Karlovy Vary	Czech. 2	16	7	4	11	16	....	....	....	....	....
	Ottawa	**NHL**	**65**	**1**	**3**	**4**	**85**	....	....	....	....	....
	NHL Totals		**671**	**33**	**94**	**127**	**1137**	**34**	**2**	**4**	**6**	**39**

Traded to **Calgary** by **Minnesota** for Brian Glynn, October 26, 1990. Traded to **Ottawa** by **Calgary** for Ottawa's fourth round choice in 1997 Entry Draft, October 7, 1995.

MYHRES, BRANTT (MIGH-uhrs) — T.B.

Left wing. Shoots right. 6'3", 220 lbs. Born, Edmonton, Alta., March 18, 1974.
(Tampa Bay's 6th choice, 97th overall, in 1992 Entry Draft).

			Regular Season					Playoffs				
Season	Club	Lea	GP	G	A	TP	PIM	GP	G	A	TP	PIM
1990-91	Portland	WHL	59	2	7	9	125	....	....	....	....	....
1991-92	Portland	WHL	4	0	2	2	22	....	....	....	....	....
	Lethbridge	WHL	53	4	11	15	359	5	0	0	0	36
1992-93	Lethbridge	WHL	64	13	35	48	277	3	0	0	0	11
1993-94	Lethbridge	WHL	34	10	21	31	103	....	....	....	....	....
	Spokane	WHL	27	10	22	32	139	3	1	4	5	7
	Atlanta	IHL	2	0	0	0	17	....	....	....	....	....
1994-95	Atlanta	IHL	40	5	5	10	213	....	....	....	....	....
	Tampa Bay	**NHL**	**15**	**2**	**0**	**2**	**81**	....	....	....	....	....
1995-96	Atlanta	IHL	12	0	2	2	58	....	....	....	....	....
	NHL Totals		**15**	**2**	**0**	**2**	**81**	....	....	....	....	....

MYRVOLD, ANDERS — COL.

Defense. Shoots left. 6'1", 178 lbs. Born, Lorenskog, Norway, August 12, 1975.
(Quebec's 6th choice, 127th overall, in 1993 Entry Draft).

			Regular Season					Playoffs				
Season	Club	Lea	GP	G	A	TP	PIM	GP	G	A	TP	PIM
1992-93	Farjestad	Swe.	2	0	0	0	0	....	....	....	....	....
1993-94	Grum	Swe. 2	24	1	0	1	59	....	....	....	....	....
1994-95	Laval	QMJHL	64	14	50	64	173	20	4	10	14	68
	Cornwall	AHL	....	....	....	....	....	3	0	1	1	2
1995-96	**Colorado**	**NHL**	**4**	**0**	**1**	**1**	**6**	....	....	....	....	....
	Cornwall	AHL	70	5	24	29	125	5	1	0	1	19
	NHL Totals		**4**	**0**	**1**	**1**	**6**	....	....	....	....	....

NABOKOV, DMITRI (nuh-BAW-kahv) — CHI.

Center. Shoots right. 6'2", 209 lbs. Born, Novosibirsk, USSR, January 4, 1977.
(Chicago's 1st choice, 19th overall, in 1995 Entry Draft).

			Regular Season					Playoffs				
Season	Club	Lea	GP	G	A	TP	PIM	GP	G	A	TP	PIM
1993-94	Soviet Wings	CIS	17	0	2	2	6	3	0	0	0	0
1994-95	Soviet Wings	CIS	49	15	12	27	32	4	5	0	5	6
1995-96	Soviet Wings	CIS	50	12	14	26	51	....	....	....	....	....

NAMESTNIKOV, YEVGENY (nah-MEST-nih-kov, yev-GAIN-ee) VAN.

Defense. Shoots right. 5'11", 190 lbs. Born, Arzamis-Ig, USSR, October 9, 1971.
(Vancouver's 6th choice, 117th overall, in 1991 Entry Draft).

			Regular Season					Playoffs				
Season	Club	Lea	GP	G	A	TP	PIM	GP	G	A	TP	PIM
1988-89	Torpedo Gorky	USSR	2	0	0	0	2	....	....	....	....	....
1989-90	Torpedo Gorky	USSR	23	0	0	0	25	....	....	....	....	....
1990-91	Torpedo Niz.	USSR	42	1	2	3	49	....	....	....	....	....
1991-92	CSKA	CIS	42	1	1	2	47	....	....	....	....	....
1992-93	CSKA	CIS	42	5	5	10	68	....	....	....	....	....
1993-94	**Vancouver**	**NHL**	**17**	**0**	**5**	**5**	**10**	....	....	....	....	....
	Hamilton	AHL	59	7	27	34	97	4	0	2	2	19
1994-95	Syracuse	AHL	59	11	22	33	59	....	....	....	....	....
	Vancouver	**NHL**	**16**	**0**	**3**	**3**	**4**	**1**	**0**	**0**	**0**	**2**
1995-96	Syracuse	AHL	59	13	34	47	85	15	1	8	9	16
	Vancouver	**NHL**	....	....	....	....	....	**1**	**0**	**0**	**0**	**0**
	NHL Totals		**33**	**0**	**8**	**8**	**14**	**2**	**0**	**0**	**0**	**2**

NASH, TYSON VAN.

Left wing. Shoots left. 6', 180 lbs. Born, Edmonton, Alta., March 11, 1975.
(Vancouver's 10th choice, 247th overall, in 1994 Entry Draft).

			Regular Season					Playoffs				
Season	Club	Lea	GP	G	A	TP	PIM	GP	G	A	TP	PIM
1991-92	Kamloops	WHL	33	1	6	7	62	4	0	0	0	0
1992-93	Kamloops	WHL	61	10	16	26	78	13	3	2	5	32
1993-94	Kamloops	WHL	65	20	36	56	135	16	3	4	7	12
1994-95	Kamloops	WHL	63	34	41	75	70	21	10	7	17	30
1995-96	Syracuse	AHL	50	4	7	11	58	4	0	0	0	11
	Raleigh	ECHL	6	1	1	2	8	....	....	....	....	....

NASLUND, MARKUS (NAZ-luhnd) VAN.

Right wing. Shoots left. 6', 186 lbs. Born, Ornskoldsvik, Sweden, July 30, 1973.
(Pittsburgh's 1st choice, 16th overall, in 1991 Entry Draft).

			Regular Season					Playoffs				
Season	Club	Lea	GP	G	A	TP	PIM	GP	G	A	TP	PIM
1990-91	MoDo	Swe.	32	10	9	19	14	....	....	....	....	....
1991-92	MoDo	Swe.	39	22	18	40	54	....	....	....	....	....
1992-93	MoDo	Swe.	39	22	17	39	67	3	3	2	5	0
1993-94	**Pittsburgh**	**NHL**	**71**	**4**	**7**	**11**	**27**	....	....	....	....	....
	Cleveland	IHL	5	1	6	7	4	....	....	....	....	....
1994-95	**Pittsburgh**	**NHL**	**14**	**2**	**2**	**4**	**2**	....	....	....	....	....
	Cleveland	IHL	7	3	4	7	6	4	1	3	4	8
1995-96	**Pittsburgh**	**NHL**	**66**	**19**	**33**	**52**	**36**	....	....	....	....	....
	Vancouver	**NHL**	**10**	**3**	**0**	**3**	**6**	**6**	**1**	**2**	**3**	**8**
	NHL Totals		**161**	**28**	**42**	**70**	**71**	**6**	**1**	**2**	**3**	**8**

Traded to **Vancouver** by **Pittsburgh** for Alek Stojanov, March 20, 1996.

NASREDDINE, ALAIN (NAS-ruh-deen, AL-ay) FLA.

Defense. Shoots left. 6'1", 201 lbs. Born, Montreal, Que., July 10, 1975.
(Florida's 8th choice, 135th overall, in 1993 Entry Draft).

			Regular Season					Playoffs				
Season	Club	Lea	GP	G	A	TP	PIM	GP	G	A	TP	PIM
1991-92	Drummondville	QMJHL	61	1	9	10	78	4	0	0	0	17
1992-93	Drummondville	QMJHL	64	0	14	14	137	10	0	1	1	36
1993-94	Chicoutimi	QMJHL	60	3	24	27	218	26	2	10	12	118
1994-95a	Chicoutimi	QMJHL	67	8	31	39	342	13	3	5	8	40
1995-96	Carolina	AHL	63	0	5	5	245	....	....	....	....	....

a QMJHL Second All-Star Team (1995)

NAUD, ERIC (NOH) BOS.

Left wing. Shoots left. 6'1", 187 lbs. Born, Lasarre, Que., October 2, 1977.
(Boston's 3rd choice, 53rd overall, in 1996 Entry Draft).

			Regular Season					Playoffs				
Season	Club	Lea	GP	G	A	TP	PIM	GP	G	A	TP	PIM
1995-96	Laval	QMJHL	9	4	3	7	37	....	....	....	....	....
	St-Hyacinthe	QMJHL	54	7	18	25	193	12	1	2	3	19

NAUMENKO, NICK ST.L.

Defense. Shoots right. 5'11", 180 lbs. Born, Chicago, IL, July 7, 1974.
(St. Louis' 9th choice, 182nd overall, in 1992 Entry Draft).

			Regular Season					Playoffs				
Season	Club	Lea	GP	G	A	TP	PIM	GP	G	A	TP	PIM
1992-93	North Dakota	WCHA	38	10	24	34	26	....	....	....	....	....
1993-94	North Dakota	WCHA	32	4	22	26	22	....	....	....	....	....
1994-95a	North Dakota	WCHA	39	13	26	39	78	....	....	....	....	....
1995-96a	North Dakota	WCHA	37	11	30	41	32	....	....	....	....	....

a WCHA First All-Star Team (1995, 1996)

NAZAROV, ANDREI (nah-ZAH-rohv) S.J.

Left wing. Shoots right. 6'5", 230 lbs. Born, Chelyabinsk, USSR, May 22, 1974.
(San Jose's 2nd choice, 10th overall, in 1992 Entry Draft).

			Regular Season					Playoffs				
Season	Club	Lea	GP	G	A	TP	PIM	GP	G	A	TP	PIM
1991-92	Moscow D'amo	CIS	2	1	0	1	2	....	....	....	....	....
1992-93	Moscow D'amo	CIS	42	8	2	10	79	10	1	1	2	8
1993-94	Moscow D'amo	CIS	6	2	2	4	0	....	....	....	....	....
	San Jose	**NHL**	**1**	**0**	**0**	**0**	**0**	....	....	....	....	....
	Kansas City	IHL	71	15	18	33	64	....	....	....	....	....
1994-95	Kansas City	IHL	43	15	10	25	55	....	....	....	....	....
	San Jose	**NHL**	**26**	**3**	**5**	**8**	**94**	**6**	**0**	**0**	**0**	**9**
1995-96	**San Jose**	**NHL**	**42**	**7**	**7**	**14**	**62**	....	....	....	....	....
	Kansas City	IHL	27	4	6	10	118	2	0	0	0	2
	NHL Totals		**69**	**10**	**12**	**22**	**156**	**6**	**0**	**0**	**0**	**9**

NDUR, RUMUN (nih-DOOR, ROO-muhn) BUF.

Defense. Shoots left. 6'2", 200 lbs. Born, Zaria, Nigeria, July 7, 1975.
(Buffalo's 3rd choice, 69th overall, in 1994 Entry Draft).

			Regular Season					Playoffs				
Season	Club	Lea	GP	G	A	TP	PIM	GP	G	A	TP	PIM
1992-93	Guelph	OHL	22	1	3	4	30	4	0	1	1	4
1993-94	Guelph	OHL	61	6	33	39	176	9	4	1	5	24
1994-95	Guelph	OHL	63	10	21	31	187	14	0	4	4	28
1995-96	Rochester	AHL	73	2	12	14	306	17	1	2	3	33

NECKAR, STANISLAV (NEHTS-kahrzh) OTT.

Defense. Shoots left. 6'1", 196 lbs. Born, Ceske Budejovice, Czech., December 22, 1975.
(Ottawa's 2nd choice, 29th overall, in 1994 Entry Draft).

			Regular Season					Playoffs				
Season	Club	Lea	GP	G	A	TP	PIM	GP	G	A	TP	PIM
1992-93	Budejovice	Czech.	42	2	9	11	12	....	....	....	....	....
1993-94	Budejovice	Czech.	12	3	2	5	2	3	0	0	0	....
1994-95	Detroit	IHL	15	2	2	4	15	....	....	....	....	....
	Ottawa	**NHL**	**48**	**1**	**3**	**4**	**37**	....	....	....	....	....
1995-96	**Ottawa**	**NHL**	**82**	**3**	**9**	**12**	**54**	....	....	....	....	....
	NHL Totals		**130**	**4**	**12**	**16**	**91**	....	....	....	....	....

NEDVED, PETR (NEHD-VEHD) PIT.

Center. Shoots left. 6'3", 195 lbs. Born, Liberec, Czech., December 9, 1971.
(Vancouver's 1st choice, 2nd overall, in 1990 Entry Draft).

			Regular Season					Playoffs				
Season	Club	Lea	GP	G	A	TP	PIM	GP	G	A	TP	PIM
1989-90a	Seattle	WHL	71	65	80	145	80	11	4	9	13	2
1990-91	**Vancouver**	**NHL**	**61**	**10**	**6**	**16**	**20**	**6**	**0**	**1**	**1**	**0**
1991-92	**Vancouver**	**NHL**	**77**	**15**	**22**	**37**	**36**	**10**	**1**	**4**	**5**	**16**
1992-93	**Vancouver**	**NHL**	**84**	**38**	**33**	**71**	**96**	**12**	**2**	**3**	**5**	**2**
1993-94	Cdn. National	....	17	19	12	31	16	....	....	....	....	....
	Cdn. Olympic	....	8	5	1	6	6	....	....	....	....	....
	St. Louis	**NHL**	**19**	**6**	**14**	**20**	**8**	**4**	**0**	**1**	**1**	**4**
1994-95	**NY Rangers**	**NHL**	**46**	**11**	**12**	**23**	**26**	**10**	**3**	**2**	**5**	**6**
1995-96	**Pittsburgh**	**NHL**	**80**	**45**	**54**	**99**	**68**	**18**	**10**	**10**	**20**	**16**
	NHL Totals		**367**	**125**	**141**	**266**	**254**	**60**	**16**	**21**	**37**	**44**

a Canadian Major Junior Rookie of the Year (1990)

Signed as a free agent by **St. Louis**, March 5, 1994. Traded to **NY Rangers** by **St. Louis** for Esa Tikkanen and Doug Lidster, July 24, 1994. Traded to **Pittsburgh** by **NY Rangers** with Sergei Zubov for Luc Robitaille and Ulf Samuelsson, August 31, 1995.

NEDVED, ZDENEK (NEHD-VEHD) TOR.

Right wing. Shoots left. 6', 180 lbs. Born, Lany, Czech., March 3, 1975.
(Toronto's 3rd choice, 123rd overall, in 1993 Entry Draft).

			Regular Season					Playoffs				
Season	Club	Lea	GP	G	A	TP	PIM	GP	G	A	TP	PIM
1991-92	Kladno	Czech.	19	15	12	27	22	....	....	....	....	....
1992-93	Sudbury	OHL	18	3	9	12	6	....	....	....	....	....
1993-94	Sudbury	OHL	60	50	50	100	42	10	7	8	15	10
1994-95	Sudbury	OHL	59	47	51	98	36	18	12	16	28	16
	Toronto	**NHL**	**1**	**0**	**0**	**0**	**2**	....	....	....	....	....
1995-96	**Toronto**	**NHL**	**7**	**1**	**1**	**2**	**6**	....	....	....	....	....
	St. John's	AHL	41	13	14	27	22	4	2	0	2	0
	NHL Totals		**8**	**1**	**1**	**2**	**8**	....	....	....	....	....

NEEDHAM, MIKE

Right wing. Shoots right. 5'10", 185 lbs. Born, Calgary, Alta., April 4, 1970.
(Pittsburgh's 7th choice, 126th overall, in 1989 Entry Draft).

			Regular Season					Playoffs				
Season	Club	Lea	GP	G	A	TP	PIM	GP	G	A	TP	PIM
1986-87	Kamloops	WHL	3	1	2	3	0	11	2	1	3	5
1987-88	Kamloops	WHL	64	31	33	64	93	5	0	1	1	5
1988-89	Kamloops	WHL	49	24	27	51	55	16	2	9	11	13
1989-90a	Kamloops	WHL	60	59	66	125	75	17	11	13	24	10
1990-91	Muskegon	IHL	65	14	31	45	17	5	2	2	4	5
1991-92	Muskegon	IHL	80	41	37	78	83	8	4	4	8	6
	Pittsburgh	**NHL**	....	....	....	....	....	**5**	**1**	**0**	**1**	**2** ♦
1992-93	**Pittsburgh**	**NHL**	**56**	**8**	**5**	**13**	**14**	**9**	**1**	**0**	**1**	**2**
	Cleveland	IHL	1	2	0	2	0	....	....	....	....	....
1993-94	**Pittsburgh**	**NHL**	**25**	**1**	**0**	**1**	**2**	....	....	....	....	....
	Cleveland	IHL	6	4	3	7	7	....	....	....	....	....
	Dallas	**NHL**	**5**	**0**	**0**	**0**	**0**	....	....	....	....	....
1994-95	Kalamazoo	IHL	37	9	9	18	31	14	5	5	10	11
1995-96	Adirondack	AHL	16	5	10	15	12	....	....	....	....	....
	NHL Totals		**86**	**9**	**5**	**14**	**16**	**14**	**2**	**0**	**2**	**4**

a WHL West First All-Star Team (1990)

Traded to **Dallas** by **Pittsburgh** for Jim McKenzie, March 21, 1994. Signed as a free agent by **Detroit**, September 20, 1995.

NEELY, CAM BOS.

Right wing. Shoots right. 6'1", 218 lbs. Born, Comox, B.C., June 6, 1965.
(Vancouver's 1st choice, 9th overall, in 1983 Entry Draft).

			Regular Season					Playoffs				
Season	Club	Lea	GP	G	A	TP	PIM	GP	G	A	TP	PIM
1982-83	Portland	WHL	72	56	64	120	130	14	9	11	20	17
1983-84	**Vancouver**	**NHL**	**56**	**16**	**15**	**31**	**57**	**4**	**2**	**0**	**2**	**2**
	Portland	WHL	19	8	18	26	29	....	....	....	....	....
1984-85	**Vancouver**	**NHL**	**72**	**21**	**18**	**39**	**137**	....	....	....	....	....
1985-86	**Vancouver**	**NHL**	**73**	**14**	**20**	**34**	**126**	**3**	**0**	**0**	**0**	**6**
1986-87	**Boston**	**NHL**	**75**	**36**	**36**	**72**	**143**	**4**	**5**	**1**	**6**	**8**
1987-88a	**Boston**	**NHL**	**69**	**42**	**27**	**69**	**175**	**23**	**9**	**8**	**17**	**51**
1988-89	**Boston**	**NHL**	**74**	**37**	**38**	**75**	**190**	**10**	**7**	**2**	**9**	**8**
1989-90a	**Boston**	**NHL**	**76**	**55**	**37**	**92**	**117**	**21**	**12**	**16**	**28**	**51**
1990-91a	**Boston**	**NHL**	**69**	**51**	**40**	**91**	**98**	**19**	**16**	**4**	**20**	**36**
1991-92	**Boston**	**NHL**	**9**	**9**	**3**	**12**	**16**	....	....	....	....	....
1992-93	**Boston**	**NHL**	**13**	**11**	**7**	**18**	**25**	**4**	**4**	**1**	**5**	**4**
1993-94ab	**Boston**	**NHL**	**49**	**50**	**24**	**74**	**54**	....	....	....	....	....
1994-95	**Boston**	**NHL**	**42**	**27**	**14**	**41**	**72**	**5**	**2**	**0**	**2**	**2**
1995-96	**Boston**	**NHL**	**49**	**26**	**20**	**46**	**31**	....	....	....	....	....
	NHL Totals		**726**	**395**	**299**	**694**	**1241**	**93**	**57**	**32**	**89**	**168**

a NHL Second All-Star Team (1988, 1990, 1991, 1994)
b Won Bill Masterton Memorial Trophy (1994)

Played in NHL All-Star Game (1988-91, 1996)

Traded to **Boston** by **Vancouver** with Vancouver's first round choice (Glen Wesley) in 1987 Entry Draft for Barry Pederson, June 6, 1986.

NELSON, JEFF — WSH.

Center. Shoots left. 6', 190 lbs. Born, Prince Albert, Sask., December 18, 1972.
(Washington's 4th choice, 36th overall, in 1991 Entry Draft).

			Regular Season					Playoffs				
Season	Club	Lea	GP	G	A	TP	PIM	GP	G	A	TP	PIM
1989-90	Prince Albert	WHL	72	28	69	97	79	14	2	11	13	10
1990-91a	Prince Albert	WHL	72	46	74	120	58	3	1	1	2	4
1991-92a	Prince Albert	WHL	64	48	65	113	84	9	7	14	21	18
1992-93	Baltimore	AHL	72	14	38	52	12	7	1	3	4	2
1993-94	Portland	AHL	80	34	73	107	92	17	10	5	15	20
1994-95	Portland	AHL	64	33	50	83	57	7	1	4	5	8
	Washington	**NHL**	**10**	**1**	**0**	**1**	**2**	....	....	....	....	....
1995-96	**Washington**	**NHL**	**33**	**0**	**7**	**7**	**16**	**3**	**0**	**0**	**0**	**4**
	Portland	AHL	39	15	32	47	62	....	....	....	....	....
	NHL Totals		**43**	**1**	**7**	**8**	**18**	**3**	**0**	**0**	**0**	**4**

a WHL East Second All-Star Team (1991, 1992)

NELSON, TODD

Defense. Shoots left. 6', 201 lbs. Born, Prince Albert, Sask., May 11, 1969.
(Pittsburgh's 4th choice, 79th overall, in 1989 Entry Draft).

			Regular Season					Playoffs				
Season	Club	Lea	GP	G	A	TP	PIM	GP	G	A	TP	PIM
1985-86	Prince Albert	WHL	4	0	0	0	0	....	....	....	....	....
1986-87	Prince Albert	WHL	35	1	6	7	10	4	0	0	0	0
1987-88	Prince Albert	WHL	72	3	21	24	59	10	3	2	5	4
1988-89a	Prince Albert	WHL	72	14	45	59	72	4	1	3	4	4
1989-90a	Prince Albert	WHL	69	13	42	55	88	14	3	12	15	12
1990-91	Muskegon	IHL	79	4	20	24	32	3	0	0	0	4
1991-92	**Pittsburgh**	**NHL**	**1**	**0**	**0**	**0**	**0**	....	....	....	....	....
	Muskegon	IHL	80	6	35	41	46	14	1	11	12	4
1992-93	Cleveland	IHL	76	7	35	42	115	4	0	2	2	4
1993-94	**Washington**	**NHL**	**2**	**1**	**0**	**1**	**2**	**4**	**0**	**0**	**0**	**0**
	Portland	AHL	80	11	34	45	69	11	0	6	6	6
1994-95	Portland	AHL	75	10	35	45	76	7	0	4	4	6
1995-96	Hershey	AHL	70	10	40	50	38	5	1	2	3	8
	NHL Totals		**3**	**1**	**0**	**1**	**2**	**4**	**0**	**0**	**0**	**0**

a WHL East Second All-Star Team (1989, 1990)

Signed as a free agent by **Washington**, August 15, 1993. Signed as a free agent by **Philadelphia**, August 1, 1995.

NEMCHINOV, SERGEI (nehm-CHEE-nahf, SAIR-gay) — NYR

Center. Shoots left. 6', 200 lbs. Born, Moscow, USSR, January 14, 1964.
(NY Rangers' 14th choice, 244th overall, in 1990 Entry Draft).

			Regular Season					Playoffs				
Season	Club	Lea	GP	G	A	TP	PIM	GP	G	A	TP	PIM
1981-82	Soviet Wings	USSR	15	1	0	1	0	....	....	....	....	....
1982-83	CSKA	USSR	11	0	0	0	2	....	....	....	....	....
1983-84	CSKA	USSR	20	6	5	11	4	....	....	....	....	....
1984-85	CSKA	USSR	31	2	4	6	4	....	....	....	....	....
1985-86	Soviet Wings	USSR	39	7	12	19	28	....	....	....	....	....
1986-87	Soviet Wings	USSR	40	13	9	22	24	....	....	....	....	....
1987-88	Soviet Wings	USSR	48	17	11	28	26	....	....	....	....	....
1988-89	Soviet Wings	USSR	43	15	14	29	28	....	....	....	....	....
1989-90	Soviet Wings	USSR	48	17	16	33	34	....	....	....	....	....
1990-91	Soviet Wings	USSR	46	21	24	45	30	....	....	....	....	....
1991-92	**NY Rangers**	**NHL**	**73**	**30**	**28**	**58**	**15**	**13**	**1**	**4**	**5**	**8**
1992-93	**NY Rangers**	**NHL**	**81**	**23**	**31**	**54**	**34**	....	....	....	....	....
1993-94	**NY Rangers**	**NHL**	**76**	**22**	**27**	**49**	**36**	**23**	**2**	**5**	**7**	**6** ♦
1994-95	**NY Rangers**	**NHL**	**47**	**7**	**6**	**13**	**16**	**10**	**4**	**5**	**9**	**2**
1995-96	**NY Rangers**	**NHL**	**78**	**17**	**15**	**32**	**38**	**6**	**0**	**1**	**1**	**2**
	NHL Totals		**355**	**99**	**107**	**206**	**139**	**52**	**7**	**15**	**22**	**18**

NEMECEK, JAN — L.A.

Defense. Shoots right. 6'1", 194 lbs. Born, Pisek, Czech., February 14, 1976.
(Los Angeles' 7th choice, 215th overall, in 1994 Entry Draft).

			Regular Season					Playoffs				
Season	Club	Lea	GP	G	A	TP	PIM	GP	G	A	TP	PIM
1992-93	Budejovice	Czech.	15	0	0	0	....	....	....	....	....	....
1993-94	Budejovice	Czech.	16	0	1	1	16	....	....	....	....	....
1994-95	Hull	QMJHL	49	10	16	26	48	21	5	9	14	10
1995-96a	Hull	QMJHL	57	17	49	66	58	17	2	13	15	10

a QMJHL Second All-Star Team (1996)

NEMIROVSKY, DAVID (nyeh-mih-ROHV-skee) — FLA.

Right wing. Shoots right. 6'1", 192 lbs. Born, Toronto, Ont., August 1, 1976.
(Florida's 5th choice, 84th overall, in 1994 Entry Draft).

			Regular Season					Playoffs				
Season	Club	Lea	GP	G	A	TP	PIM	GP	G	A	TP	PIM
1993-94	Ottawa	OHL	64	21	31	52	18	17	10	10	20	2
1994-95	Ottawa	OHL	59	27	29	56	25	....	....	....	....	....
1995-96	**Florida**	**NHL**	**9**	**0**	**2**	**2**	**2**	....	....	....	....	....
	Sarnia	OHL	26	18	27	45	14	10	8	8	16	6
	Carolina	AHL	5	1	2	3	0	....	....	....	....	....
	NHL Totals		**9**	**0**	**2**	**2**	**2**	....	....	....	....	....

NICHOL, SCOTT — BUF.

Center. Shoots right. 5'8", 160 lbs. Born, Edmonton, Alta., December 31, 1974.
(Buffalo's 9th choice, 272nd overall, in 1993 Entry Draft).

			Regular Season					Playoffs				
Season	Club	Lea	GP	G	A	TP	PIM	GP	G	A	TP	PIM
1992-93	Portland	WHL	67	31	33	64	146	16	8	8	16	41
1993-94	Portland	WHL	65	40	53	93	144	10	3	8	11	16
1994-95	Rochester	AHL	71	11	16	27	136	5	0	3	3	14
1995-96	**Buffalo**	**NHL**	**2**	**0**	**0**	**0**	**10**	....	....	....	....	....
	Rochester	AHL	62	14	18	32	170	19	7	6	13	36
	NHL Totals		**2**	**0**	**0**	**0**	**10**	....	....	....	....	....

NICHOLLS, BERNIE (NICK-els) — S.J.

Center. Shoots right. 6'1", 185 lbs. Born, Haliburton, Ont., June 24, 1961.
(Los Angeles' 6th choice, 73rd overall, in 1980 Entry Draft).

			Regular Season					Playoffs				
Season	Club	Lea	GP	G	A	TP	PIM	GP	G	A	TP	PIM
1979-80	Kingston	OHA	68	36	43	79	85	3	1	0	1	10
1980-81	Kingston	OHA	65	63	89	152	109	14	8	10	18	17
1981-82	**Los Angeles**	**NHL**	**22**	**14**	**18**	**32**	**27**	**10**	**4**	**0**	**4**	**23**
	New Haven	AHL	55	41	30	71	31	....	....	....	....	....
1982-83	**Los Angeles**	**NHL**	**71**	**28**	**22**	**50**	**124**	....	....	....	....	....
1983-84	**Los Angeles**	**NHL**	**78**	**41**	**54**	**95**	**83**	....	....	....	....	....
1984-85	**Los Angeles**	**NHL**	**80**	**46**	**54**	**100**	**76**	**3**	**1**	**1**	**2**	**9**
1985-86	**Los Angeles**	**NHL**	**80**	**36**	**61**	**97**	**78**	....	....	....	....	....
1986-87	**Los Angeles**	**NHL**	**80**	**33**	**48**	**81**	**101**	**5**	**2**	**5**	**7**	**6**
1987-88	**Los Angeles**	**NHL**	**65**	**32**	**46**	**78**	**114**	**5**	**2**	**6**	**8**	**11**
1988-89	**Los Angeles**	**NHL**	**79**	**70**	**80**	**150**	**96**	**11**	**7**	**9**	**16**	**12**
1989-90	**Los Angeles**	**NHL**	**47**	**27**	**48**	**75**	**66**	....	....	....	....	....
	NY Rangers	**NHL**	**32**	**12**	**25**	**37**	**20**	**10**	**7**	**5**	**12**	**16**
1990-91	**NY Rangers**	**NHL**	**71**	**25**	**48**	**73**	**96**	**5**	**4**	**3**	**7**	**8**
1991-92	**NY Rangers**	**NHL**	**1**	**0**	**0**	**0**	**0**	....	....	....	....	....
	Edmonton	**NHL**	**49**	**20**	**29**	**49**	**60**	**16**	**8**	**11**	**19**	**25**
1992-93	**Edmonton**	**NHL**	**46**	**8**	**32**	**40**	**40**	....	....	....	....	....
	New Jersey	**NHL**	**23**	**5**	**15**	**20**	**40**	**5**	**0**	**0**	**0**	**6**
1993-94	**New Jersey**	**NHL**	**61**	**19**	**27**	**46**	**86**	**16**	**4**	**9**	**13**	**28**
1994-95	**Chicago**	**NHL**	**48**	**22**	**29**	**51**	**32**	**16**	**1**	**11**	**12**	**8**
1995-96	**Chicago**	**NHL**	**59**	**19**	**41**	**60**	**60**	**10**	**2**	**7**	**9**	**4**
	NHL Totals		**992**	**457**	**677**	**1134**	**1199**	**112**	**42**	**67**	**109**	**156**

Played in NHL All-Star Game (1984, 1989, 1990)

Traded to **NY Rangers** by **Los Angeles** for Tomas Sandstrom and Tony Granato, January 20, 1990. Traded to **Edmonton** by **NY Rangers** with Steven Rice and Louie DeBrusk for Mark Messier and future considerations, October 4, 1991. Traded to **New Jersey** by **Edmonton** for Zdeno Ciger and Kevin Todd, January 13, 1993. Signed as a free agent by **Chicago**, July 14, 1994. Signed as a free agent by **San Jose**, August 5, 1996.

NICKULAS, ERIC — BOS.

Center. Shoots right. 5'11", 190 lbs. Born, Cape Cod, MA, March 25, 1975.
(Boston's 3rd choice, 99th overall, in 1994 Entry Draft).

			Regular Season					Playoffs				
Season	Club	Lea	GP	G	A	TP	PIM	GP	G	A	TP	PIM
1994-95	N. Hampshire	H.E.	33	15	9	24	32	....	....	....	....	....
1995-96	N. Hampshire	H.E.	34	26	12	38	66	....	....	....	....	....

NIECKAR, BARRY (NIGH-kahr)

Left wing. Shoots left. 6'3", 200 lbs. Born, Rama, Sask., December 16, 1967.

			Regular Season					Playoffs				
Season	Club	Lea	GP	G	A	TP	PIM	GP	G	A	TP	PIM
1991-92	Phoenix	IHL	5	0	0	0	9	....	....	....	....	....
	Raleigh	ECHL	46	10	18	28	229	4	4	0	4	22
1992-93	**Hartford**	**NHL**	**2**	**0**	**0**	**0**	**2**	....	....	....	....	....
	Springfield	AHL	21	2	4	6	65	6	1	0	1	14
1993-94	Springfield	AHL	30	0	2	2	67	....	....	....	....	....
	Raleigh	ECHL	18	4	6	10	126	15	5	7	12	51
1994-95	Saint John	AHL	65	8	7	15	*491	4	0	0	0	22
	Calgary	**NHL**	**3**	**0**	**0**	**0**	**12**	....	....	....	....	....
1995-96	Utah	IHL	53	9	15	24	194	....	....	....	....	....
	Peoria	IHL	10	3	3	6	72	12	4	6	10	48
	NHL Totals		**5**	**0**	**0**	**0**	**14**	....	....	....	....	....

Signed as a free agent by **Hartford**, September 25, 1992. Signed as a free agent by **Calgary**, February 11, 1995. Signed as a free agent by **NY Islanders**, August 8, 1995.

NIEDERMAYER, ROB (nee-duhr-MIGH-uhr) — FLA.

Center. Shoots left. 6'2", 201 lbs. Born, Cassiar, B.C., December 28, 1974.
(Florida's 1st choice, 5th overall, in 1993 Entry Draft).

			Regular Season					Playoffs				
Season	Club	Lea	GP	G	A	TP	PIM	GP	G	A	TP	PIM
1990-91	Medicine Hat	WHL	71	24	26	50	8	12	3	7	10	2
1991-92	Medicine Hat	WHL	71	32	46	78	77	4	2	3	5	2
1992-93a	Medicine Hat	WHL	52	43	34	77	67	....	....	....	....	....
1993-94	**Florida**	**NHL**	**65**	**9**	**17**	**26**	**51**	....	....	....	....	....
1994-95	Medicine Hat	WHL	13	9	15	24	14	....	....	....	....	....
	Florida	**NHL**	**48**	**4**	**6**	**10**	**36**	....	....	....	....	....
1995-96	**Florida**	**NHL**	**82**	**26**	**35**	**61**	**107**	**22**	**5**	**3**	**8**	**12**
	NHL Totals		**195**	**39**	**58**	**97**	**194**	**22**	**5**	**3**	**8**	**12**

a WHL East First All-Star Team (1993)

NIEDERMAYER, SCOTT (NEE-duhr-MIGH-uhr) — N.J.

Defense. Shoots left. 6', 200 lbs. Born, Edmonton, Alta., August 31, 1973.
(New Jersey's 1st choice, 3rd overall, in 1991 Entry Draft).

			Regular Season					Playoffs				
Season	Club	Lea	GP	G	A	TP	PIM	GP	G	A	TP	PIM
1989-90	Kamloops	WHL	64	14	55	69	64	17	2	14	16	35
1990-91ab	Kamloops	WHL	57	26	56	82	52	....	....	....	....	....
1991-92	**New Jersey**	**NHL**	**4**	**0**	**1**	**1**	**2**	....	....	....	....	....
acd	Kamloops	WHL	35	7	32	39	61	17	9	14	23	28
1992-93e	**New Jersey**	**NHL**	**80**	**11**	**29**	**40**	**47**	**5**	**0**	**3**	**3**	**2**
1993-94	**New Jersey**	**NHL**	**81**	**10**	**36**	**46**	**42**	**20**	**2**	**2**	**4**	**8**
1994-95	**New Jersey**	**NHL**	**48**	**4**	**15**	**19**	**18**	**20**	**4**	**7**	**11**	**10** ♦
1995-96	**New Jersey**	**NHL**	**79**	**8**	**25**	**33**	**46**	....	....	....	....	....
	NHL Totals		**292**	**33**	**106**	**139**	**155**	**45**	**6**	**12**	**18**	**20**

a WHL West First All-Star Team (1991, 1992)
b Canadian Major Junior Scholastic Player of the Year (1991)
c Memorial Cup All-Star Team (1992)
d Won Stafford Smythe Memorial Trophy (Memorial Cup Tournament MVP) (1992)
e NHL/Upper Deck All-Rookie Team (1993)

NIELSEN, JEFF — NYR

Right wing. Shoots right. 6', 200 lbs. Born, Grand Rapids, MN, September 20, 1971.
(NY Rangers' 4th choice, 69th overall, in 1990 Entry Draft).

			Regular Season					Playoffs				
Season	Club	Lea	GP	G	A	TP	PIM	GP	G	A	TP	PIM
1990-91	U. Minnesota	WCHA	45	11	14	25	50	....	....	....	....	....
1991-92	U. Minnesota	WCHA	41	14	14	28	70	....	....	....	....	....
1992-93	U. Minnesota	WCHA	42	21	20	41	80	....	....	....	....	....
1993-94a	U. Minnesota	WCHA	41	29	16	45	94	....	....	....	....	....
1994-95	Binghamton	AHL	76	24	13	37	139	7	0	0	0	22
1995-96	Binghamton	AHL	64	22	20	42	56	4	1	1	2	4

a WCHA Second All-Star Team (1994)

NIELSEN, KIRK — BOS.

Right wing. Shoots right. 6'1", 190 lbs. Born, Grand Rapids, MN, October 19, 1973.
(Philadelphia's 1st choice, 10th overall, in 1994 Supplemental Draft).

			Regular Season					Playoffs				
Season	Club	Lea	GP	G	A	TP	PIM	GP	G	A	TP	PIM
1992-93	Harvard	ECAC	30	2	2	4	38	....	....	....	....	....
1993-94	Harvard	ECAC	32	6	9	15	41	....	....	....	....	....
1994-95	Harvard	ECAC	30	13	8	21	24	....	....	....	....	....
1995-96	Harvard	ECAC	31	12	16	28	66	....	....	....	....	....

Signed as a free agent by **Boston**, June 7, 1996.

NIEMI, ANTTI-JUSSI (nee-mee, AN-tee-YOO-see) — OTT.

Defense. Shoots left. 6'1", 183 lbs. Born, Vantaa, Finland, September 22, 1977.
(Ottawa's 2nd choice, 81st overall, in 1996 Entry Draft).

			Regular Season					Playoffs				
Season	Club	Lea	GP	G	A	TP	PIM	GP	G	A	TP	PIM
1994-95	Jokerit	Fin. Jr.	24	4	8	12	74	....	....	....	....	....
1995-96	Jokerit	Fin. Jr.	34	11	18	29	56	8	0	4	4	39
	Jarvenpaa	Fin. 2	4	0	2	2	8	....	....	....	....	....
	Jokerit	Fin.	6	0	2	2	6	1	0	0	0	0

NIEUWENDYK, JOE (NOO-ihn-DIGHK) — DAL.

Center. Shoots left. 6'1", 195 lbs. Born, Oshawa, Ont., September 10, 1966.
(Calgary's 2nd choice, 27th overall, in 1985 Entry Draft).

			Regular Season					Playoffs				
Season	Club	Lea	GP	G	A	TP	PIM	GP	G	A	TP	PIM
1984-85	Cornell	ECAC	23	18	21	39	20	....	....	....	....	....
1985-86ab	Cornell	ECAC	21	21	21	42	45	....	....	....	....	....
1986-87ab	Cornell	ECAC	23	26	26	52	26	....	....	....	....	....
	Cdn. National	....	5	2	0	2	0	....	....	....	....	....
	Calgary	NHL	9	5	1	6	0	6	2	2	4	0
1987-88cde	Calgary	NHL	75	51	41	92	23	8	3	4	7	2
1988-89	Calgary	NHL	77	51	31	82	40	22	10	4	14	10 ♦
1989-90	Calgary	NHL	79	45	50	95	40	6	4	6	10	4
1990-91	Calgary	NHL	79	45	40	85	36	7	4	1	5	10
1991-92	Calgary	NHL	69	22	34	56	55	....	....	....	....	....
1992-93	Calgary	NHL	79	38	37	75	52	6	3	6	9	10
1993-94	Calgary	NHL	64	36	39	75	51	6	2	2	4	0
1994-95f	Calgary	NHL	46	21	29	50	33	5	4	3	7	0
1995-96	Dallas	NHL	52	14	18	32	41	....	....	....	....	....
	NHL Totals		629	328	320	648	371	66	32	28	60	36

a NCAA East First All-American Team (1986, 1987)
b ECAC First All-Star Team (1986, 1987)
c Won Calder Memorial Trophy (1988)
d NHL All-Rookie Team (1988)
e Won Dodge Ram Tough Award (1988)
f Won King Clancy Memorial Trophy (1995)

Played in NHL All-Star Game (1988-90, 1994)

Traded to **Dallas** by **Calgary** for Corey Millen and Jarome Iginla, December 19, 1995.

NIINIMAA, JANNE — PHI.

Defense. Shoots left. 6'1", 196 lbs. Born, Raahe, Finland, May 22, 1975.
(Philadelphia's 1st choice, 36th overall, in 1993 Entry Draft).

			Regular Season					Playoffs				
Season	Club	Lea	GP	G	A	TP	PIM	GP	G	A	TP	PIM
1991-92	Karpat	Fin. 2	41	2	11	13	49	....	....	....	....	....
1992-93	Karpat	Fin. 2	29	2	3	5	14	....	....	....	....	....
1993-94	Jokerit	Fin.	45	3	8	11	24	12	1	1	2	4
1994-95	Jokerit	Fin.	42	7	10	17	36	10	1	4	5	35
1995-96	Jokerit	Fin.	49	5	15	20	79	11	0	2	2	12

NIKOLISHIN, ANDREI (nee-koh-LEE-shin) — HFD.

Left wing. Shoots left. 5'11", 180 lbs. Born, Vorkuta, USSR, March 25, 1973.
(Hartford's 2nd choice, 47th overall, in 1992 Entry Draft).

			Regular Season					Playoffs				
Season	Club	Lea	GP	G	A	TP	PIM	GP	G	A	TP	PIM
1990-91	Moscow D'amo	USSR	2	0	0	0	0	....	....	....	....	....
1991-92	Moscow D'amo	CIS	18	1	0	1	4	....	....	....	....	....
1992-93	Moscow D'amo	CIS	42	5	7	12	30	10	2	1	3	8
1993-94	Moscow D'amo	CIS	41	8	12	20	30	9	1	3	4	4
1994-95	Moscow D'amo	CIS	12	7	2	9	6	....	....	....	....	....
	Hartford	NHL	39	8	10	18	10	....	....	....	....	....
1995-96	Hartford	NHL	61	14	37	51	34	....	....	....	....	....
	NHL Totals		100	22	47	69	44	....	....	....	....	....

NIKOLOV, ANGEL (NIH-koh-lohv) — S.J.

Defense. Shoots left. 6'1", 176 lbs. Born, Most, Czech., November 18, 1975.
(San Jose's 2nd choice, 37th overall, in 1994 Entry Draft).

			Regular Season					Playoffs				
Season	Club	Lea	GP	G	A	TP	PIM	GP	G	A	TP	PIM
1993-94	Litvinov	Czech.	10	2	2	4	....	3	0	0	0	....
1994-95	Litvinov	Czech.	41	1	4	5	18	4	0	0	0	27
1995-96	Litvinov	Czech.	40	1	7	8	....	10	0	1	1	....

NIKULIN, IGOR — ANA.

Right wing. Shoots left. 6'1", 190 lbs. Born, Cherepovets, USSR, August 26, 1972.
(Anaheim's 4th choice, 107th overall, in 1995 Entry Draft).

			Regular Season					Playoffs				
Season	Club	Lea	GP	G	A	TP	PIM	GP	G	A	TP	PIM
1992-93	Cherepovets	CIS	42	11	11	22	22	....	....	....	....	....
1993-94	Cherepovets	CIS	44	14	15	29	52	2	1	0	1	0
1994-95	Cherepovets	CIS	52	14	12	26	28	....	....	....	....	....
1995-96	Cherepovets	CIS	47	20	13	33	28	4	1	0	1	0
	Baltimore	AHL	4	2	2	4	2	....	....	....	....	....

NILSON, MARCUS — FLA.

Left wing. Shoots right. 6'1", 183 lbs. Born, Stockholm, Sweden, March 1, 1978.
(Florida's 1st choice, 20th overall, in 1996 Entry Draft).

			Regular Season					Playoffs				
Season	Club	Lea	GP	G	A	TP	PIM	GP	G	A	TP	PIM
1994-95	Djurgarden	Swe. Jr.	24	7	8	15	22	....	....	....	....	....
1995-96	Djurgarden	Swe. Jr.	25	19	17	36	46	2	1	1	2	12
	Djurgarden	Swe.	12	0	0	0	0	1	0	0	0	0

NILSSON, MAGNUS — DET.

Right wing. Shoots left. 6'1", 187 lbs. Born, Finspang, Sweden, February 1, 1978.
(Detroit's 5th choice, 144th overall, in 1996 Entry Draft).

			Regular Season					Playoffs				
Season	Club	Lea	GP	G	A	TP	PIM	GP	G	A	TP	PIM
1995-96	Vita Hasten	Swe. 2	28	3	3	6	16	....	....	....	....	....

NOBLE, STEVE — ST.L.

Center. Shoots left. 6'1", 185 lbs. Born, Sault Ste. Marie, Ont., July 17, 1976.
(St. Louis' 5th choice, 198th overall, in 1994 Entry Draft).

			Regular Season					Playoffs				
Season	Club	Lea	GP	G	A	TP	PIM	GP	G	A	TP	PIM
1994-95	Notre Dame	CCHA	37	6	8	14	25	....	....	....	....	....
1995-96	Notre Dame	CCHA	36	5	15	20	48	....	....	....	....	....

NOLAN, DOUG — TOR.

Left wing. Shoots left. 6'1", 185 lbs. Born, Quincy, MA, January 5, 1976.
(Toronto's 9th choice, 282nd overall, in 1994 Entry Draft).

			Regular Season					Playoffs				
Season	Club	Lea	GP	G	A	TP	PIM	GP	G	A	TP	PIM
1995-96	Lowell	H.E.	30	1	1	2	23	....	....	....	....	....

NOLAN, OWEN — S.J.

Right wing. Shoots right. 6'1", 201 lbs. Born, Belfast, Ireland, September 22, 1971.
(Quebec's 1st choice, 1st overall, in 1990 Entry Draft).

			Regular Season					Playoffs				
Season	Club	Lea	GP	G	A	TP	PIM	GP	G	A	TP	PIM
1988-89	Cornwall	OHL	62	34	25	59	213	18	5	11	16	41
1989-90a	Cornwall	OHL	58	51	59	110	240	6	7	5	12	26
1990-91	Quebec	NHL	59	3	10	13	109	....	....	....	....	....
	Halifax	AHL	6	4	4	8	11	....	....	....	....	....
1991-92	Quebec	NHL	75	42	31	73	183	....	....	....	....	....
1992-93	Quebec	NHL	73	36	41	77	185	5	1	0	1	2
1993-94	Quebec	NHL	6	2	2	4	8	....	....	....	....	....
1994-95	Quebec	NHL	46	30	19	49	46	6	2	3	5	6
1995-96	Colorado	NHL	9	4	4	8	9	....	....	....	....	....
	San Jose	NHL	72	29	32	61	137	....	....	....	....	....
	NHL Totals		340	146	139	285	677	11	3	3	6	8

a OHL First All-Star Team (1990)

Played in NHL All-Star Game (1992, 1996)

Traded to **San Jose** by **Colorado** for Sandis Ozolinsh, October 26, 1995.

NOONAN, BRIAN — ST.L.

Right wing. Shoots right. 6'1", 200 lbs. Born, Boston, MA, May 29, 1965.
(Chicago's 10th choice, 179th overall, in 1983 Entry Draft).

			Regular Season					Playoffs				
Season	Club	Lea	GP	G	A	TP	PIM	GP	G	A	TP	PIM
1984-85	N. Westminster	WHL	72	50	66	116	76	11	8	7	15	4
1985-86	Nova Scotia	AHL	2	0	0	0	0	....	....	....	....	....
	Saginaw	IHL	76	39	39	78	69	11	6	3	9	6
1986-87	Nova Scotia	AHL	70	25	26	51	30	5	3	1	4	4
1987-88	Chicago	NHL	77	10	20	30	44	3	0	0	0	4
1988-89	Chicago	NHL	45	4	12	16	28	1	0	0	0	0
	Saginaw	IHL	19	18	13	31	36	1	0	0	0	0
1989-90	Chicago	NHL	8	0	2	2	6	....	....	....	....	....
a	Indianapolis	IHL	56	40	36	76	85	14	6	9	15	20
1990-91	Chicago	NHL	7	0	4	4	2	....	....	....	....	....
b	Indianapolis	IHL	59	38	53	91	67	7	6	4	10	18
1991-92	Chicago	NHL	65	19	12	31	81	18	6	9	15	30
1992-93	Chicago	NHL	63	16	14	30	82	4	3	0	3	4
1993-94	Chicago	NHL	64	14	21	35	57	....	....	....	....	....
	NY Rangers	NHL	12	4	2	6	12	22	4	7	11	17 ♦
1994-95	NY Rangers	NHL	45	14	13	27	26	5	0	0	0	8
1995-96	St. Louis	NHL	81	13	22	35	84	13	4	1	5	10
	NHL Totals		467	94	122	216	422	66	17	17	34	73

a IHL Second All-Star Team (1990)
b IHL First All-Star Team (1991)

Traded to **NY Rangers** by **Chicago** with Stephane Matteau for Tony Amonte and the rights to Matt Oates, March 21, 1994. Signed as a free agent by **St. Louis**, July 24, 1995.

NORMAN, TODD — VAN.

Left wing. Shoots left. 5'11", 190 lbs. Born, Palmerston, Ont., January 29, 1977.
(Vancouver's 5th choice, 120th overall, in 1995 Entry Draft).

			Regular Season					Playoffs				
Season	Club	Lea	GP	G	A	TP	PIM	GP	G	A	TP	PIM
1993-94	Guelph	OHL	57	11	12	23	14	9	0	0	0	6
1994-95	Guelph	OHL	64	30	43	73	40	13	3	2	5	4
1995-96	Guelph	OHL	66	27	27	54	34	16	8	14	22	8

NORRIS, CLAYTON — PHI.

Right wing. Shoots right. 6'2", 205 lbs. Born, Edmonton, Alta., March 8, 1972.
(Philadelphia's 5th choice, 116th overall, in 1991 Entry Draft).

			Regular Season					Playoffs				
Season	Club	Lea	GP	G	A	TP	PIM	GP	G	A	TP	PIM
1990-91	Medicine Hat	WHL	71	26	27	53	165	12	5	4	9	41
1991-92a	Medicine Hat	WHL	69	26	39	65	300	2	0	0	0	9
1992-93	Medicine Hat	WHL	41	21	16	37	128	10	3	2	5	14
	Hershey	AHL	4	0	0	0	5	....	....	....	....	....
	Roanoke	ECHL	4	0	0	0	0	....	....	....	....	....
1993-94	Hershey	AHL	62	8	10	18	217	10	1	0	1	18
1994-95	Hershey	AHL	76	12	21	33	287	4	0	0	0	8
1995-96	Hershey	AHL	57	8	8	16	163	5	0	1	1	4

a WHL East Second All-Star Team (1992)

NORRIS, DWAYNE

Right wing. Shoots right. 5'10", 175 lbs. Born, St. John's, Nfld., January 8, 1970.
(Quebec's 5th choice, 127th overall, in 1990 Entry Draft).

				Regular Season					Playoffs			
Season	Club	Lea	GP	G	A	TP	PIM	GP	G	A	TP	PIM
1988-89	Michigan State	CCHA	40	16	21	37	32	....	....	....	....	....
1989-90	Michigan State	CCHA	33	18	25	43	30	....	....	....	....	....
1990-91	Michigan State	CCHA	40	26	25	51	60	....	....	....	....	....
1991-92ab	Michigan State	CCHA	41	40	38	78	58	....	....	....	....	....
1992-93	Halifax	AHL	50	25	28	53	62	....	....	....	....	....
1993-94	Cdn. National	....	48	18	14	32	22	....	....	....	....	....
	Cdn. Olympic	....	8	2	2	4	4	....	....	....	....	....
	Quebec	**NHL**	**4**	**1**	**1**	**2**	**4**	....	....	....	....	....
	Cornwall	AHL	9	2	9	11	0	13	7	4	11	17
1994-95c	Cornwall	AHL	60	30	43	73	61	12	7	8	15	4
	Quebec	**NHL**	**13**	**1**	**2**	**3**	**2**	....	....	....	....	....
1995-96	Los Angeles	IHL	14	7	16	23	22	....	....	....	....	....
	Anaheim	**NHL**	**3**	**0**	**1**	**1**	**2**	....	....	....	....	....
d	Baltimore	AHL	62	31	55	86	16	12	6	9	15	12
	NHL Totals		**20**	**2**	**4**	**6**	**8**	....	....	....	....	....

a CCHA First All-Star Team (1992)
b NCAA West First All-American Team (1992)
c AHL First All-Star Team (1995)
d AHL Second All-Star Team (1996)
Signed as a free agent by **Anaheim**, November 3, 1995.

NORSTROM, MATTIAS
L.A.

Defense. Shoots left. 6'1", 205 lbs. Born, Stockholm, Sweden, January 2, 1972.
(NY Rangers' 2nd choice, 48th overall, in 1992 Entry Draft).

				Regular Season					Playoffs			
Season	Club	Lea	GP	G	A	TP	PIM	GP	G	A	TP	PIM
1991-92	AIK	Swe.	39	4	3	7	28	3	0	2	2	2
1992-93	AIK	Swe.	22	0	1	1	16	....	....	....	....	....
1993-94	**NY Rangers**	**NHL**	**9**	**0**	**2**	**2**	**6**	....	....	....	....	....
	Binghamton	AHL	55	1	9	10	70	....	....	....	....	....
1994-95	Binghamton	AHL	63	9	10	19	91	....	....	....	....	....
	NY Rangers	**NHL**	**9**	**0**	**3**	**3**	**2**	**3**	**0**	**0**	**0**	**0**
1995-96	**NY Rangers**	**NHL**	**25**	**2**	**1**	**3**	**22**	....	....	....	....	....
	Los Angeles	**NHL**	**11**	**0**	**1**	**1**	**18**	....	....	....	....	....
	NHL Totals		**54**	**2**	**7**	**9**	**48**	**3**	**0**	**0**	**0**	**0**

Traded to **Los Angeles** by **NY Rangers** with Ray Ferraro, Ian Laperriere, Nathan Lafayette and NY Rangers' fourth round choice in 1997 Entry Draft for Marty McSorley, Jari Kurri and Shane Churla, March 14, 1996.

NORTON, BRAD
EDM.

Defense. Shoots left. 6'4", 225 lbs. Born, Cambridge, MA, February 13, 1975.
(Edmonton's 9th choice, 215th overall, in 1993 Entry Draft).

				Regular Season					Playoffs			
Season	Club	Lea	GP	G	A	TP	PIM	GP	G	A	TP	PIM
1994-95	Massachusetts	H.E.	30	0	6	6	89	....	....	....	....	....
1995-96	Massachusetts	H.E.	34	4	12	16	99	....	....	....	....	....

NORTON, JEFF
EDM.

Defense. Shoots left. 6'2", 200 lbs. Born, Acton, MA, November 25, 1965.
(NY Islanders' 3rd choice, 62nd overall, in 1984 Entry Draft).

				Regular Season					Playoffs			
Season	Club	Lea	GP	G	A	TP	PIM	GP	G	A	TP	PIM
1984-85	U. of Michigan	CCHA	37	8	16	24	103	....	....	....	....	....
1985-86	U. of Michigan	CCHA	37	15	30	45	99	....	....	....	....	....
1986-87a	U. of Michigan	CCHA	39	12	36	48	92	....	....	....	....	....
1987-88	U.S. National	....	54	7	22	29	52	....	....	....	....	....
	U.S. Olympic	....	6	0	4	4	4	....	....	....	....	....
	NY Islanders	**NHL**	**15**	**1**	**6**	**7**	**14**	**3**	**0**	**2**	**2**	**13**
1988-89	**NY Islanders**	**NHL**	**69**	**1**	**30**	**31**	**74**	....	....	....	....	....
1989-90	**NY Islanders**	**NHL**	**60**	**4**	**49**	**53**	**65**	**4**	**1**	**3**	**4**	**17**
1990-91	**NY Islanders**	**NHL**	**44**	**3**	**25**	**28**	**16**	....	....	....	....	....
1991-92	**NY Islanders**	**NHL**	**28**	**1**	**18**	**19**	**18**	....	....	....	....	....
1992-93	**NY Islanders**	**NHL**	**66**	**12**	**38**	**50**	**45**	**10**	**1**	**1**	**2**	**4**
1993-94	San Jose	NHL	**64**	**7**	**33**	**40**	**36**	**14**	**1**	**5**	**6**	**20**
1994-95	San Jose	NHL	**20**	**1**	**9**	**10**	**39**	....	....	....	....	....
	St. Louis	**NHL**	**28**	**2**	**18**	**20**	**33**	**7**	**1**	**1**	**2**	**11**
1995-96	**St. Louis**	**NHL**	**36**	**4**	**7**	**11**	**26**	....	....	....	....	....
	Edmonton	**NHL**	**30**	**4**	**16**	**20**	**16**	....	....	....	....	....
	NHL Totals		**460**	**40**	**249**	**289**	**382**	**38**	**4**	**12**	**16**	**65**

a CCHA Second All-Star Team (1987)
Traded to **San Jose** by **NY Islanders** for San Jose's third round choice (Jason Strudwick) in 1994 Entry Draft, June 20, 1993. Traded to **St. Louis** by **San Jose** with a conditional choice in 1997 Entry Draft for Craig Janney and cash, March 6, 1995. Traded to **Edmonton** by **St. Louis** with Donald Dufresne for Igor Kravchuk and Ken Sutton, January 4, 1996.

NUMMINEN, TEPPO
(NOO-mih-nehn, TEH-poh) PHO.

Defense. Shoots right. 6'1", 190 lbs. Born, Tampere, Finland, July 3, 1968.
(Winnipeg's 2nd choice, 29th overall, in 1986 Entry Draft).

				Regular Season					Playoffs			
Season	Club	Lea	GP	G	A	TP	PIM	GP	G	A	TP	PIM
1985-86	Tappara	Fin.	31	2	4	6	6	8	0	0	0	0
1986-87	Tappara	Fin.	44	9	9	18	16	9	4	1	5	4
1987-88	Tappara	Fin.	40	10	10	20	29	10	6	6	12	6
1988-89	**Winnipeg**	**NHL**	**69**	**1**	**14**	**15**	**36**	....	....	....	....	....
1989-90	**Winnipeg**	**NHL**	**79**	**11**	**32**	**43**	**20**	**7**	**1**	**2**	**3**	**10**
1990-91	**Winnipeg**	**NHL**	**80**	**8**	**25**	**33**	**28**	....	....	....	....	....
1991-92	**Winnipeg**	**NHL**	**80**	**5**	**34**	**39**	**32**	**7**	**0**	**0**	**0**	**0**
1992-93	**Winnipeg**	**NHL**	**66**	**7**	**30**	**37**	**33**	**6**	**1**	**1**	**2**	**2**
1993-94	**Winnipeg**	**NHL**	**57**	**5**	**18**	**23**	**28**	....	....	....	....	....
1994-95	TuTo	Fin.	12	3	8	11	4	....	....	....	....	....
	Winnipeg	**NHL**	**42**	**5**	**16**	**21**	**16**	....	....	....	....	....
1995-96	**Winnipeg**	**NHL**	**74**	**11**	**43**	**54**	**22**	**6**	**0**	**0**	**0**	**2**
	NHL Totals		**547**	**53**	**212**	**265**	**215**	**26**	**2**	**3**	**5**	**14**

NURMINEN, KAI
L.A.

Right wing. Shoots left. 6'1", 198 lbs. Born, Turku, Finland, March 29, 1969.
(Los Angeles' 9th choice, 193rd overall, in 1996 Entry Draft).

				Regular Season					Playoffs			
Season	Club	Lea	GP	G	A	TP	PIM	GP	G	A	TP	PIM
1995-96	HV 71	Fin.	40	31	24	55	....	....	....	....	....	....

NUUTINEN, SAMI
EDM.

Defense. Shoots left. 6'1", 189 lbs. Born, Espoo, Finland, June 11, 1971.
(Edmonton's 11th choice, 248th overall, in 1990 Entry Draft).

				Regular Season					Playoffs			
Season	Club	Lea	GP	G	A	TP	PIM	GP	G	A	TP	PIM
1988-89	Espoo	Fin. 2	39	18	10	28	46	....	....	....	....	....
1989-90	Espoo	Fin. 2	40	8	15	23		....	....	....	....	....
1990-91	K-Kissat	Fin. 2	3	1	0	1	0	....	....	....	....	....
	HIFK	Fin.	27	1	3	4	6	3	0	0	0	0
1991-92	HIFK	Fin.	44	5	6	11	10	9	0	1	1	4
1992-93	Kiekko-Espoo	Fin.	48	7	11	18	59	....	....	....	....	....
1993-94	Kiekko-Espoo	Fin.	46	9	15	24	36	....	....	....	....	....
1994-95	Kiekko-Espoo	Fin.	50	8	24	32	38	4	0	1	1	0
1995-96	Kiekko-Espoo	Fin.	49	7	7	14	54	....	....	....	....	....

NYLANDER, MICHAEL
(NEE-lan-duhr) CGY.

Center. Shoots left. 5'11", 190 lbs. Born, Stockholm, Sweden, October 3, 1972.
(Hartford's 4th choice, 59th overall, in 1991 Entry Draft).

				Regular Season					Playoffs			
Season	Club	Lea	GP	G	A	TP	PIM	GP	G	A	TP	PIM
1989-90	Huddinge	Swe. 2	31	7	15	22	4	....	....	....	....	....
1990-91	Huddinge	Swe. 2	33	14	20	34	10	....	....	....	....	....
1991-92	AIK	Swe.	40	11	17	28	30	3	1	4	5	4
1992-93	**Hartford**	**NHL**	**59**	**11**	**22**	**33**	**36**	....	....	....	....	....
	Springfield	AHL	....	....	....	....	....	3	3	3	6	2
1993-94	**Hartford**	**NHL**	**58**	**11**	**33**	**44**	**24**	....	....	....	....	....
	Springfield	AHL	4	0	9	9	0	....	....	....	....	....
	Calgary	**NHL**	**15**	**2**	**9**	**11**	**6**	**3**	**0**	**0**	**0**	**0**
1994-95	JyP HT	Fin.	16	11	19	30	63	....	....	....	....	....
	Calgary	**NHL**	**6**	**0**	**1**	**1**	**2**	**6**	**0**	**6**	**6**	**2**
1995-96	**Calgary**	**NHL**	**73**	**17**	**38**	**55**	**20**	**4**	**0**	**0**	**0**	**0**
	NHL Totals		**211**	**41**	**103**	**144**	**88**	**13**	**0**	**6**	**6**	**2**

Traded to **Calgary** by **Hartford** with James Patrick and Zarley Zalapski for Gary Suter, Paul Ranheim and Ted Drury, March 10, 1994.

OATES, ADAM
BOS.

Center. Shoots right. 5'11", 185 lbs. Born, Weston, Ont., August 27, 1962.

				Regular Season					Playoffs			
Season	Club	Lea	GP	G	A	TP	PIM	GP	G	A	TP	PIM
1982-83	RPI	ECAC	22	9	33	42	8	....	....	....	....	....
1983-84	RPI	ECAC	38	26	57	83	15	....	....	....	....	....
1984-85ab	RPI	ECAC	38	31	60	91	29	....	....	....	....	....
1985-86	**Detroit**	**NHL**	**38**	**9**	**11**	**20**	**10**	....	....	....	....	....
	Adirondack	AHL	34	18	28	46	4	17	7	14	21	4
1986-87	**Detroit**	**NHL**	**76**	**15**	**32**	**47**	**21**	**16**	**4**	**7**	**11**	**6**
1987-88	**Detroit**	**NHL**	**63**	**14**	**40**	**54**	**20**	**16**	**8**	**12**	**20**	**6**
1988-89	**Detroit**	**NHL**	**69**	**16**	**62**	**78**	**14**	**6**	**0**	**8**	**8**	**2**
1989-90	**St. Louis**	**NHL**	**80**	**23**	**79**	**102**	**30**	**12**	**2**	**12**	**14**	**4**
1990-91c	**St. Louis**	**NHL**	**61**	**25**	**90**	**115**	**29**	**13**	**7**	**13**	**20**	**10**
1991-92	**St. Louis**	**NHL**	**54**	**10**	**59**	**69**	**12**	....	....	....	....	....
	Boston	**NHL**	**26**	**10**	**20**	**30**	**10**	**15**	**5**	**14**	**19**	**4**
1992-93	**Boston**	**NHL**	**84**	**45**	***97**	**142**	**32**	**4**	**0**	**9**	**9**	**4**
1993-94	**Boston**	**NHL**	**77**	**32**	**80**	**112**	**45**	**13**	**3**	**9**	**12**	**8**
1994-95	**Boston**	**NHL**	**48**	**12**	**41**	**53**	**8**	**5**	**1**	**0**	**1**	**2**
1995-96	**Boston**	**NHL**	**70**	**25**	**67**	**92**	**18**	**5**	**2**	**5**	**7**	**2**
	NHL Totals		**746**	**236**	**678**	**914**	**249**	**105**	**32**	**89**	**121**	**48**

a ECAC First All-Star Team (1985)
b Named to NCAA All-American Team (1985)
c NHL Second All-Star Team (1991)
Played in NHL All-Star Game (1991-94)
Signed as a free agent by **Detroit**, June 28, 1985. Traded to **St. Louis** by **Detroit** with Paul MacLean for Bernie Federko and Tony McKegney, June 15, 1989. Traded to **Boston** by **St. Louis** for Craig Janney and Stephane Quintal, February 7, 1992.

OATES, MATT
CHI.

Left wing. Shoots left. 6'3", 208 lbs. Born, Evanston, IL, December 20, 1972.
(NY Rangers' 7th choice, 168th overall, in 1992 Entry Draft).

				Regular Season					Playoffs			
Season	Club	Lea	GP	G	A	TP	PIM	GP	G	A	TP	PIM
1991-92	Miami-Ohio	CCHA	40	8	13	21	23	....	....	....	....	....
1992-93	Miami-Ohio	CCHA	38	11	14	25	82	....	....	....	....	....
1993-94	Miami-Ohio	CCHA	33	14	12	26	60	....	....	....	....	....
1994-95	Columbus	ECHL	11	4	5	9	11	....	....	....	....	....
	Indianapolis	IHL	59	3	6	9	18	....	....	....	....	....
1995-96	Columbus	ECHL	46	12	28	40	63	3	1	0	1	4

Rights traded to **Chicago** by **NY Rangers** with Tony Amonte for Stephane Matteau and Brian Noonan, March 21, 1994.

OBSUT, JAROSLAV
PHO.

Defense. Shoots left. 6'1", 185 lbs. Born, Presov, Czech., September 3, 1976.
(Winnipeg's 9th choice, 188th overall, in 1995 Entry Draft).

				Regular Season					Playoffs			
Season	Club	Lea	GP	G	A	TP	PIM	GP	G	A	TP	PIM
1994-95	N. Battleford	Jr. A	55	21	30	51	126	....	....	....	....	....
1995-96	Swift Current	WHL	72	10	11	21	57	6	0	0	0	2

O'CONNELL, ALBERT
NYI

Left wing. Shoots left. 6', 188 lbs. Born, Cambridge, MA, May 20, 1976.
(NY Islanders' 6th choice, 116th overall, in 1994 Entry Draft).

				Regular Season					Playoffs			
Season	Club	Lea	GP	G	A	TP	PIM	GP	G	A	TP	PIM
1995-96	Boston U.	H.E.	38	9	8	17	34	....	....	....	....	....

O'CONNOR, MYLES

Defense. Shoots left. 5'11", 190 lbs. Born, Calgary, Alta., April 2, 1967.
(New Jersey's 4th choice, 45th overall, in 1985 Entry Draft).

			Regular Season					Playoffs				
Season	**Club**	**Lea**	**GP**	**G**	**A**	**TP**	**PIM**	**GP**	**G**	**A**	**TP**	**PIM**
1985-86	U. of Michigan	CCHA	37	6	19	25	73	....	....	....	....	....
	Cdn. National	....	8	0	0	0	0	....	....	....	....	....
1986-87	U. of Michigan	CCHA	39	15	39	54	111	....	....	....	....	....
1987-88	U. of Michigan	CCHA	40	9	25	34	78	....	....	....	....	....
1988-89ab	U. of Michigan	CCHA	40	3	31	34	91	....	....	....	....	....
	Utica	AHL	1	0	0	0	0	....	....	....	....	....
1989-90	Utica	AHL	76	14	33	47	124	5	1	2	3	26
1990-91	**New Jersey**	**NHL**	**22**	**3**	**1**	**4**	**41**	....	....	....	....	....
	Utica	AHL	33	6	17	23	62	....	....	....	....	....
1991-92	**New Jersey**	**NHL**	**9**	**0**	**2**	**2**	**13**	....	....	....	....	....
	Utica	AHL	66	9	39	48	184	....	....	....	....	....
1992-93	**New Jersey**	**NHL**	**7**	**0**	**0**	**0**	**9**	....	....	....	....	....
	Utica	AHL	9	1	5	6	10	....	....	....	....	....
1993-94	**Anaheim**	**NHL**	**5**	**0**	**1**	**1**	**6**	....	....	....	....	....
	San Diego	IHL	39	1	13	14	117	9	1	4	5	83
1994-95	San Diego	IHL	16	1	4	5	50	5	0	1	1	0
1995-96	Houston	IHL	80	2	24	26	256	....	....	....	....	....
	NHL Totals		**43**	**3**	**4**	**7**	**69**	....	....	....	....	....

a CCHA First All-Star Team (1989)
b NCAA West First All-American Team (1989)

Signed as a free agent by **Anaheim**, July 22, 1993.

ODELEIN, LYLE (OH-duh-LIGHN) N.J.

Defense. Shoots right. 5'11", 210 lbs. Born, Quill Lake, Sask., July 21, 1968.
(Montreal's 8th choice, 141st overall, in 1986 Entry Draft).

			Regular Season					Playoffs				
Season	**Club**	**Lea**	**GP**	**G**	**A**	**TP**	**PIM**	**GP**	**G**	**A**	**TP**	**PIM**
1985-86	Moose Jaw	WHL	67	9	37	46	117	13	1	6	7	34
1986-87	Moose Jaw	WHL	59	9	50	59	70	9	2	5	7	26
1987-88	Moose Jaw	WHL	63	15	43	58	166	....	....	....	....	....
1988-89	Sherbrooke	AHL	33	3	4	7	120	3	0	2	2	5
	Peoria	IHL	36	2	8	10	116	....	....	....	....	....
1989-90	**Montreal**	**NHL**	**8**	**0**	**2**	**2**	**33**	....	....	....	....	....
	Sherbrooke	AHL	68	7	24	31	265	12	6	5	11	79
1990-91	**Montreal**	**NHL**	**52**	**0**	**2**	**2**	**259**	**12**	**0**	**0**	**0**	**54**
1991-92	**Montreal**	**NHL**	**71**	**1**	**7**	**8**	**212**	**7**	**0**	**0**	**0**	**11**
1992-93	**Montreal**	**NHL**	**83**	**2**	**14**	**16**	**205**	**20**	**1**	**5**	**6**	**30 ♦**
1993-94	**Montreal**	**NHL**	**79**	**11**	**29**	**40**	**276**	**7**	**0**	**0**	**0**	**17**
1994-95	**Montreal**	**NHL**	**48**	**3**	**7**	**10**	**152**	....	....	....	....	....
1995-96	**Montreal**	**NHL**	**79**	**3**	**14**	**17**	**230**	**6**	**1**	**1**	**2**	**6**
	NHL Totals		**420**	**20**	**75**	**95**	**1367**	**52**	**2**	**6**	**8**	**118**

Traded to **New Jersey** by **Montreal** for Stephane Richer, August 22, 1996.

ODGERS, JEFF (AWD-juhrs) BOS.

Right wing. Shoots right. 6', 195 lbs. Born, Spy Hill, Sask., May 31, 1969.

			Regular Season					Playoffs				
Season	**Club**	**Lea**	**GP**	**G**	**A**	**TP**	**PIM**	**GP**	**G**	**A**	**TP**	**PIM**
1988-89	Brandon	WHL	71	31	29	60	277	....	....	....	....	....
1989-90	Brandon	WHL	64	37	28	65	209	....	....	....	....	....
1990-91	Kansas City	IHL	77	12	19	31	318	....	....	....	....	....
1991-92	**San Jose**	**NHL**	**61**	**7**	**4**	**11**	**217**	....	....	....	....	....
	Kansas City	IHL	12	2	2	4	56	4	2	1	3	0
1992-93	**San Jose**	**NHL**	**66**	**12**	**15**	**27**	**253**	....	....	....	....	....
1993-94	**San Jose**	**NHL**	**81**	**13**	**8**	**21**	**222**	**11**	**0**	**0**	**0**	**11**
1994-95	**San Jose**	**NHL**	**48**	**4**	**3**	**7**	**117**	**11**	**1**	**1**	**2**	**23**
1995-96	**San Jose**	**NHL**	**78**	**12**	**4**	**16**	**192**	....	....	....	....	....
	NHL Totals		**334**	**48**	**34**	**82**	**1001**	**22**	**1**	**1**	**2**	**34**

Signed as a free agent by **San Jose**, September 3, 1991. Traded to **Boston** by **San Jose** with Pittsburgh's fifth round choice (previously acquired by San Jose — Boston selected Elias Abrahamsson) in 1996 Entry Draft for Al Iafrate, June 21, 1996.

ODJICK, GINO (OH-jihk) VAN.

Left wing. Shoots left. 6'3", 210 lbs. Born, Maniwaki, Que., September 7, 1970.
(Vancouver's 5th choice, 86th overall, in 1990 Entry Draft).

			Regular Season					Playoffs				
Season	**Club**	**Lea**	**GP**	**G**	**A**	**TP**	**PIM**	**GP**	**G**	**A**	**TP**	**PIM**
1988-89	Laval	QMJHL	50	9	15	24	278	16	0	9	9	129
1989-90	Laval	QMJHL	51	12	26	38	280	....	....	....	....	....
1990-91	**Vancouver**	**NHL**	**45**	**7**	**1**	**8**	**296**	**6**	**0**	**0**	**0**	**18**
	Milwaukee	IHL	17	7	3	10	102	....	....	....	....	....
1991-92	**Vancouver**	**NHL**	**65**	**4**	**6**	**10**	**348**	**4**	**0**	**0**	**0**	**6**
1992-93	**Vancouver**	**NHL**	**75**	**4**	**13**	**17**	**370**	**1**	**0**	**0**	**0**	**0**
1993-94	**Vancouver**	**NHL**	**76**	**16**	**13**	**29**	**271**	**10**	**0**	**0**	**0**	**18**
1994-95	**Vancouver**	**NHL**	**23**	**4**	**5**	**9**	**109**	**5**	**0**	**0**	**0**	**47**
1995-96	**Vancouver**	**NHL**	**55**	**3**	**4**	**7**	**181**	**6**	**3**	**1**	**4**	**6**
	NHL Totals		**339**	**38**	**42**	**80**	**1575**	**32**	**3**	**1**	**4**	**95**

O'DONNELL, SEAN L.A.

Defense. Shoots left. 6'2", 225 lbs. Born, Ottawa, Ont., October 13, 1971.
(Buffalo's 6th choice, 123rd overall, in 1991 Entry Draft).

			Regular Season					Playoffs				
Season	**Club**	**Lea**	**GP**	**G**	**A**	**TP**	**PIM**	**GP**	**G**	**A**	**TP**	**PIM**
1990-91	Sudbury	OHL	66	8	23	31	114	5	1	4	5	10
1991-92	Rochester	AHL	73	4	9	13	193	16	1	2	3	21
1992-93	Rochester	AHL	74	3	18	21	203	17	1	6	7	38
1993-94	Rochester	AHL	64	2	10	12	242	4	0	1	1	21
1994-95	Phoenix	IHL	61	2	18	20	132	9	0	1	1	21
	Los Angeles	**NHL**	**15**	**0**	**2**	**2**	**49**	....	....	....	....	....
1995-96	**Los Angeles**	**NHL**	**71**	**2**	**5**	**7**	**127**	....	....	....	....	....
	NHL Totals		**86**	**2**	**7**	**9**	**176**	....	....	....	....	....

Traded to **Los Angeles** by **Buffalo** for Doug Houda, July 26, 1994.

ODUYA, FREDRIK S.J.

Defense. Shoots left. 6'2", 185 lbs. Born, Stockholm, Sweden, May 31, 1975.
(San Jose's 8th choice, 154th overall, in 1993 Entry Draft).

			Regular Season					Playoffs				
Season	**Club**	**Lea**	**GP**	**G**	**A**	**TP**	**PIM**	**GP**	**G**	**A**	**TP**	**PIM**
1992-93	Guelph	OHL	23	2	4	6	29	....	....	....	....	....
	Ottawa	OHL	17	0	3	3	70	....	....	....	....	....
1993-94	Ottawa	OHL	51	11	12	23	181	17	0	3	3	22
1994-95	Ottawa	OHL	61	2	13	15	175	....	....	....	....	....
1995-96	Kansas City	IHL	56	2	6	8	235	3	0	0	0	2

O'GRADY, MIKE FLA.

Defense. Shoots left. 6'3", 227 lbs. Born, Neilburg, Sask., March 22, 1977.
(Florida's 3rd choice, 62nd overall, in 1995 Entry Draft).

			Regular Season					Playoffs				
Season	**Club**	**Lea**	**GP**	**G**	**A**	**TP**	**PIM**	**GP**	**G**	**A**	**TP**	**PIM**
1993-94	Saskatoon	WHL	13	0	1	1	29	....	....	....	....	....
1994-95	Saskatoon	WHL	39	0	7	7	157	....	....	....	....	....
	Lethbridge	WHL	21	1	2	3	124	....	....	....	....	....
1995-96	Lethbridge	WHL	61	2	9	11	242	4	1	0	1	8

OHLUND, MATTIAS (EH-luhnd) VAN.

Defense. Shoots left. 6'3", 209 lbs. Born, Pitea, Sweden, September 9, 1976.
(Vancouver's 1st choice, 13th overall, in 1994 Entry Draft).

			Regular Season					Playoffs				
Season	**Club**	**Lea**	**GP**	**G**	**A**	**TP**	**PIM**	**GP**	**G**	**A**	**TP**	**PIM**
1992-93	Pitea	Swe. 2	22	0	6	6	16	....	....	....	....	....
1993-94	Pitea	Swe. 2	28	7	10	17	62	....	....	....	....	....
1994-95	Lulea	Swe.	34	6	10	16	34	9	4	0	4	16
1995-96	Lulea	Swe.	38	4	10	14	26	13	1	0	1	47

OKSIUTA, ROMAN (ohk-SEW-tah) ANA.

Right wing. Shoots left. 6'3", 229 lbs. Born, Murmansk, USSR, August 21, 1970.
(NY Rangers' 11th choice, 202nd overall, in 1989 Entry Draft).

			Regular Season					Playoffs				
Season	**Club**	**Lea**	**GP**	**G**	**A**	**TP**	**PIM**	**GP**	**G**	**A**	**TP**	**PIM**
1987-88	Khimik	USSR	11	1	0	1	4	....	....	....	....	....
1988-89	Khimik	USSR	34	13	3	16	14	....	....	....	....	....
1989-90	Khimik	USSR	37	13	6	19	16	....	....	....	....	....
1990-91	Khimik	USSR	41	12	8	20	24	....	....	....	....	....
1991-92	Khimik	CIS	42	24	20	44	28	....	....	....	....	....
1992-93	Khimik	CIS	20	11	2	13	42	....	....	....	....	....
	Cape Breton	AHL	43	26	25	51	22	16	9	19	28	12
1993-94	**Edmonton**	**NHL**	**10**	**1**	**2**	**3**	**4**	....	....	....	....	....
	Cape Breton	AHL	47	31	22	53	90	4	2	2	4	22
1994-95	Cape Breton	AHL	25	9	7	16	20	....	....	....	....	....
	Edmonton	**NHL**	**26**	**11**	**2**	**13**	**8**	....	....	....	....	....
	Vancouver	**NHL**	**12**	**5**	**2**	**7**	**2**	**10**	**2**	**3**	**5**	**0**
1995-96	**Vancouver**	**NHL**	**56**	**16**	**23**	**39**	**42**	....	....	....	....	....
	Anaheim	**NHL**	**14**	**7**	**5**	**12**	**18**	....	....	....	....	....
	NHL Totals		**118**	**40**	**34**	**74**	**74**	**10**	**2**	**3**	**5**	**0**

Traded to **Edmonton** by **NY Rangers** with NY Rangers' third round choice (Alexander Kerch) in 1993 Entry Draft for Kevin Lowe, December 11, 1992. Traded to **Vancouver** by **Edmonton** for Jiri Slegr, April 7, 1995. Traded to **Anaheim** by **Vancouver** for Mike Sillinger, March 15, 1996.

OKTYABREV, ARTUR (ohk-tib-BREE-AHV, ahr-TOOR) VAN.

Defense. Shoots left. 5'11", 183 lbs. Born, Irkutsk, USSR, November 26, 1973.
(Winnipeg's 6th choice, 155th overall, in 1992 Entry Draft).

			Regular Season					Playoffs				
Season	**Club**	**Lea**	**GP**	**G**	**A**	**TP**	**PIM**	**GP**	**G**	**A**	**TP**	**PIM**
1991-92	CSKA	CIS	38	1	2	3	19	....	....	....	....	....
1992-93	CSKA	CIS	41	0	5	5	44	....	....	....	....	....
1993-94	CSKA	CIS	45	1	1	2	46	3	0	0	0	4
	Russian Pen's	IHL	10	0	2	2	12	....	....	....	....	....
1994-95	CSKA	CIS	46	1	3	4	36	....	....	....	....	....
	Syracuse	AHL	7	1	1	2	2	....	....	....	....	....
1995-96	Syracuse	AHL	62	3	16	19	69	3	0	0	0	2

Traded to **Vancouver** by **Winnipeg** for Vancouver's sixth round choice (Steve Vezina) in 1994 Entry Draft, June 29, 1994.

OLAUSSON, FREDRIK (OHL-ah-suhn) ANA.

Defense. Shoots right. 6'2", 195 lbs. Born, Dadesjo, Sweden, October 5, 1966.
(Winnipeg's 4th choice, 81st overall, in 1985 Entry Draft).

			Regular Season					Playoffs				
Season	**Club**	**Lea**	**GP**	**G**	**A**	**TP**	**PIM**	**GP**	**G**	**A**	**TP**	**PIM**
1982-83	Nybro	Swe. 2	31	4	4	8	12	....	....	....	....	....
1983-84	Nybro	Swe. 2	28	8	14	22	32	....	....	....	....	....
1984-85	Farjestad	Swe.	29	5	12	17	22	3	1	0	1	0
1985-86	Farjestad	Swe.	33	4	12	16	22	8	3	2	5	6
1986-87	**Winnipeg**	**NHL**	**72**	**7**	**29**	**36**	**24**	**10**	**2**	**3**	**5**	**4**
1987-88	**Winnipeg**	**NHL**	**38**	**5**	**10**	**15**	**18**	**5**	**1**	**1**	**2**	**0**
1988-89	**Winnipeg**	**NHL**	**75**	**15**	**47**	**62**	**32**	....	....	....	....	....
1989-90	**Winnipeg**	**NHL**	**77**	**9**	**46**	**55**	**32**	**7**	**0**	**2**	**2**	**2**
1990-91	**Winnipeg**	**NHL**	**71**	**12**	**29**	**41**	**24**	....	....	....	....	....
1991-92	**Winnipeg**	**NHL**	**77**	**20**	**42**	**62**	**34**	**7**	**1**	**5**	**6**	**4**
1992-93	**Winnipeg**	**NHL**	**68**	**16**	**41**	**57**	**22**	**6**	**0**	**2**	**2**	**2**
1993-94	**Winnipeg**	**NHL**	**18**	**2**	**5**	**7**	**10**	....	....	....	....	....
	Edmonton	**NHL**	**55**	**9**	**19**	**28**	**20**	....	....	....	....	....
1994-95	Ehrwald	Aus.	10	4	3	7	8	....	....	....	....	....
	Edmonton	**NHL**	**33**	**0**	**10**	**10**	**20**	....	....	....	....	....
1995-96	**Edmonton**	**NHL**	**20**	**0**	**6**	**6**	**14**	....	....	....	....	....
	Anaheim	**NHL**	**36**	**2**	**16**	**18**	**24**	....	....	....	....	....
	NHL Totals		**640**	**97**	**300**	**397**	**274**	**35**	**4**	**13**	**17**	**12**

Traded to **Edmonton** by **Winnipeg** with Winnipeg's seventh round choice (Curtis Sheptak) in 1994 Entry Draft for Edmonton's third round choice (Tavis Hansen) in 1994 Entry Draft, December 6, 1993. Claimed on waivers by **Anaheim** from **Edmonton**, January 16, 1996.

OLCZYK, ED (OHL-chehk) L.A.

Center. Shoots left. 6'1", 205 lbs. Born, Chicago, IL, August 16, 1966.
(Chicago's 1st choice, 3rd overall, in 1984 Entry Draft).

			Regular Season					Playoffs				
Season	Club	Lea	GP	G	A	TP	PIM	GP	G	A	TP	PIM
1983-84	U.S. National	....	62	21	47	68	36	....	....	....	....	....
1984-85	**Chicago**	**NHL**	70	20	30	50	67	15	6	5	11	11
1985-86	**Chicago**	**NHL**	79	29	50	79	47	3	0	0	0	0
1986-87	**Chicago**	**NHL**	79	16	35	51	119	4	1	1	2	4
1987-88	**Toronto**	**NHL**	80	42	33	75	55	6	5	4	9	2
1988-89	**Toronto**	**NHL**	80	38	52	90	75	....	....	....	....	....
1989-90	**Toronto**	**NHL**	79	32	56	88	78	5	1	2	3	14
1990-91	**Toronto**	**NHL**	18	4	10	14	13	....	....	....	....	....
	Winnipeg	**NHL**	61	26	31	57	69	....	....	....	....	....
1991-92	**Winnipeg**	**NHL**	64	32	33	65	67	6	2	1	3	4
1992-93	**Winnipeg**	**NHL**	25	8	12	20	26	....	....	....	....	....
	NY Rangers	**NHL**	46	13	16	29	26	....	....	....	....	....
1993-94	**NY Rangers**	**NHL**	37	3	5	8	28	1	0	0	0	0 ♦
1994-95	**NY Rangers**	**NHL**	20	2	1	3	4	....	....	....	....	....
	Winnipeg	**NHL**	13	2	8	10	8	....	....	....	....	....
1995-96	**Winnipeg**	**NHL**	51	27	22	49	65	6	1	2	3	6
	NHL Totals		802	294	394	688	747	46	16	15	31	41

Traded to **Toronto** by **Chicago** with Al Secord for Rick Vaive, Steve Thomas and Bob McGill, September 3, 1987. Traded to **Winnipeg** by **Toronto** with Mark Osborne for Dave Ellett and Paul Fenton, November 10, 1990. Traded to **NY Rangers** by **Winnipeg** for Kris King and Tie Domi, December 28, 1992. Traded to **Winnipeg** by **NY Rangers** for Winnipeg's fifth round choice (Alexei Vasiliev) in 1995 Entry Draft, April 7, 1995. Signed as a free agent by **Los Angeles**, July 8, 1996.

OLIVER, DAVID EDM.

Right wing. Shoots right. 6', 190 lbs. Born, Sechelt, B.C., April 17, 1971.
(Edmonton's 7th choice, 144th overall, in 1991 Entry Draft).

			Regular Season					Playoffs				
Season	Club	Lea	GP	G	A	TP	PIM	GP	G	A	TP	PIM
1990-91	U. of Michigan	CCHA	27	13	11	24	34	....	....	....	....	....
1991-92	U. of Michigan	CCHA	44	31	27	58	32	....	....	....	....	....
1992-93a	U. of Michigan	CCHA	40	35	20	55	18	....	....	....	....	....
1993-94bc	U. of Michigan	CCHA	41	28	40	68	16	....	....	....	....	....
1994-95	Cape Breton	AHL	32	11	18	29	8	....	....	....	....	....
	Edmonton	**NHL**	44	16	14	30	20	....	....	....	....	....
1995-96	**Edmonton**	**NHL**	80	20	19	39	34	....	....	....	....	....
	NHL Totals		124	36	33	69	54	....	....	....	....	....

a CCHA Second All-Star Team (1993)
b CCHA First All-Star Team (1994)
c NCAA West First All-American Team (1994)

OLIWA, KRZYSZTOF (oh-LEE-vuh, KHRIH-stahf) N.J.

Left wing. Shoots left. 6'5", 235 lbs. Born, Tychy, Poland, April 12, 1973.
(New Jersey's 4th choice, 65th overall, in 1993 Entry Draft).

			Regular Season					Playoffs				
Season	Club	Lea	GP	G	A	TP	PIM	GP	G	A	TP	PIM
1991-92	GKS Tychy	Poland	10	3	7	10	6	....	....	....	....	....
1992-93	Welland	Jr.B	30	13	21	34	127	....	....	....	....	....
1993-94	Albany	AHL	33	2	4	6	151	....	....	....	....	....
	Raleigh	ECHL	15	0	2	2	65	9	0	0	0	35
1994-95	Albany	AHL	20	1	1	2	77	....	....	....	....	....
	Saint John	AHL	14	1	4	5	79	....	....	....	....	....
	Raleigh	ECHL	5	0	2	2	32	....	....	....	....	....
	Detroit	IHL	4	0	1	1	24	....	....	....	....	....
1995-96	Albany	AHL	51	5	11	16	217	....	....	....	....	....
	Raleigh	ECHL	9	1	0	1	53	....	....	....	....	....

OLSON, BOYD MTL.

Center. Shoots left. 6'1", 170 lbs. Born, Edmonton, Alta., April 4, 1976.
(Montreal's 6th choice, 138th overall, in 1995 Entry Draft).

			Regular Season					Playoffs				
Season	Club	Lea	GP	G	A	TP	PIM	GP	G	A	TP	PIM
1993-94	Tri-City	WHL	2	0	1	1	0	....	....	....	....	....
1994-95	Tri-City	WHL	69	16	16	32	87	17	6	2	8	22
1995-96	Tri-City	WHL	62	13	12	25	105	11	1	4	5	16
	Fredericton	AHL	....	....	....	....	....	2	1	0	1	0

OLSSON, CHRISTER (OOL-suhn) ST.L.

Defense. Shoots left. 5'11", 190 lbs. Born, Arboga, Sweden, July 24, 1970.
(St. Louis' 10th choice, 275th overall, in 1993 Entry Draft).

			Regular Season					Playoffs				
Season	Club	Lea	GP	G	A	TP	PIM	GP	G	A	TP	PIM
1991-92	Mora	Swe. 2	36	6	10	16	38	....	....	....	....	....
1992-93	Brynas	Swe.	22	4	4	8	18	....	....	....	....	....
1993-94	Brynas	Swe.	38	7	3	10	50	7	0	3	3	6
1994-95	Brynas	Swe.	39	6	5	11	18	14	1	3	4	8
1995-96	**St. Louis**	**NHL**	26	2	8	10	14	3	0	0	0	0
	Worcester	AHL	39	7	7	14	22	....	....	....	....	....
	NHL Totals		26	2	8	10	14	3	0	0	0	0

O'NEILL, JEFF HFD.

Center. Shoots right. 6'1", 190 lbs. Born, Richmond Hill, Ont., February 23, 1976.
(Hartford's 1st choice, 5th overall, in 1994 Entry Draft).

			Regular Season					Playoffs				
Season	Club	Lea	GP	G	A	TP	PIM	GP	G	A	TP	PIM
1992-93	Guelph	OHL	65	32	47	79	88	5	2	2	4	6
1993-94	Guelph	OHL	66	45	81	126	95	9	2	11	13	31
1994-95a	Guelph	OHL	57	43	81	124	56	14	8	18	26	34
1995-96	**Hartford**	**NHL**	65	8	19	27	40	....	....	....	....	....
	NHL Totals		65	8	19	27	40	....	....	....	....	....

a OHL First All-Star Team (1995)

ORSZAGH, VLADIMIR NYI

Right wing. Shoots left. 5'11", 173 lbs. Born, Banska Bystrica, Czech., May 24, 1977.
(NY Islanders' 4th choice, 106th overall, in 1995 Entry Draft).

			Regular Season					Playoffs				
Season	Club	Lea	GP	G	A	TP	PIM	GP	G	A	TP	PIM
1994-95	B. Bystrica	Slov. 2	38	18	12	30	....	....	....	....	....	....
1995-96	B. Bystrica	Slovak	31	9	5	14	22	....	....	....	....	....

OSADCHY, ALEXANDER (oh-SAHD-chee) S.J.

Defense. Shoots right. 5'11", 190 lbs. Born, Kharkov, USSR, July 19, 1975.
(San Jose's 5th choice, 80th overall, in 1993 Entry Draft).

			Regular Season					Playoffs				
Season	Club	Lea	GP	G	A	TP	PIM	GP	G	A	TP	PIM
1992-93	CSKA	CIS	37	0	1	1	60	....	....	....	....	....
1993-94	CSKA	CIS	46	5	2	7	33	3	0	0	0	0
	Russian Pen's	IHL	11	0	5	5	24	....	....	....	....	....
1994-95	CSKA	CIS	52	8	4	12	100	2	0	0	0	0
1995-96	Wichita	CHL	20	4	18	22	73	....	....	....	....	....
	Mobile	ECHL	12	0	4	4	27	....	....	....	....	....
	Kansas City	IHL	17	0	4	4	39	....	....	....	....	....

OSBORNE, MARK (AWS-born)

Left wing. Shoots left. 6'2", 205 lbs. Born, Toronto, Ont., August 13, 1961.
(Detroit's 2nd choice, 46th overall, in 1980 Entry Draft).

			Regular Season					Playoffs				
Season	Club	Lea	GP	G	A	TP	PIM	GP	G	A	TP	PIM
1979-80	Niagara Falls	OHA	52	10	33	43	104	10	2	1	3	23
1980-81	Niagara Falls	OHA	54	39	41	80	140	12	11	10	21	20
	Adirondack	AHL	....	....	....	....	....	13	2	3	5	2
1981-82	**Detroit**	**NHL**	80	26	41	67	61	....	....	....	....	....
1982-83	**Detroit**	**NHL**	80	19	24	43	83	....	....	....	....	....
1983-84	**NY Rangers**	**NHL**	73	23	28	51	88	5	0	1	1	7
1984-85	**NY Rangers**	**NHL**	23	4	4	8	33	3	0	0	0	4
1985-86	**NY Rangers**	**NHL**	62	16	24	40	80	15	2	3	5	26
1986-87	**NY Rangers**	**NHL**	58	17	15	32	101	....	....	....	....	....
	Toronto	**NHL**	16	5	10	15	12	9	1	3	4	6
1987-88	**Toronto**	**NHL**	79	23	37	60	102	6	1	3	4	16
1988-89	**Toronto**	**NHL**	75	16	30	46	112	....	....	....	....	....
1989-90	**Toronto**	**NHL**	78	23	50	73	91	5	2	3	5	12
1990-91	**Toronto**	**NHL**	18	3	3	6	4	....	....	....	....	....
	Winnipeg	**NHL**	37	8	8	16	59	....	....	....	....	....
1991-92	**Winnipeg**	**NHL**	43	4	12	16	65	....	....	....	....	....
	Toronto	**NHL**	11	3	1	4	8	....	....	....	....	....
1992-93	**Toronto**	**NHL**	76	12	14	26	89	19	1	1	2	16
1993-94	**Toronto**	**NHL**	73	9	15	24	145	18	4	2	6	52
1994-95	**NY Rangers**	**NHL**	37	1	3	4	19	7	1	0	1	2
1995-96	Cleveland	IHL	70	31	38	69	131	3	1	2	3	2
	NHL Totals		919	212	319	531	1152	87	12	16	28	141

Traded to **NY Rangers** by **Detroit** with Willie Huber and Mike Blaisdell for Ron Duguay, Eddie Mio and Eddie Johnstone, June 13, 1983. Traded to **Toronto** by **NY Rangers** for Jeff Jackson and Toronto's third round choice (Rod Zamuner) in 1989 Entry Draft, March 5, 1987. Traded to **Winnipeg** by **Toronto** with Ed Olczyk for Dave Ellett and Paul Fenton, November 10, 1990. Traded to **Toronto** by **Winnipeg** for Lucien Deblois, March 10, 1992. Signed as a free agent by **NY Rangers**, January 20, 1995.

O'SULLIVAN, CHRIS CGY.

Defense. Shoots left. 6'2", 185 lbs. Born, Dorchester, MA, May 15, 1974.
(Calgary's 2nd choice, 30th overall, in 1992 Entry Draft).

			Regular Season					Playoffs				
Season	Club	Lea	GP	G	A	TP	PIM	GP	G	A	TP	PIM
1992-93	Boston U.	H.E.	5	0	2	2	4	....	....	....	....	....
1993-94	Boston U.	H.E.	32	5	18	23	25	....	....	....	....	....
1994-95abcd	Boston U.	H.E.	40	23	33	56	48	....	....	....	....	....
1995-96	Boston U.	H.E.	37	12	35	47	50	....	....	....	....	....

a Hockey East First All-Star Team (1995)
b NCAA East Second All-American Team (1995)
c NCAA Final Four All-Tournament Team (1995)
d NCAA Final Four Tournament Most Valuable Player (1995)

OTTO, JOEL PHI.

Center. Shoots right. 6'4", 220 lbs. Born, Elk River, MN, October 29, 1961.

			Regular Season					Playoffs				
Season	Club	Lea	GP	G	A	TP	PIM	GP	G	A	TP	PIM
1980-81	Bemidji State	NCAA	23	5	11	16	10	....	....	....	....	....
1981-82	Bemidji State	NCAA	31	19	33	52	24	....	....	....	....	....
1982-83	Bemidji State	NCAA	37	33	28	61	68	....	....	....	....	....
1983-84	Bemidji State	NCAA	31	32	43	75	32	....	....	....	....	....
1984-85	**Calgary**	**NHL**	17	4	8	12	30	3	2	1	3	10
	Moncton	AHL	56	27	36	63	89	....	....	....	....	....
1985-86	**Calgary**	**NHL**	79	25	34	59	188	22	5	10	15	80
1986-87	**Calgary**	**NHL**	68	19	31	50	185	2	0	2	2	6
1987-88	**Calgary**	**NHL**	62	13	39	52	194	9	3	2	5	26
1988-89	**Calgary**	**NHL**	72	23	30	53	213	22	6	13	19	46 ♦
1989-90	**Calgary**	**NHL**	75	13	20	33	116	6	2	2	4	2
1990-91	**Calgary**	**NHL**	76	19	20	39	183	7	1	2	3	8
1991-92	**Calgary**	**NHL**	78	13	21	34	161	....	....	....	....	....
1992-93	**Calgary**	**NHL**	75	19	33	52	150	6	4	2	6	4
1993-94	**Calgary**	**NHL**	81	11	12	23	92	3	0	1	1	4
1994-95	**Calgary**	**NHL**	47	8	13	21	130	7	0	3	3	2
1995-96	**Philadelphia**	**NHL**	67	12	29	41	115	12	3	4	7	11
	NHL Totals		797	179	290	469	1757	99	26	42	68	199

Signed as a free agent by **Calgary**, September 11, 1984. Signed as a free agent by **Philadelphia**, July 31, 1995.

OZOLINSH, SANDIS (OH-zoh-LIHNCH, SAN-dihz) COL.

Defense. Shoots left. 6'1", 195 lbs. Born, Riga, Latvia, August 3, 1972.
(San Jose's 3rd choice, 30th overall, in 1991 Entry Draft).

			Regular Season					Playoffs				
Season	Club	Lea	GP	G	A	TP	PIM	GP	G	A	TP	PIM
1990-91	Riga	USSR	44	0	3	3	51	....	....	....	....	....
1991-92	Riga	CIS	30	6	0	6	42	....	....	....	....	....
	Kansas City	IHL	34	6	9	15	20	15	2	5	7	22
1992-93	**San Jose**	**NHL**	37	7	16	23	40	....	....	....	....	....
1993-94	**San Jose**	**NHL**	81	26	38	64	24	14	0	10	10	8
1994-95	**San Jose**	**NHL**	48	9	16	25	30	11	3	2	5	6
1995-96	San Francisco	IHL	2	1	0	1	0	....	....	....	....	....
	San Jose	**NHL**	7	1	3	4	4	....	....	....	....	....
	Colorado	**NHL**	66	13	37	50	50	22	5	14	19	16 ♦
	NHL Totals		239	56	110	166	148	47	8	26	34	30

Played in NHL All-Star Game (1994)

Traded to **Colorado** by **San Jose** for Owen Nolan, October 26, 1995.

PADEN, KEVIN — EDM.

Center/Left wing. Shoots left. 6'3", 190 lbs. Born, Woodhaven, MI, February 12, 1975.
(Edmonton's 4th choice, 59th overall, in 1993 Entry Draft).

			Regular Season					Playoffs				
Season	Club	Lea	GP	G	A	TP	PIM	GP	G	A	TP	PIM
1992-93	Detroit	OHL	54	14	9	23	41	15	1	1	2	2
1993-94	Detroit	OHL	38	10	19	29	54	....	....	....	....	....
	Windsor	OHL	24	8	11	19	30	4	0	1	1	4
1994-95	Windsor	OHL	57	15	24	39	50	....	....	....	....	....
1995-96	Cape Breton	AHL	1	1	0	1	0	....	....	....	....	....
	Tallahassee	ECHL	23	3	10	13	49	....	....	....	....	....
	Huntington	ECHL	32	4	5	9	52	....	....	....	....	....

PAEK, JIM — (PAK)

Defense. Shoots left. 6'1", 195 lbs. Born, Seoul, South Korea, April 7, 1967.
(Pittsburgh's 9th choice, 170th overall, in 1985 Entry Draft).

			Regular Season					Playoffs				
Season	Club	Lea	GP	G	A	TP	PIM	GP	G	A	TP	PIM
1984-85	Oshawa	OHL	54	2	13	15	57	5	1	0	1	9
1985-86	Oshawa	OHL	64	5	21	26	122	6	0	1	1	9
1986-87	Oshawa	OHL	57	5	17	22	75	26	1	14	15	43
1987-88	Muskegon	IHL	82	7	52	59	141	6	0	0	0	29
1988-89	Muskegon	IHL	80	3	54	57	96	14	1	10	11	24
1989-90	Muskegon	IHL	81	9	41	50	115	15	1	10	11	41
1990-91	Cdn. National	....	48	2	12	14	24	....	....	....	....	....
	Pittsburgh	**NHL**	**3**	**0**	**0**	**0**	**9**	**8**	**1**	**0**	**1**	**2 ♦**
1991-92	**Pittsburgh**	**NHL**	**49**	**1**	**7**	**8**	**36**	**19**	**0**	**4**	**4**	**6 ♦**
1992-93	**Pittsburgh**	**NHL**	**77**	**3**	**15**	**18**	**64**	....	....	....	....	....
1993-94	**Pittsburgh**	**NHL**	**41**	**0**	**4**	**4**	**8**	....	....	....	....	....
	Los Angeles	**NHL**	**18**	**1**	**1**	**2**	**10**	....	....	....	....	....
1994-95	**Ottawa**	**NHL**	**29**	**0**	**2**	**2**	**28**	....	....	....	....	....
1995-96	Houston	IHL	25	2	5	7	20	....	....	....	....	....
	Minnesota	IHL	42	1	11	12	54	....	....	....	....	....
	NHL Totals		**217**	**5**	**29**	**34**	**155**	**27**	**1**	**4**	**5**	**8**

Traded to **Los Angeles** by **Pittsburgh** with Marty McSorley for Tomas Sandstrom and Shawn McEachern, February 16, 1994. Traded to **Ottawa** by **Los Angeles** for Ottawa's seventh round choice (Benoit Larose) in 1995 Entry Draft, June 26, 1994.

PALFFY, ZIGMUND — (PAHL-fee) NYI

Left wing. Shoots left. 5'10", 183 lbs. Born, Skalica, Czech., May 5, 1972.
(NY Islanders' 2nd choice, 26th overall, in 1991 Entry Draft).

			Regular Season					Playoffs				
Season	Club	Lea	GP	G	A	TP	PIM	GP	G	A	TP	PIM
1990-91	Nitra	Czech.	50	34	16	50	18	....	....	....	....	....
1991-92	Dukla Trencin	Czech.	45	41	33	74	36	....	....	....	....	....
1992-93	Dukla Trencin	Czech.	43	38	41	79	....	....	....	....	....	....
1993-94	**NY Islanders**	**NHL**	**5**	**0**	**0**	**0**	**0**	....	....	....	....	....
	Salt Lake	IHL	57	25	32	57	83	....	....	....	....	....
1994-95	Denver	IHL	33	20	23	43	40	....	....	....	....	....
	NY Islanders	**NHL**	**33**	**10**	**7**	**17**	**6**	....	....	....	....	....
1995-96	**NY Islanders**	**NHL**	**81**	**43**	**44**	**87**	**56**	....	....	....	....	....
	NHL Totals		**119**	**53**	**51**	**104**	**62**	....	....	....	....	....

PANDOLFO, JAY — N.J.

Left wing. Shoots left. 6'1", 195 lbs. Born, Winchester, MA, December 27, 1974.
(New Jersey's 2nd choice, 32nd overall, in 1993 Entry Draft).

			Regular Season					Playoffs				
Season	Club	Lea	GP	G	A	TP	PIM	GP	G	A	TP	PIM
1992-93	Boston U.	H.E.	37	16	22	38	16	....	....	....	....	....
1993-94	Boston U.	H.E.	37	17	25	42	27	....	....	....	....	....
1994-95	Boston U.	H.E.	20	7	13	20	6	....	....	....	....	....
1995-96ab	Boston U.	H.E.	39	*38	29	67	6	....	....	....	....	....
	Albany	AHL	5	3	1	4	0	3	0	0	0	0

a Hockey East All-Star Team (1996)
b NCAA East First All-American Team (1996)

PANKEWICZ, GREG

Right wing. Shoots right. 6', 185 lbs. Born, Drayton Valley, Alta., October 6, 1970.

			Regular Season					Playoffs				
Season	Club	Lea	GP	G	A	TP	PIM	GP	G	A	TP	PIM
1989-90	Regina	WHL	63	14	24	38	136	10	1	3	4	19
1990-91	Regina	WHL	72	39	41	80	134	8	4	7	11	12
1991-92	Knoxville	ECHL	59	41	39	80	214	....	....	....	....	....
1992-93	New Haven	AHL	62	23	20	43	163	....	....	....	....	....
1993-94	**Ottawa**	**NHL**	**3**	**0**	**0**	**0**	**2**	....	....	....	....	....
	P.E.I.	AHL	69	33	29	62	241	....	....	....	....	....
1994-95	P.E.I.	AHL	75	37	30	67	161	6	1	1	2	24
1995-96	Portland	AHL	28	9	12	21	99	....	....	....	....	....
	Chicago	IHL	45	9	16	25	164	5	4	0	4	8
	NHL Totals		**3**	**0**	**0**	**0**	**2**	....	....	....	....	....

Signed as a free agent by **Ottawa**, May 27, 1993. Signed as a free agent by **Washington**, August 21, 1995.

PANTELEEV, GRIGORI — (pan-teh-LAY-ehv)

Left wing. Shoots left. 5'9", 190 lbs. Born, Gastello, USSR, November 13, 1972.
(Boston's 5th choice, 136th overall, in 1992 Entry Draft).

			Regular Season					Playoffs				
Season	Club	Lea	GP	G	A	TP	PIM	GP	G	A	TP	PIM
1990-91	Riga	USSR	23	4	1	5	4	....	....	....	....	....
1991-92	Riga	CIS	26	4	8	12	4	....	....	....	....	....
1992-93	**Boston**	**NHL**	**39**	**8**	**6**	**14**	**12**	....	....	....	....	....
	Providence	AHL	39	17	30	47	22	3	0	0	0	10
1993-94	**Boston**	**NHL**	**10**	**0**	**0**	**0**	**0**	....	....	....	....	....
	Providence	AHL	55	24	26	50	20	....	....	....	....	....
1994-95	Providence	AHL	70	20	23	43	36	13	8	11	19	6
	Boston	**NHL**	**1**	**0**	**0**	**0**	**0**	....	....	....	....	....
1995-96	**NY Islanders**	**NHL**	**4**	**0**	**0**	**0**	**0**	....	....	....	....	....
	NHL Totals		**54**	**8**	**6**	**14**	**12**	....	....	....	....	....

Signed as a free agent by **NY Islanders**, September 20, 1995.

PAQUETTE, CHARLES — (pa-KEHT) BOS.

Defense. Shoots left. 6'1", 193 lbs. Born, Lachute, Que., June 17, 1975.
(Boston's 3rd choice, 88th overall, in 1993 Entry Draft).

			Regular Season					Playoffs				
Season	Club	Lea	GP	G	A	TP	PIM	GP	G	A	TP	PIM
1991-92	Trois-Rivieres	QMJHL	60	1	7	8	101	6	0	0	0	2
1992-93	Sherbrooke	QMJHL	54	2	5	7	104	15	0	0	0	33
1993-94	Sherbrooke	QMJHL	63	5	14	19	165	8	0	2	2	15
1994-95a	Sherbrooke	QMJHL	53	15	26	41	186	5	1	1	2	18
1995-96	Providence	AHL	11	0	1	1	8	4	0	1	1	4
	Charlotte	ECHL	45	4	5	9	114	3	0	1	1	6

a QMJHL First All-Star Team (1995)

PARK, RICHARD — PIT.

Center. Shoots right. 5'11", 190 lbs. Born, Seoul, S. Korea, May 27, 1976.
(Pittsburgh's 2nd choice, 50th overall, in 1994 Entry Draft).

			Regular Season					Playoffs				
Season	Club	Lea	GP	G	A	TP	PIM	GP	G	A	TP	PIM
1992-93	Belleville	OHL	66	23	38	61	38	5	0	0	0	14
1993-94	Belleville	OHL	59	27	49	76	70	12	3	5	8	18
1994-95	Belleville	OHL	45	28	51	79	35	16	9	18	27	12
	Pittsburgh	**NHL**	**1**	**0**	**1**	**1**	**2**	**3**	**0**	**0**	**0**	**2**
1995-96	**Pittsburgh**	**NHL**	**56**	**4**	**6**	**10**	**36**	**1**	**0**	**0**	**0**	**0**
	Belleville	OHL	6	7	6	13	2	14	18	12	30	10
	NHL Totals		**57**	**4**	**7**	**11**	**38**	**4**	**0**	**0**	**0**	**2**

PARKER, SCOTT — N.J.

Right wing. Shoots right. 6'4", 220 lbs. Born, Hanford, CA, January 29, 1978.
(New Jersey's 6th choice, 63rd overall, in 1996 Entry Draft).

			Regular Season					Playoffs				
Season	Club	Lea	GP	G	A	TP	PIM	GP	G	A	TP	PIM
1995-96	Kelowna	WHL	64	3	4	7	159	6	0	0	0	12

PARRISH, MARK — COL.

Left wing. Shoots right. 6', 182 lbs. Born, Edina, MN, February 2, 1977.
(Colorado's 3rd choice, 79th overall, in 1996 Entry Draft).

			Regular Season					Playoffs				
Season	Club	Lea	GP	G	A	TP	PIM	GP	G	A	TP	PIM
1994-95	Jefferson	HS	27	40	20	60	42	....	....	....	....	....
1995-96	St. Cloud	WCHA	39	15	13	28	30	....	....	....	....	....

PATRICK, JAMES — CGY.

Defense. Shoots right. 6'2", 198 lbs. Born, Winnipeg, Man., June 14, 1963.
(NY Rangers' 1st choice, 9th overall, in 1981 Entry Draft).

			Regular Season					Playoffs				
Season	Club	Lea	GP	G	A	TP	PIM	GP	G	A	TP	PIM
1981-82ab	North Dakota	WCHA	42	5	24	29	26	....	....	....	....	....
1982-83cd	North Dakota	WCHA	36	12	36	48	29	....	....	....	....	....
1983-84	Cdn. National	....	63	7	24	31	52	....	....	....	....	....
	Cdn. Olympic	....	7	0	3	3	4	....	....	....	....	....
	NY Rangers	**NHL**	**12**	**1**	**7**	**8**	**2**	**5**	**0**	**3**	**3**	**2**
1984-85	**NY Rangers**	**NHL**	**75**	**8**	**28**	**36**	**71**	**3**	**0**	**0**	**0**	**4**
1985-86	**NY Rangers**	**NHL**	**75**	**14**	**29**	**43**	**88**	**16**	**1**	**5**	**6**	**34**
1986-87	**NY Rangers**	**NHL**	**78**	**10**	**45**	**55**	**62**	**6**	**1**	**2**	**3**	**2**
1987-88	**NY Rangers**	**NHL**	**70**	**17**	**45**	**62**	**52**	....	....	....	....	....
1988-89	**NY Rangers**	**NHL**	**68**	**11**	**36**	**47**	**41**	**4**	**0**	**1**	**1**	**2**
1989-90	**NY Rangers**	**NHL**	**73**	**14**	**43**	**57**	**50**	**10**	**3**	**8**	**11**	**0**
1990-91	**NY Rangers**	**NHL**	**74**	**10**	**49**	**59**	**58**	**6**	**0**	**0**	**0**	**6**
1991-92	**NY Rangers**	**NHL**	**80**	**14**	**57**	**71**	**54**	**13**	**0**	**7**	**7**	**12**
1992-93	**NY Rangers**	**NHL**	**60**	**5**	**21**	**26**	**61**	....	....	....	....	....
1993-94	**NY Rangers**	**NHL**	**6**	**0**	**3**	**3**	**2**	....	....	....	....	....
	Hartford	**NHL**	**47**	**8**	**20**	**28**	**32**	....	....	....	....	....
	Calgary	**NHL**	**15**	**2**	**2**	**4**	**6**	**7**	**0**	**1**	**1**	**6**
1994-95	**Calgary**	**NHL**	**43**	**0**	**10**	**10**	**14**	**5**	**0**	**1**	**1**	**0**
1995-96	**Calgary**	**NHL**	**80**	**3**	**32**	**35**	**30**	**4**	**0**	**0**	**0**	**2**
	NHL Totals		**856**	**117**	**427**	**544**	**623**	**79**	**5**	**28**	**33**	**70**

a WCHA Second All-Star Team (1982)
b NCAA All-Tournament Team (1982)
c WCHA First All-Star Team (1983)
d NCAA West All American (1983)

Traded to **Hartford** by **NY Rangers** with Darren Turcotte for Steve Larmer, Nick Kypreos, Barry Richter and Hartford's sixth round choice (Yuri Litvinov) in 1994 Entry Draft, November 2, 1993. Traded to **Calgary** by **Hartford** with Zarley Zalapski and Michael Nylander for Gary Suter, Paul Ranheim and Ted Drury, March 10, 1994.

PATTERSON, ED — PIT.

Right wing. Shoots right. 6'2", 213 lbs. Born, Delta, B.C., November 14, 1972.
(Pittsburgh's 7th choice, 148th overall, in 1991 Entry Draft).

			Regular Season					Playoffs				
Season	Club	Lea	GP	G	A	TP	PIM	GP	G	A	TP	PIM
1990-91	Swift Current	WHL	7	2	7	9	0	....	....	....	....	....
	Kamloops	WHL	55	14	33	47	134	5	0	0	0	7
1991-92	Kamloops	WHL	38	19	25	44	120	1	0	0	0	0
1992-93	Cleveland	IHL	63	4	16	20	131	3	1	1	2	2
1993-94	**Pittsburgh**	**NHL**	**27**	**3**	**1**	**4**	**10**	....	....	....	....	....
	Cleveland	IHL	55	21	32	53	73	....	....	....	....	....
1994-95	Cleveland	IHL	58	13	17	30	93	4	1	2	3	6
1995-96	**Pittsburgh**	**NHL**	**35**	**0**	**2**	**2**	**38**	....	....	....	....	....
	NHL Totals		**62**	**3**	**3**	**6**	**48**	....	....	....	....	....

PATTISON, ROB — N.J.

Right wing. Shoots left. 6', 195 lbs. Born, Sherborn, MA, September 18, 1971.

			Regular Season					Playoffs				
Season	Club	Lea	GP	G	A	TP	PIM	GP	G	A	TP	PIM
1990-91	Vermont	ECAC	24	7	3	10	14	....	....	....	....	....
1991-92	Vermont	ECAC	25	6	12	18	8	....	....	....	....	....
1992-93					DID NOT PLAY							
1993-94	Vermont	ECAC	32	8	19	27	14	....	....	....	....	....
1994-95	Vermont	ECAC	8	8	6	14	8	....	....	....	....	....
1995-96	Raleigh	ECHL	67	14	23	37	122	4	1	2	3	0
	Albany	AHL	5	4	3	7	0	2	0	0	0	0

Signed as a free agent by **New Jersey**, October 1, 1995.

PAUL, JEFF — CHI.

Defense. Shoots right. 6'3", 203 lbs. Born, London, Ont., March 1, 1978.
(Chicago's 2nd choice, 42nd overall, in 1996 Entry Draft).

			Regular Season					Playoffs				
Season	Club	Lea	GP	G	A	TP	PIM	GP	G	A	TP	PIM
1994-95	Niagara Falls	OHL	57	3	10	13	64	6	0	2	2	0
1995-96	Niagara Falls	OHL	47	1	7	8	81	10	0	4	4	37

PAYETTE, ANDRE — PHI.

Center. Shoots left. 6'2", 205 lbs. Born, Cornwall, Ont., July 29, 1976.
(Philadelphia's 9th choice, 244th overall, in 1994 Entry Draft).

			Regular Season					Playoffs				
Season	Club	Lea	GP	G	A	TP	PIM	GP	G	A	TP	PIM
1993-94	S.S. Marie	OHL	40	2	3	5	98	....	....	....	....	....
1994-95	S.S. Marie	OHL	50	15	15	30	177	....	....	....	....	....
1995-96	S.S. Marie	OHL	57	20	19	39	257	4	0	0	0	5

PAYNE, DAVIS — BOS.

Left wing. Shoots left. 6'2", 205 lbs. Born, Port Alberni, B.C., September 24, 1970.
(Edmonton's 6th choice, 140th overall, in 1989 Entry Draft).

			Regular Season					Playoffs				
Season	Club	Lea	GP	G	A	TP	PIM	GP	G	A	TP	PIM
1988-89	Michigan Tech	WCHA	35	5	3	8	39	....	....	....	....	....
1989-90	Michigan Tech	WCHA	30	11	10	21	81	....	....	....	....	....
1990-91	Michigan Tech	WCHA	41	15	20	35	82	....	....	....	....	....
1991-92	Michigan Tech	WCHA	24	6	1	7	71	....	....	....	....	....
1992-93	Greensboro	ECHL	57	15	20	35	178	1	0	0	0	4
1993-94	Greensboro	ECHL	36	17	17	34	139	8	2	1	3	27
1994-95	Greensboro	ECHL	62	25	36	61	195	17	7	10	17	38
	Providence	AHL	2	1	0	1	0	....	....	....	....	....
1995-96	**Boston**	**NHL**	**7**	**0**	**0**	**0**	**7**	....	....	....	....	....
	Providence	AHL	51	17	22	39	72	4	1	4	5	2
	NHL Totals		**7**	**0**	**0**	**0**	**7**	....	....	....	....	....

Signed as a free agent by **Boston**, September 6, 1995.

PEAKE, PAT — WSH.

Center. Shoots right. 6'1", 195 lbs. Born, Rochester, MI, May 28, 1973.
(Washington's 1st choice, 14th overall, in 1991 Entry Draft).

			Regular Season					Playoffs				
Season	Club	Lea	GP	G	A	TP	PIM	GP	G	A	TP	PIM
1990-91	Detroit	OHL	63	39	51	90	54	....	....	....	....	....
1991-92	Detroit	OHL	53	41	52	93	44	7	8	9	17	10
	Baltimore	AHL	3	1	0	1	4	....	....	....	....	....
1992-93abc	Detroit	OHL	46	58	78	136	64	2	1	3	4	2
1993-94	**Washington**	**NHL**	**49**	**11**	**18**	**29**	**39**	**8**	**0**	**1**	**1**	**8**
	Portland	AHL	4	0	5	5	2	....	....	....	....	....
1994-95	**Washington**	**NHL**	**18**	**0**	**4**	**4**	**12**	....	....	....	....	....
	Portland	AHL	5	1	3	4	2	4	0	3	3	6
1995-96	**Washington**	**NHL**	**62**	**17**	**19**	**36**	**46**	**5**	**2**	**1**	**3**	**12**
	NHL Totals		**129**	**28**	**41**	**69**	**97**	**13**	**2**	**2**	**4**	**20**

a Canadian Major Junior Player of the Year (1993)
b Canadian Major Junior First All-Star Team (1993)
c OHL First All-Star Team (1993)

PEARSON, ROB — ST.L.

Right wing. Shoots right. 6'3", 198 lbs. Born, Oshawa, Ont., March 8, 1971.
(Toronto's 2nd choice, 12th overall, in 1989 Entry Draft).

			Regular Season					Playoffs				
Season	Club	Lea	GP	G	A	TP	PIM	GP	G	A	TP	PIM
1988-89	Belleville	OHL	26	8	12	20	51	....	....	....	....	....
1989-90	Belleville	OHL	58	48	40	88	174	11	5	5	10	26
1990-91	Belleville	OHL	10	6	3	9	27	....	....	....	....	....
a	Oshawa	OHL	41	57	52	109	76	16	16	17	33	39
	Newmarket	AHL	3	0	0	0	29	....	....	....	....	....
1991-92	**Toronto**	**NHL**	**47**	**14**	**10**	**24**	**58**	....	....	....	....	....
	St. John's	AHL	27	15	14	29	107	13	5	4	9	40
1992-93	**Toronto**	**NHL**	**78**	**23**	**14**	**37**	**211**	**14**	**2**	**2**	**4**	**31**
1993-94	**Toronto**	**NHL**	**67**	**12**	**18**	**30**	**189**	**14**	**1**	**0**	**1**	**32**
1994-95	**Washington**	**NHL**	**32**	**0**	**6**	**6**	**96**	**3**	**1**	**0**	**1**	**17**
1995-96	Portland	AHL	44	18	24	42	143	....	....	....	....	....
	St. Louis	**NHL**	**27**	**6**	**4**	**10**	**54**	**2**	**0**	**0**	**0**	**14**
	NHL Totals		**251**	**55**	**52**	**107**	**608**	**33**	**4**	**2**	**6**	**94**

a OHL First All-Star Team (1991)

Traded to **Washington** by **Toronto** with Philadelphia's first round choice (previously acquired by Toronto — Washington selected Nolan Baumgartner) in 1994 Entry Draft for Mike Ridley and St. Louis' first round choice (previously acquired by Washington — Toronto selected Eric Fichaud) in 1994 Entry Draft, June 28, 1994. Traded to **St. Louis** by **Washington** for Denis Chasse, January 29, 1996.

PEARSON, SCOTT — TOR.

Left wing. Shoots left. 6'1", 205 lbs. Born, Cornwall, Ont., December 19, 1969.
(Toronto's 1st choice, 6th overall, in 1988 Entry Draft).

			Regular Season					Playoffs				
Season	Club	Lea	GP	G	A	TP	PIM	GP	G	A	TP	PIM
1986-87	Kingston	OHL	62	30	24	54	101	9	3	3	6	42
1987-88	Kingston	OHL	46	26	32	58	117	....	....	....	....	....
1988-89	**Toronto**	**NHL**	**9**	**0**	**1**	**1**	**2**	....	....	....	....	....
	Kingston	OHL	13	9	8	17	34	....	....	....	....	....
	Niagara Falls	OHL	32	26	34	60	90	17	14	10	24	53
1989-90	**Toronto**	**NHL**	**41**	**5**	**10**	**15**	**90**	**2**	**2**	**0**	**2**	**10**
	Newmarket	AHL	18	12	11	23	64	....	....	....	....	....
1990-91	**Toronto**	**NHL**	**12**	**0**	**0**	**0**	**20**	....	....	....	....	....
	Quebec	**NHL**	**35**	**11**	**4**	**15**	**86**	....	....	....	....	....
	Halifax	AHL	24	12	15	27	44	....	....	....	....	....
1991-92	**Quebec**	**NHL**	**10**	**1**	**2**	**3**	**14**	....	....	....	....	....
	Halifax	AHL	5	2	1	3	4	....	....	....	....	....
1992-93	**Quebec**	**NHL**	**41**	**13**	**1**	**14**	**95**	**3**	**0**	**0**	**0**	**0**
	Halifax	AHL	5	3	1	4	25	....	....	....	....	....
1993-94	**Edmonton**	**NHL**	**72**	**19**	**18**	**37**	**165**	....	....	....	....	....
1994-95	**Edmonton**	**NHL**	**28**	**1**	**4**	**5**	**54**	....	....	....	....	....
	Buffalo	**NHL**	**14**	**2**	**1**	**3**	**20**	**5**	**0**	**0**	**0**	**4**
1995-96	**Buffalo**	**NHL**	**27**	**4**	**0**	**4**	**67**	....	....	....	....	....
	Rochester	AHL	26	8	8	16	113	....	....	....	....	....
	NHL Totals		**289**	**56**	**41**	**97**	**613**	**10**	**2**	**0**	**2**	**14**

Traded to **Quebec** by **Toronto** with Toronto's second round choices in 1991 (later traded to Washington — Washington selected Eric Lavigne) and 1992 (Tuomas Gronman) Entry Drafts for Aaron Broten, Lucien Deblois and Michel Petit, November 17, 1990. Traded to **Edmonton** by **Quebec** for Martin Gelinas and Edmonton's sixth round choice (Nicholas Checco) in 1993 Entry Draft, June 20, 1993. Traded to **Buffalo** by **Edmonton** for Ken Sutton, April 7, 1995. Signed as a free agent by **Toronto**, July 24, 1996.

PECA, MIKE (PEH-kuh) — BUF.

Center. Shoots right. 5'11", 180 lbs. Born, Toronto, Ont., March 26, 1974.
(Vancouver's 2nd choice, 40th overall, in 1992 Entry Draft).

			Regular Season					Playoffs				
Season	Club	Lea	GP	G	A	TP	PIM	GP	G	A	TP	PIM
1990-91	Sudbury	OHL	62	14	27	41	24	5	1	0	1	7
1991-92	Sudbury	OHL	39	16	34	50	61	....	....	....	....	....
	Ottawa	OHL	27	8	17	25	32	11	6	10	16	6
1992-93	Ottawa	OHL	55	38	64	102	80	....	....	....	....	....
	Hamilton	AHL	9	6	3	9	11	....	....	....	....	....
1993-94	**Vancouver**	**NHL**	**4**	**0**	**0**	**0**	**2**	....	....	....	....	....
	Ottawa	OHL	55	50	63	113	101	17	7	22	29	30
1994-95	Syracuse	AHL	35	10	24	34	75	....	....	....	....	....
	Vancouver	**NHL**	**33**	**6**	**6**	**12**	**30**	**5**	**0**	**1**	**1**	**8**
1995-96	**Buffalo**	**NHL**	**68**	**11**	**20**	**31**	**67**	....	....	....	....	....
	NHL Totals		**105**	**17**	**26**	**43**	**99**	**5**	**0**	**1**	**1**	**8**

Traded to **Buffalo** by **Vancouver** with Mike Wilson and Vancouver's first round choice (Jay McKee) in 1995 Entry Draft for Alexander Mogilny and Buffalo's fifth round choice (Todd Norman) in 1995 Entry Draft, July 8, 1995.

PEDERSON, DENIS — N.J.

Center. Shoots right. 6'2", 190 lbs. Born, Prince Albert, Sask., September 10, 1975.
(New Jersey's 1st choice, 13th overall, in 1993 Entry Draft).

			Regular Season					Playoffs				
Season	Club	Lea	GP	G	A	TP	PIM	GP	G	A	TP	PIM
1991-92	Prince Albert	Midget	21	33	25	58	40	....	....	....	....	....
	Prince Albert	WHL	10	0	0	0	6	7	0	1	1	13
1992-93	Prince Albert	WHL	72	33	40	73	134	....	....	....	....	....
1993-94a	Prince Albert	WHL	71	53	45	98	157	....	....	....	....	....
1994-95	Prince Albert	WHL	63	30	38	68	122	15	11	14	25	14
	Albany	AHL	....	....	....	....	....	3	0	0	0	2
1995-96	**New Jersey**	**NHL**	**10**	**3**	**1**	**4**	**0**	....	....	....	....	....
	Albany	AHL	68	28	43	71	104	4	1	2	3	0
	NHL Totals		**10**	**3**	**1**	**4**	**0**	....	....	....	....	....

a WHL East Second All-Star Team (1994)

PEDERSON, TOM — S.J.

Defense. Shoots right. 5'9", 175 lbs. Born, Bloomington, MN, January 14, 1970.
(Minnesota's 12th choice, 217th overall, in 1989 Entry Draft).

			Regular Season					Playoffs				
Season	Club	Lea	GP	G	A	TP	PIM	GP	G	A	TP	PIM
1988-89	U. Minnesota	WCHA	36	4	20	24	40	....	....	....	....	....
1989-90	U. Minnesota	WCHA	43	8	30	38	58	....	....	....	....	....
1990-91	U. Minnesota	WCHA	36	12	20	32	46	....	....	....	....	....
1991-92	U.S. National	....	44	3	11	14	41	....	....	....	....	....
	Kansas City	IHL	20	6	9	15	16	13	1	6	7	14
1992-93	**San Jose**	**NHL**	**44**	**7**	**13**	**20**	**31**	....	....	....	....	....
	Kansas City	IHL	26	6	15	21	10	12	1	6	7	2
1993-94	**San Jose**	**NHL**	**74**	**6**	**19**	**25**	**31**	**14**	**1**	**6**	**7**	**2**
	Kansas City	IHL	7	3	1	4	0	....	....	....	....	....
1994-95	**San Jose**	**NHL**	**47**	**5**	**11**	**16**	**31**	**10**	**0**	**5**	**5**	**8**
1995-96	**San Jose**	**NHL**	**60**	**1**	**4**	**5**	**40**	....	....	....	....	....
	NHL Totals		**225**	**19**	**47**	**66**	**133**	**24**	**1**	**11**	**12**	**10**

Claimed by **San Jose** from **Minnesota** in Dispersal Draft, May 30, 1991.

PELLERIN, SCOTT (PEHL-ih-rihn) — ST.L.

Left wing. Shoots left. 5'11", 180 lbs. Born, Shediac, N.B., January 9, 1970.
(New Jersey's 4th choice, 47th overall, in 1989 Entry Draft).

			Regular Season					Playoffs				
Season	Club	Lea	GP	G	A	TP	PIM	GP	G	A	TP	PIM
1988-89	U. of Maine	H.E.	45	29	33	62	92	....	....	....	....	....
1989-90	U. of Maine	H.E.	42	22	34	56	68	....	....	....	....	....
1990-91	U. of Maine	H.E.	43	23	25	48	60	....	....	....	....	....
1991-92abc	U. of Maine	H.E.	37	*32	25	57	54	....	....	....	....	....
	Utica	AHL	....	....	....	....	....	3	1	0	1	0
1992-93	**New Jersey**	**NHL**	**45**	**10**	**11**	**21**	**41**	....	....	....	....	....
	Utica	AHL	27	15	18	33	33	2	0	1	1	0
1993-94	**New Jersey**	**NHL**	**1**	**0**	**0**	**0**	**2**	....	....	....	....	....
	Albany	AHL	73	28	46	74	84	5	2	1	3	11
1994-95	Albany	AHL	74	23	33	56	95	14	6	4	10	8
1995-96	**New Jersey**	**NHL**	**6**	**2**	**1**	**3**	**0**	....	....	....	....	....
	Albany	AHL	75	35	47	82	142	4	0	3	3	10
	NHL Totals		**52**	**12**	**12**	**24**	**43**	....	....	....	....	....

a Won Hobey Baker Memorial Award (Top U.S. Collegiate Player) (1992)
b Hockey East First All-Star Team (1992)
c NCAA East First All-American Team (1992)

Signed as a free agent by **St. Louis**, July 10, 1996.

PELTONEN, VILLE (PEHL-TOH-ner) — S.J.

Left wing. Shoots left. 5'11", 172 lbs. Born, Vantaa, Finland, May 24, 1973.
(San Jose's 4th choice, 58th overall, in 1993 Entry Draft).

			Regular Season					Playoffs				
Season	Club	Lea	GP	G	A	TP	PIM	GP	G	A	TP	PIM
1991-92	HIFK	Fin.	6	0	0	0	0	....	....	....	....	....
1992-93	HIFK	Fin.	46	13	24	37	16	4	0	2	2	2
1993-94	HIFK	Fin.	43	16	22	38	14	3	0	0	0	2
1994-95	HIFK	Fin.	45	20	16	36	16	3	0	0	0	0
1995-96	**San Jose**	**NHL**	**31**	**2**	**11**	**13**	**14**	....	....	....	....	....
	Kansas City	IHL	29	5	13	18	8	....	....	....	....	....
	NHL Totals		**31**	**2**	**11**	**13**	**14**	....	....	....	....	....

PELUSO, MIKE
(puh-LOO-soh) **N.J.**

Left wing. Shoots left. 6'4", 220 lbs. Born, Pengilly, MN, November 8, 1965.
(New Jersey's 10th choice, 190th overall, in 1984 Entry Draft).

				Regular Season					Playoffs			
Season	Club	Lea	GP	G	A	TP	PIM	GP	G	A	TP	PIM
1985-86	Alaska-Anch.	G.N.	32	2	11	13	59	....	....	....	....	....
1986-87	Alaska-Anch.	G.N.	30	5	21	26	68	....	....	....	....	....
1987-88	Alaska-Anch.	G.N.	35	4	33	37	76	....	....	....	....	....
1988-89	Alaska-Anch.	G.N.	33	10	27	37	75	....	....	....	....	....
1989-90	**Chicago**	**NHL**	**2**	**0**	**0**	**0**	**15**	....	....	....	....	....
	Indianapolis	IHL	75	7	10	17	279	14	0	1	1	58
1990-91	**Chicago**	**NHL**	**53**	**6**	**1**	**7**	**320**	**3**	**0**	**0**	**0**	**2**
	Indianapolis	IHL	6	2	1	3	21	5	0	2	2	40
1991-92	**Chicago**	**NHL**	**63**	**6**	**3**	**9**	***408**	**17**	**1**	**2**	**3**	**8**
	Indianapolis	IHL	4	0	1	1	15	....	....	....	....	....
1992-93	**Ottawa**	**NHL**	**81**	**15**	**10**	**25**	**318**	....	....	....	....	....
1993-94	**New Jersey**	**NHL**	**69**	**4**	**16**	**20**	**238**	**17**	**1**	**0**	**1**	***64**
1994-95	**New Jersey**	**NHL**	**46**	**2**	**9**	**11**	**167**	**20**	**1**	**2**	**3**	**8 ♦**
1995-96	**New Jersey**	**NHL**	**57**	**3**	**8**	**11**	**146**	....	....	....	....	....
	NHL Totals		**371**	**36**	**47**	**83**	**1612**	**57**	**3**	**4**	**7**	**82**

Signed as a free agent by **Chicago**, September 7, 1989. Claimed by **Ottawa** from **Chicago** in Expansion Draft, June 18, 1992. Traded to **New Jersey** by **Ottawa** to complete June 20, 1993 trade which sent Craig Billington, Troy Mallette and New Jersey's fourth round choice (Cosmo Dupaul) in 1993 Entry Draft to Ottawa for Peter Sidorkiewicz and future considerations, June 26, 1993.

PENNEY, CHAD
OTT.

Left wing. Shoots left. 6', 195 lbs. Born, Labrador City, Nfld., September 18, 1973.
(Ottawa's 2nd choice, 25th overall, in 1992 Entry Draft).

				Regular Season					Playoffs			
Season	Club	Lea	GP	G	A	TP	PIM	GP	G	A	TP	PIM
1990-91	North Bay	OHL	66	33	34	67	56	10	2	6	8	12
1991-92	North Bay	OHL	57	25	27	52	90	21	13	17	30	9
1992-93	North Bay	OHL	18	8	7	15	19	....	....	....	....	....
a	S.S. Marie	OHL	48	29	44	73	67	18	7	10	17	18
1993-94	**Ottawa**	**NHL**	**3**	**0**	**0**	**0**	**2**	....	....	....	....	....
	P.E.I.	AHL	73	20	30	50	66	....	....	....	....	....
1994-95	P.E.I.	AHL	66	16	16	32	19	11	2	2	4	2
1995-96	P.E.I.	AHL	79	23	37	60	48	3	1	1	2	0
	NHL Totals		**3**	**0**	**0**	**0**	**2**	....	....	....	....	....

a Memorial Cup All-Star Team (1993)

PEPPERALL, COLIN
NYR

Left wing. Shoots left. 5'10", 155 lbs. Born, Niagara Falls, Ont., April 28, 1978.
(NY Rangers' 4th choice, 131st overall, in 1996 Entry Draft).

				Regular Season					Playoffs			
Season	Club	Lea	GP	G	A	TP	PIM	GP	G	A	TP	PIM
1995-96	Niagara Falls	OHL	66	26	26	52	47	10	3	4	7	8

PEPPERALL, RYAN
TOR.

Right wing. Shoots right. 6'1", 185 lbs. Born, Niagara Falls, Ont., January 26, 1977.
(Toronto's 2nd choice, 54th overall, in 1995 Entry Draft).

				Regular Season					Playoffs			
Season	Club	Lea	GP	G	A	TP	PIM	GP	G	A	TP	PIM
1994-95	Kitchener	OHL	62	17	16	33	86	5	2	2	4	8
1995-96	Kitchener	OHL	66	31	26	57	173	12	3	4	7	34

PERREAULT, YANIC
(puh-ROH, YAH-nihk) **L.A.**

Center. Shoots left. 5'11", 182 lbs. Born, Sherbrooke, Que., April 4, 1971.
(Toronto's 1st choice, 47th overall, in 1991 Entry Draft).

				Regular Season					Playoffs			
Season	Club	Lea	GP	G	A	TP	PIM	GP	G	A	TP	PIM
1988-89	Trois-Rivières	QMJHL	70	53	55	108	48	....	....	....	....	....
1989-90	Trois-Rivières	QMJHL	63	51	63	114	75	7	6	5	11	19
1990-91a	Trois-Rivières	QMJHL	67	*87	98	*185	103	6	4	7	11	6
1991-92	St. John's	AHL	62	38	38	76	19	16	7	8	15	4
1992-93	St. John's	AHL	79	49	46	95	56	9	4	5	9	2
1993-94	**Toronto**	**NHL**	**13**	**3**	**3**	**6**	**0**	....	....	....	....	....
	St. John's	AHL	62	45	60	105	38	11	*12	6	18	14
1994-95	Phoenix	IHL	68	51	48	99	52	....	....	....	....	....
	Los Angeles	**NHL**	**26**	**2**	**5**	**7**	**20**	....	....	....	....	....
1995-96	**Los Angeles**	**NHL**	**78**	**25**	**24**	**49**	**16**	....	....	....	....	....
	NHL Totals		**117**	**30**	**32**	**62**	**36**	....	....	....	....	....

a QMJHL First All-Star Team (1991)

Traded to **Los Angeles** by **Toronto** for a conditional draft choice in 1996 Entry Draft, July 11, 1994.

PERROTT, NATHAN
N.J.

Right wing. Shoots right. 6', 215 lbs. Born, Owen Sound, Ont., December 8, 1976.
(New Jersey's 2nd choice, 44th overall, in 1995 Entry Draft).

				Regular Season					Playoffs			
Season	Club	Lea	GP	G	A	TP	PIM	GP	G	A	TP	PIM
1994-95	Oshawa	OHL	63	18	28	46	233	2	1	1	2	9
1995-96	Oshawa	OHL	59	30	32	62	158	5	2	3	5	8
	Albany	AHL	4	0	0	0	12	....	....	....	....	....

PERRY, TYLER
DET.

Center. Shoots right. 6'1", 170 lbs. Born, Vancouver, B.C., August 31, 1977.
(Detroit's 7th choice, 156th overall, in 1995 Entry Draft).

				Regular Season					Playoffs			
Season	Club	Lea	GP	G	A	TP	PIM	GP	G	A	TP	PIM
1994-95	Seattle	WHL	49	9	13	22	19	4	2	0	2	2
1995-96	Seattle	WHL	38	13	21	34	35	....	....	....	....	....
	Swift Current	WHL	22	11	21	32	12	6	2	2	4	4

PERSHIN, EDUARD
(PEHR-shihn, ehd-WUHRD) **T.B.**

Right wing. Shoots left. 6', 191 lbs. Born, Nizhnekamsk, USSR, September 1, 1977.
(Tampa Bay's 5th choice, 134th overall, in 1995 Entry Draft).

				Regular Season					Playoffs			
Season	Club	Lea	GP	G	A	TP	PIM	GP	G	A	TP	PIM
1994-95	Moscow D'amo	CIS	4	1	1	2	2	3	0	0	0	2
1995-96	Moscow D'amo	CIS	38	4	10	14	18	2	0	0	0	0

PERSSON, RICARD
N.J.

Defense. Shoots left. 6'2", 205 lbs. Born, Ostersund, Sweden, August 24, 1969.
(New Jersey's 2nd choice, 23rd overall, in 1987 Entry Draft).

				Regular Season					Playoffs			
Season	Club	Lea	GP	G	A	TP	PIM	GP	G	A	TP	PIM
1985-86	Ostersund	Swe. 2	24	2	2	4	16	....	....	....	....	....
1986-87	Ostersund	Swe. 2	31	10	11	21	28	....	....	....	....	....
1987-88	Leksand	Swe.	31	2	0	2	8	2	0	1	1	2
1988-89	Leksand	Swe.	33	2	4	6	28	9	0	1	1	6
1989-90	Leksand	Swe.	43	9	10	19	62	3	0	0	0	6
1990-91	Leksand	Swe.	37	6	9	15	42	....	....	....	....	....
1991-92	Leksand	Swe.	21	0	7	7	28	....	....	....	....	....
1992-93	Leksand	Swe.	36	7	15	22	63	2	0	2	2	0
1993-94	Malmo	Swe.	40	11	9	20	38	11	2	0	2	12
1994-95	Malmo	Swe.	31	3	13	16	38	9	0	2	2	8
	Albany	AHL	3	0	0	0	0	9	3	5	8	7
1995-96	**New Jersey**	**NHL**	**12**	**2**	**1**	**3**	**8**	....	....	....	....	....
	Albany	AHL	67	15	31	46	59	4	0	0	0	7
	NHL Totals		**12**	**2**	**1**	**3**	**8**	....	....	....	....	....

PETERS, GEOFF
CHI.

Center. Shoots left. 6', 180 lbs. Born, Hamilton, Ont., April 30, 1978.
(Chicago's 3rd choice, 46th overall, in 1996 Entry Draft).

				Regular Season					Playoffs			
Season	Club	Lea	GP	G	A	TP	PIM	GP	G	A	TP	PIM
1994-95	Niagara Falls	OHL	57	11	9	20	37	6	2	0	2	4
1995-96	Niagara Falls	OHL	64	25	34	59	51	10	4	4	8	8

PETERSON, BRENT
T.B.

Left wing. Shoots left. 6'3", 200 lbs. Born, Calgary, Alta., July 20, 1972.
(Tampa Bay's 1st choice, 3rd overall, in 1993 Supplemental Draft).

				Regular Season					Playoffs			
Season	Club	Lea	GP	G	A	TP	PIM	GP	G	A	TP	PIM
1991-92	Michigan Tech	WCHA	39	11	9	20	18	....	....	....	....	....
1992-93	Michigan Tech	WCHA	37	24	18	42	32	....	....	....	....	....
1993-94	Michigan Tech	WCHA	43	25	21	46	30	....	....	....	....	....
1994-95	Michigan Tech	WCHA	39	20	16	36	27	....	....	....	....	....
1995-96	Atlanta	IHL	69	9	19	28	33	3	0	0	0	0

PETERSON, KYLE
DAL.

Center. Shoots left. 6'3", 195 lbs. Born, Calgary, Alta., April 17, 1974.
(Minnesota's 5th choice, 154th overall, in 1992 Entry Draft).

				Regular Season					Playoffs			
Season	Club	Lea	GP	G	A	TP	PIM	GP	G	A	TP	PIM
1993-94	Michigan Tech	WCHA	45	5	9	14	82	....	....	....	....	....
1994-95	Michigan Tech	WCHA	36	7	11	18	52	....	....	....	....	....
1995-96	Michigan Tech	WCHA	23	8	7	15	18	....	....	....	....	....

PETERSON, MATT
ANA.

Defense. Shoots left. 6'1", 190 lbs. Born, Maple Grove, MN, February 15, 1975.
(Anaheim's 7th choice, 160th overall, in 1993 Entry Draft).

				Regular Season					Playoffs			
Season	Club	Lea	GP	G	A	TP	PIM	GP	G	A	TP	PIM
1994-95	U. Wisconsin	WCHA	20	0	0	0	10	....	....	....	....	....
1995-96	U. Wisconsin	WCHA	21	0	0	0	24	....	....	....	....	....

PETIT, MICHEL
(puh-TEE)

Defense. Shoots right. 6'1", 205 lbs. Born, St. Malo, Que., February 12, 1964.
(Vancouver's 1st choice, 11th overall, in 1982 Entry Draft).

				Regular Season					Playoffs			
Season	Club	Lea	GP	G	A	TP	PIM	GP	G	A	TP	PIM
1981-82a	Sherbrooke	QMJHL	63	10	39	49	106	22	5	20	25	24
1982-83	**Vancouver**	**NHL**	**2**	**0**	**0**	**0**	**0**	....	....	....	....	....
a	St-Jean	QMJHL	62	19	67	86	196	3	0	0	0	35
1983-84	Cdn. National	....	19	3	10	13	58	....	....	....	....	....
	Vancouver	**NHL**	**44**	**6**	**9**	**15**	**53**	**1**	**0**	**0**	**0**	**0**
1984-85	**Vancouver**	**NHL**	**69**	**5**	**26**	**31**	**127**	....	....	....	....	....
1985-86	**Vancouver**	**NHL**	**32**	**1**	**6**	**7**	**27**	....	....	....	....	....
	Fredericton	AHL	25	0	13	13	79	....	....	....	....	....
1986-87	**Vancouver**	**NHL**	**69**	**12**	**13**	**25**	**131**	....	....	....	....	....
1987-88	**Vancouver**	**NHL**	**10**	**0**	**3**	**3**	**35**	....	....	....	....	....
	NY Rangers	**NHL**	**64**	**9**	**24**	**33**	**223**	....	....	....	....	....
1988-89	**NY Rangers**	**NHL**	**69**	**8**	**25**	**33**	**154**	**4**	**0**	**2**	**2**	**27**
1989-90	**Quebec**	**NHL**	**63**	**12**	**24**	**36**	**215**	....	....	....	....	....
1990-91	**Quebec**	**NHL**	**19**	**4**	**7**	**11**	**47**	....	....	....	....	....
	Toronto	**NHL**	**54**	**9**	**19**	**28**	**132**	....	....	....	....	....
1991-92	**Toronto**	**NHL**	**34**	**1**	**13**	**14**	**85**	....	....	....	....	....
	Calgary	**NHL**	**36**	**3**	**10**	**13**	**79**	....	....	....	....	....
1992-93	**Calgary**	**NHL**	**35**	**3**	**9**	**12**	**54**	....	....	....	....	....
1993-94	**Calgary**	**NHL**	**63**	**2**	**21**	**23**	**110**	....	....	....	....	....
1994-95	**Los Angeles**	**NHL**	**40**	**5**	**12**	**17**	**84**	....	....	....	....	....
1995-96	**Los Angeles**	**NHL**	**9**	**0**	**1**	**1**	**27**	....	....	....	....	....
	Tampa Bay	**NHL**	**45**	**4**	**7**	**11**	**108**	**6**	**0**	**0**	**0**	**20**
	NHL Totals		**757**	**84**	**229**	**313**	**1691**	**11**	**0**	**2**	**2**	**47**

a QMJHL First All-Star Team (1982, 1983)

Traded to **NY Rangers** by **Vancouver** for Willie Huber and Larry Melnyk, November 4, 1987. Traded to **Quebec** by **NY Rangers** for Randy Moller, October 5, 1989. Traded to **Toronto** by **Quebec** with Aaron Broten and Lucien Deblois for Scott Pearson and Toronto's second round choices in 1991 (later traded to Washington — Washington selected Eric Lavigne) and 1992 (Tuomas Gronman) Entry Drafts, November 17, 1990. Traded to **Calgary** by **Toronto** with Craig Berube, Alexander Godynyuk, Gary Leeman and Jeff Reese for Doug Gilmour, Jamie Macoun, Ric Nattress, Rick Wamsley and Kent Manderville, January 2, 1992. Signed as a free agent by **Los Angeles**, June 16, 1994. Traded to **Tampa Bay** by **Los Angeles** for Steven Finn, November 13, 1995.

PETRAKOV, ANDREI
ST.L.

Right wing. Shoots left. 6', 198 lbs. Born, Sverdlovsk, USSR, April 26, 1976.
(St. Louis' 4th choice, 97th overall, in 1996 Entry Draft).

				Regular Season					Playoffs			
Season	Club	Lea	GP	G	A	TP	PIM	GP	G	A	TP	PIM
1992-93	Yekaterinburg	CIS	5	0	0	0	0	1	0	0	0	0
1993-94	Yekaterinburg	CIS	35	4	2	6	10	....	....	....	....	....
1994-95	Yekaterinburg	CIS	11	1	1	2	6	1	0	0	0	0
1995-96	Yekaterinburg	CIS 2	52	17	6	23	14	....	....	....	....	....

PETROCHININ, EVGENY (peht-roh-CHIH-nihn) DAL.

Defense. Shoots left. 6'2", 190 lbs. Born, Murmansk, USSR, February 7, 1976.
(Dallas' 5th choice, 150th overall, in 1994 Entry Draft).

			Regular Season					Playoffs				
Season	Club	Lea	GP	G	A	TP	PIM	GP	G	A	TP	PIM
1993-94	Spartak	CIS	2	0	0	0	0	....	....	....	....	....
1994-95	Spartak	CIS	45	0	2	2	14	....	....	....	....	....
1995-96	Spartak	CIS	50	5	17	22	18	5	3	0	3	0

PETROV, OLEG (PEH-trahf)

Right wing. Shoots left. 5'8", 175 lbs. Born, Moscow, USSR, April 18, 1971.
(Montreal's 9th choice, 127th overall, in 1991 Entry Draft).

			Regular Season					Playoffs				
Season	Club	Lea	GP	G	A	TP	PIM	GP	G	A	TP	PIM
1989-90	CSKA	USSR	30	4	7	11	4	....	....	....	....	....
1990-91	CSKA	USSR	43	7	4	11	8	....	....	....	....	....
1991-92	CSKA	CIS	42	10	16	26	8	....	....	....	....	....
1992-93	**Montreal**	**NHL**	**9**	**2**	**1**	**3**	**10**	**1**	**0**	**0**	**0**	**0**
	Fredericton	AHL	55	26	29	55	36	5	4	1	5	0
1993-94a	**Montreal**	**NHL**	**55**	**12**	**15**	**27**	**2**	**2**	**0**	**0**	**0**	**0**
	Fredericton	AHL	23	8	20	28	18	....	....	....	....	....
1994-95	**Montreal**	**NHL**	**12**	**2**	**3**	**5**	**4**	....	....	....	....	....
	Fredericton	AHL	17	7	11	18	12	17	5	6	11	10
1995-96	**Montreal**	**NHL**	**36**	**4**	**7**	**11**	**23**	**5**	**0**	**1**	**1**	**0**
	Fredericton	AHL	22	12	18	30	71	6	2	6	8	0
	NHL Totals		**112**	**20**	**26**	**46**	**39**	**8**	**0**	**1**	**1**	**0**

a NHL/Upper Deck All-Rookie Team (1994)

PETROV, SERGEI (PEH-trahf) CHI.

Left wing. Shoots left. 5'11", 185 lbs. Born, Leningrad, USSR, January 22, 1975.
(Chicago's 9th choice, 206th overall, in 1993 Entry Draft).

			Regular Season					Playoffs				
Season	Club	Lea	GP	G	A	TP	PIM	GP	G	A	TP	PIM
1993-94	Minn.-Duluth	WCHA	28	2	4	6	26	....	....	....	....	....
1994-95	Minn.-Duluth	WCHA	30	6	6	12	46	....	....	....	....	....
1995-96					UNAVAILABLE							

PETROVICKY, ROBERT (PEHT-roh-VEETS-kee)

Center. Shoots left. 5'11", 172 lbs. Born, Kosice, Czech., October 26, 1973.
(Hartford's 1st choice, 9th overall, in 1992 Entry Draft).

			Regular Season					Playoffs				
Season	Club	Lea	GP	G	A	TP	PIM	GP	G	A	TP	PIM
1990-91	Dukla Trencin	Czech.	33	9	14	23	12	....	....	....	....	....
1991-92	Dukla Trencin	Czech.	46	25	36	61	28	....	....	....	....	....
1992-93	**Hartford**	**NHL**	**42**	**3**	**6**	**9**	**45**	....	....	....	....	....
	Springfield	AHL	16	5	3	8	39	15	5	6	11	14
1993-94	Dukla Trencin	Slovak	1	0	0	0	0	....	....	....	....	....
	Hartford	**NHL**	**33**	**6**	**5**	**11**	**39**	....	....	....	....	....
	Springfield	AHL	30	16	8	24	39	4	0	2	2	4
1994-95	Springfield	AHL	74	30	52	82	121	....	....	....	....	....
	Hartford	**NHL**	**2**	**0**	**0**	**0**	**0**	....	....	....	....	....
1995-96	Springfield	AHL	9	4	8	12	18	....	....	....	....	....
	Detroit	IHL	12	5	3	8	16	....	....	....	....	....
	Dallas	**NHL**	**5**	**1**	**1**	**2**	**0**	....	....	....	....	....
	Michigan	IHL	50	23	23	46	63	7	3	1	4	16
	NHL Totals		**82**	**10**	**12**	**22**	**84**	....	....	....	....	....

Traded to **Dallas** by **Hartford** for Dan Kesa and a conditional choice in 1997 Entry Draft, November 29, 1995.

PETRUNIN, ANDREI (puh-TROO-nihn) HFD.

Right wing. Shoots left. 5'9", 169 lbs. Born, Moscow, USSR, February 2, 1978.
(Hartford's 2nd choice, 61st overall, in 1996 Entry Draft).

			Regular Season					Playoffs				
Season	Club	Lea	GP	G	A	TP	PIM	GP	G	A	TP	PIM
1994-95	CSKA	CIS	7	0	1	1	0	2	0	0	0	0
1995-96	CSKA	CIS	52	12	8	20	22	2	0	0	0	2

PHILLIPS, CHRIS OTT.

Defense. Shoots left. 6'2", 200 lbs. Born, Calgary, Alta., March 9, 1978.
(Ottawa's 1st choice, 1st overall, in 1996 Entry Draft).

			Regular Season					Playoffs				
Season	Club	Lea	GP	G	A	TP	PIM	GP	G	A	TP	PIM
1994-95	Ft. McMurray	Jr. A	48	16	32	48	127	....	....	....	....	....
1995-96	Prince Albert	WHL	61	10	30	40	97	18	2	12	14	30

PHILLIPS, GREG L.A.

Center. Shoots right. 6'1", 190 lbs. Born, Winnipeg, Man., March 27, 1978.
(Los Angeles' 3rd choice, 57th overall, in 1996 Entry Draft).

			Regular Season					Playoffs				
Season	Club	Lea	GP	G	A	TP	PIM	GP	G	A	TP	PIM
1994-95	Saskatoon	WHL	64	3	5	8	94	10	0	0	0	4
1995-96	Saskatoon	WHL	67	21	24	45	132	4	1	2	3	2

PICARD, MICHEL

Left wing. Shoots left. 5'11", 190 lbs. Born, Beauport, Que., November 7, 1969.
(Hartford's 8th choice, 178th overall, in 1989 Entry Draft).

			Regular Season					Playoffs				
Season	Club	Lea	GP	G	A	TP	PIM	GP	G	A	TP	PIM
1986-87	Trois-Rivières	QMJHL	66	33	35	68	53	....	....	....	....	....
1987-88	Trois-Rivières	QMJHL	69	40	55	95	71	....	....	....	....	....
1988-89	Trois-Rivières	QMJHL	66	59	81	140	170	4	1	3	4	2
1989-90	Binghamton	AHL	67	16	24	40	98	....	....	....	....	....
1990-91	**Hartford**	**NHL**	**5**	**1**	**0**	**1**	**2**	....	....	....	....	....
a	Springfield	AHL	77	*56	40	96	61	18	8	13	21	18
1991-92	**Hartford**	**NHL**	**25**	**3**	**5**	**8**	**6**	....	....	....	....	....
	Springfield	AHL	40	21	17	38	44	11	2	0	2	34
1992-93	**San Jose**	**NHL**	**25**	**4**	**0**	**4**	**24**	....	....	....	....	....
	Kansas City	IHL	33	7	10	17	51	12	3	2	5	20
1993-94b	Portland	AHL	61	41	44	85	99	17	11	10	21	22
1994-95a	P.E.I.	AHL	57	32	57	89	58	8	4	4	8	6
	Ottawa	**NHL**	**24**	**5**	**8**	**13**	**14**	....	....	....	....	....
1995-96	**Ottawa**	**NHL**	**17**	**2**	**6**	**8**	**10**	....	....	....	....	....
	P.E.I.	AHL	55	37	45	82	79	5	5	1	6	2
	NHL Totals		**96**	**15**	**19**	**34**	**56**	....	....	....	....	....

a AHL First All-Star Team (1991, 1995)
b AHL Second All-Star Team (1994)

Traded to **San Jose** by **Hartford** for future considerations (Yvon Corriveau, January 21, 1993), October 9, 1992. Signed as a free agent by **Ottawa**, June 16, 1994. Traded to **Washington** by **Ottawa** for cash, May 21, 1996.

PIERCE, BILL COL.

Center. Shoots left. 6'1", 190 lbs. Born, Woburn, MA, October 6, 1974.
(Quebec's 4th choice, 75th overall, in 1993 Entry Draft).

			Regular Season					Playoffs				
Season	Club	Lea	GP	G	A	TP	PIM	GP	G	A	TP	PIM
1993-94	Boston U.	H.E.	31	4	4	8	28	....	....	....	....	....
1994-95	Boston U.	H.E.	33	5	13	18	29	....	....	....	....	....
1995-96	Boston U.	H.E.	39	10	10	20	58	....	....	....	....	....

PILON, RICHARD (PEE-lahn) NYI

Defense. Shoots left. 6', 205 lbs. Born, Saskatoon, Sask., April 30, 1968.
(NY Islanders' 9th choice, 143rd overall, in 1986 Entry Draft).

			Regular Season					Playoffs				
Season	Club	Lea	GP	G	A	TP	PIM	GP	G	A	TP	PIM
1986-87	Prince Albert	WHL	68	4	21	25	192	7	1	6	7	17
1987-88	Prince Albert	WHL	65	13	34	47	177	9	0	6	6	38
1988-89	**NY Islanders**	**NHL**	**62**	**0**	**14**	**14**	**242**	....	....	....	....	....
1989-90	**NY Islanders**	**NHL**	**14**	**0**	**2**	**2**	**31**	....	....	....	....	....
1990-91	**NY Islanders**	**NHL**	**60**	**1**	**4**	**5**	**126**	....	....	....	....	....
1991-92	**NY Islanders**	**NHL**	**65**	**1**	**6**	**7**	**183**	....	....	....	....	....
1992-93	**NY Islanders**	**NHL**	**44**	**1**	**3**	**4**	**164**	**15**	**0**	**0**	**0**	**50**
	Capital Dist.	AHL	6	0	1	1	8	....	....	....	....	....
1993-94	**NY Islanders**	**NHL**	**28**	**1**	**4**	**5**	**75**	....	....	....	....	....
	Salt Lake	IHL	2	0	0	0	8	....	....	....	....	....
1994-95	**NY Islanders**	**NHL**	**20**	**1**	**1**	**2**	**40**	....	....	....	....	....
1995-96	**NY Islanders**	**NHL**	**27**	**0**	**3**	**3**	**72**	....	....	....	....	....
	NHL Totals		**320**	**5**	**37**	**42**	**933**	**15**	**0**	**0**	**0**	**50**

PITLICK, LANCE (PIHT-lihk) OTT.

Defense. Shoots right. 6', 180 lbs. Born, Minneapolis, MN, November 5, 1967.
(Minnesota's 10th choice, 108th overall, in 1986 Entry Draft).

			Regular Season					Playoffs				
Season	Club	Lea	GP	G	A	TP	PIM	GP	G	A	TP	PIM
1986-87	U. Minnesota	WCHA	45	0	9	9	88	....	....	....	....	....
1987-88	U. Minnesota	WCHA	38	3	9	12	76	....	....	....	....	....
1988-89	U. Minnesota	WCHA	47	4	9	13	95	....	....	....	....	....
1989-90	U. Minnesota	WCHA	14	3	2	5	26	....	....	....	....	....
1990-91	Hershey	AHL	64	6	15	21	75	3	0	0	0	9
1991-92	U.S. National	....	19	0	1	1	38	....	....	....	....	....
	Hershey	AHL	4	0	0	0	6	3	0	0	0	4
1992-93	Hershey	AHL	53	5	10	15	77	....	....	....	....	....
1993-94	Hershey	AHL	58	4	13	17	93	11	1	0	1	11
1994-95	P.E.I.	AHL	61	8	19	27	55	11	1	4	5	10
	Ottawa	**NHL**	**15**	**0**	**1**	**1**	**6**	....	....	....	....	....
1995-96	**Ottawa**	**NHL**	**28**	**1**	**6**	**7**	**20**	....	....	....	....	....
	P.E.I.	AHL	29	4	10	14	39	5	0	0	0	0
	NHL Totals		**43**	**1**	**7**	**8**	**26**	....	....	....	....	....

Signed as a free agent by **Philadelphia**, September 5, 1990. Signed as a free agent by **Ottawa**, June 22, 1994.

PITTIS, DOMENIC PIT.

Center. Shoots left. 5'11", 185 lbs. Born, Calgary, Alta., October 1, 1974.
(Pittsburgh's 2nd choice, 52nd overall, in 1993 Entry Draft).

			Regular Season					Playoffs				
Season	Club	Lea	GP	G	A	TP	PIM	GP	G	A	TP	PIM
1991-92	Lethbridge	WHL	65	6	17	23	48	5	0	2	2	4
1992-93	Lethbridge	WHL	66	46	73	119	69	4	3	3	6	8
1993-94a	Lethbridge	WHL	72	58	69	127	93	8	4	11	15	16
1994-95	Cleveland	IHL	62	18	32	50	66	3	0	2	2	2
1995-96	Cleveland	IHL	74	10	28	38	100	3	0	0	0	2

a WHL East Second All-Star Team (1994)

PITTMAN, MIKE CHI.

Center. Shoots right. 6', 180 lbs. Born, Placentia, Nfld., March 29, 1976.
(Chicago's 10th choice, 227th overall, in 1995 Entry Draft).

			Regular Season					Playoffs				
Season	Club	Lea	GP	G	A	TP	PIM	GP	G	A	TP	PIM
1993-94	Guelph	OHL	61	8	8	16	33	9	0	0	0	4
1994-95	Guelph	OHL	64	10	15	25	27	14	0	1	1	2
1995-96	Guelph	OHL	61	9	13	22	44	16	3	1	4	4

PIVETZ, MARK COL.

Defense. Shoots left. 6'3", 205 lbs. Born, Edmonton, Alta., December 9, 1973.
(Quebec's 12th choice, 257th overall, in 1993 Entry Draft).

			Regular Season					Playoffs				
Season	Club	Lea	GP	G	A	TP	PIM	GP	G	A	TP	PIM
1993-94	North Dakota	WCHA	36	2	5	7	96	....	....	....	....	....
1994-95	North Dakota	WCHA	39	3	11	14	38	....	....	....	....	....
1995-96	North Dakota	WCHA	28	5	9	14	42	....	....	....	....	....

PIVONKA, MICHAL (pih-VAHN-kuh) WSH.

Center. Shoots left. 6'2", 195 lbs. Born, Kladno, Czech., January 28, 1966.
(Washington's 3rd choice, 59th overall, in 1984 Entry Draft).

			Regular Season					Playoffs				
Season	Club	Lea	GP	G	A	TP	PIM	GP	G	A	TP	PIM
1984-85	Dukla Jihlava	Czech.	33	8	11	19	18	....	....	....	....	....
1985-86	Dukla Jihlava	Czech.	42	5	13	18	18	....	....	....	....	....
1986-87	**Washington**	**NHL**	**73**	**18**	**25**	**43**	**41**	**7**	**1**	**1**	**2**	**2**
1987-88	**Washington**	**NHL**	**71**	**11**	**23**	**34**	**28**	**14**	**4**	**9**	**13**	**4**
1988-89	**Washington**	**NHL**	**52**	**8**	**19**	**27**	**30**	**6**	**3**	**1**	**4**	**10**
	Baltimore	AHL	31	12	24	36	19	....	....	....	....	....
1989-90	**Washington**	**NHL**	**77**	**25**	**39**	**64**	**54**	**11**	**0**	**2**	**2**	**6**
1990-91	**Washington**	**NHL**	**79**	**20**	**50**	**70**	**34**	**11**	**2**	**3**	**5**	**8**
1991-92	**Washington**	**NHL**	**80**	**23**	**57**	**80**	**47**	**7**	**1**	**5**	**6**	**13**
1992-93	**Washington**	**NHL**	**69**	**21**	**53**	**74**	**66**	**6**	**0**	**2**	**2**	**0**
1993-94	**Washington**	**NHL**	**82**	**14**	**36**	**50**	**38**	**7**	**4**	**4**	**8**	**4**
1994-95	Klagenfurt	Aus.	7	2	4	6	4	....	....	....	....	....
	Washington	**NHL**	**46**	**10**	**23**	**33**	**50**	**7**	**1**	**4**	**5**	**21**
1995-96	Detroit	IHL	7	1	9	10	19	....	....	....	....	....
	Washington	**NHL**	**73**	**16**	**65**	**81**	**36**	**6**	**3**	**2**	**5**	**18**
	NHL Totals		**702**	**166**	**390**	**556**	**424**	**82**	**19**	**33**	**52**	**86**

PLAGER, KEVIN — ST.L.

Right wing. Shoots right. 6'1", 210 lbs. Born, St. Louis, MO, April 27, 1971.
(St. Louis' 8th choice, 156th overall, in 1989 Entry Draft).

			Regular Season					Playoffs				
Season	Club	Lea	GP	G	A	TP	PIM	GP	G	A	TP	PIM
1992-93	U. Wisc.-St. Pt.	NCAA	15	3	3	6	63	....	....	....	....	....
1993-94	U. Wisc.-St. Pt.	NCAA				UNAVAILABLE						
1994-95	U. Wisc.-St. Pt.	NCAA				UNAVAILABLE						
1995-96	U. Wisc.-St. Pt.	NCAA				UNAVAILABLE						

PLANTE, DAN — (PLAHNT) NYI

Right wing. Shoots right. 5'11", 202 lbs. Born, Hayward, WI, October 5, 1971.
(NY Islanders' 3rd choice, 48th overall, in 1990 Entry Draft).

			Regular Season					Playoffs				
Season	Club	Lea	GP	G	A	TP	PIM	GP	G	A	TP	PIM
1990-91	U. Wisconsin	WCHA	33	1	2	3	54	....	....	....	....	....
1991-92	U. Wisconsin	WCHA	36	13	13	26	107	....	....	....	....	....
1992-93	U. Wisconsin	WCHA	42	26	31	57	142	....	....	....	....	....
1993-94	**NY Islanders**	**NHL**	**12**	**0**	**1**	**1**	**4**	**1**	**1**	**0**	**1**	**2**
	Salt Lake	IHL	66	7	17	24	148	....	....	....	....	....
1994-95	Denver	IHL	2	0	0	0	4	....	....	....	....	....
1995-96	**NY Islanders**	**NHL**	**73**	**5**	**3**	**8**	**50**	....	....	....	....	....
	NHL Totals		**85**	**5**	**4**	**9**	**54**	**1**	**1**	**0**	**1**	**2**

PLANTE, DEREK — (PLAHNT) BUF.

Center. Shoots left. 5'11", 180 lbs. Born, Cloquet, MN, January 17, 1971.
(Buffalo's 7th choice, 161st overall, in 1989 Entry Draft).

			Regular Season					Playoffs				
Season	Club	Lea	GP	G	A	TP	PIM	GP	G	A	TP	PIM
1989-90	Minn.-Duluth	WCHA	28	10	11	21	12	....	....	....	....	....
1990-91	Minn.-Duluth	WCHA	36	23	20	43	6	....	....	....	....	....
1991-92a	Minn.-Duluth	WCHA	37	27	36	63	28	....	....	....	....	....
1992-93bc	Minn.-Duluth	WCHA	37	*36	*56	*92	30	....	....	....	....	....
1993-94	**Buffalo**	**NHL**	**77**	**21**	**35**	**56**	**24**	**7**	**1**	**0**	**1**	**0**
	U.S. National	....	2	0	1	1	0	....	....	....	....	....
1994-95	**Buffalo**	**NHL**	**47**	**3**	**19**	**22**	**12**	....	....	....	....	....
1995-96	**Buffalo**	**NHL**	**76**	**23**	**33**	**56**	**28**	....	....	....	....	....
	NHL Totals		**200**	**47**	**87**	**134**	**64**	**7**	**1**	**0**	**1**	**0**

a WCHA Second All-Star Team (1992)
b WCHA First All-Star Team (1993)
c NCAA West First All-American Team (1993)

PLAVSIC, ADRIEN — (PLAV-sihk) ANA.

Defense. Shoots left. 6'1", 200 lbs. Born, Montreal, Que., January 13, 1970.
(St. Louis' 2nd choice, 30th overall, in 1988 Entry Draft).

			Regular Season					Playoffs				
Season	Club	Lea	GP	G	A	TP	PIM	GP	G	A	TP	PIM
1987-88	N. Hampshire	H.E.	30	5	6	11	45	....	....	....	....	....
1988-89	Cdn. National	....	62	5	10	15	25	....	....	....	....	....
1989-90	**St. Louis**	**NHL**	**4**	**0**	**1**	**1**	**2**	....	....	....	....	....
	Peoria	IHL	51	7	14	21	87	....	....	....	....	....
	Vancouver	**NHL**	**11**	**3**	**2**	**5**	**8**	....	....	....	....	....
	Milwaukee	IHL	3	1	2	3	14	6	1	3	4	6
1990-91	**Vancouver**	**NHL**	**48**	**2**	**10**	**12**	**62**	....	....	....	....	....
1991-92	Cdn. National	....	38	7	8	15	44	....	....	....	....	....
	Cdn. Olympic	....	8	0	2	2	0	....	....	....	....	....
	Vancouver	**NHL**	**16**	**1**	**9**	**10**	**14**	**13**	**1**	**7**	**8**	**4**
1992-93	**Vancouver**	**NHL**	**57**	**6**	**21**	**27**	**53**	....	....	....	....	....
1993-94	**Vancouver**	**NHL**	**47**	**1**	**9**	**10**	**6**	....	....	....	....	....
	Hamilton	AHL	2	0	0	0	0	....	....	....	....	....
1994-95	**Vancouver**	**NHL**	**3**	**0**	**1**	**1**	**4**	....	....	....	....	....
	Tampa Bay	**NHL**	**15**	**2**	**1**	**3**	**4**	....	....	....	....	....
1995-96	**Tampa Bay**	**NHL**	**7**	**1**	**2**	**3**	**6**	....	....	....	....	....
	Atlanta	IHL	68	5	34	39	32	3	0	1	1	4
	NHL Totals		**208**	**16**	**56**	**72**	**159**	**13**	**1**	**7**	**8**	**4**

Traded to **Vancouver** by **St. Louis** with Montreal's first round choice (previously acquired by St. Louis — Vancouver selected Shawn Antoski) in 1990 Entry Draft and St. Louis' second round choice (later traded to Montreal — Montreal selected Craig Darby) in 1991 Entry Draft for Rich Sutter, Harold Snepsts and St. Louis' second round choice (previously acquired by Vancouver — St. Louis selected Craig Johnson) in 1990 Entry Draft, March 6, 1990. Traded to **Tampa Bay** by **Vancouver** for Tampa Bay's fifth round choice in 1997 Entry Draft, March 23, 1995. Signed as a free agent by **Anaheim**, August 27, 1996.

POAPST, STEVE — (POHPST) WSH.

Defense. Shoots left. 6', 200 lbs. Born, Cornwall, Ont., January 3, 1969.

			Regular Season					Playoffs				
Season	Club	Lea	GP	G	A	TP	PIM	GP	G	A	TP	PIM
1989-90	Colgate	ECAC	38	4	15	19	54	....	....	....	....	....
1990-91	Colgate	ECAC	32	6	15	21	43	....	....	....	....	....
1991-92	Hampton Rds.	ECHL	55	8	20	28	29	14	1	4	5	12
1992-93a	Hampton Rds.	ECHL	63	10	35	45	57	4	0	1	1	4
	Baltimore	AHL	7	0	1	1	4	7	0	3	3	6
1993-94	Portland	AHL	78	14	21	35	47	12	0	3	3	8
1994-95	Portland	AHL	71	8	22	30	60	7	0	1	1	16
1995-96	**Washington**	**NHL**	**3**	**1**	**0**	**1**	**0**	**6**	**0**	**0**	**0**	**0**
	Portland	AHL	70	10	24	34	79	20	2	6	8	16
	NHL Totals		**3**	**1**	**0**	**1**	**0**	**6**	**0**	**0**	**0**	**0**

a ECHL First All-Star Team (1993)

Signed as a free agent by **Washington**, February 4, 1995.

PODEIN, SHJON — (poh-DEEN, SHAWN) PHI.

Left wing. Shoots left. 6'2", 200 lbs. Born, Rochester, MN, March 5, 1968.
(Edmonton's 9th choice, 166th overall, in 1988 Entry Draft).

			Regular Season					Playoffs				
Season	Club	Lea	GP	G	A	TP	PIM	GP	G	A	TP	PIM
1987-88	Minn.-Duluth	WCHA	30	4	4	8	48	....	....	....	....	....
1988-89	Minn.-Duluth	WCHA	36	7	5	12	46	....	....	....	....	....
1989-90	Minn.-Duluth	WCHA	35	21	18	39	36	....	....	....	....	....
1990-91	Cape Breton	AHL	63	14	15	29	65	4	0	0	0	5
1991-92	Cape Breton	AHL	80	30	24	54	46	5	3	1	4	2
1992-93	**Edmonton**	**NHL**	**40**	**13**	**6**	**19**	**25**	....	....	....	....	....
	Cape Breton	AHL	38	18	21	39	32	9	2	2	4	29
1993-94	**Edmonton**	**NHL**	**28**	**3**	**5**	**8**	**8**	....	....	....	....	....
	Cape Breton	AHL	5	4	4	8	4	....	....	....	....	....
1994-95	**Philadelphia**	**NHL**	**44**	**3**	**7**	**10**	**33**	**15**	**1**	**3**	**4**	**10**
1995-96	**Philadelphia**	**NHL**	**79**	**15**	**10**	**25**	**89**	**12**	**1**	**2**	**3**	**50**
	NHL Totals		**191**	**34**	**28**	**62**	**155**	**27**	**2**	**5**	**7**	**60**

Signed as a free agent by **Philadelphia**, July 27, 1994.

PODOLLAN, JASON — FLA.

Right wing. Shoots right. 6'1", 192 lbs. Born, Vernon, B.C., February 18, 1976.
(Florida's 3rd choice, 31st overall, in 1994 Entry Draft).

			Regular Season					Playoffs				
Season	Club	Lea	GP	G	A	TP	PIM	GP	G	A	TP	PIM
1991-92	Spokane	WHL	2	0	0	0	2	10	3	1	4	16
1992-93	Spokane	WHL	72	36	33	69	108	10	4	4	8	14
1993-94	Spokane	WHL	69	29	37	66	108	3	3	0	3	2
1994-95	Spokane	WHL	72	43	41	84	102	11	5	7	12	18
1995-96a	Spokane	WHL	56	37	25	62	103	18	*21	12	33	28

a WHL West Second All-Star Team (1996)

POESCHEK, RUDY — (POH-shehk) T.B.

Right wing/Defense. Shoots right. 6'2", 218 lbs. Born, Kamloops, B.C., September 29, 1966.
(NY Rangers' 12th choice, 238th overall, in 1985 Entry Draft).

			Regular Season					Playoffs				
Season	Club	Lea	GP	G	A	TP	PIM	GP	G	A	TP	PIM
1983-84	Kamloops	WHL	47	3	9	12	93	8	0	2	2	7
1984-85	Kamloops	WHL	34	6	7	13	100	15	0	3	3	56
1985-86	Kamloops	WHL	32	3	13	16	92	16	3	7	10	40
1986-87	Kamloops	WHL	54	13	18	31	153	15	2	4	6	37
1987-88	**NY Rangers**	**NHL**	**1**	**0**	**0**	**0**	**2**	....	....	....	....	....
	Colorado	IHL	82	7	31	38	210	12	2	2	4	31
1988-89	**NY Rangers**	**NHL**	**52**	**0**	**2**	**2**	**199**	....	....	....	....	....
	Colorado	IHL	2	0	0	0	6	....	....	....	....	....
1989-90	**NY Rangers**	**NHL**	**15**	**0**	**0**	**0**	**55**	....	....	....	....	....
	Flint	IHL	38	8	13	21	109	4	0	0	0	16
1990-91	Binghamton	AHL	38	1	3	4	162	....	....	....	....	....
	Winnipeg	**NHL**	**1**	**0**	**0**	**0**	**5**	....	....	....	....	....
	Moncton	AHL	23	2	4	6	67	9	1	1	2	41
1991-92	**Winnipeg**	**NHL**	**4**	**0**	**0**	**0**	**17**	....	....	....	....	....
	Moncton	AHL	63	4	18	22	170	11	0	2	2	48
1992-93	St. John's	AHL	78	7	24	31	189	9	0	4	4	13
1993-94	**Tampa Bay**	**NHL**	**71**	**3**	**6**	**9**	**118**	....	....	....	....	....
1994-95	**Tampa Bay**	**NHL**	**25**	**1**	**1**	**2**	**92**	....	....	....	....	....
1995-96	**Tampa Bay**	**NHL**	**57**	**1**	**3**	**4**	**88**	**3**	**0**	**0**	**0**	**12**
	NHL Totals		**226**	**5**	**12**	**17**	**576**	**3**	**0**	**0**	**0**	**12**

Traded to **Winnipeg** by **NY Rangers** for Guy Larose, January 22, 1991. Signed as a free agent by **Toronto**, July 8, 1992. Signed as a free agent by **Tampa Bay**, August 10, 1993.

POIRIER, GAETAN — FLA.

Left wing. Shoots left. 6'2", 200 lbs. Born, Moncton, N.B., December 28, 1976.
(Florida's 6th choice, 156th overall, in 1996 Entry Draft).

			Regular Season					Playoffs				
Season	Club	Lea	GP	G	A	TP	PIM	GP	G	A	TP	PIM
1994-95	Merrimack	H.E.	32	8	6	14	38	....	....	....	....	....
1995-96	Merrimack	H.E.	33	10	14	24	52	....	....	....	....	....

POIRIER, JOEL — WSH.

Left wing. Shoots left. 6'1", 190 lbs. Born, Richmond Hill, Ont., January 15, 1975.
(Washington's 7th choice, 199th overall, in 1993 Entry Draft).

			Regular Season					Playoffs				
Season	Club	Lea	GP	G	A	TP	PIM	GP	G	A	TP	PIM
1992-93	Sudbury	OHL	64	18	15	33	94	14	0	2	2	8
1993-94	Sudbury	OHL	28	17	5	22	44	....	....	....	....	....
	Windsor	OHL	13	6	8	14	20	....	....	....	....	....
1994-95	Windsor	OHL	64	24	39	63	50	10	4	5	9	10
1995-96	Portland	AHL	30	5	3	8	34	1	0	0	0	0
	Hampton Rds.	ECHL	23	9	8	17	61	....	....	....	....	....

POLASEK, LIBOR — (poh-LAH-shehk) VAN.

Center. Shoots right. 6'3", 220 lbs. Born, Vitkovice, Czech., April 22, 1974.
(Vancouver's 1st choice, 21st overall, in 1992 Entry Draft).

			Regular Season					Playoffs				
Season	Club	Lea	GP	G	A	TP	PIM	GP	G	A	TP	PIM
1991-92	TJ Vitkovice	Czech.	17	2	2	4	4	....	....	....	....	....
1992-93	Hamilton	AHL	60	7	12	19	34	....	....	....	....	....
1993-94	Hamilton	AHL	76	11	12	23	40	3	0	0	0	0
1994-95	Syracuse	AHL	45	2	8	10	16	....	....	....	....	....
	S. Carolina	ECHL	7	0	0	0	6	....	....	....	....	....
1995-96	Syracuse	AHL	8	0	2	2	6	....	....	....	....	....
	HC Vitkovice	Czech.	18	4	5	9	....	3	0	0	0	

POMICHTER, MICHAEL — TOR.

Center. Shoots left. 6'1", 222 lbs. Born, New Haven, CT, September 10, 1973.
(Chicago's 2nd choice, 39th overall, in 1991 Entry Draft).

			Regular Season					Playoffs				
Season	Club	Lea	GP	G	A	TP	PIM	GP	G	A	TP	PIM
1991-92	Boston U.	H.E.	34	11	27	38	14	....	....	....	....	....
1992-93	Boston U.	H.E.	30	16	14	30	23	....	....	....	....	....
1993-94a	Boston U.	H.E.	40	*28	26	54	37	....	....	....	....	....
1994-95	Indianapolis	IHL	76	13	9	22	47	....	....	....	....	....
1995-96	Cornwall	AHL	6	0	1	1	0	....	....	....	....	....
	Indianapolis	IHL	4	0	0	0	0	....	....	....	....	....
	St. John's	AHL	19	2	4	6	4	....	....	....	....	....

a NCAA East First All-American Team (1994)

Traded to **Toronto** by **Chicago** for cash, January 29, 1996.

POPOVIC, PETER — (puh-PUH-vihch) MTL.

Defense. Shoots right. 6'6", 235 lbs. Born, Koping, Sweden, February 10, 1968.
(Montreal's 5th choice, 93rd overall, in 1988 Entry Draft).

			Regular Season					Playoffs				
Season	Club	Lea	GP	G	A	TP	PIM	GP	G	A	TP	PIM
1986-87	Vasteras	Swe. 2	24	1	2	3	10	....	....	....	....	....
1987-88	Vasteras	Swe. 2	28	3	17	20	16	....	....	....	....	....
1988-89	Vasteras	Swe.	22	1	4	5	32	....	....	....	....	....
1989-90	Vasteras	Swe.	30	2	10	12	24	2	0	1	1	2
1990-91	Vasteras	Swe.	40	3	2	5	62	4	0	0	0	4
1991-92	Vasteras	Swe.	34	7	10	17	30	....	....	....	....	....
1992-93	Vasteras	Swe.	39	6	12	18	46	3	0	1	1	2
1993-94	**Montreal**	**NHL**	**47**	**2**	**12**	**14**	**26**	**6**	**0**	**1**	**1**	**0**
1994-95	Vasteras	Swe.	11	0	3	3	10	....	....	....	....	....
	Montreal	**NHL**	**33**	**0**	**5**	**5**	**8**	....	....	....	....	....
1995-96	**Montreal**	**NHL**	**76**	**2**	**12**	**14**	**69**	**6**	**0**	**2**	**2**	**4**
	NHL Totals		**156**	**4**	**29**	**33**	**103**	**12**	**0**	**3**	**3**	**4**

POPP, KEVIN BUF.

Defense. Shoots left. 6'1", 198 lbs. Born, Surrey, B.C., February 26, 1976.
(Buffalo's 7th choice, 119th overall, in 1995 Entry Draft).

			Regular Season					Playoffs				
Season	Club	Lea	GP	G	A	TP	PIM	GP	G	A	TP	PIM
1993-94	Spokane	WHL	43	0	4	4	126	2	0	0	0	0
1994-95	Seattle	WHL	70	5	8	13	257	4	1	2	3	4
1995-96	Seattle	WHL	44	0	6	6	193	....	....	....	....	....
	Portland	WHL	23	4	4	8	61	7	0	0	0	0

POSMYK, MAREK (PAWZ-mihk) TOR.

Defense. Shoots right. 6'5", 220 lbs. Born, Jihlava, Czech., September 15, 1978.
(Toronto's 1st choice, 36th overall, in 1996 Entry Draft).

			Regular Season					Playoffs				
Season	Club	Lea	GP	G	A	TP	PIM	GP	G	A	TP	PIM
1994-95	Dukla Jihlava	Czech. Jr.	16	1	3	4	....	....	....	....	....	....
1995-96	Dukla Jihlava	Czech. Jr.	16	6	5	11	....	....	....	....	....	....
	Dukla Jihlava	Czech.	18	1	2	3	....	1	0	0	0	....

POTAPOV, VLADIMIR (poh-TAH-pohv) PHO.

Right wing. Shoots left. 6'2", 187 lbs. Born, Murmansk, USSR, June 21, 1975.
(Winnipeg's 10th choice, 217th overall, in 1993 Entry Draft).

			Regular Season					Playoffs				
Season	Club	Lea	GP	G	A	TP	PIM	GP	G	A	TP	PIM
1993-94	Elektrostal	CIS 2	41	3	3	6	4	....	....	....	....	....
1994-95	Elektrostal	CIS	51	4	7	11	24	....	....	....	....	....
1995-96	Moscow D'amo	CIS	25	1	0	1	8	....	....	....	....	....

POTI, TOM EDM.

Defense. Shoots left. 6'2", 178 lbs. Born, Worcester, MA, March 22, 1977.
(Edmonton's 4th choice, 59th overall, in 1996 Entry Draft).

			Regular Season					Playoffs				
Season	Club	Lea	GP	G	A	TP	PIM	GP	G	A	TP	PIM
1994-95	Cushing Aca.	HS	36	16	47	63	35	....	....	....	....	....
1995-96	Cushing Aca.	HS	29	14	59	73	18	....	....	....	....	....

POTOMSKI, BARRY L.A.

Left wing. Shoots left. 6'2", 215 lbs. Born, Windsor, Ont., November 24, 1972.

			Regular Season					Playoffs				
Season	Club	Lea	GP	G	A	TP	PIM	GP	G	A	TP	PIM
1989-90	London	OHL	9	0	2	2	18	....	....	....	....	....
1990-91	London	OHL	65	14	17	31	202	7	0	2	2	10
1991-92	London	OHL	61	19	32	51	224	10	5	1	6	22
1992-93	Erie	ECHL	5	1	1	2	31	....	....	....	....	....
	Toledo	ECHL	43	5	18	23	184	14	5	2	7	73
1993-94	Toledo	ECHL	13	9	4	13	81	....	....	....	....	....
	Adirondack	AHL	50	9	5	14	224	11	1	1	2	44
1994-95	Phoenix	IHL	42	5	6	11	171	....	....	....	....	....
1995-96	**Los Angeles**	**NHL**	**33**	**3**	**2**	**5**	**104**	....	....	....	....	....
	Phoenix	IHL	24	5	2	7	74	3	1	0	1	8
	NHL Totals		**33**	**3**	**2**	**5**	**104**					

Signed as a free agent by **Los Angeles**, July 7, 1994.

POTVIN, MARC (POT-vahn)

Right wing. Shoots right. 6'1", 200 lbs. Born, Ottawa, Ont., January 29, 1967.
(Detroit's 9th choice, 169th overall, in 1986 Entry Draft).

			Regular Season					Playoffs				
Season	Club	Lea	GP	G	A	TP	PIM	GP	G	A	TP	PIM
1986-87	Bowling Green	CCHA	43	5	15	20	74	....	....	....	....	....
1987-88	Bowling Green	CCHA	45	15	21	36	80	....	....	....	....	....
1988-89	Bowling Green	CCHA	46	23	12	35	63	....	....	....	....	....
1989-90	Bowling Green	CCHA	40	19	17	36	72	....	....	....	....	....
	Adirondack	AHL	5	2	1	3	9	4	0	1	1	23
1990-91	**Detroit**	**NHL**	**9**	**0**	**0**	**0**	**55**	6	0	0	0	32
	Adirondack	AHL	63	9	13	22	*365	....	....	....	....	....
1991-92	**Detroit**	**NHL**	**5**	**1**	**0**	**1**	**52**	1	0	0	0	0
	Adirondack	AHL	51	13	16	29	314	19	5	4	9	57
1992-93	Adirondack	AHL	37	8	12	20	109	....	....	....	....	....
	Los Angeles	**NHL**	**20**	**0**	**1**	**1**	**61**	1	0	0	0	0
1993-94	**Los Angeles**	**NHL**	**3**	**0**	**0**	**0**	**26**	....	....	....	....	....
	Hartford	**NHL**	**51**	**2**	**3**	**5**	**246**	....	....	....	....	....
1994-95	**Boston**	**NHL**	**6**	**0**	**1**	**1**	**4**	....	....	....	....	....
	Providence	AHL	21	4	14	18	84	12	2	4	6	25
1995-96	**Boston**	**NHL**	**27**	**0**	**0**	**0**	**12**	5	0	1	1	18
	Providence	AHL	48	9	9	18	118	....	....	....	....	....
	NHL Totals		**121**	**3**	**5**	**8**	**456**	**13**	**0**	**1**	**1**	**50**

Traded to **Los Angeles** by **Detroit** with Jimmy Carson and Gary Shuchuk for Paul Coffey, Sylvain Couturier and Jim Hiller, January 29, 1993. Traded to **Hartford** by **Los Angeles** for Doug Houda, November 3, 1993. Signed as a free agent by **Boston**, June 29, 1994.

POULIN, PATRICK (poo-LIHN) T.B.

Left wing. Shoots left. 6'1", 210 lbs. Born, Vanier, Que., April 23, 1973.
(Hartford's 1st choice, 9th overall, in 1991 Entry Draft).

			Regular Season					Playoffs				
Season	Club	Lea	GP	G	A	TP	PIM	GP	G	A	TP	PIM
1989-90	St-Hyacinthe	QMJHL	60	25	26	51	55	12	1	9	10	5
1990-91	St-Hyacinthe	QMJHL	56	32	38	70	82	4	0	2	2	23
1991-92	**Hartford**	**NHL**	**1**	**0**	**0**	**0**	**2**	7	2	1	3	0
a	St-Hyacinthe	QMJHL	56	52	86	*138	58	5	2	2	4	4
	Springfield	AHL	....	....	....	....	....	1	0	0	0	0
1992-93	**Hartford**	**NHL**	**81**	**20**	**31**	**51**	**37**	....	....	....	....	....
1993-94	**Hartford**	**NHL**	**9**	**2**	**1**	**3**	**11**	....	....	....	....	....
	Chicago	**NHL**	**58**	**12**	**13**	**25**	**40**	4	0	0	0	0
1994-95	**Chicago**	**NHL**	**45**	**15**	**15**	**30**	**53**	16	4	1	5	8
1995-96	**Chicago**	**NHL**	**38**	**7**	**8**	**15**	**16**	....	....	....	....	....
	Indianapolis	IHL	1	0	1	1	0	....	....	....	....	....
	Tampa Bay	**NHL**	**8**	**0**	**1**	**1**	**0**	2	0	0	0	0
	NHL Totals		**240**	**56**	**69**	**125**	**159**	**29**	**6**	**2**	**8**	**8**

a QMJHL First All-Star Team (1992)

Traded to **Chicago** by **Hartford** with Eric Weinrich for Steve Larmer and Bryan Marchment, November 2, 1993. Traded to **Tampa Bay** by **Chicago** with Igor Ulanov and Chicago's second round choice (later traded to New Jersey — New Jersey selected Pierre Dagenais) in 1996 Entry Draft for Enrico Ciccone and Tampa Bay's second round choice (Jeff Paul) in 1996 Entry Draft, March 20, 1996.

PRATT, NOLAN HFD.

Defense. Shoots left. 6'2", 195 lbs. Born, Fort McMurray, Alta., August 14, 1975.
(Hartford's 4th choice, 115th overall, in 1993 Entry Draft).

			Regular Season					Playoffs				
Season	Club	Lea	GP	G	A	TP	PIM	GP	G	A	TP	PIM
1991-92	Portland	WHL	22	2	9	11	13	6	1	3	4	12
1992-93	Portland	WHL	70	4	19	23	97	16	2	7	9	31
1993-94	Portland	WHL	72	4	32	36	105	10	1	2	3	14
1994-95	Portland	WHL	72	6	37	43	196	9	1	6	7	10
1995-96	Springfield	AHL	62	2	6	8	72	2	0	0	0	0
	Richmond	ECHL	4	1	0	1	2	....	....	....	....	....

PRESLEY, WAYNE TOR.

Right wing. Shoots right. 5'11", 195 lbs. Born, Dearborn, MI, March 23, 1965.
(Chicago's 2nd choice, 39th overall, in 1983 Entry Draft).

			Regular Season					Playoffs				
Season	Club	Lea	GP	G	A	TP	PIM	GP	G	A	TP	PIM
1982-83	Kitchener	OHL	70	39	48	87	99	12	1	4	5	9
1983-84a	Kitchener	OHL	70	63	76	139	156	16	12	16	28	38
1984-85	**Chicago**	**NHL**	**3**	**0**	**1**	**1**	**0**	....	....	....	....	....
	Kitchener	OHL	31	25	21	46	77	....	....	....	....	....
	S.S. Marie	OHL	11	5	9	14	14	16	13	9	22	13
1985-86	**Chicago**	**NHL**	**38**	**7**	**8**	**15**	**38**	3	0	0	0	0
	Nova Scotia	AHL	29	6	9	15	22	....	....	....	....	....
1986-87	**Chicago**	**NHL**	**80**	**32**	**29**	**61**	**114**	4	1	0	1	9
1987-88	**Chicago**	**NHL**	**42**	**12**	**10**	**22**	**52**	5	0	0	0	4
1988-89	**Chicago**	**NHL**	**72**	**21**	**19**	**40**	**100**	14	7	5	12	18
1989-90	**Chicago**	**NHL**	**49**	**6**	**7**	**13**	**69**	19	9	6	15	29
1990-91	**Chicago**	**NHL**	**71**	**15**	**19**	**34**	**122**	6	0	1	1	38
1991-92	**San Jose**	**NHL**	**47**	**8**	**14**	**22**	**76**	....	....	....	....	....
	Buffalo	**NHL**	**12**	**2**	**2**	**4**	**57**	7	3	3	6	14
1992-93	**Buffalo**	**NHL**	**79**	**15**	**17**	**32**	**96**	8	1	0	1	6
1993-94	**Buffalo**	**NHL**	**65**	**17**	**8**	**25**	**103**	7	2	1	3	14
1994-95	**Buffalo**	**NHL**	**46**	**14**	**5**	**19**	**41**	5	3	1	4	8
1995-96	**NY Rangers**	**NHL**	**61**	**4**	**6**	**10**	**71**	....	....	....	....	....
	Toronto	**NHL**	**19**	**2**	**2**	**4**	**14**	5	0	0	0	2
	NHL Totals		**684**	**155**	**147**	**302**	**953**	**83**	**26**	**17**	**43**	**142**

a OHL First All-Star Team (1984)

Traded to **San Jose** by **Chicago** for San Jose's third round choice (Bogdan Savenko) in 1993 Entry Draft, September 20, 1991. Traded to **Buffalo** by **San Jose** for Dave Snuggerud, March 9, 1992. Signed as a free agent by **NY Rangers**, August 31, 1995. Traded to **Toronto** by **NY Rangers** for Sergio Momesso, February 29, 1996.

PRIMEAU, KEITH DET.

Center. Shoots left. 6'4", 210 lbs. Born, Toronto, Ont., November 24, 1971.
(Detroit's 1st choice, 3rd overall, in 1990 Entry Draft).

			Regular Season					Playoffs				
Season	Club	Lea	GP	G	A	TP	PIM	GP	G	A	TP	PIM
1987-88	Hamilton	OHL	47	6	6	12	69	....	....	....	....	....
1988-89	Niagara Falls	OHL	48	20	35	55	56	17	9	16	25	12
1989-90a	Niagara Falls	OHL	65	*57	70	*127	97	16	*16	17	*33	49
1990-91	**Detroit**	**NHL**	**58**	**3**	**12**	**15**	**106**	5	1	1	2	25
	Adirondack	AHL	6	3	5	8	8	....	....	....	....	....
1991-92	**Detroit**	**NHL**	**35**	**6**	**10**	**16**	**83**	11	0	0	0	14
	Adirondack	AHL	42	21	24	45	89	9	1	7	8	27
1992-93	**Detroit**	**NHL**	**73**	**15**	**17**	**32**	**152**	7	0	2	2	26
1993-94	**Detroit**	**NHL**	**78**	**31**	**42**	**73**	**173**	7	0	2	2	6
1994-95	**Detroit**	**NHL**	**45**	**15**	**27**	**42**	**99**	17	4	5	9	45
1995-96	**Detroit**	**NHL**	**74**	**27**	**25**	**52**	**168**	17	1	4	5	28
	NHL Totals		**363**	**97**	**133**	**230**	**781**	**64**	**6**	**14**	**20**	**144**

a OHL Second All-Star Team (1990)

PRIMEAU, WAYNE BUF.

Center. Shoots left. 6'3", 193 lbs. Born, Scarborough, Ont., June 4, 1976.
(Buffalo's 1st choice, 17th overall, in 1994 Entry Draft).

			Regular Season					Playoffs				
Season	Club	Lea	GP	G	A	TP	PIM	GP	G	A	TP	PIM
1992-93	Owen Sound	OHL	66	10	27	37	108	8	1	4	5	0
1993-94	Owen Sound	OHL	65	25	50	75	75	9	1	6	7	8
1994-95	Owen Sound	OHL	66	34	62	96	84	10	4	9	13	15
	Buffalo	**NHL**	**1**	**1**	**0**	**1**	**0**	....	....	....	....	....
1995-96	**Buffalo**	**NHL**	**2**	**0**	**0**	**0**	**0**	....	....	....	....	....
	Owen Sound	OHL	28	15	29	44	52	....	....	....	....	....
	Oshawa	OHL	24	12	13	25	33	3	2	3	5	2
	Rochester	AHL	8	2	3	5	6	17	3	1	4	11
	NHL Totals		**3**	**1**	**0**	**1**	**0**					

PROBERT, BOB (PROH-buhrt) CHI.

Right wing. Shoots left. 6'3", 225 lbs. Born, Windsor, Ont., June 5, 1965.
(Detroit's 3rd choice, 46th overall, in 1983 Entry Draft).

			Regular Season					Playoffs				
Season	Club	Lea	GP	G	A	TP	PIM	GP	G	A	TP	PIM
1982-83	Brantford	OHL	51	12	16	28	133	8	2	2	4	23
1983-84	Brantford	OHL	65	35	38	73	189	6	0	3	3	16
1984-85	S.S. Marie	OHL	44	20	52	72	172	....	....	....	....	....
	Hamilton	OHL	4	0	1	1	21	....	....	....	....	....
1985-86	**Detroit**	**NHL**	**44**	**8**	**13**	**21**	**186**	....	....	....	....	....
	Adirondack	AHL	32	12	15	27	152	10	2	3	5	68
1986-87	**Detroit**	**NHL**	**63**	**13**	**11**	**24**	**221**	16	3	4	7	63
	Adirondack	AHL	7	1	4	5	15	....	....	....	....	....
1987-88	**Detroit**	**NHL**	**74**	**29**	**33**	**62**	***398**	16	8	13	21	51
1988-89	**Detroit**	**NHL**	**25**	**4**	**2**	**6**	**106**	....	....	....	....	....
1989-90	**Detroit**	**NHL**	**4**	**3**	**0**	**3**	**21**	....	....	....	....	....
1990-91	**Detroit**	**NHL**	**55**	**16**	**23**	**39**	**315**	6	1	2	3	50
1991-92	**Detroit**	**NHL**	**63**	**20**	**24**	**44**	**276**	11	1	6	7	28
1992-93	**Detroit**	**NHL**	**80**	**14**	**29**	**43**	**292**	7	0	3	3	10
1993-94	**Detroit**	**NHL**	**66**	**7**	**10**	**17**	**275**	7	1	1	2	8
1994-95					DID NOT PLAY							
1995-96	**Chicago**	**NHL**	**78**	**19**	**21**	**40**	**237**	10	0	2	2	23
	NHL Totals		**552**	**133**	**166**	**299**	**2327**	**73**	**14**	**31**	**45**	**233**

Played in NHL All-Star Game (1988)

Signed as a free agent by **Chicago**, July 23, 1994.

PROCHAZKA, LIBOR (proh-HAHZ-kah) ST.L.

Defense. Shoots right. 6', 185 lbs. Born, Vlasim, Czech., April 25, 1974.
(St. Louis' 8th choice, 245th overall, in 1993 Entry Draft).

			Regular Season					Playoffs				
Season	Club	Lea	GP	G	A	TP	PIM	GP	G	A	TP	PIM
1991-92	Poldi Kladno	Czech.	7	0	0	0	0	....	....	....	....	....
1992-93	Poldi Kladno	Czech.	34	2	2	4	....	....	....	....	....	....
1993-94	Poldi Kladno	Czech.	41	4	7	11	....	8	0	3	3	....
1994-95	Poldi Kladno	Czech.	40	4	16	20	81	11	2	1	3	14
1995-96	Poldi Kladno	Czech.	38	6	10	16	....	8	2	1	3	....

PROCHAZKA, MARTIN (pro-HAHS-kah) TOR.

Right wing. Shoots right. 5'11", 180 lbs. Born, Slany, Czech., March 3, 1972.
(Toronto's 8th choice, 135th overall, in 1991 Entry Draft).

			Regular Season					Playoffs				
Season	Club	Lea	GP	G	A	TP	PIM	GP	G	A	TP	PIM
1989-90	Poldi Kladno	Czech.	49	18	12	30	....	....	....	....	....	....
1990-91	Poldi Kladno	Czech.	50	19	10	29	21	....	....	....	....	....
1991-92	Dukla Jihlava	Czech.	44	18	11	29	2	....	....	....	....	....
1992-93	Poldi Kladno	Czech.	46	26	12	38	....	....	....	....	....	....
1993-94	Poldi Kladno	Czech.	43	24	16	40	0	2	2	0	2	....
1994-95	Poldi Kladno	Czech.	41	25	33	58	18	11	8	4	12	4
1995-96	Poldi Kladno	Czech.	37	15	27	42	....	8	2	4	6	....

PROKHOROV, VITALI (PROH-kohr-ohv)

Left wing. Shoots left. 5'9", 185 lbs. Born, Moscow, USSR, December 25, 1966.
(St. Louis' 3rd choice, 64th overall, in 1992 Entry Draft).

			Regular Season					Playoffs				
Season	Club	Lea	GP	G	A	TP	PIM	GP	G	A	TP	PIM
1983-84	Spartak	USSR	5	0	0	0	0	....	....	....	....	....
1984-85	Spartak	USSR	31	1	1	2	10	....	....	....	....	....
1985-86	Spartak	USSR	29	3	9	12	4	....	....	....	....	....
1986-87	Spartak	USSR	27	1	6	7	2	....	....	....	....	....
1987-88	Spartak	USSR	19	5	0	5	4	....	....	....	....	....
1988-89	Spartak	USSR	37	11	5	16	10	....	....	....	....	....
1989-90	Spartak	USSR	43	13	8	21	35	....	....	....	....	....
1990-91	Spartak	USSR	43	21	10	31	29	....	....	....	....	....
1991-92	Spartak	CIS	38	13	19	32	68	....	....	....	....	....
1992-93	**St. Louis**	**NHL**	26	4	1	5	15	....	....	....	....	....
1993-94	**St. Louis**	**NHL**	55	15	10	25	20	4	0	0	0	0
	Peoria	IHL	19	13	10	23	16	....	....	....	....	....
1994-95	Spartak	CIS	8	1	4	5	8	....	....	....	....	....
	St. Louis	**NHL**	2	0	0	0	0	....	....	....	....	....
	Peoria	IHL	20	6	3	9	6	9	4	7	11	6
1995-96	Farjestad	Swe.	37	7	11	18	61	8	2	0	2	31
	NHL Totals		**83**	**19**	**11**	**30**	**35**	**4**	**0**	**0**	**0**	**0**

PROKOPEC, MIKE CHI.

Right wing. Shoots right. 6'2", 190 lbs. Born, Toronto, Ont., May 17, 1974.
(Chicago's 7th choice, 161st overall, in 1992 Entry Draft).

			Regular Season					Playoffs				
Season	Club	Lea	GP	G	A	TP	PIM	GP	G	A	TP	PIM
1991-92	Cornwall	OHL	59	12	15	27	75	6	0	0	0	0
1992-93	Newmarket	OHL	40	6	14	20	70	....	....	....	....	....
	Guelph	OHL	28	10	14	24	27	5	1	0	1	14
1993-94	Guelph	OHL	66	52	58	110	93	9	12	4	16	17
1994-95	Indianapolis	IHL	70	21	12	33	80	....	....	....	....	....
1995-96	**Chicago**	**NHL**	9	0	0	0	5	....	....	....	....	....
	Indianapolis	IHL	67	18	22	40	131	5	2	0	2	4
	NHL Totals		**9**	**0**	**0**	**0**	**5**	....	....	....	....	....

PRONGER, CHRIS ST.L.

Defense. Shoots left. 6'5", 220 lbs. Born, Dryden, Ont., October 10, 1974.
(Hartford's 1st choice, 2nd overall, in 1993 Entry Draft).

			Regular Season					Playoffs				
Season	Club	Lea	GP	G	A	TP	PIM	GP	G	A	TP	PIM
1991-92	Peterborough	OHL	63	17	45	62	90	10	1	8	9	28
1992-93ab	Peterborough	OHL	61	15	62	77	108	21	15	25	40	51
1993-94c	**Hartford**	**NHL**	81	5	25	30	113	....	....	....	....	....
1994-95	**Hartford**	**NHL**	43	5	9	14	54	....	....	....	....	....
1995-96	**St. Louis**	**NHL**	78	7	18	25	110	13	1	5	6	16
	NHL Totals		**202**	**17**	**52**	**69**	**277**	**13**	**1**	**5**	**6**	**16**

a OHL First All-Star Team (1993)
b Canadian Major Junior First All-Star Team (1993)
c NHL/Upper Deck All-Rookie Team (1994)

Traded to **St. Louis** by **Hartford** for Brendan Shanahan, July 27, 1995.

PRONGER, SEAN ANA.

Center. Shoots left. 6'2", 205 lbs. Born, Dryden, Ont., November 30, 1972.
(Vancouver's 3rd choice, 51st overall, in 1991 Entry Draft).

			Regular Season					Playoffs				
Season	Club	Lea	GP	G	A	TP	PIM	GP	G	A	TP	PIM
1990-91	Bowling Green	CCHA	40	3	7	10	30	....	....	....	....	....
1991-92	Bowling Green	CCHA	34	9	7	16	28	....	....	....	....	....
1992-93	Bowling Green	CCHA	39	23	23	46	35	....	....	....	....	....
1993-94	Bowling Green	CCHA	38	17	17	34	38	....	....	....	....	....
1994-95	Knoxville	ECHL	34	18	23	41	55	....	....	....	....	....
	Greensboro	ECHL	2	0	2	2	0	....	....	....	....	....
	San Diego	IHL	8	0	0	0	2	....	....	....	....	....
1995-96	**Anaheim**	**NHL**	7	0	1	1	6	....	....	....	....	....
	Baltimore	AHL	72	16	17	33	61	12	3	7	10	16
	NHL Totals		**7**	**0**	**1**	**1**	**6**	....	....	....	....	....

Signed as a free agent by **Anaheim**, February 14, 1995.

PROSOFSKY, TYLER VAN.

Center. Shoots left. 5'11", 175 lbs. Born, Saskatoon, Sask., February 19, 1976.
(Chicago's 7th choice, 170th overall, in 1994 Entry Draft).

			Regular Season					Playoffs				
Season	Club	Lea	GP	G	A	TP	PIM	GP	G	A	TP	PIM
1992-93	Tacoma	WHL	62	10	9	19	79	7	0	0	0	5
1993-94	Tacoma	WHL	70	20	22	42	132	8	1	1	2	23
1994-95	Tacoma	WHL	71	20	27	47	161	4	0	1	1	21
1995-96	Kelowna	WHL	63	35	40	75	148	6	4	3	7	30

Re-entered NHL Entry Draft, **Vancouver's** 4th choice, 121st overall, in 1996 Entry Draft.

PROSPAL, VACLAV (PRAWS-pahl, VAHT-slahv) PHI.

Center. Shoots left. 6'2", 185 lbs. Born, Ceske-Budejovice, Czech., February 17, 1975.
(Philadelphia's 2nd choice, 71st overall, in 1993 Entry Draft).

			Regular Season					Playoffs				
Season	Club	Lea	GP	G	A	TP	PIM	GP	G	A	TP	PIM
1992-93	Budejovice	Czech. Jr.	32	26	31	57	24	....	....	....	....	....
1993-94	Hershey	AHL	55	14	21	35	38	2	0	0	0	2
1994-95	Hershey	AHL	69	13	32	45	36	2	1	0	1	4
1995-96	Hershey	AHL	68	15	36	51	59	5	2	4	6	2

PROTSENKO, BORIS (proht-SEHN-koh) PIT.

Right wing. Shoots right. 6', 185 lbs. Born, Kiev, USSR, August 21, 1978.
(Pittsburgh's 4th choice, 77th overall, in 1996 Entry Draft).

			Regular Season					Playoffs				
Season	Club	Lea	GP	G	A	TP	PIM	GP	G	A	TP	PIM
1994-95	Fernie	Jr. A	47	27	25	52	199	....	....	....	....	....
1995-96	Calgary	WHL	71	46	29	75	68	....	....	....	....	....

PROULX, CHRISTIAN (PROO)

Defense. Shoots left. 6', 185 lbs. Born, Sherbrooke, Que., December 10, 1973.
(Montreal's 9th choice, 164th overall, in 1992 Entry Draft).

			Regular Season					Playoffs				
Season	Club	Lea	GP	G	A	TP	PIM	GP	G	A	TP	PIM
1990-91	St-Jean	QMJHL	67	1	8	9	73	....	....	....	....	....
1991-92	St-Jean	QMJHL	68	1	17	18	180	....	....	....	....	....
1992-93	St-Jean	QMJHL	70	3	34	37	147	4	0	0	0	12
	Fredericton	AHL	2	1	0	1	2	4	0	0	0	0
1993-94	**Montreal**	**NHL**	7	1	2	3	20	....	....	....	....	....
	Fredericton	AHL	70	2	12	14	183	....	....	....	....	....
1994-95	Fredericton	AHL	75	1	9	10	184	9	0	1	1	8
1995-96	San Francisco	IHL	80	1	15	16	154	4	0	0	0	6
	NHL Totals		**7**	**1**	**2**	**3**	**20**	....	....	....	....	....

PRPIC, JOEL (puhr-PIHCH) BOS.

Center. Shoots left. 6'6", 200 lbs. Born, Sudbury, Ont., September 25, 1974.
(Boston's 9th choice, 233rd overall, in 1993 Entry Draft).

			Regular Season					Playoffs				
Season	Club	Lea	GP	G	A	TP	PIM	GP	G	A	TP	PIM
1993-94	St. Lawrence	ECAC	31	2	4	6	90	....	....	....	....	....
1994-95	St. Lawrence	ECAC	32	7	10	17	62	....	....	....	....	....
1995-96	St. Lawrence	ECAC	32	3	10	13	77	....	....	....	....	....

PURINTON, DALE NYR

Defense. Shoots left. 6'2", 190 lbs. Born, Fort Wayne, IN, October 11, 1976.
(NY Rangers' 5th choice, 117th overall, in 1995 Entry Draft).

			Regular Season					Playoffs				
Season	Club	Lea	GP	G	A	TP	PIM	GP	G	A	TP	PIM
1994-95	Tacoma	WHL	65	0	8	8	291	3	0	0	0	13
1995-96	Kelowna	WHL	22	1	4	5	88	....	....	....	....	....
	Lethbridge	WHL	37	3	6	9	144	4	1	1	2	25

PUSHOR, JAMIE (PUH-shohr) DET.

Defense. Shoots right. 6'3", 192 lbs. Born, Lethbridge, Alta., February 11, 1973.
(Detroit's 2nd choice, 32nd overall, in 1991 Entry Draft).

			Regular Season					Playoffs				
Season	Club	Lea	GP	G	A	TP	PIM	GP	G	A	TP	PIM
1989-90	Lethbridge	WHL	10	0	2	2	2	....	....	....	....	....
1990-91	Lethbridge	WHL	71	1	13	14	193	....	....	....	....	....
1991-92	Lethbridge	WHL	49	2	15	17	232	5	0	0	0	33
1992-93	Lethbridge	WHL	72	6	22	28	200	4	0	1	1	9
1993-94	Adirondack	AHL	73	1	17	18	124	12	0	0	0	22
1994-95	Adirondack	AHL	58	2	11	13	129	4	0	1	1	0
1995-96	**Detroit**	**NHL**	5	0	1	1	17	....	....	....	....	....
	Adirondack	AHL	65	2	16	18	126	3	0	0	0	5
	NHL Totals		**5**	**0**	**1**	**1**	**17**	....	....	....	....	....

PYSZ, PATRIK (PIHSH) CHI.

Center. Shoots left. 5'11", 187 lbs. Born, Nowy Targ, Poland, January 15, 1975.
(Chicago's 6th choice, 102nd overall, in 1993 Entry Draft).

			Regular Season					Playoffs				
Season	Club	Lea	GP	G	A	TP	PIM	GP	G	A	TP	PIM
1992-93	Augsburg	Ger. 2	36	7	5	12	12	8	2	1	3	0
1993-94	Augsburg	Aut.	41	7	20	27	....	9	5	5	10	8
1994-95	Augsburg	Ger.	41	5	13	18	61	5	0	2	2	6
1995-96	Mannheim	Ger.	50	14	24	38	50	8	0	2	2	26

QUINN, DAN — PIT.

Center. Shoots left. 5'11", 182 lbs. Born, Ottawa, Ont., June 1, 1965.
(Calgary's 1st choice, 13th overall, in 1983 Entry Draft).

			Regular Season					Playoffs				
Season	Club	Lea	GP	G	A	TP	PIM	GP	G	A	TP	PIM
1981-82	Belleville	OHL	67	19	32	51	41	....	....	....	....	....
1982-83	Belleville	OHL	70	59	88	147	27	4	2	6	8	2
1983-84	Calgary	NHL	54	19	33	52	20	8	3	5	8	4
	Belleville	OHL	24	23	36	59	12	....	....	....	....	....
1984-85	Calgary	NHL	74	20	38	58	22	3	0	0	0	0
1985-86	Calgary	NHL	78	30	42	72	44	18	8	7	15	10
1986-87	Calgary	NHL	16	3	6	9	14	....	....	....	....	....
	Pittsburgh	NHL	64	28	43	71	40	....	....	....	....	....
1987-88	Pittsburgh	NHL	70	40	39	79	50	....	....	....	....	....
1988-89	Pittsburgh	NHL	79	34	60	94	102	11	6	3	9	10
1989-90	Pittsburgh	NHL	41	9	20	29	22	....	....	....	....	....
	Vancouver	NHL	37	16	18	34	27	....	....	....	....	....
1990-91	Vancouver	NHL	64	18	31	49	46	....	....	....	....	....
	St. Louis	NHL	14	4	7	11	20	13	4	7	11	32
1991-92	Philadelphia	NHL	67	11	26	37	26	....	....	....	....	....
1992-93	Minnesota	NHL	11	0	4	4	6	....	....	....	....	....
1993-94	Bern	Switz.	25	13	18	31	56	....	....	....	....	....
	Ottawa	NHL	13	7	0	7	6	....	....	....	....	....
1994-95	Zug	Switz.	7	7	6	13	26	....	....	....	....	....
	Los Angeles	NHL	44	14	17	31	32	....	....	....	....	....
1995-96	Ottawa	NHL	28	6	18	24	24	....	....	....	....	....
	Detroit	IHL	4	0	5	5	2	....	....	....	....	....
	Philadelphia	NHL	35	7	14	21	22	12	1	4	5	6
	NHL Totals		789	266	416	682	523	65	22	26	48	62

Traded to **Pittsburgh** by **Calgary** for Mike Bullard, November 12, 1986. Traded to **Vancouver** by **Pittsburgh** with Dave Capuano and Andrew McBain for Rod Buskas, Barry Pederson and Tony Tanti, January 8, 1990. Traded to **St. Louis** by **Vancouver** with Garth Butcher for Geoff Courtnall, Robert Dirk, Sergio Momesso, Cliff Ronning and St. Louis' fifth round choice (Brian Loney) in 1992 Entry Draft, March 5, 1991. Traded to **Philadelphia** by **St. Louis** with Rod Brind'Amour for Ron Sutter and Murray Baron, September 22, 1991. Signed as a free agent by **Minnesota**, October 4, 1992. Signed as a free agent by **Ottawa**, March 15, 1994. Signed as a free agent by **Los Angeles**, September 3, 1994. Signed as a free agent by **Ottawa**, August 1, 1995. Traded to **Philadelphia** by **Ottawa** for cash, January 23, 1996. Signed as a free agent by **Pittsburgh**, July 17, 1996.

QUINT, DERON — PHO.

Defense. Shoots left. 6'1", 182 lbs. Born, Durham, NH, March 12, 1976.
(Winnipeg's 1st choice, 30th overall, in 1994 Entry Draft).

			Regular Season					Playoffs				
Season	Club	Lea	GP	G	A	TP	PIM	GP	G	A	TP	PIM
1993-94	Seattle	WHL	63	15	29	44	47	9	4	12	16	8
1994-95a	Seattle	WHL	65	29	60	89	82	3	1	2	3	6
1995-96	Winnipeg	NHL	51	5	13	18	22	....	....	....	....	....
	Springfield	AHL	11	2	3	5	4	10	2	3	5	6
	Seattle	WHL	....	....	....	....	....	5	4	1	5	6
	NHL Totals		51	5	13	18	22	....	....	....	....	....

a WHL West First All-Star Team (1995)

QUINTAL, STEPHANE — (KAYN-tahl) MTL.

Defense. Shoots right. 6'3", 225 lbs. Born, Boucherville, Que., October 22, 1968.
(Boston's 2nd choice, 14th overall, in 1987 Entry Draft).

			Regular Season					Playoffs				
Season	Club	Lea	GP	G	A	TP	PIM	GP	G	A	TP	PIM
1985-86	Granby	QMJHL	67	2	17	19	144	....	....	....	....	....
1986-87a	Granby	QMJHL	67	13	41	54	178	8	0	9	9	10
1987-88	Hull	QMJHL	38	13	23	36	138	19	7	12	19	30
1988-89	Boston	NHL	26	0	1	1	29	....	....	....	....	....
	Maine	AHL	16	4	10	14	28	....	....	....	....	....
1989-90	Boston	NHL	38	2	2	4	22	....	....	....	....	....
	Maine	AHL	37	4	16	20	27	....	....	....	....	....
1990-91	Boston	NHL	45	2	6	8	89	3	0	1	1	7
	Maine	AHL	23	1	5	6	30	....	....	....	....	....
1991-92	Boston	NHL	49	4	10	14	77	....	....	....	....	....
	St. Louis	NHL	26	0	6	6	32	4	1	2	3	6
1992-93	St. Louis	NHL	75	1	10	11	100	9	0	0	0	8
1993-94	Winnipeg	NHL	81	8	18	26	119	....	....	....	....	....
1994-95	Winnipeg	NHL	43	6	17	23	78	....	....	....	....	....
1995-96	Montreal	NHL	68	2	14	16	117	6	0	1	1	6
	NHL Totals		451	25	84	109	663	22	1	4	5	27

a QMJHL First All-Star Team (1987)

Traded to **St. Louis** by **Boston** with Craig Janney for Adam Oates, February 7, 1992. Traded to **Winnipeg** by **St. Louis** with Nelson Emerson for Phil Housley, September 24, 1993. Traded to **Montreal** by **Winnipeg** for Montreal's second round choice (Jason Doig) in 1995 Entry Draft, July 8, 1995.

QUINTIN, JEAN-FRANCOIS

Left wing. Shoots left. 6', 187 lbs. Born, St. Jean, Que., May 28, 1969.
(Minnesota's 4th choice, 75th overall, in 1989 Entry Draft).

			Regular Season					Playoffs				
Season	Club	Lea	GP	G	A	TP	PIM	GP	G	A	TP	PIM
1987-88	Shawinigan	QMJHL	70	28	70	98	143	11	5	8	13	26
1988-89	Shawinigan	QMJHL	69	52	100	152	105	10	9	15	24	16
1989-90	Kalamazoo	IHL	68	20	18	38	38	10	8	4	12	14
1990-91	Kalamazoo	IHL	78	31	43	74	64	9	1	5	6	11
1991-92	San Jose	NHL	8	3	0	3	0	....	....	....	....	....
	Kansas City	IHL	21	4	6	10	29	13	2	10	12	29
1992-93	San Jose	NHL	14	2	5	7	4	....	....	....	....	....
	Kansas City	IHL	64	20	29	49	169	11	2	1	3	16
1993-94	Kansas City	IHL	41	14	19	33	117	....	....	....	....	....
1994-95	Kansas City	IHL	63	23	35	58	130	19	2	9	11	57
1995-96	Kansas City	IHL	77	26	35	61	158	5	0	3	3	20
	NHL Totals		22	5	5	10	4	....	....	....	....	....

Claimed by **San Jose** from **Minnesota** in Dispersal Draft, May 30, 1991.

RABY, MATHIEU — T.B.

Defense. Shoots right. 6'2", 204 lbs. Born, Hull, Que., January 19, 1975.
(Tampa Bay's 7th choice, 159th overall, in 1993 Entry Draft).

			Regular Season					Playoffs				
Season	Club	Lea	GP	G	A	TP	PIM	GP	G	A	TP	PIM
1992-93	Victoriaville	QMJHL	53	2	2	4	103	2	0	0	0	0
1993-94	Victoriaville	QMJHL	67	3	7	10	264	5	0	0	0	22
1994-95	Victoriaville	QMJHL	38	5	11	16	238	....	....	....	....	....
	Sherbrooke	QMJHL	25	2	2	4	106	7	0	1	1	24
1995-96	Nashville	ECHL	62	4	11	15	256	5	0	0	0	28
	Atlanta	IHL	5	0	0	0	15	....	....	....	....	....

RACINE, YVES — (ruh-SEEN, EEV) S.J.

Defense. Shoots left. 6', 205 lbs. Born, Matane, Que., February 7, 1969.
(Detroit's 1st choice, 11th overall, in 1987 Entry Draft).

			Regular Season					Playoffs				
Season	Club	Lea	GP	G	A	TP	PIM	GP	G	A	TP	PIM
1986-87	Longueuil	QMJHL	70	7	43	50	50	20	3	11	14	14
1987-88a	Victoriaville	QMJHL	69	10	84	94	150	5	0	0	0	13
	Adirondack	AHL	....	....	....	....	....	9	4	2	6	2
1988-89a	Victoriaville	QMJHL	63	23	85	108	95	16	3	*30	*33	41
	Adirondack	AHL	....	....	....	....	....	2	1	1	2	0
1989-90	Detroit	NHL	28	4	9	13	23	....	....	....	....	....
	Adirondack	AHL	46	8	27	35	31	....	....	....	....	....
1990-91	Detroit	NHL	62	7	40	47	33	7	2	0	2	0
	Adirondack	AHL	16	3	9	12	10	....	....	....	....	....
1991-92	Detroit	NHL	61	2	22	24	94	11	2	1	3	10
1992-93	Detroit	NHL	80	9	31	40	80	7	1	3	4	27
1993-94	Philadelphia	NHL	67	9	43	52	48	....	....	....	....	....
1994-95	Montreal	NHL	47	4	7	11	42	....	....	....	....	....
1995-96	Montreal	NHL	25	0	3	3	26	....	....	....	....	....
	San Jose	NHL	32	1	16	17	28	....	....	....	....	....
	NHL Totals		402	36	171	207	374	25	5	4	9	37

a QMJHL First-All Star Team (1988, 1989)

Traded to **Philadelphia** by **Detroit** with Detroit's fourth round choice (Sebastien Vallee) in 1994 Entry Draft for Terry Carkner, October 5, 1993. Traded to **Montreal** by **Philadelphia** for Kevin Haller, June 29, 1994. Claimed on waivers by **San Jose** from **Montreal**, January 23, 1996.

RAGNARSSON, MARCUS — S.J.

Defense. Shoots left. 6'1", 200 lbs. Born, Ostervala, Sweden, August 13, 1971.
(San Jose's 5th choice, 99th overall, in 1992 Entry Draft).

			Regular Season					Playoffs				
Season	Club	Lea	GP	G	A	TP	PIM	GP	G	A	TP	PIM
1989-90	Djurgarden	Swe.	13	0	2	2	0	1	0	0	0	0
1990-91	Djurgarden	Swe.	35	4	1	5	12	7	0	0	0	6
1991-92	Djurgarden	Swe.	40	8	5	13	14	10	0	1	1	4
1992-93	Djurgarden	Swe.	35	3	3	6	53	6	0	3	3	8
1993-94	Djurgarden	Swe.	19	0	4	4	24	....	....	....	....	....
1994-95	Djurgarden	Swe.	38	7	9	16	20	3	0	0	0	4
1995-96	San Jose	NHL	71	8	31	39	42	....	....	....	....	....
	NHL Totals		71	8	31	39	42	....	....	....	....	....

RAJAMAKI, TOMMI — TOR.

Defense. Shoots left. 6'2", 180 lbs. Born, Pori, Finland, February 29, 1976.
(Toronto's 6th choice, 178th overall, in 1994 Entry Draft).

			Regular Season					Playoffs				
Season	Club	Lea	GP	G	A	TP	PIM	GP	G	A	TP	PIM
1994-95	Assat Jr.	Fin.	29	11	17	28	30	....	....	....	....	....
	Assat	Fin.	12	4	1	5	8	7	0	1	1	2
1995-96	Assat	Fin.	45	5	2	7	26	3	0	0	0	6

RAJNOHA, PAVEL — CGY.

Defense. Shoots right. 6', 185 lbs. Born, Gottwaldov, Czech., February 23, 1974.
(Calgary's 8th choice, 150th overall, in 1992 Entry Draft).

			Regular Season					Playoffs				
Season	Club	Lea	GP	G	A	TP	PIM	GP	G	A	TP	PIM
1990-91	TJ Zlin	Czech.	6	0	0	0	4	....	....	....	....	....
1991-92	ZPS Zlin	Czech.	24	0	1	1	4	....	....	....	....	....
1992-93	ZPS Zlin	Czech.	26	2	1	3	....	....	....	....	....	....
1993-94	ZPS Zlin	Czech.	28	2	1	3	0	3	0	4	4	....
1994-95	ZPS Zlin	Czech.	29	0	6	6	22	....	....	....	....	....
1995-96	Dukla Jihlava	Czech.	38	0	2	2	....	8	0	0	0	....

RAMSEY, MIKE

Defense. Shoots left. 6'3", 195 lbs. Born, Minneapolis, MN, December 3, 1960.
(Buffalo's 1st choice, 11th overall, in 1979 Entry Draft).

			Regular Season					Playoffs				
Season	Club	Lea	GP	G	A	TP	PIM	GP	G	A	TP	PIM
1978-79	U. Minnesota	WCHA	26	6	11	17	30	....	....	....	....	....
1979-80	U.S. National	....	56	11	22	33	55	....	....	....	....	....
	U.S. Olympic	....	7	0	2	2	8	....	....	....	....	....
	Buffalo	NHL	13	1	6	7	6	13	1	2	3	12
1980-81	Buffalo	NHL	72	3	14	17	56	8	0	3	3	20
1981-82	Buffalo	NHL	80	7	23	30	56	4	1	1	2	14
1982-83	Buffalo	NHL	77	8	30	38	55	10	4	4	8	15
1983-84	Buffalo	NHL	72	9	22	31	82	3	0	1	1	6
1984-85	Buffalo	NHL	79	8	22	30	102	5	0	1	1	23
1985-86	Buffalo	NHL	76	7	21	28	117	....	....	....	....	....
1986-87	Buffalo	NHL	80	8	31	39	109	....	....	....	....	....
1987-88	Buffalo	NHL	63	5	16	21	77	6	0	3	3	29
1988-89	Buffalo	NHL	56	2	14	16	84	5	0	1	1	11
1989-90	Buffalo	NHL	73	4	21	25	47	6	0	1	1	8
1990-91	Buffalo	NHL	71	6	14	20	46	5	1	0	1	12
1991-92	Buffalo	NHL	66	3	14	17	67	7	0	2	2	8
1992-93	Buffalo	NHL	33	2	8	10	20	....	....	....	....	....
	Pittsburgh	NHL	12	1	2	3	8	12	0	6	6	4
1993-94	Pittsburgh	NHL	65	2	2	4	22	1	0	0	0	0
1994-95	Detroit	NHL	33	1	2	3	23	15	0	1	1	4
1995-96	Detroit	NHL	47	2	4	6	35	15	0	4	4	10
	NHL Totals		1068	79	266	345	1012	115	8	29	37	176

Played in NHL All-Star Game (1982, 1983, 1985, 1986)

Traded to **Pittsburgh** by **Buffalo** for Bob Errey, March 22, 1993. Signed as a free agent by **Detroit**, August 3, 1994.

RANDALL, BRYAN — EDM.

Center. Shoots left. 6'3", 183 lbs. Born, Winnipeg, Man., August 8, 1978.
(Edmonton's 6th choice, 141st overall, in 1996 Entry Draft).

			Regular Season					Playoffs				
Season	Club	Lea	GP	G	A	TP	PIM	GP	G	A	TP	PIM
1995-96	Medicine Hat	WHL	64	4	5	9	51	5	0	0	0	7

RANHEIM, PAUL — HFD.

Left wing. Shoots right. 6'1", 210 lbs. Born, St. Louis, MO, January 25, 1966.
(Calgary's 3rd choice, 38th overall, in 1984 Entry Draft).

			Regular Season					Playoffs				
Season	Club	Lea	GP	G	A	TP	PIM	GP	G	A	TP	PIM
1984-85	U. Wisconsin	WCHA	42	11	11	22	40	....	....	....	....	....
1985-86	U. Wisconsin	WCHA	33	17	17	34	34	....	....	....	....	....
1986-87a	U. Wisconsin	WCHA	42	24	35	59	54	....	....	....	....	....
1987-88bc	U. Wisconsin	WCHA	44	36	26	62	63	....	....	....	....	....
1988-89	**Calgary**	**NHL**	**5**	**0**	**0**	**0**	**0**	....	....	....	....	....
de	Salt Lake	IHL	75	*68	29	97	16	14	5	5	10	8
1989-90	**Calgary**	**NHL**	**80**	**26**	**28**	**54**	**23**	**6**	**1**	**3**	**4**	**2**
1990-91	**Calgary**	**NHL**	**39**	**14**	**16**	**30**	**4**	**7**	**2**	**2**	**4**	**0**
1991-92	**Calgary**	**NHL**	**80**	**23**	**20**	**43**	**32**	....	....	....	....	....
1992-93	**Calgary**	**NHL**	**83**	**21**	**22**	**43**	**26**	**6**	**0**	**1**	**1**	**0**
1993-94	**Calgary**	**NHL**	**67**	**10**	**14**	**24**	**20**	....	....	....	....	....
	Hartford	**NHL**	**15**	**0**	**3**	**3**	**2**	....	....	....	....	....
1994-95	**Hartford**	**NHL**	**47**	**6**	**14**	**20**	**10**	....	....	....	....	....
1995-96	**Hartford**	**NHL**	**73**	**10**	**20**	**30**	**14**	....	....	....	....	....
	NHL Totals		**489**	**110**	**137**	**247**	**131**	**19**	**3**	**6**	**9**	**2**

a WCHA Second All-Star Team (1987)
b NCAA West First All-American Team (1988)
c WCHA First All-Star Team (1988)
d IHL Second All-Star Team (1989)
e Won Garry F. Longman Memorial Trophy (Top Rookie - IHL) (1989)

Traded to **Hartford** by **Calgary** with Gary Suter and Ted Drury for James Patrick, Zarley Zalapski and Michael Nylander, March 10, 1994.

RASMUSSEN, ERIK (RAS-moo-suhn) — BUF.

Center. Shoots left. 6'2", 191 lbs. Born, Minneapolis, MN, March 28, 1977.
(Buffalo's 1st choice, 7th overall, in 1996 Entry Draft).

			Regular Season					Playoffs				
Season	Club	Lea	GP	G	A	TP	PIM	GP	G	A	TP	PIM
1995-96	U. Minnesota	WCHA	40	16	32	48	55	....	....	....	....	....

RATCHUK, PETER (RAT-chuhk) — COL.

Defense. Shoots left. 6', 175 lbs. Born, Buffalo, NY, September 10, 1977.
(Colorado's 1st choice, 25th overall, in 1996 Entry Draft).

			Regular Season					Playoffs				
Season	Club	Lea	GP	G	A	TP	PIM	GP	G	A	TP	PIM
1994-95	Lawrence Aca.	HS	31	8	15	23	18	....	....	....	....	....
1995-96	Shattuck	HS	35	22	28	50	24	....	....	....	....	....

RATHJE, MIKE (RATH-jee) — S.J.

Defense. Shoots left. 6'6", 220 lbs. Born, Mannville, Alta., May 11, 1974.
(San Jose's 1st choice, 3rd overall, in 1992 Entry Draft).

			Regular Season					Playoffs				
Season	Club	Lea	GP	G	A	TP	PIM	GP	G	A	TP	PIM
1990-91	Medicine Hat	WHL	64	1	16	17	28	12	0	4	4	2
1991-92a	Medicine Hat	WHL	67	11	23	34	109	4	0	1	1	2
1992-93a	Medicine Hat	WHL	57	12	37	49	103	10	3	3	6	12
	Kansas City	IHL	....	....	....	....	....	5	0	0	0	12
1993-94	**San Jose**	**NHL**	**47**	**1**	**9**	**10**	**59**	**1**	**0**	**0**	**0**	**0**
	Kansas City	IHL	6	0	2	2	0	....	....	....	....	....
1994-95	**San Jose**	**NHL**	**42**	**2**	**7**	**9**	**29**	**11**	**5**	**2**	**7**	**4**
	Kansas City	IHL	6	0	1	1	7	....	....	....	....	....
1995-96	**San Jose**	**NHL**	**27**	**0**	**7**	**7**	**14**	....	....	....	....	....
	Kansas City	IHL	36	6	11	17	34	....	....	....	....	....
	NHL Totals		**116**	**3**	**23**	**26**	**102**	**12**	**5**	**2**	**7**	**4**

a WHL East Second All-Star Team (1992, 1993)

RAY, ROB — BUF.

Right wing. Shoots left. 6', 203 lbs. Born, Belleville, Ont., June 8, 1968.
(Buffalo's 5th choice, 97th overall, in 1988 Entry Draft).

			Regular Season					Playoffs				
Season	Club	Lea	GP	G	A	TP	PIM	GP	G	A	TP	PIM
1985-86	Cornwall	OHL	53	6	13	19	253	6	0	0	0	26
1986-87	Cornwall	OHL	46	17	20	37	158	5	1	1	2	16
1987-88	Cornwall	OHL	61	11	41	52	179	11	2	3	5	33
1988-89	Rochester	AHL	74	11	18	29	*446	....	....	....	....	....
1989-90	**Buffalo**	**NHL**	**27**	**2**	**1**	**3**	**99**	....	....	....	....	....
	Rochester	AHL	43	2	13	15	335	17	1	3	4	115
1990-91	**Buffalo**	**NHL**	**66**	**8**	**8**	**16**	***350**	**6**	**1**	**1**	**2**	**56**
	Rochester	AHL	8	1	1	2	15	....	....	....	....	....
1991-92	**Buffalo**	**NHL**	**63**	**5**	**3**	**8**	**354**	**7**	**0**	**0**	**0**	**2**
1992-93	**Buffalo**	**NHL**	**68**	**3**	**2**	**5**	**211**	....	....	....	....	....
1993-94	**Buffalo**	**NHL**	**82**	**3**	**4**	**7**	**274**	**7**	**1**	**0**	**1**	**43**
1994-95	**Buffalo**	**NHL**	**47**	**0**	**3**	**3**	**173**	**5**	**0**	**0**	**0**	**14**
1995-96	**Buffalo**	**NHL**	**71**	**3**	**6**	**9**	**287**	....	....	....	....	....
	NHL Totals		**424**	**24**	**27**	**51**	**1748**	**25**	**2**	**1**	**3**	**115**

REASONER, MARTY — ST.L.

Center. Shoots left. 6'1", 185 lbs. Born, Rochester, NY, February 26, 1977.
(St. Louis' 1st choice, 14th overall, in 1996 Entry Draft).

			Regular Season					Playoffs				
Season	Club	Lea	GP	G	A	TP	PIM	GP	G	A	TP	PIM
1994-95	Deerfield Aca.	HS	26	25	32	57	14	....	....	....	....	....
1995-96	Boston College	H.E.	34	16	29	45	32	....	....	....	....	....

RECCHI, MARK (REH-kee) — MTL.

Right wing. Shoots left. 5'10", 180 lbs. Born, Kamloops, B.C., February 1, 1968.
(Pittsburgh's 4th choice, 67th overall, in 1988 Entry Draft).

			Regular Season					Playoffs				
Season	Club	Lea	GP	G	A	TP	PIM	GP	G	A	TP	PIM
1985-86	N. Westminster	WHL	72	21	40	61	55	....	....	....	....	....
1986-87	Kamloops	WHL	40	26	50	76	63	13	3	16	19	17
1987-88a	Kamloops	WHL	62	61	*93	154	75	17	10	*21	*31	18
1988-89	**Pittsburgh**	**NHL**	**15**	**1**	**1**	**2**	**0**	....	....	....	....	....
b	Muskegon	IHL	63	50	49	99	86	14	7	*14	*21	28
1989-90	**Pittsburgh**	**NHL**	**74**	**30**	**37**	**67**	**44**	....	....	....	....	....
	Muskegon	IHL	4	7	4	11	2	....	....	....	....	....
1990-91	**Pittsburgh**	**NHL**	**78**	**40**	**73**	**113**	**48**	**24**	**10**	**24**	**34**	**33 ♦**
1991-92	**Pittsburgh**	**NHL**	**58**	**33**	**37**	**70**	**78**	....	....	....	....	....
c	**Philadelphia**	**NHL**	**22**	**10**	**17**	**27**	**18**	....	....	....	....	....
1992-93	**Philadelphia**	**NHL**	**84**	**53**	**70**	**123**	**95**	....	....	....	....	....
1993-94	**Philadelphia**	**NHL**	**84**	**40**	**67**	**107**	**46**	....	....	....	....	....
1994-95	**Philadelphia**	**NHL**	**10**	**2**	**3**	**5**	**12**	....	....	....	....	....
	Montreal	**NHL**	**39**	**14**	**29**	**43**	**16**	....	....	....	....	....
1995-96	**Montreal**	**NHL**	**82**	**28**	**50**	**78**	**69**	**6**	**3**	**3**	**6**	**0**
	NHL Totals		**546**	**251**	**384**	**635**	**426**	**30**	**13**	**27**	**40**	**33**

a WHL West All-Star Team (1988)
b IHL Second All-Star Team (1989)
c NHL Second All-Star Team (1992)

Played in NHL All-Star Game (1991, 1993, 1994)

Traded to **Philadelphia** by **Pittsburgh** with Brian Benning and Los Angeles' first round choice (previously acquired by Pittsburgh — Philadelphia selected Jason Bowen) in 1992 Entry Draft for Rick Tocchet, Kjell Samuelsson, Ken Wregget and Philadelphia's third round choice (Dave Roche) in 1993 Entry Draft, February 19, 1992. Traded to **Montreal** by **Philadelphia** with Philadelphia's third round choice (Martin Hohenberger) in 1995 Entry Draft for Eric Desjardins, Gilbert Dionne and John LeClair, February 9, 1995.

REDDEN, WADE — OTT.

Defense. Shoots left. 6'2", 193 lbs. Born, Lloydminster, Sask., June 12, 1977.
(NY Islanders' 1st choice, 2nd overall, in 1995 Entry Draft).

			Regular Season					Playoffs				
Season	Club	Lea	GP	G	A	TP	PIM	GP	G	A	TP	PIM
1993-94	Brandon	WHL	63	4	35	39	98	14	2	4	6	10
1994-95a	Brandon	WHL	64	14	46	60	83	18	5	10	15	8
1995-96bc	Brandon	WHL	51	9	45	54	55	19	5	10	15	19

a WHL East Second All-Star Team (1995)
b WHL East First All-Star Team (1996)
c Memorial Cup All-Star Team (1996)

Traded to **Ottawa** by **NY Islanders** with Damian Rhodes for Don Beaupre, Martin Straka and Bryan Berard, January 23, 1996.

REDMOND, KEITH

Left wing. Shoots left. 6'3", 208 lbs. Born, Richmond Hill, Ont., October 25, 1972.
(Los Angeles' 4th choice, 79th overall, in 1991 Entry Draft).

			Regular Season					Playoffs				
Season	Club	Lea	GP	G	A	TP	PIM	GP	G	A	TP	PIM
1990-91	Bowling Green	CCHA	35	1	3	4	72	....	....	....	....	....
1991-92	Bowling Green	CCHA	8	0	0	0	14	....	....	....	....	....
	Belleville	OHL	16	1	7	8	52	....	....	....	....	....
	Detroit	OHL	25	6	12	18	61	7	1	3	4	49
1992-93	Phoenix	IHL	53	6	10	16	285	....	....	....	....	....
	Muskegon	ColHL	4	1	0	1	46	....	....	....	....	....
1993-94	**Los Angeles**	**NHL**	**12**	**1**	**0**	**1**	**20**	....	....	....	....	....
	Phoenix	IHL	43	8	10	18	196	....	....	....	....	....
1994-95	Phoenix	IHL	20	0	3	3	81	6	2	1	3	29
1995-96	Phoenix	IHL	34	5	3	8	164	1	0	0	0	0
	NHL Totals		**12**	**1**	**0**	**1**	**20**	....	....	....	....	....

REEKIE, JOE — WSH.

Defense. Shoots left. 6'3", 220 lbs. Born, Victoria, B.C., February 22, 1965.
(Buffalo's 6th choice, 119th overall, in 1985 Entry Draft).

			Regular Season					Playoffs				
Season	Club	Lea	GP	G	A	TP	PIM	GP	G	A	TP	PIM
1982-83	North Bay	OHL	59	2	9	11	49	8	0	1	1	11
1983-84	North Bay	OHL	9	1	0	1	18	....	....	....	....	....
	Cornwall	OHL	53	6	27	33	166	3	0	0	0	4
1984-85	Cornwall	OHL	65	19	63	82	134	9	4	13	17	18
1985-86	**Buffalo**	**NHL**	**3**	**0**	**0**	**0**	**14**	....	....	....	....	....
	Rochester	AHL	77	3	25	28	178	....	....	....	....	....
1986-87	**Buffalo**	**NHL**	**56**	**1**	**8**	**9**	**82**	....	....	....	....	....
	Rochester	AHL	22	0	6	6	52	....	....	....	....	....
1987-88	**Buffalo**	**NHL**	**30**	**1**	**4**	**5**	**68**	**2**	**0**	**0**	**0**	**4**
1988-89	**Buffalo**	**NHL**	**15**	**1**	**3**	**4**	**26**	....	....	....	....	....
	Rochester	AHL	21	1	2	3	56	....	....	....	....	....
1989-90	**NY Islanders**	**NHL**	**31**	**1**	**8**	**9**	**43**	....	....	....	....	....
	Springfield	AHL	15	1	4	5	24	....	....	....	....	....
1990-91	**NY Islanders**	**NHL**	**66**	**3**	**16**	**19**	**96**	....	....	....	....	....
	Capital Dist.	AHL	2	1	0	1	0	....	....	....	....	....
1991-92	**NY Islanders**	**NHL**	**54**	**4**	**12**	**16**	**85**	....	....	....	....	....
	Capital Dist.	AHL	3	2	2	4	2	....	....	....	....	....
1992-93	**Tampa Bay**	**NHL**	**42**	**2**	**11**	**13**	**69**	....	....	....	....	....
1993-94	**Tampa Bay**	**NHL**	**73**	**1**	**11**	**12**	**127**	....	....	....	....	....
	Washington	**NHL**	**12**	**0**	**5**	**5**	**29**	**11**	**2**	**1**	**3**	**29**
1994-95	**Washington**	**NHL**	**48**	**1**	**6**	**7**	**97**	**7**	**0**	**0**	**0**	**2**
1995-96	**Washington**	**NHL**	**78**	**3**	**7**	**10**	**149**	....	....	....	....	....
	NHL Totals		**508**	**18**	**91**	**109**	**885**	**20**	**2**	**1**	**3**	**35**

Traded to **NY Islanders** by **Buffalo** for NY Islanders' sixth round choice (Bill Pye) in 1989 Entry Draft, June 17, 1989. Claimed by **Tampa Bay** from **NY Islanders** in Expansion Draft, June 18, 1992. Traded to **Washington** by **Tampa Bay** for Enrico Ciccone, Washington's third round choice (later traded to Anaheim — Anaheim selected Craig Reichert) in 1994 Entry Draft and the return of future draft choices transferred in the Pat Elynuik trade, March 21, 1994.

REHNBERG, HENRIK — N.J.

Defense. Shoots left. 6'2", 194 lbs. Born, Grava, Sweden, July 20, 1977.
(New Jersey's 6th choice, 96th overall, in 1995 Entry Draft).

			Regular Season					Playoffs				
Season	Club	Lea	GP	G	A	TP	PIM	GP	G	A	TP	PIM
1994-95	Farjestad	Swe. Jr.	24	1	2	3	62	....	....	....	....	....
1995-96	Farjestad	Swe. Jr.	21	1	4	5	38	....	....	....	....	....
	Farjestad	Swe.	4	0	0	0	0	....	....	....	....	....

REICHEL, MARTIN (RIGH-khul) EDM.

Right wing. Shoots left. 6'1", 183 lbs. Born, Most, Czech., November 7, 1973.
(Edmonton's 2nd choice, 37th overall, in 1992 Entry Draft).

			Regular Season					Playoffs				
Season	Club	Lea	GP	G	A	TP	PIM	GP	G	A	TP	PIM
1990-91	Freiburg	Ger.	23	7	8	15	19	....	....	....	....	....
1991-92	Freiburg	Ger.	27	15	16	31	8	4	1	1	2	4
1992-93	Freiburg	Ger.	37	13	9	22	27	9	4	4	8	11
1993-94	Rosenheim	Ger.	20	5	15	20	6	....	....	....	....	....
1994-95	Rosenheim	Ger.	43	11	26	37	36	7	3	3	6	37
1995-96	Rosenheim	Ger.	50	17	28	45	40	4	3	0	3	2

REICHEL, ROBERT (RIGH-khul) CGY.

Center. Shoots left. 5'10", 185 lbs. Born, Litvinov, Czech., June 25, 1971.
(Calgary's 5th choice, 70th overall, in 1989 Entry Draft).

			Regular Season					Playoffs				
Season	Club	Lea	GP	G	A	TP	PIM	GP	G	A	TP	PIM
1987-88	Litvinov	Czech.	36	17	10	27	8	....	....	....	....	....
1988-89	Litvinov	Czech.	44	23	25	48	32	....	....	....	....	....
1989-90	Litvinov	Czech.	52	*49	34	*83	....	....	....	....	....	....
1990-91	**Calgary**	**NHL**	**66**	**19**	**22**	**41**	**22**	**6**	**1**	**1**	**2**	**0**
1991-92	**Calgary**	**NHL**	**77**	**20**	**34**	**54**	**32**	....	....	....	....	....
1992-93	**Calgary**	**NHL**	**80**	**40**	**48**	**88**	**54**	**6**	**2**	**4**	**6**	**2**
1993-94	**Calgary**	**NHL**	**84**	**40**	**53**	**93**	**58**	**7**	**0**	**5**	**5**	**0**
1994-95	Frankfurt	Ger.	21	19	24	43	41	....	....	....	....	....
	Calgary	**NHL**	**48**	**18**	**17**	**35**	**28**	**7**	**2**	**4**	**6**	**4**
1995-96	Frankfurt	Ger.	46	47	54	101	84	3	1	3	4	0
	NHL Totals		**355**	**137**	**174**	**311**	**194**	**26**	**5**	**14**	**19**	**6**

REICHERT, CRAIG ANA.

Right wing. Shoots right. 6'1", 196 lbs. Born, Winnipeg, Man., May 11, 1974.
(Anaheim's 3rd choice, 67th overall, in 1994 Entry Draft).

			Regular Season					Playoffs				
Season	Club	Lea	GP	G	A	TP	PIM	GP	G	A	TP	PIM
1991-92	Spokane	WHL	68	13	20	33	86	4	1	0	1	4
1992-93	Red Deer	WHL	66	32	33	65	62	4	3	1	4	2
1993-94	Red Deer	WHL	72	52	67	119	153	4	2	2	4	8
1994-95	San Diego	IHL	49	4	12	16	28	....	....	....	....	....
1995-96	Baltimore	AHL	68	10	17	27	50	1	0	0	0	0

REID, DAVID DAL.

Left wing. Shoots left. 6'1", 217 lbs. Born, Toronto, Ont., May 15, 1964.
(Boston's 4th choice, 60th overall, in 1982 Entry Draft).

			Regular Season					Playoffs				
Season	Club	Lea	GP	G	A	TP	PIM	GP	G	A	TP	PIM
1981-82	Peterborough	OHL	68	10	32	42	41	9	2	3	5	11
1982-83	Peterborough	OHL	70	23	34	57	33	4	3	1	4	0
1983-84	**Boston**	**NHL**	**8**	**1**	**0**	**1**	**2**	....	....	....	....	....
	Peterborough	OHL	60	33	64	97	12	....	....	....	....	....
1984-85	**Boston**	**NHL**	**35**	**14**	**13**	**27**	**27**	**5**	**1**	**0**	**1**	**0**
	Hershey	AHL	43	10	14	24	6	....	....	....	....	....
1985-86	**Boston**	**NHL**	**37**	**10**	**10**	**20**	**10**	....	....	....	....	....
	Moncton	AHL	26	14	18	32	4	....	....	....	....	....
1986-87	**Boston**	**NHL**	**12**	**3**	**3**	**6**	**0**	**2**	**0**	**0**	**0**	**0**
	Moncton	AHL	40	12	22	34	23	5	0	1	1	0
1987-88	**Boston**	**NHL**	**3**	**0**	**0**	**0**	**0**	....	....	....	....	....
	Maine	AHL	63	21	37	58	40	10	6	7	13	0
1988-89	**Toronto**	**NHL**	**77**	**9**	**21**	**30**	**22**	....	....	....	....	....
1989-90	**Toronto**	**NHL**	**70**	**9**	**19**	**28**	**9**	**3**	**0**	**0**	**0**	**0**
1990-91	**Toronto**	**NHL**	**69**	**15**	**13**	**28**	**18**	....	....	....	....	....
1991-92	**Boston**	**NHL**	**43**	**7**	**7**	**14**	**27**	**15**	**2**	**5**	**7**	**4**
	Maine	AHL	12	1	5	6	4	....	....	....	....	....
1992-93	**Boston**	**NHL**	**65**	**20**	**16**	**36**	**10**	....	....	....	....	....
1993-94	**Boston**	**NHL**	**83**	**6**	**17**	**23**	**25**	**13**	**2**	**1**	**3**	**2**
1994-95	**Boston**	**NHL**	**38**	**5**	**5**	**10**	**10**	**5**	**0**	**0**	**0**	**0**
	Providence	AHL	7	3	0	3	0	....	....	....	....	....
1995-96	**Boston**	**NHL**	**63**	**23**	**21**	**44**	**4**	**5**	**0**	**2**	**2**	**2**
	NHL Totals		**603**	**122**	**145**	**267**	**164**	**48**	**5**	**8**	**13**	**8**

Signed as a free agent by **Toronto**, June 23, 1988. Signed as a free agent by **Boston**, December 1, 1991. Signed as a free agent by **Dallas**, July 11, 1996.

REID, SHAWN NYR

Defense. Shoots left. 6', 200 lbs. Born, Toronto, Ont., September 21, 1970.

			Regular Season					Playoffs				
Season	Club	Lea	GP	G	A	TP	PIM	GP	G	A	TP	PIM
1990-91	Colorado	WCHA	38	10	8	18	36	....	....	....	....	....
1991-92	Colorado	WCHA	41	12	22	34	64	....	....	....	....	....
1992-93	Colorado	WCHA	32	3	11	14	54	....	....	....	....	....
1993-94ab	Colorado	WCHA	39	7	20	27	25	....	....	....	....	....
1994-95	Fort Wayne	IHL	42	4	8	12	28	....	....	....	....	....
	Binghamton	AHL	18	3	4	7	8	9	0	3	3	6
1995-96	Binghamton	AHL	45	0	5	5	33	1	0	0	0	0
	Charlotte	ECHL	6	1	5	6	10	....	....	....	....	....

a WCHA First All-Star Team (1994)
b NCAA West First All-American Team (1994)

Signed as a free agent by **NY Rangers**, July 6, 1994.

RENBERG, MIKAEL (REHN-buhrg) PHI.

Right wing. Shoots left. 6'2", 218 lbs. Born, Pitea, Sweden, May 5, 1972.
(Philadelphia's 3rd choice, 40th overall, in 1990 Entry Draft).

			Regular Season					Playoffs				
Season	Club	Lea	GP	G	A	TP	PIM	GP	G	A	TP	PIM
1988-89	Pitea	Swe. 2	12	6	3	9	....	....	....	....	....	....
1989-90	Pitea	Swe. 2	29	15	19	34	....	....	....	....	....	....
1990-91	Lulea	Swe.	29	11	6	17	12	5	1	1	2	4
1991-92	Lulea	Swe.	38	8	15	23	20	2	0	0	0	0
1992-93	Lulea	Swe.	39	19	13	32	61	11	4	4	8	4
1993-94a	**Philadelphia**	**NHL**	**83**	**38**	**44**	**82**	**36**	....	....	....	....	....
1994-95	Lulea	Swe.	10	9	4	13	16	....	....	....	....	....
	Philadelphia	**NHL**	**47**	**26**	**31**	**57**	**20**	**15**	**6**	**7**	**13**	**6**
1995-96	**Philadelphia**	**NHL**	**51**	**23**	**20**	**43**	**45**	**11**	**3**	**6**	**9**	**14**
	NHL Totals		**181**	**87**	**95**	**182**	**101**	**26**	**9**	**13**	**22**	**20**

a NHL/Upper Deck All-Rookie Team (1994)

RHEAUME, PASCAL (RAY-awm) N.J.

Center. Shoots left. 6'1", 200 lbs. Born, Quebec, Que., June 21, 1973.

			Regular Season					Playoffs				
Season	Club	Lea	GP	G	A	TP	PIM	GP	G	A	TP	PIM
1991-92	Trois Rivières	QMJHL	65	17	20	37	84	14	5	4	9	23
1992-93	Sherbrooke	QMJHL	65	28	34	62	88	14	6	5	11	31
1993-94	Albany	AHL	55	17	18	35	43	5	0	1	1	0
1994-95	Albany	AHL	78	19	25	44	46	14	3	6	9	19
1995-96	Albany	AHL	68	26	42	68	50	4	1	2	3	2

Signed as a free agent by **New Jersey**, October 1, 1992.

RICCI, MIKE (REE-CHEE) COL.

Center. Shoots left. 6', 190 lbs. Born, Scarborough, Ont., October 27, 1971.
(Philadelphia's 1st choice, 4th overall, in 1990 Entry Draft).

			Regular Season					Playoffs				
Season	Club	Lea	GP	G	A	TP	PIM	GP	G	A	TP	PIM
1987-88	Peterborough	OHL	41	24	37	61	20	8	5	5	10	4
1988-89a	Peterborough	OHL	60	54	52	106	43	17	19	16	35	18
1989-90bc	Peterborough	OHL	60	52	64	116	39	12	5	7	12	26
1990-91	**Philadelphia**	**NHL**	**68**	**21**	**20**	**41**	**64**	....	....	....	....	....
1991-92	**Philadelphia**	**NHL**	**78**	**20**	**36**	**56**	**93**	....	....	....	....	....
1992-93	**Quebec**	**NHL**	**77**	**27**	**51**	**78**	**123**	**6**	**0**	**6**	**6**	**8**
1993-94	**Quebec**	**NHL**	**83**	**30**	**21**	**51**	**113**	....	....	....	....	....
1994-95	**Quebec**	**NHL**	**48**	**15**	**21**	**36**	**40**	**6**	**1**	**3**	**4**	**8**
1995-96	**Colorado**	**NHL**	**62**	**6**	**21**	**27**	**52**	**22**	**6**	**11**	**17**	**18** ♦
	NHL Totals		**416**	**119**	**170**	**289**	**485**	**34**	**7**	**20**	**27**	**34**

a OHL Second All-Star Team (1989)
b Canadian Major Junior Player of the Year (1990)
c OHL First All-Star Team (1990)

Traded to **Quebec** by **Philadelphia** with Peter Forsberg, Steve Duchesne, Kerry Huffman, Ron Hextall, Chris Simon, Philadelphia's first round choice in the 1993 (Jocelyn Thibault) and 1994 (later traded to Toronto — later traded to Washington — Washington selected Nolan Baumgartner) Entry Drafts and cash for Eric Lindros, June 30, 1992.

RICE, STEVEN HFD.

Right wing. Shoots right. 6', 217 lbs. Born, Kitchener, Ont., May 26, 1971.
(NY Rangers' 1st choice, 20th overall, in 1989 Entry Draft).

			Regular Season					Playoffs				
Season	Club	Lea	GP	G	A	TP	PIM	GP	G	A	TP	PIM
1987-88	Kitchener	OHL	59	11	14	25	43	4	0	1	1	0
1988-89	Kitchener	OHL	64	36	30	66	42	5	2	1	3	8
1989-90a	Kitchener	OHL	58	39	37	76	102	16	4	8	12	24
1990-91	**NY Rangers**	**NHL**	**11**	**1**	**1**	**2**	**4**	**2**	**2**	**1**	**3**	**6**
	Binghamton	AHL	8	4	1	5	12	5	2	0	2	2
b	Kitchener	OHL	29	30	30	60	43	6	5	6	11	2
1991-92	**Edmonton**	**NHL**	**3**	**0**	**0**	**0**	**2**	....	....	....	....	....
	Cape Breton	AHL	45	32	20	52	38	5	4	4	8	10
1992-93	**Edmonton**	**NHL**	**28**	**2**	**5**	**7**	**28**	....	....	....	....	....
c	Cape Breton	AHL	51	34	28	62	63	14	4	6	10	22
1993-94	**Edmonton**	**NHL**	**63**	**17**	**15**	**32**	**36**	....	....	....	....	....
1994-95	**Hartford**	**NHL**	**40**	**11**	**10**	**21**	**61**	....	....	....	....	....
1995-96	**Hartford**	**NHL**	**59**	**10**	**12**	**22**	**47**	....	....	....	....	....
	NHL Totals		**204**	**41**	**43**	**84**	**178**	**2**	**2**	**1**	**3**	**6**

a Memorial Cup All-Star Team (1990)
b OHL Second All-Star Team (1991)
c AHL Second All-Star Team (1993)

Traded to **Edmonton** by **NY Rangers** with Bernie Nicholls and Louie DeBrusk for Mark Messier and future considerations, October 4, 1991. Signed as a free agent by **Hartford**, August 18, 1994.

RICHARDS, TRAVIS

Defense. Shoots left. 6'1", 185 lbs. Born, Crystal, MN, March 22, 1970.
(Minnesota's 6th choice, 169th overall, in 1988 Entry Draft).

			Regular Season					Playoffs				
Season	Club	Lea	GP	G	A	TP	PIM	GP	G	A	TP	PIM
1989-90	U. Minnesota	WCHA	45	4	24	28	38	....	....	....	....	....
1990-91	U. Minnesota	WCHA	45	9	25	34	28	....	....	....	....	....
1991-92a	U. Minnesota	WCHA	41	10	22	32	65	....	....	....	....	....
1992-93a	U. Minnesota	WCHA	42	12	26	38	52	....	....	....	....	....
1993-94	U.S. National	....	51	1	11	12	38	....	....	....	....	....
	U.S. Olympic	....	8	0	0	0	2	....	....	....	....	....
	Kalamazoo	IHL	19	2	10	12	20	4	1	1	2	0
1994-95bc	Kalamazoo	IHL	63	4	16	20	53	15	1	5	6	12
	Dallas	**NHL**	**2**	**0**	**0**	**0**	**0**	....	....	....	....	....
1995-96	**Dallas**	**NHL**	**1**	**0**	**0**	**0**	**2**	....	....	....	....	....
	Michigan	IHL	65	8	15	23	55	9	2	2	4	4
	NHL Totals		**3**	**0**	**0**	**0**	**2**	....	....	....	....	....

a WCHA Second All-Star Team (1992, 1993)
b IHL First All-Star Team (1995)
c Won Governors' Trophy (Outstanding Defenseman - IHL) (1995)

RICHARDSON, LUKE EDM.

Defense. Shoots left. 6'4", 210 lbs. Born, Ottawa, Ont., March 26, 1969.
(Toronto's 1st choice, 7th overall, in 1987 Entry Draft).

			Regular Season					Playoffs				
Season	Club	Lea	GP	G	A	TP	PIM	GP	G	A	TP	PIM
1985-86	Peterborough	OHL	63	6	18	24	57	16	2	1	3	50
1986-87	Peterborough	OHL	59	13	32	45	70	12	0	5	5	24
1987-88	**Toronto**	**NHL**	**78**	**4**	**6**	**10**	**90**	**2**	**0**	**0**	**0**	**0**
1988-89	**Toronto**	**NHL**	**55**	**2**	**7**	**9**	**106**	....	....	....	....	....
1989-90	**Toronto**	**NHL**	**67**	**4**	**14**	**18**	**122**	**5**	**0**	**0**	**0**	**22**
1990-91	**Toronto**	**NHL**	**78**	**1**	**9**	**10**	**238**	....	....	....	....	....
1991-92	**Edmonton**	**NHL**	**75**	**2**	**19**	**21**	**118**	**16**	**0**	**5**	**5**	**45**
1992-93	**Edmonton**	**NHL**	**82**	**3**	**10**	**13**	**142**	....	....	....	....	....
1993-94	**Edmonton**	**NHL**	**69**	**2**	**6**	**8**	**131**	....	....	....	....	....
1994-95	**Edmonton**	**NHL**	**46**	**3**	**10**	**13**	**40**	....	....	....	....	....
1995-96	**Edmonton**	**NHL**	**82**	**2**	**9**	**11**	**108**	....	....	....	....	....
	NHL Totals		**632**	**23**	**90**	**113**	**1095**	**23**	**0**	**5**	**5**	**67**

Traded to **Edmonton** by **Toronto** with Vincent Damphousse, Peter Ing, Scott Thornton, future considerations and cash for Grant Fuhr, Glenn Anderson and Craig Berube, September 19, 1991.

RICHER, STEPHANE J. J. (REE-shay) MTL.

Right wing. Shoots right. 6'2", 215 lbs. Born, Ripon, Que., June 7, 1966.
(Montreal's 3rd choice, 29th overall, in 1984 Entry Draft).

			Regular Season					Playoffs				
Season	Club	Lea	GP	G	A	TP	PIM	GP	G	A	TP	PIM
1983-84a	Granby	QMJHL	67	39	37	76	58	3	1	1	2	4
1984-85	Granby	QMJHL	30	30	27	57	31	....	....	....	....	....
b	Chicoutimi	QMJHL	27	31	32	63	40	12	13	13	26	25
	Montreal	NHL	1	0	0	0	0	....	....	....	....	....
	Sherbrooke	AHL	....	....	....	....	....	9	6	3	9	10
1985-86	Montreal	NHL	65	21	16	37	50	16	4	1	5	23 ♦
1986-87	Montreal	NHL	57	20	19	39	80	5	3	2	5	0
	Sherbrooke	AHL	12	10	4	14	11	....	....	....	....	....
1987-88	Montreal	NHL	72	50	28	78	72	8	7	5	12	6
1988-89	Montreal	NHL	68	25	35	60	61	21	6	5	11	14
1989-90	Montreal	NHL	75	51	40	91	46	9	7	3	10	2
1990-91	Montreal	NHL	75	31	30	61	53	13	9	5	14	6
1991-92	New Jersey	NHL	74	29	35	64	25	7	1	2	3	0
1992-93	New Jersey	NHL	78	38	35	73	44	5	2	2	4	2
1993-94	New Jersey	NHL	80	36	36	72	16	20	7	5	12	6
1994-95	New Jersey	NHL	45	23	16	39	10	19	6	15	21	2 ♦
1995-96	New Jersey	NHL	73	20	12	32	30	....	....	....	....	....
	NHL Totals		763	344	302	646	487	123	52	45	97	61

a QMJHL Rookie of the Year (1984)
b QMJHL Second All-Star Team (1985)

Played in NHL All-Star Game (1990)

Traded to **New Jersey** by **Montreal** with Tom Chorske for Kirk Muller and Roland Melanson, September 20, 1991. Traded to **Montreal** by **New Jersey** for Lyle Odelein, August 22, 1996.

RICHTER, BARRY BOS.

Defense. Shoots left. 6'2", 195 lbs. Born, Madison, WI, September 11, 1970.
(Hartford's 2nd choice, 32nd overall, in 1988 Entry Draft).

			Regular Season					Playoffs				
Season	Club	Lea	GP	G	A	TP	PIM	GP	G	A	TP	PIM
1989-90	U. Wisconsin	WCHA	42	13	23	36	36	....	....	....	....	....
1990-91	U. Wisconsin	WCHA	43	15	20	35	42	....	....	....	....	....
1991-92a	U. Wisconsin	WCHA	39	10	25	35	62	....	....	....	....	....
1992-93bc	U. Wisconsin	WCHA	42	14	32	46	74	....	....	....	....	....
1993-94	U.S. National	....	56	7	16	23	50	....	....	....	....	....
	U.S. Olympic	....	8	0	3	3	4	....	....	....	....	....
	Binghamton	AHL	21	0	9	9	12	....	....	....	....	....
1994-95	Binghamton	AHL	73	15	41	56	54	11	4	5	9	12
1995-96	NY Rangers	NHL	4	0	1	1	0	....	....	....	....	....
de	Binghamton	AHL	69	20	61	81	64	3	0	3	3	0
	NHL Totals		4	0	1	1	0	....	....	....	....	....

a NCAA All-Tournament Team (1992)
b WCHA First All-Star Team (1993)
c NCAA West First All-American Team (1993)
d AHL First All-Star Team (1996)
e Won Eddie Shore Plaque (Outstanding Defenseman - AHL) (1996)

Traded to **NY Rangers** by **Hartford** with Steve Larmer, Nick Kypreos and Hartford's sixth round choice (Yuri Litvinov) in 1994 Entry Draft for Darren Turcotte and James Patrick, November 2, 1993. Signed as a free agent by **Boston**, July 19, 1996.

RIDLEY, MIKE VAN.

Center. Shoots left. 6', 195 lbs. Born, Winnipeg, Man., July 8, 1963.

			Regular Season					Playoffs				
Season	Club	Lea	GP	G	A	TP	PIM	GP	G	A	TP	PIM
1983-84a	U. of Manitoba	GPAC	46	39	41	80	....	....	....	....	....	....
1984-85b	U. of Manitoba	GPAC	30	29	38	67	48	....	....	....	....	....
1985-86c	NY Rangers	NHL	80	22	43	65	69	16	6	8	14	26
1986-87	NY Rangers	NHL	38	16	20	36	20	....	....	....	....	....
	Washington	NHL	40	15	19	34	20	7	2	1	3	6
1987-88	Washington	NHL	70	28	31	59	22	14	6	5	11	10
1988-89	Washington	NHL	80	41	48	89	49	6	0	5	5	2
1989-90	Washington	NHL	74	30	43	73	27	14	3	4	7	8
1990-91	Washington	NHL	79	23	48	71	26	11	3	4	7	8
1991-92	Washington	NHL	80	29	40	69	38	7	0	11	11	0
1992-93	Washington	NHL	84	26	56	82	44	6	1	5	6	0
1993-94	Washington	NHL	81	26	44	70	24	11	4	6	10	6
1994-95	Toronto	NHL	48	10	27	37	14	7	3	1	4	2
1995-96	Vancouver	NHL	37	6	15	21	29	5	0	0	0	2
	NHL Totals		791	272	434	706	382	104	28	50	78	70

a Canadian University Player of the Year; CIAU All-Canadian, GPAC MVP and First All-Star Team (1984)
b CIAU All-Canadian, GPAC First All-Star Team (1985)
c NHL All-Rookie Team (1986)

Played in NHL All-Star Game (1989)

Signed as a free agent by **NY Rangers**, September 26, 1985. Traded to **Washington** by **NY Rangers** with Bob Crawford and Kelly Miller for Bob Carpenter and Washington's second round choice (Jason Prosofsky) in 1989 Entry Draft, January 1, 1987. Traded to **Toronto** by **Washington** with St. Louis' first round choice (previously acquired by Washington — Toronto selected Eric Fichaud) in 1994 Entry Draft for Rob Pearson and Philadelphia's first round choice (previously acquired by Toronto — Washington selected Nolan Baumgartner) in 1994 Entry Draft, June 28, 1994. Traded to **Vancouver** by **Toronto** for Sergio Momesso, July 8, 1995.

RIIHIJARVI, TEEMO (REE-ee-hee-jahr-vee) S.J.

Left wing. Shoots left. 6'6", 202 lbs. Born, Espoo, Finland, March 1, 1977.
(San Jose's 1st choice, 12th overall, in 1995 Entry Draft).

			Regular Season					Playoffs				
Season	Club	Lea	GP	G	A	TP	PIM	GP	G	A	TP	PIM
1993-94	Kiekko-Espoo	Fin.	13	1	1	2	6	....	....	....	....	....
1994-95	Kiekko-Espoo	Fin.	13	1	0	1	4	....	....	....	....	....
1995-96	Kiekko-Espoo	Fin.	2	0	0	0	0	....	....	....	....	....
	Haukat	Div. 2	4	0	0	0	2	....	....	....	....	....
	Kiekko-Espoo	Fin. Jr.	19	2	4	6	46	4	0	2	2	6

RISIDORE, RYAN HFD.

Defense. Shoots left. 6'4", 195 lbs. Born, Hamilton, Ont., April 4, 1976.
(Hartford's 3rd choice, 109th overall, in 1994 Entry Draft).

			Regular Season					Playoffs				
Season	Club	Lea	GP	G	A	TP	PIM	GP	G	A	TP	PIM
1993-94	Guelph	OHL	51	2	9	11	39	9	0	0	0	12
1994-95	Guelph	OHL	65	2	30	32	102	14	2	2	4	19
1995-96	Guelph	OHL	66	12	38	50	186	16	4	5	9	*48

RITCHIE, BYRON HFD.

Center. Shoots left. 5'10", 180 lbs. Born, Burnaby, B.C., April 24, 1977.
(Hartford's 6th choice, 165th overall, in 1995 Entry Draft).

			Regular Season					Playoffs				
Season	Club	Lea	GP	G	A	TP	PIM	GP	G	A	TP	PIM
1993-94	Lethbridge	WHL	44	4	11	15	44	6	0	0	0	14
1994-95	Lethbridge	WHL	58	22	28	50	132	....	....	....	....	....
1995-96a	Lethbridge	WHL	66	55	51	106	163	4	0	2	2	4

a WHL East Second All-Star Team (1996)

RITCHLIN, SEAN N.J.

Right wing. Shoots right. 6', 200 lbs. Born, Rochester, NY, June 14, 1977.
(New Jersey's 10th choice, 145th overall, in 1996 Entry Draft).

			Regular Season					Playoffs				
Season	Club	Lea	GP	G	A	TP	PIM	GP	G	A	TP	PIM
1994-95	Hotchkiss	HS	25	28	31	59	26	....	....	....	....	....
1995-96	U. of Michigan	CCHA	27	7	7	14	24	....	....	....	....	....

RIVERS, JAMIE ST.L.

Defense. Shoots left. 6', 190 lbs. Born, Ottawa, Ont., March 16, 1975.
(St. Louis' 2nd choice, 63rd overall, in 1993 Entry Draft).

			Regular Season					Playoffs				
Season	Club	Lea	GP	G	A	TP	PIM	GP	G	A	TP	PIM
1991-92	Sudbury	OHL	55	3	13	16	20	8	0	0	0	0
1992-93	Sudbury	OHL	62	12	43	55	20	14	7	19	26	4
1993-94ab	Sudbury	OHL	65	32	*89	121	58	10	1	9	10	14
1994-95c	Sudbury	OHL	46	9	56	65	30	18	7	26	33	22
1995-96	St. Louis	NHL	3	0	0	0	2	....	....	....	....	....
	Worcester	AHL	75	7	45	52	130	4	0	1	1	4
	NHL Totals		3	0	0	0	2	....	....	....	....	....

a OHL First All-Star Team (1994)
b Canadian Major Junior Second All-Star Team (1994)
c OHL Second All-Star Team (1995)

RIVERS, SHAWN

Defense. Shoots left. 5'10", 185 lbs. Born, Ottawa, Ont., January 30, 1971.

			Regular Season					Playoffs				
Season	Club	Lea	GP	G	A	TP	PIM	GP	G	A	TP	PIM
1988-89	St. Lawrence	ECAC	36	3	23	26	20	....	....	....	....	....
1989-90	St. Lawrence	ECAC	26	3	14	17	29	....	....	....	....	....
1990-91	Sudbury	OHL	66	18	33	51	43	5	2	7	9	0
1991-92	Sudbury	OHL	64	26	54	80	34	11	0	4	4	10
1992-93	Tampa Bay	NHL	4	0	2	2	2	....	....	....	....	....
	Atlanta	IHL	78	9	34	43	101	9	1	3	4	8
1993-94	Atlanta	IHL	76	6	30	36	88	12	1	4	5	21
1994-95	Chicago	IHL	68	8	29	37	69	3	0	1	1	0
1995-96	Chicago	IHL	21	3	4	7	22	....	....	....	....	....
	Atlanta	IHL	45	2	16	18	22	....	....	....	....	....
	Syracuse	AHL	5	0	2	2	2	16	1	6	7	14
	NHL Totals		4	0	2	2	2	....	....	....	....	....

Signed as a free agent by **Tampa Bay**, June 29, 1992.

RIVET, CRAIG MTL.

Defense. Shoots right. 6'1", 190 lbs. Born, North Bay, Ont., September 13, 1974.
(Montreal's 4th choice, 68th overall, in 1992 Entry Draft).

			Regular Season					Playoffs				
Season	Club	Lea	GP	G	A	TP	PIM	GP	G	A	TP	PIM
1991-92	Kingston	OHL	66	5	21	26	97	....	....	....	....	....
1992-93	Kingston	OHL	64	19	55	74	117	16	5	7	12	39
1993-94	Kingston	OHL	61	12	52	64	100	6	0	3	3	6
	Fredericton	AHL	4	0	2	2	2	....	....	....	....	....
1994-95	Fredericton	AHL	78	5	27	32	126	12	0	4	4	17
	Montreal	NHL	5	0	1	1	5	....	....	....	....	....
1995-96	Montreal	NHL	19	1	4	5	54	....	....	....	....	....
	Fredericton	AHL	49	5	18	23	189	6	0	0	0	12
	NHL Totals		24	1	5	6	59	....	....	....	....	....

ROB, LUBOS NYR

Center. Shoots left. 5'11", 183 lbs. Born, Budejovice, Czech., August 5, 1970.
(NY Rangers' 7th choice, 99th overall, in 1990 Entry Draft).

			Regular Season					Playoffs				
Season	Club	Lea	GP	G	A	TP	PIM	GP	G	A	TP	PIM
1989-90	Budejovice	Czech.	42	16	24	40	....	....	....	....	....	....
1990-91						UNAVAILABLE						
1991-92						UNAVAILABLE						
1992-93	Budejovice	Czech.	40	23	21	44	....	....	....	....	....	....
1993-94	Budejovice	Czech.	33	14	20	34	0	3	0	2	2	....
1994-95	Budejovice	Czech.	41	15	21	36	16	9	2	5	7	2
1995-96	Budejovice	Czech.	40	12	26	38	....	10	6	3	9	....

ROBERTS, DAVID VAN.

Left wing. Shoots left. 6', 185 lbs. Born, Alameda, CA, May 28, 1970.
(St. Louis' 5th choice, 114th overall, in 1989 Entry Draft).

			Regular Season					Playoffs				
Season	Club	Lea	GP	G	A	TP	PIM	GP	G	A	TP	PIM
1989-90	U. of Michigan	CCHA	42	21	32	53	46	....	....	....	....	....
1990-91ab	U. of Michigan	CCHA	43	26	45	71	58	....	....	....	....	....
1991-92	U. of Michigan	CCHA	44	16	42	58	68	....	....	....	....	....
1992-93a	U. of Michigan	CCHA	40	27	38	65	40	....	....	....	....	....
1993-94	U.S. National	....	49	17	28	45	68	....	....	....	....	....
	U.S. Olympic	....	8	1	5	6	4	....	....	....	....	....
	St. Louis	NHL	1	0	0	0	2	3	0	0	0	12
	Peoria	IHL	10	4	6	10	4	....	....	....	....	....
1994-95	Peoria	IHL	65	30	38	68	65	....	....	....	....	....
	St. Louis	NHL	19	6	5	11	10	6	0	0	0	4
1995-96	St. Louis	NHL	28	1	6	7	12	....	....	....	....	....
	Worcester	AHL	22	8	17	25	46	....	....	....	....	....
	Edmonton	NHL	6	2	4	6	6	....	....	....	....	....
	NHL Totals		54	9	15	24	30	9	0	0	0	16

a CCHA Second All-Star Team (1991, 1993)
b NCAA West Second All-American Team (1991)

Traded to **Edmonton** by **St. Louis** for future considerations, March 12, 1996. Signed as a free agent by **Vancouver**, July 31, 1996.

ROBERTS, GARY

Left wing. Shoots left. 6'1", 190 lbs. Born, North York, Ont., May 23, 1966.
(Calgary's 1st choice, 12th overall, in 1984 Entry Draft).

			Regular Season					Playoffs				
Season	Club	Lea	GP	G	A	TP	PIM	GP	G	A	TP	PIM
1982-83	Ottawa	OHL	53	12	8	20	83	5	1	0	1	19
1983-84	Ottawa	OHL	48	27	30	57	144	13	10	7	17	62
1984-85	Moncton	AHL	7	4	2	6	7	....	....	....	....	....
a	Ottawa	OHL	59	44	62	106	186	5	2	8	10	10
1985-86	Ottawa	OHL	24	26	25	51	83	....	....	....	....	....
a	Guelph	OHL	23	18	15	33	65	20	18	13	31	43
1986-87	**Calgary**	**NHL**	**32**	**5**	**10**	**15**	**85**	**2**	**0**	**0**	**0**	**4**
	Moncton	AHL	38	20	18	38	72	....	....	....	....	....
1987-88	**Calgary**	**NHL**	**74**	**13**	**15**	**28**	**282**	**9**	**2**	**3**	**5**	**29**
1988-89	**Calgary**	**NHL**	**71**	**22**	**16**	**38**	**250**	**22**	**5**	**7**	**12**	**57 ◆**
1989-90	**Calgary**	**NHL**	**78**	**39**	**33**	**72**	**222**	**6**	**2**	**5**	**7**	**41**
1990-91	**Calgary**	**NHL**	**80**	**22**	**31**	**53**	**252**	**7**	**1**	**3**	**4**	**18**
1991-92	**Calgary**	**NHL**	**76**	**53**	**37**	**90**	**207**	....	....	....	....	....
1992-93	**Calgary**	**NHL**	**58**	**38**	**41**	**79**	**172**	**5**	**1**	**6**	**7**	**43**
1993-94	**Calgary**	**NHL**	**73**	**41**	**43**	**84**	**145**	**7**	**2**	**6**	**8**	**24**
1994-95	**Calgary**	**NHL**	**8**	**2**	**2**	**4**	**43**	....	....	....	....	....
1995-96b	**Calgary**	**NHL**	**35**	**22**	**20**	**42**	**78**	....	....	....	....	....
	NHL Totals		**585**	**257**	**248**	**505**	**1736**	**58**	**13**	**30**	**43**	**216**

a OHL Second All-Star Team (1985, 1986)
b Won Bill Masterton Memorial Trophy (1996)

Played in NHL All-Star Game (1992, 1993)

ROBERTSSON, BERT (ROH-behrt-suhn) VAN.

Defense. Shoots left. 6'2", 198 lbs. Born, Sodertalje, Sweden, June 30, 1974.
(Vancouver's 8th choice, 254th overall, in 1993 Entry Draft).

			Regular Season					Playoffs				
Season	Club	Lea	GP	G	A	TP	PIM	GP	G	A	TP	PIM
1992-93	Sodertalje	Swe. 2	23	2	1	3	24	....	....	....	....	....
1993-94	Sodertalje	Swe. 2	28	0	1	1	12	....	....	....	....	....
1994-95	Sodertalje	Swe. 2	23	1	2	3	24	....	....	....	....	....
1995-96	Syracuse	AHL	65	1	7	8	109	16	0	1	1	26

ROBIDAS, STEPHANE MTL.

Defense. Shoots right. 5'10", 182 lbs. Born, Sherbrooke, Que., March 3, 1977.
(Montreal's 7th choice, 164th overall, in 1995 Entry Draft).

			Regular Season					Playoffs				
Season	Club	Lea	GP	G	A	TP	PIM	GP	G	A	TP	PIM
1993-94	Shawinigan	QMJHL	67	3	18	21	33	1	0	0	0	0
1994-95	Shawinigan	QMJHL	71	13	56	69	44	15	7	12	19	4
1995-96a	Shawinigan	QMJHL	67	23	56	79	53	6	1	5	6	10

a QMJHL First All-Star Team (1996)

ROBINSON, JASON T.B.

Defense. Shoots left. 6'2", 190 lbs. Born, Goderich, Ont., August 22, 1978.
(Tampa Bay's 3rd choice, 125th overall, in 1996 Entry Draft).

			Regular Season					Playoffs				
Season	Club	Lea	GP	G	A	TP	PIM	GP	G	A	TP	PIM
1994-95	Belle River	Jr. C	39	2	11	13	87	....	....	....	....	....
1995-96	Niagara Falls	OHL	51	2	4	6	100	10	0	0	0	16

ROBITAILLE, LUC (ROH-buh-tigh) NYR

Left wing. Shoots left. 6'1", 195 lbs. Born, Montreal, Que., February 17, 1966.
(Los Angeles' 9th choice, 171st overall, in 1984 Entry Draft).

			Regular Season					Playoffs				
Season	Club	Lea	GP	G	A	TP	PIM	GP	G	A	TP	PIM
1983-84	Hull	QMJHL	70	32	53	85	48	....	....	....	....	....
1984-85a	Hull	QMJHL	64	55	94	149	115	5	4	2	6	27
1985-86bc	Hull	QMJHL	63	68	123	191	91	15	17	27	44	28
1986-87def	**Los Angeles**	**NHL**	**79**	**45**	**39**	**84**	**28**	**5**	**1**	**4**	**5**	**2**
1987-88g	**Los Angeles**	**NHL**	**80**	**53**	**58**	**111**	**82**	**5**	**2**	**5**	**7**	**18**
1988-89g	**Los Angeles**	**NHL**	**78**	**46**	**52**	**98**	**65**	**11**	**2**	**6**	**8**	**10**
1989-90g	**Los Angeles**	**NHL**	**80**	**52**	**49**	**101**	**38**	**10**	**5**	**5**	**10**	**10**
1990-91g	**Los Angeles**	**NHL**	**76**	**45**	**46**	**91**	**68**	**12**	**12**	**4**	**16**	**22**
1991-92f	**Los Angeles**	**NHL**	**80**	**44**	**63**	**107**	**95**	**6**	**3**	**4**	**7**	**12**
1992-93g	**Los Angeles**	**NHL**	**84**	**63**	**62**	**125**	**100**	**24**	**9**	**13**	**22**	**28**
1993-94	**Los Angeles**	**NHL**	**83**	**44**	**42**	**86**	**86**	....	....	....	....	....
1994-95	**Pittsburgh**	**NHL**	**46**	**23**	**19**	**42**	**37**	**12**	**7**	**4**	**11**	**26**
1995-96	**NY Rangers**	**NHL**	**77**	**23**	**46**	**69**	**80**	**11**	**1**	**5**	**6**	**8**
	NHL Totals		**763**	**438**	**476**	**914**	**679**	**96**	**42**	**50**	**92**	**136**

a QMJHL Second All-Star Team (1985)
b QMJHL First All-Star Team (1986)
c Canadian Major Junior Player of the Year (1986)
d NHL All-Rookie Team (1987)
e Won Calder Memorial Trophy (1987)
f NHL Second All-Star Team (1987, 1992)
g NHL First All-Star Team (1988, 1989, 1990, 1991, 1993)

Played in NHL All-Star Game (1988-93)

Traded to **Pittsburgh** by **Los Angeles** for Rick Tocchet and Pittsburgh's second round choice (Pavel Rosa) in 1995 Entry Draft, July 29, 1994. Traded to **NY Rangers** by **Pittsburgh** with Ulf Samuelsson for Petr Nedved and Sergei Zubov, August 31, 1995.

ROCHE, DAVE (ROHSH) PIT.

Center. Shoots left. 6'4", 224 lbs. Born, Lindsay, Ont., June 13, 1975.
(Pittsburgh's 3rd choice, 62nd overall, in 1993 Entry Draft).

			Regular Season					Playoffs				
Season	Club	Lea	GP	G	A	TP	PIM	GP	G	A	TP	PIM
1991-92	Peterborough	OHL	62	10	17	27	134	10	0	0	0	34
1992-93	Peterborough	OHL	56	40	60	100	105	21	14	15	29	42
1993-94	Peterborough	OHL	34	15	22	37	127	....	....	....	....	....
	Windsor	OHL	29	14	20	34	73	4	1	1	2	15
1994-95a	Windsor	OHL	66	55	59	114	180	10	9	6	15	16
1995-96	**Pittsburgh**	**NHL**	**71**	**7**	**7**	**14**	**130**	**16**	**2**	**7**	**9**	**26**
	NHL Totals		**71**	**7**	**7**	**14**	**130**	**16**	**2**	**7**	**9**	**26**

a OHL First All-Star Team (1995)

ROCHEFORT, NORMAND

Defense. Shoots left. 6'1", 214 lbs. Born, Trois-Rivières, Que., January 28, 1961.
(Quebec's 1st choice, 24th overall, in 1980 Entry Draft).

			Regular Season					Playoffs				
Season	Club	Lea	GP	G	A	TP	PIM	GP	G	A	TP	PIM
1978-79	Trois-Rivières	QJHL	72	17	57	74	30	13	3	11	14	17
1979-80	Trois-Rivières	QJHL	20	5	25	30	22	....	....	....	....	....
a	Quebec	QJHL	52	8	39	47	68	5	1	3	4	8
1980-81	**Quebec**	**NHL**	**56**	**3**	**7**	**10**	**51**	**5**	**0**	**0**	**0**	**4**
	Quebec	QJHL	9	2	6	8	14	....	....	....	....	....
1981-82	**Quebec**	**NHL**	**72**	**4**	**14**	**18**	**115**	**16**	**0**	**2**	**2**	**10**
1982-83	**Quebec**	**NHL**	**62**	**6**	**17**	**23**	**40**	**1**	**0**	**0**	**0**	**2**
1983-84	**Quebec**	**NHL**	**75**	**2**	**22**	**24**	**47**	**6**	**1**	**0**	**1**	**6**
1984-85	**Quebec**	**NHL**	**73**	**3**	**21**	**24**	**74**	**18**	**2**	**1**	**3**	**8**
1985-86	**Quebec**	**NHL**	**26**	**5**	**4**	**9**	**30**	....	....	....	....	....
1986-87	**Quebec**	**NHL**	**70**	**6**	**9**	**15**	**46**	**13**	**2**	**1**	**3**	**26**
1987-88	**Quebec**	**NHL**	**46**	**3**	**10**	**13**	**49**	....	....	....	....	....
1988-89	**NY Rangers**	**NHL**	**11**	**1**	**5**	**6**	**18**	....	....	....	....	....
1989-90	**NY Rangers**	**NHL**	**31**	**3**	**1**	**4**	**24**	**10**	**2**	**1**	**3**	**26**
	Flint	IHL	7	0	32	5	4	....	....	....	....	....
1990-91	**NY Rangers**	**NHL**	**44**	**3**	**7**	**10**	**35**	....	....	....	....	....
1991-92	**NY Rangers**	**NHL**	**26**	**0**	**2**	**2**	**31**	....	....	....	....	....
1992-93	Eisbaren	Ger.	17	4	2	6	21	....	....	....	....	....
1993-94	**Tampa Bay**	**NHL**	**6**	**0**	**0**	**0**	**10**	....	....	....	....	....
	Atlanta	IHL	65	5	7	12	43	13	0	2	2	6
1994-95	Denver	IHL	77	4	13	17	46	17	1	4	5	12
1995-96	San Francisco	IHL	77	3	12	15	45	4	0	0	0	2
	NHL Totals		**598**	**39**	**119**	**158**	**570**	**69**	**7**	**5**	**12**	**82**

a QMJHL Second All-Star Team (1980)

Traded to **NY Rangers** by **Quebec** with Jason Lafreniere for Bruce Bell, Jari Gronstrand, Walt Poddubny and NY Rangers' fourth round draft choice (Eric Dubois) in 1989 Entry Draft, August 1, 1988. Signed as a free agent by **Tampa Bay**, September 27, 1993.

ROCHEFORT, RICHARD N.J.

Center. Shoots right. 5'9", 180 lbs. Born, North Bay, Ont., January 7, 1977.
(New Jersey's 9th choice, 174th overall, in 1995 Entry Draft).

			Regular Season					Playoffs				
Season	Club	Lea	GP	G	A	TP	PIM	GP	G	A	TP	PIM
1994-95	Sudbury	OHL	57	21	44	65	26	13	3	7	10	6
1995-96	Sudbury	OHL	56	25	40	65	38	....	....	....	....	....

ROED, PETER S.J.

Center. Shoots left. 5'10", 210 lbs. Born, St. Paul, MN, November 15, 1976.
(San Jose's 2nd choice, 38th overall, in 1995 Entry Draft).

			Regular Season					Playoffs				
Season	Club	Lea	GP	G	A	TP	PIM	GP	G	A	TP	PIM
1994-95	White Bear Lk.	HS	28	20	39	59	22	....	....	....	....	....
1995-96	Prince George	WHL	66	18	19	37	36	....	....	....	....	....

ROENICK, JEREMY (ROH-nihk) PHO.

Center. Shoots right. 6', 170 lbs. Born, Boston, MA, January 17, 1970.
(Chicago's 1st choice, 8th overall, in 1988 Entry Draft).

			Regular Season					Playoffs				
Season	Club	Lea	GP	G	A	TP	PIM	GP	G	A	TP	PIM
1988-89a	Hull	QMJHL	28	34	36	70	14	....	....	....	....	....
	Chicago	**NHL**	**20**	**9**	**9**	**18**	**4**	**10**	**1**	**3**	**4**	**7**
1989-90	**Chicago**	**NHL**	**78**	**26**	**40**	**66**	**54**	**20**	**11**	**7**	**18**	**8**
1990-91	**Chicago**	**NHL**	**79**	**41**	**53**	**94**	**80**	**6**	**3**	**5**	**8**	**4**
1991-92	**Chicago**	**NHL**	**80**	**53**	**50**	**103**	**98**	**18**	**12**	**10**	**22**	**12**
1992-93	**Chicago**	**NHL**	**84**	**50**	**57**	**107**	**86**	**4**	**1**	**2**	**3**	**2**
1993-94	**Chicago**	**NHL**	**84**	**46**	**61**	**107**	**125**	**6**	**1**	**6**	**7**	**2**
1994-95	Koln	Ger.	3	3	1	4	2	....	....	....	....	....
	Chicago	**NHL**	**33**	**10**	**24**	**34**	**14**	**8**	**1**	**2**	**3**	**16**
1995-96	**Chicago**	**NHL**	**66**	**32**	**35**	**67**	**109**	**10**	**5**	**7**	**12**	**2**
	NHL Totals		**524**	**267**	**329**	**596**	**570**	**82**	**35**	**42**	**77**	**53**

a QMJHL Second All-Star Team (1989)

Played in NHL All-Star Game (1991-94)

Traded to **Phoenix** by **Chicago** for Alexei Zhamnov, Craig Mills and Phoenix's first round choice in 1998 Entry Draft, August 16, 1996.

ROENICK, TREVOR HFD.

Right wing. Shoots right. 6'1", 200 lbs. Born, Derby, CT, October 7, 1974.
(Hartford's 3rd choice, 84th overall, in 1993 Entry Draft).

			Regular Season					Playoffs				
Season	Club	Lea	GP	G	A	TP	PIM	GP	G	A	TP	PIM
1993-94	U. of Maine	H.E.	32	4	3	7	18	....	....	....	....	....
1994-95	U. of Maine	H.E.	36	8	12	20	42	....	....	....	....	....
1995-96	U. of Maine	H.E.	37	7	15	22	38	....	....	....	....	....

ROHLIN, LEIF (roh-LEEN) VAN.

Defense. Shoots left. 6'1", 198 lbs. Born, Vasteras, Sweden, February 26, 1968.
(Vancouver's 2nd choice, 33rd overall, in 1988 Entry Draft).

			Regular Season					Playoffs				
Season	Club	Lea	GP	G	A	TP	PIM	GP	G	A	TP	PIM
1986-87	Vasteras	Swe. 2	27	2	5	7	12	12	0	2	2	8
1987-88	Vasteras	Swe. 2	30	2	15	17	46	7	0	4	4	8
1988-89	Vasteras	Swe.	22	3	7	10	18	....	....	....	....	....
1989-90	Vasteras	Swe.	32	3	6	9	40	2	0	0	0	2
1990-91	Vasteras	Swe.	40	4	10	14	46	4	0	1	1	8
1991-92	Vasteras	Swe.	39	4	6	10	52	....	....	....	....	....
1992-93	Vasteras	Swe.	37	5	7	12	24	2	0	0	0	0
1993-94	Vasteras	Swe.	40	6	14	20	26	4	0	1	1	6
1994-95	Vasteras	Swe.	39	15	15	30	46	4	2	0	2	2
1995-96	**Vancouver**	**NHL**	**56**	**6**	**16**	**22**	**32**	**5**	**0**	**0**	**0**	**0**
	NHL Totals		**56**	**6**	**16**	**22**	**32**	**5**	**0**	**0**	**0**	**0**

ROHLOFF, JON (ROH-lohf) BOS.

Defense. Shoots right. 5'11", 220 lbs. Born, Mankato, MN, October 3, 1969.
(Boston's 7th choice, 186th overall, in 1988 Entry Draft).

			Regular Season					Playoffs				
Season	Club	Lea	GP	G	A	TP	PIM	GP	G	A	TP	PIM
1988-89	Minn.-Duluth	WCHA	39	1	2	3	44	....	....	....	....	....
1989-90	Minn.-Duluth	WCHA	5	0	1	1	6	....	....	....	....	....
1990-91	Minn.-Duluth	WCHA	32	6	11	17	38	....	....	....	....	....
1991-92	Minn.-Duluth	WCHA	27	9	9	18	48	....	....	....	....	....
1992-93a	Minn.-Duluth	WCHA	36	15	20	35	87	....	....	....	....	....
1993-94	Providence	AHL	55	12	23	35	59	....	....	....	....	....
1994-95	**Boston**	**NHL**	**34**	**3**	**8**	**11**	**39**	**5**	**0**	**0**	**0**	**6**
	Providence	AHL	4	2	1	3	6	....	....	....	....	....
1995-96	**Boston**	**NHL**	**79**	**1**	**12**	**13**	**59**	**5**	**1**	**2**	**3**	**2**
	NHL Totals		**113**	**4**	**20**	**24**	**98**	**10**	**1**	**2**	**3**	**8**

a WCHA Second All-Star Team (1993)

ROLSTON, BRIAN N.J.

Center. Shoots left. 6'2", 185 lbs. Born, Flint, MI, February 21, 1973.
(New Jersey's 2nd choice, 11th overall, in 1991 Entry Draft).

			Regular Season					Playoffs				
Season	Club	Lea	GP	G	A	TP	PIM	GP	G	A	TP	PIM
1991-92a	Lake Superior	CCHA	37	14	23	37	14	....	....	....	....	....
1992-93abc	Lake Superior	CCHA	39	33	31	64	20	....	....	....	....	....
1993-94	U.S. National	....	41	20	28	48	36	....	....	....	....	....
	U.S. Olympic	....	8	7	0	7	8	....	....	....	....	....
	Albany	AHL	17	5	5	10	8	5	1	2	3	0
1994-95	Albany	AHL	18	9	11	20	10	....	....	....	....	....
	New Jersey	**NHL**	**40**	**7**	**11**	**18**	**17**	**6**	**2**	**1**	**3**	**4 ♦**
1995-96	**New Jersey**	**NHL**	**58**	**13**	**11**	**24**	**8**	....	....	....	....	....
	NHL Totals		**98**	**20**	**22**	**42**	**25**	**6**	**2**	**1**	**3**	**4**

a NCAA Final Four All-Tournament Team (1992, 1993)
b CCHA First All-Star Team (1993)
c NCAA West Second All-American Team (1993)

ROMANIUK, RUSSELL (ROH-muh-NUHK)

Left wing. Shoots left. 6', 195 lbs. Born, Winnipeg, Man., June 9, 1970.
(Winnipeg's 2nd choice, 31st overall, in 1988 Entry Draft).

			Regular Season					Playoffs				
Season	Club	Lea	GP	G	A	TP	PIM	GP	G	A	TP	PIM
1988-89	North Dakota	WCHA	39	17	14	31	32	....	....	....	....	....
	Cdn. National	....	3	1	0	1	0	....	....	....	....	....
1989-90	North Dakota	WCHA	45	36	15	51	54	....	....	....	....	....
1990-91a	North Dakota	WCHA	39	40	28	68	30	....	....	....	....	....
1991-92	**Winnipeg**	**NHL**	**27**	**3**	**5**	**8**	**18**	....	....	....	....	....
	Moncton	AHL	45	16	15	31	25	10	5	4	9	19
1992-93	**Winnipeg**	**NHL**	**28**	**3**	**1**	**4**	**22**	**1**	**0**	**0**	**0**	**0**
	Moncton	AHL	28	18	8	26	40	5	0	4	4	2
	Fort Wayne	IHL	4	2	0	2	7	....	....	....	....	....
1993-94	Cdn. National	....	34	8	9	17	17	....	....	....	....	....
	Winnipeg	**NHL**	**24**	**4**	**8**	**12**	**6**	....	....	....	....	....
	Moncton	AHL	18	16	8	24	24	17	2	6	8	30
1994-95	**Winnipeg**	**NHL**	**6**	**0**	**0**	**0**	**0**	....	....	....	....	....
	Springfield	AHL	17	5	7	12	29	....	....	....	....	....
1995-96	**Philadelphia**	**NHL**	**17**	**3**	**0**	**3**	**17**	**1**	**0**	**0**	**0**	**0**
	Hershey	AHL	27	19	10	29	43	....	....	....	....	....
	NHL Totals		**102**	**13**	**14**	**27**	**63**	**2**	**0**	**0**	**0**	**0**

a WCHA First All-Star Team (1991)

Traded to **Philadelphia** by **Winnipeg** for Jeff Finley, June 27, 1995.

RONAN, ED (ROH-nan)

Right wing. Shoots right. 6', 197 lbs. Born, Quincy, MA, March 21, 1968.
(Montreal's 13th choice, 227th overall, in 1987 Entry Draft).

			Regular Season					Playoffs				
Season	Club	Lea	GP	G	A	TP	PIM	GP	G	A	TP	PIM
1987-88	Boston U.	H.E.	31	2	5	7	20	....	....	....	....	....
1988-89	Boston U.	H.E.	36	4	11	15	34	....	....	....	....	....
1989-90	Boston U.	H.E.	44	17	23	40	50	....	....	....	....	....
1990-91	Boston U.	H.E.	41	16	19	35	38	....	....	....	....	....
1991-92	**Montreal**	**NHL**	**3**	**0**	**0**	**0**	**0**	....	....	....	....	....
	Fredericton	AHL	78	25	34	59	82	7	5	1	6	6
1992-93	**Montreal**	**NHL**	**53**	**5**	**7**	**12**	**20**	**14**	**2**	**3**	**5**	**10 ♦**
	Fredericton	AHL	16	10	5	15	15	5	2	4	6	6
1993-94	**Montreal**	**NHL**	**61**	**6**	**8**	**14**	**42**	**7**	**1**	**0**	**1**	**0**
1994-95	**Montreal**	**NHL**	**30**	**1**	**4**	**5**	**12**	....	....	....	....	....
1995-96	**Winnipeg**	**NHL**	**17**	**0**	**0**	**0**	**16**	....	....	....	....	....
	Springfield	AHL	31	8	16	24	50	10	7	6	13	4
	NHL Totals		**164**	**12**	**19**	**31**	**90**	**21**	**3**	**3**	**6**	**10**

Signed as a free agent by **Winnipeg**, October 13, 1995.

RONNING, CLIFF PHO.

Center. Shoots left. 5'8", 170 lbs. Born, Burnaby, B.C., October 1, 1965.
(St. Louis' 9th choice, 134th overall, in 1984 Entry Draft).

			Regular Season					Playoffs				
Season	Club	Lea	GP	G	A	TP	PIM	GP	G	A	TP	PIM
1983-84	N. Westminster	WHL	71	69	67	136	10	9	8	13	21	10
1984-85a	N. Westminster	WHL	70	*89	108	*197	20	11	10	14	24	4
1985-86	Cdn. Olympic	....	71	55	63	118	53	....	....	....	....	....
	St. Louis	**NHL**	....	....	....	....	....	**5**	**1**	**1**	**2**	**2**
1986-87	**St. Louis**	**NHL**	**42**	**11**	**14**	**25**	**6**	**4**	**0**	**1**	**1**	**0**
	Cdn. National	....	26	17	16	33	12	....	....	....	....	....
1987-88	**St. Louis**	**NHL**	**26**	**5**	**8**	**13**	**12**	....	....	....	....	....
1988-89	**St. Louis**	**NHL**	**64**	**24**	**31**	**55**	**18**	**7**	**1**	**3**	**4**	**0**
	Peoria	IHL	12	11	20	31	8	....	....	....	....	....
1989-90	Asiago	Italy	36	67	49	116	25	6	7	12	19	4
1990-91	**St. Louis**	**NHL**	**48**	**14**	**18**	**32**	**10**	....	....	....	....	....
	Vancouver	**NHL**	**11**	**6**	**6**	**12**	**0**	**6**	**6**	**3**	**9**	**12**
1991-92	**Vancouver**	**NHL**	**80**	**24**	**47**	**71**	**42**	**13**	**8**	**5**	**13**	**6**
1992-93	**Vancouver**	**NHL**	**79**	**29**	**56**	**85**	**30**	**12**	**2**	**9**	**11**	**6**
1993-94	**Vancouver**	**NHL**	**76**	**25**	**43**	**68**	**42**	**24**	**5**	**10**	**15**	**16**
1994-95	**Vancouver**	**NHL**	**41**	**6**	**19**	**25**	**27**	**11**	**3**	**5**	**8**	**2**
1995-96	**Vancouver**	**NHL**	**79**	**22**	**45**	**67**	**42**	**6**	**0**	**2**	**2**	**6**
	NHL Totals		**546**	**166**	**287**	**453**	**229**	**88**	**26**	**39**	**65**	**50**

a WHL First All-Star Team (1985)

Traded to **Vancouver** by **St. Louis** with Geoff Courtnall, Robert Dirk, Sergio Momesso and St. Louis' fifth round choice (Brian Loney) in 1992 Entry Draft for Dan Quinn and Garth Butcher, March 5, 1991. Signed as a free agent by **Phoenix**, July 1, 1996.

ROSA, PAVEL L.A.

Right wing. Shoots right. 5'11", 178 lbs. Born, Most, Czech., June 7, 1977.
(Los Angeles' 3rd choice, 50th overall, in 1995 Entry Draft).

			Regular Season					Playoffs				
Season	Club	Lea	GP	G	A	TP	PIM	GP	G	A	TP	PIM
1994-95	Litvinov	Czech. Jr.	40	56	42	98	....	....	....	....	....	....
1995-96	Hull	QMJHL	61	46	70	116	39	18	14	22	36	25

ROUSE, BOB DET.

Defense. Shoots right. 6'1", 210 lbs. Born, Surrey, B.C., June 18, 1964.
(Minnesota's 3rd choice, 80th overall, in 1982 Entry Draft).

			Regular Season					Playoffs				
Season	Club	Lea	GP	G	A	TP	PIM	GP	G	A	TP	PIM
1980-81	Billings	WHL	70	0	13	13	116	5	0	0	0	2
1981-82	Billings	WHL	71	7	22	29	209	5	0	2	2	10
1982-83	Nanaimo	WHL	29	7	20	27	86	....	....	....	....	....
	Lethbridge	WHL	42	8	30	38	82	20	2	13	15	55
1983-84	**Minnesota**	**NHL**	**1**	**0**	**0**	**0**	**0**	....	....	....	....	....
a	Lethbridge	WHL	71	18	42	60	101	5	0	1	1	28
1984-85	**Minnesota**	**NHL**	**63**	**2**	**9**	**11**	**113**	....	....	....	....	....
	Springfield	AHL	8	0	3	3	6	....	....	....	....	....
1985-86	**Minnesota**	**NHL**	**75**	**1**	**14**	**15**	**151**	**3**	**0**	**0**	**0**	**0**
1986-87	**Minnesota**	**NHL**	**72**	**2**	**10**	**12**	**179**	....	....	....	....	....
1987-88	**Minnesota**	**NHL**	**74**	**0**	**12**	**12**	**168**	....	....	....	....	....
1988-89	**Minnesota**	**NHL**	**66**	**4**	**13**	**17**	**124**	....	....	....	....	....
	Washington	**NHL**	**13**	**0**	**2**	**2**	**36**	**6**	**2**	**0**	**2**	**4**
1989-90	**Washington**	**NHL**	**70**	**4**	**16**	**20**	**123**	**15**	**2**	**3**	**5**	**47**
1990-91	**Washington**	**NHL**	**47**	**5**	**15**	**20**	**65**	....	....	....	....	....
	Toronto	**NHL**	**13**	**2**	**4**	**6**	**10**	....	....	....	....	....
1991-92	**Toronto**	**NHL**	**79**	**3**	**19**	**22**	**97**	....	....	....	....	....
1992-93	**Toronto**	**NHL**	**82**	**3**	**11**	**14**	**130**	**21**	**3**	**8**	**11**	**29**
1993-94	**Toronto**	**NHL**	**63**	**5**	**11**	**16**	**101**	**18**	**0**	**3**	**3**	**29**
1994-95	**Detroit**	**NHL**	**48**	**1**	**7**	**8**	**36**	**18**	**0**	**3**	**3**	**8**
1995-96	**Detroit**	**NHL**	**58**	**0**	**6**	**6**	**48**	**7**	**0**	**1**	**1**	**4**
	NHL Totals		**824**	**32**	**149**	**181**	**1381**	**88**	**7**	**18**	**25**	**121**

a WHL East First All-Star Team (1984)

Traded to **Washington** by **Minnesota** with Dino Ciccarelli for Mike Gartner and Larry Murphy, March 7, 1989. Traded to **Toronto** by **Washington** with Peter Zezel for Al Iafrate, January 16, 1991. Signed as a free agent by **Detroit**, August 5, 1994.

ROY, ANDRE BOS.

Left wing. Shoots left. 6'3", 178 lbs. Born, Port Chester, NY, February 8, 1975.
(Boston's 5th choice, 151st overall, in 1994 Entry Draft).

			Regular Season					Playoffs				
Season	Club	Lea	GP	G	A	TP	PIM	GP	G	A	TP	PIM
1993-94	Beauport	QMJHL	33	6	7	13	125	....	....	....	....	....
	Chicoutimi	QMJHL	32	4	14	18	152	25	3	6	9	94
1994-95	Chicoutimi	QMJHL	20	15	8	23	90	....	....	....	....	....
	Drummondville	QMJHL	34	18	13	31	233	4	2	0	2	34
1995-96	**Boston**	**NHL**	**3**	**0**	**0**	**0**	**0**	....	....	....	....	....
	Providence	AHL	58	7	8	15	167	1	0	0	0	10
	NHL Totals		**3**	**0**	**0**	**0**	**0**	....	....	....	....	....

ROY, JEAN-YVES (WAH) BOS.

Right wing. Shoots left. 5'10", 180 lbs. Born, Rosemere, Que., February 17, 1969.

			Regular Season					Playoffs				
Season	Club	Lea	GP	G	A	TP	PIM	GP	G	A	TP	PIM
1989-90a	U. of Maine	H.E.	46	*39	26	65	52	....	....	....	....	....
1990-91bcd	U. of Maine	H.E.	43	37	45	82	62	....	....	....	....	....
1991-92ce	U. of Maine	H.E.	35	32	24	56	62	....	....	....	....	....
	Cdn. National	....	13	10	4	14	6	....	....	....	....	....
1992-93	Binghamton	AHL	49	13	15	28	21	14	5	2	7	4
	Cdn. National	....	23	9	6	15	35	....	....	....	....	....
1993-94	Binghamton	AHL	65	41	24	65	33	....	....	....	....	....
	Cdn. National	....	6	3	2	5	2	....	....	....	....	....
	Cdn. Olympic	....	8	1	0	1	0	....	....	....	....	....
1994-95	Binghamton	AHL	67	41	36	77	28	11	4	6	10	12
	NY Rangers	**NHL**	**3**	**1**	**0**	**1**	**2**	....	....	....	....	....
1995-96	**Ottawa**	**NHL**	**4**	**1**	**1**	**2**	**2**	....	....	....	....	....
	P.E.I.	AHL	67	40	55	95	64	5	4	8	12	6
	NHL Totals		**7**	**2**	**1**	**3**	**4**	....	....	....	....	....

a NCAA East Second All-American Team (1990)
b Hockey East First All-Star Team (1991)
c NCAA East First All-American Team (1991, 1992)
d NCAA Final Four All-Tournament Team (1991)
e Hockey East Second All-Star Team (1992)

Signed as a free agent by **NY Rangers**, July 20, 1992. Traded to **Ottawa** by **NY Rangers** for Steve Larouche, October 5, 1995. Signed as a free agent by **Boston**, July 15, 1996.

ROY, JIMMY DAL.

Center. Shoots right. 5'11", 170 lbs. Born, Sioux Lookout, Ont., September 22, 1975.
(Dallas' 7th choice, 254th overall, in 1994 Entry Draft).

			Regular Season					Playoffs				
Season	Club	Lea	GP	G	A	TP	PIM	GP	G	A	TP	PIM
1994-95	Michigan Tech.	WCHA	38	5	11	16	62	....	....	....	....	....
1995-96	Michigan Tech	WCHA	42	17	17	34	84	....	....	....	....	....

ROY, STEPHANE (WAH) ST.L.

Center. Shoots left. 5'10", 173 lbs. Born, Ste-Martine, Que., January 26, 1976.
(St. Louis' 1st choice, 68th overall, in 1994 Entry Draft).

			Regular Season					Playoffs				
Season	Club	Lea	GP	G	A	TP	PIM	GP	G	A	TP	PIM
1993-94	Val d'Or	QMJHL	72	25	28	53	116	....	....	....	....	....
1994-95	Val d'Or	QMJHL	68	19	52	71	113	....	....	....	....	....
1995-96	Val d'Or	QMJHL	62	43	72	115	89	13	9	15	24	10

ROYER, GAETAN (ROHY-uhr) CHI.

Right wing. Shoots right. 6'3", 193 lbs. Born, Donnacona, Que., March 13, 1976.

			Regular Season					Playoffs				
Season	Club	Lea	GP	G	A	TP	PIM	GP	G	A	TP	PIM
1994-95	Sherbrooke	QMJHL	65	11	25	36	194	7	0	2	2	6
1995-96	Sherbrooke	QMJHL	36	25	26	51	174	....	....	....	....	....
	Beauport	QMJHL	25	11	10	21	59	19	5	9	14	47

Signed as a free agent by **Chicago**, September 9, 1994.

ROYER, REMI (ROHY-uhr) CHI.

Defense. Shoots right. 6'2", 185 lbs. Born, Donnacona, Que., February 12, 1978.
(Chicago's 1st choice, 31st overall, in 1996 Entry Draft).

			Regular Season					Playoffs				
Season	Club	Lea	GP	G	A	TP	PIM	GP	G	A	TP	PIM
1994-95	Victoriaville	QMJHL	57	3	17	20	144	4	0	1	1	7
1995-96	Victoriaville	QMJHL	43	12	14	26	209	....	....	....	....	....
	St-Hyacinthe	QMJHL	19	10	9	19	80	12	1	4	5	29

ROZSIVAL, MICHAL PIT.

Defense. Shoots right. 6'1", 189 lbs. Born, Vlasim, Czech., September 3, 1978.
(Pittsburgh's 5th choice, 105th overall, in 1996 Entry Draft).

			Regular Season					Playoffs				
Season	Club	Lea	GP	G	A	TP	PIM	GP	G	A	TP	PIM
1994-95	Dukla Jihlava	Czech. Jr.	31	8	13	21	....	....	....	....	....	....
1995-96	Dukla Jihlava	Czech. Jr.	36	3	4	7	....	....	....	....	....	....

RUCCHIN, STEVE (ROO-chihn) ANA.

Center. Shoots left. 6'3", 210 lbs. Born, London, Ont., July 4, 1971.
(Anaheim's 1st choice, 2nd overall, in 1994 Supplemental Draft).

			Regular Season					Playoffs				
Season	Club	Lea	GP	G	A	TP	PIM	GP	G	A	TP	PIM
1990-91	Western Ont.	OUAA	34	13	16	29	14	....	....	....	....	....
1991-92	Western Ont.	OUAA	37	28	34	62	36	....	....	....	....	....
1992-93	Western Ont.	OUAA	34	22	26	48	16	....	....	....	....	....
1993-94	Western Ont.	OUAA	35	30	23	53	30	....	....	....	....	....
1994-95	San Diego	IHL	41	11	15	26	14	....	....	....	....	....
	Anaheim	**NHL**	**43**	**6**	**11**	**17**	**23**	....	....	....	....	....
1995-96	**Anaheim**	**NHL**	**64**	**19**	**25**	**44**	**12**	....	....	....	....	....
	NHL Totals		**107**	**25**	**36**	**61**	**35**	....	....	....	....	....

RUCHTY, MATTHEW (RUHK-tee) VAN.

Left wing. Shoots left. 6'1", 225 lbs. Born, Kitchener, Ont., November 27, 1969.
(New Jersey's 4th choice, 65th overall, in 1988 Entry Draft).

			Regular Season					Playoffs				
Season	Club	Lea	GP	G	A	TP	PIM	GP	G	A	TP	PIM
1987-88	Bowling Green	CCHA	41	6	15	21	78	....	....	....	....	....
1988-89	Bowling Green	CCHA	43	11	21	32	110	....	....	....	....	....
1989-90	Bowling Green	CCHA	42	28	21	49	135	....	....	....	....	....
1990-91	Bowling Green	CCHA	38	13	18	31	147	....	....	....	....	....
1991-92	Utica	AHL	73	9	14	23	250	4	0	0	0	25
1992-93	Utica	AHL	74	4	14	18	253	4	0	2	2	15
1993-94	Albany	AHL	68	11	11	22	303	5	0	1	1	18
1994-95	Albany	AHL	78	26	23	49	348	12	5	10	15	43
1995-96	Syracuse	AHL	68	12	16	28	321	....	....	....	....	....
	Atlanta	IHL	12	3	4	7	38	3	1	1	2	36

Signed as a free agent by **Vancouver**, August 25, 1995.

RUCINSKI, MIKE HFD.

Defense. Shoots left. 5'11", 179 lbs. Born, Trenton, MI, March 30, 1975.
(Hartford's 8th choice, 217th overall, in 1995 Entry Draft).

			Regular Season					Playoffs				
Season	Club	Lea	GP	G	A	TP	PIM	GP	G	A	TP	PIM
1992-93	Detroit	OHL	66	6	13	19	59	15	0	4	4	12
1993-94	Detroit	OHL	66	2	26	28	58	17	0	7	7	15
1994-95	Detroit	OHL	64	9	18	27	61	21	3	3	6	8
1995-96	Detroit	OHL	51	10	26	36	65	11	2	4	6	14

RUCINSKY, MARTIN (roo-SHIHN-skee) MTL.

Left wing. Shoots left. 6', 198 lbs. Born, Most, Czech., March 11, 1971.
(Edmonton's 2nd choice, 20th overall, in 1991 Entry Draft).

			Regular Season					Playoffs				
Season	Club	Lea	GP	G	A	TP	PIM	GP	G	A	TP	PIM
1988-89	Litvinov	Czech.	3	1	0	1	2	....	....	....	....	....
1989-90	Litvinov	Czech.	47	17	9	26	....	....	....	....	....	....
1990-91	Litvinov	Czech.	56	24	20	44	69	....	....	....	....	....
1991-92	**Edmonton**	**NHL**	**2**	**0**	**0**	**0**	**0**	....	....	....	....	....
	Cape Breton	AHL	35	11	12	23	34	....	....	....	....	....
	Quebec	**NHL**	**4**	**1**	**1**	**2**	**2**	....	....	....	....	....
	Halifax	AHL	7	1	1	2	6	....	....	....	....	....
1992-93	**Quebec**	**NHL**	**77**	**18**	**30**	**48**	**51**	**6**	**1**	**1**	**2**	**4**
1993-94	**Quebec**	**NHL**	**60**	**9**	**23**	**32**	**58**	....	....	....	....	....
1994-95	Litvinov	Czech.	13	12	10	22	54	....	....	....	....	....
	Quebec	**NHL**	**20**	**3**	**6**	**9**	**14**	....	....	....	....	....
1995-96	Vsetin	Czech.	1	1	1	2	0	....	....	....	....	....
	Colorado	**NHL**	**22**	**4**	**11**	**15**	**14**	....	....	....	....	....
	Montreal	**NHL**	**56**	**25**	**35**	**60**	**54**	....	....	....	....	....
	NHL Totals		**241**	**60**	**106**	**166**	**193**	**6**	**1**	**1**	**2**	**4**

Traded to **Quebec** by **Edmonton** for Ron Tugnutt and Brad Zavisha, March 10, 1992. Traded to **Montreal** by **Colorado** with Andrei Kovalenko and Jocelyn Thibault for Patrick Roy and Mike Keane, December 6, 1995.

RUFF, JASON

Left wing. Shoots left. 6'2", 192 lbs. Born, Kelowna, B.C., January 27, 1970.
(St Louis' 3rd choice, 96th overall, in 1990 Entry Draft).

			Regular Season					Playoffs				
Season	Club	Lea	GP	G	A	TP	PIM	GP	G	A	TP	PIM
1989-90	Lethbridge	WHL	72	55	64	119	114	19	9	10	19	18
1990-91a	Lethbridge	WHL	66	61	75	136	154	16	12	17	29	18
	Peoria	IHL	....	....	....	....	....	5	0	0	0	2
1991-92	Peoria	IHL	67	27	45	72	148	10	7	7	14	19
1992-93	**St. Louis**	**NHL**	**7**	**2**	**1**	**3**	**8**	....	....	....	....	....
	Peoria	IHL	40	22	21	43	81	....	....	....	....	....
	Tampa Bay	**NHL**	**1**	**0**	**0**	**0**	**0**	....	....	....	....	....
	Atlanta	IHL	26	11	14	25	90	7	2	1	3	26
1993-94	**Tampa Bay**	**NHL**	**6**	**1**	**2**	**3**	**2**	....	....	....	....	....
	Atlanta	IHL	71	24	25	49	122	14	6	*17	23	41
1994-95	Atlanta	IHL	64	42	34	76	161	3	3	1	4	10
1995-96	Atlanta	IHL	59	39	33	72	135	2	0	0	0	16
	NHL Totals		**14**	**3**	**3**	**6**	**10**	....	....	....	....	....

a WHL East First All-Star Team (1991)

Traded to **Tampa Bay** by **St. Louis** with future considerations for Doug Crossman, Basil McRae and Tampa Bay's fourth round choice (Andrei Petrakov) in 1996 Entry Draft, January 28, 1993.

RUHLY, DAVID MTL.

Left wing. Shoots left. 6'1", 167 lbs. Born, Baldwin, WI, January 23, 1974.
(Montreal's 9th choice, 177th overall, in 1993 Entry Draft).

			Regular Season					Playoffs				
Season	Club	Lea	GP	G	A	TP	PIM	GP	G	A	TP	PIM
1993-94	Providence	H.E.	21	2	8	10	26	....	....	....	....	....
1994-95	Providence	H.E.	24	3	0	3	8	....	....	....	....	....
1995-96					DID NOT PLAY							

RUMBLE, DARREN PHI.

Defense. Shoots left. 6'1", 200 lbs. Born, Barrie, Ont., January 23, 1969.
(Philadelphia's 1st choice, 20th overall, in 1987 Entry Draft).

			Regular Season					Playoffs				
Season	Club	Lea	GP	G	A	TP	PIM	GP	G	A	TP	PIM
1986-87	Kitchener	OHL	64	11	32	43	44	4	0	1	1	9
1987-88	Kitchener	OHL	55	15	50	65	64	....	....	....	....	....
1988-89	Kitchener	OHL	46	11	28	39	25	5	1	0	1	2
1989-90	Hershey	AHL	57	2	13	15	31	....	....	....	....	....
1990-91	**Philadelphia**	**NHL**	**3**	**1**	**0**	**1**	**0**	....	....	....	....	....
	Hershey	AHL	73	6	35	41	48	3	0	5	5	2
1991-92	Hershey	AHL	79	12	54	66	118	6	0	3	3	2
1992-93	**Ottawa**	**NHL**	**69**	**3**	**13**	**16**	**61**	....	....	....	....	....
	New Haven	AHL	2	1	0	1	0	....	....	....	....	....
1993-94	**Ottawa**	**NHL**	**70**	**6**	**9**	**15**	**116**	....	....	....	....	....
	P.E.I.	AHL	3	2	0	2	0	....	....	....	....	....
1994-95a	P.E.I.	AHL	70	7	46	53	77	11	0	6	6	4
1995-96	**Philadelphia**	**NHL**	**5**	**0**	**0**	**0**	**4**	....	....	....	....	....
	Hershey	AHL	58	13	37	50	83	5	0	0	0	6
	NHL Totals		**147**	**10**	**22**	**32**	**181**	....	....	....	....	....

a AHL Second All-Star Team (1995)

Claimed by **Ottawa** from **Philadelphia** in Expansion Draft, June 18, 1992. Signed as a free agent by **Philadelphia**, July 31, 1995.

RUSHFORTH, PAUL BUF.

Center. Shoots right. 6', 189 lbs. Born, Prince George, B.C., April 22, 1974.
(Buffalo's 8th choice, 131st overall, in 1992 Entry Draft).

			Regular Season					Playoffs				
Season	Club	Lea	GP	G	A	TP	PIM	GP	G	A	TP	PIM
1991-92	North Bay	OHL	65	8	11	19	24	19	0	2	2	6
1992-93	North Bay	OHL	21	4	10	14	24	....	....	....	....	....
	Belleville	OHL	36	21	19	40	38	7	7	2	9	4
1993-94	Belleville	OHL	63	28	35	63	109	12	6	3	9	8
1994-95	S. Carolina	ECHL	41	6	8	14	130	....	....	....	....	....
	Rochester	AHL	25	8	6	14	10	2	0	0	0	0
1995-96	S. Carolina	ECHL	56	20	26	46	141	7	1	0	1	8

RUSK, MIKE CHI.

Defense. Shoots left. 6'1", 175 lbs. Born, Milton, Ont., April 26, 1975.
(Chicago's 10th choice, 232nd overall, in 1993 Entry Draft).

			Regular Season					Playoffs				
Season	Club	Lea	GP	G	A	TP	PIM	GP	G	A	TP	PIM
1992-93	Guelph	OHL	62	3	15	18	67	5	0	1	1	8
1993-94	Guelph	OHL	48	8	26	34	59	9	2	9	11	12
1994-95	Guelph	OHL	64	9	31	40	51	14	1	4	5	8
1995-96	Columbus	ECHL	47	3	13	16	63	3	1	0	1	2

RUSSELL, CAM CHI.

Defense. Shoots left. 6'4", 206 lbs. Born, Halifax, N.S., January 12, 1969.
(Chicago's 3rd choice, 50th overall, in 1987 Entry Draft).

			Regular Season					Playoffs				
Season	Club	Lea	GP	G	A	TP	PIM	GP	G	A	TP	PIM
1985-86	Hull	QMJHL	56	3	4	7	24	15	0	2	2	4
1986-87	Hull	QMJHL	66	3	16	19	119	8	0	1	1	16
1987-88	Hull	QMJHL	53	9	18	27	141	19	2	5	7	39
1988-89	Hull	QMJHL	66	8	32	40	109	9	2	6	8	6
1989-90	**Chicago**	**NHL**	**19**	**0**	**1**	**1**	**27**	**1**	**0**	**0**	**0**	**0**
	Indianapolis	IHL	46	3	15	18	114	9	0	1	1	24
1990-91	**Chicago**	**NHL**	**3**	**0**	**0**	**0**	**5**	**1**	**0**	**0**	**0**	**0**
	Indianapolis	IHL	53	5	9	14	125	6	0	2	2	30
1991-92	**Chicago**	**NHL**	**19**	**0**	**0**	**0**	**34**	**12**	**0**	**2**	**2**	**2**
	Indianapolis	IHL	41	4	9	13	78	....	....	....	....	....
1992-93	**Chicago**	**NHL**	**67**	**2**	**4**	**6**	**151**	**4**	**0**	**0**	**0**	**0**
1993-94	**Chicago**	**NHL**	**67**	**1**	**7**	**8**	**200**	....	....	....	....	....
1994-95	**Chicago**	**NHL**	**33**	**1**	**3**	**4**	**88**	**16**	**0**	**3**	**3**	**8**
1995-96	**Chicago**	**NHL**	**61**	**2**	**2**	**4**	**129**	**6**	**0**	**0**	**0**	**2**
	NHL Totals		**269**	**6**	**17**	**23**	**634**	**40**	**0**	**5**	**5**	**12**

RUUTTU, CHRISTIAN (ROO-TOO)

Center. Shoots left. 5'11", 194 lbs. Born, Lappeenranta, Finland, February 20, 1964.
(Buffalo's 9th choice, 134th overall, in 1983 Entry Draft).

			Regular Season					Playoffs				
Season	Club	Lea	GP	G	A	TP	PIM	GP	G	A	TP	PIM
1982-83	Assat	Fin.	36	15	18	33	34	....	....	....	....	....
1983-84	Assat	Fin.	37	18	42	60	72	9	2	5	7	12
1984-85	Assat	Fin.	32	14	32	46	34	8	1	6	7	8
1985-86	HIFK	Fin.	36	16	38	54	47	10	3	6	9	8
1986-87	**Buffalo**	**NHL**	**76**	**22**	**43**	**65**	**62**	....	....	....	....	....
1987-88	**Buffalo**	**NHL**	**73**	**26**	**45**	**71**	**85**	**6**	**2**	**5**	**7**	**4**
1988-89	**Buffalo**	**NHL**	**67**	**14**	**46**	**60**	**98**	**2**	**0**	**0**	**0**	**2**
1989-90	**Buffalo**	**NHL**	**75**	**19**	**41**	**60**	**66**	**6**	**0**	**0**	**0**	**4**
1990-91	**Buffalo**	**NHL**	**77**	**16**	**34**	**50**	**96**	**6**	**1**	**3**	**4**	**29**
1991-92	**Buffalo**	**NHL**	**70**	**4**	**21**	**25**	**76**	**3**	**0**	**0**	**0**	**6**
1992-93	**Chicago**	**NHL**	**84**	**17**	**37**	**54**	**134**	**4**	**0**	**0**	**0**	**2**
1993-94	**Chicago**	**NHL**	**54**	**9**	**20**	**29**	**68**	**6**	**0**	**0**	**0**	**2**
1994-95	HIFK	Fin.	20	4	8	12	24	....	....	....	....	....
	Chicago	**NHL**	**20**	**2**	**5**	**7**	**6**	....	....	....	....	....
	Vancouver	**NHL**	**25**	**5**	**6**	**11**	**23**	**9**	**1**	**1**	**2**	**0**
1995-96	V. Frolunda	Swe.	32	13	25	38	98	12	4	7	11	24
	NHL Totals		**621**	**134**	**298**	**432**	**714**	**42**	**4**	**9**	**13**	**49**

Played in NHL All-Star Game (1988)

Traded to **Winnipeg** by **Buffalo** with future considerations for Stephane Beauregard, June 15, 1992. Traded to **Chicago** by **Winnipeg** for Stephane Beauregard, August 10, 1992. Traded to **Vancouver** by **Chicago** for Murray Craven, March 10, 1995.

RYABYKIN, DMITRI (ryah-BEE-kihn)

Defense. Shoots right. 6'1", 185 lbs. Born, Chirchik, USSR, March 24, 1976.
(Calgary's 2nd choice, 45th overall, in 1994 Entry Draft).

			Regular Season					Playoffs				
Season	Club	Lea	GP	G	A	TP	PIM	GP	G	A	TP	PIM
1994-95	Moscow D'amo	CIS	48	0	0	0	12	11	0	2	2	0
1995-96	Moscow D'amo	CIS	47	3	1	4	49	13	1	1	2	6

RYAN, TERRY — MTL.

Left wing. Shoots left. 6'1", 205 lbs. Born, St. John's, Nfld., January 14, 1977.
(Montreal's 1st choice, 8th overall, in 1995 Entry Draft).

			Regular Season					Playoffs				
Season	Club	Lea	GP	G	A	TP	PIM	GP	G	A	TP	PIM
1993-94	Tri-City	WHL	61	16	17	33	176	4	0	1	1	25
1994-95	Tri-City	WHL	70	50	60	110	207	17	12	15	27	36
1995-96	Tri-City	WHL	59	32	37	69	133	5	0	0	0	4
	Fredericton	AHL	....	....	....	....	....	3	0	0	0	2

RYCHEL, WARREN (RIGH-kuhl) ANA.

Left wing. Shoots left. 6', 202 lbs. Born, Tecumseh, Ont., May 12, 1967.

			Regular Season					Playoffs				
Season	Club	Lea	GP	G	A	TP	PIM	GP	G	A	TP	PIM
1984-85	Sudbury	OHL	35	5	8	13	74	....	....	....	....	....
	Guelph	OHL	29	1	3	4	48	....	....	....	....	....
1985-86	Guelph	OHL	38	14	5	19	119	....	....	....	....	....
	Ottawa	OHL	29	11	18	29	54	....	....	....	....	....
1986-87	Ottawa	OHL	28	11	7	18	57	....	....	....	....	....
	Kitchener	OHL	21	5	5	10	39	4	0	0	0	9
1987-88	Peoria	IHL	7	2	1	3	7	....	....	....	....	....
	Saginaw	IHL	51	2	7	9	113	1	0	0	0	0
1988-89	**Chicago**	**NHL**	**2**	**0**	**0**	**0**	**17**	....	....	....	....	....
	Saginaw	IHL	50	15	14	29	226	6	0	0	0	51
1989-90	Indianapolis	IHL	77	23	16	39	374	14	1	3	4	64
1990-91	Indianapolis	IHL	68	33	30	63	338	5	2	1	3	30
	Chicago	**NHL**	....	....	....	....	....	**3**	**1**	**3**	**4**	**2**
1991-92	Moncton	AHL	36	14	15	29	211	....	....	....	....	....
	Kalamazoo	IHL	45	15	20	35	165	8	0	3	3	51
1992-93	**Los Angeles**	**NHL**	**70**	**6**	**7**	**13**	**314**	**23**	**6**	**7**	**13**	**39**
1993-94	**Los Angeles**	**NHL**	**80**	**10**	**9**	**19**	**322**	....	....	....	....	....
1994-95	**Los Angeles**	**NHL**	**7**	**0**	**0**	**0**	**19**	....	....	....	....	....
	Toronto	**NHL**	**26**	**1**	**6**	**7**	**101**	**3**	**0**	**0**	**0**	**0**
1995-96	**Colorado**	**NHL**	**52**	**6**	**2**	**8**	**147**	**12**	**1**	**0**	**1**	**23 ♦**
	NHL Totals		**237**	**23**	**24**	**47**	**920**	**41**	**8**	**10**	**18**	**64**

Signed as a free agent by **Chicago**, September 19, 1986. Traded to **Winnipeg** by **Chicago** with Troy Murray for Bryan Marchment and Chris Norton, July 22, 1991. Traded to **Minnesota** by **Winnipeg** for Tony Joseph, December 30, 1991. Signed as a free agent by **Los Angeles**, October 1, 1992. Traded to **Washington** by **Los Angeles** for Randy Burridge, February 10, 1995. Traded to **Toronto** by **Washington** for Toronto's fourth round choice (Sebastien Charpentier) in 1995 Entry Draft, February 10, 1995. Traded to **Colorado** by **Toronto** for cash, October 2, 1995. Signed as a free agent by **Anaheim**, August 21, 1996.

SACCO, DAVID (SAK-oh)

Right wing. Shoots right. 6', 180 lbs. Born, Malden, MA, July 31, 1970.
(Toronto's 9th choice, 195th overall, in 1988 Entry Draft).

			Regular Season					Playoffs				
Season	Club	Lea	GP	G	A	TP	PIM	GP	G	A	TP	PIM
1988-89	Boston U.	H.E.	35	14	29	43	40	....	....	....	....	....
1989-90	Boston U.	H.E.	3	0	4	4	2	....	....	....	....	....
1990-91	Boston U.	H.E.	40	21	40	61	24	....	....	....	....	....
1991-92ab	Boston U.	H.E.	34	13	32	45	30	....	....	....	....	....
1992-93ab	Boston U.	H.E.	40	25	37	62	86	....	....	....	....	....
1993-94	U.S. National	....	32	8	20	28	88	....	....	....	....	....
	U.S. Olympic	....	8	3	5	8	12	....	....	....	....	....
	Toronto	**NHL**	**4**	**1**	**1**	**2**	**4**	....	....	....	....	....
	St. John's	AHL	5	3	1	4	2	....	....	....	....	....
1994-95	San Diego	IHL	45	11	25	36	57	4	3	1	4	0
	Anaheim	**NHL**	**8**	**0**	**2**	**2**	**0**	....	....	....	....	....
1995-96	**Anaheim**	**NHL**	**23**	**4**	**10**	**14**	**18**	....	....	....	....	....
	Baltimore	AHL	25	14	16	30	18	2	0	1	1	4
	NHL Totals		**35**	**5**	**13**	**18**	**22**	....	....	....	....	....

a NCAA East First All-American Team (1992, 1993)
b Hockey East First All-Star Team (1992, 1993)

Traded to **Anaheim** by **Toronto** for Terry Yake, September 28, 1994.

SACCO, JOE (SAK-oh) ANA.

Left wing. Shoots right. 6'1", 195 lbs. Born, Medford, MA, February 4, 1969.
(Toronto's 4th choice, 71st overall, in 1987 Entry Draft).

			Regular Season					Playoffs				
Season	Club	Lea	GP	G	A	TP	PIM	GP	G	A	TP	PIM
1987-88	Boston U.	H.E.	34	16	20	36	40	....	....	....	....	....
1988-89	Boston U.	H.E.	33	21	19	40	66	....	....	....	....	....
1989-90	Boston U.	H.E.	44	28	24	52	70	....	....	....	....	....
1990-91	**Toronto**	**NHL**	**20**	**0**	**5**	**5**	**2**	....	....	....	....	....
	Newmarket	AHL	49	18	17	35	24	....	....	....	....	....
1991-92	U.S. National	....	50	11	26	37	61	....	....	....	....	....
	U.S. Olympic	....	8	0	2	2	0	....	....	....	....	....
	Toronto	**NHL**	**17**	**7**	**4**	**11**	**4**	....	....	....	....	....
	St. John's	AHL	....	....	....	....	....	1	1	1	2	0
1992-93	**Toronto**	**NHL**	**23**	**4**	**4**	**8**	**8**	....	....	....	....	....
	St. John's	AHL	37	14	16	30	45	7	6	4	10	2
1993-94	**Anaheim**	**NHL**	**84**	**19**	**18**	**37**	**61**	....	....	....	....	....
1994-95	**Anaheim**	**NHL**	**41**	**10**	**8**	**18**	**23**	....	....	....	....	....
1995-96	**Anaheim**	**NHL**	**76**	**13**	**14**	**27**	**40**	....	....	....	....	....
	NHL Totals		**261**	**53**	**53**	**106**	**138**	....	....	....	....	....

Claimed by **Anaheim** from **Toronto** in Expansion Draft, June 24, 1993.

SACHL, PETER NYI

Center. Shoots left. 6'1", 194 lbs. Born, Jindrichuv Hradec, Czech., December 2, 1977.
(NY Islanders' 6th choice, 128th overall, in 1996 Entry Draft).

			Regular Season					Playoffs				
Season	Club	Lea	GP	G	A	TP	PIM	GP	G	A	TP	PIM
1994-95	Budejovice	Czech. Jr.	40	6	8	14	....	....	....	....	....	....
1995-96	Budejovice	Czech. Jr.	39	19	17	36	....	....	....	....	....	....
	Budejovice	Czech.	....	....	....	....	....	2	0	0	0	....

SAIFULLIN, RAMIL (sigh-FOO-lihn) PHO.

Center. Shoots left. 6'1", 187 lbs. Born, Izhevsk, USSR, April 8, 1976.
(Winnipeg's 8th choice, 186th overall, in 1994 Entry Draft).

			Regular Season					Playoffs				
Season	Club	Lea	GP	G	A	TP	PIM	GP	G	A	TP	PIM
1993-94	Avangard	CIS	37	1	0	1	8	3	0	0	0	0
1994-95	Avangard	CIS	32	3	4	7	....	....	....	....	....	....
1995-96	Beauport	QMJHL	62	17	37	54	18	20	12	11	23	8

SAKIC, JOE (SAK-ihk) COL.

Center. Shoots left. 5'11", 185 lbs. Born, Burnaby, B.C., July 7, 1969.
(Quebec's 2nd choice, 15th overall, in 1987 Entry Draft).

			Regular Season					Playoffs				
Season	Club	Lea	GP	G	A	TP	PIM	GP	G	A	TP	PIM
1986-87	Swift Current	WHL	72	60	73	133	31	4	0	1	1	0
	Cdn. National	....	1	0	0	0	0	....	....	....	....	....
1987-88ab	Swift Current	WHL	64	*78	82	*160	64	10	11	13	24	12
1988-89	**Quebec**	**NHL**	**70**	**23**	**39**	**62**	**24**	....	....	....	....	....
1989-90	**Quebec**	**NHL**	**80**	**39**	**63**	**102**	**27**	....	....	....	....	....
1990-91	**Quebec**	**NHL**	**80**	**48**	**61**	**109**	**24**	....	....	....	....	....
1991-92	**Quebec**	**NHL**	**69**	**29**	**65**	**94**	**20**	....	....	....	....	....
1992-93	**Quebec**	**NHL**	**78**	**48**	**57**	**105**	**40**	**6**	**3**	**3**	**6**	**2**
1993-94	**Quebec**	**NHL**	**84**	**28**	**64**	**92**	**18**	....	....	....	....	....
1994-95	**Quebec**	**NHL**	**47**	**19**	**43**	**62**	**30**	**6**	**4**	**1**	**5**	**0**
1995-96c	**Colorado**	**NHL**	**82**	**51**	**69**	**120**	**44**	**22**	***18**	**16**	***34**	**14 ♦**
	NHL Totals		**590**	**285**	**461**	**746**	**227**	**34**	**25**	**20**	**45**	**16**

a Canadian Major Junior Player of the Year (1988)
b WHL East All-Star Team (1988)
c Won Conn Smythe Trophy (1996)

Played in NHL All-Star Game (1990-94, 1996)

SALEI, RUSLAN (sah-LEE, ROOS-luhn) ANA.

Defense. Shoots left. 6'1", 200 lbs. Born, Minsk, USSR, November 2, 1974.
(Anaheim's 1st choice, 9th overall, in 1996 Entry Draft).

			Regular Season					Playoffs				
Season	Club	Lea	GP	G	A	TP	PIM	GP	G	A	TP	PIM
1992-93	Dynamo Minsk	CIS	9	1	0	1	10	....	....	....	....	....
1993-94	Tivali Minsk	CIS	39	2	3	5	50	....	....	....	....	....
1994-95	Tivali Minsk	CIS	51	4	2	6	44	....	....	....	....	....
1995-96	Las Vegas	IHL	76	7	23	30	123	15	3	7	10	18

SAMOKHALOV, ANDREI DET.

Right wing. Shoots left. 5'11", 165 lbs. Born, Ust-Kamenogorsk, USSR, May 10, 1975.
(Detroit's 9th choice, 208th overall, in 1995 Entry Draft).

			Regular Season					Playoffs				
Season	Club	Lea	GP	G	A	TP	PIM	GP	G	A	TP	PIM
1992-93	Kamenogorsk	CIS	27	6	7	13	8	1	1	1	2	0
1993-94	Kamenogorsk	CIS	33	5	5	10	16	....	....	....	....	....
1994-95	Kamenogorsk	CIS	44	13	9	22	6	2	0	0	0	2
1995-96	Kamenogorsk	CIS	49	23	8	31	20	....	....	....	....	....

SAMUELSSON, KJELL (SAM-yuhl-suhn, SHEHL) PHI.

Defense. Shoots right. 6'6", 235 lbs. Born, Tyngsryd, Sweden, October 18, 1958.
(NY Rangers' 5th choice, 119th overall, in 1984 Entry Draft).

			Regular Season					Playoffs				
Season	Club	Lea	GP	G	A	TP	PIM	GP	G	A	TP	PIM
1977-78	Tyngsryd	Swe. 2	20	3	0	3	41	....	....	....	....	....
1978-79	Tyngsryd	Swe. 2	24	3	4	7	67	....	....	....	....	....
1979-80	Tyngsryd	Swe. 2	26	5	4	9	45	....	....	....	....	....
1980-81	Tyngsryd	Swe. 2	35	6	7	13	61	2	0	1	1	14
1981-82	Tyngsryd	Swe. 2	33	11	14	25	68	3	0	2	2	2
1982-83	Tyngsryd	Swe. 2	32	11	6	17	57	....	....	....	....	....
1983-84	Leksand	Swe.	36	6	6	12	59	....	....	....	....	....
1984-85	Leksand	Swe.	35	9	5	14	34	....	....	....	....	....
1985-86	**NY Rangers**	**NHL**	**9**	**0**	**0**	**0**	**10**	**9**	**0**	**1**	**1**	**8**
	New Haven	AHL	56	6	21	27	87	3	0	0	0	10
1986-87	**NY Rangers**	**NHL**	**30**	**2**	**6**	**8**	**50**	....	....	....	....	....
	Philadelphia	**NHL**	**46**	**1**	**6**	**7**	**86**	**26**	**0**	**4**	**4**	**25**
1987-88	**Philadelphia**	**NHL**	**74**	**6**	**24**	**30**	**184**	**7**	**2**	**5**	**7**	**23**
1988-89	**Philadelphia**	**NHL**	**69**	**3**	**14**	**17**	**140**	**19**	**1**	**3**	**4**	**24**
1989-90	**Philadelphia**	**NHL**	**66**	**5**	**17**	**22**	**91**	....	....	....	....	....
1990-91	**Philadelphia**	**NHL**	**78**	**9**	**19**	**28**	**82**	....	....	....	....	....
1991-92	**Philadelphia**	**NHL**	**54**	**4**	**9**	**13**	**76**	....	....	....	....	....
	Pittsburgh	**NHL**	**20**	**1**	**2**	**3**	**34**	**15**	**0**	**3**	**3**	**12 ♦**
1992-93	**Pittsburgh**	**NHL**	**63**	**3**	**6**	**9**	**106**	**12**	**0**	**3**	**3**	**2**
1993-94	**Pittsburgh**	**NHL**	**59**	**5**	**8**	**13**	**118**	**6**	**0**	**0**	**0**	**26**
1994-95	**Pittsburgh**	**NHL**	**41**	**1**	**6**	**7**	**54**	**11**	**0**	**1**	**1**	**32**
1995-96	**Philadelphia**	**NHL**	**75**	**3**	**11**	**14**	**81**	**12**	**1**	**0**	**1**	**24**
	NHL Totals		**684**	**43**	**128**	**171**	**1112**	**117**	**4**	**20**	**24**	**176**

Played in NHL All-Star Game (1988)

Traded to **Philadelphia** by **NY Rangers** with NY Rangers' second round choice (Patrik Juhlin) in 1989 Entry Draft for Bob Froese, December 18, 1986. Traded to **Pittsburgh** by **Philadelphia** with Rick Tocchet, Ken Wregget and Philadelphia's third round choice (Dave Roche) in 1993 Entry Draft for Mark Recchi, Brian Benning and Los Angeles' first round choice (previously acquired by Pittsburgh — Philadelphia selected Jason Bowen) in 1992 Entry Draft, February 19, 1992. Signed as a free agent by **Philadelphia**, August 31, 1995.

SAMUELSSON, ULF (SAM-yuhl-suhn, UHLF) NYR

Defense. Shoots left. 6'1", 195 lbs. Born, Fagersta, Sweden, March 26, 1964.
(Hartford's 4th choice, 67th overall, in 1982 Entry Draft).

			Regular Season					Playoffs				
Season	Club	Lea	GP	G	A	TP	PIM	GP	G	A	TP	PIM
1981-82	Leksand	Swe.	31	3	1	4	40	....	....	....	....	....
1982-83	Leksand	Swe.	33	9	6	15	72	....	....	....	....	....
1983-84	Leksand	Swe.	36	5	11	16	53	....	....	....	....	....
1984-85	**Hartford**	**NHL**	**41**	**2**	**6**	**8**	**83**	....	....	....	....	....
	Binghamton	AHL	36	5	11	16	92	....	....	....	....	....
1985-86	**Hartford**	**NHL**	**80**	**5**	**19**	**24**	**174**	**10**	**1**	**2**	**3**	**38**
1986-87	**Hartford**	**NHL**	**78**	**2**	**31**	**33**	**162**	**5**	**0**	**1**	**1**	**41**
1987-88	**Hartford**	**NHL**	**76**	**8**	**33**	**41**	**159**	**5**	**0**	**0**	**0**	**8**
1988-89	**Hartford**	**NHL**	**71**	**9**	**26**	**35**	**181**	**4**	**0**	**2**	**2**	**4**
1989-90	**Hartford**	**NHL**	**55**	**2**	**11**	**13**	**177**	**7**	**1**	**0**	**1**	**2**
1990-91	**Hartford**	**NHL**	**62**	**3**	**18**	**21**	**174**	....	....	....	....	....
	Pittsburgh	**NHL**	**14**	**1**	**4**	**5**	**37**	**20**	**3**	**2**	**5**	**34 ♦**
1991-92	**Pittsburgh**	**NHL**	**62**	**1**	**14**	**15**	**206**	**21**	**0**	**2**	**2**	**39 ♦**
1992-93	**Pittsburgh**	**NHL**	**77**	**3**	**26**	**29**	**249**	**12**	**1**	**5**	**6**	**24**
1993-94	**Pittsburgh**	**NHL**	**80**	**5**	**24**	**29**	**199**	**6**	**0**	**1**	**1**	**18**
1994-95	Leksand	Swe.	2	0	0	0	8	....	....	....	....	....
	Pittsburgh	**NHL**	**44**	**1**	**15**	**16**	**113**	**7**	**0**	**2**	**2**	**8**
1995-96	**NY Rangers**	**NHL**	**74**	**1**	**18**	**19**	**122**	**11**	**1**	**5**	**6**	**16**
	NHL Totals		**814**	**43**	**245**	**288**	**2036**	**108**	**7**	**22**	**29**	**232**

Traded to **Pittsburgh** by **Hartford** with Ron Francis and Grant Jennings for John Cullen, Jeff Parker and Zarley Zalapski, March 4, 1991. Traded to **NY Rangers** by **Pittsburgh** with Luc Robitaille for Petr Nedved and Sergei Zubov, August 31, 1995.

SANDBERG, OLA NYR

Defense. Shoots left. 6'1", 189 lbs. Born, Djurgarden, Sweden, February 23, 1977.
(NY Rangers' 5th choice, 158th overall, in 1996 Entry Draft).

			Regular Season					Playoffs				
Season	Club	Lea	GP	G	A	TP	PIM	GP	G	A	TP	PIM
1995-96	Djurgarden	Swe. Jr.	26	3	5	8	46	....	....	....	....	....

SANDERSON, GEOFF — HFD.

Left wing. Shoots left. 6', 185 lbs. Born, Hay River, N.W.T., February 1, 1972.
(Hartford's 2nd choice, 36th overall, in 1990 Entry Draft).

			Regular Season					Playoffs				
Season	Club	Lea	GP	G	A	TP	PIM	GP	G	A	TP	PIM
1988-89	Swift Current	WHL	58	17	11	28	16	12	3	5	8	6
1989-90	Swift Current	WHL	70	32	62	94	56	4	1	4	5	8
1990-91	**Hartford**	**NHL**	**2**	**1**	**0**	**1**	**0**	**3**	**0**	**0**	**0**	**0**
	Swift Current	WHL	70	62	50	112	57	3	1	2	3	4
	Springfield	AHL	....	....	....	....	....	1	0	0	0	2
1991-92	**Hartford**	**NHL**	**64**	**13**	**18**	**31**	**18**	**7**	**0**	**1**	**1**	**2**
1992-93	**Hartford**	**NHL**	**82**	**46**	**43**	**89**	**28**	....	....	....	....	....
1993-94	**Hartford**	**NHL**	**82**	**41**	**26**	**67**	**42**	....	....	....	....	....
1994-95	HPK	Fin.	12	6	4	10	24	....	....	....	....	....
	Hartford	**NHL**	**46**	**18**	**14**	**32**	**24**	....	....	....	....	....
1995-96	**Hartford**	**NHL**	**81**	**34**	**31**	**65**	**40**	....	....	....	....	....
	NHL Totals		**357**	**153**	**132**	**285**	**152**	**10**	**0**	**1**	**1**	**2**

Played in NHL All-Star Game (1994)

SANDLAK, JIM

Right wing. Shoots right. 6'4", 219 lbs. Born, Kitchener, Ont., December 12, 1966.
(Vancouver's 1st choice, 4th overall, in 1985 Entry Draft).

			Regular Season					Playoffs				
Season	Club	Lea	GP	G	A	TP	PIM	GP	G	A	TP	PIM
1983-84	London	OHL	68	23	18	41	143	8	1	11	12	13
1984-85	London	OHL	58	40	24	64	128	8	3	2	5	14
1985-86	**Vancouver**	**NHL**	**23**	**1**	**3**	**4**	**10**	**3**	**0**	**1**	**1**	**0**
	London	OHL	16	8	14	22	38	5	2	3	5	24
1986-87a	**Vancouver**	**NHL**	**78**	**15**	**21**	**36**	**66**	....	....	....	....	....
1987-88	**Vancouver**	**NHL**	**49**	**16**	**15**	**31**	**81**	....	....	....	....	....
	Fredericton	AHL	24	10	15	25	47	....	....	....	....	....
1988-89	**Vancouver**	**NHL**	**72**	**20**	**20**	**40**	**99**	**6**	**1**	**1**	**2**	**2**
1989-90	**Vancouver**	**NHL**	**70**	**15**	**8**	**23**	**104**	....	....	....	....	....
1990-91	**Vancouver**	**NHL**	**59**	**7**	**6**	**13**	**125**	....	....	....	....	....
1991-92	**Vancouver**	**NHL**	**66**	**16**	**24**	**40**	**176**	**13**	**4**	**6**	**10**	**22**
1992-93	**Vancouver**	**NHL**	**59**	**10**	**18**	**28**	**122**	**6**	**2**	**2**	**4**	**4**
1993-94	**Hartford**	**NHL**	**27**	**6**	**2**	**8**	**32**	....	....	....	....	....
1994-95	**Hartford**	**NHL**	**13**	**0**	**0**	**0**	**0**	....	....	....	....	....
1995-96	**Vancouver**	**NHL**	**33**	**4**	**2**	**6**	**6**	**5**	**0**	**0**	**0**	**2**
	Syracuse	AHL	12	6	1	7	16	....	....	....	....	....
	NHL Totals		**549**	**110**	**119**	**229**	**821**	**33**	**7**	**10**	**17**	**30**

a NHL All-Rookie Team (1987)

Traded to **Hartford** by **Vancouver** to complete March 22, 1993 deal which sent Murray Craven to Vancouver by Hartford with Vancouver's fifth round choice (previously acquired by Hartford — Vancouver selected Scott Walker) in 1993 Entry Draft for Robert Kron, Vancouver's third round choice (Marek Malik) in 1993 Entry Draft and future considerations, May 17, 1993.

SANDSTROM, TOMAS (SAND-struhm) — PIT.

Right wing. Shoots left. 6'2", 205 lbs. Born, Jakobstad, Finland, September 4, 1964.
(NY Rangers' 2nd choice, 36th overall, in 1982 Entry Draft).

			Regular Season					Playoffs				
Season	Club	Lea	GP	G	A	TP	PIM	GP	G	A	TP	PIM
1981-82	Fagersta	Swe. 2	32	28	11	39	74	....	....	....	....	....
1982-83	Brynas	Swe.	36	23	14	37	50	....	....	....	....	....
1983-84	Brynas	Swe.	34	19	10	29	81	....	....	....	....	....
1984-85a	**NY Rangers**	**NHL**	**74**	**29**	**29**	**58**	**51**	**3**	**0**	**2**	**2**	**0**
1985-86	**NY Rangers**	**NHL**	**73**	**25**	**29**	**54**	**109**	**16**	**4**	**6**	**10**	**20**
1986-87	**NY Rangers**	**NHL**	**64**	**40**	**34**	**74**	**60**	**6**	**1**	**2**	**3**	**20**
1987-88	**NY Rangers**	**NHL**	**69**	**28**	**40**	**68**	**95**	....	....	....	....	....
1988-89	**NY Rangers**	**NHL**	**79**	**32**	**56**	**88**	**148**	**4**	**3**	**2**	**5**	**12**
1989-90	**NY Rangers**	**NHL**	**48**	**19**	**19**	**38**	**100**	....	....	....	....	....
	Los Angeles	**NHL**	**28**	**13**	**20**	**33**	**28**	**10**	**5**	**4**	**9**	**19**
1990-91	**Los Angeles**	**NHL**	**68**	**45**	**44**	**89**	**106**	**10**	**4**	**4**	**8**	**14**
1991-92	**Los Angeles**	**NHL**	**49**	**17**	**22**	**39**	**70**	**6**	**0**	**3**	**3**	**8**
1992-93	**Los Angeles**	**NHL**	**39**	**25**	**27**	**52**	**57**	**24**	**8**	**17**	**25**	**12**
1993-94	**Los Angeles**	**NHL**	**51**	**17**	**24**	**41**	**59**	....	....	....	....	....
	Pittsburgh	**NHL**	**27**	**6**	**11**	**17**	**24**	**6**	**0**	**0**	**0**	**4**
1994-95	Malmo	Swe.	12	10	5	15	14	....	....	....	....	....
	Pittsburgh	**NHL**	**47**	**21**	**23**	**44**	**42**	**12**	**3**	**3**	**6**	**16**
1995-96	**Pittsburgh**	**NHL**	**58**	**35**	**35**	**70**	**69**	**18**	**4**	**2**	**6**	**30**
	NHL Totals		**774**	**352**	**413**	**765**	**1018**	**115**	**32**	**45**	**77**	**155**

a NHL All-Rookie Team (1985)

Played in NHL All-Star Game (1988, 1991)

Traded to **Los Angeles** by **NY Rangers** with Tony Granato for Bernie Nicholls, January 20, 1990. Traded to **Pittsburgh** by **Los Angeles** with Shawn McEachern for Marty McSorley and Jim Paek, February 16, 1994.

SARAULT, YVES (sah-ROH, EEV)

Left wing. Shoots left. 6'1", 170 lbs. Born, Valleyfield, Que., December 23, 1972.
(Montreal's 3rd choice, 61st overall, in 1991 Entry Draft).

			Regular Season					Playoffs				
Season	Club	Lea	GP	G	A	TP	PIM	GP	G	A	TP	PIM
1989-90	Victoriaville	QMJHL	70	12	28	40	140	16	0	3	3	26
1990-91	St-Jean	QMJHL	56	22	24	46	113	....	....	....	....	....
1991-92a	St-Jean	QMJHL	50	28	38	66	96	....	....	....	....	....
a	Trois-Rivières	QMJHL	18	15	14	29	12	15	10	10	20	18
1992-93	Fredericton	AHL	59	14	17	31	41	3	0	1	1	2
	Wheeling	ECHL	2	1	3	4	0	....	....	....	....	....
1993-94	Fredericton	AHL	60	13	14	27	72	....	....	....	....	....
1994-95	Fredericton	AHL	69	24	21	45	96	13	2	1	3	33
	Montreal	**NHL**	**8**	**0**	**1**	**1**	**0**	....	....	....	....	....
1995-96	**Montreal**	**NHL**	**14**	**0**	**0**	**0**	**4**	....	....	....	....	....
	Calgary	**NHL**	**11**	**2**	**1**	**3**	**4**	....	....	....	....	....
	Saint John	AHL	26	10	12	22	34	16	6	2	8	33
	NHL Totals		**33**	**2**	**2**	**4**	**8**	....	....	....	....	....

a QMJHL Second All-Star Team (1992)

Traded to **Calgary** by **Montreal** with Craig Ferguson for a conditional choice in 1997 Entry Draft, November 26, 1995.

SARICH, CORY (SAHR-ihch) — BUF.

Defense. Shoots right. 6'3", 175 lbs. Born, Saskatoon, Sask., August 16, 1978.
(Buffalo's 2nd choice, 27th overall, in 1996 Entry Draft).

			Regular Season					Playoffs				
Season	Club	Lea	GP	G	A	TP	PIM	GP	G	A	TP	PIM
1994-95	Saskatoon	Midget	31	5	22	27	99	....	....	....	....	....
1995-96	Saskatoon	WHL	59	5	18	23	54	3	0	0	0	4

SATAN, MIROSLAV (SHA-tuhn) — EDM.

Center. Shoots left. 6'1", 185 lbs. Born, Topolcany, Czech., October 22, 1974.
(Edmonton's 6th choice, 111th overall, in 1993 Entry Draft).

			Regular Season					Playoffs				
Season	Club	Lea	GP	G	A	TP	PIM	GP	G	A	TP	PIM
1991-92	Topocalny	Czech. 2	9	2	1	3	6	....	....	....	....	....
1992-93	Dukla Trencin	Czech.	38	11	6	17	....	....	....	....	....	....
1993-94	Dukla Trencin	Slovak	30	32	16	48	16	....	....	....	....	....
1994-95	Cape Breton	AHL	25	24	16	40	15	....	....	....	....	....
	Detroit	IHL	8	1	3	4	4	....	....	....	....	....
	San Diego	IHL	6	0	2	2	6	....	....	....	....	....
1995-96	**Edmonton**	**NHL**	**62**	**18**	**17**	**35**	**22**	....	....	....	....	....
	NHL Totals		**62**	**18**	**17**	**35**	**22**	....	....	....	....	....

SAVAGE, BRIAN — MTL.

Left wing. Shoots left. 6'1", 190 lbs. Born, Sudbury, Ont., February 24, 1971.
(Montreal's 11th choice, 171st overall, in 1991 Entry Draft).

			Regular Season					Playoffs				
Season	Club	Lea	GP	G	A	TP	PIM	GP	G	A	TP	PIM
1990-91	Miami-Ohio	CCHA	28	5	6	11	26	....	....	....	....	....
1991-92	Miami-Ohio	CCHA	40	24	16	40	43	....	....	....	....	....
1992-93ab	Miami-Ohio	CCHA	38	*37	21	58	44	....	....	....	....	....
	Cdn. National	....	9	3	0	3	12	....	....	....	....	....
1993-94	Cdn. National	....	51	20	26	46	38	....	....	....	....	....
	Cdn. Olympic	....	8	2	2	4	6	....	....	....	....	....
	Montreal	**NHL**	**3**	**1**	**0**	**1**	**0**	**3**	**0**	**2**	**2**	**0**
	Fredericton	AHL	17	12	15	27	4	....	....	....	....	....
1994-95	**Montreal**	**NHL**	**37**	**12**	**7**	**19**	**27**	....	....	....	....	....
1995-96	**Montreal**	**NHL**	**75**	**25**	**8**	**33**	**28**	**6**	**0**	**2**	**2**	**2**
	NHL Totals		**115**	**38**	**15**	**53**	**55**	**9**	**0**	**4**	**4**	**2**

a CCHA First All-Star Team (1993)
b NCAA West Second All-American Team (1993)

SAVAGE, REGGIE — PHO.

Center. Shoots left. 5'10", 192 lbs. Born, Montreal, Que., May 1, 1970.
(Washington's 1st choice, 15th overall, in 1988 Entry Draft).

			Regular Season					Playoffs				
Season	Club	Lea	GP	G	A	TP	PIM	GP	G	A	TP	PIM
1987-88	Victoriaville	QMJHL	68	68	54	122	77	5	2	3	5	8
1988-89	Victoriaville	QMJHL	54	58	55	113	178	16	15	13	28	52
1989-90	Victoriaville	QMJHL	63	51	43	94	79	16	13	10	23	40
1990-91	**Washington**	**NHL**	**1**	**0**	**0**	**0**	**0**	....	....	....	....	....
	Baltimore	AHL	62	32	29	61	10	6	1	1	2	6
1991-92	Baltimore	AHL	77	42	28	70	51	....	....	....	....	....
1992-93	**Washington**	**NHL**	**16**	**2**	**3**	**5**	**12**	....	....	....	....	....
	Baltimore	AHL	40	37	18	55	28	....	....	....	....	....
1993-94	**Quebec**	**NHL**	**17**	**3**	**4**	**7**	**16**	....	....	....	....	....
	Cornwall	AHL	33	21	13	34	56	....	....	....	....	....
1994-95	Cornwall	AHL	34	13	7	20	56	14	5	6	11	40
1995-96	Atlanta	IHL	66	22	14	36	118	....	....	....	....	....
	Syracuse	AHL	10	9	5	14	28	16	9	6	15	54
	NHL Totals		**34**	**5**	**7**	**12**	**28**	....	....	....	....	....

Traded to **Quebec** by **Washington** with Paul MacDermid for Mike Hough, June 20, 1993. Signed as a free agent by **Phoenix**, August 28, 1996.

SAVARD, DENIS (sa-VARH, den-NEE) — CHI.

Center. Shoots right. 5'10", 175 lbs. Born, Pointe Gatineau, Que., February 4, 1961.
(Chicago's 1st choice, 3rd overall, in 1980 Entry Draft).

			Regular Season					Playoffs				
Season	Club	Lea	GP	G	A	TP	PIM	GP	G	A	TP	PIM
1978-79	Montreal	QJHL	70	46	*112	158	88	11	5	6	11	46
1979-80a	Montreal	QJHL	72	63	118	181	93	10	7	16	23	8
1980-81	**Chicago**	**NHL**	**76**	**28**	**47**	**75**	**47**	**3**	**0**	**0**	**0**	**0**
1981-82	**Chicago**	**NHL**	**80**	**32**	**87**	**119**	**82**	**15**	**11**	**7**	**18**	**52**
1982-83b	**Chicago**	**NHL**	**78**	**35**	**86**	**121**	**99**	**13**	**8**	**9**	**17**	**22**
1983-84	**Chicago**	**NHL**	**75**	**37**	**57**	**94**	**71**	**5**	**1**	**3**	**4**	**9**
1984-85	**Chicago**	**NHL**	**79**	**38**	**67**	**105**	**56**	**15**	**9**	**20**	**29**	**20**
1985-86	**Chicago**	**NHL**	**80**	**47**	**69**	**116**	**111**	**3**	**4**	**1**	**5**	**6**
1986-87	**Chicago**	**NHL**	**70**	**40**	**50**	**90**	**108**	**4**	**1**	**0**	**1**	**12**
1987-88	**Chicago**	**NHL**	**80**	**44**	**87**	**131**	**95**	**5**	**4**	**3**	**7**	**17**
1988-89	**Chicago**	**NHL**	**58**	**23**	**59**	**82**	**110**	**16**	**8**	**11**	**19**	**10**
1989-90	**Chicago**	**NHL**	**60**	**27**	**53**	**80**	**56**	**20**	**7**	**15**	**22**	**41**
1990-91	**Montreal**	**NHL**	**70**	**28**	**31**	**59**	**52**	**13**	**2**	**11**	**13**	**35**
1991-92	**Montreal**	**NHL**	**77**	**28**	**42**	**70**	**73**	**11**	**3**	**9**	**12**	**8**
1992-93	**Montreal**	**NHL**	**63**	**16**	**34**	**50**	**90**	**14**	**0**	**5**	**5**	**4** ♦
1993-94	**Tampa Bay**	**NHL**	**74**	**18**	**28**	**46**	**106**	....	....	....	....	....
1994-95	**Tampa Bay**	**NHL**	**31**	**6**	**11**	**17**	**10**	....	....	....	....	....
	Chicago	**NHL**	**12**	**4**	**4**	**8**	**8**	**16**	**7**	**11**	**18**	**10**
1995-96	**Chicago**	**NHL**	**69**	**13**	**35**	**48**	**102**	**10**	**1**	**2**	**3**	**8**
	NHL Totals		**1132**	**464**	**847**	**1311**	**1276**	**163**	**66**	**107**	**173**	**254**

a QMJHL First All-Star Team (1980)
b NHL Second All-Star Team (1983)

Played in NHL All-Star Game (1982-84, 1986, 1988, 1991, 1996)

Traded to **Montreal** by **Chicago** for Chris Chelios and Montreal's second round choice (Michael Pomichter) in 1991 Entry Draft, June 29, 1990. Signed as a free agent by **Tampa Bay**, July 29, 1993. Traded to **Chicago** by **Tampa Bay** for Chicago's sixth round choice (Xavier Delisle) in 1996 Entry Draft, April 6, 1995.

SAVARD, MARC — NYR

Center. Shoots left. 5'10", 177 lbs. Born, Ottawa, Ont., July 17, 1977.
(NY Rangers' 3rd choice, 91st overall, in 1995 Entry Draft).

			Regular Season					Playoffs				
Season	Club	Lea	GP	G	A	TP	PIM	GP	G	A	TP	PIM
1993-94	Oshawa	OHL	61	18	39	57	20	5	4	3	7	8
1994-95a	Oshawa	OHL	66	43	96	*139	78	7	5	6	11	8
1995-96	Oshawa	OHL	48	28	59	87	77	5	4	5	9	6

a OHL Second All-Star Team (1995)

SAVENKO, BOGDAN (sah-VEE-ehn-kah, bahg-DAHN) VAN.

Right wing. Shoots right. 6'1", 192 lbs. Born, Kiev, USSR, November 20, 1974.
(Chicago's 3rd choice, 54th overall, in 1993 Entry Draft).

			Regular Season					Playoffs				
Season	Club	Lea	GP	G	A	TP	PIM	GP	G	A	TP	PIM
1990-91	SVSM Kiev	USSR 2	40	30	18	48	24	....	....	....	....	....
1991-92	Sokol Kiev	CIS	25	3	1	4	4	....	....	....	....	....
1992-93	Niagara Falls	OHL	51	29	19	48	15	2	1	0	1	2
1993-94	Niagara Falls	OHL	62	42	49	91	22	....	....	....	....	....
1994-95	Indianapolis	IHL	62	18	17	35	49	....	....	....	....	....
1995-96	Syracuse	AHL	69	16	20	36	68	14	2	4	6	20

Traded to **Vancouver** by **Chicago** with Hartford's third round choice (previously acquired by Chicago — Vancouver selected Larry Courville) in 1995 Entry Draft for Gerald Didick, April 7, 1995.

SAVOIA, RYAN PIT.

Center. Shoots right. 6', 195 lbs. Born, Thorold, Ont., May 6, 1973.

			Regular Season					Playoffs				
Season	Club	Lea	GP	G	A	TP	PIM	GP	G	A	TP	PIM
1994-95	Brock U.	OUAA	38	35	48	83	24	....	....	....	....	....
	Cleveland	IHL	1	0	0	0	0	....	....	....	....	....
1995-96	Cleveland	IHL	49	6	7	13	31	....	....	....	....	....

Signed as a free agent by **Pittsburgh**, April 7, 1995.

SAWYER, KEVIN BOS.

Left wing. Shoots left. 6'2", 205 lbs. Born, Christina Lake, B.C., February 21, 1974.

			Regular Season					Playoffs				
Season	Club	Lea	GP	G	A	TP	PIM	GP	G	A	TP	PIM
1992-93	Spokane	WHL	62	4	3	7	274	8	1	1	2	13
1993-94	Spokane	WHL	60	10	15	25	350	3	0	1	1	6
1994-95	Spokane	WHL	54	7	9	16	365	11	2	0	2	58
1995-96	**St. Louis**	**NHL**	**6**	**0**	**0**	**0**	**23**	....	....	....	....	....
	Worcester	AHL	41	3	4	7	268	....	....	....	....	....
	Boston	**NHL**	**2**	**0**	**0**	**0**	**5**	....	....	....	....	....
	Providence	AHL	4	0	0	0	29	4	0	1	1	9
	NHL Totals		**8**	**0**	**0**	**0**	**28**	....	....	....	....	....

Signed as a free agent by **St. Louis**, February 28, 1995. Traded to **Boston** by **St. Louis** with Steve Staios for Steve Leach, March 8, 1996.

SCATCHARD, DAVE VAN.

Center. Shoots right. 6'2", 185 lbs. Born, Hinton, Alta., February 20, 1976.
(Vancouver's 3rd choice, 42nd overall, in 1994 Entry Draft).

			Regular Season					Playoffs				
Season	Club	Lea	GP	G	A	TP	PIM	GP	G	A	TP	PIM
1993-94	Portland	WHL	47	9	11	20	46	10	2	1	3	4
1994-95	Portland	WHL	71	20	30	50	148	8	0	3	3	21
1995-96	Portland	WHL	59	19	28	47	146	7	1	8	9	14
	Syracuse	AHL	1	0	0	0	0	15	2	5	7	29

SCHAEFER, PETER VAN.

Left wing. Shoots left. 5'11", 187 lbs. Born, Yellow Grass, Sask., July 12, 1977.
(Vancouver's 3rd choice, 66th overall, in 1995 Entry Draft).

			Regular Season					Playoffs				
Season	Club	Lea	GP	G	A	TP	PIM	GP	G	A	TP	PIM
1993-94	Brandon	WHL	2	1	0	1	0	....	....	....	....	....
1994-95	Brandon	WHL	68	27	32	59	34	18	5	3	8	18
1995-96a	Brandon	WHL	69	47	61	108	53	19	10	13	23	5

a WHL East First All-Star Team (1996)

SCHMIDT, CHRIS L.A.

Center. Shoots left. 6'3", 200 lbs. Born, Beaverlodge, Alta., March 1, 1976.
(Los Angeles' 4th choice, 111th overall, in 1994 Entry Draft).

			Regular Season					Playoffs				
Season	Club	Lea	GP	G	A	TP	PIM	GP	G	A	TP	PIM
1992-93	Seattle	WHL	61	6	7	13	17	5	0	1	1	0
1993-94	Seattle	WHL	68	7	17	24	26	9	3	1	4	2
1994-95	Seattle	WHL	61	21	11	32	31	3	0	0	0	0
1995-96	Seattle	WHL	61	39	23	62	135	5	1	5	6	9

SCHMIDT, COLIN EDM.

Center. Shoots left. 5'11", 185 lbs. Born, Regina, Sask., February 3, 1974.
(Edmonton's 9th choice, 190th overall, in 1992 Entry Draft).

			Regular Season					Playoffs				
Season	Club	Lea	GP	G	A	TP	PIM	GP	G	A	TP	PIM
1992-93	Colorado	WCHA	27	8	13	21	26	....	....	....	....	....
1993-94	Colorado	WCHA	38	14	22	36	49	....	....	....	....	....
1994-95a	Colorado	WCHA	43	26	31	57	61	....	....	....	....	....
1995-96a	Colorado	WCHA	41	21	37	58	101	....	....	....	....	....

a WCHA Second All-Star Team (1995, 1996)

SCHNEIDER, ANDY

Left wing. Shoots left. 5'9", 170 lbs. Born, Edmonton, Alta., March 29, 1972.

			Regular Season					Playoffs				
Season	Club	Lea	GP	G	A	TP	PIM	GP	G	A	TP	PIM
1990-91	Swift Current	WHL	69	12	74	86	103	3	0	0	0	2
1991-92	Swift Current	WHL	63	44	60	104	120	8	4	9	13	8
1992-93a	Swift Current	WHL	38	19	66	85	78	17	13	*26	*39	40
	New Haven	AHL	19	2	2	4	13	....	....	....	....	....
1993-94	**Ottawa**	**NHL**	**10**	**0**	**0**	**0**	**15**	....	....	....	....	....
	P.E.I.	AHL	61	15	46	61	119	....	....	....	....	....
1994-95	Leksand	Swe.	39	6	8	14	71	4	1	1	2	31
	Cdn. National	....	3	1	0	1	0	....	....	....	....	....
	P.E.I.	AHL	10	1	5	6	25	11	5	5	10	11
1995-96	Minnesota	IHL	81	12	28	40	85	....	....	....	....	....
	NHL Totals		**10**	**0**	**0**	**0**	**15**	....	....	....	....	....

a WHL East Second All-Star Team (1993)

Signed as a free agent by **Ottawa**, October 9, 1992.

SCHNEIDER, MATHIEU TOR.

Defense. Shoots left. 5'11", 192 lbs. Born, New York, NY, June 12, 1969.
(Montreal's 4th choice, 44th overall, in 1987 Entry Draft).

			Regular Season					Playoffs				
Season	Club	Lea	GP	G	A	TP	PIM	GP	G	A	TP	PIM
1986-87	Cornwall	OHL	63	7	29	36	75	5	0	0	0	22
1987-88	**Montreal**	**NHL**	**4**	**0**	**0**	**0**	**2**	....	....	....	....	....
a	Cornwall	OHL	48	21	40	61	83	11	2	6	8	14
	Sherbrooke	AHL	....	....	....	....	....	3	0	3	3	12
1988-89	Cornwall	OHL	59	16	57	73	96	18	7	20	27	30
1989-90	**Montreal**	**NHL**	**44**	**7**	**14**	**21**	**25**	**9**	**1**	**3**	**4**	**31**
	Sherbrooke	AHL	28	6	13	19	20	....	....	....	....	....
1990-91	**Montreal**	**NHL**	**69**	**10**	**20**	**30**	**63**	**13**	**2**	**7**	**9**	**18**
1991-92	**Montreal**	**NHL**	**78**	**8**	**24**	**32**	**72**	**10**	**1**	**4**	**5**	**6**
1992-93	**Montreal**	**NHL**	**60**	**13**	**31**	**44**	**91**	**11**	**1**	**2**	**3**	**16 ♦**
1993-94	**Montreal**	**NHL**	**75**	**20**	**32**	**52**	**62**	**1**	**0**	**0**	**0**	**0**
1994-95	**Montreal**	**NHL**	**30**	**5**	**15**	**20**	**49**	....	....	....	....	....
	NY Islanders	**NHL**	**13**	**3**	**6**	**9**	**30**	....	....	....	....	....
1995-96	**NY Islanders**	**NHL**	**65**	**11**	**36**	**47**	**93**	....	....	....	....	....
	Toronto	**NHL**	**13**	**2**	**5**	**7**	**10**	**6**	**0**	**4**	**4**	**8**
	NHL Totals		**451**	**79**	**183**	**262**	**497**	**50**	**5**	**20**	**25**	**79**

a OHL First All-Star Team (1988)

Played in NHL All-Star Game (1996)

Traded to **NY Islanders** by **Montreal** with Kirk Muller and Craig Darby for Pierre Turgeon and Vladimir Malakhov, April 5, 1995. Traded to **Toronto** by **NY Islanders** with Wendel Clark and D.J. Smith for Darby Hendrickson, Sean Haggerty, Kenny Jonsson and Toronto's first round choice in 1997 Entry Draft, March 13, 1996.

SCHULTE, PAXTON CGY.

Left wing. Shoots left. 6'2", 217 lbs. Born, Onaway, Alta., July 16, 1972.
(Quebec's 7th choice, 124th overall, in 1992 Entry Draft).

			Regular Season					Playoffs				
Season	Club	Lea	GP	G	A	TP	PIM	GP	G	A	TP	PIM
1990-91	North Dakota	WCHA	38	2	4	6	32	....	....	....	....	....
1991-92	Spokane	WHL	70	42	42	84	222	10	2	8	10	48
1992-93	Spokane	WHL	45	38	35	73	142	10	5	6	11	12
1993-94	**Quebec**	**NHL**	**1**	**0**	**0**	**0**	**2**	....	....	....	....	....
	Cornwall	AHL	56	15	15	30	102	....	....	....	....	....
1994-95	Cornwall	AHL	74	14	22	36	217	14	3	3	6	29
1995-96	Cornwall	AHL	69	25	31	56	171	....	....	....	....	....
	Saint John	AHL	14	4	5	9	25	14	4	7	11	40
	NHL Totals		**1**	**0**	**0**	**0**	**2**	....	....	....	....	....

Traded to **Calgary** by **Colorado** for Vesa Viitakoski, March 19, 1996.

SCHULTZ, RAY OTT.

Defense. Shoots left. 6'2", 199 lbs. Born, Red Deer, Alta., November 14, 1976.
(Ottawa's 8th choice, 184th overall, in 1995 Entry Draft).

			Regular Season					Playoffs				
Season	Club	Lea	GP	G	A	TP	PIM	GP	G	A	TP	PIM
1993-94	Tri-City	WHL	3	0	0	0	11	....	....	....	....	....
1994-95	Tri-City	WHL	63	1	8	9	209	11	0	0	0	16
1995-96	Calgary	WHL	66	3	17	20	282	....	....	....	....	....

SCOTT, BRIAN BUF.

Left wing. Shoots left. 6', 187 lbs. Born, Brampton, Ont., May 22, 1977.
(Buffalo's 9th choice, 172nd overall, in 1995 Entry Draft).

			Regular Season					Playoffs				
Season	Club	Lea	GP	G	A	TP	PIM	GP	G	A	TP	PIM
1993-94	Kingston	OHL	58	13	10	23	26	6	0	0	0	8
1994-95	Kingston	OHL	38	5	24	29	15	....	....	....	....	....
	Kitchener	OHL	20	6	6	12	10	5	3	0	3	4
1995-96	Kitchener	OHL	36	8	6	14	16	....	....	....	....	....
	Sudbury	OHL	24	5	5	10	8	....	....	....	....	....

SECORD, BRIAN HFD.

Center. Shoots left. 5'11", 180 lbs. Born, Ridgetown, Ont., June 19, 1975.

			Regular Season					Playoffs				
Season	Club	Lea	GP	G	A	TP	PIM	GP	G	A	TP	PIM
1992-93	Belleville	OHL	66	16	18	34	57	7	2	0	2	11
1993-94	Belleville	OHL	66	29	40	69	56	12	2	4	6	16
1994-95	Belleville	OHL	57	29	53	82	76	10	2	5	7	4
1995-96	Belleville	OHL	27	12	17	29	50	....	....	....	....	....
	S.S. Marie	OHL	32	16	28	44	50	4	0	0	0	4
	Springfield	AHL	1	0	0	0	0	....	....	....	....	....

Signed as a free agent by **Hartford**, September 27, 1995.

SELANNE, TEEMU (SEH-lahn-nay, TEE-moo) ANA.

Right wing. Shoots right. 6', 200 lbs. Born, Helsinki, Finland, July 3, 1970.
(Winnipeg's 1st choice, 10th overall, in 1988 Entry Draft).

			Regular Season					Playoffs				
Season	Club	Lea	GP	G	A	TP	PIM	GP	G	A	TP	PIM
1987-88	Jokerit	Fin. Jr.	33	43	23	66	18	5	4	3	7	2
	Jokerit	Fin. 2	5	1	1	2	0	....	....	....	....	....
1988-89	Jokerit	Fin. 2	34	35	33	68	12	5	7	3	10	4
1989-90	Jokerit	Fin.	11	4	8	12	0	....	....	....	....	....
1990-91	Jokerit	Fin.	42	33	25	58	12	....	....	....	....	....
1991-92	Jokerit	Fin.	44	*39	23	62	20	10	10	7	17	18
1992-93abc	**Winnipeg**	**NHL**	**84**	***76**	**56**	**132**	**45**	**6**	**4**	**2**	**6**	**2**
1993-94	**Winnipeg**	**NHL**	**51**	**25**	**29**	**54**	**22**	....	....	....	....	....
1994-95	Jokerit	Fin.	20	7	12	19	6	....	....	....	....	....
	Winnipeg	**NHL**	**45**	**22**	**26**	**48**	**2**	....	....	....	....	....
1995-96	**Winnipeg**	**NHL**	**51**	**24**	**48**	**72**	**18**	....	....	....	....	....
	Anaheim	**NHL**	**28**	**16**	**20**	**36**	**4**	....	....	....	....	....
	NHL Totals		**259**	**163**	**179**	**342**	**91**	**6**	**4**	**2**	**6**	**2**

a Won Calder Memorial Trophy (1993)
b NHL First All-Star Team (1993)
c NHL/Upper Deck All-Rookie Team (1993)

Played in NHL All-Star Game (1993, 1994, 1996)

Traded to **Anaheim** by **Winnipeg** with Marc Chouinard and Winnipeg's fourth round choice (later traded to Toronto — later traded to Montreal — Montreal selected Kim Staal) in 1996 Entry Draft for Chad Kilger, Oleg Tverdovsky and Anaheim's third round choice (Per-Anton Lundstrom) in 1996 Entry Draft, February 7, 1996.

SELIVANOV, ALEXANDER (seh-lih-VAH-nohv) T.B.

Right wing. Shoots left. 6'1", 206 lbs. Born, Moscow, USSR, March 23, 1971.
(Philadelphia's 4th choice, 140th overall, in 1994 Entry Draft).

			Regular Season					Playoffs				
Season	Club	Lea	GP	G	A	TP	PIM	GP	G	A	TP	PIM
1988-89	Spartak	USSR	1	0	0	0	0	....	....	....	....	....
1989-90	Spartak	USSR	4	0	0	0	0	....	....	....	....	....
1990-91	Spartak	USSR	21	3	1	4	6	....	....	....	....	....
1991-92	Spartak	CIS	31	6	7	13	16	....	....	....	....	....
1992-93	Spartak	CIS	42	12	19	31	66	3	2	0	2	2
1993-94	Spartak	CIS	45	30	11	41	50	6	5	1	6	2
1994-95	Atlanta	IHL	4	0	3	3	2	....	....	....	....	....
	Chicago	IHL	14	4	1	5	8	....	....	....	....	....
	Tampa Bay	**NHL**	**43**	**10**	**6**	**16**	**14**	....	....	....	....	....
1995-96	**Tampa Bay**	**NHL**	**79**	**31**	**21**	**52**	**93**	**6**	**2**	**2**	**4**	**6**
	NHL Totals		**122**	**41**	**27**	**68**	**107**	**6**	**2**	**2**	**4**	**6**

Traded to **Tampa Bay** by **Philadelphia** for Philadelphia's fourth round choice (previously acquired by Tampa Bay — Philadelphia selected Radovan Somik) in 1995 Entry Draft, September 6, 1994.

SEMAK, ALEXANDER (seh-MAHK) NYI

Center. Shoots right. 5'10", 185 lbs. Born, Ufa, USSR, February 11, 1966.
(New Jersey's 12th choice, 207th overall, in 1988 Entry Draft).

			Regular Season					Playoffs				
Season	Club	Lea	GP	G	A	TP	PIM	GP	G	A	TP	PIM
1982-83	Ufa Salavat	USSR	13	2	1	3	4	....	....	....	....	....
1983-84	Ufa Salavat	USSR 2			UNAVAILABLE							
1984-85	Ufa Salavat	USSR 2	47	19	17	36	64	....	....	....	....	....
1985-86	Ufa Salavat	USSR	22	9	7	16	22	....	....	....	....	....
1986-87	Moscow D'amo	USSR	40	20	8	28	32	....	....	....	....	....
1987-88	Moscow D'amo	USSR	47	21	14	35	40	....	....	....	....	....
1988-89	Moscow D'amo	USSR	44	18	10	28	22	....	....	....	....	....
1989-90	Moscow D'amo	USSR	43	23	11	34	33	....	....	....	....	....
1990-91	Moscow D'amo	USSR	46	17	21	38	48	....	....	....	....	....
1991-92	Moscow D'amo	CIS	26	10	13	23	26	....	....	....	....	....
	New Jersey	**NHL**	**25**	**5**	**6**	**11**	**0**	**1**	**0**	**0**	**0**	**0**
	Utica	AHL	7	3	2	5	0	....	....	....	....	....
1992-93	**New Jersey**	**NHL**	**82**	**37**	**42**	**79**	**70**	**5**	**1**	**1**	**2**	**0**
1993-94	**New Jersey**	**NHL**	**54**	**12**	**17**	**29**	**22**	**2**	**0**	**0**	**0**	**0**
1994-95	Ufa Salavat	CIS	9	9	6	15	4	....	....	....	....	....
	New Jersey	**NHL**	**19**	**2**	**6**	**8**	**13**	....	....	....	....	....
	Tampa Bay	**NHL**	**22**	**5**	**5**	**10**	**12**	....	....	....	....	....
1995-96	**NY Islanders**	**NHL**	**69**	**20**	**14**	**34**	**68**	....	....	....	....	....
	NHL Totals		**271**	**81**	**90**	**171**	**185**	**8**	**1**	**1**	**2**	**0**

Traded to **Tampa Bay** by **New Jersey** with Ben Hankinson for Shawn Chambers and Danton Cole, March 14, 1995. Traded to **NY Islanders** by **Tampa Bay** for NY Islanders' fifth round choice in 1997 Entry Draft, September 14, 1995.

SEMENOV, ANATOLI (seh-MEH-nahf)

Center/Left wing. Shoots left. 6'2", 190 lbs. Born, Moscow, USSR, March 5, 1962.
(Edmonton's 5th choice, 120th overall, in 1989 Entry Draft).

			Regular Season					Playoffs				
Season	Club	Lea	GP	G	A	TP	PIM	GP	G	A	TP	PIM
1979-80	Moscow D'amo	USSR	8	3	0	3	2	....	....	....	....	....
1980-81	Moscow D'amo	USSR	47	18	14	32	18	....	....	....	....	....
1981-82	Moscow D'amo	USSR	44	12	14	26	28	....	....	....	....	....
1982-83	Moscow D'amo	USSR	44	22	18	40	26	....	....	....	....	....
1983-84	Moscow D'amo	USSR	19	10	5	15	14	....	....	....	....	....
1984-85	Moscow D'amo	USSR	30	17	12	29	32	....	....	....	....	....
1985-86	Moscow D'amo	USSR	32	18	17	35	19	....	....	....	....	....
1986-87	Moscow D'amo	USSR	40	15	29	44	32	....	....	....	....	....
1987-88	Moscow D'amo	USSR	32	17	8	25	22	....	....	....	....	....
1988-89	Moscow D'amo	USSR	31	9	12	21	24	....	....	....	....	....
1989-90	Moscow D'amo	USSR	48	13	20	33	16	....	....	....	....	....
	Edmonton	**NHL**	....	....	....	....	....	**2**	**0**	**0**	**0**	**0**
1990-91	**Edmonton**	**NHL**	**57**	**15**	**16**	**31**	**26**	**12**	**5**	**5**	**10**	**6**
1991-92	**Edmonton**	**NHL**	**59**	**20**	**22**	**42**	**16**	**8**	**1**	**1**	**2**	**6**
1992-93	**Tampa Bay**	**NHL**	**13**	**2**	**3**	**5**	**4**	....	....	....	....	....
	Vancouver	**NHL**	**62**	**10**	**34**	**44**	**28**	**12**	**1**	**3**	**4**	**0**
1993-94	**Anaheim**	**NHL**	**49**	**11**	**19**	**30**	**12**	....	....	....	....	....
1994-95	**Anaheim**	**NHL**	**15**	**3**	**4**	**7**	**4**	....	....	....	....	....
	Philadelphia	**NHL**	**26**	**1**	**2**	**3**	**6**	**15**	**2**	**4**	**6**	**0**
1995-96	**Philadelphia**	**NHL**	**44**	**3**	**13**	**16**	**14**	....	....	....	....	....
	Anaheim	**NHL**	**12**	**1**	**9**	**10**	**10**	....	....	....	....	....
	NHL Totals		**337**	**66**	**122**	**188**	**120**	**49**	**9**	**13**	**22**	**12**

Claimed by **Tampa Bay** from **Edmonton** in Expansion Draft, June 18, 1992. Traded to **Vancouver** by **Tampa Bay** for Dave Capuano and Vancouver's fourth round choice (later traded to New Jersey — later traded to Calgary — Calgary selected Ryan Duthie) in 1994 Entry Draft, November 3, 1992. Claimed by **Anaheim** from **Vancouver** in Expansion Draft, June 24, 1993. Traded to **Philadelphia** by **Anaheim** for Milos Holan, March 8, 1995. Traded to **Anaheim** by **Philadelphia** with Mike Crowley for Brian Wesenberg, March 19, 1996.

SEROWIK, JEFF (sair-OH-wihk)

Defense. Shoots right. 6'1", 210 lbs. Born, Manchester, NH, January 10, 1967.
(Toronto's 5th choice, 85th overall, in 1985 Entry Draft).

			Regular Season					Playoffs				
Season	Club	Lea	GP	G	A	TP	PIM	GP	G	A	TP	PIM
1986-87	Providence	H.E.	33	3	8	11	22	....	....	....	....	....
1987-88	Providence	H.E.	33	3	9	12	44	....	....	....	....	....
1988-89	Providence	H.E.	35	3	14	17	48	....	....	....	....	....
1989-90a	Providence	H.E.	35	6	19	25	34	....	....	....	....	....
1990-91	**Toronto**	**NHL**	**1**	**0**	**0**	**0**	**0**	....	....	....	....	....
	Newmarket	AHL	60	8	15	23	45	....	....	....	....	....
1991-92	St. John's	AHL	78	11	34	45	60	16	4	9	13	22
1992-93b	St. John's	AHL	77	19	35	54	92	9	1	5	6	8
1993-94	Cincinnati	IHL	79	6	21	27	98	7	0	1	1	8
1994-95cd	Providence	AHL	78	28	34	62	102	13	4	6	10	10
	Boston	**NHL**	**1**	**0**	**0**	**0**	**0**	....	....	....	....	....
1995-96	Indianapolis	IHL	69	20	23	43	86	....	....	....	....	....
	Las Vegas	IHL	13	7	6	13	18	15	6	5	11	16
	NHL Totals		**2**	**0**	**0**	**0**	**0**	....	....	....	....	....

a Hockey East Second All-Star Team (1990)
b AHL Second All-Star Team (1993)
c AHL First All-Star Team (1995)
d Won Eddie Shore Plaque (Outstanding Defenseman - AHL) (1995)

Signed as a free agent by **Florida**, July 20, 1993. Signed as a free agent by **Boston**, June 29, 1994. Signed as a free agent by **Chicago**, August 9, 1995.

SESSA, JASON TOR.

Right wing. Shoots right. 6'1", 173 lbs. Born, Long Island, NY, July 17, 1977.
(Toronto's 5th choice, 86th overall, in 1996 Entry Draft).

			Regular Season					Playoffs				
Season	Club	Lea	GP	G	A	TP	PIM	GP	G	A	TP	PIM
1994-95	Rochester	USHL	47	45	22	67	81	....	....	....	....	....
1995-96	Lake Superior	CCHA	30	9	5	14	12	....	....	....	....	....

SEVERYN, BRENT NYI

Defense. Shoots left. 6'2", 211 lbs. Born, Vegreville, Alta., February 22, 1966.

			Regular Season					Playoffs				
Season	Club	Lea	GP	G	A	TP	PIM	GP	G	A	TP	PIM
1983-84	Seattle	WHL	72	14	22	36	49	....	....	....	....	....
1984-85	Seattle	WHL	38	8	32	40	54	....	....	....	....	....
	Brandon	WHL	26	7	16	23	57	....	....	....	....	....
1985-86	Seattle	WHL	33	11	20	31	164	....	....	....	....	....
	Saskatoon	WHL	9	1	4	5	38	....	....	....	....	....
1986-87	U. of Alberta	CWUAA	43	7	19	26	171	....	....	....	....	....
1987-88	U. of Alberta	CWUAA	46	21	29	50	178	....	....	....	....	....
1988-89	Halifax	AHL	47	2	12	14	141	....	....	....	....	....
1989-90	**Quebec**	**NHL**	**35**	**0**	**2**	**2**	**42**	....	....	....	....	....
	Halifax	AHL	43	6	9	15	105	6	1	2	3	49
1990-91	Halifax	AHL	50	7	26	33	202	....	....	....	....	....
1991-92	Utica	AHL	80	11	33	44	211	4	0	1	1	4
1992-93a	Utica	AHL	77	20	32	52	240	5	0	0	0	35
1993-94	**Florida**	**NHL**	**67**	**4**	**7**	**11**	**156**	....	....	....	....	....
1994-95	**Florida**	**NHL**	**9**	**1**	**1**	**2**	**37**	....	....	....	....	....
	NY Islanders	**NHL**	**19**	**1**	**3**	**4**	**34**	....	....	....	....	....
1995-96	**NY Islanders**	**NHL**	**65**	**1**	**8**	**9**	**180**	....	....	....	....	....
	NHL Totals		**195**	**7**	**21**	**28**	**449**	....	....	....	....	....

a AHL First All-Star Team (1993)

Signed as a free agent by **Quebec**, July 15, 1988. Traded to **New Jersey** by **Quebec** for Dave Marcinyshyn, June 3, 1991. Traded to **Winnipeg** by **New Jersey** for Winnipeg's sixth round choice (Ryan Smart) in 1994 Entry Draft, September 30, 1993. Traded to **Florida** by **Winnipeg** for Milan Tichy, October 3, 1993. Traded to **NY Islanders** by **Florida** for NY Islanders' fourth round choice (Dave Duerden) in 1995 Entry Draft, March 3, 1995.

SEVIGNY, PIERRE (seh-VIH-nee) MTL.

Left wing. Shoots left. 6', 195 lbs. Born, Trois-Rivières, Que., September 8, 1971.
(Montreal's 4th choice, 51st overall, in 1989 Entry Draft).

			Regular Season					Playoffs				
Season	Club	Lea	GP	G	A	TP	PIM	GP	G	A	TP	PIM
1988-89	Verdun	QMJHL	67	27	43	70	88	....	....	....	....	....
1989-90a	St-Hyacinthe	QMJHL	67	47	72	119	205	12	8	8	16	42
1990-91a	St-Hyacinthe	QMJHL	60	36	46	82	203	....	....	....	....	....
1991-92	Fredericton	AHL	74	22	37	59	145	7	1	1	2	26
1992-93	Fredericton	AHL	80	36	40	76	113	5	1	1	2	2
1993-94	**Montreal**	**NHL**	**43**	**4**	**5**	**9**	**42**	**3**	**0**	**1**	**1**	**0**
1994-95	**Montreal**	**NHL**	**19**	**0**	**0**	**0**	**15**	....	....	....	....	....
1995-96	Fredericton	AHL	76	39	42	81	188	10	5	9	14	20
	NHL Totals		**62**	**4**	**5**	**9**	**57**	**3**	**0**	**1**	**1**	**0**

a QMJHL Second All-Star Team (1990, 1991)

SHAFIKOV, RUSLAN PHI.

Center. Shoots right. 6'1", 176 lbs. Born, Ufa, USSR, May 11, 1976.
(Philadelphia's 8th choice, 204th overall, in 1995 Entry Draft).

			Regular Season					Playoffs				
Season	Club	Lea	GP	G	A	TP	PIM	GP	G	A	TP	PIM
1994-95	Ufa Salavat	CIS	30	2	0	2	10	7	1	1	2	4
1995-96	Ufa Salavat	CIS	51	9	2	11	18	3	0	0	0	4

SHAFRANOV, KONSTANTIN ST.L.

Left wing. Shoots left. 5'11", 176 lbs. Born, Moscow, USSR, September 11, 1968.
(St. Louis' 10th choice, 229th overall, in 1996 Entry Draft).

			Regular Season					Playoffs				
Season	Club	Lea	GP	G	A	TP	PIM	GP	G	A	TP	PIM
1995-96	Ft. Wayne	IHL	74	46	28	74	26	5	1	2	3	4

SHALDYBIN, YEVGENY BOS.

Defense. Shoots left. 6'1", 198 lbs. Born, Novosibirsk, USSR, July 29, 1975.
(Boston's 6th choice, 151st overall, in 1995 Entry Draft).

			Regular Season					Playoffs				
Season	Club	Lea	GP	G	A	TP	PIM	GP	G	A	TP	PIM
1993-94	Yaroslavl	CIS	14	0	0	0	0	....	....	....	....	....
1994-95	Yaroslavl	CIS	42	2	5	7	10	4	0	1	1	0
1995-96	Yaroslavl	CIS	41	0	2	2	10	3	0	1	1	2

SHANAHAN, BRENDAN HFD.

Left wing. Shoots right. 6'3", 218 lbs. Born, Mimico, Ont., January 23, 1969.
(New Jersey's 1st choice, 2nd overall, in 1987 Entry Draft).

			Regular Season					Playoffs				
Season	Club	Lea	GP	G	A	TP	PIM	GP	G	A	TP	PIM
1985-86	London	OHL	59	28	34	62	70	5	5	5	10	5
1986-87	London	OHL	56	39	53	92	92	....	....	....	....	....
1987-88	**New Jersey**	**NHL**	**65**	**7**	**19**	**26**	**131**	**12**	**2**	**1**	**3**	**44**
1988-89	**New Jersey**	**NHL**	**68**	**22**	**28**	**50**	**115**	....	....	....	....	....
1989-90	**New Jersey**	**NHL**	**73**	**30**	**42**	**72**	**137**	**6**	**3**	**3**	**6**	**20**
1990-91	**New Jersey**	**NHL**	**75**	**29**	**37**	**66**	**141**	**7**	**3**	**5**	**8**	**12**
1991-92	**St. Louis**	**NHL**	**80**	**33**	**36**	**69**	**171**	**6**	**2**	**3**	**5**	**14**
1992-93	**St. Louis**	**NHL**	**71**	**51**	**43**	**94**	**174**	**11**	**4**	**3**	**7**	**18**
1993-94a	**St. Louis**	**NHL**	**81**	**52**	**50**	**102**	**211**	**4**	**2**	**5**	**7**	**4**
1994-95	Dusseldorf	Ger.	3	5	3	8	4	....	....	....	....	....
	St. Louis	**NHL**	**45**	**20**	**21**	**41**	**136**	**5**	**4**	**5**	**9**	**14**
1995-96	**Hartford**	**NHL**	**74**	**44**	**34**	**78**	**125**	....	....	....	....	....
	NHL Totals		**632**	**288**	**310**	**598**	**1341**	**51**	**20**	**25**	**45**	**126**

a NHL First All-Star Team (1994)

Played in NHL All-Star Game (1994, 1996)

Signed as a free agent by **St. Louis**, July 25, 1991. Traded to **Hartford** by **St. Louis** for Chris Pronger, July 27, 1995.

SHANK, DANIEL

Right wing. Shoots right. 5'10", 190 lbs. Born, Montreal, Que., May 12, 1967.

			Regular Season					Playoffs				
Season	Club	Lea	GP	G	A	TP	PIM	GP	G	A	TP	PIM
1985-86	Shawinigan	QMJHL	51	34	38	72	184	....	....	....	....	....
1986-87	Hull	QMJHL	46	26	43	69	325	....	....	....	....	....
1987-88	Hull	QMJHL	42	23	34	57	274	5	3	2	5	16
1988-89	Adirondack	AHL	42	5	20	25	113	17	11	8	19	102
1989-90	**Detroit**	**NHL**	**57**	**11**	**13**	**24**	**143**	....	....	....	....	....
	Adirondack	AHL	14	8	8	16	36	....	....	....	....	....
1990-91	**Detroit**	**NHL**	**7**	**0**	**1**	**1**	**14**	....	....	....	....	....
	Adirondack	AHL	60	26	49	75	278	....	....	....	....	....
1991-92	Adirondack	AHL	27	13	21	34	112	....	....	....	....	....
	Hartford	**NHL**	**13**	**2**	**0**	**2**	**18**	**5**	**0**	**0**	**0**	**22**
	Springfield	AHL	31	9	19	28	83	8	8	0	8	48
1992-93a	San Diego	IHL	77	39	53	92	*495	14	5	10	15	*131
1993-94	San Diego	IHL	63	27	36	63	273	....	....	....	....	....
	Phoenix	IHL	7	4	6	10	26	....	....	....	....	....
1994-95	Minnesota	IHL	19	4	11	15	30	....	....	....	....	....
	Detroit	IHL	54	44	27	71	142	5	2	2	4	6
1995-96	Las Vegas	IHL	49	36	29	65	191	....	....	....	....	....
	Detroit	IHL	29	14	19	33	96	12	4	5	9	38
	NHL Totals		**77**	**13**	**14**	**27**	**175**	**5**	**0**	**0**	**0**	**22**

a IHL First All-Star Team (1993)

Signed as a free agent by **Detroit**, May 26, 1989. Traded to **Hartford** by **Detroit** for Chris Tancill, December 18, 1991.

SHANNON, DARRIN — PHO.

Left wing. Shoots left. 6'2", 210 lbs. Born, Barrie, Ont., December 8, 1969.
(Pittsburgh's 1st choice, 4th overall, in 1988 Entry Draft).

			Regular Season					Playoffs				
Season	Club	Lea	GP	G	A	TP	PIM	GP	G	A	TP	PIM
1986-87	Windsor	OHL	60	16	67	83	116	14	4	6	10	8
1987-88	Windsor	OHL	43	33	41	74	49	12	6	12	18	9
1988-89	**Buffalo**	**NHL**	**3**	**0**	**0**	**0**	**0**	**2**	**0**	**0**	**0**	**0**
	Windsor	OHL	54	33	48	81	47	4	1	6	7	2
1989-90	**Buffalo**	**NHL**	**17**	**2**	**7**	**9**	**4**	**6**	**0**	**1**	**1**	**4**
	Rochester	AHL	50	20	23	43	25	9	4	1	5	2
1990-91	**Buffalo**	**NHL**	**34**	**8**	**6**	**14**	**12**	**6**	**1**	**2**	**3**	**4**
	Rochester	AHL	49	26	34	60	56	10	3	5	8	22
1991-92	**Buffalo**	**NHL**	**1**	**0**	**1**	**1**	**0**	....	....	....	....	....
	Winnipeg	**NHL**	**68**	**13**	**26**	**39**	**41**	**7**	**0**	**1**	**1**	**10**
1992-93	**Winnipeg**	**NHL**	**84**	**20**	**40**	**60**	**91**	**6**	**2**	**4**	**6**	**6**
1993-94	**Winnipeg**	**NHL**	**77**	**21**	**37**	**58**	**87**	....	....	....	....	....
1994-95	**Winnipeg**	**NHL**	**19**	**5**	**3**	**8**	**14**	....	....	....	....	....
1995-96	**Winnipeg**	**NHL**	**63**	**5**	**18**	**23**	**28**	**6**	**1**	**0**	**1**	**6**
	NHL Totals		**366**	**74**	**138**	**212**	**277**	**33**	**4**	**8**	**12**	**30**

Traded to **Buffalo** by **Pittsburgh** with Doug Bodger for Tom Barrasso and Buffalo's third round choice (Joe Dziedzic) in 1990 Entry Draft, November 12, 1988. Traded to **Winnipeg** by **Buffalo** with Mike Hartman and Dean Kennedy for Dave McLlwain, Gord Donnelly, Winnipeg's fifth round choice (Yuri Khmylev) in 1992 Entry Draft and future considerations, October 11, 1991.

SHANNON, DARRYL — BUF.

Defense. Shoots left. 6'2", 200 lbs. Born, Barrie, Ont., June 21, 1968.
(Toronto's 2nd choice, 36th overall, in 1986 Entry Draft).

			Regular Season					Playoffs				
Season	Club	Lea	GP	G	A	TP	PIM	GP	G	A	TP	PIM
1985-86	Windsor	OHL	57	6	21	27	52	16	5	6	11	22
1986-87a	Windsor	OHL	64	23	27	50	83	14	4	8	12	18
1987-88b	Windsor	OHL	60	16	67	83	116	12	3	8	11	17
1988-89	**Toronto**	**NHL**	**14**	**1**	**3**	**4**	**6**	....	....	....	....	....
	Newmarket	AHL	61	5	24	29	37	5	0	3	3	10
1989-90	**Toronto**	**NHL**	**10**	**0**	**1**	**1**	**12**	....	....	....	....	....
	Newmarket	AHL	47	4	15	19	58	....	....	....	....	....
1990-91	**Toronto**	**NHL**	**10**	**0**	**1**	**1**	**0**	....	....	....	....	....
	Newmarket	AHL	47	2	14	16	51	....	....	....	....	....
1991-92	**Toronto**	**NHL**	**48**	**2**	**8**	**10**	**23**	....	....	....	....	....
1992-93	**Toronto**	**NHL**	**16**	**0**	**0**	**0**	**11**	....	....	....	....	....
	St. John's	AHL	7	1	1	2	4	....	....	....	....	....
1993-94	**Winnipeg**	**NHL**	**20**	**0**	**4**	**4**	**18**	....	....	....	....	....
	Moncton	AHL	37	1	10	11	62	20	1	7	8	32
1994-95	**Winnipeg**	**NHL**	**40**	**5**	**9**	**14**	**48**	....	....	....	....	....
1995-96	**Winnipeg**	**NHL**	**48**	**2**	**7**	**9**	**72**	....	....	....	....	....
	Buffalo	**NHL**	**26**	**2**	**6**	**8**	**20**	....	....	....	....	....
	NHL Totals		**232**	**12**	**39**	**51**	**210**	....	....	....	....	....

a OHL Second All-Star Team (1987)
b OHL First All-Star Team (1988)

Signed as a free agent by **Winnipeg**, June 30, 1993. Traded to **Buffalo** by **Winnipeg** with Michal Crosek for Craig Muni, February 15, 1996.

SHANTZ, JEFF — CHI.

Center. Shoots right. 6', 185 lbs. Born, Duchess, Alta., October 10, 1973.
(Chicago's 2nd choice, 36th overall, in 1992 Entry Draft).

			Regular Season					Playoffs				
Season	Club	Lea	GP	G	A	TP	PIM	GP	G	A	TP	PIM
1990-91	Regina	WHL	69	16	21	37	22	8	2	2	4	2
1991-92	Regina	WHL	72	39	50	89	75	....	....	....	....	....
1992-93a	Regina	WHL	64	29	54	83	75	13	2	12	14	14
1993-94	**Chicago**	**NHL**	**52**	**3**	**13**	**16**	**30**	**6**	**0**	**0**	**0**	**6**
	Indianapolis	IHL	19	5	9	14	20	....	....	....	....	....
1994-95	Indianapolis	IHL	32	9	15	24	20	....	....	....	....	....
	Chicago	**NHL**	**45**	**6**	**12**	**18**	**33**	**16**	**3**	**1**	**4**	**2**
1995-96	**Chicago**	**NHL**	**78**	**6**	**14**	**20**	**24**	**10**	**2**	**3**	**5**	**6**
	NHL Totals		**175**	**15**	**39**	**54**	**87**	**32**	**5**	**4**	**9**	**14**

a WHL East First All-Star Team (1993)

SHARIFIJANOV, VADIM (shah-rih-FYAH-nohv) — N.J.

Right wing. Shoots left. 5'11", 210 lbs. Born, Ufa, USSR, December 23, 1975.
(New Jersey's 1st choice, 25th overall, in 1994 Entry Draft).

			Regular Season					Playoffs				
Season	Club	Lea	GP	G	A	TP	PIM	GP	G	A	TP	PIM
1992-93	Ufa Salavat	CIS	37	6	4	10	16	2	1	0	1	0
1993-94	Ufa Salavat	CIS	46	10	6	16	36	5	3	0	3	4
1994-95	CSKA	CIS	34	7	3	10	26	2	0	0	0	0
	Albany	AHL	1	1	1	2	0	9	3	3	6	10
1995-96	Albany	AHL	69	14	28	42	28	....	....	....	....	....

SHAW, BRAD

Defense. Shoots right. 6', 190 lbs. Born, Cambridge, Ont., April 28, 1964.
(Detroit's 5th choice, 86th overall, in 1982 Entry Draft).

			Regular Season					Playoffs				
Season	Club	Lea	GP	G	A	TP	PIM	GP	G	A	TP	PIM
1981-82	Ottawa	OHL	68	13	59	72	24	15	1	13	14	4
1982-83	Ottawa	OHL	63	12	66	78	24	9	2	9	11	4
1983-84a	Ottawa	OHL	68	11	71	82	75	13	2	*27	29	9
1984-85	Binghamton	AHL	24	1	10	11	4	8	1	8	9	6
	Salt Lake	IHL	44	3	29	32	25	....	....	....	....	....
1985-86	**Hartford**	**NHL**	**8**	**0**	**2**	**2**	**4**	....	....	....	....	....
	Binghamton	AHL	64	10	44	54	33	5	0	2	2	6
1986-87	**Hartford**	**NHL**	**2**	**0**	**0**	**0**	**0**	....	....	....	....	....
bc	Binghamton	AHL	77	9	30	39	43	12	1	8	9	2
1987-88	**Hartford**	**NHL**	**1**	**0**	**0**	**0**	**0**	....	....	....	....	....
b	Binghamton	AHL	73	12	50	62	50	4	0	5	5	4
1988-89	Verese	Italy	35	10	30	40	44	11	4	8	12	13
	Cdn. National	....	4	1	0	1	2	....	....	....	....	....
	Hartford	**NHL**	**3**	**1**	**0**	**1**	**0**	**3**	**1**	**0**	**1**	**0**
1989-90d	**Hartford**	**NHL**	**64**	**3**	**32**	**35**	**30**	**7**	**2**	**5**	**7**	**0**
1990-91	**Hartford**	**NHL**	**72**	**4**	**28**	**32**	**29**	**6**	**1**	**2**	**3**	**2**
1991-92	**Hartford**	**NHL**	**62**	**3**	**22**	**25**	**44**	**3**	**0**	**1**	**1**	**4**
1992-93	**Ottawa**	**NHL**	**81**	**7**	**34**	**41**	**34**	....	....	....	....	....
1993-94	**Ottawa**	**NHL**	**66**	**4**	**19**	**23**	**59**	....	....	....	....	....
1994-95	**Ottawa**	**NHL**	**2**	**0**	**0**	**0**	**0**	....	....	....	....	....
	Atlanta	IHL	26	1	18	19	17	5	3	4	7	9
1995-96	Detroit	IHL	79	7	54	61	46	8	2	3	5	8
	NHL Totals		**361**	**22**	**137**	**159**	**200**	**19**	**4**	**8**	**12**	**6**

a OHL First All-Star Team (1984)
b AHL First All-Star Team (1987, 1988)
c Won Eddie Shore Plaque (AHL Outstanding Defenseman) (1987)
d NHL All-Rookie Team (1990)

Rights traded to **Hartford** by **Detroit** for Hartford's eighth round choice (Urban Nordin) in 1984 Entry Draft, May 29, 1984. Traded to **New Jersey** by **Hartford** for cash, June 13, 1992. Claimed by **Ottawa** from **New Jersey** in Expansion Draft, June 18, 1992.

SHAW, DAVID — T.B.

Defense. Shoots right. 6'2", 205 lbs. Born, St. Thomas, Ont., May 25, 1964.
(Quebec's 1st choice, 13th overall, in 1982 Entry Draft).

			Regular Season					Playoffs				
Season	Club	Lea	GP	G	A	TP	PIM	GP	G	A	TP	PIM
1981-82	Kitchener	OHL	68	6	25	31	94	15	2	2	4	51
1982-83	**Quebec**	**NHL**	**2**	**0**	**0**	**0**	**0**	....	....	....	....	....
	Kitchener	OHL	57	18	56	74	78	12	2	10	12	18
1983-84	**Quebec**	**NHL**	**3**	**0**	**0**	**0**	**0**	....	....	....	....	....
a	Kitchener	OHL	58	14	34	48	73	16	4	9	13	12
1984-85	**Quebec**	**NHL**	**14**	**0**	**0**	**0**	**11**	....	....	....	....	....
	Fredericton	AHL	48	7	6	13	73	2	0	0	0	7
1985-86	**Quebec**	**NHL**	**73**	**7**	**19**	**26**	**78**	....	....	....	....	....
1986-87	**Quebec**	**NHL**	**75**	**0**	**19**	**19**	**69**	....	....	....	....	....
1987-88	**NY Rangers**	**NHL**	**68**	**7**	**25**	**32**	**100**	....	....	....	....	....
1988-89	**NY Rangers**	**NHL**	**63**	**6**	**11**	**17**	**88**	**4**	**0**	**2**	**2**	**30**
1989-90	**NY Rangers**	**NHL**	**22**	**2**	**10**	**12**	**22**	....	....	....	....	....
1990-91	**NY Rangers**	**NHL**	**77**	**2**	**10**	**12**	**89**	**6**	**0**	**0**	**0**	**11**
1991-92	**NY Rangers**	**NHL**	**10**	**0**	**1**	**1**	**15**	....	....	....	....	....
	Edmonton	**NHL**	**12**	**1**	**1**	**2**	**8**	....	....	....	....	....
	Minnesota	**NHL**	**37**	**0**	**7**	**7**	**49**	**7**	**2**	**2**	**4**	**10**
1992-93	**Boston**	**NHL**	**77**	**10**	**14**	**24**	**108**	**4**	**0**	**1**	**1**	**6**
1993-94	**Boston**	**NHL**	**55**	**1**	**9**	**10**	**85**	**13**	**1**	**2**	**3**	**16**
1994-95	**Boston**	**NHL**	**44**	**3**	**4**	**7**	**36**	**5**	**0**	**1**	**1**	**4**
1995-96	**Tampa Bay**	**NHL**	**66**	**1**	**11**	**12**	**64**	**6**	**0**	**1**	**1**	**4**
	NHL Totals		**698**	**40**	**141**	**181**	**822**	**45**	**3**	**9**	**12**	**81**

a OHL First All-Star Team (1984)

Traded to **NY Rangers** by **Quebec** with John Ogrodnick for Jeff Jackson and Terry Carkner, September 30, 1987. Traded to **Edmonton** by **NY Rangers** for Jeff Beukeboom, November 12, 1991. Traded to **Minnesota** by **Edmonton** for Brian Glynn, January 21, 1992. Traded to **Boston** by **Minnesota** for future considerations, September 2, 1992. Traded to **Tampa Bay** by **Boston** for Detroit's third round choice (previously acquired by Tampa Bay — Boston selected Jason Doyle) in 1996 Entry Draft, August 17, 1996.

SHAW, LLOYD — VAN.

Defense. Shoots right. 6'3", 215 lbs. Born, Regina, Sask., September 26, 1976.
(Vancouver's 4th choice, 92nd overall, in 1995 Entry Draft).

			Regular Season					Playoffs				
Season	Club	Lea	GP	G	A	TP	PIM	GP	G	A	TP	PIM
1993-94	Seattle	WHL	47	0	4	4	107	8	0	0	0	23
1994-95	Seattle	WHL	66	3	12	15	313	3	0	0	0	13
1995-96	Seattle	WHL	27	0	1	1	92	....	....	....	....	....
	Red Deer	WHL	37	2	4	6	120	10	0	2	2	25

SHEPPARD, RAY — FLA.

Right wing. Shoots right. 6'1", 195 lbs. Born, Pembroke, Ont., May 27, 1966.
(Buffalo's 3rd choice, 60th overall, in 1984 Entry Draft).

			Regular Season					Playoffs				
Season	Club	Lea	GP	G	A	TP	PIM	GP	G	A	TP	PIM
1983-84	Cornwall	OHL	68	44	36	80	69	....	....	....	....	....
1984-85	Cornwall	OHL	49	25	33	58	51	9	2	12	14	4
1985-86a	Cornwall	OHL	63	*81	61	*142	25	6	7	4	11	0
1986-87	Rochester	AHL	55	18	13	31	11	15	12	3	15	2
1987-88b	**Buffalo**	**NHL**	**74**	**38**	**27**	**65**	**14**	**6**	**1**	**1**	**2**	**2**
1988-89	**Buffalo**	**NHL**	**67**	**22**	**21**	**43**	**15**	**1**	**0**	**1**	**1**	**0**
1989-90	**Buffalo**	**NHL**	**18**	**4**	**2**	**6**	**0**	....	....	....	....	....
	Rochester	AHL	5	3	5	8	2	17	8	7	15	9
1990-91	**NY Rangers**	**NHL**	**59**	**24**	**23**	**47**	**21**	....	....	....	....	....
1991-92	**Detroit**	**NHL**	**74**	**36**	**26**	**62**	**27**	**11**	**6**	**2**	**8**	**4**
1992-93	**Detroit**	**NHL**	**70**	**32**	**34**	**66**	**29**	**7**	**2**	**3**	**5**	**0**
1993-94	**Detroit**	**NHL**	**82**	**52**	**41**	**93**	**26**	**7**	**2**	**1**	**3**	**4**
1994-95	**Detroit**	**NHL**	**43**	**30**	**10**	**40**	**17**	**17**	**4**	**3**	**7**	**5**
1995-96	**Detroit**	**NHL**	**5**	**2**	**2**	**4**	**2**	....	....	....	....	....
	San Jose	**NHL**	**51**	**27**	**19**	**46**	**10**	....	....	....	....	....
	Florida	**NHL**	**14**	**8**	**2**	**10**	**4**	**21**	**8**	**8**	**16**	**4**
	NHL Totals		**557**	**275**	**207**	**482**	**165**	**70**	**23**	**19**	**42**	**19**

a OHL First All-Star Team (1986)
b NHL All-Rookie Team (1988)

Traded to **NY Rangers** by **Buffalo** for cash and future considerations, July 9, 1990. Signed as a free agent by **Detroit**, August 5, 1991. Traded to **San Jose** by **Detroit** for Igor Larionov and a conditional draft choice in 1998 Entry Draft, October 24, 1995. Traded to **Florida** by **San Jose** with San Jose's fourth round choice (Joey Tetarenko) in 1996 Entry Draft for Florida's second (later traded to Chicago — Chicago selected Geoff Peters) and fourth (Matt Bradley) round choices in 1996 Entry Draft, March 16, 1996.

SHEVALIER, JEFF (sheh-VAL-ee-ay) L.A.

Left wing. Shoots left. 5'11", 185 lbs. Born, Mississauga, Ont., March 14, 1974.
(Los Angeles' 4th choice, 111th overall, in 1992 Entry Draft).

			Regular Season					Playoffs				
Season	**Club**	**Lea**	**GP**	**G**	**A**	**TP**	**PIM**	**GP**	**G**	**A**	**TP**	**PIM**
1991-92	North Bay	OHL	64	28	29	57	26	21	5	11	16	25
1992-93	North Bay	OHL	62	59	54	113	46	2	1	2	3	4
1993-94a	North Bay	OHL	64	52	49	101	52	17	8	14	22	18
1994-95	Phoenix	IHL	68	31	39	70	44	9	5	4	9	0
	Los Angeles	**NHL**	**1**	**1**	**0**	**1**	**0**	....	....	....	....	....
1995-96	Phoenix	IHL	79	29	38	67	72	4	2	2	4	2
	NHL Totals		**1**	**1**	**0**	**1**	**0**	....	....	....	....	....

a OHL First All-Star Team (1994)

SHIRREFFS, STEVE CGY.

Defense. Shoots left. 6'3", 200 lbs. Born, Boston, MA, February 18, 1976.
(Calgary's 7th choice, 233rd overall, in 1995 Entry Draft).

			Regular Season					Playoffs				
Season	**Club**	**Lea**	**GP**	**G**	**A**	**TP**	**PIM**	**GP**	**G**	**A**	**TP**	**PIM**
1995-96	Princeton	ECAC	25	0	3	3	6	....	....	....	....	....

SHUCHUK, GARY (SHOO-chuhk)

Right wing. Shoots right. 5'11", 190 lbs. Born, Edmonton, Alta., February 17, 1967.
(Detroit's 1st choice, 22nd overall, in 1988 Supplemental Draft).

			Regular Season					Playoffs				
Season	**Club**	**Lea**	**GP**	**G**	**A**	**TP**	**PIM**	**GP**	**G**	**A**	**TP**	**PIM**
1986-87	U. Wisconsin	WCHA	42	19	11	30	72	....	....	....	....	....
1987-88	U. Wisconsin	WCHA	44	7	22	29	70	....	....	....	....	....
1988-89	U. Wisconsin	WCHA	46	18	19	37	102	....	....	....	....	....
1989-90ab	U. Wisconsin	WCHA	45	*41	39	*80	70	....	....	....	....	....
1990-91	**Detroit**	**NHL**	**6**	**1**	**2**	**3**	**6**	**3**	**0**	**0**	**0**	**0**
	Adirondack	AHL	59	23	24	47	32	....	....	....	....	....
1991-92	Adirondack	AHL	79	32	48	80	48	19	4	9	13	18
1992-93	Adirondack	AHL	47	24	53	77	66	....	....	....	....	....
	Los Angeles	**NHL**	**25**	**2**	**4**	**6**	**16**	**17**	**2**	**2**	**4**	**12**
1993-94	**Los Angeles**	**NHL**	**56**	**3**	**4**	**7**	**30**	....	....	....	....	....
1994-95	**Los Angeles**	**NHL**	**22**	**3**	**6**	**9**	**6**	....	....	....	....	....
	Phoenix	IHL	13	8	7	15	12	....	....	....	....	....
1995-96	**Los Angeles**	**NHL**	**33**	**4**	**10**	**14**	**12**	....	....	....	....	....
	Phoenix	IHL	33	8	21	29	76	4	1	0	1	4
	NHL Totals		**142**	**13**	**26**	**39**	**70**	**20**	**2**	**2**	**4**	**12**

a WCHA First All-Star Team (1990)
b NCAA West First All-American Team (1990)

Traded to **Los Angeles** by **Detroit** with Jimmy Carson and Marc Potvin for Paul Coffey, Sylvain Couturier and Jim Hiller, January 29, 1993.

SILLINGER, MIKE VAN.

Center. Shoots right. 5'10", 190 lbs. Born, Regina, Sask., June 29, 1971.
(Detroit's 1st choice, 11th overall, in 1989 Entry Draft).

			Regular Season					Playoffs				
Season	**Club**	**Lea**	**GP**	**G**	**A**	**TP**	**PIM**	**GP**	**G**	**A**	**TP**	**PIM**
1987-88	Regina	WHL	67	18	25	43	17	4	2	2	4	0
1988-89	Regina	WHL	72	53	78	131	52	....	....	....	....	....
1989-90a	Regina	WHL	70	57	72	129	41	11	12	10	22	2
	Adirondack	AHL	....	....	....	....	....	1	0	0	0	0
1990-91	**Detroit**	**NHL**	**3**	**0**	**1**	**1**	**0**	**3**	**0**	**1**	**1**	**0**
b	Regina	WHL	57	50	66	116	42	8	6	9	15	4
1991-92	Adirondack	AHL	64	25	41	66	26	15	9	*19	*28	12
	Detroit	**NHL**	....	....	....	....	....	**8**	**2**	**2**	**4**	**2**
1992-93	**Detroit**	**NHL**	**51**	**4**	**17**	**21**	**16**	....	....	....	....	....
	Adirondack	AHL	15	10	20	30	31	11	5	13	18	10
1993-94	**Detroit**	**NHL**	**62**	**8**	**21**	**29**	**10**	....	....	....	....	....
1994-95	**Detroit**	**NHL**	**13**	**2**	**6**	**8**	**2**	....	....	....	....	....
1994-95	Wien	Aus.	13	13	14	27	10	....	....	....	....	....
	Anaheim	**NHL**	**15**	**2**	**5**	**7**	**6**	....	....	....	....	....
1995-96	**Anaheim**	**NHL**	**62**	**13**	**21**	**34**	**32**	....	....	....	....	....
	Vancouver	**NHL**	**12**	**1**	**3**	**4**	**6**	**6**	**0**	**0**	**0**	**2**
	NHL Totals		**218**	**30**	**74**	**104**	**72**	**17**	**2**	**3**	**5**	**4**

a WHL East Second All-Star Team (1990)
b WHL East First All-Star Team (1991)

Traded to **Anaheim** by **Detroit** with Jason York for Stu Grimson, Mark Ferner and Anaheim's sixth round choice (Magnus Nilsson) in 1996 Entry Draft, April 4, 1995. Traded to **Vancouver** by **Anaheim** for Roman Oksiuta, March 15, 1996.

SILVERMAN, ANDREW NYR

Defense. Shoots left. 6'3", 205 lbs. Born, Beverly, MA, August 23, 1972.
(NY Rangers' 11th choice, 181st overall, in 1990 Entry Draft).

			Regular Season					Playoffs				
Season	**Club**	**Lea**	**GP**	**G**	**A**	**TP**	**PIM**	**GP**	**G**	**A**	**TP**	**PIM**
1991-92	U. of Maine	H.E.	30	2	9	11	18	....	....	....	....	....
1992-93	U. of Maine	H.E.	37	1	7	8	56	....	....	....	....	....
1993-94	U. of Maine	H.E.	35	0	3	3	80	....	....	....	....	....
1994-95	Binghamton	AHL	5	0	1	1	2	....	....	....	....	....
	Charlotte	ECHL	64	3	11	14	57	3	0	0	0	2
1995-96	Binghamton	AHL	75	5	15	20	92	4	0	0	0	6

SIM, JONATHAN DAL.

Center. Shoots left. 5'9", 175 lbs. Born, New Glasgow, N.S., September 29, 1977.
(Dallas' 2nd choice, 70th overall, in 1996 Entry Draft).

			Regular Season					Playoffs				
Season	**Club**	**Lea**	**GP**	**G**	**A**	**TP**	**PIM**	**GP**	**G**	**A**	**TP**	**PIM**
1994-95	Sarnia	OHL	25	9	12	21	19	4	3	2	5	2
1995-96	Sarnia	OHL	63	56	46	102	130	10	8	7	15	26

SIMON, CHRIS COL.

Left wing. Shoots left. 6'3", 219 lbs. Born, Wawa, Ont., January 30, 1972.
(Philadelphia's 2nd choice, 25th overall, in 1990 Entry Draft).

			Regular Season					Playoffs				
Season	**Club**	**Lea**	**GP**	**G**	**A**	**TP**	**PIM**	**GP**	**G**	**A**	**TP**	**PIM**
1988-89	Ottawa	OHL	36	4	2	6	31	....	....	....	....	....
1989-90	Ottawa	OHL	57	36	38	74	146	3	2	1	3	4
1990-91	Ottawa	OHL	20	16	6	22	69	17	5	9	14	59
1991-92	Ottawa	OHL	2	1	1	2	24	....	....	....	....	....
	S.S. Marie	OHL	31	19	25	44	143	11	5	8	13	49
1992-93	**Quebec**	**NHL**	**16**	**1**	**1**	**2**	**67**	**5**	**0**	**0**	**0**	**26**
	Halifax	AHL	36	12	6	18	131	....	....	....	....	....
1993-94	**Quebec**	**NHL**	**37**	**4**	**4**	**8**	**132**	....	....	....	....	....
1994-95	**Quebec**	**NHL**	**29**	**3**	**9**	**12**	**106**	**6**	**1**	**1**	**2**	**19**
1995-96	**Colorado**	**NHL**	**64**	**16**	**18**	**34**	**250**	**12**	**1**	**2**	**3**	**11 ♦**
	NHL Totals		**146**	**24**	**32**	**56**	**555**	**23**	**2**	**3**	**5**	**56**

Traded to **Quebec** by **Philadelphia** with Peter Forsberg, Steve Duchesne, Kerry Huffman, Mike Ricci, Ron Hextall, Philadelphia's first round choice in the 1993 (Jocelyn Thibault) and 1994 (later traded to Toronto — later traded to Washington — Washington selected Nolan Baumgartner) Entry Drafts and cash for Eric Lindros, June 30, 1992.

SIMON, JASON PHO.

Left wing. Shoots left. 6'1", 190 lbs. Born, Sarnia, Ont., March 21, 1969.
(New Jersey's 9th choice, 215th overall, in 1989 Entry Draft).

			Regular Season					Playoffs				
Season	**Club**	**Lea**	**GP**	**G**	**A**	**TP**	**PIM**	**GP**	**G**	**A**	**TP**	**PIM**
1986-87	London	OHL	33	1	2	3	33	....	....	....	....	....
	Sudbury	OHL	26	2	3	5	50	....	....	....	....	....
1987-88	Sudbury	OHL	26	5	7	12	35	....	....	....	....	....
	Hamilton	OHL	29	5	13	18	124	11	0	2	2	15
1988-89	Windsor	OHL	62	23	39	62	193	4	1	4	5	13
1989-90	Utica	AHL	16	3	4	7	28	2	0	0	0	12
	Nashville	ECHL	13	4	3	7	81	5	1	3	4	17
1990-91	Utica	AHL	50	2	12	14	189	....	....	....	....	....
	Johnstown	ECHL	22	11	9	20	55	....	....	....	....	....
1991-92	Utica	AHL	1	0	0	0	12	....	....	....	....	....
	San Diego	IHL	13	1	4	5	45	3	0	1	1	9
1992-93	Detroit	ColHL	11	7	13	20	38	....	....	....	....	....
	Flint	ColHL	44	17	32	49	202	....	....	....	....	....
1993-94	Salt Lake	IHL	50	7	7	14	*323	....	....	....	....	....
	NY Islanders	**NHL**	**4**	**0**	**0**	**0**	**34**	....	....	....	....	....
	Detroit	ColHL	13	9	16	25	87	....	....	....	....	....
1994-95	Denver	IHL	61	3	6	9	300	1	0	0	0	12
1995-96	Springfield	AHL	18	2	2	4	90	7	1	0	1	26
	NHL Totals		**4**	**0**	**0**	**0**	**34**	....	....	....	....	....

Signed as a free agent by **NY Islanders**, January 6, 1994. Signed as a free agent by **Winnipeg**, August 9, 1995.

SIMON, TODD

Center. Shoots right. 5'10", 188 lbs. Born, Toronto, Ont., April 21, 1972.
(Buffalo's 9th choice, 203rd overall, in 1992 Entry Draft).

			Regular Season					Playoffs				
Season	**Club**	**Lea**	**GP**	**G**	**A**	**TP**	**PIM**	**GP**	**G**	**A**	**TP**	**PIM**
1990-91	Niagara Falls	OHL	65	51	74	125	35	14	7	8	15	12
1991-92a	Niagara Falls	OHL	66	53	93	*146	72	17	17	24	*41	36
1992-93	Rochester	AHL	67	27	66	93	54	12	3	14	17	15
1993-94	**Buffalo**	**NHL**	**15**	**0**	**1**	**1**	**0**	**5**	**1**	**0**	**1**	**0**
	Rochester	AHL	55	33	52	85	79	....	....	....	....	....
1994-95	Rochester	AHL	69	25	65	90	78	5	0	2	2	21
1995-96b	Las Vegas	IHL	52	26	48	74	48	....	....	....	....	....
	Detroit	IHL	29	19	16	35	20	12	2	12	14	6
	NHL Totals		**15**	**0**	**1**	**1**	**0**	**5**	**1**	**0**	**1**	**0**

a OHL First All-Star Team (1992)
b IHL First All-Star Team (1996)

SIMONOV, SERGEI (SEE-muh-nahv) TOR.

Defense. Shoots left. 6'3", 194 lbs. Born, Saratov, USSR, May 20, 1974.
(Toronto's 11th choice, 221st overall, in 1992 Entry Draft).

			Regular Season					Playoffs				
Season	**Club**	**Lea**	**GP**	**G**	**A**	**TP**	**PIM**	**GP**	**G**	**A**	**TP**	**PIM**
1992-93	Saratov	CIS	40	0	2	2	34	....	....	....	....	....
1993-94	CSKA	CIS	28	0	0	0	6	....	....	....	....	....
1994-95	Magnitogorsk	CIS	44	6	3	9	8	4	0	0	0	2
1995-96	Magnitogorsk	CIS	6	0	0	0	2	....	....	....	....	....
	Saratov	CIS	10	0	0	0	6	2	0	0	0	0

SIMONS, MIKAEL L.A.

Center. Shoots left. 6'2", 187 lbs. Born, Falun, Sweden, January 15, 1978.
(Los Angeles' 4th choice, 84th overall, in 1996 Entry Draft).

			Regular Season					Playoffs				
Season	**Club**	**Lea**	**GP**	**G**	**A**	**TP**	**PIM**	**GP**	**G**	**A**	**TP**	**PIM**
1994-95	Mora	Swe. Jr.	26	5	3	8	57	....	....	....	....	....
1995-96	Mora	Swe. Jr.	10	4	4	8	12	....	....	....	....	....
	Mora	Swe. 2	33	6	3	9	22	6	0	2	2	2

SIMONTON, REID COL.

Defense. Shoots right. 6'2", 195 lbs. Born, Calgary, Alta., March 1, 1973.
(Quebec's 1st choice, 9th overall, in 1994 Supplemental Draft).

			Regular Season					Playoffs				
Season	**Club**	**Lea**	**GP**	**G**	**A**	**TP**	**PIM**	**GP**	**G**	**A**	**TP**	**PIM**
1992-93	Union	ECAC	25	7	5	12	78	....	....	....	....	....
1993-94	Union	ECAC	30	4	20	24	76	....	....	....	....	....
1994-95	Union	ECAC	27	4	9	13	63	....	....	....	....	....
1995-96	Union	ECAC	30	9	9	18	85	....	....	....	....	....
	Richmond	ECHL	4	0	1	1	21	6	0	3	3	4

SIMPSON, REID — N.J.

Left wing. Shoots left. 6'1", 210 lbs. Born, Flin Flon, Man., May 21, 1969.
(Philadelphia's 3rd choice, 72nd overall, in 1989 Entry Draft).

			Regular Season					Playoffs				
Season	Club	Lea	GP	G	A	TP	PIM	GP	G	A	TP	PIM
1987-88	Prince Albert	WHL	72	13	14	27	164	10	1	0	1	43
1988-89	Prince Albert	WHL	59	26	29	55	264	4	2	1	3	30
1989-90	Prince Albert	WHL	29	15	17	32	121	14	4	7	11	34
	Hershey	AHL	28	2	2	4	175	....	....	....	....	....
1990-91	Hershey	AHL	54	9	15	24	183	1	0	0	0	0
1991-92	**Philadelphia**	**NHL**	**1**	**0**	**0**	**0**	**0**	....	....	....	....	....
	Hershey	AHL	60	11	7	18	145	....	....	....	....	....
1992-93	**Minnesota**	**NHL**	**1**	**0**	**0**	**0**	**5**	....	....	....	....	....
	Kalamazoo	IHL	45	5	5	10	193	....	....	....	....	....
1993-94	Kalamazoo	IHL	5	0	0	0	16	....	....	....	....	....
	Albany	AHL	37	9	5	14	135	5	1	1	2	18
1994-95	Albany	AHL	70	18	25	43	268	14	1	8	9	13
	New Jersey	**NHL**	**9**	**0**	**0**	**0**	**27**	....	....	....	....	....
1995-96	**New Jersey**	**NHL**	**23**	**1**	**5**	**6**	**79**	....	....	....	....	....
	Albany	AHL	6	1	3	4	17	....	....	....	....	....
	NHL Totals		**34**	**1**	**5**	**6**	**111**	....	....	....	....	....

Signed as a free agent by **Minnesota**, December 14, 1992. Traded to **New Jersey** by **Dallas** with Roy Mitchell for future considerations, March 21, 1994.

SIMPSON, TODD — CGY.

Defense. Shoots left. 6'3", 215 lbs. Born, Edmonton, Alta., May 28, 1973.

			Regular Season					Playoffs				
Season	Club	Lea	GP	G	A	TP	PIM	GP	G	A	TP	PIM
1992-93	Tri-City	WHL	69	5	18	23	196	4	0	0	0	13
1993-94	Tri-City	WHL	12	2	3	5	32	....	....	....	....	....
	Saskatoon	WHL	51	7	19	26	175	16	0	1	1	29
1994-95	Saint John	AHL	80	3	10	13	321	5	0	0	0	4
1995-96	**Calgary**	**NHL**	**6**	**0**	**0**	**0**	**32**	....	....	....	....	....
	Saint John	AHL	66	4	13	17	277	16	2	3	5	32
	NHL Totals		**6**	**0**	**0**	**0**	**32**	....	....	....	....	....

Signed as free agent by **Calgary**, July 6, 1994.

SITTLER, RYAN — PHI.

Left wing. Shoots left. 6'2", 195 lbs. Born, London, Ont., January 28, 1974.
(Philadelphia's 1st choice, 7th overall, in 1992 Entry Draft).

			Regular Season					Playoffs				
Season	Club	Lea	GP	G	A	TP	PIM	GP	G	A	TP	PIM
1992-93	U. of Michigan	CCHA	35	9	24	33	43	....	....	....	....	....
1993-94	U. of Michigan	CCHA	26	9	9	18	14	....	....	....	....	....
1994-95	Hershey	AHL	42	2	7	9	48	....	....	....	....	....
	Johnstown	ECHL	1	1	1	2	0	....	....	....	....	....
1995-96	Hershey	AHL	6	0	1	1	6	....	....	....	....	....
	Raleigh	ECHL	12	2	8	10	8	....	....	....	....	....
	Mobile	ECHL	21	3	11	14	30	....	....	....	....	....
	St. John's	AHL	6	1	2	3	18	4	0	0	0	4

SKALDE, JARROD — (SKAHL-dee)

Center. Shoots left. 6', 175 lbs. Born, Niagara Falls, Ont., February 26, 1971.
(New Jersey's 3rd choice, 26th overall, in 1989 Entry Draft).

			Regular Season					Playoffs				
Season	Club	Lea	GP	G	A	TP	PIM	GP	G	A	TP	PIM
1987-88	Oshawa	OHL	60	12	16	28	24	7	2	1	3	2
1988-89	Oshawa	OHL	65	38	38	76	36	6	1	5	6	2
1989-90	Oshawa	OHL	62	40	52	92	66	17	10	7	17	6
1990-91	**New Jersey**	**NHL**	**1**	**0**	**1**	**1**	**0**	....	....	....	....	....
	Utica	AHL	3	3	2	5	0	....	....	....	....	....
	Oshawa	OHL	15	8	14	22	14	....	....	....	....	....
a	Belleville	OHL	40	30	52	82	21	6	9	6	15	10
1991-92	**New Jersey**	**NHL**	**15**	**2**	**4**	**6**	**4**	....	....	....	....	....
	Utica	AHL	62	20	20	40	56	4	3	1	4	8
1992-93	**New Jersey**	**NHL**	**11**	**0**	**2**	**2**	**4**	....	....	....	....	....
	Utica	AHL	59	21	39	60	76	5	0	2	2	19
	Cincinnati	IHL	4	1	2	3	4	....	....	....	....	....
1993-94	**Anaheim**	**NHL**	**20**	**5**	**4**	**9**	**10**	....	....	....	....	....
	San Diego	IHL	57	25	38	63	79	9	3	12	15	10
1994-95	Las Vegas	IHL	74	34	41	75	103	9	2	4	6	8
1995-96	Baltimore	AHL	11	2	6	8	55	....	....	....	....	....
	Calgary	**NHL**	**1**	**0**	**0**	**0**	**0**	....	....	....	....	....
	Saint John	AHL	68	27	40	67	98	16	4	9	13	6
	NHL Totals		**48**	**7**	**11**	**18**	**18**	....	....	....	....	....

a OHL Second All-Star Team (1991)

Claimed by **Anaheim** from **New Jersey** in Expansion Draft, June 24, 1993. Signed as a free agent by **Anaheim**, May 31, 1995. Traded to **Calgary** by **Anaheim** for Bobby Marshall, October 30, 1995.

SKOREPA, ZDENEK — (SKOHR-zheh-pah) N.J.

Right wing. Shoots left. 6', 185 lbs. Born, Duchcov, Czech., August 10, 1976.
(New Jersey's 4th choice, 103rd overall, in 1994 Entry Draft).

			Regular Season					Playoffs				
Season	Club	Lea	GP	G	A	TP	PIM	GP	G	A	TP	PIM
1993-94	Litvinov	Czech.	20	4	7	11	....	4	0	0	0	....
1994-95	Litvinov	Czech.	28	3	3	6	20	3	0	0	0	2
1995-96	Kingston	OHL	37	21	18	39	13	6	5	2	7	5

SKRBEK, PAVEL — (skuhr-BEHK) PIT.

Defense. Shoots left. 6'3", 191 lbs. Born, Kladno, Czech., August 9, 1978.
(Pittsburgh's 2nd choice, 28th overall, in 1996 Entry Draft).

			Regular Season					Playoffs				
Season	Club	Lea	GP	G	A	TP	PIM	GP	G	A	TP	PIM
1994-95	Kladno	Czech. Jr.	29	7	6	13	....	....	....	....	....	....
1995-96	Kladno	Czech. Jr.	29	10	12	22	....	....	....	....	....	....
	Kladno	Czech.	13	0	1	1	....	5	0	0	0	....

SKRLAC, ROB — BUF.

Left wing. Shoots left. 6'4", 230 lbs. Born, Campbell, B.C., June 10, 1976.
(Buffalo's 11th choice, 224th overall, in 1995 Entry Draft).

			Regular Season					Playoffs				
Season	Club	Lea	GP	G	A	TP	PIM	GP	G	A	TP	PIM
1994-95	Kamloops	WHL	23	0	1	1	177	....	....	....	....	....
1995-96	Kamloops	WHL	63	1	4	5	216	13	0	0	0	52

SKRUDLAND, BRIAN — (SKROOD-luhnd) FLA.

Center. Shoots left. 6', 195 lbs. Born, Peace River, Alta., July 31, 1963.

			Regular Season					Playoffs				
Season	Club	Lea	GP	G	A	TP	PIM	GP	G	A	TP	PIM
1980-81	Saskatoon	WHL	66	15	27	42	97	....	....	....	....	....
1981-82	Saskatoon	WHL	71	27	29	56	135	5	0	1	1	2
1982-83	Saskatoon	WHL	71	35	59	94	42	6	1	3	4	19
1983-84	Nova Scotia	AHL	56	13	12	25	55	12	2	8	10	14
1984-85a	Sherbrooke	AHL	70	22	28	50	109	17	9	8	17	23
1985-86	**Montreal**	**NHL**	**65**	**9**	**13**	**22**	**57**	**20**	**2**	**4**	**6**	**76 ♦**
1986-87	**Montreal**	**NHL**	**79**	**11**	**17**	**28**	**107**	**14**	**1**	**5**	**6**	**29**
1987-88	**Montreal**	**NHL**	**79**	**12**	**24**	**36**	**112**	**11**	**1**	**5**	**6**	**24**
1988-89	**Montreal**	**NHL**	**71**	**12**	**29**	**41**	**84**	**21**	**3**	**7**	**10**	**40**
1989-90	**Montreal**	**NHL**	**59**	**11**	**31**	**42**	**56**	**11**	**3**	**5**	**8**	**30**
1990-91	**Montreal**	**NHL**	**57**	**15**	**19**	**34**	**85**	**13**	**3**	**10**	**13**	**42**
1991-92	**Montreal**	**NHL**	**42**	**3**	**3**	**6**	**36**	**11**	**1**	**1**	**2**	**20**
1992-93	**Montreal**	**NHL**	**23**	**5**	**3**	**8**	**55**	....	....	....	....	....
	Calgary	**NHL**	**16**	**2**	**4**	**6**	**10**	**6**	**0**	**3**	**3**	**12**
1993-94	**Florida**	**NHL**	**79**	**15**	**25**	**40**	**136**	....	....	....	....	....
1994-95	**Florida**	**NHL**	**47**	**5**	**9**	**14**	**88**	....	....	....	....	....
1995-96	**Florida**	**NHL**	**79**	**7**	**20**	**27**	**129**	**21**	**1**	**3**	**4**	**18**
	NHL Totals		**696**	**107**	**197**	**304**	**955**	**128**	**15**	**43**	**58**	**291**

a Won Jack A. Butterfield Trophy (AHL Playoff MVP) (1985)

Signed as a free agent by **Montreal**, September 13, 1983. Traded to **Calgary** by **Montreal** for Gary Leeman, January 28, 1993. Claimed by **Florida** from **Calgary** in Expansion Draft, June 24, 1993.

SLAMIAR, PETER — (SLA-mih-eer) NYR

Left wing. Shoots right. 5'11", 174 lbs. Born, Zvolen, Czech., February 26, 1977.
(NY Rangers' 6th choice, 143rd overall, in 1995 Entry Draft).

			Regular Season					Playoffs				
Season	Club	Lea	GP	G	A	TP	PIM	GP	G	A	TP	PIM
1994-95	Zvolen	Slov. Jr.	30	19	18	37	....	....	....	....	....	....
	Zvolen	Slov. 2	11	4	1	5	....	....	....	....	....	....
1995-96	Beauport	QMJHL	37	7	10	17	40	....	....	....	....	....
	Sherbrooke	QMJHL	18	4	5	9	10	....	....	....	....	....

SLANEY, JOHN — L.A.

Defense. Shoots left. 6', 185 lbs. Born, St. John's, Nfld., February 7, 1972.
(Washington's 1st choice, 9th overall, in 1990 Entry Draft).

			Regular Season					Playoffs				
Season	Club	Lea	GP	G	A	TP	PIM	GP	G	A	TP	PIM
1988-89	Cornwall	OHL	66	16	43	59	23	18	8	16	24	10
1989-90ab	Cornwall	OHL	64	38	59	97	68	6	0	8	8	11
1990-91c	Cornwall	OHL	34	21	25	46	28	....	....	....	....	....
1991-92	Cornwall	OHL	34	19	41	60	43	6	3	8	11	0
	Baltimore	AHL	6	2	4	6	0	....	....	....	....	....
1992-93	Baltimore	AHL	79	20	46	66	60	7	0	7	7	8
1993-94	**Washington**	**NHL**	**47**	**7**	**9**	**16**	**27**	**11**	**1**	**1**	**2**	**2**
	Portland	AHL	29	14	13	27	17	....	....	....	....	....
1994-95	**Washington**	**NHL**	**16**	**0**	**3**	**3**	**6**	....	....	....	....	....
	Portland	AHL	8	3	10	13	4	7	1	3	4	4
1995-96	**Colorado**	**NHL**	**7**	**0**	**3**	**3**	**4**	....	....	....	....	....
	Cornwall	AHL	5	0	4	4	2	....	....	....	....	....
	Los Angeles	**NHL**	**31**	**6**	**11**	**17**	**10**	....	....	....	....	....
	NHL Totals		**101**	**13**	**26**	**39**	**47**	**11**	**1**	**1**	**2**	**2**

a OHL First All-Star Team (1990)
b Canadian Major Junior Defenseman of the Year (1990)
c OHL Second All-Star Team (1991)

Traded to **Colorado** by **Washington** for Philadelphia's third round choice (previously acquired by Colorado — Washington selected Shawn McNeil) in 1996 Entry Draft, July 12, 1995. Traded to **Los Angeles** by **Colorado** for Winnipeg's sixth round choice (previously acquired by Los Angeles — Colorado selected Brian Willsie) in 1996 Entry Draft, December 28, 1995.

SLEGR, JIRI — (SLAY-guhr, YOO-ree) EDM.

Defense. Shoots left. 6'1", 205 lbs. Born, Jihlava, Czech., May 30, 1971.
(Vancouver's 3rd choice, 23rd overall, in 1990 Entry Draft).

			Regular Season					Playoffs				
Season	Club	Lea	GP	G	A	TP	PIM	GP	G	A	TP	PIM
1987-88	Litvinov	Czech.	4	1	1	2	0	....	....	....	....	....
1988-89	Litvinov	Czech.	8	0	0	0	4	....	....	....	....	....
1989-90	Litvinov	Czech.	51	4	15	19	....	....	....	....	....	....
1990-91	Litvinov	Czech.	47	11	36	47	26	....	....	....	....	....
1991-92	Litvinov	Czech.	42	9	23	32	38	....	....	....	....	....
1992-93	**Vancouver**	**NHL**	**41**	**4**	**22**	**26**	**109**	**5**	**0**	**3**	**3**	**4**
	Hamilton	AHL	21	4	14	18	42	....	....	....	....	....
1993-94	**Vancouver**	**NHL**	**78**	**5**	**33**	**38**	**86**	....	....	....	....	....
1994-95	Litvinov	Czech.	11	3	10	13	80	....	....	....	....	....
	Vancouver	**NHL**	**19**	**1**	**5**	**6**	**32**	....	....	....	....	....
	Edmonton	**NHL**	**12**	**1**	**5**	**6**	**14**	....	....	....	....	....
1995-96	**Edmonton**	**NHL**	**57**	**4**	**13**	**17**	**74**	....	....	....	....	....
	Cape Breton	AHL	4	1	2	3	4	....	....	....	....	....
	NHL Totals		**207**	**15**	**78**	**93**	**315**	**5**	**0**	**3**	**3**	**4**

Traded to **Edmonton** by **Vancouver** for Roman Oksiuta, April 7, 1995.

SMART, RYAN — N.J.

Center. Shoots right. 6', 175 lbs. Born, Meadville, PA, September 22, 1975.
(New Jersey's 6th choice, 134th overall, in 1994 Entry Draft).

			Regular Season					Playoffs				
Season	Club	Lea	GP	G	A	TP	PIM	GP	G	A	TP	PIM
1994-95	Cornell	ECAC	26	13	7	20	10	....	....	....	....	....
1995-96	Cornell	ECAC	34	8	19	27	22	....	....	....	....	....

SMEHLIK, RICHARD — (SHMEH-lihk) BUF.

Defense. Shoots left. 6'3", 208 lbs. Born, Ostrava, Czech., January 23, 1970.
(Buffalo's 3rd choice, 97th overall, in 1990 Entry Draft).

			Regular Season					Playoffs				
Season	Club	Lea	GP	G	A	TP	PIM	GP	G	A	TP	PIM
1988-89	TJ Vitkovice	Czech.	38	2	5	7	12	....	....	....	....	....
1989-90	TJ Vitkovice	Czech.	51	5	4	9	....	....	....	....	....	....
1990-91	Dukla Jihlava	Czech.	58	4	3	7	22	....	....	....	....	....
1991-92	TJ Vitkovice	Czech.	47	9	10	19	42	....	....	....	....	....
1992-93	**Buffalo**	**NHL**	**80**	**4**	**27**	**31**	**59**	**8**	**0**	**4**	**4**	**2**
1993-94	**Buffalo**	**NHL**	**84**	**14**	**27**	**41**	**69**	**7**	**0**	**2**	**2**	**10**
1994-95	Vitkovice	Czech.	13	5	2	7	12	....	....	....	....	....
	Buffalo	**NHL**	**39**	**4**	**7**	**11**	**46**	**5**	**0**	**0**	**0**	**2**
1995-96			DID NOT PLAY – INJURED									
	NHL Totals		**203**	**22**	**61**	**83**	**174**	**20**	**0**	**6**	**6**	**14**

SMIRNOV, PAVEL (smihr-NAHV) CGY.

Right wing/Center. Shoots left. 6'3", 191 lbs. Born, Perm, USSR, May 12, 1977.
(Calgary's 2nd choice, 46th overall, in 1995 Entry Draft).

			Regular Season					Playoffs				
Season	Club	Lea	GP	G	A	TP	PIM	GP	G	A	TP	PIM
1993-94	Molot Perm	CIS	8	0	0	0	0	....	....	....	....	....
1994-95	Molot Perm	CIS	48	2	2	4	34	....	....	....	....	....
1995-96	CSKA	CIS	14	0	0	0	4	....	....	....	....	....
	Samara	CIS	12	0	0	0	35	....	....	....	....	....

SMIRNOV, YURI (smihr-NAHV) T.B.

Left wing. Shoots left. 5'11", 172 lbs. Born, Moscow, USSR, January 10, 1976.
(Tampa Bay's 9th choice, 216th overall, in 1994 Entry Draft).

			Regular Season					Playoffs				
Season	Club	Lea	GP	G	A	TP	PIM	GP	G	A	TP	PIM
1993-94	Spartak	CIS	27	2	3	5	4	....	....	....	....	....
1994-95	Spartak	CIS	22	1	0	1	0	....	....	....	....	....
1995-96	Spartak 2	CIS 2			UNAVAILABLE							

SMITH, ADAM NYR

Defense. Shoots left. 6', 190 lbs. Born, Digby, N.S., May 24, 1976.
(NY Rangers' 3rd choice, 78th overall, in 1994 Entry Draft).

			Regular Season					Playoffs				
Season	Club	Lea	GP	G	A	TP	PIM	GP	G	A	TP	PIM
1992-93	Tacoma	WHL	67	0	12	12	43	7	0	1	1	4
1993-94	Tacoma	WHL	66	4	19	23	119	8	0	0	0	10
1994-95	Tacoma	WHL	69	2	19	21	96	4	0	1	1	9
1995-96	Kelowna	WHL	67	8	15	23	125	6	1	1	2	8

SMITH, DAN COL.

Defense. Shoots left. 5'11", 180 lbs. Born, Vernon, B.C., May 2, 1976.
(Colorado's 7th choice, 181st overall, in 1995 Entry Draft).

			Regular Season					Playoffs				
Season	Club	Lea	GP	G	A	TP	PIM	GP	G	A	TP	PIM
1995-96					UNAVAILABLE							

SMITH, DENIS (D.J.) TOR.

Defense. Shoots left. 6'1", 200 lbs. Born, Windsor, Ont., May 13, 1977.
(NY Islanders' 3rd choice, 41st overall, in 1995 Entry Draft).

			Regular Season					Playoffs				
Season	Club	Lea	GP	G	A	TP	PIM	GP	G	A	TP	PIM
1994-95	Windsor	OHL	61	4	13	17	201	10	1	3	4	41
1995-96	Windsor	OHL	64	14	45	59	260	7	1	7	8	23

Traded to **Toronto** by **NY Islanders** with Wendel Clark and Mathieu Schneider for Darby Hendrickson, Sean Haggerty, Kenny Jonsson and Toronto's first round choice in 1997 Entry Draft, March 13, 1996.

SMITH, DERRICK

Left wing. Shoots left. 6'2", 215 lbs. Born, Scarborough, Ont., January 22, 1965.
(Philadelphia's 2nd choice, 44th overall, in 1983 Entry Draft).

			Regular Season					Playoffs				
Season	Club	Lea	GP	G	A	TP	PIM	GP	G	A	TP	PIM
1982-83	Peterborough	OHL	70	16	19	35	47	....	....	....	....	....
1983-84	Peterborough	OHL	70	30	36	66	31	8	4	4	8	7
1984-85	**Philadelphia**	**NHL**	**77**	**17**	**22**	**39**	**31**	**19**	**2**	**5**	**7**	**16**
1985-86	**Philadelphia**	**NHL**	**69**	**6**	**6**	**12**	**57**	**4**	**0**	**0**	**0**	**10**
1986-87	**Philadelphia**	**NHL**	**71**	**11**	**21**	**32**	**34**	**26**	**6**	**4**	**10**	**26**
1987-88	**Philadelphia**	**NHL**	**76**	**16**	**8**	**24**	**104**	**7**	**0**	**0**	**0**	**6**
1988-89	**Philadelphia**	**NHL**	**74**	**16**	**14**	**30**	**43**	**19**	**5**	**2**	**7**	**12**
1989-90	**Philadelphia**	**NHL**	**55**	**3**	**6**	**9**	**32**	....	....	....	....	....
1990-91	**Philadelphia**	**NHL**	**72**	**11**	**10**	**21**	**37**	....	....	....	....	....
1991-92	**Minnesota**	**NHL**	**33**	**2**	**4**	**6**	**33**	**7**	**1**	**0**	**1**	**9**
	Kalamazoo	IHL	6	1	5	6	4	....	....	....	....	....
1992-93	**Minnesota**	**NHL**	**9**	**0**	**1**	**1**	**2**	....	....	....	....	....
	Kalamazoo	IHL	52	22	13	35	43	....	....	....	....	....
1993-94	**Dallas**	**NHL**	**1**	**0**	**0**	**0**	**0**	....	....	....	....	....
a	Kalamazoo	IHL	77	44	37	81	90	5	0	0	0	18
1994-95	Kalamazoo	IHL	68	30	21	51	103	16	3	8	11	8
1995-96	Michigan	IHL	69	15	26	41	79	10	4	3	7	16
	NHL Totals		**537**	**82**	**92**	**174**	**373**	**82**	**14**	**11**	**25**	**79**

a IHL Second All-Star Team (1994)

Claimed on waivers by **Minnesota** from **Philadelphia**, October 26, 1991.

SMITH, GEOFF FLA.

Defense. Shoots left. 6'3", 194 lbs. Born, Edmonton, Alta., March 7, 1969.
(Edmonton's 3rd choice, 63rd overall, in 1987 Entry Draft).

			Regular Season					Playoffs				
Season	Club	Lea	GP	G	A	TP	PIM	GP	G	A	TP	PIM
1987-88	North Dakota	WCHA	42	4	12	16	34	....	....	....	....	....
1988-89	North Dakota	WCHA	9	0	1	1	8	....	....	....	....	....
	Kamloops	WHL	32	4	31	35	29	6	1	3	4	12
1989-90a	**Edmonton**	**NHL**	**74**	**4**	**11**	**15**	**52**	**3**	**0**	**0**	**0**	**0** ♦
1990-91	**Edmonton**	**NHL**	**59**	**1**	**12**	**13**	**55**	**4**	**0**	**0**	**0**	**0**
1991-92	**Edmonton**	**NHL**	**74**	**2**	**16**	**18**	**43**	**5**	**0**	**1**	**1**	**6**
1992-93	**Edmonton**	**NHL**	**78**	**4**	**14**	**18**	**30**	....	....	....	....	....
1993-94	**Edmonton**	**NHL**	**21**	**0**	**3**	**3**	**12**	....	....	....	....	....
	Florida	**NHL**	**56**	**1**	**5**	**6**	**38**	....	....	....	....	....
1994-95	**Florida**	**NHL**	**47**	**2**	**4**	**6**	**22**	....	....	....	....	....
1995-96	**Florida**	**NHL**	**31**	**3**	**7**	**10**	**20**	**1**	**0**	**0**	**0**	**2**
	NHL Totals		**440**	**17**	**72**	**89**	**272**	**13**	**0**	**1**	**1**	**8**

a NHL All-Rookie Team (1990)

Traded to **Florida** by **Edmonton** with Edmonton's fourth round choice (David Nemirovsky) in 1994 Entry Draft for Florida's third round choice (Corey Neilson) in 1994 Entry Draft and St. Louis' sixth round choice (previously acquired by Florida — later traded to Winnipeg — Winnipeg selected Chris Kibermanis) in 1994 Entry Draft, December 6, 1993.

SMITH, JASON N.J.

Defense. Shoots right. 6'3", 205 lbs. Born, Calgary, Alta., November 2, 1973.
(New Jersey's 1st choice, 18th overall, in 1992 Entry Draft).

			Regular Season					Playoffs				
Season	Club	Lea	GP	G	A	TP	PIM	GP	G	A	TP	PIM
1990-91	Regina	WHL	2	0	0	0	7	4	0	0	0	2
1991-92	Regina	WHL	62	9	29	38	168	....	....	....	....	....
1992-93a	Regina	WHL	64	14	52	66	175	13	4	8	12	39
	Utica	AHL	....	....	....	....	....	1	0	0	0	2
1993-94	**New Jersey**	**NHL**	**41**	**0**	**5**	**5**	**43**	**6**	**0**	**0**	**0**	**7**
	Albany	AHL	20	6	3	9	31	....	....	....	....	....
1994-95	**New Jersey**	**NHL**	**2**	**0**	**0**	**0**	**0**	....	....	....	....	....
	Albany	AHL	7	0	2	2	15	11	2	2	4	19
1995-96	**New Jersey**	**NHL**	**64**	**2**	**1**	**3**	**86**	....	....	....	....	....
	NHL Totals		**107**	**2**	**6**	**8**	**129**	**6**	**0**	**0**	**0**	**7**

a Canadian Major Junior First All-Star Team (1993).

SMITH, STEVE CHI.

Defense. Shoots left. 6'4", 215 lbs. Born, Glasgow, Scotland, April 30, 1963.
(Edmonton's 5th choice, 111th overall, in 1981 Entry Draft).

			Regular Season					Playoffs				
Season	Club	Lea	GP	G	A	TP	PIM	GP	G	A	TP	PIM
1980-81	London	OHA	62	4	12	16	141	....	....	....	....	....
1981-82	London	OHL	58	10	36	46	207	4	1	2	3	13
1982-83	Moncton	AHL	2	0	0	0	0	....	....	....	....	....
	London	OHL	50	6	35	41	133	3	1	0	1	10
1983-84	Moncton	AHL	64	1	8	9	176	....	....	....	....	....
1984-85	**Edmonton**	**NHL**	**2**	**0**	**0**	**0**	**2**	....	....	....	....	....
	Nova Scotia	AHL	68	2	28	30	161	5	0	3	3	40
1985-86	**Edmonton**	**NHL**	**55**	**4**	**20**	**24**	**166**	**6**	**0**	**1**	**1**	**14**
	Nova Scotia	AHL	4	0	2	2	11	....	....	....	....	....
1986-87	**Edmonton**	**NHL**	**62**	**7**	**15**	**22**	**165**	**15**	**1**	**3**	**4**	**45** ♦
1987-88	**Edmonton**	**NHL**	**79**	**12**	**43**	**55**	**286**	**19**	**1**	**11**	**12**	**55** ♦
1988-89	**Edmonton**	**NHL**	**35**	**3**	**19**	**22**	**97**	**7**	**2**	**2**	**4**	**20**
1989-90	**Edmonton**	**NHL**	**75**	**7**	**34**	**41**	**171**	**22**	**5**	**10**	**15**	**37** ♦
1990-91	**Edmonton**	**NHL**	**77**	**13**	**41**	**54**	**193**	**18**	**1**	**2**	**3**	**45**
1991-92	**Chicago**	**NHL**	**76**	**9**	**21**	**30**	**304**	**18**	**1**	**11**	**12**	**16**
1992-93	**Chicago**	**NHL**	**78**	**10**	**47**	**57**	**214**	**4**	**0**	**0**	**0**	**10**
1993-94	**Chicago**	**NHL**	**57**	**5**	**22**	**27**	**174**	....	....	....	....	....
1994-95	**Chicago**	**NHL**	**48**	**1**	**12**	**13**	**128**	**16**	**0**	**1**	**1**	**26**
1995-96	**Chicago**	**NHL**	**37**	**0**	**9**	**9**	**71**	**6**	**0**	**0**	**0**	**16**
	NHL Totals		**681**	**71**	**283**	**354**	**1971**	**131**	**11**	**41**	**52**	**284**

Played in NHL All-Star Game (1991)

Traded to **Chicago** by **Edmonton** for Dave Manson and Chicago's third round choice (Kirk Maltby) in 1992 Entry Draft, October 2, 1991.

SMOLINSKI, BRYAN (smoh-LIHN-skee) PIT.

Center. Shoots right. 6'1", 200 lbs. Born, Toledo, OH, December 27, 1971.
(Boston's 1st choice, 21st overall, in 1990 Entry Draft).

			Regular Season					Playoffs				
Season	Club	Lea	GP	G	A	TP	PIM	GP	G	A	TP	PIM
1989-90	Michigan State	CCHA	35	9	13	22	34	....	....	....	....	....
1990-91	Michigan State	CCHA	35	9	12	21	24	....	....	....	....	....
1991-92	Michigan State	CCHA	41	28	33	61	55	....	....	....	....	....
1992-93ab	Michigan State	CCHA	40	31	37	*68	93	....	....	....	....	....
	Boston	**NHL**	**9**	**1**	**3**	**4**	**0**	**4**	**1**	**0**	**1**	**2**
1993-94	**Boston**	**NHL**	**83**	**31**	**20**	**51**	**82**	**13**	**5**	**4**	**9**	**4**
1994-95	**Boston**	**NHL**	**44**	**18**	**13**	**31**	**31**	**5**	**0**	**1**	**1**	**4**
1995-96	**Pittsburgh**	**NHL**	**81**	**24**	**40**	**64**	**69**	**18**	**5**	**4**	**9**	**10**
	NHL Totals		**217**	**74**	**76**	**150**	**182**	**40**	**11**	**9**	**20**	**20**

a CCHA First All-Star Team (1993)
b NCAA West First All-American Team (1993)

Traded to **Pittsburgh** by **Boston** with Glen Murray and Boston's third round choice (Boyd Kane) in 1996 Entry Draft for Kevin Stevens and Shawn McEachern, August 2, 1995.

SMYTH, BRAD (SMIHTH) FLA.

Right wing. Shoots right. 6', 200 lbs. Born, Ottawa, Ont., March 13, 1973.

			Regular Season					Playoffs				
Season	Club	Lea	GP	G	A	TP	PIM	GP	G	A	TP	PIM
1990-91	London	OHL	29	2	6	8	22	....	....	....	....	....
1991-92	London	OHL	58	17	18	35	93	10	2	0	2	8
1992-93	London	OHL	66	54	55	109	118	12	7	8	15	25
1993-94	Cincinnati	IHL	30	7	3	10	54	....	....	....	....	....
	Birmingham	ECHL	29	26	30	56	38	10	8	8	16	19
1994-95	Springfield	AHL	3	0	0	0	7	....	....	....	....	....
	Birmingham	ECHL	36	33	35	68	52	3	5	2	7	0
	Cincinnati	IHL	26	2	11	13	34	1	0	0	0	2
1995-96	**Florida**	**NHL**	**7**	**1**	**1**	**2**	**4**	....	....	....	....	....
abc	Carolina	AHL	68	*68	58	*126	80	....	....	....	....	....
	NHL Totals		**7**	**1**	**1**	**2**	**4**	....	....	....	....	....

a AHL First All-Star Team (1996)
b Won John B. Sollenberger Trophy (Top Scorer - AHL) (1996)
c Won Les Cunningham Plaque (MVP - AHL) (1996)

Signed as a free agent by **Florida**, October 4, 1993.

SMYTH, GREG (SMIHTH) TOR.

Defense. Shoots right. 6'3", 212 lbs. Born, Oakville, Ont., April 23, 1966.
(Philadelphia's 1st choice, 22nd overall, in 1984 Entry Draft).

			Regular Season					Playoffs				
Season	Club	Lea	GP	G	A	TP	PIM	GP	G	A	TP	PIM
1983-84	London	OHL	64	4	21	25	252	6	1	0	1	24
1984-85	London	OHL	47	7	16	23	188	8	2	2	4	27
1985-86	Hershey	AHL	2	0	1	1	5	8	0	0	0	60
a	London	OHL	46	12	42	54	199	4	1	2	3	28
1986-87	**Philadelphia**	**NHL**	**1**	**0**	**0**	**0**	**0**	**1**	**0**	**0**	**0**	**2**
	Hershey	AHL	35	0	2	2	158	2	0	0	0	19
1987-88	**Philadelphia**	**NHL**	**48**	**1**	**6**	**7**	**192**	**5**	**0**	**0**	**0**	**38**
	Hershey	AHL	21	0	10	10	102	....	....	....	....	....
1988-89	**Quebec**	**NHL**	**10**	**0**	**1**	**1**	**70**	....	....	....	....	....
	Halifax	AHL	43	3	9	12	310	4	0	1	1	35
1989-90	**Quebec**	**NHL**	**13**	**0**	**0**	**0**	**57**	....	....	....	....	....
	Halifax	AHL	49	5	14	19	235	6	1	0	1	52
1990-91	**Quebec**	**NHL**	**1**	**0**	**0**	**0**	**0**	....	....	....	....	....
	Halifax	AHL	56	6	23	29	340	....	....	....	....	....
1991-92	**Quebec**	**NHL**	**29**	**0**	**2**	**2**	**138**	....	....	....	....	....
	Halifax	AHL	9	1	3	4	35	....	....	....	....	....
	Calgary	**NHL**	**7**	**1**	**1**	**2**	**15**	....	....	....	....	....
1992-93	**Calgary**	**NHL**	**35**	**1**	**2**	**3**	**95**	....	....	....	....	....
	Salt Lake	IHL	5	0	1	1	31	....	....	....	....	....
1993-94	**Florida**	**NHL**	**12**	**1**	**0**	**1**	**37**	....	....	....	....	....
	Toronto	**NHL**	**11**	**0**	**1**	**1**	**38**	....	....	....	....	....
	Chicago	**NHL**	**38**	**0**	**0**	**0**	**108**	**6**	**0**	**0**	**0**	**0**
1994-95	**Chicago**	**NHL**	**22**	**0**	**3**	**3**	**33**	....	....	....	....	....
	Indianapolis	IHL	2	0	0	0	0	....	....	....	....	....
1995-96	Chicago	IHL	15	1	3	4	53	....	....	....	....	....
	Los Angeles	IHL	41	2	7	9	231	....	....	....	....	....
	NHL Totals		**227**	**4**	**16**	**20**	**783**	**12**	**0**	**0**	**0**	**40**

a OHL Second All-Star Team (1986)

Traded to **Quebec** by **Philadelphia** with Philadelphia's third round choice (John Tanner) in the 1989 Entry Draft for Terry Carkner, July 25, 1988. Traded to **Calgary** by **Quebec** for Martin Simard, March 10, 1992. Signed as a free agent by **Florida**, August 10, 1993. Traded to **Toronto** by **Florida** for cash, December 7, 1993. Claimed on waivers by **Chicago** from **Toronto**, January 8, 1994. Signed as a free agent by **Toronto**, August 22, 1996.

SMYTH, KEVIN (SMIHTH) HFD.

Left wing. Shoots left. 6'2", 217 lbs. Born, Banff, Alta., November 22, 1973.
(Hartford's 4th choice, 79th overall, in 1992 Entry Draft).

			Regular Season					Playoffs				
Season	Club	Lea	GP	G	A	TP	PIM	GP	G	A	TP	PIM
1990-91	Moose Jaw	WHL	66	30	45	75	96	6	1	1	2	0
1991-92	Moose Jaw	WHL	71	30	55	85	114	4	1	3	4	6
1992-93	Moose Jaw	WHL	64	44	38	82	111	....	....	....	....	....
1993-94	**Hartford**	**NHL**	**21**	**3**	**2**	**5**	**10**	....	....	....	....	....
	Springfield	AHL	42	22	27	49	72	6	4	5	9	0
1994-95	Springfield	AHL	57	17	22	39	72	....	....	....	....	....
	Hartford	**NHL**	**16**	**1**	**5**	**6**	**13**	....	....	....	....	....
1995-96	**Hartford**	**NHL**	**21**	**2**	**1**	**3**	**8**	....	....	....	....	....
	Springfield	AHL	47	15	33	48	87	10	5	5	10	8
	NHL Totals		**58**	**6**	**8**	**14**	**31**	....	....	....	....	....

SMYTH, RYAN EDM.

Left wing. Shoots left. 6'1", 195 lbs. Born, Banff, Alta., February 21, 1976.
(Edmonton's 2nd choice, 6th overall, in 1994 Entry Draft).

			Regular Season					Playoffs				
Season	Club	Lea	GP	G	A	TP	PIM	GP	G	A	TP	PIM
1991-92	Moose Jaw	WHL	2	0	0	0	0	....	....	....	....	....
1992-93	Moose Jaw	WHL	64	19	14	33	59	....	....	....	....	....
1993-94	Moose Jaw	WHL	72	50	55	105	88	....	....	....	....	....
1994-95a	Moose Jaw	WHL	50	41	45	86	66	10	6	9	15	22
	Edmonton	**NHL**	**3**	**0**	**0**	**0**	**0**	....	....	....	....	....
1995-96	**Edmonton**	**NHL**	**48**	**2**	**9**	**11**	**28**	....	....	....	....	....
	Cape Breton	AHL	9	6	5	11	4	....	....	....	....	....
	NHL Totals		**51**	**2**	**9**	**11**	**28**	....	....	....	....	....

a WHL East Second All-Star Team (1995)

SNELL, CHRIS CHI.

Defense. Shoots left. 5'11", 200 lbs. Born, Regina, Sask., May 12, 1971.
(Buffalo's 8th choice, 145th overall, in 1991 Entry Draft).

			Regular Season					Playoffs				
Season	Club	Lea	GP	G	A	TP	PIM	GP	G	A	TP	PIM
1989-90a	Ottawa	OHL	63	18	62	80	36	3	2	4	6	4
1990-91	Ottawa	OHL	54	23	59	82	58	17	3	14	17	8
1991-92	Rochester	AHL	65	5	27	32	66	10	2	1	3	6
1992-93	Rochester	AHL	76	14	57	71	83	17	5	8	13	39
1993-94	**Toronto**	**NHL**	**2**	**0**	**0**	**0**	**2**	....	....	....	....	....
bc	St. John's	AHL	75	22	74	96	92	11	1	15	16	10
1994-95d	Phoenix	IHL	57	15	49	64	122	....	....	....	....	....
	Los Angeles	**NHL**	**32**	**2**	**7**	**9**	**22**	....	....	....	....	....
1995-96	Phoenix	IHL	40	9	22	31	113	....	....	....	....	....
	Binghamton	AHL	32	7	25	32	48	4	2	2	4	6
	NHL Totals		**34**	**2**	**7**	**9**	**24**	....	....	....	....	....

a OHL First All-Star Team (1990)
b AHL First All-Star Team (1994)
c Won Eddie Shore Plaque (Top Defenseman - AHL) (1994)
d IHL First All-Star Team (1995)

Signed as a free agent by **Toronto**, August 3, 1993. Traded to **Los Angeles** by **Toronto** with Eric Lacroix and Toronto's fourth round choice (Eric Belanger) in 1996 Entry Draft for Dixon Ward, Guy Leveque and Kelly Fairchild, October 3, 1994. Traded to **NY Rangers** by **Los Angeles** for Steve Larouche, January 14, 1996. Signed as a free agent by **Chicago**, August 16, 1996.

SNOPEK, JAN EDM.

Defense. Shoots right. 6'3", 212 lbs. Born, Prague, Czech., June 22, 1976.
(Edmonton's 5th choice, 109th overall, in 1995 Entry Draft).

			Regular Season					Playoffs				
Season	Club	Lea	GP	G	A	TP	PIM	GP	G	A	TP	PIM
1993-94	Oshawa	OHL	52	0	5	5	51	....	....	....	....	....
1994-95	Oshawa	OHL	64	14	30	44	97	7	0	1	1	4
1995-96	Oshawa	OHL	64	7	28	35	79	5	0	0	0	2

SOKOLSKY, JAMIE PHI.

Defense. Shoots right. 6'2", 202 lbs. Born, Toronto, Ont., March 11, 1977.
(Philadelphia's 5th choice, 135th overall, in 1995 Entry Draft).

			Regular Season					Playoffs				
Season	Club	Lea	GP	G	A	TP	PIM	GP	G	A	TP	PIM
1993-94	Newmarket	OHL	41	0	3	3	11	....	....	....	....	....
1994-95	Belleville	OHL	63	4	18	22	28	16	3	6	9	14
1995-96	Belleville	OHL	65	12	34	46	88	14	3	13	16	18

SOLING, JONAS VAN.

Right wing. Shoots left. 6'4", 187 lbs. Born, Stockholm, Sweden, September 7, 1978.
(Vancouver's 3rd choice, 93rd overall, in 1996 Entry Draft).

			Regular Season					Playoffs				
Season	Club	Lea	GP	G	A	TP	PIM	GP	G	A	TP	PIM
1994-95	Huddinge	Swe. Jr.	13	3	1	4	6	....	....	....	....	....
1995-96	Huddinge	Swe. Jr.	24	8	4	12	18	....	....	....	....	....
	Huddinge	Swe. 2	5	0	0	0	0	....	....	....	....	....

SOMIK, RADOVAN (SAW-mihk, RAH-doh-vahn) PHI.

Left wing. Shoots right. 6'2", 194 lbs. Born, Martin, Czech., May 5, 1977.
(Philadelphia's 3rd choice, 100th overall, in 1995 Entry Draft).

			Regular Season					Playoffs				
Season	Club	Lea	GP	G	A	TP	PIM	GP	G	A	TP	PIM
1993-94	Martin	Slovak	1	0	0	0	0	....	....	....	....	....
1994-95	Martin	Slovak	25	3	0	3	39	3	1	0	1	2
1995-96	Martin	Slovak	25	3	6	9	8	9	1	0	1	....

SOPEL, BRENT VAN.

Defense. Shoots right. 6'1", 185 lbs. Born, Calgary, Alta., January 7, 1977.
(Vancouver's 6th choice, 144th overall, in 1995 Entry Draft).

			Regular Season					Playoffs				
Season	Club	Lea	GP	G	A	TP	PIM	GP	G	A	TP	PIM
1993-94	Saskatoon	WHL	11	2	2	4	2	....	....	....	....	....
1994-95	Saskatoon	WHL	22	1	10	11	31	....	....	....	....	....
	Swift Current	WHL	41	4	19	23	50	3	0	3	3	0
1995-96	Swift Current	WHL	71	13	48	61	87	6	1	2	3	4
	Syracuse	AHL	1	0	0	0	0	....	....	....	....	....

SOROCHAN, LEE (soh-RAW-kihn) NYR

Defense. Shoots left. 6'1", 210 lbs. Born, Edmonton, Alta., September 9, 1975.
(NY Rangers' 2nd choice, 34th overall, in 1993 Entry Draft).

			Regular Season					Playoffs				
Season	Club	Lea	GP	G	A	TP	PIM	GP	G	A	TP	PIM
1991-92	Lethbridge	WHL	67	2	9	11	105	5	0	2	2	6
1992-93	Lethbridge	WHL	69	8	32	40	208	4	0	1	1	12
1993-94	Lethbridge	WHL	46	5	27	32	123	9	4	3	7	16
1994-95	Lethbridge	WHL	29	4	15	19	93	....	....	....	....	....
	Saskatoon	WHL	24	5	13	18	63	10	3	6	9	34
	Binghamton	AHL	....	....	....	....	....	8	0	0	0	11
1995-96	Binghamton	AHL	45	2	8	10	26	1	0	0	0	0

SOULLIERE, STEPHANE (SOO-lee-air) L.A.

Left wing. Shoots left. 5'11", 180 lbs. Born, Greenfield Park, Que., May 30, 1975.

			Regular Season					Playoffs				
Season	Club	Lea	GP	G	A	TP	PIM	GP	G	A	TP	PIM
1992-93	Oshawa	OHL	65	11	7	18	77	13	1	0	1	19
1993-94	Oshawa	OHL	63	25	24	49	120	5	0	1	1	12
1994-95	Oshawa	OHL	18	9	21	30	27	....	....	....	....	....
	Sarnia	OHL	22	10	9	19	38	....	....	....	....	....
	Guelph	OHL	22	10	8	18	48	14	3	2	5	21
1995-96	Knoxville	ECHL	59	26	26	52	124	5	0	2	2	16
	Phoenix	IHL	5	0	0	0	2	....	....	....	....	....

Signed as a free agent by **Los Angeles**, July 1, 1994.

SOURAY, SHELDON N.J.

Defense. Shoots left. 6'2", 210 lbs. Born, Elk Point, Alta., July 13, 1976.
(New Jersey's 3rd choice, 71st overall, in 1994 Entry Draft).

			Regular Season					Playoffs				
Season	Club	Lea	GP	G	A	TP	PIM	GP	G	A	TP	PIM
1992-93	Tri-City	WHL	2	0	0	0	0	....	....	....	....	....
1993-94	Tri-City	WHL	42	3	6	9	122	....	....	....	....	....
1994-95	Tri-City	WHL	40	2	24	26	140	....	....	....	....	....
	Prince George	WHL	11	2	3	5	23	....	....	....	....	....
	Albany	AHL	7	0	2	2	8	....	....	....	....	....
1995-96	Prince George	WHL	32	9	18	27	91	....	....	....	....	....
a	Kelowna	WHL	27	7	20	27	94	6	0	5	5	2
	Albany	AHL	6	0	2	2	12	4	0	1	1	4

a WHL West Second All-Star Team (1996)

SPAHNEL, MARTIN (SPAH-nehl) BUF.

Left wing. Shoots left. 6'2", 187 lbs. Born, Gottwaldov, Czech., July 1, 1977.
(Philadelphia's 6th choice, 152nd overall, in 1995 Entry Draft).

			Regular Season					Playoffs				
Season	Club	Lea	GP	G	A	TP	PIM	GP	G	A	TP	PIM
1994-95	Zlin	Czech. Jr.	33	25	16	41	0	....	....	....	....	....
	Zlin	Czech.	1	0	0	0	0	....	....	....	....	....
1995-96	Lethbridge	WHL	6	1	0	1	0	....	....	....	....	....
	Moose Jaw	WHL	61	4	12	16	33	....	....	....	....	....

Traded to **San Jose** by **Philadelphia** with Philadelphia's first round choice (later traded to Phoenix — Phoenix selected Daniel Briere) in 1996 Entry Draft and Philadelphia's fourth round choice (later traded to Buffalo — Buffalo selected Mike Martone) in 1996 Entry Draft for Pat Falloon, November 16, 1995. Traded to **Buffalo** by **San Jose** with Vaclav Varada, an optional first round choice in 1996 Entry Draft and Philadelphia's fourth round choice (previously acquired by San Jose — Buffalo selected Mike Martone) in 1996 Entry Draft for Doug Bodger, November 16, 1995.

SPRING, COREY T.B.

Right wing. Shoots right. 6'4", 214 lbs. Born, Cranbrook, B.C., May 31, 1971.

			Regular Season					Playoffs				
Season	Club	Lea	GP	G	A	TP	PIM	GP	G	A	TP	PIM
1991-92	Alaska-Anch.	NCAA	35	3	8	11	30	....	....	....	....	....
1992-93	Alaska-Anch.	CCHA	28	5	5	10	20	....	....	....	....	....
1993-94	Alaska-Anch.	CCHA	38	19	18	37	34	....	....	....	....	....
1994-95	Alaska-Anch.	CCHA	33	18	14	32	56	....	....	....	....	....
1995-96	Atlanta	IHL	73	14	14	28	104	2	0	0	0	0

Signed as a free agent by **Tampa Bay**, July 24, 1995.

SPROULE, DOUG — OTT.

Left wing. Shoots left. 6'3", 190 lbs. Born, Red Bank, NJ, February 16, 1976.
(Ottawa's 6th choice, 159th overall, in 1994 Entry Draft).

			Regular Season					Playoffs				
Season	Club	Lea	GP	G	A	TP	PIM	GP	G	A	TP	PIM
1994-95	Harvard	ECAC	30	7	2	9	28	....	....	....	....	....
1995-96	Harvard	ECAC	12	1	0	1	6	....	....	....	....	....

STAAL, KIM — MTL.

Center. Shoots right. 6', 185 lbs. Born, Herlev, Denmark, March 10, 1978.
(Montreal's 4th choice, 92nd overall, in 1996 Entry Draft).

			Regular Season					Playoffs				
Season	Club	Lea	GP	G	A	TP	PIM	GP	G	A	TP	PIM
1994-95	Malmo	Swe. Jr.	17	4	2	6	4	....	....	....	....	....
1995-96	Malmo	Swe. Jr.	30	24	20	44	14	....	....	....	....	....

STAIOS, STEVE (STAY-uhs) — BOS.

Defense. Shoots right. 6', 185 lbs. Born, Hamilton, Ont., July 28, 1973.
(St. Louis' 1st choice, 27th overall, in 1991 Entry Draft).

			Regular Season					Playoffs				
Season	Club	Lea	GP	G	A	TP	PIM	GP	G	A	TP	PIM
1990-91	Niagara Falls	OHL	66	17	29	46	115	12	2	3	5	10
1991-92	Niagara Falls	OHL	65	11	42	53	122	17	7	8	15	27
1992-93	Niagara Falls	OHL	12	4	14	18	30	....	....	....	....	....
	Sudbury	OHL	53	13	44	57	67	11	5	6	11	22
1993-94	Peoria	IHL	38	3	9	12	42	....	....	....	....	....
1994-95	Peoria	IHL	60	3	13	16	64	6	0	0	0	10
1995-96	Peoria	IHL	6	0	1	1	14	....	....	....	....	....
	Worcester	AHL	57	1	11	12	114	....	....	....	....	....
	Boston	**NHL**	**12**	**0**	**0**	**0**	**4**	**3**	**0**	**0**	**0**	**0**
	Providence	AHL	7	1	4	5	8	....	....	....	....	....
	NHL Totals		**12**	**0**	**0**	**0**	**4**	**3**	**0**	**0**	**0**	**0**

Traded to **Boston** by **St. Louis** with Kevin Sawyer for Steve Leach, March 8, 1996.

STAJDUHAR, NICK (STAD-joo-hahr) — EDM.

Defense. Shoots left. 6'3", 200 lbs. Born, Kitchener, Ont., December 6, 1974.
(Edmonton's 2nd choice, 16th overall, in 1993 Entry Draft).

			Regular Season					Playoffs				
Season	Club	Lea	GP	G	A	TP	PIM	GP	G	A	TP	PIM
1990-91	London	OHL	66	3	12	15	51	7	0	0	0	2
1991-92	London	OHL	66	6	15	21	62	10	1	4	5	10
1992-93	London	OHL	49	15	45	60	58	12	4	11	15	10
1993-94a	London	OHL	52	34	52	86	58	5	0	2	2	8
1994-95	Cape Breton	AHL	54	12	26	38	55	....	....	....	....	....
1995-96	**Edmonton**	**NHL**	**2**	**0**	**0**	**0**	**4**	....	....	....	....	....
	Cdn. National	....	46	7	21	28	60	....	....	....	....	....
	Cape Breton	AHL	8	2	0	2	11	....	....	....	....	....
	NHL Totals		**2**	**0**	**0**	**0**	**4**	....	....	....	....	....

a OHL First All-Star Team (1994)

STANTON, PAUL

Defense. Shoots right. 6'1", 195 lbs. Born, Boston, MA, June 22, 1967.
(Pittsburgh's 8th choice, 149th overall, in 1985 Entry Draft).

			Regular Season					Playoffs				
Season	Club	Lea	GP	G	A	TP	PIM	GP	G	A	TP	PIM
1985-86	U. Wisconsin	WCHA	36	4	6	10	16	....	....	....	....	....
1986-87	U. Wisconsin	WCHA	41	5	17	22	70	....	....	....	....	....
1987-88ab	U. Wisconsin	WCHA	45	9	38	47	98	....	....	....	....	....
1988-89c	U. Wisconsin	WCHA	45	7	29	36	126	....	....	....	....	....
1989-90	Muskegon	IHL	77	5	27	32	61	15	2	4	6	21
1990-91	**Pittsburgh**	**NHL**	**75**	**5**	**18**	**23**	**40**	**22**	**1**	**2**	**3**	**24 ♦**
1991-92	**Pittsburgh**	**NHL**	**54**	**2**	**8**	**10**	**62**	**21**	**1**	**7**	**8**	**42 ♦**
1992-93	**Pittsburgh**	**NHL**	**77**	**4**	**12**	**16**	**97**	**1**	**0**	**1**	**1**	**0**
1993-94	**Boston**	**NHL**	**71**	**3**	**7**	**10**	**54**	....	....	....	....	....
1994-95	Providence	AHL	8	4	4	8	4	....	....	....	....	....
	NY Islanders	**NHL**	**18**	**0**	**4**	**4**	**9**	....	....	....	....	....
	Denver	IHL	11	2	6	8	15	....	....	....	....	....
1995-96	Mannheim	Ger.	47	12	24	36	88	9	2	5	7	8
	NHL Totals		**295**	**14**	**49**	**63**	**262**	**44**	**2**	**10**	**12**	**66**

a NCAA West First All-American Team (1988)
b WCHA Second All-Star Team (1988)
c WCHA First All-Star Team (1989)

Traded to **Boston** by **Pittsburgh** for Boston's third round choice (Greg Crozier) in 1994 Entry Draft, October 8, 1993. Traded to **NY Islanders** by **Boston** for NY Islanders' eighth round choice (later traded to Ottawa — Ottawa selected Ray Schultz) in 1995 Entry Draft, February 10, 1995.

STAPLES, JEFF — PHI.

Defense. Shoots left. 6'2", 207 lbs. Born, Kitimat, B.C., March 4, 1975.
(Philadelphia's 10th choice, 244th overall, in 1993 Entry Draft).

			Regular Season					Playoffs				
Season	Club	Lea	GP	G	A	TP	PIM	GP	G	A	TP	PIM
1991-92	Brandon	WHL	3	0	0	0	0	....	....	....	....	....
1992-93	Brandon	WHL	40	0	5	5	114	4	0	1	1	4
1993-94	Brandon	WHL	37	0	7	7	126	....	....	....	....	....
1994-95	Brandon	WHL	57	3	16	19	176	18	0	2	2	23
1995-96	Hershey	AHL	61	7	3	10	100	5	0	1	1	0

STAPLETON, MIKE — PHO.

Center. Shoots right. 5'10", 183 lbs. Born, Sarnia, Ont., May 5, 1966.
(Chicago's 7th choice, 132nd overall, in 1984 Entry Draft).

			Regular Season					Playoffs				
Season	Club	Lea	GP	G	A	TP	PIM	GP	G	A	TP	PIM
1983-84	Cornwall	OHL	70	24	45	69	94	3	1	2	3	4
1984-85	Cornwall	OHL	56	41	44	85	68	9	2	4	6	23
1985-86	Cornwall	OHL	56	39	64	103	74	6	2	3	5	2
1986-87	**Chicago**	**NHL**	**39**	**3**	**6**	**9**	**6**	**4**	**0**	**0**	**0**	**2**
	Cdn. National	....	21	2	4	6	4	....	....	....	....	....
1987-88	**Chicago**	**NHL**	**53**	**2**	**9**	**11**	**59**	....	....	....	....	....
	Saginaw	IHL	31	11	19	30	52	10	5	6	11	10
1988-89	**Chicago**	**NHL**	**7**	**0**	**1**	**1**	**7**	....	....	....	....	....
	Saginaw	IHL	69	21	47	68	162	6	1	3	4	4
1989-90	Indianapolis	IHL	16	5	10	15	6	13	9	10	19	38
1990-91	**Chicago**	**NHL**	**7**	**0**	**1**	**1**	**2**	....	....	....	....	....
	Indianapolis	IHL	75	29	52	81	76	7	1	4	5	0
1991-92	**Chicago**	**NHL**	**19**	**4**	**4**	**8**	**8**	....	....	....	....	....
	Indianapolis	IHL	59	18	40	58	65	....	....	....	....	....
1992-93	**Pittsburgh**	**NHL**	**78**	**4**	**9**	**13**	**10**	**4**	**0**	**0**	**0**	**0**
1993-94	**Pittsburgh**	**NHL**	**58**	**7**	**4**	**11**	**18**	....	....	....	....	....
	Edmonton	**NHL**	**23**	**5**	**9**	**14**	**28**	....	....	....	....	....
1994-95	**Edmonton**	**NHL**	**46**	**6**	**11**	**17**	**21**	....	....	....	....	....
1995-96	**Winnipeg**	**NHL**	**58**	**10**	**14**	**24**	**37**	**6**	**0**	**0**	**0**	**21**
	NHL Totals		**388**	**41**	**68**	**109**	**196**	**14**	**0**	**0**	**0**	**23**

Signed as a free agent by **Pittsburgh**, September 30, 1992. Claimed on waivers by **Edmonton** from **Pittsburgh**, February 19, 1994. Signed as a free agent by **Winnipeg**, August 18, 1995.

STAROSTENKO, DIMITRI (stahr-oh-STEN-koh) — NYR

Right wing. Shoots left. 6', 195 lbs. Born, Minsk, USSR, March 18, 1973.
(NY Rangers' 5th choice, 120th overall, in 1992 Entry Draft).

			Regular Season					Playoffs				
Season	Club	Lea	GP	G	A	TP	PIM	GP	G	A	TP	PIM
1989-90	D'amo Minsk	USSR	7	0	0	0	2	....	....	....	....	....
1990-91	CSKA	USSR	20	2	1	3	4	....	....	....	....	....
1991-92	CSKA	CIS	32	3	1	4	12	....	....	....	....	....
1992-93	CSKA	CIS	42	15	12	27	22	....	....	....	....	....
1993-94	CSKA	CIS	1	0	1	1	0	....	....	....	....	....
	Binghamton	AHL	41	12	9	21	10	....	....	....	....	....
1994-95	Binghamton	AHL	69	19	22	41	40	5	1	1	2	0
1995-96	Binghamton	AHL	44	12	15	27	4	1	1	0	1	0

STASHENKOV, ILJA (stah-shehn-KOHV) — PHO.

Defense. Shoots left. 5'11", 178 lbs. Born, Odintsovo, USSR, August 26, 1974.
(Winnipeg's 11th choice, 223rd overall, in 1993 Entry Draft).

			Regular Season					Playoffs				
Season	Club	Lea	GP	G	A	TP	PIM	GP	G	A	TP	PIM
1991-92	Soviet Wings	CIS	7	0	0	0	2	....	....	....	....	....
1992-93	Soviet Wings	CIS	42	0	0	0	22	1	0	0	0	0
1993-94	Soviet Wings	CIS	46	3	0	3	10	....	....	....	....	....
1994-95	Soviet Wings	CIS	51	3	3	6	40	4	1	0	1	0
1995-96	Soviet Wings	CIS	50	5	6	11	24	....	....	....	....	....

STERN, RON — CGY.

Right wing. Shoots right. 6', 195 lbs. Born, Ste. Agathe, Que., January 11, 1967.
(Vancouver's 3rd choice, 70th overall, in 1986 Entry Draft).

			Regular Season					Playoffs				
Season	Club	Lea	GP	G	A	TP	PIM	GP	G	A	TP	PIM
1984-85	Longueuil	QMJHL	67	6	14	20	176	....	....	....	....	....
1985-86	Longueuil	QMJHL	70	39	33	72	317	....	....	....	....	....
1986-87	Longueuil	QMJHL	56	32	39	71	266	19	11	9	20	55
1987-88	**Vancouver**	**NHL**	**15**	**0**	**0**	**0**	**52**	....	....	....	....	....
	Fredericton	AHL	2	1	0	1	4	....	....	....	....	....
	Flint	IHL	55	14	19	33	294	16	8	8	16	94
1988-89	**Vancouver**	**NHL**	**17**	**1**	**0**	**1**	**49**	**3**	**0**	**1**	**1**	**17**
	Milwaukee	IHL	45	19	23	42	280	5	1	0	1	11
1989-90	**Vancouver**	**NHL**	**34**	**2**	**3**	**5**	**208**	....	....	....	....	....
	Milwaukee	IHL	26	8	9	17	165	....	....	....	....	....
1990-91	**Vancouver**	**NHL**	**31**	**2**	**3**	**5**	**171**	....	....	....	....	....
	Milwaukee	IHL	7	2	2	4	81	....	....	....	....	....
	Calgary	**NHL**	**13**	**1**	**3**	**4**	**69**	**7**	**1**	**3**	**4**	**14**
1991-92	**Calgary**	**NHL**	**72**	**13**	**9**	**22**	**338**	....	....	....	....	....
1992-93	**Calgary**	**NHL**	**70**	**10**	**15**	**25**	**207**	**6**	**0**	**0**	**0**	**43**
1993-94	**Calgary**	**NHL**	**71**	**9**	**20**	**29**	**243**	**7**	**2**	**0**	**2**	**12**
1994-95	**Calgary**	**NHL**	**39**	**9**	**4**	**13**	**163**	**7**	**3**	**1**	**4**	**8**
1995-96	**Calgary**	**NHL**	**52**	**10**	**5**	**15**	**111**	**4**	**0**	**2**	**2**	**8**
	NHL Totals		**414**	**57**	**62**	**119**	**1611**	**34**	**6**	**7**	**13**	**102**

Traded to **Calgary** by **Vancouver** with Kevan Guy for Dana Murzyn, March 5, 1991.

STEVENS, JOHN — PHI.

Defense. Shoots left. 6'1", 195 lbs. Born, Completon, N.B., May 4, 1966.
(Philadelphia's 5th choice, 47th overall, in 1984 Entry Draft).

			Regular Season					Playoffs				
Season	Club	Lea	GP	G	A	TP	PIM	GP	G	A	TP	PIM
1983-84	Oshawa	OHL	70	1	10	11	71	7	0	1	1	6
1984-85	Oshawa	OHL	44	2	10	12	61	5	0	2	2	4
	Hershey	AHL	3	0	0	0	0	....	....	....	....	....
1985-86	Oshawa	OHL	65	1	7	8	146	6	0	2	2	14
	Kalamazoo	IHL	6	0	1	1	8	6	0	3	3	9
1986-87	**Philadelphia**	**NHL**	**6**	**0**	**2**	**2**	**14**	....	....	....	....	....
	Hershey	AHL	63	1	15	16	131	3	0	0	0	7
1987-88	**Philadelphia**	**NHL**	**3**	**0**	**0**	**0**	**0**	....	....	....	....	....
	Hershey	AHL	59	1	15	16	108	....	....	....	....	....
1988-89	Hershey	AHL	78	3	13	16	129	12	1	1	2	29
1989-90	Hershey	AHL	79	3	10	13	193	....	....	....	....	....
1990-91	**Hartford**	**NHL**	**14**	**0**	**1**	**1**	**11**	....	....	....	....	....
	Springfield	AHL	65	0	12	12	139	18	0	6	6	35
1991-92	**Hartford**	**NHL**	**21**	**0**	**4**	**4**	**19**	....	....	....	....	....
	Springfield	AHL	45	1	12	13	73	11	1	3	4	27
1992-93	Springfield	AHL	74	1	19	20	111	15	0	1	1	18
1993-94	**Hartford**	**NHL**	**9**	**0**	**3**	**3**	**4**	....	....	....	....	....
	Springfield	AHL	71	3	9	12	85	3	0	0	0	0
1994-95	Springfield	AHL	79	5	15	20	122	....	....	....	....	....
1995-96	Springfield	AHL	69	0	19	19	95	10	0	1	1	31
	NHL Totals		**53**	**0**	**10**	**10**	**48**	....	....	....	....	....

Signed as a free agent by **Hartford**, July 30, 1990. Signed as a free agent by **Philadelphia**, August 6, 1996.

STEVENS, KEVIN — L.A.

Left wing. Shoots left. 6'3", 217 lbs. Born, Brockton, MA, April 15, 1965.
(Los Angeles' 6th choice, 108th overall, in 1983 Entry Draft).

			Regular Season					Playoffs				
Season	Club	Lea	GP	G	A	TP	PIM	GP	G	A	TP	PIM
1983-84	Boston College	ECAC	37	6	14	20	36	....	....	....	....	....
1984-85	Boston College	H.E.	40	13	23	36	36	....	....	....	....	....
1985-86	Boston College	H.E.	42	17	27	44	56	....	....	....	....	....
1986-87ab	Boston College	H.E.	39	35	35	70	54	....	....	....	....	....
1987-88	U.S. National	....	44	22	23	45	52	....	....	....	....	....
	U.S. Olympic	....	5	1	3	4	2	....	....	....	....	....
	Pittsburgh	NHL	16	5	2	7	8	....	....	....	....	....
1988-89	Pittsburgh	NHL	24	12	3	15	19	11	3	7	10	16
	Muskegon	IHL	45	24	41	65	113	....	....	....	....	....
1989-90	Pittsburgh	NHL	76	29	41	70	171	....	....	....	....	....
1990-91c	Pittsburgh	NHL	80	40	46	86	133	24	*17	16	33	53 ♦
1991-92d	Pittsburgh	NHL	80	54	69	123	254	21	13	15	28	28 ♦
1992-93c	Pittsburgh	NHL	72	55	56	111	177	12	5	11	16	22
1993-94	Pittsburgh	NHL	83	41	47	88	155	6	1	1	2	10
1994-95	Pittsburgh	NHL	27	15	12	27	51	12	4	7	11	21
1995-96	Boston	NHL	41	10	13	23	49	....	....	....	....	....
	Los Angeles	NHL	20	3	10	13	22	....	....	....	....	....
	NHL Totals		519	264	299	563	1039	86	43	57	100	150

a Hockey East First All-Star Team (1987)
b NCAA East Second All-American Team (1987)
c NHL Second All-Star Team (1991, 1993)
d NHL First All-Star Team (1992)

Played in NHL All-Star Game (1991-93)

Rights traded to **Pittsburgh** by **Los Angeles** for Anders Hakansson, September 9, 1983. Traded to **Boston** by **Pittsburgh** with Shawn McEachern for Glen Murray, Bryan Smolinski and Boston's third round choice (Boyd Kane) in 1996 Entry Draft, August 2, 1995. Traded to **Los Angeles** by **Boston** for Rick Tocchet, January 25, 1996.

STEVENS, ROD — VAN.

Center. Shoots left. 5'10", 175 lbs. Born, Fort St. John, B.C., April 5, 1974.

			Regular Season					Playoffs				
Season	Club	Lea	GP	G	A	TP	PIM	GP	G	A	TP	PIM
1991-92	Kamloops	WHL	57	8	13	21	20	15	2	2	4	0
1992-93	Kamloops	WHL	68	26	28	54	42	13	9	2	11	4
1993-94a	Kamloops	WHL	62	51	58	109	31	19	9	12	21	10
1994-95	Syracuse	AHL	78	21	21	42	63	....	....	....	....	....
1995-96	Syracuse	AHL	60	13	17	30	30	16	3	4	7	14

a Memorial Cup All-Star Team (1994)

Signed as a free agent by **Vancouver**, October 4, 1993.

STEVENS, SCOTT — N.J.

Defense. Shoots left. 6'2", 210 lbs. Born, Kitchener, Ont., April 1, 1964.
(Washington's 1st choice, 5th overall, in 1982 Entry Draft).

			Regular Season					Playoffs				
Season	Club	Lea	GP	G	A	TP	PIM	GP	G	A	TP	PIM
1980-81	Kitchener	OPJHL	39	7	33	40	82	....	....	....	....	....
	Kitchener	OHA	1	0	0	0	0	....	....	....	....	....
1981-82	Kitchener	OHL	68	6	36	42	158	15	1	10	11	71
1982-83a	Washington	NHL	77	9	16	25	195	4	1	0	1	26
1983-84	Washington	NHL	78	13	32	45	201	8	1	8	9	21
1984-85	Washington	NHL	80	21	44	65	221	5	0	1	1	20
1985-86	Washington	NHL	73	15	38	53	165	9	3	8	11	12
1986-87	Washington	NHL	77	10	51	61	283	7	0	5	5	19
1987-88b	Washington	NHL	80	12	60	72	184	13	1	11	12	46
1988-89	Washington	NHL	80	7	61	68	225	6	1	4	5	11
1989-90	Washington	NHL	56	11	29	40	154	15	2	7	9	25
1990-91	St. Louis	NHL	78	5	44	49	150	13	0	3	3	36
1991-92c	New Jersey	NHL	68	17	42	59	124	7	2	1	3	29
1992-93	New Jersey	NHL	81	12	45	57	120	5	2	2	4	10
1993-94bd	New Jersey	NHL	83	18	60	78	112	20	2	9	11	42
1994-95	New Jersey	NHL	48	2	20	22	56	20	1	7	8	24 ♦
1995-96	New Jersey	NHL	82	5	23	28	100	....	....	....	....	....
	NHL Totals		1041	157	565	722	2290	132	16	66	82	321

a NHL All-Rookie Team (1983)
b NHL First All-Star Team (1988, 1994)
c NHL Second All-Star Team (1992)
d Won Alka-Seltzer Plus Award (1994)

Played in NHL All-Star Game (1985, 1989, 1991-94, 1996)

Signed as a free agent by **St. Louis**, July 16, 1990. Acquired by **New Jersey** from **St. Louis** as compensation for St. Louis' signing of free agent Brendan Shanahan, September 3, 1991.

STEVENSON, JEREMY — ANA.

Left wing. Shoots left. 6'2", 215 lbs. Born, San Bernadino, CA, July 28, 1974.
(Winnipeg's 3rd choice, 60th overall, in 1992 Entry Draft).

			Regular Season					Playoffs				
Season	Club	Lea	GP	G	A	TP	PIM	GP	G	A	TP	PIM
1990-91	Cornwall	OHL	58	13	20	33	124	....	....	....	....	....
1991-92	Cornwall	OHL	63	15	23	38	176	6	3	1	4	4
1992-93	Newmarket	OHL	54	28	28	56	144	5	5	1	6	28
1993-94	Newmarket	OHL	9	2	4	6	27	....	....	....	....	....
	S.S. Marie	OHL	48	18	19	37	183	14	1	1	2	23
1994-95	Greensboro	ECHL	43	14	13	27	231	17	6	11	17	64
1995-96	Anaheim	NHL	3	0	1	1	12	....	....	....	....	....
	Baltimore	AHL	60	11	10	21	295	12	4	2	6	23
	NHL Totals		3	0	1	1	12	....	....	....	....	....

Re-entered NHL Entry Draft, **Anaheim's** 10th choice, 262nd overall in 1994 Entry Draft.

STEVENSON, TURNER — MTL.

Right wing. Shoots right. 6'3", 215 lbs. Born, Prince George, B.C., May 18, 1972.
(Montreal's 1st choice, 12th overall, in 1990 Entry Draft).

			Regular Season					Playoffs				
Season	Club	Lea	GP	G	A	TP	PIM	GP	G	A	TP	PIM
1989-90	Seattle	WHL	62	29	32	61	276	13	3	2	5	35
1990-91	Seattle	WHL	57	36	27	63	222	6	1	5	6	15
	Fredericton	AHL	....	....	....	....	....	4	0	0	0	5
1991-92ab	Seattle	WHL	58	20	32	52	264	15	9	3	12	55
1992-93	Montreal	NHL	1	0	0	0	0	....	....	....	....	....
	Fredericton	AHL	79	25	34	59	102	5	2	3	5	11
1993-94	Montreal	NHL	2	0	0	0	2	3	0	2	2	0
	Fredericton	AHL	66	19	28	47	155	....	....	....	....	....
1994-95	Fredericton	AHL	37	12	12	24	109	....	....	....	....	....
	Montreal	NHL	41	6	1	7	86	....	....	....	....	....
1995-96	Montreal	NHL	80	9	16	25	167	6	0	1	1	2
	NHL Totals		124	15	17	32	255	9	0	3	3	2

a WHL West First All-Star Team (1992)
b Memorial Cup All-Star Team (1992)

STEWART, BRIAN — L.A.

Defense. Shoots right. 6'3", 175 lbs. Born, St. Catharines, Ont., May 22, 1977.
(Los Angeles' 9th choice, 215th overall, in 1995 Entry Draft).

			Regular Season					Playoffs				
Season	Club	Lea	GP	G	A	TP	PIM	GP	G	A	TP	PIM
1994-95	S.S. Marie	OHL	44	3	7	10	6	....	....	....	....	....
1995-96	S.S. Marie	OHL	63	6	32	38	64	4	0	1	1	8

STEWART, CAM — BOS.

Left wing. Shoots left. 5'11", 196 lbs. Born, Kitchener, Ont., September 18, 1971.
(Boston's 2nd choice, 63rd overall, in 1990 Entry Draft).

			Regular Season					Playoffs				
Season	Club	Lea	GP	G	A	TP	PIM	GP	G	A	TP	PIM
1990-91	U. of Michigan	CCHA	44	8	24	32	122	....	....	....	....	....
1991-92	U. of Michigan	CCHA	44	13	15	28	106	....	....	....	....	....
1992-93	U. of Michigan	CCHA	39	20	39	59	69	....	....	....	....	....
1993-94	Boston	NHL	57	3	6	9	66	8	0	3	3	7
	Providence	AHL	14	3	2	5	5	....	....	....	....	....
1994-95	Boston	NHL	5	0	0	0	2	....	....	....	....	....
	Providence	AHL	31	13	11	24	38	9	2	5	7	0
1995-96	Boston	NHL	6	0	0	0	0	5	1	0	1	2
	Providence	AHL	54	17	25	42	39	....	....	....	....	....
	NHL Totals		68	3	6	9	68	13	1	3	4	9

STEWART, JASON — NYI

Defense. Shoots right. 5'11", 185 lbs. Born, St. Paul, MN, April 30, 1976.
(NY Islanders' 7th choice, 142nd overall, in 1994 Entry Draft).

			Regular Season					Playoffs				
Season	Club	Lea	GP	G	A	TP	PIM	GP	G	A	TP	PIM
1994-95	St. Cloud	WCHA	28	1	3	4	16	....	....	....	....	....
1995-96	St. Cloud	WCHA	36	4	7	11	40	....	....	....	....	....

STEWART, MICHAEL

Defense. Shoots left. 6'2", 210 lbs. Born, Calgary, Alta., May 30, 1972.
(NY Rangers' 1st choice, 13th overall, in 1990 Entry Draft).

			Regular Season					Playoffs				
Season	Club	Lea	GP	G	A	TP	PIM	GP	G	A	TP	PIM
1989-90	Michigan State	CCHA	40	2	6	8	39	....	....	....	....	....
1990-91	Michigan State	CCHA	37	3	12	15	58	....	....	....	....	....
1991-92	Michigan State	CCHA	8	1	3	4	6	....	....	....	....	....
1992-93	Binghamton	AHL	68	2	10	12	71	1	0	0	0	0
1993-94	Binghamton	AHL	79	8	42	50	75	....	....	....	....	....
1994-95	Binghamton	AHL	68	6	21	27	83	....	....	....	....	....
	Springfield	AHL	7	0	3	3	21	....	....	....	....	....
1995-96	Springfield	AHL	29	2	6	8	44	10	1	3	4	22
	Detroit	IHL	41	6	6	12	95	....	....	....	....	....

Traded to **Hartford** by **NY Rangers** with Glen Featherstone, NY Rangers' first round choice (Jean-Sebastien Giguere) in 1995 Entry Draft and fourth round choice (Steve Wasylko) in 1996 Entry Draft for Pat Verbeek, March 23, 1995.

STILLMAN, CORY — CGY.

Center. Shoots left. 6', 180 lbs. Born, Peterborough, Ont., December 20, 1973.
(Calgary's 1st choice, 6th overall, in 1992 Entry Draft).

			Regular Season					Playoffs				
Season	Club	Lea	GP	G	A	TP	PIM	GP	G	A	TP	PIM
1990-91	Windsor	OHL	64	31	70	101	31	11	3	6	9	8
1991-92	Windsor	OHL	53	29	61	90	59	7	2	4	6	8
1992-93	Peterborough	OHL	61	25	55	80	55	18	3	8	11	18
	Cdn. National	....	1	0	0	0	0	....	....	....	....	....
1993-94	Saint John	AHL	79	35	48	83	52	7	2	4	6	16
1994-95	Saint John	AHL	63	28	53	81	70	5	0	2	2	2
	Calgary	NHL	10	0	2	2	2	....	....	....	....	....
1995-96	Calgary	NHL	74	16	19	35	41	2	1	1	2	0
	NHL Totals		84	16	21	37	43	2	1	1	2	0

STOJANOV, ALEK (STOY-uh-nahf) — PIT.

Right wing. Shoots left. 6'4", 220 lbs. Born, Windsor, Ont., April 25, 1973.
(Vancouver's 1st choice, 7th overall, in 1991 Entry Draft).

			Regular Season					Playoffs				
Season	Club	Lea	GP	G	A	TP	PIM	GP	G	A	TP	PIM
1989-90	Hamilton	OHL	37	4	4	8	91	....	....	....	....	....
1990-91	Hamilton	OHL	62	25	20	45	181	4	1	1	2	14
1991-92	Guelph	OHL	33	12	15	27	91	....	....	....	....	....
1992-93	Guelph	OHL	36	27	28	55	62	....	....	....	....	....
	Newmarket	OHL	14	9	7	16	26	7	1	3	4	26
	Hamilton	AHL	4	4	0	4	0	....	....	....	....	....
1993-94	Hamilton	AHL	4	0	1	1	5	....	....	....	....	....
1994-95	Syracuse	AHL	73	18	12	30	270	....	....	....	....	....
	Vancouver	NHL	4	0	0	0	13	5	0	0	0	2
1995-96	Vancouver	NHL	58	0	1	1	123	....	....	....	....	....
	Pittsburgh	NHL	10	1	0	1	7	9	0	0	0	19
	NHL Totals		72	1	1	2	143	14	0	0	0	21

Traded to **Pittsburgh** by **Vancouver** for Markus Naslund, March 20, 1996.

STOREY, BEN   COL.

Defense. Shoots left. 6'2", 180 lbs.   Born, Ottawa, Ont., June 22, 1977.
(Colorado's 4th choice, 98th overall, in 1996 Entry Draft).

				Regular Season					Playoffs			
Season	Club	Lea	GP	G	A	TP	PIM	GP	G	A	TP	PIM
1994-95	Ottawa	Jr. A	51	6	33	39	83	....	....	....	....	....
1995-96	Harvard	ECAC	33	2	11	13	44	....	....	....	....	....

STORM, JIM   DAL.

Left wing. Shoots left. 6'2", 200 lbs.   Born, Milford, MI, February 5, 1971.
(Hartford's 5th choice, 75th overall, in 1991 Entry Draft).

				Regular Season					Playoffs			
Season	Club	Lea	GP	G	A	TP	PIM	GP	G	A	TP	PIM
1990-91	Michigan Tech	WCHA	36	16	18	34	46	....	....	....	....	....
1991-92	Michigan Tech	WCHA	39	25	33	58	12	....	....	....	....	....
1992-93	Michigan Tech	WCHA	33	22	32	54	30	....	....	....	....	....
1993-94	**Hartford**	**NHL**	**68**	**6**	**10**	**16**	**27**	....	....	....	....	....
	U.S. National	....	28	8	12	20	14	....	....	....	....	....
1994-95	**Hartford**	**NHL**	**6**	**0**	**3**	**3**	**0**	....	....	....	....	....
	Springfield	AHL	33	11	11	22	29	....	....	....	....	....
1995-96	**Dallas**	**NHL**	**10**	**1**	**2**	**3**	**17**	....	....	....	....	....
	Michigan	IHL	60	18	33	51	27	10	4	8	12	2
	NHL Totals		**84**	**7**	**15**	**22**	**44**	....	....	....	....	....

Signed as a free agent by **Dallas**, September 13, 1995.

STRAKA, JOSEF   CGY.

Center. Shoots right. 5'11", 183 lbs.   Born, Jindrichuv Hradec, Czech., February 11, 1978.
(Calgary's 7th choice, 122nd overall, in 1996 Entry Draft).

				Regular Season					Playoffs			
Season	Club	Lea	GP	G	A	TP	PIM	GP	G	A	TP	PIM
1994-95	Litvinov	Czech. Jr.	40	33	42	75	....	....	....	....	....	....
1995-96	Litvinov	Czech.	33	5	6	11	14	15	3	1	4	....

STRAKA, MARTIN   (STRAH-kuh) FLA.

Center. Shoots left. 5'10", 178 lbs.   Born, Plzen, Czech., September 3, 1972.
(Pittsburgh's 1st choice, 19th overall, in 1992 Entry Draft).

				Regular Season					Playoffs			
Season	Club	Lea	GP	G	A	TP	PIM	GP	G	A	TP	PIM
1989-90	Skoda Plzen	Czech.	1	0	3	3	....	....	....	....	....	....
1990-91	Skoda Plzen	Czech.	47	7	24	31	6	....	....	....	....	....
1991-92	Skoda Plzen	Czech.	50	27	28	55	20	....	....	....	....	....
1992-93	**Pittsburgh**	**NHL**	**42**	**3**	**13**	**16**	**29**	11	2	1	3	2
	Cleveland	IHL	4	4	3	7	0	....	....	....	....	....
1993-94	**Pittsburgh**	**NHL**	**84**	**30**	**34**	**64**	**24**	6	1	0	1	2
1994-95	Interconex Plzen	Czech.	19	10	11	21	18	....	....	....	....	....
	Pittsburgh	**NHL**	**31**	**4**	**12**	**16**	**16**	....	....	....	....	....
	Ottawa	**NHL**	**6**	**1**	**1**	**2**	**0**	....	....	....	....	....
1995-96	**Ottawa**	**NHL**	**43**	**9**	**16**	**25**	**29**	....	....	....	....	....
	NY Islanders	**NHL**	**22**	**2**	**10**	**12**	**6**	....	....	....	....	....
	Florida	**NHL**	**12**	**2**	**4**	**6**	**6**	13	2	2	4	2
	NHL Totals		**240**	**51**	**90**	**141**	**110**	**30**	**5**	**3**	**8**	**6**

Traded to **Ottawa** by **Pittsburgh** for Troy Murray and Norm Maciver, April 7, 1995. Traded to **NY Islanders** by **Ottawa** with Don Beaupre and Bryan Berard for Damian Rhodes and Wade Redden, January 23, 1996. Claimed on waivers by **Florida** from **NY Islanders**, March 15, 1996.

STREIT, MARTIN   PHI.

Left wing. Shoots right. 6'2", 191 lbs.   Born, Vyskov, Czech., February 2, 1977.
(Philadelphia's 7th choice, 178th overall, in 1995 Entry Draft).

				Regular Season					Playoffs			
Season	Club	Lea	GP	G	A	TP	PIM	GP	G	A	TP	PIM
1995-96	Olomouc	Czech. Jr.	19	10	6	16	....	....	....	....	....	....
	Olomouc	Czech.	10	0	0	0	....	....	....	....	....	....

STROM, PETER   (STRUHM) MTL.

Left wing. Shoots right. 6', 178 lbs.   Born, Snotorp, Sweden, January 14, 1975.
(Montreal's 10th choice, 200th overall, in 1994 Entry Draft).

				Regular Season					Playoffs			
Season	Club	Lea	GP	G	A	TP	PIM	GP	G	A	TP	PIM
1993-94	V. Frolunda	Swe.	29	0	0	0	8	....	....	....	....	....
1994-95	V. Frolunda	Swe.	16	0	3	3	10	....	....	....	....	....
	V. Frolunda	Swe. 2	12	8	10	18	10	....	....	....	....	....
1995-96	V. Frolunda	Swe.	35	7	8	15	10	13	0	3	3	0

STRUCH, DAVID   (STRUHK)

Center. Shoots left. 5'10", 180 lbs.   Born, Flin Flon, Man., February 11, 1971.
(Calgary's 10th choice, 195th overall, in 1991 Entry Draft).

				Regular Season					Playoffs			
Season	Club	Lea	GP	G	A	TP	PIM	GP	G	A	TP	PIM
1990-91	Saskatoon	WHL	72	45	57	102	69	....	....	....	....	....
1991-92	Saskatoon	WHL	47	29	26	55	34	22	8	15	23	26
	Salt Lake	IHL	12	4	1	5	8	....	....	....	....	....
1992-93	Salt Lake	IHL	78	20	22	42	73	....	....	....	....	....
1993-94	**Calgary**	**NHL**	**4**	**0**	**0**	**0**	**4**	....	....	....	....	....
	Saint John	AHL	58	18	25	43	87	7	0	1	1	4
1994-95	Saint John	AHL	7	0	1	1	4	....	....	....	....	....
1995-96	Saint John	AHL	45	10	15	25	57	3	0	1	1	4
	NHL Totals		**4**	**0**	**0**	**0**	**4**	....	....	....	....	....

STRUDWICK, JASON   NYI

Defense. Shoots left. 6'3", 207 lbs.   Born, Edmonton, Alta., July 17, 1975.
(NY Islanders' 3rd choice, 63rd overall, in 1994 Entry Draft).

				Regular Season					Playoffs			
Season	Club	Lea	GP	G	A	TP	PIM	GP	G	A	TP	PIM
1993-94	Kamloops	WHL	61	6	8	14	118	19	0	4	4	24
1994-95	Kamloops	WHL	72	3	11	14	183	21	1	1	2	39
1995-96	**NY Islanders**	**NHL**	**1**	**0**	**0**	**0**	**7**	....	....	....	....	....
	Worcester	AHL	60	2	7	9	119	4	0	1	1	0
	NHL Totals		**1**	**0**	**0**	**0**	**7**	....	....	....	....	....

STUMPEL, JOZEF   (STUM-puhl) BOS.

Center. Shoots right. 6'1", 208 lbs.   Born, Nitra, Czech., June 20, 1972.
(Boston's 2nd choice, 40th overall, in 1991 Entry Draft).

				Regular Season					Playoffs			
Season	Club	Lea	GP	G	A	TP	PIM	GP	G	A	TP	PIM
1989-90	Nitra	Czech. 2	38	12	11	23	....	....	....	....	....	....
1990-91	Nitra	Czech.	49	23	22	45	14	....	....	....	....	....
1991-92	Koln	Ger.	37	20	19	39	35	....	....	....	....	....
	Boston	**NHL**	**4**	**1**	**0**	**1**	**0**	....	....	....	....	....
1992-93	**Boston**	**NHL**	**13**	**1**	**3**	**4**	**4**	....	....	....	....	....
	Providence	AHL	56	31	61	92	26	6	4	4	8	0
1993-94	**Boston**	**NHL**	**59**	**8**	**15**	**23**	**14**	13	1	7	8	4
	Providence	AHL	17	5	12	17	4	....	....	....	....	....
1994-95	Koln	Ger.	25	16	23	39	18	....	....	....	....	....
	Boston	**NHL**	**44**	**5**	**13**	**18**	**8**	5	0	0	0	0
1995-96	**Boston**	**NHL**	**76**	**18**	**36**	**54**	**14**	5	1	2	3	0
	NHL Totals		**196**	**33**	**67**	**100**	**40**	**23**	**2**	**9**	**11**	**4**

STURM, MARCO   (STURHM) S.J.

Center. Shoots left. 5'11", 178 lbs.   Born, Dingolfing, Germany, September 8, 1978.
(San Jose's 2nd choice, 21st overall, in 1996 Entry Draft).

				Regular Season					Playoffs			
Season	Club	Lea	GP	G	A	TP	PIM	GP	G	A	TP	PIM
1995-96	Landshut	Ger.	47	12	20	32	50	11	1	3	4	18

SUBBOTIN, DMITRI   NYR

Left wing. Shoots left. 6'1", 183 lbs.   Born, Tomsk, USSR, October 20, 1977.
(NY Rangers' 3rd choice, 76th overall, in 1996 Entry Draft).

				Regular Season					Playoffs			
Season	Club	Lea	GP	G	A	TP	PIM	GP	G	A	TP	PIM
1993-94	Yekaterinburg	CIS	12	0	3	3	4	....	....	....	....	....
1994-95	Yekaterinburg	CIS	52	9	6	15	75	2	0	0	0	2
1995-96	CSKA	CIS	41	6	5	11	62	3	0	0	0	0

SUGDEN, BRANDON   TOR.

Defense. Shoots right. 6'2", 178 lbs.   Born, Toronto, Ont., June 23, 1978.
(Toronto's 8th choice, 111th overall, in 1996 Entry Draft).

				Regular Season					Playoffs			
Season	Club	Lea	GP	G	A	TP	PIM	GP	G	A	TP	PIM
1995-96	London	OHL	55	2	7	9	*264	....	....	....	....	....

SULLIVAN, MIKE   CGY.

Center. Shoots left. 6'2", 190 lbs.   Born, Marshfield, MA, February 27, 1968.
(NY Rangers' 4th choice, 69th overall, in 1987 Entry Draft).

				Regular Season					Playoffs			
Season	Club	Lea	GP	G	A	TP	PIM	GP	G	A	TP	PIM
1986-87	Boston U.	H.E.	37	13	18	31	18	....	....	....	....	....
1987-88	Boston U.	H.E.	30	18	22	40	30	....	....	....	....	....
1988-89	Boston U.	H.E.	36	19	17	36	30	....	....	....	....	....
1989-90	Boston U.	H.E.	38	11	20	31	26	....	....	....	....	....
1990-91	San Diego	IHL	74	12	23	35	27	....	....	....	....	....
1991-92	**San Jose**	**NHL**	**64**	**8**	**11**	**19**	**15**	....	....	....	....	....
	Kansas City	IHL	10	2	8	10	8	....	....	....	....	....
1992-93	**San Jose**	**NHL**	**81**	**6**	**8**	**14**	**30**	....	....	....	....	....
1993-94	**San Jose**	**NHL**	**26**	**2**	**2**	**4**	**4**	....	....	....	....	....
	Kansas City	IHL	6	3	3	6	0	....	....	....	....	....
	Calgary	**NHL**	**19**	**2**	**3**	**5**	**6**	7	1	1	2	8
	Saint John	AHL	5	2	0	2	4	....	....	....	....	....
1994-95	**Calgary**	**NHL**	**38**	**4**	**7**	**11**	**14**	7	3	5	8	2
1995-96	**Calgary**	**NHL**	**81**	**9**	**12**	**21**	**24**	4	0	0	0	0
	NHL Totals		**309**	**31**	**43**	**74**	**93**	**18**	**4**	**6**	**10**	**10**

Rights traded to **Minnesota** by **NY Rangers** with Paul Jerrard, the rights to Bret Barnett, and Los Angeles' third round choice (previously acquired by NY Rangers — Minnesota selected Murray Garbutt) in 1989 Entry Draft for Brian Lawton, Igor Liba and the rights to Eric Bennett, October 11, 1988. Signed as a free agent by **San Jose**, August 9, 1991. Claimed on waivers by **Calgary** from **San Jose**, January 6, 1994.

SULLIVAN, STEVE   N.J.

Center. Shoots right. 5'9", 155 lbs.   Born, Timmins, Ont., July 6, 1974.
(New Jersey's 10th choice, 233rd overall, in 1994 Entry Draft).

				Regular Season					Playoffs			
Season	Club	Lea	GP	G	A	TP	PIM	GP	G	A	TP	PIM
1993-94	S.S. Marie	OHL	63	51	62	113	82	14	9	16	25	22
1994-95	Albany	AHL	75	31	50	81	124	14	4	7	11	10
1995-96	**New Jersey**	**NHL**	**16**	**5**	**4**	**9**	**8**	....	....	....	....	....
a	Albany	AHL	53	33	42	75	127	4	3	0	3	6
	NHL Totals		**16**	**5**	**4**	**9**	**8**	....	....	....	....	....

a   AHL First All-Star Team (1996)

SUNDBLAD, NIKLAS   (SUHN-blad)

Right wing. Shoots right. 6'1", 200 lbs.   Born, Stockholm, Sweden, January 3, 1973.
(Calgary's 1st choice, 19th overall, in 1991 Entry Draft).

				Regular Season					Playoffs			
Season	Club	Lea	GP	G	A	TP	PIM	GP	G	A	TP	PIM
1990-91	AIK	Swe.	39	1	3	4	14	....	....	....	....	....
1991-92	AIK	Swe.	33	9	2	11	20	3	3	1	4	0
1992-93	AIK	Swe.	22	5	4	9	56	....	....	....	....	....
1993-94	Saint John	AHL	76	13	19	32	75	4	1	1	2	2
1994-95	Saint John	AHL	72	9	5	14	151	2	0	0	0	6
1995-96	**Calgary**	**NHL**	**2**	**0**	**0**	**0**	**0**	....	....	....	....	....
	Saint John	AHL	74	16	20	36	66	16	0	4	4	14
	NHL Totals		**2**	**0**	**0**	**0**	**0**	....	....	....	....	....

SUNDERLAND, MATHIEU   BUF.

Right wing. Shoots right. 6'4", 192 lbs.   Born, Quebec City, Que., November 30, 1976.
(Buffalo's 4th choice, 68th overall, in 1995 Entry Draft).

				Regular Season					Playoffs			
Season	Club	Lea	GP	G	A	TP	PIM	GP	G	A	TP	PIM
1993-94	Drummondville	QMJHL	60	19	13	32	118	5	0	0	0	19
1994-95	Drummondville	QMJHL	66	21	24	45	185	3	2	4	6	12
1995-96	Drummondville	QMJHL	30	18	17	35	90	....	....	....	....	....
	Halifax	QMJHL	18	7	4	11	51	6	0	2	2	6

SUNDIN, MATS (SUHN-deen) TOR.

Center/Right wing. Shoots right. 6'4", 215 lbs. Born, Bromma, Sweden, February 13, 1971.
(Quebec's 1st choice, 1st overall, in 1989 Entry Draft).

			Regular Season					Playoffs				
Season	Club	Lea	GP	G	A	TP	PIM	GP	G	A	TP	PIM
1988-89	Nacka	Swe. 2	25	10	8	18	18	....	....	....	....	....
1989-90	Djurgarden	Swe.	34	10	8	18	16	8	7	0	7	4
1990-91	Quebec	NHL	80	23	36	59	58	....	....	....	....	....
1991-92	Quebec	NHL	80	33	43	76	103	....	....	....	....	....
1992-93	Quebec	NHL	80	47	67	114	96	6	3	1	4	6
1993-94	Quebec	NHL	84	32	53	85	60	....	....	....	....	....
1994-95	Djurgarden	Swe.	12	7	2	9	14	....	....	....	....	....
	Toronto	NHL	47	23	24	47	14	7	5	4	9	4
1995-96	Toronto	NHL	76	33	50	83	46	6	3	1	4	4
	NHL Totals		447	191	273	464	377	19	11	6	17	14

Played in NHL All-Star Game (1996)

Traded to **Toronto** by **Quebec** with Garth Butcher, Todd Warriner and Philadelphia's first round choice (previously acquired by Quebec — later traded to Washington — Washington selected Nolan Baumgartner) in 1994 Entry Draft for Wendel Clark, Sylvain Lefebvre, Landon Wilson and Toronto's first round choice (Jeffrey Kealty) in 1994 Entry Draft, June 28, 1994.

SUNDSTROM, NIKLAS (SUHN-struhm) NYR

Left wing. Shoots left. 6', 185 lbs. Born, Ornskoldsvik, Sweden, June 6, 1975.
(NY Rangers' 1st choice, 8th overall, in 1993 Entry Draft).

			Regular Season					Playoffs				
Season	Club	Lea	GP	G	A	TP	PIM	GP	G	A	TP	PIM
1991-92	MoDo	Swe.	9	1	3	4	0	....	....	....	....	....
1992-93	MoDo	Swe.	40	7	11	18	18	3	0	0	0	0
1993-94	MoDo	Swe.	37	7	12	19	28	11	4	3	7	2
1994-95	MoDo	Swe.	33	8	13	21	30	....	....	....	....	....
1995-96	NY Rangers	NHL	82	9	12	21	14	11	4	3	7	4
	NHL Totals		82	9	12	21	14	11	4	3	7	4

SUTER, GARY (SOO-tuhr) CHI.

Defense. Shoots left. 6', 200 lbs. Born, Madison, WI, June 24, 1964.
(Calgary's 9th choice, 180th overall, in 1984 Entry Draft).

			Regular Season					Playoffs				
Season	Club	Lea	GP	G	A	TP	PIM	GP	G	A	TP	PIM
1983-84	U. Wisconsin	WCHA	35	4	18	22	32	....	....	....	....	....
1984-85	U. Wisconsin	WCHA	39	12	39	51	110	....	....	....	....	....
1985-86ab	Calgary	NHL	80	18	50	68	141	10	2	8	10	8
1986-87	Calgary	NHL	68	9	40	49	70	6	0	3	3	10
1987-88c	Calgary	NHL	75	21	70	91	124	9	1	9	10	6
1988-89	Calgary	NHL	63	13	49	62	78	5	0	3	3	10 ♦
1989-90	Calgary	NHL	76	16	60	76	97	6	0	1	1	14
1990-91	Calgary	NHL	79	12	58	70	102	7	1	6	7	12
1991-92	Calgary	NHL	70	12	43	55	128	....	....	....	....	....
1992-93	Calgary	NHL	81	23	58	81	112	6	2	3	5	8
1993-94	Calgary	NHL	25	4	9	13	20	....	....	....	....	....
	Chicago	NHL	16	2	3	5	18	6	3	2	5	6
1994-95	Chicago	NHL	48	10	27	37	42	12	2	5	7	10
1995-96	Chicago	NHL	82	20	47	67	80	10	3	3	6	8
	NHL Totals		763	160	514	674	1012	77	14	43	57	92

a Won Calder Memorial Trophy (1986)
b NHL All-Rookie Team (1986)
c NHL Second All-Star Team (1988)

Played in NHL All-Star Game (1986, 1988, 1989, 1991)

Traded to **Hartford** by **Calgary** with Paul Ranheim and Ted Drury for James Patrick, Zarley Zalapski and Michael Nylander, March 10, 1994. Traded to **Chicago** by **Hartford** with Randy Cunneyworth and Hartford's third round choice (later traded to Vancouver — Vancouver selected Larry Courville) in 1995 Entry Draft for Frantisek Kucera and Jocelyn Lemieux, March 11, 1994.

SUTTER, BRENT (SUH-tuhr) CHI.

Center. Shoots right. 5'11", 180 lbs. Born, Viking, Alta., June 10, 1962.
(NY Islanders' 1st choice, 17th overall, in 1980 Entry Draft).

			Regular Season					Playoffs				
Season	Club	Lea	GP	G	A	TP	PIM	GP	G	A	TP	PIM
1979-80	Red Deer	AJHL	59	70	101	171	....	....	....	....	....	....
	Lethbridge	WHL	5	1	0	1	2	....	....	....	....	....
1980-81	NY Islanders	NHL	3	2	2	4	0	....	....	....	....	....
	Lethbridge	WHL	68	54	54	108	116	9	6	4	10	51
1981-82	NY Islanders	NHL	43	21	22	43	114	19	2	6	8	36 ♦
	Lethbridge	WHL	34	46	33	79	162	....	....	....	....	....
1982-83	NY Islanders	NHL	80	21	19	40	128	20	10	11	21	26 ♦
1983-84	NY Islanders	NHL	69	34	15	49	69	20	4	10	14	18
1984-85	NY Islanders	NHL	72	42	60	102	51	10	3	3	6	14
1985-86	NY Islanders	NHL	61	24	31	55	74	3	0	1	1	2
1986-87	NY Islanders	NHL	69	27	36	63	73	5	1	0	1	4
1987-88	NY Islanders	NHL	70	29	31	60	55	6	2	1	3	18
1988-89	NY Islanders	NHL	77	29	34	63	77	....	....	....	....	....
1989-90	NY Islanders	NHL	67	33	35	68	65	5	2	3	5	2
1990-91	NY Islanders	NHL	75	21	32	53	49	....	....	....	....	....
1991-92	NY Islanders	NHL	8	4	6	10	6	....	....	....	....	....
	Chicago	NHL	61	18	32	50	30	18	3	5	8	22
1992-93	Chicago	NHL	65	20	34	54	67	4	1	1	2	4
1993-94	Chicago	NHL	73	9	29	38	43	6	0	0	0	2
1994-95	Chicago	NHL	47	7	8	15	51	16	1	2	3	4
1995-96	Chicago	NHL	80	13	27	40	56	10	1	1	2	6
	NHL Totals		1020	354	453	807	1008	142	30	44	74	158

Played in NHL All-Star Game (1985)

Traded to **Chicago** by **NY Islanders** with Brad Lauer for Adam Creighton and Steve Thomas, October 25, 1991.

SUTTER, RON (SUH-tuhr)

Center. Shoots right. 6', 180 lbs. Born, Viking, Alta., December 2, 1963.
(Philadelphia's 1st choice, 4th overall, in 1982 Entry Draft).

			Regular Season					Playoffs				
Season	Club	Lea	GP	G	A	TP	PIM	GP	G	A	TP	PIM
1980-81	Lethbridge	WHL	72	13	32	45	152	9	2	5	7	29
1981-82	Lethbridge	WHL	59	38	54	92	207	12	6	5	11	28
1982-83	Philadelphia	NHL	10	1	1	2	9	....	....	....	....	....
	Lethbridge	WHL	58	35	48	83	98	20	*22	*19	*41	45
1983-84	Philadelphia	NHL	79	19	32	51	101	3	0	0	0	22
1984-85	Philadelphia	NHL	73	16	29	45	94	19	4	8	12	28
1985-86	Philadelphia	NHL	75	18	42	60	159	5	0	2	2	10
1986-87	Philadelphia	NHL	39	10	17	27	69	16	1	7	8	12
1987-88	Philadelphia	NHL	69	8	25	33	146	7	0	1	1	26
1988-89	Philadelphia	NHL	55	26	22	48	80	19	1	9	10	51
1989-90	Philadelphia	NHL	75	22	26	48	104	....	....	....	....	....
1990-91	Philadelphia	NHL	80	17	28	45	92	....	....	....	....	....
1991-92	St. Louis	NHL	68	19	27	46	91	6	1	3	4	8
1992-93	St. Louis	NHL	59	12	15	27	99	....	....	....	....	....
1993-94	St. Louis	NHL	36	6	12	18	46	....	....	....	....	....
	Quebec	NHL	37	9	13	22	44	....	....	....	....	....
1994-95	NY Islanders	NHL	27	1	4	5	21	....	....	....	....	....
1995-96	Phoenix	IHL	25	6	13	19	28	....	....	....	....	....
	Boston	NHL	18	5	7	12	24	5	0	0	0	8
	NHL Totals		800	189	300	489	1179	80	7	30	37	165

Traded to **St. Louis** by **Philadelphia** with Murray Baron for Dan Quinn and Rod Brind'Amour, September 22, 1991. Traded to **Quebec** by **St. Louis** with Garth Butcher and Bob Bassen for Steve Duchesne and Denis Chasse, January 23, 1994. Traded to **NY Islanders** by **Quebec** with Quebec's first round choice (Brett Lindros) in 1994 Entry Draft for Uwe Krupp and NY Islanders' first round choice (Wade Belak) in 1994 Entry Draft, June 28, 1994. Signed as a free agent by **Boston**, March 9, 1996.

SUTTON, KEN

Defense. Shoots left. 6', 200 lbs. Born, Edmonton, Alta., November 5, 1969.
(Buffalo's 4th choice, 98th overall, in 1989 Entry Draft).

			Regular Season					Playoffs				
Season	Club	Lea	GP	G	A	TP	PIM	GP	G	A	TP	PIM
1988-89a	Saskatoon	WHL	71	22	31	53	104	8	2	5	7	12
1989-90	Rochester	AHL	57	5	14	19	83	11	1	6	7	15
1990-91	Buffalo	NHL	15	3	6	9	13	6	0	1	1	2
	Rochester	AHL	62	7	24	31	65	3	1	1	2	14
1991-92	Buffalo	NHL	64	2	18	20	71	7	0	2	2	4
1992-93	Buffalo	NHL	63	8	14	22	30	8	3	1	4	8
1993-94	Buffalo	NHL	78	4	20	24	71	4	0	0	0	2
1994-95	Buffalo	NHL	12	1	2	3	30	....	....	....	....	....
	Edmonton	NHL	12	3	1	4	12	....	....	....	....	....
1995-96	Edmonton	NHL	32	0	8	8	39	....	....	....	....	....
	St. Louis	NHL	6	0	0	0	4	1	0	0	0	0
	Worcester	AHL	32	4	16	20	60	4	0	2	2	21
	NHL Totals		282	21	69	90	270	26	3	4	7	16

a Memorial Cup All-Star Team (1989)

Traded to **Edmonton** by **Buffalo** for Scott Pearson, April 7, 1995. Traded to **St. Louis** by **Edmonton** with Igor Kravchuk for Jeff Norton and Donald Dufresne, January 4, 1996.

SUURSOO, TOIVO (SUH-uhr-soh-oh) DET.

Left wing. Shoots right. 6', 175 lbs. Born, Tallinn, USSR, November 23, 1975.
(Detroit's 10th choice, 283rd overall, in 1994 Entry Draft).

			Regular Season					Playoffs				
Season	Club	Lea	GP	G	A	TP	PIM	GP	G	A	TP	PIM
1993-94	Soviet Wings	CIS	33	3	0	3	8	....	....	....	....	....
1994-95	Soviet Wings	CIS	47	10	5	15	36	....	....	....	....	....
1995-96	Soviet Wings	CIS	47	6	4	10	36	....	....	....	....	....

SVARTVADET, PER DAL.

Center. Shoots left. 6'1", 180 lbs. Born, Solleftea, Sweden, May 17, 1975.
(Dallas' 5th choice, 139th overall, in 1993 Entry Draft).

			Regular Season					Playoffs				
Season	Club	Lea	GP	G	A	TP	PIM	GP	G	A	TP	PIM
1992-93	MoDo	Swe.	2	0	0	0	0	....	....	....	....	....
1993-94	MoDo	Swe.	36	2	1	3	4	11	0	0	0	6
1994-95	MoDo	Swe.	40	6	9	15	31	....	....	....	....	....
1995-96	MoDo	Swe.	40	9	14	23	26	8	2	3	5	0

SVEHLA, ROBERT (SCHVE-khlah) FLA.

Defense. Shoots right. 6'1", 190 lbs. Born, Martin, Czech., January 2, 1969.
(Calgary's 4th choice, 78th overall, in 1992 Entry Draft).

			Regular Season					Playoffs				
Season	Club	Lea	GP	G	A	TP	PIM	GP	G	A	TP	PIM
1989-90	Dukla Trencin	Czech.	29	4	3	7	....	....	....	....	....	....
1990-91	Dukla Trencin	Czech.	52	16	9	25	62	....	....	....	....	....
1991-92	Dukla Trencin	Czech.	51	23	28	51	74	....	....	....	....	....
1992-93	Malmo	Swe.	40	19	10	29	86	6	0	1	1	14
1993-94	Malmo	Swe.	37	14	25	39	127	10	5	1	6	23
1994-95	Malmo	Swe.	32	11	13	24	83	9	2	3	5	6
	Florida	NHL	5	1	1	2	0	....	....	....	....	....
1995-96	Florida	NHL	81	8	49	57	94	22	0	6	6	32
	NHL Totals		86	9	50	59	94	22	0	6	6	32

Traded to **Florida** by **Calgary** with Magnus Svensson for Florida's third round choice (Dmitri Vlasenkov) in 1996 Entry Draft and fourth round choice in 1997 Entry Draft, September 29, 1994.

SVEJKOVSKY, JAROSLAV (svehzh-KOHV-skee) WSH.

Right wing. Shoots right. 5'11", 185 lbs. Born, Plzen, Czech., October 1, 1976.
(Washington's 2nd choice, 17th overall, in 1996 Entry Draft).

			Regular Season					Playoffs				
Season	Club	Lea	GP	G	A	TP	PIM	GP	G	A	TP	PIM
1993-94	Plzen	Czech.	8	0	0	0	8	....	....	....	....	....
1994-95	Tabor	Czech. 2	11	6	7	13	....	....	....	....	....	....
1995-96a	Tri-City	WHL	70	58	43	101	118	11	10	9	19	8

a WHL West Second All-Star Team (1996)

SVENSSON, MAGNUS (SVEHN-suhn)

Defense. Shoots left. 5'11", 180 lbs. Born, Tranas, Sweden, March 1, 1963.
(Calgary's 13th choice, 250th overall, in 1987 Entry Draft).

			Regular Season					Playoffs				
Season	Club	Lea	GP	G	A	TP	PIM	GP	G	A	TP	PIM
1983-84	Leksand	Swe.	35	3	8	11	20	....	....	....	....	....
1984-85	Leksand	Swe.	35	8	7	15	22	....	....	....	....	....
1985-86	Leksand	Swe.	36	6	9	15	62	....	....	....	....	....
1986-87	Leksand	Swe.	33	8	16	24	42	....	....	....	....	....
1987-88	Leksand	Swe.	40	12	11	23	20	3	0	0	0	8
1988-89	Leksand	Swe.	39	15	22	37	40	9	3	5	8	8
1989-90	Leksand	Swe.	26	11	12	23	60	1	0	0	0	0
1990-91	Lugano	Switz.	33	16	20	36	....	11	3	2	5	....
1991-92	Leksand	Swe.	22	4	10	14	32	....	....	....	....	....
1992-93	Leksand	Swe.	37	10	17	27	36	2	0	2	2	0
1993-94	Leksand	Swe.	39	13	16	29	22	4	3	1	4	0
1994-95	Davos	Swiss.	35	8	25	33	46	5	2	2	4	8
	Florida	**NHL**	**19**	**2**	**5**	**7**	**10**	....	....	....	....	....
1995-96	**Florida**	**NHL**	**27**	**2**	**9**	**11**	**21**	....	....	....	....	....
	NHL Totals		**46**	**4**	**14**	**18**	**31**	....	....	....	....	....

Traded to **Florida** by **Calgary** with Robert Svehla for Florida's third round choice (Dmitri Vlasenkov) in 1996 Entry Draft and a fourth round choice in 1997 Entry Draft, September 29, 1994.

SVOBODA, PETR (svah-BOH-duh) PHI.

Defense. Shoots left. 6'1", 190 lbs. Born, Most, Czech., February 14, 1966.
(Montreal's 1st choice, 5th overall, in 1984 Entry Draft).

			Regular Season					Playoffs				
Season	Club	Lea	GP	G	A	TP	PIM	GP	G	A	TP	PIM
1982-83	Litvinov	Czech.	4	0	0	0	2	....	....	....	....	....
1983-84	Litvinov	Czech.	18	3	1	4	20	....	....	....	....	....
1984-85	**Montreal**	**NHL**	**73**	**4**	**27**	**31**	**65**	**7**	**1**	**1**	**2**	**12**
1985-86	**Montreal**	**NHL**	**73**	**1**	**18**	**19**	**93**	**8**	**0**	**0**	**0**	**21** ♦
1986-87	**Montreal**	**NHL**	**70**	**5**	**17**	**22**	**63**	**14**	**0**	**5**	**5**	**10**
1987-88	**Montreal**	**NHL**	**69**	**7**	**22**	**29**	**149**	**10**	**0**	**5**	**5**	**12**
1988-89	**Montreal**	**NHL**	**71**	**8**	**37**	**45**	**147**	**21**	**1**	**11**	**12**	**16**
1989-90	**Montreal**	**NHL**	**60**	**5**	**31**	**36**	**98**	**10**	**0**	**5**	**5**	**7**
1990-91	**Montreal**	**NHL**	**60**	**4**	**22**	**26**	**52**	**2**	**0**	**1**	**1**	**2**
1991-92	**Montreal**	**NHL**	**58**	**5**	**16**	**21**	**94**	....	....	....	....	....
	Buffalo	**NHL**	**13**	**1**	**6**	**7**	**52**	**7**	**1**	**4**	**5**	**6**
1992-93	**Buffalo**	**NHL**	**40**	**2**	**24**	**26**	**59**	....	....	....	....	....
1993-94	**Buffalo**	**NHL**	**60**	**2**	**14**	**16**	**89**	**3**	**0**	**0**	**0**	**4**
1994-95	Litvinov	Czech.	8	2	0	2	50	....	....	....	....	....
	Buffalo	**NHL**	**26**	**0**	**5**	**5**	**60**	....	....	....	....	....
	Philadelphia	**NHL**	**11**	**0**	**3**	**3**	**10**	**14**	**0**	**4**	**4**	**8**
1995-96	**Philadelphia**	**NHL**	**73**	**1**	**28**	**29**	**105**	**12**	**0**	**6**	**6**	**22**
	NHL Totals		**757**	**45**	**270**	**315**	**1136**	**108**	**3**	**42**	**45**	**120**

Traded to **Buffalo** by **Montreal** for Kevin Haller, March 10, 1992. Traded to **Philadelphia** by **Buffalo** for Garry Galley, April 7, 1995.

SWANSON, BRIAN NYR

Center. Shoots left. 5'10", 180 lbs. Born, Anchorage, AK, March 24, 1976.
(San Jose's 5th choice, 115th overall, in 1994 Entry Draft).

			Regular Season					Playoffs				
Season	Club	Lea	GP	G	A	TP	PIM	GP	G	A	TP	PIM
1994-95	Portland	WHL	65	3	18	21	91	9	2	1	3	18
1995-96a	Colorado	WCHA	40	26	33	59	24	....	....	....	....	....

a WCHA Second All-Star Team (1996)

Traded to **NY Rangers** by **San Jose** with Jayson More and a conditional choice in 1998 Entry Draft for Marty McSorley, August 20, 1996.

SWANSON, SCOTT WSH.

Defense. Shoots left. 6'2", 190 lbs. Born, St. Paul, MN, February 15, 1975.
(Washington's 10th choice, 225th overall, in 1995 Entry Draft).

			Regular Season					Playoffs				
Season	Club	Lea	GP	G	A	TP	PIM	GP	G	A	TP	PIM
1994-95	Omaha	Jr. A	48	14	46	60	22	....	....	....	....	....
1995-96	Omaha	Jr. A	1	0	0	0	0	....	....	....	....	....

SWEENEY, BOB

Center/Right wing. Shoots right. 6'3", 200 lbs. Born, Concord, MA, January 25, 1964.
(Boston's 6th choice, 123rd overall, in 1982 Entry Draft).

			Regular Season					Playoffs				
Season	Club	Lea	GP	G	A	TP	PIM	GP	G	A	TP	PIM
1982-83	Boston College	ECAC	30	17	11	28	10	....	....	....	....	....
1983-84	Boston College	ECAC	23	14	7	21	10	....	....	....	....	....
1984-85a	Boston College	ECAC	44	32	32	64	43	....	....	....	....	....
1985-86	Boston College	H.E.	41	15	24	39	52	....	....	....	....	....
1986-87	**Boston**	**NHL**	**14**	**2**	**4**	**6**	**21**	**3**	**0**	**0**	**0**	**0**
	Moncton	AHL	58	29	26	55	81	4	0	2	2	13
1987-88	**Boston**	**NHL**	**80**	**22**	**23**	**45**	**73**	**23**	**6**	**8**	**14**	**66**
1988-89	**Boston**	**NHL**	**75**	**14**	**14**	**28**	**99**	**10**	**2**	**4**	**6**	**19**
1989-90	**Boston**	**NHL**	**70**	**22**	**24**	**46**	**93**	**20**	**0**	**2**	**2**	**30**
1990-91	**Boston**	**NHL**	**80**	**15**	**33**	**48**	**115**	**17**	**4**	**2**	**6**	**45**
1991-92	**Boston**	**NHL**	**63**	**6**	**14**	**20**	**103**	**14**	**1**	**0**	**1**	**25**
	Maine	AHL	1	1	0	1	0	....	....	....	....	....
1992-93	**Buffalo**	**NHL**	**80**	**21**	**26**	**47**	**118**	**8**	**2**	**2**	**4**	**8**
1993-94	**Buffalo**	**NHL**	**60**	**11**	**14**	**25**	**94**	**1**	**0**	**0**	**0**	**0**
1994-95	**Buffalo**	**NHL**	**45**	**5**	**4**	**9**	**18**	**5**	**0**	**0**	**0**	**4**
1995-96	**NY Islanders**	**NHL**	**66**	**6**	**6**	**12**	**59**	....	....	....	....	....
	Calgary	**NHL**	**6**	**1**	**1**	**2**	**6**	**2**	**0**	**0**	**0**	**0**
	NHL Totals		**639**	**125**	**163**	**288**	**799**	**103**	**15**	**18**	**33**	**197**

a ECAC Second Team All-Star (1985)

Claimed on waivers by **Buffalo** from **Boston**, October 9, 1992. Claimed by **NY Islanders** from **Buffalo** in NHL Waiver Draft, October 2, 1995. Traded to **Calgary** by **NY Islanders** for Pat Conacher and Calgary's sixth round choice in 1997 Entry Draft, March 20, 1996.

SWEENEY, DON BOS.

Defense. Shoots left. 5'10", 188 lbs. Born, St. Stephen, N.B., August 17, 1966.
(Boston's 8th choice, 166th overall, in 1984 Entry Draft).

			Regular Season					Playoffs				
Season	Club	Lea	GP	G	A	TP	PIM	GP	G	A	TP	PIM
1984-85	Harvard	ECAC	29	3	7	10	30	....	....	....	....	....
1985-86	Harvard	ECAC	31	4	5	9	12	....	....	....	....	....
1986-87	Harvard	ECAC	34	7	4	11	22	....	....	....	....	....
1987-88ab	Harvard	ECAC	30	6	23	29	37	....	....	....	....	....
	Maine	AHL	....	....	....	....	....	6	1	3	4	0
1988-89	**Boston**	**NHL**	**36**	**3**	**5**	**8**	**20**	....	....	....	....	....
	Maine	AHL	42	8	17	25	24	....	....	....	....	....
1989-90	**Boston**	**NHL**	**58**	**3**	**5**	**8**	**58**	**21**	**1**	**5**	**6**	**18**
	Maine	AHL	11	0	8	8	8	....	....	....	....	....
1990-91	**Boston**	**NHL**	**77**	**8**	**13**	**21**	**67**	**19**	**3**	**0**	**3**	**25**
1991-92	**Boston**	**NHL**	**75**	**3**	**11**	**14**	**74**	**15**	**0**	**0**	**0**	**10**
1992-93	**Boston**	**NHL**	**84**	**7**	**27**	**34**	**68**	**4**	**0**	**0**	**0**	**4**
1993-94	**Boston**	**NHL**	**75**	**6**	**15**	**21**	**50**	**12**	**2**	**1**	**3**	**4**
1994-95	**Boston**	**NHL**	**47**	**3**	**19**	**22**	**24**	**5**	**0**	**0**	**0**	**4**
1995-96	**Boston**	**NHL**	**77**	**4**	**24**	**28**	**42**	**5**	**0**	**2**	**2**	**6**
	NHL Totals		**529**	**37**	**119**	**156**	**403**	**81**	**6**	**8**	**14**	**71**

a NCAA East All-American Team (1988)
b ECAC First All-Star Team (1988)

SWEENEY, TIM BOS.

Left wing. Shoots left. 5'11", 185 lbs. Born, Boston, MA, April 12, 1967.
(Calgary's 7th choice, 122nd overall, in 1985 Entry Draft).

			Regular Season					Playoffs				
Season	Club	Lea	GP	G	A	TP	PIM	GP	G	A	TP	PIM
1985-86	Boston College	H.E.	32	8	4	12	8	....	....	....	....	....
1986-87	Boston College	H.E.	38	31	18	49	28	....	....	....	....	....
1987-88	Boston College	H.E.	18	9	11	20	18	....	....	....	....	....
1988-89ab	Boston College	H.E.	39	29	44	73	26	....	....	....	....	....
1989-90c	Salt Lake	IHL	81	46	51	97	32	11	5	4	9	4
1990-91	**Calgary**	**NHL**	**42**	**7**	**9**	**16**	**8**	....	....	....	....	....
	Salt Lake	IHL	31	19	16	35	8	4	3	3	6	0
1991-92	U.S. National	....	21	9	11	20	10	....	....	....	....	....
	U.S. Olympic	....	8	3	4	7	6	....	....	....	....	....
	Calgary	**NHL**	**11**	**1**	**2**	**3**	**4**	....	....	....	....	....
1992-93	**Boston**	**NHL**	**14**	**1**	**7**	**8**	**6**	**3**	**0**	**0**	**0**	**0**
d	Providence	AHL	60	41	55	96	32	3	2	2	4	0
1993-94	**Anaheim**	**NHL**	**78**	**16**	**27**	**43**	**49**	....	....	....	....	....
1994-95	**Anaheim**	**NHL**	**13**	**1**	**1**	**2**	**2**	....	....	....	....	....
	Providence	AHL	2	2	2	4	0	13	8	*17	*25	6
1995-96	**Boston**	**NHL**	**41**	**8**	**8**	**16**	**14**	**1**	**0**	**0**	**0**	**2**
	Providence	AHL	34	17	22	39	12	....	....	....	....	....
	NHL Totals		**199**	**34**	**54**	**88**	**83**	**4**	**0**	**0**	**0**	**2**

a Hockey East First All-Star Team (1989)
b NCAA East Second All-American Team (1989)
c IHL Second All-Star Team (1990)
d AHL Second All-Star Team (1993)

Signed as a free agent by **Boston**, September 16, 1992. Claimed by **Anaheim** from **Boston** in Expansion Draft, June 24, 1993. Signed as a free agent by **Boston**, August 9, 1995.

SYDOR, DARRYL (sih-DOHR) DAL.

Defense. Shoots left. 6', 195 lbs. Born, Edmonton, Alta., May 13, 1972.
(Los Angeles' 1st choice, 7th overall, in 1990 Entry Draft).

			Regular Season					Playoffs				
Season	Club	Lea	GP	G	A	TP	PIM	GP	G	A	TP	PIM
1988-89	Kamloops	WHL	65	12	14	26	86	15	1	4	5	19
1989-90a	Kamloops	WHL	67	29	66	95	129	17	2	9	11	28
1990-91a	Kamloops	WHL	66	27	78	105	88	12	3	*22	25	10
1991-92	**Los Angeles**	**NHL**	**18**	**1**	**5**	**6**	**22**	....	....	....	....	....
a	Kamloops	WHL	29	9	39	48	43	17	3	15	18	18
1992-93	**Los Angeles**	**NHL**	**80**	**6**	**23**	**29**	**63**	**24**	**3**	**8**	**11**	**16**
1993-94	**Los Angeles**	**NHL**	**84**	**8**	**27**	**35**	**94**	....	....	....	....	....
1994-95	**Los Angeles**	**NHL**	**48**	**4**	**19**	**23**	**36**	....	....	....	....	....
1995-96	**Los Angeles**	**NHL**	**58**	**1**	**11**	**12**	**34**	....	....	....	....	....
	Dallas	**NHL**	**26**	**2**	**6**	**8**	**41**	....	....	....	....	....
	NHL Totals		**314**	**22**	**91**	**113**	**290**	**24**	**3**	**8**	**11**	**16**

a WHL West First All-Star Team (1990, 1991, 1992)

Traded to **Dallas** by **Los Angeles** with Los Angeles' fifth round choice (Ryan Christie) in 1996 Entry Draft for Shane Churla and Doug Zmolek, February 17, 1996.

SYKORA, MICHAL (SEE-koh-ra) S.J.

Defense. Shoots left. 6'5", 225 lbs. Born, Pardubice, Czech., July 5, 1973.
(San Jose's 6th choice, 123rd overall, in 1992 Entry Draft).

			Regular Season					Playoffs				
Season	Club	Lea	GP	G	A	TP	PIM	GP	G	A	TP	PIM
1990-91	Pardubice	Czech.	2	0	0	0	....	....	....	....	....	....
1991-92	Tacoma	WHL	61	13	23	36	66	4	0	2	2	2
1992-93a	Tacoma	WHL	70	23	50	73	73	7	4	8	12	2
1993-94	**San Jose**	**NHL**	**22**	**1**	**4**	**5**	**14**	....	....	....	....	....
	Kansas City	IHL	47	5	11	16	30	....	....	....	....	....
1994-95	Kansas City	IHL	36	1	10	11	30	....	....	....	....	....
	San Jose	**NHL**	**16**	**0**	**4**	**4**	**10**	....	....	....	....	....
1995-96	**San Jose**	**NHL**	**79**	**4**	**16**	**20**	**54**	....	....	....	....	....
	NHL Totals		**117**	**5**	**24**	**29**	**78**	....	....	....	....	....

a WHL West First All-Star Team (1993)

SYKORA, PETR (SEE-koh-ra) N.J.

Center. Shoots left. 5'11", 185 lbs. Born, Plzen, Czech., November 19, 1976.
(New Jersey's 1st choice, 18th overall, in 1995 Entry Draft).

			Regular Season					Playoffs				
Season	Club	Lea	GP	G	A	TP	PIM	GP	G	A	TP	PIM
1992-93	Skoda Plzen	Czech.	19	12	5	17	....	....	....	....	....	....
1993-94	Skoda Plzen	Czech.	37	10	16	26	....	4	0	1	1	....
	Cleveland	IHL	13	4	5	9	8	....	....	....	....	....
1994-95	Detroit	IHL	29	12	17	29	16	....	....	....	....	....
1995-96a	**New Jersey**	**NHL**	**63**	**18**	**24**	**42**	**32**	....	....	....	....	....
	Albany	AHL	5	4	1	5	0	....	....	....	....	....
	NHL Totals		**63**	**18**	**24**	**42**	**32**	....	....	....	....	....

a NHL All-Rookie Team (1996)

SYLVESTER, DEAN — S.J.

Right wing. Shoots right. 6'2", 185 lbs. Born, Hanson, MA, December 30, 1972.
(San Jose's 1st choice, 2nd overall, in 1993 Supplemental Draft).

			Regular Season					Playoffs				
Season	Club	Lea	GP	G	A	TP	PIM	GP	G	A	TP	PIM
1991-92	Kent State	CCHA	31	7	21	28	....	....	....	....	....	....
1992-93	Kent State	CCHA	38	33	20	53	28	....	....	....	....	....
1993-94	Kent State	CCHA	39	22	24	46	28	....	....	....	....	....
1994-95	Michigan State	CCHA	40	15	15	30	38	....	....	....	....	....
1995-96	Mobile	ECHL	44	24	27	51	35	....	....	....	....	....
	Kansas City	IHL	36	11	10	21	15	4	0	0	0	2

SYMES, BRAD — EDM.

Defense. Shoots left. 6'2", 210 lbs. Born, Edmonton, Alta., April 26, 1976.
(Edmonton's 5th choice, 60th overall, in 1994 Entry Draft).

			Regular Season					Playoffs				
Season	Club	Lea	GP	G	A	TP	PIM	GP	G	A	TP	PIM
1992-93	Portland	WHL	68	4	2	6	107	16	0	1	1	7
1993-94	Portland	WHL	71	7	15	22	170	7	0	0	0	21
1994-95	Portland	WHL	70	8	16	24	134	9	0	2	2	27
1995-96	Portland	WHL	62	9	12	21	118	7	1	2	3	14

TAGLIANETTI, PETER — (TAG-lee-uh-NEH-tee)

Defense. Shoots left. 6'2", 195 lbs. Born, Framingham, MA, August 15, 1963.
(Winnipeg's 4th choice, 43rd overall, in 1983 Entry Draft).

			Regular Season					Playoffs				
Season	Club	Lea	GP	G	A	TP	PIM	GP	G	A	TP	PIM
1981-82	Providence	ECAC	2	0	0	0	2	....	....	....	....	....
1982-83	Providence	ECAC	43	4	17	21	68	....	....	....	....	....
1983-84	Providence	ECAC	30	4	25	29	68	....	....	....	....	....
1984-85	**Winnipeg**	**NHL**	**1**	**0**	**0**	**0**	**0**	**1**	**0**	**0**	**0**	**0**
a	Providence	H.E.	35	6	18	24	32	....	....	....	....	....
1985-86	**Winnipeg**	**NHL**	**18**	**0**	**0**	**0**	**48**	**3**	**0**	**0**	**0**	**2**
	Sherbrooke	AHL	24	1	18	9	75	....	....	....	....	....
1986-87	**Winnipeg**	**NHL**	**3**	**0**	**0**	**0**	**12**	....	....	....	....	....
	Sherbrooke	AHL	54	5	14	19	104	10	2	5	7	25
1987-88	**Winnipeg**	**NHL**	**70**	**6**	**17**	**23**	**182**	**5**	**1**	**1**	**2**	**12**
1988-89	**Winnipeg**	**NHL**	**66**	**1**	**14**	**15**	**226**	....	....	....	....	....
1989-90	**Winnipeg**	**NHL**	**49**	**3**	**6**	**9**	**136**	**5**	**0**	**0**	**0**	**6**
	Moncton	AHL	3	0	2	2	2	....	....	....	....	....
1990-91	**Minnesota**	**NHL**	**16**	**0**	**1**	**1**	**14**	....	....	....	....	....
	Pittsburgh	**NHL**	**39**	**3**	**8**	**11**	**93**	**19**	**0**	**3**	**3**	**49 ♦**
1991-92	**Pittsburgh**	**NHL**	**44**	**1**	**3**	**4**	**57**	....	....	....	....	.... ♦
1992-93	**Tampa Bay**	**NHL**	**61**	**1**	**8**	**9**	**150**	....	....	....	....	....
	Pittsburgh	**NHL**	**11**	**1**	**4**	**5**	**34**	**11**	**1**	**2**	**3**	**16**
1993-94	**Pittsburgh**	**NHL**	**60**	**2**	**12**	**14**	**142**	**5**	**0**	**2**	**2**	**16**
1994-95	**Pittsburgh**	**NHL**	**13**	**0**	**1**	**1**	**12**	**4**	**0**	**0**	**0**	**2**
	Cleveland	IHL	3	0	1	1	7	4	0	0	0	19
1995-96	Providence	AHL	34	0	6	6	44	....	....	....	....	....
	NHL Totals		**451**	**18**	**74**	**92**	**1106**	**53**	**2**	**8**	**10**	**103**

a Hockey East First All-Star Team (1985)

Traded to **Minnesota** by **Winnipeg** for future considerations, September 30, 1990. Traded to **Pittsburgh** by **Minnesota** with Larry Murphy for Chris Dahlquist and Jim Johnson, December 11, 1990. Claimed by **Tampa Bay** from **Pittsburgh** in Expansion Draft, June 18, 1992. Traded to **Pittsburgh** by **Tampa Bay** for Pittsburgh's third round choice (later traded to Florida — Florida selected Steve Washburn) in 1993 Entry Draft, March 22, 1993. Signed as a free agent by **Boston**, August 9, 1995.

TALLAIRE, SEAN

Right wing. Shoots right. 5'10", 185 lbs. Born, Steinbach, MN, October 3, 1973.
(Vancouver's 7th choice, 202nd overall, in 1993 Entry Draft).

			Regular Season					Playoffs				
Season	Club	Lea	GP	G	A	TP	PIM	GP	G	A	TP	PIM
1992-93	Lake Superior	CCHA	43	26	26	52	26	....	....	....	....	....
1993-94	Lake Superior	CCHA	45	23	32	55	22	....	....	....	....	....
1994-95	Lake Superior	CCHA	41	21	29	50	38	....	....	....	....	....
1995-96ab	Lake Superior	CCHA	40	*32	18	50	36	....	....	....	....	....

a CCHA First All-Star Team (1996)
b NCAA West Second All-American Team (1996)

TAMER, CHRIS — (TAY-muhr) PIT.

Defense. Shoots left. 6'2", 212 lbs. Born, Dearborn, MI, November 17, 1970.
(Pittsburgh's 3rd choice, 68th overall, in 1990 Entry Draft).

			Regular Season					Playoffs				
Season	Club	Lea	GP	G	A	TP	PIM	GP	G	A	TP	PIM
1989-90	U. of Michigan	CCHA	42	2	7	9	147	....	....	....	....	....
1990-91	U. of Michigan	CCHA	45	8	19	27	130	....	....	....	....	....
1991-92	U. of Michigan	CCHA	43	4	15	19	125	....	....	....	....	....
1992-93	U. of Michigan	CCHA	39	5	18	23	113	....	....	....	....	....
1993-94	**Pittsburgh**	**NHL**	**12**	**0**	**0**	**0**	**9**	**5**	**0**	**0**	**0**	**2**
	Cleveland	IHL	53	1	2	3	160	....	....	....	....	....
1994-95	Cleveland	IHL	48	4	10	14	204	....	....	....	....	....
	Pittsburgh	**NHL**	**36**	**2**	**0**	**2**	**82**	**4**	**0**	**0**	**0**	**18**
1995-96	**Pittsburgh**	**NHL**	**70**	**4**	**10**	**14**	**153**	**18**	**0**	**7**	**7**	**24**
	NHL Totals		**118**	**6**	**10**	**16**	**244**	**27**	**0**	**7**	**7**	**44**

TANCILL, CHRIS — (TAN-sihl) S.J.

Center. Shoots left. 5'10", 185 lbs. Born, Livonia, MI, February 7, 1968.
(Hartford's 1st choice, 15th overall, in 1989 Supplemental Draft).

			Regular Season					Playoffs				
Season	Club	Lea	GP	G	A	TP	PIM	GP	G	A	TP	PIM
1986-87	U. Wisconsin	WCHA	40	9	23	32	26	....	....	....	....	....
1987-88	U. Wisconsin	WCHA	44	13	14	27	48	....	....	....	....	....
1988-89	U. Wisconsin	WCHA	44	20	23	43	50	....	....	....	....	....
1989-90a	U. Wisconsin	WCHA	45	39	32	71	44	....	....	....	....	....
1990-91	**Hartford**	**NHL**	**9**	**1**	**1**	**2**	**4**	....	....	....	....	....
	Springfield	AHL	72	37	35	72	46	17	8	4	12	32
1991-92	**Hartford**	**NHL**	**10**	**0**	**0**	**0**	**2**	....	....	....	....	....
b	Springfield	AHL	17	12	7	19	20	....	....	....	....	....
	Detroit	**NHL**	**1**	**0**	**0**	**0**	**0**	....	....	....	....	....
	Adirondack	AHL	50	36	34	70	42	19	7	9	16	31
1992-93	**Detroit**	**NHL**	**4**	**1**	**0**	**1**	**2**	....	....	....	....	....
b	Adirondack	AHL	68	*59	43	102	62	10	7	7	14	10
1993-94	**Dallas**	**NHL**	**12**	**1**	**3**	**4**	**8**	....	....	....	....	....
	Kalamazoo	IHL	60	41	54	95	55	5	0	2	2	8
1994-95	Kansas City	IHL	64	31	28	59	40	....	....	....	....	....
	San Jose	**NHL**	**26**	**3**	**11**	**14**	**10**	**11**	**1**	**1**	**2**	**8**
1995-96	**San Jose**	**NHL**	**45**	**7**	**16**	**23**	**20**	....	....	....	....	....
	Kansas City	IHL	27	12	16	28	18	....	....	....	....	....
	NHL Totals		**107**	**13**	**31**	**44**	**46**	**11**	**1**	**1**	**2**	**8**

a NCAA All-Tournament Team, Tournament MVP (1990)
b AHL First All-Star Team (1992, 1993)

Traded to **Detroit** by **Hartford** for Daniel Shank, December 18, 1991. Signed as a free agent by **Dallas**, August 28, 1993. Signed as a free agent by **San Jose**, August 24, 1994.

TARDIF, PATRICE — L.A.

Center. Shoots left. 6'2", 202 lbs. Born, Thetford Mines, Que., October 30, 1970.
(St. Louis' 2nd choice, 54th overall, in 1990 Entry Draft).

			Regular Season					Playoffs				
Season	Club	Lea	GP	G	A	TP	PIM	GP	G	A	TP	PIM
1990-91	U. of Maine	H.E.	36	13	12	25	18	....	....	....	....	....
1991-92	U. of Maine	H.E.	31	18	20	38	14	....	....	....	....	....
1992-93	U. of Maine	H.E.	45	23	25	48	22	....	....	....	....	....
1993-94	U. of Maine	H.E.	34	18	15	33	42	....	....	....	....	....
	Peoria	IHL	11	4	4	8	21	4	2	0	2	4
1994-95	Peoria	IHL	53	27	18	45	83	....	....	....	....	....
	St. Louis	**NHL**	**27**	**3**	**10**	**13**	**29**	....	....	....	....	....
1995-96	**St. Louis**	**NHL**	**23**	**3**	**0**	**3**	**12**	....	....	....	....	....
	Worcester	AHL	30	13	13	26	69	....	....	....	....	....
	Los Angeles	**NHL**	**15**	**1**	**1**	**2**	**37**	....	....	....	....	....
	NHL Totals		**65**	**7**	**11**	**18**	**78**	....	....	....	....	....

Traded to **Los Angeles** by **St. Louis** with Craig Johnson, Roman Vopat, St. Louis fifth round choice (Peter Hogan) in 1996 Entry Draft and first round choice in 1997 Entry Draft for Wayne Gretzky, February 27, 1996.

TARDIF, STEVE — CHI.

Center. Shoots left. 6'1", 180 lbs. Born, St-Agnes, Que., March 29, 1977.
(Chicago's 8th choice, 175th overall, in 1995 Entry Draft).

			Regular Season					Playoffs				
Season	Club	Lea	GP	G	A	TP	PIM	GP	G	A	TP	PIM
1993-94	Drummondville	QMJHL	71	5	16	21	117	10	0	1	1	19
1994-95	Drummondville	QMJHL	64	10	33	43	313	4	1	2	3	9
1995-96	Drummondville	QMJHL	54	17	33	50	291	6	2	3	5	58

TARNSTROM, DICK — NYI

Defense. Shoots left. 6', 180 lbs. Born, Sundbyberg, Sweden, January 20, 1975.
(NY Islanders' 12th choice, 272nd overall, in 1994 Entry Draft).

			Regular Season					Playoffs				
Season	Club	Lea	GP	G	A	TP	PIM	GP	G	A	TP	PIM
1992-93	AIK	Swe.	3	0	0	0	0	....	....	....	....	....
1993-94	AIK	Swe.	33	1	4	5	....	....	....	....	....	....
1994-95	AIK	Swe.	37	8	4	12	26	....	....	....	....	....
1995-96	AIK	Swe.	40	0	5	5	32	....	....	....	....	....

TARVAINEN, JUSSI — (tahr-VAHI-nehn) EDM.

Center. Shoots right. 6'2", 185 lbs. Born, Lahti, Finland, May 31, 1976.
(Edmonton's 7th choice, 95th overall, in 1994 Entry Draft).

			Regular Season					Playoffs				
Season	Club	Lea	GP	G	A	TP	PIM	GP	G	A	TP	PIM
1993-94	KalPa	Fin.	42	3	4	7	20	....	....	....	....	....
1994-95	KalPa	Fin.	45	10	7	17	34	3	0	0	0	2
1995-96	KalPa	Fin.	47	8	11	19	50	....	....	....	....	....

TAYLOR, ANDREW — NYI

Left wing. Shoots left. 6'1", 182 lbs. Born, Stratford, Ont., January 17, 1977.
(NY Islanders' 5th choice, 158th overall, in 1995 Entry Draft).

			Regular Season					Playoffs				
Season	Club	Lea	GP	G	A	TP	PIM	GP	G	A	TP	PIM
1993-94	Kitchener	OHL	62	1	8	9	60	5	0	1	1	6
1994-95	Kitchener	OHL	42	4	5	9	65	....	....	....	....	....
	Detroit	OHL	18	2	2	4	11	9	0	0	0	7
1995-96	Detroit	OHL	63	14	24	38	82	17	2	5	7	13

TAYLOR, CHRIS — NYI

Center. Shoots left. 6', 189 lbs. Born, Stratford, Ont., March 6, 1972.
(NY Islanders' 2nd choice, 27th overall, in 1990 Entry Draft).

			Regular Season					Playoffs				
Season	Club	Lea	GP	G	A	TP	PIM	GP	G	A	TP	PIM
1988-89	London	OHL	62	7	16	23	52	15	0	2	2	15
1989-90	London	OHL	66	45	60	105	60	6	3	2	5	6
1990-91	London	OHL	65	50	78	128	50	7	4	8	12	6
1991-92	London	OHL	66	48	74	122	57	10	8	16	24	9
1992-93	Capital Dist.	AHL	77	19	43	62	32	4	0	1	1	2
1993-94	Salt Lake	IHL	79	21	20	41	38	....	....	....	....	....
1994-95	Denver	IHL	78	38	48	86	47	14	7	6	13	10
	NY Islanders	**NHL**	**10**	**0**	**3**	**3**	**2**	....	....	....	....	....
1995-96	**NY Islanders**	**NHL**	**11**	**0**	**1**	**1**	**2**	....	....	....	....	....
	Utah	IHL	50	18	23	41	60	22	5	11	16	26
	NHL Totals		**21**	**0**	**4**	**4**	**4**	....	....	....	....	....

TAYLOR, TIM — DET.

Center. Shoots left. 6'1", 185 lbs. Born, Stratford, Ont., February 6, 1969.
(Washington's 2nd choice, 36th overall, in 1988 Entry Draft).

			Regular Season					Playoffs				
Season	Club	Lea	GP	G	A	TP	PIM	GP	G	A	TP	PIM
1986-87	London	OHL	34	7	9	16	11	....	....	....	....	....
1987-88	London	OHL	64	46	50	96	66	12	9	9	18	26
1988-89	London	OHL	61	34	80	114	93	21	*21	25	*46	58
1989-90	Baltimore	AHL	79	31	36	67	124	9	2	2	4	13
1990-91	Baltimore	AHL	79	25	42	67	75	5	0	1	1	4
1991-92	Baltimore	AHL	65	9	18	27	131	....	....	....	....	....
1992-93	Baltimore	AHL	41	15	16	31	49	....	....	....	....	....
	Hamilton	AHL	36	15	22	37	37	....	....	....	....	....
1993-94	**Detroit**	**NHL**	**1**	**1**	**0**	**1**	**0**	....	....	....	....	....
ab	Adirondack	AHL	79	36	*81	*117	86	12	2	10	12	12
1994-95	**Detroit**	**NHL**	**22**	**0**	**4**	**4**	**16**	**6**	**0**	**1**	**1**	**12**
1995-96	**Detroit**	**NHL**	**72**	**11**	**14**	**25**	**39**	**18**	**0**	**4**	**4**	**4**
	NHL Totals		**95**	**12**	**18**	**30**	**55**	**24**	**0**	**5**	**5**	**16**

a AHL First All-Star Team (1994)
b Won John B. Sollenberger Trophy (Top Scorer - AHL) (1994)

Traded to **Vancouver** by **Washington** for Eric Murano, January 29, 1993. Signed as a free agent by **Detroit**, July 28, 1993.

TERTYSHNY, DMITRY (tuhr-TIHSH-nee) — PHI.

Defense. Shoots left. 6'1", 176 lbs. Born, Chelyabinsk, USSR, December 26, 1976.
(Philadelphia's 4th choice, 132nd overall, in 1995 Entry Draft).

			Regular Season					Playoffs				
Season	Club	Lea	GP	G	A	TP	PIM	GP	G	A	TP	PIM
1994-95	Chelyabinsk	CIS	38	0	3	3	14	1	0	0	0	0
1995-96	Chelyabinsk	CIS	44	1	5	6	50	....	....	....	....	....

TETARENKO, JOEY — FLA.

Defense. Shoots right. 6'1", 205 lbs. Born, Prince Albert, Sask., March 3, 1978.
(Florida's 4th choice, 82nd overall, in 1996 Entry Draft).

			Regular Season					Playoffs				
Season	Club	Lea	GP	G	A	TP	PIM	GP	G	A	TP	PIM
1994-95	Portland	WHL	59	0	1	1	134	9	0	0	0	8
1995-96	Portland	WHL	71	4	11	15	190	7	0	1	1	17

TEZIKOV, ALEXEI — BUF.

Defense. Shoots left. 6'1", 198 lbs. Born, Togliatti, USSR, June 22, 1978.
(Buffalo's 7th choice, 115th overall, in 1996 Entry Draft).

			Regular Season					Playoffs				
Season	Club	Lea	GP	G	A	TP	PIM	GP	G	A	TP	PIM
1995-96	Lada Togliatti	CIS	14	0	0	0	8	....	....	....	....	....

THERIAULT, JOEL — WSH.

Defense. Shoots right. 6'3", 201 lbs. Born, Montreal, Que., October 30, 1976.
(Washington's 5th choice, 95th overall, in 1995 Entry Draft).

			Regular Season					Playoffs				
Season	Club	Lea	GP	G	A	TP	PIM	GP	G	A	TP	PIM
1993-94	St-Jean	QMJHL	57	3	0	3	63	5	0	1	1	0
1994-95	St-Jean	QMJHL	18	2	7	9	94	....	....	....	....	....
	Beauport	QMJHL	51	2	5	7	293	18	3	6	9	*162
1995-96	Halifax	QMJHL	39	5	15	20	*358	....	....	....	....	....
	Drummondville	QMJHL	24	1	5	6	*215	6	0	2	2	45

THERIEN, CHRIS (TEH-ree-ehn) — PHI.

Defense. Shoots left. 6'4", 230 lbs. Born, Ottawa, Ont., December 14, 1971.
(Philadelphia's 7th choice, 47th overall, in 1990 Entry Draft).

			Regular Season					Playoffs				
Season	Club	Lea	GP	G	A	TP	PIM	GP	G	A	TP	PIM
1990-91	Providence	H.E.	36	4	18	22	36	....	....	....	....	....
1991-92	Providence	H.E.	36	16	25	41	38	....	....	....	....	....
1992-93a	Providence	H.E.	33	8	11	19	52	....	....	....	....	....
	Cdn. National	....	8	1	4	5	8	....	....	....	....	....
1993-94	Cdn. National	....	59	7	15	22	46	....	....	....	....	....
	Cdn. Olympic	....	4	0	0	0	4	....	....	....	....	....
	Hershey	AHL	6	0	0	0	2	....	....	....	....	....
1994-95	Hershey	AHL	34	3	13	16	27	....	....	....	....	....
b	**Philadelphia**	**NHL**	**48**	**3**	**10**	**13**	**38**	**15**	**0**	**0**	**0**	**10**
1995-96	**Philadelphia**	**NHL**	**82**	**6**	**17**	**23**	**89**	**12**	**0**	**0**	**0**	**18**
	NHL Totals		**130**	**9**	**27**	**36**	**127**	**27**	**0**	**0**	**0**	**28**

a Hockey East Second All-Star Team (1993)
b NHL/Upper Deck All-Rookie Team (1995)

THIESSEN, TRAVIS — CHI.

Defense. Shoots left. 6'3", 203 lbs. Born, North Battleford, Sask., July 11, 1972.
(Pittsburgh's 3rd choice, 67th overall, in 1992 Entry Draft).

			Regular Season					Playoffs				
Season	Club	Lea	GP	G	A	TP	PIM	GP	G	A	TP	PIM
1990-91	Moose Jaw	WHL	69	4	14	18	80	8	0	0	0	10
1991-92	Moose Jaw	WHL	72	9	50	59	112	4	0	2	2	8
1992-93	Cleveland	IHL	64	3	7	10	69	4	0	0	0	16
1993-94	Cleveland	IHL	74	2	13	15	75	....	....	....	....	....
1994-95	Flint	ColHL	5	0	1	1	2	....	....	....	....	....
	Indianapolis	IHL	41	2	3	5	36	....	....	....	....	....
	Saint John	AHL	9	1	2	3	12	5	0	1	1	0
1995-96	Indianapolis	IHL	4	0	1	1	8	....	....	....	....	....
	Peoria	IHL	63	3	12	15	102	12	1	4	5	8

Signed as a free agent by **Chicago**, June 9, 1994.

THOMAS, SCOTT

Right wing. Shoots right. 6'2", 195 lbs. Born, Buffalo, NY, January 18, 1970.
(Buffalo's 2nd choice, 56th overall, in 1989 Entry Draft).

			Regular Season					Playoffs				
Season	Club	Lea	GP	G	A	TP	PIM	GP	G	A	TP	PIM
1989-90	Clarkson	ECAC	34	19	13	32	95	....	....	....	....	....
1990-91	Clarkson	ECAC	40	28	14	42	89	....	....	....	....	....
1991-92	Clarkson	ECAC	29	22	20	42	57	....	....	....	....	....
	Rochester	AHL	....	....	....	....	....	9	0	1	1	17
1992-93	**Buffalo**	**NHL**	**7**	**1**	**1**	**2**	**15**	....	....	....	....	....
	Rochester	AHL	65	32	27	59	38	17	8	5	13	6
1993-94	**Buffalo**	**NHL**	**32**	**2**	**2**	**4**	**8**	....	....	....	....	....
	Rochester	AHL	11	4	5	9	0	....	....	....	....	....
1994-95	Rochester	AHL	55	21	25	46	115	5	4	0	4	4
1995-96	Cincinnati	IHL	78	32	28	60	54	17	*13	2	15	4
	NHL Totals		**39**	**3**	**3**	**6**	**23**	....	....	....	....	....

THOMAS, STEVE — N.J.

Left wing. Shoots left. 5'11", 185 lbs. Born, Stockport, England, July 15, 1963.

			Regular Season					Playoffs				
Season	Club	Lea	GP	G	A	TP	PIM	GP	G	A	TP	PIM
1983-84	Toronto	OHL	70	51	54	105	77	....	....	....	....	....
1984-85	**Toronto**	**NHL**	**18**	**1**	**1**	**2**	**2**	....	....	....	....	....
ab	St. Catharines	AHL	64	42	48	90	56	....	....	....	....	....
1985-86	**Toronto**	**NHL**	**65**	**20**	**37**	**57**	**36**	**10**	**6**	**8**	**14**	**9**
	St. Catharines	AHL	19	18	14	32	35	....	....	....	....	....
1986-87	**Toronto**	**NHL**	**78**	**35**	**27**	**62**	**114**	**13**	**2**	**3**	**5**	**13**
1987-88	**Chicago**	**NHL**	**30**	**13**	**13**	**26**	**40**	**3**	**1**	**2**	**3**	**6**
1988-89	**Chicago**	**NHL**	**45**	**21**	**19**	**40**	**69**	**12**	**3**	**5**	**8**	**10**
1989-90	**Chicago**	**NHL**	**76**	**40**	**30**	**70**	**91**	**20**	**7**	**6**	**13**	**33**
1990-91	**Chicago**	**NHL**	**69**	**19**	**35**	**54**	**129**	**6**	**1**	**2**	**3**	**15**
1991-92	**Chicago**	**NHL**	**11**	**2**	**6**	**8**	**26**	....	....	....	....	....
	NY Islanders	**NHL**	**71**	**28**	**42**	**70**	**71**	....	....	....	....	....
1992-93	**NY Islanders**	**NHL**	**79**	**37**	**50**	**87**	**111**	**18**	**9**	**8**	**17**	**37**
1993-94	**NY Islanders**	**NHL**	**78**	**42**	**33**	**75**	**139**	**4**	**1**	**0**	**1**	**8**
1994-95	**NY Islanders**	**NHL**	**47**	**11**	**15**	**26**	**60**	....	....	....	....	....
1995-96	**New Jersey**	**NHL**	**81**	**26**	**35**	**61**	**98**	....	....	....	....	....
	NHL Totals		**748**	**295**	**343**	**638**	**986**	**86**	**30**	**34**	**64**	**131**

a Won Dudley "Red" Garrett Memorial Trophy (Top Rookie - AHL) (1985)
b AHL First All-Star Team (1985)

Signed as a free agent by **Toronto**, May 12, 1984. Traded to **Chicago** by **Toronto** with Rick Vaive and Bob McGill for Al Secord and Ed Olczyk, September 3, 1987. Traded to **NY Islanders** by **Chicago** with Adam Creighton for Brent Sutter and Brad Lauer, October 25, 1991. Traded to **New Jersey** by **NY Islanders** for Claude Lemieux, October 3, 1995.

THOMLINSON, DAVE

Left wing. Shoots left. 6'1", 215 lbs. Born, Edmonton, Alta., October 22, 1966.
(Toronto's 3rd choice, 43rd overall, in 1985 Entry Draft).

			Regular Season					Playoffs				
Season	Club	Lea	GP	G	A	TP	PIM	GP	G	A	TP	PIM
1984-85	Brandon	WHL	26	13	14	27	70	....	....	....	....	....
1985-86	Brandon	WHL	53	25	20	45	116	....	....	....	....	....
1986-87	Brandon	WHL	2	0	1	1	9	....	....	....	....	....
	Moose Jaw	WHL	70	44	36	80	117	9	7	3	10	19
1987-88	Peoria	IHL	74	27	30	57	56	7	4	3	7	11
1988-89	Peoria	IHL	64	27	29	56	154	3	0	1	1	8
1989-90	**St. Louis**	**NHL**	**19**	**1**	**2**	**3**	**12**	....	....	....	....	....
	Peoria	IHL	59	27	40	67	87	5	1	1	2	15
1990-91	**St. Louis**	**NHL**	**3**	**0**	**0**	**0**	**0**	**9**	**3**	**1**	**4**	**4**
	Peoria	IHL	80	53	54	107	107	11	6	7	13	28
1991-92	**Boston**	**NHL**	**12**	**0**	**1**	**1**	**17**	....	....	....	....	....
	Maine	AHL	25	9	11	20	36	....	....	....	....	....
1992-93	Binghamton	AHL	54	25	35	60	61	12	2	5	7	8
1993-94	**Los Angeles**	**NHL**	**7**	**0**	**0**	**0**	**21**	....	....	....	....	....
	Phoenix	IHL	39	10	15	25	70	....	....	....	....	....
1994-95	Phoenix	IHL	77	30	40	70	87	9	5	3	8	8
	Los Angeles	**NHL**	**1**	**0**	**0**	**0**	**0**	....	....	....	....	....
1995-96	Phoenix	IHL	48	10	13	23	65	4	1	0	1	2
	NHL Totals		**42**	**1**	**3**	**4**	**50**	**9**	**3**	**1**	**4**	**4**

Signed as a free agent by **St. Louis**, June 4, 1987. Signed as a free agent by **Boston**, July 30, 1991. Signed as a free agent by **NY Rangers**, September 4, 1992. Signed as a free agent by **Los Angeles**, July 22, 1993.

THOMPSON, BRENT — PHO.

Defense. Shoots left. 6'2", 200 lbs. Born, Calgary, Alta., January 9, 1971.
(Los Angeles' 1st choice, 39th overall, in 1989 Entry Draft).

			Regular Season					Playoffs				
Season	Club	Lea	GP	G	A	TP	PIM	GP	G	A	TP	PIM
1988-89	Medicine Hat	WHL	72	3	10	13	160	3	0	0	0	2
1989-90	Medicine Hat	WHL	68	10	35	45	167	3	0	1	1	14
1990-91a	Medicine Hat	WHL	51	5	40	45	87	12	1	7	8	16
	Phoenix	IHL	....	....	....	....	....	4	0	1	1	6
1991-92	**Los Angeles**	**NHL**	**27**	**0**	**5**	**5**	**89**	**4**	**0**	**0**	**0**	**4**
	Phoenix	IHL	42	4	13	17	139	....	....	....	....	....
1992-93	**Los Angeles**	**NHL**	**30**	**0**	**4**	**4**	**76**	....	....	....	....	....
	Phoenix	IHL	22	0	5	5	112	....	....	....	....	....
1993-94	**Los Angeles**	**NHL**	**24**	**1**	**0**	**1**	**81**	....	....	....	....	....
	Phoenix	IHL	26	1	11	12	118	....	....	....	....	....
1994-95	**Winnipeg**	**NHL**	**29**	**0**	**0**	**0**	**78**	....	....	....	....	....
1995-96	**Winnipeg**	**NHL**	**10**	**0**	**1**	**1**	**21**	....	....	....	....	....
	Springfield	AHL	58	2	10	12	203	10	1	4	5	*55
	NHL Totals		**120**	**1**	**10**	**11**	**345**	**4**	**0**	**0**	**0**	**4**

a WHL East Second All-Star Team (1991)

Traded to **Winnipeg** by **Los Angeles** with future considerations for the rights to Ruslan Batyrshin and Winnipeg's second round choice (Marian Cisar) in 1996 Entry Draft, August 8, 1994.

THOMPSON, ROCKY — CGY.

Defense. Shoots right. 6'2", 192 lbs. Born, Calgary, Alta., August 8, 1977.
(Calgary's 3rd choice, 72nd overall, in 1995 Entry Draft).

			Regular Season					Playoffs				
Season	Club	Lea	GP	G	A	TP	PIM	GP	G	A	TP	PIM
1993-94	Medicine Hat	WHL	68	1	4	5	166	3	0	0	0	2
1994-95	Medicine Hat	WHL	63	1	6	7	220	5	0	0	0	17
1995-96	Medicine Hat	WHL	71	9	20	29	260	5	2	3	5	26
	Saint John	AHL	4	0	0	0	33	....	....	....	....	....

THORNTON, SCOTT — EDM.

Center. Shoots left. 6'3", 210 lbs. Born, London, Ont., January 9, 1971.
(Toronto's 1st choice, 3rd overall, in 1989 Entry Draft).

			Regular Season					Playoffs				
Season	Club	Lea	GP	G	A	TP	PIM	GP	G	A	TP	PIM
1987-88	Belleville	OHL	62	11	19	30	54	6	0	1	1	2
1988-89	Belleville	OHL	59	28	34	62	103	5	1	1	2	6
1989-90	Belleville	OHL	47	21	28	49	91	11	2	10	12	15
1990-91	**Toronto**	**NHL**	**33**	**1**	**3**	**4**	**30**	....	....	....	....	....
	Newmarket	AHL	5	1	0	1	4	....	....	....	....	....
	Belleville	OHL	3	2	1	3	2	6	0	7	7	14
1991-92	**Edmonton**	**NHL**	**15**	**0**	**1**	**1**	**43**	**1**	**0**	**0**	**0**	**0**
	Cape Breton	AHL	49	9	14	23	40	5	1	0	1	8
1992-93	**Edmonton**	**NHL**	**9**	**0**	**1**	**1**	**0**	....	....	....	....	....
	Cape Breton	AHL	58	23	27	50	102	16	1	2	3	35
1993-94	**Edmonton**	**NHL**	**61**	**4**	**7**	**11**	**104**	....	....	....	....	....
	Cape Breton	AHL	2	1	1	2	31	....	....	....	....	....
1994-95	**Edmonton**	**NHL**	**47**	**10**	**12**	**22**	**89**	....	....	....	....	....
1995-96	**Edmonton**	**NHL**	**77**	**9**	**9**	**18**	**149**	....	....	....	....	....
	NHL Totals		**242**	**24**	**33**	**57**	**415**	**1**	**0**	**0**	**0**	**0**

Traded to **Edmonton** by **Toronto** with Vincent Damphousse, Peter Ing, Luke Richardson, future considerations and cash for Grant Fuhr, Glenn Anderson and Craig Berube, September 19, 1991.

THURESSON, MARCUS — S.J.

Center. Shoots left. 6'1", 180 lbs. Born, Jon Koping, Sweden, May 31, 1971.
(NY Islanders' 11th choice, 224th overall, in 1991 Entry Draft).

			Regular Season					Playoffs				
Season	Club	Lea	GP	G	A	TP	PIM	GP	G	A	TP	PIM
1989-90	Leksand	Swe.	28	8	7	15	18	3	2	0	2	12
1990-91	Leksand	Swe.	22	3	2	5	20					
1991-92	Leksand	Swe.	21	2	4	6	22					
1992-93	Leksand	Swe.	31	6	10	16	22	2	2	0	2	2
1993-94	Leksand	Swe.	32	3	4	7	28	4	0	1	1	0
1994-95	Leksand	Swe.	39	3	10	13	42	4	1	0	1	0
1995-96	HV-71	Swe.	32	7	6	13	28					

Rights traded to **San Jose** by **NY Islanders** for Brian Mullen, August 24, 1992.

TICHY, MILAN — (TEE-CHEE, MEE-lahn)

Defense. Shoots left. 6'3", 198 lbs. Born, Plzen, Czech., September 22, 1969.
(Chicago's 6th choice, 153rd overall, in 1989 Entry Draft).

			Regular Season					Playoffs				
Season	Club	Lea	GP	G	A	TP	PIM	GP	G	A	TP	PIM
1987-88	Skoda Plzen	Czech.	30	1	3	4	20					
1988-89	Skoda Plzen	Czech.	36	1	12	13	44					
1989-90	Dukla Trencin	Czech.	51	14	8	22	....					
1990-91	Dukla Trencin	Czech.	41	9	12	21	72					
1991-92	Indianapolis	IHL	49	6	23	29	28					
1992-93	**Chicago**	**NHL**	**13**	**0**	**1**	**1**	**30**					
	Indianapolis	IHL	49	7	32	39	62	4	0	5	5	14
1993-94	Moncton	AHL	48	1	20	21	103	20	3	3	6	12
1994-95	Denver	IHL	71	18	36	54	90	17	4	9	13	12
	NY Islanders	**NHL**	**2**	**0**	**0**	**0**	**2**					
1995-96	**NY Islanders**	**NHL**	**8**	**0**	**4**	**4**	**8**					
	Utah	IHL	21	1	12	13	26					
	ZPS Zlin	Czech.	8	0	3	3	....	4	0	0	0	....
	NHL Totals		**23**	**0**	**5**	**5**	**40**					

Claimed by **Florida** from **Chicago** in Expansion Draft, June 24, 1993. Traded to **Winnipeg** by **Florida** for Brent Severyn, October 3, 1993. Signed as a free agent by **NY Islanders**, August 2, 1994.

TIILIKAINEN, JUKKA — (REE-ee-lee-kigh-nehn, yoo-KUH) — L.A.

Left wing. Shoots left. 6', 180 lbs. Born, Espoo, Finland, April 4, 1974.
(Los Angeles' 8th choice, 255th overall, in 1992 Entry Draft).

			Regular Season					Playoffs				
Season	Club	Lea	GP	G	A	TP	PIM	GP	G	A	TP	PIM
1991-92	Kiekko	Fin. 2	1	0	0	0	0					
1992-93	Vantaa	Fin. 2	18	7	3	10	10					
	Kiekko	Fin.	5	0	0	0	4					
1993-94	Kiekko-Espoo	Fin.	33	2	4	6	12					
1994-95	TPS	Fin.	38	5	4	9	8	11	1	0	1	8
1995-96	TPS	Fin.	38	6	13	19	28	10	0	2	2	2

TIKKANEN, ESA — (TEE-kuh-nehn, EHZ-uh) — VAN.

Left wing. Shoots left. 6'1", 190 lbs. Born, Helsinki, Finland, January 25, 1965.
(Edmonton's 4th choice, 80th overall, in 1983 Entry Draft).

			Regular Season					Playoffs				
Season	Club	Lea	GP	G	A	TP	PIM	GP	G	A	TP	PIM
1981-82	Regina	SJHL	59	38	37	75	216					
	Regina	WHL	2	0	0	0	0					
1982-83	HIFK	Fin. Jr.	30	34	31	65	104	4	4	3	7	10
	HIFK	Fin.	....	....	....	....	....	1	0	0	0	2
1983-84	HIFK	Fin. Jr.	6	5	9	14	13	4	4	3	7	8
	HIFK	Fin.	36	19	11	30	30	2	0	0	0	0
1984-85	HIFK	Fin.	36	21	33	54	42					
	Edmonton	**NHL**	....	....	....	....	....	**3**	**0**	**0**	**0**	**2** ♦
1985-86	**Edmonton**	**NHL**	**35**	**7**	**6**	**13**	**28**	**8**	**3**	**2**	**5**	**7**
	Nova Scotia	AHL	15	4	8	12	17					
1986-87	**Edmonton**	**NHL**	**76**	**34**	**44**	**78**	**120**	**21**	**7**	**2**	**9**	**22** ♦
1987-88	**Edmonton**	**NHL**	**80**	**23**	**51**	**74**	**153**	**19**	**10**	**17**	**27**	**72** ♦
1988-89	**Edmonton**	**NHL**	**67**	**31**	**47**	**78**	**92**	**7**	**1**	**3**	**4**	**12**
1989-90	**Edmonton**	**NHL**	**79**	**30**	**33**	**63**	**161**	**22**	**13**	**11**	**24**	**26** ♦
1990-91	**Edmonton**	**NHL**	**79**	**27**	**42**	**69**	**85**	**18**	**12**	**8**	**20**	**24**
1991-92	**Edmonton**	**NHL**	**40**	**12**	**16**	**28**	**44**	**16**	**5**	**3**	**8**	**8**
1992-93	**Edmonton**	**NHL**	**66**	**14**	**19**	**33**	**76**					
	NY Rangers	**NHL**	**15**	**2**	**5**	**7**	**18**					
1993-94	**NY Rangers**	**NHL**	**83**	**22**	**32**	**54**	**114**	**23**	**4**	**4**	**8**	**34** ♦
1994-95	HIFK	Fin.	19	2	11	13	16					
	St. Louis	**NHL**	**43**	**12**	**23**	**35**	**22**	**7**	**2**	**2**	**4**	**20**
1995-96	**St. Louis**	**NHL**	**11**	**1**	**4**	**5**	**18**					
	New Jersey	**NHL**	**9**	**0**	**2**	**2**	**4**					
	Vancouver	**NHL**	**38**	**13**	**24**	**37**	**14**	**6**	**3**	**2**	**5**	**2**
	NHL Totals		**721**	**228**	**348**	**576**	**949**	**150**	**60**	**54**	**114**	**229**

Traded to **NY Rangers** by **Edmonton** for Doug Weight, March 17, 1993. Traded to **St. Louis** by **NY Rangers** with Doug Lidster for Petr Nedved, July 24, 1994. Traded to **New Jersey** by **St. Louis** for New Jersey's third round choice in 1997 Entry Draft, November 1, 1995. Traded to **Vancouver** by **New Jersey** for Vancouver's second round choice (Wesley Mason) in 1996 Entry Draft, November 23, 1995.

TILLEY, TOM

Defense. Shoots right. 6', 190 lbs. Born, Trenton, Ont., March 28, 1965.
(St. Louis' 13th choice, 196th overall, in 1984 Entry Draft).

			Regular Season					Playoffs				
Season	Club	Lea	GP	G	A	TP	PIM	GP	G	A	TP	PIM
1984-85	Michigan State	CCHA	37	1	5	6	58					
1985-86	Michigan State	CCHA	42	9	25	34	48					
1986-87	Michigan State	CCHA	42	7	14	21	48					
1987-88a	Michigan State	CCHA	46	8	18	26	44					
1988-89	**St. Louis**	**NHL**	**70**	**1**	**22**	**23**	**47**	**10**	**1**	**2**	**3**	**17**
1989-90	**St. Louis**	**NHL**	**34**	**0**	**5**	**5**	**6**					
	Peoria	IHL	22	1	8	9	13					
1990-91	**St. Louis**	**NHL**	**22**	**2**	**4**	**6**	**4**					
b	Peoria	IHL	48	7	38	45	53	13	2	9	11	25
1991-92	Milan Devils	Italy	18	7	13	20	12	12	5	12	17	10
	Cdn. National	....	4	0	1	1	0					
1992-93	Milan Devils	Alp.	32	5	17	22	21					
	Milan Devils	Italy	14	8	3	11	2	8	1	5	6	4
1993-94	**St. Louis**	**NHL**	**48**	**1**	**7**	**8**	**32**	**4**	**0**	**1**	**1**	**2**
1994-95	Atlanta	IHL	10	2	6	8	14					
	Indianapolis	IHL	25	2	13	15	19					
1995-96b	Milwaukee	IHL	80	11	68	79	58	4	2	2	4	4
	NHL Totals		**174**	**4**	**38**	**42**	**89**	**14**	**1**	**3**	**4**	**19**

a CCHA First All-Star Team (1988)
b IHL Second All-Star Team (1991, 1996)

Traded to **Tampa Bay** by **St. Louis** for Adam Creighton, October 6, 1994. Traded to **Chicago** by **Tampa Bay** with Jim Cummins and Jeff Buchanan for Paul Ysebaert and Rich Sutter, February 22, 1995.

TIMANDER, MATTIAS — BOS.

Defense. Shoots left. 6'1", 194 lbs. Born, Solleftea, Sweden, April 16, 1974.
(Boston's 7th choice, 208th overall, in 1992 Entry Draft).

			Regular Season					Playoffs				
Season	Club	Lea	GP	G	A	TP	PIM	GP	G	A	TP	PIM
1992-93	MoDo	Swe.	1	0	0	0	0					
1993-94	MoDo	Swe.	23	2	2	4	6	11	2	0	2	10
1994-95	MoDo	Swe.	39	8	9	17	24					
1995-96	MoDo	Swe.	37	4	10	14	34	7	1	1	2	8

TIMONEN, KIMMO — (TIH-moh-nehn) — L.A.

Defense. Shoots left. 5'9", 180 lbs. Born, Kuopio, Finland, March 18, 1975.
(Los Angeles' 11th choice, 250th overall, in 1993 Entry Draft).

			Regular Season					Playoffs				
Season	Club	Lea	GP	G	A	TP	PIM	GP	G	A	TP	PIM
1991-92	KalPa	Fin.	5	0	0	0	0					
1992-93	KalPa	Fin.	33	0	2	2	4					
1993-94	KalPa	Fin.	46	6	7	13	55					
1994-95	TPS	Fin.	45	3	4	7	10	13	0	1	1	6
1995-96	TPS	Fin.	48	3	21	24	22	9	1	2	3	12

TINORDI, MARK — WSH.

Defense. Shoots left. 6'4", 213 lbs. Born, Red Deer, Alta., May 9, 1966.

			Regular Season					Playoffs				
Season	Club	Lea	GP	G	A	TP	PIM	GP	G	A	TP	PIM
1982-83	Lethbridge	WHL	64	0	4	4	50	20	1	1	2	6
1983-84	Lethbridge	WHL	72	5	14	19	53	5	0	1	1	7
1984-85	Lethbridge	WHL	58	10	15	25	134	4	0	2	2	12
1985-86	Lethbridge	WHL	58	8	30	38	139	8	1	3	4	15
1986-87	Calgary	WHL	61	29	37	66	148					
	New Haven	AHL	2	0	0	0	2	2	0	0	0	0
1987-88	**NY Rangers**	**NHL**	**24**	**1**	**2**	**3**	**50**					
	Colorado	IHL	41	8	19	27	150	11	1	5	6	31
1988-89	**Minnesota**	**NHL**	**47**	**2**	**3**	**5**	**107**	**5**	**0**	**0**	**0**	**0**
	Kalamazoo	IHL	10	0	0	0	35					
1989-90	**Minnesota**	**NHL**	**66**	**3**	**7**	**10**	**240**	**7**	**0**	**1**	**1**	**16**
1990-91	**Minnesota**	**NHL**	**69**	**5**	**27**	**32**	**189**	**23**	**5**	**6**	**11**	**78**
1991-92	**Minnesota**	**NHL**	**63**	**4**	**24**	**28**	**179**	**7**	**1**	**2**	**3**	**11**
1992-93	**Minnesota**	**NHL**	**69**	**15**	**27**	**42**	**157**					
1993-94	**Dallas**	**NHL**	**61**	**6**	**18**	**24**	**143**					
1994-95	**Washington**	**NHL**	**42**	**3**	**9**	**12**	**71**	**1**	**0**	**0**	**0**	**2**
1995-96	**Washington**	**NHL**	**71**	**3**	**10**	**13**	**113**	**6**	**0**	**0**	**0**	**16**
	NHL Totals		**512**	**42**	**127**	**169**	**1249**	**49**	**6**	**9**	**15**	**123**

Played in NHL All-Star Game (1992)

Signed as a free agent by **NY Rangers**, January 4, 1987. Traded to **Minnesota** by **NY Rangers** with Paul Jerrard, the rights to Bret Barnett and Mike Sullivan, and Los Angeles' third round choice (previously acquired by NY Rangers — Minnesota selected Murray Garbutt) in 1989 Entry Draft for Brian Lawton, Igor Liba and the rights to Eric Bennett, October 11, 1988. Traded to **Washington** by **Dallas** with Rich Mrozik for Kevin Hatcher, January 18, 1995.

TIPLER, CURTIS — T.B.

Right wing. Shoots right. 6'5", 205 lbs. Born, Wainwright, Alta., May 9, 1978.
(Tampa Bay's 2nd choice, 69th overall, in 1996 Entry Draft).

			Regular Season					Playoffs				
Season	Club	Lea	GP	G	A	TP	PIM	GP	G	A	TP	PIM
1994-95	Leduc	Midget	36	30	32	62	36					
1995-96	Regina	WHL	69	27	38	65	65	11	3	1	4	4

TITOV, GERMAN — (TEE-tahf, GUHR-mihn) — CGY.

Center. Shoots left. 6'1", 190 lbs. Born, Moscow, USSR, October 16, 1965.
(Calgary's 10th choice, 252nd overall, in 1993 Entry Draft).

			Regular Season					Playoffs				
Season	Club	Lea	GP	G	A	TP	PIM	GP	G	A	TP	PIM
1982-83	Khimik	USSR	16	0	2	2	4					
1983-84						DID NOT PLAY						
1984-85						DID NOT PLAY						
1985-86						DID NOT PLAY						
1986-87	Khimik	USSR	23	1	0	1	10					
1987-88	Khimik	USSR	39	6	5	11	10					
1988-89	Khimik	USSR	44	10	3	13	24					
1989-90	Khimik	USSR	44	6	14	20	19					
1990-91	Khimik	USSR	45	13	11	24	28					
1991-92	Khimik	CIS	42	18	13	31	35					
1992-93	TPS	Fin.	47	25	19	44	49	12	5	12	17	10
1993-94	**Calgary**	**NHL**	**76**	**27**	**18**	**45**	**28**	**7**	**2**	**1**	**3**	**4**
1994-95	TPS	Fin.	14	6	6	12	20					
	Calgary	**NHL**	**40**	**12**	**12**	**24**	**16**	**7**	**5**	**3**	**8**	**10**
1995-96	**Calgary**	**NHL**	**82**	**28**	**39**	**67**	**24**	**4**	**0**	**2**	**2**	**0**
	NHL Totals		**198**	**67**	**69**	**136**	**68**	**18**	**7**	**6**	**13**	**14**

TJALLDEN, MIKAEL — FLA.

Defense. Shoots left. 6'2", 194 lbs. Born, Ornskoldsvik, Sweden, February 16, 1975.
(Florida's 4th choice, 67th overall, in 1993 Entry Draft).

			Regular Season					Playoffs				
Season	Club	Lea	GP	G	A	TP	PIM	GP	G	A	TP	PIM
1993-94	Sundsvall-Timra	Swe. 2	24	4	5	9	32					
1994-95	Sundsvall-Timra	Swe. 2	21	0	9	9	20					
1995-96	Sundsvall-Timra	Swe. 2	29	1	4	5	38	5	1	1	2	16

TJARNQVIST, DANIEL — (TUH-yahrn-kvihst) — FLA.

Defense. Shoots left. 6'2", 178 lbs. Born, Umea, Sweden, October 14, 1976.
(Florida's 5th choice, 88th overall, in 1995 Entry Draft).

			Regular Season					Playoffs				
Season	Club	Lea	GP	G	A	TP	PIM	GP	G	A	TP	PIM
1994-95	Rogle	Swe.	18	0	1	1	2					
	Rogle	Swe. 2	15	2	3	5	0					
1995-96	Rogle	Swe.	22	1	7	8	6					

TKACHUK, KEITH (kuh-CHUK) PHO.

Left wing. Shoots left. 6'2", 210 lbs. Born, Melrose, MA, March 28, 1972.
(Winnipeg's 1st choice, 19th overall, in 1990 Entry Draft).

			Regular Season					Playoffs				
Season	Club	Lea	GP	G	A	TP	PIM	GP	G	A	TP	PIM
1990-91	Boston U.	H.E.	36	17	23	40	70	....	....	....	....	....
1991-92	U.S. National	....	45	10	10	20	141	....	....	....	....	....
	U.S. Olympic	....	8	1	1	2	12	....	....	....	....	....
	Winnipeg	NHL	17	3	5	8	28	7	3	0	3	30
1992-93	Winnipeg	NHL	83	28	23	51	201	6	4	0	4	14
1993-94	Winnipeg	NHL	84	41	40	81	255	....	....	....	....	....
1994-95a	Winnipeg	NHL	48	22	29	51	152	....	....	....	....	....
1995-96	Winnipeg	NHL	76	50	48	98	156	6	1	2	3	22
	NHL Totals		308	144	145	289	792	19	8	2	10	66

a NHL Second All-Star Team (1995)

TOCCHET, RICK (TAH-keht) BOS.

Right wing. Shoots right. 6', 205 lbs. Born, Scarborough, Ont., April 9, 1964.
(Philadelphia's 5th choice, 121st overall, in 1983 Entry Draft).

			Regular Season					Playoffs				
Season	Club	Lea	GP	G	A	TP	PIM	GP	G	A	TP	PIM
1981-82	S.S. Marie	OHL	59	7	15	22	184	11	1	1	2	28
1982-83	S.S. Marie	OHL	66	32	34	66	146	16	4	13	17	67
1983-84	S.S. Marie	OHL	64	44	64	108	209	16	*22	14	*36	41
1984-85	Philadelphia	NHL	75	14	25	39	181	19	3	4	7	72
1985-86	Philadelphia	NHL	69	14	21	35	284	5	1	2	3	26
1986-87	Philadelphia	NHL	69	21	26	47	288	26	11	10	21	72
1987-88	Philadelphia	NHL	65	31	33	64	301	5	1	4	5	55
1988-89	Philadelphia	NHL	66	45	36	81	183	16	6	6	12	69
1989-90	Philadelphia	NHL	75	37	59	96	196	....	....	....	....	....
1990-91	Philadelphia	NHL	70	40	31	71	150	....	....	....	....	....
1991-92	Philadelphia	NHL	42	13	16	29	102	....	....	....	....	....
	Pittsburgh	NHL	19	14	16	30	49	14	6	13	19	24 ♦
1992-93	Pittsburgh	NHL	80	48	61	109	252	12	7	6	13	24
1993-94	Pittsburgh	NHL	51	14	26	40	134	6	2	3	5	20
1994-95	Los Angeles	NHL	36	18	17	35	70	....	....	....	....	....
1995-96	Los Angeles	NHL	44	13	23	36	117	....	....	....	....	....
	Boston	NHL	27	16	8	24	64	5	4	0	4	21
	NHL Totals		788	338	398	736	2371	108	41	48	89	383

Played in NHL All-Star Game (1989-91, 1993)

Traded to **Pittsburgh** by **Philadelphia** with Kjell Samuelsson, Ken Wregget and Philadelphia's third round choice (Dave Roche) in 1993 Entry Draft for Mark Recchi, Brian Benning and Los Angeles' first round choice (previously acquired by Pittsburgh — Philadelphia selected Jason Bowen) in 1992 Entry Draft, February 19, 1992 Traded to **Los Angeles** by **Pittsburgh** with Pittsburgh's second round choice (Pavel Rosa) in 1995 Entry Draft for Luc Robitaille, July 29, 1994. Traded to **Boston** by **Los Angeles** for Kevin Stevens, January 25, 1996.

TODD, KEVIN PIT.

Center. Shoots left. 5'10", 180 lbs. Born, Winnipeg, Man., May 4, 1968.
(New Jersey's 7th choice, 129th overall, in 1986 Entry Draft).

			Regular Season					Playoffs				
Season	Club	Lea	GP	G	A	TP	PIM	GP	G	A	TP	PIM
1985-86	Prince Albert	WHL	55	14	25	39	19	20	7	6	13	29
1986-87	Prince Albert	WHL	71	39	46	85	92	8	2	5	7	17
1987-88	Prince Albert	WHL	72	49	72	121	83	10	8	11	19	27
1988-89	New Jersey	NHL	1	0	0	0	0	....	....	....	....	....
	Utica	AHL	78	26	45	71	62	4	2	0	2	6
1989-90	Utica	AHL	71	18	36	54	72	5	2	4	6	2
1990-91	New Jersey	NHL	1	0	0	0	0	1	0	0	0	6
abc	Utica	AHL	75	37	*81	*118	75	....	....	....	....	....
1991-92d	New Jersey	NHL	80	21	42	63	69	7	3	2	5	8
1992-93	New Jersey	NHL	30	5	5	10	16	....	....	....	....	....
	Utica	AHL	2	2	1	3	0	....	....	....	....	....
	Edmonton	NHL	25	4	9	13	10	....	....	....	....	....
1993-94	Chicago	NHL	35	5	6	11	16	....	....	....	....	....
	Los Angeles	NHL	12	3	8	11	8	....	....	....	....	....
1994-95	Los Angeles	NHL	33	3	8	11	12	....	....	....	....	....
1995-96	Los Angeles	NHL	74	16	27	43	38	....	....	....	....	....
	NHL Totals		291	57	105	162	169	8	3	2	5	14

a AHL First All-Star Team (1991)
b Won Les Cunningham Plaque (MVP - AHL) (1991)
c Won John B. Sollenberger Trophy (Leading Scorer - AHL) (1991)
d NHL/Upper Deck All-Rookie Team (1992)

Traded to **Edmonton** by **New Jersey** with Zdeno Ciger for Bernie Nicholls, January 13, 1993. Traded to **Chicago** by **Edmonton** for Adam Bennett, October 7, 1993. Traded to **Los Angeles** by **Chicago** for Los Angeles' fourth round choice (Steve McLaren) in 1994 Entry Draft, March 21, 1994. Signed as a free agent by **Pittsburgh**, July 10, 1996.

TOMLAK, MIKE

Center/Left wing. Shoots left. 6'3", 205 lbs. Born, Thunder Bay, Ont., October 17, 1964.
(Toronto's 10th choice, 208th overall, in 1983 Entry Draft).

			Regular Season					Playoffs				
Season	Club	Lea	GP	G	A	TP	PIM	GP	G	A	TP	PIM
1982-83	Cornwall	OHL	70	18	49	67	26	....	....	....	....	....
1983-84	Cornwall	OHL	64	24	64	88	21	....	....	....	....	....
1984-85	Cornwall	OHL	66	30	70	100	9	....	....	....	....	....
1985-86	Western Ont.	OUAA	38	28	20	48	45	....	....	....	....	....
	Cdn. National	....	3	1	1	2	0	....	....	....	....	....
1986-87	Western Ont.	OUAA	38	16	30	46	10	....	....	....	....	....
1987-88	Western Ont.	OUAA	39	24	52	76	....	....	....	....	....	....
1988-89	Western Ont.	OUAA	35	16	34	50	....	....	....	....	....	....
1989-90	Hartford	NHL	70	7	14	21	48	7	0	1	1	2
1990-91	Hartford	NHL	64	8	8	16	55	3	0	0	0	2
	Springfield	AHL	15	4	9	13	15	....	....	....	....	....
1991-92	Hartford	NHL	6	0	0	0	0	....	....	....	....	....
	Springfield	AHL	39	16	21	37	24	....	....	....	....	....
1992-93	Springfield	AHL	38	16	21	37	56	5	1	1	2	2
1993-94	Hartford	NHL	1	0	0	0	0	....	....	....	....	....
	Springfield	AHL	79	44	56	100	53	4	2	5	7	4
1994-95	Milwaukee	IHL	63	27	41	68	54	15	4	5	9	8
1995-96	Milwaukee	IHL	82	11	32	43	68	5	0	2	2	6
	NHL Totals		141	15	22	37	103	10	0	1	1	4

Signed as a free agent by **Hartford**, November 14, 1988.

TOMLINSON, DAVE

Center. Shoots left. 5'11", 180 lbs. Born, North Vancouver, B.C., May 8, 1969.
(Toronto's 1st choice, 3rd overall, in 1989 Supplemental Draft).

			Regular Season					Playoffs				
Season	Club	Lea	GP	G	A	TP	PIM	GP	G	A	TP	PIM
1987-88	Boston U.	H.E.	34	16	20	36	28	....	....	....	....	....
1988-89	Boston U.	H.E.	34	16	30	46	40	....	....	....	....	....
1989-90	Boston U.	H.E.	43	15	22	37	53	....	....	....	....	....
1990-91	Boston U.	H.E.	41	30	30	60	55	....	....	....	....	....
1991-92	Toronto	NHL	3	0	0	0	2	....	....	....	....	....
	St. John's	AHL	75	23	34	57	75	12	4	5	9	6
1992-93	Toronto	NHL	3	0	0	0	2	....	....	....	....	....
	St. John's	AHL	70	36	48	84	115	9	1	4	5	8
1993-94	Winnipeg	NHL	31	1	3	4	24	....	....	....	....	....
	Moncton	AHL	39	23	23	46	38	20	6	6	12	24
1994-95	Cincinnati	IHL	78	38	72	110	79	10	7	3	10	8
	Florida	NHL	5	0	0	0	0	....	....	....	....	....
1995-96a	Cincinnati	IHL	81	39	57	96	127	17	4	12	16	18
	NHL Totals		42	1	3	4	28	....	....	....	....	....

a IHL Second All-Star Team (1996)

Traded to **Florida** by **Toronto** for cash, July 30, 1993. Traded to **Winnipeg** by **Florida** for Jason Cirone, August 3, 1993. Signed as a free agent by **Florida**, June 23, 1994.

TOMS, JEFF T.B.

Left wing. Shoots left. 6'5", 205 lbs. Born, Swift Current, Sask., June 4, 1974.
(New Jersey's 9th choice, 210th overall, in 1992 Entry Draft).

			Regular Season					Playoffs				
Season	Club	Lea	GP	G	A	TP	PIM	GP	G	A	TP	PIM
1991-92	S.S. Marie	OHL	36	9	5	14	0	16	0	1	1	2
1992-93	S.S. Marie	OHL	59	16	23	39	20	16	4	4	8	7
1993-94	S.S. Marie	OHL	64	52	45	97	19	14	11	4	15	2
1994-95	Atlanta	IHL	40	7	8	15	10	4	0	0	0	4
1995-96	Tampa Bay	NHL	1	0	0	0	0	....	....	....	....	....
	Atlanta	IHL	68	16	18	34	18	1	0	0	0	0
	NHL Totals		1	0	0	0	0	....	....	....	....	....

Traded to **Tampa Bay** by **New Jersey** for Vancouver's fourth round choice (previously acquired by Tampa Bay — later traded to Calgary — Calgary selected Ryan Duthie) in 1994 Entry Draft, May 31, 1994.

TOPOROWSKI, KERRY (toh-poh-ROW-skee) DET.

Defense. Shoots right. 6'2", 213 lbs. Born, Paddockwood, Sask., April 9, 1971.
(San Jose's 5th choice, 67th overall, in 1991 Entry Draft).

			Regular Season					Playoffs				
Season	Club	Lea	GP	G	A	TP	PIM	GP	G	A	TP	PIM
1989-90	Spokane	WHL	65	1	13	14	384	6	0	0	0	37
1990-91	Spokane	WHL	65	11	16	27	*505	15	2	2	4	*108
1991-92	Indianapolis	IHL	18	1	2	3	206	....	....	....	....	....
1992-93	Indianapolis	IHL	17	0	0	0	57	....	....	....	....	....
1993-94	Indianapolis	IHL	32	1	4	5	126	....	....	....	....	....
	Las Vegas	IHL	13	1	0	1	129	2	0	0	0	31
1994-95	Las Vegas	IHL	37	1	4	5	300	5	0	1	1	69
1995-96	Adirondack	AHL	53	1	5	6	283	....	....	....	....	....

Traded to **Chicago** by **San Jose** with San Jose's second round choice (later traded to Winnipeg — Winnipeg selected Boris Mironov) in 1992 Entry Draft for Doug Wilson, September 6, 1991. Signed as a free agent by **Detroit**, June 30, 1995.

TOPOROWSKI, SHAYNE (toh-poh-ROW-skee) TOR.

Right wing. Shoots right. 6'2", 210 lbs. Born, Paddockwood, Sask., August 6, 1975.
(Los Angeles' 1st choice, 42nd overall, in 1993 Entry Draft).

			Regular Season					Playoffs				
Season	Club	Lea	GP	G	A	TP	PIM	GP	G	A	TP	PIM
1991-92	Prince Albert	WHL	6	2	0	2	2	7	2	1	3	6
1992-93	Prince Albert	WHL	72	25	32	57	235	....	....	....	....	....
1993-94	Prince Albert	WHL	68	37	45	82	183	....	....	....	....	....
1994-95	Prince Albert	WHL	72	36	38	74	151	15	10	8	18	25
1995-96	St. John's	AHL	72	11	26	37	216	4	1	1	2	4

Traded to **Toronto** by **Los Angeles** with Dixon Ward, Guy Leveque and Kelly Fairchild for Eric Lacroix, Chris Snell and Toronto's fourth round choice (Eric Belanger) in 1996 Entry Draft, October 3, 1994.

TORGAYEV, PAVEL

Left wing. Shoots left. 6'1", 187 lbs. Born, Gorky, USSR, January 25, 1966.
(Calgary's 13th choice, 279th overall, in 1994 Entry Draft).

			Regular Season					Playoffs				
Season	Club	Lea	GP	G	A	TP	PIM	GP	G	A	TP	PIM
1982-83	Torpedo Gorky	USSR	4	0	0	0	0	....	....	....	....	....
1983-84	Torpedo Gorky	USSR	27	2	3	5	8	....	....	....	....	....
1984-85	Torpedo Gorky	USSR	47	11	5	16	52	....	....	....	....	....
1985-86	Torpedo Gorky	USSR	38	1	4	5	18	....	....	....	....	....
1986-87	Torpedo Gorky	USSR	40	6	9	15	30	....	....	....	....	....
1987-88	Torpedo Gorky	USSR	25	7	4	11	14	....	....	....	....	....
1988-89	Torpedo Gorky	USSR	26	6	3	9	17	....	....	....	....	....
1989-90	Torpedo Gorky	USSR	48	18	5	23	64	....	....	....	....	....
1990-91	Torpedo Nizhny	USSR	37	10	5	15	22	....	....	....	....	....
1991-92	Torpedo Nizhny	CIS	45	13	5	18	46	....	....	....	....	....
1992-93	Torpedo Nizhny	CIS	5	1	0	1	4	....	....	....	....	....
	Kiekko-67	Fin. 2	30	16	20	36	48	....	....	....	....	....
1993-94	TPS	Fin.	47	19	11	30	60	3	0	1	1	14
1994-95	JyP HT	Fin.	50	13	18	31	44	4	0	1	1	25
1995-96	Calgary	NHL	41	6	10	16	14	1	0	0	0	0
	Saint John	AHL	16	11	6	17	18	....	....	....	....	....
	NHL Totals		41	6	10	16	14	1	0	0	0	0

TORMANEN, ANTTI (TOHR-mah-nehn) OTT.

Right wing. Shoots left. 6'1", 198 lbs. Born, Espoo, Finland, September 19, 1970.
(Ottawa's 10th choice, 274th overall, in 1994 Entry Draft).

			Regular Season					Playoffs				
Season	Club	Lea	GP	G	A	TP	PIM	GP	G	A	TP	PIM
1990-91	Jokerit	Fin.	44	12	9	21	70	....	....	....	....	....
1991-92	Jokerit	Fin.	40	18	11	29	18	....	....	....	....	....
1992-93	Jokerit	Fin.	21	2	0	2	8	....	....	....	....	....
1993-94	Jokerit	Fin.	46	20	18	38	46	....	....	....	....	....
1994-95	Jokerit	Fin.	50	19	13	32	32	....	....	....	....	....
1995-96	Ottawa	NHL	50	7	8	15	28	....	....	....	....	....
	P.E.I.	AHL	22	6	11	17	17	5	2	3	5	2
	NHL Totals		50	7	8	15	28	....	....	....	....	....

TOWNSHEND, GRAEME (TOWN-SEHND, GRAY-ihm)

Right wing. Shoots right. 6'2", 225 lbs. Born, Kingston, Jamaica, October 2, 1965.

			Regular Season					Playoffs				
Season	Club	Lea	GP	G	A	TP	PIM	GP	G	A	TP	PIM
1985-86	RPI	ECAC	29	1	7	8	52	....	....	....	....	....
1986-87	RPI	ECAC	29	6	1	7	50	....	....	....	....	....
1987-88	RPI	ECAC	32	6	14	20	64	....	....	....	....	....
1988-89	RPI	ECAC	31	6	16	22	50	....	....	....	....	....
	Maine	AHL	5	2	1	3	11	....	....	....	....	....
1989-90	**Boston**	**NHL**	**4**	**0**	**0**	**0**	**7**	....	....	....	....	....
	Maine	AHL	64	15	13	28	162	....	....	....	....	....
1990-91	**Boston**	**NHL**	**18**	**2**	**5**	**7**	**12**	....	....	....	....	....
	Maine	AHL	46	16	10	26	119	2	2	0	2	4
1991-92	**NY Islanders**	**NHL**	**7**	**1**	**2**	**3**	**0**	....	....	....	....	....
	Capital Dist.	AHL	61	14	23	37	94	4	0	2	2	0
1992-93	**NY Islanders**	**NHL**	**2**	**0**	**0**	**0**	**0**	....	....	....	....	....
	Capital Dist.	AHL	67	29	21	50	45	2	0	0	0	0
1993-94	**Ottawa**	**NHL**	**14**	**0**	**0**	**0**	**9**	....	....	....	....	....
	P.E.I.	AHL	56	16	13	29	107	....	....	....	....	....
1994-95	Houston	IHL	71	19	21	40	204	4	0	2	2	22
1995-96	Minnesota	IHL	3	0	0	0	0	....	....	....	....	....
	Houston	IHL	63	21	11	32	97	....	....	....	....	....
	NHL Totals		**45**	**3**	**7**	**10**	**28**	....	....	....	....	....

Signed as a free agent by **Boston**, May 12, 1989. Signed as a free agent by **NY Islanders**, September 3, 1991. Signed as a free agent by **Ottawa**, August 24, 1993.

TRAVERSE, PATRICK OTT.

Defense. Shoots left. 6'3", 200 lbs. Born, Montreal, Que., March 14, 1974.
(Ottawa's 3rd choice, 50th overall, in 1992 Entry Draft).

			Regular Season					Playoffs				
Season	Club	Lea	GP	G	A	TP	PIM	GP	G	A	TP	PIM
1991-92	Shawinigan	QMJHL	59	3	11	14	12	10	0	0	0	4
1992-93	St-Jean	QMJHL	68	6	30	36	24	4	0	1	1	2
	New Haven	AHL	2	0	0	0	2	....	....	....	....	....
1993-94	St-Jean	QMJHL	66	15	37	52	30	5	0	4	4	4
	P.E.I.	AHL	3	0	1	1	2	....	....	....	....	....
1994-95	P.E.I.	AHL	70	5	13	18	19	7	0	2	2	0
1995-96	**Ottawa**	**NHL**	**5**	**0**	**0**	**0**	**2**	....	....	....	....	....
	P.E.I.	AHL	55	4	21	25	32	5	1	2	3	2
	NHL Totals		**5**	**0**	**0**	**0**	**2**	....	....	....	....	....

TRAYNOR, PAUL PHO.

Defense. Shoots left. 6'1", 170 lbs. Born, Thunder Bay, Ont., September 14, 1977.
(Winnipeg's 8th choice, 162nd overall, in 1995 Entry Draft).

			Regular Season					Playoffs				
Season	Club	Lea	GP	G	A	TP	PIM	GP	G	A	TP	PIM
1994-95	Kitchener	OHL	50	3	8	11	25	5	0	0	0	4
1995-96	Kitchener	OHL	62	7	27	34	65	12	1	6	7	23

TREBIL, DANIEL ANA.

Defense. Shoots right. 6'3", 185 lbs. Born, Edina, MN, April 10, 1974.
(New Jersey's 7th choice, 138th overall, in 1992 Entry Draft).

			Regular Season					Playoffs				
Season	Club	Lea	GP	G	A	TP	PIM	GP	G	A	TP	PIM
1992-93	U. Minnesota	WCHA	36	2	11	13	16	....	....	....	....	....
1993-94	U. Minnesota	WCHA	42	1	21	22	24	....	....	....	....	....
1994-95	U. Minnesota	WCHA	44	10	33	43	10	....	....	....	....	....
1995-96ab	U. Minnesota	WCHA	42	11	35	46	36	....	....	....	....	....

a WCHA Second All-Star Team (1996)
b NCAA West Second All-American Team (1996)

Signed as a free agent by **Anaheim**, May 30, 1996.

TREMBLAY, YANICK TOR.

Defense. Shoots right. 6'2", 185 lbs. Born, Pointe-aux-Trembles, Que., November 15, 1975.
(Toronto's 4th choice, 145th overall, in 1995 Entry Draft).

			Regular Season					Playoffs				
Season	Club	Lea	GP	G	A	TP	PIM	GP	G	A	TP	PIM
1994-95	Beauport	QMJHL	70	10	32	42	22	17	6	8	14	6
1995-96	Beauport	QMJHL	61	12	33	45	42	20	3	16	19	18
	St. John's	AHL	3	0	1	1	0	....	....	....	....	....

TREPANIER, PASCAL COL.

Defense. Shoots right. 6', 205 lbs. Born, Gaspe, Que., April 9, 1973.

			Regular Season					Playoffs				
Season	Club	Lea	GP	G	A	TP	PIM	GP	G	A	TP	PIM
1995-96	Cornwall	AHL	70	13	20	33	142	8	1	2	3	24

Signed as a free agent by **Colorado**, August 30, 1995.

TRIPP, JOHN COL.

Right wing. Shoots right. 6'2", 207 lbs. Born, Kingston, Ont., May 4, 1977.
(Colorado's 3rd choice, 77th overall, in 1995 Entry Draft).

			Regular Season					Playoffs				
Season	Club	Lea	GP	G	A	TP	PIM	GP	G	A	TP	PIM
1994-95	Oshawa	OHL	58	6	11	17	53	7	0	1	1	4
1995-96	Oshawa	OHL	56	13	14	27	95	5	1	1	2	13

TRNKA, PAVEL (tehrn-KAH) ANA.

Defense. Shoots left. 6'3", 190 lbs. Born, Plzen, Czech., July 27, 1976.
(Anaheim's 5th choice, 106th overall, in 1994 Entry Draft).

			Regular Season					Playoffs				
Season	Club	Lea	GP	G	A	TP	PIM	GP	G	A	TP	PIM
1993-94	Skoda Plzen	Czech.	12	0	1	1	....	....	....	....	....	....
1994-95	Kladno	Czech.	28	0	5	5	24	....	....	....	....	....
	Interconex Plzen	Czech.	6	0	0	0	0	....	....	....	....	....
1995-96	Baltimore	AHL	69	2	6	8	44	6	0	0	0	2

TROMBLEY, RHETT

Right wing. Shoots right. 6'3", 230 lbs. Born, Regina, Sask., August 9, 1974.

			Regular Season					Playoffs				
Season	Club	Lea	GP	G	A	TP	PIM	GP	G	A	TP	PIM
1991-92	Tacoma	WHL	7	0	0	0	32	....	....	....	....	....
	Saskatoon	WHL	50	3	4	7	181	18	1	1	2	53
1992-93	Saskatoon	WHL	27	0	0	0	47	....	....	....	....	....
	Victoria	WHL	12	0	0	0	67	....	....	....	....	....
1993-94	Victoria	WHL	21	0	3	3	67	....	....	....	....	....
1994-95	Toledo	ECHL	13	0	2	2	80	....	....	....	....	....
	Las Vegas	IHL	30	4	0	4	141	3	0	0	0	10
1995-96	Carolina	AHL	34	2	2	4	163	....	....	....	....	....
	Las Vegas	IHL	15	0	2	2	56	....	....	....	....	....

Signed as a free agent by **Florida**, April 5, 1995.

TSULYGIN, NIKOLAI (tsoo-LEE-gihn) ANA.

Defense. Shoots right. 6'4", 205 lbs. Born, Ufa, USSR, May 29, 1975.
(Anaheim's 2nd choice, 30th overall, in 1993 Entry Draft).

			Regular Season					Playoffs				
Season	Club	Lea	GP	G	A	TP	PIM	GP	G	A	TP	PIM
1992-93	Ufa Salavat	CIS	42	5	4	9	21	2	0	0	0	0
1993-94	Ufa Salavat	CIS	43	0	14	14	24	5	0	1	1	0
1994-95	CSKA	CIS	16	0	0	0	12	....	....	....	....	....
	Ufa Salavat	CIS	13	2	2	4	10	7	0	0	0	4
1995-96	Baltimore	AHL	78	3	18	21	109	12	0	5	5	18

TSYGUROV, DENIS (tsih-GOO-rawv)

Defense. Shoots left. 6'3", 198 lbs. Born, Chelyabinsk, USSR, February 26, 1971.
(Buffalo's 1st choice, 38th overall, in 1993 Entry Draft).

			Regular Season					Playoffs				
Season	Club	Lea	GP	G	A	TP	PIM	GP	G	A	TP	PIM
1988-89	Chelyabinsk	USSR	8	0	0	0	2	....	....	....	....	....
1989-90	Chelyabinsk	USSR	27	0	1	1	18	....	....	....	....	....
1990-91	Chelyabinsk	USSR	26	0	1	1	16	....	....	....	....	....
1991-92	Togliatti	CIS	29	3	2	5	6	....	....	....	....	....
1992-93a	Togliatti	CIS	37	7	13	20	29	10	1	1	2	6
1993-94	**Buffalo**	**NHL**	**8**	**0**	**0**	**0**	**8**	....	....	....	....	....
	Rochester	AHL	24	1	10	11	10	1	0	1	1	0
1994-95	Togliatti	CIS	10	3	7	10	6	....	....	....	....	....
	Buffalo	**NHL**	**4**	**0**	**0**	**0**	**4**	....	....	....	....	....
	Los Angeles	**NHL**	**21**	**0**	**0**	**0**	**11**	....	....	....	....	....
1995-96	**Los Angeles**	**NHL**	**18**	**1**	**5**	**6**	**22**	....	....	....	....	....
	Phoenix	IHL	17	1	3	4	10	....	....	....	....	....
	Togliatti	CIS	3	0	0	0	4	....	....	....	....	....
	NHL Totals		**51**	**1**	**5**	**6**	**45**	....	....	....	....	....

a CIS All-Star Team (1993)

Traded to **Los Angeles** by **Buffalo** with Philippe Boucher and Grant Fuhr for Alexei Zhitnik, Robb Stauber, Charlie Huddy and Los Angeles' fifth round choice (Marian Menhart) in 1995 Entry Draft, February 14, 1995.

TSYPLAKOV, VLADIMIR L.A.

Left wing. Shoots left. 6', 185 lbs. Born, Moscow, USSR, April 18, 1969.
(Los Angeles' 4th choice, 59th overall, in 1995 Entry Draft).

			Regular Season					Playoffs				
Season	Club	Lea	GP	G	A	TP	PIM	GP	G	A	TP	PIM
1988-89	Minsk D'amo	USSR	19	6	1	7	4	....	....	....	....	....
1989-90	Minsk D'amo	USSR	47	11	6	17	20	....	....	....	....	....
1990-91	Minsk D'amo	USSR	28	6	5	11	14	....	....	....	....	....
1991-92	Minsk D'amo	CIS	29	10	9	19	16	....	....	....	....	....
1992-93	Detroit	ColHL	44	33	43	76	20	6	5	4	9	6
	Indianapolis	IHL	11	6	7	13	4	5	1	1	2	2
1993-94	Fort Wayne	IHL	63	31	32	63	51	14	6	8	14	16
1994-95	Fort Wayne	IHL	79	38	40	78	39	4	2	4	6	2
1995-96	**Los Angeles**	**NHL**	**23**	**5**	**5**	**10**	**4**	....	....	....	....	....
	Las Vegas	IHL	9	5	6	11	4	....	....	....	....	....
	NHL Totals		**23**	**5**	**5**	**10**	**4**	....	....	....	....	....

TUCKER, DARCY MTL.

Center. Shoots left. 5'10", 170 lbs. Born, Castor, Alta., March 15, 1975.
(Montreal's 8th choice, 151st overall, in 1993 Entry Draft).

			Regular Season					Playoffs				
Season	Club	Lea	GP	G	A	TP	PIM	GP	G	A	TP	PIM
1991-92	Kamloops	WHL	26	3	10	13	32	9	0	1	1	16
1992-93	Kamloops	WHL	67	31	58	89	155	13	7	6	13	34
1993-94abcd	Kamloops	WHL	66	52	88	140	143	19	9	*18	*27	43
1994-95ac	Kamloops	WHL	64	64	73	137	94	21	*16	15	*31	19
1995-96	**Montreal**	**NHL**	**3**	**0**	**0**	**0**	**0**	....	....	....	....	....
e	Fredericton	AHL	74	29	64	93	174	7	7	3	10	14
	NHL Totals		**3**	**0**	**0**	**0**	**0**	....	....	....	....	....

a WHL West First All-Star Team (1994, 1995)
b Canadian Major Junior First All-Star Team (1994)
c Memorial Cup All-Star Team (1994, 1995)
d Won Stafford Smythe Memorial Trophy (Memorial Cup Tournament MVP) (1994)
e Won Dudley "Red" Garrett Memorial Trophy (Top Rookie - AHL) (1996)

TUCKER, JOHN

Center. Shoots right. 6', 200 lbs. Born, Windsor, Ont., September 29, 1964.
(Buffalo's 4th choice, 31st overall, in 1983 Entry Draft).

			Regular Season					Playoffs				
Season	Club	Lea	GP	G	A	TP	PIM	GP	G	A	TP	PIM
1981-82	Kitchener	OHL	67	16	32	48	32	15	2	3	5	2
1982-83	Kitchener	OHL	70	60	80	140	33	11	5	9	14	10
1983-84	**Buffalo**	**NHL**	**21**	**12**	**4**	**16**	**4**	**3**	**1**	**0**	**1**	**0**
a	Kitchener	OHL	39	40	60	100	25	12	12	18	30	8
1984-85	**Buffalo**	**NHL**	**64**	**22**	**27**	**49**	**21**	**5**	**1**	**5**	**6**	**0**
1985-86	**Buffalo**	**NHL**	**75**	**31**	**34**	**65**	**39**	....	....	....	....	....
1986-87	**Buffalo**	**NHL**	**54**	**17**	**34**	**51**	**21**	....	....	....	....	....
1987-88	**Buffalo**	**NHL**	**45**	**19**	**19**	**38**	**20**	**6**	**7**	**3**	**10**	**18**
1988-89	**Buffalo**	**NHL**	**60**	**13**	**31**	**44**	**31**	**3**	**0**	**3**	**3**	**0**
1989-90	**Buffalo**	**NHL**	**8**	**1**	**2**	**3**	**2**	....	....	....	....	....
	Washington	**NHL**	**38**	**9**	**19**	**28**	**10**	**12**	**1**	**7**	**8**	**4**
1990-91	**Buffalo**	**NHL**	**18**	**1**	**3**	**4**	**4**	....	....	....	....	....
	NY Islanders	**NHL**	**20**	**3**	**4**	**7**	**4**	....	....	....	....	....
1991-92	Asiago	Italy	18	16	21	37	6	11	7	13	20	15
1992-93	**Tampa Bay**	**NHL**	**78**	**17**	**39**	**56**	**69**	....	....	....	....	....
1993-94	**Tampa Bay**	**NHL**	**66**	**17**	**23**	**40**	**28**	....	....	....	....	....
1994-95	**Tampa Bay**	**NHL**	**46**	**12**	**13**	**25**	**14**	....	....	....	....	....
1995-96	**Tampa Bay**	**NHL**	**63**	**3**	**7**	**10**	**18**	**2**	**0**	**0**	**0**	**2**
	NHL Totals		**656**	**177**	**259**	**436**	**285**	**31**	**10**	**18**	**28**	**24**

a OHL First All-Star Team (1984)

Traded to **Washington** by **Buffalo** for future considerations, January 5, 1990. Traded to **Buffalo** by **Washington** for cash, July 3, 1990. Traded to **NY Islanders** by **Buffalo** for future considerations, January 21, 1991. Signed as a free agent by **Tampa Bay**, August 5, 1992.

TULLY, BRENT — VAN.

Defense. Shoots right. 6'3", 195 lbs. Born, Peterborough, Ont., March 26, 1974.
(Vancouver's 5th choice, 93rd overall, in 1992 Entry Draft).

			Regular Season					Playoffs				
Season	Club	Lea	GP	G	A	TP	PIM	GP	G	A	TP	PIM
1990-91	Peterborough	OHL	45	3	5	8	35	2	0	0	0	0
1991-92	Peterborough	OHL	65	9	23	32	65	10	0	0	0	2
1992-93a	Peterborough	OHL	59	15	45	60	81	21	8	24	32	32
1993-94	Peterborough	OHL	37	17	26	43	81	7	5	3	8	12
	Cdn. National	....	1	0	1	1	0	....	....	....	....	....
	Hamilton	AHL	1	0	0	0	0	1	1	0	1	0
1994-95	Syracuse	AHL	63	6	3	9	106	....	....	....	....	....
1995-96	Syracuse	AHL	52	3	13	16	114	....	....	....	....	....

a OHL Second All-Star Team (1993)

TUOHY, JOHN — WSH.

Defense. Shoots left. 6'2", 190 lbs. Born, Baldwin, NY, February 2, 1976.
(Washington's 9th choice, 223rd overall, in 1994 Entry Draft).

			Regular Season					Playoffs				
Season	Club	Lea	GP	G	A	TP	PIM	GP	G	A	TP	PIM
1994-95	Providence	H.E.	16	1	1	2	18	....	....	....	....	....
1995-96	Providence	H.E.	32	0	6	6	28	....	....	....	....	....

TUOMAINEN, MARKO — (TOO-oh-migh-nehn) EDM.

Right wing. Shoots right. 6'3", 203 lbs. Born, Kuopio, Finland, April 25, 1972.
(Edmonton's 10th choice, 205th overall, in 1992 Entry Draft).

			Regular Season					Playoffs				
Season	Club	Lea	GP	G	A	TP	PIM	GP	G	A	TP	PIM
1989-90	KalPa	Fin.	5	0	0	0	0	....	....	....	....	....
1990-91	KalPa	Fin.	30	2	1	3	2	8	0	0	0	6
1991-92	Clarkson	ECAC	28	11	12	23	32	....	....	....	....	....
1992-93a	Clarkson	ECAC	35	25	30	55	26	....	....	....	....	....
1993-94	Clarkson	ECAC	34	23	29	52	60	....	....	....	....	....
1994-95ab	Clarkson	ECAC	37	23	38	61	34	....	....	....	....	....
	Edmonton	**NHL**	**4**	**0**	**0**	**0**	**0**	....	....	....	....	....
1995-96	Cape Breton	AHL	58	25	35	60	71	....	....	....	....	....
	NHL Totals		**4**	**0**	**0**	**0**	**0**	....	....	....	....	....

a ECAC First All-Star Team (1993, 1995)
b NCAA East Second All-American Team (1995)

TURCOTTE, DARREN — S.J.

Center. Shoots left. 6', 178 lbs. Born, Boston, MA, March 2, 1968.
(NY Rangers' 6th choice, 114th overall, in 1986 Entry Draft).

			Regular Season					Playoffs				
Season	Club	Lea	GP	G	A	TP	PIM	GP	G	A	TP	PIM
1984-85	North Bay	OHL	62	33	32	65	28	8	0	2	2	0
1985-86	North Bay	OHL	62	35	37	72	35	10	3	4	7	8
1986-87	North Bay	OHL	55	30	48	78	20	18	12	8	20	6
1987-88	North Bay	OHL	32	30	33	63	16	4	3	0	3	4
	Colorado	IHL	8	4	3	7	9	6	2	6	8	8
1988-89	**NY Rangers**	**NHL**	**20**	**7**	**3**	**10**	**4**	**1**	**0**	**0**	**0**	**0**
	Denver	IHL	40	21	28	49	32	....	....	....	....	....
1989-90	**NY Rangers**	**NHL**	**76**	**32**	**34**	**66**	**32**	**10**	**1**	**6**	**7**	**4**
1990-91	**NY Rangers**	**NHL**	**74**	**26**	**41**	**67**	**37**	**6**	**1**	**2**	**3**	**0**
1991-92	**NY Rangers**	**NHL**	**71**	**30**	**23**	**53**	**57**	**8**	**4**	**0**	**4**	**6**
1992-93	**NY Rangers**	**NHL**	**71**	**25**	**28**	**53**	**40**	....	....	....	....	....
1993-94	**NY Rangers**	**NHL**	**13**	**2**	**4**	**6**	**13**	....	....	....	....	....
	Hartford	**NHL**	**19**	**2**	**11**	**13**	**4**	....	....	....	....	....
1994-95	**Hartford**	**NHL**	**47**	**17**	**18**	**35**	**22**	....	....	....	....	....
1995-96	**Winnipeg**	**NHL**	**59**	**16**	**16**	**32**	**26**	....	....	....	....	....
	San Jose	**NHL**	**9**	**6**	**5**	**11**	**4**	....	....	....	....	....
	NHL Totals		**459**	**163**	**183**	**346**	**239**	**25**	**6**	**8**	**14**	**10**

Played in NHL All-Star Game (1991)

Traded to **Hartford** by **NY Rangers** with James Patrick for Steve Larmer, Nick Kypreos, Barry Richter and Hartford's sixth round choice (Yuri Litvinov) in 1994 Entry Draft, November 2, 1993. Traded to **Winnipeg** by **Hartford** for Nelson Emerson, October 6, 1995. Traded to **San Jose** by **Winnipeg** with Dallas' second round choice (previously acquired by Winnipeg — later traded to Chicago — Chicago selected Remi Royer) in 1996 Entry Draft for Craig Janney, March 18, 1996.

TURGEON, PIERRE — (TUHR-zhaw) MTL.

Center. Shoots left. 6'1", 195 lbs. Born, Rouyn, Que., August 28, 1969.
(Buffalo's 1st choice, 1st overall, in 1987 Entry Draft).

			Regular Season					Playoffs				
Season	Club	Lea	GP	G	A	TP	PIM	GP	G	A	TP	PIM
1985-86	Granby	QMJHL	69	47	67	114	31	....	....	....	....	....
	Cdn. National	....	11	2	4	6	2	....	....	....	....	....
1986-87	Granby	QMJHL	58	69	85	154	8	7	9	6	15	15
1987-88	**Buffalo**	**NHL**	**76**	**14**	**28**	**42**	**34**	**6**	**4**	**3**	**7**	**4**
1988-89	**Buffalo**	**NHL**	**80**	**34**	**54**	**88**	**26**	**5**	**3**	**5**	**8**	**2**
1989-90	**Buffalo**	**NHL**	**80**	**40**	**66**	**106**	**29**	**6**	**2**	**4**	**6**	**2**
1990-91	**Buffalo**	**NHL**	**78**	**32**	**47**	**79**	**26**	**6**	**3**	**1**	**4**	**6**
1991-92	**Buffalo**	**NHL**	**8**	**2**	**6**	**8**	**4**	....	....	....	....	....
	NY Islanders	**NHL**	**69**	**38**	**49**	**87**	**16**	....	....	....	....	....
1992-93a	**NY Islanders**	**NHL**	**83**	**58**	**74**	**132**	**26**	**11**	**6**	**7**	**13**	**0**
1993-94	**NY Islanders**	**NHL**	**69**	**38**	**56**	**94**	**18**	**4**	**0**	**1**	**1**	**0**
1994-95	**NY Islanders**	**NHL**	**34**	**13**	**14**	**27**	**10**	....	....	....	....	....
	Montreal	**NHL**	**15**	**11**	**9**	**20**	**4**	....	....	....	....	....
1995-96	**Montreal**	**NHL**	**80**	**38**	**58**	**96**	**44**	**6**	**2**	**4**	**6**	**2**
	NHL Totals		**672**	**318**	**461**	**779**	**237**	**44**	**20**	**25**	**45**	**16**

a Won Lady Byng Memorial Trophy (1993)

Played in NHL All-Star Game (1990, 1993, 1994, 1996)

Traded to **NY Islanders** by **Buffalo** with Uwe Krupp, Benoit Hogue and Dave McLlwain for Pat Lafontaine, Randy Hillier, Randy Wood and NY Islanders' fourth round choice (Dean Melanson) in 1992 Entry Draft, October 25, 1991. Traded to **Montreal** by **NY Islanders** with Vladimir Malakhov for Kirk Muller, Mathieu Schneider and Craig Darby, April 5, 1995.

TURGEON, SYLVAIN — (TUHR-zhaw)

Left wing. Shoots left. 6', 200 lbs. Born, Noranda, Que., January 17, 1965.
(Hartford's 1st choice, 2nd overall, in 1983 Entry Draft).

			Regular Season					Playoffs				
Season	Club	Lea	GP	G	A	TP	PIM	GP	G	A	TP	PIM
1981-82	Hull	QMJHL	57	33	40	73	78	14	11	11	22	16
1982-83a	Hull	QMJHL	67	54	109	163	103	7	8	7	15	10
1983-84b	**Hartford**	**NHL**	**76**	**40**	**32**	**72**	**55**	....	....	....	....	....
1984-85	**Hartford**	**NHL**	**64**	**31**	**31**	**62**	**67**	....	....	....	....	....
1985-86	**Hartford**	**NHL**	**76**	**45**	**34**	**79**	**88**	**9**	**2**	**3**	**5**	**4**
1986-87	**Hartford**	**NHL**	**41**	**23**	**13**	**36**	**45**	**6**	**1**	**2**	**3**	**4**
1987-88	**Hartford**	**NHL**	**71**	**23**	**26**	**49**	**71**	**6**	**0**	**0**	**0**	**4**
1988-89	**Hartford**	**NHL**	**42**	**16**	**14**	**30**	**40**	**4**	**0**	**2**	**2**	**4**
1989-90	**New Jersey**	**NHL**	**72**	**30**	**17**	**47**	**81**	**1**	**0**	**0**	**0**	**0**
1990-91	**Montreal**	**NHL**	**19**	**5**	**7**	**12**	**20**	**5**	**0**	**0**	**0**	**2**
1991-92	**Montreal**	**NHL**	**56**	**9**	**11**	**20**	**39**	**5**	**1**	**0**	**1**	**4**
1992-93	**Ottawa**	**NHL**	**72**	**25**	**18**	**43**	**104**	....	....	....	....	....
1993-94	**Ottawa**	**NHL**	**47**	**11**	**15**	**26**	**52**	....	....	....	....	....
1994-95	**Ottawa**	**NHL**	**33**	**11**	**8**	**19**	**29**	....	....	....	....	....
1995-96	Houston	IHL	65	28	31	59	66	....	....	....	....	....
	NHL Totals		**669**	**269**	**226**	**495**	**691**	**36**	**4**	**7**	**11**	**22**

a QMJHL First All-Star Team (1983)
b NHL All-Rookie Team (1984)

Played in NHL All-Star Game (1986)

Traded to **New Jersey** by **Hartford** for Pat Verbeek, June 17, 1989. Traded to **Montreal** by **New Jersey** for Claude Lemieux, September 4, 1990. Claimed by **Ottawa** from **Montreal** in Expansion Draft, June 18, 1992.

TURKOVSKY, VASILI — WSH.

Defense. Shoots left. 6'2", 198 lbs. Born, Saratov, USSR, September 3, 1974.
(Washington's 9th choice, 199th overall, in 1995 Entry Draft).

			Regular Season					Playoffs				
Season	Club	Lea	GP	G	A	TP	PIM	GP	G	A	TP	PIM
1992-93	Saratov	CIS	41	0	0	0	50	....	....	....	....	....
1993-94	CSKA	CIS	46	0	2	2	60	3	0	0	0	0
1994-95	CSKA	CIS	46	1	2	3	22	3	0	0	0	2
1995-96	CSKA	CIS	51	0	1	1	88	3	0	0	0	0

TUZZOLINO, TONY — COL.

Right wing. Shoots right. 6'2", 180 lbs. Born, Buffalo, NY, October 9, 1975.
(Quebec's 7th choice, 113th overall, in 1994 Entry Draft).

			Regular Season					Playoffs				
Season	Club	Lea	GP	G	A	TP	PIM	GP	G	A	TP	PIM
1993-94	Michigan State	CCHA	35	4	3	7	46	....	....	....	....	....
1994-95	Michigan State	CCHA	39	9	18	27	81	....	....	....	....	....
1995-96	Michigan State	CCHA	41	12	17	29	120	....	....	....	....	....

TVERDOVSKY, OLEG — (tvehr-DOHV-skee) PHO.

Defense. Shoots left. 6', 185 lbs. Born, Donetsk, USSR, May 18, 1976.
(Anaheim's 1st choice, 2nd overall, in 1994 Entry Draft).

			Regular Season					Playoffs				
Season	Club	Lea	GP	G	A	TP	PIM	GP	G	A	TP	PIM
1992-93	Soviet Wings	CIS	21	0	1	1	6	6	0	0	0	0
1993-94	Soviet Wings	CIS	46	4	10	14	22	3	1	0	1	2
1994-95	Brandon	WHL	7	1	4	5	4	....	....	....	....	....
	Anaheim	**NHL**	**36**	**3**	**9**	**12**	**14**	....	....	....	....	....
1995-96	**Anaheim**	**NHL**	**51**	**7**	**15**	**22**	**35**	....	....	....	....	....
	Winnipeg	**NHL**	**31**	**0**	**8**	**8**	**6**	**6**	**0**	**1**	**1**	**0**
	NHL Totals		**118**	**10**	**32**	**42**	**55**	**6**	**0**	**1**	**1**	**0**

Traded to **Winnipeg** by **Anaheim** with Chad Kilger and Anaheim's third round choice (Per-Anton Lundstrom) in 1996 Entry Draft for Teemu Selanne, Marc Chouinard and Winnipeg's fourth round choice (later traded to Toronto — later traded to Montreal — Montreal selected Kim Staal) in 1996 Entry Draft, February 7, 1996.

TWIST, TONY — ST.L.

Left wing/Defense. Shoots left. 6'1", 220 lbs. Born, Sherwood Park, Alta., May 9, 1968.
(St. Louis' 9th choice, 177th overall, in 1988 Entry Draft).

			Regular Season					Playoffs				
Season	Club	Lea	GP	G	A	TP	PIM	GP	G	A	TP	PIM
1987-88	Saskatoon	WHL	55	1	8	9	226	10	1	1	2	6
1988-89	Peoria	IHL	67	3	8	11	312	....	....	....	....	....
1989-90	**St. Louis**	**NHL**	**28**	**0**	**0**	**0**	**124**	....	....	....	....	....
	Peoria	IHL	36	1	5	6	200	5	0	1	1	8
1990-91	Peoria	IHL	38	2	10	12	244	....	....	....	....	....
	Quebec	**NHL**	**24**	**0**	**0**	**0**	**104**	....	....	....	....	....
1991-92	**Quebec**	**NHL**	**44**	**0**	**1**	**1**	**164**	....	....	....	....	....
1992-93	**Quebec**	**NHL**	**34**	**0**	**2**	**2**	**64**	....	....	....	....	....
1993-94	**Quebec**	**NHL**	**49**	**0**	**4**	**4**	**101**	....	....	....	....	....
1994-95	**St. Louis**	**NHL**	**28**	**3**	**0**	**3**	**89**	**1**	**0**	**0**	**0**	**6**
1995-96	**St. Louis**	**NHL**	**51**	**3**	**2**	**5**	**100**	**10**	**1**	**1**	**2**	**16**
	NHL Totals		**258**	**6**	**9**	**15**	**746**	**11**	**1**	**1**	**2**	**22**

Traded to **Quebec** by **St. Louis** with Herb Raglan and Andy Rymsha for Darin Kimble, February 4, 1991. Signed as a free agent by **St. Louis**, August 16, 1994.

TYSBUK, EVGENY — DAL.

Defense. Shoots left. 6', 183 lbs. Born, Chebarkul, USSR, February 2, 1978.
(Dallas' 5th choice, 113th overall, in 1996 Entry Draft).

			Regular Season					Playoffs				
Season	Club	Lea	GP	G	A	TP	PIM	GP	G	A	TP	PIM
1995-96	Yaroslavl 2	CIS 2				UNAVAILABLE						

ULANOV, IGOR (oo-LAH-nahf, EE-gohr) — T.B.

Defense. Shoots left. 6'1", 205 lbs. Born, Krasnokamsk, USSR, October 1, 1969.
(Winnipeg's 8th choice, 203rd overall, in 1991 Entry Draft).

			Regular Season					Playoffs				
Season	Club	Lea	GP	G	A	TP	PIM	GP	G	A	TP	PIM
1990-91	Khimik	USSR	41	2	2	4	52	....	....	....	....	....
1991-92	Khimik	CIS	27	1	4	5	24	....	....	....	....	....
	Winnipeg	**NHL**	**27**	**2**	**9**	**11**	**67**	**7**	**0**	**0**	**0**	**39**
	Moncton	AHL	3	0	1	1	16	....	....	....	....	....
1992-93	**Winnipeg**	**NHL**	**56**	**2**	**14**	**16**	**124**	**4**	**0**	**0**	**0**	**4**
	Moncton	AHL	9	1	3	4	26	....	....	....	....	....
	Fort Wayne	IHL	3	0	1	1	29	....	....	....	....	....
1993-94	**Winnipeg**	**NHL**	**74**	**0**	**17**	**17**	**165**	....	....	....	....	....
1994-95	**Winnipeg**	**NHL**	**19**	**1**	**3**	**4**	**27**	....	....	....	....	....
	Washington	**NHL**	**3**	**0**	**1**	**1**	**2**	**2**	**0**	**0**	**0**	**4**
1995-96	**Chicago**	**NHL**	**53**	**1**	**8**	**9**	**92**	....	....	....	....	....
	Indianapolis	IHL	1	0	0	0	0	....	....	....	....	....
	Tampa Bay	**NHL**	**11**	**2**	**1**	**3**	**24**	**5**	**0**	**0**	**0**	**15**
	NHL Totals		**243**	**8**	**53**	**61**	**501**	**18**	**0**	**0**	**0**	**62**

Traded to **Washington** by **Winnipeg** with Mike Eagles for Washington's third (later traded to Dallas — Dallas selected Sergei Gusev) and fifth (Brian Elder) round choices in 1995 Entry Draft, April 7, 1995. Traded to **Chicago** by **Washington** for Chicago's third round choice (Dave Weninger) in 1996 Entry Draft, October 17, 1995. Traded to **Tampa Bay** by **Chicago** with Patrick Poulin and Chicago's second round choice (later traded to New Jersey — New Jersey selected Pierre Dagenais) in 1996 Entry Draft for Enrico Ciccone and Tampa Bay's second round choice (Jeff Paul) in 1996 Entry Draft, March 20, 1996.

URICK, BRIAN — EDM.

Right wing. Shoots right. 6'1", 190 lbs. Born, Minneapolis, MN, January 25, 1977.
(Edmonton's 5th choice, 114th overall, in 1996 Entry Draft).

			Regular Season					Playoffs				
Season	Club	Lea	GP	G	A	TP	PIM	GP	G	A	TP	PIM
1994-95	Minnetonka	HS	24	30	29	59	28	....	....	....	....	....
1995-96	Nortre Dame	CCHA	36	12	15	27	66	....	....	....	....	....

USTORF, STEFAN (OOSH-tohrf, SHTEH-fuhn) — WSH.

Center. Shoots left. 6', 185 lbs. Born, Kaufbeuren, Germany, January 3, 1974.
(Washington's 3rd choice, 53rd overall, in 1992 Entry Draft).

			Regular Season					Playoffs				
Season	Club	Lea	GP	G	A	TP	PIM	GP	G	A	TP	PIM
1991-92	Kaufbeuren	Ger.	41	2	22	24	46	5	2	7	9	6
1992-93	Kaufbeuren	Ger.	37	14	18	32	32	3	1	0	1	10
1993-94	Kaufbeuren	Ger.	38	10	20	30	21	3	0	0	0	4
1994-95	Portland	AHL	63	21	38	59	51	7	1	6	7	7
1995-96	**Washington**	**NHL**	**48**	**7**	**10**	**17**	**14**	**5**	**0**	**0**	**0**	**0**
	Portland	AHL	8	1	4	5	6	....	....	....	....	....
	NHL Totals		**48**	**7**	**10**	**17**	**14**	**5**	**0**	**0**	**0**	**0**

USTUGOV, ANATOLY — DET.

Left wing. Shoots left. 5'10", 165 lbs. Born, Yaroslavl, USSR, June 26, 1977.
(Detroit's 4th choice, 104th overall, in 1995 Entry Draft).

			Regular Season					Playoffs				
Season	Club	Lea	GP	G	A	TP	PIM	GP	G	A	TP	PIM
1994-95	Yaroslavl	CIS	5	0	0	0	0	....	....	....	....	....
1995-96	Yaroslavl	CIS	9	1	0	1	4	....	....	....	....	....

VACHON, NICK — L.A.

Center. Shoots left. 5'10", 185 lbs. Born, Montreal, Que., July 20, 1972.
(Toronto's 11th choice, 241st overall, in 1990 Entry Draft).

			Regular Season					Playoffs				
Season	Club	Lea	GP	G	A	TP	PIM	GP	G	A	TP	PIM
1990-91	Boston U.	H.E.	8	0	1	1	4	....	....	....	....	....
1991-92	Boston U.	H.E.	16	6	7	13	10	....	....	....	....	....
	Portland	WHL	25	9	19	28	46	6	0	3	3	14
1992-93	Portland	WHL	66	33	58	91	100	16	11	7	18	34
1993-94	Atlanta	IHL	3	1	1	2	0	....	....	....	....	....
	Knoxville	ECHL	61	29	57	86	139	3	0	0	0	2
1994-95	Phoenix	IHL	64	13	26	39	137	9	1	2	3	24
1995-96	Phoenix	IHL	73	13	17	30	168	1	0	0	0	2

Signed as a free agent by **Los Angeles**, September 12, 1995.

VALK, GARRY (VAHLK) — ANA.

Left wing. Shoots left. 6'1", 205 lbs. Born, Edmonton, Alta., November 27, 1967.
(Vancouver's 5th choice, 108th overall, in 1987 Entry Draft).

			Regular Season					Playoffs				
Season	Club	Lea	GP	G	A	TP	PIM	GP	G	A	TP	PIM
1987-88	North Dakota	WCHA	38	23	12	35	64	....	....	....	....	....
1988-89	North Dakota	WCHA	40	14	17	31	71	....	....	....	....	....
1989-90	North Dakota	WCHA	43	22	17	39	92	....	....	....	....	....
1990-91	**Vancouver**	**NHL**	**59**	**10**	**11**	**21**	**67**	**5**	**0**	**0**	**0**	**20**
	Milwaukee	IHL	10	12	4	16	13	3	0	0	0	2
1991-92	**Vancouver**	**NHL**	**65**	**8**	**17**	**25**	**56**	**4**	**0**	**0**	**0**	**5**
1992-93	**Vancouver**	**NHL**	**48**	**6**	**7**	**13**	**77**	**7**	**0**	**1**	**1**	**12**
	Hamilton	AHL	7	3	6	9	6	....	....	....	....	....
1993-94	**Anaheim**	**NHL**	**78**	**18**	**27**	**45**	**100**	....	....	....	....	....
1994-95	**Anaheim**	**NHL**	**36**	**3**	**6**	**9**	**34**	....	....	....	....	....
1995-96	**Anaheim**	**NHL**	**79**	**12**	**12**	**24**	**125**	....	....	....	....	....
	NHL Totals		**365**	**57**	**80**	**137**	**459**	**16**	**0**	**1**	**1**	**37**

Claimed by **Anaheim** from **Vancouver** in NHL Waiver Draft, October 3, 1993.

VAN ALLEN, SHAUN — ANA.

Center. Shoots left. 6'1", 200 lbs. Born, Shaunavon, Sask., August 29, 1967.
(Edmonton's 5th choice, 105th overall, in 1987 Entry Draft).

			Regular Season					Playoffs				
Season	Club	Lea	GP	G	A	TP	PIM	GP	G	A	TP	PIM
1984-85	Swift Current	WHL	61	12	20	32	136	....	....	....	....	....
1985-86	Saskatoon	WHL	55	12	11	23	43	13	4	8	12	28
1986-87	Saskatoon	WHL	72	38	59	97	116	11	4	6	10	24
1987-88	Milwaukee	IHL	40	14	28	42	34	....	....	....	....	....
	Nova Scotia	AHL	19	4	10	14	17	4	1	1	2	4
1988-89	Cape Breton	AHL	76	32	42	74	81	....	....	....	....	....
1989-90	Cape Breton	AHL	61	25	44	69	83	4	0	2	2	8
1990-91	**Edmonton**	**NHL**	**2**	**0**	**0**	**0**	**0**	....	....	....	....	....
a	Cape Breton	AHL	76	25	75	100	182	4	0	1	1	8
1991-92bc	Cape Breton	AHL	77	29	*84	*113	80	5	3	7	10	14
1992-93	**Edmonton**	**NHL**	**21**	**1**	**4**	**5**	**6**	....	....	....	....	....
	Cape Breton	AHL	43	14	62	76	68	15	8	9	17	18
1993-94	**Anaheim**	**NHL**	**80**	**8**	**25**	**33**	**64**	....	....	....	....	....
1994-95	**Anaheim**	**NHL**	**45**	**8**	**21**	**29**	**32**	....	....	....	....	....
1995-96	**Anaheim**	**NHL**	**49**	**8**	**17**	**25**	**41**	....	....	....	....	....
	NHL Totals		**197**	**25**	**67**	**92**	**143**	....	....	....	....	....

a AHL Second All-Star Team (1991)
b Won John B. Sollenberger Trophy (Top Scorer - AHL) (1992)
c AHL First All-Star Team (1992)

Signed as a free agent by **Anaheim**, July 22, 1993.

VAN BRUGGEN, ANDREW — WSH.

Right wing. Shoots right. 6'5", 220 lbs. Born, Iowa City, IA, April 24, 1977.
(Washington's 9th choice, 153rd overall, in 1996 Entry Draft).

			Regular Season					Playoffs				
Season	Club	Lea	GP	G	A	TP	PIM	GP	G	A	TP	PIM
1994-95	Sioux City	USHL	47	7	20	27	143	....	....	....	....	....
1995-96	N. Michigan	WCHA	36	1	7	8	63	....	....	....	....	....

VANDENBUSSCHE, RYAN (van-dehn-BUHSH) — NYR

Right wing. Shoots right. 5'11", 187 lbs. Born, Simcoe, Ont., February 28, 1973.
(Toronto's 8th choice, 173rd overall, in 1992 Entry Draft).

			Regular Season					Playoffs				
Season	Club	Lea	GP	G	A	TP	PIM	GP	G	A	TP	PIM
1990-91	Cornwall	OHL	49	3	8	11	139	....	....	....	....	....
1991-92	Cornwall	OHL	61	13	15	28	232	6	0	2	2	9
1992-93	Newmarket	OHL	30	15	12	27	161	....	....	....	....	....
	Guelph	OHL	29	3	14	17	99	5	1	3	4	13
	St. John's	AHL	1	0	0	0	0	....	....	....	....	....
1993-94	St. John's	AHL	44	4	10	14	124	....	....	....	....	....
	Springfield	AHL	9	1	2	3	29	5	0	0	0	16
1994-95	St. John's	AHL	53	2	13	15	239	....	....	....	....	....
1995-96	Binghamton	AHL	68	3	17	20	240	4	0	0	0	9

Signed as a free agent by **NY Rangers**, August 22, 1995.

VAN DYK, CHRIS (van-DIGHK) — CHI.

Defense. Shoots right. 6'2", 185 lbs. Born, Welland, Ont., February 18, 1977.
(Chicago's 4th choice, 82nd overall, in 1995 Entry Draft).

			Regular Season					Playoffs				
Season	Club	Lea	GP	G	A	TP	PIM	GP	G	A	TP	PIM
1994-95	Windsor	OHL	51	4	23	27	55	10	0	2	2	4
1995-96	Windsor	OHL	28	1	12	13	36	....	....	....	....	....

VAN IMPE, DARREN — ANA.

Defense. Shoots left. 6', 195 lbs. Born, Saskatoon, Sask., May 18, 1973.
(NY Islanders' 7th choice, 170th overall, in 1993 Entry Draft).

			Regular Season					Playoffs				
Season	Club	Lea	GP	G	A	TP	PIM	GP	G	A	TP	PIM
1990-91	Prince Albert	WHL	70	15	45	60	57	3	1	1	2	2
1991-92	Prince Albert	WHL	69	9	37	46	129	8	1	5	6	10
1992-93a	Red Deer	WHL	54	23	47	70	118	4	2	5	7	16
1993-94a	Red Deer	WHL	58	20	64	84	125	4	2	4	6	6
1994-95	San Diego	IHL	76	6	17	23	74	5	0	0	0	0
	Anaheim	**NHL**	**1**	**0**	**1**	**1**	**4**	....	....	....	....	....
1995-96	**Anaheim**	**NHL**	**16**	**1**	**2**	**3**	**14**	....	....	....	....	....
	Baltimore	AHL	63	11	47	58	79	....	....	....	....	....
	NHL Totals		**17**	**1**	**3**	**4**	**18**	....	....	....	....	....

a WHL First All-Star Team (1993, 1994)

Traded to **Anaheim** by **NY Islanders** for Anaheim's eighth round choice (Mike Broda) in 1995 Entry Draft, August 31, 1994.

VAN OENE, DARREN (van OH-uhn) — BUF.

Left wing. Shoots left. 6'3", 207 lbs. Born, Edmonton, Alta., January 18, 1978.
(Buffalo's 3rd choice, 33rd overall, in 1996 Entry Draft).

			Regular Season					Playoffs				
Season	Club	Lea	GP	G	A	TP	PIM	GP	G	A	TP	PIM
1994-95	Brandon	WHL	58	5	13	18	106	18	1	1	2	34
1995-96	Brandon	WHL	47	10	18	28	126	18	1	6	7	*78

VARADA, VACLAV (VAH-rah-dah) — BUF.

Right wing. Shoots left. 6', 200 lbs. Born, Vsetin, Czech., April 26, 1976.
(San Jose's 4th choice, 89th overall, in 1994 Entry Draft).

			Regular Season					Playoffs				
Season	Club	Lea	GP	G	A	TP	PIM	GP	G	A	TP	PIM
1992-93	Vitkovice	Czech.	1	0	0	0	....	....	....	....	....	....
1993-94	Vitkovice	Czech.	24	6	7	13	....	5	1	1	2	....
1994-95	Tacoma	WHL	68	50	38	88	108	4	4	3	7	11
1995-96	Kelowna	WHL	59	39	46	85	100	6	3	3	6	16
	Buffalo	**NHL**	**1**	**0**	**0**	**0**	**0**	....	....	....	....	....
	Rochester	AHL	5	3	0	3	4	....	....	....	....	....
	NHL Totals		**1**	**0**	**0**	**0**	**0**	....	....	....	....	....

Traded to **Buffalo** by **San Jose** with Martin Spahnel, an optional first round choice in 1996 Entry Draft and Philadelphia's fourth round choice (previously acquired by San Jose — Buffalo selected Mike Martone) in 1996 Entry Draft for Doug Bodger, November 16, 1995.

VARIS, PETRI — S.J.

Left wing. Shoots left. 6'1", 200 lbs. Born, Varkaus, Finland, May 13, 1969.
(San Jose's 7th choice, 132nd overall, in 1993 Entry Draft).

			Regular Season					Playoffs				
Season	Club	Lea	GP	G	A	TP	PIM	GP	G	A	TP	PIM
1990-91	KooKoo	Fin. 2	44	20	31	51	42	....	....	....	....	....
1991-92a	Assat	Fin.	36	13	23	36	24	....	....	....	....	....
1992-93	Assat	Fin.	46	14	35	49	42	8	2	2	4	12
1993-94	Jokerit	Fin.	31	14	15	29	16	11	3	4	7	6
1994-95	Jokerit	Fin.	47	21	20	41	53	11	7	2	9	10
1995-96	Jokerit	Fin.	50	28	28	56	22	11	12	7	19	6

a Finnish Rookie of the Year (1992)

VARVIO, JARKKO — (VAHR-vee-oh, YAHR-koh)

Right wing. Shoots right. 5'9", 175 lbs. Born, Tampere, Finland, April 28, 1972.
(Minnesota's 1st choice, 34th overall, in 1992 Entry Draft).

			Regular Season					Playoffs				
Season	Club	Lea	GP	G	A	TP	PIM	GP	G	A	TP	PIM
1989-90	Ilves	Fin.	1	0	0	0	0	....	....	....	....	....
1990-91	Ilves	Fin.	37	10	7	17	6	....	....	....	....	....
1991-92	HPK	Fin.	41	25	9	34	6	....	....	....	....	....
1992-93	HPK	Fin.	40	29	19	48	16	12	3	2	5	8
1993-94	**Dallas**	**NHL**	**8**	**2**	**3**	**5**	**4**	....	....	....	....	....
	Kalamazoo	IHL	58	29	16	45	18	1	0	0	0	0
1994-95	HPK	Fin.	19	7	8	15	4	....	....	....	....	....
	Dallas	**NHL**	**5**	**1**	**1**	**2**	**0**	....	....	....	....	....
	Kalamazoo	IHL	7	0	0	0	2	....	....	....	....	....
1995-96	Lukko	Fin.	47	14	13	27	32	8	5	0	5	4
	NHL Totals		**13**	**3**	**4**	**7**	**4**	....	....	....	....	....

VASILEVSKII, ALEXANDER — (vah-sih-LEHV-skee) ST.L.

Right wing. Shoots left. 5'11", 190 lbs. Born, Kiev, USSR, January 8, 1975.
(St. Louis' 9th choice, 271st overall, in 1993 Entry Draft).

			Regular Season					Playoffs				
Season	Club	Lea	GP	G	A	TP	PIM	GP	G	A	TP	PIM
1992-93	Victoria	WHL	71	27	25	52	52	....	....	....	....	....
1993-94	Victoria	WHL	69	34	51	85	78	....	....	....	....	....
1994-95	Prince George	WHL	48	32	34	66	52	....	....	....	....	....
	Brandon	WHL	23	6	11	17	39	18	3	6	9	34
1995-96	**St. Louis**	**NHL**	**1**	**0**	**0**	**0**	**0**	....	....	....	....	....
	Worcester	AHL	69	18	21	39	112	4	2	1	3	10
	NHL Totals		**1**	**0**	**0**	**0**	**0**					

VASILIEV, ALEXEI — (vah-SEE-lee-ehf) NYR

Defense. Shoots left. 6'1", 189 lbs. Born, Yaroslavl, USSR, September 1, 1977.
(NY Rangers' 4th choice, 110th overall, in 1995 Entry Draft).

			Regular Season					Playoffs				
Season	Club	Lea	GP	G	A	TP	PIM	GP	G	A	TP	PIM
1993-94	Yaroslavl	CIS	2	0	1	1	4	....	....	....	....	....
1994-95	Yaroslavl-2	CIS 2				UNAVAILABLE						
1995-96	Yaroslavl	CIS	40	4	7	11	4	....	....	....	....	....

VASILIEV, ANDREI — (vah-SEE-lee-ehf)

Left wing. Shoots right. 5'9", 180 lbs. Born, Voskresensk, USSR, March 30, 1972.
(NY Islanders' 11th choice, 248th overall, in 1992 Entry Draft).

			Regular Season					Playoffs				
Season	Club	Lea	GP	G	A	TP	PIM	GP	G	A	TP	PIM
1991-92	CSKA	CIS	28	7	2	9	2	....	....	....	....	....
1992-93	Khimik	CIS	34	4	8	12	20	....	....	....	....	....
1993-94	CSKA	CIS	46	17	6	23	8	3	1	0	1	0
1994-95	Denver	IHL	74	28	37	65	48	13	9	4	13	22
	NY Islanders	**NHL**	**2**	**0**	**0**	**0**	**2**	....	....	....	....	....
1995-96	**NY Islanders**	**NHL**	**10**	**2**	**5**	**7**	**2**	....	....	....	....	....
	Utah	IHL	43	26	20	46	34	22	12	4	16	18
	NHL Totals		**12**	**2**	**5**	**7**	**4**	....	....	....	....	....

VASKE, DENNIS — (VAS-kee) NYI

Defense. Shoots left. 6'2", 210 lbs. Born, Rockford, IL, October 11, 1967.
(NY Islanders' 2nd choice, 38th overall, in 1986 Entry Draft).

			Regular Season					Playoffs				
Season	Club	Lea	GP	G	A	TP	PIM	GP	G	A	TP	PIM
1986-87	Minn.-Duluth	WCHA	33	0	2	2	40	....	....	....	....	....
1987-88	Minn.-Duluth	WCHA	39	1	6	7	90	....	....	....	....	....
1988-89	Minn.-Duluth	WCHA	37	9	19	28	86	....	....	....	....	....
1989-90	Minn.-Duluth	WCHA	37	5	24	29	72	....	....	....	....	....
1990-91	**NY Islanders**	**NHL**	**5**	**0**	**0**	**0**	**2**	....	....	....	....	....
	Capital Dist.	AHL	67	10	10	20	65	....	....	....	....	....
1991-92	**NY Islanders**	**NHL**	**39**	**0**	**1**	**1**	**39**	....	....	....	....	....
	Capital Dist.	AHL	31	1	11	12	59	....	....	....	....	....
1992-93	**NY Islanders**	**NHL**	**27**	**1**	**5**	**6**	**32**	**18**	**0**	**6**	**6**	**14**
	Capital Dist.	AHL	42	4	15	19	70	....	....	....	....	....
1993-94	**NY Islanders**	**NHL**	**65**	**2**	**11**	**13**	**76**	**4**	**0**	**1**	**1**	**2**
1994-95	**NY Islanders**	**NHL**	**41**	**1**	**11**	**12**	**53**	....	....	....	....	....
1995-96	**NY Islanders**	**NHL**	**19**	**1**	**6**	**7**	**21**	....	....	....	....	....
	NHL Totals		**196**	**5**	**34**	**39**	**223**	**22**	**0**	**7**	**7**	**16**

VEILLEUX, ERIC — (VAY-yew) COL.

Center. Shoots left. 5'7", 148 lbs. Born, Quebec, Que., February 20, 1972.

			Regular Season					Playoffs				
Season	Club	Lea	GP	G	A	TP	PIM	GP	G	A	TP	PIM
1991-92	Laval	QMJHL	60	31	40	71	87	10	3	5	8	27
1992-93	Laval	QMJHL	70	55	70	125	100	13	9	11	20	19
1993-94	Cornwall	AHL	77	8	19	27	69	13	1	7	8	20
1994-95	Cornwall	AHL	70	13	23	36	93	13	1	1	2	20
1995-96	Cornwall	AHL	71	25	35	60	119	8	2	6	8	2

Signed as a free agent by **Quebec**, October 6, 1993.

VERBEEK, PAT — (vuhr-BEEK) DAL.

Right/Left wing. Shoots right. 5'9", 192 lbs. Born, Sarnia, Ont., May 24, 1964.
(New Jersey's 3rd choice, 43rd overall, in 1982 Entry Draft).

			Regular Season					Playoffs				
Season	Club	Lea	GP	G	A	TP	PIM	GP	G	A	TP	PIM
1981-82	Sudbury	OHL	66	37	51	88	180	....	....	....	....	....
1982-83	**New Jersey**	**NHL**	**6**	**3**	**2**	**5**	**8**	....	....	....	....	....
	Sudbury	OHL	61	40	67	107	184	....	....	....	....	....
1983-84	**New Jersey**	**NHL**	**79**	**20**	**27**	**47**	**158**	....	....	....	....	....
1984-85	**New Jersey**	**NHL**	**78**	**15**	**18**	**33**	**162**	....	....	....	....	....
1985-86	**New Jersey**	**NHL**	**76**	**25**	**28**	**53**	**79**	....	....	....	....	....
1986-87	**New Jersey**	**NHL**	**74**	**35**	**24**	**59**	**120**	....	....	....	....	....
1987-88	**New Jersey**	**NHL**	**73**	**46**	**31**	**77**	**227**	**20**	**4**	**8**	**12**	**51**
1988-89	**New Jersey**	**NHL**	**77**	**26**	**21**	**47**	**189**	....	....	....	....	....
1989-90	**Hartford**	**NHL**	**80**	**44**	**45**	**89**	**228**	**7**	**2**	**2**	**4**	**26**
1990-91	**Hartford**	**NHL**	**80**	**43**	**39**	**82**	**246**	**6**	**3**	**2**	**5**	**40**
1991-92	**Hartford**	**NHL**	**76**	**22**	**35**	**57**	**243**	**7**	**0**	**2**	**2**	**12**
1992-93	**Hartford**	**NHL**	**84**	**39**	**43**	**82**	**197**	....	....	....	....	....
1993-94	**Hartford**	**NHL**	**84**	**37**	**38**	**75**	**177**	....	....	....	....	....
1994-95	**Hartford**	**NHL**	**29**	**7**	**11**	**18**	**53**	....	....	....	....	....
	NY Rangers	**NHL**	**19**	**10**	**5**	**15**	**18**	**10**	**4**	**6**	**10**	**20**
1995-96	**NY Rangers**	**NHL**	**69**	**41**	**41**	**82**	**129**	**11**	**3**	**6**	**9**	**12**
	NHL Totals		**984**	**413**	**408**	**821**	**2234**	**61**	**16**	**26**	**42**	**161**

Played in NHL All-Star Game (1991, 1996)

Traded to **Hartford** by **New Jersey** for Sylvain Turgeon, June 17, 1989. Traded to **NY Rangers** by **Hartford** for Glen Featherstone, Michael Stewart, NY Rangers' first round choice (Jean-Sebastien Giguere) in 1995 Entry Draft and fourth round choice (Steve Wasylko) in 1996 Entry Draft, March 23, 1995. Signed as a free agent by **Dallas**, August 21, 1996.

VERCIK, RUDOLF — (VEHR-chihk) NYR

Left wing. Shoots left. 6'1", 189 lbs. Born, Bratislava, Czech., March 19, 1976.
(NY Rangers' 2nd choice, 52nd overall, in 1994 Entry Draft).

			Regular Season					Playoffs				
Season	Club	Lea	GP	G	A	TP	PIM	GP	G	A	TP	PIM
1993-94	Bratislava	Slovak	17	1	4	5	14	....	....	....	....	....
1994-95	Bratislava	Slovak	33	14	9	23	22	....	....	....	....	....
1995-96	Bratislava	Slovak	28	7	3	10	61	13	1	0	1	....

VIAL, DENNIS — (vee-AL) OTT.

Left wing. Shoots left. 6'2", 218 lbs. Born, Sault Ste. Marie, Ont., April 10, 1969.
(NY Rangers' 5th choice, 110th overall, in 1988 Entry Draft).

			Regular Season					Playoffs				
Season	Club	Lea	GP	G	A	TP	PIM	GP	G	A	TP	PIM
1985-86	Hamilton	OHL	31	1	1	2	66	....	....	....	....	....
1986-87	Hamilton	OHL	53	1	8	9	194	8	0	0	0	8
1987-88	Hamilton	OHL	52	3	17	20	229	13	2	2	4	49
1988-89	Niagara Falls	OHL	50	10	27	37	227	15	1	7	8	44
1989-90	Flint	IHL	79	6	29	35	351	4	0	0	0	10
1990-91	**NY Rangers**	**NHL**	**21**	**0**	**0**	**0**	**61**	....	....	....	....	....
	Binghamton	AHL	40	2	7	9	250	....	....	....	....	....
	Detroit	**NHL**	**9**	**0**	**0**	**0**	**16**	....	....	....	....	....
1991-92	**Detroit**	**NHL**	**27**	**1**	**0**	**1**	**72**	....	....	....	....	....
	Adirondack	AHL	20	2	4	6	107	17	1	3	4	43
1992-93	**Detroit**	**NHL**	**9**	**0**	**1**	**1**	**20**	....	....	....	....	....
	Adirondack	AHL	30	2	11	13	177	11	1	1	2	14
1993-94	**Ottawa**	**NHL**	**55**	**2**	**5**	**7**	**214**	....	....	....	....	....
1994-95	**Ottawa**	**NHL**	**27**	**0**	**4**	**4**	**65**	....	....	....	....	....
1995-96	**Ottawa**	**NHL**	**64**	**1**	**4**	**5**	**276**	....	....	....	....	....
	NHL Totals		**212**	**4**	**14**	**18**	**724**	....	....	....	....	....

Traded to **Detroit** by **NY Rangers** with Kevin Miller and Jim Cummins for Joey Kocur and Per Djoos, March 5, 1991. Traded to **Quebec** by **Detroit** with Doug Crossman for cash, June 15, 1992. Traded to **Detroit** by **Quebec** for cash, September 9, 1992. Traded to **Tampa Bay** by **Detroit** for Steve Maltais, June 8, 1993. Claimed by **Anaheim** from **Tampa Bay** in Expansion Draft, June 24, 1993. Claimed by **Ottawa** from **Anaheim** in Phase II of Expansion Draft, June 25, 1993.

VIITAKOSKI, VESA — (VEE-ee-tah-kohs-kee)

Left wing. Shoots left. 6'3", 215 lbs. Born, Lappeenranta, Finland, February 13, 1971.
(Calgary's 3rd choice, 32nd overall, in 1990 Entry Draft).

			Regular Season					Playoffs				
Season	Club	Lea	GP	G	A	TP	PIM	GP	G	A	TP	PIM
1988-89	SaiPa	Fin.	11	4	1	5	6	....	....	....	....	....
1989-90	SaiPa	Fin.	44	24	10	34	8	....	....	....	....	....
1990-91	Tappara	Fin.	41	17	23	40	14	3	2	0	2	4
1991-92	Tappara	Fin.	44	19	19	38	39	....	....	....	....	....
1992-93	Tappara	Fin.	48	27	27	54	28	....	....	....	....	....
1993-94	**Calgary**	**NHL**	**8**	**1**	**2**	**3**	**0**	....	....	....	....	....
	Saint John	AHL	67	28	39	67	24	5	1	2	3	2
1994-95	Saint John	AHL	56	17	26	43	8	4	0	1	1	2
	Calgary	**NHL**	**10**	**1**	**2**	**3**	**6**	....	....	....	....	....
1995-96	**Calgary**	**NHL**	**5**	**0**	**0**	**0**	**2**	....	....	....	....	....
	Saint John	AHL	48	18	29	47	48	....	....	....	....	....
	Cornwall	AHL	10	7	6	13	4	8	1	3	4	2
	NHL Totals		**23**	**2**	**4**	**6**	**8**	....	....	....	....	....

Traded to **Colorado** by **Calgary** for Paxton Schulte, March 19, 1996.

VINCENT, PAUL — TOR.

Center. Shoots left. 6'4", 200 lbs. Born, Utica, NY, January 4, 1975.
(Toronto's 4th choice, 149th overall, in 1993 Entry Draft).

			Regular Season					Playoffs				
Season	Club	Lea	GP	G	A	TP	PIM	GP	G	A	TP	PIM
1993-94	Seattle	WHL	66	27	26	53	57	8	1	3	4	8
1994-95	Seattle	WHL	3	0	2	2	2	....	....	....	....	....
	Swift Current	WHL	62	59	39	98	85	6	3	2	5	17
	St. John's	AHL	2	0	2	2	0	....	....	....	....	....
1995-96	St. John's	AHL	16	2	3	5	2	1	0	0	0	2
	Raleigh	ECHL	30	12	9	21	29	....	....	....	....	....

VIRTUE, TERRY — ST.L.

Defense. Shoots right. 6', 200 lbs. Born, Scarborough, Ont., August 12, 1970.

			Regular Season					Playoffs				
Season	Club	Lea	GP	G	A	TP	PIM	GP	G	A	TP	PIM
1988-89	Victoria	WHL	8	1	1	2	13	....	....	....	....	....
1989-90	Tri-City	WHL	58	2	19	21	167	....	....	....	....	....
1990-91	Tri-City	WHL	11	1	8	9	24	....	....	....	....	....
	Portland	WHL	59	9	44	53	127	....	....	....	....	....
1991-92	Roanoke	ECHL	38	4	22	26	165	....	....	....	....	....
	Louisville	ECHL	23	1	15	16	58	13	0	8	8	49
1992-93	Louisville	ECHL	28	0	17	17	84	....	....	....	....	....
	Wheeling	ECHL	31	3	15	18	86	16	3	5	8	18
1993-94	Wheeling	ECHL	34	5	28	33	61	6	2	2	4	4
	Cape Breton	AHL	26	4	6	10	10	5	0	0	0	17
1994-95	Worcester	AHL	73	14	25	39	183	....	....	....	....	....
1995-96	Worcester	AHL	76	7	31	38	234	4	0	0	0	4

Signed as a free agent by **St. Louis**, January 29, 1996.

VISHEAU, MARK — (VEE-SHOO) PHO.

Defense. Shoots right. 6'4", 200 lbs. Born, Burlington, Ont., June 27, 1973.
(Winnipeg's 4th choice, 84th overall, in 1992 Entry Draft).

			Regular Season					Playoffs				
Season	Club	Lea	GP	G	A	TP	PIM	GP	G	A	TP	PIM
1990-91	London	OHL	59	4	11	15	40	7	0	1	1	6
1991-92	London	OHL	66	5	31	36	104	10	0	4	4	27
1992-93	London	OHL	62	8	52	60	88	12	0	5	5	26
1993-94	**Winnipeg**	**NHL**	**1**	**0**	**0**	**0**	**0**	....	....	....	....	....
	Moncton	AHL	48	4	5	9	58	....	....	....	....	....
1994-95	Springfield	AHL	35	0	4	4	94	....	....	....	....	....
1995-96	Cape Breton	AHL	8	0	0	0	30	....	....	....	....	....
	Minnesota	IHL	10	0	0	0	25	....	....	....	....	....
	Wheeling	ECHL	7	1	2	3	14	7	0	3	3	4
	NHL Totals		**1**	**0**	**0**	**0**	**0**	....	....	....	....	....

VLASAK, TOMAS — L.A.

Center. Shoots right. 5'10", 175 lbs. Born, Prague, Czech., February 1, 1975.
(Los Angeles' 6th choice, 120th overall, in 1993 Entry Draft).

			Regular Season					Playoffs				
Season	Club	Lea	GP	G	A	TP	PIM	GP	G	A	TP	PIM
1992-93	Slavia Praha	Czech. 2	31	17	6	23	....	....	....	....	....	....
1993-94	Litvinov	Czech.	41	16	11	27	0	4	0	1	1	....
1994-95	Litvinov	Czech.	35	6	14	20	4	4	0	0	0	4
1995-96	Litvinov	Czech.	35	10	22	32	....	15	5	5	10	....

VLASEKKOV, DMITRI — (vlah-SEHN-kahv) CGY.

Left wing. Shoots left. 5'11", 183 lbs. Born, Olenigorsk, USSR, January 1, 1978.
(Calgary's 4th choice, 73rd overall, in 1996 Entry Draft.)

			Regular Season					Playoffs				
Season	Club	Lea	GP	G	A	TP	PIM	GP	G	A	TP	PIM
1995-96	Yaroslavl	CIS	17	1	1	2	4	1	0	0	0	0

VOLCHKOV, ALEXANDER — (VOHLCH-kahf) WSH.

Center. Shoots left. 6'1", 194 lbs. Born, Moscow, USSR, September 25, 1977.
(Washington's 1st choice, 4th overall, in 1996 Entry Draft).

			Regular Season					Playoffs				
Season	Club	Lea	GP	G	A	TP	PIM	GP	G	A	TP	PIM
1994-95	CSKA	CIS Jr.	50	20	30	50	20	....	....	....	....	....
1995-96	Barrie	OHL	47	37	27	64	36	7	2	3	5	12

VON STEFENELLI, PHIL — OTT.

Defense. Shoots left. 6'1", 200 lbs. Born, Vancouver, B.C., April 10, 1969.
(Vancouver's 5th choice, 122nd overall, in 1988 Entry Draft).

			Regular Season					Playoffs				
Season	Club	Lea	GP	G	A	TP	PIM	GP	G	A	TP	PIM
1987-88	Boston U.	H.E.	34	3	13	16	38	....	....	....	....	....
1988-89	Boston U.	H.E.	33	2	6	8	34	....	....	....	....	....
1989-90	Boston U.	H.E.	44	8	20	28	40	....	....	....	....	....
1990-91	Boston U.	H.E.	41	7	23	30	32	....	....	....	....	....
1991-92	Milwaukee	IHL	80	2	34	36	40	5	1	2	3	2
1992-93	Hamilton	AHL	78	11	20	31	75	....	....	....	....	....
1993-94	Hamilton	AHL	80	10	31	41	89	4	1	0	1	2
1994-95	Providence	AHL	75	6	13	19	93	13	2	4	6	6
1995-96	**Boston**	**NHL**	**37**	**0**	**4**	**4**	**16**	....	....	....	....	....
	Providence	AHL	42	9	21	30	52	....	....	....	....	....
	NHL Totals		**37**	**0**	**4**	**4**	**16**	....	....	....	....	....

Signed as a free agent by **Boston**, September 10, 1994. Signed as a free agent by **Ottawa**, July 17, 1996.

VOPAT, JAN — (VOH-paht) L.A.

Defense. Shoots left. 6', 198 lbs. Born, Most, Czech., March 22, 1973.
(Hartford's 3rd choice, 57th overall, in 1992 Entry Draft).

			Regular Season					Playoffs				
Season	Club	Lea	GP	G	A	TP	PIM	GP	G	A	TP	PIM
1990-91	Litvinov	Czech.	25	1	4	5	4	....	....	....	....	....
1991-92	Litvinov	Czech.	46	4	2	6	16	....	....	....	....	....
1992-93	Litvinov	Czech.	45	12	10	22	....	....	....	....	....	....
1993-94	Litvinov	Czech.	41	9	19	28	0	4	1	1	2	....
1994-95	Litvinov	Czech.	42	7	18	25	49	4	0	2	2	2
1995-96	**Los Angeles**	**NHL**	**11**	**1**	**4**	**5**	**4**	....	....	....	....	....
	Phoenix	IHL	47	0	9	9	34	4	0	2	2	4
	NHL Totals		**11**	**1**	**4**	**5**	**4**	....	....	....	....	....

Rights traded to **Los Angeles** by **Hartford** for Los Angeles' fourth round choice (Ian MacNeil) in 1995 Entry Draft, May 31, 1995.

VOPAT, ROMAN — (VOH-paht) L.A.

Center. Shoots left. 6'3", 216 lbs. Born, Litvinov, Czech., April 21, 1976.
(St. Louis' 4th choice, 172nd overall, in 1994 Entry Draft).

			Regular Season					Playoffs				
Season	Club	Lea	GP	G	A	TP	PIM	GP	G	A	TP	PIM
1993-94	Litvinov	Czech.	7	0	0	0	0	....	....	....	....	....
1994-95	Moose Jaw	WHL	72	23	20	43	141	10	4	1	5	28
1995-96	**St. Louis**	**NHL**	**25**	**2**	**3**	**5**	**48**	....	....	....	....	....
	Worcester	AHL	5	2	0	2	14	....	....	....	....	....
	Moose Jaw	WHL	7	0	4	4	34	....	....	....	....	....
	Prince Albert	WHL	22	15	5	20	81	18	9	8	17	57
	NHL Totals		**25**	**2**	**3**	**5**	**48**	....	....	....	....	....

Traded to **Los Angeles** by **St. Louis** with Craig Johnson, Patrice Tardif, St. Louis fifth round choice (Peter Hogan) in 1996 Entry Draft and first round choice in 1997 Entry Draft for Wayne Gretzky, February 27, 1996.

VOROBIEV, VLADIMIR — NYR

Left wing. Shoots right. 5'11", 185 lbs. Born, Cherepovets, USSR, October 2, 1972.
(NY Rangers' 10th choice, 240th overall, in 1992 Entry Draft).

			Regular Season					Playoffs				
Season	Club	Lea	GP	G	A	TP	PIM	GP	G	A	TP	PIM
1992-93	Cherepovets	CIS	42	18	5	23	18	....	....	....	....	....
1993-94	Moscow D'amo	CIS	11	3	1	4	2	....	....	....	....	....
1994-95	Moscow D'amo	CIS	48	9	20	29	28	14	1	7	8	2
1995-96	Moscow D'amo	CIS	42	19	9	28	49	9	2	8	10	2

VORONOV, SERGEI — PIT.

Defense. Shoots left. 6'2", 200 lbs. Born, Moscow, USSR, February 5, 1971.
(Pittsburgh's 7th choice, 206th overall, in 1995 Entry Draft).

			Regular Season					Playoffs				
Season	Club	Lea	GP	G	A	TP	PIM	GP	G	A	TP	PIM
1992-93	Moscow D'amo	CIS	36	1	0	1	25	....	....	....	....	....
1993-94	Moscow D'amo	CIS	44	5	6	11	72	....	....	....	....	....
1994-95	Moscow D'amo	CIS	44	3	4	7	80	12	4	1	5	26
1995-96	Cleveland	IHL	2	0	0	0	4	....	....	....	....	....
	Hampton Rds.	ECHL	57	6	23	29	241	2	0	0	0	6

VUKOTA, MICK — (vuh-KOH-tuh) NYI

Right wing. Shoots right. 6'1", 225 lbs. Born, Saskatoon, Sask., September 14, 1966.

			Regular Season					Playoffs				
Season	Club	Lea	GP	G	A	TP	PIM	GP	G	A	TP	PIM
1983-84	Winnipeg	WHL	3	1	1	2	10	....	....	....	....	....
1984-85	Kelowna	WHL	66	10	6	16	247	....	....	....	....	....
1985-86	Spokane	WHL	64	19	14	33	369	9	6	4	10	68
1986-87	Spokane	WHL	61	25	28	53	*337	4	0	0	0	40
1987-88	**NY Islanders**	**NHL**	**17**	**1**	**0**	**1**	**82**	**2**	**0**	**0**	**0**	**23**
	Springfield	AHL	52	7	9	16	375	....	....	....	....	....
1988-89	**NY Islanders**	**NHL**	**48**	**2**	**2**	**4**	**237**	....	....	....	....	....
	Springfield	AHL	3	1	0	1	33	....	....	....	....	....
1989-90	**NY Islanders**	**NHL**	**76**	**4**	**8**	**12**	**290**	**1**	**0**	**0**	**0**	**17**
1990-91	**NY Islanders**	**NHL**	**60**	**2**	**4**	**6**	**238**	....	....	....	....	....
	Capital Dist.	AHL	2	0	0	0	9	....	....	....	....	....
1991-92	**NY Islanders**	**NHL**	**74**	**0**	**6**	**6**	**293**	....	....	....	....	....
1992-93	**NY Islanders**	**NHL**	**74**	**2**	**5**	**7**	**216**	**15**	**0**	**0**	**0**	**16**
1993-94	**NY Islanders**	**NHL**	**72**	**3**	**1**	**4**	**237**	**4**	**0**	**0**	**0**	**17**
1994-95	**NY Islanders**	**NHL**	**40**	**0**	**2**	**2**	**109**	....	....	....	....	....
1995-96	**NY Islanders**	**NHL**	**32**	**1**	**1**	**2**	**106**	....	....	....	....	....
	NHL Totals		**493**	**15**	**29**	**44**	**1808**	**22**	**0**	**0**	**0**	**73**

Signed as a free agent by **NY Islanders**, March 2, 1987.

VUORIVIRTA, JUHA — L.A.

Center. Shoots left. 6'3", 189 lbs. Born, Oulu, Finland, May 3, 1976.
(Los Angeles' 8th choice, 163rd overall, in 1995 Entry Draft).

			Regular Season					Playoffs				
Season	Club	Lea	GP	G	A	TP	PIM	GP	G	A	TP	PIM
1994-95	Tappara	Fin.	39	2	3	5	12	....	....	....	....	....
1995-96	Tappara	Fin. Jr.	4	2	5	7	0	....	....	....	....	....
	Tappara	Fin.	47	6	3	9	20	4	0	0	0	0

VYSHEDKEVICH, SERGEI — (vee-shehd-KAY-vihch) N.J.

Defense. Shoots left. 6', 185 lbs. Born, Dedovsk, USSR, January 3, 1975.
(New Jersey's 3rd choice, 70th overall, in 1995 Entry Draft).

			Regular Season					Playoffs				
Season	Club	Lea	GP	G	A	TP	PIM	GP	G	A	TP	PIM
1994-95	Moscow D'amo	CIS	49	6	7	13	67	14	2	0	2	12
1995-96	Moscow D'amo	CIS	49	5	4	9	12	13	1	1	2	6

WAINWRIGHT, DAVID — NYI

Defense. Shoots left. 6', 193 lbs. Born, Boston, MA, January 17, 1974.
(NY Islanders' 10th choice, 224th overall, in 1992 Entry Draft).

			Regular Season					Playoffs				
Season	Club	Lea	GP	G	A	TP	PIM	GP	G	A	TP	PIM
1993-94	Boston College	H.E.	36	2	1	3	38	....	....	....	....	....
1994-95	Boston College	H.E.	33	3	5	8	48	....	....	....	....	....
1995-96	Boston College	H.E.	29	2	6	8	38	....	....	....	....	....

WALKER, SCOTT — VAN.

Defense. Shoots right. 5'9", 180 lbs. Born, Montreal, Que., July 19, 1973.
(Vancouver's 4th choice, 124th overall, in 1993 Entry Draft).

			Regular Season					Playoffs				
Season	Club	Lea	GP	G	A	TP	PIM	GP	G	A	TP	PIM
1991-92	Owen Sound	OHL	53	7	31	38	128	5	0	7	7	8
1992-93a	Owen Sound	OHL	57	23	68	91	110	8	1	5	6	16
	Cdn. National	....	2	3	0	3	0	....	....	....	....	....
1993-94	Hamilton	AHL	77	10	29	39	272	4	0	1	1	25
1994-95	Syracuse	AHL	74	14	38	52	334	....	....	....	....	....
	Vancouver	**NHL**	**11**	**0**	**1**	**1**	**33**	....	....	....	....	....
1995-96	**Vancouver**	**NHL**	**63**	**4**	**8**	**12**	**137**	....	....	....	....	....
	Syracuse	AHL	15	3	12	15	52	16	9	8	17	39
	NHL Totals		**74**	**4**	**9**	**13**	**170**	....	....	....	....	....

a OHL Second All-Star Team (1993)

WALLIN, JESSE — DET.

Defense. Shoots left. 6'2", 190 lbs. Born, Saskatoon, Sask., March 10, 1978.
(Detroit's 1st choice, 26th overall, in 1996 Entry Draft).

			Regular Season					Playoffs				
Season	Club	Lea	GP	G	A	TP	PIM	GP	G	A	TP	PIM
1994-95	Prince Albert	WHL	72	4	20	24	72	....	....	....	....	....
1995-96	Red Deer	WHL	70	5	19	24	61	9	0	3	3	4

WALSH, GORD — NYI

Left wing. Shoots left. 6'1", 186 lbs. Born, St. John's, Nfld., December 12, 1975.
(NY Islanders' 10th choice, 220th overall, in 1994 Entry Draft).

			Regular Season					Playoffs				
Season	Club	Lea	GP	G	A	TP	PIM	GP	G	A	TP	PIM
1992-93	Guelph	OHL	55	2	9	11	12	5	0	0	0	2
1993-94	Guelph	OHL	8	0	1	1	9	....	....	....	....	....
	Kingston	OHL	55	14	19	33	52	6	0	1	1	4
1994-95	Kingston	OHL	61	27	37	64	43	6	1	0	1	6
1995-96	Kingston	OHL	57	33	26	59	40	....	....	....	....	....

WALSH, KURT — BUF.

Right wing. Shoots right. 6'2", 205 lbs. Born, St. John's, Nfld., September 26, 1977.
(Buffalo's 5th choice, 87th overall, in 1996 Entry Draft).

			Regular Season					Playoffs				
Season	Club	Lea	GP	G	A	TP	PIM	GP	G	A	TP	PIM
1993-94	Newmarket	OHL	35	1	2	3	23	....	....	....	....	....
1994-95	Sarnia	OHL	17	0	4	4	18	....	....	....	....	....
	Oshawa	OHL	42	6	10	16	31	....	....	....	....	....
1995-96	Oshawa	OHL	41	19	18	37	63	....	....	....	....	....
	Owen Sound	OHL	26	8	9	17	20	6	0	2	2	4

WALZ, WES — (WAHLS)

Center. Shoots right. 5'10", 185 lbs. Born, Calgary, Alta., May 15, 1970.
(Boston's 3rd choice, 57th overall, in 1989 Entry Draft).

			Regular Season					Playoffs				
Season	Club	Lea	GP	G	A	TP	PIM	GP	G	A	TP	PIM
1988-89	Lethbridge	WHL	63	29	75	104	32	8	1	5	6	6
1989-90	**Boston**	**NHL**	**2**	**1**	**1**	**2**	**0**	....	....	....	....	....
a	Lethbridge	WHL	56	54	86	140	69	19	13	*24	*37	33
1990-91	**Boston**	**NHL**	**56**	**8**	**8**	**16**	**32**	**2**	**0**	**0**	**0**	**0**
	Maine	AHL	20	8	12	20	19	2	0	0	0	21
1991-92	**Boston**	**NHL**	**15**	**0**	**3**	**3**	**12**	....	....	....	....	....
	Maine	AHL	21	13	11	24	38	....	....	....	....	....
	Philadelphia	**NHL**	**2**	**1**	**0**	**1**	**0**	....	....	....	....	....
	Hershey	AHL	41	13	28	41	37	6	1	2	3	0
1992-93	Hershey	AHL	78	35	45	80	106	....	....	....	....	....
1993-94	**Calgary**	**NHL**	**53**	**11**	**27**	**38**	**16**	**6**	**3**	**0**	**3**	**2**
	Saint John	AHL	15	6	6	12	14	....	....	....	....	....
1994-95	**Calgary**	**NHL**	**39**	**6**	**12**	**18**	**11**	**1**	**0**	**0**	**0**	**0**
1995-96	**Detroit**	**NHL**	**2**	**0**	**0**	**0**	**0**	....	....	....	....	....
	Adirondack	AHL	38	20	35	55	58	....	....	....	....	....
	NHL Totals		**169**	**27**	**51**	**78**	**71**	**9**	**3**	**0**	**3**	**2**

a WHL East First All-Star Team (1990)

Traded to **Philadelphia** by **Boston** with Garry Galley and Boston's third round choice (Milos Holan) in 1993 Entry Draft for Gord Murphy, Brian Dobbin, Philadelphia's third round choice (Sergei Zholtok) in 1992 Entry Draft and Philadelphia's fourth round choice (Charles Paquette) in 1993 Entry Draft, January 2, 1992. Signed as a free agent by **Calgary**, August 26, 1993. Signed as a free agent by **Detroit**, September 6, 1995.

WARD, AARON — DET.

Defense. Shoots right. 6'2", 200 lbs. Born, Windsor, Ont., January 17, 1973.
(Winnipeg's 1st choice, 5th overall, in 1991 Entry Draft).

			Regular Season					Playoffs				
Season	Club	Lea	GP	G	A	TP	PIM	GP	G	A	TP	PIM
1990-91	U. of Michigan	CCHA	46	8	11	19	126	....	....	....	....	....
1991-92	U. of Michigan	CCHA	42	7	12	19	64	....	....	....	....	....
1992-93	U. of Michigan	CCHA	30	5	8	13	73	....	....	....	....	....
	Cdn. National	....	4	0	0	0	8	....	....	....	....	....
1993-94	**Detroit**	**NHL**	**5**	**1**	**0**	**1**	**4**	....	....	....	....	....
	Adirondack	AHL	58	4	12	16	87	9	2	6	8	6
1994-95	Adirondack	AHL	76	11	24	35	87	4	0	1	1	0
	Detroit	**NHL**	**1**	**0**	**1**	**1**	**2**	....	....	....	....	....
1995-96	Adirondack	AHL	74	5	10	15	133	3	0	0	0	6
	NHL Totals		**6**	**1**	**1**	**2**	**6**	....	....	....	....	....

Traded to **Detroit** by **Winnipeg** with Toronto's fourth round choice (previously acquired by Winnipeg — later traded to Detroit — Detroit selected John Jakopin) in 1993 Entry Draft for Paul Ysebaert and future considerations (Alan Kerr, June 18, 1993), June 11, 1993.

WARD, DIXON — BUF.

Right wing. Shoots right. 6', 200 lbs. Born, Leduc, Alta., September 23, 1968.
(Vancouver's 6th choice, 128th overall, in 1988 Entry Draft).

			Regular Season					Playoffs				
Season	Club	Lea	GP	G	A	TP	PIM	GP	G	A	TP	PIM
1988-89	North Dakota	WCHA	37	8	9	17	26	....	....	....	....	....
1989-90	North Dakota	WCHA	45	35	34	69	44	....	....	....	....	....
1990-91a	North Dakota	WCHA	43	34	35	69	84	....	....	....	....	....
1991-92a	North Dakota	WCHA	38	33	31	64	90	....	....	....	....	....
1992-93	**Vancouver**	**NHL**	**70**	**22**	**30**	**52**	**82**	**9**	**2**	**3**	**5**	**0**
1993-94	**Vancouver**	**NHL**	**33**	**6**	**1**	**7**	**37**	....	....	....	....	....
	Los Angeles	**NHL**	**34**	**6**	**2**	**8**	**45**	....	....	....	....	....
1994-95	**Toronto**	**NHL**	**22**	**0**	**3**	**3**	**31**	....	....	....	....	....
	St. John's	AHL	6	3	3	6	19	....	....	....	....	....
	Detroit	IHL	7	3	6	9	7	5	3	0	3	7
1995-96	**Buffalo**	**NHL**	**8**	**2**	**2**	**4**	**6**	....	....	....	....	....
b	Rochester	AHL	71	38	56	94	74	19	11	*24	*35	8
	NHL Totals		**167**	**36**	**38**	**74**	**201**	**9**	**2**	**3**	**5**	**0**

a WCHA Second All-Star Team (1991, 1992)
b Won Jack A. Butterfield Trophy (Playoff MVP - AHL) (1996)

Traded to **Los Angeles** by **Vancouver** with a conditional draft choice in 1995 Entry Draft for Jimmy Carson, January 8, 1994. Traded to **Toronto** by **Los Angeles** with Guy Leveque, Kelly Fairchild and Shayne Toporowski for Eric Lacroix, Chris Snell and Toronto's fourth round choice (Eric Belanger) in 1996 Entry draft, October 3, 1994. Signed as a free agent by **Buffalo**, September 20, 1995.

WARD, ED

Right wing. Shoots right. 6'3", 205 lbs. Born, Edmonton, Alta., November 10, 1969.
(Quebec's 7th choice, 108th overall, in 1988 Entry Draft).

			Regular Season					Playoffs				
Season	Club	Lea	GP	G	A	TP	PIM	GP	G	A	TP	PIM
1987-88	N. Michigan	WCHA	25	0	2	2	40	....	....	....	....	....
1988-89	N. Michigan	WCHA	42	5	15	20	36	....	....	....	....	....
1989-90	N. Michigan	WCHA	39	5	11	16	77	....	....	....	....	....
1990-91	N. Michigan	WCHA	46	13	18	31	109	....	....	....	....	....
1991-92	Greensboro	ECHL	12	4	8	12	21	....	....	....	....	....
	Halifax	AHL	51	7	11	18	65	....	....	....	....	....
1992-93	Halifax	AHL	70	13	19	32	56	....	....	....	....	....
1993-94	**Quebec**	**NHL**	**7**	**1**	**0**	**1**	**5**	....	....	....	....	....
	Cornwall	AHL	60	12	30	42	65	12	1	3	4	14
1994-95	Cornwall	AHL	56	10	14	24	118	....	....	....	....	....
	Calgary	**NHL**	**2**	**1**	**1**	**2**	**2**	....	....	....	....	....
	Saint John	AHL	11	4	5	9	20	5	1	0	1	10
1995-96	**Calgary**	**NHL**	**41**	**3**	**5**	**8**	**44**	....	....	....	....	....
	Saint John	AHL	12	1	2	3	45	16	4	4	8	27
	NHL Totals		**50**	**5**	**6**	**11**	**51**	....	....	....	....	....

Traded to **Calgary** by **Quebec** for Francois Groleau, March 23, 1995.

WARD, LANCE — N.J.

Defense. Shoots left. 6'3", 195 lbs. Born, Lloydminster, Alta., June 2, 1978.
(New Jersey's 1st choice, 10th overall, in 1996 Entry Draft).

			Regular Season					Playoffs				
Season	Club	Lea	GP	G	A	TP	PIM	GP	G	A	TP	PIM
1994-95	Red Deer	WHL	28	0	0	0	57	....	....	....	....	....
1995-96	Red Deer	WHL	72	4	13	17	127	10	0	4	4	10

WARE, JEFF — (WAIR) TOR.

Defense. Shoots left. 6'4", 220 lbs. Born, Toronto, Ont., May 19, 1977.
(Toronto's 1st choice, 15th overall, in 1995 Entry Draft).

			Regular Season					Playoffs				
Season	Club	Lea	GP	G	A	TP	PIM	GP	G	A	TP	PIM
1994-95	Oshawa	OHL	55	2	11	13	86	7	1	1	2	6
1995-96	Oshawa	OHL	62	4	19	23	128	5	0	1	1	8
	St. John's	AHL	4	0	0	0	4	4	0	0	0	2

WARE, MIKE — (WAIR) TOR.

Left wing. Shoots left. 6'1", 193 lbs. Born, Toronto, Ont., February 27, 1974.

			Regular Season					Playoffs				
Season	Club	Lea	GP	G	A	TP	PIM	GP	G	A	TP	PIM
1994-95	Kingston	OHL	64	25	41	66	98	6	3	4	7	9
	St. John's	AHL	1	2	0	2	0	....	....	....	....	....
1995-96	St. John's	AHL	58	4	9	13	95	2	0	1	1	2

Signed as a free agent by **Toronto**, August 2, 1994.

WARRENER, RHETT — FLA.

Defense. Shoots left. 6'1", 209 lbs. Born, Shaunavon, Sask., January 27, 1976.
(Florida's 2nd choice, 27th overall, in 1994 Entry Draft).

			Regular Season					Playoffs				
Season	Club	Lea	GP	G	A	TP	PIM	GP	G	A	TP	PIM
1991-92	Saskatoon	WHL	2	0	0	0	0	....	....	....	....	....
1992-93	Saskatoon	WHL	68	2	17	19	100	9	0	0	0	14
1993-94	Saskatoon	WHL	61	7	19	26	131	16	0	5	5	33
1994-95	Saskatoon	WHL	66	13	26	39	137	10	0	3	3	6
1995-96	**Florida**	**NHL**	**28**	**0**	**3**	**3**	**46**	**21**	**0**	**1**	**1**	**0**
	Carolina	AHL	9	0	0	0	4	....	....	....	....	....
	NHL Totals		**28**	**0**	**3**	**3**	**46**	**21**	**0**	**1**	**1**	**0**

WARRINER, TODD — TOR.

Left wing. Shoots left. 6'1", 188 lbs. Born, Blenheim, Ont., January 3, 1974.
(Quebec's 1st choice, 4th overall, in 1992 Entry Draft).

			Regular Season					Playoffs				
Season	Club	Lea	GP	G	A	TP	PIM	GP	G	A	TP	PIM
1990-91	Windsor	OHL	57	36	28	64	26	11	5	6	11	12
1991-92a	Windsor	OHL	50	41	41	82	64	7	5	4	9	6
1992-93	Windsor	OHL	23	13	21	34	29	....	....	....	....	....
	Kitchener	OHL	32	19	24	43	35	7	5	14	19	14
1993-94	Cdn. National	....	50	11	20	31	33	....	....	....	....	....
	Cdn. Olympic	....	4	1	1	2	0	....	....	....	....	....
	Kitchener	OHL	....	....	....	....	....	1	0	1	1	0
	Cornwall	AHL	....	....	....	....	....	10	1	4	5	4
1994-95	St. John's	AHL	46	8	10	18	22	4	1	0	1	2
	Toronto	**NHL**	**5**	**0**	**0**	**0**	**0**	....	....	....	....	....
1995-96	**Toronto**	**NHL**	**57**	**7**	**8**	**15**	**26**	**6**	**1**	**1**	**2**	**2**
	St. John's	AHL	11	5	6	11	16	....	....	....	....	....
	NHL Totals		**62**	**7**	**8**	**15**	**26**	**6**	**1**	**1**	**2**	**2**

a OHL First All-Star Team (1992)

Traded to **Toronto** by **Quebec** with Mats Sundin, Garth Butcher and Philadelphia's first round choice (previously acquired by Quebec — later traded to Washington — Washington selected Nolan Baumgartner) in 1994 Entry Draft for Wendel Clark, Sylvain Lefebvre, Landon Wilson and Toronto's first round choice (Jeffrey Kealty) in 1994 Entry Draft, June 28, 1994.

WASHBURN, STEVE — FLA.

Center. Shoots left. 6'2", 191 lbs. Born, Ottawa, Ont., April 10, 1975.
(Florida's 5th choice, 78th overall, in 1993 Entry Draft).

			Regular Season					Playoffs				
Season	Club	Lea	GP	G	A	TP	PIM	GP	G	A	TP	PIM
1991-92	Ottawa	OHL	59	5	17	22	10	11	2	3	5	4
1992-93	Ottawa	OHL	66	20	38	58	54	....	....	....	....	....
1993-94	Ottawa	OHL	65	30	50	80	88	17	7	16	23	10
1994-95	Ottawa	OHL	63	43	63	106	72	....	....	....	....	....
	Cincinnati	IHL	6	3	1	4	0	9	1	3	4	4
1995-96	**Florida**	**NHL**	**1**	**0**	**1**	**1**	**0**	**1**	**0**	**1**	**1**	**0**
	Carolina	AHL	78	29	54	83	45	....	....	....	....	....
	NHL Totals		**1**	**0**	**1**	**1**	**0**	**1**	**0**	**1**	**1**	**0**

WASYLKO, STEVE — HFD.

Center. Shoots left. 6'1", 173 lbs. Born, Ottawa, Ont., July 11, 1978.
(Hartford's 4th choice, 104th overall, in 1996 Entry Draft).

			Regular Season					Playoffs				
Season	Club	Lea	GP	G	A	TP	PIM	GP	G	A	TP	PIM
1994-95	Kanata	Jr. A	51	8	11	19	16	....	....	....	....	....
1995-96	Detroit	OHL	65	18	30	48	33	9	0	1	1	6

WASYLUK, TREVOR — (WAHZ-ah-luhk) HFD.

Left wing. Shoots left. 6'1", 187 lbs. Born, Saskatoon, Sask., May 4, 1978.
(Hartford's 1st choice, 34th overall, in 1996 Entry Draft).

			Regular Season					Playoffs				
Season	Club	Lea	GP	G	A	TP	PIM	GP	G	A	TP	PIM
1994-95	Medicine Hat	WHL	67	6	4	10	75	5	0	2	2	4
1995-96	Medicine Hat	WHL	69	25	21	46	59	5	0	2	2	15

WATT, MIKE — EDM.

Left wing. Shoots left. 6'2", 210 lbs. Born, Seaforth, Ont., March 31, 1976.
(Edmonton's 3rd choice, 32nd overall, in 1994 Entry Draft).

			Regular Season					Playoffs				
Season	Club	Lea	GP	G	A	TP	PIM	GP	G	A	TP	PIM
1994-95	Michigan State	CCHA	39	12	6	18	64	....	....	....	....	....
1995-96	Michigan State	CCHA	37	17	22	39	60	....	....	....	....	....

WEIGHT, DOUG (WAYT) EDM.

Center. Shoots left. 5'11", 191 lbs. Born, Warren, MI, January 21, 1971.
(NY Rangers' 2nd choice, 34th overall, in 1990 Entry Draft).

				Regul	ar Sea	son			Pla	yoffs		
Season	Club	Lea	GP	G	A	TP	PIM	GP	G	A	TP	PIM
1989-90	Lake Superior	CCHA	46	21	48	69	44	....	....	....	....	....
1990-91ab	Lake Superior	CCHA	42	29	46	75	86	....	....	....	....	....
	NY Rangers	NHL	....	....	....	....	....	1	0	0	0	0
1991-92	NY Rangers	NHL	53	8	22	30	23	7	2	2	4	0
	Binghamton	AHL	9	3	14	17	2	4	1	4	5	6
1992-93	NY Rangers	NHL	65	15	25	40	55	....	....	....	....	....
	Edmonton	NHL	13	2	6	8	10	....	....	....	....	....
1993-94	Edmonton	NHL	84	24	50	74	47	....	....	....	....	....
1994-95	Rosenheim	Ger.	8	2	3	5	18	....	....	....	....	....
	Edmonton	NHL	48	7	33	40	69	....	....	....	....	....
1995-96	Edmonton	NHL	82	25	79	104	95	....	....	....	....	....
	NHL Totals		345	81	215	296	299	8	2	2	4	0

a CCHA First All-Star Team (1991)
b NCAA West Second All-American Team (1991)

Played in NHL All-Star Game (1996)

Traded to **Edmonton** by **NY Rangers** for Esa Tikkanen, March 17, 1993.

WEINRICH, ERIC (WIGHN-rihc) CHI.

Defense. Shoots left. 6'1", 210 lbs. Born, Roanoke, VA, December 19, 1966.
(New Jersey's 3rd choice, 32nd overall, in 1985 Entry Draft).

				Regul	ar Sea	son			Pla	yoffs		
Season	Club	Lea	GP	G	A	TP	PIM	GP	G	A	TP	PIM
1985-86	U. of Maine	H.E.	34	0	15	15	26	....	....	....	....	....
1986-87ab	U. of Maine	H.E.	41	12	32	44	59	....	....	....	....	....
1987-88	U. of Maine	H.E.	8	4	7	11	22	....	....	....	....	....
	U.S. National	....	38	3	9	12	24	....	....	....	....	....
	U.S. Olympic	....	3	0	0	0	0	....	....	....	....	....
1988-89	New Jersey	NHL	2	0	0	0	0	....	....	....	....	....
	Utica	AHL	80	17	27	44	70	5	0	1	1	4
1989-90	New Jersey	NHL	19	2	7	9	11	6	1	3	4	17
cd	Utica	AHL	57	12	48	60	38	....	....	....	....	....
1990-91e	New Jersey	NHL	76	4	34	38	48	7	1	2	3	6
1991-92	New Jersey	NHL	76	7	25	32	55	7	0	2	2	4
1992-93	Hartford	NHL	79	7	29	36	76	....	....	....	....	....
1993-94	Hartford	NHL	8	1	1	2	2	....	....	....	....	....
	Chicago	NHL	54	3	23	26	31	6	0	2	2	6
1994-95	Chicago	NHL	48	3	10	13	33	16	1	5	6	4
1995-96	Chicago	NHL	77	5	10	15	65	10	1	4	5	10
	NHL Totals		439	32	139	171	321	52	4	18	22	47

a Hockey East First All-Star Team (1987)
b NCAA East Second All-American Team (1987)
c AHL First All-Star Team (1990)
d Won Eddie Shore Plaque (Outstanding Defenseman - AHL) (1990)
e NHL/Upper Deck All-Rookie Team (1991)

Traded to **Hartford** by **New Jersey** with Sean Burke for Bobby Holik, Hartford's second round choice (Jay Pandolfo) in 1993 Entry Draft and future considerations, August 28, 1992. Traded to **Chicago** by **Hartford** with Patrick Poulin for Steve Larmer and Bryan Marchment, November 2, 1993.

WELLS, CHRIS PIT.

Center. Shoots left. 6'6", 223 lbs. Born, Calgary, Alta., November 12, 1975.
(Pittsburgh's 1st choice, 24th overall, in 1994 Entry Draft).

				Regul	ar Sea	son			Pla	yoffs		
Season	Club	Lea	GP	G	A	TP	PIM	GP	G	A	TP	PIM
1991-92	Seattle	WHL	64	13	8	21	80	11	0	0	0	15
1992-93	Seattle	WHL	63	18	37	55	111	5	2	3	5	4
1993-94	Seattle	WHL	69	30	44	74	150	9	6	5	11	23
1994-95a	Seattle	WHL	69	45	63	108	148	3	0	1	1	4
	Cleveland	IHL	3	0	1	1	2	....	....	....	....	....
1995-96	Pittsburgh	NHL	54	2	2	4	59	....	....	....	....	....
	NHL Totals		54	2	2	4	59					

a WHL West First All-Star Team (1995)

WELLS, JAY T.B.

Defense. Shoots left. 6'1", 210 lbs. Born, Paris, Ont., May 18, 1959.
(Los Angeles' 1st choice, 16th overall, in 1979 Entry Draft).

				Regul	ar Sea	son			Pla	yoffs		
Season	Club	Lea	GP	G	A	TP	PIM	GP	G	A	TP	PIM
1977-78	Kingston	OHA	68	9	13	22	195	5	1	2	3	6
1978-79a	Kingston	OHA	48	6	21	27	100	11	2	7	9	29
1979-80	Los Angeles	NHL	43	0	0	0	113	4	0	0	0	11
	Binghamton	AHL	28	0	6	6	48	....	....	....	....	....
1980-81	Los Angeles	NHL	72	5	13	18	155	4	0	0	0	27
1981-82	Los Angeles	NHL	60	1	8	9	145	10	1	3	4	41
1982-83	Los Angeles	NHL	69	3	12	15	167	....	....	....	....	....
1983-84	Los Angeles	NHL	69	3	18	21	141	....	....	....	....	....
1984-85	Los Angeles	NHL	77	2	9	11	185	3	0	1	1	0
1985-86	Los Angeles	NHL	79	11	31	42	226	....	....	....	....	....
1986-87	Los Angeles	NHL	77	7	29	36	155	5	1	2	3	10
1987-88	Los Angeles	NHL	58	2	23	25	159	5	1	2	3	21
1988-89	Philadelphia	NHL	67	2	19	21	184	18	0	2	2	51
1989-90	Philadelphia	NHL	59	3	16	19	129	....	....	....	....	....
	Buffalo	NHL	1	0	1	1	0	6	0	0	0	12
1990-91	Buffalo	NHL	43	1	2	3	86	1	0	1	1	0
1991-92	Buffalo	NHL	41	2	9	11	157	....	....	....	....	....
	NY Rangers	NHL	11	0	0	0	24	13	0	2	2	10
1992-93	NY Rangers	NHL	53	1	9	10	107	....	....	....	....	....
1993-94	NY Rangers	NHL	79	2	7	9	110	23	0	0	0	20 ♦
1994-95	NY Rangers	NHL	43	2	7	9	36	10	0	0	0	8
1995-96	St. Louis	NHL	76	0	3	3	67	12	0	1	1	2
	NHL Totals		1077	47	216	263	2346	114	3	14	17	213

a OHA First All-Star Team (1979)

Traded to **Philadelphia** by **Los Angeles** for Doug Crossman, September 29, 1988. Traded to **Buffalo** by **Philadelphia** with Philadelphia's fourth round choice (Peter Ambroziak) in 1991 Entry Draft for Kevin Maguire and Buffalo's second round choice (Mikael Renberg) in 1990 Entry Draft, March 5, 1990. Traded to **NY Rangers** by **Buffalo** for Randy Moller, March 9, 1992. Traded to **St. Louis** by **NY Rangers** for Doug Lidster, July 31, 1995. Signed as a free agent by **Tampa Bay**, August 3, 1996.

WELSING, MARK (ROCKY) ANA.

Defense. Shoots left. 6'3", 196 lbs. Born, Beloit, WI, February 8, 1976.
(Anaheim's 7th choice, 158th overall, in 1994 Entry Draft).

				Regul	ar Sea	son			Pla	yoffs		
Season	Club	Lea	GP	G	A	TP	PIM	GP	G	A	TP	PIM
1994-95	N. Michigan	WCHA	38	0	8	8	129	....	....	....	....	....
1995-96	N. Michigan	WCHA	38	0	6	6	84	....	....	....	....	....

WERENKA, BRAD (wuh-REHN-kuh) CHI.

Defense. Shoots left. 6'2", 210 lbs. Born, Two Hills, Alta., February 12, 1969.
(Edmonton's 2nd choice, 42nd overall, in 1987 Entry Draft).

				Regul	ar Sea	son			Pla	yoffs		
Season	Club	Lea	GP	G	A	TP	PIM	GP	G	A	TP	PIM
1986-87	N. Michigan	WCHA	30	4	4	8	35	....	....	....	....	....
1987-88	N. Michigan	WCHA	34	7	23	30	26	....	....	....	....	....
1988-89	N. Michigan	WCHA	28	7	13	20	16	....	....	....	....	....
1989-90	N. Michigan	WCHA	8	2	5	7	8	....	....	....	....	....
1990-91abc	N. Michigan	WCHA	47	20	43	63	36	....	....	....	....	....
1991-92	Cape Breton	AHL	66	6	21	27	95	5	0	3	3	6
1992-93	Edmonton	NHL	27	5	3	8	24	....	....	....	....	....
	Cdn. National	....	18	3	7	10	10	....	....	....	....	....
	Cape Breton	AHL	4	1	1	2	4	16	4	17	21	12
1993-94	Edmonton	NHL	15	0	4	4	14	....	....	....	....	....
	Cape Breton	AHL	25	6	17	23	19	....	....	....	....	....
	Cdn. Olympic	....	8	2	2	4	8	....	....	....	....	....
	Quebec	NHL	11	0	7	7	8	....	....	....	....	....
	Cornwall	AHL	....	....	....	....	....	12	2	10	12	22
1994-95	Milwaukee	IHL	80	8	45	53	161	15	3	10	13	36
1995-96	Chicago	NHL	9	0	0	0	8	....	....	....	....	....
	Indianapolis	IHL	73	15	42	57	85	5	1	3	4	8
	NHL Totals		62	5	14	19	54					

a WCHA First All-Star Team (1991)
b NCAA West First All-American Team (1991)
c NCAA Final Four All-Tournament Team (1991)

Traded to **Quebec** by **Edmonton** for Steve Passmore, March 21, 1994. Signed as a free agent by **Chicago**, July 20, 1995.

WERNBLOM, MAGNUS L.A.

Right wing. Shoots left. 6', 187 lbs. Born, Kramfors, Sweden, February 3, 1973.
(Los Angeles' 6th choice, 207th overall, in 1992 Entry Draft).

				Regul	ar Sea	son			Pla	yoffs		
Season	Club	Lea	GP	G	A	TP	PIM	GP	G	A	TP	PIM
1990-91	MoDo	Swe.	16	4	2	6	8	....	....	....	....	....
1991-92	MoDo	Swe.	35	7	6	13	50	....	....	....	....	....
1992-93	MoDo	Swe.	37	8	3	11	36	3	0	0	0	0
1993-94	MoDo	Swe.	39	14	9	23	46	11	2	3	5	12
1994-95	MoDo	Swe.	38	12	10	22	50	....	....	....	....	....
1995-96	MoDo	Swe.	28	16	8	24	50	8	3	0	3	14

WESENBERG, BRIAN PHI.

Right wing. Shoots right. 6'3", 173 lbs. Born, Peterborough, Ont., May 9, 1977.
(Anaheim's 2nd choice, 29th overall, in 1995 Entry Draft).

				Regul	ar Sea	son			Pla	yoffs		
Season	Club	Lea	GP	G	A	TP	PIM	GP	G	A	TP	PIM
1994-95	Guelph	OHL	66	17	27	44	81	14	2	3	5	18
1995-96	Guelph	OHL	66	25	33	58	161	16	4	11	15	34

Traded to **Philadelphia** by **Anaheim** for Anatoli Semenov and Mike Crowley, March 19, 1996.

WESLEY, GLEN HFD.

Defense. Shoots left. 6'1", 197 lbs. Born, Red Deer, Alta., October 2, 1968.
(Boston's 1st choice, 3rd overall, in 1987 Entry Draft).

				Regul	ar Sea	son			Pla	yoffs		
Season	Club	Lea	GP	G	A	TP	PIM	GP	G	A	TP	PIM
1983-84	Portland	WHL	3	1	2	3	0	....	....	....	....	....
1984-85	Portland	WHL	67	16	52	68	76	6	1	6	7	8
1985-86a	Portland	WHL	69	16	75	91	96	15	3	11	14	29
1986-87a	Portland	WHL	63	16	46	62	72	20	8	18	26	27
1987-88b	Boston	NHL	79	7	30	37	69	23	6	8	14	22
1988-89	Boston	NHL	77	19	35	54	61	10	0	2	2	4
1989-90	Boston	NHL	78	9	27	36	48	21	2	6	8	36
1990-91	Boston	NHL	80	11	32	43	78	19	2	9	11	19
1991-92	Boston	NHL	78	9	37	46	54	15	2	4	6	16
1992-93	Boston	NHL	64	8	25	33	47	4	0	0	0	0
1993-94	Boston	NHL	81	14	44	58	64	13	3	3	6	12
1994-95	Hartford	NHL	48	2	14	16	50	....	....	....	....	....
1995-96	Hartford	NHL	68	8	16	24	88	....	....	....	....	....
	NHL Totals		653	87	260	347	559	105	15	32	47	109

a WHL West All-Star Team (1986, 1987)
b NHL All-Rookie Team (1988)

Played in NHL All-Star Game (1989)

Traded to **Hartford** by **Boston** for Hartford's first round choices in 1995 (Kyle McLaren), 1996 (Jonathan Aitken) and 1997 Entry Draft, August 26, 1994.

WHITE, BRIAN T.B.

Defense. Shoots right. 6'1", 180 lbs. Born, Winchester, MA, February 7, 1976.
(Tampa Bay's 11th choice, 268th overall, in 1994 Entry Draft).

				Regul	ar Sea	son			Pla	yoffs		
Season	Club	Lea	GP	G	A	TP	PIM	GP	G	A	TP	PIM
1994-95	U. of Maine	H.E.	28	1	1	2	16	....	....	....	....	....
1995-96	U. of Maine	H.E.	39	0	4	4	18	....	....	....	....	....

WHITE, COLIN N.J.

Defense. Shoots left. 6'3", 190 lbs. Born, New Glasgow, N.S., December 12, 1977.
(New Jersey's 5th choice, 49th overall, in 1996 Entry Draft).

				Regul	ar Sea	son			Pla	yoffs		
Season	Club	Lea	GP	G	A	TP	PIM	GP	G	A	TP	PIM
1994-95	Laval	QMJHL	7	0	1	1	32	....	....	....	....	....
	Hull	QMJHL	5	0	1	1	4	12	0	0	0	23
1995-96	Hull	QMJHL	62	2	8	10	303	18	0	4	4	42

WHITE, PETER — PHI.

Center. Shoots left. 5'11", 200 lbs. Born, Montreal, Que., March 15, 1969.
(Edmonton's 4th choice, 92nd overall, in 1989 Entry Draft).

			Regular Season					Playoffs				
Season	Club	Lea	GP	G	A	TP	PIM	GP	G	A	TP	PIM
1988-89	Michigan State	CCHA	46	20	33	53	17	....	....	....	....	....
1989-90	Michigan State	CCHA	45	22	40	62	6	....	....	....	....	....
1990-91	Michigan State	CCHA	37	7	31	38	28	....	....	....	....	....
1991-92	Michigan State	CCHA	41	26	49	75	32	....	....	....	....	....
1992-93	Cape Breton	AHL	64	12	28	40	10	16	3	3	6	12
1993-94	**Edmonton**	**NHL**	**26**	**3**	**5**	**8**	**2**	....	....	....	....	....
	Cape Breton	AHL	45	21	49	70	12	5	2	3	5	2
1994-95ab	Cape Breton	AHL	65	36	*69	*105	30	....	....	....	....	....
	Edmonton	**NHL**	**9**	**2**	**4**	**6**	**0**	....	....	....	....	....
1995-96	**Edmonton**	**NHL**	**26**	**5**	**3**	**8**	**0**	....	....	....	....	....
	Toronto	**NHL**	**1**	**0**	**0**	**0**	**0**	....	....	....	....	....
	St. John's	AHL	17	6	7	13	6	....	....	....	....	....
	Atlanta	IHL	36	21	20	41	4	3	0	3	3	2
	NHL Totals		**62**	**10**	**12**	**22**	**2**	....	....	....	....	....

a AHL Second All-Star Team (1995)
b Won John B. Sollenberger Trophy (Top Scorer - AHL) (1995)

Traded to **Toronto** by **Edmonton** with Edmonton's fourth round choice (Jason Sessa) in 1996 Entry Draft for Kent Manderville, December 4, 1995. Signed as a free agent by **Philadelphia**, August 19, 1996.

WHITE, TOM — CHI.

Center. Shoots left. 6'1", 185 lbs. Born, Chicago, IL, August 25, 1975.

			Regular Season					Playoffs				
Season	Club	Lea	GP	G	A	TP	PIM	GP	G	A	TP	PIM
1993-94	Miami-Ohio	CCHA	31	1	6	7	26	....	....	....	....	....
1994-95	Miami-Ohio	CCHA	35	2	5	7	24	....	....	....	....	....
1995-96	Miami-Ohio	CCHA	36	7	4	11	56	....	....	....	....	....

WHITFIELD, TRENT — BOS.

Center. Shoots left. 5'10", 176 lbs. Born, Estevan, Sask., June 17, 1977.
(Boston's 5th choice, 100th overall, in 1996 Entry Draft).

			Regular Season					Playoffs				
Season	Club	Lea	GP	G	A	TP	PIM	GP	G	A	TP	PIM
1993-94	Spokane	WHL	5	1	1	2	0	....	....	....	....	....
1994-95	Spokane	WHL	48	8	17	25	26	11	7	6	13	5
1995-96	Spokane	WHL	72	33	51	84	75	18	8	10	18	10

WHITNEY, RAY — S.J.

Center. Shoots right. 5'9", 160 lbs. Born, Fort Saskatchewan, Alta., May 8, 1972.
(San Jose's 2nd choice, 23rd overall, in 1991 Entry Draft).

			Regular Season					Playoffs				
Season	Club	Lea	GP	G	A	TP	PIM	GP	G	A	TP	PIM
1988-89	Spokane	WHL	71	17	33	50	16	....	....	....	....	....
1989-90	Spokane	WHL	71	57	56	113	50	6	3	4	7	6
1990-91abc	Spokane	WHL	72	67	118	*185	36	15	13	18	*31	12
1991-92	Koln	Ger.	10	3	6	9	4	....	....	....	....	....
	Cdn. National	....	5	1	0	1	6	....	....	....	....	....
	San Diego	IHL	63	36	54	90	12	4	0	0	0	0
	San Jose	**NHL**	**2**	**0**	**3**	**3**	**0**	....	....	....	....	....
1992-93	**San Jose**	**NHL**	**26**	**4**	**6**	**10**	**4**	....	....	....	....	....
	Kansas City	IHL	46	20	33	53	14	12	5	7	12	2
1993-94	**San Jose**	**NHL**	**61**	**14**	**26**	**40**	**14**	**14**	**0**	**4**	**4**	**8**
1994-95	**San Jose**	**NHL**	**39**	**13**	**12**	**25**	**14**	**11**	**4**	**4**	**8**	**2**
1995-96	**San Jose**	**NHL**	**60**	**17**	**24**	**41**	**16**	....	....	....	....	....
	NHL Totals		**188**	**48**	**71**	**119**	**48**	**25**	**4**	**8**	**12**	**10**

a WHL West First All-Star Team (1991)
b Memorial Cup All-Star Team (1991)
c Won George Parsons Trophy (Memorial Cup Tournament Most Sportsmanlike Player) (1991)

WIDMER, JASON — S.J.

Defense. Shoots left. 6', 205 lbs. Born, Calgary, Alta., August 1, 1973.
(NY Islanders' 8th choice, 176th overall, in 1992 Entry Draft).

			Regular Season					Playoffs				
Season	Club	Lea	GP	G	A	TP	PIM	GP	G	A	TP	PIM
1990-91	Lethbridge	WHL	58	2	12	14	55	16	0	1	1	12
1991-92	Lethbridge	WHL	40	2	19	21	181	5	0	4	4	9
1992-93	Lethbridge	WHL	55	3	15	18	140	4	0	3	3	2
	Capital Dist.	AHL	4	0	0	0	2	....	....	....	....	....
1993-94	Lethbridge	WHL	64	11	31	42	191	9	3	5	8	34
1994-95	Worcester	AHL	73	8	26	34	136	....	....	....	....	....
	Cdn. National	....	6	1	4	5	4	....	....	....	....	....
	NY Islanders	**NHL**	**1**	**0**	**0**	**0**	**0**	....	....	....	....	....
1995-96	**NY Islanders**	**NHL**	**4**	**0**	**0**	**0**	**7**	....	....	....	....	....
	Worcester	AHL	76	6	21	27	129	4	2	0	2	9
	NHL Totals		**5**	**0**	**0**	**0**	**7**	....	....	....	....	....

Signed as a free agent by **San Jose**, August 26, 1996.

WIEMER, JASON — (WEE-muhr) — T.B.

Center. Shoots left. 6'1", 215 lbs. Born, Kimberley, B.C., April 14, 1976.
(Tampa Bay's 1st choice, 8th overall, in 1994 Entry Draft).

			Regular Season					Playoffs				
Season	Club	Lea	GP	G	A	TP	PIM	GP	G	A	TP	PIM
1991-92	Portland	WHL	2	0	1	1	0	....	....	....	....	....
1992-93	Portland	WHL	68	18	34	52	159	16	7	3	10	27
1993-94	Portland	WHL	72	45	51	96	236	10	4	4	8	32
1994-95	Portland	WHL	16	10	14	24	63	....	....	....	....	....
	Tampa Bay	**NHL**	**36**	**1**	**4**	**5**	**44**	....	....	....	....	....
1995-96	**Tampa Bay**	**NHL**	**66**	**9**	**9**	**18**	**81**	**6**	**1**	**0**	**1**	**28**
	NHL Totals		**102**	**10**	**13**	**23**	**125**	**6**	**1**	**0**	**1**	**28**

WIESEL, ADAM — MTL.

Defense. Shoots right. 6'3", 210 lbs. Born, Holyoke, MA, January 25, 1975.
(Montreal's 4th choice, 85th overall, in 1993 Entry Draft).

			Regular Season					Playoffs				
Season	Club	Lea	GP	G	A	TP	PIM	GP	G	A	TP	PIM
1993-94	Clarkson	ECAC	33	3	7	10	26	....	....	....	....	....
1994-95	Clarkson	ECAC	36	6	13	19	28	....	....	....	....	....
1995-96	Fredericton	AHL	69	6	13	19	12	2	0	0	0	0

WILCHYNSKI, CHAD — DET.

Defense. Shoots left. 6'3", 179 lbs. Born, Regina, Sask., April 4, 1977.
(Detroit's 5th choice, 125th overall, in 1995 Entry Draft).

			Regular Season					Playoffs				
Season	Club	Lea	GP	G	A	TP	PIM	GP	G	A	TP	PIM
1994-95	Regina	WHL	70	7	15	22	96	4	0	1	1	4
1995-96	Regina	WHL	....	....	....	....	....	11	0	2	2	18

WILFORD, MARTY — CHI.

Defense. Shoots left. 6', 216 lbs. Born, Cobourg, Ont., April 17, 1977.
(Chicago's 7th choice, 149th overall, in 1995 Entry Draft).

			Regular Season					Playoffs				
Season	Club	Lea	GP	G	A	TP	PIM	GP	G	A	TP	PIM
1994-95	Oshawa	OHL	63	1	6	7	95	7	1	1	2	4
1995-96	Oshawa	OHL	65	3	24	27	107	5	0	1	1	4

WILKIE, BOB

Defense. Shoots right. 6'2", 215 lbs. Born, Calgary, Alta., February 11, 1969.
(Detroit's 3rd choice, 41st overall, in 1987 Entry Draft).

			Regular Season					Playoffs				
Season	Club	Lea	GP	G	A	TP	PIM	GP	G	A	TP	PIM
1985-86	Calgary	WHL	63	8	19	27	56	....	....	....	....	....
1986-87	Swift Current	WHL	65	12	38	50	50	4	1	3	4	2
1987-88	Swift Current	WHL	67	12	68	80	124	10	4	12	16	8
1988-89	Swift Current	WHL	62	18	67	85	89	12	1	11	12	47
1989-90	Adirondack	AHL	58	5	33	38	64	6	1	4	5	2
1990-91	**Detroit**	**NHL**	**8**	**1**	**2**	**3**	**2**	....	....	....	....	....
	Adirondack	AHL	43	6	18	24	71	2	1	0	1	2
1991-92	Adirondack	AHL	7	1	4	5	6	16	2	5	7	12
1992-93	Adirondack	AHL	14	0	5	5	20	....	....	....	....	....
	Fort Wayne	IHL	32	7	14	21	82	12	4	6	10	10
	Hershey	AHL	28	7	25	32	18	....	....	....	....	....
1993-94	**Philadelphia**	**NHL**	**10**	**1**	**3**	**4**	**8**	....	....	....	....	....
a	Hershey	AHL	69	8	53	61	100	9	1	4	5	8
1994-95	Hershey	AHL	50	9	30	39	46	....	....	....	....	....
	Indianapolis	IHL	29	5	22	27	30	....	....	....	....	....
1995-96	Augsburg	Ger.	6	0	1	1	43	....	....	....	....	....
	Cincinnati	IHL	22	4	6	10	32	....	....	....	....	....
	NHL Totals		**18**	**2**	**5**	**7**	**10**	....	....	....	....	....

a AHL Second All-Star Team (1994)

Traded to **Philadelphia** by **Detroit** for future considerations, February 2, 1993. Traded to **Chicago** by **Philadelphia** with a possible conditional choice in 1997 Entry Draft for Karl Dykhuis, February 16, 1995.

WILKIE, DAVID — MTL.

Defense. Shoots right. 6'2", 210 lbs. Born, Ellensburgh, WA, May 30, 1974.
(Montreal's 1st choice, 20th overall, in 1992 Entry Draft).

			Regular Season					Playoffs				
Season	Club	Lea	GP	G	A	TP	PIM	GP	G	A	TP	PIM
1990-91	Seattle	WHL	25	1	1	2	22	....	....	....	....	....
1991-92	Kamloops	WHL	71	12	28	40	153	16	6	5	11	19
1992-93	Kamloops	WHL	53	11	26	37	109	6	4	2	6	2
1993-94	Kamloops	WHL	27	11	18	29	18	....	....	....	....	....
	Regina	WHL	29	27	21	48	16	4	1	4	5	4
1994-95	Fredericton	AHL	70	10	43	53	34	1	0	0	0	0
	Montreal	**NHL**	**1**	**0**	**0**	**0**	**0**	....	....	....	....	....
1995-96	**Montreal**	**NHL**	**24**	**1**	**5**	**6**	**10**	**6**	**1**	**2**	**3**	**12**
	Fredericton	AHL	23	5	12	17	20	....	....	....	....	....
	NHL Totals		**25**	**1**	**5**	**6**	**10**	**6**	**1**	**2**	**3**	**12**

WILKINSON, NEIL — PIT.

Defense. Shoots right. 6'3", 190 lbs. Born, Selkirk, Man., August 15, 1967.
(Minnesota's 2nd choice, 30th overall, in 1986 Entry Draft).

			Regular Season					Playoffs				
Season	Club	Lea	GP	G	A	TP	PIM	GP	G	A	TP	PIM
1986-87	Michigan State	CCHA	19	3	4	7	18	....	....	....	....	....
1987-88	Medicine Hat	WHL	55	11	21	32	157	5	1	0	1	2
1988-89	Kalamazoo	IHL	39	5	15	20	96	....	....	....	....	....
1989-90	**Minnesota**	**NHL**	**36**	**0**	**5**	**5**	**100**	**7**	**0**	**2**	**2**	**11**
	Kalamazoo	IHL	20	6	7	13	62	....	....	....	....	....
1990-91	**Minnesota**	**NHL**	**50**	**2**	**9**	**11**	**117**	**22**	**3**	**3**	**6**	**12**
	Kalamazoo	IHL	10	0	3	3	38	....	....	....	....	....
1991-92	**San Jose**	**NHL**	**60**	**4**	**15**	**19**	**107**	....	....	....	....	....
1992-93	**San Jose**	**NHL**	**59**	**1**	**7**	**8**	**96**	....	....	....	....	....
1993-94	**Chicago**	**NHL**	**72**	**3**	**9**	**12**	**116**	**4**	**0**	**0**	**0**	**0**
1994-95	**Winnipeg**	**NHL**	**40**	**1**	**4**	**5**	**75**	....	....	....	....	....
1995-96	**Winnipeg**	**NHL**	**21**	**1**	**4**	**5**	**33**	....	....	....	....	....
	Pittsburgh	**NHL**	**41**	**2**	**10**	**12**	**87**	**15**	**0**	**1**	**1**	**14**
	NHL Totals		**379**	**14**	**63**	**77**	**731**	**48**	**3**	**6**	**9**	**37**

Claimed by **San Jose** from **Minnesota** in Dispersal Draft, May 30, 1991. Traded to **Chicago** by **San Jose** as future considerations to complete June 18, 1993 trade for Jimmy Waite, July 9, 1993. Traded to **Winnipeg** by **Chicago** for Chicago's third round choice (previously acquired by Winnipeg) in 1995 Entry Draft, June 3, 1994. Traded to **Pittsburgh** by **Winnipeg** for Norm Maciver, December 28, 1995.

WILLIAMS, DAVID — ST.L.

Defense. Shoots right. 6'2", 195 lbs. Born, Plainfield, NJ, August 25, 1967.
(New Jersey's 12th choice, 234th overall, in 1985 Entry Draft).

			Regular Season					Playoffs				
Season	Club	Lea	GP	G	A	TP	PIM	GP	G	A	TP	PIM
1986-87	Dartmouth	ECAC	23	2	19	21	20	....	....	....	....	....
1987-88	Dartmouth	ECAC	25	8	14	22	30	....	....	....	....	....
1988-89ab	Dartmouth	ECAC	25	4	11	15	28	....	....	....	....	....
1989-90	Dartmouth	ECAC	26	3	12	15	32	....	....	....	....	....
1990-91	Muskegon	IHL	14	1	2	3	4	....	....	....	....	....
	Knoxville	ECHL	38	12	15	27	40	3	0	0	0	4
1991-92	**San Jose**	**NHL**	**56**	**3**	**25**	**28**	**40**	....	....	....	....	....
	Kansas City	IHL	18	2	3	5	22	....	....	....	....	....
1992-93	**San Jose**	**NHL**	**40**	**1**	**11**	**12**	**49**	....	....	....	....	....
	Kansas City	IHL	31	1	11	12	28	....	....	....	....	....
1993-94	**Anaheim**	**NHL**	**56**	**5**	**15**	**20**	**42**	....	....	....	....	....
	San Diego	IHL	16	1	6	7	17	....	....	....	....	....
1994-95	**Anaheim**	**NHL**	**21**	**2**	**2**	**4**	**26**	....	....	....	....	....
	San Diego	IHL	2	0	1	1	0	5	1	0	1	0
1995-96	Detroit	IHL	81	5	14	19	81	11	1	3	4	6
	NHL Totals		**173**	**11**	**53**	**64**	**157**	....	....	....	....	....

a ECAC First All-Star Team (1989)
b NCAA East Second All-American Team (1989)

Signed as a free agent by **San Jose**, August 9, 1991. Claimed by **Anaheim** from **San Jose** in Expansion Draft, June 24, 1993. Signed as a free agent by **Hartford**, August 25, 1995. Signed as a free agent by **St. Louis**, July 29, 1996.

WILLIAMS, JEFF N.J.

Center. Shoots left. 6', 175 lbs. Born, Pointe-Claire, Que., February 11, 1976.
(New Jersey's 8th choice, 181st overall, in 1994 Entry Draft).

			Regular Season					Playoffs				
Season	Club	Lea	GP	G	A	TP	PIM	GP	G	A	TP	PIM
1993-94	Guelph	OHL	62	14	12	26	19	9	2	1	3	4
1994-95	Guelph	OHL	52	15	32	47	21	14	5	5	10	0
1995-96a	Guelph	OHL	63	15	49	64	42	16	13	15	28	10

a Canadian Major Junior Most Sportsmanlike Player of the Year (1996)

WILLIS, RICK NYR

Left wing. Shoots left. 6', 190 lbs. Born, Lynn, MA, January 12, 1972.
(NY Rangers' 5th choice, 76th overall, in 1990 Entry Draft).

			Regular Season					Playoffs				
Season	Club	Lea	GP	G	A	TP	PIM	GP	G	A	TP	PIM
1991-92	U. of Michigan	CCHA	32	1	4	5	42	....	....	....	....	....
1992-93	U. of Michigan	CCHA	39	3	8	11	67	....	....	....	....	....
1993-94	U. of Michigan	CCHA	40	8	5	13	83	....	....	....	....	....
1994-95	U. of Michigan	CCHA	35	3	6	9	78	....	....	....	....	....
1995-96	Charlotte	ECHL	11	3	1	4	49	....	....	....	....	....
	Binghamton	AHL	39	3	2	5	62	2	0	0	0	0

WILLIS, SHANE T.B.

Right wing. Shoots right. 6', 176 lbs. Born, Edmonton, Alta., June 13, 1977.
(Tampa Bay's 3rd choice, 56th overall, in 1995 Entry Draft).

			Regular Season					Playoffs				
Season	Club	Lea	GP	G	A	TP	PIM	GP	G	A	TP	PIM
1994-95	Prince Albert	WHL	65	24	19	43	38	13	3	4	7	6
1995-96	Prince Albert	WHL	69	41	40	81	47	18	11	10	21	18

WILLIS, TYLER VAN.

Right wing. Shoots right. 5'8", 160 lbs. Born, Princeton, B.C., April 30, 1977.
(Vancouver's 8th choice, 196th overall, in 1995 Entry Draft).

			Regular Season					Playoffs				
Season	Club	Lea	GP	G	A	TP	PIM	GP	G	A	TP	PIM
1993-94	Swift Current	WHL	71	19	26	45	263	....	....	....	....	....
1994-95	Swift Current	WHL	71	21	29	50	284	6	0	0	0	20
1995-96	Swift Current	WHL	40	9	38	47	196	....	....	....	....	....
	Seattle	WHL	15	1	3	4	71	5	1	5	6	13

WILLSIE, BRIAN COL.

Right wing. Shoots right. 6', 179 lbs. Born, London, Ont., March 16, 1978.
(Colorado's 7th choice, 146th overall, in 1996 Entry Draft).

			Regular Season					Playoffs				
Season	Club	Lea	GP	G	A	TP	PIM	GP	G	A	TP	PIM
1995-96	Guelph	OHL	65	13	21	34	18	16	4	2	6	6

WILM, CLARKE CGY.

Center. Shoots left. 6', 202 lbs. Born, Central Butte, Sask., October 24, 1976.
(Calgary's 5th choice, 150th overall, in 1995 Entry Draft).

			Regular Season					Playoffs				
Season	Club	Lea	GP	G	A	TP	PIM	GP	G	A	TP	PIM
1992-93	Saskatoon	WHL	69	14	19	33	71	9	4	2	6	13
1993-94	Saskatoon	WHL	70	18	32	50	181	16	0	9	9	19
1994-95	Saskatoon	WHL	71	20	39	59	179	10	6	1	7	21
1995-96	Saskatoon	WHL	72	49	61	110	83	4	1	1	2	4

WILSON, LANDON COL.

Right wing. Shoots right. 6'2", 202 lbs. Born, St. Louis, MO, March 13, 1975.
(Toronto's 2nd choice, 19th overall, in 1993 Entry Draft).

			Regular Season					Playoffs				
Season	Club	Lea	GP	G	A	TP	PIM	GP	G	A	TP	PIM
1993-94	North Dakota	WCHA	35	18	15	33	*147	....	....	....	....	....
1994-95	North Dakota	WCHA	31	7	16	23	141	....	....	....	....	....
	Cornwall	AHL	8	4	4	8	25	13	3	4	7	68
1995-96	**Colorado**	**NHL**	**7**	**1**	**0**	**1**	**6**	....	....	....	....	....
	Cornwall	AHL	53	21	13	34	154	8	1	3	4	22
	NHL Totals		**7**	**1**	**0**	**1**	**6**	....	....	....	....	....

Traded to **Quebec** by **Toronto** with Wendel Clark, Sylvain Lefebvre and Toronto's first round choice (Jeffrey Kealty) in 1994 Entry Draft for Mats Sundin, Garth Butcher, Todd Warriner and Philadelphia's first round choice (previously acquired by Quebec — later traded to Washington — Washington selected Nolan Baumgartner) in 1994 Entry Draft, June 28, 1994.

WILSON, MIKE BUF.

Defense. Shoots left. 6'6", 210 lbs. Born, Brampton, Ont., February 26, 1975.
(Vancouver's 1st choice, 20th overall, in 1993 Entry Draft).

			Regular Season					Playoffs				
Season	Club	Lea	GP	G	A	TP	PIM	GP	G	A	TP	PIM
1992-93	Sudbury	OHL	53	6	7	13	58	14	1	1	2	2
1993-94	Sudbury	OHL	60	4	22	26	62	9	1	3	4	8
1994-95	Sudbury	OHL	64	13	34	47	46	18	1	8	9	10
1995-96	**Buffalo**	**NHL**	**58**	**4**	**8**	**12**	**41**	....	....	....	....	....
	Rochester	AHL	15	0	5	5	38	....	....	....	....	....
	NHL Totals		**58**	**4**	**8**	**12**	**41**	....	....	....	....	....

Traded to **Buffalo** by **Vancouver** with Mike Peca and Vancouver's first round choice (Jay McKee) in 1995 Entry Draft for Alexander Mogilny and Buffalo's fifth round choice (Todd Norman) in 1995 Entry Draft, July 8, 1995.

WILSON, RON

Center. Shoots left. 5'9", 180 lbs. Born, Toronto, Ont., May 13, 1956.
(Montreal's 15th choice, 133rd overall, in 1976 Amateur Draft).

			Regular Season					Playoffs				
Season	Club	Lea	GP	G	A	TP	PIM	GP	G	A	TP	PIM
1974-75	Toronto	OMJHL	16	6	12	18	6	23	9	17	26	6
1975-76	St. Catharines	OHA	64	37	62	99	44	4	1	6	7	7
1976-77	Nova Scotia	AHL	67	15	21	36	18	6	0	0	0	0
1977-78	Nova Scotia	AHL	59	15	25	40	17	11	4	4	8	9
1978-79	Nova Scotia	AHL	77	33	42	75	91	10	5	6	11	14
1979-80	**Winnipeg**	**NHL**	**79**	**21**	**36**	**57**	**28**	....	....	....	....	....
1980-81	**Winnipeg**	**NHL**	**77**	**18**	**33**	**51**	**55**	....	....	....	....	....
1981-82	**Winnipeg**	**NHL**	**39**	**3**	**13**	**16**	**49**	....	....	....	....	....
	Tulsa	CHL	41	20	38	58	22	3	1	0	1	2
1982-83	**Winnipeg**	**NHL**	**12**	**6**	**3**	**9**	**4**	**3**	**2**	**2**	**4**	**2**
	Sherbrooke	AHL	65	30	55	85	71	....	....	....	....	....
1983-84	**Winnipeg**	**NHL**	**51**	**3**	**12**	**15**	**12**	....	....	....	....	....
	Sherbrooke	AHL	22	10	30	40	16	....	....	....	....	....
1984-85	**Winnipeg**	**NHL**	**75**	**10**	**9**	**19**	**31**	**8**	**4**	**2**	**6**	**2**
1985-86	**Winnipeg**	**NHL**	**54**	**6**	**7**	**13**	**16**	**1**	**0**	**0**	**0**	**0**
	Sherbrooke	AHL	10	9	8	17	9	....	....	....	....	....
1986-87	**Winnipeg**	**NHL**	**80**	**3**	**13**	**16**	**13**	**10**	**1**	**2**	**3**	**0**
1987-88	**Winnipeg**	**NHL**	**69**	**5**	**8**	**13**	**28**	**1**	**0**	**0**	**0**	**2**
1988-89a	Moncton	AHL	80	31	61	92	110	8	1	4	5	20
1989-90	Moncton	AHL	47	16	37	53	39	....	....	....	....	....
	St. Louis	**NHL**	**33**	**3**	**17**	**20**	**23**	**12**	**3**	**5**	**8**	**18**
1990-91	**St. Louis**	**NHL**	**73**	**10**	**27**	**37**	**54**	**7**	**0**	**0**	**0**	**28**
1991-92	**St. Louis**	**NHL**	**64**	**12**	**17**	**29**	**46**	**6**	**0**	**1**	**1**	**0**
1992-93	**St. Louis**	**NHL**	**78**	**8**	**11**	**19**	**44**	**11**	**0**	**0**	**0**	**12**
1993-94	**Montreal**	**NHL**	**48**	**2**	**10**	**12**	**12**	**4**	**0**	**0**	**0**	**0**
1994-95	Detroit	IHL	12	6	9	15	10	....	....	....	....	....
	San Diego	IHL	58	8	25	33	60	5	2	0	2	8
1995-96	Wheeling	ECHL	46	12	30	42	72	2	0	3	3	6
	NHL Totals		**832**	**110**	**216**	**326**	**415**	**63**	**10**	**12**	**22**	**64**

a AHL Second All-Star Team (1989)

Sold to **Winnipeg** by **Montreal**, October 4, 1979. Traded to **St. Louis** by **Winnipeg** for Doug Evans, January 22, 1990. Signed as a free agent by **Montreal**, August 20, 1993.

WINDSOR, NICHOLAS COL.

Defense. Shoots left. 6'1", 165 lbs. Born, Granby, Que., January 19, 1976.
(Quebec's 8th choice, 139th overall, in 1994 Entry Draft).

			Regular Season					Playoffs				
Season	Club	Lea	GP	G	A	TP	PIM	GP	G	A	TP	PIM
1994-95	Clarkson	ECAC	26	1	10	11	20	....	....	....	....	....
1995-96	Clarkson	ECAC	38	4	16	20	60	....	....	....	....	....

WINNES, CHRIS (WIHN-ehs)

Right wing. Shoots right. 6', 201 lbs. Born, Ridgefield, CT, February 12, 1968.
(Boston's 9th choice, 161st overall, in 1987 Entry Draft).

			Regular Season					Playoffs				
Season	Club	Lea	GP	G	A	TP	PIM	GP	G	A	TP	PIM
1987-88	N. Hampshire	H.E.	30	17	19	36	28	....	....	....	....	....
1988-89	N. Hampshire	H.E.	30	11	20	31	22	....	....	....	....	....
1989-90	N. Hampshire	H.E.	24	10	13	23	12	....	....	....	....	....
1990-91	N. Hampshire	H.E.	33	15	16	31	24	....	....	....	....	....
	Maine	AHL	7	3	1	4	0	1	0	2	2	0
	Boston	**NHL**	....	....	....	....	....	**1**	**0**	**0**	**0**	**0**
1991-92	**Boston**	**NHL**	**24**	**1**	**3**	**4**	**6**	....	....	....	....	....
	Maine	AHL	45	12	35	47	30	....	....	....	....	....
1992-93	**Boston**	**NHL**	**5**	**0**	**1**	**1**	**0**	....	....	....	....	....
	Providence	AHL	64	23	36	59	34	4	0	2	2	5
1993-94	**Philadelphia**	**NHL**	**4**	**0**	**2**	**2**	**0**	....	....	....	....	....
	Hershey	AHL	70	29	21	50	20	7	1	3	4	0
1994-95	Hershey	AHL	78	26	40	66	39	6	2	2	4	17
1995-96	Michigan	IHL	27	6	13	19	14	....	....	....	....	....
	Fort Wayne	IHL	39	6	7	13	12	2	0	0	0	0
	NHL Totals		**33**	**1**	**6**	**7**	**6**	**1**	**0**	**0**	**0**	**0**

Signed as a free agent by **Philadelphia**, August 4, 1993.

WITT, BRENDAN WSH.

Defense. Shoots left. 6'1", 205 lbs. Born, Humbolt, Sask., February 20, 1975.
(Washington's 1st choice, 11th overall, in 1993 Entry Draft).

			Regular Season					Playoffs				
Season	Club	Lea	GP	G	A	TP	PIM	GP	G	A	TP	PIM
1991-92	Seattle	WHL	67	3	9	12	212	15	1	1	2	84
1992-93a	Seattle	WHL	70	2	26	28	239	5	1	2	3	30
1993-94ab	Seattle	WHL	56	8	31	39	235	9	3	8	11	23
1994-95			DID NOT PLAY									
1995-96	**Washington**	**NHL**	**48**	**2**	**3**	**5**	**85**	....	....	....	....	....
	NHL Totals		**48**	**2**	**3**	**5**	**85**	....	....	....	....	....

a WHL West First All-Star Team (1993, 1994)
b Canadian Major Junior First All-Star Team (1994)

WOLANIN, CRAIG (wuh-LAN-ihn) T.B.

Defense. Shoots left. 6'4", 215 lbs. Born, Grosse Pointe, MI, July 27, 1967.
(New Jersey's 1st choice, 3rd overall, in 1985 Entry Draft).

			Regular Season					Playoffs				
Season	Club	Lea	GP	G	A	TP	PIM	GP	G	A	TP	PIM
1984-85	Kitchener	OHL	60	5	16	21	95	4	1	1	2	2
1985-86	**New Jersey**	**NHL**	**44**	**2**	**16**	**18**	**74**	....	....	....	....	....
1986-87	**New Jersey**	**NHL**	**68**	**4**	**6**	**10**	**109**	....	....	....	....	....
1987-88	**New Jersey**	**NHL**	**78**	**6**	**25**	**31**	**170**	**18**	**2**	**5**	**7**	**51**
1988-89	**New Jersey**	**NHL**	**56**	**3**	**8**	**11**	**69**	....	....	....	....	....
1989-90	**New Jersey**	**NHL**	**37**	**1**	**7**	**8**	**47**	....	....	....	....	....
	Utica	AHL	6	2	4	6	2	....	....	....	....	....
	Quebec	**NHL**	**13**	**0**	**3**	**3**	**10**	....	....	....	....	....
1990-91	**Quebec**	**NHL**	**80**	**5**	**13**	**18**	**89**	....	....	....	....	....
1991-92	**Quebec**	**NHL**	**69**	**2**	**11**	**13**	**80**	....	....	....	....	....
1992-93	**Quebec**	**NHL**	**24**	**1**	**4**	**5**	**49**	**4**	**0**	**0**	**0**	**4**
1993-94	**Quebec**	**NHL**	**63**	**6**	**10**	**16**	**80**	....	....	....	....	....
1994-95	**Quebec**	**NHL**	**40**	**3**	**6**	**9**	**40**	**6**	**1**	**1**	**2**	**4**
1995-96	**Colorado**	**NHL**	**75**	**7**	**20**	**27**	**50**	**7**	**1**	**0**	**1**	**8** ♦
	NHL Totals		**647**	**40**	**129**	**169**	**867**	**35**	**4**	**6**	**10**	**67**

Traded to **Quebec** by **New Jersey** with future considerations (Randy Velischek, August 13, 1990) for Peter Stastny, March 6, 1990. Traded to **Tampa Bay** by **Colorado** for Tampa Bay's second round choice in 1998 Entry Draft, July 29, 1996.

WOOD, DODY — S.J.

Center. Shoots left. 5'11", 181 lbs. Born, Chetwynd, B.C., March 10, 1972.
(San Jose's 4th choice, 45th overall, in 1991 Entry Draft).

			Regular Season					Playoffs				
Season	Club	Lea	GP	G	A	TP	PIM	GP	G	A	TP	PIM
1989-90	Ft. St. John	Jr. A	44	51	73	124	270	....	....	....	....	....
	Seattle	WHL	....	....	....	....	....	5	0	0	0	2
1990-91	Seattle	WHL	69	28	37	65	272	6	0	1	1	2
1991-92	Seattle	WHL	37	13	19	32	232	....	....	....	....	....
	Swift Current	WHL	3	0	2	2	14	7	2	1	3	37
1992-93	**San Jose**	**NHL**	**13**	**1**	**1**	**2**	**71**	....	....	....	....	....
	Kansas City	IHL	36	3	2	5	216	6	0	1	1	15
1993-94	Kansas City	IHL	48	5	15	20	320	....	....	....	....	....
1994-95	Kansas City	IHL	44	5	13	18	255	21	7	10	17	87
	San Jose	**NHL**	**9**	**1**	**1**	**2**	**29**	....	....	....	....	....
1995-96	**San Jose**	**NHL**	**32**	**3**	**6**	**9**	**138**	....	....	....	....	....
	NHL Totals		**54**	**5**	**8**	**13**	**238**	....	....	....	....	....

WOOD, RANDY

Left wing/Center. Shoots left. 6', 195 lbs. Born, Princeton, NJ, October 12, 1963.

			Regular Season					Playoffs				
Season	Club	Lea	GP	G	A	TP	PIM	GP	G	A	TP	PIM
1982-83	Yale	ECAC	26	5	14	19	10	....	....	....	....	....
1983-84	Yale	ECAC	18	7	7	14	10	....	....	....	....	....
1984-85a	Yale	ECAC	32	25	28	53	23	....	....	....	....	....
1985-86bc	Yale	ECAC	31	25	30	55	26	....	....	....	....	....
1986-87	**NY Islanders**	**NHL**	**6**	**1**	**0**	**1**	**4**	**13**	**1**	**3**	**4**	**14**
	Springfield	AHL	75	23	24	47	57	....	....	....	....	....
1987-88	**NY Islanders**	**NHL**	**75**	**22**	**16**	**38**	**80**	**5**	**1**	**0**	**1**	**6**
	Springfield	AHL	1	0	1	1	0	....	....	....	....	....
1988-89	**NY Islanders**	**NHL**	**77**	**15**	**13**	**28**	**44**	....	....	....	....	....
	Springfield	AHL	1	1	1	2	0	....	....	....	....	....
1989-90	**NY Islanders**	**NHL**	**74**	**24**	**24**	**48**	**39**	**5**	**1**	**1**	**2**	**4**
1990-91	**NY Islanders**	**NHL**	**76**	**24**	**18**	**42**	**45**	....	....	....	....	....
1991-92	**NY Islanders**	**NHL**	**8**	**2**	**2**	**4**	**21**	....	....	....	....	....
	Buffalo	**NHL**	**70**	**20**	**16**	**36**	**65**	**7**	**2**	**1**	**3**	**6**
1992-93	**Buffalo**	**NHL**	**82**	**18**	**25**	**43**	**77**	**8**	**1**	**4**	**5**	**4**
1993-94	**Buffalo**	**NHL**	**84**	**22**	**16**	**38**	**71**	**6**	**0**	**0**	**0**	**0**
1994-95	**Toronto**	**NHL**	**48**	**13**	**11**	**24**	**34**	**7**	**2**	**0**	**2**	**6**
1995-96	**Toronto**	**NHL**	**46**	**7**	**9**	**16**	**36**	....	....	....	....	....
	Dallas	**NHL**	**30**	**1**	**4**	**5**	**26**	....	....	....	....	....
	NHL Totals		**676**	**169**	**154**	**323**	**542**	**51**	**8**	**9**	**17**	**40**

a ECAC Second All-Star Team (1985)
b ECAC First All-Star Team (1986)
c NCAA East Second All-Star Team (1986)

Signed as a free agent by **NY Islanders**, September 17, 1986. Traded to **Buffalo** by **NY Islanders** with Pat Lafontaine, Randy Hillier and NY Islanders' fourth round choice (Dean Melanson) in 1992 Entry Draft for Pierre Turgeon, Uwe Krupp, Benoit Hogue and Dave McLlwain, October 25, 1991. Claimed by **Toronto** from **Buffalo** in NHL Waiver Draft, January 18, 1995. Traded to **Dallas** by **Toronto** with Benoit Hogue for Dave Gagner and Dallas' sixth round choice (Dmitriy Yakushin) in 1996 Entry Draft, January 29, 1996.

WOOLLEY, JASON — (WOO-lee) FLA.

Defense. Shoots left. 6', 188 lbs. Born, Toronto, Ont., July 27, 1969.
(Washington's 4th choice, 61st overall, in 1989 Entry Draft).

			Regular Season					Playoffs				
Season	Club	Lea	GP	G	A	TP	PIM	GP	G	A	TP	PIM
1988-89	Michigan State	CCHA	47	12	25	37	26	....	....	....	....	....
1989-90	Michigan State	CCHA	45	10	38	48	26	....	....	....	....	....
1990-91ab	Michigan State	CCHA	40	15	44	59	24	....	....	....	....	....
1991-92	Cdn. National	....	60	14	30	44	36	....	....	....	....	....
	Cdn. Olympic	....	8	0	5	5	4	....	....	....	....	....
	Washington	**NHL**	**1**	**0**	**0**	**0**	**0**	....	....	....	....	....
	Baltimore	AHL	15	1	10	11	6	....	....	....	....	....
1992-93	**Washington**	**NHL**	**26**	**0**	**2**	**2**	**10**	....	....	....	....	....
	Baltimore	AHL	29	14	27	41	22	1	0	2	2	0
1993-94	**Washington**	**NHL**	**10**	**1**	**2**	**3**	**4**	**4**	**1**	**0**	**1**	**4**
	Portland	AHL	41	12	29	41	14	9	2	2	4	4
1994-95	Detroit	IHL	48	8	28	36	38	....	....	....	....	....
	Florida	**NHL**	**34**	**4**	**9**	**13**	**18**	....	....	....	....	....
1995-96	**Florida**	**NHL**	**52**	**6**	**28**	**34**	**32**	**13**	**2**	**6**	**8**	**14**
	NHL Totals		**123**	**11**	**41**	**52**	**64**	**17**	**3**	**6**	**9**	**18**

a CCHA First All-Star Team (1991)
b NCAA West First All-American Team (1991)

Signed as a free agent by **Florida**, February 15, 1995.

WORRELL, PETER — FLA.

Left wing. Shoots left. 6'6", 249 lbs. Born, Pierre Fonds, Que., August 18, 1977.
(Florida's 7th choice, 166th overall, in 1995 Entry Draft).

			Regular Season					Playoffs				
Season	Club	Lea	GP	G	A	TP	PIM	GP	G	A	TP	PIM
1994-95	Hull	QMJHL	56	1	8	9	243	21	0	1	1	91
1995-96	Hull	QMJHL	63	23	36	59	464	18	11	8	19	81

WORTMAN, KEVIN

Defense. Shoots right. 6', 200 lbs. Born, Sagus, MA, February 22, 1969.
(Calgary's 9th choice, 168th overall, in 1989 Entry Draft).

			Regular Season					Playoffs				
Season	Club	Lea	GP	G	A	TP	PIM	GP	G	A	TP	PIM
1990-91	American Int'l	NCAA	28	21	25	46	6	....	....	....	....	....
1991-92	Salt Lake	IHL	82	12	34	46	34	5	1	0	1	0
1992-93a	Salt Lake	IHL	82	13	50	63	24	....	....	....	....	....
1993-94	**Calgary**	**NHL**	**5**	**0**	**0**	**0**	**2**	....	....	....	....	....
	Saint John	AHL	72	17	32	49	32	7	1	5	6	16
1994-95	Kansas City	IHL	80	6	28	34	22	21	1	1	2	4
1995-96	Fort Wayne	IHL	82	12	21	33	26	5	2	4	6	4
	NHL Totals		**5**	**0**	**0**	**0**	**2**	....	....	....	....	....

a IHL Second All-Star Team (1993)

Signed as a free agent by **San Jose**, August 25, 1994.

WOTTON, MARK — (WAH-tuhn) VAN.

Defense. Shoots left. 5'11", 187 lbs. Born, Foxwarren, Man., November 16, 1973.
(Vancouver's 11th choice, 237th overall, in 1992 Entry Draft).

			Regular Season					Playoffs				
Season	Club	Lea	GP	G	A	TP	PIM	GP	G	A	TP	PIM
1990-91	Saskatoon	WHL	45	4	11	15	37	....	....	....	....	....
1991-92	Saskatoon	WHL	64	11	25	36	92	....	....	....	....	....
1992-93	Saskatoon	WHL	71	15	51	66	90	9	6	5	11	18
1993-94a	Saskatoon	WHL	65	12	34	46	108	16	3	12	15	32
1994-95	Syracuse	AHL	75	12	29	41	50	....	....	....	....	....
	Vancouver	**NHL**	**1**	**0**	**0**	**0**	**0**	**5**	**0**	**0**	**0**	**4**
1995-96	Syracuse	AHL	80	10	35	45	96	15	1	12	13	20
	NHL Totals		**1**	**0**	**0**	**0**	**0**	**5**	**0**	**0**	**0**	**4**

a WHL East Second All-Star Team (1994)

WRIGHT, JAMIE — DAL.

Left wing. Shoots left. 6', 172 lbs. Born, Kitchener, Ont., May 13, 1976.
(Dallas' 3rd choice, 98th overall, in 1994 Entry Draft).

			Regular Season					Playoffs				
Season	Club	Lea	GP	G	A	TP	PIM	GP	G	A	TP	PIM
1993-94	Guelph	OHL	65	17	15	32	34	8	2	1	3	10
1994-95	Guelph	OHL	65	43	39	82	36	14	6	8	14	6
1995-96	Guelph	OHL	55	30	36	66	45	16	10	12	22	35

WRIGHT, SHAYNE — BUF.

Defense. Shoots left. 6', 189 lbs. Born, Welland, Ont., June 30, 1975.
(Buffalo's 12th choice, 277th overall, in 1994 Entry Draft).

			Regular Season					Playoffs				
Season	Club	Lea	GP	G	A	TP	PIM	GP	G	A	TP	PIM
1992-93	Owen Sound	OHL	62	9	21	30	101	8	2	0	2	5
1993-94	Owen Sound	OHL	64	11	24	35	95	9	1	10	11	4
1994-95	Owen Sound	OHL	63	11	50	61	114	10	1	9	10	34
1995-96	Rochester	AHL	48	0	7	7	99	5	0	1	1	8

WRIGHT, TYLER — PIT.

Center. Shoots right. 5'11", 185 lbs. Born, Canora, Sask., April 6, 1973.
(Edmonton's 1st choice, 12th overall, in 1991 Entry Draft).

			Regular Season					Playoffs				
Season	Club	Lea	GP	G	A	TP	PIM	GP	G	A	TP	PIM
1989-90	Swift Current	WHL	67	14	18	32	139	4	0	0	0	12
1990-91	Swift Current	WHL	66	41	51	92	157	3	0	0	0	6
1991-92	Swift Current	WHL	63	36	46	82	295	8	2	5	7	16
1992-93	**Edmonton**	**NHL**	**7**	**1**	**1**	**2**	**19**	....	....	....	....	....
	Swift Current	WHL	37	24	41	65	76	17	9	17	26	*49
1993-94	**Edmonton**	**NHL**	**5**	**0**	**0**	**0**	**4**	....	....	....	....	....
	Cape Breton	AHL	65	14	27	41	160	5	2	0	2	11
1994-95	Cape Breton	AHL	70	16	15	31	184	....	....	....	....	....
	Edmonton	**NHL**	**6**	**1**	**0**	**1**	**14**	....	....	....	....	....
1995-96	**Edmonton**	**NHL**	**23**	**1**	**0**	**1**	**33**	....	....	....	....	....
	Cape Breton	AHL	31	6	12	18	158	....	....	....	....	....
	NHL Totals		**41**	**3**	**1**	**4**	**70**	....	....	....	....	....

Traded to **Pittsburgh** by **Edmonton** for Pittsburgh's seventh round choice (Brandon Lafrance) in 1996 Entry Draft, June 22, 1996.

YACHMENEV, VITALI — (yach-meh-NEHV) L.A.

Right wing. Shoots left. 5'9", 180 lbs. Born, Chelyabinsk, USSR, January 8, 1975.
(Los Angeles' 3rd choice, 59th overall, in 1994 Entry Draft).

			Regular Season					Playoffs				
Season	Club	Lea	GP	G	A	TP	PIM	GP	G	A	TP	PIM
1992-93	Chelyabinsk	CIS 2	51	23	20	43	12	....	....	....	....	....
1993-94a	North Bay	OHL	66	*61	52	113	18	18	13	19	32	12
1994-95	North Bay	OHL	59	53	52	105	8	6	1	8	9	2
	Phoenix	IHL	....	....	....	....	....	4	1	0	1	0
1995-96	**Los Angeles**	**NHL**	**80**	**19**	**34**	**53**	**16**	....	....	....	....	....
	NHL Totals		**80**	**19**	**34**	**53**	**16**	....	....	....	....	....

a Canadian Major Junior Rookie of the Year (1994)

YAKE, TERRY — (YAYK) BUF.

Right wing. Shoots right. 5'11", 190 lbs. Born, New Westminster, B.C., October 22, 1968.
(Hartford's 3rd choice, 81st overall, in 1987 Entry Draft).

			Regular Season					Playoffs				
Season	Club	Lea	GP	G	A	TP	PIM	GP	G	A	TP	PIM
1984-85	Brandon	WHL	11	1	1	2	0	....	....	....	....	....
1985-86	Brandon	WHL	72	26	26	52	49	....	....	....	....	....
1986-87	Brandon	WHL	71	44	58	102	64	....	....	....	....	....
1987-88	Brandon	WHL	72	55	85	140	59	3	4	2	6	7
1988-89	**Hartford**	**NHL**	**2**	**0**	**0**	**0**	**0**	....	....	....	....	....
	Binghamton	AHL	75	39	56	95	57	....	....	....	....	....
1989-90	**Hartford**	**NHL**	**2**	**0**	**1**	**1**	**0**	....	....	....	....	....
	Binghamton	AHL	77	13	42	55	37	....	....	....	....	....
1990-91	**Hartford**	**NHL**	**19**	**1**	**4**	**5**	**10**	**6**	**1**	**1**	**2**	**16**
	Springfield	AHL	60	35	42	77	56	15	9	9	18	10
1991-92	**Hartford**	**NHL**	**15**	**1**	**1**	**2**	**4**	....	....	....	....	....
	Springfield	AHL	53	21	34	55	63	8	3	4	7	2
1992-93	**Hartford**	**NHL**	**66**	**22**	**31**	**53**	**46**	....	....	....	....	....
	Springfield	AHL	16	8	14	22	27	....	....	....	....	....
1993-94	**Anaheim**	**NHL**	**82**	**21**	**31**	**52**	**44**	....	....	....	....	....
1994-95	**Toronto**	**NHL**	**19**	**3**	**2**	**5**	**2**	....	....	....	....	....
	Denver	IHL	2	0	3	3	2	17	4	11	15	16
1995-96	Milwaukee	IHL	70	32	56	88	70	5	3	6	9	4
	NHL Totals		**205**	**48**	**70**	**118**	**106**	**6**	**1**	**1**	**2**	**16**

Claimed by **Anaheim** from **Hartford** in Expansion Draft, June 24, 1993. Traded to **Toronto** by **Anaheim** for David Sacco, September 28, 1994. Signed as a free agent by **Buffalo**, August 5, 1996.

YAKHANOV, ANDREI — BOS.

Defense. Shoots right. 5'11", 187 lbs. Born, Ufa, USSR, July 23, 1973.
(Boston's 9th choice, 281st overall, in 1994 Entry Draft).

			Regular Season					Playoffs				
Season	Club	Lea	GP	G	A	TP	PIM	GP	G	A	TP	PIM
1992-93	Ufa Salavat	CIS	41	1	3	4	16	2	0	0	0	2
1993-94	Ufa Salavat	CIS	44	1	3	4	44	5	0	0	0	2
1994-95	Ufa Salavat	CIS	52	3	7	10	50	7	1	0	1	10
1995-96	Ufa Salavat	CIS	51	7	7	14	82	4	1	1	2	0

YAKUBOV, RAVIL (yah-KOO-bohv, rah-VEEL) CGY.

Center. Shoots left. 6'1", 190 lbs. Born, Moscow, USSR, July 26, 1970.
(Calgary's 6th choice, 126th overall, in 1992 Entry Draft).

			Regular Season					Playoffs				
Season	Club	Lea	GP	G	A	TP	PIM	GP	G	A	TP	PIM
1990-91	Moscow D'amo	USSR	31	4	4	8	6	....	....	....	....	....
1991-92	Moscow D'amo	CIS	39	14	1	15	29	....	....	....	....	....
1992-93	Moscow D'amo	CIS	40	7	13	20	26	10	1	2	3	6
1993-94	Moscow D'amo	CIS	44	12	12	24	30	10	3	1	4	4
1994-95	Moscow D'amo	CIS	49	15	8	23	38	14	4	3	7	20
1995-96	Moscow D'amo	CIS	45	12	16	28	34	13	2	2	4	6

YAKUSHIN, DMITRI TOR.

Defense. Shoots left. 6', 198 lbs. Born, Kharkov, USSR, January 21, 1978.
(Toronto's 9th choice, 140th overall, in 1996 Entry Draft).

			Regular Season					Playoffs				
Season	Club	Lea	GP	G	A	TP	PIM	GP	G	A	TP	PIM
1995-96	Pembroke	Jr. A	31	8	5	13	62	....	....	....	....	....

YASHIN, ALEXEI (YAH-shin) OTT.

Center. Shoots right. 6'3", 215 lbs. Born, Sverdlovsk, USSR, November 5, 1973.
(Ottawa's 1st choice, 2nd overall, in 1992 Entry Draft).

			Regular Season					Playoffs				
Season	Club	Lea	GP	G	A	TP	PIM	GP	G	A	TP	PIM
1990-91	Sverdlovsk	USSR	26	2	1	3	10	....	....	....	....	....
1991-92	Moscow D'amo	CIS	35	7	5	12	19	....	....	....	....	....
1992-93	Moscow D'amo	CIS	27	10	12	22	18	10	7	3	10	18
1993-94	**Ottawa**	**NHL**	**83**	**30**	**49**	**79**	**22**	....	....	....	....	....
1994-95	Las Vegas	IHL	24	15	20	35	32	....	....	....	....	....
	Ottawa	**NHL**	**47**	**21**	**23**	**44**	**20**	....	....	....	....	....
1995-96	CSKA	CIS	4	2	2	4	4	....	....	....	....	....
	Ottawa	**NHL**	**46**	**15**	**24**	**39**	**28**	....	....	....	....	....
	NHL Totals		**176**	**66**	**96**	**162**	**70**	....	....	....	....	....

Played in NHL All-Star Game (1994)

YAWNEY, TRENT (YAW-nee) ST.L.

Defense. Shoots left. 6'3", 195 lbs. Born, Hudson Bay, Sask., September 29, 1965.
(Chicago's 2nd choice, 45th overall, in 1984 Entry Draft).

			Regular Season					Playoffs				
Season	Club	Lea	GP	G	A	TP	PIM	GP	G	A	TP	PIM
1982-83	Saskatoon	WHL	59	6	31	37	44	6	0	2	2	0
1983-84	Saskatoon	WHL	73	13	46	59	81	....	....	....	....	....
1984-85	Saskatoon	WHL	72	16	51	67	158	3	1	6	7	7
1985-86	Cdn. National	....	73	6	15	21	60	....	....	....	....	....
1986-87	Cdn. National	....	51	4	15	19	37	....	....	....	....	....
1987-88	Cdn. National	....	60	4	12	16	81	....	....	....	....	....
	Cdn. Olympic	....	8	1	1	2	6	....	....	....	....	....
	Chicago	**NHL**	**15**	**2**	**8**	**10**	**15**	**5**	**0**	**4**	**4**	**8**
1988-89	**Chicago**	**NHL**	**69**	**5**	**19**	**24**	**116**	**15**	**3**	**6**	**9**	**20**
1989-90	**Chicago**	**NHL**	**70**	**5**	**15**	**20**	**82**	**20**	**3**	**5**	**8**	**27**
1990-91	**Chicago**	**NHL**	**61**	**3**	**13**	**16**	**77**	**1**	**0**	**0**	**0**	**0**
1991-92	**Calgary**	**NHL**	**47**	**4**	**9**	**13**	**45**	....	....	....	....	....
	Indianapolis	IHL	9	2	3	5	12	....	....	....	....	....
1992-93	**Calgary**	**NHL**	**63**	**1**	**16**	**17**	**67**	**6**	**3**	**2**	**5**	**6**
1993-94	**Calgary**	**NHL**	**58**	**6**	**15**	**21**	**60**	**7**	**0**	**0**	**0**	**16**
1994-95	**Calgary**	**NHL**	**37**	**0**	**2**	**2**	**108**	**2**	**0**	**0**	**0**	**2**
1995-96	**Calgary**	**NHL**	**69**	**0**	**3**	**3**	**88**	**4**	**0**	**0**	**0**	**2**
	NHL Totals		**489**	**26**	**100**	**126**	**658**	**60**	**9**	**17**	**26**	**81**

Traded to **Calgary** by **Chicago** for Stephane Matteau, December 16, 1991. Signed as a free agent by **St. Louis**, July 31, 1996.

YEGOROV, ALEXEI (yeh-GOH-rohv) S.J.

Center. Shoots left. 5'11", 185 lbs. Born, St. Petersburg, USSR, May 21, 1975.
(San Jose's 3rd choice, 66th overall, in 1994 Entry Draft).

			Regular Season					Playoffs				
Season	Club	Lea	GP	G	A	TP	PIM	GP	G	A	TP	PIM
1992-93	St. Peterburg	CIS	17	1	2	3	10	6	3	1	4	6
1993-94	St. Peterburg	CIS	23	5	3	8	18	6	0	0	0	4
1994-95	St. Peterburg	CIS	10	2	1	3	10	....	....	....	....	....
	Fort Worth	CHL	18	4	10	14	15	....	....	....	....	....
1995-96	**San Jose**	**NHL**	**9**	**3**	**2**	**5**	**2**	....	....	....	....	....
	Kansas City	IHL	65	31	25	56	84	5	2	0	2	8
	NHL Totals		**9**	**3**	**2**	**5**	**2**	....	....	....	....	....

YELLE, STEPHANE (YEHL-ee) COL.

Center. Shoots left. 6'1", 162 lbs. Born, Ottawa, Ont., May 9, 1974.
(New Jersey's 8th choice, 186th overall, in 1992 Entry Draft).

			Regular Season					Playoffs				
Season	Club	Lea	GP	G	A	TP	PIM	GP	G	A	TP	PIM
1991-92	Oshawa	OHL	55	12	14	26	20	7	2	0	2	1
1992-93	Oshawa	OHL	66	24	50	74	20	10	2	4	6	4
1993-94	Oshawa	OHL	66	35	69	104	22	5	1	7	8	2
1994-95	Cornwall	AHL	40	18	15	33	22	13	7	7	14	8
1995-96	**Colorado**	**NHL**	**71**	**13**	**14**	**27**	**30**	**22**	**1**	**4**	**5**	**8** ♦
	NHL Totals		**71**	**13**	**14**	**27**	**30**	**22**	**1**	**4**	**5**	**8**

Traded to **Quebec** by **New Jersey** with New Jersey's eleventh round choice (Steven Low) in 1994 Entry Draft for Quebec's eleventh round choice (Mike Hansen) in 1994 Entry Draft, June 1, 1994.

YERESKO, YURI (yeh-REHS-koh) DET.

Defense. Shoots left. 5'11", 178 lbs. Born, Moscow, USSR, August 30, 1975.
(Detroit's 8th choice, 178th overall, in 1993 Entry Draft).

			Regular Season					Playoffs				
Season	Club	Lea	GP	G	A	TP	PIM	GP	G	A	TP	PIM
1992-93	CSKA	CIS	35	0	0	0	8	....	....	....	....	....
1993-94	CSKA	CIS	45	0	0	0	16	3	0	1	1	0
1994-95	CSKA	CIS	38	0	1	1	8	2	0	0	0	0
1995-96	CSKA	CIS	42	1	1	2	31	3	0	0	0	2

YLONEN, JUHA (YOO-lih-nehn, YOO-hah) PHO.

Center. Shoots left. 6', 180 lbs. Born, Helsinki, Finland, February 13, 1972.
(Winnipeg's 5th choice, 91st overall, in 1991 Entry Draft).

			Regular Season					Playoffs				
Season	Club	Lea	GP	G	A	TP	PIM	GP	G	A	TP	PIM
1990-91	Espoo	Fin. 2	40	12	21	33	4	....	....	....	....	....
1991-92	HPK	Fin.	43	7	11	18	8	....	....	....	....	....
1992-93	HPK	Fin.	48	8	18	26	22	12	3	5	8	2
1993-94	Jokerit	Fin.	37	5	11	16	2	12	1	3	4	8
1994-95	Jokerit	Fin.	50	13	15	28	10	11	3	2	5	0
1995-96	Jokerit	Fin.	24	3	13	16	20	11	4	5	9	4

YORK, HARRY ST.L.

Center. Shoots left. 6'2", 215 lbs. Born, Panoka, Alta., April 16, 1974.

			Regular Season					Playoffs				
Season	Club	Lea	GP	G	A	TP	PIM	GP	G	A	TP	PIM
1995-96	Nashville	ECHL	64	33	50	83	122	....	....	....	....	....
	Worcester	AHL	13	8	5	13	2	4	0	4	4	4

Signed as a free agent by **St. Louis**, May 1, 1996.

YORK, JASON ANA.

Defense. Shoots right. 6'2", 195 lbs. Born, Nepean, Ont., May 20, 1970.
(Detroit's 6th choice, 129th overall, in 1990 Entry Draft).

			Regular Season					Playoffs				
Season	Club	Lea	GP	G	A	TP	PIM	GP	G	A	TP	PIM
1989-90	Windsor	OHL	39	9	30	39	38	....	....	....	....	....
	Kitchener	OHL	25	11	25	36	17	17	3	19	22	10
1990-91	Windsor	OHL	66	13	80	93	40	11	3	10	13	12
1991-92	Adirondack	AHL	49	4	20	24	32	5	0	1	1	0
1992-93	**Detroit**	**NHL**	**2**	**0**	**0**	**0**	**0**	....	....	....	....	....
	Adirondack	AHL	77	15	40	55	86	11	0	3	3	18
1993-94	**Detroit**	**NHL**	**7**	**1**	**2**	**3**	**2**	....	....	....	....	....
a	Adirondack	AHL	74	10	56	66	98	12	3	11	14	22
1994-95	**Detroit**	**NHL**	**10**	**1**	**2**	**3**	**2**	....	....	....	....	....
	Adirondack	AHL	5	1	3	4	4	....	....	....	....	....
	Anaheim	**NHL**	**15**	**0**	**8**	**8**	**12**	....	....	....	....	....
1995-96	**Anaheim**	**NHL**	**79**	**3**	**21**	**24**	**88**	....	....	....	....	....
	NHL Totals		**113**	**5**	**33**	**38**	**104**	....	....	....	....	....

a AHL First All-Star Team (1994)

Traded to **Anaheim** by **Detroit** with Mike Sillinger for Stu Grimson, Mark Ferner and Anaheim's sixth round choice (Magnus Nilsson) in 1996 Entry Draft, April 4, 1995.

YOUNG, SCOTT COL.

Right wing. Shoots right. 6', 190 lbs. Born, Clinton, MA, October 1, 1967.
(Hartford's 1st choice, 11th overall, in 1986 Entry Draft).

			Regular Season					Playoffs				
Season	Club	Lea	GP	G	A	TP	PIM	GP	G	A	TP	PIM
1985-86	Boston U.	H.E.	38	16	13	29	31	....	....	....	....	....
1986-87	Boston U.	H.E.	33	15	21	36	24	....	....	....	....	....
1987-88	U.S. National	....	56	11	47	58	31	....	....	....	....	....
	U.S. Olympic	....	6	2	6	8	4	....	....	....	....	....
	Hartford	**NHL**	**7**	**0**	**0**	**0**	**2**	**4**	**1**	**0**	**1**	**0**
1988-89	**Hartford**	**NHL**	**76**	**19**	**40**	**59**	**27**	**4**	**2**	**0**	**2**	**4**
1989-90	**Hartford**	**NHL**	**80**	**24**	**40**	**64**	**47**	**7**	**2**	**0**	**2**	**2**
1990-91	**Hartford**	**NHL**	**34**	**6**	**9**	**15**	**8**	....	....	....	....	....
	Pittsburgh	**NHL**	**43**	**11**	**16**	**27**	**33**	**17**	**1**	**6**	**7**	**2** ♦
1991-92	Bolzano	Italy	18	22	17	39	6	5	4	3	7	7
	U.S. National	....	10	2	4	6	21	....	....	....	....	....
	U.S. Olympic	....	8	2	1	3	2	....	....	....	....	....
1992-93	**Quebec**	**NHL**	**82**	**30**	**30**	**60**	**20**	**6**	**4**	**1**	**5**	**0**
1993-94	**Quebec**	**NHL**	**76**	**26**	**25**	**51**	**14**	....	....	....	....	....
1994-95	Landshut	Ger.	4	6	1	7	6	....	....	....	....	....
	Frankfurt	Ger.	1	1	0	1	0	....	....	....	....	....
	Quebec	**NHL**	**48**	**18**	**21**	**39**	**14**	**6**	**3**	**3**	**6**	**2**
1995-96	**Colorado**	**NHL**	**81**	**21**	**39**	**60**	**50**	**22**	**3**	**12**	**15**	**10** ♦
	NHL Totals		**527**	**155**	**220**	**375**	**215**	**66**	**16**	**22**	**38**	**20**

Traded to **Pittsburgh** by **Hartford** for Rob Brown, December 21, 1990. Traded to **Quebec** by **Pittsburgh** for Bryan Fogarty, March 10, 1992.

YSEBAERT, PAUL (IGHS-bahrt) T.B.

Center. Shoots left. 6'1", 190 lbs. Born, Sarnia, Ont., May 15, 1966.
(New Jersey's 4th choice, 74th overall, in 1984 Entry Draft).

			Regular Season					Playoffs				
Season	Club	Lea	GP	G	A	TP	PIM	GP	G	A	TP	PIM
1984-85	Bowling Green	CCHA	42	23	32	55	54	....	....	....	....	....
1985-86a	Bowling Green	CCHA	42	23	45	68	50	....	....	....	....	....
1986-87a	Bowling Green	CCHA	45	27	58	85	44	....	....	....	....	....
	Cdn. National	....	5	1	0	1	4	....	....	....	....	....
1987-88	Utica	AHL	78	30	49	79	60	....	....	....	....	....
1988-89	**New Jersey**	**NHL**	**5**	**0**	**4**	**4**	**0**	....	....	....	....	....
	Utica	AHL	56	36	44	80	22	5	0	1	1	4
1989-90	**New Jersey**	**NHL**	**5**	**1**	**2**	**3**	**0**	....	....	....	....	....
bcd	Utica	AHL	74	53	52	*105	61	5	2	4	6	0
1990-91	**New Jersey**	**NHL**	**11**	**4**	**3**	**7**	**6**	....	....	....	....	....
	Detroit	**NHL**	**51**	**15**	**18**	**33**	**16**	**2**	**0**	**2**	**2**	**0**
1991-92e	**Detroit**	**NHL**	**79**	**35**	**40**	**75**	**55**	**10**	**1**	**0**	**1**	**10**
1992-93	**Detroit**	**NHL**	**80**	**34**	**28**	**62**	**42**	**7**	**3**	**1**	**4**	**2**
1993-94	**Winnipeg**	**NHL**	**60**	**9**	**18**	**27**	**18**	....	....	....	....	....
	Chicago	**NHL**	**11**	**5**	**3**	**8**	**8**	**6**	**0**	**0**	**0**	**8**
1994-95	**Chicago**	**NHL**	**15**	**4**	**5**	**9**	**6**	....	....	....	....	....
	Tampa Bay	**NHL**	**29**	**8**	**11**	**19**	**12**	....	....	....	....	....
1995-96	**Tampa Bay**	**NHL**	**55**	**16**	**15**	**31**	**16**	**5**	**0**	**0**	**0**	**0**
	NHL Totals		**401**	**131**	**147**	**278**	**179**	**30**	**4**	**3**	**7**	**20**

a CCHA Second All-Star Team (1986, 1987)
b AHL First All-Star Team (1990)
c Won John B. Sollenberger Trophy (Top Scorer - AHL) (1990)
d Won Les Cunningham Plaque (MVP - AHL) (1990)
e Won Alka-Seltzer Plus Award (1992)

Traded to **Detroit** by **New Jersey** for Lee Norwood and Detroit's fourth round choice (Scott McCabe) in 1992 Entry Draft, November 27, 1990. Traded to **Winnipeg** by **Detroit** with future considerations (Alan Kerr, June 18, 1993) for Aaron Ward and Toronto's fourth round choice (previously acquired by Winnipeg — later traded to Detroit — Detroit selected John Jakopin) in 1993 Entry Draft, June 11, 1993. Traded to **Chicago** by **Winnipeg** for Chicago's third round choice in 1995 Entry Draft, March 21, 1994. Traded to **Tampa Bay** by **Chicago** with Rich Sutter for Jim Cummins, Tom Tilley and Jeff Buchanan, February 22, 1995.

YUSHKEVICH, DIMITRI (yoosh-KAY-vihch) TOR.

Defense. Shoots right. 5'11", 208 lbs. Born, Yaroslavl, USSR, November 19, 1971.
(Philadelphia's 6th choice, 122nd overall, in 1991 Entry Draft).

				Regular Season					Playoffs			
Season	Club	Lea	GP	G	A	TP	PIM	GP	G	A	TP	PIM
1988-89	Torpedo Yaro.	USSR	23	2	1	3	8	....	....	....	....	....
1989-90	Torpedo Yaro.	USSR	41	2	3	5	39	....	....	....	....	....
1990-91	Torpedo Yaro.	USSR	41	10	4	14	22	....	....	....	....	....
1991-92	Moscow D'amo	CIS	35	5	7	12	14	....	....	....	....	....
1992-93	**Philadelphia**	NHL	82	5	27	32	71	....	....	....	....	....
1993-94	**Philadelphia**	NHL	75	5	25	30	86	....	....	....	....	....
1994-95	Torpedo Yaro.	CIS	10	3	4	7	8	....	....	....	....	....
	Philadelphia	NHL	40	5	9	14	47	15	1	5	6	12
1995-96	**Toronto**	NHL	69	1	10	11	54	4	0	0	0	0
	NHL Totals		**266**	**16**	**71**	**87**	**258**	**19**	**1**	**5**	**6**	**12**

Traded to **Toronto** by **Philadelphia** with Philadelphia's second round choice (Francis Larivee) in 1996 Entry Draft for Toronto's first round choice (Dainius Zubrus) in 1996 Entry Draft, second round choice in 1997 Entry Draft and Los Angeles' fourth round choice (previously acquired by Toronto — later traded to Los Angeles — Los Angeles selected Mikael Simons) in 1996 Entry Draft, August 30, 1995.

YZERMAN, STEVE (IGH-zuhr-muhn) DET.

Center. Shoots right. 5'11", 185 lbs. Born, Cranbrook, B.C., May 9, 1965.
(Detroit's 1st choice, 4th overall, in 1983 Entry Draft).

				Regular Season					Playoffs			
Season	Club	Lea	GP	G	A	TP	PIM	GP	G	A	TP	PIM
1981-82	Peterborough	OHL	58	21	43	64	65	6	0	1	1	16
1982-83	Peterborough	OHL	56	42	49	91	33	4	1	4	5	0
1983-84a	**Detroit**	NHL	80	39	48	87	33	4	3	3	6	0
1984-85	**Detroit**	NHL	80	30	59	89	58	3	2	1	3	2
1985-86	**Detroit**	NHL	51	14	28	42	16	....	....	....	....	....
1986-87	**Detroit**	NHL	80	31	59	90	43	16	5	13	18	8
1987-88	**Detroit**	NHL	64	50	52	102	44	3	1	3	4	6
1988-89b	**Detroit**	NHL	80	65	90	155	61	6	5	5	10	2
1989-90	**Detroit**	NHL	79	62	65	127	79	....	....	....	....	....
1990-91	**Detroit**	NHL	80	51	57	108	34	7	3	3	6	4
1991-92	**Detroit**	NHL	79	45	58	103	64	11	3	5	8	12
1992-93	**Detroit**	NHL	84	58	79	137	44	7	4	3	7	4
1993-94	**Detroit**	NHL	58	24	58	82	36	3	1	3	4	0
1994-95	**Detroit**	NHL	47	12	26	38	40	15	4	8	12	0
1995-96	**Detroit**	NHL	80	36	59	95	64	18	8	12	20	4
	NHL Totals		**942**	**517**	**738**	**1255**	**616**	**93**	**39**	**59**	**98**	**42**

a NHL All-Rookie Team (1984)
b Won Lester B. Pearson Award (1989)
Played in NHL All-Star Game (1984, 1988-93)

ZABRANSKY, LIBOR ST.L.

Defense. Shoots left. 6'3", 196 lbs. Born, Brno, Czech., November 25, 1973.
(St. Louis' 7th choice, 209th overall, in 1995 Entry Draft).

				Regular Season					Playoffs			
Season	Club	Lea	GP	G	A	TP	PIM	GP	G	A	TP	PIM
1994-95	Budejovice	Czech.	44	2	6	8	54	9	0	4	4	6
1995-96	Budejovice	Czech.	40	4	7	11	....	10	0	1	1	....

ZALAPSKI, ZARLEY CGY.

Defense. Shoots left. 6'1", 215 lbs. Born, Edmonton, Alta., April 22, 1968.
(Pittsburgh's 1st choice, 4th overall, in 1986 Entry Draft).

				Regular Season					Playoffs			
Season	Club	Lea	GP	G	A	TP	PIM	GP	G	A	TP	PIM
1985-86	Cdn. National	....	32	2	4	6	10	....	....	....	....	....
1986-87	Cdn. National	....	74	11	29	40	28	....	....	....	....	....
1987-88	Cdn. National	....	47	3	13	16	32	....	....	....	....	....
	Cdn. Olympic	....	8	1	3	4	2	....	....	....	....	....
	Pittsburgh	NHL	15	3	8	11	7	....	....	....	....	....
1988-89a	**Pittsburgh**	NHL	58	12	33	45	57	11	1	8	9	13
1989-90	**Pittsburgh**	NHL	51	6	25	31	37	....	....	....	....	....
1990-91	**Pittsburgh**	NHL	66	12	36	48	59	....	....	....	....	....
	Hartford	NHL	11	3	3	6	6	6	1	3	4	8
1991-92	**Hartford**	NHL	79	20	37	57	120	7	2	3	5	6
1992-93	**Hartford**	NHL	83	14	51	65	94	....	....	....	....	....
1993-94	**Hartford**	NHL	56	7	30	37	56	....	....	....	....	....
	Calgary	NHL	13	3	7	10	18	7	0	3	3	2
1994-95	**Calgary**	NHL	48	4	24	28	46	7	0	4	4	4
1995-96	**Calgary**	NHL	80	12	17	29	115	4	0	1	1	10
	NHL Totals		**560**	**96**	**271**	**367**	**615**	**42**	**4**	**22**	**26**	**43**

a NHL All-Rookie Team (1989)
Played in NHL All-Star Game (1993)

Traded to **Hartford** by **Pittsburgh** with John Cullen and Jeff Parker for Ron Francis, Grant Jennings and Ulf Samuelsson, March 4, 1991. Traded to **Calgary** by **Hartford** with James Patrick and Michael Nylander for Gary Suter, Paul Ranheim and Ted Drury, March 10, 1994.

ZAMUNER, ROB (ZAM-nuhr) T.B.

Left wing. Shoots left. 6'2", 202 lbs. Born, Oakville, Ont., September 17, 1969.
(NY Rangers' 3rd choice, 45th overall, in 1989 Entry Draft).

				Regular Season					Playoffs			
Season	Club	Lea	GP	G	A	TP	PIM	GP	G	A	TP	PIM
1986-87	Guelph	OHL	62	6	15	21	8	....	....	....	....	....
1987-88	Guelph	OHL	58	20	41	61	18	....	....	....	....	....
1988-89	Guelph	OHL	66	46	65	111	38	7	5	5	10	9
1989-90	Flint	IHL	77	44	35	79	32	4	1	0	1	6
1990-91	Binghamton	AHL	80	25	58	83	50	9	7	6	13	35
1991-92	**NY Rangers**	NHL	9	1	2	3	2	....	....	....	....	....
	Binghamton	AHL	61	19	53	72	42	11	8	9	17	8
1992-93	**Tampa Bay**	NHL	84	15	28	43	74	....	....	....	....	....
1993-94	**Tampa Bay**	NHL	59	6	6	12	42	....	....	....	....	....
1994-95	**Tampa Bay**	NHL	43	9	6	15	24	....	....	....	....	....
1995-96	**Tampa Bay**	NHL	72	15	20	35	62	6	2	3	5	10
	NHL Totals		**267**	**46**	**62**	**108**	**204**	**6**	**2**	**3**	**5**	**10**

Signed as a free agent by **Tampa Bay**, July 13, 1992.

ZANUTTO, MIKE BUF.

Center. Shoots left. 6', 190 lbs. Born, Burlington, Ont., January 1, 1977.
(Buffalo's 10th choice, 198th overall, in 1995 Entry Draft).

				Regular Season					Playoffs			
Season	Club	Lea	GP	G	A	TP	PIM	GP	G	A	TP	PIM
1994-95	North Bay	OHL	13	1	1	2	2	....	....	....	....	....
	Oshawa	OHL	42	13	17	30	2	7	4	1	5	0
1995-96	Oshawa	OHL	66	32	38	70	6	5	0	2	2	0

ZAVISHA, BRAD (zuh-VIH-shuh)

Left wing. Shoots left. 6'2", 205 lbs. Born, Hines Creek, Alta., January 4, 1972.
(Quebec's 3rd choice, 43rd overall, in 1990 Entry Draft).

				Regular Season					Playoffs			
Season	Club	Lea	GP	G	A	TP	PIM	GP	G	A	TP	PIM
1988-89	Seattle	WHL	52	8	13	21	43	....	....	....	....	....
1989-90	Seattle	WHL	69	22	38	60	124	13	1	6	7	16
1990-91	Seattle	WHL	24	15	12	27	40	....	....	....	....	....
	Portland	WHL	48	25	22	47	41	....	....	....	....	....
1991-92a	Portland	WHL	11	7	4	11	18	....	....	....	....	....
	Lethbridge	WHL	59	44	40	84	160	5	3	1	4	18
1992-93				DID NOT PLAY – INJURED								
1993-94	**Edmonton**	NHL	2	0	0	0	0	....	....	....	....	....
	Cape Breton	AHL	58	19	15	34	114	2	0	0	0	2
1994-95	Cape Breton	AHL	62	13	20	33	55	....	....	....	....	....
	Hershey	AHL	9	3	0	3	12	....	....	....	....	....
1995-96	Hershey	AHL	5	1	0	1	2	....	....	....	....	....
	Michigan	IHL	5	1	0	1	2	....	....	....	....	....
	NHL Totals		**2**	**0**	**0**	**0**	**0**					

a WHL East First All-Star Team (1992)

Traded to **Edmonton** by **Quebec** with Ron Tugnutt for Martin Rucinsky, March 10, 1992. Traded to **Philadelphia** by **Edmonton** with Edmonton's sixth round choice (Jamie Sokolosky) in 1995 Entry Draft for Ryan McGill, March 13, 1995.

ZEDNIK, RICHARD WSH.

Left wing. Shoots left. 5'11", 172 lbs. Born, Bystrica, Czech., January 6, 1976.
(Washington's 10th choice, 249th overall, in 1994 Entry Draft).

				Regular Season					Playoffs			
Season	Club	Lea	GP	G	A	TP	PIM	GP	G	A	TP	PIM
1993-94	Bystrica	Slov. 2	25	3	6	9	....	....	....	....	....	....
1994-95	Portland	WHL	65	35	51	86	89	9	5	5	10	20
1995-96	**Washington**	NHL	1	0	0	0	0	....	....	....	....	....
a	Portland	WHL	61	44	37	81	154	7	8	4	12	23
	Portland	AHL	1	1	1	2	0	21	4	5	9	26
	NHL Totals		**1**	**0**	**0**	**0**	**0**					

a WHL West Second All-Star Team (1996)

ZELENKO, BORIS PIT.

Left wing. Shoots right. 6'1", 172 lbs. Born, Moscow, USSR, September 12, 1975.
(Pittsburgh's 11th choice, 206th overall, in 1994 Entry Draft).

				Regular Season					Playoffs			
Season	Club	Lea	GP	G	A	TP	PIM	GP	G	A	TP	PIM
1993-94	CSKA	CIS	34	5	1	6	10	1	0	0	0	0
1994-95	CSKA	CIS	35	5	1	6	12	1	0	0	0	0
1995-96	CSKA	CIS	26	4	2	6	8	3	1	0	1	0

ZELEPUKIN, VALERI (zeh-leh-POO-kin) N.J.

Left wing. Shoots left. 5'11", 190 lbs. Born, Voskresensk, USSR, September 17, 1968.
(New Jersey's 13th choice, 221st overall, in 1990 Entry Draft).

				Regular Season					Playoffs			
Season	Club	Lea	GP	G	A	TP	PIM	GP	G	A	TP	PIM
1984-85	Khimik	USSR	5	0	0	0	2	....	....	....	....	....
1985-86	Khimik	USSR	33	2	2	4	10	....	....	....	....	....
1986-87	Khimik	USSR	19	1	0	1	4	....	....	....	....	....
1987-88	SKA MVO	USSR 2	18	18	6	24	....	....	....	....	....	....
	CSKA	USSR	19	3	1	4	8	....	....	....	....	....
1988-89	CSKA	USSR	17	2	3	5	2	....	....	....	....	....
1989-90	Khimik	USSR	46	17	14	31	26	....	....	....	....	....
1990-91	Khimik	USSR	34	11	6	17	38	....	....	....	....	....
1991-92	**New Jersey**	NHL	44	13	18	31	28	4	1	1	2	2
	Utica	AHL	22	20	9	29	8	....	....	....	....	....
1992-93	**New Jersey**	NHL	78	23	41	64	70	5	0	2	2	0
1993-94	**New Jersey**	NHL	82	26	31	57	70	20	5	2	7	14
1994-95	**New Jersey**	NHL	4	1	2	3	6	18	1	2	3	12 ◆
1995-96	**New Jersey**	NHL	61	6	9	15	107	....	....	....	....	....
	NHL Totals		**269**	**69**	**101**	**170**	**281**	**47**	**7**	**7**	**14**	**28**

ZENT, JASON OTT.

Left wing. Shoots left. 5'11", 180 lbs. Born, Buffalo, NY, April 15, 1971.
(NY Islanders' 3rd choice, 44th overall, in 1989 Entry Draft).

				Regular Season					Playoffs			
Season	Club	Lea	GP	G	A	TP	PIM	GP	G	A	TP	PIM
1990-91	U. Wisconsin	WCHA	39	19	18	37	51	....	....	....	....	....
1991-92a	U. Wisconsin	WCHA	39	22	17	39	128	....	....	....	....	....
1992-93	U. Wisconsin	WCHA	40	26	12	38	92	....	....	....	....	....
1993-94	U. Wisconsin	WCHA	42	20	21	41	120	....	....	....	....	....
1994-95	P.E.I.	AHL	55	15	11	26	46	9	6	1	7	6
1995-96	P.E.I.	AHL	68	14	5	19	61	5	2	1	3	4

a NCAA All-Tournament Team (1992)

Traded to **Ottawa** by **NY Islanders** for Ottawa's fifth round choice (Andy Berenzweig) in 1996 Entry Draft, October 15, 1994.

ZETTLER, ROB TOR.

Defense. Shoots left. 6'3", 200 lbs. Born, Sept Iles, Que., March 8, 1968.
(Minnesota's 5th choice, 55th overall, in 1986 Entry Draft).

				Regular Season					Playoffs			
Season	Club	Lea	GP	G	A	TP	PIM	GP	G	A	TP	PIM
1985-86	S.S. Marie	OHL	57	5	23	28	92	....	....	....	....	....
1986-87	S.S. Marie	OHL	64	13	22	35	89	4	0	0	0	0
1987-88	Kalamazoo	IHL	2	0	1	1	0	7	0	2	2	2
	S.S. Marie	OHL	64	7	41	48	77	6	2	2	4	9
1988-89	**Minnesota**	NHL	2	0	0	0	0	....	....	....	....	....
	Kalamazoo	IHL	80	5	21	26	79	6	0	1	1	26
1989-90	**Minnesota**	NHL	31	0	8	8	45	....	....	....	....	....
	Kalamazoo	IHL	41	6	10	16	64	7	0	0	0	6
1990-91	**Minnesota**	NHL	47	1	4	5	119	....	....	....	....	....
	Kalamazoo	IHL	1	0	0	0	2	....	....	....	....	....
1991-92	**San Jose**	NHL	74	1	8	9	99	....	....	....	....	....
1992-93	**San Jose**	NHL	80	0	7	7	150	....	....	....	....	....
1993-94	**San Jose**	NHL	42	0	3	3	65	....	....	....	....	....
	Philadelphia	NHL	33	0	4	4	69	....	....	....	....	....
1994-95	**Philadelphia**	NHL	32	0	1	1	34	1	0	0	0	2
1995-96	**Toronto**	NHL	29	0	1	1	48	2	0	0	0	0
	NHL Totals		**370**	**2**	**36**	**38**	**629**	**3**	**0**	**0**	**0**	**2**

Claimed by **San Jose** from **Minnesota** in Dispersal Draft, May 30, 1991. Traded to **Philadelphia** by **San Jose** for Viacheslav Butsayev, February 1, 1994. Traded to **Toronto** by **Philadelphia** for Toronto's fifth round choice (Per-Ragna Bergqvist) in 1996 Entry Draft, July 8, 1995.

ZEZEL, PETER (ZEH-zehl) ST.L.

Center. Shoots left. 5'11", 200 lbs. Born, Toronto, Ont., April 22, 1965.
(Philadelphia's 1st choice, 41st overall, in 1983 Entry Draft).

			Regular Season					Playoffs				
Season	Club	Lea	GP	G	A	TP	PIM	GP	G	A	TP	PIM
1982-83	Toronto	OHL	66	35	39	74	28	4	2	4	6	0
1983-84	Toronto	OHL	68	47	86	133	31	9	7	5	12	4
1984-85	**Philadelphia**	**NHL**	**65**	**15**	**46**	**61**	**26**	**19**	**1**	**8**	**9**	**28**
1985-86	**Philadelphia**	**NHL**	**79**	**17**	**37**	**54**	**76**	**5**	**3**	**1**	**4**	**4**
1986-87	**Philadelphia**	**NHL**	**71**	**33**	**39**	**72**	**71**	**25**	**3**	**10**	**13**	**10**
1987-88	**Philadelphia**	**NHL**	**69**	**22**	**35**	**57**	**42**	**7**	**3**	**2**	**5**	**7**
1988-89	**Philadelphia**	**NHL**	**26**	**4**	**13**	**17**	**15**	....	....	....	....	....
	St. Louis	**NHL**	**52**	**17**	**36**	**53**	**27**	**10**	**6**	**6**	**12**	**4**
1989-90	**St. Louis**	**NHL**	**73**	**25**	**47**	**72**	**30**	**12**	**1**	**7**	**8**	**4**
1990-91	**Washington**	**NHL**	**20**	**7**	**5**	**12**	**10**	....	....	....	....	....
	Toronto	**NHL**	**32**	**14**	**14**	**28**	**4**	....	....	....	....	....
1991-92	**Toronto**	**NHL**	**64**	**16**	**33**	**49**	**26**	....	....	....	....	....
1992-93	**Toronto**	**NHL**	**70**	**12**	**23**	**35**	**24**	**20**	**2**	**1**	**3**	**6**
1993-94	**Toronto**	**NHL**	**41**	**8**	**8**	**16**	**19**	**18**	**2**	**4**	**6**	**8**
1994-95	**Dallas**	**NHL**	**30**	**6**	**5**	**11**	**19**	**3**	**1**	**0**	**1**	**0**
	Kalamazoo	IHL	2	0	0	0	0	....	....	....	....	....
1995-96	**St. Louis**	**NHL**	**57**	**8**	**13**	**21**	**12**	**10**	**3**	**0**	**3**	**2**
	NHL Totals		**749**	**204**	**354**	**558**	**401**	**129**	**25**	**39**	**64**	**73**

Traded to **St. Louis** by **Philadelphia** for Mike Bullard, November 29, 1988. Traded to **Washington** by **St. Louis** with Mike Lalor for Geoff Courtnall, July 13, 1990. Traded to **Toronto** by **Washington** with Bob Rouse for Al Iafrate, January 16, 1991. Acquired by **Dallas** from **Toronto** with Grant Marshall as compensation for Toronto's signing of free agent Mike Craig, August 10, 1994.

ZHAMNOV, ALEXEI (ZHAHM-nahf) CHI.

Center. Shoots left. 6'1", 195 lbs. Born, Moscow, USSR, October 1, 1970.
(Winnipeg's 5th choice, 77th overall, in 1990 Entry Draft).

			Regular Season					Playoffs				
Season	Club	Lea	GP	G	A	TP	PIM	GP	G	A	TP	PIM
1988-89	Moscow D'amo	USSR	4	0	0	0	0	....	....	....	....	....
1989-90	Moscow D'amo	USSR	43	11	6	17	21	....	....	....	....	....
1990-91	Moscow D'amo	USSR	46	16	12	28	24	....	....	....	....	....
1991-92	Moscow D'amo	CIS	39	15	21	36	28	....	....	....	....	....
1992-93	**Winnipeg**	**NHL**	**68**	**25**	**47**	**72**	**58**	**6**	**0**	**2**	**2**	**2**
1993-94	**Winnipeg**	**NHL**	**61**	**26**	**45**	**71**	**62**	....	....	....	....	....
1994-95a	**Winnipeg**	**NHL**	**48**	**30**	**35**	**65**	**20**	....	....	....	....	....
1995-96	**Winnipeg**	**NHL**	**58**	**22**	**37**	**59**	**65**	**6**	**2**	**1**	**3**	**8**
	NHL Totals		**235**	**103**	**164**	**267**	**205**	**12**	**2**	**3**	**5**	**10**

a NHL Second All-Star Team (1995)

Traded to **Chicago** by **Phoenix** with Craig Mills and Phoenix's first round choice in 1998 Entry Draft for Jeremy Roenick, August 16, 1996.

ZHITNIK, ALEXEI (ZHIHT-nihk) BUF.

Defense. Shoots left. 5'11", 204 lbs. Born, Kiev, USSR, October 10, 1972.
(Los Angeles' 3rd choice, 81st overall, in 1991 Entry Draft).

			Regular Season					Playoffs				
Season	Club	Lea	GP	G	A	TP	PIM	GP	G	A	TP	PIM
1989-90	Sokol Kiev	USSR	31	3	4	7	16	....	....	....	....	....
1990-91	Sokol Kiev	USSR	46	1	4	5	46	....	....	....	....	....
1991-92	CSKA	CIS	44	2	7	9	52	....	....	....	....	....
1992-93	**Los Angeles**	**NHL**	**78**	**12**	**36**	**48**	**80**	**24**	**3**	**9**	**12**	**26**
1993-94	**Los Angeles**	**NHL**	**81**	**12**	**40**	**52**	**101**	....	....	....	....	....
1994-95	**Los Angeles**	**NHL**	**11**	**2**	**5**	**7**	**27**	....	....	....	....	....
	Buffalo	**NHL**	**21**	**2**	**5**	**7**	**34**	**5**	**0**	**1**	**1**	**14**
1995-96	**Buffalo**	**NHL**	**80**	**6**	**30**	**36**	**58**	....	....	....	....	....
	NHL Totals		**271**	**34**	**116**	**150**	**300**	**29**	**3**	**10**	**13**	**40**

Traded to **Buffalo** by **Los Angeles** with Robb Stauber, Charlie Huddy and Los Angeles' fifth round choice (Marian Menhart) in 1995 Entry Draft for Philippe Boucher, Denis Tsygurov and Grant Fuhr, February 14, 1995.

ZHOLTOK, SERGEI (ZHOL-tok) OTT.

Center. Shoots right. 6', 190 lbs. Born, Riga, Latvia, December 2, 1972.
(Boston's 2nd choice, 55th overall, in 1992 Entry Draft).

			Regular Season					Playoffs				
Season	Club	Lea	GP	G	A	TP	PIM	GP	G	A	TP	PIM
1990-91	Dynamo Riga	USSR	39	4	0	4	16	....	....	....	....	....
1991-92	Riga	CIS	27	6	3	9	6	....	....	....	....	....
1992-93	**Boston**	**NHL**	**1**	**0**	**1**	**1**	**0**	....	....	....	....	....
	Providence	AHL	64	31	35	66	57	6	3	5	8	4
1993-94	**Boston**	**NHL**	**24**	**2**	**1**	**3**	**2**	....	....	....	....	....
	Providence	AHL	54	29	33	62	16	....	....	....	....	....
1994-95	Providence	AHL	78	23	35	58	42	13	8	5	13	6
1995-96	Las Vegas	IHL	82	51	50	101	30	15	7	13	20	6
	NHL Totals		**25**	**2**	**2**	**4**	**2**	....	....	....	....	....

Signed as a free agent by **Ottawa**, August, 1996.

ZHURIK, ALEXANDER (ZHUH-rihk) EDM.

Defense. Shoots left. 6'3", 195 lbs. Born, Minsk, USSR, May 29, 1975.
(Edmonton's 7th choice, 163rd overall, in 1993 Entry Draft).

			Regular Season					Playoffs				
Season	Club	Lea	GP	G	A	TP	PIM	GP	G	A	TP	PIM
1993-94	Kingston	OHL	59	7	23	30	92	6	0	0	0	4
1994-95	Kingston	OHL	54	3	21	24	51	6	0	0	0	0
1995-96	Cape Breton	AHL	80	5	36	41	85	....	....	....	....	....

ZIB, LUKAS (ZIHB, LOO-kahsh) EDM.

Defense. Shoots right. 6'1", 200 lbs. Born, Ceske Budejovice, Czech., February 24, 1977.
(Edmonton's 3rd choice, 57th overall, in 1995 Entry Draft).

			Regular Season					Playoffs				
Season	Club	Lea	GP	G	A	TP	PIM	GP	G	A	TP	PIM
1994-95	Budejovice	Czech.	13	2	0	2	16	9	1	0	1	6
1995-96	Budejovice	Czech. Jr.	11	5	1	6	....	....	....	....	....	....
	Budejovice	Czech.	7	1	0	1	....	2	0	0	0	....

ZIMAKOV, SERGEI (zih-MAH-kahv) WSH.

Defense. Shoots left. 6'1", 194 lbs. Born, Moscow, USSR, January 15, 1978.
(Washington's 4th choice, 58th overall, in 1996 Entry Draft).

			Regular Season					Playoffs				
Season	Club	Lea	GP	G	A	TP	PIM	GP	G	A	TP	PIM
1995-96	Soviet Wings	CIS	49	2	7	9	36	....	....	....	....	....

ZMOLEK, DOUG (zuh-MOH-lehk) L.A.

Defense. Shoots left. 6'2", 220 lbs. Born, Rochester, MN, November 3, 1970.
(Minnesota's 1st choice, 7th overall, in 1989 Entry Draft).

			Regular Season					Playoffs				
Season	Club	Lea	GP	G	A	TP	PIM	GP	G	A	TP	PIM
1989-90	U. Minnesota	WCHA	40	1	10	11	52	....	....	....	....	....
1990-91	U. Minnesota	WCHA	34	11	6	17	38	....	....	....	....	....
1991-92ab	U. Minnesota	WCHA	41	6	20	26	84	....	....	....	....	....
1992-93	**San Jose**	**NHL**	**84**	**5**	**10**	**15**	**229**	....	....	....	....	....
1993-94	**San Jose**	**NHL**	**68**	**0**	**4**	**4**	**122**	....	....	....	....	....
	Dallas	**NHL**	**7**	**1**	**0**	**1**	**11**	**7**	**0**	**1**	**1**	**4**
1994-95	**Dallas**	**NHL**	**42**	**0**	**5**	**5**	**67**	**5**	**0**	**0**	**0**	**10**
1995-96	**Dallas**	**NHL**	**42**	**1**	**5**	**6**	**65**	....	....	....	....	....
	Los Angeles	**NHL**	**16**	**1**	**0**	**1**	**22**	....	....	....	....	....
	NHL Totals		**259**	**8**	**24**	**32**	**516**	**12**	**0**	**1**	**1**	**14**

a WCHA Second All-Star Team (1992)
b NCAA West Second All-American Team (1992)

Claimed by **San Jose** from **Minnesota** in Dispersal Draft, May 30, 1991. Traded to **Dallas** by **San Jose** with Mike Lalor and cash for Ulf Dahlen and Dallas' seventh round choice (Brad Mehalko) in 1995 Entry Draft, March 19, 1994. Traded to **Los Angeles** by **Dallas** with Shane Churla for Darryl Sydor and Los Angeles' fifth round choice (Ryan Christie) in 1996 Entry Draft, February 17, 1996.

ZOLOTOV, ROMAN (ZOH-loh-tov) PHI.

Defense. Shoots left. 6'1", 191 lbs. Born, Moscow, USSR, February 13, 1974.
(Philadelphia's 5th choice, 127th overall, in 1992 Entry Draft).

			Regular Season					Playoffs				
Season	Club	Lea	GP	G	A	TP	PIM	GP	G	A	TP	PIM
1991-92	Moscow D'amo	CIS	1	0	0	0	0	....	....	....	....	....
1992-93	Moscow D'amo	CIS Jr.				UNAVAILABLE						
1993-94	Moscow D'amo	CIS	33	0	2	2	20	5	0	1	1	6
1994-95	Moscow D'amo	CIS	25	0	2	2	24	8	1	2	3	6
1995-96	Moscow D'amo	CIS	41	0	2	2	94	9	0	1	1	6

ZOMBO, RICK

Defense. Shoots right. 6'1", 202 lbs. Born, Des Plaines, IL, May 8, 1963.
(Detroit's 6th choice, 149th overall, in 1981 Entry Draft).

			Regular Season					Playoffs				
Season	Club	Lea	GP	G	A	TP	PIM	GP	G	A	TP	PIM
1981-82	North Dakota	WCHA	45	1	15	16	31	....	....	....	....	....
1982-83	North Dakota	WCHA	35	5	11	16	41	....	....	....	....	....
1983-84	North Dakota	WCHA	34	7	24	31	40	....	....	....	....	....
1984-85	**Detroit**	**NHL**	**1**	**0**	**0**	**0**	**0**	....	....	....	....	....
	Adirondack	AHL	56	3	32	35	70	....	....	....	....	....
1985-86	**Detroit**	**NHL**	**14**	**0**	**1**	**1**	**16**	....	....	....	....	....
	Adirondack	AHL	69	7	34	41	94	17	0	4	4	40
1986-87	**Detroit**	**NHL**	**44**	**1**	**4**	**5**	**59**	**7**	**0**	**1**	**1**	**9**
	Adirondack	AHL	25	0	6	6	22	....	....	....	....	....
1987-88	**Detroit**	**NHL**	**62**	**3**	**14**	**17**	**96**	**16**	**0**	**6**	**6**	**55**
1988-89	**Detroit**	**NHL**	**75**	**1**	**20**	**21**	**106**	**6**	**0**	**1**	**1**	**16**
1989-90	**Detroit**	**NHL**	**77**	**5**	**20**	**25**	**95**	....	....	....	....	....
1990-91	**Detroit**	**NHL**	**77**	**4**	**19**	**23**	**55**	**7**	**1**	**0**	**1**	**10**
1991-92	**Detroit**	**NHL**	**3**	**0**	**0**	**0**	**15**	....	....	....	....	....
	St. Louis	**NHL**	**64**	**3**	**15**	**18**	**46**	**6**	**0**	**2**	**2**	**12**
1992-93	**St. Louis**	**NHL**	**71**	**0**	**15**	**15**	**78**	**11**	**0**	**1**	**1**	**12**
1993-94	**St. Louis**	**NHL**	**74**	**2**	**8**	**10**	**85**	**4**	**0**	**0**	**0**	**11**
1994-95	**St. Louis**	**NHL**	**23**	**1**	**4**	**5**	**24**	**3**	**0**	**0**	**0**	**2**
1995-96	**Boston**	**NHL**	**67**	**4**	**10**	**14**	**53**	....	....	....	....	....
	NHL Totals		**652**	**24**	**130**	**154**	**728**	**60**	**1**	**11**	**12**	**127**

Traded to **St. Louis** by **Detroit** for Vincent Riendeau, October 18, 1991. Traded to **Boston** by **St. Louis** for Fred Knipscheer, October 2, 1995.

ZUBOV, SERGEI (ZOO-bahf) DAL.

Defense. Shoots right. 6'1", 200 lbs. Born, Moscow, USSR, July 22, 1970.
(NY Rangers' 6th choice, 85th overall, in 1990 Entry Draft).

			Regular Season					Playoffs				
Season	Club	Lea	GP	G	A	TP	PIM	GP	G	A	TP	PIM
1988-89	CSKA	USSR	29	1	4	5	10	....	....	....	....	....
1989-90	CSKA	USSR	48	6	2	8	16	....	....	....	....	....
1990-91	CSKA	USSR	41	6	5	11	12	....	....	....	....	....
1991-92	CSKA	CIS	44	4	7	11	8	....	....	....	....	....
1992-93	CSKA	CIS	1	0	1	1	0	....	....	....	....	....
	NY Rangers	**NHL**	**49**	**8**	**23**	**31**	**4**	....	....	....	....	....
	Binghamton	AHL	30	7	29	36	14	11	5	5	10	2
1993-94	**NY Rangers**	**NHL**	**78**	**12**	**77**	**89**	**39**	**22**	**5**	**14**	**19**	**0 ♦**
	Binghamton	AHL	2	1	2	3	0	....	....	....	....	....
1994-95	**NY Rangers**	**NHL**	**38**	**10**	**26**	**36**	**18**	**10**	**3**	**8**	**11**	**2**
1995-96	**Pittsburgh**	**NHL**	**64**	**11**	**55**	**66**	**22**	**18**	**1**	**14**	**15**	**26**
	NHL Totals		**229**	**41**	**181**	**222**	**83**	**50**	**9**	**36**	**45**	**28**

Traded to **Pittsburgh** by **NY Rangers** with Petr Nedved for Luc Robitaille and Ulf Samuelsson, August 31, 1995. Traded to **Dallas** by **Pittsburgh** for Kevin Hatcher, June 22, 1996.

ZUBRUS, DAINIUS (ZOO-bruhs) PHI.

Right wing. Shoots left. 6'3", 215 lbs. Born, Elektrenai, USSR, June 16, 1978.
(Philadelphia's 1st choice, 15th overall, in 1996 Entry Draft).

			Regular Season					Playoffs				
Season	Club	Lea	GP	G	A	TP	PIM	GP	G	A	TP	PIM
1995-96	Pembroke	Jr. A	28	19	13	32	73	....	....	....	....	....
	Caledon	Jr. A	7	3	7	10	2	17	11	12	23	4

ZUKIWSKY, JONATHAN ST.L.

Center. Shoots left. 6'2", 185 lbs. Born, St. Paul, Alta., October 7, 1977.
(St. Louis' 3rd choice, 95th overall, in 1996 Entry Draft).

			Regular Season					Playoffs				
Season	Club	Lea	GP	G	A	TP	PIM	GP	G	A	TP	PIM
1993-94	Red Deer	WHL	59	12	15	27	38	4	0	2	2	0
1994-95	Red Deer	WHL	71	19	24	43	45	....	....	....	....	....
1995-96	Red Deer	WHL	72	20	28	48	38	10	5	2	7	6

ZYUZIN, ANDREI (ZYOO-zin) S.J.

Defense. Shoots left. 6'1", 187 lbs. Born, Ufa, USSR, January 21, 1978.
(San Jose's 1st choice, 2nd overall, in 1996 Entry Draft).

			Regular Season					Playoffs				
Season	Club	Lea	GP	G	A	TP	PIM	GP	G	A	TP	PIM
1994-95	Ufa Salavat	CIS	30	3	0	3	16	....	....	....	....	....
1995-96	Ufa Salavat	CIS	41	6	3	9	24	....	....	....	....	....

Retired NHL Player Index

Abbreviations: Teams/Cities: — **Ana.** – Anaheim; **Atl.** – Atlanta; **Bos.** – Boston, **Bro.** – Brooklyn; **Buf.** – Buffalo; **Cal.** – California; **Cgy.** – Calgary; **Cle.** – Cleveland; **Col.** – Colorado; **Dal.** – Dallas; **Det.** – Detroit; **Edm.** – Edmonton; **Fla.** – Florida; **Ham.** – Hamilton; **Hfd.** – Hartford; **K.C.** – Kansas City; **L.A.** – Los Angeles; **Min.** — Minnesota; **Mtl.** – Montreal; **Mtl. M.** – Montreal Maroons; **Mtl. W.** – Montreal Wanderers; **N.J.** – New Jersey; **NYA** – NY Americans; **NYI** – New York Islanders; **NYR** – New York Rangers; **Oak.** – Oakland; **Ott.** – Ottawa; **Phi.** – Philadelphia; **Pit.** – Pittsburgh; **Que.** – Quebec; **St. L.** – St. Louis; **S.J.** – San Jose; **T.B.** – Tampa Bay; **Tor.** – Toronto; **Van.** – Vancouver; **Wpg.** – Winnipeg; **Wsh.** – Washington.

Total seasons are rounded off to the nearest full season. **A** – assists; **G** – goals; **GP** – games played; **PIM** – penalties in minutes; **TP** – total points. • – deceased. Assists not recorded during 1917-18 season.

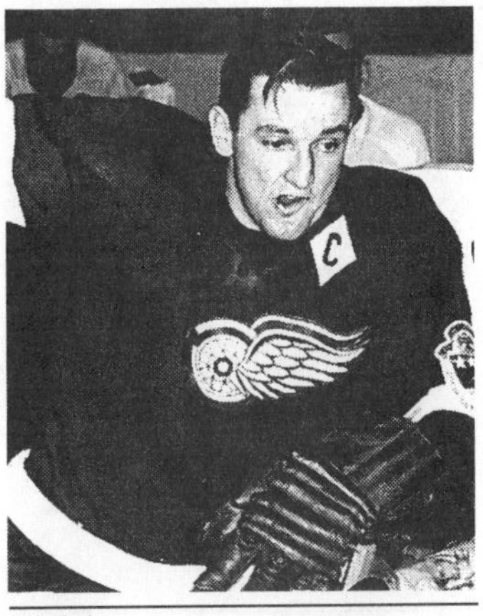
Sid Abel

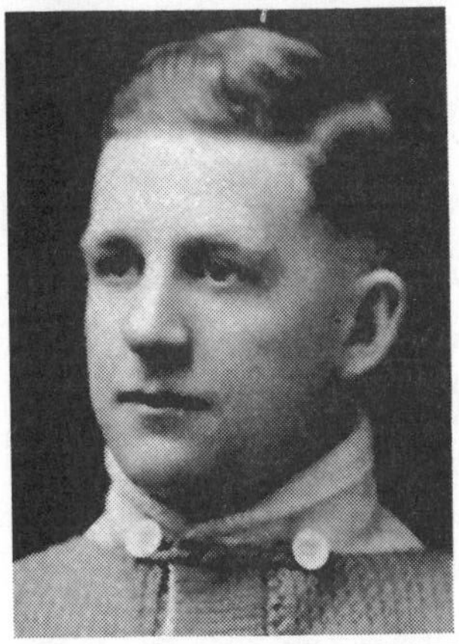
Jack Adams

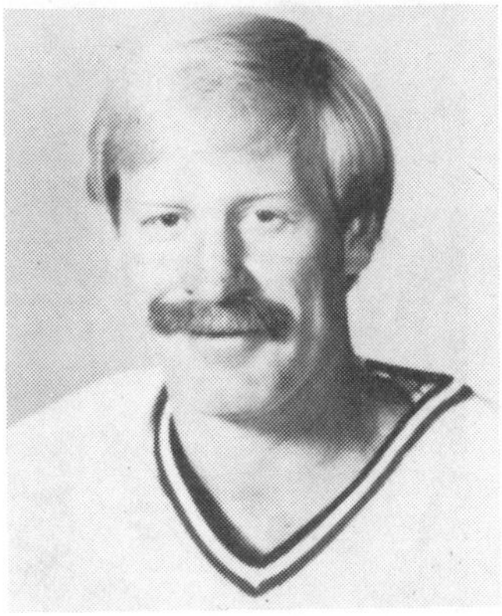
John Anderson

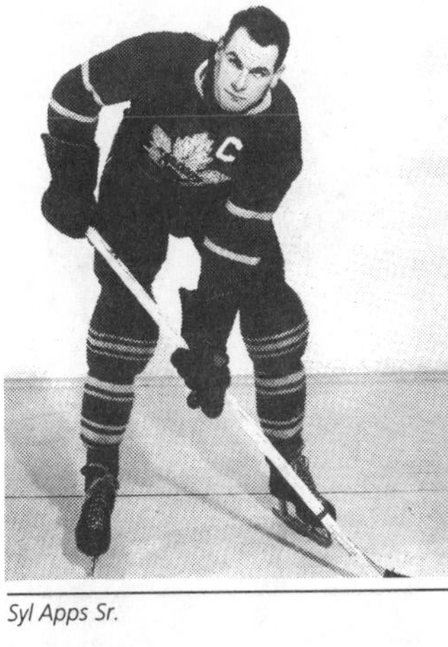
Syl Apps Sr.

A

Name	NHL Teams	NHL Seasons	Regular Schedule					Playoffs					NHL Cup Wins	First NHL Season	Last NHL Season
			GP	G	A	TP	PIM	GP	G	A	TP	PIM			
Abbott, Reg	Mtl.	1	3	0	0	0	0	....	....	....	....	....		1952-53	1952-53
• Abel, Clarence	NYR, Chi.	8	333	18	18	36	359	38	1	1	2	58	2	1926-27	1933-34
Abel, Gerry	Det.	1	1	0	0	0	0	....	....	....	....	....		1966-67	1966-67
Abel, Sid	Det., Chi.	14	612	189	283	472	376	97	28	30	58	79	3	1938-39	1953-54
Abgrall, Dennis	L.A.	1	13	0	2	2	4	....	....	....	....	....		1975-76	1975-76
Abrahamsson, Thommy	Hfd.	1	32	6	11	17	16	....	....	....	....	....		1980-81	1980-81
Achtymichuk, Gene	Mtl., Det.	4	32	3	5	8	2	....	....	....	....	....		1951-52	1958-59
Acomb, Doug	Tor.	1	2	0	1	1	0	....	....	....	....	....		1969-70	1969-70
Acton, Keith	Mtl., Min., Edm., Phi., Wsh., NYI	15	1023	226	358	584	1172	66	12	21	33	88	1	1979-80	1993-94
Adam, Douglas	NYR	1	4	0	1	1	0	....	....	....	....	....		1949-50	1949-50
Adam, Russ	Tor.	1	8	1	2	3	11	....	....	....	....	....		1982-83	1982-83
Adams, Greg C.	Phi., Hfd., Wsh., Edm., Van., Que., Det.	10	545	84	143	227	1173	43	2	11	13	153		1980-81	1989-90
Adams, Jack	Mtl.	1	42	6	12	18	11	3	0	0	0	0		1940-41	1940-41
• Adams, Jack J.	Tor., Ott.	7	173	82	29	111	307	10	3	0	3	12	2	1917-18	1926-27
• Adams, Stewart	Chi., Tor.	4	106	9	26	35	60	11	3	3	6	14		1929-30	1932-33
Adduono, Rick	Bos., Atl.	2	4	0	0	0	2	....	....	....	....	....		1975-76	1979-80
Affleck, Bruce	St.L., Van., NYI	7	280	14	66	80	86	8	0	0	0	0		1974-75	1983-84
Agnew, Jim	Van., Hfd.	6	81	0	1	1	257	4	0	0	0	6		1986-87	1992-93
Ahern, Fred	Cal., Cle., Col.	4	146	31	30	61	130	2	0	1	1	2		1974-75	1977-78
Ahlin, Tony	Chi.	1	1	0	0	0	0	....	....	....	....	....		1937-38	1937-38
Ahola, Peter	L.A., Pit., S.J., Cgy.	3	123	10	17	27	137	6	0	0	0	2		1991-92	1993-94
Ahrens, Chris	Min.	6	52	0	3	3	84	1	0	0	0	0		1973-74	1977-78
Ailsby, Lloyd	NYR	1	3	0	0	0	2	....	....	....	....	....		1951-52	1951-52
Aitken, Brad	Pit., Edm.	2	14	1	3	4	25	....	....	....	....	....		1987-88	1990-91
Albright, Clint	NYR	1	59	14	5	19	19	....	....	....	....	....		1948-49	1948-49
Aldcorn, Gary	Tor., Det., Bos.	5	226	41	56	97	78	6	1	2	3	4		1956-57	1960-61
Alexander, Claire	Tor., Van.	4	155	18	47	65	36	16	2	4	6	4		1974-75	1977-78
• Alexandre, Art	Mtl.	2	11	0	2	2	8	4	0	0	0	0		1931-32	1932-33
Allen, George	NYR, Chi., Mtl.	8	339	82	115	197	179	41	9	10	19	32		1938-39	1946-47
Allen, Jeff	Cle.	1	4	0	0	0	0	....	....	....	....	....		1977-78	1977-78
Allen, Keith	Det.	2	28	0	4	4	8	5	0	0	0	0	1	1953-54	1954-55
Allen, Viv	NYA	1	6	0	1	1	0	....	....	....	....	....		1940-41	1940-41
Alley, Steve	Hfd.	2	15	3	3	6	11	3	0	1	1	0		1979-80	1980-81
Allison, Dave	Mtl.	1	3	0	0	0	12	....	....	....	....	....		1983-84	1983-84
Allison, Mike	NYR, Tor., L.A.	10	499	102	166	268	630	82	9	17	26	135		1980-81	1989-90
Allison, Ray	Hfd., Phi.	7	238	64	93	157	223	12	2	3	5	20		1979-80	1986-87
Allum, Bill	Chi, NYR	1	1	0	1	1	0	....	....	....	....	....		1939-40	1940-41
• Amadio, Dave	Det., L.A.	3	125	5	11	16	163	16	1	2	3	18		1957-58	1968-69
Amodeo, Mike	Wpg.	1	19	0	0	0	2	....	....	....	....	....		1979-80	1979-80
Anderson, Bill	Bos.	1	....	....	....	....	....	1	0	0	0	0		1942-43	1942-43
Anderson, Dale	Det.	1	13	0	0	0	6	2	0	0	0	0		1956-57	1956-57
Anderson, Doug	Mtl.	1	....	....	....	....	....	2	0	0	0	0	1	1952-53	1952-53
Anderson, Earl	Det., Bos.	3	109	19	19	38	22	5	0	1	1	0		1974-75	1976-77
Anderson, Jim	L.A.	1	7	1	2	3	2	....	....	....	....	....		1967-68	1967-68
Anderson, John	Tor., Que., Hfd.	12	814	282	349	631	263	37	9	18	27	2		1977-78	1988-89
Anderson, Murray	Wsh.	1	40	0	1	1	68	....	....	....	....	....		1974-75	1974-75
Anderson, Perry	St. L., N.J., S.J.	10	400	50	59	109	1051	36	2	1	3	161		1981-82	1991-92
Anderson, Ron C.	Det., L.A., St.L., Buf.	5	251	28	30	58	118	5	0	0	0	4		1967-68	1971-72
Anderson, Ron H.	Wsh.	1	28	9	7	16	8	....	....	....	....	....		1974-75	1974-75
Anderson, Russ	Pit., Hfd., L.A.	9	519	22	99	121	1086	10	0	3	3	28		1976-77	1984-85
• Anderson, Tom	Det., NYA, Bro.	8	319	62	127	189	190	16	2	7	9	8		1934-35	1941-42
Andersson, Kent-Erik	Min., NYR	7	456	72	103	175	78	50	4	11	15	4		1977-78	1983-84
Andersson, Peter	Wsh., Que.	3	172	10	41	51	81	7	0	2	2	2		1983-84	1985-86
Andersson, Peter	NYR, Fla.	2	47	6	13	19	20	....	....	....	....	....		1992-93	1993-94
Andrascik, Steve	NYR	1	....	....	....	....	....	1	0	0	0	0		1971-72	1971-72
Andrea, Paul	NYR, Pit., Cal., Buf.	4	175	38	55	93	12	....	....	....	....	....		1965-66	1970-71
Andrews, Lloyd	Tor.	4	53	8	5	13	10	7	2	0	2	5		1921-22	1924-25
Andrijevski, Alexander	Chi.	1	1	0	0	0	0	....	....	....	....	....		1992-93	1992-93
Andruff, Ron	Mtl., Col.,	5	153	19	36	55	54	2	0	0	0	0		1974-75	1978-79
Angotti, Lou	NYR, Chi., Phi., Pit., St.L.	10	653	103	186	289	228	65	8	8	16	17		1964-65	1973-74
Anholt, Darrel	Chi.	1	1	0	0	0	0	....	....	....	....	....		1983-84	1983-84
Anslow, Bert	NYR	1	2	0	0	0	0	....	....	....	....	....		1947-48	1947-48
Antonovich, Mike	Min., Hfd., N.J.	5	87	10	15	25	37	....	....	....	....	....		1975-76	1983-84
Apps, Syl (Jr.)	NYR, Pit., L.A.	10	727	183	423	606	311	23	5	5	10	23		1970-71	1979-80
Apps, Syl (Sr.)	Tor.	10	423	201	231	432	56	69	25	29	54	8	3	1936-37	1947-48
Arbour, Al	Det., Chi., Tor., St.L.	16	626	12	58	70	617	86	1	8	9	92	3	1953-54	1970-71
• Arbour, Amos	Mtl., Ham., Tor.	6	109	51	13	64	66	....	....	....	....	....		1918-19	1923-24
Arbour, Jack	Det., Tor.	2	47	5	1	6	56	....	....	....	....	....		1926-27	1928-29
Arbour, John	Bos., Pit., Van., St.L.	5	106	1	9	10	149	5	0	0	0	0		1965-66	1971-72
Arbour, Ty	Pit., Chi.	5	207	28	28	56	112	11	2	0	2	6		1926-27	1930-31
Archambault, Michel	Chi.	1	3	0	0	0	0	....	....	....	....	....		1976-77	1976-77
Archibald, Jim	Min.	3	16	1	2	3	45	....	....	....	....	....		1984-85	1986-87
Areshenkoff, Ronald	Edm.	1	4	0	0	0	0	....	....	....	....	....		1979-80	1979-80
• Armstrong, Bob	Bos.	12	542	13	86	99	671	42	1	7	8	28		1950-51	1961-62
Armstrong, George	Tor.	21	1187	296	417	713	721	110	26	34	60	52	4	1949-50	1970-71
Armstrong, Murray	Tor., NYA, Bro., Det.	8	270	67	121	188	72	30	4	6	10	2		1937-38	1945-46
• Armstrong, Red	Tor.	1	7	1	1	2	2	....	....	....	....	....		1962-63	1962-63
Armstrong, Tim	Tor.	1	11	1	0	1	6	....	....	....	....	....		1988-89	1988-89
Arnason, Chuck	Mtl., Atl., Pit., K.C., Col., Cle., Min., Wsh.	8	401	109	90	199	122	9	2	4	6	4		1971-72	1978-79
Arniel, Scott	Wpg., Buf., Bos.	11	730	149	189	338	599	34	3	3	6	39		1981-82	1991-92
Arthur, Fred	Hfd., Phi.	3	80	1	8	9	49	4	0	0	0	2		1980-81	1982-83
Arundel, John	Tor.	1	3	0	0	0	9	....	....	....	....	....		1949-50	1949-50
• Ashbee, Barry	Bos., Phi.	5	284	15	70	85	291	17	0	4	4	22	1	1965-66	1973-74
• Ashby, Don	Tor., Col., Edm.	6	188	40	56	96	40	12	1	0	1	4		1975-76	1980-81
Ashton, Brent	Van., Col., N.J., Min., Que., Det., Wpg., Bos., Cgy.	14	998	284	345	629	635	85	24	25	49	70		1979-80	1992-93
Ashworth, Frank	Chi.	1	18	5	4	9	2	....	....	....	....	....		1946-47	1946-47
Asmundson, Oscar	NYR, Det., St.L., NYA, Mtl.	5	111	11	23	34	30	9	0	2	2	4	1	1932-33	1937-38
Atanas, Walt	NYR	1	49	13	8	21	40	....	....	....	....	....		1944-45	1944-45
Atcheynum, Blair	Ott.	1	4	0	1	1	0	....	....	....	....	....		1992-93	1992-93
Atkinson, Steve	Bos., Buf., Wsh.	6	302	60	51	111	104	1	0	0	0	0		1968-69	1974-75
Attwell, Bob	Col.	2	22	1	5	6	0	....	....	....	....	....		1979-80	1980-81
Attwell, Ron	St.L., NYR	1	22	1	7	8	8	....	....	....	....	....		1967-68	1967-68
Aubin, Norm	Tor.	2	69	18	13	31	30	1	0	0	0	0		1981-82	1982-83
Aubry, Pierre	Que., Det.	5	202	24	26	50	133	20	1	1	2	32		1980-81	1984-85
Aubuchon, Ossie	Bos., NYR	2	50	19	12	31	4	6	1	0	1	0		1942-43	1943-44
Auge, Les	Col.	1	6	0	3	3	4	....	....	....	....	....		1980-81	1980-81
• Aurie, Larry	Det.	12	489	147	129	276	279	24	6	9	15	10	2	1927-28	1938-39
Awrey, Don	Bos., St.L., Mtl., Pit., NYR, Col.	16	979	31	158	189	1065	71	0	18	18	150	2	1963-64	1978-79
• Ayres, Vern	NYA, Mtl.M., St.L., NYR	6	211	6	14	20	350	....	....	....	....	....		1930-31	1935-36

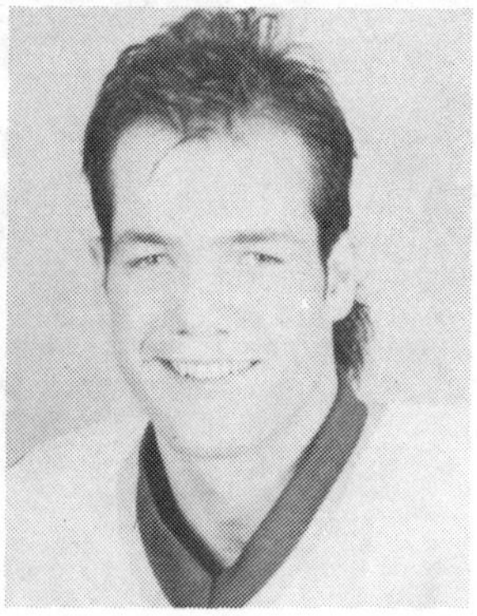

Jeff Batters

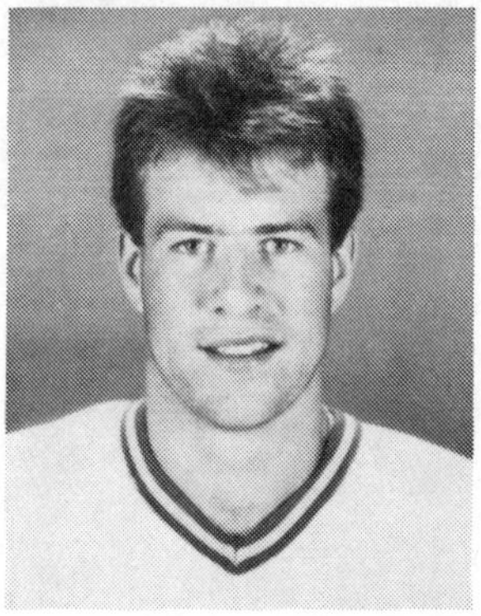

Brian Benning

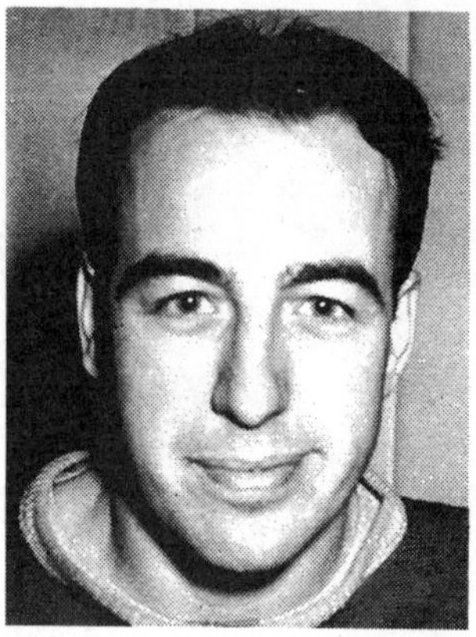

Toe Blake

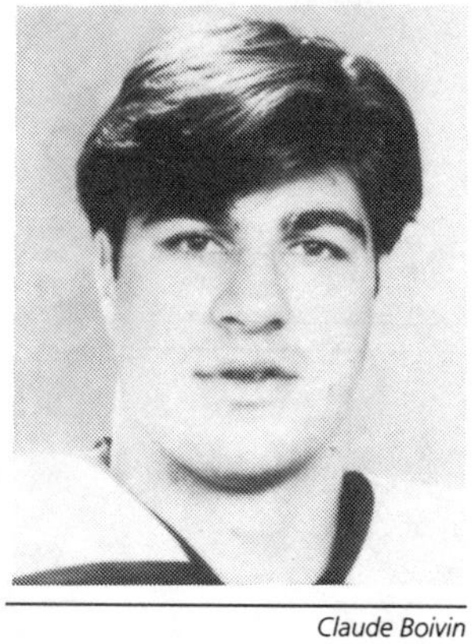

Claude Boivin

Name	NHL Teams	NHL Seasons	Regular Schedule GP	G	A	TP	PIM	Playoffs GP	G	A	TP	PIM	NHL Cup Wins	First NHL Season	Last NHL Season
B															
Babando, Pete	Bos., Det., Chi., NYR	6	351	86	73	159	194	17	3	3	6	6		1947-48	1952-53
Babcock, Bobby	Wsh.	2	2	0	0	0	2	....	....	....	....	....		1990-91	1992-93
Babe, Warren	Min.	3	21	2	5	7	23	2	0	0	0	0		1987-88	1990-91
Babin, Mitch	St.L.	1	8	0	0	0	0	....	....	....	....	....		1975-76	1975-76
Baby, John	Cle., Min.	2	26	2	8	10	26	....	....	....	....	....		1977-78	1978-79
Babych, Wayne	St.L., Pit., Que., Hfd.	9	519	192	246	438	498	41	7	9	16	24		1978-79	1986-87
Baca, Jergus	Hfd.	2	10	0	2	2	14	....	....	....	....	....		1990-91	1991-92
Backman, Mike	NYR	3	18	1	6	7	18	10	2	2	4	2		1981-82	1983-84
Backor, Peter	Tor.	1	36	4	5	9	6	....	....	....	....	....	1	1944-45	1944-45
Backstrom, Ralph	Mtl., L.A., Chi.	17	1032	278	361	639	386	116	27	32	59	68	6	1956-57	1972-73
Bailey, Ace (G.)	Bos., Det., St.L., Wsh.	10	568	107	201	278	633	15	2	4	6	18	1	1968-69	1977-78
● Bailey, Ace (I.)	Tor.	8	313	111	82	193	472	21	3	4	7	12	1	1926-27	1933-34
Bailey, Bob	Tor., Det., Chi.	5	150	15	21	36	197	15	0	4	4	22		1953-54	1957-58
Bailey, Reid	Phi., Tor., Hfd.	4	40	1	3	4	105	16	0	2	2	25		1980-81	1983-84
Baillargeon, Joel	Wpg., Que.	3	20	0	2	2	31	....	....	....	....	....		1986-87	1988-89
Baird, Ken	Cal.	1	10	0	2	2	15	....	....	....	....	....		1971-72	1971-72
Baker, Bill	Mtl., Col., St.L., NYR	3	143	7	25	32	175	6	0	0	0	0		1980-81	1982-83
Bakovic, Peter	Van.	1	10	2	0	2	48	....	....	....	....	....		1987-88	1987-88
Balderis, Helmut	Min.	1	26	3	6	9	2	....	....	....	....	....		1989-90	1989-90
Baldwin, Doug	Tor., Det., Chi.	3	24	0	1	1	8	....	....	....	....	....		1945-46	1947-48
Balfour, Earl	Tor., Chi.,	7	288	30	22	52	78	26	0	3	3	4	1	1951-52	1960-61
● Balfour, Murray	Mtl., Chi., Bos.	8	306	67	90	157	393	40	9	10	19	45	1	1956-57	1964-65
Ball, Terry	Phi., Buf.	4	74	7	19	26	26	....	....	....	....	....		1967-68	1971-72
Balon, Dave	NYR, Mtl., Min., Van.	14	776	192	222	414	607	78	14	21	35	109	2	1959-60	1972-73
Baltimore, Byron	Edm.	1	2	0	0	0	4	....	....	....	....	....		1979-80	1979-80
Baluik, Stanley	Bos.	1	7	0	0	0	2	....	....	....	....	....		1959-60	1959-60
Bandura, Jeff	NYR	1	2	0	1	1	0	....	....	....	....	....		1980-81	1980-81
Banks, Darren	Bos.	2	20	2	2	4	73	....	....	....	....	....		1992-93	1993-94
Barahona, Ralph	Bos.	2	6	2	2	4	0	....	....	....	....	....		1990-91	1991-92
Barbe, Andy	Tor.	1	1	0	0	0	2	....	....	....	....	....		1950-51	1950-51
Barber, Bill	Phi.	12	903	420	463	883	623	129	53	55	108	109	2	1972-73	1984-85
Barber, Don	Min., Wpg., Que., S.J.	4	115	25	32	57	64	11	4	4	8	10		1988-89	1991-92
● Barilko, Bill	Tor.	5	252	26	36	62	456	47	5	7	12	104	4	1946-47	1950-51
Barkley, Doug	Chi., Det.	6	253	24	80	104	382	30	0	9	9	63		1957-58	1965-66
Barlow, Bob	Min.	2	77	16	17	33	10	6	2	2	4	6		1969-70	1970-71
Barnes, Blair	L.A.	1	1	0	0	0	0	....	....	....	....	....		1982-83	1982-83
Barnes, Norm	Phi., Hfd.	5	156	6	38	44	178	12	0	0	0	8		1976-77	1981-82
Baron, Normand	Mtl., St.L.	2	27	2	0	2	51	3	0	0	0	22		1983-84	1985-86
Barrett, Fred	Min., L.A.	13	745	25	123	148	671	44	0	2	2	60		1970-71	1983-84
Barrett, John	Det., Wsh., Min.	8	488	20	77	97	604	16	2	2	4	50		1980-81	1987-88
Barrie, Doug	Pit., Buf., L.A.	3	158	10	42	52	268	....	....	....	....	....		1968-69	1971-72
Barry, Ed	Bos.	1	19	1	3	4	2	....	....	....	....	....		1946-47	1946-47
● Barry, Marty	NYA, Bos., Det., Mtl.	12	509	195	192	387	231	43	15	18	33	34	2	1927-28	1939-40
Barry, Ray	Bos.	1	18	1	2	3	6	....	....	....	....	....		1951-52	1951-52
Bartel, Robin	Cgy., Van.	2	41	0	1	1	14	6	0	0	0	16		1985-86	1986-87
Bartlett, Jim	Mtl., NYR, Bos.	5	191	34	23	57	273	2	0	0	0	0		1954-55	1960-61
● Barton, Cliff	Pit., Phi., NYR	3	85	10	9	19	22	....	....	....	....	....		1929-30	1939-40
Bathe, Frank	Det., Phi.,	9	224	3	28	31	542	27	1	3	4	42		1974-75	1983-84
Bathgate, Andy	NYR, Tor., Det., Pit.	17	1069	349	624	973	624	54	21	14	35	76	1	1952-53	1970-71
Bathgate, Frank	NYR	1	2	0	0	0	2	....	....	....	....	....		1952-53	1952-53
● Batters, Jeff	St. L.	2	16	0	0	0	28	....	....	....	....	....		1993-94	1994-95
● Bauer, Bobby	Bos.	9	327	123	137	260	36	48	11	8	19	6	2	1935-36	1951-52
Baumgartner, Mike	K.C.	1	17	0	0	0	0	....	....	....	....	....		1974-75	1974-75
Baun, Bob	Tor., Oak., Det.	17	964	37	187	224	1493	96	3	12	17	171	4	1956-57	1972-73
Baxter, Paul	Que., Pit., Cgy.	8	472	48	121	169	1564	40	0	5	5	162		1979-80	1986-87
Beadle, Sandy	Wpg.	1	6	1	0	1	2	....	....	....	....	....		1980-81	1980-81
Beaton, Frank	NYR	2	25	1	1	2	43	....	....	....	....	....		1978-79	1979-80
Beattie, Red	Bos., Det., NYA	8	333	62	85	147	137	22	4	2	6	8		1930-31	1938-39
Beaudin, Norm	St.L., Min.	2	25	1	2	3	4	....	....	....	....	....		1967-68	1970-71
Beaudoin, Serge	Atl.	1	3	0	0	0	0	....	....	....	....	....		1979-80	1979-80
Beaudoin, Yves	Wsh.	3	11	0	0	0	5	....	....	....	....	....		1985-86	1987-88
Beck, Barry	Col., NYR, L.A.	10	615	104	251	355	1016	51	10	23	33	77		1977-78	1989-90
Beckett, Bob	Bos.	4	68	7	6	13	18	....	....	....	....	....		1956-57	1963-64
Bedard, James	Chi.	2	22	1	1	2	8	....	....	....	....	....		1949-50	1950-51
Bednarski, John	NYR, Edm.	4	100	2	18	20	114	1	0	0	0	17		1974-75	1979-80
Beers, Eddy	Cgy., St.L.	5	250	94	116	210	256	41	7	10	17	47		1981-82	1985-86
Behling, Dick	Det.	2	5	1	0	1	2	....	....	....	....	....		1940-41	1942-43
Beisler, Frank	NYA	2	2	0	0	0	0	....	....	....	....	....		1936-37	1939-40
Belanger, Alain	Tor.	1	9	0	1	1	6	....	....	....	....	....		1977-78	1977-78
Belanger, Roger	Pit.	1	44	3	5	8	32	....	....	....	....	....		1984-85	1984-85
Belisle, Danny	NYR	1	4	2	0	2	0	....	....	....	....	....		1960-61	1960-61
Beliveau, Jean	Mtl.	20	1125	507	712	1219	1029	162	79	97	176	211	10	1950-51	1970-71
● Bell, Billy	Mtl.W, Mtl., Ott.	6	61	3	1	4	7	9	0	0	0	0	1	1917-18	1923-24
Bell, Bruce	Que., St. L., NYR, Edm.	5	209	12	64	76	113	34	3	5	8	41		1984-85	1989-90
Bell, Harry	NYR	1	1	0	1	1	0	....	....	....	....	....		1946-47	1946-47
Bell, Joe	NYR	2	62	8	9	17	18	....	....	....	....	....		1942-43	1946-47
Belland, Neil	Van., Pit.	6	109	13	32	45	54	21	2	9	11	23		1981-82	1986-87
● Bellefeuille, Pete	Tor., Det.	4	92	26	4	30	58	....	....	....	....	....		1925-26	1929-30
● Bellemer, Andy	Mtl.M.	1	15	0	0	0	0	....	....	....	....	....		1932-33	1932-33
Bend, Lin	NYR	1	8	3	1	4	2	....	....	....	....	....		1942-43	1942-43
Bennett, Adam	Chi., Edm.	3	69	3	8	11	69	....	....	....	....	....		1991-92	1993-94
Bennett, Bill	Bos., Hfd.	2	31	4	7	11	65	....	....	....	....	....		1978-79	1979-80
Bennett, Curt	St.L., NYR, Atl.	10	580	152	182	334	347	21	1	1	2	57		1970-71	1979-80
Bennett, Frank	Det.	1	7	0	1	1	2	....	....	....	....	....		1943-44	1943-44
Bennett, Harvey	Pit., Wsh., Phi., Min., St.L.	5	268	44	46	90	347	4	0	0	0	2		1974-75	1978-79
● Bennett, Max	Mtl.	1	1	0	0	0	0	....	....	....	....	....		1935-36	1935-36
Bennett, Rick	NYR	3	15	1	1	2	13	....	....	....	....	....		1989-90	1991-92
Benning, Brian	St. L., L.A., Phi., Edm., Fla.	11	568	63	233	296	963	48	3	20	23	74		1984-85	1994-95
Benning, Jim	Tor., Van.	9	605	52	191	243	461	7	1	1	2	2		1981-82	1989-90
● Benoit, Joe	Mtl.	5	185	75	69	144	94	11	6	3	9	11	1	1940-41	1946-47
Benson, Bill	NYA, Bro.	2	67	11	25	36	35	....	....	....	....	....		1940-41	1941-42
Benson, Bobby	Bos.	1	8	0	1	1	4	....	....	....	....	....		1924-25	1924-25
● Bentley, Doug	Chi., NYR	13	566	219	324	543	217	23	9	8	17	8		1939-40	1953-54
● Bentley, Max	Chi., Tor., NYR	12	646	245	299	544	179	51	18	27	45	14	3	1940-41	1953-54
Bentley, Reggie	Chi.	1	11	1	2	3	2	....	....	....	....	....		1942-43	1942-43
Beraldo, Paul	Bos.	2	10	0	0	0	4	....	....	....	....	....		1987-88	1988-89
Berenson, Red	Mtl., NYR, St.L., Det.	17	987	261	397	658	305	85	23	14	37	49	2	1961-62	1977-78
Berezan, Perry	Cgy., Min., S.J.	9	378	61	75	136	279	31	4	7	11	34		1984-85	1992-93
Bergdinon, Fred	Bos.	1	2	0	0	0	0	....	....	....	....	....		1925-26	1925-26
Bergen, Todd	Phi.	1	14	11	5	16	4	17	4	9	13	8		1984-85	1984-85
Berger, Mike	Min.	2	30	3	1	4	67	....	....	....	....	....		1987-88	1988-89
Bergeron, Michel	Det., NYI, Wsh.	5	229	80	58	138	165	....	....	....	....	....		1974-75	1978-79
Bergeron, Yves	Pit.	2	3	0	0	0	0	....	....	....	....	....		1974-75	1976-77
Bergland, Tim	Wsh., T.B.	5	182	17	26	43	75	26	2	2	4	22		1989-90	1993-94
Bergloff, Bob	Min.	1	2	0	0	0	5	....	....	....	....	....		1982-83	1982-83
Berglund, Bo	Que., Min., Phi.	3	130	28	39	67	40	9	2	0	2	6		1983-84	1985-86
Bergman, Gary	Det., Min., K.C.	12	838	68	299	367	1249	21	0	5	5	20		1964-65	1975-76
Bergman, Thommie	Det.	6	246	21	44	65	243	7	0	2	2	2		1972-73	1979-80
Bergqvist, Jonas	Cgy.	1	22	2	5	7	10	....	....	....	....	....		1989-90	1989-90
● Berlinquette, Louis	Mtl., Mtl.M., Pit.	8	193	44	29	73	120	16	1	1	2	9		1917-18	1925-26
Bernier, Serge	Phi., L.A., Que.	7	302	78	119	197	234	5	1	1	2	0		1968-69	1980-81
Berry, Bob	Mtl., L.A.	8	541	159	191	350	344	26	2	6	8	6		1968-69	1976-77
Berry, Doug	Col.	2	121	10	33	43	25	....	....	....	....	....		1979-80	1980-81
Berry, Fred	Det.	1	3	0	0	0	0	....	....	....	....	....		1976-77	1976-77
Berry, Ken	Edm., Van.	4	55	8	10	18	30	....	....	....	....	....		1981-82	1988-89
Besler, Phil	Bos., Chi., Det.	2	30	1	4	5	18	....	....	....	....	....		1935-36	1938-39
● Bessone, Pete	Det.	1	6	0	1	1	6	....	....	....	....	....		1937-38	1937-38
Bethel, John	Wpg.	1	17	0	2	2	4	....	....	....	....	....		1979-80	1979-80
Bettio, Sam	Bos.	1	44	9	12	21	32	....	....	....	....	....		1949-50	1949-50
Beverley, Nick	Bos., Pit., NYR, Min., L.A., Col.	11	502	18	94	112	156	7	0	1	1	0		1966-67	1979-80

Name	NHL Teams	NHL Seasons	Regular Schedule GP	G	A	TP	PIM	Playoffs GP	G	A	TP	PIM	NHL Cup Wins	First NHL Season	Last NHL Season
Bialowas, Dwight	Atl., Min.	4	164	11	46	57	46	....	....	....	....	....		1973-74	1976-77
Bianchin, Wayne	Pit., Edm.	7	276	68	41	109	137	3	0	1	1	6		1973-74	1979-80
Bidner, Todd	Wsh.	1	12	2	1	3	7	....	....	....	....	....		1981-82	1981-82
Biggs, Don	Min.	2	12	2	0	2	8	....	....	....	....	....		1984-85	1984-85
Bignell, Larry	Pit.	2	20	0	3	3	2	3	0	0	0	2		1973-74	1974-75
Bilodeau, Gilles	Que.	1	9	0	1	1	25	....	....	....	....	....		1979-80	1979-80
Bionda, Jack	Tor., Bos.	4	93	3	9	12	113	11	0	1	1	14		1955-56	1958-59
Bissett, Tom	Det.	1	5	0	0	0	0	....	....	....	....	....		1990-91	1990-91
Bjugstad, Scott	Min., Pit., L.A.	9	317	76	68	144	144	9	0	1	1	2		1983-84	1991-92
Black, Stephen	Det., Chi.	2	113	11	20	31	77	13	0	0	0	13	1	1949-50	1950-51
Blackburn, Bob	NYR., Pit.	3	135	8	12	20	105	6	0	0	0	4		1968-69	1970-71
Blackburn, Don	Bos., Phi., NYR, NYI, Min.	6	185	23	44	67	87	12	3	0	3	10		1962-63	1972-73
Blade, Hank	Chi.	2	24	2	3	5	2	....	....	....	....	....		1946-47	1947-48
Bladon, Tom	Phi., Pit., Edm., Wpg., Det.	9	610	73	197	270	392	86	8	29	37	70	2	1972-73	1980-81
Blaine, Gary	Mtl.	1	1	0	0	0	0	....	....	....	....	....		1954-55	1954-55
• Blair, Andy	Tor., Chi.	9	402	74	86	160	323	38	6	6	12	32	1	1928-29	1936-37
Blair, Chuck	Tor.	2	3	0	0	0	0	....	....	....	....	....		1948-49	1950-51
Blair, George	Tor.	1	2	0	0	0	0	....	....	....	....	....		1950-51	1950-51
Blaisdell, Mike	Det., NYR, Pit., Tor.	9	343	70	84	154	166	6	1	2	3	10		1980-81	1988-89
Blake, Mickey	St.L., Bos., Tor.	2	16	1	1	2	6	....	....	....	....	....		1934-35	1935-36
• Blake, Toe	Mtl.M., Mtl.	15	578	235	292	527	272	58	25	37	62	23	3	1932-33	1947-48
Blight, Rick	Van., L.A.	7	326	96	125	221	170	5	0	5	5	2		1975-76	1982-83
Blinco, Russ	Mtl.M, Chi.	6	268	59	66	125	24	19	3	3	6	4	1	1933-34	1938-39
Block, Ken	Van.	1	1	0	0	0	0	....	....	....	....	....		1970-71	1970-71
Blomqvist, Timo	Wsh., N.J.	5	243	4	53	57	293	13	0	0	0	24		1981-82	1986-87
Bloom, Mike	Wsh., Det.	3	201	30	47	77	215	....	....	....	....	....		1974-75	1976-77
Blum, John	Edm., Bos., Wsh., Det.	8	250	7	34	41	610	20	0	2	2	27		1982-83	1989-90
Bodak, Bob	Cgy., Hfd.	2	4	0	0	0	29	....	....	....	....	....		1987-88	1989-90
Boddy, Gregg	Van.	5	273	23	44	67	263	3	0	0	0	0		1971-72	1975-76
Bodnar, Gus	Tor., Chi., Bos.	12	667	142	254	396	207	32	4	3	7	10	2	1943-44	1954-55
Boehm, Ron	Oak.	1	16	2	1	3	10	....	....	....	....	....		1967-68	1967-68
Boesch, Garth	Tor.	4	197	9	28	37	205	34	2	5	7	18	3	1946-47	1949-50
Boh, Rick	Min.	1	8	2	1	3	4	....	....	....	....	....		1987-88	1987-88
Boileau, Marc	Det.	1	54	5	6	11	8	....	....	....	....	....		1961-62	1961-62
Boileau, Rene	NYA	1	7	0	0	0	0	....	....	....	....	....		1925-26	1925-26
Boimistruck, Fred	Tor.	2	83	4	14	18	45	....	....	....	....	....		1981-82	1982-83
Boisvert, Serge	Tor., Mtl.	5	46	5	7	12	8	23	3	7	10	4	1	1982-83	1987-88
Boivin, Claude	Phi., Ott.	4	132	12	19	31	364	....	....	....	....	....		1991-92	1994-95
Boivin, Leo	Tor., Bos., Det., Pit., Min.	19	1150	72	250	322	1192	54	3	10	13	59		1951-52	1969-70
Boland, Mike A.	Phi.	1	2	0	0	0	0	....	....	....	....	....		1974-75	1974-75
Boland, Mike J.	K.C., Buf.	2	23	1	2	3	29	3	1	0	1	2		1974-75	1978-79
Boldirev, Ivan	Bos., Cal., Chi., Atl., Van., Det.	15	1052	361	505	866	507	48	13	20	33	14		1970-71	1984-85
Bolduc, Danny	Det., Cgy.	3	102	22	19	41	33	1	0	0	0	0		1978-79	1983-84
Bolduc, Michel	Que.	2	10	0	0	0	6	....	....	....	....	....		1981-82	1982-83
Boll, Buzz	Tor., NYA, Bro., Bos.	12	437	133	130	263	148	31	7	3	10	13		1933-34	1943-44
Bolonchuk, Larry	Van., Wsh.	4	74	3	9	12	97	....	....	....	....	....		1972-73	1977-78
Bolton, Hughie	Tor.	8	235	10	51	61	221	17	0	5	5	14		1949-50	1956-57
Bonar, Dan	L.A.	3	170	25	39	64	208	14	3	4	7	22		1980-81	1982-83
Bonin, Marcel	Det., Bos., Mtl.	9	454	97	175	272	336	50	11	14	25	51	4	1952-53	1961-62
Boo, Jim	Min.	1	6	0	0	0	22	....	....	....	....	....		1977-78	1977-78
Boone, Buddy	Bos.	2	34	5	3	8	28	22	2	1	3	25		1956-57	1957-58
Boothman, George	Tor.	2	58	17	19	36	18	5	2	1	3	2		1942-43	1943-44
Bordeleau, Chris	Mtl., St.L., Chi.,	4	205	38	65	103	82	19	4	7	11	17	1	1968-69	1971-72
Bordeleau, J.P.	Chi.	10	519	97	126	223	143	48	3	6	9	12		1969-70	1979-80
Bordeleau, Paulin	Van.	3	183	33	56	89	47	5	2	1	3	0		1973-74	1975-76
Borotsik, Jack	St.L.	1	1	0	0	0	0	....	....	....	....	....		1974-75	1974-75
Boschman, Laurie	Tor., Edm., Wpg., N.J., Ott.	14	1009	229	348	577	2265	57	8	13	21	140		1979-80	1992-93
Bossy, Mike	NYI	10	752	573	553	1126	210	129	85	75	160	38	4	1977-78	1986-87
Bostrom, Helge	Chi.	4	96	3	3	6	58	13	0	0	0	16		1929-30	1932-33
Botell, Mark	Phi.	1	32	4	10	14	31	....	....	....	....	....		1981-82	1981-82
Bothwell, Tim	NYR, St.L., Hfd.	11	502	28	93	121	382	49	0	3	3	56		1978-79	1988-89
Botting, Cam	Atl.	1	2	0	1	1	0	....	....	....	....	....		1975-76	1975-76
Boucha, Henry	Det., Min., K.C., Col.	6	247	53	49	102	157	....	....	....	....	....		1971-72	1976-77
Bouchard, Dick	NYR	1	1	0	0	0	0	....	....	....	....	....		1954-55	1954-55
Bouchard, Edmond	Mtl., Ham., NYA, Pit.	8	220	19	20	39	105	....	....	....	....	....		1921-22	1928-29
Bouchard, Emile (Butch)	Mtl.	15	785	49	144	193	863	113	11	21	32	121	4	1941-42	1955-56
Bouchard, Pierre	Mtl., Wsh.	12	595	24	82	106	433	76	3	10	13	56	5	1970-71	1981-82
• Boucher, Billy	Mtl., Bos., NYA	7	213	93	35	128	391	21	9	3	12	35	1	1921-22	1927-28
• Boucher, Frank	Ott., NYR	14	557	161	262	423	119	56	16	18	34	12	2	1921-22	1943-44
• Boucher, George	Ott., Mtl.M, Chi.	15	449	122	62	184	739	44	11	3	14	105	4	1917-18	1931-32
• Boucher, Robert	Mtl.	1	12	0	0	0	0	....	....	....	....	....	1	1923-24	1923-24
Boudreau, Bruce	Tor., Chi.	8	141	28	42	70	46	9	2	0	2	0		1976-77	1985-86
Boudrias, Andre	Mtl., Min., Chi., St.L., Van.	12	662	151	340	491	218	34	6	10	16	12		1963-64	1975-76
Boughner, Barry	Oak., Cal.	2	20	0	0	0	11	....	....	....	....	....		1969-70	1970-71
Bourbonnais, Dan	Hfd.	2	59	3	25	28	11	....	....	....	....	....		1981-82	1983-84
Bourbonnais, Rick	St.L.	3	71	9	15	24	29	4	0	1	1	0		1975-76	1977-78
Bourcier, Conrad	Mtl.	1	6	0	0	0	0	....	....	....	....	....		1935-36	1935-36
Bourcier, Jean	Mtl.	1	9	0	1	1	0	....	....	....	....	....		1935-36	1935-36
• Bourgeault, Leo	Tor. NYR, Ott., Mtl.	8	307	24	20	44	269	24	1	1	2	18	1	1926-27	1934-35
Bourgeois, Charlie	Cgy., St.L., Hfd.	7	290	16	54	70	788	40	2	3	5	194		1981-82	1987-88
Bourne, Bob	NYI, L.A.	14	964	258	324	582	605	139	40	56	96	108	4	1974-75	1987-88
Boutette, Pat	Tor., Hfd., Pit.	10	756	171	282	453	1354	46	10	14	24	109		1975-76	1984-85
Boutilier, Paul	NYI, Bos., Min., NYR, Wpg.	8	288	27	83	110	358	41	1	9	10	45	1	1981-82	1988-89
Bowcher, Clarence	NYA	2	47	2	2	4	133	....	....	....	....	....		1926-27	1927-28
Bowman, Kirk	Chi.	3	88	11	17	28	19	7	1	0	1	0		1976-77	1978-79
• Bowman, Ralph	Ott., St.L., Det.	7	274	8	17	25	260	22	2	2	4	6	2	1933-34	1939-40
Bownass, Jack	Mtl., NYR	4	80	3	8	11	58	....	....	....	....	....		1957-58	1961-62
Bowness, Rick	Atl., Det., St. L, Wpg.	7	173	18	37	55	191	5	0	0	0	2		1975-76	1981-82
• Boyd, Bill	NYR, NYA	4	138	15	7	22	72	9	0	0	0	2	1	1926-27	1929-30
Boyd, Irwin	Bos., Det.	4	97	18	19	37	51	15	0	1	1	4		1931-32	1943-44
Boyd, Randy	Pit., Chi., NYI, Van.	8	257	20	67	87	328	13	0	2	2	26		1981-82	1988-89
Boyer, Wally	Tor., Chi., Oak. Pit.	7	365	54	105	159	163	15	1	3	4	0		1965-66	1971-72
Boyko, Darren	Wpg.	1	1	0	0	0	0	....	....	....	....	....		1988-89	1988-89
Bozek, Steve	L.A., Cgy., St. L., Van., S.J.	11	641	164	167	331	309	58	12	11	23	69		1981-82	1991-92
Bozon, Philippe	St. L.	4	144	16	25	41	101	19	2	0	2	31		1991-92	1994-95
• Brackenborough, John	Bos.	1	7	0	0	0	0	....	....	....	....	....		1925-26	1925-26
Brackenbury, Curt	Que., Edm., St.L.	4	141	9	17	26	226	2	0	0	0	0		1979-80	1982-83
Bradley, Barton	Bos.	1	1	0	0	0	0	....	....	....	....	....		1949-50	1949-50
Bradley, Lyle	Cal. Cle.	2	6	1	0	1	2	....	....	....	....	....		1973-74	1976-77
Bragnalo, Rick	Wsh.	4	145	15	35	50	46	....	....	....	....	....		1975-76	1978-79
Brannigan, Andy	NYA, Bro.	2	27	1	2	3	31	....	....	....	....	....		1940-41	1941-42
Brasar, Per-Olov	Min., Van.	5	348	64	142	206	33	13	1	2	3	0		1977-78	1981-82
Brayshaw, Russ	Chi.	1	43	5	9	14	24	....	....	....	....	....		1944-45	1944-45
Breault, Francois	L.A.	3	27	2	4	6	42	....	....	....	....	....		1990-91	1992-93
Breitenbach, Ken	Buf.	3	68	1	13	14	49	8	0	1	1	4		1975-76	1978-79
Brennan, Dan	L.A.	2	8	0	1	1	9	....	....	....	....	....		1983-84	1985-86
Brennan, Doug	NYR	3	123	9	7	16	152	16	1	0	1	21	1	1931-32	1933-34
Brennan, Tom	Bos.	2	22	2	2	4	2	....	....	....	....	....		1943-44	1944-45
Brenneman, John	Chi., NYR, Tor., Det., Oak.	5	152	21	19	40	46	....	....	....	....	....		1964-65	1968-69
Bretto, Joe	Chi.	1	3	0	0	0	4	....	....	....	....	....		1944-45	1944-45
Brewer, Carl	Tor., Det., St.L.	12	604	25	198	223	1037	72	3	17	20	146	3	1957-58	1979-80
Briden, Archie	Det., Pit.	2	72	9	5	14	56	....	....	....	....	....		1926-27	1929-30
Bridgman, Mel	Phi., Cgy., N.J., Det., Van.	14	977	252	449	701	1625	125	28	39	67	298		1975-76	1988-89
• Briere, Michel	Pit.	1	76	12	32	44	20	10	5	3	8	17		1969-70	1969-70
Brindley, Doug	Tor.	1	3	0	0	0	0	....	....	....	....	....		1970-71	1970-71
Brink, Milt	Chi.	1	5	0	0	0	0	....	....	....	....	....		1936-37	1936-37
Brisson, Gerry	Mtl.	1	4	0	2	2	4	....	....	....	....	....		1962-63	1962-63
Britz, Greg	Tor., Hfd.	3	8	0	0	0	4	....	....	....	....	....		1983-84	1986-87
• Broadbent, Harry	Ott. Mt.M, NYA	11	302	122	45	167	553	42	12	1	13	81	4	1918-19	1928-29
Brochu, Stephane	NYR	1	1	0	0	0	0	....	....	....	....	....		1988-89	1988-89
Broden, Connie	Mtl.	3	6	2	1	3	2	7	0	1	1	0	2	1955-56	1957-58
Brooke, Bob	NYR, Min., N.J.	7	447	69	97	166	520	34	9	9	18	59		1983-84	1989-90
Brooks, Gord	St.L., Wsh.	3	70	7	18	25	37	....	....	....	....	....		1971-72	1974-75
• Brophy, Bernie	Mtl.M, Det.	3	62	4	4	8	25	2	0	0	0	2		1925-26	1929-30

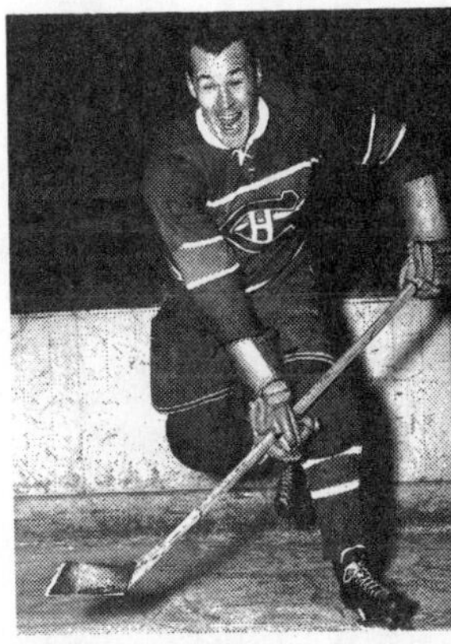

Butch Bouchard

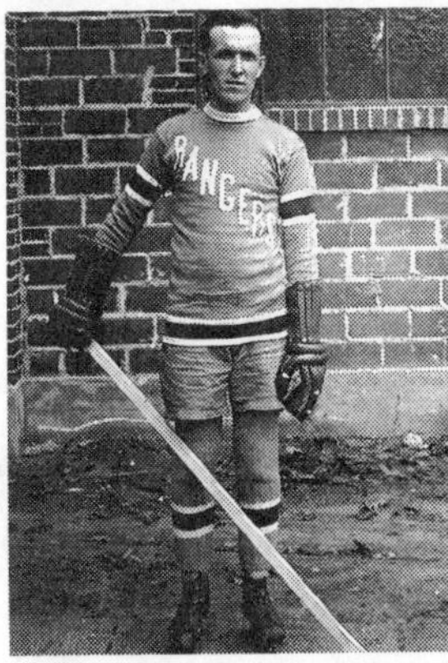

Frank Boucher

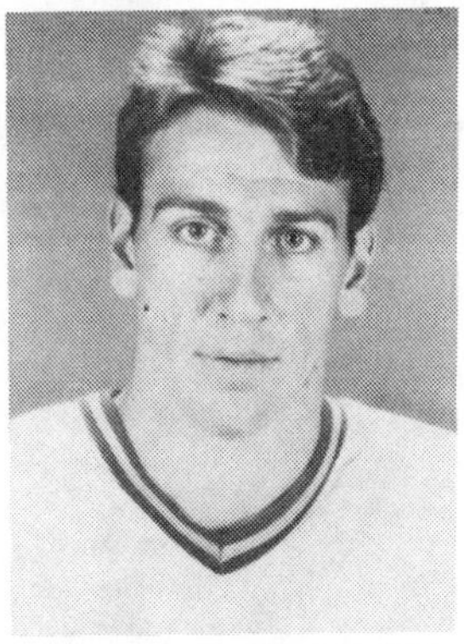

Charlie Bourgeois

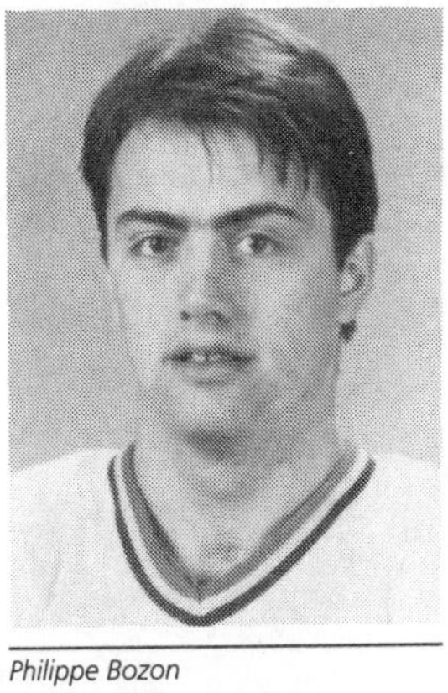

Philippe Bozon

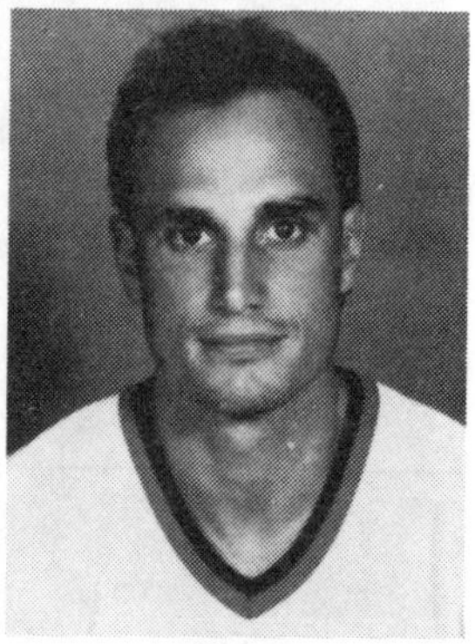

Keith Brown

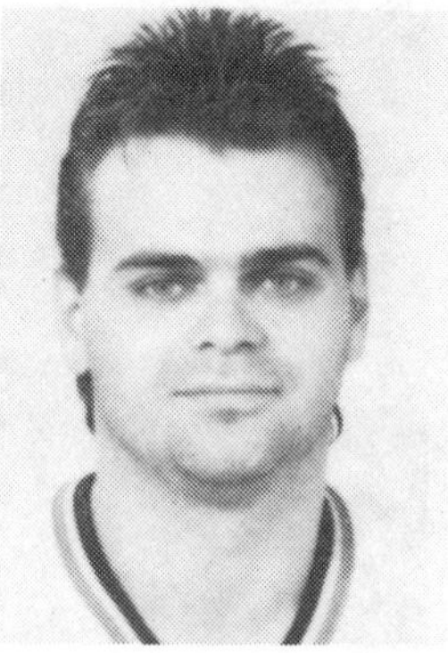

Garth Butcher

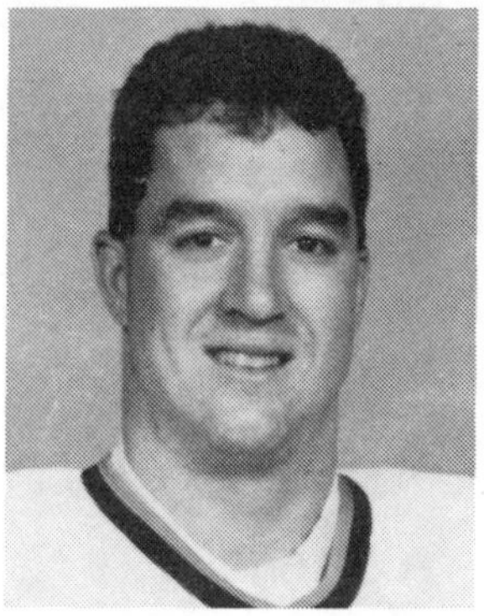

John Carter

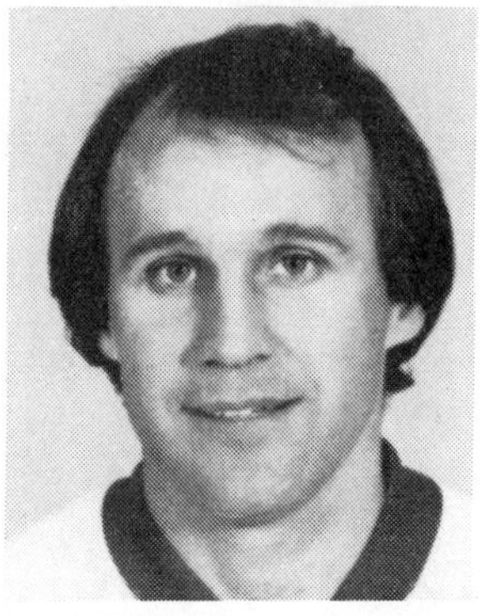

Colin Campbell

Name	NHL Teams	NHL Seasons	Regular Schedule GP	G	A	TP	PIM	Playoffs GP	G	A	TP	PIM	NHL Cup Wins	First NHL Season	Last NHL Season
Brossart, Willie	Phi., Tor., Wsh.	6	129	1	14	15	88	1	0	0	0	0		1970-71	1975-76
Broten, Aaron	Col., N.J., Min., Que., Tor., Wpg.	12	748	186	329	515	441	34	7	18	25	40		1980-81	1991-92
• Brown, Adam	Det. Chi. Bos.	10	391	104	113	217	333	26	2	4	6	14	1	1941-42	1951-52
Brown, Arnie	Tor. NYR, Det., NYI, Atl.	12	681	44	141	185	738	22	0	6	6	23		1961-62	1973-74
Brown, Cam	Van.	1	1	0	0	0	7	....	....	....	....	....		1990-91	1990-91
Brown, Connie	Det.	5	91	15	24	39	12	14	2	3	5	0		1938-39	1942-43
Brown, Fred	Mtl.M	1	19	1	0	1	0	9	0	0	0	0		1927-28	1927-28
Brown, George	Mtl.	3	79	6	22	28	34	7	0	0	0	2		1936-37	1938-39
Brown, Gerry	Det.	2	23	4	5	9	2	12	2	1	3	4		1941-42	1945-46
Brown, Harold	NYR	1	13	2	1	3	2	....	....	....	....	....		1945-46	1945-46
Brown, Jim	L.A.	1	3	0	1	1	5	....	....	....	....	....		1982-83	1982-83
Brown, Keith	Chi., Fla.	16	876	68	274	342	916	103	4	32	36	184		1979-80	1994-95
Brown, Larry	NYR, Det., Phi., L.A.	9	455	7	53	60	180	35	0	4	4	10		1969-70	1977-78
Brown, Stan	NYR, Det.	2	48	8	2	10	18	2	0	0	0	0		1926-27	1927-28
Brown, Wayne	Bos.	1	....	....	....	....	....	4	0	0	0	2		1953-54	1953-54
• Browne, Cecil	Chi.	1	13	2	0	2	4	....	....	....	....	....		1927-28	1927-28
Brownschidle, Jack	St.L., Hfd.	9	494	39	162	201	151	26	0	5	5	18		1977-78	1985-86
Brownschidle, Jeff	Hfd.	2	7	0	1	1	2	....	....	....	....	....		1981-82	1982-83
Brubaker, Jeff	Hfd., Mtl., Cgy., Tor., Edm., NYR, Det.	8	178	16	9	25	512	2	0	0	0	27		1979-80	1988-89
Bruce, Gordie	Bos.	3	28	4	9	13	13	7	2	3	5	4		1940-41	1945-46
Bruce, Morley	Ott.	4	72	8	1	9	27	12	0	0	0	2	2	1917-18	1921-22
Brumwell, Murray	Min., N.J.,	7	128	12	31	43	70	2	0	0	0	2		1980-81	1987-88
Bruneteau, Eddie	Det.	7	180	40	42	82	35	31	7	6	13	0		1940-41	1948-49
• Bruneteau, Mud	Det.	11	411	139	138	277	80	77	23	14	37	22	3	1935-36	1945-46
• Brydge, Bill	Tor., Det., NYA	9	368	26	52	78	506	2	0	0	0	4		1926-27	1935-36
Brydges, Paul	Buf.	1	15	2	2	4	6	....	....	....	....	....		1986-87	1986-87
• Brydson, Glenn	Mtl.M, St.L., NYR, Chi.	8	299	56	79	135	203	11	0	0	0	8		1930-31	1937-38
Brydson, Gord	Tor.	1	8	2	0	2	8	....	....	....	....	....		1929-30	1929-30
Bubla, Jiri	Van.	5	256	17	101	118	202	6	0	0	0	7		1981-82	1985-86
Buchanan, Al	Tor.	2	4	0	1	1	2	....	....	....	....	....		1948-49	1949-50
Buchanan, Bucky	NYR	1	2	0	0	0	0	....	....	....	....	....		1948-49	1948-49
Buchanan, Mike	Chi.	1	1	0	0	0	0	....	....	....	....	....		1951-52	1951-52
Buchanan, Ron	Bos., St.L.	2	5	0	0	0	0	....	....	....	....	....		1966-67	1969-70
Bucyk, John	Det., Bos.,	23	1540	556	813	1369	497	124	41	62	103	42	2	1955-56	1977-78
Bucyk, Randy	Mtl., Cgy.	2	19	4	2	6	8	2	0	0	0	0		1985-86	1987-88
Buhr, Doug	K.C.	1	6	0	2	2	4	....	....	....	....	....		1974-75	1974-75
Bukovich, Tony	Det.	2	17	7	3	10	6	6	0	1	1	0		1943-44	1944-45
Bullard, Mike	Pit., Cgy., St.L., Phi., Tor.	11	727	329	345	674	703	40	11	18	29	44		1980-81	1991-92
• Buller, Hy	Det., NYR	5	188	22	58	80	215	....	....	....	....	....		1943-44	1953-54
Bulley, Ted	Chi., Wsh., Pit.	8	414	101	113	214	704	29	5	5	10	24		1976-77	1983-84
Burakovsky, Robert	Ott.	1	23	2	3	5	6	....	....	....	....	....		1993-94	1993-94
• Burch, Billy	Ham., NYA, Bos., Chi.	11	390	137	53	190	251	2	0	0	0	0		1922-23	1932-33
Burchell, Fred	Mtl.	2	4	0	0	0	2	....	....	....	....	....		1950-51	1953-54
Burdon, Glen	K.C.	1	11	0	2	2	0	....	....	....	....	....		1974-75	1974-75
Burega, Bill	Tor.	1	4	0	1	1	4	....	....	....	....	....		1955-56	1955-56
Burke, Eddie	Bos., NYA	4	106	29	20	49	55	....	....	....	....	....		1931-32	1934-35
• Burke, Marty	Mtl., Pit., Ott., Chi.	11	494	19	47	66	560	31	2	4	6	44	2	1927-28	1937-38
Burmeister, Roy	NYA	3	67	4	3	7	2	....	....	....	....	....		1929-30	1931-32
Burnett, Kelly	NYR	1	3	1	0	1	0	....	....	....	....	....		1952-53	1952-53
Burns, Bobby	Chi.	3	20	1	0	1	8	....	....	....	....	....		1927-28	1929-30
Burns, Charlie	Det., Bos., Oak., Pit., Min.	11	749	106	198	304	252	31	5	4	9	6		1958-59	1972-73
Burns, Gary	NYR	2	11	2	2	4	18	5	0	0	0	2		1980-81	1981-82
• Burns, Norm	NYR	1	11	0	4	4	2	....	....	....	....	....		1941-42	1941-42
Burns, Robin	Pit., K.C.	5	190	31	38	69	139	....	....	....	....	....		1970-71	1975-76
Burrows, Dave	Pit., Tor.	10	724	29	135	164	373	29	1	5	6	25		1971-72	1980-81
Burry, Bert	Ott.	1	4	0	0	0	0	....	....	....	....	....		1932-33	1932-33
Burton, Cummy	Det.	3	43	0	2	2	21	3	0	0	0	0		1955-56	1958-59
Burton, Nelson	Wsh.	2	8	1	0	1	21	....	....	....	....	....		1977-78	1978-79
• Bush, Eddie	Det.	2	26	4	6	10	40	12	1	6	7	23		1938-39	1941-42
Buskas, Rod	Pit., Van., L.A., Chi.	11	556	19	63	82	1294	18	0	3	3	45		1982-83	1992-93
Busniuk, Mike	Phi.	2	143	3	23	26	297	25	2	5	7	34		1979-80	1980-81
Busniuk, Ron	Buf.	2	6	0	3	3	13	....	....	....	....	....		1972-73	1973-74
• Buswell, Walt	Det., Mtl.	8	368	10	40	50	164	24	2	1	3	10		1932-33	1939-40
Butcher, Garth	Van., St. L., Que., Tor.	14	897	48	158	206	2302	50	6	5	11	122		1981-82	1994-95
Butler, Dick	Chi.	1	7	2	0	2	0	....	....	....	....	....		1947-48	1947-48
Butler, Jerry	NYR, St.L., Tor., Van., Wpg.	11	641	99	120	219	515	48	3	3	6	79		1972-73	1982-83
Butters, Bill	Min.	2	72	1	4	5	77	....	....	....	....	....		1977-78	1978-79
Buttrey, Gord	Chi.	1	10	0	0	0	0	....	....	....	....	....		1943-44	1943-44
Buynak, Gordon	St. L	1	4	0	0	0	2	....	....	....	....	....		1974-75	1974-75
Byce, John	Bos.	3	21	2	3	5	6	8	2	0	2	2		1989-90	1991-92
Byers, Gord	Bos.	1	1	0	1	1	0	....	....	....	....	....		1949-50	1949-50
Byers, Jerry	Min., Atl, NYR	4	43	3	4	7	15	....	....	....	....	....		1972-73	1977-78
Byers, Lyndon	Bos., S.J.	10	279	28	43	71	1081	37	2	2	4	96		1983-84	1992-93
Byers, Mike	Tor., Phi., Buf., L.A.	4	166	42	34	76	39	4	0	1	1	0		1967-68	1971-72
Byram, Shawn	NYI, Chi.	2	5	0	0	0	14	....	....	....	....	....		1990-91	1991-92

C

Name	NHL Teams	NHL Seasons	Regular Schedule GP	G	A	TP	PIM	Playoffs GP	G	A	TP	PIM	NHL Cup Wins	First NHL Season	Last NHL Season
• Caffery, Jack	Tor., Bos.	3	57	3	2	5	22	10	1	0	1	4		1954-55	1957-58
Caffery, Terry	Chi., Min.	2	14	0	0	0	0	1	0	0	0	0		1969-70	1970-71
• Cahan, Larry	Tor., NYR, Oak., L.A.	13	666	38	92	130	700	29	1	1	2	38		1954-55	1970-71
Cahill, Chuck	Bos.	2	32	0	1	1	4	....	....	....	....	....		1925-26	1926-27
• Cain, Herb	Mtl.M, Mtl., Bos.	13	570	206	194	400	178	67	16	13	29	13	2	1933-34	1945-46
• Cain, Jim	Mtl.M, Tor.	2	61	4	0	4	35	....	....	....	....	....	1	1924-25	1925-26
Cairns, Don	K.C., Col.	2	9	0	1	1	2	....	....	....	....	....		1975-76	1976-77
Calder, Eric	Wsh.	2	2	0	0	0	0	....	....	....	....	....		1981-82	1982-83
Calladine, Norm	Bos.	3	63	19	29	48	8	....	....	....	....	....		1942-43	1944-45
Callander, Drew	Phi., Van.	4	39	6	2	8	7	....	....	....	....	....		1976-77	1979-80
Callander, John (Jock)	Pit., T.B.	5	109	22	29	51	116	22	3	8	11	12	1	1987-88	1992-93
Callighen, Brett	Edm.	3	160	56	89	145	132	14	4	6	10	8		1979-80	1981-82
Callighen, Patsy	NYR	1	36	0	0	0	32	9	0	0	0	0	1	1927-28	1927-28
Camazzola, James	Chi.	2	3	0	0	0	0	....	....	....	....	....		1983-84	1986-87
Camazzola, Tony	Wsh.	1	3	0	0	0	4	....	....	....	....	....		1981-82	1981-82
Cameron, Al	Det., Wpg.	6	282	11	44	55	356	7	0	1	1	2		1975-76	1980-81
Cameron, Billy	Mtl., NYA	2	39	0	0	0	2	6	0	0	0	0	1	1923-24	1925-26
Cameron, Craig	Det., St.L., Min., NYI	9	552	87	65	152	196	27	3	1	4	17		1966-67	1975-76
Cameron, Dave	Col., N.J.	3	168	25	28	53	238	....	....	....	....	....		1981-82	1983-84
• Cameron, Harry	Tor., Ott., Mtl.	6	127	85	32	117	137	21	7	0	7	36	2	1917-18	1922-23
Cameron, Scotty	NYR	1	35	8	11	19	0	....	....	....	....	....		1942-43	1942-43
Campbell, Bryan	L.A., Chi.	5	260	35	71	106	74	22	3	4	7	2		1967-68	1971-72
Campbell, Colin	Pit., Col., Edm., Van., Det.	11	636	25	103	128	1292	45	4	10	14	181		1974-75	1984-85
• Campbell, Dave	Mtl.	1	3	0	0	0	0	....	....	....	....	....		1920-21	1920-21
Campbell, Don	Chi.	1	17	1	3	4	8	....	....	....	....	....		1943-44	1943-44
Campbell, Earl (Spiff)	Ott., NYA	3	77	5	1	6	12	2	0	0	0	0		1923-24	1925-26
Campbell, Scott	Wpg., St.L.	3	80	4	21	25	243	....	....	....	....	....		1979-80	1981-82
Campbell, Wade	Wpg., Bos.	6	213	9	27	36	305	10	0	0	0	20		1982-83	1987-88
Campeau, Tod	Mtl.	3	42	5	9	14	16	1	0	0	0	0		1943-44	1948-49
Campedelli, Dom	Mtl.	1	2	0	0	0	0	....	....	....	....	....		1985-86	1985-86
Capuano, Dave	Pit., Van., T.B., S.J.	4	104	17	38	55	56	6	1	1	2	5		1989-90	1993-94
Capuano, Jack	Tor., Van., Bos.	3	6	0	0	0	0	....	....	....	....	....		1989-90	1991-92
Carbol, Leo	Chi.	1	6	0	1	1	4	....	....	....	....	....		1942-43	1942-43
Cardin, Claude	St.L.	1	1	0	0	0	0	....	....	....	....	....		1967-68	1967-68
Cardwell, Steve	Pit.	3	53	9	11	20	35	4	0	0	0	2		1970-71	1972-73
• Carey, George	Que, Ham., Tor.	5	72	22	8	30	14	....	....	....	....	....		1919-20	1923-24
Carleton, Wayne	Tor., Bos., Cal.	7	278	55	73	128	172	18	2	4	6	14	1	1965-66	1971-72
Carlin, Brian	L.A.	1	5	1	0	1	0	....	....	....	....	....		1971-72	1971-72
Carlson, Jack	Min., St.L.	5	228	30	15	45	404	25	1	2	3	72		1978-79	1986-87
Carlson, Kent	Mtl., St.L., Wsh.	5	113	7	11	18	148	8	0	0	0	13		1983-84	1988-89
Carlson, Steve	L.A.	1	52	9	12	21	23	4	1	1	2	7		1979-80	1979-80
Carlsson, Anders	N.J.	3	104	7	26	33	34	3	1	0	1	2		1986-87	1988-89
Carlyle, Randy	Tor., Pit., Wpg.	17	1055	148	499	647	1400	69	9	24	33	120		1976-77	1992-93
• Caron, Alain	Oak., Mtl.	2	60	9	13	22	18	....	....	....	....	....		1967-68	1968-69
• Carpenter, Eddie	Que, Ham.	2	44	10	4	14	23	....	....	....	....	....		1919-20	1920-21

			Regular Schedule					Playoffs					NHL	First	Last
Name	NHL Teams	NHL Seasons	GP	G	A	TP	PIM	GP	G	A	TP	PIM	Cup Wins	NHL Season	NHL Season
Carr,	Que.	1	1	0	0	0	0	....	....	....	....	....		1919-20	1919-20
Carr, Al	Tor.	1	5	0	1	1	2	....	....	....	....	....		1943-44	1943-44
Carr, Gene	St.L., NYR, L.A., Pit., Atl.	8	465	79	136	215	365	35	5	8	13	66		1971-72	1978-79
Carr, Lorne	NYR, NYA, Tor.	11	524	189	214	403	130	53	10	9	19	13	2	1933-34	1945-46
Carriere, Larry	Buf. Atl, Van., L.A., Tor.	7	367	16	74	90	462	27	0	3	3	42		1972-73	1979-80
• Carrigan, Gene	NYR, StL, Det.	3	37	2	1	3	13	4	0	0	0	0		1930-31	1934-35
Carroll, Billy	NYI, Edm., Det.	7	322	30	54	84	113	71	6	12	18	18	4	1980-81	1986-87
Carroll, George	Mtl.M, Bos.	1	15	0	0	0	9	....	....	....	....	....		1924-25	1924-25
Carroll, Greg	Wsh., Det., Hfd.	2	131	20	34	54	44	....	....	....	....	....		1978-79	1979-80
Carruthers, Dwight	Det. Phi.	2	2	0	0	0	0	....	....	....	....	....		1965-66	1967-68
Carse, Bill	NYR, Chi.	4	124	28	43	71	38	16	3	2	5	0		1938-39	1941-42
Carse, Bob	Chi., Mtl.	5	167	32	55	87	52	10	0	2	2	2		1939-40	1947-48
• Carson, Bill	Tor., Bos.	4	159	54	24	78	156	11	3	0	3	14	1	1926-27	1929-30
• Carson, Frank	Mtl.M., NYA, Det.	7	248	42	48	90	166	31	0	2	2	9	1	1925-26	1933-34
• Carson, Gerry	Mtl., NYR, Mtl.M.	6	261	12	11	23	205	22	0	0	0	12	1	1928-29	1936-37
Carson, Lindsay	Phi., Hfd.	7	373	66	80	146	524	49	4	10	14	56		1981-82	1987-88
Carter, Billy	Mtl., Bos.	3	16	0	0	0	6	....	....	....	....	....		1957-58	1961-62
Carter, John	Bos., S.J.	8	244	40	50	90	201	31	7	5	12	51		1985-86	1992-93
Carter, Ron	Edm.	1	2	0	0	0	0	....	....	....	....	....		1979-80	1979-80
• Carveth, Joe	Det., Bos., Mtl.	11	504	150	189	339	81	69	21	16	37	28	2	1940-41	1950-51
Cashman, Wayne	Bos.	17	1027	277	516	793	1041	145	31	57	88	250	2	1964-65	1982-83
Cassidy, Tom	Pit.	1	26	3	4	7	15	....	....	....	....	....		1977-78	1977-78
Cassolato, Tony	Wsh.	3	23	1	6	7	4	....	....	....	....	....		1979-80	1981-82
Caufield, Jay	NYR, Min., Pit.	7	208	5	8	13	759	17	0	0	0	42	2	1986-87	1992-93
Ceresino, Ray	Tor.	1	12	1	1	2	2	....	....	....	....	....		1948-49	1948-49
Cernik, Frantisek	Det.	1	49	5	4	9	13	....	....	....	....	....		1984-85	1984-85
Chabot, John	Mtl., Pit., Det.	8	508	84	228	312	85	33	6	20	26	2		1983-84	1990-91
Chad, John	Chi.	3	80	15	22	37	29	10	0	1	1	2		1939-40	1945-46
Chalmers, Bill	NYR	1	1	0	0	0	0	....	....	....	....	....		1953-54	1953-54
Chalupa, Milan	Det.	1	14	0	5	5	6	....	....	....	....	....		1984-85	1984-85
• Chamberlain, Murph	Tor., Mtl., Bro., Bos.	12	510	100	175	275	769	66	14	17	31	96	2	1937-38	1948-49
Champagne, Andre	Tor.	1	2	0	0	0	0	....	....	....	....	....		1962-63	1962-63
Chapdelaine, Rene	L.A.	3	32	0	2	2	32	....	....	....	....	....		1990-91	1992-93
• Chapman, Art	Bos., NYA	10	438	112	176	247	140	26	1	5	6	9		1930-31	1939-40
Chapman, Blair	Pit., St.L.	7	402	106	125	231	158	25	4	6	10	15		1976-77	1982-83
Chapman, Brian	Hfd.	1	3	0	0	0	29	....	....	....	....	....		1990-91	1990-91
Charbonneau, Stephane	Que.	1	2	0	0	0	0	....	....	....	....	....		1991-92	1991-92
Charlebois, Bob	Min.	1	7	1	0	1	0	....	....	....	....	....		1967-68	1967-68
Charlesworth, Todd	Pit., NYR	6	93	3	9	12	47	....	....	....	....	....		1983-84	1989-90
Charron, Guy	Mtl., Det., K.C., Wsh.	12	734	221	309	530	146	....	....	....	....	....		1969-70	1980-81
Chartier, Dave	Wpg.	1	1	0	0	0	0	....	....	....	....	....		1980-81	1980-81
Chartraw, Rick	Mtl., L.A., NYR, Edm.	10	420	28	64	92	399	75	7	9	16	80	4	1974-75	1983-84
Check, Lude	Det., Chi.	2	27	6	2	8	4	....	....	....	....	....		1943-44	1944-45
Chernoff, Mike	Min.	1	1	0	0	0	0	....	....	....	....	....		1968-69	1968-69
Chernomaz, Rich	Col., N.J., Cgy.	7	51	9	7	16	18	....	....	....	....	....		1981-82	1991-92
Cherry, Dick	Bos., Phi.	3	145	12	10	22	45	4	1	0	1	4		1956-57	1969-70
Cherry, Don	Bos.	1	....	....	....	....	....	1	0	0	0	0		1954-55	1954-55
• Chevrefils, Real	Bos., Det.	8	387	104	97	201	185	30	5	4	9	20		1951-52	1958-59
Chibirev, Igor	Hfd.	2	45	7	12	19	2	....	....	....	....	....		1993-94	1994-95
Chicoine, Dan	Cle. Min.	3	31	1	2	3	12	1	0	0	0	0		1977-78	1979-80
Chinnick, Rick	Min.	2	4	0	2	2	0	....	....	....	....	....		1973-74	1974-75
Chipperfield, Ron	Edm., Que.,	2	83	22	24	46	34	....	....	....	....	....		1979-80	1980-81
Chisholm, Art	Bos.	1	3	0	0	0	0	....	....	....	....	....		1960-61	1960-61
Chisholm, Colin	Min.	1	1	0	0	0	0	....	....	....	....	....		1986-87	1986-87
• Chisholm, Lex	Tor.	2	54	10	8	18	19	3	1	0	1	0		1939-40	1940-41
Chorney, Marc	Pit. L.A.	4	210	8	27	35	209	7	0	1	1	2		1980-81	1983-84
• Chouinard, Gene	Ott.	1	8	0	0	0	0	....	....	....	....	....		1927-28	1927-28
Chouinard, Guy	Atl, Cgy., St.L.	10	578	205	370	575	120	46	9	28	37	12		1974-75	1983-84
Christie, Mike	Cal., Cle., Col., Van.	7	412	15	101	116	550	2	0	0	0	0		1974-75	1980-81
Christoff, Steve	Min. Cgy., L.A.	5	248	77	64	141	108	35	16	12	28	25		1979-80	1983-84
Chrystal, Bob	NYR	2	132	11	14	25	112	....	....	....	....	....		1953-54	1954-55
• Church, Jack	Tor., Bro., Bos.	5	130	4	19	23	154	25	1	1	2	18		1938-39	1945-46
Chychrun, Jeff	Phi., L.A., Pit., Edm.	8	262	3	22	25	744	19	0	2	2	65	1	1986-87	1993-94
Cichocki, Chris	Det., N.J.	4	68	11	12	23	27	....	....	....	....	....		1985-86	1988-89
• Ciesla, Hank	Chi., NYR	4	269	26	51	77	87	6	0	2	2	0		1955-56	1958-59
Cimellaro, Tony	Ott.	1	2	0	0	0	0	....	....	....	....	....		1992-93	1992-93
Cimetta, Robert	Bos., Tor.	4	103	16	16	32	66	1	0	0	0	15		1988-89	1991-92
Cirone, Jason	Wpg.	1	3	0	0	0	2	....	....	....	....	....		1991-92	1991-92
Clackson, Kim	Pit., Que.	2	106	0	8	8	370	8	0	0	0	70		1979-80	1980-81
• Clancy, Francis (King)	Ott., Tor.	16	593	137	143	280	904	61	9	8	17	92	3	1921-22	1936-37
Clancy, Terry	Oak., Tor.	4	93	6	6	12	39	....	....	....	....	....		1967-68	1972-73
• Clapper, Dit	Bos.	20	833	228	246	474	462	82	13	17	30	50	3	1927-28	1946-47
Clark, Andy	Bos.	1	5	0	0	0	0	....	....	....	....	....		1927-28	1927-28
Clark, Dan	NYR	1	4	0	1	1	6	....	....	....	....	....		1978-79	1978-79
Clark, Dean	Edm.	1	1	0	0	0	0	....	....	....	....	....		1983-84	1983-84
Clark, Gordie	Bos.	2	8	0	1	1	0	1	0	0	0	0		1974-75	1975-76
Clarke, Bobby	Phi.	15	1144	358	852	1210	1433	136	42	77	119	152	2	1969-70	1983-84
• Cleghorn, Odie	Mtl., Pit.	10	180	95	29	124	147	24	9	3	12	13	1	1918-19	1927-28
• Cleghorn, Sprague	Ott. Tor. Mtl., Bos.	10	262	84	39	123	489	39	7	8	15	48	3	1918-19	1927-28
Clement, Bill	Phi., Wsh., Atl., Cgy.	11	719	148	208	356	383	50	5	3	8	26	2	1971-72	1981-82
Cline, Bruce	NYR	1	30	2	3	5	10	....	....	....	....	....		1956-57	1956-57
Clippingdale, Steve	L.A., Wsh.	2	19	1	2	3	9	1	0	0	0	0		1976-77	1979-80
Cloutier, Real	Que. Buf.	6	317	146	198	344	119	25	7	5	12	20		1979-80	1984-85
Cloutier, Rejean	Det.	2	5	0	2	2	2	....	....	....	....	....		1979-80	1981-82
Cloutier, Roland	Det., Que.	3	34	8	9	17	2	....	....	....	....	....		1977-78	1979-80
Clune, Wally	Mtl.	1	5	0	0	0	6	....	....	....	....	....		1955-56	1955-56
Coalter, Gary	Cal., K.C.	2	34	2	4	6	2	....	....	....	....	....		1973-74	1974-75
Coates, Steve	Det.	1	5	1	0	1	24	....	....	....	....	....		1976-77	1976-77
Cochrane, Glen	Phi., Van., Chi., Edm.	10	411	17	72	89	1556	18	1	1	2	31		1978-79	1988-89
Coflin, Hughie	Chi.	1	31	0	3	3	33	....	....	....	....	....		1950-51	1950-51
Colley, Tom	Min.	1	1	0	0	0	2	....	....	....	....	....		1974-75	1974-75
Collings, Norm	Mtl.	1	1	0	1	1	0	....	....	....	....	....		1934-35	1934-35
Collins, Bill	Min., Mtl., Det., St. L, NYR, Phi., Wsh.	11	768	157	154	311	415	18	3	5	8	12		1967-68	1977-78
Collins, Gary	Tor.	1	....	....	....	....	....	2	0	0	0	0		1958-59	1958-59
Collyard, Bob	St.L.	1	10	1	3	4	4	....	....	....	....	....		1973-74	1973-74
• Colman, Michael	S.J.	1	15	0	1	1	32	....	....	....	....	....		1991-92	1991-92
Colville, Mac	NYR	9	353	71	104	175	130	40	9	10	19	14	1	1935-36	1946-47
• Colville, Neil	NYR	12	464	99	166	265	213	46	7	19	26	32	1	1935-36	1948-49
Colwill, Les	NYR	1	69	7	6	13	16	....	....	....	....	....		1958-59	1958-59
Comeau, Rey	Mtl., Atl, Col.	9	564	98	141	239	175	9	2	1	3	8		1971-72	1979-80
Conacher, Brian	Tor., Det.	5	155	28	28	56	84	12	3	2	5	21	1	1961-62	1971-72
• Conacher, Charlie	Tor., Det., NYA	12	459	225	173	398	523	49	17	18	35	0	1	1929-30	1940-41
Conacher, Jim	Det., Chi., NYR	8	328	85	117	202	91	19	5	2	7	4		1945-46	1952-53
• Conacher, Lionel	Pit., NYA, Mtl.M., Chi.	12	498	80	105	185	882	35	2	2	4	34	2	1925-26	1936-37
Conacher, Pete	Chi., NYR, Tor.	6	229	47	39	86	57	7	0	0	0	0		1951-52	1957-58
• Conacher, Roy	Bos., Det., Chi.	11	490	226	200	426	90	42	15	15	30	14	2	1938-39	1951-52
Conn, Hugh	NYA	2	96	9	28	21	22	....	....	....	....	....		1933-34	1934-35
Connelly, Wayne	Mtl., Bos., Min., Det., St. L, Van.	10	543	133	174	307	156	24	11	7	18	4		1960-61	1971-72
Connolly, Bert	NYR, Chi.	3	87	13	15	28	37	14	1	0	1	0	1	1934-35	1937-38
Connor, Cam	Mtl., Edm., NYR	5	89	9	22	31	256	20	5	0	5	6	1	1978-79	1982-83
• Connor, Harry	Bos., NYA, Ott.	4	134	16	5	21	149	10	0	0	0	2		1927-28	1930-31
• Connors, Bobby	NYA, Det.	3	78	17	10	27	110	2	0	0	0	10		1926-27	1929-30
Contini, Joe	Col., Min.	3	68	17	21	38	34	2	0	0	0	0		1977-78	1980-81
• Convey, Eddie	NYR	3	36	1	1	2	33	....	....	....	....	....		1930-31	1932-33
• Cook, Bill	NYR	11	474	229	138	367	386	46	13	11	24	72	2	1926-27	1936-37
• Cook, Bob	Van., Det., NYI, Min.	4	72	13	9	22	22	....	....	....	....	....		1970-71	1974-75
• Cook, Bud	Bos., Ott., St.L.	3	51	5	4	9	22	....	....	....	....	....		1931-32	1934-35
• Cook, Bun	NYR, Bos.	11	473	158	144	302	444	46	15	3	18	50	2	1926-27	1936-37
Cook, Lloyd	Bos.	1	4	1	0	1	0	....	....	....	....	....		1924-25	1924-25
• Cook, Tom	Chi., Mtl.M.	9	311	77	98	175	184	24	2	4	6	19	1	1929-30	1937-38
• Cooper, Carson	Bos., Mtl., Det.	8	294	110	57	167	111	7	0	0	0	2		1924-25	1931-32
Cooper, Ed	Col.	2	49	8	7	15	46	....	....	....	....	....		1980-81	1981-82
• Cooper, Hal	NYR	1	8	0	0	0	2	....	....	....	....	....		1944-45	1944-45

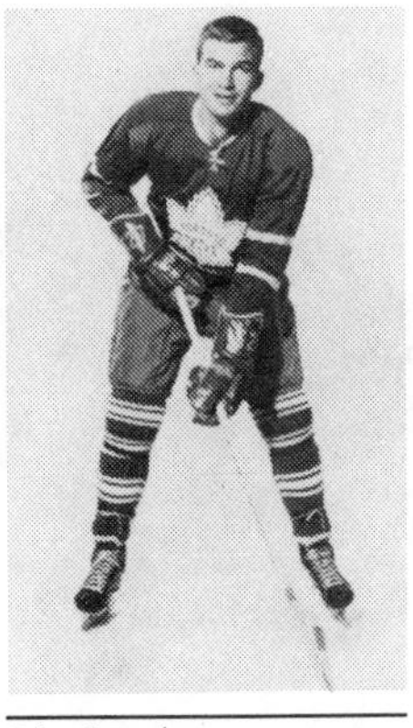

Brian Conacher

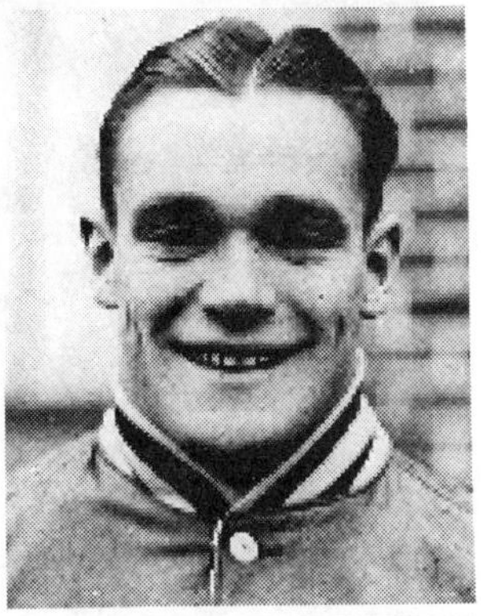

Charlie Conacher

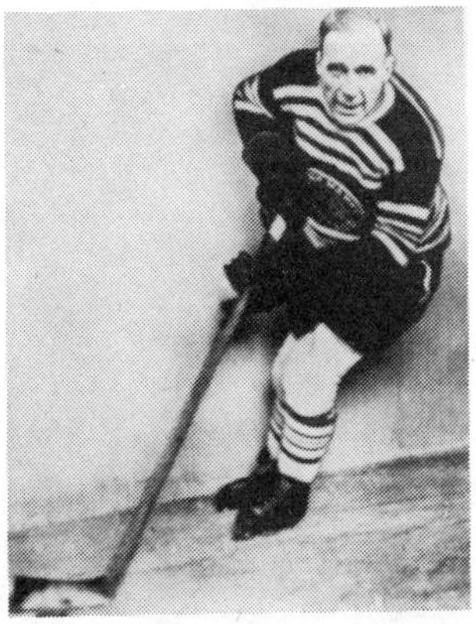

Lionel Conacher

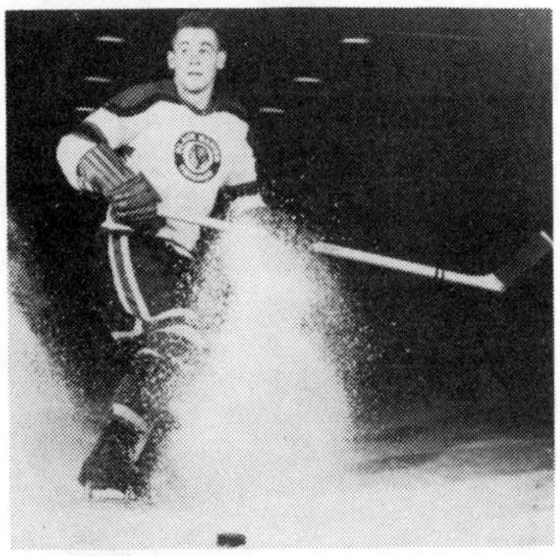

Pete Conacher

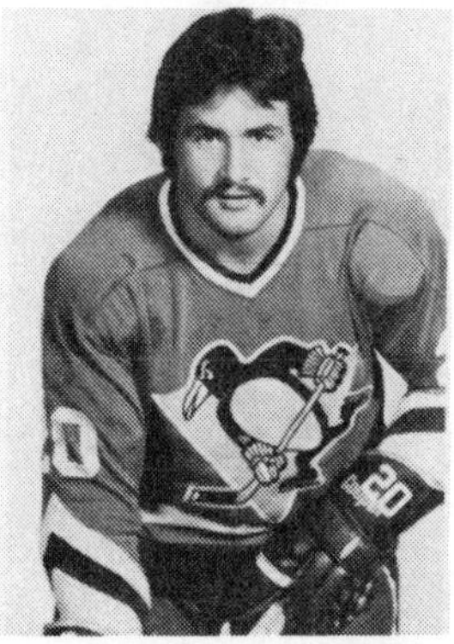

Jacques Cossette

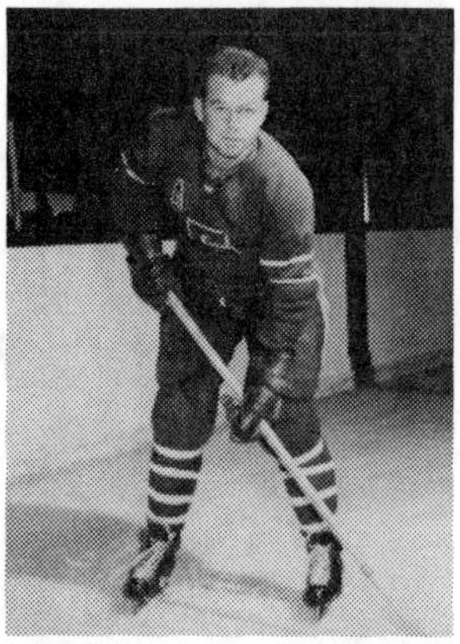

Don Cherry

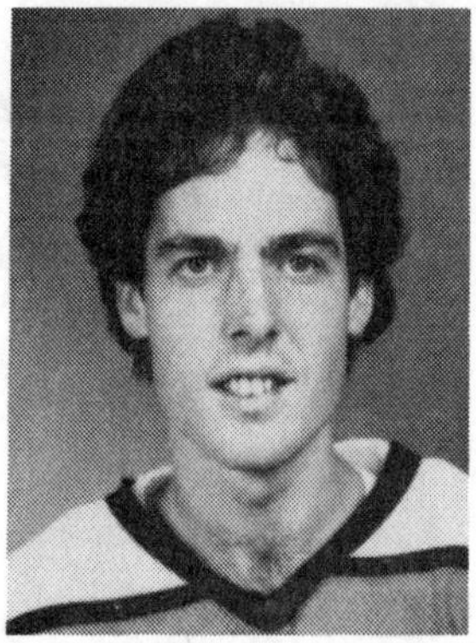

Doug Crossman

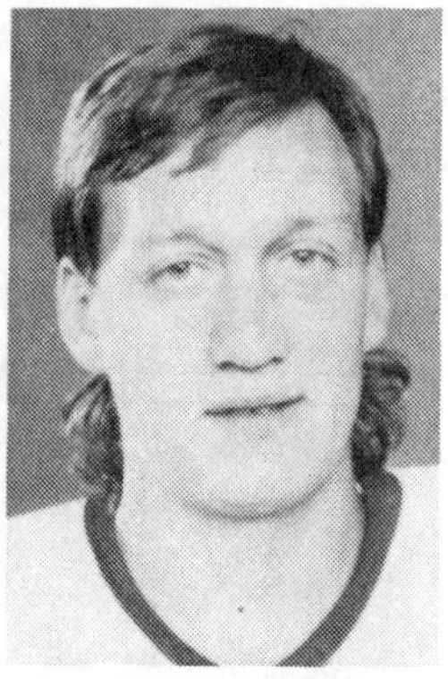

Evgeny Davydov

Name	NHL Teams	NHL Seasons	Regular Schedule GP	G	A	TP	PIM	Playoffs GP	G	A	TP	PIM	NHL Cup Wins	First NHL Season	Last NHL Season
• Cooper, Joe	NYR, Chi.	11	420	30	66	96	442	35	3	5	8	58		1935-36	1946-47
Copp, Bob	Tor.	2	40	3	9	12	26	....	....	....	....	....		1942-43	1950-51
• Corbeau, Bert	Mtl., Ham., Tor.,	10	257	65	33	98	611	14	2	0	2	10		1917-18	1926-27
Corbett, Michael	L.A.	1	....	....	....	....	....	2	0	1	1	2		1967-68	1967-68
Corcoran, Norm	Bos., Det., Chi.	4	29	1	3	4	21	4	0	0	0	6		1949-50	1955-56
Cormier, Roger	Mtl.	1	1	0	0	0	0	....	....	....	....	....		1925-26	1925-26
Corrigan, Charlie	Tor., NYA	2	19	2	2	4	2	....	....	....	....	....		1937-38	1940-41
Corrigan, Mike	L.A., Van., Pit.	10	594	152	195	347	698	17	2	3	5	20		1967-68	1977-78
Corriveau, Andre	Mtl.	1	3	0	1	1	0	....	....	....	....	....		1953-54	1953-54
Cory, Ross	Wpg.	2	51	2	10	12	41	....	....	....	....	....		1979-80	1980-81
Cossete, Jacques	Pit.	3	64	8	6	14	29	3	0	1	1	4		1975-76	1978-79
Costello, Les	Tor.	3	15	2	3	5	11	6	2	2	4	2	1	1947-48	1949-50
Costello, Murray	Chi., Bos., Det.	4	162	13	19	32	54	5	0	0	0	2		1953-54	1956-57
Costello, Rich	Tor.	2	12	2	2	4	2	....	....	....	....	....		1983-84	1985-86
Cotch, Charlie	Ham.	1	11	1	0	1	0	....	....	....	....	....		1924-25	1924-25
Cote, Alain	Bos., Wsh., Mtl., T.B., Que.	9	119	2	18	20	124	11	0	2	2	26		1985-86	1993-94
Cote, Alain	Que.	10	696	103	190	293	383	67	9	15	24	44		1979-80	1988-89
Cote, Ray	Edm.	3	15	0	0	0	4	14	3	2	5	0		1982-83	1984-85
• Cotton, Baldy	Pit., Tor., NYA	12	503	101	103	204	419	43	4	9	13	46	1	1925-26	1936-37
• Coughlin, Jack	Tor., Que, Mtl., Ham.	3	19	2	0	2	0	....	....	....	....	....		1917-18	1920-21
Coulis, Tim	Wsh., Min.	4	47	4	5	9	138	3	1	0	1	2		1979-80	1985-86
Coulson, D'arcy	Phi.	1	28	0	0	0	103	....	....	....	....	....		1930-31	1930-31
Coulter, Art	Chi., NYR	11	465	30	82	112	543	49	4	5	9	61	2	1931-32	1941-42
Coulter, Neal	NYI	3	26	5	5	10	11	....	....	....	....	....		1985-86	1987-88
Coulter, Tommy	Chi.	1	2	0	0	0	0	....	....	....	....	....		1933-34	1933-34
Cournoyer, Yvan	Mtl.	16	968	428	435	863	255	147	64	63	127	47	10	1963-64	1978-79
Courteau, Yves	Cgy., Hfd.	3	22	2	5	7	4	1	0	0	0	0		1984-85	1986-87
Courtenay, Edward	S.J.	2	44	7	13	20	10	....	....	....	....	....		1991-92	1992-93
• Coutu, Billy	Mtl., Ham., Bos.	10	239	33	18	51	350	32	2	0	2	42	1	1917-18	1926-27
• Couture, Gerry	Det., Mtl., Chi.,	10	385	86	70	156	89	45	9	7	16	4	1	1944-45	1953-54
• Couture, Rosie	Chi., Mtl.	8	309	48	56	104	184	23	1	5	6	15		1928-29	1935-36
Cowan, Tommy	Phi.	1	1	0	0	0	0	....	....	....	....	....		1930-31	1930-31
Cowick, Bruce	Phi., Wsh., St.L.	3	70	5	6	11	43	8	0	0	0	9	1	1973-74	1975-76
• Cowley, Bill	St.L., Bos.	13	549	195	353	548	143	64	12	34	46	22	2	1934-35	1946-47
• Cox, Danny	Tor., Ott., Det., NYR, St.L.	8	319	47	49	96	128	8	0	1	1	6		1926-27	1934-35
Coxe, Craig	Van., Cgy., St. L., S.J.	8	235	14	31	45	713	5	1	0	1	18		1984-85	1991-92
Crashley, Bart	Det., K.C., L.A.	6	140	7	36	43	50	....	....	....	....	....		1965-66	1975-76
Crawford, Bob	St.L., Hfd., NYR, Wsh.	7	246	71	71	142	72	11	0	1	1	8		1979-80	1986-87
Crawford, Bobby	Col., Det.	2	16	1	3	4	6	....	....	....	....	....		1980-81	1982-83
• Crawford, John	Bos.	13	548	38	140	178	202	66	4	13	17	36	2	1937-38	1949-50
Crawford, Lou	Bos.	2	26	2	1	3	29	....	....	....	....	....		1989-90	1991-92
Crawford, Marc	Van.	6	176	19	31	50	229	20	1	2	3	44		1981-82	1986-87
• Crawford, Rusty	Ott., Tor.,	2	38	10	3	13	84	2	2	1	3	0	1	1917-18	1918-19
Creighton, Dave	Bos., Chi., Tor., NYR	12	616	140	174	314	223	51	11	13	24	20		1948-49	1959-60
• Creighton, Jimmy	Det.,	1	11	1	0	1	2	....	....	....	....	....		1930-31	1930-31
Cressman, Dave	Min.	2	85	6	8	14	37	....	....	....	....	....		1974-75	1975-76
Cressman, Glen	Mtl.	1	4	0	0	0	2	....	....	....	....	....		1956-57	1956-57
Crisp, Terry	Bos., St.L., Phi., NYI	11	536	67	134	201	135	110	15	28	43	40	2	1965-66	1976-77
Cristofoli, Ed	Mtl.	1	9	0	1	1	4	....	....	....	....	....		1989-90	1989-90
Croghen, Maurice	Mtl.M.	1	16	0	0	0	4	....	....	....	....	....		1937-38	1937-38
Crombeen, Mike	Cle., St.L., Hfd.	8	475	55	68	123	218	27	6	2	8	32		1977-78	1984-85
Crossett, Stan	Phi.,	1	21	0	0	0	10	....	....	....	....	....		1930-31	1930-31
Crossman, Doug	Chi., Phi., NYI, Hfd., Det., T.B., St. L.	14	914	105	359	464	534	97	12	39	51	105		1980-81	1993-94
Croteau, Gary	L.A., Det., Cal., K.C., Col.	12	684	144	175	319	143	11	3	2	5	8		1968-69	1979-80
Crowder, Bruce	Bos., Pit.	4	243	47	51	98	156	31	8	4	12	41		1981-82	1984-85
Crowder, Keith	Bos., L.A.	10	662	223	271	494	1344	85	14	22	36	218		1980-81	1989-90
Crozier, Joe	Tor.,	1	5	0	3	3	2	....	....	....	....	....		1959-60	1959-60
Crutchfield, Nels	Mtl.	1	41	5	5	10	20	2	0	1	1	22		1934-35	1934-35
Culhane, Jim	Hfd.	1	6	0	1	1	4	....	....	....	....	....		1989-90	1989-90
Cullen, Barry	Tor., Det.	5	219	32	52	84	111	6	0	0	0	2		1955-56	1959-60
Cullen, Brian	Tor., NYR	7	326	56	100	156	92	19	3	0	3	2		1954-55	1960-61
Cullen, Ray	NYR, Det., Min., Van.	6	313	92	123	215	120	20	3	10	13	2		1965-66	1970-71
Cummins, Barry	Cal.	1	36	1	2	3	39	....	....	....	....	....		1973-74	1973-74
Cunningham, Bob	NYR	2	4	0	1	1	0	....	....	....	....	....		1960-61	1961-62
Cunningham, Jim	Phi.	1	1	0	0	0	4	....	....	....	....	....		1977-78	1977-78
Cunningham, Les	NYA, Chi.	2	60	7	19	26	21	1	0	0	0	2		1936-37	1939-40
Cupolo, Bill	Bos.	1	47	11	13	24	10	7	1	2	3	0		1944-45	1944-45
Currie, Glen	Wsh., L.A.	8	326	39	79	118	100	12	1	3	4	4		1979-80	1987-88
Currie, Hugh	Mtl.	1	1	0	0	0	0	....	....	....	....	....		1950-51	1950-51
Currie, Tony	St.L., Hfd., Van.	8	290	92	119	211	83	16	4	12	16	14		1977-78	1984-85
Curry, Floyd	Mtl.	11	601	105	99	204	147	91	23	17	40	38	4	1947-48	1957-58
Curtale, Tony	Cgy.	1	2	0	0	0	0	....	....	....	....	....		1980-81	1980-81
Curtis, Paul	Mtl., L.A., St.L.	4	185	3	34	37	161	5	0	0	0	2		1969-70	1972-73
Cushenan, Ian	Chi., Mtl., NYR, Det.	5	129	3	11	14	134	....	....	....	....	....		1956-57	1963-64
Cusson, Jean	Oak.	1	2	0	0	0	0	....	....	....	....	....		1967-68	1967-68
Cyr, Denis	Cgy., Chi., St.L.	6	193	41	43	84	36	4	0	0	0	0		1980-81	1985-86
Cyr, Paul	Buf., NYR, Hfd.	9	470	101	140	241	623	24	4	6	10	31		1982-83	1991-92

D

Name	NHL Teams	NHL Seasons	Regular Schedule GP	G	A	TP	PIM	Playoffs GP	G	A	TP	PIM	NHL Cup Wins	First NHL Season	Last NHL Season
Dahlin, Kjell	Mtl.	3	166	57	59	116	10	35	6	11	17	6	1	1985-86	1987-88
Dahlstrom, Cully	Chi.	8	342	88	118	206	58	29	6	8	14	4	1	1937-38	1944-45
Daigle, Alain	Chi.	6	389	56	50	106	122	17	0	1	1	0		1974-75	1979-80
Dailey, Bob	Van., Phi.	9	561	94	231	325	814	63	12	34	46	105		1973-74	1981-82
Daley, Frank	Det.	1	5	0	0	0	0	2	0	0	0	0		1928-29	1928-29
Daley, Pat	Wpg.	2	12	1	0	1	13	....	....	....	....	....		1979-80	1980-81
Dallman, Marty	Tor.	2	6	0	1	1	0	....	....	....	....	....		1987-88	1988-89
Dallman, Rod	NYI, Phi.	4	6	1	0	1	26	1	0	1	1	0		1987-88	1991-92
Dame, Bunny	Mtl.	1	34	2	5	7	4	....	....	....	....	....		1941-42	1941-42
Damore, Hank	NYR	1	4	1	0	1	2	....	....	....	....	....		1943-44	1943-44
Daniels, Kimbi	Phi.	2	27	1	2	3	4	....	....	....	....	....		1990-91	1991-92
Daoust, Dan	Mtl., Tor.	8	522	87	167	254	544	32	7	5	12	83		1982-83	1989-90
Dark, Michael	St.L.	2	43	5	6	11	14	....	....	....	....	....		1986-87	1987-88
• Darragh, Harry	Pit., Phi., Bos., Tor.	8	308	68	49	117	50	16	1	3	4	4	1	1925-26	1932-33
• Darragh, Jack	Ott.	6	120	68	21	89	87	21	14	2	16	13	3	1917-18	1923-24
David, Richard	Que.	3	31	4	4	8	10	1	0	0	0	0		1979-80	1982-83
Davidson, Bob	Tor.,	12	491	94	160	254	398	82	5	17	22	79	2	1934-35	1945-46
Davidson, Gord	NYR	2	51	3	6	9	8	....	....	....	....	....		1942-43	1943-44
• Davie, Bob	Bos.	3	41	0	1	1	25	....	....	....	....	....		1933-34	1935-36
Davies, Ken	NYR	1	....	....	....	....	....	1	0	0	0	0		1947-48	1947-48
Davis, Bob	Det.	1	3	0	0	0	0	....	....	....	....	....		1932-33	1932-33
Davis, Kim	Pit., Tor.	4	36	5	7	12	51	4	0	0	0	0		1977-78	1980-81
Davis, Lorne	Mtl., Chi., Det., Bos.	6	95	8	12	20	20	18	3	1	4	10	1	1951-52	1959-60
Davis, Mal	Det., Buf.	6	100	31	22	53	34	7	1	0	1	0		1980-81	1985-86
Davison, Murray	Bos.	1	1	0	0	0	0	....	....	....	....	....		1965-66	1965-66
Davydov, Evgeny	Wpg., Fla., Ott.	4	155	40	39	79	120	11	2	2	4	2		1991-92	1994-95
Dawes, Robert	Tor., Mtl.	4	32	2	7	9	6	10	0	0	0	2	1	1946-47	1950-51
• Day, Hap	Tor., NYA	14	581	86	116	202	601	53	4	7	11	56	1	1924-25	1937-38
Dea, Billy	Chi., NYR, Det., Pit.	8	397	67	54	121	44	11	2	1	3	6		1953-54	1970-71
Deacon, Don	Det.	3	30	6	4	10	6	2	2	1	3	0		1936-37	1939-40
Deadmarsh, Butch	Buf., ATL, K.C.	5	137	12	5	17	155	4	0	0	0	17		1970-71	1974-75
Dean, Barry	Col., Phi.	3	165	25	56	81	146	....	....	....	....	....		1976-77	1978-79
Debenedet, Nelson	Det., Pit.	2	46	10	4	14	13	....	....	....	....	....		1973-74	1974-75
DeBlois, Lucien	NYR, Col., Wpg., Mtl., Que., Tor.	15	993	249	276	525	814	52	7	6	13	38		1977-78	1991-92
Debol, David	Hfd.	2	92	26	26	52	4	3	0	0	0	0		1979-80	1980-81
Defazio, Dean	Pit.	1	22	0	2	2	28	....	....	....	....	....		1983-84	1983-84
DeGray, Dale	Cgy., Tor. L.A., Buf.	5	153	18	47	65	195	13	1	3	4	28		1985-86	1989-90
Delmonte, Armand	Bos.	1	1	0	0	0	0	....	....	....	....	....		1945-46	1945-46
Delorme, Gilbert	Mtl., St. L., Que., Det., Pit.	9	541	31	92	123	520	56	1	9	10	56		1981-82	1989-90
Delorme, Ron	Col., Van.	9	524	83	83	166	667	25	1	2	3	59		1976-77	1984-85
Delory, Valentine	NYR	1	1	0	0	0	0	....	....	....	....	....		1948-49	1948-49
Delparte, Guy	Col.	1	48	1	8	9	18	....	....	....	....	....		1976-77	1976-77
Delvecchio, Alex	Det.	24	1549	456	825	1281	383	121	35	69	104	29	3	1950-51	1973-74

Name	NHL Teams	NHL Seasons	Regular Schedule GP	G	A	TP	PIM	Playoffs GP	G	A	TP	PIM	NHL Cup Wins	First NHL Season	Last NHL Season
• DeMarco, Ab	Chi., Tor., Bos., NYR	7	209	72	93	165	53	11	3	0	3	2		1938-39	1946-47
DeMarco, Albert	NYR, St.L., Pit., Van., L.A., Bos.	9	344	44	80	124	75	25	1	2	3	17		1969-70	1978-79
DeMeres, Tony	Mtl., NYR	6	83	20	22	42	23	3	0	0	0	0		1937-38	1943-44
Denis, Johnny	NYR	2	10	0	2	2	2	....	....	....	....	....		1946-47	1949-50
Denis, Lulu	Mtl.	2	3	0	1	1	0	....	....	....	....	....		1949-50	1950-51
• Denneny, Corbett	Tor., Ham., Chi.	9	175	99	29	128	138	15	7	4	11	9	2	1917-18	1927-28
• Denneny, Cy	Ott., Bos.	12	326	246	69	315	210	41	18	3	21	31	5	1917-18	1928-29
Dennis, Norm	St.L.	4	12	3	0	3	11	5	0	0	0	2		1968-69	1971-72
Denoird, Gerry	Tor.	1	15	0	0	0	0	....	....	....	....	....		1922-23	1922-23
DePalma, Larry	Min., S.J., Pit.	7	148	21	20	41	408	3	0	0	0	6		1985-86	1993-94
Derlago, Bill	Van., Bos., Wpg., Que., Tor.	9	555	189	227	416	247	13	5	0	5	8		1978-79	1986-87
• Desaulniers, Gerard	Mtl.	3	8	0	2	2	4	....	....	....	....	....		1950-51	1953-54
• Desilets, Joffre	Mtl., Chi.	5	....	....	....	....	....	....	....	....	....	....		1935-36	1939-40
Desjardins, Martin	Mtl.	1	8	0	2	2	2	....	....	....	....	....		1989-90	1989-90
• Desjardins, Vic	Chi., NYR	2	87	6	15	21	27	16	0	0	0	0		1930-31	1931-32
Deslauriers, Jacques	Mtl.	1	2	0	0	0	0	....	....	....	....	....		1955-56	1955-56
Devine, Kevin	NYI	1	2	0	1	1	8	....	....	....	....	....		1982-83	1982-83
• Dewar, Tom	NYR	1	9	0	2	2	4	....	....	....	....	....		1943-44	1943-44
Dewsbury, Al	Det., Chi.	9	347	30	78	108	365	14	1	5	6	16	1	1946-47	1955-56
Deziel, Michel	Buf.	1	....	....	....	....	....	1	0	0	0	0		1974-75	1974-75
Dheere, Marcel	Mtl.	1	11	1	2	3	2	5	0	0	0	6		1942-43	1942-43
Diachuk, Edward	Det.	1	12	0	0	0	19	....	....	....	....	....		1960-61	1960-61
Dick, Harry	Chi.	1	12	0	1	1	12	....	....	....	....	....		1946-47	1946-47
Dickens, Ernie	Tor., Chi.	6	278	12	44	56	98	13	0	0	0	4	1	1941-42	1950-51
Dickenson, Herb	NYR	2	48	18	17	35	10	....	....	....	....	....		1951-52	1952-53
Dietrich, Don	Chi., N.J.	2	28	0	7	7	10	....	....	....	....	....		1983-84	1985-86
• Dill, Bob	NYR	2	76	15	15	30	135	....	....	....	....	....		1943-44	1944-45
Dillabough, Bob	Det., Bos., Pit., Oak.	9	407	54	98	152	112	26	5	5	10	8		1961-62	1969-70
• Dillon, Cecil	NYR, Det.	10	453	167	131	298	105	43	14	9	23	14	1	1930-31	1939-40
Dillon, Gary	Col.	1	13	1	1	2	29	....	....	....	....	....		1980-81	1980-81
Dillon, Wayne	NYR, Wpg.	4	229	43	66	109	60	3	0	1	1	0		1975-76	1979-80
Dineen, Bill	Det., Chi.	5	323	51	44	95	122	37	1	1	2	18	2	1953-54	1957-58
Dineen, Gary	Min.	1	4	0	1	1	0	....	....	....	....	....		1968-69	1968-69
Dineen, Peter	L.A., Det.	2	13	0	2	2	13	....	....	....	....	....		1986-87	1989-90
Dinsmore, Chuck	Mtl.M	4	102	6	2	8	50	12	1	0	1	6	1	1924-25	1929-30
Dionne, Marcel	Det., L.A., NYR	18	1348	731	1040	1771	600	49	21	24	45	17		1971-72	1988-89
Djoos, Per	Det., NYR	3	82	2	31	33	58	....	....	....	....	....		1990-91	1992-93
Doak, Gary	Det., Bos., Van., NYR	16	789	23	107	130	908	78	2	4	6	121	1	1965-66	1980-81
Dobbin, Brian	Phi., Bos.	5	63	7	8	15	61	2	0	0	0	17		1986-87	1991-92
Dobson, Jim	Min., Col.	4	12	0	0	0	6	....	....	....	....	....		1979-80	1981-82
• Doherty, Fred	Mtl.	1	3	0	0	0	0	....	....	....	....	....		1918-19	1918-19
Donaldson, Gary	Chi.	1	1	0	0	0	0	....	....	....	....	....		1973-74	1973-74
Donatelli, Clark	Min., Bos.	2	35	3	4	7	39	2	0	0	0	0		1989-90	1991-92
Donnelly, Babe	Mtl.M.	1	34	0	1	1	14	2	0	0	0	0		1926-27	1926-27
Donnelly, Dave	Bos., Chi., Edm.	5	137	15	24	39	150	5	0	0	0	0		1983-84	1987-88
Doran, Red (I.)	Det.	1	24	3	2	5	10	....	....	....	....	....		1946-47	1946-47
• Doran, Red (J.)	NYA., Det., Mtl.	5	98	5	10	15	110	3	0	0	0	0		1933-34	1939-40
• Doraty, Ken	Chi., Tor., Det.	5	103	15	26	41	24	15	7	2	9	2		1926-27	1937-38
Dore, Andre	NYR, St.L., Que.	7	257	14	81	95	261	23	1	2	3	32		1978-79	1984-85
Dore, Daniel	Que.	2	17	2	3	5	59	....	....	....	....	....		1989-90	1990-91
Dorey, Jim	Tor., NYR	4	232	25	74	99	553	11	0	2	2	40		1968-69	1971-72
Dorion, Dan	N.J.	2	4	1	1	2	2	....	....	....	....	....		1985-86	1987-88
Dornhoefer, Gary	Bos., Phi.	14	787	214	328	542	1291	80	17	19	36	203	2	1963-64	1977-78
Dorohoy, Eddie	Mtl.	1	16	0	0	0	6	....	....	....	....	....		1948-49	1948-49
Douglas, Jordy	Hfd., Min., Wpg.	6	268	76	62	138	160	6	0	0	0	4		1979-80	1984-85
Douglas, Kent	Tor., Oak., Det.	7	428	33	115	148	631	19	1	3	4	33	1	1962-63	1968-69
Douglas, Les	Det.	4	52	6	12	18	8	10	3	2	5	2	1	1940-41	1946-47
Downie, Dave	Tor.	1	11	0	1	1	2	....	....	....	....	....		1932-33	1932-33
Doyon, Mario	Chi., Que.	3	28	3	4	7	16	....	....	....	....	....		1988-89	1990-91
• Draper, Bruce	Tor.	1	1	0	0	0	0	....	....	....	....	....		1962-63	1962-63
• Drillon, Gordie	Tor., Mtl.	7	311	155	139	294	56	50	26	15	41	10	1	1936-37	1942-43
Driscoll, Pete	Edm.	2	60	3	8	11	97	3	0	0	0	0		1979-80	1980-81
Drolet, Rene	Phi., Det.	2	2	0	0	0	0	....	....	....	....	....		1971-72	1974-75
Drouillard, Clarence	Det.	1	10	0	1	1	0	....	....	....	....	....		1937-38	1937-38
Drouin, Jude	Mtl., Min., NYI, Wpg.	12	666	151	305	456	346	72	27	41	68	33		1968-69	1980-81
• Drouin, Polly	Mtl.	5	142	23	50	73	80	5	0	1	1	5		1935-36	1940-41
Drulia, Stan	T.B.	1	24	2	1	3	10	....	....	....	....	....		1992-93	1992-93
Drummond, John	NYR	1	2	0	0	0	2	....	....	....	....	....		1944-45	1944-45
Drury, Herb	Pit., Phi.	6	213	24	13	37	203	4	1	1	2	0		1925-26	1930-31
Dube, Gilles	Mtl., Det.	2	12	1	2	3	2	2	0	0	0	0	1	1949-50	1953-54
Dube, Norm	K.C.	2	57	8	10	18	54	....	....	....	....	....		1974-75	1975-76
Duberman, Justin	Pit.	1	4	0	0	0	0	....	....	....	....	....		1993-94	1993-94
Duchesne, Gaetan	Wsh., Que., Min., S.J., Fla.	14	1028	179	254	433	617	84	14	13	27	97		1981-82	1994-95
Dudley, Rick	Buf., Wpg.	6	309	75	99	174	292	25	7	2	9	69		1972-73	1980-81
Duff, Dick	Tor., NYR, Mtl., L.A., Buf.	18	1030	283	289	572	743	114	30	49	79	78	6	1954-55	1971-72
Dufour, Luc	Bos., Que., St.L.	3	167	23	21	44	199	18	1	0	1	32		1982-83	1984-85
Dufour, Marc	NYR, L.A.	3	14	1	0	1	2	....	....	....	....	....		1963-64	1968-69
Duggan, Jack	Ott.	1	27	0	0	0	0	2	0	0	0	0		1925-26	1925-26
Duggan, Ken	Min.	1	1	0	0	0	0	....	....	....	....	....		1987-88	1987-88
Duguay, Ron	NYR, Det., Pit., L.A.	12	864	274	346	620	582	89	31	22	53	118		1977-78	1988-89
• Duguid, Lorne	Mtl.M, Det., Bos.	6	135	9	15	24	57	2	0	0	0	4		1931-32	1936-37
Dumart, Woody	Bos.	16	772	211	218	429	99	88	12	15	27	23	2	1935-36	1953-54
Dunbar, Dale	Van., Bos.	2	2	0	0	0	2	....	....	....	....	....		1985-86	1988-89
• Duncan, Art	Det., Tor.	5	156	18	16	34	225	5	0	0	0	4		1926-27	1930-31
Duncan, Iain	Wpg.	4	127	34	55	89	149	11	0	3	3	6		1986-87	1990-91
Dundas, Rocky	Tor.	1	5	0	0	0	14	....	....	....	....	....		1989-90	1989-90
Dunlap, Frank	Tor.	1	15	0	1	1	2	....	....	....	....	....		1943-44	1943-44
Dunlop, Blake	Min., Phi., St.L., Det.	11	550	130	274	404	172	40	4	10	14	18		1973-74	1983-84
Dunn, Dave	Van., Tor.	3	184	14	41	55	313	10	1	1	2	41		1973-74	1975-76
Dunn, Richie	Buf., Cgy., Hfd.	12	483	36	140	176	314	36	3	15	18	24		1977-78	1988-89
Dupere, Denis	Tor., Wsh., St.L., K.C., Col.	8	421	80	99	179	66	16	1	0	1	0		1970-71	1977-78
Dupont, Andre	NYR, St.L., Phi., Que.	13	800	59	185	244	1986	140	14	18	32	352	2	1970-71	1982-83
Dupont, Jerome	Chi., Tor.	6	214	7	29	36	468	20	0	2	2	56		1981-82	1986-87
Dupont, Norm	Mtl., Wpg., Hfd.	5	256	55	85	140	52	13	4	2	6	0		1979-80	1983-84
Durbano, Steve	St.L., Pit., K.C., Col.	6	220	13	60	73	1127	5	0	2	2	8		1972-73	1978-79
Duris, Vitezslav	Tor.	2	89	3	20	23	62	3	0	1	1	2		1980-81	1982-83
Dussault, Norm	Mtl.	4	206	31	62	93	47	7	3	1	4	0		1947-48	1950-51
• Dutkowski, Duke	Chi., NYA, NYR	5	200	16	30	46	172	6	0	0	0	6		1926-27	1933-34
• Dutton, Red	Mtl.M, NYA	10	449	29	67	96	871	18	1	0	1	33		1926-27	1935-36
Dvorak, Miroslav	Phi.	3	193	11	74	85	51	18	0	2	2	6		1982-83	1984-85
Dwyer, Mike	Col., Cgy.	4	31	2	6	8	25	1	1	0	1	0		1978-79	1981-82
Dyck, Henry	NYR	1	1	0	0	0	0	....	....	....	....	....		1943-44	1943-44
• Dye, Babe	Tor., Ham., Chi., NYA	11	269	202	41	243	200	15	11	2	13	18	1	1919-20	1930-31
Dykstra, Steven	Buf., Edm., Pit., Hfd.	5	217	8	32	40	545	1	0	0	0	2		1985-86	1989-90
Dyte, John	Chi.	1	27	1	0	1	31	....	....	....	....	....		1943-44	1943-44

E

Name	NHL Teams	NHL Seasons	Regular Schedule GP	G	A	TP	PIM	Playoffs GP	G	A	TP	PIM	NHL Cup Wins	First NHL Season	Last NHL Season
Eakin, Bruce	Cgy., Det.	4	13	2	2	4	4	....	....	....	....	....		1981-82	1985-86
Eatough, Jeff	Buf.	1	1	0	0	0	0	....	....	....	....	....		1981-82	1981-82
Eaves, Mike	Min., Cgy.	8	324	83	143	226	80	43	7	10	17	14		1978-79	1985-86
Eaves, Murray	Wpg., Det.	8	57	4	13	17	9	4	0	1	1	2		1980-81	1989-90
Ecclestone, Tim	St.L., Det., Tor., Atl.	11	692	126	233	359	344	48	6	11	17	76		1967-68	1977-78
Edberg, Rolf	Wsh.	3	184	45	58	103	24	....	....	....	....	....		1978-79	1980-81
• Eddolls, Frank	Mtl., NYR	8	317	23	43	66	114	31	0	2	2	10	1	1944-45	1951-52
Edestrand, Darryl	St.L., Phi., Pit., Bos., L.A.	10	455	34	90	124	404	42	3	9	12	57		1967-68	1978-79
Edmundson, Garry	Mtl., Tor.	3	43	4	6	10	49	11	0	1	1	8		1951-52	1960-61
Edur, Tom	Col., Pit	2	158	17	70	87	67	....	....	....	....	....		1976-77	1977-78
Egan, Pat	Bro., Det., Bos., NYR	11	554	77	153	230	776	44	9	4	13	44		1939-40	1950-51
Egers, Jack	NYR, St.L., Wsh.	7	284	64	69	133	154	32	5	6	11	32		1969-70	1975-76
Ehman, Gerry	Bos., Det., Tor., Oak, Cal.	9	429	96	118	214	100	41	10	10	20	12	1	1957-58	1970-71
Eklund, Pelle	Phi., Dal.	9	594	120	335	455	109	66	10	36	46	8		1985-86	1993-94
Eldebrink, Anders	Van., Que.	2	55	3	11	14	29	14	0	0	0	10		1981-82	1982-83

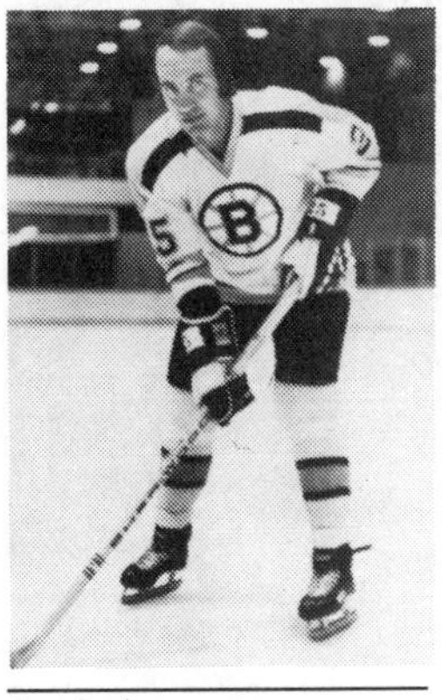

Gary Doak

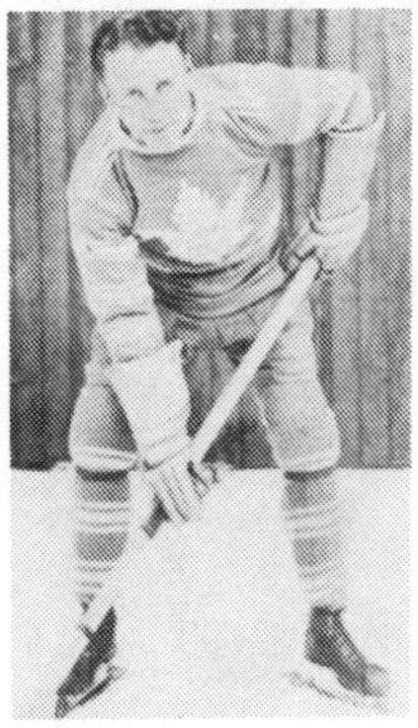

Ken Doraty

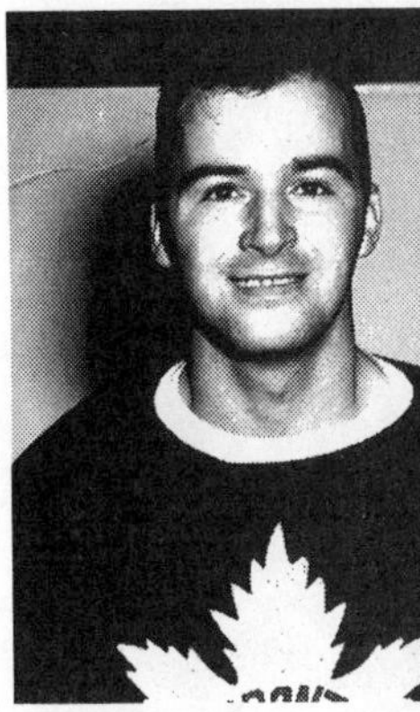

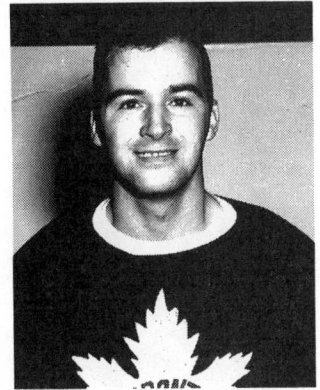

Gordie Drillon

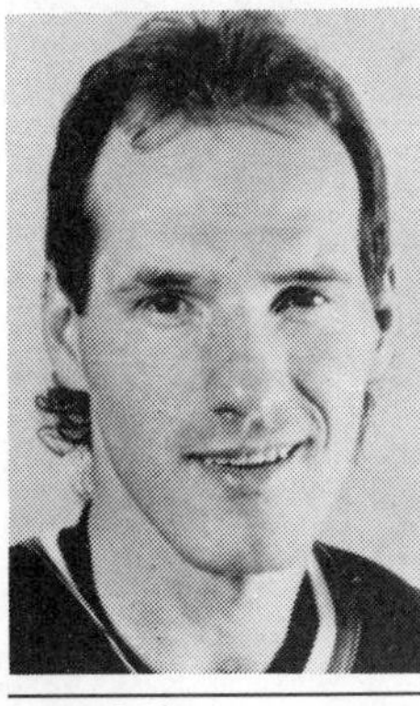

Gaetan Duchesne

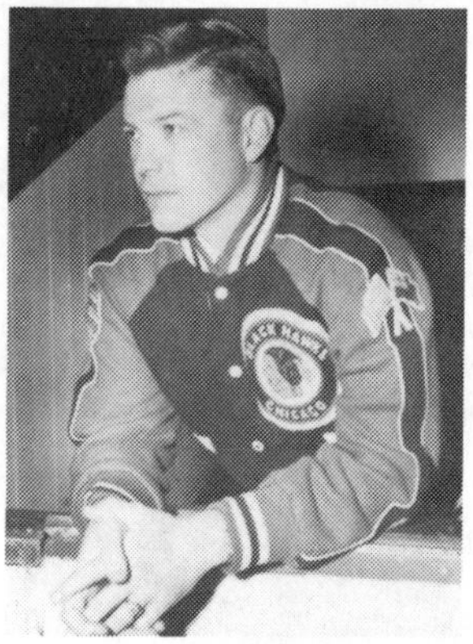
Frank Eddolls

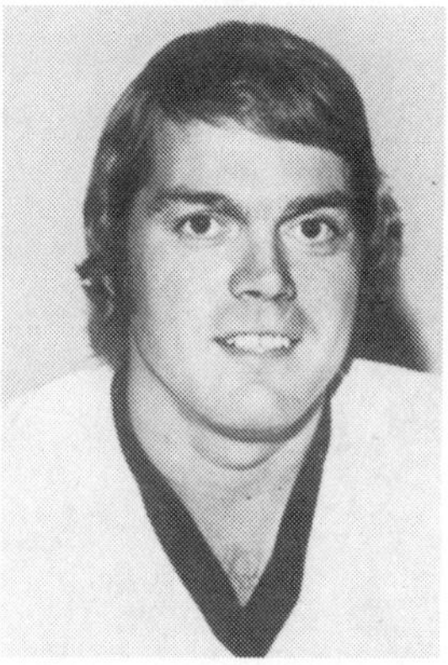
Darryl Edestrand

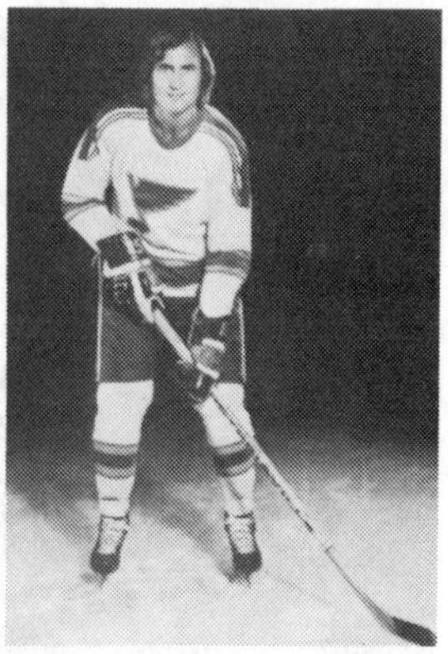
Jack Egers

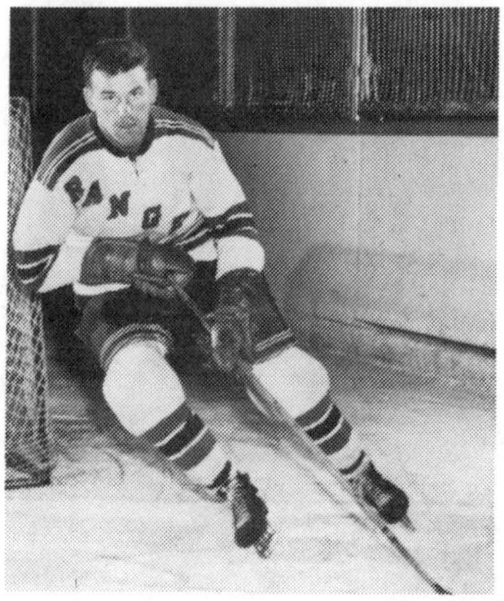
Jack Evans

Name	NHL Teams	NHL Seasons	Regular Schedule					Playoffs					NHL Cup Wins	First NHL Season	Last NHL Season
			GP	G	A	TP	PIM	GP	G	A	TP	PIM			
Elik, Boris	Det.	1	3	0	0	0	0	....	....	....	....	....		1962-63	1962-63
Elliot, Fred	Ott.	1	43	2	0	2	6	....	....	....	....	....		1928-29	1928-29
Ellis, Ron	Tor.	16	1034	332	308	640	207	70	18	8	26	20	1	1963-64	1980-81
Eloranta, Kari	Cgy., St.L.	5	267	13	103	116	155	26	1	7	8	19		1981-82	1986-87
Emberg, Eddie	Mtl.	1	....	....	....	....	....	2	1	0	1	0		1944-45	1944-45
Emmons, Gary	S.J.	1	3	1	0	1	0	....	....	....	....	....		1993-94	1993-94
● Emms, Hap	Mtl.M, NYA, Det., Bos.	10	320	36	53	89	311	14	0	0	0	12		1926-27	1937-38
Endean, Craig	Wpg.	1	2	0	1	1	0	....	....	....	....	....		1986-87	1986-87
Engblom, Brian	Mtl., Wsh., L.A., Buf., Cgy.	11	659	29	177	206	599	48	3	9	12	43	3	1976-77	1986-87
Engele, Jerry	Min.	3	100	2	13	15	162	2	0	1	1	0		1975-76	1977-78
English, John	L.A.	1	3	1	3	4	4	1	0	0	0	0		1987-88	1987-88
Ennis, Jim	Edm.	1	5	1	0	1	10	....	....	....	....	....		1987-88	1987-88
Erickson, Aut	Bos., Chi., Oak., Tor.	7	226	7	24	31	182	7	0	0	0	2	1	1959-60	1969-70
Erickson, Bryan	Wsh., L.A., Pit., Wpg.	9	351	80	125	205	141	14	3	4	7	7		1983-84	1993-94
Erickson, Grant	Bos., Min.	2	6	1	0	1	0	....	....	....	....	....		1968-69	1969-70
Eriksson, Peter	Edm.	1	20	3	3	6	24	....	....	....	....	....		1989-90	1989-90
Eriksson, Rolie	Min., Van.	3	193	48	95	143	26	3	1	0	1	0		1976-77	1978-79
Eriksson, Thomas	Phi.	5	208	22	76	98	107	19	0	3	3	12		1980-81	1985-86
Erixon, Jan	NYR	10	556	57	159	216	167	58	7	7	14	16		1983-84	1992-93
Esposito, Phil	Chi., Bos., NYR	18	1282	717	873	1590	910	130	61	76	137	138	2	1963-64	1980-81
Evans, Chris	Tor., Buf., St.L., Det., K.C.	5	241	19	42	61	143	12	1	1	2	8		1969-70	1974-75
Evans, Daryl	L.A., Wsh., Tor.	6	113	22	30	52	25	11	5	8	13	12		1981-82	1986-87
Evans, Doug	St.L., Wpg., Phi.	8	355	48	87	135	502	22	3	4	7	38		1985-86	1992-93
Evans, Jack	NYR, Chi.	14	752	19	80	99	989	56	2	2	4	97	1	1948-49	1962-63
Evans, John	Phi.	3	103	14	25	39	34	1	0	0	0	0		1978-79	1982-83
Evans, Kevin	Min., S.J.	2	9	0	1	1	44	....	....	....	....	....		1990-91	1991-92
Evans, Paul	Tor.	2	11	1	1	2	21	2	0	0	0	0		1976-77	1977-78
Evans, Shawn	St. L., NYI	2	9	1	0	1	2	....	....	....	....	....		1985-86	1989-90
● Evans, Stewart	Det., Mtl.M., Mtl.	8	367	28	49	77	425	26	0	0	0	20	1	1930-31	1938-39
Ezinicki, Bill	Tor., Bos., NYR	9	368	79	105	184	713	40	5	8	13	87	3	1944-45	1954-55

F

Name	NHL Teams	NHL Seasons	GP	G	A	TP	PIM	GP	G	A	TP	PIM	NHL Cup Wins	First NHL Season	Last NHL Season
Fahey, Trevor	NYR	1	1	0	0	0	0	....	....	....	....	....		1964-65	1964-65
Fairbairn, Bill	NYR, Min. St.L.	11	658	162	261	423	173	54	13	22	35	42		1968-69	1978-79
Falkenberg, Bob	Det.	5	54	1	5	6	26	....	....	....	....	....		1966-67	1971-72
Farrant, Walt	Chi.	1	1	0	0	0	0	....	....	....	....	....		1943-44	1943-44
Farrish, Dave	NYR, Que, Tor.	7	430	17	110	127	440	14	0	2	2	24		1976-77	1983-84
Fashoway, Gordie	Chi.	1	13	3	2	5	14	....	....	....	....	....		1950-51	1950-51
Faubert, Mario	Pit.	7	231	21	90	111	292	10	2	2	4	6		1974-75	1981-82
Faulkner, Alex	Tor., Det.	3	101	15	17	32	15	12	5	0	5	2		1961-62	1963-64
Fauss, Ted	Tor.	2	28	0	2	2	15	....	....	....	....	....		1986-87	1987-88
Feamster, Dave	Chi.	4	169	13	24	37	154	33	3	5	8	61		1981-82	1984-85
Featherstone, Tony	Oak., Cal., Min.	3	130	17	21	38	65	2	0	0	0	0		1969-70	1973-74
Federko, Bernie	St.L., Det.	14	1000	369	761	1130	487	91	35	66	101	83		1976-77	1989-90
Fedotov, Anatoli	Wpg., Ana.	2	4	0	2	2	0	....	....	....	....	....		1992-93	1993-94
Felix, Chris	Wsh.	4	35	1	12	13	10	2	0	1	1	0		1987-88	1990-91
Feltrin, Tony	Pit., NYR	4	48	3	3	6	65	....	....	....	....	....		1980-81	1985-86
Fenton, Paul	Hfd., NYR, L.A., Wpg., Tor., Cgy., S.J.	8	411	100	83	183	198	17	4	1	5	27		1984-85	1991-92
Fenyves, David	Buf., Phi.	9	206	3	32	35	119	11	0	0	0	9		1982-83	1990-91
Fergus, Tom	Bos., Tor., Van.	12	726	235	346	581	499	65	21	17	38	48		1981-82	1992-93
Ferguson, George	Tor., Pit, Min	12	797	160	238	398	431	86	14	23	37	44		1972-73	1983-84
Ferguson, John	Mtl.	8	500	145	158	303	1214	85	20	18	38	260	5	1963-64	1970-71
Ferguson, Lorne	Bos., Det., Chi.	8	422	82	80	162	193	31	6	3	9	24		1949-50	1958-59
Ferguson, Norm	Oak., Cal.	4	279	73	66	139	72	10	1	4	5	7		1968-69	1971-72
Fidler, Mike	Cle., Min, Hfd., Chi.	7	271	84	97	181	124	....	....	....	....	....		1976-77	1982-83
Field, Wilf	Bro., Mtl., Chi.	6	219	17	25	42	151	5	0	0	0	2		1936-37	1944-45
Fielder, Guyle	Det., Chi., Bos.	4	9	0	0	0	2	6	0	0	0	2		1950-51	1957-58
Filimonov, Dmitri	Ott.	1	30	1	4	5	18	....	....	....	....	....		1993-94	1993-94
Fillion, Bob	Mtl.	7	327	42	61	103	84	33	7	4	11	10	2	1943-44	1949-50
Fillion, Marcel	Bos.	1	1	0	0	0	0	....	....	....	....	....		1944-45	1944-45
● Filmore, Tommy	Det., NYA, Bos.	4	117	15	12	27	33	....	....	....	....	....		1930-31	1933-34
Finkbeiner, Lloyd	NYA	1	1	0	0	0	0	....	....	....	....	....		1940-41	1940-41
Finney, Sid	Chi.	3	59	10	7	17	4	7	0	2	2	0		1951-52	1953-54
Finnigan, Ed	Bos.	2	15	1	1	2	2	....	....	....	....	....		1935-36	1935-36
● Finnigan, Frank	Ott., Tor., St.L.	14	553	115	88	203	405	37	6	9	15	22	2	1923-24	1936-37
Fischer, Ron	Buf.	2	18	0	7	7	6	....	....	....	....	....		1981-82	1982-83
Fisher, Alvin	Tor.	1	9	1	0	1	4	....	....	....	....	....		1924-25	1924-25
Fisher, Dunc	NYR, Bos., Det.	7	275	45	70	115	104	21	4	4	8	14	1	1947-48	1958-59
Fisher, Joe	Det.	4	66	8	12	20	13	15	2	1	3	6		1939-40	1942-43
Fitchner, Bob	Que	2	78	12	20	32	59	3	0	0	0	10		1979-80	1980-81
Fitzpatrick, Ross	Phi.	4	20	5	2	7	0	....	....	....	....	....		1982-83	1985-86
Fitzpatrick, Sandy	NYR, Min.	2	22	3	6	9	8	12	0	0	0	0		1964-65	1967-68
Flaman, Fern	Bos., Tor.	17	910	34	174	208	1370	63	4	8	12	93	1	1944-45	1960-61
Fleming, Reggie	Mtl., Chi., Bos., NYR, Phi., Buf.	12	749	108	132	240	1468	50	3	6	9	106	1	1959-60	1970-71
Flesch,	Ham.	1	1	0	0	0	0	....	....	....	....	....		1920-21	1920-21
Flesch, John	Min, Pit, Col.	4	124	18	23	41	117	....	....	....	....	....		1974-75	1979-80
Fletcher, Steven	Mtl., Wpg.	2	3	0	0	0	5	1	0	0	0	5		1987-88	1988-89
Flett, Bill	L.A., Phi., Tor., Atl, Edm.	11	689	202	215	417	501	52	7	16	23	42	1	1967-68	1979-80
Flichel, Todd	Wpg.	3	6	0	1	1	4	....	....	....	....	....		1987-88	1989-90
Flockhart, Rob	Van., Min	5	55	2	5	7	14	1	1	0	1	2		1976-77	1980-81
Flockhart, Ron	Phi., Pit., Mtl., St.L., Bos.	9	453	145	183	328	208	19	4	6	10	14		1980-81	1988-89
Floyd, Larry	N.J.	2	12	2	3	5	9	....	....	....	....	....		1982-83	1983-84
Fogolin, Lee	Buf., Edm.	13	924	44	195	239	1318	108	5	19	24	173	2	1974-75	1986-87
Fogolin, Lidio (Lee)	Det., Chi.	9	427	10	48	58	575	28	0	2	2	30	1	1947-48	1955-56
Folco, Peter	Van.	1	2	0	0	0	0	....	....	....	....	....		1973-74	1973-74
Foley, Gerry	Tor., NYR, L.A.	4	142	9	14	23	99	9	0	1	1	2		1954-55	1968-69
Foley, Rick	Chi., Phi., Det.	3	67	11	26	37	180	4	0	1	1	4		1970-71	1973-74
Foligno, Mike	Det., Buf., Tor., Fla.	15	1018	355	372	727	2049	57	15	17	32	185		1979-80	1993-94
Folk, Bill	Det.	2	12	0	0	0	4	....	....	....	....	....		1951-52	1952-53
Fontaine, Len	Det.	2	46	8	11	19	10	....	....	....	....	....		1972-73	1973-74
Fontas, Jon	Min.	2	2	0	0	0	0	....	....	....	....	....		1979-80	1980-81
Fonteyne, Val	Det., NYR, Pit.	13	820	75	154	229	26	59	3	10	13	8		1959-60	1971-72
Fontinato, Lou	NYR, Mtl.	9	535	26	78	104	1247	21	0	2	2	42		1954-55	1962-63
Forbes, Dave	Bos., Wsh.	6	363	64	64	128	341	45	1	4	5	13		1973-74	1978-79
Forbes, Mike	Bos., Edm.	3	50	1	11	12	41	....	....	....	....	....		1977-78	1981-82
Forey, Connie	St.L.	1	4	0	0	0	2	....	....	....	....	....		1973-74	1973-74
Forsey, Jack	Tor.	1	19	7	9	16	10	3	0	1	1	0		1942-43	1942-43
Forslund, Gus	Ott.	1	48	4	9	13	2	....	....	....	....	....		1932-33	1932-33
Forslund, Tomas	Cgy.	2	44	5	11	16	12	....	....	....	....	....		1991-92	1992-93
Forsyth, Alex	Wsh.	1	1	0	0	0	0	....	....	....	....	....		1976-77	1976-77
Fortier, Charles	Mtl.	1	1	0	0	0	0	....	....	....	....	....		1923-24	1923-24
Fortier, Dave	Tor., NYI, Van.	4	205	8	21	29	335	20	0	2	2	33		1972-73	1976-77
Fortier, Marc	Que., Ott., L.A.	6	212	42	60	102	135	....	....	....	....	....		1987-88	1992-93
Fortin, Ray	St.L.	3	92	2	6	8	33	6	0	0	0	8		1967-68	1969-70
Foster, Dwight	Bos., Col., N.J., Det.	10	541	111	163	274	420	35	5	12	17	4		1977-78	1986-87
● Foster, Harry	NYR, Bos., Det.	5	83	4	2	6	37	....	....	....	....	....		1929-31	1934-35
Foster, Herb	NYR	2	5	1	0	1	5	....	....	....	....	....		1940-41	1947-48
Fotiu, Nick	NYR, Hfd., Cgy., Phi., Edm.	13	646	60	77	137	1362	38	0	4	4	67		1976-77	1988-89
● Fowler, Jimmy	Tor.	3	135	18	29	47	39	18	0	3	3	2		1936-37	1938-39
Fowler, Tom	Chi.	1	24	0	1	1	18	....	....	....	....	....		1946-47	1946-47
Fox, Greg	Atl, Chi., Pit.	8	494	14	92	106	637	44	1	9	10	67		1977-78	1984-85
Fox, Jim	L.A.	9	578	186	293	479	143	22	4	8	12	0		1980-81	1989-90
● Foyston, Frank	Det.	2	64	17	7	24	32	....	....	....	....	....		1926-27	1927-28
Frampton, Bob	Mtl.	1	2	0	0	0	0	3	0	0	0	0		1949-50	1949-50
Franceschetti, Lou	Wsh., Tor., Buf.	10	459	59	81	140	747	44	3	2	5	111		1981-82	1991-92
Francis, Bobby	Det.	1	14	2	0	2	0	....	....	....	....	....		1982-83	1982-83
● Fraser, Archie	NYR	1	3	0	1	1	0	....	....	....	....	....		1943-44	1943-44
Fraser, Curt	Van., Chi., Min.	12	704	193	240	433	1306	65	15	18	33	198		1978-79	1989-90
Fraser, Gord	Chi., Det., Mtl., Pit., Phi.	5	144	24	12	36	224	2	1	0	1	6		1926-27	1930-31
Fraser, Harry	Chi.	1	21	5	4	9	0	....	....	....	....	....		1944-45	1944-45
Fraser, Jack	Ham.	1	1	0	0	0	0	....	....	....	....	....		1923-24	1923-24
Frawley, Dan	Chi., Pit.	6	273	37	40	77	674	1	0	0	0	0		1983-84	1988-89
● Fredrickson, Frank	Det., Bos., Pit.	5	165	37	36	73	206	10	2	5	7	26	1	1926-27	1930-31

Name	NHL Teams	NHL Seasons	Regular Schedule GP	G	A	TP	PIM	Playoffs GP	G	A	TP	PIM	NHL Cup Wins	First NHL Season	Last NHL Season
Frew, Irv	Mtl.M, St.L., Mtl.	3	98	2	5	7	146	4	0	0	0	6		1933-34	1935-36
Friday, Tim	Det.	1	23	0	3	3	6	....	....	....	....	....		1985-86	1985-86
Fridgen, Dan	Hfd.	2	13	2	3	5	2	....	....	....	....	....		1981-82	1982-83
Friest, Ron	Min.	3	64	7	7	14	191	6	1	0	1	7		1980-81	1982-83
Frig, Len	Chi., Cal., Cle., St.L.	7	311	13	51	64	479	14	2	1	3	0		1972-73	1979-80
Frost, Harry	Bos.	1	3	0	0	0	0	1	0	0	0	0		1938-39	1938-39
Frycer, Miroslav	Que., Tor., Det., Edm.	8	415	147	183	330	486	17	3	8	11	16		1981-82	1988-89
Fryday, Bob	Mtl.	2	5	1	0	1	0	....	....	....	....	....		1949-50	1951-52
Ftorek, Robbie	Det., Que, NYR	8	334	77	150	227	262	19	9	6	15	28		1972-73	1984-85
Fullan, Lawrence	Wsh.	1	4	1	0	1	0	....	....	....	....	....		1974-75	1974-75
Fusco, Mark	Hfd.	2	80	3	12	15	42	....	....	....	....	....		1983-84	1984-85

G

Name	NHL Teams	NHL Seasons	Regular Schedule GP	G	A	TP	PIM	Playoffs GP	G	A	TP	PIM	NHL Cup Wins	First NHL Season	Last NHL Season
Gadsby, Bill	Chi., NYR, Det.	20	1248	130	438	568	1539	67	4	23	27	92		1946-47	1965-66
Gaetz, Link	Min., S.J.	3	65	6	8	14	412	....	....	....	....	....		1988-89	1991-92
Gage, Jody	Det., Buf.	6	68	14	15	29	26	....	....	....	....	....		1980-81	1991-92
Gagne, Art	Mtl., Bos., Ott., Det.	6	228	67	33	100	257	11	2	1	3	20		1926-27	1931-32
Gagne, Paul	Col., N.J., Tor., NYI	8	400	110	101	211	127	....	....	....	....	....		1980-81	1989-90
Gagne, Pierre	Bos.	1	2	0	0	0	0	....	....	....	....	....		1959-60	1959-60
Gagnon, Germaine	Mtl., NYI, Chi., K.C.	5	259	40	101	141	72	19	2	3	5	2		1971-72	1975-76
• Gagnon, Johnny	Mtl., Bos., NYA	10	454	120	141	261	295	32	12	12	24	37	1	1930-31	1939-40
Gainey, Bob	Mtl.	16	1160	239	262	501	585	182	25	48	73	151	5	1973-74	1988-89
• Gainor, Dutch	Bos., NYR, Ott., Mtl.M	7	246	51	56	107	129	25	2	1	3	14	2	1927-28	1934-35
Galarneau, Michel	Hfd.	3	78	7	10	17	34	....	....	....	....	....		1980-81	1982-83
• Galbraith, Percy	Bos., Ott.	8	347	29	31	60	224	31	4	7	11	24		1926-27	1933-34
• Gallagher, John	Mtl.M, Det., NYA	7	204	14	19	33	153	22	2	3	5	27	1	1930-31	1938-39
Gallant, Gerard	Det., T.B.	11	615	211	269	480	1674	58	18	21	39	178		1984-85	1994-95
Gallimore, Jamie	Min.	1	2	0	0	0	0	....	....	....	....	....		1977-78	1977-78
• Gallinger, Don	Bos.	5	222	65	88	153	89	23	5	5	10	19		1942-43	1947-48
Gamble, Dick	Mtl., Chi., Tor.	8	195	41	41	82	66	14	1	2	3	4	2	1950-51	1966-67
Gambucci, Gary	Min.	2	51	2	7	9	9	....	....	....	....	....		1971-72	1973-74
Ganchar, Perry	St. L., Mtl., Pit.	4	42	3	7	10	36	7	3	1	4	0		1983-84	1988-89
Gans, Dave	L.A.	2	6	0	0	0	2	....	....	....	....	....		1982-83	1985-86
• Gardiner, Herb	Mtl., Chi.	3	101	10	9	19	52	7	0	1	1	14		1926-27	1928-29
Gardner, Bill	Chi., Hfd.	9	380	73	115	188	68	45	3	8	11	17		1980-81	1988-89
Gardner, Cal	NYR, Tor., Chi., Bos.	12	696	154	238	392	517	61	7	10	17	20	2	1945-46	1956-57
Gardner, Dave	Mtl., St.L., Cal., Cle., Phi.	7	350	75	115	190	41	....	....	....	....	....		1972-73	1979-80
Gardner, Paul	Col., Tor., Pit., Wsh., Buf.	10	447	201	201	402	207	16	2	6	8	14		1976-77	1985-86
Gare, Danny	Buf., Det., Edm.	13	827	354	331	685	1285	64	25	21	46	195		1974-75	1986-87
Gariepy, Ray	Bos., Tor.	2	36	1	6	7	43	....	....	....	....	....		1953-54	1955-56
• Garland, Scott	Tor., L.A.	3	91	13	24	37	115	7	1	2	3	35		1975-76	1978-79
Garner, Bob	Pit.	1	1	0	0	0	0	....	....	....	....	....		1982-83	1982-83
• Garrett, Red	NYR	1	23	1	1	2	18	....	....	....	....	....		1942-43	1942-43
• Gassoff, Bob	St.L.	4	245	11	47	58	866	9	0	1	1	16		1973-74	1976-77
Gassoff, Brad	Van.	4	122	19	17	36	163	3	0	0	0	0		1975-76	1978-79
Gatzos, Steve	Pit.	4	89	15	20	35	83	1	0	0	0	0		1981-82	1984-85
Gaudreault, Armand	Bos.	1	44	15	9	24	27	7	0	2	2	8		1944-45	1944-45
• Gaudreault, Leo	Mtl.	3	67	8	4	12	30	....	....	....	....	....		1927-28	1932-33
Gaulin, Jean-Marc	Que.	4	26	4	3	7	8	1	0	0	0	0		1982-83	1985-86
Gaume, Dallas	Hfd.	1	4	1	1	2	0	....	....	....	....	....		1988-89	1988-89
Gauthier, Art	Mtl.	1	13	0	0	0	0	1	0	0	0	0		1926-27	1926-27
• Gauthier, Fern	NYR, Mtl., Det.	6	229	46	50	96	35	22	5	1	6	7		1943-44	1948-49
Gauthier, Jean	Mtl., Phi., Bos.	10	166	6	29	35	150	14	1	3	4	22	1	1960-61	1969-70
Gauthier, Luc	Mtl.	1	3	0	0	0	2	....	....	....	....	....		1990-91	1990-91
Gauvreau, Jocelyn	Mtl.	1	2	0	0	0	0	....	....	....	....	....		1983-84	1983-84
Gavin, Stewart	Tor., Hfd., Min.	13	768	130	155	285	584	66	14	20	34	75		1980-81	1992-93
Geale, Bob	Pit.	1	1	0	0	0	2	....	....	....	....	....		1984-85	1984-85
• Gee, George	Chi., Det.	9	551	135	183	318	345	41	6	13	19	32	1	1945-46	1953-54
Geldart, Gary	Min.	1	4	0	0	0	5	....	....	....	....	....		1970-71	1970-71
Gendron, Jean-Guy	NYR, Mtl., Bos., Phi.	14	863	182	201	383	701	42	7	4	11	47		1955-56	1971-72
Geoffrion, Bernie	Mtl., NYR	16	883	393	429	822	689	132	58	60	118	88	6	1950-51	1967-68
Geoffrion, Danny	Mtl., Wpg.	3	111	20	32	52	99	2	0	0	0	7		1979-80	1981-82
• Geran, Gerry	Mtl.W., Bos.	2	37	5	1	6	6	....	....	....	....	....		1917-18	1925-26
• Gerard, Eddie	Ott.	6	129	50	30	80	106	26	7	3	10	23	4	1917-18	1922-23
Germain, Eric	L.A.	1	4	0	1	1	13	1	0	0	0	4		1987-88	1987-88
Getliffe, Ray	Bos., Mtl.	10	393	136	137	273	250	45	9	10	19	30	2	1935-36	1944-45
Giallonardo, Mario	Col.	2	23	0	3	3	6	....	....	....	....	....		1979-80	1980-81
Gibbs, Barry	Bos., Min., Atl., St.L., L.A.	13	797	58	224	282	945	36	4	2	6	67		1967-68	1979-80
Gibson, Don	Van.	1	14	0	3	3	20	....	....	....	....	....		1990-91	1990-91
Gibson, Doug	Bos., Wsh.	3	63	9	19	28	0	1	0	0	0	0		1973-74	1977-78
Gibson, John	L.A., Tor., Wpg.	3	48	0	2	2	120	....	....	....	....	....		1980-81	1983-84
Giesebrecht, Gus	Det.	4	135	27	51	78	13	17	2	3	5	0		1938-39	1941-42
Giffin, Lee	Pit.	2	27	1	3	4	9	....	....	....	....	....		1986-87	1987-88
Gilbert, Ed	K.C., Pit.	3	166	21	31	52	22	....	....	....	....	....		1974-75	1976-77
Gilbert, Jean	Bos.	2	9	0	1	1	4	....	....	....	....	....		1962-63	1964-65
Gilbert, Rod	NYR	18	1065	406	615	1021	508	79	34	33	67	43		1960-61	1977-78
Gilbertson, Stan	Cal., St.L., Wsh., Pit.	6	428	85	89	174	148	3	1	1	2	2		1971-72	1976-77
Giles, Curt	Min., NYR, St.L.	14	895	43	199	242	733	103	6	16	22	118		1979-80	1992-93
Gillen, Don	Phi., Hfd.	2	35	2	4	6	22	....	....	....	....	....		1979-80	1981-82
Gillie, Ferrand	Det.	1	1	0	0	0	0	....	....	....	....	....		1928-29	1928-29
Gillies, Clark	NYI, Buf.	14	958	319	378	697	1023	164	47	47	94	287	4	1974-75	1987-88
Gillis, Jere	Que., Buf., Phi., Van., NYR	9	386	78	95	173	230	19	4	7	11	9		1977-78	1986-87
Gillis, Mike	Col., Bos.	6	246	33	43	76	186	27	2	5	7	10		1978-79	1983-84
Gillis, Paul	Que., Chi., Hfd.	11	624	88	154	242	1498	42	3	14	17	156		1982-83	1992-93
Gingras, Gaston	Mtl., Tor., St.L.	10	476	61	174	235	161	52	6	18	24	20	1	1979-80	1988-89
Girard, Bob	Cal., Cle., Wsh.	5	305	45	69	114	140	....	....	....	....	....		1975-76	1979-80
Girard, Kenny	Tor.	3	7	0	1	1	2	....	....	....	....	....		1956-57	1959-60
Giroux, Art	Mtl., Bos., Det.	3	54	6	4	10	14	2	0	0	0	0		1932-33	1935-36
Giroux, Larry	St.L., K.C., Det., Hfd.	7	274	15	74	89	333	5	0	0	0	4		1973-74	1979-80
Giroux, Pierre	L.A.	1	6	1	0	1	17	....	....	....	....	....		1982-83	1982-83
Gladney, Bob	L.A., Pit.	2	14	1	5	6	4	....	....	....	....	....		1982-83	1983-84
Gladu, Jean	Bos.	1	40	6	14	20	2	7	2	2	4	0		1944-45	1944-45
Glennie, Brian	Tor., L.A.	10	572	14	100	114	621	32	0	1	1	66		1969-70	1978-79
Glennon, Matt	Bos.	1	3	0	0	0	2	....	....	....	....	....		1991-92	1991-92
Gloeckner, Lorry	Det.	1	13	0	2	2	6	....	....	....	....	....		1978-79	1978-79
Gloor, Dan	Van.	1	2	0	0	0	0	....	....	....	....	....		1973-74	1973-74
Glover, Fred	Det., Chi.	5	92	13	11	24	62	4	0	0	0	0	1	1948-49	1952-53
Glover, Howie	Chi., Det., NYR, Mtl.	5	144	29	17	46	101	11	1	2	3	2		1958-59	1968-69
Godden, Ernie	Tor.	1	5	1	1	2	6	....	....	....	....	....		1981-82	1981-82
Godfrey, Warren	Bos., Det.	16	786	32	125	157	752	52	1	4	5	42		1952-53	1967-68
Godin, Eddy	Wsh.	2	27	3	6	9	12	....	....	....	....	....		1977-78	1978-79
Godin, Sammy	Ott., Mtl.	3	83	4	3	7	36	....	....	....	....	....		1927-28	1933-34
Goegan, Peter	Det., NYR, Min.	12	383	19	67	86	365	33	1	3	4	61		1957-58	1967-68
Goertz, Dave	Pit.	1	2	0	0	0	2	....	....	....	....	....		1987-88	1987-88
• Goldham, Bob	Tor., Chi., Det.	12	650	28	143	171	400	66	3	14	17	53	5	1941-42	1955-56
• Goldsworthy, Bill	Bos., Min., NYR	14	771	283	258	541	793	40	18	19	37	30		1964-65	1977-78
• Goldsworthy, Leroy	NYR, Det., Chi., Mtl., Bos., NYA	10	336	66	57	123	79	24	1	0	1	4	1	1929-30	1938-39
Goldup, Glenn	Mtl., L.A.	9	291	52	67	119	303	16	4	3	7	22		1973-74	1981-82
Goldup, Hank	Tor., NYR	6	202	63	80	143	97	19	5	1	6	6	1	1939-40	1945-46
Gooden, Bill	NYR	2	53	9	11	20	15	....	....	....	....	....		1942-43	1943-44
Goodenough, Larry	Phi., Van.	6	242	22	77	99	179	22	3	15	18	10	1	1974-75	1979-80
• Goodfellow, Ebbie	Det.	14	557	134	190	324	511	45	8	8	16	65	3	1929-30	1942-43
Gordon, Fred	Det., Bos.	2	81	8	7	15	68	2	0	0	0	0		1926-27	1927-28
Gordon, Jackie	NYR	3	36	3	10	13	0	9	1	1	2	7		1948-49	1950-51
Gorence, Tom	Phi., Edm.	6	303	58	53	111	89	37	9	6	15	47		1978-79	1983-84
Goring, Butch	L.A., NYI, Bos.	16	1107	375	513	888	102	134	38	50	88	32	4	1969-70	1984-85
Gorman, Dave	Atl.	1	3	0	0	0	0	....	....	....	....	....		1979-80	1979-80
• Gorman, Ed	Ott., Tor.	4	113	14	5	19	108	8	0	0	0	2	1	1924-25	1927-28
Gosselin, Benoit	NYR	1	7	0	0	0	33	....	....	....	....	....		1977-78	1977-78
Gosselin, Guy	Wpg.	1	5	0	0	0	6	....	....	....	....	....		1987-88	1987-88
Gotaas, Steve	Pit., Min.	3	49	6	9	15	53	3	0	1	1	5		1987-88	1990-91
• Gottselig, Johnny	Chi.	16	589	176	195	371	203	43	13	13	26	18	2	1928-29	1944-45

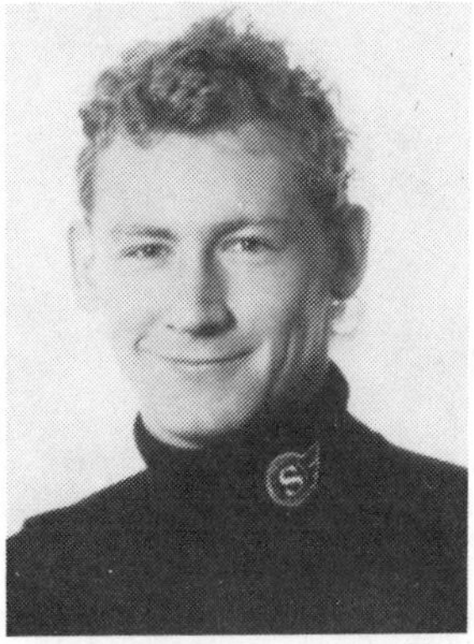
Dmitri Filimonov

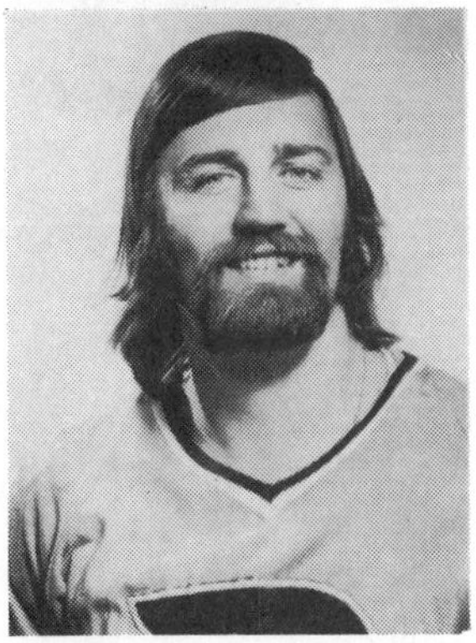
Bill Flett

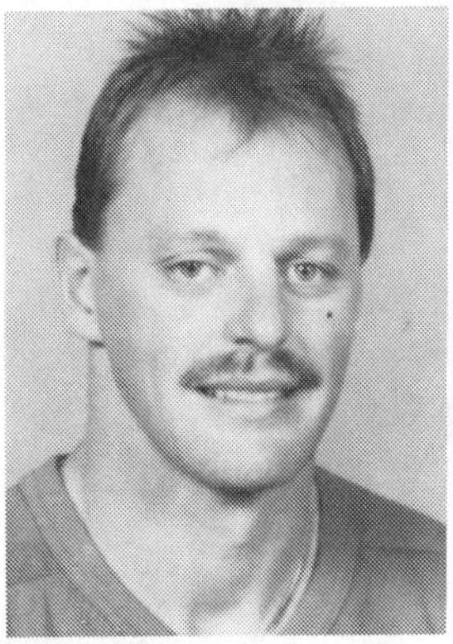
Gerard Gallant

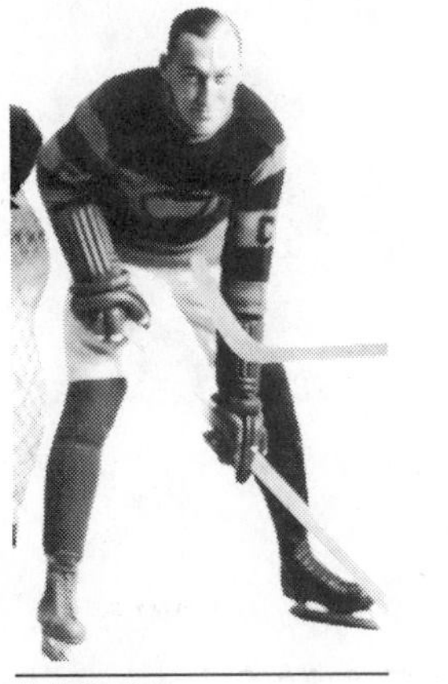
Herb Gardiner

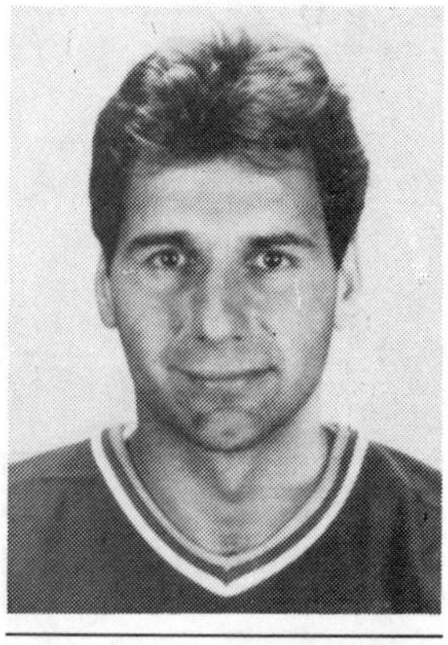

Gaston Gingras

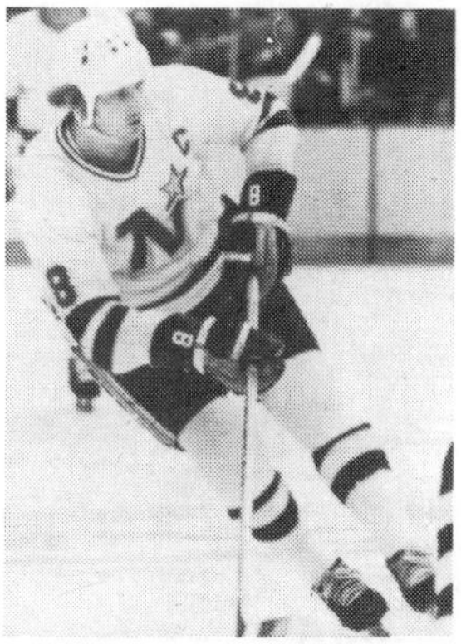

Bill Goldsworthy

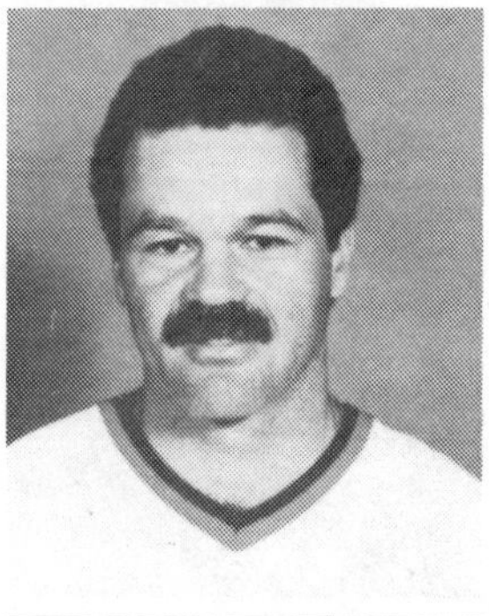

Dirk Graham

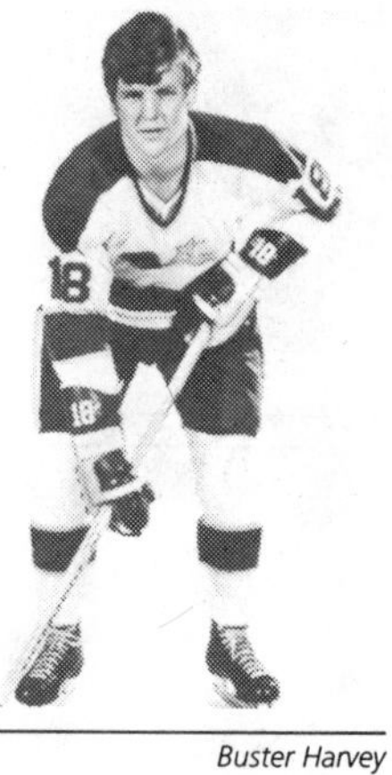

Buster Harvey

			Regular Schedule					Playoffs							
Name	NHL Teams	NHL Seasons	GP	G	A	TP	PIM	GP	G	A	TP	PIM	NHL Cup Wins	First NHL Season	Last NHL Season
Gould, Bobby	Atl., Cgy., Wsh., Bos.	11	697	145	159	304	572	78	15	13	28	58		1979-80	1989-90
Gould, John	Buf., Van., Atl.	9	504	131	138	269	113	14	3	2	5	4		1971-72	1979-80
Gould, Larry	Van.	1	2	0	0	0	0	....	....	....	....	....		1973-74	1973-74
Goulet, Michel	Que., Chi.	15	1089	548	604	1152	825	92	39	39	78	110		1979-80	1993-94
Goupille, Red	Mtl.	8	222	12	28	40	256	8	2	0	2	6		1935-36	1942-43
Goyer, Gerry	Chi.	1	40	1	2	3	4	3	0	0	0	2		1967-68	1967-68
Goyette, Phil	Mtl., NYR, St.L., Buf.	16	941	207	467	674	131	94	17	29	46	26	4	1956-57	1971-72
Graboski, Tony	Mtl.	3	66	6	10	16	24	3	0	0	0	6		1940-41	1942-43
• Gracie, Bob	Tor., Bos., NYA, Mtl.M., Mtl., Chi.	9	379	82	109	191	205	33	4	7	11	4	2	1930-31	1938-39
Gradin, Thomas	Van., Bos.	9	677	209	384	593	298	42	17	25	42	20		1978-79	1986-87
Graham, Dirk	Min., Chi.	12	772	219	270	489	917	90	17	27	44	92		1983-84	1994-95
• Graham, Leth	Ott., Ham.	6	26	3	0	3	0	1	0	0	0	0	1	1920-21	1925-26
Graham, Pat	Pit., Tor.	3	103	11	17	28	136	4	0	0	0	2		1981-82	1983-84
Graham, Rod	Bos.	1	14	2	1	3	7	....	....	....	....	....		1974-75	1974-75
Graham, Ted	Chi., Mtl.M., Det., St.L., Bos., NYA	9	343	14	25	39	300	23	3	1	4	34		1927-28	1936-37
Grant, Danny	Mtl., Min., Det., L.A.	13	736	263	273	536	239	43	10	14	24	19	1	1965-66	1978-79
Gratton, Dan	L.A.	1	7	1	0	1	5	....	....	....	....	....		1987-88	1987-88
Gratton, Norm	NYR, Atl., Buf., Min.	5	201	39	44	83	64	6	0	1	1	2		1971-72	1975-76
Gravelle, Leo	Mtl., Det.	5	223	44	34	78	42	17	4	1	5	2		1946-47	1950-51
Graves, Hilliard	Cal., Atl., Van., Wpg.	9	556	118	163	281	209	2	0	0	0	0		1970-71	1979-80
Graves, Steve	Edm.	3	35	5	4	9	10	....	....	....	....	....		1983-84	1987-88
• Gray, Alex	NYR, Tor.	2	50	7	0	7	32	13	1	0	1	0	1	1927-28	1928-29
Gray, Terry	Bos., Mtl., L.A., St.L.	6	147	26	28	54	64	35	5	5	10	22		1961-62	1970-71
Green, Red	Ham., NYA, Bos., Det.	6	195	59	13	72	261	1	0	0	0	0	1	1923-24	1928-29
Green, Rick	Wsh., Mtl., Det., NYI	15	845	43	220	263	588	100	3	16	19	73	1	1976-77	1991-92
Green, Ted	Bos.	11	620	48	206	254	1029	31	4	8	12	54	1	1960-61	1971-72
• Green, Wilf	Ham., NYA	4	103	33	8	41	151	....	....	....	....	....		1923-24	1926-27
Gregg, Randy	Edm., Van.	10	474	41	152	193	333	137	13	38	51	127	5	1981-82	1991-92
Greig, Bruce	Cal.	2	9	0	1	1	46	....	....	....	....	....		1973-74	1974-75
Grenier, Lucien	Mtl., L.A.	4	151	14	14	28	18	2	0	0	0	0	1	1968-69	1971-72
Grenier, Richard	NYI	1	10	1	1	2	2	....	....	....	....	....		1972-73	1972-73
Greschner, Ron	NYR	16	982	179	431	610	1226	84	17	32	49	106		1974-75	1989-90
Grigor, George	Chi.	1	2	1	0	1	0	1	0	0	0	0		1943-44	1943-44
Grisdale, John	Tor., Van.	6	250	4	39	43	346	10	0	1	1	15		1972-73	1978-79
Gronsdahl, Lloyd	Bos.	1	10	1	2	3	0	....	....	....	....	....		1941-42	1941-42
Gronstrand, Jari	Min., NYR, Que., NYI	5	185	8	26	34	135	3	0	0	0	4		1986-87	1990-91
Gross, Lloyd	Tor., NYA, Bos., Det.	3	52	11	5	16	20	1	0	0	0	0		1926-27	1934-35
• Grosso, Don	Det., Chi., Bos.	9	336	87	117	204	90	49	15	14	29	63	1	1938-39	1946-47
Grosvenar, Len	Ott., NYA, Mtl.	6	147	9	11	20	78	4	0	0	0	2		1927-28	1932-33
Groulx, Wayne	Que.	1	1	0	0	0	0	....	....	....	....	....		1984-85	1984-85
Gruen, Danny	Det., Col.	3	49	9	13	22	19	....	....	....	....	....		1972-73	1976-77
Gruhl, Scott	L.A., Pit.	3	20	3	3	6	6	....	....	....	....	....		1981-82	1987-88
Gryp, Bob	Bos., Wsh.	3	74	11	13	24	33	....	....	....	....	....		1973-74	1975-76
Guay, Francois	Buf.	1	1	0	0	0	0	....	....	....	....	....		1989-90	1989-90
Guay, Paul	Phi., L.A., Bos., NYI	7	117	11	23	34	92	9	0	1	1	12		1983-84	1990-91
Guerard, Stephane	Que.	2	34	0	0	0	40	....	....	....	....	....		1987-88	1989-90
Guevremont, Jocelyn	Van., Buf., NYR	9	571	84	223	307	319	40	4	17	21	18		1971-72	1979-80
Guidolin, Aldo	NYR	4	182	9	15	24	117	....	....	....	....	....		1952-53	1955-56
Guidolin, Bep	Bos., Det., Chi.	9	519	107	171	278	606	24	5	7	12	35		1942-43	1951-52
Guindon, Bobby	Wpg.	1	6	0	1	1	0	....	....	....	....	....		1979-80	1979-80
Gustafsson, Bengt	Wsh.	9	629	196	359	555	196	32	9	19	28	16		1979-80	1988-89
Gustavsson, Peter	Col.	1	2	0	0	0	0	....	....	....	....	....		1981-82	1981-82
Guy, Kevan	Cgy., Van.	6	156	5	20	25	138	5	0	1	1	23		1986-87	1991-92

H

Name	NHL Teams	NHL Seasons	GP	G	A	TP	PIM	GP	G	A	TP	PIM	NHL Cup Wins	First NHL Season	Last NHL Season
Haanpaa, Ari	NYI	3	60	6	11	17	37	6	0	0	0	10		1985-86	1987-88
Haas, David	Edm., Cgy.	2	7	2	1	3	7	....	....	....	....	....		1990-91	1993-94
Habscheid, Marc	Edm., Min., Det., Cgy.	11	345	72	91	163	171	12	1	3	4	13		1981-82	1991-92
Hachborn, Len	Phi., L.A.	3	102	20	39	59	29	7	0	3	3	7		1983-84	1985-86
Haddon, Lloyd	Det.	1	8	0	0	0	2	1	0	0	0	0		1959-60	1959-60
Hadfield, Vic	NYR, Pit.	16	1002	323	389	712	1154	73	27	21	48	117		1961-62	1976-77
Haggarty, Jim	Mtl.	1	5	1	1	2	0	3	2	1	3	0		1941-42	1941-42
• Hagglund, Roger	Que.	1	....	....	....	....	....	....	....	....	....	....		1984-85	1984-85
Hagman, Matti	Bos., Edm.	4	237	56	89	145	36	20	5	2	7	6		1976-77	1981-82
Haidy, Gord	Det.	1	....	....	....	....	....	1	0	0	0	0	1	1949-50	1949-50
Hajdu, Richard	Buf.	2	5	0	0	0	4	....	....	....	....	....		1985-86	1986-87
Hajt, Bill	Buf.	14	854	42	202	244	433	80	2	16	18	70		1973-74	1986-87
Hakansson, Anders	Min., Pit., L.A.	5	330	52	46	98	141	6	0	0	0	2		1981-82	1985-86
• Halderson, Slim	Det., Tor.	1	44	3	2	5	65	....	....	....	....	....		1926-27	1926-27
Hale, Larry	Phi.	4	196	5	37	42	90	8	0	0	0	12		1968-69	1971-72
Haley, Len	Det.	2	30	2	2	4	14	6	1	3	4	6		1959-60	1960-61
Hall, Bob	NYA	1	8	0	0	0	0	....	....	....	....	....		1925-26	1925-26
Hall, Del	Cal.	3	9	2	0	2	2	....	....	....	....	....		1971-72	1973-74
• Hall, Joe	Mtl.	2	37	15	1	16	145	12	0	2	2	31		1917-18	1918-19
Hall, Murray	Chi., Det., Min., Van.	9	164	35	48	83	46	6	0	0	0	0		1961-62	1971-72
Hall, Taylor	Van., Bos.	5	41	7	9	16	29	....	....	....	....	....		1983-84	1987-88
Hall, Wayne	NYR	1	4	0	0	0	0	....	....	....	....	....		1960-61	1960-61
• Halliday, Milt	Ott.	3	67	1	0	1	4	6	0	0	0	0	1	1926-27	1928-29
Hallin, Mats	NYI, Min.	5	152	17	14	31	193	15	1	0	1	13	1	1982-83	1986-87
Halward, Doug	Bos., L.A., Van., Det., Edm.	14	653	69	224	293	774	47	7	10	17	113		1975-76	1988-89
Hamel, Gilles	Buf., Wpg., L.A.	9	519	127	147	274	276	27	4	5	9	10		1980-81	1988-89
Hamel, Herb	Tor.	1	4	0	0	0	14	....	....	....	....	....		1930-31	1930-31
Hamel, Jean	St.L., Det., Que., Mtl.	12	699	26	95	121	766	33	0	2	2	44		1972-73	1983-84
• Hamill, Red	Bos., Chi.	12	419	128	94	222	160	24	1	2	3	20	2	1937-38	1950-51
Hamilton, Al	NYR, Buf., Edm.	7	257	10	78	88	258	7	0	0	0	0		1965-66	1979-80
Hamilton, Chuck	Mtl., St.L.	2	4	0	2	2	2	....	....	....	....	....		1961-62	1972-73
• Hamilton, Jack	Tor.	3	138	31	48	79	76	11	2	1	3	0		1942-43	1945-46
Hamilton, Jim	Pit.	8	95	14	18	32	28	6	3	0	3	0		1977-78	1984-85
• Hamilton, Reg	Tor., Chi.	12	424	21	87	108	412	57	3	8	11	54	2	1935-36	1946-47
Hammarstrom, Inge	Tor., St.L.	6	427	116	123	239	86	13	2	3	5	4		1973-74	1978-79
Hammond, Ken	L.A., Edm., NYR, Tor., Bos., S.J., Van., Ott.	8	193	18	29	47	290	15	0	0	0	24		1984-85	1992-93
Hampson, Gord	Cgy.	1	4	0	0	0	5	....	....	....	....	....		1982-83	1982-83
Hampson, Ted	Tor., NYR, Det., Oak., Cal., Min.	12	676	108	245	353	94	35	7	10	17	2		1959-60	1971-72
Hampton, Rick	Cal., Cle., L.A.	6	337	59	113	172	147	2	0	0	0	0		1974-75	1979-80
Hamway, Mark	NYI	3	53	5	13	18	9	1	0	0	0	0		1984-85	1986-87
Handy, Ron	NYI, St.L.	2	14	0	3	3	0	....	....	....	....	....		1984-85	1987-88
Hangsleben, Al	Hfd., Wsh., L.A.	3	185	21	48	69	396	....	....	....	....	....		1979-80	1981-82
Hanna, John	NYR, Mtl., Phi.	5	198	6	26	32	206	....	....	....	....	....		1958-59	1967-68
• Hannigan, Gord	Tor.	4	161	29	31	60	117	9	2	0	2	8		1952-53	1955-56
Hannigan, Pat	Tor., NYR, Phi.	5	182	30	39	69	116	11	1	2	3	11		1959-60	1968-69
Hannigan, Ray	Tor.	1	3	0	0	0	2	....	....	....	....	....		1948-49	1948-49
Hansen, Ritchie	NYI, St.L.	4	20	2	8	10	4	....	....	....	....	....		1976-77	1981-82
Hanson, Dave	Det., Min.	2	33	1	1	2	65	....	....	....	....	....		1978-79	1979-80
Hanson, Emil	Det.	1	7	0	0	0	6	....	....	....	....	....		1932-33	1932-33
Hanson, Keith	Cgy.	1	25	0	2	2	77	....	....	....	....	....		1983-84	1983-84
Hanson, Ossie	Chi.	1	7	0	0	0	0	....	....	....	....	....		1937-38	1937-38
Harbaruk, Nick	Pit., St.L.	5	364	45	75	120	273	14	3	1	4	20		1969-70	1973-74
Harding, Jeff	Phi.	2	15	0	0	0	47	....	....	....	....	....		1988-89	1989-90
Hardy, Joe	Oak., Cal.	2	63	9	14	23	51	4	0	0	0	0		1969-70	1970-71
Hardy, Mark	L.A., NYR, Min.	15	915	62	306	368	1293	67	5	16	21	158		1979-80	1993-94
Hargreaves, Jim	Van.	2	66	1	7	8	105	....	....	....	....	....		1970-71	1972-73
Harlow, Scott	St.L.	1	1	0	1	1	0	....	....	....	....	....		1987-88	1987-88
Harmon, Glen	Mtl.	9	452	50	96	146	334	53	5	10	15	37	2	1942-43	1950-51
Harms, John	Chi.	2	44	5	5	10	21	3	3	0	3	2		1943-44	1944-45
Harnott, Happy	Bos.	1	6	0	0	0	6	....	....	....	....	....		1933-34	1933-34
Harper, Terry	Mtl., L.A., Det., St.L., Col.	19	1066	35	221	256	1362	112	4	13	17	140	5	1962-63	1980-81
Harrer, Tim	Cgy.	1	3	0	0	0	2	....	....	....	....	....		1982-83	1982-83
• Harrington, Hago	Bos., Mtl.	3	72	9	3	12	15	4	1	0	1	2		1925-26	1932-33
Harris, Billy	Tor., Det., Oak., Cal., Pit.	13	769	126	219	345	205	62	8	10	18	30	3	1955-56	1968-69
Harris, Billy	NYI, L.A., Tor.	12	897	231	327	558	394	71	19	19	38	48		1972-73	1983-84
Harris, Duke	Min., Tor.	1	26	1	4	5	4	....	....	....	....	....		1967-68	1967-68
Harris, Hugh	Buf.	1	60	12	26	38	17	3	0	0	0	0		1972-73	1972-73

			Regular Schedule					Playoffs					NHL	First	Last
Name	**NHL Teams**	**NHL Seasons**	**GP**	**G**	**A**	**TP**	**PIM**	**GP**	**G**	**A**	**TP**	**PIM**	**Cup Wins**	**NHL Season**	**NHL Season**
Harris, Ron	Det., Oak., Atl., NYR	11	476	20	91	111	474	28	4	3	7	33		1962-63	1975-76
Harris, Smokey	Bos.	2	40	5	5	10	28	2	0	0	0	0		1924-25	1930-31
Harris, Ted	Mtl., Min., Det., St.L., Phi.	12	788	30	168	198	1000	100	1	22	23	230	5	1963-64	1974-75
Harrison, Ed	Bos., NYR	4	194	27	24	51	53	9	1	0	1	2		1947-48	1950-51
Harrison, Jim	Bos., Tor., Chi., Edm.	8	324	67	86	153	435	13	1	1	2	43		1968-69	1979-80
Hart, Gerry	Det., NYI, Que., St.L.	15	730	29	150	179	1240	78	3	12	15	175		1968-69	1982-83
● Hart, Gizzy	Det., Mtl.	3	100	6	8	14	12	8	0	1	1	0		1926-27	1932-33
Hartsburg, Craig	Min.	10	570	98	315	413	818	61	15	27	42	70		1979-80	1988-89
● Harvey, Doug	Mtl., NYR, Det., St.L.	20	1113	88	452	540	1216	137	8	64	72	152	6	1947-48	1968-69
Harvey, Fred	Min., Atl., K.C., Det.	7	407	90	118	208	131	14	0	2	2	8		1970-71	1976-77
Harvey, Hugh	K.C.	2	18	1	1	2	4	....	....	....	....	....		1974-75	1975-76
Hassard, Bob	Tor., Chi.	5	126	9	28	37	22	....	....	....	....	....		1949-50	1954-55
Hatoum, Ed	Det., Van.	3	47	3	6	9	25	....	....	....	....	....		1968-69	1970-71
Haworth, Alan	Buf., Wsh., Que.	8	524	189	211	400	425	42	12	16	28	28		1980-81	1987-88
Haworth, Gord	NYR	1	2	0	1	1	0	....	....	....	....	....		1952-53	1952-53
Hawryliw, Neil	NYI	1	1	0	0	0	0	....	....	....	....	....		1981-82	1981-82
Hay, Bill	Chi.	8	506	113	273	386	244	67	15	21	36	62		1959-60	1966-67
● Hay, George	Chi., Det.	7	242	74	60	134	84	8	2	3	5	2		1926-27	1933-34
Hay, Jim	Det.	3	75	1	5	6	22	9	1	0	1	2	1	1952-53	1954-55
Hayek, Peter	Min.	1	1	0	0	0	0	....	....	....	....	....		1981-82	1981-82
Hayes, Chris	Bos.	1	....	....	....	....	....	1	0	0	0	0	1	1971-72	1971-72
Haynes, Paul	Mtl.M., Bos., Mtl.	11	391	61	134	195	164	23	2	8	10	14		1930-31	1940-41
Hayward, Rick	L.A.	1	4	0	0	0	5	....	....	....	....	....		1990-91	1990-91
Hazlett, Steve	Van.	1	1	0	0	0	0	....	....	....	....	....		1979-80	1979-80
Head, Galen	Det.	1	1	0	0	0	0	....	....	....	....	....		1967-68	1967-68
Headley, Fern	Bos., Mtl.	1	27	1	1	2	6	5	0	0	0	0		1924-25	1924-25
Healey, Dick	Det.	1	1	0	0	0	2	....	....	....	....	....		1960-61	1960-61
Heaphy, Shawn	Cgy.	1	1	0	0	0	0	....	....	....	....	....		1992-93	1992-93
Heaslip, Mark	NYR, L.A.	3	117	10	19	29	110	5	0	0	0	2		1976-77	1978-79
Heath, Randy	NYR	2	13	2	4	6	15	....	....	....	....	....		1984-85	1985-86
Hebenton, Andy	NYR, Bos.	9	630	189	202	391	83	22	6	5	11	8		1955-56	1963-64
Hedberg, Anders	NYR	7	465	172	225	397	144	58	22	24	46	31		1978-79	1984-85
● Heffernan, Frank	Tor.	1	17	0	0	0	4	....	....	....	....	....		1919-20	1919-20
Heffernan, Gerry	Mtl.	3	83	33	35	68	27	11	3	3	6	8	1	1941-42	1943-44
Heidt, Mike	L.A.	1	6	0	1	1	7	....	....	....	....	....		1983-84	1983-84
Heindl, Bill	Min., NYR	3	18	2	1	3	0	....	....	....	....	....		1970-71	1972-73
Heinrich, Lionel	Bos.	1	35	1	1	2	33	....	....	....	....	....		1955-56	1955-56
Heiskala, Earl	Phi.	3	127	13	11	24	294	....	....	....	....	....		1968-69	1970-71
Helander, Peter	L.A.	1	7	0	1	1	0	....	....	....	....	....		1982-83	1982-83
● Heller, Ott	NYR	15	647	55	176	231	465	61	6	8	14	61	2	1931-32	1945-46
Helman, Harry	Ott.	3	42	1	0	1	7	5	0	0	0	0	1	1922-23	1924-25
Helminen, Raimo	NYR, Min., NYI	3	117	13	46	59	16	2	0	0	0	0		1985-86	1988-89
Hemmerling, Tony	NYA	2	24	3	3	6	4	....	....	....	....	....		1935-36	1936-37
Henderson, Archie	Wsh., Min., Hfd.	3	23	3	1	4	92	....	....	....	....	....		1980-81	1982-83
Henderson, Murray	Bos.	8	405	24	62	86	305	41	2	3	5	23		1944-45	1951-52
Henderson, Paul	Det., Tor., Atl.	13	707	236	241	477	304	56	11	14	25	28		1962-63	1979-80
Hendrickson, John	Det.	3	5	0	0	0	4	....	....	....	....	....		1957-58	1961-62
Henning, Lorne	NYI	9	544	73	111	184	102	81	7	7	14	8	2	1972-73	1980-81
Henry, Camille	NYR, Chi., St.L.	14	727	279	249	528	88	47	6	12	18	7		1953-54	1969-70
Henry, Dale	NYI	6	132	13	26	39	263	14	1	0	1	19		1984-85	1989-90
Hepple, Alan	N.J.	3	3	0	0	0	7	....	....	....	....	....		1983-84	1985-86
● Herberts, Jimmy	Bos., Tor., Det.	6	206	83	29	112	250	9	3	0	3	10		1924-25	1929-30
Herchenratter, Art	Det.	1	10	1	2	3	2	....	....	....	....	....		1940-41	1940-41
Hergerts, Fred	NYA	2	20	2	4	6	2	....	....	....	....	....		1934-35	1935-36
Hergesheimer, Philip	Chi., Bos.	4	125	21	41	62	19	7	0	0	0	2		1939-40	1942-43
Hergesheimer, Wally	NYR, Chi.	7	351	114	85	199	106	5	1	0	1	0		1951-52	1958-59
Heron, Red	Tor., Bro., Mtl.	4	106	21	19	40	38	21	2	2	4	6		1938-39	1941-42
Heroux, Yves	Que.	1	1	0	0	0	0	....	....	....	....	....		1986-87	1986-87
Hervey, Matt	Wpg., Bos., T.B.	3	35	0	5	5	97	5	0	0	0	6		1988-89	1992-93
Hess, Bob	St.L., Buf., Hfd.	8	329	27	95	122	178	4	1	1	2	2		1974-75	1983-84
Heximer, Orville	NYR, Bos., NYA	3	85	13	7	20	28	5	0	0	0	2		1929-30	1934-35
Hextall, Bryan Jr.	NYR, Pit., Atl., Det., Min.	8	549	99	161	260	738	18	0	4	4	59		1962-63	1975-76
● Hextall, Bryan Sr.	NYR	11	449	187	175	362	227	37	8	9	17	19	1	1936-37	1947-48
Hextall, Dennis	NYR, L.A., Cal., Min., Det., Wsh.	13	684	153	350	503	1398	22	3	3	6	45		1968-69	1979-80
Heyliger, Vic	Chi.	2	34	2	3	5	2	....	....	....	....	....		1937-38	1943-44
Hicke, Bill	Mtl., NYR, Oak.	14	729	168	234	402	395	42	3	10	13	41	2	1958-59	1971-72
Hicke, Ernie	Cal., Atl., NYI, Min., L.A.	8	520	132	140	272	407	2	1	0	1	0		1970-71	1977-78
Hickey, Greg	NYR	1	1	0	0	0	0	....	....	....	....	....		1977-78	1977-78
Hickey, Pat	NYR, Col., Tor., Que., St.L.	10	646	192	212	404	351	55	5	11	16	37		1975-76	1984-85
Hicks, Doug	Min., Chi., Edm., Wsh.	9	561	37	131	168	442	18	2	1	3	15		1974-75	1982-83
Hicks, Glenn	Det.	2	108	6	12	18	127	....	....	....	....	....		1979-80	1980-81
● Hicks, Hal	Mtl.M., Det.	3	110	7	2	9	72	....	....	....	....	....		1928-29	1930-31
Hicks, Wayne	Chi., Bos., Mtl., Phi., Pit.	5	115	13	23	36	22	2	0	1	1	2	1	1959-60	1967-68
Hidi, Andre	Wsh.	2	7	2	1	3	9	2	0	0	0	0		1983-84	1984-85
Hiemer, Uli	N.J.	3	143	19	54	73	176	....	....	....	....	....		1984-85	1986-87
Higgins, Paul	Tor.	2	25	0	0	0	152	1	0	0	0	0		1981-82	1982-83
Higgins, Tim	Chi., N.J., Det.	11	706	154	198	352	719	65	5	8	13	77		1978-79	1988-89
Hildebrand, Ike	NYR, Chi.	2	41	7	11	18	16	....	....	....	....	....		1953-54	1954-55
Hill, Al	Phi.	8	251	40	55	95	227	51	8	11	19	43		1976-77	1987-88
Hill, Brian	Hfd.	1	19	1	1	2	4	....	....	....	....	....		1979-80	1979-80
● Hill, Mel	Bos., Bro., Tor.	9	324	89	109	198	128	43	12	7	19	18	3	1937-38	1945-46
Hiller, Dutch	NYR, Det., Bos., Mtl.	9	383	91	113	204	163	48	9	8	17	21	2	1937-38	1945-46
Hillier, Randy	Bos., Pit., NYI, Buf.	11	543	16	110	126	906	28	0	2	2	93	1	1981-82	1991-92
Hillman, Floyd	Bos.	1	6	0	0	0	10	....	....	....	....	....		1956-57	1956-57
Hillman, Larry	Det., Bos., Tor., Min., Mtl., Phi., L.A., Buf.	19	790	36	196	232	579	74	2	9	11	30	6	1954-55	1972-73
● Hillman, Wayne	Chi., NYR, Min., Phi.	13	691	18	86	104	534	28	0	3	3	19	1	1960-61	1972-73
Hilworth, John	Det.	3	57	1	1	2	89	....	....	....	....	....		1977-78	1979-80
Himes, Normie	NYA	9	402	106	113	219	127	2	0	0	0	0		1926-27	1934-35
Hindmarch, Dave	Cgy.	4	99	21	17	38	25	10	0	0	0	6		1980-81	1983-84
Hinse, Andre	Tor.	1	4	0	0	0	0	....	....	....	....	....		1967-68	1967-68
Hinton, Dan	Chi.	1	14	0	0	0	16	....	....	....	....	....		1976-77	1976-77
Hirsch, Tom	Min.	3	31	1	7	8	30	12	0	0	0	6		1983-84	1987-88
● Hirschfeld, Bert	Mtl.	2	33	1	4	5	2	5	1	0	1	0		1949-50	1950-51
Hislop, Jamie	Que., Cgy.	5	345	75	103	178	86	28	3	2	5	11		1979-80	1983-84
● Hitchman, Lionel	Ott., Bos.	12	416	28	33	61	523	40	4	1	5	77	2	1922-23	1933-34
Hlinka, Ivan	Van.	2	137	42	81	123	28	16	3	10	13	8		1981-82	1982-83
Hodge, Ken	Min., Bos., T.B.	4	142	39	48	87	32	15	4	6	10	6		1988-89	1992-93
Hodge, Ken	Chi., Bos., NYR	14	881	328	472	800	785	97	34	47	81	120	2	1965-66	1977-78
Hodgson, Dan	Tor., Van.	4	114	29	45	74	64	....	....	....	....	....		1985-86	1988-89
Hodgson, Rick	Hfd.	1	6	0	0	0	6	1	0	0	0	0		1979-80	1979-80
Hodgson, Ted	Bos.	1	4	0	0	0	0	....	....	....	....	....		1966-67	1966-67
Hoekstra, Cecil	Mtl.	1	4	0	0	0	0	....	....	....	....	....		1959-60	1959-60
Hoekstra, Ed	Phi.	1	70	15	21	36	6	7	0	1	1	0		1967-68	1967-68
Hoene, Phil	L.A.	3	37	2	4	6	22	....	....	....	....	....		1972-73	1974-75
Hoffinger, Vic	Chi.	2	28	0	1	1	30	....	....	....	....	....		1927-28	1928-29
Hoffman, Mike	Hfd.	3	9	1	3	4	2	....	....	....	....	....		1982-83	1985-86
Hoffmeyer, Bob	Chi., Phi., N.J.	6	198	14	52	66	325	3	0	1	1	25		1977-78	1984-85
Hofford, Jim	Buf., L.A.	3	18	0	0	0	47	....	....	....	....	....		1985-86	1988-89
Hogaboam, Bill	Atl., Det., Min.	8	332	80	109	189	100	2	0	0	0	0		1972-73	1979-80
Hoganson, Dale	L.A., Mtl., Que.	7	343	13	77	90	186	11	0	3	3	12		1969-70	1981-82
Holbrook, Terry	Min.	2	43	3	6	9	4	6	0	0	0	0		1972-73	1973-74
Holland, Jerry	NYR	2	37	8	4	12	6	....	....	....	....	....		1974-75	1975-76
Hollett, Frank	Tor., Ott., Bos., Det.	13	562	132	181	313	358	79	8	26	34	38	2	1933-34	1945-46
● Hollingworth, Gord	Chi., Det.	4	163	4	14	18	201	3	0	0	0	2		1954-55	1957-58
Holloway, Bruce	Van.	1	2	0	0	0	0	....	....	....	....	....		1984-85	1984-85
● Holmes, Bill	Mtl., NYA.	3	52	6	4	10	35	....	....	....	....	....		1925-26	1929-30
Holmes, Chuck	Det.	2	23	1	3	4	10	....	....	....	....	....		1958-59	1961-62
Holmes, Lou	Chi.	2	59	1	4	5	6	2	0	0	0	2		1931-32	1932-33
Holmes, Warren	L.A.	3	45	8	18	26	7	....	....	....	....	....		1981-82	1983-84
Holmgren, Paul	Phi., Min.	10	527	144	179	323	1684	82	19	32	51	195		1975-76	1984-85
● Holota, John	Det.	2	15	2	0	2	0	....	....	....	....	....		1942-43	1945-46
Holst, Greg	NYR	3	11	0	0	0	0	....	....	....	....	....		1975-76	1977-78
Holt, Gary	Cal., Clev., St.L.	5	101	13	11	24	133	....	....	....	....	....		1973-74	1977-78

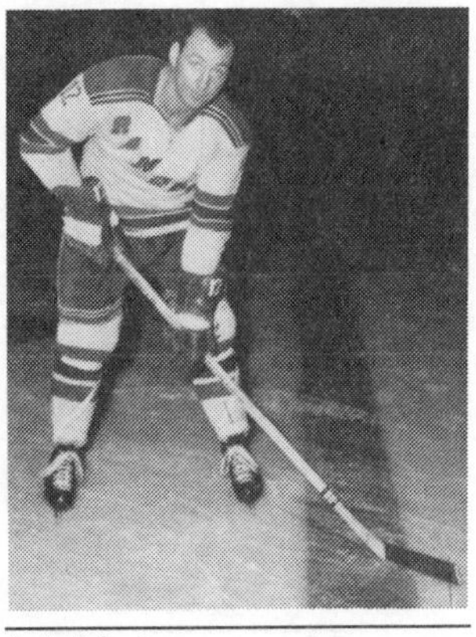

Andy Hebenton

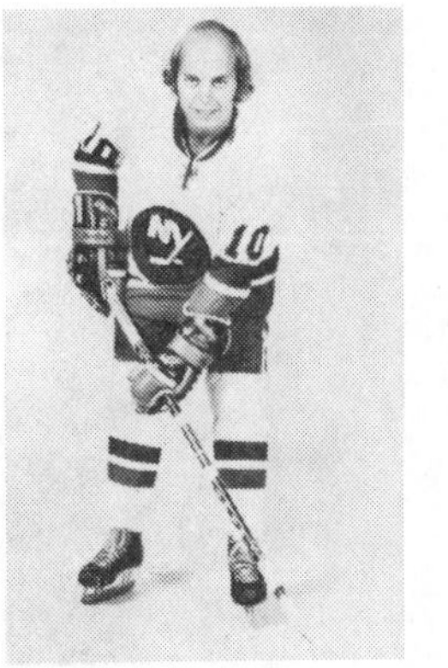

Lorne Henning

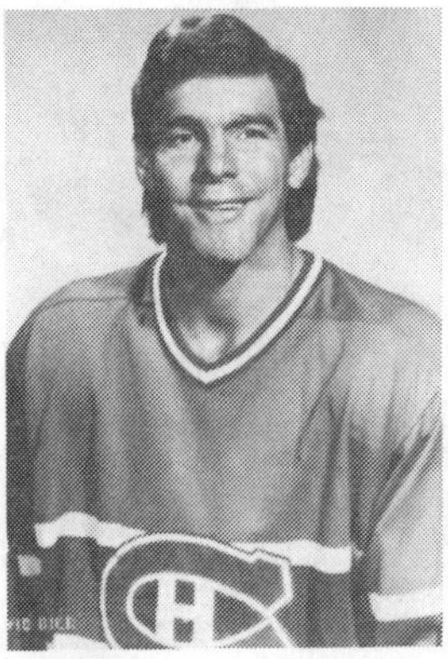

Rejean Houle

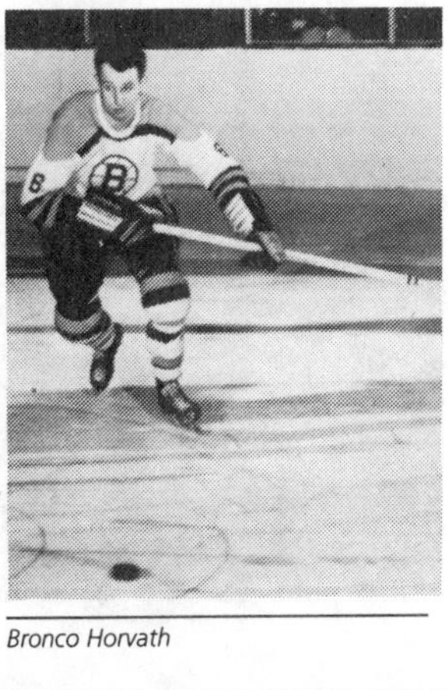

Bronco Horvath

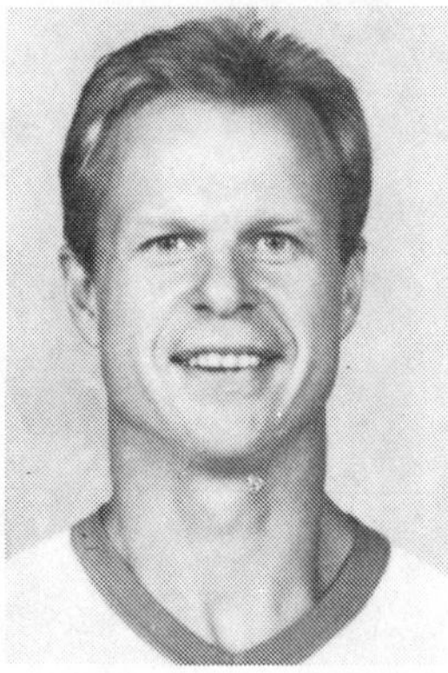
Mark Howe

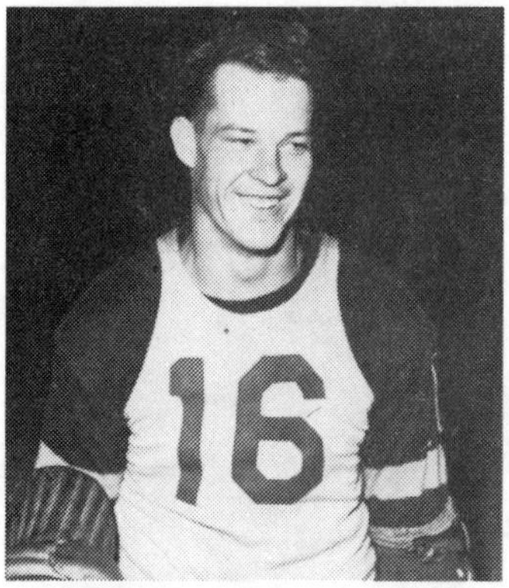
Gordie Howe

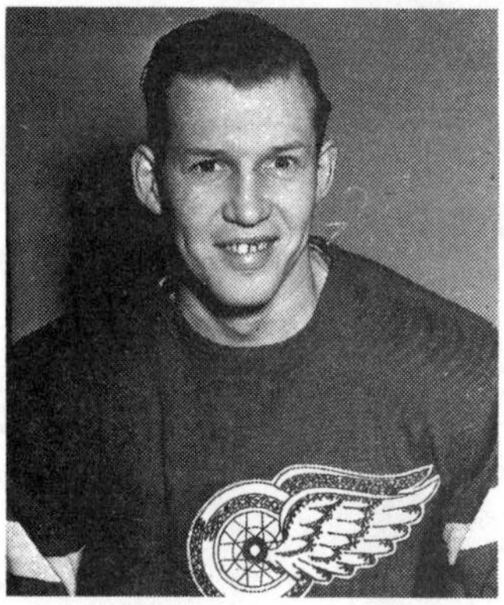
Syd Howe

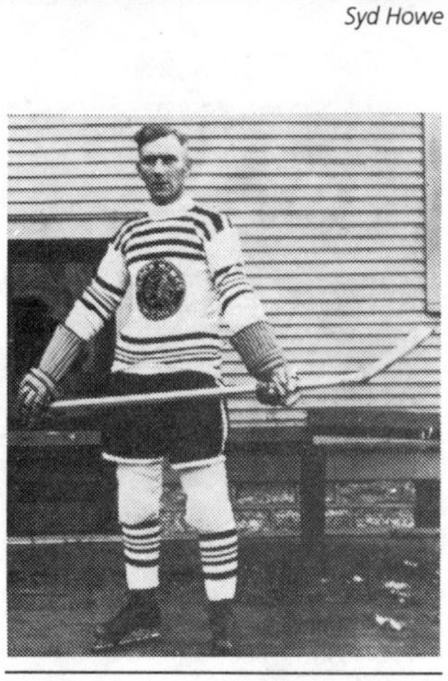
Dick Irvin

Name	NHL Teams	NHL Seasons	Regular Schedule GP	G	A	TP	PIM	Playoffs GP	G	A	TP	PIM	NHL Cup Wins	First NHL Season	Last NHL Season
Holt, Randy	Chi., Clev., Van., L.A., Cgy., Wsh., Phi.	10	393	4	37	41	1438	21	2	3	5	83		1974-75	1983-84
• Holway, Albert	Tor., Mtl.M., Pit.	5	113	7	2	9	48	8	0	0	0	2	1	1923-24	1928-29
Homenuke, Ron	Van.	1	1	0	0	0	0	....	....	....	....	....		1972-73	1972-73
Hoover, Ron	Bos., St.L.	3	18	4	0	4	31	8	0	0	0	18		1989-90	1991-92
Hopkins, Dean	L.A., Edm., Que.	6	223	23	51	74	306	18	1	5	6	29		1979-80	1988-89
Hopkins, Larry	Tor., Wpg.	4	60	13	16	29	26	6	0	0	0	2		1977-78	1982-83
Horava, Miloslav	NYR	3	80	5	17	22	38	2	0	1	1	0		1988-89	1990-91
Horbul, Doug	K.C.	1	4	1	0	1	2	....	....	....	....	....		1974-75	1974-75
Hordy, Mike	NYI	2	11	0	0	0	7	....	....	....	....	....		1978-79	1979-80
Horeck, Pete	Chi., Det., Bos.	8	426	106	118	224	340	34	6	8	14	43		1944-45	1951-52
• Horne, George	Mtl.M, Tor.	3	54	9	3	12	34	4	0	0	0	4		1925-26	1928-29
Horner, Red	Tor.	12	489	42	110	152	1254	71	7	10	17	170	1	1928-29	1939-40
Hornung, Larry	St.L.	2	48	2	9	11	10	11	0	2	2	2		1970-71	1971-72
• Horton, Tim	Tor., NYR, Buf., Pit.	24	1446	115	403	518	1611	126	11	39	50	183	4	1949-50	1973-74
Horvath, Bronco	NYR, Mtl., Bos., Chi., Tor., Min.	9	434	141	185	326	319	36	12	9	21	18		1955-56	1967-68
Hospodar, Ed	NYR, Hfd., Phi., Min., Buf.	9	480	17	51	68	1314	44	4	1	5	208		1979-80	1987-88
Hostak, Martin	Phi.	2	55	3	11	14	24	....	....	....	....	....		1990-91	1991-92
Hotham, Greg	Tor., Pit.	6	230	15	74	89	139	5	0	3	3	6		1979-80	1984-85
Houck, Paul	Min.	3	16	1	2	3	2	....	....	....	....	....		1985-86	1987-88
Houde, Claude	K.C.	2	59	3	6	9	40	....	....	....	....	....		1974-75	1975-76
Houle, Rejean	Mtl.	11	635	161	247	408	395	90	14	34	48	66	5	1969-70	1982-83
Houston, Ken	Atl., Cgy., Wsh., L.A.	9	570	161	167	328	624	35	10	9	19	66		1975-76	1983-84
Howard, Frank	Tor.	1	2	0	0	0	0	....	....	....	....	....		1936-37	1936-37
Howatt, Garry	NYI, Hfd., N.J.	12	720	112	156	268	1836	87	12	14	26	289	2	1972-73	1983-84
Howe, Gordie	Det., Hfd.	26	1767	801	1049	1846	1675	157	68	92	160	220	4	1946-47	1979-80
Howe, Mark	Hfd., Phi., Det.	16	929	197	545	742	455	101	10	51	61	34		1979-80	1994-95
Howe, Marty	Hfd., Bos.	6	197	2	29	31	99	15	1	2	3	9		1979-80	1984-85
• Howe, Syd	Ott., Phi., Tor., St.L., Det.	17	698	237	291	528	212	70	17	27	44	10	3	1929-30	1945-46
Howe, Vic	NYR	3	33	3	4	7	10	....	....	....	....	....		1950-51	1954-55
Howell, Harry	NYR, Oak., L.A.	21	1411	94	324	418	1298	38	3	3	6	32		1952-53	1972-73
Howell, Ron	NYR	2	4	0	0	0	0	....	....	....	....	....		1954-55	1955-56
Howse, Don	L.A.	1	33	2	5	7	6	2	0	0	0	0		1979-80	1979-80
Howson, Scott	NYI	2	18	5	3	8	4	....	....	....	....	....		1984-85	1985-86
Hoyda, Dave	Phi., Wpg.	4	132	6	17	23	299	12	0	0	0	17		1977-78	1980-81
Hrdina, Jiri	Cgy., Pit.	5	250	45	85	130	92	46	2	5	7	24	3	1987-88	1991-92
Hrechkosy, Dave	Cal., St.L.	4	140	42	24	66	41	3	1	0	1	2		1973-74	1976-77
Hrycuik, Jim	Wsh.	1	21	5	5	10	12	....	....	....	....	....		1974-75	1974-75
Hrymnak, Steve	Chi., Det.	2	18	2	1	3	4	2	0	0	0	0		1951-52	1952-53
Hrynewich, Tim	Pit.	2	55	6	8	14	82	....	....	....	....	....		1982-83	1983-84
Huard, Rolly	Tor.	1	1	1	0	1	0	....	....	....	....	....		1930-31	1930-31
Huber, Willie	Det., NYR, Van., Phi.	10	655	104	217	321	950	33	5	5	10	35		1978-79	1987-88
Hubick, Greg	Tor., Van.	2	77	6	9	15	10	....	....	....	....	....		1975-76	1979-80
Huck, Fran	Mtl., St.L.	3	94	24	30	54	38	11	3	4	7	2		1969-70	1972-73
Hucul, Fred	Chi., St.L.	5	164	11	30	41	113	6	1	0	1	10		1950-51	1967-68
Hudson, Dave	NYI, K.C., Col.	6	409	59	124	183	89	2	1	1	2	0		1972-73	1977-78
Hudson, Lex	Pit.	1	2	0	0	0	0	2	0	0	0	0		1978-79	1978-79
Hudson, Ron	Det.	2	33	5	2	7	2	....	....	....	....	....		1937-38	1939-40
Huggins, Al	Mtl.M	1	20	1	1	2	2	....	....	....	....	....		1930-31	1930-31
Hughes, Al	NYA	2	60	6	8	14	22	....	....	....	....	....		1930-31	1931-32
Hughes, Brent	L.A., Phi., St.L., Det., K.C.	8	435	15	117	132	440	22	1	3	4	53		1967-68	1974-75
Hughes, Frank	Cal.	1	5	0	0	0	0	....	....	....	....	....		1971-72	1971-72
Hughes, Howie	L.A.	3	168	25	32	57	30	14	2	0	2	2		1967-68	1969-70
Hughes, Jack	Col.	2	46	2	5	7	104	....	....	....	....	....		1980-81	1981-82
Hughes, John	Van., Edm., NYR	2	70	2	14	16	211	7	0	1	1	16		1979-80	1980-81
Hughes, Pat	Mtl., Pit., Edm., Buf., St.L., Hfd.	10	573	130	128	258	646	71	8	20	28	65	3	1977-78	1986-87
Hughes, Rusty	Det.	1	40	0	1	1	48	....	....	....	....	....		1929-30	1929-30
Hull, Bobby	Chi., Wpg., Hfd.	16	1063	610	560	1170	640	119	62	67	129	102	1	1957-58	1979-80
Hull, Dennis	Chi., Det.	14	959	303	351	654	261	104	33	34	67	30		1964-65	1977-78
• Hunt, Fred	NYA, NYR	2	59	15	14	29	6	....	....	....	....	....		1940-41	1944-45
Hunter, Dave	Edm., Pit., Wpg.	10	746	133	190	323	918	105	16	24	40	211	3	1979-80	1988-89
Hunter, Mark	Mtl., St.L., Cgy., Hfd., Wsh.	12	628	213	171	384	1426	79	18	20	38	230	1	1981-82	1992-93
Huras, Larry	NYR	1	2	0	0	0	0	....	....	....	....	....		1976-77	1976-77
Hurlburt, Bob	Van.	1	1	0	0	0	2	....	....	....	....	....		1974-75	1974-75
Hurley, Paul	Bos.	1	1	0	1	1	0	....	....	....	....	....		1968-69	1968-69
Hurst, Ron	Tor.	2	64	9	7	16	70	3	0	2	2	4		1955-56	1956-57
Huston, Ron	Cal.	2	79	15	31	46	8	....	....	....	....	....		1973-74	1974-75
Hutchinson, Ronald	NYR	1	9	0	0	0	0	....	....	....	....	....		1960-61	1960-61
Hutchison, Dave	L.A., Tor., Chi., N.J.	10	584	19	97	116	1550	48	2	12	14	149		1974-75	1983-84
• Hutton, William	Bos., Ott., Phi.	2	64	3	2	5	8	2	0	0	0	0		1929-30	1930-31
• Hyland, Harry	Mtl.W, Ott.	1	16	14	0	14	9	....	....	....	....	....		1917-18	1917-18
Hynes, Dave	Bos.	2	22	4	0	4	2	....	....	....	....	....		1973-74	1974-75
Hynes, Gord	Bos., Phi.	2	52	3	9	12	22	12	1	2	3	6		1991-92	1992-93

I

Name	NHL Teams	NHL Seasons	Regular Schedule GP	G	A	TP	PIM	Playoffs GP	G	A	TP	PIM	NHL Cup Wins	First NHL Season	Last NHL Season
Ihnacak, Miroslav	Tor., Det.	3	56	8	9	17	39	1	0	0	0	0		1985-86	1988-89
Ihnacak, Peter	Tor.	8	417	102	165	267	175	28	4	10	14	25		1982-83	1989-90
Imlach, Brent	Tor.	2	3	0	0	0	0	....	....	....	....	....		1965-66	1966-67
Ingarfield, Earl	NYR, Pit., Oak., Cal.	13	746	179	226	405	239	21	9	8	17	10		1958-59	1970-71
Ingarfield, Earl Jr.	Atl., Cgy., Det.	2	39	4	4	8	22	2	0	1	1	0		1979-80	1980-81
Inglis, Bill	L.A., Buf.	3	36	1	3	4	4	11	1	2	3	4		1967-68	1970-71
• Ingoldsby, Johnny	Tor.	2	29	5	1	6	15	....	....	....	....	....		1942-43	1943-44
Ingram, Frank	Bos., Chi.	4	102	24	16	40	69	11	0	1	1	2		1924-25	1931-32
Ingram, Ron	Chi., Det., NYR	4	114	5	15	20	81	2	0	0	0	0		1956-57	1964-65
• Irvin, Dick	Chi.	3	94	29	23	52	78	2	2	0	2	4		1926-27	1928-29
Irvine, Ted	Bos., L.A., NYR, St.L.	11	724	154	177	331	657	83	16	24	40	115		1963-64	1976-77
Irwin, Ivan	Mtl., NYR	5	155	2	27	29	214	5	0	0	0	8		1952-53	1957-58
Isaksson, Ulf	L.A.	1	50	7	15	22	10	....	....	....	....	....		1982-83	1982-83
Issel, Kim	Edm.	1	4	0	0	0	0	....	....	....	....	....		1988-89	1988-89

J

Name	NHL Teams	NHL Seasons	Regular Schedule GP	G	A	TP	PIM	Playoffs GP	G	A	TP	PIM	NHL Cup Wins	First NHL Season	Last NHL Season
• Jackson, Art	Bos., Tor.	11	468	123	178	301	144	52	8	12	20	29	2	1934-35	1944-45
Jackson, Don	Min., Edm., NYR	10	311	16	52	68	640	53	4	5	9	147	2	1977-78	1986-87
Jackson, Hal	Chi., Det.	8	219	17	34	51	208	31	1	2	3	33	2	1936-37	1946-47
• Jackson, Harvey	Tor., Bos., NYA	15	633	241	234	475	437	71	18	12	30	53	1	1929-30	1943-44
Jackson, Jeff	Tor., NYR, Que., Chi.	8	263	38	48	86	313	6	1	1	2	16		1984-85	1991-92
Jackson, Jim	Cgy., Buf.	4	112	17	30	47	20	14	3	2	5	6		1982-83	1987-88
Jackson, John	Chi.	1	48	2	5	7	38	....	....	....	....	....		1946-47	1946-47
Jackson, Lloyd	NYA	1	14	1	1	2	0	....	....	....	....	....		1936-37	1936-37
Jackson, Stan	Tor., Bos., Ott.	5	85	9	4	13	74	....	....	....	....	....	1	1921-22	1926-27
Jackson, Walt	NYA	3	82	16	11	27	18	....	....	....	....	....		1932-33	1934-35
• Jacobs, Paul	Tor.	1	1	0	0	0	0	....	....	....	....	....		1918-19	1918-19
Jacobs, Tim	Cal.	1	46	0	10	10	35	....	....	....	....	....		1975-76	1975-76
Jalo, Risto	Edm.	1	3	0	3	3	0	....	....	....	....	....		1985-86	1985-86
Jalonen, Kari	Cgy., Edm.	2	37	9	6	15	4	5	1	0	1	0		1982-83	1983-84
James, Gerry	Tor.	5	149	14	26	40	257	15	1	0	1	8		1954-55	1959-60
James, Val	Buf., Tor.	2	11	0	0	0	30	....	....	....	....	....		1981-82	1986-87
Jamieson, Jim	NYR	1	1	0	1	1	0	....	....	....	....	....		1943-44	1943-44
Jankowski, Lou	Det., Chi.	4	127	19	18	37	15	1	0	0	0	0		1950-51	1954-55
Jarrett, Doug	Chi., NYR	13	775	38	182	220	631	99	7	16	23	82		1964-65	1976-77
Jarrett, Gary	Tor., Det., Oak., Cal.	7	341	72	92	164	131	11	3	1	4	9		1960-61	1971-72
Jarry, Pierre	NYR, Tor., Det., Min.	7	344	88	117	205	142	5	0	1	1	0		1971-72	1977-78
Jarvenpaa, Hannu	Wpg.	3	114	11	26	37	83	....	....	....	....	....		1986-87	1988-89
Jarvi, Iiro	Que.	2	116	18	43	61	58	....	....	....	....	....		1988-89	1989-90
Jarvis, Doug	Mtl., Wsh., Hfd.	13	964	139	264	403	263	105	14	27	41	42	4	1975-76	1987-88
Jarvis, Jim	Pit., Phi., Tor.	3	112	17	15	32	62	....	....	....	....	....		1929-30	1936-37
Jarvis, Wes	Wsh., Min., L.A., Tor.	9	237	31	55	86	98	2	0	0	0	2		1979-80	1987-88
Javanainen, Arto	Pit.	1	14	4	1	5	2	....	....	....	....	....		1984-85	1984-85
Jay, Bob	L.A.	1	3	0	1	1	0	....	....	....	....	....		1993-94	1993-94
Jeffrey, Larry	Det., Tor., NYR	8	368	39	62	101	293	38	4	10	14	42	1	1961-62	1968-69
Jelinek, Tomas	Ott.	1	49	7	6	13	52	....	....	....	....	....		1992-93	1992-93
Jenkins, Dean	L.A.	1	5	0	0	0	2	....	....	....	....	....		1983-84	1983-84

Name	NHL Teams	NHL Seasons	Regular Schedule					Playoffs					NHL Cup Wins	First NHL Season	Last NHL Season
			GP	G	A	TP	PIM	GP	G	A	TP	PIM			
Jenkins, Roger	Tor., Chi., Mtl., Bos., Mtl.M., NYA	8	325	15	39	54	253	25	1	7	8	12	2	1930-31	1938-39
Jennings, Bill	Det., Bos.	5	108	32	33	65	45	20	4	4	8	6		1940-41	1944-45
Jensen, Chris	NYR, Phi.	6	74	9	12	21	27	....	....	....	....	....		1985-86	1991-92
Jensen, David A.	Hfd., Wsh.	4	69	9	13	22	22	11	0	0	0	2		1983-84	1987-88
Jensen, David H.	Min.	3	18	0	2	2	11	....	....	....	....	....		1983-84	1985-86
Jensen, Steve	Min., L.A.	7	438	113	107	220	318	12	0	3	3	9		1975-76	1981-82
• Jeremiah, Ed	NYA, Bos.	1	15	0	1	1	0	....	....	....	....	....		1931-32	1931-32
Jerrard, Paul	Min.	1	5	0	0	0	4	....	....	....	....	....		1988-89	1988-89
Jerwa, Frank	Bos.	4	91	11	16	27	61	....	....	....	....	....		1931-32	1931-32
• Jerwa, Joe	NYR, Bos., St.L., NYA	9	293	36	69	105	338	17	2	3	5	16		1930-31	1938-39
Jirik, Jaroslav	St.L.	1	3	0	0	0	0	....	....	....	....	....		1969-70	1969-70
Joanette, Rosario	Mtl.	1	2	0	1	1	4	....	....	....	....	....		1944-45	1944-45
Jodzio, Rick	Col., Clev.	1	70	2	8	10	71	....	....	....	....	....		1977-78	1977-78
Johannesen, Glenn	NYI	1	2	0	0	0	0	....	....	....	....	....		1985-86	1985-86
Johannson, John	N.J.	1	5	0	0	0	0	....	....	....	....	....		1983-84	1983-84
Johansen, Trevor	Tor., Col., L.A.	5	286	11	46	57	282	13	0	3	3	21		1977-78	1981-82
Johansson, Bjorn	Clev.	2	15	1	1	2	10	....	....	....	....	....		1976-77	1977-78
Johns, Don	NYR, Mtl., Min.	6	153	2	21	23	76	....	....	....	....	....		1960-61	1967-68
Johnson, Al	Mtl., Det.	4	105	21	28	49	30	11	2	2	4	6		1956-57	1962-63
Johnson, Brian	Det.	1	3	0	0	0	5	....	....	....	....	....		1983-84	1983-84
• Johnson, Danny	Tor., Van., Det.	3	121	18	19	37	24	....	....	....	....	....		1969-70	1971-72
Johnson, Earl	Det.	1	1	0	0	0	0	....	....	....	....	....		1953-54	1953-54
• Johnson, Ivan	NYR, NYA	12	436	38	48	86	808	61	5	2	7	161	2	1926-27	1937-38
Johnson, Jim	NYR, Phi., L.A.	8	302	75	111	186	73	7	0	2	2	2		1964-65	1971-72
Johnson, Mark	Pit., Min., Hfd., St.L., N.J.	11	669	203	305	508	260	37	16	12	28	10		1979-80	1989-90
Johnson, Norm J.	NYR, Phi., L.A.	8	302	75	111	186	73	7	0	2	2	2		1964-65	1971-72
Johnson, Norman B.	Bos., Chi.	3	61	5	20	25	41	14	4	0	4	6		1957-58	1959-60
Johnson, Terry	Que., St.L., Cgy., Tor.	9	285	3	24	27	580	38	0	4	4	118		1979-80	1987-88
Johnson, Tom	Mtl., Bos.	17	978	51	213	264	960	111	8	15	23	109	6	1947-48	1964-65
Johnson, Virgil	Chi.	3	75	2	9	11	27	19	0	3	3	4	1	1937-38	1944-45
Johnson, William	Tor.	1	1	0	0	0	0	....	....	....	....	....		1949-50	1949-50
Johnston, Bernie	Hfd.	2	57	12	24	36	16	3	0	1	1	0		1979-80	1980-81
Johnston, George	Chi.	4	58	20	12	32	2	....	....	....	....	....		1941-42	1946-47
Johnston, Greg	Bos., Tor.	9	187	26	30	56	124	22	2	1	3	12		1983-84	1991-92
Johnston, Jay	Wsh.	2	8	0	0	0	13	....	....	....	....	....		1980-81	1981-82
Johnston, Joey	Min., Cal., Chi.	6	331	85	106	191	320	....	....	....	....	....		1968-69	1975-76
Johnston, Larry	L.A., Det., K.C., Col.	7	320	9	64	73	580	....	....	....	....	....		1967-68	1976-77
Johnston, Marshall	Min., Cal.	7	251	14	52	66	58	6	0	0	0	2		1967-68	1973-74
Johnston, Randy	NYI	1	4	0	0	0	4	....	....	....	....	....		1979-80	1979-80
Johnstone, Eddie	NYR, Det.	10	426	122	136	258	375	55	13	10	23	83		1975-76	1986-87
Johnstone, Ross	Tor.	2	42	5	4	9	14	3	0	0	0	0	1	1943-44	1944-45
• Joliat, Aurel	Mtl.	16	654	270	190	460	757	54	14	19	33	89	3	1922-23	1937-38
Joliat, Bobby	Mtl.	1	1	0	0	0	0	....	....	....	....	....		1924-25	1924-25
Joly, Greg	Wsh., Det.	9	365	21	76	97	250	5	0	0	0	8		1974-75	1982-83
Joly, Yvan	Mtl.	3	2	0	0	0	0	1	0	0	0	0		1979-80	1982-83
Jonathon, Stan	Bos., Pit.	8	411	91	110	201	751	63	8	4	12	137		1975-76	1982-83
Jones, Bob	NYR	1	2	0	0	0	0	....	....	....	....	....		1968-69	1968-69
Jones, Buck	Det., Tor.	4	50	2	2	4	36	12	0	1	1	18		1938-39	1942-43
Jones, Jim	Cal.	1	2	0	0	0	0	....	....	....	....	....		1971-72	1971-72
Jones, Jimmy	Tor.	3	148	13	18	31	68	19	1	5	6	11		1977-78	1979-80
Jones, Ron	Bos., Pit., Wsh.	5	54	1	4	5	31	....	....	....	....	....		1971-72	1975-76
Jonsson, Tomas	NYI, Edm.	8	552	85	259	344	482	80	11	26	37	97	2	1981-82	1988-89
Joseph, Anthony	Wpg.	1	2	1	0	1	0	....	....	....	....	....		1988-89	1988-89
Joyal, Eddie	Det., Tor., L.A., Phi.	9	466	128	134	262	103	50	11	8	19	18		1962-63	1971-72
Joyce, Bob	Bos., Wsh., Wpg.	6	158	34	49	83	90	46	15	9	24	29		1987-88	1992-93
Joyce, Duane	Dal.	1	3	0	0	0	0	....	....	....	....	....		1993-94	1993-94
Juckes, Bing	NYR	2	16	2	1	3	6	....	....	....	....	....		1947-48	1949-50
Julien, Claude	Que.	2	14	0	1	1	25	....	....	....	....	....		1984-85	1985-86
Jutila, Timo	Buf.	1	10	1	5	6	13	....	....	....	....	....		1984-85	1984-85
Juzda, Bill	NYR, Tor.	9	398	14	54	68	398	42	0	3	3	46	2	1940-41	1951-52

K

Name	NHL Teams	NHL Seasons	GP	G	A	TP	PIM	GP	G	A	TP	PIM	NHL Cup Wins	First NHL Season	Last NHL Season
Kabel, Bob	NYR	2	48	5	13	18	34	....	....	....	....	....		1959-60	1960-61
Kachowski, Mark	Pit.	3	64	6	5	11	209	....	....	....	....	....		1987-88	1989-90
Kachur, Ed	Chi.	2	96	10	14	24	35	....	....	....	....	....		1956-57	1957-58
Kaese, Trent	Buf.	1	1	0	0	0	0	....	....	....	....	....		1988-89	1988-89
Kaiser, Vern	Mtl.	1	50	7	5	12	33	2	0	0	0	0		1950-51	1950-51
Kalbfleish, Walter	Ott., St.L., NYA, Bos.	4	36	0	4	4	32	5	0	0	0	2		1933-34	1936-37
• Kaleta, Alex	Chi., NYR	7	387	92	121	213	190	17	1	6	7	2		1941-42	1950-51
Kallur, Anders	NYI	6	383	101	110	211	149	78	12	23	35	32	4	1979-80	1984-85
• Kaminsky, Max	Ott., St.L., Bos., Mtl.M.	4	130	22	34	56	38	4	0	0	0	0		1933-34	1936-37
• Kampman, Bingo	Tor.	5	189	14	30	44	287	47	1	4	5	38	1	1937-38	1941-42
Kane, Frank	Det.	1	2	0	0	0	0	....	....	....	....	....		1943-44	1943-44
Kannegiesser, Gord	St.L.	2	23	0	1	1	15	....	....	....	....	....		1967-68	1971-72
Kannegiesser, Sheldon	Pit., NYR, L.A., Van.	8	366	14	67	81	292	18	0	2	2	10		1970-71	1977-78
Karjalainen, Kyosti	L.A.	1	28	1	8	9	12	3	0	1	1	2		1991-92	1991-92
Karlander, Al	Det.	4	212	36	56	92	70	4	0	1	1	0		1969-70	1972-73
Kasper, Steve	Bos., L.A., Phi., T.B.	13	821	177	291	468	554	94	20	28	48	82		1980-81	1992-93
Kastelic, Ed	Wsh., Hfd.	7	220	11	10	21	719	8	1	0	1	32		1985-86	1991-92
Kaszycki, Mike	NYI, Wsh., Tor.	5	226	42	80	122	108	19	2	6	8	10		1977-78	1982-83
Kea, Ed	Atl., St.L.	10	583	30	145	175	508	32	2	4	6	39		1973-74	1982-83
Kearns, Dennis	Van.	10	677	31	290	321	386	11	1	2	3	8		1971-72	1980-81
• Keating, Jack	NYA	2	35	5	5	10	17	....	....	....	....	....		1931-32	1932-33
Keating, John	Det.	2	11	2	1	3	4	....	....	....	....	....		1938-39	1939-40
Keating, Mike	NYR	1	1	0	0	0	0	....	....	....	....	....		1977-78	1977-78
• Keats, Duke	Det., Chi.	3	80	30	19	49	113	....	....	....	....	....		1926-27	1928-29
• Keeling, Butch	Tor., NYR	12	525	157	63	220	331	47	11	11	22	34	1	1926-27	1937-38
Keenan, Larry	Tor., St.L., Buf., Phi.	6	233	38	64	102	28	46	15	16	31	12		1961-62	1971-72
Kehoe, Rick	Tor., Pit.	14	906	371	396	767	120	39	4	17	21	4		1971-72	1984-85
Kekalainen, Jarmo	Bos., Ott.	3	55	5	8	13	28	....	....	....	....	....		1989-90	1993-94
Keller, Ralph	NYR	1	3	1	0	1	6	....	....	....	....	....		1962-63	1962-63
Kellgren, Christer	Col.	1	5	0	0	0	0	....	....	....	....	....		1981-82	1981-82
Kelly, Bob	St.L., Pit., Chi.	6	425	87	109	196	687	23	6	3	9	40		1973-74	1978-79
Kelly, Bob	Phi., Wsh.	11	837	154	208	362	1454	101	9	14	23	172	2	1970-71	1981-82
Kelly, Dave	Det.	1	16	2	0	2	4	....	....	....	....	....		1976-77	1976-77
Kelly, John Paul	L.A.	7	400	54	70	124	366	18	1	1	2	41		1979-80	1985-86
Kelly, Pete	St.L., Det., NYA, Bro.	7	177	21	38	59	68	19	3	1	4	2	2	1934-35	1941-42
Kelly, Red	Det., Tor.	20	1316	281	542	823	327	164	33	59	92	51	8	1947-48	1966-67
• Kelly, Reg	Tor., Chi., Bro.	8	288	74	53	127	105	38	7	6	13	10		1934-35	1941-42
Kemp, Kevin	Hfd.	1	3	0	0	0	4	....	....	....	....	....		1980-81	1980-81
Kemp, Stan	Tor.	1	1	0	0	0	2	....	....	....	....	....		1948-49	1948-49
Kendall, William	Chi., Tor.	5	131	16	10	26	28	6	0	0	0	0	1	1933-34	1937-38
Kennedy, Dean	L.A., NYR, Buf., Wpg., Edm.	12	717	26	110	136	1118	36	1	7	8	59		1982-83	1994-95
Kennedy, Forbes	Chi., Det., Bos., Phi., Tor.	11	603	70	108	178	988	12	2	4	6	64		1956-57	1968-69
Kennedy, Ted	Tor.	14	696	231	329	560	432	78	29	31	60	32	5	1942-43	1956-57
• Kenny, Eddie	NYR, Chi.	2	10	0	0	0	18	....	....	....	....	....		1930-31	1934-35
Keon, Dave	Tor., Hfd.	18	1296	396	590	986	117	92	32	36	68	6	4	1960-61	1981-82
Kerch, Alexander	Edm.	1	5	0	0	0	2	....	....	....	....	....		1993-94	1993-94
Kerr, Alan	NYI, Det., Wpg.	9	391	72	94	166	826	38	5	4	9	70		1984-85	1992-93
Kerr, Reg	Cle., Chi., Edm.	6	263	66	94	160	169	7	1	0	1	7		1977-78	1983-84
Kerr, Tim	Phi., NYR, Hfd.	13	655	370	304	674	596	81	40	31	71	58		1980-81	1992-93
Kessell, Rick	Pit., Cal.	5	135	4	24	28	6	....	....	....	....	....		1969-70	1973-74
Ketola, Veli-Pekka	Col.	1	44	9	5	14	4	....	....	....	....	....		1981-82	1981-82
Ketter, Kerry	Atl.	1	41	0	2	2	58	....	....	....	....	....		1972-73	1972-73
Kharin, Sergei	Wpg.	1	7	2	3	5	2	....	....	....	....	....		1990-91	1990-91
Kidd, Ian	Van.	2	20	4	7	11	25	....	....	....	....	....		1987-88	1988-89
Kiessling, Udo	Min.	1	1	0	0	0	2	....	....	....	....	....		1981-82	1981-82
Kilrea, Brian	Det., L.A.	2	26	3	5	8	12	....	....	....	....	....		1957-58	1967-68
• Kilrea, Hec	Ott., Det., Tor.	15	633	167	129	296	438	48	8	7	15	18	3	1925-26	1939-40
• Kilrea, Ken	Det.	5	91	16	23	39	8	15	2	2	4	4		1938-39	1943-44
Kilrea, Wally	Ott., Phi., NYA, Mtl.M., Det.	9	329	35	58	93	87	25	2	4	6	6	2	1929-30	1937-38
Kindrachuk, Orest	Phi., Pit., Wsh.	10	508	118	261	379	648	76	20	20	40	53	2	1972-73	1981-82
King, Frank	Mtl.	1	10	1	0	1	2	....	....	....	....	....		1950-51	1950-51

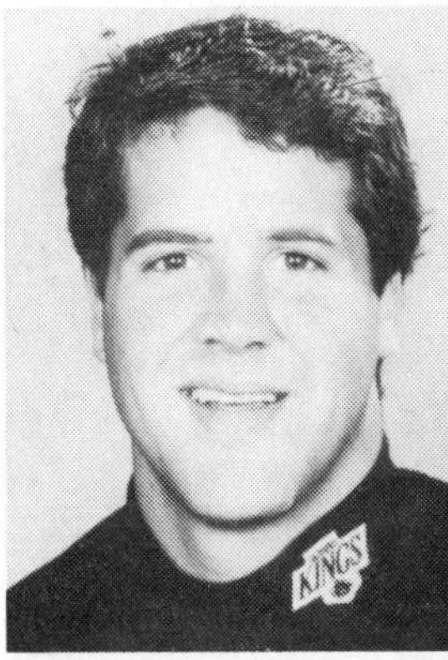

Bobby Jay

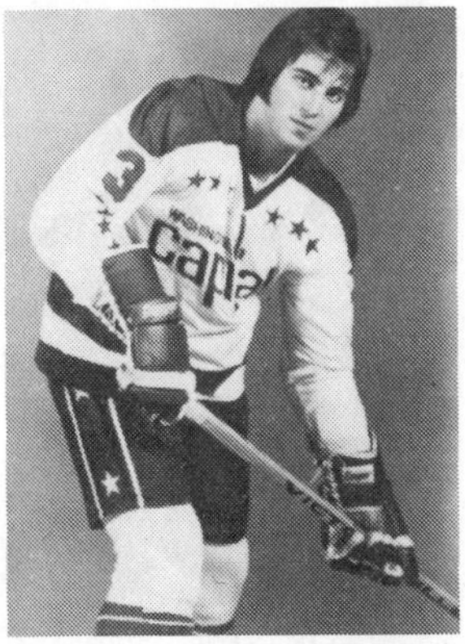

Greg Joly

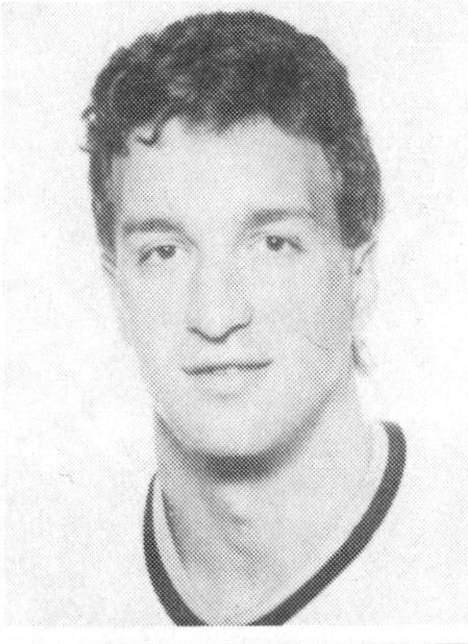

Dean Kennedy

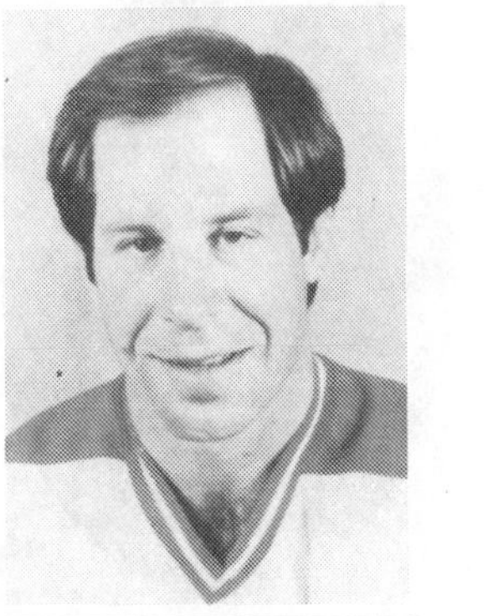

Kelly Kisio

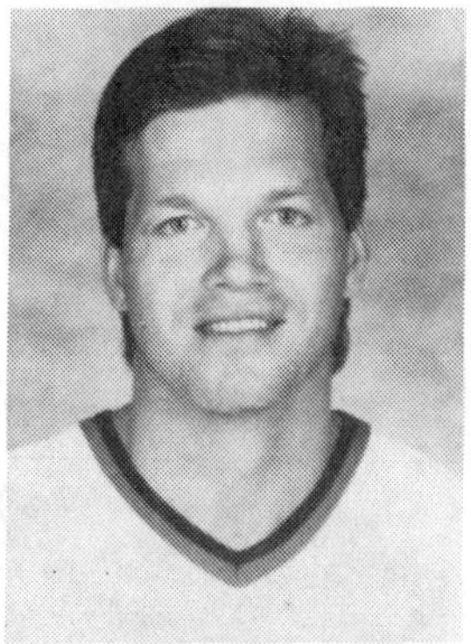

Steve Konroyd

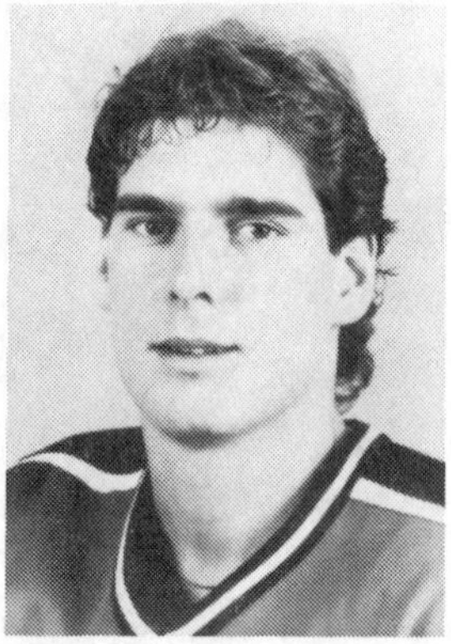

Tom Kurvers

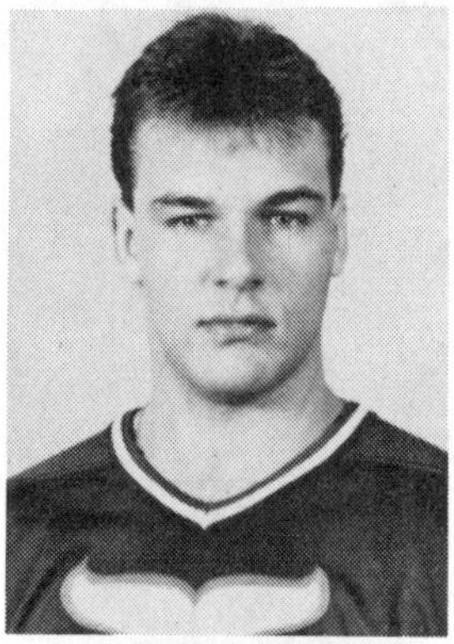

Marc LaForge

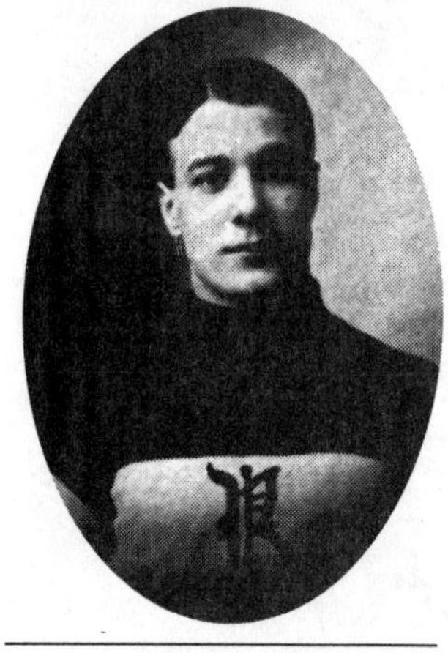

Newsy Lalonde

			Regular Schedule					Playoffs					NHL	First	Last
Name	**NHL Teams**	**NHL Seasons**	**GP**	**G**	**A**	**TP**	**PIM**	**GP**	**G**	**A**	**TP**	**PIM**	**Cup Wins**	**NHL Season**	**NHL Season**
King, Wayne	Cal.	3	73	5	18	23	34	....	....	....	....	....		1973-74	1975-76
Kinsella, Brian	Wsh.	2	10	0	1	1	0	....	....	....	....	....		1975-76	1976-77
Kinsella, Ray	Ott.	1	14	0	0	0	0	....	....	....	....	....		1930-31	1930-31
• Kirk, Bobby	NYR	1	39	4	8	12	14	....	....	....	....	....		1937-38	1937-38
Kirkpatrick, Bob	NYR	1	49	12	12	24	6	....	....	....	....	....		1942-43	1942-43
Kirton, Mark	Tor., Det., Van.	6	266	57	56	113	121	4	1	2	3	7		1979-80	1984-85
Kisio, Kelly	Det., NYR, S.J., Cgy.	13	761	229	429	658	768	39	6	15	21	52		1982-83	1994-95
Kitchen, Bill	Mtl., Tor.	4	41	1	4	5	40	3	0	1	1	0		1981-82	1984-85
• Kitchen, Hobie	Mtl.M., Det.	2	48	5	4	9	58	....	....	....	....	....		1925-26	1926-27
Kitchen, Mike	Col., N.J.	8	474	12	62	74	370	2	0	0	0	2		1976-77	1983-84
Kjellberg, Patrik	Mtl.	1	7	0	0	0	2	....	....	....	....	....		1992-93	1992-93
Klassen, Ralph	Cal., Clev., Col., St.L.	9	497	52	93	145	120	26	4	2	6	12		1975-76	1983-84
Klein, Jim	Bos., NYA	8	164	30	24	54	68	6	0	0	0	2	1	1928-29	1937-38
Kleinendorst, Scot	NYR, Hfd., Wsh.	8	281	12	46	58	452	26	2	7	9	40		1982-83	1989-90
Klingbeil, Ike	Chi.	1	5	1	2	3	2	....	....	....	....	....		1936-37	1936-37
Klukay, Joe	Tor., Bos.	11	566	109	127	236	189	71	13	10	23	23	4	1942-43	1955-56
Kluzak, Gord	Bos.	7	299	25	98	123	543	46	6	13	19	129		1982-83	1990-91
Knibbs, Bill	Bos.	1	53	7	10	17	4	....	....	....	....	....		1964-65	1964-65
• Knott, Nick	Bro.	1	14	3	1	4	9	....	....	....	....	....		1941-42	1941-42
Knox, Paul	Tor.	1	1	0	0	0	0	....	....	....	....	....		1954-55	1954-55
Kolstad, Dean	Min., S.J.	3	40	1	7	8	69	....	....	....	....	....		1988-89	1992-93
Komadoski, Neil	L.A., St.L.	8	502	16	76	92	632	23	0	2	2	47		1972-73	1979-80
Konik, George	Pit.	1	52	7	8	15	26	....	....	....	....	....		1967-68	1967-68
Konroyd, Steve	Cgy., NYI, Chi., Hfd., Det., Ott.	15	895	41	195	236	863	97	10	15	25	99		1980-81	1994-95
Kopak, Russ	Bos.	1	24	7	9	16	0	....	....	....	....	....		1943-44	1943-44
Korab, Jerry	Chi., Van., Buf., L.A.	15	975	114	341	455	1629	93	8	18	26	201		1970-71	1984-85
• Kordic, John	Mtl., Tor., Wsh., Que.	7	244	17	18	35	997	41	4	3	7	131	1	1985-86	1991-92
Korn, Jim	Det., Tor., Buf., N.J., Cgy.	10	597	66	122	188	1801	16	1	2	3	109		1979-80	1989-90
Korney, Mike	Det., NYR	4	77	9	10	19	59	....	....	....	....	....		1973-74	1978-79
Koroll, Cliff	Chi.	11	814	208	254	462	376	85	19	29	48	67		1969-70	1979-80
Kortko, Roger	NYI	2	79	7	17	24	28	10	0	3	3	17		1984-85	1985-86
Kostynski, Doug	Bos.	2	15	3	1	4	4	....	....	....	....	....		1983-84	1984-85
Kotanen, Dick	Det., NYR	2	2	0	1	1	0	....	....	....	....	....		1948-49	1950-51
Kotsopoulos, Chris	NYR, Hfd.,Tor., Det.	9	479	44	109	153	827	31	1	3	4	91		1980-81	1989-90
Kowal, Joe	Buf.	2	22	0	5	5	13	2	0	0	0	0		1976-77	1977-78
Kozak, Don	L.A., Van.	7	437	96	86	182	480	29	7	2	9	69		1972-73	1978-79
Kozak, Les	Tor.	1	12	1	0	1	2	....	....	....	....	....		1961-62	1961-62
Kraftcheck, Stephen	Bos., NYR, Tor.	4	157	11	18	29	83	6	0	0	0	7		1950-51	1958-59
Krake, Skip	Bos., L.A., Buf.	7	249	23	40	63	182	10	1	0	1	17		1963-64	1970-71
Kravets, Mikhail	S.J.	2	2	0	0	0	0	....	....	....	....	....		1991-92	1992-93
Krentz, Dale	Det.	3	30	5	3	8	9	2	0	0	0	0		1986-87	1988-89
Krol, Joe	NYR, Bro.	3	26	10	4	14	8	....	....	....	....	....		1936-37	1941-42
Kromm, Rich	Cgy., NYI	9	372	70	103	173	138	36	2	6	8	22		1983-84	1992-93
Krook, Kevin	Col.	1	3	0	0	0	2	....	....	....	....	....		1978-79	1978-79
Krulicki, Jim	NYR, Det.	1	41	0	3	3	6	....	....	....	....	....		1970-71	1970-71
Krushelnyski, Mike	Bos., Edm., L.A., Tor., Det.	14	897	241	328	569	699	139	29	43	72	106	3	1981-82	1994-95
Krutov, Vladimir	Van.	1	61	11	23	34	20	....	....	....	....	....		1989-90	1989-90
Kryskow, Dave	Chi., Wsh., Det., Atl.	4	231	33	56	89	174	12	2	0	2	4		1972-73	1975-76
Kryznowski, Edward	Bos., Chi.	5	237	15	22	37	65	18	0	1	1	4		1948-49	1952-53
Kuhn, Gord	NYA	1	12	1	1	2	4	....	....	....	....	....		1932-33	1932-33
Kukulowicz, Adolph	NYR	2	4	1	0	1	0	....	....	....	....	....		1952-53	1953-54
Kulak, Stu	Van., Edm., NYR, Que., Wpg.	4	90	8	4	12	130	3	0	0	0	2		1982-83	1988-89
Kullman, Arnie	Bos.	2	13	0	1	1	11	....	....	....	....	....		1947-48	1949-50
Kullman, Eddie	NYR	6	343	56	70	126	298	6	1	0	1	2		1947-48	1953-54
Kumpel, Mark	Que., Det., Wpg.	6	288	38	46	84	113	39	6	4	10	14		1984-85	1990-91
Kuntz, Alan	NYR	2	45	10	12	22	12	6	1	0	1	2		1941-42	1945-46
Kuntz, Murray	St.L.	1	7	1	2	3	0	....	....	....	....	....		1974-75	1974-75
Kurtenbach, Orland	NYR, Bos., Tor., Van.	13	639	119	213	332	628	19	2	4	6	70		1960-61	1973-74
Kurvers, Tom	Mtl., Buf., N.J., Tor., Van., NYI, Ana.	11	659	93	328	421	350	57	8	22	30	68	1	1984-85	1994-95
Kuryluk, Mervin	Chi.	1	....	....	....	....	....	2	0	0	0	0		1961-62	1961-62
Kushner, Dale	NYI, Phi.	3	84	10	13	23	215	....	....	....	....	....		1989-90	1991-92
Kuzyk, Ken	Clev.	2	41	5	9	14	8	....	....	....	....	....		1976-77	1977-78
Kvartalnov, Dmitri	Bos.	2	112	42	49	91	26	4	0	0	0	0		1992-93	1993-94
Kwong, Larry	NYR	1	1	0	0	0	0	....	....	....	....	....		1947-48	1947-48
• Kyle, Bill	NYR	2	3	0	3	3	0	....	....	....	....	....		1949-50	1950-51
Kyle, Gus	NYR, Bos.	3	203	6	20	26	362	14	1	2	3	34		1949-50	1951-52
Kyllonen, Marku	Wpg.	1	9	0	2	2	2	....	....	....	....	....		1988-89	1988-89

L

Labadie, Mike	NYR	1	3	0	0	0	0	....	....	....	....	....		1952-53	1952-53
Labatte, Neil	St.L.	2	26	0	2	2	19	....	....	....	....	....		1978-79	1981-82
L'Abbe, Moe	Chi.	1	5	0	1	1	0	....	....	....	....	....		1972-73	1972-73
Labine, Leo	Bos., Det.	11	643	128	193	321	730	60	11	12	23	82		1951-52	1961-62
Labossierre, Gord	NYR, L.A., Min.	6	215	44	62	106	75	10	2	3	5	28		1963-64	1971-72
Labovitch, Max	NYR	1	5	0	0	0	4	....	....	....	....	....		1943-44	1943-44
Labraaten, Dan	Det., Cgy.	4	268	71	73	144	47	8	1	0	1	4		1978-79	1981-82
Labre, Yvon	Pit., Wsh.	9	371	14	87	101	788	....	....	....	....	....		1970-71	1980-81
Labrie, Guy	Bos., NYR	2	42	4	9	13	16	....	....	....	....	....		1943-44	1944-45
Lach, Elmer	Mtl.	14	664	215	408	623	478	76	19	45	64	36	3	1940-41	1953-54
Lachance, Earl	Mtl.	1	1	0	0	0	0	....	....	....	....	....		1926-27	1926-27
Lachance, Michel	Col.	1	21	0	4	4	22	....	....	....	....	....		1978-79	1978-79
Lacombe, Francois	Oak., Buf., Que.	4	78	2	17	19	54	3	1	0	1	0		1968-69	1979-80
Lacombe, Normand	Buf., Edm., Phi	7	319	53	62	115	196	26	5	1	6	49	1	1984-85	1990-91
Lacroix, Andre	Phi., Chi., Hfd.	6	325	79	119	198	44	16	2	5	7	0		1967-68	1979-80
Lacroix, Pierre	Que., Hfd.	4	274	24	108	132	197	8	0	2	2	10		1979-80	1982-83
Lafleur, Guy	Mtl., NYR, Que.	17	1126	560	793	1353	399	128	58	76	134	67	5	1971-72	1990-91
Lafleur, Rene	Mtl.	1	1	0	0	0	0	....	....	....	....	....		1924-25	1924-25
Laforce, Ernie	Mtl.	1	1	0	0	0	0	....	....	....	....	....		1942-43	1942-43
LaForest, Bob	L.A.	1	5	1	0	1	2	....	....	....	....	....		1983-84	1983-84
Laforge, Claude	Mtl., Det., Phi.	8	193	24	33	57	82	5	1	2	3	15		1957-58	1968-69
LaForge, Marc	Hfd., Edm.	2	14	0	0	0	64	....	....	....	....	....		1989-90	1993-94
Laframboise, Pete	Cal., Wsh., Pit.	4	227	33	55	88	70	9	1	0	1	0		1971-72	1974-75
Lafrance, Adie	Mtl.	1	3	0	0	0	2	2	0	0	0	0		1933-34	1933-34
Lafrance, Leo	Mtl., Chi.	2	33	2	0	2	6	....	....	....	....	....		1926-27	1927-28
Lafreniere, Jason	Que., NYR, T.B.	5	146	34	53	87	22	15	1	5	6	19		1986-87	1993-94
Lafreniere, Roger	Det., St.L.	2	13	0	0	0	4	....	....	....	....	....		1962-63	1972-73
Lagace, Jean-Guy	Pit., Buf., K.C.	6	197	9	39	48	251	....	....	....	....	....		1968-69	1975-76
Laidlaw, Tom	NYR, L.A.	10	705	25	139	164	717	69	4	17	21	78		1980-81	1989-90
Laird, Robbie	Min.	1	1	0	0	0	0	....	....	....	....	....		1979-80	1979-80
Lajeunesse, Serge	Det., Phi.	5	103	1	4	5	103	....	....	....	....	....		1970-71	1974-75
Lalande, Hec	Chi., Det.	4	151	21	39	60	120	....	....	....	....	....		1953-54	1957-58
Lalonde, Bobby	Van., Atl., Bos., Cgy.	11	641	124	210	334	298	16	4	2	6	6		1971-72	1981-82
• Lalonde, Newsy	Mtl., NYA	6	99	124	27	151	122	12	22	1	23	19		1917-18	1926-27
Lalonde, Ron	Pit., Wsh.	7	397	45	78	123	106	....	....	....	....	....		1972-73	1978-79
• Lamb, Joe	Mtl.M., Ott., NYA, Bos., Mtl., St.L., Det.	11	443	108	101	209	601	18	1	1	2	51		1927-28	1937-38
Lambert, Lane	Det., NYR, Que.	6	283	58	66	124	521	17	2	4	6	40		1983-84	1988-89
Lambert, Yvon	Mtl., Buf.	10	683	206	273	479	340	90	27	22	49	67	4	1972-73	1981-82
Lamby, Dick	St.L.	3	22	0	5	5	22	....	....	....	....	....		1978-79	1980-81
• Lamirande, Jean-Paul	NYR, Mtl.	4	49	5	5	10	26	8	0	0	0	4		1946-47	1954-55
Lammens, Hank	Ott.	1	27	1	2	3	22	....	....	....	....	....		1993-94	1993-94
• Lamoureux, Leo	Mtl.	6	235	19	79	98	175	28	1	6	7	16	2	1941-42	1946-47
Lamoureux, Mitch	Pit., Phi.	3	73	11	9	20	59	....	....	....	....	....		1983-84	1987-88
Lampman, Mike	St.L., Van., Wsh.	4	96	17	20	37	34	....	....	....	....	....		1972-73	1976-77
Lancien, Jack	NYR	4	63	1	5	6	35	6	0	1	1	2		1946-47	1950-51
Landon, Larry	Mtl., Tor.	2	9	0	0	0	2	....	....	....	....	....		1983-84	1984-85
Lane, Gord	Wsh., NYI	10	539	19	94	113	1228	75	3	14	17	214	4	1975-76	1984-85
• Lane, Myles	NYR, Bos.	3	71	4	1	5	41	11	0	0	0	0	1	1928-29	1933-34
Langdon, Steve	Bos.	3	7	0	1	1	2	4	0	0	0	0		1974-75	1977-78
Langelle, Pete	Tor.	4	136	22	51	73	11	39	5	9	14	4	1	1938-39	1941-42
Langevin, Chris	Buf.	2	22	3	1	4	22	....	....	....	....	....		1983-84	1985-86
Langevin, Dave	NYI, Min., L.A.	8	513	12	107	119	530	87	2	17	19	106	4	1979-80	1986-87
Langlais, Alain	Min.	2	25	4	4	8	10	....	....	....	....	....		1973-74	1974-75
Langlois, Al	Mtl., NYR, Det., Bos.	9	497	21	91	112	488	53	1	5	6	50	3	1957-58	1965-66

			Regular Schedule					Playoffs							
Name	NHL Teams	NHL Seasons	GP	G	A	TP	PIM	GP	G	A	TP	PIM	NHL Cup Wins	First NHL Season	Last NHL Season
Langlois, Charlie	Ham., NYA., Pit., Mtl.	4	151	22	3	25	201	2	0	0	0	0		1924-25	1927-28
Langway, Rod	Mtl., Wsh.	15	994	51	278	329	849	104	5	22	27	97	1	1978-79	1992-93
Lanthier, Jean-Marc	Van.	4	105	16	16	32	29	....	....	....	....	....		1983-84	1987-88
Lanyon, Ted	Pit.	1	5	0	0	0	4	....	....	....	....	....		1967-68	1967-68
Lanz, Rick	Van., Tor., Chi.	10	569	65	221	286	448	28	3	8	11	35		1980-81	1991-92
Laperriere, Jacques	Mtl.	12	691	40	242	282	674	88	9	22	31	101	6	1962-63	1973-74
Lapointe, Guy	Mtl., St.L., Bos.	16	884	171	451	622	893	123	26	44	70	138	6	1968-69	1983-84
Lapointe, Rick	Det., Phi., St.L., Que., L.A.	11	664	44	176	220	831	46	2	7	9	64		1975-76	1985-86
Lappin, Peter	Min., S.J.	2	7	0	0	0	2	....	....	....	....	....		1989-90	1991-92
Laprade, Edgar	NYR	10	501	108	172	280	42	18	4	9	13	4		1945-46	1954-55
LaPrairie, Ben	Chi.	1	7	0	0	0	0	....	....	....	....	....		1936-37	1936-37
Lariviere, Garry	Que., Edm.	4	219	6	57	63	167	14	0	5	5	8		1979-80	1982-83
Larmer, Jeff	Col., N.J., Chi.	5	158	37	51	88	57	5	1	0	1	2		1981-82	1985-86
Larmer, Steve	Chi., NYR	15	1006	441	571	1012	532	140	56	75	131	89	1	1980-81	1994-95
• Larochelle, Wildor	Mtl., Chi.	12	474	92	74	166	211	34	6	4	10	24	2	1925-26	1936-37
Larocque, Denis	L.A.	1	8	0	1	1	18	....	....	....	....	....		1987-88	1987-88
Larose, Bonner	Bos.	1	6	0	0	0	0	....	....	....	....	....		1925-26	1925-26
Larose, Claude	NYR	2	25	4	7	11	2	2	0	0	0	0		1979-80	1981-82
Larose, Claude	Mtl., Min., St.L.	16	943	226	257	483	887	97	14	18	32	143	5	1962-63	1977-78
Larouche, Pierre	Pit., Mtl., Hfd., NYR	14	812	395	427	822	237	64	20	34	54	16	2	1974-75	1987-88
Larson, Norman	NYA., Bro., NYR	3	89	25	18	43	12	....	....	....	....	....		1940-41	1946-47
Larson, Reed	Det., Bos., Edm., NYI, Min., Buf.	14	904	222	463	685	1391	32	4	7	11	63		1976-77	1989-90
Larter, Tyler	Wsh.	1	1	0	0	0	0	....	....	....	....	....		1989-90	1989-90
Latal, Jiri	Phi.	3	92	12	36	48	24	....	....	....	....	....		1989-90	1990-91
Latos, James	NYR	1	1	0	0	0	0	....	....	....	....	....		1988-89	1988-89
Latreille, Phil	NYR	1	4	0	0	0	2	....	....	....	....	....		1960-61	1960-61
Latta, David	Que.	4	36	4	8	12	4	....	....	....	....	....		1985-86	1990-91
Lauder, Marty	Bos.	1	3	0	0	0	2	....	....	....	....	....		1927-28	1927-28
Lauen, Mike	Wpg.	1	4	0	1	1	0	....	....	....	....	....		1983-84	1983-84
Laughlin, Craig	Mtl., Wsh., L.A., Tor.	8	549	136	205	341	364	33	6	6	12	20		1981-82	1988-89
Laughton, Mike	Oak., Cal.	4	189	39	48	87	101	11	2	4	6	0		1967-68	1970-71
Laurence, Red	Atl., St.L.	2	79	15	22	37	14	....	....	....	....	....		1978-79	1979-80
LaVallee, Kevin	Cgy., L.A., St.L., Pit.	7	366	110	125	235	85	32	5	8	13	21		1980-81	1986-87
Lavarre, Mark	Chi.	3	78	9	16	25	58	1	0	0	0	2		1985-86	1987-88
Lavender, Brian	St.L., NYI, Det., Cal.	4	184	16	26	42	174	3	0	0	0	2		1971-72	1974-75
• Laviolette, Jack	Mtl.	1	18	2	0	2	6	2	0	0	0	0		1917-18	1917-18
Laviolette, Peter	NYR	1	12	0	0	0	6	....	....	....	....	....		1988-89	1988-89
Lavoie, Dominic	St.L., Ott., Bos., L.A.	6	38	5	8	13	32	....	....	....	....	....		1988-89	1993-94
Lawless, Paul	Hfd., Phi., Van., Tor.	7	181	27	47	74	42	1	0	0	0	0		1982-83	1989-90
Lawson, Danny	Det., Min., Buf.	5	219	28	29	57	61	16	0	1	1	2		1967-68	1971-72
Lawton, Brian	Min., NYR, Hfd., Que., Bos., S.J.	9	483	112	154	266	401	11	1	1	2	12		1983-84	1992-93
Laxdal, Derek	Tor., NYI	6	67	12	7	19	90	1	0	2	2	2		1984-85	1990-91
Laycoe, Hal	NYR, Mtl., Bos.	11	531	25	77	102	292	40	2	5	7	39		1945-46	1955-56
Lazaro, Jeff	Bos., Ott.	3	102	14	23	37	114	28	3	3	6	32		1990-91	1992-93
Leach, Larry	Bos.	3	126	13	29	42	91	7	1	1	2	8		1958-59	1961-62
Leach, Reggie	Bos., Cal., Phi., Det.	13	934	381	285	666	387	94	47	22	69	22	1	1970-71	1982-83
Leavins, Jim	Det., NYR	2	41	2	12	14	30	....	....	....	....	....		1985-86	1986-87
Lebeau, Patrick	Mtl., Cgy., Fla.	3	7	2	2	4	4	....	....	....	....	....		1990-91	1993-94
LeBlanc, Fern	Det.	3	34	5	6	11	0	....	....	....	....	....		1976-77	1978-79
LeBlanc, J.P.	Chi., Det.	5	153	14	30	44	87	2	0	0	0	0		1968-69	1978-79
LeBrun, Al	NYR	2	6	0	2	2	4	....	....	....	....	....		1960-61	1965-66
Lecaine, Bill	Pit.	1	4	0	0	0	0	....	....	....	....	....		1968-69	1968-69
Leclair, Jackie	Mtl.	3	160	20	40	60	56	20	6	1	7	6	1	1954-55	1956-57
Leclerc, Rene	Det.	2	87	10	11	21	105	....	....	....	....	....		1968-69	1970-71
Lecuyer, Doug	Chi., Wpg., Pit.	4	126	11	31	42	178	7	4	0	4	15		1978-79	1982-83
Ledingham, Walt	Chi., NYI	3	15	0	2	2	4	....	....	....	....	....		1972-73	1976-77
• LeDuc, Albert	Mtl., Ott., NYR	10	383	57	35	92	614	28	5	6	11	32	2	1925-26	1934-35
LeDuc, Rich	Bos., Que.	4	130	28	38	66	69	5	0	0	0	9		1972-73	1980-81
• Lee, Bobby	Mtl.	1	1	0	0	0	0	....	....	....	....	....		1942-43	1942-43
Lee, Edward	Que.	1	2	0	0	0	5	....	....	....	....	....		1984-85	1984-85
Lee, Peter	Pit.	6	431	114	131	245	257	19	0	8	8	4		1977-78	1982-83
Leeman, Gary	Tor., Cgy., Mtl., Van.	13	665	199	266	465	531	36	8	16	24	36	1	1982-83	1994-95
Lefley, Bryan	N.Y.I., K.C., Col.	5	228	7	29	36	101	2	0	0	0	0		1972-73	1977-78
Lefley, Chuck	Mtl., St.L.	9	407	128	164	292	137	29	5	8	13	10	2	1970-71	1980-81
• Leger, Roger	NYR, Mtl.	5	187	18	53	71	71	20	0	7	7	14		1943-44	1949-50
Legge, Barry	Que., Wpg.	3	107	1	11	12	144	....	....	....	....	....		1979-80	1981-82
Legge, Randy	NYR	1	12	0	2	2	2	....	....	....	....	....		1972-73	1972-73
Lehmann, Tommy	Bos., Edm.	3	36	5	5	10	16	....	....	....	....	....		1987-88	1989-90
Lehto, Petteri	Pit.	1	6	0	0	0	4	....	....	....	....	....		1984-85	1984-85
Lehtonen, Antero	Wsh.	1	65	9	12	21	14	....	....	....	....	....		1979-80	1979-80
Lehvonen, Henri	K.C.	1	4	0	0	0	0	....	....	....	....	....		1974-75	1974-75
Leier, Edward	Chi.	2	16	2	1	3	2	....	....	....	....	....		1949-50	1950-51
Leinonen, Mikko	NYR, Wsh.	4	162	31	78	109	71	20	2	11	13	28		1981-82	1984-85
Leiter, Bobby	Bos., Pit., Atl.	10	447	98	126	224	144	8	3	0	3	2		1962-63	1975-76
Leiter, Ken	NYI, Min.	5	143	14	36	50	62	15	0	6	6	8		1984-85	1989-90
Lemaire, Jacques	Mtl.	12	853	366	469	835	217	145	61	78	139	63	8	1967-68	1978-79
Lemay, Moe	Van., Edm., Bos., Wpg.	8	317	72	94	166	442	28	6	3	9	55	1	1981-82	1988-89
Lemelin, Roger	K.C., Col.	4	36	1	2	3	27	....	....	....	....	....		1974-75	1977-78
Lemieux, Alain	St.L., Que., Pit.	6	119	28	44	72	38	19	4	6	10	0		1981-82	1986-87
Lemieux, Bob	Oak.	1	19	0	1	1	12	....	....	....	....	....		1967-68	1967-68
Lemieux, Jacques	L.A.	3	19	0	4	4	8	1	0	0	0	0		1967-68	1969-70
Lemieux, Jean	L.A., Atl., Wsh.	5	204	23	63	86	39	3	1	1	2	0		1969-70	1977-78
• Lemieux, Real	Det., L.A., NYR, Buf.	8	456	51	104	155	262	18	2	4	6	10		1966-67	1973-74
Lemieux, Richard	Van., K.C., Atl.	5	274	39	82	121	132	2	0	0	0	0		1971-72	1975-76
Lenardon, Tim	N.J., Van.	2	15	2	1	3	4	....	....	....	....	....		1986-87	1989-90
• Lepine, Hec	Mtl.	1	33	5	2	7	2	....	....	....	....	....		1925-26	1925-26
• Lepine, Pit	Mtl.	13	526	143	98	241	392	41	7	5	12	26	2	1925-26	1937-38
Leroux, Gaston	Mtl.	1	2	0	0	0	0	....	....	....	....	....		1935-36	1935-36
Lesieur, Art	Mtl., Chi.	5	100	4	2	6	50	14	0	0	0	4	1	1928-29	1935-36
Lessard, Rick	Cgy., S.J.	3	15	0	4	4	18	....	....	....	....	....		1988-89	1991-92
Lesuk, Bill	Bos., Phi., L.A., Wsh., Wpg.	8	388	44	63	107	368	9	1	0	1	12	1	1968-69	1979-80
Leswick, Jack	Chi.	1	47	1	7	8	16	....	....	....	....	....	1	1933-34	1933-34
Leswick, Peter	NYA, Bos.	2	3	1	0	1	0	....	....	....	....	....		1936-37	1944-45
Leswick, Tony	NYR, Det., Chi.	12	740	165	159	324	900	59	13	10	23	91	3	1945-46	1957-58
Levandoski, Joseph	NYR	1	8	1	1	2	0	....	....	....	....	....		1946-47	1946-47
Leveille, Norm	Bos.	2	75	17	25	42	49	....	....	....	....	....		1981-82	1982-83
Lever, Don	Van., Atl., Cgy., Col., N.J., Buf.	15	1020	313	367	680	593	30	7	10	17	26		1972-73	1986-87
Levie, Craig	Wpg., Min., Van., St.L.	6	183	22	53	75	177	16	2	3	5	32		1981-82	1986-87
• Levinsky, Alex	Tor., Chi., NYR	9	368	19	49	68	307	37	2	1	3	26	2	1930-31	1938-39
Levo, Tapio	Col., N.J.,	2	107	16	53	69	36	....	....	....	....	....		1981-82	1982-83
Lewicki, Danny	Tor., NYR, Chi.	9	461	105	135	240	177	28	0	4	4	8	1	1950-51	1958-59
Lewis, Bob	NYR	1	....	....	....	....	....	....	....	....	....	....		1975-76	1975-76
Lewis, Dave	NYI, L.A., N.J., Det.	15	1008	36	187	223	953	91	1	20	21	143		1973-74	1987-88
Lewis, Douglas	Mtl.	1	3	0	0	0	0	....	....	....	....	....		1946-47	1946-47
• Lewis, Herbie	Det.	11	483	148	161	309	248	38	13	10	23	6	2	1928-29	1938-39
Ley, Rick	Tor., Hfd.	6	310	12	72	84	528	14	0	2	2	20		1968-69	1980-81
Liba, Igor	NYR, L.A.	1	37	7	18	25	36	2	0	0	0	2		1988-89	1988-89
Libett, Nick	Det., K.C., Pit.	14	982	237	268	505	472	16	6	2	8	2		1967-68	1980-81
Licari, Anthony	Det.	1	9	0	1	1	0	....	....	....	....	....		1946-47	1946-47
Liddington, Bob	Tor.	1	11	0	1	1	2	....	....	....	....	....		1970-71	1970-71
Lindberg, Chris	Cgy., Que.	3	116	17	25	42	47	2	0	1	1	2		1991-92	1993-94
Lindgren, Lars	Van., Min.	6	394	25	113	138	325	40	5	6	11	20		1978-79	1983-84
Lindholm, Mikael	L.A.	1	18	2	2	4	2	....	....	....	....	....		1989-90	1989-90
Lindsay, Ted	Det., Chi.	17	1068	379	472	851	1808	133	47	49	96	194	4	1944-45	1964-65
Lindstrom, Willy	Wpg., Edm., Pit.	8	582	161	162	323	200	57	14	18	32	24	2	1979-80	1986-87
Linseman, Ken	Phi., Edm., Bos., Tor.	14	860	256	551	807	1727	113	43	77	120	325	1	1978-79	1991-92
Liscombe, Carl	Det.	9	373	137	140	277	117	57	22	20	42	20	1	1937-38	1945-46
Litzenberger, Ed	Mtl., Chi., Det., Tor.	12	618	178	238	416	283	40	5	13	18	34	4	1952-53	1963-64
• Locas, Jacques	Mtl.	2	59	7	8	15	66	....	....	....	....	....		1947-48	1948-49
Lochead, Bill	NYR, Det., Col.	6	330	69	62	131	180	7	3	0	3	6		1974-75	1979-80
• Locking, Norm	Chi.	2	48	2	6	8	26	....	....	....	....	....		1934-35	1935-36
Lofthouse, Mark	Wsh., Det.	6	181	42	38	80	73	....	....	....	....	....		1977-78	1982-83
Logan, Dave	Chi., Van.	6	218	5	29	34	470	12	0	0	0	10		1975-76	1980-81
Logan, Robert	Buf., L.A.	3	42	10	5	15	0	....	....	....	....	....		1986-87	1988-89

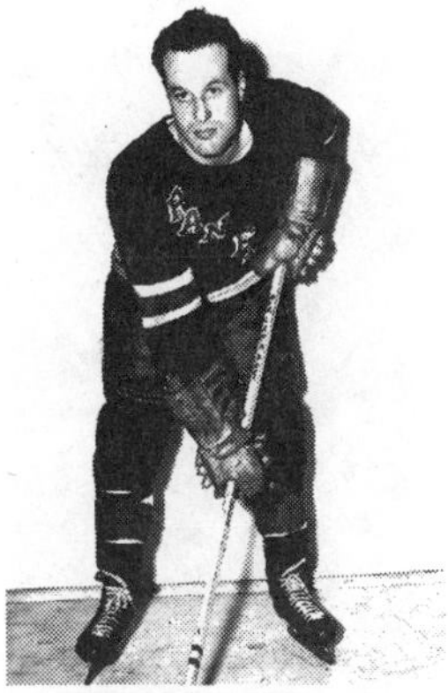
Edgar Laprade

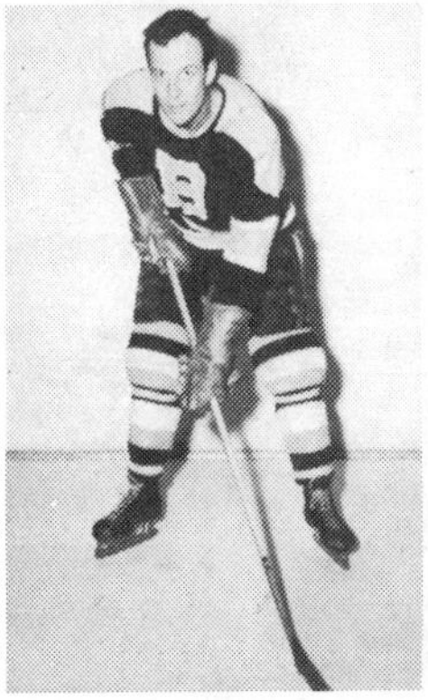
Hal Laycoe

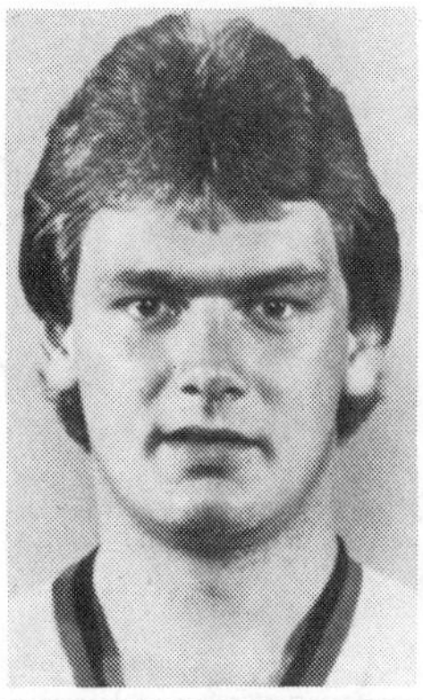
Steve Larmer

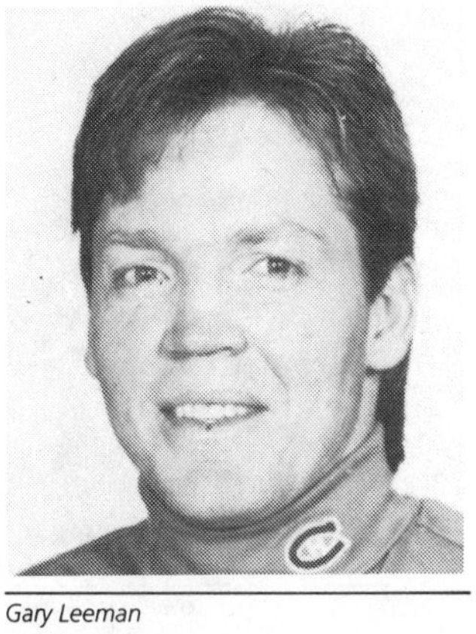
Gary Leeman

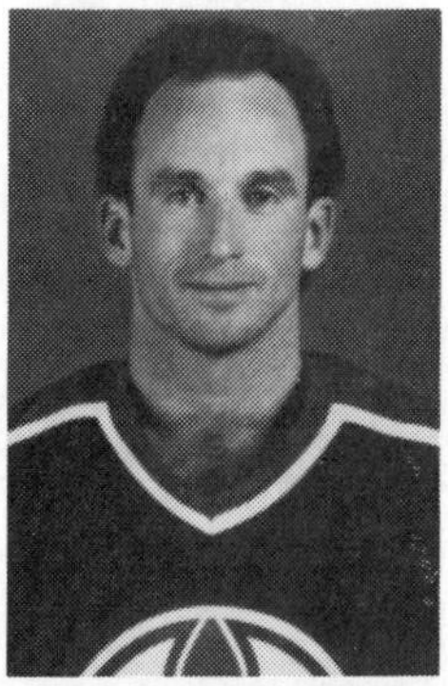

Ken Linseman

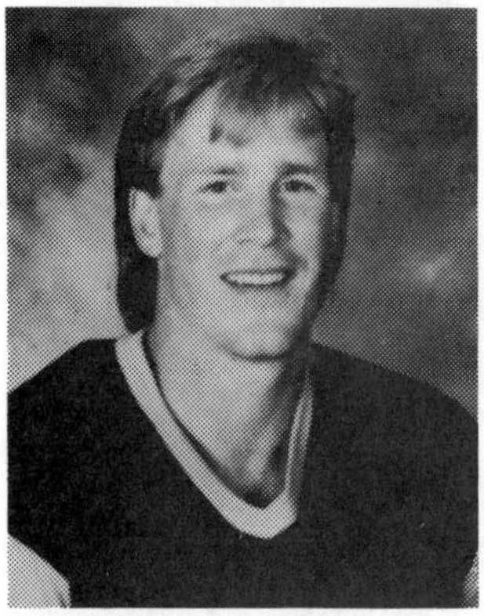

Troy Loney

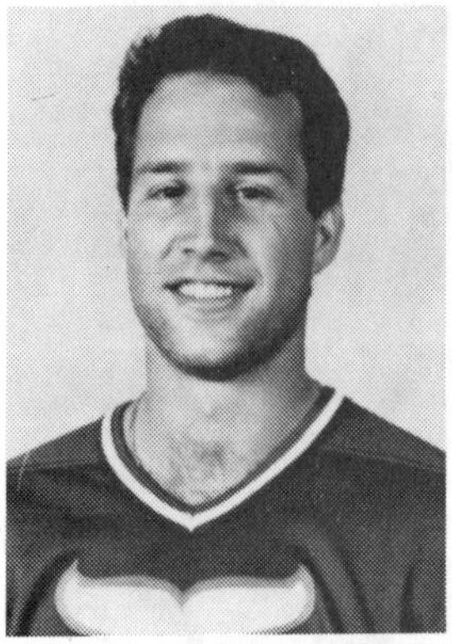

Paul MacDermid

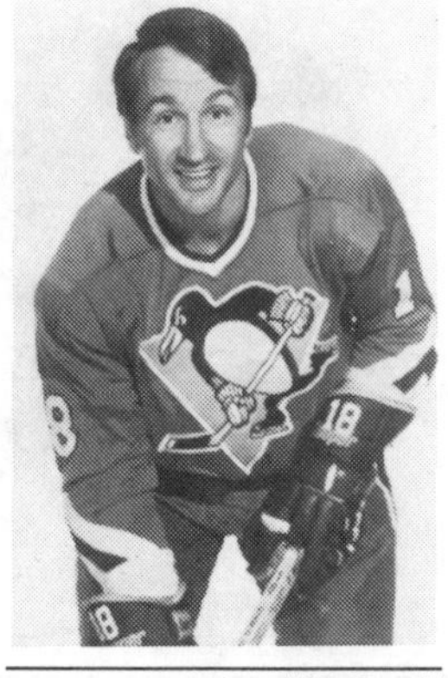

Lowell MacDonald

Name	NHL Teams	NHL Seasons	Regular Schedule GP	G	A	TP	PIM	Playoffs GP	G	A	TP	PIM	NHL Cup Wins	First NHL Season	Last NHL Season
Loiselle, Claude	Det., N.J., Que., Tor., NYI	13	616	92	117	209	1149	41	4	11	15	60		1981-82	1993-94
Lomakin, Andrei	Phi., Fla.	4	215	42	62	104	92	....	....	....	....	....		1991-92	1994-95
Loney, Troy	Pit., Ana., NYI, NYR	12	624	87	110	197	1091	67	8	14	22	97	2	1983-84	1994-95
Long, Barry	L.A., Det., Wpg.	5	280	11	68	79	250	5	0	1	1	18		1972-73	1981-82
• Long, Stanley	Mtl.	1	....	....	....	....	....	3	0	0	0	0		1951-52	1951-52
Lonsberry, Ross	Phi., Pit., Bos., L.A.	15	968	256	310	566	806	100	21	25	46	87	2	1966-67	1980-81
Loob, Hakan	Cgy.	6	450	193	236	429	189	73	26	28	54	16	1	1983-84	1988-89
Loob, Peter	Que.	1	8	1	2	3	0	....	....	....	....	....		1984-85	1984-85
Lorentz, Jim	NYR, Buf., Bos., St.L.	10	659	161	238	399	208	54	12	10	22	30	1	1968-69	1977-78
Lorimer, Bob	NYI, Col., N.J.	10	529	22	90	112	431	49	3	10	13	83	2	1976-77	1985-86
Lorrain, Rod	Mtl.	6	179	28	39	67	30	11	0	3	3	0		1935-36	1941-42
Loughlin, Clem	Det., Chi.	3	101	8	6	14	77	....	....	....	....	....		1926-27	1928-29
Loughlin, Wilf	Tor.	1	14	0	0	0	2	....	....	....	....	....		1923-24	1923-24
Lovsin, Ken	Wsh.	1	1	0	0	0	0	....	....	....	....	....		1990-91	1990-91
Lowdermilk, Dwayne	Wsh.	1	2	0	1	1	2	....	....	....	....	....		1980-81	1980-81
Lowe, Darren	Pit.	1	8	1	2	3	0	....	....	....	....	....		1983-84	1983-84
Lowe, Norm	NYR	1	4	1	1	2	0	....	....	....	....	....		1948-49	1949-50
• Lowe, Ross	Bos., Mtl.	3	77	6	8	14	82	2	0	0	0	0		1949-50	1951-52
• Lowery, Fred	Mtl.M., Pit.	2	54	1	0	1	10	2	0	0	0	6		1924-25	1925-26
• Lowrey, Eddie	Ott., Ham.	3	24	2	0	2	3	....	....	....	....	....		1917-18	1920-21
• Lowrey, Gerry	Chi., Ott., Tor., Phi., Pit.	7	226	48	48	96	170	4	1	0	1	8		1927-28	1932-33
Lucas, Danny	Phi.	1	6	1	0	1	0	....	....	....	....	....		1978-79	1978-79
Lucas, Dave	Det.	1	1	0	0	0	0	....	....	....	....	....		1962-63	1962-63
Luce, Don	NYR, Det., Buf., L.A., Tor.	13	894	225	329	554	364	71	17	22	39	52		1969-70	1981-82
Ludvig, Jan	N.J., Buf.	7	314	54	87	141	418	....	....	....	....	....		1982-83	1988-89
Ludzik, Steve	Chi., Buf.	9	424	46	93	139	333	44	4	8	12	70		1981-82	1989-90
Lukowich, Bernie	Pit., St.L.	2	79	13	15	28	34	2	0	0	0	0		1973-74	1974-75
Lukowich, Morris	Wpg., Bos., L.A.	8	582	199	219	418	584	11	0	2	2	24		1979-80	1986-87
Luksa, Charlie	Hfd.	1	8	0	1	1	4	....	....	....	....	....		1979-80	1979-80
Lumley, Dave	Mtl., Edm., Hfd.	9	437	98	160	258	680	61	6	8	14	131	2	1978-79	1986-87
Lund, Pentti	NYR, Bos.	7	259	44	55	99	40	19	7	5	12	0		1946-47	1952-53
Lundberg, Brian	Pit.	1	....	....	....	....	....	....	....	....	....	....		1982-83	1982-83
Lunde, Len	Min., Van., Det., Chi.	8	321	39	83	122	75	20	3	2	5	2		1958-59	1970-71
Lundholm, Bengt	Wpg.	5	275	48	95	143	72	14	3	4	7	14		1981-82	1985-86
Lundrigan, Joe	Tor., Wsh.	2	52	2	8	10	22	....	....	....	....	....		1972-73	1974-75
Lundstrom, Tord	Det.	1	11	1	1	2	0	....	....	....	....	....		1973-74	1973-74
Lundy, Pat	Det. Chi.	5	150	37	32	69	31	16	2	2	4	2		1945-46	1950-51
Lupien, Gilles	Mtl., Pit., Hfd.	5	226	5	25	30	416	25	0	0	0	21	2	1977-78	1981-82
Lupul, Gary	Van.	7	293	70	75	145	243	25	4	7	11	11		1979-80	1985-86
Lyle, George	Det., Hfd.	4	99	24	38	62	51	....	....	....	....	....		1979-80	1982-83
Lynch, Jack	Pit., Det., Wsh.	7	382	24	106	130	336	....	....	....	....	....		1972-73	1978-79
Lynn, Vic	Det., Mtl., Tor., Bos., Chi.	10	326	49	76	125	274	47	7	10	17	46	3	1943-44	1953-54
Lyon, Steve	Pit.	1	3	0	0	0	2	....	....	....	....	....		1976-77	1976-77
Lyons, Ron	Bos., Phi.	1	36	2	4	6	29	5	0	0	0	0		1930-31	1930-31
Lysiak, Tom	Atl., Chi.	13	919	292	551	843	567	76	25	38	63	49		1973-74	1985-86

M

Name	NHL Teams	NHL Seasons	Regular Schedule GP	G	A	TP	PIM	Playoffs GP	G	A	TP	PIM	NHL Cup Wins	First NHL Season	Last NHL Season
MacAdam, Al	Phi., Cal., Cle., Min., Van.	12	864	240	351	591	509	64	20	24	44	21		1973-74	1984-85
MacDermid, Paul	Hfd., Wpg., Wsh., Que.	14	690	116	142	258	1303	43	5	11	16	116		1981-82	1994-95
MacDonald, Blair	Edm., Van.	4	219	91	100	191	65	11	0	6	6	2		1979-80	1982-83
MacDonald, Brett	Van.	1	1	0	0	0	0	....	....	....	....	....		1987-88	1987-88
MacDonald, Kevin	Ott.	1	1	0	0	0	2	....	....	....	....	....		1993-94	1993-94
• MacDonald, Kilby	NYR	4	151	36	34	70	47	15	1	2	3	4	1	1939-40	1944-45
MacDonald, Lowell	Det., L.A., Pit.	13	506	180	210	390	92	30	11	11	22	12		1961-62	1977-78
MacDonald, Parker	Tor., NYR, Det., Bos., Min.	14	676	144	179	323	253	75	14	14	28	20		1952-53	1968-69
MacDougall, Kim	Min.	1	1	0	0	0	0	....	....	....	....	....		1974-75	1974-75
MacEachern, Shane	St.L.	1	1	0	0	0	0	....	....	....	....	....		1987-88	1987-88
Macey, Hubert	NYR, Mtl.	3	30	6	9	15	0	8	0	0	0	0		1941-42	1946-47
MacGregor, Bruce	Det., NYR	14	893	213	257	470	217	107	19	28	47	44		1960-61	1973-74
MacGregor, Randy	Hfd.	1	2	1	1	2	2	....	....	....	....	....		1981-82	1981-82
MacGuigan, Garth	NYI	2	5	0	1	1	2	....	....	....	....	....		1979-80	1979-80
MacIntosh, Ian	NYR	1	4	0	0	0	4	....	....	....	....	....		1952-53	1952-53
MacIver, Don	Wpg.	1	6	0	0	0	2	....	....	....	....	....		1979-80	1979-80
MacKasey, Blair	Tor.	1	1	0	0	0	2	....	....	....	....	....		1976-77	1976-77
MacKay, Calum	Det., Mtl.	8	237	50	55	105	214	38	5	13	18	20	1	1946-47	1954-55
Mackay, Dave	Chi.	1	29	3	0	3	26	5	0	1	1	2		1940-41	1940-41
• MacKay, Mickey	Chi., Pit., Bos.	4	147	44	19	63	79	11	0	0	0	6	1	1926-27	1929-30
MacKay, Murdo	Mtl.	4	19	0	3	3	0	15	1	2	3	0		1945-46	1947-48
Mackell, Fleming	Tor., Bos.	13	665	149	220	369	562	80	22	41	63	75	2	1947-48	1959-60
MacKenzie, Barry	Min.	1	6	0	1	1	6	....	....	....	....	....		1968-69	1968-69
• MacKenzie, Bill	Chi., Mtl.M., Mtl., NYR	7	264	15	14	29	145	21	1	1	2	11	1	1932-33	1939-40
Mackey, David	Chi., Min., St. L.	6	126	8	12	20	305	3	0	0	0	2		1987-88	1993-94
MacKey, Reggie	NYR	1	34	0	0	0	16	1	0	0	0	0		1926-27	1926-27
Mackie, Howie	Det.	2	20	1	0	1	4	8	0	0	0	0	1	1936-37	1937-38
MacKinnon, Paul	Wsh.	5	147	5	23	28	91	....	....	....	....	....		1979-80	1983-84
MacLean, Paul	St.L., Wpg., Det.	11	719	324	349	673	968	53	21	14	35	110		1980-81	1990-91
MacLeish, Rick	Phi., Hfd., Pit., Det.	14	846	349	410	759	434	114	54	53	107	38	2	1970-71	1983-84
MacLellan, Brian	L.A., NYR, Min., Cgy., Det.	10	606	172	241	413	551	47	5	9	14	42		1982-83	1991-92
MacMillan, Billy	Tor., Atl., NYI	7	446	74	77	151	184	53	6	6	12	40		1970-71	1976-77
MacMillan, Bob	NYR, St.L., Atl., Cgy., Col., N.J., Chi.	11	753	228	349	577	260	31	8	11	19	16		1974-75	1984-85
MacMillan, John	Tor., Det.	5	104	5	10	15	32	12	0	1	1	2	2	1960-61	1964-65
MacNeil, Al	Tor., Mtl., Chi., NYR, Pit.	11	524	17	75	92	617	37	0	4	4	67		1955-56	1967-68
MacNeil, Bernie	St.L.	1	4	0	0	0	0	....	....	....	....	....		1973-74	1973-74
• MacPherson, Bud	Mtl.	7	259	5	33	38	233	29	0	3	3	21	1	1948-49	1956-57
• MacSweyn, Ralph	Phi.	5	47	0	5	5	10	8	0	0	0	6		1967-68	1971-72
Madigan, Connie	St.L.	1	20	0	3	3	25	5	0	0	0	4		1972-73	1972-73
Madill, Jeff	N.J.	1	14	4	0	4	46	7	0	2	2	8		1990-91	1990-91
Magee, Dean	Min.	1	7	0	0	0	4	....	....	....	....	....		1977-78	1977-78
Maggs, Daryl	Chi., Cal., Tor.	3	135	14	19	33	54	4	0	0	0	0		1971-72	1979-80
Magnan, Marc	Tor.	1	4	0	1	1	5	....	....	....	....	....		1982-83	1982-83
Magnuson, Keith	Chi.	11	589	14	125	139	1442	68	3	9	12	164		1969-70	1979-80
Maguire, Kevin	Tor., Buf., Phi.	6	260	29	30	59	782	11	0	0	0	86		1986-87	1991-92
Mahaffy, John	Mtl., NYR	3	37	11	25	36	4	1	0	1	1	0		1942-43	1944-45
Mahovlich, Frank	Tor., Det., Mtl.	18	1181	533	570	1103	1056	137	51	67	118	163	6	1956-57	1973-74
Mahovlich, Pete	Det., Mtl., Pit.	16	884	288	485	773	916	88	30	42	72	134	4	1965-66	1980-81
Mailhot, Jacques	Que.	1	5	0	0	0	33	....	....	....	....	....		1988-89	1988-89
Mailley, Frank	Mtl.	1	1	0	0	0	0	....	....	....	....	....		1942-43	1942-43
Mair, Jim	Phi., NYI, Van.	5	76	4	15	19	49	3	1	2	3	4		1970-71	1974-75
• Majeau, Fern	Mtl.	2	56	22	24	46	43	1	0	0	0	0	1	1943-44	1944-45
Major, Bruce	Que.	1	4	0	0	0	0	....	....	....	....	....		1990-91	1990-91
Makarov, Sergei	Cgy., S.J.	6	420	134	250	384	317	34	12	11	23	8		1989-90	1994-95
Makela, Mikko	NYI, L.A., Buf., Bos.	7	423	118	147	265	139	18	3	8	11	14		1985-86	1994-95
Maki, Chico	Chi.	15	841	143	292	435	345	113	17	36	53	43	1	1960-61	1975-76
• Maki, Wayne	Chi., St.L., Van.	6	246	57	79	136	184	2	1	0	1	2		1967-68	1972-73
Makkonen, Karl	Edm.	1	9	2	2	4	0	....	....	....	....	....		1979-80	1979-80
Maley, David	Mtl., N.J., Edm., S.J., NYI	9	466	43	81	124	1043	46	5	5	10	111	1	1985-86	1993-94
Malinowski, Merlin	Col., N.J., Hfd.	5	282	54	111	165	121	....	....	....	....	....		1978-79	1982-83
Malone, Cliff	Mtl.	1	3	0	0	0	0	....	....	....	....	....		1951-52	1951-52
Malone, Greg	Pit., Hfd., Que.	11	704	191	310	501	661	20	3	5	8	32		1976-77	1986-87
• Malone, Joe	Mtl., Que., Ham.	7	125	146	21	167	35	9	5	0	5	0		1917-18	1923-24
Maloney, Dan	Chi., L.A., Det., Tor.	11	737	192	259	451	1489	40	4	7	11	35		1970-71	1981-82
Maloney, Dave	NYR, Buf.	11	657	71	246	317	1154	49	7	17	24	91		1974-75	1984-85
Maloney, Don	NYR, Hfd., NYI	13	765	214	350	564	815	94	22	35	57	101		1978-79	1990-91
Maloney, Phil	Bos., Tor., Chi.	5	158	28	43	71	16	6	0	0	0	0		1949-50	1959-60
Maluta, Ray	Bos.	2	25	2	3	5	6	2	0	0	0	0		1975-76	1976-77
Manastersky, Tom	Mtl.	1	6	0	0	0	11	....	....	....	....	....		1950-51	1950-51
Mancuso, Gus	Mtl., NYR	4	42	7	9	16	17	....	....	....	....	....		1937-38	1942-43
Mandich, Dan	Min.	4	111	5	11	16	303	7	0	0	0	2		1982-83	1985-86
Manery, Kris	Van., Wpg., Clev., Min.	4	250	63	64	127	91	....	....	....	....	....		1977-78	1980-81
Manery, Randy	L.A., Det., Atl.	10	582	50	206	256	415	13	0	2	2	12		1970-71	1979-80
Mann, Jack	NYR	2	9	3	4	7	0	....	....	....	....	....		1943-44	1944-45
Mann, Jimmy	Wpg., Que., Pit.	8	293	10	20	30	895	22	0	0	0	89		1979-80	1987-88
Mann, Ken	Det.	1	1	0	0	0	0	....	....	....	....	....		1975-76	1975-76

Name	NHL Teams	NHL Seasons	Regular Schedule GP	G	A	TP	PIM	Playoffs GP	G	A	TP	PIM	NHL Cup Wins	First NHL Season	Last NHL Season
Mann, Norm	Tor.	2	31	0	3	3	4	1	0	0	0	0		1938-39	1940-41
Manners, Rennison	Pit., Phi.	2	37	3	2	5	14	....	....	....	....	....		1929-30	1930-31
Manno, Bob	Van., Tor., Det.	8	371	41	131	172	274	17	2	4	6	12		1976-77	1984-85
Manson, Ray	Bos., NYR	2	2	0	1	1	0	....	....	....	....	....		1947-48	1948-49
● Mantha, Georges	Mtl.	13	488	89	102	191	148	36	6	2	8	24	2	1928-29	1940-41
Mantha, Moe	Wpg., Pit., Edm., Min., Phi.	12	656	81	289	370	501	17	5	10	15	18		1980-81	1991-92
● Mantha, Sylvio	Mtl., Bos.	14	542	63	72	135	667	46	5	4	9	66	3	1923-24	1936-37
Maracle, Buddy	NYR	1	11	1	3	4	4	4	0	0	0	0		1930-31	1930-31
Marcetta, Milan	Tor., Min.	3	54	7	15	22	10	17	7	7	14	4	1	1966-67	1968-69
March, Mush	Chi.	17	759	153	230	383	540	45	12	15	27	41	2	1928-29	1944-45
Marchinko, Brian	Tor., NYI	4	47	2	6	8	0	....	....	....	....	....		1970-71	1973-74
Marcinyshyn, David	N.J., Que., NYR	3	16	0	1	1	49	....	....	....	....	....		1990-91	1992-93
Marcon, Lou	Det.	3	60	0	4	4	42	....	....	....	....	....		1958-59	1962-63
Marcotte, Don	Bos.	15	868	230	254	484	317	132	34	27	61	81	2	1965-66	1981-82
Marini, Hector	NYI, N.J.	5	154	27	46	73	246	10	3	6	9	14	2	1978-79	1983-84
Mario, Frank	Bos.	2	53	9	19	28	24	....	....	....	....	....		1941-42	1944-45
● Mariucci, John	Chi.	5	223	11	34	45	308	12	0	3	3	26		1940-41	1947-48
Markell, John	Wpg., St. L., Min.	4	55	11	10	21	36	....	....	....	....	....		1979-80	1984-85
Marker, Gus	Det., Mtl.M., Tor., Bro.	10	322	64	69	133	133	46	5	7	12	36	1	1932-33	1941-42
Markham, Ray	NYR	1	14	1	1	2	21	7	1	0	1	24		1979-80	1979-80
Markle, Jack	Tor.	1	8	0	1	1	0	....	....	....	....	....		1935-36	1935-36
● Marks, Jack	Mtl.W, Tor., Que.	2	7	0	0	0	4	....	....	....	....	....		1917-18	1919-20
Marks, John	Chi.	10	657	112	163	275	330	57	5	9	14	60		1972-73	1981-82
Markwart, Nevin	Bos., Cgy.	8	309	41	68	109	794	19	1	0	1	33		1983-84	1991-92
Marois, Mario	NYR, Van., Que., Wpg., St.L.	15	955	76	357	433	1746	100	4	34	38	182		1977-78	1991-92
Marotte, Gilles	Bos., Chi., L.A., NYR, St.L.	12	808	56	265	321	872	29	3	3	6	26		1965-66	1976-77
Marquess, Mark	Bos.	1	27	5	4	9	6	4	0	0	0	0		1946-47	1946-47
Marsh, Brad	Atl., Cgy., Phi., Tor., Det., Ott.	15	1086	23	175	198	1241	97	6	18	24	124		1978-79	1992-93
Marsh, Gary	Det., Tor.	2	7	1	3	4	4	....	....	....	....	....		1967-68	1968-69
Marsh, Peter	Wpg., Chi.	5	278	48	71	119	224	26	1	5	6	33		1979-80	1983-84
Marshall, Bert	Det., Oak., Cal., NYR, NYI	14	868	17	181	198	926	72	4	22	26	99		1965-66	1978-79
Marshall, Don	Mtl., NYR, Buf., Tor.	19	1176	265	324	589	127	94	8	15	23	14	5	1951-52	1971-72
Marshall, Paul	Pit., Tor., Hfd.	4	95	15	18	33	17	1	0	0	0	0		1979-80	1982-83
Marshall, Willie	Tor.	4	33	1	5	6	2	....	....	....	....	....		1952-53	1958-59
Marson, Mike	Wsh., L.A.	6	196	24	24	48	233	....	....	....	....	....		1974-75	1979-80
● Martin, Clare	Bos., Det., Chi., NYR	6	237	12	28	40	78	27	0	2	2	6	1	1941-42	1951-52
Martin, Frank	Bos., Chi.	6	282	11	46	57	122	10	0	2	2	2		1952-53	1957-58
Martin, Grant	Van., Wsh.	4	44	0	4	4	55	1	1	0	1	2		1983-84	1986-87
Martin, Jack	Tor.	1	1	0	0	0	0	....	....	....	....	....		1960-61	1960-61
Martin, Pit	Det., Bos., Chi., Van.	17	1101	324	485	809	609	100	27	31	58	56		1961-62	1978-79
Martin, Rick	Buf., L.A.	11	685	384	317	701	477	63	24	29	53	74		1971-72	1981-82
Martin, Ron	NYA	2	94	13	16	29	36	....	....	....	....	....		1932-33	1933-34
Martin, Terry	Buf., Que., Tor., Edm., Min.	10	479	104	101	235	202	21	4	2	6	26		1975-76	1984-85
Martin, Tom	Wpg., Hfd., Min.	6	92	12	11	23	249	4	0	0	0	6		1984-85	1989-90
Martin, Tom	Tor.	1	3	1	0	1	0	....	....	....	....	....		1967-68	1967-68
Martineau, Don	Atl., Min., Det.	4	90	6	10	16	63	....	....	....	....	....		1973-74	1976-77
Martinson, Steven	Det., Mtl., Min.	4	49	2	1	3	244	1	0	0	0	10		1987-88	1991-92
Maruk, Dennis	Cal., Clev., Min., Wsh.	14	888	356	522	878	761	34	14	22	36	26		1975-76	1988-89
Masnick, Paul	Mtl., Chi., Tor.	6	232	18	41	59	139	33	4	5	9	27	1	1950-51	1957-58
● Mason, Charley	NYR, NYA, Det., Chi.	4	95	7	18	25	44	4	0	1	1	0		1934-35	1938-39
Massecar, George	NYA	3	100	12	11	23	46	....	....	....	....	....		1929-30	1931-32
Masters, Jamie	St.L.	3	33	1	13	14	2	2	0	0	0	0		1975-76	1978-79
● Masterton, Bill	Min.	1	38	4	8	12	4	....	....	....	....	....		1967-68	1967-68
Mathers, Frank	Tor.	3	23	1	3	4	4	....	....	....	....	....		1948-49	1951-52
Mathiasen, Dwight	Pit.	3	33	1	7	8	18	....	....	....	....	....		1985-86	1987-88
Mathieson, Jim	Wsh.	1	2	0	0	0	4	....	....	....	....	....		1989-90	1989-90
● Matte, Joe	Tor., Ham., Bos., Mtl.	4	64	18	14	32	43	....	....	....	....	....		1919-20	1925-26
Matte, Joe	Chi.	2	24	0	3	3	8	....	....	....	....	....		1942-43	1942-43
Mattiussi, Dick	Pit., Oak., Cal.	4	200	8	31	39	124	8	0	1	1	6		1967-68	1970-71
Matz, Johnny	Mtl.	1	30	3	2	5	0	5	0	0	0	2		1924-25	1924-25
Maxner, Wayne	Bos.	2	62	8	9	17	48	....	....	....	....	....		1964-65	1965-66
Maxwell, Brad	Min., Que., Tor., Van., NYR	10	612	98	270	368	1270	79	12	49	61	178		1977-78	1986-87
Maxwell, Bryan	Min., St.L., Wpg., Pit.	8	331	18	77	95	745	15	1	1	2	86		1977-78	1984-85
Maxwell, Kevin	Min., Col., N.J.	3	66	6	15	21	61	16	3	4	7	24		1980-81	1983-84
Maxwell, Wally	Tor.	1	2	0	0	0	0	....	....	....	....	....		1952-53	1952-53
Mayer, Jim	NYR	1	4	0	0	0	0	....	....	....	....	....		1979-80	1979-80
Mayer, Pat	Pit.	1	1	0	0	0	4	....	....	....	....	....		1987-88	1987-88
Mayer, Shep	Tor.	1	2	1	2	3	4	....	....	....	....	....		1942-43	1942-43
● Mazur, Eddie	Mtl., Chi.	6	107	8	20	28	120	25	4	5	9	22	1	1950-51	1956-57
Mazur, Jay	Van.	4	47	11	7	18	20	6	0	1	1	8		1988-89	1991-92
McAdam, Gary	Buf., Pit., Det., Cal., Wsh., N.J., Tor.	11	534	96	132	228	243	30	6	5	11	16		1975-76	1985-86
McAdam, Sam	NYR	1	5	0	0	0	0	....	....	....	....	....		1930-31	1930-31
McAndrew, Hazen	Bro.	1	7	0	1	1	6	....	....	....	....	....		1941-42	1941-42
McAneeley, Ted	Cal.	3	158	8	35	43	141	....	....	....	....	....		1972-73	1974-75
McAtee, Jud	Det.	3	46	15	13	28	6	14	2	1	3	0		1942-43	1944-45
McAtee, Norm	Bos.	1	13	0	1	1	0	....	....	....	....	....		1946-47	1946-47
McAvoy, George	Mtl.	1	....	....	....	....	....	4	0	0	0	0		1954-55	1954-55
McBain, Andrew	Wpg., Pit., Van., Ott.	11	608	129	172	301	633	24	5	7	12	39		1983-84	1993-94
McBean, Wayne	L.A., NYI, Wpg.	6	211	10	39	49	168	2	1	1	2	0		1987-88	1993-94
McBride, Cliff	Mtl.M., Tor.	2	2	0	0	0	0	....	....	....	....	....		1928-29	1929-30
McBurney, Jim	Chi.	1	1	0	1	1	0	....	....	....	....	....		1952-53	1952-53
McCabe, Stan	Det., Mtl.M.	4	78	9	4	13	49	....	....	....	....	....		1929-30	1933-34
● McCaffrey, Bert	Tor., Pit., Mtl.	7	260	42	30	72	202	8	2	1	3	12	2	1924-25	1930-31
McCahill, John	Col.	1	1	0	0	0	0	....	....	....	....	....		1977-78	1977-78
McCaig, Douglas	Det., Chi.	7	263	8	21	29	255	7	0	1	1	10		1941-42	1950-51
● McCallum, Dunc	NYR, Pit.	5	187	14	35	49	230	10	1	2	3	12		1965-66	1970-71
McCalmon, Eddie	Chi., Phi.	2	39	5	0	5	14	....	....	....	....	....		1927-28	1930-31
McCann, Rick	Det.	6	43	1	4	5	6	....	....	....	....	....		1967-68	1974-75
McCarthy, Dan	NYR	1	5	4	0	4	4	....	....	....	....	....		1980-81	1980-81
McCarthy, Kevin	Phi., Van., Pit.	10	537	67	191	258	527	21	2	3	5	20		1977-78	1986-87
● McCarthy, Tom	Que., Ham.	2	34	19	3	22	10	....	....	....	....	....		1919-20	1920-21
McCarthy, Tom	Det., Bos.	4	60	8	9	17	8	....	....	....	....	....		1956-57	1960-61
McCarthy, Tom	Min., Bos.	9	460	178	221	399	330	68	12	26	38	67		1979-80	1987-88
McCartney, Walt	Mtl.	1	2	0	0	0	0	....	....	....	....	....		1932-33	1932-33
McCaskill, Ted	Min.	1	4	0	2	2	0	....	....	....	....	....		1967-68	1967-68
McClanahan, Rob	Buf., Hfd., NYR	5	224	38	63	101	126	34	4	12	16	31		1979-80	1983-84
McClelland, Kevin	Pit., Edm., Det., Tor., Wpg.	12	588	68	112	180	1672	98	11	18	29	281	4	1981-82	1993-94
McCord, Bob	Bos., Det., Min., St.L.	7	316	10	58	68	262	14	2	5	7	10		1963-64	1972-73
McCord, Dennis	Van.	1	3	0	0	0	6	....	....	....	....	....		1973-74	1973-74
McCormack, John	Tor., Mtl., Chi.	8	311	25	49	74	35	22	1	1	2	0	2	1947-48	1954-55
McCourt, Dale	Det., Buf., Tor.	7	532	194	284	478	124	21	9	7	16	6		1977-78	1983-84
McCreary, Bill	Tor.	1	12	1	0	1	4	....	....	....	....	....		1980-81	1980-81
McCreary, Bill E.	NYR, Det., Mtl., St.L.	8	309	53	62	115	108	48	6	16	22	14		1953-54	1970-71
McCreary, Keith	Mtl., Pit., Atl.	10	532	131	112	243	294	16	0	4	4	6		1961-62	1974-75
● McCreedy, Johnny	Tor.	2	64	17	12	29	25	21	4	3	7	16	2	1941-42	1944-45
McCrimmon, Jim	St.L.	1	2	0	0	0	0	....	....	....	....	....		1974-75	1974-75
McCulley, Bob	Mtl.	1	1	0	0	0	0	....	....	....	....	....		1934-35	1934-35
McCurry, Duke	Pit.	4	148	21	11	32	119	4	0	2	2	4		1925-26	1928-29
McCutcheon, Brian	Det.	3	37	3	1	4	7	....	....	....	....	....		1974-75	1976-77
McCutcheon, Darwin	Tor.	1	1	0	0	0	2	....	....	....	....	....		1981-82	1981-82
McDill, Jeff	Chi.	1	1	0	0	0	0	....	....	....	....	....		1976-77	1976-77
McDonagh, Bill	NYR	1	4	0	0	0	2	....	....	....	....	....		1949-50	1949-50
McDonald, Ab	Mtl., Chi., Bos., Det., Pit., St.L.	15	762	182	248	430	200	84	21	29	50	42	4	1957-58	1971-72
McDonald, Brian	Chi., Buf.	2	12	0	0	0	29	8	0	0	0	2		1967-68	1970-71
● McDonald, Bucko	Det., Tor., NYR	11	446	35	88	123	206	50	6	1	7	24	3	1934-35	1944-45
McDonald, Butch	Det., Chi.	2	66	8	20	28	2	5	0	2	2	10		1939-40	1944-45
McDonald, Gerry	Hfd.	2	8	0	0	0	4	....	....	....	....	....		1981-82	1981-82
● McDonald, Jack	Mtl.W, Mtl., Que., Tor.	5	73	27	11	38	22	12	2	0	2	5		1917-18	1921-22
McDonald, John	NYR	1	43	10	9	19	6	....	....	....	....	....		1943-44	1943-44
McDonald, Lanny	Tor., Col., Cgy.	16	1111	500	506	1006	899	117	44	40	84	114	1	1973-74	1988-89
McDonald, Robert	NYR	1	1	0	0	0	0	....	....	....	....	....		1943-44	1943-44
McDonald, Terry	K.C.	1	8	0	1	1	6	....	....	....	....	....		1975-76	1975-76
McDonnell, Joe	Van., Pit.	3	50	2	10	12	34	....	....	....	....	....		1981-82	1985-86
● McDonnell, Moylan	Ham.	1	20	1	1	2	0	....	....	....	....	....		1920-21	1920-21

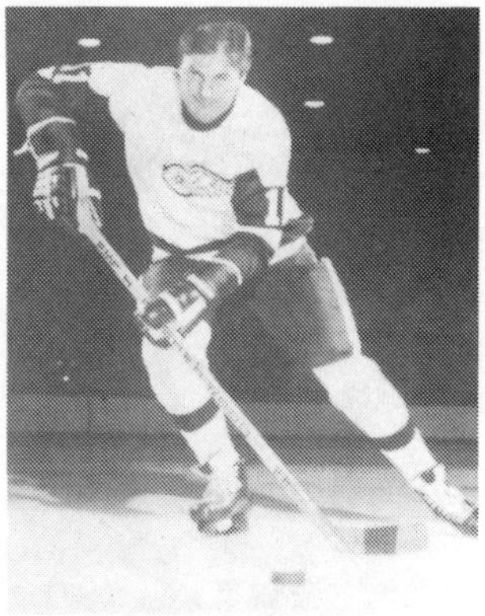

Peter Mahovlich

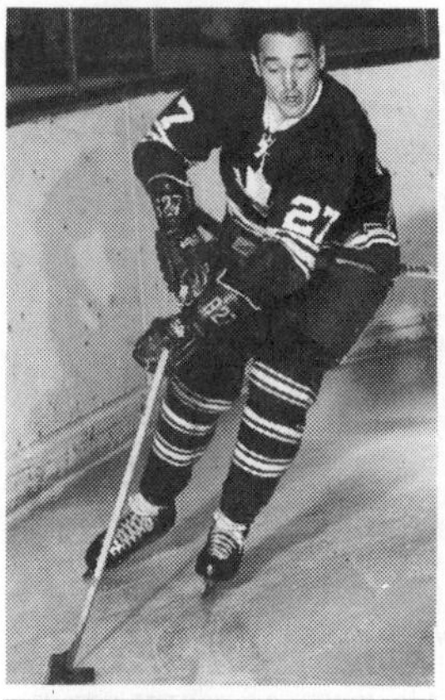

Frank Mahovlich

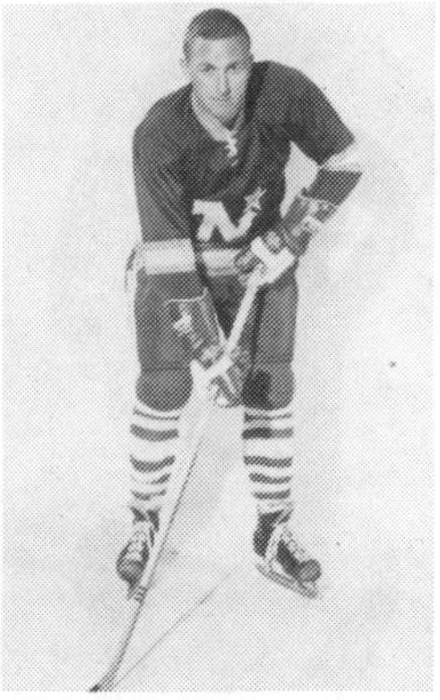

Bill Masterton

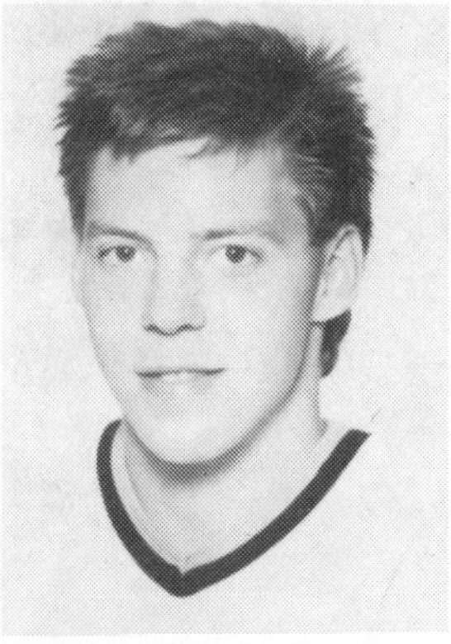

Wayne McBean

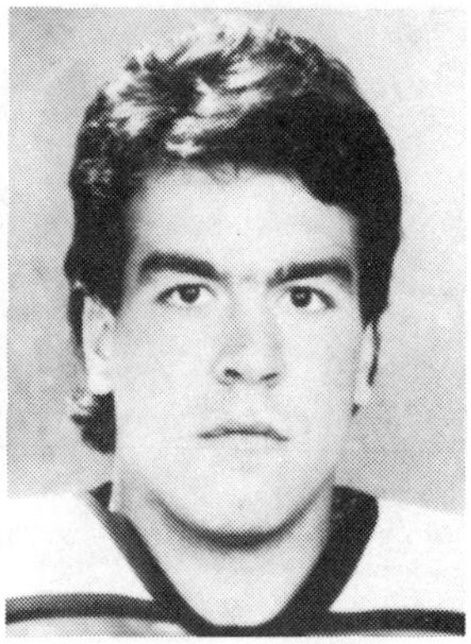
Ryan McGill

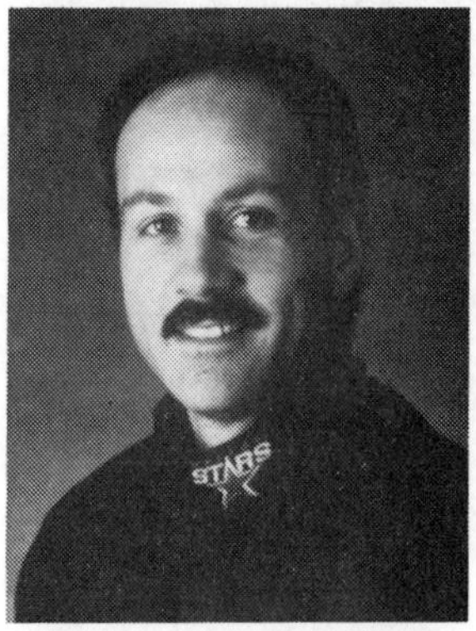
Mike McPhee

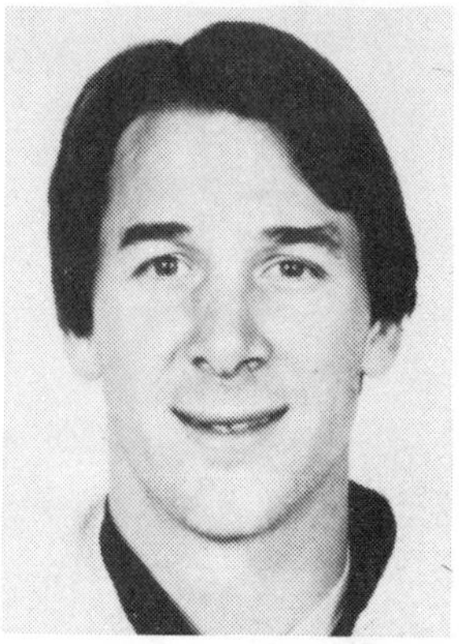
Mike Milbury

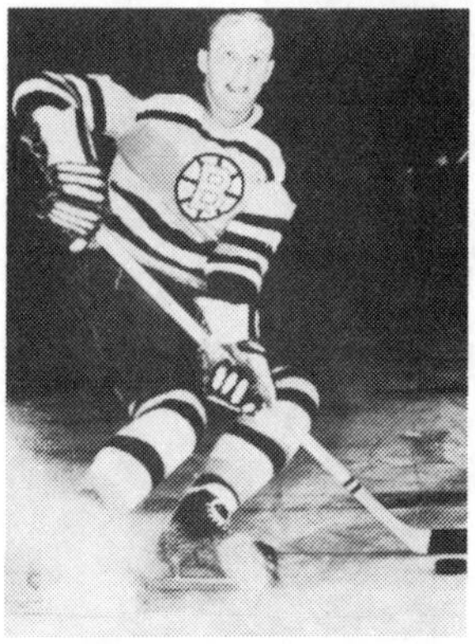
Doug Mohns

			Regular Schedule					Playoffs					NHL	First	Last
Name	NHL Teams	NHL Seasons	GP	G	A	TP	PIM	GP	G	A	TP	PIM	Cup Wins	NHL Season	NHL Season
McDonough, Al	L.A., Pit., Atl., Det.	5	237	73	88	161	73	8	0	1	1	2		1970-71	1977-78
McDougal, Mike	NYR, Hfd.	4	61	8	10	18	43	....	....	....	....	....		1978-79	1982-83
McDougall, Bill	Det., Edm., T.B.	3	28	5	5	10	12	1	0	0	0	0		1990-91	1993-94
McElmury, Jim	Min., K.C., Col.	5	180	14	47	61	49	....	....	....	....	....		1972-73	1977-78
McEwen, Mike	NYR, Col., NYI, L.A., Wsh., Det., Hfd.	12	716	108	296	404	460	78	12	36	48	48	3	1976-77	1987-88
McFadden, Jim	Det., Chi.	8	412	100	126	226	89	49	10	9	19	30	1	1947-48	1953-54
McFadyen, Don	Chi.	4	179	12	33	45	77	11	2	2	4	5	1	1932-33	1935-36
McFall, Dan	Wpg.	2	9	0	1	1	0	....	....	....	....	....		1984-85	1985-86
McFarland, George	Chi.	1	2	0	0	0	0	....	....	....	....	....		1926-27	1926-27
McGeough, Jim	Wsh., Pit.	4	57	7	10	17	32	....	....	....	....	....		1981-82	1986-87
McGibbon, John	Mtl.	1	1	0	0	0	2	....	....	....	....	....		1942-43	1942-43
McGill, Bob	Tor., Chi., S.J., Det., NYI, Hfd.	13	705	17	55	72	1766	49	0	0	0	88		1981-82	1993-94
McGill, Jack	Mtl.	3	134	27	10	37	71	3	2	0	2	0		1934-35	1936-37
McGill, Jack G.	Bos.	4	97	23	36	59	42	27	7	4	11	17		1941-42	1946-47
McGill, Ryan	Chi., Phi., Edm.	4	151	4	15	19	391	....	....	....	....	....		1991-92	1994-95
McGregor, Sandy	NYR	1	2	0	0	0	2	....	....	....	....	....		1963-64	1963-64
McGuire, Mickey	Pit.	2	36	3	0	3	6	....	....	....	....	....		1926-27	1927-28
McHugh, Mike	Min., S.J.	4	20	1	0	1	16	....	....	....	....	....		1988-89	1991-92
McIlhargey, Jack	Phi., Van., Hfd.	8	393	11	36	47	1102	27	0	3	3	68		1974-75	1981-82
• McInenly, Bert	Det., NYA, Ott., Bos.	6	166	19	15	34	144	4	0	0	0	2		1930-31	1935-36
McIntosh, Bruce	Min.	1	2	0	0	0	0	....	....	....	....	....		1972-73	1972-73
McIntosh, Paul	Buf.	2	48	0	2	2	66	2	0	0	0	7		1974-75	1975-76
McIntyre, Jack	Bos., Chi., Det.	11	499	109	102	211	173	29	7	6	13	4		1949-50	1959-60
McIntyre, Larry	Tor.	2	41	0	3	3	26	....	....	....	....	....		1969-70	1972-73
McKay, Doug	Det.	1	....	....	....	....	....	1	0	0	0	0	1	1949-50	1949-50
McKay, Ray	Chi., Buf., Cal.	6	140	2	16	18	102	....	....	....	....	....		1968-69	1973-74
McKay, Scott	Ana.	1	1	0	0	0	0	....	....	....	....	....		1993-94	1993-94
McKechnie, Walt	Min., Cal., Bos., Det., Wsh., Clev., Tor., Col.	16	955	214	392	606	469	15	7	5	12	7		1967-68	1982-83
McKee, Mike	Que.	1	48	3	12	15	41	....	....	....	....	....		1993-94	1993-94
McKegney, Ian	Chi.	1	3	0	0	0	2	....	....	....	....	....		1976-77	1976-77
McKegney, Tony	Buf., Que., Min., NYR, St. L., Det., Chi.	13	912	320	319	639	517	79	24	23	47	56		1978-79	1990-91
• McKell, Jack	Ott.	2	42	4	1	5	42	12	0	0	0	0	1	1919-20	1920-21
McKendry, Alex	NYI, Cgy.	4	46	3	6	9	21	6	2	2	4	0	1	1977-78	1980-81
McKenna, Sean	Buf., L.A., Tor.	9	414	82	80	162	181	15	1	2	3	2		1981-82	1989-90
McKenney, Don	Bos., NYR, Tor., Det., St.L.	13	798	237	345	582	230	58	18	29	47	10	1	1954-55	1967-68
McKenny, Jim	Tor., Min.	14	604	82	247	329	294	37	7	9	16	10		1965-66	1978-79
McKenzie, Brian	Pit.	1	6	1	1	2	4	....	....	....	....	....		1971-72	1971-72
McKenzie, John	Chi., Det., NYR, Bos.	12	691	206	268	474	917	69	15	32	47	133	2	1958-59	1971-72
McKinnon, Alex	Ham., NYA, Chi.	5	194	19	10	29	235	....	....	....	....	....		1924-25	1928-29
McKinnon, Bob	Chi.	1	2	0	0	0	0	....	....	....	....	....		1928-29	1928-29
• McKinnon, John	Mtl., Pit., Phi.	6	208	28	11	39	224	2	0	0	0	4		1925-26	1930-31
McLean, Don	Wsh.	1	9	0	0	0	6	....	....	....	....	....		1975-76	1975-76
• McLean, Fred	Que., Ham.	2	9	0	0	0	2	....	....	....	....	....		1919-20	1920-21
McLean, Jack	Tor.	3	67	14	24	38	76	13	2	2	4	8	1	1942-43	1944-45
McLean, Jeff	S.J.	1	6	1	0	1	0	....	....	....	....	....		1993-94	1993-94
• McLellan, John	Tor.	1	2	0	0	0	0	....	....	....	....	....		1951-52	1951-52
McLellan, Scott	Bos.	1	2	0	0	0	0	....	....	....	....	....		1982-83	1982-83
McLellan, Todd	NYI	1	5	1	1	2	0	....	....	....	....	....		1987-88	1987-88
• McLenahan, Roly	Det.	1	9	2	1	3	10	2	0	0	0	0		1945-46	1945-46
McLeod, Al	Det.	1	26	2	2	4	24	....	....	....	....	....		1973-74	1973-74
McLeod, Jackie	NYR	5	106	14	23	37	12	7	0	0	0	0		1949-50	1954-55
McMahon, Mike	NYR, Min., Chi., Det., Pit., Buf.	8	224	15	68	83	171	14	3	7	10	4		1963-64	1971-72
• McMahon, Mike C.	Mtl., Bos.	3	57	7	18	25	102	13	1	2	3	30	1	1942-43	1945-46
McManama, Bob	Pit.	3	99	11	25	36	28	8	0	1	1	6		1973-74	1975-76
McManus, Sammy	Mtl.M., Bos.	2	26	0	1	1	8	1	0	0	0	0	1	1934-35	1936-37
McMurchy, Tom	Chi., Edm.	4	55	8	4	12	65	....	....	....	....	....		1983-84	1987-88
McNab, Max	Det.	4	128	16	19	35	24	25	1	0	1	4	1	1947-48	1950-51
McNab, Peter	Buf., Bos., Van., N.J.	14	954	363	450	813	179	107	40	42	82	20		1973-74	1986-87
McNabney, Sid	Mtl.	1	....	....	....	....	....	5	0	1	1	2		1950-51	1950-51
• McNamara, Howard	Mtl.	1	11	1	0	1	2	....	....	....	....	....		1919-20	1919-20
• McNaughton, George	Que.B.	1	1	0	0	0	0	....	....	....	....	....		1919-20	1919-20
McNeill, Billy	Det.	6	257	21	46	67	142	4	1	1	2	4		1956-57	1963-64
McNeill, Michael	Chi., Que.	2	63	5	11	16	18	....	....	....	....	....		1990-91	1991-92
McNeill, Stu	Det.	3	10	1	1	2	2	....	....	....	....	....		1957-58	1959-60
McPhee, George	NYR, N.J.	7	115	24	25	49	257	29	5	3	8	69		1982-83	1988-89
McPhee, Mike	Mtl., Min., Dal.	11	744	200	199	399	661	134	28	27	55	193	1	1983-84	1993-94
McRae, Chris	Tor., Det.	3	21	1	0	1	122	....	....	....	....	....		1987-88	1989-90
McReavy, Pat	Bos., Det.	4	55	5	10	15	4	22	3	3	6	9	1	1938-39	1941-42
McReynolds, Brian	Wpg., NYR, L.A.	3	30	1	5	6	8	....	....	....	....	....		1989-90	1993-94
McSheffrey, Bryan	Van., Buf.	3	90	13	7	20	44	....	....	....	....	....		1972-73	1974-75
McTaggart, Jim	Wsh.	2	71	3	10	13	205	....	....	....	....	....		1980-81	1981-82
McTavish, Gordon	St.L., Wpg.	2	11	1	3	4	2	....	....	....	....	....		1978-79	1979-80
• McVeigh, Charley	Chi., NYA	9	397	84	88	172	138	4	0	0	0	2		1926-27	1934-35
McVicar, Jack	Mtl.M.	2	88	2	4	6	63	6	0	0	0	2		1930-31	1931-32
Meagher, Rick	Mtl., Hfd., N.J., St.L.	12	691	144	165	309	383	62	8	7	15	41		1979-80	1990-91
Meehan, Gerry	Tor., Phi., Buf., Van., Atl., Wsh.	10	670	180	243	423	111	10	0	1	1	0		1968-69	1978-79
Meeke, Brent	Cal., Clev.	5	75	9	22	31	8	....	....	....	....	....		1972-73	1976-77
Meeker, Howie	Tor.	8	346	83	102	185	329	42	6	9	15	50	4	1946-47	1953-54
Meeker, Mike	Pit.	1	4	0	0	0	5	....	....	....	....	....		1978-79	1978-79
• Meeking, Harry	Tor., Det., Bos.	3	63	18	3	21	57	14	4	2	6	24	1	1917-18	1926-27
Meger, Paul	Mtl.	6	212	39	52	91	118	35	3	8	11	16	1	1949-50	1954-55
Meighan, Ron	Min., Pit.	2	48	3	7	10	18	....	....	....	....	....		1981-82	1982-83
Meissner, Barrie	Min.	2	6	0	1	1	4	....	....	....	....	....		1967-68	1968-69
Meissner, Dick	Bos., NYR	5	171	11	15	26	37	....	....	....	....	....		1959-60	1964-65
Melametsa, Anssi	Wpg.	1	27	0	3	3	2	....	....	....	....	....		1985-86	1985-86
Melin, Roger	Min.	2	3	0	0	0	0	....	....	....	....	....		1980-81	1981-82
Mellor, Tom	Det.	2	26	2	4	6	25	....	....	....	....	....		1973-74	1974-75
Melnyk, Gerry	Det., Chi., St.L.	6	269	39	77	116	34	53	6	6	12	6		1955-56	1967-68
Melnyk, Larry	Bos., Edm., NYR, Van.	10	432	11	63	74	686	66	2	9	11	127	1	1980-81	1989-90
Melrose, Barry	Wpg., Tor., Det.	6	300	10	23	33	728	7	0	2	2	38		1979-80	1985-86
Menard, Hillary	Chi.	1	1	0	0	0	0	....	....	....	....	....		1953-54	1953-54
Menard, Howie	Det., L.A., Chi., Oak.	4	151	23	42	65	87	19	3	7	10	36		1963-64	1969-70
Mercredi, Vic	Atl.	1	2	0	0	0	0	....	....	....	....	....		1974-75	1974-75
Meredith, Greg	Cgy.	2	38	6	4	10	8	5	3	1	4	4		1980-81	1982-83
Merkosky, Glenn	Hfd., N.J., Det.	5	66	5	12	17	22	....	....	....	....	....		1981-82	1989-90
Meronek, Bill	Mtl.	2	19	5	8	13	0	1	0	0	0	0		1939-40	1942-43
Merrick, Wayne	St.L., Cal., Clev., NYI	12	774	191	265	456	303	102	19	30	49	30	4	1972-73	1983-84
• Merrill, Horace	Ott.	2	11	0	0	0	0	....	....	....	....	....	1	1917-18	1919-20
Messier, Mitch	Min.	4	20	0	2	2	11	....	....	....	....	....		1987-88	1990-91
Messier, Paul	Col.	1	9	0	0	0	4	....	....	....	....	....		1978-79	1978-79
Metcalfe, Scott	Edm., Buf.	3	19	1	2	3	18	....	....	....	....	....		1987-88	1989-90
Metz, Don	Tor.	9	172	20	35	55	42	42	7	8	15	12	5	1939-40	1948-49
• Metz, Nick	Tor.	12	518	131	119	250	149	76	19	20	39	31	4	1934-35	1947-48
Michaluk, Art	Chi.	1	5	0	0	0	0	....	....	....	....	....		1947-48	1947-48
Michaluk, John	Chi.	1	1	0	0	0	0	....	....	....	....	....		1950-51	1950-51
Michayluk, Dave	Phi., Pit.	3	14	2	6	8	8	7	1	1	2	0	1	1981-82	1991-92
Micheletii, Pat	Min.	1	12	2	0	2	8	....	....	....	....	....		1987-88	1987-88
Micheletti, Joe	St.L., Col.	3	158	11	60	71	114	11	1	11	12	10		1979-80	1981-82
• Mickey, Larry	Chi., NYR., Tor., Mtl., L.A., Phi., Buf.	11	292	39	53	92	160	9	1	0	1	10		1964-65	1974-75
Mickoski, Nick	NYR, Chi., Det., Bos.	13	703	158	185	343	319	18	1	6	7	6		1947-48	1959-60
Middendorf, Max	Que., Edm.	4	13	2	4	6	6	....	....	....	....	....		1986-87	1990-91
Middleton, Rick	NYR, Bos.	14	1005	448	540	988	157	114	45	55	100	19		1974-75	1987-88
Miehm, Kevin	St.L.	2	22	1	4	5	8	2	0	1	1	0		1992-93	1993-94
Migay, Rudy	Tor.	10	418	59	92	151	293	15	1	0	1	20		1949-50	1959-60
Mikita, Stan	Chi.	22	1394	541	926	1467	1270	155	59	91	150	169	1	1958-59	1979-80
Mikkelson, Bill	L.A., N.Y.I., Wsh.	4	147	4	18	22	105	....	....	....	....	....		1971-72	1976-77
Mikol, Jim	Tor., NYR	2	34	1	4	5	8	....	....	....	....	....		1962-63	1964-65
Milbury, Mike	Bos.	12	754	49	189	238	1552	86	4	24	28	219		1975-76	1986-87
• Milks, Hib	Pit., Phi., NYR, Ott.	8	317	87	41	128	179	9	0	0	0	2		1925-26	1932-33
Millar, Hugh	Det.	1	4	0	0	0	0	1	0	0	0	0		1946-47	1946-47
Millar, Mike	Hfd., Wsh., Bos., Tor.	5	78	18	18	36	12	....	....	....	....	....		1986-87	1990-91
Miller, Bill	Mtl.M., Mtl.	3	95	7	3	10	16	12	0	0	0	0	1	1934-35	1936-37
Miller, Bob	Bos., Col., L.A.	6	404	75	119	194	220	36	4	7	11	27		1977-78	1984-85

Name	NHL Teams	NHL Seasons	Regular Schedule GP	G	A	TP	PIM	Playoffs GP	G	A	TP	PIM	NHL Cup Wins	First NHL Season	Last NHL Season
Miller, Brad	Buf., Ott., Cgy.	6	82	1	5	6	321	....	....	....	....	....		1988-89	1993-94
• Miller, Earl	Chi., Tor.	5	109	19	14	33	124	10	1	0	1	6	1	1927-28	1931-32
Miller, Jack	Chi.	2	17	0	0	0	4	....	....	....	....	....		1949-50	1950-51
Miller, Jay	Bos., L.A.	7	446	40	44	84	1723	48	2	3	5	243		1985-86	1991-92
Miller, Paul	Col.	1	3	0	3	3	0	....	....	....	....	....		1981-82	1981-82
Miller, Perry	Det.	4	217	10	51	61	387	....	....	....	....	....		1977-78	1980-81
Miller, Tom	Det., NYI	4	118	16	25	41	34	....	....	....	....	....		1970-71	1974-75
Miller, Warren	NYR, Hfd.	4	262	40	50	90	137	6	1	0	1	0		1979-80	1982-83
Miner, John	Edm.	1	14	2	3	5	16	....	....	....	....	....		1987-88	1987-88
Minor, Gerry	Van.	5	140	11	21	32	173	12	1	3	4	25		1979-80	1983-84
Miszuk, John	Det., Chi., Phi., Min.	6	237	7	39	46	232	19	0	3	3	19		1963-64	1969-70
Mitchell, Bill	Det.	1	1	0	0	0	0	....	....	....	....	....		1963-64	1963-64
Mitchell, Herb	Bos.	2	53	6	0	6	38	....	....	....	....	....		1924-25	1925-26
Mitchell, Red	Chi.	3	83	4	5	9	67	....	....	....	....	....		1941-42	1944-45
Mitchell, Roy	Min.	1	3	0	0	0	0	....	....	....	....	....		1992-93	1992-93
Moe, Billy	NYR	5	261	11	42	53	163	1	0	0	0	0		1944-45	1948-49
Moffat, Lyle	Tor., Wpg.	3	97	12	16	28	51	....	....	....	....	....		1972-73	1979-80
Moffat, Ron	Det.	3	37	1	1	2	8	7	0	0	0	0		1932-33	1934-35
Moher, Mike	N.J.	1	9	0	1	1	28	....	....	....	....	....		1982-83	1982-83
Mohns, Doug	Bos., Chi., Min., Atl., Wsh.	22	1390	248	462	710	1250	94	14	36	50	122		1953-54	1974-75
Mohns, Lloyd	NYR	1	1	0	0	0	0	....	....	....	....	....		1943-44	1943-44
Mokosak, Carl	Cgy., L.A., Phi., Pit., Bos.	6	83	11	15	26	170	1	0	0	0	0		1981-82	1988-89
Mokosak, John	Det.	2	41	0	2	2	96	....	....	....	....	....		1988-89	1989-90
Molin, Lars	Van.	3	172	33	65	98	37	19	2	9	11	7		1981-82	1983-84
Moller, Mike	Buf., Edm.	7	134	15	28	43	41	3	0	1	1	0		1980-81	1986-87
Moller, Randy	Que., NYR, Buf., Fla.	14	815	45	180	225	1692	78	6	16	22	197		1981-82	1994-95
Molloy, Mitch	Buf.	1	2	0	0	0	10	....	....	....	....	....		1989-90	1989-90
Molyneaux, Larry	NYR	2	45	0	1	1	20	10	0	0	0	8		1937-38	1938-39
Monahan, Garry	Mtl., Det., L.A., Tor., Van.	12	748	116	169	285	484	22	3	1	4	13		1967-68	1978-79
Monahan, Hartland	Cal., NYR, Wsh., Pit., L.A., St.L.	7	334	61	80	141	163	6	0	0	0	4		1973-74	1980-81
• Mondou, Armand	Mtl.	11	386	47	71	118	99	32	3	5	8	12	2	1928-29	1939-40
Mondou, Pierre	Mtl.	9	548	194	262	456	179	69	17	28	45	26	3	1976-77	1984-85
Mongeau, Michel	St. L., T.B.	4	54	6	19	25	10	2	0	1	1	0		1989-90	1992-93
Mongrain, Bob	Buf., L.A.	6	81	13	14	27	14	11	1	2	3	2		1979-80	1985-86
Monteith, Hank	Det.	3	77	5	12	17	6	4	0	0	0	0		1968-69	1970-71
Moore, Dickie	Mtl., Tor., St.L.	14	719	261	347	608	652	135	46	64	110	122	6	1951-52	1967-68
Moran, Amby	Mtl., Chi.	2	35	1	1	2	24	....	....	....	....	....		1926-27	1927-28
• Morenz, Howie	Mtl., Chi., NYR	14	550	270	197	467	563	47	21	11	32	68	3	1923-24	1936-37
Moretto, Angelo	Clev.	1	5	1	2	3	2	....	....	....	....	....		1976-77	1976-77
Morin, Pete	Mtl.	1	31	10	12	22	7	1	0	0	0	0		1941-42	1941-42
Morris, Bernie	Bos.	1	6	2	0	2	0	....	....	....	....	....		1924-25	1924-25
Morris, Elwyn	Tor., NYR	4	135	13	29	42	58	18	4	2	6	16	1	1943-44	1948-49
Morris, Jon	N.J., S.J., Bos.	6	103	16	33	49	47	11	1	7	8	25		1988-89	1993-94
Morrison, Dave	L.A., Van.	4	39	3	3	6	4	....	....	....	....	....		1980-81	1984-85
Morrison, Don	Det., Chi.	3	112	18	28	46	12	3	0	1	1	0		1947-48	1950-51
Morrison, Doug	Bos.	4	23	7	3	10	15	....	....	....	....	....		1979-80	1984-85
Morrison, Gary	Phi.	3	43	1	15	16	70	5	0	1	1	2		1979-80	1981-82
Morrison, George	St.L.	2	115	17	21	38	13	3	0	0	0	0		1970-71	1971-72
Morrison, Jim	Bos., Tor., Det., NYR, Pit.	12	704	40	160	200	542	36	0	12	12	38		1951-52	1970-71
Morrison, John	NYA	1	18	0	0	0	0	....	....	....	....	....		1925-26	1925-26
Morrison, Kevin	Col.	1	41	4	11	15	23	....	....	....	....	....		1979-80	1979-80
Morrison, Lew	Phi., Atl., Wsh., Pit.	9	564	39	52	91	107	17	0	0	0	2		1969-70	1977-78
Morrison, Mark	NYR	2	10	1	1	2	0	....	....	....	....	....		1981-82	1983-84
Morrison, Roderick	Det.	1	34	8	7	15	4	3	0	0	0	0		1947-48	1947-48
Morrow, Ken	NYI	10	550	17	88	105	309	127	11	22	33	97	4	1979-80	1988-89
Morton, Dean	Det.	1	1	1	0	1	2	....	....	....	....	....		1989-90	1989-90
Mortson, Gus	Tor., Chi., Det.	13	797	46	152	198	1380	54	5	8	13	65	4	1946-47	1958-59
Mosdell, Kenny	Bro., Mtl., Chi.	16	693	141	168	309	475	80	16	13	29	48	4	1941-42	1958-59
• Mosienko, Bill	Chi.	14	710	258	282	540	121	22	10	4	14	15		1941-42	1954-55
Mott, Morris	Cal.	3	199	18	32	50	49	....	....	....	....	....		1972-73	1974-75
Motter, Alex	Bos., Det.	8	256	39	64	103	135	41	3	9	12	41	1	1934-35	1942-43
Moxey, Jim	Cal., Clev., L.A.	3	127	22	27	49	59	....	....	....	....	....		1974-75	1976-77
Mulhern, Richard	Atl., L.A., Tor., Wpg.	6	303	27	93	120	217	7	0	3	3	5		1975-76	1980-81
Mullen, Brian	Wpg., NYR, S.J., NYI	11	832	260	362	622	414	62	12	18	30	30		1982-83	1992-93
Muloin, Wayne	Det., Oak., Cal., Min.	3	147	3	21	24	93	11	0	0	0	2		1963-64	1970-71
Mulvenna, Glenn	Pit., Phi.	2	2	0	0	0	4	....	....	....	....	....		1991-92	1992-93
Mulvey, Grant	Chi., N.J.	10	586	149	135	284	816	42	10	5	15	70		1974-75	1983-84
Mulvey, Paul	Wsh., Pit., L.A.	4	225	30	51	81	613	....	....	....	....	....		1978-79	1981-82
• Mummery, Harry	Tor., Que., Mtl., Ham.	6	106	33	13	46	185	7	1	4	5	0	1	1917-18	1922-23
• Munro, Dunc	Mtl.	8	239	28	18	46	170	25	3	2	5	24	1	1924-25	1931-32
Munro, Gerry	Mtl., Tor.	2	33	1	0	1	22	....	....	....	....	....		1924-25	1925-26
Murdoch, Bob J.	Mtl., L.A., Atl., Cgy.	12	757	60	218	278	764	69	4	18	22	92	2	1970-71	1981-82
Murdoch, Bob L.	Cal., Clev., St.L.	4	260	72	85	157	127	....	....	....	....	....		1975-76	1978-79
Murdoch, Don	NYR, Edm., Det.	6	320	121	117	238	155	24	10	8	18	16		1976-77	1981-82
Murdoch, Murray	NYR	11	507	84	108	192	197	55	9	12	21	28	2	1926-27	1936-37
Murphy, Brian	Det.	1	1	0	0	0	0	....	....	....	....	....		1974-75	1974-75
Murphy, Mike	St.L. NYR, L.A.	12	831	238	318	556	514	66	13	23	36	54		1971-72	1982-83
Murphy, Rob	Van., Ott., L.A.	7	125	9	12	21	152	4	0	0	0	2		1987-88	1993-94
Murphy, Ron	NYR, Chi., Det., Bos.	18	889	205	274	479	460	53	7	8	15	26	1	1952-53	1969-70
Murray, Allan	NYA	7	271	5	9	14	163	....	....	....	....	....		1933-34	1939-40
Murray, Bob F.	Chi.	15	1008	132	382	514	873	112	19	37	56	106		1975-76	1989-90
Murray, Bob J.	Atl., Van.	4	194	6	16	22	98	10	1	1	2	15		1973-74	1976-77
Murray, Jim	L.A.	1	30	0	2	2	14	....	....	....	....	....		1967-68	1967-68
Murray, Ken	Tor., N.Y.I., Det., K.C.	5	106	1	10	11	135	....	....	....	....	....		1969-70	1975-76
Murray, Leo	Mtl.	1	6	0	0	0	2	....	....	....	....	....		1932-33	1932-33
Murray, Mike	Phi.	1	1	0	0	0	0	....	....	....	....	....		1987-88	1987-88
Murray, Pat	Phi.	2	25	3	1	4	15	....	....	....	....	....		1990-91	1991-92
Murray, Randy	Tor.	1	3	0	0	0	2	....	....	....	....	....		1969-70	1969-70
Murray, Terry	Cal., Phi., Det., Wsh.	8	302	4	76	80	199	18	2	2	4	10		1972-73	1981-82
Myers, Hap	Buf.	1	13	0	0	0	6	....	....	....	....	....		1970-71	1970-71
Myles, Vic	NYR	1	45	6	9	15	57	....	....	....	....	....		1942-43	1942-43

N

Name	NHL Teams	NHL Seasons	Regular Schedule GP	G	A	TP	PIM	Playoffs GP	G	A	TP	PIM	NHL Cup Wins	First NHL Season	Last NHL Season
Nachbaur, Don	Hfd., Edm., Phi.	8	223	23	46	69	465	11	1	1	2	24		1980-81	1989-90
Nahrgang, Jim	Det.	3	57	5	12	17	34	....	....	....	....	....		1974-75	1976-77
Nanne, Lou	Min.	11	635	68	157	225	356	32	4	10	14	8		1967-68	1977-78
Nantais, Richard	Min.	3	63	5	4	9	79	....	....	....	....	....		1974-75	1976-77
Napier, Mark	Mtl., Min., Edm., Buf.	11	767	235	306	541	157	82	18	24	42	11	2	1978-79	1988-89
Naslund, Mats	Mtl., Bos.	9	651	251	383	634	111	102	35	57	92	33	1	1982-83	1994-95
Nattrass, Ralph	Chi.	4	223	18	38	56	308	....	....	....	....	....		1946-47	1949-50
Nattress, Ric	Mtl., St.L., Cgy., Tor., Phi.	11	536	29	135	164	377	67	5	10	15	60	1	1982-83	1992-93
Natyshak, Mike	Que.	1	4	0	0	0	0	....	....	....	....	....		1987-88	1987-88
Neaton, Pat	Pit.	1	9	1	1	2	12	....	....	....	....	....		1993-94	1993-94
Nechaev, Victor	L.A.	1	3	1	0	1	0	....	....	....	....	....		1982-83	1982-83
Nedomansky, Vaclav	Det., NYR, St.L.	6	421	123	156	279	88	7	3	5	8	0		1977-78	1982-83
Neely, Bob	Tor., Col.	5	283	39	59	98	266	26	5	7	12	15		1973-74	1977-78
Neilson, Jim	NYR, Cal., Clev.	16	1023	69	299	368	904	65	1	17	18	61		1962-63	1977-78
Nelson, Gordie	Tor.	1	3	0	0	0	11	....	....	....	....	....		1969-70	1969-70
Nemeth, Steve	NYR	1	12	2	0	2	2	....	....	....	....	....		1987-88	1987-88
Nesterenko, Eric	Tor., Chi.	21	1219	250	324	574	1273	124	13	24	37	127	1	1951-52	1971-72
Nethery, Lance	NYR, Edm.	2	41	11	14	25	14	14	5	3	8	9		1980-81	1981-82
Neufeld, Ray	Hfd., Win., Bos.	11	595	157	200	357	816	28	8	6	14	55		1979-80	1989-90
• Neville, Mike	Tor., NYA	4	65	6	3	9	15	2	0	0	0	0	1	1917-18	1930-31
Nevin, Bob	Tor., NYR, Min., L.A.	18	1128	307	419	726	211	84	16	18	34	24	2	1957-58	1975-76
Newberry, John	Mtl., Hfd.	4	22	0	4	4	6	2	0	0	0	0		1982-83	1985-86
Newell, Rick	Det.	2	6	0	0	0	0	....	....	....	....	....		1972-73	1973-74
Newman, Dan	NYR, Mtl., Edm.	4	126	17	24	41	63	3	0	0	0	4		1976-77	1979-80
Newman, John	Det.	1	8	1	1	2	0	....	....	....	....	....		1930-31	1930-31
Nicholson, Al	Bos.	2	19	0	1	1	4	....	....	....	....	....		1955-56	1956-57
Nicholson, Edward	Det.	1	1	0	0	0	0	....	....	....	....	....		1947-48	1947-48
Nicholson, Graeme	Bos., Col., NYR	3	52	2	7	9	60	....	....	....	....	....		1978-79	1982-83
Nicholson, John	Chi.	1	2	1	0	1	0	....	....	....	....	....		1937-38	1937-38
Nicholson, Neil	Oak., N.Y.I.	4	39	3	1	4	23	2	0	0	0	0		1969-70	1977-78

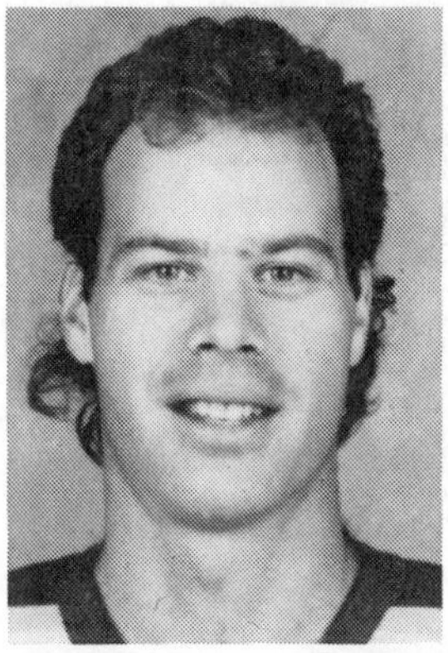

Randy Moller

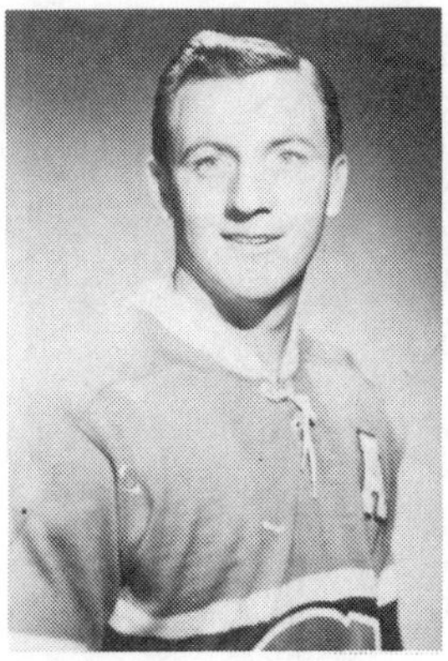

Dickie Moore

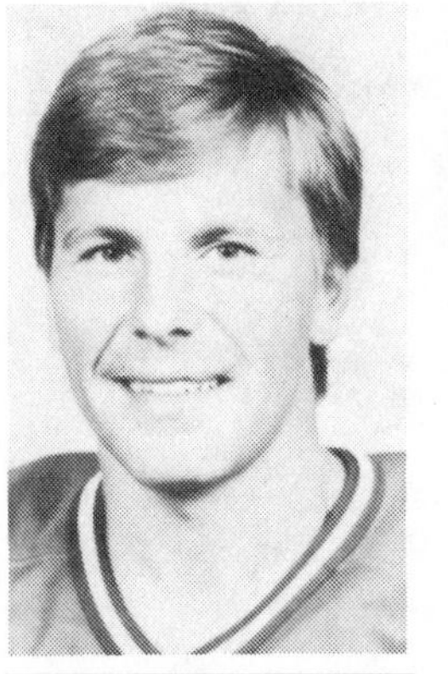

Mats Naslund

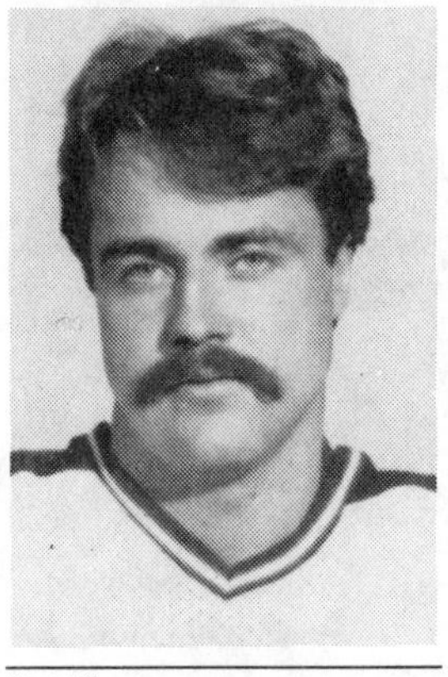

Kent Nilsson

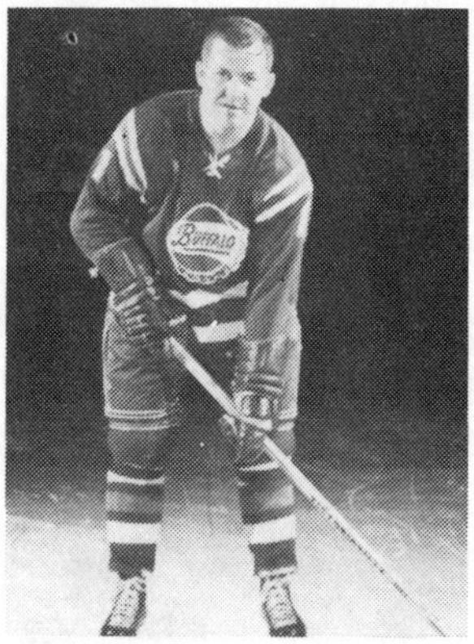

Gerry Ouelette

Name	NHL Teams	NHL Seasons	Regular Schedule GP	G	A	TP	PIM	Playoffs GP	G	A	TP	PIM	NHL Cup Wins	First NHL Season	Last NHL Season
Nicholson, Paul	Wsh.	3	62	4	8	12	18	....	....	....	....	....		1974-75	1976-77
Niekamp, Jim	Det.	2	29	0	2	2	37	....	....	....	....	....		1970-71	1971-72
Nienhuis, Kraig	Bos.	3	87	20	16	36	39	2	0	0	0	14		1985-86	1987-88
• Nighbor, Frank	Ott., Tor.	13	348	136	60	196	244	36	11	11	22	25	4	1917-18	1929-30
Nigro, Frank	Tor.	2	68	8	18	26	39	3	0	0	0	2		1982-83	1983-84
Nilan, Chris	Mtl., NYR, Bos.	13	688	110	115	225	3043	111	8	9	17	541	1	1979-80	1991-92
Nill, Jim	St.L., Van., Bos., Wpg., Det.	9	524	58	87	145	854	59	10	5	15	203		1981-82	1989-90
Nilsson, Kent	Atl., Cgy., Min., Edm.	9	553	264	422	686	116	59	11	41	52	14	1	1979-80	1994-95
Nilsson, Ulf	NYR	4	170	57	112	169	85	25	8	14	22	27		1978-79	1982-83
Nistico, Lou	Col.	1	3	0	0	0	0	....	....	....	....	....		1977-78	1977-78
• Noble, Reg	Tor., Mtl.M., Det.	16	509	167	79	246	830	32	4	5	9	33	3	1917-18	1932-33
Noel, Claude	Wsh.	1	7	0	0	0	0	....	....	....	....	....		1979-80	1979-80
Nolan, Pat	Tor.	1	2	0	0	0	0	....	....	....	....	....	1	1921-22	1921-22
Nolan, Ted	Det., Pit.	3	78	6	16	22	105	....	....	....	....	....		1981-82	1985-86
Nolet, Simon	Phi., K.C., Pit., Col.	10	562	150	182	332	187	34	6	3	9	8	1	1967-68	1976-77
Nordmark, Robert	St. L., Van.	4	236	13	70	83	254	7	3	2	5	8		1987-88	1990-91
Noris, Joe	Pit., St.L., Buf.	3	55	2	5	7	22	....	....	....	....	....		1971-72	1973-74
Norrish, Rod	Min.	2	21	3	3	6	2	....	....	....	....	....		1973-74	1974-75
• Northcott, Baldy	Mtl.M., Chi.	11	446	133	112	245	273	31	8	5	13	14	1	1928-29	1938-39
Norwich, Craig	Wpg., St.L., Col.	2	104	17	58	75	60	....	....	....	....	....		1979-80	1980-81
Norwood, Lee	Que., Wsh., St.L., Det., N.J., Hfd., Cgy.	12	503	58	153	211	1099	65	6	22	28	171		1980-81	1993-94
Novy, Milan	Wsh.	1	73	18	30	48	16	2	0	0	0	0		1982-83	1982-83
Nowak, Hank	Pit., Det., Bos.	4	180	26	29	55	161	13	1	0	1	8		1973-74	1976-77
Nykoluk, Mike	Tor.	1	32	3	1	4	20	....	....	....	....	....		1956-57	1956-57
Nylund, Gary	Tor., Chi., NYI	11	608	32	139	171	1235	24	0	6	6	63		1982-83	1992-93
• Nyrop, Bill	Mtl., Min.	4	207	12	51	63	101	35	1	7	8	22	3	1975-76	1981-82
Nystrom, Bob	NYI	14	900	235	278	513	1248	157	39	44	83	236	4	1972-73	1985-86

O

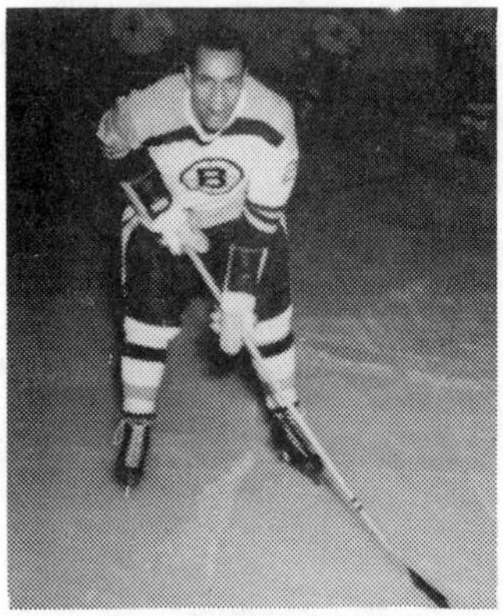

Willie O'Ree

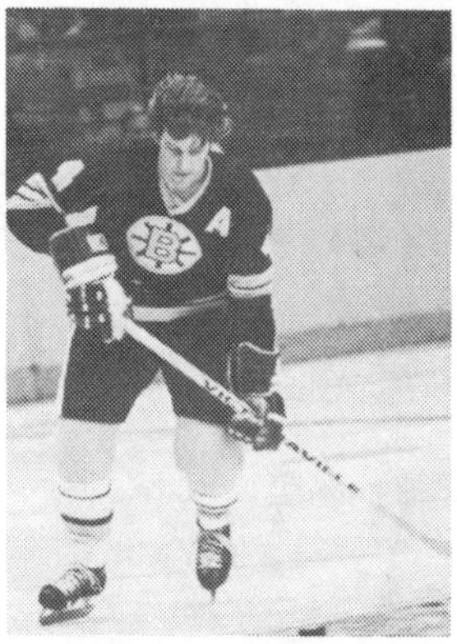

Bobby Orr

Name	NHL Teams	NHL Seasons	Regular Schedule GP	G	A	TP	PIM	Playoffs GP	G	A	TP	PIM	NHL Cup Wins	First NHL Season	Last NHL Season
• Oatman, Russell	Det., Mtl.M., NYR	3	120	20	9	29	100	15	1	0	1	18		1926-27	1928-29
O'Brien, Dennis	Min., Col., Clev., Bos.	10	592	31	91	122	1017	34	1	2	3	101		1970-71	1979-80
O'Brien, Obie	Bos.	1	2	0	0	0	0	....	....	....	....	....		1955-56	1955-56
O'Callahan, Jack	Chi., N.J.	7	389	27	104	131	541	32	4	11	15	41		1982-83	1988-89
O'Connell, Mike	Chi., Bos., Det.	13	860	105	334	439	605	82	8	24	32	64		1977-78	1989-90
• O'Connor, Buddy	Mtl., NYR	10	509	140	257	397	34	53	15	21	36	6	2	1941-42	1950-51
Oddleifson, Chris	Bos., Van.	9	524	95	191	286	464	14	1	6	7	8		1972-73	1980-81
Odelein, Selmar	Edm.	3	18	0	2	2	35	....	....	....	....	....		1985-86	1988-89
O'Donnell, Fred	Bos.	2	115	15	11	26	98	5	0	1	1	5		1972-73	1973-74
O'Donoghue, Don	Oak., Cal.	3	125	18	17	35	35	3	0	0	0	0		1969-70	1971-72
Odrowski, Gerry	Det., Oak., St.L.	6	309	12	19	31	111	30	0	1	1	16		1960-61	1971-72
O'Dwyer, Bill	L.A., Bos.	5	120	9	13	22	113	10	0	0	0	2		1983-84	1989-90
O'Flaherty, Gerry	Tor., Van., Atl.	8	438	99	95	194	168	7	2	2	4	6		1971-72	1978-79
O'Flaherty, John	NYA, Bro.	2	21	5	1	6	0	....	....	....	....	....		1940-41	1941-42
Ogilvie, Brian	Chi., St.L.	6	90	15	21	36	29	....	....	....	....	....		1972-73	1978-79
O'Grady, George	Mtl.M.	1	4	0	0	0	0	....	....	....	....	....		1917-18	1917-18
Ogrodnick, John	Det., Que., NYR	14	928	402	425	827	260	41	18	8	26	6		1979-80	1992-93
Ojanen, Janne	N.J.	4	98	21	23	44	28	3	0	2	2	0		1988-89	1992-93
Okerlund, Todd	NYI	1	4	0	0	0	2	....	....	....	....	....		1987-88	1987-88
• Oliver, Harry	Bos., NYA	11	463	127	85	212	147	35	10	6	16	24	1	1926-27	1936-37
Oliver, Murray	Det., Bos., Tor., Min.	17	1127	274	454	728	320	35	9	16	25	10		1957-58	1974-75
Olmstead, Bert	Chi., Mtl., Tor.	14	848	181	421	602	884	115	16	43	59	101	5	1948-49	1961-62
Olsen, Darryl	Cgy.	1	1	0	0	0	0	....	....	....	....	....		1991-92	1991-92
Olson, Dennis	Det.	1	4	0	0	0	0	....	....	....	....	....		1957-58	1957-58
O'Neil, Paul	Van., Bos.	2	6	0	0	0	0	....	....	....	....	....		1973-74	1975-76
O'Neill, Jim	Bos., Mtl.	6	156	6	30	36	109	9	1	1	2	13		1933-34	1941-42
• O'Neill, Tom	Tor.	2	66	10	12	22	53	4	0	0	0	6	1	1943-44	1944-45
Orban, Bill	Chi., Min.	3	114	8	15	23	67	3	0	0	0	0		1967-68	1969-70
O'Ree, Willie	Bos.	2	45	4	10	14	26	....	....	....	....	....		1957-58	1960-61
O'Regan, Tom	Pit.	3	61	5	12	17	10	....	....	....	....	....		1983-84	1985-86
O'Reilly, Terry	Bos.	14	891	204	402	606	2095	108	25	42	67	335		1971-72	1984-85
Orlando, Gaetano	Buf.	3	98	18	26	44	51	5	0	4	4	14		1984-85	1986-87
Orlando, Jimmy	Det.	6	199	6	25	31	375	36	0	9	9	105	1	1936-37	1942-43
Orleski, Dave	Mtl.	2	2	0	0	0	0	....	....	....	....	....		1980-81	1981-82
Orr, Bobby	Bos., Chi.	12	657	270	645	915	953	74	26	66	92	107	2	1966-67	1978-79
Osborne, Keith	St.L., T.B.	2	16	1	3	4	16	....	....	....	....	....		1989-90	1992-93
Osburn, Randy	Tor., Phi.	2	27	0	2	2	0	....	....	....	....	....		1972-73	1974-75
O'Shea, Danny	Min., Chi., St.L.	5	369	64	115	179	265	39	3	7	10	61		1968-69	1972-73
O'Shea, Kevin	Buf., St.L.	3	134	13	18	31	85	12	2	1	3	10		1970-71	1972-73
Osiecki, Mark	Cgy., Ott., Wpg., Min.	2	93	3	11	14	43	....	....	....	....	....		1991-92	1992-93
Otevrel, Jaroslav	S.J.	2	16	3	4	7	2	....	....	....	....	....		1992-93	1993-94
Ouelette, Eddie	Chi.	1	43	3	2	5	11	1	0	0	0	0		1935-36	1935-36
Ouelette, Gerry	Bos.	1	34	5	4	9	0	....	....	....	....	....		1960-61	1960-61
Owchar, Dennis	Pit., Col.	6	288	30	85	115	200	10	1	1	2	8		1974-75	1979-80
• Owen, George	Bos.	5	183	44	33	77	151	21	2	5	7	25	1	1928-29	1932-33

P

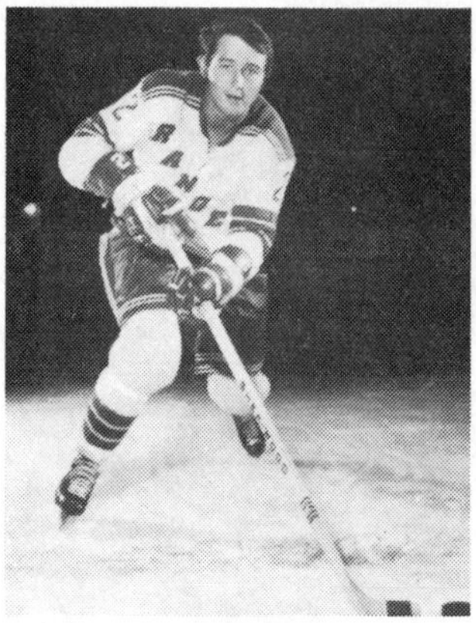

Brad Park

Name	NHL Teams	NHL Seasons	Regular Schedule GP	G	A	TP	PIM	Playoffs GP	G	A	TP	PIM	NHL Cup Wins	First NHL Season	Last NHL Season
Pachal, Clayton	Bos., Col.	3	35	2	3	5	95	....	....	....	....	....		1976-77	1978-79
Paddock, John	Wsh., Phi., Que.	5	87	8	14	22	86	5	2	0	2	0		1975-76	1982-83
Paiement, Rosaire	Phi., Van.	5	190	48	52	100	343	3	3	0	3	0		1967-68	1971-72
Paiement, Wilf	K.C. Col., Tor., Que., NYR, Buf., Pit.	14	946	356	458	814	1757	69	18	17	35	185		1974-75	1987-88
Palangio, Peter	Mtl., Det., Chi.	4	71	13	10	23	28	7	0	0	0	0	1	1926-27	1937-38
Palazzari, Aldo	Bos., NYR	1	35	8	3	11	4	....	....	....	....	....		1943-44	1943-44
Palazzari, Doug	St.L.	4	108	18	20	38	23	2	0	0	0	0		1974-75	1978-79
Palmer, Brad	Min., Bos.	3	168	32	38	70	58	29	9	5	14	16		1980-81	1982-83
Palmer, Rob H.	Chi.	3	16	0	3	3	2	....	....	....	....	....		1973-74	1975-76
Palmer, Rob R.	L.A., N.J.	7	320	9	101	110	115	8	1	2	3	6		1977-78	1983-84
• Panagabko, Ed	Bos.	2	29	0	3	3	38	....	....	....	....	....		1955-56	1956-57
Papike, Joe	Chi.	3	20	3	3	6	4	5	0	2	2	0		1940-41	1944-45
Pappin, Jim	Tor., Chi., Cal., Clev.	14	767	278	295	573	667	92	33	34	67	101	2	1963-64	1976-77
Paradise, Bob	Min., Atl., Pit., Wsh.	8	368	8	54	62	393	12	0	1	1	19		1971-72	1978-79
Pargeter, George	Mtl.	1	4	0	0	0	0	....	....	....	....	....		1946-47	1946-47
Parise, J.P.	Bos., Tor., Min., NYI, Clev.	14	890	238	356	594	706	86	27	31	58	87		1965-66	1978-79
Parizeau, Michel	St.L., Phi.	1	58	3	14	17	18	....	....	....	....	....		1971-72	1971-72
Park, Brad	NYR, Bos., Det.	17	1113	213	683	896	1429	161	35	90	125	217		1968-69	1984-85
Parker, Jeff	Buf., Hfd.	5	141	16	19	35	163	5	0	0	0	26		1986-87	1990-91
Parkes, Ernie	Mtl.M.	1	17	0	0	0	2	....	....	....	....	....		1924-25	1924-25
Parks, Greg	NYI	3	23	1	2	3	6	2	0	0	0	0		1990-91	1992-93
Parsons, George	Tor.	3	78	12	13	25	20	7	3	2	5	11		1936-37	1938-39
Pasek, Dusan	Min.	1	48	4	10	14	30	2	1	0	1	0		1988-89	1988-89
Pasin, Dave	Bos., L.A.	2	76	18	19	37	50	3	0	1	1	0		1985-86	1988-89
Paslawski, Greg	Mtl., St.L., Wpg., Buf., Que., Phi., Cgy.	11	650	187	185	372	169	60	19	13	32	25		1983-84	1993-94
Paterson, Joe	Det., Phi., L.A., NYR	9	291	19	37	56	829	22	3	4	7	77		1980-81	1988-89
Paterson, Mark	Hfd.	4	29	3	3	6	33	....	....	....	....	....		1982-83	1985-86
Paterson, Rick	Chi.	9	430	50	43	93	136	61	7	10	17	51		1978-79	1986-87
Patey, Doug	Wsh.	3	45	4	2	6	8	....	....	....	....	....		1976-77	1978-79
Patey, Larry	Cal., St.L., NYR	12	717	153	163	316	631	40	8	10	18	57		1973-74	1984-85
Patrick, Craig	Cal., St.L., K.C., Min. Wsh.	8	401	72	91	163	61	2	0	1	1	0		1971-72	1978-79
Patrick, Glenn	St.L., Cal., Clev.	3	38	2	3	5	72	....	....	....	....	....		1973-74	1976-77
• Patrick, Lester	NYR	1	1	0	0	0	2	....	....	....	....	....		1926-27	1926-27
• Patrick, Lynn	NYR	10	455	145	190	335	240	44	10	6	16	22	1	1934-35	1945-46
Patrick, Muzz	NYR	5	166	5	26	31	133	25	4	0	4	34	1	1937-38	1945-46
Patrick, Steve	Buf., NYR, Que.	6	250	40	68	108	242	12	0	1	1	12		1980-81	1985-86
Patterson, Colin	Cgy., Buf.	10	504	96	109	205	239	85	12	17	29	57	1	1983-84	1992-93
Patterson, Dennis	K.C., Phi.	3	138	6	22	28	67	....	....	....	....	....		1974-75	1979-80
• Patterson, George	Bos., Det., St.L., Tor., Mtl., NYA	9	284	51	27	78	218	3	0	0	0	2		1926-27	1934-35
• Paul, Butch	Det.	1	3	0	0	0	0	....	....	....	....	....		1964-65	1964-65
• Paulhus, Rollie	Mtl.	1	33	0	0	0	0	....	....	....	....	....		1925-26	1925-26
Pavelich, Mark	NYR, Min., S.J.	7	355	137	192	329	340	23	7	17	24	14		1981-82	1991-92
Pavelich, Marty	Det.	10	634	93	159	252	454	91	13	15	28	74	4	1947-48	1956-57
Pavese, Jim	St.L., NYR, Det., Hfd.	8	328	13	44	57	689	34	0	6	6	81		1981-82	1988-89
• Payer, Evariste	Mtl.	1	1	0	0	0	0	....	....	....	....	....		1917-18	1917-18

Name	NHL Teams	NHL Seasons	Regular Schedule GP	G	A	TP	PIM	Playoffs GP	G	A	TP	PIM	NHL Cup Wins	First NHL Season	Last NHL Season
Payne, Steve	Min.	10	613	228	238	466	435	71	35	35	70	60		1978-79	1987-88
Paynter, Kent	Chi., Wsh., Wpg., Ott.	7	37	1	3	4	69	4	0	0	0	10		1987-88	1993-94
Pearson, Mel	NYR, Pit.	5	38	2	6	8	25	....	....	....	....	....		1949-50	1967-68
Pedersen, Allen	Bos., Min., Hfd.	8	428	5	36	41	487	64	0	0	0	91		1986-87	1993-94
Pederson, Barry	Bos., Van., Pit., Hfd.	12	701	238	416	654	472	34	22	30	52	25		1980-81	1991-92
Pederson, Mark	Mtl., Phi., S.J., Det.	5	169	35	50	85	77	2	0	0	0	0		1989-90	1993-94
Peer, Bert	Det.	1	1	0	0	0	0	....	....	....	....	....		1939-40	1939-40
Peirson, Johnny	Bos.	11	545	153	173	326	315	49	9	17	26	26		1946-47	1957-58
Pelensky, Perry	Chi.	1	4	0	0	0	5	....	....	....	....	....		1983-84	1983-84
Pelletier, Roger	Phi.	1	1	0	0	0	0	....	....	....	....	....		1967-68	1967-68
Peloffy, Andre	Wsh.	1	9	0	0	0	0	....	....	....	....	....		1974-75	1974-75
Pelyk, Mike	Tor.	9	441	26	88	114	566	40	0	3	3	41		1967-68	1977-78
Pennington, Cliff	Mtl., Bos.	3	101	17	42	59	6	....	....	....	....	....		1960-61	1962-63
Peplinski, Jim	Cgy.	11	711	161	263	424	1467	99	15	31	46	382	1	1980-81	1994-95
Perlini, Fred	Tor.	2	8	2	3	5	0	....	....	....	....	....		1981-82	1983-84
Perreault, Fern	NYR	2	3	0	0	0	0	....	....	....	....	....		1947-48	1949-50
Perreault, Gilbert	Buf.	17	1191	512	814	1326	500	90	33	70	103	44		1970-71	1986-87
Perry, Brian	Oak., Buf.	3	96	16	29	45	24	8	1	1	2	4		1968-69	1970-71
Persson, Stefan	NYI	9	622	52	317	369	574	102	7	50	57	69	4	1977-78	1985-86
Pesut, George	Cal.	2	92	3	22	25	130	....	....	....	....	....		1974-75	1975-76
• Peters, Frank	NYR	1	43	0	0	0	59	4	0	0	0	2		1930-31	1930-31
Peters, Garry	Mtl., NYR, Phi., Bos.	8	311	34	34	68	261	9	2	2	4	31	1	1964-65	1971-72
Peters, Jim	Det., Chi., Mtl., Bos.	9	574	125	150	275	186	60	5	9	14	22	3	1945-46	1953-54
Peters, Jimmy	Det., L.A.	9	309	37	36	73	48	11	0	2	2	2		1964-65	1974-75
Peters, Steve	Col.	1	2	0	1	1	0	....	....	....	....	....		1979-80	1979-80
Peterson, Brent	Det., Buf., Van., Hfd.	11	620	72	141	213	484	31	4	4	8	65		1979-80	1988-89
Petrenko, Sergei	Buf.	1	14	0	4	4	0	....	....	....	....	....		1993-94	1993-94
Pettersson, Jorgen	St.L., Hfd., Wsh.	6	435	174	192	366	117	44	15	12	27	4		1980-81	1985-86
• Pettinger, Eric	Ott., Bos., Tor.	3	98	7	12	19	83	4	1	0	1	8		1928-29	1930-31
Pettinger, Gord	Det., NYR, Bos.	8	292	42	74	116	77	47	4	5	9	11	4	1932-33	1939-40
Phair, Lyle	L.A.	3	48	6	7	13	12	1	0	0	0	0		1985-86	1987-88
Phillipoff, Harold	Atl., Chi.,	3	141	26	57	83	267	6	0	2	2	9		1977-78	1979-80
Phillips, Bat	Mtl.M.	1	27	1	1	2	6	4	0	0	0	2		1929-30	1929-30
• Phillips, Bill	Mtl.M., NYA.	8	302	52	31	83	232	28	6	2	8	19	1	1925-26	1932-33
Phillips, Charlie	Mtl.	1	17	0	0	0	6	....	....	....	....	....		1942-43	1942-43
Picard, Noel	Atl., Mtl., St.L.	7	335	12	63	75	616	50	2	11	13	167	1	1964-65	1972-73
Picard, Robert	Wsh. Tor., Mtl., Wpg., Que., Det.	13	899	104	319	423	1025	36	5	15	20	39		1977-78	1989-90
Picard, Roger	St.L.	1	15	2	2	4	21	....	....	....	....	....		1967-68	1967-68
Pichette, Dave	Que., St.L., N.J., NYR	7	322	41	140	181	348	28	3	7	10	54		1980-81	1987-88
Picketts, Hal	NYA.	1	48	3	1	4	32	....	....	....	....	....		1933-34	1933-34
Pidhirny, Harry	Bos.	1	2	0	0	0	0	....	....	....	....	....		1957-58	1957-58
Pierce, Randy	Col., N.J., Hfd.	8	277	62	76	138	223	2	0	0	0	0		1977-78	1984-85
Pike, Alf	NYR	6	234	42	77	119	145	21	4	2	6	12	1	1939-40	1946-47
Pilote, Pierre	Chi., Tor.	14	890	80	418	498	1251	86	8	53	61	102	1	1955-56	1968-69
Pinder, Gerry	Chi., Cal.	3	223	55	69	124	135	17	0	4	4	6		1969-70	1971-72
Pirus, Alex	Min., Det.	4	159	30	28	58	94	2	0	1	1	2		1976-77	1979-80
• Pitre, Didier	Mtl.	6	127	64	17	81	59	12	2	2	4	3		1917-18	1922-23
• Plager, Barclay	St.L.	10	614	44	187	231	1115	68	3	20	23	182		1967-68	1976-77
Plager, Bill	Min., St.L., Atl.	9	263	4	34	38	294	31	0	2	2	26		1967-68	1975-76
Plager, Bob	NYR, St.L.	14	644	20	126	146	802	74	2	17	19	195		1964-65	1977-78
Plamondon, Gerry	Mtl.	5	74	7	13	20	10	11	5	2	7	2	1	1945-46	1950-51
Plante, Cam	Tor.	1	2	0	0	0	0	....	....	....	....	....		1984-85	1984-85
Plante, Pierre	NYR, Que., Phi., St.L., Chi.	9	599	125	172	297	599	33	2	6	8	51		1971-72	1979-80
Plantery, Mark	Wpg.	1	25	1	5	6	14	....	....	....	....	....		1980-81	1980-81
Plaxton, Hugh	Mtl.M.	1	15	1	2	3	4	....	....	....	....	....		1932-33	1932-33
Playfair, Jim	Edm., Chi.	3	21	2	4	6	51	....	....	....	....	....		1983-84	1988-89
Playfair, Larry	Buf., L.A.	12	688	26	94	120	1812	43	0	6	6	111		1978-79	1989-90
Pleau, Larry	Mtl.	3	94	9	15	24	27	4	0	0	0	0		1969-70	1971-72
Plett, Willi	Atl., Cgy., Min., Bos.	13	834	222	215	437	2574	83	24	22	46	466		1975-76	1987-88
Plumb, Rob	Det.	2	14	3	2	5	2	....	....	....	....	....		1977-78	1977-78
Plumb, Ron	Hfd.	1	26	3	4	7	14	....	....	....	....	....		1979-80	1979-80
Pocza, Harvie	Wsh.	2	3	0	0	0	2	....	....	....	....	....		1979-80	1981-82
Poddubny, Walt	Edm., Tor., NYR, Que., N.J.	11	468	184	238	422	454	19	7	2	9	12		1981-82	1991-92
Podloski, Ray	Bos.	1	8	0	1	1	22	....	....	....	....	....		1988-89	1988-89
Podolsky, Nels	Det.	1	1	0	0	0	0	7	0	0	0	4		1948-49	1948-49
Poeta, Anthony	Chi.	1	1	0	0	0	0	....	....	....	....	....		1951-52	1951-52
Poile, Bud	NYR, Bos., Det., Tor., Chi.,	7	311	107	122	229	91	23	4	5	9	8	1	1942-43	1949-50
Poile, Don	Det.	2	66	7	9	16	12	4	0	0	0	0		1954-55	1957-58
Poirer, Gordie	Mtl.	1	10	0	0	0	0	....	....	....	....	....		1939-40	1939-40
Polanic, Tom	Min.	2	19	0	2	2	53	5	1	1	2	4		1969-70	1970-71
Polich, John	NYR	2	3	0	1	1	0	....	....	....	....	....		1939-40	1940-41
Polich, Mike	Mtl., Min.	5	226	24	29	53	57	23	2	1	3	2	1	1976-77	1980-81
Polis, Greg	Pit., St.L., NYR, Wsh.	10	615	174	169	343	391	7	0	2	2	6		1970-71	1979-80
Poliziani, Daniel	Bos.	1	1	0	0	0	0	3	0	0	0	0		1958-59	1958-59
Polonich, Dennis	Det.	8	390	59	82	141	1242	7	1	0	1	19		1974-75	1982-83
Pooley, Paul	Wpg.	2	15	0	3	3	0	....	....	....	....	....		1984-85	1985-86
Popein, Larry	NYR, Oak.	8	449	80	141	221	162	16	1	4	5	6		1954-55	1967-68
Popiel, Paul	Bos., L.A., Det., Van., Edm.	7	224	13	41	54	210	4	1	0	1	4		1965-66	1979-80
Portland, Jack	Chi., Mtl., Bos.	10	381	15	56	71	323	33	1	3	4	25	1	1933-34	1942-43
Porvari, Jukka	Col., N.J.	2	39	3	9	12	4	....	....	....	....	....		1981-82	1982-83
Posa, Victor	Chi.	1	2	0	0	0	2	....	....	....	....	....		1985-86	1985-86
Posavad, Mike	St.L.	2	8	0	0	0	0	....	....	....	....	....		1985-86	1986-87
Potvin, Denis	NYI	15	1066	310	742	1052	1354	185	56	108	164	253	4	1973-74	1987-88
Potvin, Jean	L.A., Min., Phi., NYI, Cle.	11	613	63	224	287	466	39	2	9	11	17	1	1970-71	1980-81
Poudrier, Daniel	Que.	3	25	1	5	6	10	....	....	....	....	....		1985-86	1987-88
Poulin, Dan	Min.	1	3	1	1	2	2	....	....	....	....	....		1981-82	1981-82
Poulin, Dave	Phi., Bos., Wsh.	13	724	205	325	530	482	129	31	42	73	132		1982-83	1994-95
Pouzar, Jaroslav	Edm.	4	186	34	48	82	135	29	6	4	10	16	3	1982-83	1986-87
Powell, Ray	Chi.	1	31	7	15	22	2	....	....	....	....	....		1950-51	1950-51
Powis, Geoff	Chi.	1	2	0	0	0	0	....	....	....	....	....		1967-68	1967-68
Powis, Lynn	Chi., K.C.	2	130	19	33	52	25	1	0	0	0	0		1973-74	1974-75
Prajsler, Petr	L.A., Bos.	4	46	3	10	13	51	4	0	0	0	0		1987-88	1991-92
• Pratt, Babe	Bos., NYR, Tor.	12	518	83	209	292	463	63	12	17	29	90	2	1935-36	1946-47
Pratt, Jack	Bos.	2	37	2	0	2	42	4	0	0	0	0		1930-31	1931-32
Pratt, Kelly	Pit.	1	22	0	6	6	15	....	....	....	....	....		1974-75	1974-75
Pratt, Tracy	Van., Col., Buf., Pit. Tor., Oak.	10	580	17	97	114	1026	25	0	1	1	62		1967-68	1976-77
Prentice, Dean	Pit., Min., Det., NYR, Bos.	22	1378	391	469	860	484	54	13	17	30	38		1952-53	1973-74
Prentice, Eric	Tor.	1	5	0	0	0	4	....	....	....	....	....		1943-44	1943-44
Preston, Rich	Chi., N.J.	8	580	127	164	291	348	47	4	18	22	56		1979-80	1986-87
Preston, Yves	Phi.	2	28	7	3	10	4	....	....	....	....	....		1978-79	1980-81
Priakin, Sergei	Cgy.	3	46	3	8	11	2	1	0	0	0	0		1988-89	1990-91
• Price, Bob	Ott.	1	1	0	0	0	0	....	....	....	....	....		1919-20	1919-20
Price, Jack	Chi.	3	57	4	6	10	24	4	0	0	0	0		1951-52	1953-54
Price, Noel	Pit., L.A., Det., Tor., NYR, Mtl., Atl.	14	499	14	114	128	333	12	0	1	1	8	1	1957-58	1975-76
Price, Pat	NYI, Edm., Pit., Que., NYR, Min.	13	726	43	218	261	1456	74	2	10	12	195		1975-76	1987-88
Price, Tom	Cal., Clev., Pit.	5	29	0	2	2	12	....	....	....	....	....		1974-75	1978-79
Priestlay, Ken	Buf., Pit.	6	168	27	34	61	63	14	0	0	0	21	1	1986-87	1991-92
• Primeau, Joe	Tor.	9	310	66	177	243	105	38	5	18	23	12	1	1927-28	1935-36
Primeau, Kevin	Van.	1	2	0	0	0	4	....	....	....	....	....		1980-81	1980-81
Pringle, Ellie	NYA	1	6	0	0	0	0	....	....	....	....	....		1930-31	1930-31
• Prodgers, Goldie	Tor., Ham.	6	110	63	22	85	33	....	....	....	....	....		1919-20	1924-25
Pronovost, Andre	Mtl., Bos., Det., Min.	10	556	94	104	198	408	70	11	11	22	58	4	1956-57	1967-68
Pronovost, Jean	Wsh., Pit., Atl.	14	998	391	383	774	413	35	11	9	20	14		1968-69	1981-82
Pronovost, Marcel	Det., Tor.	21	1206	88	257	345	851	134	8	23	31	104	5	1950-51	1969-70
Propp, Brian	Phi., Bos., Min., Hfd.	15	1016	425	579	1004	830	160	64	84	148	151		1979-80	1993-94
• Provost, Claude	Mtl.	15	1005	254	335	589	469	126	25	38	63	86	9	1955-56	1969-70
Pryor, Chris	Min., NYI	6	82	1	4	5	122	....	....	....	....	....		1984-85	1989-90
Prystai, Metro	Chi., Det.	11	674	151	179	330	231	43	12	14	26	8	2	1947-48	1957-58
• Pudas, Al	Tor.	1	3	0	0	0	0	....	....	....	....	....		1926-27	1926-27
Pulford, Bob	Tor., L.A.	16	1079	281	362	643	792	89	25	26	51	126	4	1956-57	1971-72
Pulkkinen, Dave	NYI	1	2	0	0	0	0	....	....	....	....	....		1972-73	1972-73
Purpur, Cliff (Fido)	Det., Chi., St.L.	5	144	25	35	60	46	16	1	2	3	4		1934-35	1944-45
Purves, John	Wsh.	1	7	1	0	1	0	....	....	....	....	....		1990-91	1990-91
• Pusie, Jean	Mtl., NYR, Bos.	5	61	1	4	5	28	7	0	0	0	0	1	1930-31	1935-36

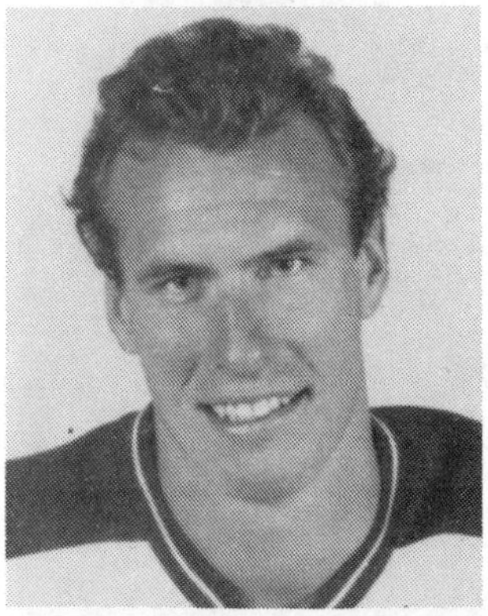
Jim Peplinski

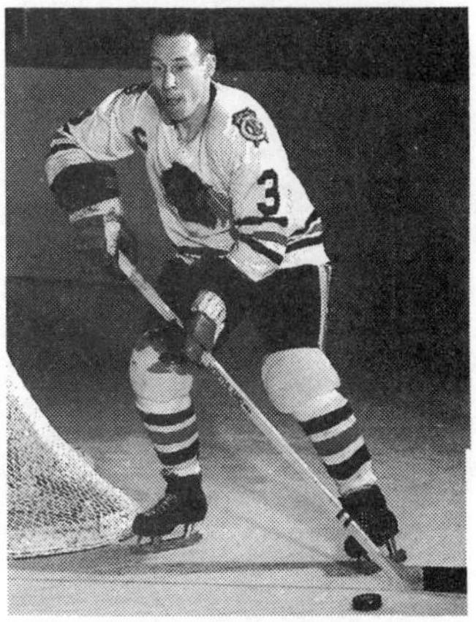
Pierre Pilote

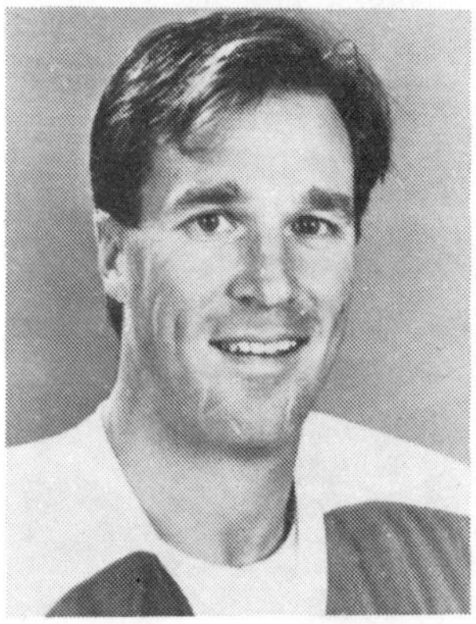
Dave Poulin

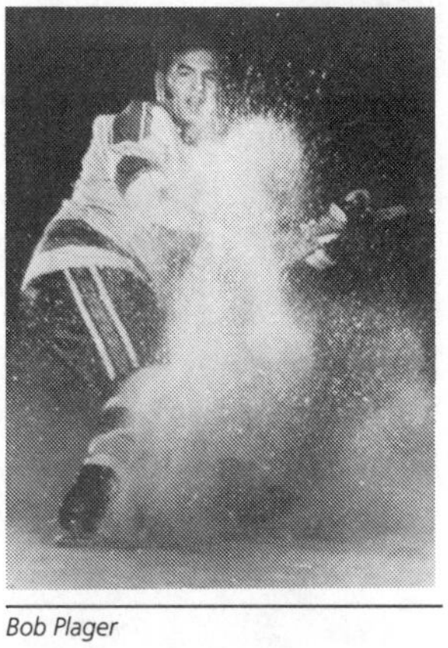
Bob Plager

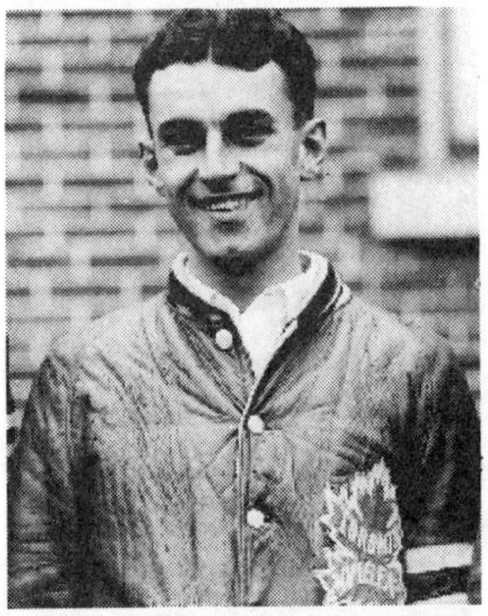
Joe Primeau

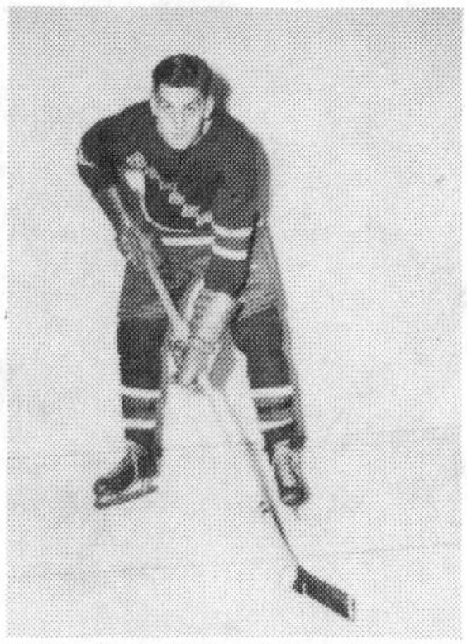
Don Raleigh

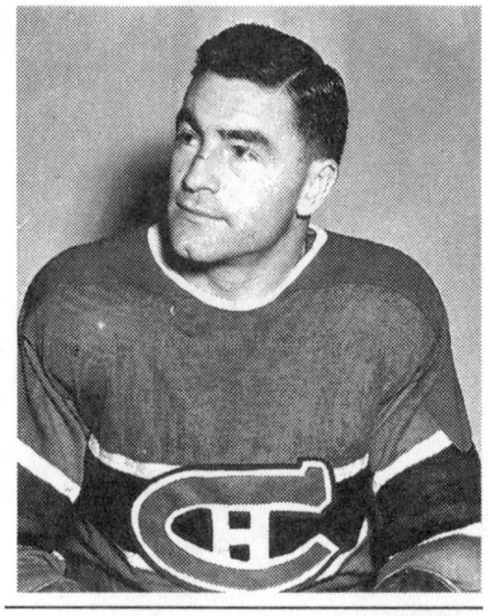
Ken Reardon

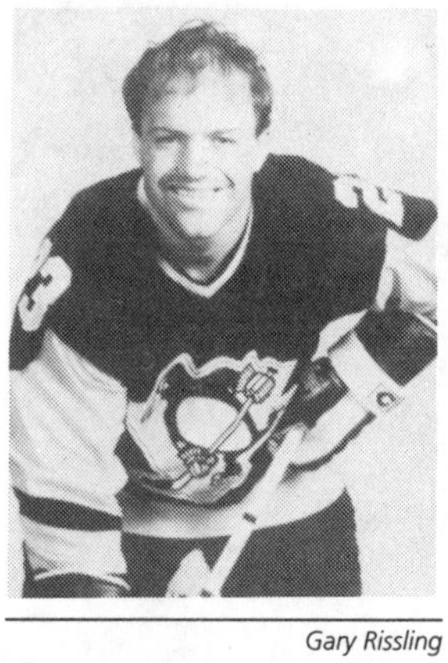
Gary Rissling

Name	NHL Teams	NHL Seasons	Regular Schedule GP	G	A	TP	PIM	Playoffs GP	G	A	TP	PIM	NHL Cup Wins	First NHL Season	Last NHL Season
Pyatt, Nelson	Det., Wsh., Col.	7	296	71	63	134	69	....	....	....	....	....		1973-74	1979-80

Q

Name	NHL Teams	NHL Seasons	Regular Schedule GP	G	A	TP	PIM	Playoffs GP	G	A	TP	PIM	NHL Cup Wins	First NHL Season	Last NHL Season
Quackenbush, Bill	Det., Bos.	14	774	62	222	284	95	80	2	19	21	8		1942-43	1955-56
Quackenbush, Max	Bos., Chi.,	2	61	4	7	11	30	6	0	0	0	4		1950-51	1951-52
Quenneville, Joel	Tor., Col., N.J., Hfd., Wsh.	13	803	54	136	190	705	32	0	8	8	22		1978-79	1990-91
• Quenneville, Leo	NYR	1	25	0	3	3	10	3	0	0	0	0		1929-30	1929-30
• Quilty, John	Mtl., Bos.	4	125	36	34	70	81	13	3	5	8	9		1940-41	1947-48
Quinn, Pat	Tor., Van., Atl.	9	606	18	113	131	950	11	0	1	1	21		1968-69	1976-77
Quinney, Ken	Que.	3	59	7	13	20	23	....	....	....	....	....		1986-87	1990-91

R

Name	NHL Teams	NHL Seasons	Regular Schedule GP	G	A	TP	PIM	Playoffs GP	G	A	TP	PIM	NHL Cup Wins	First NHL Season	Last NHL Season
Radley, Yip	NYA, Mtl.M.	2	18	0	1	1	13	....	....	....	....	....		1930-31	1936-37
Raglan, Clare	Det., Chi.	3	100	4	9	13	52	3	0	0	0	0		1950-51	1952-53
Raglan, Herb	St.L., Que., T.B., Ott.	9	343	33	56	89	775	32	3	6	9	50		1985-86	1993-94
Raleigh, Don	NYR	10	535	101	219	320	96	18	6	5	11	6		1943-44	1955-56
Ramage, Rob	Col., St.L., Cgy., Tor., Min., T.B., Mtl., Phi.	15	1044	139	425	564	2226	84	8	42	50	218	2	1979-80	1993-94
• Ramsay, Beattie	Tor.,	1	43	0	2	2	10	....	....	....	....	....		1927-28	1927-28
Ramsay, Craig	Buf.	14	1070	252	420	672	201	89	17	31	48	27		1971-72	1984-85
Ramsay, Wayne	Buf.	1	2	0	0	0	0	....	....	....	....	....		1977-78	1977-78
Ramsey, Les	Chi.	1	11	2	2	4	2	....	....	....	....	....		1944-45	1944-45
• Randall, Ken	Tor., Ham., NYA	10	215	67	28	95	415	14	3	1	4	43	2	1917-18	1926-27
Ranieri, George	Bos.	1	2	0	0	0	0	....	....	....	....	....		1956-57	1956-57
Ratelle, Jean	NYR, Bos.	21	1281	491	776	1267	276	123	32	66	98	24		1960-61	1980-81
Rathwell, John	Bos.	1	1	0	0	0	0	....	....	....	....	....		1974-75	1974-75
Rausse, Errol	Wsh.	3	31	7	3	10	0	....	....	....	....	....		1979-80	1981-82
Rautakallio, Pekka	Atl., Cgy.	3	235	33	121	154	122	23	2	5	7	8		1979-80	1981-82
Ravlich, Matt	Bos., Chi., Det., L.A.	10	410	12	78	90	364	24	1	5	6	16		1962-63	1972-73
Raymond, Armand	Mtl.	2	22	0	2	2	10	....	....	....	....	....		1937-38	1939-40
Raymond, Paul	Mtl.	4	76	2	3	5	6	5	0	0	0	2		1932-33	1937-38
Read, Mel	NYR	1	1	0	0	0	0	....	....	....	....	....		1946-47	1946-47
Reardon, Ken	Mtl.	7	341	26	96	122	604	31	2	5	7	62	1	1940-41	1949-50
Reardon, Terry	Bos., Mtl.	7	193	47	53	100	73	30	8	10	18	12	1	1938-39	1946-47
Reaume, Marc	Tor., Det., Mtl., Van.	9	344	8	43	51	273	21	0	2	2	8		1954-55	1970-71
Reay, Billy	Det., Mtl.	10	479	105	162	267	202	63	13	16	29	43	2	1943-44	1952-53
Redahl, Gord	Bos.	1	18	0	1	1	2	....	....	....	....	....		1958-59	1958-59
Redding, George	Bos.	2	35	3	2	5	10	....	....	....	....	....		1924-25	1925-26
Redmond, Craig	L.A., Edm.	5	191	16	68	84	134	3	1	0	1	2		1984-85	1988-89
Redmond, Dick	Min., Cal., Chi., St.L., Atl., Bos.	13	771	133	312	445	504	66	9	22	31	27		1969-70	1981-82
Redmond, Mickey	Mtl., Det.	9	538	233	195	428	219	16	2	3	5	2	2	1967-68	1975-76
Reeds, Mark	St.L., Hfd.	8	365	45	114	159	135	53	8	9	17	23		1981-82	1988-89
• Regan, Bill	NYR, NYA	3	67	3	2	5	67	8	0	0	0	2		1929-30	1932-33
Regan, Larry	Bos., Tor.,	5	280	41	95	136	71	42	7	14	21	18		1956-57	1960-61
Regier, Darcy	Clev., NYI	3	26	0	2	2	35	....	....	....	....	....		1977-78	1983-84
Reibel, Earl	Det., Chi., Bos.	6	409	84	161	245	75	39	6	14	20	4	2	1953-54	1958-59
Reid, Dave	Tor.	3	7	0	0	0	0	....	....	....	....	....		1952-53	1955-56
Reid, Gerry	Det.	1	....	....	....	....	....	2	0	0	0	2		1948-49	1948-49
Reid, Gordie	NYA	1	1	0	0	0	2	....	....	....	....	....		1936-37	1936-37
Reid, Reg	Tor.	2	40	2	0	2	4	2	0	0	0	0		1924-25	1925-26
Reid, Tom	Chi., Min.	11	701	17	113	130	652	42	1	13	14	49		1967-68	1977-78
Reierson, Dave	Cgy.	1	2	0	0	0	2	....	....	....	....	....		1988-89	1988-89
Reigle, Ed	Bos.	1	17	0	2	2	25	....	....	....	....	....		1950-51	1950-51
Reinhart, Paul	Atl., Cgy., Van.	11	648	133	426	559	277	83	23	54	77	42		1979-80	1989-90
Reinikka, Ollie	NYR	1	16	0	0	0	0	....	....	....	....	....		1926-27	1926-27
Reise, Leo Jr.	Chi., Det., NYR	9	494	28	81	109	399	52	8	5	13	68	2	1945-46	1953-54
• Reise, Leo Sr.	Ham., NYA, NYR	8	223	36	29	65	177	6	0	0	0	16		1920-21	1929-30
Renaud, Mark	Hfd., Buf.	5	152	6	50	56	86	....	....	....	....	....		1979-80	1983-84
Reynolds, Bobby	Tor.	1	7	1	1	2	0	....	....	....	....	....		1989-90	1989-90
Ribble, Pat	Atl., Chi., Tor., Wsh., Cgy.	8	349	19	60	79	365	8	0	1	1	12		1975-76	1982-83
Richard, Henri	Mtl.	20	1256	358	688	1046	928	180	49	80	129	181	11	1955-56	1974-75
Richard, Jacques	Alt., Buf., Que.	10	556	160	187	347	307	35	5	5	10	34		1972-73	1982-83
Richard, Jean-Marc	Que.	2	5	2	1	3	2	....	....	....	....	....		1987-88	1989-90
Richard, Maurice	Mtl.	18	978	544	421	965	1285	133	82	44	126	188	8	1942-43	1959-60
Richard, Mike	Wsh.	2	7	0	2	2	0	....	....	....	....	....		1987-88	1989-90
Richards, Todd	Hfd.	2	8	0	4	4	4	11	0	3	3	6		1990-91	1991-92
Richardson, Dave	NYR, Chi., Det.	4	45	3	2	5	27	....	....	....	....	....		1963-64	1967-68
Richardson, Glen	Van.	1	24	3	6	9	19	....	....	....	....	....		1975-76	1975-76
Richardson, Ken	St.L.	3	49	8	13	21	16	....	....	....	....	....		1974-75	1978-79
Richer, Bob	Buf.	1	3	0	0	0	0	....	....	....	....	....		1972-73	1972-73
Richer, Stephane J. G.	T.B., Bos., Fla.	3	27	1	5	6	20	3	0	0	0	0		1992-93	1994-95
Richmond, Steve	NYR, Det., N.J., L.A.	5	159	4	23	27	514	4	0	0	0	12		1983-84	1988-89
Richter, Dave	Min., Phi., Van., St.L.	9	365	9	40	49	1030	22	1	0	1	80		1981-82	1989-90
Riley, Bill	Wsh., Wpg.	5	139	31	30	61	320	....	....	....	....	....		1974-75	1979-80
Riley, Jack	Det., Mtl., Bos.,	4	104	10	22	32	8	4	0	3	3	0		1932-33	1935-36
Riley, Jim	Det.	1	17	0	2	2	14	....	....	....	....	....		1926-27	1926-27
Riopellie, Howard	Mtl.	3	169	27	16	43	73	8	1	1	2	2		1947-48	1949-50
Rioux, Gerry	Wpg.	1	8	0	0	0	6	....	....	....	....	....		1979-80	1979-80
Rioux, Pierre	Cgy.	1	14	1	2	3	4	....	....	....	....	....		1982-83	1982-83
• Ripley, Vic	Chi., Bos., NYR, St.L.	7	278	51	49	100	173	20	4	1	5	10		1928-29	1934-35
Risebrough, Doug	Mtl., Cgy.	13	740	185	286	471	1542	124	21	37	58	238	4	1974-75	1986-87
Rissling, Gary	Wsh., Pit.	7	221	23	30	53	1008	5	0	1	1	4		1978-79	1984-85
Ritchie, Bob	Phi., Det.	2	29	8	4	12	10	....	....	....	....	....		1976-77	1977-78
• Ritchie, Dave	Mtl.W, Ott., Tor., Que., Mtl.	6	54	15	3	18	39	1	0	0	0	0		1917-18	1925-26
Ritson, Alex	NYR	1	1	0	0	0	0	....	....	....	....	....		1944-45	1944-45
Rittinger, Alan	Bos.	1	19	3	7	10	0	....	....	....	....	....		1943-44	1943-44
Rivard, Bob	Pit.	1	27	5	12	17	4	....	....	....	....	....		1967-68	1967-68
• Rivers, Gus	Mtl.	3	88	4	5	9	12	16	2	0	2	2	2	1929-30	1931-32
Rivers, Wayne	Det., Bos., St.L., NYR	7	108	15	30	45	94	....	....	....	....	....		1961-62	1968-69
Rizzuto, Garth	Van.	1	37	3	4	7	16	....	....	....	....	....		1970-71	1970-71
• Roach, Mickey	Tor., Ham., NYA	8	209	75	27	102	41	....	....	....	....	....		1919-20	1926-27
Roberge, Mario	Mtl.	5	112	7	7	14	314	15	0	0	0	24	1	1990-91	1994-95
Roberge, Serge	Que.	1	9	0	0	0	24	....	....	....	....	....		1990-91	1990-91
Robert, Claude	Mtl.	1	23	1	0	1	9	....	....	....	....	....		1950-51	1950-51
Robert, Rene	Tor., Pit., Buf., Col.	12	744	284	418	702	597	50	22	19	41	73		1970-71	1981-82
• Robert, Sammy	Ott.	1	1	0	0	0	0	....	....	....	....	....		1917-18	1917-18
Roberto, Phil	Mtl., St.L., Det., K.C., Col., Clev.	8	385	75	106	181	464	31	9	8	17	69	1	1969-70	1976-77
Roberts, Doug	Det., Dak., Cal., Bos.	10	419	43	104	147	342	16	2	3	5	46		1965-66	1974-75
Roberts, Gordie	Hfd., Min., Phi., St. L., Pit., Bos.	15	1097	61	359	420	1582	153	10	47	57	273	2	1979-80	1993-94
Roberts, Jim	Mtl., St.L.	15	1006	126	194	320	621	153	20	16	36	160	5	1963-64	1977-78
Roberts, Jimmy	Min.	3	106	17	23	40	33	2	0	0	0	0		1976-77	1978-79
Robertson, Fred	Tor., Det.,	2	34	1	0	1	35	7	0	0	0	0	1	1931-32	1933-34
Robertson, George	Mtl.	2	31	2	5	7	6	....	....	....	....	....		1947-48	1948-49
Robertson, Gordie	Buf.	1	5	1	2	3	7	....	....	....	....	....		1982-83	1982-83
Robertson, Torrie	Wsh., Hfd., Det.	10	442	49	99	148	1751	22	2	1	3	90		1980-81	1989-90
Robidoux, Florent	Chi.	3	52	7	4	11	75	....	....	....	....	....		1980-81	1983-84
Robinson, Doug	Chi., NYR, L.A.	7	239	44	67	111	34	11	4	3	7	0		1963-64	1970-71
Robinson, Earl	Mtl.M., Chi., Mtl.	11	417	83	98	181	133	25	5	4	9	0	1	1928-29	1939-40
Robinson, Larry	Mtl., L.A.	20	1384	208	750	958	793	227	28	116	144	211	6	1972-73	1991-92
Robinson, Moe	Mtl	1	1	0	0	0	0	....	....	....	....	....		1979-80	1979-80
Robinson, Rob	St.L.	1	22	0	1	1	8	....	....	....	....	....		1991-92	1991-92
Robinson, Scott	Min.	1	1	0	0	0	2	....	....	....	....	....		1989-90	1989-90
Robitaille, Mike	NYR, Det., Buf., Van.	8	382	23	105	128	280	13	0	1	1	4		1969-70	1976-77
• Roche, Earl	Mtl.M., Bos., Ott., St.L., Det.	4	147	25	27	52	48	2	0	0	0	0		1930-31	1934-35
Roche, Ernest	Mtl.	1	4	0	0	0	2	....	....	....	....	....		1950-51	1950-51
Roche, Michel	Mtl.M., Ott., St.L., Mtl., Det.	4	113	20	18	38	44	....	....	....	....	....		1930-31	1934-35
Rochefort, Dave	Det	1	1	0	0	0	0	....	....	....	....	....		1966-67	1966-67
Rochefort, Leon	NYR, Mtl., Phi., L.A., Det., Atl., Van.	15	617	121	147	268	93	39	4	4	8	16	2	1960-61	1975-76
Rockburn, Harvey	Det., Ott.	3	94	4	2	6	254	....	....	....	....	....		1929-30	1932-33
• Rodden, Eddie	Chi., Tor., Bos., NYR	4	98	6	14	20	152	2	0	1	1	0	1	1926-27	1930-31

Name	NHL Teams	NHL Seasons	Regular Schedule GP	G	A	TP	PIM	Playoffs GP	G	A	TP	PIM	NHL Cup Wins	First NHL Season	Last NHL Season
Rogers, Alfred (John)	Min.	2	14	2	4	6	0	....	....	....	....	....		1973-74	1974-75
Rogers, Mike	Hfd., NYR, Edm.	7	484	202	317	519	184	17	1	13	14	6		1979-80	1985-86
Rohlicek, Jeff	Van.	2	9	0	0	0	8	....	....	....	....	....		1987-88	1988-89
Rolfe, Dale	Bos., L.A., Det., NYR	9	509	25	125	150	556	71	5	24	29	89		1959-60	1974-75
Romanchych, Larry	Chi., Atl	6	298	68	97	165	102	7	2	2	4	4		1970-71	1976-77
Rombough, Doug	Buf., NYI, Min.	4	150	24	27	51	80	....	....	....	....	....		1972-73	1975-76
• Romnes, Doc	Chi., Tor., NYA	10	360	68	136	204	42	43	7	18	25	4	2	1930-31	1939-40
• Ronan, Skene	Ott.	1	11	0	0	0	0	....	....	....	....	....		1918-19	1918-19
Ronson, Len	NYR, Oak.	2	18	2	1	3	10	....	....	....	....	....		1960-61	1968-69
Ronty, Paul	Bos., NYR, Mtl.	8	488	101	211	312	103	21	1	7	8	6		1947-48	1954-55
Rooney, Steve	Mtl., Wpg., N.J.	5	154	15	13	28	496	25	3	2	5	86	1	1984-85	1988-89
Root, Bill	Mtl., Tor., St.L., Phi.	6	247	11	23	34	180	22	1	2	3	25		1982-83	1987-88
• Ross, Art	Mtl.W	1	3	1	0	1	0	....	....	....	....	....		1917-18	1917-18
Ross, Jim	NYR	2	62	2	11	13	29	....	....	....	....	....		1951-52	1952-53
Rossignol, Roland	Det., Mtl.	3	14	3	5	8	6	1	0	0	0	2		1943-44	1945-46
Rota, Darcy	Chi., Atl., Van.	11	794	256	239	495	973	60	14	7	21	147		1973-74	1983-84
Rota, Randy	Mtl., L.A., K.C., Col.	5	212	38	39	77	60	5	0	1	1	0		1972-73	1976-77
• Rothschild, Sam	Mtl.M., NYA	4	92	8	6	14	24	10	0	0	0	0	1	1924-25	1927-28
• Roulston, Rolly	Det.	3	24	0	6	6	10	....	....	....	....	....		1935-36	1937-38
Roulston, Tom	Edm., Pit.	5	195	47	49	96	74	21	2	2	4	2		1980-81	1985-86
Roupe, Magnus	Phi.	2	40	3	5	8	42	....	....	....	....	....		1987-88	1988-89
Rousseau, Bobby	Mtl., Min., NYR	15	942	245	458	703	359	128	27	57	84	69	4	1960-61	1974-75
Rousseau, Guy	Mtl.	2	4	0	1	1	0	....	....	....	....	....		1954-55	1956-57
Rousseau, Roland	Mtl.	1	2	0	0	0	0	....	....	....	....	....		1952-53	1952-53
Routhier, Jean-Marc	Que.	1	8	0	0	0	9	....	....	....	....	....		1989-90	1989-90
Rowe, Bobby	Bos.	1	4	1	0	1	0	....	....	....	....	....		1924-25	1924-25
Rowe, Mike	Pit.	3	11	0	0	0	11	....	....	....	....	....		1984-85	1986-87
Rowe, Ron	NYR	1	5	1	0	1	0	....	....	....	....	....		1947-48	1947-48
Rowe, Tom	Wsh., Hfd., Det.	7	357	85	100	185	615	3	2	0	2	0		1976-77	1982-83
Roy, Stephane	Min.	1	12	1	0	1	0	....	....	....	....	....		1987-88	1987-88
Rozzini, Gino	Bos.	1	31	5	10	15	20	6	1	2	3	6		1944-45	1944-45
Rucinski, Mike	Chi.	2	1	0	0	0	0	2	0	0	0	0		1987-88	1988-89
Ruelle, Bernard	Det.	1	2	1	0	1	0	....	....	....	....	....		1943-44	1943-44
Ruff, Lindy	Buf., NYR	12	691	105	195	300	1264	52	11	13	24	193		1979-80	1990-91
Ruhnke, Kent	Bos.	1	2	0	1	1	0	....	....	....	....	....		1975-76	1975-76
Rundqvist, Thomas	Mtl.	1	2	0	1	1	0	....	....	....	....	....		1984-85	1984-85
• Runge, Paul	Bos., Mtl.M., Mtl.	7	140	18	22	40	57	7	0	0	0	6		1930-31	1937-38
Ruotsalainen, Reijo	NYR, Edm., N.J.	7	446	107	237	344	180	86	15	32	47	44	2	1981-82	1989-90
Rupp, Duane	NYR, Tor., Min., Pit.	10	374	24	93	117	220	10	2	2	4	8		1962-63	1972-73
Ruskowski, Terry	Chi., L.A., Pit., Min.	10	630	113	313	426	1354	21	1	6	7	86		1979-80	1988-89
• Russell, Churchill	NYR	3	90	20	16	36	12	....	....	....	....	....		1945-46	1947-48
Russell, Phil	Chi., Atl., Cgy., N.J., Buf.	15	1016	99	325	424	2038	73	4	22	26	202		1972-73	1986-87
Ruzicka, Vladimir	Edm., Bos., Ott.	5	233	82	85	167	129	30	4	14	18	2		1989-90	1993-94
Rymsha, Andy	Que.	1	6	0	0	0	23	....	....	....	....	....		1991-92	1991-92
S															
Saarinen, Simo	NYR	1	8	0	0	0	0	....	....	....	....	....		1984-85	1984-85
Sabol, Shaun	Phi.	1	2	0	0	0	0	....	....	....	....	....		1989-90	1989-90
Sabourin, Bob	Tor.	1	1	0	0	0	2	....	....	....	....	....		1951-52	1951-52
Sabourin, Gary	St.L., Tor., Cal., Clev.	10	627	169	188	357	397	62	19	11	30	58		1967-68	1976-77
Sabourin, Ken	Cgy., Wsh.	4	74	2	8	10	201	12	0	0	0	34	1	1988-89	1991-92
Sacharuk, Larry	NYR, St.L.	5	151	29	33	62	42	2	1	1	2	2		1972-73	1976-77
Saganiuk, Rocky	Tor., Pit.	6	259	57	65	122	201	6	1	0	1	15		1978-79	1983-84
St. Amour, Martin	Ott.	1	1	0	0	0	2	....	....	....	....	....		1992-93	1992-93
St. Laurent, Andre	NYI, Det., L.A., Pit.	11	644	129	187	316	749	59	8	12	20	48		1973-74	1983-84
St. Laurent, Dollard	Mtl., Chi.	12	652	29	133	162	496	92	2	22	24	87	5	1950-51	1961-62
St. Marseille, Frank	St.L., L.A.	10	707	140	285	425	242	88	20	25	45	18		1967-68	1976-77
St. Sauveur, Claude	Atl.	1	79	24	24	48	23	2	0	0	0	0		1975-76	1975-76
Saleski, Don	Phi., Col.	9	543	128	125	253	629	82	13	17	30	131	2	1971-72	1979-80
Salming, Borje	Tor., Det.	17	1148	150	637	787	1344	81	12	37	49	91		1973-74	1989-90
Salovaara, John Barry	Det.	2	90	2	13	15	70	....	....	....	....	....		1974-75	1975-76
Salvian, Dave	NYI	1	....	....	....	....	....	1	0	1	1	2		1976-77	1976-77
Samis, Phil	Tor.	2	2	0	0	0	0	5	0	1	1	2	1	1947-48	1949-50
Sampson, Gary	Wsh.	4	105	13	22	35	25	12	1	0	1	0		1983-84	1986-87
Sandelin, Scott	Mtl., Phi., Min.	4	25	0	4	4	2	....	....	....	....	....		1986-87	1991-92
Sanderson, Derek	Bos., NYR, St.L., Van., Pit.	13	598	202	250	452	911	56	18	12	30	187	2	1965-66	1977-78
Sandford, Ed	Bos., Det., Chi.	9	502	106	145	251	355	42	13	11	24	27		1947-48	1955-56
• Sands, Charlie	Tor., Bos., Mtl., NYR	12	427	99	109	208	58	33	6	6	12	4	1	1932-33	1943-44
Sanipass, Everett	Chi., Que.	5	164	25	34	59	358	5	2	0	2	4		1986-87	1990-91
Sargent, Gary	L.A., Min.	8	402	61	161	222	273	20	5	7	12	8		1975-76	1982-83
Sarner, Craig	Bos.	1	7	0	0	0	0	....	....	....	....	....		1974-75	1974-75
Sarrazin, Dick	Phi.	3	100	20	35	55	22	4	0	0	0	0		1968-69	1971-72
Saskamoose, Fred	Chi.	1	11	0	0	0	6	....	....	....	....	....		1953-54	1953-54
Sasser, Grant	Pit.	1	3	0	0	0	0	....	....	....	....	....		1983-84	1983-84
Sather, Glen	Bos., Pit., NYR, St.L., Mtl., Min.	10	658	80	113	193	724	72	1	5	6	86		1966-67	1975-76
Saunders, Bernie	Que.	2	10	0	1	1	8	....	....	....	....	....		1979-80	1980-81
Saunders, Bud	Ott.	1	18	1	3	4	4	....	....	....	....	....		1933-34	1933-34
Saunders, David	Van.	1	56	7	13	20	10	....	....	....	....	....		1987-88	1987-88
Sauve, Jean-Francois	Buf., Que.	7	290	65	138	203	117	36	9	12	21	10		1980-81	1986-87
Savage, Joel	Buf.	1	3	0	1	1	0	....	....	....	....	....		1990-91	1990-91
• Savage, Tony	Bos., Mtl.	1	49	1	5	6	6	2	0	0	0	0		1934-35	1934-35
Savard, Andre	Bos., Buf., Que.	12	790	211	271	482	411	85	13	18	31	77		1973-74	1984-85
Savard, Jean	Chi, Hfd.	3	43	7	12	19	29	....	....	....	....	....		1977-78	1979-80
Savard, Serge	Mtl., Wpg.	17	1040	106	333	439	592	130	19	49	68	88	7	1966-67	1982-83
Scamurra, Peter	Wsh.	4	132	8	25	33	59	....	....	....	....	....		1975-76	1979-80
Sceviour, Darin	Chi.	1	1	0	0	0	0	....	....	....	....	....		1986-87	1986-87
Schaeffer, Butch	Chi.,	1	5	0	0	0	6	....	....	....	....	....		1936-37	1936-37
Schamehorn, Kevin	Det., L.A.	3	10	0	0	0	17	....	....	....	....	....		1976-77	1980-81
Schella, John	Van.	2	115	2	18	20	224	....	....	....	....	....		1970-71	1971-72
Scherza, Chuck	Bos., NYR	2	56	6	6	12	35	....	....	....	....	....		1943-44	1944-45
Schinkel, Ken	NYR, Pit.	12	636	127	198	325	163	19	7	2	9	4		1959-60	1972-73
Schlegel, Brad	Wsh., Cgy.	3	48	1	8	9	10	7	0	1	1	2		1991-92	1993-94
Schliebener, Andy	Van.	3	84	2	11	13	74	6	0	0	0	0		1981-82	1984-85
Schmautz, Bobby	Chi., Bos., Edm., Col., Van.	13	764	271	286	557	988	84	28	33	61	92		1967-68	1980-81
Schmautz, Cliff	Buf., Phi.	1	56	13	19	32	33	....	....	....	....	....		1970-71	1970-71
Schmidt, Clarence	Bos.,	1	7	1	0	1	2	....	....	....	....	....		1943-44	1943-44
Schmidt, Jackie	Bos.	1	45	6	7	13	6	5	0	0	0	0		1942-43	1942-43
Schmidt, Joseph	Bos.	1	2	0	0	0	0	....	....	....	....	....		1943-44	1943-44
Schmidt, Milt	Bos.	16	776	229	346	575	466	86	24	25	49	60	2	1936-37	1954-55
Schmidt, Norm	Pit.	4	125	23	33	56	73	....	....	....	....	....		1983-84	1987-88
Schnarr, Werner	Bos.	2	25	0	0	0	0	....	....	....	....	....		1924-25	1925-26
Schock, Danny	Bos., Phi.	2	20	1	2	3	0	1	0	0	0	0	1	1969-70	1970-71
Schock, Ron	Bos., St.L., Pit., Buf.	15	909	166	351	517	261	55	4	16	20	29		1963-64	1977-78
Schoenfeld, Jim	Buf., Det., Bos.	13	719	51	204	255	1132	75	3	13	16	151		1972-73	1984-85
Schofield, Dwight	Det., Mtl., St.L., Wsh., Pit., Wpg.	7	211	8	22	30	631	9	0	0	0	55		1976-77	1987-88
Schreiber, Wally	Min.	2	41	8	10	18	12	....	....	....	....	....		1987-88	1988-89
• Schriner, Sweeney	NYA, Tor.	11	484	201	204	405	148	59	18	11	29	54	2	1934-35	1945-46
Schultz, Dave	Phi., L.A., Pit., Buf.	9	535	79	121	200	2294	73	8	12	20	412	2	1971-72	1979-80
Schurman, Maynard	Hfd.	1	7	0	0	0	0	....	....	....	....	....		1979-80	1979-80
Schutt, Rod	Mtl., Pit., Tor.	8	286	77	92	169	177	22	8	6	14	26		1977-78	1985-86
Scissons, Scott	NYI	3	2	0	0	0	0	1	0	0	0	0		1990-91	1993-94
Sclisizzi, Enio	Det., Chi.	6	81	12	11	23	26	13	0	0	0	6		1946-47	1952-53
Scott, Ganton	Tor., Ham., Mtl.M.	3	53	1	1	2	0	....	....	....	....	....		1922-23	1924-25
• Scott, Laurie	NYA, NYR	2	62	6	3	9	28	....	....	....	....	....	1	1926-27	1927-28
Scremin, Claudio	S.J.	2	17	0	1	1	29	....	....	....	....	....		1991-92	1992-93
Scruton, Howard	L.A.	1	4	0	4	4	9	....	....	....	....	....		1982-83	1982-83
Seabrooke, Glen	Phi.	3	19	1	6	7	4	....	....	....	....	....		1986-87	1988-89
Secord, Al	Bos., Chi., Tor, Phi.	12	766	273	222	495	2093	102	21	34	55	382		1978-79	1989-90
Sedlbauer, Ron	Van., Chi., Tor.	7	430	143	86	229	210	19	1	3	4	27		1974-75	1980-81
Seftel, Steve	Wsh.	1	4	0	0	0	2	....	....	....	....	....		1990-91	1990-91
Seguin, Dan	Min., Van.	2	37	2	6	8	50	....	....	....	....	....		1970-71	1973-74
Seguin, Steve	L.A.	1	5	0	0	0	9	....	....	....	....	....		1984-85	1984-85
• Seibert, Earl	NYR, Chi., Det.	15	645	89	184	273	683	65	9	8	17	76	2	1931-32	1945-46

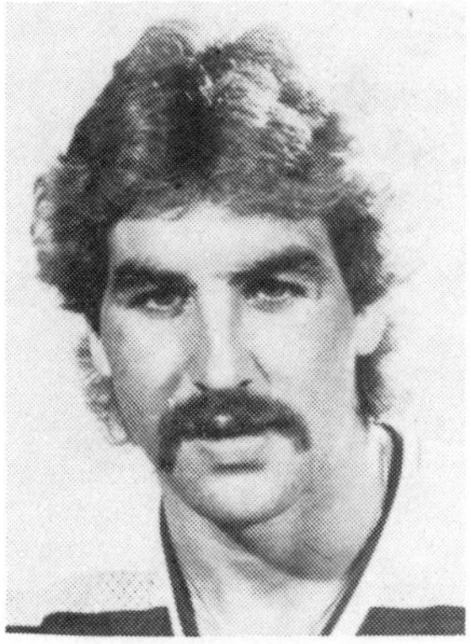

Gordie Roberts

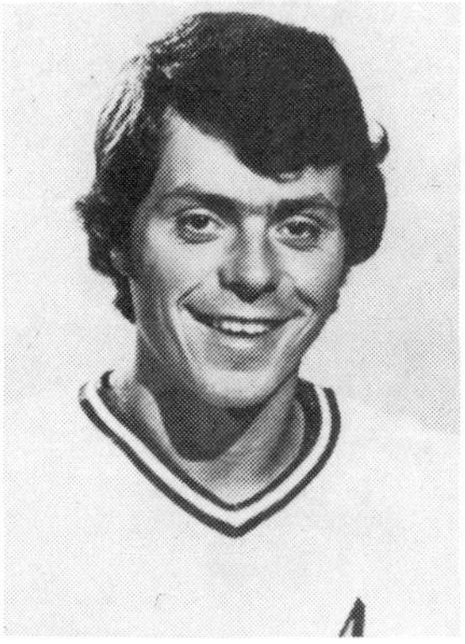

Jimmy Roberts

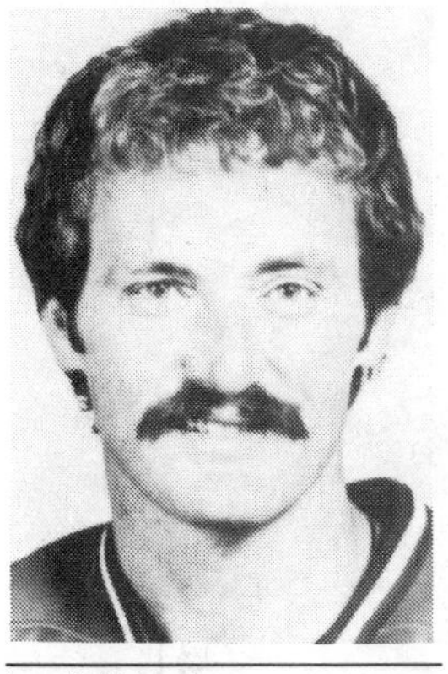

Larry Robinson

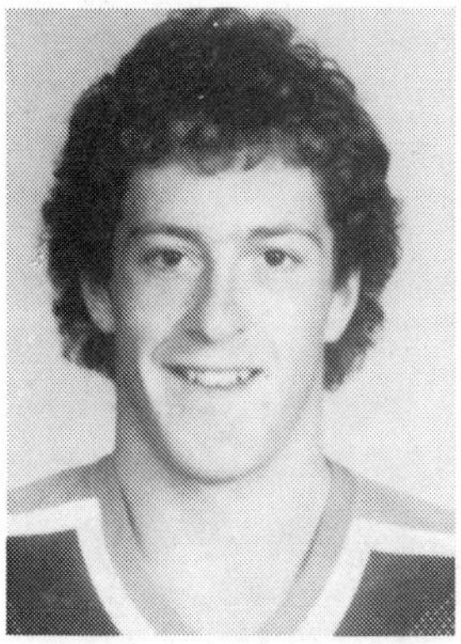

Tom Roulston

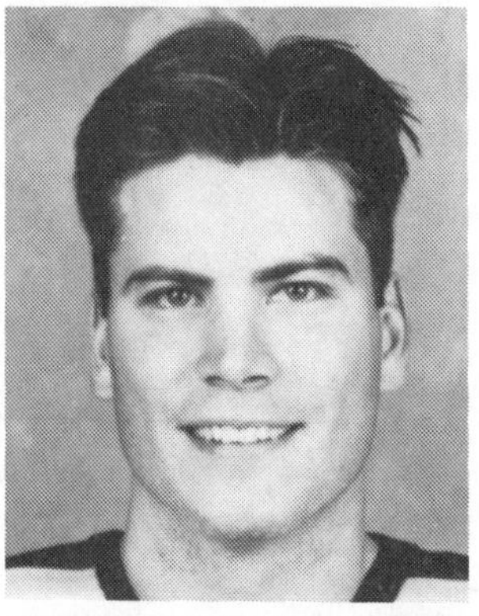

Craig Simpson

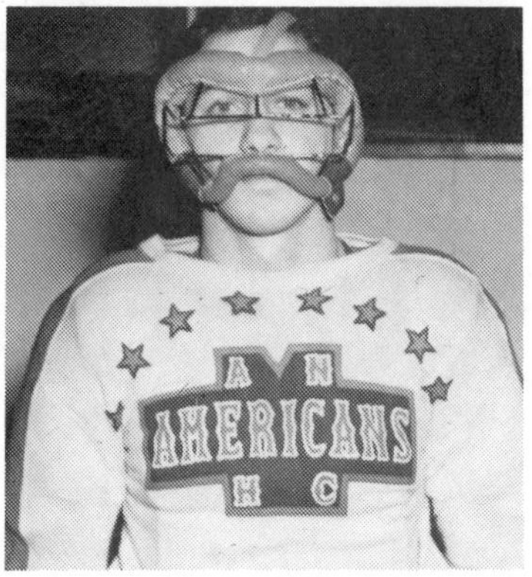

Peter Slobodzian

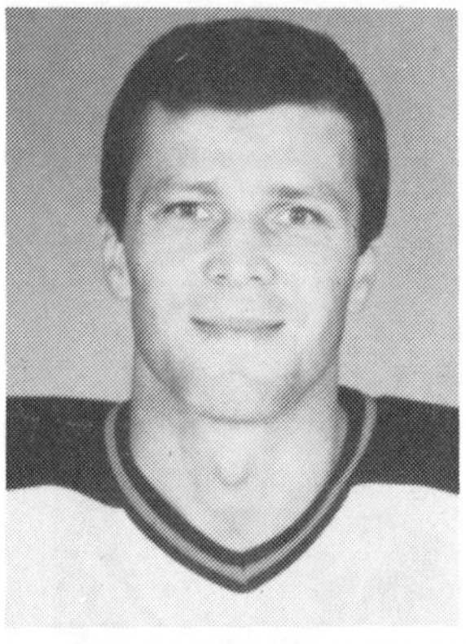

Peter Stastny

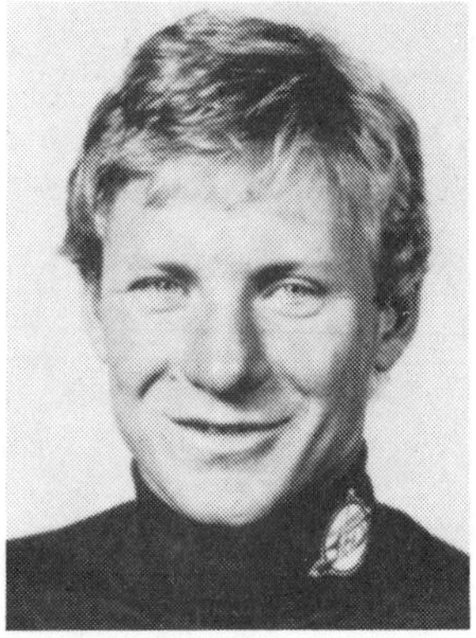

Thomas Steen

Name	NHL Teams	NHL Seasons	Regular Schedule					Playoffs					NHL Cup Wins	First NHL Season	Last NHL Season
			GP	G	A	TP	PIM	GP	G	A	TP	PIM			
Seiling, Ric	Buf., Det.	10	738	179	208	387	573	62	14	14	28	36		1977-78	1986-87
Seiling, Rod	Tor., NYR, Wsh., St.L., Atl.	17	979	62	269	331	601	77	4	8	12	55		1962-63	1978-79
Sejba, Jiri	Buf.	1	11	0	2	2	8	....	....	....	....	....		1990-91	1990-91
Selby, Brit	Tor., Phi., St.L.	8	350	55	62	117	163	16	1	1	2	8		1964-65	1971-72
Self, Steve	Wsh.	1	3	0	0	0	0	....	....	....	....	....		1976-77	1976-77
Selwood, Brad	Tor., L.A.	3	163	7	40	47	153	6	0	0	0	4		1970-71	1979-80
Semchuk, Brandy	L.A.	1	1	0	0	0	2	....	....	....	....	....		1992-93	1992-93
Semenko, Dave	Edm., Hfd., Tor.	9	575	65	88	153	1175	73	6	6	12	208	2	1979-80	1987-88
Senick, George	NYR	1	13	2	3	5	8	....	....	....	....	....		1952-53	1952-53
Seppa, Jyrki	Wpg.	1	13	0	2	2	6	....	....	....	....	....		1983-84	1983-84
Serafini, Ron	Cal.	1	2	0	0	0	2	....	....	....	....	....		1973-74	1973-74
Servinis, George	Min.	1	5	0	0	0	0	....	....	....	....	....		1987-88	1987-88
Sevcik, Jaroslav	Que.	1	13	0	2	2	2	....	....	....	....	....		1989-90	1989-90
Shack, Eddie	NYR, Tor., Bos., L.A., Buf., Pit.	17	1047	239	226	465	1437	74	6	7	13	151	4	1958-59	1974-75
• Shack, Joe	NYR	2	70	23	13	36	20	....	....	....	....	....		1942-43	1944-45
Shakes, Paul	Cal.	1	21	0	4	4	12	....	....	....	....	....		1973-74	1973-74
Shanahan, Sean	Mtl., Col., Bos.	3	40	1	3	4	47	....	....	....	....	....		1975-76	1977-78
Shand, Dave	Atl., Tor., Wsh.	8	421	19	84	103	544	26	1	2	3	83		1976-77	1984-85
Shannon, Charles	NYA	1	4	0	0	0	2	....	....	....	....	....		1939-40	1939-40
• Shannon, Gerry	Ott., St.L., Bos., Mtl.M.	5	180	23	29	52	80	9	0	1	1	2		1933-34	1937-38
Sharples, Jeff	Det.	3	105	14	35	49	70	7	0	3	3	6		1986-87	1988-89
Sharpley, Glen	Min., Chi.	6	389	117	161	278	199	27	7	11	18	24		1976-77	1981-82
Shaunessy, Scott	Que.	2	7	0	0	0	23	....	....	....	....	....		1986-87	1988-89
Shay, Norman	Bos., Tor.	2	53	5	2	7	34	....	....	....	....	....		1924-25	1925-26
Shea, Pat	Chi.	1	14	0	1	1	0	....	....	....	....	....		1931-32	1931-32
Shedden, Doug	Pit., Det., Que., Tor.	8	416	139	186	325	176	....	....	....	....	....		1981-82	1990-91
Sheehan, Bobby	Mtl., Cal., Chi., Det., NYR, Col., L.A.	9	310	48	63	111	50	25	4	3	7	8	1	1969-70	1981-82
Sheehy, Neil	Cgy., Hfd., Wsh.	9	379	18	47	65	1311	54	0	3	3	241		1983-84	1991-92
Sheehy, Tim	Det., Hfd.	2	27	2	1	3	0	....	....	....	....	....		1977-78	1979-80
Shelton, Doug	Chi.	1	5	0	1	1	2	....	....	....	....	....		1967-68	1967-68
Sheppard, Frank	Det.	1	8	1	1	2	0	....	....	....	....	....		1927-28	1927-28
Sheppard, Gregg	Bos., Pit.	10	657	205	293	498	243	82	32	40	72	31		1972-73	1981-82
Sheppard, Johnny	Det., NYA, Bos., Chi.	8	311	68	58	126	224	10	0	0	0	0	1	1926-27	1933-34
Sherf, John	Det.	5	19	0	0	0	8	8	0	1	1	2	1	1935-36	1943-44
• Shero, Fred	NYR	3	145	6	14	20	137	13	0	2	2	8		1947-48	1949-50
Sherritt, Gordon	Det.	1	8	0	0	0	12	....	....	....	....	....		1943-44	1943-44
Sherven, Gord	Edm., Min., Hfd.	5	97	13	22	35	33	3	0	0	0	0		1983-84	1987-88
• Shewchuck, Jack	Bos.	6	187	9	19	28	160	20	0	1	1	19	1	1938-39	1944-45
Shibicky, Alex	NYR	8	322	110	91	201	161	39	12	12	24	12	1	1935-36	1945-46
• Shields, Al	Ott., Phi., NYA, Mtl.M., Bos.	11	460	42	46	88	637	15	0	1	1	14	1	1927-28	1937-38
Shill, Bill	Bos.	3	79	21	13	34	18	7	1	2	3	2		1942-43	1946-47
• Shill, Jack	Tor., Bos., NYA, Chi.	6	163	15	20	35	70	27	1	6	7	13	1	1933-34	1938-39
Shinske, Rick	Clev., St.L.	3	63	5	16	21	10	....	....	....	....	....		1976-77	1978-79
Shires, Jim	Det., St.L., Pit.	3	56	3	6	9	32	....	....	....	....	....		1970-71	1972-73
Shmyr, Paul	Chi., Cal., Min., Hfd.	7	343	13	72	85	528	34	3	3	6	44		1968-69	1981-82
Shoebottom, Bruce	Bos.	4	35	1	4	5	53	14	1	2	3	77		1987-88	1990-91
• Shore, Eddie	Bos., NYA	14	553	105	179	284	1047	55	6	13	19	179	2	1926-27	1939-40
• Shore, Hamby	Ott.	1	18	3	0	3	17	....	....	....	....	....		1917-18	1917-18
Shores, Aubrey	Phi.	1	1	0	0	0	0	....	....	....	....	....		1930-31	1930-31
Short, Steve	L.A., Det.	2	6	0	0	0	2	....	....	....	....	....		1977-78	1978-79
Shudra, Ron	Edm.	1	10	0	5	5	6	....	....	....	....	....		1987-88	1987-88
Shutt, Steve	Mtl., L.A.	13	930	424	393	817	410	99	50	48	98	65	5	1972-73	1984-85
• Siebert, Babe	Mtl.M., NYR, Bos., Mtl.	14	596	140	156	296	982	53	8	7	15	64	2	1925-26	1938-39
Silk, Dave	NYR, Bos., Wpg., Det.	7	249	54	59	113	271	13	2	4	6	13		1979-80	1985-86
Siltala, Mike	Wsh., NYR	3	7	1	0	1	2	....	....	....	....	....		1981-82	1987-88
Siltanen, Risto	Edm., Hfd., Que.	8	562	90	265	355	266	32	6	12	18	30		1979-80	1986-87
Sim, Trevor	Edm.	1	3	0	1	1	2	....	....	....	....	....		1989-90	1989-90
Simard, Martin	Cgy., T.B.	3	44	1	5	6	183	....	....	....	....	....		1990-91	1992-93
Simmer, Charlie	Cal., Cle., L.A., Bos., Pit.	14	712	342	369	711	554	24	9	9	18	32		1974-75	1987-88
Simmons, Al	Cal., Bos.	3	11	0	1	1	21	1	0	0	0	0		1971-72	1975-76
Simon, Cully	Det., Chi.	3	130	4	11	15	121	14	0	1	1	6	1	1942-43	1944-45
Simon, Thain	Det.	1	3	0	0	0	0	....	....	....	....	....		1946-47	1946-47
Simonetti, Frank	Bos.	4	115	5	8	13	76	12	0	1	1	8		1984-85	1987-88
Simpson, Bobby	Atl., St.L., Pit.	5	175	35	29	64	98	6	0	1	1	2		1976-77	1982-83
• Simpson, Cliff	Det.	2	6	0	1	1	0	2	0	0	0	2		1946-47	1947-48
Simpson, Craig	Pit., Edm., Buf.	10	634	247	250	497	659	67	36	32	68	56	2	1985-86	1994-95
• Simpson, Joe	NYA	6	228	21	19	40	156	2	0	0	0	0		1925-26	1930-31
Sims, Al	Bos., Hfd., L.A.	10	475	49	116	165	286	41	0	2	2	14		1973-74	1982-83
Sinclair, Reg	NYR, Det.	3	208	49	43	92	139	3	1	0	1	0		1950-51	1952-53
Singbush, Alex	Mtl.	1	32	0	5	5	15	3	0	0	0	4		1940-41	1940-41
Sinisalo, Ilkka	Phi., Min., L.A.	11	582	204	222	426	208	68	21	11	32	6		1981-82	1991-92
Siren, Ville	Pit., Min.	5	290	14	68	82	276	7	0	0	0	6		1985-86	1989-90
Sirois, Bob	Phi., Wsh.	6	286	92	120	212	42	....	....	....	....	....		1974-75	1979-80
Sittler, Darryl	Tor., Phi., Det.	15	1096	484	637	1121	948	76	29	45	74	137		1970-71	1984-85
• Sjoberg, Lars-Erik	Wpg.	1	79	7	27	34	48	....	....	....	....	....		1979-80	1979-80
Sjodin, Tommy	Min., Dal., Que.	2	106	8	40	48	52	....	....	....	....	....		1992-93	1993-94
• Skaare, Bjorne	Det.	1	1	0	0	0	0	....	....	....	....	....		1978-79	1978-79
Skarda, Randy	St. L.	2	26	0	5	5	11	....	....	....	....	....		1989-90	1991-92
• Skilton, Raymie	Mtl.W	1	1	1	0	1	0	....	....	....	....	....		1917-18	1917-18
• Skinner, Alf	Tor., Bos., Mtl.M., Pit.	4	70	26	4	30	76	7	8	1	9	0	1	1917-18	1925-26
Skinner, Larry	Col.	4	47	10	12	22	8	2	0	0	0	0		1976-77	1979-80
Skov, Glen	Det., Chi., Mtl.	12	650	106	136	242	413	53	7	7	14	48	3	1949-50	1960-61
Skriko, Petri	Van., Bos., Wpg., S.J.	9	541	183	222	405	246	28	5	9	14	4		1984-85	1992-93
Sleaver, John	Chi.	2	13	1	0	1	6	....	....	....	....	....		1953-54	1956-57
Sleigher, Louis	Que., Bos.	6	194	46	53	99	146	17	1	1	2	64		1979-80	1985-86
Sloan, Tod	Tor., Chi.	13	745	220	262	482	831	47	9	12	21	47	2	1947-48	1960-61
• Slobodzian, Peter	NYA	1	41	3	2	5	54	....	....	....	....	....		1940-41	1940-41
Slowinski, Eddie	NYR	6	291	58	74	132	63	16	2	6	8	6		1947-48	1952-53
Sly, Darryl	Tor., Min., Van.	4	79	1	2	3	20	....	....	....	....	....		1965-66	1970-71
Smail, Doug	Wpg., Min., Que., Ott.	13	845	210	249	459	602	42	9	2	11	49		1980-81	1992-93
Smart, Alex	Mtl.	1	8	5	2	7	0	....	....	....	....	....		1942-43	1942-43
Smedsmo, Dale	Tor.	1	4	0	0	0	0	....	....	....	....	....		1972-73	1972-73
Smillie, Don	Bos.	1	12	2	2	4	4	....	....	....	....	....		1933-34	1933-34
• Smith, Alex	Ott., Det., Bos., NYA	11	443	41	50	91	643	19	0	2	2	40	1	1924-25	1934-35
• Smith, Arthur	Tor., Ott.	4	144	15	10	25	249	4	1	1	2	8		1927-28	1930-31
Smith, Barry	Bos., Col.	3	114	7	7	14	10	....	....	....	....	....		1975-76	1980-81
Smith, Bobby	Min., Mtl.	15	1077	357	679	1036	917	184	64	96	160	245	1	1978-79	1992-93
Smith, Brad	Van., Atl., Cgy., Det., Tor.	9	222	28	34	62	591	20	3	3	6	49		1978-79	1986-87
• Smith, Brian D.	L.A., Min.	2	67	10	10	20	33	7	0	0	0	0		1967-68	1968-69
Smith, Brian S.	Det.	3	61	2	8	10	12	5	0	0	0	0		1957-58	1960-61
Smith, Carl	Det.	1	7	1	1	2	2	....	....	....	....	....		1943-44	1943-44
Smith, Clint	NYR, Chi.	11	483	161	236	397	24	42	10	14	24	2	1	1936-37	1946-47
Smith, Dallas	Bos., NYR	16	890	55	252	307	959	86	3	29	32	128	2	1959-60	1977-78
Smith, Dalton	NYA, Det.	1	10	1	2	3	0	....	....	....	....	....		1936-37	1943-44
Smith, Dennis	Wsh., L.A.	2	8	0	0	0	4	....	....	....	....	....		1989-90	1990-91
Smith, Derek	Buf., Det.	8	335	78	116	194	60	30	9	14	23	13		1975-76	1982-83
Smith, Des	Mtl.M., Mtl., Chi., Bos.	5	196	22	25	47	236	25	1	4	5	18	1	1937-38	1941-42
• Smith, Don	Mtl.	1	10	1	0	1	4	....	....	....	....	....		1919-20	1919-20
Smith, Don A.	NYR	1	11	1	1	2	0	1	0	0	0	0		1949-50	1949-50
Smith, Doug	L.A., Buf., Edm., Van., Pit.	9	535	115	138	253	624	18	4	2	6	21		1981-82	1989-90
Smith, Floyd	Bos., NYR, Det., Tor., Buf.	13	616	129	178	307	207	48	12	11	23	16		1954-55	1971-72
Smith, George	Tor.	1	9	0	0	0	0	....	....	....	....	....		1921-22	1921-22
Smith, Glen	Chi.	1	2	0	0	0	0	....	....	....	....	....		1950-51	1950-51
Smith, Glenn	Tor.	1	9	0	0	0	0	....	....	....	....	....		1922-23	1922-23
Smith, Gord	Wsh., Wpg.	6	299	9	30	39	284	....	....	....	....	....		1974-75	1979-80
Smith, Greg	Cal., Clev., Min., Det., Wsh.	13	829	56	232	288	1110	63	4	7	11	106		1975-76	1987-88
• Smith, Hooley	Ott., Mtl.M., Bos., NYA	17	715	200	215	415	1013	54	11	8	19	109	2	1924-25	1940-41
Smith, Kenny	Bos.	7	331	78	93	171	49	30	8	13	21	6		1944-45	1950-51
Smith, Randy	Min.	2	3	0	0	0	0	....	....	....	....	....		1985-86	1986-87
Smith, Rick	Bos., Cal., St.L., Det., Wsh.	11	687	52	167	219	560	78	3	23	26	73	1	1968-69	1980-81
• Smith, Roger	Pit., Phi.	6	210	20	4	24	172	4	3	0	3	0		1925-26	1930-31
Smith, Ron	NYI	1	11	1	1	2	14	....	....	....	....	....		1972-73	1972-73
Smith, Sid	Tor.	12	601	186	183	369	94	44	17	10	27	2	3	1946-47	1957-58
Smith, Stan	NYR	2	9	2	1	3	0	....	....	....	....	....		1939-40	1940-41

Name	NHL Teams	NHL Seasons	Regular Schedule GP	G	A	TP	PIM	Playoffs GP	G	A	TP	PIM	NHL Cup Wins	First NHL Season	Last NHL Season
Smith, Steve	Phi., Buf.	6	18	0	1	1	15	....	....	....	....	....		1981-82	1988-89
Smith, Stu E.	Mtl.	2	17	2	2	4	2	1	0	0	0	0		1940-41	1941-42
Smith, Stu G.	Hfd.	4	77	2	10	12	95	....	....	....	....	....		1979-80	1982-83
• Smith, Tommy	Que.B.	1	10	0	0	0	9	....	....	....	....	....		1919-20	1919-20
Smith, Vern	NYI	1	1	0	0	0	0	....	....	....	....	....		1984-85	1984-85
Smith, Wayne	Chi.	1	2	1	1	2	2	1	0	0	0	0		1966-67	1966-67
Smrke, John	St.L., Que.	3	103	11	17	28	33	....	....	....	....	....		1977-78	1979-80
• Smrke, Stan	Mtl.	2	9	0	3	3	0	....	....	....	....	....		1956-57	1957-58
Smyl, Stan	Van.	13	896	262	411	673	1556	41	16	17	33	64		1978-79	1990-91
• Smylie, Rod	Tor., Ott.	6	76	3	1	4	10	9	1	2	3	2	1	1920-21	1925-26
Snell, Ron	Pit.	2	7	3	2	5	6	....	....	....	....	....		1968-69	1969-70
Snell, Ted	Pit., K.C., Det.	2	104	7	18	25	32	....	....	....	....	....		1973-74	1974-75
Snepsts, Harold	Van., Min., Det., St.L.	17	1033	38	195	233	2009	93	1	14	15	231		1974-75	1990-91
Snow, Sandy	Det.	1	3	0	0	0	2	....	....	....	....	....		1968-69	1968-69
Snuggerud, Dave	Buf., S.J., Phi.	4	265	30	54	84	127	12	1	3	4	6		1989-90	1992-93
Sobchuk, Dennis	Det., Que.	1	33	4	6	10	0	....	....	....	....	....		1979-80	1982-83
Sobchuk, Gene	Van.	1	1	0	0	0	0	....	....	....	....	....		1973-74	1973-74
Solheim, Ken	Chi., Min., Det., Edm.	5	135	19	20	39	34	3	1	1	2	2		1980-81	1985-86
Solinger, Bob	Tor., Det.	5	99	10	11	21	19	....	....	....	....	....		1951-52	1959-60
• Somers, Art	Chi., NYR	6	222	33	56	89	189	30	1	5	6	20	1	1929-30	1934-35
Sommer, Roy	Edm.	1	3	1	0	1	7	....	....	....	....	....		1980-81	1980-81
Songin, Tom	Bos.	3	43	5	5	10	22	....	....	....	....	....		1978-79	1980-81
Sonmor, Glen	NYR	2	28	2	0	2	21	....	....	....	....	....		1953-54	1954-55
• Sorrell, John	Det., NYA	11	490	127	119	246	100	42	12	15	27	10	2	1930-31	1940-41
Sparrow, Emory	Bos.	1	6	0	0	0	4	....	....	....	....	....		1924-25	1924-25
Speck, Fred	Det., Van.	3	28	1	2	3	2	....	....	....	....	....		1968-69	1971-72
• Speer, Bill	Pit., Bos.	4	130	5	20	25	79	8	1	0	1	4	1	1967-68	1970-71
Speers, Ted	Det.	1	4	1	1	2	0	....	....	....	....	....		1985-86	1985-86
• Spencer, Brian	Tor., NYI, Buf., Pit.	10	553	80	143	223	634	37	1	5	6	29		1969-70	1978-79
Spencer, Irv	NYR, Bos., Det.	8	230	12	38	50	127	16	0	0	0	8		1959-60	1967-68
Speyer, Chris	Tor., NYA	3	14	0	0	0	0	....	....	....	....	....		1923-24	1933-34
Spring, Don	Wpg.	4	259	1	54	55	80	6	0	0	0	4		1980-81	1983-84
Spring, Frank	Bos., St.L., Cal., Clev.	5	61	14	20	34	12	....	....	....	....	....		1969-70	1976-77
• Spring, Jesse	Ham., Pit., Tor., NYA	6	162	11	2	13	62	2	0	2	2	2		1923-24	1929-30
Spruce, Andy	Van., Col.	3	172	31	42	73	111	2	0	2	2	0		1976-77	1978-79
Srsen, Tomas	Edm.	1	2	0	0	0	0	....	....	....	....	....		1990-91	1990-91
Stackhouse, Ron	Cal., Det., Pit.	12	889	87	372	459	824	32	5	8	13	38		1970-71	1981-82
Stackhouse, Ted	Tor.	1	12	0	0	0	2	5	0	0	0	0	1	1921-22	1921-22
Stahan, Butch	Mtl.	1	....	....	....	....	....	3	0	1	1	2		1944-45	1944-45
Staley, Al	NYR	2	11	0	3	3	11	....	....	....	....	....		1948-49	1948-49
Stamler, Lorne	L.A., Tor., Wpg.	4	116	14	11	25	16	....	....	....	....	....		1976-77	1979-80
Standing, George	Min.	1	2	0	0	0	0	....	....	....	....	....		1967-68	1967-68
Stanfield, Fred	Chi., Bos., Min., Buf.	14	914	211	405	616	134	106	21	35	56	10	2	1964-65	1977-78
Stanfield, Jack	Chi.	1	....	....	....	....	....	1	0	0	0	0		1965-66	1965-66
Stanfield, Jim	L.A.	3	7	0	1	1	0	....	....	....	....	....		1969-70	1971-72
Stankiewicz, Edward	Det.	2	6	0	0	0	2	....	....	....	....	....		1953-54	1955-56
Stankiewicz, Myron	St.L., Phi.	1	35	0	7	7	36	1	0	0	0	0		1968-69	1968-69
Stanley, Allan	NYR, Chi., Bos., Tor., Phi.	21	1244	100	333	433	792	109	7	36	43	80	4	1948-49	1968-69
• Stanley, Barney	Chi.	1	1	0	0	0	0	....	....	....	....	....		1927-28	1927-28
Stanley, Daryl	Phi., Van.	6	189	8	17	25	408	17	0	0	0	30		1983-84	1989-90
Stanowski, Wally	Tor., NYR	10	428	23	88	111	160	60	3	14	17	13	4	1939-40	1950-51
Stapleton, Brian	Wsh.	1	1	0	0	0	0	....	....	....	....	....		1975-76	1975-76
Stapleton, Pat	Bos., Chi.	10	635	43	294	337	353	65	10	39	49	38		1961-62	1972-73
Starikov, Sergei	N.J.	1	16	0	1	1	8	....	....	....	....	....		1989-90	1989-90
Starr, Harold	Ott., Mtl.M., Mtl., NYR	7	205	6	5	11	186	15	1	0	1	4		1929-30	1935-36
Starr, Wilf	NYA, Det.	4	87	8	6	14	25	7	0	2	2	2	1	1932-33	1935-36
Stasiuk, Vic	Chi., Det., Bos.	14	745	183	254	437	669	69	16	18	34	40	2	1949-50	1962-63
Stastny, Anton	Que.	9	650	252	384	636	150	66	20	32	52	31		1980-81	1988-89
Stastny, Marian	Que., Tor.	5	322	121	173	294	110	32	5	17	22	7		1981-82	1985-86
Stastny, Peter	Que., N.J., St. L.	15	977	450	789	1239	824	93	33	72	105	123		1980-81	1994-95
Staszak, Ray	Det.	1	4	0	1	1	7	....	....	....	....	....		1985-86	1985-86
Steele, Frank	Det.	1	1	0	0	0	0	....	....	....	....	....		1930-31	1930-31
Steen, Anders	Wpg.	1	42	5	11	16	22	....	....	....	....	....		1980-81	1980-81
Steen, Thomas	Wpg.	14	950	264	553	817	753	56	12	32	44	62		1981-82	1994-95
Stefaniw, Morris	Atl.	1	13	1	1	2	2	....	....	....	....	....		1972-73	1972-73
Stefanski, Bud	NYR	1	1	0	0	0	0	....	....	....	....	....		1977-78	1977-78
Steinburg, Trevor	Que.	4	71	8	4	12	161	1	0	0	0	0		1985-86	1988-89
Stemkowski, Pete	Tor., Det., NYR, L.A.	15	967	206	349	555	866	83	25	29	54	136	1	1963-64	1977-78
Stenlund, Vern	Clev.	1	4	0	0	0	0	....	....	....	....	....		1976-77	1976-77
• Stephens, Phil	Mtl.W, Mtl.	2	8	1	0	1	0	....	....	....	....	....		1917-18	1921-22
Stephenson, Bob	Hfd., Tor.	1	18	2	3	5	4	....	....	....	....	....		1979-80	1979-80
Sterner, Ulf	NYR	1	4	0	0	0	0	....	....	....	....	....		1964-65	1964-65
Stevens, Mike	Van., NYI, Tor.	4	23	1	4	5	29	....	....	....	....	....		1984-85	1989-90
Stevens, Paul	Bos.	1	17	0	0	0	0	....	....	....	....	....		1925-26	1925-26
Stevenson, Shayne	Bos., T.B.	3	27	0	2	2	35	....	....	....	....	....		1990-91	1992-93
Stewart, Allan	N.J., Bos.	6	64	6	4	10	243	....	....	....	....	....		1985-86	1991-92
Stewart, Bill	Buf., St.L., Tor., Min.	8	261	7	64	71	424	13	1	3	4	11		1977-78	1985-86
Stewart, Blair	Det., Wsh., Que.	7	229	34	44	78	326	....	....	....	....	....		1973-74	1979-80
Stewart, Gaye	Tor., Chi., Det., NYR, Mtl.	11	502	185	159	344	274	25	2	9	11	16	2	1941-42	1953-54
• Stewart, Jack	Det., Chi.	12	565	31	84	115	765	80	5	14	19	143	2	1938-39	1951-52
Stewart, John	Pit., Atl., Cal., Que.	5	258	58	60	118	158	4	0	0	0	10		1970-71	1979-80
Stewart, Ken	Chi.	1	6	1	1	2	2	....	....	....	....	....		1941-42	1941-42
• Stewart, Nels	Mtl.M., Bos., NYA	15	650	324	191	515	953	54	15	13	28	61	1	1925-26	1939-40
Stewart, Paul	Que.	1	21	2	0	2	74	....	....	....	....	....		1979-80	1979-80
Stewart, Ralph	Van., NYI	7	252	57	73	130	28	19	4	4	8	2		1970-71	1977-78
Stewart, Robert	Bos., Cal., Clev., St.L., Pit.	9	575	27	101	128	809	5	1	1	2	2		1971-72	1979-80
Stewart, Ron	Tor., Bos., St.L., NYR, Van., NYI	21	1353	276	253	529	560	119	14	21	35	60	3	1952-53	1972-73
Stewart, Ryan	Wpg.	1	3	1	0	1	0	....	....	....	....	....		1985-86	1985-86
Stiles, Tony	Cgy.	1	30	2	7	9	20	....	....	....	....	....		1983-84	1983-84
Stoddard, Jack	NYR	2	80	16	15	31	31	....	....	....	....	....		1951-52	1952-53
Stoltz, Roland	Wsh.	1	14	2	2	4	14	....	....	....	....	....		1981-82	1981-82
Stone, Steve	Van.	1	2	0	0	0	0	....	....	....	....	....		1973-74	1973-74
Stothers, Mike	Phi., Tor.	4	30	0	2	2	65	5	0	0	0	11		1984-85	1987-88
Stoughton, Blaine	Pit., Tor., Hfd., NYR	8	526	258	191	449	204	8	4	2	6	2		1973-74	1983-84
Stoyanovich, Steve	Hfd.	1	23	3	5	8	11	....	....	....	....	....		1983-84	1983-84
• Strain, Neil	NYR	1	52	11	13	24	12	....	....	....	....	....		1952-53	1952-53
Strate, Gord	Det.	3	61	0	0	0	34	....	....	....	....	....		1956-57	1958-59
Stratton, Art	NYR, Det., Chi., Pit., Phi.	4	95	18	33	51	24	5	0	0	0	0		1959-60	1967-68
Strobel, Art	NYR	1	7	0	0	0	0	....	....	....	....	....		1943-44	1943-44
Strong, Ken	Tor.	3	15	2	2	4	6	....	....	....	....	....		1982-83	1984-85
Strueby, Todd	Edm.	3	5	0	1	1	2	....	....	....	....	....		1981-82	1983-84
• Stuart, Billy	Tor., Bos.	7	194	30	17	47	145	17	1	0	0	12	1	1920-21	1926-27
Stumpf, Robert	St.L., Pit.	1	10	1	1	2	20	....	....	....	....	....		1974-75	1974-75
Sturgeon, Peter	Col.	2	6	0	1	1	2	....	....	....	....	....		1979-80	1980-81
Suikkanen, Kai	Buf.	2	2	0	0	0	0	....	....	....	....	....		1981-82	1982-83
Sulliman, Doug	NYR, Hfd., N.J., Phi.	11	631	160	168	328	175	16	1	3	4	2		1979-80	1989-90
Sullivan, Barry	Det.	1	1	0	0	0	0	....	....	....	....	....		1947-48	1947-48
Sullivan, Bob	Hfd.	1	62	18	19	37	18	....	....	....	....	....		1982-83	1982-83
Sullivan, Brian	N.J.	1	2	0	1	1	0	....	....	....	....	....		1992-93	1992-93
Sullivan, Frank	Tor., Chi.	4	8	0	0	0	2	....	....	....	....	....		1949-50	1955-56
Sullivan, Peter	Wpg.	2	126	28	54	82	40	....	....	....	....	....		1979-80	1980-81
Sullivan, Red	Bos., Chi., NYR	11	557	107	239	346	441	18	1	2	3	6		1949-50	1960-61
Summanen, Raimo	Edm., Van.	5	151	36	40	76	35	10	2	5	7	0		1983-84	1987-88
• Summerhill, Bill	Mtl., Bro.	3	72	14	17	31	70	3	0	0	0	2		1938-39	1941-42
Sundstrom, Patrik	Van., N.J.	10	679	219	369	588	349	37	9	17	26	25		1982-83	1991-92
Sundstrom, Peter	NYR, Wsh., N.J.	6	338	61	83	144	120	23	3	3	6	8		1983-84	1989-90
Suomi, Al	Chi.	1	5	0	0	0	0	....	....	....	....	....		1936-37	1936-37
Sutherland, Bill	Mtl., Phi., Tor., St.L., Det.	6	250	70	58	128	99	14	2	4	6	0		1962-63	1971-72
Sutherland, Ron	Bos.	1	2	0	0	0	0	....	....	....	....	....		1931-32	1931-32
Sutter, Brian	St.L.	12	779	303	333	636	1786	65	21	21	42	249		1976-77	1987-88
Sutter, Darryl	Chi.	8	406	161	118	279	288	51	24	19	43	26		1979-80	1986-87
Sutter, Duane	NYI, Chi.	11	731	139	203	342	1333	161	26	32	58	405	4	1979-80	1989-90
Sutter, Rich	Pit., Phi., Van., St. L., Chi., T.B., Tor.	13	874	149	166	315	1411	78	13	5	18	133		1982-83	1994-95
Suzor, Mark	Phi., Col.	2	64	4	16	20	60	....	....	....	....	....		1976-77	1977-78

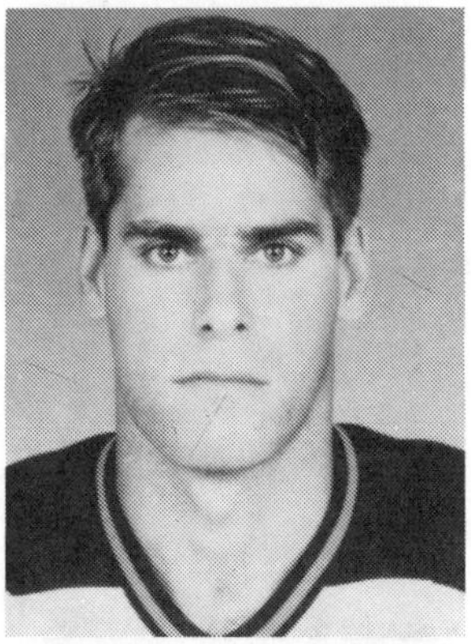
Brian Sullivan

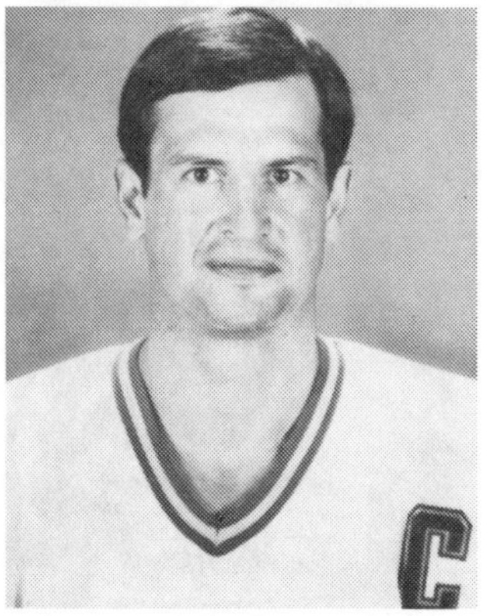
Brian Sutter

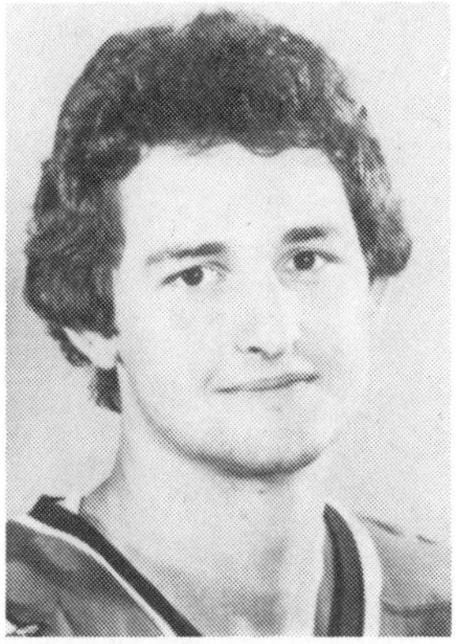
Darryl Sutter

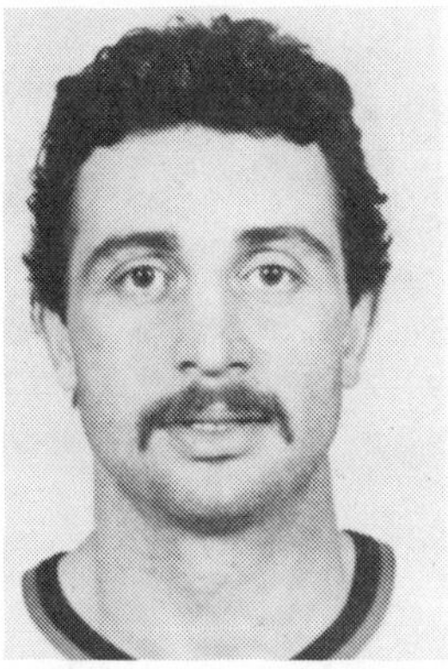
Duane Sutter

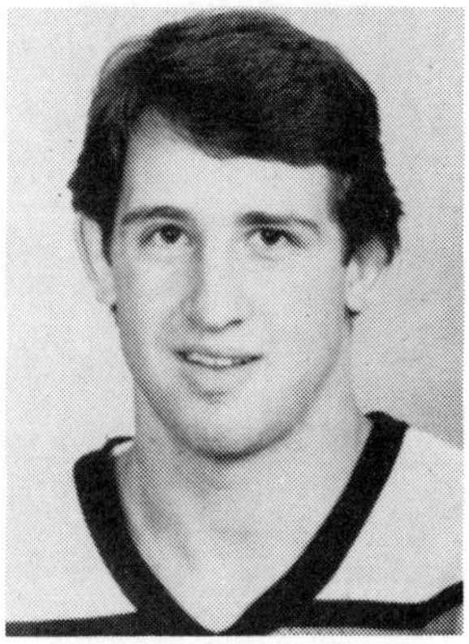

Rich Sutter

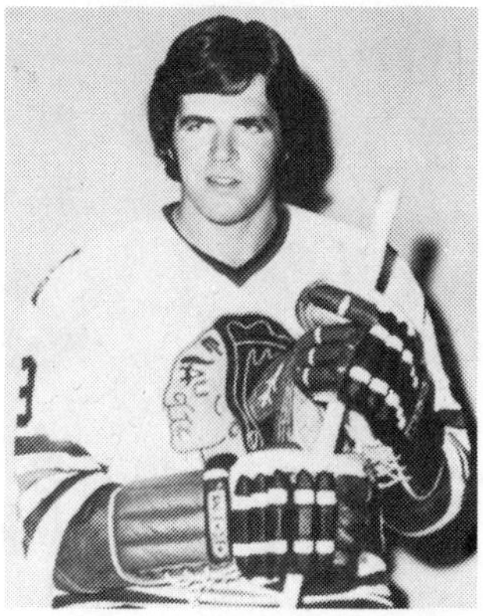

Dale Tallon

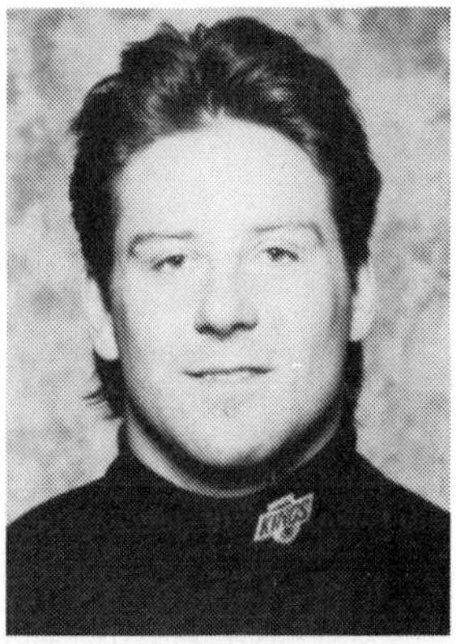

Jim Thomson

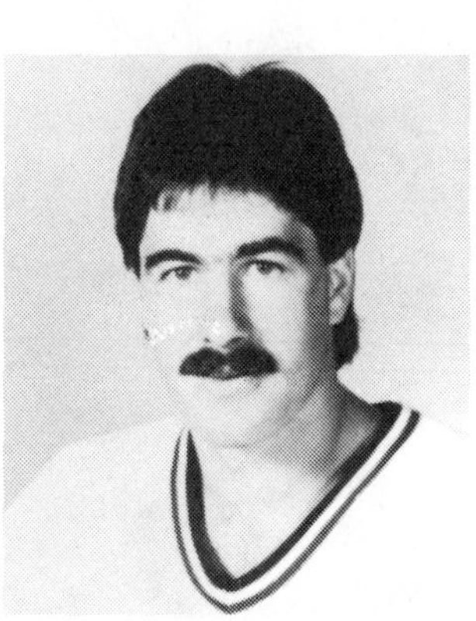

Dave Tippett

Name	NHL Teams	NHL Seasons	Regular Schedule GP	G	A	TP	PIM	Playoffs GP	G	A	TP	PIM	NHL Cup Wins	First NHL Season	Last NHL Season
Svensson, Leif	Wsh.	2	121	6	40	46	49	....	....	....	....	....		1978-79	1979-80
Swain, Garry	Pit.	1	9	1	1	2	0	....	....	....	....	....		1968-69	1968-69
Swarbrick, George	Oak., Pit., Phi.	4	132	17	25	42	173	....	....	....	....	....		1967-68	1970-71
● Sweeney, Bill	NYR	1	4	1	0	1	0	....	....	....	....	....		1959-60	1959-60
Sykes, Bob	Tor.	1	2	0	0	0	0	....	....	....	....	....		1974-75	1974-75
Sykes, Phil	L.A., Wpg.	10	456	79	85	164	519	26	0	3	3	29		1982-83	1991-92
Szura, Joe	Oak.	2	90	10	15	25	30	7	2	3	5	2		1967-68	1968-69

T

Name	NHL Teams	NHL Seasons	Regular Schedule GP	G	A	TP	PIM	Playoffs GP	G	A	TP	PIM	NHL Cup Wins	First NHL Season	Last NHL Season
Taft, John	Det.	1	15	0	2	2	4	....	....	....	....	....		1978-79	1978-79
Talafous, Dean	Atl., Min., NYR	9	497	104	154	258	163	21	4	7	11	11		1974-75	1981-82
Talakoski, Ron	NYR	2	9	0	1	1	33	....	....	....	....	....		1986-87	1987-88
Talbot, Jean-Guy	Mtl., Min., Det., St.L., Buf.	17	1056	43	242	285	1006	150	4	26	30	142	7	1954-55	1970-71
Tallon, Dale	Van., Chi., Pit.	10	642	98	238	336	568	33	2	10	12	45		1970-71	1979-80
Tambellini, Steve	NYI, Col., N.J., Cgy., Van.	10	553	160	150	310	105	2	0	1	1	0	1	1978-79	1987-88
Tanguay, Chris	Que.	1	2	0	0	0	0	....	....	....	....	....		1981-82	1981-82
Tannahill, Don	Van.	2	111	30	33	63	25	....	....	....	....	....		1972-73	1973-74
Tanti, Tony	Chi., Van., Pit., Buf.	11	697	287	273	560	661	30	3	12	15	27		1981-82	1991-92
Tardif, Marc	Mtl., Que.	8	517	194	207	401	443	62	13	15	28	75	2	1969-70	1982-83
Tatarinov, Mikhail	Wsh., Que., Bos.	4	161	21	48	69	184	....	....	....	....	....		1990-91	1993-94
● Taylor, Billy	Tor., Det., Bos., NYR	7	323	87	180	267	120	33	6	18	24	13	1	1939-40	1947-48
● Taylor, Billy	NYR	1	2	0	0	0	0	....	....	....	....	....		1964-65	1964-65
● Taylor, Bob	Bos.	1	8	0	0	0	6	....	....	....	....	....		1929-30	1929-30
Taylor, Dave	L.A.	17	1111	431	638	1069	1589	92	26	33	59	145		1977-78	1993-94
Taylor, Harry	Tor., Chi.	3	66	5	10	15	30	1	0	0	0	0	1	1946-47	1951-52
Taylor, Mark	Phi., Pit., Wsh.	5	209	42	68	110	73	6	0	0	0	0		1981-82	1985-86
● Taylor, Ralph	Chi., NYR	3	99	4	1	5	169	4	0	0	0	10		1927-28	1929-30
Taylor, Ted	NYR, Det., Min., Van.	6	166	23	35	58	181	....	....	....	....	....		1964-65	1971-72
Teal, Jeff	Mtl.	1	6	0	1	1	0	....	....	....	....	....		1984-85	1984-85
Teal, Skip	Bos.	1	1	0	0	0	0	....	....	....	....	....		1954-55	1954-55
Teal, Victor	NYI	1	1	0	0	0	0	....	....	....	....	....		1973-74	1973-74
Tebbutt, Greg	Que., Pit.	2	26	0	3	3	35	....	....	....	....	....		1979-80	1983-84
Tepper, Stephen	Chi.	1	1	0	0	0	0	....	....	....	....	....		1992-93	1992-93
Terbenche, Paul	Chi., Buf.	5	189	5	26	31	28	12	0	0	0	0		1967-68	1973-74
Terrion, Greg	L.A., Tor.	8	561	93	150	243	339	35	2	9	11	41		1980-81	1987-88
Terry, Bill	Min.	1	5	0	0	0	0	....	....	....	....	....		1987-88	1987-88
Tessier, Orval	Mtl., Bos.	3	59	5	7	12	6	....	....	....	....	....		1954-55	1960-61
Thatchell, Spence	NYR	1	1	0	0	0	0	....	....	....	....	....		1942-43	1942-43
Theberge, Greg	Wsh.	5	153	15	63	78	73	4	0	1	1	0		1979-80	1983-84
Thelin, Mats	Bos.	3	163	8	19	27	107	5	0	0	0	6		1984-85	1986-87
Thelven, Michael	Bos.	5	207	20	80	100	217	34	4	10	14	34		1985-86	1989-90
Therrien, Gaston	Que.	3	22	0	8	8	12	9	0	1	1	4		1980-81	1982-83
Thibaudeau, Gilles	Mtl., NYI, Tor.	5	119	25	37	62	40	8	3	3	6	2		1986-87	1990-91
Thibeault, Laurence	Det., Mtl.	2	5	0	2	2	2	....	....	....	....	....		1944-45	1945-46
Thiffault, Leo	Min.	1	....	....	....	....	....	5	0	0	0	0		1967-68	1967-68
Thomas, Cy	Chi., Tor.	1	6	2	2	4	12	....	....	....	....	....		1947-48	1947-48
Thomas, Reg	Que.	1	39	9	7	16	6	....	....	....	....	....		1979-80	1979-80
Thompson, Cliff	Bos.	2	13	0	1	1	2	....	....	....	....	....		1941-42	1948-49
Thompson, Errol	Tor., Det., Pit.	10	599	208	185	393	184	34	7	5	12	11		1970-71	1980-81
● Thompson, Kenneth	Mtl.W	1	1	0	0	0	0	....	....	....	....	....		1917-18	1917-18
● Thompson, Paul	NYR, Chi.	13	582	153	179	332	336	48	11	11	22	54	3	1926-27	1938-39
● Thoms, Bill	Tor., Chi., Bos.	13	548	135	206	341	153	44	6	10	16	6		1932-33	1944-45
Thomson, Bill	Det., Chi.	2	10	2	2	4	0	2	0	0	0	0		1938-39	1943-44
Thomson, Floyd	St.L.	8	411	56	97	153	341	10	0	2	2	6		1971-72	1979-80
Thomson, Jim	Wsh., Hfd., N.J., L.A., Ott., Ana.	7	115	4	3	7	416	1	0	0	0	0		1986-87	1993-94
● Thomson, Jimmy	Tor., Chi.	13	787	19	215	234	920	63	2	13	15	135	4	1945-46	1957-58
● Thomson, Rhys	Mtl., Tor.	2	25	0	2	2	38	....	....	....	....	....		1939-40	1942-43
Thornbury, Tom	Pit.	1	14	1	8	9	16	....	....	....	....	....		1983-84	1983-84
Thorsteinson, Joe	NYA	1	4	0	0	0	0	....	....	....	....	....		1932-33	1932-33
● Thurier, Fred	NYA, Bro., NYR	3	80	25	27	52	18	....	....	....	....	....		1940-41	1944-45
Thurlby, Tom	Oak.	1	20	1	1	2	4	....	....	....	....	....		1967-68	1967-68
Thyer, Mario	Min.	1	5	0	0	0	0	1	0	0	0	2		1989-90	1989-90
Tidey, Alex	Buf., Edm.	3	9	0	0	0	8	2	0	0	0	0		1976-77	1979-80
Timgren, Ray	Tor., Chi.	6	251	14	44	58	68	30	3	9	12	6	2	1948-49	1954-55
Tippett, Dave	Hfd., Wsh., Pit., Phi.	11	721	93	169	262	317	62	6	16	22	34		1983-84	1993-94
Titanic, Morris	Buf.	2	19	0	0	0	0	....	....	....	....	....		1974-75	1975-76
Tkaczuk, Walt	NYR	14	945	227	451	678	556	93	19	32	51	119		1967-68	1980-81
Toal, Mike	Edm.	1	3	0	0	0	0	....	....	....	....	....		1979-80	1979-80
Tomalty, Glenn	Wpg.	1	1	0	0	0	0	....	....	....	....	....		1979-80	1979-80
Tomlinson, Kirk	Min.	1	1	0	0	0	0	....	....	....	....	....		1987-88	1987-88
Tomson, Jack	NYA	3	....	....	....	....	....	....	....	....	....	....		1938-39	1940-41
Tonelli, John	NYI, Cgy., L.A., Chi., Que.	14	1028	325	511	836	911	172	40	75	115	200	4	1978-79	1991-92
Tookey, Tim	Wsh., Que., Pit., Phi., L.A.	7	106	22	36	58	71	10	1	3	4	2		1980-81	1988-89
Toomey, Sean	Min.	1	1	0	0	0	0	....	....	....	....	....		1986-87	1986-87
Toppazzini, Jerry	Bos., Chi., Det.	12	783	163	244	407	436	40	13	9	22	13		1952-53	1963-64
Toppazzini, Zellio	Bos., NYR, Chi.	5	123	21	21	42	49	2	0	0	0	0		1948-49	1956-57
Torkki, Jari	Chi.	1	4	1	0	1	0	....	....	....	....	....		1988-89	1988-89
Touhey, Bill	Mtl.M., Ott., Bos.	7	280	65	40	105	107	2	1	0	1	0		1927-28	1933-34
Toupin, Jacques	Chi.	1	8	1	2	3	0	4	0	0	0	0		1943-44	1943-44
Townsend, Art	Chi.	1	5	0	0	0	0	....	....	....	....	....		1926-27	1926-27
Trader, Larry	Det., St.L., Mtl.	4	91	5	13	18	74	3	0	0	0	0		1982-83	1987-88
Trainor, Wes	NYR	1	17	1	2	3	6	....	....	....	....	....		1948-49	1948-49
● Trapp, Bobby	Chi.	2	82	4	4	8	129	2	0	0	0	4		1926-27	1927-28
Trapp, Doug	Buf.	1	2	0	0	0	0	....	....	....	....	....		1986-87	1986-87
Traub, Percy	Chi., Det.	3	130	3	3	6	217	4	0	0	0	6		1926-27	1928-29
Tredway, Brock	L.A.	1	....	....	....	....	....	1	0	0	0	0		1981-82	1981-82
Tremblay, Brent	Wsh.	2	10	1	0	1	6	....	....	....	....	....		1978-79	1979-80
Tremblay, Gilles	Mtl.	9	509	168	162	330	161	48	9	14	23	4	2	1960-61	1968-69
● Tremblay, J.C.	Mtl.	13	794	57	306	363	204	108	14	51	65	58	5	1959-60	1971-72
Tremblay, Marcel	Mtl.	1	10	0	2	2	0	....	....	....	....	....		1938-39	1938-39
Tremblay, Mario	Mtl.	12	852	258	326	584	1043	101	20	29	49	187	5	1974-75	1985-86
● Tremblay, Nels	Mtl.	2	3	0	1	1	0	2	0	0	0	0		1944-45	1945-46
Trimper, Tim	Chi., Wpg., Min.	6	190	30	36	66	153	2	0	0	0	2		1979-80	1984-85
Trottier, Bryan	NYI, Pit.	18	1279	524	901	1425	912	221	71	113	184	277	6	1975-76	1993-94
● Trottier, Dave	Mtl.M., Det.	11	446	121	113	234	517	31	4	3	7	39	1	1928-29	1938-39
Trottier, Guy	NYR, Tor.	3	115	28	17	45	37	9	1	0	1	16		1968-69	1971-72
Trottier, Rocky	N.J.	2	38	6	4	10	2	....	....	....	....	....		1983-84	1984-85
● Trudel, Louis	Chi., Mtl.	8	306	49	69	118	122	24	1	3	4	4	2	1933-34	1940-41
Trudell, Rene	NYR	3	129	24	28	52	72	5	0	0	0	2		1945-46	1947-48
● Tudin, Connie	Mtl.	1	4	0	1	1	4	....	....	....	....	....		1941-42	1941-42
Tudor, Rob	Van., St.L.	3	28	4	4	8	19	3	0	0	0	0		1978-79	1982-83
Tuer, Allan	L.A., Min., Hfd.	4	57	1	1	2	208	....	....	....	....	....		1985-86	1989-90
Turcotte, Alfie	Mtl., Wpg., Wsh.	7	112	17	29	46	49	5	0	0	0	0		1983-84	1990-91
Turlick, Gord	Bos.	1	2	0	0	0	2	....	....	....	....	....		1959-60	1959-60
Turnbull, Ian	Tor., L.A., Pit.	10	628	123	317	440	736	55	13	32	45	94		1973-74	1982-83
Turnbull, Perry	St.L., Mtl., Wpg.	9	608	188	163	351	1245	34	6	7	13	86		1979-80	1987-88
Turnbull, Randy	Cgy.	1	1	0	0	0	2	....	....	....	....	....		1981-82	1981-82
Turner, Bob	Mtl., Chi.	8	478	19	51	70	307	68	1	4	5	44	5	1955-56	1962-63
Turner, Brad	NYI	1	3	0	0	0	0	....	....	....	....	....		1991-92	1991-92
Turner, Dean	NYR, Col., L.A.	4	35	1	0	1	59	....	....	....	....	....		1978-79	1982-83
Tustin, Norman	NYR	1	18	2	4	6	0	....	....	....	....	....		1941-42	1941-42
Tuten, Audley	Chi.	2	39	4	8	12	48	....	....	....	....	....		1941-42	1942-43
Tutt, Brian	Wsh.	1	7	1	0	1	2	....	....	....	....	....		1989-90	1989-90
Tuttle, Steve	St.L.	3	144	28	28	56	12	17	1	6	7	2		1988-89	1990-91

UV

Name	NHL Teams	NHL Seasons	Regular Schedule GP	G	A	TP	PIM	Playoffs GP	G	A	TP	PIM	NHL Cup Wins	First NHL Season	Last NHL Season
Ubriaco, Gene	Pit., Oak., Chi.	3	177	39	35	74	50	11	2	0	2	4		1967-68	1969-70
Ullman, Norm	Det., Tor.	20	1410	476	719	1195	774	106	29	52	81	75		1955-56	1974-75
Unger, Garry	Tor., Det., St.L., Atl., L.A., Edm.	16	1105	413	391	804	1075	52	12	18	30	105		1967-68	1982-83
Vadnais, Carol	Mtl., Oak., Cal., Bos., NYR, N.J.	17	1087	169	418	587	1813	106	10	40	50	185	2	1966-67	1982-83
Vail, Eric	Atl, Cgy., Det.	9	591	216	260	476	281	20	5	6	11	6		1973-74	1981-82

Name	NHL Teams	NHL Seasons	Regular Schedule GP	G	A	TP	PIM	Playoffs GP	G	A	TP	PIM	NHL Cup Wins	First NHL Season	Last NHL Season
• Vail, Melville	NYR	2	50	4	1	5	18	10	0	0	0	2		1928-29	1929-30
Vaive, Rick	Van., Tor., Chi., Buf.	13	876	441	347	788	1445	54	27	16	43	111		1979-80	1991-92
Valentine, Chris	Wsh.	3	105	43	52	95	127	2	0	0	0	4		1981-82	1983-84
Valiquette, Jack	Tor., Col.	7	350	84	134	218	79	23	3	6	9	4		1974-75	1980-81
Vallis, Lindsay	Mtl.	1	1	0	0	0	0	....	....	....	....	....		1993-94	1993-94
Van Boxmeer, John	Mtl., Col., Buf., Que.	11	588	84	274	358	462	38	5	15	20	37		1973-74	1983-84
Van Dorp, Wayne	Edm., Pit., Chi., Que.	6	125	12	12	24	565	27	0	1	1	42		1986-87	1991-92
Van Impe, Ed	Chi., Phi., Pit.	11	700	27	126	153	1025	66	1	12	13	131	2	1966-67	1976-77
Vasko, Elmer	Chi., Min.	13	786	34	166	200	719	78	2	7	9	73	1	1956-57	1969-70
Vasko, Rick	Det.	3	31	3	7	10	29	....	....	....	....	....		1977-78	1980-81
Vautour, Yvon	NYI, Col., N.J., Que.	6	204	26	33	59	401	....	....	....	....	....		1979-80	1984-85
Vaydik, Greg	Chi.	1	5	0	0	0	0	....	....	....	....	....		1976-77	1976-77
Veitch, Darren	Wsh., Det., Tor.	10	511	48	209	257	296	33	4	11	15	33		1980-81	1990-91
Velischek, Randy	Min., N.J., Que.	10	509	21	76	97	401	44	2	5	7	32		1982-83	1991-92
Venasky, Vic	L.A.	7	430	61	101	162	66	21	1	5	6	12		1972-73	1978-79
Veneruzzo, Gary	St.L.	2	7	1	1	2	0	9	0	2	2	2		1967-68	1971-72
Vermette, Mark	Que.	4	67	5	13	18	33	....	....	....	....	....		1988-89	1991-92
Verret, Claude	Buf.	2	14	2	5	7	2	....	....	....	....	....		1983-84	1984-85
Verstraete, Leigh	Tor.	3	8	0	1	1	14	....	....	....	....	....		1982-83	1987-88
Ververgaert, Dennis	Van., Phi., Wsh.	8	583	176	216	392	247	8	1	2	3	6		1973-74	1980-81
Vesey, Jim	St.L., Bos.	3	15	1	2	3	7	....	....	....	....	....		1988-89	1991-92
Veysey, Sid	Van.	1	1	0	0	0	0	....	....	....	....	....		1977-78	1977-78
Vickers, Steve	NYR	10	698	246	340	586	330	68	24	25	49	58		1972-73	1981-82
Vigneault, Alain	St.L.	2	42	2	5	7	82	4	0	1	1	26		1981-82	1982-83
Vilgrain, Claude	Van., N.J., Phi.	5	89	21	32	53	78	11	1	1	2	17		1987-88	1993-94
Vincelette, Daniel	Chi., Que.	6	193	20	22	42	351	12	0	0	0	4		1986-87	1991-92
Vipond, Pete	Cal.	1	3	0	0	0	0	....	....	....	....	....		1972-73	1972-73
Virta, Hannu	Buf.	5	245	25	101	126	66	17	1	3	4	6		1981-82	1985-86
Vitolinsh, Harijs	Wpg.	1	8	0	0	0	4	....	....	....	....	....		1993-94	1993-94
Viveiros, Emanuel	Min.	3	29	1	11	12	6	....	....	....	....	....		1985-86	1987-88
Vokes, Ed	Chi.	1	5	0	0	0	0	....	....	....	....	....		1930-31	1930-31
Volcan, Mickey	Hfd., Cgy.	4	162	8	33	41	146	....	....	....	....	....		1980-81	1983-84
Volek, David	NYI	6	396	95	154	249	201	15	5	5	10	2		1988-89	1993-94
Volmar, Doug	Det., L.A.	4	62	13	8	21	26	2	1	0	1	0		1969-70	1972-73
• Voss, Carl	Tor., NYR, Det., Ott., St.L., Mtl.M., NYA, Chi.	8	261	34	70	104	50	24	5	3	8	0	1	1926-27	1937-38
Vujtek, Vladimir	Mtl., Edm.	3	72	5	25	30	22	....	....	....	....	....		1991-92	1993-94
Vyazmikin, Igor	Edm.	1	4	1	0	1	0	....	....	....	....	....		1990-91	1990-91

W

Name	NHL Teams	NHL Seasons	Regular Schedule GP	G	A	TP	PIM	Playoffs GP	G	A	TP	PIM	NHL Cup Wins	First NHL Season	Last NHL Season
Waddell, Don	L.A.	1	1	0	0	0	0	....	....	....	....	....		1980-81	1980-81
• Waite, Frank	NYR	1	17	1	3	4	4	....	....	....	....	....		1930-31	1930-31
Walker, Gord	NYR, L.A.	4	31	3	4	7	23	....	....	....	....	....		1986-87	1989-90
Walker, Howard	Wsh., Cal.	3	83	2	13	15	133	....	....	....	....	....		1980-81	1982-83
• Walker, Jack	Det.	2	80	5	8	13	18	....	....	....	....	....		1926-27	1927-28
Walker, Kurt	Tor.	3	71	4	5	9	142	16	0	0	0	34		1975-76	1977-78
Walker, Russ	L.A.	2	17	1	0	1	41	....	....	....	....	....		1976-77	1977-78
Wall, Bob	Det., L.A., St.L.	8	322	30	55	85	155	23	0	3	3	2		1964-65	1971-72
Wallin, Peter	NYR	2	52	3	14	17	14	14	2	6	8	6		1980-81	1981-82
Walsh, Jim	Buf.	1	4	0	1	1	4	....	....	....	....	....		1981-82	1981-82
Walsh, Mike	NYI	2	14	2	0	2	4	....	....	....	....	....		1987-88	1988-89
Walter, Ryan	Wsh., Mtl., Van.	15	1003	264	382	646	946	113	16	35	51	62	1	1978-79	1992-93
Walton, Bobby	Mtl.	1	4	0	0	0	0	....	....	....	....	....		1943-44	1943-44
Walton, Mike	Tor., Bos., Van., Chi., St.L.	12	588	201	247	448	357	47	14	10	24	45	2	1965-66	1978-79
Wappel, Gord	Atl., Cgy.	3	20	1	1	2	10	2	0	0	0	4		1979-80	1981-82
Ward, Don	Chi., Bos.	2	34	0	1	1	16	....	....	....	....	....		1957-58	1959-60
• Ward, Jimmy	Mtl.M., Mtl.	12	527	147	127	274	455	36	4	4	8	26	1	1927-28	1938-39
Ward, Joe	Col.	1	4	0	0	0	2	....	....	....	....	....		1980-81	1980-81
Ward, Ron	Tor., Van.,	2	89	2	5	7	6	....	....	....	....	....		1969-70	1971-72
Ware, Michael	Edm.	2	5	0	1	1	15	....	....	....	....	....		1988-89	1989-90
Wares, Eddie	NYR, Det., Chi.	9	321	60	102	162	161	45	5	7	12	34	1	1936-37	1946-47
Warner, Bob	Tor.	2	10	1	1	2	4	4	0	0	0	0		1975-76	1976-77
Warner, Jim	Hfd.	1	32	0	3	3	10	....	....	....	....	....		1979-80	1979-80
Warwick, Bill	NYR	2	14	3	3	6	16	....	....	....	....	....		1942-43	1943-44
Warwick, Grant	NYR, Bos., Mtl.	9	395	147	142	289	220	16	2	4	6	6		1941-42	1949-50
• Wasnie, Nick	Chi., Mtl., NYA, Ott., St.L.	7	248	57	34	91	176	14	6	3	9	20	2	1927-28	1934-35
Watson, Bill	Chi.	4	115	23	36	59	12	6	0	2	2	0		1985-86	1988-89
Watson, Bryan	Mtl., Oak., Pit., Det., St.L., Wsh.	16	878	17	135	152	2212	32	2	0	2	70		1963-64	1978-79
Watson, Dave	Col.	2	18	0	1	1	10	....	....	....	....	....		1979-80	1980-81
Watson, Harry	Bro., Det., Tor., Chi.	14	809	236	207	443	150	62	16	9	25	27	5	1941-42	1956-57
Watson, Jim	Det., Buf.	8	221	4	19	23	345	....	....	....	....	....		1963-64	1971-72
Watson, Jimmy	Phi.	10	613	38	148	186	492	101	5	34	39	89	2	1972-73	1981-82
Watson, Joe	Bos., Phi., Col.	14	835	38	178	216	447	84	3	12	15	82	2	1964-65	1978-79
• Watson, Phil	NYR, Mtl.	13	590	144	265	409	532	45	10	25	35	67	2	1935-36	1947-48
Watters, Tim	Wpg., L.A.	14	741	26	151	177	1289	82	1	5	6	115		1981-82	1994-95
Watts, Brian	Det.	1	4	0	0	0	0	....	....	....	....	....		1975-76	1975-76
Webster, Aubrey	Phi., Mtl.M.	2	5	0	0	0	0	....	....	....	....	....		1930-31	1934-35
• Webster, Don	Tor.	1	27	7	6	13	28	5	0	0	0	12		1943-44	1943-44
Webster, John	NYR	1	14	0	0	0	4	....	....	....	....	....		1949-50	1949-50
Webster, Tom	Bos., Det., Cal.	5	102	33	42	75	61	1	0	0	0	0		1968-69	1979-80
• Weiland, Cooney	Bos., Ott., Det.	11	557	188	179	367	157	54	14	12	26	16	2	1928-29	1938-39
Weir, Stan	Cal., Tor., Edm., Col., Det.	10	642	139	207	346	183	37	6	5	11	4		1972-73	1982-83
Weir, Wally	Que., Hfd., Pit.	6	320	21	45	66	625	23	0	1	1	96		1979-80	1984-85
• Wellington, Duke	Que.	1	1	0	0	0	0	....	....	....	....	....		1919-20	1919-20
Wensink, John	Bos., Que., Col., N.J., St.L.	8	403	70	68	138	840	43	2	6	8	86		1973-74	1982-83
• Wentworth, Cy	Chi., Mtl.M., Mtl.	13	575	39	68	107	355	35	5	6	11	20	1	1927-28	1939-40
Wesley, Blake	Phi., Hfd., Que., Tor.	7	298	18	46	64	486	19	2	2	4	30		1979-80	1985-86
Westfall, Ed	Bos., NYI	18	1220	231	394	625	544	95	22	37	59	41	2	1961-62	1978-79
Wharram, Kenny	Chi.	14	766	252	281	533	222	80	16	27	43	38	1	1951-52	1968-69
Wharton, Len	NYR	1	1	0	0	0	0	....	....	....	....	....		1944-45	1944-45
Wheeldon, Simon	NYR, Wpg.	3	15	0	2	2	10	....	....	....	....	....		1987-88	1990-91
• Wheldon, Donald	St.L.	1	2	0	0	0	0	....	....	....	....	....		1974-75	1974-75
Whelton, Bill	Wpg.	1	2	0	0	0	0	....	....	....	....	....		1980-81	1980-81
Whistle, Rob	NYR, St.L.	2	51	7	5	12	16	4	0	0	0	2		1985-86	1987-88
White, Bill	L.A., Chi.	9	604	50	215	265	495	91	7	32	39	76		1967-68	1975-76
White, Moe	Mtl.	1	4	0	1	1	2	....	....	....	....	....		1945-46	1945-46
• White, Sherman	NYR	2	4	0	2	2	0	....	....	....	....	....		1946-47	1949-50
• White, Tex	Pit., NYA, Phi.	6	203	33	12	45	141	4	0	0	0	4		1925-26	1930-31
White, Tony	Wsh., Min.	5	164	37	28	65	104	....	....	....	....	....		1974-75	1979-80
Whitelaw, Bob	Det.	2	32	0	2	2	2	8	0	0	0	0		1940-41	1941-42
Whitlock, Bob	Min.	1	1	0	0	0	0	....	....	....	....	....		1969-70	1969-70
Whyte, Sean	L.A.	2	21	0	2	2	12	....	....	....	....	....		1991-92	1992-93
Wickenheiser, Doug	Mtl., St.L., Van., NYR, Wsh.	10	556	111	165	276	286	41	4	7	11	18		1980-81	1989-90
• Widing, Juha	NYR, L.A., Clev.	8	575	144	226	370	208	8	1	2	3	2		1969-70	1976-77
• Wiebe, Art	Chi.	11	414	14	27	41	201	31	1	3	4	10	1	1932-33	1943-44
Wiemer, Jim	Buf., NYR, Edm., L.A., Bos.	11	325	29	72	101	378	62	5	8	13	63	1	1982-83	1993-94
• Wilcox, Archie	Mtl.M., Bos., St.L.	6	208	8	14	22	158	12	1	0	1	8		1929-30	1934-35
Wilcox, Barry	Van.	2	33	3	2	5	15	....	....	....	....	....		1972-73	1974-75
Wilder, Arch	Det.	1	18	0	2	2	2	....	....	....	....	....		1940-41	1940-41
Wiley, Jim	Pit., Van.	5	63	4	10	14	8	....	....	....	....	....		1972-73	1976-77
Wilkins, Barry	Bos., Van., Pit.	9	418	27	125	152	663	6	0	1	1	4		1966-67	1975-76
Wilkinson, John	Bos.	1	9	0	0	0	6	....	....	....	....	....		1943-44	1943-44
Wilks, Brian	L.A.	4	48	4	8	12	27	....	....	....	....	....		1984-85	1988-89
Willard, Rod	Tor.	1	1	0	0	0	0	....	....	....	....	....		1982-83	1982-83
Williams, Burr	Det., St.L., Bos.	4	19	0	1	1	28	2	0	0	0	8		1933-34	1936-37
Williams, Darryl	L.A.	1	2	0	0	0	10	....	....	....	....	....		1992-93	1992-93
Williams, Dave	Tor., Van., Det., L.A., Hfd.	14	962	241	272	513	3966	83	12	23	35	455		1974-75	1987-88
Williams, Fred	Det.	1	44	2	5	7	10	....	....	....	....	....		1976-77	1976-77
Williams, Gord	Phi.	2	2	0	0	0	2	....	....	....	....	....		1981-82	1982-83
Williams, Sean	Chi.	1	2	0	0	0	4	....	....	....	....	....		1991-92	1991-92
• Williams, Tom	Bos., Min., Cal., Wsh.	13	663	161	269	430	177	10	2	5	7	2		1961-62	1975-76
Williams, Tommy	NYR, L.A.	8	397	115	138	253	73	29	8	7	15	4		1971-72	1978-79

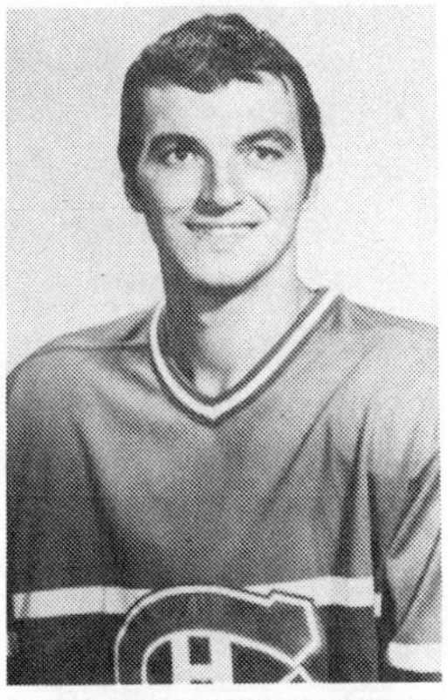
Mario Tremblay

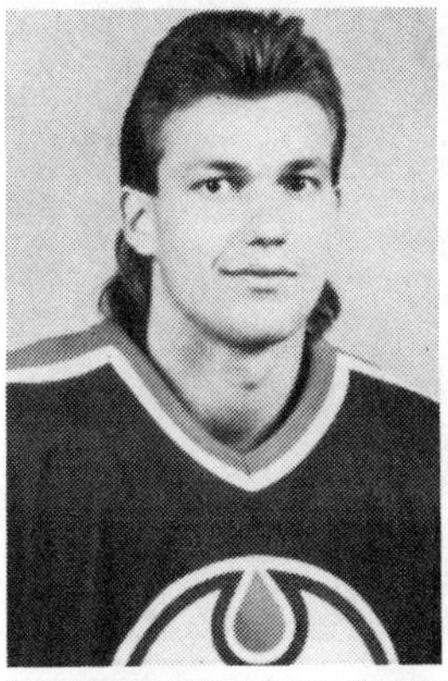
Vladimir Vujtek

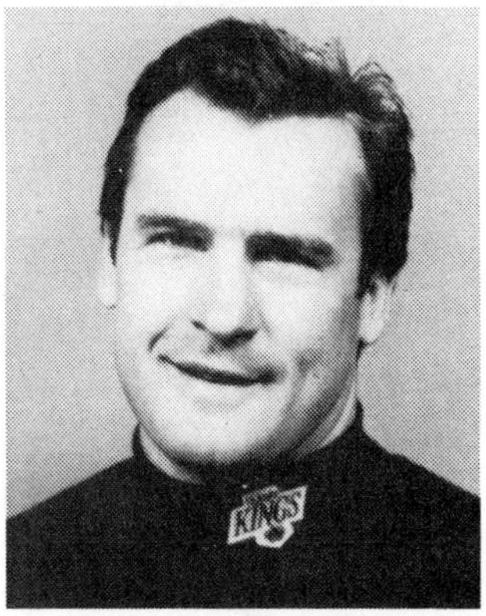

Tim Watters

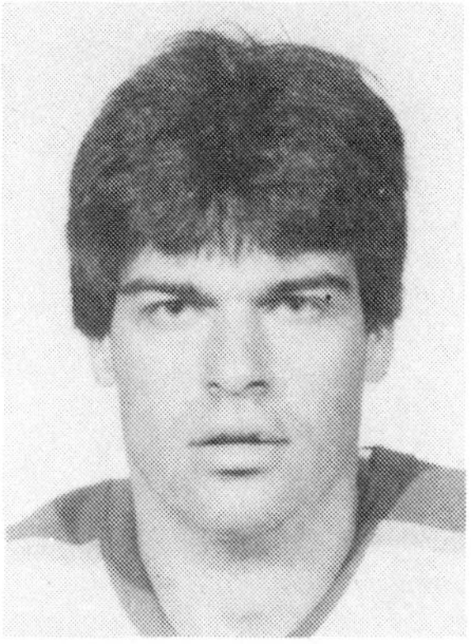
Jim Wiemer

Behn Wilson

Steve Wojciechowski

Name	NHL Teams	NHL Seasons	Regular Schedule					Playoffs					NHL Cup Wins	First NHL Season	Last NHL Season
			GP	G	A	TP	PIM	GP	G	A	TP	PIM			
Williams, Warren	St.L., Cal.	3	108	14	35	49	131	....	....	....	....	....		1973-74	1975-76
Willson, Don	Mtl.	2	22	2	7	9	0	3	0	0	0	0		1937-38	1938-39
Wilson, Behn	Phi., Chi.	9	601	98	260	358	1480	67	12	29	41	190		1978-79	1987-88
• Wilson, Bert	NYR, L.A., St.L., Cgy.	8	478	37	44	81	646	21	0	2	2	42		1973-74	1980-81
Wilson, Bob	Chi.	1	1	0	0	0	0	....	....	....	....	....		1953-54	1953-54
Wilson, Carey	Cgy., Hfd., NYR	10	552	169	258	427	314	52	11	13	24	14		1983-84	1992-93
Wilson, Cully	Tor., Mtl., Ham., Chi.	5	125	60	23	83	232	2	1	0	1	6		1919-20	1926-27
Wilson, Doug	Chi., S.J.	16	1024	237	590	827	830	95	19	61	80	88		1977-78	1992-93
Wilson, Gord	Bos.	1						2	0	0	0	0		1954-55	1954-55
Wilson, Hub	NYA	1	2	0	0	0	0	....	....	....	....	....		1931-32	1931-32
Wilson, Jerry	Mtl.	1	3	0	0	0	2	....	....	....	....	....		1956-57	1956-57
Wilson, Johnny	Det., Chi., Tor., NYR	13	688	161	171	332	190	66	14	13	27	11	4	1949-50	1961-62
• Wilson, Larry	Det., Chi.	6	152	21	48	69	75	4	0	0	0	0	1	1949-50	1955-56
Wilson, Mitch	N.J., Pit.	2	26	2	3	5	104	....	....	....	....	....		1984-85	1986-87
Wilson, Murray	Mtl., L.A.	7	386	94	95	189	162	53	5	14	19	32	4	1972-73	1978-79
Wilson, Rick	Mtl., St.L., Det.	4	239	6	26	32	165	3	0	0	0	0		1973-74	1976-77
Wilson, Rik	St.L., Cgy., Chi.	6	251	25	65	90	220	22	0	4	4	23		1981-82	1987-88
Wilson, Roger	Chi.	1	7	0	2	2	6	....	....	....	....	....		1974-75	1974-75
Wilson, Ron	Tor., Min.	7	177	26	67	93	68	20	4	13	17	8		1977-78	1987-88
Wilson, Wally	Bos.	1	53	11	8	19	18	1	0	0	0	0		1947-48	1947-48
Wing, Murray	Det.	1	1	0	1	1	0	....	....	....	....	....		1973-74	1973-74
• Wiseman, Eddie	Det., NYA, Bos.	10	456	115	165	280	136	43	10	10	20	16	1	1932-33	1941-42
Wiste, Jim	Chi., Van.	3	52	1	10	11	8	....	....	....	....	....		1968-69	1970-71
Witherspoon, Jim	L.A.	1	2	0	0	0	2	....	....	....	....	....		1975-76	1975-76
Witiuk, Steve	Chi.	1	33	3	8	11	14	....	....	....	....	....		1951-52	1951-52
Woit, Benny	Det., Chi.	7	334	7	26	33	170	41	2	6	8	18	3	1950-51	1956-57
Wojciechowski, Steven	Det.	2	54	19	20	39	17	6	0	1	1	0		1944-45	1946-47
Wolf, Bennett	Pit.	3	30	0	1	1	133	....	....	....	....	....		1980-81	1982-83
Wong, Mike	Det.	1	22	1	1	2	12	....	....	....	....	....		1975-76	1975-76
Wood, Robert	NYR	1	1	0	0	0	0	....	....	....	....	....		1950-51	1950-51
Woodley, Dan	Van.	1	5	2	0	2	17	....	....	....	....	....		1987-88	1987-88
Woods, Paul	Det.	7	501	72	124	196	276	7	0	5	5	4		1977-78	1983-84
• Woytowich, Bob	Bos., Min., Pit., L.A.	8	503	32	126	158	352	24	1	3	4	20		1964-65	1971-72
Wright, John	Van., St.L., K.C.	3	127	16	36	52	67	....	....	....	....	....		1972-73	1974-75
Wright, Keith	Phi.	1	1	0	0	0	0	....	....	....	....	....		1967-68	1967-68
Wright, Larry	Phi., Cal., Det.	5	106	4	8	12	19	....	....	....	....	....		1971-72	1977-78
Wycherley, Ralph	NYA, Bro.	2	28	4	7	11	6	....	....	....	....	....		1940-41	1941-42
Wylie, Duane	Chi.	2	14	3	3	6	2	....	....	....	....	....		1974-75	1976-77
• Wylie, William	NYR	1	1	0	0	0	0	....	....	....	....	....		1950-51	1950-51
Wyrozub, Randy	Buf.	4	100	8	10	18	10	....	....	....	....	....		1970-71	1973-74

YZ

Name	NHL Teams	NHL Seasons	GP	G	A	TP	PIM	GP	G	A	TP	PIM	NHL Cup Wins	First NHL Season	Last NHL Season
Yackel, Ken	Bos.	1	6	0	0	0	2	2	0	0	0	2		1958-59	1958-59
Yaremchuk, Gary	Tor.	4	34	1	4	5	28	....	....	....	....	....		1981-82	1984-85
Yaremchuk, Ken	Chi., Tor.	6	235	36	56	92	106	31	6	8	14	49		1983-84	1988-89
Yates, Ross	Hfd.	1	7	1	1	2	4	....	....	....	....	....		1983-84	1983-84
Young, Brian	Chi.	1	8	0	2	2	6	....	....	....	....	....		1980-81	1980-81
Young, C.J.	Cgy., Bos.	1	43	7	7	14	32	....	....	....	....	....		1992-93	1992-93
• Young, Doug	Mtl., Det.	10	388	35	45	80	303	28	1	5	6	16	2	1931-32	1940-41
Young, Howie	Det., Chi., Van.	8	336	12	62	74	851	19	2	4	6	46		1960-61	1970-71
Young, Tim	Min., Wpg., Phi.	10	628	195	341	536	438	36	7	24	31	27		1975-76	1984-85
Young, Warren	Min., Pit., Det.	7	236	72	77	149	472	....	....	....	....	....		1981-82	1987-88
Younghans, Tom	Min., NYR	6	429	44	41	85	373	24	2	1	3	21		1976-77	1981-82
Zabroski, Marty	Chi.	1	1	0	0	0	0	....	....	....	....	....		1944-45	1944-45
Zaharko, Miles	Atl., Chi.	4	129	5	32	37	84	3	0	0	0	0		1977-78	1981-82
Zaine, Rod	Pit., Buf.	2	61	10	6	16	25	....	....	....	....	....		1970-71	1971-72
Zanussi, Joe	NYR, Bos., St.L.	3	87	1	13	14	46	4	0	1	1	2		1974-75	1976-77
Zanussi, Ron	Min., Tor.	5	299	52	83	135	373	17	0	4	4	17		1977-78	1981-82
Zeidel, Larry	Det., Chi., Phi.	5	158	3	16	19	198	12	0	1	1	12	1	1951-52	1968-69
Zemlak, Richard	Que., Min., Pit., Cgy.	5	132	2	12	14	587	1	0	0	0	10		1986-87	1991-92
Zeniuk, Ed	Det.	1	2	0	0	0	0	....	....	....	....	....		1954-55	1954-55
Zetterstrom, Lars	Van.	1	14	0	1	1	2	....	....	....	....	....		1978-79	1978-79
Zuke, Mike	St.L., Hfd.	8	455	86	196	282	220	26	6	6	12	12		1978-79	1985-86
Zunich, Ruby	Det.	1	2	0	0	0	2	....	....	....	....	....		1943-44	1943-44

NOTE: Some players added to the Retired NHL Player Index remain active in other hockey leagues in North America or Europe. Players with NHL experience playing outside the NHL are placed in the Retired NHL Player Index when they have completed one or more seasons of play after having been removed from an NHL club's reserve list. A player's age and his performance outside the NHL are considered in determining when he is moved from the active Player Register to the Retired NHL Player Index.

1996-97 Goaltender Register

Note: The 1996-97 Goaltender Register lists every goaltender who appeared in an NHL game in the 1995-96 season, every goaltender drafted in the first six rounds of the 1996 Entry Draft, goaltenders on NHL Reserve Lists and other goaltenders.

Trades and roster changes are current as of August 28, 1996

To calculate a goaltender's goals-against-per-game average **(AVG)**, divide goals against **(GA)** by minutes played **(Mins)** and multiply this result by **60**.

Abbreviations: A list of league names can be found at the beginning of the Player Register. **Avg.** – goals against per game average; **GA** – goals against; **GP** – games played; **L** – losses; **Lea** – league; **SO** – shutouts; **T** – ties; **W** – wins; ♦ – member of Stanley Cup-winning team.

Player Register begins on page 247.

ARSENAULT, DAVID — DET.

Goaltender. Catches left. 6'2", 165 lbs. Born, Frankfurt, Germany, March 21, 1977.
(Detroit's 6th choice, 126th overall, in 1995 Entry Draft).

			Regular Season								Playoffs						
Season	**Club**	**Lea**	**GP**	**W**	**L**	**T**	**Mins**	**GA**	**SO**	**Avg**	**GP**	**W**	**L**	**Mins**	**GA**	**SO**	**Avg**
1994-95	St-Hyacinthe	QMJHL	19	3	10	0	862	75	0	5.22	....	....	....	....	....	....	....
	Drummondville	QMJHL	12	2	5	0	478	40	0	5.02	2	0	2	122	8	0	3.93
1995-96	Drummondville	QMJHL	21	8	10	1	1177	89	0	4.54	....	....	....	....	....	....	....
	Chicoutimi	QMJHL	6	1	1	1	207	14	0	4.06	5	0	1	....	....	....	5.61

ASKEY, TOM — ANA.

Goaltender. Catches left. 6'2", 185 lbs. Born, Kenmore, NY, October 4, 1974.
(Anaheim's 8th choice, 186th overall, in 1993 Entry Draft).

			Regular Season								Playoffs						
Season	**Club**	**Lea**	**GP**	**W**	**L**	**T**	**Mins**	**GA**	**SO**	**Avg**	**GP**	**W**	**L**	**Mins**	**GA**	**SO**	**Avg**
1992-93	Ohio State	NCAA	25	2	19	0	1235	125	....	6.07	....	....	....	....	....	....	....
1993-94	Ohio State	CCHA	27	3	19	4	1488	103	....	4.15	....	....	....	....	....	....	....
1994-95	Ohio State	CCHA	26	4	19	2	1387	121	0	5.23	....	....	....	....	....	....	....
1995-96a	Ohio State	CCHA	26	8	11	4	1340	68	....	3.05	....	....	....	....	....	....	....

a CCHA Second All-Star Team (1996)

AUBIN, JEAN-SEBASTIEN (OH-behn) — PIT.

Goaltender. Catches right. 5'11", 179 lbs. Born, Montreal, Que., July 19, 1977.
(Pittsburgh's 2nd choice, 76th overall, in 1995 Entry Draft).

			Regular Season								Playoffs						
Season	**Club**	**Lea**	**GP**	**W**	**L**	**T**	**Mins**	**GA**	**SO**	**Avg**	**GP**	**W**	**L**	**Mins**	**GA**	**SO**	**Avg**
1994-95	Sherbrooke	QMJHL	27	13	10	1	1287	73	1	3.40	3	1	2	185	11	0	3.57
1995-96	Sherbrooke	QMJHL	40	18	14	2	2140	127	0	3.57	4	1	3	....	....	....	5.55

BACH, RYAN — DET.

Goaltender. Catches left. 6'1", 180 lbs. Born, Sherwood Park, Alta., October 21, 1973.
(Detroit's 11th choice, 262nd overall, in 1992 Entry Draft).

			Regular Season								Playoffs						
Season	**Club**	**Lea**	**GP**	**W**	**L**	**T**	**Mins**	**GA**	**SO**	**Avg**	**GP**	**W**	**L**	**Mins**	**GA**	**SO**	**Avg**
1992-93	Colorado	WCHA	4	1	3	0	239	11	0	2.76	....	....	....	....	....	....	....
1993-94	Colorado	WCHA	30	17	7	5	1733	105	0	3.64	....	....	....	....	....	....	....
1994-95ab	Colorado	WCHA	27	18	5	1	1522	83	0	3.27	....	....	....	....	....	....	....
1995-96ac	Colorado	WCHA	23	*17	4	2	1390	62	2	2.68	....	....	....	....	....	....	....

a WCHA First All-Star Team (1995, 1996)
b NCAA West Second All-American Team (1995)
c NCAA West First All-American (1996)

BAILEY, SCOTT — BOS.

Goaltender. Catches left. 6', 195 lbs. Born, Calgary, Alta., May 2, 1972.
(Boston's 3rd choice, 112th overall, in 1992 Entry Draft).

			Regular Season								Playoffs						
Season	**Club**	**Lea**	**GP**	**W**	**L**	**T**	**Mins**	**GA**	**SO**	**Avg**	**GP**	**W**	**L**	**Mins**	**GA**	**SO**	**Avg**
1990-91a	Spokane	WHL	46	33	11	0	2537	157	*4	3.71	....	....	....	....	....	....	....
1991-92a	Spokane	WHL	65	34	23	5	3798	206	1	3.30	10	5	5	605	43	0	4.26
1992-93	Johnstown	ECHL	36	13	15	3	1750	112	1	3.84	....	....	....	....	....	....	....
1993-94	Providence	AHL	7	2	2	2	377	24	0	3.82	....	....	....	....	....	....	....
	Charlotte	ECHL	36	22	11	3	2180	130	1	3.58	3	1	2	187	12	0	3.83
1994-95	Providence	AHL	52	25	16	9	2936	147	2	3.00	9	4	4	504	31	*2	3.69
1995-96	**Boston**	**NHL**	**11**	**5**	**1**	**2**	**571**	**31**	**0**	**3.26**	....	....	....	....	....	....	....
	Providence	AHL	37	15	19	3	2210	120	1	3.26	2	1	1	119	6	0	3.03
	NHL Totals		**11**	**5**	**1**	**2**	**571**	**31**	**0**	**3.26**	....	....	....	....	....	....	....

a WHL West Second All-Star Team (1991, 1992)

BAKER, AARON — HFD.

Goaltender. Catches right. 6'1", 174 lbs. Born, Eckville, Alta., February 17, 1978.
(Hartford's 6th choice, 143rd overall, in 1996 Entry Draft).

			Regular Season								Playoffs						
Season	**Club**	**Lea**	**GP**	**W**	**L**	**T**	**Mins**	**GA**	**SO**	**Avg**	**GP**	**W**	**L**	**Mins**	**GA**	**SO**	**Avg**
1995-96	Tri-City	WHL	20	11	6	0	1082	61	2	3.38	1	0	0	20	1	....	3.00

BALES, MICHAEL — OTT.

Goaltender. Catches left. 6'1", 180 lbs. Born, Prince Albert, Sask., August 6, 1971.
(Boston's 4th choice, 105th overall, in 1990 Entry Draft).

			Regular Season								Playoffs						
Season	**Club**	**Lea**	**GP**	**W**	**L**	**T**	**Mins**	**GA**	**SO**	**Avg**	**GP**	**W**	**L**	**Mins**	**GA**	**SO**	**Avg**
1989-90	Ohio State	CCHA	21	6	13	2	1117	95	0	5.11	....	....	....	....	....	....	....
1990-91	Ohio State	CCHA	*39	11	24	3	*2180	184	0	5.06	....	....	....	....	....	....	....
1991-92	Ohio State	CCHA	36	11	20	5	2060	180	0	5.24	....	....	....	....	....	....	....
1992-93	**Boston**	**NHL**	**1**	**0**	**0**	**0**	**25**	**1**	**0**	**2.40**	....	....	....	....	....	....	....
	Providence	AHL	44	22	17	0	2363	166	1	4.21	2	0	2	118	8	0	4.07
1993-94	Providence	AHL	33	9	15	4	1757	130	0	4.44	....	....	....	....	....	....	....
1994-95	P.E.I.	AHL	45	25	16	3	2649	160	2	3.62	9	6	3	530	24	*2	2.72
	Ottawa	**NHL**	**1**	**0**	**0**	**0**	**3**	**0**	**0**	**0.00**	....	....	....	....	....	....	....
1995-96	**Ottawa**	**NHL**	**20**	**2**	**14**	**1**	**1040**	**72**	**0**	**4.15**	....	....	....	....	....	....	....
	P.E.I.	AHL	2	0	2	0	118	11	0	5.58	....	....	....	....	....	....	....
	NHL Totals		**22**	**2**	**14**	**1**	**1068**	**73**	**0**	**4.10**	....	....	....	....	....	....	....

Signed as a free agent by **Ottawa**, July 4, 1994.

BARRASSO, TOM (buh-RAH-soh) — PIT.

Goaltender. Catches right. 6'3", 211 lbs. Born, Boston, MA, March 31, 1965.
(Buffalo's 1st choice, 5th overall, in 1983 Entry Draft).

			Regular Season								Playoffs							
Season	**Club**	**Lea**	**GP**	**W**	**L**	**T**	**Mins**	**GA**	**SO**	**Avg**	**GP**	**W**	**L**	**Mins**	**GA**	**SO**	**Avg**	
1982-83	Acton-Boxboro	HS	23	....	....	....	1035	17	10	0.73	....	....	....	....	....	....	....	
1983-84 abcd	**Buffalo**	**NHL**	**42**	**26**	**12**	**3**	**2475**	**117**	**2**	**2.84**	**3**	**0**	**2**	**139**	**8**	**0**	**3.45**	
1984-85ef	**Buffalo**	**NHL**	**54**	**25**	**18**	**10**	**3248**	**144**	***5**	***2.66**	**5**	**2**	**3**	**300**	**22**	**0**	**4.40**	
	Rochester	AHL	5	3	1	1	267	6	1	1.35	....	....	....	....	....	....	....	
1985-86	**Buffalo**	**NHL**	**60**	**29**	**24**	**5**	**3561**	**214**	**2**	**3.61**	....	....	....	....	....	....	....	
1986-87	**Buffalo**	**NHL**	**46**	**17**	**23**	**2**	**2501**	**152**	**2**	**3.65**	....	....	....	....	....	....	....	
1987-88	**Buffalo**	**NHL**	**54**	**25**	**18**	**8**	**3133**	**173**	**2**	**3.31**	**4**	**1**	**3**	**224**	**16**	**0**	**4.29**	
1988-89	**Buffalo**	**NHL**	**10**	**2**	**7**	**0**	**545**	**45**	**0**	**4.95**	....	....	....	....	....	....	....	
	Pittsburgh	**NHL**	**44**	**18**	**15**	**7**	**2406**	**162**	**0**	**4.04**	**11**	**7**	**4**	**631**	**40**	**0**	**3.80**	
1989-90	**Pittsburgh**	**NHL**	**24**	**7**	**12**	**3**	**1294**	**101**	**0**	**4.68**	....	....	....	....	....	....	....	
1990-91	**Pittsburgh**	**NHL**	**48**	**27**	**16**	**3**	**2754**	**165**	**1**	**3.59**	**20**	**12**	**7**	**1175**	**51**	***1**	***2.60**	♦
1991-92	**Pittsburgh**	**NHL**	**57**	**25**	**22**	**9**	**3329**	**196**	**1**	**3.53**	***21**	***16**	**5**	***1233**	**58**	**1**	**2.82**	♦
1992-93e	**Pittsburgh**	**NHL**	**63**	***43**	**14**	**5**	**3702**	**186**	**4**	**3.01**	**12**	**7**	**5**	**722**	**35**	***2**	**2.91**	
1993-94	**Pittsburgh**	**NHL**	**44**	**22**	**15**	**5**	**2482**	**139**	**2**	**3.36**	**6**	**2**	**4**	**356**	**17**	**0**	**2.87**	
1994-95	**Pittsburgh**	**NHL**	**2**	**0**	**1**	**1**	**125**	**8**	**0**	**3.84**	**2**	**0**	**1**	**80**	**8**	**0**	**6.00**	
1995-96	**Pittsburgh**	**NHL**	**49**	**29**	**16**	**2**	**2799**	**160**	**2**	**3.43**	**10**	**4**	**5**	**558**	**26**	**1**	**2.80**	
	NHL Totals		**597**	**295**	**213**	**63**	**34354**	**1962**	**23**	**3.43**	**94**	**51**	**39**	**5418**	**281**	**5**	**3.11**	

a NHL First All-Star Team (1984)
b Won Vezina Trophy (1984)
c Won Calder Memorial Trophy (1984)
d NHL All-Rookie Team (1984)
e NHL Second All-Star Team (1985, 1993)
f Shared William Jennings Trophy with Bob Sauve (1985)

Played in NHL All-Star Game (1985)

Traded to **Pittsburgh** by **Buffalo** with Buffalo's third round choice (Joe Dziedzic) in 1990 Entry Draft for Doug Bodger and Darrin Shannon, November 12, 1988.

BEAUBIEN, FREDERICK (boh-BEE-yehn) — L.A.

Goaltender. Catches left. 6'1", 204 lbs. Born, Lauzon, Que., April 1, 1975.
(Los Angeles' 4th choice, 105th overall, in 1993 Entry Draft).

			Regular Season								Playoffs						
Season	**Club**	**Lea**	**GP**	**W**	**L**	**T**	**Mins**	**GA**	**SO**	**Avg**	**GP**	**W**	**L**	**Mins**	**GA**	**SO**	**Avg**
1992-93	St-Hyacinthe	QMJHL	33	8	16	3	1702	133	0	4.69	....	....	....	....	....	....	....
1993-94	St-Hyacinthe	QMJHL	47	19	19	5	2663	168	1	3.79	7	3	4	411	33	0	4.82
1994-95	St-Hyacinthe	QMJHL	51	19	24	4	2697	178	1	3.96	3	1	2	176	9	0	3.07
1995-96	Phoenix	IHL	36	13	9	7	1832	100	1	3.28	2	0	2	119	9	0	4.52

BEAUPRE, DON (boh-PRAY) — TOR.

Goaltender. Catches left. 5'10", 172 lbs. Born, Waterloo, Ont., September 19, 1961.
(Minnesota's 2nd choice, 37th overall, in 1980 Entry Draft).

			Regular Season								Playoffs						
Season	**Club**	**Lea**	**GP**	**W**	**L**	**T**	**Mins**	**GA**	**SO**	**Avg**	**GP**	**W**	**L**	**Mins**	**GA**	**SO**	**Avg**
1978-79	Sudbury	OHA	54	....	....	....	3248	260	2	4.78	10	....	....	600	44	0	4.20
1979-80a	Sudbury	OHA	59	28	29	2	3447	248	0	4.32	9	5	4	552	38	0	4.13
1980-81	**Minnesota**	**NHL**	**44**	**18**	**14**	**11**	**2585**	**138**	**0**	**3.20**	**6**	**4**	**2**	**360**	**26**	**0**	**4.33**
1981-82	**Minnesota**	**NHL**	**29**	**11**	**8**	**9**	**1634**	**101**	**0**	**3.71**	**2**	**0**	**1**	**60**	**4**	**0**	**4.00**
	Nashville	CHL	5	2	3	0	299	25	0	5.02	....	....	....	....	....	....	....
1982-83	**Minnesota**	**NHL**	**36**	**19**	**10**	**5**	**2011**	**120**	**0**	**3.58**	**4**	**2**	**2**	**245**	**20**	**0**	**4.90**
	Birmingham	CHL	10	8	2	0	599	31	0	3.11	....	....	....	....	....	....	....
1983-84	**Minnesota**	**NHL**	**33**	**16**	**13**	**2**	**1791**	**123**	**0**	**4.12**	**13**	**6**	**7**	**782**	**40**	**1**	**3.07**
	Salt Lake	CHL	7	2	5	0	419	30	0	4.30	....	....	....	....	....	....	....
1984-85	**Minnesota**	**NHL**	**31**	**10**	**17**	**3**	**1770**	**109**	**1**	**3.69**	**4**	**1**	**1**	**184**	**12**	**0**	**3.91**
1985-86	**Minnesota**	**NHL**	**52**	**25**	**20**	**6**	**3073**	**182**	**1**	**3.55**	**5**	**2**	**3**	**300**	**17**	**0**	**3.40**
1986-87	**Minnesota**	**NHL**	**47**	**17**	**20**	**6**	**2622**	**174**	**1**	**3.98**	....	....	....	....	....	....	....
1987-88	**Minnesota**	**NHL**	**43**	**10**	**22**	**3**	**2288**	**161**	**0**	**4.22**	....	....	....	....	....	....	....
1988-89	**Minnesota**	**NHL**	**1**	**0**	**1**	**0**	**59**	**3**	**0**	**3.05**	....	....	....	....	....	....	....
	Kalamazoo	IHL	3	1	2	0	179	9	1	3.02	....	....	....	....	....	....	....
	Washington	**NHL**	**11**	**5**	**4**	**0**	**578**	**28**	**1**	**2.91**	....	....	....	....	....	....	....
	Baltimore	AHL	30	14	12	2	1715	102	0	3.57	....	....	....	....	....	....	....
1989-90	**Washington**	**NHL**	**48**	**23**	**18**	**5**	**2793**	**150**	**2**	**3.22**	**8**	**4**	**3**	**401**	**18**	**0**	**2.69**
1990-91	**Washington**	**NHL**	**45**	**20**	**18**	**3**	**2572**	**113**	***5**	**2.64**	**11**	**5**	**5**	**624**	**29**	***1**	**2.79**
	Baltimore	AHL	2	2	0	0	120	3	0	1.50	....	....	....	....	....	....	....
1991-92	**Washington**	**NHL**	**54**	**29**	**17**	**6**	**3108**	**166**	**1**	**3.20**	**7**	**3**	**4**	**419**	**22**	**0**	**3.15**
	Baltimore	AHL	3	1	1	1	184	10	0	3.26	....	....	....	....	....	....	....
1992-93	**Washington**	**NHL**	**58**	**27**	**23**	**5**	**3282**	**181**	**1**	**3.31**	**2**	**1**	**1**	**119**	**9**	**0**	**4.54**
1993-94	**Washington**	**NHL**	**53**	**24**	**16**	**8**	**2853**	**135**	**2**	**2.84**	**8**	**5**	**2**	**429**	**21**	**1**	**2.94**
1994-95	**Ottawa**	**NHL**	**38**	**8**	**25**	**3**	**2161**	**121**	**1**	**3.36**	....	....	....	....	....	....	....
1995-96	**Ottawa**	**NHL**	**33**	**6**	**23**	**0**	**1770**	**110**	**1**	**3.73**	....	....	....	....	....	....	....
	Toronto	**NHL**	**8**	**0**	**5**	**0**	**336**	**26**	**0**	**4.64**	**2**	**0**	**0**	**20**	**2**	**0**	**6.00**
	NHL Totals		**664**	**268**	**274**	**75**	**37286**	**2141**	**17**	**3.45**	**72**	**33**	**31**	**3943**	**220**	**3**	**3.35**

a OHA First All-Star Team (1980)

Played in NHL All-Star Game (1981, 1992)

Traded to **Washington** by **Minnesota** for rights to Claudio Scremin, November 1, 1988. Traded to **Ottawa** by **Washington** for Ottawa's fifth round choice (Benoit Gratton) in 1995 Entry Draft, January 18, 1995. Traded to **NY Islanders** by **Ottawa** with Martin Straka and Bryan Berard for Damian Rhodes and Wade Redden, January 23, 1996. Traded to **Toronto** by **NY Islanders** with Kirk Muller for future considerations, January 23, 1996.

BEAUREGARD, STEPHANE

Goaltender. Catches right. 5'11", 190 lbs. Born, Cowansville, Que., January 10, 1968.
(Winnipeg's 3rd choice, 52nd overall, in 1988 Entry Draft).

			Regular Season								Playoffs						
Season	Club	Lea	GP	W	L	T	Mins	GA	SO	Avg	GP	W	L	Mins	GA	SO	Avg
1986-87	St-Jean	QMJHL	13	6	7	0	785	58	0	4.43	5	1	3	260	26	0	6.00
1987-88ab	St-Jean	QMJHL	66	38	20	3	3766	229	2	3.65	7	3	4	423	34	0	4.82
1988-89	Moncton	AHL	15	4	8	2	824	62	0	4.51	....	....	....	....	....	....	....
	Fort Wayne	IHL	16	9	5	0	830	43	0	3.10	9	4	4	484	21	*1	*2.60
1989-90	**Winnipeg**	**NHL**	**19**	**7**	**8**	**3**	**1079**	**59**	**0**	**3.28**	**4**	**1**	**3**	**238**	**12**	**0**	**3.03**
	Fort Wayne	IHL	33	20	8	3	1949	115	0	3.54	....	....	....	....	....	....	....
1990-91	**Winnipeg**	**NHL**	**16**	**3**	**10**	**1**	**836**	**55**	**0**	**3.95**	....	....	....	....	....	....	....
	Moncton	AHL	9	3	4	1	504	20	1	2.38	1	1	0	60	1	0	1.00
	Fort Wayne	IHL	32	14	13	2	1761	109	0	3.71	*19	*10	9	*1158	57	0	2.95
1991-92	**Winnipeg**	**NHL**	**26**	**6**	**8**	**6**	**1267**	**61**	**2**	**2.89**	....	....	....	....	....	....	....
1992-93	**Philadelphia**	**NHL**	**16**	**3**	**9**	**0**	**802**	**59**	**0**	**4.41**	....	....	....	....	....	....	....
	Hershey	AHL	13	5	5	3	794	48	0	3.63	....	....	....	....	....	....	....
1993-94	**Winnipeg**	**NHL**	**13**	**0**	**4**	**1**	**418**	**34**	**0**	**4.88**	....	....	....	....	....	....	....
	Moncton	AHL	37	18	11	6	2082	121	1	3.49	*21	*12	9	*1305	57	*2	2.62
1994-95	Springfield	AHL	24	10	11	3	1381	73	2	3.17	....	....	....	....	....	....	....
1995-96cd	San Francisco	IHL	*69	*36	24	8	*4022	207	1	3.09	4	1	3	241	10	0	2.49
	NHL Totals		**90**	**19**	**39**	**11**	**4402**	**268**	**2**	**3.65**	**4**	**1**	**3**	**238**	**12**	**0**	**3.03**

a QMJHL First All-Star Team (1988)
b Canadian Major Junior Goaltender of the year (1988)
c IHL First All-Star Team (1996)
d Won James Gatschene Memorial Trophy (MVP - IHL) (1996)

Traded to **Buffalo** by **Winnipeg** for Christian Ruuttu and future considerations, June 15, 1992. Traded to **Chicago** by **Buffalo** with Buffalo's fourth round choice (Eric Dazel) in 1993 Entry Draft for Dominik Hasek, August 7, 1992. Traded to **Winnipeg** by **Chicago** for Christian Ruuttu, August 10, 1992. Traded to **Philadelphia** by **Winnipeg** for future considerations, October 1, 1992. Traded to **Winnipeg** by **Philadelphia** for future considerations, June 11, 1993.

BELFOUR, ED — CHI.

Goaltender. Catches left. 5'11", 182 lbs. Born, Carman, Man., April 21, 1965.

			Regular Season								Playoffs						
Season	Club	Lea	GP	W	L	T	Mins	GA	SO	Avg	GP	W	L	Mins	GA	SO	Avg
1986-87a	North Dakota	WCHA	34	29	4	0	2049	81	3	2.43	....	....	....	....	....	....	....
1987-88bc	Saginaw	IHL	61	32	25	0	*3446	183	3	3.19	9	4	5	561	33	0	3.53
1988-89	**Chicago**	**NHL**	**23**	**4**	**12**	**3**	**1148**	**74**	**0**	**3.87**	....	....	....	....	....	....	....
	Saginaw	IHL	29	12	10	0	1760	92	0	3.10	5	2	3	298	14	0	2.82
1989-90	Cdn. National	....	33	13	12	6	1808	93	0	3.08	....	....	....	....	....	....	....
	Chicago	**NHL**	....	....	....	....	....	....	....	....	**9**	**4**	**2**	**409**	**17**	**0**	**2.49**
1990-91 defghi	**Chicago**	**NHL**	***74**	***43**	**19**	**7**	***4127**	**170**	**4**	***2.47**	**6**	**2**	**4**	**295**	**20**	**0**	**4.07**
1991-92	**Chicago**	**NHL**	**52**	**21**	**18**	**10**	**2928**	**132**	***5**	**2.70**	**18**	**12**	**4**	**949**	**39**	**1**	***2.47**
1992-93deg	**Chicago**	**NHL**	***71**	**41**	**18**	**11**	***4106**	**177**	***7**	**2.59**	**4**	**0**	**4**	**249**	**13**	**0**	**3.13**
1993-94	**Chicago**	**NHL**	**70**	**37**	**24**	**6**	**3998**	**178**	***7**	**2.67**	**6**	**2**	**4**	**360**	**15**	**0**	**2.50**
1994-95gj	**Chicago**	**NHL**	**42**	**22**	**15**	**3**	**2450**	**93**	***5**	**2.28**	**16**	**9**	**7**	**1014**	**37**	**1**	**2.19**
1995-96	**Chicago**	**NHL**	**50**	**22**	**17**	**10**	**2956**	**135**	**1**	**2.74**	**9**	**6**	**3**	**666**	**23**	**1**	**2.07**
	NHL Totals		**382**	**190**	**123**	**50**	**21713**	**959**	**29**	**2.65**	**68**	**35**	**28**	**3942**	**164**	**3**	**2.50**

a WCHA First All-Star Team (1987)
b IHL First All-Star Team (1988)
c Shared Garry F. Longman Memorial Trophy (Top Rookie - IHL) (1988)
d NHL First All-Star Team (1991, 1993)
e Won Vezina Trophy (1991, 1993)
f Won Calder Memorial Trophy (1991)
g Won William M. Jennings Trophy (1991, 1993, 1995)
h Won Trico Goaltender Award (1991)
i NHL/Upper Deck All-Rookie Team (1991)
j NHL Second All-Star Team (1995)

Played in NHL All-Star Game (1992, 1993, 1996)

Signed as a free agent by **Chicago**, September 25, 1987.

BERGERON, JEAN-CLAUDE — L.A.

Goaltender. Catches left. 6'2", 192 lbs. Born, Hauterive, Que., October 14, 1968.
(Montreal's 5th choice, 104th overall, in 1988 Entry Draft).

			Regular Season								Playoffs						
Season	Club	Lea	GP	W	L	T	Mins	GA	SO	Avg	GP	W	L	Mins	GA	SO	Avg
1987-88	Verdun	QMJHL	49	13	31	3	2715	265	0	5.86	....	....	....	....	....	....	....
1988-89	Verdun	QMJHL	44	8	34	1	2417	199	0	4.94	....	....	....	....	....	....	....
	Sherbrooke	AHL	5	4	1	0	302	18	0	3.58	....	....	....	....	....	....	....
1989-90abc	Sherbrooke	AHL	40	21	8	7	2254	103	2	*2.74	9	6	2	497	28	0	3.38
1990-91	**Montreal**	**NHL**	**18**	**7**	**6**	**2**	**941**	**59**	**0**	**3.76**	....	....	....	....	....	....	....
	Fredericton	AHL	18	12	6	0	1083	59	1	3.27	10	5	5	546	32	0	3.52
1991-92	Fredericton	AHL	13	5	7	1	791	57	0	4.32	....	....	....	....	....	....	....
	Peoria	IHL	27	14	9	3	1632	96	1	3.53	6	3	3	352	24	0	4.09
1992-93	**Tampa Bay**	**NHL**	**21**	**8**	**10**	**1**	**1163**	**71**	**0**	**3.66**	....	....	....	....	....	....	....
	Atlanta	IHL	31	21	7	1	1722	92	1	3.21	6	3	3	368	19	0	3.10
1993-94	**Tampa Bay**	**NHL**	**3**	**1**	**1**	**1**	**134**	**7**	**0**	**3.13**	....	....	....	....	....	....	....
d	Atlanta	IHL	48	27	11	7	2755	141	0	3.07	2	1	1	153	6	0	2.34
1994-95	Atlanta	IHL	6	3	3	0	324	24	0	4.44	....	....	....	....	....	....	....
	Tampa Bay	**NHL**	**17**	**3**	**9**	**1**	**883**	**49**	**1**	**3.33**	....	....	....	....	....	....	....
1995-96	**Tampa Bay**	**NHL**	**12**	**2**	**6**	**2**	**595**	**42**	**0**	**4.24**	....	....	....	....	....	....	....
	Atlanta	IHL	25	9	10	3	1326	92	0	4.16	....	....	....	....	....	....	....
	NHL Totals		**71**	**21**	**32**	**7**	**3716**	**228**	**1**	**3.68**	....	....	....	....	....	....	....

a AHL First All-Star Team (1990)
b Shared Harry "Hap" Holmes Trophy (fewest goals-against - AHL) with Andre Racicot (1990)
c Won Baz Bastien Memorial Trophy (Top Goaltender - AHL) (1990)
d Shared James Norris Memorial Trophy (fewest goals-against - IHL) with Mike Greenlay (1994)

Traded to **Tampa Bay** by **Montreal** for Frederic Chabot, June 19, 1992. Signed as a free agent by **Los Angeles**, August 28, 1996.

BERGQVIST, PER-RAGNAR — PHI.

Goaltender. Catches left. 5'11", 183 lbs. Born, Leksand, Sweden, April 11, 1976.
(Philadelphia's 3rd choice, 124th overall, in 1996 Entry Draft).

			Regular Season								Playoffs						
Season	Club	Lea	GP	W	L	T	Mins	GA	SO	Avg	GP	W	L	Mins	GA	SO	Avg
1995-96	Leksand	Swe. Jr.	3	....	....	....	180	17	0	5.67	....	....	....	....	....	....	....
	Leksand	Swe.	6	....	....	....	327	17	0	3.12	1	....	....	60	1	0	1.00

BERTHIAUME, DANIEL — (bairt-YOHM)

Goaltender. Catches left. 5'9", 155 lbs. Born, Longueuil, Que., January 26, 1966.
(Winnipeg's 3rd choice, 60th overall, in 1985 Entry Draft).

			Regular Season								Playoffs						
Season	Club	Lea	GP	W	L	T	Mins	GA	SO	Avg	GP	W	L	Mins	GA	SO	Avg
1984-85	Chicoutimi	QMJHL	59	40	11	2	2177	149	0	4.11	14	8	6	770	51	0	3.97
1985-86	Chicoutimi	QMJHL	66	34	29	3	3718	286	1	4.62	9	4	5	580	36	0	3.72
	Winnipeg	**NHL**	....	....	....	....	....	....	....	....	**1**	**0**	**1**	**68**	**4**	**0**	**3.53**
1986-87	**Winnipeg**	**NHL**	**31**	**18**	**7**	**3**	**1758**	**93**	**1**	**3.17**	**8**	**4**	**4**	**439**	**21**	**0**	**2.87**
	Sherbrooke	AHL	7	4	3	0	420	23	0	3.29	....	....	....	....	....	....	....
1987-88	**Winnipeg**	**NHL**	**56**	**22**	**19**	**7**	**3010**	**176**	**2**	**3.51**	**5**	**1**	**4**	**300**	**25**	**0**	**5.00**
1988-89	**Winnipeg**	**NHL**	**9**	**0**	**8**	**0**	**443**	**44**	**0**	**5.96**	....	....	....	....	....	....	....
	Moncton	AHL	21	6	9	2	1083	76	0	4.21	3	1	2	180	11	0	3.67
1989-90	**Winnipeg**	**NHL**	**24**	**10**	**11**	**3**	**1387**	**86**	**1**	**3.72**	....	....	....	....	....	....	....
	Minnesota	**NHL**	**5**	**1**	**3**	**0**	**240**	**14**	**0**	**3.50**	....	....	....	....	....	....	....
1990-91	**Los Angeles**	**NHL**	**37**	**20**	**11**	**4**	**2119**	**117**	**1**	**3.31**	....	....	....	....	....	....	....
1991-92	**Los Angeles**	**NHL**	**19**	**7**	**10**	**1**	**979**	**66**	**0**	**4.04**	....	....	....	....	....	....	....
	Boston	**NHL**	**8**	**1**	**4**	**2**	**399**	**21**	**0**	**3.16**	....	....	....	....	....	....	....
1992-93	Graz	Alp.	28	....	....	....	....	110	0	4.07	....	....	....	....	....	....	....
	Ottawa	**NHL**	**25**	**2**	**17**	**1**	**1326**	**95**	**0**	**4.30**	....	....	....	....	....	....	....
1993-94	**Ottawa**	**NHL**	**1**	**0**	**0**	**0**	**1**	**2**	**0**	**120.00**	....	....	....	....	....	....	....
	PEI	AHL	30	8	16	3	1640	130	0	4.76	....	....	....	....	....	....	....
	Adirondack	AHL	11	7	2	0	552	35	0	3.80	11	6	4	632	30	0	2.85
1994-95	Providence	AHL	2	0	1	1	126	7	0	3.32	....	....	....	....	....	....	....
	Wheeling	ECHL	10	6	1	1	599	41	0	4.10	....	....	....	....	....	....	....
	Roanoke	ECHL	21	15	4	2	1196	47	0	2.36	8	4	4	464	23	1	2.97
	Detroit	IHL	....	....	....	....	....	....	....	....	5	2	3	331	14	0	2.53
1995-96	Detroit	IHL	7	4	3	0	401	19	2	2.84	....	....	....	....	....	....	....
	Roanoke	ECHL	39	22	13	3	2109	112	*2	3.19	2	0	2	116	6	0	3.09
	NHL Totals		**215**	**81**	**90**	**21**	**11662**	**714**	**5**	**3.67**	**14**	**5**	**9**	**807**	**50**	**0**	**3.72**

Traded to **Minnesota** by **Winnipeg** for future considerations, January 22, 1990. Traded to **Los Angeles** by **Minnesota** for Craig Duncanson, September 6, 1990. Traded to **Boston** by **Los Angeles** for future considerations, January 18, 1992. Traded to **Winnipeg** by **Boston** for Doug Evans, June 10, 1992. Signed as a free agent by **Ottawa**, December 15, 1992. Traded to **Detroit** by **Ottawa** for Steve Konroyd, March 21, 1994.

BESTER, ALLAN

Goaltender. Catches left. 5'7", 155 lbs. Born, Hamilton, Ont., March 26, 1964.
(Toronto's 3rd choice, 48th overall, in 1983 Entry Draft).

			Regular Season								Playoffs						
Season	Club	Lea	GP	W	L	T	Mins	GA	SO	Avg	GP	W	L	Mins	GA	SO	Avg
1981-82	Brantford	OHL	19	4	11	0	970	68	0	4.21	....	....	....	....	....	....	....
1982-83a	Brantford	OHL	56	29	21	3	3210	188	0	3.51	8	3	3	480	20	*1	*2.50
1983-84	**Toronto**	**NHL**	**32**	**11**	**16**	**4**	**1848**	**134**	**0**	**4.35**	....	....	....	....	....	....	....
	Brantford	OHL	23	12	9	1	1271	71	1	3.35	1	0	1	60	5	0	5.00
1984-85	**Toronto**	**NHL**	**15**	**3**	**9**	**1**	**767**	**54**	**1**	**4.22**	....	....	....	....	....	....	....
	St. Catharines	AHL	30	9	18	1	1669	133	0	4.78	....	....	....	....	....	....	....
1985-86	**Toronto**	**NHL**	**1**	**0**	**0**	**0**	**20**	**2**	**0**	**6.00**	....	....	....	....	....	....	....
	St. Catharines	AHL	50	23	23	3	2855	173	1	3.64	11	7	3	637	27	0	2.54
1986-87	**Toronto**	**NHL**	**36**	**10**	**14**	**3**	**1808**	**110**	**2**	**3.65**	**1**	**0**	**0**	**39**	**1**	**0**	**1.54**
	Newmarket	AHL	3	1	0	0	190	6	0	1.89	....	....	....	....	....	....	....
1987-88	**Toronto**	**NHL**	**30**	**8**	**12**	**5**	**1607**	**102**	**2**	**3.81**	**5**	**2**	**3**	**253**	**21**	**0**	**4.98**
1988-89	**Toronto**	**NHL**	**43**	**17**	**20**	**3**	**2460**	**156**	**2**	**3.80**	....	....	....	....	....	....	....
1989-90	**Toronto**	**NHL**	**42**	**20**	**16**	**0**	**2206**	**165**	**0**	**4.49**	**4**	**0**	**3**	**196**	**14**	**0**	**4.29**
	Newmarket	AHL	5	2	1	1	264	18	0	4.09	....	....	....	....	....	....	....
1990-91	**Toronto**	**NHL**	**6**	**0**	**4**	**0**	**247**	**18**	**0**	**4.37**	....	....	....	....	....	....	....
	Newmarket	AHL	19	7	8	4	1157	58	1	3.01	....	....	....	....	....	....	....
	Detroit	**NHL**	**3**	**0**	**3**	**0**	**178**	**13**	**0**	**4.38**	**1**	**0**	**0**	**20**	**1**	**0**	**3.00**
1991-92	**Detroit**	**NHL**	**1**	**0**	**0**	**0**	**31**	**2**	**0**	**3.87**	....	....	....	....	....	....	....
b	Adirondack	AHL	22	13	8	0	1268	78	0	3.69	*19	*14	5	1174	50	*1	*2.56
1992-93	Adirondack	AHL	41	16	15	5	2268	133	1	3.52	10	7	3	633	26	*1	2.46
1993-94	San Diego	IHL	46	22	14	6	2543	150	1	3.54	8	4	4	419	28	0	4.00
1994-95	San Diego	IHL	58	28	23	5	3250	183	1	3.38	4	2	2	272	13	0	2.86
1995-96	Orlando	IHL	51	32	16	2	2947	176	1	3.58	*23	11	12	*1343	65	2	2.90
	Dallas	**NHL**	**10**	**4**	**5**	**1**	**601**	**30**	**0**	**3.00**	....	....	....	....	....	....	....
	NHL Totals		**219**	**73**	**99**	**17**	**11773**	**786**	**7**	**4.01**	**11**	**2**	**6**	**508**	**37**	**0**	**4.37**

a OHL First All-Star Team (1983)
b Won Jack Butterfield Trophy (Playoff MVP - AHL) (1992)

Traded to **Detroit** by **Toronto** for Detroit's sixth round choice (Alexander Kuzminsky) in 1991 Entry Draft, March 5, 1991. Signed as a free agent by **Anaheim**, September 9, 1993. Signed as a free agent by **Dallas**, January 21, 1996.

BIERK, ZAC — T.B.

Goaltender. Catches left. 6'4", 186 lbs. Born, Peterborough, Ont., September 17, 1976.
(Tampa Bay's 8th choice, 212th overall, in 1995 Entry Draft).

			Regular Season								Playoffs						
Season	Club	Lea	GP	W	L	T	Mins	GA	SO	Avg	GP	W	L	Mins	GA	SO	Avg
1993-94	Peterborough	OHL	9	0	4	2	423	37	0	5.22	1	0	0	33	7	0	12.70
1994-95	Peterborough	OHL	35	11	15	5	1779	117	0	3.95	6	2	3	301	24	0	4.78
1995-96	Peterborough	OHL	58	31	16	6	3292	174	2	3.17	*22	*14	7	*1383	83	0	3.60

BILLINGTON, CRAIG

Goaltender. Catches left. 5'10", 170 lbs. Born, London, Ont., September 11, 1966.
(New Jersey's 2nd choice, 23rd overall, in 1984 Entry Draft).

			Regular Season								Playoffs						
Season	Club	Lea	GP	W	L	T	Mins	GA	SO	Avg	GP	W	L	Mins	GA	SO	Avg
1983-84	Belleville	OHL	44	20	19	0	2335	162	1	4.16	1	0	0	30	3	0	6.00
1984-85a	Belleville	OHL	47	26	19	0	2544	180	1	4.25	14	7	5	761	47	1	3.71
1985-86	**New Jersey**	**NHL**	**18**	**4**	**9**	**1**	**901**	**77**	**0**	**5.13**	....	....	....	....	....	....	....
	Belleville	OHL	3	2	1	0	180	11	0	3.67	20	9	6	1133	68	0	3.60
1986-87	**New Jersey**	**NHL**	**22**	**4**	**13**	**2**	**1114**	**89**	**0**	**4.79**	....	....	....	....	....	....	....
	Maine	AHL	20	9	8	2	1151	70	0	3.65	....	....	....	....	....	....	....
1987-88	Utica	AHL	*59	22	27	8	*3404	208	1	3.67	....	....	....	....	....	....	....
1988-89	**New Jersey**	**NHL**	**3**	**1**	**1**	**0**	**140**	**11**	**0**	**4.71**	....	....	....	....	....	....	....
	Utica	AHL	41	17	18	6	2432	150	2	3.70	4	1	3	220	18	0	4.91
1989-90	Utica	AHL	38	20	13	1	2087	138	0	3.97	....	....	....	....	....	....	....
1990-91	Cdn. National	....	34	17	14	2	1879	110	2	3.51	....	....	....	....	....	....	....
1991-92	**New Jersey**	**NHL**	**26**	**13**	**7**	**1**	**1363**	**69**	**2**	**3.04**	....	....	....	....	....	....	....
1992-93	**New Jersey**	**NHL**	**42**	**21**	**16**	**4**	**2389**	**146**	**2**	**3.67**	**2**	**0**	**1**	**78**	**5**	**0**	**3.85**
1993-94	**Ottawa**	**NHL**	**63**	**11**	**41**	**4**	**3319**	**254**	**0**	**4.59**	....	....	....	....	....	....	....
1994-95	**Ottawa**	**NHL**	**9**	**0**	**6**	**2**	**472**	**32**	**0**	**4.07**	....	....	....	....	....	....	....
	Boston	**NHL**	**8**	**5**	**1**	**0**	**373**	**19**	**0**	**3.06**	**1**	**0**	**0**	**25**	**1**	**0**	**2.40**
1995-96	**Boston**	**NHL**	**27**	**10**	**13**	**3**	**1380**	**79**	**1**	**3.43**	**1**	**0**	**1**	**60**	**6**	**0**	**6.00**
	NHL Totals		**218**	**69**	**107**	**17**	**11451**	**776**	**5**	**4.07**	**4**	**0**	**2**	**163**	**12**	**0**	**4.42**

a OHL First All-Star Team (1985)

Played in NHL All-Star Game (1993)

Traded to **Ottawa** by **New Jersey** with Troy Mallette and New Jersey's fourth round choice (Cosmo Dupaul) in 1993 Entry Draft for Peter Sidorkiewicz and future considerations (Mike Peluso, June 26, 1993), June 20, 1993. Traded to **Boston** by **Ottawa** for NY Islanders' eighth round choice (previously acquired by Boston — Ottawa selected Ray Schultz) in 1995 Entry Draft, April 7, 1995.

BIRON, MARTIN (BIH-rohn) BUF.

Goaltender. Catches left. 6'1", 154 lbs. Born, Lac St. Charles, Que., August 15, 1977.
(Buffalo's 2nd choice, 16th overall, in 1995 Entry Draft).

			Regular Season								Playoffs						
Season	Club	Lea	GP	W	L	T	Mins	GA	SO	Avg	GP	W	L	Mins	GA	SO	Avg
1994-95ab	Beauport	QMJHL	56	29	16	9	3193	132	3	*2.48	16	8	7	900	37	*4	2.47
1995-96	**Buffalo**	**NHL**	**3**	**0**	**2**	**0**	**119**	**10**	**0**	**5.04**	....	....	....	....	....	....	....
	Beauport	QMJHL	55	29	17	7	3201	152	1	2.85	*19	*12	7	....	....	....	3.39
	NHL Totals		**3**	**0**	**2**	**0**	**119**	**10**	**0**	**5.04**	....	....	....	....	....	....	....

a Canadian Major Junior First All-Star Team (1995)
b Canadian Major Junior Goaltender of the Year (1995)

BLUE, JOHN

Goaltender. Catches left. 5'10", 185 lbs. Born, Huntington Beach, CA, February 19, 1966.
(Winnipeg's 9th choice, 197th overall, in 1986 Entry Draft).

			Regular Season								Playoffs						
Season	Club	Lea	GP	W	L	T	Mins	GA	SO	Avg	GP	W	L	Mins	GA	SO	Avg
1984-85	U. Minnesota	WCHA	34	23	10	0	1964	111	2	3.39	....	....	....	....	....	....	....
1985-86a	U. Minnesota	WCHA	29	20	6	0	1588	80	2	3.02	....	....	....	....	....	....	....
1986-87	U. Minnesota	WCHA	33	21	9	1	1889	99	3	3.14	....	....	....	....	....	....	....
1987-88	Kalamazoo	IHL	15	3	8	4	847	65	0	4.60	1	0	1	40	6	0	9.00
	U.S. National	....	13	3	4	1	588	33	0	3.37	....	....	....	....	....	....	....
1988-89	Kalamazoo	IHL	17	8	6	0	970	69	0	4.27	....	....	....	....	....	....	....
	Virginia	ECHL	10	....	....	....	570	38	0	4.00	....	....	....	....	....	....	....
1989-90	Phoenix	IHL	19	5	10	3	986	92	0	5.65	....	....	....	....	....	....	....
	Knoxville	ECHL	19	6	10	1	1000	85	0	5.15	....	....	....	....	....	....	....
	Kalamazoo	IHL	4	2	1	1	232	18	0	4.65	....	....	....	....	....	....	....
1990-91	Maine	AHL	10	3	4	2	545	22	0	2.42	1	0	1	40	7	0	10.50
	Albany	IHL	19	11	6	0	1077	71	0	3.96	....	....	....	....	....	....	....
	Kalamazoo	IHL	1	1	0	0	64	2	0	1.88	....	....	....	....	....	....	....
	Peoria	IHL	4	4	0	0	240	12	0	3.00	....	....	....	....	....	....	....
	Knoxville	ECHL	3	1	1	0	149	13	0	5.23	....	....	....	....	....	....	....
1991-92	Maine	AHL	43	11	23	6	2168	165	1	4.57	....	....	....	....	....	....	....
1992-93	**Boston**	**NHL**	**23**	**9**	**8**	**4**	**1322**	**64**	**1**	**2.90**	**2**	**0**	**1**	**96**	**5**	**0**	**3.13**
	Providence	AHL	19	14	4	1	1159	67	0	3.47	....	....	....	....	....	....	....
1993-94	**Boston**	**NHL**	**18**	**5**	**8**	**3**	**944**	**47**	**0**	**2.99**	....	....	....	....	....	....	....
	Providence	AHL	24	7	11	4	1298	76	1	3.51	....	....	....	....	....	....	....
1994-95	Providence	AHL	10	6	3	0	577	30	0	3.11	4	1	3	219	19	0	5.19
1995-96	Phoenix	IHL	8	1	5	0	309	21	0	4.07	....	....	....	....	....	....	....
	Fort Wayne	IHL	5	1	2	2	249	19	0	4.58	....	....	....	....	....	....	....
	Buffalo	**NHL**	**5**	**2**	**2**	**0**	**255**	**15**	**0**	**3.53**	....	....	....	....	....	....	....
	Rochester	AHL	14	4	6	1	672	41	0	3.66	1	0	1	27	1	0	2.24
	NHL Totals		**46**	**16**	**18**	**7**	**2521**	**126**	**1**	**3.00**	**2**	**0**	**1**	**96**	**5**	**0**	**3.13**

a WCHA First All-Star Team (1986)

Traded to **Minnesota** by **Winnipeg** for Winnipeg's seventh round choice (Markus Akerblom) in 1988 Entry Draft, March 7, 1988. Signed as a free agent by **Boston**, August 1, 1991. Signed as a free agent by **Buffalo**, December 28, 1995.

BONNER, DOUG TOR.

Goaltender. Catches left. 5'10", 175 lbs. Born, Tacoma, WA, October 15, 1976.
(Toronto's 3rd choice, 139th overall, in 1995 Entry Draft).

			Regular Season								Playoffs						
Season	Club	Lea	GP	W	L	T	Mins	GA	SO	Avg	GP	W	L	Mins	GA	SO	Avg
1992-93	Seattle	WHL	30	7	15	0	1212	93	1	4.60	....	....	....	....	....	....	....
1993-94	Seattle	WHL	29	9	15	0	1481	111	1	4.50	....	....	....	....	....	....	....
1994-95	Seattle	WHL	59	33	23	1	3386	205	1	3.63	3	0	3	193	10	0	3.11
1995-96	Seattle	WHL	58	20	27	7	3219	190	2	3.54	5	1	4	317	19	0	3.60

BOUCHER, BRIAN (BOO-shay) PHI.

Goaltender. Catches left. 6'1", 190 lbs. Born, Woonsocket, RI, January 2, 1977.
(Philadelphia's 1st choice, 22nd overall, in 1995 Entry Draft).

			Regular Season								Playoffs						
Season	Club	Lea	GP	W	L	T	Mins	GA	SO	Avg	GP	W	L	Mins	GA	SO	Avg
1994-95	Tri-City	WHL	35	17	11	2	1969	108	1	3.29	13	6	5	795	50	0	3.77
1995-96	Tri-City	WHL	55	33	19	2	3183	181	1	3.41	11	6	5	653	37	*2	3.40

BRATHWAITE, FRED (BRAYTH-wayt)

Goaltender. Catches left. 5'7", 170 lbs. Born, Ottawa, Ont., November 24, 1972.

			Regular Season								Playoffs						
Season	Club	Lea	GP	W	L	T	Mins	GA	SO	Avg	GP	W	L	Mins	GA	SO	Avg
1989-90	Oshawa	OHL	20	11	2	1	886	43	1	2.91	10	4	2	451	22	0	*2.93
1990-91	Oshawa	OHL	39	25	6	3	1986	112	1	3.38	13	*9	2	677	43	0	3.81
1991-92	Oshawa	OHL	24	12	7	2	1248	81	0	3.89	....	....	....	....	....	....	....
	London	OHL	23	15	6	2	1325	61	*4	2.76	10	5	5	615	36	0	3.51
1992-93	Detroit	OHL	37	23	10	4	2192	134	0	3.67	15	9	6	858	48	1	3.36
1993-94	**Edmonton**	**NHL**	**19**	**3**	**10**	**3**	**982**	**58**	**0**	**3.54**	....	....	....	....	....	....	....
	Cape Breton	AHL	2	1	1	0	119	6	0	3.04	....	....	....	....	....	....	....
1994-95	**Edmonton**	**NHL**	**14**	**2**	**5**	**1**	**601**	**40**	**0**	**3.99**	....	....	....	....	....	....	....
1995-96	**Edmonton**	**NHL**	**7**	**0**	**2**	**0**	**293**	**12**	**0**	**2.46**	....	....	....	....	....	....	....
	Cape Breton	AHL	31	12	16	0	1699	110	1	3.88	....	....	....	....	....	....	....
	NHL Totals		**40**	**5**	**17**	**4**	**1876**	**110**	**0**	**3.52**	....	....	....	....	....	....	....

Signed as a free agent by **Edmonton**, October 6, 1993.

BROCHU, MARTIN (broh-shoo)

Goaltender. Catches left. 5'10", 200 lbs. Born, Anjou, Que., March 10, 1973.

			Regular Season								Playoffs						
Season	Club	Lea	GP	W	L	T	Mins	GA	SO	Avg	GP	W	L	Mins	GA	SO	Avg
1991-92	Granby	QMJHL	52	15	29	2	2772	278	0	4.72	....	....	....	....	....	....	....
1992-93	Hull	QMJHL	29	9	15	1	1453	137	0	5.66	2	0	1	69	7	0	6.07
1993-94	Fredericton	AHL	32	10	11	3	1505	76	2	3.03	....	....	....	....	....	....	....
1994-95	Fredericton	AHL	44	18	18	4	2475	145	0	3.51	....	....	....	....	....	....	....
1995-96	Fredericton	AHL	17	6	8	2	986	70	0	4.26	....	....	....	....	....	....	....
	Wheeling	ECHL	19	10	6	2	1060	51	1	2.89	....	....	....	....	....	....	....
	Portland	AHL	5	2	2	1	287	15	0	3.14	12	7	4	700	28	*2	*2.40

Signed as a free agent by **Montreal**, September 22, 1992. Traded to **Washington** by **Montreal** for future considerations, March 15, 1996.

BRODEUR, MARTIN (broh-DOOR, MAHR-tihn) N.J.

Goaltender. Catches left. 6'1", 205 lbs. Born, Montreal, Que., May 6, 1972.
(New Jersey's 1st choice, 20th overall, in 1990 Entry Draft).

			Regular Season								Playoffs							
Season	Club	Lea	GP	W	L	T	Mins	GA	SO	Avg	GP	W	L	Mins	GA	SO	Avg	
1989-90	St-Hyacinthe	QMJHL	42	23	13	2	2333	156	0	4.01	12	5	7	678	46	0	4.07	
1990-91	St-Hyacinthe	QMJHL	52	22	24	4	2946	162	2	3.30	4	0	4	232	16	0	4.14	
1991-92	**New Jersey**	**NHL**	**4**	**2**	**1**	**0**	**179**	**10**	**0**	**3.35**	**1**	**0**	**1**	**32**	**3**	**0**	**5.63**	
a	St-Hyacinthe	QMJHL	48	27	16	4	2846	161	2	3.39	5	2	3	317	14	0	2.65	
1992-93	Utica	AHL	32	14	13	5	1952	131	0	4.03	4	1	3	258	18	0	4.19	
1993-94bc	**New Jersey**	**NHL**	**47**	**27**	**11**	**8**	**2625**	**105**	**3**	**2.40**	**17**	**8**	**9**	**1171**	**38**	**1**	**1.95**	
1994-95	**New Jersey**	**NHL**	**40**	**19**	**11**	**6**	**2184**	**89**	**3**	**2.45**	***20**	***16**	**4**	***1222**	**34**	***3**	***1.67**	♦
1995-96	**New Jersey**	**NHL**	**77**	**34**	**30**	**12**	***4433**	**173**	**6**	**2.34**	....	....	....	....	....	....	....	
	NHL Totals		**168**	**82**	**53**	**26**	**9421**	**377**	**12**	**2.40**	**38**	**24**	**14**	**2425**	**75**	**4**	**1.86**	

a QMJHL Second All-Star Team (1992)
b NHL/Upper Deck All-Rookie Team (1994)
c Won Calder Memorial Trophy (1994)

Played in NHL All-Star Game (1996)

BURKE, SEAN HFD.

Goaltender. Catches left. 6'4", 208 lbs. Born, Windsor, Ont., January 29, 1967.
(New Jersey's 2nd choice, 24th overall, in 1985 Entry Draft).

			Regular Season								Playoffs						
Season	Club	Lea	GP	W	L	T	Mins	GA	SO	Avg	GP	W	L	Mins	GA	SO	Avg
1984-85	Toronto	OHL	49	25	21	3	2987	211	0	4.24	5	1	3	266	25	0	5.64
1985-86	Toronto	OHL	47	16	27	3	2840	233	0	4.92	4	0	4	238	24	0	6.05
1986-87	Cdn. National	....	42	27	13	2	2550	130	0	3.05	....	....	....	....	....	....	....
1987-88	Cdn. National	....	37	19	9	2	1962	92	1	2.81	....	....	....	....	....	....	....
	Cdn. Olympic	....	4	1	2	1	238	12	0	3.02	....	....	....	....	....	....	....
	New Jersey	**NHL**	**13**	**10**	**1**	**0**	**689**	**35**	**1**	**3.05**	**17**	**9**	**8**	**1001**	**57**	***1**	**3.42**
1988-89	**New Jersey**	**NHL**	**62**	**22**	**31**	**9**	**3590**	**230**	**3**	**3.84**	....	....	....	....	....	....	....
1989-90	**New Jersey**	**NHL**	**52**	**22**	**22**	**6**	**2914**	**175**	**0**	**3.60**	**2**	**0**	**2**	**125**	**8**	**0**	**3.84**
1990-91	**New Jersey**	**NHL**	**35**	**8**	**12**	**8**	**1870**	**112**	**0**	**3.59**	....	....	....	....	....	....	....
1991-92	Cdn. National	....	31	18	6	4	1721	75	1	2.61	....	....	....	....	....	....	....
	Cdn. Olympic	....	7	5	2	0	429	17	0	2.37	....	....	....	....	....	....	....
	San Diego	IHL	7	4	2	1	424	17	0	2.41	3	0	3	160	13	0	4.88
1992-93	**Hartford**	**NHL**	**50**	**16**	**27**	**3**	**2656**	**184**	**0**	**4.16**	....	....	....	....	....	....	....
1993-94	**Hartford**	**NHL**	**47**	**17**	**24**	**5**	**2750**	**137**	**2**	**2.99**	....	....	....	....	....	....	....
1994-95	**Hartford**	**NHL**	**42**	**17**	**19**	**4**	**2418**	**108**	**0**	**2.68**	....	....	....	....	....	....	....
1995-96	**Hartford**	**NHL**	**66**	**28**	**28**	**6**	**3669**	**190**	**4**	**3.11**	....	....	....	....	....	....	....
	NHL Totals		**367**	**140**	**164**	**41**	**20556**	**1171**	**10**	**3.42**	**19**	**9**	**10**	**1126**	**65**	**1**	**3.46**

Played in NHL All-Star Game (1989)

Traded to **Hartford** by **New Jersey** with Eric Weinrich for Bobby Holik, Hartford's second round choice (Jay Pandolfo) in 1993 Entry Draft and future considerations, August 28, 1992.

BUZAK, MIKE ST.L.

Goaltender. Catches left. 6'3", 183 lbs. Born, Edson, Alta., February 10, 1973.
(St. Louis' 5th choice, 167th overall, in 1993 Entry Draft).

			Regular Season								Playoffs						
Season	Club	Lea	GP	W	L	T	Mins	GA	SO	Avg	GP	W	L	Mins	GA	SO	Avg
1991-92	Michigan State	CCHA	7	4	0	0	311	22	0	4.25	....	....	....	....	....	....	....
1992-93	Michigan State	CCHA	38	22	10	2	*2090	102	0	2.93	....	....	....	....	....	....	....
1993-94a	Michigan State	CCHA	*39	21	12	5	*2297	104	2	2.72	....	....	....	....	....	....	....
1994-95a	Michigan State	CCHA	31	17	10	3	1796	94	0	3.14	....	....	....	....	....	....	....
1995-96	Worcester	AHL	30	9	10	5	1672	85	0	3.05	....	....	....	....	....	....	....

a CCHA Second All-Star Team (1994, 1995)

CARAVAGGIO, LUCIANO N.J.

Goaltender. Catches left. 5'11", 175 lbs. Born, Etobicoke, Ont., October 3, 1975.
(New Jersey's 7th choice, 155th overall, in 1994 Entry Draft).

			Regular Season								Playoffs						
Season	Club	Lea	GP	W	L	T	Mins	GA	SO	Avg	GP	W	L	Mins	GA	SO	Avg
1993-94	Michigan Tech	WCHA	13	1	7	0	538	37	*1	4.13	....	....	....	....	....	....	....
1994-95	Michigan Tech	WCHA	31	12	5	3	1776	119	*1	4.02	....	....	....	....	....	....	....
1995-96	Michigan Tech	WCHA	25	7	11	4	1280	85	0	3.98	....	....	....	....	....	....	....

CAREY, JIM WSH.

Goaltender. Catches left. 6'2", 205 lbs. Born, Dorchester, MA, May 31, 1974.
(Washington's 2nd choice, 32nd overall, in 1992 Entry Draft).

			Regular Season								Playoffs						
Season	Club	Lea	GP	W	L	T	Mins	GA	SO	Avg	GP	W	L	Mins	GA	SO	Avg
1992-93a	U. Wisconsin	WCHA	26	15	8	1	1525	78	1	3.07	....	....	....	....	....	....	....
1993-94	U. Wisconsin	WCHA	*40	*24	13	1	*2247	114	*1	*3.04	....	....	....	....	....	....	....
1994-95bcd	Portland	AHL	55	30	14	11	3281	151	*6	2.76	....	....	....	....	....	....	....
e	**Washington**	**NHL**	**28**	**18**	**6**	**3**	**1604**	**57**	**4**	**2.13**	**7**	**2**	**4**	**358**	**25**	**0**	**4.19**
1995-96fg	**Washington**	**NHL**	**71**	**35**	**24**	**9**	**4069**	**153**	***9**	**2.26**	**3**	**0**	**1**	**97**	**10**	**0**	**6.19**
	NHL Totals		**99**	**53**	**30**	**12**	**5673**	**210**	**13**	**2.22**	**10**	**2**	**5**	**455**	**35**	**0**	**4.62**

a WCHA Second All-Star Team (1993)
b AHL First All-Star Team (1995)
c Won Baz Bastien Memorial Trophy (Top Goaltender - AHL) (1995)
d Won Dudley "Red" Garrett Memorial Trophy (Top Rookie - AHL) (1995)
e NHL/Upper Deck All-Rookie Team (1995)
f NHL First All-Star Team (1996)
g Won Vezina Trophy (1996)

CASEY, JON — ST.L.

Goaltender. Catches left. 5'10", 155 lbs. Born, Grand Rapids, MN, March 29, 1962.

						Regular Season								Playoffs			
Season	Club	Lea	GP	W	L	T	Mins	GA	SO	Avg	GP	W	L	Mins	GA	SO	Avg
1980-81	North Dakota	WCHA	5	3	1	0	300	19	0	3.80	....	....	....	....	....	....	....
1981-82	North Dakota	WCHA	18	15	3	0	1038	48	1	2.77	....	....	....	....	....	....	....
1982-83	North Dakota	WCHA	17	9	6	2	1020	42	0	2.51	....	....	....	....	....	....	....
1983-84	North Dakota	WCHA	37	25	10	2	2180	115	2	3.13	....	....	....	....	....	....	....
	Minnesota	**NHL**	**2**	**1**	**0**	**0**	**84**	**6**	**0**	**4.29**	....	....	....	....	....	....	....
1984-85abc	Baltimore	AHL	46	30	11	4	2646	116	*4	*2.63	*13	8	3	689	38	0	3.31
1985-86	**Minnesota**	**NHL**	**26**	**11**	**11**	**1**	**1402**	**91**	**0**	**3.89**	....	....	....	....	....	....	....
	Springfield	AHL	9	4	3	1	464	30	0	3.88	....	....	....	....	....	....	....
1986-87	Springfield	AHL	13	1	8	0	770	56	0	4.36	....	....	....	....	....	....	....
	Indianapolis	IHL	31	14	15	0	1794	133	0	4.45	....	....	....	....	....	....	....
1987-88	**Minnesota**	**NHL**	**14**	**1**	**7**	**4**	**663**	**41**	**0**	**3.71**	....	....	....	....	....	....	....
	Kalamazoo	IHL	42	24	13	5	2541	154	2	3.64	7	3	3	382	26	0	4.08
1988-89	**Minnesota**	**NHL**	**55**	**18**	**17**	**12**	**2961**	**151**	**1**	**3.06**	**4**	**1**	**3**	**211**	**16**	**0**	**4.55**
1989-90	**Minnesota**	**NHL**	**61**	***31**	**22**	**4**	**3407**	**183**	**3**	**3.22**	**7**	**3**	**4**	**415**	**21**	**1**	**3.04**
1990-91	**Minnesota**	**NHL**	**55**	**21**	**20**	**11**	**3185**	**158**	**3**	**2.98**	***23**	***14**	**7**	***1205**	**61**	***1**	**3.04**
1991-92	**Minnesota**	**NHL**	**52**	**19**	**23**	**5**	**2911**	**165**	**2**	**3.40**	**7**	**3**	**4**	**437**	**22**	**0**	**3.02**
	Kalamazoo	IHL	4	2	1	1	250	11	0	2.64	....	....	....	....	....	....	....
1992-93	**Minnesota**	**NHL**	**60**	**26**	**26**	**5**	**3476**	**193**	**3**	**3.33**	....	....	....	....	....	....	....
1993-94	**Boston**	**NHL**	**57**	**30**	**15**	**9**	**3192**	**153**	**4**	**2.88**	**11**	**5**	**6**	**698**	**34**	**0**	**2.92**
1994-95	**St. Louis**	**NHL**	**19**	**7**	**5**	**4**	**872**	**40**	**0**	**2.75**	**2**	**0**	**1**	**30**	**2**	**0**	**4.00**
1995-96	**St. Louis**	**NHL**	**9**	**2**	**3**	**0**	**395**	**25**	**0**	**3.80**	**12**	**6**	**6**	**747**	**36**	**1**	**2.89**
	Peoria	IHL	43	21	19	2	2514	128	3	3.05	....	....	....	....	....	....	....
	NHL Totals		**410**	**167**	**149**	**55**	**22548**	**1206**	**16**	**3.21**	**66**	**32**	**31**	**3743**	**192**	**3**	**3.08**

a Won Baz Bastien Memorial Trophy (Top Goaltender - AHL) (1985)
b Won Harry "Hap" Holmes Memorial Trophy (fewest goals against - AHL) (1985)
c AHL First All-Star Team (1985)

Played in NHL All-Star Game (1993)

Signed as a free agent by **Minnesota**, April 1, 1984. Traded to **Boston** by **Dallas** for Andy Moog to complete June 20, 1993 trade which sent Gord Murphy to Dallas for future considerations, June 25, 1993. Signed as a free agent by **St. Louis**, June 29, 1994.

CASSIVI, FREDERIC — OTT.

Goaltender. Catches left. 6'3", 193 lbs. Born, Sorel, Que., June 12, 1975.
(Ottawa's 7th choice, 210th overall, in 1994 Entry Draft).

						Regular Season								Playoffs			
Season	Club	Lea	GP	W	L	T	Mins	GA	SO	Avg	GP	W	L	Mins	GA	SO	Avg
1993-94	St-Hyacinthe	QMJHL	35	15	13	3	1751	127	1	4.35	....	....	....	....	....	....	....
1994-95	Halifax	QMJHL	24	9	12	1	1362	105	0	4.63	....	....	....	....	....	....	....
	St-Jean	QMJHL	19	12	6	0	1021	55	1	3.23	5	2	3	258	18	0	4.19
1995-96	Thunder Bay	ColHL	12	6	4	2	715	51	0	4.28	....	....	....	....	....	....	....
	P.E.I.	AHL	41	20	14	3	2347	128	1	3.27	5	2	3	317	24	0	4.54

CAVICCHI, TRENT — MTL.

Goaltender. Catches left. 6'3", 180 lbs. Born, Halifax, N.S., August 11, 1974.
(Montreal's 12th choice, 236th overall, in 1992 Entry Draft).

						Regular Season								Playoffs			
Season	Club	Lea	GP	W	L	T	Mins	GA	SO	Avg	GP	W	L	Mins	GA	SO	Avg
1992-93	N. Hampshire	H.E.	9	3	2	1	391	32	0	4.91	....	....	....	....	....	....	....
1993-94	N. Hampshire	H.E.	25	14	7	1	1324	65	1	2.95	....	....	....	....	....	....	....
1994-95	N. Hampshire	H.E.	23	14	6	1	1276	71	0	3.34	....	....	....	....	....	....	....
1995-96	N. Hampshire	H.E.	24	9	12	3	1340	95	0	4.25	....	....	....	....	....	....	....

CHABOT, FREDERIC — (shah-BOH)

Goaltender. Catches left. 5'11", 175 lbs. Born, Hebertville-Station, Que., February 12, 1968.
(New Jersey's 10th choice, 192nd overall, in 1986 Entry Draft).

						Regular Season								Playoffs			
Season	Club	Lea	GP	W	L	T	Mins	GA	SO	Avg	GP	W	L	Mins	GA	SO	Avg
1986-87	Drummondville	QMJHL	62	31	29	0	3508	293	1	5.01	8	2	6	481	40	0	4.99
1987-88	Drummondville	QMJHL	58	27	24	4	3276	237	1	4.34	16	10	6	1019	56	*1	*3.30
1988-89a	Prince Albert	WHL	54	21	29	0	2957	202	2	4.10	4	1	1	199	16	0	4.82
1989-90	Sherbrooke	AHL	2	1	1	0	119	8	0	4.03	....	....	....	....	....	....	....
	Fort Wayne	IHL	23	6	13	3	1208	87	1	4.32	....	....	....	....	....	....	....
1990-91	**Montreal**	**NHL**	**3**	**0**	**0**	**1**	**108**	**6**	**0**	**3.33**	....	....	....	....	....	....	....
	Fredericton	AHL	35	9	15	5	1800	122	0	4.07	....	....	....	....	....	....	....
1991-92	Fredericton	AHL	30	17	9	4	1761	79	2	*2.69	7	3	4	457	20	0	2.63
	Winston-Salem	ECHL	24	15	7	2	1449	71	0	*2.94	....	....	....	....	....	....	....
1992-93	**Montreal**	**NHL**	**1**	**0**	**0**	**0**	**40**	**1**	**0**	**1.50**	....	....	....	....	....	....	....
	Fredericton	AHL	45	22	17	4	2544	141	0	3.33	4	1	3	261	16	0	3.68
1993-94	**Montreal**	**NHL**	**1**	**0**	**1**	**0**	**60**	**5**	**0**	**5.00**	....	....	....	....	....	....	....
	Fredericton	AHL	3	0	1	1	143	12	0	5.03	....	....	....	....	....	....	....
	Las Vegas	IHL	2	1	1	0	110	5	0	2.72	....	....	....	....	....	....	....
	Philadelphia	**NHL**	**4**	**0**	**1**	**1**	**70**	**5**	**0**	**4.29**	....	....	....	....	....	....	....
b	Hershey	AHL	28	13	5	6	1464	63	2	*2.58	11	7	4	665	32	0	2.89
1994-95	Cincinnati	IHL	48	25	12	7	2622	128	1	2.93	5	3	2	326	16	0	2.94
1995-96c	Cincinnati	IHL	38	23	9	4	2147	88	3	*2.46	14	9	5	854	37	1	2.60
	NHL Totals		**9**	**0**	**2**	**2**	**278**	**17**	**0**	**3.67**	....	....	....	....	....	....	....

a WHL East All-Star Team (1989)
b Won Baz Bastien Award (Top Goaltender - AHL) (1994)
c IHL Second All-Star Team (1996)

Signed as a free agent by **Montreal**, January 16, 1990. Claimed by **Tampa Bay** from **Montreal** in Expansion Draft, June 18, 1992. Traded to **Montreal** by **Tampa Bay** for J.C. Bergeron, June 19, 1992. Traded to **Philadelphia** by **Montreal** for cash, February 21, 1994. Signed as a free agent by **Florida**, August 11, 1994.

CHARBONNEAU, PATRICK — OTT.

Goaltender. Catches left. 5'11", 205 lbs. Born, St-Jean sur Richelieu, Que., July 22, 1975.
(Ottawa's 3rd choice, 53rd overall, in 1993 Entry Draft).

						Regular Season								Playoffs			
Season	Club	Lea	GP	W	L	T	Mins	GA	SO	Avg	GP	W	L	Mins	GA	SO	Avg
1991-92	Victoriaville	QMJHL	37	9	23	2	1943	163	0	5.03	....	....	....	....	....	....	....
1992-93	Victoriaville	QMJHL	59	*35	22	0	3121	216	0	4.15	2	1	0	92	4	0	2.61
1993-94	Victoriaville	QMJHL	56	11	34	2	2948	261	0	5.31	5	1	4	212	24	0	6.79
	P.E.I.	AHL	3	2	1	0	180	11	0	3.67	....	....	....	....	....	....	....
1994-95	Victoriaville	QMJHL	47	15	27	1	2339	201	0	5.16	4	0	3	142	20	0	8.45
	P.E.I.	AHL	2	2	0	0	120	4	0	2.00	3	0	2	137	12	0	5.24
1995-96	Thunder Bay	ColHL	29	16	7	3	1587	86	1	3.25	*19	*10	8	*942	63	0	4.01
	P.E.I.	AHL	17	5	8	0	864	69	0	4.79	....	....	....	....	....	....	....

CHARPENTIER, SEBASTIEN — WSH.

Goaltender. Catches left. 5'9", 161 lbs. Born, Drummondville, Que., April 18, 1977.
(Washington's 4th choice, 93rd overall, in 1995 Entry Draft).

						Regular Season								Playoffs			
Season	Club	Lea	GP	W	L	T	Mins	GA	SO	Avg	GP	W	L	Mins	GA	SO	Avg
1994-95	Laval	QMJHL	41	25	12	1	2152	99	2	2.76	16	9	4	886	45	0	3.05
1995-96	Laval	QMJHL	18	4	10	0	938	97	0	6.20	....	....	....	....	....	....	....
	Val d'Or	QMJHL	33	21	9	1	1906	87	1	2.74	13	7	5	....	....	....	3.64

CHEVELDAE, TIM — (SHEH-vehl-day) BOS.

Goaltender. Catches left. 5'10", 195 lbs. Born, Melville, Sask., February 15, 1968.
(Detroit's 4th choice, 64th overall, in 1986 Entry Draft).

						Regular Season								Playoffs			
Season	Club	Lea	GP	W	L	T	Mins	GA	SO	Avg	GP	W	L	Mins	GA	SO	Avg
1985-86	Saskatoon	WHL	36	21	10	3	2030	165	0	4.88	8	6	2	480	29	0	3.63
1986-87	Saskatoon	WHL	33	20	11	0	1909	133	2	4.18	5	4	1	308	20	0	3.90
1987-88a	Saskatoon	WHL	66	44	19	3	3798	235	1	3.71	6	4	2	364	27	0	4.45
1988-89	**Detroit**	**NHL**	**2**	**0**	**2**	**0**	**122**	**9**	**0**	**4.43**	....	....	....	....	....	....	....
	Adirondack	AHL	30	20	8	0	1694	98	1	3.47	2	1	0	99	9	0	5.45
1989-90	**Detroit**	**NHL**	**28**	**10**	**9**	**8**	**1600**	**101**	**0**	**3.79**	....	....	....	....	....	....	....
	Adirondack	AHL	31	17	8	6	1848	116	0	3.77	....	....	....	....	....	....	....
1990-91	**Detroit**	**NHL**	**65**	**30**	**26**	**5**	**3615**	**214**	**2**	**3.55**	**7**	**3**	**4**	**398**	**22**	**0**	**3.32**
1991-92	**Detroit**	**NHL**	***72**	***38**	**23**	**9**	***4236**	**226**	**2**	**3.20**	**11**	**3**	**7**	**597**	**25**	***2**	**2.51**
1992-93	**Detroit**	**NHL**	**67**	**34**	**24**	**7**	**3880**	**210**	**4**	**3.25**	**7**	**3**	**4**	**423**	**24**	**0**	**3.40**
1993-94	**Detroit**	**NHL**	**30**	**16**	**9**	**1**	**1572**	**91**	**1**	**3.47**	....	....	....	....	....	....	....
	Adirondack	AHL	2	1	0	1	125	7	0	3.36	....	....	....	....	....	....	....
	Winnipeg	**NHL**	**14**	**5**	**8**	**1**	**788**	**52**	**1**	**3.96**	....	....	....	....	....	....	....
1994-95	**Winnipeg**	**NHL**	**30**	**8**	**16**	**3**	**1571**	**97**	**0**	**3.70**	....	....	....	....	....	....	....
1995-96	**Winnipeg**	**NHL**	**30**	**8**	**18**	**3**	**1695**	**111**	**0**	**3.93**	....	....	....	....	....	....	....
	Hershey	AHL	8	4	3	0	457	31	0	4.07	4	2	2	250	14	0	3.36
	NHL Totals		**338**	**149**	**135**	**37**	**19079**	**1111**	**10**	**3.49**	**25**	**9**	**15**	**1418**	**71**	**2**	**3.00**

a WHL East All-Star Team (1988)

Played in NHL All-Star Game (1992)

Traded to **Winnipeg** by **Detroit** with Dallas Drake for Bob Essensa and Sergei Bautin, March 8, 1994. Traded to **Philadelphia** by **Winnipeg** with Winnipeg's third round choice (Chester Gallant) in 1996 Entry Draft, February 27, 1996. Signed as a free agent by **Boston**, August 27, 1996.

CLOUTIER, DAN — NYR

Goaltender. Catches left. 6'1", 182 lbs. Born, Mont-Laurier, Que., April 22, 1976.
(NY Rangers' 1st choice, 26th overall, in 1994 Entry Draft).

						Regular Season								Playoffs			
Season	Club	Lea	GP	W	L	T	Mins	GA	SO	Avg	GP	W	L	Mins	GA	SO	Avg
1992-93	S.S. Marie	OHL	12	4	6	0	572	44	0	4.62	4	1	2	231	12	0	3.12
1993-94	S.S. Marie	OHL	55	28	14	6	2934	174	*2	3.56	14	*10	4	833	52	0	3.75
1994-95	S.S. Marie	OHL	45	15	26	2	2518	185	1	4.41	....	....	....	....	....	....	....
1995-96	S.S. Marie	OHL	13	9	3	0	641	43	0	4.02	....	....	....	....	....	....	....
a	Guelph	OHL	17	12	2	2	1004	35	2	2.09	16	11	5	993	52	*2	3.14

a OHL Second All-Star Team (1996)

COUSINEAU, MARCEL — (koo-ZEE-noh) TOR.

Goaltender. Catches left. 5'9", 180 lbs. Born, Delson, Que., April 30, 1973.
(Boston's 3rd choice, 62nd overall, in 1991 Entry Draft).

						Regular Season								Playoffs			
Season	Club	Lea	GP	W	L	T	Mins	GA	SO	Avg	GP	W	L	Mins	GA	SO	Avg
1990-91	Beauport	QMJHL	49	13	29	3	2739	196	1	4.29	....	....	....	....	....	....	....
1991-92	Beauport	QMJHL	*67	26	32	5	*3673	241	0	3.94	....	....	....	....	....	....	....
1992-93	Drummondville	QMJHL	60	20	32	2	3298	225	0	4.09	9	3	6	498	37	*1	4.45
1993-94	St. John's	AHL	37	13	11	9	2015	118	0	3.51	....	....	....	....	....	....	....
1994-95	St. John's	AHL	58	22	27	6	3342	171	4	3.07	3	0	3	179	9	0	3.01
1995-96	St. John's	AHL	62	21	26	13	3629	192	1	3.17	4	1	3	258	11	0	2.56

Signed as a free agent by **Toronto**, November 13, 1993.

CUGNET, JASON — VAN.

Goaltender. Catches left. 6'1", 176 lbs. Born, North Battleford, Sask., July 31, 1976.
(Vancouver's 9th choice, 222nd overall, in 1995 Entry Draft).

						Regular Season								Playoffs			
Season	Club	Lea	GP	W	L	T	Mins	GA	SO	Avg	GP	W	L	Mins	GA	SO	Avg
1994-95	Kelowna	BCJHL	24	18	4	0	1391	77	1	3.32	....	....	....	....	....	....	....
1995-96	Kelowna	BCJHL	1	1	0	0	60	5	0	5.00	....	....	....	....	....	....	....

DAFOE, BYRON — (day-FOH) L.A.

Goaltender. Catches left. 5'11", 175 lbs. Born, Sussex, England, February 25, 1971.
(Washington's 2nd choice, 35th overall, in 1989 Entry Draft).

						Regular Season								Playoffs			
Season	Club	Lea	GP	W	L	T	Mins	GA	SO	Avg	GP	W	L	Mins	GA	SO	Avg
1988-89	Portland	WHL	59	29	24	3	3279	291	1	5.32	*18	10	8	*1091	81	*1	4.45
1989-90	Portland	WHL	40	14	21	3	2265	193	0	5.11	....	....	....	....	....	....	....
1990-91	Portland	WHL	8	1	5	1	414	41	0	5.94	....	....	....	....	....	....	....
	Prince Albert	WHL	32	13	12	4	1839	124	0	4.05	....	....	....	....	....	....	....
1991-92	New Haven	AHL	7	3	2	1	364	22	0	3.63	....	....	....	....	....	....	....
	Baltimore	AHL	33	12	16	4	1847	119	0	3.87	....	....	....	....	....	....	....
	Hampton Rds.	ECHL	10	6	4	0	562	26	0	2.78	....	....	....	....	....	....	....
1992-93	**Washington**	**NHL**	**1**	**0**	**0**	**0**	**1**	**0**	**0**	**0.00**	....	....	....	....	....	....	....
	Baltimore	AHL	48	16	20	7	2617	191	1	4.38	5	2	3	241	22	0	5.48
1993-94	**Washington**	**NHL**	**5**	**2**	**2**	**0**	**230**	**13**	**0**	**3.39**	**2**	**0**	**2**	**118**	**5**	**0**	**2.54**
ab	Portland	AHL	47	24	16	4	2661	148	1	3.34	1	0	0	9	1	0	6.79
1994-95	Phoenix	IHL	49	25	16	6	2743	169	2	3.70	....	....	....	....	....	....	....
	Washington	**NHL**	**4**	**1**	**1**	**1**	**187**	**11**	**0**	**3.53**	**1**	**0**	**0**	**20**	**1**	**0**	**3.00**
	Portland	AHL	6	5	0	0	330	16	0	2.91	7	3	4	416	29	0	4.18
1995-96	**Los Angeles**	**NHL**	**47**	**14**	**24**	**8**	**2666**	**172**	**1**	**3.87**	....	....	....	....	....	....	....
	NHL Totals		**57**	**17**	**27**	**9**	**3084**	**196**	**1**	**3.81**	**3**	**0**	**2**	**138**	**6**	**0**	**2.61**

a AHL First All-Star Team (1994)
b Share Harry "Hap" Holmes Trophy (fewest goals-against - AHL) with Olaf Kolzig (1994)

Traded to **Los Angeles** by **Washington** with Dimitri Khristich for Los Angeles' first round choice (Alexander Volchkov) and Dallas' fourth round choice (previously acquired by Los Angeles — Washington selected Justin Davis) in 1996 Entry Draft, July 8, 1995.

DAIGLE, SYLVAIN — (DAYG) PHO.

Goaltender. Catches right. 5'8", 185 lbs. Born, St-Hyacinthe, Que., October 20, 1976.
(Winnipeg's 7th choice, 136th overall, in 1995 Entry Draft).

						Regular Season								Playoffs			
Season	Club	Lea	GP	W	L	T	Mins	GA	SO	Avg	GP	W	L	Mins	GA	SO	Avg
1993-94	Shawinigan	QMJHL	31	....	....	....	1645	113	0	4.12	....	....	....	....	....	....	....
1994-95	Shawinigan	QMJHL	48	27	17	3	2831	159	3	3.37	14	7	6	824	57	0	4.15
1995-96	Shawinigan	QMJHL	49	23	14	5	2708	159	*3	3.52	6	2	4	....	....	....	3.39

DAUBENSPECK, KIRK — OTT.

Goaltender. Catches left. 6'1", 170 lbs. Born, Madison, WI, July 16, 1974.
(Philadelphia's 7th choice, 151st overall, in 1992 Entry Draft).

						Regular Season								Playoffs			
Season	Club	Lea	GP	W	L	T	Mins	GA	SO	Avg	GP	W	L	Mins	GA	SO	Avg
1993-94	U. Wisconsin	WCHA	7	2	2	0	280	19	0	4.07	....	....	....	....	....	....	....
1994-95	U. Wisconsin	WCHA	42	*23	15	4	*2503	146	0	3.51	....	....	....	....	....	....	....
1995-96	U. Wisconsin	WCHA	*39	*17	20	2	*2357	151	0	3.84	....	....	....	....	....	....	....

Traded to **Ottawa** by **Philadelphia** with Claude Boivin for Mark Lamb, March 5, 1994.

DAVIS, CHRIS — BUF.

Goaltender. Catches left. 6'3", 177 lbs. Born, Calgary, Alta., December 1, 1974.
(Buffalo's 8th choice, 246th overall, in 1993 Entry Draft).

			Regular Season								Playoffs						
Season	Club	Lea	GP	W	L	T	Mins	GA	SO	Avg	GP	W	L	Mins	GA	SO	Avg
1993-94	Alaska-Anch.	WCHA	9	2	4	0	390	27	0	4.15	....	....	....	....	....	....	....
1994-95	Alaska-Anch.	WCHA	14	4	6	0	670	49	0	4.39	....	....	....	....	....	....	....
1995-96	Alaska-Anch.	WCHA	22	6	10	3	1146	80	1	4.19	....	....	....	....	....	....	....

DENIS, MARC — COL.

Goaltender. Catches left. 6', 188 lbs. Born, Montreal, Que., August 1, 1977.
(Colorado's 1st choice, 25th overall, in 1995 Entry Draft).

			Regular Season								Playoffs						
Season	Club	Lea	GP	W	L	T	Mins	GA	SO	Avg	GP	W	L	Mins	GA	SO	Avg
1994-95	Chicoutimi	QMJHL	32	17	9	1	1688	98	0	3.48	6	4	2	372	19	1	3.06
1995-96	Chicoutimi	QMJHL	51	23	21	4	2951	157	2	3.19	16	8	8	....	....	....	4.33

DeROUVILLE, PHILIPPE (deh-ROO-vihl) — PIT.

Goaltender. Catches left. 6'1", 185 lbs. Born, Victoriaville, Que., August 7, 1974.
(Pittsburgh's 5th choice, 115th overall, in 1992 Entry Draft).

			Regular Season								Playoffs						
Season	Club	Lea	GP	W	L	T	Mins	GA	SO	Avg	GP	W	L	Mins	GA	SO	Avg
1990-91	Longueuil	QMJHL	20	13	6	0	1030	50	0	2.91	....	....	....	....	....	....	....
1991-92	Verdun	QMJHL	34	20	6	3	1854	99	2	3.20	11	7	3	593	28	1	2.83
1992-93a	Verdun	QMJHL	61	30	27	2	3491	210	1	3.61	4	0	4	256	18	0	3.61
1993-94a	Verdun	QMJHL	51	28	22	0	2845	145	1	*3.06	4	0	4	210	14	0	4.00
1994-95	Cleveland	IHL	41	24	10	5	2369	131	1	3.32	4	1	3	263	18	0	4.09
	Pittsburgh	**NHL**	**1**	**1**	**0**	**0**	**60**	**3**	**0**	**3.00**	....	....	....	....	....	....	....
1995-96	Cleveland	IHL	38	19	11	3	2008	129	1	3.86	....	....	....	....	....	....	....
	NHL Totals		**1**	**1**	**0**	**0**	**60**	**3**	**0**	**3.00**	....	....	....	....	....	....	....

a QMJHL Second All-Star Team (1993, 1994)

DESCHENES, FREDERIC — DET.

Goaltender. Catches left. 5'9", 164 lbs. Born, Quebec, Que., January 12, 1976.
(Detroit's 4th choice, 114th overall, in 1994 Entry Draft).

			Regular Season								Playoffs						
Season	Club	Lea	GP	W	L	T	Mins	GA	SO	Avg	GP	W	L	Mins	GA	SO	Avg
1993-94	Granby	QMJHL	35	14	15	1	1861	132	0	4.26	7	3	4	372	27	0	4.35
1994-95	Granby	QMJHL	45	16	23	1	2375	160	0	4.04	11	3	7	553	35	1	3.80
1995-96 abcde	Granby	QMJHL	47	*34	7	0	2505	110	2	*2.63	14	8	2	....	....	....	2.98

a QMJHL First All-Star Team (1996)
b Canadian Major Junior First All-Star Team (1996)
c Canadian Major Junior Goaltender of the Year (1996)
d Memorial Cup All-Star Team (1996)
e Won Hap Emms Memorial Trophy (Memorial Cup Tournament Top Goaltender) (1996)

DOPSON, ROBERT

Goaltender. Catches left. 6', 200 lbs. Born, Smiths Falls, Ont., August 21, 1967.

			Regular Season								Playoffs						
Season	Club	Lea	GP	W	L	T	Mins	GA	SO	Avg	GP	W	L	Mins	GA	SO	Avg
1989-90	Wilfred Laurier	OUAA	22	....	....	....	1319	57	0	2.59	....	....	....	....	....	....	....
1990-91	Muskegon	IHL	24	10	10	0	1243	90	0	4.34	....	....	....	....	....	....	....
	Louisville	ECHL	3	3	0	0	180	12	0	4.00	5	3	1	270	16	0	3.55
1991-92	Muskegon	IHL	28	13	12	2	1655	90	4	3.26	12	8	4	697	40	0	3.44
1992-93	Cleveland	IHL	50	26	15	3	2825	167	1	3.55	4	0	4	203	20	0	5.91
1993-94	**Pittsburgh**	**NHL**	**2**	**0**	**0**	**0**	**45**	**3**	**0**	**4.00**	....	....	....	....	....	....	....
	Cleveland	IHL	32	9	10	8	1681	109	0	3.89	....	....	....	....	....	....	....
1994-95	Houston	IHL	41	17	16	2	2102	119	0	3.40	1	0	0	40	6	0	9.00
1995-96	Louisiana	ECHL	2	1	0	1	120	4	0	2.00	....	....	....	....	....	....	....
	Kansas City	IHL	5	1	0	1	183	10	0	3.28	....	....	....	....	....	....	....
	Houston	IHL	33	9	13	2	1518	96	0	3.79	....	....	....	....	....	....	....
	NHL Totals		**2**	**0**	**0**	**0**	**45**	**3**	**0**	**4.00**	....	....	....	....	....	....	....

Signed as a free agent by **Pittsburgh**, July 6, 1991.

DRAPER, TOM

Goaltender. Catches left. 5'11", 185 lbs. Born, Outremont, Que., November 20, 1966.
(Winnipeg's 8th choice, 165th overall, in 1985 Entry Draft).

			Regular Season								Playoffs						
Season	Club	Lea	GP	W	L	T	Mins	GA	SO	Avg	GP	W	L	Mins	GA	SO	Avg
1983-84	U. of Vermont	ECAC	20	8	12	0	1205	82	0	4.08	....	....	....	....	....	....	....
1984-85	U. of Vermont	ECAC	24	5	17	0	1316	90	0	4.11	....	....	....	....	....	....	....
1985-86	U. of Vermont	ECAC	29	15	12	1	1697	87	1	3.08	....	....	....	....	....	....	....
1986-87a	U. of Vermont	ECAC	29	16	13	0	1662	96	2	3.47	....	....	....	....	....	....	....
1987-88	Tappara	Fin.	28	16	3	9	1619	87	0	3.22	....	....	....	....	....	....	....
1988-89	**Winnipeg**	**NHL**	**2**	**1**	**1**	**0**	**120**	**12**	**0**	**6.00**	....	....	....	....	....	....	....
b	Moncton	AHL	*54	27	17	5	*2962	171	2	3.46	7	5	2	419	24	0	3.44
1989-90	**Winnipeg**	**NHL**	**6**	**2**	**4**	**0**	**359**	**26**	**0**	**4.35**	....	....	....	....	....	....	....
	Moncton	AHL	51	20	24	3	2844	167	1	3.52	....	....	....	....	....	....	....
1990-91	Moncton	AHL	30	15	13	2	1779	95	1	3.20	....	....	....	....	....	....	....
	Fort Wayne	IHL	10	5	3	1	564	32	0	3.40	....	....	....	....	....	....	....
	Peoria	IHL	10	6	3	1	584	36	0	3.70	4	2	1	214	10	0	2.80
1991-92	**Buffalo**	**NHL**	**26**	**10**	**9**	**5**	**1403**	**75**	**1**	**3.21**	**7**	**3**	**4**	**433**	**19**	**1**	**2.63**
	Rochester	AHL	9	4	3	2	531	28	0	3.16	....	....	....	....	....	....	....
1992-93	**Buffalo**	**NHL**	**11**	**5**	**6**	**0**	**664**	**41**	**0**	**3.70**	....	....	....	....	....	....	....
	Rochester	AHL	5	3	2	0	303	22	0	4.36	....	....	....	....	....	....	....
1993-94	**NY Islanders**	**NHL**	**7**	**1**	**3**	**0**	**227**	**16**	**0**	**4.23**	....	....	....	....	....	....	....
	Salt Lake	IHL	35	7	23	3	1933	140	0	4.34	....	....	....	....	....	....	....
1994-95	Minnesota	IHL	59	25	20	6	3063	187	1	3.66	2	0	2	118	10	0	5.07
1995-96	**Winnipeg**	**NHL**	**1**	**0**	**0**	**0**	**34**	**3**	**0**	**5.29**	....	....	....	....	....	....	....
	Milwaukee	IHL	31	14	12	3	1793	101	1	3.38	....	....	....	....	....	....	....
	NHL Totals		**53**	**19**	**23**	**5**	**2807**	**173**	**1**	**3.70**	**7**	**3**	**4**	**433**	**19**	**1**	**2.63**

a ECAC First All-Star Team (1987)
b AHL Second All-Star Team (1989)

Traded to **St. Louis** by **Winnipeg** for future considerations (Jim Vesey, May 24, 1991), February 28, 1991. Traded to **Winnipeg** by **St. Louis** for future considerations, May 24, 1991. Traded to **Buffalo** by **Winnipeg** for Buffalo's seventh round choice (Artur Oktyabrev) in 1992 Entry Draft, June 22, 1991. Traded to **NY Islanders** by **Buffalo** for NY Islanders' seventh round choice (Stev Plouffe) in 1994 Entry Draft, September 30, 1993. Signed as a free agent by **Winnipeg**, December 14, 1995.

DUFFUS, PARRIS (DOO-fihz, PAIR-ihz) — PHO.

Goaltender. Catches left. 6'2", 192 lbs. Born, Denver, CO, January 27, 1970.
(St. Louis' 6th choice, 180th overall, in 1990 Entry Draft).

			Regular Season								Playoffs						
Season	Club	Lea	GP	W	L	T	Mins	GA	SO	Avg	GP	W	L	Mins	GA	SO	Avg
1990-91	Cornell	ECAC	4	0	0	0	37	3	0	4.86	....	....	....	....	....	....	....
1991-92ab	Cornell	ECAC	28	14	11	3	1677	74	1	2.65	....	....	....	....	....	....	....
1992-93	Hampton Rds.	ECHL	4	3	1	0	245	13	0	3.18	....	....	....	....	....	....	....
	Peoria	IHL	37	16	15	4	2149	142	0	3.96	1	0	1	59	5	0	5.08
1993-94	Peoria	IHL	36	19	10	3	1845	141	0	4.58	2	0	1	92	6	0	3.88
1994-95	Peoria	IHL	29	17	7	3	1581	71	*3	2.69	7	4	2	409	17	0	2.49
1995-96	Minnesota	IHL	35	10	17	2	1812	100	1	3.31	....	....	....	....	....	....	....

a NCAA East First All-American Team (1992)
b ECAC Second All-Star Team (1992)

Signed as a free agent by **Winnipeg**, August 4, 1995.

DUNHAM, MICHAEL (DUHN-uhm) — N.J.

Goaltender. Catches left. 6'3", 185 lbs. Born, Johnson City, NY, June 1, 1972.
(New Jersey's 4th choice, 53rd overall, in 1990 Entry Draft).

			Regular Season								Playoffs						
Season	Club	Lea	GP	W	L	T	Mins	GA	SO	Avg	GP	W	L	Mins	GA	SO	Avg
1990-91	U. of Maine	H.E.	23	14	5	2	1275	63	0	*2.96	....	....	....	....	....	....	....
1991-92	U. of Maine	H.E.	7	6	0	0	382	14	1	2.20	....	....	....	....	....	....	....
	U.S. National	....	3	0	1	1	157	10	0	3.82	....	....	....	....	....	....	....
1992-93ab	U. of Maine	H.E.	25	*21	1	1	1429	63	0	2.65	....	....	....	....	....	....	....
1993-94	U.S. National	....	33	22	9	2	1983	125	2	3.78	....	....	....	....	....	....	....
	U.S. Olympic	....	3	0	2	1	180	15	0	5.02	....	....	....	....	....	....	....
	Albany	AHL	5	2	2	1	304	26	0	5.12	....	....	....	....	....	....	....
1994-95cd	Albany	AHL	35	20	7	8	2120	99	1	2.80	7	6	1	419	20	1	2.86
1995-96e	Albany	AHL	44	30	10	2	2592	109	1	2.52	3	1	2	182	5	1	1.65

a Hockey East First All-Star Team (1993)
b NCAA East First All-American Team (1993)
c Shared Harry "Hap" Holmes Memorial Trophy (fewest goals against - AHL) with Corey Schwab (1995)
d Shared Jack A. Butterfield Trophy (Playoff MVP - AHL) with Corey Schwab (1995)
e AHL Second All-Star Team (1996)

ELDER, BRIAN — PHO.

Goaltender. Catches left. 6', 175 lbs. Born, Oak Lake, Man., June 8, 1976.
(Winnipeg's 6th choice, 121st overall, in 1995 Entry Draft).

			Regular Season								Playoffs						
Season	Club	Lea	GP	W	L	T	Mins	GA	SO	Avg	GP	W	L	Mins	GA	SO	Avg
1994-95	Brandon	WHL	23	16	5	1	1325	69	0	3.12	13	6	7	756	38	*1	3.02
1995-96	Brandon	WHL	34	23	9	1	1962	113	3	3.46	....	....	....	....	....	....	....

ELLIOT, JASON — DET.

Goaltender. Catches left. 6'2", 183 lbs. Born, Inovik, N.W.T., November 10, 1975.
(Detroit's 7th choice, 205th overall, in 1994 Entry Draft).

			Regular Season								Playoffs						
Season	Club	Lea	GP	W	L	T	Mins	GA	SO	Avg	GP	W	L	Mins	GA	SO	Avg
1994-95	Cornell	ECAC	16	3	11	1	877	62	0	4.24	....	....	....	....	....	....	....
1995-96	Cornell	ECAC	19	12	2	1	971	38	2	2.35	....	....	....	....	....	....	....

ESCHE, ROBERT — PHO.

Goaltender. Catches left. 6', 188 lbs. Born, Utica, NY, January 22, 1978.
(Phoenix's 5th choice, 139th overall, in 1996 Entry Draft).

			Regular Season								Playoffs						
Season	Club	Lea	GP	W	L	T	Mins	GA	SO	Avg	GP	W	L	Mins	GA	SO	Avg
1995-96	Detroit	OHL	23	13	6	0	1219	76	1	3.74	3	0	2	105	4	0	2.29

ESSENSA, BOB (EH-sehn-suh) — EDM.

Goaltender. Catches left. 6', 185 lbs. Born, Toronto, Ont., January 14, 1965.
(Winnipeg's 5th choice, 69th overall, in 1983 Entry Draft).

			Regular Season								Playoffs						
Season	Club	Lea	GP	W	L	T	Mins	GA	SO	Avg	GP	W	L	Mins	GA	SO	Avg
1983-84	Michigan State	CCHA	17	11	4	0	946	44	2	2.79	....	....	....	....	....	....	....
1984-85	Michigan State	CCHA	18	15	2	0	1059	29	2	1.64	....	....	....	....	....	....	....
1985-86a	Michigan State	CCHA	23	17	4	1	1333	74	1	3.33	....	....	....	....	....	....	....
1986-87	Michigan State	CCHA	25	19	3	1	1383	64	2	2.78	....	....	....	....	....	....	....
1987-88	Moncton	AHL	27	7	11	1	1287	100	1	4.66	....	....	....	....	....	....	....
1988-89	**Winnipeg**	**NHL**	**20**	**6**	**8**	**3**	**1102**	**68**	**1**	**3.70**	....	....	....	....	....	....	....
	Fort Wayne	IHL	22	14	7	0	1287	70	0	3.26	....	....	....	....	....	....	....
1989-90b	**Winnipeg**	**NHL**	**36**	**18**	**9**	**5**	**2035**	**107**	**1**	**3.15**	**4**	**2**	**1**	**206**	**12**	**0**	**3.50**
	Moncton	AHL	6	3	3	0	358	15	0	2.51	....	....	....	....	....	....	....
1990-91	**Winnipeg**	**NHL**	**55**	**19**	**24**	**6**	**2916**	**153**	**4**	**3.15**	....	....	....	....	....	....	....
	Moncton	AHL	2	1	0	1	125	6	0	2.88	....	....	....	....	....	....	....
1991-92	**Winnipeg**	**NHL**	**47**	**21**	**17**	**6**	**2627**	**126**	***5**	**2.88**	**1**	**0**	**0**	**33**	**3**	**0**	**5.45**
1992-93	**Winnipeg**	**NHL**	**67**	**33**	**26**	**6**	**3855**	**227**	**2**	**3.53**	**6**	**2**	**4**	**367**	**20**	**0**	**3.27**
1993-94	**Winnipeg**	**NHL**	**56**	**19**	**30**	**6**	**3136**	**201**	**1**	**3.85**	....	....	....	....	....	....	....
	Detroit	**NHL**	**13**	**4**	**7**	**2**	**778**	**34**	**1**	**2.62**	**2**	**0**	**2**	**109**	**9**	**0**	**4.95**
1994-95	San Diego	IHL	16	6	8	1	919	52	0	3.39	1	0	1	59	3	0	3.05
1995-96	Adirondack	AHL	3	1	2	0	179	11	0	3.69	....	....	....	....	....	....	....
	Fort Wayne	IHL	45	24	14	5	2529	122	1	2.89	5	2	3	299	12	0	2.41
	NHL Totals		**294**	**120**	**121**	**34**	**16449**	**916**	**15**	**3.34**	**13**	**4**	**7**	**715**	**44**	**0**	**3.69**

a CCHA Second All-Star Team (1986)
b NHL All-Rookie Team (1990)

Traded to **Detroit** by **Winnipeg** with Sergei Bautin for Tim Cheveldae and Dallas Drake, March 8, 1994. Traded to **Edmonton** by **Detroit** for future considerations, June 14, 1996.

FANKHOUSER, SCOTT — ST.L.

Goaltender. Catches left. 6'2", 195 lbs. Born, Bismark, ND, July 1, 1975.
(St. Louis' 8th choice, 276th overall, in 1994 Entry Draft).

			Regular Season								Playoffs						
Season	Club	Lea	GP	W	L	T	Mins	GA	SO	Avg	GP	W	L	Mins	GA	SO	Avg
1994-95	Lowell	H.E.	11	4	4	1	499	37	0	4.44	....	....	....	....	....	....	....
1995-96								UNAVAILABLE									

FERNANDEZ, EMMANUEL — DAL.

Goaltender. Catches left. 6', 185 lbs. Born, Etobicoke, Ont., August 27, 1974.
(Quebec's 4th choice, 52nd overall, in 1992 Entry Draft).

			Regular Season								Playoffs						
Season	Club	Lea	GP	W	L	T	Mins	GA	SO	Avg	GP	W	L	Mins	GA	SO	Avg
1991-92	Laval	QMJHL	31	14	13	2	1593	99	1	3.73	9	3	5	468	39	0	5.00
1992-93	Laval	QMJHL	43	26	14	2	2347	141	1	3.60	13	*12	1	818	42	0	3.08
1993-94a	Laval	QMJHL	51	29	14	1	2776	143	*5	3.09	19	14	5	1116	49	*1	*2.63
1994-95b	Kalamazoo	IHL	46	21	10	9	2470	115	2	2.79	14	10	2	753	34	1	2.71
	Dallas	**NHL**	**1**	**0**	**1**	**0**	**59**	**3**	**0**	**3.05**	....	....	....	....	....	....	....
1995-96	**Dallas**	**NHL**	**5**	**0**	**1**	**1**	**249**	**19**	**0**	**4.58**	....	....	....	....	....	....	....
	Michigan	IHL	47	22	15	9	2664	133	*4	3.00	6	5	1	372	14	0	*2.26
	NHL Totals		**6**	**0**	**2**	**1**	**308**	**22**	**0**	**4.29**	....	....	....	....	....	....	....

a QMJHL First All-Star Team (1994)
b IHL Second All-Star Team (1995)

Rights traded to **Dallas** by **Quebec** for Tommy Sjodin and Dallas' third round draft choice (Chris Drury) in 1994 Entry Draft, February 13, 1994.

FICHAUD, ERIC — NYI

Goaltender. Catches left. 5'11", 171 lbs. Born, Anjou, Que., November 4, 1975.
(Toronto's 1st choice, 16th overall, in 1994 Entry Draft).

			Regular Season								Playoffs						
Season	Club	Lea	GP	W	L	T	Mins	GA	SO	Avg	GP	W	L	Mins	GA	SO	Avg
1992-93	Chicoutimi	QMJHL	43	18	13	1	2039	149	0	4.38	....	....	....	....	....	....	....
1993-94abc	Chicoutimi	QMJHL	*63	*37	21	3	*3493	192	4	3.30	*26	*16	10	*1560	86	*1	3.31
1994-95d	Chicoutimi	QMJHL	46	21	19	4	2637	151	4	3.44	7	2	5	428	20	0	2.80
1995-96	**NY Islanders**	**NHL**	**24**	**7**	**12**	**2**	**1234**	**68**	**1**	**3.31**	....	....	....	....	....	....	....
	Worcester	AHL	34	13	15	6	1989	97	1	2.93	2	1	1	127	7	0	3.30
	NHL Totals		**24**	**7**	**12**	**2**	**1234**	**68**	**1**	**3.31**	....	....	....	....	....	....	....

a Canadian Major Junior Second All-Star Team (1994)
b Memorial Cup All-Star Team (1994)
c Won Hap Emms Memorial Trophy (Memorial Cup Tournament Top Goaltender) (1994)
d QMJHL First All-Star Team (1995)

Traded to **NY Islanders** by **Toronto** for Benoit Hogue, NY Islanders' third round choice (Brian Pepperall) in 1995 Entry Draft and fifth round choice in 1996 Entry Draft, April 6, 1995.

FISCHER, KAI — COL.

Goaltender. Catches left. 5'11", 176 lbs. Born, Forst, Germany, March 25, 1977.
(Colorado's 8th choice, 160th overall, in 1996 Entry Draft).

			Regular Season								Playoffs						
Season	Club	Lea	GP	W	L	T	Mins	GA	SO	Avg	GP	W	L	Mins	GA	SO	Avg
1995-96	Dusseldorf	Ger. Jr.							UNAVAILABLE								

FISET, STEPHANE (fih-SEHT) — L.A.

Goaltender. Catches left. 6'1", 195 lbs. Born, Montreal, Que., June 17, 1970.
(Quebec's 3rd choice, 24th overall, in 1988 Entry Draft).

			Regular Season								Playoffs						
Season	Club	Lea	GP	W	L	T	Mins	GA	SO	Avg	GP	W	L	Mins	GA	SO	Avg
1987-88	Victoriaville	QMJHL	40	15	17	4	2221	146	1	3.94	2	0	2	163	10	0	3.68
1988-89ab	Victoriaville	QMJHL	43	25	14	0	2401	138	1	*3.45	12	*9	2	711	33	0	*2.78
1989-90	**Quebec**	**NHL**	**6**	**0**	**5**	**1**	**342**	**34**	**0**	**5.96**	....	....	....	....	....	....	....
	Victoriaville	QMJHL	24	14	6	3	1383	63	1	*2.73	*14	7	6	*790	49	0	3.72
1990-91	**Quebec**	**NHL**	**3**	**0**	**2**	**1**	**186**	**12**	**0**	**3.87**	....	....	....	....	....	....	....
	Halifax	AHL	36	10	15	8	1902	131	0	4.13	....	....	....	....	....	....	....
1991-92	**Quebec**	**NHL**	**23**	**7**	**10**	**2**	**1133**	**71**	**1**	**3.76**	....	....	....	....	....	....	....
	Halifax	AHL	29	8	14	6	1675	110	*3	3.94	....	....	....	....	....	....	....
1992-93	**Quebec**	**NHL**	**37**	**18**	**9**	**4**	**1939**	**110**	**0**	**3.40**	**1**	**0**	**0**	**21**	**1**	**0**	**2.86**
	Halifax	AHL	3	2	1	0	180	11	0	3.67	....	....	....	....	....	....	....
1993-94	**Quebec**	**NHL**	**50**	**20**	**25**	**4**	**2798**	**158**	**2**	**3.39**	....	....	....	....	....	....	....
	Cornwall	AHL	1	0	1	0	60	4	0	4.00	....	....	....	....	....	....	....
1994-95	**Quebec**	**NHL**	**32**	**17**	**10**	**3**	**1879**	**87**	**2**	**2.78**	**4**	**1**	**2**	**209**	**16**	**0**	**4.59**
1995-96	**Colorado**	**NHL**	**37**	**22**	**6**	**7**	**2107**	**103**	**1**	**2.93**	**1**	**0**	**0**	**1**	**0**	**0**	**0.00** ◆
	NHL Totals		**188**	**84**	**67**	**22**	**10384**	**575**	**6**	**3.32**	**6**	**1**	**2**	**231**	**17**	**0**	**4.42**

a QMJHL First All-Star Team (1989)
b Canadian Major Junior Goaltender of the Year (1989)

Traded to **Los Angeles** by **Colorado** with Colorado's first round choice in 1998 Entry Draft for Eric Lacroix and Los Angeles' first round choice in 1998 Entry Draft, June 20, 1996.

FITZPATRICK, MARK — FLA.

Goaltender. Catches left. 6'2", 198 lbs. Born, Toronto, Ont., November 13, 1968.
(Los Angeles' 2nd choice, 27th overall, in 1987 Entry Draft).

			Regular Season								Playoffs						
Season	Club	Lea	GP	W	L	T	Mins	GA	SO	Avg	GP	W	L	Mins	GA	SO	Avg
1985-86	Medicine Hat	WHL	41	26	6	1	2074	99	1	2.86	19	12	5	986	58	0	3.53
1986-87a	Medicine Hat	WHL	50	31	11	4	2844	159	4	3.35	20	12	8	1224	71	1	3.48
1987-88a	Medicine Hat	WHL	63	36	15	6	3600	194	2	3.23	16	12	4	959	52	*1	*3.25
1988-89	**Los Angeles**	**NHL**	**17**	**6**	**7**	**3**	**957**	**64**	**0**	**4.01**	....	....	....	....	....	....	....
	New Haven	AHL	18	10	5	1	980	54	1	3.31	....	....	....	....	....	....	....
	NY Islanders	**NHL**	**11**	**3**	**5**	**2**	**627**	**41**	**0**	**3.92**	....	....	....	....	....	....	....
1989-90	**NY Islanders**	**NHL**	**47**	**19**	**19**	**5**	**2653**	**150**	**3**	**3.39**	**4**	**0**	**2**	**152**	**13**	**0**	**5.13**
1990-91	**NY Islanders**	**NHL**	**2**	**1**	**1**	**0**	**120**	**6**	**0**	**3.00**	....	....	....	....	....	....	....
	Capital Dist.	AHL	12	3	7	2	734	47	0	3.84	....	....	....	....	....	....	....
1991-92b	**NY Islanders**	**NHL**	**30**	**11**	**13**	**5**	**1743**	**93**	**0**	**3.20**	....	....	....	....	....	....	....
	Capital Dist.	AHL	14	6	5	1	782	39	0	2.99	....	....	....	....	....	....	....
1992-93	**NY Islanders**	**NHL**	**39**	**17**	**15**	**5**	**2253**	**130**	**0**	**3.46**	**3**	**0**	**1**	**77**	**4**	**0**	**3.12**
	Capital Dist.	AHL	5	1	3	1	284	18	0	3.80	....	....	....	....	....	....	....
1993-94	**Florida**	**NHL**	**28**	**12**	**8**	**6**	**1603**	**73**	**1**	**2.73**	....	....	....	....	....	....	....
1994-95	**Florida**	**NHL**	**15**	**6**	**7**	**2**	**819**	**36**	**2**	**2.64**	....	....	....	....	....	....	....
1995-96	**Florida**	**NHL**	**34**	**15**	**11**	**3**	**1786**	**88**	**0**	**2.96**	**2**	**0**	**0**	**60**	**6**	**0**	**6.00**
	NHL Totals		**223**	**90**	**86**	**31**	**12561**	**681**	**6**	**3.25**	**9**	**0**	**3**	**289**	**23**	**0**	**4.78**

a Won Hap Emms Memorial Trophy (Memorial Cup Tournament Top Goaltender) (1987, 1988)
b Won Bill Masterton Memorial Trophy (1992)

Traded to **NY Islanders** by **Los Angeles** with Wayne McBean and future considerations (Doug Crossman, May 23, 1989) for Kelly Hrudey, February 22, 1989. Traded to **Quebec** by **NY Islanders** with NY Islanders' first round choice (Adam Deadmarsh) in 1993 Entry Draft for Ron Hextall and Quebec's first round choice (Todd Bertuzzi) in 1993 Entry Draft, June 20, 1993. Claimed by **Florida** from **Quebec** in Expansion Draft, June 24, 1993.

FLAHERTY, WADE (FLAY-uhr-tee) — S.J.

Goaltender. Catches left. 6', 170 lbs. Born, Terrace, B.C., January 11, 1968.
(Buffalo's 10th choice, 181st overall, in 1988 Entry Draft).

			Regular Season								Playoffs						
Season	Club	Lea	GP	W	L	T	Mins	GA	SO	Avg	GP	W	L	Mins	GA	SO	Avg
1988-89	Victoria	WHL	42	21	19	0	2408	180	4	4.49	....	....	....	....	....	....	....
1989-90	Greensboro	ECHL	27	12	10	0	1308	96	0	4.40	....	....	....	....	....	....	....
1990-91	Kansas City	IHL	*56	16	31	4	2990	224	0	4.49	....	....	....	....	....	....	....
1991-92	**San Jose**	**NHL**	**3**	**0**	**3**	**0**	**178**	**13**	**0**	**4.38**	....	....	....	....	....	....	....
	Kansas City	IHL	43	26	14	3	2603	140	1	3.23	1	0	0	1	0	0	0.00
1992-93	**San Jose**	**NHL**	**1**	**0**	**1**	**0**	**60**	**5**	**0**	**5.00**	....	....	....	....	....	....	....
a	Kansas City	IHL	*61	*34	19	7	*3642	195	2	3.21	*12	6	6	733	34	*1	2.78
1993-94ab	Kansas City	IHL	*60	32	19	9	*3564	202	0	3.40	....	....	....	....	....	....	....
1994-95	**San Jose**	**NHL**	**18**	**5**	**6**	**1**	**852**	**44**	**1**	**3.10**	**7**	**2**	**3**	**377**	**31**	**0**	**4.93**
1995-96	**San Jose**	**NHL**	**24**	**3**	**12**	**1**	**1137**	**92**	**0**	**4.85**	....	....	....	....	....	....	....
	NHL Totals		**46**	**8**	**22**	**2**	**2227**	**154**	**1**	**4.15**	**7**	**2**	**3**	**377**	**31**	**0**	**4.93**

a Shared James Norris Memorial Trophy (fewest goals against - IHL) with Arturs Irbe (1992)
b IHL Second All-Star Team (1993, 1994)

Signed as a free agent by **San Jose**, September 3, 1991.

FORSBERG, JONAS (FOHRS-behrg) — S.J.

Goaltender. Catches left. 5'10", 150 lbs. Born, Stockholm, Sweden, June 15, 1975.
(San Jose's 11th choice, 210th overall, in 1993 Entry Draft).

			Regular Season								Playoffs						
Season	Club	Lea	GP	W	L	T	Mins	GA	SO	Avg	GP	W	L	Mins	GA	SO	Avg
1993-94	Djurgarden	Swe.	1	....	....	....	60	4	0	4.00	....	....	....	....	....	....	....
1994-95	Djurgarden	Swe.	1	....	....	....	60	1	0	1.00	....	....	....	....	....	....	....
1995-96	Djurgarden	Swe. Jr.							UNAVAILABLE								

FOUNTAIN, MIKE — VAN.

Goaltender. Catches left. 6'1", 176 lbs. Born, North York, Ont., January 26, 1972.
(Vancouver's 4th choice, 69th overall, in 1992 Entry Draft).

			Regular Season								Playoffs						
Season	Club	Lea	GP	W	L	T	Mins	GA	SO	Avg	GP	W	L	Mins	GA	SO	Avg
1990-91	S.S. Marie	OHL	7	5	2	0	380	19	....	3.00	....	....	....	....	....	....	....
	Oshawa	OHL	30	17	5	1	1483	84	....	3.40	8	1	4	292	26	0	5.34
1991-92a	Oshawa	OHL	40	18	13	6	2260	149	1	3.96	7	3	4	429	26	0	3.64
1992-93	Cdn. National	....	13	7	5	1	745	37	1	2.98	....	....	....	....	....	....	....
	Hamilton	AHL	12	2	8	0	618	46	0	4.47	....	....	....	....	....	....	....
1993-94b	Hamilton	AHL	*70	*34	28	6	*4005	241	*4	3.61	3	0	2	146	12	0	4.92
1994-95	Syracuse	AHL	61	25	29	7	3618	225	2	3.73	....	....	....	....	....	....	....
1995-96	Syracuse	AHL	54	21	27	3	3060	184	1	3.61	15	8	7	915	57	*2	3.74

a OHL First All-Star Team (1992)
b AHL Second All-Star Team (1994)

FRANEK, PETR (FRAH-nehk) — COL.

Goaltender. Catches left. 5'11", 187 lbs. Born, Most, Czech., April 6, 1975.
(Quebec's 10th choice, 205th overall, in 1993 Entry Draft).

			Regular Season								Playoffs						
Season	Club	Lea	GP	W	L	T	Mins	GA	SO	Avg	GP	W	L	Mins	GA	SO	Avg
1992-93	Litvinov	Czech.	5	....	....	....	273	15	....	3.29	....	....	....	....	....	....	....
1993-94	Litvinov	Czech.	11	....	....	....	535	34	....	3.81	2	....	....	61	10	....	9.83
1994-95	Litvinov	Czech.	12	....	....	....	657	47	....	4.29	1	0	0	16	0	0	0.00
1995-96	Litvinov	Czech.	36	....	....	....	2096	85	3	2.43	16	....	....	948	47	....	2.97

FRIESEN, TERRY — S.J.

Goaltender. Catches left. 5'11", 185 lbs. Born, Winkler, Man., October 29, 1977.
(San Jose's 3rd choice, 55th overall, in 1996 Entry Draft).

			Regular Season								Playoffs						
Season	Club	Lea	GP	W	L	T	Mins	GA	SO	Avg	GP	W	L	Mins	GA	SO	Avg
1994-95	Winkler	Jr. A	24	....	....	....	1164	72	1	3.71	....	....	....	....	....	....	....
1995-96a	Swift Current	WHL	42	19	17	3	2504	155	2	3.71	6	2	4	338	21	0	3.73

a WHL East Second All-Star Team (1996)

FUHR, GRANT (FYOOR) — ST.L.

Goaltender. Catches right. 5'9", 190 lbs. Born, Spruce Grove, Alta., September 28, 1962.
(Edmonton's 1st choice, 8th overall, in 1981 Entry Draft).

			Regular Season								Playoffs						
Season	Club	Lea	GP	W	L	T	Mins	GA	SO	Avg	GP	W	L	Mins	GA	SO	Avg
1979-80a	Victoria	WHL	43	30	12	0	2488	130	2	3.14	8	5	3	465	22	0	2.84
1980-81a	Victoria	WHL	59	48	9	1	3448	160	*4	*2.78	15	12	3	899	45	*1	*3.00
1981-82b	**Edmonton**	**NHL**	**48**	**28**	**5**	**14**	**2847**	**157**	**0**	**3.31**	**5**	**2**	**3**	**309**	**26**	**0**	**5.05**
1982-83	**Edmonton**	**NHL**	**32**	**13**	**12**	**5**	**1803**	**129**	**0**	**4.29**	**1**	**0**	**0**	**11**	**0**	**0**	**0.00**
	Moncton	AHL	10	4	5	1	604	40	0	3.98	....	....	....	....	....	....	....
1983-84	**Edmonton**	**NHL**	**45**	**30**	**10**	**4**	**2625**	**171**	**1**	**3.91**	**16**	**11**	**4**	**883**	**44**	**1**	**2.99** ◆
1984-85	**Edmonton**	**NHL**	**46**	**26**	**8**	**7**	**2559**	**165**	**1**	**3.87**	***18**	***15**	**3**	**1064**	**55**	**0**	**3.10** ◆
1985-86	**Edmonton**	**NHL**	**40**	**29**	**8**	**0**	**2184**	**143**	**0**	**3.93**	**9**	**5**	**4**	**541**	**28**	**0**	**3.11**
1986-87	**Edmonton**	**NHL**	**44**	**22**	**13**	**3**	**2388**	**137**	**0**	**3.44**	**19**	**14**	**5**	**1148**	**47**	**0**	**2.46** ◆
1987-88cd	**Edmonton**	**NHL**	***75**	***40**	**24**	**9**	***4304**	**246**	***4**	**3.43**	***19**	***16**	**2**	***1136**	**55**	**0**	**2.90** ◆
1988-89	**Edmonton**	**NHL**	**59**	**23**	**26**	**6**	**3341**	**213**	**1**	**3.83**	**7**	**3**	**4**	**417**	**24**	**1**	**3.45**
1989-90	**Edmonton**	**NHL**	**21**	**9**	**7**	**3**	**1081**	**70**	**1**	**3.89**	....	....	....	....	....	....	.... ◆
	Cape Breton	AHL	2	2	0	0	120	6	0	3.01	....	....	....	....	....	....	....
1990-91	**Edmonton**	**NHL**	**13**	**6**	**4**	**3**	**778**	**39**	**1**	**3.01**	**17**	**8**	**7**	**1019**	**51**	**0**	**3.00**
	Cape Breton	AHL	4	2	2	0	240	17	0	4.25	....	....	....	....	....	....	....
1991-92	**Toronto**	**NHL**	**66**	**25**	**33**	**5**	**3774**	**230**	**2**	**3.66**	....	....	....	....	....	....	....
1992-93	**Toronto**	**NHL**	**29**	**13**	**9**	**4**	**1665**	**87**	**1**	**3.14**	....	....	....	....	....	....	....
	Buffalo	**NHL**	**29**	**11**	**15**	**2**	**1694**	**98**	**0**	**3.47**	**8**	**3**	**4**	**474**	**27**	**1**	**3.42**
1993-94e	**Buffalo**	**NHL**	**32**	**13**	**12**	**3**	**1726**	**106**	**2**	**3.68**	....	....	....	....	....	....	....
	Rochester	AHL	5	3	0	2	310	10	0	1.94	....	....	....	....	....	....	....
1994-95	**Buffalo**	**NHL**	**3**	**1**	**2**	**0**	**180**	**12**	**0**	**4.00**	....	....	....	....	....	....	....
	Los Angeles	**NHL**	**14**	**1**	**7**	**3**	**698**	**47**	**0**	**4.04**	....	....	....	....	....	....	....
1995-96	**St. Louis**	**NHL**	***79**	**30**	**28**	**16**	**4365**	**209**	**3**	**2.87**	**2**	**1**	**0**	**69**	**1**	**0**	**0.87**
	NHL Totals		**675**	**320**	**223**	**87**	**38012**	**2259**	**17**	**3.57**	**121**	**78**	**36**	**7071**	**358**	**3**	**3.04**

a WHL First All-Star Team (1980, 1981)
b NHL Second All-Star Team (1982)
c NHL First All-Star Team (1988)
d Won Vezina Trophy (1988)
e Shared William M. Jennings Trophy with Dominik Hasek (1994)

Played in NHL All-Star Game (1982, 1984-86, 1988-89)

Traded to **Toronto** by **Edmonton** with Glenn Anderson and Craig Berube for Vincent Damphousse, Peter Ing, Scott Thornton, Luke Richardson, future considerations and cash, September 19, 1991. Traded to **Buffalo** by **Toronto** with Toronto's fifth round choice (Kevin Popp) in 1995 Entry Draft for Dave Andreychuk, Daren Puppa and Buffalo's first round choice (Kenny Jonsson) in 1993 Entry Draft, February 2, 1993. Traded to **Los Angeles** by **Buffalo** with Philippe Boucher and Denis Tsygurov for Alexei Zhitnik, Robb Stauber, Charlie Huddy and Los Angeles' fifth round choice (Marian Menhart) in 1995 Entry Draft, February 14, 1995. Signed as a free agent by **St. Louis**, July 14, 1995.

GAGE, JOAQUIN — EDM.

Goaltender. Catches left. 6', 200 lbs. Born, Vancouver, B.C., October 19, 1973.
(Edmonton's 6th choice, 109th overall, in 1992 Entry Draft).

			Regular Season								Playoffs						
Season	Club	Lea	GP	W	L	T	Mins	GA	SO	Avg	GP	W	L	Mins	GA	SO	Avg
1990-91	Portland	WHL	3	0	3	0	180	17	0	5.70	....	....	....	....	....	....	....
1991-92	Portland	WHL	63	27	30	4	3635	269	2	4.44	6	2	4	366	28	0	4.59
1992-93	Portland	WHL	38	21	16	1	2302	153	2	3.99	8	5	2	427	30	0	4.22
1993-94	Prince Albert	WHL	53	24	25	3	3041	212	1	4.18	....	....	....	....	....	....	....
1994-95	Cape Breton	AHL	54	17	28	5	3010	207	0	4.13	....	....	....	....	....	....	....
	Edmonton	**NHL**	**2**	**0**	**2**	**0**	**99**	**7**	**0**	**4.24**	....	....	....	....	....	....	....
1995-96	**Edmonton**	**NHL**	**16**	**2**	**8**	**1**	**717**	**45**	**0**	**3.77**	....	....	....	....	....	....	....
	Cape Breton	AHL	21	8	11	0	1162	80	0	4.13	....	....	....	....	....	....	....
	NHL Totals		**18**	**2**	**10**	**1**	**816**	**52**	**0**	**3.82**	....	....	....	....	....	....	....

GAMBLE, TROY

Goaltender. Catches left. 5'11", 195 lbs. Born, New Glasgow, N.S., April 7, 1967.
(Vancouver's 2nd choice, 25th overall, in 1985 Entry Draft).

			Regular Season								Playoffs						
Season	Club	Lea	GP	W	L	T	Mins	GA	SO	Avg	GP	W	L	Mins	GA	SO	Avg
1984-85a	Medicine Hat	WHL	37	27	6	2	2095	100	3	2.86	2	1	1	120	9	0	4.50
1985-86	Medicine Hat	WHL	45	28	11	0	2264	142	0	3.76	11	5	4	530	31	0	3.51
1986-87	**Vancouver**	**NHL**	**1**	**0**	**1**	**0**	**60**	**4**	**0**	**4.00**	....	....	....	....	....	....	....
	Medicine Hat	WHL	11	7	3	0	646	46	0	4.27	....	....	....	....	....	....	....
	Spokane	WHL	38	17	17	1	2155	163	0	4.54	5	0	5	298	35	0	7.05
1987-88b	Spokane	WHL	67	36	26	1	3824	235	0	3.69	15	7	8	875	56	1	3.84
1988-89	**Vancouver**	**NHL**	**5**	**2**	**3**	**0**	**302**	**12**	**0**	**2.38**	....	....	....	....	....	....	....
	Milwaukee	IHL	42	23	9	0	2198	138	0	3.77	11	5	5	640	35	0	3.28
1989-90	Milwaukee	IHL	*56	22	21	4	2779	160	2	4.21	5	2	2	216	19	0	5.28
1990-91	**Vancouver**	**NHL**	**47**	**16**	**16**	**6**	**2433**	**140**	**1**	**3.45**	**4**	**1**	**3**	**249**	**16**	**0**	**3.86**
1991-92	**Vancouver**	**NHL**	**19**	**4**	**9**	**3**	**1009**	**73**	**0**	**4.34**	....	....	....	....	....	....	....
	Milwaukee	IHL	9	2	4	2	521	31	0	3.57	....	....	....	....	....	....	....
1992-93	Hamilton	AHL	14	1	10	2	769	62	0	4.84	....	....	....	....	....	....	....
	Cincinnati	IHL	33	11	18	2	1762	134	0	4.56	....	....	....	....	....	....	....
1993-94	Kalamazoo	IHL	48	25	13	5	2607	146	*2	3.36	2	0	1	80	7	0	5.25
1994-95	Houston	IHL	43	18	17	5	2421	132	1	3.27	4	1	3	203	16	0	4.72
1995-96	Houston	IHL	52	16	25	5	2722	174	0	3.83	....	....	....	....	....	....	....
	NHL Totals		**72**	**22**	**29**	**9**	**3804**	**229**	**1**	**3.61**	**4**	**1**	**3**	**249**	**16**	**0**	**3.86**

a WHL East First All-Star Team (1985)
b WHL West First All-Star Team (1988)

Signed as a free agent by **Dallas**, August 28, 1993.

GARNER, TYRONE — NYI

Goaltender. Catches left. 6'1", 164 lbs. Born, Stoney Creek, Ont., July 27, 1978.
(NY Islanders' 4th choice, 83rd overall, in 1996 Entry Draft).

			Regular Season								Playoffs						
Season	Club	Lea	GP	W	L	T	Mins	GA	SO	Avg	GP	W	L	Mins	GA	SO	Avg
1995-96	Oshawa	OHL	32	11	15	4	1697	112	0	3.96	....	....	....	....	....	....	....

GARON, MATHIEU — (gah-ROHN) MTL.

Goaltender. Catches right. 6'1", 175 lbs. Born, Chandler, Que., January 9, 1978.
(Montreal's 2nd choice, 44th overall, in 1996 Entry Draft).

			Regular Season								Playoffs						
Season	Club	Lea	GP	W	L	T	Mins	GA	SO	Avg	GP	W	L	Mins	GA	SO	Avg
1994-95	Jonquiere	Midget	27	13	13	1	1548	94	5	3.63	9	4	5	557	35	1	3.77
1995-96	Victoriaville	QMJHL	51	18	27	0	2709	189	1	4.19	12	7	4	676	38	1	3.39

GIGUERE, JEAN-SEBASTIEN — (ZHEE-gair) HFD.

Goaltender. Catches left. 6', 175 lbs. Born, Montreal, Que., May 16, 1977.
(Hartford's 1st choice, 13th overall, in 1995 Entry Draft).

			Regular Season								Playoffs						
Season	Club	Lea	GP	W	L	T	Mins	GA	SO	Avg	GP	W	L	Mins	GA	SO	Avg
1993-94	Verdun	QMJHL	25	....	....	....	1234	66	1	3.21	....	....	....	....	....	....	....
1994-95	Halifax	QMJHL	47	14	27	5	2755	181	2	3.94	7	3	4	417	17	1	*2.15
1995-96	Halifax	QMJHL	55	26	23	2	3230	185	1	3.44	6	1	5	....	....	....	4.07

GOVERDE, DAVID — (goh-VEHR-deh)

Goaltender. Catches right. 6', 210 lbs. Born, Toronto, Ont., April 9, 1970.
(Los Angeles' 4th choice, 91st overall, in 1990 Entry Draft).

			Regular Season								Playoffs						
Season	Club	Lea	GP	W	L	T	Mins	GA	SO	Avg	GP	W	L	Mins	GA	SO	Avg
1989-90	Sudbury	OHL	52	28	12	7	2941	182	0	3.71	7	3	3	394	25	0	3.81
1990-91	Phoenix	IHL	40	11	19	5	2007	137	0	4.10	....	....	....	....	....	....	....
1991-92	**Los Angeles**	**NHL**	**2**	**1**	**1**	**0**	**120**	**9**	**0**	**4.50**	....	....	....	....	....	....	....
	Phoenix	IHL	35	11	19	3	1951	129	1	3.97	....	....	....	....	....	....	....
	New Haven	AHL	5	1	3	0	248	17	0	4.11	....	....	....	....	....	....	....
1992-93	**Los Angeles**	**NHL**	**2**	**0**	**2**	**0**	**98**	**13**	**0**	**7.96**	....	....	....	....	....	....	....
	Phoenix	IHL	45	18	21	3	2569	173	1	4.04	....	....	....	....	....	....	....
1993-94	**Los Angeles**	**NHL**	**1**	**0**	**1**	**0**	**60**	**7**	**0**	**7.00**	....	....	....	....	....	....	....
	Phoenix	IHL	30	15	13	1	1716	93	0	3.25	....	....	....	....	....	....	....
	Portland	AHL	1	0	1	0	59	4	0	4.01	....	....	....	....	....	....	....
	Peoria	IHL	5	4	1	0	299	13	0	2.61	1	0	1	59	7	0	7.05
1994-95	Detroit	ColHL	4	4	0	0	240	10	0	2.50	....	....	....	....	....	....	....
	Phoenix	IHL	2	0	2	0	76	5	0	3.95	....	....	....	....	....	....	....
	Detroit	IHL	15	8	5	0	814	49	0	3.61	....	....	....	....	....	....	....
1995-96	Saint John	AHL	1	0	0	0	47	9	0	11.40	....	....	....	....	....	....	....
	Louisville	ECHL	12	5	5	1	697	46	*1	3.96	....	....	....	....	....	....	....
	Toledo	ECHL	31	23	3	4	1817	79	*1	2.61	11	8	3	666	32	0	2.88
	NHL Totals		**5**	**1**	**4**	**0**	**278**	**29**	**0**	**6.26**	....	....	....	....	....	....	....

GRAHAME, JOHN — BOS.

Goaltender. Catches left. 6'2", 195 lbs. Born, Denver, CO, August 31, 1975.
(Boston's 7th choice, 229th overall, in 1994 Entry Draft).

			Regular Season								Playoffs						
Season	Club	Lea	GP	W	L	T	Mins	GA	SO	Avg	GP	W	L	Mins	GA	SO	Avg
1994-95	Lake Superior	CCHA	28	16	7	3	1616	75	2	2.79	....	....	....	....	....	....	....
1995-96	Lake Superior	CCHA	29	21	4	2	1558	66	2	2.54	....	....	....	....	....	....	....

GUZDA, BRAD — L.A.

Goaltender. Catches left. 6'3", 180 lbs. Born, Banff, Alta., April 28, 1973.

			Regular Season								Playoffs						
Season	Club	Lea	GP	W	L	T	Mins	GA	SO	Avg	GP	W	L	Mins	GA	SO	Avg
1995-96	Knoxville	ECHL	19	16	1	0	1083	69	0	3.82	7	3	4	433	24	0	3.33
	Muskegon	ColHL	2	0	0	0	12	5	0	24.50	....	....	....	....	....	....	....

Signed as a free agent by **Los Angeles**, May 28, 1996.

HACKETT, JEFF — CHI.

Goaltender. Catches left. 6'1", 180 lbs. Born, London, Ont., June 1, 1968.
(NY Islanders' 2nd choice, 34th overall, in 1987 Entry Draft).

			Regular Season								Playoffs						
Season	Club	Lea	GP	W	L	T	Mins	GA	SO	Avg	GP	W	L	Mins	GA	SO	Avg
1986-87	Oshawa	OHL	31	18	9	2	1672	85	2	3.05	15	8	7	895	40	0	2.68
1987-88	Oshawa	OHL	53	30	21	2	3165	205	0	3.89	7	3	4	438	31	0	4.25
1988-89	**NY Islanders**	**NHL**	**13**	**4**	**7**	**0**	**662**	**39**	**0**	**3.53**	....	....	....	....	....	....	....
	Springfield	AHL	29	12	14	2	1677	116	0	4.15	....	....	....	....	....	....	....
1989-90a	Springfield	AHL	54	24	25	3	3045	187	1	3.68	*17	*10	5	934	60	0	3.85
1990-91	**NY Islanders**	**NHL**	**30**	**5**	**18**	**1**	**1508**	**91**	**0**	**3.62**	....	....	....	....	....	....	....
1991-92	**San Jose**	**NHL**	**42**	**11**	**27**	**1**	**2314**	**148**	**0**	**3.84**	....	....	....	....	....	....	....
1992-93	**San Jose**	**NHL**	**36**	**2**	**30**	**1**	**2000**	**176**	**0**	**5.28**	....	....	....	....	....	....	....
1993-94	**Chicago**	**NHL**	**22**	**2**	**12**	**3**	**1084**	**62**	**0**	**3.43**	....	....	....	....	....	....	....
1994-95	**Chicago**	**NHL**	**7**	**1**	**3**	**2**	**328**	**13**	**0**	**2.38**	**2**	**0**	**0**	**26**	**1**	**0**	**2.31**
1995-96	**Chicago**	**NHL**	**35**	**18**	**11**	**4**	**2000**	**80**	**4**	**2.40**	**1**	**0**	**1**	**60**	**5**	**0**	**5.00**
	NHL Totals		**185**	**43**	**108**	**12**	**9896**	**609**	**4**	**3.69**	**3**	**0**	**1**	**86**	**6**	**0**	**4.19**

a Won Jack A. Butterfield Trophy (Playoff MVP - AHL) (1990)

Claimed by **San Jose** from **NY Islanders** in Expansion Draft, May 30, 1991. Traded to **Chicago** by **San Jose** for Chicago's third round choice (Alexei Yegorov) in 1994 Entry Draft, July 13, 1993.

HALTIA, PATRIK — (HAHL-tih-ah) CGY.

Goaltender. Catches left. 6'1", 176 lbs. Born, Karlstad, Sweden, March 29, 1973.
(Calgary's 8th choice, 149th overall, in 1994 Entry Draft).

			Regular Season								Playoffs						
Season	Club	Lea	GP	W	L	T	Mins	GA	SO	Avg	GP	W	L	Mins	GA	SO	Avg
1994-95	Farjestad	Swe.	17	....	....	....	956	44	0	2.76	2	0	0	120	7	0	3.50
1995-96	Farjestad	Swe.	11	....	....	....	640	31	....	2.91	....	....	....	....	....	....	....

HASEK, DOMINIK — (HAH-shihk) BUF.

Goaltender. Catches left. 5'11", 168 lbs. Born, Pardubice, Czech., January 29, 1965.
(Chicago's 11th choice, 199th overall, in 1983 Entry Draft).

			Regular Season								Playoffs						
Season	Club	Lea	GP	W	L	T	Mins	GA	SO	Avg	GP	W	L	Mins	GA	SO	Avg
1981-82	Pardubice	Czech.	12	....	....	....	661	34	....	3.09	....	....	....	....	....	....	....
1982-83	Pardubice	Czech.	42	....	....	....	2358	105	....	2.67	....	....	....	....	....	....	....
1983-84	Pardubice	Czech.	40	....	....	....	2304	108	....	2.81	....	....	....	....	....	....	....
1984-85	Pardubice	Czech.	42	....	....	....	2419	131	....	3.25	....	....	....	....	....	....	....
1985-86a	Pardubice	Czech.	45	....	....	....	2689	138	....	3.08	....	....	....	....	....	....	....
1986-87ab	Pardubice	Czech.	43	....	....	....	2515	103	....	2.46	....	....	....	....	....	....	....
1987-88ac	Pardubice	Czech.	31	....	....	....	1862	93	....	3.00	....	....	....	....	....	....	....
1988-89abc	Pardubice	Czech.	42	....	....	....	2507	114	....	2.73	....	....	....	....	....	....	....
1989-90abc	Dukla Jihlava	Czech.	40	....	....	....	2251	80	....	2.13	....	....	....	....	....	....	....
1990-91	**Chicago**	**NHL**	**5**	**3**	**0**	**1**	**195**	**8**	**0**	**2.46**	**3**	**0**	**0**	**69**	**3**	**0**	**2.61**
d	Indianapolis	IHL	33	20	11	1	1903	80	*5	*2.52	1	1	0	60	3	0	3.00
1991-92e	**Chicago**	**NHL**	**20**	**10**	**4**	**1**	**1014**	**44**	**1**	**2.60**	**3**	**0**	**2**	**158**	**8**	**0**	**3.04**
	Indianapolis	IHL	20	7	10	3	1162	69	1	3.56	....	....	....	....	....	....	....
1992-93	**Buffalo**	**NHL**	**28**	**11**	**10**	**4**	**1429**	**75**	**0**	**3.15**	**1**	**1**	**0**	**45**	**1**	**0**	**1.33**
1993-94fgh	**Buffalo**	**NHL**	**58**	**30**	**20**	**6**	**3358**	**109**	***7**	***1.95**	**7**	**3**	**4**	**484**	**13**	**2**	***1.61**
1994-95	Pardubice	Czech.	2	....	....	....	124	6	0	2.90	....	....	....	....	....	....	....
fg	**Buffalo**	**NHL**	**41**	**19**	**14**	**7**	**2416**	**85**	***5**	***2.11**	**5**	**1**	**4**	**309**	**18**	**0**	**3.50**
1995-96	**Buffalo**	**NHL**	**59**	**22**	**30**	**6**	**3417**	**161**	**2**	**2.83**	....	....	....	....	....	....	....
	NHL Totals		**211**	**95**	**78**	**25**	**11829**	**482**	**15**	**2.44**	**19**	**5**	**10**	**1065**	**43**	**2**	**2.42**

a Czechoslovakian Goaltender-of-the-Year (1986, 1987, 1988, 1989, 1990)
b Czechoslovakian Player-of-the-Year (1987, 1989, 1990)
c Czechoslovakian First-Team All-Star (1988, 1989, 1990)
d IHL First All-Star Team (1991)
e NHL/Upper Deck All-Rookie Team (1992)
f NHL First All-Star Team (1994, 1995)
g Won Vezina Trophy (1994, 1995)
h Shared William M. Jennings Trophy with Grant Fuhr (1994)

Played in NHL All-Star Game (1996)

Traded to **Buffalo** by **Chicago** for Stephane Beauregard and Buffalo's fourth round choice (Eric Daze) in 1993 Entry Draft, August 7, 1992.

HEALY, GLENN — NYR

Goaltender. Catches left. 5'10", 185 lbs. Born, Pickering, Ont., August 23, 1962.

			Regular Season								Playoffs						
Season	Club	Lea	GP	W	L	T	Mins	GA	SO	Avg	GP	W	L	Mins	GA	SO	Avg
1981-82	W. Michigan	CCHA	27	7	19	1	1569	116	0	4.44	....	....	....	....	....	....	....
1982-83	W. Michigan	CCHA	30	8	19	2	1732	116	0	4.01	....	....	....	....	....	....	....
1983-84	W. Michigan	CCHA	38	19	16	3	2241	146	0	3.90	....	....	....	....	....	....	....
1984-85	W. Michigan	CCHA	37	21	14	2	2171	118	0	3.26	....	....	....	....	....	....	....
1985-86	**Los Angeles**	**NHL**	**1**	**0**	**0**	**0**	**51**	**6**	**0**	**7.06**	....	....	....	....	....	....	....
	New Haven	AHL	43	21	15	4	2410	160	0	3.98	2	0	2	49	11	0	5.55
1986-87	New Haven	AHL	47	21	15	0	2828	173	1	3.67	7	3	4	427	19	0	2.67
1987-88	**Los Angeles**	**NHL**	**34**	**12**	**18**	**1**	**1869**	**135**	**1**	**4.33**	**4**	**1**	**3**	**240**	**20**	**0**	**5.00**
1988-89	**Los Angeles**	**NHL**	**48**	**25**	**19**	**2**	**2699**	**192**	**0**	**4.27**	**3**	**0**	**1**	**97**	**6**	**0**	**3.71**
1989-90	**NY Islanders**	**NHL**	**39**	**12**	**19**	**6**	**2197**	**128**	**2**	**3.50**	**4**	**1**	**2**	**166**	**9**	**0**	**3.25**
1990-91	**NY Islanders**	**NHL**	**53**	**18**	**24**	**9**	**2999**	**166**	**0**	**3.32**	....	....	....	....	....	....	....
1991-92	**NY Islanders**	**NHL**	**37**	**14**	**16**	**4**	**1960**	**124**	**1**	**3.80**	....	....	....	....	....	....	....
1992-93	**NY Islanders**	**NHL**	**47**	**22**	**20**	**2**	**2655**	**146**	**1**	**3.30**	**18**	**9**	**8**	**1109**	**59**	**0**	**3.19**
1993-94	**NY Rangers**	**NHL**	**29**	**10**	**12**	**2**	**1368**	**69**	**2**	**3.03**	**2**	**0**	**0**	**68**	**1**	**0**	**0.88** ♦
1994-95	**NY Rangers**	**NHL**	**17**	**8**	**6**	**1**	**888**	**35**	**1**	**2.36**	**5**	**2**	**1**	**230**	**13**	**0**	**3.39**
1995-96	**NY Rangers**	**NHL**	**44**	**17**	**14**	**11**	**2564**	**124**	**2**	**2.90**	....	....	....	....	....	....	....
	NHL Totals		**349**	**138**	**148**	**38**	**19250**	**1125**	**10**	**3.51**	**36**	**13**	**15**	**1910**	**108**	**0**	**3.39**

Signed as a free agent by **Los Angeles**, June 13, 1985. Signed as a free agent by **NY Islanders**, August 16, 1989. Claimed by **Anaheim** from **NY Islanders** in Expansion Draft, June 24, 1993. Claimed by **Tampa Bay** from **Anaheim** in Phase II of Expansion Draft, June 25, 1993. Traded to **NY Rangers** by **Tampa Bay** for Tampa Bay's third round choice (previously acquired by NY Rangers — Tampa Bay selected Allan Egeland) in 1993 Entry Draft, June 25, 1993.

HEBERT, GUY (ay-BAIR, GEE) ANA.

Goaltender. Catches left. 5'11", 185 lbs. Born, Troy, NY, January 7, 1967.
(St. Louis' 8th choice, 159th overall, in 1987 Entry Draft).

			Regular Season								Playoffs						
Season	Club	Lea	GP	W	L	T	Mins	GA	SO	Avg	GP	W	L	Mins	GA	SO	Avg
1985-86	Hamilton Coll.	NCAA	18	4	12	2	1011	69	2	4.09	....	....	....	....	....	....	....
1986-87	Hamilton Coll.	NCAA	18	12	5	0	1070	40	3	2.19	2	1	1	134	6	0	2.69
1987-88	Hamilton Coll.	NCAA	9	5	3	0	510	22	1	2.58	1	0	1	60	3	0	3.00
1988-89	Hamilton Coll.	NCAA	25	18	7	0	1454	62	2	2.56	2	1	1	126	4	0	1.90
1989-90	Peoria	IHL	30	7	13	7	1706	124	1	4.36	2	0	1	76	5	0	3.95
1990-91ab	Peoria	IHL	36	24	10	1	2093	100	2	2.87	8	3	4	458	32	0	4.19
1991-92	**St. Louis**	**NHL**	**13**	**5**	**5**	**1**	**738**	**36**	**0**	**2.93**	....	....	....	....	....	....	....
	Peoria	IHL	29	20	9	0	1731	98	0	3.40	4	3	1	239	9	0	2.26
1992-93	**St. Louis**	**NHL**	**24**	**8**	**8**	**2**	**1210**	**74**	**1**	**3.67**	**1**	**0**	**0**	**2**	**0**	**0**	**0.00**
1993-94	**Anaheim**	**NHL**	**52**	**20**	**27**	**3**	**2991**	**141**	**2**	**2.83**	....	....	....	....	....	....	....
1994-95	**Anaheim**	**NHL**	**39**	**12**	**20**	**4**	**2092**	**109**	**2**	**3.13**	....	....	....	....	....	....	....
1995-96	**Anaheim**	**NHL**	**59**	**28**	**23**	**5**	**3326**	**157**	**4**	**2.83**	....	....	....	....	....	....	....
	NHL Totals		**187**	**73**	**83**	**15**	**10357**	**517**	**9**	**3.00**	**1**	**0**	**0**	**2**	**0**	**0**	**0.00**

a Shared James Norris Memorial Trophy (fewest goals against - IHL) with Pat Jablonski (1991)
b IHL Second All-Star Team (1991)

Claimed by **Anaheim** from **St. Louis** in Expansion Draft, June 24, 1993.

HEDBERG, JOHAN PHI.

Goaltender. Catches left. 5'11", 180 lbs. Born, Leksand, Sweden, May 5, 1973.
(Philadelphia's 8th choice, 218th overall, in 1994 Entry Draft).

			Regular Season								Playoffs						
Season	Club	Lea	GP	W	L	T	Mins	GA	SO	Avg	GP	W	L	Mins	GA	SO	Avg
1992-93	Leksand	Swe.	10	....	....	....	600	24	....	2.40	....	....	....	....	....	....	....
1993-94	Leksand	Swe.	17	....	....	....	1020	48	....	2.81	....	....	....	....	....	....	....
1994-95	Leksand	Swe.	17	....	....	....	986	58	....	3.53	....	....	....	....	....	....	....
1995-96	Leksand	Swe.	34	....	....	....	2013	95	....	2.83	4	....	....	240	13	....	3.25

HEIL, JEFF NYR

Goaltender. Catches left. 6'1", 190 lbs. Born, Bloomington, MN, September 17, 1975.
(NY Rangers' 7th choice, 169th overall, in 1995 Entry Draft).

			Regular Season								Playoffs						
Season	Club	Lea	GP	W	L	T	Mins	GA	SO	Avg	GP	W	L	Mins	GA	SO	Avg
1994-95	Wisc.-River Falls	WCHA	25	13	7	3	1399	64	2	2.74	....	....	....	....	....	....	....
1995-96	Wisc.-River Falls	WCHA	16	13	2	0	943	28	2	1.78	....	....	....	....	....	....	....

HENRY, FREDERIC N.J.

Goaltender. Catches left. 5'11", 155 lbs. Born, Cap-Rouge, Que., August 9, 1977.
(New Jersey's 10th choice, 200th overall, in 1995 Entry Draft).

			Regular Season								Playoffs						
Season	Club	Lea	GP	W	L	T	Mins	GA	SO	Avg	GP	W	L	Mins	GA	SO	Avg
1994-95	Granby	QMJHL	15	8	5	0	866	47	0	3.26	6	1	2	232	21	0	5.43
1995-96	Granby	QMJHL	28	19	5	2	1530	69	*3	2.71	12	9	2	610	21	2	*2.08

HEXTALL, RON PHI.

Goaltender. Catches left. 6'3", 192 lbs. Born, Brandon, Man., May 3, 1964.
(Philadelphia's 6th choice, 119th overall, in 1982 Entry Draft).

			Regular Season								Playoffs						
Season	Club	Lea	GP	W	L	T	Mins	GA	SO	Avg	GP	W	L	Mins	GA	SO	Avg
1981-82	Brandon	WHL	30	12	11	0	1398	133	0	5.71	3	0	2	103	16	0	9.32
1982-83	Brandon	WHL	44	13	30	0	2589	249	0	5.77	....	....	....	....	....	....	....
1983-84	Brandon	WHL	46	29	13	2	2670	190	0	4.27	10	5	5	592	37	0	3.75
1984-85	Hershey	AHL	11	4	6	0	555	34	0	3.68	....	....	....	....	....	....	....
	Kalamazoo	IHL	19	6	11	1	1103	80	0	4.35	....	....	....	....	....	....	....
1985-86ab	Hershey	AHL	*53	30	19	2	*3061	174	*5	3.41	13	5	7	780	42	*1	3.23
1986-87																	
cdef	**Philadelphia**	**NHL**	***66**	**37**	**21**	**6**	***3799**	**190**	**1**	**3.00**	***26**	**15**	**11**	***1540**	**71**	***2**	**2.77**
1987-88g	**Philadelphia**	**NHL**	**62**	**30**	**22**	**7**	**3561**	**208**	**0**	**3.50**	**7**	**2**	**4**	**379**	**30**	**0**	**4.75**
1988-89h	**Philadelphia**	**NHL**	***64**	**30**	**28**	**6**	***3756**	**202**	**0**	**3.23**	**15**	**8**	**7**	**886**	**49**	**0**	**3.32**
1989-90	**Philadelphia**	**NHL**	**8**	**4**	**2**	**1**	**419**	**29**	**0**	**4.15**	....	....	....	....	....	....	....
	Hershey	AHL	1	1	0	0	49	3	0	3.67	....	....	....	....	....	....	....
1990-91	**Philadelphia**	**NHL**	**36**	**13**	**16**	**5**	**2035**	**106**	**0**	**3.13**	....	....	....	....	....	....	....
1991-92	**Philadelphia**	**NHL**	**45**	**16**	**21**	**6**	**2668**	**151**	**3**	**3.40**	....	....	....	....	....	....	....
1992-93	**Quebec**	**NHL**	**54**	**29**	**16**	**5**	**2988**	**172**	**0**	**3.45**	**6**	**2**	**4**	**372**	**18**	**0**	**2.90**
1993-94	**NY Islanders**	**NHL**	**65**	**27**	**26**	**6**	**3581**	**184**	**5**	**3.08**	**3**	**0**	**3**	**158**	**16**	**0**	**6.08**
1994-95	**Philadelphia**	**NHL**	**31**	**17**	**9**	**4**	**1824**	**88**	**1**	**2.89**	**15**	**10**	**5**	**897**	**42**	**0**	**2.81**
1995-96	**Philadelphia**	**NHL**	**53**	**31**	**13**	**7**	**3102**	**112**	**4**	***2.17**	**12**	**6**	**6**	**760**	**27**	**0**	**2.13**
	NHL Totals		**484**	**234**	**174**	**53**	**27733**	**1442**	**14**	**3.12**	**84**	**43**	**40**	**4992**	**253**	**2**	**3.04**

a AHL First All-Star Team (1986)
b Won Dudley "Red" Garrett Memorial Trophy (Top Rookie - AHL) (1986)
c NHL First All-Star Team (1987)
d Won Vezina Trophy (1987)
e Won Conn Smythe Trophy (1987)
f NHL All-Rookie Team (1987)
g Scored a goal vs. Boston, December 8, 1987
h Scored a goal in playoffs vs. Washington, April 11, 1989

Played in NHL All-Star Game (1988)

Traded to **Quebec** by **Philadelphia** with Peter Forsberg, Steve Duchesne, Kerry Huffman, Mike Ricci, Chris Simon, Philadelphia's first round choice in the 1993 (Jocelyn Thibault) and 1994 (later traded to Toronto — later traded to Washington — Washington selected Nolan Baumgartner) Entry Drafts and cash for Eric Lindros, June 30, 1992. Traded to **NY Islanders** by **Quebec** with Quebec's first round choice (Todd Bertuzzi) in 1993 Entry Draft for Mark Fitzpatrick and NY Islanders' first round choice (Adam Deadmarsh) in 1993 Entry Draft, June 20, 1993. Traded to **Philadelphia** by **NY Islanders** with NY Islanders' sixth round choice (Dimitri Tertyshny) in 1995 Entry Draft for Tommy Soderstrom, September 22, 1994.

HILLEBRANDT, JON NYR

Goaltender. Catches left. 5'10", 185 lbs. Born, Cottage Grove, WI, December 18, 1971.
(NY Rangers' 12th choice, 202nd overall, in 1990 Entry Draft).

			Regular Season								Playoffs						
Season	Club	Lea	GP	W	L	T	Mins	GA	SO	Avg	GP	W	L	Mins	GA	SO	Avg
1991-92a	Ill.-Chicago	CCHA	31	7	19	....	1754	121	0	4.14	....	....	....	....	....	....	....
1992-93	Ill.-Chicago	CCHA	33	8	22	2	1783	134	0	4.51	....	....	....	....	....	....	....
1993-94	U.S. National	....	2	1	1	0	120	10	0	5.00	....	....	....	....	....	....	....
	Binghamton	AHL	7	1	3	0	294	18	0	3.67	....	....	....	....	....	....	....
	Erie	ECHL	3	2	0	1	189	8	1	2.53	....	....	....	....	....	....	....
1994-95	Charlotte	ECHL	32	14	11	5	1790	121	0	4.05	3	0	2	179	12	0	4.01
	San Diego	IHL	1	0	1	0	40	6	0	9.00	....	....	....	....	....	....	....
	Binghamton	AHL	....	....	....	....	....	....	....	....	1	0	0	5	1	0	10.20
1995-96	Binghamton	AHL	36	15	14	2	1845	136	0	4.42	2	1	1	47	8	0	10.10

a CCHA Second All-Star Team (1992)

HILLIER, CRAIG PIT.

Goaltender. Catches left. 6'1", 174 lbs. Born, Cole Harbour, N.S., February 28, 1978.
(Pittsburgh's 1st choice, 23rd overall, in 1996 Entry Draft).

			Regular Season								Playoffs						
Season	Club	Lea	GP	W	L	T	Mins	GA	SO	Avg	GP	W	L	Mins	GA	SO	Avg
1994-95	Ottawa	OHL	24	6	7	2	1078	69	1	3.84	....	....	....	....	....	....	....
1995-96a	Ottawa	OHL	44	24	14	3	2439	117	2	2.88	3	0	2	130	12	0	5.54

a OHL First All-Star Team (1996)

HIRSCH, COREY (HUHRSH) VAN.

Goaltender. Catches left. 5'10", 160 lbs. Born, Medicine Hat, Alta., July 1, 1972.
(NY Rangers' 8th choice, 169th overall, in 1991 Entry Draft).

			Regular Season								Playoffs						
Season	Club	Lea	GP	W	L	T	Mins	GA	SO	Avg	GP	W	L	Mins	GA	SO	Avg
1988-89	Kamloops	WHL	32	11	12	2	1516	106	2	4.20	5	3	2	245	19	0	4.65
1989-90	Kamloops	WHL	*63	*48	13	0	3608	230	*3	3.82	*17	*14	3	*1043	60	0	*3.45
1990-91a	Kamloops	WHL	38	26	7	1	1970	100	3	*3.05	11	5	6	623	42	0	4.04
1991-92																	
abcd	Kamloops	WHL	48	35	10	2	2732	124	*5	*2.72	*16	*11	5	954	35	*2	*2.20
1992-93	**NY Rangers**	**NHL**	**4**	**1**	**2**	**1**	**224**	**14**	**0**	**3.75**	....	....	....	....	....	....	....
efg	Binghamton	AHL	46	*35	4	5	2692	125	1	*2.79	14	7	7	831	46	0	3.32
1993-94	Cdn. National	....	45	24	17	3	2653	124	0	2.80	....	....	....	....	....	....	....
	Cdn. Olympic	....	8	5	2	1	495	17	0	2.06	....	....	....	....	....	....	....
	Binghamton	AHL	10	5	4	1	610	38	0	3.73	....	....	....	....	....	....	....
1994-95	Binghamton	AHL	57	31	20	5	3371	175	0	3.11	....	....	....	....	....	....	....
1995-96h	**Vancouver**	**NHL**	**41**	**17**	**14**	**6**	**2338**	**114**	**1**	**2.93**	**6**	**2**	**3**	**338**	**21**	**0**	**3.73**
	NHL Totals		**45**	**18**	**16**	**7**	**2562**	**128**	**1**	**3.00**	**6**	**2**	**3**	**338**	**21**	**0**	**3.73**

a WHL West First All-Star Team (1991, 1992)
b Canadian Major Junior Goaltender of the Year (1992)
c Memorial Cup All-Star Team (1992)
d Memorial Cup Tournament Top Goaltender (1992)
e Won Dudley "Red" Garrett Memorial Trophy (AHL Rookie of the Year) (1993)
f Shared Harry "Hap" Holmes Memorial Trophy (fewest goals-against - AHL) with Boris Rousson (1993)
g AHL First All-Star Team (1993)
h NHL All-Rookie Team (1996)

Traded to **Vancouver** by **NY Rangers** for Nathan Lafayette, April 7, 1995.

HODSON, KEVIN DET.

Goaltender. Catches left. 6', 182 lbs. Born, Winnipeg, Man., March 27, 1972.

			Regular Season								Playoffs						
Season	Club	Lea	GP	W	L	T	Mins	GA	SO	Avg	GP	W	L	Mins	GA	SO	Avg
1990-91	S.S. Marie	OHL	30	18	11	0	1638	88	0	*3.22	10	*9	1	581	28	0	*2.89
1991-92	S.S. Marie	OHL	50	28	12	4	2722	151	0	3.33	18	12	6	1116	54	1	2.90
1992-93ab	S.S. Marie	OHL	26	18	5	2	1470	76	1	*3.10	14	11	2	755	34	0	2.70
	Indianapolis	IHL	14	5	9	0	777	53	0	4.09	....	....	....	....	....	....	....
1993-94	Adirondack	AHL	37	20	10	5	2082	102	2	2.94	3	0	2	89	10	0	6.77
1994-95	Adirondack	AHL	51	19	22	8	2731	161	1	3.54	4	0	4	237	14	0	3.53
1995-96	**Detroit**	**NHL**	**4**	**2**	**0**	**0**	**163**	**3**	**1**	**1.10**	....	....	....	....	....	....	....
	Adirondack	AHL	32	13	13	2	1654	87	0	3.16	3	0	2	150	8	0	3.21
	NHL Totals		**4**	**2**	**0**	**0**	**163**	**3**	**1**	**1.10**	....	....	....	....	....	....	....

a Memorial Cup All-Star Team (1993)
b Won Hap Emms Memorial Trophy (Memorial Cup Tournament Top Goaltender) (1993)

Signed as a free agent by **Chicago**, August 17, 1992. Signed as a free agent by **Detroit**, June 16, 1993.

HRIVNAK, JIM (RIV-NAK)

Goaltender. Catches left. 6'2", 195 lbs. Born, Montreal, Que., May 28, 1968.
(Washington's 4th choice, 61st overall, in 1986 Entry Draft).

			Regular Season								Playoffs						
Season	Club	Lea	GP	W	L	T	Mins	GA	SO	Avg	GP	W	L	Mins	GA	SO	Avg
1985-86	Merrimack	NCAA	21	12	8	0	1230	75	0	3.66	....	....	....	....	....	....	....
1986-87	Merrimack	NCAA	34	27	7	0	1618	58	3	2.14	....	....	....	....	....	....	....
1987-88	Merrimack	NCAA	37	31	6	0	2119	84	4	2.38	....	....	....	....	....	....	....
1988-89	Merrimack	NCAA	22	....	....	....	1295	52	4	2.41	....	....	....	....	....	....	....
	Baltimore	AHL	10	1	8	0	502	55	0	6.57	....	....	....	....	....	....	....
1989-90	**Washington**	**NHL**	**11**	**5**	**5**	**0**	**609**	**36**	**0**	**3.55**	....	....	....	....	....	....	....
a	Baltimore	AHL	47	24	19	2	2722	139	*4	3.06	6	4	2	360	19	0	3.17
1990-91	**Washington**	**NHL**	**9**	**4**	**2**	**1**	**432**	**26**	**0**	**3.61**	....	....	....	....	....	....	....
	Baltimore	AHL	42	20	16	6	2481	134	1	3.24	6	2	3	324	21	0	3.89
1991-92	**Washington**	**NHL**	**12**	**6**	**3**	**0**	**605**	**35**	**0**	**3.47**	....	....	....	....	....	....	....
	Baltimore	AHL	22	10	8	3	1303	73	0	3.36	....	....	....	....	....	....	....
1992-93	**Washington**	**NHL**	**27**	**13**	**9**	**2**	**1421**	**83**	**0**	**3.50**	....	....	....	....	....	....	....
	Winnipeg	**NHL**	**3**	**2**	**1**	**0**	**180**	**13**	**0**	**4.33**	....	....	....	....	....	....	....
1993-94	**St. Louis**	**NHL**	**23**	**4**	**10**	**0**	**970**	**69**	**0**	**4.27**	....	....	....	....	....	....	....
1994-95	Milwaukee	IHL	28	17	10	1	1634	106	0	3.89	....	....	....	....	....	....	....
	Kansas City	IHL	10	3	5	2	550	35	0	3.81	2	0	2	118	7	0	3.55
1995-96	Carolina	AHL	11	1	4	1	458	27	0	3.54	....	....	....	....	....	....	....
	Las Vegas	IHL	13	10	1	1	713	34	0	2.86	....	....	....	....	....	....	....
	Kansas City	IHL	4	1	1	0	154	11	0	4.29	....	....	....	....	....	....	....
	NHL Totals		**85**	**34**	**30**	**3**	**4217**	**262**	**0**	**3.73**	....	....	....	....	....	....	....

a AHL Second All-Star Team (1990)

Traded to **Winnipeg** by **Washington** with Washington's second round choice (Alexei Budayev) in 1993 Entry Draft for Rick Tabaracci, March 22, 1993. Traded to **St. Louis** by **Winnipeg** for St. Louis' seventh round choice (later traded to Florida — later traded to Edmonton — later traded to Winnipeg — Winnipeg selected Chris Kibermanis) in 1994 Entry Draft and future considerations, July 29, 1993.

HRUDEY, KELLY (ROO-dee) S.J.

Goaltender. Catches left. 5'10", 189 lbs. Born, Edmonton, Alta., January 13, 1961.
(NY Islanders' 2nd choice, 38th overall, in 1980 Entry Draft).

			Regular Season								Playoffs						
Season	Club	Lea	GP	W	L	T	Mins	GA	SO	Avg	GP	W	L	Mins	GA	SO	Avg
1978-79	Medicine Hat	WHL	57	12	34	7	3093	318	0	6.17	....	....	....	....	....	....	....
1979-80	Medicine Hat	WHL	57	25	23	4	3049	212	1	4.17	13	6	6	638	48	0	4.51
1980-81a	Medicine Hat	WHL	55	32	19	1	3023	200	4	3.97	4	1	3	244	17	0	4.18
	Indianapolis	CHL	....	....	....	....	....	....	....	....	2	....	....	135	8	0	3.56
1981-82bc	Indianapolis	CHL	51	27	19	4	3033	149	1	*2.95	13	11	2	842	34	*1	*2.42
1982-83bcd	Indianapolis	CHL	47	*26	17	1	2744	139	2	3.04	10	*7	3	*637	28	0	*2.64
1983-84	NY Islanders	NHL	12	7	2	0	535	28	0	3.14	....	....	....	....	....	....	....
	Indianapolis	CHL	6	3	2	1	370	21	0	3.40	....	....	....	....	....	....	....
1984-85	NY Islanders	NHL	41	19	17	3	2335	141	2	3.62	5	1	3	281	8	0	1.71
1985-86	NY Islanders	NHL	45	19	15	8	2563	137	1	3.21	2	0	2	120	6	0	3.00
1986-87	NY Islanders	NHL	46	21	15	7	2634	145	0	3.30	14	7	7	842	38	0	2.71
1987-88	NY Islanders	NHL	47	22	17	5	2751	153	3	3.34	6	2	4	381	23	0	3.62
1988-89	NY Islanders	NHL	50	18	24	3	2800	183	0	3.92	....	....	....	....	....	....	....
	Los Angeles	NHL	16	10	4	2	974	47	1	2.90	10	4	6	566	35	0	3.71
1989-90	Los Angeles	NHL	52	22	21	6	2860	194	2	4.07	9	4	4	539	39	0	4.34
1990-91	Los Angeles	NHL	47	26	13	6	2730	132	3	2.90	12	6	6	798	37	0	2.78
1991-92	Los Angeles	NHL	60	26	17	13	3509	197	1	3.37	6	2	4	355	22	0	3.72
1992-93	Los Angeles	NHL	50	18	21	6	2718	175	2	3.86	20	10	10	1261	74	0	3.52
1993-94	Los Angeles	NHL	64	22	31	7	3713	228	1	3.68	....	....	....	....	....	....	....
1994-95	Los Angeles	NHL	35	14	13	5	1894	99	0	3.14	....	....	....	....	....	....	....
1995-96	Los Angeles	NHL	36	7	15	10	2077	113	0	3.26	....	....	....	....	....	....	....
	Phoenix	IHL	1	0	1	0	50	5	0	5.95	....	....	....	....	....	....	....
	NHL Totals		601	251	225	81	34093	1972	16	3.47	84	36	46	5143	282	0	3.29

a WHL Second All-Star Team (1981)
b CHL First All-Star Team (1982, 1983)
c Shared Terry Sawchuk Trophy (CHL's Leading Goaltender) with Rob Holland (1982, 1983)
d Won Tommy Ivan Trophy (CHL's Most Valuable Player) (1983)

Traded to **Los Angeles** by **NY Islanders** for Mark Fitzpatrick, Wayne McBean and future considerations (Doug Crossman, May 23, 1989) February 22, 1989. Signed as a free agent by **San Jose**, August 18, 1996.

ING, PETER

Goaltender. Catches left. 6'2", 170 lbs. Born, Toronto, Ont., April 28, 1969.
(Toronto's 3rd choice, 48th overall, in 1988 Entry Draft).

			Regular Season								Playoffs						
Season	Club	Lea	GP	W	L	T	Mins	GA	SO	Avg	GP	W	L	Mins	GA	SO	Avg
1986-87	Windsor	OHL	28	13	11	3	1615	105	0	3.90	5	4	0	161	9	0	3.35
1987-88	Windsor	OHL	43	30	7	1	2422	125	2	3.10	3	2	0	225	7	0	1.87
1988-89	Windsor	OHL	19	7	7	3	1043	76	*1	4.37	....	....	....	....	....	....	....
	London	OHL	32	18	11	2	1848	104	*2	3.38	21	11	9	1093	82	0	4.50
1989-90	Toronto	NHL	3	0	2	1	182	18	0	5.93	....	....	....	....	....	....	....
	Newmarket	AHL	48	16	19	12	2829	184	0	3.90	....	....	....	....	....	....	....
	Cdn. National	....	10	2	2	4	460	29	....	3.78	....	....	....	....	....	....	....
	London	OHL	8	6	2	0	480	27	0	3.38	....	....	....	....	....	....	....
1990-91	Toronto	NHL	56	16	29	8	3126	200	1	3.84	....	....	....	....	....	....	....
1991-92	Edmonton	NHL	12	3	4	0	463	33	0	4.28	....	....	....	....	....	....	....
	Cape Breton	AHL	24	9	10	4	1411	92	0	3.91	1	0	1	60	9	0	9.00
1992-93	Detroit	ColHL	3	2	1	0	136	6	0	2.65	....	....	....	....	....	....	....
	San Diego	IHL	17	11	4	1	882	53	0	3.61	4	2	2	183	13	0	4.26
1993-94	Detroit	NHL	3	1	2	0	170	15	0	5.29	....	....	....	....	....	....	....
	Adirondack	AHL	7	3	3	1	425	26	1	3.67	....	....	....	....	....	....	....
	Las Vegas	IHL	30	16	7	4	1627	91	0	3.36	2	0	1	40	4	0	5.87
1994-95	Fort Wayne	IHL	36	15	18	2	2018	119	2	3.54	2	0	1	94	5	0	3.19
1995-96	Fort Wayne	IHL	31	12	16	0	1674	109	2	3.91	....	....	....	....	....	....	....
	Cincinnati	IHL	1	0	1	0	60	8	0	8.00	....	....	....	....	....	....	....
	NHL Totals		74	20	37	9	3941	266	1	4.05	....	....	....	....	....	....	....

Traded to **Edmonton** by **Toronto** with Vincent Damphousse, Scott Thornton, Luke Richardson, future considerations and cash for Grant Fuhr, Glenn Anderson and Craig Berube, September 19, 1991. Traded to **Detroit** by **Edmonton** for Detroit's seventh round choice (Chris Wickenheiser) in 1994 Entry Draft and future considerations, August 30, 1993.

IRBE, ARTURS (UHR-bay, AHR-tuhrs) DAL.

Goaltender. Catches left. 5'8", 175 lbs. Born, Riga, Latvia, February 2, 1967.
(Minnesota's 11th choice, 196th overall, in 1989 Entry Draft).

			Regular Season								Playoffs						
Season	Club	Lea	GP	W	L	T	Mins	GA	SO	Avg	GP	W	L	Mins	GA	SO	Avg
1986-87	Dynamo Riga	USSR	2	....	....	....	27	1	0	2.22	....	....	....	....	....	....	....
1987-88a	Dynamo Riga	USSR	34	....	....	....	1870	86	4	2.69	....	....	....	....	....	....	....
1988-89	Dynamo Riga	USSR	40	....	....	....	2460	116	4	2.85	....	....	....	....	....	....	....
1989-90	Dynamo Riga	USSR	48	....	....	....	2880	115	2	2.42	....	....	....	....	....	....	....
1990-91	Dynamo Riga	USSR	46	....	....	....	2713	133	5	2.94	....	....	....	....	....	....	....
1991-92	San Jose	NHL	13	2	6	3	645	48	0	4.47	....	....	....	....	....	....	....
bc	Kansas City	IHL	32	24	7	1	1955	80	0	*2.46	*15	*12	3	914	44	0	*2.89
1992-93	San Jose	NHL	36	7	26	0	2074	142	1	4.11	....	....	....	....	....	....	....
	Kansas City	IHL	6	3	3	0	364	20	0	3.30	....	....	....	....	....	....	....
1993-94	San Jose	NHL	*74	30	28	16	*4412	209	3	2.84	14	7	7	806	50	0	3.72
1994-95	San Jose	NHL	38	14	19	3	2043	111	4	3.26	6	2	4	316	27	0	5.13
1995-96	San Jose	NHL	22	4	12	4	1112	85	0	4.59	....	....	....	....	....	....	....
	Kansas City	IHL	4	1	2	1	226	16	0	4.24	....	....	....	....	....	....	....
	NHL Totals		183	57	91	26	10286	595	8	3.47	20	9	11	1122	77	0	4.12

a Soviet National League Rookie-of-the-Year (1988)
b IHL First All-Star Team (1992)
c Shared James Norris Memorial Trophy (fewest goals against - IHL) with Wade Flaherty (1992)

Played in NHL All-Star Game (1994)

Claimed by **San Jose** from **Minnesota** in Dispersal Draft, May 30, 1991. Signed as a free agent by **Dallas**, August 19, 1996.

JABLONSKI, PAT MTL.

Goaltender. Catches right. 6', 180 lbs. Born, Toledo, OH, June 20, 1967.
(St. Louis' 6th choice, 138th overall, in 1985 Entry Draft).

			Regular Season								Playoffs						
Season	Club	Lea	GP	W	L	T	Mins	GA	SO	Avg	GP	W	L	Mins	GA	SO	Avg
1985-86	Windsor	OHL	29	6	16	4	1600	119	1	4.46	6	0	3	263	20	0	4.56
1986-87	Windsor	OHL	41	22	14	2	2328	128	*3	3.30	12	8	4	710	38	0	3.21
1987-88	Peoria	IHL	5	2	2	1	285	17	0	3.58	....	....	....	....	....	....	....
	Windsor	OHL	18	14	3	0	994	48	2	*2.90	9	*8	0	537	28	0	3.13
1988-89	Peoria	IHL	35	11	20	0	2051	163	1	4.77	3	0	2	130	13	0	6.00
1989-90	St. Louis	NHL	4	0	3	0	208	17	0	4.90	....	....	....	....	....	....	....
	Peoria	IHL	36	14	17	4	2023	165	0	4.89	4	1	3	223	19	0	5.11
1990-91	St. Louis	NHL	8	2	3	3	492	25	0	3.05	3	0	0	90	5	0	3.33
a	Peoria	IHL	29	23	3	2	1738	87	0	3.00	10	7	2	532	23	0	2.59
1991-92	St. Louis	NHL	10	3	6	0	468	38	0	4.87	....	....	....	....	....	....	....
	Peoria	IHL	8	6	1	1	493	29	1	3.53	....	....	....	....	....	....	....
1992-93	Tampa Bay	NHL	43	8	24	4	2268	150	1	3.97	....	....	....	....	....	....	....
1993-94	Tampa Bay	NHL	15	5	6	3	834	54	0	3.88	....	....	....	....	....	....	....
	St. John's	AHL	16	12	3	1	962	49	1	3.05	11	6	5	676	36	0	3.19
1994-95	Chicago	IHL	4	0	4	0	216	17	0	4.71	....	....	....	....	....	....	....
	Houston	IHL	3	1	1	1	179	9	0	3.01	....	....	....	....	....	....	....
1995-96	St. Louis	NHL	1	0	0	0	8	1	0	7.50	....	....	....	....	....	....	....
	Montreal	NHL	23	5	9	6	1264	62	0	2.94	1	0	0	49	1	0	1.22
	NHL Totals		104	23	51	16	5542	347	1	3.76	4	0	0	139	6	0	2.59

a Shared James Norris Memorial Trophy (fewest goals against - IHL) with Guy Hebert (1991)

Traded to **Tampa Bay** by **St. Louis** with Steve Tuttle and Darin Kimble for future considerations, June 19, 1992. Traded to **Toronto** by **Tampa Bay** for cash, February 21, 1994. Claimed by **St. Louis** from **Toronto** in NHL Waiver Draft, October 2, 1995. Traded to **Montreal** by **St. Louis** for J.J. Daigneault, November 7, 1995.

JAKS, PAULI (YAHKS, POW-lee)

Goaltender. Catches left. 6', 194 lbs. Born, Schaffhausen, Switz., January 25, 1972.
(Los Angeles' 5th choice, 108th overall, in 1991 Entry Draft).

			Regular Season								Playoffs						
Season	Club	Lea	GP	W	L	T	Mins	GA	SO	Avg	GP	W	L	Mins	GA	SO	Avg
1990-91	Ambri-Piotta	Switz.	22	....	....	....	1247	100	0	4.81	....	....	....	....	....	....	....
1991-92	Ambri-Piotta	Switz.	33	25	7	1	1890	97	2	2.93	....	....	....	....	....	....	....
1992-93	Ambri-Piotta	Switz.	29	....	....	....	....	92	....	3.17	....	....	....	....	....	....	....
1993-94	Phoenix	IHL	33	16	13	1	1712	101	0	3.54	....	....	....	....	....	....	....
1994-95	Phoenix	IHL	15	2	4	4	635	44	0	4.15	....	....	....	....	....	....	....
	Los Angeles	NHL	1	0	0	0	40	2	0	3.00	....	....	....	....	....	....	....
1995-96	Ambri-Piotta	Switz.	30	....	....	....	1799	106	....	3.53	....	....	....	....	....	....	....
	NHL Totals		1	0	0	0	40	2	0	3.00	....	....	....	....	....	....	....

JOHNSON, BRENT COL.

Goaltender. Catches left. 6'1", 175 lbs. Born, Farmington, MI, March 12, 1977.
(Colorado's 5th choice, 129th overall, in 1995 Entry Draft).

			Regular Season								Playoffs						
Season	Club	Lea	GP	W	L	T	Mins	GA	SO	Avg	GP	W	L	Mins	GA	SO	Avg
1994-95	Owen Sound	OHL	18	3	9	1	904	75	0	4.98	....	....	....	....	....	....	....
1995-96	Owen Sound	OHL	58	24	28	1	3211	243	1	4.54	6	2	4	371	29	0	4.69

JOSEPH, CURTIS EDM.

Goaltender. Catches left. 5'10", 182 lbs. Born, Keswick, Ont., April 29, 1967.

			Regular Season								Playoffs						
Season	Club	Lea	GP	W	L	T	Mins	GA	SO	Avg	GP	W	L	Mins	GA	SO	Avg
1988-89a	U. Wisconsin	WCHA	38	21	11	5	2267	94	1	2.49	....	....	....	....	....	....	....
1989-90	St. Louis	NHL	15	9	5	1	852	48	0	3.38	6	4	1	327	18	0	3.30
	Peoria	IHL	23	10	8	2	1241	80	0	3.87	....	....	....	....	....	....	....
1990-91	St. Louis	NHL	30	16	10	2	1710	89	0	3.12	....	....	....	....	....	....	....
1991-92	St. Louis	NHL	60	27	20	10	3494	175	2	3.01	6	2	4	379	23	0	3.64
1992-93	St. Louis	NHL	68	29	28	9	3890	196	1	3.02	11	7	4	715	27	*2	2.27
1993-94	St. Louis	NHL	71	36	23	11	4127	213	1	3.10	4	0	4	246	15	0	3.66
1994-95	St. Louis	NHL	36	20	10	1	1914	89	1	2.79	7	3	3	392	24	0	3.67
1995-96	Las Vegas	IHL	15	12	2	1	874	29	1	1.99	....	....	....	....	....	....	....
	Edmonton	NHL	34	15	16	2	1936	111	0	3.44	....	....	....	....	....	....	....
	NHL Totals		314	152	112	36	17923	921	5	3.08	34	16	16	2059	107	2	3.12

a WCHA First All-Star Team (1989)

Played in NHL All-Star Game (1994)

Signed as a free agent by **St. Louis**, June 16, 1989. Traded to **Edmonton** by **St. Louis** with the rights to Michael Grier for St. Louis' first round choices (previously acquired by Edmonton) in 1996 (Marty Reasoner) and 1997 Entry Drafts, August 4, 1995.

KARPENKO, IGOR ANA.

Goaltender. Catches left. 5'8", 158 lbs. Born, Kiev, USSR, July 23, 1976.
(Anaheim's 7th choice, 185th overall, in 1995 Entry Draft).

			Regular Season								Playoffs						
Season	Club	Lea	GP	W	L	T	Mins	GA	SO	Avg	GP	W	L	Mins	GA	SO	Avg
1993-94	Sokol-Kiev	CIS	5	....	....	....	88	3	....	2.05	....	....	....	....	....	....	....
1994-95	Sokol-Kiev	CIS	23	....	....	....	1292	67	....	3.11	....	....	....	....	....	....	....
1995-96	Sokol-Kiev	CIS	23	....	....	....	1269	62	....	2.93	....	....	....	....	....	....	....

KHABIBULIN, NIKOLAI (khah-bee-BOO-lihn) PHO.

Goaltender. Catches left. 6'1", 176 lbs. Born, Sverdlovsk, USSR, January 13, 1973.
(Winnipeg's 8th choice, 204th overall, in 1992 Entry Draft).

			Regular Season								Playoffs						
Season	Club	Lea	GP	W	L	T	Mins	GA	SO	Avg	GP	W	L	Mins	GA	SO	Avg
1988-89	Sverdlovsk	USSR	1	....	....	....	3	0	0	0.00	....	....	....	....	....	....	....
1989-90	Sverdlovsk Jrs.	USSR								UNAVAILABLE							
1990-91	Sputnik	USSR 3								UNAVAILABLE							
1991-92	CSKA	CIS	2	....	....	....	34	2	....	3.52	....	....	....	....	....	....	....
1992-93	CSKA	CIS	13	....	....	....	491	27	....	3.29	....	....	....	....	....	....	....
1993-94	CSKA	CIS	46	....	....	....	2625	116	....	2.65	3	....	....	193	11	....	3.42
	Russian Pen's	IHL	12	2	7	2	639	47	0	4.41	....	....	....	....	....	....	....
1994-95	Springfield	AHL	23	9	9	3	1240	80	0	3.87	....	....	....	....	....	....	....
	Winnipeg	NHL	26	8	9	4	1339	76	0	3.41	....	....	....	....	....	....	....
1995-96	Winnipeg	NHL	53	26	20	3	2914	152	2	3.13	6	2	4	359	19	0	3.18
	NHL Totals		79	34	29	7	4253	228	2	3.22	6	2	4	359	19	0	3.18

KIDD, TREVOR — CGY.

Goaltender. Catches left. 6'2", 190 lbs. Born, Dugald, Man., March 29, 1972.
(Calgary's 1st choice, 11th overall, in 1990 Entry Draft).

			Regular Season								Playoffs						
Season	Club	Lea	GP	W	L	T	Mins	GA	SO	Avg	GP	W	L	Mins	GA	SO	Avg
1988-89	Brandon	WHL	32	11	13	1	1509	102	0	4.06	....	....	....	....	....	....	....
1989-90a	Brandon	WHL	*63	24	32	2	*3676	254	2	4.15	....	....	....	....	....	....	....
1990-91	Brandon	WHL	30	10	19	1	1730	117	0	4.06	....	....	....	....	....	....	....
	Spokane	WHL	14	8	3	0	749	44	0	3.52	15	*14	1	926	32	2	*2.07
1991-92	Cdn. National	....	28	18	4	4	1349	79	2	3.51	....	....	....	....	....	....	....
	Cdn. Olympic	....	1	1	0	0	60	0	1	0.00	....	....	....	....	....	....	....
	Calgary	**NHL**	**2**	**1**	**1**	**0**	**120**	**8**	**0**	**4.00**	....	....	....	....	....	....	....
1992-93	Salt Lake	IHL	29	10	16	1	1696	111	1	3.93	....	....	....	....	....	....	....
1993-94	**Calgary**	**NHL**	**31**	**13**	**7**	**6**	**1614**	**85**	**0**	**3.16**	....	....	....	....	....	....	....
1994-95	**Calgary**	**NHL**	***43**	**22**	**14**	**6**	***2463**	**107**	**3**	**2.61**	**7**	**3**	**4**	**434**	**26**	**1**	**3.59**
1995-96	**Calgary**	**NHL**	**47**	**15**	**21**	**8**	**2570**	**119**	**3**	**2.78**	**2**	**0**	**1**	**83**	**9**	**0**	**6.51**
	NHL Totals		**123**	**51**	**43**	**20**	**6767**	**319**	**6**	**2.83**	**9**	**3**	**5**	**517**	**35**	**1**	**4.06**

a WHL East First All-Star Team (1990)

KIPRUSOFF, MIIKKA — S.J.

Goaltender. Catches left. 6', 176 lbs. Born, Turku, Finland, October 26, 1976.
(San Jose's 5th choice, 116th overall, in 1995 Entry Draft).

			Regular Season								Playoffs						
Season	Club	Lea	GP	W	L	T	Mins	GA	SO	Avg	GP	W	L	Mins	GA	SO	Avg
1994-95	TPS	Fin. Jr.	31	....	....	....	1896	92	....	2.91	....	....	....	....	....	....	....
	TPS	Fin.	4	....	....	....	240	12	0	3.00	2	....	....	120	7	....	3.50
1995-96	TPS	Fin. Jr.	3	....	....	....	180	9	....	3.00	....	....	....	....	....	....	....
	Kiekko-67	Fin. 2	5	....	....	....	300	7	....	1.40	....	....	....	....	....	....	....
	TPS	Fin.	12	....	....	....	550	38	0	4.14	3	....	....	114	4	....	2.11

KNICKLE, RICK — (kuh-NIHK-uhl)

Goaltender. Catches left. 5'10", 175 lbs. Born, Chatham, N.B., February 26, 1960.
(Buffalo's 7th choice, 116th overall, in 1979 Entry Draft).

			Regular Season								Playoffs						
Season	Club	Lea	GP	W	L	T	Mins	GA	SO	Avg	GP	W	L	Mins	GA	SO	Avg
1977-78	Brandon	WHL	49	34	5	7	2806	182	0	3.89	8	....	....	450	36	0	4.82
1978-79a	Brandon	WHL	38	26	3	8	2240	118	1	*3.16	16	12	3	886	41	*1	*2.78
1979-80	Brandon	WHL	33	11	14	1	1604	125	0	4.68	....	....	....	....	....	....	....
	Muskegon	IHL	16	....	....	....	829	52	0	3.76	3	....	....	156	17	0	6.54
1980-81b	Erie	EHL	43	....	....	....	2347	125	1	*3.20	8	....	....	446	14	0	*1.88
1981-82	Rochester	AHL	31	10	12	5	1753	108	1	3.70	3	0	2	125	7	0	3.37
1982-83	Flint	IHL	27	....	....	....	1638	92	2	3.37	3	....	....	193	10	0	3.11
	Rochester	AHL	4	0	3	0	143	11	0	4.64	....	....	....	....	....	....	....
1983-84c	Flint	IHL	60	32	21	5	3518	203	3	3.46	8	8	0	480	24	0	3.00
1984-85	Sherbrooke	AHL	14	7	6	0	780	53	0	4.08	....	....	....	....	....	....	....
	Flint	IHL	36	18	11	3	2018	115	2	3.42	7	3	4	401	27	0	4.04
1985-86	Saginaw	IHL	39	16	15	0	2235	135	2	3.62	3	2	1	193	12	0	3.73
1986-87	Saginaw	IHL	26	9	13	0	1413	113	0	4.80	5	1	4	329	21	0	3.83
1987-88	Flint	IHL	1	0	1	0	60	4	0	4.00	....	....	....	....	....	....	....
	Peoria	IHL	13	2	8	1	705	58	0	4.94	6	3	3	294	20	....	4.08
1988-89de	Fort Wayne	IHL	47	22	16	0	2716	141	1	*3.11	4	1	2	173	15	0	5.20
1989-90	Flint	IHL	55	25	24	1	2998	210	1	4.20	2	0	2	101	13	0	7.72
1990-91	Albany	IHL	14	4	6	2	679	52	0	4.59	....	....	....	....	....	....	....
	Springfield	AHL	9	6	0	2	509	28	0	3.30	....	....	....	....	....	....	....
1991-92c	San Diego	IHL	46	*28	13	4	2686	155	0	3.46	2	0	1	78	3	0	2.31
1992-93df	San Diego	IHL	41	33	4	4	2437	88	*4	*2.17	....	....	....	....	....	....	....
	Los Angeles	**NHL**	**10**	**6**	**4**	**0**	**532**	**35**	**0**	**3.95**	....	....	....	....	....	....	....
1993-94	**Los Angeles**	**NHL**	**4**	**1**	**2**	**0**	**174**	**9**	**0**	**3.10**	....	....	....	....	....	....	....
	Phoenix	IHL	25	8	9	3	1292	89	1	4.13	....	....	....	....	....	....	....
1994-95	Detroit	IHL	49	24	15	5	2725	134	*3	2.95	....	....	....	....	....	....	....
1995-96	Detroit	IHL	18	9	5	1	872	50	0	3.44	....	....	....	....	....	....	....
	Las Vegas	IHL	7	6	1	0	420	27	0	3.86	4	1	0	126	7	0	3.33
	NHL Totals		**14**	**7**	**6**	**0**	**706**	**44**	**0**	**3.74**	....	....	....	....	....	....	....

a WHL First All-Star Team (1979)
b EHL First All-Star Team (1981)
c IHL Second All-Star Team (1984, 1992)
d IHL First All-Star Team (1989, 1993)
e Won James Norris Memorial Trophy (fewest goals against - IHL) (1989)
f Shared James Norris Memorial Trophy (fewest goals against - IHL) with Clint Malarchuk (1993)

Signed as a free agent by **Montreal**, February 8, 1985. Signed as a free agent by **Los Angeles**, February 16, 1993.

KOCHAN, DIETER — VAN.

Goaltender. Catches left. 6'1", 170 lbs. Born, Saskatoon, Sask., November 5, 1974.
(Vancouver's 3rd choice, 98th overall, in 1993 Entry Draft).

			Regular Season								Playoffs						
Season	Club	Lea	GP	W	L	T	Mins	GA	SO	Avg	GP	W	L	Mins	GA	SO	Avg
1993-94	N. Michigan	WCHA	20	9	7	0	686	44	0	3.85	....	....	....	....	....	....	....
1994-95	N. Michigan	WCHA	29	8	17	3	1511	107	0	4.25	....	....	....	....	....	....	....
1995-96	N. Michigan	WCHA	31	7	21	2	1627	123	0	4.54	....	....	....	....	....	....	....

KOLZIG, OLAF — (KOHLT-zihg, OH-lahf) WSH.

Goaltender. Catches left. 6'3", 225 lbs. Born, Johannesburg, South Africa, April 9, 1970.
(Washington's 1st choice, 19th overall, in 1989 Entry Draft).

			Regular Season								Playoffs						
Season	Club	Lea	GP	W	L	T	Mins	GA	SO	Avg	GP	W	L	Mins	GA	SO	Avg
1987-88	N. Westminster	WHL	15	6	5	0	650	48	1	4.43	3	0	3	149	11	0	4.43
1988-89	Tri-Cities	WHL	30	16	10	2	1671	97	1	*3.48	....	....	....	....	....	....	....
1989-90	**Washington**	**NHL**	**2**	**0**	**2**	**0**	**120**	**12**	**0**	**6.00**	....	....	....	....	....	....	....
	Tri-Cities	WHL	48	27	27	3	2504	250	1	4.38	6	4	0	318	27	0	5.09
1990-91	Baltimore	AHL	26	10	12	1	1367	72	0	3.16	....	....	....	....	....	....	....
	Hampton Rds.	ECHL	21	11	9	1	1248	71	2	3.41	3	1	2	180	14	0	4.66
1991-92	Baltimore	AHL	28	5	17	2	1503	105	1	4.19	....	....	....	....	....	....	....
	Hampton Rds.	ECHL	14	11	3	0	847	41	0	2.90	....	....	....	....	....	....	....
1992-93	**Washington**	**NHL**	**1**	**0**	**0**	**0**	**20**	**2**	**0**	**6.00**	....	....	....	....	....	....	....
	Rochester	AHL	49	25	16	4	2737	168	0	3.68	*17	9	8	*1040	61	0	3.52
1993-94	**Washington**	**NHL**	**7**	**0**	**3**	**0**	**224**	**20**	**0**	**5.36**	....	....	....	....	....	....	....
ab	Portland	AHL	29	16	8	5	1725	88	3	3.06	17	*12	5	1035	44	0	*2.55
1994-95	**Washington**	**NHL**	**14**	**2**	**8**	**2**	**724**	**30**	**0**	**2.49**	**2**	**1**	**0**	**44**	**1**	**0**	**1.36**
	Portland	AHL	2	1	0	1	125	3	0	1.44	....	....	....	....	....	....	....
1995-96	**Washington**	**NHL**	**18**	**4**	**8**	**2**	**897**	**46**	**0**	**3.08**	**5**	**2**	**3**	**341**	**11**	**0**	***1.94**
	Portland	AHL	5	5	0	0	300	7	1	1.40	....	....	....	....	....	....	....
	NHL Totals		**42**	**6**	**21**	**4**	**1985**	**110**	**0**	**3.32**	**7**	**3**	**3**	**385**	**12**	**0**	**1.87**

a Shared Harry "Hap" Holmes Trophy (fewest goals-against - AHL) with Byron Dafoe (1994)
b Won Jack Butterfield Trophy (Playoff MVP - IHL) (1994)

KUNTAR, LES — (KOON-tahr) PHI.

Goaltender. Catches left. 6'2", 195 lbs. Born, Elma, NY, July 28, 1969.
(Montreal's 8th choice, 122nd overall, in 1987 Entry Draft).

			Regular Season								Playoffs						
Season	Club	Lea	GP	W	L	T	Mins	GA	SO	Avg	GP	W	L	Mins	GA	SO	Avg
1987-88	St. Lawrence	ECAC	10	6	1	0	488	27	0	3.31	....	....	....	....	....	....	....
1988-89	St. Lawrence	ECAC	14	11	2	0	786	31	0	2.37	....	....	....	....	....	....	....
1989-90	St. Lawrence	ECAC	20	7	11	1	1136	80	0	4.23	....	....	....	....	....	....	....
1990-91ab	St. Lawrence	ECAC	*33	*19	11	1	*1797	97	*1	*3.24	....	....	....	....	....	....	....
1991-92	Fredericton	AHL	11	7	3	0	638	26	0	2.45	....	....	....	....	....	....	....
	U.S. National	....	2	0	1	0	100	4	0	2.40	....	....	....	....	....	....	....
1992-93	Fredericton	AHL	42	16	14	7	2315	130	0	3.37	1	0	1	64	6	0	5.63
1993-94	**Montreal**	**NHL**	**6**	**2**	**2**	**0**	**302**	**16**	**0**	**3.18**	....	....	....	....	....	....	....
	Fredericton	AHL	34	10	17	3	1804	109	1	3.62	....	....	....	....	....	....	....
1994-95	Worcester	AHL	24	6	10	5	1241	77	2	3.72	....	....	....	....	....	....	....
	Hershey	AHL	32	15	13	2	1802	89	0	2.96	2	0	1	70	5	0	4.28
1995-96	Hershey	AHL	20	7	8	2	1020	71	0	4.18	....	....	....	....	....	....	....
	Fort Wayne	IHL	8	2	3	1	387	26	1	4.03	....	....	....	....	....	....	....
	NHL Totals		**6**	**2**	**2**	**0**	**302**	**16**	**0**	**3.18**	....	....	....	....	....	....	....

a ECAC First All-Star Team (1991)
b NCAA East First All-American Team (1991)

Signed as a free agent by **Philadelphia**, June 30, 1995.

KVALEVOG, TOBY — OTT.

Goaltender. Catches left. 5'11", 170 lbs. Born, Fargo, ND, December 22, 1974.
(Ottawa's 8th choice, 209th overall, in 1993 Entry Draft).

			Regular Season								Playoffs						
Season	Club	Lea	GP	W	L	T	Mins	GA	SO	Avg	GP	W	L	Mins	GA	SO	Avg
1993-94	North Dakota	WCHA	32	11	17	3	1813	120	0	3.97	....	....	....	....	....	....	....
1994-95	North Dakota	WCHA	32	14	13	3	1828	120	*1	3.94	....	....	....	....	....	....	....
1995-96	North Dakota	WCHA	35	15	15	1	1889	123	0	3.91	....	....	....	....	....	....	....

LABBE, JEAN-FRANCOIS — COL.

Goaltender. Catches left. 5'9", 170 lbs. Born, Sherbrooke, Que., June 15, 1972.

			Regular Season								Playoffs						
Season	Club	Lea	GP	W	L	T	Mins	GA	SO	Avg	GP	W	L	Mins	GA	SO	Avg
1989-90	Trois-Rivieres	QMJHL	28	13	10	0	1499	106	1	4.24	3	1	1	132	8	0	3.64
1990-91	Trois-Rivieres	QMJHL	54	*35	14	0	2870	158	5	3.30	5	1	4	230	19	0	4.96
1991-92a	Trois-Rivieres	QMJHL	48	*31	13	3	2749	142	1	3.10	*15	*10	3	791	33	*1	*2.50
1992-93	Hull	QMJHL	46	26	18	2	2701	156	2	3.46	10	6	3	518	24	*1	*2.78
1993-94bcd	Thunder Bay	ColHL	52	*35	11	4	*2900	150	*2	*3.10	8	7	1	493	18	*2	*2.19
	P.E.I.	AHL	7	4	3	0	389	22	0	3.39	....	....	....	....	....	....	....
1994-95	P.E.I.	AHL	32	13	14	3	1817	94	2	3.10	....	....	....	....	....	....	....
1995-96	Cornwall	AHL	55	25	21	5	2972	144	3	2.91	8	3	5	471	21	1	2.68

a QMJHL First All-Star Team (1992)
b ColHL First All-Star Team (1994)
c Named ColHL's Rookie of the Year (1994)
d Named ColHL's Outstanding Goaltender (1994)

Signed as a free agent by **Ottawa**, May 12, 1994. Traded to **Colorado** by **Ottawa** for a conditional draft choice, September 20, 1995.

LABRECQUE, PATRICK — MTL.

Goaltender. Catches left. 6', 190 lbs. Born, Laval, Que., March 6, 1971.
(Quebec's 5th choice, 90th overall, in 1991 Entry Draft).

			Regular Season								Playoffs						
Season	Club	Lea	GP	W	L	T	Mins	GA	SO	Avg	GP	W	L	Mins	GA	SO	Avg
1990-91	St-Jean	QMJHL	59	17	34	6	3375	216	1	3.84	....	....	....	....	....	....	....
1991-92	Halifax	AHL	29	5	12	8	1570	114	0	4.36	....	....	....	....	....	....	....
1992-93	Greensboro	ECHL	11	6	3	2	650	31	0	2.86	1	0	1	59	5	0	5.08
	Halifax	AHL	20	3	12	2	914	76	0	4.99	....	....	....	....	....	....	....
1993-94	Cornwall	AHL	4	1	2	0	198	8	1	2.42	....	....	....	....	....	....	....
	Greensboro	ECHL	29	17	8	2	1609	89	0	3.32	1	0	0	22	4	0	10.80
1994-95	Fredericton	AHL	35	15	17	1	1913	104	1	3.26	*16	*10	6	*967	40	1	2.48
	Wheeling	ECHL	5	2	3	0	281	22	0	4.69	....	....	....	....	....	....	....
1995-96	**Montreal**	**NHL**	**2**	**0**	**1**	**0**	**98**	**7**	**0**	**4.29**	....	....	....	....	....	....	....
	Fredericton	AHL	48	23	18	6	2686	153	3	3.42	7	3	3	405	31	0	4.59
	NHL Totals		**2**	**0**	**1**	**0**	**98**	**7**	**0**	**4.29**	....	....	....	....	....	....	....

Signed as a free agent by **Montreal**, June 21, 1994.

LACHER, BLAINE — (LAW-kuhr)

Goaltender. Catches left. 6'1", 205 lbs. Born, Medicine Hat, Alta., September 5, 1970.

			Regular Season								Playoffs						
Season	Club	Lea	GP	W	L	T	Mins	GA	SO	Avg	GP	W	L	Mins	GA	SO	Avg
1991-92	Lake Superior	CCHA	9	5	3	0	410	22	0	3.22	....	....	....	....	....	....	....
1992-93	Lake Superior	CCHA	34	24	5	3	1915	86	2	2.70	....	....	....	....	....	....	....
1993-94	Lake Superior	CCHA	30	20	5	4	1785	59	6	*1.98	....	....	....	....	....	....	....
1994-95	**Boston**	**NHL**	**35**	**19**	**11**	**2**	**1965**	**79**	**4**	**2.41**	**5**	**1**	**4**	**283**	**12**	**0**	**2.54**
	Providence	AHL	1	0	1	0	59	3	0	3.03	....	....	....	....	....	....	....
1995-96	**Boston**	**NHL**	**12**	**3**	**5**	**2**	**671**	**44**	**0**	**3.93**	....	....	....	....	....	....	....
	Providence	AHL	9	3	5	0	462	30	0	3.90	....	....	....	....	....	....	....
	Cleveland	IHL	8	3	4	1	478	28	0	3.51	3	0	3	191	10	0	3.14
	NHL Totals		**47**	**22**	**16**	**4**	**2636**	**123**	**4**	**2.80**	**5**	**1**	**4**	**283**	**12**	**0**	**2.54**

Signed as a free agent by **Boston**, June 2, 1994.

LaFOREST, MARK

Goaltender. Catches left. 5'11", 190 lbs. Born, Welland, Ont., July 10, 1962.

			Regular Season								Playoffs						
Season	Club	Lea	GP	W	L	T	Mins	GA	SO	Avg	GP	W	L	Mins	GA	SO	Avg
1981-82	Niagara Falls	OHL	24	10	13	1	1365	105	1	4.62	5	1	2	300	19	0	3.80
1982-83	North Bay	OHL	54	34	17	1	3140	195	0	3.73	8	4	4	474	31	0	3.92
1983-84	Adirondack	AHL	7	3	3	1	351	29	0	4.96							
	Kalamazoo	IHL	13	4	5	2	718	48	1	4.01							
1984-85	Adirondack	AHL	11	2	3	1	430	35	0	4.88							
1985-86	**Detroit**	**NHL**	**28**	**4**	**21**	**0**	**1383**	**114**	**1**	**4.95**							
	Adirondack	AHL	19	13	5	1	1142	57	0	2.99	*17	*12	5	*1075	58	0	3.24
1986-87	**Detroit**	**NHL**	**5**	**2**	**1**	**0**	**219**	**12**	**0**	**3.29**							
a	Adirondack	AHL	37	23	8	0	2229	105	*3	2.83							
1987-88	**Philadelphia**	**NHL**	**21**	**5**	**9**	**2**	**972**	**60**	**1**	**3.70**	**2**	**1**	**0**	**48**	**1**	**0**	**1.25**
	Hershey	AHL	5	2	1	2	309	13	0	2.52							
1988-89	**Philadelphia**	**NHL**	**17**	**5**	**7**	**2**	**933**	**64**	**0**	**4.12**							
	Hershey	AHL	3	2	0	0	185	9	0	2.92	12	7	5	744	27	1	2.18
1989-90	**Toronto**	**NHL**	**27**	**9**	**14**	**0**	**1343**	**87**	**0**	**3.89**							
	Newmarket	AHL	10	6	4	0	604	33	1	3.28							
1990-91ab	Binghamton	AHL	45	25	14	2	2452	129	0	3.16	9	3	4	442	28	1	3.80
1991-92	Binghamton	AHL	43	25	15	3	2559	146	1	3.42	11	7	4	662	34	0	3.08
1992-93	New Haven	AHL	30	10	18	1	1688	121	1	4.30							
	Brantford	Col.	10	5	3	1	565	35	1	3.72							
1993-94	**Ottawa**	**NHL**	**5**	**0**	**2**	**0**	**182**	**17**	**0**	**5.60**							
	P.E.I.	AHL	43	9	25	5	2359	161	0	4.09							
1994-95	Milwaukee	IHL	42	19	13	7	2325	123	2	3.17	15	8	7	937	40	*2	2.56
1995-96	Milwaukee	IHL	53	26	20	7	3079	191	0	3.72	5	2	3	315	18	0	3.42
	NHL Totals		**103**	**25**	**54**	**4**	**5032**	**354**	**2**	**4.22**	**2**	**1**	**0**	**48**	**1**	**0**	**1.25**

a Won Baz Bastien Memorial Trophy (Top Goaltender - AHL) (1987, 1991)
b AHL Second All-Star Team (1991)

Signed as a free agent by **Detroit**, April 29, 1983. Traded to **Philadelphia** by **Detroit** for Philadelphia's second round choice (Bob Wilkie) in 1987 Entry Draft, June 13, 1987. Traded to **Toronto** by **Philadelphia** for Toronto's sixth round choice in 1991 Entry Draft and its seventh round choice in 1991 Entry Draft, September 8, 1989. Traded to **NY Rangers** by **Toronto** with Tie Domi for Greg Johnston, June 28, 1990. Claimed by **Ottawa** from **NY Rangers** in Expansion Draft, June 18, 1992.

LAGRAND, SCOTT

Goaltender. Catches left. 6', 165 lbs. Born, Potsdam, NY, February 11, 1970.
(Philadelphia's 5th choice, 77th overall, in 1988 Entry Draft).

			Regular Season								Playoffs						
Season	Club	Lea	GP	W	L	T	Mins	GA	SO	Avg	GP	W	L	Mins	GA	SO	Avg
1989-90	Boston College	H.E.	24	17	4	0	1268	57	0	2.70							
1990-91a	Boston College	H.E.	23	12	8	0	1153	63	2	3.28							
1991-92b	Boston College	H.E.	30	11	16	2	1750	108	1	3.70							
1992-93	Hershey	AHL	32	8	17	4	1854	145	0	4.69							
1993-94	Hershey	AHL	40	16	13	3	2032	117	2	3.45							
1994-95	Hershey	AHL	21	7	9	3	1104	71	1	3.86							
	Atlanta	IHL	21	7	7	3	993	67	0	4.04	3	0	2	101	10	0	5.91
1995-96	Orlando	IHL	33	17	7	3	1618	103	1	3.82	3	0	0	51	1	0	1.17

a Hockey East First All-Star Team (1991)
b NCAA East Second All-American Team (1992)

Traded to **Tampa Bay** by **Philadelphia** for Mike Greenlay, February 2, 1995.

LALIME, PATRICK — PIT.

Goaltender. Catches left. 6'2", 170 lbs. Born, St. Bonaventure, Que., July 7, 1974.
(Pittsburgh's 6th choice, 156th overall, in 1993 Entry Draft).

			Regular Season								Playoffs						
Season	Club	Lea	GP	W	L	T	Mins	GA	SO	Avg	GP	W	L	Mins	GA	SO	Avg
1992-93	Shawinigan	QMJHL	44	10	24	4	2467	192	0	4.67							
1993-94	Shawinigan	QMJHL	48	22	20	0	2733	192	1	4.22	5	1	3	223	25	0	6.73
1994-95	Hampton Rds.	ECHL	26	15	7	3	1470	82	2	3.35							
	Cleveland	IHL	23	7	10	4	1230	91	0	4.44							
1995-96	Cleveland	IHL	41	20	12	7	2314	149	0	3.86							

LAMBERT, JUDD — N.J.

Goaltender. Catches left. 6', 165 lbs. Born, Richmond, B.C., June 3, 1974.
(New Jersey's 9th choice, 221st overall, in 1993 Entry Draft).

			Regular Season								Playoffs						
Season	Club	Lea	GP	W	L	T	Mins	GA	SO	Avg	GP	W	L	Mins	GA	SO	Avg
1993-94	Colorado	WCHA	11	6	4	0	620	33	0	3.19							
1994-95	Colorado	WCHA	21	12	7	0	1060	57	*1	3.23							
1995-96	Colorado	WCHA	19	16	1	2	1179	43	1	*2.19							

LAMOTHE, MARC — MTL.

Goaltender. Catches left. 6'1", 204 lbs. Born, New Liskeard, Ont., February 27, 1974.
(Montreal's 6th choice, 92nd overall, in 1992 Entry Draft).

			Regular Season								Playoffs						
Season	Club	Lea	GP	W	L	T	Mins	GA	SO	Avg	GP	W	L	Mins	GA	SO	Avg
1991-92	Kingston	OHL	42	10	25	2	2378	189	1	4.77							
1992-93	Kingston	OHL	45	23	12	6	2489	162	1	3.91	15	8	5	753	48	1	3.82
1993-94	Kingston	OHL	48	23	20	5	2828	177	*2	3.76	6	2	2	224	12	0	3.21
1994-95	Fredericton	AHL	9	2	5	0	428	32	0	4.48							
	Wheeling	ECHL	13	9	2	1	736	38	0	3.10							
1995-96	Fredericton	AHL	23	5	9	3	1166	73	1	3.76	3	1	2	161	9	0	3.36

LANGKOW, SCOTT (LAING-kow) — PHO.

Goaltender. Catches left. 5'11", 190 lbs. Born, Sherwood Park, Alta., April 21, 1975.
(Winnipeg's 2nd choice, 31st overall, in 1993 Entry Draft).

			Regular Season								Playoffs						
Season	Club	Lea	GP	W	L	T	Mins	GA	SO	Avg	GP	W	L	Mins	GA	SO	Avg
1991-92	Portland	WHL	1	0	0	0	33	2	0	3.46							
1992-93	Portland	WHL	34	24	8	2	2064	119	2	3.46	9	6	3	535	31	0	3.48
1993-94a	Portland	WHL	39	27	9	1	2302	121	2	3.15	10	6	4	600	34	0	3.40
1994-95a	Portland	WHL	63	20	36	5	*3638	240	1	3.96	8	3	5	510	30	0	3.53
1995-96	**Winnipeg**	**NHL**	**1**	**0**	**0**	**0**	**6**	**0**	**0**	**0.00**							
b	Springfield	AHL	39	18	15	6	2329	116	3	2.99	7	4	2	393	23	0	3.51
	NHL Totals		**1**	**0**	**0**	**0**	**6**	**0**	**0**	**0.00**							

a WHL West Second All-Star Team (1994, 1995)
b Shared Harry "Hap" Holmes Memorial Trophy (fewest goals against - AHL) with Manny Legace (1996)

LARIVEE, FRANCIS (la-RIHV-ay) — TOR.

Goaltender. Catches left. 6'2", 198 lbs. Born, Montreal, Que., November 8, 1977.
(Toronto's 2nd choice, 50th overall, in 1996 Entry Draft).

			Regular Season								Playoffs						
Season	Club	Lea	GP	W	L	T	Mins	GA	SO	Avg	GP	W	L	Mins	GA	SO	Avg
1993-94	Val d'Or	QMJHL	36				1706	162	0	5.71							
1994-95	Val d'Or	QMJHL	38	9	21	1	1795	132	0	4.41							
1995-96	Val d'Or	QMJHL	*22	12	4	2	1162	73	0	3.77							
	Laval	QMJHL	*39	9	24	1	2085	178	0	5.12							

LAROCHELLE, BRIAN — MTL.

Goaltender. Catches right. 6'1", 185 lbs. Born, Manchester, NH, August 8, 1974.
(Montreal's 12th choice, 255th overall, in 1993 Entry Draft).

			Regular Season								Playoffs						
Season	Club	Lea	GP	W	L	T	Mins	GA	SO	Avg	GP	W	L	Mins	GA	SO	Avg
1994-95	N. Hampshire	H.E.	1	0	0	0	3	0	0	0.00							
1995-96	N. Hampshire	H.E.	13	3	6	1	717	49	1	4.10							

LAROCQUE, MICHEL — S.J.

Goaltender. Catches left. 5'11", 198 lbs. Born, Lahr, West Germany, October 3, 1976.
(San Jose's 5th choice, 137th overall, in 1996 Entry Draft).

			Regular Season								Playoffs						
Season	Club	Lea	GP	W	L	T	Mins	GA	SO	Avg	GP	W	L	Mins	GA	SO	Avg
1995-96	Boston U.	H.E.	14	10	1	1	735	42	0	3.43							

LEBLANC, RAYMOND (luh-BLAHNK)

Goaltender. Catches right. 5'10", 170 lbs. Born, Fitchburg, MA, October 24, 1964.

			Regular Season								Playoffs						
Season	Club	Lea	GP	W	L	T	Mins	GA	SO	Avg	GP	W	L	Mins	GA	SO	Avg
1983-84	Kitchener	OHL	54				2965	185	1	3.74							
1984-85	Pinebridge	ACHL	40				2178	150	0	4.13							
1985-86	Carolina	ACHL	42				2505	133	3	3.19							
1986-87	Flint	IHL	64	33	23	1	3417	222	0	3.90	4	1	3				4.38
1987-88	Flint	IHL	62	27	19	8	3269	239	1	4.39	16	10	6	925	55	1	3.57
1988-89	Flint	IHL	15	5	9	0	852	67	0	4.72							
	New Haven	AHL	1	0	0	0	20	3	0	9.00							
	Saginaw	IHL	29	19	7	2	1655	99	0	3.59	1	0	1	5	9	0	3.05
1989-90	Indianapolis	IHL	23	15	6	2	1334	71	2	3.19							
	Fort Wayne	IHL	15	3	3	3	680	44	0	3.88	3	0	2	139	11	0	4.75
1990-91	Fort Wayne	IHL	21	10	8	0	1072	69	0	3.86							
	Indianapolis	IHL	3	2	0	0	145	7	0	2.90	1	0	0	19	1	0	3.20
1991-92	U.S. National	....	17	5	10	1	891	54	0	3.63							
	U.S. Olympic	....	8	5	2	1	463	17	2	2.20							
	Chicago	**NHL**	**1**	**1**	**0**	**0**	**60**	**1**	**0**	**1.00**							
	Indianapolis	IHL	25	14	9	2	1468	84	2	3.43							
1992-93	Indianapolis	IHL	56	23	22	7	3201	206	0	3.86	5	1	4	276	23	0	5.00
1993-94	Indianapolis	IHL	2	0	1	0	112	8	0	4.25							
	Cincinnati	IHL	34	17	9	3	1779	104	1	3.51	5	0	3	159	9	0	3.39
1994-95	Chicago	IHL	44	19	14	6	2375	129	1	3.26	3	0	3	177	14	0	4.73
1995-96	Chicago	IHL	31	10	14	2	1614	97	0	3.61							
	NHL Totals		**1**	**1**	**0**	**0**	**60**	**1**	**0**	**1.00**							

Signed as a free agent by **Chicago**, July 5, 1989.

LEGACE, MANNY (leh-GAH-see) — HFD.

Goaltender. Catches left. 5'9", 162 lbs. Born, Toronto, Ont., February 4, 1973.
(Hartford's 5th choice, 188th overall, in 1993 Entry Draft).

			Regular Season								Playoffs						
Season	Club	Lea	GP	W	L	T	Mins	GA	SO	Avg	GP	W	L	Mins	GA	SO	Avg
1990-91	Niagara Falls	OHL	30	13	11	2	1515	107	0	4.24	4	1	1	119	10	0	5.04
1991-92	Niagara Falls	OHL	43	21	16	3	2384	143	0	3.60	14	8	5	791	56	0	4.25
1992-93a	Niagara Falls	OHL	48	22	19	3	2630	171	0	3.90	4	0	4	240	18	0	4.50
1993-94	Cdn. National	....	16	8	6	0	859	36	2	2.51							
1994-95	Springfield	AHL	39	12	17	6	2169	128	2	3.54							
1995-96bcd	Springfield	AHL	37	20	12	4	2196	83	*5	*2.27	4	1	3	220	18	0	4.91

a OHL First All-Star Team (1993)
b AHL First All-Star Team (1996)
c Shared Harry "Hap" Holmes Memorial Trophy (fewest goals against - AHL) with Scott Langkow (1996)
d Won Baz Bastien Memorial Trophy (Top Goaltender - AHL) (1996)

LEITZA, BRIAN — PIT.

Goaltender. Catches left. 6'2", 185 lbs. Born, Waukegin, IL, March 16, 1974.
(Pittsburgh's 14th choice, 284th overall, in 1994 Entry Draft).

			Regular Season								Playoffs						
Season	Club	Lea	GP	W	L	T	Mins	GA	SO	Avg	GP	W	L	Mins	GA	SO	Avg
1994-95	St. Cloud	WCHA	30	13	15	0	1626	93	....	3.43							
1995-96	St. Cloud	WCHA	35	12	19	4	2064	131	2	3.81							

LEMANOWICZ, DAVID — FLA.

Goaltender. Catches left. 6'2", 190 lbs. Born, Edmonton, Alta., March 8, 1976.
(Florida's 9th choice, 218th overall, in 1996 Entry Draft).

			Regular Season								Playoffs						
Season	Club	Lea	GP	W	L	T	Mins	GA	SO	Avg	GP	W	L	Mins	GA	SO	Avg
1992-93	Spokane	WHL	16	3	11	0	738	61	1	4.96							
1993-94	Spokane	WHL	6	1	2	0	256	21	0	4.92							
1994-95	Spokane	WHL	16	5	5	1	761	41	2	3.23							
1995-96a	Spokane	WHL	*62	*42	10	2	3362	162	*4	*2.89	18	9	6	1036	59	*2	3.42

a WHL West First All-Star Team (1996)

LENARDUZZI, MIKE

Goaltender. Catches left. 6'1", 165 lbs. Born, London, Ont., September 14, 1972.
(Hartford's 3rd choice, 57th overall, in 1990 Entry Draft).

			Regular Season								Playoffs						
Season	Club	Lea	GP	W	L	T	Mins	GA	SO	Avg	GP	W	L	Mins	GA	SO	Avg
1989-90	Oshawa	OHL	12	6	3	1	444	32	0	4.32							
	S.S. Marie	OHL	20				1117	66	0	3.55							
1990-91	S.S. Marie	OHL	35	19	8	3	1966	107	0	3.27	5	3	1	268	13	*1	2.91
1991-92	S.S. Marie	OHL	9	5	3	0	486	33	0	4.07							
	Ottawa	OHL	18	5	12	1	986	60	1	3.65							
	Sudbury	OHL	22	11	5	4	1201	84	2	4.20	11	4	7	651	38	0	3.50
	Springfield	AHL									1	0	0	39	2	0	3.08
1992-93	**Hartford**	**NHL**	**3**	**1**	**1**	**1**	**168**	**9**	**0**	**3.21**							
	Springfield	AHL	36	10	17	5	1945	142	0	4.38	2	1	0	100	5	0	3.00
1993-94	**Hartford**	**NHL**	**1**	**0**	**0**	**0**	**21**	**1**	**0**	**2.86**							
	Springfield	AHL	22	5	7	2	984	73	0	4.45							
	Salt Lake	IHL	4	0	4	0	211	22	0	6.25							
1994-95	London	ColHL	43	19	16	3	2198	172	0	4.69	5	1	2	274	20	0	4.37
1995-96	Saginaw	ColHL	43	14	15	3	2153	155	0	4.32	5	1	4	299	19	0	3.82
	NHL Totals		**4**	**1**	**1**	**1**	**189**	**10**	**0**	**3.17**							

LESLIE, LANCE

Goaltender. Catches left. 5'10", 160 lbs. Born, Dawson Creek, B.C., June 21, 1974.

			Regular Season								Playoffs						
Season	Club	Lea	GP	W	L	T	Mins	GA	SO	Avg	GP	W	L	Mins	GA	SO	Avg
1992-93	Tri-City	WHL	49	15	25	3	2620	163	*3	3.73	....	....	....	....	....	....	....
1993-94	Tri-City	WHL	41	10	26	2	2273	189	2	4.99	2	0	2	120	9	0	4.50
1994-95ab	Thunder Bay	ColHL	42	*29	10	3	2420	130	*2	3.22	10	*7	2	587	35	*1	3.58
	P.E.I.	AHL	1	0	0	1	65	2	0	1.85	....	....	....	....	....	....	....
1995-96	Thunder Bay	ColHL	11	5	3	2	588	35	0	3.57	....	....	....	....	....	....	....
	P.E.I.	AHL	28	12	12	3	1444	93	1	3.86	....	....	....	....	....	....	....
	Toledo	ECHL	4	3	0	0	212	10	0	2.83	....	....	....	....	....	....	....

a ColHL First All-Star Team (1995)
b ColHL's Rookie of the Year (1995)

Signed as a free agent by **Ottawa**, October 4, 1993.

LINDFORS, SAKARI (LIHND-fohrs) COL.

Goaltender. Catches left. 5'7", 150 lbs. Born, Helsinki, Finland, April 27, 1966.
(Quebec's 9th choice, 150th overall, in 1988 Entry Draft).

			Regular Season								Playoffs						
Season	Club	Lea	GP	W	L	T	Mins	GA	SO	Avg	GP	W	L	Mins	GA	SO	Avg
1986-87	HIFK	Fin.	20	....	....	....	1009	65	0	3.86	....	....	....	....	....	....	....
1987-88	HIFK	Fin.	39	....	....	....	2346	....	....	....	6	....	....	340	....	....	....
1988-89	HIFK	Fin.	24	11	11	2	1433	89	1	3.75	2	....	....	118	7	....	3.53
1989-90	HIFK	Fin.	42	23	15	4	2518	146	2	3.48	....	....	....	....	....	....	....
1990-91	HIFK	Fin.	41	....	....	....	2445	142	2	3.48	3	....	....	180	14	0	4.67
1991-92	HIFK	Fin.	38	....	....	....	2222	127	4	3.43	9	....	....	538	28	0	3.12
1992-93	HIFK	Fin.	39	....	....	....	2293	123	0	3.22	4	....	....	236	12	0	3.04
1993-94	HIFK	Fin.	43	....	....	....	2465	128	3	3.11	3	....	....	175	11	....	3.76
1994-95	HIFK	Fin.	44	28	13	3	2597	119	2	2.75	3	0	3	178	6	0	2.02
1995-96	HIFK	Fin.	38	....	....	....	2217	110	3	2.98	3	....	....	180	11	....	3.67

LITTLE, NEIL PHI.

Goaltender. Catches left. 6'1", 193 lbs. Born, Medicine Hat, Alta., December 18, 1971.
(Philadelphia's 10th choice, 226th overall, in 1991 Entry Draft).

			Regular Season								Playoffs						
Season	Club	Lea	GP	W	L	T	Mins	GA	SO	Avg	GP	W	L	Mins	GA	SO	Avg
1990-91	RPI	ECAC	18	9	8	0	1032	71	0	4.13	....	....	....	....	....	....	....
1991-92	RPI	ECAC	28	11	11	3	1532	96	0	3.76	....	....	....	....	....	....	....
1992-93ab	RPI	ECAC	*31	*19	9	3	*1801	88	0	2.93	....	....	....	....	....	....	....
1993-94	RPI	ECAC	27	16	7	4	1570	88	0	3.36	....	....	....	....	....	....	....
	Hershey	AHL	1	0	0	0	18	1	0	3.33	....	....	....	....	....	....	....
1994-95	Hershey	AHL	19	5	7	3	919	60	0	3.91	....	....	....	....	....	....	....
	Johnstown	ECHL	16	7	6	1	897	55	0	3.68	3	0	2	144	11	0	4.55
1995-96	Hershey	AHL	48	21	18	6	2680	149	0	3.34	1	0	1	60	4	0	4.02

a ECAC First All-Star Team (1993)
b NCAA East Second All-American Team (1993)

LITTMAN, DAVID

Goaltender. Catches left. 6', 183 lbs. Born, Cranston, RI, June 13, 1967.
(Buffalo's 12th choice, 211th overall, in 1987 Entry Draft).

			Regular Season								Playoffs						
Season	Club	Lea	GP	W	L	T	Mins	GA	SO	Avg	GP	W	L	Mins	GA	SO	Avg
1985-86	Boston College	H.E.	7	4	0	1	312	18	0	3.46	....	....	....	....	....	....	....
1986-87	Boston College	H.E.	21	15	5	0	1182	68	0	3.45	....	....	....	....	....	....	....
1987-88a	Boston College	H.E.	30	11	16	2	1726	116	0	4.03	....	....	....	....	....	....	....
1988-89bc	Boston College	H.E.	*32	19	9	4	*1945	107	0	3.30	....	....	....	....	....	....	....
1989-90	Rochester	AHL	14	5	6	1	681	37	0	3.26	....	....	....	....	....	....	....
	Phoenix	IHL	18	8	7	2	1047	64	0	3.67	....	....	....	....	....	....	....
1990-91	**Buffalo**	**NHL**	**1**	**0**	**0**	**0**	**36**	**3**	**0**	**5.00**	....	....	....	....	....	....	....
de	Rochester	AHL	*56	*33	13	5	*3155	160	3	3.04	8	4	2	378	16	0	2.54
1991-92	**Buffalo**	**NHL**	**1**	**0**	**1**	**0**	**60**	**4**	**0**	**4.00**	....	....	....	....	....	....	....
fg	Rochester	AHL	*61	*29	20	9	*3558	174	*3	2.93	15	8	7	879	43	*1	2.94
1992-93	**Tampa Bay**	**NHL**	**1**	**0**	**1**	**0**	**45**	**7**	**0**	**9.33**	....	....	....	....	....	....	....
	Atlanta	IHL	44	23	12	4	2390	134	0	3.36	3	1	2	178	8	0	2.70
1993-94	Fredericton	AHL	16	8	7	0	872	63	0	4.33	....	....	....	....	....	....	....
	Providence	AHL	25	10	11	3	1385	83	0	3.60	....	....	....	....	....	....	....
1994-95	Richmond	ECHL	8	4	2	0	346	13	1	2.25	*17	*12	4	*952	37	*3	*2.33
1995-96	Los Angeles	IHL	43	17	16	5	2245	145	1	3.88	....	....	....	....	....	....	....
	NHL Totals		**3**	**0**	**2**	**0**	**141**	**14**	**0**	**5.96**	....	....	....	....	....	....	....

a Hockey East Second All-Star Team (1988)
b Hockey East First All-Star Team (1989)
c NCAA East Second All-American Team (1989)
d Shared Harry "Hap" Holmes Memorial Trophy (fewest goals against - AHL) with Darcy Wakaluk (1991)
e AHL First All-Star Team (1991)
f Won Harry "Hap" Holmes Memorial Trophy (fewest goals against - AHL) (1992)
g AHL Second All-Star Team (1992)

Signed as a free agent by **Tampa Bay**, August 27, 1992. Signed as a free agent by **Boston**, August 6, 1993.

LORENZ, DANNY

Goaltender. Catches left. 5'10", 187 lbs. Born, Murrayville, B.C., December 12, 1969.
(NY Islanders' 4th choice, 58th overall, in 1988 Entry Draft).

			Regular Season								Playoffs						
Season	Club	Lea	GP	W	L	T	Mins	GA	SO	Avg	GP	W	L	Mins	GA	SO	Avg
1986-87	Seattle	WHL	38	12	21	2	2103	199	0	5.68	....	....	....	....	....	....	....
1987-88	Seattle	WHL	62	20	37	2	3302	314	0	5.71	....	....	....	....	....	....	....
1988-89	Springfield	AHL	4	2	1	0	210	12	0	3.43	....	....	....	....	....	....	....
a	Seattle	WHL	*68	31	33	4	*4003	240	*3	3.60	....	....	....	....	....	....	....
1989-90a	Seattle	WHL	56	37	15	2	3226	221	0	4.11	13	6	7	751	40	0	3.21
1990-91	**NY Islanders**	**NHL**	**2**	**0**	**1**	**0**	**80**	**5**	**0**	**3.75**	....	....	....	....	....	....	....
	Capital Dist.	AHL	17	5	9	2	940	70	0	4.47	....	....	....	....	....	....	....
	Richmond	ECHL	20	6	9	2	1020	75	0	4.41	....	....	....	....	....	....	....
1991-92	**NY Islanders**	**NHL**	**2**	**0**	**2**	**0**	**120**	**10**	**0**	**5.00**	....	....	....	....	....	....	....
	Capital Dist.	AHL	53	22	22	7	3050	181	2	3.56	7	3	4	442	25	0	3.39
1992-93	**NY Islanders**	**NHL**	**4**	**1**	**2**	**0**	**157**	**10**	**0**	**3.82**	....	....	....	....	....	....	....
	Capital Dist.	AHL	44	16	17	5	2412	146	1	3.63	4	0	3	219	12	0	3.29
1993-94	Salt Lake	IHL	20	4	12	0	982	91	0	5.56	....	....	....	....	....	....	....
	Springfield	AHL	14	5	7	1	801	59	0	4.42	2	0	0	35	0	0	0.00
1994-95	Cincinnati	IHL	41	24	10	3	2222	126	0	3.40	5	2	3	308	16	0	3.12
1995-96	Cincinnati	IHL	46	28	12	2	2694	139	1	3.10	5	1	2	199	11	0	3.31
	NHL Totals		**8**	**1**	**5**	**0**	**357**	**25**	**0**	**4.20**	....	....	....	....	....	....	....

a WHL West First All-Star Team (1989, 1990)

Signed as a free agent by **Florida**, June 14, 1994.

MacDONALD, AARON FLA.

Goaltender. Catches left. 6'1", 193 lbs. Born, Grand Prairie, Alta., August 29, 1977.
(Florida's 2nd choice, 36th overall, in 1995 Entry Draft).

			Regular Season								Playoffs						
Season	Club	Lea	GP	W	L	T	Mins	GA	SO	Avg	GP	W	L	Mins	GA	SO	Avg
1993-94	Swift Current	WHL	18	6	6	0	710	48	0	4.06	....	....	....	....	....	....	....
1994-95	Swift Current	WHL	53	24	20	6	2957	177	4	3.59	6	2	4	393	18	0	2.75
1995-96	Swift Current	WHL	29	14	12	2	1657	98	0	3.55	....	....	....	....	....	....	....
	Calgary	WHL	19	2	14	1	1025	84	0	4.92	....	....	....	....	....	....	....

MacDONALD, DAVID NYI

Goaltender. Catches left. 5'10", 185 lbs. Born, St. Thomas, Ont., September 23, 1976.
(NY Islander's 6th choice, 210th overall, in 1995 Entry Draft).

			Regular Season								Playoffs						
Season	Club	Lea	GP	W	L	T	Mins	GA	SO	Avg	GP	W	L	Mins	GA	SO	Avg
1993-94	Sudbury	OHL	1	0	1	0	60	6	0	6.00	....	....	....	....	....	....	....
1994-95	Sudbury	OHL	26	14	7	2	1327	68	1	3.07	4	1	0	117	9	0	4.62
1995-96	Sudbury	OHL	40	14	20	1	2093	162	0	4.64	....	....	....	....	....	....	....

MacDONALD, TODD FLA.

Goaltender. Catches left. 6', 167 lbs. Born, Charlottetown, P.E.I., July 5, 1975.
(Florida's 7th choice, 109th overall, in 1993 Entry Draft).

			Regular Season								Playoffs						
Season	Club	Lea	GP	W	L	T	Mins	GA	SO	Avg	GP	W	L	Mins	GA	SO	Avg
1992-93	Tacoma	WHL	19	6	6	0	823	59	0	4.30	....	....	....	....	....	....	....
1993-94	Tacoma	WHL	29	13	10	2	1606	109	1	4.07	....	....	....	....	....	....	....
1994-95a	Tacoma	WHL	60	*35	21	2	3433	179	3	3.13	4	1	3	255	13	0	3.06
1995-96	Carolina	AHL	18	3	12	2	980	78	0	4.78	....	....	....	....	....	....	....
	Detroit	ColHL	2	1	1	0	120	8	0	4.01	2	1	1	133	3	0	1.36

a WHL West First All-Star Team (1995)

MADELEY, DARRIN (MAY-duh-lee)

Goaltender. Catches left. 5'11", 170 lbs. Born, Holland Landing, Ont., February 25, 1968.

			Regular Season								Playoffs						
Season	Club	Lea	GP	W	L	T	Mins	GA	SO	Avg	GP	W	L	Mins	GA	SO	Avg
1989-90	Lake Superior	CCHA	30	21	7	1	1683	68	1	2.42	....	....	....	....	....	....	....
1990-91a	Lake Superior	CCHA	36	*29	3	3	2137	93	1	*2.61	....	....	....	....	....	....	....
1991-92abc	Lake Superior	CCHA	36	23	6	4	2144	69	2	*2.05	....	....	....	....	....	....	....
1992-93	**Ottawa**	**NHL**	**2**	**0**	**2**	**0**	**90**	**10**	**0**	**6.67**	....	....	....	....	....	....	....
	New Haven	AHL	41	10	16	9	2295	127	0	3.32	....	....	....	....	....	....	....
1993-94	**Ottawa**	**NHL**	**32**	**3**	**18**	**5**	**1583**	**115**	**0**	**4.36**	....	....	....	....	....	....	....
	P.E.I.	AHL	6	0	4	0	270	26	0	5.77	....	....	....	....	....	....	....
1994-95	**Ottawa**	**NHL**	**5**	**1**	**3**	**0**	**255**	**15**	**0**	**3.53**	....	....	....	....	....	....	....
	P.E.I.	AHL	3	1	1	1	185	8	0	2.59	....	....	....	....	....	....	....
	Detroit	IHL	9	7	2	0	498	20	1	2.41	....	....	....	....	....	....	....
1995-96	P.E.I.	AHL	1	1	0	0	60	4	0	4.00	....	....	....	....	....	....	....
	Detroit	IHL	40	16	14	4	2047	108	0	3.17	7	3	3	355	23	0	3.89
	NHL Totals		**39**	**4**	**23**	**5**	**1928**	**140**	**0**	**4.36**	....	....	....	....	....	....	....

a NCAA West First All-American Team (1991, 1992)
b NCAA Final Four All-Tournament Team (1992)
c CCHA First All-Star Team (1992)
d AHL Second All-Star Team (1993)

Signed as a free agent by **Ottawa**, June 20, 1992.

MAGLIARDITI, MARC CHI.

Goaltender. Catches left. 5'11", 170 lbs. Born, Niagara Falls, NY, July 9, 1976.
(Chicago's 6th choice, 146th overall, in 1995 Entry Draft).

			Regular Season								Playoffs						
Season	Club	Lea	GP	W	L	T	Mins	GA	SO	Avg	GP	W	L	Mins	GA	SO	Avg
1994-95	Des Moines	Jr. A	29	21	2	4	1727	82	....	2.85	....	....	....	....	....	....	....
1995-96ab	W. Michigan	CCHA	36	23	11	2	2111	92	*5	2.62	....	....	....	....	....	....	....

a CCHA First All-Star Team (1996)
b NCAA West Second All-American Team (1996)

MARACLE, NORM DET.

Goaltender. Catches left. 5'9", 175 lbs. Born, Belleville, Ont., October 2, 1974.
(Detroit's 6th choice, 126th overall, in 1993 Entry Draft).

			Regular Season								Playoffs						
Season	Club	Lea	GP	W	L	T	Mins	GA	SO	Avg	GP	W	L	Mins	GA	SO	Avg
1991-92	Saskatoon	WHL	29	13	6	3	1529	87	1	3.41	15	9	5	860	37	0	3.38
1992-93a	Saskatoon	WHL	53	27	18	3	1939	160	1	3.27	9	4	5	569	33	0	3.48
1993-94bcd	Saskatoon	WHL	56	*41	13	1	3219	148	2	2.76	16	*11	5	940	48	*1	3.06
1994-95	Adirondack	AHL	39	12	15	2	1997	119	0	3.57	....	....	....	....	....	....	....
1995-96	Adirondack	AHL	54	24	18	6	2949	135	2	2.75	1	0	1	30	4	0	8.11

a WHL East Second All-Star Team (1993)
b WHL East First All-Star Team (1994)
c Canadian Major Junior First All-Star Team (1994)
d Canadian Major Junior Goaltender of the Year (1994)

MASON, CHRIS N.J.

Goaltender. Catches left. 5'11", 180 lbs. Born, Red Deer, Alta., April 20, 1976.
(New Jersey's 7th choice, 122nd overall, in 1995 Entry Draft).

			Regular Season								Playoffs						
Season	Club	Lea	GP	W	L	T	Mins	GA	SO	Avg	GP	W	L	Mins	GA	SO	Avg
1993-94	Victoria	WHL	3	0	3	0	129	16	0	7.44	....	....	....	....	....	....	....
1994-95	Prince George	WHL	44	8	30	1	2288	192	1	5.03	....	....	....	....	....	....	....
1995-96	Prince George	WHL	59	16	37	1	3289	236	1	4.31	....	....	....	....	....	....	....

MASOTTA, BRYAN OTT.

Goaltender. Catches left. 6'2", 195 lbs. Born, New Haven, CT, May 30, 1975.
(Ottawa's 3rd choice, 81st overall, in 1994 Entry Draft).

			Regular Season								Playoffs						
Season	Club	Lea	GP	W	L	T	Mins	GA	SO	Avg	GP	W	L	Mins	GA	SO	Avg
1994-95	RPI	ECAC	13	5	6	0	646	46	0	4.27	....	....	....	....	....	....	....
1995-96	RPI	ECAC	7	2	2	0	193	18	....	5.59	....	....	....	....	....	....	....

McARTHUR, MARK NYI

Goaltender. Catches left. 5'10", 175 lbs. Born, East York, Ont., November 16, 1975.
(NY Islanders' 5th choice, 112th overall, in 1994 Entry Draft).

			Regular Season								Playoffs						
Season	Club	Lea	GP	W	L	T	Mins	GA	SO	Avg	GP	W	L	Mins	GA	SO	Avg
1992-93	Guelph	OHL	35	14	14	3	1853	180	0	5.83	....	....	....	....	....	....	....
1993-94	Guelph	OHL	51	25	18	5	2936	201	0	4.11	9	4	5	561	38	0	4.06
1994-95a	Guelph	OHL	48	*34	8	4	2776	130	1	*2.81	13	9	4	797	44	0	3.31
1995-96b	Utah	IHL	26	12	12	0	1482	77	0	3.12	....	....	....	....	....	....	....

a OHL Second All-Star Team (1995)
b Shared James Norris Memorial Trophy (fewest goals against - IHL) with Tommy Salo (1996)

McDONALD, NOLAN — VAN.

Goaltender. Catches left. 6'2", 185 lbs. Born, Thunder Bay, Ont., July 29, 1977.
(Vancouver's 5th choice, 147th overall, in 1996 Entry Draft).

			Regular Season								Playoffs						
Season	Club	Lea	GP	W	L	T	Mins	GA	SO	Avg	GP	W	L	Mins	GA	SO	Avg
1995-96	Vermont	ECAC	2	1	0	0	40	1	0	1.49	....	....	....	....	....	....	....

McLEAN, KIRK — VAN.

Goaltender. Catches left. 6', 195 lbs. Born, Willowdale, Ont., June 26, 1966.
(New Jersey's 6th choice, 107th overall, in 1984 Entry Draft).

			Regular Season								Playoffs						
Season	Club	Lea	GP	W	L	T	Mins	GA	SO	Avg	GP	W	L	Mins	GA	SO	Avg
1983-84	Oshawa	OHL	17	5	9	0	940	67	0	4.28	....	....	....	....	....	....	....
1984-85	Oshawa	OHL	47	23	17	2	2581	143	1	*3.32	5	1	3	271	21	0	4.65
1985-86	**New Jersey**	**NHL**	**2**	**1**	**1**	**0**	**111**	**11**	**0**	**5.95**	....	....	....	....	....	....	....
	Oshawa	OHL	51	24	21	2	2830	169	1	3.58	4	1	2	201	18	0	5.37
1986-87	**New Jersey**	**NHL**	**4**	**1**	**1**	**0**	**160**	**10**	**0**	**3.75**	....	....	....	....	....	....	....
	Maine	AHL	45	15	23	4	2606	140	1	3.22	....	....	....	....	....	....	....
1987-88	**Vancouver**	**NHL**	**41**	**11**	**27**	**3**	**2380**	**147**	**1**	**3.71**	....	....	....	....	....	....	....
1988-89	**Vancouver**	**NHL**	**42**	**20**	**17**	**3**	**2477**	**127**	**4**	**3.08**	**5**	**2**	**3**	**302**	**18**	**0**	**3.58**
1989-90	**Vancouver**	**NHL**	***63**	**21**	**30**	**10**	***3739**	**216**	**0**	**3.47**	....	....	....	....	....	....	....
1990-91	**Vancouver**	**NHL**	**41**	**10**	**22**	**3**	**1969**	**131**	**0**	**3.99**	**2**	**1**	**1**	**123**	**7**	**0**	**3.41**
1991-92a	**Vancouver**	**NHL**	**65**	***38**	**17**	**9**	**3852**	**176**	***5**	**2.74**	**13**	**6**	**7**	**785**	**33**	***2**	**2.52**
1992-93	**Vancouver**	**NHL**	**54**	**28**	**21**	**5**	**3261**	**184**	**3**	**3.39**	**12**	**6**	**6**	**754**	**42**	**0**	**3.34**
1993-94	**Vancouver**	**NHL**	**52**	**23**	**26**	**3**	**3128**	**156**	**3**	**2.99**	***24**	**15**	**9**	***1544**	**59**	***4**	**2.29**
1994-95	**Vancouver**	**NHL**	**40**	**18**	**12**	**10**	**2374**	**109**	**1**	**2.75**	**11**	**4**	**7**	**660**	**36**	**0**	**3.27**
1995-96	**Vancouver**	**NHL**	**45**	**15**	**21**	**9**	**2645**	**156**	**2**	**3.54**	**1**	**0**	**1**	**21**	**3**	**0**	**8.57**
	NHL Totals		**449**	**186**	**195**	**55**	**26096**	**1423**	**19**	**3.27**	**68**	**34**	**34**	**4189**	**198**	**6**	**2.84**

a NHL Second All-Star Team (1992)

Played in NHL All-Star Game (1990, 1992)

Traded to **Vancouver** by **New Jersey** with Greg Adams for Patrik Sundstrom and Vancouver's fourth round choice (Matt Ruchty) in 1988 Entry Draft, September 15, 1987.

McLENNAN, JAMIE — ST.L.

Goaltender. Catches left. 6', 190 lbs. Born, Edmonton, Alta., June 30, 1971.
(NY Islanders' 3rd choice, 48th overall, in 1991 Entry Draft).

			Regular Season								Playoffs						
Season	Club	Lea	GP	W	L	T	Mins	GA	SO	Avg	GP	W	L	Mins	GA	SO	Avg
1989-90	Lethbridge	WHL	34	20	4	2	1690	110	1	3.91	13	6	5	677	44	0	3.90
1990-91a	Lethbridge	WHL	56	32	18	4	3230	205	0	3.81	*16	8	8	*970	56	0	3.46
1991-92	Capital Dist.	AHL	18	4	10	2	952	60	1	3.78	....	....	....	....	....	....	....
	Richmond	ECHL	32	16	12	2	1837	114	0	3.72	....	....	....	....	....	....	....
1992-93	Capital Dist.	AHL	38	17	14	6	2171	117	1	3.23	1	0	1	20	5	0	15.00
1993-94	**NY Islanders**	**NHL**	**22**	**8**	**7**	**6**	**1287**	**61**	**0**	**2.84**	**2**	**0**	**1**	**82**	**6**	**0**	**4.39**
	Salt Lake	IHL	24	8	12	2	1320	80	0	3.64	....	....	....	....	....	....	....
1994-95	**NY Islanders**	**NHL**	**21**	**6**	**11**	**2**	**1185**	**67**	**0**	**3.39**	....	....	....	....	....	....	....
	Denver	IHL	4	3	0	1	239	12	0	3.00	11	8	2	640	23	1	*2.15
1995-96	**NY Islanders**	**NHL**	**13**	**3**	**9**	**1**	**636**	**39**	**0**	**3.68**	....	....	....	....	....	....	....
	Utah	IHL	14	9	2	2	728	29	0	2.39	....	....	....	....	....	....	....
	Worcester	AHL	22	14	7	1	1216	57	0	2.81	2	0	2	119	8	0	4.04
	NHL Totals		**56**	**17**	**27**	**9**	**3108**	**167**	**0**	**3.22**	**2**	**0**	**1**	**82**	**6**	**0**	**4.39**

a WHL East First All-Star Team (1991)

Signed as a free agent by **St. Louis**, July 15, 1996.

MIKLENDA, JAROSLAV — OTT.

Goaltender. Catches left. 6'1", 176 lbs. Born, Uherske Hradiste, Czech., March 7, 1974.
(Ottawa's 7th choice, 146th overall, in 1992 Entry Draft).

			Regular Season								Playoffs						
Season	Club	Lea	GP	W	L	T	Mins	GA	SO	Avg	GP	W	L	Mins	GA	SO	Avg
1991-92	Olomouc	Czech.	1	....	....	....	36	6	0	9.99	....	....	....	....	....	....	....
1992-93	Olomouc	Czech.	5	....	....	....	285	22	....	4.63	....	....	....	....	....	....	....
1993-94	TJ Vitkovice	Czech.	10	....	....	....	555	25	0	2.71	....	....	....	....	....	....	....
1994-95	Presov	Czech. 2	8	....	....	....	....	20	....	2.80	....	....	....	....	....	....	....
1995-96	Olomouc	Czech.	1	....	....	....	60	6	0	6.00	....	....	....	....	....	....	....
	Sumperk	Czech. 2	20	....	....	....	1200	54	....	2.70	....	....	....	....	....	....	....

MILLER, AREN — DET.

Goaltender. Catches left. 6'2", 208 lbs. Born, Oxbow, Sask., January 13, 1978.
(Detroit's 2nd choice, 52nd overall, in 1996 Entry Draft).

			Regular Season								Playoffs						
Season	Club	Lea	GP	W	L	T	Mins	GA	SO	Avg	GP	W	L	Mins	GA	SO	Avg
1994-95	Saskatoon	Midget	18	....	....	....	977	70	0	4.30	....	....	....	....	....	....	....
1995-96	Spokane	WHL	23	8	7	2	965	50	1	3.11	....	....	....	....	....	....	....

MINARD, MIKE — EDM.

Goaltender. Catches left. 6'3", 205 lbs. Born, Owen Sound, Ont., November 1, 1976.
(Edmonton's 4th choice, 83rd overall, in 1995 Entry Draft).

			Regular Season								Playoffs						
Season	Club	Lea	GP	W	L	T	Mins	GA	SO	Avg	GP	W	L	Mins	GA	SO	Avg
1994-95	Chilliwack	Jr. A	40	....	....	....	2330	136	0	3.50	....	....	....	....	....	....	....
1995-96	Barrie	OHL	1	0	1	0	52	8	0	9.23	....	....	....	....	....	....	....
	Detroit	OHL	42	25	10	4	2314	128	2	3.32	17	9	6	922	55	1	3.58

MOOG, ANDY — (MOHG) — DAL.

Goaltender. Catches left. 5'8", 175 lbs. Born, Penticton, B.C., February 18, 1960.
(Edmonton's 6th choice, 132nd overall, in 1980 Entry Draft).

			Regular Season								Playoffs						
Season	Club	Lea	GP	W	L	T	Mins	GA	SO	Avg	GP	W	L	Mins	GA	SO	Avg
1978-79	Billings	WHL	26	13	5	4	1306	90	4	4.13	5	1	3	229	21	0	5.50
1979-80a	Billings	WHL	46	23	14	1	2435	149	1	3.67	3	2	1	190	10	0	3.16
1980-81	**Edmonton**	**NHL**	**7**	**3**	**3**	**0**	**313**	**20**	**0**	**3.83**	**9**	**5**	**4**	**526**	**32**	**0**	**3.65**
	Wichita	CHL	29	14	13	1	1602	89	0	3.33	5	3	2	300	16	0	3.20
1981-82	**Edmonton**	**NHL**	**8**	**3**	**5**	**0**	**399**	**32**	**0**	**4.81**	....	....	....	....	....	....	....
b	Wichita	CHL	40	23	13	3	2391	119	1	2.99	7	3	4	434	23	0	3.18
1982-83	**Edmonton**	**NHL**	**50**	**33**	**8**	**7**	**2833**	**167**	**1**	**3.54**	**16**	**11**	**5**	**949**	**48**	**0**	**3.03**
1983-84	**Edmonton**	**NHL**	**38**	**27**	**8**	**1**	**2212**	**139**	**1**	**3.77**	**7**	**4**	**0**	**263**	**12**	**0**	**2.74 ♦**
1984-85	**Edmonton**	**NHL**	**39**	**22**	**9**	**3**	**2019**	**111**	**1**	**3.30**	**2**	**0**	**0**	**20**	**0**	**0**	**0.00 ♦**
1985-86	**Edmonton**	**NHL**	**47**	**27**	**9**	**7**	**2664**	**164**	**1**	**3.69**	**1**	**1**	**0**	**60**	**1**	**0**	**1.00**
1986-87	**Edmonton**	**NHL**	**46**	**28**	**11**	**3**	**2461**	**144**	**0**	**3.51**	**2**	**2**	**0**	**120**	**8**	**0**	**4.00 ♦**
1987-88	Cdn. National	....	27	10	7	5	1438	86	0	3.58	....	....	....	....	....	....	....
	Cdn. Olympic	....	4	4	0	0	240	9	1	2.25	....	....	....	....	....	....	....
	Boston	**NHL**	**6**	**4**	**2**	**0**	**360**	**17**	**1**	**2.83**	**7**	**1**	**4**	**354**	**25**	**0**	**4.24**
1988-89	**Boston**	**NHL**	**41**	**18**	**14**	**8**	**2482**	**133**	**1**	**3.22**	**6**	**4**	**2**	**359**	**14**	**0**	**2.34**
1989-90c	**Boston**	**NHL**	**46**	**24**	**10**	**7**	**2536**	**122**	**3**	**2.89**	**20**	**13**	**7**	**1195**	**44**	***2**	***2.21**
1990-91	**Boston**	**NHL**	**51**	**25**	**13**	**9**	**2844**	**136**	**4**	**2.87**	**19**	**10**	**9**	**1133**	**60**	**0**	**3.18**
1991-92	**Boston**	**NHL**	**62**	**28**	**22**	**9**	**3640**	**196**	**1**	**3.23**	**15**	**8**	**7**	**866**	**46**	**1**	**3.19**
1992-93	**Boston**	**NHL**	**55**	**37**	**14**	**3**	**3194**	**168**	**3**	**3.16**	**3**	**0**	**3**	**161**	**14**	**0**	**5.22**
1993-94	**Dallas**	**NHL**	**55**	**24**	**20**	**7**	**3121**	**170**	**2**	**3.27**	**4**	**1**	**3**	**246**	**12**	**0**	**2.93**
1994-95	**Dallas**	**NHL**	**31**	**10**	**12**	**7**	**1770**	**72**	**2**	**2.44**	**5**	**1**	**4**	**277**	**16**	**0**	**3.47**
1995-96	**Dallas**	**NHL**	**41**	**13**	**19**	**7**	**2228**	**111**	**1**	**2.99**	....	....	....	....	....	....	....
	NHL Totals		**623**	**326**	**179**	**78**	**35076**	**1902**	**22**	**3.25**	**116**	**61**	**48**	**6529**	**332**	**3**	**3.05**

a WHL Second All-Star Team (1980)
b CHL Second All-Star Team (1982)
c Shared William Jennings Trophy with Rejean Lemelin (1990)

Played in NHL All-Star Game (1985, 1986, 1991)

Traded to **Boston** by **Edmonton** for Geoff Courtnall, Bill Ranford and Boston's second choice (Petro Koivunen) in 1988 Entry Draft, March 8, 1988. Traded to **Dallas** by **Boston** for Jon Casey to complete June 20, 1993 trade which sent Gord Murphy to Dallas for future considerations, June 25, 1993.

MOSS, TYLER — T.B.

Goaltender. Catches right. 6', 184 lbs. Born, Ottawa, Ont., June 29, 1975.
(Tampa Bay's 2nd choice, 29th overall, in 1993 Entry Draft).

			Regular Season								Playoffs						
Season	Club	Lea	GP	W	L	T	Mins	GA	SO	Avg	GP	W	L	Mins	GA	SO	Avg
1992-93	Kingston	OHL	31	13	7	5	1537	97	0	3.79	6	1	2	228	19	0	5.00
1993-94	Kingston	OHL	13	6	4	3	795	42	1	3.17	3	0	2	136	8	0	3.53
1994-95a	Kingston	OHL	*57	33	17	5	*3249	164	1	3.03	6	2	4	333	27	0	4.86
1995-96	Atlanta	IHL	40	11	19	4	2030	138	1	4.08	3	0	3	213	11	0	3.10

a OHL First All-Star Team (1995)

MUZZATTI, JASON — (moo-ZAH-tee) — HFD.

Goaltender. Catches left. 6'1", 190 lbs. Born, Toronto, Ont., February 3, 1970.
(Calgary's 1st choice, 21st overall, in 1988 Entry Draft).

			Regular Season								Playoffs						
Season	Club	Lea	GP	W	L	T	Mins	GA	SO	Avg	GP	W	L	Mins	GA	SO	Avg
1987-88a	Michigan State	CCHA	33	19	9	3	1915	109	0	3.41	....	....	....	....	....	....	....
1988-89	Michigan State	CCHA	42	32	9	1	2515	127	3	*3.03	....	....	....	....	....	....	....
1989-90bc	Michigan State	CCHA	33	*24	6	0	1976	99	0	3.01	....	....	....	....	....	....	....
1990-91	Michigan State	CCHA	22	8	10	2	1204	75	1	3.74	....	....	....	....	....	....	....
1991-92	Salt Lake	IHL	52	24	22	5	3033	167	2	3.30	4	1	3	247	18	0	4.37
1992-93	Cdn. National	....	16	6	9	0	880	53	0	3.84	....	....	....	....	....	....	....
	Indianapolis	IHL	12	5	6	1	707	48	0	4.07	....	....	....	....	....	....	....
	Salt Lake	IHL	13	5	6	1	747	52	0	4.18	....	....	....	....	....	....	....
1993-94	**Calgary**	**NHL**	**1**	**0**	**1**	**0**	**60**	**8**	**0**	**8.00**	....	....	....	....	....	....	....
	Saint John	AHL	51	26	21	3	2939	183	2	3.74	7	3	4	415	19	0	2.75
1994-95	Saint John	AHL	31	10	14	4	1741	101	2	3.48	....	....	....	....	....	....	....
	Calgary	**NHL**	**1**	**0**	**0**	**0**	**10**	**0**	**0**	**0.00**	....	....	....	....	....	....	....
1995-96	**Hartford**	**NHL**	**22**	**4**	**8**	**3**	**1013**	**49**	**1**	**2.90**	....	....	....	....	....	....	....
	Springfield	AHL	5	4	0	1	300	12	1	2.40	....	....	....	....	....	....	....
	NHL Totals		**24**	**4**	**9**	**3**	**1083**	**57**	**1**	**3.16**	....	....	....	....	....	....	....

a CCHA Second All-Star Team (1988)
b CCHA First All-Star Team (1990)
c NCAA West Second All-American Team (1990)

Claimed on waivers by **Hartford** from **Calgary**, October 6, 1995.

NABOKOV, YEVGENI — (nuh-BAW-kahv, yehv-GEH-nee) — S.J.

Goaltender. Catches left. 6', 180 lbs. Born, Ust-Kamenogorsk, USSR, July 25, 1975.
(San Jose's 9th choice, 219th overall, in 1994 Entry Draft).

			Regular Season								Playoffs						
Season	Club	Lea	GP	W	L	T	Mins	GA	SO	Avg	GP	W	L	Mins	GA	SO	Avg
1992-93	Kamenogorsk	CIS	4	....	....	....	109	5	0	2.75	....	....	....	....	....	....	....
1993-94	Kamenogorsk	CIS	11	....	....	....	539	29	0	3.22	....	....	....	....	....	....	....
1994-95	Moscow D'amo	CIS	24	....	....	....	1265	40	....	1.89	....	....	....	....	....	....	....
1995-96	Moscow D'amo	CIS	39	....	....	....	2008	67	5	2.00	6	....	....	298	7	....	1.41

NOBLE, TOM — CHI.

Goaltender. Catches left. 5'10", 165 lbs. Born, Quincy, MA, March 21, 1975.
(Chicago's 12th choice, 284th overall, in 1993 Entry Draft).

			Regular Season								Playoffs						
Season	Club	Lea	GP	W	L	T	Mins	GA	SO	Avg	GP	W	L	Mins	GA	SO	Avg
1994-95	Boston U.	H.E.	18	15	2	0	1003	46	0	2.75	....	....	....	....	....	....	....
1995-96	Boston U.	H.E.	28	19	5	2	1536	77	....	3.01	....	....	....	....	....	....	....

O'NEILL, MIKE — ANA.

Goaltender. Catches left. 5'7", 160 lbs. Born, LaSalle, Que., November 3, 1967.
(Winnipeg's 1st choice, 15th overall, in 1988 Supplemental Draft).

			Regular Season								Playoffs						
Season	Club	Lea	GP	W	L	T	Mins	GA	SO	Avg	GP	W	L	Mins	GA	SO	Avg
1985-86	Yale	ECAC	6	3	1	0	389	17	0	3.53	....	....	....	....	....	....	....
1986-87a	Yale	ECAC	16	9	6	1	964	55	2	3.42	....	....	....	....	....	....	....
1987-88	Yale	ECAC	24	6	17	0	1385	101	0	4.37	....	....	....	....	....	....	....
1988-89ab	Yale	ECAC	25	10	14	1	1490	93	0	3.74	....	....	....	....	....	....	....
1989-90	Tappara	Fin.	41	23	13	5	2369	127	2	3.22	....	....	....	....	....	....	....
1990-91	Fort Wayne	IHL	8	5	2	1	490	31	0	3.80	....	....	....	....	....	....	....
	Moncton	AHL	30	13	7	6	1613	84	0	3.12	8	3	4	435	29	0	4.00
1991-92	**Winnipeg**	**NHL**	**1**	**0**	**0**	**0**	**13**	**1**	**0**	**4.62**	....	....	....	....	....	....	....
	Moncton	AHL	32	14	16	2	1902	108	1	3.41	11	4	7	670	43	*1	3.85
	Fort Wayne	IHL	33	22	6	3	1858	97	*4	3.13	....	....	....	....	....	....	....
1992-93	**Winnipeg**	**NHL**	**2**	**0**	**0**	**1**	**73**	**6**	**0**	**4.93**	....	....	....	....	....	....	....
	Moncton	AHL	30	13	10	4	1649	88	1	3.20	....	....	....	....	....	....	....
1993-94	**Winnipeg**	**NHL**	**17**	**0**	**9**	**1**	**738**	**51**	**0**	**4.15**	....	....	....	....	....	....	....
	Moncton	AHL	12	8	4	0	716	33	1	2.76	....	....	....	....	....	....	....
	Ft. Wayne	IHL	11	4	4	3	642	38	0	3.55	....	....	....	....	....	....	....
1994-95	Ft. Wayne	IHL	28	11	12	4	1603	109	0	4.08	....	....	....	....	....	....	....
	Phoenix	IHL	21	13	4	4	1256	64	1	3.06	9	4	5	535	33	0	3.70
1995-96	Baltimore	AHL	*74	31	31	7	*4250	250	2	3.53	12	6	6	689	43	0	3.75
	NHL Totals		**20**	**0**	**9**	**2**	**824**	**58**	**0**	**4.22**	....	....	....	....	....	....	....

a ECAC First All-Star Team (1987, 1989)
b NCAA East First All-American Team (1989)

Signed as a free agent by **Anaheim**, July 14, 1995.

OSGOOD, CHRIS (AWS-gud) — DET.

Goaltender. Catches left. 5'10", 160 lbs. Born, Peace River, Alta., November 26, 1972.
(Detroit's 3rd choice, 54th overall, in 1991 Entry Draft).

			Regular Season								Playoffs						
Season	Club	Lea	GP	W	L	T	Mins	GA	SO	Avg	GP	W	L	Mins	GA	SO	Avg
1989-90	Medicine Hat	WHL	57	24	28	2	3094	228	0	4.42	3	0	3	173	17	0	5.91
1990-91a	Medicine Hat	WHL	46	23	18	3	2630	173	2	3.95	12	7	5	712	42	0	3.54
1991-92	Medicine Hat	WHL	15	10	3	0	819	44	0	3.22	....	....	....	....	....	....	....
	Brandon	WHL	16	3	10	1	890	60	1	4.04	....	....	....	....	....	....	....
	Seattle	WHL	21	12	7	1	1217	65	1	3.20	15	9	6	904	51	0	3.38
1992-93	Adirondack	AHL	45	19	19	4	2438	159	0	3.91	1	0	1	59	2	0	2.03
1993-94	**Detroit**	**NHL**	**41**	**23**	**8**	**5**	**2206**	**105**	**2**	**2.86**	**6**	**3**	**2**	**307**	**12**	**1**	**2.35**
	Adirondack	AHL	4	3	1	0	239	13	0	3.26	....	....	....	....	....	....	....
1994-95	**Detroit**	**NHL**	**19**	**14**	**5**	**0**	**1087**	**41**	**1**	**2.26**	**2**	**0**	**0**	**68**	**2**	**0**	**1.76**
	Adirondack	AHL	2	1	1	0	120	6	0	3.00	....	....	....	....	....	....	....
1995-96bc	**Detroit**	**NHL**	**50**	***39**	**6**	**5**	**2933**	**106**	**5**	**2.17**	**15**	**8**	**7**	**936**	**33**	**2**	**2.12**
	NHL Totals		**110**	**76**	**19**	**10**	**6226**	**252**	**8**	**2.43**	**23**	**11**	**9**	**1311**	**47**	**3**	**2.15**

a WHL East Second All-Star Team (1991)
b NHL Second All-Star Team (1996)
c Shared William M. Jennings Trophy with Mike Vernon (1996)

Played in NHL All-Star Game (1996)

PASSMORE, STEVE — EDM.

Goaltender. Catches left. 5'9", 165 lbs. Born, Thunder Bay, Ont., January 29, 1973.
(Quebec's 9th choice, 196th overall, in 1992 Entry Draft).

			Regular Season								Playoffs						
Season	Club	Lea	GP	W	L	T	Mins	GA	SO	Avg	GP	W	L	Mins	GA	SO	Avg
1990-91	Victoria	WHL	35	3	25	1	1838	190	0	6.20	....	....	....	....	....	....	....
1991-92	Victoria	WHL	*71	15	50	5	*4228	347	0	4.92	....	....	....	....	....	....	....
1992-93a	Victoria	WHL	43	14	24	2	2402	150	1	3.75	....	....	....	....	....	....	....
	Kamloops	WHL	25	19	6	0	1479	69	1	2.80	7	4	2	401	22	1	3.29
1993-94a	Kamloops	WHL	36	22	9	2	1927	88	1	*2.74	*18	*11	7	*1099	60	0	3.28
1994-95	Cape Breton	AHL	25	8	13	3	1455	93	0	3.83	....	....	....	....	....	....	....
1995-96	Cape Breton	AHL	2	1	0	0	90	2	0	1.33	....	....	....	....	....	....	....

a WHL West First All-Star Team (1993, 1994)

Traded to **Edmonton** by **Quebec** for Brad Werenka, March 21, 1994.

PENSTOCK, BYRON

Goaltender. Catches left. 5'9", 180 lbs. Born, Regina, Sask., September 9, 1974.

			Regular Season								Playoffs						
Season	Club	Lea	GP	W	L	T	Mins	GA	SO	Avg	GP	W	L	Mins	GA	SO	Avg
1991-92	Tri-City	WHL	33	8	15	2	1644	151	0	5.51	....	....	....	....	....	....	....
1992-93	Brandon	WHL	17	7	8	0	882	68	1	4.63	....	....	....	....	....	....	....
1993-94	Brandon	WHL	58	35	18	4	3447	182	2	3.17	14	8	6	869	49	0	3.38
1994-95a	Brandon	WHL	48	27	16	4	2813	148	4	3.16	6	4	1	342	24	0	4.21
1995-96	Baltimore	AHL	11	0	6	1	332	28	0	5.06	....	....	....	....	....	....	....
	Raleigh	ECHL	8	2	4	2	459	32	0	4.19	....	....	....	....	....	....	....

a WHL East Second All-Star Team (1995)

Signed as a free agent by **Anaheim**, June 30, 1995.

PERSSON, JOAKIM (PEHR-suhn) — BOS.

Goaltender. Catches left. 5'11", 176 lbs. Born, Ostervala, Sweden, May 4, 1970.
(Boston's 10th choice, 259th overall, in 1993 Entry Draft).

			Regular Season								Playoffs						
Season	Club	Lea	GP	W	L	T	Mins	GA	SO	Avg	GP	W	L	Mins	GA	SO	Avg
1992-93	Hammarby	Swe. 2	40	....	....	....	....	....	....	2.71	....	....	....	....	....	....	....
1993-94	Hammarby	Swe. 2	23	....	....	....	....	59	....	2.57	....	....	....	....	....	....	....
	Providence	AHL	1	0	0	0	24	0	0	0.00	....	....	....	....	....	....	....
1994-95	AIK	Swe.	30	....	....	....	1800	103	1	3.43	....	....	....	....	....	....	....
1995-96	AIK	Swe.	24	....	....	....	1344	64	....	2.86	....	....	....	....	....	....	....

PETRUK, RANDY — COL.

Goaltender. Catches right. 5'9", 178 lbs. Born, Cranbrook, B.C., April 23, 1978.
(Colorado's 5th choice, 107th overall, in 1996 Entry Draft).

			Regular Season								Playoffs						
Season	Club	Lea	GP	W	L	T	Mins	GA	SO	Avg	GP	W	L	Mins	GA	SO	Avg
1994-95	Kamloops	WHL	27	16	3	4	1462	71	1	2.91	7	5	2	423	19	0	2.70
1995-96	Kamloops	WHL	52	34	15	1	3071	181	1	3.54	16	9	6	990	58	0	3.52

PODOLKA, MICHAL — DET.

Goaltender. Catches right. 5'11", 146 lbs. Born, Most, Czech., August 11, 1977.
(Detroit's 4th choice, 135th overall, in 1996 Entry Draft).

			Regular Season								Playoffs						
Season	Club	Lea	GP	W	L	T	Mins	GA	SO	Avg	GP	W	L	Mins	GA	SO	Avg
1995-96	S.S. Marie	OHL	44	20	15	4	2391	149	1	3.74	1	0	1	60	6	0	6.00

POTVIN, FELIX (PAHT-vihn) — TOR.

Goaltender. Catches left. 6', 190 lbs. Born, Anjou, Que., June 23, 1971.
(Toronto's 2nd choice, 31st overall, in 1990 Entry Draft).

			Regular Season								Playoffs						
Season	Club	Lea	GP	W	L	T	Mins	GA	SO	Avg	GP	W	L	Mins	GA	SO	Avg
1988-89	Chicoutimi	QMJHL	*65	25	31	1	*3489	271	*2	4.66	....	....	....	....	....	....	....
1989-90a	Chicoutimi	QMJHL	*62	*31	26	2	*3478	231	*2	3.99	....	....	....	....	....	....	....
1990-91 bcde	Chicoutimi	QMJHL	54	33	15	4	3216	145	*6	*2.70	*16	*11	5	*992	46	0	*2.78
1991-92	**Toronto**	**NHL**	**4**	**0**	**2**	**1**	**210**	**8**	**0**	**2.29**	....	....	....	....	....	....	....
fgh	St. John's	AHL	35	18	10	6	2070	101	2	2.93	11	7	4	642	41	0	3.83
1992-93i	**Toronto**	**NHL**	**48**	**25**	**15**	**7**	**2781**	**116**	**2**	***2.50**	***21**	**11**	**10**	***1308**	**62**	**1**	**2.84**
	St. John's	AHL	5	3	0	2	309	18	0	3.50	....	....	....	....	....	....	....
1993-94	**Toronto**	**NHL**	**66**	**34**	**22**	**9**	**3883**	**187**	**3**	**2.89**	**18**	**9**	**9**	**1124**	**46**	**3**	**2.46**
1994-95	**Toronto**	**NHL**	**36**	**15**	**13**	**7**	**2144**	**104**	**0**	**2.91**	**7**	**3**	**4**	**424**	**20**	**1**	**2.83**
1995-96	**Toronto**	**NHL**	**69**	**30**	**26**	**11**	**4009**	**192**	**2**	**2.87**	**6**	**2**	**4**	**350**	**19**	**0**	**3.26**
	NHL Totals		**223**	**104**	**78**	**35**	**13027**	**607**	**7**	**2.80**	**52**	**25**	**27**	**3206**	**147**	**5**	**2.75**

a QMJHL Second All-Star Team (1990)
b QMJHL First All-Star Team (1991)
c Canadian Major Junior Goaltender of the Year (1991)
d Memorial Cup All-Star Team (1991)
e Won Hap Emms Memorial Trophy (Memorial Cup Top Goaltender) (1991)
f Won Baz Bastien Memorial Trophy (Top Goaltender - AHL) (1992)
g Won Dudley "Red" Garrett Memorial Trophy (Top Rookie - AHL) (1992)
h AHL First All-Star Team (1992)
i NHL/Upper Deck All-Rookie Team (1993)

Played in NHL All-Star Game (1994, 1996)

PUPPA, DAREN (POO-puh) — T.B.

Goaltender. Catches right. 6'3", 205 lbs. Born, Kirkland Lake, Ont., March 23, 1965.
(Buffalo's 6th choice, 74th overall, in 1983 Entry Draft).

			Regular Season								Playoffs						
Season	Club	Lea	GP	W	L	T	Mins	GA	SO	Avg	GP	W	L	Mins	GA	SO	Avg
1983-84	RPI	ECAC	32	24	6	0	....	....	....	2.94	....	....	....	....	....	....	....
1984-85	RPI	ECAC	32	31	1	0	1830	78	0	2.56	....	....	....	....	....	....	....
1985-86	**Buffalo**	**NHL**	**7**	**3**	**4**	**0**	**401**	**21**	**1**	**3.14**	....	....	....	....	....	....	....
	Rochester	AHL	20	8	11	0	1092	79	0	4.34	....	....	....	....	....	....	....
1986-87	**Buffalo**	**NHL**	**3**	**0**	**2**	**1**	**185**	**13**	**0**	**4.22**	....	....	....	....	....	....	....
a	Rochester	AHL	57	*33	14	0	3129	146	1	2.80	*16	*10	6	*944	48	*1	3.05
1987-88	**Buffalo**	**NHL**	**17**	**8**	**6**	**1**	**874**	**61**	**0**	**4.19**	**3**	**1**	**1**	**142**	**11**	**0**	**4.65**
	Rochester	AHL	26	14	8	2	1415	65	2	2.76	2	0	1	108	5	0	2.78
1988-89	**Buffalo**	**NHL**	**37**	**17**	**10**	**6**	**1908**	**107**	**1**	**3.36**	....	....	....	....	....	....	....
1989-90b	**Buffalo**	**NHL**	**56**	***31**	**16**	**6**	**3241**	**156**	**1**	**2.89**	**6**	**2**	**4**	**370**	**15**	**0**	**2.43**
1990-91	**Buffalo**	**NHL**	**38**	**15**	**11**	**6**	**2092**	**118**	**2**	**3.38**	**2**	**0**	**1**	**81**	**10**	**0**	**7.41**
1991-92	**Buffalo**	**NHL**	**33**	**11**	**14**	**4**	**1757**	**114**	**0**	**3.89**	....	....	....	....	....	....	....
	Rochester	AHL	2	0	2	0	119	9	0	4.54	....	....	....	....	....	....	....
1992-93	**Buffalo**	**NHL**	**24**	**11**	**5**	**4**	**1306**	**78**	**0**	**3.58**	....	....	....	....	....	....	....
	Toronto	**NHL**	**8**	**6**	**2**	**0**	**479**	**18**	**2**	**2.25**	**1**	**0**	**0**	**20**	**1**	**0**	**3.00**
1993-94	**Tampa Bay**	**NHL**	**63**	**22**	**33**	**6**	**3653**	**165**	**4**	**2.71**	....	....	....	....	....	....	....
1994-95	**Tampa Bay**	**NHL**	**36**	**14**	**19**	**2**	**2013**	**90**	**1**	**2.68**	....	....	....	....	....	....	....
1995-96	**Tampa Bay**	**NHL**	**57**	**29**	**16**	**9**	**3189**	**131**	**5**	**2.46**	**4**	**1**	**3**	**173**	**14**	**0**	**4.86**
	NHL Totals		**379**	**167**	**138**	**45**	**21098**	**1072**	**17**	**3.05**	**16**	**4**	**9**	**786**	**51**	**0**	**3.89**

a AHL First All-Star Team (1987)
b NHL Second All-Star Team (1990)

Played in NHL All-Star Game (1990)

Traded to **Toronto** by **Buffalo** with Dave Andreychuk and Buffalo's first round choice (Kenny Jonsson) in 1993 Entry Draft for Grant Fuhr and Toronto's fifth round choice (Kevin Popp) in 1995 Entry Draft, February 2, 1993. Claimed by **Florida** from **Toronto** in Expansion Draft, June 24, 1993. Claimed by **Tampa Bay** from **Florida** in Phase II of Expansion Draft, June 25, 1993.

RACICOT, ANDRE (RAH-sih-KOH) — CHI.

Goaltender. Catches left. 5'11", 165 lbs. Born, Rouyn-Noranda, Que., June 9, 1969.
(Montreal's 5th choice, 83rd overall, in 1989 Entry Draft).

			Regular Season								Playoffs						
Season	Club	Lea	GP	W	L	T	Mins	GA	SO	Avg	GP	W	L	Mins	GA	SO	Avg
1986-87	Longueuil	QMJHL	3	1	2	0	180	19	0	6.33	....	....	....	....	....	....	....
1987-88	Granby	QMJHL	30	15	11	1	1547	105	1	4.07	5	1	4	298	23	0	4.63
1988-89a	Granby	QMJHL	54	22	24	3	2944	198	0	4.04	4	0	4	218	18	0	4.95
1989-90	**Montreal**	**NHL**	**1**	**0**	**0**	**0**	**13**	**3**	**0**	**13.85**	....	....	....	....	....	....	....
b	Sherbrooke	AHL	33	19	11	2	1948	97	1	2.99	5	0	4	227	18	0	4.76
1990-91	**Montreal**	**NHL**	**21**	**7**	**9**	**2**	**975**	**52**	**1**	**3.20**	**2**	**0**	**1**	**12**	**2**	**0**	**10.00**
	Fredericton	AHL	22	13	8	1	1252	60	1	2.88	....	....	....	....	....	....	....
1991-92	**Montreal**	**NHL**	**9**	**0**	**3**	**3**	**436**	**23**	**0**	**3.17**	**1**	**0**	**0**	**1**	**0**	**0**	**0.00**
	Fredericton	AHL	28	14	8	5	1666	86	0	3.10	....	....	....	....	....	....	....
1992-93	**Montreal**	**NHL**	**26**	**17**	**5**	**1**	**1433**	**81**	**1**	**3.39**	**1**	**0**	**0**	**18**	**2**	**0**	**6.67** ♦
1993-94	**Montreal**	**NHL**	**11**	**2**	**6**	**2**	**500**	**37**	**0**	**4.44**	....	....	....	....	....	....	....
	Fredericton	AHL	6	1	4	0	292	16	0	3.28	....	....	....	....	....	....	....
1994-95	Portland	AHL	19	10	7	0	1080	53	1	2.94	....	....	....	....	....	....	....
	Phoenix	IHL	3	1	0	0	132	8	0	3.62	2	0	0	20	0	0	0.00
1995-96	Albany	AHL	2	2	0	0	120	4	0	2.00	....	....	....	....	....	....	....
	Columbus	ECHL	1	1	0	0	60	2	0	2.00	....	....	....	....	....	....	....
	Indianapolis	IHL	11	3	6	0	547	43	0	4.71	....	....	....	....	....	....	....
	Peoria	IHL	4	2	1	1	240	14	0	3.50	11	6	5	654	34	1	3.12
	NHL Totals		**68**	**26**	**23**	**8**	**3357**	**196**	**2**	**3.50**	**4**	**0**	**1**	**31**	**4**	**0**	**7.74**

a QMJHL Second All-Star Team (1989)
b Shared Harry "Hap" Holmes Trophy (fewest goals-against - AHL) with J.C. Bergeron (1990)

Signed as a free agent by **Los Angeles**, September 22, 1994. Signed as a free agent by **Chicago**, August 25, 1995.

RACINE, BRUCE

Goaltender. Catches left. 6', 170 lbs. Born, Cornwall, Ont., August 9, 1966.
(Pittsburgh's 3rd choice, 58th overall, in 1985 Entry Draft).

			Regular Season								Playoffs						
Season	Club	Lea	GP	W	L	T	Mins	GA	SO	Avg	GP	W	L	Mins	GA	SO	Avg
1984-85	Northeastern	H.E.	26	11	14	1	1615	103	1	3.83							
1985-86	Northeastern	H.E.	32	17	14	1	1920	147	0	4.56	....	....	....	....	....	....	....
1986-87ab	Northeastern	H.E.	33	12	18	3	1966	133	0	4.06	....	....	....	....	....	....	....
1987-88b	Northeastern	H.E.	30	15	11	4	1808	108	1	3.58	....	....	....	....	....	....	....
1988-89	Muskegon	IHL	51	*37	11	0	*3039	184	*3	3.63	5	4	1	300	15	0	3.00
1989-90	Muskegon	IHL	49	29	15	4	2911	182	1	3.75	9	5	4	566	32	1	3.34
1990-91	Albany	IHL	29	7	18	1	1567	104	0	3.98	....	....	....	....	....	....	....
	Muskegon	IHL	9	4	4	1	516	40	0	4.65	....	....	....	....	....	....	....
1991-92	Muskegon	IHL	27	13	10	3	1559	91	1	3.50	1	0	1	60	6	0	6.00
1992-93	Cleveland	IHL	35	13	16	6	1949	140	1	4.31	2	0	0	37	2	0	3.24
1993-94	St. John's	AHL	37	20	9	2	1875	116	0	3.71	1	0	0	20	1	0	0.00
1994-95	St. John's	AHL	27	11	10	4	1492	85	1	3.42	2	1	1	119	3	0	1.51
1995-96	**St. Louis**	**NHL**	**11**	**0**	**3**	**0**	**230**	**12**	**0**	**3.13**	**1**	**0**	**0**	**1**	**0**	**0**	**0.00**
	Peoria	IHL	22	11	10	1	1228	69	1	3.37	1	0	1	59	3	0	3.05
	NHL Totals		**11**	**0**	**3**	**0**	**230**	**12**	**0**	**3.13**	**1**	**0**	**0**	**1**	**0**	**0**	**0.00**

a Hockey East First All-Star Team (1987)
b NCAA East First All-American Team (1987, 1988)

Signed as a free agent by **Toronto**, August 11, 1993. Signed as a free agent by **St. Louis**, August 10, 1995.

RAM, JAMIE — NYR

Goaltender. Catches left. 5'11", 175 lbs. Born, Scarborough, Ont., January 18, 1971.
(NY Rangers' 10th choice, 213th overall, in 1991 Entry Draft).

			Regular Season								Playoffs						
Season	Club	Lea	GP	W	L	T	Mins	GA	SO	Avg	GP	W	L	Mins	GA	SO	Avg
1990-91	Michigan Tech	WCHA	14	5	9	0	826	57	0	4.14	....	....	....	....	....	....	....
1991-92	Michigan Tech	WCHA	23	9	9	1	1144	83	0	4.35	....	....	....	....	....	....	....
1992-93ab	Michigan Tech	WCHA	*36	16	14	5	*2078	115	0	3.32	....	....	....	....	....	....	....
1993-94ab	Michigan Tech	WCHA	39	12	20	5	2192	117	*1	3.20	....	....	....	....	....	....	....
1994-95	Binghamton	AHL	26	12	10	2	1472	81	1	3.30	11	6	5	663	29	1	2.62
1995-96	**NY Rangers**	**NHL**	**1**	**0**	**0**	**0**	**27**	**0**	**0**	**0.00**	....	....	....	....	....	....	....
	Binghamton	AHL	40	18	16	3	2262	151	1	4.01	1	0	0	34	1	0	1.75
	NHL Totals		**1**	**0**	**0**	**0**	**27**	**0**	**0**	**0.00**	....	....	....	....	....	....	....

a WCHA First All-Star Team (1993, 1994)
b NCAA West First All-American Team (1993, 1994)

RANFORD, BILL — BOS.

Goaltender. Catches left. 5'11", 185 lbs. Born, Brandon, Man., December 14, 1966.
(Boston's 2nd choice, 52nd overall, in 1985 Entry Draft).

			Regular Season								Playoffs						
Season	Club	Lea	GP	W	L	T	Mins	GA	SO	Avg	GP	W	L	Mins	GA	SO	Avg
1983-84	N. Westminster	WHL	27	10	14	0	1450	130	0	5.38	1	0	0	27	2	0	4.44
1984-85	N. Westminster	WHL	38	19	17	0	2034	142	0	4.19	7	2	3	309	26	0	5.05
1985-86	**Boston**	**NHL**	**4**	**3**	**1**	**0**	**240**	**10**	**0**	**2.50**	**2**	**0**	**2**	**120**	**7**	**0**	**3.50**
	N. Westminster	WHL	53	17	29	1	2791	225	0	4.84	....	....	....	....	....	....	....
1986-87	**Boston**	**NHL**	**41**	**16**	**20**	**2**	**2234**	**124**	**3**	**3.33**	**2**	**0**	**2**	**123**	**8**	**0**	**3.90**
	Moncton	AHL	3	3	0	0	180	6	0	2.00	....	....	....	....	....	....	....
1987-88	Maine	AHL	51	27	16	6	2856	165	1	3.47	....	....	....	....	....	....	....
	Edmonton	**NHL**	**6**	**3**	**0**	**2**	**325**	**16**	**0**	**2.95**	....	....	....	....	....	....	.... ◆
1988-89	**Edmonton**	**NHL**	**29**	**15**	**8**	**2**	**1509**	**88**	**1**	**3.50**	....	....	....	....	....	....	....
1989-90a	**Edmonton**	**NHL**	**56**	**24**	**16**	**9**	**3107**	**165**	**1**	**3.19**	***22**	***16**	**6**	***1401**	**59**	**1**	**2.53** ◆
1990-91	**Edmonton**	**NHL**	**60**	**27**	**27**	**3**	**3415**	**182**	**0**	**3.20**	**3**	**1**	**2**	**135**	**8**	**0**	**3.56**
1991-92	**Edmonton**	**NHL**	**67**	**27**	**26**	**10**	**3822**	**228**	**1**	**3.58**	**16**	**8**	**8**	**909**	**51**	***2**	**3.37**
1992-93	**Edmonton**	**NHL**	**67**	**17**	**38**	**6**	**3753**	**240**	**1**	**3.84**	....	....	....	....	....	....	....
1993-94	**Edmonton**	**NHL**	**71**	**22**	**34**	**11**	**4070**	**236**	**1**	**3.48**	....	....	....	....	....	....	....
1994-95	**Edmonton**	**NHL**	**40**	**15**	**20**	**3**	**2203**	**133**	**2**	**3.62**	....	....	....	....	....	....	....
1995-96	**Edmonton**	**NHL**	**37**	**13**	**18**	**5**	**2015**	**128**	**1**	**3.81**	....	....	....	....	....	....	....
	Boston	**NHL**	**40**	**21**	**12**	**4**	**2307**	**109**	**1**	**2.83**	**4**	**1**	**3**	**239**	**16**	**0**	**4.02**
	NHL Totals		**518**	**203**	**220**	**57**	**29000**	**1659**	**12**	**3.43**	**49**	**26**	**23**	**2927**	**149**	**3**	**3.05**

a Won Conn Smythe Trophy (1990)

Played in NHL All-Star Game (1991)

Traded to **Edmonton** by **Boston** with Geoff Courtnall and future considerations for Andy Moog, March 8, 1988. Traded to **Boston** by **Edmonton** for Mariusz Czerkawski, Sean Brown and Boston's first round choice (Matthieu Descoteaux) in 1996 Entry Draft, January 11, 1996.

REDDICK, ELDON (POKEY)

Goaltender. Catches left. 5'8", 170 lbs. Born, Halifax, N.S., October 6, 1964.

			Regular Season								Playoffs						
Season	Club	Lea	GP	W	L	T	Mins	GA	SO	Avg	GP	W	L	Mins	GA	SO	Avg
1982-83	Nanaimo	WHL	66	19	38	1	3549	383	0	6.46	....	....	....	....	....	....	....
1983-84	N. Westminster	WHL	50	24	22	2	2930	215	0	4.40	9	4	5	542	53	0	5.87
1984-85	Brandon	WHL	47	14	30	1	2585	243	0	5.64	....	....	....	....	....	....	....
1985-86a	Ft. Wayne	IHL	29	15	11	0	1674	86	*3	3.00	....	....	....	....	....	....	....
1986-87	**Winnipeg**	**NHL**	**48**	**21**	**21**	**4**	**2762**	**149**	**0**	**3.24**	**3**	**0**	**2**	**166**	**10**	**0**	**3.61**
1987-88	**Winnipeg**	**NHL**	**28**	**9**	**13**	**3**	**1487**	**102**	**0**	**4.12**	....	....	....	....	....	....	....
	Moncton	AHL	9	2	6	1	545	26	0	2.86	....	....	....	....	....	....	....
1988-89	**Winnipeg**	**NHL**	**41**	**11**	**17**	**7**	**2109**	**144**	**0**	**4.10**	....	....	....	....	....	....	....
1989-90	**Edmonton**	**NHL**	**11**	**5**	**4**	**2**	**604**	**31**	**0**	**3.08**	**1**	**0**	**0**	**2**	**0**	**0**	**0.00** ◆
	Cape Breton	AHL	15	9	4	1	821	54	0	3.95	....	....	....	....	....	....	....
	Phoenix	IHL	3	2	1	0	185	7	0	2.27	....	....	....	....	....	....	....
1990-91	**Edmonton**	**NHL**	**2**	**0**	**2**	**0**	**120**	**9**	**0**	**4.50**	....	....	....	....	....	....	....
	Cape Breton	AHL	31	19	10	0	1673	97	2	3.48	2	0	2	124	10	0	4.84
1991-92	Cape Breton	AHL	16	5	3	3	765	45	0	3.53	....	....	....	....	....	....	....
	Ft. Wayne	IHL	14	6	5	2	787	40	1	3.05	7	3	4	369	18	0	2.93
1992-93b	Ft. Wayne	IHL	54	33	16	4	3043	156	3	3.08	*12	*12	0	723	18	0	*1.49
1993-94	**Florida**	**NHL**	**2**	**0**	**1**	**0**	**80**	**8**	**0**	**6.00**	....	....	....	....	....	....	....
	Cincinnati	IHL	54	31	12	6	2894	147	*2	3.05	10	6	2	498	21	*1	2.53
1994-95	Las Vegas	IHL	40	23	13	1	2075	104	*3	3.01	10	4	6	592	31	0	3.14
1995-96	Las Vegas	IHL	47	27	12	4	2636	129	1	2.94	15	8	6	770	43	0	3.35
	NHL Totals		**132**	**46**	**58**	**16**	**7162**	**443**	**0**	**3.71**	**4**	**0**	**2**	**168**	**10**	**0**	**3.57**

a Shared James Norris Memorial Trophy (fewest goals against - IHL) with Rick St. Croix (1986)
b Won "Bud" Poile Trophy (Playoff MVP - IHL) (1993)

Signed as a free agent by **Winnipeg**, September 27, 1985. Traded to **Edmonton** by **Winnipeg** for future considerations, September 28, 1989. Signed as a free agent by **Florida**, July 12, 1993.

REESE, JEFF — N.J.

Goaltender. Catches left. 5'9", 180 lbs. Born, Brantford, Ont., March 24, 1966.
(Toronto's 3rd choice, 67th overall, in 1984 Entry Draft).

			Regular Season								Playoffs						
Season	Club	Lea	GP	W	L	T	Mins	GA	SO	Avg	GP	W	L	Mins	GA	SO	Avg
1983-84	London	OHL	43	18	19	0	2308	173	0	4.50	6	3	3	327	27	0	4.95
1984-85	London	OHL	50	31	15	1	2878	186	1	3.88	8	5	2	440	20	1	2.73
1985-86	London	OHL	57	25	26	3	3281	215	0	3.93	5	0	4	299	25	0	5.02
1986-87	Newmarket	AHL	50	11	29	0	2822	193	1	4.10	....	....	....	....	....	....	....
1987-88	**Toronto**	**NHL**	**5**	**1**	**2**	**1**	**249**	**17**	**0**	**4.10**	....	....	....	....	....	....	....
	Newmarket	AHL	28	10	14	3	1587	103	0	3.89	....	....	....	....	....	....	....
1988-89	**Toronto**	**NHL**	**10**	**2**	**6**	**1**	**486**	**40**	**0**	**4.94**	....	....	....	....	....	....	....
	Newmarket	AHL	37	17	14	3	2072	132	0	3.82	....	....	....	....	....	....	....
1989-90	**Toronto**	**NHL**	**21**	**9**	**6**	**3**	**1101**	**81**	**0**	**4.41**	**2**	**1**	**1**	**108**	**6**	**0**	**3.33**
	Newmarket	AHL	7	3	2	2	431	29	0	4.04	....	....	....	....	....	....	....
1990-91	**Toronto**	**NHL**	**30**	**6**	**13**	**3**	**1430**	**92**	**1**	**3.86**	....	....	....	....	....	....	....
	Newmarket	AHL	3	2	1	0	180	7	0	2.33	....	....	....	....	....	....	....
1991-92	**Toronto**	**NHL**	**8**	**1**	**5**	**1**	**413**	**20**	**1**	**2.91**	....	....	....	....	....	....	....
	Calgary	**NHL**	**12**	**3**	**2**	**2**	**587**	**37**	**0**	**3.78**	....	....	....	....	....	....	....
1992-93	**Calgary**	**NHL**	**26**	**14**	**4**	**1**	**1311**	**70**	**1**	**3.20**	**4**	**1**	**3**	**209**	**17**	**0**	**4.88**
1993-94	**Calgary**	**NHL**	**1**	**0**	**0**	**0**	**13**	**1**	**0**	**4.62**	....	....	....	....	....	....	....
	Hartford	**NHL**	**19**	**5**	**9**	**3**	**1086**	**56**	**1**	**3.09**	....	....	....	....	....	....	....
1994-95	**Hartford**	**NHL**	**11**	**2**	**5**	**1**	**477**	**26**	**0**	**3.27**	....	....	....	....	....	....	....
1995-96	**Hartford**	**NHL**	**7**	**2**	**3**	**0**	**275**	**14**	**1**	**3.05**	....	....	....	....	....	....	....
	Tampa Bay	**NHL**	**19**	**7**	**7**	**1**	**994**	**54**	**0**	**3.26**	**5**	**1**	**1**	**198**	**12**	**0**	**3.64**
	NHL Totals		**169**	**52**	**62**	**17**	**8422**	**508**	**5**	**3.62**	**11**	**3**	**5**	**515**	**35**	**0**	**4.08**

Traded to **Calgary** with Craig Berube, Alexander Godynyuk, Gary Leeman and Michel Petit for Doug Gilmour, Jamie Macoun, Ric Nattress, Rick Wamsley and Kent Manderville, January 2, 1992. Traded to **Hartford** by **Calgary** for Dan Keczmer, November 19, 1993. Traded to **Tampa Bay** by **Hartford** for Tampa Bay's ninth round choice (Ashhat Rakhmatullin) in 1996 Entry Draft, December 1, 1995. Traded to **New Jersey** by **Tampa Bay** with Chicago's second round choice (previously acquired by Tampa Bay — New Jersey selected Pierre Dagenais) in 1996 Entry Draft and Tampa Bay's eighth round choice (Jason Bertsch) in 1996 Entry Draft for Corey Schwab, June 22, 1996.

RHODES, DAMIAN — OTT.

Goaltender. Catches left. 6', 190 lbs. Born, St. Paul, MN, May 28, 1969.
(Toronto's 6th choice, 112th overall, in 1987 Entry Draft).

			Regular Season								Playoffs						
Season	Club	Lea	GP	W	L	T	Mins	GA	SO	Avg	GP	W	L	Mins	GA	SO	Avg
1987-88	Michigan Tech	WCHA	29	16	10	1	1625	114	0	4.20	....	....	....	....	....	....	....
1988-89	Michigan Tech	WCHA	37	15	22	0	2216	163	0	4.41	....	....	....	....	....	....	....
1989-90	Michigan Tech	WCHA	25	6	17	0	1358	119	0	6.26	....	....	....	....	....	....	....
1990-91	**Toronto**	**NHL**	**1**	**1**	**0**	**0**	**60**	**1**	**0**	**1.00**	....	....	....	....	....	....	....
	Newmarket	AHL	38	8	24	3	2154	144	1	4.01	....	....	....	....	....	....	....
1991-92	St. John's	AHL	43	20	16	5	2454	148	0	3.62	6	4	1	331	16	0	2.90
1992-93	St. John's	AHL	*52	27	16	8	*3074	184	1	3.59	9	4	5	538	37	0	4.13
1993-94	**Toronto**	**NHL**	**22**	**9**	**7**	**3**	**1213**	**53**	**0**	**2.62**	**1**	**0**	**0**	**1**	**0**	**0**	**0.00**
1994-95	**Toronto**	**NHL**	**13**	**6**	**6**	**1**	**760**	**34**	**0**	**2.68**	....	....	....	....	....	....	....
1995-96	**Toronto**	**NHL**	**11**	**4**	**5**	**1**	**624**	**29**	**0**	**2.79**	....	....	....	....	....	....	....
	Ottawa	**NHL**	**36**	**10**	**22**	**4**	**2123**	**98**	**2**	**2.77**	....	....	....	....	....	....	....
	NHL Totals		**83**	**30**	**40**	**9**	**4780**	**215**	**2**	**2.70**	**1**	**0**	**0**	**1**	**0**	**0**	**0.00**

Note: Played 10 seconds in playoff game vs. San Jose, May 6, 1994. Traded to **NY Islanders** by **Toronto** with Ken Belanger for future considerations, January 23, 1996. Traded to **Ottawa** by **NY Islanders** with Wade Redden for Don Beaupre, Martin Straka and Bryan Berard, January 23, 1996.

RICHTER, MIKE — (RIHK-tuhr) NYR

Goaltender. Catches left. 5'11", 185 lbs. Born, Abington, PA, September 22, 1966.
(NY Rangers' 2nd choice, 28th overall, in 1985 Entry Draft).

			Regular Season								Playoffs						
Season	Club	Lea	GP	W	L	T	Mins	GA	SO	Avg	GP	W	L	Mins	GA	SO	Avg
1985-86	U. Wisconsin	WCHA	24	14	9	0	1394	92	1	3.96	....	....	....	....	....	....	....
1986-87a	U. Wisconsin	WCHA	36	19	16	1	2136	126	0	3.54	....	....	....	....	....	....	....
1987-88	Colorado	IHL	22	16	5	0	1298	68	1	3.14	10	5	3	536	35	0	3.92
	U.S. National	....	29	17	7	2	1559	86	0	3.31	....	....	....	....	....	....	....
	U.S. Olympic	....	4	2	2	0	230	15	0	3.91	....	....	....	....	....	....	....
1988-89	Denver	IHL	*57	23	26	0	3031	217	1	4.30	4	0	4	210	21	0	6.00
	NY Rangers	**NHL**	....	....	....	....	....	....	....	....	**1**	**0**	**1**	**58**	**4**	**0**	**4.14**
1989-90	**NY Rangers**	**NHL**	**23**	**12**	**5**	**5**	**1320**	**66**	**0**	**3.00**	**6**	**3**	**2**	**330**	**19**	**0**	**3.45**
	Flint	IHL	13	7	4	2	782	49	0	3.76	....	....	....	....	....	....	....
1990-91	**NY Rangers**	**NHL**	**45**	**21**	**13**	**7**	**2596**	**135**	**0**	**3.12**	**6**	**2**	**4**	**313**	**14**	***1**	**2.68**
1991-92	**NY Rangers**	**NHL**	**41**	**23**	**12**	**2**	**2298**	**119**	**3**	**3.11**	**7**	**4**	**2**	**412**	**24**	**1**	**3.50**
1992-93	**NY Rangers**	**NHL**	**38**	**13**	**19**	**3**	**2105**	**134**	**1**	**3.82**	....	....	....	....	....	....	....
	Binghamton	AHL	5	4	0	1	305	6	0	1.18	....	....	....	....	....	....	....
1993-94	**NY Rangers**	**NHL**	**68**	***42**	**12**	**6**	**3710**	**159**	**5**	**2.57**	**23**	***16**	**7**	**1417**	**49**	***4**	**2.07** ◆
1994-95	**NY Rangers**	**NHL**	**35**	**14**	**17**	**2**	**1993**	**97**	**2**	**2.92**	**7**	**2**	**5**	**384**	**23**	**0**	**3.59**
1995-96	**NY Rangers**	**NHL**	**41**	**24**	**13**	**3**	**2396**	**107**	**3**	**2.68**	**11**	**5**	**6**	**661**	**36**	**0**	**3.27**
	NHL Totals		**291**	**149**	**91**	**28**	**16418**	**817**	**14**	**2.99**	**61**	**32**	**27**	**3575**	**169**	**6**	**2.84**

a WCHA Second All-Star Team (1987)

Played in NHL All-Star Game (1992, 1994)

RIENDEAU, VINCENT — (ree-EHN-doh)

Goaltender. Catches left. 5'10", 185 lbs. Born, St. Hyacinthe, Que., April 20, 1966.

			Regular Season								Playoffs						
Season	Club	Lea	GP	W	L	T	Mins	GA	SO	Avg	GP	W	L	Mins	GA	SO	Avg
1985-86a	Drummondville	QMJHL	57	33	20	3	3336	215	2	3.87	23	10	13	1271	106	1	5.00
1986-87b	Sherbrooke	AHL	41	25	14	0	2363	114	2	2.89	13	8	5	742	47	0	3.80
1987-88	**Montreal**	**NHL**	**1**	**0**	**0**	**0**	**36**	**5**	**0**	**8.33**	....	....	....	....	....	....	....
cd	Sherbrooke	AHL	44	27	13	3	2521	112	*4	*2.67	2	0	2	127	7	0	3.31
1988-89	**St. Louis**	**NHL**	**32**	**11**	**15**	**5**	**1842**	**108**	**0**	**3.52**	....	....	....	....	....	....	....
1989-90	**St. Louis**	**NHL**	**43**	**17**	**19**	**5**	**2551**	**149**	**1**	**3.50**	**8**	**3**	**4**	**397**	**24**	**0**	**3.63**
1990-91	**St. Louis**	**NHL**	**44**	**29**	**9**	**6**	**2671**	**134**	**3**	**3.01**	**13**	**6**	**7**	**687**	**35**	***1**	**3.06**
1991-92	**St. Louis**	**NHL**	**3**	**1**	**2**	**0**	**157**	**11**	**0**	**4.20**	....	....	....	....	....	....	....
	Detroit	**NHL**	**2**	**2**	**0**	**0**	**87**	**2**	**0**	**1.38**	**2**	**1**	**0**	**73**	**4**	**0**	**3.29**
	Adirondack	AHL	3	2	1	0	179	8	0	2.68	....	....	....	....	....	....	....
1992-93	**Detroit**	**NHL**	**22**	**13**	**4**	**2**	**1193**	**64**	**0**	**3.22**	....	....	....	....	....	....	....
1993-94	**Detroit**	**NHL**	**8**	**2**	**4**	**0**	**345**	**23**	**0**	**4.00**	....	....	....	....	....	....	....
	Adirondack	AHL	10	6	3	0	582	30	0	3.09	....	....	....	....	....	....	....
	Boston	**NHL**	**18**	**7**	**6**	**1**	**976**	**50**	**1**	**3.07**	**2**	**1**	**1**	**120**	**8**	**0**	**4.00**
1994-95	**Boston**	**NHL**	**11**	**3**	**6**	**1**	**565**	**27**	**0**	**2.87**	....	....	....	....	....	....	....
	Providence	AHL	....	....	....	....	....	....	....	....	1	1	0	60	3	0	3.00
1995-96	Riessersee	Ger.	47	....	....	....	2776	184	....	4.00	3	....	....	189	20	0	6.35
	NHL Totals		**184**	**85**	**65**	**20**	**10423**	**573**	**5**	**3.30**	**25**	**11**	**12**	**1277**	**71**	**1**	**3.34**

a QMJHL Second All-Star Team (1986)
b Won Harry "Hap" Holmes Memorial Trophy (fewest goals-against - AHL) (1987)
c Shared Harry "Hap" Holmes Memorial Trophy (fewest goals-against - AHL) with Jocelyn Perreault (1988)
d AHL Second All-Star Team (1988)

Signed as a free agent by **Montreal**, October 9, 1985. Traded to **St. Louis** by **Montreal** with Sergio Momesso for Jocelyn Lemieux, Darrell May and St. Louis' second round choice (Patrice Brisebois) in 1989 Entry Draft, August 9, 1988. Traded to **Detroit** by **St. Louis** for Rick Zombo, October 18, 1991. Traded to **Boston** by **Detroit** for Boston's fifth round choice (Chad Wilchynski) in 1995 Entry Draft, January 17, 1994.

ROCHE, SCOTT — ST.L.

Goaltender. Catches left. 6'4", 220 lbs. Born, Lindsay, Ont., March 19, 1977.
(St. Louis' 2nd choice, 75th overall, in 1995 Entry Draft).

			Regular Season								Playoffs						
Season	Club	Lea	GP	W	L	T	Mins	GA	SO	Avg	GP	W	L	Mins	GA	SO	Avg
1993-94	North Bay	OHL	32	15	5	4	1587	93	0	3.52	5	2	1	191	10	0	*3.14
1994-95	North Bay	OHL	47	24	17	2	2599	167	2	3.86	6	2	4	348	30	0	5.17
1995-96	North Bay	OHL	53	12	29	5	2859	232	1	4.87	....	....	....	....	....	....	....

ROLOSON, DWAYNE — CGY.

Goaltender. Catches left. 6'1", 180 lbs. Born, Simcoe, Ont., October 12, 1969.

			Regular Season								Playoffs						
Season	Club	Lea	GP	W	L	T	Mins	GA	SO	Avg	GP	W	L	Mins	GA	SO	Avg
1990-91	Lowell	H.E.	15	5	9	0	823	63	0	4.59	....	....	....	....	....	....	....
1991-92	Lowell	H.E.	12	3	8	0	660	52	0	4.73	....	....	....	....	....	....	....
1992-93	Lowell	H.E.	*39	20	17	2	*2342	150	0	3.84	....	....	....	....	....	....	....
1993-94ab	Lowell	H.E.	*40	*23	10	7	*2305	106	0	2.76	....	....	....	....	....	....	....
1994-95	Saint John	AHL	46	16	21	8	2734	156	1	3.42	5	1	4	298	13	0	2.61
1995-96	Saint John	AHL	67	*33	22	11	4026	190	1	2.83	16	10	6	1027	49	1	2.86

a Hockey East First All-Star Team (1994)
b NCAA East First All-Ameircan Team (1994)

Signed as a free agent by **Calgary**, July 4, 1994.

RONNQVIST, PETTER

Goaltender. Catches left. 5'10", 154 lbs. Born, Stockholm, Sweden, February 7, 1973.
(Ottawa's 12th choice, 264th overall, in 1992 Entry Draft).

			Regular Season								Playoffs						
Season	Club	Lea	GP	W	L	T	Mins	GA	SO	Avg	GP	W	L	Mins	GA	SO	Avg
1992-93	Djurgarden	Swe.	7	....	....	....	380	20	0	3.15	1	....	....	60	5	0	5.00
1993-94	Djurgarden	Swe.	12	....	....	....	680	39	0	3.21	....	....	....	....	....	....	....
1994-95	MoDo	Swe.	28	....	....	....	1600	94	1	3.52	....	....	....	....	....	....	....
1995-96	MoDo	Swe.	30	....	....	....	1700	96	....	3.39	6	....	....	360	16	....	2.67

ROUSSEL, DOMINIC (roo-SEHL) PHI.

Goaltender. Catches left. 6'1", 191 lbs. Born, Hull, Que., February 22, 1970.
(Philadelphia's 4th choice, 63rd overall, in 1988 Entry Draft).

			Regular Season								Playoffs						
Season	**Club**	**Lea**	**GP**	**W**	**L**	**T**	**Mins**	**GA**	**SO**	**Avg**	**GP**	**W**	**L**	**Mins**	**GA**	**SO**	**Avg**
1987-88	Trois-Rivières	QMJHL	51	18	25	4	2905	251	0	5.18	....	....	....	....	....	....	....
1988-89	Shawinigan	QMJHL	46	24	15	2	2555	171	0	4.02	10	6	4	638	36	0	3.39
1989-90	Shawinigan	QMJHL	37	20	14	1	1985	133	0	4.02	2	1	1	120	12	0	6.00
1990-91	Hershey	AHL	45	20	14	7	2507	151	1	3.61	7	3	4	366	21	0	3.44
1991-92	**Philadelphia**	**NHL**	**17**	**7**	**8**	**2**	**922**	**40**	**1**	**2.60**	....	....	....	....	....	....	....
	Hershey	AHL	35	15	11	6	2040	121	1	3.56	....	....	....	....	....	....	....
1992-93	**Philadelphia**	**NHL**	**34**	**13**	**11**	**5**	**1769**	**111**	**1**	**3.76**	....	....	....	....	....	....	....
	Hershey	AHL	6	0	3	3	372	23	0	3.71	....	....	....	....	....	....	....
1993-94	**Philadelphia**	**NHL**	**60**	**29**	**20**	**5**	**3285**	**183**	**1**	**3.34**	....	....	....	....	....	....	....
1994-95	**Philadelphia**	**NHL**	**19**	**11**	**7**	**0**	**1075**	**42**	**1**	**2.34**	**1**	**0**	**0**	**23**	**0**	**0**	**0.00**
	Hershey	AHL	1	0	1	0	59	5	0	5.07	....	....	....	....	....	....	....
1995-96	**Philadelphia**	**NHL**	**9**	**2**	**3**	**2**	**456**	**22**	**1**	**2.89**	....	....	....	....	....	....	....
	Hershey	AHL	12	4	4	3	690	32	0	2.78	....	....	....	....	....	....	....
	Winnipeg	**NHL**	**7**	**2**	**2**	**0**	**285**	**16**	**0**	**3.37**	....	....	....	....	....	....	....
	NHL Totals		**146**	**64**	**51**	**14**	**7792**	**414**	**5**	**3.19**	**1**	**0**	**0**	**23**	**0**	**0**	**0.00**

Traded to **Winnipeg** by **Philadelphia** for Tim Cheveldae and Winnipeg's third round choice (Chester Gallant) in 1996 Entry Draft, February 27, 1996. Signed as a free agent by **Philadelphia**, July 3, 1996.

ROY, PATRICK (WAH) COL.

Goaltender. Catches left. 6', 192 lbs. Born, Quebec City, Que., October 5, 1965.
(Montreal's 4th choice, 51st overall, in 1984 Entry Draft).

			Regular Season								Playoffs						
Season	**Club**	**Lea**	**GP**	**W**	**L**	**T**	**Mins**	**GA**	**SO**	**Avg**	**GP**	**W**	**L**	**Mins**	**GA**	**SO**	**Avg**
1982-83	Granby	QMJHL	54	13	35	1	2808	293	0	6.26	....	....	....	....	....	....	....
1983-84	Granby	QMJHL	61	29	29	1	3585	265	0	4.44	4	0	4	244	22	0	5.41
1984-85	**Montreal**	**NHL**	**1**	**1**	**0**	**0**	**20**	**0**	**0**	**0.00**	....	....	....	....	....	....	....
	Granby	QMJHL	44	16	25	1	2463	228	0	5.55	....	....	....	....	....	....	....
	Sherbrooke	AHL	1	1	0	0	60	4	0	4.00	13	10	3	*769	37	0	*2.89
1985-86ab	**Montreal**	**NHL**	**47**	**23**	**18**	**3**	**2651**	**148**	**1**	**3.35**	**20**	***15**	**5**	**1218**	**39**	***1**	**1.92** ♦
1986-87c	**Montreal**	**NHL**	**46**	**22**	**16**	**6**	**2686**	**131**	**1**	**2.93**	**6**	**4**	**2**	**330**	**22**	**0**	**4.00**
1987-88cd	**Montreal**	**NHL**	**45**	**23**	**12**	**9**	**2586**	**125**	**3**	**2.90**	**8**	**3**	**4**	**430**	**24**	**0**	**3.35**
1988-89 cefg	**Montreal**	**NHL**	**48**	**33**	**5**	**6**	**2744**	**113**	**4**	***2.47**	**19**	**13**	**6**	**1206**	**42**	**2**	***2.09**
1989-90efg	**Montreal**	**NHL**	**54**	***31**	**16**	**5**	**3173**	**134**	**3**	**2.53**	**11**	**5**	**6**	**641**	**26**	**1**	**2.43**
1990-91d	**Montreal**	**NHL**	**48**	**25**	**15**	**6**	**2835**	**128**	**1**	**2.71**	**13**	**7**	**5**	**785**	**40**	**0**	**3.06**
1991-92efh	**Montreal**	**NHL**	**67**	**36**	**22**	**8**	**3935**	**155**	***5**	***2.36**	**11**	**4**	**7**	**686**	**30**	**1**	**2.62**
1992-93a	**Montreal**	**NHL**	**62**	**31**	**25**	**5**	**3595**	**192**	**2**	**3.20**	**20**	***16**	**4**	**1293**	**46**	**0**	***2.13** ♦
1993-94	**Montreal**	**NHL**	**68**	**35**	**17**	**11**	**3867**	**161**	***7**	**2.50**	**6**	**3**	**3**	**375**	**16**	**0**	**2.56**
1994-95	**Montreal**	**NHL**	**43**	**17**	**20**	**6**	**2566**	**127**	**1**	**2.97**	....	....	....	....	....	....	....
1995-96	**Montreal**	**NHL**	**22**	**12**	**9**	**1**	**1260**	**62**	**1**	**2.95**	....	....	....	....	....	....	....
	Colorado	**NHL**	**39**	**22**	**15**	**1**	**2305**	**103**	**1**	**2.68**	***22**	***16**	**6**	***1454**	**51**	***3**	**2.10** ♦
	NHL Totals		**590**	**311**	**190**	**67**	**34223**	**1579**	**30**	**2.77**	**136**	**86**	**48**	**8418**	**336**	**8**	**2.39**

a Won Conn Smythe Trophy (1986, 1993)
b NHL All-Rookie Team (1986)
c Shared William Jennings Trophy with Brian Hayward (1987, 1988, 1989)
d NHL Second All-Star Team (1988, 1991)
e Won Vezina Trophy (1989, 1990, 1992)
f NHL First All-Star Team (1989, 1990, 1992)
g Won Trico Goaltending Award (1989, 1990)
h Won William M. Jennings Award (1992)

Played in NHL All-Star Game (1988, 1990-94)

Traded to **Colorado** by **Montreal** with Mike Keane for Andrei Kovalenko, Martin Rucinsky and Jocelyn Thibault, December 6, 1995.

RUSSELL, BLAINE ANA.

Goaltender. Catches left. 5'11", 180 lbs. Born, Wetaskawin, Sask., January 11, 1977.
(Anaheim's 4th choice, 149th overall, in 1996 Entry Draft).

			Regular Season								Playoffs						
Season	**Club**	**Lea**	**GP**	**W**	**L**	**T**	**Mins**	**GA**	**SO**	**Avg**	**GP**	**W**	**L**	**Mins**	**GA**	**SO**	**Avg**
1995-96	Prince Albert	WHL	34	25	5	2	1920	98	2	3.06	7	4	2	380	20	0	3.16

RYABCHIKOV, EVGENY (RYAB-chih-kohv) BOS.

Goaltender. Catches left. 5'11", 167 lbs. Born, Yaroslavl, Soviet Union, January 16, 1974.
(Boston's 1st choice, 21st overall, in 1994 Entry Draft).

			Regular Season								Playoffs						
Season	**Club**	**Lea**	**GP**	**W**	**L**	**T**	**Mins**	**GA**	**SO**	**Avg**	**GP**	**W**	**L**	**Mins**	**GA**	**SO**	**Avg**
1993-94	Molot Perm	CIS	28	....	....	....	1572	96	....	3.66	....	....	....	....	....	....	....
1994-95	Providence	AHL	14	6	3	1	721	42	0	3.49	....	....	....	....	....	....	....
	Magnitogorsk	CIS	1	....	....	....	60	1	0	1.00	....	....	....	....	....	....	....
1995-96	Charlotte	ECHL	1	0	1	0	29	4	0	8.24	....	....	....	....	....	....	....
	Huntington	ECHL	8	3	3	0	360	25	0	4.17	....	....	....	....	....	....	....
	Erie	ECHL	16	2	7	1	858	50	0	3.50	....	....	....	....	....	....	....
	Providence	AHL	1	0	0	0	40	2	0	3.00	....	....	....	....	....	....	....

SAAL, JASON TOR.

Goaltender. Catches left. 5'11", 175 lbs. Born, Sterling Heights, MI, February 1, 1975.
(Los Angeles' 5th choice, 117th overall, in 1993 Entry Draft).

			Regular Season								Playoffs						
Season	**Club**	**Lea**	**GP**	**W**	**L**	**T**	**Mins**	**GA**	**SO**	**Avg**	**GP**	**W**	**L**	**Mins**	**GA**	**SO**	**Avg**
1992-93	Detroit	OHL	23	11	8	1	1289	85	0	3.96	3	0	0	42	2	0	2.86
1993-94	Detroit	OHL	45	28	11	3	2551	143	0	3.36	7	5	0	346	23	0	3.99
1994-95	Detroit	OHL	51	32	13	3	2887	153	1	3.18	18	13	4	1083	52	3	2.88
1995-96	S. Carolina	ECHL	8	5	3	0	428	25	0	3.51	....	....	....	....	....	....	....
	St. John's	AHL	24	9	8	1	1084	68	0	3.76	1	0	0	13	0	0	0.00

a Memorial Cup All-Star Team
b Won Hap Emms Memorial Trophy (Memorial Cup Tournament Top Goaltender) (1995)

Signed as a free agent by **Toronto**, August 3, 1995.

SALO, TOMMY (SAH-loh) NYI

Goaltender. Catches left. 5'11", 173 lbs. Born, Surahammar, Sweden, February 1, 1971.
(NY Islanders' 5th choice, 118th overall, in 1993 Entry Draft).

			Regular Season								Playoffs						
Season	**Club**	**Lea**	**GP**	**W**	**L**	**T**	**Mins**	**GA**	**SO**	**Avg**	**GP**	**W**	**L**	**Mins**	**GA**	**SO**	**Avg**
1990-91	Vasteras	Swe.	2	....	....	....	100	11	0	6.60	....	....	....	....	....	....	....
1991-92	Vasteras	Swe.	UNAVAILABLE														
1992-93	Vasteras	Swe.	24	....	....	....	1431	59	2	2.47	2	....	....	120	6	0	3.00
1993-94	Vasteras	Swe.	32	....	....	....	1896	106	0	3.35	....	....	....	....	....	....	....
1994-95 abcd	Denver	IHL	*65	*45	14	4	*3810	165	*3	*2.60	8	7	0	390	20	0	3.07
	NY Islanders	**NHL**	**6**	**1**	**5**	**0**	**358**	**18**	**0**	**3.02**	....	....	....	....	....	....	....
1995-96	**NY Islanders**	**NHL**	**10**	**1**	**7**	**1**	**523**	**35**	**0**	**4.02**	....	....	....	....	....	....	....
e	Utah	IHL	45	28	15	2	2695	119	*4	2.65	22	*15	7	1342	51	*3	2.28
	NHL Totals		**16**	**2**	**12**	**1**	**881**	**53**	**0**	**3.61**	....	....	....	....	....	....	....

a IHL First All-Star Team (1995)
b Won James Norris Memorial Trophy (Fewest goals against - IHL) (1995)
c Won Garry F. Longman Memorial Trophy (Top Rookie - IHL) (1995)
d Won James Gatschene Memorial Trophy (MVP - IHL) (1995)
e Shared James Norris Memorial Trophy (fewest goals against - IHL) with Mark McArthur (1996)

SALZMAN, WADE ST.L.

Goaltender. Catches right. 6'3", 195 lbs. Born, Duluth, MN, May 30, 1974.
(St. Louis' 12th choice, 259th overall, in 1992 Entry Draft).

			Regular Season								Playoffs						
Season	**Club**	**Lea**	**GP**	**W**	**L**	**T**	**Mins**	**GA**	**SO**	**Avg**	**GP**	**W**	**L**	**Mins**	**GA**	**SO**	**Avg**
1992-93	Notre Dame	CCHA	DID NOT PLAY														
1993-94	Notre Dame	CCHA	10	2	3	1	452	30	0	3.98	....	....	....	....	....	....	....
1994-95	Notre Dame	CCHA	16	2	12	1	777	59	1	4.55	....	....	....	....	....	....	....
1995-96	Notre Dame	CCHA	14	2	3	3	716	40	....	3.35	....	....	....	....	....	....	....

SARJEANT, GEOFF (SAHR-jehnt)

Goaltender. Catches left. 5'9", 180 lbs. Born, Newmarket, Ont., November 30, 1969.
(St. Louis' 1st choice, 17th overall, in 1990 Supplemental Draft).

			Regular Season								Playoffs						
Season	**Club**	**Lea**	**GP**	**W**	**L**	**T**	**Mins**	**GA**	**SO**	**Avg**	**GP**	**W**	**L**	**Mins**	**GA**	**SO**	**Avg**
1988-89	Michigan Tech	WCHA	6	0	3	2	329	22	0	4.01	....	....	....	....	....	....	....
1989-90	Michigan Tech	WCHA	19	4	13	0	1043	94	0	5.41	....	....	....	....	....	....	....
1990-91	Michigan Tech	WCHA	23	5	15	3	1540	97	0	3.78	....	....	....	....	....	....	....
1991-92	Michigan Tech	WCHA	23	7	13	0	1201	90	1	4.50	....	....	....	....	....	....	....
1992-93	Peoria	IHL	41	22	14	3	2356	130	0	3.31	3	0	3	179	13	0	4.36
1993-94a	Peoria	IHL	41	25	9	2	2275	93	*2	*2.45	4	2	2	211	13	0	3.69
1994-95	Peoria	IHL	55	32	12	8	3146	158	0	3.01	4	0	3	206	20	0	5.81
	St. Louis	**NHL**	**4**	**1**	**0**	**0**	**120**	**6**	**0**	**3.00**	....	....	....	....	....	....	....
1995-96	**San Jose**	**NHL**	**4**	**0**	**2**	**1**	**171**	**14**	**0**	**4.91**	....	....	....	....	....	....	....
	Kansas City	IHL	41	18	18	1	2167	140	1	3.88	2	0	1	99	3	0	1.82
	NHL Totals		**8**	**1**	**2**	**1**	**291**	**20**	**0**	**4.12**	....	....	....	....	....	....	....

a IHL First All-Star Team (1994)

Signed as a free agent by **San Jose**, September 23, 1995.

SAVARY, NEIL

Goaltender. Catches left. 6', 170 lbs. Born, Halifax, N.S., April 3, 1976.
(Boston's 8th choice, 255th overall, in 1994 Entry Draft).

			Regular Season								Playoffs						
Season	**Club**	**Lea**	**GP**	**W**	**L**	**T**	**Mins**	**GA**	**SO**	**Avg**	**GP**	**W**	**L**	**Mins**	**GA**	**SO**	**Avg**
1993-94	Hull	QMJHL	32	....	....	....	1708	118	2	4.15	6	0	2	158	14	0	5.32
1994-95	Hull	QMJHL	30	14	12	1	1525	118	0	4.64	1	0	0	20	1	0	3.00
1995-96	Drummondville	QMJHL	8	4	4	0	435	28	0	3.86	....	....	....	....	....	....	....
	Halifax	QMJHL	15	6	9	0	755	50	0	3.97	1	0	0	....	....	....	10.70

SCHAFER, PAXTON BOS.

Goaltender. Catches left. 5'9", 152 lbs. Born, Medicine Hat, Alta., February 26, 1976.
(Boston's 3rd choice, 47th overall, in 1995 Entry Draft).

			Regular Season								Playoffs						
Season	**Club**	**Lea**	**GP**	**W**	**L**	**T**	**Mins**	**GA**	**SO**	**Avg**	**GP**	**W**	**L**	**Mins**	**GA**	**SO**	**Avg**
1993-94	Medicine Hat	WHL	19	6	9	1	909	67	0	4.42	....	....	....	....	....	....	....
1994-95a	Medicine Hat	WHL	61	32	26	2	3519	185	0	3.15	5	1	4	339	18	0	3.19
1995-96	Medicine Hat	WHL	60	24	30	3	3256	200	1	3.69	5	1	4	251	25	0	5.98

a WHL East First All-Star Team (1995)

SCHWAB, COREY (SHWAHB) T.B.

Goaltender. Catches left. 6', 180 lbs. Born, North Battleford, Sask., November 4, 1970.
(New Jersey's 12th choice, 200th overall, in 1990 Entry Draft).

			Regular Season								Playoffs						
Season	**Club**	**Lea**	**GP**	**W**	**L**	**T**	**Mins**	**GA**	**SO**	**Avg**	**GP**	**W**	**L**	**Mins**	**GA**	**SO**	**Avg**
1988-89	Seattle	WHL	10	2	2	0	386	31	0	4.82	....	....	....	....	....	....	....
1989-90	Seattle	WHL	27	15	2	1	1150	69	1	3.60	3	0	0	49	2	0	2.45
1990-91	Seattle	WHL	*58	32	18	3	*3289	224	0	4.09	6	1	5	382	25	0	3.93
1991-92	Utica	AHL	24	9	12	1	1322	95	0	4.31	....	....	....	....	....	....	....
	Cincinnati	ECHL	8	6	0	1	450	31	0	4.13	9	6	3	540	29	0	3.22
1992-93	Utica	AHL	40	18	16	5	2387	169	*2	4.25	1	0	1	59	6	0	6.10
	Cincinnati	IHL	3	1	2	0	185	17	0	5.51	....	....	....	....	....	....	....
1993-94	Albany	AHL	51	27	21	3	3058	184	0	3.61	5	1	4	298	20	0	4.02
1994-95abc	Albany	AHL	45	25	10	9	2711	117	3	*2.59	7	6	1	425	19	0	2.68
1995-96	**New Jersey**	**NHL**	**10**	**0**	**3**	**0**	**331**	**12**	**0**	**2.18**	....	....	....	....	....	....	....
	Albany	AHL	5	3	2	0	299	13	0	2.61	....	....	....	....	....	....	....
	NHL Totals		**10**	**0**	**3**	**0**	**331**	**12**	**0**	**2.18**	....	....	....	....	....	....	....

a AHL Second All-Star Team (1995)
b Shared Harry "Hap" Holmes Memorial Trophy (fewest goals against - AHL) with Mike Dunham (1995)
c Shared Jack A. Butterfield Trophy (Playoff MVP - AHL) with Mike Dunham (1995)

Traded to **Tampa Bay** by **New Jersey** for Jeff Reese, Chicago's second round choice (previously acquired by Tampa Bay — New Jersey selected Pierre Dagenais) in 1996 Entry Draft and Tampa Bay's eighth round choice (Jason Bertsch) in 1996 Entry Draft, June 22, 1996.

SELIGER, MARC (ZEH-lih-gehr) WSH.

Goaltender. Catches left. 5'11", 165 lbs. Born, Rosenheim, Germany, May 1, 1974.
(Washington's 9th choice, 251st overall, in 1993 Entry Draft).

			Regular Season								Playoffs						
Season	**Club**	**Lea**	**GP**	**W**	**L**	**T**	**Mins**	**GA**	**SO**	**Avg**	**GP**	**W**	**L**	**Mins**	**GA**	**SO**	**Avg**
1992-93	Rosenheim	Ger.	42	....	....	....	1264	75	1	3.56	....	....	....	....	....	....	....
1993-94	Rosenheim	Ger.	27	....	....	....	....	....	....	....	....	....	....	....	....	....	....
1994-95	Rosenheim	Ger.	34	....	....	....	1859	....	3	....	7	....	....	428	31	....	4.34
1995-96	Frankfurt	Ger.	15	....	....	....	858	53	....	3.70	....	....	....	....	....	....	....

SHEPARD, KEN — NYR

Goaltender. Catches left. 5'10", 192 lbs. Born, Toronto, Ont., January 20, 1974.
(NY Rangers' 10th choice, 216th overall, in 1993 Entry Draft).

			Regular Season								Playoffs						
Season	Club	Lea	GP	W	L	T	Mins	GA	SO	Avg	GP	W	L	Mins	GA	SO	Avg
1991-92	Oshawa	OHL	7	1	2	0	265	16	1	3.62	1	0	0	2	0	0	0.00
1992-93	Oshawa	OHL	31	12	7	4	1483	86	0	3.48	11	3	7	512	34	0	3.98
1993-94	Oshawa	OHL	45	20	15	5	2383	157	0	3.95	5	1	4	309	18	0	3.50
1994-95	Oshawa	OHL	42	24	11	3	2404	128	2	3.19	5	1	4	299	26	0	5.22
1995-96	Binghamton	AHL	14	6	4	2	726	38	1	3.14	1	0	0	38	2	0	3.13
	Charlotte	ECHL	17	10	4	1	952	50	0	3.15	8	6	1	374	18	0	2.89

SHIELDS, STEVE — BUF.

Goaltender. Catches left. 6'3", 210 lbs. Born, Toronto, Ont., July 19, 1972.
(Buffalo's 5th choice, 101st overall, in 1991 Entry Draft).

			Regular Season								Playoffs						
Season	Club	Lea	GP	W	L	T	Mins	GA	SO	Avg	GP	W	L	Mins	GA	SO	Avg
1990-91	U. of Michigan	CCHA	37	26	6	3	1963	106	0	3.24	....	....	....	....	....	....	....
1991-92	U. of Michigan	CCHA	*37	*27	7	2	*2090	99	1	2.84	....	....	....	....	....	....	....
1992-93ab	U. of Michigan	CCHA	*39	*30	6	2	2027	75	2	*2.22	....	....	....	....	....	....	....
1993-94ab	U. of Michigan	CCHA	36	*28	6	1	1961	87	0	2.66	....	....	....	....	....	....	....
1994-95	Rochester	AHL	13	3	8	0	673	53	0	4.72	1	0	0	20	3	0	9.00
	S. Carolina	ECHL	21	11	5	2	1157	52	2	2.69	3	0	2	144	11	0	4.58
1995-96	**Buffalo**	**NHL**	**2**	**1**	**0**	**0**	**75**	**4**	**0**	**3.20**	....	....	....	....	....	....	....
	Rochester	AHL	43	20	17	2	2357	140	1	3.56	*19	*15	3	*1127	47	1	2.50
	NHL Totals		**2**	**1**	**0**	**0**	**75**	**4**	**0**	**3.20**	....	....	....	....	....	....	....

a CCHA First All-Star Team (1993, 1994)
b NCAA West Second All-American Team (1993, 1994)

SHTALENKOV, MIKHAIL — (shtuh-LEHN-kahf, mihk-HIGHL) ANA.

Goaltender. Catches left. 6'2", 180 lbs. Born, Moscow, USSR, October 20, 1965.
(Anaheim's 5th choice, 108th overall, in 1993 Entry Draft).

			Regular Season								Playoffs						
Season	Club	Lea	GP	W	L	T	Mins	GA	SO	Avg	GP	W	L	Mins	GA	SO	Avg
1986-87a	Moscow D'amo	USSR	17	....	....	....	893	36	1	2.41	....	....	....	....	....	....	....
1987-88	Moscow D'amo	USSR	25	....	....	....	1302	72	1	3.31	....	....	....	....	....	....	....
1988-89	Moscow D'amo	USSR	4	....	....	....	80	3	0	2.25	....	....	....	....	....	....	....
1989-90	Moscow D'amo	USSR	6	....	....	....	20	1	0	3.00	....	....	....	....	....	....	....
1990-91	Moscow D'amo	USSR	31	....	....	....	1568	56	2	2.14	....	....	....	....	....	....	....
1991-92	Moscow D'amo	CIS	27	....	....	....	1268	45	1	2.12	....	....	....	....	....	....	....
1992-93b	Milwaukee	IHL	47	26	14	5	2669	135	2	3.03	3	1	2	209	11	0	3.16
1993-94	**Anaheim**	**NHL**	**10**	**3**	**4**	**1**	**543**	**24**	**0**	**2.65**	....	....	....	....	....	....	....
	San Diego	IHL	28	15	11	2	1616	93	0	3.45	....	....	....	....	....	....	....
1994-95	**Anaheim**	**NHL**	**18**	**4**	**7**	**1**	**810**	**49**	**0**	**3.63**	....	....	....	....	....	....	....
1995-96	**Anaheim**	**NHL**	**30**	**7**	**16**	**3**	**1637**	**85**	**0**	**3.12**	....	....	....	....	....	....	....
	NHL Totals		**58**	**14**	**27**	**5**	**2990**	**158**	**0**	**3.17**	....	....	....	....	....	....	....

a Soviet Rookie of the Year (1987)
b Won Garry F. Longman Memorial Trophy (Top Rookie - IHL) (1993)

SHULMISTRA, RICHARD

Goaltender. Catches right. 6'2", 186 lbs. Born, Sudbury, Ont., April 1, 1971.
(Quebec's 1st choice, 4th overall, in 1992 Supplemental Draft).

			Regular Season								Playoffs						
Season	Club	Lea	GP	W	L	T	Mins	GA	SO	Avg	GP	W	L	Mins	GA	SO	Avg
1990-91	Miami-Ohio	CCHA	20	2	12	2	920	80	0	5.21	....	....	....	....	....	....	....
1991-92	Miami-Ohio	CCHA	19	3	5	2	850	67	0	4.72	....	....	....	....	....	....	....
1992-93a	Miami-Ohio	CCHA	33	22	6	4	1949	88	1	2.71	....	....	....	....	....	....	....
1993-94	Miami-Ohio	CCHA	27	13	12	1	1521	74	0	2.92	....	....	....	....	....	....	....
1994-95	Cornwall	AHL	20	4	9	2	937	58	0	3.71	8	4	3	446	22	0	2.95
1995-96	Cornwall	AHL	36	9	18	2	1844	100	0	3.25	1	0	0	9	1	0	6.76

a CCHA Second All-Star Team (1993)

SIDORKIEWICZ, PETER — (sih-DOHR-kuh-vihch) N.J.

Goaltender. Catches left. 5'9", 180 lbs. Born, Dabrowa Bialostocka, Pol., June 29, 1963.
(Washington's 5th choice, 91st overall, in 1981 Entry Draft).

			Regular Season								Playoffs						
Season	Club	Lea	GP	W	L	T	Mins	GA	SO	Avg	GP	W	L	Mins	GA	SO	Avg
1980-81	Oshawa	OHA	7	3	3	0	308	24	0	4.68	5	2	2	266	20	0	4.52
1981-82	Oshawa	OHL	29	14	11	1	1553	123	*2	4.75	1	0	0	13	1	0	4.62
1982-83	Oshawa	OHL	60	36	20	3	3536	213	0	3.61	17	15	1	1020	60	0	3.53
1983-84	Oshawa	OHL	52	28	21	1	2966	250	1	4.15	7	3	4	420	27	*1	3.86
1984-85	Binghamton	AHL	45	31	9	5	2691	137	3	3.05	8	4	4	481	31	0	3.87
	Fort Wayne	IHL	10	4	4	2	590	43	0	4.37	....	....	....	....	....	....	....
1985-86	Binghamton	AHL	49	21	22	3	2819	150	2	*3.19	4	1	3	235	12	0	3.06
1986-87a	Binghamton	AHL	57	23	16	0	3304	161	4	2.92	13	6	7	794	36	0	*2.72
1987-88	**Hartford**	**NHL**	**1**	**0**	**1**	**0**	**60**	**6**	**0**	**6.00**	....	....	....	....	....	....	....
	Binghamton	AHL	42	19	17	3	2345	144	0	3.68	3	0	2	147	8	0	3.27
1988-89b	**Hartford**	**NHL**	**44**	**22**	**18**	**4**	**2635**	**133**	**4**	**3.03**	**2**	**0**	**2**	**124**	**8**	**0**	**3.87**
1989-90	**Hartford**	**NHL**	**46**	**19**	**19**	**7**	**2703**	**161**	**1**	**3.57**	**7**	**3**	**4**	**429**	**23**	**0**	**3.22**
1990-91	**Hartford**	**NHL**	**52**	**21**	**22**	**7**	**2953**	**164**	**1**	**3.33**	**6**	**2**	**4**	**359**	**24**	**0**	**4.01**
1991-92	**Hartford**	**NHL**	**35**	**9**	**19**	**6**	**1995**	**111**	**2**	**3.34**	....	....	....	....	....	....	....
1992-93	**Ottawa**	**NHL**	**64**	**8**	**46**	**3**	**3388**	**250**	**0**	**4.43**	....	....	....	....	....	....	....
1993-94	**New Jersey**	**NHL**	**3**	**0**	**3**	**0**	**130**	**6**	**0**	**2.77**	....	....	....	....	....	....	....
	Albany	AHL	15	6	7	2	907	60	0	3.97	....	....	....	....	....	....	....
	Fort Wayne	IHL	11	6	3	0	591	27	*2	2.74	*18	10	8	*1054	59	*1	3.36
1994-95	Fort Wayne	IHL	16	8	6	1	941	58	1	3.70	3	1	2	144	12	0	5.00
1995-96	Albany	AHL	32	19	7	5	1809	89	3	2.95	1	0	1	59	3	0	3.06
	NHL Totals		**245**	**79**	**128**	**27**	**13864**	**831**	**8**	**3.60**	**15**	**5**	**10**	**912**	**55**	**0**	**3.62**

a AHL Second All-Star Team (1987)
b NHL All-Rookie Team (1989)

Played in NHL All-Star Game (1993)

Traded to **Hartford** by **Washington** with Dean Evason for David Jensen, March 12, 1985. Claimed by **Ottawa** from **Hartford** in Expansion Draft, June 18, 1992. Traded to **New Jersey** by **Ottawa** with future considerations (Mike Peluso, June 26, 1993) for Craig Billington, Troy Mallette and New Jersey's fourth round choice (Cosmo Dupaul) in 1993 Entry Draft, June 20, 1993.

SMANGS, HENRIK — (SMOHNGS) PHO.

Goaltender. Catches left. 5'11", 174 lbs. Born, Leksand, Sweden, January 19, 1976.
(Winnipeg's 9th choice, 212th overall, in 1994 Entry Draft).

			Regular Season								Playoffs						
Season	Club	Lea	GP	W	L	T	Mins	GA	SO	Avg	GP	W	L	Mins	GA	SO	Avg
1994-95	Leksand	Swe. Jr.					UNAVAILABLE										
1995-96	Leksand	Swe. Jr.					UNAVAILABLE										

SNOW, GARTH — PHI.

Goaltender. Catches left. 6'3", 200 lbs. Born, Wrentham, MA, July 28, 1969.
(Quebec's 6th choice, 114th overall, in 1987 Entry Draft).

			Regular Season								Playoffs						
Season	Club	Lea	GP	W	L	T	Mins	GA	SO	Avg	GP	W	L	Mins	GA	SO	Avg
1988-89	U. of Maine	H.E.	5	2	2	0	241	14	1	3.49	....	....	....	....	....	....	....
1989-90									DID NOT PLAY								
1990-91	U. of Maine	H.E.	25	*18	4	0	1290	64	2	2.98	....	....	....	....	....	....	....
1991-92a	U. of Maine	H.E.	31	*25	4	2	1792	73	*2	*2.44	....	....	....	....	....	....	....
1992-93b	U. of Maine	H.E.	23	*21	0	1	1210	42	1	*2.08	....	....	....	....	....	....	....
1993-94	U.S. National	....	23	13	5	3	1324	71	1	3.22	....	....	....	....	....	....	....
	U.S. Olympic	....	5	....	....	....	299	17	0	3.41	....	....	....	....	....	....	....
	Quebec	**NHL**	**5**	**3**	**2**	**0**	**279**	**16**	**0**	**3.44**	....	....	....	....	....	....	....
	Cornwall	AHL	16	6	5	3	927	51	0	3.30	13	8	5	790	42	0	3.19
1994-95	Cornwall	AHL	*62	*32	20	7	*3558	162	3	2.73	8	4	3	402	14	*2	*2.09
	Quebec	**NHL**	**2**	**1**	**1**	**0**	**119**	**11**	**0**	**5.55**	**1**	**0**	**0**	**9**	**1**	**0**	**6.67**
1995-96	**Philadelphia**	**NHL**	**26**	**12**	**8**	**4**	**1437**	**69**	**0**	**2.88**	**1**	**0**	**0**	**1**	**0**	**0**	**0.00**
	NHL Totals		**33**	**16**	**11**	**4**	**1835**	**96**	**0**	**3.14**	**2**	**0**	**0**	**10**	**1**	**0**	**6.00**

a Hockey East Second All-Star Team (1992)
b NCAA Final Four All-Tournament Team (1993)

Traded to **Philadelphia** by **Colorado** for Philadelphia's third (later traded to Washington — Washington selected Shawn McNeil) and sixth (Kai Fischer) round choices in 1996 Entry Draft, July 12, 1995.

SODERSTROM, TOMMY — (SAH-duhr-struhm) NYI

Goaltender. Catches left. 5'7", 157 lbs. Born, Stockholm, Sweden, July 17, 1969.
(Philadelphia's 14th choice, 214th overall, in 1990 Entry Draft).

			Regular Season								Playoffs						
Season	Club	Lea	GP	W	L	T	Mins	GA	SO	Avg	GP	W	L	Mins	GA	SO	Avg
1989-90	Djurgarden	Swe.	4	....	....	....	240	14	0	3.50	....	....	....	....	....	....	....
1990-91	Djurgarden	Swe.	39	....	....	....	2340	104	3	2.67	7	....	....	423	10	2	1.42
1991-92	Djurgarden	Swe.	39	15	8	11	2340	109	4	2.79	10	....	....	635	28	0	2.65
1992-93	**Philadelphia**	**NHL**	**44**	**20**	**17**	**6**	**2512**	**143**	**5**	**3.42**	....	....	....	....	....	....	....
	Hershey	AHL	7	4	1	0	373	15	0	2.41	....	....	....	....	....	....	....
1993-94	**Philadelphia**	**NHL**	**34**	**6**	**18**	**4**	**1736**	**116**	**2**	**4.01**	....	....	....	....	....	....	....
	Hershey	AHL	9	3	4	1	461	37	0	4.81	....	....	....	....	....	....	....
1994-95	**NY Islanders**	**NHL**	**26**	**8**	**12**	**3**	**1350**	**70**	**1**	**3.11**	....	....	....	....	....	....	....
1995-96	**NY Islanders**	**NHL**	**51**	**11**	**22**	**6**	**2590**	**167**	**2**	**3.87**	....	....	....	....	....	....	....
	NHL Totals		**155**	**45**	**69**	**19**	**8188**	**496**	**10**	**3.63**	....	....	....	....	....	....	....

Traded to **NY Islanders** by **Philadelphia** for Ron Hextall and NY Islanders' sixth round choice (Dmitry Tertyshny) in 1995 Entry Draft, September 22, 1994.

SOUCY, CHRISTIAN — (SOO-see)

Goaltender. Catches left. 5'11", 160 lbs. Born, Gatineau, Que., September 14, 1970.

			Regular Season								Playoffs						
Season	Club	Lea	GP	W	L	T	Mins	GA	SO	Avg	GP	W	L	Mins	GA	SO	Avg
1991-92	Vermont	ECAC	*30	15	11	3	*1783	81	0	2.83	....	....	....	....	....	....	....
1992-93a	Vermont	ECAC	29	11	15	3	1708	90	1	3.16	....	....	....	....	....	....	....
1993-94	**Chicago**	**NHL**	**1**	**0**	**0**	**0**	**3**	**0**	**0**	**0.00**	....	....	....	....	....	....	....
	Indianapolis	IHL	46	14	25	1	2302	159	1	4.14	....	....	....	....	....	....	....
1994-95	Indianapolis	IHL	42	15	17	5	2216	148	0	4.01	....	....	....	....	....	....	....
1995-96	Fort Worth	CHL	5	3	2	0	300	19	0	3.80	....	....	....	....	....	....	....
	Jacksonville	ECHL	3	2	1	0	179	11	0	3.68	....	....	....	....	....	....	....
	Indianapolis	IHL	22	12	9	0	1198	62	0	3.11	....	....	....	....	....	....	....
	NHL Totals		**1**	**0**	**0**	**0**	**3**	**0**	**0**	**0.00**	....	....	....	....	....	....	....

a ECAC Second All-Star Team (1993)

Signed as a free agent by **Chicago**, June 21, 1993.

STAUBER, ROBB — (STAW-buhr) WSH.

Goaltender. Catches left. 5'11", 180 lbs. Born, Duluth, MN, November 25, 1967.
(Los Angeles' 5th choice, 107th overall, in 1986 Entry Draft).

			Regular Season								Playoffs						
Season	Club	Lea	GP	W	L	T	Mins	GA	SO	Avg	GP	W	L	Mins	GA	SO	Avg
1986-87	U. Minnesota	WCHA	20	13	5	0	1072	63	0	3.53	....	....	....	....	....	....	....
1987-88abc	U. Minnesota	WCHA	44	34	10	0	2621	119	5	2.72	....	....	....	....	....	....	....
1988-89d	U. Minnesota	WCHA	34	26	8	0	2024	82	0	2.43	....	....	....	....	....	....	....
1989-90	**Los Angeles**	**NHL**	**2**	**0**	**1**	**0**	**83**	**11**	**0**	**7.95**	....	....	....	....	....	....	....
	New Haven	AHL	14	6	6	2	851	43	0	3.03	5	2	3	302	24	0	4.77
1990-91	New Haven	AHL	33	13	16	4	1882	115	1	3.67	....	....	....	....	....	....	....
	Phoenix	IHL	4	1	2	0	160	11	0	4.13	....	....	....	....	....	....	....
1991-92	Phoenix	IHL	22	8	12	1	1242	80	0	3.86	....	....	....	....	....	....	....
1992-93	**Los Angeles**	**NHL**	**31**	**15**	**8**	**4**	**1735**	**111**	**0**	**3.84**	**4**	**3**	**1**	**240**	**16**	**0**	**4.00**
1993-94	**Los Angeles**	**NHL**	**22**	**4**	**11**	**5**	**1144**	**65**	**1**	**3.41**	....	....	....	....	....	....	....
	Phoenix	IHL	3	1	1	0	121	13	0	6.42	....	....	....	....	....	....	....
1994-95	**Los Angeles**	**NHL**	**1**	**0**	**0**	**0**	**16**	**2**	**0**	**7.50**	....	....	....	....	....	....	....
	Buffalo	**NHL**	**6**	**2**	**3**	**0**	**317**	**20**	**0**	**3.79**	....	....	....	....	....	....	....
1995-96	Rochester	AHL	16	6	7	1	833	49	0	3.53	....	....	....	....	....	....	....
	NHL Totals		**62**	**21**	**23**	**9**	**3295**	**209**	**1**	**3.81**	**4**	**3**	**1**	**240**	**16**	**0**	**4.00**

a Won Hobey Baker Memorial Award (Top U.S. Collegiate Player) (1988)
b NCAA West First All-American Team (1988)
c WCHA First All-Star Team (1988)
d WCHA Second All-Star Team (1989)

Traded to **Buffalo** by **Los Angeles** with Alexei Zhitnik, Charlie Huddy and Los Angeles' fifth round choice (Marian Menhart) in 1995 Entry Draft for Philippe Boucher, Denis Tsygurov and Grant Fuhr, February 14, 1995. Signed as a free agent by **Washington**, August 20, 1996.

STORR, JAMIE — (STOHR) L.A.

Goaltender. Catches left. 6', 170 lbs. Born, Brampton, Ont., December 28, 1975.
(Los Angeles' 1st choice, 7th overall, in 1994 Entry Draft).

			Regular Season								Playoffs						
Season	Club	Lea	GP	W	L	T	Mins	GA	SO	Avg	GP	W	L	Mins	GA	SO	Avg
1991-92	Owen Sound	OHL	34	11	16	1	1732	128	0	4.43	5	1	4	299	28	0	5.62
1992-93	Owen Sound	OHL	41	20	17	3	2362	180	0	4.57	8	4	4	454	35	0	4.63
1993-94a	Owen Sound	OHL	35	21	11	1	2004	120	1	3.59	9	4	5	547	44	0	4.83
1994-95	Owen Sound	OHL	17	5	9	2	977	64	0	3.93	....	....	....	....	....	....	....
	Los Angeles	**NHL**	**5**	**1**	**3**	**1**	**263**	**17**	**0**	**3.88**	....	....	....	....	....	....	....
	Windsor	OHL	4	3	1	0	241	8	1	1.99	10	6	3	520	34	1	3.92
1995-96	**Los Angeles**	**NHL**	**5**	**3**	**1**	**0**	**262**	**12**	**0**	**2.75**	....	....	....	....	....	....	....
	Phoenix	IHL	48	22	20	4	2711	139	2	3.08	2	1	1	118	4	1	2.03
	NHL Totals		**10**	**4**	**4**	**1**	**525**	**29**	**0**	**3.31**	....	....	....	....	....	....	....

a OHL First All-Star Team (1994)

SWANJORD, SCOTT — N.J.

Goaltender. Catches left. 6'4", 210 lbs. Born, Sioux Falls, SD, October 8, 1975.
(New Jersey's 11th choice, 259th overall, in 1994 Entry Draft).

			Regular Season								Playoffs						
Season	Club	Lea	GP	W	L	T	Mins	GA	SO	Avg	GP	W	L	Mins	GA	SO	Avg
1994-95	Sioux City	USHL	24	7	14	0	1206	70	0	3.48	....	....	....	....	....	....	....
1995-96	Providence	H.E.	2	1	1	0	85	8	....	5.63	....	....	....	....	....	....	....

TABARACCI, RICK (tab-uh-RA-chee) CGY.

Goaltender. Catches left. 6'1", 180 lbs. Born, Toronto, Ont., January 2, 1969.
(Pittsburgh's 2nd choice, 26th overall, in 1987 Entry Draft).

			Regular Season								Playoffs						
Season	**Club**	**Lea**	**GP**	**W**	**L**	**T**	**Mins**	**GA**	**SO**	**Avg**	**GP**	**W**	**L**	**Mins**	**GA**	**SO**	**Avg**
1986-87	Cornwall	OHL	59	23	32	3	3347	290	1	5.20	5	1	4	303	26	0	3.17
1987-88a	Cornwall	OHL	58	*33	18	6	3448	200	*3	3.48	11	5	6	642	37	0	3.46
	Muskegon	IHL	....	....	....	....	....	....	....	....	1	0	0	13	1	0	4.62
1988-89	**Pittsburgh**	**NHL**	**1**	**0**	**0**	**0**	**33**	**4**	**0**	**7.27**	....	....	....	....	....	....	....
b	Cornwall	OHL	50	24	20	5	2974	210	1	4.24	18	10	8	1080	65	*1	3.61
1989-90	Moncton	AHL	27	10	15	2	1580	107	2	4.06	....	....	....	....	....	....	....
	Fort Wayne	IHL	22	8	9	1	1064	73	0	4.12	3	1	2	159	19	0	7.17
1990-91	**Winnipeg**	**NHL**	**24**	**4**	**9**	**4**	**1093**	**71**	**1**	**3.90**	....	....	....	....	....	....	....
	Moncton	AHL	11	4	5	2	645	41	0	3.81	....	....	....	....	....	....	....
1991-92	**Winnipeg**	**NHL**	**18**	**6**	**7**	**3**	**966**	**52**	**0**	**3.23**	**7**	**3**	**4**	**387**	**26**	**0**	**4.03**
	Moncton	AHL	23	10	11	1	1313	80	0	3.66	....	....	....	....	....	....	....
1992-93	**Winnipeg**	**NHL**	**19**	**5**	**10**	**0**	**959**	**70**	**0**	**4.38**	....	....	....	....	....	....	....
	Moncton	AHL	5	2	1	2	290	18	0	3.72	....	....	....	....	....	....	....
	Washington	**NHL**	**6**	**3**	**2**	**0**	**343**	**10**	**2**	**1.75**	**4**	**1**	**3**	**304**	**14**	**0**	**2.76**
1993-94	**Washington**	**NHL**	**32**	**13**	**14**	**2**	**1770**	**91**	**2**	**3.08**	**2**	**0**	**2**	**111**	**6**	**0**	**3.24**
	Portland	AHL	3	3	0	0	176	8	0	2.72	....	....	....	....	....	....	....
1994-95	**Washington**	**NHL**	**8**	**1**	**3**	**2**	**394**	**16**	**0**	**2.44**	....	....	....	....	....	....	....
	Chicago	IHL	2	1	1	0	119	9	0	4.51	....	....	....	....	....	....	....
	Calgary	**NHL**	**5**	**2**	**0**	**1**	**202**	**5**	**0**	**1.49**	**1**	**0**	**0**	**19**	**0**	**0**	**0.00**
1995-96	**Calgary**	**NHL**	**43**	**19**	**16**	**3**	**2391**	**117**	**3**	**2.94**	**3**	**0**	**3**	**204**	**7**	**0**	**2.06**
	NHL Totals		**156**	**53**	**61**	**15**	**8151**	**436**	**8**	**3.21**	**17**	**4**	**12**	**1025**	**53**	**0**	**3.10**

a OHL First All-Star Team (1988)
b OHL Second All-Star Team (1989)

Traded to **Winnipeg** by **Pittsburgh** with Randy Cunneyworth and Dave McLlwain for Jim Kyte, Andrew McBain and Randy Gilhen, June 17, 1989. Traded to **Washington** by **Winnipeg** for Jim Hrivnak and Washington's second round choice (Alexei Budayev) in 1993 Entry Draft, March 22, 1993. Traded to **Calgary** by **Washington** for a conditional fifth round draft choice, April 7, 1995.

TALLAS, ROBBIE BOS.

Goaltender. Catches left. 6', 178 lbs. Born, Edmonton, Alta., March 20, 1973.

			Regular Season								Playoffs						
Season	**Club**	**Lea**	**GP**	**W**	**L**	**T**	**Mins**	**GA**	**SO**	**Avg**	**GP**	**W**	**L**	**Mins**	**GA**	**SO**	**Avg**
1991-92	Seattle	WHL	14	4	7	0	708	52	0	4.41	....	....	....	....	....	....	....
1992-93	Seattle	WHL	58	24	23	3	3151	194	2	3.69	5	1	4	333	18	0	3.24
1993-94	Seattle	WHL	51	23	21	3	2849	188	0	3.96	9	5	4	567	40	0	4.23
1994-95	Charlotte	ECHL	36	21	9	3	2011	114	0	3.40	....	....	....	....	....	....	....
	Providence	AHL	2	1	0	0	82	4	1	2.90	....	....	....	....	....	....	....
1995-96	**Boston**	**NHL**	**1**	**1**	**0**	**0**	**60**	**3**	**0**	**3.00**	....	....	....	....	....	....	....
	Providence	AHL	37	12	16	7	2136	117	1	3.29	2	0	2	135	9	0	4.01
	NHL Totals		**1**	**1**	**0**	**0**	**60**	**3**	**0**	**3.00**	....	....	....	....	....	....	....

Signed as a free agent by **Boston**, September 13, 1995.

TANNER, JOHN

Goaltender. Catches left. 6'3", 182 lbs. Born, Cambridge, Ont., March 17, 1971.
(Quebec's 4th choice, 54th overall, in 1989 Entry Draft).

			Regular Season								Playoffs						
Season	**Club**	**Lea**	**GP**	**W**	**L**	**T**	**Mins**	**GA**	**SO**	**Avg**	**GP**	**W**	**L**	**Mins**	**GA**	**SO**	**Avg**
1987-88a	Peterborough	OHL	26	18	4	3	1532	88	0	3.45	2	1	0	98	3	0	1.84
1988-89a	Peterborough	OHL	34	22	10	0	1923	107	2	*3.34	8	4	3	369	23	0	3.74
1989-90	**Quebec**	**NHL**	**1**	**0**	**1**	**0**	**60**	**3**	**0**	**3.00**	....	....	....	....	....	....	....
	Peterborough	OHL	18	6	8	2	1037	70	0	4.05	....	....	....	....	....	....	....
	London	OHL	19	12	5	1	1097	53	1	2.90	6	2	4	341	24	0	4.22
1990-91	**Quebec**	**NHL**	**6**	**1**	**3**	**1**	**228**	**16**	**0**	**4.21**	....	....	....	....	....	....	....
	London	OHL	7	3	3	1	427	29	0	4.07	....	....	....	....	....	....	....
	Sudbury	OHL	19	10	8	0	1043	60	0	3.45	5	1	4	274	21	0	4.60
1991-92	**Quebec**	**NHL**	**14**	**1**	**7**	**4**	**796**	**46**	**1**	**3.47**	....	....	....	....	....	....	....
	Halifax	AHL	12	6	5	1	672	29	2	2.59	....	....	....	....	....	....	....
	New Haven	AHL	16	7	6	2	908	57	0	3.77	....	....	....	....	....	....	....
1992-93	Halifax	AHL	51	20	18	7	2852	199	0	4.19	....	....	....	....	....	....	....
1993-94	Cornwall	AHL	38	14	15	4	2035	123	1	3.63	....	....	....	....	....	....	....
	San Diego	IHL	13	5	3	2	629	37	0	3.53	3	0	1	118	5	0	2.53
1994-95	Greensboro	ECHL	6	0	4	1	342	27	0	4.73	....	....	....	....	....	....	....
	San Diego	IHL	8	1	3	1	344	28	0	4.87	....	....	....	....	....	....	....
1995-96	Detroit	ColHL	2	1	0	0	112	8	0	4.27	....	....	....	....	....	....	....
	Muskegon	ColHL	2	0	2	0	89	8	0	5.38	....	....	....	....	....	....	....
	Rochester	AHL	10	3	6	1	579	38	0	3.94	....	....	....	....	....	....	....
	NHL Totals		**21**	**2**	**11**	**5**	**1084**	**65**	**1**	**3.60**	....	....	....	....	....	....	....

a Won Dave Pinkney Trophy (Top Team Goaltending, OHL) shared with Todd Bojcun (1988, 1989)

Traded to **Anaheim** by **Quebec** for Anaheim's fourth round choice (Tomi Kallio) in 1995 Entry Draft, February 20, 1994.

TERRERI, CHRIS (tuh-RAIR-ee) S.J.

Goaltender. Catches left. 5'8", 160 lbs. Born, Providence, RI, November 15, 1964.
(New Jersey's 3rd choice, 87th overall, in 1983 Entry Draft).

			Regular Season								Playoffs						
Season	**Club**	**Lea**	**GP**	**W**	**L**	**T**	**Mins**	**GA**	**SO**	**Avg**	**GP**	**W**	**L**	**Mins**	**GA**	**SO**	**Avg**
1982-83	Providence	ECAC	11	7	1	0	528	17	2	1.93	....	....	....	....	....	....	....
1983-84	Providence	ECAC	10	4	2	0	391	20	0	3.07	....	....	....	....	....	....	....
1984-85ab	Providence	H.E.	33	15	13	5	1956	116	1	3.35	....	....	....	....	....	....	....
1985-86	Providence	H.E.	22	6	16	0	1320	84	0	3.74	....	....	....	....	....	....	....
1986-87	**New Jersey**	**NHL**	**7**	**0**	**3**	**1**	**286**	**21**	**0**	**4.41**	....	....	....	....	....	....	....
	Maine	AHL	14	4	9	1	765	57	0	4.47	....	....	....	....	....	....	....
1987-88	Utica	AHL	7	5	1	0	399	18	0	2.71	....	....	....	....	....	....	....
	U.S. National	....	26	17	7	2	1430	81	0	3.40	....	....	....	....	....	....	....
	U.S. Olympic	....	3	1	1	0	128	14	0	6.56	....	....	....	....	....	....	....
1988-89	**New Jersey**	**NHL**	**8**	**0**	**4**	**2**	**402**	**18**	**0**	**2.69**	....	....	....	....	....	....	....
	Utica	AHL	39	20	15	3	2314	132	0	3.42	2	0	1	80	6	0	4.50
1989-90	**New Jersey**	**NHL**	**35**	**15**	**12**	**3**	**1931**	**110**	**0**	**3.42**	**4**	**2**	**2**	**238**	**13**	**0**	**3.28**
1990-91	**New Jersey**	**NHL**	**53**	**24**	**21**	**7**	**2970**	**144**	**1**	**2.91**	**7**	**3**	**4**	**428**	**21**	**0**	**2.94**
1991-92	**New Jersey**	**NHL**	**54**	**22**	**22**	**10**	**3186**	**169**	**1**	**3.18**	**7**	**3**	**3**	**386**	**23**	**0**	**3.58**
1992-93	**New Jersey**	**NHL**	**48**	**19**	**21**	**3**	**2672**	**151**	**2**	**3.39**	**4**	**1**	**3**	**219**	**17**	**0**	**4.66**
1993-94	**New Jersey**	**NHL**	**44**	**20**	**11**	**4**	**2340**	**106**	**2**	**2.72**	**4**	**3**	**0**	**200**	**9**	**0**	**2.70**
1994-95	**New Jersey**	**NHL**	**15**	**3**	**7**	**2**	**734**	**31**	**0**	**2.53**	**1**	**0**	**0**	**8**	**0**	**0**	**0.00** ♦
1995-96	**New Jersey**	**NHL**	**4**	**3**	**0**	**0**	**210**	**9**	**0**	**2.57**	....	....	....	....	....	....	....
	San Jose	**NHL**	**46**	**13**	**29**	**1**	**2516**	**155**	**0**	**3.70**	....	....	....	....	....	....	....
	NHL Totals		**314**	**119**	**130**	**33**	**17247**	**914**	**6**	**3.18**	**27**	**12**	**12**	**1479**	**83**	**0**	**3.37**

a Hockey East All-Star Team (1985)
b NCAA All-American Team (1985)

Traded to **San Jose** by **New Jersey** for San Jose's second round choice (later traded to Pittsburgh — Pittsburgh selected Pavel Skrbek) in 1996 Entry Draft, November 15, 1995.

THEODORE, JOSE (THEE-uh-dohr, joh-SAY) MTL.

Goaltender. Catches right. 5'11", 180 lbs. Born, Laval, Que., September 13, 1976.
(Montreal's 2nd choice, 44th overall, in 1994 Entry Draft).

			Regular Season								Playoffs						
Season	**Club**	**Lea**	**GP**	**W**	**L**	**T**	**Mins**	**GA**	**SO**	**Avg**	**GP**	**W**	**L**	**Mins**	**GA**	**SO**	**Avg**
1992-93	St-Jean	QMJHL	34	12	16	2	1776	112	0	3.78	3	0	2	175	11	0	3.77
1993-94	St-Jean	QMJHL	57	20	29	6	3225	194	0	3.61	5	1	4	296	18	0	3.65
1994-95	Hull	QMJHL	*58	*32	22	2	*3348	193	5	3.46	*21	*15	6	*1263	59	*1	2.80
	Fredericton	AHL	....	....	....	....	....	....	....	....	1	0	1	60	3	0	3.00
1995-96	**Montreal**	**NHL**	**1**	**0**	**0**	**0**	**9**	**1**	**0**	**6.67**	....	....	....	....	....	....	....
a	Hull	QMJHL	48	33	11	2	2807	158	0	3.38	5	2	3	....	....	....	4.01
	NHL Totals		**1**	**0**	**0**	**0**	**9**	**1**	**0**	**6.67**	....	....	....	....	....	....	....

a QMJHL Second All-Star Team (1996)

THIBAULT, JOCELYN (tee-BOW) MTL.

Goaltender. Catches left. 5'11", 170 lbs. Born, Montreal, Que., January 12, 1975.
(Quebec's 1st choice, 10th overall, in 1993 Entry Draft).

			Regular Season								Playoffs						
Season	**Club**	**Lea**	**GP**	**W**	**L**	**T**	**Mins**	**GA**	**SO**	**Avg**	**GP**	**W**	**L**	**Mins**	**GA**	**SO**	**Avg**
1991-92	Trois Rivieres	QMJHL	30	14	7	1	1496	77	0	3.09	3	1	1	110	4	0	2.19
1992-93abc	Sherbrooke	QMJHL	56	34	14	5	3190	159	3	2.99	15	9	6	882	57	0	3.87
1993-94	**Quebec**	**NHL**	**29**	**8**	**13**	**3**	**1504**	**83**	**0**	**3.31**	....	....	....	....	....	....	....
	Cornwall	AHL	4	4	0	0	240	9	1	2.25	....	....	....	....	....	....	....
1994-95	Sherbrooke	QMJHL	13	6	6	1	776	38	1	2.94	....	....	....	....	....	....	....
	Quebec	**NHL**	**18**	**12**	**2**	**2**	**898**	**35**	**1**	**2.34**	**3**	**1**	**2**	**148**	**8**	**0**	**3.24**
1995-96	**Colorado**	**NHL**	**10**	**3**	**4**	**2**	**558**	**28**	**0**	**3.01**	....	....	....	....	....	....	....
	Montreal	**NHL**	**40**	**23**	**13**	**3**	**2334**	**110**	**3**	**2.83**	**6**	**2**	**4**	**311**	**18**	**0**	**3.47**
	NHL Totals		**97**	**46**	**32**	**10**	**5294**	**256**	**4**	**2.90**	**9**	**3**	**6**	**459**	**26**	**0**	**3.40**

a QMJHL First All-Star Team (1993)
b Canadian Major Junior First All-Star Team (1993)
c Canadian Major Junior Goaltender of the Year (1993)

Traded to **Montreal** by **Colorado** with Andrei Kovalenko and Martin Rucinsky for Patrick Roy and Mike Keane, December 6, 1995.

THOMAS, TIM COL.

Goaltender. Catches left. 5'11", 180 lbs. Born, Flint, MI, April 15, 1974.
(Quebec's 11th choice, 217th overall, in 1994 Entry Draft).

			Regular Season								Playoffs						
Season	**Club**	**Lea**	**GP**	**W**	**L**	**T**	**Mins**	**GA**	**SO**	**Avg**	**GP**	**W**	**L**	**Mins**	**GA**	**SO**	**Avg**
1993-94	U. of Vermont	ECAC	*33	15	12	6	1864	94	0	3.03	....	....	....	....	....	....	....
1994-95ab	U. of Vermont	ECAC	34	18	13	2	2010	90	*4	*2.69	....	....	....	....	....	....	....
1995-96ac	U. of Vermont	ECAC	37	*26	7	4	*2254	88	*3	*2.34	....	....	....	....	....	....	....

a ECAC First All-Star Team (1995, 1996)
b NCAA East Second All-American Team (1995)
c NCAA East First All-American Team (1996)

TKACHENKO, SERGEI (kuh-CHEHN-koh, SAIR-gay) VAN.

Goaltender. Catches left. 6'2", 198 lbs. Born, Kiev, USSR, June 6, 1971.
(Vancouver's 9th choice, 280th overall, in 1993 Entry Draft).

			Regular Season								Playoffs						
Season	**Club**	**Lea**	**GP**	**W**	**L**	**T**	**Mins**	**GA**	**SO**	**Avg**	**GP**	**W**	**L**	**Mins**	**GA**	**SO**	**Avg**
1989-90	Sokol Kiev	USSR	1	....	....	....	10	0	0	0.00	....	....	....	....	....	....	....
1990-91	Sokol Kiev	USSR	14	....	....	....	220	14	0	3.37	....	....	....	....	....	....	....
1991-92	Sokol Kiev	CIS	24	....	....	....	1305	91	0	4.18	....	....	....	....	....	....	....
1992-93	Brantford	ColHL	4	0	1	0	96	11	0	6.88	....	....	....	....	....	....	....
	Hamilton	AHL	1	1	0	0	60	3	0	3.00	....	....	....	....	....	....	....
1993-94	Hamilton	AHL	2	0	1	1	125	9	0	4.32	....	....	....	....	....	....	....
	Columbus	ECHL	34	18	7	4	1884	129	0	4.11	4	1	2	182	16	0	5.27
1994-95	Syracuse	AHL	2	0	2	0	118	9	0	4.57	....	....	....	....	....	....	....
	S. Carolina	ECHL	16	7	7	1	868	47	0	3.25	....	....	....	....	....	....	....
	Birmingham	ECHL	6	2	4	0	359	25	0	4.17	....	....	....	....	....	....	....
1995-96	Oklahoma City	CHL	16	12	3	1	944	37	1	*2.35	1	0	1	63	5	0	4.73
	Syracuse	AHL	14	2	8	1	733	52	2	4.26	1	0	1	60	5	0	5.00
	Raleigh	ECHL	3	0	2	1	179	14	0	4.69	....	....	....	....	....	....	....

TORCHIA, MIKE (TOR-chee-ah) ANA.

Goaltender. Catches left. 5'11", 215 lbs. Born, Toronto, Ont., February 23, 1972.
(Minnesota's 2nd choice, 74th overall, in 1991 Entry Draft).

			Regular Season								Playoffs						
Season	**Club**	**Lea**	**GP**	**W**	**L**	**T**	**Mins**	**GA**	**SO**	**Avg**	**GP**	**W**	**L**	**Mins**	**GA**	**SO**	**Avg**
1988-89	Kitchener	OHL	30	14	9	4	1472	102	0	4.02	2	0	2	126	8	0	3.81
1989-90ab	Kitchener	OHL	40	25	11	2	2280	136	1	3.58	*17	*11	6	*1023	60	0	3.52
1990-91	Kitchener	OHL	57	25	24	7	*3317	219	0	3.95	6	2	4	382	30	0	4.71
1991-92	Kitchener	OHL	*55	25	24	3	*3042	203	1	4.00	14	7	7	900	47	0	3.13
1992-93	Cdn. National	....	5	5	0	0	300	11	1	2.20	....	....	....	....	....	....	....
	Kalamazoo	IHL	48	19	17	9	2729	173	0	3.80	....	....	....	....	....	....	....
1993-94	Kalamazoo	IHL	43	23	12	2	2168	133	0	3.68	4	1	3	221	14	*1	3.80
1994-95	Kalamazoo	IHL	41	19	14	5	2140	106	*3	2.97	6	0	4	257	17	0	3.97
	Dallas	**NHL**	**6**	**3**	**2**	**1**	**327**	**18**	**0**	**3.30**	....	....	....	....	....	....	....
1995-96	Portland	AHL	12	2	6	2	577	46	0	4.79	....	....	....	....	....	....	....
	Hampton Rds.	ECHL	5	2	2	0	260	17	0	3.92	....	....	....	....	....	....	....
	Michigan	IHL	1	1	0	0	60	1	0	1.00	....	....	....	....	....	....	....
	Orlando	IHL	7	3	1	1	341	17	0	2.99	....	....	....	....	....	....	....
	Baltimore	AHL	5	2	1	1	256	18	0	4.21	1	0	0	40	0	0	0.00
	NHL Totals		**6**	**3**	**2**	**1**	**327**	**18**	**0**	**3.30**	....	....	....	....	....	....	....

a Memorial Cup All-Star Team (1990)
b Won Hap Emms Memorial Memorial Trophy (Memorial Cup Tournament Top Goaltender) (1990)

Traded to **Washington** by **Dallas** for future considerations, July 14, 1995. Traded to **Anaheim** by **Washington** for Todd Krygier, March 8, 1996.

TOSKALA, VESA (TAWS-kah-lah) S.J.

Goaltender. Catches left. 5'9", 172 lbs. Born, Tampere, Finland, May 20, 1977.
(San Jose's 4th choice, 90th overall, in 1995 Entry Draft).

			Regular Season								Playoffs						
Season	**Club**	**Lea**	**GP**	**W**	**L**	**T**	**Mins**	**GA**	**SO**	**Avg**	**GP**	**W**	**L**	**Mins**	**GA**	**SO**	**Avg**
1994-95	Ilves	Fin. Jr.	17	....	....	....	956	36	....	2.26	....	....	....	....	....	....	....
1995-96	Ilves	Fin. Jr.	3	....	....	....	180	3	....	1.00	....	....	....	....	....	....	....
	Koo-Vee	Fin. 2	2	....	....	....	119	5	....	2.51	....	....	....	....	....	....	....
	Ilves	Fin.	37	....	....	....	2073	109	1	3.16	2	....	....	78	11	....	8.49

TREFILOV, ANDREI (TREH-fee-lahf) BUF.

Goaltender. Catches left. 6', 180 lbs. Born, Kirovo-Chepetsk, USSR, August 31, 1969.
(Calgary's 14th choice, 261st overall, in 1991 Entry Draft).

			Regular Season								Playoffs						
Season	Club	Lea	GP	W	L	T	Mins	GA	SO	Avg	GP	W	L	Mins	GA	SO	Avg
1990-91	Moscow D'amo	USSR	20	....	....	....	1070	36	0	2.01	....	....	....	....	....	....	....
1991-92	Moscow D'amo	CIS	28	....	....	....	1326	35	0	1.58	....	....	....	....	....	....	....
1992-93	**Calgary**	**NHL**	**1**	**0**	**0**	**1**	**65**	**5**	**0**	**4.62**	....	....	....	....	....	....	....
	Salt Lake	IHL	44	23	17	3	2536	135	0	3.19	....	....	....	....	....	....	....
1993-94	**Calgary**	**NHL**	**11**	**3**	**4**	**2**	**623**	**26**	**2**	**2.50**	....	....	....	....	....	....	....
	Saint John	AHL	28	10	10	7	1629	93	0	3.42	....	....	....	....	....	....	....
1994-95	**Calgary**	**NHL**	**6**	**0**	**3**	**0**	**236**	**16**	**0**	**4.07**	....	....	....	....	....	....	....
	Saint John	AHL	7	1	5	1	383	20	0	3.13	....	....	....	....	....	....	....
1995-96	**Buffalo**	**NHL**	**22**	**8**	**8**	**1**	**1094**	**64**	**0**	**3.51**	....	....	....	....	....	....	....
	Rochester	AHL	5	4	1	0	299	13	0	2.61	....	....	....	....	....	....	....
	NHL Totals		**40**	**11**	**15**	**4**	**2018**	**111**	**2**	**3.30**	....	....	....	....	....	....	....

Signed as a free agent by **Buffalo**, July 11, 1995.

TUGNUTT, RON OTT.

Goaltender. Catches left. 5'11", 155 lbs. Born, Scarborough, Ont., October 22, 1967.
(Quebec's 4th choice, 81st overall, in 1986 Entry Draft).

			Regular Season								Playoffs						
Season	Club	Lea	GP	W	L	T	Mins	GA	SO	Avg	GP	W	L	Mins	GA	SO	Avg
1984-85	Peterborough	OHL	18	7	4	2	938	59	0	3.77	....	....	....	....	....	....	....
1985-86	Peterborough	OHL	26	18	7	0	1543	74	1	2.88	3	2	0	133	6	0	2.71
1986-87a	Peterborough	OHL	31	21	7	2	1891	88	2	*2.79	6	3	3	374	21	1	3.37
1987-88	**Quebec**	**NHL**	**6**	**2**	**3**	**0**	**284**	**16**	**0**	**3.38**	....	....	....	....	....	....	....
	Fredericton	AHL	34	20	9	4	1964	118	1	3.60	4	1	2	204	11	0	3.24
1988-89	**Quebec**	**NHL**	**26**	**10**	**10**	**3**	**1367**	**82**	**0**	**3.60**	....	....	....	....	....	....	....
	Halifax	AHL	24	14	7	2	1368	79	1	3.46	....	....	....	....	....	....	....
1989-90	**Quebec**	**NHL**	**35**	**5**	**24**	**3**	**1978**	**152**	**0**	**4.61**	....	....	....	....	....	....	....
	Halifax	AHL	6	1	5	0	366	23	0	3.77	....	....	....	....	....	....	....
1990-91	**Quebec**	**NHL**	**56**	**12**	**29**	**10**	**3144**	**212**	**0**	**4.05**	....	....	....	....	....	....	....
	Halifax	AHL	2	0	1	0	100	8	0	4.80	....	....	....	....	....	....	....
1991-92	**Quebec**	**NHL**	**30**	**6**	**17**	**3**	**1583**	**106**	**1**	**4.02**	....	....	....	....	....	....	....
	Halifax	AHL	8	3	3	1	447	30	0	4.03	....	....	....	....	....	....	....
	Edmonton	**NHL**	**3**	**1**	**1**	**0**	**124**	**10**	**0**	**4.84**	**2**	**0**	**0**	**60**	**3**	**0**	**3.00**
1992-93	**Edmonton**	**NHL**	**26**	**9**	**12**	**2**	**1338**	**93**	**0**	**4.17**	....	....	....	....	....	....	....
1993-94	**Anaheim**	**NHL**	**28**	**10**	**15**	**1**	**1520**	**76**	**1**	**3.00**	....	....	....	....	....	....	....
	Montreal	**NHL**	**8**	**2**	**3**	**1**	**378**	**24**	**0**	**3.81**	**1**	**0**	**1**	**59**	**5**	**0**	**5.08**
1994-95	**Montreal**	**NHL**	**7**	**1**	**3**	**1**	**346**	**18**	**0**	**3.12**	....	....	....	....	....	....	....
1995-96	Portland	AHL	58	21	23	6	3068	171	2	3.34	13	7	6	782	36	1	2.76
	NHL Totals		**225**	**58**	**117**	**24**	**12062**	**789**	**2**	**3.92**	**3**	**0**	**1**	**119**	**8**	**0**	**4.03**

a OHL First All-Star Team (1987)

Traded to **Edmonton** by **Quebec** with Brad Zavisha for Martin Rucinsky, March 10, 1992. Claimed by **Anaheim** from **Edmonton** in Expansion Draft, June 24, 1993. Traded to **Montreal** by **Anaheim** for Stephan Lebeau, February 20, 1994. Signed as a free agent by **Ottawa**, August 14, 1996.

TURCO, MARTY DAL.

Goaltender. Catches left. 5'11", 175 lbs. Born, Sault Ste. Marie, Ont., August 13, 1975.
(Dallas' 4th choice, 124th overall, in 1994 Entry Draft).

			Regular Season								Playoffs						
Season	Club	Lea	GP	W	L	T	Mins	GA	SO	Avg	GP	W	L	Mins	GA	SO	Avg
1994-95	U. of Michigan	CCHA	37	*27	7	1	2063	95	1	2.76	....	....	....	....	....	....	....
1995-96	U. of Michigan	CCHA	*42	*34	7	1	*2335	84	*5	*2.16	....	....	....	....	....	....	....

TUREK, ROMAN (TOOR-ehk) DAL.

Goaltender. Catches right. 6'3", 193 lbs. Born, Pisek, Czechoslovakia, May 21, 1970.
(Minnesota's 6th choice, 113th overall, in 1990 Entry Draft

			Regular Season								Playoffs						
Season	Club	Lea	GP	W	L	T	Mins	GA	SO	Avg	GP	W	L	Mins	GA	SO	Avg
1990-91	Budejovice	Czech.	26	....	....	....	1244	98	0	4.70	....	....	....	....	....	....	....
1991-92	Budejovice	Czech.2	....	....	....	....	....	....	....	....	....	....	....	....	....	....	....
1992-93	Budejovice	Czech.	43	....	....	....	2555	121	....	2.84	....	....	....	....	....	....	....
1993-94	Budejovice	Czech.	44	....	....	....	2584	111	....	2.51	3	....	....	180	12	0	4.00
1994-95	Budejovice	Czech.	44	....	....	....	2587	119	....	2.76	9	....	....	498	25	....	3.01
1995-96	Nurnberg	Ger.	48	....	....	....	2787	154	....	3.31	5	....	....	338	14	....	2.48

VANBIESBROUCK, JOHN (van-BEES-bruhk) FLA.

Goaltender. Catches left. 5'8", 176 lbs. Born, Detroit, MI, September 4, 1963.
(NY Rangers' 5th choice, 72nd overall, in 1981 Entry Draft).

			Regular Season								Playoffs						
Season	Club	Lea	GP	W	L	T	Mins	GA	SO	Avg	GP	W	L	Mins	GA	SO	Avg
1980-81	S.S. Marie	OHA	56	31	16	1	2941	203	0	4.14	11	3	3	457	24	1	3.15
1981-82	**NY Rangers**	**NHL**	**1**	**1**	**0**	**0**	**60**	**1**	**0**	**1.00**	....	....	....	....	....	....	....
	S.S. Marie	OHL	31	12	12	2	1686	102	0	3.62	7	1	4	276	20	0	4.35
1982-83a	S.S. Marie	OHL	62	39	21	1	3471	209	0	3.61	16	7	6	944	56	*1	3.56
1983-84	**NY Rangers**	**NHL**	**3**	**2**	**1**	**0**	**180**	**10**	**0**	**3.33**	**1**	**0**	**0**	**1**	**0**	**0**	**0.00**
bcd	Tulsa	CHL	37	20	13	2	2153	124	*3	3.46	4	4	0	240	10	0	*2.50
1984-85	**NY Rangers**	**NHL**	**42**	**12**	**24**	**3**	**2358**	**166**	**1**	**4.22**	**1**	**0**	**0**	**20**	**0**	**0**	**0.00**
1985-86ef	**NY Rangers**	**NHL**	**61**	***31**	**21**	**5**	**3326**	**184**	**3**	**3.32**	**16**	**8**	**8**	**899**	**49**	***1**	**3.27**
1986-87	**NY Rangers**	**NHL**	**50**	**18**	**20**	**5**	**2656**	**161**	**0**	**3.64**	**4**	**1**	**3**	**195**	**11**	**1**	**3.38**
1987-88	**NY Rangers**	**NHL**	**56**	**27**	**22**	**7**	**3319**	**187**	**2**	**3.38**	....	....	....	....	....	....	....
1988-89	**NY Rangers**	**NHL**	**56**	**28**	**21**	**4**	**3207**	**197**	**0**	**3.69**	**2**	**0**	**1**	**107**	**6**	**0**	**3.36**
1989-90	**NY Rangers**	**NHL**	**47**	**19**	**19**	**7**	**2734**	**154**	**1**	**3.38**	**6**	**2**	**3**	**298**	**15**	**0**	**3.02**
1990-91	**NY Rangers**	**NHL**	**40**	**15**	**18**	**6**	**2257**	**126**	**3**	**3.35**	**1**	**0**	**0**	**52**	**1**	**0**	**1.15**
1991-92	**NY Rangers**	**NHL**	**45**	**27**	**13**	**3**	**2526**	**120**	**2**	**2.85**	**7**	**2**	**5**	**368**	**23**	**0**	**3.75**
1992-93	**NY Rangers**	**NHL**	**48**	**20**	**18**	**7**	**2757**	**152**	**4**	**3.31**	....	....	....	....	....	....	....
1993-94g	**Florida**	**NHL**	**57**	**21**	**25**	**11**	**3440**	**145**	**1**	**2.53**	....	....	....	....	....	....	....
1994-95	**Florida**	**NHL**	**37**	**14**	**15**	**4**	**2087**	**86**	**4**	**2.47**	....	....	....	....	....	....	....
1995-96	**Florida**	**NHL**	**57**	**26**	**20**	**7**	**3178**	**142**	**2**	**2.68**	***22**	**12**	**10**	**1332**	**50**	**1**	**2.25**
	NHL Totals		**600**	**261**	**237**	**69**	**34085**	**1831**	**23**	**3.22**	**60**	**25**	**30**	**3272**	**155**	**3**	**2.84**

a OHL Second All-Star Team (1983)
b CHL First All-Star Team (1984)
c Shared Terry Sawchuk Trophy (CHL's Leading Goaltender) with Ron Scott (1984)
d Shared Tommy Ivan Trophy (CHL's Most Valuable Player) with Bruce Affleck of Indianapolis (1984)
e Won Vezina Trophy (1986)
f NHL First All-Star Team (1986)
g NHL Second All-Star Team (1994)

Played in NHL All-Star Game (1994, 1996)

Traded to **Vancouver** by **NY Rangers** for future considerations (Doug Lidster, June 25, 1993), June 20, 1993. Claimed by **Florida** from **Vancouver** in Expansion Draft, June 24, 1993.

VEISOR, MIKE (VIGH-awr) ST.L.

Goaltender. Catches right. 6'2", 195 lbs. Born, Dallas, TX, December 7, 1972.
(St. Louis' 12th choice, 263rd overall, in 1991 Entry Draft).

			Regular Season								Playoffs						
Season	Club	Lea	GP	W	L	T	Mins	GA	SO	Avg	GP	W	L	Mins	GA	SO	Avg
1992-93	Northeastern	H.E.	30	8	19	1	1699	151	0	5.33	....	....	....	....	....	....	....
1993-94	Northeastern	H.E.	15	7	3	2	775	55	0	4.26	....	....	....	....	....	....	....
1994-95	Northeastern	H.E.	24	12	5	3	1289	73	0	3.41	....	....	....	....	....	....	....
1995-96	Northeastern	H.E.	21	5	11	3	1139	80	0	4.22	....	....	....	....	....	....	....

VERNON, MIKE DET.

Goaltender. Catches left. 5'9", 165 lbs. Born, Calgary, Alta., February 24, 1963.
(Calgary's 2nd choice, 56th overall, in 1981 Entry Draft).

			Regular Season								Playoffs						
Season	Club	Lea	GP	W	L	T	Mins	GA	SO	Avg	GP	W	L	Mins	GA	SO	Avg
1980-81	Calgary	WHL	59	33	17	1	3154	198	1	3.77	22	14	8	1271	82	1	3.87
1981-82a	Calgary	WHL	42	22	14	2	2329	143	3	3.68	9	5	4	527	30	0	3.42
	Oklahoma City	CHL	....	....	....	....	....	....	....	....	1	0	1	70	4	0	3.43
1982-83	**Calgary**	**NHL**	**2**	**0**	**2**	**0**	**100**	**11**	**0**	**6.59**	....	....	....	....	....	....	....
ab	Calgary	WHL	50	19	18	2	2856	155	3	3.26	16	9	7	925	60	0	3.89
1983-84	**Calgary**	**NHL**	**1**	**0**	**1**	**0**	**11**	**4**	**0**	**22.22**	....	....	....	....	....	....	....
c	Colorado	CHL	46	30	13	2	2648	148	1	*3.35	6	2	4	347	21	0	3.63
1984-85	Moncton	AHL	41	10	20	4	2050	134	0	3.92	....	....	....	....	....	....	....
1985-86	**Calgary**	**NHL**	**18**	**9**	**3**	**3**	**921**	**52**	**1**	**3.39**	***21**	**12**	***9**	**1229**	**60**	**0**	**2.93**
	Moncton	AHL	6	3	1	2	374	21	0	3.37	....	....	....	....	....	....	....
	Salt Lake	IHL	10	6	4	0	600	34	1	3.40	....	....	....	....	....	....	....
1986-87	**Calgary**	**NHL**	**54**	**30**	**21**	**1**	**2957**	**178**	**1**	**3.61**	**5**	**2**	**3**	**263**	**16**	**0**	**3.65**
1987-88	**Calgary**	**NHL**	**64**	**39**	**16**	**7**	**3565**	**210**	**1**	**3.53**	**9**	**4**	**4**	**515**	**34**	**0**	**3.96**
1988-89d	**Calgary**	**NHL**	**52**	***37**	**6**	**5**	**2938**	**130**	**0**	**2.65**	***22**	***16**	**5**	***1381**	**52**	***3**	**2.26** ◆
1989-90	**Calgary**	**NHL**	**47**	**23**	**14**	**9**	**2795**	**146**	**0**	**3.13**	**6**	**2**	**3**	**342**	**19**	**0**	**3.33**
1990-91	**Calgary**	**NHL**	**54**	**31**	**19**	**3**	**3121**	**172**	**1**	**3.31**	**7**	**3**	**4**	**427**	**21**	**0**	**2.95**
1991-92	**Calgary**	**NHL**	**63**	**24**	**30**	**9**	**3640**	**217**	**0**	**3.58**	....	....	....	....	....	....	....
1992-93	**Calgary**	**NHL**	**64**	**29**	**26**	**9**	**3732**	**203**	**2**	**3.26**	**4**	**1**	**1**	**150**	**15**	**0**	**6.00**
1993-94	**Calgary**	**NHL**	**48**	**26**	**17**	**5**	**2798**	**131**	**3**	**2.81**	**7**	**3**	**4**	**466**	**23**	**0**	**2.96**
1994-95	**Detroit**	**NHL**	**30**	**19**	**6**	**4**	**1807**	**76**	**1**	**2.52**	**18**	**12**	**6**	**1063**	**41**	**1**	**2.31**
1995-96e	**Detroit**	**NHL**	**32**	**21**	**7**	**2**	**1855**	**70**	**3**	**2.26**	**4**	**2**	**2**	**243**	**11**	**0**	**2.72**
	NHL Totals		**529**	**288**	**168**	**57**	**30240**	**1600**	**13**	**3.17**	**103**	**57**	**41**	**6079**	**292**	**4**	**2.88**

a WHL First All-Star Team (1982, 1983)
b Won Hap Emms Memorial Trophy (Memorial Cup Tournament Top Goaltender) (1983)
c CHL Second All-Star Team (1984)
d NHL Second All-Star Team (1989)
e Shared William M. Jennings Trophy with Chris Osgood (1996)

Played in NHL All-Star Game (1988-91, 1993)

Traded to **Detroit** by **Calgary** for Steve Chiasson, June 29, 1994.

VOKOUN, TOMAS MTL.

Goaltender. Catches right. 5'11", 180 lbs. Born, Karlovy Vary, Czech., July 2, 1976.
(Montreal's 11th choice, 226th overall, in 1994 Entry Draft).

			Regular Season								Playoffs						
Season	Club	Lea	GP	W	L	T	Mins	GA	SO	Avg	GP	W	L	Mins	GA	SO	Avg
1993-94	Kladno	Czech.	1	0	0	0	20	2	0	6.01	....	....	....	....	....	....	....
1994-95	Kladno	Czech.	26	....	....	....	1368	70	....	3.07	5	....	....	240	19	....	4.75
1995-96	Wheeling	ECHL	35	20	10	2	1912	117	0	3.67	7	4	3	436	19	0	2.61
	Fredericton	AHL	....	....	....	....	....	....	....	....	1	0	1	59	4	0	4.09

WAGNER, STEPHEN ST.L.

Goaltender. Catches left. 6'2", 200 lbs. Born, Red Deer, Alta., January 17, 1977.
(St. Louis' 5th choice, 159th overall, in 1996 Entry Draft).

			Regular Season								Playoffs						
Season	Club	Lea	GP	W	L	T	Mins	GA	SO	Avg	GP	W	L	Mins	GA	SO	Avg
1995-96	Olds	Jr. A	47	....	....	....	2787	139	2	2.99	....	....	....	....	....	....	....

WAITE, JIMMY (WAYT) CHI.

Goaltender. Catches left. 6'1", 180 lbs. Born, Sherbrooke, Que., April 15, 1969.
(Chicago's 1st choice, 8th overall, in 1987 Entry Draft).

			Regular Season								Playoffs						
Season	Club	Lea	GP	W	L	T	Mins	GA	SO	Avg	GP	W	L	Mins	GA	SO	Avg
1986-87a	Chicoutimi	QMJHL	50	23	17	3	2569	209	2	4.48	11	4	6	576	54	1	5.63
1987-88	Chicoutimi	QMJHL	36	17	16	1	2000	150	0	4.50	4	1	2	222	17	0	4.59
1988-89	**Chicago**	**NHL**	**11**	**0**	**7**	**1**	**494**	**43**	**0**	**5.22**	....	....	....	....	....	....	....
	Saginaw	IHL	5	3	1	0	304	10	0	1.97	....	....	....	....	....	....	....
1989-90	**Chicago**	**NHL**	**4**	**2**	**0**	**0**	**183**	**14**	**0**	**4.59**	....	....	....	....	....	....	....
bc	Indianapolis	IHL	54	*34	14	5	*3207	135	*5	*2.53	*10	*9	1	*602	19	*1	*1.89
1990-91	**Chicago**	**NHL**	**1**	**1**	**0**	**0**	**60**	**2**	**0**	**2.00**	....	....	....	....	....	....	....
	Indianapolis	IHL	49	*26	18	4	2888	167	3	3.47	6	2	4	369	20	0	3.25
1991-92	**Chicago**	**NHL**	**17**	**4**	**7**	**4**	**877**	**54**	**0**	**3.69**	....	....	....	....	....	....	....
	Indianapolis	IHL	13	4	7	1	702	53	0	4.53	....	....	....	....	....	....	....
	Hershey	AHL	11	6	4	1	631	44	0	4.18	6	2	4	360	19	0	3.17
1992-93	**Chicago**	**NHL**	**20**	**6**	**7**	**1**	**996**	**49**	**2**	**2.95**	....	....	....	....	....	....	....
1993-94	**San Jose**	**NHL**	**15**	**3**	**7**	**0**	**697**	**50**	**0**	**4.30**	**2**	**0**	**0**	**40**	**3**	**0**	**4.50**
1994-95	**Chicago**	**NHL**	**2**	**1**	**1**	**0**	**119**	**5**	**0**	**2.52**	....	....	....	....	....	....	....
	Indianapolis	IHL	4	2	1	1	239	13	0	3.25	....	....	....	....	....	....	....
1995-96	**Chicago**	**NHL**	**1**	**0**	**0**	**0**	**31**	**0**	**0**	**0.00**	....	....	....	....	....	....	....
	Indianapolis	IHL	56	28	18	6	3157	179	0	3.40	5	2	3	298	15	1	3.02
	NHL Totals		**71**	**17**	**29**	**6**	**3457**	**217**	**2**	**3.77**	**2**	**0**	**0**	**40**	**3**	**0**	**4.50**

a QMJHL Second All-Star Team (1987)
b IHL First All-Star Team (1990)
c Won James Norris Memorial Trophy (fewest goals against - IHL) (1990)

Traded to **San Jose** by **Chicago** for future considerations (Neil Wilkinson, July 9, 1993), June 19, 1993. Traded to **Chicago** by **San Jose** for a conditional choice in 1997 Entry Draft, February 6, 1995.

WAKALUK, DARCY (WAHK-uh-luhk) PHO.

Goaltender. Catches left. 5'11", 180 lbs. Born, Pincher Creek, Alta., March 14, 1966.
(Buffalo's 7th choice, 144th overall, in 1984 Entry Draft).

			Regular Season								Playoffs						
Season	Club	Lea	GP	W	L	T	Mins	GA	SO	Avg	GP	W	L	Mins	GA	SO	Avg
1983-84	Kelowna	WHL	31	2	22	0	1555	163	0	6.29	....	....	....	....	....	....	....
1984-85	Kelowna	WHL	54	19	30	4	3094	244	0	4.73	5	1	4	282	22	0	4.68
1985-86	Spokane	WHL	47	21	22	1	2562	224	1	5.25	7	3	4	419	37	0	5.30
1986-87	Rochester	AHL	11	2	2	0	545	26	0	2.86	5	2	0	141	11	0	4.68
1987-88	Rochester	AHL	55	27	16	3	2763	159	0	3.45	6	3	3	328	22	0	4.02
1988-89	**Buffalo**	**NHL**	**6**	**1**	**3**	**0**	**214**	**15**	**0**	**4.21**	....	....	....	....	....	....	....
	Rochester	AHL	33	11	14	0	1566	97	1	3.72	....	....	....	....	....	....	....
1989-90	Rochester	AHL	56	31	16	4	3095	173	2	3.35	*17	*10	6	*1001	50	0	*3.01
1990-91	**Buffalo**	**NHL**	**16**	**4**	**5**	**3**	**630**	**35**	**0**	**3.33**	**2**	**0**	**1**	**37**	**2**	**0**	**3.24**
a	Rochester	AHL	26	10	10	3	1363	68	4	*2.99	9	6	3	544	30	0	3.31
1991-92	**Minnesota**	**NHL**	**36**	**13**	**19**	**1**	**1905**	**104**	**1**	**3.28**	....	....	....	....	....	....	....
	Kalamazoo	IHL	1	1	0	0	60	7	0	7.00	....	....	....	....	....	....	....
1992-93	**Minnesota**	**NHL**	**29**	**10**	**12**	**5**	**1596**	**97**	**1**	**3.65**	....	....	....	....	....	....	....
1993-94	**Dallas**	**NHL**	**36**	**18**	**9**	**6**	**2000**	**88**	**3**	**2.64**	**5**	**4**	**1**	**307**	**15**	**0**	**2.93**
1994-95	**Dallas**	**NHL**	**15**	**4**	**8**	**0**	**754**	**40**	**2**	**3.18**	**1**	**0**	**0**	**20**	**1**	**0**	**3.00**
1995-96	**Dallas**	**NHL**	**37**	**9**	**16**	**5**	**1875**	**106**	**1**	**3.39**	....	....	....	....	....	....	....
	NHL Totals		**175**	**59**	**72**	**20**	**8974**	**485**	**8**	**3.24**	**8**	**4**	**2**	**364**	**18**	**0**	**2.97**

a Shared Harry "Hap" Holmes Memorial Trophy (fewest goals against - AHL) with David Littman (1991)

Traded to **Minnesota** by **Buffalo** for Minnesota's eighth round choice (Jiri Kuntos) in 1991 Entry Draft and Minnesota's fifth round choice (later traded to Toronto — Toronto selected Chris Deruiter) in 1992 Entry Draft, May 26, 1991. Signed as a free agent by **Phoenix**, July 23, 1996.

WEEKES, KEVIN — FLA.

Goaltender. Catches left. 6', 158 lbs. Born, Toronto, Ont., April 4, 1975.
(Florida's 2nd choice, 41st overall, in 1993 Entry Draft).

			Regular Season								Playoffs						
Season	Club	Lea	GP	W	L	T	Mins	GA	SO	Avg	GP	W	L	Mins	GA	SO	Avg
1992-93	Owen Sound	OHL	29	9	12	5	1645	143	0	5.22	1	0	0	26	5	0	11.50
1993-94	Owen Sound	OHL	34	13	19	1	1974	158	0	4.80	....	....	....	....	....	....	....
1994-95	Ottawa	OHL	41	13	23	4	2266	153	1	4.05	....	....	....	....	....	....	....
1995-96	Carolina	AHL	60	24	25	8	3404	229	2	4.04	....	....	....	....	....	....	....

WEIBEL, LARS (VIGH-behl) — CHI.

Goaltender. Catches left. 6', 178 lbs. Born, Rapperswil, Switz., May 20, 1974.
(Chicago's 10th choice, 248th overall, in 1994 Entry Draft).

			Regular Season								Playoffs						
Season	Club	Lea	GP	W	L	T	Mins	GA	SO	Avg	GP	W	L	Mins	GA	SO	Avg
1992-93	Biel-Bienne	Switz.	14	....	....	....	674	54	....	4.80	....	....	....	....	....	....	....
1993-94	Lugano	Switz.	25	....	....	....	....	....	....	....	9	....	....	560	23	....	2.46
1994-95	Lugano	Switz.	35	....	....	....	2076	95	....	2.74	....	....	....	....	....	....	....
1995-96	Lugano	Switz.	36	....	....	....	2122	107	....	3.02	4	....	....	240	9	....	2.25

WENINGER, DAVE — WSH.

Goaltender. Catches left. 6'1", 160 lbs. Born, Calgary, Alta., February 8, 1976.
(Washington's 5th choice, 74th overall, in 1996 Entry Draft).

			Regular Season								Playoffs						
Season	Club	Lea	GP	W	L	T	Mins	GA	SO	Avg	GP	W	L	Mins	GA	SO	Avg
1995-96	Michigan Tech.	WCHA	25	11	7	2	1300	70	0	3.23	....	....	....	....	....	....	....

WHITMORE, KAY

Goaltender. Catches left. 5'11", 175 lbs. Born, Sudbury, Ont., April 10, 1967.
(Hartford's 2nd choice, 26th overall, in 1985 Entry Draft).

			Regular Season								Playoffs						
Season	Club	Lea	GP	W	L	T	Mins	GA	SO	Avg	GP	W	L	Mins	GA	SO	Avg
1983-84	Peterborough	OHL	29	17	8	0	1471	110	0	4.49	....	....	....	....	....	....	....
1984-85	Peterborough	OHL	53	*35	16	2	3077	172	*2	3.35	17	10	4	1020	58	0	3.41
1985-86a	Peterborough	OHL	41	27	12	2	2467	114	*3	*2.77	14	8	5	837	40	0	2.87
1986-87	Peterborough	OHL	36	14	17	5	2159	118	1	3.28	7	3	3	366	17	1	2.79
1987-88	Binghamton	AHL	38	17	15	4	2137	121	*3	3.40	2	0	2	118	10	0	5.08
1988-89	**Hartford**	**NHL**	**3**	**2**	**1**	**0**	**180**	**10**	**0**	**3.33**	**2**	**0**	**2**	**135**	**10**	**0**	**4.44**
	Binghamton	AHL	*56	21	29	4	*3200	241	1	4.52	....	....	....	....	....	....	....
1989-90	**Hartford**	**NHL**	**9**	**4**	**2**	**1**	**442**	**26**	**0**	**3.53**	....	....	....	....	....	....	....
	Binghamton	AHL	24	3	19	2	1386	109	0	4.72	....	....	....	....	....	....	....
1990-91	**Hartford**	**NHL**	**18**	**3**	**9**	**3**	**850**	**52**	**0**	**3.67**	....	....	....	....	....	....	....
b	Springfield	AHL	33	22	9	1	1916	98	1	3.07	*15	*11	4	*926	37	0	*2.40
1991-92	**Hartford**	**NHL**	**45**	**14**	**21**	**6**	**2567**	**155**	**3**	**3.62**	**1**	**0**	**0**	**19**	**1**	**0**	**3.16**
1992-93	**Vancouver**	**NHL**	**31**	**18**	**8**	**4**	**1817**	**94**	**1**	**3.10**	....	....	....	....	....	....	....
1993-94	**Vancouver**	**NHL**	**32**	**18**	**14**	**0**	**1921**	**113**	**0**	**3.53**	....	....	....	....	....	....	....
1994-95	**Vancouver**	**NHL**	**11**	**0**	**6**	**2**	**558**	**37**	**0**	**3.98**	**1**	**0**	**0**	**20**	**2**	**0**	**6.00**
1995-96	Los Angeles	IHL	40	13	14	7	2064	132	1	3.84	....	....	....	....	....	....	....
	Binghamton	AHL	11	6	4	1	663	37	0	3.35	2	0	2	127	9	0	4.27
	NHL Totals		**149**	**59**	**61**	**16**	**8335**	**487**	**4**	**3.51**	**4**	**0**	**2**	**174**	**13**	**0**	**4.48**

a OHL First All-Star Team (1986)
b Won Jack A. Butterfield Trophy (Playoff MVP - AHL) (1991)

Traded to **Vancouver** by **Hartford** for Corrie D'Alessio and future considerations, October 1, 1992. Traded to **NY Rangers** by **Vancouver** for Joe Kocur, March 20, 1996.

WICKENHEISER, CHRIS — EDM.

Goaltender. Catches left. 6'1", 185 lbs. Born, Lethbridge, Alta., January 20, 1976.
(Edmonton's 12th choice, 179th overall, in 1994 Entry Draft).

			Regular Season								Playoffs						
Season	Club	Lea	GP	W	L	T	Mins	GA	SO	Avg	GP	W	L	Mins	GA	SO	Avg
1993-94	Red Deer	WHL	29	11	13	0	1356	114	0	5.04	....	....	....	....	....	....	....
1994-95	Red Deer	WHL	47	13	26	3	2429	181	1	4.47	....	....	....	....	....	....	....
1995-96	Red Deer	WHL	48	17	27	2	2666	183	1	4.12	10	3	6	550	34	1	3.71

WILKINSON, DEREK — T.B.

Goaltender. Catches left. 6', 170 lbs. Born, Lasalle, Que., July 29, 1974.
(Tampa Bay's 7th choice, 145th overall, in 1992 Entry Draft).

			Regular Season								Playoffs						
Season	Club	Lea	GP	W	L	T	Mins	GA	SO	Avg	GP	W	L	Mins	GA	SO	Avg
1991-92	Detroit	OHL	38	16	17	1	1943	138	1	4.26	7	3	2	313	28	0	5.37
1992-93	Detroit	OHL	*4	1	2	1	*245	18	0	4.41	....	....	....	....	....	....	....
	Belleville	OHL	*59	21	24	11	*3370	237	0	4.22	7	3	4	434	29	0	4.01
1993-94	Belleville	OHL	*56	24	16	4	2860	179	*2	3.76	12	6	6	700	39	*1	3.34
1994-95	Atlanta	IHL	46	22	17	2	2414	121	1	3.01	4	2	1	197	8	0	2.43
1995-96	**Tampa Bay**	**NHL**	**4**	**0**	**3**	**0**	**200**	**15**	**0**	**4.50**	....	....	....	....	....	....	....
	Atlanta	IHL	28	11	11	2	1433	98	1	4.10	....	....	....	....	....	....	....
	NHL Totals		**4**	**0**	**3**	**0**	**200**	**15**	**0**	**4.50**	....	....	....	....	....	....	....

WILLIS, JORDAN — DAL.

Goaltender. Catches left. 5'9", 155 lbs. Born, Kincardine, Ont., February 28, 1975.
(Dallas' 8th choice, 243rd overall, in 1993 Entry Draft).

			Regular Season								Playoffs						
Season	Club	Lea	GP	W	L	T	Mins	GA	SO	Avg	GP	W	L	Mins	GA	SO	Avg
1992-93	London	OHL	26	13	6	3	1428	101	1	4.24	7	....	....	355	19	0	3.21
1993-94	London	OHL	44	20	19	2	2428	158	1	3.90	1	0	0	8	1	0	7.50
1994-95	London	OHL	53	16	29	3	2824	202	0	4.29	3	0	3	165	15	0	5.45
1995-96	**Dallas**	**NHL**	**1**	**0**	**1**	**0**	**19**	**1**	**0**	**3.16**	....	....	....	....	....	....	....
	Michigan	IHL	38	17	9	9	2184	118	1	3.24	4	1	3	238	17	0	4.29
	NHL Totals		**1**	**0**	**1**	**0**	**19**	**1**	**0**	**3.16**	....	....	....	....	....	....	....

WREGGET, KEN (REHG-eht) — PIT.

Goaltender. Catches left. 6'1", 200 lbs. Born, Brandon, Man., March 25, 1964.
(Toronto's 4th choice, 45th overall, in 1982 Entry Draft).

			Regular Season								Playoffs						
Season	Club	Lea	GP	W	L	T	Mins	GA	SO	Avg	GP	W	L	Mins	GA	SO	Avg
1981-82	Lethbridge	WHL	36	19	12	0	1713	118	0	4.13	3	2	0	84	3	0	2.14
1982-83	Lethbridge	WHL	48	26	17	1	2696	157	0	3.49	20	14	5	1154	58	1	3.02
1983-84	**Toronto**	**NHL**	**3**	**1**	**1**	**1**	**165**	**14**	**0**	**5.09**	....	....	....	....	....	....	....
a	Lethbridge	WHL	53	32	20	0	3053	161	0	*3.16	4	1	3	210	18	0	5.14
1984-85	**Toronto**	**NHL**	**23**	**2**	**15**	**3**	**1278**	**103**	**0**	**4.84**	....	....	....	....	....	....	....
	St. Catharines	AHL	12	2	8	1	688	48	0	4.19	....	....	....	....	....	....	....
1985-86	**Toronto**	**NHL**	**30**	**9**	**13**	**4**	**1566**	**113**	**0**	**4.33**	**10**	**6**	**4**	**607**	**32**	***1**	**3.16**
	St. Catharines	AHL	18	8	9	0	1058	78	1	4.42	....	....	....	....	....	....	....
1986-87	**Toronto**	**NHL**	**56**	**22**	**28**	**3**	**3026**	**200**	**0**	**3.97**	**13**	**7**	**6**	**761**	**29**	**1**	**2.29**
1987-88	**Toronto**	**NHL**	**56**	**12**	**35**	**4**	**3000**	**222**	**2**	**4.44**	**2**	**0**	**1**	**108**	**11**	**0**	**6.11**
1988-89	**Toronto**	**NHL**	**32**	**9**	**20**	**2**	**1888**	**139**	**0**	**4.42**	....	....	....	....	....	....	....
	Philadelphia	**NHL**	**3**	**1**	**1**	**0**	**130**	**13**	**0**	**6.00**	**5**	**2**	**2**	**268**	**10**	**0**	**2.24**
1989-90	**Philadelphia**	**NHL**	**51**	**22**	**24**	**3**	**2961**	**169**	**0**	**3.42**	....	....	....	....	....	....	....
1990-91	**Philadelphia**	**NHL**	**30**	**10**	**14**	**3**	**1484**	**88**	**0**	**3.56**	....	....	....	....	....	....	....
1991-92	**Philadelphia**	**NHL**	**23**	**9**	**8**	**3**	**1259**	**75**	**0**	**3.57**	....	....	....	....	....	....	....
	Pittsburgh	**NHL**	**9**	**5**	**3**	**0**	**448**	**31**	**0**	**4.15**	**1**	**0**	**0**	**40**	**4**	**0**	**6.00** ◆
1992-93	**Pittsburgh**	**NHL**	**25**	**13**	**7**	**2**	**1368**	**78**	**0**	**3.42**	....	....	....	....	....	....	....
1993-94	**Pittsburgh**	**NHL**	**42**	**21**	**12**	**7**	**2456**	**138**	**1**	**3.37**	....	....	....	....	....	....	....
1994-95	**Pittsburgh**	**NHL**	**38**	***25**	**9**	**2**	**2208**	**118**	**0**	**3.21**	**11**	**5**	**6**	**661**	**33**	**1**	**3.00**
1995-96	**Pittsburgh**	**NHL**	**37**	**20**	**13**	**2**	**2132**	**115**	**3**	**3.24**	**9**	**7**	**2**	**599**	**23**	**0**	**2.30**
	NHL Totals		**458**	**181**	**203**	**39**	**25369**	**1616**	**6**	**3.82**	**51**	**27**	**21**	**3044**	**142**	**3**	**2.80**

a WHL East First All-Star Team (1984)

Traded to **Philadelphia** by **Toronto** for Philadelphia's first round choice (Rob Pearson) and Calgary's first round choice (previously acquired by Philadelphia — Toronto selected Steve Bancroft) in 1989 Entry Draft, March 6, 1989. Traded to **Pittsburgh** by **Philadelphia** with Rick Tocchet, Kjell Samuelsson and Philadelphia's third round choice (Dave Roche) in 1993 Entry Draft for Mark Recchi, Brian Benning and Los Angeles' first round choice (previously acquired by Pittsburgh — Philadelphia selected Jason Bowen) in 1992 Entry Draft, February 19, 1992.

YEREMEYEV, VITALI (yehr-eh-MAY-ehv) — NYR

Goaltender. Catches left. 5'10", 167 lbs. Born, Ust-Kamenogorsk, USSR, September 23, 1975.
(NY Rangers' 11th choice, 209th overall, in 1994 Entry Draft).

			Regular Season								Playoffs						
Season	Club	Lea	GP	W	L	T	Mins	GA	SO	Avg	GP	W	L	Mins	GA	SO	Avg
1993-94	Kamenogorsk	CIS	19	....	....	....	1015	38	....	2.24	....	....	....	....	....	....	....
1994-95	CSKA	CIS	49	....	....	....	2733	97	....	2.13	....	....	....	....	....	....	....
1995-96	CSKA	CIS	25	....	....	....	1339	37	5	1.66	3	....	....	179	7	....	2.34

YOUNG, WENDELL

Goaltender. Catches left. 5'9", 181 lbs. Born, Halifax, N.S., August 1, 1963.
(Vancouver's 3rd choice, 73rd overall, in 1981 Entry Draft).

			Regular Season								Playoffs						
Season	Club	Lea	GP	W	L	T	Mins	GA	SO	Avg	GP	W	L	Mins	GA	SO	Avg
1980-81	Kitchener	OHA	42	19	15	0	2215	164	1	4.44	14	9	1	800	42	*1	3.15
1981-82	Kitchener	OHL	60	38	17	2	3470	195	1	3.37	15	12	1	900	35	*1	*2.33
1982-83	Kitchener	OHL	61	41	19	0	3611	231	1	3.84	12	6	5	720	43	0	3.58
1983-84	Fredericton	AHL	11	7	3	0	569	39	1	4.11	....	....	....	....	....	....	....
	Milwaukee	IHL	6	4	1	1	339	17	0	3.01	....	....	....	....	....	....	....
	Salt Lake	CHL	20	11	6	0	1094	80	0	4.39	4	0	2	122	11	0	5.42
1984-85	Fredericton	AHL	22	7	11	3	1242	83	0	4.01	....	....	....	....	....	....	....
1985-86	**Vancouver**	**NHL**	**22**	**4**	**9**	**3**	**1023**	**61**	**0**	**3.58**	**1**	**0**	**1**	**60**	**5**	**0**	**5.00**
	Fredericton	AHL	24	12	8	4	1457	78	0	3.21	....	....	....	....	....	....	....
1986-87	**Vancouver**	**NHL**	**8**	**1**	**6**	**1**	**420**	**35**	**0**	**5.00**	....	....	....	....	....	....	....
	Fredericton	AHL	30	11	16	0	1676	118	0	4.22	....	....	....	....	....	....	....
1987-88	**Philadelphia**	**NHL**	**6**	**3**	**2**	**0**	**320**	**20**	**0**	**3.75**	....	....	....	....	....	....	....
abc	Hershey	AHL	51	*33	15	1	2922	135	1	2.77	12	*12	0	*767	28	*1	*2.19
1988-89	**Pittsburgh**	**NHL**	**22**	**12**	**9**	**0**	**1150**	**92**	**0**	**4.80**	**1**	**0**	**0**	**39**	**1**	**0**	**1.54**
	Muskegon	IHL	2	1	0	1	125	7	0	3.36	....	....	....	....	....	....	....
1989-90	**Pittsburgh**	**NHL**	**43**	**16**	**20**	**3**	**2318**	**161**	**1**	**4.17**	....	....	....	....	....	....	....
1990-91	**Pittsburgh**	**NHL**	**18**	**4**	**6**	**2**	**773**	**52**	**0**	**4.04**	....	....	....	....	....	....	.... ◆
1991-92	**Pittsburgh**	**NHL**	**18**	**7**	**6**	**0**	**838**	**53**	**0**	**3.79**	....	....	....	....	....	....	.... ◆
1992-93	**Tampa Bay**	**NHL**	**31**	**7**	**19**	**2**	**1591**	**97**	**0**	**3.66**	....	....	....	....	....	....	....
	Atlanta	IHL	3	3	0	0	183	8	0	2.62	....	....	....	....	....	....	....
1993-94	**Tampa Bay**	**NHL**	**9**	**2**	**3**	**1**	**480**	**20**	**1**	**2.50**	....	....	....	....	....	....	....
	Atlanta	IHL	2	2	0	0	120	6	0	3.00	....	....	....	....	....	....	....
1994-95	Chicago	IHL	37	14	11	7	1882	112	0	3.57	....	....	....	....	....	....	....
	Pittsburgh	**NHL**	**10**	**3**	**6**	**0**	**497**	**27**	**0**	**3.26**	....	....	....	....	....	....	....
1995-96	Chicago	IHL	61	30	20	6	3285	199	1	3.63	9	4	5	540	30	0	3.33
	NHL Totals		**187**	**59**	**86**	**12**	**9410**	**618**	**2**	**3.94**	**2**	**0**	**1**	**99**	**6**	**0**	**3.64**

a AHL First All-Star Team (1988)
b Won Baz Bastien Memorial Trophy (Top Goaltender - AHL) (1988)
c Won Jack Butterfield Trophy (Playoff MVP - AHL) (1988)

Traded to **Philadelphia** by **Vancouver** with Vancouver's third round choice (Kimbi Daniels) in 1990 Entry Draft for Darren Jensen and Daryl Stanley, August 28, 1987. Traded to **Pittsburgh** by **Philadelphia** with Philadelphia's seventh round choice (Mika Valila) in 1990 Entry Draft for Pittsburgh's third round choice (Chris Therien) in 1990 Entry Draft, Steptember 1, 1988. Claimed by **Tampa Bay** from **Pittsburgh** in Expansion Draft, June 18, 1992. Traded to **Pittsburgh** by **Tampa Bay** for future considerations, February 16, 1995.

Notes

Hank Bassen

Jim Henry

Jacques Plante

Frank Brimsek

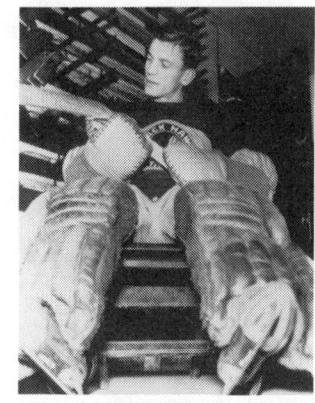

Mike Karakas

Dennis Riggin

Len Broderick

Clint Malarchuk

Al Rollins

Roger Crozier

Greg Millen

Tiny Thompson

Retired NHL Goaltender Index

Abbreviations: Teams/Cities: — **Ana.** – Anaheim; **Atl.** – Atlanta; **Bos.** – Boston, **Bro.** – Brooklyn; **Buf.** – Buffalo; **Cal.** – California; **Cgy.** – Calgary; **Cle.** – Cleveland; **Col.** – Colorado; **Dal.** – Dallas; **Det.** – Detroit; **Edm.** – Edmonton; **Fla.** – Florida; **Ham.** – Hamilton; **Hfd.** – Hartford; **K.C.** – Kansas City; **L.A.** – Los Angeles; **Min.** — Minnesota; **Mtl.** - Montreal; **Mtl. M.** – Montreal Maroons; **Mtl. W.** – Montreal Wanderers; **N.J.** – New Jersey; **NYA** – NY Americans; **NYI** – New York Islanders; **NYR** – New York Rangers; **Oak.** – Oakland; **Ott.** – Ottawa; **Phi.** – Philadelphia; **Pit.** – Pittsburgh; **Que.** – Quebec; **St. L.** – St. Louis; **S.J.** – San Jose; **T.B.** – Tampa Bay; **Tor.** – Toronto; **Van.** – Vancouver; **Wpg.** – Winnipeg; **Wsh.** – Washington.

Avg. – goals against per 60 minutes played; **GA** – goals against; **GP** – games played; **Mins** – minutes played; **SO** – shutouts.
• – deceased.

			Regular Schedule								Playoffs										
Name	NHL Teams	NHL Seasons	GP	W	L	T	Mins	GA	SO	Avg	GP	W	L	T	Mins	GA	SO	Avg	NHL Cup Wins	First NHL Season	Last NHL Season
Abbott, George	Bos.	1	1	0	1	0	60	7	0	7.00	....	....	....	....	....	....	....	....		1943-44	1943-44
Adams, John	Bos., Wsh.	2	22	9	10	1	1180	85	1	4.32	....	....	....	....	....	....	....	....		1972-73	1974-75
Aiken, Don	Mtl.	1	1	0	1	0	34	6	0	10.59	....	....	....	....	....	....	....	....		1957-58	1957-58
Aikenhead, Andy	NYR	3	106	47	43	16	6570	257	11	2.35	10	6	3	1	608	15	3	1.48	1	1932-33	1934-35
Almas, Red	Det., Chi.	3	3	0	2	1	180	13	0	4.33	5	1	3	0	263	13	0	2.97		1946-47	1952-53
• Anderson, Lorne	NYR	1	3	1	2	0	180	18	0	6.00	....	....	....	....	....	....	....	....		1951-52	1951-52
Astrom, Hardy	NYR, Col.	3	83	17	44	12	4456	278	0	3.74	....	....	....	....	....	....	....	....		1977-78	1980-81
Baker, Steve	NYR	4	57	20	20	11	3081	190	3	3.70	14	7	7	0	826	55	0	4.00		1979-80	1982-83
Bannerman, Murray	Van., Chi.	8	289	116	125	33	16470	1051	8	3.83	40	20	18	0	2322	165	0	4.26		1977-78	1986-87
Baron, Marco	Bos., L.A., Edm.	6	86	34	39	9	4822	292	1	3.63	1	0	1	0	20	3	0	9.00		1979-80	1984-85
Bassen, Hank	Chi., Det., Pit.	9	157	47	65	31	8779	441	5	3.01	5	1	4	0	274	11	0	2.41		1954-55	1967-68
• Bastien, Baz	Tor.	1	5	0	4	1	300	20	0	4.00	....	....	....	....	....	....	....	....		1945-46	1945-46
Bauman, Gary	Mtl., Min.	3	35	6	18	6	1718	102	0	3.56	....	....	....	....	....	....	....	....		1966-67	1968-69
Bedard, Jim	Wsh.	2	73	17	40	13	4232	278	1	3.94	....	....	....	....	....	....	....	....		1977-78	1978-79
Behrend, Marc	Wpg.	3	39	12	19	3	1991	160	1	4.82	7	1	3	0	312	19	0	3.65		1983-84	1985-86
Belanger, Yves	St.L., Atl., Bos.	6	78	29	33	6	4134	259	2	3.76	....	....	....	....	....	....	....	....		1974-75	1979-80
Belhumeur, Michel	Phi., Wsh.	3	65	9	36	7	3306	254	0	4.61	1	0	0	0	10	1	0	6.00		1972-73	1975-76
• Bell, Gordie	Tor., NYR	2	8	3	5	0	480	31	0	3.88	2	1	1	0	120	9	0	4.50		1945-46	1955-56
• Benedict, Clint	Ott., Mtl.M.	13	360	190	43	28	22321	859	58	2.31	48	25	18	4	2907	87	13	1.80	4	1917-18	1929-30
Bennett, Harvey	Bos.	1	24	10	12	2	1440	103	0	4.29	....	....	....	....	....	....	....	....		1944-45	1944-45
Bernhardt, Tim	Cgy., Tor.	4	67	17	36	7	3748	267	0	4.27	....	....	....	....	....	....	....	....		1982-83	1986-87
• Beveridge, Bill	Det., Ott., St.L., Mtl.M., NYR	7	297	87	166	42	18375	879	17	2.87	4	2	3	0	300	11	0	2.20		1929-30	1942-43
• Bibeault, Paul	Mtl., Tor., Bos., Chi.	7	214	81	107	25	12890	785	10	3.65	20	6	14	0	1237	71	2	3.44		1940-41	1946-47
Binette, Andre	Mtl.	1	1	1	0	0	60	4	0	4.00	....	....	....	....	....	....	....	....		1954-55	1954-55
Binkley, Les	Pit.	5	196	58	94	34	11046	575	11	3.12	7	5	2	0	428	15	0	2.10		1967-68	1971-72
Bittner, Richard	Bos.	1	1	0	0	1	60	3	0	3.00	....	....	....	....	....	....	....	....		1949-50	1949-50
Blake, Mike	L.A.	3	40	13	15	5	2117	150	0	4.25	....	....	....	....	....	....	....	....		1981-82	1983-84
Boisvert, Gilles	Det.	1	3	0	3	0	180	9	0	3.00	....	....	....	....	....	....	....	....		1959-60	1959-60
Bouchard, Dan	Atl., Cgy., Que., Wpg.	14	655	286	232	113	37919	2061	27	3.26	43	13	30	0	2549	147	1	3.46		1972-73	1985-86
• Bourque, Claude	Mtl., Det.	2	62	16	38	8	3830	192	5	3.01	3	1	2	0	188	8	1	2.55		1938-39	1939-40
Boutin, Rollie	Wsh.	3	22	7	10	1	1137	75	0	3.96	....	....	....	....	....	....	....	....		1978-79	1980-81
Bouvrette, Lionel	NYR	1	1	0	1	0	60	6	0	6.00	....	....	....	....	....	....	....	....		1942-43	1942-43
Bower, Johnny	NYR, Tor.	15	552	251	196	90	32016	1347	37	2.52	74	35	34	0	4350	184	5	2.54	4	1953-54	1969-70
Brannigan, Andy	NYA	1	1	0	0	0	7	0	0	0.00	....	....	....	....	....	....	....	....		1940-41	1940-41
Brimsek, Frank	Bos., Chi.	10	514	252	182	80	31210	1404	40	2.70	68	32	36	0	4365	186	2	2.56	2	1938-39	1949-50
• Broda, Turk	Tor.	14	629	302	224	101	38168	1609	62	2.53	102	58	43	1	6406	211	13	1.98	5	1936-37	1951-52
Broderick, Ken	Min., Bos.	3	27	11	12	1	1464	74	1	3.03	....	....	....	....	....	....	....	....		1969-70	1974-75
Broderick, Len	Mtl.	1	1	1	0	0	60	2	0	2.00	....	....	....	....	....	....	....	....		1957-58	1957-58
Brodeur, Richard	NYI, Van., Hfd.	9	385	131	176	62	21968	1410	6	3.85	33	13	20	0	2009	111	1	3.32		1979-80	1987-88
Bromley, Gary	Buf., Van.	6	136	54	44	28	7427	425	7	3.43	7	2	5	0	360	25	0	4.17		1973-74	1980-81
• Brooks, Arthur	Tor.	1	4	2	1	0	220	23	0	6.27	....	....	....	....	....	....	....	....		1917-18	1917-18
Brooks, Ross	Bos.	3	54	37	7	6	3047	134	4	2.64	1	0	0	0	20	3	0	9.00		1972-73	1974-75
• Brophy, Frank	Que.	1	21	3	18	0	1247	148	0	7.12	....	....	....	....	....	....	....	....		1919-20	1919-20
Brown, Andy	Det., Pit.	3	62	22	26	9	3373	213	1	3.79	....	....	....	....	....	....	....	....		1971-72	1973-74
Brown, Ken	Chi.	1	1	0	0	0	18	1	0	3.33	....	....	....	....	....	....	....	....		1970-71	1970-71
Brunetta, Mario	Que.	3	40	12	17	1	1967	128	0	3.90	....	....	....	....	....	....	....	....		1987-88	1989-90
Bullock, Bruce	Van.	3	16	3	9	3	927	74	0	4.79	....	....	....	....	....	....	....	....		1972-73	1976-77
Buzinski, Steve	NYR	1	9	2	6	1	560	55	0	5.89	....	....	....	....	....	....	....	....		1942-43	1942-43
Caley, Don	St.L.	1	1	0	0	0	30	3	0	6.00	....	....	....	....	....	....	....	....		1967-68	1967-68
Caprice, Frank	Van.	6	102	31	40	11	5589	391	1	4.20	....	....	....	....	....	....	....	....		1982-83	1987-88
Caron, Jacques	L.A., St.L., Van.	5	72	24	29	11	3846	211	2	3.29	12	4	7	0	639	34	0	3.19		1967-68	1973-74
Carter, Lyle	Cal.	1	15	4	7	0	721	50	0	4.16	....	....	....	....	....	....	....	....		1971-72	1971-72
• Chabot, Lorne	NYR, Tor., Mtl., Chi., Mtl.M., NYA	11	411	206	140	65	25309	861	73	2.04	37	13	16	6	2558	64	5	1.50	2	1926-27	1936-37
Chadwick, Ed	Tor., Bos.	6	184	57	92	35	10980	551	14	3.01	....	....	....	....	....	....	....	....		1955-56	1961-62
Champoux, Bob	Det., Cal.	2	17	2	11	3	923	80	0	5.20	1	1	0	0	55	4	0	4.36		1963-64	1973-74
Cheevers, Gerry	Tor., Bos.	13	418	230	103	74	24394	1175	26	2.89	88	47	35	0	5396	242	8	2.69	2	1961-62	1979-80
Chevrier, Alain	N.J., Wpg., Chi., Pit., Det.	6	234	91	100	14	12202	845	2	4.16	16	9	7	0	1013	44	0	2.61		1985-86	1990-91
Clancy, Frank	Tor.	1	1	0	0	0	1	1	0	60.00	....	....	....	....	....	....	....	....		1931-32	1931-32
Cleghorn, Odie	Pit.	1	1	1	0	0	60	2	0	2.00	....	....	....	....	....	....	....	....		1925-26	1925-26
Clifford, Chris	Chi.	2	2	0	0	0	24	0	0	0.00	....	....	....	....	....	....	....	....		1984-85	1988-89
Cloutier, Jacques	Buf., Chi., Que.	12	255	82	102	24	12826	778	3	3.64	8	1	5	0	413	18	1	2.62		1981-82	1993-94
Colvin, Les	Bos.	1	1	0	1	0	60	4	0	4.00	....	....	....	....	....	....	....	....		1948-49	1948-49
Conacher, Charlie	Tor., Det.	3	3	0	0	0	9	0	0	0.00	....	....	....	....	....	....	....	....		1929-30	1940-41
• Connell, Alex	Ott., Det., NYA, Mtl.M.	12	417	199	155	59	26030	830	81	1.91	21	9	5	7	1309	26	4	1.19	2	1924-25	1936-37
Corsi, Jim	Edm.	1	26	8	14	3	1366	83	0	3.65	....	....	....	....	....	....	....	....		1979-80	1979-80
Courteau, Maurice	Bos.	1	6	2	4	0	360	33	0	5.50	....	....	....	....	....	....	....	....		1943-44	1943-44
Cowley, Wayne	Edmonton	1	1	0	1	0	57	3	0	3.16	....	....	....	....	....	....	....	....		1993-94	1993-94
Cox, Abbie	Mtl.M., Det., NYA, Mtl.	3	5	1	1	2	263	11	0	2.51	....	....	....	....	....	....	....	....		1929-30	1935-36
Craig, Jim	Atl., Bos., Min.	3	30	11	10	7	1588	100	0	3.78	....	....	....	....	....	....	....	....		1979-80	1983-84
Crha, Jiri	Tor.	2	69	28	27	11	3942	261	0	3.97	5	0	4	0	186	21	0	6.77		1979-80	1980-81
• Crozier, Roger	Det., Buf., Wsh.	14	518	206	198	70	28567	1446	30	3.04	31	14	15	0	1769	82	1	2.78		1963-64	1976-77
• Cude, Wilf	Phi., Bos., Chi., Det., Mtl.	10	282	100	129	49	17486	798	24	2.74	19	7	11	1	1317	51	1	2.32		1930-31	1940-41
Cutts, Don	Edm.	1	6	1	2	1	269	16	0	3.57	....	....	....	....	....	....	....	....		1979-80	1979-80
• Cyr, Claude	Mtl.	1	1	0	0	0	20	1	0	3.00	....	....	....	....	....	....	....	....		1958-59	1958-59
Dadswell, Doug	Cgy.	2	27	8	8	3	1346	99	0	4.41	....	....	....	....	....	....	....	....		1986-87	1987-88
D'Alessio, Corrie	Hfd.	1	1	0	0	0	11	0	0	0.00	....	....	....	....	....	....	....	....		1992-93	1992-93
Daley, Joe	Pit., Buf., Det.	4	105	34	44	19	5836	326	3	3.35	....	....	....	....	....	....	....	....		1968-69	1971-72
Damore, Nick	Bos.	1	1	0	1	0	60	3	0	3.00	....	....	....	....	....	....	....	....		1941-42	1941-42
D'Amour, Marc	Cgy., Phi.	2	16	2	4	2	579	32	0	3.32	....	....	....	....	....	....	....	....		1985-86	1988-89
Daskalakis, Cleon	Bos.	3	12	3	4	1	506	41	0	4.86	....	....	....	....	....	....	....	....		1984-85	1986-87
Davidson, John	St.L., NYR	10	301	123	124	39	17109	1004	7	3.52	31	16	14	0	1862	77	1	2.48		1973-74	1982-83
Decourcy, Robert	NYR	1	1	0	1	0	29	6	0	12.41	....	....	....	....	....	....	....	....		1947-48	1947-48
Defelice, Norman	Bos.	1	10	3	5	2	600	30	0	3.00	....	....	....	....	....	....	....	....		1956-57	1956-57
DeJordy, Denis	Chi., L.A., Mtl., Det.	11	316	124	127	51	17798	929	15	3.13	18	6	9	0	946	55	0	3.49		1962-63	1973-74
DelGuidice, Matt	Bos.	2	11	2	5	1	434	28	0	3.87	....	....	....	....	....	....	....	....		1990-91	1991-92
Desjardins, Gerry	L.A., Chi., NYI, Buf.	10	331	122	153	44	19014	1042	12	3.29	35	15	15	0	1874	108	0	3.46		1968-69	1977-78
Dickie, Bill	Chi.	1	1	1	0	0	60	3	0	3.00	....	....	....	....	....	....	....	....		1941-42	1941-42
Dion, Connie	Det.	2	38	23	11	4	2280	119	0	3.13	5	1	4	0	300	17	0	3.40		1943-44	1944-45
Dion, Michel	Que., Wpg., Pit.	6	227	60	118	32	12695	898	2	4.24	5	2	3	0	304	22	0	4.34		1979-80	1984-85
Dolson, Clarence	Det.	3	93	35	44	13	5820	192	16	1.98	2	0	2	0	120	7	0	3.50		1928-29	1930-31
Dowie, Bruce	Tor.	1	2	0	1	0	72	4	0	3.33	....	....	....	....	....	....	....	....		1983-84	1983-84
Dryden, Dave	NYR, Chi., Buf., Edm.	9	203	66	76	31	10424	555	9	3.19	3	0	2	0	133	9	0	4.06		1961-62	1979-80
Dryden, Ken	Mtl.	8	397	258	57	74	23352	870	46	2.24	112	80	32	0	6846	274	10	2.40	6	1970-71	1978-79
Dumas, Michel	Chi.	2	8	2	1	2	362	24	0	3.98	1	0	0	0	19	1	0	3.16		1974-75	1976-77
Dupuis, Bob	Edm.	1	1	0	1	0	60	4	0	4.00	....	....	....	....	....	....	....	....		1979-80	1979-80
• Durnan, Bill	Mtl.	7	383	208	112	62	22945	901	34	2.36	45	27	18	0	2851	99	2	2.08	2	1943-44	1949-50
Dyck, Ed	Van.	3	49	8	28	5	2453	178	1	4.35	....	....	....	....	....	....	....	....		1971-72	1973-74
Edwards, Don	Buf., Cgy., Tor.	10	459	208	155	77	26181	1449	16	3.32	42	16	24	0	2302	132	1	3.44		1976-77	1985-86
Edwards, Gary	St.L., L.A., Clev., Min., Edm., Pit.	13	286	88	125	43	16002	973	11	3.65	11	5	4	0	537	34	0	3.80		1968-69	1981-82
Edwards, Marv	Pit., Tor., Cal.	4	61	15	34	7	3467	218	2	3.77	....	....	....	....	....	....	....	....		1968-69	1973-74
Edwards, Roy	Det., Pit.	7	236	92	88	38	13109	637	12	2.92	4	0	3	0	206	11	0	3.20		1967-68	1973-74

Name	NHL Teams	NHL Seasons	Regular Schedule								Playoffs								NHL Cup Wins	First NHL Season	Last NHL Season
			GP	W	L	T	Mins	GA	SO	Avg	GP	W	L	T	Mins	GA	SO	Avg			
Eliot, Darren	L.A., Det., Buf.	5	89	25	41	12	4931	377	1	4.59	1	0	0	0	40	7	0	10.50		1984-85	1988-89
Ellacott, Ken	Van.	1	12	2	3	4	555	41	0	4.43	....	....	....	....	....	....	....	....		1982-83	1982-83
Erickson, Chad	N.J.	1	2	1	1	0	120	9	0	4.50	....	....	....	....	....	....	....	....		1991-92	1991-92
Esposito, Tony	Mtl., Chi.	16	886	423	306	152	52585	2563	76	2.92	99	45	53	0	6017	308	6	3.07	1	1968-69	1983-84
• Evans, Claude	Mtl., Bos.	2	5	2	2	1	280	16	0	3.43	....	....	....	....	....	....	....	....		1954-55	1957-58
Exelby, Randy	Mtl., Edm.	2	2	0	1	0	63	5	0	4.76	....	....	....	....	....	....	....	....		1988-89	1989-90
Farr, Rocky	Buf.	3	19	2	6	3	722	42	0	3.49	....	....	....	....	....	....	....	....		1972-73	1974-75
Favell, Doug	Phi., Tor., Col.	12	373	123	153	69	20771	1096	18	3.17	21	5	16	0	1270	66	1	3.12		1967-68	1978-79
• Forbes, Jake	Tor., Ham., NYA, Phi.	13	210	84	114	11	12922	594	19	2.76	2	0	2	0	120	7	0	3.50		1919-20	1932-33
Ford, Brian	Que., Pit.	2	11	3	7	0	580	61	0	6.31	....	....	....	....	....	....	....	....		1983-84	1984-85
Foster, Norm	Bos., Edm.	2	13	7	4	0	623	34	0	3.27	....	....	....	....	....	....	....	....		1990-91	1991-92
Fowler, Hec	Bos.	1	7	1	6	0	420	43	0	6.14	....	....	....	....	....	....	....	....		1924-25	1924-25
Francis, Emile	Chi., NYR	6	95	31	52	11	5660	355	1	3.76	....	....	....	....	....	....	....	....		1946-47	1951-52
• Franks, Jim	Det., NYR, Bos.	4	43	12	23	7	2580	185	1	4.30	1	0	1	0	30	2	0	4.00	1	1936-37	1943-44
Frederick, Ray	Chi.	1	5	0	4	1	300	22	0	4.40	....	....	....	....	....	....	....	....		1954-55	1954-55
Friesen, Karl	N.J.	1	4	0	2	1	130	16	0	7.38	....	....	....	....	....	....	....	....		1986-87	1986-87
Froese, Bob	Phi., NYR	8	242	128	72	20	13451	694	13	3.10	18	3	9	0	830	55	0	3.98		1982-83	1990-91
Gagnon, David	Det.	1	2	0	1	0	35	6	0	10.29	....	....	....	....	....	....	....	....		1990-91	1990-91
• Gamble, Bruce	NYR, Bos., Tor., Phi.	10	327	109	149	47	18442	992	22	3.23	5	0	4	0	206	25	0	7.28		1958-59	1971-72
Gardiner, Bert	NYR, Mtl., Chi., Bos.	6	144	49	68	27	8760	554	3	3.79	9	4	5	0	647	20	0	1.85		1935-36	1943-44
• Gardiner, Chuck	Chi.	7	316	112	152	52	19687	664	42	2.02	21	12	6	3	1532	35	5	1.37	1	1927-28	1933-34
Gardner, George	Det., Van.	5	66	16	30	6	3313	207	0	3.75	....	....	....	....	....	....	....	....		1965-66	1971-72
Garrett, John	Hfd., Que., Van.	6	207	68	91	37	11763	837	1	4.27	9	4	3	0	461	33	0	4.30		1979-80	1984-85
Gatherum, Dave	Det.	1	3	2	0	1	180	3	1	1.00	....	....	....	....	....	....	....	....		1953-54	1953-54
Gauthier, Paul	Mtl.	1	1	0	0	1	70	2	0	1.71	....	....	....	....	....	....	....	....		1937-38	1937-38
Gelineau, Jack	Bos., Chi.	4	143	46	64	33	8580	447	7	3.13	4	2	2	0	260	7	1	1.62		1948-49	1953-54
Giacomin, Ed	NYR, Det.	13	610	289	206	97	35693	1675	54	2.82	65	29	35	0	3834	180	1	2.82		1965-66	1977-78
Gilbert, Gilles	Min., Bos., Det.	14	416	192	143	60	23677	1290	18	3.27	32	17	15	0	1919	97	3	3.03		1969-70	1982-83
Gill, Andre	Bos.	1	5	3	2	0	270	13	1	2.89	....	....	....	....	....	....	....	....		1967-68	1967-68
• Goodman, Paul	Chi.	3	52	23	20	9	3240	117	6	2.17	3	0	3	0	187	10	0	3.21	1	1937-38	1940-41
Gordon, Scott	Que.	2	23	2	16	0	1082	101	0	5.60	....	....	....	....	....	....	....	....		1989-90	1990-91
Gosselin, Mario	Que., L.A., Hfd.	9	241	91	107	14	12857	801	6	3.74	32	16	15	0	1816	99	0	3.27		1983-84	1993-94
Grahame, Ron	Bos., L.A., Que.	4	114	50	43	15	6472	409	5	3.79	4	2	1	0	202	7	0	2.08		1977-78	1980-81
• Grant, Ben	Tor., NYA., Bos.	6	50	17	26	4	2990	188	4	3.77	....	....	....	....	....	....	....	....		1928-29	1943-44
Grant, Doug	Det., St.L.	7	77	27	34	8	4199	280	2	4.00	....	....	....	....	....	....	....	....		1973-74	1979-80
Gratton, Gilles	St.L., NYR	2	47	13	18	9	2299	154	0	4.02	....	....	....	....	....	....	....	....		1975-76	1976-77
Gray, Gerry	Det., NYI	2	8	1	5	1	440	35	0	4.77	....	....	....	....	....	....	....	....		1970-71	1972-73
Gray, Harrison	Det.	1	1	0	0	0	40	5	0	7.50	....	....	....	....	....	....	....	....		1963-64	1963-64
Greenlay, Mike	Edm.	1	2	0	0	0	20	4	0	12.00	....	....	....	....	....	....	....	....		1989-90	1989-90
Guenette, Steve	Pit., Cgy.	5	35	19	16	0	1958	122	1	3.74	....	....	....	....	....	....	....	....		1986-87	1990-91
• Hainsworth, George	Mtl., Tor.	11	465	246	145	74	29415	937	94	1.91	52	21	26	5	3486	112	8	1.93	2	1926-27	1936-37
Hall, Glenn	Det., Chi., St.L.	18	906	407	327	163	53484	2239	84	2.51	115	49	65	0	6899	321	6	2.79	1	1952-53	1970-71
Hamel, Pierre	Tor., Wpg.	4	69	13	41	7	3766	276	0	4.40	....	....	....	....	....	....	....	....		1974-75	1980-81
Hanlon, Glen	Van., St.L., NYR, Det.	14	477	167	202	61	26037	1561	13	3.60	35	11	15	0	1756	92	4	3.14		1977-78	1990-91
Harrison, Paul	Min., Tor., Pit., Buf.	7	109	28	59	9	5806	408	2	4.22	4	0	1	0	157	9	0	3.44		1975-76	1981-82
Hayward, Brian	Wpg., Mtl., Min., S.J.	11	357	143	156	37	20025	1242	8	3.72	37	11	18	0	1803	104	0	3.46		1982-83	1992-93
Head, Don	Bos.	1	38	9	26	3	2280	161	2	4.24	....	....	....	....	....	....	....	....	1	1961-62	1961-62
• Hebert, Sammy	Tor., Ott.	2	4	1	3	0	200	19	0	5.70	....	....	....	....	....	....	....	....		1917-18	1923-24
Heinz, Rick	St.L., Van.	5	49	14	19	5	2356	159	2	4.05	1	0	0	0	8	1	0	7.50		1980-81	1984-85
Henderson, John	Bos.	2	45	15	15	15	2688	113	5	2.52	2	0	2	0	120	8	0	4.00		1954-55	1955-56
• Henry, Gord	Bos.	4	3	1	2	0	180	5	1	1.67	5	0	4	0	283	21	0	4.45		1948-49	1952-53
Henry, Jim	NYR, Chi., Bos.	9	405	161	173	70	24315	1166	28	2.88	29	11	18	0	1741	81	2	2.79		1941-42	1954-55
Herron, Denis	Pit., K.C., Mtl.	14	462	146	203	76	25608	1579	10	3.70	15	5	10	0	901	50	0	3.33		1972-73	1985-86
Highton, Hec	Chi.	1	24	10	14	0	1440	108	0	4.50	....	....	....	....	....	....	....	....		1943-44	1943-44
Himes, Normie	NYA	2	2	0	0	1	79	3	0	2.28	....	....	....	....	....	....	....	....		1927-28	1928-29
Hodge, Charlie	Mtl., Oak., Van.	13	358	152	124	60	20593	927	24	2.70	16	6	8	0	803	32	2	2.39	4	1954-55	1970-71
Hoffort, Bruce	Phi.	2	9	4	0	3	368	22	0	3.59	....	....	....	....	....	....	....	....		1989-90	1990-91
Hoganson, Paul	Pit.	1	2	0	1	0	57	7	0	7.37	....	....	....	....	....	....	....	....		1970-71	1970-71
Hogosta, Goran	NYI, Que.	2	22	5	12	3	1208	83	1	4.12	....	....	....	....	....	....	....	....		1977-78	1979-80
Holden, Mark	Mtl., Wpg.	4	8	3	2	1	372	25	0	4.03	....	....	....	....	....	....	....	....		1981-82	1984-85
Holland, Ken	Hfd.	2	4	0	2	1	206	17	0	4.95	....	....	....	....	....	....	....	....		1980-81	1980-81
Holland, Robbie	Pit.	2	44	11	22	9	2513	171	1	4.08	....	....	....	....	....	....	....	....		1979-80	1980-81
• Holmes, Harry	Tor., Det.	4	103	40	53	10	6510	264	17	2.43	7	4	3	0	420	38	1	5.43		1917-18	1927-28
Horner, Red	Tor.	1	1	0	0	0	1	1	0	60.00	....	....	....	....	....	....	....	....		1932-33	1932-33
Inness, Gary	Pit., Phi., Wsh.	7	162	58	61	27	8710	494	2	3.40	9	5	4	0	540	24	0	2.67		1973-74	1980-81
Ireland, Randy	Buf.	1	2	0	0	0	30	3	0	6.00	....	....	....	....	....	....	....	....		1978-79	1978-79
Irons, Robbie	St.L.	1	1	0	0	0	3	0	0	0.00	....	....	....	....	....	....	....	....		1968-69	1968-69
• Ironstone, Joe	NYA, Tor.	2	2	0	1	1	110	3	1	1.64	....	....	....	....	....	....	....	....		1925-26	1927-28
Jackson, Doug	Chi.	1	6	2	3	1	360	42	0	7.00	....	....	....	....	....	....	....	....		1947-48	1947-48
Jackson, Percy	Bos., NYA, NYR	4	7	1	3	1	392	26	0	3.98	....	....	....	....	....	....	....	....		1931-32	1935-36
Janaszak, Steve	Min., Col.	2	3	0	1	1	160	15	0	5.62	....	....	....	....	....	....	....	....		1979-80	1981-82
Janecyk, Bob	Chi., L.A.	6	110	43	47	13	6250	432	2	4.15	3	0	3	0	184	10	0	3.26		1983-84	1988-89
Jenkins, Roger	NYA	1	1	0	1	0	30	7	0	14.00	....	....	....	....	....	....	....	....		1938-39	1938-39
Jensen, Al	Det., Wsh., L.A.	7	179	95	53	18	9974	557	8	3.35	12	5	5	0	598	32	0	3.21		1980-81	1986-87
Jensen, Darren	Phi.	2	30	15	10	1	1496	95	2	3.81	....	....	....	....	....	....	....	....		1984-85	1985-86
Johnson, Bob	St.L., Pit.	2	24	9	9	1	1059	66	0	3.74	....	....	....	....	....	....	....	....		1972-73	1974-75
Johnston, Eddie	Bos., Tor., St.L., Chi.	16	592	236	256	81	34215	1855	32	3.25	18	7	10	0	1023	57	1	3.34	2	1962-63	1977-78
Junkin, Joe	Bos.	1	1	0	0	0	8	0	0	0.00	....	....	....	....	....	....	....	....		1968-69	1968-69
Kaarela, Jari	Col.	1	5	2	2	0	220	22	0	6.00	....	....	....	....	....	....	....	....		1980-81	1980-81
Kampurri, Hannu	N.J.	1	13	1	10	1	645	54	0	5.02	....	....	....	....	....	....	....	....		1984-85	1984-85
• Karakas, Mike	Chi., Mtl.	8	336	114	169	53	20616	1002	28	2.92	23	11	12	0	1434	72	3	3.01	1	1935-36	1945-46
Keans, Doug	L.A., Bos.	9	210	96	64	26	11388	666	4	3.51	9	2	6	0	432	34	0	4.72		1979-80	1987-88
Keenan, Don	Bos.	1	1	0	1	0	60	4	0	4.00	....	....	....	....	....	....	....	....		1958-59	1958-59
• Kerr, Dave	Mtl.M., NYA, NYR	11	426	203	148	75	26519	960	51	2.17	40	18	19	3	2616	76	8	1.74	1	1930-31	1940-41
King, Scott	Det.	2	2	0	0	0	61	3	0	2.95	....	....	....	....	....	....	....	....		1990-91	1991-92
Kleisinger, Terry	NYR	1	4	0	2	0	191	14	0	4.40	....	....	....	....	....	....	....	....		1985-86	1985-86
Klymkiw, Julian	NYR	1	1	0	0	0	19	2	0	6.32	....	....	....	....	....	....	....	....		1958-59	1958-59
Kurt, Gary	Cal.	1	16	1	7	0	838	60	0	4.30	....	....	....	....	....	....	....	....		1971-72	1971-72
Lacroix, Al	Mtl.	1	5	1	4	0	280	15	0	3.21	....	....	....	....	....	....	....	....		1925-26	1925-26
LaFerriere, Rick	Col.	1	1	0	0	0	20	1	0	3.00	....	....	....	....	....	....	....	....		1981-82	1981-82
• Larocque, Michel	Mtl., Tor., Phi., St.L.	11	312	160	89	45	17615	978	17	3.33	14	6	6	0	759	37	1	2.92	4	1973-74	1983-84
Laskowski, Gary	L.A.	2	59	19	27	5	2942	228	0	4.65	....	....	....	....	....	....	....	....		1982-83	1983-84
Laxton, Gord	Pit.	4	17	4	9	0	800	74	0	5.55	....	....	....	....	....	....	....	....		1975-76	1978-79
LeDuc, Albert	Mtl.	1	1	0	0	0	2	1	0	30.00	....	....	....	....	....	....	....	....		1931-32	1931-32
Legris, Claude	Det.	2	4	0	1	1	91	4	0	2.64	....	....	....	....	....	....	....	....		1980-81	1981-82
• Lehman, Hugh	Chi.	2	48	20	23	4	3047	136	6	2.68	2	0	1	1	120	10	0	5.00		1926-27	1927-28
Lemelin, Reggie	Atl., Cgy., Bos.	15	507	236	162	63	28006	1613	12	3.46	59	23	25	0	3119	186	2	3.58		1978-79	1992-93
Lessard, Mario	L.A.	6	240	92	97	39	13529	843	9	3.74	20	6	12	0	1136	83	0	4.38		1978-79	1983-84
Levasseur, Jean-Louis	Min.	1	1	0	1	0	60	7	0	7.00	....	....	....	....	....	....	....	....		1979-80	1979-80
Levinsky, Alex	Tor.	1	1	0	0	0	1	1	0	60.00	....	....	....	....	....	....	....	....		1932-33	1932-33
• Lindbergh, Pelle	Phi.	5	157	87	49	15	9151	503	7	3.30	23	12	10	0	1214	63	3	3.11		1981-82	1985-86
• Lindsay, Bert	Mtl.W., Tor.	2	20	6	14	0	1200	118	0	5.90	....	....	....	....	....	....	....	....		1917-18	1918-19
Liut, Mike	St. L., Hfd., Wsh.	13	663	294	271	74	38155	2219	25	3.49	67	29	32	0	3814	215	2	3.38		1979-80	1991-92
Lockett, Ken	Van.	2	55	13	15	8	2348	131	2	3.35	1	0	1	0	60	6	0	6.00		1974-75	1975-76
• Lockhart, Howie	Tor., Que., Ham., Bos.	5	57	17	39	0	3371	281	1	5.00	....	....	....	....	....	....	....	....		1919-20	1924-25
LoPresti, Pete	Min., Edm.	6	175	43	102	20	9858	668	5	4.07	2	0	2	0	77	6	0	4.68		1974-75	1980-81
• LoPresti, Sam	Chi.	2	74	30	38	6	4530	236	4	3.13	8	3	5	0	530	17	1	1.92		1940-41	1941-42
Loustel, Ron	Wpg.	1	1	0	1	0	60	10	0	10.00	....	....	....	....	....	....	....	....		1980-81	1980-81
Low, Ron	Tor., Wsh., Det., Que., Edm., NJ	11	382	102	203	38	20502	1463	4	4.28	7	1	6	0	452	29	0	3.85		1972-73	1984-85
Lozinski, Larry	Det.	1	30	6	11	7	1459	105	0	4.32	....	....	....	....	....	....	....	....		1980-81	1980-81
Lumley, Harry	Det., NYR, Chi., Tor., Bos.	16	804	333	326	143	48100	2210	71	2.76	76	29	47	0	4760	199	7	2.51	1	1943-44	1959-60
MacKenzie, Shawn	N.J.	1	4	0	1	0	130	15	0	6.92	....	....	....	....	....	....	....	....		1982-83	1982-83
Malarchuk, Clint	Que., Wsh., Buf.	10	338	141	130	45	19030	1100	12	3.47	15	2	9	0	781	56	0	4.30		1981-82	1991-92
Maneluk, George	NYI	1	4	1	1	0	140	15	0	6.43	....	....	....	....	....	....	....	....		1990-91	1990-91

Name	NHL Teams	NHL Seasons	Regular Schedule GP	W	L	T	Mins	GA	SO	Avg	Playoffs GP	W	L	T	Mins	GA	SO	Avg	NHL Cup Wins	First NHL Season	Last NHL Season
Maniago, Cesare	Tor., Mtl., NYR, Min., Van.	15	568	189	261	96	32570	1774	30	3.27	36	15	21	0	2245	100	3	2.67		1960-61	1977-78
Marios, Jean	Tor., Chi.	2	3	1	2	0	180	15	0	5.00	....	....	....	....	....	....	....	....		1943-44	1953-54
Martin, Seth	St.L.	1	30	8	10	7	1552	67	1	2.59	2	0	0	0	73	5	0	4.11		1967-68	1967-68
Mason, Bob	Wsh., Chi., Que., Van.	8	145	55	65	16	7988	500	1	3.76	5	2	3	0	369	12	1	1.95		1983-84	1990-91
Mattsson, Markus	Wpg., Min., L.A.	4	92	21	46	14	5007	343	6	4.11	....	....	....	....	....	....	....	....		1979-80	1983-84
May, Darrell	St. L.	2	6	1	5	0	364	31	0	5.11	....	....	....	....	....	....	....	....		1985-86	1987-88
Mayer, Gilles	Tor.	4	9	1	7	1	540	25	0	2.78	....	....	....	....	....	....	....	....		1949-50	1955-56
McAuley, Ken	NYR	2	96	17	64	15	5740	537	1	5.61	....	....	....	....	....	....	....	....		1943-44	1944-45
McCartan, Jack	NYR	2	12	3	7	2	680	43	1	3.79	....	....	....	....	....	....	....	....		1959-60	1960-61
• McCool, Frank	Tor.	2	72	34	31	7	4320	242	4	3.36	13	8	5	0	807	30	4	2.23	1	1944-45	1945-46
McDuffe, Pete	St.L., NYR, K.C., Det.	5	57	11	36	6	3207	218	0	4.08	1	0	0	0	60	7	0	7.00		1971-72	1975-76
McGrattan, Tom	Det.	1	1	0	0	0	8	0	0	0.00	....	....	....	....	....	....	....	....		1947-48	1947-48
McKay, Ross	Hfd.	1	1	0	0	0	35	3	0	5.14	....	....	....	....	....	....	....	....		1990-91	1990-91
McKenzie, Bill	Det., K.C., Col.	6	91	18	49	13	4776	326	2	4.10	....	....	....	....	....	....	....	....		1973-74	1979-80
McKichan, Steve	Van.	1	1	0	0	0	20	2	0	6.00	....	....	....	....	....	....	....	....		1990-91	1990-91
McLachlan, Murray	Tor.	1	2	0	1	0	25	4	0	9.60	....	....	....	....	....	....	....	....		1970-71	1970-71
McLelland, Dave	Van.	1	2	1	1	0	120	10	0	5.00	....	....	....	....	....	....	....	....		1972-73	1972-73
McLeod, Don	Det., Phi.	2	18	3	10	1	879	74	0	5.05	....	....	....	....	....	....	....	....		1970-71	1971-72
McLeod, Jim	St.L.	1	16	6	6	4	880	44	0	3.00	....	....	....	....	....	....	....	....		1971-72	1971-72
McNamara, Gerry	Tor.	2	7	2	2	1	323	15	0	2.79	....	....	....	....	....	....	....	....		1960-61	1969-70
McNeil, Gerry	Mtl.	7	276	119	105	52	16535	650	28	2.36	35	17	18	0	2284	72	5	1.89	3	1947-48	1956-57
McRae, Gord	Tor.	5	71	30	22	10	3799	221	1	3.49	8	2	5	0	454	22	0	2.91		1972-73	1977-78
Melanson, Rollie	NYI, Min., L.A., N.J., Mtl.	11	291	129	106	33	16452	995	6	3.63	23	4	9	0	801	59	0	4.42	3	1980-81	1991-92
Meloche, Gilles	Chi., Cal., Cle., Min., Pit.	18	788	270	351	131	45401	2756	20	3.64	45	21	19	0	2464	143	2	3.48		1970-71	1987-88
Micalef, Corrado	Det.	5	113	26	59	15	5794	409	2	4.24	3	0	0	0	49	8	0	9.80		1981-82	1985-86
Middlebrook, Lindsay	Wpg., Min., N.J., Edm.	4	37	3	25	4	1845	152	0	4.94	....	....	....	....	....	....	....	....		1979-80	1982-83
• Millar, Al	Bos.	1	6	1	3	2	360	25	0	4.17	....	....	....	....	....	....	....	....		1957-58	1957-58
Millen, Greg	Pit., Hfd., St. L., Que., Chi., Det.	14	604	215	284	89	35377	2281	17	3.87	59	27	29	0	3383	193	0	3.42		1978-79	1991-92
• Miller, Joe	NYA, NYR, Pit., Phi.	4	130	24	90	16	7981	386	16	2.90	3	2	1	0	180	3	1	1.00	1	1927-28	1930-31
Mio, Eddie	Edm., NYR, Det.	7	192	64	73	30	10428	705	4	4.06	17	9	7	0	986	63	0	3.83		1979-80	1985-86
• Mitchell, Ivan	Tor.	3	20	11	9	0	1232	96	0	4.68	....	....	....	....	....	....	....	....		1919-20	1921-22
Moffat, Mike	Bos.	3	19	7	7	2	979	70	0	4.29	11	6	5	0	663	38	0	3.44		1981-82	1983-84
Moore, Alfie	NYA, Det., Chi.,	4	21	7	14	0	1290	81	1	3.77	3	1	2	0	180	7	0	2.33	1	1936-37	1939-40
Moore, Robbie	Phi., Wsh.	2	6	3	1	1	257	8	2	1.87	5	3	2	0	268	18	0	4.03		1978-79	1982-83
Morissette, Jean	Mtl.	1	1	0	1	0	36	4	0	6.67	....	....	....	....	....	....	....	....		1963-64	1963-64
• Mowers, Johnny	Det.	4	152	65	61	26	9350	399	15	2.56	32	19	13	0	2000	85	2	2.55	1	1940-41	1946-47
Mrazek, Jerry	Phi.	1	1	0	0	0	6	1	0	10.00	....	....	....	....	....	....	....	....		1975-76	1975-76
• Mummery, Harry	Que., Ham.	2	4	2	1	0	191	20	0	6.28	....	....	....	....	....	....	....	....		1919-20	1921-22
• Murphy, Hal	Mtl.	1	1	1	0	0	60	4	0	4.00	....	....	....	....	....	....	....	....		1952-53	1952-53
Murray, Tom	Mtl.	1	1	0	1	0	60	4	0	4.00	....	....	....	....	....	....	....	....		1929-30	1929-30
Myllys, Jarmo	Min., S.J.	4	39	4	27	1	1846	161	0	5.23	....	....	....	....	....	....	....	....		1988-89	1991-92
Mylnikov, Sergei	Que.	1	10	1	7	2	568	47	0	4.96	....	....	....	....	....	....	....	....		1989-90	1989-90
Myre, Phil	Mtl., Atl., St.L., Phi., Col., Buf.	14	439	149	198	74	25220	1482	14	3.53	12	6	5	0	747	41	1	3.29		1969-70	1982-83
Newton, Cam	Pit.	2	16	4	7	1	814	51	0	3.76	....	....	....	....	....	....	....	....		1970-71	1972-73
Norris, Jack	Bos., Chi., L.A.	4	58	19	26	4	3119	202	2	3.89	....	....	....	....	....	....	....	....		1964-65	1970-71
Oleschuk, Bill	K.C., Col.	4	55	7	28	10	2835	188	1	3.98	....	....	....	....	....	....	....	....		1975-76	1979-80
• Olesevich, Dan	NYR	1	1	0	0	1	40	2	0	3.00	....	....	....	....	....	....	....	....		1961-62	1961-62
Ouimet, Ted	St.L.	1	1	0	1	0	60	2	0	2.00	....	....	....	....	....	....	....	....		1968-69	1968-69
Pageau, Paul	L.A.	1	1	0	1	0	60	8	0	8.00	....	....	....	....	....	....	....	....		1980-81	1980-81
Paille, Marcel	NYR	7	107	33	52	21	6342	362	2	3.42	....	....	....	....	....	....	....	....		1957-58	1964-65
Palmateer, Mike	Tor., Wsh.	8	356	149	138	52	20131	1183	17	3.53	29	12	17	0	1765	89	2	3.03		1976-77	1983-84
Pang, Darren	Chi.	3	81	27	35	7	4252	287	0	4.05	6	1	3	0	250	18	0	4.32		1984-85	1988-89
Parent, Bernie	Bos., Tor., Phi.	13	608	270	197	121	35136	1493	55	2.55	71	38	33	0	4302	174	6	2.43	2	1965-66	1978-79
Parent, Bob	Tor.	2	3	0	2	0	160	15	0	5.62	....	....	....	....	....	....	....	....		1981-82	1982-83
Parro, Dave	Wsh.	4	77	21	36	10	4015	274	2	4.09	....	....	....	....	....	....	....	....		1980-81	1983-84
• Patrick, Lester	NYR	1	....	....	....	....	....	....	....	....	1	1	0	0	46	1	0	1.30	1	1927-28	1927-28
Peeters, Pete	Phi., Bos., Wsh.	13	489	246	155	51	27699	1424	21	3.08	71	35	35	0	4200	232	2	3.31		1978-79	1990-91
Pelletier, Marcel	Chi., NYR	2	8	1	6	1	395	33	0	5.01	....	....	....	....	....	....	....	....		1950-51	1962-63
Penney, Steve	Mtl., Wpg.	5	91	35	38	12	5194	313	1	3.62	27	15	12	0	1604	72	4	2.69		1983-84	1987-88
• Perreault, Robert	Mtl., Det., Bos.	3	31	8	16	6	1827	106	3	3.48	....	....	....	....	....	....	....	....		1955-56	1962-63
Pettie, Jim	Bos.	3	21	9	7	2	1157	71	1	3.68	....	....	....	....	....	....	....	....		1976-77	1978-79
Pietrangelo, Frank	Pit., Hfd.	7	141	46	59	6	7141	490	1	4.12	12	7	5	0	713	34	1	2.86	1	1987-88	1993-94
• Plante, Jacques	Mtl., NYR, St.L., Tor., Bos.	18	837	434	246	147	49533	1965	82	2.38	112	71	37	0	6651	240	14	2.17	6	1952-53	1972-73
Plasse, Michel	St.L., Mtl., K.C., Pit., Col., Que.	12	299	92	136	54	16760	1058	2	3.79	4	1	2	0	195	9	1	2.77	1	1970-71	1981-82
Plaxton, Hugh	Mtl.M.	1	1	0	1	0	59	5	0	5.08	....	....	....	....	....	....	....	....		1932-33	1932-33
Pronovost, Claude	Bos., Mtl.	2	3	1	1	0	120	7	1	3.50	....	....	....	....	....	....	....	....		1955-56	1958-59
Pusey, Chris	Det.	1	1	0	0	0	40	3	0	4.50	....	....	....	....	....	....	....	....		1985-86	1985-86
Raymond, Alain	Wsh.	1	1	0	1	0	40	2	0	3.00	....	....	....	....	....	....	....	....		1987-88	1987-88
Rayner, Chuck	NYA, Bro., NYR	10	424	138	209	77	25491	1294	25	3.05	18	9	9	0	1135	46	1	2.43		1940-41	1952-53
Reaugh, Daryl	Edm., Hfd.	3	27	8	9	1	1246	72	1	3.47	....	....	....	....	....	....	....	....		1984-85	1990-91
Redquest, Greg	Pit.	1	1	0	0	0	13	3	0	13.85	....	....	....	....	....	....	....	....		1977-78	1977-78
Reece, Dave	Bos.	1	14	7	5	2	777	43	2	3.32	....	....	....	....	....	....	....	....		1975-76	1975-76
Resch, Glenn	NYI, Col., N.J., Phi.	14	571	231	224	82	32279	1761	26	3.27	41	17	17	0	2044	85	2	2.50	1	1973-74	1986-87
Rheaume, Herb	Mtl.	1	31	10	19	1	1889	92	0	2.92	....	....	....	....	....	....	....	....		1925-26	1925-26
Ricci, Nick	Pit.	4	19	7	12	0	1087	79	0	4.36	....	....	....	....	....	....	....	....		1979-80	1982-83
Richardson, Terry	Det., St.L.	5	20	3	11	0	906	85	0	5.63	....	....	....	....	....	....	....	....		1973-74	1978-79
Ridley, Curt	NYR, Van., Tor.	6	104	27	47	16	5498	355	1	3.87	2	0	2	0	120	8	0	4.00		1974-75	1980-81
Riggin, Dennis	Det.	2	18	5	10	2	985	54	1	3.29	....	....	....	....	....	....	....	....		1959-60	1962-63
Riggin, Pat	Atl., Cgy., Wsh., Bos., Pit.	9	350	153	120	52	19872	1135	11	3.43	25	8	13	0	1336	72	0	3.23		1979-80	1987-88
Ring, Bob	Bos.	1	1	0	0	0	34	4	0	7.06	....	....	....	....	....	....	....	....		1965-66	1965-66
Rivard, Fern	Min.	4	55	9	27	11	2865	190	2	3.98	....	....	....	....	....	....	....	....		1968-69	1974-75
• Roach, John	Tor., NYR, Det.	14	491	219	204	68	30423	1246	58	2.46	34	15	16	3	2206	69	7	1.88	1	1921-22	1934-35
• Roberts, Moe	Bos., NYA, Chi.	4	10	2	5	0	506	31	0	3.68	....	....	....	....	....	....	....	....		1925-26	1951-52
• Robertson, Earl	NYA, Bro., Det.	6	190	60	95	34	11820	575	16	2.92	15	6	7	0	995	29	0	1.75	1	1936-37	1941-42
• Rollins, Al	Tor., Chi., NYR	9	430	139	206	84	25743	1196	28	2.79	13	6	7	0	755	30	0	2.38	1	1949-50	1959-60
Romano, Roberto	Pit., Bos.	6	126	46	63	8	7111	471	4	3.97	....	....	....	....	....	....	....	....		1982-83	1993-94
Rupp, Pat	Det.	1	1	0	1	0	60	4	0	4.00	....	....	....	....	....	....	....	....		1963-64	1963-64
Rutherford, Jim	Det., Pit., Tor., L.A.	13	457	151	227	59	25895	1576	14	3.65	8	2	5	0	440	28	0	3.82		1970-71	1982-83
Rutledge, Wayne	L.A.	3	82	27	41	6	4325	241	2	3.34	8	2	2	0	378	20	0	3.17		1967-68	1969-70
St. Laurent, Sam	N.J., Det.	5	34	7	12	4	1572	92	1	3.51	1	0	0	0	10	1	0	6.00		1985-86	1989-90
Sands, Charlie	Mtl.	1	1	0	0	0	25	5	0	12.00	....	....	....	....	....	....	....	....		1939-40	1939-40
Sands, Mike	Min.	2	6	0	5	0	302	26	0	5.17	....	....	....	....	....	....	....	....		1984-85	1986-87
Sauve, Bob	Buf., Det., Chi., N.J.	12	420	182	154	54	23711	1377	8	3.48	34	15	16	0	1850	95	4	3.08		1976-77	1987-88
• Sawchuk, Terry	Det., Bos., Tor., L.A., NYR	21	971	447	330	173	57184	2401	103	2.52	106	54	48	0	6306	267	12	2.54	4	1949-50	1969-70
Schaefer, Joe	NYR	2	2	0	1	0	86	8	0	5.58	....	....	....	....	....	....	....	....		1959-60	1960-61
Scott, Ron	NYR, L.A.	5	28	8	13	4	1450	91	0	3.77	1	0	0	0	32	4	0	7.50	1	1983-84	1989-90
Sevigny, Richard	Mtl., Que.	8	176	80	44	20	9485	507	5	3.21	4	0	3	0	208	13	0	3.75		1979-80	1986-87
Sharples, Scott	Cgy.	1	1	0	0	1	65	4	0	3.69	....	....	....	....	....	....	....	....		1991-92	1991-92
Shields, Al	NYA	1	2	0	0	0	41	9	0	13.17	....	....	....	....	....	....	....	....		1931-32	1931-32
Simmons, Don	Bos., Tor., NYR	11	247	98	104	39	14436	705	20	2.93	24	13	11	0	1436	64	3	2.67	2	1956-57	1968-69
Simmons, Gary	Cal., Clev., L.A.	4	107	30	57	15	6162	366	5	3.56	1	0	0	0	20	1	0	3.00		1974-75	1977-78
Skidmore, Paul	St.L.	1	2	1	1	0	120	6	0	3.00	....	....	....	....	....	....	....	....		1981-82	1981-82
Skorodenski, Warren	Chi., Edm.	5	35	12	11	4	1732	100	2	3.46	2	0	0	0	33	6	0	10.91		1981-82	1987-88
Smith, Al	Tor., Pit., Det., Buf., Hfd., Col.	10	233	74	99	36	12752	735	10	3.46	6	1	4	0	317	21	0	3.97		1965-66	1980-81
Smith, Billy	L.A., NYI	18	680	305	233	105	38431	2031	22	3.17	132	88	36	0	7645	348	5	2.73	4	1971-72	1988-89
Smith, Gary	Tor., Oak., Cal., Chi., Van., Min., Wsh., Wpg.	14	532	173	261	74	29619	1675	26	3.39	20	5	13	0	1153	62	1	3.23		1965-66	1979-80
• Smith, Norman	Mtl.M., Det.	8	199	81	83	35	12297	475	17	2.32	12	9	2	0	880	18	3	1.23	2	1931-32	1944-45
Sneddon, Bob	Cal.	1	5	0	2	0	225	21	0	5.60	....	....	....	....	....	....	....	....		1970-71	1970-71
Soetaert, Doug	NYR, Wpg., Mtl.	12	284	110	104	42	15583	1030	6	3.97	5	1	2	0	180	14	0	4.67	1	1975-76	1986-87
• Spooner, Red	Pit.	1	1	0	1	0	60	6	0	6.00	....	....	....	....	....	....	....	....		1929-30	1929-30
St.Croix, Rick	Phi., Tor.	8	129	49	54	18	7275	450	2	3.71	11	4	6	0	562	29	1	3.10		1977-78	1984-85
Staniowski, Ed	St.L., Wpg., Hfd.	10	219	67	104	21	12075	818	2	4.06	8	1	6	0	428	28	0	3.93		1975-76	1984-85
Starr, Harold	Mtl.M.	1	1	0	0	0	3	0	0	0.00	....	....	....	....	....	....	....	....		1931-32	1931-32

			Regular Schedule								Playoffs										
Name	NHL Teams	NHL Seasons	GP	W	L	T	Mins	GA	SO	Avg	GP	W	L	T	Mins	GA	SO	Avg	NHL Cup Wins	First NHL Season	Last NHL Season
Stefan, Greg	Det.	9	299	115	127	30	16333	1068	5	3.92	30	12	17	0	1681	99	1	3.53		1981-82	1989-90
Stein, Phil	Tor.	1	1	0	0	1	70	2	0	1.71	....	....	....	....	....	....	....	....		1939-40	1939-40
Stephenson, Wayne	St.L., Phi., Wsh.	10	328	146	103	49	18343	937	14	3.06	26	11	12	0	1522	79	2	3.11	1	1971-72	1980-81
Stevenson, Doug	NYR, Chi.	2	8	2	6	0	480	39	0	4.88	....	....	....	....	....	....	....	....		1944-45	1945-46
Stewart, Charles	Bos.	3	77	31	41	5	4737	194	10	2.46	....	....	....	....	....	....	....	....		1924-25	1926-27
Stewart, Jim	Bos.	1	1	0	1	0	20	5	0	15.00	....	....	....	....	....	....	....	....		1979-80	1979-80
Stuart, Herb	Det.	1	3	1	2	0	180	5	0	1.67	....	....	....	....	....	....	....	....		1926-27	1926-27
Sylvestri, Don	Bos.	1	3	0	0	2	102	6	0	3.53	....	....	....	....	....	....	....	....		1984-85	1984-85
Takko, Kari	Min., Edm.	6	142	37	71	14	7317	475	1	3.90	4	0	1	0	109	7	0	3.85		1985-86	1990-91
Tataryn, Dave	NYR	1	2	1	1	0	80	10	0	7.50	....	....	....	....	....	....	....	....		1976-77	1976-77
Taylor, Bobby	Phi., Pit.	5	46	15	17	6	2268	155	0	4.10	....	....	....	....	....	....	....	....	1	1971-72	1975-76
Teno, Harvey	Det.	1	5	2	3	0	300	15	0	3.00	....	....	....	....	....	....	....	....		1938-39	1938-39
Thomas, Wayne	Mtl., Tor., NYR	8	243	103	93	34	13768	766	10	3.34	15	6	8	0	849	50	1	3.53		1972-73	1980-81
• Thompson, Tiny	Bos., Det.	12	553	284	194	75	34174	1183	81	2.08	44	20	24	0	2968	93	7	1.88	1	1928-29	1939-40
Tremblay, Vince	Tor., Pit.	5	58	12	26	8	2785	223	1	4.80	....	....	....	....	....	....	....	....		1979-80	1983-84
Tucker, Ted	Cal.	1	5	1	1	1	177	10	0	3.39	....	....	....	....	....	....	....	....		1973-74	1973-74
Turner, Joe	Det.	1	1	0	0	1	60	3	0	3.00	....	....	....	....	....	....	....	....		1941-42	1941-42
Vachon, Rogatien	Mtl., L.A., Det., Bos.	16	795	355	291	127	46298	2310	51	2.99	48	23	23	0	2876	133	2	2.77	3	1966-67	1981-82
Veisor, Mike	Chi., Hfd., Wpg.	10	139	41	62	26	7806	532	5	4.09	4	0	2	0	180	15	0	5.00		1973-74	1983-84
• Vezina, Georges	Mtl.	9	191	104	81	5	11564	633	13	3.28	26	17	8	0	1596	74	4	2.78	2	1917-18	1925-26
Villemure, Gilles	NYR, Chi.	10	205	100	65	28	11581	542	13	2.81	14	5	5	0	656	32	0	2.93		1963-64	1976-77
Wakely, Ernie	Mtl., St.L.	5	113	41	42	17	6244	290	8	2.79	10	2	6	0	509	37	1	4.36		1962-63	1971-72
• Walsh, James	Mtl.M., NYA	7	108	48	43	16	6461	250	12	2.32	8	2	4	2	570	16	2	1.68		1926-27	1932-33
Wamsley, Rick	Mtl., St.L., Cgy., Tor.	13	407	204	131	46	23123	1287	12	3.34	27	7	18	0	1397	81	0	3.48	1	1980-81	1992-93
Watt, Jim	St.L.	1	1	0	0	0	20	2	0	6.00	....	....	....	....	....	....	....	....		1973-74	1973-74
Weeks, Steve	NYR, Hfd., Van., NYI, L.A., Ott.	13	290	111	119	33	15879	989	5	3.74	12	3	5	0	486	27	0	3.33		1980-81	1992-93
Wetzel, Carl	Det., Min.	2	7	1	3	1	302	22	0	4.37	....	....	....	....	....	....	....	....		1964-65	1967-68
Wilson, Dunc	Phi., Van., Tor., NYR, Pit.	10	287	80	150	33	15851	988	8	3.74	....	....	....	....	....	....	....	....		1969-70	1978-79
Wilson, Lefty	Det., Tor., Bos.	3	3	0	0	1	85	1	0	0.71	....	....	....	....	....	....	....	....		1953-54	1957-58
• Winkler, Hal	NYR, Bos.	2	75	35	26	14	4739	126	21	1.60	10	2	3	5	640	18	2	1.69		1926-27	1927-28
Wolfe, Bernie	Wsh.	4	120	20	61	21	6104	424	1	4.17	....	....	....	....	....	....	....	....		1975-76	1978-79
Woods, Alec	NYA	1	1	0	1	0	70	3	0	2.57	....	....	....	....	....	....	....	....		1936-37	1936-37
Worsley, Gump	NYR, Mtl., Min.	21	861	335	353	150	50201	2432	43	2.91	70	41	25	0	4080	192	5	2.82	4	1952-53	1973-74
• Worters, Roy	Pit., NYA, Mtl.	12	484	171	233	68	30175	1143	66	2.27	11	3	6	2	690	24	3	2.09		1925-26	1936-37
Worthy, Chris	Oak., Cal.	3	26	5	10	4	1326	98	0	4.43	....	....	....	....	....	....	....	....		1968-69	1970-71
Young, Doug	Det.	1	1	0	0	0	21	1	0	2.86	....	....	....	....	....	....	....	....		1933-34	1933-34
Zanier, Mike	Edm.	1	3	1	1	1	185	12	0	3.89	....	....	....	....	....	....	....	....		1984-85	1984-85

1995-96 Transactions

August, 1995

17 – LW **Shawn Burr** and Detroit's 3rd round choice in 1996 Entry Draft traded from Detrot to Tampa Bay for D **Marc Bergevin** and RW **Ben Hankinson**.

17 – D **David Shaw** and a conditional draft choice in 1996 Entry Draft traded from Boston to Tampa Bay for Detroit's 3rd round choice in 1996 Entry Draft (previously acquired) and a conditional draft choice in 1996 Entry Draft.

24 – D **Brett Hauer** traded from Vancouver to Edmonton for a conditional draft pick.

30 – D **Dimitri Yushkevich** and Philadelphia's 2nd round choice in 1996 Entry Draft traded from Philadelphia to Toronto for Toronto's 1st round choice in 1996 Entry Draft, 2nd round choice in 1997 Entry Draft and Los Angeles' 4th round choice in 1996 Entry Draft (previously acquired).

31 – LW **Luc Robitaille** and D **Ulf Samuelsson** traded from Pittsburgh to NY Rangers for C **Petr Nedved** and D **Sergei Zubov**.

September

14 – C **Alexander Semak** traded from Tampa Bay to NY Islanders for the NY Islanders' 5th round choice in the 1997 Entry Draft.

20 – C **Andre Faust** traded from Philadelphia to Winnipeg for Winnipeg's 7th round choice in 1997 Entry Draft.

20 – G **Jean-Francois Labbe** traded from Ottawa to Colorado for a conditional draft pick.

21 – D **Jason Herter** traded from Dallas to NY Islanders for cash.

28 – D **Dallas Eakins** traded from Florida to St. Louis for St. Louis' 4th round choice in 1997 Entry Draft.

October

2 – **1996 Waiver Draft**

- RW **Jim McKenzie** to Winnipeg from NY Islanders
- C **Ted Drury** to Ottawa from Colorado
- LW **Bill Huard** to Dallas from Colorado
- LW **Brent Hughes** to Buffalo from Boston
- G **Pat Jablonski** to St. Louis from Toronto
- D **Justin Hocking** to Ottawa from Los Angeles
- RW **Rob Conn** to Buffalo from New Jersey
- C **Bob Sweeney** to NY Islanders from Buffalo

2 – RW **Paul Broten** traded from Dallas to St. Louis for C **Guy Carbonneau**.

2 – D **Rick Zombo** traded from St. Louis to Boston for C **Fred Knipscheer**.

2 – LW **Warren Rychel** traded from Toronto to Colorado for cash.

3 – RW **Claude Lemieux** traded from New Jersey to NY Islanders for LW **Steve Thomas**.

3 – RW **Claude Lemieux** traded from NY Islanders to Colorado for LW **Wendel Clark**.

5 – D **Steven Finn** traded from Colorado to **Tampa Bay** for Tampa Bay's 4th round choice in 1997 Entry Draft.

5 – C **Steve Larouche** traded from Ottawa to NY Rangers for RW **Jean-Yves Roy**.

6 – RW **Nelson Emerson** traded from Winnipeg to Hartford for C **Darren Turcotte**.

7 – D **Frank Musil** traded from Calgary to Ottawa for Ottawa's 4th round choice in 1997 Entry Draft.

17 – D **Igor Ulanov** traded from Washington to Chicago for Chicago's 3rd round choice in 1996 Entry Draft.

24 – RW **Ray Sheppard** traded from Detroit to San Jose for C **Igor Larionov** and a conditional draft choice in 1998 Entry Draft.

26 – RW **Owen Nolan** traded from Colorado to San Jose for D **Sandis Ozolinsh**.

30 – D **Bobby Marshall** traded from Calgary to Anaheim for C **Jarrod Skalde**.

November

1 – RW **Darin Kimble** traded from Chicago to New Jersey for C **Michael Vukonich** and C **Bill Armstrong**.

1 – LW **Esa Tikkanen** traded from St. Louis to New Jersey for New Jersey's 3rd round choice in 1997 Entry Draft.

1 – C **Claude Lapointe** traded from Colorado to Calgary for Calgary's 7th round choice in 1996 Entry Draft.

7 – G **Pat Jablonski** traded from St. Louis to Montreal for D **Jean-Jacques Daigneault**.

13 – D **Michel Petit** traded from Los Angeles to Tampa Bay for D **Steven Finn**.

15 – G **Chris Terreri** traded from New Jersey to San Jose for San Jose's 2nd round choice in 1996 Entry Draft.

16 – RW **Pat Falloon** traded from San Jose to Philadelphia for an optional 1st round choice in 1996 Entry Draft, Philadelphia's 4th round choice in 1996 Entry Draft and LW **Martin Spanhel**.

16 – D **Doug Bodger** traded from Buffalo to San Jose for an optional 1st round choice in 1996 Entry Draft, San Jose's 4th round choice in 1996 Entry Draft, RW **Vaclav Varada** and LW **Martin Spanhel**.

16 – D **Eric Charron** traded from Tampa Bay to Washington for a conditional draft choice in 1997 Entry Draft.

23 – LW **Esa Tikkanen** traded from New Jersey to Vancouver for Vancouver's 2nd round choice in 1996 Entry Draft.

26 – C **Craig Ferguson** and LW **Yves Sarault** traded from Montreal to Calgary for a conditional draft choice in 1997 Entry Draft.

29 – RW **Dan Kesa** and a conditional draft choice in 1997 Entry Draft traded from Dallas to Hartford for C **Robert Petrovicky**.

December

1 – G **Jeff Reese** traded from Hartford to Tampa Bay for Tampa Bay's 9th round choice in 1996 Entry Draft.

4 – C **Peter White** and Edmonton's 4th round choice in 1996 Entry Draft traded from Edmonton to Toronto for LW **Kent Manderville**.

6 – G **Patrick Roy** and RW **Mike Keane** traded from Montreal to Colorado for RW **Andrei Kovalenko**, LW **Martin Rucinsky** and G **Jocelyn Thibault**.

9 – D **Dean Chynoweth** traded from NY Islanders to Boston for Boston's 5th round choice in 1996 Entry Draft.

13 – RW **Trent Klatt** traded from Dallas to Philadelphia for LW **Brent Fedyk**.

19 – C **Jim Dowd** and New Jersey's 2nd round choice in 1997 Entry Draft traded from New Jersey to Hartford for RW **Jocelyn Lemieux** and Hartford's 2nd round choice in 1998 Entry Draft.

19 – C **Jim Dowd**, D **Frantisek Kucera** and Hartford's 2nd round choice in 1997 Entry Draft traded from Hartford to Vancouver for D **Jeff Brown** and Vancouver's 3rd round choice in 1998 Entry Draft.

19 – C **Joe Nieuwendyk** traded from Calgary to Dallas for C **Corey Millen** and RW **Jarome Iginla**.

28 – D **Neil Wilkinson** traded from Winnipeg to Pittsburgh for D **Norm Maciver**.

28 – C **Ian Laperriere** traded from St. Louis to NY Rangers for LW **Stephane Matteau**.

28 – RW **Kevin Dineen** traded from Philadelphia to Hartford for a conditional draft choice in 1997 Entry Draft.

28 – D **John Slaney** traded from Colorado to Los Angeles for conditional draft choice in 1996 Entry Draft.

January, 1996

4 – D **Jeff Norton** and D **Donald Dufresne** traded from St. Louis to Edmonton for D **Igor Kravchuk** and D **Ken Sutton**.

11 – G **Bill Ranford** traded from Edmonton to Boston for LW **Mariusz Czerkawski**, D **Sean Brown** and Boston's 1st round choice in 1996 Entry Draft.

14 – C **Steve Larouche** traded from NY Rangers to Los Angeles for D **Chris Snell**.

21 – C **Jim Campbell** traded from Montreal to Anaheim for D **Robert Dirk**.

23 – C **Dan Quinn** traded from Ottawa to Philadelphia for cash.

23 –G **Damian Rhodes** and LW **Ken Belanger** traded from Toronto to NY Islanders for future considerations.

23 –G **Damian Rhodes** and D **Wade Redden** traded from NY Islanders to Ottawa for G **Don Beaupre**, RW **Martin Straka** and D **Bryan Berard**.

23 –G **Don Beaupre** and C **Kirk Muller** traded from NY Islanders to Toronto for future considerations.

25 –RW **Rick Tocchet** traded from Los Angeles to Boston for LW **Kevin Stevens**.

26 –D **Janne Laukkanen** traded from Colorado to Ottawa for LW **Brad Larsen**.

29 –C **Benoit Hogue** and LW **Randy Wood** traded from Toronto to Dallas for C **Dave Gagner** and Dallas' 6th round choice in 1996 Entry Draft.

29 –C **Mike Pomichter** traded from Chicago to Toronto for cash.

29 –RW **Denis Chasse** traded from St. Louis to Washington for RW **Rob Pearson**.

February

1 –D **Bob Boughner** traded from Florida to Buffalo for a conditional draft choice in 1996 Entry Draft.

2 –D **Bob Halkidis** traded from Chicago to NY Islanders for C/RW **Danton Cole**.

6 –LW **Chris Herperger** and Winnipeg's 7th round choice in 1997 Entry Draft (previously acquired) traded from Philadelphia to Anaheim for C **Bob Corkum**.

7 –C **Chad Kilger**, D **Oleg Tverdovsky** and Anaheim's 3rd round choice in 1996 Entry Draft traded from Anaheim to Winnipeg for RW **Teemu Selanne**, C **Marc Chouinard** and Winnipeg's 4th round choice in 1996 Entry Draft.

10 –C **Craig Ferguson** traded from Calgary to Los Angeles for LW **Pat Conacher**.

15 –D **Stewart Malgunas** traded from Winnipeg to Washington for RW **Denis Chasse**.

15 –D **Darryl Shannon** and LW **Michal Grosek** traded from Winnipeg to Buffalo for D **Craig Muni** and a 1st round choice in 1996 Entry Draft.

17 –RW **Shane Churla** and D **Doug Zmolek** traded from Dallas to Los Angeles for D **Darryl Sydor** and Los Angeles' 5th round choice in 1996 Entry Draft.

26 –D **Tommy Albelin**, D **Cale Hulse** and RW **Jocelyn Lemieux** traded from New Jersey to Calgary for D **Phil Housley** and D **Dan Keczmer**.

27 –G **Tim Cheveldae** and Winnipeg's 3rd round choice in 1996 Entry Draft traded from Winnipeg to Philadelphia for G **Dominic Roussel**.

27 –C **Wayne Gretzky** traded from Los Angeles to St. Louis for LW **Craig Johnson**, C **Patrice Tardif**, C **Roman Vopat**, St. Louis' 1st round choice in 1997 Entry Draft and 5th round choice in 1996 Entry Draft.

29 –LW **Nick Kypreos** traded from NY Rangers to Toronto for LW **Bill Berg**.

29 –RW **Wayne Presley** traded from NY Rangers to Toronto for LW **Sergio Momesso**.

March

1 –C **Dave McLlwain** traded from Ottawa to Pittsburgh for Pittsburgh's 8th round choice in 1996 Entry Draft.

8 –LW **Kevin Sawyer** and D **Steve Staios** traded from St. Louis to Boston for RW **Steve Leach**.

8 –G **Mike Torchia** traded from Washington to Anaheim for LW **Todd Krygier**.

12 –LW **David Roberts** traded from St. Louis to Edmonton for future considerations.

13 –C **Darby Hendrickson**, D **Kenny Jonsson**, C **Sean Haggerty** and Toronto's 1st round choice in 1997 Entry Draft traded from Toronto to NY Islanders for LW **Wendel Clark**, D **Mathieu Schneider** and D **D.J. Smith**.

13 –LW **Dave Andreychuk** traded from Toronto to New Jersey for a 2nd round draft choice in 1996 Entry Draft and a conditional draft choice in 1998 or 1999 Entry Drafts.

14 –C **Ray Ferraro**, C **Ian Laperriere**, D **Mattias Norstrom**, C **Nathan Lafayette** and NY Rangers' 4th round choice in 1997 Entry Draft traded from NY Rangers to Los Angeles for D **Marty McSorley**, RW **Jari Kurri** and RW **Shane Churla**.

15 –G **Martin Brochu** traded from Montreal to Washington for future considerations.

15 –RW **Mike Sillinger** traded from Anaheim to Vancouver for RW **Roman Oksiuta**.

15 –C **Dale Hawerchuk** traded from St. Louis to Philadelphia for C **Craig MacTavish**.

16 –RW **Ray Sheppard** and San Jose's 4th round choice in 1996 Entry Draft traded from San Jose to Florida for Florida's 2nd and 4th round draft choices in 1996 Entry Draft.

18 –C **Darren Turcotte** and Dallas' 2nd round choice in 1996 Entry Draft (previously acquired) traded from Winnipeg to San Jose for C **Craig Janney**.

19 –D **Kerry Huffman** traded from Ottawa to Philadelphia for future consideratons.

19 –C **Anatoli Semenov** and D **Mike Crowley** traded from Philadelphia to Anaheim for RW **Brian Wesenberg**.

19 –LW **Vesa Viitakoski** traded from Calgary to Colorado for LW **Paxton Schulte**.

19 –RW **John Druce** and Los Angeles' 7th round choice in 1997 Entry Draft traded from Los Angeles to Philadelphia for Los Angeles' 4th round choice in 1996 Entry Draft (previously acquired).

19 –D **Charlie Huddy** and Buffalo's 7th round choice in 1996 Entry Draft traded from Buffalo to St. Louis for LW **Denis Hamel**.

20 –C **Jesse Belanger** traded from Florida to Vancouver for Vancouver's 3rd round choice in 1996 Entry Draft and future considerations.

20 –LW **Ken Baumgartner** traded from Toronto to Anaheim for Winnipeg's 4th round choice in 1996 Entry Draft (previously acquired).

20 –D **J-J Daigneault** traded from St. Louis to Pittsburgh for Pittsburgh's 6th round choice in 1996 Entry Draft.

20 –LW **Kevin Miller** traded from San Jose to Pittsburgh for Pittsburgh's 5th round choice in 1996 Entry Draft and future considerations.

20 –LW **Pat Conacher** and Calgary's 6th round choice in 1997 Entry Draft traded from Calgary to NY Islanders for C **Bob Sweeney**.

20 –RW **Kirk Maltby** traded from Edmonton to Detroit for D **Dan McGillis**.

20 –D **Jaroslav Modry** and Ottawa's 8th round choice in 1996 Entry Draft traded from Ottawa to Los Angeles for RW **Kevin Brown**.

20 –LW **Patrick Poulin**, D **Igor Ulanov** and Chicago's 2nd round choice in 1996 Entry Draft traded from Chicago to Tampa Bay for D **Enrico Ciccone** and Tampa Bay's 2nd round choice in 1996 Entry Draft.

20 –LW **Yuri Khmylev** and Buffalo's 8th round choice in 1996 Entry Draft traded from Buffalo to St. Louis for D **Jean-Luc Grand Pierre**, Ottawa's 2nd round choice in 1996 Entry Draft (previously acquired) and St. Louis' 3rd round choice in 1997 **Entry Draft**.

20 –C **Dave Hannan** traded from Buffalo to Colorado for Colorado's 6th round choice in 1996 Entry Draft.

20 –RW **Alek Stojanov** traded from Vancouver to Pittsburgh for RW **Markus Naslund**.

20 –RW **Ravil Gusmanov** traded from Winnipeg to Chicago for Chicago's 4th round choice in 1996 Entry Draft.

20 –RW **Joe Kocur** traded from NY Rangers to Vancouver for G **Kay Whitmore**.

April

3 –C **Anson Carter** traded from Colorado to Washington for Washington's 4th round choice in 1996 Entry Draft.

May

21 –LW **Michel Picard** traded from Ottawa to Washington for cash.

June

1 –D **Brad Lukowich** traded from NY Islanders to Dallas for Dallas' 3rd round choice in 1997 Entry Draft.

14 –G **Bob Essensa** traded from Detroit to Edmonton for future considerations.

14 –C **Jamie Baker** and a 5th round choice in 1996 Entry Draft traded from San Jose to Toronto for D **Todd Gill**.

14 –D **Todd Gill** traded from Toronto to San Jose for C **Jamie Baker** and a fifth round choice in 1996 Entry Draft.

20 –LW **Eric Lacroix** and Los Angeles' 1st round choice in 1998 Entry Draft traded from Los Angeles to Colorado for G **Stephane Fiset** and Colorado's 1st round choice in 1998 Entry Draft.

21 –D **Al Iafrate** traded from Boston to San Jose for LW **Jeff Odgers** and Pittsburgh's 5th round choice in 1996 Entry Draft (previously acquired).

22 –C **Shawn McEachern** traded from Boston to Ottawa for RW **Trent McCleary** and Ottawa's 3rd round choice in 1996 Entry Draft.

22 –G **Jeff Reese**, Chicago's 2nd round choice in 1996 Entry Draft (previously acquired) and Tampa Bay's 8th round choice in 1996 Entry Draft traded from Tampa Bay to New Jersey for G **Corey Schwab**.

22 –C **Tyler Wright** traded from Edmonton to Pittsburgh for Pittsburgh's 7th round choice in 1996 Entry Draft.

22 –Dallas trades its 3rd round choice in 1996 Entry Draft (#58) to Washington for Washington's 3rd round choice in 1996 (#70) and Anaheim's 4th round choice in 1996 (#90, previously acquired).

22 –RW **Mike Gartner** traded from Toronto to Phoenix for Chicago's 4th round choice in 1996 Entry Draft (previously acquired).

22 –Toronto cedes Phoenix's 4th round choice in 1996 Entry Draft (previously acquired) to Montreal to complete trade of April 6, 1995 in which Toronto acquired C **Paul DiPietro**.

22 –C **Dave Gagner** traded from Toronto to Calgary for Calgary's 3rd round choice in 1996 Entry Draft.

22 –D **Sergei Zubov** traded from Pittsburgh to Dallas for D **Kevin Hatcher**.

22 –Chicago trades its 1st round choice in 1996 Entry Draft to San Jose for two second round choices in 1996 Entry Draft (#31 and #46).

22 –New Jersey trades San Jose's 2nd round choice in 1996 Entry Draft (previously acquired) to Pittsburgh for two second round choices in 1996 Entry Draft (#41 and #49).

28 –LW **Mike Maneluk** traded from Anaheim to Ottawa for RW **Kevin Brown**.

July

10 –D **Tuomas Gronman** traded from Colorado to Chicago for Chicago's 2nd round choice in 1998 Entry Draft.

18 –D **Frank Bialowas** traded from Washington to Philadelphia for future considerations.

29 –D **Craig Wolanin** traded from Colorado to Tampa Bay for Tampa Bay's 2nd round choice in 1998 Entry Draft.

August

15 –RW **Sergei Gorbachev** traded from San Jose to Dallas for Dallas' 5th round choice in 1998 Entry Draft.

16 –C **Jeremy Roenick** traded from Chicago to Phoenix for C **Alexei Zhamnov**, RW **Craig Mills** and Phoenix's 1st round choice in 1998 Entry Draft.

20 –D **Marty McSorley** traded from NY Rangers to San Jose for D **Jayson More**, C **Brian Swanson** and a conditional choice in 1998 Entry Draft.

22 –D **Lyle Odelein** traded from Montreal to New Jersey for RW **Stephane Richer**.

22 –RW **Petr Klima** traded from Tampa Bay to Los Angeles for a conditional choice in 1997 Entry Draft.

28 –RW **Dino Ciccarelli** traded from Detroit to Tampa Bay for a conditional choice in 1998 Entry Draft.

Trades and free agent signings that occurred after August 28, 1996 are listed on page 246.

THREE STAR SELECTION...

NHL PUBLICATIONS
ORDER FORM

Please send

☐ copies of **next** year's
NHL Guide & Record Book/97-98 (available Sept. 97)

☐ copies of **this** year's
NHL Guide & Record Book/96-97 (available now)

☐ copies of **next** year's
NHL Yearbook 1998 magazine (available Sept. 97)

☐ copies of **this** year's
NHL Yearbook 1997 magazine (available now)

☐ copies of **next** year's
NHL Rule Book and Schedule/97-98 (available Sept. 97)

☐ copies of **this** year's
NHL Rule Book and Schedule/96-97 (available now)

PRICES:	CANADA	USA	OVERSEAS
GUIDE & RECORD BOOK	$21.95	$18.95	$21.95 CDN
Handling (per copy)	$ 4.50	$ 8.00	$ 9.00 CDN
7% GST	$ 1.85	–	
Total (per copy)	**$28.30**	**$26.95**	**$30.95 CDN**
Add Extra for airmail	$ 8.00	$ 9.00	$27.00 CDN
YEARBOOK	$ 7.95	$ 7.95	$ 7.95 CDN
Handling (per copy)	$ 2.94	$ 3.50	$ 5.00 CDN
7% GST	$ .76	—	—
Total (per copy)	**$11.65**	**$11.45**	**$12.95 CDN**
RULE BOOK	$ 9.95	$ 7.95	$ 9.95 CDN
Handling (per copy)	$ 1.73	$ 3.00	$ 4.00 CDN
7% GST	$ .82	–	–
Total (per copy)	**$12.50**	**$10.95**	**$13.95 CDN**

☐ Enclosed is my cheque or money order.

Charge my   ☐ Visa   ☐ MasterCard   ☐ Am Ex

_____

Credit Card Account Number   Expiry Date (important)

_____

Signature

_____

Name

_____

Address

_____

Province/State   Postal/Zip Code

IN CANADA	*IN USA*	*OVERSEAS*
Mail completed form to:	Mail completed form to:	Mail completed form to:
NHL Publishing	NHL Publishing	NHL Publishing
194 Dovercourt Rd.	194 Dovercourt Rd.	194 Dovercourt Rd.
Toronto, Ontario	Toronto, Ontario	Toronto, Ontario
M6J 3C8	CANADA M6J 3C8	CANADA M6J 3C8
	Remit in U.S. funds	**Money order or credit card only. No cheques please.**

DELIVERY: Canada & USA – up to three weeks. Overseas – up to five weeks.

NHL PUBLISHING
IS PLEASED TO OFFER
THREE OF THE GAME'S
LEADING ANNUAL
PUBLICATIONS

1. THE NHL OFFICIAL GUIDE & RECORD BOOK
The NHL's authoritative information source.
65th year in print.
448 pages.
The "Bible of Hockey".
Read worldwide.

2. THE NHL YEARBOOK
200-page, full-color magazine with features on each club. Award winners, All-Stars and special statistics.

3. THE NHL RULE BOOK
Complete playing rules, including numerous rule changes for 1996-97.

Free Book List with each order.